Mathematics
for the international student
Mathematics HL (Core)
Also suitable for HL & SL combined classes

second edition

Paul Urban
David Martin
Robert Haese
Sandra Haese
Michael Haese
Mark Humphries

for use with
IB Diploma Programme

Roger Dixon
Valerie Frost
Robert Haese
Michael Haese
Sandra Haese
Mark Humphries

Haese & Harris Publications

WORKED SOLUTIONS

MATHEMATICS FOR THE INTERNATIONAL STUDENT
Mathematics HL (Core) second edition – WORKED SOLUTIONS
IB Diploma Programme

Roger Dixon	B.Ed.
Valerie Frost	B.Sc., Dip.Ed.
Robert Haese	B.Sc.
Michael Haese	B.Sc.(Hons.), Ph.D.
Sandra Haese	B.Sc.
Mark Humphries	B.Sc.(Hons.)

Haese & Harris Publications
3 Frank Collopy Court, Adelaide Airport, SA 5950, AUSTRALIA
Telephone: +61 8 8355 9444, Fax: +61 8 8355 9471
Email: info@haeseandharris.com.au
Web: www.haeseandharris.com.au

National Library of Australia Card Number & ISBN 978-1-876543-95-2

© Haese & Harris Publications 2009

Published by Raksar Nominees Pty Ltd
3 Frank Collopy Court, Adelaide Airport, SA 5950, AUSTRALIA

First Edition	2005
Second Edition	2009

Artwork and cover design by Piotr Poturaj

Typeset in Australia by Susan Haese and Charlotte Sabel (Raksar Nominees).
Typeset in Times Roman $8\frac{1}{2}/10$

The textbook, its accompanying CD and this book of fully worked solutions have been developed independently of the International Baccalaureate Organization (IBO). These publications are in no way connected with, or endorsed by, the IBO.

This book is copyright. Except as permitted by the Copyright Act (any fair dealing for the purposes of private study, research, criticism or review), no part of this publication may be reproduced, stored in a retrieval system, or transmitted in any form or by any means, electronic, mechanical, photocopying, recording or otherwise, without the prior permission of the publisher. Enquiries to be made to Haese & Harris Publications.

Copying for educational purposes: Where copies of part or the whole of the book are made under Part VB of the Copyright Act, the law requires that the educational institution or the body that administers it has given a remuneration notice to Copyright Agency Limited (CAL). For information, contact the Copyright Agency Limited.

Acknowledgements: While every attempt has been made to trace and acknowledge copyright, the authors and publishers apologise for any accidental infringement where copyright has proved untraceable. They would be pleased to come to a suitable agreement with the rightful owner.

Disclaimer: All the internet addresses (URL's) given in this book were valid at the time of printing. While the authors and publisher regret any inconvenience that changes of address may cause readers, no responsibility for any such changes can be accepted by either the authors or the publisher.

FOREWORD

This book gives you fully worked solutions for every question in each chapter of our textbook *Mathematics HL (Core) second edition* which is one of the textbooks in our series **Mathematics for the International Student** intended for use with IB Diploma and Middle Years courses.

Correct answers can sometimes be obtained by different methods. In this book, where applicable, each worked solution is modelled on the worked example in the textbook.

Be aware of the limitations of calculators and computer modelling packages. Understand that when your calculator gives an answer that is different from the answer you find in the book, you have not necessarily made a mistake, but the book may not be wrong either.

We have a list of errata for our books on our website. Please contact us if you notice any errors in this book.

RLD VF RCH
PMH SHH MAH

e-mail: info@haeseandharris.com.au
web: www.haeseandharris.com.au

TABLE OF CONTENTS

Chapter 1	FUNCTIONS	5
Chapter 2	SEQUENCES AND SERIES	44
Chapter 3	EXPONENTIALS	74
Chapter 4	LOGARITHMS	92
Chapter 5	GRAPHING AND TRANSFORMING FUNCTIONS	118
Chapter 6	QUADRATIC EQUATIONS AND FUNCTIONS	136
Chapter 7	COMPLEX NUMBERS AND POLYNOMIALS	181
Chapter 8	COUNTING AND THE BINOMIAL EXPANSION	220
Chapter 9	MATHEMATICAL INDUCTION	237
Chapter 10	THE UNIT CIRCLE AND RADIAN MEASURE	260
Chapter 11	NON-RIGHT ANGLED TRIANGLE TRIGONOMETRY	275
Chapter 12	ADVANCED TRIGONOMETRY	287
Chapter 13	MATRICES	326
Chapter 14	VECTORS IN 2 AND 3 DIMENSIONS	375
Chapter 15	COMPLEX NUMBERS	423
Chapter 16	LINES AND PLANES IN SPACE	461
Chapter 17	DESCRIPTIVE STATISTICS	506
Chapter 18	PROBABILITY	528
Chapter 19	INTRODUCTION TO CALCULUS	558
Chapter 20	DIFFERENTIAL CALCULUS	572
Chapter 21	APPLICATIONS OF DIFFERENTIAL CALCULUS	610
Chapter 22	DERIVATIVES OF EXPONENTIAL AND LOGARITHMIC FUNCTIONS	650
Chapter 23	DERIVATIVES OF CIRCULAR FUNCTIONS AND RELATED RATES	677
Chapter 24	INTEGRATION	704
Chapter 25	APPLICATIONS OF INTEGRATION	735
Chapter 26	VOLUMES OF REVOLUTION	760
Chapter 27	FURTHER INTEGRATION AND DIFFERENTIAL EQUATIONS	770
Chapter 28	STATISTICAL DISTRIBUTIONS OF DISCRETE RANDOM VARIABLES	798
Chapter 29	STATISTICAL DISTRIBUTIONS OF CONTINUOUS RANDOM VARIABLES	821
Chapter 30	MISCELLANEOUS QUESTIONS	839

Chapter 1
FUNCTIONS

EXERCISE 1A

1 **a** $\{(1, 3), (2, 4), (3, 5), (4, 6)\}$ is a function since no two ordered pairs have the same x-coordinate.
   b $\{(1, 3), (3, 2), (1, 7), (-1, 4)\}$ is not a function since two of the ordered pairs, $(1, 3)$ and $(1, 7)$, have the same x-coordinate 1.
   c $\{(2, -1), (2, 0), (2, 3), (2, 11)\}$ is not a function since each ordered pair has the same x-coordinate 2.
   d $\{(7, 6), (5, 6), (3, 6), (-4, 6)\}$ is a function since no two ordered pairs have the same x-coordinate.
   e $\{(0, 0), (1, 0), (3, 0), (5, 0)\}$ is a function since no two ordered pairs have the same x-coordinate.
   f $\{(0,0), (0,-2), (0,2), (0,4)\}$ is not a function since each ordered pair has the same x-coordinate 0.

2 **a** 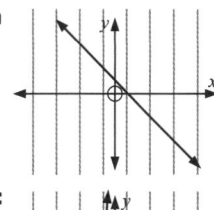 Each line cuts the graph no more than once, so it is a function.

   b 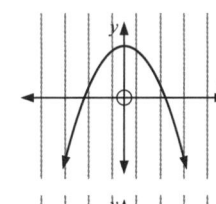 Each line cuts the graph no more than once, so it is a function.

   c 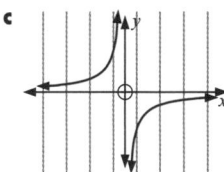 Each line cuts the graph no more than once, so it is a function.

   d 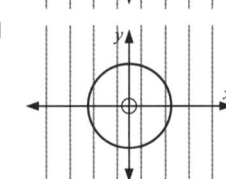 Some lines cut the graph more than once, so it is not a function.

   e 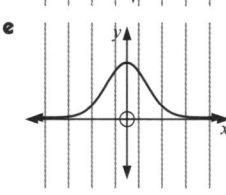 Each line cuts the graph no more than once, so it is a function.

   f 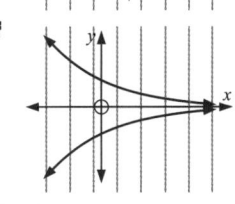 The lines cut the graph more than once, so it is not a function.

   g 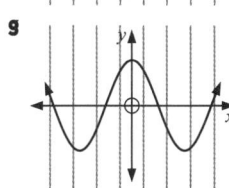 Each line cuts the graph no more than once, so it is a function.

   h 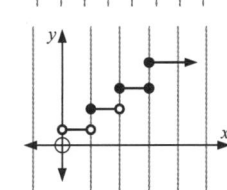 One line cuts the graph more than once, so it is not a function.

3 The graph of a straight line is not a function if the graph is a vertical line, i.e., $x = a$ for all a.
The vertical line through $x = a$ cuts the graph at every point, so it is not a function.

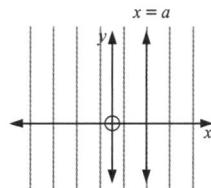

4 $x^2 + y^2 = 9$ is the equation of a circle, centre $(0, 0)$ and radius 3.
Now $x^2 + y^2 = 9$
$\therefore \quad y^2 = 9 - x^2$
$\therefore \quad y = \pm\sqrt{9 - x^2}$
For any value of x where $-3 < x < 3$, y has two real values. Hence $x^2 + y^2 = 9$ is not a function.

EXERCISE 1B.1

1 **a** $f(0) = 3(0) + 2 = 2$ **b** $f(2) = 3(2) + 2 = 8$ **c** $f(-1) = 3(-1) + 2 = -1$
d $f(-5) = 3(-5) + 2 = -13$ **e** $f(-\frac{1}{3}) = 3(-\frac{1}{3}) + 2 = 1$

2 **a** $f(0) = 3(0) - 0^2 + 2$ **b** $f(3) = 3(3) - 3^2 + 2$ **c** $f(-3) = 3(-3) - (-3)^2 + 2$
$= 2$ $= 9 - 9 + 2$ $= -9 - 9 + 2$
      $= 2$ $= -16$

d $f(-7) = 3(-7) - (-7)^2 + 2$ **e** $f(\frac{3}{2}) = 3(\frac{3}{2}) - (\frac{3}{2})^2 + 2$
$= -21 - 49 + 2$ $= \frac{9}{2} - \frac{9}{4} + 2$
$= -68$ $= \frac{17}{4}$

3 **a** $f(a) = 7 - 3a$ **b** $f(-a) = 7 - 3(-a)$ **c** $f(a+3) = 7 - 3(a+3)$
        $= 7 + 3a$ $= 7 - 3a - 9$
              $= -3a - 2$

d $f(b-1) = 7 - 3(b-1)$ **e** $f(x+2) = 7 - 3(x+2)$ **f** $f(x+h) = 7 - 3(x+h)$
$= 7 - 3b + 3$ $= 7 - 3x - 6$ $= 7 - 3x - 3h$
$= 10 - 3b$ $= 1 - 3x$

4 **a** $F(x+4)$ **b** $F(2-x)$
$= 2(x+4)^2 + 3(x+4) - 1$ $= 2(2-x)^2 + 3(2-x) - 1$
$= 2(x^2 + 8x + 16) + 3x + 12 - 1$ $= 2(4 - 4x + x^2) + 6 - 3x - 1$
$= 2x^2 + 16x + 32 + 3x + 11$ $= 8 - 8x + 2x^2 + 5 - 3x$
$= 2x^2 + 19x + 43$ $= 2x^2 - 11x + 13$

c $F(-x)$ **d** $F(x^2)$
$= 2(-x)^2 + 3(-x) - 1$ $= 2(x^2)^2 + 3(x^2) - 1$
$= 2x^2 - 3x - 1$ $= 2x^4 + 3x^2 - 1$

e $F(x^2 - 1)$ **f** $F(x+h)$
$= 2(x^2 - 1)^2 + 3(x^2 - 1) - 1$ $= 2(x+h)^2 + 3(x+h) - 1$
$= 2(x^4 - 2x^2 + 1) + 3x^2 - 3 - 1$ $= 2(x^2 + 2xh + h^2) + 3x + 3h - 1$
$= 2x^4 - 4x^2 + 2 + 3x^2 - 4$ $= 2x^2 + 4xh + 2h^2 + 3x + 3h - 1$
$= 2x^4 - x^2 - 2$

5 **a** **i** $G(2) = \dfrac{2(2)+3}{2-4}$ **ii** $G(0) = \dfrac{2(0)+3}{0-4}$ **iii** $G(-\frac{1}{2}) = \dfrac{2(-\frac{1}{2})+3}{-\frac{1}{2}-4}$
$= \frac{7}{-2}$ $= \frac{3}{-4}$ $= \dfrac{-1+3}{(-\frac{9}{2})}$
$= -\frac{7}{2}$ $= -\frac{3}{4}$ $= \dfrac{2}{(-\frac{9}{2})}$
            $= -\frac{4}{9}$

b $G(x) = \dfrac{2x+3}{x-4}$ is undefined when $x - 4 = 0$
$\therefore \quad x = 4$
So, when $x = 4$, $G(x)$ does not exist.

c $G(x+2) = \dfrac{2(x+2)+3}{(x+2)-4} = \dfrac{2x+4+3}{x+2-4} = \dfrac{2x+7}{x-2}$

d $G(x) = -3$, so $\dfrac{2x+3}{x-4} = -3$ $\therefore \quad 2x + 3 = -3(x-4)$
$\therefore \quad 2x + 3 = -3x + 12$
$\therefore \quad 5x = 9$ and so $x = \frac{9}{5}$

6 f is the function which converts x into $f(x)$ whereas $f(x)$ is the value of the function at any value of x.

7 a $V(4) = 9650 - 860(4)$
          $= 9650 - 3440$
          $= 6210$
   The value of the photocopier 4 years after purchase is 6210 euros.

b If $V(t) = 5780$,
   then $9650 - 860t = 5780$
   $\therefore\ 860t = 3870$
   $\therefore\ t = 4.5$
   The value of the photocopier $4\frac{1}{2}$ years after purchase is 5780 euros.

c Original purchase price is when $t = 0$,
   $V(0) = 9650 - 860(0)$
          $= 9650$
   The original purchase price was 9650 euros.

8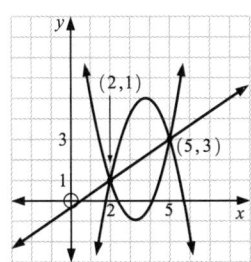

First sketch the linear function which passes through the two points (2, 1) and (5, 3).
Then sketch two quadratic functions which also pass through the two points.

9 $f(x) = ax + b$ where $f(2) = 1$ and $f(-3) = 11$
So, $a(2) + b = 1$ and $a(-3) + b = 11$
$\therefore\ 2a + b = 1$ $\therefore\ -3a + b = 11$
$\therefore\ b = 1 - 2a$ ..... (1) $\therefore\ b = 11 + 3a$ .....(2)

Solving (1) and (2) simultaneously, $1 - 2a = 11 + 3a$
$\therefore\ 5a = -10$
$\therefore\ a = -2$

Substituting $a = -2$ into (1) gives $b = 1 - 2(-2) = 5$. So, $a = -2$, $b = 5$
Hence $f(x) = -2x + 5$

10 $T(x) = ax^2 + bx + c$ where $T(0) = -4$, $T(1) = -2$ and $T(2) = 6$
So, $a(0)^2 + b(0) + c = -4$
$\therefore\ c = -4$
Also, $a(1)^2 + b(1) + c = -2$ and $a(2)^2 + b(2) + c = 6$
$\therefore\ a + b + c = -2$ $\therefore\ 4a + 2b + c = 6$

Substituting $c = -4$ into both equations gives
$a + b + (-4) = -2$
$\therefore\ a + b = 2$
$\therefore\ a = 2 - b$ .....(1)
and $4a + 2b + (-4) = 6$
$\therefore\ 4a + 2b = 10$ .....(2)

Substituting (1) into (2) gives $4(2 - b) + 2b = 10$ $\therefore\ 8 - 4b + 2b = 10$
$\therefore\ -2b = 2$
$\therefore\ b = -1$

Now, substituting $b = -1$ into (1) gives $a = 2 - (-1) = 3$. So, $a = 3$, $b = -1$, $c = -4$

EXERCISE 1B.2

1 a The permissible values for x are 1, 2 and 3, so the domain is $\{1, 2, 3\}$.
   The permissible values for y are 3, 5 and 7, so the range is $\{3, 5, 7\}$.

b The permissible values for x are -1, 0 and 2, so the domain is $\{-1, 0, 2\}$.
The permissible values for y are 3 and 5, so the range is $\{3, 5\}$.

c The permissible values for x are -3, -2, -1 and 3, so the domain is $\{-3, -2, -1, 3\}$.
The only permissible value for y is 1, so the range is $\{1\}$.

d The only solutions (x, y) to $x^2 + y^2 = 4$, where $x \in \mathbb{Z}$ and $y \geqslant 0$, are $(-2, 0)$, $(-1, \sqrt{3})$, $(0, 2)$, $(1, \sqrt{3})$ and $(2, 0)$.
$\therefore$ the domain is $\{-2, -1, 0, 1, 2\}$ and the range is $\{0, \sqrt{3}, 2\}$.

2 **a** Domain is $\{x \mid -1 < x \leqslant 5\}$
Range is $\{y \mid 1 < y \leqslant 3\}$

b Domain is $\{x \mid x \neq 2\}$
Range is $\{y \mid y \neq -1\}$

c Domain is $\{x \mid x \in \mathbb{R}\}$
Range is $\{y \mid 0 < y \leqslant 2\}$

d Domain is $\{x \mid x \in \mathbb{R}\}$
Range is $\{y \mid y \geqslant -1\}$

e Domain is $\{x \mid x \geqslant -4\}$
Range is $\{y \mid y \geqslant -3\}$

f Domain is $\{x \mid x \neq \pm 2\}$
Range is $\{y \mid y \leqslant -1 \text{ or } y > 0\}$

3 **a** $y = 2x - 1$ can take any x-value and any y-value.
$\therefore$ the domain is $\{x \mid x \in \mathbb{R}\}$ and the range is $\{y \mid y \in \mathbb{R}\}$.

b $y = 3$ can take any value of x, but the only permissible value for y is 3
$\therefore$ the domain is $\{x \mid x \in \mathbb{R}\}$ and the range is $\{3\}$.

c $y = |3x - 1| + 2$ can take any value of x, but $|3x - 1| \geqslant 0$ and so $|3x - 1| + 2 \geqslant 2$
$\therefore$ the domain is $\{x \mid x \in \mathbb{R}\}$ and the range is $\{y \mid y \geqslant 2\}$.

d $y = \sqrt{x^2 + 4}$ can take any value of x, as $x^2 + 4 \geqslant 0$ for all real x.
In fact, $x^2 + 4 \geqslant 4$, so $\sqrt{x^2 + 4} \geqslant 2$
$\therefore$ the domain is $\{x \mid x \in \mathbb{R}\}$ and the range is $\{y \mid y \geqslant 2\}$.

e $y = \sqrt{x^2 - 4}$ is defined when $x^2 - 4 \geqslant 0$,
which is when $x \leqslant -2$ or $x \geqslant 2$.
Also, $\sqrt{x^2 - 4} \geqslant 0$
$\therefore$ the domain is $\{x \mid x \leqslant -2, \, x \geqslant 2\}$ and the range is $\{y \mid y \geqslant 0\}$.

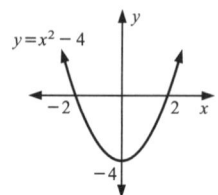

f $y = \dfrac{5}{x - 2}$ is undefined when $x - 2 = 0$, or when $x = 2$
$y = \dfrac{5}{x - 2}$ cannot be 0 for any value of x.
$\therefore$ the domain is $\{x \mid x \neq 2\}$ and the range is $\{y \mid y \neq 0\}$.

g $y = \sqrt{2 - x}$ is defined when $2 - x \geqslant 0$, or when $x \leqslant 2$
Also, $\sqrt{2 - x} \geqslant 0$ for all $x \leqslant 2$.
$\therefore$ the domain is $\{x \mid x \leq 2\}$ and the range is $\{y \mid y \geqslant 0\}$.

h $y = \dfrac{3}{\sqrt{2x - 5}}$ is defined when $2x - 5 > 0$, or when $x > \tfrac{5}{2}$
Since $\sqrt{2x - 5} > 0$, $\dfrac{3}{\sqrt{2x - 5}} > 0$
$\therefore$ the domain is $\{x \mid x > \tfrac{5}{2}\}$ and the range is $\{y \mid y > 0\}$.

i $y = 2 + \dfrac{3}{5 - x}$ is undefined when $5 - x = 0$, or when $x = 5$
Since $\dfrac{3}{5 - x} \neq 0$, $2 + \dfrac{3}{5 - x} \neq 2$
$\therefore$ the domain is $\{x \mid x \neq 5\}$ and the range is $\{y \mid y \neq 2\}$.

4 **a** 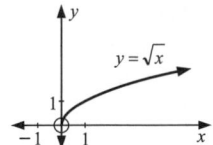 Domain is $\{x \mid x \geqslant 0\}$
Range is $\{y \mid y \geqslant 0\}$

b 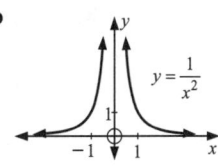 Domain is $\{x \mid x \neq 0\}$
Range is $\{y \mid y > 0\}$

c 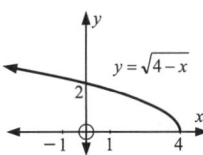 Domain is $\{x \mid x \leqslant 4\}$
Range is $\{y \mid y \geqslant 0\}$

d 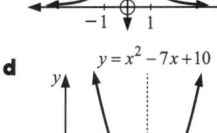 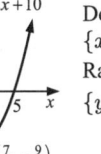 Domain is $\{x \mid x \in \mathbb{R}\}$
Range is $\{y \mid y \geqslant -2\tfrac{1}{4}\}$

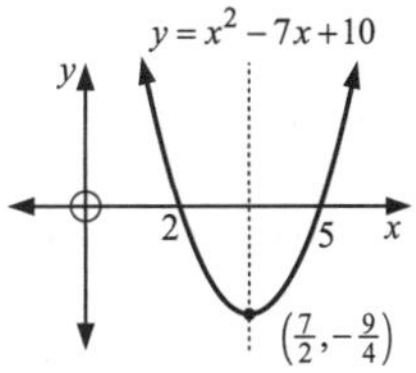

e 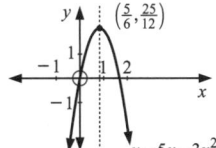 Domain is $\{x \mid x \in \mathbb{R}\}$
Range is $\{y \mid y \leqslant \tfrac{25}{12}\}$

f 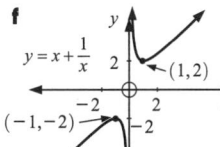 Domain is $\{x \mid x \neq 0\}$
Range is $\{y \mid y \leqslant -2 \text{ or } y \geqslant 2\}$

g 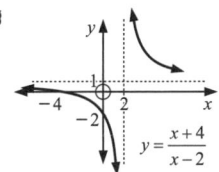 Domain is $\{x \mid x \neq 2\}$
Range is $\{y \mid y \neq 1\}$

h Domain is $\{x \mid x \in \mathbb{R}\}$
Range is $\{y \mid y \in \mathbb{R}\}$

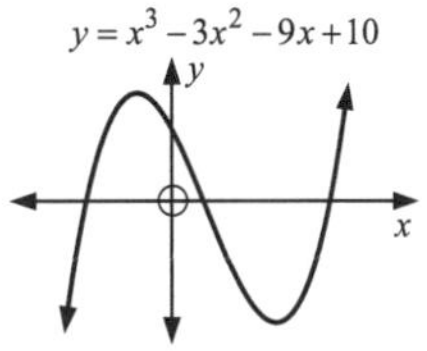

i Domain is $\{x \mid x \neq -1,\ x \neq 2\}$
Range is $\{y \mid y \leqslant \tfrac{1}{3} \text{ or } y \geqslant 3\}$

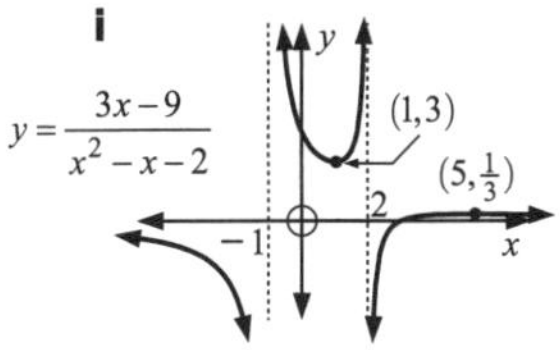

j Domain is $\{x \mid x \neq 0\}$
Range is $\{y \mid y \geqslant 2\}$

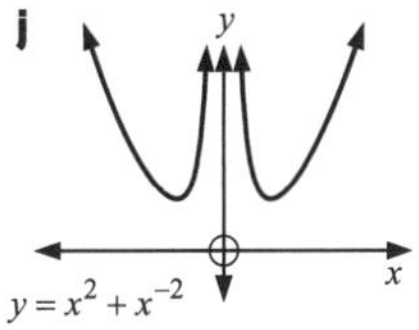

k 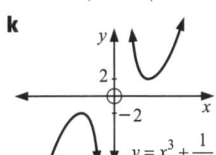 Domain is $\{x \mid x \neq 0\}$
Range is $\{y \mid y \leqslant -2 \text{ or } y \geqslant 2\}$

l Domain is $\{x \mid x \in \mathbb{R}\}$
Range is $\{y \mid y \geqslant -8\}$

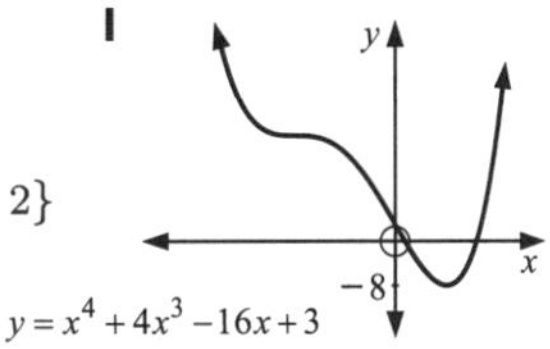

EXERCISE 1C

1 **a** $(f \circ g)(x)$
$= f(g(x))$
$= f(1-x)$
$= 2(1-x) + 3$
$= 2 - 2x + 3$
$= 5 - 2x$

b $(g \circ f)(x)$
$= g(f(x))$
$= g(2x+3)$
$= 1 - (2x+3)$
$= 1 - 2x - 3$
$= -2x - 2$

c $(f \circ g)(-3)$
$= 5 - 2(-3)$ {from **a**}
$= 11$

2 $(f \circ g)(x) = f(g(x))$
$= f(2-x)$
$= (2-x)^2$

Domain is $\{x \mid x \in \mathbb{R}\}$
Range is $\{y \mid y \geqslant 0\}$

$(g \circ f)(x) = g(f(x))$
$= g(x^2)$
$= 2 - x^2$

Domain is $\{x \mid x \in \mathbb{R}\}$
Range is $\{y \mid y \leqslant 2\}$

3 **a** $(f \circ g)(x)$
$= f(g(x))$
$= f(3-x)$
$= (3-x)^2 + 1$
$= 9 - 6x + x^2 + 1$
$= x^2 - 6x + 10$

b $(g \circ f)(x)$
$= g(f(x))$
$= g(x^2 + 1)$
$= 3 - (x^2 + 1)$
$= 3 - x^2 - 1$
$= 2 - x^2$

c $(g \circ f)(x) = f(x)$
$\therefore \quad 2 - x^2 = f(x) \quad \{\text{from } \mathbf{b}\}$
$\therefore \quad 2 - x^2 = x^2 + 1$
$\therefore \quad 2x^2 = 1$
$\therefore \quad x^2 = \frac{1}{2}$
$\therefore \quad x = \pm \frac{1}{\sqrt{2}}$

4 **a** $(f \circ g)(0) = f(g(0)) = f(3) = 1$
$(f \circ g)(1) = f(g(1)) = f(2) = 0$
$(f \circ g)(2) = f(g(2)) = f(1) = 3$
$(f \circ g)(3) = f(g(3)) = f(0) = 2$
$\therefore \quad f \circ g = \{(0, 1), (1, 0), (2, 3), (3, 2)\}$

b $(g \circ f)(0) = g(f(0)) = f(2) = 1$
$(g \circ f)(1) = g(f(1)) = f(3) = 0$
$(g \circ f)(2) = g(f(2)) = f(0) = 3$
$(g \circ f)(3) = g(f(3)) = f(1) = 2$
$\therefore \quad g \circ f = \{(0, 1), (1, 0), (2, 3), (3, 2)\}$

c $(f \circ f)(0) = f(f(0)) = f(2) = 0$
$(f \circ f)(1) = f(f(1)) = f(3) = 1$
$(f \circ f)(2) = f(f(2)) = f(0) = 2$
$(f \circ f)(3) = f(f(3)) = f(1) = 3$
$\therefore \quad f \circ f = \{(0, 0), (1, 1), (2, 2), (3, 3)\}$

5 $(f \circ g)(0) = f(g(0)) = f(1) = 0$
$(f \circ g)(1) = f(g(1)) = f(2) = 1$
$(f \circ g)(2) = f(g(2)) = f(3) = 2$
$(f \circ g)(3) = f(g(3)) = f(0) = 3$
$\therefore \quad f \circ g = \{(0, 0), (1, 1), (2, 2), (3, 3)\}$

6 **a** $(f \circ g)(2) = f(g(2)) = f(2) = 7$
$(f \circ g)(5) = f(g(5)) = f(0) = 2$
$(f \circ g)(7) = f(g(7)) = f(1) = 5$
$(f \circ g)(9) = f(g(9)) = f(3) = 9$
$\therefore \quad f \circ g = \{(2, 7), (5, 2), (7, 5), (9, 9)\}$

b $(g \circ f)(0) = g(f(0)) = f(2) = 2$
$(g \circ f)(1) = g(f(1)) = f(5) = 0$
$(g \circ f)(2) = g(f(2)) = f(7) = 1$
$(g \circ f)(3) = g(f(3)) = f(9) = 3$
$\therefore \quad g \circ f = \{(0, 2), (1, 0), (2, 1), (3, 3)\}$

7 **a** $(f \circ g)(x)$
$= f(g(x))$
$= f\left(\dfrac{x+1}{x-1}\right)$
$= \dfrac{\left(\frac{x+1}{x-1}\right) + 3}{\left(\frac{x+1}{x-1}\right) + 2} \times \dfrac{(x-1)}{(x-1)}$
$= \dfrac{x + 1 + 3(x-1)}{x + 1 + 2(x-1)}$
$= \dfrac{4x - 2}{3x - 1}, \quad x \neq 1$

$(f \circ g)(x)$ is undefined when $3x - 1 = 0$, which is when $x = \frac{1}{3}$
$\therefore \quad$ domain is $\{x \mid x \neq \frac{1}{3} \text{ or } 1\}$

b $(g \circ f)(x)$
$= g(f(x))$
$= g\left(\dfrac{x+3}{x+2}\right)$
$= \dfrac{\left(\frac{x+3}{x+2}\right) + 1}{\left(\frac{x+3}{x+2}\right) - 1} \times \dfrac{(x+2)}{(x+2)}$
$= \dfrac{x + 3 + (x+2)}{x + 3 - (x+2)}$
$= \dfrac{2x + 5}{1}$
$= 2x + 5, \quad x \neq -2$
$\therefore \quad$ domain is $\{x \mid x \neq -2\}$

c $(g \circ g)(x)$
$= g(g(x))$
$= g\left(\dfrac{x+1}{x-1}\right)$
$= \dfrac{\left(\frac{x+1}{x-1}\right) + 1}{\left(\frac{x+1}{x-1}\right) - 1} \times \dfrac{(x-1)}{(x-1)}$
$= \dfrac{x + 1 + (x-1)}{x + 1 - (x-1)}$
$= \dfrac{2x}{2}$
$= x, \quad x \neq 1$
$\therefore \quad$ domain is $\{x \mid x \neq 1\}$

8 **a** $ax + b = cx + d$ is true for all x $\{\text{given}\}$
When $x = 0$,
$a(0) + b = c(0) + d$
$\therefore \quad b = d \quad .....(1)$

When $x = 1$, $a(1) + b = c(1) + d$
$\therefore \quad a + b = c + d$
but $b = d \quad \{\text{from (1)}\}$
$\therefore \quad a + d = c + d$
$\therefore \quad a = c$

b $(f \circ g)(x) = x$ for all x {given}
$\therefore \quad f(g(x)) = x$
$\therefore \quad f(ax + b) = x$
$\therefore \quad 2(ax + b) + 3 = x$
$\therefore \quad 2ax + 2b + 3 = x$ for all x
$\therefore \quad 2a = 1$ and $2b + 3 = 0$ {using **a**}
$\therefore \quad a = \frac{1}{2}$ and $2b = -3$
So, $a = \frac{1}{2}$ and $b = -\frac{3}{2}$ as required.

c If $(g \circ f)(x) = x$
then $g(f(x)) = x$
$\therefore \quad g(2x + 3) = x$
$\therefore \quad a(2x + 3) + b = x$
$\therefore \quad 2ax + 3a + b = x$
$\therefore \quad 2a = 1$ and $3a + b = 0$ {using **a**}
$\therefore \quad a = \frac{1}{2}$ and $b = -3a$
So, $a = \frac{1}{2}$ and $b = -\frac{3}{2}$ as required.
$\therefore$ the result in **b** is also true if $(g \circ f)(x) = x$ for all x.

EXERCISE 1D

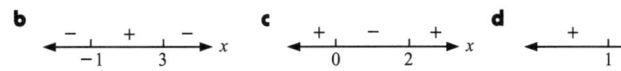

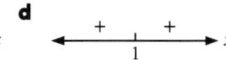

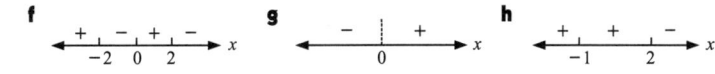

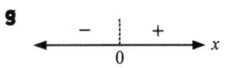

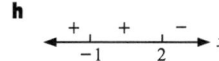

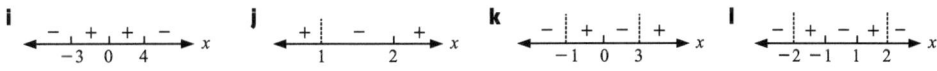

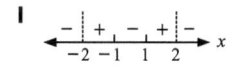

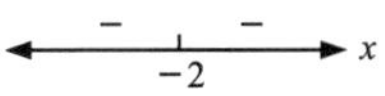

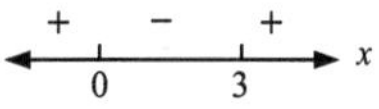

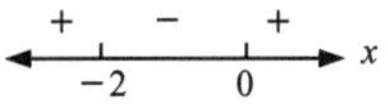

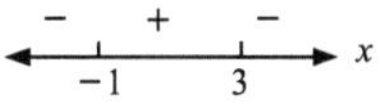

1 a sign diagram with $-$ / $+$ at 2

b sign diagram with $-$ / $+$ / $-$ at $-1, 3$

c sign diagram with $+$ / $-$ / $+$ at $0, 2$

d sign diagram with $+$ / $+$ at 1

e sign diagram with $-$ / $-$ at -2

f sign diagram with $+$ / $-$ / $+$ / $-$ at $-2, 0, 2$

g sign diagram with $-$ / $+$ at 0

h sign diagram with $+$ / $+$ / $-$ at $-1, 2$

i sign diagram with $-$ / $+$ / $+$ / $-$ at $-3, 0, 4$

j sign diagram with $+$ / $-$ / $+$ at $1, 2$

k sign diagram with $-$ / $+$ / $-$ / $+$ at $-1, 0, 3$

l sign diagram with $-$ / $+$ / $-$ / $+$ / $-$ at $-2, -1, 1, 2$

2 a $y = (x + 4)(x - 2)$ is zero when $x = -4$ or 2.
When $x = 0$, $y = (4)(-2) = -8 < 0$.
The factors are single, so the signs alternate.
$\therefore$ sign diagram is: $+ / - / +$ at $-4, 2$

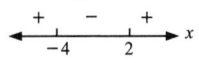

b $y = x(x - 3)$ is zero when $x = 0$ or 3.
When $x = 10$, $y = 10(7) = 70 > 0$.
The factors are single, so the signs alternate.
$\therefore$ sign diagram is: $+ / - / +$ at $0, 3$

c $y = x(x + 2)$ is zero when $x = -2$ or 0.
When $x = 10$, $y = 10(12) = 120 > 0$.
The factors are single, so the signs alternate.
$\therefore$ sign diagram is: $+ / - / +$ at $-2, 0$

d $y = -(x + 1)(x - 3)$ is zero when $x = -1$ or 3.
When $x = 0$, $y = -(1)(-3) = 3 > 0$.
The factors are single, so the signs alternate.
$\therefore$ sign diagram is: $- / + / -$ at $-1, 3$

e $y = (2x - 1)(3 - x)$ is zero when $x = \frac{1}{2}$ or 3.
When $x = 0$, $y = (-1)(3) = -3 < 0$.
The factors are single, so the signs alternate.
$\therefore$ sign diagram is: $- / + / -$ at $\frac{1}{2}, 3$

f $y = (5 - x)(1 - 2x)$ is zero when $x = \frac{1}{2}$ or 5.
When $x = 0$, $y = (5)(1) = 5 > 0$.
The factors are single, so the signs alternate.
$\therefore$ sign diagram is: $+ / - / +$ at $\frac{1}{2}, 5$

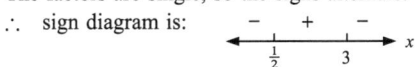

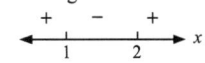

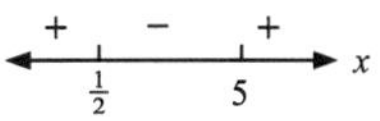

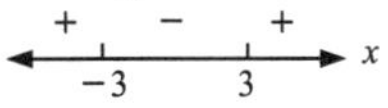

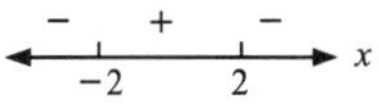

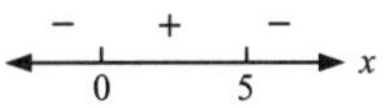

g $y = x^2 - 9 = (x + 3)(x - 3)$ is zero when $x = -3$ or 3.
When $x = 0$, $y = (3)(-3) = -9 < 0$.
The factors are single, so the signs alternate.
$\therefore$ sign diagram is: $+ / - / +$ at $-3, 3$

h $y = 4 - x^2 = (2 + x)(2 - x)$ is zero when $x = -2$ or 2.
When $x = 0$, $y = (2)(2) = 4 > 0$.
The factors are single, so the signs alternate.
$\therefore$ sign diagram is: $- / + / -$ at $-2, 2$

i $y = 5x - x^2 = x(5 - x)$ is zero when $x = 0$ or 5.
When $x = 10$, $y = 10(-5) = -50 < 0$.
The factors are single, so the signs alternate.
$\therefore$ sign diagram is: $- / + / -$ at $0, 5$

j $y = x^2 - 3x + 2 = (x - 1)(x - 2)$ is zero when $x = 1$ or 2.
When $x = 0$, $y = (-1)(-2) = 2 > 0$.
The factors are single, so the signs alternate.
$\therefore$ sign diagram is: $+ / - / +$ at $1, 2$

k $y = 2 - 8x^2 = 2(1+2x)(1-2x)$ is zero when $x = -\frac{1}{2}$ or $\frac{1}{2}$.
When $x = 0$, $y = 2(1)(1) = 2 > 0$.
The factors are single, so the signs alternate.
$\therefore$ sign diagram is: $\quad\begin{array}{c}-\quad+\quad-\\ \xleftarrow{\quad\bullet\quad\bullet\quad}\to x\\ \;-\frac{1}{2}\quad\frac{1}{2}\end{array}$

l $y = 6x^2 + x - 2 = (3x+2)(2x-1)$ is zero when $x = -\frac{2}{3}$ or $\frac{1}{2}$.
When $x = 0$, $y = (2)(-1) = -2 < 0$.
The factors are single, so the signs alternate.
$\therefore$ sign diagram is: $\quad\begin{array}{c}+\quad-\quad+\\ \xleftarrow{\quad\bullet\quad\bullet\quad}\to x\\ \;-\frac{2}{3}\quad\frac{1}{2}\end{array}$

m $y = 6 - 16x - 6x^2 = 2(3+x)(1-3x)$ is zero when $x = -3$ or $\frac{1}{3}$.
When $x = 0$, $y = 2(3)(1) = 6 > 0$.
The factors are single, so the signs alternate.
$\therefore$ sign diagram is: $\quad\begin{array}{c}-\quad+\quad-\\ \xleftarrow{\quad\bullet\quad\bullet\quad}\to x\\ \;-3\quad\frac{1}{3}\end{array}$

n $y = -2x^2 + 9x + 5 = (2x+1)(5-x)$ is zero when $x = -\frac{1}{2}$ or 5.
When $x = 0$, $y = (1)(5) = 5 > 0$.
The factors are single, so the signs alternate.
$\therefore$ sign diagram is: $\quad\begin{array}{c}-\quad+\quad-\\ \xleftarrow{\quad\bullet\quad\bullet\quad}\to x\\ \;-\frac{1}{2}\quad 5\end{array}$

o $y = -15x^2 - x + 2 = (5x+2)(1-3x)$ is zero when $x = -\frac{2}{5}$ or $\frac{1}{3}$
When $x = 0$, $y = (2)(1) = 2 > 0$.
The factors are single, so the signs alternate.
$\therefore$ sign diagram is: $\quad\begin{array}{c}-\quad+\quad-\\ \xleftarrow{\quad\bullet\quad\bullet\quad}\to x\\ \;-\frac{2}{5}\quad\frac{1}{3}\end{array}$

3 a $y = (x+2)^2$ is zero when $x = -2$.
When $x = 0$, $y = 2^2 = 4 > 0$.
The factor is squared, so the sign does not change.
$\therefore$ sign diagram is: $\quad\begin{array}{c}+\quad\quad+\\ \xleftarrow{\quad\bullet\quad}\to x\\ \;-2\end{array}$

b $y = (x-3)^2$ is zero when $x = 3$.
When $x = 0$, $y = (-3)^2 = 9 > 0$.
The factor is squared, so the sign does not change.
$\therefore$ sign diagram is: $\quad\begin{array}{c}+\quad\quad+\\ \xleftarrow{\quad\bullet\quad}\to x\\ \;3\end{array}$

c $y = -(x+2)^2$ is zero when $x = -2$.
When $x = 0$, $y = -(2^2) = -4 < 0$.
The factor is squared, so the sign does not change.
$\therefore$ sign diagram is: $\quad\begin{array}{c}-\quad\quad-\\ \xleftarrow{\quad\bullet\quad}\to x\\ \;-2\end{array}$

d $y = -(x-4)^2$ is zero when $x = 4$.
When $x = 0$, $y = -(-4)^2 = -16 < 0$.
The factor is squared, so the sign does not change.
$\therefore$ sign diagram is: $\quad\begin{array}{c}-\quad\quad-\\ \xleftarrow{\quad\bullet\quad}\to x\\ \;4\end{array}$

e $y = x^2 - 2x + 1 = (x-1)^2$ is zero when $x = 1$.
When $x = 0$, $y = (-1)^2 = 1 > 0$.
The factor is squared, so the sign does not change.
$\therefore$ sign diagram is: $\quad\begin{array}{c}+\quad\quad+\\ \xleftarrow{\quad\bullet\quad}\to x\\ \;1\end{array}$

f $y = -x^2 + 4x - 4 = -(x-2)^2$ is zero when $x = 2$.
When $x = 0$, $y = -(-2)^2 = -4 < 0$.
The factor is squared, so the sign does not change.
$\therefore$ sign diagram is: $\quad\begin{array}{c}-\quad\quad-\\ \xleftarrow{\quad\bullet\quad}\to x\\ \;2\end{array}$

g $y = 4x^2 - 4x + 1 = (2x-1)^2$ is zero when $x = \frac{1}{2}$.
When $x = 0$, $y = (-1)^2 = 1 > 0$.
The factor is squared, so the sign does not change.
$\therefore$ sign diagram is: $\quad\begin{array}{c}+\quad\quad+\\ \xleftarrow{\quad\bullet\quad}\to x\\ \;\frac{1}{2}\end{array}$

h $y = -x^2 - 6x - 9 = -(x+3)^2$ is zero when $x = -3$.
When $x = 0$, $y = -(3^2) = -9 < 0$.
The factor is squared, so the sign does not change.
$\therefore$ sign diagram is: $\quad\begin{array}{c}-\quad\quad-\\ \xleftarrow{\quad\bullet\quad}\to x\\ \;-3\end{array}$

i $y = -4x^2 + 12x - 9 = -(2x-3)^2$ is zero when $x = \frac{3}{2}$.
When $x = 0$, $y = -(-3)^2 = -9 < 0$.
The factor is squared, so the sign does not change.
$\therefore$ sign diagram is: $\quad\begin{array}{c}-\quad\quad-\\ \xleftarrow{\quad\bullet\quad}\to x\\ \;\frac{3}{2}\end{array}$

4 a $y = \dfrac{x+2}{x-1}$ is zero when $x = -2$ and undefined when $x = 1$.
When $x = 0$, $y = \dfrac{2}{-1} = -2 < 0$.
Since the factors are single, the signs alternate.
∴ sign diagram is:

```
  +     -   +
←——•————⋮——•——→ x
  -2        1
```

b $y = \dfrac{x}{x+3}$ is zero when $x = 0$ and undefined when $x = -3$.
When $x = 10$, $y = \dfrac{10}{13} > 0$.
Since the factors are single, the signs alternate.
∴ sign diagram is:

```
  +  ⋮  -   +
←——•————•——→ x
  -3     0
```

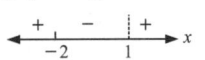

c $y = \dfrac{2x+3}{4-x}$ is zero when $x = -\tfrac{3}{2}$ and undefined when $x = 4$.
When $x = 0$, $y = \tfrac{3}{4} > 0$.
Since the factors are single, the signs alternate.
∴ sign diagram is:

```
  -     +   ⋮ -
←——•————————•——→ x
  -3/2       4
```

d $y = \dfrac{4x-1}{2-x}$ is zero when $x = \tfrac{1}{4}$ and undefined when $x = 2$.
When $x = 0$, $y = \dfrac{-1}{2} = -\tfrac{1}{2} < 0$.
Since the factors are single, the signs alternate.
∴ sign diagram is:

```
  -     +   ⋮ -
←——•————————•——→ x
  1/4        2
```

e $y = \dfrac{3x}{x-2}$ is zero when $x = 0$ and undefined when $x = 2$.
When $x = 5$, $y = \tfrac{15}{3} = 5 > 0$.
Since the factors are single, the signs alternate.
∴ sign diagram is:

```
  +   -  ⋮ +
←——•————•——→ x
  0       2
```

f $y = \dfrac{-8x}{3-x}$ is zero when $x = 0$ and undefined when $x = 3$.
When $x = 5$, $y = \dfrac{-40}{-2} = 20 > 0$.
Since the factors are single, the signs alternate.
∴ sign diagram is:

```
  +   -   ⋮ +
←——•————•——→ x
  0       3
```

g $y = \dfrac{(x-1)^2}{x}$ is zero when $x = 1$ and undefined when $x = 0$.
When $x = 2$, $y = \dfrac{1^2}{2} = \tfrac{1}{2} > 0$.
Since the $(x-1)$ factor is squared, the sign does not change at $x = 1$.
∴ sign diagram is:

```
  - ⋮  +   +
←——•————•——→ x
   0    1
```

h $y = \dfrac{4x}{(x+1)^2}$ is zero when $x = 0$ and undefined when $x = -1$.
When $x = 1$, $y = \tfrac{4}{2^2} = 1 > 0$.
Since the $(x+1)$ factor is squared, the sign does not change at $x = -1$.
∴ sign diagram is:

```
  - ⋮ -     +
←——•————•——→ x
  -1     0
```

i $y = \dfrac{(x+2)(x-1)}{3-x}$ is zero when $x = -2$ or 1 and undefined when $x = 3$.
When $x = 0$, $y = \dfrac{(2)(-1)}{3} = -\tfrac{2}{3} < 0$.
Since the factors are single, the signs alternate.
∴ sign diagram is:

```
  +   -  +  ⋮ -
←—•———•———•——→ x
 -2   1   3
```

j $y = \dfrac{x(x-1)}{2-x}$ is zero when $x = 0$ or 1 and undefined when $x = 2$.
When $x = 3$, $y = \dfrac{3(2)}{-1} = -6 < 0$.
Since the factors are single, the signs alternate.
∴ sign diagram is:

```
  +   -  +  ⋮ -
←—•———•———•——→ x
  0   1   2
```

k $y = \dfrac{x^2-4}{-x} = \dfrac{(x-2)(x+2)}{-x}$ is zero when $x = \pm 2$ and undefined when $x = 0$.
When $x = 1$, $y = \dfrac{(-1)(3)}{-1} = 3 > 0$.
Since the factors are single, the signs alternate.
∴ sign diagram is:

```
  +   -  ⋮ +   -
←—•———•————•——→ x
 -2   0    2
```

l $y = \dfrac{3-x}{2x^2-x-6} = \dfrac{3-x}{(2x+3)(x-2)}$ is zero when $x = 3$ and undefined when $x = -\tfrac{3}{2}$ or 2.
When $x = 0$, $y = \dfrac{3}{-6} = -\tfrac{1}{2} < 0$.
Since the factors are single, the signs alternate.
∴ sign diagram is:

```
  +  ⋮ -  ⋮ +   -
←—•————•————•——→ x
 -3/2   2   3
```

m $y = \dfrac{x^2-3}{x+1} = \dfrac{(x+\sqrt{3})(x-\sqrt{3})}{x+1}$ is zero when $x = \pm\sqrt{3}$ and undefined when $x = -1$.
When $x = 0$, $y = \dfrac{-3}{1} = -3 < 0$.
Since the factors are single, the signs alternate.
∴ sign diagram is:

```
  -   + ⋮ -   +
←—•———•———•——→ x
 -√3  -1  √3
```

n $y = \dfrac{x^2+1}{x}$ is never zero (since $x^2 + 1 > 0$ for all real x), and undefined when $x = 0$.
When $x = 1$, $y = \tfrac{2}{1} = 2 > 0$.
Since the factor is single, the sign alternates.
∴ sign diagram is:

```
  -  ⋮  +
←————•————→ x
     0
```

- $y = \dfrac{x^2 + 2x + 4}{x + 1}$ is never zero (since $x^2 + 2x + 4 > 0$ for all real x), and undefined when $x = -1$.
  When $x = 0$, $y = \frac{4}{1} = 4 > 0$.
  Since the factor is single, the sign alternates.
  $\therefore$ sign diagram is:

  $\xleftarrow{\quad - \quad | \quad + \quad}\rightarrow x$
  $\qquad\qquad -1$

p $y = \dfrac{-(x-3)^2(x^2+2)}{x+3}$ is zero when $x = 3$ and undefined when $x = -3$.
  When $x = 0$, $y = \dfrac{-(-3)^2(2)}{3} = -6 < 0$.
  Since the $(x-3)$ factor is squared, the sign does not change at $x = 3$.
  $\therefore$ sign diagram is:

  $\xleftarrow{\quad + \quad | \quad - \quad | \quad - \quad}\rightarrow x$
  $\qquad\qquad -3 \qquad\quad 3$

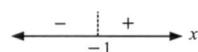

q $y = \dfrac{-x^2(x+2)}{5-x}$ is zero when $x = 0$ or -2 and undefined when $x = 5$.
  When $x = 1$, $y = \dfrac{-1^2(3)}{4} = -\frac{3}{4} < 0$.
  Since the x factor is squared, the sign does not change at $x = 0$.
  $\therefore$ sign diagram is:

  $\xleftarrow{\quad + \quad | \quad - \quad | \quad - \quad | \quad + \quad}\rightarrow x$
  $\qquad\quad -2 \quad 0 \qquad 5$

r $y = \dfrac{x^2+4}{(x-3)^2(x-1)}$ is never zero (since $x^2 + 4 > 0$ for all real x) and undefined when $x = 3$ or 1.
  When $x = 0$, $y = \dfrac{4}{(-3)^2(-1)} = -\frac{4}{9} < 0$.
  Since the $(x-3)$ factor is squared, the sign does not change at $x = 3$.
  $\therefore$ sign diagram is:

  $\xleftarrow{\quad - \quad | \quad + \quad | \quad + \quad}\rightarrow x$
  $\qquad\qquad 1 \qquad\quad 3$

s $y = \dfrac{x-5}{x+1} + 3\dfrac{(x+1)}{(x+1)}$
  $= \dfrac{x - 5 + 3x + 3}{x + 1}$
  $= \dfrac{4x - 2}{x + 1}$
  which is zero when $x = \frac{1}{2}$ and undefined when $x = -1$.
  When $x = 0$, $y = \frac{-2}{1} = -2 < 0$.
  Since the factors are single, the signs alternate.
  $\therefore$ sign diagram is:

  $\xleftarrow{\quad + \quad | \quad - \quad | \quad + \quad}\rightarrow x$
  $\qquad\quad -1 \qquad \frac{1}{2}$

t $y = \dfrac{x-2}{x+3} - 4\dfrac{(x+3)}{(x+3)}$
  $= \dfrac{x - 2 - 4x - 12}{x + 3}$
  $= \dfrac{-3x - 14}{x + 3}$
  which is zero when $x = -\frac{14}{3}$ and undefined when $x = -3$.
  When $x = 0$, $y = \frac{-14}{3} < 0$.
  Since the factors are single, the signs alternate.
  $\therefore$ sign diagram is:

  $\xleftarrow{\quad - \quad | \quad + \quad | \quad - \quad}\rightarrow x$
  $\qquad\quad -\frac{14}{3} \quad -3$

u $y = \dfrac{3x+2}{x-2} - \dfrac{x-3}{x+3}$
  $= \dfrac{(3x+2)(x+3) - (x-3)(x-2)}{(x-2)(x+3)}$
  $= \dfrac{3x^2 + 11x + 6 - (x^2 - 5x + 6)}{(x-2)(x+3)}$
  $= \dfrac{2x^2 + 16x}{(x-2)(x+3)}$
  $= \dfrac{2x(x+8)}{(x-2)(x+3)}$

  which is zero when $x = 0$ or -8 and undefined when $x = 2$ or -3.
  When $x = 1$, $y = \dfrac{2(1)(9)}{(-1)(4)} = -\frac{18}{4} < 0$.
  Since the factors are single, the signs alternate.
  $\therefore$ sign diagram is:

  $\xleftarrow{\quad + \quad | \quad - \quad | \quad + \quad | \quad - \quad | \quad + \quad}\rightarrow x$
  $\qquad -8 \quad -3 \quad 0 \qquad 2$

EXERCISE 1E

1 a Sign diagram of $(2-x)(x+3)$ is

  $\xleftarrow{\quad - \quad | \quad + \quad | \quad - \quad}\rightarrow x$
  $\qquad -3 \qquad 2$

  $\therefore$ $(2-x)(x+3) \geqslant 0$ when $x \in [-3, 2]$

b Sign diagram of $(x-1)^2$ is

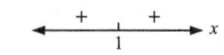

  $\xleftarrow{\quad + \quad | \quad + \quad}\rightarrow x$
  $\qquad\qquad 1$

  $\therefore$ $(x-1)^2 < 0$ is never true

c Sign diagram of $(2x+1)(3-x)$ is

$$\begin{array}{c|c|c|c} - & + & - \\ \hline & -\tfrac{1}{2} & & 3 & \end{array} \to x$$

$\therefore (2x+1)(3-x) > 0$ when $x \in \,]-\tfrac{1}{2}, 3[$

d $x^2 \geqslant x$
$\therefore x^2 - x \geqslant 0$
$\therefore x(x-1) \geqslant 0$
Sign diagram of LHS is

$$\begin{array}{c|c|c} + & - & + \\ \hline 0 & & 1 \end{array} \to x$$

$\therefore x \in \,]-\infty, 0]$ or $[1, \infty[$

e $x^2 \geqslant 3x$
$\therefore x^2 - 3x \geqslant 0$
$\therefore x(x-3) \geqslant 0$
Sign diagram of LHS is

$$\begin{array}{c|c|c} + & - & + \\ \hline 0 & & 3 \end{array} \to x$$

$\therefore$ LHS $\geqslant 0$ when $x \in \,]-\infty, 0]$ or $[3, \infty[$

f $3x^2 + 2x < 0$
$\therefore x(3x+2) < 0$
Sign diagram of LHS is

$$\begin{array}{c|c|c} + & - & + \\ \hline -\tfrac{2}{3} & & 0 \end{array} \to x$$

$\therefore$ LHS < 0 when $x \in \,]-\tfrac{2}{3}, 0[$

g $x^2 < 4$
$\therefore x^2 - 4 < 0$
$\therefore (x+2)(x-2) < 0$
Sign diagram of LHS is

$$\begin{array}{c|c|c} + & - & + \\ \hline -2 & & 2 \end{array} \to x$$

$\therefore$ LHS < 0 when $x \in \,]-2, 2[$

h $2x^2 \geqslant 4$
$\therefore 2x^2 - 4 \geqslant 0$
$\therefore 2(x+\sqrt{2})(x-\sqrt{2}) \geqslant 0$
Sign diagram of LHS is

$$\begin{array}{c|c|c} + & - & + \\ \hline -\sqrt{2} & & \sqrt{2} \end{array} \to x$$

$\therefore$ LHS $\geqslant 0$ when $x \in \,]-\infty, -\sqrt{2}]$ or $[\sqrt{2}, \infty[$

i $x^2 + 4x + 4 > 0$
$\therefore (x+2)^2 > 0$
Sign diagram of LHS is

$$\begin{array}{c|c} + & + \\ \hline & -2 \end{array} \to x$$

$\therefore$ LHS > 0 when $x \neq -2$

j $2x^2 \geqslant x + 3$
$\therefore 2x^2 - x - 3 \geqslant 0$
$\therefore (2x-3)(x+1) \geqslant 0$
Sign diagram of LHS is

$$\begin{array}{c|c|c} + & - & + \\ \hline -1 & & \tfrac{3}{2} \end{array} \to x$$

$\therefore$ LHS $\geqslant 0$ when $x \in \,]-\infty, -1]$ or $[\tfrac{3}{2}, \infty[$

k $4x^2 - 4x + 1 < 0$
$\therefore (2x-1)^2 < 0$
Sign diagram of LHS is

$$\begin{array}{c|c} + & + \\ \hline & \tfrac{1}{2} \end{array} \to x$$

$\therefore$ LHS < 0 is never true

l $6x^2 + 7x < 3$
$\therefore 6x^2 + 7x - 3 < 0$
$\therefore (3x-1)(2x+3) < 0$
Sign diagram of LHS is

$$\begin{array}{c|c|c} + & - & + \\ \hline -\tfrac{3}{2} & & \tfrac{1}{3} \end{array} \to x$$

$\therefore$ LHS < 0 when $x \in \,]-\tfrac{3}{2}, \tfrac{1}{3}[$

m $3x^2 > 8(x+2)$
$\therefore 3x^2 - 8x - 16 > 0$
$\therefore (3x+4)(x-4) > 0$
Sign diagram of LHS is

$$\begin{array}{c|c|c} + & - & + \\ \hline -\tfrac{4}{3} & & 4 \end{array} \to x$$

$\therefore$ LHS > 0 when $x \in \,]-\infty, -\tfrac{4}{3}[$ or $]4, \infty[$

n $2x^2 - 4x + 2 > 0$
$\therefore 2(x^2 - 2x + 1) > 0$
$\therefore 2(x-1)^2 > 0$
Sign diagram of LHS is

$$\begin{array}{c|c} + & + \\ \hline & 1 \end{array} \to x$$

$\therefore$ LHS > 0 when $x \neq 1$

o $\quad 6x^2 + 1 \leq 5x$
$\therefore \quad 6x^2 - 5x + 1 \leq 0$
$\therefore \quad (3x-1)(2x-1) \leq 0$
Sign diagram of LHS is

$$\begin{array}{c} + \quad - \quad + \\ \xleftarrow{} \underset{\frac{1}{3}}{|} \underset{\frac{1}{2}}{|} \xrightarrow{} x \end{array}$$

$\therefore$ LHS ≤ 0 when $x \in [\frac{1}{3}, \frac{1}{2}]$

p $\quad 1 + 5x < 6x^2$
$\therefore \quad -6x^2 + 5x + 1 < 0$
$\therefore \quad 6x^2 - 5x - 1 > 0$
$\therefore \quad (6x+1)(x-1) > 0$
Sign diagram of LHS is

$$\begin{array}{c} + \quad - \quad + \\ \xleftarrow{} \underset{-\frac{1}{6}}{|} \underset{1}{|} \xrightarrow{} x \end{array}$$

$\therefore$ LHS > 0 when $x \in \,]-\infty, -\frac{1}{6}[$
or $\,]1, \infty[$

q $\quad 12x^2 \geq 5x + 2$
$\therefore \quad 12x^2 - 5x - 2 \geq 0$
$\therefore \quad (3x-2)(4x+1) \geq 0$
Sign diagram of LHS is

$$\begin{array}{c} + \quad - \quad + \\ \xleftarrow{} \underset{-\frac{1}{4}}{|} \underset{\frac{2}{3}}{|} \xrightarrow{} x \end{array}$$

$\therefore$ LHS ≥ 0 when $x \in \,]-\infty, -\frac{1}{4}]$
or $[\frac{2}{3}, \infty[$

r $\quad 2x^2 + 9 > 9x$
$\therefore \quad 2x^2 - 9x + 9 > 0$
$\therefore \quad (2x-3)(x-3) > 0$
Sign diagram of LHS is

$$\begin{array}{c} + \quad - \quad + \\ \xleftarrow{} \underset{\frac{3}{2}}{|} \underset{3}{|} \xrightarrow{} x \end{array}$$

$\therefore$ LHS > 0 when $x \in \,]-\infty, \frac{3}{2}[$
or $\,]3, \infty[$

2 a $\dfrac{x+4}{2x-1} > 0$
Sign diagram of LHS is

$$\begin{array}{c} + \quad - \quad + \\ \xleftarrow{} \underset{-4}{|} \underset{\frac{1}{2}}{|} \xrightarrow{} x \end{array}$$

$\therefore$ LHS > 0 when $x \in \,]-\infty, -4[$
or $\,]\frac{1}{2}, \infty[$

b $\dfrac{x+1}{4-x} < 0$
Sign diagram of LHS is

$$\begin{array}{c} - \quad + \quad - \\ \xleftarrow{} \underset{-1}{|} \underset{4}{|} \xrightarrow{} x \end{array}$$

$\therefore$ LHS < 0 when $x \in \,]-\infty, -1[$
or $\,]4, \infty[$

c $\dfrac{x+3}{2x+3} \geq 0$
Sign diagram of LHS is

$$\begin{array}{c} + \quad - \quad + \\ \xleftarrow{} \underset{-3}{|} \underset{-\frac{3}{2}}{|} \xrightarrow{} x \end{array}$$

$\therefore$ LHS ≥ 0 when $x \in \,]-\infty, -3]$
or $\,]-\frac{3}{2}, \infty[$

d $\quad \dfrac{2x}{x-3} \geq 1$
$\therefore \quad \dfrac{2x}{x-3} - \dfrac{x-3}{x-3} \geq 0$
$\therefore \quad \dfrac{x+3}{x-3} \geq 0$
Sign diagram of LHS is

$$\begin{array}{c} + \quad - \quad + \\ \xleftarrow{} \underset{-3}{|} \underset{3}{|} \xrightarrow{} x \end{array}$$

$\therefore$ LHS ≥ 0 when $x \in \,]-\infty, -3]$
or $\,]3, \infty[$

e $\quad \dfrac{x+2}{x-1} \geq -3$
$\therefore \quad \dfrac{x+2}{x-1} + \dfrac{3(x-1)}{x-1} \geq 0$
$\quad \dfrac{4x-1}{x-1} \geq 0$
Sign diagram of LHS is

$$\begin{array}{c} + \quad - \quad + \\ \xleftarrow{} \underset{\frac{1}{4}}{|} \underset{1}{|} \xrightarrow{} x \end{array}$$

$\therefore$ LHS ≥ 0 when $x \in \,]-\infty, \frac{1}{4}]$
or $\,]1, \infty[$

f $\quad \dfrac{x+2}{2x-1} < \frac{1}{2}$
$\therefore \quad \dfrac{x+2}{2x-1} - \frac{1}{2} < 0$
$\therefore \quad \dfrac{2(x+2) - 1(2x-1)}{2(2x-1)} < 0$
$\therefore \quad \dfrac{5}{2(2x-1)} < 0$
Sign diagram of LHS is

$$\begin{array}{c} - \quad + \\ \xleftarrow{} \underset{\frac{1}{2}}{|} \xrightarrow{} x \end{array}$$

$\therefore$ LHS < 0 when $x \in \,]-\infty, \frac{1}{2}[$

g $\dfrac{1}{x} > 100$

$\therefore \dfrac{1}{x} - 100 > 0$

$\therefore \dfrac{1 - 100x}{x} > 0$

Sign diagram of LHS is

```
  − │ +    −
◄───┼───┬──────► x
    0  1/100
```

$\therefore$ LHS > 0 when $x \in \,]0, \tfrac{1}{100}[$

h $\dfrac{x}{2x - 1} \geqslant 5$

$\therefore \dfrac{x}{2x - 1} - \dfrac{5(2x - 1)}{2x - 1} \geqslant 0$

$\therefore \dfrac{-9x + 5}{2x - 1} \geqslant 0$

Sign diagram of LHS is

```
  − │ +    −
◄───┼────┬────► x
   1/2  5/9
```

$\therefore$ LHS $\geqslant 0$ when $x \in \,]\tfrac{1}{2}, \tfrac{5}{9}]$

i $\dfrac{1 - x}{1 + x} < 4$

$\therefore \dfrac{1 - x}{1 + x} - \dfrac{4(1 + x)}{1 + x} < 0$

$\therefore \dfrac{-5x - 3}{1 + x} < 0$

Sign diagram of LHS is

```
   −  │  +    −
◄─────┼─────┬────► x
     −1   −3/5
```

$\therefore$ LHS < 0 when $x \in \,]-\infty, -1[$
or $\,]-\tfrac{3}{5}, \infty[$

j $\dfrac{2}{2x - 5} < \dfrac{1}{x + 7}$

$\therefore \dfrac{2}{2x - 5} - \dfrac{1}{x + 7} < 0$

$\therefore \dfrac{2(x + 7) - 1(2x - 5)}{(2x - 5)(x + 7)} < 0$

$\therefore \dfrac{19}{(2x - 5)(x + 7)} < 0$

Sign diagram of LHS is

```
  +  │  −  │  +
◄────┬─────┬────► x
    −7    5/2
```

$\therefore$ LHS < 0 when $x \in \,]-7, \tfrac{5}{2}[$

k $\dfrac{x^2 - 2x}{x + 3} > 0$

$\therefore \dfrac{x(x - 2)}{x + 3} > 0$

Sign diagram of LHS is

```
  − │ +   −   +
◄───┼─────┬───┬──► x
   −3    0   2
```

$\therefore$ LHS > 0 when $x \in \,]-3, 0[$
or $\,]2, \infty[$

l $\dfrac{x^2 + 5x}{x^2 - 4} \leqslant 0$

$\therefore \dfrac{x(x + 5)}{(x + 2)(x - 2)} \leqslant 0$

Sign diagram of LHS is

```
  +  │ −  │ +  │ −  │ +
◄────┬────┬────┬────┬──► x
    −5   −2   0    2
```

$\therefore$ LHS $\leqslant 0$ when $x \in [-5, -2[$
or $[0, 2[$

m $\dfrac{x}{x + 2} > \dfrac{1}{x}$

$\therefore \dfrac{x}{x + 2} - \dfrac{1}{x} > 0$

$\therefore \dfrac{x^2 - (x + 2)}{x(x + 2)} > 0$

$\therefore \dfrac{x^2 - x - 2}{x(x + 2)} > 0$

$\therefore \dfrac{(x + 1)(x - 2)}{x(x + 2)} > 0$

Sign diagram of LHS is

```
  +  │ −  │ +  │ −  │ +
◄────┬────┬────┬────┬──► x
    −2   −1   0    2
```

$\therefore$ LHS > 0 when $x \in \,]-\infty, -2[$
or $\,]-1, 0[$ or $\,]2, \infty[$

n $x > \dfrac{4}{x}$

$\therefore x - \dfrac{4}{x} > 0$

$\therefore \dfrac{x^2 - 4}{x} > 0$

$\therefore \dfrac{(x + 2)(x - 2)}{x} > 0$

Sign diagram of LHS is

```
  − │ +   −   +
◄───┬─────┬───┬──► x
   −2    0   2
```

$\therefore$ LHS > 0 when $x \in \,]-2, 0[$
or $\,]2, \infty[$

o $\dfrac{1}{x} \leqslant x$

$\therefore \ \dfrac{1}{x} - x \leqslant 0$

$\therefore \ \dfrac{1-x^2}{x} \leqslant 0$

$\therefore \ \dfrac{(1-x)(1+x)}{x} \leqslant 0$

Sign diagram of LHS is

```
  +  |  -  |  +  |  -
----- --- ----- ------→ x
    -1   0   1
```

$\therefore$ LHS $\leqslant 0$ when $x \in [-1, 0[$ or $[1, \infty[$

q $\dfrac{2x-3}{x+2} < \dfrac{2x}{x-2}$

$\therefore \ \dfrac{2x-3}{x+2} - \dfrac{2x}{x-2} < 0$

$\therefore \ \dfrac{(2x-3)(x-2) - 2x(x+2)}{(x+2)(x-2)} < 0$

$\therefore \ \dfrac{2x^2 - 7x + 6 - 2x^2 - 4x}{(x+2)(x-2)} < 0$

$\therefore \ \dfrac{6 - 11x}{(x+2)(x-2)} < 0$

Sign diagram of LHS is

```
  +  |  -  |  +  |  -
----- --- ----- ------→ x
   -2   6/11  2
```

$\therefore$ LHS < 0 when $x \in\,]-2, \tfrac{6}{11}[$ or $]2, \infty[$

p $x^3 \geqslant x$

$\therefore \ x^3 - x \geqslant 0$

$\therefore \ x(x^2 - 1) \geqslant 0$

$\therefore \ x(x+1)(x-1) \geqslant 0$

Sign diagram of LHS is

```
  -  |  +  |  -  |  +
----- --- ----- ------→ x
   -1   0   1
```

$\therefore$ LHS $\geqslant 0$ when $x \in [-1, 0]$ or $[1, \infty[$

r $\dfrac{x^2}{3x-2} \leqslant 1$

$\therefore \ \dfrac{x^2}{3x-2} - \dfrac{3x-2}{3x-2} \leqslant 0$

$\therefore \ \dfrac{x^2 - 3x + 2}{3x-2} \leqslant 0$

$\therefore \ \dfrac{(x-1)(x-2)}{3x-2} \leqslant 0$

Sign diagram of LHS is

```
  -  |  +  |  -  |  +
----- --- ----- ------→ x
   2/3   1   2
```

$\therefore$ LHS $\leqslant 0$ when $x \in\,]-\infty, \tfrac{2}{3}[$ or $[1, 2]$

EXERCISE 1F.1

1 a $|a| = |-2|$
       $= 2$

b $|b| = |3|$
       $= 3$

c $|a|\,|b| = |-2|\,|3|$
       $= 2 \times 3$
       $= 6$

d $|ab| = |-2 \times 3|$
       $= |-6|$
       $= 6$

e $|a - b| = |-2 - 3|$
       $= |-5|$
       $= 5$

f $|a| - |b| = |-2| - |3|$
       $= 2 - 3$
       $= -1$

g $|a + b| = |-2 + 3|$
       $= |1|$
       $= 1$

h $|a| + |b| = |-2| + |3|$
       $= 2 + 3$
       $= 5$

i $|a|^2 = |-2|^2$
       $= 2^2$
       $= 4$

j $a^2 = (-2)^2$
       $= 4$

k $\left|\dfrac{c}{a}\right| = \left|\dfrac{-4}{-2}\right|$
       $= |2|$
       $= 2$

l $\dfrac{|c|}{|a|} = \dfrac{|-4|}{|-2|}$
       $= \dfrac{4}{2}$
       $= 2$

2 a $|5 - x| = |5 - (-3)|$
       $= |8|$
       $= 8$

b $|5| - |x| = |5| - |-3|$
       $= 5 - 3$
       $= 2$

c $\left|\dfrac{2x+1}{1-x}\right| = \left|\dfrac{2(-3)+1}{1-(-3)}\right|$
       $= \left|\dfrac{-5}{4}\right|$
       $= \dfrac{5}{4}$

d $|3 - 2x - x^2| = |3 - 2(-3) - (-3)^2|$
       $= |0|$
       $= 0$

3 **a** No (compare questions **1g** and **1h**)   **b** No (compare questions **1e** and **1f**)

4

a	b	$\|ab\|$	$\|a\|\,\|b\|$	$\left\|\dfrac{a}{b}\right\|$	$\dfrac{\|a\|}{\|b\|}$
6	2	12	12	3	3
6	-2	12	12	3	3
-6	2	12	12	3	3
-6	-2	12	12	3	3

5 **a** $|ab| = \sqrt{(ab)^2}$
$= \sqrt{a^2 b^2}$
$= \sqrt{a^2}\sqrt{b^2}$
$= |a|\,|b|$

b $\left|\dfrac{a}{b}\right| = \sqrt{\left(\dfrac{a}{b}\right)^2}$
$= \sqrt{\dfrac{a^2}{b^2}}$
$= \dfrac{\sqrt{a^2}}{\sqrt{b^2}}$
$= \dfrac{|a|}{|b|}$

c $|a - b| = \sqrt{(a-b)^2}$
$= \sqrt{(b-a)^2}$
$= |b - a|$

6 **a** $y = |x - 2|$
When $x \geqslant 2$, $x - 2 \geqslant 0$,
so $y = x - 2$
When $x < 2$, $x - 2 < 0$,
so $y = -(x - 2)$
$= 2 - x$
$\therefore\ y = \begin{cases} x - 2 & \text{when } x \geqslant 2 \\ 2 - x & \text{when } x < 2 \end{cases}$

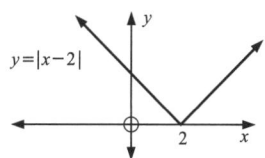

b $y = |x + 1|$
When $x \geqslant -1$, $x + 1 \geqslant 0$,
so $y = x + 1$
When $x < -1$, $x + 1 < 0$,
so $y = -(x + 1)$
$= -x - 1$
$\therefore\ y = \begin{cases} x + 1 & \text{when } x \geqslant -1 \\ -x - 1 & \text{when } x < -1 \end{cases}$

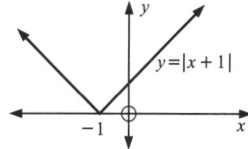

c $y = -|x|$
When $x \geqslant 0$, $y = -x$
When $x < 0$, $y = -(-x)$
$= x$
$\therefore\ y = \begin{cases} -x & \text{when } x \geqslant 0 \\ x & \text{when } x < 0 \end{cases}$

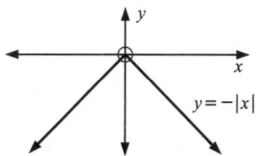

d $y = |x| + x$
When $x \geqslant 0$, $y = x + x$
$= 2x$
When $x < 0$, $y = -x + x$
$= 0$
$\therefore\ y = \begin{cases} 2x & \text{when } x \geqslant 0 \\ 0 & \text{when } x < 0 \end{cases}$

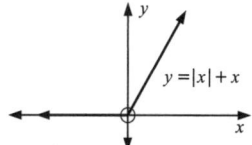

e $y = \dfrac{|x|}{x}$

When $x > 0$, $y = \dfrac{x}{x} = 1$

When $x < 0$, $y = \dfrac{-x}{x} = -1$

When $x = 0$, y is undefined

$\therefore\ y = \begin{cases} 1 & \text{when } x > 0 \\ \text{undefined} & \text{when } x = 0 \\ -1 & \text{when } x < 0 \end{cases}$

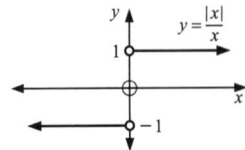

f $y = x - 2|x|$

When $x \geqslant 0$, $y = x - 2x$
$ = -x$

When $x < 0$, $y = x - 2(-x)$
$\phantom{When x < 0, y} = 3x$

$\therefore\ y = \begin{cases} -x & \text{when } x \geqslant 0 \\ 3x & \text{when } x < 0 \end{cases}$

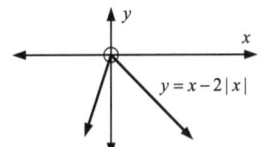

g $y = |x| + |x - 2|$

When $x \geqslant 2$, $x - 2 \geqslant 0$ and $x \geqslant 0$
$\therefore\ y = x + (x - 2)$
$ = 2x - 2$

When $0 \leqslant x < 2$, $x \geqslant 0$ and $x - 2 < 0$
$\therefore\ y = x - (x - 2)$
$ = 2$

When $x < 0$, $x - 2 < 0$
$\therefore\ y = -x - (x - 2)$
$ = 2 - 2x$

$\therefore\ y = \begin{cases} 2x - 2 & \text{when } x \geqslant 2 \\ 2 & \text{when } 0 \leqslant x < 2 \\ 2 - 2x & \text{when } x < 0 \end{cases}$

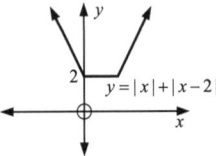

h $y = |x| - |x - 1|$

When $x \geqslant 1$, $x - 1 \geqslant 0$ and $x \geqslant 0$
$\therefore\ y = x - (x - 1)$
$ = 1$

When $0 \leqslant x < 1$, $x \geqslant 0$ and $x - 1 < 0$
$\therefore\ y = x + (x - 1)$
$ = 2x - 1$

When $x < 0$, $x - 1 < 0$
$\therefore\ y = -x + (x - 1)$
$ = -1$

$\therefore\ y = \begin{cases} 1 & \text{when } x \geqslant 1 \\ 2x - 1 & \text{when } 0 \leqslant x < 1 \\ -1 & \text{when } x < 0 \end{cases}$

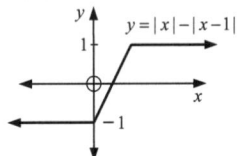

i $y = |x^2 + 1|$

$x^2 + 1 > 0$ for all real x

$\therefore\ y = x^2 + 1$ for all x

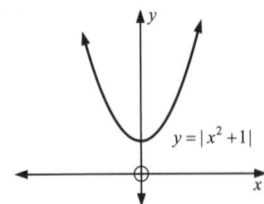

j $y = |x^2 - 1| = |(x + 1)(x - 1)|$

$\therefore\ x^2 - 1$ has sign diagram

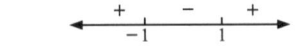

When $x \leqslant -1$ or $\geqslant 1$, $x^2 - 1 \geqslant 0$
$\therefore\ y = x^2 - 1$

When $-1 < x < 1$, $x^2 - 1 < 0$
$\therefore\ y = -(x^2 - 1)$
$ = 1 - x^2$

$\therefore\ y = \begin{cases} x^2 - 1 & \text{when } x \geqslant 1,\ x \leqslant -1 \\ 1 - x^2 & \text{when } -1 < x < 1 \end{cases}$

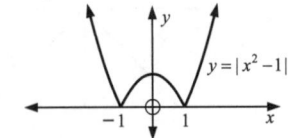

k $y = |x^2 - 2x| = |x(x-2)|$
∴ $x^2 - 2x$ has sign diagram

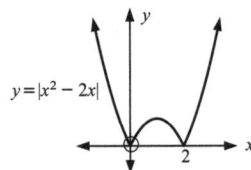

When $x \leqslant 0$ or $\geqslant 2$, $x^2 - 2x \geqslant 0$
∴ $y = x^2 - 2x$
When $0 < x < 2$, $x^2 - 2x < 0$
∴ $y = -(x^2 - 2x)$
$= 2x - x^2$

∴ $y = \begin{cases} x^2 - 2x & \text{when } x \geqslant 2,\ x \leqslant 0 \\ 2x - x^2 & \text{when } 0 < x < 2 \end{cases}$

$y = |x^2 - 2x|$

l $y = |x^2 + 3x + 2| = |(x+2)(x+1)|$
∴ $x^2 + 3x + 2$ has sign diagram

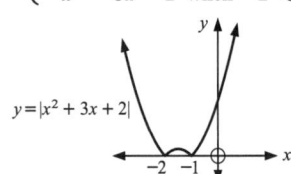

When $x \leqslant -2$ or $x \geqslant -1$,
$x^2 + 3x + 2 \geqslant 0$
∴ $y = x^2 + 3x + 2$
When $-2 < x < -1$, $x^2 + 3x + 2 < 0$
∴ $y = -(x^2 + 3x + 2)$
$= -x^2 - 3x - 2$

∴ $y = \begin{cases} x^2 + 3x + 2 & \text{when } x \geqslant -1,\ x \leqslant -2 \\ -x^2 - 3x - 2 & \text{when } -2 < x < -1 \end{cases}$

$y = |x^2 + 3x + 2|$

EXERCISE 1F.2

1 a $|x| = 3$
∴ $x = \pm 3$

b $|x| = -5$ has no solution as $|x|$ is never negative.

c $|x| = 0$
∴ $x = 0$

d $|x-1| = 3$
∴ $x - 1 = \pm 3$
∴ $x = 1 + 3$ or $1 - 3$
∴ $x = 4$ or -2

e $|3 - x| = 4$
∴ $3 - x = \pm 4$
∴ $x - 3 = \pm 4$
∴ $x = 3 + 4$ or $3 - 4$
∴ $x = 7$ or -1

f $|x + 5| = -1$ has no solution as $|x + 5|$ is never negative.

g $|3x - 2| = 1$
∴ $3x - 2 = \pm 1$
∴ $3x = 2 + 1$ or $2 - 1$
∴ $3x = 3$ or 1
∴ $x = 1$ or $\frac{1}{3}$

h $|3 - 2x| = 3$
∴ $3 - 2x = \pm 3$
∴ $-2x = -3 + 3$
  or $-3 - 3$
∴ $-2x = 0$ or -6
∴ $x = 0$ or 3

i $|2 - 5x| = 12$
∴ $2 - 5x = \pm 12$
∴ $-5x = -2 + 12$
  or $-2 - 12$
∴ $-5x = 10$ or -14
∴ $x = -2$ or $\frac{14}{5}$

2 a $\left|\dfrac{x}{x-1}\right| = 3$
∴ $\dfrac{x}{x-1} = \pm 3$
If $\dfrac{x}{x-1} = 3$
then $x = 3x - 3$
∴ $-2x = -3$
∴ $x = \frac{3}{2}$
If $\dfrac{x}{x-1} = -3$
then $x = -3x + 3$
∴ $4x = 3$
∴ $x = \frac{3}{4}$
So, $x = \frac{3}{2}$ or $\frac{3}{4}$

b $\left|\dfrac{2x-1}{x+1}\right| = 5$
∴ $\dfrac{2x-1}{x+1} = \pm 5$
If $\dfrac{2x-1}{x+1} = 5$
then $2x - 1 = 5x + 5$
∴ $-3x = 6$
∴ $x = -2$
If $\dfrac{2x-1}{x+1} = -5$
then $2x - 1 = -5x - 5$
∴ $7x = -4$
∴ $x = -\frac{4}{7}$
So, $x = -2$ or $-\frac{4}{7}$

c $\left|\dfrac{x+3}{1-3x}\right| = \frac{1}{2}$
∴ $\dfrac{x+3}{1-3x} = \pm\frac{1}{2}$
If $\dfrac{x+3}{1-3x} = \frac{1}{2}$
then $2(x + 3) = 1 - 3x$
∴ $5x = -5$
∴ $x = -1$
If $\dfrac{x+3}{1-3x} = -\frac{1}{2}$
then $2(x + 3) = -(1 - 3x)$
∴ $-x = -7$
∴ $x = 7$
So, $x = -1$ or 7

3 a $|x+1| = |2-x|$
$\therefore x+1 = \pm(2-x)$
If $x+1 = 2-x$
then $2x = 1$
$\therefore x = \frac{1}{2}$
If $x+1 = -(2-x)$
then $x+1 = -2+x$
$\therefore 1 = -2$
which is false.
So, $x = \frac{1}{2}$ is the only solution.

b $|x| = |5-x|$
$\therefore x = \pm(5-x)$
If $x = 5-x$
then $2x = 5$
$\therefore x = \frac{5}{2}$
If $x = -(5-x)$
then $x = -5+x$
$\therefore 0 = -5$
which is false.
So, $x = \frac{5}{2}$ is the only solution.

c $|3x-1| = |x+2|$
$\therefore 3x-1 = \pm(x+2)$
If $3x-1 = x+2$
then $2x = 3$
$\therefore x = \frac{3}{2}$
If $3x-1 = -x-2$
$\therefore 4x = -1$
$\therefore x = -\frac{1}{4}$
So, $x = \frac{3}{2}$ or $-\frac{1}{4}$

d $|2x+5| = |1-x|$
$\therefore 2x+5 = \pm(1-x)$
If $2x+5 = 1-x$
then $3x = -4$
$\therefore x = -\frac{4}{3}$
If $2x+5 = -(1-x)$
then $2x+5 = -1+x$
$\therefore x = -6$
So, $x = -\frac{4}{3}$ or -6

e $|1-4x| = 2|x-1|$
$\therefore 1-4x = \pm 2(x-1)$
If $1-4x = 2(x-1)$
then $1-4x = 2x-2$
$\therefore -6x = -3$
$\therefore x = \frac{1}{2}$
If $1-4x = -2(x-1)$
then $1-4x = -2x+2$
$\therefore -2x = 1$
$\therefore x = -\frac{1}{2}$
So, $x = \pm\frac{1}{2}$

f $|3x+2| = 2|2-x|$
$\therefore 3x+2 = \pm 2(2-x)$
If $3x+2 = 2(2-x)$
then $3x+2 = 4-2x$
$\therefore 5x = 2$
$\therefore x = \frac{2}{5}$
If $3x+2 = -2(2-x)$
then $3x+2 = -4+2x$
$\therefore x = -6$
So, $x = \frac{2}{5}$ or -6

4 a i

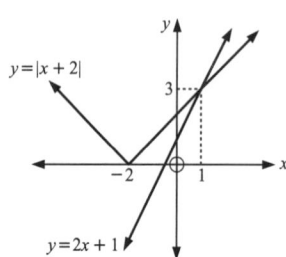

The lines $y = |x+2|$ and $y = 2x+1$ intersect at $(1, 3)$.
$\therefore$ the solution is $x = 1$.

ii $|x+2| = 2x+1$
$\therefore x+2 = \pm(2x+1)$
If $x+2 = 2x+1$
then $-x = -1$
$\therefore x = 1$
If $x+2 = -(2x+1)$
then $x+2 = -2x-1$
$\therefore 3x = -3$
$\therefore x = -1$
However, $x = -1$ is not a valid solution, because when $x = -1$, $2x+1 < 0$, and $|x+2|$ is never negative.
$\therefore x = 1$ is the only solution.

b i

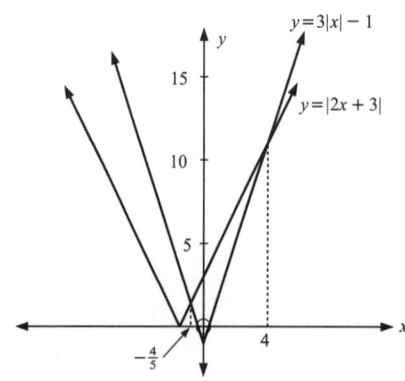

The lines $y = |2x+3|$ and $y = 3|x|-1$ intersect at $(-\frac{4}{5}, \frac{7}{5})$ and $(4, 11)$.
$\therefore$ the solution is $x = -\frac{4}{5}$ or 4

ii Let $y_1 = |2x+3|$, $y_2 = 3|x| - 1$
When $x < -\frac{3}{2}$, $y_1 = -(2x+3)$
and $y_2 = 3(-x) - 1$
$\therefore -(2x+3) = 3(-x) - 1$
$\therefore -2x - 3 = -3x - 1$
$\therefore x = 2$

This is not in the domain $x < -\frac{3}{2}$, so is not a valid solution.

When $-\frac{3}{2} \leqslant x < 0$, $y_1 = 2x + 3$
and $y_2 = 3(-x) - 1$
$\therefore 2x + 3 = 3(-x) - 1$
$\therefore 2x + 3 = -3x - 1$
$\therefore 5x = -4$
$\therefore x = -\frac{4}{5}$

When $x \geqslant 0$, $y_1 = 2x + 3$
and $y_2 = 3x - 1$
$\therefore 2x + 3 = 3x - 1$
$\therefore -x = -4$
$\therefore x = 4$

So, the solution is $x = -\frac{4}{5}$ or 4

c i

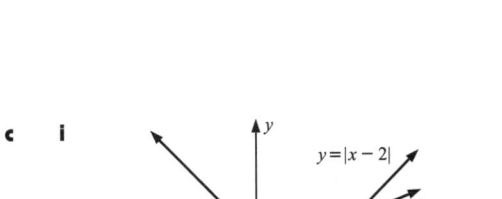

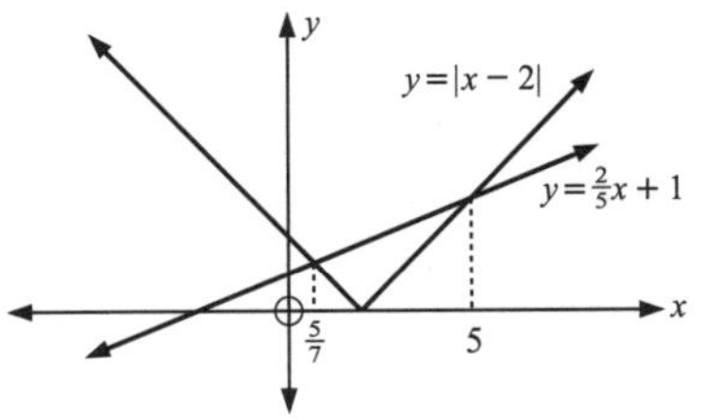

The lines $y = |x - 2|$ and $y = \frac{2}{5}x + 1$ intersect at $(\frac{5}{7}, \frac{9}{7})$ and $(5, 3)$.
$\therefore$ the solution is $x = \frac{5}{7}$ or 5

ii $|x - 2| = \frac{2}{5}x + 1$
$\therefore x - 2 = \pm(\frac{2}{5}x + 1)$
If $x - 2 = \frac{2}{5}x + 1$
then $\frac{3}{5}x = 3$
$\therefore x = 5$
If $x - 2 = -(\frac{2}{5}x + 1)$
then $x - 2 = -\frac{2}{5}x - 1$
$\therefore \frac{7}{5}x = 1$
$\therefore x = \frac{5}{7}$
So, the solution is $x = \frac{5}{7}$ or 5

EXERCISE 1F.3

1 a $|x| < 4$
$\therefore -4 < x < 4$
$\therefore x \in \,]-4, 4[$

b $|x| \geqslant 3$
$\therefore x \leqslant -3$ or $x \geqslant 3$
$\therefore x \in \,]-\infty, -3]$ or $[3, \infty[$

c $|x + 3| \leqslant 1$
$\therefore -1 \leqslant x + 3 \leqslant 1$
$\therefore -4 \leqslant x \leqslant -2$
$\therefore x \in [-4, -2]$

d $|x + 4| \geqslant 2$
$\therefore x + 4 \leqslant -2$ or $x + 4 \geqslant 2$
$\therefore x \leqslant -6$ or $x \geqslant -2$
$\therefore x \in \,]-\infty, -6]$ or $[-2, \infty[$

e $|2x - 1| < 3$
$\therefore -3 < 2x - 1 < 3$
$\therefore -2 < 2x < 4$
$\therefore -1 < x < 2$
$\therefore x \in \,]-1, 2[$

f $|3 - 4x| > 2$
$\therefore |4x - 3| > 2$
$\therefore 4x - 3 < -2$ or $4x - 3 > 2$
$\therefore 4x < 1$ $\qquad \therefore 4x > 5$
$\therefore x < \frac{1}{4}$ $\qquad \therefore x > \frac{5}{4}$
$\therefore x \in \,]-\infty, \frac{1}{4}[$ or $]\frac{5}{4}, \infty[$

g $|2x + 1| < 4$
$\therefore -4 < 2x + 1 < 4$
$\therefore -5 < 2x < 3$
$\therefore -\frac{5}{2} < x < \frac{3}{2}$
$\therefore x \in \,]-\frac{5}{2}, \frac{3}{2}[$

h $2 \geqslant |x - 1|$
$\therefore |x - 1| \leqslant 2$
$\therefore -2 \leqslant x - 1 \leqslant 2$
$\therefore -1 \leqslant x \leqslant 3$
$\therefore x \in [-1, 3]$

i $|3 - 7x| < 4$
$\therefore |7x - 3| < 4$
$\therefore -4 < 7x - 3 < 4$
$\therefore -1 < 7x < 7$
$\therefore -\frac{1}{7} < x < 1$
$\therefore x \in \,]-\frac{1}{7}, 1[$

j $|2 - 7x| \geqslant 5$
$\therefore |7x - 2| \geqslant 5$
$\therefore 7x - 2 \leqslant -5$ or $7x - 2 \geqslant 5$
$\therefore 7x \leqslant -3$ $\qquad \therefore 7x \geqslant 7$
$\therefore x \leqslant -\frac{3}{7}$ $\qquad \therefore x \geqslant 1$
$\therefore x \in \,]-\infty, -\frac{3}{7}]$ or $[1, \infty[$

k $\quad |5 - 3x| \leqslant 1$
$\therefore \quad |3x - 5| \leqslant 1$
$\therefore \quad -1 \leqslant 3x - 5 \leqslant 1$
$\therefore \quad 4 \leqslant 3x \leqslant 6$
$\therefore \quad \frac{4}{3} \leqslant x \leqslant 2$
$\therefore \quad x \in [\frac{4}{3}, 2]$

l $\quad 5 \geqslant |3 - x|$
$\therefore \quad |x - 3| \leqslant 5$
$\therefore \quad -5 \leqslant x - 3 \leqslant 5$
$\therefore \quad -2 \leqslant x \leqslant 8$
$\therefore \quad x \in [-2, 8]$

2 a $\quad |x - 3| \leqslant 4$
$\therefore \quad (x - 3)^2 \leqslant 4^2$
$\therefore \quad (x - 3)^2 - 4^2 \leqslant 0$
$\therefore \quad (x - 3 + 4)(x - 3 - 4) \leqslant 0$
$\therefore \quad (x + 1)(x - 7) \leqslant 0$

$\xrightarrow[\;-1\;\;\;\;\;\;\;\;\;7\;]{+\;\;\;|\;-\;|\;+} x$

So, $-1 \leqslant x \leqslant 7$ or $x \in [-1, 7]$

b $\quad |2x - 1| \leqslant 3$
$\therefore \quad (2x - 1)^2 \leqslant 3^2$
$\therefore \quad (2x - 1)^2 - 3^2 \leqslant 0$
$\therefore \quad (2x - 1 + 3)(2x - 1 - 3) \leqslant 0$
$\therefore \quad (2x + 2)(2x - 4) \leqslant 0$

$\xrightarrow[\;-1\;\;\;\;\;\;\;\;\;2\;]{+\;\;\;|\;-\;|\;+} x$

So, $-1 \leqslant x \leqslant 2$ or $x \in [-1, 2]$

c $\quad |3x + 1| > 2$
$\therefore \quad (3x + 1)^2 > 2^2$
$\therefore \quad (3x + 1)^2 - 2^2 > 0$
$\therefore \quad (3x + 1 + 2)(3x + 1 - 2) > 0$
$\therefore \quad (3x + 3)(3x - 1) > 0$

$\xrightarrow[\;-1\;\;\;\;\;\;\;\;\;\frac{1}{3}\;]{+\;\;\;|\;-\;|\;+} x$

$\therefore \quad x < -1$ or $x > \frac{1}{3}$
So, $x \in \;]-\infty, -1[\;$ or $\;]\frac{1}{3}, \infty[$

d $\quad |5 - 2x| \geqslant 7$
$\therefore \quad (5 - 2x)^2 \geqslant 7^2$
$\therefore \quad (5 - 2x)^2 - 7^2 \geqslant 0$
$\therefore \quad (5 - 2x + 7)(5 - 2x - 7) \geqslant 0$
$\therefore \quad (-2x + 12)(-2x - 2) \geqslant 0$

$\xrightarrow[\;-1\;\;\;\;\;\;\;\;\;6\;]{+\;\;\;|\;-\;|\;+} x$

$\therefore \quad x \leqslant -1$ or $x \geqslant 6$
So, $x \in \;]-\infty, -1]\;$ or $[6, \infty[$

e $\quad |x| \geqslant |2 - x|$
$\therefore \quad x^2 \geqslant (2 - x)^2$
$\therefore \quad x^2 - (2 - x)^2 \geqslant 0$
$\therefore \quad [x + (2 - x)][x - (2 - x)] \geqslant 0$
$\therefore \quad 2(2x - 2) \geqslant 0$

$\xrightarrow[\;\;\;\;\;\;\;1\;\;\;\;\;\;\;]{-\;\;\;|\;+} x$

$\therefore \quad x \geqslant 1$
So, $x \in [1, \infty[$

f $\quad 3|x| \leqslant |1 - 2x|$
$\therefore \quad 9x^2 \leqslant (1 - 2x)^2$
$\therefore \quad 9x^2 - (1 - 2x)^2 \leqslant 0$
$\therefore \quad [3x + (1 - 2x)][3x - (1 - 2x)] \leqslant 0$
$\therefore \quad (x + 1)(5x - 1) \leqslant 0$

$\xrightarrow[\;-1\;\;\;\;\;\;\;\;\;\frac{1}{5}\;]{+\;\;\;|\;-\;|\;+} x$

$\therefore \quad -1 \leqslant x \leqslant \frac{1}{5}$
So, $x \in [-1, \frac{1}{5}]$

g $\quad \left|\dfrac{x}{x-2}\right| \geqslant 3$
$\therefore \quad \left(\dfrac{x}{x-2}\right)^2 \geqslant 3^2$
$\therefore \quad \left(\dfrac{x}{x-2}\right)^2 - 3^2 \geqslant 0$
$\therefore \quad \left(\dfrac{x}{x-2} + 3\right)\left(\dfrac{x}{x-2} - 3\right) \geqslant 0$
$\therefore \quad \left(\dfrac{x + 3x - 6}{x - 2}\right)\left(\dfrac{x - 3x + 6}{x - 2}\right) \geqslant 0$
$\therefore \quad \dfrac{(4x - 6)(-2x + 6)}{(x - 2)^2} \geqslant 0$

$\xrightarrow[\;\;\;\frac{3}{2}\;\;\;\;\;\;2\;\;\;\;\;\;3\;\;]{-\;\;|\;+\;\;|\;+\;\;|\;-} x$

$\therefore \quad x \in [\frac{3}{2}, 3]$ but $x \neq 2$

h $\quad \left|\dfrac{2x + 3}{x - 1}\right| \geqslant 2$
$\therefore \quad \left(\dfrac{2x + 3}{x - 1}\right)^2 \geqslant 2^2$
$\therefore \quad \left(\dfrac{2x + 3}{x - 1}\right)^2 - 2^2 \geqslant 0$
$\therefore \quad \left(\dfrac{2x + 3}{x - 1} + 2\right)\left(\dfrac{2x + 3}{x - 1} - 2\right) \geqslant 0$
$\therefore \quad \left(\dfrac{2x + 3 + 2x - 2}{x - 1}\right)\left(\dfrac{2x + 3 - 2x + 2}{x - 1}\right) \geqslant 0$
$\therefore \quad \dfrac{(4x + 1)(5)}{(x - 1)^2} \geqslant 0$

$\xrightarrow[\;\;-\frac{1}{4}\;\;\;\;\;\;1\;\;\;\;\;]{-\;\;|\;+\;\;|\;+} x$

$\therefore \quad x \in [-\frac{1}{4}, \infty[$ but $x \neq 1$

3 a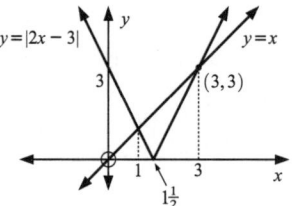

$|2x - 3| < x$ when the modulus graph is below the line.
∴ $1 < x < 3$
∴ $x \in \;]1, 3[$

b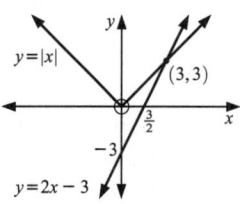

$2x - 3 < |x|$ when the line is below the modulus graph
∴ $x < 3$
∴ $x \in \;]-\infty, 3\,[$

c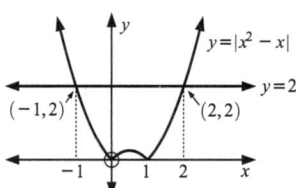

$|x^2 - x| > 2$ when the modulus graph is above the line.
∴ $x < -1$ or $x > 2$
∴ $x \in \;]-\infty, -1\,[\;$ or $\;]\,2, \infty\,[$

d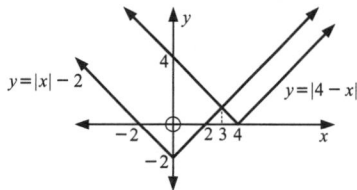

$|x| - 2 \geqslant |4 - x|$ when the graph of $y = |x| - 2$ is above or on the graph of $y = |4 - x|$.
∴ $x \geqslant 3$
∴ $x \in [\,3, \infty\,[$

4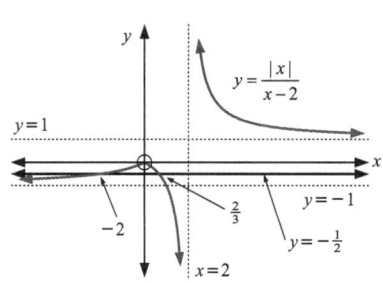

If $\dfrac{|x|}{x - 2} \geqslant -\dfrac{1}{2}$ then the graph of $y = f(x)$ is above or on $y = -\dfrac{1}{2}$.

They intersect at -2 and $\dfrac{2}{3}$

∴ $-2 \leqslant x \leqslant \dfrac{2}{3}\;$ or $\;x > 2$
∴ $x \in [\,-2, \dfrac{2}{3}\,]\;$ or $\;]\,2, \infty\,[$

5 a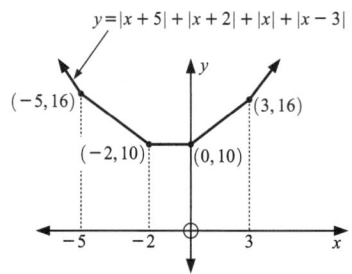

b i If x is a position along (AB) then:
  XP $= |x - (-5)| = |x + 5|$
  XQ $= |x - (-2)| = |x + 2|$
  XO $= |x - 0| = |x|$
  XR $= |x - 3|$
The total length is
  $|x + 5| + |x + 2| + |x| + |x - 3|$

ii The minimum length is 10 km when $-2 \leqslant x \leqslant 0$, so x can be anywhere between O and Q.

iii We need to graph
  $y = |x + 5| + |x + 2| + |x| + |x - 3| + |x - 7|$
From technology, the minimum cable length is 17 km when $x = 0$, so x is at O.

6 a $|x+y|^2 = (x+y)^2$
$= x^2 + 2xy + y^2$
and $(|x| + |y|)^2 = |x|^2 + 2|x||y| + |y|^2$
$= x^2 + 2|x||y| + y^2$
Now $xy \leqslant |x||y|$
$\therefore\ x^2 + 2xy + y^2 \leqslant x^2 + 2|x||y| + y^2$
$\therefore\ |x+y|^2 \leqslant (|x| + |y|)^2$
$\therefore\ |x+y| \leqslant |x| + |y|$ {both sides $\geqslant 0$}
$\therefore$ the statement is true for all $x,\ y$.

b $|x-y|^2 = (x-y)^2$
$= x^2 - 2xy + y^2$
and $(|x| - |y|)^2 = |x|^2 - 2|x||y| + |y|^2$
$= x^2 - 2|x||y| + y^2$
Now $xy \leqslant |x||y|$
$\therefore\ -2xy \geqslant -2|x||y|$
$\therefore\ x^2 - 2xy + y^2 \geqslant x^2 - 2|x||y| + y^2$
$\therefore\ |x-y|^2 \geqslant (|x| - |y|)^2$
$\therefore\ |x-y| \geqslant |x| - |y|$ {both sides $\geqslant 0$}
$\therefore$ the statement is true for all $x,\ y$.

EXERCISE 1G

1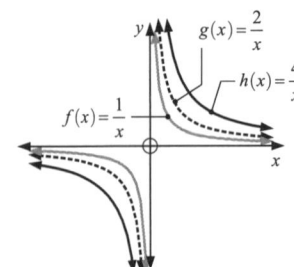

$f(x)$, $g(x)$ and $h(x)$ are all reciprocal functions which are all asymptotic about the x- and y-axes.
The graphs all lie in the 1st and 3rd quadrants.
The smaller the numerator, the closer is the graph to the axes.
Thus the graph of $f(x) = \dfrac{1}{x}$ is closer to the axes than $g(x) = \dfrac{2}{x}$ for corresponding values of x, and $g(x) = \dfrac{2}{x}$ is closer to the axes than $h(x) = \dfrac{4}{x}$.

2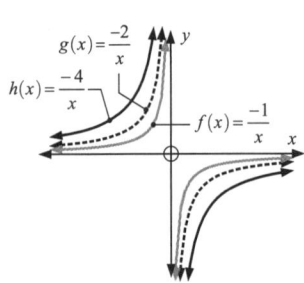

$f(x)$, $g(x)$ and $h(x)$ are all reciprocal functions which are all asymptotic about the x- and y-axes.
The graphs all lie in the 2nd and 4th quadrants.
The smaller the numerator, the closer is the graph to the axes.
Thus the graph of $f(x) = -\dfrac{1}{x}$ is closer to the axes than $g(x) = -\dfrac{2}{x}$ for corresponding values of x, and $g(x) = -\dfrac{2}{x}$ is closer to the axes than $h(x) = -\dfrac{4}{x}$.

EXERCISE 1H

1 a i $f : x \mapsto \dfrac{3}{x-2}$ is undefined when $x = 2$, so $x = 2$ is a vertical asymptote.
As $|x| \to \infty$, $f(x) \to 0$, so $y = 0$ is a horizontal asymptote.

ii As $x \to 2^-$, $y \to -\infty$.
As $x \to 2^+$, $y \to \infty$.
As $x \to \infty$, $y \to 0^+$.
As $x \to -\infty$, $y \to 0^-$.

iii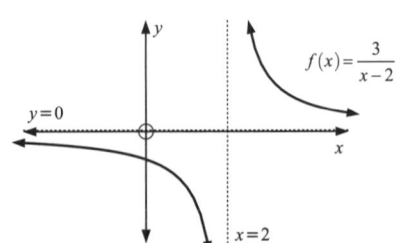

iv $f(x)$ crosses the horizontal asymptote when $\dfrac{3}{x-2} = 0$, which has no solutions
$\therefore$ the function does not cross its asymptotes.

b i $f(x) = 2 - \dfrac{3}{x+1}$ is undefined when $x = -1$, so $x = -1$ is a vertical asymptote.

As $|x| \to \infty$, $\dfrac{3}{x+1} \to 0$, so $f(x) \to 2$ $\therefore$ $y = 2$ is a horizontal asymptote.

ii As $x \to -1^-$, $y \to \infty$.
As $x \to -1^+$, $y \to -\infty$.
As $x \to \infty$, $y \to 2^-$.
As $x \to -\infty$, $y \to 2^+$.

iii

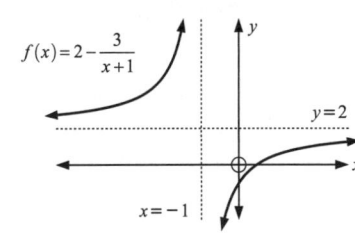

iv $f(x)$ crosses the horizontal asymptote when $2 - \dfrac{3}{x+1} = 2$

$\therefore$ $-\dfrac{3}{x+1} = 0$, which has no solutions.

$\therefore$ the function does not cross its asymptotes.

c i $f : x \mapsto \dfrac{x+3}{(x+1)(x-2)}$ is undefined when $x = -1$ or 2, so $x = -1$ and $x = 2$ are vertical asymptotes.

Now $f(x) = \dfrac{x+3}{x^2 - x - 2} = \dfrac{\frac{1}{x} + \frac{3}{x^2}}{1 - \frac{1}{x} - \frac{2}{x^2}}$

$\therefore$ as $|x| \to \infty$, $f(x) \to \dfrac{0}{1} = 0$, and so $y = 0$ is a horizontal asymptote.

ii As $x \to -1^-$, $y \to \infty$.
As $x \to -1^+$, $y \to -\infty$.
As $x \to 2^-$, $y \to -\infty$.
As $x \to 2^+$, $y \to \infty$.
As $x \to \infty$, $y \to 0^+$.
As $x \to -\infty$, $y \to 0^-$.

iii

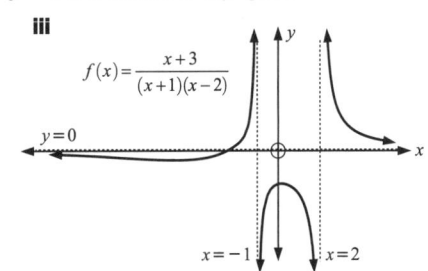

iv $f(x)$ crosses the horizontal asymptote when $\dfrac{x+3}{(x+1)(x-2)} = 0$, or $x = -3$.

$\therefore$ the function crosses the horizontal asymptote at $(-3, 0)$.

d i $f(x) = x + \dfrac{2}{x-3}$ is undefined when $x = 3$, so $x = 3$ is a vertical asymptote.

As $|x| \to \infty$, $\dfrac{2}{x-3} \to 0$, so $f(x) \to x$. $\therefore$ $y = x$ is an oblique asymptote.

ii As $x \to 3^-$, $y \to -\infty$.
As $x \to 3^+$, $y \to \infty$.
As $x \to \infty$, $y \to x^+$.
As $x \to -\infty$, $y \to x^-$.

iii

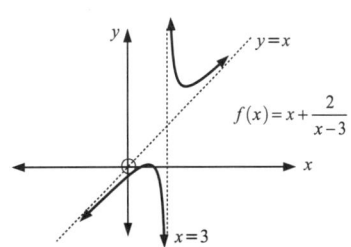

iv $f(x)$ crosses the oblique asymptote when $x + \dfrac{2}{x-3} = x$

$\therefore$ $\dfrac{2}{x-3} = 0$, which has no solutions.

$\therefore$ the function does not cross its asymptotes.

e **i** $y = \dfrac{x^2 - 4}{x^2 + 4}$ is never undefined since $x^2 + 4 > 0$ for all real x.

So, the function has no vertical asymptotes.

Now $y = \dfrac{x^2 - 4}{x^2 + 4} = \dfrac{1 - \frac{4}{x^2}}{1 + \frac{4}{x^2}}$

$\therefore$ as $|x| \to \infty$, $y \to \frac{1}{1} = 1$

$\therefore$ $y = 1$ is a horizontal asymptote.

ii As $x \to \infty$, $y \to 1^-$.
As $x \to -\infty$, $y \to 1^-$.

iii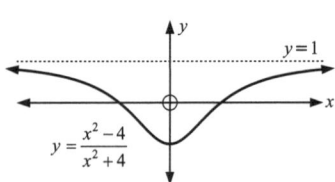

iv $y = \dfrac{x^2 - 4}{x^2 + 4}$ crosses the horizontal

asymptote when $\dfrac{x^2 - 4}{x^2 + 4} = 1$

$\therefore$ $x^2 - 4 = x^2 + 4$, which has no solutions
$\therefore$ the function does not cross its asymptotes.

f **i** $y = \dfrac{2x^2 + 1}{x^2 - 4}$ is undefined when $x = -2$ or 2

$\therefore$ $x = -2$ and $x = 2$ are vertical asymptotes.

Now $y = \dfrac{2x^2 + 1}{x^2 - 4} = \dfrac{2 + \frac{1}{x^2}}{1 - \frac{4}{x^2}}$

As $|x| \to \infty$, $y \to \frac{2}{1} = 2$, so $y = 2$ is a horizontal asymptote.

ii As $x \to -2^-$, $y \to \infty$.
As $x \to -2^+$, $y \to -\infty$.
As $x \to 2^-$, $y \to -\infty$.
As $x \to 2^+$, $y \to \infty$.
As $x \to \infty$, $y \to 2^+$.
As $x \to -\infty$, $y \to 2^+$.

iii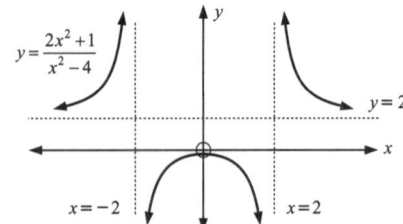

iv $y = \dfrac{2x^2 + 1}{x^2 - 4}$ crosses the horizontal asymptote when $\dfrac{2x^2 + 1}{x^2 - 4} = 2$

$\therefore$ $2x^2 + 1 = 2x^2 - 8$, which has no solutions
$\therefore$ the function does not cross its asymptotes.

g **i** $f : x \mapsto x + 2 + \dfrac{x - 2}{x + 1}$ is undefined when $x = -1$

$\therefore$ $x = -1$ is a vertical asymptote.

Now $f(x) = x + 2 + \dfrac{x - 2}{x + 1} = x + 2 + \dfrac{1 - \frac{2}{x}}{1 + \frac{1}{x}}$

As $|x| \to \infty$, $\dfrac{1 - \frac{2}{x}}{1 + \frac{1}{x}} \to \frac{1}{1} = 1$, so $f(x) \to x + 2 + 1 = x + 3$

$\therefore$ $y = x + 3$ is an oblique asymptote.

ii As $x \to -1^-$, $y \to \infty$.
As $x \to -1^+$, $y \to -\infty$.
As $x \to \infty$, $y \to (x + 3)^-$.
As $x \to -\infty$, $y \to (x + 3)^+$.

iii

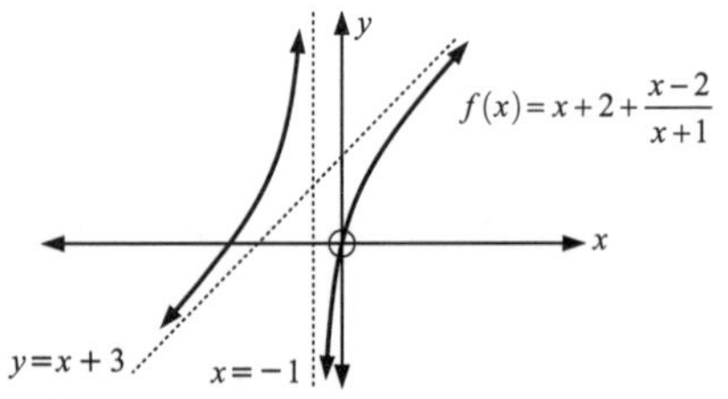

iv $f(x)$ crosses the oblique asymptote when $x + 2 + \dfrac{x-2}{x+1} = x + 3$

$\therefore \dfrac{x-2}{x+1} = 1$

$\therefore x - 2 = x + 1$, which has no solutions.

$\therefore$ the function does not cross its asymptotes.

h **i** $g : x \mapsto 2x - \dfrac{2x}{x^2+1}$ is never undefined, since $x^2 + 1 > 0$ for all real x.

So, the function has no vertical asymptotes.

Now $g(x) = 2x - \dfrac{2x}{x^2+1} = 2x - \dfrac{2}{x + \frac{1}{x}}$

As $|x| \to \infty$, $\dfrac{2}{x + \frac{1}{x}} \to 0$, so $g(x) \to 2x$ $\therefore$ $y = 2x$ is an oblique asymptote.

ii As $x \to \infty$, $y \to (2x)^-$.
As $x \to -\infty$, $y \to (2x)^+$.

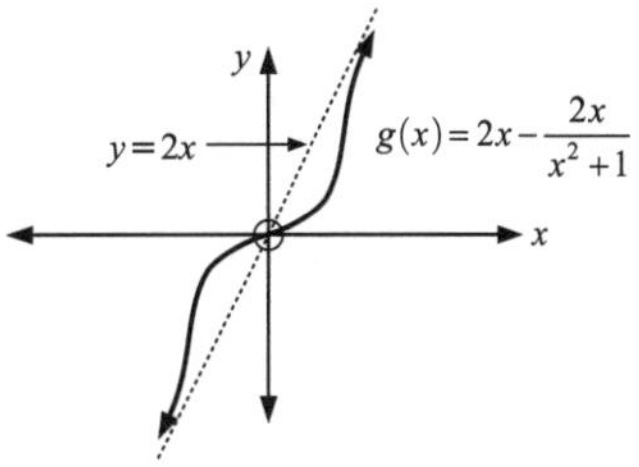

iv $g(x)$ crosses the oblique asymptote when

$2x - \dfrac{2x}{x^2+1} = 2x$

$\therefore \dfrac{2x}{x^2+1} = 0$

$\therefore x = 0$

$\therefore$ the function crosses the oblique asymptote at $(0, 0)$.

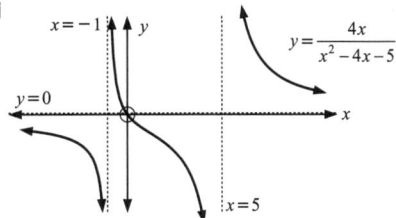

i **i** $y = \dfrac{4x}{x^2 - 4x - 5} = \dfrac{4x}{(x+1)(x-5)}$ is undefined when $x = -1$ or 5.

$\therefore x = -1$ and $x = 5$ are vertical asymptotes.

Now $y = \dfrac{4x}{x^2 - 4x - 5} = \dfrac{\frac{4}{x}}{1 - \frac{4}{x} - \frac{5}{x^2}}$.

As $|x| \to \infty$, $y \to \dfrac{0}{1} = 0$, and so $y = 0$ is a horizontal asymptote.

ii As $x \to -1^-$, $y \to -\infty$.
As $x \to -1^+$, $y \to \infty$.
As $x \to 5^-$, $y \to -\infty$.
As $x \to 5^+$, $y \to \infty$.
As $x \to \infty$, $y \to 0^+$.
As $x \to -\infty$, $y \to 0^-$.

iv $y = \dfrac{4x}{x^2 - 4x - 5}$ crosses the horizontal asymptote when $\dfrac{4x}{x^2 - 4x - 5} = 0$

$\therefore x = 0$

$\therefore$ the function crosses the horizontal asymptote at $(0, 0)$.

j **i** $y = x^2 - \dfrac{4}{x}$ is undefined when $x = 0$, so $x = 0$ is a vertical asymptote.

As $|x| \to \infty$, $\dfrac{4}{x} \to 0$, so $y = x^2$. $\therefore y = x^2$ is a parabolic asymptote.

ii As $x \to 0^-$, $y \to \infty$.
As $x \to 0^+$, $y \to -\infty$.
As $x \to \infty$, $y \to (x^2)^-$.
As $x \to -\infty$, $y \to (x^2)^+$.

iii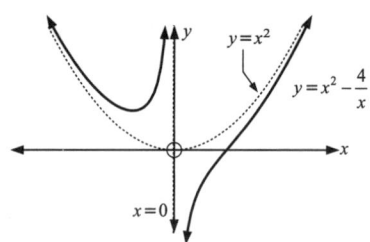

iv $y = x^2 - \dfrac{4}{x}$ crosses the parabolic asymptote when $x^2 - \dfrac{4}{x} = x^2$

$\therefore \dfrac{4}{x} = 0$, which has no solutions.

$\therefore$ the function does not cross its asymptotes.

EXERCISE 1I

1 a i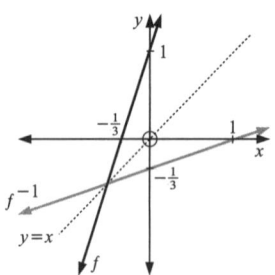

ii $f(x)$ passes through $(0, 1)$ and $(-\tfrac{1}{3}, 0)$

$\therefore f^{-1}(x)$ passes through $(1, 0)$ and $(0, -\tfrac{1}{3})$

$f^{-1}(x)$ has slope $\dfrac{-\tfrac{1}{3} - 0}{0 - 1} = \dfrac{-\tfrac{1}{3}}{-1} = \dfrac{1}{3}$

So, its equation is $\dfrac{y - 0}{x - 1} = \dfrac{1}{3}$

which is $y = \dfrac{x - 1}{3}$.

So, $f^{-1}(x) = \dfrac{x - 1}{3}$

iii f is $y = 3x + 1$
so f^{-1} is $x = 3y + 1$
$\therefore x - 1 = 3y$
$\therefore y = \dfrac{x - 1}{3}$. So, $f^{-1}(x) = \dfrac{x - 1}{3}$

b i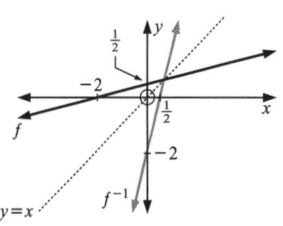

ii $f(x)$ passes through $(0, \tfrac{1}{2})$ and $(-2, 0)$

$\therefore f^{-1}(x)$ passes through $(\tfrac{1}{2}, 0)$ and $(0, -2)$

$f^{-1}(x)$ has slope $\dfrac{-2 - 0}{0 - \tfrac{1}{2}} = \dfrac{-2}{-\tfrac{1}{2}} = 4$

So, its equation is $\dfrac{y - 0}{x - \tfrac{1}{2}} = 4$

which is $y = 4x - 2$.

So, $f^{-1}(x) = 4x - 2$

iii f is $y = \dfrac{x + 2}{4}$

so f^{-1} is $x = \dfrac{y + 2}{4}$

$\therefore 4x = y + 2$

$\therefore y = 4x - 2$. So, $f^{-1}(x) = 4x - 2$

2 a i f is $y = 2x + 5$
so f^{-1} is $x = 2y + 5$
$\therefore \quad x - 5 = 2y$
$\therefore \quad y = \dfrac{x-5}{2}$
So, $f^{-1}(x) = \dfrac{x-5}{2}$

ii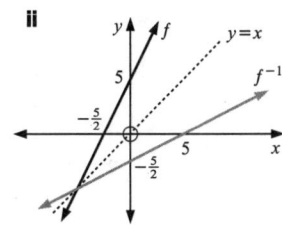

$f(x)$ passes through $(0, 5)$ and $(-\frac{5}{2}, 0)$
$\therefore \quad f^{-1}(x)$ passes through $(5, 0)$ and $(0, -\frac{5}{2})$.

iii $(f^{-1} \circ f)(x)$ and $(f \circ f^{-1})(x)$
$= f^{-1}(2x + 5)$ $= f(f^{-1}(x))$
$= \dfrac{2x + 5 - 5}{2}$ $= f\left(\dfrac{x-5}{2}\right)$
$= \dfrac{2x}{2}$ $= 2\left(\dfrac{x-5}{2}\right) + 5$
$= x$ $= x - 5 + 5$
    $= x$

b i f is $y = \dfrac{3 - 2x}{4}$
so f^{-1} is $x = \dfrac{3 - 2y}{4}$
$\therefore \quad 4x = 3 - 2y$
$\therefore \quad 4x - 3 = -2y$
$\therefore \quad y = -2x + \frac{3}{2}$
So, $f^{-1}(x) = -2x + \frac{3}{2}$

ii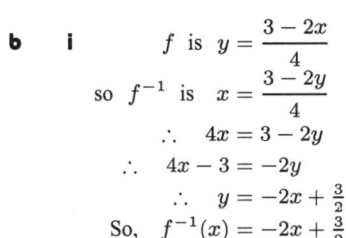

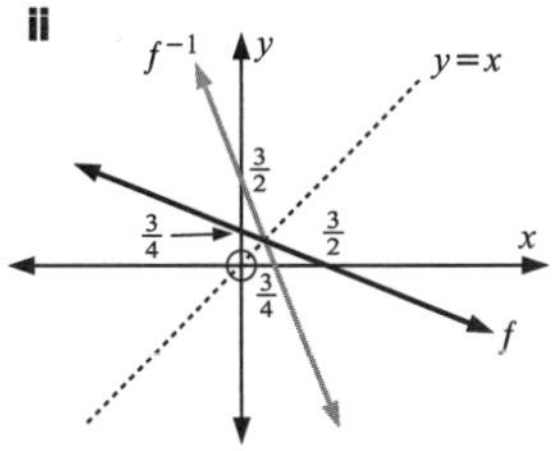

$f(x)$ passes through $(0, \frac{3}{4})$ and $(\frac{3}{2}, 0)$
$\therefore \quad f^{-1}(x)$ passes through $(\frac{3}{4}, 0)$ and $(0, \frac{3}{2})$.

iii $(f^{-1} \circ f)(x)$ and $(f \circ f^{-1})(x)$
$= f^{-1}(f(x))$ $= f(f^{-1}(x))$
$= f^{-1}\left(\dfrac{3 - 2x}{4}\right)$ $= f\left(-2x + \frac{3}{2}\right)$
$= -2\left(\dfrac{3 - 2x}{4}\right) + \frac{3}{2}$ $= \dfrac{3 - 2(-2x + \frac{3}{2})}{4}$
$= \dfrac{3 - 2x}{-2} + \frac{3}{2}$ $= \dfrac{3 + 4x - 3}{4}$
$= -\frac{3}{2} + x + \frac{3}{2}$ $= \dfrac{4x}{4}$
$= x$ $= x$

c i f is $y = x + 3$
so f^{-1} is $x = y + 3$
$\therefore \quad y = x - 3$
So, $f^{-1}(x) = x - 3$

ii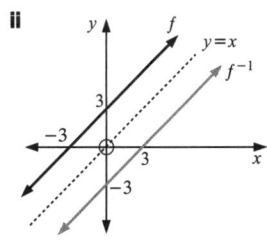

$f(x)$ passes through $(0, 3)$ and $(-3, 0)$
$\therefore \quad f^{-1}(x)$ passes through $(3, 0)$ and $(0, -3)$.

iii $(f^{-1} \circ f)(x)$ and $(f \circ f^{-1})(x)$
$= f^{-1}(f(x))$ $= f(f^{-1}(x))$
$= f^{-1}(x + 3)$ $= f(x - 3)$
$= (x + 3) - 3$ $= (x - 3) + 3$
$= x$ $= x$

3 **a** 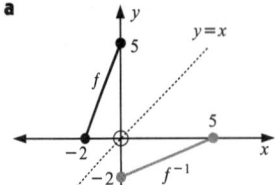   **b** 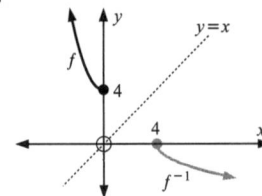   **c**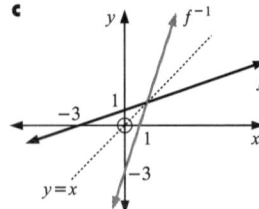

d 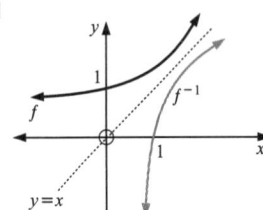   **e** 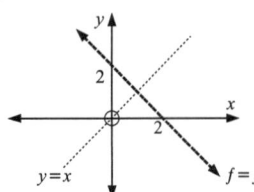   **f**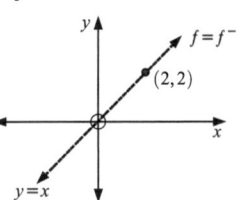

4 **a**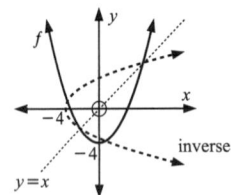

  b Using the 'horizontal line test', f does not have an inverse function as a horizontal line through $y = x^2 - 4$ cuts it more than once.

  c For $x \geqslant 0$, any horizontal line cuts it only once.
  $\therefore$ f does have an inverse function for $x \geqslant 0$.

5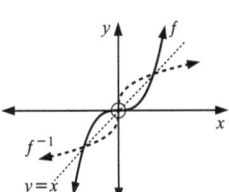

EXERCISE 1J

1 **a** For $\{(1, 2), (2, 4), (3, 5)\}$, there is at most one x-value corresponding to each y-value, so the function has an inverse. The inverse function is $\{(2, 1), (4, 2), (5, 3)\}$.

  b For $\{(-1, 3), (0, 2), (1, 3)\}$, there are two x-values corresponding to the y-value of 3. So, the function does not have an inverse.

  c For $\{(2, 1), (-1, 0), (0, 2), (1, 3)\}$, there is at most one x-value corresponding to each y-value, so the function has an inverse. The inverse function is $\{(0, -1), (1, 2), (2, 0), (3, 1)\}$.

  d For $\{(-1, -1), (0, 0), (1, 1)\}$, there is at most one x-value corresponding to each y-value, so the function has an inverse. The inverse function is $\{(-1, -1), (0, 0), (1, 1)\}$.

2 **a** $f(x) = \dfrac{1}{x}$ has graph

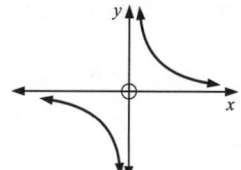

No vertical line cuts the graph more than once, so it is a function.
No horizontal line cuts the graph more than once.
Hence, $f(x) = \dfrac{1}{x}$, $x \neq 0$ has an inverse function.

b $f(x) = \dfrac{1}{x}$ has inverse function $x = \dfrac{1}{y}$ or $y = \dfrac{1}{x}$

So, $f^{-1}(x) = \dfrac{1}{x}$, which means $f(x)$ is a self-inverse function.

3 **a** $f(x) = \dfrac{3x-8}{x-3}$ has graph

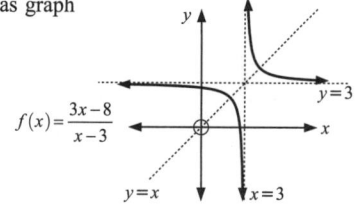

The vertical line test shows it to be a function.
The horizontal line test shows it has an inverse function.
Symmetry about $y = x$ shows it is a self-inverse function.

b $f(x) = \dfrac{3x-8}{x-3}$ has inverse function $x = \dfrac{3y-8}{y-3}$

$\therefore \ x(y-3) = 3y - 8$
$\therefore \ xy - 3x = 3y - 8$
$\therefore \ y(x-3) = 3x - 8$
$\therefore \ y = \dfrac{3x-8}{x-3}$

So, $f(x) = f^{-1}(x)$, which means $f(x)$ is a self-inverse function.

4 **a** If $y = f(x)$ has an inverse function, then the inverse function must also be a function. Thus, it must satisfy the 'vertical line test', i.e., no vertical line can cut it more than once. This condition for the inverse function cannot be satisfied if the original function does not satisfy the 'horizontal line test'. Thus, the 'horizontal line test' is a valid test for the existence of an inverse function.

b **i** This graph satisfies the 'horizontal line test' and therefore has an inverse function.
ii, iii These graphs both fail the 'horizontal line test' so neither of these have inverse functions.

c **ii** Domain $\{x \mid x \geqslant 1\}$ or $\{x \mid x \leqslant 1\}$ **iii** Domain $\{x \mid x \geqslant 1\}$ or $\{x \mid x \leqslant -2\}$

5 **a** f is $y = x^2$, $x \leqslant 0$
so f^{-1} is $x = y^2$, $y \leqslant 0$
$\therefore \ y = -\sqrt{x}$
So, $f^{-1}(x) = -\sqrt{x}$

b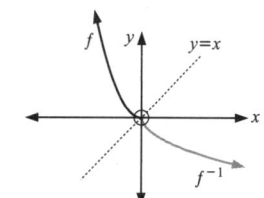

6 **a**

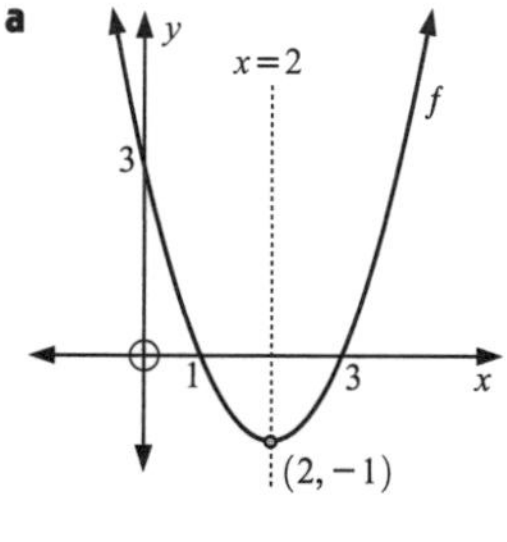

$f : x \mapsto x^2 - 4x + 3$ satisfies the 'vertical line test' so is therefore a function. It does not however satisfy the horizontal line test as any horizontal line above the vertex cuts the graph twice. Therefore it does not have an inverse function.

b For $x \geqslant 2$, all horizontal lines cut the graph no more than once. Therefore f has an inverse function for $x \geqslant 2$.

c f is $y = x^2 - 4x + 3$, $x \geqslant 2$
so f^{-1} is $x = y^2 - 4y + 3$, $y \geqslant 2$
$\therefore \quad x = (y-2)^2 - 4 + 3$, $y \geqslant 2$
$\therefore \quad x = (y-2)^2 - 1$, $y \geqslant 2$
$\therefore \quad x + 1 = (y-2)^2$, $y \geqslant 2$
$\therefore \quad y - 2 = \sqrt{x+1}$, $y \geqslant 2$
$\therefore \quad y = 2 + \sqrt{1+x}$, $y \geqslant 2$
So, $f^{-1}(x) = 2 + \sqrt{1+x}$ as required.

d i Domain of f is $\{x \mid x \geqslant 2\}$.
Range is $\{y \mid y \geqslant -1\}$
ii Domain of f^{-1} is $\{x \mid x \geqslant -1\}$.
Range is $\{y \mid y \geqslant 2\}$

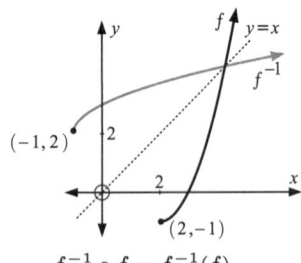

e $f \circ f^{-1} = f(f^{-1})$
$= \left(2 + \sqrt{1+x}\right)^2 - 4\left(2 + \sqrt{1+x}\right) + 3$
$= 4 + 4\sqrt{1+x} + 1 + x - 8 - 4\sqrt{1+x} + 3$
$= x$

$f^{-1} \circ f = f^{-1}(f)$
$= 2 + \sqrt{1 + x^2 - 4x + 3}$
$= 2 + \sqrt{(x-2)^2}$
$= 2 + x - 2$
$= x$

7 a f is $y = (x+1)^2 + 3$, $x \geqslant -1$
so f^{-1} is $x = (y+1)^2 + 3$, $y \geqslant -1$
$\therefore \quad x - 3 = (y+1)^2$, $y \geqslant -1$
$\therefore \quad y + 1 = \sqrt{x-3}$, $y \geqslant -1$
$\therefore \quad y = \sqrt{x-3} - 1$, $y \geqslant -1$

b

c i Domain $\{x \mid x \geqslant -1\}$. Range $\{y \mid y \geqslant 3\}$.
ii Domain $\{x \mid x \geqslant 3\}$. Range $\{y \mid y \geqslant -1\}$.

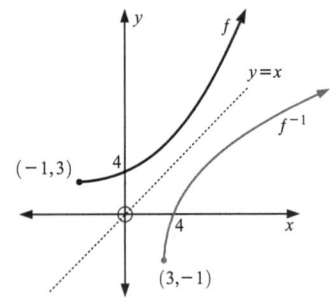

8 a g is $y = \dfrac{8-x}{2}$
so g^{-1} is $x = \dfrac{8-y}{2}$
$\therefore \quad 2x = 8 - y$
$\therefore \quad y = 8 - 2x$
So, $g^{-1}(x) = 8 - 2x$
$\therefore \quad g^{-1}(-1) = 8 - 2(-1) = 10$

b $(f \circ g^{-1})(x) = 9$
$\therefore \quad f(g^{-1}(x)) = 9$
$\therefore \quad f(8 - 2x) = 9$
$\therefore \quad 2(8 - 2x) + 5 = 9$
$\therefore \quad 16 - 4x + 5 = 9$
$\therefore \quad -4x = -12$
$\therefore \quad x = 3$

9 a i f is $y = 5^x$
so $f(2) = 5^2$
$= 25$

ii g is $y = \sqrt{x}$
so g^{-1} is $x = \sqrt{y}$
$\therefore \quad y = x^2$
$\therefore \quad g^{-1}(x) = x^2$, $x \geqslant 0$
$\therefore \quad g^{-1}(4) = 4^2$
$\therefore \quad g^{-1}(4) = 16$

b $(g^{-1} \circ f)(x) = 25$
$\therefore \quad g^{-1}(f(x)) = 25$
$\therefore \quad g^{-1}(5^x) = 25$
$\therefore \quad (5^x)^2 = 25$ {as $g^{-1}(x) = x^2$, $x \geqslant 0$}
$\therefore \quad 5^{2x} = 5^2$
$\therefore \quad 2x = 2$
$\therefore \quad x = 1$

10 f is $y = 2x$
so f^{-1} is $x = 2y$
$\therefore\ y = \dfrac{x}{2}$
$\therefore\ f^{-1}(x) = \dfrac{x}{2}$

g is $y = 4x - 3$
so g^{-1} is $x = 4y - 3$
$\therefore\ 4y = x + 3$
$\therefore\ y = \dfrac{x+3}{4}$
$\therefore\ g^{-1}(x) = \dfrac{x+3}{4}$

$(g \circ f)(x) = g(f(x))$
$= g(2x)$
$= 4(2x) - 3$
$\therefore\ (g \circ f)(x) = 8x - 3$
$\therefore\ g \circ f$ is $y = 8x - 3$
so $(g \circ f)^{-1}$ is $x = 8y - 3$
$\therefore\ y = \dfrac{x+3}{8}$
So, $(g \circ f)^{-1}(x) = \dfrac{x+3}{8}$

Now $(f^{-1} \circ g^{-1})(x) = f^{-1}(g^{-1}(x))$
$= f^{-1}\left(\dfrac{x+3}{4}\right)$
$= \dfrac{\left(\dfrac{x+3}{4}\right)}{2}$
$\therefore\ (f^{-1} \circ g^{-1})(x) = \dfrac{x+3}{8} = (g \circ f)^{-1}(x)$ as required

11 a f is $y = 2x$
so f^{-1} is $x = 2y$
$\therefore\ y = \dfrac{x}{2}$
so $f^{-1}(x) = \dfrac{x}{2} \neq 2x$
So, $f^{-1}(x) \neq f(x)$

b f is $y = x$
so f^{-1} is $x = y$
$\therefore\ y = x$
so $f^{-1}(x) = x$
So, $f^{-1}(x) = f(x)$

c f is $y = -x$
so f^{-1} is $x = -y$
$\therefore\ y = -x$
so $f^{-1}(x) = -x$
So, $f^{-1}(x) = f(x)$

d f is $y = \dfrac{2}{x}$
so f^{-1} is $x = \dfrac{2}{y}$
$\therefore\ y = \dfrac{2}{x}$
so $f^{-1}(x) = \dfrac{2}{x}$
So, $f^{-1}(x) = f(x)$

e f is $y = -\dfrac{6}{x}$
so f^{-1} is $x = -\dfrac{6}{y}$
$\therefore\ y = -\dfrac{6}{x}$
so $f^{-1}(x) = -\dfrac{6}{x}$
So, $f^{-1}(x) = f(x)$

So, $f^{-1}(x) = f(x)$ is true for parts **b, c, d** and **e**.

12 a f is $y = 3x + 1$
so f^{-1} is $x = 3y + 1$
$\therefore\ y = \dfrac{x-1}{3}$
$\therefore\ f^{-1}(x) = \dfrac{x-1}{3}$

$(f \circ f^{-1})(x) = f(f^{-1}(x))$
$= f\left(\dfrac{x-1}{3}\right)$
$= 3\left(\dfrac{x-1}{3}\right) + 1$
$= x - 1 + 1$
$\therefore\ (f \circ f^{-1})(x) = x$

$(f^{-1} \circ f)(x) = f^{-1}(f(x))$
$= f^{-1}(3x + 1)$
$= \dfrac{3x + 1 - 1}{3}$
$= \dfrac{3x}{3}$
$\therefore\ (f^{-1} \circ f)(x) = x = (f \circ f^{-1})(x)$ as required.

b f is $y = \dfrac{x+3}{4}$ so f^{-1} is $x = \dfrac{y+3}{4}$

$\therefore\ 4x = y + 3$

$\therefore\ y = 4x - 3$

$\therefore\ f^{-1}(x) = 4x - 3$

$(f \circ f^{-1})(x) = f(f^{-1}(x))$
$= f(4x - 3)$
$= \dfrac{4x - 3 + 3}{4}$
$= \dfrac{4x}{4}$

$\therefore\ (f \circ f^{-1})(x) = x$

$(f^{-1} \circ f)(x) = f^{-1}(f(x))$
$= f^{-1}\left(\dfrac{x+3}{4}\right)$
$= 4\left(\dfrac{x+3}{4}\right) - 3$
$= x + 3 - 3$

$\therefore\ (f^{-1} \circ f)(x) = x = (f \circ f^{-1})(x)$ as required.

c f is $y = \sqrt{x}$ for $x \geqslant 0$ so f^{-1} is $x = \sqrt{y}$

$\therefore\ y = x^2$

$\therefore\ f^{-1}(x) = x^2$ for $x \geqslant 0$

$(f \circ f^{-1})(x) = f(f^{-1}(x))$
$= f(x^2)$
$= \sqrt{x^2}$

$\therefore\ (f \circ f^{-1})(x) = x \ \{x \geqslant 0\}$

$(f^{-1} \circ f)(x) = f^{-1}(f(x))$
$= f^{-1}(\sqrt{x})$
$= (\sqrt{x})^2$

$\therefore\ (f^{-1} \circ f)(x) = x = (f \circ f^{-1})(x)$ as required.

13 a $f(x)$ passes through $A(x, f(x))$, so $f^{-1}(x)$ passes through $B(f(x), x)$.

b Substituting the coordinates of $B(f(x), x)$ into $y = f^{-1}(x)$ gives
$x = f^{-1}(f(x)) = (f^{-1} \circ f)(x)$.

c B has coordinates $(x, f^{-1}(x))$ since it lies on $y = f^{-1}(x)$,
so A has coordinates $(f^{-1}(x), x)$ as $f(x)$ is the inverse of $f^{-1}(x)$.
Substituting the coordinates of $A(f^{-1}(x), x)$ into $y = f(x)$ gives $x = f(f^{-1}(x))$.

$\therefore\ f(f^{-1}(x)) = x$ as required.

REVIEW SET 1A

1 a $f(x) = 2x - x^2$
$f(2) = 2(2) - 2^2$
$= 0$

b $f(-3) = 2(-3) - (-3)^2$
$= -6 - 9$
$= -15$

c $f(-\tfrac{1}{2}) = 2(-\tfrac{1}{2}) - (-\tfrac{1}{2})^2$
$= -1 - \tfrac{1}{4}$
$= -\tfrac{5}{4}$

2 a i range is $\{y \mid y \geqslant -5\}$, domain is $\{x \mid x \in \mathbb{R}\}$
   ii x-intercepts are -1 and 5, y-intercept is $-\tfrac{25}{9}$
   iii The graph passes the 'vertical line test' so is therefore a function.
   iv No, as it fails the horizontal line test.

b i range is $\{y \mid y = 1 \text{ or } -3\}$, domain is $\{x \mid x \in \mathbb{R}\}$
   ii there are no x-intercepts; y-intercept is 1
   iii The graph passes the 'vertical line test' so is therefore a function.
   iv No, as it fails the horizontal line test.

3 $f(x) = ax^2 + bx + c$, where $f(0) = 5$, $f(-2) = 21$ and $f(3) = -4$

When $f(0) = 5$,
$5 = a(0)^2 + b(0) + c$
$\therefore\ 5 = c$
$\therefore\ c = 5$ .....(1)

When $f(-2) = 21$,
$21 = a(-2)^2 + b(-2) + c$
$= 4a - 2b + c$
$= 4a - 2b + 5$ {using (1)}

$\therefore\ 4a - 2b = 16$

$\therefore\ 2a - b = 8$ and so $b = 2a - 8$ .....(2)

When $f(3) = -4$, $\quad -4 = a(3)^2 + b(3) + c$
$\therefore \quad -4 = 9a + 3b + c$
$\therefore \quad -4 = 9a + 3b + 5 \quad$ {using (1)}
$\therefore \quad -4 = 9a + 3(2a - 8) + 5 \quad$ {using (2)}
$\therefore \quad -4 = 9a + 6a - 24 + 5$
$\therefore \quad 15 = 15a \quad$ and so $\quad a = 1$

Now, substituting $a = 1$ into (2) gives $b = 2(1) - 8 = -6$
So, $a = 1$, $b = -6$, $c = 5$

4 **a** $y = (3x + 2)(4 - x)$ is zero when $x = -\frac{2}{3}$ or 4.
When $x = 0$, $y = (2)(4) = 8 > 0$.
Since the factors are single, the signs alternate.
$\therefore$ sign diagram is

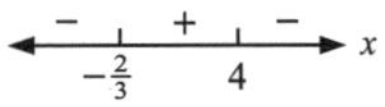

$\xleftarrow{\quad - \quad | \quad + \quad | \quad - \quad}{\quad -\frac{2}{3} \quad \quad 4 \quad} x$

b $y = \dfrac{x - 3}{x^2 + 4x + 4} = \dfrac{x - 3}{(x + 2)^2}$ is zero when $x = 3$ and undefined when $x = -2$.

When $x = 0$, $y = \dfrac{-3}{2^2} = -\dfrac{3}{4} < 0$.

Since the $(x + 2)$ factor is squared, the sign does not change at $x = -2$
$\therefore$ sign diagram is

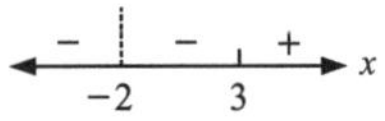

$\xleftarrow{\quad - \quad | \quad - \quad | \quad + \quad}{\quad -2 \quad \quad 3 \quad} x$

5 **a** $f(g(x)) = f(x^2 + 2)$
$= 2(x^2 + 2) - 3$
$= 2x^2 + 4 - 3$
$= 2x^2 + 1$

b $g(f(x)) = g(2x - 3)$
$= (2x - 3)^2 + 2$
$= 4x^2 - 12x + 9 + 2$
$= 4x^2 - 12x + 11$

6 **a** $\dfrac{x(x + 8)}{x + 2} \leqslant 5$

$\therefore \dfrac{x(x + 8)}{x + 2} - \dfrac{5(x + 2)}{x + 2} \leqslant 0$

$\therefore \dfrac{x^2 + 3x - 10}{x + 2} \leqslant 0$

$\therefore \dfrac{(x + 5)(x - 2)}{x + 2} \leqslant 0$

Sign diagram of LHS is

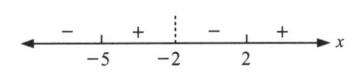

$\xleftarrow{\quad - \quad | \quad + \quad | \quad - \quad | \quad + \quad}{\quad -5 \quad -2 \quad 2 \quad} x$

$\therefore$ LHS $\leqslant 0$ when $x \in]-\infty, -5]$ or $]-2, 2]$

b $\dfrac{3}{x - 1} > \dfrac{5}{2x + 1}$

$\therefore \dfrac{3}{x - 1} - \dfrac{5}{2x + 1} > 0$

$\therefore \dfrac{3(2x + 1) - 5(x - 1)}{(x - 1)(2x + 1)} > 0$

$\therefore \dfrac{x + 8}{(x - 1)(2x + 1)} > 0$

Sign diagram of LHS is

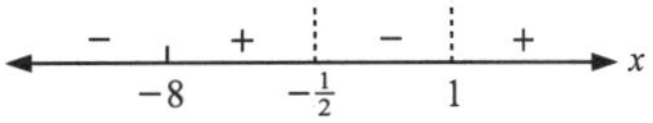

$\xleftarrow{\quad - \quad | \quad + \quad | \quad - \quad | \quad + \quad}{\quad -8 \quad -\frac{1}{2} \quad 1 \quad} x$

$\therefore$ LHS > 0 when $x \in]-8, -\frac{1}{2}[$ or $]1, \infty[$

7 **a** [graph showing $y = x$, f, and f^{-1} with intercepts at $\frac{7}{2}$, $-\frac{7}{2}$, -7, and 7]

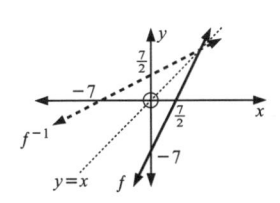

b The function f is $y = 2x - 7$
so f^{-1} is $x = 2y - 7$

$\therefore \quad y = \dfrac{x + 7}{2}$

So, $f^{-1}(x) = \dfrac{x + 7}{2}$

c $f \circ f^{-1}$ and $f^{-1} \circ f$
$= f\left(f^{-1}(x)\right)$ $= f^{-1}(f(x))$
$= f\left(\dfrac{x+7}{2}\right)$ $= f^{-1}(2x-7)$
$= 2\left(\dfrac{x+7}{2}\right) - 7$ $= \dfrac{2x-7+7}{2}$
$= x + 7 - 7$ $= \dfrac{2x}{2}$
$= x$ $= x$ So, $f \circ f^{-1} = f^{-1} \circ f = x$

8 a $\left|\dfrac{2x+1}{x-2}\right| = 3$

$\therefore \dfrac{2x+1}{x-2} = \pm 3$

If $\dfrac{2x+1}{x-2} = 3$
then $2x+1 = 3x - 6$
$\therefore -x = -7$
$\therefore x = 7$

If $\dfrac{2x+1}{x-2} = -3$
then $2x+1 = -3x + 6$
$\therefore 5x = 5$
$\therefore x = 1$
So, $x = 1$ or 7

b $|3x-2| \geqslant |2x+3|$
$\therefore |3x-2|^2 \geqslant |2x+3|^2$
$\therefore (3x-2)^2 - (2x+3)^2 \geqslant 0$
$\therefore 9x^2 - 12x + 4 - (4x^2 + 12x + 9) \geqslant 0$
$\therefore 5x^2 - 24x - 5 \geqslant 0$
$\therefore (5x+1)(x-5) \geqslant 0$

Sign diagram of LHS is

```
    +        -        +
  ──┼────────┼────────►  x
   -1/5      5
```

$\therefore$ LHS $\geqslant 0$ when $x \in]-\infty, -\tfrac{1}{5}]$ or $[5, \infty[$

9 a $f: x \mapsto \dfrac{4x+1}{x^2+x-6} = \dfrac{4x+1}{(x+3)(x-2)}$ is undefined when $x = -3$ or 2

$\therefore x = -3$ and $x = 2$ are vertical asymptotes.

Now $f(x) = \dfrac{4x+1}{x^2+x-6} = \dfrac{\tfrac{4}{x} + \tfrac{1}{x^2}}{1 + \tfrac{1}{x} - \tfrac{6}{x^2}}$

As $|x| \to \infty$, $f(x) \to \tfrac{0}{1} = 0$, and so $y = 0$ is a horizontal asymptote.

b As $x \to -3^-$, $y \to -\infty$.
As $x \to -3^+$, $y \to \infty$.
As $x \to 2^-$, $y \to -\infty$.
As $x \to 2^+$, $y \to \infty$.
As $x \to \infty$, $y \to 0^+$.
As $x \to -\infty$, $y \to 0^-$.

c

Graph of $f(x) = \dfrac{4x+1}{x^2+x-6}$ with asymptotes $x = -3$, $x = 2$, $y = 0$.

10 $f(x) = 3x + 6$
$\therefore y = 3x + 6$
$\therefore f^{-1}(x)$ is $x = 3y + 6$
$\therefore y = \dfrac{x-6}{3}$
So, $f^{-1}(x) = \dfrac{x-6}{3}$

$h(x) = \dfrac{x}{3}$
$\therefore y = \dfrac{x}{3}$
$\therefore h^{-1}(x)$ is $x = \dfrac{y}{3}$
$\therefore y = 3x$
So, $h^{-1}(x) = 3x$

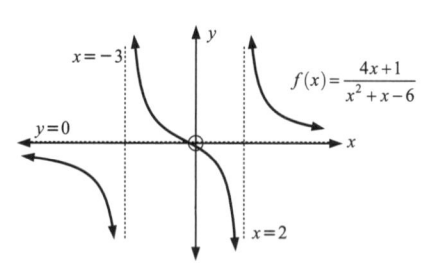

Now $(f^{-1} \circ h^{-1})(x) = f^{-1}(h^{-1}(x))$
$= f^{-1}(3x)$
$= \dfrac{3x - 6}{3}$
$= x - 2$

$(h \circ f)(x) = h(f(x))$
$= h(3x + 6)$
$= \dfrac{3x + 6}{3}$
So, $y = x + 2$
$\therefore (h \circ f)^{-1}(x)$ is $x = y + 2$
$\therefore y = x - 2$
So, $(h \circ f)^{-1}(x) = x - 2$

Hence $(f^{-1} \circ h^{-1})(x) = (h \circ f)^{-1}(x)$ as required.

REVIEW SET 1B

1 $g(x) = x^2 - 3x$

a $g(x + 1) = (x + 1)^2 - 3(x + 1)$
$= x^2 + 2x + 1 - 3x - 3$
$= x^2 - x - 2$

b $g(x^2 - 2) = (x^2 - 2)^2 - 3(x^2 - 2)$
$= x^4 - 4x^2 + 4 - 3x^2 + 6$
$= x^4 - 7x^2 + 10$

2 a $f(x) = 7 - 4x$
$\therefore y = 7 - 4x$
$\therefore f^{-1}(x)$ is $x = 7 - 4y$
$\therefore y = \dfrac{7 - x}{4}$
So, $f^{-1}(x) = \dfrac{7 - x}{4}$

b $f(x) = \dfrac{3 + 2x}{5}$
$\therefore y = \dfrac{3 + 2x}{5}$
$\therefore f^{-1}(x)$ is $x = \dfrac{3 + 2y}{5}$
$\therefore 5x = 3 + 2y$
$\therefore y = \dfrac{5x - 3}{2}$ So, $f^{-1}(x) = \dfrac{5x - 3}{2}$

3 a $y = (x - 1)(x - 5)$
$\therefore$ the x-intercepts are $x = 1$ and 5
The vertex is at $x = 3$, with $y = (3 - 1)(3 - 5) = 2 \times (-2) = -4$
$\therefore$ the vertex is at $(3, -4)$
The domain is $\{x \mid x \in \mathbb{R}\}$. The range is $\{y \mid y \geqslant -4\}$.

b From the graph, the domain is $\{x \mid x \neq 0, 2\}$ and the range is $\{y \mid y \leqslant -1$ or $y > 0\}$.

4 a

b

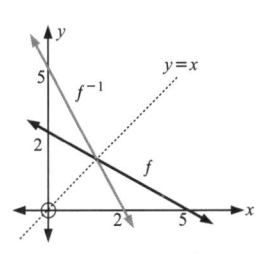

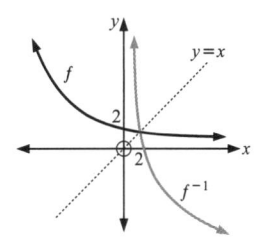

5 a $y = \dfrac{x^2 - 6x - 16}{x - 3} = \dfrac{(x + 2)(x - 8)}{x - 3}$ is zero when $x = -2$ or 8 and undefined when $x = 3$.
When $x = 0$, $y = \dfrac{-16}{-3} > 0$.
Since the factors are single, the signs alternate. So, the sign diagram is

b $y = \dfrac{x + 9}{x + 5} + x \left(\dfrac{x + 5}{x + 5} \right) = \dfrac{x^2 + 6x + 9}{x + 5} = \dfrac{(x + 3)^2}{x + 5}$ is zero when $x = -3$ and undefined when $x = -5$.
When $x = 0$, $y = \dfrac{3^2}{5} > 0$. The $(x + 3)$ factor is squared, so the sign does not change at $x = -3$.
So, the sign diagram is

6 **a** $2x^2 + x \leqslant 10$
$\therefore\ 2x^2 + x - 10 \leqslant 0$
$\therefore\ (2x+5)(x-2) \leqslant 0$
Sign diagram of LHS is

$$\begin{array}{c} + \quad - \quad + \\ \xleftarrow{\hspace{1cm}}\bullet\xrightarrow{\hspace{1cm}}\bullet\xrightarrow{\hspace{1cm}} x \\ -\tfrac{5}{2} \qquad 2 \end{array}$$

$\therefore$ LHS $\leqslant 0$ when $x \in [-\tfrac{5}{2}, 2]$

b $\dfrac{x^2 - 3x - 4}{x+2} > 0$
$\therefore\ \dfrac{(x+1)(x-4)}{x+2} > 0$
Sign diagram of LHS is

$$\begin{array}{c} - \quad + \quad - \quad + \\ \xleftarrow{\hspace{0.5cm}}\bullet\xrightarrow{\hspace{0.5cm}}\bullet\xrightarrow{\hspace{0.5cm}}\bullet\xrightarrow{\hspace{0.5cm}} x \\ -2 \quad -1 \quad\quad 4 \end{array}$$

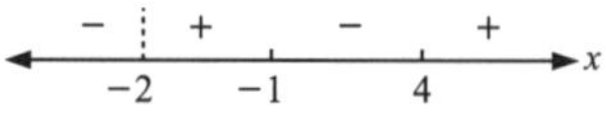

$\therefore$ LHS > 0 when $x \in\ ]-2, -1[$ or $]4, \infty[$

7 **a** $f(g(x)) = \sqrt{1-x^2}$
$\qquad\qquad = f(1-x^2)$
So, $f(x) = \sqrt{x}$
$\qquad g(x) = 1 - x^2$

Note: There are other possible functions f and g.

b $g(f(x)) = \left(\dfrac{x-2}{x+1}\right)^2$
$\qquad\qquad = g\left(\dfrac{x-2}{x+1}\right)$
So, $g(x) = x^2$
$\qquad f(x) = \dfrac{x-2}{x+1}$

8 **a** $|4x - 2| = |x + 7|$
$\therefore\ 4x - 2 = \pm(x+7)$

If $4x - 2 = x + 7$
then $3x = 9$
$\therefore\ x = 3$

If $4x - 2 = -(x+7)$
then $4x - 2 = -x - 7$
$\therefore\ 5x = -5$
$\therefore\ x = -1$
So, $x = -1$ or 3

b $|7 - 3x| \geqslant 8$
$\therefore\ 7 - 3x \leqslant -8$ or $7 - 3x \geqslant 8$
$\therefore\ -3x \leqslant -15$ or $-3x \geqslant 1$
$\therefore\ x \geqslant 5$ or $x \leqslant -\tfrac{1}{3}$ So, $x \in\ ]-\infty, -\tfrac{1}{3}]$ or $[5, \infty[$

9 **a** $f(x) = 3 + \dfrac{3x-2}{x^2-4}$ is undefined when $x^2 - 4 = 0$, which is when $x = \pm 2$
$\therefore\ x = -2$ and $x = 2$ are vertical asymptotes.
As $|x| \to \infty$, $\dfrac{3x-2}{x^2-4} \to 0$, so $f(x) \to 3$. Hence $y = 3$ is a horizontal asymptote.

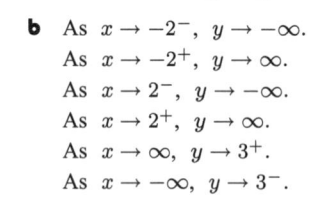

b As $x \to -2^-$, $y \to -\infty$.
As $x \to -2^+$, $y \to \infty$.
As $x \to 2^-$, $y \to -\infty$.
As $x \to 2^+$, $y \to \infty$.
As $x \to \infty$, $y \to 3^+$.
As $x \to -\infty$, $y \to 3^-$.

c

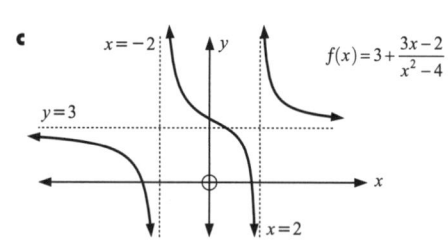

d $f(x)$ crosses the horizontal asymptote when $3 + \dfrac{3x-2}{x^2-4} = 3$
$\therefore\ \dfrac{3x-2}{x^2-4} = 0$
$\therefore\ 3x - 2 = 0$
$\therefore\ x = \tfrac{2}{3}$

$\therefore$ the function crosses the horizontal asymptote at $(\tfrac{2}{3}, 3)$.

10 a $h(x) = (x-4)^2 + 3, \quad x \geq 4$
$\therefore \quad y = (x-4)^2 + 3, \quad x \geq 4$
$\therefore \quad h^{-1}(x)$ is $x = (y-4)^2 + 3, \quad y \geq 4$
$\therefore \quad x - 3 = (y-4)^2$
$\therefore \quad y - 4 = \pm\sqrt{x-3}$
$\therefore \quad y = 4 \pm \sqrt{x-3}$
But $y \geq 4$, so $y = 4 + \sqrt{x-3}$
$\therefore \quad h^{-1}(x) = 4 + \sqrt{x-3}, \quad x \geq 3$

b
$h \circ h^{-1}$
$= h\left(h^{-1}(x)\right)$
$= h(4 + \sqrt{x-3})$
$= (4 + \sqrt{x-3} - 4)^2 + 3$
$= \left(\sqrt{x-3}\right)^2 + 3$
$= x - 3 + 3$
$= x$

$h^{-1} \circ h$
$= h^{-1}(h(x))$
$= h^{-1}\left((x-4)^2 + 3\right)$
$= 4 + \sqrt{(x-4)^2 + 3 - 3}$
$= 4 + \sqrt{(x-4)^2}$
$= 4 + x - 4 \quad \{\text{as } x \geq 4\}$
$= x$

$\therefore \quad h \circ h^{-1} = h^{-1} \circ h = x$

REVIEW SET 1C

1 $h(x) = 7 - 3x$

a $h(2x - 1) = 7 - 3(2x - 1)$
$= 7 - 6x + 3$
$= 10 - 6x$

b $h(2x - 1) = -2$
$\therefore \quad 10 - 6x = -2$
$\therefore \quad -6x = -12$
$\therefore \quad x = 2$

2 a Domain is $\{x \mid x > -3\}$.
Range is $\{y \mid -3 < y < 5\}$.

b Domain is $\{x \mid x \neq 1\}$.
Range is $\{y \mid y \leq -3 \text{ or } y \geq 5\}$.

3 a i $(f \circ g)(x) = f(g(x))$
$= f(\sqrt{x})$
$= 1 - 2\sqrt{x}$

ii $(g \circ f)(x) = g(f(x))$
$= g(1 - 2x)$
$= \sqrt{1 - 2x}$

b The domain of $f \circ g$ is $\{x \mid x \geq 0\}$ for $\sqrt{x}$ to be defined.
The range of $f \circ g$ is $\{y \mid y \leq 1\}$.
The domain of $g \circ f$ is obtained by noticing that $1 - 2x$ must be ≥ 0.
$\therefore \quad 2x \leq 1$
$\therefore \quad x \leq \frac{1}{2}$
$\therefore \quad$ the domain is $\{x \mid x \leq \frac{1}{2}\}$
and the range is $\{y \mid y \geq 0\}$.

4 **a** $\dfrac{x^2-3}{x-2}<6$

$\therefore\ \dfrac{x^2-3}{x-2}-\dfrac{6(x-2)}{x-2}<0$

$\therefore\ \dfrac{x^2-6x+9}{x-2}<0$

$\therefore\ \dfrac{(x-3)^2}{x-2}<0$

Sign diagram of LHS is

$\begin{array}{c|c|c|c}\ -\ & \ +\ & \ +\ \\ \hline & 2 & 3 & \end{array} \longrightarrow x$

$\therefore$ LHS <0 when $x\in\ ]-\infty,2[$

b $\dfrac{2x+1}{x-1}\geqslant\dfrac{2x+3}{x+2}$

$\therefore\ \dfrac{2x+1}{x-1}-\dfrac{2x+3}{x+2}\geqslant 0$

$\therefore\ \dfrac{(2x+1)(x+2)-(2x+3)(x-1)}{(x-1)(x+2)}\geqslant 0$

$\therefore\ \dfrac{2x^2+4x+x+2-2x^2+2x-3x+3}{(x-1)(x+2)}\geqslant 0$

$\therefore\ \dfrac{4x+5}{(x-1)(x+2)}\geqslant 0$

Sign diagram of LHS is

$\begin{array}{c|c|c|c|c}\ -\ & \ +\ & \ -\ & \ +\ \\ \hline -2 & -\tfrac{5}{4} & 1 & \end{array} \longrightarrow x$

$\therefore$ LHS $\geqslant 0$ when $x\in\ ]-2,-\tfrac{5}{4}]$ or $]1,\infty[$

5 **a** $f(x)=\dfrac{1}{x^2}$ is meaningless when $x=0$.

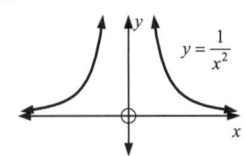

b [graph of $y=\dfrac{1}{x^2}$]

c Domain of $f(x)$ is $\{x\mid x\neq 0\}$.
Range of $f(x)$ is $\{y\mid y>0\}$.

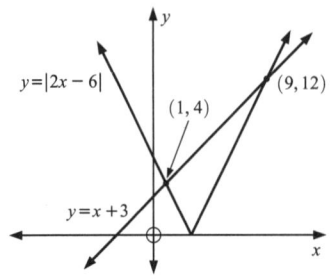

6 **a** [graph showing $y=|2x-6|$ and $y=x+3$ intersecting at $(1,4)$ and $(9,12)$]

$y=|2x-6|$ and $y=x+3$ intersect at $x=1$ and $x=9$.
$\therefore$ from the graph, $|2x-6|>x+3$ when $x\in\ ]-\infty,1[$ or $]9,\infty[$.

b [graph of $y=\dfrac{x}{|x|+1}$ with asymptote $y=\tfrac{1}{3}$ and point $(\tfrac{1}{2},\tfrac{1}{3})$]

$\therefore\ \dfrac{x}{|x|+1}\geqslant\tfrac{1}{3}$ for $x\in[\tfrac{1}{2},\infty[$

7 **a** $y=\dfrac{(x+2)(x-3)}{x-1}$ is zero when
$x=-2$ or 3, and undefined when $x=1$.
When $x=0$, $y=\dfrac{(2)(-3)}{-1}=6>0$.
Since the factors are single, the signs alternate.
$\therefore$ the sign diagram is

$\begin{array}{c|c|c|c|c}\ -\ & \ +\ & \ -\ & \ +\ \\ \hline -2 & 1 & 3 & \end{array} \longrightarrow x$

b $\dfrac{x^2+x-8}{x-1}<2$

$\therefore\ \dfrac{x^2+x-8}{x-1}-\dfrac{2(x-1)}{(x-1)}<0$

$\therefore\ \dfrac{x^2-x-6}{x-1}<0$

$\therefore\ \dfrac{(x+2)(x-3)}{x-1}<0$

From **a**, sign diagram of LHS is

$\begin{array}{c|c|c|c|c}\ -\ & \ +\ & \ -\ & \ +\ \\ \hline -2 & 1 & 3 & \end{array} \longrightarrow x$

$\therefore$ LHS <0 when $x\in\ ]-\infty,-2[$ or $]1,3[$

8 **a** $f(x) = x - 2 + \dfrac{5}{(x-1)^2}$ is undefined when $x = 1$, so $x = 1$ is a vertical asymptote.

As $|x| \to \infty$, $\dfrac{5}{(x-1)^2} \to 0$, so $f(x) \to x - 2$. $\therefore$ $y = x - 2$ is an oblique asymptote.

b As $x \to 1^-$, $y \to \infty$.
As $x \to 1^+$, $y \to \infty$.
As $x \to \infty$, $y \to (x - 2)^+$.
As $x \to -\infty$, $y \to (x - 2)^+$.

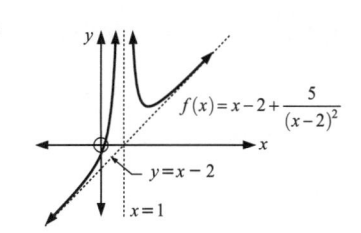

c

[Graph showing $f(x) = x - 2 + \dfrac{5}{(x-2)^2}$, asymptote $y = x - 2$, and $x = 1$]

9 **a** $f(x) = 4x + 2$
$\therefore \ y = 4x + 2$
$\therefore \ f^{-1}(x)$ is $x = 4y + 2$
$\therefore \ y = \dfrac{x - 2}{4}$
So, $f^{-1}(x) = \dfrac{x - 2}{4}$

b $f(x) = \dfrac{3 - 5x}{4}$ so $y = \dfrac{3 - 5x}{4}$
$\therefore \ f^{-1}(x)$ is $x = \dfrac{3 - 5y}{4}$
$\therefore \ 4x = 3 - 5y$
$\therefore \ y = \dfrac{3 - 4x}{5}$
So, $f^{-1}(x) = \dfrac{3 - 4x}{5}$

10 a/d

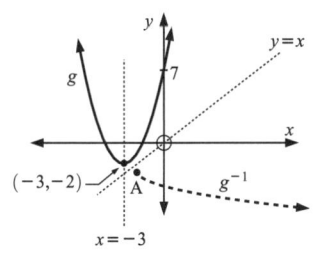

[Graph showing parabola g with vertex at $(-3, -2)$, passing through y-axis at 7, line $y = x$, point A, curve g^{-1}, and vertical line $x = -3$]

b If $x \leqslant -3$, we have the graph to the left of $x = -3$, and any horizontal line through the graph cuts it no more than once. Therefore it has an inverse function.

c $\qquad g(x) = x^2 + 6x + 7, \quad x \leqslant -3$
$\therefore \qquad y = x^2 + 6x + 7, \quad x \leqslant -3$
$\therefore \ g^{-1}(x)$ is $\ x = y^2 + 6y + 7, \quad y \leqslant -3$
$\qquad \qquad = (y + 3)^2 - 9 + 7$
$\therefore \qquad x + 2 = (y + 3)^2$
$\therefore \qquad y + 3 = \pm\sqrt{x + 2}$
$\therefore \qquad y = -3 \pm \sqrt{x + 2}$
but $y \leqslant -3$, so $y = -3 - \sqrt{x + 2}$
So, $g^{-1}(x) = -3 - \sqrt{x + 2}$

e The range of g is $\{y \mid y \geqslant -2\}$, so the domain of g^{-1} is $\{x \mid x \geqslant -2\}$
and the range of g^{-1} is $\{y \mid y \leqslant -3\}$.

Chapter 2
SEQUENCES AND SERIES

EXERCISE 2A

1 **a** 4, 13, 22, 31   **b** 45, 39, 33, 27   **c** 2, 6, 18, 54   **d** 96, 48, 24, 12

2 **a** The sequence starts at 8 and each term is 8 more than the previous term. The next two terms are 40 and 48.
   b The sequence starts at 2 and each term is 3 more than the previous term. The next two terms are 14 and 17.
   c The sequence starts at 36 and each term is 5 less than the previous term. The next two terms are 16 and 11.
   d The sequence starts at 96 and each term is 7 less than the previous term. The next two terms are 68 and 61.
   e The sequence starts at 1 and each term is 4 times the previous term. The next two terms are 256 and 1024.
   f The sequence starts at 2 and each term is 3 times the previous term. The next two terms are 162 and 486.
   g The sequence starts at 480 and each term is half the previous term. The next two terms are 30 and 15.
   h The sequence starts at 243 and each term is one third of the previous term. The next two terms are 3 and 1.
   i The sequence starts at 50 000 and each term is one fifth of the previous term. The next two terms are 80 and 16.

3 **a** Each term is the square of the number of the term. The next three terms are 25, 36 and 49.
   b Each term is the cube of the number of the term. The next three terms are 125, 216 and 343.
   c Each term is $n \times (n+1)$ where n is the number of the term. The next three terms are 30, 42 and 56.

EXERCISE 2B

1 **a** The sequence $\{2n\}$ begins 2, 4, 6, 8, 10 (letting $n = 1, 2, 3, 4, 5, \ldots$).
   b The sequence $\{2n+2\}$ begins 4, 6, 8, 10, 12 (letting $n = 1, 2, 3, 4, 5, \ldots$).
   c The sequence $\{2n-1\}$ begins 1, 3, 5, 7, 9 (letting $n = 1, 2, 3, 4, 5, \ldots$).
   d The sequence $\{2n-3\}$ begins $-1, 1, 3, 5, 7$ (letting $n = 1, 2, 3, 4, 5, \ldots$).
   e The sequence $\{2n+3\}$ begins 5, 7, 9, 11, 13 (letting $n = 1, 2, 3, 4, 5, \ldots$).
   f The sequence $\{2n+11\}$ begins 13, 15, 17, 19, 21 (letting $n = 1, 2, 3, 4, 5, \ldots$).
   g The sequence $\{3n+1\}$ begins 4, 7, 10, 13, 16 (letting $n = 1, 2, 3, 4, 5, \ldots$).
   h The sequence $\{4n-3\}$ begins 1, 5, 9, 13, 17 (letting $n = 1, 2, 3, 4, 5, \ldots$).

2 **a** The sequence $\{2^n\}$ begins 2, 4, 8, 16, 32 (letting $n = 1, 2, 3, 4, 5, \ldots$).
   b The sequence $\{3 \times 2^n\}$ begins 6, 12, 24, 48, 96 (letting $n = 1, 2, 3, 4, 5, \ldots$).
   c The sequence $\{6 \times (\frac{1}{2})^n\}$ begins $3, \frac{3}{2}, \frac{3}{4}, \frac{3}{8}, \frac{3}{16}$ (letting $n = 1, 2, 3, 4, 5, \ldots$).
   d The sequence $\{(-2)^n\}$ begins $-2, 4, -8, 16, -32$ (letting $n = 1, 2, 3, 4, 5, \ldots$).

3 $\{15 - (-2)^n\}$ generates the sequence with first five terms:
   $t_1 = 15 - (-2)^1 = 17,$ $t_2 = 15 - (-2)^2 = 11,$ $t_3 = 15 - (-2)^3 = 23,$
   $t_4 = 15 - (-2)^4 = -1,$ $t_5 = 15 - (-2)^5 = 47$

EXERCISE 2C

1 a $17 - 6 = 11$
$28 - 17 = 11$
$39 - 28 = 11$ Assuming that the pattern continues, consecutive terms differ by 11.
$50 - 39 = 11$ $\therefore$ the sequence is arithmetic with $u_1 = 6$, $d = 11$.

b $u_n = u_1 + (n-1)d$ **c** $u_{50} = 11(50) - 5$ **d** Let $u_n = 325 = 11n - 5$
$= 6 + (n-1)11$ $= 545$ $\therefore \quad 330 = 11n$
$= 11n - 5$ $\therefore \quad n = 30$
                                                          So, 325 is the 30th member.

e Let $u_n = 761 = 11n - 5$
$\therefore \quad 766 = 11n$
$\therefore \quad n = 69\frac{7}{11}$, but n must be an integer, so 761 is not a member of the sequence.

2 a $83 - 87 = -4$ Assuming that the pattern continues, consecutive terms differ by -4.
$79 - 83 = -4$ $\therefore$ the sequence is arithmetic with $u_1 = 87$, $d = -4$.
$75 - 79 = -4$

b $u_n = u_1 + (n-1)d$ **c** $u_{40} = 91 - 4(40)$ **d** Let $u_n = -143 = 91 - 4n$
$= 87 + (n-1)(-4)$ $= 91 - 160$ $\therefore \quad 4n = 234$
$= 87 - 4n + 4$ $= -69$ $\therefore \quad n = 58\frac{1}{2}$
$= 91 - 4n$ But n must be an integer, so
                                                          -143 is not a member
                                                          of the sequence.

3 a $u_n = 3n - 2$, $u_1 = 3(1) - 2 = 1$ and $u_{n+1} = 3(n+1) - 2 = 3n + 1$
$u_{n+1} - u_n = (3n+1) - (3n-2)$ Consecutive terms differ by 3.
$= 3$, a constant $\therefore$ the sequence is arithmetic with $u_1 = 1$ and $d = 3$.

b $u_1 = 1$, $d = 3$ **c** $u_{57} = 3(57) - 2 = 169$

d Let $u_n = 450 = 3n - 2$, so $3n = 452$ and hence $n = 150\frac{2}{3}$.
We try the two values on either side of $n = 150\frac{2}{3}$, which are $n = 150$ and $n = 151$:
$u_{150} = 3(150) - 2 = 448$ and $u_{151} = 3(151) - 2 = 451$
So, $u_{151} = 451$ is the least term which is greater than 450.

4 a $u_n = \dfrac{71 - 7n}{2} = 35\frac{1}{2} - \frac{7}{2}n$ $u_1 = \dfrac{71 - 7(1)}{2} = 32$

$u_{n+1} = \dfrac{71 - 7(n+1)}{2} = \dfrac{71 - 7n - 7}{2} = \dfrac{64 - 7n}{2} = 32 - \frac{7}{2}n$

$u_{n+1} - u_n = (32 - \frac{7}{2}n) - (35\frac{1}{2} - \frac{7}{2}n) = -\frac{7}{2}$, a constant

So, consecutive terms differ by $-\frac{7}{2}$.
$\therefore$ the sequence is arithmetic with $u_1 = 32$, $d = -\frac{7}{2}$.

b $u_1 = 32$, $d = -\frac{7}{2}$ **c** $u_{75} = \dfrac{71 - 7(75)}{2} = -227$

d Let $u_n = -200 = \dfrac{71 - 7n}{2}$ so $-400 = 71 - 7n$ $\therefore$ $7n = 471$
$\therefore$ $n = 67\frac{2}{7}$

We try the two values on either side of $n = 67\frac{2}{7}$, which are $n = 67$ and $n = 68$:
$u_{67} = \dfrac{71 - 7(67)}{2} = -199$ and $u_{68} = \dfrac{71 - 7(68)}{2} = -202\frac{1}{2}$
So, the terms of the sequence are less than -200 for $n \geqslant 68$.

5 **a** The terms are consecutive,
$\therefore$ $k - 32 = 3 - k$
{equating common differences}
$\therefore$ $2k = 35$ and so $k = 17\frac{1}{2}$

b The terms are consecutive,
$\therefore$ $(2k+1) - (k+1) = 13 - (2k+1)$
$\therefore$ $k = 12 - 2k$
$\therefore$ $3k = 12$ and so $k = 4$

c The terms are consecutive,
$k - 5 = k^2 - 8 - k$
{equating common differences}
$\therefore$ $k^2 - 2k - 3 = 0$
$\therefore$ $(k-3)(k+1) = 0$
$\therefore$ $k = -1$ or 3

6 **a** $u_7 = 41$ $\therefore$ $u_1 + 6d = 41$ .... (1)
$u_{13} = 77$ $\therefore$ $u_1 + 12d = 77$ .... (2)
Solving simultaneously,
$-u_1 - 6d = -41$
$u_1 + 12d = 77$
$\therefore$ $6d = 36$ {adding the
$\therefore$ $d = 6$ equations}
So in (1), $u_1 + 6(6) = 41$
$\therefore$ $u_1 + 36 = 41$
$\therefore$ $u_1 = 5$
Now $u_n = u_1 + (n-1)d$
$\therefore$ $u_n = 5 + (n-1)6$
$\therefore$ $u_n = 6n - 1$

b $u_5 = -2$ $\therefore$ $u_1 + 4d = -2$ .... (1)
$u_{12} = -12\frac{1}{2}$ $\therefore$ $u_1 + 11d = -12\frac{1}{2}$ .... (2)
Solving simultaneously,
$-u_1 - 4d = 2$
$u_1 + 11d = -12\frac{1}{2}$
$\therefore$ $7d = -10\frac{1}{2}$ {adding the
$\therefore$ $d = -\frac{3}{2}$ equations}
So in (1), $u_1 + 4(-\frac{3}{2}) = -2$
$\therefore$ $u_1 = 4$
Now $u_n = u_1 + (n-1)d$
$\therefore$ $u_n = 4 + (n-1)(-\frac{3}{2})$
$\therefore$ $u_n = -\frac{3}{2}n + \frac{11}{2}$

c $u_7 = 1$ $\therefore$ $u_1 + 6d = 1$ .... (1)
$u_{15} = -39$ $\therefore$ $u_1 + 14d = -39$ .... (2)
Solving simultaneously,
$-u_1 - 6d = -1$
$u_1 + 14d = -39$
$\therefore$ $8d = -40$ {adding the
$\therefore$ $d = -5$ equations}
So in (1), $u_1 + 6(-5) = 1$
$\therefore$ $u_1 - 30 = 1$
$\therefore$ $u_1 = 31$
Now $u_n = u_1 + (n-1)d$
$\therefore$ $u_n = 31 + (n-1)(-5)$
$\therefore$ $u_n = 31 - 5n + 5$
$\therefore$ $u_n = -5n + 36$

d $u_{11} = -16$ $\therefore$ $u_1 + 10d = -16$ .... (1)
$u_8 = -11\frac{1}{2}$ $\therefore$ $u_1 + 7d = -11\frac{1}{2}$ .... (2)
Solving simultaneously,
$-u_1 - 10d = 16$
$u_1 + 7d = -11\frac{1}{2}$
$\therefore$ $-3d = 4\frac{1}{2}$ {adding the
$\therefore$ $d = -\frac{3}{2}$ equations}
So in (1), $u_1 + 10(-\frac{3}{2}) = -16$
$\therefore$ $u_1 - 15 = -16$
$\therefore$ $u_1 = -1$
Now $u_n = u_1 + (n-1)d$
$\therefore$ $u_n = -1 + (n-1)(-\frac{3}{2})$
$\therefore$ $u_n = -\frac{3}{2}n + \frac{1}{2}$

7 **a** Let the numbers be 5, $5 + d$, $5 + 2d$, $5 + 3d$, 10.
Then $5 + 4d = 10$
$\therefore$ $4d = 5$
$\therefore$ $d = \frac{5}{4} = 1\frac{1}{4}$
So, the numbers are $5, 6\frac{1}{4}, 7\frac{1}{2}, 8\frac{3}{4}, 10$.

b Let the numbers be -1, $-1 + d$, $-1 + 2d$, $-1 + 3d$, $-1 + 4d$, $-1 + 5d$, $-1 + 6d$, 32.
Then $-1 + 7d = 32$
$\therefore$ $7d = 33$
$\therefore$ $d = \frac{33}{7} = 4\frac{5}{7}$
So, the numbers are $-1, 3\frac{5}{7}, 8\frac{3}{7}, 13\frac{1}{7}, 17\frac{6}{7}, 22\frac{4}{7}, 27\frac{2}{7}, 32$.

8 **a** $u_1 = 36$, $35\frac{1}{3} - 36 = -\frac{2}{3}$, $34\frac{2}{3} - 35\frac{1}{3} = -\frac{2}{3}$, so $d = -\frac{2}{3}$

b $u_n = u_1 + (n-1)d$
$\therefore$ $-30 = 36 + (n-1)(-\frac{2}{3})$ {letting $u_n = -30$, the last term of the sequence}
$\therefore$ $-66 = -\frac{2}{3}n + \frac{2}{3}$
$\therefore$ $\frac{2}{3}n = 66\frac{2}{3}$
$\therefore$ $n = 100$ So, the sequence has 100 terms.

9 $u_1 = 23$, $36 - 23 = 13$
       $49 - 36 = 13$
       $62 - 49 = 13$, so $d = 13$

$\therefore$ $u_n = u_1 + (n-1)d$
$\therefore$ $u_n = 23 + (n-1)13$
       $= 23 + 13n - 13$
$\therefore$ $u_n = 13n + 10$

Let $u_n = 100\,000 = 13n + 10$
$\therefore$ $99\,990 = 13n$
$\therefore$ $n = 7691\frac{7}{13}$

We try the two values on either side of $n = 7691\frac{7}{13}$, which are $n = 7691$ and $n = 7692$:
$u_{7691} = 13(7691) + 10 = 99\,993$ and $u_{7692} = 13(7692) + 10 = 100\,006$
So, the first term to exceed $100\,000$ is $u_{7692} = 100\,006$.

EXERCISE 2D.1

1 a $\frac{6}{2} = 3$ $\therefore$ $r = 3$, $u_1 = 2$ $\therefore$ $b = 6 \times 3 = 18$ and $c = 18 \times 3 = 54$

b $\frac{5}{10} = \frac{1}{2}$ $\therefore$ $r = \frac{1}{2}$, $u_1 = 10$ $\therefore$ $b = 5 \times \frac{1}{2} = 2\frac{1}{2}$ and $c = 2\frac{1}{2} \times \frac{1}{2} = 1\frac{1}{4}$

c $\frac{-6}{12} = -\frac{1}{2}$ $\therefore$ $r = -\frac{1}{2}$, $u_1 = 12$ $\therefore$ $b = -6 \times -\frac{1}{2} = 3$ and $c = 3 \times -\frac{1}{2} = -1\frac{1}{2}$

2 a $\frac{10}{5} = \frac{20}{10} = \frac{40}{20} = 2$ Assuming the pattern continues, consecutive terms have a common ratio of 2.
b $u_n = u_1 r^{n-1}$ $\therefore$ the sequence is geometric with $u_1 = 5$ and $r = 2$.
$\therefore$ $u_n = 5 \times 2^{n-1}$
so $u_{15} = 5 \times 2^{14} = 81\,920$

3 a $\frac{-6}{12} = -\frac{1}{2}$ Assuming the pattern continues, consecutive terms have a common ratio of $-\frac{1}{2}$.
$\frac{3}{-6} = -\frac{1}{2}$
$\frac{(-\frac{3}{2})}{3} = -\frac{1}{2}$ $\therefore$ the sequence is geometric with $u_1 = 12$ and $r = -\frac{1}{2}$.

b $u_n = u_1 r^{n-1}$ so $u_{13} = 12 \times (-\frac{1}{2})^{13-1}$
$\therefore$ $u_n = 12 \times (-\frac{1}{2})^{n-1}$
       $= 12 \times (-\frac{1}{2})^{12}$
       $= 12 \times \frac{1}{4096}$
       $= 3 \times \frac{1}{1024} = \frac{3}{1024}$

4 $\frac{-6}{8} = -\frac{3}{4}$ Assuming the pattern continues, consecutive terms have a common ratio of $-\frac{3}{4}$.
$\frac{4.5}{-6} = \frac{(\frac{9}{2})}{6} = -\frac{3}{4}$ $\therefore$ the sequence is geometric with $u_1 = 8$ and $r = -\frac{3}{4}$.

$\frac{-3.375}{4.5} = \frac{(-\frac{27}{8})}{(\frac{9}{2})} = -\frac{3}{4}$

$u_n = u_1 r^{n-1} = 8 \times (-\frac{3}{4})^{n-1}$ So, $u_{10} = 8 \times (-\frac{3}{4})^9 \approx -0.601$

5 $\dfrac{4\sqrt{2}}{8} = \dfrac{\sqrt{2}}{2} = \dfrac{1}{\sqrt{2}}$ Assuming the pattern continues, consecutive terms have a common ratio of $\dfrac{1}{\sqrt{2}}$.

$\dfrac{4}{4\sqrt{2}} = \dfrac{1}{\sqrt{2}}$ $\therefore$ the sequence is geometric with $u_1 = 8$ and $r = \dfrac{1}{\sqrt{2}}$.

$\dfrac{2\sqrt{2}}{4} = \dfrac{\sqrt{2}}{2} = \dfrac{1}{\sqrt{2}}$

$u_n = u_1 r^{n-1} = 8 \left(\dfrac{1}{\sqrt{2}}\right)^{n-1} = 2^3 \times \left(2^{-\frac{1}{2}}\right)^{n-1} = 2^3 \times 2^{-\frac{1}{2}n + \frac{1}{2}}$

So, $u_n = 2^{\frac{7}{2} - \frac{n}{2}}$

6 a Since the terms are geometric,
$\dfrac{k}{7} = \dfrac{28}{k}$ $\therefore$ $k^2 = 196$
$\therefore$ $k = \pm 14$

b Since the terms are geometric,
$\dfrac{3k}{k} = \dfrac{20 - k}{3k} = 3$
$\therefore$ $20 - k = 9k$
$\therefore$ $20 = 10k$
$\therefore$ $k = 2$

c Since the terms are geometric,
$\dfrac{k + 8}{k} = \dfrac{9k}{k + 8}$
$\therefore$ $(k + 8)^2 = 9k^2$
$\therefore$ $k^2 + 16k + 64 = 9k^2$
$\therefore$ $8k^2 - 16k - 64 = 0$
$\therefore$ $8(k^2 - 2k - 8) = 0$
$\therefore$ $8(k + 2)(k - 4) = 0$ and so $k = -2$ or 4

7 a $u_4 = 24$ $\therefore$ $u_1 \times r^3 = 24$ .... (1)
$u_7 = 192$ $\therefore$ $u_1 \times r^6 = 192$ .... (2)

So, $\dfrac{u_1 r^6}{u_1 r^3} = \dfrac{192}{24}$ $\{(2) \div (1)\}$

$\therefore$ $r^3 = 8$ $\therefore$ $r = 2$

So in (1), $u_1 \times 2^3 = 24$
$\therefore$ $u_1 \times 8 = 24$
$\therefore$ $u_1 = 3$
$\therefore$ $u_n = 3 \times 2^{n-1}$

b $u_3 = 8$ $\therefore$ $u_1 \times r^2 = 8$ .... (1)
$u_6 = -1$ $\therefore$ $u_1 \times r^5 = -1$ .... (2)

So, $\dfrac{u_1 r^5}{u_1 r^2} = -\dfrac{1}{8}$ $\{(2) \div (1)\}$

$\therefore$ $r^3 = -\dfrac{1}{8}$ $\therefore$ $r = -\dfrac{1}{2}$

So in (1), $u_1 \times \left(-\dfrac{1}{2}\right)^2 = 8$
$\therefore$ $u_1 \times \dfrac{1}{4} = 8$
$\therefore$ $u_1 = 32$
$\therefore$ $u_n = 32 \times \left(-\dfrac{1}{2}\right)^{n-1}$

c $u_7 = 24$ $\therefore$ $u_1 \times r^6 = 24$ .... (1)
$u_{15} = 384$ $\therefore$ $u_1 \times r^{14} = 384$ .... (2)

So, $\dfrac{u_1 r^{14}}{u_1 r^6} = \dfrac{384}{24}$ $\{(2) \div (1)\}$

$\therefore$ $r^8 = 16$ $\therefore$ $r = \pm\sqrt{2}$

So in (1), $u_1 \times (\pm\sqrt{2})^6 = 24$
$\therefore$ $u_1 \times 8 = 24$
$\therefore$ $u_1 = 3$

Now $u_n = u_1 r^{n-1}$
$\therefore$ $u_n = 3 \times (\sqrt{2})^{n-1}$
or $u_n = 3 \times (-\sqrt{2})^{n-1}$

d $u_3 = 5$ $\therefore$ $u_1 \times r^2 = 5$ .... (1)
$u_7 = \dfrac{5}{4}$ $\therefore$ $u_1 \times r^6 = \dfrac{5}{4}$ .... (2)

So, $\dfrac{u_1 r^6}{u_1 r^2} = \dfrac{\left(\frac{5}{4}\right)}{5}$ $\{(2) \div (1)\}$

$\therefore$ $r^4 = \dfrac{1}{4}$ $\therefore$ $r = \pm\dfrac{1}{\sqrt{2}}$

So in (1), $u_1 \times \left(\pm\dfrac{1}{\sqrt{2}}\right)^2 = 5$
$\therefore$ $u_1 \times \dfrac{1}{2} = 5$
$\therefore$ $u_1 = 10$

Now $u_n = u_1 r^{n-1}$
$\therefore$ $u_n = 10 \times \left(\dfrac{1}{\sqrt{2}}\right)^{n-1}$
$= 10 \times (\sqrt{2})^{1-n}$
or $u_n = 10 \times \left(-\dfrac{1}{\sqrt{2}}\right)^{n-1}$
$= 10 \times (-\sqrt{2})^{1-n}$

8 **a** 2, 6, 18, 54, ... has $u_1 = 2$ and $r = 3$
$u_n = u_1 r^{n-1}$ ∴ $u_n = 2 \times 3^{n-1}$
Let $u_n = 10\,000 = 2 \times 3^{n-1}$, so $5000 = 3^{n-1}$
∴ $n \approx 8.7527$ {using technology}
We try the two values on either side of $n = 8.7527$, which are $n = 8$ and $n = 9$:
$u_8 = 2 \times 3^7$ and $u_9 = 2 \times 3^8$
$= 4374$ $= 13\,122$
So, the first term to exceed $10\,000$ is $u_9 = 13\,122$.

b 4, $4\sqrt{3}$, 12, $12\sqrt{3}$, ... has $u_1 = 4$ and $r = \sqrt{3}$
$u_n = u_1 r^{n-1}$ ∴ $u_n = 4 \times (\sqrt{3})^{n-1}$
Let $u_n = 4800 = 4 \times (\sqrt{3})^{n-1}$, so $1200 = (\sqrt{3})^{n-1}$
∴ $n \approx 13.91$ {using technology}
We try the two values on either side of $n \approx 13.91$, which are $n = 13$ and $n = 14$:
$u_{13} = 4 \times (\sqrt{3})^{12}$ and $u_{14} = 4 \times (\sqrt{3})^{13}$
$= 2916$ ≈ 5050.66
So, the first term to exceed 4800 is $u_{14} \approx 5050$.

c 12, 6, 3, 1.5, ... has $u_1 = 12$ and $r = \frac{1}{2}$
$u_n = u_1 r^{n-1}$ ∴ $u_n = 12 \times (\frac{1}{2})^{n-1}$
Let $0.0001 = u_n = 12 \times (\frac{1}{2})^{n-1}$
∴ $0.000\,008\overline{3} = (\frac{1}{2})^{n-1}$
∴ $n \approx 17.87$ {using technology}
We try the two values on either side of $n \approx 17.87$, which are $n = 17$ and $n = 18$:
$u_{17} = 12 \times (\frac{1}{2})^{16}$ and $u_{18} = 12 \times (\frac{1}{2})^{17}$
$\approx 0.000\,1831$ $\approx 0.000\,091\,55$
So, the first term of the sequence which is less than 0.0001 is $u_{18} \approx 0.000\,091\,6$.

EXERCISE 2D.2

1 **a** $u_{n+1} = u_1 \times r^n$
where $u_1 = 3000$, $r = 1.1$, $n = 3$
∴ $u_4 = 3000 \times (1.1)^3$
$= 3993$
So it amounts to $3993.

b Interest $=$ amount after 3 years $-$ initial amount
$= \$3993 - \$3000$
$= \$993$

2 $u_{n+1} = u_1 \times r^n$ where $u_1 = 20\,000$, $r = 1.12$, $n = 4$
∴ $u_5 = 20\,000 \times (1.12)^4$
$\approx 31\,470.39$
Interest $= 31\,470.39 - 20\,000$ euro
$= 11\,470.39$ euro

3 **a** $u_{n+1} = u_1 \times r^n$ where $u_1 = 30\,000$, $r = 1.1$, $n = 4$
∴ $u_5 = 30\,000 \times (1.1)^4$
$= 43\,923$ The investment amounts to $43\,923$ yen.

b Interest $=$ amount after 4 years $-$ initial amount
$= 43\,923 - 30\,000$ yen.
$= 13\,923$ yen

4 $u_{n+1} = u_1 \times r^n$ where $u_1 = 80\,000$, $r = 1.09$, $n = 3$
$\therefore \quad u_4 = 80\,000 \times (1.09)^3$
$= 103\,602.32$
Interest $=$ amount after 3 years $-$ initial amount
$= \$103\,602.32 - \$80\,000$
$= \$23\,602.32$

5 $u_{n+1} = u_1 \times r^n$ where $u_1 = 100\,000$, $r = 1 + \dfrac{0.08}{2} = 1.04$, $n = 10$
$\therefore \quad u_{11} = 100\,000 \times (1.04)^{10}$
$\approx 148\,024.43$ It amounts to $148\,024.43$ yen.

6 $u_{n+1} = u_1 \times r^n$ where $u_1 = 45\,000$, $r = 1 + \dfrac{0.075}{4} = 1.018\,75$,
$n = 7$ {21 months $=$ 7 'quarters'}
$\therefore \quad u_{10} = 45\,000 \times (1.018\,75)^7$
$\approx 51\,249.06$ It amounts to £51 249.06

7 $u_{n+1} = u_1 \times r^n$ where $u_{n+1} = 20\,000$, $r = 1.075$, $n = 4$
$\therefore \quad 20\,000 = u_1 \times (1.075)^4$
$\therefore \quad u_1 \approx 14\,976.01$ $\$14\,976.01$ should be invested now.

8 $u_{n+1} = u_1 \times r^n$ where $u_{n+1} = 15\,000$, $r = 1.055$, $n = \frac{60}{12} = 5$
$\therefore \quad 15\,000 = u_1 \times (1.055)^5$
$\therefore \quad u_1 \approx 11\,477.02$ The initial investment required is £11 477.02.

9 $u_{n+1} = u_1 \times r^n$ where $u_{n+1} = 25\,000$, $r = 1 + \dfrac{0.08}{4} = 1.02$, $n = 3 \times 4 = 12$
$\therefore \quad 25\,000 = u_1 \times (1.02)^{12}$
$\therefore \quad u_1 \approx 19\,712.33$ I should invest 19 712.33 euro now.

10 $u_{n+1} = u_1 \times r^n$ where $u_{n+1} = 40\,000$, $r = 1 + \dfrac{0.09}{12} = 1.0075$, $n = 8 \times 12 = 96$
$\therefore \quad 40\,000 = u_1 \times (1.0075)^{96}$
$\therefore \quad u_1 \approx 19\,522.47$ The initial investment should be 19 522.47 yen.

EXERCISE 2D.3

1 $u_{n+1} = u_1 \times r^n$, where $u_1 = 500$, $r = 1.12$

  a   **i** $u_{11} = 500 \times (1.12)^{10}$ **ii** $u_{21} = 500 \times (1.12)^{20}$
                 ≈ 1552.92 ≈ 4823.15
           There will be approximately 1550 ants.   There will be approximately 4820 ants.

  b   For the population to reach 2000, $u_{n+1} = 500 \times (1.12)^n = 2000$
$\therefore \quad (1.12)^n = 4$
$\therefore \quad n \approx 12.23$ {using technology}
       It will take approximately 12.2 weeks.

2 $u_{n+1} = u_1 \times r^n$, where $u_1 = 555$, $r = 0.955$

  a $u_{16} = 555 \times (0.955)^{15}$
       ≈ 278.19 The population is approximately 278 animals in the year 2007.

  b   For the population to have declined to 50,
       $u_{n+1} = 555 \times (0.955)^n = 50$
$\therefore \quad (0.955)^n = 0.0\overline{900}$
$\therefore \quad n \approx 52.3$ {using technology}
     So, after approximately 52 years the population is 50. This is the year 2044.

EXERCISE 2E.1

1 a i $3, 11, 19, 27, \ldots\ldots$ is arithmetic with $u_1 = 3, d = 8$, so $u_n = 3 + (n-1)8 = 8n - 5$
$S_n = 3 + 11 + 19 + 27 + \ldots\ldots + (8n - 5)$
ii $S_5 = 3 + 11 + 19 + 27 + 35 = 95$

b i $42, 37, 32, 27, \ldots\ldots$ is arithmetic with $u_1 = 42, d = -5$,
so $u_n = 42 + (n-1)(-5) = 47 - 5n$
$\therefore \quad S_n = 42 + 37 + 32 + 27 + \ldots\ldots + (47 - 5n)$
ii $S_5 = 42 + 37 + 32 + 27 + 22 = 160$

c i $12, 6, 3, 1\frac{1}{2}, \ldots\ldots$ is geometric with $u_1 = 12, r = \frac{1}{2}$, so $u_n = 12 \times (\frac{1}{2})^{n-1}$
$S_n = 12 + 6 + 3 + 1\frac{1}{2} + \ldots\ldots + 12(\frac{1}{2})^{n-1}$
ii $S_5 = 12 + 6 + 3 + 1\frac{1}{2} + \frac{3}{4} = 23\frac{1}{4}$

d i $2, 3, 4\frac{1}{2}, 6\frac{3}{4}, \ldots\ldots$ is geometric with $u_1 = 2, r = \frac{3}{2}$, so $u_n = 2 \times (\frac{3}{2})^{n-1}$
$S_n = 2 + 3 + 4\frac{1}{2} + 6\frac{3}{4} + \ldots\ldots + 2(\frac{3}{2})^{n-1}$
ii $S_5 = 2 + 3 + 4\frac{1}{2} + 6\frac{3}{4} + 10\frac{1}{8} = 26\frac{3}{8}$

e i $1, \frac{1}{2}, \frac{1}{4}, \frac{1}{8}, \ldots\ldots$ is geometric with $u_1 = 1, r = \frac{1}{2}$, so $u_n = 1 \times (\frac{1}{2})^{n-1} = 2^{1-n}$
$S_n = 1 + \frac{1}{2} + \frac{1}{4} + \frac{1}{8} + \ldots\ldots + 2^{1-n}$
ii $S_5 = 1 + \frac{1}{2} + \frac{1}{4} + \frac{1}{8} + \frac{1}{16} = 1\frac{15}{16}$

f i $1, 8, 27, 64, \ldots\ldots$
$S_n = 1 + 8 + 27 + 64 + \ldots\ldots + n^3$ {since $1 = 1^3, \ 8 = 2^3, \ 27 = 3^3, \ 64 = 4^3$}
ii $S_5 = 1 + 8 + 27 + 64 + 125 = 225$

2 a $\displaystyle\sum_{k=1}^{4}(3k - 5) = -2 + 1 + 4 + 7 = 10$ **b** $\displaystyle\sum_{k=1}^{5}(11 - 2k) = 9 + 7 + 5 + 3 + 1 = 25$

c $\displaystyle\sum_{k=1}^{7} k(k+1) = 2 + 6 + 12 + 20 + 30 + 42 + 56 = 168$

d $\displaystyle\sum_{k=1}^{5} 10 \times 2^{k-1} = 10 + 20 + 40 + 80 + 160 = 310$

3 $u_n = 3n - 1$
$\therefore \quad u_1 + u_2 + u_3 + \ldots\ldots + u_{20} = \displaystyle\sum_{n=1}^{20}(3n - 1)$
$= 2 + 5 + 8 + 11 + 14 + 17 + 20 + 23 + 26 + 29 + 32 + 35$
$\quad + 38 + 41 + 44 + 47 + 50 + 53 + 56 + 59$
$= 610$

4 a $\displaystyle\sum_{k=1}^{n} c = \underbrace{c + c + c + \ldots. + c}_{n \text{ times}} = cn$ **b** $\displaystyle\sum_{k=1}^{n} ca_k = ca_1 + ca_2 + \ldots. + ca_n$
$= c(a_1 + a_2 + \ldots. + a_n)$
$= c \displaystyle\sum_{k=1}^{n} a_k$

c $\displaystyle\sum_{k=1}^{n}(a_k + b_k) = (a_1 + b_1) + (a_2 + b_2) + \ldots. + (a_k + b_k)$
$= (a_1 + a_2 + \ldots. + a_k) + (b_1 + b_2 + \ldots. + b_k)$
$= \displaystyle\sum_{k=1}^{n} a_k + \displaystyle\sum_{k=1}^{n} b_k$

5 a $\displaystyle\sum_{k=1}^{n}(3k^2 + 4k - 3) = \displaystyle\sum_{k=1}^{n} 3k^2 + \displaystyle\sum_{k=1}^{n} 4k - \displaystyle\sum_{k=1}^{n} 3$ {using **4 c**}
$= 3\displaystyle\sum_{k=1}^{n} k^2 + 4\displaystyle\sum_{k=1}^{n} k - 3n$ {using **4 a, b**}

b $\sum_{k=1}^{n}(k+1)(k+2)$

$= \sum_{k=1}^{n}(k^2+3k+2)$

$= \sum_{k=1}^{n}k^2 + 3\sum_{k=1}^{n}k + 2n$

$= \dfrac{n(n+1)(2n+1)}{6} + 3\dfrac{n(n+1)}{2} + 2n$

$= \dfrac{n(n+1)(2n+1) + 9n(n+1) + 12n}{6}$

$= \dfrac{2n^3 + n^2 + 2n^2 + n + 9n^2 + 9n + 12n}{6}$

$= \dfrac{2n^3 + 12n^2 + 22n}{6}$

$= \dfrac{n(n^2 + 6n + 11)}{3}$

When $n = 10$,

LHS $= \sum_{k=1}^{10}(k+1)(k+2)$
$= 2 \times 3 + 3 \times 4 + 4 \times 5 + 5 \times 6$
$\quad + 6 \times 7 + 7 \times 8 + 8 \times 9$
$\quad + 9 \times 10 + 10 \times 11 + 11 \times 12$
$= 6 + 12 + 20 + 30 + 42 + 56$
$\quad + 72 + 90 + 110 + 132$
$= 570$

RHS $= \dfrac{10(10^2 + 6(10) + 11)}{3}$
$= \dfrac{10 \times 171}{3}$
$= 570$ ✓

EXERCISE 2E.2

1 a The series is arithmetic with
$u_1 = 3, \quad d = 4, \quad n = 20$

$S_n = \dfrac{n}{2}(2u_1 + (n-1)d)$

So, $S_{20} = \dfrac{20}{2}(2 \times 3 + 19 \times 4)$
$= 10(6 + 76)$
$= 820$

c The series is arithmetic with
$u_1 = 100, \quad d = -7, \quad n = 40$

$S_n = \dfrac{n}{2}(2u_1 + (n-1)d)$

So, $S_{40} = \dfrac{40}{2}(2 \times 100 + 39 \times (-7))$
$= 20(200 - 273)$
$= -1460$

b The series is arithmetic with
$u_1 = \tfrac{1}{2}, \quad d = \tfrac{5}{2}, \quad n = 50$

$S_n = \dfrac{n}{2}(2u_1 + (n-1)d)$

So, $S_{50} = \dfrac{50}{2}\left(2 \times \tfrac{1}{2} + 49 \times \tfrac{5}{2}\right)$
$= 25(1 + 122\tfrac{1}{2})$
$= 3087\tfrac{1}{2}$

d The series is arithmetic with
$u_1 = 50, \quad d = -\tfrac{3}{2}, \quad n = 80$

$S_n = \dfrac{n}{2}(2u_1 + (n-1)d)$

So, $S_{80} = \dfrac{80}{2}\left(2 \times 50 + 79 \times (-\tfrac{3}{2})\right)$
$= 40(100 - \tfrac{237}{2})$
$= -740$

2 a The series is arithmetic with
$u_1 = 5, \quad d = 3, \quad u_n = 101$
Since $u_n = 101$,
then $u_1 + (n-1)d = 101$
$\therefore \quad 5 + 3(n-1) = 101$
$\therefore \quad 5 + 3n - 3 = 101$
$\therefore \quad 3n = 99$
$\therefore \quad n = 33$

So, $S_n = \dfrac{n}{2}(u_1 + u_n)$
$= \dfrac{33}{2}(5 + 101)$
$= 1749$

b The series is arithmetic with
$u_1 = 50, \quad d = -\tfrac{1}{2}, \quad u_n = -20$
Since $u_n = -20$,
then $u_1 + (n-1)d = -20$
$\therefore \quad 50 + (-\tfrac{1}{2})(n-1) = -20$
$\therefore \quad -\tfrac{1}{2}n + \tfrac{1}{2} = -70$
$\therefore \quad -\tfrac{1}{2}n = -\tfrac{141}{2}$
$\therefore \quad n = 141$

So, $S_n = \dfrac{n}{2}(u_1 + u_n)$
$= \dfrac{141}{2}(50 + (-20))$
$= 2115$

c The series is arithmetic with
$u_1 = 8$, $d = \frac{5}{2}$, $u_n = 83$
Since $u_n = 83$,
then $u_1 + (n-1)d = 83$
$\therefore \ 8 + \frac{5}{2}(n-1) = 83$
$\therefore \ \frac{5}{2}n - \frac{5}{2} = 75$
$\therefore \ \frac{5}{2}n = \frac{155}{2}$
$\therefore \ n = 31$

So, $S_n = \frac{n}{2}(u_1 + u_n)$
$= \frac{31}{2}(8 + 83)$
$= 1410\frac{1}{2}$

3 a $\sum_{k=1}^{10}(2k+5) = 7 + 9 + 11 + \ldots + 21 + 23 + 25$
This series is arithmetic with $u_1 = 7$, $d = 2$ and $n = 10$.
$\therefore \ \text{sum} = \frac{n}{2}[2u_1 + (n-1)d] = \frac{10}{2}[14 + 9 \times 2] = 160$

b $\sum_{k=1}^{15}(k-50) = (-49) + (-48) + (-47) + \ldots + (-37) + (-36) + (-35)$
This series is arithmetic with $u_1 = -49$, $d = 1$ and $n = 15$.
$\therefore \ \text{sum} = \frac{n}{2}[2u_1 + (n-1)d] = \frac{15}{2}[-98 + 14 \times 1] = -630$

c $\sum_{k=1}^{20}\left(\frac{k+3}{2}\right) = 2 + \frac{5}{2} + 3 + \ldots + \frac{21}{2} + 11 + \frac{23}{2}$
This series is arithmetic with $u_1 = 2$, $r = \frac{1}{2}$ and $n = 20$.
$\therefore \ \text{sum} = \frac{n}{2}[2u_1 + (n-1)d] = \frac{20}{2}[4 + 19 \times \frac{1}{2}] = 135$

4 $u_1 = 5$, $n = 7$, $u_n = 53$
$S_n = \frac{n}{2}(u_1 + u_n)$
$= \frac{7}{2}(5 + 53)$
$= 203$

5 $u_1 = 6$, $n = 11$, $u_n = -27$
$S_n = \frac{n}{2}(u_1 + u_n)$
$= \frac{11}{2}(6 + (-27))$
$= -115\frac{1}{2}$

6 The total number of bricks can be expressed as an arithmetic series:
$1 + 2 + 3 + 4 + \ldots + n$
We know that the total number of bricks is 171, so $S_n = 171$.
Also, $u_1 = 1$, $d = 1$ and we need to find n, the number of members (layers) of the series.
$S_n = \frac{n}{2}(2u_1 + (n-1)d) = 171$
$\therefore \ \frac{n}{2}(2 \times 1 + (n-1) \times 1) = 171$
$\therefore \ n(2 + n - 1) = 342$
$\therefore \ n(n+1) = 342$
$\therefore \ n^2 + n - 342 = 0$
$\therefore \ (n-18)(n+19) = 0$
$\therefore \ n = -19 \text{ or } 18$
But $n > 0$, so $n = 18$. So, there are 18 layers placed.

7 The total number of seats in n rows can be expressed as an arithmetic series:
$22 + 23 + 24 + \ldots + u_n$
Row 1 has 22 seats, so $u_1 = 22$. Row 2 has 23 seats, so $d = 1$.

$S_n = \dfrac{n}{2}(2u_1 + (n-1)d)$

$ = \dfrac{n}{2}(2 \times 22 + 1(n-1))$

$ = \dfrac{n}{2}(44 + n - 1)$

$\therefore\quad S_n = \dfrac{n}{2}(n + 43)\quad$ which is the total number of seats in n rows.

a Number of seats in row 44 = total no. of seats in every row $-$ no. of seats in the first 43 rows
$= S_{44} - S_{43}$
$= \frac{44}{2}(44 + 43) - \frac{43}{2}(43 + 43)$
$= 1914 - 1849$
$= 65$

b Number of seats in a section $= S_{44} = 1914\quad$ (from **a**)

c Number of seats in 25 sections $= S_{44} \times 25 = 1914 \times 25 = 47\,850$

8 **a** The first 50 multiples of 11 can be expressed as an arithmetic series:
$11 + 22 + 33 + \ldots\ldots + u_{50}\quad$ where $\quad u_1 = 11, \quad d = 11, \quad n = 50$
$S_n = \dfrac{n}{2}(2u_1 + (n-1)d) \quad \therefore \quad S_{50} = \dfrac{50}{2}(2 \times 11 + 11(50 - 1))$
$\phantom{S_{50}} = 25(22 + 539)$
$\phantom{S_{50}} = 14\,025$

b The multiples of 7 between 0 and 1000 can be expressed as an arithmetic series:
$7 + 14 + 21 + 28 + \ldots\ldots + u_n\quad$ where $\quad u_1 = 7, \quad d = 7$
To find u_n, we need to find the largest multiple of 7 less than 1000.
Now $\quad \dfrac{1000}{7} \approx 142.9, \quad$ so $\quad u_n = 142 \times 7 = 994$
But $\quad u_n = u_1 + (n-1)d$
$\therefore \quad 994 = 7 + 7(n-1)$
$\therefore \quad 987 = 7n - 7$
$\therefore \quad 7n = 994$
$\therefore \quad n = 142$
So, $\quad S_{142} = \dfrac{142}{2}(7 + 994) = 71\,071$

c The integers between 1 and 100 which are not divisible by 3 can be expressed as:
$1, 2, 4, 5, 7, 8, \ldots\ldots, 100\quad$ where $\quad u_1 = 1, \quad u_n = 100.$
Alternatively, these integers can be expressed as two separate arithmetic series:
$S_1 = 1 + 4 + 7 + \ldots\ldots + 97 + 100\quad$ where $\quad u_1 = 1, \quad d = 3, \quad u_n = 100$
and $\quad S_2 = 2 + 5 + 8 + \ldots\ldots + 95 + 98 \quad$ where $\quad u_1 = 2, \quad d = 3, \quad u_n = 98$
Now for S_1, $\quad u_n = u_1 + (n-1)d \qquad$ and for S_2, $\quad u_n = u_1 + (n-1)d$
$\therefore \quad 100 = 1 + 3(n-1) \qquad\qquad\qquad \therefore \quad 98 = 2 + 3(n-1)$
$\therefore \quad 99 = 3n - 3 \qquad\qquad\qquad\qquad \therefore \quad 96 = 3n - 3$
$\therefore \quad 3n = 102 \qquad\qquad\qquad\qquad\quad \therefore \quad 3n = 99$
$\therefore \quad n = 34 \qquad\qquad\qquad\qquad\qquad \therefore \quad n = 33$
So, $S_1 = \dfrac{34}{2}(1 + 100) = 1717\quad$ and $\quad S_2 = \dfrac{33}{2}(2 + 98) = 1650$
The total sum $= S_1 + S_2 = 1717 + 1650 = 3367$

9 We need to show that $\quad 1 + 2 + 3 + 4 + \ldots\ldots + n = \dfrac{n(n+1)}{2}$

The sum of the first n positive integers can be expressed as an arithmetic series:
$1 + 2 + 3 + 4 + \ldots\ldots + n$, where $\quad u_1 = 1, \quad d = 1, \quad u_n = n.$

So the sum of the series is $S_n = \dfrac{n}{2}(u_1 + u_n)$

$= \dfrac{n}{2}(1 + n)$ 　　Hence $S_n = \dfrac{n(n+1)}{2}$ as required.

10 The series of odd numbers can be expressed as an arithmetic series:
$1 + 3 + 5 + 7 + \ldots$ where $u_1 = 1$, $d = 2$

a Now $u_n = u_1 + (n-1)d = 1 + 2(n-1)$
∴ $u_n = 2n - 1$

b We need to show that S_n is n^2.
The sum of the first n odd numbers can be expressed as an arithmetic series:
$1 + 3 + 5 + 7 + \ldots (2n-1)$ 　　{using $u_n = 2n - 1$ from **a**}

So, $S_n = \dfrac{n}{2}(u_1 + u_n)$

$= \dfrac{n}{2}(1 + (2n-1))$

$= \dfrac{n}{2}(2n)$ 　　Hence $S_n = n^2$ as required.

c $S_1 = \tfrac{1}{2}(1+1) = 1 = 1^2 = n^2$ for $n = 1$ ✓
　$S_2 = \tfrac{2}{2}(1+3) = 4 = 2^2 = n^2$ for $n = 2$ ✓
　$S_3 = \tfrac{3}{2}(1+5) = 9 = 3^2 = n^2$ for $n = 3$ ✓
　$S_4 = \tfrac{4}{2}(1+7) = 16 = 4^2 = n^2$ for $n = 4$ ✓

11 $u_6 = 21$, $S_{17} = 0$. 　　We need to find u_1 and u_2.

$S_n = \dfrac{n}{2}(2u_1 + (n-1)d)$ 　　　　　　Also, $u_n = u_1 + (n-1)d$
∴ $S_{17} = \tfrac{17}{2}(2u_1 + 16d) = 0$ 　　　　　∴ $u_6 = u_1 + 5d$
∴ $u_1 + 8d = 0$ 　　　　　　　　　　　　∴ $21 = -8d + 5d$ 　{using (1)}
∴ $u_1 = -8d$ 　…… (1) 　　　　　　　　∴ $21 = -3d$
　　　　　　　　　　　　　　　　　　∴ $d = -7$
　　　　　　　　　　　　　　and $u_1 = -8(-7) = 56$
　　　　　　　　　　　　　　so $u_2 = 56 - 7 = 49$

The first two terms are 56 and 49.

12 Let the three consecutive terms be $x - d$, x and $x + d$.

Now, sum of terms $= 12$ 　　　　　Also, product of terms $= -80$
∴ $(x - d) + x + (x + d) = 12$ 　　　∴ $(4 - d)4(4 + d) = -80$
∴ $3x = 12$ 　　　　　　　　　　∴ $4(4^2 - d^2) = -80$
∴ $x = 4$ 　　　　　　　　　　　∴ $16 - d^2 = -20$
So, the terms are 　$4 - d$, 4, $4 + d$ 　　∴ $d^2 = 36$
　　　　　　　　　　　　　　　　∴ $d = \pm 6$

So, the three terms could be 　$4 - 6$, 4, $4 + 6$, 　which is $-2, 4, 10$
　　　　　　　　or 　$4 - (-6)$, 4, $4 + (-6)$, 　which is $10, 4, -2$

13 Let the five consecutive terms be 　$n - 2d$, $n - d$, n, $n + d$, $n + 2d$.

Now, sum of terms $= 40$
∴ $(n - 2d) + (n - d) + n + (n + d) + (n + 2d) = 40$
∴ $5n = 40$
∴ $n = 8$

So the terms are 　$8 - 2d$, $8 - d$, 8, $8 + d$, $8 + 2d$

Also, the product of the middle and end terms $= 8 \times (8-2d) \times (8+2d) = 224$
$$\therefore \quad 8(8^2 - 4d^2) = 224$$
$$\therefore \quad 64 - 4d^2 = 28$$
$$\therefore \quad 4d^2 = 36$$
$$\therefore \quad d^2 = 9$$
$$\therefore \quad d = \pm 3$$

So, the five terms could be $8-2(3), \ 8-3, \ 8, \ 8+3, \ 8+2(3),$ which is 2, 5, 8, 11, 14
or $8-2(-3), \ 8-(-3), \ 8, \ 8+(-3), \ 8+2(-3),$ which is 14, 11, 8, 5, 2.

EXERCISE 2E.3

1 a The series is geometric with
$u_1 = 12, \quad r = \tfrac{1}{2}, \quad n = 10$

Now $S_n = \dfrac{u_1(1-r^n)}{1-r}$

$\therefore \ S_{10} = \dfrac{12\left(1-(\tfrac{1}{2})^{10}\right)}{1-\tfrac{1}{2}}$

≈ 23.9766
≈ 24.0 (3 s.f.)

b The series is geometric with
$u_1 = \sqrt{7}, \quad r = \sqrt{7}, \quad n = 12$

Now $S_n = \dfrac{u_1(r^n - 1)}{r - 1}$

$\therefore \ S_{12} = \dfrac{\sqrt{7}\left((\sqrt{7})^{12} - 1\right)}{\sqrt{7} - 1}$

$\approx 189\,134$
$\approx 189\,000$

c The series is geometric with
$u_1 = 6, \quad r = -\tfrac{1}{2}, \quad n = 15$

Now $S_n = \dfrac{u_1(1-r^n)}{1-r}$

$\therefore \ S_{15} = \dfrac{6\left(1-(-\tfrac{1}{2})^{15}\right)}{1-(-\tfrac{1}{2})}$

≈ 4.00

d The series is geometric with
$u_1 = 1, \quad r = -\tfrac{1}{\sqrt{2}}, \quad n = 20$

Now $S_n = \dfrac{u_1(1-r^n)}{1-r}$

$\therefore \ S_{20} = \dfrac{1\left(1-(-\tfrac{1}{\sqrt{2}})^{20}\right)}{1-(-\tfrac{1}{\sqrt{2}})}$

≈ 0.585

2 a The series is geometric with
$u_1 = \sqrt{3}, \quad r = \sqrt{3}$
$S_n = \dfrac{u_1(r^n - 1)}{r - 1}$

$= \dfrac{\sqrt{3}\left((\sqrt{3})^n - 1\right)}{\sqrt{3} - 1} \times \left(\dfrac{\sqrt{3}+1}{\sqrt{3}+1}\right)$

$= \dfrac{(3+\sqrt{3})\left((\sqrt{3})^n - 1\right)}{3 - 1}$

$= \dfrac{3+\sqrt{3}}{2}\left((\sqrt{3})^n - 1\right)$

b The series is geometric with
$u_1 = 12, \quad r = \tfrac{1}{2}$
$S_n = \dfrac{u_1(1-r^n)}{1-r}$

$= \dfrac{12\left(1-(\tfrac{1}{2})^n\right)}{1-\tfrac{1}{2}}$

$= 24\left(1-(\tfrac{1}{2})^n\right)$

c The series is geometric with
$u_1 = 0.9, \quad r = 0.1$
$S_n = \dfrac{u_1(1-r^n)}{1-r}$

$= \dfrac{0.9\,(1-(0.1)^n)}{1-0.1}$

$= 1 - (0.1)^n$

d The series is geometric with
$u_1 = 20, \quad r = -\tfrac{1}{2}$
$S_n = \dfrac{u_1(1-r^n)}{1-r}$

$= \dfrac{20\left(1-(-\tfrac{1}{2})^n\right)}{1-(-\tfrac{1}{2})}$

$= \dfrac{20\left(1-(-\tfrac{1}{2})^n\right)}{(\tfrac{3}{2})}$

$= \tfrac{40}{3}\left(1-(-\tfrac{1}{2})^n\right)$

3 **a** $\sum_{k=1}^{10} \left(3 \times 2^{k-1}\right) = 3 + 6 + 12 + \ldots\ldots + 384 + 768 + 1536$

This series is geometric with $u_1 = 3$, $r = 2$ and $n = 10$.

$\therefore$ sum $= \dfrac{u_1(r^n - 1)}{r - 1} = \dfrac{3(2^{10} - 1)}{1} = 3069$

b $\sum_{k=1}^{12} \left(\tfrac{1}{2}\right)^{k-2} = 2 + 1 + \tfrac{1}{2} + \ldots\ldots + \tfrac{1}{256} + \tfrac{1}{512} + \tfrac{1}{1024}$

This series is geometric with $u_1 = 2$, $r = \tfrac{1}{2}$ and $n = 12$.

$\therefore$ sum $= \dfrac{u_1(1 - r^n)}{1 - r} = \dfrac{2\left(1 - \left(\tfrac{1}{2}\right)^{12}\right)}{\tfrac{1}{2}} = 4\left(1 - \left(\tfrac{1}{2}\right)^{12}\right) = \dfrac{2^{12} - 1}{2^{10}}$

$\therefore$ sum $= \dfrac{4095}{1024} \approx 4.00$

c $\sum_{k=1}^{25} \left(6 \times (-2)^k\right) = -12 + 24 + (-48) + \ldots + 100\,663\,296 + (-201\,326\,592)$

This series is geometric with $u_1 = -12$, $r = -2$ and $n = 25$.

$\therefore$ sum $= \dfrac{u_1(1 - r^n)}{1 - r} = \dfrac{-12\left(1 - (-2)^{25}\right)}{1 + 2} = -4\left(1 - (-2)^{25}\right)$

$\therefore$ sum $= -134\,217\,732$

4 **a** $A_2 = A_1 \times 1.06 + 2000$
$= (A_0 \times 1.06 + 2000) \times 1.06 + 2000$
$= (2000 \times 1.06 + 2000) \times 1.06 + 2000$

$\therefore$ $A_2 = 2000 + 2000 \times 1.06 + 2000 \times (1.06)^2$ as required.

b $A_3 = A_2 \times 1.06 + 2000$
$= \left[2000 + 2000 \times 1.06 + 2000 \times (1.06)^2\right] \times 1.06 + 2000$ {from **a**}

$\therefore$ $A_3 = 2000\left[1 + 1.06 + (1.06)^2 + (1.06)^3\right]$ as required.

c $A_9 = 2000[1 + 1.06 + (1.06)^2 + (1.06)^3 + (1.06)^4 + (1.06)^5 + (1.06)^6 + (1.06)^7 + (1.06)^8 + (1.06)^9]$

$\therefore$ $A_9 \approx 26\,361.59$

$\therefore$ the total bank balance after 10 years is $26\,361.59

5 **a** $S_1 = \tfrac{1}{2}$, $S_2 = \tfrac{1}{2} + \tfrac{1}{4} = \tfrac{3}{4}$, $S_3 = \tfrac{1}{2} + \tfrac{1}{4} + \tfrac{1}{8} = \tfrac{7}{8}$, $S_4 = \tfrac{1}{2} + \tfrac{1}{4} + \tfrac{1}{8} + \tfrac{1}{16} = \tfrac{15}{16}$,
$S_5 = \tfrac{1}{2} + \tfrac{1}{4} + \tfrac{1}{8} + \tfrac{1}{16} + \tfrac{1}{32} = \tfrac{31}{32}$

b $S_n = \dfrac{2^n - 1}{2^n}$

c $S_n = \dfrac{u_1(1 - r^n)}{1 - r}$, where $u_1 = \tfrac{1}{2}$, $r = \tfrac{1}{2}$

$= \dfrac{\tfrac{1}{2}\left(1 - \left(\tfrac{1}{2}\right)^n\right)}{1 - \tfrac{1}{2}}$

$\therefore$ $S_n = 1 - \left(\tfrac{1}{2}\right)^n = 1 - \dfrac{1}{2^n} = \dfrac{2^n - 1}{2^n}$

d As $n \to \infty$, $\left(\tfrac{1}{2}\right)^n \to 0$, and so $S_n \to 1$ (from below)

e The diagram represents one whole unit divided into smaller and smaller fractions.
As $n \to \infty$, the area which the fraction represents becomes smaller and smaller, and the total area approaches one whole unit.

EXERCISE 2E.4

1 a **i** $u_1 = \frac{3}{10}$

ii $r = \dfrac{\left(\frac{3}{100}\right)}{\left(\frac{3}{10}\right)} = \frac{1}{10}$

b We need to show that $0.\overline{3} = \frac{1}{3}$.

Now $0.\overline{3} = \frac{3}{10} + \frac{3}{100} + \frac{3}{1000} + \ldots\ldots$

So, let $S_n = \frac{3}{10} + \frac{3}{100} + \frac{3}{1000} + \ldots\ldots$

Since $n \to \infty$, then $S = \dfrac{u_1}{1-r} = \dfrac{\frac{3}{10}}{1-\left(\frac{1}{10}\right)} = \frac{1}{3}$

So, $0.\overline{3} = \frac{1}{3}$ as required.

2 a $0.\overline{4} = 0.444444\ldots.$

$= \frac{4}{10} + \frac{4}{100} + \frac{4}{1000} + \ldots\ldots$

which is a geometric series with
$u_1 = 0.4, \quad r = 0.1$

$\therefore \ S = \dfrac{u_1}{1-r} = \dfrac{0.4}{1-0.1} = \dfrac{0.4}{0.9}$

$= \frac{4}{9}$

So, $0.\overline{4} = \frac{4}{9}$

b $0.\overline{16} = 0.161616\ldots.$

$= \frac{16}{10^2} + \frac{16}{10^4} + \frac{16}{10^6} + \ldots\ldots$

which is a geometric series with
$u_1 = 0.16, \quad r = 0.01$

$\therefore \ S = \dfrac{u_1}{1-r} = \dfrac{0.16}{0.99} = \dfrac{16}{99}$

So, $0.\overline{16} = \frac{16}{99}$

c $0.\overline{312} = 0.312\,312\,312\ldots.$

$= \frac{312}{10^3} + \frac{312}{10^6} + \frac{312}{10^9} + \ldots\ldots$

which is a geometric series with $u_1 = 0.312, \quad r = 0.001$

$\therefore \ S = \dfrac{u_1}{1-r} = \dfrac{0.312}{0.999} = \dfrac{312}{999} = \dfrac{104}{333}$ So, $0.\overline{312} = \dfrac{104}{333}$

3 Checking **5 d** : $\quad S = \dfrac{u_1}{1-r} = \dfrac{\frac{1}{2}}{1-\frac{1}{2}}$

$\therefore \ S = 1 \ \checkmark$

4 a $18 + 12 + 8 + \ldots.$ is an infinite geometric series with $u_1 = 18, \ r = \frac{2}{3}$.

$\therefore \ S = \dfrac{u_1}{1-r}$

$= \dfrac{18}{\frac{1}{3}}$

$= 54$

b $18.9 - 6.3 + 2.1 - \ldots.$ is an infinite geometric series with $u_1 = 18.9, \ r = -\frac{1}{3}$.

$\therefore \ S = \dfrac{u_1}{1-r}$

$= \dfrac{18.9}{\frac{4}{3}}$

$= 14.175$

5 a $\displaystyle\sum_{k=1}^{\infty} \frac{3}{4^k} = \frac{3}{4} + \frac{3}{16} + \frac{3}{64} + \ldots.$ is an infinite geometric series with $u_1 = \frac{3}{4}$, $r = \frac{1}{4}$.

$\therefore \ S = \dfrac{u_1}{1-r}$

$= \dfrac{\frac{3}{4}}{\frac{3}{4}}$

$= 1$

b $\displaystyle\sum_{k=0}^{\infty} 6\left(-\frac{2}{5}\right)^k = 6 - 6 \times \left(\frac{2}{5}\right) + 6 \times \left(\frac{2}{5}\right)^2 - \ldots.$
is an infinite geometric series with $u_1 = 6$, $r = -\frac{2}{5}$.

$\therefore \ S = \dfrac{u_1}{1-r}$

$= \dfrac{6}{\frac{7}{5}}$

$= \frac{30}{7}$ or $4\frac{2}{7}$

6 **a** $18 - 9 + 4.5 - \ldots$ is an infinite geometric series with $u_1 = 18$, $r = -\frac{1}{2}$.
Since $|r| < 1$, the series converges.

$\therefore \quad S = \dfrac{u_1}{1-r}$

$= \dfrac{18}{\frac{3}{2}}$

$= 12$

$\therefore$ the series is convergent, and its sum is 12.

b $1.2 + 1.8 + 2.7 + \ldots$ is an infinite geometric series with $u_1 = 1.2$, $r = 1.5$.
Since $|r| > 1$, the series is divergent.

$S_n > 100$ when $\dfrac{u_1(r^n - 1)}{r - 1} > 100$

$\therefore \quad \dfrac{1.2(1.5^n - 1)}{\frac{1}{2}} > 100$

$\therefore \quad 2.4(1.5^n - 1) > 100$

$\therefore \quad 1.5^n - 1 > \dfrac{125}{3}$

$\therefore \quad 1.5^n > \dfrac{128}{3}$

$\therefore \quad n > 9.26$

{using technology}

$\therefore \quad n = 10$ is the smallest value of n such that $S_n > 100$.

7 Let the terms of the geometric series be $u_1,\ u_1r,\ u_1r^2,\ \ldots$

Then $u_1 + u_1r + u_1r^2 = 19$ and $\dfrac{u_1}{1-r} = 27$

$\therefore \quad u_1(1 + r + r^2) = 19$

$\therefore \quad u_1 = \dfrac{19}{1 + r + r^2}$ ...... (1)

$\therefore \quad u_1 = 27(1 - r)$ ...... (2)

Equating (1) and (2), $\dfrac{19}{1 + r + r^2} = 27(1 - r)$

$\therefore \quad \dfrac{19}{27} = (1 - r)(1 + r + r^2)$

$\therefore \quad \dfrac{19}{27} = 1 + r + r^2 - r - r^2 - r^3$

$\therefore \quad \dfrac{19}{27} = 1 - r^3$

$\therefore \quad r^3 = \dfrac{8}{27}$

$\therefore \quad r = \dfrac{2}{3}$

Substituting $r = \dfrac{2}{3}$ into (2) gives $u_1 = 27(1 - \dfrac{2}{3}) = 9$

$\therefore$ the first term is 9 and the common ratio is $\dfrac{2}{3}$.

8 Let the terms of the geometric series be $u_1,\ u_1r,\ u_1r^2,\ \ldots$

Then $u_1 r = \dfrac{8}{5}$ and $\dfrac{u_1}{1-r} = 10$

$\therefore \quad u_1 = \dfrac{8}{5r}$ ...... (1)

$\therefore \quad u_1 = 10 - 10r$ ...... (2)

Equating (1) and (2), $\dfrac{8}{5r} = 10 - 10r$

$\therefore \quad 8 = 50r - 50r^2$

$\therefore \quad 50r^2 - 50r + 8 = 0$

$\therefore \quad 2(25r^2 - 25r + 4) = 0$

$\therefore \quad 2(5r - 1)(5r - 4) = 0$

$\therefore \quad r = \dfrac{1}{5}$ or $\dfrac{4}{5}$

Using (2), if $r = \dfrac{1}{5}$, $u_1 = 10 - 10(\dfrac{1}{5}) = 8$

if $r = \dfrac{4}{5}$, $u_1 = 10 - 10(\dfrac{4}{5}) = 2$

$\therefore$ either $u_1 = 8$, $r = \dfrac{1}{5}$ or $u_1 = 2$, $r = \dfrac{4}{5}$

9 a Total time of motion $= 1 + (90\% \times 1) + (90\% \times 1) + (90\% \times 90\% \times 1)$
$\qquad \qquad \qquad \qquad \qquad + (90\% \times 90\% \times 1) + (90\% \times 90\% \times 90\% \times 1) + \ .....$
$\qquad \qquad \qquad \quad = 1 + 0.9 + 0.9 + (0.9)^2 + (0.9)^2 + (0.9)^3 + \ ......$
$\qquad \qquad \qquad \quad = 1 + 2(0.9) + 2(0.9)^2 + 2(0.9)^3 + \ ......$ as required.

b $S_n = \dfrac{u_1(1-r^n)}{1-r}$, where $u_1 = 2(0.9)$, $r = 0.9$, 'n' $= n-1$

{since the term u_1, used in calculating S_n, is the second term of the series, not the first}

$\therefore \ S_n = \dfrac{2(0.9)\left(1-(0.9)^{n-1}\right)}{1-0.9} + 1$

$\qquad = \dfrac{1.8\left(1-(0.9)^{n-1}\right)}{0.1} + 1$

$\qquad = 1 + 18\left(1-(0.9)^{n-1}\right)$

c For the ball to come to rest, n must approach infinity

$\therefore \ (0.9)^{n-1} \to 0$ and so $\left(1-(0.9)^{n-1}\right) \to 1$ (from below)

$\therefore \ S_n \to 1 + 18(1) = 19$

So, it takes 19 seconds for the ball to come to rest.

EXERCISE 2F

1 11, 14, 17, 20, ... is arithmetic with $u_1 = 11$, $d = 3$

$\therefore \ S_n = \dfrac{n}{2}[2u_1 + (n-1)d]$

$\qquad = \dfrac{n}{2}[22 + 3(n-1)]$

$\qquad = \dfrac{n}{2}[3n + 19]$

Suppose $S_n = 2000$

$\therefore \ \dfrac{n}{2}[3n + 19] = 2000$

$\therefore \ 3n^2 + 19n = 4000$

Using technology to list the terms of $3n^2 + 19n$:
$n = 33$ gives $3n^2 + 19n = 3894$
$n = 34$ gives $3n^2 + 19n = 4114$ $\therefore \ S_{34} = 2057$
$\therefore$ Henk would sell the 2000th TV set in week 34.

2 $u_1 = \$2795$, $r = 0.98$, $u_n = 500$

Now $u_n = u_1 \times r^{n-1}$

$\therefore \quad 500 = 2795 \times (0.98)^{n-1}$

$\therefore \ (0.98)^{n-1} = 0.178\,89$

Using technology to list the terms of $(0.98)^{n-1}$, $n \approx 86$.
When $n = 86$, $u_{86} = 2795 \times (0.98)^{85} \approx 501.88$ (after 85 months)
When $n = 87$, $u_{87} = 2795 \times (0.98)^{86} \approx 491.84$ (after 86 months)
So, it is $500 during the 86th month.

3 $u_2 = u_1 r = 6$ and so $u_1 = \dfrac{6}{r}$

$S_3 = u_1 + u_1 r + u_1 r^2 = -14$

$\therefore \ \dfrac{6}{r} + 6 + 6r = -14$

$\therefore \ \dfrac{6}{r} + 20 + 6r = 0$

$\therefore \ 6 + 20r + 6r^2 = 0$

$\therefore \ 3r^2 + 10r + 3 = 0$

$\therefore \ (3r+1)(r+3) = 0$

$\therefore \ r = -\tfrac{1}{3}$ or -3

When $r = -\tfrac{1}{3}$, $u_1 = -18$
When $r = -3$, $u_1 = -2$

Since $u_4 = u_1 r^3$,

$u_4 = -18 \times \left(-\tfrac{1}{3}\right)^3$ or $-2 \times (-3)^3$

$\therefore \ u_4 = \tfrac{2}{3}$ or 54

4 Total distance travelled

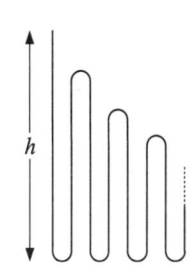

$= h + 2\left(\frac{3}{4}\right)h + 2\left(\frac{3}{4}\right)\left(\frac{3}{4}\right)h + \ldots$

$= h + 2\left(\frac{3}{4}\right)h\left[1 + \frac{3}{4} + \left(\frac{3}{4}\right)^2 + \left(\frac{3}{4}\right)^3 + \ldots\right]$

$= h + \frac{3}{2}h\left(\dfrac{1}{1-\frac{3}{4}}\right)\quad\left\{\text{as }|r|=\left|\frac{3}{4}\right|<1\text{ and }S=\dfrac{u_1}{1-r}\right\}$

$= h + \frac{3}{2}h(4)$

$= 7h$

But $7h = 490$, so $h = 70$. The table top is 70 cm above the floor.

---

5 $u_1 = 1$

Now $u_2 = u_1 + d$ {for arithmetic}   Also, $u_{14} = u_1 + 13d$ {for arithmetic}

and $u_2 = u_1 r$ {for geometric}   and $u_3 = u_1 r^2$ {for geometric}

$\therefore\ u_1 + d = u_1 r$ $\therefore\ u_1 + 13d = 3u_1 r^2$

$\therefore\ 1 + d = r$ ......(1) $\therefore\ 1 + 13d = 3r^2$ ......(2)

From (1), $d = r - 1$ $\therefore$ in (2) $1 + 13(r - 1) = 3r^2$

$\therefore\ 1 + 13r - 13 = 3r^2$

$\therefore\ 3r^2 - 13r + 12 = 0$

$\therefore\ (3r - 4)(r - 3) = 0$

$\therefore\ r = \frac{4}{3}$ or 3

When $r = \frac{4}{3}$, $d = \frac{1}{3}$: $u_{20} = u_1 + 19d = 1 + 19(\frac{1}{3}) = \frac{22}{3} = 7\frac{1}{3}$ {arithmetic}

$u_{20} = u_1 r^{19} = 1 \times \left(\frac{4}{3}\right)^{19} = \left(\frac{4}{3}\right)^{19}$ {geometric}

When $r = 3$, $d = 2$: $u_{20} = u_1 + 19d = 1 + 19(2) = 39$ {arithmetic}

$u_{20} = u_1 r^{19} = 1 \times 3^{19} = 3^{19}$ {geometric}

So, the 20th terms are $7\frac{1}{3}$ for arithmetic and $\left(\frac{4}{3}\right)^{19}$ for geometric   or

39 for arithmetic and 3^{19} for geometric.

---

6 a This series is neither arithmetic nor geometric so the sum is found by adding the 5 terms.

$\displaystyle\sum_{k=1}^{5} k(k+1)(k+2) = 6 + 24 + 60 + 120 + 210 = 420$

b $\displaystyle\sum_{k=6}^{12}\left(100(1.2)^{k-3}\right) = 172.8 + 207.36 + 248.832 + 298.5984 + 358.318\,08$
$+\ 429.981\,696 + 515.978\,0352$

This series is geometric with $u_1 = 172.8$, $r = 1.2$ and $n = 7$

$\therefore\ \text{sum} = \dfrac{u_1(r^n - 1)}{r - 1} = \dfrac{172.8\,((1.2)^7 - 1)}{0.2} \approx 2230$

---

7 a The LHS is arithmetic with $u_1 = 5$, $d = 2$,   **b** The LHS is geometric with $u_1 = 2$, $r = 3$,
'n' = n.   'n' = n.

Now $\dfrac{n}{2}[2u_1 + (n-1)d] = 1517$ Now $u_1\left(\dfrac{r^n - 1}{r - 1}\right) = 177\,146$

$\therefore\ \dfrac{n}{2}[10 + 2(n-1)] = 1517$ $\therefore\ 2\left(\dfrac{3^n - 1}{3 - 1}\right) = 177\,146$

$\therefore\ \dfrac{n}{2}[2n + 8] = 1517$ $\therefore\ 3^n - 1 = 177\,146$

$\therefore\ n(n + 4) - 1517 = 0$ $\therefore\ 3^n = 177\,147$

$\therefore\ n^2 + 4n - 1517 = 0$ where $n > 1$ $\therefore\ n = 11$ {using technology}

and $n = 37$ {using technology}

8 $\sum_{k=1}^{\infty} \left(\dfrac{3x}{2}\right)^{k-1} = \left(\dfrac{3x}{2}\right)^0 + \left(\dfrac{3x}{2}\right)^1 + \left(\dfrac{3x}{2}\right)^2 + \left(\dfrac{3x}{2}\right)^3 + \ldots$

$= 1 + \dfrac{3x}{2} + \left(\dfrac{3x}{2}\right)^2 + \left(\dfrac{3x}{2}\right)^3 + \ldots$

$= \dfrac{u_1}{1-r}$ {as it converges to 4 and is geometric}

$= \dfrac{1}{1 - \frac{3x}{2}} = \dfrac{2}{2-3x}$

$\therefore \ \dfrac{2}{2-3x} = 4$ and so $2 - 3x = \dfrac{1}{2}$

$\therefore \ 3x = 1\dfrac{1}{2}$

$\therefore \ x = \dfrac{1}{2}$

9 a $S_n = \dfrac{n(3n+11)}{2}$

$\therefore \ S_1 = u_1 = \dfrac{1(14)}{2} = 7$

and $S_2 = u_1 + u_2 = \dfrac{2(17)}{2} = 17$

$\therefore \ u_1 = 7$ and $u_2 = 10$

b $u_1 = 7$ and $d = 3$

$\therefore \ u_{20} = u_1 + 19d = 7 + 19 \times 3 = 64$

$\therefore \ $ the twentieth term is 64.

10 a $A_3 = A_2 \times 1.03 - R$
$= \left(\$8000 \times (1.03)^2 - 1.03R - R\right) \times 1.03 - R$
$= \$8000 \times (1.03)^3 - (1.03)^2 R - (1.03)R - R$

b $A_8 = \$8000 \times (1.03)^8 - (1.03)^7 R - (1.03)^6 R - (1.05)^5 R - \ldots - 1.03R - R$
We want A_8 to have a value of 0

$\therefore \ R\left(1 + 1.03 + (1.03)^2 + (1.03)^3 + \ldots + (1.03)^7\right) = \$8000 \times (1.03)^8$

$\therefore \ R\left(1\left[\dfrac{(1.03)^8 - 1}{1.03 - 1}\right]\right) = \$8000 \times (1.03)^8$

$\therefore \ R = \dfrac{\$8000 \times (1.03)^8 \times 0.03}{(1.03)^8 - 1} \approx \$1139.65$

c Notice in **b** that $\$8000 = P$ and $(1.03)^8 = \left(1 + \dfrac{3}{100}\right)^8 = \left(1 + \dfrac{r}{100}\right)^m$

$0.03 = \dfrac{3}{100} = \dfrac{r}{100}$

and $(1.03)^8 - 1 = \left(1 + \dfrac{r}{100}\right)^m - 1$

So, in the general case $R = \dfrac{P \times \left(1 + \frac{r}{100}\right)^m \times \frac{r}{100}}{\left(1 + \frac{r}{100}\right)^m - 1}$

REVIEW SET 2A

1 a $u_n = 3^{n-2}$ $\therefore \ u_1 = 3^{-1} = \dfrac{1}{3}, \ u_2 = 3^0 = 1, \ u_3 = 3^1 = 3, \ u_4 = 3^2 = 9$

b $u_n = \dfrac{3n+2}{n+3}$ $\therefore \ u_1 = \dfrac{5}{4}, \ u_2 = \dfrac{8}{5}, \ u_3 = \dfrac{11}{6}, \ u_4 = \dfrac{14}{7} = 2$

c $u_n = 2^n - (-3)^n$
$\therefore \ u_1 = 2 - (-3) = 5, \ u_2 = 4 - 9 = -5, \ u_3 = 8 - (-27) = 35, \ u_4 = 16 - 81 = -65$

2 $u_n = 68 - 5n$

a $u_{n+1} - u_n = [68 - 5(n+1)] - [68 - 5n]$
$= 68 - 5n - 5 - 68 + 5n$
$= -5$ for all n
$\therefore$ the sequence is arithmetic with common difference $d = -5$.

b $u_1 = 68 - 5(1) = 63$, $\quad d = -5$

c $u_{37} = 68 - 5(37) = -117$

d Let $u_n = -200$, and we need to find n.
$u_n = 68 - 5n = -200$
$\therefore \quad 5n = 268$
$\therefore \quad n = 53\frac{3}{5}$

We try the two values on either side of $n = 53\frac{3}{5}$, which are $n = 53$ and $n = 54$:
$u_{53} = 68 - 5(53)$ and $\quad u_{54} = 68 - 5(54)$
$= -197 \qquad\qquad\qquad = -202$
So, the first term of the sequence less than -200 is $u_{54} = -202$.

3 a 3, 12, 48, 192, ...
$\frac{12}{3} = 4 \qquad \frac{48}{12} = 4 \qquad \frac{192}{48} = 4$
Assuming the pattern continues, consecutive terms have a common ratio of 4.
$\therefore$ the sequence is geometric with $u_1 = 3$ and $r = 4$.

b $\quad u_n = u_1 r^{n-1}$
$\therefore \quad u_n = 3 \times 4^{n-1}$
$\therefore \quad u_9 = 3 \times 4^8 = 196\,608$

4 Since the terms are consecutive,
$(k-2) - 3k = k + 7 - (k-2)$ {equating common differences}
$\therefore \quad k - 2 - 3k = k + 7 - k + 2$
$\therefore \quad -2 - 2k = 9$
$\therefore \quad 2k = -11$
$\therefore \quad k = -\frac{11}{2}$

5 $u_7 = 31 \qquad \therefore \quad u_1 + 6d = 31 \quad$ ..... (1)
$u_{15} = -17 \quad \therefore \quad u_1 + 14d = -17 \quad$ ..... (2)
So, $(u_1 + 14d) - (u_1 + 6d) = -17 - 31 \quad \{(2) - (1)\}$
$\therefore \quad 8d = -48$
$\therefore \quad d = -6$

So in (1), $u_1 + 6(-6) = 31 \qquad$ Now $u_n = u_1 + (n-1)d$
$\therefore \quad u_1 - 36 = 31 \qquad \therefore \quad u_n = 67 + (n-1)(-6)$
$\therefore \quad u_1 = 67 \qquad\qquad \therefore \quad u_n = 67 - 6n + 6$
$\qquad\qquad\qquad\qquad\qquad \therefore \quad u_n = -6n + 73$
$\qquad\qquad\qquad\qquad$ So, $u_{34} = -6(34) + 73 = -131$

6 $u_n = 6\left(\frac{1}{2}\right)^{n-1}$

a $\dfrac{u_{n+1}}{u_n} = \dfrac{6\left(\frac{1}{2}\right)^{n+1-1}}{6\left(\frac{1}{2}\right)^{n-1}} = \frac{1}{2}$ for all n

b $u_1 = 6$,
$r = \frac{1}{2}$

c $u_{16} = 6\left(\frac{1}{2}\right)^{15}$
$= 0.000\,183$

$\therefore$ $\{u_n\}$ is a geometric sequence.

7 28, 23, 18, 13, ...
$23 - 28 = -5 \qquad$ Assuming that the pattern continues, consecutive terms differ by -5.
$18 - 23 = -5 \qquad \therefore$ the sequence is arithmetic with $u_1 = 28$, $d = -5$.
$13 - 18 = -5$

$u_n = u_1 + (n-1)d$ $S_n = \dfrac{n}{2}(2u_1 + (n-1)d)$
$= 28 + (n-1)(-5)$
$= 28 - 5n + 5$ $= \dfrac{n}{2}(2 \times 28 + (n-1)(-5))$
$= -5n + 33$
$= \dfrac{n}{2}(56 - 5n + 5)$

$= \dfrac{n}{2}(61 - 5n)$

8 Since the terms are geometric, then $\dfrac{k}{4} = \dfrac{k^2 - 1}{k}$

$\therefore\ k^2 = 4(k^2 - 1)$
$\therefore\ k^2 = 4k^2 - 4$
$\therefore\ 3k^2 = 4$
$\therefore\ k^2 = \dfrac{4}{3}$
$\therefore\ k = \pm \dfrac{2}{\sqrt{3}}$
$\therefore\ k = \pm \dfrac{2\sqrt{3}}{3}$

9 $u_6 = \dfrac{16}{3}$ $\therefore\ u_1 \times r^5 = \dfrac{16}{3}$ ..... (1)   So, $\dfrac{u_1 r^9}{u_1 r^5} = \dfrac{\left(\dfrac{256}{3}\right)}{\left(\dfrac{16}{3}\right)}$ $\{(2) \div (1)\}$

$u_{10} = \dfrac{256}{3}$ $\therefore\ u_1 \times r^9 = \dfrac{256}{3}$ ..... (2)

$\therefore\ r^4 = 16$
$\therefore\ r = \pm 2$

Substituting $r = 2$ into (1) gives   Substituting $r = -2$ into (1) gives
$u_1 \times 2^5 = \dfrac{16}{3}$ $u_1 \times (-2)^5 = \dfrac{16}{3}$
$\therefore\ u_1 \times 32 = \dfrac{16}{3}$ $\therefore\ u_1 \times (-32) = \dfrac{16}{3}$
$\therefore\ u_1 = \dfrac{1}{6}$ $\therefore\ u_1 = -\dfrac{1}{6}$

Now $u_n = u_1 r^{n-1}$ $\therefore\ u_n = \dfrac{1}{6} \times 2^{n-1}$ or $-\dfrac{1}{6} \times (-2)^{n-1}$

10 a $1.21 - 1.1 + 1 - ....$ is an infinite geometric series with $u_1 = 1.21$, $r = -\dfrac{10}{11}$.

$\therefore\ S = \dfrac{u_1}{1 - r}$

$= \dfrac{1.21}{\dfrac{21}{11}}$

$= \dfrac{1331}{2100} \approx 0.634$

b $\dfrac{14}{3} + \dfrac{4}{3} + \dfrac{8}{21} + ...$ is an infinite geometric series with $u_1 = \dfrac{14}{3}$, $r = \dfrac{2}{7}$.

$\therefore\ S = \dfrac{u_1}{1 - r}$

$= \dfrac{\dfrac{14}{3}}{\dfrac{5}{7}}$

$= \dfrac{98}{15} = 6\dfrac{8}{15}$

11 $u_1 = x + 3$, $u_2 = u_1 r = x - 2$

$\therefore\ r = \dfrac{u_2}{u_1} = \dfrac{x - 2}{x + 3}$

The series will converge if $|r| < 1$

$\therefore\ \left| \dfrac{x - 2}{x + 3} \right| < 1$

$\therefore\ |x - 2| < |x + 3|$ $\left\{ \left|\dfrac{a}{b}\right| = \dfrac{|a|}{|b|} \right\}$

$\therefore\ (x - 2)^2 < (x + 3)^2$
$\therefore\ x^2 - 4x + 4 < x^2 + 6x + 9$
$\therefore\ -10x < 5$
$\therefore\ x > -\dfrac{1}{2}$

12 **a** Let the terms of the geometric series be $u_1, u_1r, u_1r^2, \ldots$
Then $u_1 + u_1r = 90$ and $u_1r^2 = 24$
$\therefore \quad u_1(1+r) = 90$
$\therefore \quad u_1 = \dfrac{90}{1+r}$ ...... (1)
$\therefore \quad u_1 = \dfrac{24}{r^2}$ ...... (2)

Equating (1) and (2) gives $\dfrac{90}{1+r} = \dfrac{24}{r^2}$
$\therefore \quad 90r^2 = 24r + 24$
$\therefore \quad 90r^2 - 24r - 24 = 0$
$\therefore \quad 6(15r^2 - 4r - 4) = 0$
$\therefore \quad 6(5r+2)(3r-2) = 0$
$\therefore \quad r = -\tfrac{2}{5} \text{ or } \tfrac{2}{3}$

Using (2), if $r = -\tfrac{2}{5}$ then $u_1 = \dfrac{24}{(-\tfrac{2}{5})^2} = \dfrac{24}{\tfrac{4}{25}} = 150$

if $r = \tfrac{2}{3}$ then $u_1 = \dfrac{24}{(\tfrac{2}{3})^2} = \dfrac{24}{\tfrac{4}{9}} = 54$

$\therefore$ either $u_1 = 150,\ r = -\tfrac{2}{5}$ or $u_1 = 54,\ r = \tfrac{2}{3}$

b Since $|r| < 1$ in each case, both series converge.
When $u_1 = 150,\ r = -\tfrac{2}{5}$ \quad\quad When $u_1 = 54,\ r = \tfrac{2}{3}$
$\therefore \quad S = \dfrac{u_1}{1-r}$ \quad\quad\quad\quad\quad\quad $\therefore \quad S = \dfrac{u_1}{1-r}$
$\quad\quad = \dfrac{150}{\tfrac{7}{5}}$ \quad\quad\quad\quad\quad\quad\quad\quad $= \dfrac{54}{\tfrac{1}{3}}$
$\quad\quad = \tfrac{750}{7}$ or $107\tfrac{1}{7}$ \quad\quad\quad\quad\quad $= 162$

13 If a, b and c are consecutive terms of a geometric sequence with constant ratio r,
then $b = ar$ and $c = ar^2$ ...... (1)
If a, b and c are consecutive terms of an arithmetic sequence then
$\quad\quad b - a = c - b$
$\therefore \quad ar - a = ar^2 - ar$ \quad {using (1)}
$\therefore \quad ar^2 - 2ar + a = 0$
$\therefore \quad a(r^2 - 2r + 1) = 0$
$\therefore \quad a(r-1)^2 = 0$
$\therefore \quad a = 0$ or $r = 1$

If $a = 0$ then $b = 0$ and $c = 0$ {using (1)}
If $r = 1$ then $b = a(1) = a$ and $c = a(1)^2 = a$
In either case, $a = b = c$.

14 If x, y and z are consecutive terms of a geometric sequence, then
$\quad\quad \dfrac{y}{x} = \dfrac{z}{y}$ \quad {equating constant ratios}
$\therefore \quad y^2 = xz$ ...... (1)
Now $x + y + z = \tfrac{7}{3}$ ...... (2)
$\therefore \quad (x + y + z)^2 = \tfrac{49}{9}$
$\therefore \quad x^2 + y^2 + z^2 + 2xy + 2xz + 2yz = \tfrac{49}{9}$ {expanding LHS}
$\therefore \quad \tfrac{91}{9} + 2(xy + xz + yz) = \tfrac{49}{9}$ \quad $\{x^2 + y^2 + z^2 = \tfrac{91}{9}\}$
$\therefore \quad 2(xy + xz + yz) = -\tfrac{42}{9}$

$\therefore \quad xy + xz + yz = -\frac{7}{3}$

$\therefore \quad xy + y^2 + yz = -\frac{7}{3}$ {using (1)}

$\therefore \quad y(x + y + z) = -(x + y + z)$ $\quad \{x + y + z = \frac{7}{3}\}$

$\therefore \quad y = -1$

Substituting $y = -1$ into (1) and (2) gives $xz = 1$ and $x + z = \frac{10}{3}$ ...... (4)

$$\therefore \quad z = \frac{1}{x} \quad ...... (3)$$

Substituting (3) into (4) gives $x + \frac{1}{x} = \frac{10}{3}$

$\therefore \quad 3x^2 - 10x + 3 = 0$

$\therefore \quad (3x - 1)(x - 3) = 0$

$\therefore \quad x = \frac{1}{3}$ or 3

Using (3), if $x = \frac{1}{3}$, $z = 3$ and if $x = 3$, $z = \frac{1}{3}$

$\therefore \quad x = \frac{1}{3}, \; y = -1, \; z = 3$ or $x = 3, \; y = -1, \; z = \frac{1}{3}$

REVIEW SET 2B

1 a Given $24, 23\frac{1}{4}, 22\frac{1}{2}, \ldots, -36$ we have $u_1 = 24$, $u_n = -36$, and we need to find n.
The sequence is arithmetic with $d = -\frac{3}{4}$.

Now $u_n = u_1 + (n-1)d$

$\therefore \quad -36 = 24 + (n-1)(-\frac{3}{4})$

$\therefore \quad -60 = -\frac{3}{4}n + \frac{3}{4}$

$\therefore \quad \frac{3}{4}n = \frac{243}{4}$

$\therefore \quad n = 81$ So, there are 81 terms in the sequence.

b $u_{35} = 24 + (35 - 1)(-\frac{3}{4})$

$= 24 - \frac{102}{4}$

$= -\frac{3}{2}$

c $S_n = \frac{n}{2}(u_1 + u_n)$

$\therefore \quad S_{81} = \frac{81}{2}(24 + (-36))$

$= -486$

2 Let the numbers be $23, \; 23+d, \; 23+2d, \; 23+3d, \; 23+4d, \; 23+5d, \; 23+6d, \; 9$

Then $23 + 7d = 9$

$\therefore \quad 7d = -14$

$\therefore \quad d = -2$ So, the numbers are $23, 21, 19, 17, 15, 13, 11, 9$.

3 a The sequence $86, 83, 80, 77, \ldots$ is arithmetic with $u_1 = 86, \; d = -3$.

$u_n = u_1 + (n-1)d$

$\therefore \quad u_n = 86 + (n-1)(-3) = 86 - 3n + 3$

$\therefore \quad u_n = 89 - 3n$

b $\frac{3}{4}, 1, \frac{7}{6}, \frac{9}{7}, \ldots$ can also be written as $\frac{3}{4}, \frac{5}{5}, \frac{7}{6}, \frac{9}{7}, \ldots$
So, the numerator starts at 3 and increases by 2 each time,
whilst the denominator starts at 4 and increases by 1 each time.

The nth term is $\frac{2n+1}{n+3}$, and so $u_n = \frac{2n+1}{n+3}$

c The sequence $100, 90, 81, 72.9, \ldots$ is geometric with $u_1 = 100$, $r = \frac{90}{100} = 0.9$

$u_n = u_1 r^{n-1}$

$\therefore \quad u_n = 100(0.9)^{n-1}$

4 a $\sum_{k=1}^{7} k^2 = 1^2 + 2^2 + 3^2 + 4^2 + 5^2 + 6^2 + 7^2$
$= 1 + 4 + 9 + 16 + 25 + 36 + 49$

b $\sum_{k=1}^{8} \dfrac{k+3}{k+2} = \dfrac{4}{3} + \dfrac{5}{4} + \dfrac{6}{5} + \dfrac{7}{6} + \dfrac{8}{7} + \dfrac{9}{8} + \dfrac{10}{9} + \dfrac{11}{10}$

5 a $4 + 11 + 18 + 25 + \ldots\ldots$
The series is arithmetic with $u_1 = 4$, $d = 7$, $u_k = u_1 + (k-1)d$
$= 4 + 7(k-1)$
$= 7k - 3$

So, the series is $\sum_{k=1}^{n}(7k - 3)$

b $\dfrac{1}{4} + \dfrac{1}{8} + \dfrac{1}{16} + \dfrac{1}{32} + \ldots\ldots$
The series is geometric with $u_1 = \dfrac{1}{4}$, $r = \dfrac{1}{2}$,
$u_k = u_1 r^{k-1} = \dfrac{1}{4} \times \left(\dfrac{1}{2}\right)^{k-1} = \left(\dfrac{1}{2}\right)^2 \left(\dfrac{1}{2}\right)^{k-1} = \left(\dfrac{1}{2}\right)^{k+1}$

So, the series is $\sum_{k=1}^{n}\left(\dfrac{1}{2}\right)^{k+1}$

6 a $3 + 9 + 15 + 21 + \ldots\ldots$
The series is arithmetic with
$u_1 = 3$, $d = 6$, $n = 23$

Now $S_n = \dfrac{n}{2}(2u_1 + (n-1)d)$

$\therefore\ S_{23} = \dfrac{23}{2}(2 \times 3 + 6(23 - 1))$

$\therefore\ S_{23} = \dfrac{23}{2}(6 + 132)$

$= 1587$

b $24 + 12 + 6 + 3 + \ldots\ldots$
The series is geometric with
$u_1 = 24$, $r = \dfrac{1}{2}$, $n = 12$

$S_n = \dfrac{u_1(1 - r^n)}{1 - r}$

$\therefore\ S_{12} = \dfrac{24\left(1 - \left(\dfrac{1}{2}\right)^{12}\right)}{1 - \dfrac{1}{2}}$

$= 48\left(1 - \left(\dfrac{1}{2}\right)^{12}\right)$

$= 47\dfrac{253}{256}$

7 a $\sum_{k=1}^{8}\left(\dfrac{31 - 3k}{2}\right) = 14 + 12\tfrac{1}{2} + 11 + 9\tfrac{1}{2} + 8 + 6\tfrac{1}{2} + 5 + 3\tfrac{1}{2}$

This series is arithmetic with $u_1 = 14$, $d = -1\tfrac{1}{2}$ and $n = 8$.

$\therefore\ $ the sum is $\dfrac{8}{2}(14 + 3\tfrac{1}{2}) = 70$

b $\sum_{r=1}^{15} 50(0.8)^{r-1} \approx 50 + 40 + 32 + \ldots\ldots + 3.436 + 2.749 + 2.199$

This series is geometric with $u_1 = 50$, $r = 0.8$ and $n = 15$.

$\therefore\ $ the sum is $\dfrac{50[1 - (0.8)^{15}]}{1 - 0.8} \approx 241$

8 $5, 10, 20, 40, \ldots\ldots$ The sequence is geometric with $u_1 = 5$, $r = 2$
$u_n = u_1 r^{n-1} = 5 \times 2^{n-1}$
Let $u_n = 10\,000 = 5 \times 2^{n-1}$
$\therefore\ 2000 = 2^{n-1}$
$\therefore\ n \approx 11.97$ {using technology}

We try the two values on either side of $n \approx 11.97$, which are $n = 11$ and $n = 12$:
$u_{11} = 5 \times 2^{10}$ and $u_{12} = 5 \times 2^{11}$
$= 5120$ $= 10\,240$

So, the first term to exceed $10\,000$ is $u_{12} = 10\,240$.

9 a $u_6 = u_1 \times r^5$ is the amount after 5 years, where $u_1 = 6000$, $r = 1.07$
   $= 6000 \times (1.07)^5$
   ≈ 8415.31 So, the value of the investment will be €8415.31

b If interest is compounded quarterly, then $r = 1 + \dfrac{0.07}{4} = 1.0175$

   and $n = 5 \times 4 = 20$

   $\therefore \quad u_{21} = u_1 \times r^{20}$
   $= 6000 \times (1.0175)^{20}$
   ≈ 8488.67 So, the value of the investment will be €8488.67

c If interest is compounded monthly, then $r = 1 + \dfrac{0.07}{12} = 1.005\,8\bar{3}$

   and $n = 5 \times 12 = 60$

   $\therefore \quad u_{61} = u_1 \times r^{60}$
   $= 6000 \times (1.005\,8\bar{3})^{60}$
   ≈ 8505.75 So, the value of the investment will be €8505.75

10 a $18 - 12 + 8 - \dots$
   The series is geometric with $u_1 = 18$,
   $r = -\dfrac{2}{3}$

   $\therefore \quad S = \dfrac{u_1}{1-r}$

   $= \dfrac{18}{\frac{5}{3}}$

   $= \dfrac{54}{5}$ or $10\frac{4}{5}$

b $8 + 4\sqrt{2} + 4 + \dots$
   The series is geometric with $u_1 = 8$,
   $r = \dfrac{1}{\sqrt{2}}$

   $\therefore \quad S = \dfrac{u_1}{1-r}$

   $= \dfrac{8}{(1-\frac{1}{\sqrt{2}})} \times \dfrac{(1+\frac{1}{\sqrt{2}})}{(1+\frac{1}{\sqrt{2}})}$

   $= \dfrac{8 + \frac{8}{\sqrt{2}}}{1 - \frac{1}{2}}$

   $= \dfrac{8 + 4\sqrt{2}}{\frac{1}{2}}$

   $= 16 + 8\sqrt{2}$

11 The first two terms of a geometric series are $2x$ and $x-2$, so $u_1 = 2x$ and $r = \dfrac{x-2}{2x}$

Now $S = \dfrac{u_1}{1-r} = \dfrac{2x}{1-(\frac{x-2}{2x})}$

$= \dfrac{4x^2}{2x - (x-2)}$

$= \dfrac{4x^2}{x+2}$

The sum of the series is $\dfrac{18}{7}$, so $\dfrac{4x^2}{x+2} = \dfrac{18}{7}$

$\therefore \quad 28x^2 = 18x + 36$
$\therefore \quad 28x^2 - 18x - 36 = 0$
$\therefore \quad 2(14x^2 - 9x - 18) = 0$
$\therefore \quad 2(7x+6)(2x-3) = 0$
$\therefore \quad x = -\dfrac{6}{7}$ or $\dfrac{3}{2}$

When $x = -\dfrac{6}{7}$, $r = \dfrac{-\frac{6}{7} - 2}{2(-\frac{6}{7})}$

$= \dfrac{-\frac{20}{7}}{-\frac{12}{7}}$

$= \dfrac{5}{3}$

When $x = \dfrac{3}{2}$, $r = \dfrac{\frac{3}{2} - 2}{2(\frac{3}{2})}$

$= \dfrac{-\frac{1}{2}}{3}$

$= -\dfrac{1}{6}$

$|r| < 1$ only when $x = \dfrac{3}{2}$, so $x = \dfrac{3}{2}$ is the only solution.

12 $\sum_{k=7}^{\infty} 5(\frac{2}{5})^{k-1} = 5(\frac{2}{5})^6 + 5(\frac{2}{5})^7 + 5(\frac{2}{5})^8 + \ldots$

The series is an infinite geometric series
with $u_1 = 5(\frac{2}{5})^6$, $r = \frac{2}{5}$

$\therefore S = \dfrac{u_1}{1-r} = \dfrac{5(\frac{2}{5})^6}{\frac{3}{5}}$

$= \dfrac{2^6}{3 \times 5^4}$

$= \dfrac{64}{1875}$

13 Since a, b, c, d and e are consecutive terms of an arithmetic sequence,
$b - a = c - b = d - c = e - d$

Taking the first and last equalities, $\quad b - a = e - d$
$\therefore \quad b + d = a + e$

Taking the middle equalities, $\quad c - b = d - c$
$\therefore \quad 2c = b + d$

$\therefore \quad a + e = b + d = 2c$

14 Let the geometric sequence be $\quad 1, \underbrace{r, r^2, r^3, \ldots\ldots, r^{n-1}, r^n}_{n \text{ terms}}, 2$

$\therefore \quad r^{n+1} = 2 \quad$ and so $\quad r = 2^{\frac{1}{n+1}}$

The required sum is $\quad r + r^2 + r^3 + \ldots\ldots + r^{n-1} + r^n$,
which is geometric with $\quad u_1 = r$, 'r' $= r$ and 'n' $= n$.

$\therefore \quad S_n = \dfrac{u_1(r^n - 1)}{r - 1}$

$= \dfrac{r(r^n - 1)}{r - 1}$

$= \dfrac{r^{n+1} - r}{r - 1}$

$= \dfrac{2 - 2^{\frac{1}{n+1}}}{2^{\frac{1}{n+1}} - 1}$

15 Let the first three terms of the arithmetic sequence be u_1, $u_1 + d$, $u_1 + 2d$,
and the first three terms of the geometric sequence be u_1, $u_1 r$, $u_1 r^2$.

The second terms are equal
$\therefore \quad u_1 + d = u_1 r$
$\therefore \quad d = u_1(r - 1)$
$\therefore \quad u_1 = \dfrac{d}{r - 1} \quad \ldots\ldots \text{ (1)}$

Now $\dfrac{u_1 r^2}{u_1 + 2d} = \dfrac{(\frac{d}{r-1})r^2}{(\frac{d}{r-1}) + 2d} \quad \{\text{using (1)}\}$

$= \dfrac{dr^2}{d + 2d(r - 1)}$

$= \dfrac{dr^2}{d(2r - 1)}$

$= \dfrac{r^2}{2r - 1}$

$\therefore \quad$ the third term of the geometric sequence is $\dfrac{r^2}{2r - 1}$ times the third term of the arithmetic sequence.

REVIEW SET 2C

1 $u_6 = 24$
$u_{11} = 768$

$\therefore \quad u_1 \times r^5 = 24 \quad \ldots\ldots \text{ (1)}$
$\therefore \quad u_1 \times r^{10} = 768 \quad \ldots\ldots \text{ (2)}$

So $\dfrac{u_1 r^{10}}{u_1 r^5} = \dfrac{768}{24} \quad \{(2) \div (1)\}$

$\therefore \quad r^5 = 32$

$\therefore \quad r = 2$

Substituting $r = 2$ into (1) gives $u_1 \times 2^5 = 24$

$$\therefore \quad u_1 = \frac{24}{32} = \frac{3}{4}$$

$$u_n = u_1 r^{n-1} = \left(\frac{3}{4}\right) 2^{n-1}$$

a $u_{17} = \left(\frac{3}{4}\right) 2^{17-1}$
$= 49\,152$

b $S_n = \dfrac{u_1(r^n - 1)}{r - 1}$

$= \dfrac{\frac{3}{4}(2^n - 1)}{2 - 1}$

$= \frac{3}{4}(2^n - 1)$

$\therefore \quad S_{15} = \frac{3}{4}(2^{15} - 1)$
$= 24\,575.25$

2 $11 + 16 + 21 + 26 + \ldots$ is arithmetic with $u_1 = 11$, $d = 5$

$\therefore \quad S_n = \dfrac{n}{2}(2u_1 + (n-1)d)$

$= \dfrac{n}{2}(2 \times 11 + 5(n-1))$

$= \dfrac{n}{2}(22 + 5n - 5)$

$= \dfrac{n}{2}(5n + 17)$

Given $S_n = 450$, we need to find n,

so $S_n = \dfrac{n}{2}(5n + 17) = 450$

$\therefore \quad \frac{5}{2}n^2 + \frac{17}{2}n - 450 = 0$

$\therefore \quad 5n^2 + 17n - 900 = 0$

$\therefore \quad n \approx -15.2, \; 11.8 \quad \{\text{using technology}\}$

But $n > 0$, so $n \approx 11.8$

We try the two values on either side of $n \approx 11.8$, which are $n = 11$ and $n = 12$:

$S_{11} = \frac{11}{2}(5(11) + 17) = 396$ and $S_{12} = \frac{12}{2}(5(12) + 17) = 462$

$\therefore$ 12 terms of the series are required to exceed a sum of 450.

3 $24, 8, \frac{8}{3}, \frac{8}{9}, \ldots$ is geometric with $u_1 = 24$, $r = \frac{1}{3}$

$u_n = u_1 r^{n-1} = 24 \left(\frac{1}{3}\right)^{n-1}$

Given $u_n = 0.001$, we need to find n, so $u_n = 24 \left(\frac{1}{3}\right)^{n-1} = 0.001$

$\therefore \quad \left(\frac{1}{3}\right)^{n-1} = \dfrac{0.001}{24}$

$\therefore \quad n \approx 10.18 \quad \{\text{using technology}\}$

We try the two values on either side of $n \approx 10.18$, which are $n = 10$ and $n = 11$:

$u_{10} = 24 \left(\frac{1}{3}\right)^9$ and $u_{11} = 24 \left(\frac{1}{3}\right)^{10}$

$\approx 0.001\,22$ $\approx 0.000\,406$

$\therefore \quad u_{11} \approx 0.000\,406$ is the first term of the sequence which is less than 0.001.

4 a $128, 64, 32, 16, \ldots, \frac{1}{512}$ is geometric with:

$u_1 = 128$, $r = \frac{1}{2}$, $u_n = \frac{1}{512}$

$u_n = u_1 r^{n-1}$

$= 128 \left(\frac{1}{2}\right)^{n-1}$

$= 2^7 \times 2^{1-n}$

$\therefore \quad \frac{1}{512} = 2^7 \times 2^{1-n}$

$\therefore \quad 2^{-9} = 2^{8-n}$

$\therefore \quad -9 = 8 - n$

$\therefore \quad n = 17$ So, there are 17 terms in the sequence.

b $S_n = \dfrac{u_1(1 - r^n)}{1 - r}$

$\therefore \quad S_{17} = \dfrac{128\left(1 - \left(\frac{1}{2}\right)^{17}\right)}{1 - \frac{1}{2}}$

≈ 255.998

≈ 256

5 **a** $u_{n+1} = u_1 \times r^n$ where $u_1 = 12\,500$, $r = 1 + \dfrac{0.0825}{2} = 1.04125$, $n = 5 \times 2 = 10$

So, $u_{n+1} = 12\,500 \times (1.04125)^{10}$

$\approx 18\,726.65$ The value of the investment is $18\,726.65.

b $u_{n+1} = u_1 \times r^n$ where $u_1 = 12\,500$, $r = 1 + \dfrac{0.0825}{12} = 1.006\,875$, $n = 5 \times 12 = 60$

So, $u_{n+1} = 12\,500 \times (1.006\,875)^{60}$

$\approx 18\,855.74$ The value of the investment is $18\,855.74.

6 $u_{n+1} = u_1 \times r^n$ where $u_{n+1} = 20\,000$, $r = 1 + \dfrac{0.09}{12} = 1.0075$, $n = 4 \times 12 = 48$

$\therefore \quad 20\,000 = u_1 \times (1.0075)^{48}$

$\therefore \quad u_1 \approx 13\,972.28$ So, $13\,972.28 should be invested.

7 **a** $u_{n+1} = u_1 \times r^n$ where $u_1 = 3000$, $r = 1.05$, $n = 3$

$\therefore \quad u_{n+1} = 3000 \times (1.05)^3$

$= 3472.875$ There were approximately 3470 koalas.

b $u_{n+1} = u_1 \times r^n$ where $u_1 = 3000$, $u_{n+1} = 5000$, $r = 1.05$

$\therefore \quad 5000 = 3000 \times (1.05)^n$

$\therefore \quad n \approx 10.47$ {using technology}

After 10.47 years the population will exceed 5000. This is during the year 2014.

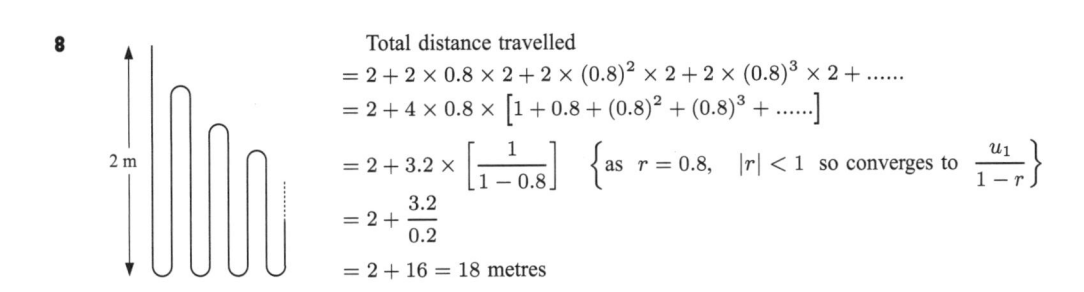

8 Total distance travelled

$= 2 + 2 \times 0.8 \times 2 + 2 \times (0.8)^2 \times 2 + 2 \times (0.8)^3 \times 2 + \ldots\ldots$

$= 2 + 4 \times 0.8 \times \left[1 + 0.8 + (0.8)^2 + (0.8)^3 + \ldots\ldots\right]$

$= 2 + 3.2 \times \left[\dfrac{1}{1 - 0.8}\right]$ $\left\{\text{as } r = 0.8,\ |r| < 1 \text{ so converges to } \dfrac{u_1}{1-r}\right\}$

$= 2 + \dfrac{3.2}{0.2}$

$= 2 + 16 = 18$ metres

9 **a** $\displaystyle\sum_{k=1}^{\infty} 50(2x - 1)^{k-1}$ is a geometric series with $r = 2x - 1$ and converges if $-1 < r < 1$

$\therefore \quad -1 < 2x - 1 < 1$

$\therefore \quad 0 < 2x < 2$

$\therefore \quad 0 < x < 1$

b When $x = 0.3$, $2x - 1 = 0.6 - 1 = -0.4$

and $\displaystyle\sum_{k=1}^{\infty} 50(2x-1)^{k-1} = 50(-0.4)^0 + 50(-0.4)^1 + 50(-0.4)^2 + \ldots\ldots$

which is geometric with $u_1 = 50$, $r = -0.4$

Now as $0 < 0.3 < 1$, the series converges and $S = \dfrac{u_1}{1-r} = \dfrac{50}{1 + 0.4} = \dfrac{50}{\frac{7}{5}} = 35\dfrac{5}{7}$

10 a $S_n = \dfrac{3n^2 + 5n}{2}$

$\therefore \quad u_n = S_n - S_{n-1}$

$= \dfrac{3n^2 + 5n}{2} - \dfrac{3(n-1)^2 + 5(n-1)}{2}$

$= \dfrac{3n^2 + 5n - 3(n^2 - 2n + 1) - 5(n-1)}{2}$

$= \dfrac{3n^2 + 5n - 3n^2 + 6n - 3 - 5n + 5}{2}$

$= \dfrac{6n + 2}{2}$

$\therefore \quad u_n = 3n + 1$

b Using part **a**,

$u_n - u_{n-1} = [3n + 1] - [3(n-1) + 1]$
$= 3n + 1 - 3n + 3 - 1$
$= 3$

The difference between consecutive terms is constant for all n, so the sequence is arithmetic.

11 a, b and c are arithmetic, so $a - b = b - c = d$ where d is a constant.

a $(c + a) - (b + c) = c + a - b - c$
$= a - b$
$= d$

$(a + b) - (c + a) = a + b - c - a$
$= b - c$
$= d$

$\therefore$ the differences between the terms are equal.

$\therefore \quad b + c$, $c + a$ and $a + b$ are also consecutive terms of an arithmetic sequence.

b $\dfrac{1}{\sqrt{b}+\sqrt{c}} = \dfrac{1}{(\sqrt{b}+\sqrt{c})} \cdot \dfrac{(\sqrt{b}-\sqrt{c})}{(\sqrt{b}-\sqrt{c})} = \dfrac{\sqrt{b}-\sqrt{c}}{b-c} = \dfrac{\sqrt{b}-\sqrt{c}}{d}$ ...... (1)

$\dfrac{1}{\sqrt{c}+\sqrt{a}} = \dfrac{1}{(\sqrt{c}+\sqrt{a})} \cdot \dfrac{(\sqrt{c}-\sqrt{a})}{(\sqrt{c}-\sqrt{a})} = \dfrac{\sqrt{c}-\sqrt{a}}{c-a} = \dfrac{\sqrt{c}-\sqrt{a}}{-2d}$ ...... (2)

$\dfrac{1}{\sqrt{a}+\sqrt{b}} = \dfrac{1}{(\sqrt{a}+\sqrt{b})} \cdot \dfrac{(\sqrt{a}-\sqrt{b})}{(\sqrt{a}-\sqrt{b})} = \dfrac{\sqrt{a}-\sqrt{b}}{a-b} = \dfrac{\sqrt{a}-\sqrt{b}}{d}$ ...... (3)

Using (2) and (1):

$\dfrac{1}{\sqrt{c}+\sqrt{a}} - \dfrac{1}{\sqrt{b}+\sqrt{c}} = \dfrac{\sqrt{c}-\sqrt{a}}{-2d} - \dfrac{\sqrt{b}-\sqrt{c}}{d} = \dfrac{\sqrt{a}-\sqrt{c}-2\sqrt{b}+2\sqrt{c}}{2d}$

$= \dfrac{\sqrt{a}-2\sqrt{b}+\sqrt{c}}{2d}$

Using (3) and (2):

$\dfrac{1}{\sqrt{a}+\sqrt{b}} - \dfrac{1}{\sqrt{c}+\sqrt{a}} = \dfrac{\sqrt{a}-\sqrt{b}}{d} - \dfrac{\sqrt{c}-\sqrt{a}}{-2d} = \dfrac{2\sqrt{a}-2\sqrt{b}+\sqrt{c}-\sqrt{a}}{2d}$

$= \dfrac{\sqrt{a}-2\sqrt{b}+\sqrt{c}}{2d}$

$\therefore$ the differences between the terms are equal.

$\therefore \quad \dfrac{1}{\sqrt{b}+\sqrt{c}}$, $\dfrac{1}{\sqrt{c}+\sqrt{a}}$ and $\dfrac{1}{\sqrt{a}+\sqrt{b}}$ are also consecutive terms of an arithmetic sequence.

12 The value of $\underbrace{111....11}_{2n \text{ lots of } 1}$ is $1 + 10 + 10^2 + ... + 10^{2n-1}$, which is a geometric series with $u_1 = 1$, $r = 10$, 'n' $= 2n$.

$\therefore$ the value of this sum is $S_1 = \dfrac{u_1(r^n - 1)}{r - 1} = \dfrac{1(10^{2n} - 1)}{10 - 1}$

$= \dfrac{10^{2n} - 1}{9}$

The value of $\underbrace{222....22}_{n \text{ lots of } 2}$ is $2 + 2 \times 10 + 2 \times 10^2 + ... + 2 \times 10^{n-1}$,

which is a geometric series with $u_1 = 2, \ r = 10, \ \text{'}n\text{'} = n$.

$\therefore$ the value of this sum is $S_2 = \dfrac{u_1(r^n - 1)}{r - 1} = \dfrac{2(10^n - 1)}{10 - 1}$

$$= \dfrac{2 \times 10^n - 2}{9}$$

$\therefore$ the value of $\underbrace{111....11}_{2n \text{ lots of } 1} - \underbrace{222....22}_{n \text{ lots of } 2} = S_1 - S_2 = \dfrac{10^{2n} - 1}{9} - \dfrac{2 \times 10^n - 2}{9}$

$$= \dfrac{10^{2n} - 1 - 2 \times 10^n + 2}{9}$$

$$= \dfrac{10^{2n} - 2 \times 10^n + 1}{9}$$

$$= \dfrac{(10^n - 1)^2}{3^2}$$

$$= \left(\dfrac{10^n - 1}{3}\right)^2$$

$10^n - 1 = \underbrace{99....9}_{n \text{ lots of } 9}$ is divisible by 3, so $\dfrac{10^n - 1}{3}$ is an integer

$\therefore \ \underbrace{111....11}_{2n \text{ lots of } 1} - \underbrace{222....22}_{n \text{ lots of } 2}$ is a perfect square.

Chapter 3
EXPONENTIALS

EXERCISE 3A

1
  a $2^1 = 2$, $2^2 = 4$, $2^3 = 8$, $2^4 = 16$, $2^5 = 32$, $2^6 = 64$
  b $3^1 = 3$, $3^2 = 9$, $3^3 = 27$, $3^4 = 81$, $3^5 = 243$, $3^6 = 729$
  c $4^1 = 4$, $4^2 = 16$, $4^3 = 64$, $4^4 = 256$, $4^5 = 1024$, $4^6 = 4096$

2
  a $5^1 = 5$, $5^2 = 25$, $5^3 = 125$, $5^4 = 625$ **b** $6^1 = 6$, $6^2 = 36$, $6^3 = 216$, $6^4 = 1296$
  c $7^1 = 7$, $7^2 = 49$, $7^3 = 343$, $7^4 = 2401$

EXERCISE 3B

1
  a $(-1)^5$
  $= (-1) \times (-1) \times (-1) \times (-1) \times (-1)$
  $= 1 \times 1 \times (-1)$
  $= -1$

  b $(-1)^6$
  $= (-1)^5 \times (-1)$
  $= (-1) \times (-1)$
  $= 1$

  c $(-1)^{14}$
  $= 1$

  d $(-1)^{19}$
  $= -1$

  e $(-1)^8$
  $= 1$

  f -1^8
  $= -(1^8)$
  $= -1$

  g $-(-1)^8$
  $= -(1)$
  $= -1$

  h $(-2)^5$
  $= (-2) \times (-2) \times (-2) \times (-2) \times (-2)$
  $= 4 \times 4 \times (-2)$
  $= -32$

  i -2^5
  $= -(2^5)$
  $= -32$

  j $-(-2)^6$
  $= -(-2)^5 \times (-2)$
  $= 32 \times (-2)$
  $= -64$

  k $(-5)^4$
  $= (-5) \times (-5) \times (-5) \times (-5)$
  $= 25 \times 25$
  $= 625$

  l $-(-5)^4$
  $= -(-5) \times (-5) \times (-5) \times (-5)$
  $= -25 \times 25$
  $= -625$

2
  a $4^7 = 16\,384$ **b** $7^4 = 2401$ **c** $-5^5 = -3125$ **d** $(-5)^5 = -3125$
  e $8^6 = 262\,144$ **f** $(-8)^6 = 262\,144$ **g** $-8^6 = -262\,144$
  h $2.13^9 = 902.436\,039\,6$ **i** $-2.13^9 = -902.436\,039\,6$ **j** $(-2.13)^9 = -902.436\,039\,6$

3
  a $9^{-1} = 0.\overline{1}$ **b** $\dfrac{1}{9^1} = 0.\overline{1}$ **c** $6^{-2} = 0.02\overline{7}$ **d** $\dfrac{1}{6^2} = 0.02\overline{7}$
  e $3^{-4} \approx 0.012\,345\,679$ **f** $\dfrac{1}{3^4} \approx 0.012\,345\,679$ **g** $17^0 = 1$ **h** $(0.366)^0 = 1$

We notice that $a^{-n} = \dfrac{1}{a^n}$ and $a^0 = 1$ for $a \neq 0$.

4 $3^{101} = \underbrace{3^4 \times 3^4 \times 3^4 \times \ldots \times 3^4}_{25 \text{ of these}} \times 3^1$ But $3^4 = 81$ which ends in a 1
$\therefore \underbrace{3^4 \times 3^4 \times 3^4 \times \ldots \times 3^4}_{25 \text{ of these}}$ ends in a 1
$\therefore \; 3^{101}$ ends in a 3

5 $7^1 = 7$, $\; 7^2 = 49$, $\; 7^3 = 343$, $\; 7^4 = 2401$, $\; 7^5 = 16\,807$
Now $\; 7^{217} = \underbrace{7^4 \times 7^4 \times 7^4 \times \ldots \times 7^4}_{54 \text{ of these so this part ends in a 1}} \times 7^1$

$\therefore \; 7^{217}$ ends in $\; 1 \times 7 = 7$.

6 **a** On the first square, there is $1 = 2^0$ grains of rice.
On the second square, there are $2 = 2^1$ grains of rice.
On the third square, there are $4 = 2^2$ grains of rice.
$\therefore$ in general, on the sth square, there are $n = 2^{s-1}$ grains of rice.

b When $s = 40$, $n = 2^{40-1} = 2^{39}$
$\therefore$ on the 40th square, there are $2^{39} \approx 5.50 \times 10^{11}$ grains of rice.

c Total number of grains of rice $= 2^0 + 2^1 + 2^2 + 2^3 + ... + 2^{63}$, which is a geometric series with $u_1 = 1$, $r = 2$, $n = 64$.

$\therefore$ sum $= \dfrac{u_1(r^n - 1)}{r - 1}$

$= \dfrac{1(2^{64} - 1)}{2 - 1}$

$= 2^{64} - 1$

$\therefore$ the king owes a total of $2^{64} - 1 \approx 1.84 \times 10^{19}$ grains of rice.

EXERCISE 3C.1

1 **a** $4 = 2 \times 2$
$= 2^2$

b $\dfrac{1}{4} = \dfrac{1}{2^2}$
$= 2^{-2}$

c $8 = 2 \times 2 \times 2$
$= 2^3$

d $\dfrac{1}{8} = \dfrac{1}{2^3}$
$= 2^{-3}$

e $32 = 2 \times 2 \times 2 \times 2 \times 2$
$= 2^5$

f $\dfrac{1}{32} = \dfrac{1}{2^5}$
$= 2^{-5}$

g $2 = 2^1$

h $\dfrac{1}{2} = \dfrac{1}{2^1}$
$= 2^{-1}$

i $64 = 32 \times 2$
$= 2^5 \times 2^1$
$= 2^6$

j $\dfrac{1}{64} = \dfrac{1}{2^6}$
$= 2^{-6}$

k $128 = 64 \times 2$
$= 2^6 \times 2^1$
$= 2^7$

l $\dfrac{1}{128} = \dfrac{1}{2^7}$
$= 2^{-7}$

2 **a** $9 = 3 \times 3$
$= 3^2$

b $\dfrac{1}{9} = \dfrac{1}{3^2}$
$= 3^{-2}$

c $27 = 3 \times 3 \times 3$
$= 3^3$

d $\dfrac{1}{27} = \dfrac{1}{3^3}$
$= 3^{-3}$

e $3 = 3^1$

f $\dfrac{1}{3} = \dfrac{1}{3^1}$
$= 3^{-1}$

g $81 = 3 \times 3 \times 3 \times 3$
$= 3^4$

h $\dfrac{1}{81} = \dfrac{1}{3^4}$
$= 3^{-4}$

i $1 = 3^0$

j $243 = 81 \times 3$
$= 3^4 \times 3^1$
$= 3^5$

k $\dfrac{1}{243} = \dfrac{1}{3^5}$
$= 3^{-5}$

3 **a** $2 \times 2^a = 2^1 \times 2^a$
$= 2^{a+1}$

b $4 \times 2^b = 2^2 \times 2^b$
$= 2^{b+2}$

c $8 \times 2^t = 2^3 \times 2^t$
$= 2^{t+3}$

d $(2^{x+1})^2 = 2^{2(x+1)}$
$= 2^{2x+2}$

e $(2^{1-n})^{-1} = 2^{-(1-n)}$
$= 2^{n-1}$

f $\dfrac{2^c}{4} = \dfrac{2^c}{2^2}$
$= 2^{c-2}$

g $\dfrac{2^m}{2^{-m}} = 2^{m-(-m)}$
$= 2^{2m}$

h $\dfrac{4}{2^{1-n}} = \dfrac{2^2}{2^{1-n}}$
$= 2^{2-(1-n)}$
$= 2^{n+1}$

i $\dfrac{2^{x+1}}{2^x} = 2^{x+1-x}$
$= 2^1$

j $\dfrac{4^x}{2^{1-x}} = \dfrac{(2^2)^x}{2^{1-x}}$
$= 2^{2x-(1-x)}$
$= 2^{3x-1}$

4 **a** $9 \times 3^p = 3^2 \times 3^p$
$= 3^{p+2}$

b $27^a = (3^3)^a$
$= 3^{3a}$

c $3 \times 9^n = 3^1 \times (3^2)^n$
$= 3^{2n+1}$

d $27 \times 3^d = 3^3 \times 3^d$
$= 3^{d+3}$

e $9 \times 27^t = 3^2 \times (3^3)^t$
$= 3^{3t+2}$

f $\dfrac{3^y}{3} = \dfrac{3^y}{3^1}$
$= 3^{y-1}$

g $\dfrac{3}{3^y} = \dfrac{3^1}{3^y}$
$= 3^{1-y}$

h $\dfrac{9}{27^t} = \dfrac{3^2}{(3^3)^t}$
$= 3^{2-3t}$

i $\dfrac{9^a}{3^{1-a}} = \dfrac{(3^2)^a}{3^{1-a}}$
$= 3^{2a-(1-a)}$
$= 3^{3a-1}$

j $\dfrac{9^{n+1}}{3^{2n-1}} = \dfrac{(3^2)^{n+1}}{3^{2n-1}}$
$= 3^{2n+2-(2n-1)}$
$= 3^3$

5 **a** $ab^{-2} = \dfrac{a}{b^2}$

b $(ab)^{-2} = \dfrac{1}{(ab)^2}$
$= \dfrac{1}{a^2b^2}$

c $(2ab^{-1})^2 = 2^2 a^2 b^{-2}$
$= \dfrac{4a^2}{b^2}$

d $(3a^{-2}b)^2 = 3^2 a^{-4} b^2$
$= \dfrac{9b^2}{a^4}$

e $\dfrac{a^2 b^{-1}}{c^2} = \dfrac{a^2}{bc^2}$

f $\dfrac{a^2 b^{-1}}{c^{-2}} = \dfrac{a^2 c^2}{b}$

g $\dfrac{1}{a^{-3}} = a^3$

h $\dfrac{a^{-2}}{b^{-3}} = \dfrac{b^3}{a^2}$

i $\dfrac{2a^{-1}}{d^2} = \dfrac{2}{ad^2}$

j $\dfrac{12a}{m^{-3}} = 12am^3$

6 **a** $\dfrac{1}{a^n} = a^{-n}$

b $\dfrac{1}{b^{-n}} = b^n$

c $\dfrac{1}{3^{2-n}} = 3^{n-2}$

d $\dfrac{a^n}{b^{-m}} = a^n b^m$

e $\dfrac{a^{-n}}{a^{2+n}} = a^{-n-(2+n)}$
$= a^{-2n-2}$

EXERCISE 3C.2

1 **a** $\sqrt[5]{2} = 2^{\frac{1}{5}}$

b $\dfrac{1}{\sqrt[5]{2}} = \dfrac{1}{2^{\frac{1}{5}}}$
$= 2^{-\frac{1}{5}}$

c $2\sqrt{2} = 2^1 \times 2^{\frac{1}{2}}$
$= 2^{\frac{3}{2}}$

d $4\sqrt{2} = 2^2 \times 2^{\frac{1}{2}}$
$= 2^{\frac{5}{2}}$

e $\dfrac{1}{\sqrt[3]{2}} = \dfrac{1}{2^{\frac{1}{3}}}$
$= 2^{-\frac{1}{3}}$

f $2 \times \sqrt[3]{2} = 2^1 \times 2^{\frac{1}{3}}$
$= 2^{\frac{4}{3}}$

g $\dfrac{4}{\sqrt{2}} = \dfrac{2^2}{2^{\frac{1}{2}}}$
$= 2^{\frac{3}{2}}$

h $(\sqrt{2})^3 = (2^{\frac{1}{2}})^3$
$= 2^{\frac{3}{2}}$

i $\dfrac{1}{\sqrt[3]{16}} = \dfrac{1}{\sqrt[3]{2^4}}$
$= \dfrac{1}{2^{\frac{4}{3}}}$
$= 2^{-\frac{4}{3}}$

j $\dfrac{1}{\sqrt{8}} = \dfrac{1}{\sqrt{2^3}}$
$= \dfrac{1}{2^{\frac{3}{2}}}$
$= 2^{-\frac{3}{2}}$

2 **a** $\sqrt[3]{3} = 3^{\frac{1}{3}}$

b $\dfrac{1}{\sqrt[3]{3}} = \dfrac{1}{3^{\frac{1}{3}}}$
$= 3^{-\frac{1}{3}}$

c $\sqrt[4]{3} = 3^{\frac{1}{4}}$

d $3\sqrt{3} = 3^1 \times 3^{\frac{1}{2}}$
$= 3^{\frac{3}{2}}$

e $\dfrac{1}{9\sqrt{3}} = \dfrac{1}{3^2 \times 3^{\frac{1}{2}}}$
$= \dfrac{1}{3^{\frac{5}{2}}}$
$= 3^{-\frac{5}{2}}$

3 **a** $\sqrt[3]{7} = 7^{\frac{1}{3}}$ **b** $\sqrt[4]{27} = \sqrt[4]{3^3}$ **c** $\sqrt[5]{16} = \sqrt[5]{2^4}$ **d** $\sqrt[3]{32} = \sqrt[3]{2^5}$
$= 3^{\frac{3}{4}}$ $= 2^{\frac{4}{5}}$ $= 2^{\frac{5}{3}}$

e $\sqrt[7]{49} = \sqrt[7]{7^2}$ **f** $\dfrac{1}{\sqrt[3]{7}} = \dfrac{1}{7^{\frac{1}{3}}}$ **g** $\dfrac{1}{\sqrt[4]{27}} = \dfrac{1}{3^{\frac{3}{4}}}$ **h** $\dfrac{1}{\sqrt[5]{16}} = \dfrac{1}{2^{\frac{4}{5}}}$
$= 7^{\frac{2}{7}}$ $= 7^{-\frac{1}{3}}$ $= 3^{-\frac{3}{4}}$ $= 2^{-\frac{4}{5}}$

i $\dfrac{1}{\sqrt[3]{32}} = \dfrac{1}{2^{\frac{5}{3}}}$ **j** $\dfrac{1}{\sqrt[7]{49}} = \dfrac{1}{7^{\frac{2}{7}}}$
$= 2^{-\frac{5}{3}}$ $= 7^{-\frac{2}{7}}$

4 **a** $3^{\frac{3}{4}} \approx 2.28$ **b** $2^{\frac{7}{8}} \approx 1.83$ **c** $2^{-\frac{1}{3}} \approx 0.794$ **d** $4^{-\frac{3}{5}} \approx 0.435$

5 **a** $\sqrt{9} = 3$ **b** $\sqrt[4]{8} \approx 1.68$ **c** $\sqrt[5]{27} \approx 1.93$ **d** $\dfrac{1}{\sqrt[3]{7}} \approx 0.523$

6 **a** $4^{\frac{3}{2}} = (2^2)^{\frac{3}{2}}$ **b** $8^{\frac{5}{3}} = (2^3)^{\frac{5}{3}}$ **c** $16^{\frac{3}{4}} = (2^4)^{\frac{3}{4}}$ **d** $25^{\frac{3}{2}} = (5^2)^{\frac{3}{2}}$
$= 2^3$ $= 2^5$ $= 2^3$ $= 5^3$
$= 8$ $= 32$ $= 8$ $= 125$

e $32^{\frac{2}{5}} = (2^5)^{\frac{2}{5}}$ **f** $4^{-\frac{1}{2}} = (2^2)^{-\frac{1}{2}}$ **g** $9^{-\frac{3}{2}} = (3^2)^{-\frac{3}{2}}$ **h** $8^{-\frac{4}{3}} = (2^3)^{-\frac{4}{3}}$
$= 2^2$ $= 2^{-1}$ $= 3^{-3}$ $= 2^{-4}$
$= 4$ $= \frac{1}{2}$ $= \frac{1}{27}$ $= \frac{1}{16}$

i $27^{-\frac{4}{3}} = (3^3)^{-\frac{4}{3}}$ **j** $125^{-\frac{2}{3}} = (5^3)^{-\frac{2}{3}}$
$= 3^{-4}$ $= 5^{-2}$
$= \frac{1}{81}$ $= \frac{1}{25}$

EXERCISE 3D.1

1 **a** $x^2(x^3 + 2x^2 + 1)$ **b** $2^x(2^x + 1)$
$= x^2 \times x^3 + x^2 \times 2x^2 + x^2 \times 1$ $= 2^x \times 2^x + 2^x \times 1$
$= x^5 + 2x^4 + x^2$ $= 2^{2x} + 2^x$

c $x^{\frac{1}{2}}(x^{\frac{1}{2}} + x^{-\frac{1}{2}})$ **d** $e^x(e^x + 2)$ **e** $3^x(2 - 3^{-x})$
$= x^{\frac{1}{2}} \times x^{\frac{1}{2}} + x^{\frac{1}{2}} \times x^{-\frac{1}{2}}$ $= e^x \times e^x + e^x \times 2$ $= 3^x \times 2 - 3^x \times 3^{-x}$
$= x^1 + x^0$ $= e^{2x} + 2e^x$ $= 2(3^x) - 3^0$
$= x + 1$ $= 2(3^x) - 1$

f $x^{\frac{1}{2}}(x^{\frac{3}{2}} + 2x^{\frac{1}{2}} + 3x^{-\frac{1}{2}})$ **g** $2^{-x}(2^x + 5)$
$= x^{\frac{1}{2}} \times x^{\frac{3}{2}} + x^{\frac{1}{2}} \times 2x^{\frac{1}{2}} + x^{\frac{1}{2}} \times 3x^{-\frac{1}{2}}$ $= 2^{-x} \times 2^x + 2^{-x} \times 5$
$= x^2 + 2x^1 + 3x^0$ $= 2^0 + 5(2^{-x})$
$= x^2 + 2x + 3$ $= 1 + 5(2^{-x})$

h $5^{-x}(5^{2x} + 5^x)$ **i** $x^{-\frac{1}{2}}(x^2 + x + x^{\frac{1}{2}})$
$= 5^{-x} \times 5^{2x} + 5^{-x} \times 5^x$ $= x^{-\frac{1}{2}} \times x^2 + x^{-\frac{1}{2}} \times x^1 + x^{-\frac{1}{2}} \times x^{\frac{1}{2}}$
$= 5^x + 5^0$ $= x^{\frac{3}{2}} + x^{\frac{1}{2}} + x^0$
$= 5^x + 1$ $= x^{\frac{3}{2}} + x^{\frac{1}{2}} + 1$

2 **a** $(2^x + 1)(2^x + 3)$
$= 2^x \times 2^x + 2^x \times 3 + 1 \times 2^x + 3$
$= 2^{2x} + 4(2^x) + 3$
$= 4^x + 2^{2+x} + 3$

b $(3^x + 2)(3^x + 5)$
$= 3^x \times 3^x + 3^x \times 5 + 2 \times 3^x + 10$
$= 3^{2x} + 7(3^x) + 10$
$= 9^x + 7(3^x) + 10$

c $(5^x - 2)(5^x - 4)$
$= 5^x \times 5^x - 5^x \times 4 - 2 \times 5^x + 8$
$= 5^{2x} - 6(5^x) + 8$
$= 25^x - 6(5^x) + 8$

d $(2^x + 3)^2$
$= (2^x)^2 + 2 \times 2^x \times 3 + 3^2$
$= 2^{2x} + 6(2^x) + 9$
$= 4^x + 6(2^x) + 9$

e $(3^x - 1)^2$
$= (3^x)^2 - 2 \times 3^x \times 1 + 1^2$
$= 3^{2x} - 2(3^x) + 1$
$= 9^x - 2(3^x) + 1$

f $(4^x + 7)^2$
$= (4^x)^2 + 2 \times 4^x \times 7 + 7^2$
$= 4^{2x} + 14(4^x) + 49$
$= 16^x + 14(4^x) + 49$

g $(x^{\frac{1}{2}} + 2)(x^{\frac{1}{2}} - 2)$
$= (x^{\frac{1}{2}})^2 - 2^2$
$= x - 4$

h $(2^x + 3)(2^x - 3)$
$= (2^x)^2 - 3^2$
$= 2^{2x} - 9$
$= 4^x - 9$

i $(x^{\frac{1}{2}} + x^{-\frac{1}{2}})(x^{\frac{1}{2}} - x^{-\frac{1}{2}})$
$= (x^{\frac{1}{2}})^2 - (x^{-\frac{1}{2}})^2$
$= x^1 - x^{-1}$
$= x - x^{-1}$

j $\left(x + \dfrac{2}{x}\right)^2$
$= x^2 + 2 \times x \times \left(\dfrac{2}{x}\right) + \left(\dfrac{2}{x}\right)^2$
$= x^2 + 4 + \dfrac{4}{x^2}$

k $(e^x - e^{-x})^2$
$= (e^x)^2 - 2 \times e^x \times e^{-x} + (e^{-x})^2$
$= e^{2x} - 2e^0 + e^{-2x}$
$= e^{2x} - 2 + e^{-2x}$

l $(5 - 2^{-x})^2$
$= 5^2 - 2 \times 5 \times 2^{-x} + (2^{-x})^2$
$= 25 - 10(2^{-x}) + 2^{-2x}$
$= 25 - 10(2^{-x}) + 4^{-x}$

EXERCISE 3D.2

1 **a** $5^{2x} + 5^x$
$= 5^x \times 5^x + 5^x$
$= 5^x(5^x + 1)$

b $3^{n+2} + 3^n$
$= 3^n \times 3^2 + 3^n$
$= 3^n(3^2 + 1)$
$= 10(3^n)$

c $e^n + e^{3n}$
$= e^n + e^n \times e^{2n}$
$= e^n(1 + e^{2n})$

d $5^{n+1} - 5$
$= 5 \times 5^n - 5$
$= 5(5^n - 1)$

e $6^{n+2} - 6$
$= 6 \times 6^{n+1} - 6$
$= 6(6^{n+1} - 1)$

f $4^{n+2} - 16$
$= 4^2 \times 4^n - 16$
$= 16 \times 4^n - 16$
$= 16(4^n - 1)$

g $3(2^n) + 2^{n+1}$
$= 3(2^n) + 2 \times 2^n$
$= 5(2^n)$

h $2^{n+2} + 2^{n+1} + 2^n$
$= 2^n \times 2^2 + 2^n \times 2 + 2^n$
$= 2^n(2^2 + 2 + 1)$
$= 7(2^n)$

i $3^{n+1} + 2(3^n) + 3^{n-1}$
$= 3^{n-1} \times 3^2 + 2 \times (3 \times 3^{n-1}) + 3^{n-1}$
$= 3^{n-1}(3^2 + 2 \times 3 + 1)$
$= 16(3^{n-1})$

2 **a** $9^x - 4$
$= (3^x)^2 - 2^2$
$= (3^x + 2)(3^x - 2)$

b $4^x - 25$
$= (2^x)^2 - 5^2$
$= (2^x + 5)(2^x - 5)$

c $16 - 9^x$
$= 4^2 - (3^x)^2$
$= (4 + 3^x)(4 - 3^x)$

d $25 - 4^x$
$= 5^2 - (2^x)^2$
$= (5 + 2^x)(5 - 2^x)$

e $9^x - 4^x$
$= (3^x)^2 - (2^x)^2$
$= (3^x + 2^x)(3^x - 2^x)$

f $4^x + 6(2^x) + 9$
$= (2^x)^2 + 6(2^x) + 9$
$= (2^x + 3)^2$
$\{a^2 + 6a + 9 = (a + 3)^2\}$

g $9^x + 10(3^x) + 25$
$= (3^x)^2 + 10(3^x) + 25$
$= (3^x + 5)^2$
$\{a^2 + 10a + 25 = (a + 5)^2\}$

h $4^x - 14(2^x) + 49$
$= (2^x)^2 - 14(2^x) + 49$
$= (2^x - 7)^2$
$\{a^2 - 14a + 49 = (a - 7)^2\}$

i $25^x - 4(5^x) + 4$
$= (5^x)^2 - 4(5^x) + 4$
$= (5^x - 2)^2$
$\{a^2 - 4a + 4 = (a - 2)^2\}$

3 a $4^x + 9(2^x) + 18$
$= (2^x)^2 + 9(2^x) + 18$
$= (2^x + 3)(2^x + 6)$
$\{a^2 + 9a + 18 = (a + 3)(a + 6)\}$

b $4^x - 2^x - 20$
$= (2^x)^2 - 2^x - 20$
$= (2^x + 4)(2^x - 5)$
$\{a^2 - a - 20 = (a + 4)(a - 5)\}$

c $9^x + 9(3^x) + 14$
$= (3^x)^2 + 9(3^x) + 14$
$= (3^x + 2)(3^x + 7)$
$\{a^2 + 9a + 14 = (a + 2)(a + 7)\}$

d $9^x + 4(3^x) - 5$
$= (3^x)^2 + 4(3^x) - 5$
$= (3^x + 5)(3^x - 1)$
$\{a^2 + 4a - 5 = (a + 5)(a - 1)\}$

e $25^x + 5^x - 2$
$= (5^x)^2 + 5^x - 2$
$= (5^x + 2)(5^x - 1)$
$\{a^2 + a - 2 = (a + 2)(a - 1)\}$

f $49^x - 7^{x+1} + 12$
$= (7^x)^2 - 7(7^x) + 12$
$= (7^x - 4)(7^x - 3)$
$\{a^2 - 7a + 12 = (a - 4)(a - 3)\}$

4 a $\dfrac{12^n}{6^n} = \left(\dfrac{12}{6}\right)^n$
$= 2^n$

b $\dfrac{20^a}{2^a} = \left(\dfrac{20}{2}\right)^a$
$= 10^a$

c $\dfrac{6^b}{2^b} = \left(\dfrac{6}{2}\right)^b$
$= 3^b$

d $\dfrac{4^n}{20^n} = \left(\dfrac{4}{20}\right)^n$
$= \left(\dfrac{1}{5}\right)^n$
$= \dfrac{1}{5^n}$

e $\dfrac{35^x}{7^x} = \left(\dfrac{35}{7}\right)^x$
$= 5^x$

f $\dfrac{6^a}{8^a} = \left(\dfrac{6}{8}\right)^a$
$= \left(\dfrac{3}{4}\right)^a$

g $\dfrac{5^{n+1}}{5^n} = \dfrac{5 \times 5^n}{5^n}$
$= 5$

h $\dfrac{5^{n+1}}{5} = \dfrac{5 \times 5^n}{5}$
$= 5^n$

5 a $\dfrac{6^m + 2^m}{2^m}$
$= \dfrac{2^m 3^m + 2^m}{2^m}$
$= \dfrac{2^m(3^m + 1)}{2^m}$
$= 3^m + 1$

b $\dfrac{2^n + 12^n}{2^n}$
$= \dfrac{2^n + 2^n 6^n}{2^n}$
$= \dfrac{2^n(1 + 6^n)}{2^n}$
$= 1 + 6^n$

c $\dfrac{8^n + 4^n}{2^n}$
$= \dfrac{2^n 4^n + 2^n 2^n}{2^n}$
$= \dfrac{2^n(4^n + 2^n)}{2^n}$
$= 4^n + 2^n$

d $\dfrac{6^n + 12^n}{1 + 2^n}$
$= \dfrac{6^n + 6^n 2^n}{1 + 2^n}$
$= \dfrac{6^n(1 + 2^n)}{1 + 2^n}$
$= 6^n$

e $\dfrac{5^{n+1} - 5^n}{4}$
$= \dfrac{5^n \times 5 - 5^n}{4}$
$= \dfrac{5^n(5 - 1)}{4}$
$= 5^n$

f $\dfrac{5^{n+1} - 5^n}{5^n}$
$= \dfrac{5^n \times 5 - 5^n}{5^n}$
$= \dfrac{5^n(5 - 1)}{5^n}$
$= 4$

g $\dfrac{2^n - 2^{n-1}}{2^n}$

$= \dfrac{2^{n-1} \times 2 - 2^{n-1}}{2^{n-1} \times 2}$

$= \dfrac{2^{n-1}(2 - 1)}{2^{n-1} \times 2}$

$= \dfrac{1}{2}$

h $\dfrac{2^n + 2^{n-1}}{2^n + 2^{n+1}}$

$= \dfrac{2^{n-1} \times 2 + 2^{n-1}}{2^{n-1} \times 2 + 2^{n-1} \times 2^2}$

$= \dfrac{2^{n-1}(2 + 1)}{2^{n-1}(2 + 2^2)}$

$= \dfrac{1}{2}$

i $\dfrac{3^{n+1} - 3^n}{3^n + 3^{n-1}}$

$= \dfrac{3^{n-1}3^2 - 3^{n-1} \times 3}{3^{n-1} \times 3 + 3^{n-1}}$

$= \dfrac{3^{n-1}(3^2 - 3)}{3^{n-1}(3 + 1)}$

$= \dfrac{3}{2}$

6 a $2^n(n+1) + 2^n(n-1)$
$= 2^n(n + 1 + n - 1)$
$= 2^n(2n)$
$= n2^{n+1}$

b $3^n\left(\dfrac{n-1}{6}\right) - 3^n\left(\dfrac{n+1}{6}\right)$

$= 3^n\left(\dfrac{n-1}{6} - \dfrac{n+1}{6}\right)$

$= 3^n(-\tfrac{1}{3})$

$= 3^n \times -3^{-1}$

$= -3^{n-1}$

7 a $4^x - 6(2^x) + 8 = 0$
$\therefore\ (2^x)^2 - 6(2^x) + 8 = 0$
$\therefore\ (2^x - 2)(2^x - 4) = 0 \quad \{a^2 - 6a + 8 = (a-2)(a-4)\}$
$\therefore\quad 2^x = 2 \quad \text{or}\quad 2^x = 4$
$\therefore\quad 2^x = 2^1 \quad \text{or}\quad 2^x = 2^2$
$\therefore\quad x = 1 \quad \text{or}\quad 2$

b $4^x - 2^x - 2 = 0$
$\therefore\ (2^x)^2 - 2^x - 2 = 0$
$\therefore\ (2^x - 2)(2^x + 1) = 0 \quad \{a^2 - a - 2 = (a-2)(a+1)\}$
$\therefore\quad 2^x = 2 \quad \text{or}\quad 2^x = -1$
$\therefore\quad 2^x = 2^1 \quad \{2^x \text{ cannot be negative}\}$
$\therefore\quad x = 1$

c $9^x - 12(3^x) + 27 = 0$
$\therefore\ (3^x)^2 - 12(3^x) + 27 = 0$
$\therefore\ (3^x - 3)(3^x - 9) = 0 \quad \{a^2 - 12a + 27 = (a-3)(a-9)\}$
$\therefore\quad 3^x = 3 \quad \text{or}\quad 3^x = 9$
$\therefore\quad 3^x = 3^1 \quad \text{or}\quad 3^x = 3^2$
$\therefore\quad x = 1 \quad \text{or}\quad 2$

d $9^x = 3^x + 6$
$\therefore\ (3^x)^2 - 3^x - 6 = 0$
$\therefore\ (3^x - 3)(3^x + 2) = 0 \quad \{a^2 - a - 6 = (a-3)(a+2)\}$
$\therefore\quad 3^x = 3 \quad \text{or}\quad 3^x = -2$
$\therefore\quad 3^x = 3^1 \quad \{3^x \text{ cannot be negative}\}$
$\therefore\quad x = 1$

e $25^x - 23(5^x) - 50 = 0$
$\therefore\ (5^x)^2 - 23(5^x) - 50 = 0$
$\therefore\ (5^x - 25)(5^x + 2) = 0 \quad \{a^2 - 23a - 50 = (a-25)(a+2)\}$
$\therefore\quad 5^x = 25 \quad \text{or}\quad 5^x = -2$
$\therefore\quad 5^x = 5^2 \quad \{5^x \text{ cannot be negative}\}$
$\therefore\quad x = 2$

f
$$49^x + 1 = 2(7^x)$$
$$\therefore \quad (7^x)^2 - 2(7^x) + 1 = 0$$
$$\therefore \quad (7^x - 1)^2 = 0 \quad \{a^2 - 2a + 1 = (a-1)^2\}$$
$$\therefore \quad 7^x = 1$$
$$\therefore \quad 7^x = 7^0$$
$$\therefore \quad x = 0$$

EXERCISE 3E

1 a $2^x = 2$
$\therefore \quad 2^x = 2^1$
$\therefore \quad x = 1$

b $2^x = 4$
$\therefore \quad 2^x = 2^2$
$\therefore \quad x = 2$

c $3^x = 27$
$\therefore \quad 3^x = 3^3$
$\therefore \quad x = 3$

d $2^x = 1$
$\therefore \quad 2^x = 2^0$
$\therefore \quad x = 0$

e $2^x = \frac{1}{2}$
$\therefore \quad 2^x = 2^{-1}$
$\therefore \quad x = -1$

f $3^x = \frac{1}{3}$
$\therefore \quad 3^x = 3^{-1}$
$\therefore \quad x = -1$

g $2^x = \frac{1}{8}$
$\therefore \quad 2^x = 2^{-3}$
$\therefore \quad x = -3$

h $2^{x+1} = 8$
$\therefore \quad 2^{x+1} = 2^3$
$\therefore \quad x + 1 = 3$
$\therefore \quad x = 2$

i $2^{x-2} = \frac{1}{4}$
$\therefore \quad 2^{x-2} = 2^{-2}$
$\therefore \quad x - 2 = -2$
$\therefore \quad x = 0$

j $3^{x+1} = \frac{1}{27}$
$\therefore \quad 3^{x+1} = 3^{-3}$
$\therefore \quad x + 1 = -3$
$\therefore \quad x = -4$

k $2^{x+1} = 64$
$\therefore \quad 2^{x+1} = 2^6$
$\therefore \quad x + 1 = 6$
$\therefore \quad x = 5$

l $2^{1-2x} = \frac{1}{2}$
$\therefore \quad 2^{1-2x} = 2^{-1}$
$\therefore \quad 1 - 2x = -1$
$\therefore \quad -2x = -2$
$\therefore \quad x = 1$

2 a $4^x = 32$
$\therefore \quad 2^{2x} = 2^5$
$\therefore \quad 2x = 5$
$\therefore \quad x = \frac{5}{2}$

b $8^x = \frac{1}{4}$
$\therefore \quad 2^{3x} = 2^{-2}$
$\therefore \quad 3x = -2$
$\therefore \quad x = -\frac{2}{3}$

c $9^x = \frac{1}{3}$
$\therefore \quad 3^{2x} = 3^{-1}$
$\therefore \quad 2x = -1$
$\therefore \quad x = -\frac{1}{2}$

d $49^x = \frac{1}{7}$
$\therefore \quad 7^{2x} = 7^{-1}$
$\therefore \quad 2x = -1$
$\therefore \quad x = -\frac{1}{2}$

e $4^x = \frac{1}{8}$
$\therefore \quad 2^{2x} = 2^{-3}$
$\therefore \quad 2x = -3$
$\therefore \quad x = -\frac{3}{2}$

f $25^x = \frac{1}{5}$
$\therefore \quad 5^{2x} = 5^{-1}$
$\therefore \quad 2x = -1$
$\therefore \quad x = -\frac{1}{2}$

g $8^{x+2} = 32$
$\therefore \quad 2^{3(x+2)} = 2^5$
$\therefore \quad 3x + 6 = 5$
$\therefore \quad 3x = -1$
$\therefore \quad x = -\frac{1}{3}$

h $8^{1-x} = \frac{1}{4}$
$\therefore \quad 2^{3(1-x)} = 2^{-2}$
$\therefore \quad 3 - 3x = -2$
$\therefore \quad -3x = -5$
$\therefore \quad x = \frac{5}{3}$

i $4^{2x-1} = \frac{1}{2}$
$\therefore \quad 2^{2(2x-1)} = 2^{-1}$
$\therefore \quad 4x - 2 = -1$
$\therefore \quad 4x = 1$
$\therefore \quad x = \frac{1}{4}$

j $9^{x-3} = 3$
$\therefore \quad 3^{2(x-3)} = 3^1$
$\therefore \quad 2x - 6 = 1$
$\therefore \quad 2x = 7$
$\therefore \quad x = \frac{7}{2}$

k $\left(\frac{1}{2}\right)^{x+1} = 2$
$\therefore \quad \left(2^{-1}\right)^{x+1} = 2^1$
$\therefore \quad -x - 1 = 1$
$\therefore \quad -x = 2$
$\therefore \quad x = -2$

l $\left(\frac{1}{3}\right)^{x+2} = 9$
$\therefore \quad \left(3^{-1}\right)^{x+2} = 3^2$
$\therefore \quad -x - 2 = 2$
$\therefore \quad -x = 4$
$\therefore \quad x = -4$

m $4^x = 8^{-x}$
$\therefore \quad 2^{2x} = \left(2^3\right)^{-x}$
$\therefore \quad 2x = -3x$
$\therefore \quad 5x = 0$
$\therefore \quad x = 0$

n $\left(\frac{1}{4}\right)^{1-x} = 8$
$\therefore \quad \left(2^{-2}\right)^{1-x} = 2^3$
$\therefore \quad -2 + 2x = 3$
$\therefore \quad 2x = 5$
$\therefore \quad x = \frac{5}{2}$

o $\left(\frac{1}{7}\right)^x = 49$
$\therefore \quad \left(7^{-1}\right)^x = 7^2$
$\therefore \quad -x = 2$
$\therefore \quad x = -2$

p $\left(\frac{1}{2}\right)^{x+1} = 32$
$\therefore \quad \left(2^{-1}\right)^{x+1} = 2^5$
$\therefore \quad -x - 1 = 5$
$\therefore \quad -x = 6$
$\therefore \quad x = -6$

3 a $4^{2x+1} = 8^{1-x}$

$\therefore (2^2)^{2x+1} = (2^3)^{1-x}$

$\therefore 4x + 2 = 3 - 3x$

$\therefore 7x = 1$

$\therefore x = \frac{1}{7}$

b $9^{2-x} = \left(\frac{1}{3}\right)^{2x+1}$

$\therefore (3^2)^{2-x} = (3^{-1})^{2x+1}$

$\therefore 4 - 2x = -2x - 1$

$\therefore 4 = -1$

This is clearly false, so no solutions exist.

c $2^x \times 8^{1-x} = \frac{1}{4}$

$\therefore 2^x \times (2^3)^{1-x} = 2^{-2}$

$\therefore x + 3 - 3x = -2$

$\therefore -2x = -5$

$\therefore x = \frac{5}{2}$

4 a $3 \times 2^x = 24$

$\therefore 2^x = 8$

$\therefore 2^x = 2^3$

$\therefore x = 3$

b $7 \times 2^x = 56$

$\therefore 2^x = 8$

$\therefore 2^x = 2^3$

$\therefore x = 3$

c $3 \times 2^{x+1} = 24$

$\therefore 2^{x+1} = 8$

$\therefore 2^{x+1} = 2^3$

$\therefore x + 1 = 3$

$\therefore x = 2$

d $12 \times 3^{-x} = \frac{4}{3}$

$\therefore 3^{-x} = \frac{4}{3} \div 12$

$\therefore 3^{-x} = \frac{4}{3} \times \frac{1}{12}$

$\therefore 3^{-x} = \frac{1}{9}$

$\therefore 3^{-x} = 3^{-2}$

$\therefore x = 2$

e $4 \times \left(\frac{1}{3}\right)^x = 36$

$\therefore \left(\frac{1}{3}\right)^x = 9$

$\therefore (3^{-1})^x = 3^2$

$\therefore 3^{-x} = 3^2$

$\therefore -x = 2$

$\therefore x = -2$

f $5 \times \left(\frac{1}{2}\right)^x = 20$

$\therefore \left(\frac{1}{2}\right)^x = 4$

$\therefore (2^{-1})^x = 2^2$

$\therefore -x = 2$

$\therefore x = -2$

EXERCISE 3F

1 a When $x = \frac{1}{2}$, $y = 2^{\frac{1}{2}}$
From point A, $y \approx 1.4$
$\therefore 2^{\frac{1}{2}} \approx 1.4$

b When $x = 0.8$, $y = 2^{0.8}$
From point B, $y \approx 1.7$
$\therefore 2^{0.8} \approx 1.7$

c When $x = 1.5$, $y = 2^{1.5}$
From point C, $y \approx 2.8$
$\therefore 2^{1.5} \approx 2.8$

d When $x = -1.6$, $y = 2^{-1.6}$
From point D, $y \approx 0.3$
$\therefore 2^{-1.6} \approx 0.3$

e When $x = \sqrt{2}$, $y = 2^{\sqrt{2}}$
Using **a** we know $x \approx 1.4$
From point E, $y \approx 2.7$
$\therefore 2^{\sqrt{2}} \approx 2.7$

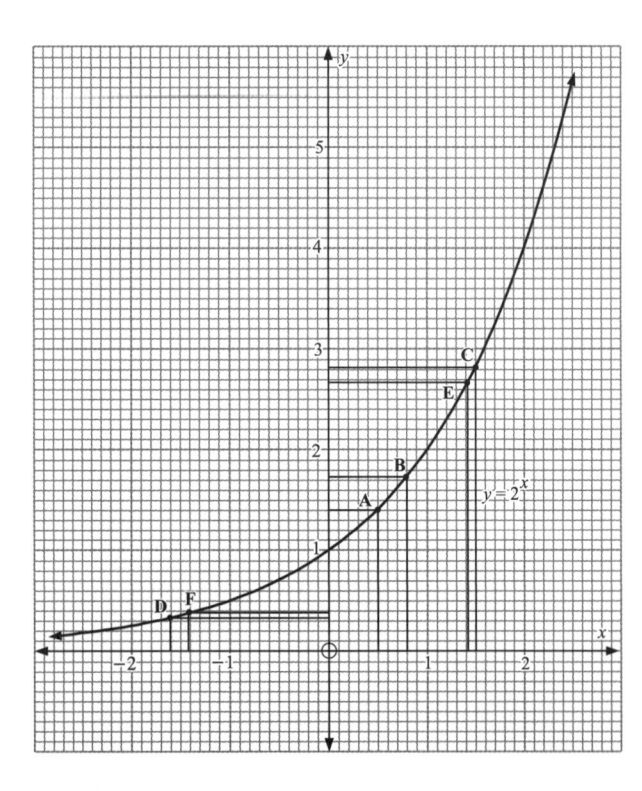

f When $x = -\sqrt{2}$, $y = 2^{-\sqrt{2}}$
Using **a** we know $x \approx -1.4$
From point F, $y \approx 0.4$
$\therefore 2^{-\sqrt{2}} \approx 0.4$

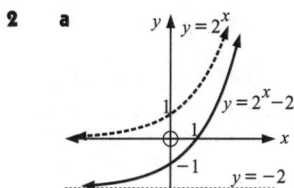

2 a a vertical translation of 2 units downwards $y = -2$ is the HA

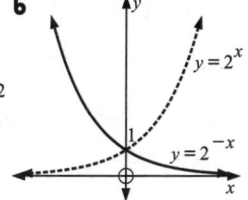

b a reflection in the y-axis

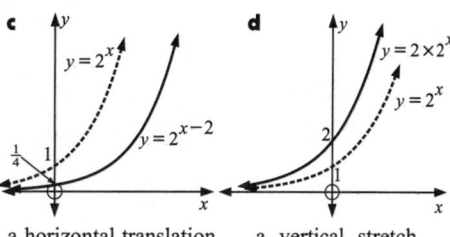

c a horizontal translation of 2 units right

d a vertical stretch of factor 2

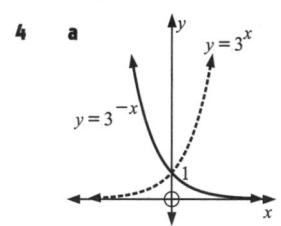

4 a a reflection in the y-axis

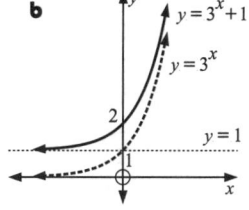

b a vertical translation of 1 unit upwards $y = 1$ is the HA

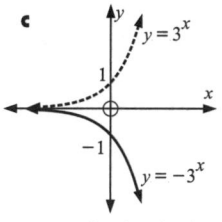

c a reflection in the x-axis

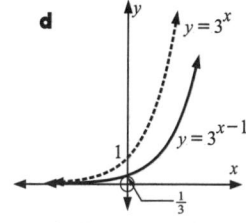

d a horizontal translation of 1 unit right

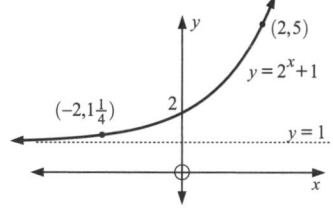

5 a a vertical translation of 1 unit upwards
When $x = 2$, $y = 4 + 1 = 5$
When $x = -2$, $y = \frac{1}{4} + 1 = 1\frac{1}{4}$

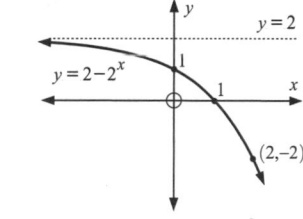

b When $x = 0$, $y = 2 - 2^0 = 2 - 1 = 1$
∴ y-intercept is 1
When $x = 1$, $y = 2 - 2 = 0$
When $x = 2$, $y = 2 - 4 = -2$
When $x = -2$, $y = 2 - \frac{1}{4} = 1\frac{3}{4}$

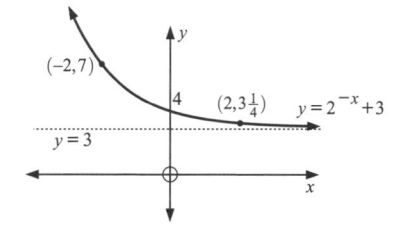

c When $x = 0$, $y = 1 + 3 = 4$
When $x = 2$, $y = \frac{1}{4} + 3 = 3\frac{1}{4}$
When $x = -2$, $y = 2^2 + 3 = 7$

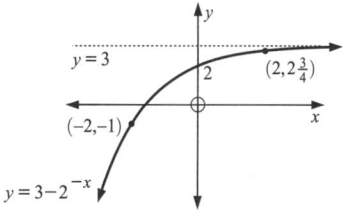

d When $x = 0$, $y = 3 - 1 = 2$
When $x = 2$, $y = 3 - \frac{1}{4} = 2\frac{3}{4}$
When $x = -2$, $y = 3 - 4 = -1$

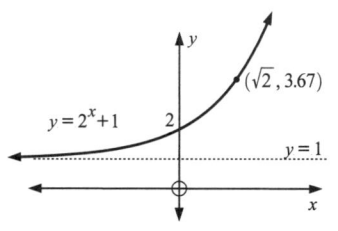

6 a Using technology, when $x = \sqrt{2}$, $y \approx 3.67$

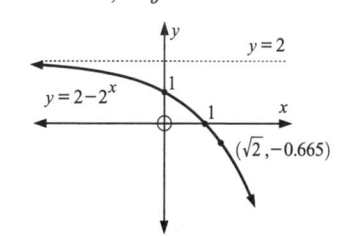

b Using technology, when $x = \sqrt{2}$, $y \approx -0.665$

c

$y = 2^{-x} + 3$

$(\sqrt{2}, 3.38)$

$y = 3$

Using technology, when
$x = \sqrt{2}$, $y \approx 3.38$

d

$y = 3$

$(\sqrt{2}, 2.62)$

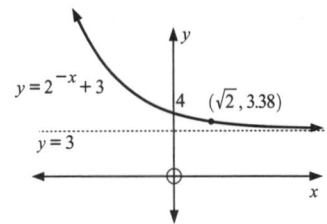

$y = 3 - 2^{-x}$

Using technology, when
$x = \sqrt{2}$, $y \approx 2.62$

7 a As $x \to \infty$, $y \to \infty$
As $x \to -\infty$, $y \to 1$ (from above)
HA is $y = 1$

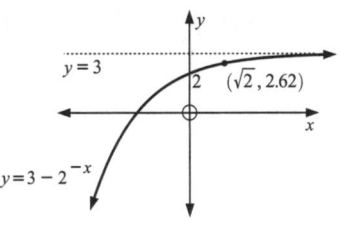

b As $x \to \infty$, $y \to -\infty$
As $x \to -\infty$, $y \to 2$ (from below)
HA is $y = 2$

c As $x \to \infty$, $y \to 3$ (from above)
As $x \to -\infty$, $y \to \infty$
HA is $y = 3$

d As $x \to \infty$, $y \to 3$ (from below)
As $x \to -\infty$, $y \to -\infty$
HA is $y = 3$

EXERCISE 3G.1

1 a When $t = 0$, $W_0 = 100$ grams = the initial weight

b i When $t = 4$,
$W_4 = 100 \times 2^{0.1 \times 4}$
$= 100 \times 2^{0.4}$
≈ 132 grams

ii When $t = 10$,
$W_{10} = 100 \times 2^1$
$= 200$ grams

iii When $t = 24$, $W_{24} = 100 \times 2^{0.1 \times 24}$
$= 100 \times 2^{2.4}$
≈ 528 grams

c W_t (grams)   (24, 528)

$W_t = 100 \times 2^{0.1t}$

(10, 200)

100 (4, 132)

t (hours)

2 a $P_0 = 50$ (the initial population)

b i When $n = 2$,
$P_2 = 50 \times 2^{0.3 \times 2}$
$= 50 \times 2^{0.6}$
≈ 75.785
So, the expected population is 76 possums.

ii When $n = 5$,
$P_5 = 50 \times 2^{0.3 \times 5}$
$= 50 \times 2^{1.5}$
≈ 141.421
So, the expected population is 141 possums.

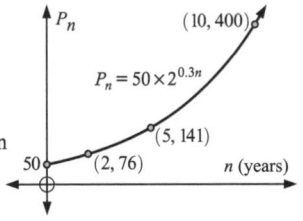

c P_n (10, 400)

$P_n = 50 \times 2^{0.3n}$

(5, 141)

50 (2, 76) n (years)

iii When $n = 10$, $P_{10} = 50 \times 2^{0.3 \times 10}$
$= 50 \times 2^3 = 400$ So, the expected population is 400 possums.

3 a When $t = 0$,
$V_0 = V_0 \times 2^0$
$= V_0$
So, the speed is V_0.

b When $t = 20$,
$V_{20} = V_0 \times 2^{0.05 \times 20}$
$= V_0 \times 2^1$
$= 2V_0$
So, the speed is $2V_0$.

c V_0 becomes $2V_0$
a 100% increase.

d $\left(\dfrac{V_{50} - V_{20}}{V_{20}}\right) \times 100\%$

$= \left(\dfrac{V_0 \times 2^{2.5} - V_0 \times 2^1}{V_0 \times 2^1}\right) \times 100\%$

$= \left(\dfrac{2^{2.5} - 2^1}{2^1}\right) \times 100\%$

$\approx 183\%$

This expression is the percentage increase in the speed from the speed at $20°C$ to the speed at $50°C$.
($V_{50} - V_{20}$ is the increase in speed.)

4 a $B_0 = 6$ pairs $= 12$ bears

b At year 2018, $t = 20$
$\therefore B_{20} = 12 \times 2^{0.18 \times 20}$
$= 12 \times 2^{3.6}$
≈ 145.508
≈ 146 bears

c At year 2008, $t = 10$
$\therefore$ % increase $= \left(\dfrac{B_{20} - B_{10}}{B_{10}}\right) \times 100\%$
$= \left(\dfrac{12 \times 2^{3.6} - 12 \times 2^{1.8}}{12 \times 2^{1.8}}\right) \times 100\%$
$= \left(\dfrac{2^{3.6} - 2^{1.8}}{2^{1.8}}\right) \times 100\%$
$\approx 248\%$

EXERCISE 3G.2

1 $W(t) = 250 \times (0.998)^t$ grams

a $W(0) = 250 \times (0.998)^0$
$= 250 \times 1$
$= 250$ grams $\quad \therefore$ 250 g of radioactive substance was put aside.

b i When $t = 400$
$W(400)$
$= 250 \times (0.998)^{400}$
≈ 112 grams

ii When $t = 800$
$W(800)$
$= 250 \times (0.998)^{800}$
≈ 50.4 grams

iii When $t = 1200$
$W(1200)$
$= 250 \times (0.998)^{1200}$
≈ 22.6 grams

c [Graph of $W(t) = 250 \times (0.998)^t$ with points $(400, 112)$, $(800, 50.4)$, $(1200, 22.6)$, axes $W(t)$ (grams) vs t (years)]

d When $W(t) = 125$
$250 \times (0.998)^t = 125$
$\therefore (0.998)^t = 0.5$
$\therefore t \approx 346.2$ {using technology}
It takes approximately 346 years

2 $T(t) = 100 \times 2^{-0.02t}$

a $T(0) = 100 \times 2^0$
$= 100 \times 1$
$= 100°C$

b i $T(15) = 100 \times 2^{-0.02 \times 15}$
$= 100 \times 2^{-0.3}$
$\approx 81.2°C$

ii $T(20) = 100 \times 2^{-0.02 \times 20}$
$= 100 \times 2^{-0.4}$
$\approx 75.8°C$

iii $T(78) = 100 \times 2^{-0.02 \times 78}$
$= 100 \times 2^{-1.56}$
$\approx 33.9°C$

c [Graph of $T(t) = 100 \times 2^{-0.02t}$ with points $(15, 81.2)$, $(20, 75.8)$, $(78, 33.9)$, axes $T(t)$ (°C) vs t (min)]

3 $W_t = 1000 \times 2^{-0.03t}$

a $W_0 = 1000 \times 2^0$
$= 1000 \times 1$
$= 1000$ g

b i W_{10}
$= 1000 \times 2^{-0.3}$
≈ 812 g

ii W_{100}
$= 1000 \times 2^{-3}$
$= 125$ g

iii W_{1000}
$= 1000 \times 2^{-30}$
$\approx 9.31 \times 10^{-7}$ g

c [Graph of $W_t = 1000 \times 2^{-0.03t}$ with points $(10, 812)$, $(100, 125)$, axes W_t (grams) vs t (years)]

4 a When $t = 0$, $W_0 = W_0 2^0$
$= W_0$ grams
∴ the original weight was W_0 grams

b % change $= \left(\dfrac{W_{1000} - W_0}{W_0}\right) \times 100\%$
$= \left(\dfrac{W_0 \times 2^{-0.2} - W_0}{W_0}\right) \times 100\%$
$= (2^{-0.2} - 1) \times 100\%$
$\approx -12.9\%$
The weight loss was about 12.9%.

EXERCISE 3H

1 $e^1 \approx 2.718\,281\,828$

2

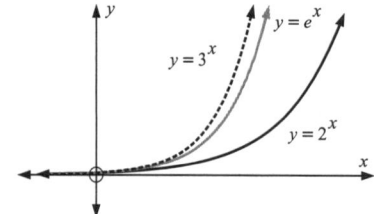

The graph of $y = e^x$ lies between $y = 2^x$ and $y = 3^x$.

3

One is the other reflected in the y-axis.

4 When $x = 0$, $y = ae^0 = a \times 1 = a$ ∴ the y-intercept is a.

5 a The graph of $y = e^x$ is entirely above the x-axis.
$y > 0$ for all x
∴ $e^x > 0$ for all x
∴ $2e^x > 0$ for all x
∴ $y = 2e^x$ cannot be negative.

b i When $x = -20$, $y = 2e^{-20} \approx 4.12 \times 10^{-9}$
  ii When $x = 20$, $y = 2e^{20} \approx 9.70 \times 10^8$

6 a ≈ 7.39 **b** ≈ 20.1 **c** ≈ 2.01 **d** ≈ 1.65 **e** ≈ 0.368

7 a $\sqrt{e} = e^{\frac{1}{2}}$
  b $e\sqrt{e} = e^1 e^{\frac{1}{2}} = e^{\frac{3}{2}}$
  c $\dfrac{1}{\sqrt{e}} = \dfrac{1}{e^{\frac{1}{2}}} = e^{-\frac{1}{2}}$
  d $\dfrac{1}{e^2} = e^{-2}$

8 a $\left(e^{0.36}\right)^{\frac{t}{2}} = e^{0.36 \times \frac{t}{2}} = e^{0.18t}$
  b $\left(e^{0.064}\right)^{\frac{t}{16}} = e^{0.064 \times \frac{t}{16}} = e^{0.004t}$
  c $\left(e^{-0.04}\right)^{\frac{t}{8}} = e^{-0.04 \times \frac{t}{8}} = e^{-0.005t}$
  d $\left(e^{-0.836}\right)^{\frac{t}{5}} = e^{-0.836 \times \frac{t}{5}} \approx e^{-0.167t}$

9 a ≈ 10.074 **b** $\approx 0.099\,261$ **c** ≈ 125.09 **d** $\approx 0.007\,994\,5$
   e ≈ 41.914 **f** ≈ 42.429 **g** ≈ 3540.3 **h** $\approx 0.006\,342\,4$

10

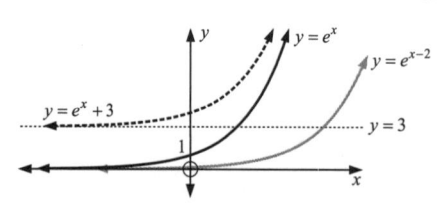

Domain of f, g and h is $\{x \mid x \in \mathbb{R}\}$
Range of f is $\{y \mid y > 0\}$
Range of g is $\{y \mid y > 0\}$
Range of h is $\{y \mid y > 3\}$

11 Domain of f, g and h is $\{x \mid x \in \mathbb{R}\}$
Range of f is $\{y \mid y > 0\}$
Range of g is $\{y \mid y < 0\}$
Range of h is $\{y \mid y < 10\}$

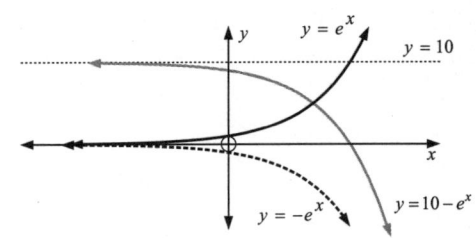

12 $W(t) = 2e^{\frac{t}{2}}$ grams

a **i** $W(0) = 2e^0$
        $= 2 \times 1$
        $= 2$ g

  ii $W(\tfrac{1}{2}) = 2e^{\frac{1}{4}}$
        ≈ 2.57 g

  iii $W(1\tfrac{1}{2}) = 2e^{\frac{3}{4}}$
        ≈ 4.23 g

  iv $W(6) = 2e^3$
        ≈ 40.2 g

b Graph of $W(t) = 2e^{\frac{t}{2}}$ with points $(\tfrac{1}{2}, 2.57)$, $(1\tfrac{1}{2}, 4.23)$, $(6, 40.2)$.

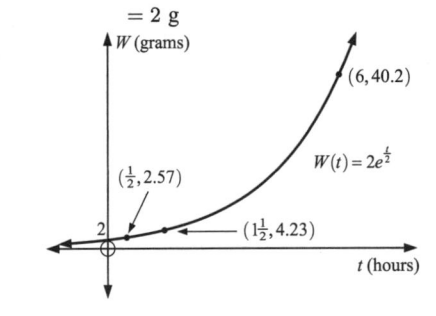

13 $I(t) = 75e^{-0.15t}$

a **i** $I(1) = 75e^{-0.15}$
        ≈ 64.6 amps

  ii $I(10) = 75e^{-1.5}$
        ≈ 16.7 amps

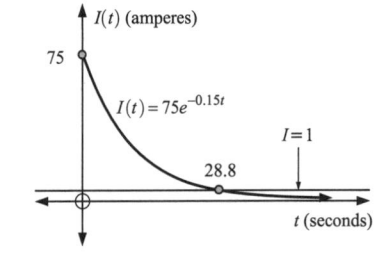

c We need to solve $75e^{-0.15t} = 1$.
Using technology, $t \approx 28.8$ s

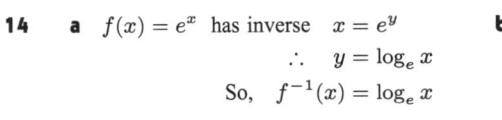

b Graph showing $I(t) = 75e^{-0.15t}$, with $I = 75$ at $t = 0$ and $I \approx 28.8$ when $t = 1$.

14 a $f(x) = e^x$ has inverse $x = e^y$
$\therefore \ y = \log_e x$
So, $f^{-1}(x) = \log_e x$

b Graph of f and f^{-1} with line $y = x$.

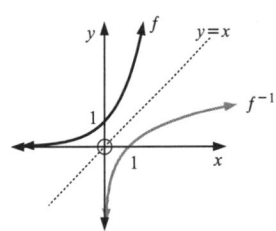

REVIEW SET 3A

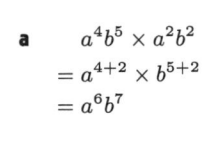

1 a $-(-1)^{10}$
$= -1$

  b $-(-3)^3$
$= -(-27)$
$= 27$

  c $3^0 - 3^{-1}$
$= 1 - \tfrac{1}{3}$
$= \tfrac{2}{3}$

2 a $a^4 b^5 \times a^2 b^2$
$= a^{4+2} \times b^{5+2}$
$= a^6 b^7$

  b $6xy^5 \div 9x^2 y^5$
$= \tfrac{6}{9} x^{1-2} y^{5-5}$
$= \tfrac{2}{3} x^{-1} y^0$
$= \dfrac{2}{3x}$

  c $\dfrac{5(x^2 y)^2}{(5x^2)^2}$
$= \dfrac{5 \times x^4 y^2}{25 x^4}$
$= \tfrac{1}{5} x^0 y^2 = \dfrac{y^2}{5}$

3 **a** 2×2^{-4}
$= 2^1 \times 2^{-4}$
$= 2^{1+(-4)}$
$= 2^{-3}$

b $16 \div 2^{-3}$
$= 2^4 \div 2^{-3}$
$= 2^{4-(-3)}$
$= 2^7$

c 8^4
$= (2^3)^4$
$= 2^{12}$

4 **a** b^{-3}
$= \dfrac{1}{b^3}$

b $(ab)^{-1}$
$= \left(\dfrac{1}{ab}\right)$
$= \dfrac{1}{ab}$

c ab^{-1}
$= a \times \dfrac{1}{b}$
$= \dfrac{a}{b}$

5 **a** $2^{x-3} = \tfrac{1}{32}$
$\therefore\ 2^{x-3} = 2^{-5}$
$\therefore\ x - 3 = -5$
$\therefore\ x = -2$

b $9^x = 27^{2-2x}$
$\therefore\ (3^2)^x = (3^3)^{2-2x}$
$\therefore\ 2x = 6 - 6x$
$\therefore\ 8x = 6$
$\therefore\ x = \tfrac{6}{8} = \tfrac{3}{4}$

6 **a** $8^{\frac{2}{3}} = (2^3)^{\frac{2}{3}} = 2^2 = 4$

b $27^{-\frac{2}{3}} = (3^3)^{-\frac{2}{3}} = 3^{-2} = \dfrac{1}{3^2} = \tfrac{1}{9}$

7 **a** ≈ 2.28 **b** ≈ 0.517 **c** ≈ 3.16

8 $f(x) = 3 \times 2^x$

a $f(0) = 3 \times 2^0$
$= 3 \times 1$
$= 3$

b $f(3) = 3 \times 2^3$
$= 3 \times 8$
$= 24$

c $f(-2) = 3 \times 2^{-2}$
$= 3 \times \dfrac{1}{2^2} = \tfrac{3}{4}$

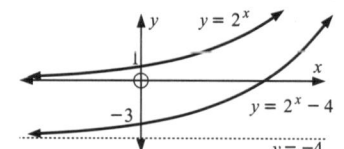

9

a $y = 2^x$ has y-intercept 1 and horizontal asymptote $y = 0$

b $y = 2^x - 4$ has y-intercept -3 and horizontal asymptote $y = -4$

10 $T = 80 \times (0.913)^t$ °C

a When $t = 0$, $T = 80 \times (0.913)^0$
$= 80 \times 1$
$= 80$ $\therefore$ the initial temperature was $80°C$.

b **i** When $t = 12$,
$T = 80 \times (0.913)^{12}$
$\approx 26.8°C$

ii When $t = 24$,
$T = 80 \times (0.913)^{24}$
$\approx 9.00°C$

iii When $t = 36$,
$T = 80 \times (0.913)^{36}$
$\approx 3.02°C$

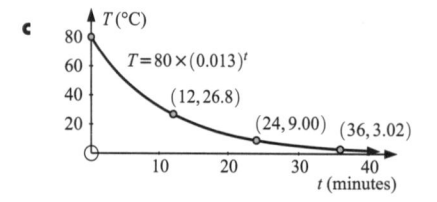

c [Graph of $T = 80 \times (0.913)^t$ showing points $(12, 26.8)$, $(24, 9.00)$, $(36, 3.02)$ with T(°C) axis and t (minutes) axis]

d When $T = 25$
$80 \times (0.913)^t = 25$
$\therefore\ 0.913^t = 0.3125$
$\therefore\ t \approx 12.8$ min {using technology}

REVIEW SET 3B

1 **a** $-(-2)^3$
$= -(-8)$
$= 8$

b $5^{-1} - 5^0$
$= \tfrac{1}{5} - 1$
$= -\tfrac{4}{5}$

2 a $(a^7)^3$
$= a^{7 \times 3}$
$= a^{21}$

b $pq^2 \times p^3 q^4$
$= p^{1+3} q^{2+4}$
$= p^4 q^6$

c $\dfrac{8ab^5}{2a^4 b^4}$
$= \tfrac{8}{2} a^{1-4} b^{5-4}$
$= 4a^{-3} b^1$
$= \dfrac{4b}{a^3}$

3 a $\dfrac{1}{16}$
$= \dfrac{1}{2^4}$
$= 2^{-4}$

b $2^x \times 4$
$= 2^x \times 2^2$
$= 2^{x+2}$

c $4^x \div 8$
$= (2^2)^x \div 2^3$
$= 2^{2x} \div 2^3$
$= 2^{2x-3}$

4 a $x^{-2} \times x^{-3}$
$= x^{-2+(-3)}$
$= x^{-5}$
$= \dfrac{1}{x^5}$

b $2(ab)^{-2}$
$= 2 \times \dfrac{1}{(ab)^2}$
$= \dfrac{2}{a^2 b^2}$

c $2ab^{-2}$
$= 2a \times \left(\dfrac{1}{b^2}\right)$
$= \dfrac{2a}{b^2}$

5 a $2^{x+1} = 32$
$\therefore \ 2^{x+1} = 2^5$
$\therefore \ x + 1 = 5$
$\therefore \ x = 4$

b $4^{x+1} = \left(\tfrac{1}{8}\right)^x$
$\therefore \ (2^2)^{x+1} = (2^{-3})^x$
$\therefore \ 2x + 2 = -3x$
$\therefore \ 5x = -2$
$\therefore \ x = -\tfrac{2}{5}$

6 a $81 = 3^4$
b $1 = 3^0$
c $\dfrac{1}{27} = \dfrac{1}{3^3} = 3^{-3}$
d $\dfrac{1}{243} = \dfrac{1}{3^5} = 3^{-5}$

7 a $\dfrac{27}{9^a} = \dfrac{3^3}{(3^2)^a}$
$= 3^{3-2a}$

b $(\sqrt{3})^{1-x} \times 9^{1-2x} = (3^{\frac{1}{2}})^{1-x} \times (3^2)^{1-2x}$
$= 3^{\frac{1}{2} - \frac{1}{2}x + 2 - 4x}$
$= 3^{\frac{5}{2} - \frac{9}{2}x}$

8 a When $x = 0$, $y = 3^0 - 5 = 1 - 5 = -4$
When $x = 1$, $y = 3^1 - 5 = 3 - 5 = -2$
When $x = 2$, $y = 3^2 - 5 = 9 - 5 = 4$
When $x = -1$, $y = 3^{-1} - 5 = \tfrac{1}{3} - 5 = -4\tfrac{2}{3}$
When $x = -2$, $y = 3^{-2} - 5 = \tfrac{1}{9} - 5 = -4\tfrac{8}{9}$

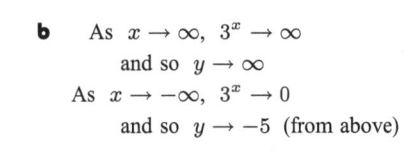

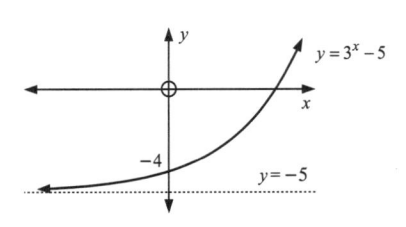

b As $x \to \infty$, $3^x \to \infty$
and so $y \to \infty$
As $x \to -\infty$, $3^x \to 0$
and so $y \to -5$ (from above)

d $y = -5$ is the horizontal asymptote.

c

9 a $27^x = 3$
$\therefore \ (3^3)^x = 3^1$
$\therefore \ 3x = 1$
$\therefore \ x = \tfrac{1}{3}$

b $9^{1-x} = 27^{x+2}$
$\therefore \ (3^2)^{1-x} = (3^3)^{x+2}$
$\therefore \ 2 - 2x = 3x + 6$
$\therefore \ -5x = 4$ and so $x = -\tfrac{4}{5}$

10

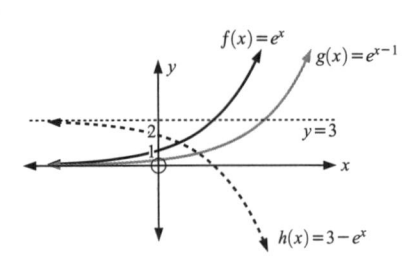

Domain of f, g and h is $\{x \mid x \in \mathbb{R}\}$
Range of f is $\{y \mid y > 0\}$
Range of g is $\{y \mid y > 0\}$
Range of h is $\{y \mid y < 3\}$

REVIEW SET 3C

1 **a** $\quad 4 \times 2^n$
$= 2^2 \times 2^n$
$= 2^{n+2}$

b $\quad 7^{-1} - 7^0$
$= \frac{1}{7} - 1$
$= -\frac{6}{7}$

c $\quad \left(\frac{2}{3}\right)^{-3}$
$= \left(\frac{3}{2}\right)^3$
$= \frac{27}{8}$
$= 3\frac{3}{8}$

d $\quad \left(\frac{2a^{-1}}{b^2}\right)^2$
$= \frac{2^2 a^{-2}}{b^4}$
$= \frac{4}{a^2 b^4}$

2 **a**

2	288
2	144
2	72
2	36
2	18
3	9
	3

$\therefore \ 288 = 2^5 \times 3^2$

b $\quad \dfrac{2^{x+1}}{2^{1-x}} = 2^{x+1-(1-x)}$
$= 2^{x+1-1+x}$
$= 2^{2x}$

3 **a** $\quad 1 = 5^0$

b $\quad 5\sqrt{5}$
$= 5^1 \times 5^{\frac{1}{2}}$
$= 5^{\frac{3}{2}}$

c $\quad \dfrac{1}{\sqrt[4]{5}}$
$= \dfrac{1}{5^{\frac{1}{4}}}$
$= 5^{-\frac{1}{4}}$

d $\quad 25^{a+3}$
$= (5^2)^{a+3}$
$= 5^{2a+6}$

4 **a** $\quad -(-2)^2$
$= -(4)$
$= -4$

b $\quad \left(-\frac{1}{2}a^{-3}\right)^2$
$= \left(-\frac{1}{2}\right)^2 a^{-6}$
$= \frac{1}{4}a^{-6}$
$= \frac{1}{4} \times \frac{1}{a^6}$
$= \frac{1}{4a^6}$

c $\quad (-3b^{-1})^{-3}$
$= (-3)^{-3} b^3$
$= \frac{1}{(-3)^3} b^3$
$= \frac{1}{-27} b^3$
$= -\frac{b^3}{27}$

5 **a** $\quad e^x(e^{-x} + e^x)$
$= e^0 + e^{2x}$
$= 1 + e^{2x}$

b $\quad (2^x + 5)^2$
$= (2^x)^2 + 2 \times 2^x \times 5 + 5^2$
$= 2^{2x} + 5 \times 2^{x+1} + 25$
$= 4^x + 5 \times 2^{x+1} + 25$
{or $\ 2^{2x} + 10(2^x) + 25$}

c $\quad (x^{\frac{1}{2}} - 7)(x^{\frac{1}{2}} + 7)$
$= (x^{\frac{1}{2}})^2 - 7^2$
$= x^1 - 49$
$= x - 49$

6 a $(3 - 2^a)^2$
$= 3^2 - 2 \times 3 \times 2^a + (2^a)^2$
$= 9 - 3 \times 2^{a+1} + 2^{2a}$
{or $9 - 6(2^a) + 2^{2a}$}

b $(\sqrt{x} + 2)(\sqrt{x} - 2)$
$= (\sqrt{x})^2 - 2^2$
$= x - 4$

c $2^{-x}(2^{2x} + 2^x)$
$= 2^{-x+2x} + 2^{-x+x}$
$= 2^x + 2^0$
$= 2^x + 1$

7 a $6 \times 2^x = 192$
$\therefore \ 2^x = 32$
$\therefore \ 2^x = 2^5$
$\therefore \ x = 5$

b $4 \times (\frac{1}{3})^x = 324$
$\therefore \ (\frac{1}{3})^x = 81$
$\therefore \ (3^{-1})^x = 3^4$
$\therefore \ 3^{-x} = 3^4$
$\therefore \ x = -4$

8 $W = 1500 \times (0.993)^t$ grams

a When $t = 0$,
$W = 1500 \times (0.993)^0$
$= 1500 \times 1$
$= 1500$ grams

b i When $t = 400$,
$W = 1500 \times (0.993)^{400}$
≈ 90.3 grams

ii When $t = 800$,
$W = 1500 \times (0.993)^{800}$
≈ 5.44 grams

c

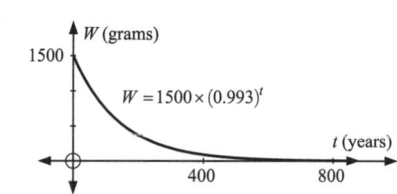

d When $W = 100$,
$1500 \times (0.993)^t = 100$
$\therefore \ (0.993)^t \approx 0.0667$
$\therefore \ t \approx 385.5$ {using technology}
So, it will take about 386 years.

9 $4^a 2^b = 1$
$\therefore \ (2^2)^a \times 2^b = 2^0$
$\therefore \ 2^{2a+b} = 2^0$
$\therefore \ 2a + b = 0$
$\therefore \ b = -2a$ ...... (1)

Now $\dfrac{8^a}{4^b} = \dfrac{1}{128}$
$\therefore \ \dfrac{(2^3)^a}{(2^2)^b} = \dfrac{1}{2^7}$
$\therefore \ 2^{3a-2b} = 2^{-7}$
$\therefore \ 3a - 2b = -7$
$\therefore \ 3a - 2(-2a) = -7$ {substituting (1)}
$\therefore \ 7a = -7$
$\therefore \ a = -1$
Substituting $a = -1$ into (1) gives $b = -2(-1) = 2$

So, $\dfrac{16^a}{2^b} = \dfrac{16^{-1}}{2^2} = \dfrac{1}{16 \times 4} = \dfrac{1}{64}$.

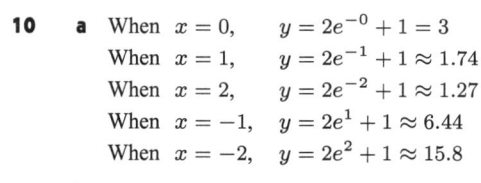

10 a When $x = 0$, $y = 2e^{-0} + 1 = 3$
When $x = 1$, $y = 2e^{-1} + 1 \approx 1.74$
When $x = 2$, $y = 2e^{-2} + 1 \approx 1.27$
When $x = -1$, $y = 2e^1 + 1 \approx 6.44$
When $x = -2$, $y = 2e^2 + 1 \approx 15.8$

b As $x \to \infty$, $y \to 1$ (from above)
As $x \to -\infty$, $y \to \infty$

c

d $y = 1$ is a horizontal asymptote.

Chapter 4
LOGARITHMS

EXERCISE 4A

1
  a $10^4 = 10\,000$
  b $10^{-1} = 0.1$
  c $10^{\frac{1}{2}} = \sqrt{10}$
  d $2^3 = 8$
  e $2^{-2} = \frac{1}{4}$
  f $3^{1.5} = \sqrt{27}$

2
  a $\log_2 4 = 2$
  b $\log_2(\frac{1}{8}) = -3$
  c $\log_{10}(0.01) = -2$
  d $\log_7 49 = 2$
  e $\log_2 64 = 6$
  f $\log_3(\frac{1}{27}) = -3$

3
  a $10^5 = 100\,000$
    so $\log_{10}(100\,000) = 5$
  b $10^{-2} = 0.01$
    so $\log_{10}(0.01) = -2$
  c $3^{\frac{1}{2}} = \sqrt{3}$
    so $\log_3(\sqrt{3}) = \frac{1}{2}$

  d $2^3 = 8$
    so $\log_2 8 = 3$
  e $2^6 = 64$
    so $\log_2 64 = 6$
  f $2^7 = 128$
    so $\log_2 128 = 7$

  g $5^2 = 25$
    so $\log_5 25 = 2$
  h $5^3 = 125$
    so $\log_5 125 = 3$
  i $2^{-3} = \frac{1}{8} = 0.125$
    so $\log_2(0.125) = -3$

  j $9^{\frac{1}{2}} = \sqrt{9} = 3$
    so $\log_9 3 = \frac{1}{2}$
  k $4^2 = 16$
    so $\log_4 16 = 2$
  l $36^{\frac{1}{2}} = \sqrt{36} = 6$
    so $\log_{36} 6 = \frac{1}{2}$

  m $243 = 3^5$
    so $\log_3 243 = 5$
  n $\sqrt[3]{2} = 2^{\frac{1}{3}}$
    so $\log_2 \sqrt[3]{2} = \frac{1}{3}$
  o $\log_a a^n = n$

  p $2 = 8^{\frac{1}{3}}$
    so $\log_8 2 = \frac{1}{3}$
  q $\frac{1}{t} = t^{-1}$
    so $\log_t\left(\frac{1}{t}\right) = -1$
  r $6\sqrt{6} = 6^1 \times 6^{\frac{1}{2}} = 6^{\frac{3}{2}}$
    so $\log_6(6\sqrt{6}) = \frac{3}{2}$

  s $1 = 4^0$
    so $\log_4 1 = 0$
  t $9 = 9^1$
    so $\log_9 9 = 1$

4
  a ≈ 2.18
  b ≈ 1.40
  c ≈ 1.87
  d ≈ -0.0969

5
  a $\log_2 x = 3$
    $\therefore x = 2^3$
    $\therefore x = 8$

  b $\log_4 x = \frac{1}{2}$
    $\therefore x = 4^{\frac{1}{2}}$
    $\therefore x = 2$

  c $\log_x 81 = 4$
    $\therefore 81 = x^4$
    $\therefore x = \pm\sqrt[4]{81}$
    $\therefore x = \pm 3$
    $\therefore x = 3$ {as $x > 0$}

  d $\log_2(x - 6) = 3$
    $\therefore x - 6 = 2^3$
    $\therefore x - 6 = 8$
    $\therefore x = 14$

6
  a Let $\log_a a^n = x$
      $\therefore a^x = a^n$
      $\therefore x = n$, so $\log_a a^n = n$.

  b
    i $\log_4 16$
      $= \log_4 4^2$
      $= 2$

    ii $\log_2 4$
      $= \log_2 2^2$
      $= 2$

    iii $\log_3(\frac{1}{3})$
      $= \log_3 3^{-1}$
      $= -1$

    iv $\log_{10} \sqrt[5]{100}$
      $= \log_{10}(10^2)^{\frac{1}{5}}$
      $= \log_{10} 10^{\frac{2}{5}}$
      $= \frac{2}{5}$

v $\log_2\left(\frac{1}{\sqrt{2}}\right)$ **vi** $\log_5(25\sqrt{5})$ **vii** $\log_3\left(\frac{1}{\sqrt{3}}\right)$ **viii** $\log_4\left(\frac{1}{2\sqrt{2}}\right)$

$= \log_2 2^{-\frac{1}{2}}$ $= \log_5\left(5^2 5^{\frac{1}{2}}\right)$ $= \log_3 3^{-\frac{1}{2}}$ $= \log_4\left(2^{-\frac{3}{2}}\right)$

$= -\frac{1}{2}$ $= \log_5 5^{\frac{5}{2}}$ $= -\frac{1}{2}$ $= \log_4\left((2^2)^{-\frac{3}{4}}\right)$

     $= \frac{5}{2}$ $= \log_4 4^{-\frac{3}{4}}$

             $= -\frac{3}{4}$

EXERCISE 4B

1 a $\log 10\,000$ **b** $\log 0.001$ **c** $\log 10$ **d** $\log 1$

$= \log_{10} 10^4$ $= \log_{10} 10^{-3}$ $= \log_{10} 10^1$ $= \log_{10} 10^0$

$= 4$ $= -3$ $= 1$ $= 0$

e $\log\sqrt{10}$ **f** $\log\sqrt[3]{10}$ **g** $\log\left(\frac{1}{\sqrt[4]{10}}\right)$ **h** $\log 10\sqrt{10}$

$= \log_{10} 10^{\frac{1}{2}}$ $= \log_{10} 10^{\frac{1}{3}}$ $= \log_{10} 10^{-\frac{1}{4}}$ $= \log_{10} 10^{\frac{3}{2}}$

$= \frac{1}{2}$ $= \frac{1}{3}$ $= -\frac{1}{4}$ $= \frac{3}{2}$

i $\log\sqrt[3]{100}$ **j** $\log\left(\frac{100}{\sqrt{10}}\right)$ **k** $\log\left(10 \times \sqrt[3]{10}\right)$

$= \log_{10}(10^2)^{\frac{1}{3}}$ $= \log_{10}\left(\frac{10^2}{10^{\frac{1}{2}}}\right)$ $= \log_{10}\left(10^1 \times 10^{\frac{1}{3}}\right)$

$= \log_{10} 10^{\frac{2}{3}}$ $= \log_{10} 10^{\frac{3}{2}}$ $= \log_{10} 10^{\frac{4}{3}}$

$= \frac{2}{3}$ $= \frac{3}{2}$ $= \frac{4}{3}$

l $\log 1000\sqrt{10}$ **m** $\log 10^n$ **n** $\log(10^a \times 100)$

$= \log_{10}(10^3 \times 10^{\frac{1}{2}})$ $= \log_{10} 10^n$ $= \log_{10}\left(10^a \times 10^2\right)$

$= \log_{10} 10^{\frac{7}{2}}$ $= n$ $= \log_{10}\left(10^{a+2}\right)$

$= \frac{7}{2}$ $= a + 2$

o $\log\left(\frac{10}{10^m}\right)$ **p** $\log\left(\frac{10^a}{10^b}\right)$

$= \log_{10}(10^{1-m})$ $= \log_{10}(10^{a-b})$

$= 1 - m$ $= a - b$

2 Instructions given for a TI-84 plus:

    a `log` 10 000 `ENTER` , 4   **b** `log` 0.001 `ENTER` , -3

    c `log` `2nd` `√` 10 `)` `)` `ENTER` , 0.5

    d `log` 10 `^` `(` 1 `÷` 3 `)` `)` `ENTER` , $0.\overline{3}$

    e `log` 100 `^` `(` 1 `÷` 3 `)` `)` `ENTER` , $0.\overline{6}$

    f `log` 10 `×` `2nd` `√` 10 `)` `)` `ENTER` , 1.5

    g `log` 1 `÷` `2nd` `√` 10 `)` `)` `ENTER` , -0.5

    h `log` 1 `÷` 10 `^` 0.25 `)` `ENTER` , -0.25

3 **a** 6
$= 10^{\log 6}$
$\approx 10^{0.7782}$

b 60
$= 10^{\log 60}$
$\approx 10^{1.7782}$

c 6000
$= 10^{\log 6000}$
$\approx 10^{3.7782}$

d 0.6
$= 10^{\log(0.6)}$
$\approx 10^{-0.2218}$

e 0.006
$= 10^{\log(0.006)}$
$\approx 10^{-2.2218}$

f 15
$= 10^{\log 15}$
$\approx 10^{1.1761}$

g 1500
$= 10^{\log 1500}$
$\approx 10^{3.1761}$

h 1.5
$= 10^{\log 1.5}$
$\approx 10^{0.1761}$

i 0.15
$= 10^{\log(0.15)}$
$\approx 10^{-0.8239}$

j 0.00015
$= 10^{\log(0.00015)}$
$\approx 10^{-3.8239}$

4 a i $\log 3$
≈ 0.477

ii $\log 300$
≈ 2.477

b $300 = 3 \times 10^2$
$= 10^{\log 3} \times 10^2$
$= 10^{\log 3 + 2}$
$\therefore \ \log 300 = \log 3 + 2$

5 a i $\log 5$
≈ 0.699

ii $\log 0.05$
≈ -1.301

b $0.05 = 5 \times 10^{-2}$
$= 10^{\log 5} \times 10^{-2}$
$= 10^{\log 5 - 2}$
$\therefore \ \log 0.05 = \log 5 - 2$

6 a $\log x = 2$
$\therefore \ x = 10^2$
$\therefore \ x = 100$

b $\log x = 1$
$\therefore \ x = 10^1$
$\therefore \ x = 10$

c $\log x = 0$
$\therefore \ x = 10^0$
$\therefore \ x = 1$

d $\log x = -1$
$\therefore \ x = 10^{-1}$
$\therefore \ x = \frac{1}{10}$

e $\log x = \frac{1}{2}$
$\therefore \ x = 10^{\frac{1}{2}}$
$\therefore \ x = \sqrt{10}$

f $\log x = -\frac{1}{2}$
$\therefore \ x = 10^{-\frac{1}{2}}$
$\therefore \ x = \frac{1}{10^{\frac{1}{2}}}$
$\therefore \ x = \frac{1}{\sqrt{10}}$

g $\log x \approx 0.8351$
$\therefore \ x \approx 10^{0.8351}$
$\therefore \ x \approx 6.84$

h $\log x \approx -3.1997$
$\therefore \ x \approx 10^{-3.1997}$
$\therefore \ x \approx 0.000631$

EXERCISE 4C.1

1 a $\log 8 + \log 2$
$= \log(8 \times 2)$
$= \log 16$

b $\log 8 - \log 2$
$= \log(\frac{8}{2})$
$= \log 4$

c $\log 40 - \log 5$
$= \log(\frac{40}{5})$
$= \log 8$

d $\log 4 + \log 5$
$= \log(4 \times 5)$
$= \log 20$

e $\log 5 + \log(0.4)$
$= \log(5 \times 0.4)$
$= \log 2$

f $\log 2 + \log 3 + \log 4$
$= \log(2 \times 3 \times 4)$
$= \log 24$

g $1 + \log 3$
$= \log 10^1 + \log 3$
$= \log(10 \times 3)$
$= \log 30$

h $\log 4 - 1$
$= \log 4 - \log 10^1$
$= \log(\frac{4}{10})$
$= \log(0.4)$

i $\log 5 + \log 4 - \log 2$
$= \log\left(\frac{5 \times 4}{2}\right)$
$= \log 10$

j $2 + \log 2$
$= \log 10^2 + \log 2$
$= \log(100 \times 2)$
$= \log 200$

k $\log 40 - 2$
$= \log 40 - \log 10^2$
$= \log\left(\frac{40}{100}\right)$
$= \log(0.4)$

l $\log 6 - \log 2 - \log 3$
$= \log(6 \div 2 \div 3)$
$= \log 1$

m $\log 50 - 4$
$= \log 50 - \log 10^4$
$= \log\left(\frac{50}{10^4}\right)$
$= \log(0.005)$

n $3 - \log 50$
$= \log 10^3 - \log 50$
$= \log\left(\frac{1000}{50}\right)$
$= \log 20$

o $\log(\frac{4}{3}) + \log 3 + \log 7$
$= \log\left(\frac{4}{3} \times 3 \times 7\right)$
$= \log 28$

2 a $5\log 2 + \log 3$
$= \log 2^5 + \log 3$
$= \log(2^5 \times 3)$
$= \log 96$

b $2\log 3 + 3\log 2$
$= \log 3^2 + \log 2^3$
$= \log(9 \times 8)$
$= \log 72$

c $3\log 4 - \log 8$
$= \log 4^3 - \log 8$
$= \log(\frac{64}{8})$
$= \log 8$

d $2\log 5 - 3\log 2$
$= \log 5^2 - \log 2^3$
$= \log\left(\frac{25}{8}\right)$

e $\frac{1}{2}\log 4 + \log 3$
$= \log 4^{\frac{1}{2}} + \log 3$
$= \log(2 \times 3)$
$= \log 6$

f $\frac{1}{3}\log\left(\frac{1}{8}\right)$
$= \log\left(\frac{1}{8}\right)^{\frac{1}{3}}$
$= \log\left(2^{-3}\right)^{\frac{1}{3}}$
$= \log 2^{-1}$
$= \log(\frac{1}{2})$ or $-\log 2$

g $3 - \log 2 - 2\log 5$
$= \log 10^3 - \log 2 - \log 5^2$
$= \log(1000 \div 2 \div 25)$
$= \log 20$

h $1 - 3\log 2 + \log 20$
$= \log 10^1 - \log 2^3 + \log 20$
$= \log(10 \div 8 \times 20)$
$= \log 25$

i $2 - \frac{1}{2}\log 4 - \log 5$
$= \log 10^2 - \log 4^{\frac{1}{2}} - \log 5$
$= \log(100 \div 2 \div 5)$
$= \log 10$
$= 1$

3 a $\dfrac{\log 4}{\log 2}$
$= \dfrac{\log 2^2}{\log 2}$
$= \dfrac{2\log 2}{\log 2}$
$= 2$

b $\dfrac{\log 27}{\log 9}$
$= \dfrac{\log 3^3}{\log 3^2}$
$= \dfrac{3\log 3}{2\log 3}$
$= \dfrac{3}{2}$

c $\dfrac{\log 8}{\log 2}$
$= \dfrac{\log 2^3}{\log 2}$
$= \dfrac{3\log 2}{\log 2}$
$= 3$

d $\dfrac{\log 3}{\log 9}$
$= \dfrac{\log 3}{\log 3^2}$
$= \dfrac{\log 3}{2\log 3}$
$= \dfrac{1}{2}$

e $\dfrac{\log 25}{\log(0.2)}$
$= \dfrac{\log 5^2}{\log 5^{-1}}$
$= \dfrac{2\log 5}{-1\log 5}$
$= -2$

f $\dfrac{\log 8}{\log(0.25)}$
$= \dfrac{\log 2^3}{\log 2^{-2}}$ $\{0.25 = \frac{1}{4} = \frac{1}{2^2}\}$
$= \dfrac{3\log 2}{-2\log 2}$
$= -\dfrac{3}{2}$

4 a $\log 9 = \log 3^2$
$= 2\log 3$

b $\log \sqrt{2} = \log 2^{\frac{1}{2}}$
$= \frac{1}{2}\log 2$

c $\log\left(\frac{1}{8}\right) = \log\left(\dfrac{1}{2^3}\right)$
$= \log 2^{-3}$
$= -3\log 2$

d $\log\left(\frac{1}{5}\right) = \log 5^{-1}$
$= -1\log 5$
$= -\log 5$

e $\log 5 = \log\left(\frac{10}{2}\right)$
$= \log 10^1 - \log 2$
$= 1 - \log 2$

f $\log 5000 = \log\left(\frac{10\,000}{2}\right)$
$= \log 10^4 - \log 2$
$= 4 - \log 2$

5 a $\log_b 6$
$= \log_b(2 \times 3)$
$= \log_b 2 + \log_b 3$
$= p + q$

b $\log_b 108$
$= \log_b(2^2 3^3)$
$= 2\log_b 2 + 3\log_b 3$
$= 2p + 3q$

c $\log_b 45$
$= \log_b(3^2 5)$
$= 2\log_b 3 + \log_b 5$
$= 2q + r$

d $\log_b\left(\frac{5\sqrt{3}}{2}\right)$
$= \log_b(5 \times 3^{\frac{1}{2}}) - \log_b 2$
$= \log_b 5 + \frac{1}{2}\log_b 3 - \log_b 2$
$= r + \frac{1}{2}q - p$

e $\log_b\left(\frac{5}{32}\right)$
$= \log_b 5 - \log_b 2^5$
$= \log_b 5 - 5\log_b 2$
$= r - 5p$

f $\log_b(0.\overline{2})$
$= \log_b\left(\frac{2}{9}\right)$
$= \log_b 2 - \log_b 3^2$
$= p - 2q$

6 **a** $\log_2(PR)$
$= \log_2 P + \log_2 R$
$= x + z$

b $\log_2(RQ^2)$
$= \log_2 R + \log_2 Q^2$
$= \log_2 R + 2\log_2 Q$
$= z + 2y$

c $\log_2\left(\dfrac{PR}{Q}\right)$
$= \log_2(PR) - \log_2 Q$
$= \log_2 P + \log_2 R - \log_2 Q$
$= x + z - y$

d $\log_2\left(P^2\sqrt{Q}\right)$
$= \log_2 P^2 + \log_2 Q^{\frac{1}{2}}$
$= 2\log_2 P + \frac{1}{2}\log_2 Q$
$= 2x + \frac{1}{2}y$

e $\log_2\left(\dfrac{Q^3}{\sqrt{R}}\right)$
$= \log_2 Q^3 - \log_2 R^{\frac{1}{2}}$
$= 3\log_2 Q - \frac{1}{2}\log_2 R$
$= 3y - \frac{1}{2}z$

f $\log_2\left(\dfrac{R^2\sqrt{Q}}{P^3}\right)$
$= \log_2 R^2 + \log_2 Q^{\frac{1}{2}} - \log_2 P^3$
$= 2\log_2 R + \frac{1}{2}\log_2 Q - 3\log_2 P$
$= 2z + \frac{1}{2}y - 3x$

7 **a** $\log_t N^2 = 1.72$
$\therefore\ 2\log_t N = 1.72$
$\therefore\ \log_t N = 1.72 \div 2$
$\qquad\quad\ = 0.86$

b $\log_t(MN)$
$= \log_t M + \log_t N$
$= 1.29 + 0.86$
$= 2.15$

c $\log_t\left(\dfrac{N^2}{\sqrt{M}}\right)$
$= \log_t N^2 - \log_t M^{\frac{1}{2}}$
$= 1.72 - \frac{1}{2}\log_t M$
$= 1.72 - \frac{1}{2}(1.29)$
$= 1.075$

EXERCISE 4C.2

1 **a** $y = 2^x$
$\therefore\ \log y = \log 2^x$
$\therefore\ \log y = x\log 2$

b $y = 20b^3$
$\therefore\ \log y = \log(20b^3)$
$\therefore\ \log y = \log 20 + \log b^3$
$\therefore\ \log y \approx 1.30 + 3\log b$

c $M = ad^4$
$\therefore\ \log M = \log(ad^4)$
$\therefore\ \log M = \log a + \log d^4$
$\therefore\ \log M = \log a + 4\log d$

d $T = 5\sqrt{d} = 5d^{\frac{1}{2}}$
$\therefore\ \log T = \log(5d^{\frac{1}{2}})$
$\therefore\ \log T = \log 5 + \log d^{\frac{1}{2}}$
$\therefore\ \log T \approx 0.699 + \frac{1}{2}\log d$

e $R = b\sqrt{l} = bl^{\frac{1}{2}}$
$\therefore\ \log R = \log(bl^{\frac{1}{2}})$
$\therefore\ \log R = \log b + \log l^{\frac{1}{2}}$
$\therefore\ \log R = \log b + \frac{1}{2}\log l$

f $Q = \dfrac{a}{b^n}$
$\therefore\ \log Q = \log\left(\dfrac{a}{b^n}\right)$
$\therefore\ \log Q = \log a - \log b^n$
$\therefore\ \log Q = \log a - n\log b$

g $y = ab^x$
$\therefore\ \log y = \log(ab^x)$
$\therefore\ \log y = \log a + \log b^x$
$\therefore\ \log y = \log a + x\log b$

h $F = \dfrac{20}{\sqrt{n}} = \dfrac{20}{n^{\frac{1}{2}}}$
$\therefore\ \log F = \log\left(\dfrac{20}{n^{\frac{1}{2}}}\right)$
$\therefore\ \log F = \log 20 - \log n^{\frac{1}{2}}$
$\therefore\ \log F \approx 1.30 - \frac{1}{2}\log n$

i $L = \dfrac{ab}{c}$
$\therefore\ \log L = \log\left(\dfrac{ab}{c}\right)$
$\therefore\ \log L = \log ab - \log c$
$\therefore\ \log L = \log a + \log b$
$\qquad\qquad\quad - \log c$

j $N = \sqrt{\dfrac{a}{b}}$
$\therefore\ N = \left(\dfrac{a}{b}\right)^{\frac{1}{2}}$
$\therefore\ \log N = \log\left(\dfrac{a}{b}\right)^{\frac{1}{2}}$
$\therefore\ \log N = \frac{1}{2}\log\left(\dfrac{a}{b}\right)$
$\therefore\ \log N = \frac{1}{2}\log a - \frac{1}{2}\log b$

k $S = 200 \times 2^t$
$\therefore\ \log S = \log(200 \times 2^t)$
$\therefore\ \log S = \log 200 + \log 2^t$
$\therefore\ \log S = \log 200 + t\log 2$
$\therefore\ \log S \approx 2.30 + 0.301t$

l $y = \dfrac{a^m}{b^n}$
$\therefore\ \log y = \log\left(\dfrac{a^m}{b^n}\right)$
$\therefore\ \log y = \log a^m - \log b^n$
$\therefore\ \log y = m\log a - n\log b$

2 a $\log D = \log e + \log 2$
$= \log(e \times 2)$
$\therefore \ D = 2e$

b $\log F = \log 5 - \log t$
$= \log\left(\dfrac{5}{t}\right)$
$\therefore \ F = \dfrac{5}{t}$

c $\log P = \frac{1}{2} \log x$
$= \log x^{\frac{1}{2}}$
$\therefore \ P = \sqrt{x}$

d $\log M = 2\log b + \log c$
$= \log b^2 + \log c$
$= \log(b^2 c)$
$\therefore \ M = b^2 c$

e $\log B = 3\log m - 2\log n$
$= \log m^3 - \log n^2$
$= \log\left(\dfrac{m^3}{n^2}\right)$
$\therefore \ B = \dfrac{m^3}{n^2}$

f $\log N = -\frac{1}{3}\log p$
$= \log p^{-\frac{1}{3}}$
$= \log\left(\dfrac{1}{\sqrt[3]{p}}\right)$
$\therefore \ N = \dfrac{1}{\sqrt[3]{p}}$

g $\log P = 3\log x + 1$
$= \log x^3 + \log 10^1$
$= \log(10x^3)$
$\therefore \ P = 10x^3$

h $\log Q = 2 - \log x$
$= \log 10^2 - \log x$
$= \log\left(\dfrac{100}{x}\right)$
$\therefore \ Q = \dfrac{100}{x}$

3 a $\log_3 27 + \log_3(\frac{1}{3}) = \log_3 x$
$\therefore \ \log_3(27 \times \frac{1}{3}) = \log_3 x$
$\therefore \ \log_3 9 = \log_3 x$
$\therefore \ x = 9$

b $\log_5 x = \log_5 8 - \log_5(6-x)$
$\therefore \ \log_5 x = \log_5\left(\dfrac{8}{6-x}\right)$
$\therefore \ x = \dfrac{8}{6-x}$
$\therefore \ 6x - x^2 = 8$
$\therefore \ x^2 - 6x + 8 = 0$
$\therefore \ (x-2)(x-4) = 0$
$\therefore \ x = 2 \text{ or } 4$

Note: $x > 0$
and $6-x > 0$
so $0 < x < 6$

c $\log_5 125 - \log_5 \sqrt{5} = \log_5 x$
$\therefore \ \log_5\left(\dfrac{125}{\sqrt{5}}\right) = \log_5 x$
$\therefore \ x = \dfrac{125}{\sqrt{5}} \text{ or } 25\sqrt{5}$

d $\log_{20} x = 1 + \log_{20} 10$
$\therefore \ \log_{20} x = \log_{20} 20^1 + \log_{20} 10$
$= \log_{20} 200$
$\therefore \ x = 200$

e $\log x + \log(x+1) = \log 30$
$\therefore \ \log[x(x+1)] = \log 30$
$\therefore \ x^2 + x = 30$
$\therefore \ x^2 + x - 30 = 0$
$\therefore \ (x+6)(x-5) = 0$
$\therefore \ x = -6 \text{ or } 5$
but $x > 0$ for $\log x$ to exist
$\therefore \ x = 5$

f $\log(x+2) - \log(x-2) = \log 5$
$\therefore \ \log\left(\dfrac{x+2}{x-2}\right) = \log 5$
$\therefore \ \dfrac{x+2}{x-2} = 5$
$\therefore \ x+2 = 5x - 10$
$\therefore \ -4x = -12$
$\therefore \ x = 3$
Note: $x+2 > 0$ and $x-2 > 0$
$\therefore \ x > 2$ ✓

EXERCISE 4D

1 a $\ln e^3$
$= 3 \quad \{\ln e^a = a\}$

b $\ln 1$
$= \ln e^0$
$= 0$

c $\ln \sqrt[3]{e}$
$= \ln e^{\frac{1}{3}}$
$= \frac{1}{3}$

d $\ln\left(\dfrac{1}{e^2}\right)$
$= \ln e^{-2}$
$= -2$

3 $\ln x$ exists only when $x > 0$.
$\therefore \ \ln(-2)$ and $\ln(0)$ do not exist.

Note: If $\ln(-2) = a$ then $-2 = e^a$
and $e^a = -2$ has no solutions as $e^a > 0$ for all a.

4 **a** $\ln e^a$
       $= a$

   b $\ln(e \times e^a)$
       $= \ln e^{1+a}$
       $= a + 1$

   c $\ln(e^a \times e^b)$
       $= \ln(e^{a+b})$
       $= a + b$

   d $\ln(e^a)^b$
       $= \ln e^{ab}$
       $= ab$

   e $\ln\left(\dfrac{e^a}{e^b}\right)$
       $= \ln(e^{a-b})$
       $= a - b$

5 **a** $e^{1.7918}$ **b** $e^{4.0943}$ **c** $e^{8.6995}$ **d** $e^{-0.5108}$ **e** $e^{-5.1160}$
     f $e^{2.7081}$ **g** $e^{7.3132}$ **h** $e^{0.4055}$ **i** $e^{-1.8971}$ **j** $e^{-8.8049}$

6 **a** $\ln x = 3$
       $\therefore\ x = e^3$
       $\therefore\ x \approx 20.1$

   b $\ln x = 1$
       $\therefore\ x = e^1$
       $\therefore\ x = e \approx 2.72$

   c $\ln x = 0$
       $\therefore\ x = e^0$
       $\therefore\ x = 1$

   d $\ln x = -1$
       $\therefore\ x = e^{-1}$
       $\therefore\ x \approx 0.368$

   e $\ln x = -5$
       $\therefore\ x = e^{-5}$
       $\therefore\ x \approx 0.00674$

   f $\ln x \approx 0.835$
       $\therefore\ x \approx e^{0.835}$
       $\therefore\ x \approx 2.30$

   g $\ln x \approx 2.145$
       $\therefore\ x \approx e^{2.145}$
       $\therefore\ x \approx 8.54$

   h $\ln x \approx -3.2971$
       $\therefore\ x \approx e^{-3.2971}$
       $\therefore\ x \approx 0.0370$

7 **a** $\ln 15 + \ln 3$
       $= \ln(15 \times 3)$
       $= \ln 45$

   b $\ln 15 - \ln 3$
       $= \ln(\tfrac{15}{3})$
       $= \ln 5$

   c $\ln 20 - \ln 5$
       $= \ln(\tfrac{20}{5})$
       $= \ln 4$

   d $\ln 4 + \ln 6$
       $= \ln(4 \times 6)$
       $= \ln 24$

   e $\ln 5 + \ln(0.2)$
       $= \ln(5 \times 0.2)$
       $= \ln 1$

   f $\ln 2 + \ln 3 + \ln 5$
       $= \ln(2 \times 3 \times 5)$
       $= \ln 30$

   g $1 + \ln 4$
       $= \ln e^1 + \ln 4$
       $= \ln(e \times 4)$
       $= \ln 4e$

   h $\ln 6 - 1$
       $= \ln 6 - \ln e^1$
       $= \ln(\tfrac{6}{e})$

   i $\ln 5 + \ln 8 - \ln 2$
       $= \ln(5 \times 8 \div 2)$
       $= \ln 20$

   j $2 + \ln 4$
       $= \ln e^2 + \ln 4$
       $= \ln(e^2 \times 4)$
       $= \ln 4e^2$

   k $\ln 20 - 2$
       $= \ln 20 - \ln e^2$
       $= \ln\left(\dfrac{20}{e^2}\right)$

   l $\ln 12 - \ln 4 - \ln 3$
       $= \ln(12 \div 4 \div 3)$
       $= \ln 1$

8 **a** $5\ln 3 + \ln 4$
       $= \ln(3^5) + \ln 4$
       $= \ln(3^5 \times 4)$
       $= \ln 972$

   b $3\ln 2 + 2\ln 5$
       $= \ln(2^3) + \ln(5^2)$
       $= \ln(2^3 \times 5^2)$
       $= \ln 200$

   c $3\ln 2 - \ln 8$
       $= \ln(2^3) - \ln 8$
       $= \ln(\tfrac{2^3}{8})$
       $= \ln 1$

   d $3\ln 4 - 2\ln 2$
       $= \ln(4^3) - \ln(2^2)$
       $= \ln(\tfrac{64}{4})$
       $= \ln 16$

   e $\tfrac{1}{3}\ln 8 + \ln 3$
       $= \ln(8^{\frac{1}{3}}) + \ln 3$
       $= \ln(8^{\frac{1}{3}} \times 3)$
       $= \ln 6$

   f $\tfrac{1}{3}\ln(\tfrac{1}{27})$
       $= \ln\left((\tfrac{1}{27})^{\frac{1}{3}}\right)$
       $= \ln\left(\dfrac{1}{27^{\frac{1}{3}}}\right)$
       $= \ln(\tfrac{1}{3})$

   g $-\ln 2$
       $= \ln(2^{-1})$
       $= \ln \tfrac{1}{2}$

   h $-\ln(\tfrac{1}{2})$
       $= \ln((\tfrac{1}{2})^{-1})$
       $= \ln 2$

   i $-2\ln(\tfrac{1}{4})$
       $= \ln((\tfrac{1}{4})^{-2})$
       $= \ln(4^2)$
       $= \ln 16$

9 **a** $\ln 27$
$= \ln 3^3$
$= 3\ln 3$

b $\ln \sqrt{3}$
$= \ln 3^{\frac{1}{2}}$
$= \frac{1}{2}\ln 3$

c $\ln(\frac{1}{16})$
$= \ln\left(\frac{1}{2^4}\right)$
$= \ln(2^{-4})$
$= -4\ln 2$

d $\ln(\frac{1}{6})$
$= \ln 6^{-1}$
$= -1\ln 6$
$= -\ln 6$

e $\ln\left(\frac{1}{\sqrt{2}}\right)$
$= \ln 2^{-\frac{1}{2}}$
$= -\frac{1}{2}\ln 2$

f $\ln\left(\frac{e}{5}\right)$
$= \ln e^1 - \ln 5$
$= 1 - \ln 5$

g $\ln \sqrt[3]{5}$
$= \ln 5^{\frac{1}{3}}$
$= \frac{1}{3}\ln 5$

h $\ln(\frac{1}{32})$
$= \ln 2^{-5}$
$= -5\ln 2$

i $\ln\left(\frac{1}{\sqrt[5]{2}}\right)$
$= \ln\left(\frac{1}{2^{\frac{1}{5}}}\right)$
$= \ln 2^{-\frac{1}{5}}$
$= -\frac{1}{5}\ln 2$

10 **a** $\ln D = \ln x + 1$
$\therefore \ln D - \ln x = 1$
$\therefore \ln\left(\frac{D}{x}\right) = 1$
$\therefore \frac{D}{x} = e^1$
$\therefore D = ex$

b $\ln F = -\ln p + 2$
$\therefore \ln F + \ln p = 2$
$\therefore \ln(Fp) = 2$
$\therefore Fp = e^2$
$\therefore F = \frac{e^2}{p}$

c $\ln P = \frac{1}{2}\ln x$
$\therefore \ln P = \ln x^{\frac{1}{2}}$
$\therefore P = \sqrt{x}$

d $\ln M = 2\ln y + 3$
$\therefore \ln M - 2\ln y = 3$
$\therefore \ln\left(\frac{M}{y^2}\right) = 3$
$\therefore \frac{M}{y^2} = e^3$
$\therefore M = e^3 y^2$

e $\ln B = 3\ln t - 1$
$\therefore \ln B - \ln t^3 = -1$
$\therefore \ln\left(\frac{B}{t^3}\right) = -1$
$\therefore \frac{B}{t^3} = e^{-1}$
$\therefore B = \frac{t^3}{e}$

f $\ln N = -\frac{1}{3}\ln g$
$\therefore \ln N = \ln g^{-\frac{1}{3}}$
$\therefore N = g^{-\frac{1}{3}}$
$\therefore N = \frac{1}{\sqrt[3]{g}}$

g $\ln Q \approx 3\ln x + 2.159$
$\therefore \ln Q - 3\ln x \approx 2.159$
$\therefore \ln\left(\frac{Q}{x^3}\right) \approx 2.159$
$\therefore \frac{Q}{x^3} \approx e^{2.159}$
$\therefore \frac{Q}{x^3} \approx 8.66$
$\therefore Q \approx 8.66 x^3$

h $\ln D \approx 0.4\ln n - 0.6582$
$\therefore \ln D - \ln n^{0.4} \approx -0.6582$
$\therefore \ln\left(\frac{D}{n^{0.4}}\right) \approx -0.6582$
$\therefore \frac{D}{n^{0.4}} \approx e^{-0.6582}$
$\therefore \frac{D}{n^{0.4}} \approx 0.518$
$\therefore D \approx 0.518 n^{0.4}$

EXERCISE 4E

1 **a** $2^x = 10$
$\therefore \log 2^x = \log 10$
$\therefore x\log 2 = \log 10$
$\therefore x = \frac{\log 10}{\log 2} \approx 3.32$

b $3^x = 20$
$\therefore \log 3^x = \log 20$
$\therefore x\log 3 = \log 20$
$\therefore x = \frac{\log 20}{\log 3} \approx 2.73$

c $4^x = 100$
$\therefore \log 4^x = \log 100$
$\therefore x\log 4 = \log 100$
$\therefore x = \frac{\log 100}{\log 4}$
≈ 3.32

d $(1.2)^x = 1000$
$\therefore\ x \log(1.2) = \log 1000$
$\therefore\ x = \dfrac{\log 1000}{\log(1.2)}$
$\therefore\ x \approx 37.9$

e $2^x = 0.08$
$\therefore\ \log 2^x = \log(0.08)$
$\therefore\ x \log 2 = \log(0.08)$
$\therefore\ x = \dfrac{\log(0.08)}{\log 2}$
$\therefore\ x \approx -3.64$

f $3^x = 0.000\,25$
$\therefore\ \log 3^x = \log(0.000\,25)$
$\therefore\ x \log 3 = \log(0.000\,25)$
$\therefore\ x = \dfrac{\log(0.000\,25)}{\log 3}$
≈ -7.55

g $\left(\tfrac{1}{2}\right)^x = 0.005$
$\therefore\ \log(0.5)^x = \log(0.005)$
$\therefore\ x \log(0.5) = \log(0.005)$
$\therefore\ x = \dfrac{\log(0.005)}{\log(0.5)}$
≈ 7.64

h $\left(\tfrac{3}{4}\right)^x = 10^{-4}$
$\therefore\ \log(0.75)^x = -4$
$\therefore\ x \log(0.75) = -4$
$\therefore\ x = \dfrac{-4}{\log(0.75)}$
≈ 32.0

i $(0.99)^x = 0.000\,01$
$\therefore\ \log(0.99)^x = \log(0.000\,01)$
$\therefore\ x \log(0.99) = \log(0.000\,01)$
$\therefore\ x = \dfrac{\log(0.000\,01)}{\log(0.99)}$
$\therefore\ x \approx 1146$
or 1150 (3 s.f.)

2 **a** $200 \times 2^{0.25t} = 600$
$\therefore\ 2^{0.25t} = 3$
$\therefore\ \log(2^{0.25t}) = \log 3$
$\therefore\ 0.25t \log 2 = \log 3$
$\therefore\ t = \dfrac{\log 3}{0.25 \times \log 2}$
$\therefore\ t \approx 6.340$

b $20 \times 2^{0.06t} = 450$
$\therefore\ 2^{0.06t} = 22.5$
$\therefore\ \log(2^{0.06t}) = \log(22.5)$
$\therefore\ 0.06t \log 2 = \log(22.5)$
$\therefore\ t = \dfrac{\log(22.5)}{0.06 \times \log 2}$
$\therefore\ t \approx 74.86$

c $30 \times 3^{-0.25t} = 3$
$\therefore\ 3^{-0.25t} = \tfrac{1}{10}$
$\therefore\ \log 3^{-0.25t} = \log(0.1)$
$\therefore\ -0.25t \log 3 = \log(0.1)$
$\therefore\ t = \dfrac{\log(0.1)}{-0.25 \times \log 3}$
≈ 8.384

d $12 \times 2^{-0.05t} = 0.12$
$\therefore\ 2^{-0.05t} = \tfrac{1}{100}$
$\therefore\ \log 2^{-0.05t} = \log(0.01)$
$\therefore\ -0.05t \log 2 = \log(0.01)$
$\therefore\ t = \dfrac{\log(0.01)}{-0.05 \times \log 2}$
≈ 132.9

e $50 \times 5^{-0.02t} = 1$
$\therefore\ 5^{-0.02t} = \tfrac{1}{50} = 0.02$
$\therefore\ \log 5^{-0.02t} = \log(0.02)$
$\therefore\ -0.02t \log 5 = \log(0.02)$
$\therefore\ t = \dfrac{\log(0.02)}{-0.02 \times \log 5}$
$\therefore\ t \approx 121.5$

f $300 \times 2^{0.005t} = 1000$
$\therefore\ 2^{0.005t} = \tfrac{10}{3}$
$\therefore\ \log 2^{0.005t} = \log(\tfrac{10}{3})$
$\therefore\ 0.005t \log 2 = \log(\tfrac{10}{3})$
$\therefore\ t = \dfrac{\log(\tfrac{10}{3})}{0.005 \times \log 2}$
$\therefore\ t \approx 347.4$

3 **a** $e^x = 10$
$\therefore\ x = \ln 10$
$\therefore\ x \approx 2.303$

b $e^x = 1000$
$\therefore\ x = \ln 1000$
$\therefore\ x \approx 6.908$

c $e^x = 0.008\,62$
$\therefore\ x = \ln(0.008\,62)$
$\therefore\ x \approx -4.754$

d $e^{\frac{x}{2}} = 5$
$\therefore \dfrac{x}{2} = \ln 5$
$\therefore x = 2\ln 5$
$\therefore x \approx 3.219$

e $e^{\frac{x}{3}} = 157.8$
$\therefore \dfrac{x}{3} = \ln(157.8)$
$\therefore x = 3\ln(157.8)$
$\therefore x \approx 15.18$

f $e^{\frac{x}{10}} = 0.01682$
$\therefore \dfrac{x}{10} = \ln(0.01682)$
$\therefore x = 10\ln(0.01682)$
$\therefore x \approx -40.85$

g $20 \times e^{0.06x} = 8.312$
$\therefore e^{0.06x} = 0.4156$
$\therefore 0.06x = \ln(0.4156)$
$\therefore x = \dfrac{\ln(0.4156)}{0.06}$
$\therefore x \approx -14.63$

h $50e^{-0.03x} = 0.816$
$\therefore e^{-0.03x} = 0.01632$
$\therefore -0.03x = \ln(0.01632)$
$\therefore x = \dfrac{\ln(0.01632)}{-0.03}$
$\therefore x \approx 137.2$

i $41.83e^{0.652x} = 1000$
$\therefore e^{0.652x} \approx 23.91$
$\therefore 0.652x \approx \ln(23.91)$
$\therefore x \approx \dfrac{\ln(23.91)}{0.652}$
$\therefore x \approx 4.868$

EXERCISE 4F

1 a $\log_3 12$
$= \dfrac{\log_{10} 12}{\log_{10} 3}$
≈ 2.26

b $\log_{\frac{1}{2}} 1250$
$= \dfrac{\log_{10} 1250}{\log_{10}(0.5)}$
≈ -10.3

c $\log_3 (0.067)$
$= \dfrac{\log_{10}(0.067)}{\log_{10} 3}$
≈ -2.46

d $\log_{0.4}(0.006\,984)$
$= \dfrac{\log_{10}(0.006\,984)}{\log_{10}(0.4)}$
≈ 5.42

2 a $2^x = 0.051$
$\therefore x = \log_2(0.051)$
$\therefore x = \dfrac{\ln(0.051)}{\ln 2}$
$\therefore x \approx -4.29$

b $4^x = 213.8$
$\therefore x = \log_4 213.8$
$\therefore x = \dfrac{\ln(213.8)}{\ln 4}$
$\therefore x \approx 3.87$

c $3^{2x+1} = 4.069$
$\therefore 2x + 1 = \log_3(4.069)$
$\therefore 2x + 1 = \dfrac{\ln(4.069)}{\ln 3}$
$\therefore 2x + 1 \approx 1.2774$
$\therefore 2x \approx 0.2774$
$\therefore x \approx 0.139$

3 a $25^x - 3(5^x) = 0$
$\therefore 5^{2x} - 3(5^x) = 0$
$\therefore 5^x(5^x - 3) = 0$
$\therefore 5^x = 3$ {as $5^x > 0$ for all x}
$\therefore x = \log_5 3$
$\therefore x = \dfrac{\log 3}{\log 5}$
$\therefore x \approx 0.683$

b $8(9^x) - 3^x = 0$
$\therefore 8 \times 3^{2x} - 3^x = 0$
$\therefore 3^x(8 \times 3^x - 1) = 0$
$\therefore 8 \times 3^x - 1 = 0$ {as $3^x > 0$ for all x}
$\therefore 3^x = \tfrac{1}{8}$
$\therefore x = \log_3(\tfrac{1}{8})$
$\therefore x = \dfrac{\log(\tfrac{1}{8})}{\log 3} \approx -1.89$

4 a $\log_4 x^3 + \log_2 \sqrt{x} = 8$
$\therefore \dfrac{\log x^3}{\log 4} + \dfrac{\log x^{\frac{1}{2}}}{\log 2} = 8$
$\therefore \dfrac{3\log x}{2\log 2} + \dfrac{\tfrac{1}{2}\log x}{\log 2} = 8$
$\therefore \dfrac{3\log x}{2\log 2} + \dfrac{\log x}{2\log 2} = 8$
$\therefore \dfrac{4\log x}{2\log 2} = 8$
$\therefore \log x = 4\log 2$
$\therefore \log x = \log 2^4$
$\therefore x = 16$

b $\log_{16} x^5 = \log_{64} 125 - \log_4 \sqrt{x}$
$\therefore \dfrac{\log x^5}{\log 16} = \dfrac{\log 125}{\log 64} - \dfrac{\log x^{\frac{1}{2}}}{\log 4}$
$\therefore \dfrac{5\log x}{4\log 2} = \dfrac{\log 125}{6\log 2} - \dfrac{\tfrac{1}{2}\log x}{2\log 2}$
$\therefore \dfrac{15\log x}{12\log 2} = \dfrac{2\log 125}{12\log 2} - \dfrac{3\log x}{12\log 2}$
$\therefore 15\log x = 2\log 125 - 3\log x$
$\therefore 18\log x = 2\log 125$
$\therefore \log x = \tfrac{1}{9}\log 5^3$
$\therefore \log x = \log(5^3)^{\frac{1}{9}}$
$\therefore x = 5^{\frac{1}{3}} \approx 1.71$

5
$$4^x \times 5^{4x+3} = 10^{2x+3}$$
$$\therefore \quad \log(4^x \times 5^{4x+3}) = \log 10^{2x+3}$$
$$\therefore \quad x \log 4 + (4x+3) \log 5 = 2x + 3$$
$$\therefore \quad x \log 4 + 4x \log 5 + 3 \log 5 = 2x + 3$$
$$\therefore \quad x[\log 4 + 4 \log 5 - 2] = 3 - 3 \log 5$$

$$\therefore \quad x = \frac{3 - 3 \log 5}{\log 4 + 4 \log 5 - 2}$$

$$\therefore \quad x = \frac{\log 10^3 - \log 5^3}{\log 4 + \log 5^4 - \log 10^2}$$

$$\therefore \quad x = \frac{\log(\frac{1000}{125})}{\log\left(\frac{4 \times 5^4}{10^2}\right)}$$

$$\therefore \quad x = \frac{\log 8}{\log 25} \quad \text{or} \quad \log_{25} 8$$

EXERCISE 4G.1

1 a $f(x) = \log_3(x+1)$

  i We require $x + 1 > 0$ $\therefore$ $x > -1$ So, the domain is $x \in \,]-1, \infty[$ and the range is $y \in \mathbb{R}$.

  ii As $x \to -1$ (from the right), $y \to -\infty$, so $x = -1$ is a vertical asymptote.
  As $x \to \infty$, $y \to \infty$.
  When $x = 0$, $y = \log_3 1 = 0$
  $\therefore$ y-intercept is 0.
  When $y = 0$, $\log_3(x+1) = 0$
  $\therefore$ $x + 1 = 3^0$, so $x + 1 = 1$, $x = 0$
  $\therefore$ x-intercept is 0.

  iii We graph, using $y = \dfrac{\log(x+1)}{\log 3}$

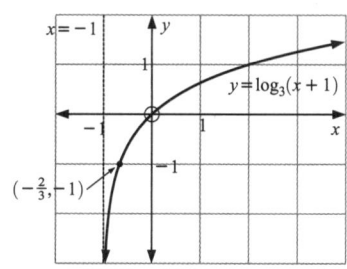

  iv If $f(x) = -1$
  then $\log_3(x+1) = -1$
  $\therefore$ $x + 1 = 3^{-1}$
  $\therefore$ $x = \frac{1}{3} - 1$
  $\therefore$ $x = -\frac{2}{3}$
  which checks with the graph

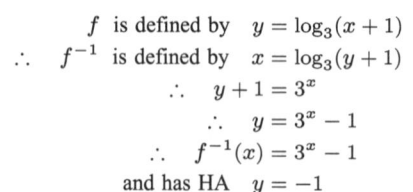

  v f is defined by $y = \log_3(x+1)$
  $\therefore$ f^{-1} is defined by $x = \log_3(y+1)$
  $\therefore$ $y + 1 = 3^x$
  $\therefore$ $y = 3^x - 1$
  $\therefore$ $f^{-1}(x) = 3^x - 1$
  and has HA $y = -1$
  Its domain is $x \in \mathbb{R}$
  and range is $y \in \,]-1, \infty[$.
  We can verify the inverse function by checking that $(f^{-1} \circ f)(x) = x$.

b $f(x) = 1 - \log_3(x+1)$

  i We require $x + 1 > 0$ $\therefore$ $x > -1$ So, domain is $x \in \,]-1, \infty[$ and range is $y \in \mathbb{R}$.

  ii As $x \to -1$ (right), $y \to \infty$, so $x = -1$ is a vertical asymptote.
  As $x \to \infty$, $y \to -\infty$.
  When $x = 0$, $y = 1 - \log_3 1 = 1 - 0 = 1$
  $\therefore$ y-intercept is 1.
  When $y = 0$, $1 - \log_3(x+1) = 0$
  $\therefore$ $\log_3(x+1) = 1$
  $\therefore$ $x + 1 = 3^1 = 3$
  $\therefore$ $x = 2$
  So, the x-intercept is 2.

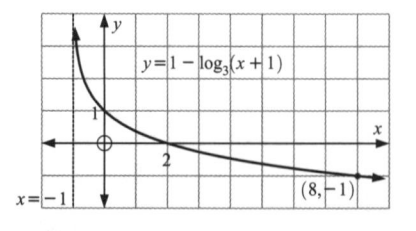

  iii We graph using $y = 1 - \dfrac{\log(x+1)}{\log 3}$

iv If $f(x) = -1$, $\quad 1 - \log_3(x+1) = -1$
$\quad\quad\therefore \log_3(x+1) = 2$
$\quad\quad\therefore x + 1 = 3^2$
$\quad\quad\therefore x = 8$

v $\quad f$ is defined by $\quad y = 1 - \log_3(x+1)$ $\quad\quad$ HA is $y = -1$.
$\therefore f^{-1}$ is defined by $\quad x = 1 - \log_3(y+1)$ $\quad\quad$ Domain is $x \in \mathbb{R}$.
$\quad\quad\therefore \log_3(y+1) = 1 - x$ $\quad\quad\quad\quad\quad\quad\quad\quad$ Range is $y \in\ ]-1, \infty[$.
$\quad\quad\therefore y + 1 = 3^{1-x}$
$\quad\quad\therefore y = 3^{1-x} - 1$
$\quad\quad\therefore f^{-1}(x) = 3^{1-x} - 1$

c $f(x) = \log_5(x-2) - 2$

i We require $x - 2 > 0 \quad\therefore x > 2$. $\quad$ So, domain is $x \in\ ]2, \infty[$
$\quad\quad\quad\quad\quad\quad\quad\quad\quad\quad\quad\quad\quad\quad\quad\quad$ and range is $y \in \mathbb{R}$.

ii As $x \to 2$ (right), $y \to -\infty$. So, $x = 2$ is a vertical asymptote.
As $x \to \infty$, $y \to \infty$.
When $x = 0$, y is undefined $\therefore$ no y-intercept.
When $y = 0$, $\log_5(x-2) = 2 \quad\therefore x - 2 = 5^2 = 25$
$\quad\quad\quad\quad\quad\quad\quad\quad\quad\quad\quad\quad\therefore x = 27$
$\quad\quad\quad\quad\quad\quad\quad\quad\quad\quad\quad\quad\therefore x$-intercept is 27

iii We graph using $\quad y = \dfrac{\log(x-2)}{\log 5} - 2$

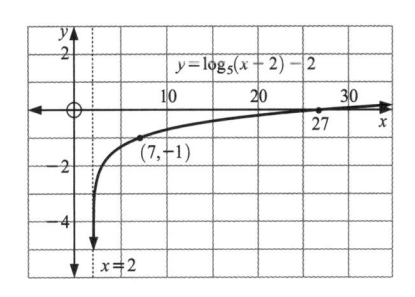

iv $\quad$ If $f(x) = -1$
$\log_5(x-2) - 2 = -1$
$\therefore \log_5(x-2) = 1$
$\quad\therefore x - 2 = 5^1$
$\quad\quad\therefore x = 5 + 2 = 7$

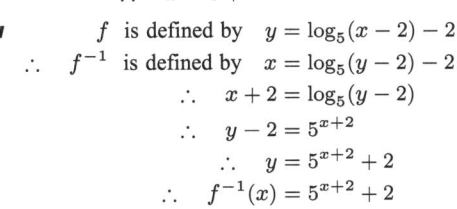

v $\quad f$ is defined by $\quad y = \log_5(x-2) - 2$
$\therefore f^{-1}$ is defined by $\quad x = \log_5(y-2) - 2$
$\quad\quad\therefore x + 2 = \log_5(y-2)$
$\quad\quad\therefore y - 2 = 5^{x+2}$
$\quad\quad\therefore y = 5^{x+2} + 2$
$\quad\quad\therefore f^{-1}(x) = 5^{x+2} + 2$

HA is $y = 2$.
Domain is $x \in \mathbb{R}$.
Range is $y \in\ ]2, \infty[$.

d $f(x) = 1 - \log_5(x-2)$

i We require $x - 2 > 0 \quad\therefore x > 2 \quad$ So, domain is $x \in\ ]2, \infty[$
$\quad\quad\quad\quad\quad\quad\quad\quad\quad\quad\quad\quad\quad\quad\quad$ and range is $y \in \mathbb{R}$.

ii As $x \to 2$ (right), $y \to \infty$. $\quad\therefore x = 2$ is a VA.
As $x \to \infty$, $y \to -\infty$.
When $x = 0$, y is undefined $\therefore$ no y-intercept.
When $y = 0$, $1 - \log_5(x-2) = 0$
$\quad\quad\therefore \log_5(x-2) = 1$
$\quad\quad\therefore x - 2 = 5^1$
$\quad\quad\therefore x = 7$

So, x-intercept is 7.

iii We graph using $\quad y = 1 - \dfrac{\log(x-2)}{\log 5}$

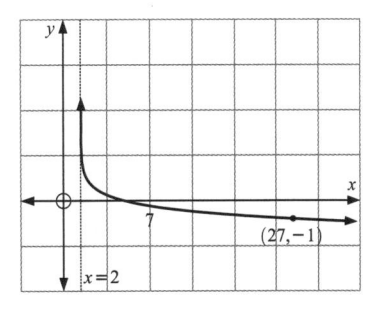

iv If $f(x) = -1$, then $1 - \log_5(x-2) = -1$
$\quad\quad\quad\quad\quad\quad\quad\quad\therefore \log_5(x-2) = 2$
$\quad\quad\quad\quad\quad\quad\quad\quad\therefore x - 2 = 5^2$
$\quad\quad\quad\quad\quad\quad\quad\quad\therefore x = 27$

v f is defined by $y = 1 - \log_5(x - 2)$ HA is $y = 2$.
∴ f^{-1} is defined by $x = 1 - \log_5(y - 2)$ Domain is $x \in \mathbb{R}$.
∴ $\log_5(y - 2) = 1 - x$ Range is $y \in \,]2, \infty[$.
∴ $y - 2 = 5^{1-x}$
∴ $y = 5^{1-x} + 2$
∴ $f^{-1}(x) = 5^{1-x} + 2$

e $f(x) = 1 - \log_2 x^2$

  i We require $x^2 > 0$ which is true for all x except $x = 0$
   ∴ domain is $x \in \mathbb{R}$, but $x \neq 0$,   range is $y \in \mathbb{R}$.

  ii As $x \to 0$ (right or left), $y \to \infty$ **iii** We graph using $y = 1 - \dfrac{\log x^2}{\log 2}$
   ∴ $x = 0$ is a VA.
   As $x \to \infty$, $y \to -\infty$,
   as $x \to -\infty$, $y \to -\infty$.
   When $x = 0$, $y = 1 - \log_2 0$
   which is undefined ∴ no y-intercept.
   When $y = 0$, $\log_2 x^2 = 1$
   ∴ $x^2 = 2^1 = 2$
   ∴ $x = \pm\sqrt{2}$
   ∴ x-intercepts are $\sqrt{2}$ and $-\sqrt{2}$

  iv When $f(x) = -1$ ∴ $x^2 = 2^2$
   $1 - \log_2 x^2 = -1$ ∴ $x^2 = 4$
   ∴ $\log_2 x^2 = 2$ ∴ $x = \pm 2$

  v If $f(x) = 1 - \log_2 x^2$, $x > 0$ If $f(x) = 1 - \log_2 x^2$, $x < 0$
   then $f^{-1}(x)$ exists and is defined   then $f^{-1}(x)$ also exists and is defined
   by $x = 1 - \log_2 y^2$, $y > 0$ by $x = 1 - \log_2 y^2$, $y < 0$
   ∴ $\log_2 y^2 = 1 - x$ ∴ $\log_2 y^2 = 1 - x$
   ∴ $y^2 = 2^{1-x}$ ∴ $y^2 = 2^{1-x}$
   ∴ $y = 2^{\frac{1-x}{2}}$ as $y > 0$ ∴ $y = -2^{\frac{1-x}{2}}$ as $y < 0$
   So, $f^{-1}(x) = 2^{\frac{1-x}{2}}$ So, $f^{-1}(x) = -2^{\frac{1-x}{2}}$

f $f(x) = \log_2(x^2 - 3x - 4)$

  i We require $x^2 - 3x - 4 > 0$ ∴ domain is $x \in \,]-\infty, -1[$ or $]4, \infty[$
   ∴ $(x - 4)(x + 1) > 0$ range is $y \in \mathbb{R}$

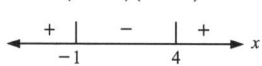

   ```
   + |   -   | +
   ──────────────→ x
     -1      4
   ```

  ii As $x \to -1$ (left), $y \to -\infty$
   As $x \to 4$ (right), $y \to -\infty$ ∴ $x = -1$, $x = 4$ are VAs.
   As $x \to \infty$, $y \to \infty$ and as $x \to -\infty$, $y \to \infty$.
   When $x = 0$, $y = \log_2(-4)$ which is undefined ∴ no y-intercept.
   When $y = 0$, $x^2 - 3x - 4 = 2^0 = 1$
   ∴ $x^2 - 3x - 5 = 0$
   ∴ $x \approx -1.19$ or 4.19 {using technology}
   So, the x-intercepts are ≈ -1.19, 4.19

  iii We graph using $y = \dfrac{\log(x^2 - 3x - 4)}{\log 2}$

  iv If $f(x) = -1$ then
   $\log_2(x^2 - 3x - 4) = -1$
   ∴ $x^2 - 3x - 4 = 2^{-1}$
   ∴ $x^2 - 3x - 4.5 = 0$
   ∴ $x \approx -1.10$ or 4.10 {using technology}

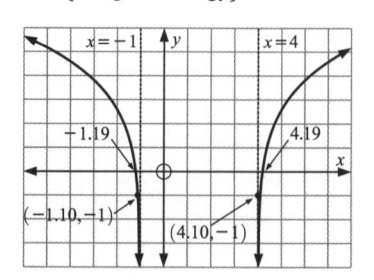

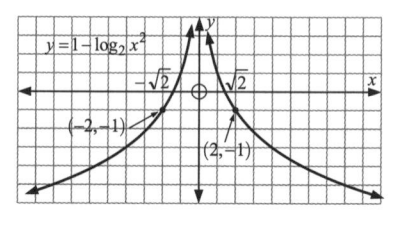

v If $f(x) = \log_2(x^2 - 3x - 4)$, $x > 4$ then f^{-1} is defined by
$x = \log_2(y^2 - 3y - 4)$, $y > 4$

$\therefore \quad y^2 - 3y - 4 = 2^x$, $y > 4$

$\therefore \quad y^2 - 3y - [4 + 2^x] = 0$, $y > 4$

$\therefore \quad y = \dfrac{3 \pm \sqrt{9 + 4[4 + 2^x]}}{2}$, $y > 4$

$\therefore \quad y = \dfrac{3 + \sqrt{25 + 2^{x+2}}}{2}$ as $y > 4$

$\therefore \quad f^{-1}(x) = \dfrac{3 + \sqrt{25 + 2^{x+2}}}{2}$

If $f(x) = \log_2(x^2 - 3x - 4)$, $x < -1$ then by the same working

$y = \dfrac{3 - \sqrt{25 + 2^{x+2}}}{2}$ as $y < -1$

$\therefore \quad f^{-1}(x) = \dfrac{3 - \sqrt{25 + 2^{x+2}}}{2}$

2 a i $f(x) = e^x + 5$
or $y = e^x + 5$
has inverse function
$x = e^y + 5$
$\therefore \quad x - 5 = e^y$
$\therefore \quad y = \ln(x - 5)$
$\therefore \quad f^{-1}(x) = \ln(x - 5)$

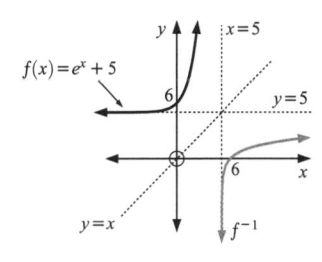

iii domain of f is $\{x \mid x \in \mathbb{R}\}$, range is $\{y \mid y > 5\}$
domain of f^{-1} is $\{x \mid x > 5\}$, range is $\{y \mid y \in \mathbb{R}\}$

iv f has a HA $y = 5$. f^{-1} has a VA $x = 5$.

b i $f(x) = e^{x+1} - 3$
or $y = e^{x+1} - 3$
has inverse function
$x = e^{y+1} - 3$
$\therefore \quad x + 3 = e^{y+1}$
$\therefore \quad y + 1 = \ln(x + 3)$
$\therefore \quad f^{-1}(x) = \ln(x + 3) - 1$

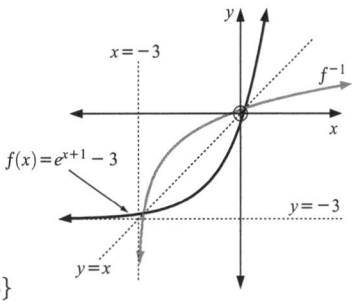

iii domain of f is $\{x \mid x \in \mathbb{R}\}$, range is $\{y \mid y > -3\}$
domain of f^{-1} is $\{x \mid x > -3\}$, range is $\{y \mid y \in \mathbb{R}\}$

iv f has a HA $y = -3$. f^{-1} has a VA $x = -3$.

c i $f(x) = \ln x - 4$
$\therefore \quad y = \ln x - 4$
and has inverse function
$x = \ln y - 4$
$\therefore \quad x + 4 = \ln y$
$\therefore \quad y = e^{x+4}$
$\therefore \quad f^{-1}(x) = e^{x+4}$

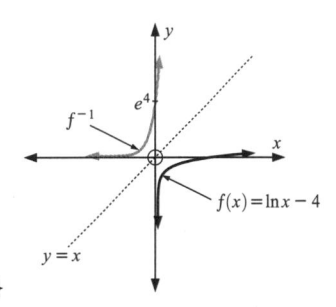

iii domain of f is $\{x \mid x > 0\}$, range is $\{y \mid y \in \mathbb{R}\}$
domain of f^{-1} is $\{x \mid x \in \mathbb{R}\}$, range is $\{y \mid y > 0\}$

iv f has a VA $x = 0$. f^{-1} has a HA $y = 0$.

d **i** $f(x) = \ln(x-1) + 2$, $x > 1$

$\therefore \quad y = \ln(x-1) + 2$

and has inverse function

$x = \ln(y-1) + 2$

$\therefore \quad \ln(y-1) = x - 2$

$\therefore \quad y - 1 = e^{x-2}$

$\therefore \quad y = e^{x-2} + 1$

$\therefore \quad f^{-1}(x) = e^{x-2} + 1$

ii (graph showing $f(x) = \ln(x-1) + 2$, f^{-1}, line $y = x$, asymptotes $x = 1$ and $y = 1$)

iii domain of f is $\{x \mid x > 1\}$, range is $\{y \mid y \in \mathbb{R}\}$

domain of f^{-1} is $\{x \mid x \in \mathbb{R}\}$, range is $\{y \mid y > 1\}$

iv f has a VA $x = 1$. f^{-1} has a HA $y = 1$.

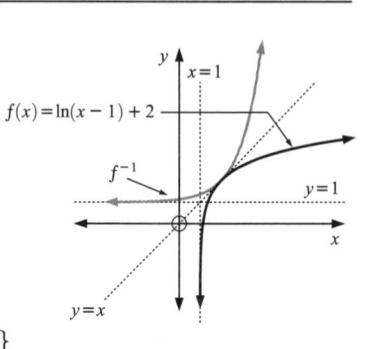

3 a Now for $f(x) = e^{2x}$, i.e., $y = e^{2x}$

the inverse function is

$x = e^{2y}$

$\therefore \quad 2y = \ln x$

$\therefore \quad y = \frac{1}{2} \ln x$

$\therefore \quad f^{-1}(x) = \frac{1}{2} \ln x$

$\therefore \quad (f^{-1} \circ g)(x) = f^{-1}(g(x))$

$= f^{-1}(2x - 1)$

$= \frac{1}{2} \ln(2x - 1)$

b $(g \circ f)(x) = g(f(x))$

$= g(e^{2x})$

$= 2(e^{2x}) - 1$

So, $y = 2e^{2x} - 1$ which has inverse

$x = 2e^{2y} - 1$

$\therefore \quad x + 1 = 2e^{2y}$

$\therefore \quad \frac{1}{2}(x+1) = e^{2y}$

$\therefore \quad 2y = \ln\left(\frac{x+1}{2}\right)$

$\therefore \quad y = \frac{1}{2} \ln\left(\frac{x+1}{2}\right)$

$\therefore \quad (g \circ f)^{-1}(x) = \frac{1}{2} \ln\left(\frac{x+1}{2}\right)$

4 a $y = \ln x$ cuts the x-axis when $y = 0$

$\therefore \quad \ln x = 0$

$\therefore \quad x = e^0 = 1$

So, graph A is that of $y = \ln x$.

Note: x-intercept of $y = \ln(x - 2)$

is when $x - 2 = e^0 = 1$

$\therefore \quad x = 3$

c $y = \ln x$ has a VA of $x = 0$.

$y = \ln(x - 2)$ has a VA of $x = 2$.

$y = \ln(x + 2)$ has a VA of $x = -2$.

b The x-intercept of $y = \ln(x + 2)$

occurs when $x + 2 = e^0 = 1$

$\therefore \quad x = -1$

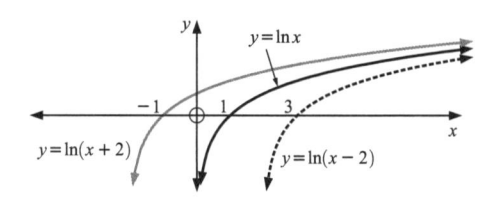

(graph showing $y = \ln x$, $y = \ln(x+2)$, $y = \ln(x-2)$)

5 Since $y = \ln x^2$ then $y = 2 \ln x$ {log law}

$\therefore$ the new y-values are $2 \times$ old y-values. So, she is partly correct.

However, unlike $y = \ln x$, $y = \ln x^2$ is also defined for $x < 0$, so she must find $\ln x^2$ for $x < 0$ too.

6 a $f(x) = e^{x+3} + 2$

or $y = e^{x+3} + 2$ has inverse function

$x = e^{y+3} + 2$

$\therefore \quad x - 2 = e^{y+3}$

$\therefore \quad \ln(x - 2) = y + 3$

$\therefore \quad y = \ln(x - 2) - 3$

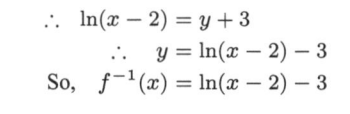

So, $f^{-1}(x) = \ln(x - 2) - 3$

b i $f(x) < 2.1$ when

$e^{x+3} + 2 < 2.1$

$\therefore \quad e^{x+3} < 0.1$

$\therefore \quad x + 3 < \ln(0.1)$

$\therefore \quad x < \ln(0.1) - 3$

$\therefore \quad x < -5.30$

ii Similarly, $f(x) < 2.01$ when

$x < \ln(0.01) - 3$

$\therefore \quad x < -7.61$

iii $f(x) < 2.001$ when
$x < \ln(0.001) - 3$
$\therefore \quad x < -9.91$

iv $f(x) < 2.0001$ when
$x < \ln(0.0001) - 3$
$\therefore \quad x < -12.2$
We conjecture that the HA is $y = 2$.

c As $x \to \infty$, $y \to \infty$
As $x \to -\infty$, $e^{x+3} \to 0$ $\therefore$ $y \to 2$
$\therefore$ $y = 2$ is a HA.

d f has a HA $y = 2$ and range $\{y \mid y > 2\}$
$\therefore$ f^{-1} has a VA $x = 2$ and
domain $\{x \mid x > 2\}$

EXERCISE 4G.2

1 a $x^2 > e^x \Rightarrow x^2 - e^x > 0$
$\therefore$ to solve $x^2 > e^x$, we find where the
graph of $y = x^2 - e^x$ is above the x-axis.
The graph cuts the x-axis when $x \approx -0.703$
$\therefore$ $x^2 > e^x$ when $x < -0.703$

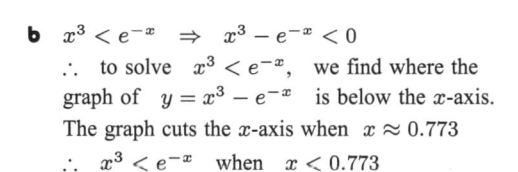

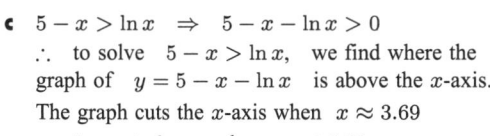

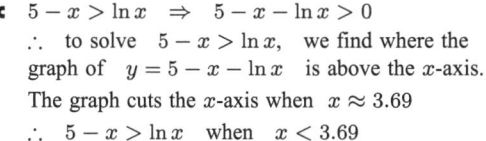

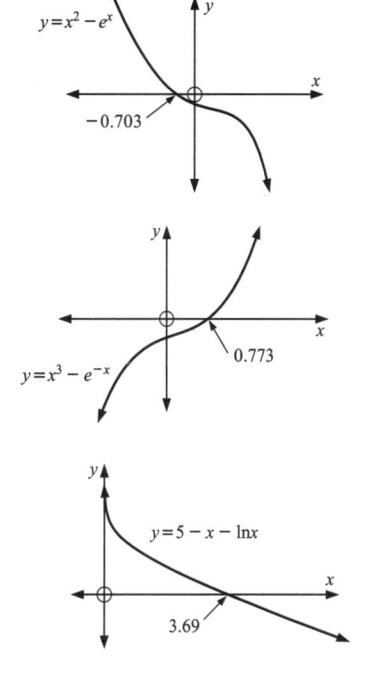

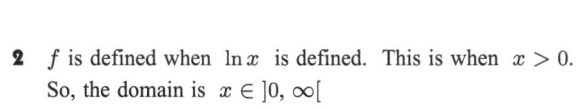

b $x^3 < e^{-x} \Rightarrow x^3 - e^{-x} < 0$
$\therefore$ to solve $x^3 < e^{-x}$, we find where the
graph of $y = x^3 - e^{-x}$ is below the x-axis.
The graph cuts the x-axis when $x \approx 0.773$
$\therefore$ $x^3 < e^{-x}$ when $x < 0.773$

c $5 - x > \ln x \Rightarrow 5 - x - \ln x > 0$
$\therefore$ to solve $5 - x > \ln x$, we find where the
graph of $y = 5 - x - \ln x$ is above the x-axis.
The graph cuts the x-axis when $x \approx 3.69$
$\therefore$ $5 - x > \ln x$ when $x < 3.69$

2 f is defined when $\ln x$ is defined. This is when $x > 0$.
So, the domain is $x \in \,]0, \infty[$

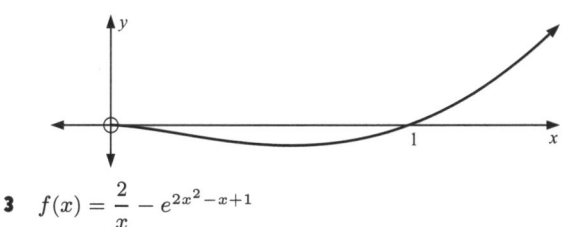

If $f(x) \leqslant 0$ then $x^2 \ln x \leqslant 0$
$\therefore$ the graph of $y = x^2 \ln x$
is on or below $y = 0$.
$\therefore$ $0 < x \leqslant 1$ $\therefore$ $x \in \,]0, 1]$

3 $f(x) = \dfrac{2}{x} - e^{2x^2 - x + 1}$

a

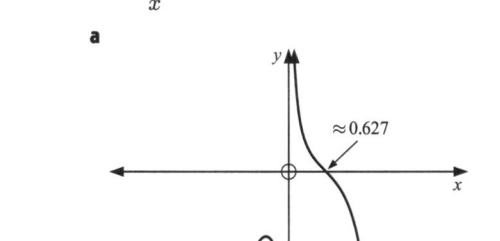

b domain is $\{x \mid x \in \mathbb{R}, \ x \neq 0\}$
range is $\{y \mid y \in \mathbb{R}\}$

c If $e^{2x^2 - x + 1} > \dfrac{2}{x}$
then $\dfrac{2}{x} - e^{2x^2 - x + 1} < 0$
So, we want x such that $f(x) < 0$.
This is for $x < 0$ or $x > 0.627$
$\therefore$ $x \in \,]-\infty, 0[$ or $x \in \,]0.627, \infty[$

EXERCISE 4H.1

1 $W_t = 20 \times 2^{0.15t}$ grams

    a When $W_t = 30$,
$$20 \times 2^{0.15t} = 30$$
$$\therefore \quad 2^{0.15t} = 1.5$$
$$\therefore \quad \log 2^{0.15t} = \log(1.5)$$
$$\therefore \quad 0.15t \log 2 = \log(1.5)$$
$$\therefore \quad t = \frac{\log(1.5)}{0.15 \times \log 2}$$
$$\therefore \quad t \approx 3.90 \text{ hours}$$
$\therefore$ it takes about 3.90 hours to reach 30 g.

    b When $W_t = 100$,
$$20 \times 2^{0.15t} = 100$$
$$\therefore \quad 2^{0.15t} = 5$$
$$\therefore \quad \log 2^{0.15t} = \log 5$$
$$\therefore \quad 0.15t \log 2 = \log 5$$
$$\therefore \quad t = \frac{\log 5}{0.15 \times \log 2}$$
$$\therefore \quad t \approx 15.5 \text{ hours}$$
$\therefore$ it takes about 15.5 hours to reach 100 g.

2   **a** When $M_t = 50$, $25 \times e^{0.1t} = 50$
$$\therefore \quad e^{0.1t} = 2$$
$$\therefore \quad \ln e^{0.1t} = \ln 2$$
$$\therefore \quad 0.1t = \ln 2$$
$$\therefore \quad t = 10 \times \ln 2$$
$$\therefore \quad t \approx 6.93$$
$\therefore$ it takes about 6.93 hours to reach 50 g.

    b When $M_t = 100$, $25 \times e^{0.1t} = 100$
$$\therefore \quad e^{0.1t} = 4$$
$$\therefore \quad \ln e^{0.1t} = \ln 4$$
$$\therefore \quad 0.1t = \ln 4$$
$$\therefore \quad t = 10 \times \ln 4$$
$$\therefore \quad t \approx 13.9$$
$\therefore$ it takes about 13.9 hours to reach 100 g.

3   **a**

[Graph showing $A_n = 2000e^{0.57n}$ with axes A_n (0 to 12000) and n (1 to 4), dashed lines indicating approximately 2.8 weeks]

$\therefore$ approximately 2.8 weeks

When $A_n = 10\,000$, $t \approx 2.8$
$\therefore$ we estimate that it will take 2.8 weeks for the infested area to reach 10 000 ha.

    b When $A_n = 10\,000$, $2000 \times e^{0.57n} = 10\,000$
$$\therefore \quad e^{0.57n} = 5$$
$$\therefore \quad \ln e^{0.57n} = \ln 5$$
$$\therefore \quad 0.57n = \ln 5$$
$$\therefore \quad n = \frac{\ln 5}{0.57}$$
$$\therefore \quad n \approx 2.82$$
$\therefore$ it takes about 2.82 weeks for the infested area to reach 10 000 hectares.

EXERCISE 4H.2

1 $r = 107.5\% = 1.075$,
$u_1 = 160\,000$,
$u_{n+1} = 250\,000$

$$u_{n+1} = u_1 \times r^n$$
$$\therefore \quad 250\,000 = 160\,000 \times (1.075)^n$$
$$\therefore \quad (1.075)^n = \tfrac{25}{16}$$
$$\therefore \quad \log(1.075)^n = \log(\tfrac{25}{16})$$
$$\therefore \quad n \log(1.075) = \log(\tfrac{25}{16})$$
$$\therefore \quad n = \frac{\log(\tfrac{25}{16})}{\log(1.075)} \approx 6.1709$$
$\therefore$ it would take 6.17 years or 6 years 62 days.

2 $u_1 = 10\,000$,
$u_{n+1} = 15\,000$,
$r = 104.8\% = 1.048$

$$u_{n+1} = u_1 \times r^n$$
$$\therefore \quad 15\,000 = 10\,000 \times (1.048)^n$$
$$\therefore \quad (1.048)^n = 1.5$$
$$\therefore \quad \log(1.048)^n = \log(1.5)$$
$$\therefore \quad n \log(1.048) = \log(1.5)$$
$$\therefore \quad n = \frac{\log(1.5)}{\log(1.048)}$$
$$\therefore \quad n \approx 8.648$$
$\therefore$ it would take 9 years.

3 a 8.4% p.a. compounded monthly

is $\dfrac{8.4\%}{12} = 0.7\%$ a month

So $T = 100\% + 0.7\%$
$= 100.7\%$
$= 1.007$

b $u_1 = 15\,000$ and $u_{n+1} = 25\,000$

$u_{n+1} = u_1 \times r^n$

$\therefore\ 25\,000 = 15\,000 \times (1.007)^n$

$\therefore\ (1.007)^n = \dfrac{25}{15} = \dfrac{5}{3}$

$\therefore\ \log(1.007)^n = \log(\tfrac{5}{3})$

$\therefore\ n\log(1.007) = \log(\tfrac{5}{3})$

$\therefore\ n = \dfrac{\log(\tfrac{5}{3})}{\log(1.007)} \approx 73.23$

$\therefore$ it would take 74 months.

4 a $A_{n+1} = 12\,000 \times (1.0835)^n$

$\therefore$ when $n = 0$, $A_1 = 12\,000 \times (1.0835)^0$

$\therefore\ A_1 = 12\,000$ euros

This is the initial investment.

b When $n = 5$, $A_6 = 12\,000 \times (1.0835)^5$
$\approx 17\,919.50$

$\therefore$ the value of the investment after 5 years is €17 919.50

c $A_{3.25}$ is the value of the investment after 2.25 years, or after 2 years 3 months.

d When $A_{n+1} = 24\,000$,
$12\,000 \times (1.0835)^n = 24\,000$

$\therefore\ (1.0835)^n = 2$

$\therefore\ \log(1.0835)^n = \log 2$

$\therefore\ n\log 1.0835 = \log 2$

$\therefore\ n = \dfrac{\log 2}{\log 1.0835}$

$\therefore\ n \approx 8.64$

$\therefore$ it takes 9 years for the investment to double in value.

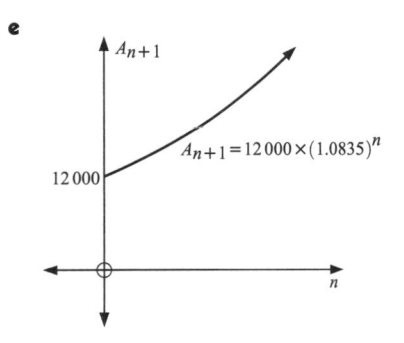

e

Graph showing A_{n+1} vs n, passing through $(0, 12\,000)$, labelled $A_{n+1} = 12\,000 \times (1.0835)^n$.

EXERCISE 4H.3

1 $M_t = 1000e^{-0.04t}$ $\quad\therefore\ M_0 = 1000e^0 = 1000$ g

a For M_t to halve,
$M_t = 500$

$\therefore\ 1000e^{-0.04t} = 500$

$\therefore\ e^{-0.04t} = 0.5$

$\therefore\ -0.04t = \ln(0.5)$

$\therefore\ t = \dfrac{\ln(0.5)}{-0.04}$

$\therefore\ t \approx 17.3$ years

b For $M_t = 25$ g,

$\therefore\ 1000e^{-0.04t} = 25$

$\therefore\ e^{-0.04t} = 0.025$

$\therefore\ -0.04t = \ln(0.025)$

$\therefore\ t = \dfrac{\ln(0.025)}{-0.04}$

$\therefore\ t \approx 92.2$ years

c For $M_t = 1\%$ of M_0

$\therefore\ 1000e^{-0.04t} = 0.01 \times 1000$

$\therefore\ e^{-0.04t} = 0.01$

$\therefore\ -0.04t = \ln(0.01)$

$\therefore\ t = \dfrac{\ln(0.01)}{-0.04}$

$\therefore\ t \approx 115$ years

2 $V = 50(1 - e^{-0.2t})$ m s^{-1}

So, when $V = 40$, $50(1 - e^{-0.2t}) = 40$

$\therefore \quad 1 - e^{-0.2t} = 0.8$

$\therefore \quad e^{-0.2t} = 0.2$

$\therefore \quad -0.2t = \ln(0.2)$

$\therefore \quad t = \dfrac{\ln(0.2)}{-0.2}$

$\therefore \quad t \approx 8.05$ s

So, it would take 8.05 s.

3 $T = 4 + 96 \times e^{-0.03t}$ °C

a When $T = 25$,

$4 + 96 \times e^{-0.03t} = 25$

$\therefore \quad 96 \times e^{-0.03t} = 21$

$\therefore \quad e^{-0.03t} = \dfrac{21}{96}$

$\therefore \quad -0.03t = \ln(\tfrac{21}{96})$

$\therefore \quad t = \dfrac{\ln(\tfrac{21}{96})}{-0.03}$

$\therefore \quad t \approx 50.7$ minutes

b When $T = 5$,

$4 + 96 \times e^{-0.03t} = 5$

$\therefore \quad 96 \times e^{-0.03t} = 1$

$\therefore \quad e^{-0.03t} = \dfrac{1}{96}$

$\therefore \quad -0.03t = \ln(\tfrac{1}{96})$

$\therefore \quad t = \dfrac{\ln(\tfrac{1}{96})}{-0.03}$

$\therefore \quad t \approx 152$ minutes

4 $W_t = 1000 \times 2^{-0.04t}$ has $W_0 = 1000 \times 2^0 = 1000$ grams

a For the weight to halve,

$W_t = 500$

$\therefore \quad 1000 \times 2^{-0.04t} = 500$

$\therefore \quad 2^{-0.04t} = \tfrac{1}{2} = 2^{-1}$

$\therefore \quad -0.04t = -1$

$\therefore \quad t = \dfrac{1}{0.04}$

$\therefore \quad t = 25$ years

b For $W_t = 20$,

$1000 \times 2^{-0.04t} = 20$

$\therefore \quad 2^{-0.04t} = 0.02$

$\therefore \quad \log 2^{-0.04t} = \log(0.02)$

$\therefore \quad -0.04t \log 2 = \log(0.02)$

$\therefore \quad t = \dfrac{\log(0.02)}{-0.04 \times \log 2}$

$\therefore \quad t \approx 141$ years

c When $W_t = 1\%$ of 1000 grams $= 10$ g,

$1000 \times 2^{-0.04t} = 10$

$\therefore \quad 2^{-0.04t} = 0.01$

$\therefore \quad \log 2^{-0.04t} = \log(0.01)$

and so $-0.04 \log 2 = \log(0.01)$

$\therefore \quad t = \dfrac{\log(0.01)}{-0.04 \times \log 2}$

$\therefore \quad t \approx 166$ years

5 $W = W_0 \times 2^{-0.0002t}$ grams

a When W is 25% of original,

$W = \tfrac{1}{4}$ of W_0

$\therefore \quad W_0 \times 2^{-0.0002t} = \tfrac{1}{4} \times W_0$

$\therefore \quad 2^{-0.0002t} = 2^{-2}$

$\therefore \quad 0.0002t = 2$

$\therefore \quad t = \dfrac{2}{0.0002}$

$\therefore \quad t = 10\,000$

$\therefore$ it would take 10 000 years.

b When W is 0.1% of original,

$W = \dfrac{0.1}{100}$ of W_0

$\therefore \quad W_0 \times 2^{-0.0002t} = \dfrac{1}{1000} \times W_0$

$\therefore \quad \log 2^{-0.0002t} = \log(0.001)$

$\therefore \quad -0.0002t \log 2 = \log(0.001)$

$\therefore \quad t = \dfrac{\log(0.001)}{-0.0002 \times \log 2}$

$\therefore \quad t \approx 49\,829$

$\therefore$ it would take about 49 800 years.

6 $I = I_0 \times 2^{-0.02t}$ amps
When I is 10% of its original value,
$I = 10\%$ of I_0
$\therefore \quad I_0 \times 2^{-0.02t} = 0.1 \times I_0$
$\therefore \quad 2^{-0.02t} = 0.1$
$\therefore \quad \log 2^{-0.02t} = \log(0.1)$
$\therefore \quad -0.02t \log 2 = \log(0.1)$
$\therefore \quad t = \dfrac{\log(0.1)}{-0.02 \times \log 2}$
$\therefore \quad t \approx 166$ seconds

7 $V = 50(1 - 2^{-0.2t})$ m s^{-1}
When $V = 40$, $50(1 - 2^{-0.2t}) = 40$
$\therefore \quad 1 - 2^{-0.2t} = 0.8$
$\therefore \quad 2^{-0.2t} = 0.2$
$\therefore \quad \log 2^{-0.2t} = \log 0.2$
$\therefore \quad -0.2t \log 2 = \log 0.2$
$\therefore \quad t = \dfrac{\log 0.2}{-0.2 \times \log 2}$
$\therefore \quad t \approx 11.6$ seconds

REVIEW SET 4A

1 a $\log_4 64$
$= \log_4 4^3$
$= 3$

b $\log_2 256$
$= \log_2 2^8$
$= 8$

c $\log_2(0.25)$
$= \log_2(\tfrac{1}{4})$
$= \log_2 2^{-2}$
$= -2$

d $\log_{25} 5$
$= \log_{25} 25^{\frac{1}{2}}$
$= \tfrac{1}{2}$

e $\log_8 1$
$= \log_8 8^0$
$= 0$

f $\log_6 6$
$= \log_6 6^1$
$= 1$

g $\log_{81} 3$
$= \log_{81} 81^{\frac{1}{4}}$
$= \tfrac{1}{4}$

h $\log_9(0.\overline{1})$
$= \log_9(\tfrac{1}{9})$
$= \log_9 9^{-1}$
$= -1$

i $\log_{27} 3$
$= \log_{27} 27^{\frac{1}{3}}$
$= \tfrac{1}{3}$

j $\log_k \sqrt{k}$
$= \log_k k^{\frac{1}{2}}$
$= \tfrac{1}{2}$ provided $k > 0$, $k \neq 1$

2 a $\log \sqrt{10}$
$= \log 10^{\frac{1}{2}}$
$= \tfrac{1}{2}$

b $\log\left(\dfrac{1}{\sqrt[3]{10}}\right)$
$= \log 10^{-\frac{1}{3}}$
$= -\tfrac{1}{3}$

c $\log(10^a \times 10^{b+1})$
$= \log 10^{a+b+1}$
$= a + b + 1$

3 a $\log_2 x = -3$
$\therefore \quad x = 2^{-3}$
$\therefore \quad x = \tfrac{1}{8}$

b $\log_5 x \approx 2.743$
$\therefore \quad x \approx 5^{2.743}$
$\therefore \quad x \approx 82.7$

c $\log_3 x \approx -3.145$
$\therefore \quad x \approx 3^{-3.145}$
$\therefore \quad x \approx 0.0316$

4 a $P = 3 \times b^x$
$\therefore \quad \log P = \log(3 \times b^x)$
$\therefore \quad \log P = \log 3 + \log b^x$
$\therefore \quad \log P = \log 3 + x \log b$

b $m = \dfrac{n^3}{p^2}$
$\therefore \quad \log m = \log\left(\dfrac{n^3}{p^2}\right)$
$\therefore \quad \log m = \log n^3 - \log p^2$
$\therefore \quad \log m = 3 \log n - 2 \log p$

5 a $\log_2 k \approx 1.699 + x$
$\therefore \quad k \approx 2^{1.699+x}$
$\therefore \quad k \approx 2^{1.699} \times 2^x$
$\therefore \quad k \approx 3.25 \times 2^x$

b $\log_a Q = 3 \log_a P + \log_a R$
$= \log_a P^3 + \log_a R$
$= \log_a(P^3 \times R)$
$\therefore \quad Q = P^3 R$

c $\log A \approx 5 \log B - 2.602$
$\therefore \quad \log A - \log B^5 \approx -2.602$
$\therefore \quad \log\left(\dfrac{A}{B^5}\right) \approx -2.602$
$\therefore \quad \dfrac{A}{B^5} \approx 10^{-2.602} \approx 0.0025$
$\therefore \quad A \approx \dfrac{B^5}{400}$

6 a $5^x = 7$
$\therefore \log 5^x = \log 7$
$\therefore x \log 5 = \log 7$
$\therefore x = \dfrac{\log 7}{\log 5}$
$\therefore x \approx 1.209$

b $20 \times 2^{2x+1} = 500$
$\therefore 2^{2x+1} = 25$
$\therefore \log 2^{2x+1} = \log 25$
$\therefore (2x+1) \log 2 = \log 25$
$\therefore 2x + 1 = \dfrac{\log 25}{\log 2} \approx 4.6439$
$\therefore 2x \approx 3.6439$
$\therefore x \approx 1.822$

7 $W_t = 2500 \times 3^{-\frac{t}{3000}}$ grams

a $W_0 = 2500 \times 3^0$
$= 2500 \times 1$
$= 2500$ grams

b We need t when $W_t = 30\%$ of 2500 g
$\therefore 2500 \times 3^{-\frac{t}{3000}} = 0.3 \times 2500$
$\therefore \log 3^{-\frac{t}{3000}} = \log(0.3)$
$\therefore -\dfrac{t}{3000} \times \log 3 = \log(0.3)$
$\therefore t = \dfrac{-\log(0.3) \times 3000}{\log 3}$
$\therefore t \approx 3287.7$
$\therefore$ about 3290 years

c % change
$= \left(\dfrac{W_{1500} - W_0}{W_0}\right) \times 100\%$
$= \left(\dfrac{2500 \times 3^{-\frac{1500}{3000}} - 2500}{2500}\right) \times 100\%$
$= (3^{-\frac{1}{2}} - 1) \times 100\%$
$\approx -42.3\%$
So, a loss of 42.3%.

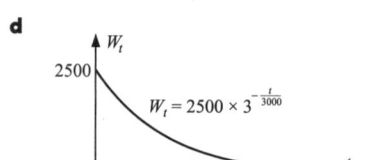

d
Graph showing W_t vs t, starting at 2500, decaying curve $W_t = 2500 \times 3^{-\frac{t}{3000}}$.

8 $16^x - 5 \times 8^x = 0$
$\therefore 2^x \times 8^x - 5 \times 8^x = 0$
$\therefore 8^x(2^x - 5) = 0$
$\therefore 2^x = 5$ as $8^x > 0$ for all x
$\therefore x = \log_2 5 = \dfrac{\log 5}{\log 2} \approx 2.32$

9 $\log_3(10x^2 - x - 2) = 2 + 2\log_3 x$
$\therefore \log_3(10x^2 - x - 2) = \log_3 3^2 + \log_3 x^2$
$\therefore \log_3(10x^2 - x - 2) = \log_3(9x^2)$
$\therefore 10x^2 - x - 2 = 9x^2$
$\therefore x^2 - x - 2 = 0$
$\therefore (x-2)(x+1) = 0$
$\therefore x = 2$ or -1
but $\log_3 x$ is undefined when $x = -1$
$\therefore x = 2$

10 $5^{3a} \times 4^{2a+1} = 10^{3a+2}$
$\therefore 4^{2a+1} = \dfrac{100 \times 10^{3a}}{5^{3a}}$
$\therefore (2^2)^{2a+1} = 100 \times 2^{3a}$
$\therefore \dfrac{2^{4a+2}}{2^{3a}} = 100$
$\therefore 2^{a+2} = 100$
$\therefore 2^a \times 2^2 = 100$
$\therefore 2^a = 25$
$\therefore a = \dfrac{\ln 25}{\ln 2}$ {change of base rule}

REVIEW SET 4B

1 a $\log \sqrt{1000}$
$= \log \left(10^3\right)^{\frac{1}{2}}$
$= \log 10^{\frac{3}{2}}$
$= \frac{3}{2}$

b $\log \left(\dfrac{10}{\sqrt[3]{10}}\right)$
$= \log \left(\dfrac{10^1}{10^{\frac{1}{3}}}\right)$
$= \log 10^{\frac{2}{3}} = \frac{2}{3}$

c $\log \left(\dfrac{10^a}{10^{-b}}\right)$
$= \log \left(10^{a-(-b)}\right)$
$= \log 10^{a+b}$
$= a + b$

2 a $\log x = 3$
$\therefore \ x = 10^3$
$\therefore \ x = 1000$

b $\log_3(x+2) = 1.732$
$\therefore \ x + 2 = 3^{1.732}$
$\therefore \ x + 2 \approx 6.7046$
$\therefore \ x \approx 4.7046$
$\therefore \ x \approx 4.70$

c $\log_2 \left(\dfrac{x}{10}\right) = -0.671$
$\therefore \ \dfrac{x}{10} = 2^{-0.671}$
$\therefore \ \dfrac{x}{10} \approx 0.628\,07$
$\therefore \ x \approx 6.28$

3 a $\log 16 + 2 \log 3$
$= \log 16 + \log 3^2$
$= \log(16 \times 9)$
$= \log 144$

b $\log_2 16 - 2\log_2 3$
$= \log_2 16 - \log_2 3^2$
$= \log_2 \left(\dfrac{16}{9}\right)$

c $2 + \log_4 5$
$= \log_4 4^2 + \log_4 5$
$= \log_4 (16 \times 5)$
$= \log_4 80$

4 a $\log T = 2 \log x - \log y$
$\therefore \ \log T = \log x^2 - \log y$
$\therefore \ \log T = \log \left(\dfrac{x^2}{y}\right)$
$\therefore \ T = \dfrac{x^2}{y}$

b $\log_2 K = \log_2 n + \frac{1}{2} \log_2 t$
$\therefore \ \log_2 K = \log_2 n + \log_2 t^{\frac{1}{2}}$
$\therefore \ \log_2 K = \log_2 (n \times \sqrt{t})$
$\therefore \ K = n\sqrt{t}$

5 a $3^x = 300$
$\therefore \ \log 3^x = \log 300$
$\therefore \ x \log 3 = \log 300$
$\therefore \ x = \dfrac{\log 300}{\log 3}$
$\therefore \ x \approx 5.19$

b $30 \times 5^{1-x} = 0.15$
$\therefore \ 5^{1-x} = 0.005$
$\therefore \ \log 5^{1-x} = \log(0.005)$
$\therefore \ (1-x)\log 5 = \log(0.005)$
$\therefore \ 1 - x = \dfrac{\log(0.005)}{\log 5}$
$\therefore \ 1 - x \approx -3.292$
$\therefore \ x \approx 4.29$

c $3^{x+2} = 2^{1-x}$
$\therefore \ \log 3^{x+2} = \log 2^{1-x}$
$\therefore \ (x+2)\log 3 = (1-x)\log 2$
$\therefore \ x \log 3 + 2 \log 3 = \log 2 - x \log 2$
$\therefore \ x(\log 3 + \log 2) = \log 2 - 2 \log 3$
$\therefore \ x \log 6 = \log\left(\frac{2}{9}\right)$
$\therefore \ x = \dfrac{\log\left(\frac{2}{9}\right)}{\log 6}$
≈ -0.839

6 a $\log_2 36$
$= \log_2(2^2 \times 3^2)$
$= \log_2 2^2 + \log_2 3^2$
$= 2\log_2 2 + 2\log_2 3$
$= 2A + 2B$

b $\log 54$
$= \log_2(2 \times 3^3)$
$= \log_2 2 + \log_2 3^3$
$= \log_2 2 + 3\log_2 3$
$= A + 3B$

c $\log_2(8\sqrt{3})$
$= \log_2(2^3 \times 3^{\frac{1}{2}})$
$= \log_2 2^3 + \log_2 3^{\frac{1}{2}}$
$= 3\log_2 2 + \frac{1}{2}\log_2 3$
$= 3A + \frac{1}{2}B$

d $\log_2(20.25)$
$= \log_2(\frac{81}{4})$
$= \log_2\left(\frac{3^4}{2^2}\right)$
$= \log_2 3^4 - \log_2 2^2$
$= 4\log_2 3 - 2\log_2 2$
$= 4B - 2A$

e $\log_2(0.\overline{8})$
$= \log_2(\frac{8}{9})$
$= \log_2\left(\frac{2^3}{3^2}\right)$
$= \log_2 2^3 - \log_2 3^2$
$= 3\log_2 2 - 2\log_2 3$
$= 3A - 2B$

7 $g(x) = \log_3(x+2) - 2$

  a We require $x + 2 > 0$, so $x > -2$ $\therefore$ domain is $x \in\ ]-2,\ \infty[$ range is $y \in \mathbb{R}$
  b If $x \to -2$ (right), $y \to -\infty$ $\therefore$ VA is $x = -2$.
  As $x \to \infty$, $y \to \infty$.
  When $x = 0$, $g(0) = \log_3 2 - 2 \approx -1.37$ $\therefore$ y-intercept ≈ -1.37
  When $y = 0$, $\log_3(x+2) = 2$ $\therefore$ $x + 2 = 3^2$
  $\therefore$ $x = 7$ So, the x-intercept is 7.

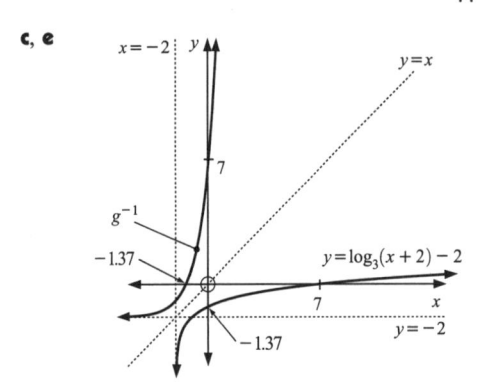

  c, e [graph showing $x=-2$, $y=\log_3(x+2)-2$, $y=x$, g^{-1}, points -1.37, 7, $y=-2$]

  d g^{-1} is defined by $x = \log_3(y+2) - 2$
  $\therefore$ $\log_3(y+2) = x + 2$
  $\therefore$ $y + 2 = 3^{x+2}$
  $\therefore$ $y = 3^{x+2} - 2$
  $\therefore$ $g^{-1}(x) = 3^{x+2} - 2$
  We can verify this by checking that
  $(g^{-1} \circ g)(x) = (g \circ g^{-1})(x) = x$.

8 $\log_4 a^5 + \log_2 a^{\frac{3}{2}} = \log_8 625$

$\therefore$ $\dfrac{\log a^5}{\log 4} + \dfrac{\log a^{\frac{3}{2}}}{\log 2} = \dfrac{\log 5^4}{\log 8}$

$\therefore$ $\dfrac{5 \log a}{2 \log 2} + \dfrac{\frac{3}{2} \log a}{\log 2} = \dfrac{4 \log 5}{3 \log 2}$

$\therefore$ $\frac{5}{2} \log a + \frac{3}{2} \log a = \frac{4}{3} \log 5$

$\therefore$ $4 \log a = \frac{4}{3} \log 5$

$\therefore$ $\log a = \frac{1}{3} \log 5$

$\therefore$ $\log a = \log \sqrt[3]{5}$ and so $a = \sqrt[3]{5}$

9 a $y = mx + c$
its gradient is -2 $\therefore$ $m = -2$
$\therefore$ $y = -2x + c$
it passes through $(1, \log_5(\frac{3}{25}))$, so
$\log_5(\frac{3}{25}) = -2(1) + c$
$\therefore$ $\log_5 3 - \log_5 25 = -2 + c$
$\therefore$ $\log_5 3 - 2 = -2 + c$
$\therefore$ $c = \log_5 3$
$\therefore$ the equation is $y = -2x + \log_5 3$

b If $y = \log_5 M$, then
$-2x + \log_5 3 = \log_5 M$
$\therefore$ $\log_5 5^{-2x} + \log_5 3 = \log_5 M$
$\therefore$ $\log_5(5^{-2x} \times 3) = \log_5 M$
$\therefore$ $M = 3(5^{-2x})$

c When $M = 25$, $y = \log_5 25 = 2$
$\therefore$ $-2x + \log_5 3 = 2$
$\therefore$ $2x = \log_5 3 - 2$
$\therefore$ $x = \frac{1}{2}\log_5 3 - 1$

10 $4^x \times 2^y = 16$
$\therefore \ 2^{2x} \times 2^y = 2^4$
$\therefore \ 2x + y = 4$ .... (1)
and $8^x = 2^{\frac{y}{2}}$
$\therefore \ 2^{3x} = 2^{\frac{y}{2}}$
$\therefore \ 3x = \dfrac{y}{2}$
$\therefore \ y = 6x$ .... (2)

Substituting (2) into (1) gives
$2x + 6x = 4$
$\therefore \ 8x = 4$
$\therefore \ x = \frac{1}{2}$
and using (2), $y = 6(\frac{1}{2}) = 3$
$\therefore \ x = \frac{1}{2}, \ y = 3$

11 $\log_8 \sqrt[4]{x^2 + 7} = \frac{1}{3}$
$\therefore \ 8^{\frac{1}{3}} = \sqrt[4]{x^2 + 7}$
$\therefore \ 2 = \sqrt[4]{x^2 + 7}$
$\therefore \ x^2 + 7 = 16$
$\therefore \ x^2 = 9$
$\therefore \ x = \pm 3$

REVIEW SET 4C

1 a

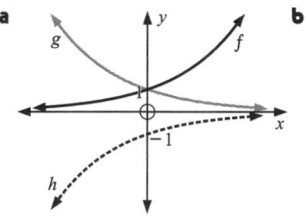

b **i** g is the reflection of f in the y-axis
ii h is the reflection of g in the x-axis

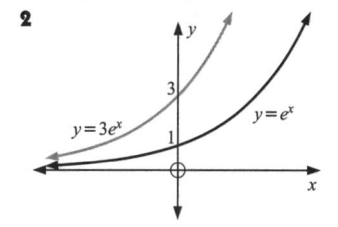

2

3 $s(t) = 120t - 40e^{-\frac{t}{5}}$ metres

a **i** $s(0) = 0 - 40e^0$
$= -40$ m

ii $s(5) = 600 - 40e^{-1}$
≈ 585 m

iii $s(20) = 2400 - 40e^{-4}$
≈ 2400 m

b

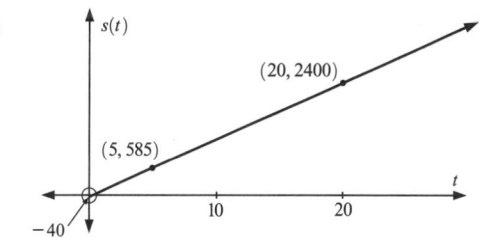

4 a $\ln(e^5) = 5$
{as $\ln e^a = a$}

b $\ln(\sqrt{e}) = \ln e^{\frac{1}{2}}$
$= \frac{1}{2}$

c $\ln\left(\frac{1}{e}\right) = \ln e^{-1}$
$= -1$

5 a $\ln(e^{2x}) = 2x$

b $\ln(e^2 e^x) = \ln(e^{2+x})$
$= 2 + x$

c $\ln\left(\dfrac{e}{e^x}\right) = \ln(e^{1-x})$
$= 1 - x$

6 a $\ln 6 + \ln 4$
$= \ln(6 \times 4)$
$= \ln 24$

b $\ln 60 - \ln 20$
$= \ln(\frac{60}{20})$
$= \ln 3$

c $\ln 4 + \ln 1$
$= \ln 4 + 0$
$= \ln 4$

d $\ln 200 - \ln 8 + \ln 5$
$= \ln(\frac{200}{8}) + \ln 5$
$= \ln\left(\frac{200}{8} \times 5\right)$
$= \ln 125$

7 a $\ln 32 = \ln 2^5$
$= 5 \ln 2$

b $\ln 125 = \ln 5^3$
$= 3 \ln 5$

c $\ln 729 = \ln 3^6$
$= 6 \ln 3$

8 a $e^x = 400$
$\therefore \ x = \ln 400$
$\therefore \ x \approx 5.99$

b $e^{2x+1} = 11$
$\therefore \ 2x + 1 = \ln 11$
$\therefore \ 2x = \ln 11 - 1$
$\therefore \ x = \dfrac{\ln 11 - 1}{2}$
$\therefore \ x \approx 0.699$

c $25e^{\frac{x}{2}} = 750$
$\therefore \ e^{\frac{x}{2}} = 30$
$\therefore \ \dfrac{x}{2} = \ln 30$
$\therefore \ x = 2 \ln 30$
$\therefore \ x \approx 6.80$

d $e^{2x} = 7e^x - 12$
$\therefore\ e^{2x} - 7e^x + 12 = 0$
$\therefore\ (e^x - 3)(e^x - 4) = 0$
$\therefore\ e^x = 3$ or $e^x = 4$
$\therefore\ x = \ln 3$ or $\ln 4$
$\therefore\ x \approx 1.10$ or 1.39

9 $12(2^x) = 7 + \dfrac{10}{2^x}$
$\therefore\ 12(2^{2x}) = 7(2^x) + 10$
$\therefore\ 12(2^{2x}) - 7(2^x) - 10 = 0$
$\therefore\ [4(2^x) - 5][3(2^x) + 2] = 0$
$\therefore\ 4(2^x) = 5$ or $3(2^x) = -2$
$\therefore\ 2^x = \tfrac{5}{4}$ $\{2^x > 0$ for all $x\}$
$\therefore\ x = \log_2(\tfrac{5}{4})$
$\therefore\ x = \log_2 5 - \log_2 4$
$\therefore\ x = -2 + \log_2 5$

REVIEW SET 4D

1

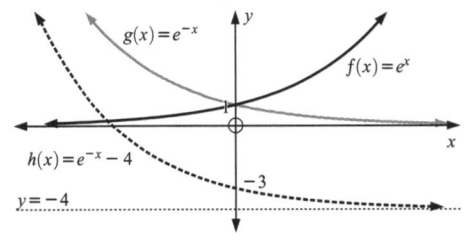

Each function has domain $\{x \mid x \in \mathbb{R}\}$
Range of f is $\{y \mid y > 0\}$
Range of g is $\{y \mid y > 0\}$
Range of h is $\{y \mid y > -4\}$

2

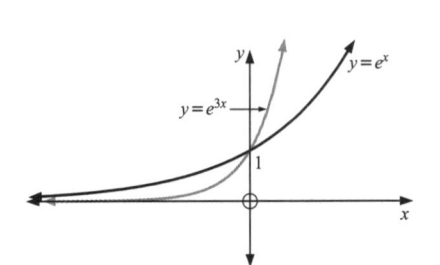

3 a $\ln\left(e\sqrt{e}\right)$
$= \ln(e^1 e^{\frac{1}{2}})$
$= \ln e^{\frac{3}{2}}$
$= \tfrac{3}{2}$

b $\ln\left(\dfrac{1}{e^3}\right)$
$= \ln e^{-3}$
$= -3$

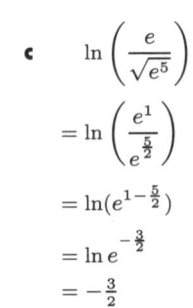

c $\ln\left(\dfrac{e}{\sqrt{e^5}}\right)$
$= \ln\left(\dfrac{e^1}{e^{\frac{5}{2}}}\right)$
$= \ln(e^{1-\frac{5}{2}})$
$= \ln e^{-\frac{3}{2}}$
$= -\tfrac{3}{2}$

4 a $20 = e^{\ln 20}$
$\approx e^{3.00}$

b $3000 = e^{\ln 3000}$
$\approx e^{8.01}$

c $0.075 = e^{\ln(0.075)}$
$\approx e^{-2.59}$

5 a $4\ln 2 + 2\ln 3$
$= \ln 2^4 + \ln 3^2$
$= \ln(16 \times 9)$
$= \ln 144$

b $\tfrac{1}{2}\ln 9 - \ln 2$
$= \ln 9^{\frac{1}{2}} - \ln 2$
$= \ln 3 - \ln 2$
$= \ln(\tfrac{3}{2})$

c $2\ln 5 - 1$
$= \ln 5^2 - \ln e^1$
$= \ln\left(\dfrac{25}{e}\right)$

d $\tfrac{1}{4}\ln 81$
$= \ln\left(3^4\right)^{\frac{1}{4}}$
$= \ln 3^1$
$= \ln 3$

6 a $\ln P = 1.5 \ln Q + \ln T$
$\therefore\ \ln P = \ln Q^{1.5} + \ln T$
$= \ln(TQ^{1.5})$
$\therefore\ P = TQ^{1.5}$

b $\ln M = 1.2 - 0.5 \ln N$
$\therefore\ \ln M + \ln N^{\frac{1}{2}} = 1.2$
$\therefore\ \ln\left(M\sqrt{N}\right) = 1.2$
$\therefore\ M\sqrt{N} = e^{1.2}$
$\therefore\ M = \dfrac{e^{1.2}}{\sqrt{N}}$

7 a $g(x) = 2e^x - 5$ has inverse function $x = 2e^y - 5$
$\therefore \quad 2e^y = x + 5$
$\therefore \quad e^y = \dfrac{x+5}{2}$
$\therefore \quad y = \ln\left(\dfrac{x+5}{2}\right)$
$\therefore \quad g^{-1}(x) = \ln\left(\dfrac{x+5}{2}\right)$

b Graph showing $x = -5$, g^{-1}, $g(x) = 2e^x - 5$, $y = -5$.

c domain of g is $\{x \mid x \in \mathbb{R}\}$, range is $\{y \mid y > -5\}$
domain of g^{-1} is $\{x \mid x > -5\}$, range is $\{y \mid y \in \mathbb{R}\}$

8 $W_t = 8000 \times e^{-\frac{t}{20}}$ grams
$W_0 = 8000e^0$
$= 8000 \times 1$
$= 8000$ grams

a When $W_t = \frac{1}{2} \times 8000$ grams,
$8000e^{-\frac{t}{20}} = 4000$
$\therefore \quad e^{-\frac{t}{20}} = 0.5$
$\therefore \quad -\dfrac{t}{20} = \ln(0.5)$
$\therefore \quad t = -20\ln(0.5) \approx 13.9$ weeks

b When $W_t = 1000$,
$8000e^{-\frac{t}{20}} = 1000$
$\therefore \quad e^{-\frac{t}{20}} = \frac{1}{8}$
$\therefore \quad -\dfrac{t}{20} = \ln(\frac{1}{8})$
$\therefore \quad t = -20\ln(\frac{1}{8})$
$\therefore \quad t \approx 41.6$ weeks

c When $W_t = 0.1\%$ of W_0
$= \frac{1}{1000}$ of 8000 g
$= 8$ g,
$8000e^{-\frac{t}{20}} = 8$
$\therefore \quad e^{-\frac{t}{20}} = 0.001$
$\therefore \quad -\dfrac{t}{20} = \ln(0.001)$
$\therefore \quad t = -20\ln(0.001) \approx 138$ weeks

9 a $f(x) = \ln(x^2 - 16) - \ln x - \ln(x - 4)$, $x > 4$
$= \ln\left(\dfrac{x^2 - 16}{x(x-4)}\right)$
$= \ln\left(\dfrac{(x+4)(x-4)}{x(x-4)}\right)$
$= \ln\left(\dfrac{x+4}{x}\right)$ {So $a = 4$}

b $y = \ln\left(\dfrac{x+4}{x}\right)$ has inverse
$x = \ln\left(\dfrac{y+4}{y}\right)$
$\therefore \quad x = \ln\left(1 + \dfrac{4}{y}\right)$
$\therefore \quad e^x = 1 + \dfrac{4}{y}$
$\therefore \quad e^x - 1 = \dfrac{4}{y}$
$\therefore \quad y = \dfrac{4}{e^x - 1}$
$\therefore \quad f^{-1}(x) = \dfrac{4}{e^x - 1}$

Note: f has domain $\{x \mid x > 4\}$ and range $\{y \mid 0 < y < \ln 2\}$, so f^{-1} has domain $\{x \mid 0 < x < \ln 2\}$ and range $\{y \mid y > 4\}$

Chapter 5
GRAPHING AND TRANSFORMING FUNCTIONS

EXERCISE 5A

1 $f(x) = x$

   a $f(2x) = 2x$ **b** $f(x) + 2$ **c** $\frac{1}{2}f(x) = \frac{x}{2}$ **d** $2f(x) + 3$
$$= x + 2 \qquad\qquad\qquad\qquad\qquad\qquad = 2x + 3$$

2 $f(x) = x^3$

   a $f(4x)$ **b** $\frac{1}{2}f(2x)$ **c** $f(x+1)$ **d** $2f(x+1) - 3$
$$\begin{aligned}
&= (4x)^3 &&= \tfrac{1}{2}(2x)^3 &&= (x+1)^3 &&= 2(x+1)^3 - 3\\
&= 64x^3 &&= \tfrac{1}{2} \times 8x^3 &&= x^3 + 3x^2 + 3x + 1 &&= 2(x^3 + 3x^2 + 3x + 1) - 3\\
& &&= 4x^3 && &&= 2x^3 + 6x^2 + 6x - 1
\end{aligned}$$

3 $f(x) = 2^x$

   a $f(2x) = 2^{2x}$ **b** $f(-x) + 1$ **c** $f(x-2) + 3$ **d** $2f(x) + 3$
$$\begin{aligned}
&= 4^x &&= 2^{-x} + 1 &&= 2^{x-2} + 3 &&= 2 \times 2^x + 3\\
& && && &&= 2^{x+1} + 3
\end{aligned}$$

4 $f(x) = \dfrac{1}{x}$

   a $f(-x)$ **b** $f(\tfrac{1}{2}x)$ **c** $2f(x) + 3$ **d** $3f(x-1) + 2$
$$\begin{aligned}
&= \tfrac{1}{(-x)} &&= \tfrac{1}{\frac{1}{2}x} &&= 2\left(\tfrac{1}{x}\right) + 3 &&= 3\left(\tfrac{1}{x-1}\right) + 2\\
&= -\tfrac{1}{x} &&= \tfrac{2}{x} &&= \tfrac{2}{x} + 3 &&= \tfrac{3 + 2(x-1)}{x-1}\\
& && &&= \tfrac{2 + 3x}{x} &&= \tfrac{2x+1}{x-1}
\end{aligned}$$

5 a Graph of $y = 2x + 3$ with y-intercept 3 and x-intercept $-1\tfrac{1}{2}$.

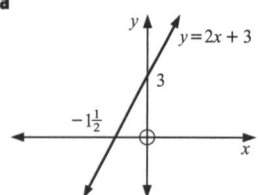

   b
     i When $y = 0$, $2x + 3 = 0$ $\therefore$ $x = -\tfrac{3}{2}$
$\therefore$ x-intercept is $-1\tfrac{1}{2}$
     ii When $x = 0$, $y = 0 + 3 = 3$
$\therefore$ y-intercept is 3
     iii As $y = 2x + 3$, the slope is 2 {the coefficient of x}

6 a Graph of $y = (x-2)^2 - 9$ with x-intercepts -1 and 5, y-intercept -5.

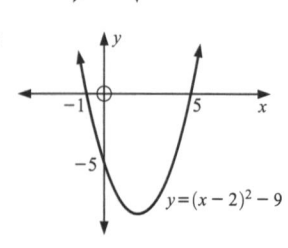

   b When $y = 0$,   When $x = 0$,
$(x-2)^2 - 9 = 0$ $y = (-2)^2 - 9$
$\therefore$ $(x-2)^2 = 9$ $= 4 - 9$
$\therefore$ $x - 2 = \pm 3$ $= -5$
$\therefore$ $x = 2 + 3$ or $2 - 3$ $\therefore$ y-intercept is -5
$\therefore$ $x = 5$ or -1
$\therefore$ x-intercepts are 5 and -1

7 a, b Graph of $y = 2x^3 - 9x^2 + 12x - 5$ with points $(1, 0)$, $(\tfrac{5}{2}, ?)$, $(2, -1)$, and y-intercept -5.

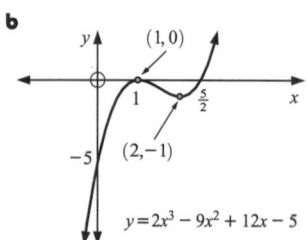

8 Graph of $y = |x|$.

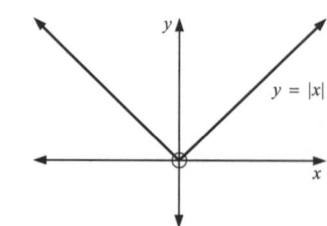

9 [Graph of $y = 2^x$ passing through $(0, 1)$]

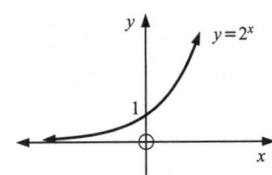

c When $x = 0$,
$y = 2^0 = 1$ ✓

d $2^x > 0$ for all x as the graph is always above the y-axis. ✓

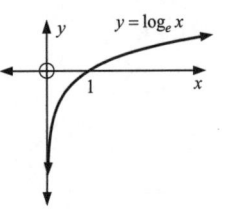

10 [Graph of $y = \log_e x$ passing through $(1, 0)$]

EXERCISE 5B.1

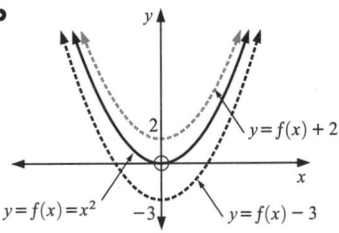

1 a, b [Graphs of $y = f(x) = x^2$, $y = f(x) + 2$, and $y = f(x) - 3$]

c
  i If $b > 0$, the function is translated vertically upwards through b units.
  ii If $b < 0$, the function is translated vertically downwards $|b|$ units.

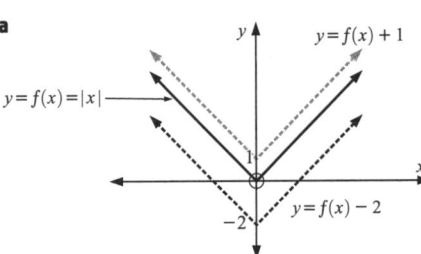

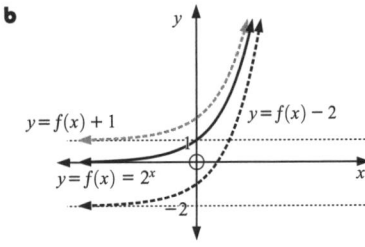

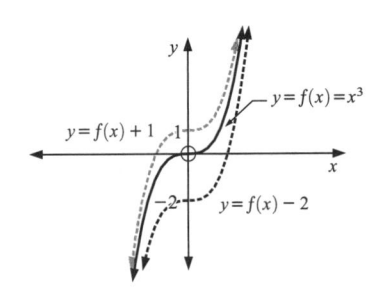

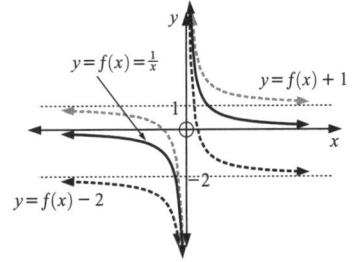

2 a [Graphs of $y = f(x) = |x|$, $y = f(x) + 1$, and $y = f(x) - 2$]

b [Graphs of $y = f(x) = 2^x$, $y = f(x) + 1$, and $y = f(x) - 2$]

c [Graphs of $y = f(x) = x^3$, $y = f(x) + 1$, and $y = f(x) - 2$]

d [Graphs of $y = f(x) = \frac{1}{x}$, $y = f(x) + 1$, and $y = f(x) - 2$]

Summary: For $y = f(x) + b$, $y = f(x)$ is translated upwards b units.
If $b > 0$ movement is vertically upwards.
If $b < 0$ movement is vertically downwards.

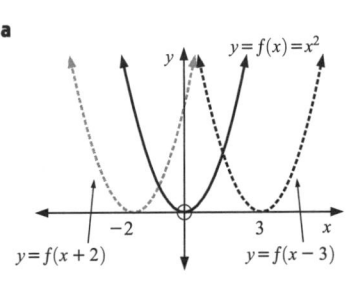

3 a [Graphs of $y = f(x) = x^2$, $y = f(x + 2)$, and $y = f(x - 3)$]

b
  i If $a > 0$, the graph is translated a units right.
  ii If $a < 0$, the graph is translated $|a|$ units left.

4 **a, b, c, d** (graphs)

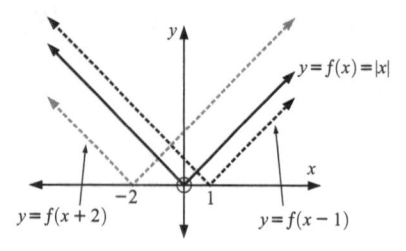

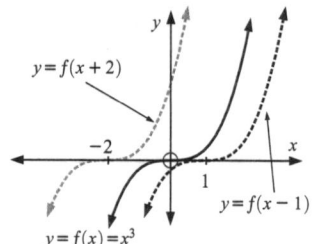

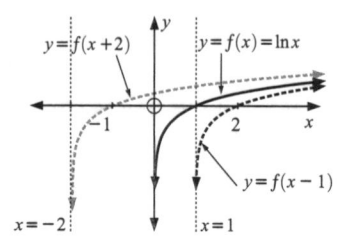

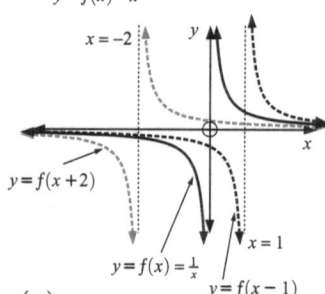

$y = f(x-a)$ is a horizontal translation of $y = f(x)$ through $\begin{pmatrix} a \\ 0 \end{pmatrix}$.

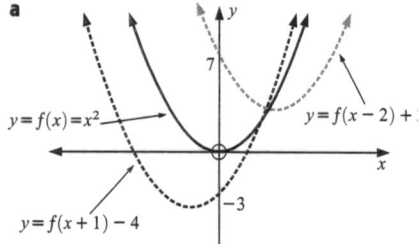

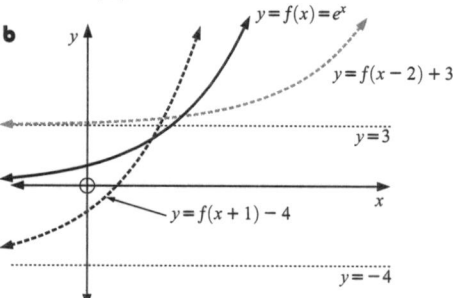

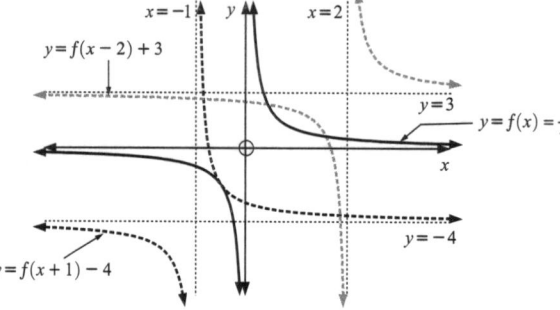

5 **a, b, c** (graphs)

6 A translation of $\begin{pmatrix} 2 \\ -3 \end{pmatrix}$.   **a, b** (graphs)

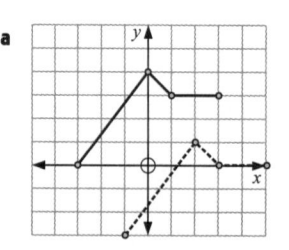

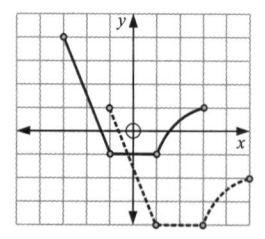

7 **a** The transformation from $f(x) = x^2$ to $g(x) = (x-3)^2 + 2$ is a translation of $\begin{pmatrix} 3 \\ 2 \end{pmatrix}$.

    i $(0, 0)$ is translated to $(3, 2)$.

    ii $f(-3) = (-3)^2 = 9$
       ∴ $(-3, 9)$ is translated to $(0, 11)$.

    iii $f(2) = 2^2 = 4$
       ∴ $(2, 4)$ is translated to $(5, 6)$.

b The transformation from $g(x)$ back to $f(x)$ is a translation of $\begin{pmatrix} -3 \\ -2 \end{pmatrix}$.

i $(1, 6)$ is translated to $(-2, 4)$.

ii $(-2, 27)$ is translated to $(-5, 25)$.

iii $(1\frac{1}{2}, 4\frac{1}{4})$ is translated to $(-1\frac{1}{2}, 2\frac{1}{4})$.

EXERCISE 5B.2

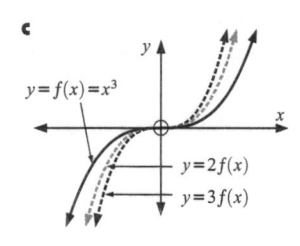

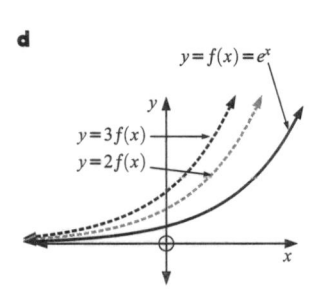

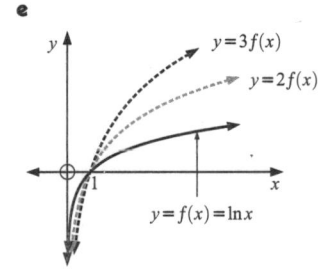

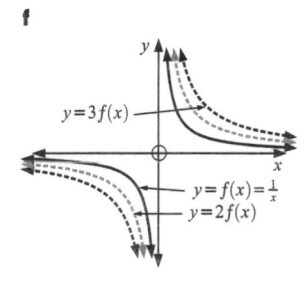

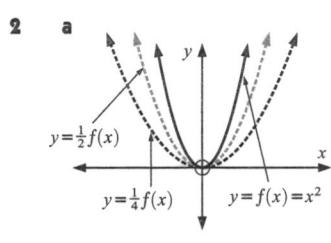

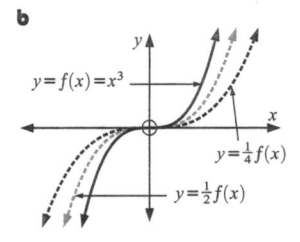

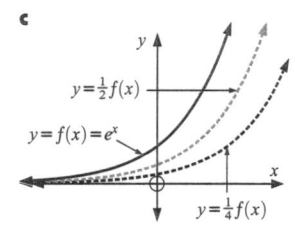

1 a $y = f(x) = x^2$; shows $y = 2f(x)$ and $y = 3f(x)$

b $y = f(x) = |x|$; shows $y = 2f(x)$ and $y = 3f(x)$

c $y = f(x) = x^3$; shows $y = 2f(x)$ and $y = 3f(x)$

d $y = f(x) = e^x$; shows $y = 3f(x)$ and $y = 2f(x)$

e $y = f(x) = \ln x$; shows $y = 3f(x)$ and $y = 2f(x)$

f $y = f(x) = \frac{1}{x}$; shows $y = 3f(x)$ and $y = 2f(x)$

2 a $y = f(x) = x^2$; shows $y = \frac{1}{2}f(x)$ and $y = \frac{1}{4}f(x)$

b $y = f(x) = x^3$; shows $y = \frac{1}{2}f(x)$ and $y = \frac{1}{4}f(x)$

c $y = f(x) = e^x$; shows $y = \frac{1}{2}f(x)$ and $y = \frac{1}{4}f(x)$

3 p affects the vertical stretching or compression of the graph of $y = f(x)$ by a factor of p. If $p > 1$, stretching occurs. If $0 < p < 1$, compression occurs.

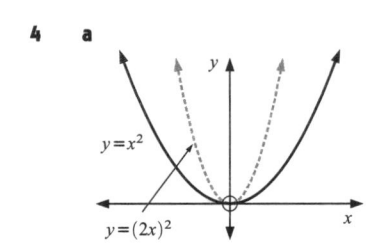

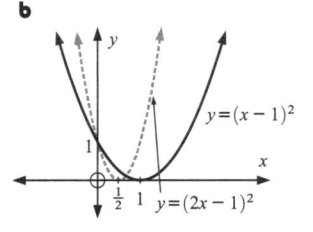

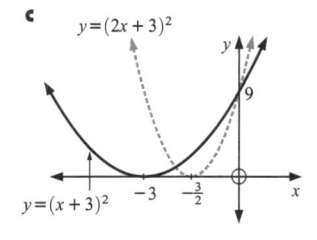

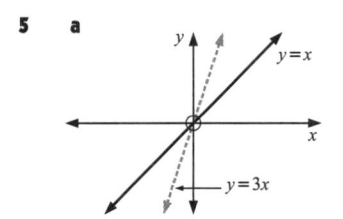

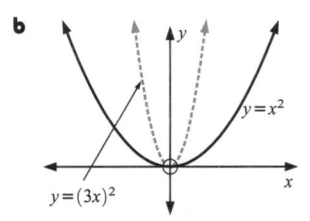

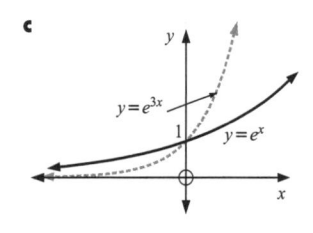

4 a $y = x^2$ and $y = (2x)^2$

b $y = (x-1)^2$ and $y = (2x-1)^2$

c $y = (2x+3)^2$ and $y = (x+3)^2$

5 a $y = x$ and $y = 3x$

b $y = x^2$ and $y = (3x)^2$

c $y = e^x$ and $y = e^{3x}$

6 **a** $y=x^2$, $y=\left(\frac{x}{2}\right)^2$

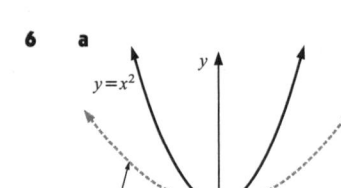

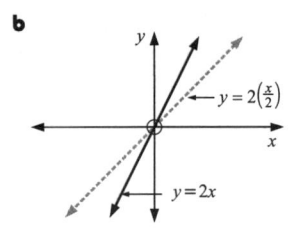

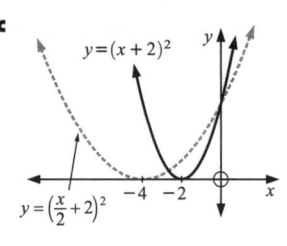

b $y=2\left(\frac{x}{2}\right)$, $y=2x$

c $y=(x+2)^2$, $y=\left(\frac{x}{2}+2\right)^2$

7 k affects the horizontal compression of $y = f(x)$ by a factor of k.
If $k > 1$, it moves closer to the y-axis. If $0 < k < 1$, it moves further from the y-axis.

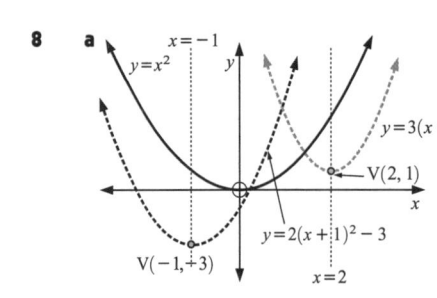

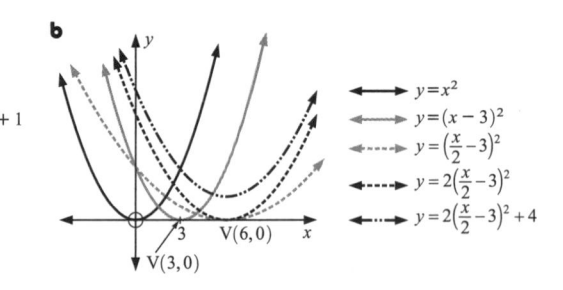

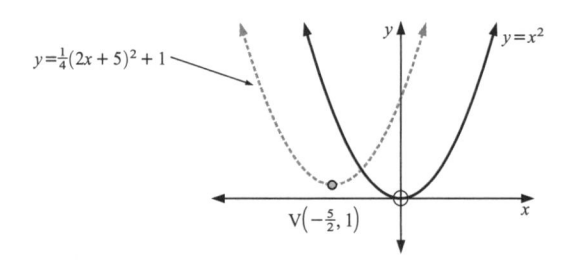

8 **a** $y=x^2$, $y=3(x-2)^2+1$ V(2, 1), $y=2(x+1)^2-3$ V(−1, −3), $x=-1$, $x=2$

b $y=x^2$, $y=(x-3)^2$, $y=\left(\frac{x}{2}-3\right)^2$, $y=2\left(\frac{x}{2}-3\right)^2$, $y=2\left(\frac{x}{2}-3\right)^2+4$, V(3, 0), V(6, 0)

c $y=\frac{1}{4}(2x+5)^2+1$, V$\left(-\frac{5}{2},1\right)$, $y=x^2$

9 **a** The transformation from $y = f(x)$ to $y = 3f(2x)$ is a horizontal compression of factor 2 followed by a vertical stretch of factor 3.

   i $(3, -5) \to \left(\frac{3}{2}, -5\right) \to \left(\frac{3}{2}, -15\right)$ $\therefore$ $(3, -5)$ is translated to $\left(\frac{3}{2}, -15\right)$

   ii $(1, 2) \to \left(\frac{1}{2}, 2\right) \to \left(\frac{1}{2}, 6\right)$ $\therefore$ $(1, 2)$ is translated to $\left(\frac{1}{2}, 6\right)$

   iii $(-2, 1) \to (-1, 1) \to (-1, 3)$ $\therefore$ $(-2, 1)$ is translated to $(-1, 3)$

b The translation from $y = 3f(2x)$ back to $y = f(x)$ is a vertical compression of factor 3 followed by a horizontal stretch of factor 2.

   i $(2, 1) \to \left(2, \frac{1}{3}\right) \to \left(4, \frac{1}{3}\right)$ $\therefore$ $\left(4, \frac{1}{3}\right)$ is the point on $y = f(x)$

   ii $(-3, 2) \to \left(-3, \frac{2}{3}\right) \to \left(-6, \frac{2}{3}\right)$ $\therefore$ $\left(-6, \frac{2}{3}\right)$ is the point on $y = f(x)$

   iii $(-7, 3) \to (-7, 1) \to (-14, 1)$ $\therefore$ $(-14, 1)$ is the point on $y = f(x)$

10 **a** $f(x) \to f(x+1) \to f\left(\frac{1}{2}x+1\right) \to 2f\left(\frac{1}{2}x+1\right) \to 3+2f\left(\frac{1}{2}x+1\right)$
              horizontal   horizontal   vertical   vertical
              translation   stretch   stretch   translation

   $\therefore$ $f(x)$ is translated horizontally 1 unit left, then horizontally stretched by a factor of 2, then vertically stretched by a factor of 2, then translated 3 units upwards.

b **i** $(1, -3) \to (0, -3) \to (0, -3) \to (0, -6) \to (0, -3)$ $\therefore$ $(1, -3)$ is translated to $(0, -3)$

   ii $(2, 1) \to (1, 1) \to (2, 1) \to (2, 2) \to (2, 5)$ $\therefore$ $(2, 1)$ is translated to $(2, 5)$

   iii $(-1, -2) \to (-2, -2) \to (-4, -2) \to (-4, -4) \to (-4, -1)$
     $\therefore$ $(-1, -2)$ is translated to $(-4, -1)$

c To transform points on $g(x)$ back to points on $f(x)$, we translate 3 units downwards, then vertically compress by a factor of 2, then horizontally compress by a factor of 2, then translate 1 unit right.

  i $(-2, -5) \to (-2, -8) \to (-2, -4) \to (-1, -4) \to (0, -4)$
  $\therefore$ the point on $f(x)$ is $(0, -4)$.

  ii $(1, -1) \to (1, -4) \to (1, -2) \to (\frac{1}{2}, -2) \to (\frac{3}{2}, -2)$ $\therefore$ the point on $f(x)$ is $(\frac{3}{2}, -2)$.

  iii $(5, 0) \to (5, -3) \to (5, -\frac{3}{2}) \to (\frac{5}{2}, -\frac{3}{2}) \to (\frac{7}{2}, -\frac{3}{2})$ $\therefore$ the point on $f(x)$ is $(\frac{7}{2}, -\frac{3}{2})$.

EXERCISE 5B.3

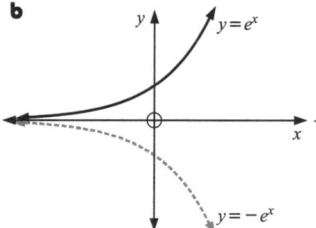

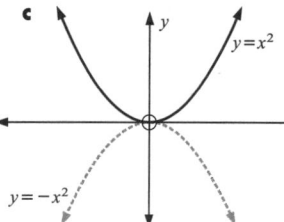

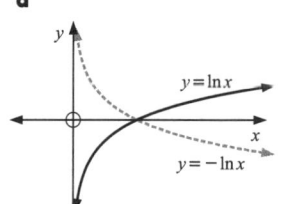

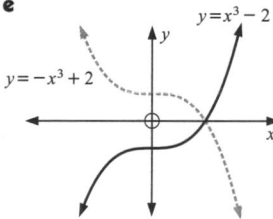

1 a graph showing $y = 3x$ and $y = -3x$
  b graph showing $y = e^x$ and $y = -e^x$
  c graph showing $y = x^2$ and $y = -x^2$
  d graph showing $y = \ln x$ and $y = -\ln x$
  e graph showing $y = x^3 - 2$ and $y = -x^3 + 2$
  f graph showing $y = 2(x+1)^2$ and $y = -2(x+1)^2$

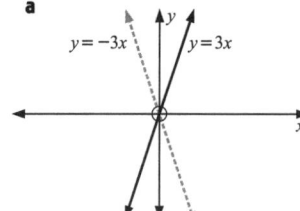

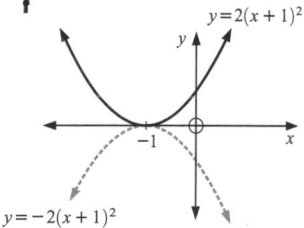

2 $y = -f(x)$ is the reflection of $y = f(x)$ in the x-axis.

3 a i $f(x) = 2x + 1$
$\therefore f(-x) = 2(-x) + 1$
$= -2x + 1$

  ii $f(x) = x^2 + 2x + 1$
$\therefore f(-x) = (-x)^2 + 2(-x) + 1$
$= x^2 - 2x + 1$

  iii $f(x) = |x - 3|$
$\therefore f(-x) = |-x - 3|$
$= |x + 3|$

  b i graph showing $y = 2x + 1$ and $y = -2x + 1$
  ii graph showing $y = x^2 + 2x + 1$ and $y = x^2 - 2x + 1$
  iii graph showing $y = |-x - 3|$ and $y = |x - 3|$

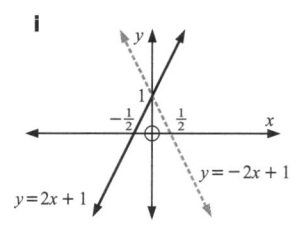

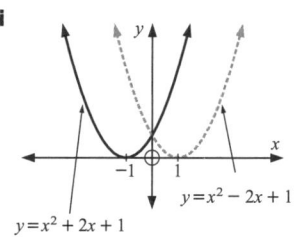

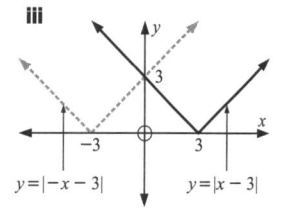

4 $y = f(-x)$ is the reflection of $y = f(x)$ in the y-axis.

5 a To transform $y = f(x)$ to $g(x) = -f(x)$, we reflect $y = f(x)$ in the x-axis. To do this we keep the x-coordinates the same and take the negative of the y-coordinates.

  i $(3, 0)$ is transformed to $(3, 0)$
  ii $(2, -1)$ is transformed to $(2, 1)$
  iii $(-3, 2)$ is transformed to $(-3, -2)$

  b To find the points on $f(x)$ corresponding to $g(x)$, we again take the negative of the y-coordinates.

  i The point transformed to $(7, -1)$ is $(7, 1)$.
  ii The point transformed to $(-5, 0)$ is $(-5, 0)$.
  iii The point transformed to $(-3, -2)$ is $(-3, 2)$.

6 a To transform $y = f(x)$ to $h(x) = f(-x)$, we reflect $y = f(x)$ in the y-axis.
To do this we keep the y-coordinates the same and take the negative of the x-coordinates.
i $(2, -1)$ is transformed to $(-2, -1)$. **ii** $(0, 3)$ is transformed to $(0, 3)$.
iii $(-1, 2)$ is transformed to $(1, 2)$.

b To find the points on $f(x)$ corresponding to $h(x)$, we again take the negative of the x-coordinates.
i The point transformed to $(5, -4)$ is $(-5, -4)$.
ii The point transformed to $(0, 3)$ is $(0, 3)$.
iii The point transformed to $(2, 3)$ is $(-2, 3)$.

7 a $f(x)$ is reflected in the y-axis, then reflected in the x-axis. This has the effect of rotating the point about the origin through $180°$.

b The point (a, b) is transformed to the point $(-a, -b)$.
i $(3, -7)$ is transformed to $(-3, 7)$.
ii The point that transforms to $(-5, -1)$ is $(5, 1)$.

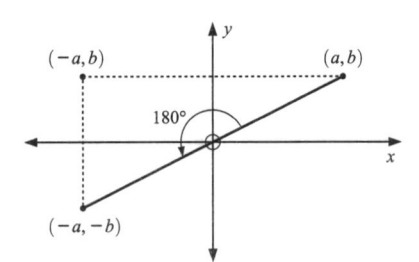

EXERCISE 5B.4

1 $y = -f(x)$ is obtained from $y = f(x)$ by reflecting it in the x-axis.

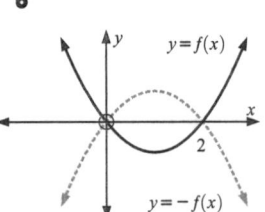

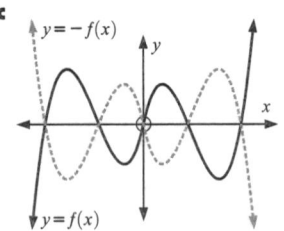

2 $y = f(-x)$ is obtained from $y = f(x)$ by reflecting it in the y-axis.

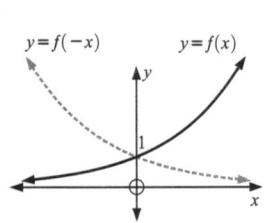

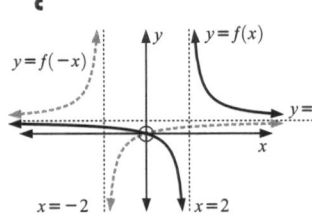

3 $y = 2x^4$ and $y = 6x^4$ are 'thinner' than $y = x^4$ and $y = \frac{1}{2}x^4$ is 'fatter'
$\therefore$ **a** is A, **b** is B, **c** is D and **d** is C

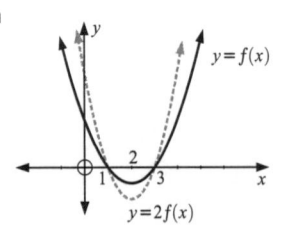

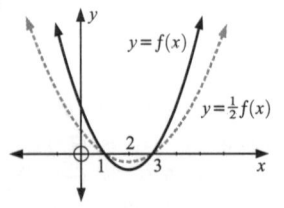

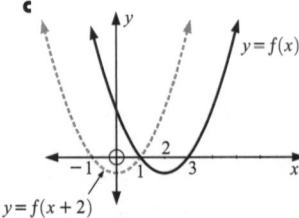

4

d [Graph showing $y=f(x)$ and $y=f(2x)$ with points 1, 2, 3]

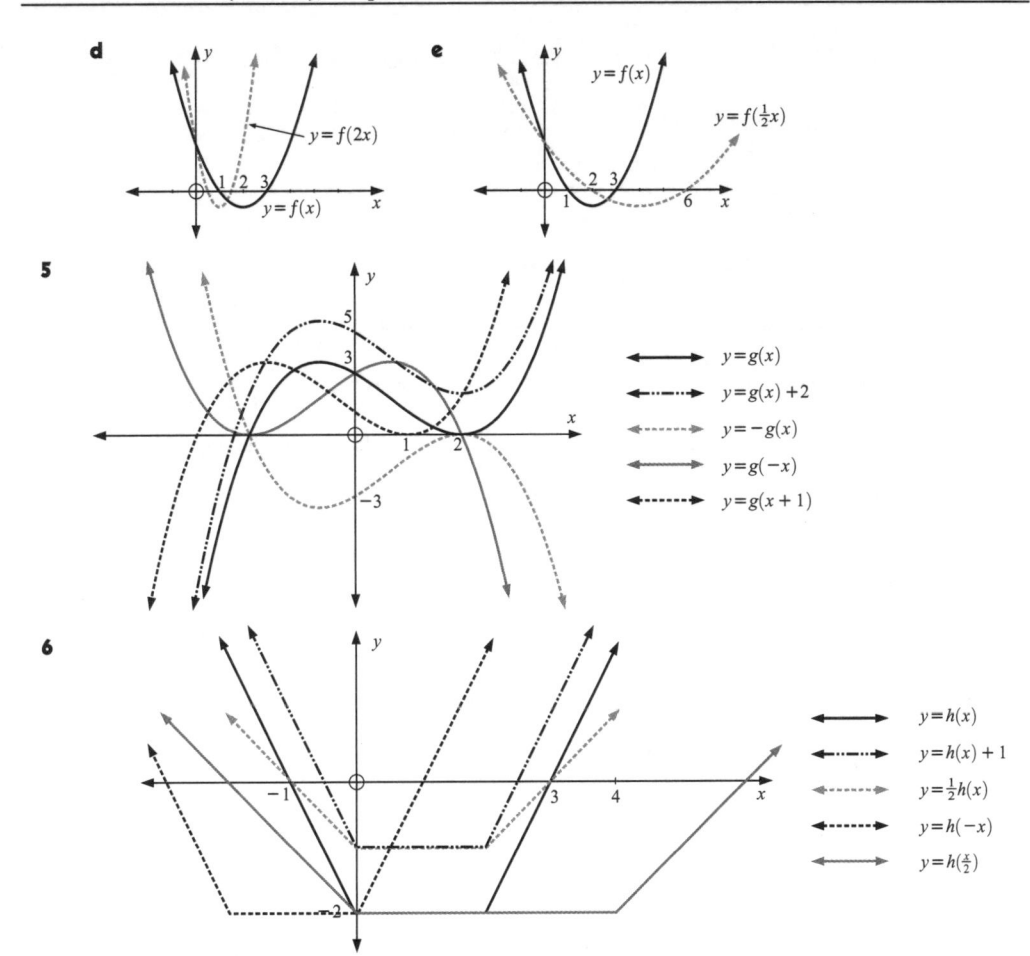

e [Graph showing $y=f(x)$ and $y=f(\tfrac{1}{2}x)$ with points 2, 3, 6]

5 [Graph showing $y=g(x)$, $y=g(x)+2$, $y=-g(x)$, $y=g(-x)$, $y=g(x+1)$]

6 [Graph showing $y=h(x)$, $y=h(x)+1$, $y=\tfrac{1}{2}h(x)$, $y=h(-x)$, $y=h(\tfrac{x}{2})$]

EXERCISE 5C

1 a i Under a vertical stretch of factor $\tfrac{1}{2}$, $y = \dfrac{1}{x}$ becomes $y = \tfrac{1}{2}\left(\dfrac{1}{x}\right)$. $\therefore\ y = \dfrac{1}{2x}$

  ii Under a horizontal stretch of factor 3, $y = \dfrac{1}{x}$ becomes $y = \dfrac{1}{\left(\tfrac{x}{3}\right)}$. $\therefore\ y = \dfrac{3}{x}$

  iii Under a horizontal translation of -3, $y = \dfrac{1}{x}$ becomes $y = \dfrac{1}{x+3}$.

  iv Under a vertical translation of 4, $y = \dfrac{1}{x}$ becomes $y = \dfrac{1}{x} + 4$. $\therefore\ y = \dfrac{4x+1}{x}$

  v Under all four transformations,

  $\dfrac{1}{x}$ becomes $\dfrac{1}{2x}$ becomes $\dfrac{1}{2\left(\tfrac{x}{3}\right)}$ or $\dfrac{3}{2x}$, which becomes $\dfrac{3}{2(x+3)}$.

  So, finally $y = \dfrac{3}{2(x+3)} + 4 = \dfrac{3 + 8(x+3)}{2x+6} = \dfrac{8x+27}{2x+6}$

b From $y = \dfrac{3}{2(x+3)} + 4$ we see that y is undefined when $x+3=0$ or $x=-3$

  $\therefore$ VA is $x=-3$.   Domain is $\{x \mid x \in \mathbb{R},\ x \neq -3\}$

  Also, if $y=4$, $\dfrac{3}{2(x+3)} = 0$ which is not possible as $3 \neq 0$

  $\therefore\ y=4$ is the HA.   Range is $\{y \mid y \in \mathbb{R},\ y \neq 4\}$

2 a i $y = \dfrac{2x+4}{x-1}$

$= \dfrac{2(x-1)+6}{x-1}$

$= 2 + \dfrac{6}{x-1}$

$2 + \dfrac{6}{x-1}$ is undefined when $x = 1$.

As $|x| \to \infty$, $f(x) \to 2$.

$\therefore$ VA is $x = 1$, HA is $y = 2$.

ii To get $y = \dfrac{2x+4}{x-1} = 2 + \dfrac{6}{x-1}$ from $y = \dfrac{1}{x}$

we vertically stretch by factor 6 $\quad \{\dfrac{1}{x}$ becomes $6\left(\dfrac{1}{x}\right) = \dfrac{6}{x}\}$

then translate by $\binom{1}{2}$ $\quad \{\dfrac{6}{x}$ becomes $2 + \dfrac{6}{x-1}\}$.

To transform $y = 2 + \dfrac{6}{x-1}$ to give $y = \dfrac{1}{x}$ we do the opposite.

So, we translate by $\binom{-1}{-2}$, then vertically stretch by factor $\tfrac{1}{6}$.

b i $y = \dfrac{3x-2}{x+1}$

$= \dfrac{3(x+1)-5}{x+1}$

$= 3 - \dfrac{5}{x+1}$

$3 - \dfrac{5}{x+1}$ is undefined when $x = -1$.

As $|x| \to \infty$, $f(x) \to 3$.

$\therefore$ VA is $x = -1$, HA is $y = 3$.

ii To get $y = \dfrac{3x-2}{x+1} = 3 - \dfrac{5}{x+1}$ from $y = \dfrac{1}{x}$

we vertically stretch by factor 5 $\quad \{\dfrac{1}{x}$ becomes $\dfrac{5}{x}\}$,

reflect in the x-axis $\quad \{\dfrac{5}{x}$ becomes $-\dfrac{5}{x}\}$,

then translate by $\binom{-1}{3}$ $\quad \{-\dfrac{5}{x}$ becomes $3 - \dfrac{5}{x+1}\}$.

To transform $y = 3 - \dfrac{5}{x+1}$ to give $y = \dfrac{1}{x}$ we do the opposite.

So, we translate by $\binom{1}{-3}$, reflect in the x-axis, then vertically stretch by factor $\tfrac{1}{5}$.

c i $y = \dfrac{2x+1}{2-x}$

$= \dfrac{-2(2-x)+5}{2-x}$

$= -2 + \dfrac{5}{2-x}$

$-2 + \dfrac{5}{2-x}$ is undefined when $x = 2$.

As $|x| \to \infty$, $f(x) \to -2$.

$\therefore$ VA is $x = 2$, HA is $y = -2$.

ii To get $y = \dfrac{2x+1}{2-x} = -2 + \dfrac{5}{2-x} = -2 - \dfrac{5}{x-2}$ from $y = \dfrac{1}{x}$

we vertically stretch by factor 5 $\quad \{\dfrac{1}{x}$ becomes $\dfrac{5}{x}\}$,

reflect in the x-axis $\quad \{\dfrac{5}{x}$ becomes $-\dfrac{5}{x}\}$,

then translate by $\binom{2}{-2}$ $\quad \{-\dfrac{5}{x}$ becomes $-2 - \dfrac{5}{x-2}\}$.

To transform $y = -2 - \dfrac{5}{x-2}$ to give $y = \dfrac{1}{x}$ we do the opposite.

So, we translate by $\binom{-2}{2}$, reflect in the x-axis, then vertically stretch by factor $\tfrac{1}{5}$.

3 a i $y = \dfrac{2x+3}{x+1}$

$\therefore y = \dfrac{2(x+1)+1}{x+1}$

$\therefore y = 2 + \dfrac{1}{x+1}$

VA is $x = -1$,
HA is $y = 2$

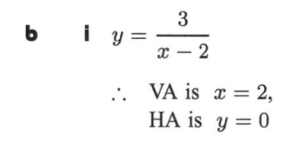

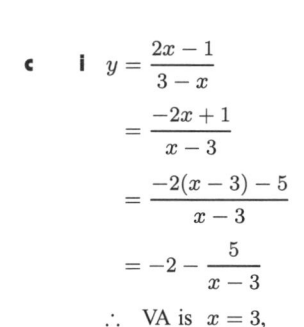

ii Cuts x-axis when $y = 0$
$\therefore 2x + 3 = 0$
$\therefore x = -\tfrac{3}{2}$
$\therefore x$-intercept is $-\tfrac{3}{2}$
Cuts y-axis when $x = 0$
$\therefore y = \tfrac{3}{1} = 3$
$\therefore y$-intercept is 3

iii As $x \to -1$ (from left), $y \to -\infty$
As $x \to -1$ (from right), $y \to \infty$
As $x \to -\infty$, $y \to 2$ (from below)
As $x \to \infty$, $y \to 2$ (from above)

iv [graph with $x = -1$, $y = 2$, intercepts $-\tfrac{3}{2}$ and 3]

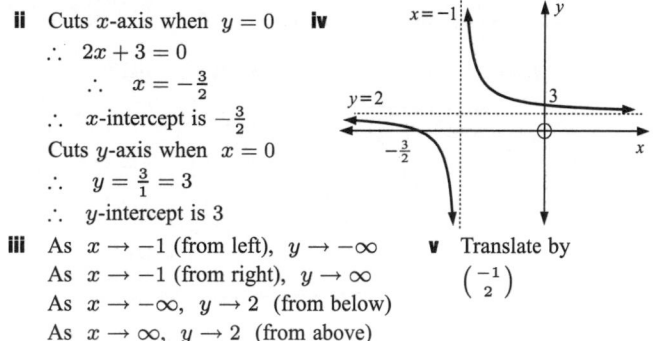

v Translate by $\begin{pmatrix} -1 \\ 2 \end{pmatrix}$

b i $y = \dfrac{3}{x-2}$

$\therefore$ VA is $x = 2$,
HA is $y = 0$

ii Cuts x-axis when $y = 0$
$\therefore \dfrac{3}{x-2} = 0$
which is not possible.
$\therefore$ no x-intercept
Cuts y-axis when $x = 0$
$\therefore y = \tfrac{3}{-2} = -1\tfrac{1}{2}$
$\therefore y$-intercept is $-1\tfrac{1}{2}$

iii As $x \to 2$ (from left), $y \to -\infty$
As $x \to 2$ (from right), $y \to \infty$
As $x \to \infty$, $y \to 0$ (from above)
As $x \to -\infty$, $y \to 0$ (from below)

iv [graph with $x = 2$, intercept $-1\tfrac{1}{2}$]

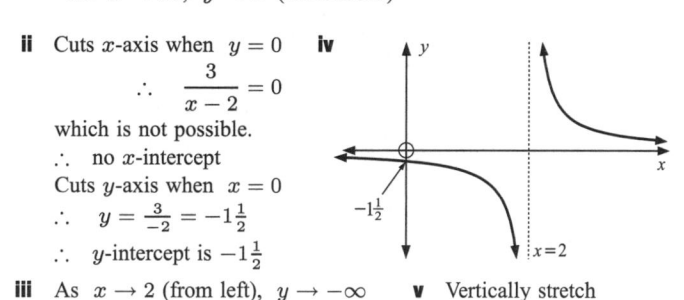

v Vertically stretch with factor 3, then translate by $\begin{pmatrix} 2 \\ 0 \end{pmatrix}$.

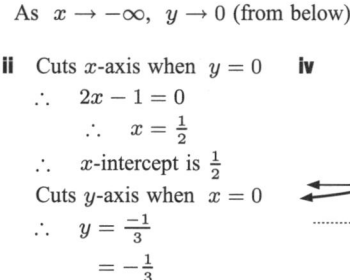

c i $y = \dfrac{2x-1}{3-x}$

$= \dfrac{-2x+1}{x-3}$

$= \dfrac{-2(x-3)-5}{x-3}$

$= -2 - \dfrac{5}{x-3}$

$\therefore$ VA is $x = 3$,
HA is $y = -2$

ii Cuts x-axis when $y = 0$
$\therefore 2x - 1 = 0$
$\therefore x = \tfrac{1}{2}$
$\therefore x$-intercept is $\tfrac{1}{2}$
Cuts y-axis when $x = 0$
$\therefore y = \tfrac{-1}{3}$
$= -\tfrac{1}{3}$
$\therefore y$-intercept is $-\tfrac{1}{3}$

iii As $x \to 3$ (from left), $y \to \infty$
As $x \to 3$ (from right), $y \to -\infty$
As $x \to -\infty$, $y \to -2$ (from above)
As $x \to \infty$, $y \to -2$ (from below)

iv [graph with $x = 3$, $y = -2$, intercepts $\tfrac{1}{2}$ and $-\tfrac{1}{3}$]

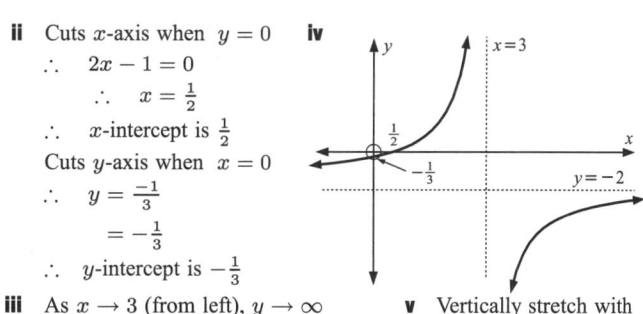

v Vertically stretch with factor 5, reflect in x-axis, then translate by $\begin{pmatrix} 3 \\ -2 \end{pmatrix}$.

d i $y = \dfrac{5x-1}{2x+1}$

$= \dfrac{\tfrac{5}{2}x - \tfrac{1}{2}}{x + \tfrac{1}{2}}$

$= \dfrac{\tfrac{5}{2}\left(x + \tfrac{1}{2}\right) - \tfrac{7}{4}}{x + \tfrac{1}{2}}$

$= \tfrac{5}{2} - \dfrac{\tfrac{7}{4}}{x + \tfrac{1}{2}}$

$\therefore$ VA is $x = -\tfrac{1}{2}$,
HA is $y = \tfrac{5}{2}$

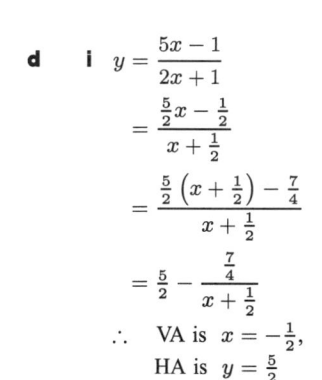

ii Cuts x-axis when $y = 0$
$\therefore 5x - 1 = 0$
$\therefore x = \tfrac{1}{5}$
$\therefore x$-intercept is $\tfrac{1}{5}$
Cuts y-axis when $x = 0$
$\therefore y = \tfrac{-1}{1}$
$= -1$
$\therefore y$-intercept is -1

iii As $x \to -\tfrac{1}{2}$ (from left), $y \to \infty$
As $x \to -\tfrac{1}{2}$ (from right), $y \to -\infty$
As $x \to \infty$, $y \to 2\tfrac{1}{2}$ (from below)
As $x \to -\infty$, $y \to 2\tfrac{1}{2}$ (from above)

iv [graph with $x = -\tfrac{1}{2}$, $y = 2\tfrac{1}{2}$, intercepts $\tfrac{1}{5}$ and -1]

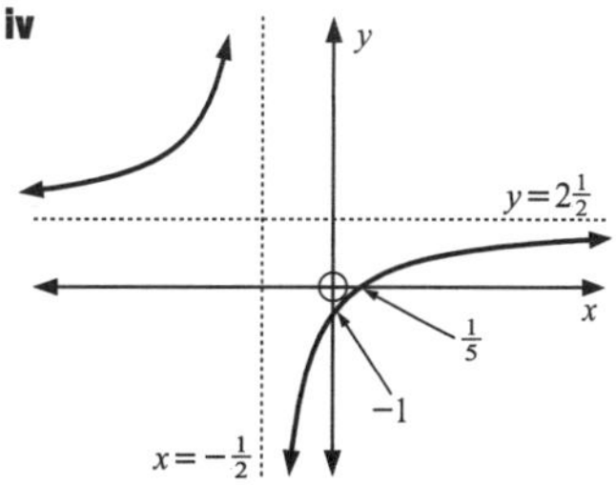

v Vertically stretch with factor $\tfrac{7}{4}$, reflect in x-axis, then translate by $\begin{pmatrix} -\tfrac{1}{2} \\ \tfrac{5}{2} \end{pmatrix}$.

4 $N = 20 + \dfrac{100}{t+2}$ weeds per hectare

a When $t=0$,
$N = 20 + \frac{100}{2}$
$= 20 + 50$
$= 70$ weeds/ha

b When $t=8$,
$N = 20 + \frac{100}{10}$
$= 20 + 10$
$= 30$ weeds/ha

c When $N = 40$,
$20 + \dfrac{100}{t+2} = 40$
$\therefore \dfrac{100}{t+2} = 20$
$\therefore t+2 = 5$
$\therefore t = 3$ days

d [Graph of $N = 20 + \dfrac{100}{t+2}$, with horizontal asymptote at $N = 20$, shown with t-axis marked at 20, 40, 60, 80.]

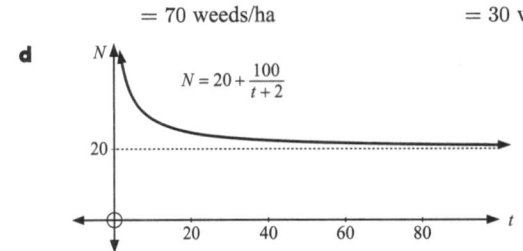

e No, the number of weeds per hectare will approach 20 (from above).

EXERCISE 5D.1

1 **a** [Graphs of $y = -x^2$ and $y = \frac{-1}{x^2}$ with invariant points $(-1,-1)$ and $(1,-1)$.]

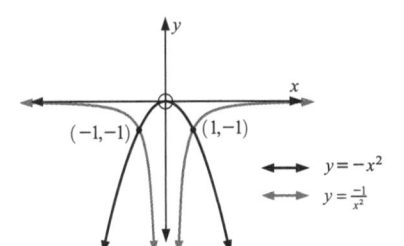

b [Graphs of $y = (x-1)(x-3)$ and $y = \dfrac{1}{(x-1)(x-3)}$.]

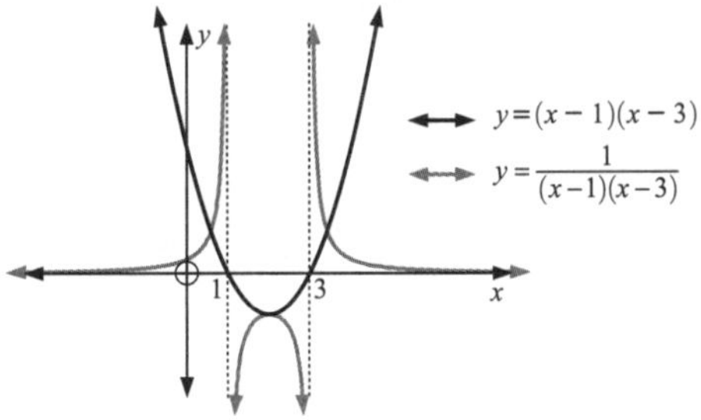

2 Notice that $f(x) = \dfrac{1}{f(x)}$ when $y = \dfrac{1}{y}$ $\therefore$ $y^2 = 1$ $\therefore$ $y = \pm 1$.

For **1 a**: When $y = 1$, $-x^2 = 1$ which has no real solutions
When $y = -1$, $-x^2 = -1$ $\therefore$ $x^2 = 1$ $\therefore$ $x = \pm 1$
So invariant points are $(1, -1)$ and $(-1, -1)$.

For **1 b**: When $y = 1$, $(x-1)(x-3) = 1$
$\therefore x^2 - 4x + 3 = 1$
$\therefore x^2 - 4x + 2 = 0$
$\therefore x = \dfrac{4 \pm \sqrt{8}}{2} = 2 \pm \sqrt{2}$

When $y = -1$, $(x-1)(x-3) = -1$
$\therefore x^2 - 4x + 3 = -1$
$\therefore x^2 - 4x + 4 = 0$
$\therefore (x-2)^2 = 0$
$\therefore x = 2$

$\therefore$ invariant points are $(2 - \sqrt{2}, 1)$, $(2, -1)$, $(2 + \sqrt{2}, 1)$

EXERCISE 5D.2

1 **a** [Graphs of $y = x(x+2)$ and $y = |f(x)|$.]

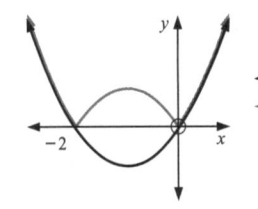

b [Graphs of $y = x(x+2)$ and $y = f(|x|)$.]

2 **a** [Graphs of $f(x)$ and $\dfrac{1}{f(x)}$.]

b [Graphs of $f(x)$ and $\dfrac{1}{f(x)}$ with points $(1\tfrac{1}{2}, -\tfrac{1}{2})$ and $(1\tfrac{1}{2}, -2)$.]

c [Graphs of $f(x)$ and $\dfrac{1}{f(x)}$ with asymptotes $y = 1$ and $x = 4$.]

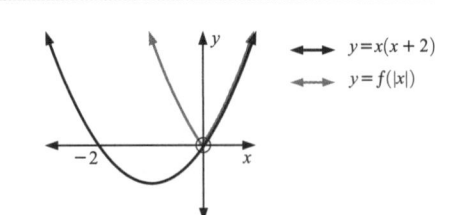

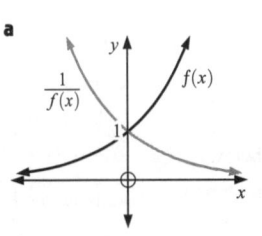

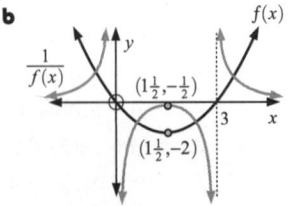

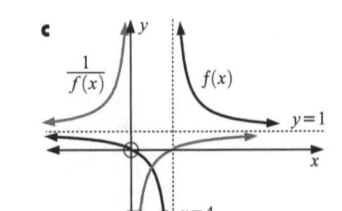

3 a, b, 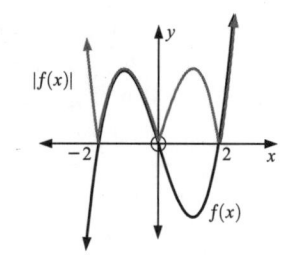 c (graphs)

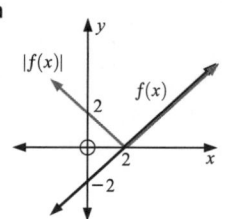

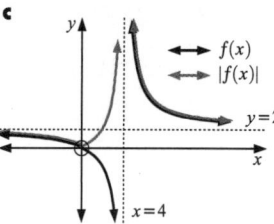

4 a, 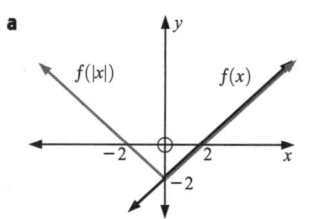 b, 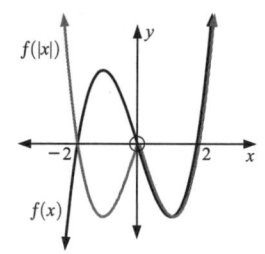 c (graphs)

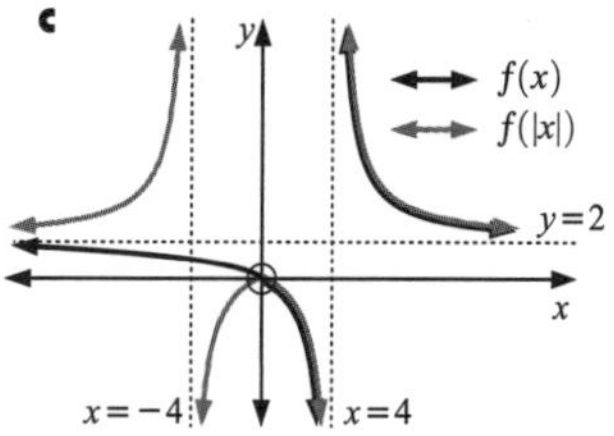

5 To transform $f(x)$ to $|f(x)|$, the point (a, b) on $f(x)$ is transformed to $(a, |b|)$.

    a $(3, 0)$ is transformed to $(3, 0)$ **b** $(5, -2)$ is transformed to $(5, 2)$

    c $(0, 7)$ is transformed to $(0, 7)$ **d** $(2, 2)$ is transformed to $(2, 2)$

6   **a** For any point (a, b), $a \geqslant 0$, on $f(x)$, (a, b) is also a point on $f(|x|)$, and (a, b) is also transformed to $(-a, b)$.

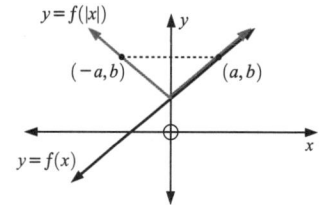

    i $(0, 3)$ is transformed to $(0, 3)$

    ii $(1, 3)$ is transformed to $(1, 3)$ and $(-1, 3)$

    iii $(7, -4)$ is transformed to $(7, -4)$ and $(-7, -4)$

  b The point (a, b) on $f(|x|)$ has been transformed by the point $(|a|, b)$ on $f(x)$.

    i $(0, 3)$ has been transformed from $(0, 3)$

    ii $(-1, 3)$ has been transformed from $(1, 3)$

    iii $(10, -8)$ has been transformed from $(10, -8)$

REVIEW SET 5A

1 $f(x) = x^2 - 2x$

  a $f(3)$ **b** $f(-2)$ **c** $f(2x)$

     $= 3^2 - 2(3)$ $= (-2)^2 - 2(-2)$ $= (2x)^2 - 2(2x)$

     $= 9 - 6$ $= 4 + 4$ $= 4x^2 - 4x$

     $= 3$ $= 8$

  d $f(-x)$ **e** $3f(x) - 2$

     $= (-x)^2 - 2(-x)$ $= 3(x^2 - 2x) - 2$

     $= x^2 + 2x$ $= 3x^2 - 6x - 2$

2 $f(x) = 5 - x - x^2$

  a $f(4)$ **b** $f(-1)$ **c** $f(x - 1)$

     $= 5 - 4 - 4^2$ $= 5 - (-1) - (-1)^2$ $= 5 - (x - 1) - (x - 1)^2$

     $= 1 - 16$ $= 5 + 1 - 1$ $= 5 - x + 1 - [x^2 - 2x + 1]$

     $= -15$ $= 5$ $= 6 - x - x^2 + 2x - 1$

                                                                                        $= -x^2 + x + 5$

d $f\left(\frac{x}{2}\right)$
$= 5 - \left(\frac{x}{2}\right) - \left(\frac{x}{2}\right)^2$
$= 5 - \frac{x}{2} - \frac{x^2}{4}$

e $2f(x) - f(-x)$
$= 2(5 - x - x^2) - \left[5 - (-x) - (-x)^2\right]$
$= 10 - 2x - 2x^2 - [5 + x - x^2]$
$= 10 - 2x - 2x^2 - 5 - x + x^2$
$= -x^2 - 3x + 5$

3

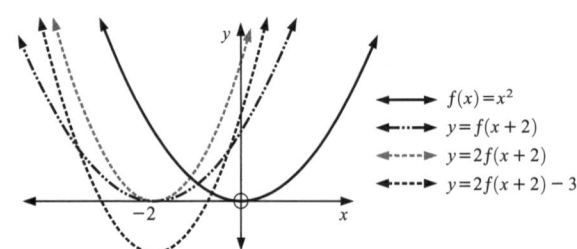

$\longleftrightarrow f(x) = x^2$
$\longleftarrow\cdots\longrightarrow y = f(x+2)$
$\longleftarrow\cdots\cdots\longrightarrow y = 2f(x+2)$
$\longleftarrow\cdot\cdot\cdot\cdot\longrightarrow y = 2f(x+2) - 3$

4 $f(x) = 3x^3 - 2x^2 + x + 2$

If $g(x)$ is $f(x)$ translated $\begin{pmatrix}1\\-2\end{pmatrix}$, then $g(x) = f(x-1) - 2$
$= 3(x-1)^3 - 2(x-1)^2 + (x-1) + 2 - 2$
$= 3(x^3 - 3x^2 + 3x - 1) - 2(x^2 - 2x + 1) + x - 1$
$= 3x^3 - 9x^2 + 9x - 3 - 2x^2 + 4x - 2 + x - 1$
$\therefore\ g(x) = 3x^3 - 11x^2 + 14x - 6$

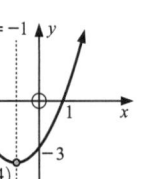

5 a

$y = (x+1)^2 - 4$
$V(-1, -4)$

b i When $y = 0$,
$(x+1)^2 - 4 = 0$
$\therefore\ (x+1)^2 = 4$
$\therefore\ x + 1 = \pm 2$
$\therefore\ x = 2 - 1$ or $-2 - 1$
$\therefore\ x = 1$ or -3
$\therefore\ x$-intercepts are $1, -3$

ii When $x = 0$,
$y = 1^2 - 4$
$= -3$
$\therefore\ y$-intercept is -3

c $y = (x+1)^2 - 4$ is obtained from $y = x^2$ under a translation of $\begin{pmatrix}-1\\-4\end{pmatrix}$. So, the vertex must be $(-1, -4)$.

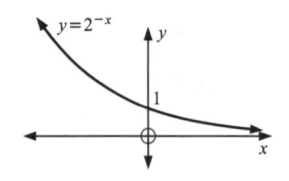

6 a

$y = 2^{-x}$

b i $x \to \infty$ means x is very large and positive.
We see the graph approaching the x-axis
$\therefore\ y \to 0\ \therefore$ **true**.

ii $x \to -\infty$ means x is very large and negative.
We see the graph heading for ∞
$\therefore$ statement is **false**.

iii When $x = 0$, $y = 2^0 = 1 \neq \frac{1}{2}\ \therefore$ **false**.

iv The graph is above the x-axis for all $x\ \therefore\ 2^{-x} > 0$ for all $x\ \therefore$ **true**.

7 So that you can see the answers more easily, they have been drawn on two graphs.

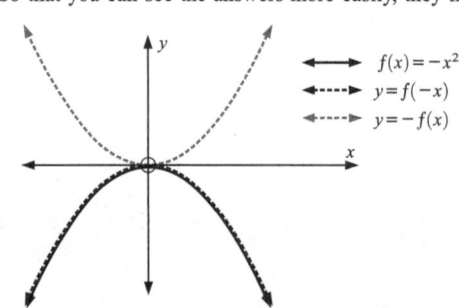

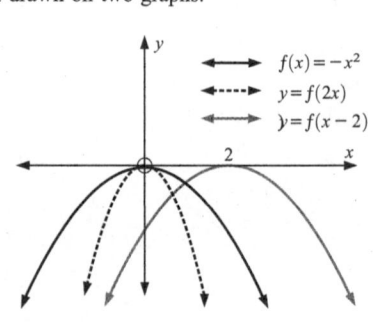

$\longleftrightarrow f(x) = -x^2$
$\longleftarrow\cdots\longrightarrow y = f(-x)$
$\longleftarrow\cdots\cdots\longrightarrow y = -f(x)$

$\longleftrightarrow f(x) = -x^2$
$\longleftarrow\cdots\longrightarrow y = f(2x)$
$\longleftrightarrow y = f(x-2)$

8

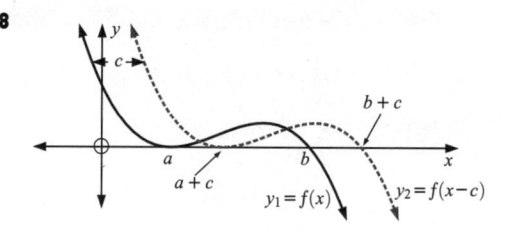

y_2 is obtained by shifting y_1 c units to the right.

9 a

b When $x = 0$,
$$\frac{1}{f(x)} = \frac{1}{f(0)}$$
$$= \frac{1}{1}$$
$$= 1$$

$\therefore$ the y-intercept of $\dfrac{1}{f(x)}$ is 1

c Invariant points for $\dfrac{1}{f(x)}$ occur

when $f(x) = \pm 1$.
$f(x) = -1$ for all $x \in [2, 3]$
$f(x) = 1$ when $x = 0$ and at point P.
To find the point P where $f(x) = 1$,

note that the gradient of $[AB] = \dfrac{2 - (-1)}{4 - 3} = 3$,

so $\dfrac{2 - 1}{4 - x} = 3$

$\therefore \quad 1 = 12 - 3x$
$\therefore \quad 3x = 11$
$\therefore \quad x = \dfrac{11}{3}$

$\therefore$ $f(x)$ is invariant for $\dfrac{1}{f(x)}$ at $(0, 1)$, $(\dfrac{11}{3}, 1)$, and all the points on $y = -1$, $x \in [2, 3]$.

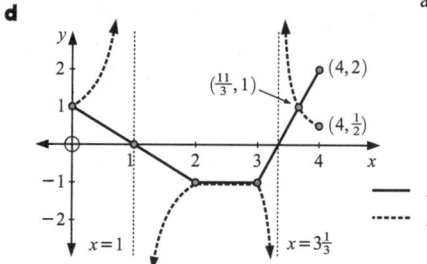

d

10 a $f(x) = x + 2$
stretching $f(x)$ vertically by a factor of 2 becomes $\quad 2f(x) = 2x + 4$
compressing the function horizontally by a factor of 2 becomes $\quad 2f(2x) = 2(2x) + 4$
$= 4x + 4$

translating $\frac{1}{2}$ horizontally and -3 vertically, the function becomes $\quad 4(x - \frac{1}{2}) + 4 - 3$
$= 4x - 2 + 1$
$\therefore \quad F(x) = 4x - 1$

b i $(1, 3) \to (1, 6) \to (\frac{1}{2}, 6) \to (1, 6) \to (1, 3)$
$\therefore$ $(1, 3)$ remains invariant under the transformation.
ii $(0, 2) \to (0, 4) \to (0, 4) \to (\frac{1}{2}, 4) \to (\frac{1}{2}, 1)$ $\therefore$ $(0, 2)$ transforms to $(\frac{1}{2}, 1)$.
$(-1, 1) \to (-1, 2) \to (-\frac{1}{2}, 2) \to (0, 2) \to (0, -1)$ $\therefore$ $(-1, 1)$ transforms to $(0, -1)$.
iii When $x = \frac{1}{2}$, $F(x) = 4(\frac{1}{2}) - 1 = 1$ $\therefore$ $(\frac{1}{2}, 1)$ lies on $F(x)$.
When $x = 0$, $F(x) = 4(0) - 1 = -1$ $\therefore$ $(0, -1)$ lies on $F(x)$.

11 $f(x) = x^2$ is first reflected in the x-axis to become $\quad -f(x) = -x^2$
The function is then translated by $\begin{pmatrix} -3 \\ 2 \end{pmatrix}$ to become $\quad -f(x + 3) + 2 = -(x + 3)^2 + 2$
$= -(x^2 + 6x + 9) + 2$
$\therefore \quad g(x) = -x^2 - 6x - 7$

REVIEW SET 5B

1 $f(x) = \dfrac{4}{x}$

a $f(-4)$
$= \dfrac{4}{-4}$
$= -1$

b $f(2x)$
$= \dfrac{4}{2x}$
$= \dfrac{2}{x}$

c $f\left(\dfrac{x}{2}\right)$
$= \dfrac{4}{\frac{x}{2}}$
$= 4 \times \dfrac{2}{x}$
$= \dfrac{8}{x}$

d $4f(x+2) - 3$
$= 4\left(\dfrac{4}{x+2}\right) - 3$
$= \dfrac{16}{x+2} - 3$

$\left(\text{or } \dfrac{16 - 3(x+2)}{x+2} = \dfrac{10 - 3x}{x+2}\right)$

2 a

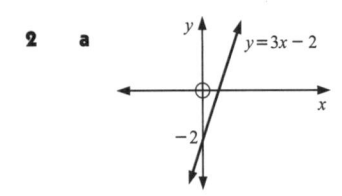

[Graph of $y = 3x - 2$ with x-intercept and y-intercept at -2]

b i When $y = 0$,
$3x - 2 = 0$
$\therefore x = \dfrac{2}{3}$
$\therefore x$-intercept is $\dfrac{2}{3}$

ii When $x = 0$,
$y = 0 - 2 = -2$
$\therefore y$-intercept is -2

iii As $y = 3x - 2$, the slope is 3 {coefficient of x}

c i When $x = 0.3$,
$y = 3(0.3) - 2$
$= 0.9 - 2$
$= -1.1$

ii When $y = 0.7$,
$3x - 2 = 0.7$
$\therefore 3x = 2.7$
$\therefore x = 0.9$

3 $|x - a| = \begin{cases} x - a, & x \geqslant a \\ -x + a, & x < a \end{cases}$ and $|x| - a = \begin{cases} x - a, & x \geqslant 0 \\ -x - a, & x < 0 \end{cases}$

$\therefore |x - a| = |x| - a$ when $x \geqslant a$ and $x \geqslant 0$ {both $= x - a$}
$\therefore$ when $x \geqslant a$ $\{a > 0\}$

4

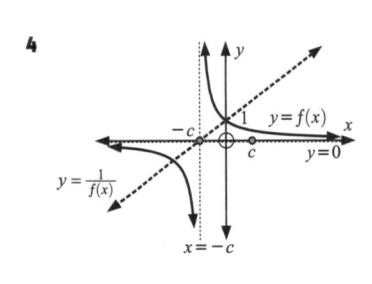

[Graph showing $y = f(x)$, $y = \dfrac{1}{f(x)}$, with $x = -c$ vertical asymptote and $y = 0$ horizontal asymptote]

a $f(x) = \dfrac{c}{x + c}$ has a VA $x = -c$ $\{f(x)$ is undefined$\}$

and a HA $y = 0$ {as $|x| \to \infty$, $f(x) \to 0$}

$f(0) = \dfrac{c}{0 + c} = 1$ $\therefore$ the y-intercept is 1

There are no x-intercepts $\{\dfrac{c}{x+c} \neq 0$ for $c > 0\}$

b $\dfrac{1}{f(x)} = \dfrac{x+c}{c}$

$\dfrac{1}{f(0)} = \dfrac{0+c}{c} = 1$ $\therefore$ the y-intercept of $\dfrac{1}{f(x)}$ is 1

$\dfrac{1}{f(x)} = 0$ when $x + c = 0$ or $x = -c$

$\therefore$ the x-intercept of $\dfrac{1}{f(x)}$ is $-c$.

5

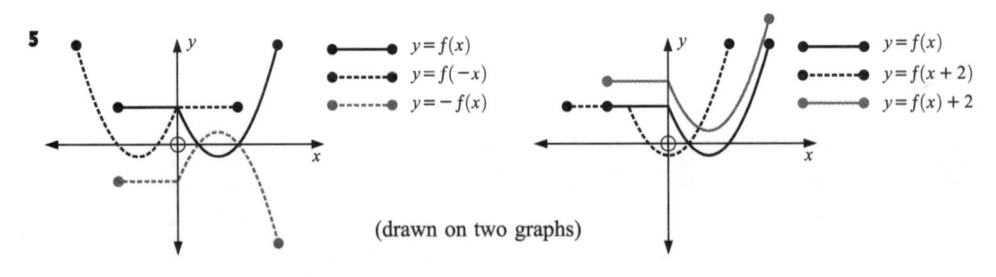

[Two graphs: first showing $y = f(x)$, $y = f(-x)$, $y = -f(x)$; second showing $y = f(x)$, $y = f(x+2)$, $y = f(x) + 2$]

(drawn on two graphs)

6 **a**

$y = f(x)$, $y = 1$, $(2,-2)$, $(4,-1)$, $x=2$, $x=4$, $x=6$, $y = f(x-2)+1$

b

$y = \dfrac{1}{f(x)}$, $y = f(x)$, $(2,-\tfrac{1}{2})$, $(2,-2)$, $x=4$

c

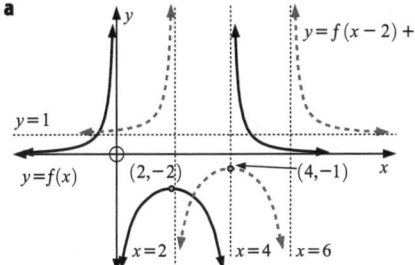

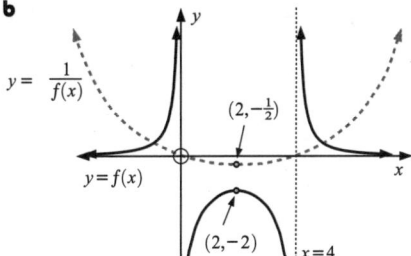

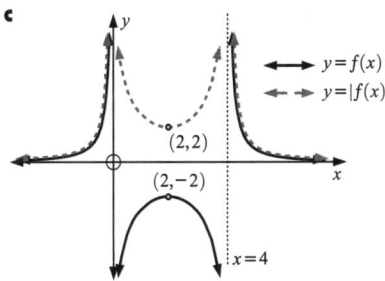

$y = f(x)$, $y = |f(x)|$, $(2,2)$, $(2,-2)$, $x=4$

7 **a** $y = \dfrac{1}{x}$ under a reflection in the y-axis becomes $y = \dfrac{1}{(-x)} = -\dfrac{1}{x}$

$y = -\dfrac{1}{x}$ under a vertical stretch of factor 3 becomes $y = 3\left(-\dfrac{1}{x}\right) = -\dfrac{3}{x}$

$y = -\dfrac{3}{x}$ under a horizontal compression of factor 2 becomes $y = \dfrac{-3}{(2x)} = \dfrac{-3}{2x}$

$y = -\dfrac{3}{2x}$ under a translation of $\binom{1}{1}$ becomes $y = 1 - \dfrac{3}{2(x-1)}$

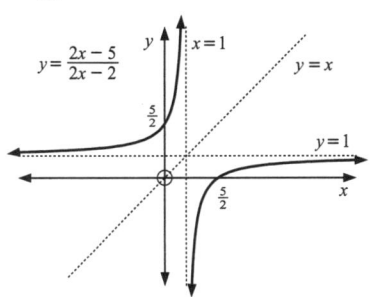

b $y = \dfrac{2x-5}{2x-2}$, $x=1$, $y=x$, $y=1$, $\tfrac{5}{2}$

$\therefore\ y = 1 - \dfrac{3}{2x-2}$

$\therefore\ y = \dfrac{(2x-2) - 3}{2x-2}$

$\therefore\ y = \dfrac{2x-5}{2x-2}$

domain of $f(x)$ is $\{x \mid x \neq 1\}$
range of $f(x)$ is $\{y \mid y \neq 1\}$

c Yes, since it is a one-to-one function (passes both the vertical and horizontal line tests).

d $f(x) = y = \dfrac{2x-5}{2x-2}$

$\therefore$ inverse function is $x = \dfrac{2y-5}{2y-2}$

So, $(2y-2)x = 2y-5$
$\therefore\ 2xy - 2x = 2y - 5$
$\therefore\ y(2x-2) = 2x-5$
$\therefore\ y = \dfrac{2x-5}{2x-2}$

$\therefore\ f^{-1}(x) = f(x) = \dfrac{2x-5}{2x-2}$

$\therefore$ it is a self-inverse function.
Also, the graph of $f(x)$ is symmetrical about the line $y = x$.

8 $y = \dfrac{2x-3}{3x+5}$

$= \dfrac{\frac{2}{3}x - 1}{x + \frac{5}{3}}$

$= \dfrac{\frac{2}{3}\left(x + \frac{5}{3}\right) - 1 - \frac{10}{9}}{x + \frac{5}{3}}$

$= \dfrac{\frac{2}{3}\left(x + \frac{5}{3}\right) - \frac{19}{9}}{x + \frac{5}{3}}$

$\therefore\ y = \dfrac{2}{3} - \dfrac{\frac{19}{9}}{\left(x + \frac{5}{3}\right)}$

$\therefore$ VA is $x = -\dfrac{5}{3}$, HA is $y = \dfrac{2}{3}$

When $x = 0$, $y = -\dfrac{3}{5}$ $\therefore$ y-intercept is $-\dfrac{3}{5}$

When $y = 0$, $2x - 3 = 0$ $\therefore$ $x = \dfrac{3}{2}$

$\therefore$ x-intercept is $\dfrac{3}{2}$

As $x \to +\infty$, $y \to \dfrac{2}{3}$ (from below)

As $x \to -\infty$, $y \to \dfrac{2}{3}$ (from above)

As $x \to -\dfrac{5}{3}$ (from the left), $y \to +\infty$

As $x \to -\dfrac{5}{3}$ (from the right), $y \to -\infty$

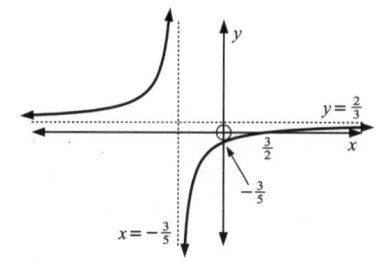

9 VA is $x = 3$, HA is $y = -2$

$\therefore$ function has form $y = -2 + \dfrac{k}{x-3}$

where k is a constant.

But $(0, 0)$ lies on the curve

$\therefore$ $0 = -2 - \dfrac{k}{3}$

$\therefore$ $\dfrac{k}{3} = -2$

$\therefore$ $k = -6$

$\therefore$ the curve is $y = -2 - \dfrac{6}{x-3}$

So, $y = \dfrac{-2(x-3) - 6}{x-3}$

$\therefore$ $y = \dfrac{-2x + 6 - 6}{x-3}$

$\therefore$ $y = \dfrac{-2x}{x-3}$

10 a i Under translation $\begin{pmatrix} 1 \\ -2 \end{pmatrix}$,

$y = 2^x$

becomes $y = 2^{x-1} - 2$

ii

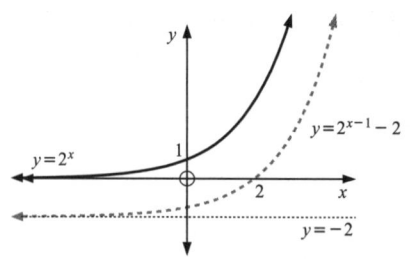

iii For $y = 2^x$, HA is $y = 0$, no VA.
For $y = 2^{x-1} - 2$, HA is $y = -2$, no VA.

iv For $y = 2^x$,
domain is $\{x \mid x \in \mathbb{R}\}$,
range is $\{y \mid y > 0\}$.
For $y = 2^{x-1} - 2$,
domain is $\{x \mid x \in \mathbb{R}\}$,
range is $\{y \mid y > -2\}$.

b i Under translation $\begin{pmatrix} 1 \\ -2 \end{pmatrix}$,

$y = \log_4 x$

becomes $y = \log_4(x - 1) - 2$

ii

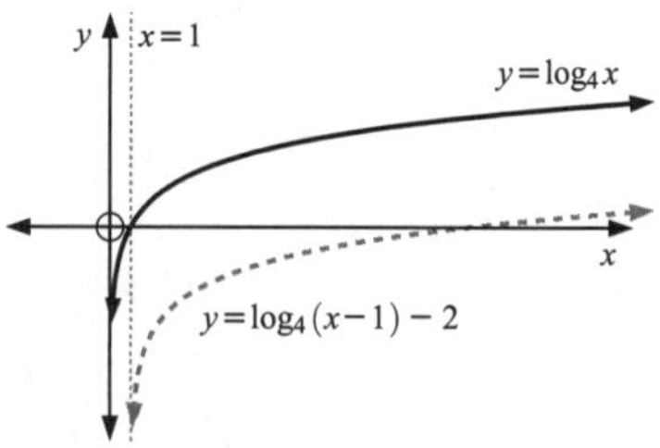

iii For $y = \log_4 x$, VA is $x = 0$, no HA.
For $y = \log_4(x - 1) - 2$, VA is $x = 1$, no HA.

iv For $y = \log_4 x$,
domain is $\{x \mid x > 0\}$,
range is $\{y \mid y \in \mathbb{R}\}$.
For $y = \log_4(x - 1) - 2$,
domain is $\{x \mid x > 1\}$,
range is $\{y \mid y \in \mathbb{R}\}$.

11 a, d

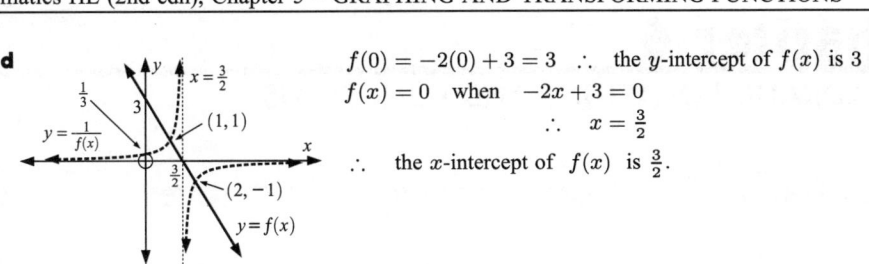

$f(0) = -2(0) + 3 = 3$ ∴ the y-intercept of $f(x)$ is 3
$f(x) = 0$ when $-2x + 3 = 0$
∴ $x = \frac{3}{2}$
∴ the x-intercept of $f(x)$ is $\frac{3}{2}$.

b The invariant points for $y = \dfrac{1}{f(x)}$ occur when $f(x) = \pm 1$

$f(x) = 1$ when $-2x + 3 = 1$ $f(x) = -1$ when $-2x + 3 = -1$
∴ $2x = 2$ ∴ $2x = 4$
∴ $x = 1$ ∴ $x = 2$
∴ the invariant points are $(1, 1)$ and $(2, -1)$.

c $\dfrac{1}{f(x)}$ is undefined when $f(x) = 0$

∴ the vertical asymptote of $y = \dfrac{1}{f(x)}$ is $x = \dfrac{3}{2}$

The y-intercept of $y = \dfrac{1}{f(x)}$ is $\dfrac{1}{f(0)} = \dfrac{1}{3}$

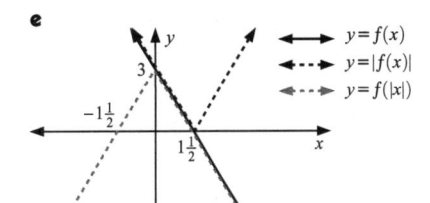

Chapter 6
QUADRATIC EQUATIONS AND FUNCTIONS

EXERCISE 6A.1

1 **a** $\quad 4x^2 + 7x = 0$
$\therefore \quad x(4x + 7) = 0$
$\therefore \quad x = 0 \text{ or } 4x + 7 = 0$
$\quad\quad$ {Null Factor law}
$\therefore \quad x = 0 \text{ or } -\frac{7}{4}$

b $\quad 6x^2 + 2x = 0$
$\therefore \quad 2x(3x + 1) = 0$
$\therefore \quad x = 0 \text{ or } 3x + 1 = 0$
$\quad\quad$ {Null Factor law}
$\therefore \quad x = 0 \text{ or } -\frac{1}{3}$

c $\quad 3x^2 - 7x = 0$
$\therefore \quad x(3x - 7) = 0$
$\therefore \quad x = 0 \text{ or } 3x - 7 = 0$
$\quad\quad$ {Null Factor law}
$\therefore \quad x = 0 \text{ or } \frac{7}{3}$

d $\quad 2x^2 - 11x = 0$
$\therefore \quad x(2x - 11) = 0$
$\therefore \quad x = 0 \text{ or } 2x - 11 = 0$
$\quad\quad$ {Null Factor law}
$\therefore \quad x = 0 \text{ or } \frac{11}{2}$

e $\quad 3x^2 = 8x$
$\therefore \quad 3x^2 - 8x = 0$
$\therefore \quad x(3x - 8) = 0$
$\therefore \quad x = 0 \text{ or } 3x - 8 = 0$
$\quad\quad$ {Null Factor law}
$\therefore \quad x = 0 \text{ or } \frac{8}{3}$

f $\quad 9x = 6x^2$
$\therefore \quad 6x^2 - 9x = 0$
$\therefore \quad 3x(2x - 3) = 0$
$\therefore \quad x = 0 \text{ or } 2x - 3 = 0$
$\quad\quad$ {Null Factor law}
$\therefore \quad x = 0 \text{ or } \frac{3}{2}$

g $\quad x^2 - 5x + 6 = 0$
$\therefore \quad (x - 2)(x - 3) = 0$
$\therefore \quad x - 2 = 0 \text{ or } x - 3 = 0$
$\quad\quad$ {Null Factor law}
$\therefore \quad x = 2 \text{ or } 3$

h $\quad x^2 = 2x + 8$
$\therefore \quad x^2 - 2x - 8 = 0$
$\therefore \quad (x - 4)(x + 2) = 0$
$\therefore \quad x - 4 = 0 \text{ or } x + 2 = 0$
$\quad\quad$ {Null Factor law}
$\therefore \quad x = -2 \text{ or } 4$

i $\quad x^2 + 21 = 10x$
$\therefore \quad x^2 - 10x + 21 = 0$
$\therefore \quad (x - 3)(x - 7) = 0$
$\therefore \quad x - 3 = 0 \text{ or } x - 7 = 0$
$\quad\quad$ {Null Factor law}
$\therefore \quad x = 3 \text{ or } 7$

j $\quad 9 + x^2 = 6x$
$\therefore \quad x^2 - 6x + 9 = 0$
$\therefore \quad (x - 3)^2 = 0$
$\therefore \quad x - 3 = 0$
$\therefore \quad x = 3$

k $\quad x^2 + x = 12$
$\therefore \quad x^2 + x - 12 = 0$
$\therefore \quad (x + 4)(x - 3) = 0$
$\therefore \quad x + 4 = 0 \text{ or } x - 3 = 0$
$\quad\quad$ {Null Factor law}
$\therefore \quad x = -4 \text{ or } 3$

l $\quad x^2 + 8x = 33$
$\therefore \quad x^2 + 8x - 33 = 0$
$\therefore \quad (x + 11)(x - 3) = 0$
$\therefore \quad x + 11 = 0 \text{ or } x - 3 = 0$
$\quad\quad$ {Null Factor law}
$\therefore \quad x = -11 \text{ or } 3$

2 **a** $\quad 9x^2 - 12x + 4 = 0$
$\therefore \quad (3x - 2)^2 = 0$
$\therefore \quad x = \frac{2}{3}$

b $\quad 2x^2 - 13x - 7 = 0$
$\therefore \quad (2x + 1)(x - 7) = 0$
$\therefore \quad x = -\frac{1}{2} \text{ or } 7$

c $\quad 3x^2 = 16x + 12$
$\therefore \quad 3x^2 - 16x - 12 = 0$
$\therefore \quad (3x + 2)(x - 6) = 0$
$\therefore \quad x = -\frac{2}{3} \text{ or } 6$

d $\quad 3x^2 + 5x = 2$
$\therefore \quad 3x^2 + 5x - 2 = 0$
$\therefore \quad (3x - 1)(x + 2) = 0$
$\therefore \quad x = \frac{1}{3} \text{ or } -2$

e $\quad 2x^2 + 3 = 5x$
$\therefore \quad 2x^2 - 5x + 3 = 0$
$\therefore \quad (2x - 3)(x - 1) = 0$
$\therefore \quad x = \frac{3}{2} \text{ or } 1$

f $\quad 3x^2 = 4x + 4$
$\therefore \quad 3x^2 - 4x - 4 = 0$
$\therefore \quad (3x + 2)(x - 2) = 0$
$\therefore \quad x = -\frac{2}{3} \text{ or } 2$

g $\quad 3x^2 = 10x + 8$
$\therefore \quad 3x^2 - 10x - 8 = 0$
$\therefore \quad (3x + 2)(x - 4) = 0$
$\therefore \quad x = -\frac{2}{3} \text{ or } 4$

h $\quad 4x^2 + 4x = 3$
$\therefore \quad 4x^2 + 4x - 3 = 0$
$\therefore \quad (2x + 3)(2x - 1) = 0$
$\therefore \quad x = -\frac{3}{2} \text{ or } \frac{1}{2}$

i $\quad 4x^2 = 11x + 3$
$\therefore \quad 4x^2 - 11x - 3 = 0$
$\therefore \quad (4x + 1)(x - 3) = 0$
$\therefore \quad x = -\frac{1}{4} \text{ or } 3$

j $\quad 12x^2 = 11x + 15$
$\therefore \quad 12x^2 - 11x - 15 = 0$
$\therefore \quad (4x + 3)(3x - 5) = 0$
$\therefore \quad x = -\frac{3}{4} \text{ or } \frac{5}{3}$

k $\quad 7x^2 + 6x = 1$
$\therefore \quad 7x^2 + 6x - 1 = 0$
$\therefore \quad (7x - 1)(x + 1) = 0$
$\therefore \quad x = \frac{1}{7} \text{ or } -1$

l $\quad 15x^2 + 2x = 56$
$\therefore \quad 15x^2 + 2x - 56 = 0$
$\therefore \quad (15x - 28)(x + 2) = 0$
$\therefore \quad x = \frac{28}{15} \text{ or } -2$

3 **a** $(x+1)^2 = 2x^2 - 5x + 11$
$\therefore \quad x^2 + 2x + 1 = 2x^2 - 5x + 11$
$\therefore \quad x^2 - 7x + 10 = 0$
$\therefore \quad (x-2)(x-5) = 0$
$\therefore \quad x = 2 \text{ or } 5$

b $(x+2)(1-x) = -4$
$\therefore \quad x - x^2 + 2 - 2x = -4$
$\therefore \quad x^2 + x - 6 = 0$
$\therefore \quad (x+3)(x-2) = 0$
$\therefore \quad x = -3 \text{ or } 2$

c $5 - 4x^2 = 3(2x+1) + 2$
$\therefore \quad 5 - 4x^2 = 6x + 3 + 2$
$\therefore \quad 4x^2 + 6x = 0$
$\therefore \quad 2x(2x+3) = 0$
$\therefore \quad x = 0 \text{ or } -\frac{3}{2}$

d $x + \dfrac{2}{x} = 3$
$\therefore \quad x^2 + 2 = 3x$
$\therefore \quad x^2 - 3x + 2 = 0$
$\therefore \quad (x-1)(x-2) = 0$
$\therefore \quad x = 1 \text{ or } 2$

e $2x - \dfrac{1}{x} = -1$
$\therefore \quad 2x^2 - 1 = -x$
$\therefore \quad 2x^2 + x - 1 = 0$
$\therefore \quad (2x-1)(x+1) = 0$
$\therefore \quad x = \tfrac{1}{2} \text{ or } -1$

f $\dfrac{x+3}{1-x} = -\dfrac{9}{x}$
$\therefore \quad x(x+3) = -9(1-x)$
$\therefore \quad x^2 + 3x = -9 + 9x$
$\therefore \quad x^2 - 6x + 9 = 0$
$\therefore \quad (x-3)^2 = 0$
$\therefore \quad x = 3$

EXERCISE 6A.2

1 **a** $(x+5)^2 = 2$
$\therefore \quad x+5 = \pm\sqrt{2}$
$\therefore \quad x = -5 \pm \sqrt{2}$

b $(x+6)^2 = -11$
has no real solutions as $(x+6)^2$ cannot be negative.

c $(x-4)^2 = 8$
$\therefore \quad x-4 = \pm\sqrt{8}$
$\therefore \quad x = 4 \pm 2\sqrt{2}$

d $(x-8)^2 = 7$
$\therefore \quad x-8 = \pm\sqrt{7}$
$\therefore \quad x = 8 \pm \sqrt{7}$

e $2(x+3)^2 = 10$
$\therefore \quad (x+3)^2 = 5$
$\therefore \quad x+3 = \pm\sqrt{5}$
$\therefore \quad x = -3 \pm \sqrt{5}$

f $3(x-2)^2 = 18$
$\therefore \quad (x-2)^2 = 6$
$\therefore \quad x-2 = \pm\sqrt{6}$
$\therefore \quad x = 2 \pm \sqrt{6}$

g $(x+1)^2 + 1 = 11$
$\therefore \quad (x+1)^2 = 10$
$\therefore \quad x+1 = \pm\sqrt{10}$
$\therefore \quad x = -1 \pm \sqrt{10}$

h $(2x+1)^2 = 3$
$\therefore \quad 2x+1 = \pm\sqrt{3}$
$\therefore \quad 2x = -1 \pm \sqrt{3}$
$\therefore \quad x = -\tfrac{1}{2} \pm \tfrac{1}{2}\sqrt{3}$

i $(1-3x)^2 - 7 = 0$
$\therefore \quad (1-3x)^2 = 7$
$\therefore \quad 1-3x = \pm\sqrt{7}$
$\therefore \quad 3x = 1 \pm \sqrt{7}$
$\therefore \quad x = \tfrac{1}{3} \pm \tfrac{\sqrt{7}}{3}$

2 **a** $x^2 - 4x + 1 = 0$
$\therefore \quad x^2 - 4x = -1$
$\therefore \quad x^2 - 4x + (-2)^2 = -1 + (-2)^2$
$\therefore \quad (x-2)^2 = 3$
$\therefore \quad x-2 = \pm\sqrt{3}$
$\therefore \quad x = 2 \pm \sqrt{3}$

b $x^2 + 6x + 2 = 0$
$\therefore \quad x^2 + 6x = -2$
$\therefore \quad x^2 + 6x + 3^2 = -2 + 3^2$
$\therefore \quad (x+3)^2 = 7$
$\therefore \quad x+3 = \pm\sqrt{7}$
$\therefore \quad x = -3 \pm \sqrt{7}$

c $x^2 - 14x + 46 = 0$
$\therefore \quad x^2 - 14x = -46$
$\therefore \quad x^2 - 14x + (-7)^2 = -46 + (-7)^2$
$\therefore \quad (x-7)^2 = 3$
$\therefore \quad x-7 = \pm\sqrt{3}$
$\therefore \quad x = 7 \pm \sqrt{3}$

d $x^2 = 4x + 3$
$\therefore \quad x^2 - 4x = 3$
$\therefore \quad x^2 - 4x + (-2)^2 = 3 + (-2)^2$
$\therefore \quad (x-2)^2 = 7$
$\therefore \quad x-2 = \pm\sqrt{7}$
$\therefore \quad x = 2 \pm \sqrt{7}$

e $\quad x^2 + 6x + 7 = 0$
$\therefore \quad x^2 + 6x = -7$
$\therefore \quad x^2 + 6x + 3^2 = -7 + 3^2$
$\therefore \quad (x+3)^2 = 2$
$\therefore \quad x + 3 = \pm\sqrt{2}$
$\therefore \quad x = -3 \pm \sqrt{2}$

f $\quad x^2 = 2x + 6$
$\therefore \quad x^2 - 2x = 6$
$\therefore \quad x^2 - 2x + (-1)^2 = 6 + (-1)^2$
$\therefore \quad (x-1)^2 = 7$
$\therefore \quad x - 1 = \pm\sqrt{7}$
$\therefore \quad x = 1 \pm \sqrt{7}$

g $\quad x^2 + 6x = 2$
$\therefore \quad x^2 + 6x + 3^2 = 2 + 3^2$
$\therefore \quad (x+3)^2 = 11$
$\therefore \quad x + 3 = \pm\sqrt{11}$
$\therefore \quad x = -3 \pm \sqrt{11}$

h $\quad x^2 + 10 = 8x$
$\therefore \quad x^2 - 8x = -10$
$\therefore \quad x^2 - 8x + (-4)^2 = -10 + (-4)^2$
$\therefore \quad (x-4)^2 = 6$
$\therefore \quad x - 4 = \pm\sqrt{6}$
$\therefore \quad x = 4 \pm \sqrt{6}$

i $\quad x^2 + 6x = -11$
$\therefore \quad x^2 + 6x + 3^2 = -11 + 3^2$
$\therefore \quad (x+3)^2 = -2$
$\therefore \quad x$ has no real solutions, since the perfect square cannot be negative.

3 a $\quad 2x^2 + 4x + 1 = 0$
$\therefore \quad x^2 + 2x + \frac{1}{2} = 0$
$\therefore \quad x^2 + 2x = -\frac{1}{2}$
$\therefore \quad x^2 + 2x + 1^2 = -\frac{1}{2} + 1^2$
$\therefore \quad (x+1)^2 = \frac{1}{2}$
$\therefore \quad x + 1 = \pm\frac{1}{\sqrt{2}}$
$\therefore \quad x = -1 \pm \frac{1}{\sqrt{2}}$

b $\quad 2x^2 - 10x + 3 = 0$
$\therefore \quad x^2 - 5x + \frac{3}{2} = 0$
$\therefore \quad x^2 - 5x = -\frac{3}{2}$
$\therefore \quad x^2 - 5x + (-\frac{5}{2})^2 = -\frac{3}{2} + (-\frac{5}{2})^2$
$\therefore \quad (x - \frac{5}{2})^2 = -\frac{3}{2} + \frac{25}{4}$
$\therefore \quad (x - \frac{5}{2})^2 = \frac{19}{4}$
$\therefore \quad x - \frac{5}{2} = \pm\frac{\sqrt{19}}{2}$
$\therefore \quad x = \frac{5}{2} \pm \frac{\sqrt{19}}{2}$

c $\quad 3x^2 + 12x + 5 = 0$
$\therefore \quad x^2 + 4x + \frac{5}{3} = 0$
$\therefore \quad x^2 + 4x = -\frac{5}{3}$
$\therefore \quad x^2 + 4x + 2^2 = -\frac{5}{3} + 2^2$
$\therefore \quad (x+2)^2 = \frac{7}{3}$
$\therefore \quad x + 2 = \pm\sqrt{\frac{7}{3}}$
$\therefore \quad x = -2 \pm \sqrt{\frac{7}{3}}$

d $\quad 3x^2 = 6x + 4$
$\therefore \quad x^2 = 2x + \frac{4}{3}$
$\therefore \quad x^2 - 2x = \frac{4}{3}$
$\therefore \quad x^2 - 2x + (-1)^2 = \frac{4}{3} + (-1)^2$
$\therefore \quad (x-1)^2 = \frac{7}{3}$
$\therefore \quad x - 1 = \pm\sqrt{\frac{7}{3}}$
$\therefore \quad x = 1 \pm \sqrt{\frac{7}{3}}$

e $\quad 5x^2 - 15x + 2 = 0$
$\therefore \quad x^2 - 3x + \frac{2}{5} = 0$
$\therefore \quad x^2 - 3x = -\frac{2}{5}$
$\therefore \quad x^2 - 3x + (-\frac{3}{2})^2 = -\frac{2}{5} + (-\frac{3}{2})^2$
$\therefore \quad (x - \frac{3}{2})^2 = -\frac{2}{5} + \frac{9}{4} = \frac{37}{20}$
$\therefore \quad x - \frac{3}{2} = \pm\sqrt{\frac{37}{20}}$
$\therefore \quad x = \frac{3}{2} \pm \sqrt{\frac{37}{20}}$

f $\quad 4x^2 + 4x = 5$
$\therefore \quad x^2 + x = \frac{5}{4}$
$\therefore \quad x^2 + x + (\frac{1}{2})^2 = \frac{5}{4} + (\frac{1}{2})^2$
$\therefore \quad (x + \frac{1}{2})^2 = \frac{6}{4}$
$\therefore \quad x + \frac{1}{2} = \pm\frac{\sqrt{6}}{2}$
$\therefore \quad x = -\frac{1}{2} \pm \frac{\sqrt{6}}{2}$

EXERCISE 6A.3

1 a $x^2 - 4x - 3 = 0$
has $a = 1$, $b = -4$, $c = -3$

$$\therefore x = \frac{-(-4) \pm \sqrt{(-4)^2 - 4(1)(-3)}}{2(1)}$$

$$= \frac{4 \pm \sqrt{28}}{2}$$

$$= \frac{4 \pm 2\sqrt{7}}{2}$$

$$= 2 \pm \sqrt{7}$$

b $x^2 + 6x + 7 = 0$
has $a = 1$, $b = 6$, $c = 7$

$$\therefore x = \frac{-6 \pm \sqrt{6^2 - 4(1)(7)}}{2(1)}$$

$$= \frac{-6 \pm \sqrt{8}}{2}$$

$$= \frac{-6 \pm 2\sqrt{2}}{2}$$

$$= -3 \pm \sqrt{2}$$

c $x^2 + 1 = 4x$
$\therefore x^2 - 4x + 1 = 0$
which has $a = 1$, $b = -4$, $c = 1$

$$\therefore x = \frac{-(-4) \pm \sqrt{(-4)^2 - 4(1)(1)}}{2(1)}$$

$$= \frac{4 \pm \sqrt{12}}{2}$$

$$= \frac{4 \pm 2\sqrt{3}}{2}$$

$$= 2 \pm \sqrt{3}$$

d $x^2 + 4x = 1$
$\therefore x^2 + 4x - 1 = 0$
which has $a = 1$, $b = 4$, $c = -1$

$$\therefore x = \frac{-4 \pm \sqrt{4^2 - 4(1)(-1)}}{2(1)}$$

$$= \frac{-4 \pm \sqrt{20}}{2}$$

$$= \frac{-4 \pm 2\sqrt{5}}{2}$$

$$= -2 \pm \sqrt{5}$$

e $x^2 - 4x + 2 = 0$
has $a = 1$, $b = -4$, $c = 2$

$$\therefore x = \frac{-(-4) \pm \sqrt{(-4)^2 - 4(1)(2)}}{2(1)}$$

$$= \frac{4 \pm \sqrt{8}}{2}$$

$$= \frac{4 \pm 2\sqrt{2}}{2}$$

$$= 2 \pm \sqrt{2}$$

f $2x^2 - 2x - 3 = 0$
has $a = 2$, $b = -2$, $c = -3$

$$\therefore x = \frac{-(-2) \pm \sqrt{(-2)^2 - 4(2)(-3)}}{2(2)}$$

$$= \frac{2 \pm \sqrt{28}}{4}$$

$$= \frac{2 \pm 2\sqrt{7}}{4}$$

$$= \tfrac{1}{2} \pm \tfrac{\sqrt{7}}{2}$$

g $x^2 - 2\sqrt{2}x + 2 = 0$ has $a = 1$, $b = -2\sqrt{2}$, $c = 2$

$$\therefore x = \frac{-(-2\sqrt{2}) \pm \sqrt{(-2\sqrt{2})^2 - 4(1)(2)}}{2(1)}$$

$$= \frac{2\sqrt{2} \pm \sqrt{8-8}}{2} = \sqrt{2}$$

h $(3x + 1)^2 = -2x$
$\therefore 9x^2 + 6x + 1 = -2x$
$\therefore 9x^2 + 8x + 1 = 0$
which has $a = 9$, $b = 8$, $c = 1$

$$\therefore x = \frac{-8 \pm \sqrt{8^2 - 4(9)(1)}}{2(9)}$$

$$= \frac{-8 \pm \sqrt{28}}{18}$$

$$= \frac{-8 \pm 2\sqrt{7}}{18} \quad \text{or} \quad -\tfrac{4}{9} \pm \tfrac{\sqrt{7}}{9}$$

i $(x + 3)(2x + 1) = 9$
$\therefore 2x^2 + x + 6x + 3 = 9$
$\therefore 2x^2 + 7x - 6 = 0$
which has $a = 2$, $b = 7$, $c = -6$

$$\therefore x = \frac{-7 \pm \sqrt{7^2 - 4(2)(-6)}}{2(2)}$$

$$= \frac{-7 \pm \sqrt{49 + 48}}{4}$$

$$= -\tfrac{7}{4} \pm \tfrac{\sqrt{97}}{4}$$

2 a $(x+2)(x-1) = 2 - 3x$
$\therefore \quad x^2 - x + 2x - 2 = 2 - 3x$
$\therefore \quad x^2 + 4x - 4 = 0$
which has $a = 1$, $b = 4$, $c = -4$

$\therefore \quad x = \dfrac{-4 \pm \sqrt{4^2 - 4(1)(-4)}}{2(1)}$

$= \dfrac{-4 \pm \sqrt{32}}{2}$

$= \dfrac{-4 \pm 4\sqrt{2}}{2}$

$= -2 \pm 2\sqrt{2}$

b $(2x+1)^2 = 3 - x$
$\therefore \quad 4x^2 + 4x + 1 = 3 - x$
$\therefore \quad 4x^2 + 5x - 2 = 0$
which has $a = 4$, $b = 5$, $c = -2$

$\therefore \quad x = \dfrac{-5 \pm \sqrt{5^2 - 4(4)(-2)}}{2(4)}$

$= \dfrac{-5 \pm \sqrt{25 + 32}}{8}$

$= -\dfrac{5}{8} \pm \dfrac{\sqrt{57}}{8}$

c $(x-2)^2 = 1 + x$
$\therefore \quad x^2 - 4x + 4 = 1 + x$
$\therefore \quad x^2 - 5x + 3 = 0$
which has $a = 1$, $b = -5$, $c = 3$

$\therefore \quad x = \dfrac{-(-5) \pm \sqrt{(-5)^2 - 4(1)(3)}}{2(1)}$

$= \dfrac{5 \pm \sqrt{25 - 12}}{2}$

$= \dfrac{5}{2} \pm \dfrac{\sqrt{13}}{2}$

d $\dfrac{x-1}{2-x} = 2x + 1$

$\therefore \quad x - 1 = (2x+1)(2-x)$
$\therefore \quad x - 1 = 4x - 2x^2 + 2 - x$
$\therefore \quad 2x^2 - 2x - 3 = 0$
which has $a = 2$, $b = -2$, $c = -3$

$\therefore \quad x = \dfrac{-(-2) \pm \sqrt{(-2)^2 - 4(2)(-3)}}{2(2)}$

$= \dfrac{2 \pm \sqrt{28}}{4}$

$= \dfrac{2 \pm 2\sqrt{7}}{4}$ or $\dfrac{1}{2} \pm \dfrac{\sqrt{7}}{2}$

e $x - \dfrac{1}{x} = 1$
$\therefore \quad x^2 - 1 = x$
$\therefore \quad x^2 - x - 1 = 0$
which has $a = 1$, $b = -1$, $c = -1$

$\therefore \quad x = \dfrac{-(-1) \pm \sqrt{(-1)^2 - 4(1)(-1)}}{2(1)}$

$= \dfrac{1 \pm \sqrt{1+4}}{2}$

$= \dfrac{1}{2} \pm \dfrac{\sqrt{5}}{2}$

f $2x - \dfrac{1}{x} = 3$
$\therefore \quad 2x^2 - 1 = 3x$
$\therefore \quad 2x^2 - 3x - 1 = 0$
which has $a = 2$, $b = -3$, $c = -1$

$\therefore \quad x = \dfrac{-(-3) \pm \sqrt{(-3)^2 - 4(2)(-1)}}{2(2)}$

$= \dfrac{3 \pm \sqrt{9+8}}{4}$

$= \dfrac{3}{4} \pm \dfrac{\sqrt{17}}{4}$

EXERCISE 6B

1 a $x^2 + 7x - 3 = 0$
has $a = 1$, $b = 7$, $c = -3$
$\therefore \quad \Delta = b^2 - 4ac$
$= 7^2 - 4(1)(-3)$
$= 61$
Since $\Delta > 0$, there are two distinct real solutions.

b $x^2 + 2\sqrt{3}x + 3 = 0$
has $a = 1$, $b = 2\sqrt{3}$, $c = 3$
$\therefore \quad \Delta = b^2 - 4ac$
$= (2\sqrt{3})^2 - 4(1)(3)$
$= 12 - 12$
$= 0$
$\therefore$ there is one repeated real root.

c $3x^2 + 2x - 1 = 0$
has $a = 3$, $b = 2$, $c = -1$
$\therefore \Delta = b^2 - 4ac$
$= 2^2 - 4(3)(-1)$
$= 16$
Since $\Delta > 0$, there are two distinct real solutions.

e $x^2 + x + 5 = 0$
has $a = 1$, $b = 1$, $c = 5$
$\therefore \Delta = b^2 - 4ac$
$= 1^2 - 4(1)(5)$
$= -19$
Since $\Delta < 0$, there are no real roots.

d $5x^2 + 4x - 3 = 0$
has $a = 5$, $b = 4$, $c = -3$
$\therefore \Delta = b^2 - 4ac$
$= 4^2 - 4(5)(-3)$
$= 76$
Since $\Delta > 0$, there are two distinct real solutions.

f $16x^2 - 8x + 1 = 0$
has $a = 16$, $b = -8$, $c = 1$
$\therefore \Delta = b^2 - 4ac$
$= (-8)^2 - 4(16)(1)$
$= 0$
$\therefore$ there is one repeated real root.

2 a $6x^2 - 5x - 6 = 0$
has $a = 6$, $b = -5$, $c = -6$
$\therefore \Delta = b^2 - 4ac$
$= (-5)^2 - 4(6)(-6)$
$= 169$
$\therefore \sqrt{\Delta} = 13$, so the equation has rational roots.

c $3x^2 + 4x + 1 = 0$
has $a = 3$, $b = 4$, $c = 1$
$\therefore \Delta = b^2 - 4ac$
$= 4^2 - 4(3)(1)$
$= 4$
$\therefore \sqrt{\Delta} = 2$, so the equation has rational roots.

e $4x^2 - 3x + 2 = 0$
has $a = 4$, $b = -3$, $c = 2$
$\therefore \Delta = b^2 - 4ac$
$= (-3)^2 - 4(4)2$
$= -23$
Since $\Delta < 0$, the equation does not have rational roots.

b $2x^2 - 7x - 5 = 0$
has $a = 2$, $b = -7$, $c = -5$
$\therefore \Delta = b^2 - 4ac$
$= (-7)^2 - 4(2)(-5)$
$= 89$
$\therefore \sqrt{\Delta} = \sqrt{89}$, so the equation does not have rational roots.

d $6x^2 - 47x - 8 = 0$
has $a = 6$, $b = -47$, $c = -8$
$\therefore \Delta = b^2 - 4ac$
$= (-47)^2 - 4(6)(-8)$
$= 2401$
$\therefore \sqrt{\Delta} = 49$,
so the equation has rational roots.

f $8x^2 + 2x - 3 = 0$
has $a = 8$, $b = 2$, $c = -3$
$\therefore \Delta = b^2 - 4ac$
$= 2^2 - 4(8)(-3)$
$= 100$
$\therefore \sqrt{\Delta} = 10$, so the equation has rational roots.

3 a For $x^2 + 4x + m = 0$,
$a = 1$, $b = 4$, $c = m$
So, $\Delta = b^2 - 4ac$
$= 4^2 - 4(1)(m)$
$= 16 - 4m$
which has sign diagram

$\xleftarrow{\qquad +\qquad}\underset{4}{|}\xrightarrow{\quad -\quad} m$

i For a repeated root, $\Delta = 0$
$\therefore m = 4$
ii For two distinct real roots, $\Delta > 0$
$\therefore m < 4$
iii For no real roots, $\Delta < 0$
$\therefore m > 4$

b For $mx^2 + 3x + 2 = 0$,
$a = m$, $b = 3$, $c = 2$
So, $\Delta = b^2 - 4ac$
$= 3^2 - 4(m)(2)$
$= 9 - 8m$
which has sign diagram

$\xleftarrow{\qquad +\qquad}\underset{\frac{9}{8}}{|}\xrightarrow{\quad -\quad} m$

i For a repeated root, $\Delta = 0$
$\therefore m = \frac{9}{8}$
ii For two distinct real roots, $\Delta > 0$
$\therefore m < \frac{9}{8}$
iii For no real roots, $\Delta < 0$
$\therefore m > \frac{9}{8}$

c For $mx^2 - 3x + 1 = 0$, which has sign diagram

$a = m$, $b = -3$, $c = 1$

So, $\Delta = b^2 - 4ac$
$= (-3)^2 - 4(m)(1)$
$= 9 - 4m$

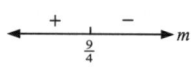

$\xrightarrow{\quad + \quad | \quad - \quad} m$
$\qquad\qquad \frac{9}{4}$

i For a repeated root, $\Delta = 0$ $\quad\therefore\ m = \frac{9}{4}$
ii For two distinct real roots, $\Delta > 0$ $\quad\therefore\ m < \frac{9}{4}$
iii For no real roots, $\Delta < 0$ $\quad\therefore\ m > \frac{9}{4}$

4 a For $2x^2 + kx - k = 0$,
$a = 2$, $b = k$, $c = -k$
So, $\Delta = b^2 - 4ac$
$= k^2 - 4(2)(-k)$
$= k^2 + 8k$
$= k(k+8)$

which has sign diagram

$\xrightarrow{\quad + \quad | \quad - \quad | \quad + \quad} k$
$\qquad -8 \qquad 0$

i For two distinct real roots, $\Delta > 0$
$\therefore\ k < -8$ or $k > 0$
ii For two real roots, $\Delta \geqslant 0$
$\therefore\ k \leqslant -8$ or $k \geqslant 0$
iii For a repeated root, $\Delta = 0$
$\therefore\ k = -8$ or 0
iv For no real roots, $\Delta < 0$
$\therefore\ -8 < k < 0$

b For $kx^2 - 2x + k = 0$,
$a = k$, $b = -2$, $c = k$
So, $\Delta = b^2 - 4ac$
$= (-2)^2 - 4(k)(k)$
$= 4 - 4k^2$
$= 4(1+k)(1-k)$

which has sign diagram

$\xrightarrow{\quad - \quad | \quad + \quad | \quad - \quad} k$
$\qquad -1 \qquad 1$

i For two distinct real roots, $\Delta > 0$
$\therefore\ -1 < k < 1$
ii For two real roots, $\Delta \geqslant 0$
$\therefore\ -1 \leqslant k \leqslant 1$
iii For a repeated root, $\Delta = 0$
$\therefore\ k = -1$ or 1
iv For no real roots, $\Delta < 0$
$\therefore\ k < -1$ or $k > 1$

c For $x^2 + [k+2]x + 4 = 0$,
$a = 1$, $b = k+2$, $c = 4$
So, $\Delta = b^2 - 4ac$
$= (k+2)^2 - 4(1)(4)$
$= k^2 + 4k + 4 - 16$
$= k^2 + 4k - 12$
$= (k+6)(k-2)$

which has sign diagram

$\xrightarrow{\quad + \quad | \quad - \quad | \quad + \quad} k$
$\qquad -6 \qquad 2$

i For two distinct real roots, $\Delta > 0$
$\therefore\ k < -6$ or $k > 2$
ii For two real roots, $\Delta \geqslant 0$
$\therefore\ k \leqslant -6$ or $k \geqslant 2$
iii For a repeated root, $\Delta = 0$
$\therefore\ k = -6$ or 2
iv For no real roots, $\Delta < 0$
$\therefore\ -6 < k < 2$

d For $2x^2 + [k-2]x + 2 = 0$,
$a = 2$, $b = k-2$, $c = 2$
So, $\Delta = b^2 - 4ac$
$= (k-2)^2 - 4(2)(2)$
$= k^2 - 4k + 4 - 16$
$= k^2 - 4k - 12$
$= (k-6)(k+2)$

which has sign diagram

$\xrightarrow{\quad + \quad | \quad - \quad | \quad + \quad} k$
$\qquad -2 \qquad 6$

i For two distinct real roots, $\Delta > 0$
$\therefore\ k < -2$ or $k > 6$
ii For two real roots, $\Delta \geqslant 0$
$\therefore\ k \leqslant -2$ or $k \geqslant 6$
iii For a repeated root, $\Delta = 0$
$\therefore\ k = -2$ or 6
iv For no real roots, $\Delta < 0$
$\therefore\ -2 < k < 6$

e For $x^2 + [3k-1]x + [2k+10] = 0$,
$a = 1$, $b = 3k-1$, $c = 2k+10$
So, $\Delta = b^2 - 4ac$
$= (3k-1)^2 - 4(1)(2k+10)$
$= 9k^2 - 6k + 1 - 8k - 40$
$= 9k^2 - 14k - 39$
$= (9k+13)(k-3)$

which has sign diagram

$\xrightarrow{\quad + \quad | \quad - \quad | \quad + \quad} k$
$\qquad -\frac{13}{9} \qquad 3$

i For two distinct real roots, $\Delta > 0$
$\therefore\ k < -\frac{13}{9}$ or $k > 3$
ii For two real roots, $\Delta \geqslant 0$
$\therefore\ k \leqslant -\frac{13}{9}$ or $k \geqslant 3$
iii For a repeated root, $\Delta = 0$
$\therefore\ k = -\frac{13}{9}$ or 3
iv For no real roots, $\Delta < 0$
$\therefore\ -\frac{13}{9} < k < 3$

f For $[k+1]x^2 + kx + k = 0$,
$a = k+1$, $b = k$, $c = k$
So, $\Delta = b^2 - 4ac$
$= k^2 - 4(k+1)(k)$
$= k^2 - 4k^2 - 4k$
$= -3k^2 - 4k$
$= -k(3k+4)$
which has sign diagram

```
───────┬────┬───────→ k
  -    -4/3  +  0  -
```

i For two distinct real roots, $\Delta > 0$
$\therefore -\frac{4}{3} < k < 0$

ii For two real roots, $\Delta \geqslant 0$
$\therefore -\frac{4}{3} \leqslant k \leqslant 0$

iii For a repeated root, $\Delta = 0$
$\therefore k = -\frac{4}{3}$ or 0

iv For no real roots, $\Delta < 0$
$\therefore k < -\frac{4}{3}$ or $k > 0$

EXERCISE 6C

1 a For $3x^2 - 2x + 7 = 0$:
sum of roots $= -\frac{b}{a} = -\frac{(-2)}{3} = \frac{2}{3}$
product of roots $= \frac{c}{a} = \frac{7}{3}$

b For $x^2 + 11x - 13 = 0$:
sum of roots $= -\frac{b}{a} = -\frac{11}{1} = -11$
product of roots $= \frac{c}{a} = \frac{-13}{1} = -13$

c For $5x^2 - 6x - 14 = 0$: sum of roots $= -\frac{b}{a} = -\frac{(-6)}{5} = \frac{6}{5}$
product of roots $= \frac{c}{a} = -\frac{14}{5}$

2 For $kx^2 - (1+k)x + (3k+2) = 0$, $a = k$, $b = -(1+k)$, $c = 3k+2$
$\therefore$ sum of roots $= -\frac{b}{a} = -\frac{-(1+k)}{k} = \frac{k+1}{k}$, product of roots $= \frac{c}{a} = \frac{3k+2}{k}$

Now sum of the roots is twice their product
$\therefore \frac{k+1}{k} = 2\left(\frac{3k+2}{k}\right)$
$\therefore k+1 = 2(3k+2)$
$\therefore k+1 = 6k+4$
$\therefore -3 = 5k$
$\therefore k = -\frac{3}{5}$

Substituting $k = -\frac{3}{5}$ into the equation gives
$-\frac{3}{5}x^2 - (1 - \frac{3}{5})x + (-\frac{9}{5} + 2) = 0$
$\therefore -\frac{3}{5}x^2 - \frac{2}{5}x + \frac{1}{5} = 0$
$\therefore -\frac{1}{5}(3x^2 + 2x - 1) = 0$
$\therefore -\frac{1}{5}(3x - 1)(x + 1) = 0$
$\therefore x = \frac{1}{3}$ or -1
$\therefore$ the roots of the equation are $\frac{1}{3}$ and -1

3 For $ax^2 - 6x + a - 2 = 0$, "a" $= a$, $b = -6$, $c = a-2$

a sum of roots $= -\frac{b}{a}$
$\therefore \alpha + 2\alpha = -\frac{(-6)}{a}$
$\therefore 3\alpha = \frac{6}{a}$
$\{$or $\alpha = \frac{2}{a}$ .... (1)$\}$

product of roots $= \frac{c}{a}$
$\therefore \alpha \times 2\alpha = \frac{a-2}{a}$
$\therefore 2\alpha^2 = \frac{a-2}{a}$ .... (2)

b Substituting (1) into (2) gives
$2\left(\frac{2}{a}\right)^2 = \frac{a-2}{a}$
$\therefore 2\left(\frac{4}{a^2}\right) = \frac{a-2}{a}$
$\therefore \frac{8}{a} = a - 2$

$\therefore 8 = a^2 - 2a$
$\therefore a^2 - 2a - 8 = 0$
$\therefore (a-4)(a+2) = 0$
$\therefore a = 4$ or -2

If $a = 4$, then $\alpha = \frac{2}{4}$ {using (1)}   If $a = -2$, then $\alpha = \frac{2}{-2}$ {using (1)}

$\qquad\qquad\qquad = \frac{1}{2}$ $\qquad\qquad\qquad\qquad\qquad\qquad = -1$

and $2\alpha = 1$ $\qquad\qquad\qquad\qquad\qquad$ and $2\alpha = -2$

$\therefore$ $a = 4$ and the roots are $\frac{1}{2}$ and 1 $\quad$ or $\quad$ $a = -2$ and the roots are -1 and -2.

4 For $kx^2 + (k-8)x + (1-k) = 0$, $\quad a = k$, $\ b = k - 8$, $\ c = 1 - k$

Let the roots of the equation be m and $m + 2$ $\qquad$ Substituting (1) into (2) gives

sum of roots $= -\dfrac{b}{a}$ $\qquad\qquad\qquad\qquad\qquad\left(\dfrac{8-3k}{2k}\right)\left(\dfrac{8-3k}{2k} + 2\right) = \dfrac{1-k}{k}$

$\therefore$ $m + (m+2) = -\dfrac{k-8}{k}$ $\qquad\qquad\qquad \therefore\ \left(\dfrac{8-3k}{2k}\right)\left(\dfrac{8+k}{2k}\right) = \dfrac{1-k}{k}$

$\therefore$ $2m + 2 = \dfrac{8-k}{k}$ $\qquad\qquad\qquad\qquad \therefore\ \dfrac{64 - 16k - 3k^2}{4k^2} = \dfrac{1-k}{k}$

$\therefore$ $2m = \dfrac{8-3k}{k}$ $\qquad\qquad\qquad\qquad\quad \therefore\ \dfrac{64 - 16k - 3k^2}{4k} = 1 - k$

$\therefore$ $m = \dfrac{8-3k}{2k}$ $\quad$.... (1) $\qquad\qquad\qquad \therefore\ 64 - 16k - 3k^2 = 4k - 4k^2$

$\qquad\qquad\qquad\qquad\qquad\qquad\qquad\qquad \therefore\ k^2 - 20k + 64 = 0$

and product of roots $= \dfrac{c}{a}$ $\qquad\qquad\qquad \therefore\ (k-4)(k-16) = 0$

$\qquad\qquad\qquad\qquad\qquad\qquad\qquad\qquad\qquad\qquad \therefore\ k = 4 \text{ or } 16$

$\therefore$ $m(m+2) = \dfrac{1-k}{k}$ $\quad$.... (2)

Using (1), if $k = 4$ then $m = \dfrac{8 - 3(4)}{2(4)} = \dfrac{-4}{8} = -\dfrac{1}{2}$, and $m + 2 = \dfrac{3}{2}$

and if $k = 16$ then $m = \dfrac{8 - 3(16)}{2(16)} = \dfrac{-40}{32} = -\dfrac{5}{4}$, and $m + 2 = \dfrac{3}{4}$

$\therefore$ $k = 4$ and the roots are $-\dfrac{1}{2}$ and $\dfrac{3}{2}$ $\quad$ or $\quad$ $k = 16$ and the roots are $-\dfrac{5}{4}$ and $\dfrac{3}{4}$.

5 The roots of $x^2 - 6x + 7 = 0$ are α and β.

sum of roots $= -\dfrac{-6}{1}$ $\quad$ and $\quad$ product of roots $= \dfrac{7}{1}$

$\therefore$ $\alpha + \beta = 6$ $\qquad\qquad\qquad\qquad \therefore\ \alpha\beta = 7$

Now consider a quadratic equation with roots $\alpha + \dfrac{1}{\beta}$ and $\beta + \dfrac{1}{\alpha}$

sum of roots $= \alpha + \dfrac{1}{\beta} + \beta + \dfrac{1}{\alpha}$ $\qquad\qquad$ product of roots $= \left(\alpha + \dfrac{1}{\beta}\right)\left(\beta + \dfrac{1}{\alpha}\right)$

$\qquad\qquad = (\alpha + \beta) + \left(\dfrac{1}{\alpha} + \dfrac{1}{\beta}\right)$ $\qquad\qquad\qquad\quad = \alpha\beta + 1 + 1 + \dfrac{1}{\alpha\beta}$

$\qquad\qquad\qquad\qquad\qquad\qquad\qquad\qquad\qquad\qquad = 7 + 2 + \dfrac{1}{7}$

$\qquad\qquad = (\alpha + \beta) + \dfrac{\alpha + \beta}{\alpha\beta}$ $\qquad\qquad\qquad\qquad\ = 9 + \dfrac{1}{7}$

$\qquad\qquad = 6 + \dfrac{6}{7}$ $\qquad\qquad\qquad\qquad\qquad\qquad\quad = \dfrac{64}{7}$

$\qquad\qquad = \dfrac{48}{7}$

$\therefore$ a quadratic equation $ax^2 + bx + c = 0$ with roots $\alpha + \dfrac{1}{\beta}$ and $\beta + \dfrac{1}{\alpha}$ has $-\dfrac{b}{a} = \dfrac{48}{7}$ and $\dfrac{c}{a} = \dfrac{64}{7}$.

The simplest solution to this is $a = 7$, $b = -48$, $c = 64$.

$\therefore$ the simplest quadratic equation with roots $\alpha + \dfrac{1}{\beta}$ and $\beta + \dfrac{1}{\alpha}$ is $7x^2 - 48x + 64 = 0$.

6 The roots of $2x^2 - 3x - 5 = 0$ are p and q.

∴ sum of roots $= -\frac{-3}{2}$ and product of roots $= \frac{-5}{2}$

∴ $p + q = \frac{3}{2}$ ∴ $pq = -\frac{5}{2}$

Now consider a quadratic equation with roots $p^2 + q$ and $q^2 + p$.

sum of roots $= p^2 + q + q^2 + p$
$= (p^2 + q^2) + (p + q)$
$= [(p+q)^2 - 2pq] + (p+q)$
$= (\frac{3}{2})^2 - 2(-\frac{5}{2}) + \frac{3}{2}$
$= \frac{9}{4} + 5 + \frac{3}{2}$
$= \frac{35}{4}$

product of roots $= (p^2 + q)(q^2 + p)$
$= p^2q^2 + p^3 + q^3 + qp$
$= (pq)^2 + [(p+q)^3 - 3p^2q - 3pq^2] + pq$
$= (pq)^2 + [(p+q)^3 - 3pq(p+q)] + pq$
$= (-\frac{5}{2})^2 + (\frac{3}{2})^3 - 3(-\frac{5}{2})(\frac{3}{2}) + (-\frac{5}{2})$
$= \frac{25}{4} + \frac{27}{8} + \frac{45}{4} - \frac{5}{2}$
$= \frac{147}{8}$

∴ a quadratic equation $ax^2 + bx + c = 0$ with roots $p^2 + q$ and $q^2 + p$

has $-\frac{b}{a} = \frac{35}{4}$ and $\frac{c}{a} = \frac{147}{8}$.

∴ $b = -\frac{35}{4}a$ and $c = \frac{147}{8}a$

∴ the quadratic equation is $ax^2 - \frac{35}{4}ax + \frac{147}{8}a = 0$, $a \neq 0$

∴ $a(x^2 - \frac{35}{4}x + \frac{147}{8}) = 0$, $a \neq 0$

∴ $a(8x^2 - 70x + 147) = 0$, $a \neq 0$

7 $kx^2 + [k+2]x - 3 = 0$ will have roots which are real and positive if:

(1) $\Delta > 0$ (2) sum of roots > 0 (3) product of roots > 0

(1) $\Delta > 0$
∴ $(k+2)^2 - 4(k)(-3) > 0$
∴ $k^2 + 4k + 4 + 12k > 0$
∴ $k^2 + 16k + 4 > 0$

Now $k^2 + 16k + 4 = 0$ when

$k = \dfrac{-16 \pm \sqrt{16^2 - 4(1)(4)}}{2(1)}$

$= \dfrac{-16 \pm \sqrt{240}}{2}$

$= \dfrac{-16 \pm 2\sqrt{60}}{2}$

$= -8 \pm \sqrt{60}$

∴ $k^2 + 16k + 4$ has sign diagram

```
   +        -         +
<--|--------|-------->  k
 -8-√60   -8+√60
```

∴ $\Delta > 0$ when

$k < -8 - \sqrt{60}$ or $k > -8 + \sqrt{60}$

(2)   sum of roots > 0

∴ $-\dfrac{k+2}{k} > 0$

$-\dfrac{k+2}{k}$ has sign diagram

```
   -    +    -
<--|----|---->  k
  -2    0
```

∴ sum of roots > 0 when
$-2 < k < 0$

(3) product of roots > 0

∴ $\dfrac{-3}{k} > 0$

$-\dfrac{3}{k}$ has sign diagram

```
   +    -
<--|---->  k
   0
```

∴ product of roots > 0 when
$k < 0$

∴ the only values of k which satisfy all three conditions are $-8 + \sqrt{60} < k < 0$.

EXERCISE 6D.1

1 a $y = (x-4)(x+2)$
has x-intercepts
-2 and 4
and y-intercept
-8

b $y = -(x-4)(x+2)$
has x-intercepts
-2 and 4
and y-intercept 8

c $y = 2(x+3)(x+5)$
has x-intercepts
-5 and -3
and y-intercept
30

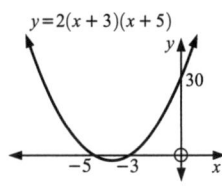

d $y = -3x(x+4)$
has x-intercepts
0 and -4
and y-intercept 0

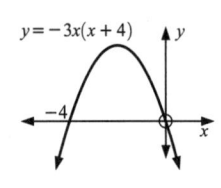

e $y = 2(x+3)^2$
has x-intercept
-3
and y-intercept
18

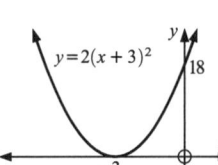

f $y = -\frac{1}{4}(x+2)^2$
has x-intercept
-2
and y-intercept
-1

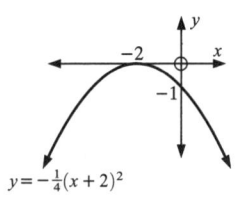

2 a The average of the x-intercepts is 1 ∴ the axis of symmetry is $x = 1$.
b The average of the x-intercepts is 1 ∴ the axis of symmetry is $x = 1$.
c The average of the x-intercepts is -4 ∴ the axis of symmetry is $x = -4$.
d The average of the x-intercepts is -2 ∴ the axis of symmetry is $x = -2$.
e The only x-intercept is -3, so the axis of symmetry is $x = -3$.
f The only x-intercept is -2, so the axis of symmetry is $x = -2$.

3 a The vertex is $(1, 3)$.
The axis of symmetry is $x = 1$.
The y-intercept is 4.

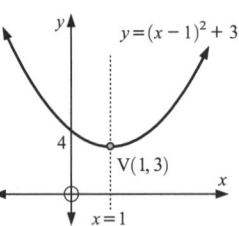

b The vertex is $(-2, 1)$.
The axis of symmetry is $x = -2$.
The y-intercept is 9.

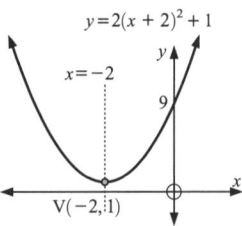

c The vertex is $(1, -3)$.
The axis of symmetry is $x = 1$.
The y-intercept is -5.

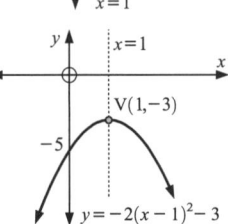

d The vertex is $(3, 2)$.
The axis of symmetry is $x = 3$.
The y-intercept is $\frac{13}{2}$.

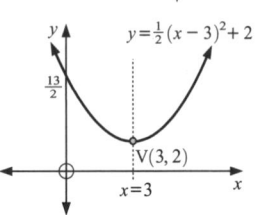

e The vertex is $(1, 4)$.
The axis of symmetry is $x = 1$.
The y-intercept is $3\frac{2}{3}$.

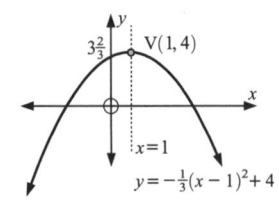

f The vertex is $(-2, -3)$.
The axis of symmetry is $x = -2$.
The y-intercept is $-3\frac{2}{5}$.

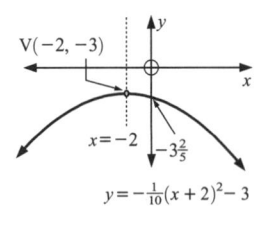

4 a $y = x^2 - 4x + 2$
has $a = 1$, $b = -4$, $c = 2$
∴ $-\dfrac{b}{2a} = -\dfrac{(-4)}{2(1)} = 2$
∴ the axis of symmetry is $x = 2$.
When $x = 2$,
$y = 2^2 - 4 \times 2 + 2 = -2$
∴ the vertex is at $(2, -2)$.

b $y = x^2 + 2x - 3$
has $a = 1$, $b = 2$, $c = -3$
∴ $-\dfrac{b}{2a} = -\dfrac{2}{2(1)} = -1$
∴ the axis of symmetry is $x = -1$.
When $x = -1$,
$y = (-1)^2 + 2(-1) - 3 = -4$
∴ the vertex is at $(-1, -4)$.

c $y = 2x^2 + 4$
has $a = 2$, $b = 0$, $c = 4$
$\therefore \quad -\dfrac{b}{2a} = -\dfrac{0}{2(2)} = 0$
$\therefore$ the axis of symmetry is $x = 0$.
When $x = 0$, $y = 4$
$\therefore$ the vertex is at $(0, 4)$.

e $y = 2x^2 + 8x - 7$
has $a = 2$, $b = 8$, $c = -7$
$\therefore \quad -\dfrac{b}{2a} = -\dfrac{8}{2(2)} = -2$
$\therefore$ the axis of symmetry is $x = -2$.
When $x = -2$,
$y = 2(-2)^2 + 8(-2) - 7 = -15$
$\therefore$ the vertex is at $(-2, -15)$.

g $y = 2x^2 + 6x - 1$
has $a = 2$, $b = 6$, $c = -1$
$\therefore \quad -\dfrac{b}{2a} = -\dfrac{6}{2(2)} = -\dfrac{3}{2}$
$\therefore$ the axis of symmetry is $x = -\dfrac{3}{2}$.
When $x = -\dfrac{3}{2}$, $y = 2(-\dfrac{3}{2})^2 + 6(-\dfrac{3}{2}) - 1$
$= \dfrac{9}{2} - 9 - 1$
$= -\dfrac{11}{2}$
$\therefore$ the vertex is at $(-\dfrac{3}{2}, -\dfrac{11}{2})$.

i $y = -\dfrac{1}{2}x^2 + x - 5$
has $a = -\dfrac{1}{2}$, $b = 1$, $c = -5$
$\therefore \quad -\dfrac{b}{2a} = -\dfrac{1}{2(-\frac{1}{2})} = 1$
$\therefore$ the axis of symmetry is $x = 1$.
When $x = 1$, $y = -\dfrac{1}{2}(1)^2 + 1 - 5 = -\dfrac{9}{2}$
$\therefore$ the vertex is at $(1, -\dfrac{9}{2})$.

d $y = -3x^2 + 1$
has $a = -3$, $b = 0$, $c = 1$
$\therefore \quad -\dfrac{b}{2a} = -\dfrac{0}{2(-3)} = 0$
$\therefore$ the axis of symmetry is $x = 0$.
When $x = 0$, $y = 1$
$\therefore$ the vertex is at $(0, 1)$.

f $y = -x^2 - 4x - 9$
has $a = -1$, $b = -4$, $c = -9$
$\therefore \quad -\dfrac{b}{2a} = -\dfrac{(-4)}{2(-1)} = -2$
$\therefore$ the axis of symmetry is $x = -2$.
When $x = -2$, $y = -(-2)^2 - 4(-2) - 9$
$= -4 + 8 - 9$
$= -5$
$\therefore$ the vertex is at $(-2, -5)$.

h $y = 2x^2 - 10x + 3$
has $a = 2$, $b = -10$, $c = 3$
$\therefore \quad -\dfrac{b}{2a} = -\dfrac{(-10)}{2(2)} = \dfrac{5}{2}$
$\therefore$ the axis of symmetry is $x = \dfrac{5}{2}$.
When $x = \dfrac{5}{2}$, $y = 2(\dfrac{5}{2})^2 - 10(\dfrac{5}{2}) + 3$
$= \dfrac{25}{2} - \dfrac{50}{2} + 3$
$= -\dfrac{19}{2}$
$\therefore$ the vertex is at $(\dfrac{5}{2}, -\dfrac{19}{2})$.

5 a When $y = 0$, $x^2 - 9 = 0$
$\therefore \quad (x + 3)(x - 3) = 0$
$\therefore \quad x = \pm 3$
$\therefore$ the x-intercepts are ± 3

c When $y = 0$, $x^2 + 7x + 10 = 0$
$\therefore \quad (x + 5)(x + 2) = 0$
$\therefore \quad x = -5$ or -2
$\therefore$ the x-intercepts are -5 and -2

e When $y = 0$, $4x - x^2 = 0$
$\therefore \quad x(4 - x) = 0$
$\therefore \quad x = 0$ or 4
$\therefore$ the x-intercepts are 0 and 4

b When $y = 0$, $2x^2 - 6 = 0$
$\therefore \quad x^2 - 3 = 0$
$\therefore \quad (x + \sqrt{3})(x - \sqrt{3}) = 0$
$\therefore \quad x = \pm\sqrt{3}$
$\therefore$ the x-intercepts are $\pm\sqrt{3}$

d When $y = 0$, $x^2 + x - 12 = 0$
$\therefore \quad (x + 4)(x - 3) = 0$
$\therefore \quad x = -4$ or 3
$\therefore$ the x-intercepts are -4 and 3

f When $y = 0$, $-x^2 - 6x - 8 = 0$
$\therefore \quad x^2 + 6x + 8 = 0$
$\therefore \quad (x + 4)(x + 2) = 0$
$\therefore \quad x = -4$ or -2
$\therefore$ the x-intercepts are -4 and -2

g When $y = 0$, $-2x^2 - 4x - 2 = 0$
$\therefore \quad x^2 + 2x + 1 = 0$
$\therefore \quad (x+1)^2 = 0$
$\therefore \quad x = -1$
$\therefore$ the x-intercept is -1 (touching)

i When $y = 0$, $x^2 - 4x + 1 = 0$
$a = 1$, $b = -4$ and $c = 1$
$\therefore \quad x = \dfrac{-(-4) \pm \sqrt{(-4)^2 - 4(1)(1)}}{2(1)}$
$= \dfrac{4 \pm \sqrt{12}}{2}$
$= \dfrac{4 \pm 2\sqrt{3}}{2}$
$= 2 \pm \sqrt{3}$
$\therefore$ the x-intercepts are $2 \pm \sqrt{3}$

k When $y = 0$, $x^2 - 6x - 2 = 0$
$a = 1$, $b = -6$ and $c = -2$
$\therefore \quad x = \dfrac{-(-6) \pm \sqrt{(-6)^2 - 4(1)(-2)}}{2(1)}$
$= \dfrac{6 \pm \sqrt{44}}{2}$
$= \dfrac{6 \pm 2\sqrt{11}}{2}$
$= 3 \pm \sqrt{11}$
$\therefore$ the x-intercepts are $3 \pm \sqrt{11}$

h When $y = 0$, $4x^2 - 24x + 36 = 0$
$\therefore \quad x^2 - 6x + 9 = 0$
$\therefore \quad (x-3)^2 = 0$
$\therefore \quad x = 3$
$\therefore$ the x-intercept is 3 (touching)

j When $y = 0$, $x^2 + 4x - 3 = 0$
$a = 1$, $b = 4$ and $c = -3$
$\therefore \quad x = \dfrac{-4 \pm \sqrt{4^2 - 4(1)(-3)}}{2(1)}$
$= \dfrac{-4 \pm \sqrt{28}}{2}$
$= \dfrac{-4 \pm 2\sqrt{7}}{2}$
$= -2 \pm \sqrt{7}$
$\therefore$ the x-intercepts are $-2 \pm \sqrt{7}$

l When $y = 0$, $x^2 + 8x + 11 = 0$
$a = 1$, $b = 8$ and $c = 11$
$\therefore \quad x = \dfrac{-8 \pm \sqrt{8^2 - 4(1)(11)}}{2(1)}$
$= \dfrac{-8 \pm \sqrt{20}}{2}$
$= \dfrac{-8 \pm 2\sqrt{5}}{2}$
$= -4 \pm \sqrt{5}$
$\therefore$ the x-intercepts are $-4 \pm \sqrt{5}$

6 a i $y = x^2 - 2x + 5$
has $a = 1$, $b = -2$, $c = 5$
$\therefore \quad -\dfrac{b}{2a} = -\dfrac{(-2)}{2(1)} = 1$
$\therefore$ the axis of symmetry is $x = 1$

iii When $x = 0$, $y = 5$,
so the y-intercept is 5
When $y = 0$, $x^2 - 2x + 5 = 0$
$\therefore \quad x = \dfrac{-(-2) \pm \sqrt{(-2)^2 - 4(1)(5)}}{2(1)}$
$= \dfrac{2 \pm \sqrt{4 - 20}}{2}$
This has no real solutions,
so there are no x-intercepts.

b i $y = x^2 + 4x - 1$
has $a = 1$, $b = 4$, $c = -1$
$\therefore \quad -\dfrac{b}{2a} = -\dfrac{4}{2(1)} = -2$
$\therefore$ the axis of symmetry is $x = -2$

ii When $x = 1$,
$y = 1^2 - 2(1) + 5$
$= 1 - 2 + 5$
$= 4$
$\therefore$ the vertex is at $(1, 4)$

iv

ii When $x = -2$,
$y = (-2)^2 + 4(-2) - 1$
$= 4 - 8 - 1$
$= -5$
$\therefore$ the vertex is at $(-2, -5)$

iii When $x = 0$, $y = -1$,
so the y-intercept is -1.
When $y = 0$, $x^2 + 4x - 1 = 0$

$$\therefore \quad x = \frac{-4 \pm \sqrt{4^2 - 4(1)(-1)}}{2(1)}$$

$$= \frac{-4 \pm \sqrt{20}}{2}$$

$$= \frac{-4 \pm 2\sqrt{5}}{2}$$

$$= -2 \pm \sqrt{5}$$

$\therefore$ the x-intercepts are $-2 \pm \sqrt{5}$

iv [graph showing parabola with $x = -2$, points $-2-\sqrt{5}$, -1, $-2+\sqrt{5}$, $V(-2, -5)$]

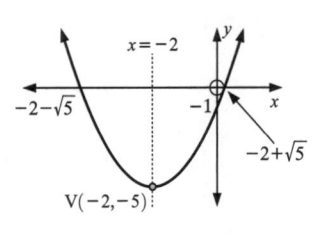

c **i** $y = 2x^2 - 5x + 2$
has $a = 2$, $b = -5$, $c = 2$

$$\therefore \quad -\frac{b}{2a} = -\frac{(-5)}{2(2)} = \frac{5}{4}$$

$\therefore$ the axis of symmetry is $x = \frac{5}{4}$

ii When $x = \frac{5}{4}$,
$y = 2(\frac{5}{4})^2 - 5(\frac{5}{4}) + 2$
$= \frac{25}{8} - \frac{25}{4} + 2$
$= -\frac{9}{8}$

$\therefore$ the vertex is at $(\frac{5}{4}, -\frac{9}{8})$

iii When $x = 0$, $y = 2$,
so the y-intercept is 2.
When $y = 0$, $2x^2 - 5x + 2 = 0$
$\therefore \quad (2x-1)(x-2) = 0$
$\therefore \quad x = \frac{1}{2}$ or 2

$\therefore$ the x-intercepts are $\frac{1}{2}$ and 2

iv [graph with $x = \frac{5}{4}$, points $\frac{1}{2}$, 2, vertex $V(\frac{5}{4}, -\frac{9}{8})$]

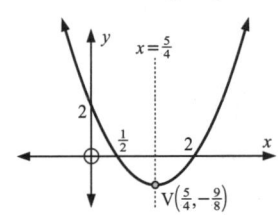

d **i** $y = -x^2 + 3x - 2$
has $a = -1$, $b = 3$, $c = -2$

$$\therefore \quad -\frac{b}{2a} = -\frac{3}{2(-1)} = \frac{3}{2}$$

$\therefore$ the axis of symmetry is $x = \frac{3}{2}$

iii When $x = 0$, $y = -2$,
so the y-intercept is -2.
When $y = 0$, $-x^2 + 3x - 2 = 0$
$\therefore \quad x^2 - 3x + 2 = 0$
$\therefore \quad (x-1)(x-2) = 0$
$\therefore \quad x = 1$ or 2

$\therefore$ the x-intercepts are 1 and 2

ii When $x = \frac{3}{2}$, $y = -(\frac{3}{2})^2 + 3(\frac{3}{2}) - 2$
$= -\frac{9}{4} + \frac{9}{2} - 2$
$= \frac{1}{4}$

$\therefore$ the vertex is at $(\frac{3}{2}, \frac{1}{4})$

iv [graph with vertex $V(\frac{3}{2}, \frac{1}{4})$, points 1, 2, -2, axis $x = \frac{3}{2}$]

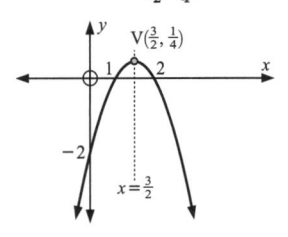

e **i** $y = -3x^2 + 4x - 1$
has $a = -3$, $b = 4$, $c = -1$

$$\therefore \quad -\frac{b}{2a} = -\frac{4}{2(-3)} = \frac{2}{3}$$

$\therefore$ the axis of symmetry is $x = \frac{2}{3}$

iii When $x = 0$, $y = -1$,
so the y-intercept is -1.
When $y = 0$, $-3x^2 + 4x - 1 = 0$
$\therefore \quad 3x^2 - 4x + 1 = 0$
$\therefore \quad (3x-1)(x-1) = 0$
$\therefore \quad x = \frac{1}{3}$ or 1

$\therefore$ the x-intercepts are $\frac{1}{3}$ and 1

ii When $x = \frac{2}{3}$, $y = -3(\frac{2}{3})^2 + 4(\frac{2}{3}) - 1$
$= -\frac{4}{3} + \frac{8}{3} - 1$
$= \frac{1}{3}$

$\therefore$ the vertex is at $(\frac{2}{3}, \frac{1}{3})$

iv [graph with vertex $V(\frac{2}{3}, \frac{1}{3})$, points $\frac{1}{3}$, 1, -1, axis $x = \frac{2}{3}$]

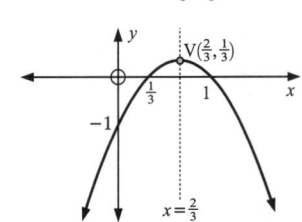

f **i** $y = -2x^2 + x + 1$
has $a = -2$, $b = 1$, $c = 1$
$\therefore -\dfrac{b}{2a} = -\dfrac{1}{2(-2)} = \dfrac{1}{4}$
$\therefore$ the axis of symmetry is $x = \dfrac{1}{4}$

ii When $x = \dfrac{1}{4}$, $y = -2(\dfrac{1}{4})^2 + \dfrac{1}{4} + 1$
$= -\dfrac{1}{8} + \dfrac{1}{4} + 1$
$= \dfrac{9}{8}$
$\therefore$ the vertex is at $(\dfrac{1}{4}, \dfrac{9}{8})$

iii When $x = 0$, $y = 1$,
so the y-intercept is 1.
When $y = 0$, $-2x^2 + x + 1 = 0$
$\therefore\ 2x^2 - x - 1 = 0$
$\therefore\ (2x + 1)(x - 1) = 0$
$\therefore\ x = -\dfrac{1}{2}$ or 1
$\therefore$ the x-intercepts are $-\dfrac{1}{2}$ and 1

iv [Graph: downward parabola with vertex $V(\dfrac{1}{4}, \dfrac{9}{8})$, axis $x = \dfrac{1}{4}$, x-intercepts $-\dfrac{1}{2}$ and 1, y-intercept 1]

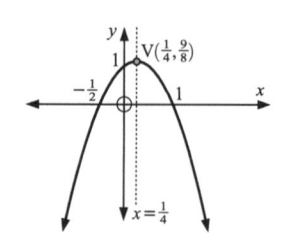

g **i** $y = 6x - x^2$
has $a = -1$, $b = 6$, $c = 0$
$\therefore -\dfrac{b}{2a} = -\dfrac{6}{2(-1)} = 3$
$\therefore$ the axis of symmetry is $x = 3$

ii When $x = 3$, $y = 6 \times 3 - 3^2$
$= 9$
$\therefore$ the vertex is at $(3, 9)$

iii When $x = 0$, $y = 0$,
so the y-intercept is 0.
When $y = 0$, $6x - x^2 = 0$
$\therefore\ x(6 - x) = 0$
$\therefore\ x = 0$ or 6
$\therefore$ the x-intercepts are 0 and 6

iv [Graph: downward parabola with vertex $V(3, 9)$, axis $x = 3$, x-intercepts 0 and 6]

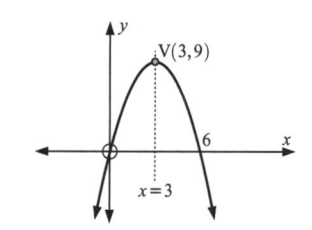

h **i** $y = -x^2 - 6x - 8$
has $a = -1$, $b = -6$, $c = -8$
$\therefore -\dfrac{b}{2a} = -\dfrac{(-6)}{2(-1)} = -3$
$\therefore$ the axis of symmetry is $x = -3$

ii When $x = -3$,
$y = -(-3)^2 - 6(-3) - 8$
$= -9 + 18 - 8$
$= 1$
$\therefore$ the vertex is at $(-3, 1)$

iii When $x = 0$, $y = -8$,
so the y-intercept is -8.
When $y = 0$, $-x^2 - 6x - 8 = 0$
$\therefore\ x^2 + 6x + 8 = 0$
$\therefore\ (x + 4)(x + 2) = 0$
$\therefore\ x = -4$ or -2
$\therefore$ the x-intercepts are -4 and -2

iv [Graph: downward parabola with vertex $V(-3, 1)$, axis $x = -3$, x-intercepts -4 and -2, y-intercept -8]

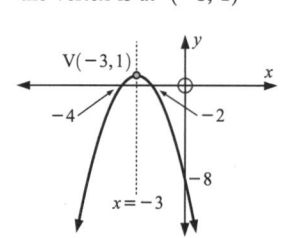

i **i** $y = -\dfrac{1}{4}x^2 + 2x + 1$
has $a = -\dfrac{1}{4}$, $b = 2$, $c = 1$
$\therefore -\dfrac{b}{2a} = -\dfrac{2}{2(-\frac{1}{4})} = 4$
$\therefore$ the axis of symmetry is $x = 4$

ii When $x = 4$, $y = -\dfrac{1}{4}(4)^2 + 2(4) + 1$
$= -4 + 8 + 1$
$= 5$
$\therefore$ the vertex is at $(4, 5)$

iii When $x = 0$, $y = 1$,
so the y-intercept is 1.
When $y = 0$, $-\frac{1}{4}x^2 + 2x + 1 = 0$
$\therefore \quad x^2 - 8x - 4 = 0$
which has $a = 1$, $b = -8$, $c = -4$

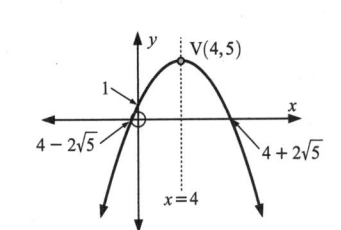

$\therefore \quad x = \dfrac{-(-8) \pm \sqrt{(-8)^2 - 4(1)(-4)}}{2(1)}$

$= \dfrac{8 \pm \sqrt{80}}{2}$

$= \dfrac{8 \pm 4\sqrt{5}}{2}$

$= 4 \pm 2\sqrt{5}$

$\therefore$ the x-intercepts are $4 \pm 2\sqrt{5}$.

iv

EXERCISE 6D.2

1 a $y = x^2 - 2x + 3$
$\therefore \quad y = x^2 - 2x + 1^2 + 3 - 1^2$
$\therefore \quad y = (x - 1)^2 + 2$
$\therefore$ vertex is $(1, 2)$, y-intercept is 3

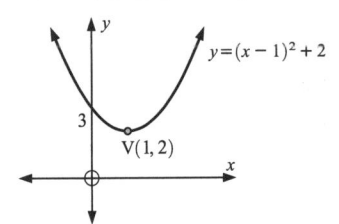

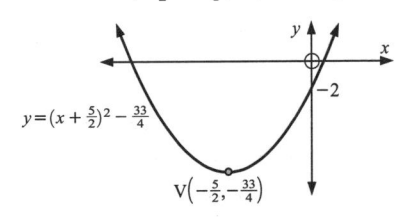

b $y = x^2 + 4x - 2$
$\therefore \quad y = x^2 + 4x + 2^2 - 2 - 2^2$
$\therefore \quad y = (x + 2)^2 - 6$
$\therefore$ vertex is $(-2, -6)$, y-intercept is -2

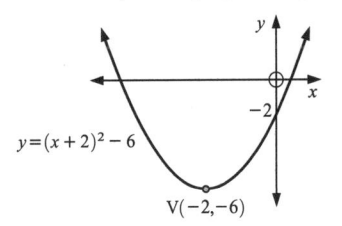

c $y = x^2 - 4x$
$\therefore \quad y = x^2 - 4x + 2^2 - 2^2$
$\therefore \quad y = (x - 2)^2 - 4$
$\therefore$ vertex is $(2, -4)$, y-intercept is 0

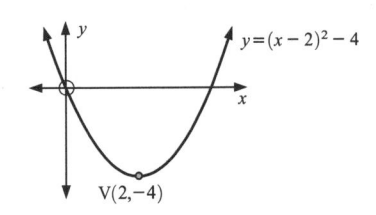

d $y = x^2 + 3x$
$\therefore \quad y = x^2 + 3x + (\frac{3}{2})^2 - (\frac{3}{2})^2$
$\therefore \quad y = (x + \frac{3}{2})^2 - \frac{9}{4}$
$\therefore$ vertex is $(-\frac{3}{2}, -\frac{9}{4})$, y-intercept is 0

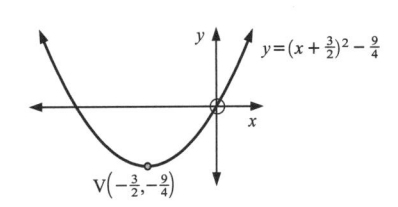

e $y = x^2 + 5x - 2$
$\therefore \quad y = x^2 + 5x + (\frac{5}{2})^2 - 2 - (\frac{5}{2})^2$
$\therefore \quad y = (x + \frac{5}{2})^2 - \frac{33}{4}$
$\therefore$ vertex is $(-\frac{5}{2}, -\frac{33}{4})$, y-intercept is -2

f $y = x^2 - 3x + 2$
$\therefore \quad y = x^2 - 3x + (\frac{3}{2})^2 + 2 - (\frac{3}{2})^2$
$\therefore \quad y = (x - \frac{3}{2})^2 - \frac{1}{4}$
$\therefore$ vertex is $(\frac{3}{2}, -\frac{1}{4})$, y-intercept is 2

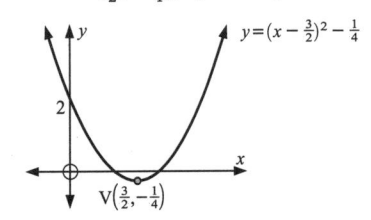

g $y = x^2 - 6x + 5$
∴ $y = x^2 - 6x + 3^2 + 5 - 3^2$
∴ $y = (x-3)^2 - 4$
∴ vertex is $(3, -4)$, y-intercept is 5

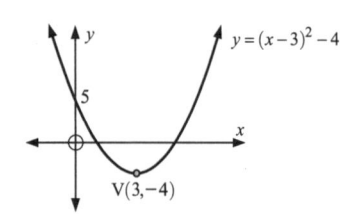

h $y = x^2 + 8x - 2$
∴ $y = x^2 + 8x + 4^2 - 2 - 4^2$
∴ $y = (x+4)^2 - 18$
∴ vertex is $(-4, -18)$, y-intercept is -2

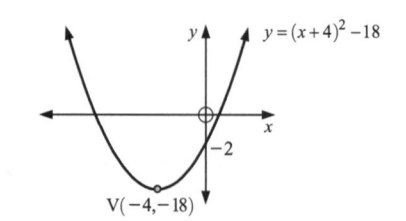

i $y = x^2 - 5x + 1$
∴ $y = x^2 - 5x + (\frac{5}{2})^2 + 1 - (\frac{5}{2})^2$
∴ $y = (x - \frac{5}{2})^2 - \frac{21}{4}$
∴ vertex is $(\frac{5}{2}, -5\frac{1}{4})$, y-intercept is 1

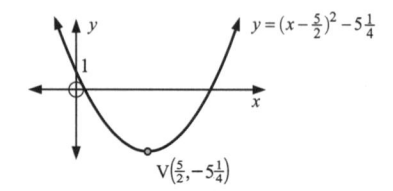

2 a   i $y = 2x^2 + 4x + 5$
$= 2[x^2 + 2x + \frac{5}{2}]$
$= 2[x^2 + 2x + 1^2 - 1^2 + \frac{5}{2}]$
$= 2[(x+1)^2 + \frac{3}{2}]$
$= 2(x+1)^2 + 3$

ii The vertex is $(-1, 3)$.

iii When $x = 0$, $y = 5$
∴ the y-intercept is 5

iv

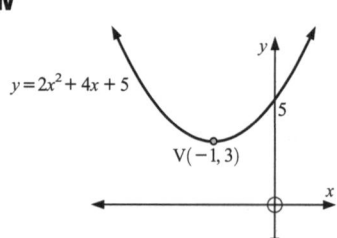

b   i $y = 2x^2 - 8x + 3$
$= 2[x^2 - 4x + \frac{3}{2}]$
$= 2[x^2 - 4x + 2^2 - 2^2 + \frac{3}{2}]$
$= 2[(x-2)^2 - \frac{5}{2}]$
$= 2(x-2)^2 - 5$

ii The vertex is $(2, -5)$.

iii When $x = 0$, $y = 3$
∴ the y-intercept is 3

iv

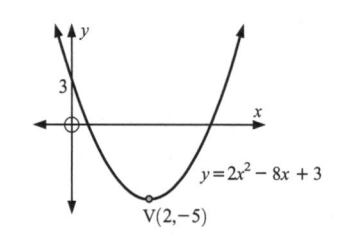

c   i $y = 2x^2 - 6x + 1$
$= 2[x^2 - 3x + \frac{1}{2}]$
$= 2[x^2 - 3x + (\frac{3}{2})^2 - (\frac{3}{2})^2 + \frac{1}{2}]$
$= 2[(x - \frac{3}{2})^2 - \frac{7}{4}]$
$= 2(x - \frac{3}{2})^2 - \frac{7}{2}$

ii The vertex is $(\frac{3}{2}, -\frac{7}{2})$.

iii When $x = 0$, $y = 1$
∴ the y-intercept is 1

iv

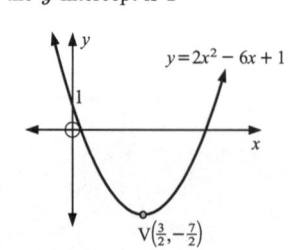

d **i** $y = 3x^2 - 6x + 5$
$= 3[x^2 - 2x + \frac{5}{3}]$
$= 3[x^2 - 2x + 1^2 - 1^2 + \frac{5}{3}]$
$= 3[(x-1)^2 + \frac{2}{3}]$
$= 3(x-1)^2 + 2$

ii The vertex is $(1, 2)$.

iii When $x = 0$, $y = 5$
∴ the y-intercept is 5

iv Graph of $y = 3x^2 - 6x + 5$, vertex $V(1, 2)$, y-intercept 5.

e **i** $y = -x^2 + 4x + 2$
$= -[x^2 - 4x - 2]$
$= -[x^2 - 4x + 2^2 - 2^2 - 2]$
$= -[(x-2)^2 - 6]$
$= -(x-2)^2 + 6$

ii The vertex is $(2, 6)$.

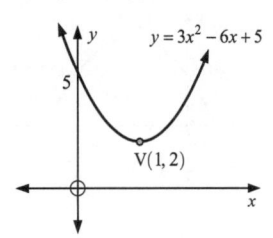

iii When $x = 0$, $y = 2$
∴ the y-intercept is 2

iv Graph of $y = -x^2 + 4x + 2$, vertex $V(2, 6)$, y-intercept 2.

f **i** $y = -2x^2 - 5x + 3$
$= -2[x^2 + \frac{5}{2}x - \frac{3}{2}]$
$= -2[x^2 + \frac{5}{2}x + (\frac{5}{4})^2 - (\frac{5}{4})^2 - \frac{3}{2}]$
$= -2[(x + \frac{5}{4})^2 - \frac{25}{16} - \frac{24}{16}]$
$= -2[(x + \frac{5}{4})^2 - \frac{49}{16}]$
$= -2(x + \frac{5}{4})^2 + \frac{49}{8}$

ii The vertex is $(-\frac{5}{4}, \frac{49}{8})$.

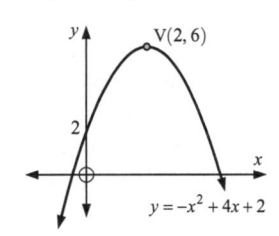

iii When $x = 0$, $y = 3$
∴ the y-intercept is 3

iv Graph of $y = -2x^2 - 5x + 3$, vertex $V(-\frac{5}{4}, \frac{49}{8})$, y-intercept 3.

3 a Using technology, the graph is

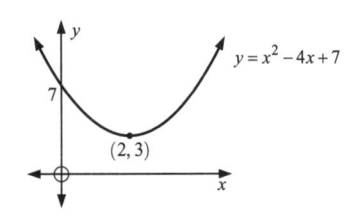

Graph of $y = x^2 - 4x + 7$, vertex $(2, 3)$, y-intercept 7.

Since the vertex is at $(2, 3)$,
the function must be of the form
$y = a(x-2)^2 + 3$ for some a.
∴ when $x = 0$,
$y = a(-2)^2 + 3 = 4a + 3$
but the y-intercept is 7
∴ $4a + 3 = 7$
∴ $a = 1$
∴ the equation is $y = (x-2)^2 + 3$

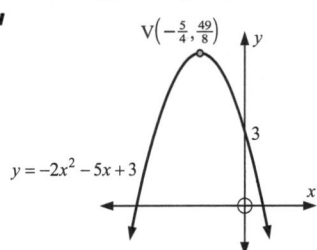

b Using technology, the graph is

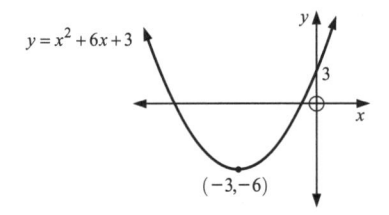

Graph of $y = x^2 + 6x + 3$, vertex $(-3, -6)$, y-intercept 3.

Since the vertex is at $(-3, -6)$,
the function must be of the form
$y = a(x+3)^2 - 6$ for some a.
∴ when $x = 0$,
$y = a \times 3^2 - 6 = 9a - 6$
but the y-intercept is 3
∴ $9a - 6 = 3$
∴ $a = 1$
∴ the equation is $y = (x+3)^2 - 6$

c Using technology, the graph is

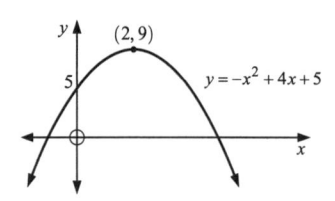

Since the vertex is at $(2, 9)$,
the function must be of the form
$$y = a(x-2)^2 + 9 \quad \text{for some } a.$$
$\therefore$ when $x = 0$,
$$y = a(-2)^2 + 9 = 4a + 9$$
but the y-intercept is 5
$\therefore \quad 4a + 9 = 5$
$\therefore \quad a = -1$
$\therefore$ the equation is $y = -(x-2)^2 + 9$

d Using technology, the graph is

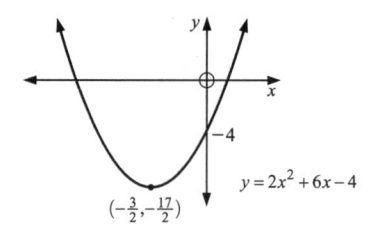

Since the vertex is at $(-\frac{3}{2}, -\frac{17}{2})$,
the function must be of the form
$$y = a(x + \frac{3}{2})^2 - \frac{17}{2} \quad \text{for some } a.$$
$\therefore$ when $x = 0$,
$$y = a(\frac{3}{2})^2 - \frac{17}{2} = \frac{9}{4}a - \frac{17}{2}$$
but the y-intercept is -4
$\therefore \quad \frac{9}{4}a - \frac{17}{2} = -4$
$\therefore \quad \frac{9}{4}a = \frac{9}{2}$
$\therefore \quad a = 2$
$\therefore$ the equation is $y = 2(x + \frac{3}{2})^2 - \frac{17}{2}$

e Using technology, the graph is

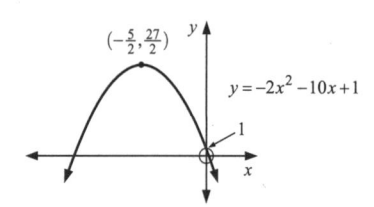

Since the vertex is at $(-\frac{5}{2}, \frac{27}{2})$,
the function must be of the form
$$y = a(x + \frac{5}{2})^2 + \frac{27}{2} \quad \text{for some } a.$$
$\therefore$ when $x = 0$,
$$y = a(\frac{5}{2})^2 + \frac{27}{2} = \frac{25}{4}a + \frac{27}{2}$$
but the y-intercept is 1
$\therefore \quad \frac{25}{4}a + \frac{27}{2} = 1$
$\therefore \quad \frac{25}{4}a = -\frac{25}{2}$
$\therefore \quad a = -2$
$\therefore$ the equation is $y = -2(x + \frac{5}{2})^2 + \frac{27}{2}$

f Using technology, the graph is

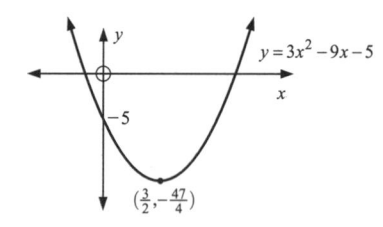

Since the vertex is at $(\frac{3}{2}, -\frac{47}{4})$,
the function must be of the form
$$y = a(x - \frac{3}{2})^2 - \frac{47}{4} \quad \text{for some } a.$$
$\therefore$ when $x = 0$,
$$y = a(-\frac{3}{2})^2 - \frac{47}{4} = \frac{9}{4}a - \frac{47}{4}$$
but the y-intercept is -5
$\therefore \quad \frac{9}{4}a - \frac{47}{4} = -5$
$\therefore \quad \frac{9}{4}a = \frac{27}{4}$
$\therefore \quad a = 3$
$\therefore$ the equation is $y = 3(x - \frac{3}{2})^2 - \frac{47}{4}$

EXERCISE 6D.3

1 a $y = x^2 + 7x - 2$
has $a = 1$, $b = 7$, $c = -2$
$\therefore \quad \Delta = b^2 - 4ac$
$\quad = 7^2 - 4(1)(-2)$
$\quad = 57 > 0$
$\therefore$ the graph cuts the x-axis twice.

b $y = x^2 + 4\sqrt{2}x + 8$
has $a = 1$, $b = 4\sqrt{2}$, $c = 8$
$\therefore \quad \Delta = b^2 - 4ac$
$\quad = (4\sqrt{2})^2 - 4(1)(8)$
$\quad = 0$
$\therefore$ the graph touches the x-axis.

   c $y = -2x^2 + 3x + 1$
       has $a = -2$, $b = 3$, $c = 1$
      $\therefore \quad \Delta = b^2 - 4ac$
           $= 3^2 - 4(-2)(1)$
           $= 17 > 0$
      $\therefore$ the graph cuts the x-axis twice.

   e $y = -x^2 + x + 6$
       has $a = -1$, $b = 1$, $c = 6$
      $\therefore \quad \Delta = b^2 - 4ac$
           $= 1^2 - 4(-1)(6)$
           $= 25 > 0$
      $\therefore$ the graph cuts the x-axis twice.

   d $y = 6x^2 + 5x - 4$
       has $a = 6$, $b = 5$, $c = -4$
      $\therefore \quad \Delta = b^2 - 4ac$
           $= 5^2 - 4(6)(-4)$
           $= 121 > 0$
      $\therefore$ the graph cuts the x-axis twice.

   f $y = 9x^2 + 6x + 1$
       has $a = 9$, $b = 6$, $c = 1$
      $\therefore \quad \Delta = b^2 - 4ac$
           $= 6^2 - 4(9)(1)$
           $= 0$
      $\therefore$ the graph touches the x-axis.

2   **a** $x^2 - 3x + 6$
       has $a = 1$, $b = -3$, $c = 6$
      $\therefore \quad \Delta = b^2 - 4ac$
           $= (-3)^2 - 4(1)(6)$
           $= -15$
      $\therefore$ since $a > 0$ and $\Delta < 0$,
      $x^2 - 3x + 6 > 0$ for all x.

   c $2x^2 - 4x + 7$
       has $a = 2$, $b = -4$, $c = 7$
      $\therefore \quad \Delta = b^2 - 4ac$
           $= (-4)^2 - 4(2)(7)$
           $= -40$
      $\therefore$ since $a > 0$ and $\Delta < 0$,
      $2x^2 - 4x + 7 > 0$ for all x.
      $\therefore$ it is positive definite.

   b $4x - x^2 - 6$
       has $a = -1$, $b = 4$, $c = -6$
      $\therefore \quad \Delta = b^2 - 4ac$
           $= 4^2 - 4(-1)(-6)$
           $= -8$
      $\therefore$ since $a < 0$ and $\Delta < 0$,
      $4x - x^2 - 6 < 0$ for all x.

   d $-2x^2 + 3x - 4$
       has $a = -2$, $b = 3$, $c = -4$
      $\therefore \quad \Delta = b^2 - 4ac$
           $= 3^2 - 4(-2)(-4)$
           $= -23$
      $\therefore$ since $a < 0$ and $\Delta < 0$,
      $-2x^2 + 3x - 4 < 0$ for all x.
      $\therefore$ it is negative definite.

3 $3x^2 + kx - 1$
   has $a = 3$, $b = k$, $c = -1$
   $\therefore \quad \Delta = b^2 - 4ac$
        $= k^2 - 4(3)(-1)$
        $= k^2 + 12$
   $\therefore \quad \Delta > 0$ for all k
   {as $k^2 \geqslant 0$ for all k}
   $\therefore \quad 3x^2 + kx - 1$ has two real distinct
   roots for all k.
   $\therefore$ it can never be positive definite.

4 $2x^2 + kx + 2$
   has $a = 2$, $b = k$, $c = 2$
   $\therefore \quad \Delta = b^2 - 4ac$
        $= k^2 - 4(2)(2)$
        $= k^2 - 16$
   Now $2x^2 + kx + 2$ has $a > 0$.
   $\therefore$ it is positive definite provided $k^2 - 16 < 0$
                                        $\therefore \quad k^2 < 16$
                                        $\therefore \quad -4 < k < 4$

EXERCISE 6E

1   **a**   The x-intercepts are 1 and 2.
      $\therefore \quad y = a(x - 1)(x - 2)$
      for some $a \neq 0$.
      But the y-intercept is 4.
      $\therefore \quad a(-1)(-2) = 4$
      $\therefore \quad 2a = 4$
      $\therefore \quad a = 2$
      $\therefore \quad y = 2(x - 1)(x - 2)$

   b   The graph touches the
      x-axis when $x = 2$.
      $\therefore \quad y = a(x - 2)^2$
      for some $a \neq 0$.
      But the y-intercept is 8.
      $\therefore \quad a(-2)^2 = 8$
      $\therefore \quad 4a = 8$
      $\therefore \quad a = 2$
      $\therefore \quad y = 2(x - 2)^2$

   c   The x-intercepts are 1 and 3.
      $\therefore \quad y = a(x - 1)(x - 3)$
      for some $a \neq 0$.
      But the y-intercept is 3.
      $\therefore \quad a(-1)(-3) = 3$
      $\therefore \quad 3a = 3$
      $\therefore \quad a = 1$
      $\therefore \quad y = (x - 1)(x - 3)$

d The x-intercepts are -1 and 3.
$\therefore \ y = a(x+1)(x-3)$ for some $a \neq 0$.
But the y-intercept is 3.
$\therefore \ a(1)(-3) = 3$
$\therefore \ -3a = 3$
$\therefore \ a = -1$
$\therefore \ y = -(x+1)(x-3)$

e The graph touches the x-axis when $x = 1$.
$\therefore \ y = a(x-1)^2$ for some $a \neq 0$.
But the y-intercept is -3.
$\therefore \ a(-1)^2 = -3$
$\therefore \ a = -3$
$\therefore \ y = -3(x-1)^2$

f The x-intercepts are -2 and 3.
$\therefore \ y = a(x+2)(x-3)$ for some $a \neq 0$.
But the y-intercept is 12.
$\therefore \ a(2)(-3) = 12$
$\therefore \ -6a = 12$
$\therefore \ a = -2$
$\therefore \ y = -2(x+2)(x-3)$

2 a As the axis of symmetry is $x = 3$, the other x-intercept is 4.
$\therefore \ y = a(x-2)(x-4)$ for some $a \neq 0$.
But the y-intercept $= 12$
$\therefore \ a(-2)(-4) = 12$
$\therefore \ 8a = 12$
$\therefore \ a = \frac{12}{8} = \frac{3}{2}$
$\therefore \ y = \frac{3}{2}(x-2)(x-4)$

b As the axis of symmetry is $x = -1$, the other x-intercept is 2.
$\therefore \ y = a(x+4)(x-2)$ for some $a \neq 0$.
But the y-intercept $= 4$
$\therefore \ a(4)(-2) = 4$
$\therefore \ -8a = 4$
$\therefore \ a = -\frac{1}{2}$
$\therefore \ y = -\frac{1}{2}(x+4)(x-2)$

c The graph touches the x-axis at $x = -3$,
$\therefore \ y = a(x+3)^2$ for some $a \neq 0$.
But the y-intercept is -12, so $a(3)^2 = -12$
$\therefore \ 9a = -12$
$\therefore \ a = -\frac{12}{9} = -\frac{4}{3}$
$\therefore \ y = -\frac{4}{3}(x+3)^2$

3 a Since the x-intercepts are 5 and 1, the equation is $y = a(x-5)(x-1)$ for some $a \neq 0$.
But when $x = 2$, $y = -9$
$\therefore \ -9 = a(2-5)(2-1)$
$\therefore \ -9 = a(-3)(1)$
$\therefore \ -3a = -9$
$\therefore \ a = 3$
$\therefore$ the equation is $y = 3(x-5)(x-1)$
$\therefore \ y = 3(x^2 - 6x + 5)$
$\therefore \ y = 3x^2 - 18x + 15$

b Since the x-intercepts are 2 and $-\frac{1}{2}$, the equation is $y = a(x-2)(x+\frac{1}{2})$ for some $a \neq 0$.
But when $x = 3$, $y = -14$
$\therefore \ -14 = a(3-2)(3+\frac{1}{2})$
$\therefore \ -14 = a(1)(\frac{7}{2})$
$\therefore \ \frac{7}{2}a = -14$
$\therefore \ a = -4$
$\therefore$ the equation is $y = -4(x-2)(x+\frac{1}{2})$
$\therefore \ y = -4(x^2 - \frac{3}{2}x - 1)$
$\therefore \ y = -4x^2 + 6x + 4$

c Since the graph touches the x-axis at 3, its equation is $y = a(x-3)^2$, for some $a \neq 0$.
But when $x = -2$, $y = -25$
$\therefore \ -25 = a(-2-3)^2$
$\therefore \ -25 = 25a$
$\therefore \ a = -1$
$\therefore$ the equation is $y = -(x-3)^2$
$\therefore \ y = -(x^2 - 6x + 9)$
$\therefore \ y = -x^2 + 6x - 9$

d Since the graph touches the x-axis at -2, its equation is $y = a(x+2)^2$, for some $a \neq 0$.
But when $x = -1$, $y = 4$
$\therefore \ 4 = a(-1+2)^2$
$\therefore \ 4 = a$
$\therefore$ the equation is $y = 4(x+2)^2$
$\therefore \ y = 4(x^2 + 4x + 4)$
$\therefore \ y = 4x^2 + 16x + 16$

e Since the graph cuts the x-axis at 3 and has axis of symmetry $x = 2$, it must also cut the x-axis at 1.
∴ the x-intercepts are 3 and 1, and the equation is $y = a(x - 3)(x - 1)$ for some $a \neq 0$.
But when $x = 5$, $y = 12$
∴ $12 = a(5 - 3)(5 - 1)$
∴ $12 = a(2)(4)$
∴ $8a = 12$
∴ $a = \frac{3}{2}$
∴ the equation is $y = \frac{3}{2}(x - 3)(x - 1)$
∴ $y = \frac{3}{2}(x^2 - 4x + 3)$
∴ $y = \frac{3}{2}x^2 - 6x + \frac{9}{2}$

f Since the graph cuts the x-axis at 5 and has axis of symmetry $x = 1$, it must also cut the x-axis at -3.
∴ the x-intercepts are 5 and -3, and the equation is $y = a(x - 5)(x + 3)$ for some $a \neq 0$.
But when $x = 2$, $y = 5$
∴ $5 = a(2 - 5)(2 + 3)$
∴ $5 = a(-3)(5)$
∴ $-15a = 5$
∴ $a = -\frac{1}{3}$
∴ the equation is $y = -\frac{1}{3}(x - 5)(x + 3)$
∴ $y = -\frac{1}{3}(x^2 - 2x - 15)$
∴ $y = -\frac{1}{3}x^2 + \frac{2}{3}x + 5$

4 a The vertex is $(2, 4)$, so the quadratic has equation
$y = a(x - 2)^2 + 4$ for some $a \neq 0$.
But the graph passes through the origin
∴ $0 = a(0 - 2)^2 + 4$
∴ $4a + 4 = 0$
∴ $a = -1$
∴ the equation is $y = -(x - 2)^2 + 4$

c The vertex is $(3, 8)$, so the quadratic has equation
$y = a(x - 3)^2 + 8$ for some $a \neq 0$.
But the graph passes through $(1, 0)$
∴ $0 = a(1 - 3)^2 + 8$
∴ $0 = 4a + 8$
∴ $a = -2$
∴ the equation is $y = -2(x - 3)^2 + 8$

e The vertex is $(2, 3)$, so the quadratic has equation
$y = a(x - 2)^2 + 3$ for some $a \neq 0$.
But the graph passes through $(3, 1)$
∴ $1 = a(3 - 2)^2 + 3$
∴ $1 = a + 3$
∴ $a = -2$
∴ the equation is $y = -2(x - 2)^2 + 3$

b The vertex is $(2, -1)$, so the quadratic has equation
$y = a(x - 2)^2 - 1$ for some $a \neq 0$.
But the graph passes through $(0, 7)$
∴ $7 = a(0 - 2)^2 - 1$
∴ $7 = 4a - 1$
∴ $a = 2$
∴ the equation is $y = 2(x - 2)^2 - 1$

d The vertex is $(4, -6)$, so the quadratic has equation
$y = a(x - 4)^2 - 6$ for some $a \neq 0$.
But the graph passes through $(7, 0)$
∴ $0 = a(7 - 4)^2 - 6$
∴ $9a - 6 = 0$
∴ $a = \frac{2}{3}$
∴ the equation is $y = \frac{2}{3}(x - 4)^2 - 6$

f The vertex is $(\frac{1}{2}, -\frac{3}{2})$, so the quadratic has equation
$y = a(x - \frac{1}{2})^2 - \frac{3}{2}$ for some $a \neq 0$.
But the graph passes through $(\frac{3}{2}, \frac{1}{2})$
∴ $\frac{1}{2} = a(\frac{3}{2} - \frac{1}{2})^2 - \frac{3}{2}$
∴ $\frac{1}{2} = a - \frac{3}{2}$
∴ $a = 2$
∴ the equation is $y = 2(x - \frac{1}{2})^2 - \frac{3}{2}$

EXERCISE 6F

1 a $y = x^2 - 2x + 8$ meets $y = x + 6$
when $x^2 - 2x + 8 = x + 6$
∴ $x^2 - 3x + 2 = 0$
∴ $(x - 1)(x - 2) = 0$
∴ $x = 1$ or 2

Substituting into $y = x + 6$,
when $x = 1$, $y = 7$
and when $x = 2$, $y = 8$
∴ the graphs meet at $(1, 7)$ and $(2, 8)$

b $y = -x^2 + 3x + 9$ meets $y = 2x - 3$
when $-x^2 + 3x + 9 = 2x - 3$
$\therefore \quad x^2 - x - 12 = 0$
$\therefore \quad (x - 4)(x + 3) = 0$
$\therefore \quad x = 4$ or -3

Substituting into $y = 2x - 3$,
when $x = -3$, $y = 2(-3) - 3 = -9$
and when $x = 4$, $y = 2(4) - 3 = 5$
$\therefore$ the graphs meet at $(-3, -9)$ and $(4, 5)$

c $y = x^2 - 4x + 3$ meets $y = 2x - 6$
when $x^2 - 4x + 3 = 2x - 6$
$\therefore \quad x^2 - 6x + 9 = 0$
$\therefore \quad (x - 3)^2 = 0$
$\therefore \quad x = 3$
Substituting into $y = 2x - 6$,
when $x = 3$, $y = 0$
$\therefore$ the graphs touch at $(3, 0)$

d $y = -x^2 + 4x - 7$ meets $y = 5x - 4$
when $-x^2 + 4x - 7 = 5x - 4$
$\therefore \quad x^2 + x + 3 = 0$
which has $a = 1$, $b = 1$, $c = 3$
$\therefore \quad x = \dfrac{-1 \pm \sqrt{1^2 - 4(1)(3)}}{2}$
$= \dfrac{-1 \pm \sqrt{-11}}{2}$
$\therefore$ there are no real solutions
$\therefore$ the graphs do not meet.

2 a $(0.59, 5.59)$ and $(3.41, 8.41)$ **b** $(3, -4)$ touching
c graphs do not meet   **d** $(-2.56, -18.81)$ and $(1.56, 1.81)$

3 a $y = x^2$ meets $y = x + 2$
when $x^2 = x + 2$
$\therefore \quad x^2 - x - 2 = 0$
$\therefore \quad (x + 1)(x - 2) = 0$
$\therefore \quad x = -1$ or 2
Substituting into $y = x + 2$,
when $x = -1$, $y = 1$
and when $x = 2$, $y = 4$
$\therefore$ the graphs meet at $(-1, 1)$ and $(2, 4)$.

b $y = x^2 + 2x - 3$ meets $y = x - 1$
when $x^2 + 2x - 3 = x - 1$
$\therefore \quad x^2 + x - 2 = 0$
$\therefore \quad (x - 1)(x + 2) = 0$
$\therefore \quad x = 1$ or -2
Substituting into $y = x - 1$,
when $x = 1$, $y = 0$
and when $x = -2$, $y = -3$
$\therefore$ the graphs meet at $(1, 0)$ and $(-2, -3)$.

c $y = 2x^2 - x + 3$ meets $y = 2 + x + x^2$
when $2x^2 - x + 3 = 2 + x + x^2$
$\therefore \quad x^2 - 2x + 1 = 0$
$\therefore \quad (x - 1)^2 = 0$
$\therefore \quad x = 1$
Substituting into $y = 2 + x + x^2$
when $x = 1$, $y = 2 + 1 + 1 = 4$
$\therefore$ the graphs meet at $(1, 4)$.

d Substituting $y = x + 3$ into $xy = 4$
gives $x(x + 3) = 4$
$\therefore \quad x^2 + 3x - 4 = 0$
$\therefore \quad (x + 4)(x - 1) = 0$
$\therefore \quad x = -4$ or 1
Substituting into $y = x + 3$,
when $x = -4$, $y = -1$
and when $x = 1$, $y = 4$
$\therefore$ the graphs meet at $(-4, -1)$ and $(1, 4)$.

5 $y = 3x + c$ is a tangent to $y = x^2 - 5x + 7$ if they meet at exactly one point (touch).
$y = x^2 - 5x + 7$ meets $y = 3x + c$ when $x^2 - 5x + 7 = 3x + c$
$\therefore \quad x^2 - 8x + 7 - c = 0$
The graphs meet exactly once when this equation has a repeated root $\therefore \Delta = 0$
$\therefore \quad (-8)^2 - 4(1)(7 - c) = 0$
$\therefore \quad 64 - 28 + 4c = 0$
$\therefore \quad 4c = -36$
$\therefore \quad c = -9$

6 $y = mx - 2$ is a tangent to $y = x^2 - 4x + 2$ if they meet at exactly one point (touch).
$y = x^2 - 4x + 2$ meets $y = mx - 2$ when $x^2 - 4x + 2 = mx - 2$
$\therefore \quad x^2 - (m+4)x + 4 = 0$
The graphs meet exactly once when this equation has a repeated root $\quad \therefore \quad \Delta = 0$
$\therefore \quad (m+4)^2 - 4(1)(4) = 0$
$\therefore \quad m^2 + 8m + 16 - 16 = 0$
$\therefore \quad m(m+8) = 0$
$\therefore \quad m = 0$ or -8

7 Lines with y-intercept 1 have the form $y = mx + 1$.
$y = mx + 1$ is a tangent to $y = 3x^2 + 5x + 4$ if they meet at exactly one point (touch).
$y = 3x^2 + 5x + 4$ meets $y = mx + 1$ when $3x^2 + 5x + 4 = mx + 1$
$\therefore \quad 3x^2 + (5 - m)x + 3 = 0$
The graphs meet exactly once when this equation has a repeated root $\quad \therefore \quad \Delta = 0$
$\therefore \quad (5 - m)^2 - 4(3)(3) = 0$
$\therefore \quad 25 - 10m + m^2 - 36 = 0$
$\therefore \quad m^2 - 10m - 11 = 0$
$\therefore \quad (m+1)(m-11) = 0$
$\therefore \quad m = -1$ or 11
$\therefore \quad$ the required lines have gradient -1 or 11.

8 a $y = x + c$ meets $y = 2x^2 - 3x - 7$
when $2x^2 - 3x - 7 = x + c$
$\therefore \quad 2x^2 - 4x - 7 - c = 0$
The graphs will never meet if this equation has no real roots $\quad \therefore \quad \Delta < 0$
$\therefore \quad (-4)^2 - 4(2)(-7 - c) < 0$
$\therefore \quad 16 + 56 + 8c < 0$
$\therefore \quad 8c < -72$
$\therefore \quad c < -9$

b Choose c such that $c < -9$, for example $c = -10$:

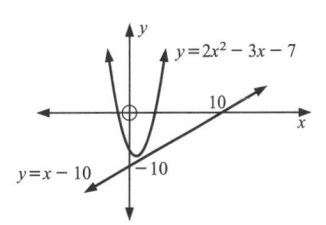

EXERCISE 6G

1 Let the smaller of the integers be x.
The other integer is $(x + 12)$.
$\therefore$ the sum of their squares is
$x^2 + (x + 12)^2 = 74$
$\therefore \quad x^2 + x^2 + 24x + 144 = 74$
$\therefore \quad 2x^2 + 24x + 70 = 0$
$\therefore \quad x^2 + 12x + 35 = 0$
$\therefore \quad (x + 7)(x + 5) = 0$
$\therefore \quad x = -7$ or -5
So, the integers are -7 and 5, or -5 and 7.

2 Let the number be x, so its reciprocal is $\dfrac{1}{x}$.
They have sum $x + \dfrac{1}{x} = 5\dfrac{1}{5}$
$\therefore \quad x^2 + 1 = \dfrac{26}{5}x$
$\therefore \quad x^2 - \dfrac{26}{5}x + 1 = 0$
$\therefore \quad 5x^2 - 26x + 5 = 0$
$\therefore \quad (5x - 1)(x - 5) = 0$
$\therefore \quad x = \dfrac{1}{5}$ or 5
So, the number is either $\dfrac{1}{5}$ or 5.

3 Let the number be x so its square is x^2.
$\therefore$ the sum is $x + x^2 = 210$
$\therefore \quad x^2 + x - 210 = 0$
$\therefore \quad (x + 15)(x - 14) = 0$
$\therefore \quad x = -15$ or 14
But x is a natural number, so $x > 0$,
$\therefore$ the number is 14.

4 Suppose the numbers are x and $(x + 2)$.
Then $x(x + 2) = 360$
$\therefore \quad x^2 + 2x - 360 = 0$
$\therefore \quad (x + 20)(x - 18) = 0$
$\therefore \quad x = -20$ or 18
$\therefore$ the numbers are -20 and -18, or 18 and 20.

5 Suppose the numbers are x and $(x+2)$.
Then $x(x+2) = 255$
$\therefore \quad x^2 + 2x - 255 = 0$
$\therefore \quad (x+17)(x-15) = 0$
$\therefore \quad x = -17$ or 15
$\therefore$ the numbers are -17 and -15,
or 15 and 17.

6 If the polygon has n sides, then
$\dfrac{n}{2}(n-3) = 90$
$\therefore \quad \frac{1}{2}n^2 - \frac{3}{2}n = 90$
$\therefore \quad n^2 - 3n - 180 = 0$
$\therefore \quad (n-15)(n+12) = 0$
$\therefore \quad n = -12$ or 15
$\therefore$ the polygon has 15 sides. $\{$as $n > 0\}$

7 If the width of the rectangle is w cm, then its length is $(w+4)$ cm.
$\therefore$ the area is $w(w+4) = 26$
$\therefore \quad w^2 + 4w - 26 = 0$
which has $a = 1$, $b = 4$, $c = -26$
$\therefore \quad w = \dfrac{-4 \pm \sqrt{4^2 - 4(1)(-26)}}{2(1)}$
$= \dfrac{-4 \pm \sqrt{120}}{2} = -2 \pm \sqrt{30}$
But $w > 0$, so $w = -2 + \sqrt{30}$
≈ 3.477 cm
So, the width is approximately 3.48 cm.

8 a The base has sides of length x cm, so the areas of the top and bottom surfaces are both x^2 cm^2.

The box has height $(x+1)$ cm, so the area of each of the side faces is $x(x+1)$ cm^2.

$\therefore$ the total surface area is
$A = 2x^2 + 4x(x+1)$
$= 2x^2 + 4x^2 + 4x$
$= 6x^2 + 4x$ cm^2

b $\qquad 6x^2 + 4x = 240$
$\therefore \quad 3x^2 + 2x - 120 = 0$
$\therefore \quad (3x + 20)(x - 6) = 0$
$\therefore \quad x = -\frac{20}{3}$ or 6
but $x > 0$, so $x = 6$ cm
$\therefore$ the box is 6 cm $\times$ 6 cm $\times$ 7 cm

9 Suppose the tin plate was x cm $\times$ x cm. When 3 cm $\times$ 3 cm squares are cut from the corners, the base of the open box formed is $(x-6)$ cm $\times$ $(x-6)$ cm.
The open box has height 3 cm, so its volume is $3 \times (x-6) \times (x-6) = 80$
$\therefore \quad 3(x^2 - 12x + 36) = 80$
$\quad 3x^2 - 36x + 108 = 80$
$\therefore \quad 3x^2 - 36x + 28 = 0$
which has $a = 3$, $b = -36$, $c = 28$

$\therefore \quad x = \dfrac{-(-36) \pm \sqrt{(-36)^2 - 4(3)(28)}}{2(3)}$
$= \dfrac{36 \pm \sqrt{960}}{6}$ and since $x > 6$,
$x = 6 + \dfrac{\sqrt{960}}{6} \approx 11.16$ cm
$\therefore$ the original piece of tinplate was about 11.2 cm square.

10

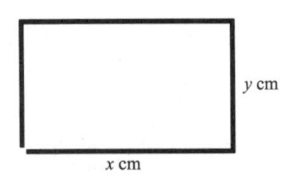

Suppose one side of the rectangle has length x cm and the other has length y cm.
The perimeter is $(2x + 2y)$ cm,
so $2x + 2y = 20$
$\therefore \quad 2y = 20 - 2x$
$\therefore \quad y = 10 - x$
The area of the rectangle is therefore $x(10 - x)$ cm^2.

If the area is 30 cm^2, then
$x(10 - x) = 30$
$\therefore \quad 10x - x^2 = 30$
$\therefore \quad x^2 - 10x + 30 = 0$
which has $a = 1$, $b = -10$, $c = 30$
$\therefore \quad x = \dfrac{-(-10) \pm \sqrt{(-10)^2 - 4(1)(30)}}{2(1)}$
$= \dfrac{10 \pm \sqrt{100 - 120}}{2}$
$= \dfrac{10 \pm \sqrt{-120}}{2}$
$\therefore \quad x$ has no real solutions, so it is not possible.

11 The smaller rectangle is similar to the original rectangle.

$$\therefore \quad \frac{AB}{AD} = \frac{BC}{BY}$$

Suppose $AB = x$ units, and $AD = BC = 1$ unit

$$\therefore \quad \frac{x}{1} = \frac{1}{x-1}$$

$$\therefore \quad x(x-1) = 1$$

$$\therefore \quad x^2 - x - 1 = 0$$

which has $a = 1$, $b = -1$, $c = -1$

$$\therefore \quad x = \frac{-(-1) \pm \sqrt{(-1)^2 - 4(1)(-1)}}{2(1)}$$

$$= \frac{1 \pm \sqrt{1+4}}{2}$$

$$= \frac{1 \pm \sqrt{5}}{2}$$

$$\therefore \quad x = \frac{1 + \sqrt{5}}{2}, \text{ since } x > 0$$

But $x = \frac{AB}{AD}$, which is the golden ratio

$\therefore$ the golden ratio is $\frac{1 + \sqrt{5}}{2}$

12

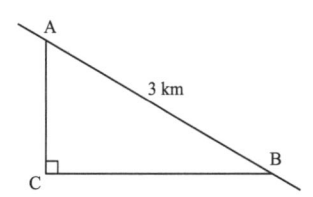

Suppose AC is x hundred metres, so BC is $(x + 4)$ hundred metres.

Now $AC^2 + BC^2 = AB^2$ {Pythagoras}

$$\therefore \quad x^2 + (x+4)^2 = 30^2$$

$$\therefore \quad x^2 + x^2 + 8x + 16 = 900$$

$$\therefore \quad 2x^2 + 8x - 884 = 0$$

$$\therefore \quad x^2 + 4x - 442 = 0$$

which has $a = 1$, $b = 4$, $c = -442$

$$\therefore \quad x = \frac{-4 \pm \sqrt{4^2 - 4(1)(-442)}}{2(1)}$$

$$= \frac{-4 \pm \sqrt{1784}}{2}$$

$$= \frac{-4 + \sqrt{1784}}{2} \approx 19.12 \quad \{\text{as } x > 0\}$$

$\therefore$ AC ≈ 19.12 hundred metres and BC ≈ 23.12 hundred metres

$\therefore$ since the paddock is triangular, its area is $\frac{1}{2} \times$ AC $\times$ BC $= 221$ hectares.

13

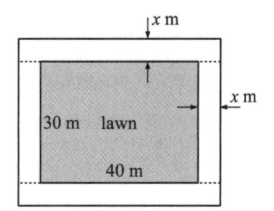

Suppose the concrete has width x m around the lawn. We divide the concrete up into four regions as shown.

The smaller regions have area $30x$ m^2, whilst the larger regions have area $x(40 + 2x)$ m^2.

Now the total area of concrete is one quarter the area of the lawn.

$$\therefore \quad 2 \times 30x + 2 \times x(40 + 2x) = \tfrac{1}{4} \times 30 \times 40$$

$$\therefore \quad 60x + 80x + 4x^2 = 300$$

$$\therefore \quad 4x^2 + 140x - 300 = 0$$

$$\therefore \quad x^2 + 35x - 75 = 0$$

which has $a = 1$, $b = 35$, $c = -75$

$$\therefore \quad x = \frac{-35 \pm \sqrt{35^2 - 4(1)(-75)}}{2(1)}$$

$$= \frac{-35 \pm \sqrt{1525}}{2}$$

But $x > 0$,

so $x = \frac{-35 + \sqrt{1525}}{2} \approx 2.026$ m

$\therefore$ the path is about 2.03 m wide.

14 Suppose Hassan's speed is h km h^{-1}. We know that speed $= \frac{\text{distance}}{\text{time}}$, so time $= \frac{\text{distance}}{\text{speed}}$

$\therefore$ if it takes Hassan t hours, $t = \frac{40}{h}$ .... (1)

Now Chuong says he will drive home at speed $(h + 40)$ km h^{-1} and arrive in time $(t - \tfrac{1}{3})$ hrs.

$\therefore \quad t - \tfrac{1}{3} = \frac{40}{h + 40}$, and so $t = \frac{40}{h + 40} + \tfrac{1}{3}$ .... (2)

Using (1) and (2), $\dfrac{40}{h} = \dfrac{40}{h+40} + \dfrac{1}{3}$

$\therefore \quad 40(h+40) = 40h + \dfrac{1}{3}h(h+40)$

$\therefore \quad 40h + 1600 = 40h + \dfrac{1}{3}h^2 + \dfrac{40}{3}h$

$\therefore \quad h^2 + 40h - 4800 = 0$

which has $a = 1$, $b = 40$, $c = -4800$.

$\therefore \quad h = \dfrac{-40 \pm \sqrt{40^2 - 4(1)(-4800)}}{2(1)}$

$= \dfrac{-40 \pm \sqrt{1600 + 19\,200}}{2}$

$= \dfrac{-40 \pm \sqrt{20\,800}}{2}$

But $h > 0$, so $h = \dfrac{-40 + \sqrt{20\,800}}{2} \approx 52.1$ km h^{-1}.

So, Hassan's speed is approximately 52.1 km h^{-1}.

15 Suppose the speed of the plane is x km h^{-1}. We know speed $= \dfrac{\text{distance}}{\text{time}}$, so time $= \dfrac{\text{distance}}{\text{speed}}$.

Using the information given, $\dfrac{1000}{x} = \dfrac{1000}{x - 120} - \dfrac{1}{2}$

$\therefore \quad 1000(x - 120) = 1000x - \dfrac{1}{2}x(x - 120)$

$\therefore \quad 1000x - 120\,000 = 1000x - \dfrac{1}{2}x^2 + 60x$

$\therefore \quad x^2 - 120x - 240\,000 = 0$ which has $a = 1$, $b = -120$, $c = -240\,000$

$\therefore \quad x = \dfrac{-(-120) \pm \sqrt{(-120)^2 - 4(1)(-240\,000)}}{2(1)} = \dfrac{120 \pm \sqrt{974\,400}}{2}$

But $x > 0$, so $x = \dfrac{120 + \sqrt{974\,400}}{2} \approx 553.6$ km h^{-1}.

$\therefore$ the plane has speed approximately 554 km h^{-1}.

16 Suppose the express train travels at x km h^{-1}. We know speed $= \dfrac{\text{distance}}{\text{time}}$, so time $= \dfrac{\text{distance}}{\text{speed}}$.

$\therefore$ it takes the express train $\dfrac{160}{x}$ hours and the normal train $\dfrac{160}{x - 10}$ hours.

$\therefore \quad \dfrac{160}{x} + \dfrac{1}{2} = \dfrac{160}{x - 10}$

$\therefore \quad 160(x - 10) + \dfrac{1}{2}x(x - 10) = 160x$

$\therefore \quad 160x - 1600 + \dfrac{1}{2}x^2 - 5x = 160x$

$\therefore \quad x^2 - 10x - 3200 = 0$ which has $a = 1$, $b = -10$, $c = -3200$

$\therefore \quad x = \dfrac{-(-10) \pm \sqrt{(-10)^2 - 4(1)(-3200)}}{2(1)} = \dfrac{10 \pm \sqrt{12\,900}}{2}$

But $x > 0$, so $x = \dfrac{10 + \sqrt{12\,900}}{2} \approx 61.8$ km h^{-1}

$\therefore$ the express train travels on average at about 61.8 km h^{-1}.

17 Suppose n elderly citizens ended up going on the trip, so the cost per person was $\$\dfrac{160}{n}$.

If the original number of elderly citizens had gone, there would have been $(n + 8)$,

and the cost per person would have been $\$\dfrac{160}{n + 8}$.

Hence $\dfrac{160}{n} = \dfrac{160}{n + 8} + 1$

$\therefore \quad 160(n + 8) = 160n + n(n + 8)$

$\therefore \quad 160n + 1280 = 160n + n^2 + 8n$

$\therefore \quad n^2 + 8n - 1280 = 0$

$\therefore \quad (n - 32)(n + 40) = 0$

$\therefore$ since $n > 0$, $n = 32$. So, 32 elderly citizens went on the trip.

18 We fit a set of axes to the tunnel, with the origin at ground level at the midpoint of the tunnel.

The parabola has vertex $(0, 8)$, so it has equation
$$y = a(x - 0)^2 + 8$$
$$\therefore \quad y = ax^2 + 8$$

When $x = 3$, $y = 0$, so
$$0 = a(3^2) + 8$$
$$\therefore \quad 9a = -8$$
$$\therefore \quad a = -\tfrac{8}{9}$$

$\therefore$ the equation of the parabola is $y = -\tfrac{8}{9}x^2 + 8$.

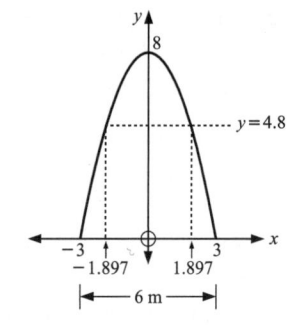

We use this equation to find the width of the tunnel 4.8 m above ground level (at the top of the truck).

When $y = 4.8$, $-\tfrac{8}{9}x^2 + 8 = 4.8$
$$\therefore \quad 3.2 = \tfrac{8}{9}x^2$$
$$\therefore \quad x^2 = 3.6$$
$$\therefore \quad x \approx \pm 1.897$$

$\therefore$ width of tunnel $\approx 2 \times 1.897$
≈ 3.79 m

$\therefore$ at 4.8 m above ground level, the tunnel is only 3.79 m wide, and the truck is 3.9 m wide.

$\therefore$ the truck will not fit through the tunnel.

19 a With the axes as described, the parabola has vertex $(0, 70)$.

$\therefore$ its equation is $y = ax^2 + 70$ for some $a \neq 0$.

The end of the bridge is 80 m from A, so the arch meets the vertical end supports at the point $(80, 6)$.

$(80, 6)$ must lie on the curve, so $6 = a(80)^2 + 70$
$$\therefore \quad 6400a = -64 \quad \text{and so} \quad a = -\tfrac{1}{100}$$

$\therefore$ the arch has equation $y = -\tfrac{1}{100}x^2 + 70$

b The supports occur every 10 m.

When $x = 10$, $y = -\tfrac{1}{100} \times 10^2 + 70 = 69$ m
When $x = 20$, $y = -\tfrac{1}{100} \times 20^2 + 70 = 66$ m
When $x = 30$, $y = -\tfrac{1}{100} \times 30^2 + 70 = 61$ m
When $x = 40$, $y = -\tfrac{1}{100} \times 40^2 + 70 = 54$ m
When $x = 50$, $y = -\tfrac{1}{100} \times 50^2 + 70 = 45$ m
When $x = 60$, $y = -\tfrac{1}{100} \times 60^2 + 70 = 34$ m
When $x = 70$, $y = -\tfrac{1}{100} \times 70^2 + 70 = 21$ m

and the supports at $x = -10, -20, \ldots, -70$ m have the same lengths.

$\therefore$ the other supports have lengths 21 m, 34 m, 45 m, 54 m, 61 m, 66 m and 69 m.

EXERCISE 6H

1 a For $y = x^2 - 2x$,
$a = 1$, $b = -2$, $c = 0$.
As $a > 0$, the shape is ∪

$\therefore$ the minimum value occurs when
$$x = \frac{-b}{2a} = \frac{2}{2} = 1$$
and $y = 1^2 - 2(1)$
$= -1$

$\therefore$ the minimum value of $y = x^2 - 2x$ is -1, occurring when $x = 1$.

b For $y = 7 - 2x - x^2$,
$a = -1$, $b = -2$, $c = 7$.
As $a < 0$, the shape is ∩

$\therefore$ the maximum value occurs when
$$x = \frac{-b}{2a} = -\frac{-2}{2(-1)} = -1$$
and $y = 7 - 2(-1) - (-1)^2$
$= 8$

$\therefore$ the maximum value of $y = 7 - 2x - x^2$ is 8, occuring when $x = -1$.

c For $y = 8 + 2x - 3x^2$,
$a = -3$, $b = 2$, $c = 8$.

As $a < 0$, the shape is ⌢

∴ the maximum value occurs when

$$x = \frac{-b}{2a} = \frac{-2}{-6} = \tfrac{1}{3}$$

and $y = 8 + 2(\tfrac{1}{3}) - 3(\tfrac{1}{3})^2$
$= 8\tfrac{1}{3}$

∴ the maximum value of $y = 8 + 2x - 3x^2$ is $8\tfrac{1}{3}$, occuring when $x = \tfrac{1}{3}$.

d For $y = 2x^2 + x - 1$,
$a = 2$, $b = 1$, $c = -1$.

As $a > 0$, the shape is ⌣

∴ the minimum value occurs when

$$x = \frac{-b}{2a} = -\tfrac{1}{4}$$

and $y = 2(-\tfrac{1}{4})^2 + (-\tfrac{1}{4}) - 1$
$= \tfrac{1}{8} - \tfrac{1}{4} - 1$
$= -1\tfrac{1}{8}$

∴ the minimum value of $y = 2x^2 + x - 1$ is $-1\tfrac{1}{8}$, occuring when $x = -\tfrac{1}{4}$.

e For $y = 4x^2 - x + 5$,
$a = 4$, $b = -1$, $c = 5$.

As $a > 0$, the shape is ⌣

∴ the minimum value occurs when

$$x = \frac{-b}{2a} = \tfrac{1}{8}$$

and $y = 4(\tfrac{1}{8})^2 - \tfrac{1}{8} + 5$
$= \tfrac{1}{16} - \tfrac{1}{8} + 5$
$= 4\tfrac{15}{16}$

∴ the minimum value of $y = 4x^2 - x + 5$ is $4\tfrac{15}{16}$, occuring when $x = \tfrac{1}{8}$.

f For $y = 7x - 2x^2$,
$a = -2$, $b = 7$, $c = 0$.

As $a < 0$, the shape is ⌢

∴ the maximum value occurs when

$$x = \frac{-b}{2a} = \frac{-7}{-4} = \tfrac{7}{4}$$

and $y = 7(\tfrac{7}{4}) - 2(\tfrac{7}{4})^2$
$= \tfrac{49}{4} - \tfrac{49}{8}$
$= \tfrac{49}{8}$ or $6\tfrac{1}{8}$

∴ the maximum value of $y = 7x - 2x^2$ is $6\tfrac{1}{8}$, occuring when $x = \tfrac{7}{4}$.

2 For $P = -3x^2 + 240x - 800$,
$a = -3$, $b = 240$, $c = -800$.

As $a < 0$, the shape is ⌢

∴ the maximum profit occurs when

$$x = \frac{-b}{2a} = \frac{-240}{-6} = 40$$

and $P = -3(40)^2 + 240(40) - 800$
$= 4000$

∴ 40 refrigerators should be made each day, for a maximum profit of $4000.

3 a Let the other side be y m long.
The perimeter is 200 m.

∴ $2x + 2y = 200$
∴ $x + y = 100$
∴ $y = 100 - x$
∴ the area $A = xy$
∴ $A = x(100 - x)$
∴ $A = 100x - x^2$

b $A = 100x - x^2$ is a quadratic function with
$a = -1$, $b = 100$, $c = 0$.

As $a < 0$, the shape is ⌢

∴ the area is maximised when

$$x = \frac{-b}{2a} = \frac{-100}{-2} = 50$$

and $y = 100 - 50 = 50$

∴ the area of the rectangle is maximised when $x = y = 50$, which is when the rectangle is a square.

4 Let the dimensions of the paddock be x m $\times$ y m. 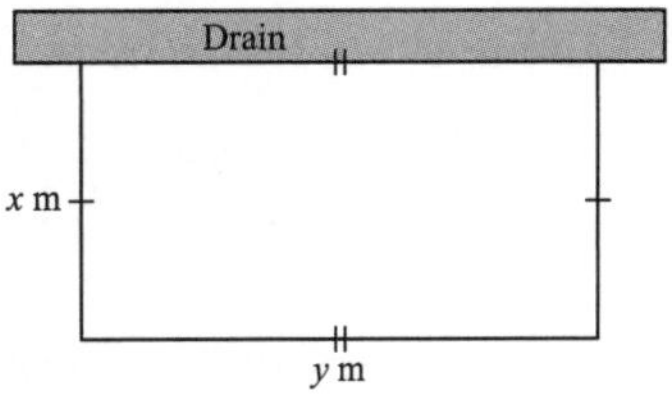
If 1000 m of fence is available, then
$2x + y = 1000$ {perimeter}
$\therefore \quad y = 1000 - 2x$ ...... (1)
The area of the enclosure $A = xy$
Since $y = 1000 - 2x$, $A = x(1000 - 2x)$
$= 1000x - 2x^2$
$\therefore \quad A = -2x^2 + 1000x$

A is a quadratic and $a < 0$, so its shape is ⌢

So, area is maximised when $x = \dfrac{-b}{2a} = \dfrac{-1000}{2 \times (-2)} = 250$

and when $x = 250$, $y = 1000 - 2(250) = 500$
$\therefore$ the paddock has a maximum area when the dimensions are 250 m $\times$ 500 m.

5 a The length of fence required for this enclosure is $9x + 8y$. If 1800 m is available for this enclosure, then $9x + 8y = 1800$.

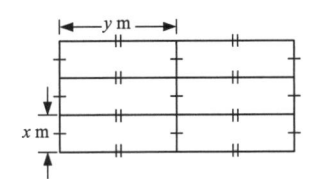

b If $9x + 8y = 1800$, then $y = \dfrac{1800 - 9x}{8}$.

The area of each pen is $A = xy$. Substituting $y = \dfrac{1800 - 9x}{8}$ into A we get

$A = x\left(\dfrac{1800 - 9x}{8}\right)$

$\therefore \quad A = \dfrac{1800x}{8} - \dfrac{9x^2}{8}$

$\therefore \quad A = -\dfrac{9}{8}x^2 + 225x$

c The area is a quadratic function with $a < 0$, so its shape is ⌢

So, at $x = \dfrac{-b}{2a}$ we have a maximum

$\therefore \quad x = \dfrac{-225}{2 \times (-\frac{9}{8})} = 100$, and when $x = 100$, $y = \dfrac{1800 - 9(100)}{8} = 112.5$

Hence, the area is maximised when the dimensions are 100 m $\times$ 112.5 m.

6 a Let x m $\times$ y m be the dimensions of a single pen as shown below.
Hence, the total length of fence required is $6x + 6y$. 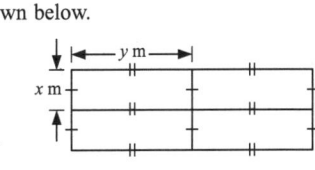
If there is 500 m of fence available, then $6x + 6y = 500$
$\therefore \quad x + y = 83\frac{1}{3}$
$\therefore \quad y = 83\frac{1}{3} - x$ ...... (1)
The area of each pen will be $A = xy$ and substituting equation (1), we have
$A = x(83\frac{1}{3} - x)$
$\therefore \quad A = -x^2 + 83\frac{1}{3}x$

which is a quadratic with $a < 0$ $\therefore$ its shape is ⌢

Hence, at $x = \dfrac{-b}{2a}$ we have a maximum value of A.

$\therefore \quad x = \dfrac{-83\frac{1}{3}}{2(-1)} = 41\frac{2}{3}$ substituting $x = 41\frac{2}{3}$ into $y = 83\frac{1}{3} - x$, we have

$$y = 41\frac{2}{3}$$

$\therefore$ the dimensions that maximise the area are $41\frac{2}{3}$ m $\times$ $41\frac{2}{3}$ m.

b Let x m $\times$ y m be the dimensions of a single pen as shown below.
Hence, the total length of fence required is $5x + 8y$.
If there is 500 m of fence available, then
$5x + 8y = 500$
$\therefore \quad 8y = 500 - 5x$
$\therefore \quad y = \dfrac{500 - 5x}{8}$
$\therefore \quad y = 62\frac{1}{2} - \frac{5}{8}x$ ...... (1)

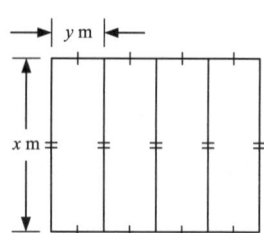

The area of each pen will be $A = xy$ and substituting equation (1), we have
$A = x(62\frac{1}{2} - \frac{5}{8}x)$
$\therefore \quad A = -\frac{5}{8}x^2 + 62\frac{1}{2}x$ which is a quadratic with $a < 0$, $\therefore$ its shape is ⌒

Hence, when $x = \dfrac{-b}{2a}$ we have a maximum value of A.

$\therefore \quad x = \dfrac{-62\frac{1}{2}}{2 \times (-\frac{5}{8})} = 50$ and substituting $x = 50$ into $y = 62\frac{1}{2} - \frac{5}{8}x$, we have

$$y = 31\frac{1}{4}$$

$\therefore$ the dimensions that maximise the area are 50 m $\times$ $31\frac{1}{4}$ m.

7 a The graphs of $y = x^2 - 3x$ and $y = 2x - x^2$ meet
where $x^2 - 3x = 2x - x^2$
$\therefore \quad 2x^2 - 5x = 0$
$\therefore \quad x(2x - 5) = 0$
$\therefore \quad x = 0$ or $2\frac{1}{2}$

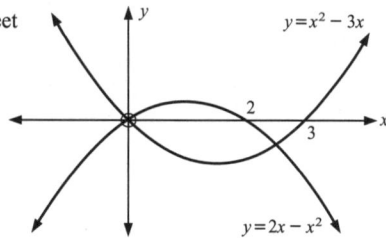

b The vertical separation between the curves is given by
$S = (2x - x^2) - (x^2 - 3x)$ $\{y = 2x - x^2$ is above $y = x^2 - 3x$ for $0 \leqslant x \leqslant 2\frac{1}{2}\}$
$\therefore \quad S = 2x - x^2 - x^2 + 3x$
$\therefore \quad S = -2x^2 + 5x$
Thus S is a quadratic function with $a < 0$ so the shape is ⌒

$\therefore$ the maximum separation occurs when $x = \dfrac{-b}{2a} = \dfrac{-5}{-4} = \dfrac{5}{4}$

and $S = -2(\frac{5}{4})^2 + 5(\frac{5}{4})$
$= -\frac{25}{8} + \frac{25}{4}$
$= \frac{25}{8}$ or $3\frac{1}{8}$

$\therefore$ the maximum vertical separation between the curves for $0 \leqslant x \leqslant 2\frac{1}{2}$ is $3\frac{1}{8}$ units.

8 **a**

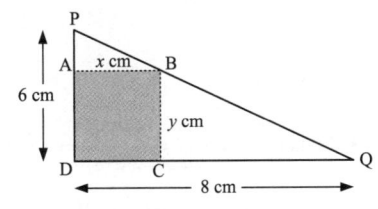

$\triangle$s PAB and PDQ are similar

{$A\hat{P}B$ is common,

$A\hat{B}P = D\hat{Q}P$ as AB $\parallel$ DQ}

$\therefore \quad \dfrac{PA}{PD} = \dfrac{AB}{DQ}$

$\therefore \quad \dfrac{6-y}{6} = \dfrac{x}{8}$

$\therefore \quad 6 - y = \tfrac{3}{4}x$

$\therefore \quad y = 6 - \tfrac{3}{4}x$

b Rectangle ABCD has area $A = xy$
$$= x(6 - \tfrac{3}{4}x)$$
$$= -\tfrac{3}{4}x^2 + 6x$$

which is a quadratic with $a < 0$

$\therefore$ the shape is $\frown$

$\therefore$ the area is maximised when $x = \dfrac{-b}{2a}$

$$= \dfrac{-6}{-\tfrac{3}{2}} = 4$$

and when $x = 4$, $y = 6 - \tfrac{3}{4}(4)$
$$= 3$$

$\therefore$ the dimensions of rectangle ABCD of maximum area is 4 cm $\times$ 3 cm.

9 Total profit, P = receipts $-$ costs

$\therefore \quad P = (550x - 2x^2) - \underbrace{\left(50 + \dfrac{400}{x}\right)}_{\text{cost for one}} \underbrace{x}_{x \text{ of them}}$

$\therefore \quad P = 550x - 2x^2 - 50x - 400$

$\therefore \quad P = -2x^2 + 500x - 400$ dollars

which is a quadratic in x, with $a = -2$, $b = 500$, $c = -400$.

Since $a < 0$, the shape is $\frown$

$\therefore \quad P$ is maximised when $x = \dfrac{-b}{2a} = \dfrac{-500}{-4} = 125$

$\therefore$ profit is maximised when 125 are produced per week.

10 Total profit, P = total selling price $-$ cost

$$= \underbrace{x}_{x \text{ of them}} \underbrace{(44 - \tfrac{1}{5}x)}_{\text{selling price of each}} - (\tfrac{1}{10}x^2 + 20x + 25)$$

$\therefore \quad P = 44x - \tfrac{1}{5}x^2 - \tfrac{1}{10}x^2 - 20x - 25$

$\therefore \quad P = -\tfrac{3}{10}x^2 + 24x - 25$

which is a quadratic in x, with $a = -\tfrac{3}{10}$, $b = 24$, $c = -25$.

Since $a < 0$, the shape is $\frown$, so P is maximised when $x = \dfrac{-b}{2a} = \dfrac{-24}{2(-\tfrac{3}{10})} = 40$

$\therefore$ profit is maximised when 40 toasters are produced each day.

11 Total profit, P = receipts $-$ costs

$$= (1000x - 3x^2) - \underbrace{\left(60 + \dfrac{800}{x}\right)}_{\text{cost for one}} \underbrace{x}_{x \text{ of them}}$$

$\therefore \quad P = 1000x - 3x^2 - 60x - 800$
$\therefore \quad P = -3x^2 + 940x - 800$
which is a quadratic in x, with $a = -3$, $b = 940$ and $c = -800$.

Since $a < 0$, the shape is ⌢, so P is maximised when $x = \dfrac{-b}{2a} = \dfrac{-940}{2(-3)} = 156\tfrac{2}{3}$

But only a whole number can be produced, so $x = 157$.
$\therefore$ need to make 157 barbeques per week to maximise profits.

12 Let the 'line of best fit' through $(0, 0)$ have slope m.
$\therefore$ the line has equation $y = mx$.
$\therefore$ for $P_1(a_1, b_1)$, the coordinates of M_1 are (a_1, ma_1).
$\therefore$ the distance between P_1 and M_1 is $b_1 - ma_1$.
In general, $P_i M_i = |b_i - ma_i|$, $i = 1, 2, ..., n$.
$\therefore \quad (P_1 M_1)^2 + (P_2 M_2)^2 + ... + (P_n M_n)^2$
$= |b_1 - ma_1|^2 + |b_2 - ma_2|^2 + ... + |b_n - ma_n|^2$
$= (b_1 - ma_1)^2 + (b_2 - ma_2)^2 + ... + (b_n - ma_n)^2 \quad \{|z|^2 = z^2\}$
$= b_1^2 - 2b_1 ma_1 + m^2 a_1^2 + b_2^2 - 2b_2 ma_2 + m^2 a_2^2 + ... + b_n^2 - 2b_n ma_n + m^2 a_n^2$
$= m^2(a_1^2 + a_2^2 + ... + a_n^2) - m(2a_1 b_1 + 2a_2 b_2 + ... + 2a_n b_n) + (b_1^2 + b_2^2 + ... + b_n^2)$
which is a quadratic in m, with $a = a_1^2 + a_2^2 + ... + a_n^2$, $b = -(2a_1 b_1 + 2a_2 b_2 + ... + 2a_n b_n)$, $c = b_1^2 + b_2^2 + ... + b_n^2$.
$a = a_1^2 + a_2^2 + ... + a_n^2 > 0$, so the quadratic has shape ⌣

$\therefore$ the sum $(P_1 M_1)^2 + (P_2 M_2)^2 + ... + (P_n M_n)^2$ is minimised when

$m = \dfrac{-b}{2a} = \dfrac{2a_1 b_1 + 2a_2 b_2 + ... + 2a_n b_n}{2a_1^2 + 2a_2^2 + ... + 2a_n^2}$

$\therefore \quad m = \dfrac{a_1 b_1 + a_2 b_2 + ... + a_n b_n}{a_1^2 + a_2^2 + ... + a_n^2}$

13 $f(x) = (x - a - b)(x - a + b)(x + a - b)(x + a + b)$
$= [x - (a + b)][x + (a + b)][x - (a - b)][x + (a - b)] \quad \{\text{rearranging}\}$
$= [x^2 - (a + b)^2][x^2 - (a - b)^2]$
$= x^4 - x^2(a - b)^2 - x^2(a + b)^2 + (a + b)^2(a - b)^2$
$= x^4 - x^2[(a - b)^2 + (a + b)^2] + [(a + b)(a - b)]^2$
$= x^4 - x^2(a^2 \cancel{-2ab} + b^2 + a^2 \cancel{+2ab} + b^2) + (a^2 - b^2)^2$
$= x^4 - 2(a^2 + b^2)x^2 + (a^2 - b^2)^2$
which is a quadratic in x^2 with "a" $= 1$, "b" $= -2(a^2 + b^2)$, "c" $= (a^2 - b^2)^2$
"a" > 0, so the quadratic has shape ⌣

$\therefore \quad f(x)$ is minimised when $x^2 = \dfrac{2(a^2 + b^2)}{2} = a^2 + b^2$

When $x^2 = a^2 + b^2$, $f(x) = (a^2 + b^2)^2 - 2(a^2 + b^2)(a^2 + b^2) + (a^2 - b^2)^2$
$= (a^2 + b^2)^2 - 2(a^2 + b^2)^2 + (a^2 - b^2)^2$
$= (a^2 - b^2)^2 - (a^2 + b^2)^2$
$= a^4 - 2a^2 b^2 + b^4 - a^4 - 2a^2 b^2 - b^4$
$= -4a^2 b^2$

$\therefore$ the least value of $f(x)$ is $-4a^2 b^2$.

14 $f(x) = (a_1x - b_1)^2 + (a_2x - b_2)^2$
$= a_1^2 x^2 - 2a_1b_1x + b_1^2 + a_2^2 x^2 - 2a_2b_2x + b_2^2$
$= (a_1^2 + a_2^2)x^2 - 2(a_1b_1 + a_2b_2)x + (b_1^2 + b_2^2)$

which is a quadratic in x with $a = a_1^2 + a_2^2 > 0$, so it has shape $\smile$

$\therefore$ $f(x)$ is minimised when $x = \dfrac{-b}{2a} = \dfrac{2(a_1b_1 + a_2b_2)}{2(a_1^2 + a_2^2)} = \dfrac{a_1b_1 + a_2b_2}{a_1^2 + a_2^2}$

When $x = \dfrac{a_1b_1 + a_2b_2}{a_1^2 + a_2^2}$,

$f(x) = \left(a_1^2 + a_2^2\right)\left(\dfrac{a_1b_1 + a_2b_2}{a_1^2 + a_2^2}\right)^2 - 2(a_1b_1 + a_2b_2)\left(\dfrac{a_1b_1 + a_2b_2}{a_1^2 + a_2^2}\right) + b_1^2 + b_2^2$

$= \dfrac{(a_1b_1 + a_2b_2)^2}{a_1^2 + a_2^2} - \dfrac{2(a_1b_1 + a_2b_2)^2}{a_1^2 + a_2^2} + b_1^2 + b_2^2$

$= b_1^2 + b_2^2 - \dfrac{(a_1b_1 + a_2b_2)^2}{a_1^2 + a_2^2}$

But since $f(x) = (a_1x - b_1)^2 + (a_2x - b_2)^2$, $f(x) \geqslant 0$ for all x {sum of 2 squared terms}

$\therefore$ $b_1^2 + b_2^2 - \dfrac{(a_1b_1 + a_2b_2)^2}{a_1^2 + a_2^2} \geqslant 0$

$\therefore$ $b_1^2 + b_2^2 \geqslant \dfrac{(a_1b_1 + a_2b_2)^2}{a_1^2 + a_2^2}$

$\therefore$ $(a_1^2 + a_2^2)(b_1^2 + b_2^2) \geqslant (a_1b_1 + a_2b_2)^2$ $\{a_1^2 + a_2^2 \geqslant 0\}$

$\therefore$ $\sqrt{a_1^2 + a_2^2}\sqrt{b_1^2 + b_2^2} \geqslant \sqrt{(a_1b_1 + a_2b_2)^2}$

$\therefore$ $|a_1b_1 + a_2b_2| \leqslant \sqrt{a_1^2 + a_2^2}\sqrt{b_1^2 + b_2^2}$

15 Suppose one of the equations, say $x^2 + b_1x + c_1 = 0$ does not have two real roots.

$\therefore$ its discriminant $\Delta < 0$
$\therefore$ $b_1^2 - 4(1)(c_1) < 0$
$\therefore$ $b_1^2 < 4c_1$ .... (1)
$\therefore$ $\left(\dfrac{2(c_1 + c_2)}{b_2}\right)^2 < 4c_1$ $\{b_1b_2 = 2(c_1 + c_2)\}$
$\therefore$ $\dfrac{4(c_1 + c_2)^2}{b_2^2} < 4c_1$ $\{b_2^2 > 0\}$
$\therefore$ $c_1^2 + 2c_1c_2 + c_2^2 < c_1b_2^2$
$\therefore$ $c_1^2 - 2c_1c_2 + c_2^2 < c_1b_2^2 - 4c_1c_2$ {subtract $4c_1c_2$ from both sides}
$\therefore$ $(c_1 - c_2)^2 < c_1(b_2^2 - 4c_2)$
$\therefore$ $c_1(b_2^2 - 4c_2) > (c_1 - c_2)^2$

Now $(c_1 - c_2)^2 \geqslant 0$ $\therefore$ $c_1(b_2^2 - 4c_2) > 0$

We know $c_1 > 0$ $\{4c_1 > b_1^2 > 0$ using (1)$\}$
$\therefore$ $b_2^2 - 4c_2 > 0$

$\therefore$ $x^2 + b_2x + c_2$ has two real roots $\{b_2^2 - 4c_2$ is the discriminant$\}$
$\therefore$ if one of the equations does not have two real roots, the other equation does have two real roots.
$\therefore$ at least one of the equations has two real roots.

REVIEW SET 6A

1   **a** The x-intercepts are -2 and 1.
   b The axis of symmetry lies midway between the x-intercepts, so its equation is $x = -\frac{1}{2}$.
   c When $x = -\frac{1}{2}$, $y = -2(-\frac{1}{2} + 2)(-\frac{1}{2} - 1)$
   $\qquad = -2(\frac{3}{2})(-\frac{3}{2})$
   $\qquad = \frac{9}{2}$
   $\therefore$ the vertex is $(-\frac{1}{2}, \frac{9}{2})$
   d When $x = 0$, $y = -2(2)(-1) = 4$
   $\therefore$ the y-intercept is 4
   e [graph: $y = -2(x+2)(x-1)$, vertex $(-\frac{1}{2}, \frac{9}{2})$, x-intercepts -2 and 1, y-intercept 4, axis $x = -\frac{1}{2}$]

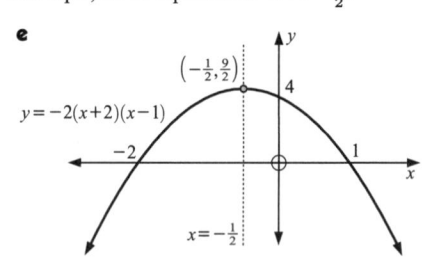

2   **a** The axis of symmetry is $x = 2$.
   b When $x = 2$, $y = \frac{1}{2}(2 - 2)^2 - 4$
   $\qquad = -4$
   $\therefore$ the vertex is $(2, -4)$
   c When $x = 0$, $y = \frac{1}{2}(-2)^2 - 4$
   $\qquad = -2$
   $\therefore$ the y-intercept is -2
   d [graph: $y = \frac{1}{2}(x-2)^2 - 4$, vertex $(2, -4)$, axis $x = 2$]

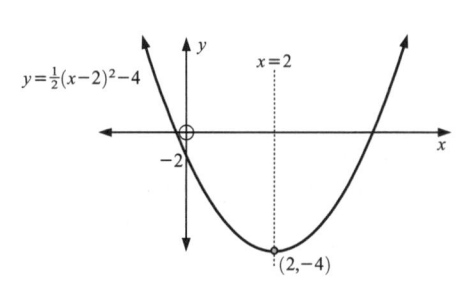

3   **a** $y = 2x^2 + 6x - 3$
   $\quad = 2[x^2 + 3x - \frac{3}{2}]$
   $\quad = 2[x^2 + 3x + (\frac{3}{2})^2 - (\frac{3}{2})^2 - \frac{3}{2}]$
   $\quad = 2[(x + \frac{3}{2})^2 - \frac{9}{4} - \frac{3}{2}]$
   $\quad = 2[(x + \frac{3}{2})^2 - \frac{15}{4}]$
   $\quad = 2(x + \frac{3}{2})^2 - \frac{15}{2}$
   b The vertex is $(-\frac{3}{2}, -\frac{15}{2})$.
   c When $x = 0$, $y = -3$
   $\therefore$ the y-intercept is -3.
   d [graph: $y = 2x^2 + 6x - 3$, vertex $(-\frac{3}{2}, -\frac{15}{2})$, y-intercept -3]

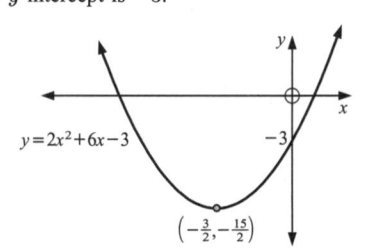

4   **a** $\qquad x^2 - 11x = 60$
   $\therefore\ x^2 - 11x - 60 = 0$
   $\therefore\ (x + 4)(x - 15) = 0$
   $\therefore\qquad x = -4$ or 15
   b $\qquad 3x^2 - x - 10 = 0$
   $\therefore\ (3x + 5)(x - 2) = 0$
   $\therefore\qquad x = -\frac{5}{3}$ or 2
   c $\qquad 3x^2 - 12x = 0$
   $\therefore\ 3x(x - 4) = 0$
   $\therefore\qquad x = 0$ or 4

5   **a** $\qquad x^2 + 10 = 7x$
   $\therefore\ x^2 - 7x + 10 = 0$
   $\therefore\ (x - 2)(x - 5) = 0$
   $\therefore\qquad x = 2$ or 5
   b $\qquad x + \dfrac{12}{x} = 7$
   $\therefore\ x^2 + 12 = 7x$
   $\therefore\ x^2 - 7x + 12 = 0$
   $\therefore\ (x - 3)(x - 4) = 0$
   $\therefore\qquad x = 3$ or 4
   c $\qquad 2x^2 - 7x + 3 = 0$
   $\therefore\ (2x - 1)(x - 3) = 0$
   $\therefore\qquad x = \frac{1}{2}$ or 3

6 $\qquad x^2 + 7x - 4 = 0$
   $\therefore\ x^2 + 7x + (\frac{7}{2})^2 - (\frac{7}{2})^2 - 4 = 0$
   $\therefore\ (x + \frac{7}{2})^2 - \frac{49}{4} - 4 = 0$
   $\therefore\ (x + \frac{7}{2})^2 = \frac{65}{4}$
   $\therefore\ x + \frac{7}{2} = \pm \frac{\sqrt{65}}{2}$
   $\therefore\ x = -\frac{7}{2} \pm \frac{\sqrt{65}}{2}$

7 **a** $x^2 - 7x + 3 = 0$
has $a = 1$, $b = -7$ and $c = 3$

$$\therefore \quad x = \frac{-(-7) \pm \sqrt{(-7)^2 - 4(1)(3)}}{2(1)}$$

$$= \frac{7 \pm \sqrt{49 - 12}}{2}$$

$$= \frac{7 \pm \sqrt{37}}{2}$$

$$\therefore \quad x = \frac{7}{2} \pm \frac{\sqrt{37}}{2}$$

b $2x^2 - 5x + 4 = 0$
has $a = 2$, $b = -5$ and $c = 4$

$$\therefore \quad x = \frac{-(-5) \pm \sqrt{(-5)^2 - 4(2)(4)}}{2(2)}$$

$$= \frac{5 \pm \sqrt{25 - 32}}{4}$$

$$\therefore \quad x = \frac{5 \pm \sqrt{-7}}{4}$$

$\therefore$ x has no real solutions.

8 **a** $y = 3x + c$ intersects the parabola $y = x^2 + x - 5$ when $x^2 + x - 5 = 3x + c$
$$\therefore \quad x^2 - 2x - 5 - c = 0$$

The graphs meet in two distinct points when this equation has two distinct real roots.
$$\therefore \quad \Delta > 0$$
$$\therefore \quad (-2)^2 - 4(1)(-5 - c) > 0$$
$$\therefore \quad 4 + 20 + 4c > 0$$
$$\therefore \quad 4c > -24$$
$$\therefore \quad c > -6$$

b Choose c such that $c > -6$, for example, $c = -2$.
The graphs meet where $x^2 + x - 5 - 3x - 2$
$$\therefore \quad x^2 - 2x - 3 = 0$$
$$\therefore \quad (x + 1)(x - 3) = 0$$
$$\therefore \quad x = -1 \text{ or } 3$$

Using the line $y = 3x - 2$, when $x = -1$, $y = 3(-1) - 2 = -5$
and when $x = 3$, $y = 3(3) - 2 = 7$
$\therefore$ the points of intersection are $(-1, -5)$ and $(3, 7)$.

9 The roots of $2x^2 - 3x = 4$ or $2x^2 - 3x - 4 = 0$ are α and β.

sum of roots $= -\frac{b}{a}$ and product of roots $= \frac{c}{a}$

$$\therefore \quad \alpha + \beta = -\frac{-3}{2} \qquad \therefore \quad \alpha\beta = \frac{-4}{2}$$

$$\therefore \quad \alpha + \beta = \frac{3}{2} \qquad \therefore \quad \alpha\beta = -2$$

Now consider a quadratic equation with roots $\frac{1}{\alpha}$ and $\frac{1}{\beta}$.

sum of roots $= \frac{1}{\alpha} + \frac{1}{\beta} = \frac{\beta}{\alpha\beta} + \frac{\alpha}{\alpha\beta}$ and product of roots $= \frac{1}{\alpha} \times \frac{1}{\beta}$

$$= \frac{\alpha + \beta}{\alpha\beta} \qquad\qquad = \frac{1}{\alpha\beta}$$

$$= \frac{\frac{3}{2}}{-2} \qquad\qquad = \frac{1}{-2}$$

$$= -\frac{3}{4} \qquad\qquad = -\frac{1}{2}$$

$\therefore$ a quadratic equation $ax^2 + bx + c = 0$ with roots $\frac{1}{\alpha}$ and $\frac{1}{\beta}$ has $-\frac{b}{a} = -\frac{3}{4}$ and $\frac{c}{a} = -\frac{1}{2}$

$\therefore$ $b = \frac{3}{4}a$ and $c = -\frac{1}{2}a$

The simplest solution to this is $a = 4$, $\therefore$ $b = 3$ and $c = -2$.

$\therefore$ the simplest quadratic equation with roots $\frac{1}{\alpha}$ and $\frac{1}{\beta}$ is $4x^2 + 3x - 2 = 0$.

REVIEW SET 6B

1 $y = -x^2 + 2x = x(2-x)$
$\therefore$ the graph has x-intercepts 0 and 2, and y-intercept 0
Its axis of symmetry is midway between the x-intercepts,
    at $x = 1$
and when $x = 1$, $y = -1^2 + 2 = 1$
$\therefore$ the vertex is $(1, 1)$

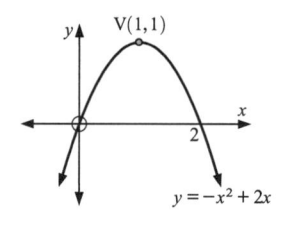

2 $y = -3x^2 + 8x + 7$ has $a = -3$, $b = 8$ and $c = 7$

The axis of symmetry is $x = -\dfrac{b}{2a} = -\dfrac{8}{2(-3)} = \dfrac{4}{3}$

$\therefore$ the axis of symmetry is $x = \frac{4}{3}$ and the vertex is $(\frac{4}{3}, \frac{37}{3})$.

When $x = \frac{4}{3}$, $y = -3(\frac{4}{3})^2 + 8(\frac{4}{3}) + 7$
$= -\frac{16}{3} + \frac{32}{3} + 7$
$= \frac{37}{3}$

3 **a** $3x^2 - 5x + 7 = 0$
has $a = 3$, $b = -5$ and $c = 7$
$\therefore \Delta = b^2 - 4ac$
$= (-5)^2 - 4(3)(7)$
$= -59$
Since $\Delta < 0$, there are no real solutions.

b $-2x^2 - 4x + 3 = 0$
has $a = -2$, $b = -4$ and $c = 3$
$\therefore \Delta = b^2 - 4ac$
$= (-4)^2 - 4(-2)(3)$
$= 40$
Since $\Delta > 0$, there are two real solutions.

4 $y = -2x^2 + 4x + 3$ has $a = -2$, $b = 4$ and $c = 3$
Since $a < 0$, the graph has shape ⌢ and will have a maximum.

The axis of symmetry is $x = -\dfrac{b}{2a} = -\dfrac{4}{2(-2)} = 1$

When $x = 1$, $y = -2(1)^2 + 4(1) + 3$
$= 5$

$\therefore$ the maximum is 5, and this occurs when $x = 1$.

5 $y = x^2 - 3x$ meets $y = 3x^2 - 5x - 24$
when $x^2 - 3x = 3x^2 - 5x - 24$
$\therefore 2x^2 - 2x - 24 = 0$
$\therefore x^2 - x - 12 = 0$
$\therefore (x-4)(x+3) = 0$
$\therefore x = 4$ or -3
Substituting into $y = x^2 - 3x$,
when $x = 4$, $y = 4^2 - 3 \times 4 = 4$
and when $x = -3$, $y = (-3)^2 - 3(-3)$
$= 9 + 9 = 18$
$\therefore$ the graphs meet at $(4, 4)$ and $(-3, 18)$.

6 $y = -2x^2 + 5x + k$
has $a = -2$, $b = 5$ and $c = k$.
$\therefore \Delta = b^2 - 4ac$
$= 5^2 - 4(-2)k$
$= 25 + 8k$

The graph does not cut the x-axis if $\Delta < 0$
$\therefore 25 + 8k < 0$
$\therefore 8k < -25$
$\therefore k < -\frac{25}{8}$
So, $k < -3\frac{1}{8}$

7 a The total length of wire for the fence is 60 m.
$\therefore$ $AB + BC + CD = 60$
Since the enclosure is rectangular,
$CD = AB$
$\therefore$ $2AB + x = 60$
$\therefore$ $2AB = 60 - x$
$\therefore$ $AB = 30 - \frac{1}{2}x$
$\therefore$ the area of the rectangle is
$A = x\left(30 - \frac{1}{2}x\right)$
$= \left(30x - \frac{1}{2}x^2\right)$ m^2

b $A = 30x - \frac{1}{2}x^2$
has $a = -\frac{1}{2}$ and $b = 30$.
Since $a < 0$, A has a maximum at the axis of symmetry, and this is at
$x = -\frac{b}{2a} = -\frac{30}{2(-\frac{1}{2})} = 30$
When $x = 30$, $AB = 30 - \frac{1}{2} \times 30$
$= 15$ m
$\therefore$ the enclosure is 15 m by 30 m.

8 $y = mx - 10$ is a tangent to $y = 3x^2 + 7x + 2$ if they meet at exactly one point (touch).
$y = 3x^2 + 7x + 2$ meets $y = mx - 10$ when $3x^2 + 7x + 2 = mx - 10$
$\therefore$ $3x^2 + (7 - m)x + 12 = 0$
The graphs meet exactly once when this equation has a repeated root $\therefore$ $\Delta = 0$
$\therefore$ $(7 - m)^2 - 4(3)(12) = 0$
$\therefore$ $49 - 14m + m^2 - 144 = 0$
$\therefore$ $m^2 - 14m - 95 = 0$
$\therefore$ $(m + 5)(m - 19) = 0$
$\therefore$ $m = -5$ or 19

9 $kx^2 + (1 - 3k)x + (k - 6) = 0$ has $a = k$, $b = 1 - 3k$ and $c = k - 6$.
Let the roots be α and $-\dfrac{1}{\alpha}$.
$\therefore$ product of roots $= -1$
$\therefore$ $\dfrac{c}{a} = \dfrac{k - 6}{k} = -1$
$\therefore$ $k - 6 = -k$
$\therefore$ $2k = 6$
$\therefore$ $k = 3$

For $k = 3$ the equation is
$3x^2 + (1 - 3(3))x + (3 - 6) = 0$
$\therefore$ $3x^2 - 8x - 3 = 0$
$\therefore$ $(3x + 1)(x - 3) = 0$
$\therefore$ $x = -\frac{1}{3}$ or 3

$\therefore$ $k = 3$, and the two roots of the equation are $-\frac{1}{3}$ and 3.

REVIEW SET 6C

1 a $x^2 + 5x + 3 = 0$
has $a = 1$, $b = 5$, $c = 3$
$\therefore$ $x = \dfrac{-5 \pm \sqrt{5^2 - 4(1)(3)}}{2(1)}$
$= -\frac{5}{2} \pm \dfrac{\sqrt{13}}{2}$

b $3x^2 + 11x - 2 = 0$
has $a = 3$, $b = 11$, $c = -2$
$\therefore$ $x = \dfrac{-11 \pm \sqrt{11^2 - 4(3)(-2)}}{2(3)}$
$= -\frac{11}{6} \pm \dfrac{\sqrt{145}}{6}$

2 a $x^2 - 5x - 3 = 0$
has $a = 1$, $b = -5$, $c = -3$
$\therefore$ $x = \dfrac{-(-5) \pm \sqrt{(-5)^2 - 4(1)(-3)}}{2(1)}$
$= \frac{5}{2} \pm \dfrac{\sqrt{37}}{2}$

b $2x^2 - 7x - 3 = 0$
has $a = 2$, $b = -7$, $c = -3$
$\therefore$ $x = \dfrac{-(-7) \pm \sqrt{(-7)^2 - 4(2)(-3)}}{2(2)}$
$= \frac{7}{4} \pm \dfrac{\sqrt{73}}{4}$

3 a $x \approx 0.586$ or 3.414

b $x \approx -0.186$ or 2.686

4 a $2x^2 - 5x - 7 = 0$
has $a = 2$, $b = -5$, $c = -7$
$\therefore \Delta = b^2 - 4ac$
$= (-5)^2 - 4(2)(-7)$
$= 25 + 56$
$= 81$
$\therefore \Delta > 0$ and $\sqrt{\Delta} = 9$
$\therefore$ there are two distinct real rational roots

b $3x^2 - 24x + 48 = 0$
has $a = 3$, $b = -24$, $c = 48$
$\therefore \Delta = b^2 - 4ac$
$= (-24)^2 - 4(3)(48)$
$= 576 - 576$
$= 0$
$\therefore$ there is a repeated real root

5 $2x^2 - 3x + m = 0$
has $a = 2$, $b = -3$ and $c = m$
$\therefore \Delta = b^2 - 4ac$
$= (-3)^2 - 4(2)m$
$= 9 - 8m$

a There is a repeated root if $\Delta = 0$
$\therefore 9 - 8m = 0$
$\therefore m = \frac{9}{8}$

b There are two distinct real roots if $\Delta > 0$
$\therefore 9 - 8m > 0$
$\therefore 8m < 9$
$\therefore m < \frac{9}{8}$

c There are no real roots if $\Delta < 0$
$\therefore 9 - 8m < 0$
$\therefore 8m > 9$
$\therefore m > \frac{9}{8}$

6 Suppose AB is x cm in length. Then, using the information given, we can label the diagram:

Now by similar triangles, $\dfrac{BE}{AB} = \dfrac{CD}{AC}$

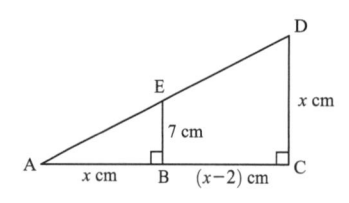

$\therefore \dfrac{7}{x} = \dfrac{x}{x + (x-2)}$

$\therefore \dfrac{7}{x} = \dfrac{x}{2x - 2}$

$\therefore 7(2x - 2) = x^2$
$\therefore 14x - 14 = x^2$
$\therefore x^2 - 14x + 14 = 0$

which has $a = 1$, $b = -14$ and $c = 14$

$\therefore x = \dfrac{-(-14) \pm \sqrt{(-14)^2 - 4(1)(14)}}{2(1)} = \dfrac{14 \pm \sqrt{140}}{2}$

Now $x - 2 > 0$, so $x = \dfrac{14 + \sqrt{140}}{2} \approx 12.92$ cm

$\therefore$ AB is approximately 12.9 cm long.

7 Let the hypotenuse have length x cm.
$\therefore$ the longer of the remaining sides has length $(x - 2)$ cm,
and the third side has length $(x - 9)$ cm.
By Pythagoras' theorem, $(x - 2)^2 + (x - 9)^2 = x^2$
$\therefore x^2 - 4x + 4 + x^2 - 18x + 81 = x^2$
$\therefore x^2 - 22x + 85 = 0$
$\therefore (x - 5)(x - 17) = 0$
$\therefore x = 5$ or 17

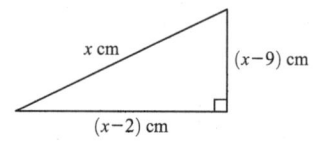

But if x was 5, the shortest side would have negative length $\therefore$ the hypotenuse has length 17 cm.

8 Let the line with gradient -3 and y-intercept c have equation $y = -3x + c$.
$y = -3x + c$ is tangential to $y = 2x^2 - 5x + 1$ if they meet at exactly one point.
$y = 2x^2 - 5x + 1$ meets $y = -3x + c$ when $2x^2 - 5x + 1 = -3x + c$
$\therefore 2x^2 - 2x + 1 - c = 0$

The graphs meet exactly once when this equation has a repeated root $\therefore \Delta = 0$
$$\therefore (-2)^2 - 4(2)(1-c) = 0$$
$$\therefore 4 - 8 + 8c = 0$$
$$\therefore 8c = 4$$
$$\therefore c = \tfrac{1}{2}$$

$\therefore$ the y-intercept of the line is $\tfrac{1}{2}$.

9 $ax^2 + [3-a]x - 4 = 0$ will have roots which are real and positive if:
(1) $\Delta > 0$ (2) sum of roots > 0 (3) product of roots > 0

(1) $\Delta > 0$ (2)   sum of roots > 0
$\therefore (3-a)^2 - 4(a)(-4) > 0$ $\therefore -\dfrac{3-a}{a} > 0$
$\therefore 9 - 6a + a^2 + 16a > 0$
$\therefore a^2 + 10a + 9 > 0$ $-\dfrac{3-a}{a}$ has sign diagram
$\therefore (a+9)(a+1) > 0$

$(a+9)(a+1)$ has sign diagram

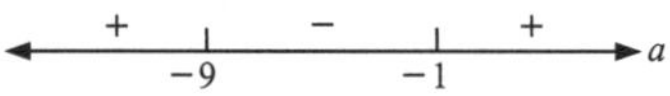

$\xleftarrow{+}\underset{-9}{\bullet}\xleftarrow{-}\underset{-1}{\bullet}\xrightarrow{+}a$

$\therefore \Delta > 0$ when $a < -9$ or $a > -1$

$\xleftarrow{+}\underset{0}{|}\xleftarrow{-}\underset{3}{|}\xrightarrow{+}a$

$\therefore$ sum of roots > 0 when $a < 0$
     or $a > 3$

(3) product of roots > 0
$$\therefore \dfrac{-4}{a} > 0$$

$-\dfrac{4}{a}$ has sign diagram

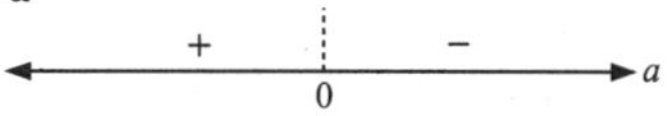

$\xleftarrow{+}\underset{0}{|}\xrightarrow{-}a$

$\therefore$ product of roots > 0 when $a < 0$

$\therefore$ the only values of a which satisfy all three conditions are $a < -9$ and $-1 < a < 0$.

REVIEW SET 6D

1 a $y = (x-2)^2 - 4$ has vertex $(2, -4)$ and axis of symmetry $x = 2$.
When $x = 0$, $y = (-2)^2 - 4 = 0$
so the y-intercept is 0.

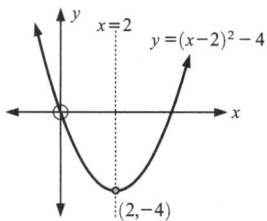

b $y = -\tfrac{1}{2}(x+4)^2 + 6$ has vertex $(-4, 6)$ and axis of symmetry $x = -4$.
When $x = 0$, $y = -\tfrac{1}{2}(4)^2 + 6 = -2$
so the y-intercept is -2.

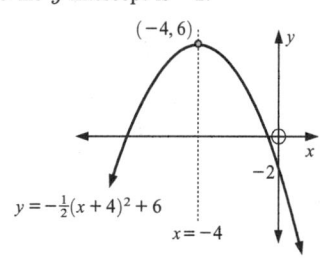

2 a $y = 2x^2 + 4x - 1$
has $a = 2$, $b = 4$ and $c = -1$
The axis of symmetry is $x = -\dfrac{b}{2a}$
$\therefore x = -\dfrac{4}{2 \times 2}$
$\therefore x = -1$

b When $x = -1$, $y = 2(-1)^2 + 4(-1) - 1$
$= 2 - 4 - 1$
$= -3$
$\therefore$ the vertex is $(-1, -3)$

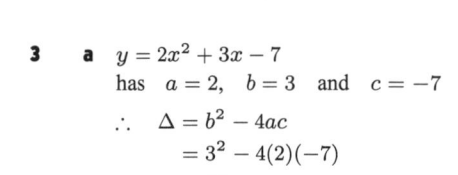

c When $x = 0$, $y = -1$,
so the y-intercept is -1
When $y = 0$, $2x^2 + 4x - 1 = 0$

$$\therefore \quad x = \frac{-4 \pm \sqrt{4^2 - 4(2)(-1)}}{2(2)}$$

$$= \frac{-4 \pm \sqrt{24}}{4}$$

$$= \frac{-4 \pm 2\sqrt{6}}{4} = -1 \pm \tfrac{1}{2}\sqrt{6} \quad \therefore \quad \text{the } x\text{-intercepts are } -1 \pm \tfrac{1}{2}\sqrt{6}.$$

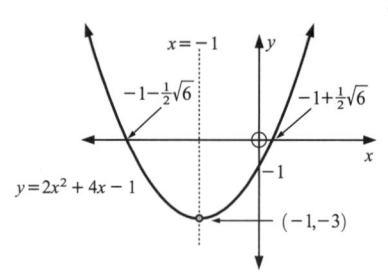

d

3 a $y = 2x^2 + 3x - 7$
has $a = 2$, $b = 3$ and $c = -7$

$\therefore \quad \Delta = b^2 - 4ac$
$= 3^2 - 4(2)(-7)$
$= 65$

Since $\Delta > 0$, the graph cuts the x-axis twice.
Note that since $a > 0$, the graph is

b $y = -3x^2 - 7x + 4$
has $a = -3$, $b = -7$ and $c = 4$

$\therefore \quad \Delta = b^2 - 4ac$
$= (-7)^2 - 4(-3)4$
$= 97$

Since $\Delta > 0$, the graph cuts the x-axis twice.
Note that since $a < 0$, the graph is

4 a $y = -2x^2 + 3x + 2$
has $a = -2$, $b = 3$ and $c = 2$

$\therefore \quad \Delta = b^2 - 4ac$
$= 3^2 - 4(-2)(2)$
$= 25$

Since $\Delta > 0$, the function is neither positive definite nor negative definite.

b $y = 3x^2 + x + 11$
has $a = 3$, $b = 1$ and $c = 11$

$\therefore \quad \Delta = b^2 - 4ac$
$= 1^2 - 4(3)(11)$
$= -131$

$\therefore \quad \Delta < 0$, and since $a > 0$, the function is positive definite.

5 a The graph has x-intercepts ± 3, so its equation is
$y = a(x + 3)(x - 3)$ for some $a \neq 0$.
Its y-intercept is -27, so
$a(3)(-3) = -27$
$\therefore \quad -9a = -27$
$\therefore \quad a = 3$
$\therefore \quad$ the equation is $y = 3(x + 3)(x - 3)$

b The quadratic has vertex $(2, 25)$
$\therefore \quad$ its equation is $y = a(x - 2)^2 + 25$
The y-intercept is 1, so
$a(-2)^2 + 25 = 1$
$\therefore \quad 4a = -24$
$\therefore \quad a = -6$
$\therefore \quad$ the equation is $y = -6(x - 2)^2 + 25$

6 Let the number be x, so its reciprocal is $\dfrac{1}{x}$.

$\therefore \quad x + \dfrac{1}{x} = 2\tfrac{1}{30} = \tfrac{61}{30}$

$\therefore \quad x^2 + 1 = \tfrac{61}{30}x$

$\therefore \quad 30x^2 + 30 = 61x$

$\therefore \quad 30x^2 - 61x + 30 = 0$

$\therefore \quad (6x - 5)(5x - 6) = 0$

$\therefore \quad x = \tfrac{5}{6}$ or $\tfrac{6}{5}$

$\therefore \quad$ the number is $\tfrac{5}{6}$ or $\tfrac{6}{5}$

7 Since the container has a square base, the original tinplate must have been square.
Suppose its side was x cm long, so the base of the container is $(x-8)$ cm by $(x-8)$ cm.
The height of the container is 4 cm, so its capacity is $4(x-8)(x-8)$ cm^3.

$\therefore \quad 4(x-8)^2 = 120$
$\therefore \quad (x-8)^2 = 30$
$\therefore \quad x - 8 = \pm\sqrt{30}$
$\therefore \quad x = 8 \pm \sqrt{30}$

Clearly, $x > 8$, so $x = 8 + \sqrt{30} \approx 13.48$
$\therefore$ the tinplate was about 13.5 cm by 13.5 cm.

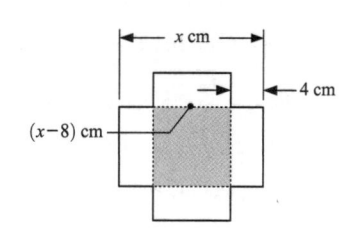

8 $y = -x^2 - 5x + 3$ meets $y = x^2 + 3x + 11$
when $\quad -x^2 - 5x + 3 = x^2 + 3x + 11$
$\therefore \quad 2x^2 + 8x + 8 = 0$
$\therefore \quad x^2 + 4x + 4 = 0$
$\therefore \quad (x+2)^2 = 0$
$\therefore \quad x = -2$

Substituting into $y = x^2 + 3x + 11$,
when $x = -2$, $y = (-2)^2 + 3(-2) + 11$
$= 4 - 6 + 11$
$= 9$

$\therefore$ the graphs touch at $(-2, 9)$.

9 Let the line with y-intercept $(0, 10)$ have equation $y = mx + 10$.
$y = 3x^2 + 7x - 2$ meets this line when $3x^2 + 7x - 2 = mx + 10$
$\therefore \quad 3x^2 + (7-m)x - 12 = 0$

For $y = mx + 10$ to be tangential to $y = 3x^2 + 7x - 2$, this equation must have exactly one solution, so there is a repeated root.

$\therefore \quad \Delta = 0$
$\therefore \quad (7-m)^2 - 4(3)(-12) = 0$
$\therefore \quad 49 - 14m + m^2 + 144 = 0$
$\therefore \quad m^2 - 14m + 193 = 0$

$\therefore \quad m = \dfrac{14 \pm \sqrt{(-14)^2 - 4(1)(193)}}{2}$

$\therefore \quad m = \dfrac{14 \pm \sqrt{-576}}{2}$ which has no real solutions.

$\therefore$ no line with y-intercept $(0, 10)$ can be tangential to $y = 3x^2 + 7x - 2$.

10 The roots of $3x^2 - 2x - 2 = 0$ are m and n.

$\therefore$ sum of roots $= -\dfrac{-2}{3}$ and product of roots $= \dfrac{-2}{3}$
$\therefore \quad m + n = \dfrac{2}{3}$ $\qquad \therefore \quad mn = -\dfrac{2}{3}$

Now consider a quadratic equation with roots $m - \dfrac{1}{n}$ and $n - \dfrac{1}{m}$.

sum of roots $= m - \dfrac{1}{n} + n - \dfrac{1}{m}$
$= (m+n) - \left(\dfrac{1}{m} + \dfrac{1}{n}\right)$
$= (m+n) - \left(\dfrac{m+n}{mn}\right)$
$= \dfrac{2}{3} - \dfrac{\frac{2}{3}}{-\frac{2}{3}}$
$= \dfrac{2}{3} + 1$
$= \dfrac{5}{3}$

product of roots $= \left(m - \dfrac{1}{n}\right)\left(n - \dfrac{1}{m}\right)$
$= mn - 1 - 1 + \dfrac{1}{mn}$
$= -\dfrac{2}{3} - 2 - \dfrac{3}{2}$
$= -\dfrac{4}{6} - \dfrac{12}{6} - \dfrac{9}{6}$
$= -\dfrac{25}{6}$

$\therefore\quad$ a quadratic equation $ax^2 + bx + c = 0$ with roots $m - \dfrac{1}{n}$ and $n - \dfrac{1}{m}$

has $-\dfrac{b}{a} = \dfrac{5}{3}$ and $\dfrac{c}{a} = -\dfrac{25}{6}$

$\therefore\quad b = -\dfrac{5}{3}a$ and $c = -\dfrac{25}{6}a$

$\therefore\quad$ the quadratic equation is $ax^2 - \dfrac{5}{3}ax - \dfrac{25}{6}a = 0,\ a \neq 0$

$\therefore\quad a(x^2 - \dfrac{5}{3}x - \dfrac{25}{6}) = 0,\ a \neq 0$

$\therefore\quad a(6x^2 - 10x - 25) = 0,\ a \neq 0$

REVIEW SET 6E

1 a The graph has x-intercepts -3 and 1, so its equation is
$y = a(x + 3)(x - 1)$ for some $a \neq 0$.
Its y-intercept is 18, so $a(3)(-1) = 18$
$\therefore\quad a = -6$
So the equation is
$y = -6(x + 3)(x - 1)$.

b The graph has vertex $(2, -20)$, so its equation is
$y = a(x - 2)^2 - 20$ for some $a \neq 0$.
Now an x-intercept is 5
$\therefore\quad a(5 - 2)^2 - 20 = 0$
$\therefore\quad 9a = 20$ and so $a = \dfrac{20}{9}$
So the equation is $y = \dfrac{20}{9}(x - 2)^2 - 20$.

c Since one x-intercept is 7 and the axis of symmetry is $x = 4$, the other x-intercept is $x = 1$.
$\therefore\quad$ the graph has equation
$y = a(x - 7)(x - 1)$ for some $a \neq 0$.
The y-intercept is -2
$\therefore\quad a(-7)(-1) = -2$
$\therefore\quad a = -\dfrac{2}{7}$
$\therefore\quad$ the equation is $y = -\dfrac{2}{7}(x - 7)(x - 1)$.

d The graph has vertex $(-3, 0)$, so its equation is
$y = a(x + 3)^2$ for some $a \neq 0$.
The y-intercept is 2
$\therefore\quad a(3)^2 = 2$
$\therefore\quad 9a = 2$ and so $a = \dfrac{2}{9}$
So the equation is $y = \dfrac{2}{9}(x + 3)^2$.

2 The x-intercepts are 3 and -2, so the equation is $y = a(x - 3)(x + 2)$ for some $a \neq 0$.
But the y-intercept is 24 $\quad\therefore\quad a(-3)(2) = 24$
$\therefore\quad -6a = 24$
$\therefore\quad a = -4$

$\therefore\quad$ the equation is $y = -4(x - 3)(x + 2)$ $\quad\therefore\quad y = -4(x^2 - x - 6)$
$\therefore\quad y = -4x^2 + 4x + 24$

3 a The graph touches the x-axis at 4, so its vertex is $(4, 0)$.
$\therefore\quad$ its equation is $y = a(x - 4)^2$ for some $a \neq 0$.
The graph also passes through $(2, 12)$ $\quad\therefore\quad a(2 - 4)^2 = 12$
$\therefore\quad 4a = 12$
$\therefore\quad a = 3$
$\therefore\quad$ the equation is $y = 3(x - 4)^2$ $\quad\therefore\quad y = 3(x^2 - 8x + 16)$
$\therefore\quad y = 3x^2 - 24x + 48$

b The quadratic has vertex $(-4, 1)$, so its equation is $y = a(x + 4)^2 + 1$ for some $a \neq 0$.
The graph also passes through $(1, 11)$ $\quad\therefore\quad 11 = a(1 + 4)^2 + 1$
$\therefore\quad 25a = 10$
$\therefore\quad a = \dfrac{2}{5}$

$\therefore\quad$ the equation is $y = \dfrac{2}{5}(x + 4)^2 + 1$ $\quad\therefore\quad y = \dfrac{2}{5}(x^2 + 8x + 16) + 1$
$\therefore\quad y = \dfrac{2}{5}x^2 + \dfrac{16}{5}x + \dfrac{37}{5}$

4 **a** $y = 3x^2 + 4x + 7$
has $a = 3$, $b = 4$ and $c = 7$
Since $a > 0$,
the graph has shape ∪

and so has a minimum.
This occurs on the axis of symmetry
$$x = -\frac{b}{2a}$$
$$\therefore \quad x = -\frac{4}{2(3)} = -\frac{2}{3}$$
When $x = -\frac{2}{3}$,
$$y = 3(-\tfrac{2}{3})^2 + 4(-\tfrac{2}{3}) + 7$$
$$= \tfrac{4}{3} - \tfrac{8}{3} + 7$$
$$= \tfrac{17}{3}$$
$\therefore$ the minimum is $\frac{17}{3}$ when $x = -\frac{2}{3}$

b $y = -2x^2 - 5x + 2$
has $a = -2$, $b = -5$ and $c = 2$
Since $a < 0$,
the graph has shape ∩

and so has a maximum.
This occurs on the axis of symmetry
$$x = -\frac{b}{2a}$$
$$\therefore \quad x = -\frac{-5}{2(-2)} = -\frac{5}{4}$$
When $x = -\frac{5}{4}$,
$$y = -2(-\tfrac{5}{4})^2 - 5(-\tfrac{5}{4}) + 2$$
$$= -\tfrac{25}{8} + \tfrac{25}{4} + 2$$
$$= \frac{-25 + 50 + 16}{8}$$
$$= \tfrac{41}{8}$$
$\therefore$ the maximum is $\frac{41}{8}$ when $x = -\frac{5}{4}$

5 $y = x^2 - 2x + k$
has $a = 1$, $b = -2$ and $c = k$
$\therefore \quad \Delta = b^2 - 4ac$
$= (-2)^2 - 4(1)k$
$= 4 - 4k$

The graph cuts the x-axis twice if $\Delta > 0$
$\therefore \quad 4 - 4k > 0$
$\therefore \quad 4k < 4$
$\therefore \quad k < 1$

6 **a** The total length of fencing is $(8x + 9y)$ m
$\therefore \quad 8x + 9y = 600$
$\therefore \quad 9y = 600 - 8x$
$\therefore \quad y = \frac{600 - 8x}{9}$

b The area of each pen is
$A = xy$
$= x\left(\frac{600 - 8x}{9}\right)$ m^2

d The maximum area of each pen is
$37\tfrac{1}{2} \times 33\tfrac{1}{3}$
$= \tfrac{75}{2} \times \tfrac{100}{3}$
$= 1250$ m^2

c $A = x\left(\dfrac{600 - 8x}{9}\right)$
$= \tfrac{600}{9}x - \tfrac{8}{9}x^2$
which has $a = -\tfrac{8}{9}$, $b = \tfrac{600}{9}$
Since $a < 0$, A is maximised at the axis of symmetry, which is $x = -\dfrac{b}{2a}$
$\therefore \quad x = -\dfrac{\tfrac{600}{9}}{2(-\tfrac{8}{9})} = \dfrac{600}{16}$
$\therefore \quad x = \tfrac{75}{2}$
When $x = \tfrac{75}{2}$, $y = \dfrac{600 - 8(\tfrac{75}{2})}{9} = 33\tfrac{1}{3}$
$\therefore$ for maximum area, each pen should be $37\tfrac{1}{2}$ m $\times$ $33\tfrac{1}{3}$ m.

7 $y = -5x + k$ meets $y = x^2 - 3x + c$ when $x^2 - 3x + c = -5x + k$
$\therefore \quad x^2 + 2x + c - k = 0$
For $y = -5x + k$ to be a tangent to $y = x^2 - 3x + c$, this equation must have exactly one solution, so there is a repeated root.
$\therefore \quad \Delta = 0$
$\therefore \quad 2^2 - 4(1)(c - k) = 0$
$\therefore \quad 4 = 4(c - k)$
$\therefore \quad c - k = 1$

8 The roots of $4x^2 - 3x - 3 = 0$ are p and q.

$\therefore$ sum of roots $= -\dfrac{-3}{4}$ and $\therefore$ product of roots $= \dfrac{-3}{4}$

$\therefore \quad p + q = \dfrac{3}{4}$ $\qquad\qquad\qquad\qquad \therefore \quad pq = -\dfrac{3}{4}$

Now consider a quadratic equation with roots p^3 and q^3.

sum of roots $= p^3 + q^3$ $\qquad\qquad\qquad$ product of roots $= p^3 \times q^3$
$= (p+q)^3 - 3p^2q - 3pq^2$ $\qquad\qquad\qquad = (pq)^3$
$= (p+q)^3 - 3pq(p+q)$ $\qquad\qquad\qquad\quad = (-\tfrac{3}{4})^3$
$= (\tfrac{3}{4})^3 - 3(-\tfrac{3}{4})(\tfrac{3}{4})$ $\qquad\qquad\qquad\quad = -\dfrac{27}{64}$
$= \dfrac{27}{64} + \dfrac{27}{16}$
$= \dfrac{135}{64}$

$\therefore$ a quadratic equation $ax^2 + bx + c = 0$ with roots p^3 and q^3 has $-\dfrac{b}{a} = \dfrac{135}{64}$ and $\dfrac{c}{a} = -\dfrac{27}{64}$

$\therefore \quad b = -\dfrac{135}{64}a$ and $c = -\dfrac{27}{64}a$

$\therefore$ the quadratic equation is $ax^2 - \dfrac{135}{64}ax - \dfrac{27}{64}a = 0, \quad a \neq 0$

$\therefore \qquad a(x^2 - \dfrac{135}{64}x - \dfrac{27}{64}) = 0, \quad a \neq 0$

$\therefore \qquad a(64x^2 - 135x - 27) = 0, \quad a \neq 0$

Chapter 7
COMPLEX NUMBERS AND POLYNOMIALS

EXERCISE 7A

1 a $\sqrt{-9}$
$= \sqrt{9} \times \sqrt{-1}$
$= 3i$

b $\sqrt{-64}$
$= \sqrt{64} \times \sqrt{-1}$
$= 8i$

c $\sqrt{-\frac{1}{4}}$
$= \sqrt{\frac{1}{4}} \times \sqrt{-1}$
$= \frac{1}{2}i$

d $\sqrt{-5}$
$= \sqrt{5} \times \sqrt{-1}$
$= i\sqrt{5}$

e $\sqrt{-8}$
$= \sqrt{8} \times \sqrt{-1}$
$= i\sqrt{8}$

2 a $x^2 - 9$
$= (x+3)(x-3)$

b $x^2 + 9$
$= x^2 - 9i^2$
$= (x+3i)(x-3i)$

c $x^2 - 7$
$= (x+\sqrt{7})(x-\sqrt{7})$

d $x^2 + 7$
$= x^2 - (i\sqrt{7})^2$
$= (x+i\sqrt{7})(x-i\sqrt{7})$

e $4x^2 - 1$
$= (2x+1)(2x-1)$

f $4x^2 + 1$
$= 4x^2 - i^2$
$= (2x+i)(2x-i)$

g $2x^2 - 9$
$= (\sqrt{2}x+3)(\sqrt{2}x-3)$

h $2x^2 + 9$
$= 2x^2 - 9i^2$
$= (\sqrt{2}x+3i)(\sqrt{2}x-3i)$

i $x^3 - x$
$= x(x^2 - 1)$
$= x(x+1)(x-1)$

j $x^3 + x$
$= x(x^2 + 1)$
$= x(x^2 - i^2)$
$= x(x+i)(x-i)$

k $x^4 - 1$
$= (x^2+1)(x^2-1)$
$= (x^2-i^2)(x^2-1)$
$= (x+i)(x-i)(x+1)(x-1)$

l $x^4 - 16$
$= (x^2+4)(x^2-4)$
$= (x^2-4i^2)(x^2-4)$
$= (x+2i)(x-2i)(x+2)(x-2)$

3 a $x^2 - 25 = 0$
$\therefore (x+5)(x-5) = 0$
$\therefore x = \pm 5$

b $x^2 + 25 = 0$
$\therefore x^2 - 25i^2 = 0$
$\therefore (x+5i)(x-5i) = 0$
$\therefore x = \pm 5i$

c $x^2 - 5 = 0$
$\therefore (x+\sqrt{5})(x-\sqrt{5}) = 0$
$\therefore x = \pm\sqrt{5}$

d $x^2 + 5 = 0$
$\therefore x^2 - 5i^2 = 0$
$\therefore (x+i\sqrt{5})(x-i\sqrt{5}) = 0$
$\therefore x = \pm i\sqrt{5}$

e $4x^2 - 9 = 0$
$\therefore (2x+3)(2x-3) = 0$
$\therefore x = \pm\frac{3}{2}$

f $4x^2 + 9 = 0$
$\therefore 4x^2 - 9i^2 = 0$
$\therefore (2x+3i)(2x-3i) = 0$
$\therefore x = \pm\frac{3}{2}i$

g $x^3 - 4x = 0$
$\therefore x(x^2 - 4) = 0$
$\therefore x(x+2)(x-2) = 0$
$\therefore x = 0 \text{ or } \pm 2$

h $x^3 + 4x = 0$
$\therefore x(x^2 + 4) = 0$
$\therefore x(x^2 - 4i^2) = 0$
$\therefore x(x+2i)(x-2i) = 0$
$\therefore x = 0 \text{ or } \pm 2i$

i $\quad x^3 - 3x = 0$
$\therefore \quad x(x^2 - 3) = 0$
$\therefore \quad x(x + \sqrt{3})(x - \sqrt{3}) = 0$
$\therefore \quad x = 0 \text{ or } \pm\sqrt{3}$

j $\quad x^3 + 3x = 0$
$\therefore \quad x(x^2 + 3) = 0$
$\therefore \quad x(x^2 - 3i^2) = 0$
$\therefore \quad x(x + i\sqrt{3})(x - i\sqrt{3}) = 0$
$\therefore \quad x = 0 \text{ or } \pm i\sqrt{3}$

k $\quad x^4 - 1 = 0$
$\therefore \quad (x^2 + 1)(x^2 - 1) = 0$
$\therefore \quad (x^2 - i^2)(x^2 - 1) = 0$
$\therefore \quad (x + i)(x - i)(x + 1)(x - 1) = 0$
$\therefore \quad x = \pm i \text{ or } \pm 1$

l $\quad x^4 = 81$
$\therefore \quad x^4 - 81 = 0$
$\therefore \quad (x^2 + 9)(x^2 - 9) = 0$
$\therefore \quad (x^2 - 9i^2)(x^2 - 9) = 0$
$\therefore \quad (x + 3i)(x - 3i)(x + 3)(x - 3) = 0$
$\therefore \quad x = \pm 3i \text{ or } \pm 3$

4 a If $x^2 - 10x + 29 = 0$

then $x = \dfrac{10 \pm \sqrt{100 - 4 \times 1 \times 29}}{2}$

$= \dfrac{10 \pm \sqrt{-16}}{2}$

$= 5 \pm \sqrt{-4}$

$= 5 \pm 2i$

b If $x^2 + 6x + 25 = 0$

then $x = \dfrac{-6 \pm \sqrt{36 - 4 \times 1 \times 25}}{2}$

$= \dfrac{-6 \pm \sqrt{-64}}{2}$

$= -3 \pm \sqrt{-16}$

$= -3 \pm 4i$

c If $x^2 + 14x + 50 = 0$,

then $x = \dfrac{-14 \pm \sqrt{14^2 - 4 \times 1 \times 50}}{2}$

$= \dfrac{-14 \pm \sqrt{-4}}{2}$

$= -7 \pm \sqrt{-1}$

$= -7 \pm i$

d If $2x^2 + 5 = 6x$,

then $2x^2 - 6x + 5 = 0$

$x = \dfrac{6 \pm \sqrt{36 - 4 \times 2 \times 5}}{4}$

$= \dfrac{6 \pm \sqrt{-4}}{4}$

$= \dfrac{3 \pm \sqrt{-1}}{2}$

$= \tfrac{3}{2} \pm \tfrac{1}{2}i$

e If $x^2 - 2\sqrt{3}x + 4 = 0$,

then $x = \dfrac{2\sqrt{3} \pm \sqrt{12 - 4 \times 1 \times 4}}{2}$

$= \dfrac{2\sqrt{3} \pm \sqrt{-4}}{2}$

$= \sqrt{3} \pm \sqrt{-1}$

$= \sqrt{3} \pm i$

f If $2x + \dfrac{1}{x} = 1$,

then $2x^2 + 1 = x$
$\therefore \quad 2x^2 - x + 1 = 0$

$x = \dfrac{1 \pm \sqrt{1 - 4 \times 2 \times 1}}{4}$

$= \dfrac{1 \pm \sqrt{-7}}{4}$

$= \tfrac{1}{4} \pm i\tfrac{\sqrt{7}}{4}$

5 a $\quad x^4 + 2x^2 = 3$
$\therefore \quad x^4 + 2x^2 - 3 = 0$
$\therefore \quad (x^2 + 3)(x^2 - 1) = 0$
$\therefore \quad (x^2 - 3i^2)(x^2 - 1) = 0$
$\therefore \quad (x + i\sqrt{3})(x - i\sqrt{3})(x + 1)(x - 1) = 0$
$\therefore \quad x = \pm i\sqrt{3} \text{ or } \pm 1$

b $\quad x^4 = x^2 + 6$
$\therefore \quad x^4 - x^2 - 6 = 0$
$\therefore \quad (x^2 - 3)(x^2 + 2) = 0$
$\therefore \quad (x^2 - 3)(x^2 - 2i^2) = 0$
$\therefore \quad (x + \sqrt{3})(x - \sqrt{3})(x + i\sqrt{2})(x - i\sqrt{2}) = 0$
$\therefore \quad x = \pm\sqrt{3} \text{ or } \pm i\sqrt{2}$

c
$$x^4 + 5x^2 = 36$$
$$\therefore \quad x^4 + 5x^2 - 36 = 0$$
$$\therefore \quad (x^2 + 9)(x^2 - 4) = 0$$
$$\therefore \quad (x^2 - 9i^2)(x^2 - 4) = 0$$
$$\therefore \quad (x + 3i)(x - 3i)(x + 2)(x - 2) = 0$$
$$\therefore \quad x = \pm 3i \text{ or } \pm 2$$

d
$$x^4 + 9x^2 + 14 = 0$$
$$\therefore \quad (x^2 + 7)(x^2 + 2) = 0$$
$$\therefore \quad (x^2 - 7i^2)(x^2 - 2i^2) = 0$$
$$\therefore \quad (x + i\sqrt{7})(x - i\sqrt{7})(x + i\sqrt{2})(x - i\sqrt{2}) = 0$$
$$\therefore \quad x = \pm i\sqrt{7} \text{ or } \pm i\sqrt{2}$$

e
$$x^4 + 1 = 2x^2$$
$$\therefore \quad x^4 - 2x^2 + 1 = 0$$
$$\therefore \quad (x^2 - 1)^2 = 0$$
$$\therefore \quad (x + 1)^2(x - 1)^2 = 0$$
$$\therefore \quad x = \pm 1$$

f
$$x^4 + 2x^2 + 1 = 0$$
$$\therefore \quad (x^2 + 1)^2 = 0$$
$$\therefore \quad (x^2 - i^2)^2 = 0$$
$$\therefore \quad (x + i)^2(x - i)^2 = 0$$
$$\therefore \quad x = \pm i$$

EXERCISE 7B.1

1

z	$\mathcal{R}e(z)$	$\mathcal{I}m(z)$	z	$\mathcal{R}e(z)$	$\mathcal{I}m(z)$
$3 + 2i$	3	2	$-3 + 4i$	-3	4
$5 - i$	5	-1	$-7 - 2i$	-7	-2
3	3	0	$-11i$	0	-11
0	0	0	$i\sqrt{3}$	0	$\sqrt{3}$

2 a $z + w$
$= (5 - 2i) + (2 + i)$
$= 7 - i$

b $2z$
$= 2(5 - 2i)$
$= 10 - 4i$

c $iw = i(2 + i)$
$= 2i + i^2$
$= -1 + 2i$

d $z - w$
$= (5 - 2i) - (2 + i)$
$= 5 - 2i - 2 - i$
$= 3 - 3i$

e $2z - 3w$
$= 2(5 - 2i) - 3(2 + i)$
$= 10 - 4i - 6 - 3i$
$= 4 - 7i$

f zw
$= (5 - 2i)(2 + i)$
$= 10 - 4i + 5i - 2i^2$
$= 12 + i$

g $w^2 = (2 + i)^2$
$= 4 + 4i + i^2$
$= 3 + 4i$

h $z^2 = (5 - 2i)^2$
$= 25 - 20i + 4i^2$
$= 21 - 20i$

3 a $z + 2w$
$= (1 + i) + 2(-2 + 3i)$
$= 1 + i - 4 + 6i$
$= -3 + 7i$

b z^2
$= (1 + i)^2$
$= 1 + 2i + i^2$
$= 2i$

c $z^3 = z^2 \times z$
$= 2i(1 + i)$
$= 2i + 2i^2$
$= -2 + 2i$

d $iz = i(1 + i)$
$= i + i^2$
$= -1 + i$

e $w^2 = (-2 + 3i)^2$
$= 4 - 12i + 9i^2$
$= -5 - 12i$

f zw
$= (1 + i)(-2 + 3i)$
$= -2 + 3i - 2i + 3i^2$
$= -5 + i$

g $z^2w = (1 + i)^2(-2 + 3i)$
$= 2i(-2 + 3i)$
$= -4i + 6i^2$
$= -6 - 4i$

h $izw = i(1 + i)(-2 + 3i)$
$= i(-5 + i)$
$= -5i + i^2$
$= -1 - 5i$

4 $i^0 = 1$ $i^4 = 1$ $i^8 = 1$ $i^{-1} = -i$
$i^1 = i$ $i^5 = i$ $i^9 = i$ $i^{-2} = -1$
$i^2 = -1$ $i^6 = -1$ $i^{-3} = i$
$i^3 = -i$ $i^7 = -i$ $i^{-4} = 1$
$i^{-5} = -i$ $\therefore$ $i^{4n+3} = -i$ where n is any integer

5 $(1+i)^4 = [(1+i)^2]^2$ $(1+i)^{101} = (1+i)^{100} \times (1+i)$
$= (1 + 2i + i^2)^2$ $= \left[(1+i)^4\right]^{25} \times (1+i)$
$= (2i)^2$ $= [-4]^{25}(1+i)$
$= -4$ $= -2^{50}(1+i)$

6 $(a+bi)^2 = -16 - 30i$ $\therefore$ $a^2 - \dfrac{225}{a^2} = -16$
$a^2 + 2abi + b^2i^2 = -16 - 30i$ $\therefore$ $a^4 + 16a^2 - 225 = 0$
$\therefore$ $a^2 - b^2 = -16$ and $2ab = -30$, $\therefore$ $(a^2 + 25)(a^2 - 9) = 0$
$\therefore$ $ab = -15$ and $\therefore$ $b = -\dfrac{15}{a}$ $\therefore$ $a = \pm 3$ or $\pm 5i$
But a is real and > 0
So, $a^2 - \left(-\dfrac{15}{a}\right)^2 = -16$ $\therefore$ $a = 3$ and $b = -\dfrac{15}{3} = -5$

7 **a** $\dfrac{z}{w} = \dfrac{2-i}{1+3i} \times \dfrac{1-3i}{1-3i}$ **b** $\dfrac{i}{z} = \dfrac{i}{2-i} \times \dfrac{2+i}{2+i}$

$= \dfrac{2 - 6i - i + 3i^2}{1 - 9i^2}$ $= \dfrac{2i + i^2}{4 - i^2}$

$= \dfrac{-1 - 7i}{10}$ $= \dfrac{-1 + 2i}{5}$

$= -\dfrac{1}{10} - \dfrac{7}{10}i$ $= -\dfrac{1}{5} + \dfrac{2}{5}i$

c $\dfrac{w}{iz} = \dfrac{1+3i}{i(2-i)}$ **d** $z^{-2} = \dfrac{1}{(2-i)^2}$

$= \dfrac{1+3i}{2i - i^2}$ $= \dfrac{1}{4 - 4i + i^2}$

$= \dfrac{1+3i}{1+2i} \times \dfrac{1-2i}{1-2i}$ $= \dfrac{1}{3-4i} \times \dfrac{3+4i}{3+4i}$

$= \dfrac{1 - 2i + 3i - 6i^2}{1 - 4i^2}$ $= \dfrac{3+4i}{9 - 16i^2}$

$= \dfrac{7+i}{5}$ $= \dfrac{3+4i}{25}$

$= \dfrac{7}{5} + \dfrac{1}{5}i$ $= \dfrac{3}{25} + \dfrac{4}{25}i$

8 **a** $\dfrac{i}{1-2i}$ **b** $\dfrac{i(2-i)}{3-2i}$ **c** $\dfrac{1}{2-i} - \dfrac{2}{2+i}$

$= \dfrac{i}{1-2i} \times \dfrac{1+2i}{1+2i}$ $= \dfrac{2i - i^2}{3-2i}$ $= \dfrac{1}{2-i}\left(\dfrac{2+i}{2+i}\right) - \dfrac{2}{2+i}\left(\dfrac{2-i}{2-i}\right)$

$= \dfrac{i + 2i^2}{1 - 4i^2}$ $= \dfrac{1+2i}{3-2i} \times \dfrac{3+2i}{3+2i}$ $= \dfrac{2 + i - 2(2-i)}{(2-i)(2+i)}$

$= \dfrac{-2+i}{5}$ $= \dfrac{3 + 2i + 6i + 4i^2}{9 - 4i^2}$ $= \dfrac{2 + i - 4 + 2i}{4 - i^2}$

$= -\dfrac{2}{5} + \dfrac{1}{5}i$ $= \dfrac{-1 + 8i}{13}$ $= \dfrac{-2 + 3i}{5}$

                           $= -\dfrac{1}{13} + \dfrac{8}{13}i$ $= -\dfrac{2}{5} + \dfrac{3}{5}i$

9 a $\quad 4z - 3w = 4(2+i) - 3(-1+2i)$
$\qquad\qquad\quad = 8 + 4i + 3 - 6i$
$\qquad\qquad\quad = 11 - 2i$
$\quad\therefore\ \mathcal{I}m\,(4z - 3w) = -2$

b $\quad zw = (2+i)(-1+2i)$
$\qquad\quad = -2 + 4i - i + 2i^2$
$\qquad\quad = -4 + 3i$
$\therefore\ \mathcal{R}e\,(zw) = -4$

c $\quad iz^2 = i(2+i)^2$
$\qquad\quad = i(4 + 4i + i^2)$
$\qquad\quad = i(3 + 4i)$
$\qquad\quad = 3i + 4i^2$
$\qquad\quad = -4 + 3i$
$\therefore\ \mathcal{I}m\,(iz^2) = 3$

d $\quad \dfrac{z}{w} = \dfrac{2+i}{-1+2i} \times \dfrac{-1-2i}{-1-2i}$
$\qquad\quad = \dfrac{-2 - 4i - i - 2i^2}{1 - 4i^2}$
$\qquad\quad = \dfrac{0 - 5i}{5}$
$\qquad\quad = -i$
$\therefore\ \mathcal{R}e\left(\dfrac{z}{w}\right) = 0$

EXERCISE 7B.2

1 a $2x + 3iy = -x - 6i$
Equating real and imaginary parts,
$\quad 2x = -x\ \text{and}\ 3y = -6$
$\quad \{x, y\ \text{are real}\}$
$\therefore\quad 3x = 0\ \text{and}\ y = -2$
$\therefore\quad x = 0\ \text{and}\ y = -2$

b $x^2 + ix = 4 - 2i$
Equating real and imaginary parts,
$\quad x^2 = 4\ \text{and}\ x = -2\ \{x\ \text{is real}\}$
$\therefore\quad x = \pm 2\ \text{and}\ x = -2$
$\therefore\quad x = -2$

c $(x + iy)(2 - i) = 8 + i$
$\therefore\quad x + iy = \dfrac{8+i}{2-i} \times \dfrac{2+i}{2+i}$
$\therefore\quad x + iy = \dfrac{16 + 8i + 2i + i^2}{4 - i^2}$
$\therefore\quad x + iy = \dfrac{15 + 10i}{5}$
$\therefore\quad x + iy = 3 + 2i$
Equating real and imag. parts, for real x, y
$\quad x = 3\ \text{and}\ y = 2$

d $(3 + 2i)(x + iy) = -i$
$\therefore\quad x + iy = \dfrac{-i}{3+2i} \times \dfrac{3-2i}{3-2i}$
$\therefore\quad x + iy = \dfrac{-3i + 2i^2}{9 - 4i^2}$
$\therefore\quad x + iy = \dfrac{-2 - 3i}{13}$
Equating real and imag. parts, for real x, y
$\quad x = -\dfrac{2}{13}\ \text{and}\ y = -\dfrac{3}{13}$

2 a $2(x + iy) = x - iy$
$\therefore\quad 2x + 2iy = x - iy$
Equating real and imaginary parts,
$\quad 2x = x\ \text{and}\ 2y = -y$
$\therefore\quad x = 0\ \text{and}\ 3y = 0$
$\therefore\quad x = 0\ \text{and}\ y = 0$

b $\quad (x + 2i)(y - i) = -4 - 7i$
$\therefore\quad xy - ix + 2iy - 2i^2 = -4 - 7i$
$\therefore\quad (xy + 2) + i(2y - x) = -4 - 7i$
Equating real and imaginary parts,
$\quad xy + 2 = -4\ \text{and}\ 2y - x = -7$
$\therefore\quad xy = -6\ \text{and}\ x = 2y + 7$
$\therefore\quad (2y + 7)y = -6$
$\therefore\quad 2y^2 + 7y = -6$
$\therefore\quad 2y^2 + 7y + 6 = 0$
$\therefore\quad (2y + 3)(y + 2) = 0$
$\therefore\quad y = -\dfrac{3}{2}\ \text{or}\ y = -2$
When $y = -2$, $x = 2(-2) + 7 = 3$
When $y = -\dfrac{3}{2}$, $x = 2(-\dfrac{3}{2}) + 7 = 4$
$\therefore\quad x = 3\ \text{and}\ y = -2$
$\quad \text{or}\quad x = 4\ \text{and}\ y = -\dfrac{3}{2}$

c $\quad (x+i)(3-iy) = 1 + 13i$
$\therefore \quad 3x - ixy + 3i - i^2y = 1 + 13i$
$\therefore \quad (3x+y) + i(3-xy) = 1 + 13i$
Equating real and imaginary parts,
$3x + y = 1 \quad$ and $\quad 3 - xy = 13$
$\therefore \quad y = 1 - 3x \quad$ and $\quad xy = -10$
$\therefore \quad x(1 - 3x) = -10$
$\therefore \quad x - 3x^2 = -10$
$\therefore \quad 0 = 3x^2 - x - 10$
$\therefore \quad 0 = (3x+5)(x-2)$
$\therefore \quad x = -\frac{5}{3} \quad$ or $\quad x = 2$
When $x = -\frac{5}{3}$, $y = 1 - 3(-\frac{5}{3}) = 6$
and when $x = 2$, $y = 1 - 3 \times 2 = -5$
$\therefore \quad x = -\frac{5}{3} \quad$ and $\quad y = 6$
or $\quad x = 2 \quad$ and $\quad y = -5$

d $\quad (x+iy)(2+i) = 2x - i(y+1)$
$\therefore \quad 2x + ix + 2iy + yi^2 = 2x + i(-y-1)$
$\therefore \quad (2x-y) + i(x+2y) = 2x + i(-y-1)$
Equating real and imaginary parts,
$2x - y = 2x \quad$ and $\quad x + 2y = -y - 1$
$\therefore \quad -y = 2x - 2x$
$\therefore \quad y = 0 \quad$ and consequently
$x + 0 = 0 - 1 = -1$
$\therefore \quad x = -1 \quad$ and $\quad y = 0$

3 $\quad 3z + 17i = iz + 11$
$\therefore \quad z(3-i) = 11 - 17i$
$\therefore \quad z = \dfrac{11 - 17i}{3 - i} \times \dfrac{(3+i)}{(3+i)}$
$= \dfrac{33 + 11i - 51i - 17i^2}{9 - i^2}$
$= \dfrac{50 - 40i}{10}$
$= 5 - 4i$

4 $\quad \dfrac{4}{1+i} = \dfrac{4}{(1+i)} \times \dfrac{(1-i)}{(1-i)}$
$= \dfrac{4 - 4i}{1 - i^2}$
$= \dfrac{4 - 4i}{2} = 2 - 2i$
$\therefore \quad \sqrt{z} = (2 - 2i) + 7 - 2i$
$= 9 - 4i$
$\therefore \quad z = (9 - 4i)^2$
$= 81 - 72i + 16i^2$
$= 65 - 72i$

5 $\quad 3(m + ni) = n - 2mi - (1 - 2i)$
$\therefore \quad 3m + 3ni = n - 2mi - 1 + 2i$
$\therefore \quad 3m + 3ni = (n - 1) + i(2 - 2m)$
Equating real and imaginary parts,
$3m = n - 1 \quad$ and $\quad 3n = 2 - 2m$
$\therefore \quad n = 3m + 1 \quad$ and $\quad 3n = 2 - 2m$
$\therefore \quad 3(3m + 1) = 2 - 2m$
$\therefore \quad 9m + 3 = 2 - 2m$
$\therefore \quad 11m = -1$
$\therefore \quad m = -\frac{1}{11}$
and $\quad n = 3(-\frac{1}{11}) + 1 = \frac{8}{11}$

6 $\quad z = \dfrac{3i}{\sqrt{2} - i} + 1$
$= \left(\dfrac{3i}{\sqrt{2} - i}\right)\left(\dfrac{\sqrt{2} + i}{\sqrt{2} + i}\right) + 1$
$= \dfrac{3i\sqrt{2} + 3i^2}{2 - i^2} + 1$
$= \dfrac{3i\sqrt{2} - 3}{3} + \dfrac{3}{3}$
$= \dfrac{3i\sqrt{2}}{3}$
$= i\sqrt{2}$

EXERCISE 7B.3

1 **a** roots α and β are $3 \pm i \qquad \therefore \quad \alpha + \beta = 6$ and $\alpha\beta = 9 - i^2 = 10$
$\therefore \quad$ quadratics have form $\quad a(x^2 - 6x + 10) = 0, \quad a \neq 0$

b roots α and β are $1 \pm 3i \qquad \therefore \quad \alpha + \beta = 2$ and $\alpha\beta = 1 - 9i^2 = 10$
$\therefore \quad$ quadratics have form $\quad a(x^2 - 2x + 10) = 0, \quad a \neq 0$

   c roots α and β are $-2 \pm 5i$ $\therefore$ $\alpha + \beta = -4$ and $\alpha\beta = 4 - 25i^2 = 29$
      $\therefore$ quadratics have form $a(x^2 + 4x + 29) = 0, \quad a \neq 0$

   d roots α and β are $\sqrt{2} \pm i$ $\therefore$ $\alpha + \beta = 2\sqrt{2}$ and $\alpha\beta = 2 - i^2 = 3$
      $\therefore$ quadratics have form $a(x^2 - 2\sqrt{2}x + 3) = 0, \quad a \neq 0$

   e roots α and β are $2 \pm \sqrt{3}$ $\therefore$ $\alpha + \beta = 4$ and $\alpha\beta = 4 - 3 = 1$
      $\therefore$ quadratics have form $a(x^2 - 4x + 1) = 0, \quad a \neq 0$

   f roots α and β are 0 and $-\frac{2}{3}$ $\therefore$ factors are x, $3x + 2$
      $\therefore$ quadratics have form $ax(3x + 2) = 0$
                       $\therefore$ $a(3x^2 + 2x) = 0, \quad a \neq 0$

   g roots α and β are $\pm i\sqrt{2}$ $\therefore$ $\alpha + \beta = 0$ and $\alpha\beta = -2i^2 = 2$
      $\therefore$ quadratics have form $a(x^2 + 2) = 0, \quad a \neq 0$

   h roots α and β are $-6 \pm i$ $\therefore$ $\alpha + \beta = -12$ and $\alpha\beta = 36 - i^2 = 37$
      $\therefore$ quadratics have form $a(x^2 + 12x + 37) = 0, \quad a \neq 0$

2   **a** If $3 + i$ is a root then so is $3 - i$ (if a and b are real)
      $\therefore$ $\alpha + \beta = 6$ and $\alpha\beta = 9 - i^2 = 10$
      $\therefore$ $x^2 - 6x + 10 = 0$ and so $a = -6, \quad b = 10$

   b If $1 - \sqrt{2}$ is a root then so is $1 + \sqrt{2}$ if a, b are rational.
      $\therefore$ $\alpha + \beta = 2$ and $\alpha\beta = 1 - 2 = -1$
      $\therefore$ $x^2 - 2x - 1 = 0$
             $\therefore$ $a = -2$ and $b = -1$

   c If $a + ai$ is a root then so is $a - ai$ (if a and b are real and $a \neq 0$.)
      $\therefore$ $\alpha + \beta = 2a$
      and $\alpha\beta = (a + ai)(a - ai)$ $\therefore$ $x^2 - 2ax + 2a^2 = x^2 + 4x + b$
                $= a^2 - (ai)^2$ $\therefore$ $-2a = 4$ and $b = 2a^2$
                $= 2a^2$ $\therefore$ $a = -2$ and $b = 8$

      However, if $a = 0$, $a + ai = 0$, which is *not* complex, so the other root could be any real number.
      But $\alpha\beta = 0$ $\therefore$ $b = 0$
                      $\therefore$ $a = 0, \quad b = 0$ is also a solution.

EXERCISE 7B.4

1 To Prove: $(z_1 - z_2)^* = z_1{}^* - z_2{}^*$
    Let $z_1 = a + ib$, and $z_2 = c + id$.
    $\therefore$ $(z_1 - z_2)^* = [(a + ib) - (c + id)]^*$
                          $= [(a - c) + i(b - d)]^*$
                          $= (a - c) - i(b - d)$
                          $= a - c - bi + di$
                          $= (a - bi) - (c - di)$
                          $= z_1{}^* - z_2{}^*$

2 $(w^* - z)^* - (w - 2z^*)$
    $= w^{**} - z^* - w + 2z^*$
    $= w - z^* - w + 2z^*$
    $= -z^* + 2z^*$
    $= z^*$

3   Let $z = a + bi$ $\therefore$ $z^* = a - bi$
    If $z^* = -z$, then $a - bi = -a - bi$
                    $\therefore$ $a = -a$
                    $\therefore$ $2a = 0$
                    $\therefore$ $a = 0$ and b is any real number
  $\therefore$ z is purely imaginary
  or $a = 0, \quad b = 0$ $\therefore$ z is zero.

4 **a** Let $z_1 = a + bi$ $z_2 = c + di$

$\therefore \dfrac{z_1}{z_2} = \dfrac{a+bi}{c+di} \times \dfrac{c-di}{c-di}$

$= \dfrac{(a+bi)(c-di)}{(c+di)(c-di)}$

$= \dfrac{ac - adi + bci - bdi^2}{c^2 - i^2 d^2}$

$= \dfrac{(ac+bd) + i(-ad+bc)}{c^2 + d^2}$

$= \left[\dfrac{ac+bd}{c^2+d^2}\right] + \left[\dfrac{bc-ad}{c^2+d^2}\right] i$

b $\dfrac{z_1{}^*}{z_2{}^*} = \dfrac{a-bi}{c-di} \times \dfrac{c+di}{c+di}$

$= \dfrac{(a-bi)(c+di)}{(c-di)(c+di)}$

$= \dfrac{ac + adi - bci - bdi^2}{c^2 - i^2 d^2}$

$= \dfrac{(ac+bd) - i(bc-ad)}{c^2 + d^2}$

$= \left[\dfrac{(ac+bd)}{c^2+d^2}\right] - \left[\dfrac{bc-ad}{c^2+d^2}\right] i$

$= \left(\dfrac{z_1}{z_2}\right)^*$ for all $z_2 \neq 0$

5 $\left(\dfrac{z_1}{z_2}\right)^* \times z_2{}^* = \left(\dfrac{z_1}{z_2} \times z_2\right)^*$ (from **Example 13**)

$= z_1{}^*$

$\therefore \left(\dfrac{z_1}{z_2}\right)^* = \dfrac{z_1{}^*}{z_2{}^*}$ {dividing both sides by $z_2{}^*$}

6 **a**   Let $z = a+bi$ and $w = c+di$

$\therefore \ zw^* + z^*w = (a+bi)(c-di) + (a-bi)(c+di)$

$= ac - adi + bci + bd + ac + adi - bci + bd$

$= ac + bd + ac + bd$

$= 2ac + 2bd$ which is a real number

b   Let $z = a+bi$ and $w = c+di$

$\therefore \ zw^* - z^*w = (a+bi)(c-di) - (a-bi)(c+di)$

$= ac - adi + bci + bd - [ac + adi - bci + bd]$

$= 2bci - 2adi$

$= (2bc - 2ad)i$ which is purely imaginary or zero

7 **a** If $z = a+bi$
then $z^2 = (a+bi)(a+bi)$
$= a^2 + 2abi + b^2 i^2$
$= (a^2 - b^2) + 2abi$

b $(z^*)^2 = (a-bi)^2$
$= a^2 - 2abi + b^2 i^2$
$= (a^2 - b^2) - 2abi$
and $(z^2)^* = (a^2 - b^2) - 2abi$ (from **a**)
$\therefore \ (z^2)^* = (z^*)^2$ as required

c $z^3 = (z^2)z$
$= ((a^2 - b^2) + 2abi)(a+bi)$
$= a(a^2 - b^2) + b(a^2 - b^2)i + 2a^2 bi + 2ab^2 i^2$
$= a^3 - ab^2 + a^2 bi - b^3 i + 2a^2 bi - 2ab^2$
$= (a^3 - 3ab^2) + (3a^2 b - b^3)i$

$\therefore \ (z^3)^* = (a^3 - 3ab^2) - (3a^2 b - b^3)i$

$(z^*)^3 = (z^*)^2 \, z^*$
$= \left[(a^2 - b^2) - 2abi\right](a - bi)$
$= a(a^2 - b^2) - b(a^2 - b^2)i - 2a^2 bi + 2ab^2 i^2$
$= a^3 - ab^2 - a^2 bi + b^3 i - 2a^2 bi - 2ab^2$
$= (a^3 - 3ab^2) - (3a^2 b - b^3)i$ which is $(z^3)^*$ as required

8 $w = \dfrac{z-1}{z^*+1}$ where $z = a + bi$

$\therefore\ w = \dfrac{(a-1)+bi}{(a+1)-bi} \times \dfrac{(a+1)+bi}{(a+1)+bi}$

$= \dfrac{(a^2-1)+(a-1)bi+(a+1)bi+b^2i^2}{(a+1)^2-b^2i^2}$

$= \dfrac{(a^2-b^2-1)+2abi}{(a+1)^2+b^2}$

a w is real if $2ab = 0$,
that is, if $a = 0$ or $b = 0$, $a \neq -1$
However, if $b = 0$ and $a = -1$,
w is undefined and hence is not real.
$\therefore\quad a = 0\ \ $ or $\ \ (b = 0,\ a \neq -1)$.

b w is purely imaginary if
$a^2 - b^2 - 1 = 0$, and $2ab \neq 0$
$\therefore\quad a^2 - b^2 = 1$
and neither a nor b is zero.

EXERCISE 7B.5

1 a $(z_1 z_2 z_3)^* = [z_1 \times (z_2 \times z_3)]^*$
$= z_1^* (z_2 \times z_3)^*$ \{as $(zw)^* = z^* w^*$\}
$= z_1^* \times z_2^* \times z_3^*$ \{as $(zw)^* = z^* w^*$ again\}

b $(z_1 z_2 z_3 z_4)^* = (z_1 z_2 z_3)^* \times z_4^*$ \{as $(zw)^* = z^* w^*$\}
$= z_1^* \times z_2^* \times z_3^* \times z_4^*$ \{using **a**\}

c $(z_1 \times z_2 \times z_3 \ldots z_n)^* = z_1^* \times z_2^* \times z_3^* \ldots z_n^*$

d $(z^n)^* = (z \times z \times z \times \ldots \times z)^*$
$= z^* \times z^* \times z^* \times \ldots \times z^*$ \{using **c**\}
$= (z^*)^n$

EXERCISE 7C.1

1 a $3P(x)$
$= 3(x^2 + 2x + 3)$
$= 3x^2 + 6x + 9$

b $P(x) + Q(x)$
$= (x^2 + 2x + 3) + (4x^2 + 5x + 6)$
$= 5x^2 + 7x + 9$

c $P(x) - 2Q(x)$
$= (x^2 + 2x + 3) - 2(4x^2 + 5x + 6)$
$= x^2 + 2x + 3 - 8x^2 - 10x - 12$
$= -7x^2 - 8x - 9$

d $P(x) Q(x)$
$= (x^2 + 2x + 3)(4x^2 + 5x + 6)$
$= 4x^4 + 8x^3 + 12x^2 + 5x^3 + 10x^2$
$\quad + 15x + 6x^2 + 12x + 18$
$= 4x^4 + 13x^3 + 28x^2 + 27x + 18$

2 a $f(x) + g(x)$
$= (x^2 - x + 2) + (x^3 - 3x + 5)$
$= x^3 + x^2 - 4x + 7$

b $g(x) - f(x)$
$= (x^3 - 3x + 5) - (x^2 - x + 2)$
$= x^3 - 3x + 5 - x^2 + x - 2$
$= x^3 - x^2 - 2x + 3$

c $2f(x) + 3g(x)$
$= 2(x^2 - x + 2) + 3(x^3 - 3x + 5)$
$= 2x^2 - 2x + 4 + 3x^3 - 9x + 15$
$= 3x^3 + 2x^2 - 11x + 19$

d $g(x) + x f(x)$
$= (x^3 - 3x + 5) + x(x^2 - x + 2)$
$= x^3 - 3x + 5 + x^3 - x^2 + 2x$
$= 2x^3 - x^2 - x + 5$

e $f(x) g(x)$
$= (x^2 - x + 2)(x^3 - 3x + 5)$
$= x^5 - x^4 + 2x^3 - 3x^3 + 3x^2$
$\quad - 6x + 5x^2 - 5x + 10$
$= x^5 - x^4 - x^3 + 8x^2 - 11x + 10$

f $[f(x)]^2$
$= (x^2 - x + 2)(x^2 - x + 2)$
$= x^4 - x^3 + 2x^2 - x^3 + x^2$
$\quad - 2x + 2x^2 - 2x + 4$
$= x^4 - 2x^3 + 5x^2 - 4x + 4$

3 a $(x^2 - 2x + 3)(2x + 1)$
$= 2x^3 - 4x^2 + 6x + x^2 - 2x + 3$
$= 2x^3 - 3x^2 + 4x + 3$

b $(x - 1)^2(x^2 + 3x - 2)$
$= (x^2 - 2x + 1)(x^2 + 3x - 2)$
$= x^4 - 2x^3 + x^2 + 3x^3 - 6x^2$
$\quad + 3x - 2x^2 + 4x - 2$
$= x^4 + x^3 - 7x^2 + 7x - 2$

c $(x + 2)^3$
$= (x + 2)(x + 2)^2$
$= (x + 2)(x^2 + 4x + 4)$
$= x^3 + 2x^2 + 4x^2 + 8x + 4x + 8$
$= x^3 + 6x^2 + 12x + 8$

d $(2x^2 - x + 3)^2$
$= (2x^2 - x + 3)(2x^2 - x + 3)$
$= 4x^4 - 2x^3 + 6x^2 - 2x^3 + x^2$
$\quad - 3x + 6x^2 - 3x + 9$
$= 4x^4 - 4x^3 + 13x^2 - 6x + 9$

e $(2x - 1)^4$
$= (2x - 1)^2(2x - 1)^2$
$= (4x^2 - 4x + 1)(4x^2 - 4x + 1)$
$= 16x^4 - 16x^3 + 4x^2 - 16x^3 + 16x^2$
$\quad - 4x + 4x^2 - 4x + 1$
$= 16x^4 - 32x^3 + 24x^2 - 8x + 1$

f $(3x - 2)^2(2x + 1)(x - 4)$
$= (9x^2 - 12x + 4)(2x^2 - 7x - 4)$
$= 18x^4 - 24x^3 + 8x^2 - 63x^3 + 84x^2$
$\quad - 28x - 36x^2 + 48x - 16$
$= 18x^4 - 87x^3 + 56x^2 + 20x - 16$

4 a $(2x^2 - 3x + 5)(3x - 1)$
$= 6x^3 - 11x^2 + 18x - 5$

as

		2	−3	5
×			3	−1
		−2	3	−5
	6	−9	15	
	6	−11	18	−5

b $(4x^2 - x + 2)(2x + 5)$
$= 8x^3 + 18x^2 - x + 10$

as

		4	−1	2
×			2	5
		20	−5	10
	8	−2	4	
	8	18	−1	10

c $(2x^2 + 3x + 2)(5 - x)$
$= -2x^3 + 7x^2 + 13x + 10$

as

		2	3	2
×			−1	5
		10	15	10
	−2	−3	−2	
	−2	7	13	10

d $(x - 2)^2(2x + 1)$
$= (x^2 - 4x + 4)(2x + 1)$
$= 2x^3 - 7x^2 + 4x + 4$

as

		1	−4	4
×			2	1
		1	−4	4
	2	−8	8	
	2	−7	4	4

e $(x^2 - 3x + 2)(2x^2 + 4x - 1)$
$= 2x^4 - 2x^3 - 9x^2 + 11x - 2$

as

			1	−3	2
×				2	4	−1
			−1	3	−2
		4	−12	8	
	2	−6	4		
	2	−2	−9	11	−2

f $(3x^2 - x + 2)(5x^2 + 2x - 3)$
$= 15x^4 + x^3 - x^2 + 7x - 6$

as

			3	−1	2
×				5	2	−3
			−9	3	−6
		6	−2	4	
	15	−5	10		
	15	1	−1	7	−6

g $(x^2 - x + 3)^2$
$= x^4 - 2x^3 + 7x^2 - 6x + 9$

as

			1	−1	3
×				1	−1	3
			3	−3	9
		−1	1	−3	
	1	−1	3		
	1	−2	7	−6	9

h $(2x^2 + x - 4)^2$
$= 4x^4 + 4x^3 - 15x^2 - 8x + 16$

as

			2	1	−4
×				2	1	−4
			−8	−4	16
		2	1	−4	
	4	2	−8		
	4	4	−15	−8	16

i $(2x+5)^3$
$= (2x+5)^2(2x+5)$
$= (4x^2 + 20x + 25)(2x+5)$
$= 8x^3 + 60x^2 + 150x + 125$

as

	4	20	25	
×		2	5	
	20	100	125	
8	40	50		
8	60	150	125	

j $(x^3 + x^2 - 2)^2$
$= x^6 + 2x^5 + x^4 - 4x^3 - 4x^2 + 4$

as

		1	1	0	-2		
×			1	1	0	-2	
			-2	-2	0	4	
		0	0	0	0		
	1	1	0	-2			
1	1	0	-2				
1	2	1	-4	-4	0	4	

EXERCISE 7C.2

1 a
$$\begin{array}{r} x \phantom{{}+2x-3} \\ x+2 \overline{\smash{)}\, x^2 + 2x - 3} \\ -(x^2 + 2x) \\ \hline -3 \end{array}$$

$\therefore\ Q(x) = x, \quad R = -3$

b
$$\begin{array}{r} x - 4 \phantom{{}+1} \\ x-1 \overline{\smash{)}\, x^2 - 5x + 1} \\ -(x^2 - x) \\ \hline -4x + 1 \\ -(-4x + 4) \\ \hline -3 \end{array}$$

$\therefore\ Q(x) = x - 4$
$R = -3$

c
$$\begin{array}{r} 2x^2 + 10x + 16 \\ x-2 \overline{\smash{)}\, 2x^3 + 6x^2 - 4x + 3} \\ -(2x^3 - 4x^2) \\ \hline 10x^2 - 4x \\ -(10x^2 - 20x) \\ \hline 16x + 3 \\ -(16x - 32) \\ \hline 35 \end{array}$$

$\therefore\ Q(x) = 2x^2 + 10x + 16$
$R = 35$

2 a
$$\begin{array}{r} x + 1 \\ x-4 \overline{\smash{)}\, x^2 - 3x + 6} \\ -(x^2 - 4x) \\ \hline x + 6 \\ -(x - 4) \\ \hline 10 \end{array}$$

$\therefore\ D(x) = x + 1 + \dfrac{10}{x-4}$

b
$$\begin{array}{r} x + 1 \\ x+3 \overline{\smash{)}\, x^2 + 4x - 11} \\ -(x^2 + 3x) \\ \hline x - 11 \\ -(x + 3) \\ \hline -14 \end{array}$$

$\therefore\ D(x) = x + 1 - \dfrac{14}{x+3}$

c
$$\begin{array}{r} 2x - 3 \\ x-2 \overline{\smash{)}\, 2x^2 - 7x + 2} \\ -(2x^2 - 4x) \\ \hline -3x + 2 \\ -(-3x + 6) \\ \hline -4 \end{array}$$

$\therefore\ D(x) = 2x - 3 - \dfrac{4}{x-2}$

d
$$\begin{array}{r} x^2 + x - 2 \\ 2x+1 \overline{\smash{)}\, 2x^3 + 3x^2 - 3x - 2} \\ -(2x^3 + x^2) \\ \hline 2x^2 - 3x \\ -(2x^2 + x) \\ \hline -4x - 2 \\ -(-4x - 2) \\ \hline 0 \end{array}$$

$\therefore\ D(x) = x^2 + x - 2$

e

$$\begin{array}{r} x^2 + 4x + 4 \\ 3x-1 \overline{\smash{\big)}\ 3x^3 + 11x^2 + 8x + 7} \\ \underline{-(3x^3 - x^2)} \\ 12x^2 + 8x \\ \underline{-(12x^2 - 4x)} \\ 12x + 7 \\ \underline{-(12x - 4)} \\ 11 \end{array}$$

$\therefore\ D(x) = x^2 + 4x + 4 + \dfrac{11}{3x-1}$

f

$$\begin{array}{r} x^3 - 2x^2 + \tfrac{5}{2}x - \tfrac{1}{4} \\ 2x+3 \overline{\smash{\big)}\ 2x^4 - x^3 - x^2 + 7x + 4} \\ \underline{-(2x^4 + 3x^3)} \\ -4x^3 - x^2 \\ \underline{-(-4x^3 - 6x^2)} \\ 5x^2 + 7x \\ \underline{-(5x^2 + \tfrac{15}{2}x)} \\ -\tfrac{1}{2}x + 4 \\ \underline{-(-\tfrac{1}{2}x - \tfrac{3}{4})} \\ \tfrac{19}{4} \end{array}$$

$\therefore\ D(x) = x^3 - 2x^2 + \tfrac{5}{2}x - \tfrac{1}{4} + \dfrac{\tfrac{19}{4}}{2x+3}$

3 a

$$\begin{array}{r} x + 2 \\ x-2 \overline{\smash{\big)}\ x^2 + 0x + 5} \\ \underline{-(x^2 - 2x)} \\ 2x + 5 \\ \underline{-(2x - 4)} \\ 9 \end{array}$$

$\therefore\ D(x) = x + 2 + \dfrac{9}{x-2}$

b

$$\begin{array}{r} 2x + 1 \\ x+1 \overline{\smash{\big)}\ 2x^2 + 3x + 0} \\ \underline{-(2x^2 + 2x)} \\ x + 0 \\ \underline{-(x + 1)} \\ -1 \end{array}$$

$\therefore\ D(x) = 2x + 1 - \dfrac{1}{x+1}$

c

$$\begin{array}{r} 3x - 4 \\ x+2 \overline{\smash{\big)}\ 3x^2 + 2x - 5} \\ \underline{-(3x^2 + 6x)} \\ -4x - 5 \\ \underline{-(-4x - 8)} \\ 3 \end{array}$$

$\therefore\ D(x) = 3x - 4 + \dfrac{3}{x+2}$

d

$$\begin{array}{r} x^2 + 3x - 2 \\ x-1 \overline{\smash{\big)}\ x^3 + 2x^2 - 5x + 2} \\ \underline{-(x^3 - x^2)} \\ 3x^2 - 5x \\ \underline{-(3x^2 - 3x)} \\ -2x + 2 \\ \underline{-(-2x + 2)} \\ 0 \end{array}$$

$\therefore\ D(x) = x^2 + 3x - 2$

e

$$\begin{array}{r} 2x^2 - 8x + 31 \\ x+4 \overline{\smash{\big)}\ 2x^3 + 0x^2 - x + 0} \\ \underline{-(2x^3 + 8x^2)} \\ -8x^2 - x \\ \underline{-(-8x^2 - 32x)} \\ 31x + 0 \\ \underline{-(31x + 124)} \\ -124 \end{array}$$

$\therefore\ D(x) = 2x^2 - 8x + 31 - \dfrac{124}{x+4}$

f

$$\begin{array}{r} x^2 + 3x + 6 \\ x-2 \overline{\smash{\big)}\ x^3 + x^2 + 0x - 5} \\ \underline{-(x^3 - 2x^2)} \\ 3x^2 + 0x \\ \underline{-(3x^2 - 6x)} \\ 6x - 5 \\ \underline{-(6x - 12)} \\ 7 \end{array}$$

$\therefore\ D(x) = x^2 + 3x + 6 + \dfrac{7}{x-2}$

EXERCISE 7C.3

1 a
$$\begin{array}{r} x+1 \\ x^2+x+1 \overline{\smash{\big)}\, x^3+2x^2+x-3} \\ -(x^3+x^2+x) \\ \hline x^2+0x-3 \\ -(x^2+x+1) \\ \hline -x-4 \end{array}$$
$\therefore\quad Q(x)=x+1,\quad R(x)=-x-4$

b
$$\begin{array}{r} 3 \\ x^2-1 \overline{\smash{\big)}\, 3x^2-x+0} \\ -(3x^2-3) \\ \hline -x+3 \end{array}$$
$\therefore\quad Q(x)=3,\quad R(x)=-x+3$

c
$$\begin{array}{r} 3x \\ x^2+1 \overline{\smash{\big)}\, 3x^3+0x^2+x-1} \\ -(3x^3+3x) \\ \hline -2x-1 \end{array}$$
$\therefore\quad Q(x)=3x,\quad R(x)=-2x-1$

d $Q(x)=0,\quad R(x)=x-4$

2 a
$$\begin{array}{r} 1 \\ x^2+x+1 \overline{\smash{\big)}\, x^2-x+1} \\ -(x^2+x+1) \\ \hline -2x \end{array}$$
$\therefore\quad x^2-x+1=(x^2+x+1)-2x$

b
$$\begin{array}{r} x \\ x^2+2 \overline{\smash{\big)}\, x^3+0x^2+0x+0} \\ -(x^3+2x) \\ \hline -2x+0 \end{array}$$
$\therefore\quad x^3=(x^2+2)x-2x$

c
$$\begin{array}{r} x^2+x+3 \\ x^2-x+1 \overline{\smash{\big)}\, x^4+0x^3+3x^2+x-1} \\ -(x^4-x^3+x^2) \\ \hline x^3+2x^2+x \\ -(x^3-x^2+x) \\ \hline 3x^2+0x-1 \\ -(3x^2-3x+3) \\ \hline 3x-4 \end{array}$$
$\therefore\quad x^4+3x^2+x-1$
$=(x^2-x+1)(x^2+x+3)+3x-4$

d $\dfrac{2x^3-x+6}{(x-1)^2}=\dfrac{2x^3-x+6}{x^2-2x+1}$
$$\begin{array}{r} 2x+4 \\ x^2-2x+1 \overline{\smash{\big)}\, 2x^3+0x^2-x+6} \\ -(2x^3-4x^2+2x) \\ \hline 4x^2-3x+6 \\ -(4x^2-8x+4) \\ \hline 5x+2 \end{array}$$
$\therefore\quad 2x^3-x+6$
$=(x-1)^2(2x+4)+5x+2$

e $\dfrac{x^4}{(x+1)^2}=\dfrac{x^4}{x^2+2x+1}$
$$\begin{array}{r} x^2-2x+3 \\ x^2+2x+1 \overline{\smash{\big)}\, x^4+0x^3+0x^2+0x+0} \\ -(x^4+2x^3+x^2) \\ \hline -2x^3-x^2+0x \\ -(-2x^3-4x^2-2x) \\ \hline 3x^2+2x+0 \\ -(3x^2+6x+3) \\ \hline -4x-3 \end{array}$$
$\therefore\quad x^4=(x+1)^2(x^2-2x+3)-4x-3$

f $\dfrac{x^4-2x^3+x+5}{(x-1)(x+2)}=\dfrac{x^4-2x^3+x+5}{x^2+x-2}$
$$\begin{array}{r} x^2-3x+5 \\ x^2+x-2 \overline{\smash{\big)}\, x^4-2x^3+0x^2+x+5} \\ -(x^4+x^3-2x^2) \\ \hline -3x^3+2x^2+x \\ -(-3x^3-3x^2+6x) \\ \hline 5x^2-5x+5 \\ -(5x^2+5x-10) \\ \hline -10x+15 \end{array}$$
$\therefore\quad x^4-2x^3+x+5$
$=(x-1)(x+2)(x^2-3x+5)-10x+15$

3 $\dfrac{P(x)}{x-2} = \dfrac{(x-2)(x^2+2x+3)+7}{x-2}$

$= x^2 + 2x + 3 + \dfrac{7}{x-2}$

$\therefore$ quotient is $x^2 + 2x + 3$, remainder is 7

4 $\dfrac{f(x)}{x^2+x-2} = \dfrac{(x-1)(x+2)(x^2-3x+5)+15-10x}{(x-1)(x+2)}$

$= x^2 - 3x + 5 + \dfrac{15-10x}{(x-1)(x+2)}$

$\therefore$ quotient is $x^2 - 3x + 5$, remainder is $15 - 10x$

EXERCISE 7D.1

1 a $2x^2 - 5x - 12$ has zeros

$x = \dfrac{5 \pm \sqrt{25 - 4(2)(-12)}}{4}$

$= \dfrac{5 \pm \sqrt{121}}{4}$

$= \dfrac{5 \pm 11}{4}$

$= 4, \ -\tfrac{6}{4}$

$\therefore$ zeros are $4, \ -\tfrac{3}{2}$

b $x^2 + 6x + 10$ has zeros

$x = \dfrac{-6 \pm \sqrt{36 - 4(1)(10)}}{2}$

$= \dfrac{-6 \pm \sqrt{-4}}{2}$

$= -3 \pm i$

$\therefore$ zeros are $-3 \pm i$

c $z^2 - 6z + 6$ has zeros

$z = \dfrac{6 \pm \sqrt{36 - 4(1)(6)}}{2}$

$= \dfrac{6 \pm \sqrt{12}}{2}$

$= 3 \pm \sqrt{3}$

$\therefore$ zeros are $3 \pm \sqrt{3}$

d $x^3 - 4x$

$= x(x^2 - 4)$

$= x(x+2)(x-2)$

$\therefore$ zeros are $0, \pm 2$

e $z^3 + 2z$
$= z(z^2 + 2)$
$= z(z^2 - 2i^2)$
$= z(z + i\sqrt{2})(z - i\sqrt{2})$
$\therefore$ zeros are $0, \pm i\sqrt{2}$

f $z^4 + 4z^2 - 5$
$= (z^2 + 5)(z^2 - 1)$
$= (z^2 - 5i^2)(z^2 - 1)$
$= (z + i\sqrt{5})(z - i\sqrt{5})(z+1)(z-1)$
$\therefore$ zeros are $\pm i\sqrt{5}, \pm 1$

2 a $ 5x^2 = 3x + 2$
$\therefore 5x^2 - 3x - 2 = 0$
$\therefore (5x+2)(x-1) = 0$
$\therefore$ roots are $1, -\tfrac{2}{5}$

b $ (2x+1)(x^2+3) = 0$
$\therefore (2x+1)(x^2-3i^2) = 0$
$\therefore (2x+1)(x+i\sqrt{3})(x-i\sqrt{3}) = 0$
$\therefore$ roots are $-\tfrac{1}{2}, \pm i\sqrt{3}$

c $-2z(z^2 - 2z + 2) = 0$

$z = 0$ or $\dfrac{2 \pm \sqrt{4 - 4(1)(2)}}{2}$

$= 0$ or $\dfrac{2 \pm \sqrt{-4}}{2}$

$= 0$ or $1 \pm i$

$\therefore$ roots are $0, 1 \pm i$

d $ x^3 = 5x$
$\therefore x^3 - 5x = 0$
$ x(x^2 - 5) = 0$
$ x(x + \sqrt{5})(x - \sqrt{5}) = 0$
$\therefore$ roots are $0, \pm \sqrt{5}$

e $ z^3 + 5z = 0$
$ z(z^2 + 5) = 0$
$ z(z^2 - 5i^2) = 0$
$z(z + i\sqrt{5})(z - i\sqrt{5}) = 0$
$\therefore$ roots are $0, \pm i\sqrt{5}$

f $ z^4 = 3z^2 + 10$
$\therefore z^4 - 3z^2 - 10 = 0$
$ (z^2 - 5)(z^2 + 2) = 0$
$ (z^2 - 5)(z^2 - 2i^2) = 0$
$(z + \sqrt{5})(z - \sqrt{5})(z + i\sqrt{2})(z - i\sqrt{2}) = 0$
$\therefore$ roots are $\pm \sqrt{5}, \pm i\sqrt{2}$

3 **a** $\quad 2x^2 - 7x - 15$
$\quad\quad = (2x+3)(x-5)$

c $\quad x^3 + 2x^2 - 4x$
$\quad\quad = x(x^2 + 2x - 4)$
$\quad x^2 + 2x - 4$ is zero when
$$x = \frac{-2 \pm \sqrt{4+16}}{2}$$
$\quad\quad = -1 \pm \sqrt{5}$
$\therefore \quad x^3 + 2x^2 - 4x$
$\quad\quad = x(x + 1 + \sqrt{5})(x + 1 - \sqrt{5})$

e $\quad z^4 - 6z^2 + 5$
$\quad\quad = (z^2 - 1)(z^2 - 5)$
$\quad\quad = (z+1)(z-1)(z+\sqrt{5})(z-\sqrt{5})$

b $\quad z^2 - 6z + 16$ is zero when
$$z = \frac{6 \pm \sqrt{36 - 4(1)(16)}}{2}$$
$\quad\quad = 3 \pm i\sqrt{7}$
$\therefore \quad z^2 - 6z + 16$
$\quad\quad = (z - 3 + i\sqrt{7})(z - 3 - i\sqrt{7})$

d $\quad 6z^3 - z^2 - 2z$
$\quad\quad = z(6z^2 - z - 2)$
$\quad\quad = z(2z+1)(3z-2)$

f $\quad z^4 - z^2 - 2$
$\quad\quad = (z^2 - 2)(z^2 + 1)$
$\quad\quad = (z + \sqrt{2})(z - \sqrt{2})(z+i)(z-i)$

4 $\quad P(x) = a(x-\alpha)(x-\beta)(x-\gamma)$
$\therefore \quad P(\alpha) = a \times 0 \times (\alpha - \beta)(\alpha - \gamma) = 0$
and $\quad P(\beta) = a(\beta - \alpha) \times 0 \times (\beta - \gamma) = 0$
and $\quad P(\gamma) = a(\gamma - \alpha)(\gamma - \beta) \times 0 = 0$
$\therefore \quad \alpha, \beta$ and γ all satisfy $P(x) = 0$
$\therefore \quad \alpha, \beta$ and γ are zeros of $P(x)$

5 **a** The zeros ± 2
have sum $= 0$ and product $= -4$
$\therefore$ come from quadratic factor $z^2 - 4$
and zero 3 comes from $(z - 3)$
$\therefore \quad P(z) = a(z^2 - 4)(z - 3)$, $a \neq 0$

c The zeros $-1 \pm i$
have sum $= -2$ and product $= 2$
$\therefore$ come from quadratic factor $z^2 + 2z + 2$
and zero 3 comes from $(z - 3)$
$\therefore \quad P(z) = a(z - 3)(z^2 + 2z + 2)$, $a \neq 0$

b The zeros $\pm i$
have sum $= 0$ and product $= 1$
$\therefore$ come from quadratic factor $z^2 + 1$
and zero -2 comes from $(z + 2)$
$\therefore \quad P(z) = a(z^2 + 1)(z + 2)$, $a \neq 0$

d The zeros $-2 \pm \sqrt{2}$
have sum $= -4$ and product $= 2$
$\therefore$ come from quadratic factor $z^2 + 4z + 2$
and zero -1 comes from $(z + 1)$
$\therefore \quad P(z) = a(z + 1)(z^2 + 4z + 2)$, $a \neq 0$

6 **a** For zeros of ± 1, sum $= 0$ and product $= -1$ $\therefore$ come from $z^2 - 1$
For zeros of $\pm \sqrt{2}$, sum $= 0$ and product $= -2$ $\therefore$ come from $z^2 - 2$
$\therefore \quad P(z) = a(z^2 - 1)(z^2 - 2)$, $a \neq 0$

b For zeros of $\pm i\sqrt{3}$, sum $= 0$ and product $= 3$ $\therefore$ come from $z^2 + 3$
zeros of $2, -1$ come from $(z - 2)(z + 1)$
$\therefore \quad P(z) = a(z - 2)(z + 1)(z^2 + 3)$, $a \neq 0$

c For zeros of $\pm \sqrt{3}$, sum $= 0$ and product $= -3$ $\therefore$ come from $z^2 - 3$
For zeros of $1 \pm i$, sum $= 2$ and product $= 2$ $\therefore$ come from $z^2 - 2z + 2$
$\therefore \quad P(z) = a(z^2 - 3)(z^2 - 2z + 2)$, $a \neq 0$

d For zeros of $2 \pm \sqrt{5}$, sum $= 4$ and product $= -1$ $\therefore$ come from $z^2 - 4z - 1$
For zeros of $-2 \pm 3i$, sum $= -4$ and product $= 13$ $\therefore$ come from $z^2 + 4z + 13$
$\therefore \quad P(z) = a(z^2 - 4z - 1)(z^2 + 4z + 13)$, $a \neq 0$

EXERCISE 7D.2

1 **a** $2x^2 + 4x + 5 = ax^2 + [2b - 6]x + c$
Equating coefficients gives
$a = 2$, $2b - 6 = 4$, and $c = 5$

$\therefore \quad 2b = 10$
$\therefore \quad b = 5$
$\therefore \quad a = 2$, $b = 5$, $c = 5$

b $2x^3 - x^2 + 6 = (x-1)^2(2x+a) + bx + c$
$= (x^2 - 2x + 1)(2x+a) + bx + c$
$= 2x^3 + [a-4]x^2 + [2-2a]x + a + bx + c$
$= 2x^3 + [a-4]x^2 + [2-2a+b]x + [a+c]$

Equating coefficients gives $\quad a - 4 = -1 \qquad 2 - 2a + b = 0 \qquad a + c = 6$
$\qquad \qquad \qquad \qquad \qquad \therefore \quad a = 3 \qquad \therefore \quad b = 2a - 2 \qquad \therefore \quad c = 6 - a$
$\qquad \qquad \qquad \qquad \qquad \qquad \qquad \qquad \qquad \therefore \quad b = 4 \qquad \qquad \therefore \quad c = 3$

2 a $z^4 + 4 = (z^2 + az + 2)(z^2 + bz + 2)$
$= z^4 + [a+b]z^3 + [4+ab]z^2 + [2a+2b]z + 4$

Equating coefficients gives: $\quad a + b = 0 \qquad 4 + ab = 0$
$\qquad \qquad \qquad \qquad \qquad \quad \therefore \quad a = -b \quad \therefore \quad ab = -4$
$\qquad \qquad \qquad \text{By inspection} \quad a = 2 \quad \text{and} \quad b = -2$
$\qquad \qquad \qquad \qquad \text{or} \quad a = -2 \quad \text{and} \quad b = 2$

		1	a	2
×		1	b	2
		2	2a	4
	b	ab	2b	
1	a	2		
1	a+b	4+ab	2a+2b	4

b $2z^4 + 5z^3 + 4z^2 + 7z + 6$
$= (z^2 + az + 2)(2z^2 + bz + 3)$
$= 2z^4 + [2a+b]z^3 + [ab+7]z^2 + [3a+2b]z + 6$

Equating coefficients gives: $2a + b = 5$ .... (1)
$\qquad \qquad \qquad \qquad \qquad \quad 3a + 2b = 7$ .... (2)
$\qquad \qquad \qquad \qquad \qquad \quad ab + 7 = 4$ .... (3)
$\qquad \qquad \therefore \quad 4a + 2b = 10 \quad \{(1) \times 2\}$
$\qquad \qquad \text{and} \quad 3a + 2b = 7$

and solving these two equations gives $a = 3, \ b = -1$
which checks with (3) as $\ ab + 7 = -3 + 7 = 4 \ \checkmark$

		1	a	2
×		2	b	3
		3	3a	6
	b	ab	2b	
2	2a	4		
2	2a+b	ab+7	3a+2b	6

3 Consider
$z^4 + 64 = (z^2 + az + 8)(z^2 + bz + 8)$
$= z^4 + [a+b]z^3 + [ab+16]z^2 + [8a+8b]z + 64$

Equating coefficients gives:
$a + b = 0 \quad \text{and} \quad ab + 16 = 0$
$\therefore \quad a = -b \qquad \therefore \quad ab = -16$
$\therefore \quad$ by inspection $a = 4 \quad \text{and} \quad b = -4$
$\qquad \qquad \text{or} \quad a = -4 \quad \text{and} \quad b = 4$
$\therefore \quad z^4 + 64$ can be factorised into $(z^2 + 4z + 8)(z^2 - 4z + 8)$

		1	a	8
×		1	b	8
		8	8a	64
	b	ab	8b	
1	a	8		
1	a+b	ab+16	8a+8b	64

Now consider
$z^4 + 64 = (z^2 + az + 16)(z^2 + bz + 4)$
$= z^4 + [a+b]z^3 + [ab+20]z^2 + [4a+16b]z + 64$

Equating coefficients gives:
$a + b = 0$ .... (1) and $ab + 20 = 0$
$4a + 16b = 0$ .... (2) $\qquad \therefore \quad ab = -20$ .... (3)
Solution to (1), (2) is $a = b = 0$
But this does not satisfy (3)
$\therefore \quad$ no values of a and b exist which obey the original assumption
$\therefore \quad$ cannot be factorised in this way.

		1	a	16
×		1	b	4
		4	4a	64
	b	ab	16b	
1	a	16		
1	a+b	ab+20	4a+16b	64

4 Consider
$x^4 - 4x^2 + 8x - 4$
$= (x^2 + ax + 2)(x^2 + bx - 2)$
$= x^4 + [a+b]x^3 + [ab]x^2 + [2b - 2a]x - 4$
Equating coefficients gives:
$\quad a + b = 0$ and $ab = -4$ and $-2a + 2b = 8$
$\therefore \quad 2a + 2b = 0$ .... (1)
$\quad -2a + 2b = 8$ .... (2)

		1	a	2
×		1	b	-2
		-2	$-2a$	-4
	b	ab	$2b$	
1	a	2		
1	$a+b$	ab	$2b-2a$	-4

Adding (1) and (2) gives $4b = 8$ $\therefore$ $b = 2$ and hence $a = -2$, which checks with $ab = -4$ ✓
$\therefore \quad P(x) = (x^2 - 2x + 2)(x^2 + 2x - 2)$
$\quad$ Now if $\quad x^4 + 8x = 4x^2 + 4$
$\quad$ then $\quad x^4 - 4x^2 + 8x - 4 = 0$
$\therefore \quad (x^2 - 2x + 2)(x^2 + 2x - 2) = 0$
$\therefore \quad x^2 - 2x + 2 = 0$ or $x^2 + 2x - 2 = 0$
$\therefore \quad x = \dfrac{2 \pm \sqrt{4-8}}{2} = 1 \pm i$ or $x = \dfrac{-2 \pm \sqrt{4+8}}{2} = -1 \pm \sqrt{3}$
$\therefore \quad x = 1 \pm i, \; -1 \pm \sqrt{3}$

5 a $P(z) = 2z^3 - z^2 + az - 3$
$\quad = (2z - 3)(z^2 + bz + 1)$ for some value b
$\quad = 2z^3 + [2b - 3]z^2 + [2 - 3b]z - 3$
Equating coefficients gives:
$2b - 3 = -1$ and $2 - 3b = a$
$2b = 2 \quad\quad \therefore \; a = 2 - 3$
$b = 1 \quad\quad\quad a = -1$
$\therefore \quad P(z) = (2z - 3)\underbrace{(z^2 + z + 1)}$

	1	b	1
×		2	-3
	-3	$-3b$	-3
2	$2b$	2	
2	$2b-3$	$2-3b$	-3

$\quad$ this quadratic has zeros $z = \dfrac{-1 \pm \sqrt{1-4}}{2} = \dfrac{-1 \pm i\sqrt{3}}{2}$
$\therefore \quad a = -1$ and zeros are $\frac{3}{2}, \; -\frac{1}{2} \pm i\frac{\sqrt{3}}{2}$

b $P(z) = 3z^3 - z^2 + [a + 1]z + a$
$\quad = (3z + 2)(z^2 + bz + c)$
$\quad = 3z^3 + [2 + 3b]z^2 + [2b + 3c]z + 2c$
Equating coefficients gives:
$\therefore \quad 2 + 3b = -1, \quad 2b + 3c = a + 1$ and $2c = a$
Now as $2 + 3b = -1$
$\therefore \quad 3b = -3$
$\therefore \quad b = -1$

	1	b	c
×		3	2
	2	$2b$	$2c$
3	$3b$	$3c$	
3	$2+3b$	$2b+3c$	$2c$

Substituting $b = -1$ and $a = 2c$ into $2b + 3c = a + 1$ gives $2(-1) + 3c = 2c + 1$
$\therefore \quad -2 + 3c = 2c + 1$
$\quad\quad c = 3$
and so $a = 6$
$\therefore \quad P(z) = (3z + 2)\underbrace{(z^2 - z + 3)}$
$\quad$ this quadratic has zeros $\dfrac{1 \pm \sqrt{1 - 4(3)(1)}}{2} = \dfrac{1 \pm i\sqrt{11}}{2}$
So, $a = 6$ and the zeros are $-\frac{2}{3}, \; \frac{1}{2} \pm i\frac{\sqrt{11}}{2}$.

6 a $P(x) = 2x^4 + ax^3 + bx^2 - 12x - 8$
$= (2x+1)(x-2)(x^2+cx+4)$
$= (2x^2 - 3x - 2)(x^2 + cx + 4)$

Equating coefficients: $2c - 3 = a$,
$6 - 3c = b$ and $-2c - 12 = -12$
The last equation has solution $c = 0$, and consequently,
$a = -3$ and $b = 6$
$\therefore$ $P(x) = (2x+1)(x-2)(x^2+4) = (2x+1)(x-2)(x+2i)(x-2i)$
$\therefore$ zeros are $-\tfrac{1}{2}, 2$ and $\pm 2i$ and $a = -3$, $b = 6$.

			2	-3	-2
	$\times$		1	c	4
			8	-12	-8
		$2c$	$-3c$	$-2c$	
	2	-3	-2		
	2	$2c-3$	$6-3c$	$-2c-12$	-8

b $P(x) = 2x^4 + ax^3 + bx^2 + ax + 3$
$= (x+3)(2x-1)(x^2+cx-1)$
$= (2x^2 + 5x - 3)(x^2 + cx - 1)$

Equating coefficients: $a = 2c + 5$,
$b = 5c - 5$, $a = -5 - 3c$
$\therefore$ $2c + 5 = -5 - 3c$ {equating a's}
$\therefore$ $5c = -10$
$\therefore$ $c = -2$ and so, $a = 1$ $b = -15$
$\therefore$ $P(x) = (x+3)(2x-1)\underbrace{(x^2 - 2x - 1)}$

this quadratic has zeros $\dfrac{2 \pm \sqrt{4+4}}{2} = 1 \pm \sqrt{2}$

$\therefore$ zeros are $-3, \tfrac{1}{2}, 1 \pm \sqrt{2}$ and $a = 1$, $b = -15$

			2	5	-3
	$\times$		1	c	-1
			-2	-5	3
		$2c$	$5c$	$-3c$	
	2	5	-3		
	2	$2c+5$	$5c-5$	$-5-3c$	3

7 a $x^3 + 3x^2 - 9x + c$
$= (x+a)^2(x+b)$
$= (x^2 + 2ax + a^2)(x+b)$
$= x^3 + [b+2a]x^2 + [a^2 + 2ab]x + a^2b$

Equating coefficients gives
$2a + b = 3$, $a^2 + 2ab = -9$ and $c = a^2b$
Substituting $b = 3 - 2a$ into the second equation gives:
$a^2 + 2a(3-2a) = -9$
$\therefore$ $a^2 + 6a - 4a^2 = -9$
$\therefore$ $-3a^2 + 6a = -9$
$\therefore$ $3a^2 - 6a - 9 = 0$
$\therefore$ $a^2 - 2a - 3 = 0$
$\therefore$ $(a-3)(a+1) = 0$

$\therefore$ $\begin{cases} a = 3 \\ b = -3 \\ c = -27 \end{cases}$ or $\begin{cases} a = -1 \\ b = 5 \\ c = 5 \end{cases}$

If $c = -27$, $P(x) = (x+3)^2(x-3)$
If $c = 5$, $P(x) = (x-1)^2(x+5)$

		1	$2a$	a^2
	$\times$		1	b
		b	$2ab$	a^2b
	1	$2a$	a^2	
	1	$b+2a$	a^2+2ab	a^2b

b $3x^3 + 4x^2 - x + m$
$= (x+a)^2(3x+b)$
$= (x^2 + 2ax + a^2)(3x+b)$
$= x^3 + [6a+b]x^2 + [3a^2 + 2ab]x + a^2b$

Equating coefficients gives
$6a + b = 4$, $3a^2 + 2ab = -1$ and $a^2b = m$
Substituting $b = 4 - 6a$ into the second equation gives:
$3a^2 + 2a(4 - 6a) = -1$
$\therefore$ $3a^2 + 8a - 12a^2 = -1$
$\therefore$ $9a^2 - 8a - 1 = 0$
$\therefore$ $(9a+1)(a-1) = 0$
$\therefore$ $a = -\tfrac{1}{9}$ or $a = 1$

		1	$2a$	a^2
	$\times$		3	b
		b	$2ab$	a^2b
	3	$6a$	$3a^2$	
	3	$6a+b$	$3a^2+2ab$	a^2b

When $a = 1$, $b = -2$ and $m = -2$. So, $P(x) = (x+1)^2(3x-2)$ $\therefore$ zeros are $-1, \tfrac{2}{3}$
When $a = -\tfrac{1}{9}$, $b = \tfrac{14}{3}$ and $m = \tfrac{14}{243}$. So, $P(x) = (x - \tfrac{1}{9})^2(3x + \tfrac{14}{3})$
$\therefore$ zeros are $\tfrac{1}{9}, -\tfrac{14}{9}$

EXERCISE 7D.3

1 **a** If $P(2) = 7$, then $P(x) = (x-2)Q(x) + 7$ and $P(x)$ divided by $(x-2)$ leaves a remainder of 7.
   b If $P(x) = (x+3)Q(x) - 8$, then $P(-3) = -8$ and $P(x)$ divided by $(x+3)$ leaves a remainder of -8.
   c If $P(x)$ when divided by $(x-5)$ has a remainder of 11, then $P(5) = 11$ and $P(x) = (x-5)Q(x) + 11$.

2 **a** $P(x) = x^3 + 2x^2 - 7x + 5$
   $\therefore R = P(1)$ {Remainder theorem}
   $= 1^3 + 2(1)^2 - 7 + 5$
   $= 1$

   b $P(x) = x^4 - 2x^2 + 3x - 1$
   $\therefore R = P(-2)$ {Remainder theorem}
   $= (-2)^4 - 2(-2)^2 + 3(-2) - 1$
   $= 16 - 8 - 6 - 1$
   $= 1$

3 **a** $P(x) = x^3 - 2x + a$
   Now $P(2) = 7$ {Remainder theorem}
   $\therefore 2^3 - 2(2) + a = 7$
   $4 + a = 7$
   $\therefore a = 3$

   b $P(x) = 2x^3 + x^2 + ax - 5$
   Now $P(-1) = -8$
   $\therefore 2(-1)^3 + (-1)^2 + a(-1) - 5 = -8$
   $-2 + 1 - a - 5 = -8$
   $\therefore -a - 6 = -8$
   $-a = -2$
   $\therefore a = 2$

4 $P(x) = x^3 + 2x^2 + ax + b$
Now $P(1) = 4$ and $P(-2) = 16$ {Remainder theorem}
If $P(1) = 4$ then $1 + 2 + a + b = 4$ and so $a + b = 1$ ...... (1)
If $P(-2) = 16$ then $(-2)^3 + 2(-2)^2 + a(-2) + b = 16$
$\therefore -8 + 8 - 2a + b = 16$
$\therefore -2a + b = 16$ ...... (2)
Solving (1) and (2) $-a - b = -1$
$-2a + b = 16$
$\therefore -3a = 15$ {adding}
$\therefore a = -5$ and so $b = 6$
$\therefore a = -5$ and $b = 6$

5 $P(x) = 2x^n + ax^2 - 6$
By the Remainder theorem, $P(1) = -7$ $\therefore$ $2(1)^n + a(1)^2 - 6 = -7$
$\therefore 2 + a - 6 = -7$
$\therefore a = -3$
So, $P(x) = 2x^n - 3x^2 - 6$
and since $P(-3) = 129$, $\therefore$ $2(-3)^n - 3(-3)^2 - 6 = 129$
$2(-3)^n - 27 - 6 = 129$
$2(-3)^n = 162$
$(-3)^n = 81$
$\therefore n = 4$
$\therefore a = -3$ and $n = 4$

6 $P(z) = Q(z)(z^2 - 3z + 2) + (4z - 7) = Q(z)(z-2)(z-1) + (4z-7)$
   a Remainder is $P(1)$ {Remainder theorem}
   $\therefore R = Q(1) \times (1-2) \times 0 + (4-7)$
   $= -3$

   b Remainder is $P(2)$ {Remainder theorem}
   $\therefore R = Q(2) \times 0 \times (2-1) + [4(2) - 7]$
   $= 0 + 1$
   $= 1$

7 Suppose $P(z)$ is divided by $(z-3)(z+1)$
$\therefore \quad P(z) = Q(z) \times (z-3)(z+1) + (Az+B)$
$\qquad\qquad\qquad\qquad\qquad\qquad\uparrow$
$\qquad\qquad\qquad$ the remainder must be of this form

Now $P(-1) = -8 \qquad \therefore \quad Q(-1) \times 0 + (-A+B) = -8$
$\qquad\qquad\qquad\qquad\qquad\therefore \quad -A+B = -8 \quad \ldots\ldots \text{ (1)}$

and $P(3) = 4 \qquad \therefore \quad Q(3) \times 0 + (3A+B) = 4$
$\qquad\qquad\qquad\qquad\qquad\therefore \quad 3A+B = 4 \quad \ldots\ldots \text{ (2)}$

Solving (1) and (2) $\quad -A+B = -8$
$\qquad\qquad\qquad\qquad\quad -3A-B = -4$
$\qquad\qquad\qquad\qquad\overline{\quad -4A = -12 \quad}$
$\qquad\qquad\qquad\qquad\therefore \quad A = 3 \text{ and so } B = -5$
$\qquad\qquad\qquad\qquad\therefore \quad R(z) = 3z - 5$

8 Suppose $P(x)$ is divided by $(x-a)(x-b)$ and has remainder $Ex+F$
hence $P(x) = Q(x) \times (x-a)(x-b) + Ex+F$
Now $\quad P(a) = Ea+F \quad \ldots\ldots \text{ (1)} \quad$ and $\quad P(b) = Eb+F \quad \ldots\ldots \text{ (2)}$
Subtracting (2) and (1), $P(b) - P(a) = Eb - Ea = E(b-a)$

$\qquad\qquad\qquad\therefore \quad E = \dfrac{P(b) - P(a)}{b-a}$

$\qquad\therefore \quad$ from (1) $\quad F = P(a) - Ea = P(a) - \left(\dfrac{P(b) - P(a)}{b-a}\right) a$

$\qquad\qquad\qquad$ Now $R(x) = Ex + F$

$\qquad\qquad\therefore \quad R(x) = \left(\dfrac{P(b) - P(a)}{b-a}\right) x + P(a) - \left(\dfrac{P(b) - P(a)}{b-a}\right) a$

$\qquad\qquad\therefore \quad R(x) = \left(\dfrac{P(b) - P(a)}{b-a}\right)(x-a) + P(a)$

EXERCISE 7D.4

1 a $P(x) = 2x^3 + x^2 + kx - 4$
if $x+2$ is a factor then $P(-2) = 0$
$\therefore \quad -2k - 16 = 0$
$\therefore \quad k = -8$
$\therefore \quad P(x) = 2x^3 + x^2 - 8x - 4$
$\qquad\quad = (x+2)(2x^2 - 3x - 2) \quad$ {as when $k = -8$, $k+6 = -2$}
$\therefore \quad P(x) = (x+2)(2x+1)(x-2) \quad$ and $\quad k = -8$

-2	2	1	k	-4
	0	-4	6	$-2k-12$
	2	-3	$k+6$	$-2k-16$

b $P(x) = x^4 - 3x^3 - kx^2 + 6x$
if $x-3$ is a factor then $P(3) = 0$
$\therefore \quad 18 - 9k = 0$
$\therefore \quad 9k = 18$
$\therefore \quad k = 2$
$\therefore \quad P(x) = x^4 - 3x^3 - 2x^2 + 6x$
$\therefore \quad P(x) = (x-3)(x^3 - 2x) \quad$ {as when $k = 2$, $-k = -2$ and $6 - 3k = 0$}
$\qquad\quad = x(x-3)(x^2 - 2)$
$\qquad\quad = x(x-3)(x+\sqrt{2})(x-\sqrt{2}) \quad$ and $\quad k = 2$

3	1	-3	$-k$	6	0
	0	3	0	$-3k$	$18-9k$
	1	0	$-k$	$6-3k$	$18-9k$

2 $P(x) = 2x^3 + ax^2 + bx + 5$

if $x - 1$ is a factor, $P(1) = 0$
$\therefore \quad 2(1)^3 + a(1)^2 + b(1) + 5 = 0$
$\qquad 2 + a + b + 5 = 0$
$\therefore \quad a + b = -7$ ...... (1)

if $x + 5$ is a factor, $P(-5) = 0$
$2(-5)^3 + a(-5)^2 + b(-5) + 5 = 0$
$-250 + 25a - 5b + 5 = 0$
$25a - 5b = 245$
$\therefore \quad 5a - b = 49$ ...... (2)

Adding (1) and (2) gives: $6a = 42$
$\therefore \quad a = 7$ and $b = -14$

3 a $P(z) = z^3 - z^2 + [k-5]z + [k^2 - 7]$
if 3 is a zero, $R = P(3) = 0$
$\therefore \quad k^2 + 3k - 4 = 0$
$(k+4)(k-1) = 0$
$\therefore \quad k = -4$ or $k = 1$

3	1	-1	$k-5$	k^2-7
	0	3	6	$3k+3$
	1	2	$k+1$	k^2+3k-4

if $k = 1$, $P(z) = (z-3)(z^2 + 2z + 2)$

the quadratic has zeros: $\dfrac{-2 \pm \sqrt{4-8}}{2} = -1 \pm i$

$\therefore$ zeros are $3, -1 \pm i$

if $k = -4$, $P(z) = (z-3)(z^2 + 2z - 3)$
$\qquad = (z-3)(z+3)(z-1)$

$\therefore$ zeros are $3, -3$ and 1

b $P(z) = z^3 + mz^2 + (3m-2)z - 10m - 4$
if $z - 2$ is a factor, $P(2) = 0$
since $* - 0$ R_1 is always 0
$\therefore \quad z - 2$ is always a factor
now for $(z-2)^2$ to be a factor
$7m + 10 = 0$ $\{R_2$ is also $0\}$ $\therefore \quad m = -\dfrac{10}{7}$

2	1	m	$3m-2$	$-10m-4$
	0	2	$2m+4$	$10m+4$
2	1	$m+2$	$5m+2$	0 ... (*)
	0	2	$2m+8$	
	1	$m+4$	$7m+10$	

4 a i $P(x) = x^3 - a^3$
$P(a) = a^3 - a^3$
$\qquad = 0$
$\therefore \quad x - a$ is a linear factor of $P(x)$ for all a

ii
a	1	0	0	$-a^3$
	0	a	a^2	a^3
	1	a	a^2	0

$\therefore \quad P(x) = (x-a)(x^2 + ax + a^2)$

b i $P(x) = x^3 + a^3$
$P(-a) = -a^3 + a^3$
$\qquad = 0$
$\therefore \quad x + a$ is a factor of $P(x)$ for all a

ii
$-a$	1	0	0	a^3
	0	$-a$	a^2	$-a^3$
	1	$-a$	a^2	0

$\therefore \quad P(x) = (x+a)(x^2 - ax + a^2)$

5 a Consider $P(x) = x^n + 1$
if $x + 1$ is a factor then
$P(-1) = 0$
$\therefore \quad (-1)^n + 1 = 0$
$\therefore \quad (-1)^n = -1$
which is only true if n is odd
$\therefore \quad x + 1$ is a factor of $x^n + 1 \Leftrightarrow n$ is odd.

if n is odd $(-1)^n = -1$
$\therefore \quad (-1)^n + 1 = 0$
then $P(-1) = 0$ if $P(x) = x^n + 1$
$\therefore \quad x = -1$ is a zero of $P(x)$
$\therefore \quad x + 1$ is a factor of $P(x)$

b $P(x) = x^3 - 3ax - 9$ and if $x - 1 - a$ is a factor then $P(1+a) = 0$

$1+a$	1	0	$-3a$	-9
	0	$1+a$	$1+2a+a^2$	a^3+1
	1	$1+a$	a^2-a+1	a^3-8

$\therefore \quad a^3 - 8 = 0$
$\therefore \quad a = 2$ {the only real soln.}

EXERCISE 7E.1

1 **a** A single factor such as $(x - \alpha)$ indicates that the graph *cuts* the x-axis at α.
   b A squared factor such as $(x - \alpha)^2$ indicates that the graph *touches* the x-axis at α.
   c A cubed factor such as $(x - \alpha)^3$ indicates that the graph *cuts* the x-axis at α, and at α the graph changes shape.

2 **a** The x-intercepts are: -1, 2 and 3 $\quad \therefore \quad y = a(x+1)(x-2)(x-3), \ a \neq 0$
   As the curve passes through $(0, 12)$, $\quad 12 = a(1)(-2)(-3) \quad \therefore \quad a = 2$
   $\therefore \quad y = 2(x+1)(x-2)(x-3)$

   b The x-intercepts are: -3, $-\frac{1}{2}$ and $\frac{1}{2}$ $\quad \therefore \quad y = a(x+3)(2x+1)(2x-1), \ a \neq 0$
   As the curve passes through $(0, 6)$, $\quad 6 = a(3)(1)(-1) \quad \therefore \quad a = -2$
   $\therefore \quad y = -2(x+3)(2x+1)(2x-1)$

   c The x-intercepts are: -4, -4 and 3 $\quad \therefore \quad y = a(x+4)^2(x-3), \ a \neq 0$
   As the curve passes through $(0, -12)$, $\quad -12 = a(4)^2(-3) \quad \therefore \quad a = \frac{1}{4}$
   $\therefore \quad y = \frac{1}{4}(x+4)^2(x-3)$

   d The x-intercepts are: -5, -2 and 5 $\quad \therefore \quad y = a(x+5)(x+2)(x-5), \ a \neq 0$
   As the curve passes through $(0, -5)$, $\quad -5 = a(5)(2)(-5) \quad \therefore \quad a = \frac{1}{10}$
   $\therefore \quad y = \frac{1}{10}(x+5)(x+2)(x-5)$

   e The x-intercepts are: -4, 3 and 3 $\quad \therefore \quad y = a(x+4)(x-3)^2, \ a \neq 0$
   As the curve passes through $(0, 9)$, $\quad 9 = a(4)(-3)^2 \quad \therefore \quad a = \frac{1}{4}$
   $\therefore \quad y = \frac{1}{4}(x+4)(x-3)^2$

   f The x-intercepts are: -3, -2 and $-\frac{1}{2}$ $\quad \therefore \quad y = a(x+3)(x+2)(2x+1), \ a \neq 0$
   As the curve passes through $(0, -12)$, $\quad -12 = a(3)(2)(1) \quad \therefore \quad a = -2$
   $\therefore \quad y = -2(x+3)(x+2)(2x+1)$

3 **a** $P(x) = a(x-3)(x-1)(x+2)$
   Since $P(x)$ passes through $(2, -4)$
   $\quad -4 = a(-1)(1)(4)$
   $\therefore \quad -4 = -4a$
   $\therefore \quad a = 1$
   $\therefore \quad P(x) = (x-3)(x-1)(x+2)$

   b $P(x) = ax(x+2)(2x-1)$
   Since $P(x)$ passes through $(-3, -21)$
   $\quad -21 = -3a(-1)(-7)$
   $\therefore \quad -21 = -21a$
   $\therefore \quad a = 1$
   $\therefore \quad P(x) = x(x+2)(2x-1)$

   c $P(x) = a(x-1)^2(x+2)$
   Since $P(x)$ passes through $(4, 54)$
   $\quad 54 = a(9)(6)$
   $\therefore \quad a = 1$
   $\therefore \quad P(x) = (x-1)^2(x+2)$

   d $P(x) = a(3x+2)^2(x-4)$
   Since $P(x)$ passes through $(-1, -5)$
   $\quad -5 = a(1)(-5)$
   $\therefore \quad a = 1$
   $\therefore \quad P(x) = (3x+2)^2(x-4)$

4 **a** $y = 2(x-1)(x+2)(x+4)$
   has x-intercepts $1, -2, -4$
   has y-intercept $2(-1)(2)(4) = -16$
   $\therefore$ matches graph **F**

   b $y = -(x+1)(x-2)(x-4)$
   has x-intercepts $-1, 2, 4$
   has y-intercept $-(1)(-2)(-4) = -8$
   $\therefore$ matches graph **C**

   c $y = (x-1)(x-2)(x+4)$
   has x-intercepts $1, 2, -4$
   has y-intercept $(-1)(-2)(4) = 8$
   $\therefore$ matches graph **A**

   d $y = -2(x-1)(x+2)(x+4)$
   has x-intercepts $1, -2, -4$
   has y-intercept $-2(-1)(2)(4) = 16$
   $\therefore$ matches graph **E**

e $y = -(x-1)(x+2)(x+4)$
has x-intercepts $1, -2, -4$
has y-intercept $-(-1)(2)(4) = 8$
$\therefore$ matches graph **D**

f $y = 2(x-1)(x-2)(x+4)$
has x-intercepts $1, 2, -4$
has y-intercept $2(-1)(-2)(4) = 16$
$\therefore$ matches graph **B**

5 a $\frac{1}{2}$ and -3 are zeros, and so $(2x-1)$ and $(x+3)$ are factors
$\therefore P(x) = (2x-1)(x+3)(ax+b)$
But $P(0) = 30 \quad \therefore \quad b(-1)(3) = 30$ and so $b = -10$
$\therefore P(x) = (2x-1)(x+3)(ax-10)$
Now $P(1) = (1)(4)(a-10) = -20$
$\therefore a - 10 = -5$ and so $a = 5$
$\therefore P(x) = (2x-1)(x+3)(5x-10)$
$\therefore P(x) = 5(x-2)(2x-1)(x+3)$

b 1 is a zero and so $(x-1)$ is a factor, touches at -2 indicates that $(x+2)^2$ is a factor
$\therefore P(x) = k(x-1)(x+2)^2$
But $P(0) = 8 \quad \therefore \quad 8 = k(-1)(2)^2$ and so $k = -2$
$\therefore P(x) = -2(x-1)(x+2)^2$

c cuts the x-axis at $(2, 0)$ and so $(x-2)$ is a factor
$\therefore P(x) = (x-2)(ax^2 + bx + c)$
But $P(0) = -4 \quad \therefore \quad -2c = -4$ and so $c = 2$
Also $P(1) = -1 \quad \therefore \quad (-1)(a+b+2) = -1$
$\therefore a + b + 2 = 1 \quad \therefore \quad a + b = -1$ ..... (1)
Also $P(-1) = -21 \quad \therefore \quad (-3)(a-b+2) = -21$
$\therefore a - b + 2 = 7 \quad \therefore \quad a - b = 5$ ..... (2)
Adding (1) and (2) gives $2a = 4$
$\therefore a = 2$ and so $b = -3$
$\therefore P(x) = (x-2)(2x^2 - 3x + 2)$

EXERCISE 7E.2

1 a $P(x) = a(x+1)^2(x-1)^2$
where $a \neq 0$, and passes through $(0, 2)$
$2 = a(1)(1)$
$\therefore a = 2$
$\therefore P(x) = 2(x+1)^2(x-1)^2$

b $P(x) = a(x+3)(x+1)^2(3x-2)$
where $a \neq 0$, and passes through $(0, -6)$
$-6 = a(3)(1)(-2)$
$\therefore a = 1$
$\therefore P(x) = (x+3)(x+1)^2(3x-2)$

c $P(x) = a(x+2)(x+1)(x-2)^2$
where $a \neq 0$, and passes through $(0, -16)$
$-16 = a(2)(1)(4)$
$\therefore a = -2$
$\therefore P(x) = -2(x+2)(x+1)(x-2)^2$

d $P(x) = a(x+3)(x+1)(2x-3)(x-3)$
where $a \neq 0$, and passes through $(0, -9)$
$-9 = a(3)(1)(-3)(-3)$
$\therefore a = -\frac{1}{3}$
$\therefore P(x) = -\frac{1}{3}(x+3)(x+1)(2x-3)(x-3)$

e $P(x) = a(x+1)(x-4)^3$
where $a \neq 0$, and passes through $(0, -16)$
$-16 = a(1)(-4)^3$
$\therefore a = \frac{1}{4}$
$\therefore P(x) = \frac{1}{4}(x+1)(x-4)^3$

f $P(x) = ax^2(x+2)(x-3)$
where $a \neq 0$, and passes through $(-3, 54)$
$54 = a(9)(-1)(-6)$
$\therefore 54 = 54a$
$\therefore a = 1$
$\therefore P(x) = x^2(x+2)(x-3)$

2 **a** $y = (x-1)^2(x+1)(x+3)$
has x-intercepts $-1, -3$, touches at 1
has y-intercept $(-1)^2(1)(3) = 3$ (> 0)
$\therefore$ matches graph **C**

b $y = -2(x-1)^2(x+1)(x+3)$
has x-intercepts $-1, -3$, touches at 1
has y-intercept $-2(-1)^2(1)(3) = -6$ (< 0)
$\therefore$ matches graph **F**

c $y = (x-1)(x+1)^2(x+3)$
has x-intercepts $1, -3$, touches at -1
has y-intercept $(-1)(1)^2(3) = -3$ (< 0)
$\therefore$ matches graph **A**

d $y = (x-1)(x+1)^2(x-3)$
has x-intercepts $1, 3$, touches at -1
has y-intercept $(-1)(1)^2(-3) = 3$ (> 0)
$\therefore$ matches graph **E**

e $y = -\frac{1}{3}(x-1)(x+1)(x+3)^2$
has x-intercepts $1, -1$, touches at -3
has y-intercept $-\frac{1}{3}(-1)(1)(3)^2 = 3$ (> 0)
$\therefore$ matches graph **B**

f $y = -(x-1)(x+1)(x-3)^2$
has x-intercepts $1, -1$, touches at 3
has y-intercept $-(-1)(1)(3)^2 = 9$ (> 0)
$\therefore$ matches graph **D**

3 **a** $P(x) = a(x+4)(2x-1)(x-2)^2$
where $a \neq 0$, and passes through $(1, 5)$
$5 = a \times 5 \times 1 \times 1$
$\therefore$ $a = 1$
$\therefore$ $P(x) = (x+4)(2x-1)(x-2)^2$

b $P(x) = a(3x-2)^2(x+3)^2$
where $a \neq 0$, and passes through $(-4, 49)$
$49 = a(-14)^2(1)$
$\therefore$ $a = \frac{1}{4}$
$\therefore$ $P(x) = \frac{1}{4}(3x-2)^2(x+3)^2$

c $P(x) = a(2x+1)(2x-1)(x+2)(x-2)$
where $a \neq 0$, and passes through $(1, -18)$
$-18 = a(3)(1)(3)(-1)$
$\therefore$ $a = 2$
$\therefore$ $P(x) = 2(2x+1)(2x-1)(x+2)(x-2)$

d $P(x) = (x-1)^2(ax^2 + bx + c)$
where $a \neq 0$, and cuts y-axis at $(0, -1)$
$-1 = 1 \times (0+0+c)$
$\therefore$ $c = -1$
$\therefore$ $P(x) = (x-1)^2(ax^2 + bx - 1)$
But $P(-1) = -4$
$\therefore$ $-4 = 4(a-b-1)$
$\therefore$ $a - b = 0$ ......(1)
Also $P(2) = 15$
$\therefore$ $15 = 1(4a + 2b - 1)$
$\therefore$ $16 = 4a + 2b$
$\therefore$ $2a + b = 8$ ......(2)
Adding (1) and (2) we get:
$\therefore$ $a = \frac{8}{3}$ and so $b = \frac{8}{3}$ also
$\therefore$ $P(x) = (x-1)^2(\frac{8}{3}x^2 + \frac{8}{3}x - 1)$

EXERCISE 7E.3

1 **a** $P(x) = x^3 - 3x^2 - 3x + 1$
From technology, -1 is a zero.
Check: $P(-1) = -1 - 3 + 3 + 1 = 0$ ✓
$\therefore$ $x + 1$ is a factor
$\therefore$ $x^3 - 3x^2 - 3x + 1 = (x+1)(x^2 - 4x + 1)$
and the quadratic has zeros of $\dfrac{4 \pm \sqrt{16-4}}{2} = 2 \pm \sqrt{3}$
$\therefore$ zeros are $-1, 2 \pm \sqrt{3}$

-1	1	-3	-3	1
	0	-1	4	-1
	1	-4	1	0

b $P(x) = x^3 - 3x^2 + 4x - 2$
From technology, 1 is a zero
Check: $P(1) = 1 - 3 + 4 - 2 = 0$ ✓
$\therefore$ $x - 1$ is a factor
From the division process $x^2 - 2x + 2$ is a quadratic factor
and it has zeros of $\dfrac{2 \pm \sqrt{4 - 4 \times 2}}{2} = \dfrac{2 \pm \sqrt{-4}}{2} = 1 \pm i$
$\therefore$ zeros are $1, 1 \pm i$

1	1	-3	4	-2
	0	1	-2	2
	1	-2	2	0

c $P(x) = 2x^3 - 3x^2 - 4x - 35$
From technology, $\frac{7}{2}$ is a zero.

Check: $P(\frac{7}{2}) = \frac{343}{4} - \frac{147}{4} - 14 - 35$
$= \frac{343 - 147 - 56 - 140}{4}$
$= 0$ ✓

$\frac{7}{2}$	2	-3	-4	-35
	0	7	14	35
	2	4	10	0

From the division process $2x^2 + 4x + 10$ is a quadratic factor
$\therefore\ P(x) = (x - \frac{7}{2})(2x^2 + 4x + 10)$
$= (2x - 7)(x^2 + 2x + 5)$

where the quadratic has zeros $\dfrac{-2 \pm \sqrt{4 - 20}}{2} = -1 \pm 2i$

$\therefore$ zeros are $\frac{7}{2}, -1 \pm 2i$

d $P(x) = 2x^3 - x^2 + 20x - 10$
From technology, $\frac{1}{2}$ is a zero.

Check: $P(\frac{1}{2}) = \frac{1}{4} - \frac{1}{4} + 10 - 10 = 0$ ✓

$\frac{1}{2}$	2	-1	20	-10
	0	1	0	10
	2	0	20	0

$\therefore\ P(x) = (x - \frac{1}{2})(2x^2 + 20)$
$= (2x - 1)(x^2 + 10)$

$\therefore$ zeros are $\frac{1}{2}, \pm i\sqrt{10}$

e $P(x) = 4x^4 - 4x^3 - 25x^2 + x + 6$
From technology, -2 and 3 are zeros
Check: $P(-2) = 64 + 32 - 100 - 2 + 6 = 0$ ✓
$P(3) = 324 - 108 - 225 + 3 + 6 = 0$ ✓
$\therefore\ P(x) = (x + 2)(x - 3)(4x^2 - 1)$
$\therefore$ zeros are $-2, 3, \pm\frac{1}{2}$

-2	4	-4	-25	1	6
	0	-8	24	2	-6
3	4	-12	-1	3	0
	0	12	0	-3	
	4	0	-1	0	

f $P(x) = x^4 - 6x^3 + 22x^2 - 48x + 40$
From technology, 2 seems to be a double zero.
{Graph touches the x-axis at 2}
Check: $P(2) = 16 - 48 + 88 - 96 + 40 = 0$ ✓
$\therefore\ P(x) = (x - 2)^2(x^2 - 2x + 10)$

where the quadratic has zeros of $\dfrac{2 \pm \sqrt{4 - 40}}{2}$
$= 1 \pm 3i$

$\therefore$ zeros are $2, 2, 1 \pm 3i$

2	1	-6	22	-48	40
	0	2	-8	28	-40
2	1	-4	14	-20	0
	0	2	-4	20	
	1	-2	10	0	

2 a $P(x) = x^3 + 2x^2 + 3x + 6$
From technology, -2 is a zero.
Check: $P(-2) = -8 + 8 - 6 + 6 = 0$ ✓
$\therefore\ P(x) = (x + 2)(x^2 + 3)$
$= (x + 2)(x + i\sqrt{3})(x - i\sqrt{3})$
$\therefore$ roots of $P(x) = 0$ are $x = -2$ and $x = \pm i\sqrt{3}$

-2	1	2	3	6
	0	-2	0	-6
	1	0	3	0

b $P(x) = 2x^3 + 3x^2 - 3x - 2$
From technology, 1 is a zero.
Check: $P(1) = 2 + 3 - 3 - 2 = 0$ ✓
$\therefore\ P(x) = (x - 1)(2x^2 + 5x + 2)$
$= (x - 1)(2x + 1)(x + 2)$
$\therefore$ roots of $P(x) = 0$ are $1, -\frac{1}{2}, -2$

1	2	3	-3	-2
	0	2	5	2
	2	5	2	0

c $P(x) = x^3 - 6x^2 + 12x - 8$
From technology, 2 is a zero.
Check: $P(2) = 8 - 24 + 24 - 8 = 0$ ✓
∴ $P(x) = (x - 2)(x^2 - 4x + 4)$
$= (x - 2)(x - 2)(x - 2)$
∴ only root of $P(x) = 0$ is $x = 2$ (a treble root)

2	1	−6	12	−8
	0	2	−8	8
	1	−4	4	0

d $P(x) = 2x^3 - 5x^2 - 9x + 18$
From technology, 3 is a zero.
Check: $P(3) = 54 - 45 - 27 + 18 = 0$ ✓
∴ $P(x) = (x - 3)(2x^2 + x - 6)$
$= (x - 3)(2x - 3)(x + 2)$
∴ roots of $P(x) = 0$ are $3, \frac{3}{2}$ and -2

3	2	−5	−9	18
	0	6	3	−18
	2	1	−6	0

e $P(x) = x^4 - x^3 - 9x^2 + 11x + 6$
From technology, 2 and −3 are zeros.
Check: $P(2) = 16 - 8 - 36 + 22 + 6 = 0$ ✓
$P(-3) = 81 + 27 - 81 - 33 + 6 = 0$ ✓
∴ $P(x) = (x - 2)(x + 3)(x^2 - 2x - 1)$
where the quadratic has zeros of $\dfrac{2 \pm \sqrt{4 + 4}}{2} = 1 \pm \sqrt{2}$
∴ roots of $P(x) = 0$ are $2, -3, 1 \pm \sqrt{2}$

2	1	−1	−9	11	6
	0	2	2	−14	−6
−3	1	1	−7	−3	0
	0	−3	6	3	
	1	−2	−1	0	

f $P(x) = 2x^4 - 13x^3 + 27x^2 - 13x - 15$
From technology, $-\frac{1}{2}$ and 3 are zeros.
Check: $P(-\frac{1}{2}) = \frac{1}{8} + \frac{13}{8} + \frac{27}{4} + \frac{13}{2} - 15 = 0$ ✓
$P(3) = 162 - 351 + 243 - 39 - 15 = 0$ ✓
∴ $P(x) = (x + \frac{1}{2})(x - 3)(2x^2 - 8x + 10)$
$= (2x + 1)(x - 3)(x^2 - 4x + 5)$
where the quadratic has zeros of $\dfrac{4 \pm \sqrt{16 - 20}}{2} = 2 \pm i$
∴ roots of $P(x) = 0$ are $-\frac{1}{2}, 3, 2 \pm i$

$-\frac{1}{2}$	2	−13	27	−13	−15
	0	−1	7	−17	15
3	2	−14	34	−30	0
	0	6	−24	30	
	2	−8	10	0	

3 a Consider $P(x) = x^3 - 3x^2 + 4x - 2$
From technology, 1 is a zero.
Check: $P(1) = 1 - 3 + 4 - 2 = 0$ ✓
Now $P(x) = (x - 1)(x^2 - 2x + 2)$
where the quadratic has zeros of $\dfrac{2 \pm \sqrt{4 - 8}}{2} = 1 \pm i$
∴ $P(x) = (x - 1)(x - [1 + i])(x - [1 - i])$

1	1	−3	4	−2
	0	1	−2	2
	1	−2	2	0

b Consider $P(x) = x^3 + 3x^2 + 4x + 12$
From technology, −3 is a zero.
Check: $P(-3) = -27 + 27 - 12 + 12 = 0$ ✓
Now $P(x) = (x + 3)(x^2 + 4)$
∴ $P(x) = (x + 3)(x - 2i)(x + 2i)$

−3	1	3	4	12
	0	−3	0	−12
	1	0	4	0

c Consider $P(x) = 2x^3 - 9x^2 + 6x - 1$
From technology, $\frac{1}{2}$ is a zero.
Check: $P(\frac{1}{2}) = \frac{1}{4} - \frac{9}{4} + 3 - 1 = 0$ ✓

$\frac{1}{2}$	2	−9	6	−1
	0	1	−4	1
	2	−8	2	0

Now $P(x) = (x - \frac{1}{2})(2x^2 - 8x + 2)$
$= (2x - 1)(x^2 - 4x + 1)$

where the quadratic has zeros of $\dfrac{4 \pm \sqrt{16 - 4}}{2} = 2 \pm \sqrt{3}$

$\therefore \quad P(x) = (2x - 1)(x - [2 + \sqrt{3}])(x - [2 - \sqrt{3}])$

d $P(x) = x^3 - 4x^2 + 9x - 10$
From technology, 2 is a zero.
Check: $P(2) = 8 - 16 + 18 - 10 = 0$ ✓
Now $P(x) = (x - 2)(x^2 - 2x + 5)$

where the quadratic has zeros of $\dfrac{2 \pm \sqrt{4 - 20}}{2} = 1 \pm 2i$

$\therefore \quad P(x) = (x - 2)(x - [1 + 2i])(x - [1 - 2i])$

2	1	−4	9	−10
	0	2	−4	10
	1	−2	5	0

e $P(x) = 4x^3 - 8x^2 + x + 3$
From technology, 1 is a zero.
Check: $P(1) = 4 - 8 + 1 + 3 = 0$ ✓
Now $P(x) = (x - 1)(4x^2 - 4x - 3)$
$= (x - 1)(2x - 3)(2x + 1)$
$\therefore \quad P(x) = (x - 1)(2x + 1)(2x - 3)$

1	4	−8	1	3
	0	4	−4	−3
	4	−4	−3	0

f $P(x) = 3x^4 + 4x^3 + 5x^2 + 12x - 12$
From technology, -2 and $\frac{2}{3}$ are zeros.
Check: $P(-2) = 48 - 32 + 20 - 24 - 12 = 0$ ✓
$P(\frac{2}{3}) = \frac{16}{27} + \frac{32}{27} + \frac{20}{9} + 8 - 12 = 0$ ✓
Now $P(x) = (x + 2)(x - \frac{2}{3})(3x^2 + 9)$
$= (x + 2)(3x - 2)(x^2 + 3)$
$\therefore \quad P(x) = (x + 2)(3x - 2)(x + i\sqrt{3})(x - i\sqrt{3})$

−2	3	4	5	12	−12
	0	−6	4	−18	12
$\frac{2}{3}$	3	−2	9	−6	0
	0	2	0	6	
	3	0	9	0	

g $P(x) = 2x^4 - 3x^3 + 5x^2 + 6x - 4$
From technology, -1 and $\frac{1}{2}$ are zeros.
Check: $P(-1) = 2 + 3 + 5 - 6 - 4 = 0$ ✓
$P(\frac{1}{2}) = \frac{1}{8} - \frac{3}{8} + \frac{5}{4} + 3 - 4 = 0$ ✓
Now $P(x) = (x + 1)(x - \frac{1}{2})(2x^2 - 4x + 8)$
$= (x + 1)(2x - 1)(x^2 - 2x + 4)$

where the quadratic has zeros of $\dfrac{2 \pm \sqrt{4 - 16}}{2} = 1 \pm i\sqrt{3}$

$\therefore \quad P(x) = (x + 1)(2x - 1)(x - [1 + i\sqrt{3}])(x - [1 - i\sqrt{3}])$

−1	2	−3	5	6	−4
	0	−2	5	−10	4
$\frac{1}{2}$	2	−5	10	−4	0
	0	1	−2	4	
	2	−4	8	0	

h $P(x) = 2x^3 + 5x^2 + 8x + 20$
From technology, $-\frac{5}{2}$ is a zero.
Check: $P(-\frac{5}{2}) = -\frac{125}{4} + \frac{125}{4} - 20 + 20 = 0$ ✓
Now $P(x) = (x + \frac{5}{2})(2x^2 + 8)$
$= (2x + 5)(x^2 + 4)$
$\therefore \quad P(x) = (2x + 5)(x - 2i)(x + 2i)$

$-\frac{5}{2}$	2	5	8	20
	0	−5	0	−20
	2	0	8	0

4 a Using technology, $x^3 + 2x^2 - 6x - 6$ has zeros of -0.860, 2.133 and -3.273
  b Using technology, $x^3 + x^2 - 7x - 8$ has zeros of -2.518, -1.178 and 2.696

EXERCISE 7F

1 Since it is a real polynomial, the zeros must be $-\frac{1}{2}$, $1-3i$ and $1+3i$.
For $1 \pm 3i$, $\alpha + \beta = 2$ and $\alpha\beta = 1 - 9i^2 = 10$
$\therefore$ factors are $(2x+1)$ and $(x^2 - 2x + 10)$
$\therefore$ $P(x) = a(2x+1)(x^2 - 2x + 10)$, $a \neq 0$

2 $p(1) = p(2+i) = 0$
Hence zeros of $p(x)$ must be $1, 2 \pm i$ {as $p(x)$ is real}
For $2 \pm i$, $\alpha + \beta = 4$ and $\alpha\beta = 4 - i^2 = 5$
$\therefore$ factors must be $(x-1)$ and $(x^2 - 4x + 5)$
$\therefore$ $p(x) = k(x-1)(x^2 - 4x + 5)$
Since $p(0) = -20$ then $-20 = k(-1)(5)$
$\therefore$ $k = 4$
$\therefore$ $p(x) = 4(x-1)(x^2 - 4x + 5)$
$\therefore$ $p(x) = 4x^3 - 20x^2 + 36x - 20$

	1	-4	5
$\times$		4	-4
	-4	16	-20
4	-16	20	
4	-20	36	-20

3 $2-3i$ is a zero of $z^3 + pz + q$ and as the cubic has real coefficients, $2+3i$ is also a zero.
For $2 \pm 3i$, $\alpha + \beta = 4$ and $\alpha\beta = 4 - 9i^2 = 13$
$\therefore$ $z^2 - 4z + 13$ is a factor
$\therefore$ $z^3 + pz + q = (z^2 - 4z + 13)(z + a)$ for some a.
Equating coefficients:
$a - 4 = 0$, $\quad 13 - 4a = p$ and $13a = q$
$\therefore$ $a = 4$, $\quad p = -3$, $\quad q = 52$
$\therefore$ the other zeros are -4 and $2+3i$

	1	-4	13
$\times$		1	a
	a	$-4a$	$13a$
1	-4	13	
1	$a-4$	$13-4a$	$13a$

Check: Since $P(2-3i) = 0$, $(2-3i)^3 + p(2-3i) + q = 0$
Expanding, $(-46 - 9i) + p(2 - 3i) + q = 0$
$\therefore$ $(-46 + 2p + q) + (-9 - 3p)i = 0$
Equating real and imaginary parts, $-46 + 2p + q = 0$ ..... (1)
and $-9 - 3p = 0$ ..... (2)
From (2), $p = -3$, so in (1), $-46 - 6 + q = 0$ $\therefore$ $p = -3$, $q = 52$ ✓

4 $3 + i$ is a root of $z^4 - 2z^3 + az^2 + bz + 10 = 0$ where the coefficients are real.
$\therefore$ $3 - i$ is also a root
For $3 \pm i$, $\alpha + \beta = 6$ and $\alpha\beta = 9 - i^2 = 10$
$\therefore$ $z^2 - 6z + 10$ is a factor
$\therefore$ $z^4 - 2z^3 + az^2 + bz + 10$
$= (z^2 - 6z + 10)(z^2 + sz + 1)$ for some s.
Equating coefficients:
$s - 6 = -2$, $\quad 11 - 6s = a$ and $10s - 6 = b$
$\therefore$ $s = 4$ $\quad\quad a = 11 - 6(4) = -13$ $\quad\quad b = 10(4) - 6 = 34$
$\therefore$ the other factor is $z^2 + 4z + 1$ which has zeros $\dfrac{-4 \pm \sqrt{16-4}}{2} = -2 \pm \sqrt{3}$
$\therefore$ $a = -13$, $b = 34$ and the other roots are $3 - i$, $-2 \pm \sqrt{3}$.

	1	-6	10
$\times$		1	s	1
		1	-6	10
	s	$-6s$	$10s$	
1	-6	10		
1	$s-6$	$11-6s$	$10s-6$	10

5 Let the purely imaginary zero be bi. Since $P(z)$ is real, another zero is $-bi$, (b is real)
$\therefore$ $z^2 + b^2$ is a factor of $P(z)$
$\therefore$ $z^3 + az^2 + 3z + 9 = (z^2 + b^2)(z + c)$
$= z^3 + cz^2 + b^2 z + b^2 c$

Equating coefficients, $b^2 = 3$, $b^2c = 9$ and $a = c$
$\therefore \quad c = 3$ and $a = 3$ and $b = \pm\sqrt{3}$
$\therefore \quad P(z) = (z+3)(z^2+3)$
$\therefore \quad P(z) = (z+3)(z+i\sqrt{3})(z-i\sqrt{3})$, $a = 3$

6 Let ai be the purely imaginary zero of $3x^3 + kx^2 + 15x + 10$
$\therefore$ as $P(x)$ is real, $-ai$ is also a zero
For $\pm ai$, $\alpha + \beta = 0$ and $\alpha\beta = -a^2i^2 = a^2$
$\therefore \quad x^2 + a^2$ is a factor
$\therefore \quad 3x^3 + kx^2 + 15x + 10 = (x^2 + a^2)(3x + b)$
$\qquad\qquad\qquad\qquad\qquad\quad = 3x^3 + bx^2 + 3a^2x + a^2b$

	1	0	a^2
×		3	b
	b	0	a^2b
	3	0	$3a^2$
	3	b	$3a^2$	a^2b

Equating coefficients $k = b$
and $3a^2 = 15$ $\therefore$ $a^2 = 5$
and $a^2b = 10$ $\therefore$ $b = 2$ $\therefore$ $k = 2$
$\therefore \quad P(x) = (x^2 + 5)(3x + 2)$
$\therefore \quad P(x) = (3x + 2)(x - i\sqrt{5})(x + i\sqrt{5})$, $k = 2$

7 a $f(t) = kt(t-a)^2$
From the graph a is the t-value at the point where the graph touches the t-axis.
$\therefore \quad a = 700$ milliseconds
This represents the time when the barrier has returned to its original position.

b when $t = 100$ ms $f(t) = 85$ mm
$\therefore \quad 85 = k \times 100(100 - 700)^2$
$85 = 100 \times k \times 360\,000$
$k = \dfrac{85}{36\,000\,000}$
$\therefore \quad f(t) = \dfrac{85t}{36\,000\,000}(t - 700)^2$

c Using technology to find the maximum, on $0 \leqslant t \leqslant 700$, the maximum occurs when $t \approx 233$ ms
$\therefore$ when $f(t) \approx 120$ mm

8 $V(t) = -t^3 + 30t^2 - 131t + 250$
We graph $V(t)$ against t and add the graph of $V(t) = 100$.
From the graph, the level drops below 100 ML when $t = 2$ and rises above 100 ML again when $t = 3$.
Now as $t = 0$ is Jan 1st,
$0 \leqslant t < 1$ is January.
$\therefore$ as irrigation is prohibited for $2 < t < 3$, it is banned during March.

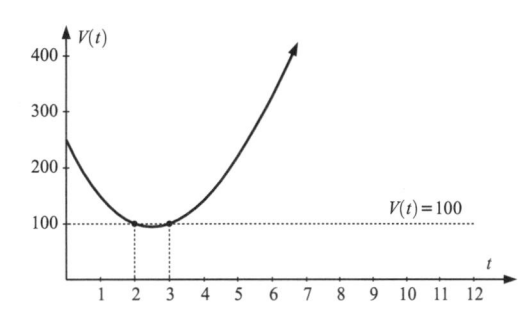

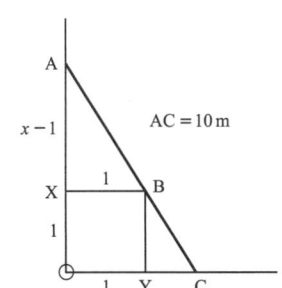

9 Let the height of the wall where the ladder touches be x m.
Using similar triangles AXB, AOC:
$\dfrac{x-1}{1} = \dfrac{x}{OC}$
$\therefore \quad OC = \dfrac{x}{x-1}$
but $x^2 + OC^2 = 10^2$
$x^2 + \left(\dfrac{x}{x-1}\right)^2 = 100$

Using technology to find the intersection of $y = x^2 + \left(\dfrac{x}{x-1}\right)^2$ and $y = 100$
$x \approx 1.112$ or 9.938
So, distance ≈ 9.94 m or 1.11 m

REVIEW SET 7A

1 **a** $a + bi = 4 = 4 + 0i$, $\therefore$ $a = 4$, $b = 0$

b $(1 - 2i)(a + bi) = -5 - 10i$

$\therefore \quad a + bi = \dfrac{-5 - 10i}{1 - 2i} \times \dfrac{1 + 2i}{1 + 2i}$

$= \dfrac{-5 - 10i - 10i - 20i^2}{1 - 4i^2}$

$= \dfrac{15 - 20i}{5}$

$= 3 - 4i$

$\therefore \quad a = 3 \quad b = -4$

c $\quad (a + 2i)(1 + bi) = 17 - 19i$

$\therefore \quad a + 2i + abi + 2i^2 b = 17 - 19i$

$\therefore \quad (a - 2b) + i(ab + 2) = 17 - 19i$

Equating real and imaginary parts,

$a - 2b = 17$ and $ab + 2 = -19$

$\therefore \quad a = 2b + 17 \qquad ab = -21$

$\therefore \quad b(2b + 17) = -21$

$\therefore \quad 2b^2 + 17b + 21 = 0$

$\therefore \quad (2b + 3)(b + 7) = 0$

$\therefore \quad b = -\tfrac{3}{2}$ or $b = -7$

When $b = -7$, $a = 3$ and when $b = -\tfrac{3}{2}$, $a = 14$

2 $z = 3 + i \qquad w = -2 - i$

a $2z - 3w$
$= 2(3 + i) - 3(-2 - i)$
$= 6 + 2i + 6 + 3i$
$= 12 + 5i$

b $\dfrac{z^*}{w}$

$= \dfrac{3 - i}{-2 - i} \times \dfrac{-2 + i}{-2 + i}$

$= \dfrac{-6 + 2i + 3i - i^2}{4 - i^2}$

$= \dfrac{-5 + 5i}{5}$

$= -1 + i$

c z^3
$= (3 + i)^3$
$= 3^3 + 3(3^2)(i) + 3(3)(i^2) + i^3$
$= 27 + 27i + 9i^2 - i$
$= 27 - 9 + 26i$
$= 18 + 26i$

3 $z = \dfrac{3}{i + \sqrt{3}} + \sqrt{3}$

$= \dfrac{3}{i + \sqrt{3}} \dfrac{(i - \sqrt{3})}{(i - \sqrt{3})} + \sqrt{3}$

$= \dfrac{3i - 3\sqrt{3}}{i^2 - 3} + \sqrt{3}$

$= \dfrac{3i - 3\sqrt{3}}{-4} - \dfrac{4\sqrt{3}}{-4}$

$= \dfrac{3i - 7\sqrt{3}}{-4}$

$\therefore \quad \mathcal{Re}(z) = \dfrac{7\sqrt{3}}{4}, \quad \mathcal{Im}(z) = -\dfrac{3}{4}$

4 $\qquad 2z - 1 = iz - i$

$\therefore \quad 2(a + bi) - 1 = i(a + bi) - i$

$\therefore \quad 2a + 2bi - 1 = ai + bi^2 - i$

$\therefore \quad (2a - 1) + 2bi = -b + i(a - 1)$

Equating real and imaginary parts,

$2a - 1 = -b$ and $2b = a - 1$

$\therefore \quad b = 1 - 2a$ and $2b = a - 1$

$\therefore \quad 2(1 - 2a) = a - 1$

$\therefore \quad 2 - 4a = a - 1$

$\therefore \quad 3 = 5a$

$\therefore \quad a = \tfrac{3}{5}$

and $b = 1 - 2(\tfrac{3}{5}) = -\tfrac{1}{5}$

$\therefore \quad z = \tfrac{3}{5} - \tfrac{1}{5}i$

5 Let $z = a + bi$, $w = c + di$

$\therefore \quad zw^* - z^*w = (a + bi)(c - di) - (a - bi)(c + di)$

$= ac - adi + bci - bdi^2 - ac - adi + bci + bdi^2$

$= 2bci - 2adi$

$= 2i(bc - ad)$

which is purely imaginary if $bc - ad \neq 0$ and zero if $bc - ad = 0$.

6 $w = \dfrac{z+1}{z^*+1}$

$= \dfrac{a+1+bi}{a+1-bi} \times \dfrac{(a+1+bi)}{(a+1+bi)}$

$= \dfrac{(a+1)^2 + 2(a+1)bi + b^2 i^2}{(a+1)^2 - b^2 i^2}$

$= \dfrac{(a+1)^2 + 2(a+1)bi - b^2}{(a+1)^2 + b^2}$

$= \dfrac{(a+1)^2 - b^2}{(a+1)^2 + b^2} + i\left(\dfrac{2(a+1)b}{(a+1)^2 + b^2}\right)$

w is purely imaginary when
$(a+1)^2 - b^2 = 0$ and $2(a+1)b \neq 0$
$\therefore\ b^2 = (a+1)^2$ and $a \neq -1,\ b \neq 0$
$\therefore\ b = \pm(a+1),\ a \neq -1$

7 a $(3x^3 + 2x - 5)(4x - 3)$
$= 12x^4 - 9x^3 + 8x^2 - 6x - 20x + 15$
$= 12x^4 - 9x^3 + 8x^2 - 26x + 15$

b $(2x^2 - x + 3)^2 = 4x^4 - 4x^3 + 13x^2 - 6x + 9$

		2	−1	3
	×	2	−1	3
		6	−3	9
	−2	1	−3	
4	−2	6		
4	−4	13	−6	9

8 a

$$\begin{array}{r}x^2 - 2x + 4\\ x+2\ \overline{\smash{\big)}\ x^3 + 0x^2 + 0x + 0}\\ -(x^3 + 2x^2)\\ \hline -2x^2 + 0x\\ -(-2x^2 - 4x)\\ \hline 4x + 0\\ -(4x + 8)\\ \hline -8\end{array}$$

$\therefore\ \dfrac{x^3}{x+2} = x^2 - 2x + 4 - \dfrac{8}{x+2}$

b $(x+2)(x+3) = x^2 + 5x + 6$

$$\begin{array}{r}x - 5\\ x^2 + 5x + 6\ \overline{\smash{\big)}\ x^3 + 0x^2 + 0x + 0}\\ -(x^3 + 5x^2 + 6x)\\ \hline -5x^2 - 6x + 0\\ -(-5x^2 - 25x - 30)\\ \hline 19x + 30\end{array}$$

$\therefore\ \dfrac{x^3}{(x+2)(x+3)} = x - 5 + \dfrac{19x + 30}{(x+2)(x+3)}$

9 The Remainder theorem:
"When a polynomial $P(x)$ is divided by $x - k$ until a constant remainder R is obtained then $R = P(k)$."
Proof From the division process, $P(x) = (x - k)Q(x) + R$
Now, letting $x = k$, $P(k) = (k - k) \times Q(k) + R$
$\therefore\quad P(k) = 0 \times Q(k) + R$
$\therefore\quad P(k) = R$
$\therefore\quad R = P(k)$

10 Let $P(z) = z^2 + az + [3 + a]$
if $-2 + bi$ is a zero then $P(-2 + bi) = 0$
$\therefore\ (-2+bi)^2 + a(-2+bi) + 3 + a = 0$
$4 - 4bi + b^2 i^2 - 2a + abi + 3 + a = 0$
$(4 - b^2 - 2a + 3 + a) + i(-4b + ab) = 0$

$\therefore\ 4 - b^2 - 2a + 3 + a = 0$ and $-4b + ab = 0$
$a = 7 - b^2$ $\therefore\ b(a - 4) = 0$
$\therefore\ b = 0$ or $a = 4$

If $b = 0$ then $a = 7 - 0 = 7$.
If $a = 4$ then $b^2 = 3$ and so $b = \pm\sqrt{3}$.

11 Let $P(z) = 2z^4 - 5z^3 + 13z^2 - 4z - 6$
From technology, 1 and $-\frac{1}{2}$ are zeros.
Check: $P(1) = 2 - 5 + 13 - 4 - 6 = 0$ ✓
$P(-\frac{1}{2}) = \frac{1}{8} + \frac{5}{8} + \frac{13}{4} + 2 - 6 = 0$ ✓

∴ $P(z) = (z-1)(z+\frac{1}{2})(2z^2 - 4z + 12)$
$= (z-1)(2z+1)(z^2 - 2z + 6)$

where the quadratic has zeros of $\dfrac{2 \pm \sqrt{4-24}}{2} = 1 \pm i\sqrt{5}$. ∴ zeros are $1, -\frac{1}{2}, 1 \pm i\sqrt{5}$.

	2	−5	13	−4	−6
1		2	−3	10	6
	2	−3	10	6	0
$-\frac{1}{2}$		−1	2	−6	
	2	−4	12	0	

12 Let $P(z) = z^4 + 2z^3 - 2z^2 + 8$
From technology, -2 seems to be a double zero.
Check: $P(-2) = 16 - 16 - 8 + 8 = 0$ ✓
∴ $P(z) = (z+2)^2(z^2 - 2z + 2)$

where the quadratic has zeros of $\dfrac{2 \pm \sqrt{4-8}}{2} = 1 \pm i$

∴ $P(z) = (z+2)^2(z - [1+i])(z - [1-i])$

	1	2	−2	0	8
−2		−2	0	4	−8
	1	0	−2	4	0
−2		−2	4	−4	
	1	−2	2	0	

13 $2 - i\sqrt{3}$ and $\sqrt{2} + 1$
Since the quartic has real rational coefficients, $2 - i\sqrt{3}$ and $2 + i\sqrt{3}$ are zeros
$\sqrt{2} + 1$ and $-\sqrt{2} + 1$ are zeros
∴ the four zeros are: $2 \pm i\sqrt{3}$ and $\pm\sqrt{2} + 1$

For $2 \pm i\sqrt{3}$, $\alpha + \beta = 4$
$\alpha\beta = 4 - 3i^2 = 7$

∴ $P(z) = (z^2 - 4z + 7)(z^2 - 2z - 1)$
∴ $P(z) = z^4 - 6z^3 + 14z^2 - 10z - 7$

For $\pm\sqrt{2} + 1$, $\alpha + \beta = 2$
$\alpha\beta = -2 + 1 = -1$

		1	−4	7
×		1	−2	−1
		−1	4	−7
	−2	8	−14	
1	−4	7		
1	−6	14	−10	−7

14 $f(x) = x^3 - 3x^2 - 9x + b$ ...... (1)
$= (x-k)^2(x+a)$
$= (x^2 - 2kx + k^2)(x+a)$
$= x^3 + [a - 2k]x^2 + [k^2 - 2ak]x + ak^2$ ...... (2)

		1	−2k	k^2
×			1	a
		a	−2ak	ak^2
1	−2k	k^2		
1	a − 2k	$k^2 - 2ak$	ak^2	

Equating coefficients of (1) and (2) gives
∴ $a - 2k = -3$, $k^2 - 2ak = -9$ and $ak^2 = b$
Since $a = 2k - 3$, then as $k^2 - 2ak = -9$
$k^2 - 2k(2k-3) = -9$
$k^2 - 4k^2 + 6k = -9$
∴ $3k^2 - 6k - 9 = 0$
$k^2 - 2k - 3 = 0$
$(k-3)(k+1) = 0$
∴ $k = -1$ or $k = 3$

If $k = -1$, $a = -5$ and $b = ak^2 = -5$ and so $f(x) = (x+1)^2(x-5)$
and the roots of $f(x) = 0$ are $-1, 5$
If $k = 3$, $a = 3$ and $b = ak^2 = 3 \times 9 = 27$ and so $f(x) = (x-3)^2(x+3)$
and the roots of $f(x) = 0$ are $3, -3$

15 They meet where $x^2 + (2x+k)^2 + 8x - 4(2x+k) + 2 = 0$
$\therefore \quad x^2 + 4x^2 + 4kx + k^2 + 8x - 8x - 4k + 2 = 0$
$\therefore \quad 5x^2 + 4kx + [k^2 - 4k + 2] = 0$

Now $\Delta = (4k)^2 - 4(5)(k^2 - 4k + 2)$ and $\Delta < 0$ when $-4k^2 + 80k - 40 < 0$
$= 16k^2 - 20k^2 + 80k - 40$ $\therefore \quad k^2 - 20k + 10 > 0$
$= -4k^2 + 80k - 40$ $\therefore \quad k^2 - 20k + 10^2 + 10 - 10^2 > 0$
$\therefore \quad (k-10)^2 - 90 > 0$
$\therefore \quad [k - 10 + 3\sqrt{10}][k - 10 - 3\sqrt{10}] > 0$

$\therefore \quad k \in \;]-\infty,\, 10 - 3\sqrt{10}[\;$ or $\;k \in \;]10 + 3\sqrt{10},\, \infty[$

```
   +        -        +
←——————|————————|——————→ k
     10−3√10  10+3√10
```

16 $P(x) = x^n + 3x^2 + kx + 6$
$P(-1) = 12$ {Remainder Theorem} $\therefore \quad 12 = (-1)^n + 3 - k + 6$
$\therefore \quad k = (-1)^n - 3$ ...... (1)

$P(1) = 8$ {Remainder Theorem} $\therefore \quad 8 = 1^n + 3 + k + 6$
$\therefore \quad 8 = 10 + k$
$\therefore \quad k = -2$

$\therefore$ (1) becomes $-2 = (-1)^n - 3$
$(-1)^n = 1$ $\therefore \quad n$ is even
If $34 < n < 38$, then $n = 36$.

17 Let $x^3 - x + 1 = (x - \alpha)(x - \beta)(x - \gamma)$
$= (x^2 - [\alpha + \beta]x + \alpha\beta)(x - \gamma)$
$= x^3 - [\alpha + \beta + \gamma]x^2 + [\alpha\beta + \beta\gamma + \alpha\gamma] - \alpha\beta\gamma$

$\alpha + \beta + \gamma = 0$ Now $\gamma = \dfrac{-1}{\alpha\beta}$ ...... (1) and $\alpha\beta + \gamma(\alpha + \beta) = -1$ ...... (2)
$\alpha\beta + \beta\gamma + \alpha\gamma = -1$ $\therefore \quad \alpha\beta + \gamma(-\gamma) = -1$
$\therefore \quad \alpha\beta\gamma = -1$ $\therefore \quad \alpha\beta - \gamma^2 = -1$
$\therefore \quad \alpha\beta - \dfrac{1}{(\alpha\beta)^2} = -1$ {using (1)}
$\therefore \quad (\alpha\beta)^3 - 1 = -(\alpha\beta)^2$
$\therefore \quad (\alpha\beta)^3 + (\alpha\beta)^2 - 1 = 0$
$\therefore \quad \alpha\beta$ is a root of $x^3 + x^2 - 1 = 0$

REVIEW SET 7B

1 $\dfrac{5}{2-i} = \dfrac{5}{2-i} \dfrac{(2+i)}{(2+i)}$ $\therefore \quad z = (-1-i)^3$
$= \dfrac{10 + 5i}{4 - i^2}$ $= -(i+1)^3$
$= \dfrac{10 + 5i}{5} = 2 + i$ $= -(i^3 + 3i^2 + 3i + 1)$
$= -(-i - 3 + 3i + 1)$
$\therefore \quad \sqrt[3]{z} = (2+i) - 3 - 2i$ $= -(2i - 2)$
$= -1 - i$ $= 2 - 2i$
$\therefore \quad x = 2,\; y = -2$

2 Let $z = a + bi = \sqrt{5 - 12i}$, a, b real
$\therefore$ $(a + bi)^2 = 5 - 12i$
$\therefore$ $a^2 + 2abi + b^2 i^2 = 5 - 12i$
$\therefore$ $a^2 - b^2 + 2abi = 5 - 12i$
Equating real and imaginary parts,
$a^2 - b^2 = 5$ and $2ab = -12$
$\therefore$ $a^2 - b^2 = 5$ and $b = -\dfrac{6}{a}$

$\therefore$ $a^2 - \left(-\dfrac{6}{a}\right)^2 = 5$

$\therefore$ $a^2 - \dfrac{36}{a^2} = 5$

$\therefore$ $a^4 - 36 = 5a^2$
$\therefore$ $a^4 - 5a^2 - 36 = 0$
$\therefore$ $(a^2 - 9)(a^2 + 4) = 0$
$\therefore$ $a = \pm 3$ (a real)

using $b = -\dfrac{6}{a}$, if $a = 3$, $b = -2$
and if $a = -3$, $b = 2$

$\therefore$ $\sqrt{5 - 12i} = 3 - 2i$ (positive real part)

3 Let $z = a + bi$, $w = c + di$
$\therefore$ $zw^* - z^*w = (a + bi)(c - di) - (a - bi)(c + di)$
$= ac - adi + bci - bdi^2 - ac - adi + bci + bdi^2$
$= 2bci - 2adi$
$= 2i(bc - ad)$

which is purely imaginary if $bc - ad \neq 0$ and zero if $bc - ad = 0$.

4 If $z = a + bi$
then $z + z^* = (a + bi) + (a - bi)$
$= 2a$ which is real.

Also, $zz^* = (a + bi)(a - bi)$
$= a^2 + abi - abi - b^2 i^2$
$= a^2 + b^2$ which is real.

5 $z = 4 + i$ $w = 3 - 2i$ $2w^* - iz = 2(3 + 2i) - i(4 + i)$
$= 6 + 4i - 4i - i^2$
$= 7$

6 If $\dfrac{2 - 3i}{2a + bi} = 3 + 2i$ then $2a + bi = \dfrac{2 - 3i}{3 + 2i} \times \dfrac{3 - 2i}{3 - 2i}$

$\therefore$ $2a + bi = \dfrac{6 - 4i - 9i + 6i^2}{9 - 4i^2} = \dfrac{-13i}{13}$

$\therefore$ $2a + bi = 0 - i$

$\therefore$ $a = 0$ and $b = -1$

7 If $a + ai$ is a root of $x^2 - 6x + b = 0$ then $(a + ai)^2 - 6(a + ai) + b = 0$
$\therefore$ $a^2 + 2a^2 i - a^2 - 6a - 6ai + b = 0$
$\therefore$ $(b - 6a) + (2a^2 - 6a)i = 0$
$\therefore$ $b = 6a$ and $2a^2 - 6a = 0$
$\therefore$ $b = 6a$ and $2a(a - 3) = 0$
$\therefore$ $a = 0$ or 3, and when $a = 0$, $b = 0$
and when $a = 3$, $b = 18$

8 Let $P(x) = x^{47} - 3x^{26} + 5x^3 + 11$ $\therefore$ $R = P(-1)$ {Remainder theorem}
$= (-1)^{47} - 3(-1)^{26} + 5(-1)^3 + 11$
$= -1 - 3 - 5 + 11$
$\therefore$ remainder $= 2$

9 Touches the x-axis at $(-2, 0)$ and cuts it at $(1, 0)$.
$\therefore$ $P(x) = (x + 2)^2 (x - 1)(ax + b)$
But $P(0) = 12$ $\therefore$ $4(-1)b = 12$ $\therefore$ $b = -3$
$\therefore$ $P(x) = (x + 2)^2 (x - 1)(ax - 3)$

Also $P(2) = 80$ $\therefore$ $80 = 16(1)(2a - 3)$
$\therefore$ $2a - 3 = 5$
$\therefore$ $2a = 8$
$\therefore$ $a = 4$
$\therefore$ $P(x) = (x + 2)^2(x - 1)(4x - 3)$

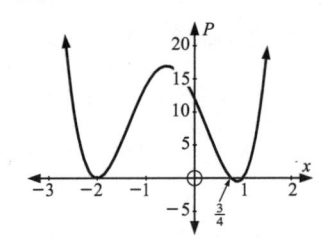

10 As $(x - 3)(x + 2) = x^2 - x - 6$,
$P(x) = Q(x)(x^2 - x - 6) + (Ax + B)$, where $Q(x)$ is the quotient and $Ax + B$ is the remainder.
Now $P(x)$ has remainder 2 when divided by $x - 3$ and so $P(3) = 2$ {Remainder theorem}
$\therefore$ $Q(3)(9 - 3 - 6) + (3A + B) = 2$
$\therefore$ $3A + B = 2$ ...... (1)
Also $P(x)$ has remainder -13 when divided by $x + 2$ and so $P(-2) = -13$
$\therefore$ $Q(-2)(4 + 2 - 6) + (-2A + B) = -13$
$\therefore$ $-2A + B = -13$ ...... (2)
Solving (1) and (2): $5A = 15$
$\therefore$ $A = 3$ and $B = -7$
$\therefore$ $R(x) = 3x - 7$

11 Since the coefficients are rational, $3 + i\sqrt{2}$ and $1 + \sqrt{2}$ also have to be zeros.
For zeros of $3 \pm i\sqrt{2}$, $\alpha + \beta = 6$ and $\alpha\beta = 9 - 2i^2 = 11$
For zeros of $1 \pm \sqrt{2}$, $\alpha + \beta = 2$ and $\alpha\beta = 1 - 2 = -1$
$\therefore$ $P(x) = a(x^2 - 6x + 11)(x^2 - 2x - 1)$, $a \neq 0$
$\therefore$ $P(x) = a(x^4 - 8x^3 + 22x^2 - 16x - 11)$, $a \neq 0$

		1	-6	11
×		1	-2	-1
		-1	6	-11
	-2	12	-22	
1	-6	11		
1	-8	22	-16	-11

12 $P(z) = 2z^3 + z^2 + 10z + 5$
Using technology, $-\frac{1}{2}$ is a zero.
Check: $P(-\frac{1}{2}) = -\frac{1}{4} + \frac{1}{4} - 5 + 5 = 0$ ✓
$\therefore$ $P(z) = (z + \frac{1}{2})(2z^2 + 10)$
$P(z) = (2z + 1)(z^2 + 5)$
$P(z) = (2z + 1)(z - i\sqrt{5})(z + i\sqrt{5})$

$-\frac{1}{2}$	2	1	10	5
	0	-1	0	-5
	2	0	10	0

13 Zeros are $2 + i$ and $-1 + 3i$.
Since we have a real polynomial, the other zeros are $2 - i$ and $-1 - 3i$.
For zeros of $2 \pm i$, $\alpha + \beta = 4$ and $\alpha\beta = 4 - i^2 = 5$
For zeros of $-1 \pm 3i$, $\alpha + \beta = -2$ and $\alpha\beta = 1 - 9i^2 = 10$
$\therefore$ $P(z) = a(z^2 - 4z + 5)(z^2 + 2z + 10)$, $a \neq 0$

14 Since $3 - 2i$ is a zero, so is $3 + 2i$. These have $\alpha + \beta = 6$ and $\alpha\beta = 9 - 4i^2 = 13$.
$\therefore$ $z^2 - 6z + 13$ is a factor
$\therefore$ $P(z) = (z^2 - 6z + 13)(z^2 + Az + B)$
     $= z^4 + kz^3 + 32z + 3k - 1$
Equating coefficients gives
$\begin{cases} A - 6 = k \\ B - 6A + 13 = 0 \\ 13A - 6B = 32 \\ 3k - 1 = 13B \end{cases}$

	1	-6	13	
×	1	A	B	
	B	$-6B$	$13B$	
	A	$-6A$	$13A$	
1	-6	13		
1	$A - 6$	$B - 6A + 13$	$13A - 6B$	$13B$

$\therefore$ $-6A + B = -13$ ...... (1)
and $13A - 6B = 32$ ...... (2)
(1) × 6 gives $-36A + 6B = -78$ ...... (3)

Adding (2) and (3) gives: $-23A = -46$ $\therefore$ $A = 2$
$\therefore$ $k = A - 6 = 2 - 6 = -4$ and $B = 6A - 13 = 12 - 13 = -1$
$\therefore$ $P(z) = (z^2 - 6z + 13)\underbrace{(z^2 + 2z - 1)}$

this quadratic has zeros $\dfrac{-2 \pm \sqrt{4+4}}{2} = -1 \pm \sqrt{2}$

$\therefore$ $k = -4$, zeros are $3 \pm 2i$, $-1 \pm \sqrt{2}$

15 Consider $P(z) = z^4 + 2z^3 + 6z^2 + 8z + 8$.
If one zero is purely imaginary, for example, ai, then $-ai$ is also a zero (a is real).
$\pm ai$ have $\alpha + \beta = 0$ and $\alpha\beta = -a^2 i^2 = a^2$
$\therefore$ $z^2 + a^2$ is a factor, $\therefore$ $z^2 + A$ is a factor
$\therefore$ $P(z) = (z^2 + A)(z^2 + Bz + C)$
$\qquad = z^4 + Bz^3 + [A + C]z^2 + ABz + AC$
Equating coefficients gives:
$B = 2$, $A + C = 6$, $AB = 8$ and $AC = 8$
$\therefore$ $B = 2$ $\therefore$ $A = 4$ $\therefore$ $C = 2$
$\therefore$ $P(z) = (z^2 + 4)\underbrace{(z^2 + 2z + 2)}$

		B	C
×	1	0	A
	A	AB	AC
1	B	C	
1	B	A+C	AB	AC

this quadratic has zeros $\dfrac{-2 \pm \sqrt{4-8}}{2} = -1 \pm i$

$\therefore$ zeros are $\pm 2i$, $-1 \pm i$

16 $\dfrac{P(x)}{x^2 - 3x + 2} = Q(x) + \dfrac{2x + 3}{x^2 - 3x + 2}$ $\therefore$ $P(x) = Q(x)(x^2 - 3x + 2) + 2x + 3$
and $P(2) = Q(2)(4 - 6 + 2) + 4 + 3$
$\qquad = Q(2) \times (0) + 7$
$\qquad = 7$, so the remainder is 7.

REVIEW SET 7C

1 $(3x + 2yi)(1 - i) = (3y + 1)i - x$
$\therefore$ $3x - 3xi + 2yi - 2yi^2 = 3yi + i - x$
$\therefore$ $(3x + 2y) + i(2y - 3x) = -x + i(3y + 1)$
Equating real and imaginary parts,
$3x + 2y = -x$ and $2y - 3x = 3y + 1$

$\therefore$ $4x = -2y$ and $-1 - 3x = y$
$\therefore$ $4x = -2(-1 - 3x)$
$\therefore$ $4x = 2 + 6x$
$\therefore$ $-2x = 2$
$\therefore$ $x = -1$ and $y = -1 - 3(-1) = 2$

2 $z^2 + iz + 10 = 6z$
$\therefore$ $z^2 + (i - 6)z + 10 = 0$
$\therefore$ $z = \dfrac{6 - i \pm \sqrt{(i - 6)^2 - 4(10)}}{2}$
$\qquad = \dfrac{6 - i \pm \sqrt{i^2 - 12i + 36 - 40}}{2}$
$\qquad = \dfrac{6 - i \pm \sqrt{-5 - 12i}}{2}$
We must now find $\sqrt{-5 - 12i}$
Let $z = a + bi = \sqrt{-5 - 12i}$, a, b real
$\therefore$ $(a + bi)^2 = -5 - 12i$
$\therefore$ $a^2 + 2abi + b^2 i^2 = -5 - 12i$
$\therefore$ $a^2 - b^2 + 2abi = -5 - 12i$

Equating real and imaginary parts,
$\qquad a^2 - b^2 = -5$ and $2ab = -12$
$\therefore$ $a^2 - b^2 = -5$ and $b = -\dfrac{6}{a}$
$\therefore$ $a^2 - \left(-\dfrac{6}{a}\right)^2 = -5$
$\therefore$ $a^2 - \dfrac{36}{a^2} = -5$
$\therefore$ $a^4 + 5a^2 - 36 = 0$
$\therefore$ $(a^2 + 9)(a^2 - 4) = 0$
$\therefore$ $a = 2$ (a real, $a > 0$)
and $b = \dfrac{-6}{2} = -3$
$\therefore$ $\sqrt{-5 - 12i} = 2 - 3i$
so $z = \dfrac{6 - i \pm (2 - 3i)}{2}$
$\therefore$ $z = \dfrac{8 - 4i}{2}$ or $\dfrac{4 + 2i}{2}$
$\therefore$ $z = 4 - 2i$ or $2 + i$

3 Let $z = a + bi$ and $w = c + di$
∴ $zw^* + z^*w$
$= (a + bi)(c - di) + (a - bi)(c + di)$
$= ac - adi + bci - bdi^2 + ac + adi - bci - bdi^2$
$= ac + bd + ac + bd$
$= 2ac + 2bd$ which is a real number

4 a If $x + iy = 0$ then $x = 0$ and $y = 0$
{equating real and imaginary parts}

b $(3 - 2i)(x + i) = 17 + yi$
$3x + 3i - 2xi - 2i^2 = 17 + yi$
$(3x + 2) + i(3 - 2x) = 17 + yi$
∴ $3x + 2 = 17$ and $y = 3 - 2x$
∴ $3x = 15$
∴ $x = 5$
and so ∴ $y = 3 - 10$
∴ $y = -7$

c $(x + iy)^2 = x - iy$
$x^2 + i^2y^2 + 2xyi = x - iy$
$x^2 - y^2 = x$ and $2xy = -y$
Now if $2xy + y = 0$
then $y(2x + 1) = 0$
∴ $y = 0$ or $x = -\frac{1}{2}$
If $y = 0$, then $x^2 = x$ and so $x = 0$ or 1
If $x = -\frac{1}{2}$, then $\frac{1}{4} - y^2 = -\frac{1}{2}$,
∴ $y^2 = \frac{3}{4}$
and so $y = \pm\frac{\sqrt{3}}{2}$

Possible solutions are:

x	0	1	$-\frac{1}{2}$	$-\frac{1}{2}$
y	0	0	$\frac{\sqrt{3}}{2}$	$-\frac{\sqrt{3}}{2}$

5 Let $z = a + bi$ and $w = c + di$ where $b \neq 0$ and $d \neq 0$ ...... (1)
Now $z + w = (a + c) + (b + d)i$ and $zw = (a + bi)(c + di)$
$= (ac - bd) + i(bc + ad)$
As $z + w$ is real, $b + d = 0$ ∴ $b = -d$ ...... (2)
As zw is real, $bc + ad = 0$ ...... (3)
Substituting (2) into (3) $-dc + ad = 0$
∴ $d(a - c) = 0$
Since $d \neq 0$ {from (1)}
∴ $a = c$ and $b = -d$
∴ $z^* = a - bi = c + di = w$

6 $\sqrt{z} = \dfrac{2}{3 - 2i} + 2 + 5i$

$= \dfrac{2}{3 - 2i} \times \dfrac{3 + 2i}{3 + 2i} + 2 + 5i$

$= \dfrac{6 + 4i}{9 - 4i^2} + 2 + 5i$

$= \dfrac{6 + 4i}{13} + 2 + 5i$

$= \frac{32}{13} + \frac{69}{13}i$

∴ $z = \left(\frac{32}{13} + \frac{69}{13}i\right)^2$

$= \dfrac{32^2 - 69^2}{169} + \dfrac{2 \times 32 \times 69}{169}i$

$= -\dfrac{3737}{169} + \dfrac{4416}{169}i$

7 Let $P(x) = 2x^{17} + 5x^{10} - 7x^3 + 6$
Now $R = P(2)$ {Remainder theorem}
$= 2^{18} + 5 \times 2^{10} - 7 \times 2^3 + 6$
$= 267\,214$

8 Let $P(z) = 2z^3 + az^2 + 62z + [a - 5]$
If $5 - i$ is a zero, then so is $5 + i$
{as $P(z)$ is a real polynomial}
and for these zeros $\alpha + \beta = 10$
$\alpha\beta = 25 - i^2 = 26$
∴ $P(z) = (z^2 - 10z + 26)(2z + b)$

	1	−10	26
×		2	b
	b	−10b	26b
2	−20	52	
2	b − 20	52 − 10b	26b

Equating coefficients gives $a = b - 20$, $52 - 10b = 62$ and $a - 5 = 26b$.

From $52 - 10b = 62$

$-10b = 10$

$\therefore\ b = -1$, and since $a = b - 20$ we find $a = -21$.

Check: $a - 5 = -26$ and $26b = -26$ ✓

$\therefore\ P(z) = 2z^3 - 21z^2 + 62z - 26$
$= (z^2 - 10z + 26)(2z - 1)$

$\therefore$ other two zeros are $\frac{1}{2}$, $5 + i$ and $a = -21$.

9 a Two zeros are $i\sqrt{2}$ and $\frac{1}{2}$, so another zero must be $-i\sqrt{2}$

Now $\pm i\sqrt{2}$ have $\alpha + \beta = 0$ and $\alpha\beta = -2i^2 = 2$

$\therefore\ x^2 + 2$ is a factor

$\therefore\ P(x) = a(2x - 1)(x^2 + 2)$, $a \neq 0$

b Two zeros are $1 - i$ and $-3 - i$

$\therefore$ the other zeros must be $1 + i$ and $-3 + i$

$1 \pm i$ have $\alpha + \beta = 2$ and $-3 \pm i$ have $\alpha + \beta = -6$

and $\alpha\beta = 1 - i^2 = 2$ and $\alpha\beta = 9 - i^2 = 10$

$\therefore\ P(x) = a(x^2 - 2x + 2)(x^2 + 6x + 10)$, $a \neq 0$

10 $P(x) = 2x^3 + 7x^2 + kx - k$ ...... (1)
$= (x + a)^2(2x + b)$ ...... (2)
$= (x^2 + 2ax + a^2)(2x + b)$
$= 2x^3 + [b + 4a]x^2 + [2ab + 2a^2]x + a^2b$ ...... (3)

	1	2a	a^2
×		2	b
	b	2ab	a^2b
2	4a	$2a^2$	
2	$b + 4a$	$2ab + 2a^2$	a^2b

Equating coefficients gives in (1) and (3):

$b + 4a = 7$, $2ab + 2a^2 = k$ and $a^2b = -k$

$\therefore\ 2ab + 2a^2 = -a^2b$ {equating ks}

$\therefore\ 2a(7 - 4a) + 2a^2 = -a^2(7 - 4a)$

$\therefore\ 14a - 8a^2 + 2a^2 + 7a^2 - 4a^3 = 0$

$\therefore\ 4a^3 - a^2 - 14a = 0$

$\therefore\ a(4a^2 - a - 14) = 0$

$\therefore\ a(4a + 7)(a - 2) = 0$

$\therefore\ a = 0, -\frac{7}{4}$ or 2

If $a = 0$, $b = 7$ and $k = 0$.
If $a = 2$, $b = -1$ and $k = 4$.
If $a = -\frac{7}{4}$, $b = 14$ and $k = -\frac{343}{8}$.

$\therefore$ largest value of k is $k = 4$ and $P(x) = (x + 2)^2(2x - 1)$. {substituting into (2)}

11 $2z^4 - 3z^3 + 2z^2 = 6z + 4$

$\therefore\ 2z^4 - 3z^3 + 2z^2 - 6z - 4 = 0$

From technology, 2 and $-\frac{1}{2}$ are solutions.

Check: $P(2) = 32 - 24 + 8 - 12 - 4 = 0$ ✓

$P(-\frac{1}{2}) = \frac{1}{8} + \frac{3}{8} + \frac{1}{2} + 3 - 4 = 0$ ✓

$\therefore\ P(z) = (z - 2)(z + \frac{1}{2})(2z^2 + 4)$
$= (z - 2)(2z + 1)(z^2 + 2)$ $\therefore$ roots are $2, -\frac{1}{2}, \pm i\sqrt{2}$

	2	-3	2	-6	-4
2	0	4	2	8	4
$-\frac{1}{2}$	2	1	4	2	0
	0	-1	0	-2	
	2	0	4	0	

12 $P(z) = z^3 + az^2 + kz + ka$

$P(-a) = -a^3 + a^3 - ka + ka = 0$

$\therefore\ z + a$ is a factor

$-a$	1	a	k	ka
	0	-a	0	-ka
	1	0	k	0

$\therefore\ P(z) = (z + a)(z^2 + k)$

or $P(z) = z^3 + az^2 + kz + ka$
$= z^2(z + a) + k(z + a)$
$= (z + a)(z^2 + k)$

    a $P(z) = 0$ has one real root if $k > 0$, $a \in \mathbb{R}$

    b and 3 real roots if $k \leqslant 0$, $a \in \mathbb{R}$

13 Let $P(x) = 6x^3 + ax^2 - 4ax + b$

$3x + 2$ and $x - 2$ are factors

$\therefore \quad 6x^3 + ax^2 - 4ax + b = (3x + 2)(x - 2)(2x + c)$
$$= (3x^2 - 4x - 4)(2x + c)$$
$$= 6x^3 - 8x^2 - 8x + 3cx^2 - 4cx - 4c$$
$$= 6x^3 + [3c - 8]x^2 + [-8 - 4c]x - 4c$$

Equating coefficients gives: $a = 3c - 8$, $\quad -4a = -8 - 4c$ and $b = -4c$

Equating a's gives: $\quad 3c - 8 = 2 + c$

$\therefore \quad 2c = 10$

$\therefore \quad c = 5$

Consequently, $a = 3(5) - 8 = 7$ and $b = -20$.

14 $y = x - k$ meets $(x - 2)^2 + (y + 3)^2 = 4$ where
$$(x - 2)^2 + (x - k + 3)^2 = 4$$

$\therefore \quad x^2 - 4x + 4 + (x - k)^2 + 6(x - k) + 9 - 4 = 0$

$\therefore \quad x^2 - 4x + 4 + x^2 - 2kx + k^2 + 6x - 6k + 5 = 0$

$\therefore \quad 2x^2 + [-4 - 2k + 6]x + [4 + k^2 - 6k + 5] = 0$

$\therefore \quad 2x^2 + [2 - 2k]x + [k^2 - 6k + 9] = 0$

which is a quadratic in x and in the tangent case $\Delta = 0$

$\therefore \quad [2 - 2k]^2 - 4(2)(k^2 - 6k + 9) = 0$

$\therefore \quad 4 - 8k + 4k^2 - 8k^2 + 48k - 72 = 0$

$\therefore \quad -4k^2 + 40k - 68 = 0$

$\therefore \quad k^2 - 10k + 17 = 0$

$\therefore \quad k = 5 \pm 2\sqrt{2}$

15

$$\begin{array}{r}
x^2 + 3x - 9 \\
x^2 + 2 \,\overline{\smash{\big)}\, x^4 + 3x^3 - 7x^2 + 11x - 1} \\
\underline{-(x^4 + 2x^2)} \\
3x^3 - 9x^2 + 11x \\
\underline{-(3x^3 + 6x)} \\
-9x^2 + 5x - 1 \\
\underline{-(-9x^2 - 18)} \\
5x + 17
\end{array}$$

$\therefore \quad Q(x) = x^2 + 3x - 9 \quad R(x) = 5x + 17$ and the new function would be divisible by $x^2 + 2$ if $x^4 + 3x^3 - 7x^2 + (2 + a)x + b = P(x) - R(x)$

and as $P(x) - R(x) = x^4 + 3x^3 - 7x^2 + 11x - 1 - (5x + 17)$
$$= x^4 + 3x^3 - 7x^2 + 6x - 18$$

then $2 + a = 6$ and $b = -18$ {equating coefficients}

$\therefore \quad a = 4$ and $b = -18$

Chapter 8

COUNTING AND THE BINOMIAL EXPANSION

EXERCISE 8A

1 There are 3 paths from P to Q
   4 paths from Q to R
   2 paths from R to S
   ∴ number of routes possible
   $= 3 \times 4 \times 2$ {product principle}
   $= 24$

2 a There are 4 choices for A. But once A is located, there is 1 choice for B, 1 for C and 1 for D
   ∴ there are $4 \times 1 \times 1 \times 1 = 4$ ways.

  b There are 4 choices for A. But once A is located there are 2 choices for B.
   Once B is located there is 1 choice for C and 1 for D
   ∴ there are $4 \times 2 \times 1 \times 1 = 8$ ways.

  c There are 4 choices for A. Once A is located there are 3 choices for B. Once B is located there are 2 choices for C and then 1 for D
   ∴ there are $4 \times 3 \times 2 \times 1 = 24$ ways.

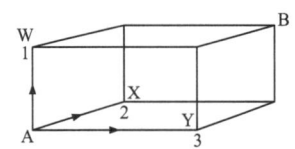

3 From A there are 3 possible first leg paths, to W, X or Y. Then there are 2 second leg paths to B
   ∴ total number $= 3 \times 2 = 6$ paths.

4 Any of the 7 teams could be in 'top' position.
   Then there are 6 left which could be in the 'second' position.
   So, there are $7 \times 6 = 42$ possible ways.

5 Any of the 8 teams could be 'top'.
   Any of the remaining 7 could be second.
   Any of the remaining 6 could be third.
   Any of the remaining 5 could be fourth
   ∴ there are $8 \times 7 \times 6 \times 5$
   $= 1680$ ways.

6 There are 5 digits to choose from.
   a Number of ways $= 5 \times 5 \times 5 = 125$
   b Number of ways $= 5 \times 4 \times 3 = 60$

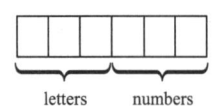

7 Repetitions are allowed.
   ∴ total number of ways
   $= 26 \times 26 \times 26 \times 10 \times 10 \times 10$
   $= 17\,576\,000$

8 a The 1st letter could go into either of the 2 boxes, and the second could go into either of the 2 boxes,
   ∴ there are $2 \times 2 = 4$ ways.
   These are:

Box X	Box Y
A, B	-
A	B
B	A
-	A, B

  b There are $3 \times 3 = 9$ ways.
  c There are $3 \times 3 \times 3 \times 3 = 81$ ways.

EXERCISE 8B

1 a There are $\quad 2 \times 2 + 3 \times 3$
         $= 13$ different paths

  b There are $\quad 4 \times 2 + 3 \times 2 \times 2$
         $= 20$ different paths

  c There are $\quad 2 + 4 \times 2 + 3 \times 3$
         $= 19$ different paths

  d There are $\quad 2 \times 2 + 2 \times 2 + 2 \times 3 \times 4$
         $= 32$ different paths

EXERCISE 8C

1 $0! = 1$
$1! = 1$
$2! = 2 \times 1 = 2$
$3! = 3 \times 2 \times 1 = 6$
$4! = 4 \times 3 \times 2 \times 1 = 24$
$5! = 5 \times 4 \times 3 \times 2 \times 1 = 120$

$6! = 6 \times 5! = 6 \times 120 = 720$
$7! = 7 \times 6! = 7 \times 720 = 5040$
$8! = 8 \times 7! = 8 \times 5040 = 40\,320$
$9! = 9 \times 8! = 9 \times 40\,320 = 362\,880$
$10! = 10 \times 9! = 10 \times 362\,880 = 3\,628\,800$

2 **a** $\dfrac{6!}{5!} = \dfrac{6 \times \cancel{5!}}{\cancel{5!}_1} = 6$

b $\dfrac{6!}{4!} = \dfrac{6 \times 5 \times \cancel{4!}}{\cancel{4!}_1} = 30$

c $\dfrac{6!}{7!} = \dfrac{\cancel{6!}^{\,1}}{7 \times \cancel{6!}} = \dfrac{1}{7}$

d $\dfrac{4!}{6!} = \dfrac{\cancel{4!}^{\,1}}{6 \times 5 \times \cancel{4!}} = \dfrac{1}{30}$

e $\dfrac{100!}{99!} = \dfrac{100 \times \cancel{99!}}{\cancel{99!}_1} = 100$

f $\dfrac{7!}{5! \times 2!} = \dfrac{7 \times 6 \times \cancel{5!}}{\cancel{5!} \times 2} = 21$

3 **a** $\dfrac{n!}{(n-1)!}$
$= \dfrac{n \times \cancel{(n-1)!}}{\cancel{(n-1)!}_1}$
$= n$

b $\dfrac{(n+2)!}{n!}$
$= \dfrac{(n+2)(n+1)\cancel{n!}}{\cancel{n!}_1}$
$= (n+2)(n+1)$

c $\dfrac{(n+1)!}{(n-1)!}$
$= \dfrac{(n+1)(n)\cancel{(n-1)!}}{\cancel{(n-1)!}_1}$
$= n(n+1)$

4 **a** $7 \times 6 \times 5$
$= \dfrac{7 \times 6 \times 5 \times 4 \times 3 \times 2 \times 1}{4 \times 3 \times 2 \times 1}$
$= \dfrac{7!}{4!}$

b 10×9
$= \dfrac{10 \times 9 \times 8!}{8!}$
$= \dfrac{10!}{8!}$

c $11 \times 10 \times 9 \times 8 \times 7$
$= \dfrac{11 \times 10 \times 9 \times 8 \times 7 \times 6!}{6!}$
$= \dfrac{11!}{6!}$

d $\dfrac{13 \times 12 \times 11}{3 \times 2 \times 1}$
$= \dfrac{13 \times 12 \times 11 \times 10!}{10! \times 3 \times 2 \times 1}$
$= \dfrac{13!}{10! \times 3!}$

e $\dfrac{1}{6 \times 5 \times 4}$
$= \dfrac{3!}{6 \times 5 \times 4 \times 3!}$
$= \dfrac{3!}{6!}$

f $\dfrac{4 \times 3 \times 2 \times 1}{20 \times 19 \times 18 \times 17}$
$= \dfrac{4! \times 16!}{20 \times 19 \times 18 \times 17 \times 16!}$
$= \dfrac{4! \times 16!}{20!}$

5 **a** $5! + 4!$
$= 5 \times 4! + 4!$
$= 4!(5+1)$
$= 6 \times 4!$

b $11! - 10!$
$= 11 \times 10! - 10!$
$= 10!(11-1)$
$= 10 \times 10!$

c $6! + 8!$
$= 6! + 8 \times 7 \times 6!$
$= 6!(1 + 8 \times 7)$
$= 57 \times 6!$

d $12! - 10!$
$= 12 \times 11 \times 10! - 10!$
$= 10!(12 \times 11 - 1)$
$= 131 \times 10!$

e $9! + 8! + 7!$
$= 9 \times 8 \times 7! + 8 \times 7! + 7!$
$= 7!(72 + 8 + 1)$
$= 81 \times 7!$

f $7! - 6! + 8!$
$= 7 \times 6! - 6! + 8 \times 7 \times 6!$
$= 6!(7 - 1 + 56)$
$= 62 \times 6!$

g $12! - 2 \times 11!$
$= 12 \times 11! - 2 \times 11!$
$= 11!(12 - 2)$
$= 10 \times 11!$

h $3 \times 9! + 5 \times 8!$
$= 3 \times 9 \times 8! + 5 \times 8!$
$= 8!(27 + 5)$
$= 32 \times 8!$

6 a $\dfrac{12! - 11!}{11}$

$= \dfrac{12 \times 11! - 11!}{11}$

$= \dfrac{11!(12 - 1)}{11}$

$= \dfrac{11! \times 11}{11}$

$= 11!$

b $\dfrac{10! + 9!}{11}$

$= \dfrac{10 \times 9! + 9!}{11}$

$= \dfrac{9!(10 + 1)}{11}$

$= \dfrac{9! \times 11}{11}$

$= 9!$

c $\dfrac{10! - 8!}{89}$

$= \dfrac{10 \times 9 \times 8! - 8!}{89}$

$= \dfrac{8!(90 - 1)}{89}$

$= \dfrac{8! \times 89}{89}$

$= 8!$

d $\dfrac{10! - 9!}{9!}$

$= \dfrac{10 \times 9! - 9!}{9!}$

$= \dfrac{9!(10 - 1)}{9!}$

$= 9$

e $\dfrac{6! + 5! - 4!}{4!}$

$= \dfrac{6 \times 5 \times 4! + 5 \times 4! - 4!}{4!}$

$= \dfrac{4!(30 + 5 - 1)}{4!}$

$= 34$

f $\dfrac{n! + (n-1)!}{(n-1)!}$

$= \dfrac{n \times (n-1)! + (n-1)!}{(n-1)!}$

$= \dfrac{(n-1)!(n+1)}{(n-1)!}$

$= n + 1$

g $\dfrac{n! - (n-1)!}{n-1}$

$= \dfrac{n \times (n-1)! - (n-1)!}{n-1}$

$= \dfrac{(n-1)!(n-1)}{n-1}$

$= (n-1)!$

h $\dfrac{(n+2)! + (n+1)!}{n+3}$

$= \dfrac{(n+2)(n+1)! + (n+1)!}{n+3}$

$= \dfrac{(n+1)!(n+2+1)}{n+3}$

$= (n+1)!$

EXERCISE 8D

1 a W, X, Y, Z

b WX, WY, WZ, XW, XY, XZ, YW, YX, YZ, ZW, ZX, ZY

c WXY, WXZ, WYX, WYZ, WZX, WZY, XWY, XWZ, XYW, XYZ, XZW, XZY, YWX, YWZ, YXW, YXZ, YZW, YZX, ZWX, ZWY, ZXW, ZXY, ZYW, ZYX

2 a AB, AC, AD, AE, BA, BC, BD, BE, CA, CB, CD, CE, DA, DB, DC, DE, EA, EB, EC, ED

b ABC, ABD, ABE, ACB, ACD, ACE, ADB, ADC, ADE, AEB, AEC, AED, BAC, BAD, BAE, BCA, BCD, BCE, BDA, BDC, BDE, BEA, BEC, BED, CAB, CAD, CAE, CBA, CBD, CBE, CDA, CDB, CDE, CEA, CEB, CED, DAB, DAC, DAE, DBA, DBC, DBE, DCA, DCB, DCE, DEA, DEB, DEC, EAB, EAC, EAD, EBA, EBC, EBD, ECA, ECB, ECD, EDA, EDB, EDC

(2 at a time: 20   3 at a time: 60)

3 a There are $5! = 120$ different orderings. **b** There are $8 \times 7 \times 6 = 336$ different orderings.
c There are $10 \times 9 \times 8 \times 7 = 5040$ different signals.

4 a $\boxed{4\ |\ 3}$ $\therefore$ there are $4 \times 3 = 12$ different signals

b $\boxed{4\ |\ 3\ |\ 2}$ $\therefore$ there are $4 \times 3 \times 2 = 24$ different signals

c $12 + 24 = 36$ different signals {using **a** and **b**}

5 There are 6 different letters $\therefore$ $6! = 720$ permutations.

a $\boxed{4\ |\ 3\ |\ 2\ |\ 1\ |\ 1\ |\ 1}$ with arrows pointing to positions E, D $\therefore$ there are $4 \times 3 \times 2 \times 1 \times 1 \times 1 = 24$ permutations

b $\boxed{1\ |\ 4\ |\ 3\ |\ 2\ |\ 1\ |\ 1}$ with arrows pointing to positions F, A $\therefore$ there are $1 \times 4 \times 3 \times 2 \times 1 \times 1 = 24$ permutations

$\quad$ **c** $\boxed{2\ |\ 4\ |\ 3\ |\ 2\ |\ 1\ |\ 1}\quad \therefore\ $ there are $\ 2\times 4\times 3\times 2\times 1\times 1 = 48\ $ permutations
$\qquad\ \ \uparrow\qquad\qquad\ \ \uparrow$
$\qquad$ A or E $\qquad$ the other one

6 a $\boxed{7\ |\ 7\ |\ 7}\quad$ So, there are $\ 7^3 = 343\ $ different numbers.

$\quad$ **b** $\boxed{7\ |\ 6\ |\ 5}\quad$ So, there are $\ 7 \times 6 \times 5 = 210\ $ different numbers.

$\quad$ **c** $\boxed{6\ |\ 5\ |\ 4}\quad$ So, there are $\ 6 \times 5 \times 4 = 120\ $ different numbers.
$\qquad\ \ \uparrow\quad\ \uparrow$
$\qquad$ 6 remain $\ \ $ fill 1st with any of 4 odds

7 $\ $ There are no restrictions $\ \therefore\ 6! = 720\ $ different ways

$\quad\boxed{3\ |\ 3\ |\ 2\ |\ 2\ |\ 1\ |\ 1}\ $ or $\ \boxed{3\ |\ 3\ |\ 2\ |\ 2\ |\ 1\ |\ 1}$
$\quad\ \ $ B $\ $ G $\ $ B $\ $ G $\ $ B $\ $ G $\qquad$ G $\ $ B $\ $ G $\ $ B $\ $ G $\ $ B

$\quad$ So, there are $\ 3 \times 3 \times 2 \times 2 \times 1 \times 1 + 3 \times 3 \times 2 \times 2 \times 1 \times 1 = 72\ $ different ways.

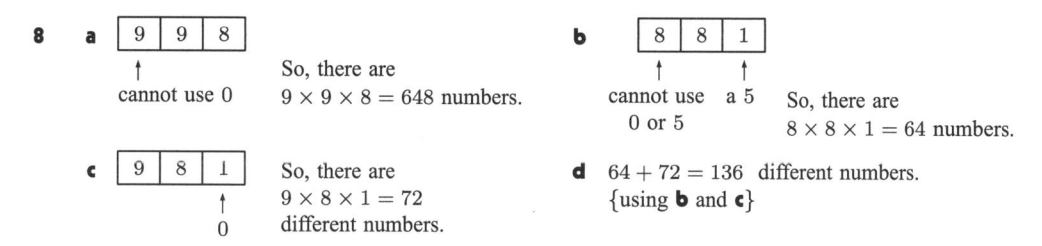

8 a $\boxed{9\ |\ 9\ |\ 8}\qquad\qquad\qquad\qquad\qquad$ **b** $\boxed{8\ |\ 8\ |\ 1}$
$\qquad\ \uparrow\qquad\qquad$ So, there are $\qquad\qquad\qquad\ \ \uparrow\qquad\ \uparrow$
$\qquad$ cannot use 0 $\ \ 9 \times 9 \times 8 = 648\ $ numbers. $\quad$ cannot use $\ $ a 5 $\ \ $ So, there are
$\qquad\qquad\qquad\qquad\qquad\qquad\qquad\qquad\qquad\qquad$ 0 or 5 $\qquad\qquad\quad 8 \times 8 \times 1 = 64\ $ numbers.

$\quad$ **c** $\boxed{9\ |\ 8\ |\ 1}\quad$ So, there are $\qquad$ **d** $\ 64 + 72 = 136\ $ different numbers.
$\qquad\qquad\quad\ \uparrow\qquad\ 9 \times 8 \times 1 = 72 \qquad\qquad\quad$ {using **b** and **c**}
$\qquad\qquad\quad\ 0\qquad\ \ $ different numbers.

9 a $\ $ As there are no restrictions, the number of ways is $\ 5! = 120$.

$\quad$ **b** $\ $ X and Y are together in 2! ways $\ $ {XY or YX}
$\qquad$ They, together with the other three books can be permutated in 4! ways.
$\qquad \therefore\ $ total number $= 2! \times 4! = 48\ $ ways.

$\quad$ **c** $\ 120 - 48 = 72\ $ ways $\ $ {using **a** and **b**}

10 a $\ $ As there are no restrictions, the number of ways is $\ 10! = 3\,628\,800$.

$\quad$ **b** $\ $ A, B and C are together in 3! ways $\ $ {ABC, ACB, BAC, BCA, CAB, CBA}
$\qquad$ They, together with the other 7 can be permutated in 8! ways.
$\qquad \therefore\ $ total number is $\ 3! \times 8! = 241\,920\ $ ways.

11 a $\boxed{4\ |\ 4\ |\ 3}\qquad$ So, there are $\qquad\qquad$ **b** $\boxed{2\ |\ 4\ |\ 3}\qquad$ So, there are
$\qquad\ \uparrow\qquad\qquad\quad 4 \times 4 \times 3 = 48\qquad\qquad\qquad\ \uparrow\qquad\qquad\qquad\quad 2 \times 4 \times 3 = 24$
$\qquad$ not 0 $\qquad\qquad$ different numbers. $\qquad\qquad\qquad$ 1 or 3 $\qquad\qquad\qquad$ different numbers.

$\quad$ **c** $\ $ The last digit must be a 0 or 8.

$\qquad$ If it is 0: $\ \boxed{3\ |\ 3\ |\ 1}\qquad\qquad\ \therefore\ 3 \times 3 \times 1 = 9\ $ different numbers
$\qquad\qquad\qquad\qquad\ \uparrow\qquad\ \ \uparrow$
$\qquad\qquad\qquad\ \ $ 3, 5 or 8 $\quad$ 0

$\qquad$ If it is 8: $\ \boxed{2\ |\ 3\ |\ 1}\qquad\qquad\ \therefore\ 2 \times 3 \times 1 = 6\ $ different numbers
$\qquad\qquad\qquad\qquad\ \uparrow\qquad\quad\uparrow$
$\qquad\qquad\qquad\quad$ 3 or 5 $\qquad$ 8 $\qquad \therefore\ $ in total there are $\ 9 + 6 = 15\ $ different numbers.

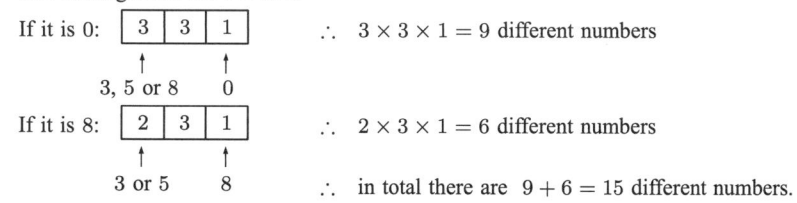

12 a $\boxed{6\ |\ 5\ |\ 4\ |\ 3}\quad$ So, there are $\ 6 \times 5 \times 4 \times 3 = 360\ $ different arrangements.

$\quad$ **b** $\ $ If no vowels are used, there are 4 letters to choose from.

$\qquad\qquad\therefore\ \boxed{4\ |\ 3\ |\ 2\ |\ 1}\quad$ So, there are $\ 4! = 24\ $ different arrangements.

∴ if at least one vowel must be used, there are   360 − 24   {from **a**}
= 336 different arrangements

c We first count the number of ways two vowels are adjacent.
A and O can be put together in 2! ways   {AO or OA}
These vowels can be placed in any one of 3 positions   {1st and 2nd, 2nd and 3rd, or 3rd and 4th}
The remaining 2 places can be filled from the other 4 letters in 4×3 different ways.
∴ two vowels are adjacent in $2! \times 3 \times 4 \times 3 = 72$ ways
∴ no two vowels are adjacent in $360 − 72 = 288$ ways

13 a | 9 | 8 | 7 | 6 | 5 | So, there are $9 \times 8 \times 7 \times 6 \times 5 = 15\,120$ different ways.

b | 4 | 3 | 2 | 6 | 5 | So, there are $4 \times 3 \times 2 \times 6 \times 5 = 720$ different ways.
         ↑
    2, 4, 6 or 8

14 a i | 10 | 9 | 8 | 7 | 6 | 5 | 4 | 3 | 2 | 1 | ∴ $10! = 3\,628\,800$ different ways.

ii | 10 | 5 | 4 | 4 | 3 | 3 | 2 | 2 | 1 | 1 | ∴ $10 \times 5 \times 4 \times 4 \times 3 \times 3 \times 2 \times 2 \times 1 \times 1 = 28\,800$ ways
         ↑   ↑
   opposite gender   same gender
   to first person   as first person

b i | 10 | 9 | 8 | 7 | 6 | 5 | ∴ $10 \times 9 \times 8 \times 7 \times 6 \times 5 = 151\,200$ different ways
         ↑   ↑
   Alice can sit in any   Her friend can sit
   of the 10 seats   in any of the
                          remaining 9 seats

ii Alice can sit in any of the 8 middle seats.
She can choose the two friends to sit next to her in 5×4 different ways.
The remaining 3 friends can occupy the other 7 seats in $7 \times 6 \times 5$ different ways.
∴ there are $8 \times 5 \times 4 \times 7 \times 6 \times 5 = 33\,600$ different ways.

15 a | 8 | 7 | 6 | 5 | 4 | 3 | 2 | 1 | So, there are $8! = 40\,320$ different ways.

b | 8 | 1 | 6 | 5 | 4 | 3 | 2 | 1 | So, there are $8 \times 1 \times 6! = 5760$ different ways.
       ↑   ↑
   1st person   2nd person sits
   sits anywhere directly opposite

c Two people can sit next to each other in $6 \times 2 = 12$ different ways.
{6 possible positions, and 2 possible orderings for each position}
The remaining 6 people can be seated in 6! ways
∴ there are $12 \times 6! = 8640$ different ways.

EXERCISE 8E

1 a $C_1^8 = \frac{8}{1}$
         $= 8$

b $C_2^8 = \frac{8 \times 7}{2 \times 1}$
       $= 28$

c $C_3^8 = \frac{8 \times 7 \times 6}{3 \times 2 \times 1}$
       $= 56$

d $C_6^8 = \frac{8 \times 7 \times \cancel{6} \times \cancel{5} \times \cancel{4} \times \cancel{3}}{\cancel{6} \times \cancel{5} \times \cancel{4} \times \cancel{3} \times 2 \times 1}$
       $= 28$

  e C_8^8

   $= \dfrac{8 \times 7 \times 6 \times 5 \times 4 \times 3 \times 2 \times 1}{8 \times 7 \times 6 \times 5 \times 4 \times 3 \times 2 \times 1}$

   $= 1,$ as expected

2 $C_{n-r}^n = \dfrac{n!}{(n-r)!(n-[n-r])!}$

  $= \dfrac{n!}{(n-r)!r!} = C_r^n$

3 $\binom{9}{k} = 4\binom{7}{k-1}$

  $\therefore \dfrac{9!}{k!(9-k)!} = 4\left(\dfrac{7!}{(k-1)!(7-[k-1])!}\right)$

  $\therefore \dfrac{9!}{k!(9-k)!} = \dfrac{4 \times 7!}{(k-1)!(8-k)!}$

  $\therefore \dfrac{9!}{4 \times 7!} = \dfrac{k!(9-k)!}{(k-1)!(8-k)!}$

  $\therefore \dfrac{9 \times 8 \times \cancel{7!}}{4 \times \cancel{7!}} = \dfrac{k\cancel{(k-1)!} \times (9-k)\cancel{(8-k)!}}{\cancel{(k-1)!}\cancel{(8-k)!}}$

  $\therefore \dfrac{9 \times 8}{4} = k(9-k)$

  $\therefore 18 = 9k - k^2$

  $\therefore k^2 - 9k + 18 = 0$

  $\therefore (k-3)(k-6) = 0$

  $\therefore k = 3$ or 6

4 ABCD, ABCE, ABCF, ABDE, ABDF, ABEF, ACDE, ACDF, ACEF, ADEF, BCDE, BCDF, BCEF, BDEF, CDEF, and $C_4^6 = 15$ ✓

5 There are $C_{11}^{17} = 12\,376$ different teams.

6 There are $C_5^9 = 126$ different possible selections.
  If question 1 is compulsory there are
  $C_1^1 C_4^8 = 1 \times 70 = 70$ possible selections.

7 If no restrictions, there are $C_3^{13} = 286$ different committees.
  $C_1^1 C_2^{12} = 66$ of them consist of the president and two others.

8 If no restrictions, there are $C_5^{12} = 792$ different teams.

 a Those containing the captain and vice-captain number $C_2^2 C_3^{10} = 1 \times 120 = 120$.

 b Those containing exactly one of the captain and vice captain number $C_1^2 C_4^{10} = 2 \times 210 = 420$.

9 Number of different teams $= C_3^3 C_0^1 C_6^{11} = 1 \times 1 \times 462 = 462$.

10 **a** If 1 person is always in the selection, number of ways $= C_1^1 C_3^9 = 84$

 b If 2 are always excluded, the number of ways $= C_0^2 C_4^8 = 70$

 c If 1 is always 'in' and 2 are always 'out', the number of ways is $C_1^1 C_0^2 C_3^7 = 35$

11 **a** If there are no restrictions the number of ways $= C_5^{16} = 4368$

 b The three men can be chosen in C_3^{10} ways and the 2 women in C_2^6 ways.
  $\therefore$ total number of ways $= C_3^{10} \times C_2^6 = 120 \times 15 = 1800$ ways.

 c If it contains all men, the number of ways $= C_5^{10} \times C_0^6 = 252$

 d If it contains at least 3 men it would contain
  3 men and 2 women or 4 men and 1 woman or 5 men and 0 women
  and this can be done in $C_3^{10}C_2^6 + C_4^{10}C_1^6 + C_5^{10}C_0^6$ ways $= 3312$ ways.

 e If it contains at least one of each sex, the total number of ways
  $= C_1^{10}C_4^6 + C_2^{10}C_3^6 + C_3^{10}C_2^6 + C_4^{10}C_1^6 = 4110$ or $C_5^{16} - C_0^{10}C_5^6 - C_5^{10}C_0^6 = 4110$

12 **a** The 2 doctors can be chosen in C_2^6 ways
  The 1 dentist can be chosen in C_1^3 ways
  The 2 others can be chosen in C_2^7 ways
  $\therefore$ the total number of ways $= C_2^6 \times C_1^3 \times C_2^7 = 945$

 b If it contains 2 doctors, 3 must be chosen from the other 10, $\therefore$ there are $C_2^6 C_3^{10} = 1800$ ways.

 c If it contains at least one of the two professions this can be done in
  $C_1^9 C_4^7 + C_2^9 C_3^7 + C_3^9 C_2^7 + C_4^9 C_1^7 = 4347$ or $C_5^{16} - C_0^9 C_5^7 = 4347$

13 There are 20 points (for vertices) to choose from and any 2 form a line.
This can be done in C_2^{20} ways. But this count includes the 20 lines joining the vertices.
$\therefore$ the number of diagonals $= C_2^{20} - 20 = 190 - 20 = 170$

14 a **i** $C_2^{12} = 66$ lines can be determined.
  ii Of the lines in **a i** $C_1^1 C_1^{11} = 11$ pass through B.
  b **i** $C_3^{12} = 220$ triangles can be determined.
  ii Of the triangles in **b i** $C_1^1 C_2^{11} = 55$ have one vertex B.

15 The digits must be from 1 to 9. So, there are 9 of them, and we want any 4.
This can be done in $C_4^9 = 126$ ways.
Once they have been selected they can be put in one ascending order
$\therefore$ total number $= 126 \times 1 = 126$.

16 a The different committees of 4, consisting of selections from 5 men and 6 women *in all possible ways* are
(4 men, 0 women) or (3 men, 1 woman) or (2 men, 2 women) or (1 man, 3 women) or (0 men, 4 women)
$\therefore$ $C_4^5 C_0^6 + C_3^5 C_1^6 + C_2^5 C_2^6 + C_1^5 C_3^6 + C_0^5 C_4^6 = C_4^{11}$ $\longleftarrow$ total number unrestricted.

b The generalisation is:
$C_0^m C_r^n + C_1^m C_{r-1}^n + C_2^m C_{r-2}^n + \ldots\ldots + C_{r-2}^m C_2^n + C_{r-1}^m C_1^n + C_r^m C_0^n = C_r^{m+n}$

17 a Consider a simpler case of 4 people (A, B, C and D) going into two equal groups.
AB CD (1)   (1) and (6) are the same division.
AC BD (2)   (2) and (5) are the same division
AD BC (3)   (3) and (4) are the same division
BC AD (4)
BD AC (5)   So, the number of ways is $\frac{1}{2}$ of C_3^6.
CD AB (6)
So, for 2 equal groups of 6, the number of ways $\frac{1}{2}$ of $C_6^{12} C_6^6$
$= \frac{1}{2} \times 924$
$= 462$

b For 3 equal groups of 4, the number of ways $= \dfrac{1}{3!} \times C_4^{12} \times C_4^8 \times C_4^4$
$= 5775$

18 There is one point of intersection for every combination of 4 points (2 from A, 2 from B) as shown.
There are $C_2^{10} \times C_2^7$ ways to choose these points.
$\therefore$ the maximum number of points of intersection (when none of the intersection points coincide) is $C_2^{10} \times C_2^7 = 945$

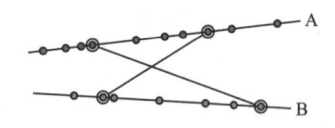

19 There is one point of intersection for every combination of 4 points (no more than 2 from any one line) as shown.
$\therefore$ the maximum number of points of intersection (when none of the intersection points coincide) is
$C_2^{10} C_2^9 C_0^8 + C_2^{10} C_0^9 C_2^8 + C_0^{10} C_2^9 C_2^8 + C_2^{10} C_1^9 C_1^8 +$
$C_1^{10} C_2^9 C_1^8 + C_1^{10} C_1^9 C_2^8 = 12\,528$

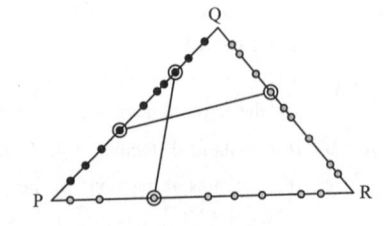

EXERCISE 8F

1 a $(x+1)^3$
$= x^3 + 3x^2(1)^1 + 3x(1)^2 + (1)^3$
$= x^3 + 3x^2 + 3x + 1$

b $(3x-1)^3$
$= (3x)^3 + 3(3x)^2(-1) + 3(3x)(-1)^2 + (-1)^3$
$= 27x^3 - 27x^2 + 9x - 1$

c $(2x+5)^3$
$= (2x)^3 + 3(2x)^2(5) + 3(2x)(5)^2 + (5)^3$
$= 8x^3 + 60x^2 + 150x + 125$

d $\left(2x + \dfrac{1}{x}\right)^3$
$= (2x)^3 + 3(2x)^2\left(\dfrac{1}{x}\right) + 3(2x)\left(\dfrac{1}{x}\right)^2 + \left(\dfrac{1}{x}\right)^3$
$= 8x^3 + 12x + \dfrac{6}{x} + \dfrac{1}{x^3}$

2 a $(x-2)^4 = x^4 + 4x^3(-2)^1 + 6x^2(-2)^2 + 4x(-2)^3 + (-2)^4$
$= x^4 - 8x^3 + 24x^2 - 32x + 16$

b $(2x+3)^4 = (2x)^4 + 4(2x)^3(3)^1 + 6(2x)^2(3)^2 + 4(2x)(3)^3 + (3)^4$
$= 16x^4 + 12 \times 8x^3 + 54 \times 4x^2 + 108 \times 2x + 81$
$= 16x^4 + 96x^3 + 216x^2 + 216x + 81$

c $\left(x + \dfrac{1}{x}\right)^4 = x^4 + 4x^3\left(\dfrac{1}{x}\right) + 6x^2\left(\dfrac{1}{x}\right)^2 + 4x\left(\dfrac{1}{x}\right)^3 + \left(\dfrac{1}{x}\right)^4$
$= x^4 + 4x^2 + 6 + \dfrac{4}{x^2} + \dfrac{1}{x^4}$

d $\left(2x - \dfrac{1}{x}\right)^4 = (2x)^4 + 4(2x)^3\left(-\dfrac{1}{x}\right) + 6(2x)^2\left(-\dfrac{1}{x}\right)^2 + 4(2x)\left(-\dfrac{1}{x}\right)^3 + \left(-\dfrac{1}{x}\right)^4$
$= 16x^4 - 32x^2 + 24 - \dfrac{8}{x^2} + \dfrac{1}{x^4}$

3 a 1 5 10 10 5 1 ← the 5th row
1 6 15 20 15 6 1 ← the 6th row

b i $(x+2)^6 = x^6 + 6x^5(2) + 15x^4(2)^2 + 20x^3(2)^3 + 15x^2(2)^4 + 6x(2)^5 + (2)^6$
$= x^6 + 12x^5 + 60x^4 + 160x^3 + 240x^2 + 192x + 64$

ii $(2x-1)^6 = (2x)^6 + 6(2x)^5(-1) + 15(2x)^4(-1)^2 + 20(2x)^3(-1)^3 + 15(2x)^2(-1)^4$
$\qquad + 6(2x)(-1)^5 + (-1)^6$
$= 64x^6 - 6 \times 32x^5 + 15 \times 16x^4 - 20 \times 8x^3 + 15 \times 4x^2 - 6 \times 2x + 1$
$= 64x^6 - 192x^5 + 240x^4 - 160x^3 + 60x^2 - 12x + 1$

iii $\left(x + \dfrac{1}{x}\right)^6$
$= x^6 + 6x^5\left(\dfrac{1}{x}\right) + 15x^4\left(\dfrac{1}{x}\right)^2 + 20x^3\left(\dfrac{1}{x}\right)^3 + 15x^2\left(\dfrac{1}{x}\right)^4 + 6x\left(\dfrac{1}{x}\right)^5 + \left(\dfrac{1}{x}\right)^6$
$= x^6 + 6x^4 + 15x^2 + 20 + \dfrac{15}{x^2} + \dfrac{6}{x^4} + \dfrac{1}{x^6}$

4 a $\left(1+\sqrt{2}\right)^3 = (1)^3 + 3(1)^2\left(\sqrt{2}\right) + 3(1)\left(\sqrt{2}\right)^2 + \left(\sqrt{2}\right)^3$
$= 1 + 3\sqrt{2} + 3 \times 2 + 2 \times \sqrt{2}$
$= 1 + 3\sqrt{2} + 6 + 2\sqrt{2}$
$= 7 + 5\sqrt{2}$

b $\left(1+\sqrt{5}\right)^4 = (1)^4 + 4(1)^3\left(\sqrt{5}\right) + 6(1)^2\left(\sqrt{5}\right)^2 + 4(1)\left(\sqrt{5}\right)^3 + \left(\sqrt{5}\right)^4$
$= 1 + 4\sqrt{5} + 30 + 20\sqrt{5} + 25$
$= 56 + 24\sqrt{5}$

c $(2-\sqrt{2})^5$
$= (2)^5 + 5(2)^4(-\sqrt{2}) + 10(2)^3(-\sqrt{2})^2 + 10(2)^2(-\sqrt{2})^3 + 5(2)^1(-\sqrt{2})^4 + (-\sqrt{2})^5$
$= 32 - 80\sqrt{2} + 160 - 80\sqrt{2} + 40 - 4\sqrt{2}$
$= 232 - 164\sqrt{2}$

5 a $(2+x)^6 = (2)^6 + 6(2)^5 x + 15(2)^4 x^2 + 20(2)^3 x^3 + 15(2)^2 x^4 + 6(2)x^5 + x^6$
$= 64 + 192x + 240x^2 + 160x^3 + 60x^4 + 12x^5 + x^6$

b $(2.01)^6$ is obtained by letting $x = 0.01$
$\therefore (2.01)^6 = 64 + 192 \times (0.01) + 240 \times (0.01)^2 + 160 \times (0.01)^3$
$\qquad + 60 \times (0.01)^4 + 12 \times (0.01)^5 + (0.01)^6$
$= 65.944\,160\,601\,201$

```
        64
        1.92
        0.024
        0.000 16
        0.000 000 6
        0.000 000 001 2
      + 0.000 000 000 001
      ───────────────────
        65.944 160 601 201
```

6 $(2x+3)(x+1)^4$
$= (2x+3)(x^4 + 4x^3 + 6x^2 + 4x + 1)$
$= 2x^5 + 8x^4 + 12x^3 + 8x^2 + 2x + 3x^4 + 12x^3 + 18x^2 + 12x + 3$
$= 2x^5 + 11x^4 + 24x^3 + 26x^2 + 14x + 3$

7 a $(3a+b)^5 = (3a)^5 + 5(3a)^4 b + 10(3a)^3 b^2 + \ldots$
$\therefore$ the coefficient of $a^3 b^2$ is $10 \times 3^3 = 270$

b $(2a+3b)^6 = (2a)^6 + 6(2a)^5(3b) + 15(2a)^4(3b)^2 + 20(2a)^3(3b)^3 + \ldots$
$\therefore$ the coefficient of $a^3 b^3$ is $20 \times 2^3 \times 3^3 = 4320$

EXERCISE 8G

1 a $(1+2x)^{11} = 1^{11} + \binom{11}{1} 1^{10}(2x)^1 + \binom{11}{2} 1^9 (2x)^2 + \ldots + \binom{11}{10} 1^1 (2x)^{10} + \binom{11}{11}(2x)^{11}$
$= 1 + \binom{11}{1}(2x) + \binom{11}{2}(2x)^2 + \ldots + \binom{11}{10}(2x)^{10} + \binom{11}{11}(2x)^{11}$

b $\left(3x + \dfrac{2}{x}\right)^{15}$
$= (3x)^{15} + \binom{15}{1}(3x)^{14}\left(\dfrac{2}{x}\right) + \binom{15}{2}(3x)^{13}\left(\dfrac{2}{x}\right)^2 + \ldots + \binom{15}{14}(3x)\left(\dfrac{2}{x}\right)^{14} + \binom{15}{15}\left(\dfrac{2}{x}\right)^{15}$

c $\left(2x - \dfrac{3}{x}\right)^{20}$
$= (2x)^{20} + \binom{20}{1}(2x)^{19}\left(-\dfrac{3}{x}\right) + \binom{20}{2}(2x)^{18}\left(-\dfrac{3}{x}\right)^2 + \ldots + \binom{20}{19}(2x)\left(-\dfrac{3}{x}\right)^{19} + \binom{20}{20}\left(-\dfrac{3}{x}\right)^{20}$

2 a For $(2x+5)^{15}$, $a = (2x)$, $b = 5$ and $n = 15$
Now $T_{r+1} = \binom{n}{r} a^{n-r} b^r$ and letting $r = 5$ gives $T_6 = \binom{15}{5}(2x)^{10} 5^5$.

b For $\left(x^2 + \dfrac{5}{x}\right)^9$, $a = (x^2)$, $b = \left(\dfrac{5}{x}\right)$ and $n = 9$
Now $T_{r+1} = \binom{n}{r} a^{n-r} b^r$ and letting $r = 3$ gives $T_4 = \binom{9}{3}(x^2)^6 \left(\dfrac{5}{x}\right)^3$.

c For $\left(x - \dfrac{2}{x}\right)^{17}$, $a = x$, $b = \left(-\dfrac{2}{x}\right)$ and $n = 17$
Now $T_{r+1} = \binom{n}{r} a^{n-r} b^r$ and letting $r = 9$ gives $T_{10} = \binom{17}{9} x^8 \left(-\dfrac{2}{x}\right)^9$.

d For $\left(2x^2 - \dfrac{1}{x}\right)^{21}$, $a = (2x^2)$, $b = \left(-\dfrac{1}{x}\right)$ and $n = 21$
Now $T_{r+1} = \binom{n}{r} a^{n-r} b^r$ and letting $r = 8$ gives $T_9 = \binom{21}{8}(2x^2)^{13} \left(-\dfrac{1}{x}\right)^8$.

3 a In $(3 + 2x^2)^{10}$, $a = 3$, $b = (2x^2)$ and $n = 10$

Now $T_{r+1} = \binom{n}{r} a^{n-r} b^r$

$= \binom{10}{r} 3^{10-r} (2x^2)^r$

$= \binom{10}{r} 3^{10-r} 2^r x^{2r}$

We now let $2r = 10$
$\therefore \ r = 5$

So, $T_6 = \underbrace{\binom{10}{5} 3^5 2^5}\, x^{10}$

$\therefore$ the coefficient is $\binom{10}{5} 3^5 2^5$.

b In $\left(2x^2 - \dfrac{3}{x}\right)^6$, $a = (2x^2)$, $b = \left(-\dfrac{3}{x}\right)$ and $n = 6$

Now $T_{r+1} = \binom{n}{r} a^{n-r} b^r$

$= \binom{6}{r} (2x^2)^{6-r} \left(-\dfrac{3}{x}\right)^r$

$= \binom{6}{r} 2^{6-r} x^{12-2r} \dfrac{(-3)^r}{x^r}$

$= \binom{6}{r} 2^{6-r} (-3)^r x^{12-3r}$

We now let $12 - 3r = 3$
$\therefore \ 3r = 9$
$\therefore \ r = 3$

So, $T_4 = \underbrace{\binom{6}{3} 2^3 (-3)^3}\, x^3$

$\therefore$ the coefficient is $\binom{6}{3} 2^3 (-3)^3$.

c In $\left(2x^2 - \dfrac{1}{x}\right)^{12}$, $a = (2x^2)$, $b = \left(-\dfrac{1}{x}\right)$ and $n = 12$

Now $T_{r+1} = \binom{n}{r} a^{n-r} b^r$

$= \binom{12}{r} (2x^2)^{12-r} \left(-\dfrac{1}{x}\right)^r$

$= \binom{12}{r} 2^{12-r} x^{24-2r} \dfrac{(-1)^r}{x^r}$

$= \binom{12}{r} 2^{12-r} (-1)^r x^{24-3r}$

We now let $24 - 3r = 12$
$\therefore \ 3r = 12$
$\therefore \ r = 4$

So, $T_5 = \underbrace{\binom{12}{4} 2^8 (-1)^4}\, x^{12}$

$\therefore$ the coefficient is $\binom{12}{4} 2^8 (-1)^4$.

4 a For $\left(x + \dfrac{2}{x^2}\right)^{15}$, $a = x$, $b = \dfrac{2}{x^2}$ and $n = 15$

Now $T_{r+1} = \binom{n}{r} a^{n-r} b^r = \binom{15}{r} x^{15-r} \left(\dfrac{2}{x^2}\right)^r = \binom{15}{r} x^{15-r} \dfrac{2^r}{x^{2r}} = \binom{15}{r} 2^r x^{15-3r}$

The constant term does not contain x. $\therefore \ 15 - 3r = 0$ $\therefore \ r = 5$

so $T_6 = \binom{15}{5} 2^5 x^0$ $\therefore$ the constant term is $\binom{15}{5} 2^5$.

b For $\left(x - \dfrac{3}{x^2}\right)^9$, $a = x$, $b = \left(-\dfrac{3}{x^2}\right)$ and $n = 9$

Now $T_{r+1} = \binom{n}{r} a^{n-r} b^r$

$= \binom{9}{r} x^{9-r} \left(-\dfrac{3}{x^2}\right)^r$

$= \binom{9}{r} x^{9-r} \dfrac{(-3)^r}{x^{2r}}$

$= \binom{9}{r} (-3)^r x^{9-3r}$

The constant term does not contain x.
$\therefore \ 9 - 3r = 0$
$\therefore \ r = 3$

so $T_4 = \binom{9}{3} (-3)^3 x^0$

$\therefore$ the constant term is $\binom{9}{3} (-3)^3$.

5 a, b
Row 1	1 1	sum $= 1 + 1 = 2$	$= 2^1$
Row 2	1 2 1	sum $= 1 + 2 + 1 = 4$	$= 2^2$
Row 3	1 3 3 1	sum $= 1 + 3 + 3 + 1 = 8$	$= 2^3$
Row 4	1 4 6 4 1	sum $= 1 + 4 + 6 + 4 + 1 = 16$	$= 2^4$
Row 5	1 5 10 10 5 1	sum $= 1 + 5 + 10 + 10 + 5 + 1 = 32$	$= 2^5$

c The sum of the numbers in row n of Pascal's triangle is 2^n.

d $(1 + x)^n$

$= \binom{n}{0} 1^n + \binom{n}{1} 1^{n-1} x + \binom{n}{2} 1^{n-2} x^2 + \binom{n}{3} 1^{n-3} x^3 + \ldots + \binom{n}{n-1} 1^1 x^{n-1} + \binom{n}{n} x^n$

$= \binom{n}{0} + \binom{n}{1} x + \binom{n}{2} x^2 + \binom{n}{3} x^3 + \ldots + \binom{n}{n-1} x^{n-1} + \binom{n}{n} x^n$ {as all powers of 1 are 1}

Now letting $x = 1$ gives LHS $= (1+1)^n = 2^n$

and RHS $= \binom{n}{0} + \binom{n}{1} + \binom{n}{2} + \binom{n}{3} + \ldots + \binom{n}{n-1} + \binom{n}{n}$

$\therefore \binom{n}{0} + \binom{n}{1} + \binom{n}{2} + \ldots + \binom{n}{n-1} + \binom{n}{n} = 2^n$

6 a $(x+2)(x^2+1)^8$

$= (x+2)\left[(x^2)^8 + \binom{8}{1}(x^2)^7 1 + \binom{8}{2}(x^2)^6 1^2 + \ldots + \binom{8}{6}(x^2)^2 1^6 + \binom{8}{7}(x^2)^1 1^7 + \binom{8}{8} 1^8\right]$

only terms which when multiplied give an x^5

$\therefore$ coefficient of x^5 is $1 \times \binom{8}{6} = \binom{8}{6} = 28$.

b $(2-x)(3x+1)^9$

$= (2-x)\left[(3x)^9 + \binom{9}{1}(3x)^8 + \binom{9}{2}(3x)^7 + \binom{9}{3}(3x)^6 + \binom{9}{4}(3x)^5 + \ldots\right]$

$\therefore$ coefficient of x^6 is $2 \times \binom{9}{3} \times 3^6 + (-1) \times \binom{9}{4} \times 3^5 = 2\binom{9}{3}3^6 - \binom{9}{4}3^5 = 91\,854$

7 $(1 + 2x - x^2)^5$

$= \left([1 + 2x] - x^2\right)^5$

$= (1+2x)^5 + 5(1+2x)^4(-x^2) + 10(1+2x)^3(-x^2)^2 + \ldots$

{all further terms contain higher powers of x than x^4}

$= 1^5 + 5(1^4)(2x) + 10(1^3)(2x)^2 + 10(1^2)(2x)^3 + 5(1)(2x)^4 + \ldots$

$\quad - 5x^2(1^4 + 4(1^3)(2x) + 6(1^2)(2x)^2 + \ldots) + 10x^4(1^3 + \ldots) + \ldots$

$= 1 + 10x + 40x^2 + 80x^3 + 80x^4 - 5x^2 - 40x^3 - 120x^4 + 10x^4 + \ldots$

$= 1 + 10x + 35x^2 + 40x^3 - 30x^4 + \ldots$

8 a $\binom{n}{1} = C_1^n = \dfrac{n}{1} = n$ and $\binom{n}{2} = C_2^n = \dfrac{n(n-1)}{2 \times 1} = \dfrac{n(n-1)}{2}$

b $(1+x)^n$ has $T_3 = \binom{n}{2} 1^{n-2} x^2 = \binom{n}{2} x^2$ and $n \geqslant 2$

But this term is $36x^2$ $\therefore \binom{n}{2} = 36$

$\therefore \dfrac{n(n-1)}{2} = 36$ But $n \geqslant 2$ $\therefore$ $n = 9$ or -8

$\therefore n(n-1) = 72$ $\therefore n = 9$

$\therefore n^2 - n - 72 = 0$ and $T_4 = \binom{n}{3} 1^{n-3} x^3$

$\therefore (n-9)(n+8) = 0$ $= \binom{9}{3} x^3$

$= 84x^3$

c $(1+kx)^n = 1^n + \binom{n}{1} 1^{n-1}(kx)^1 + \binom{n}{2} 1^{n-2}(kx)^2 + \ldots$

$= 1 + \binom{n}{1} kx + \binom{n}{2} k^2 x^2 + \ldots$

$\therefore \binom{n}{1} k = -12$ and $\binom{n}{2} k^2 = 60$

$\therefore nk = -12$ and $\dfrac{n(n-1)}{2} k^2 = 60$

$\therefore n(n-1)k^2 = 120$

But $k = -\dfrac{12}{n}$ $\therefore n(n-1) \dfrac{144}{n^2} = 120$

$\therefore 144(n-1) = 120n$ $\{n \geqslant 2\}$

$\therefore 144n - 120n = 144$

$\therefore 24n = 144$

$\therefore n = 6$ and so $k = -2$

9 $T_{r+1} = \binom{n}{r} a^{n-r} b^r$ where $n = 10$, $a = (x^2)$, $b = \left(\dfrac{1}{ax}\right)$

$= \binom{10}{r}(x^2)^{10-r}\left(\dfrac{1}{ax}\right)^r$

$= \binom{10}{r} x^{20-2r} \times \dfrac{1}{a^r x^r}$

$= \binom{10}{r} x^{20-3r} \times \dfrac{1}{a^r}$

We let $20 - 3r = 11$

$\therefore \ 3r = 9$

$\therefore \ r = 3$

and $T_4 = \binom{10}{3} x^{11} \times \dfrac{1}{a^3}$

$= \dfrac{\binom{10}{3}}{a^3} x^{11}$

So, $\dfrac{\binom{10}{3}}{a^3} = 15$

$\therefore \ \dfrac{120}{a^3} = 15$

$\therefore \ a^3 = 8$

$\therefore \ a = 2$

10 a From **5 d**, $(1+x)^n = \binom{n}{0} + \binom{n}{1}x + \binom{n}{2}x^2 + \binom{n}{3}x^3 + \ldots + \binom{n}{n-1}x^{n-1} + \binom{n}{n}x^n$

Now, letting $x = -1$ gives LHS $= (1+(-1))^n = 0$

and RHS $= \binom{n}{0} + \binom{n}{1}(-1) + \binom{n}{2}(-1)^2 + \binom{n}{3}(-1)^3 + \ldots$

$+ \binom{n}{n-1}(-1)^{n-1} + \binom{n}{n}(-1)^n$

$= \binom{n}{0} - \binom{n}{1} + \binom{n}{2} - \binom{n}{3} + \ldots + (-1)^n \binom{n}{n}$

$\therefore \ \binom{n}{0} - \binom{n}{1} + \binom{n}{2} - \binom{n}{3} + \ldots + (-1)^n \binom{n}{n} = 0$

b As $(1+x)^n = \binom{n}{0} + \binom{n}{1}x + \binom{n}{2}x^2 + \binom{n}{3}x^3 + \ldots + \binom{n}{n-1}x^{n-1} + \binom{n}{n}x^n$,

$(1+x)^{2n+1} = \binom{2n+1}{0} + \binom{2n+1}{1}x + \binom{2n+1}{2}x^2 + \ldots + \binom{2n+1}{2n}x^{2n} + \binom{2n+1}{2n+1}x^{2n+1}$

Now letting $x = 1$ gives LHS $= 2^{2n+1} = 2^{2n} \times 2^1 = 4^n \times 2$

and RHS $= \binom{2n+1}{0} + \binom{2n+1}{1} + \binom{2n+1}{2} + \ldots + \binom{2n+1}{2n} + \binom{2n+1}{2n+1}$

$= 2\left[\binom{2n+1}{0} + \binom{2n+1}{1} + \binom{2n+1}{2} + \ldots + \binom{2n+1}{n}\right]$

$\left\{\binom{2n+1}{2n+1} = \binom{2n+1}{0}, \binom{2n+1}{2n} = \binom{2n+1}{1}, \ldots, \binom{2n+1}{n+1} = \binom{2n+1}{n}\right\}$

$\therefore \ 2\left[\binom{2n+1}{0} + \binom{2n+1}{1} + \binom{2n+1}{2} + \ldots + \binom{2n+1}{n}\right] = 4^n \times 2$

$\therefore \ \binom{2n+1}{0} + \binom{2n+1}{1} + \binom{2n+1}{2} + \ldots + \binom{2n+1}{n} = 4^n$

11 $\displaystyle\sum_{r=0}^{n} 2^r \binom{n}{r} = 2^0 \binom{n}{0} + 2^1 \binom{n}{1} + 2^2 \binom{n}{2} + \ldots + 2^{n-1} \binom{n}{n-1} + 2^n \binom{n}{n}$

Using **5 d**, $(1+x)^n = \binom{n}{0} + \binom{n}{1}x + \binom{n}{2}x^2 + \ldots + \binom{n}{n-1}x^{n-1} + \binom{n}{n}x^n$

$\therefore$ letting $x = 2$, $(1+2)^n = \binom{n}{0} + \binom{n}{1}2 + \binom{n}{2}2^2 + \ldots + \binom{n}{n-1}2^{n-1} + \binom{n}{n}2^n$

$\therefore \ 3^n = 2^0 \binom{n}{0} + 2^1 \binom{n}{1} + 2^2 \binom{n}{2} + \ldots + 2^{n-1} \binom{n}{n-1} + 2^n \binom{n}{n}$

$\therefore \ \displaystyle\sum_{r=0}^{n} 2^r \binom{n}{r} = 3^n$

12 For any polynomial $f(x)$, the sum of its coefficients is $f(1)$.

Let $f(x) = x^3 + 2x^2 + 3x - 7$

$\therefore$ the sum of the coefficients of $f(x) = f(1)$

$= 1^3 + 2(1)^2 + 3(1) - 7$

$= 1 + 2 + 3 - 7 = -1$

Now consider the function $g(x) = (x^3 + 2x^2 + 3x - 7)^{100}$
$= [f(x)]^{100}$

The sum of the coefficients of $g(x) = g(1)$
$= [f(1)]^{100}$
$= (-1)^{100} = 1$

$\therefore$ the sum of the coefficients of $(x^3 + 2x^2 + 3x - 7)^{100}$ is 1.

13 From **5 d**, $(1+x)^n = \binom{n}{0} + \binom{n}{1}x + \dots + \binom{n}{n-1}x^{n-1} + \binom{n}{n}x^n$

$\therefore (1+x)^{2n} = \binom{2n}{0} + \binom{2n}{1}x + \dots + \binom{2n}{n-1}x^{n-1} + \binom{2n}{n}x^n + \dots + \binom{2n}{2n-1}x^{2n-1} + \binom{2n}{2n}x^{2n}$

Now $(1+x)^n(1+x)^n = (1+x)^{2n}$

$\therefore \left[\binom{n}{0} + \binom{n}{1}x + \dots + \binom{n}{n-1}x^{n-1} + \binom{n}{n}x^n\right]\left[\binom{n}{0} + \binom{n}{1}x + \dots + \binom{n}{n-1}x^{n-1} + \binom{n}{n}x^n\right]$
$= \binom{2n}{0} + \binom{2n}{1}x + \dots + \binom{2n}{n-1}x^{n-1} + \binom{2n}{n}x^n + \dots + \binom{2n}{2n-1}x^{2n-1} + \binom{2n}{2n}x^{2n}$

Equating coefficients of x^n,

$\binom{n}{0}\binom{n}{n} + \binom{n}{1}\binom{n}{n-1} + \dots + \binom{n}{n-1}\binom{n}{1} + \binom{n}{n}\binom{n}{0} = \binom{2n}{n}$

But $\binom{n}{n} = \binom{n}{0}$, $\binom{n}{n-1} = \binom{n}{1}$, and so on.

$\therefore \binom{n}{0}^2 + \binom{n}{1}^2 + \binom{n}{2}^2 + \dots + \binom{n}{n-1}^2 + \binom{n}{n}^2 = \binom{2n}{n}$

14 a $n\binom{n-1}{r-1} = n\dfrac{(n-1)!}{(r-1)!(n-1-[r-1])!}$

$= \dfrac{n \times (n-1)!}{(r-1)!(n-r)!}$

$= r \times \dfrac{n!}{r!(n-r)!}$

$= r\binom{n}{r}$

b $\binom{n}{1} + 2\binom{n}{2} + 3\binom{n}{3} + \dots + n\binom{n}{n}$

$= n\binom{n-1}{0} + n\binom{n-1}{1} + n\binom{n-1}{2} + \dots + n\binom{n-1}{n-1}$

{using **a**}

$= n\left[\binom{n-1}{0} + \binom{n-1}{1} + \binom{n-1}{2} + \dots + \binom{n-1}{n-1}\right]$

$= n\,2^{n-1}$ {second part of **5 d**}

c i $\displaystyle\sum_{r=0}^{n} P_r = P_0 + P_1 + P_2 + \dots + P_n$

$= \binom{n}{0}p^0(1-p)^n + \binom{n}{1}p^1(1-p)^{n-1} + \binom{n}{2}p^2(1-p)^{n-2} + \dots + \binom{n}{n}p^n(1-p)^0$

$= (p + [1-p])^n$ {binomial expansion}

$= 1^n = 1$

ii $\displaystyle\sum_{r=1}^{n} rP_r = 1P_1 + 2P_2 + 3P_3 + \dots + nP_n$

$= 1\binom{n}{1}p^1(1-p)^{n-1} + 2\binom{n}{2}p^2(1-p)^{n-2} + 3\binom{n}{3}p^3(1-p)^{n-3} + \dots$
$\quad + n\binom{n}{n}p^n(1-p)^0$

$= n\binom{n-1}{0}p^1(1-p)^{n-1} + n\binom{n-1}{1}p^2(1-p)^{n-2} + n\binom{n-1}{2}p^3(1-p)^{n-3} + \dots$
$\quad + n\binom{n-1}{n-1}p^n$ {using **a**}

$= np[\binom{n-1}{0}p^0(1-p)^{n-1} + \binom{n-1}{1}p^1(1-p)^{n-2} + \binom{n-1}{2}p^2(1-p)^{n-3} + \dots$
$\quad + \binom{n-1}{n-1}p^{n-1}]$

$= np\left[(p + (1-p))^{n-1}\right]$

$= np \times 1^{n-1}$

$= np$

Mathematics HL (2nd edn), Chapter 8 – COUNTING AND THE BINOMIAL EXPANSION   233

REVIEW SET 8A

1 a | 26 | 26 | 10 | 10 | 10 | 10 | $\therefore$ there are $26^2 \times 10^4 = 6\,760\,000$ if there are no restrictions

b | 5 | 26 | 10 | 10 | 10 | 10 | $\therefore$ there are $5 \times 26 \times 10^4 = 1\,300\,000$ possibilities
   $\uparrow$
   a vowel
   if the first letter is a vowel

c | 26 | 25 | 10 | 9 | 8 | 7 | $\therefore$ there are $26 \times 25 \times 10 \times 9 \times 8 \times 7 = 3\,276\,000$, if there are no repetitions

2 a To form a line we need to select any two points from the 10.
   $\therefore$ total is $C_2^{10} = 45$ lines.

b To form a triangle we need to select any three points from the 10.
   $\therefore$ total is $C_3^{10} = 120$ triangles.

3 a $\dfrac{n!}{(n-2)!} = \dfrac{n(n-1)(n-2)!}{(n-2)!}$
   $= n(n-1)$

b $\dfrac{n! + (n+1)!}{n!} = \dfrac{n! + (n+1)n!}{n!}$
   $= \dfrac{n![1 + n + 1]}{n!}$
   $= n + 2$

4 a Total number $= C_5^{8+7} = C_5^{15} = 3003$ committees
b Total with 2 men and 3 women $= C_2^8 C_3^7 = 980$ committees
c Total with at least one man = total unrestricted − total with all women
   $= 3003 - C_0^8 C_5^7 = 2982$ committees

5 There are $C_2^8 = 28$ handshakes made.

6 a $(x - 2y)^3 = x^3 + 3x^2(-2y) + 3x(-2y)^2 + (-2y)^3$
   $= x^3 - 6x^2 y + 12xy^2 - 8y^3$

b $(3x + 2)^4 = (3x)^4 + 4(3x)^3(2) + 6(3x)^2(2)^2 + 4(3x)(2)^3 + (2)^4$
   $= 81x^4 + 216x^3 + 216x^2 + 96x + 16$

7 a With no restrictions there are $C_5^{10} = 252$ different teams.
b Those consisting of at least one of each sex
   $= C_5^{10} - C_5^6 C_0^4$ {there are no committees consisting of 5 women}
   $= 246$

8 a | 4 | 3 | 2 | 1 | 1 | $\therefore$ $4 \times 3 \times 2 \times 1 \times 1 = 24$ arrangements end in T
                $\uparrow$
                T

b | 1 | 3 | 2 | 1 | 1 | $\therefore$ $1 \times 3 \times 2 \times 1 \times 1 = 6$ arrangements begin with P and end with T
   $\uparrow$ $\uparrow$
   P   T

9 In the expansion of $(2x + 5)^6$, $a = (2x)$, $b = 5$, $n = 6$
   $T_{r+1} = \binom{n}{r} a^{n-r} b^r$ For the coefficient of x^3 we let $6 - r = 3$
   $= \binom{6}{r}(2x)^{6-r} 5^r$ $\therefore$ $r = 3$
   $= \binom{6}{r} 2^{6-r} x^{6-r} 5^r$ and $T_4 = \binom{6}{3} 2^3 5^3 x^3$

   $\therefore$ the coefficient is $\binom{6}{3} 2^3 5^3 = 20\,000$.

10 In the expansion of $\left(2x^2 - \dfrac{1}{x}\right)^6$, $a = 2x^2$, $b = -\dfrac{1}{x}$, $n = 6$

$T_{r+1} = \binom{n}{r} a^{n-r} b^r$

$\phantom{T_{r+1}} = \binom{6}{r}(2x^2)^{6-r}\left(-\dfrac{1}{x}\right)^r$

$\phantom{T_{r+1}} = \binom{6}{r} 2^{6-r} x^{12-2r} (-1)^r x^{-r}$

$\phantom{T_{r+1}} = \binom{6}{r} 2^{6-r} (-1)^r x^{12-3r}$

For the constant term we let $12 - 2r = 0$

$\therefore \quad r = 4$

and $T_5 = \binom{6}{4} 2^2 (-1)^4 \, x^0$

$\therefore$ the constant term is $\binom{6}{4} 2^2 (-1)^4 = 60$.

11 $(1 + kx)^n = 1^n + \binom{n}{1} 1^{n-1}(kx)^1 + \binom{n}{2} 1^{n-2}(kx)^2 + \ldots$

$ = 1 + nkx + \binom{n}{2} k^2 x^2 + \ldots$

$\therefore \quad nk = -4$ and $\binom{n}{2} k^2 = \dfrac{15}{2}$

$\therefore \quad k = -\dfrac{4}{n}$ and $\dfrac{n(n-1)}{2} k^2 = \dfrac{15}{2}$

$\therefore \quad n(n-1)k^2 = 15$

Using $k = -\dfrac{4}{n}$, $n(n-1)\left(\dfrac{16}{n^2}\right) = 15$

$\therefore \quad 16(n-1) = 15n \quad \{n \geqslant 2\}$

$\therefore \quad 16n - 16 = 15n$

$\therefore \quad n = 16$ and so $k = \dfrac{-4}{16} = -\dfrac{1}{4}$

12 The three sisters can sit together in 3! ways. They as a group, plus the other 5 people, make 6 items which can be permutated in 6! ways.

$\therefore$ total number of orderings $= 3! \times 6! = 4320$

13 a $\boxed{9 \;|\; 10 \;|\; 10}$ So, $9 \times 10 \times 10 = 900$ three digit numbers can be formed.
  ↑
  can't use 0

b To be divisible by 5 the last digit must be 0 or 5.

either $\boxed{9 \;|\; 10 \;|\; 1}$ or $\boxed{9 \;|\; 10 \;|\; 1}$ $\therefore \quad 9 \times 10 \times 1 + 9 \times 10 \times 1 = 180$ of them
                ↑   ↑   are divisible by 5.
                0   5

REVIEW SET 8B

1 a If no restrictions there are $C_8^{18} = 43\,758$ different teams possible.

b If 4 of each sex are needed there are $C_4^{11} \times C_4^7 = 11\,550$ different teams.

c If at least 2 women are needed, total number $= C_8^{18} - C_8^{11} C_0^7 - C_7^{11} C_1^7$
$\phantom{\text{If at least 2 women are needed, total number}} = 41\,283$ different teams

2 a $\boxed{9 \;|\; 9 \;|\; 8 \;|\; 7}$ So, $9 \times 9 \times 8 \times 7 = 4536$ numbers are possible.
  ↑
  can't use 0

b Either they end in 0 or in 5

$\boxed{9 \;|\; 8 \;|\; 7 \;|\; 1}$ or $\boxed{8 \;|\; 8 \;|\; 7 \;|\; 1}$ So, $9 \times 8 \times 7 \times 1 + 8 \times 8 \times 7 \times 1$
              ↑   ↑   ↑ $= 952$ numbers are possible.
              0   can't use 0   5

3 The sixth row of Pascal's triangle is $\quad 1 \quad 6 \quad 15 \quad 20 \quad 15 \quad 6 \quad 1$
$\therefore \quad (a+b)^6 = a^6 + 6a^5b + 15a^4b^2 + 20a^3b^3 + 15a^2b^4 + 6ab^5 + b^6$

a $(x-3)^6 = x^6 + 6x^5(-3) + 15x^4(-3)^2 + 20x^3(-3)^3 + 15x^2(-3)^4 + 6x(-3)^5 + (-3)^6$
$= x^6 - 18x^5 + 135x^4 - 540x^3 + 1215x^2 - 1458x + 729$

b $\left(1 + \dfrac{1}{x}\right)^6$

$= (1)^6 + 6(1)^5 \left(\dfrac{1}{x}\right) + 15(1)^4 \left(\dfrac{1}{x}\right)^2 + 20(1)^3 \left(\dfrac{1}{x}\right)^3 + 15(1)^2 \left(\dfrac{1}{x}\right)^4 + 6(1) \left(\dfrac{1}{x}\right)^5 + \left(\dfrac{1}{x}\right)^6$

$= 1 + \dfrac{6}{x} + \dfrac{15}{x^2} + \dfrac{20}{x^3} + \dfrac{15}{x^4} + \dfrac{6}{x^5} + \dfrac{1}{x^6}$

4 $(\sqrt{3}+2)^5 = (\sqrt{3})^5 + 5(\sqrt{3})^4(2) + 10(\sqrt{3})^3(2)^2 + 10(\sqrt{3})^2(2)^3 + 5(\sqrt{3})^1(2)^4 + 2^5$
$= 9\sqrt{3} + 90 + 120\sqrt{3} + 240 + 80\sqrt{3} + 32$
$= 362 + 209\sqrt{3}$

5 $(4+x)^3 = 4^3 + 3(4)^2 x^1 + 3(4)^1 x^2 + x^3$
$= 64 + 48x + 12x^2 + x^3$

Letting $x = 0.02$ gives $(4.02)^3 = 64 + 48(0.02) + 12(0.02)^2 + (0.02)^3$
$= 64 + 0.96 + 0.0048 + 0.000\,008$
$= 64.964\,808$

6 For $\left(3x^2 + \dfrac{1}{x}\right)^8$, $a = (3x^2)$, $b = \left(\dfrac{1}{x}\right)$, $n = 8$

$T_{r+1} = \binom{n}{r} a^{n-r} b^r \qquad$ Now a constant term does not contain x
$= \binom{8}{r}(3x^2)^{8-r}\left(\dfrac{1}{x}\right)^r \qquad \therefore \quad 16 - 3r = 0$
$= \binom{8}{r} 3^{8-r} x^{16-2r-r} \qquad \therefore \quad 3r = 16$
$= \binom{8}{r} 3^{8-r} x^{16-3r} \qquad \therefore \quad r = 5\tfrac{1}{3}$

which is impossible as r is in $\mathbb{Z}$
$\therefore$ no constant term exists.

7 In $\left(2x - \dfrac{3}{x^2}\right)^{12}$, $a = (2x)$, $b = \left(-\dfrac{3}{x^2}\right)$, $n = 12$

$T_{r+1} = \binom{n}{r} a^{n-r} b^r \qquad$ For the coefficient of x^{-6} we let $\quad 12 - 3r = -6$
$= \binom{12}{r}(2x)^{12-r}\left(-\dfrac{3}{x^2}\right)^r \qquad\qquad\qquad\qquad\qquad \therefore \quad 3r = 18$
$= \binom{12}{r} 2^{12-r} x^{12-r} \dfrac{(-3)^r}{x^{2r}} \qquad$ So, $T_7 = \underbrace{\binom{12}{6} 2^6 (-3)^6}\, x^{-6}$
$\hphantom{\therefore \quad r = 6}$
$= \binom{12}{r} 2^{12-r} (-3)^r x^{12-3r} \qquad \therefore$ the coefficient is $\binom{12}{6} 2^6 (-3)^6 = 43\,110\,144$.

8 $(2x+3)(x-2)^6$
$= (2x+3)\left[x^6 + \binom{6}{1}x^5(-2) + \binom{6}{2}x^4(-2)^2 + \ldots\right]$

$\therefore$ coefficient of x^5 is $\quad 2 \times \binom{6}{2} \times (-2)^2 + 3 \times \binom{6}{1} \times (-2) = 8\binom{6}{2} - 6\binom{6}{1} = 84$

9 $T_{r+1} = C_r^9 (2x)^{9-r} \left(\dfrac{1}{ax^2}\right)^r \qquad$ Letting $r = 2$, $T_3 = \underbrace{C_2^9\, 2^7 a^{-2}}\, x^3$

$= C_r^9\, 2^{9-r} x^{9-r} \times \dfrac{1}{a^r x^{2r}} \qquad \therefore \quad \dfrac{C_2^9\, 2^7}{a^2} = 288$

$= C_r^9\, 2^{9-r} a^{-r} x^{9-3r} \qquad\qquad \therefore \quad a^2 = \dfrac{C_2^9\, 2^7}{288} = 16$

$\hphantom{= C_r^9\, 2^{9-r} a^{-r} x^{9-3r} \qquad\qquad} \therefore \quad a = \pm 4$

10
$$T_{r+1} = C_r^6 (3x)^{6-r} \left(\frac{-2}{x^2}\right)^r$$
$$= C_r^6 \, 3^{6-r} x^{6-r} (-2)^r x^{-2r}$$
$$= C_r^6 \, 3^{6-r} x^{6-3r} (-2)^r$$

If we let $6 - 3r = 0$ then $r = 2$
$$\therefore \quad T_3 = \underbrace{C_2^6 \, 3^4 (-2)^2}_{} x^0$$
$$\therefore \quad \text{constant term} = C_2^6 \, 3^4 (-2)^2 = 4860$$

11 $\left(x^3 + \dfrac{q}{x^3}\right)^8$ has $T_{r+1} = C_r^8 (x^3)^{8-r} \left(\dfrac{q}{x^3}\right)^r$
$$= C_r^8 \, x^{24-3r} \, \frac{q^r}{x^{3r}}$$
$$= C_r^8 \, x^{24-6r} q^r$$

which has constant term $C_4^8 q^4$ $\{24 - 6r = 0$ when $r = 4\}$

$\left(x^3 + \dfrac{q}{x^3}\right)^4$ has $T_{r+1} = C_r^4 (x^3)^{4-r} \left(\dfrac{q}{x^3}\right)^r$
$$= C_r^4 \, x^{12-3r} q^r x^{-3r}$$
$$= C_r^4 \, x^{12-6r} q^r$$

which has constant term $C_2^4 q^2$ $\{12 - 6r = 0$ when $r = 2\}$
$$\therefore \quad C_4^8 q^4 = C_2^4 q^2$$
$$\therefore \quad 70q^4 - 6q^2 = 0$$
$$\therefore \quad q^2(70q^2 - 6) = 0$$
$$\therefore \quad 70q^2 - 6 = 0 \quad \{q = 0 \text{ gives a trivial solution}\}$$
$$\therefore \quad q^2 = \tfrac{6}{70}$$
$$\therefore \quad q = \pm\sqrt{\tfrac{6}{70}}$$

Chapter 9
MATHEMATICAL INDUCTION

EXERCISE 9A

1 a $3 = 4 \times 1 - 1$
   $7 = 4 \times 2 - 1$
   $11 = 4 \times 3 - 1$
   $15 = 4 \times 4 - 1$
   $19 = 4 \times 5 - 1$ and so on.

   Our proposition is:
   The nth term of the sequence 3, 7, 11, 15, 19, ... is $4n - 1$
   for $n = 1, 2, 3, 4, $ ......

b $3^1 = 3$ $1 + 2(1) = 3$
   $3^2 = 9$ $1 + 2(2) = 5$
   $3^3 = 27$ $1 + 2(3) = 7$
   $3^4 = 81$ $1 + 2(4) = 9$

   Our proposition is:
   $3^n > 1 + 2n$ for $n = 2, 3, 4, 5, $ ......
   or $n \geqslant 2$, $n \in \mathbb{Z}^+$

c $11^1 - 1 = 10$
   $11^2 - 1 = 121 - 1 = 120$
   $11^3 - 1 = 1331 - 1 = 1330$
   $11^4 - 1 = 14\,641 - 1 = 14\,640$

   Our proposition is:
   $11^n - 1$ is divisible by 10 for all $n \in \mathbb{Z}^+$

d $2 = 2 = 1 \times 2$
   $2 + 4 = 6 = 2 \times 3$
   $2 + 4 + 6 = 12 = 3 \times 4$
   $2 + 4 + 6 + 8 = 20 = 4 \times 5$
   $2 + 4 + 6 + 8 + 10 = 30 = 5 \times 6$

   Our proposition is:
   $2 + 4 + 6 + 8 + 10 + \ldots + 2n = n(n+1)$ for all $n \in \mathbb{Z}^+$
   ↑
   nth term

e $1! = 1$
   $1! + 2 \times 2! = 1 + 2(2) = 5$
   $1! + 2 \times 2! + 3 \times 3! = 1 + 4 + 18 = 23$
   $1! + 2 \times 2! + 3 \times 3! + 4 \times 4! = 1 + 4 + 18 + 96 = 119$
   where each number result is 1 less than a factorial number
   $1 = 2! - 1$
   $5 = 3! - 1$
   $23 = 4! - 1$
   $119 = 5! - 1$

   Our proposition is:
   $1! + 2 \times 2! + 3 \times 3! + 4 \times 4! + \ldots + n \times n! = (n+1)! - 1$
   for all $n \in \mathbb{Z}^+$

f $\dfrac{1}{2!} = \dfrac{1}{2} = \dfrac{2! - 1}{2!}$

   $\dfrac{1}{2!} + \dfrac{2}{3!} = \dfrac{1}{2} + \dfrac{2}{6} = \dfrac{5}{6} = \dfrac{3! - 1}{3!}$

   $\dfrac{1}{2!} + \dfrac{2}{3!} + \dfrac{3}{4!} = \dfrac{1}{2} + \dfrac{2}{6} + \dfrac{3}{24} = \dfrac{23}{24} = \dfrac{4! - 1}{4!}$

   $\dfrac{1}{2!} + \dfrac{2}{3!} + \dfrac{3}{4!} + \dfrac{4}{5!} = \dfrac{1}{2} + \dfrac{2}{6} + \dfrac{3}{24} + \dfrac{4}{120} = \dfrac{119}{120} = \dfrac{5! - 1}{5!}$

   Our proposition is: $\dfrac{1}{2!} + \dfrac{2}{3!} + \dfrac{3}{4!} + \dfrac{4}{5!} + \ldots + \dfrac{n}{(n+1)!} = \dfrac{(n+1)! - 1}{(n+1)!}$, $n \in \mathbb{Z}^+$

g $7^1 + 2 = 7 + 2 = 9 = 3 \times 3$
   $7^2 + 2 = 49 + 2 = 51 = 3 \times 17$
   $7^3 + 2 = 343 + 2 = 345 = 3 \times 115$
   $7^4 + 2 = 2401 + 2 = 2403 = 3 \times 801$

   Our proposition is:
   $7^n + 2$ is divisible by 3 for all $n \in \mathbb{Z}^+$

h $(1 - \frac{1}{2}) = \frac{1}{2}$

$(1 - \frac{1}{2})(1 - \frac{1}{3}) = \frac{1}{2} \times \frac{2}{3} = \frac{1}{3}$

$(1 - \frac{1}{2})(1 - \frac{1}{3})(1 - \frac{1}{4}) = \frac{1}{2} \times \frac{2}{3} \times \frac{3}{4} = \frac{1}{4}$

$(1 - \frac{1}{2})(1 - \frac{1}{3})(1 - \frac{1}{4})(1 - \frac{1}{5}) = \frac{1}{2} \times \frac{2}{3} \times \frac{3}{4} \times \frac{4}{5} = \frac{1}{5}$

Our proposition is: $(1 - \frac{1}{2})(1 - \frac{1}{3})(1 - \frac{1}{4})......\left(1 - \frac{1}{n+1}\right) = \frac{1}{n+1}$, $n \in \mathbb{Z}^+$

i $\frac{1}{2 \times 5} = \frac{1}{10}$

$\frac{1}{2 \times 5} + \frac{1}{5 \times 8} = \frac{1}{10} + \frac{1}{40} = \frac{5}{40} = \frac{1}{8} = \frac{2}{16}$

$\frac{1}{2 \times 5} + \frac{1}{5 \times 8} + \frac{1}{8 \times 11} = \frac{1}{10} + \frac{1}{40} + \frac{1}{88} = \frac{3}{22}$

$\frac{1}{2 \times 5} + \frac{1}{5 \times 8} + \frac{1}{8 \times 11} + \frac{1}{11 \times 14} = \frac{1}{7} = \frac{4}{28}$

10, 16, 22, 28 is arithmetic
with $u_1 = 10$, $d = 6$
$u_n = u_1 + (n-1)d$
$= 10 + 6(n-1)$
$= 6n + 4$

Our proposition is:

$\frac{1}{2 \times 5} + \frac{1}{5 \times 8} + \frac{1}{8 \times 11} + \frac{1}{11 \times 14} + ... + \frac{1}{(3n-1)(3n+2)} = \frac{n}{6n+4}$ for all $n \in \mathbb{Z}^+$

{2, 5, 8, 11 are arithmetic with $u_1 = 2$, $d = 3$ $\therefore$ $u_n = 2 + (n-1)3 = 3n - 1$}

2 For $n = 1$ For $n = 2$ For $n = 3$

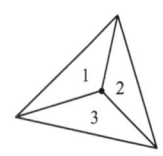

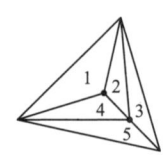

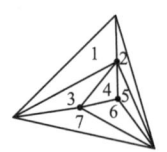

$T_1 = 3$ $T_2 = 5$ $T_3 = 7$
$= 2 \times 1 + 1$ $= 2 \times 2 + 1$ $= 2 \times 3 + 1$

Our proposition is:
The number of triangular partitions for n dots within the triangle is $T_n = 2n + 1$, $n \in \mathbb{Z}^+$.

EXERCISE 9B

1 a P_n is "$1 + 2 + 3 + 4 + ... + n = \frac{n(n+1)}{2}$" for all $n \in \mathbb{Z}^+$

Proof: (By the principle of mathematical induction)

(1) If $n = 1$, LHS $= 1$ and RHS $= \frac{1(2)}{2} = 1$, $\therefore$ P_1 is true

(2) If P_k is true then $1 + 2 + 3 + 4 + ... + k = \frac{k(k+1)}{2}$

Thus $1 + 2 + 3 + 4 + ... + k + (k+1)$

$= \frac{k(k+1)}{2} + k + 1$ {using P_k}

$= \frac{k(k+1)}{2} + \frac{2(k+1)}{2}$ {to equalise denominators}

$= \frac{(k+1)[k+2]}{2}$ {common factor of $\frac{(k+1)}{2}$}

$= \frac{(k+1)([k+1]+1)}{2}$

Thus P_{k+1} is true whenever P_k is true and P_1 is true
$\therefore$ P_n is true for all $n \in \mathbb{Z}^+$ {Principle of mathematical induction}

b P_n is "$1 \times 2 + 2 \times 3 + 3 \times 4 + \ldots\ldots + n(n+1) = \dfrac{n(n+1)(n+2)}{3}$" for all $n \in \mathbb{Z}^+$

Proof: (By the principle of mathematical induction)

(1) If $n = 1$, LHS $= 1 \times 2 = 2$ and RHS $= \dfrac{1(2)(3)}{3} = 2$, $\therefore$ P_1 is true

(2) If P_k is true then
$$1 \times 2 + 2 \times 3 + 3 \times 4 + \ldots\ldots + k(k+1) = \dfrac{k(k+1)(k+2)}{3}$$
$\therefore$ $1 \times 2 + 2 \times 3 + 3 \times 4 + \ldots\ldots + k(k+1) + (k+1)(k+2)$

$= \dfrac{k(k+1)(k+2)}{3} + (k+1)(k+2)$ \qquad {using P_k}

$= \dfrac{k(k+1)(k+2)}{3} + \dfrac{3(k+1)(k+2)}{3}$ \qquad {to equalise denominators}

$= \dfrac{(k+1)(k+2)[k+3]}{3}$ \qquad {common factor of $(k+1)(k+2)$}

$= \dfrac{[k+1]([k+1]+1)([k+1]+2)}{3}$

Thus P_{k+1} is true whenever P_k is true and P_1 is true
$\therefore$ P_n is true for all $n \in \mathbb{Z}^+$ \quad {Principle of mathematical induction}

c P_n is "$3 \times 5 + 6 \times 6 + 9 \times 7 + 12 \times 8 + \ldots\ldots + 3n(n+4) = \dfrac{n(n+1)(2n+13)}{2}$"
for all $n \in \mathbb{Z}^+$

Proof: (By the principle of mathematical induction)

(1) If $n = 1$, LHS $= 3 \times 5 = 15$, RHS $= \dfrac{1 \times 2 \times (2+13)}{2} = 15$, $\therefore$ P_1 is true

(2) If P_k is true, then
$$3 \times 5 + 6 \times 6 + 9 \times 7 + \ldots\ldots + 3k(k+4) = \dfrac{k(k+1)(2k+13)}{2}$$

Now $3 \times 5 + 6 \times 6 + 9 \times 7 + \ldots\ldots + 3k(k+4) + 3(k+1)(k+5)$

$= \dfrac{k(k+1)(2k+13)}{2} + 3(k+1)(k+5)$ \qquad {using P_k}

$= \dfrac{k(k+1)(2k+13)}{2} + \dfrac{6(k+1)(k+5)}{2}$ \qquad {to equalise denominators}

$= \dfrac{(k+1)[k(2k+13) + 6(k+5)]}{2}$ \qquad {common factor}

$= \dfrac{(k+1)[2k^2 + 19k + 30]}{2}$

$= \dfrac{(k+1)(k+2)(2k+15)}{2}$

$= \dfrac{(k+1)([k+1]+1)(2[k+1]+13)}{2}$

Thus P_{k+1} is true whenever P_k is true and P_1 is true
$\therefore$ P_n is true for all $n \in \mathbb{Z}^+$ \quad {Principle of mathematical induction}

d P_n is "$1^3 + 2^3 + 3^3 + 4^3 + \ldots\ldots + n^3 = \dfrac{n^2(n+1)^2}{4}$" for all $n \in \mathbb{Z}^+$

Proof: (By the principle of mathematical induction)

(1) If $n = 1$, LHS $= 1^3 = 1$, RHS $= \dfrac{1^2(2)^2}{4} = 1$ $\therefore$ P_1 is true

(2) If P_k is true, then $1^3 + 2^3 + 3^3 + \ldots\ldots + k^3 = \dfrac{k^2(k+1)^2}{4}$

Now $1^3 + 2^3 + 3^3 + \ldots\ldots + k^3 + (k+1)^3$

$= \dfrac{k^2(k+1)^2}{4} + (k+1)^3 \qquad$ {using P_k}

$= \dfrac{k^2(k+1)^2}{4} + \dfrac{4(k+1)^3}{4} \qquad$ {equalising denominators}

$= \dfrac{(k+1)^2[k^2 + 4(k+1)]}{4} \qquad$ {common factor}

$= \dfrac{(k+1)^2[k^2 + 4k + 4]}{4}$

$= \dfrac{(k+1)^2(k+2)^2}{4} \qquad$ Thus P_{k+1} is true whenever P_k is true and P_1 is true

$\therefore$ P_n is true for all $n \in \mathbb{Z}^+$ {Principle of mathematical induction}

2 P_n is "$1 \times 2^0 + 2 \times 2 + 3 \times 2^2 + 4 \times 2^3 + \ldots\ldots + n \times 2^{n-1} = (n-1) \times 2^n + 1$" for all $n \in \mathbb{Z}^+$

Proof: (By the principle of mathematical induction)

(1) If $n = 1$, LHS $= 1$, RHS $= (0)2^0 + 1 = 1$, $\therefore$ P_1 is true

(2) If P_k is true, then

$1 \times 2^0 + 2 \times 2 + 3 \times 2^2 + 4 \times 2^3 + \ldots\ldots + k \times 2^{k-1} = (k-1)2^k + 1$

Now $1 \times 2^0 + 2 \times 2 + 3 \times 2^2 + 4 \times 2^3 \ldots\ldots + k\, 2^{k-1} + (k+1)2^k$

$= (k-1)2^k + 1 + (k+1)2^k \qquad$ {using P_k}

$= 2^k[k-1+k+1] + 1$

$= 2^k[2k] + 1 \qquad$ Thus P_{k+1} is true whenever P_k is true and P_1 is true

$= k\,2^{k+1} + 1 \qquad \therefore$ P_n is true for all $n \in \mathbb{Z}^+$ {Principle of mathematical induction}

3 a P_n is "$\dfrac{1}{1 \times 2} + \dfrac{1}{2 \times 3} + \dfrac{1}{3 \times 4} + \ldots\ldots + \dfrac{1}{n(n+1)} = \dfrac{n}{n+1}$" for all $n \in \mathbb{Z}^+$

Proof: (By the principle of mathematical induction)

(1) If $n = 1$, LHS $= \dfrac{1}{1 \times 2} = \dfrac{1}{2}$, RHS $= \dfrac{1}{1+1} = \dfrac{1}{2}$ $\therefore$ P_1 is true

(2) If P_k is true, then $\dfrac{1}{1 \times 2} + \dfrac{1}{2 \times 3} + \dfrac{1}{3 \times 4} + \ldots\ldots + \dfrac{1}{k(k+1)} = \dfrac{k}{k+1}$

Now $\dfrac{1}{1 \times 2} + \dfrac{1}{2 \times 3} + \dfrac{1}{3 \times 4} + \ldots\ldots + \dfrac{1}{k(k+1)} + \dfrac{1}{(k+1)(k+2)}$

$= \dfrac{k}{k+1} + \dfrac{1}{(k+1)(k+2)} \qquad$ {using P_k}

$= \dfrac{k}{k+1}\left(\dfrac{k+2}{k+2}\right) + \dfrac{1}{(k+1)(k+2)} \qquad$ {equalising denominators}

$= \dfrac{k(k+2) + 1}{(k+1)(k+2)}$

$= \dfrac{k^2 + 2k + 1}{(k+1)(k+2)}$

$= \dfrac{(k+1)^2}{(k+1)(k+2)}$

$= \dfrac{k+1}{k+2}$

$= \dfrac{k+1}{[k+1]+1} \qquad$ Thus P_{k+1} is true whenever P_k is true and P_1 is true

$\therefore$ P_n is true for all $n \in \mathbb{Z}^+$ {Principle of mathematical induction}

So, $\dfrac{1}{10 \times 11} + \dfrac{1}{11 \times 12} + \dfrac{1}{12 \times 13} + \ldots\ldots + \dfrac{1}{20 \times 21} = S_{20} - S_9 = \dfrac{20}{21} - \dfrac{9}{10} = \dfrac{11}{210}$

b P_n is "$\dfrac{1}{1 \times 2 \times 3} + \dfrac{1}{2 \times 3 \times 4} + \dfrac{1}{3 \times 4 \times 5} + \ldots\ldots + \dfrac{1}{n(n+1)(n+2)} = \dfrac{n(n+3)}{4(n+1)(n+2)}$"
for all $n \in \mathbb{Z}^+$

Proof: (By the principle of mathematical induction)

(1) If $n = 1$, LHS $= \dfrac{1}{1 \times 2 \times 3} = \dfrac{1}{6}$, RHS $= \dfrac{1(4)}{4(2)(3)} = \dfrac{1}{6}$ $\therefore$ P_1 is true

(2) If P_k is true, then

$$\dfrac{1}{1 \times 2 \times 3} + \dfrac{1}{2 \times 3 \times 4} + \dfrac{1}{3 \times 4 \times 5} + \ldots + \dfrac{1}{k(k+1)(k+2)} = \dfrac{k(k+3)}{4(k+1)(k+2)}$$

Now $\dfrac{1}{1 \times 2 \times 3} + \dfrac{1}{2 \times 3 \times 4} + \dfrac{1}{3 \times 4 \times 5} + \ldots + \dfrac{1}{k(k+1)(k+2)} + \dfrac{1}{(k+1)(k+2)(k+3)}$

$= \dfrac{k(k+3)}{4(k+1)(k+2)} + \dfrac{1}{(k+1)(k+2)(k+3)}$ {using P_k}

$= \dfrac{k(k+3)}{4(k+1)(k+2)} \left(\dfrac{k+3}{k+3}\right) + \dfrac{4}{4(k+1)(k+2)(k+3)}$ {equalising denominators}

$= \dfrac{k(k+3)^2 + 4}{4(k+1)(k+2)(k+3)}$

$= \dfrac{k(k^2 + 6k + 9) + 4}{4(k+1)(k+2)(k+3)}$

$= \dfrac{k^3 + 6k^2 + 9k + 4}{4(k+1)(k+2)(k+3)} \quad \begin{array}{r|rrrr} -1 & 1 & 6 & 9 & 4 \\ & 0 & -1 & -5 & -4 \\ \hline & 1 & 5 & 4 & 0 \end{array}$

$= \dfrac{(k+1)(k^2 + 5k + 4)}{4(k+1)(k+2)(k+3)}$

$= \dfrac{(k+1)(k+4)}{4(k+2)(k+3)}$ Thus P_{k+1} is true whenever P_k is true and P_1 is true
$\therefore$ P_n is true for all $n \in \mathbb{Z}^+$ {Principle of mathematical induction}

4 a P_n is "$1 \times 1! + 2 \times 2! + 3 \times 3! + \ldots\ldots + n \times n! = (n+1)! - 1$" for all $n \in \mathbb{Z}^+$

Proof: (By the principle of mathematical induction)

(1) If $n = 1$, LHS $= 1 \times 1!$ RHS $= 2! - 1$
$ = 1 \times 1 = 2 - 1$
$ = 1 = 1$ $\therefore$ P_1 is true

(2) If P_k is true, then $1 \times 1! + 2 \times 2! + 3 \times 3! + \ldots\ldots + k \times k! = (k+1)! - 1$
Now $\quad 1 \times 1! + 2 \times 2! + 3 \times 3! + \ldots\ldots + k \times k! + (k+1)(k+1)!$
$= (k+1)! - 1 + (k+1)(k+1)!$ {using P_k}
$= (k+1)![1 + k + 1] - 1$
$= (k+1)!(k+2) - 1$ Thus P_{k+1} is true whenever P_k is true and P_1 is true
$= (k+2)! - 1$ $\therefore$ P_n is true for all $n \in \mathbb{Z}^+$ {Principle of mathematical induction}

b P_n is "$\dfrac{1}{2!} + \dfrac{2}{3!} + \dfrac{3}{4!} + \ldots\ldots + \dfrac{n}{(n+1)!} = \dfrac{(n+1)! - 1}{(n+1)!}$" for all $n \in \mathbb{Z}^+$

Proof: (By the principle of mathematical induction)

(1) If $n = 1$, LHS $= \dfrac{1}{2!} = \dfrac{1}{2}$, RHS $= \dfrac{2! - 1}{2!} = \dfrac{2 - 1}{2} = \dfrac{1}{2}$ $\therefore$ P_1 is true

(2) If P_k is true, then $\dfrac{1}{2!} + \dfrac{2}{3!} + \dfrac{3}{4!} + \ldots\ldots + \dfrac{k}{(k+1)!} = \dfrac{(k+1)! - 1}{(k+1)!}$

Now $\quad \dfrac{1}{2!} + \dfrac{2}{3!} + \dfrac{3}{4!} + \ldots\ldots + \dfrac{k}{(k+1)!} + \dfrac{k+1}{(k+2)!}$

$= \dfrac{(k+1)! - 1}{(k+1)!} + \dfrac{k+1}{(k+2)!}$ {using P_k}

$$= \left(\frac{k+2}{k+2}\right)\left[\frac{(k+1)!-1}{(k+1)!}\right] + \frac{k+1}{(k+2)!} \quad \text{\{equalising denominators\}}$$

$$= \frac{(k+2)! - (k+2) + k + 1}{(k+2)!}$$

$$= \frac{(k+2)! - k - 2 + k + 1}{(k+2)!}$$

$$= \frac{(k+2)! - 1}{(k+2)!}$$

Thus P_{k+1} is true whenever P_k is true and P_1 is true

∴ P_n is true for all $n \in \mathbb{Z}^+$ \{Principle of mathematical induction\}

and $\dfrac{1}{2!} + \dfrac{2}{3!} + \dfrac{3}{4!} + \ldots\ldots + \dfrac{9}{10!} = \dfrac{10! - 1}{10!} = \dfrac{3\,628\,799}{3\,628\,800}$

5 P_n is "$1 \times n + 2 \times (n-1) + 3 \times (n-2) + \ldots\ldots + (n-1) \times 2 + n \times 1 = \dfrac{n(n+1)(n+2)}{6}$"

for all $n \in \mathbb{Z}^+$

Proof: (By the principle of mathematical induction)

(1) If $n = 1$, LHS $= 1 \times 1 = 1$, RHS $= \dfrac{1(2)(3)}{6} = 1$ ∴ P_1 is true

(2) If P_k is true, then $1 \times k + 2(k-1) + 3(k-2) + \ldots\ldots + (k-1)2 + k \times 1 = \dfrac{k(k+1)(k+2)}{6}$

Now $1(k+1) + 2(k) + 3(k-1) + \ldots\ldots + k2 + (k+1)1$

$= 1(k) + 2(k-1) + 3(k-2) + \ldots\ldots + k1 + 1 + 2 + 3 + \ldots\ldots + k + k + 1$

\{using the hint\}

$= \dfrac{k(k+1)(k+2)}{6} + \dfrac{(k+1)(k+2)}{2}$ \{using P_k and the sum of an arithmetic series\}

$= \dfrac{k(k+1)(k+2)}{6} + \dfrac{3(k+1)(k+2)}{6}$ \{equalising denominators\}

$= \dfrac{(k+1)(k+2)[k+3]}{6}$

Thus P_{k+1} is true whenever P_k is true and P_1 is true

∴ P_n is true for all $n \in \mathbb{Z}^+$ \{Principle of mathematical induction\}

6 a P_n is "$n^3 + 2n$ is divisible by 3" for all $n \in \mathbb{Z}^+$

Proof: (By the principle of mathematical induction)

(1) If $n = 1$, $1^3 + 2(1) = 3$ which is divisible by 3

(2) If P_k is true, then $k^3 + 2k = 3A$ where $A \in \mathbb{Z}$

Now $(k+1)^3 + 2(k+1)$

$= k^3 + 3k^2 + 3k + 1 + 2k + 2$

$= (k^3 + 2k) + 3k^2 + 3k + 3$

$= 3A + 3k^2 + 3k + 3$ \{using P_k\}

$= 3[A + k^2 + k + 1]$ where $A + k^2 + k + 1$ is an integer

as A and k are integers

∴ $(k+1)^3 + 2(k+1)$ is divisible by 3

Thus P_{k+1} is true whenever P_k is true and P_1 is true

∴ P_n is true for all $n \in \mathbb{Z}^+$ \{Principle of mathematical induction\}

b P_n is "$n(n^2 + 5)$ is divisible by 6" for all $n \in \mathbb{Z}^+$
   Proof: (By the principle of mathematical induction)
   (1) If $n = 1$, $1(1^2 + 5) = 1 \times 6 = 6$ which is divisible by 6 $\therefore$ P_1 is true
   (2) If P_k is true, then $k(k^2 + 5) = 6A$ where A is an integer
   Now $(k + 1)[(k + 1)^2 + 5] = (k + 1)(k^2 + 2k + 1 + 5)$
   $= (k + 1)(k^2 + 2k + 6)$
   $= k^3 + 2k^2 + 6k + k^2 + 2k + 6$
   $= k^3 + 5k + [3k^2 + 3k + 6]$
   $= k(k^2 + 5) + 3k(k + 1) + 6$
   $= 6A + 6 + 3k(k + 1)$

   We notice that $k(k + 1)$ is the product of consecutive integers, one of which must be even $\therefore$ $k(k + 1) = 2B$ where $B \in \mathbb{Z}$
   $\therefore$ $(k + 1)[(k + 1)^2 + 5] = 6A + 6 + 3(2B)$
   $= 6(A + 1 + B)$ where $A + 1 + B \in \mathbb{Z}$
   $\therefore$ $(k + 1)[(k + 1)^2 + 5]$ is divisible by 6

   Thus P_{k+1} is true whenever P_k is true and P_1 is true
   $\therefore$ P_n is true for all $n \in \mathbb{Z}^+$ {Principle of mathematical induction}

c P_n is "$6^n - 1$ is divisible by 5" for all $n \in \mathbb{N}$
   Proof: (By the principle of mathematical induction)
   (1) If $n = 0$, $6^0 - 1 = 0$ which is divisible by 5 $\therefore$ P_0 is true
   (2) If P_k is true, then $6^k - 1 = 5A$ where $A \in \mathbb{N}$
   Now $6^{k+1} - 1$
   $= 6^k \times 6 - 1$
   $= 6[5A + 1] - 1$ {using P_k}
   $= 30A + 6 - 1$
   $= 30A + 5$
   $= 5(6A + 1)$ where $6A + 1 \in \mathbb{N}$
   So, $6^{k+1} - 1$ is divisible by 5

   Thus P_{k+1} is true whenever P_k is true and P_0 is true
   $\therefore$ P_n is true for all $n \in \mathbb{N}$ {Principle of mathematical induction}

d P_n is "$7^n - 4^n - 3^n$ is divisible by 12" for all $n \in \mathbb{Z}^+$
   Proof: (By the principle of mathematical induction)
   (1) If $n = 1$, $7^1 - 4^1 - 3^1 = 0$ which is divisible by 12 $\therefore$ P_1 is true
   (2) If P_k is true, then $7^k - 4^k - 3^k = 12A$ where $A \in \mathbb{Z}$
   Now $7^{k+1} - 4^{k+1} - 3^{k+1}$
   $= 7(7^k) - 4(4^k) - 3(3^k)$
   $= 7[12A + 4^k + 3^k] - 4(4^k) - 3(3^k)$ {using P_k}
   $= 84A + 7(4^k) + 7(3^k) - 4(4^k) - 3(3^k)$
   $= 84A + 3(4^k) + 4(3^k)$
   $= 84A + 3 \times 4 \times 4^{k-1} + 4 \times 3 \times 3^{k-1}$
   $= 12(7A + 4^{k-1} + 3^{k-1})$ where $k \geqslant 2$, $k \in \mathbb{Z}^+$
   $= 12 \times$ an integer {as 4^{k-1} and 3^{k-1} are integers}
   $\therefore$ $7^{k+1} - 4^{k+1} - 3^{k+1}$ is divisible by 12

   Thus P_{k+1} is true whenever P_k is true and P_1 is true
   $\therefore$ P_n is true for all $n \in \mathbb{Z}^+$ {Principle of mathematical induction}

7 **a** P_n is "if $u_1 = 5$ and $u_{n+1} = u_n + 8n + 5$ for all $n \in \mathbb{Z}^+$, then $u_n = 4n^2 + n$"
Proof: (By the principle of mathematical induction)
(1) If $n = 1$, $u_1 = 4(1)^2 + 1 = 5$ which is true and so P_1 is true.
(2) If P_k is true, then $u_k = 4k^2 + k$ and $u_{k+1} = u_k + 8k + 5$
$= 4k^2 + k + 8k + 5$ {using P_k}
$= 4(k^2 + 2k + 1) + k + 1$
$= 4(k+1)^2 + (k+1)$

$\therefore$ P_{k+1} is also true.
Thus, P_1 is true and P_{k+1} is true whenever P_k is true,
so P_n is true for all $n \in \mathbb{Z}^+$ {Principle of mathematical induction}

b P_n is "if $u_1 = 1$ and $u_{n+1} = 2 + 3u_n$ for all $n \in \mathbb{Z}^+$, then $u_n = 2(3^{n-1}) - 1$"
Proof: (By the principle of mathematical induction)
(1) If $n = 1$, $u_1 = 2(3^{1-1}) - 1 = 1$ which is true and so P_1 is true.
(2) If P_k is true, then $u_k = 2(3^{k-1}) - 1$ and $u_{k+1} = 2 + 3u_k$
$= 2 + 3(2[3^{k-1}] - 1)$ {using P_k}
$= 2 + 2 \times 3^k - 3$
$= 2(3^k) - 1$

$\therefore$ P_{k+1} is also true.
Thus, P_1 is true and P_{k+1} is true whenever P_k is true,
so P_n is true for all $n \in \mathbb{Z}^+$ {Principle of mathematical induction}

c P_n is "if $u_1 = 2$ and $u_{n+1} = \dfrac{u_n}{2(n+1)}$ for all $n \in \mathbb{Z}^+$, then $u_n = \dfrac{2^{2-n}}{n!}$"
Proof: (By the principle of mathematical induction)
(1) If $n = 1$, $u_1 = \dfrac{2^{2-1}}{1!} = 2^1 = 2$ which is true and so P_1 is true.
(2) If P_k is true, then $u_k = \dfrac{2^{2-k}}{k!}$ and $u_{k+1} = \dfrac{u_k}{2(k+1)} = \dfrac{2^{2-k}}{k!\, 2(k+1)}$ {using P_k}
$= \dfrac{2^{2-k-1}}{(k+1)k!}$
$= \dfrac{2^{2-(k+1)}}{(k+1)!}$

$\therefore$ P_{k+1} is also true.
Thus, P_1 is true and P_{k+1} is true whenever P_k is true,
so P_n is true for all $n \in \mathbb{Z}^+$ {Principle of mathematical induction}

d P_n is "if $u_1 = 1$ and $u_{n+1} = u_n + (-1)^n(n+1)^2$ for all $n \in \mathbb{Z}^+$,
then $u_n = \dfrac{(-1)^{n-1}n(n+1)}{2}$"
Proof: (By the principle of mathematical induction)
(1) If $n = 1$, $u_1 = \dfrac{(-1)^0 \times 1 \times 2}{2} = 1$ which is true and so P_1 is true.
(2) If P_k is true, then $u_k = \dfrac{(-1)^{k-1}k(k+1)}{2}$
and $u_{k+1} = u_k + (-1)^k(k+1)^2$
$= \dfrac{(-1)^{k-1}k(k+1)}{2} + (-1)^k(k+1)^2$ {using P_k}
$= \dfrac{(-1)^{k-1}k(k+1) + 2(-1)^k(k+1)^2}{2}$

$$= \frac{2(-1)^k(k+1)^2 - (-1)^k k(k+1)}{2}$$

$$= \frac{(-1)^k(k+1)[2(k+1)-k]}{2}$$

$$= \frac{(-1)^k(k+1)(k+2)}{2} \qquad \therefore \ P_{k+1} \text{ is also true.}$$

Thus, P_1 is true and P_{k+1} is true whenever P_k is true,
so P_n is true for all $n \in \mathbb{Z}^+$ {Principle of mathematical induction}

8 $u_1 = 1 = 1^2$
$u_2 = u_1 + 2(1) + 1 = 1 + 2 + 1 = 4 = 2^2$
$u_3 = u_2 + 2(2) + 1 = 4 + 4 + 1 = 9 = 3^2$
$u_4 = u_3 + 2(3) + 1 = 9 + 6 + 1 = 16 = 4^2$

We conjecture that $u_n = n^2$ for all $n \in \mathbb{Z}^+$

P_n is "if $u_1 = 1$ and $u_{n+1} = u_n + (2n+1)$ for all $n \in \mathbb{Z}^+$, then $u_n = n^2$"

Proof: (By the principle of mathematical induction)

(1) If $n = 1$, then $u_1 = 1 = 1^2$, so P_1 is true.

(2) If P_k is true, then $u_k = k^2$ and $u_{k+1} = u_k + (2k+1)$
$$= k^2 + 2k + 1 \quad \{\text{using } P_k\}$$
$$= (k+1)^2$$

$\therefore \ P_{k+1}$ is also true.

Thus, P_1 is true and P_{k+1} is true whenever P_k is true,
so P_n is true for all $n \in \mathbb{Z}^+$ {Principle of mathematical induction}

9 $u_1 = \frac{1}{3}$ $\quad u_2 = u_1 + \frac{1}{(2(1)+1)(2(1)+3)} = \frac{1}{3} + \frac{1}{3 \times 5} = \frac{5+1}{15} = \frac{6}{15} = \frac{2}{5}$

$u_3 = u_2 + \frac{1}{(2(2)+1)(2(2)+3)} = \frac{2}{5} + \frac{1}{5 \times 7} = \frac{14+1}{35} = \frac{15}{35} = \frac{3}{7}$

$u_4 = u_3 + \frac{1}{(2(3)+1)(2(3)+3)} = \frac{3}{7} + \frac{1}{7 \times 9} = \frac{27+1}{63} = \frac{28}{63} = \frac{4}{9}$

We conjecture that $u_n = \frac{n}{2n+1}$ for all $n \in \mathbb{Z}^+$

P_n is "if $u_1 = \frac{1}{3}$ and $u_{n+1} = u_n + \frac{1}{(2n+1)(2n+3)}$ for all $n \in \mathbb{Z}^+$, then $u_n = \frac{n}{2n+1}$"

Proof: (By the principle of mathematical induction)

(1) If $n = 1$, then $u_1 = \frac{1}{3} = \frac{1}{2(1)+1}$, so P_1 is true.

(2) If P_k is true, then $u_k = \frac{k}{2k+1}$

and $u_{k+1} = u_k + \frac{1}{(2k+1)(2k+3)}$

$$= \frac{k}{2k+1} + \frac{1}{(2k+1)(2k+3)} \quad \{\text{using } P_k\}$$

$$= \frac{k(2k+3)+1}{(2k+1)(2k+3)}$$

$$= \frac{2k^2+3k+1}{(2k+1)(2k+3)}$$

$$= \frac{\cancel{(2k+1)}(k+1)}{\cancel{(2k+1)}(2k+3)}$$

$$= \frac{k+1}{2(k+1)+1}$$

$\therefore \ P_{k+1}$ is also true.

Thus, P_1 is true and P_{k+1} is true whenever P_k is true, so P_n is true for all $n \in \mathbb{Z}^+$.

{Principle of mathematical induction}

10 **a** $(2+\sqrt{3})^1 = 2+\sqrt{3}$ $\qquad \therefore \quad A_1 = 2, \; B_1 = 1$

$(2+\sqrt{3})^2 = 4 + 4\sqrt{3} + 3$
$= 7 + 4\sqrt{3} \qquad \therefore \quad A_2 = 7, \; B_2 = 4$

$(2+\sqrt{3})^3 = (7+4\sqrt{3})(2+\sqrt{3})$
$= 14 + 7\sqrt{3} + 8\sqrt{3} + 4(3)$
$= 26 + 15\sqrt{3} \qquad \therefore \quad A_3 = 26, \; B_3 = 15$

$(2+\sqrt{3})^4 = (7+4\sqrt{3})^2$
$= 49 + 56\sqrt{3} + 16(3)$
$= 97 + 56\sqrt{3} \qquad \therefore \quad A_4 = 97, \; B_4 = 56$

b $(2+\sqrt{3})^n = A_n + B_n\sqrt{3}$

$\therefore \quad (2+\sqrt{3})^{n+1} = (2+\sqrt{3})^n (2+\sqrt{3})$
$= (A_n + B_n\sqrt{3})(2+\sqrt{3})$
$= 2A_n + A_n\sqrt{3} + 2B_n\sqrt{3} + B_n(3)$
$= 2A_n + 3B_n + (A_n + 2B_n)\sqrt{3}$

$\therefore \quad A_{n+1} = 2A_n + 3B_n, \quad B_{n+1} = A_n + 2B_n$

c $A_1^2 - 3B_1^2 = 2^2 - 3(1)^2 = 4 - 3 = 1$
$A_2^2 - 3B_2^2 = 7^2 - 3(4)^2 = 49 - 3 \times 16 = 1$
$A_3^2 - 3B_3^2 = 26^2 - 3(15)^2 = 676 - 3 \times 225 = 1$
$A_4^2 - 3B_4^2 = 97^2 - 3(56)^2 = 9409 - 3 \times 3136 = 1$

$\therefore$ we conjecture $(A_n)^2 - 3(B_n)^2 = 1$ for all $n \in \mathbb{Z}^+$

d P_n is "if $(2+\sqrt{3})^n = A_n + B_n\sqrt{3}$ for all $n \in \mathbb{Z}^+$, then $A_n^2 - 3B_n^2 = 1$"

Proof: (By the principle of mathematical induction)

(1) If $n = 1$, $A_1 = 2$, $B_1 = 1$, and $A_1^2 - 3B_1^2 = 2^2 - 3(1)^2 = 1$, so P_1 is true.

(2) If P_k is true, then $A_k^2 - 3B_k^2 = 1$, and
$A_{k+1}^2 - 3B_{k+1}^2 = (2A_k + 3B_k)^2 - 3(A_k + 2B_k)^2 \quad \{\text{using } \textbf{b}\}$
$= 4A_k^2 + 12A_kB_k + 9B_k^2 - 3(A_k^2 + 4A_kB_k + 4B_k^2)$
$= 4A_k^2 + \cancel{12A_kB_k} + 9B_k^2 - 3A_k^2 - \cancel{12A_kB_k} - 12B_k^2$
$= A_k^2 - 3B_k^2$
$= 1 \quad \{\text{using } P_k\}$

$\therefore \quad P_{k+1}$ is true.
Thus, P_1 is true and P_{k+1} is true whenever P_k is true,
so P_n is true for all $n \in \mathbb{Z}^+$ {Principle of mathematical induction}

11 P_n is "$\dfrac{2^n - (-1)^n}{3}$ is an odd number" for all $n \in \mathbb{Z}^+$

Proof: (By the principle of mathematical induction)

(1) If $n = 1$, $\dfrac{2^1 - (-1)^1}{3} = \dfrac{3}{3} = 1$ which is odd $\therefore \; P_1$ is true

(2) If P_k is true, then $\dfrac{2^k - (-1)^k}{3} = 2A + 1$ where $A \in \mathbb{Z}$

Now $\dfrac{2^{k+1} - (-1)^{k+1}}{3} = \dfrac{2(2^k) - (-1)^{k+1}}{3}$

$= \dfrac{2[6A + 3 + (-1)^k] - (-1)^{k+1}}{3} \quad \{\text{using } P_k\}$

$$= \frac{12A + 6 + 2(-1)^k - (-1)(-1)^k}{3}$$
$$= \frac{12A + 6 + 2(-1)^k + (-1)^k}{3}$$
$$= \frac{12A + 6 + 3(-1)^k}{3}$$
$$= 4A + 2 + (-1)^k$$

Now $4A + 2$ is always even and $(-1)^k$ is either $+1$ or -1

∴ $4A + 2 + (-1)^k$ is odd

∴ $\dfrac{2^{k+1} - (-1)^{k+1}}{3}$ is odd

Thus P_{k+1} is true whenever P_k is true and P_1 is true

∴ P_n is true for all $n \in \mathbb{Z}^+$ {Principle of mathematical induction}

12 a P_n is "if $u_1 = 11$, $u_2 = 37$ and $u_{n+2} = 5u_{n+1} - 6u_n$ for all $n \in \mathbb{Z}^+$, then $u_n = 5(3^n) - 2^{n+1}$"

Proof: (By the principle of mathematical induction)

(1) If $n = 1$, $5(3^1) - 2^{1+1} = 15 - 2^2 = 11 = u_1$, so P_1 is true.

If $n = 2$, $5(3^2) - 2^{2+1} = 5 \times 9 - 2^3 = 37 = u_2$, so P_2 is true.

(2) If P_k and P_{k+1} are true, then $u_k = 5(3^k) - 2^{k+1}$ and $u_{k+1} = 5(3^{k+1}) - 2^{k+2}$

and $u_{k+2} = 5u_{k+1} - 6u_k$
$$= 5[5(3^{k+1}) - 2^{k+2}] - 6[5(3^k) - 2^{k+1}] \quad \{\text{using } P_k \text{ and } P_{k+1}\}$$
$$= 25(3^{k+1}) - 5(2^{k+2}) - 30(3^k) + 6(2^{k+1})$$
$$= 25(3^{k+1}) - 5(2^{k+2}) - 10(3^{k+1}) + 3(2^{k+2})$$
$$= 15(3^{k+1}) - 2(2^{k+2})$$
$$= 5(3^{k+2}) - 2^{k+3}$$

∴ P_{k+2} is true.

Thus, P_1 and P_2 are true, and P_{k+2} is true whenever P_k and P_{k+1} are true, so P_n is true for all $n \in \mathbb{Z}^+$ {Principle of mathematical induction}

b $u_{n+2} = au_{n+1} + bu_n$

∴ $(3 + \sqrt{5})^{n+2} + (3 - \sqrt{5})^{n+2} = a\left[(3 + \sqrt{5})^{n+1} + (3 - \sqrt{5})^{n+1}\right]$
$$+ b\left[(3 + \sqrt{5})^n + (3 - \sqrt{5})^n\right]$$

∴ $(3 + \sqrt{5})^2 (3 + \sqrt{5})^n + (3 - \sqrt{5})^2 (3 - \sqrt{5})^n = a[(3 + \sqrt{5})(3 + \sqrt{5})^n$
$$+ (3 - \sqrt{5})(3 - \sqrt{5})^n]$$
$$+ b\left[(3 + \sqrt{5})^n + (3 - \sqrt{5})^n\right]$$

∴ $(14 + 6\sqrt{5})(3 + \sqrt{5})^n + (14 - 6\sqrt{5})(3 - \sqrt{5})^n = (3a + a\sqrt{5})(3 + \sqrt{5})^n$
$$+ (3a - a\sqrt{5})(3 - \sqrt{5})^n$$
$$+ b(3 + \sqrt{5})^n + b(3 - \sqrt{5})^n$$

∴ $(14 + 6\sqrt{5})(3 + \sqrt{5})^n + (14 - 6\sqrt{5})(3 - \sqrt{5})^n = (3a + b + a\sqrt{5})(3 + \sqrt{5})^n$
$$+ (3a + b - a\sqrt{5})(3 - \sqrt{5})^n$$

Equating coefficients of $(3 + \sqrt{5})^n$, $14 + 6\sqrt{5} = 3a + b + a\sqrt{5}$

Equating rational and irrational parts,

$3a + b = 14$ and $a = 6$

∴ $a = 6$ and $b = -4$ {this checks with the coefficients of $(3 - \sqrt{5})^n$}

∴ $u_{n+2} = 6u_{n+1} - 4u_n$

P_n is "if $u_n = (3+\sqrt{5})^n + (3-\sqrt{5})^n$ where $n \in \mathbb{Z}^+$, then u_n is a multiple of 2^n"

Proof: (By the principle of mathematical induction)

(1) If $n = 1$, $u_1 = (3+\sqrt{5}) + (3-\sqrt{5})$
$= 6$ which is a multiple of $2^1 = 2$, so P_1 is true.

If $n = 2$, $u_2 = (3+\sqrt{5})^2 + (3-\sqrt{5})^2$
$= 9 + 6\sqrt{5} + 5 + 9 - 6\sqrt{5} + 5$
$= 28$ which is a multiple of $2^2 = 4$, so P_2 is true.

(2) If P_k and P_{k+1} are true, then $u_k = A \times 2^k$, where $A \in \mathbb{Z}$
and $u_{k+1} = B \times 2^{k+1}$, where $B \in \mathbb{Z}$

Now $u_{k+2} = 6u_{k+1} - 4u_k$ {using the above result}
$= 6(B \times 2^{k+1}) - 4(A \times 2^k)$
$= 3B \times 2^{k+2} - A \times 2^{k+2}$
$= (3B - A) \times 2^{k+2}$

which is a multiple of 2^{k+2} since $3B - A \in \mathbb{Z}$ {as $A, B \in \mathbb{Z}$}
$\therefore$ P_{k+2} is true.

Thus P_1 and P_2 are true, and P_{k+2} is true whenever P_k and P_{k+1} are true, so P_n is true for all $n \in \mathbb{Z}^+$ {Principle of mathematical induction}

13 a P_n is "$\left(1-\frac{1}{2}\right)\left(1-\frac{1}{3}\right)\left(1-\frac{1}{4}\right)\ldots\ldots\left(1-\frac{1}{n+1}\right) = \frac{1}{n+1}$" for all $n \in \mathbb{Z}^+$

Proof: (By the principle of mathematical induction)

(1) If $n = 1$, LHS $= \left(1-\frac{1}{2}\right) = \frac{1}{2}$, RHS $= \frac{1}{1+1} = \frac{1}{2}$ $\therefore$ P_1 is true

(2) If P_k is true, then $\left(1-\frac{1}{2}\right)\left(1-\frac{1}{3}\right)\left(1-\frac{1}{4}\right)\ldots\ldots\left(1-\frac{1}{k+1}\right) = \frac{1}{k+1}$

$\therefore$ $\left(1-\frac{1}{2}\right)\left(1-\frac{1}{3}\right)\left(1-\frac{1}{4}\right)\ldots\ldots\left(1-\frac{1}{k+1}\right)\left(1-\frac{1}{k+2}\right)$

$= \frac{1}{k+1}\left(1-\frac{1}{k+2}\right)$ {using P_k}

$= \frac{1}{k+1}\left(\frac{k+2-1}{k+2}\right)$

$= \frac{1}{k+1}\left(\frac{k+1}{k+2}\right)$

$= \frac{1}{k+2}$

Thus P_{k+1} is true when ever P_k is true and P_1 is true
$\therefore$ P_n is true for all $n \in \mathbb{Z}^+$ {Principle of mathematical induction}

b

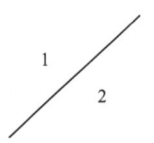

1 line, $R_1 = 2$ 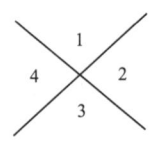   2 lines, $R_2 = 4$ 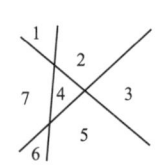   3 lines, $R_3 = 7$, and so on.

P_n is "For n lines as described, $R_n = \dfrac{n(n+1)}{2} + 1$" for all $n \in \mathbb{Z}^+$

Proof: (By the principle of mathematical induction)

(1) If $n = 1$, $R_1 = \dfrac{1(2)}{2} + 1 = 1 + 1 = 2$ $\therefore$ P_1 is true

(2) If P_k is true, then $R_k = \dfrac{k(k+1)}{2} + 1$

The addition of another line creates another $k+1$ regions

$\therefore \quad R_{k+1} = \dfrac{k(k+1)}{2} + 1 + k + 1 \qquad \{\text{using } P_k\}$

$= \dfrac{k(k+1)}{2} + \dfrac{2(k+1)}{2} + 1$

$= \dfrac{k^2 + k + 2k + 2}{2} + 1$

$= \dfrac{k^2 + 3k + 2}{2} + 1$

$= \dfrac{(k+1)(k+2)}{2} + 1$

Thus P_{k+1} is true whenever P_k is true and P_1 is true
$\therefore \quad P_n$ is true for all $n \in \mathbb{Z}^+$ {Principle of mathematical induction}

c

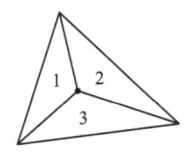

$n = 1, \; T_1 = 3 \qquad\qquad n = 2, \; T_2 = 5$

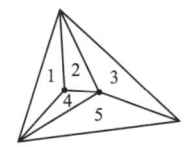

P_n is "For n points inside the triangle (as described) there are $T_n = 2n + 1$ triangular partitions" for all $n \in \mathbb{Z}^+$.

Proof: (By the principle of mathematical induction)

(1) If $n = 1$, $T_1 = 2(1) + 1 = 3 \quad \therefore \quad P_1$ is true

(2) If P_k is true, then $T_k = 2k + 1$
Adding an extra point within the triangle gives the $k + 1^{\text{th}}$ case.
This point could be either

- in an existing triangle or - on an existing line between 2 triangles

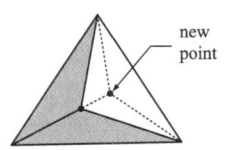

So, 1 triangle becomes 3, a net increase of 2.
So, 2 triangles become 4, a net increase of 2. 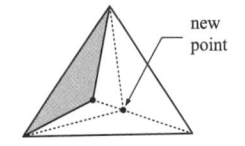

In each case 2 triangles are added

$\therefore \quad T_{k+1} = T_k + 2$

$= 2k + 1 + 2 \qquad \{\text{using } P_k\}$

$= 2(k+1) + 1$

Thus P_{k+1} is true whenever P_k is true and P_1 is true
$\therefore \quad P_n$ is true for all $n \in \mathbb{Z}^+$ {Principle of mathematical induction}

d P_n is "$\left(1 - \dfrac{1}{2^2}\right)\left(1 - \dfrac{1}{3^2}\right)\left(1 - \dfrac{1}{4^2}\right) \ldots \left(1 - \dfrac{1}{n^2}\right) = \dfrac{n+1}{2n}$" for all $n \geqslant 2$, $n \in \mathbb{Z}$.

Proof: (By the principle of mathematical induction)

(1) If $n = 2$, LHS $= 1 - \dfrac{1}{2^2}\qquad$ RHS $= \dfrac{2+1}{2(2)}$

$= 1 - \dfrac{1}{4}\qquad\qquad\quad = \dfrac{3}{4}\quad \therefore \quad P_2$ is true

$= \dfrac{3}{4}$

(2) If P_k is true, then $\left(1 - \dfrac{1}{2^2}\right)\left(1 - \dfrac{1}{3^2}\right)\left(1 - \dfrac{1}{4^2}\right)\ldots\left(1 - \dfrac{1}{k^2}\right) = \dfrac{k+1}{2k}$

Now $\left(1 - \dfrac{1}{2^2}\right)\left(1 - \dfrac{1}{3^2}\right)\left(1 - \dfrac{1}{4^2}\right)\ldots\left(1 - \dfrac{1}{k^2}\right)\left(1 - \dfrac{1}{(k+1)^2}\right)$

$= \dfrac{k+1}{2k}\left(1 - \dfrac{1}{(k+1)^2}\right)$ {using P_k}

$= \dfrac{k+1}{2k}\left(\dfrac{(k+1)^2 - 1}{(k+1)^2}\right)$

$= \dfrac{k+1}{2k}\left(\dfrac{k^2 + 2k + 1 - 1}{(k+1)^2}\right)$

$= \dfrac{k^2 + 2k}{2k(k+1)}$

$= \dfrac{k(k+2)}{2k(k+1)}$

$= \dfrac{k+2}{2(k+1)}$

Thus P_{k+1} is true whenever P_k is true and P_2 is true.

$\therefore\ P_n$ is true for all $n \geqslant 2$, $n \in \mathbb{Z}$ {Principle of mathematical induction}

14 a P_n is "$3^n \geqslant 1 + 2n$" for $n \in \mathbb{Z}$, $n \geqslant 0$

Proof: (By the principle of mathematical induction)

(1) If $n = 0$, we have $3^0 \geqslant 1 + 2(0)$

$\therefore\ 1 \geqslant 1$ which is true $\therefore\ P_0$ is true

(2) If P_k is true, then $3^k \geqslant 1 + 2k$

Now $3^{k+1} = 3^k \times 3$

$\geqslant (1 + 2k) \times 3$ {using P_k}

$\geqslant 3 + 6k$

$\geqslant 3 + 2k$ $\{k \geqslant 0\}$

$\geqslant 1 + 2(k+1)$

$\therefore\ P_{k+1}$ is true.

Thus P_0 is true and P_{k+1} is true whenever P_k is true, so P_n is true for all $n \in \mathbb{Z}$, $n \geqslant 0$ {Principle of mathematical induction}

b P_n is "$n! \geqslant 2^n$" for $n \in \mathbb{Z}$, $n \geqslant 4$

Proof: (By the principle of mathematical induction)

(1) If $n = 4$, we have $4! \geqslant 2^4$

$\therefore\ 24 \geqslant 16$ which is true $\therefore\ P_4$ is true

(2) If P_k is true then $k! \geqslant 2^k$

Now $(k+1)! = (k+1) \times k!$

$\geqslant (k+1) \times 2^k$ {using P_k}

$\geqslant 2 \times 2^k$ $\{k \geqslant 4\}$

$\geqslant 2^{k+1}$

$\therefore\ P_{k+1}$ is true.

Thus P_4 is true and P_{k+1} is true whenever P_k is true, so P_n is true for all $n \in \mathbb{Z}$, $n \geqslant 4$ {Principle of mathematical induction}

c P_n is "$8^n \geqslant n^3$" for $n \in \mathbb{Z}^+$

Proof: (By the principle of mathematical induction)

(1) If $n = 1$, we have $8^1 \geqslant 1^3$

$\therefore\ 8 \geqslant 1$ which is true, so P_1 is true

(2) If P_k is true then $8^k \geqslant k^3$

$$\begin{aligned}
\text{Now } 8^{k+1} &= 8 \times 8^k \\
&\geqslant 8 \times k^3 \quad \{\text{using } P_k\} \\
&\geqslant (2k)^3 \quad \{k \geqslant 4\} \\
&\geqslant (k+1)^3 \quad \{k \geqslant 1, \text{ so } 2k \geqslant k+1\}
\end{aligned}$$

$\therefore$ P_{k+1} is true.
Thus P_1 is true and P_{k+1} is true whenever P_k is true,
so P_n is true for all $n \in \mathbb{Z}^+$ {Principle of mathematical induction}

d P_n is "$(1-h)^n \leqslant \dfrac{1}{1+nh}$ for $0 \leqslant h \leqslant 1$" for $n \in \mathbb{Z}^+$

Proof: (By the principle of mathematical induction)

(1) If $n = 1$, we have $(1-h) \leqslant \dfrac{1}{1+h}$

$\therefore$ $(1-h)(1+h) \leqslant 1 \quad \{1+h \geqslant 0\}$
$\therefore$ $1 - h^2 \leqslant 1$
$\therefore$ $h^2 \geqslant 0$

which is true for $0 \leqslant h \leqslant 1$, so P_1 is true

(2) If P_k is true then $(1-h)^k \leqslant \dfrac{1}{1+kh}$ for $0 \leqslant h \leqslant 1$

Now $(1-h)^{k+1} = (1-h)(1-h)^k$

$\therefore$ $(1-h)^{k+1} \leqslant (1-h)\left(\dfrac{1}{1+kh}\right) \quad \{\text{using } P_k\}$

$\therefore$ $(1-h)^{k+1} \leqslant \left(\dfrac{1-h}{1+kh}\right) \times \left(\dfrac{1+kh+h}{1+kh+h}\right)$

$\therefore$ $(1-h)^{k+1} \leqslant \dfrac{1+kh+h-h-kh^2-h^2}{(1+kh)(1+kh+h)}$

$\therefore$ $(1-h)^{k+1} \leqslant \dfrac{(1+kh)-(kh^2+h^2)}{(1+kh)(1+(k+1)h)}$

$\therefore$ $(1-h)^{k+1} \leqslant \dfrac{1 - \frac{kh^2+h^2}{1+kh}}{1+(k+1)h}$

$\therefore$ $(1-h)^{k+1} \leqslant \dfrac{1}{1+(k+1)h} \quad \{k, h \geqslant 0, \text{ so } \dfrac{kh^2+h^2}{1+kh} \geqslant 0\}$

$\therefore$ P_{k+1} is true.
Thus P_1 is true and P_{k+1} is true whenever P_k is true,
so P_n is true for all $n \in \mathbb{Z}^+$ {Principle of mathematical induction}

EXERCISE 9C

1 a Proof: (By contradiction)

Let x be the positive number, so we need to prove that $x + 9\left(\dfrac{1}{x}\right) \geqslant 6$

So, we suppose the opposite, $\therefore$ $x + \dfrac{9}{x} < 6$ for all x

$\therefore$ $x\left(x + \dfrac{9}{x}\right) < 6x$ as $x > 0$

$\therefore$ $x^2 + 9 < 6x$
$\therefore$ $x^2 - 6x + 9 < 0$
$\therefore$ $(x-3)^2 < 0$

which is false as no square of a real number can be negative.

Hence, the supposition is false and its opposite is true, so $x + 9\left(\dfrac{1}{x}\right) \geqslant 6$ for all x

So, the sum of a positive number and 9 times its reciprocal is at least 6.

b **Proof:** (By contradiction)

Suppose the solution of $3^x = 4$ is rational $\therefore$ $x = \dfrac{p}{q}$, $q \neq 0$ where p and q are integers having no common factors.

$\therefore$ $3^{\frac{p}{q}} = 4$

$\therefore$ $(3^{\frac{p}{q}})^q = 4^q$

$\therefore$ $3^p = 4^q$

which is a contradiction as 3^p is odd and 4^q is even

$\therefore$ the supposition is false and so the solution of $3^x = 4$ is irrational.

c **Proof:** (By contradiction)

Suppose $\log_2 5$ is rational $\therefore$ $\log_2 5 = \dfrac{p}{q}$ where p and q are integers, $q \neq 0$ and p and q have no common factors.

$\therefore$ $5 = 2^{\frac{p}{q}}$

$\therefore$ $5^q = (2^{\frac{p}{q}})^q$

$\therefore$ $5^q = 2^p$

which is a contradiction as 5^q is odd and 2^p is even

$\therefore$ the supposition is false $\therefore$ $\log_2 5$ is irrational.

2 **Proof:** (By contradiction)

Suppose $\sqrt{2}$ is rational $\therefore$ $\sqrt{2} = \dfrac{p}{q}$ where p and q are $\in \mathbb{Z}$, $q \neq 0$ and p and q have no common factors. ...... (1)

$\therefore$ $2 = \dfrac{p^2}{q^2}$ and so $p^2 = 2q^2$ ...... (2)

$\therefore$ p^2 is even

$\therefore$ p is even {the only even perfect squares come from squaring evens}

$\therefore$ $p = 2a$ where $a \in \mathbb{Z}$

Back into (2) $(2a)^2 = 2q^2$

$\therefore$ $4a^2 = 2q^2$

$\therefore$ $q^2 = 2a^2$ $\therefore$ q^2 is even

$\therefore$ q is even

So, on the supposition, p and q are even and so have a common factor of 2. This contradicts (1), so the supposition is false $\therefore$ $\sqrt{2}$ is irrational.

REVIEW SET 9A

1 P_n is "$1 + 3 + 5 + 7 + \ldots\ldots + (2n - 1) = n^2$" for all $n \in \mathbb{Z}^+$

Proof: (By the principle of mathematical induction)

(1) If $n = 1$, LHS $= 1$ and RHS $= 1^2 = 1$ $\therefore$ P_1 is true

(2) If P_k is true, then $1 + 3 + 5 + 7 + \ldots\ldots + (2k - 1) = k^2$

$\therefore$ $1 + 3 + 5 + 7 + \ldots\ldots + (2k - 1) + (2[k + 1] - 1)$
$= k^2 + 2k + 2 - 1$ {using P_k}
$= k^2 + 2k + 1$
$= (k + 1)^2$

Thus P_{k+1} is true whenever P_k is true and P_1 is true

$\therefore$ P_n is true for all $n \in \mathbb{Z}^+$ {Principle of mathematical induction}

2 P_n is "$7^n + 2$ is divisible by 3" for all $n \in \mathbb{Z}^+$
   Proof: (By the principle of mathematical induction)
   (1) If $n = 1$, $7^1 + 2 = 9$ which is divisible by 3 $\therefore$ P_1 is true
   (2) If P_k is true, then $7^k + 2 = 3A$ where $A \in \mathbb{Z}$
   $\therefore$ $7^{k+1} + 2 = 7 \times 7^k + 2$
   $= 7[3A - 2] + 2$ {using P_k}
   $= 21A - 14 + 2$
   $= 21A - 12$
   $= 3(7A - 4)$ where $7A - 4$ is an integer as A is an integer
   $\therefore$ $7^{k+1} + 2$ is divisible by 3
   Thus P_{k+1} is true whenever P_k is true and P_1 is true
   $\therefore$ P_n is true for all $n \in \mathbb{Z}^+$ {Principle of mathematical induction}

3 P_n is "$1 \times 2 \times 3 + 2 \times 3 \times 4 + 3 \times 4 \times 5 + \ldots\ldots + n(n+1)(n+2) = \dfrac{n(n+1)(n+2)(n+3)}{4}$,"
   for all $n \in \mathbb{Z}^+$
   Proof: (By the principle of mathematical induction)
   (1) If $n = 1$, LHS $= 1 \times 2 \times 3 = 6$, RHS $= \dfrac{1 \times 2 \times 3 \times 4}{4} = 6$ $\therefore$ P_1 is true
   (2) If P_k is true, then
   $1 \times 2 \times 3 + 2 \times 3 \times 4 + \ldots\ldots + k(k+1)(k+2) = \dfrac{k(k+1)(k+2)(k+3)}{4}$
   $\therefore$ $1 \times 2 \times 3 + 2 \times 3 \times 4 + \ldots\ldots + k(k+1)(k+2) + (k+1)(k+2)(k+3)$
   $= \dfrac{k(k+1)(k+2)(k+3)}{4} + (k+1)(k+2)(k+3)$ {using P_k}
   $= \dfrac{k(k+1)(k+2)(k+3)}{4} + \dfrac{4(k+1)(k+2)(k+3)}{4}$ {equalising denominators}
   $= \dfrac{(k+1)(k+2)(k+3)[k+4]}{4}$
   Thus P_{k+1} is true whenever P_k is true and P_1 is true
   $\therefore$ P_n is true for all $n \in \mathbb{Z}^+$ {Principle of mathematical induction}

4 P_n is "$1 + r + r^2 + r^3 + \ldots\ldots + r^{n-1} = \dfrac{1 - r^n}{1 - r}$," for all $n \in \mathbb{Z}^+$, $r \neq 1$
   Proof: (By the principle of mathematical induction)
   (1) If $n = 1$, LHS $= 1$ and RHS $= \dfrac{1 - r}{1 - r} = 1$ as $r \neq 1$ $\therefore$ P_1 is true
   (2) If P_k is true, then $1 + r + r^2 + r^3 + \ldots\ldots r^{k-1} = \dfrac{1 - r^k}{1 - r}$
   Now $1 + r + r^2 + r^3 + \ldots\ldots + r^{k-1} + r^k$
   $= \dfrac{1 - r^k}{1 - r} + r^k$ {using P_k}
   $= \dfrac{1 - r^k}{1 - r} + r^k \left(\dfrac{1 - r}{1 - r}\right)$ {equalising denominators}
   $= \dfrac{1 - r^k + r^k - r^{k+1}}{1 - r}$
   $= \dfrac{1 - r^{k+1}}{1 - r}$ Thus P_{k+1} is true whenever P_k is true and P_1 is true
   $\therefore$ P_n is true for all $n \in \mathbb{Z}^+$ {Principle of mathematical induction}

5 P_n is "$5^{2n} - 1$ is divisible by 24" for all $n \in \mathbb{Z}^+$
   Proof: (By the principle of mathematical induction)
   (1) If $n = 1$, $5^2 - 1 = 25 - 1 = 24$ is divisible by 24 $\therefore$ P_1 is true
   (2) If P_k is true, then $5^{2k} - 1 = 24A$ where $A \in \mathbb{Z}$
   Now $5^{2(k+1)} - 1 = 5^{2k} 5^2 - 1$
   $= 25[24A + 1] - 1$ {using P_k}
   $= 25 \times 24A + 25 - 1$
   $= 25 \times 24A + 24$
   $= 24(25A + 1)$ where $25A + 1$ is an integer
   $\therefore$ $5^{2(k+1)} - 1$ is divisible by 24

   Thus P_{k+1} is true whenever P_k is true and P_1 is true
   $\therefore$ P_n is true for all $n \in \mathbb{Z}^+$ {Principle of mathematical induction}

6 P_n is "$5^n \geqslant 1 + 4n$" for all $n \in \mathbb{Z}^+$
   Proof: (By the principle of mathematical induction)
   (1) If $n = 1$, we have $5^1 \geqslant 1 + 4(1)$
   $\therefore$ $5 \geqslant 5$ which is true, so P_1 is true

   (2) If P_k is true, then $5^k \geqslant 1 + 4k$
   Now $5^{k+1} = 5 \times 5^k$
   $\geqslant 5 \times (1 + 4k)$ {using P_k}
   $\geqslant 5 + 20k$
   $\geqslant 5 + 4k$ {$k \geqslant 0$}
   $\geqslant 1 + 4(k+1)$
   $\therefore$ P_{k+1} is true.

   Thus P_1 is true and P_{k+1} is true whenever P_k is true,
   so P_n is true for all $n \in \mathbb{Z}^+$ {Principle of mathematical induction}

7 P_n is "if $u_1 = 1$ and $u_{n+1} = 3u_n + 2$" for all $n \in \mathbb{Z}^+$, then $u_n = 3^n - 2^n$"
   Proof: (By the principle of mathematical induction)
   (1) If $n = 1$, $u_1 = 1 = 3^1 - 2^1$, so P_1 is true
   (2) If P_k is true, then $u_k = 3^k - 2^k$ and $u_{k+1} = 3u_k + 2^k$
   $= 3(3^k - 2^k) + 2^k$ {using P_k}
   $= 3^{k+1} - 3 \times 2^k + 2^k$
   $= 3^{k+1} - 2 \times 2^k$
   $= 3^{k+1} - 2^{k+1}$
   $\therefore$ P_{k+1} is true.

   Thus P_1 is true and P_k is true whenever P_{k+1} is true,
   so P_n is true for all $n \in \mathbb{Z}^+$ {Principle of mathematical induction}

REVIEW SET 9B

1 P_n is "$1^2 + 3^2 + 5^2 + 7^2 + \ldots\ldots + (2n-1)^2 = \dfrac{n(2n+1)(2n-1)}{3}$" for all $n \in \mathbb{Z}^+$
   Proof: (By the principle of mathematical induction)
   (1) If $n = 1$, LHS $= 1^2 = 1$, RHS $= \dfrac{1 \times 3 \times 1}{3} = 1$ $\therefore$ P_1 is true

(2) If P_k is true, then $1^2 + 3^2 + 5^2 + \ldots\ldots + (2k-1)^2 = \dfrac{k(2k+1)(2k-1)}{3}$

$\therefore\quad 1^2 + 3^2 + 5^2 + \ldots\ldots + (2k-1)^2 + (2k+1)^2$

$= \dfrac{k(2k+1)(2k-1)}{3} + (2k+1)^2 \quad$ {using P_k}

$= \dfrac{k(2k+1)(2k-1)}{3} + \dfrac{3(2k+1)^2}{3} \quad$ {equalising denominators}

$= \dfrac{(2k+1)[k(2k-1) + 3(2k+1)]}{3}$

$= \dfrac{(2k+1)[2k^2 - k + 6k + 3]}{3}$

$= \dfrac{(2k+1)(2k^2 + 5k + 3)}{3}$

$= \dfrac{(2k+1)(k+1)(2k+3)}{3}$

$= \dfrac{[k+1](2[k+1]+1)(2[k+1]-1)}{3}$

Thus P_{k+1} is true whenever P_k is true and P_1 is true

$\therefore\quad P_n$ is true for all $n \in \mathbb{Z}^+$ {Principle of mathematical induction}

2 P_n is "$3^{2n+2} - 8n - 9$ is divisible by 64" for all $n \in \mathbb{Z}^+$
Proof: (By the principle of mathematical induction)

(1) If $n = 1$, $3^4 - 8 - 9 = 81 - 17 = 64$ which is divisible by 64 $\therefore\ P_1$ is true

(2) If P_k is true, then $3^{2k+2} - 8k - 9 = 64A$ where $A \in \mathbb{Z}$
Now $3^{2(k+1)+2} - 8(k+1) - 9$
$= 3^{2k+2} \times 3^2 - 8k - 8 - 9$
$= 9[64A + 8k + 9] - 8k - 17 \quad$ {using P_k}
$= 9 \times 64A + 72k + 81 - 8k - 17$
$= 9 \times 64A + 64k + 64$
$= 64(9A + k + 1)$ where $9A + k + 1$ is $\in \mathbb{Z}$ as $A, k \in \mathbb{Z}$
$\therefore\quad 3^{2(k+1)+2} - 8(k+1) - 9$ is divisible by 64

Thus P_{k+1} is true whenever P_k is true and P_1 is true
$\therefore\quad P_n$ is true for all $n \in \mathbb{Z}^+$ {Principle of mathematical induction}

3 P_n is "$3 + 5 \times 2 + 7 \times 2^2 + 9 \times 2^3 + \ldots\ldots + (2n+1)2^{n-1} = 1 + (2n-1) \times 2^n$" for all $n \in \mathbb{Z}^+$
Proof: (By the principle of mathematical induction)

(1) If $n = 1$, LHS $= 3$ and RHS $= 1 + 1 \times 2^1 = 1 + 2 = 3$ $\therefore\ P_1$ is true

(2) If P_k is true, then $3 + 5 \times 2 + 7 \times 2^2 + 9 \times 2^3 + \ldots\ldots + (2k+1)2^{k-1} = 1 + (2k-1) \times 2^k$
$\therefore\quad 3 + 5 \times 2 + 7 \times 2^2 + 9 \times 2^3 + \ldots\ldots + (2k+1)2^{k-1} + (2k+3)2^k$
$= 1 + (2k-1)2^k + (2k+3)2^k \quad$ {using P_k}
$= 1 + 2^k[2k - 1 + 2k + 3]$
$= 1 + 2^k[4k + 2]$
$= 1 + 2^k(2)(2k+1)$
$= 1 + (2k+1)2^{k+1}$
$= 1 + (2[k+1] - 1)2^{[k+1]}$

Thus P_{k+1} is true whenever P_k is true and P_1 is true
$\therefore\quad P_n$ is true for all $n \in \mathbb{Z}^+$ {Principle of mathematical induction}

4 P_n is "$5^n + 3$ is divisible by 4" for all $n \in \mathbb{Z}$, $n \geq 0$
  Proof: (By the principle of mathematical induction)
  (1) If $n = 0$, $5^0 + 3 = 4$ which is divisible by 4 $\therefore$ P_0 is true
  (2) If P_k is true, then $5^k + 3 = 4A$ where A is in $\mathbb{Z}$
  Now $5^{k+1} + 3 = 5 \times 5^k + 3$
  $= 5[4A - 3] + 3$ {using P_k}
  $= 20A - 15 + 3$
  $= 20A - 12$
  $= 4(5A - 3)$ where $5A - 3$ is in $\mathbb{Z}$, as A is in $\mathbb{Z}$
  So, $5^{k+1} + 3$ is divisible by 4
  Thus P_{k+1} is true whenever P_k is true and P_0 is true
  $\therefore$ P_n is true for all $n \in \mathbb{Z}$, $n \geq 0$ {Principle of mathematical induction}

5 P_n is "$1 \times 2^2 + 2 \times 3^2 + 3 \times 4^2 + \ldots + n(n+1)^2 = \dfrac{n(n+1)(n+2)(3n+5)}{12}$" for all $n \in \mathbb{Z}^+$
  Proof: (By the principle of mathematical induction)
  (1) If $n = 1$, LHS $= 1 \times 2^2 = 4$ and RHS $= \dfrac{1 \times 2 \times 3 \times 8}{12} = \dfrac{48}{12} = 4$ $\therefore$ P_1 is true
  (2) If P_k is true, then $1 \times 2^2 + 2 \times 3^2 + 3 \times 4^2 + \ldots + k(k+1)^2 = \dfrac{k(k+1)(k+2)(3k+5)}{12}$
  $\therefore$ $1 \times 2^2 + 2 \times 3^2 + 3 \times 4^2 + \ldots + k(k+1)^2 + (k+1)(k+2)^2$
  $= \dfrac{k(k+1)(k+2)(3k+5)}{12} + (k+1)(k+2)^2$ {using P_k}
  $= \dfrac{k(k+1)(k+2)(3k+5)}{12} + \dfrac{12(k+1)(k+2)^2}{12}$ {equalising denominators}
  $= \dfrac{(k+1)(k+2)[k(3k+5) + 12(k+2)]}{12}$
  $= \dfrac{(k+1)(k+2)[3k^2 + 5k + 12k + 24]}{12}$
  $= \dfrac{(k+1)(k+2)(3k^2 + 17k + 24)}{12}$
  $= \dfrac{(k+1)(k+2)(k+3)(3k+8)}{12}$
  $= \dfrac{[k+1]([k+1]+1)([k+1]+2)(3[k+1]+5)}{12}$
  Thus P_{k+1} is true whenever P_k is true and P_1 is true
  $\therefore$ P_n is true for all $n \in \mathbb{Z}^+$ {Principle of mathematical induction}

6 P_n is "$5^n + 3^n \geq 2^{2n+1}$" for all $n \in \mathbb{Z}^+$
  Proof: (By the principle of mathematical induction)
  (1) If $n = 1$, we have $5^1 + 3^1 \geq 2^3$
  $\therefore$ $8 \geq 8$ which is true, so P_1 is true
  (2) If P_k is true, then $5^k + 3^k \geq 2^{2k+1}$, so $5^k \geq 2^{2k+1} - 3^k$
  Now $5^{k+1} + 3^{k+1} = 5 \times 5^k + 3 \times 3^k$
  $\geq 5(2^{2k+1} - 3^k) + 3 \times 3^k$ {using P_k}
  $\therefore$ $5^{k+1} + 3^{k+1} \geq 5 \times 2^{2k+1} - 5 \times 3^k + 3 \times 3^k$
  $\therefore$ $5^{k+1} + 3^{k+1} \geq 5 \times 2^{2k+1} - 2 \times 3^k$
  $\geq 5 \times 2^{2k+1} - 2 \times 4^k$ {$4^k \geq 3^k$ as $k \geq 0$}
  $\therefore$ $5^{k+1} + 3^{k+1} \geq 5 \times 2^{2k+1} - 2^{2k+1}$
  $\therefore$ $5^{k+1} + 3^{k+1} \geq 4 \times 2^{2k+1}$

$\therefore \quad 5^{k+1} + 3^{k+1} \geqslant 2^{2k+3}$
$\therefore \quad 5^{k+1} + 3^{k+1} \geqslant 2^{2(k+1)+1} \quad \therefore \quad P_{k+1}$ is true.

Thus P_1 is true and P_{k+1} is true whenever P_k is true,
so P_n is true for all $n \in \mathbb{Z}^+$ {Principle of mathematical induction}

7 P_n is "if $u_1 = 9$ and $u_{n+1} = 2u_n + 3(5^n)$ then $u_n = 2^{n+1} + 5^n$" for all $n \in \mathbb{Z}^+$.
Proof: (By the principle of mathematical induction)
(1) If $n = 1$, $u_1 = 2^2 + 5^1 = 9$ ✓ so P_1 is true
(2) If P_k is true, then $u_k = 2^{k+1} + 5^k$ and $u_{k+1} = 2u_k + 3(5^k)$
$\qquad\qquad\qquad\qquad\qquad\qquad\quad = 2(2^{k+1} + 5^k) + 3(5^k) \quad$ {using P_k}
$\qquad\qquad\qquad\qquad\qquad\qquad\quad = 2^{k+2} + 2(5^k) + 3(5^k)$
$\qquad\qquad\qquad\qquad\qquad\qquad\quad = 2^{k+2} + 5(5^k)$
$\qquad\qquad\qquad\qquad\qquad\qquad\quad = 2^{k+2} + 5^{k+1} \quad \therefore \quad P_{k+1}$ is true.

Thus P_1 is true and P_{k+1} is true whenever P_k is true,
so P_n is true for all $n \in \mathbb{Z}^+$ {Principle of mathematical induction}

REVIEW SET 9C

1 P_n is "$1 \times 3 + 2 \times 4 + 3 \times 5 + 4 \times 6 + \ldots + n(n+2) = \dfrac{n(n+1)(2n+7)}{6}$" for all $n \in \mathbb{Z}^+$
Proof: (By the principle of mathematical induction)
(1) If $n = 1$, LHS $= 1 \times 3 = 3$ and RHS $= \dfrac{1 \times 2 \times 9}{6} = \dfrac{18}{6} = 3 \quad \therefore \quad P_1$ is true

(2) If P_k is true, then $1 \times 3 + 2 \times 4 + 3 \times 5 + \ldots + k(k+2) = \dfrac{k(k+1)(2k+7)}{6}$

$\therefore \quad 1 \times 3 + 2 \times 4 + 3 \times 5 + \ldots + k(k+2) + (k+1)(k+3)$
$= \dfrac{k(k+1)(2k+7)}{6} + (k+1)(k+3) \quad$ {using P_k}
$= \dfrac{k(k+1)(2k+7)}{6} + \dfrac{6(k+1)(k+3)}{6} \quad$ {equalising denominators}
$= \dfrac{(k+1)[k(2k+7) + 6(k+3)]}{6}$
$= \dfrac{(k+1)[2k^2 + 13k + 18]}{6}$
$= \dfrac{(k+1)(k+2)(2k+9)}{6}$
$= \dfrac{[k+1]([k+1]+1)(2[k+1]+7)}{6} \quad \therefore \quad P_{k+1}$ is true.

Thus P_{k+1} is true whenever P_k is true and P_1 is true
$\therefore \quad P_n$ is true for all $n \in \mathbb{Z}^+$ {Principle of mathematical induction}

2 P_n is "$7^n - 1$ is divisible by 6" for all $n \in \mathbb{Z}^+$
Proof: (By the principle of mathematical induction)
(1) If $n = 1$, $7^1 - 1 = 6$ which is divisible by 6 $\quad \therefore \quad P_1$ is true
(2) If P_k is true, then $7^k - 1 = 6A$ where $A \in \mathbb{Z}$
$\quad$ Now $7^{k+1} - 1 = 7 \times 7^k - 1$
$\qquad\qquad\qquad\quad = 7[6A + 1] - 1 \quad$ {using P_k}
$\qquad\qquad\qquad\quad = 42A + 7 - 1$
$\qquad\qquad\qquad\quad = 42A + 6$
$\qquad\qquad\qquad\quad = 6(7A + 1)$ where $7A + 1$ is in $\mathbb{Z}$.

Thus $7^{k+1} - 1$ is divisible by 6
Thus P_{k+1} is true whenever P_k is true and P_1 is true
$\therefore$ P_n is true for all $n \in \mathbb{Z}^+$ {Principle of mathematical induction}

3 P_n is "$1^3 + 3^3 + 5^3 + ... + (2n-1)^3 = n^2(2n^2 - 1)$" for all $n \in \mathbb{Z}^+$
Proof: (By the principle of mathematical induction)
(1) If $n = 1$, LHS $= 1^3 = 1$ and RHS $= 1^2(2-1) = 1 \times 1 = 1$ $\therefore$ P_1 is true
(2) If P_k is true, then $1^3 + 3^3 + 5^3 + ... + (2k-1)^3 = k^2(2k^2 - 1)$
$\therefore$ $1^3 + 3^3 + 5^3 + ... + (2k-1)^3 + (2k+1)^3$
$= k^2(2k^2 - 1) + (2k+1)^3$ {using P_k}
$= 2k^4 - k^2 + (2k)^3 + 3(2k)^2 1 + 3(2k)1^2 + 1^3$
$= 2k^4 - k^2 + 8k^3 + 12k^2 + 6k + 1$
$= 2k^4 + 8k^3 + 11k^2 + 6k + 1$
$= (k+1)^2(2k^2 + 4k + 1)$
$= (k+1)^2(2[k^2 + 2k + 1] - 1)$
$= (k+1)^2(2[k+1]^2 - 1)$

	−1	2	8	11	6	1
		0	−2	−6	−5	−1
	−1	2	6	5	1	0
		0	−2	−4	−1	
		2	4	1	0	

Thus P_{k+1} is true whenever P_k is true and P_1 is true
$\therefore$ P_n is true for all $n \in \mathbb{Z}^+$ {Principle of mathematical induction}

4 P_n is "$3^n - 1 - 2n$ is divisible by 4" for all $n \in \mathbb{N}$.
Proof: (By the principle of mathematical induction)
(1) If $n = 0$, $3^0 - 1 - 2(0) = 1 - 1 - 0 = 0$ which is divisible by 4 $\therefore$ P_0 is true
(2) If P_k is true, then $3^k - 1 - 2k = 4A$ where $A \in \mathbb{Z}$
Now $3^{k+1} - 1 - 2(k+1)$
$= 3 \times 3^k - 1 - 2k - 2$
$= 3[4A + 1 + 2k] - 2k - 3$ {using P_k}
$= 12A + 3 + 6k - 2k - 3$
$= 12A + 4k$
$= 4(3A + k)$ where $3A + k$ is in $\mathbb{Z}$
$\therefore$ $3^{k+1} - 1 - 2(k+1)$ is divisible by 4
Thus P_{k+1} is true whenever P_k is true and P_0 is true
$\therefore$ P_n is true for all $n \in \mathbb{N}$ {Principle of mathematical induction}

5 P_n is "$\dfrac{1}{1 \times 3} + \dfrac{1}{3 \times 5} + \dfrac{1}{5 \times 7} + ... + \dfrac{1}{(2n-1)(2n+1)} = \dfrac{n}{2n+1}$" for all $n \in \mathbb{Z}^+$
Proof: (By the principle of mathematical induction)
(1) If $n = 1$, LHS $= \dfrac{1}{1 \times 3} = \dfrac{1}{3}$, RHS $= \dfrac{1}{2+1} = \dfrac{1}{3}$ $\therefore$ P_1 is true
(2) If P_k is true, then $\dfrac{1}{1 \times 3} + \dfrac{1}{3 \times 5} + \dfrac{1}{5 \times 7} + ... + \dfrac{1}{(2k-1)(2k+1)} = \dfrac{k}{2k+1}$
$\therefore$ $\dfrac{1}{1 \times 3} + \dfrac{1}{3 \times 5} + \dfrac{1}{5 \times 7} + ... + \dfrac{1}{(2k-1)(2k+1)} + \dfrac{1}{(2k+1)(2k+3)}$
$= \dfrac{k}{2k+1} + \dfrac{1}{(2k+1)(2k+3)}$ {using P_k}
$= \dfrac{k}{2k+1}\left(\dfrac{2k+3}{2k+3}\right) + \dfrac{1}{(2k+1)(2k+3)}$ {equalising denominators}
$= \dfrac{2k^2 + 3k + 1}{(2k+1)(2k+3)}$

$$= \frac{(k+1)(2k+1)}{(2k+1)(2k+3)}$$

$$= \frac{[k+1]}{2[k+1]+1}$$

Thus P_{k+1} is true whenever P_k is true and P_1 is true

∴ P_n is true for all $n \in \mathbb{Z}^+$ {Principle of mathematical induction}

6 P_n is "if $u_1 = 5$ and $u_{n+1} = 2u_n - 3(-1)^n$ for $n \in \mathbb{Z}^+$, then $u_n = 3(2^n) + (-1)^n$"

Proof: (By the principle of mathematical induction)

(1) If $n = 1$, $3(2^1) + (-1)^1 = 6 - 1 = 5 = u_1$, so P_1 is true

(2) If P_k is true, then $u_k = 3(2^k) + (-1)^k$, and $u_{k+1} = 2u_k - 3(-1)^k$
$$= 2[3(2^k) + (-1)^k] - 3(-1)^k \quad \{\text{using } P_k\}$$
$$= 6(2^k) + 2(-1)^k - 3(-1)^k$$
$$= 3(2^{k+1}) - (-1)^k$$
$$= 3(2^{k+1}) + (-1)^{k+1}$$

∴ P_{k+1} is true.

Thus P_1 is true and P_{k+1} is true whenever P_k is true,

so P_n is true for all $n \in \mathbb{Z}^+$ {Principle of mathematical induction}

7 $\sqrt[n]{n!} \leqslant \frac{n+1}{2} \Leftrightarrow n! \leqslant \left(\frac{n+1}{2}\right)^n$

∴ P_n is "$n! \leqslant \left(\frac{n+1}{2}\right)^n$" for $n \in \mathbb{Z}^+$

Proof: (By the principle of mathematical induction)

(1) If $n = 1$, we have $1! \leqslant \left(\frac{1+1}{2}\right)^1$

∴ $1 \leqslant 1$ which is true, so P_1 is true

(2) If P_k is true, then $k! \leqslant \left(\frac{k+1}{2}\right)^k$

Now $(k+1)! = (k+1)k!$
$$\leqslant (k+1)\left(\frac{k+1}{2}\right)^k$$
$$\leqslant \frac{(k+1)^{k+1}}{2^k} \quad .....(1)$$

Also, $(k+1)^k = k^k + \binom{k}{1}k^{k-1} + ...$
$$= k^k + k^k + ...$$
$$= 2k^k + ...$$

∴ $(k+1)^k \geqslant 2k^k$ for $k \geqslant 1$

∴ $\left(\frac{k+1}{k}\right)^k \geqslant 2$

∴ $\frac{1}{2}\left(\frac{k+1}{k}\right)^k \geqslant 1$

∴ $\frac{1}{2}\left(\frac{k+2}{k+1}\right)^{k+1} \geqslant 1$ .....(2)

{replacing k with $k+1$}

Using (1) and (2),
$$(k+1)! \leqslant \frac{(k+1)^{k+1}}{2^k} \times \frac{1}{2}\left(\frac{k+2}{k+1}\right)^{k+1}$$
$$\leqslant \frac{(k+1)^{k+1}}{2^{k+1}} \times \frac{(k+2)^{k+1}}{(k+1)^{k+1}}$$
$$\leqslant \frac{(k+2)^{k+1}}{2^{k+1}}$$
$$\leqslant \left(\frac{[k+1]+1}{2}\right)^{k+1}$$

Thus P_{k+1} is true whenever P_k is true and P_1 is true

∴ P_n is true for all $n \in \mathbb{Z}^+$

{Principle of mathematical induction}

Chapter 10
THE UNIT CIRCLE AND RADIAN MEASURE

EXERCISE 10A

1 **a** $180° = \pi$ radians
$\therefore\ 90° = \frac{\pi}{2}$ radians

b $180° = \pi$ radians
$\therefore\ 60° = \frac{\pi}{3}$ radians

c $180° = \pi$ radians
$\therefore\ 30° = \frac{\pi}{6}$ radians

d $180° = \pi$ radians
$\therefore\ 18° = \frac{\pi}{10}$ radians

e $180° = \pi$ radians
$\therefore\ 9° = \frac{\pi}{20}$ radians

f $180° = \pi$ radians
$\therefore\ 45° = \frac{\pi}{4}$ radians
$\therefore\ 135° = \frac{3\pi}{4}$ radians

g $180° = \pi$ radians
$\therefore\ 45° = \frac{\pi}{4}$ radians
$\therefore\ 225° = \frac{5\pi}{4}$ radians

h $180° = \pi$ radians
$\therefore\ 90° = \frac{\pi}{2}$ radians
$\therefore\ 270° = \frac{3\pi}{2}$ radians

i $360° = 2 \times 180°$
$= 2\pi$ radians

j $720° = 4 \times 180°$
$= 4\pi$ radians

k $180° = \pi$ radians
$\therefore\ 45° = \frac{\pi}{4}$ radians
$\therefore\ 315° = \frac{7\pi}{4}$ radians

l $180° = \pi$ radians
$\therefore\ 540° = 3\pi$ radians

m $180° = \pi$ radians
$\therefore\ 36° = \frac{\pi}{5}$ radians

n $180° = \pi$ radians
$\therefore\ 10° = \frac{\pi}{18}$ radians
$\therefore\ 80° = \frac{8\pi}{18}$ radians
$= \frac{4\pi}{9}$ radians

o $180° = \pi$ radians
$\therefore\ 10° = \frac{\pi}{18}$ radians
$\therefore\ 230° = \frac{23\pi}{18}$ radians

2 **a** $36.7°$
$= 36.7 \times \frac{\pi}{180}$ radians
≈ 0.641 radians

b $137.2°$
$= 137.2 \times \frac{\pi}{180}$ radians
≈ 2.39 radians

c $317.9°$
$= 317.9 \times \frac{\pi}{180}$ radians
≈ 5.55 radians

d $219.6°$
$= 219.6 \times \frac{\pi}{180}$ radians
≈ 3.83 radians

e $396.7°$
$= 396.7 \times \frac{\pi}{180}$ radians
≈ 6.92 radians

3 **a** $\frac{\pi}{5}$
$= \frac{180°}{5}$
$= 36°$

b $\frac{3\pi}{5}$
$= \frac{3 \times 180°}{5}$
$= 108°$

c $\frac{3\pi}{4}$
$= \frac{3 \times 180°}{4}$
$= 135°$

d $\frac{\pi}{18}$
$= \frac{180°}{18}$
$= 10°$

e $\frac{\pi}{9}$
$= \frac{180°}{9}$
$= 20°$

f $\frac{7\pi}{9}$
$= \frac{7 \times 180°}{9}$
$= 140°$

g $\frac{\pi}{10}$
$= \frac{180°}{10}$
$= 18°$

h $\frac{3\pi}{20}$
$= \frac{3 \times 180°}{20}$
$= 27°$

i $\frac{5\pi}{6}$
$= \frac{5 \times 180°}{6}$
$= 150°$

j $\frac{\pi}{8}$
$= \frac{180°}{8}$
$= 22.5°$

4 **a** 2^c
$= 2 \times \frac{180}{\pi}$ degrees
$\approx 114.59°$

b 1.53^c
$= 1.53 \times \frac{180}{\pi}$ degrees
$\approx 87.66°$

c 0.867^c
$= 0.867 \times \frac{180}{\pi}$ degrees
$\approx 49.68°$

d 3.179^c
$= 3.179 \times \frac{180}{\pi}$ degrees
$\approx 182.14°$

e 5.267^c
$= 5.267 \times \frac{180}{\pi}$ degrees
$\approx 301.78°$

5 **a**

Degrees	0	45	90	135	180	225	270	315	360
Radians	0	$\frac{\pi}{4}$	$\frac{\pi}{2}$	$\frac{3\pi}{4}$	π	$\frac{5\pi}{4}$	$\frac{3\pi}{2}$	$\frac{7\pi}{4}$	2π

b

Degrees	0	30	60	90	120	150	180	210	240	270	300	330	360
Radians	0	$\frac{\pi}{6}$	$\frac{\pi}{3}$	$\frac{\pi}{2}$	$\frac{2\pi}{3}$	$\frac{5\pi}{6}$	π	$\frac{7\pi}{6}$	$\frac{4\pi}{3}$	$\frac{3\pi}{2}$	$\frac{5\pi}{3}$	$\frac{11\pi}{6}$	2π

EXERCISE 10B

1 a i arc length $= \left(\frac{41.6}{360}\right) \times 2\pi \times 9$
≈ 6.53 cm

ii area $= \left(\frac{41.6}{360}\right) \times \pi \times 9^2$
≈ 29.4 cm^2

b i arc length $= \left(\frac{122}{360}\right) \times 2\pi \times 4.93$
≈ 10.5 cm

ii area $= \left(\frac{122}{360}\right) \times \pi \times 4.93^2$
≈ 25.9 cm^2

2 a $\theta = 107.9°$, $l = 5.92$
$\therefore \left(\frac{107.9}{360}\right) \times 2\pi \times r = 5.92$
$\therefore r = \frac{5.92 \times 360}{107.9 \times 2 \times \pi}$
$\therefore r \approx 3.14$ m

b area $= \left(\frac{107.9}{360}\right) \times \pi \times (3.1436)^2$
≈ 9.30 m^2

3 a area $= \left(\frac{\theta}{360}\right) \times \pi r^2$
$\therefore 20.8 = \left(\frac{68.2}{360}\right) \times \pi r^2$
$\therefore \frac{20.8 \times 360}{68.2 \times \pi} = r^2$
$\therefore r = \sqrt{\frac{20.8 \times 360}{68.2 \times \pi}}$
$\therefore r \approx 5.91$ cm

b perimeter
$= l + 2r$
$= \left(\frac{68.2}{360}\right) \times 2\pi \times 5.912 + 2 \times 5.912$
≈ 18.9 cm

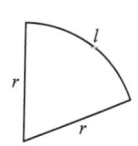

4 a 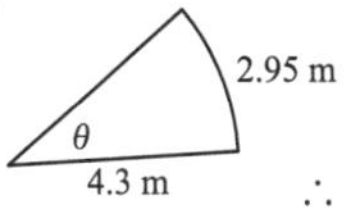 $l = \left(\frac{\theta}{360}\right) \times 2\pi \times r$
$\therefore 2.95 = \left(\frac{\theta}{360}\right) \times 2\pi \times 4.3$
$\therefore \frac{2.95 \times 360}{2 \times \pi \times 4.3} = \theta$
$\therefore \theta \approx 39.3°$

b area $= \left(\frac{\theta}{360}\right) \times \pi r^2$
$\therefore 30 = \left(\frac{\theta}{360}\right) \times \pi \times 10^2$
$\therefore \frac{30 \times 360}{\pi \times 100} = \theta$
$\therefore \theta \approx 34.4°$

5 a $l = \theta r$
$\therefore 6 = \theta \times 8$
$\therefore \theta = \frac{6}{8}$
$\therefore \theta = 0.75^c$

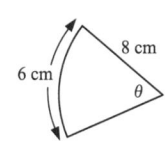

area $= \frac{1}{2}\theta r^2$
$= \frac{1}{2}(0.75) \times 8^2$
$= 24$ cm^2

b $l = \theta r$
$\therefore 8.4 = \theta \times 5$
$\therefore \theta = \frac{8.4}{5}$
$\therefore \theta = 1.68^c$

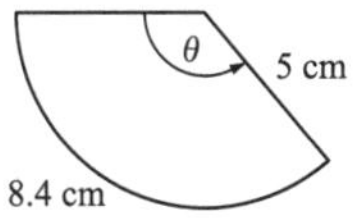

area $= \frac{1}{2}\theta r^2$
$= \frac{1}{2}(1.68) \times 5^2$
$= 21$ cm^2

c $l = \phi r$
$\therefore 31.7 = \phi \times 8$
$\therefore \phi = \frac{31.7}{8}$
$\therefore \phi \approx 3.96^c$
But $\theta = 2\pi - \phi$
$\therefore \theta \approx 2.32^c$

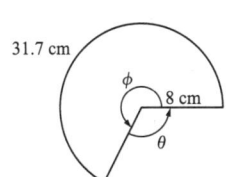

area $= \frac{1}{2}\phi r^2$
$= \frac{1}{2} \times \frac{31.7}{8} \times 8^2$
$= 126.8$ cm^2

6 arc length $= r\theta$ area
$= 5 \times 2$ $= \frac{1}{2}r^2\theta$
$= 10$ cm $= \frac{1}{2} \times 5^2 \times 2$
     $= 25$ cm^2

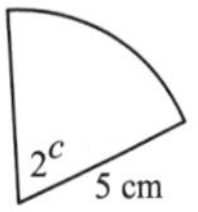

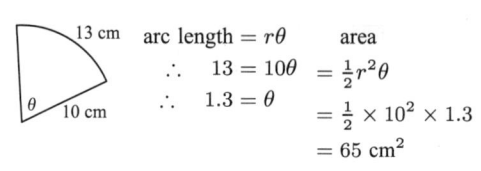

7 arc length $= r\theta$ area
$\therefore\ 13 = 10\theta$ $= \frac{1}{2}r^2\theta$
$\therefore\ 1.3 = \theta$ $= \frac{1}{2} \times 10^2 \times 1.3$
     $= 65$ cm^2

8 a $s^2 = 6^2 + 10^2$ {Pythagoras}
$\therefore\ s = \sqrt{6^2 + 10^2}$
$\therefore\ s \approx 11.6619$
$\therefore\ s \approx 11.7$

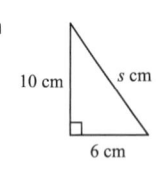

d arc length $= \left(\frac{\theta}{360}\right) \times 2\pi r$
$\therefore\ 37.6991 \approx \frac{\theta}{360} \times 2 \times \pi \times 11.6619$
$\therefore\ \theta \approx \frac{37.6991 \times 360}{2 \times \pi \times 11.6619}$
$\therefore\ \theta \approx 185°$

b $r = s \approx 11.7$

c arc length $= 2\pi \times 6 \approx 37.6991 \approx 37.7$ cm

9 a $\tan\alpha = \frac{5}{15}$
$\therefore\ \alpha = \tan^{-1}\left(\frac{1}{3}\right)$
$\therefore\ \alpha \approx 18.43$

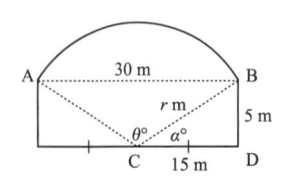

b $\theta + 2\alpha = 180$ {angles on a line}
$\therefore\ \theta \approx 180 - 2 \times 18.43$
$\therefore\ \theta \approx 143.1$

Note: $r^2 = 5^2 + 15^2$
$\therefore\ r^2 = 250$

c area $= 2 \times$ area of $\triangle CDB +$ area of sector
$\approx 2 \times \frac{1}{2} \times 15 \times 5 + \left(\frac{143.1}{360}\right) \times \pi \times 250$
≈ 387 m^2

10 a $l = \left(\frac{\theta}{360}\right) \times 2\pi r$
$= \frac{\frac{1}{60}}{360} \times 2 \times \pi \times 6370$ km
$\approx 1.852\,957$ km
≈ 1.853 km

b speed $= \dfrac{\text{distance}}{\text{time}}$ $\therefore$ time $= \dfrac{\text{distance}}{\text{speed}}$

$= \dfrac{2130 \text{ km}}{480 \text{ n miles h}^{-1}}$

$= \dfrac{2130 \text{ km}}{480 \times 1.853 \text{ km h}^{-1}}$

≈ 2.3947 hours
≈ 2 hours 24 min

11 $\cos\theta = \frac{6}{9} = \frac{2}{3}$
$\therefore\ \theta = \cos^{-1}\left(\frac{2}{3}\right)$
$\therefore\ \theta \approx 48.19°$
So, $360 - 2\theta \approx 263.62°$
Now MB $= \sqrt{9^2 - 6^2}$
$= \sqrt{45}$

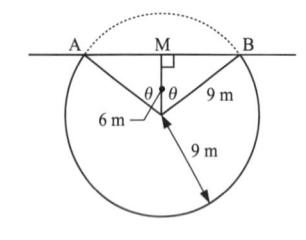

$\therefore$ available feeding area
$=$ area of $\triangle +$ area of sector
$= \frac{1}{2} \times 2 \times \sqrt{45} \times 6$
$+ \left(\frac{263.62}{360}\right) \times \pi \times 9^2$
≈ 227 m^2

12 a $\sin\alpha = \frac{2}{20} = 0.1$
$\therefore\ \alpha = \sin^{-1}(0.1)$
$\therefore\ \alpha \approx 5.739$

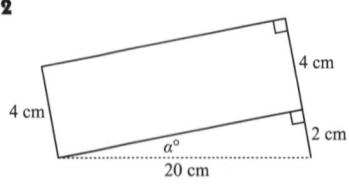

b $\theta + 90 + 90 + 2\alpha = 360$
$\therefore\ \theta = 180 - 2\alpha$
$\approx 180 - 2 \times 5.739$
≈ 168.5

c $\phi + \theta = 360$
$\therefore\ \phi \approx 360 - 168.5$
$\therefore\ \phi \approx 191.5$

d length of belt
$= 2 \times \sqrt{20^2 - 2^2}$
$+ \frac{\theta}{360} \times 2\pi \times 4$
$+ \frac{\phi}{360} \times 2\pi \times 6$
≈ 71.62 cm

EXERCISE 10C.1

1 **a**, **b**, 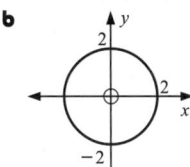 **c** (unit circle diagrams)

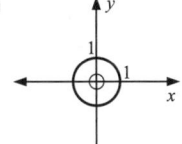

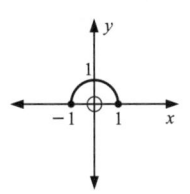

2 **a** **i** A(cos 26°, sin 26°), B(cos 146°, sin 146°), C(cos 199°, sin 199°)

  ii A(0.899, 0.438), B(−0.829, 0.559), C(−0.946, −0.326)

 b **i** A(cos 123°, sin 123°), B(cos 251°, sin 251°), C(cos(−35°), sin(−35°))

  ii A(−0.545, 0.839), B(−0.326, −0.946), C(0.819, −0.574)

3

θ (degrees)	0°	90°	180°	270°	360°	450°
θ (radians)	0	$\frac{\pi}{2}$	π	$\frac{3\pi}{2}$	2π	$\frac{5\pi}{2}$
sine	0	1	0	−1	0	1
cosine	1	0	−1	0	1	0
tangent	0	undef.	0	undef.	0	undef.

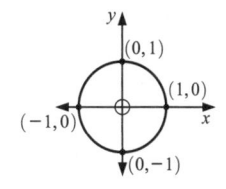

4 **a** P(a, b) is such that [OP] makes an angle of θ with the positive
  x-axis. $\therefore$ $a = \cos\theta$, $b = \sin\theta$.
  [OQ] makes an angle of $\pi + \theta$ with the positive x-axis.
  Now $\triangle$s POS and QOR are congruent {AAcorrS}
  $\therefore$ OR = a and RQ = b
  $\therefore$ Q has coordinates $(-a, -b)$, and so $\sin(\pi + \theta) = -b$
  $\qquad\qquad\qquad\qquad\qquad\qquad\qquad\qquad = -\sin\theta$

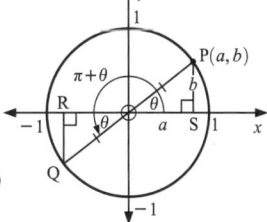

 b P(a, b) is such that [OP] makes an angle of θ with the positive
  x-axis. $\therefore$ $a = \cos\theta$, $b = \sin\theta$.
  [OQ] makes an angle of $\frac{3\pi}{2} + \theta$ with the positive x-axis.
  Now $\triangle$s POS and QOR are congruent {AAcorrS}
  $\therefore$ OR = a and RQ = b
  $\therefore$ Q has coordinates $(b, -a)$, and so $\sin(\frac{3\pi}{2} + \theta) = -a$
  $\qquad\qquad\qquad\qquad\qquad\qquad\qquad\qquad = -\cos\theta$

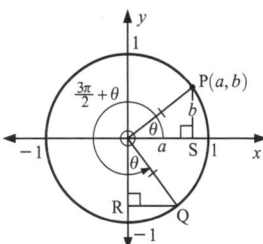

5 **a** sin 137°
   $= \sin(180 - 137)°$
   $= \sin 43°$
   ≈ 0.6820

 b sin 59°
   $= \sin(180 - 59)°$
   $= \sin 121°$
   ≈ 0.8572

 c cos 143°
   $= -\cos(180 - 143)°$
   $= -\cos 37°$
   ≈ -0.7986

 d cos 24°
   $= -\cos(180 - 24)°$
   $= -\cos 156°$
   ≈ 0.9135

 e sin 115°
   $= \sin(180 - 115)°$
   $= \sin 65°$
   ≈ 0.9063

 f cos 132°
   $= -\cos(180 - 132)°$
   $= -\cos 48°$
   ≈ -0.6691

6 **a** $\cos^2\theta + \sin^2\theta = 1$
   $\therefore \cos^2\theta + \frac{1}{4} = 1$
   $\therefore \cos^2\theta = \frac{3}{4}$
   $\therefore \cos\theta = \pm\frac{\sqrt{3}}{2}$

 b $\cos^2\theta + \sin^2\theta = 1$
   $\therefore \cos^2\theta + \frac{1}{9} = 1$
   $\therefore \cos^2\theta = \frac{8}{9}$
   $\therefore \cos\theta = \pm\frac{\sqrt{8}}{3}$
   $\qquad = \pm\frac{2\sqrt{2}}{3}$

 c $\cos^2\theta + \sin^2\theta = 1$
   $\therefore \cos^2\theta + 0 = 1$
   $\therefore \cos\theta = \pm 1$

 d $\cos^2\theta + \sin^2\theta = 1$
   $\therefore \cos^2\theta + 1 = 1$
   $\therefore \cos\theta = 0$

7 **a** $\cos^2\theta + \sin^2\theta = 1$
$\therefore \frac{16}{25} + \sin^2\theta = 1$
$\therefore \sin^2\theta = \frac{9}{25}$
$\therefore \sin\theta = \pm\frac{3}{5}$

b $\cos^2\theta + \sin^2\theta = 1$
$\therefore \frac{9}{16} + \sin^2\theta = 1$
$\therefore \sin^2\theta = \frac{7}{16}$
$\therefore \sin\theta = \pm\frac{\sqrt{7}}{4}$

c $\cos^2\theta + \sin^2\theta = 1$
$\therefore 1 + \sin^2\theta = 1$
$\therefore \sin^2\theta = 0$
$\therefore \sin\theta = 0$

d $\cos^2\theta + \sin^2\theta = 1$
$\therefore 0 + \sin^2\theta = 1$
$\therefore \sin^2\theta = 1$
$\therefore \sin\theta = \pm 1$

8 **a**

Quadrant	Degree measure	Radian measure	$\cos\theta$	$\sin\theta$	$\tan\theta$
1	$0 < \theta < 90$	$0 < \theta < \frac{\pi}{2}$	+ve	+ve	+ve
2	$90 < \theta < 180$	$\frac{\pi}{2} < \theta < \pi$	−ve	+ve	−ve
3	$180 < \theta < 270$	$\pi < \theta < \frac{3\pi}{2}$	−ve	−ve	+ve
4	$270 < \theta < 360$	$\frac{3\pi}{2} < \theta < 2\pi$	+ve	−ve	−ve

b **i** 1 and 4
ii 2 and 3
iii 3
iv 2

9 **a** $\cos^2\theta + \sin^2\theta = 1$
$\therefore \frac{4}{9} + \sin^2\theta = 1$
$\therefore \sin^2\theta = \frac{5}{9}$
$\therefore \sin\theta = \pm\frac{\sqrt{5}}{3}$
But θ is in quadrant 1
where $\sin\theta > 0$
$\therefore \sin\theta = \frac{\sqrt{5}}{3}$

b $\cos^2\theta + \sin^2\theta = 1$
$\therefore \cos^2\theta + \frac{4}{25} = 1$
$\therefore \cos^2\theta = \frac{21}{25}$
$\therefore \cos\theta = \pm\frac{\sqrt{21}}{5}$
But θ is in quadrant 2
where $\cos\theta < 1$
$\therefore \cos\theta = -\frac{\sqrt{21}}{5}$

c $\cos^2\theta + \sin^2\theta = 1$
$\therefore \cos^2\theta + \frac{9}{25} = 1$
$\therefore \cos^2\theta = \frac{16}{25}$
$\therefore \cos\theta = \pm\frac{4}{5}$
But θ is in quadrant 4
where $\cos\theta > 0$
$\therefore \cos\theta = \frac{4}{5}$

d $\cos^2\theta + \sin^2\theta = 1$
$\therefore \frac{25}{169} + \sin^2\theta = 1$
$\therefore \sin^2\theta = \frac{144}{169}$
$\therefore \sin\theta = \pm\frac{12}{13}$
But θ is in quadrant 3
where $\sin\theta < 0$
$\therefore \sin\theta = -\frac{12}{13}$

10 **a** $\sin x = \frac{1}{3}$

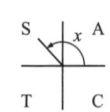

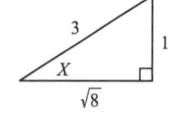

$\tan X = \frac{1}{\sqrt{8}}$
$\therefore \tan x = -\frac{1}{\sqrt{8}} = -\frac{1}{2\sqrt{2}}$

b $\cos x = \frac{1}{5}$

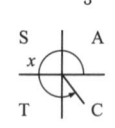

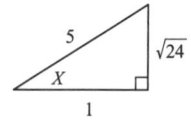

$\tan X = \frac{\sqrt{24}}{1}$
$\therefore \tan x = -\frac{\sqrt{24}}{1} = -2\sqrt{6}$

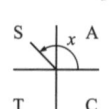

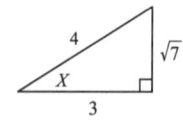

c $\sin x = -\frac{1}{\sqrt{3}}$

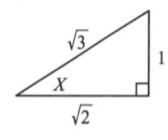

$\tan X = \frac{1}{\sqrt{2}}$
$\therefore \tan x = \frac{1}{\sqrt{2}}$

d $\cos x = -\frac{3}{4}$

$\tan X = \frac{\sqrt{7}}{3}$
$\therefore \tan x = -\frac{\sqrt{7}}{3}$

11 **a** $\tan x = \frac{2}{3}$

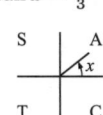

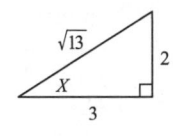

$\sin X = \frac{2}{\sqrt{13}}, \quad \cos X = \frac{3}{\sqrt{13}}$

$\therefore \quad \sin x = \frac{2}{\sqrt{13}}, \quad \cos x = \frac{3}{\sqrt{13}}$

b $\tan x = -\frac{4}{3}$

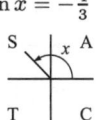

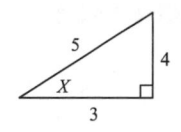

$\sin X = \frac{4}{5}, \quad \cos X = \frac{3}{5}$

$\therefore \quad \sin x = \frac{4}{5}, \quad \cos x = -\frac{3}{5}$

c $\tan x = \frac{\sqrt{5}}{3}$

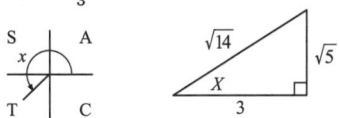

$\sin X = \frac{\sqrt{5}}{\sqrt{14}}, \quad \cos X = \frac{3}{\sqrt{14}}$

$\therefore \quad \sin x = -\frac{\sqrt{5}}{\sqrt{14}}, \quad \cos x = -\frac{3}{\sqrt{14}}$

d $\tan x = -\frac{12}{5}$

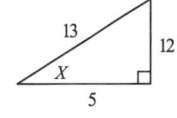

$\sin X = \frac{12}{13}, \quad \cos X = \frac{5}{13}$

$\therefore \quad \sin x = -\frac{12}{13}, \quad \cos x = \frac{5}{13}$

EXERCISE 10C.2

1 **a** $\sin\theta + \sin(-\theta)$
$= \sin\theta - \sin\theta$
$= 0$

b $\tan(-\theta) - \tan\theta$
$= -\tan\theta - \tan\theta$
$= -2\tan\theta$

c $2\cos\theta + \cos(-\theta)$
$= 2\cos\theta + \cos\theta$
$= 3\cos\theta$

d $3\sin\theta - \sin(-\theta)$
$= 3\sin\theta - -\sin\theta$
$= 3\sin\theta + \sin\theta$
$= 4\sin\theta$

e $\cos^2(-\alpha)$
$= \cos(-\alpha) \times \cos(-\alpha)$
$= \cos\alpha \times \cos\alpha$
$= \cos^2\alpha$

f $\sin^2(-\alpha)$
$= \sin(-\alpha) \times \sin(-\alpha)$
$= -\sin\alpha \times -\sin\alpha$
$= \sin^2\alpha$

g $\cos(-\alpha)\cos\alpha - \sin(-\alpha)\sin\alpha$
$= \cos\alpha\cos\alpha - -\sin\alpha\sin\alpha$
$= \cos^2\alpha + \sin^2\alpha$
$= 1$

2 **a** $2\sin\theta - \cos(90° - \theta)$
$= 2\sin\theta - \sin\theta$
$= \sin\theta$

b $\sin(-\theta) - \cos(90° - \theta)$
$= -\sin\theta - \sin\theta$
$= -2\sin\theta$

c $\sin(90° - \theta) - \cos\theta$
$= \cos\theta - \cos\theta$
$= 0$

d $3\cos(-\theta) - 4\sin(\frac{\pi}{2} - \theta)$
$= 3\cos\theta - 4\cos\theta$
$= -\cos\theta$

e $3\cos\theta + \sin(\frac{\pi}{2} - \theta)$
$= 3\cos\theta + \cos\theta$
$= 4\cos\theta$

f $\cos(\frac{\pi}{2} - \theta) + 4\sin\theta$
$= \sin\theta + 4\sin\theta$
$= 5\sin\theta$

3 $\sin(\theta - \phi) = \sin(-(\phi - \theta))$ and $\cos(\theta - \phi) = \cos(-(\phi - \theta))$
$= -\sin(\phi - \theta)$ $= \cos(\phi - \theta)$

4 **a** $\dfrac{\sin\theta}{\cos\theta} = \tan\theta$

b $\dfrac{\sin(-\theta)}{\cos(-\theta)} = \dfrac{-\sin\theta}{\cos\theta}$
$= -\tan\theta$

c $\dfrac{\sin(\frac{\pi}{2} - \theta)}{\cos\theta} = \dfrac{\cos\theta}{\cos\theta}$
$= 1$

d $\dfrac{-\sin(-\theta)}{\cos\theta} = \dfrac{\sin\theta}{\cos\theta}$
$= \tan\theta$

e $\dfrac{\cos(\frac{\pi}{2} - \theta)}{\sin(\frac{\pi}{2} - \theta)} = \dfrac{\sin\theta}{\cos\theta}$
$= \tan\theta$

f $\dfrac{\cos(\frac{\pi}{2} - \theta)}{\cos\theta} = \dfrac{\sin\theta}{\cos\theta}$
$= \tan\theta$

EXERCISE 10C.3

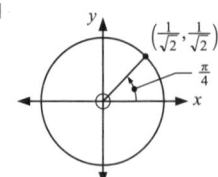

1 So $\cos(\frac{\pi}{4}) = \frac{1}{\sqrt{2}}$

$\sin(\frac{\pi}{4}) = \frac{1}{\sqrt{2}}$

$\tan(\frac{\pi}{4}) = \frac{\frac{1}{\sqrt{2}}}{\frac{1}{\sqrt{2}}} = 1$

You should draw separate unit circle diagrams for each case.

	a	b	c	d	e
$\sin\theta$	$\frac{1}{\sqrt{2}}$	$-\frac{1}{\sqrt{2}}$	$-\frac{1}{\sqrt{2}}$	0	$-\frac{1}{\sqrt{2}}$
$\cos\theta$	$\frac{1}{\sqrt{2}}$	$-\frac{1}{\sqrt{2}}$	$\frac{1}{\sqrt{2}}$	-1	$-\frac{1}{\sqrt{2}}$
$\tan\theta$	1	1	-1	0	1

2 You should draw separate unit circle diagrams for each case.

	a	b	c	d	e
$\sin\beta$	$\frac{1}{2}$	$\frac{\sqrt{3}}{2}$	$-\frac{1}{2}$	$-\frac{\sqrt{3}}{2}$	$-\frac{1}{2}$
$\cos\beta$	$\frac{\sqrt{3}}{2}$	$-\frac{1}{2}$	$-\frac{\sqrt{3}}{2}$	$\frac{1}{2}$	$\frac{\sqrt{3}}{2}$
$\tan\beta$	$\frac{1}{\sqrt{3}}$	$-\sqrt{3}$	$\frac{1}{\sqrt{3}}$	$-\sqrt{3}$	$-\frac{1}{\sqrt{3}}$

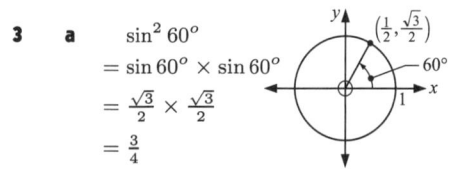

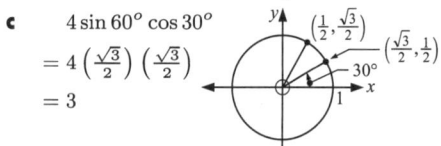

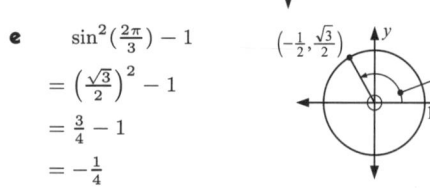

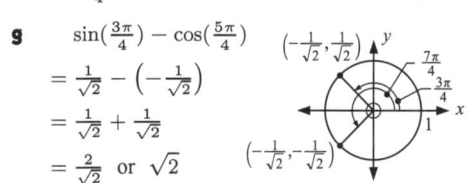

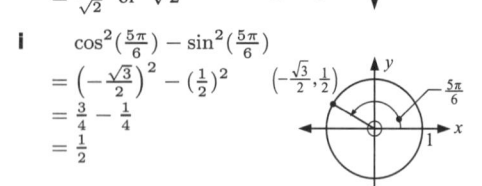

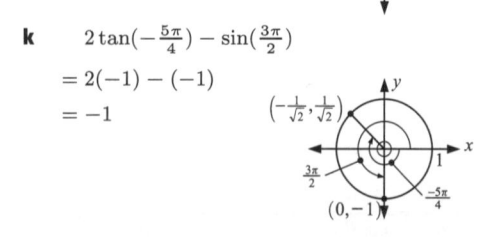

3 a $\sin^2 60°$
$= \sin 60° \times \sin 60°$
$= \frac{\sqrt{3}}{2} \times \frac{\sqrt{3}}{2}$
$= \frac{3}{4}$

b $\sin 30° \cos 60°$
$= \frac{1}{2} \times \frac{1}{2}$
$= \frac{1}{4}$

c $4\sin 60° \cos 30°$
$= 4\left(\frac{\sqrt{3}}{2}\right)\left(\frac{\sqrt{3}}{2}\right)$
$= 3$

d $1 - \cos^2(\frac{\pi}{6})$
$= 1 - \left(\frac{\sqrt{3}}{2}\right)^2$
$= 1 - \frac{3}{4}$
$= \frac{1}{4}$

e $\sin^2(\frac{2\pi}{3}) - 1$
$= \left(\frac{\sqrt{3}}{2}\right)^2 - 1$
$= \frac{3}{4} - 1$
$= -\frac{1}{4}$

f $\cos^2(\frac{\pi}{4}) - \sin(\frac{7\pi}{6})$
$= \left(\frac{1}{\sqrt{2}}\right)^2 - \left(-\frac{1}{2}\right)$
$= \frac{1}{2} + \frac{1}{2}$
$= 1$

g $\sin(\frac{3\pi}{4}) - \cos(\frac{5\pi}{4})$
$= \frac{1}{\sqrt{2}} - \left(-\frac{1}{\sqrt{2}}\right)$
$= \frac{1}{\sqrt{2}} + \frac{1}{\sqrt{2}}$
$= \frac{2}{\sqrt{2}}$ or $\sqrt{2}$

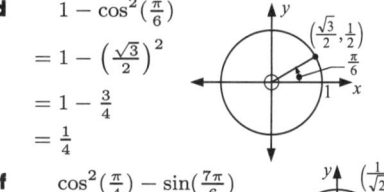

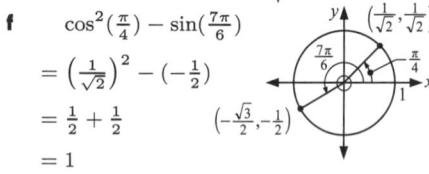

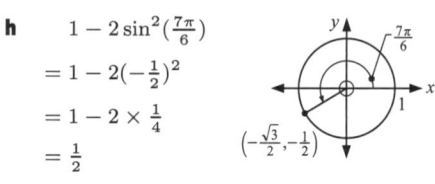

h $1 - 2\sin^2(\frac{7\pi}{6})$
$= 1 - 2(-\frac{1}{2})^2$
$= 1 - 2 \times \frac{1}{4}$
$= \frac{1}{2}$

i $\cos^2(\frac{5\pi}{6}) - \sin^2(\frac{5\pi}{6})$
$= \left(-\frac{\sqrt{3}}{2}\right)^2 - (\frac{1}{2})^2$
$= \frac{3}{4} - \frac{1}{4}$
$= \frac{1}{2}$

j $\tan^2(\frac{\pi}{3}) - 2\sin^2(\frac{\pi}{4})$
$= \left(\sqrt{3}\right)^2 - 2\left(\frac{1}{\sqrt{2}}\right)^2$
$= 3 - 2(\frac{1}{2})$
$= 2$

k $2\tan(-\frac{5\pi}{4}) - \sin(\frac{3\pi}{2})$
$= 2(-1) - (-1)$
$= -1$

l $\dfrac{2\tan 150°}{1 - \tan^2 150°}$
$= \dfrac{2(-\frac{1}{\sqrt{3}})}{1 - (-\frac{1}{\sqrt{3}})^2}$
$= \dfrac{-\frac{2}{\sqrt{3}}}{1 - \frac{1}{3}}$
$= \dfrac{-\frac{2}{\sqrt{3}}}{\frac{2}{3}} = -\frac{3}{\sqrt{3}} = -\sqrt{3}$

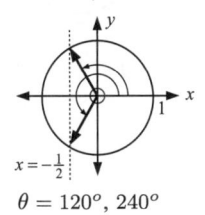

4
a $\theta = 30°, 150°$
b $\theta = 60°, 120°$
c $\theta = 45°, 315°$
d $\theta = 120°, 240°$
e $\theta = 135°, 225°$
f $\theta = 240°, 300°$

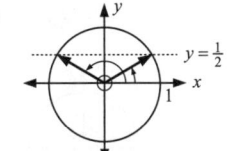

5
a $\theta = \frac{\pi}{4}, \frac{5\pi}{4}$
b $\theta = \frac{3\pi}{4}, \frac{7\pi}{4}$
c $\theta = \frac{\pi}{3}, \frac{4\pi}{3}$
d $\theta = 0, \pi, 2\pi$
e $\theta = \frac{\pi}{6}, \frac{7\pi}{6}$
f $\theta = \frac{2\pi}{3}, \frac{5\pi}{3}$

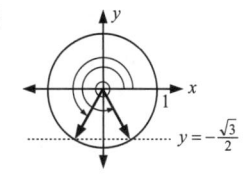

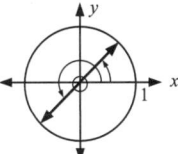

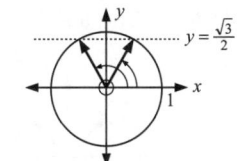

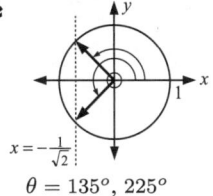

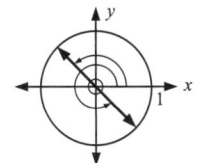

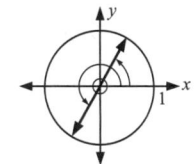

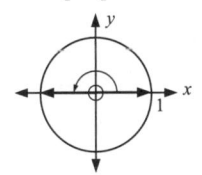

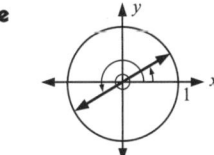

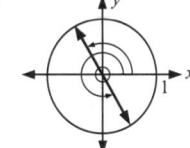

6
a $\theta = \frac{\pi}{6}, \frac{11\pi}{6}, \frac{13\pi}{6}, \frac{23\pi}{6}$
b $\theta = \frac{7\pi}{6}, \frac{11\pi}{6}, \frac{19\pi}{6}, \frac{23\pi}{6}$
c $\theta = \frac{3\pi}{2}, \frac{7\pi}{2}$

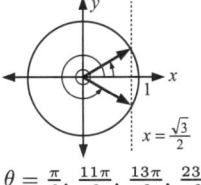

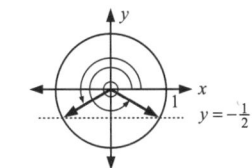

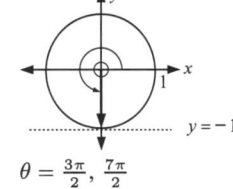

7
a $\cos\theta = \frac{1}{2}$ 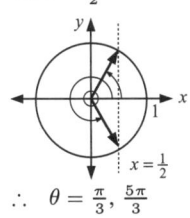
∴ $\theta = \frac{\pi}{3}, \frac{5\pi}{3}$

b $\sin\theta = \frac{\sqrt{3}}{2}$ 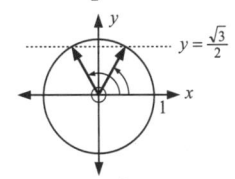
∴ $\theta = \frac{\pi}{3}, \frac{2\pi}{3}$

c $\cos\theta = -1$
∴ $\theta = \pi$

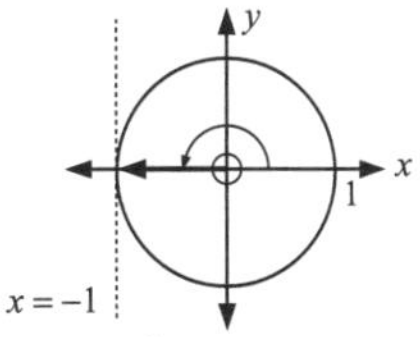

d $\sin\theta = 1$
∴ $\theta = \frac{\pi}{2}$ 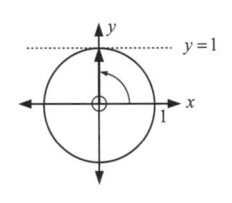

e $\cos\theta = -\frac{1}{\sqrt{2}}$ 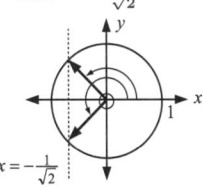
∴ $\theta = \frac{3\pi}{4}, \frac{5\pi}{4}$

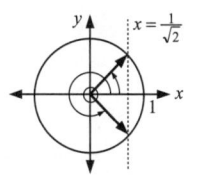

f $\sin^2\theta = 1$
∴ $\sin\theta = \pm 1$ 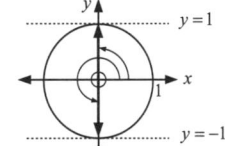
∴ $\theta = \frac{\pi}{2}, \frac{3\pi}{2}$

g $\cos^2\theta = 1$
  $\therefore\ \cos\theta = \pm 1$ 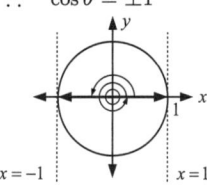

  $\therefore\ \theta = 0,\ \pi,\ 2\pi$

h $\cos^2\theta = \frac{1}{2}$
  $\therefore\ \cos\theta = \pm\frac{1}{\sqrt{2}}$ 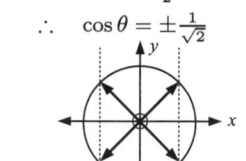

  $\therefore\ \theta = \frac{\pi}{4},\ \frac{3\pi}{4},\ \frac{5\pi}{4},\ \frac{7\pi}{4}$

i $\tan\theta = -\frac{1}{\sqrt{3}}$ 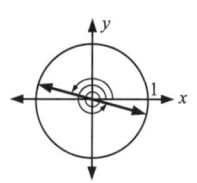

  $\therefore\ \theta = \frac{5\pi}{6},\ \frac{11\pi}{6}$

j $\tan^2\theta = 3$
  $\therefore\ \tan\theta = \pm\sqrt{3}$ 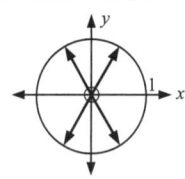

  $\therefore\ \theta = \frac{\pi}{3},\ \frac{2\pi}{3},\ \frac{4\pi}{3},\ \frac{5\pi}{3}$

EXERCISE 10D

1 a area
   $= \frac{1}{2} \times 9 \times 10 \times \sin 40°$
   ≈ 28.9 cm^2

b area
   $= \frac{1}{2} \times 25 \times 31 \times \sin 82°$
   ≈ 384 km^2

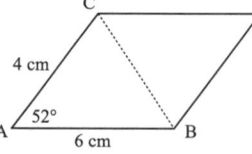

c area
   $= \frac{1}{2} \times 10.2 \times 6.4 \times \sin\frac{2\pi}{3}$
   ≈ 28.3 cm^2

2 area $= 150$ cm^2
   $\therefore\ \frac{1}{2} \times 17 \times x \times \sin 68° = 150$
   $\therefore\ x = \frac{2 \times 150}{17 \times \sin 68°}$
   $\therefore\ x \approx 19.0$

3 area
   $= 2 \times$ area $\triangle ABC$
   $= 2 \times \frac{1}{2} \times 4 \times 6 \times \sin 52°$
   ≈ 18.9 cm^2

4 area
   $= 2 \times$ area $\triangle ABC$
   $= 2 \times \frac{1}{2} \times 12^2 \times \sin 72°$
   ≈ 137 cm^2

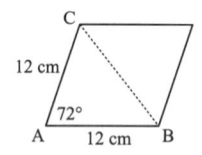

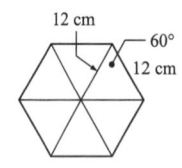

5 area $= 6 \times$ area of $\triangle$
   $= 6 \times \frac{1}{2} \times 12^2 \times \sin 60°$
   ≈ 374 cm^2

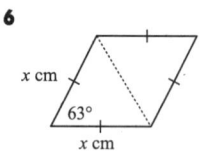

6 area $= 2 \times \frac{1}{2}x^2 \sin 63°$
   $\therefore\ x^2 \sin 63° = 50$
   $\therefore\ x^2 = \frac{50}{\sin 63°}$
   $\therefore\ x = \sqrt{\frac{50}{\sin 63°}}$
   $\therefore\ x \approx 7.49$
   So, sides are 7.49 cm long.

7 area of $\triangle = \frac{338}{5}$
   $\therefore\ \frac{1}{2}x^2 \sin 72° = \frac{338}{5}$
   $\therefore\ x^2 = \frac{2 \times 338}{5 \times \sin 72°}$
   $\therefore\ x = \sqrt{\frac{2 \times 338}{5 \times \sin 72°}}$
   $\therefore\ x \approx 11.9$
   So, OA ≈ 11.9 m long.

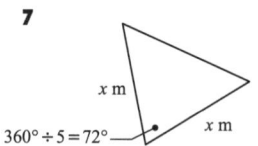

8 a If the included angle is θ

then $\frac{1}{2} \times 5 \times 8 \times \sin \theta = 15$

$\therefore \quad 20 \sin \theta = 15$

$\therefore \quad \sin \theta = \frac{3}{4}$

Now $\arcsin(\frac{3}{4}) \approx 48.6°$

$\therefore \quad \theta \approx 48.6°$ or $(180 - 48.6)°$

$\therefore \quad \theta \approx 48.6°$ or $131.4°$

b Likewise,

$\frac{1}{2} \times 45 \times 53 \times \sin \theta = 800$

$\therefore \quad \sin \theta = \frac{800 \times 2}{45 \times 53}$

Now $\arcsin \left(\frac{800 \times 2}{45 \times 53} \right) \approx 42.1°$

$\therefore \quad \theta \approx 42.1°$ or $(180 - 42.1)°$

$\therefore \quad \theta \approx 42.1°$ or $137.9°$

9

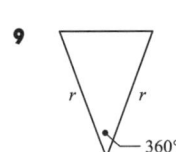

$360° \div 12° = 30°$

total area of 8 coins
$= 8 \times 12 \times \frac{1}{2} r^2 \sin 30°$
$= 48r^2(\frac{1}{2})$
$= 24r^2$

area of $10 note
$= 8r \times 4r$
$= 32r^2$

fraction covered
$= \frac{24r^2}{32r^2}$
$= \frac{3}{4} \quad \therefore \quad \frac{1}{4}$ is uncovered

10 a shaded area
$=$ area of sector $-$ area of triangle
$= \frac{1}{2} \times 1.5 \times 12^2 - \frac{1}{2} \times 12^2 \times \sin(1.5)$
≈ 36.2 cm^2

b shaded area
$=$ area of triangle $-$ area of sector
$= \frac{1}{2} \times 12 \times 30 \times \sin(0.66) - \frac{1}{2} \times 0.66 \times 12^2$
≈ 62.8 cm^2

11 a i area $= \frac{1}{2}$ base $\times$ altitude
$= \frac{1}{2} \times 4 \times 3$
$= 6$ cm^2

ii $s = \frac{3+4+5}{2} = 6$

$\therefore$ area $= \sqrt{6(6-3)(6-4)(6-5)}$
$= \sqrt{6 \times 3 \times 2 \times 1}$
$= 6$ cm^2

b i $s = \frac{6+8+12}{2} = 13$

$\therefore A = \sqrt{13(13-6)(13-8)(13-12)}$
$= \sqrt{13 \times 7 \times 5 \times 1}$
≈ 21.3 cm^2

ii $s = \frac{7.2 + 8.9 + 9.7}{2} = 12.9$

$\therefore A = \sqrt{12.9(12.9 - 7.2)(12.9 - 8.9)(12.9 - 9.7)}$
$= \sqrt{12.9 \times 5.7 \times 4 \times 3.2}$
≈ 30.7 cm^2

REVIEW SET 10A

1 area $= \frac{1}{2} \times 7.3 \times 9.4 \times \sin 38°$
≈ 21.1 km^2

2 a area $= \left(\frac{80}{360} \right) \times \pi \times 13^2 \approx 118$ cm^2

b area $= \frac{1}{2} \times 11 \times 9 \times \sin 65° \approx 44.9$ cm^2

3 M$(\cos 73°, \sin 73°) \approx (0.292, 0.956)$, N$(\cos 190°, \sin 190°) \approx (-0.985, -0.174)$,
P$(\cos(-53°), \sin(-53°)) \approx (0.602, -0.799)$

4 The x-coordinate of A $= -0.222$

$\therefore \quad \cos \theta = -0.222$

$\therefore \quad \theta = \cos^{-1}(-0.222)$

$\therefore \quad \theta \approx 102.8°, \ 257.2°$

5 a $\sin \frac{2\pi}{3} = \sin(\pi - \frac{2\pi}{3}) = \sin \frac{\pi}{3}$

$\therefore \quad \theta = \frac{\pi}{3}$

b $\sin 165° = \sin(180 - 165)° = \sin 15°$

$\therefore \quad \theta = 15°$

c $\cos 276° = \cos(360 - 276)° = \cos 84°$

$\therefore \quad \theta = 84°$

6 **a** $\sin 47°$
$= \sin(180 - 47)°$
$= \sin 133°$
$\therefore \theta = 133°$

b $\sin \frac{\pi}{15}$
$= \sin(\pi - \frac{\pi}{15})$
$= \sin \frac{14\pi}{15}$
$\therefore \theta = \frac{14\pi}{15}$

c $\cos 186°$
$= \cos(360 - 186)°$
$= \cos 174°$
$\therefore \theta = 174°$

7 **a** $\sin 159°$
$= \sin(180 - 159)°$
$= \sin 21°$
≈ 0.358

b $\cos 92°$
$= -\cos(180 - 92)°$
$= -\cos 88°$
≈ -0.035

c $\cos 75°$
$= -\cos(180 - 75)°$
$= -\cos 105°$
≈ 0.259

d $\sin 227° = \sin(-47)°$
$= -\sin 47°$
≈ -0.731

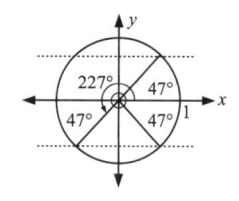

8 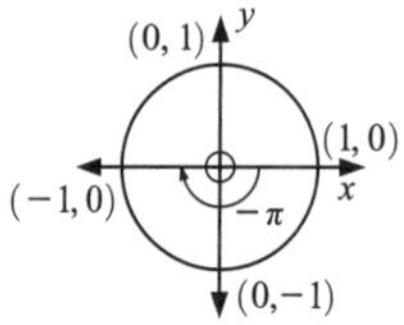 **a** $\cos 360° = 1$, $\sin 360° = 0$
b $\cos(-\pi) = -1$, $\sin(-\pi) = 0$

9 when $\cos \theta = -\sin \theta$
$\frac{\sin \theta}{\cos \theta} = -1$
$\therefore \tan \theta = -1$

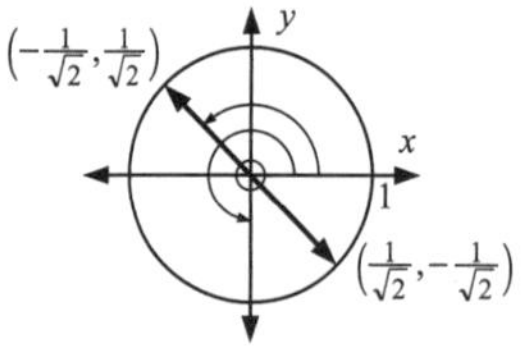

and this only occurs at the two points shown.
So, $\theta = \frac{3\pi}{4}, \frac{7\pi}{4}$

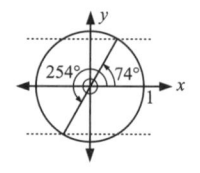

10 **a** $\sin 106°$
$= \sin(180 - 106)°$
$= \sin 74°$
≈ 0.961

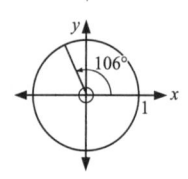

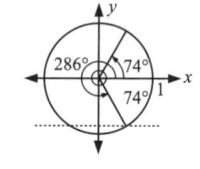

b $254° = 74° + 180°$
$\therefore \sin 254° = -\sin 74°$
≈ -0.961

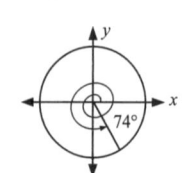

c $\sin 286° = -\sin 74°$
≈ -0.961

d $646° = 360° + 286°$
$\therefore \sin 646° = \sin 286°$
≈ -0.961 {from **c**}

11 **a** $\tan^2(\frac{2\pi}{3})$
$= (-\sqrt{3})^2$
$= 3$

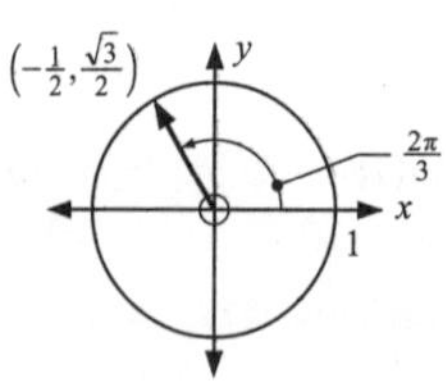

b $\cos(\frac{3\pi}{4}) - \sin(\frac{3\pi}{4})$
$= -\frac{1}{\sqrt{2}} - \frac{1}{\sqrt{2}}$
$= -\frac{2}{\sqrt{2}}$
$= -\sqrt{2}$

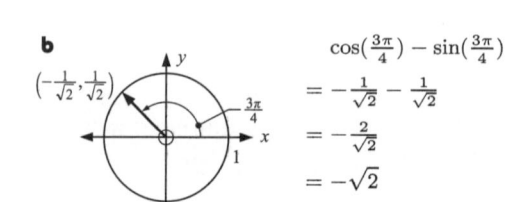

12 $\sin x = -\frac{1}{4}$

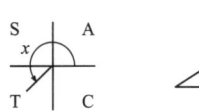

$\tan X = \frac{1}{\sqrt{15}}$

$\therefore \tan x = \frac{1}{\sqrt{15}}$

REVIEW SET 10B

1 a $120°$
$= \left(120 \times \frac{\pi}{180}\right)^c$
$= \frac{2\pi}{3}^c$

  b $225°$
$= 5 \times 45°$
$= 5 \times \frac{\pi}{4}^c$
$= \frac{5\pi}{4}^c$

  c $150°$
$= 5 \times 30°$
$= 5 \times \frac{\pi}{6}^c$
$= \frac{5\pi}{6}^c$

  d $540°$
$= 3 \times 180°$
$= 3\pi^c$

2 a $71°$
$= \left(71 \times \frac{\pi}{180}\right)^c$
$\approx 1.239^c$

  b $124.6°$
$= \left(124.6 \times \frac{\pi}{180}\right)^c$
$\approx 2.175^c$

  c $-142°$
$= \left(-142 \times \frac{\pi}{180}\right)^c$
$\approx -2.478^c$

  d $-25.3°$
$= \left(-25.3 \times \frac{\pi}{180}\right)^c$
$\approx -0.4416^c$

3 a $\frac{2\pi}{5}$
$= \frac{2 \times 180°}{5}$
$= 72°$

  b $\frac{5\pi}{4}$
$= \frac{5 \times 180°}{4}$
$= 225°$

  c $\frac{7\pi}{9}$
$= \frac{7 \times 180°}{9}$
$= 140°$

  d $\frac{11\pi}{6}$
$= \frac{11 \times 180°}{6}$
$= 330°$

4 a 3^c
$= \left(3 \times \frac{180}{\pi}\right)°$
$\approx 171.89°$

  b 1.46^c
$= \left(1.46 \times \frac{180}{\pi}\right)°$
$\approx 83.65°$

  c 0.435^c
$= \left(0.435 \times \frac{180}{\pi}\right)°$
$\approx 24.92°$

  d -5.271^c
$= \left(-5.271 \times \frac{180}{\pi}\right)°$
$\approx -302.01°$

5 perimeter $= 2 \times 11 + \left(\frac{63}{360}\right) \times 2\pi \times 11$
≈ 34.1 cm

area $= \left(\frac{63}{360}\right) \times \pi \times 11^2$
≈ 66.5 cm^2

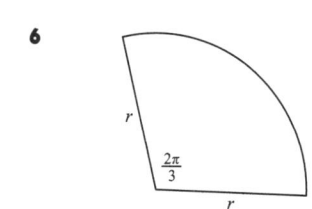

6 perimeter $= 2r + \left(\frac{2\pi}{3}\right)r$
$\therefore 36 = r\left(2 + \frac{2\pi}{3}\right)$
$\therefore r = \frac{36}{2 + \frac{2\pi}{3}}$ cm
$\therefore r \approx 8.79$ cm

area $= \frac{1}{2}\left(\frac{2\pi}{3}\right) \times (8.7925)^2$
≈ 81.0 cm^2

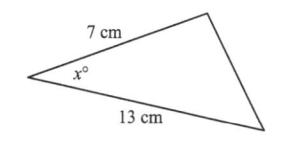

7 area $= 42$ cm^2

$\therefore \frac{1}{2} \times 7 \times 13 \times \sin x = 42$
$\therefore \sin x = \frac{42 \times 2}{7 \times 13}$

Now $\arcsin\left(\frac{42 \times 2}{7 \times 13}\right) \approx 67.4°$
$\therefore x \approx 67.4$ or $180 - 67.4$
$\therefore x \approx 67.4$ or 112.6

$\therefore$ the included angle is $67.4°$ or $112.6°$ {assuming the figure is not drawn accurately}

8 a We construct a perpendicular from B to (AD).

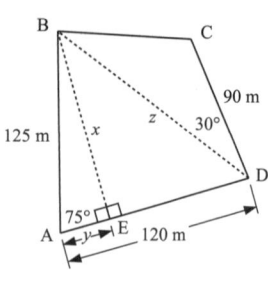

$\sin 75° = \dfrac{x}{125}$ ∴ $x \approx 120.7$ m

$\cos 75° = \dfrac{y}{125}$ ∴ $y \approx 32.4$ m

Using Pythagoras' theorem, $z^2 = x^2 + (120-y)^2$
$\approx 120.7^2 + (120 - 32.4)^2$
∴ $z \approx 149.2$ m

The area of the block = area of $\triangle ABD$ + area of $\triangle BCD$
$\approx \tfrac{1}{2} \times 120 \times 125 \times \sin 75° + \tfrac{1}{2} \times 149.2 \times 90 \times \sin 30°$
$\approx 10\,600$ m^2

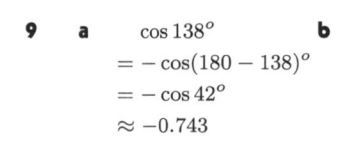

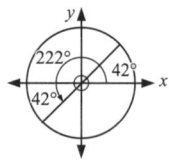

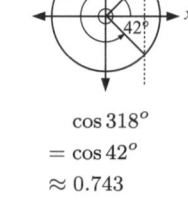

b ≈ 1.06 ha $\{10\,000$ m$^2 = 1$ ha$\}$

9 a $\cos 138°$
$= -\cos(180 - 138)°$
$= -\cos 42°$
≈ -0.743

b $\cos 222°$
$= -\cos 42°$
≈ -0.743

c $\cos 318°$
$= \cos 42°$
≈ 0.743

d $\cos(-222)°$
$= -\cos 42°$
≈ -0.743

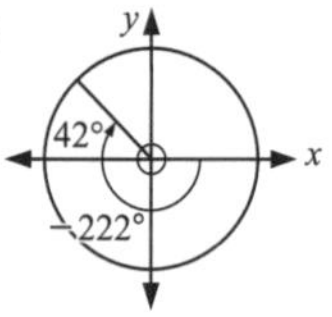

10 $\cos^2 \theta + \sin^2 \theta = 1$
∴ $\dfrac{9}{16} + \sin^2 \theta = 1$
∴ $\sin^2 \theta = \dfrac{7}{16}$
∴ $\sin \theta = \pm \dfrac{\sqrt{7}}{4}$

11 a $2\sin(\tfrac{\pi}{3})\cos(\tfrac{\pi}{3})$
$= 2(\tfrac{\sqrt{3}}{2})(\tfrac{1}{2})$
$= \dfrac{\sqrt{3}}{2}$

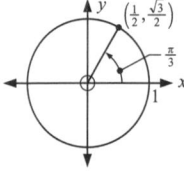

b $\tan^2(\tfrac{\pi}{4}) - 1$
$= 1^2 - 1$
$= 0$

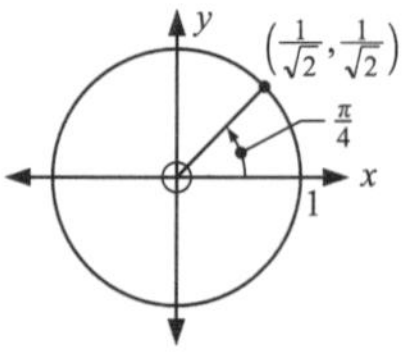

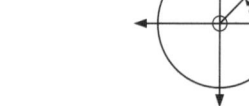

c $\cos^2(\tfrac{\pi}{6}) - \sin^2(\tfrac{\pi}{6})$
$= \left(\tfrac{\sqrt{3}}{2}\right)^2 - \left(\tfrac{1}{2}\right)^2$
$= \tfrac{3}{4} - \tfrac{1}{4} = \tfrac{1}{2}$

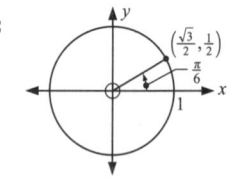

12 $\tan x = -\dfrac{3}{2}$

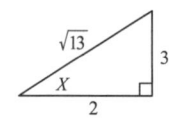

a $\sin X = \dfrac{3}{\sqrt{13}}$
∴ $\sin x = -\dfrac{3}{\sqrt{13}}$

b $\cos X = \dfrac{2}{\sqrt{13}}$
∴ $\cos x = \dfrac{2}{\sqrt{13}}$

REVIEW SET 10C

1 a The point is $(\cos 320°, \sin 320°)$
$\approx (0.766, -0.643)$.

b The point is $(\cos 163°, \sin 163°)$
$\approx (-0.956, 0.292)$.

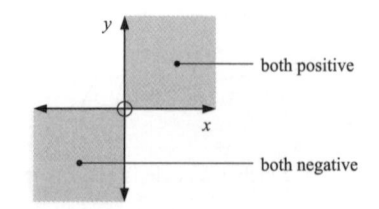

3 a $\therefore \sin\left(\frac{2\pi}{3}\right) = \frac{\sqrt{3}}{2}$
$\cos\left(\frac{2\pi}{3}\right) = -\frac{1}{2}$

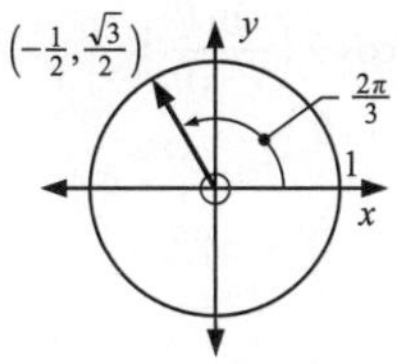

b $\therefore \sin\left(\frac{8\pi}{3}\right) = \frac{\sqrt{3}}{2}$
$\cos\left(\frac{8\pi}{3}\right) = -\frac{1}{2}$

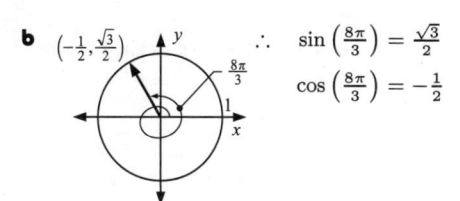

4 a $\therefore \cos\left(\frac{3\pi}{2}\right) = 0$
$\sin\left(\frac{3\pi}{2}\right) = -1$

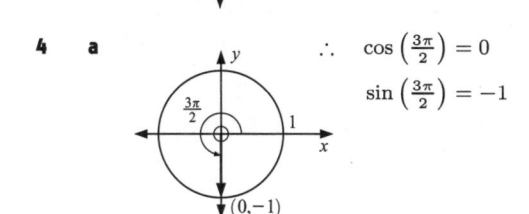

b $\therefore \cos\left(-\frac{\pi}{2}\right) = 0$
$\sin\left(-\frac{\pi}{2}\right) = -1$

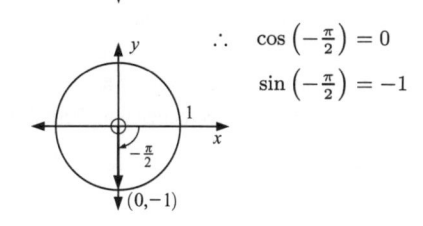

5 $\cos\theta = -\frac{3}{4}$

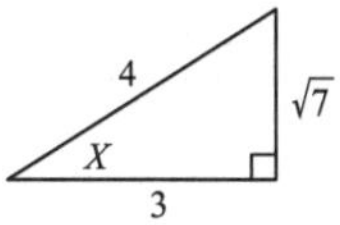

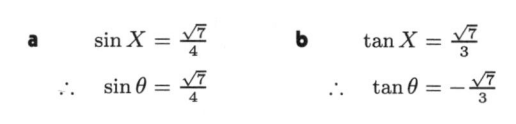

a $\sin X = \frac{\sqrt{7}}{4}$
$\therefore \sin\theta = \frac{\sqrt{7}}{4}$

b $\tan X = \frac{\sqrt{7}}{3}$
$\therefore \tan\theta = -\frac{\sqrt{7}}{3}$

6 a $\therefore \theta = 150°$ or $210°$

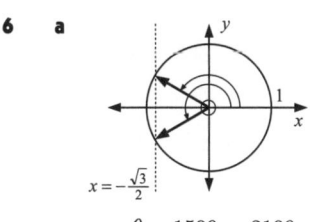

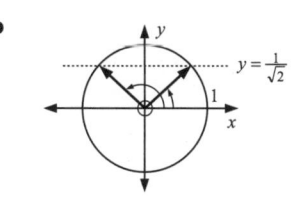

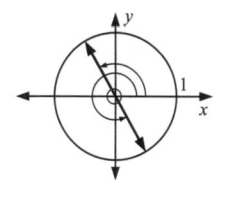

b $\therefore \theta = 45°$ or $135°$

c $\therefore \theta = 120°$ or $300°$

7 a $\therefore \theta = \pi + k2\pi, \quad k \in \mathbb{Z}$

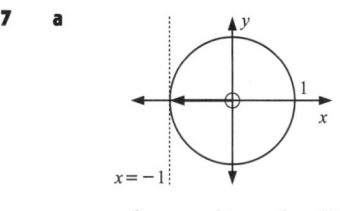

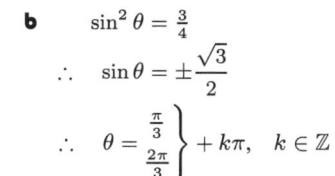

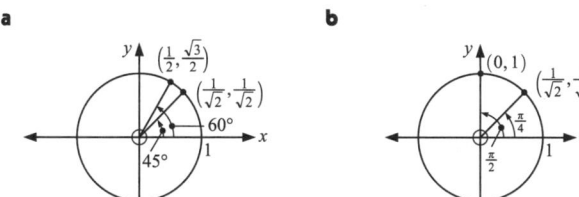

b $\sin^2\theta = \frac{3}{4}$
$\therefore \sin\theta = \pm\frac{\sqrt{3}}{2}$
$\therefore \theta = \left.\begin{matrix}\frac{\pi}{3}\\\frac{2\pi}{3}\end{matrix}\right\} + k\pi, \quad k \in \mathbb{Z}$

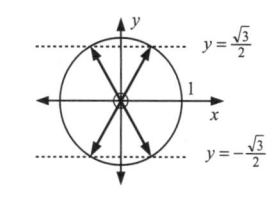

8 a
$\tan^2 60° - \sin^2 45°$
$= (\sqrt{3})^2 - \left(\frac{1}{\sqrt{2}}\right)^2$
$= 3 - \frac{1}{2}$
$= 2\frac{1}{2}$

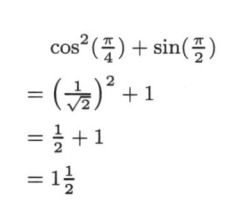

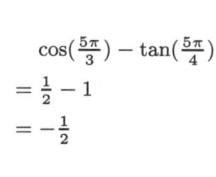

b
$\cos^2\left(\frac{\pi}{4}\right) + \sin\left(\frac{\pi}{2}\right)$
$= \left(\frac{1}{\sqrt{2}}\right)^2 + 1$
$= \frac{1}{2} + 1$
$= 1\frac{1}{2}$

c 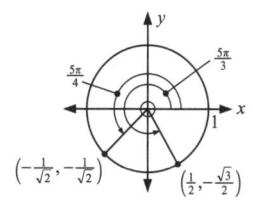
$\cos\left(\frac{5\pi}{3}\right) - \tan\left(\frac{5\pi}{4}\right)$
$= \frac{1}{2} - 1$
$= -\frac{1}{2}$

9 a $\cos(\frac{\pi}{2} - \theta) - \sin\theta = \sin\theta - \sin\theta$
$= 0$

b $\cos\theta \tan\theta = \cos\theta \left(\dfrac{\sin\theta}{\cos\theta}\right)$
$= \sin\theta$

10 area = 80 cm^2
$\therefore \ \frac{1}{2} \times 11.3 \times 19.2 \sin x° = 80$
$\therefore \ \sin x° = \dfrac{160}{11.3 \times 19.2}$

Now $\arcsin\left(\dfrac{160}{11.3 \times 19.2}\right) \approx 47.5°$
$\therefore \ x \approx 47.5$ or $180 - 47.5$
$\therefore \ x \approx 47.5$ or 132.5

Consider the case $x \approx 47.5$.
We construct a perpendicular from A to (BC).
$\sin 47.5° = \dfrac{AD}{19.2}$ and $\cos 47.5° = \dfrac{BD}{19.2}$.

Using Pythagoras' theorem,
$AC^2 = AD^2 + CD^2$
$\quad = AD^2 + (BC - BD)^2$
$\therefore \ AC \approx \sqrt{(19.2 \sin 47.5°)^2 + (11.3 - 19.2 \cos 47.5°)^2}$
$\quad \approx 14.3$ cm

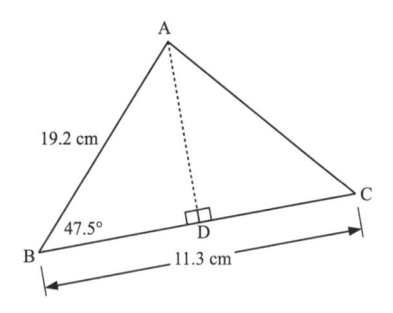

We can similarly construct a perpendicular from A to the extension (BC) in the case $x \approx 132.5$. In this case we obtain $AC \approx 28.1$ cm.

11 shaded area
= area of sector − area of Δ
$= \frac{1}{2} \times \frac{13\pi}{18} \times 7^2 - \frac{1}{2} \times 7 \times 7 \times \sin\frac{13\pi}{18}$
≈ 36.8 cm^2

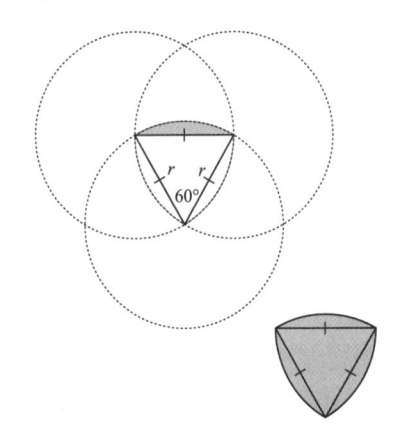

12

shaded area of sector
= area of sector − area of Δ
$= \dfrac{60}{360}\pi r^2 - \frac{1}{2} \times r \times r \times \sin 60°$
$= \frac{\pi}{6}r^2 - \frac{1}{2}r^2 \left(\frac{\sqrt{3}}{2}\right)$

$\therefore$ shaded area of figure
$= 3\left[\frac{\pi}{6}r^2 - \frac{\sqrt{3}}{4}r^2\right] + \frac{1}{2}r^2 \left(\frac{\sqrt{3}}{2}\right)$
$= \frac{\pi}{2}r^2 - \frac{3\sqrt{3}}{4}r^2 + \frac{\sqrt{3}}{4}r^2$
$= \frac{\pi}{2}r^2 - \frac{1}{2}\sqrt{3}r^2$
$= \dfrac{r^2}{2}\left(\pi - \sqrt{3}\right)$

Chapter 11
NON-RIGHT ANGLED TRIANGLE TRIGONOMETRY

EXERCISE 11A

1 **a** $BC^2 = 21^2 + 15^2 - 2 \times 21 \times 15 \times \cos 105°$

$\therefore BC = \sqrt{21^2 + 15^2 - 2 \times 21 \times 15 \times \cos 105°} \approx 28.8$ cm

b $PQ^2 = 6.3^2 + 4.8^2 - 2 \times 6.3 \times 4.8 \times \cos 32°$

$\therefore PQ = \sqrt{6.3^2 + 4.8^2 - 2 \times 6.3 \times 4.8 \times \cos 32°} \approx 3.38$ km

c $KM^2 = 6.2^2 + 14.8^2 - 2 \times 6.2 \times 14.8 \times \cos 72°$

$\therefore KM = \sqrt{6.2^2 + 14.8^2 - 2 \times 6.2 \times 14.8 \times \cos 72°} \approx 14.2$ m

2 $\cos A = \dfrac{12^2 + 13^2 - 11^2}{2 \times 12 \times 13}$ $\qquad \cos B = \dfrac{13^2 + 11^2 - 12^2}{2 \times 13 \times 11}$ $\qquad C = 180° - A - B$

$\therefore A = \cos^{-1}\left(\dfrac{192}{312}\right)$ $\qquad \therefore B = \cos^{-1}\left(\dfrac{146}{286}\right)$ $\qquad \approx 68.7°$

$\therefore A \approx 52.0°$ $\qquad \therefore B \approx 59.3°$

3 $\cos Q = \dfrac{5^2 + 7^2 - 10^2}{2 \times 5 \times 7}$

$\therefore Q = \cos^{-1}\left(\dfrac{-26}{70}\right)$

$\therefore Q \approx 112°$

4 **a**

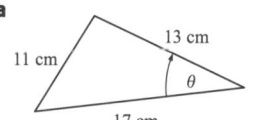

The smallest angle is opposite the shortest side.

$\cos \theta = \dfrac{13^2 + 17^2 - 11^2}{2 \times 13 \times 17}$

$\therefore \theta = \cos^{-1}\left(\dfrac{337}{442}\right)$

$\therefore \theta \approx 40.3$

So, the smallest angle measures 40.3°.

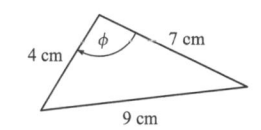

b

The largest angle is opposite the longest side.

$\cos \phi = \dfrac{4^2 + 7^2 - 9^2}{2 \times 4 \times 7}$

$\therefore \phi = \cos^{-1}\left(-\dfrac{16}{56}\right)$

$\therefore \phi \approx 106.60$

So, the largest angle measures about 107°.

5 **a** $\cos \theta = \dfrac{2^2 + 5^2 - 4^2}{2 \times 2 \times 5}$

$= \dfrac{13}{20}$

$= 0.65$

b $x^2 = 5^2 + 3^2 - 2 \times 5 \times 3 \times \cos \theta$

$\therefore x = \sqrt{5^2 + 3^2 - 2 \times 5 \times 3 \times 0.65}$

$\therefore x \approx 3.81$

6 **a** $7^2 = x^2 + 6^2 - 2 \times x \times 6 \times \cos 60°$

$\therefore 49 = x^2 + 36 - 12x \times \left(\tfrac{1}{2}\right)$

$\therefore x^2 - 6x - 13 = 0$

$\therefore x = \dfrac{6 \pm \sqrt{36 - 4(1)(-13)}}{2}$

$= \dfrac{6 \pm \sqrt{88}}{2}$

$= 3 \pm \sqrt{22}$

But $x > 0$, so $x = 3 + \sqrt{22}$.

b $5^2 = x^2 + 3^2 - 2 \times x \times 3 \times \cos 120°$

$\therefore 25 = x^2 + 9 - 6x \times \left(-\tfrac{1}{2}\right)$

$\therefore x^2 + 3x - 16 = 0$

$\therefore x = \dfrac{-3 \pm \sqrt{9 - 4(1)(-16)}}{2}$

$= \dfrac{-3 \pm \sqrt{73}}{2}$

But $x > 0$, so $x = \dfrac{-3 + \sqrt{73}}{2}$.

c $5^2 = (2x)^2 + x^2 - 2 \times (2x) \times x \times \cos 60°$
$\therefore \quad 25 = 4x^2 + x^2 - 4x^2(\frac{1}{2})$
$\therefore \quad 3x^2 = 25$
$\therefore \quad x^2 = \frac{25}{3}$
$\therefore \quad x = \pm\frac{5}{\sqrt{3}}$ But $x > 0$, so $x = \frac{5}{\sqrt{3}}$.

7 a $11^2 = x^2 + 8^2 - 2 \times x \times 8 \times \cos 70°$
$\therefore \quad 121 = x^2 + 64 - 16x \cos 70°$
$\therefore \quad x^2 - (16 \cos 70°)x - 57 = 0$
Using the quadratic formula or technology,
$x \approx -5.29$ or 10.8.
But $x > 0$, so $x \approx 10.8$.

b $13^2 = x^2 + 5^2 - 2 \times x \times 5 \times \cos 130°$
$\therefore \quad 169 = x^2 + 25 - 10x \cos 130°$
$\therefore \quad x^2 - (10 \cos 130°)x - 144 = 0$
Using the quadratic formula or technology,
$x \approx -15.6$ or 9.21.
But $x > 0$, so $x \approx 9.21$.

8 a $(3x+1)^2 = (x+2)^2 + (x+3)^2 - 2(x+2)(x+3) \cos \theta$
$\therefore \quad 9x^2 + 6x + 1 = x^2 + 4x + 4 + x^2 + 6x + 9 - 2(x^2 + 5x + 6)(-\frac{1}{5})$
$\therefore \quad 9x^2 + 6x + 1 = 2x^2 + 10x + 13 + \frac{2}{5}x^2 + 2x + \frac{12}{5}$
$\therefore \quad \frac{33}{5}x^2 - 6x - \frac{72}{5} = 0$
$\therefore \quad 33x^2 - 30x - 72 = 0$
$\therefore \quad 3(11x + 12)(x - 2) = 0$
$\therefore \quad x = -\frac{12}{11}$ or 2
But $3x + 1 > 0$, so $x = 2$.

b $\cos^2 \theta + \sin^2 \theta = 1$
$\therefore \quad \frac{1}{25} + \sin^2 \theta = 1$
$\therefore \quad \sin^2 \theta = \frac{24}{25}$
$\therefore \quad \sin \theta = \pm \frac{\sqrt{24}}{5}$
But $0° < \theta < 180°$, so $\sin \theta > 0$.
$\therefore \quad \sin \theta = \frac{\sqrt{24}}{5}$

$\therefore$ area $= \frac{1}{2} \times (x+2) \times (x+3) \times \sin \theta$
$= \frac{1}{2} \times 4 \times 5 \times \frac{\sqrt{24}}{5}$
$= 2\sqrt{24}$ cm^2

EXERCISE 11B.1

1 a By the sine rule,
$\frac{x}{\sin 48°} = \frac{23}{\sin 37°}$
$\therefore \quad x = \frac{23 \times \sin 48°}{\sin 37°}$
$\therefore \quad x \approx 28.4$

b By the sine rule,
$\frac{x}{\sin 115°} = \frac{11}{\sin 48°}$
$\therefore \quad x = \frac{11 \times \sin 115°}{\sin 48°}$
$\therefore \quad x \approx 13.4$

c By the sine rule,
$\frac{x}{\sin 51°} = \frac{4.8}{\sin 80°}$
$\therefore \quad x = \frac{4.8 \times \sin 51°}{\sin 80°}$
$\therefore \quad x \approx 3.79$

2 a

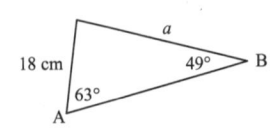

$\frac{a}{\sin 63°} = \frac{18}{\sin 49°}$ {sine rule}
$\therefore \quad a = \frac{18 \times \sin 63°}{\sin 49°}$
$\therefore \quad a \approx 21.3$ cm

b $(180 - 82 - 25)° = 73°$

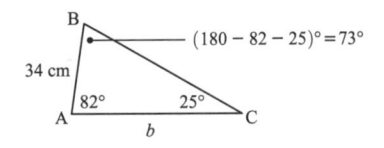

By the sine rule, $\frac{b}{\sin 73°} = \frac{34}{\sin 25°}$
$\therefore \quad b = \frac{34 \times \sin 73°}{\sin 25°}$
$\therefore \quad b \approx 76.9$ cm

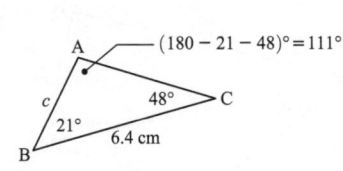

By the sine rule, $\dfrac{c}{\sin 48°} = \dfrac{6.4}{\sin 111°}$

$\therefore \ c = \dfrac{6.4 \times \sin 48°}{\sin 111°}$

$\therefore \ c \approx 5.09$ cm

$(180 - 21 - 48)° = 111°$

EXERCISE 11B.2

1 By the sine rule, $\dfrac{\sin C}{11} = \dfrac{\sin 40°}{8}$

$\therefore \ \sin C = \dfrac{11 \times \sin 40°}{8}$

$\therefore \ C = \sin^{-1}\left(\dfrac{11 \times \sin 40°}{8}\right)$ or its supplement

$\therefore \ C \approx 62.1°$ or $(180 - 62.1)°$

$\therefore \ C \approx 62.1°$ or $117.9°$

2 a $\dfrac{\sin A}{a} = \dfrac{\sin B}{b}$

$\therefore \ \sin A = \dfrac{14.6 \times \sin 65°}{17.4}$

$\therefore \ A = \sin^{-1}\left(\dfrac{14.6 \times \sin 65°}{17.4}\right)$

or its supplement

$\therefore \ A \approx 49.5°$ or $180° - 49.5°$

$\therefore \ A \approx 49.5°$ or $130.5°$

Check: $A = 130.5°$ is impossible as $A + B = 130.5° + 65°$ is already over $180°$. $\therefore \ A \approx 49.5°$

b $\dfrac{\sin B}{43.8} = \dfrac{\sin 43°}{31.4}$

$\therefore \ \sin B = \dfrac{43.8 \times \sin 43°}{31.4}$

$\therefore \ B = \sin^{-1}\left(\dfrac{43.8 \times \sin 43°}{31.4}\right)$

or its supplement

$\therefore \ B \approx 72.0°$ or $108°$

both of which are possible as $108 + 43 = 151$ which is < 180.

c $\dfrac{\sin C}{4.8} = \dfrac{\sin 71°}{6.5}$

$\therefore \ \sin C = \dfrac{4.8 \times \sin 71°}{6.5}$

$\therefore \ C = \sin^{-1}\left(\dfrac{4.8 \times \sin 71°}{6.5}\right)$ or its supplement

$\therefore \ C \approx 44.3°$ or $135.7°$

But $135.7 + 71 > 180$ $\therefore$ this case is impossible $\therefore \ C \approx 44.3°$

3 The third angle is $180° - 85° - 68° = 27°$

$\dfrac{\sin 85°}{11.4}$ and $\dfrac{\sin 27°}{9.8}$

$\approx 0.087\,38$ $\approx 0.046\,32$

$\therefore$ it is not possible as $\dfrac{\sin 85°}{11.4} \neq \dfrac{\sin 27°}{9.8}$

$\therefore$ the sine rule is violated.

4 In $\triangle ABD$,

$\theta = 78 - 12$

$\therefore \ \widehat{ABC} = 66°$

Now $\dfrac{x}{\sin 12°} = \dfrac{20}{\sin 66°}$

$\therefore \ x = \dfrac{20 \times \sin 12°}{\sin 66°}$

$\therefore \ x \approx 4.55$

$\therefore$ [BD] is 4.55 cm long

5 First we find the length of the diagonal, d m.

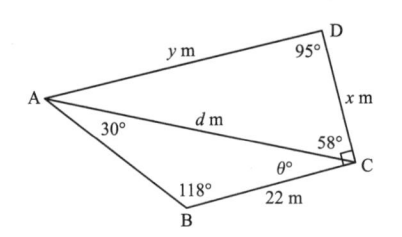

$$\frac{d}{\sin 118°} = \frac{22}{\sin 30°}$$

$$\therefore \quad d = \frac{22 \times \sin 118°}{\sin 30°}$$

$$\therefore \quad d \approx 38.85$$

Using the sine rule

$$\frac{y}{\sin 58°} = \frac{38.85}{\sin 95°}$$

$$\therefore \quad y \approx \frac{38.85 \times \sin 58°}{\sin 95°}$$

$$\therefore \quad y \approx 33.1$$

$\theta = 180 - 30 - 118 = 32$

$\therefore \quad \widehat{ACD} = 58°$

and $\quad \dfrac{x}{\sin(180 - 95 - 58)°} \approx \dfrac{38.85}{\sin 95°}$

$$\therefore \quad x \approx \frac{38.85 \times \sin 27°}{\sin 95°}$$

$$\therefore \quad x \approx 17.7$$

6 a $(180 - 58 - C)° = (122 - C)°$

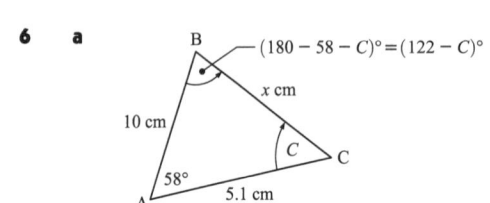

$$\frac{\sin C}{10} = \frac{\sin(122 - C)}{5.1}$$

$\therefore \quad 5.1 \sin C = 10 \sin(122 - C)$

Using technology,

$C \approx 88.7°$ or $(180 - 88.7)°$

$\therefore \quad C \approx 88.7°$ or $91.3°$

b Let $BC = x$ cm $\quad \therefore \quad x^2 = 10^2 + 5.1^2 - 2 \times 10 \times 5.1 \cos 58°$

$$\therefore \quad x = \sqrt{10^2 + 5.1^2 - 20 \times 5.1 \times \cos 58°}$$

$$\therefore \quad x \approx 8.4828$$

and $\quad \cos C = \dfrac{5.1^2 + 8.4828^2 - 10^2}{2 \times 5.1 \times 8.4828} \approx -0.023\,09$

$$\therefore \quad C \approx \arccos(-0.02309) \approx 91.3°$$

c "When faced with using either the sine rule or the cosine rule it is better to use the *cosine rule* as it avoids *the ambiguous case*."

7 $\quad 9^2 = x^2 + 7^2 - 2 \times x \times 7 \times \cos 30°$

$$\therefore \quad 81 = x^2 + 49 - 14x\left(\tfrac{\sqrt{3}}{2}\right)$$

$$\therefore \quad x^2 - \tfrac{14\sqrt{3}}{2}x - 32 = 0$$

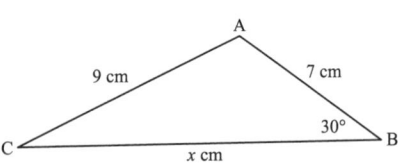

Using the quadratic formula or technology,

$x \approx -2.23$ or 14.35

but $x > 0$, so $x \approx 14.35$

$\therefore \quad$ area of triangle $\approx \tfrac{1}{2} \times 7 \times 14.35 \times \sin 30° \approx 25.1$ cm^2

8 $\quad \dfrac{2x - 5}{\sin 45°} = \dfrac{x + 3}{\sin 30°}$

$\therefore \quad (2x - 5)\sin 30° = (x + 3)\sin 45°$

$\therefore \quad \dfrac{2x - 5}{2} = \dfrac{x + 3}{\sqrt{2}}$

$\therefore \quad 2\sqrt{2}x - 5\sqrt{2} = 2x + 6$

$\therefore \quad -6 - 5\sqrt{2} = x(2 - 2\sqrt{2})$

$$\therefore \quad x = \left(\frac{-6 - 5\sqrt{2}}{2 - 2\sqrt{2}}\right)\left(\frac{2 + 2\sqrt{2}}{2 + 2\sqrt{2}}\right)$$

$$= \frac{-12 - 12\sqrt{2} - 10\sqrt{2} - 10(2)}{4 - 4(2)}$$

$$= \frac{-32 - 22\sqrt{2}}{-4}$$

$$= 8 + \tfrac{11}{2}\sqrt{2}$$

EXERCISE 11C

1

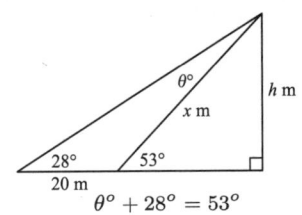

$\theta° + 28° = 53°$
{exterior angle of a $\triangle$ theorem}
$\therefore \ \theta = 25$

By the sine rule,
$$\frac{x}{\sin 28°} = \frac{20}{\sin 25°}$$
$$\therefore \ x \approx \frac{20 \times \sin 28°}{\sin 25°}$$
$$\therefore \ x \approx 22.22$$

and $\sin 53° = \dfrac{h}{x}$
$\therefore \ h = x \sin 53°$
$\quad \approx 22.22 \times \sin 53°$
$\quad \approx 17.7$ m
$\therefore$ the pole is 17.7 m high.

2 $PR^2 = 63^2 + 175^2 - 2 \times 63 \times 175 \times \cos 112°$
$\therefore \ PR = \sqrt{63^2 + 175^2 - 2 \times 63 \times 175 \times \cos 112°}$
$\therefore \ PR \approx 207$ m

3 $\cos T = \dfrac{220^2 + 340^2 - 165^2}{2 \times 220 \times 340}$
$\therefore \ T = \cos^{-1}\left(\dfrac{136\,775}{149\,600}\right)$
$\therefore \ T \approx 23.9$
$\therefore$ the tee shot was 23.9° off line.

4

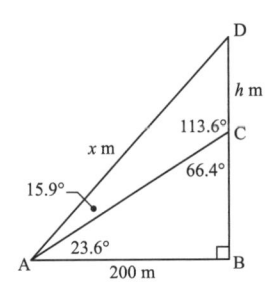

In $\triangle ABD$,
$\cos(23.6 + 15.9)° = \dfrac{200}{x}$
$\therefore \ x = \dfrac{200}{\cos 39.5°}$
$\therefore \ x \approx 259.2$

In $\triangle ACD$,
$\dfrac{h}{\sin 15.9°} = \dfrac{x}{\sin 113.6°}$
$\therefore \ h \approx \dfrac{259.2 \times \sin 15.9°}{\sin 113.6°}$
$\therefore \ h \approx 77.5$
$\therefore$ the tower is 77.5 m high.

5

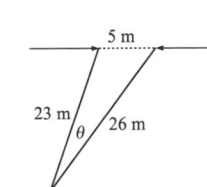

$\cos \theta = \dfrac{23^2 + 26^2 - 5^2}{2 \times 23 \times 26}$
$\therefore \ \theta = \cos^{-1}\left(\dfrac{1180}{1196}\right)$
$\therefore \ \theta \approx 9.38°$
$\therefore$ the angle of view is 9.38°.

6

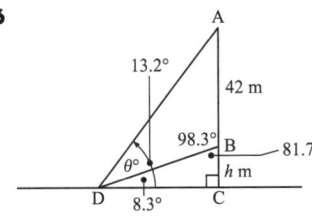

$\theta = 13.2° - 8.3° = 4.9°$

In $\triangle ABD$,
$\dfrac{AD}{\sin 98.3°} = \dfrac{42}{\sin 4.9°}$
$\therefore \ AD = \dfrac{42 \times \sin 98.3°}{\sin 4.9°}$
$\therefore \ AD \approx 486.56$ m

In $\triangle ADC$,
$\sin 13.2° = \dfrac{h + 42}{AD}$
$\therefore \ h + 42 \approx 486.56 \times \sin 13.2°$
$\therefore \ h + 42 \approx 111.1$
$\therefore \ h \approx 69.1$
$\therefore$ the hill is 69.1 m high.

7 a, b

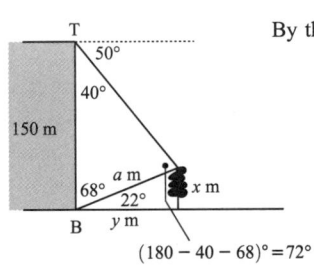

$(180 - 40 - 68)° = 72°$

By the sine rule, $\dfrac{a}{\sin 40°} = \dfrac{150}{\sin 72°}$
$\therefore \ a = \dfrac{150 \times \sin 40°}{\sin 72°}$
$\therefore \ a \approx 101.38$

Now $\sin 22° \approx \dfrac{x}{101.38}$ and $\cos 22° \approx \dfrac{y}{101.38}$

$\therefore \quad x \approx 101.38 \times \sin 22°$ $\qquad \therefore \quad y \approx 101.38 \times \cos 22°$

$\therefore \quad x \approx 38.0$ $\qquad \qquad \therefore \quad y \approx 94.0$

$\therefore$ the tree is 38.0 m high and 94.0 m from the building.

8 Using Pythagoras' theorem

$RQ = \sqrt{4^2 + 7^2} = \sqrt{65}$ m

$PQ = \sqrt{8^2 + 7^2} = \sqrt{113}$ cm

$PR = \sqrt{8^2 + 4^2} = \sqrt{80}$ cm

Now $\cos Q = \dfrac{(\sqrt{113})^2 + (\sqrt{65})^2 - (\sqrt{80})^2}{2 \times \sqrt{113} \times \sqrt{65}}$

$\therefore \quad \cos \theta \approx \left(\dfrac{98}{171.4}\right)$

$\therefore \quad \theta \approx \cos^{-1}\left(\dfrac{98}{171.4}\right)$

$\therefore \quad \theta \approx 55.1 \qquad$ So, $P\widehat{Q}R$ measures 55.1°

9 $(180 - 42 - 67)° = 71°$

$\dfrac{x}{\sin 67°} = \dfrac{12}{\sin 71°} = \dfrac{y}{\sin 42°}$

$\therefore \quad x = \dfrac{12 \times \sin 67°}{\sin 71°} \quad$ and $\quad y = \dfrac{12 \times \sin 42°}{\sin 71°}$

$\therefore \quad x \approx 11.7 \qquad \qquad \therefore \quad y \approx 8.49$

So, C is 11.7 km from A and 8.49 km from B.

10 a $QS = \sqrt{8^2 + 12^2 - 2 \times 8 \times 12 \times \cos 70°}$

≈ 11.93

$\therefore$ area $\approx \tfrac{1}{2} \times 8 \times 12 \times \sin 70° + \tfrac{1}{2} \times 10 \times 11.93 \times \sin 30°$

≈ 74.9 km²

b 1 ha is 100 m × 100 m

$= 0.1$ km × 0.1 km

$= 0.01$ km²

$\therefore \quad 1$ km² $= 100$ ha

$\therefore$ area ≈ 7490 ha

11

Distance = speed × time

So, after 45 min = 0.75 h

$AT = 6 \times 0.75 = 4.5$ km

$AP = 8 \times 0.75 = 6$ km

Now $PT = \sqrt{4.5^2 + 6^2 - 2 \times 4.5 \times 6 \times \cos 120°}$

$\therefore \quad PT \approx 9.12$

So, they are 9.12 km apart.

12 In $\triangle ABC$, $\dfrac{AC}{\sin 110°} = \dfrac{200}{\sin 38°}$

$\therefore \quad AC = \dfrac{200 \times \sin 110°}{\sin 38°} \approx 305.26$

and in $\triangle ACD$, $\dfrac{x}{\sin 8°} \approx \dfrac{305.26}{\sin 30°}$

$\therefore \quad x \approx \dfrac{305.26 \times \sin 8°}{\sin 30°} \approx 84.968$

$\therefore$ the metal strip is 85.0 mm wide.

13 $x = \sqrt{6^2 + (4.5)^2 - 2 \times 6 \times 4.5 \times \cos 148°}$

$\therefore \quad x \approx 10.1$

$\therefore$ the orienteer is 10.1 km from the start.

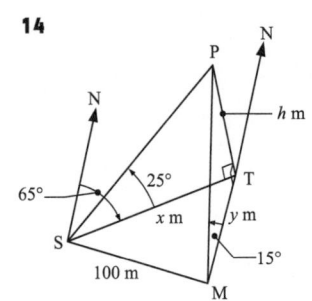

14 In $\triangle$PST, $\tan 25° = \dfrac{h}{x}$ In $\triangle$PMT, $\tan 15° = \dfrac{h}{y}$

$\therefore \ x = \dfrac{h}{\tan 25°}$ $\therefore \ y = \dfrac{h}{\tan 15°}$

$\approx 2.145h$ $\approx 3.732h$

But $\widehat{\text{STM}} = 65°$ {equal alternate angles}

and $100^2 = x^2 + y^2 - 2xy \cos 65°$

$\therefore \ 10\,000 \approx (2.145h)^2 + (3.732h)^2 - 2 \times (2.145)(3.732)h^2 \cos 65°$

$\therefore \ 10\,000 \approx 11.762\,h^2$

$\therefore \ h^2 \approx 850.17$

$\therefore \ h \approx 29.2$ So, the tree is 29.2 m high.

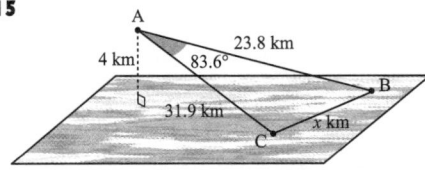

15 By the cosine rule

$x^2 = 23.8^2 + 31.9^2 - 2 \times 23.8 \times 31.9 \times \cos 83.6°$

$\therefore \ x = \sqrt{23.8^2 + 31.9^2 - 2 \times 23.8 \times 31.9 \times \cos 83.6°}$

$\therefore \ x \approx 37.6$

$\therefore$ B and C are 37.6 km apart.

REVIEW SET 11A

1 a $\cos x° = \dfrac{13^2 + 19^2 - 11^2}{2 \times 13 \times 19}$ **b** $x = \sqrt{15^2 + 17^2 - 2 \times 15 \times 17 \times \cos 72°}$

$\therefore \ \cos x° = \dfrac{409}{494}$ $\therefore \ x \approx 18.9$

$\therefore \ x° = \cos^{-1}\left(\dfrac{409}{494}\right)$

$\therefore \ x \approx 34.1$

2 a $\cos x° = \dfrac{11^2 + 19^2 - 13^2}{2 \times 11 \times 19}$ **b** $x = \sqrt{14^2 + 21^2 - 2 \times 14 \times 21 \times \cos 47°}$

$\therefore \ \cos x° = \dfrac{313}{418}$ $\therefore \ x \approx 15.4$

$\therefore \ x° = \cos^{-1}\left(\dfrac{313}{418}\right)$

$\therefore \ x \approx 41.5$

3 $AC = \sqrt{11^2 + 9.8^2 - 2 \times 11 \times 9.8 \times \cos 74°}$ Now $\dfrac{\sin C}{11} = \dfrac{\sin 74°}{AC}$

$\therefore \ AC \approx 12.554$ cm

$\therefore \ AC \approx 12.6$ cm $\therefore \ \sin C \approx \dfrac{11 \times \sin 74°}{12.554}$

$\therefore \ C \approx \sin^{-1}\left(\dfrac{11 \times \sin 74°}{12.554}\right)$ or its supplement

$\therefore \ C \approx 57.4°$ or $122.6°$

$\uparrow$

impossible as $122.6 + 74 > 180$

$\therefore \ C$ measures 57.4°

$\therefore \ A$ measures 48.6°.

4 $DB = \sqrt{7^2 + 11^2 - 2 \times 7 \times 11 \times \cos 110°} \approx 14.922$ cm

$\therefore$ total area $\approx \tfrac{1}{2} \times 7 \times 11 \times \sin 110° + \tfrac{1}{2} \times 16 \times 14.922 \times \sin 40°$

≈ 113 cm^2

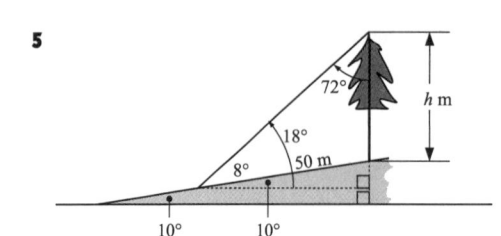

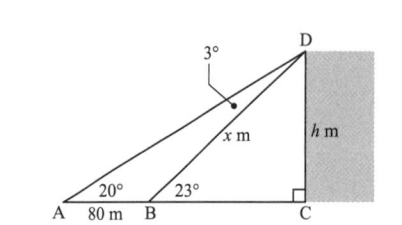

5

$$\frac{h}{\sin 8°} = \frac{50}{\sin 72°}$$

$$\therefore\ h = \frac{50 \times \sin 8°}{\sin 72°}$$

$$\therefore\ h \approx 7.32$$

So, the tree is 7.32 m high.

6

In $\triangle ABD$, $\dfrac{x}{\sin 20°} = \dfrac{80}{\sin 3°}$

$$\therefore\ x = \frac{80 \times \sin 20°}{\sin 3°} \approx 522.8$$

Now $\sin 23° = \dfrac{h}{x}$

$$\therefore\ h \approx 522.8 \times \sin 23°$$
$$\therefore\ h \approx 204$$

So the building is 204 m tall.

7

$A\hat{S}P = 203° - 113° = 90°$

$$\therefore\ x^2 = 310^2 + 430^2 \quad \{\text{Pythagoras}\}$$
$$\therefore\ x = \sqrt{310^2 + 430^2}$$
$$\therefore\ x \approx 530$$

$\therefore\ $ they are 530 m apart.

and $\tan\theta = \dfrac{430}{310}$

$$\therefore\ \theta = \tan^{-1}\left(\frac{430}{310}\right) \approx 54.2$$

and $23 + \theta = 77.2$

$\therefore\ $ the bearing of Peter from Alix is 077.2°.

8

In 45 minutes, $140 \times \tfrac{3}{4} = 105$ km is travelled.

In 40 minutes, $180 \times \tfrac{2}{3} = 120$ km is travelled.

We notice that $\theta + 43 + 32 = 180$ $\{\text{co-interior angles add to 180°}\}$
$$\therefore\ \theta = 105$$

and so, $x = \sqrt{120^2 + 105^2 - 2 \times 120 \times 105 \times \cos 105°}$
$$\therefore\ x \approx 178.74$$

So, the car is 179 km from the start.

Now $\dfrac{\sin\phi}{105} \approx \dfrac{\sin 105°}{178.74}$

$$\therefore\ \sin\phi \approx \frac{105 \times \sin 105°}{178.74}$$

$$\therefore\ \phi \approx 34.6$$
$$\therefore\ \alpha \approx 180 - 105 - 34.6 - 32 \approx 8.4 \approx 8$$

So, the bearing from its starting point is 352°.

9 If the unknown is an angle, use the cosine rule to avoid the ambiguous case.

10 a By the cosine rule, $7^2 = 8^2 + x^2 - 2 \times 8 \times x \times \cos 60°$

$$\therefore\ 49 = 64 + x^2 - 16x\left(\tfrac{1}{2}\right)$$
$$\therefore\ 49 = 64 + x^2 - 8x$$
$$\therefore\ x^2 - 8x + 15 = 0$$
$$\therefore\ (x-3)(x-5) = 0$$
$$\therefore\ x = 3 \text{ or } 5$$

b Kady's response should be "Please supply me with additional information as there are two possibilities. Which one do you want?"

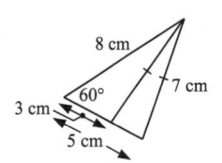

11 a 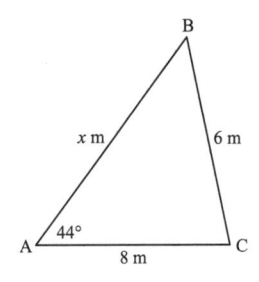 By the cosine rule, $6^2 = x^2 + 8^2 - 2 \times x \times 8 \times \cos 44°$
$\therefore \quad 36 = x^2 + 64 - 16x \times \cos 44°$
$\therefore \quad x^2 - 11.51x + 28 \approx 0$
$\therefore \quad x \approx \dfrac{11.51 \pm \sqrt{11.51^2 - 4(1)(28)}}{2}$
$\therefore \quad x \approx \dfrac{11.51 \pm 4.524}{2}$
$\therefore \quad x \approx 8.02 \text{ or } 3.49$

Frank needs additional information as there are two possible cases:
(1) when $AB \approx 8.02$ m and
(2) when $AB \approx 3.49$ m

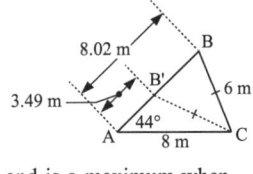

b Volume = area × depth
$= \tfrac{1}{2} \times 8 \times x \times \sin 44° \times 0.1$ and is a maximum when $AB \approx 8.02$ m
$\approx 4 \times 8.02 \times \sin 44° \times 0.1$
$\approx 2.23 \text{ m}^3$

REVIEW SET 11B

1 Using Pythagoras,
$ED = \sqrt{6^2 + 3^2} = \sqrt{45}$ m
$DG = \sqrt{4^2 + 3^2} = \sqrt{25} = 5$ m
$EG = \sqrt{6^2 + 4^2} = \sqrt{52}$ m

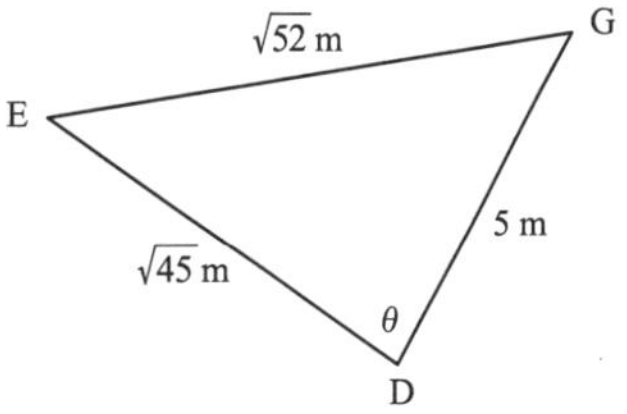

Using the cosine rule, $\cos \theta = \dfrac{(\sqrt{45})^2 + 5^2 - (\sqrt{52})^2}{2 \times \sqrt{45} \times 5}$
$\therefore \quad \theta = \cos^{-1}\left(\dfrac{18}{10\sqrt{45}}\right)$
$\therefore \quad \theta \approx 74.4°$ Thus $E\widehat{D}G$ measures $74.4°$.

2 $x^2 = 8^2 + 3^2 - 2 \times 8 \times 3 \times \cos 100°$
$\therefore \quad x = \sqrt{8^2 + 3^2 - 48 \cos 100°}$
$\therefore \quad x \approx 9.0186$

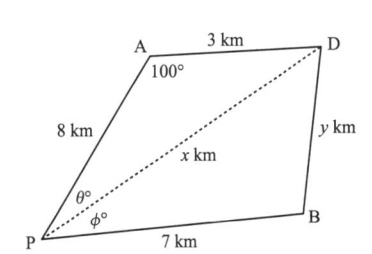

Now $\dfrac{\sin \theta°}{3} \approx \dfrac{\sin 100°}{9.0186}$
$\therefore \quad \sin \theta° \approx \dfrac{3 \times \sin 100°}{9.0186}$
$\therefore \quad \theta = \sin^{-1}\left(\dfrac{3 \times \sin 100°}{9.0186}\right)$
or its supplement
$\therefore \quad \theta \approx 19.1 \text{ or } 160.9$
        ↑
    impossible
$\therefore \quad \theta \approx 19.1$

$\therefore \quad \phi \approx 40 - 19.1 \approx 20.9$
$\therefore \quad y^2 = x^2 + 7^2 - 2 \times x \times 7 \times \cos \phi°$
$\therefore \quad y \approx \sqrt{(9.0186)^2 + 7^2 - 2 \times (9.0186) \times 7 \times \cos 20.9°}$
$\therefore \quad y \approx 3.52$

So, Brett has to walk 3.52 km.

3 a

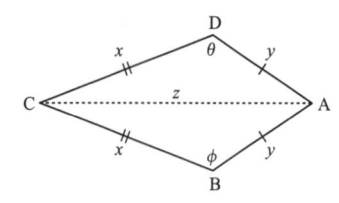

Using $\triangle ADC$,
$$z^2 = x^2 + y^2 - 2xy\cos\theta \quad \ldots\ldots (1)$$
Using $\triangle ABC$,
$$z^2 = x^2 + y^2 - 2xy\cos\phi \quad \ldots\ldots (2)$$
Equating (1) and (2),
$$\cos\theta = \cos\phi$$
and since $0 < \theta, \phi < 180$,
$$\theta = \phi$$
$$\therefore \quad A\widehat{D}C = A\widehat{B}C$$

b

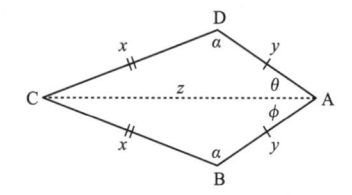

Using $\triangle DAC$,
$$\frac{\sin\theta}{x} = \frac{\sin\alpha}{z} \quad \ldots\ldots (1)$$
Using $\triangle BAC$,
$$\frac{\sin\phi}{x} = \frac{\sin\alpha}{z} \quad \ldots\ldots (2)$$
$\{A\widehat{D}C = A\widehat{B}C \text{ from } \mathbf{a}\}$
Equating (1) and (2),
$$\sin\theta = \sin\phi$$
$\therefore \quad \theta = \phi \text{ or } \theta = 180 - \phi$
but $D\widehat{A}B = \theta + \phi < 180°$
$\therefore \quad \theta = \phi$
$\therefore \quad D\widehat{A}C = B\widehat{A}C$

4 Total distance travelled $= x + 10$ km
$\therefore \quad AB = (x + 10) - 4 = x + 6$ km
Now $(x + 6)^2 = x^2 + 10^2 - 2 \times x \times 10 \times \cos 120°$
$\therefore \quad x^2 + 12x + 36 = x^2 + 100 - 20x(-\frac{1}{2})$
$\therefore \quad 12x + 36 = 100 + 10x$
$\therefore \quad 2x = 64$
$\therefore \quad x = 32$
$\therefore$ the boat travelled $x + 10 = 42$ km.

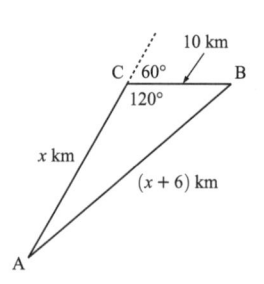

5 a speed $= \dfrac{\text{distance}}{\text{time}}$ $\quad \therefore$ distance $=$ speed $\times$ time
$\therefore$ in t hours, runner A travels $14 \times t = 14t$ km
and runner B travels $12 \times t = 12t$ km
Now $A\widehat{S}B = 97° - 25° = 72°$
$\therefore \quad 20^2 = (14t)^2 + (12t)^2 - 2(14t)(12t)\cos 72°$
$\therefore \quad 400 = 196t^2 + 144t^2 - 336t^2 \cos 72°$
$\therefore \quad 400 \approx 236.2t^2$
$\therefore \quad t^2 \approx 1.69$
$\therefore \quad t \approx 1.30 \quad \{t > 0\}$
$\therefore$ A and B are 20 km apart after 1 hour 18 minutes, at 2:18 pm.

b When $t \approx 1.30$, $SA \approx 14 \times 1.30 \approx 18.22$ km
and $SB \approx 12 \times 1.30 \approx 15.62$ km
$\therefore \quad \cos\theta° \approx \dfrac{18.22^2 + 20^2 - 15.62^2}{2 \times 18.22 \times 20}$
$\therefore \quad \theta° \approx \cos^{-1}\left(\dfrac{488.1}{728.8}\right)$
$\therefore \quad \theta \approx 48.0$
$\therefore \quad \phi \approx 360 - 155 - 48$
$\qquad \approx 157$
$\therefore$ B is on a bearing of 157° from A.

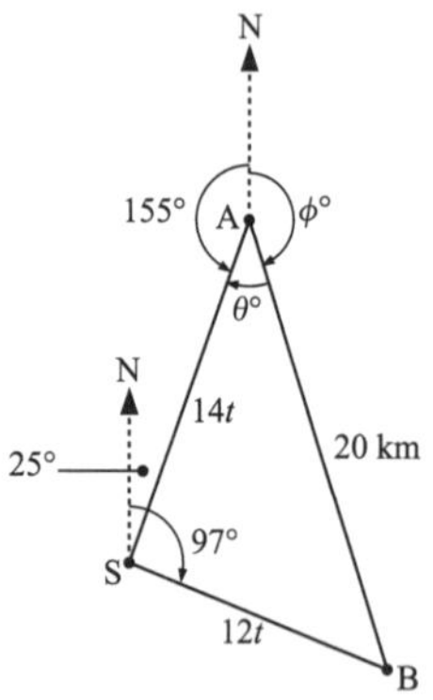

6 a $d^2 = x^2 + 5^2 - 2 \times x \times 5 \times \cos 20°$
∴ $d^2 = x^2 - (10 \cos 20°)x + 25$

b d^2 is minimised when $x = \dfrac{-b}{2a}$

∴ $x = \dfrac{10 \cos 20°}{2}$

∴ $x = 5 \cos 20°$

∴ d is minimised when $x = 5 \cos 20°$

c If $B\widehat{C}A$ is a right angle, then we have

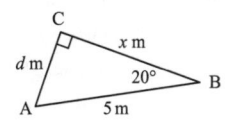

[diagram: triangle with C at top, A bottom-left, B bottom-right; d m from A to C, x m from C to B, 5 m from A to B, angle $20°$ at B]

Now $\cos 20° = \dfrac{x}{5}$

∴ $x = 5 \cos 20°$

and from **b**, d is minimised when $x = 5 \cos 20°$

∴ d is minimised when $B\widehat{C}A$ is a right angle.

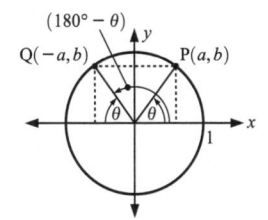

7 a [diagram: unit circle with $P(a,b)$ and $Q(-a,b)$, angle θ and $(180° - \theta)$]

∴ $\cos(180° - \theta) = -a$
$\qquad\qquad\qquad = -\cos\theta$

b **i** Using $\triangle JLM$,
$x^2 = 10^2 + 15^2 - 2 \times 10 \times 15 \cos d°$
∴ $x^2 = 325 - 300 \cos d°$ ..... (1)

Using $\triangle JLK$,
$x^2 = 12^2 + 8^2 - 2 \times 12 \times 8 \cos b°$
∴ $x^2 = 208 - 192 \cos b°$ ..... (2)

Equating (1) and (2), $325 - 300 \cos d° = 208 - 192 \cos b°$
∴ $300 \cos d° - 192 \cos b° = 117$

[diagram: quadrilateral JMLK with JK = 12 m, KL = 8 m, ML = 15 m, JM = 10 m, diagonal JL = x m, angle $d°$ at M, angle $b°$ at K]

ii If $b + d = 180$, then $b = 180 - d$
∴ $300 \cos d° - 192 \cos(180 - d)° = 117$
∴ $300 \cos d° + 192 \cos d° = 117$ {from **a**}
∴ $492 \cos d° = 117$
∴ $d = \cos^{-1}\left(\dfrac{117}{492}\right)$
∴ $d \approx 76.2$
and $b = 180 - d \approx 103.8$

iii If $b + d = 180$, then $a + c = 180$ also
{angles in a quadrilateral}

If $d \approx 76.2$, then $x \approx \sqrt{325 - 300 \cos(76.2)°}$ {from (1)}
∴ $x \approx 15.93$

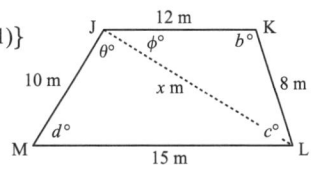

[diagram: same quadrilateral with angles $\theta°$, $\phi°$, $b°$, $d°$, $c°$ labelled]

In $\triangle JLM$, $\cos\theta° \approx \dfrac{10^2 + 15.93^2 - 15^2}{2 \times 10 \times 15.93}$

∴ $\theta° \approx \cos^{-1}\left(\dfrac{128.7}{318.5}\right)$
∴ $\theta \approx 66.2$

In $\triangle JLK$, $\cos\phi° \approx \dfrac{12^2 + 15.93^2 - 8^2}{2 \times 12 \times 15.93}$

∴ $\phi° \approx \cos^{-1}\left(\dfrac{333.7}{382.2}\right)$
∴ $\phi \approx 29.2$

∴ $a = \theta + \phi \approx 95.4$ and $c = 180 - a \approx 84.6$.

8 a $y = -x^2 + 12x - 20$ has $a = -1 < 0$

∴ its shape is ⌢, and y is maximised when $x = \dfrac{-b}{2a} = \dfrac{-12}{-2} = 6$.

When $x = 6$, $y = -6^2 + 12(6) - 20 = -36 + 72 - 20 = 16$

$\therefore$ the maximum value of $y = -x^2 + 12x - 20$ is 16, which occurs when $x = 6$.

b **i** The perimeter is 20

$\therefore \quad x + y + 8 = 20$

$\therefore \quad y = 12 - x$

ii $y^2 = x^2 + 8^2 - 2 \times x \times 8 \times \cos\theta$

$\therefore \quad y^2 = x^2 + 64 - 16x\cos\theta$

iii Since $y = 12 - x$, $(12 - x)^2 = x^2 + 64 - 16x\cos\theta$

$\therefore \quad 144 - 24x + x^2 = x^2 + 64 - 16x\cos\theta$

$\therefore \quad 16x\cos\theta = 24x - 80$

$\therefore \quad \cos\theta = \dfrac{24x - 80}{16x}$

$= \dfrac{3x - 10}{2x}$

c Area $A = \frac{1}{2} \times x \times 8 \times \sin\theta$

$= 4x\sin\theta$

$\therefore \quad A^2 = 16x^2 \sin^2\theta$

$= 16x^2(1 - \cos^2\theta)$

$= 16x^2 \left[1 - \left(\dfrac{3x - 10}{2x}\right)^2\right]$

$= 16x^2 \left[1 - \dfrac{9x^2 - 60x + 100}{4x^2}\right]$

$= 16x^2 - 4(9x^2 - 60x + 100)$

$= 16x^2 - 36x^2 + 240x - 400$

$= -20x^2 + 240x - 400$

$= 20(-x^2 + 12x - 20)$

d A is maximised when A^2 is maximised since $A > 0$.

From **a**, $-x^2 + 12x - 20$ has a maximum value of 16 when $x = 6$.

When $x = 6$, $A^2 = 20(16)$

$= 320$

$\therefore \quad A = \sqrt{320} \quad \{A > 0\}$

$= 8\sqrt{5}$

Also, when $x = 6$, $y = 12 - 6$

$= 6$

$\therefore$ the maximum area of the triangle is $8\sqrt{5}$ units^2, and the triangle is isosceles when this occurs.

9 a $QS^2 = 6^2 + 3^2 - 2 \times 6 \times 3 \times \cos\phi$

$\therefore \quad QS = \sqrt{45 - 36\cos\phi}$

b **i** If $\phi = 50°$, $QS = \sqrt{45 - 36\cos 50°}$

≈ 4.675

$\therefore \quad \dfrac{\sin\theta}{7} \approx \dfrac{\sin 32°}{4.675}$

$\therefore \quad \sin\theta \approx \dfrac{7 \times \sin 32°}{4.675}$

$\therefore \quad \theta \approx \sin^{-1}\left(\dfrac{7 \times \sin 32°}{4.675}\right)$ or its supplement

$\therefore \quad \theta \approx 52.5°$ or $(180 - 52.5)°$

$\therefore \quad \widehat{RSQ} \approx 52.5°$ or $127.5°$

ii If θ is acute, then $\theta \approx 52.5°$

and $\alpha = 180° - 32° - \theta$

$\approx 95.5°$

$\therefore \quad \dfrac{x}{\sin 95.5°} \approx \dfrac{7}{\sin 52.5°}$

$\therefore \quad x \approx \dfrac{7 \times \sin 95.5°}{\sin 52.5°}$

$\therefore \quad x \approx 8.78$

$\therefore$ perimeter $\approx 6 + 3 + 7 + 8.78$

≈ 24.8 units

c area of PQRS $= \frac{1}{2} \times 3 \times 6 \times \sin 50° + \frac{1}{2} \times 7 \times 8.78 \times \sin 32°$

≈ 23.2 units^2

or if θ is obtuse we can similarly calculate that the area of PQRS ≈ 12.6 units^2.

Chapter 12
ADVANCED TRIGONOMETRY

EXERCISE 12A

1 **a** Data exhibits periodic behaviour.

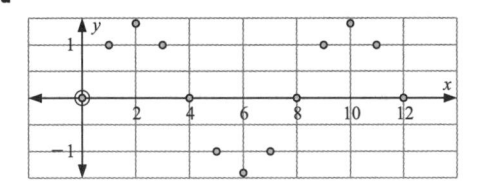

b Not enough information to say data is periodic. It may in fact be quadratic.

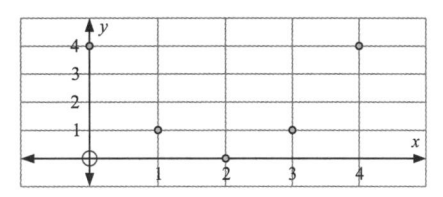

c Not enough information to say data is periodic. It may in fact be quadratic.

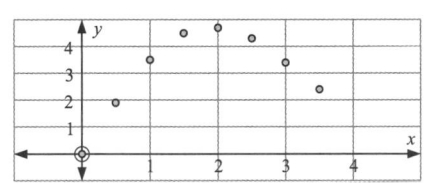

d Not enough information to say data is periodic.

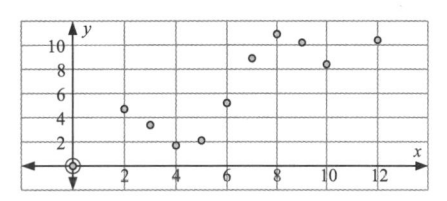

2 **a**

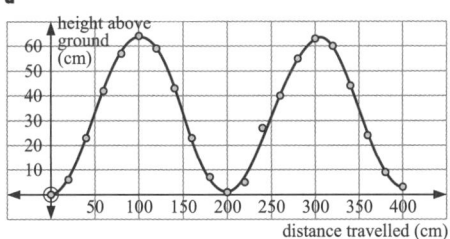

b The data is periodic.
  i The minimum value from the table is 0 and the maximum value is 64. So, the principal axis is $y \approx \frac{0+64}{2}$, $\therefore y \approx 32$.
  ii The maximum value is ≈ 64 cm.
  iii The period is ≈ 200 cm.
  iv The amplitude is ≈ 32 cm.

c A curve can be fitted to the data as the distance travelled is continuous.

3 **a** periodic **b** periodic **c** periodic **d** not periodic **e** periodic **f** periodic

EXERCISE 12B.1

1 **a** $y = 3 \sin x$
has amplitude 3 and period $\frac{2\pi}{1} = 2\pi$
When $x = 0$, $y = 0$.

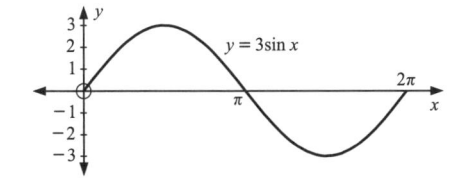

b $y = -3 \sin x$
has amplitude $|-3| = 3$
and period $\frac{2\pi}{1} = 2\pi$.
When $x = 0$, $y = 0$.

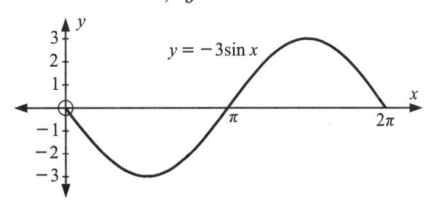

It is the reflection of $y = 3 \sin x$ in the x-axis.

c $y = \frac{3}{2}\sin x$

has amplitude $\frac{3}{2}$ and period $\frac{2\pi}{1} = 2\pi$.

When $x = 0$, $y = 0$.

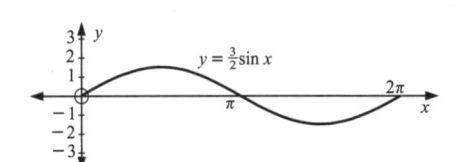

d $y = -\frac{3}{2}\sin x$

has amplitude $\left|-\frac{3}{2}\right| = \frac{3}{2}$

and period $\frac{2\pi}{1} = 2\pi$.

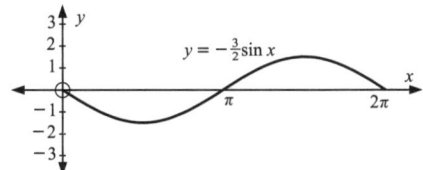

It is the reflection of $y = \frac{3}{2}\sin x$ in the x-axis.

2 a $y = \sin 3x$

has amplitude 1 and period $\frac{2\pi}{3}$.

When $x = 0$, $y = 0$.

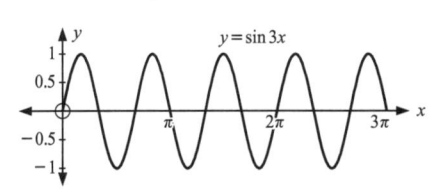

b $y = \sin\left(\frac{x}{2}\right)$

has amplitude 1 and period $\frac{2\pi}{\frac{1}{2}} = 4\pi$.

When $x = 0$, $y = 0$.

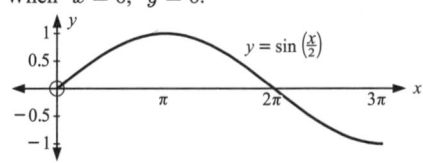

c $y = \sin(-2x)$

has amplitude 1 and period $\frac{2\pi}{|-2|} = \pi$.

When $x = 0$, $y = 0$.

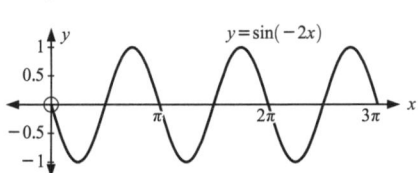

It is the reflection of $y = \sin 2x$ in the y-axis.

3 a period $= \dfrac{2\pi}{|4|}$

$= \dfrac{\pi}{2}$

b period $= \dfrac{2\pi}{|-4|}$

$= \dfrac{\pi}{2}$

c period $= \dfrac{2\pi}{\left|\frac{1}{3}\right|}$

$= 6\pi$

d period $= \dfrac{2\pi}{0.6}$

$= \dfrac{20\pi}{6} = \dfrac{10\pi}{3}$

4 a $\dfrac{2\pi}{B} = 5\pi$

$\therefore B = \frac{2}{5}$

b $\dfrac{2\pi}{B} = \dfrac{2\pi}{3}$

$\therefore B = 3$

c $\dfrac{2\pi}{B} = 12\pi$

$\therefore B = \frac{1}{6}$

d $\dfrac{2\pi}{B} = 4$

$\therefore B = \frac{\pi}{2}$

e $\dfrac{2\pi}{B} = 100$

$\therefore B = \dfrac{2\pi}{100} = \dfrac{\pi}{50}$

5 a, **b**, **c** (graphs)

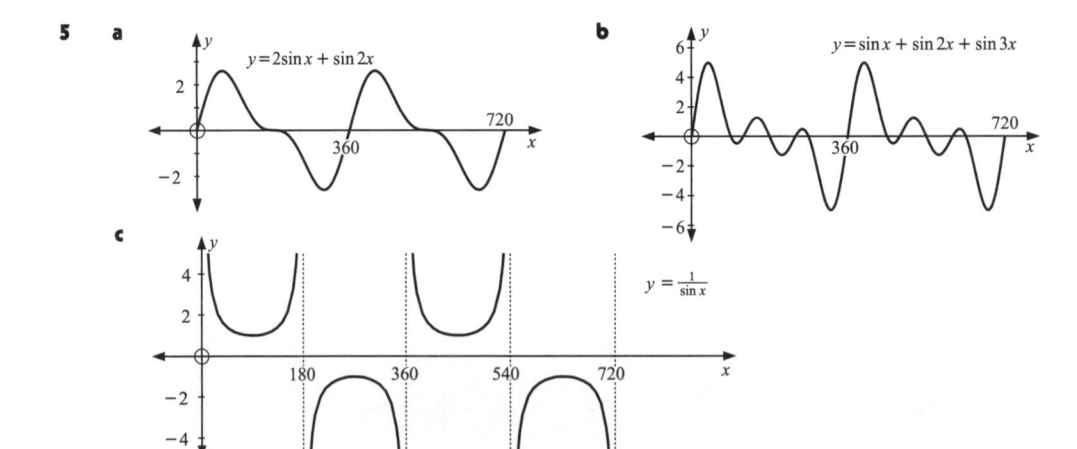

6 a [graph] b [graph]

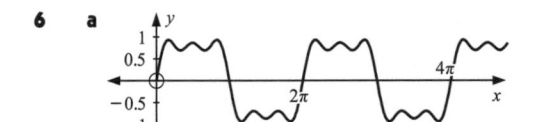

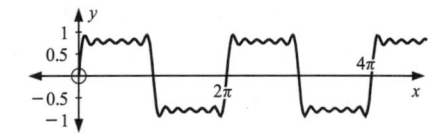

Prediction: [graph]

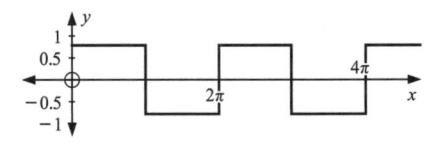

EXERCISE 12B.2

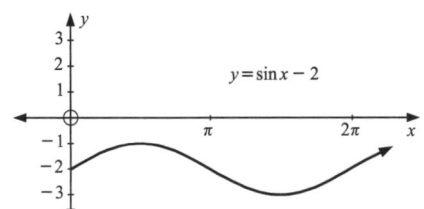

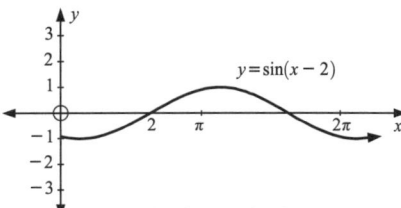

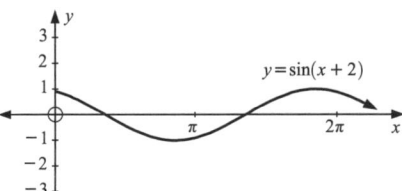

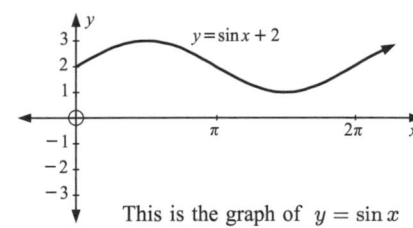

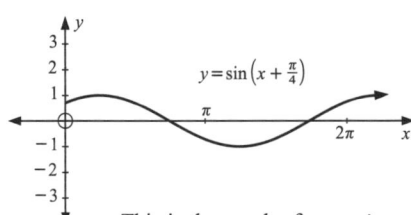

1 a [graph] This is the graph of $y = \sin x$ translated by $\begin{pmatrix} 0 \\ -2 \end{pmatrix}$.

b [graph] This is the graph of $y = \sin x$ translated by $\begin{pmatrix} 2 \\ 0 \end{pmatrix}$.

c [graph] This is the graph of $y = \sin x$ translated by $\begin{pmatrix} -2 \\ 0 \end{pmatrix}$.

d [graph] This is the graph of $y = \sin x$ translated by $\begin{pmatrix} 0 \\ 2 \end{pmatrix}$.

e [graph] This is the graph of $y = \sin x$ translated by $\begin{pmatrix} -\frac{\pi}{4} \\ 0 \end{pmatrix}$.

f [graph] This is the graph of $y = \sin x$ translated by $\begin{pmatrix} \frac{\pi}{6} \\ 1 \end{pmatrix}$.

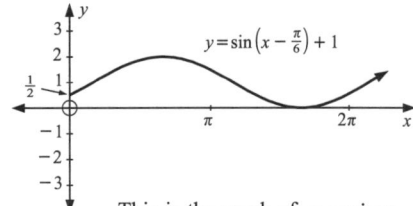

3 a period $= \dfrac{2\pi}{|5|} = \dfrac{2\pi}{5}$ **b** period $= \dfrac{2\pi}{\left|\frac{1}{4}\right|} = 8\pi$ **c** period $= \dfrac{2\pi}{|-2|} = \pi$

4 a $\dfrac{2\pi}{B} = 3\pi$ **b** $\dfrac{2\pi}{B} = \dfrac{\pi}{10}$ **c** $\dfrac{2\pi}{B} = 100\pi$ **d** $\dfrac{2\pi}{B} = 50$

$\therefore B = \dfrac{2}{3}$ $\therefore B = 20$ $\therefore B = \dfrac{2}{100} = \dfrac{1}{50}$ $\therefore B = \dfrac{2\pi}{50} = \dfrac{\pi}{25}$

5 a A translation of $\begin{pmatrix} 0 \\ -1 \end{pmatrix}$, or vertically down 1 unit.

b A translation of $\begin{pmatrix} \frac{\pi}{4} \\ 0 \end{pmatrix}$, or horizontally $\frac{\pi}{4}$ units right.

c A vertical stretch of factor 2.
d A horizontal compression of factor 4.
e A vertical stretch of factor $\frac{1}{2}$.
f A horizontal stretch of factor 4.
g A reflection in the x-axis.
h A translation of $\begin{pmatrix} -2 \\ -3 \end{pmatrix}$.
i A vertical stretch of factor 2 followed by a horizontal compression of factor 3.
j A translation of $\begin{pmatrix} \frac{\pi}{3} \\ 2 \end{pmatrix}$.

EXERCISE 12C

1 a

Month, t	1	2	3	4	5	6	7	8	9	10	11	12
Temp, T	15	14	15	18	21	25	27	26	24	20	18	16

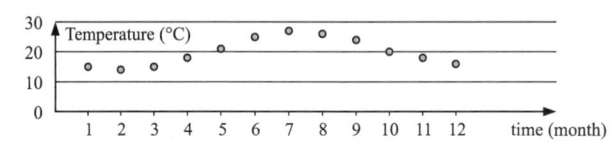

The period is 12 months so $\dfrac{2\pi}{B} = 12$ ∴ $B = \frac{\pi}{6}$ {assuming $B > 0$}.

Amplitude, $A \approx \dfrac{\text{max.} - \text{min.}}{2} \approx \dfrac{27 - 14}{2} \approx 6.5$

As the principal axis is midway between min. and max., then $D \approx \dfrac{27 + 14}{2} \approx 20.5$

When T is 20.5 (midway between min. and max.)

$C \approx \dfrac{2 + 7}{2} \approx 4.5$ {average of t values}

∴ $T \approx 6.5 \sin \frac{\pi}{6}(t - 4.5) + 20.5$ where $\frac{\pi}{6} \approx 0.524$.

b Using technology, $T \approx 6.14 \sin(0.575t - 2.70) + 20.4$
∴ $T \approx 6.14 \sin 0.575(t - 4.70) + 20.4$

2 a

Month, t	1	2	3	4	5	6	7	8	9	10	11	12
Temp, T	15	16	$14\frac{1}{2}$	12	10	$7\frac{1}{2}$	7	$7\frac{1}{2}$	$8\frac{1}{2}$	$10\frac{1}{2}$	$12\frac{1}{2}$	14

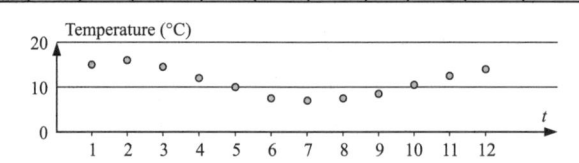

The period is $\dfrac{2\pi}{B} = 12$ ∴ $B = \frac{\pi}{6}$ {$B > 0$}

Amplitude, $A \approx \dfrac{\text{max.} - \text{min.}}{2} \approx \dfrac{16 - 7}{2} \approx 4.5$

As the principal axis is midway between min. and max. then $D \approx \dfrac{16 + 7}{2} \approx 11.5$

At min., $t = 7$ and at max., $t = 2 + 12 = 14$ ∴ $C = \dfrac{7 + 14}{2} = 10.5$

So, $T \approx 4.5 \sin \frac{\pi}{6}(t - 10.5) + 11.5$

b Using tech., $T \approx 4.29 \sin(0.533t + 0.769) + 11.2$
∴ $T \approx 4.29 \sin 0.533(t + 1.44) + 11.2$

Note: (1) $\frac{\pi}{6} \approx 0.524$ ✓
(2) $1.44 - (-10.5) = 11.94 \approx 12$

3

Month, t	1	2	3	4	5	6	7	8	9	10	11	12
Temp, T	0	−4	−10	−15	−16	−17	−18	−19	−17	−13	−6	−1

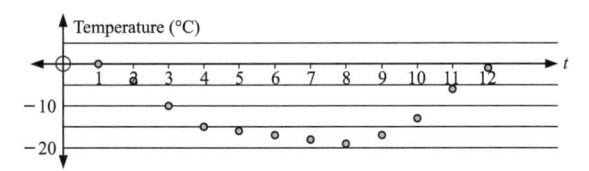

The period is $\dfrac{2\pi}{B} = 12$ $\therefore$ $B = \dfrac{\pi}{6}$ $\{B > 0\}$

Amplitude, $A \approx \dfrac{\text{max.} - \text{min.}}{2} \approx \dfrac{0 - (-19)}{2} \approx 9.5$

$D \approx \dfrac{\text{max.} + \text{min.}}{2} \approx \dfrac{0 + (-19)}{2} \approx -9.5$

At min., $t = 8$ and at max., $t = 1 + 12 = 13$ $\therefore$ $C \approx \dfrac{8 + 13}{2} \approx 10.5$

So, $T \approx 9.5 \sin \dfrac{\pi}{6}(t - 10.5) - 9.5$ ...... (1)

From technology, $T \approx 13.1 \sin(0.345t + 2.37) - 5.43$

$\therefore$ $T \approx 13.1 \sin 0.345(t + 6.87) - 5.43$ ...... (2)

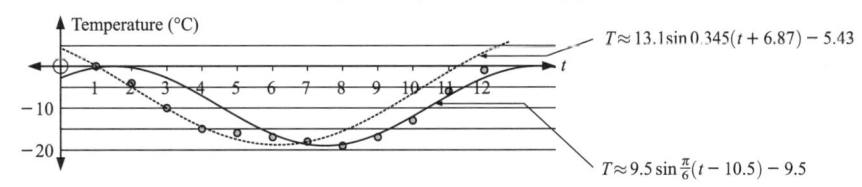

Neither model seems appropriate.

4 a For the model $H = A \sin B(t - C) + D$

$\text{period} = \dfrac{2\pi}{B} = 12.4$ hours $\therefore$ $B = \dfrac{2\pi}{12.4} \approx 0.507$

We let the principal axis be 0, so $D = 0$

$\therefore$ the amplitude $A = 7$, so the min. is -7, and the max. is $+7$

Let $t = 0$ correspond to 'low tide' $\therefore$ $t = 6.2$ corresponds to 'high tide'

$\therefore$ $C = \dfrac{0 + 6.2}{2} = 3.1$

So, $H \approx 7 \sin 0.507(t - 3.1) + 0$

$\therefore$ $H \approx 7 \sin 0.507(t - 3.1)$

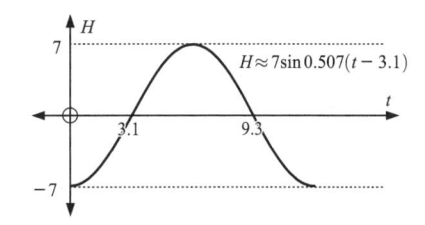

b

5 Let the model be $H = A \sin B(t - C) + D$ metres

When $t = 0$, $H = 2$ and when $t = 50$, $H = 22$

$\uparrow$ $\qquad\qquad\qquad$ $\uparrow$

min. $\qquad\qquad\qquad$ max.

$\text{period} = \dfrac{2\pi}{B} = 100$ $\therefore$ $B = \dfrac{2\pi}{100} = \dfrac{\pi}{50}$

$A = 10$ {from the diagram} $\qquad D = \dfrac{\text{max.} + \text{min.}}{2} = \dfrac{22 + 2}{2} = 12$

$C = \dfrac{0 + 50}{2} = 25$ {values of t at min. and max.} $\therefore$ $H = 10 \sin \dfrac{\pi}{50}(t - 25) + 12$

EXERCISE 12D

1 a $y = \cos x + 2$

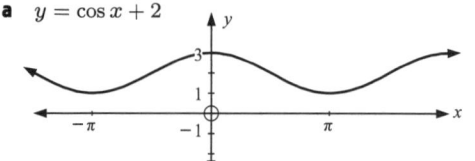

This is a vertical translation of $y = \cos x$ through $\begin{pmatrix} 0 \\ 2 \end{pmatrix}$.

b $y = \cos x - 1$

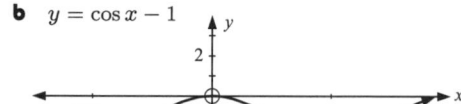

This is a vertical translation of $y = \cos x$ through $\begin{pmatrix} 0 \\ -1 \end{pmatrix}$.

c $y = \cos(x - \frac{\pi}{4})$

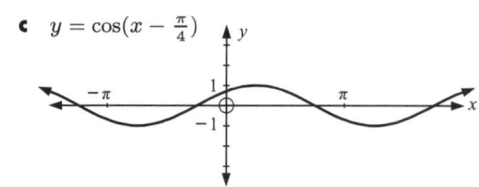

This is a horizontal translation of $y = \cos x$ through $\begin{pmatrix} \frac{\pi}{4} \\ 0 \end{pmatrix}$.

d $y = \cos(x + \frac{\pi}{6})$

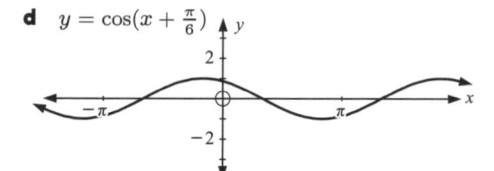

This is a horizontal translation of $y = \cos x$ through $\begin{pmatrix} -\frac{\pi}{6} \\ 0 \end{pmatrix}$.

e $y = \frac{2}{3} \cos x$

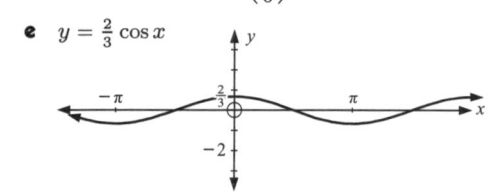

This is a vertical stretch of $y = \cos x$ with factor $\frac{2}{3}$.

f $y = \frac{3}{2} \cos x$

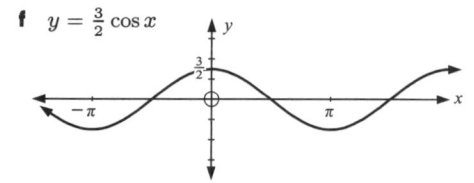

This is a vertical stretch of $y = \cos x$ with factor $\frac{3}{2}$.

g $y = -\cos x$

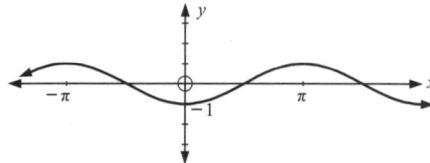

This is a reflection of $y = \cos x$ in the x-axis.

h $y = \cos(x - \frac{\pi}{6}) + 1$

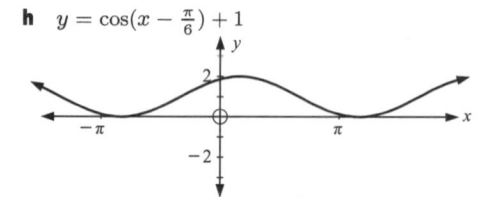

This is a translation of $\begin{pmatrix} \frac{\pi}{6} \\ 1 \end{pmatrix}$.

i $y = \cos(x + \frac{\pi}{4}) - 1$

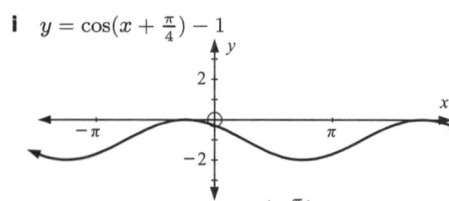

This is a translation of $\begin{pmatrix} -\frac{\pi}{4} \\ -1 \end{pmatrix}$.

j $y = \cos(2x)$

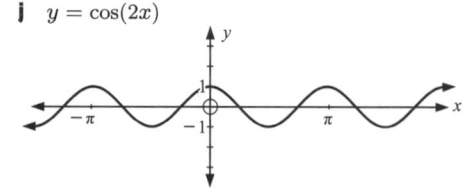

This is a horizontal compression of factor 2.

k $y = \cos\left(\frac{x}{2}\right)$

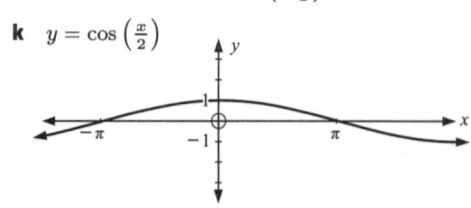

This is a horizontal stretch of factor 2.

l $y = 3\cos(2x)$

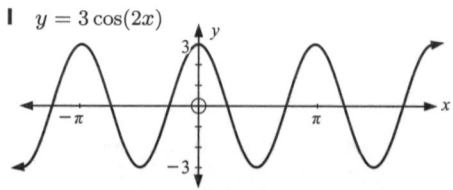

This is a horizontal compression of factor 2 followed by a vertical stretch of factor 3.

2 a period $= \frac{2\pi}{3}$ **b** period $= \frac{2\pi}{\frac{1}{3}} = 6\pi$ **c** period $= \frac{2\pi}{\frac{\pi}{50}} = 100$

3 A controls the amplitude. B controls the period $\{$period $= \frac{2\pi}{|B|}\}$. C controls the horizontal translation. D controls the vertical translation.

4 a If $y = A\cos B(x - C) + D$, then $A = 2$, $\pi = \frac{2\pi}{B}$ $\therefore$ $B = 2$
C and D are 0 as there is no horizontal or vertical shift. $\therefore$ $y = 2\cos(2x)$

b If $y = A\cos B(x - C) + D$, then $A = 1$, $4\pi = \frac{2\pi}{B}$ $\therefore$ $B = \frac{1}{2}$
A vertical shift of 2 units, no horizontal shift $\therefore$ $D = 2$, $C = 0$.
So, $y = \cos(\frac{1}{2}x) + 2$ or $y = \cos\left(\frac{x}{2}\right) + 2$.

c If $y = A\cos B(x - C) + D$, then $A = -5$, $6 = \frac{2\pi}{B}$ $\therefore$ $B = \frac{\pi}{3}$
$C = D = 0$ $\{$as there is no translation$\}$ $\therefore$ $y = -5\cos\left(\frac{\pi}{3}x\right)$

EXERCISE 12E.1

1 a $\tan 0°$ $= 0$ **b** $\tan 15° \approx 0.268$ **c** $\tan 20° \approx 0.364$ **d** $\tan 25° \approx 0.466$
e $\tan 35° \approx 0.700$ **f** $\tan 45° = 1$ **g** $\tan 50° \approx 1.19$ **h** $\tan 55° \approx 1.43$

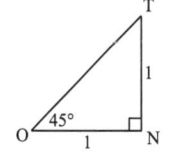

2 In $\triangle TON$, $ON = NT = 1$ $\{\triangle$ is isosceles$\}$ $\tan 45° = \frac{NT}{ON} = \frac{1}{1} = 1$

EXERCISE 12E.2

1 a i $y = \tan(x - \frac{\pi}{2})$ is $y = \tan x$ translated $\begin{pmatrix} \frac{\pi}{2} \\ 0 \end{pmatrix}$.

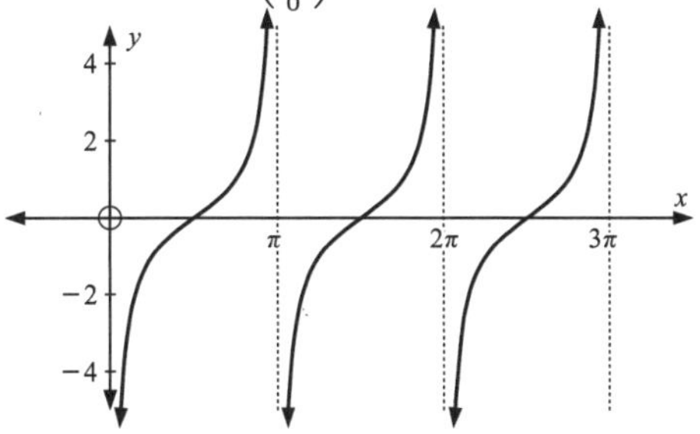

ii $y = -\tan x$ is $y = \tan x$ reflected in the x-axis.

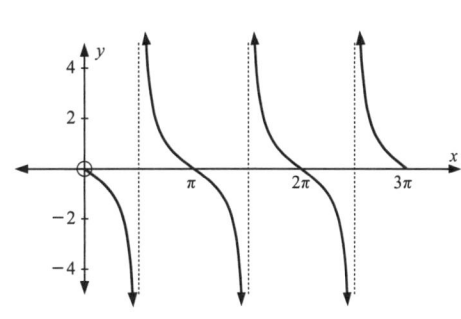

iii $y = \tan 2x$ comes from $y = \tan x$ under a horizontal compression of factor 2.

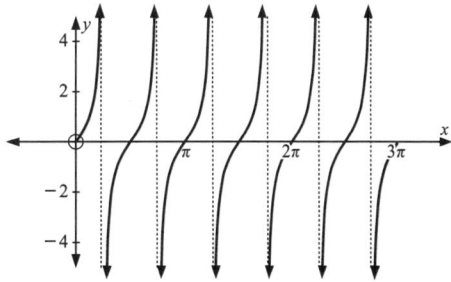

2 a translation through $\begin{pmatrix} 1 \\ 0 \end{pmatrix}$ **b** reflection in x-axis **c** horizontal stretch, factor 2

3 a period $= \frac{\pi}{1} = \pi$ **b** period $= \frac{\pi}{2}$ **c** period $= \frac{\pi}{n}$

EXERCISE 12F.1

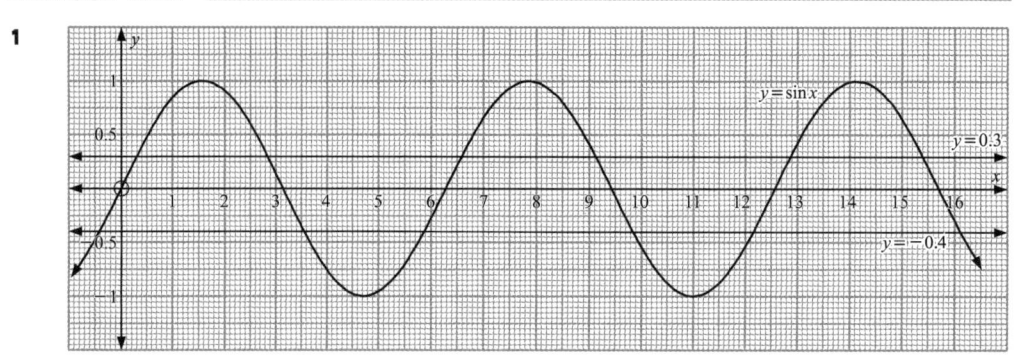

1

a When $\sin x = 0.3$, $x \approx 0.3, 2.8, 6.6, 9.1, 12.9$ **b** When $\sin x = -0.4$, $x \approx 5.9, 9.8, 12.2$

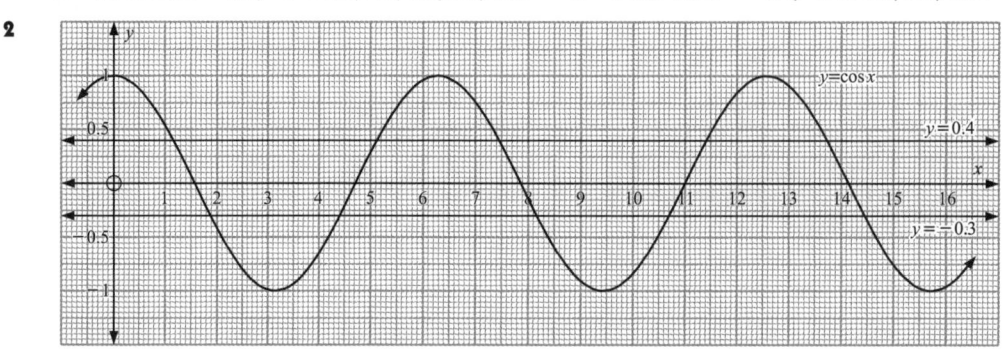

2

a When $\cos x = 0.4$, $x \approx 1.2, 5.1, 7.4$ **b** When $\cos x = -0.3$, $x \approx 4.4, 8.2, 10.7$

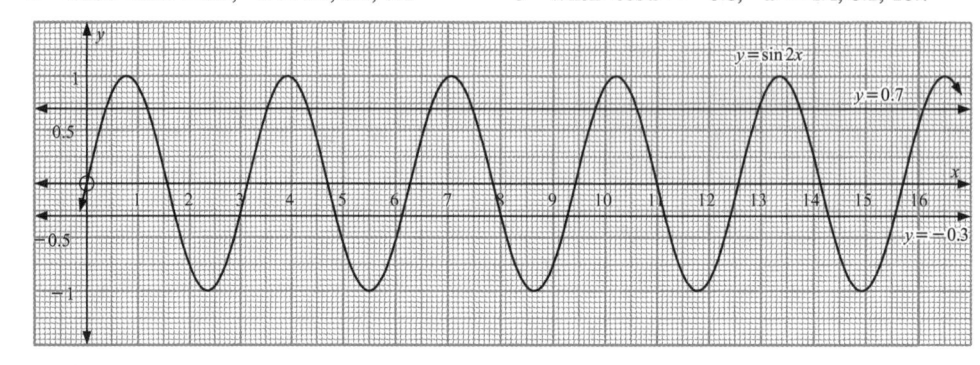

3

a When $\sin(2x) = 0.7$, $x \approx 0.4, 1.2, 3.5, 4.3, 6.7, 7.5, 9.8, 10.6, 13.0, 13.7$
b When $\sin(2x) = -0.3$, $x \approx 1.7, 3.0, 4.9, 6.1, 8.0, 9.3, 11.1, 12.4, 14.3, 15.6$

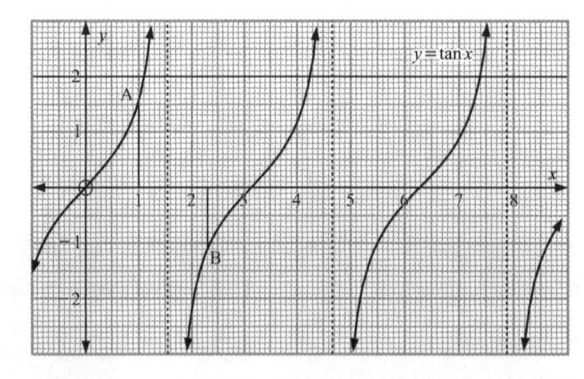

4

a **i** $\tan 1 \approx 1.6$ {point A}
  ii $\tan 2.3 \approx -1.1$ {point B}
b **i** $\tan 1 \approx 1.557$
  ii $\tan 2.3 \approx -1.119$
c **i** When $\tan x = 2$, $x \approx 1.1, 4.2, 7.4$
  ii When $\tan x = -1.4$, $x \approx 2.2, 5.3$

EXERCISE 12F.2

1 Using technology:
   a $\sin(x+2) = 0.0652$ when $x \approx 1.08, 4.35$ **b** $\sin^2 x + \sin x - 1 = 0$ when $x \approx 0.666, 2.48$
   c $x \tan(\frac{x^2}{10}) = x^2 - 6x + 1$ when $x \approx 0.171, 4.92$
   d $2\sin(2x)\cos x = \ln x$ when $x \approx 1.31, 2.03, 2.85$

2 $\cos(x-1) + \sin(x+1) = 6x + 5x^2 - x^3$ when $x \approx -0.951, 0.234, 5.98$

EXERCISE 12F.3

1 a $x = \frac{\pi}{6} + \frac{k12\pi}{6}$ and $0 \leqslant x \leqslant \frac{36\pi}{6}$
   $\therefore x = \frac{\pi}{6}, \frac{13\pi}{6}, \frac{25\pi}{6}$

b $x = -\frac{\pi}{3} + \frac{k6\pi}{3}$ and $-\frac{6\pi}{3} \leqslant x \leqslant \frac{6\pi}{3}$
   $\therefore x = -\frac{\pi}{3}, \frac{5\pi}{3}$

c $x = -\frac{\pi}{2} + \frac{k2\pi}{2}$ and $-\frac{8\pi}{2} \leqslant x \leqslant \frac{8\pi}{2}$
   $\therefore x = -\frac{\pi}{2}, \frac{\pi}{2}, \frac{3\pi}{2}, \frac{5\pi}{2}, \frac{7\pi}{2}, -\frac{3\pi}{2}, -\frac{5\pi}{2}, -\frac{7\pi}{2}$

d $x = \frac{5\pi}{6} + \frac{k3\pi}{6}$ and $0 \leqslant x \leqslant \frac{24\pi}{6}$
   $\therefore x = \frac{2\pi}{6}, \frac{5\pi}{6}, \frac{8\pi}{6}, \frac{11\pi}{6}, \frac{14\pi}{6}, \frac{17\pi}{6}, \frac{20\pi}{6}, \frac{23\pi}{6}$
   $\therefore x = \frac{\pi}{3}, \frac{5\pi}{6}, \frac{4\pi}{3}, \frac{11\pi}{6}, \frac{7\pi}{3}, \frac{17\pi}{6}, \frac{10\pi}{3}, \frac{23\pi}{6}$

2 a $\cos x = -\frac{1}{2}$, $x \in [0, 5\pi]$

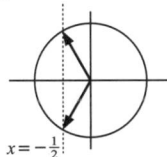

   $\therefore x = \left.\begin{array}{c}\frac{2\pi}{3} \\ \frac{4\pi}{3}\end{array}\right\} + k2\pi$

   $\therefore x = \frac{2\pi}{3}, \frac{4\pi}{3}, \frac{8\pi}{3}, \frac{10\pi}{3}, \frac{14\pi}{3}$

b $2\sin x - 1 = 0$, $-2\pi \leqslant x \leqslant 2\pi$
   $\therefore \sin x = \frac{1}{2}$

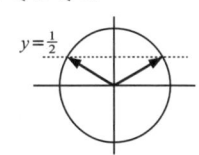

   $\therefore x = \left.\begin{array}{c}\frac{\pi}{6} \\ \frac{5\pi}{6}\end{array}\right\} + k2\pi$

   $\therefore x = -\frac{11\pi}{6}, -\frac{7\pi}{6}, \frac{\pi}{6}, \frac{5\pi}{6}$

c $2\cos x + \sqrt{3} = 0$, $0 \leqslant x \leqslant 3\pi$
   $\therefore \cos x = -\frac{\sqrt{3}}{2}$

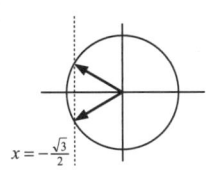

   $\therefore x = \left.\begin{array}{c}\frac{5\pi}{6} \\ \frac{7\pi}{6}\end{array}\right\} + k2\pi$

   $\therefore x = \frac{5\pi}{6}, \frac{7\pi}{6}, \frac{17\pi}{6}$

d $\cos(x - \frac{2\pi}{3}) = \frac{1}{2}$, $x \in [-2\pi, 2\pi]$

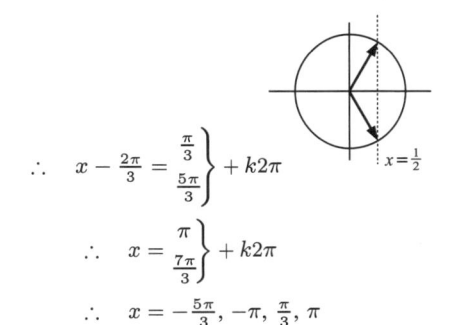

   $\therefore x - \frac{2\pi}{3} = \left.\begin{array}{c}\frac{\pi}{3} \\ \frac{5\pi}{3}\end{array}\right\} + k2\pi$

   $\therefore x = \left.\begin{array}{c}\pi \\ \frac{7\pi}{3}\end{array}\right\} + k2\pi$

   $\therefore x = -\frac{5\pi}{3}, -\pi, \frac{\pi}{3}, \pi$

e $2\sin(x + \frac{\pi}{3}) = 1$, $x \in [-3\pi, 3\pi]$
   $\therefore \sin(x + \frac{\pi}{3}) = \frac{1}{2}$

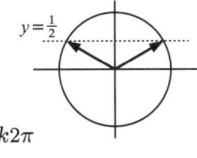

   $\therefore x + \frac{\pi}{3} = \left.\begin{array}{c}\frac{\pi}{6} \\ \frac{5\pi}{6}\end{array}\right\} + k2\pi$

   $\therefore x = \left.\begin{array}{c}-\frac{\pi}{6} \\ \frac{\pi}{2}\end{array}\right\} + k2\pi$

   $\therefore x = -\frac{13\pi}{6}, -\frac{3\pi}{2}, -\frac{\pi}{6}, \frac{\pi}{2}, \frac{11\pi}{6}, \frac{5\pi}{2}$

f $\sqrt{2}\sin(x - \frac{\pi}{4}) + 1 = 0$, $x \in [0, 3\pi]$
   $\therefore \sin(x - \frac{\pi}{4}) = -\frac{1}{\sqrt{2}}$

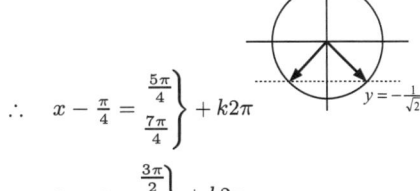

   $\therefore x - \frac{\pi}{4} = \left.\begin{array}{c}\frac{5\pi}{4} \\ \frac{7\pi}{4}\end{array}\right\} + k2\pi$

   $\therefore x = \left.\begin{array}{c}\frac{3\pi}{2} \\ 2\pi\end{array}\right\} + k2\pi$

   $\therefore x = 0, \frac{3\pi}{2}, 2\pi$

3 $X = \tan^{-1}(\sqrt{3}) = \frac{\pi}{3} + k\pi$

  a $\tan(x - \frac{\pi}{6}) = \sqrt{3}$
    $\therefore \ x - \frac{\pi}{6} = \frac{\pi}{3} + k\pi$
    $\therefore \ x = \frac{\pi}{2} + k\pi$

  b $\tan 4x = \sqrt{3}$
    $\therefore \ 4x = \frac{\pi}{3} + k\pi$
    $\therefore \ x = \frac{\pi}{12} + \frac{k\pi}{4}$

  c $\tan^2 x = 3$
    $\therefore \ \tan x = \pm\sqrt{3}$
    $\therefore \ x = \left.\begin{array}{c}\frac{\pi}{3} \\ -\frac{\pi}{3}\end{array}\right\} + k\pi$

4 **a** The zeros of $y = \sin 2x$ are the solutions of $\sin 2x = 0$ $\{0 \leqslant x \leqslant \pi\}$

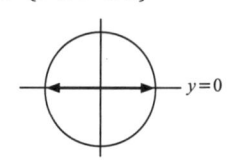

  $\therefore \ 2x = 0 + k\pi$
  $\therefore \ x = 0 + k\frac{\pi}{2}$
  $\therefore \ x = 0, \frac{\pi}{2}, \pi$

 b The zeros of $y = \sin(x - \frac{\pi}{4})$ are the solutions of $\sin(x - \frac{\pi}{4}) = 0$ $\{0 \leqslant x \leqslant 3\pi\}$

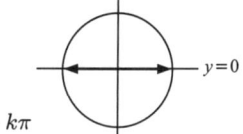

  $\therefore \ x - \frac{\pi}{4} = 0 + k\pi$
  $\therefore \ x = \frac{\pi}{4} + k\pi$
  $\therefore \ x = \frac{\pi}{4}, \frac{5\pi}{4}, \frac{9\pi}{4}$

5 **a** [graph of $y = \sin x$ and $y = \cos x$ with intersection points at $\frac{5\pi}{4}$ marked, and $\frac{\pi}{4}, \frac{\pi}{2}, \pi, \frac{3\pi}{2}, 2\pi$ on x-axis]

 b $x = \frac{\pi}{4}$ or $\frac{5\pi}{4}$

 c If $\sin x = \cos x$ then $\dfrac{\sin x}{\cos x} = 1$
  $\therefore \ \tan x = 1$
  $\therefore \ x = \frac{\pi}{4} + k\pi$
  $\therefore \ x = \frac{\pi}{4}, \frac{5\pi}{4}$

6 **a** $\sin x = -\cos x, \ 0 \leqslant x \leqslant 2\pi$
  $\therefore \ \dfrac{\sin x}{\cos x} = \dfrac{-\cos x}{\cos x}$
  $\therefore \ \tan x = -1$
  $\therefore \ x = \frac{3\pi}{4} + k\pi$
  $\therefore \ x = \frac{3\pi}{4}, \frac{7\pi}{4}$

 c $\sin(2x) = \sqrt{3}\cos(2x), \ 0 \leqslant x \leqslant 2\pi$
  $\therefore \ \dfrac{\sin(2x)}{\cos(2x)} = \sqrt{3}$
  $\therefore \ \tan(2x) = \sqrt{3}$
  $\therefore \ 2x = \frac{\pi}{3} + k\pi$
  $\therefore \ x = \frac{\pi}{6} + \frac{k\pi}{2}$
  $\therefore \ x = \frac{\pi}{6}, \frac{4\pi}{6}, \frac{7\pi}{6}, \frac{10\pi}{6}$
  $\therefore \ x = \frac{\pi}{6}, \frac{2\pi}{3}, \frac{7\pi}{6}, \frac{5\pi}{3}$

 b $\sin(3x) = \cos(3x), \ 0 \leqslant x \leqslant 2\pi$
  $\therefore \ \dfrac{\sin(3x)}{\cos(3x)} = 1$
  $\therefore \ \tan(3x) = 1$
  $\therefore \ 3x = \frac{\pi}{4} + k\pi$
  $\therefore \ x = \frac{\pi}{12} + \frac{k\pi}{3}$
  $\therefore \ x = \frac{\pi}{12}, \frac{5\pi}{12}, \frac{9\pi}{12}, \frac{13\pi}{12}, \frac{17\pi}{12}, \frac{21\pi}{12}$
  $\therefore \ x = \frac{\pi}{12}, \frac{5\pi}{12}, \frac{3\pi}{4}, \frac{13\pi}{12}, \frac{17\pi}{12}, \frac{7\pi}{4}$

EXERCISE 12G

1 **a** $P(t) = 7500 + 3000\sin(\frac{\pi t}{8}), \ 0 \leqslant t \leqslant 12$

  i $P(0) = 7500 + 3000\sin 0$
    $= 7500 + 0$
    $= 7500$ grasshoppers

  ii $P(5) = 7500 + 3000\sin(\frac{5\pi}{8})$
    $\approx 10\,271.63\,....$
    $\approx 10\,300$ grasshoppers

b The greatest value of $P(t)$ occurs when $\sin\left(\frac{\pi t}{8}\right) = 1$, so the greatest population is $7500 + 3000 = 10\,500$ grasshoppers when $\frac{\pi t}{8} = \frac{\pi}{2} + k2\pi$

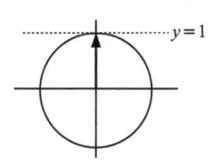

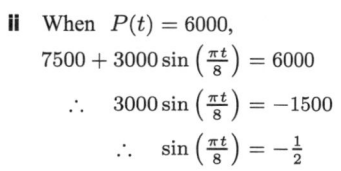

$\therefore \quad \frac{t}{8} = \frac{1}{2} + 2k$

$\therefore \quad t = 4 + 16k$

$\therefore \quad t = 4 \quad \{\text{as } 0 \leqslant t \leqslant 12\}$

So the greatest population occurs after 4 weeks.

c i When $P(t) = 9000$,

$7500 + 3000\sin\left(\frac{\pi t}{8}\right) = 9000$

$\therefore \quad 3000\sin\left(\frac{\pi t}{8}\right) = 1500$

$\therefore \quad \sin\left(\frac{\pi t}{8}\right) = \frac{1}{2}$

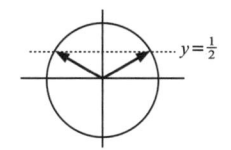

$\therefore \quad \frac{\pi t}{8} = \left.\begin{matrix}\frac{\pi}{6}\\ \frac{5\pi}{6}\end{matrix}\right\} + k2\pi$

$\therefore \quad \frac{t}{8} = \left.\begin{matrix}\frac{1}{6}\\ \frac{5}{6}\end{matrix}\right\} + k\,2$

$\therefore \quad t = \left.\begin{matrix}\frac{4}{3}\\ \frac{20}{3}\end{matrix}\right\} + k\,16$

$\therefore \quad t = 1\frac{1}{3} \text{ or } 6\frac{2}{3}$

So, the population is 9000 at $1\frac{1}{3}$ weeks and $6\frac{2}{3}$ weeks.

ii When $P(t) = 6000$,

$7500 + 3000\sin\left(\frac{\pi t}{8}\right) = 6000$

$\therefore \quad 3000\sin\left(\frac{\pi t}{8}\right) = -1500$

$\therefore \quad \sin\left(\frac{\pi t}{8}\right) = -\frac{1}{2}$

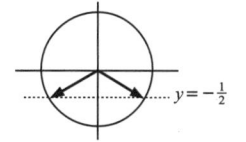

$\therefore \quad \frac{\pi t}{8} = \left.\begin{matrix}\frac{7\pi}{6}\\ \frac{11\pi}{6}\end{matrix}\right\} + k2\pi$

$\therefore \quad \frac{t}{8} = \left.\begin{matrix}\frac{7}{6}\\ \frac{11}{6}\end{matrix}\right\} + k\,2$

$\therefore \quad t = \left.\begin{matrix}\frac{28}{3}\\ \frac{44}{3}\end{matrix}\right\} + k\,16$

$\therefore \quad t = 9\frac{1}{3}$

So, the population is 6000 at $9\frac{1}{3}$ weeks.

d If $P(t) > 10\,000$, then

$7500 + 3000\sin\left(\frac{\pi t}{8}\right) > 10\,000$

$\therefore \quad 3000\sin\left(\frac{\pi t}{8}\right) > 2500$

$\therefore \quad \sin\left(\frac{\pi t}{8}\right) > \frac{5}{6}$

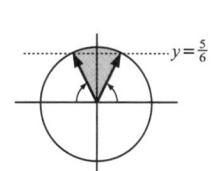

Solving $\sin\left(\frac{\pi t}{8}\right) = \frac{5}{6}$ using technology

$t \approx 2.51$ or 5.49 So, $2.51 \leqslant t \leqslant 5.49$ weeks.

2 $H(t) = 20 - 19\sin\left(\frac{2\pi t}{3}\right)$

a $H(0) = 20 - 19(0)$
$= 20$ m

So, at time $t = 0$, the light is 20 m above the ground.

b H is smallest when $\sin\left(\frac{2\pi t}{3}\right) = 1$

$\therefore \quad \frac{2\pi t}{3} = \frac{\pi}{2} + k2\pi$

$\therefore \quad \frac{2t}{3} = \frac{1}{2} + k\,2$

$\therefore \quad t = \frac{3}{4} + k\,3$

$\therefore \quad t = \frac{3}{4}$ min $\{\text{as } k = 0\}$

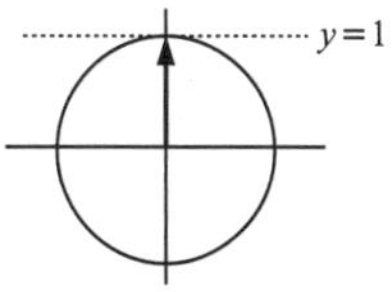

c period = $\dfrac{2\pi}{\frac{2\pi}{3}}$ = 3 min

∴ one revolution takes 3 min

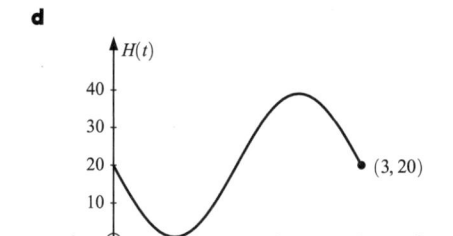

d

3 $P(t) = 400 + 250 \sin\left(\dfrac{\pi t}{2}\right)$ years

a $P(0) = 400 + 250(0)$
= 400 water buffalo

c $P(1) = 400 + 250 \sin(\dfrac{\pi}{2})$
= $400 + 250 \times 1$
= 650 water buffalo
This is the maximum herd size.

b i $P(\tfrac{1}{2}) = 400 + 250 \sin\left(\dfrac{\pi(\frac{1}{2})}{2}\right)$
= $400 + 250 \sin(\dfrac{\pi}{4})$
= $400 + 250 \times \dfrac{1}{\sqrt{2}}$
≈ 577 water buffalo

ii $P(2) = 400 + 250 \sin \pi$
= $400 + 250(0)$
= 400 water buffalo

d $P(t)$ is smallest when $\sin\left(\dfrac{\pi t}{2}\right) = -1$
and is $400 - 250 = 150$ water buffalo.

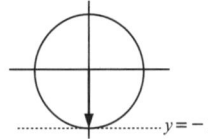

It occurs when $\dfrac{\pi t}{2} = \dfrac{3\pi}{2} + k2\pi$

∴ $\dfrac{t}{2} = \dfrac{3}{2} + k2$

∴ $t = 3 + 4k$

So, the first time is after 3 years.

e If $P(t) > 500$ then
$400 + 250 \sin\left(\dfrac{\pi t}{2}\right) > 500$
∴ $250 \sin\left(\dfrac{\pi t}{2}\right) > 100$
∴ $\sin\left(\dfrac{\pi t}{2}\right) > \dfrac{2}{5}$

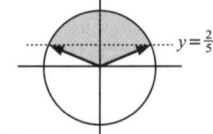

$\sin\left(\dfrac{\pi t}{2}\right) = \dfrac{2}{5}$ when
$\dfrac{\pi t}{2} = 0.4115$ or $\pi - 0.4115$
∴ $t \approx 0.262$ or 1.74

So, for $\sin\left(\dfrac{\pi t}{2}\right) > \dfrac{2}{5}$, $0.26 < t < 1.74$
∴ the herd first exceeded 500 when $t \approx 0.262$ years.

4 a The period is 4 seconds.
∴ $\dfrac{2\pi}{B} = 4$
∴ $B = \dfrac{\pi}{2}$
Amplitude is 3
∴ $A = 3$

$D = 1 + 3 = 4$
$C = 0$
∴ $H(t) = 3 \cos \dfrac{\pi}{2}(t - 0) + 4$ metres
∴ $H(t) = 3 \cos(\dfrac{\pi}{2}t) + 4$ metres
Check: When $t = 0$, $H(0) = 3 \cos 0 + 4 = 7$ ✓

b X enters the water when $H(t) = 2$
∴ $3 \cos\left(\dfrac{\pi t}{2}\right) + 4 = 2$
∴ $\cos\left(\dfrac{\pi t}{2}\right) = -\dfrac{2}{3}$
Using technology, $t \approx 1.46$ sec

5 $C(t) = 9.2 \sin \frac{\pi}{7}(t-4) + 107.8$ cents L^{-1}

a **i** 107.8 is the median value. Values are between $107.8 - 9.2$ and $107.8 + 9.2$
$= 98.6$ cents L^{-1} and 117.0 cents L^{-1}
↑ min.   ↑ max.

∴ the statement is true.

ii period $= \dfrac{2\pi}{\frac{\pi}{7}} = 14$ days ∴ true

b $C(7) = 9.2 \sin \frac{\pi}{7}(3) + 107.8 \approx 116.8$ cents L^{-1}

c When $C(t) = \$1.10$ L^{-1} then $9.2 \sin \frac{\pi}{7}(t-4) + 107.8 = 110$

∴ $\sin \frac{\pi}{7}(t-4) = \dfrac{2.2}{9.2} \approx 0.23913$

∴ $\frac{\pi}{7}(t-4) \approx 0.23913$ or $\pi - 0.23913$

∴ $t - 4 \approx 0.533$ or 6.467

∴ $t \approx 4.53$ or 10.47

So, the price is $1.10 per litre on the 5th and 11th days.

d The min. cost per litre is $-9.2 + 107.8 = 98.6$ cents L^{-1}
when $\sin \frac{\pi}{7}(t-4) = -1$ ∴ $2t - 8 = 21$
∴ $\frac{\pi}{7}(t-4) = \frac{3\pi}{2}$ ∴ $2t = 29$
∴ $\dfrac{t-4}{7} = \dfrac{3}{2}$ ∴ $t = 14.5 \pm 14k$
{period is 14 days}

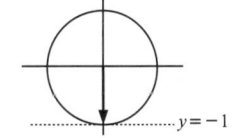

So, the minimum occurred on the 1st day and the 15th day.

EXERCISE 12H

1 a $\sin x = \frac{3}{5}$, $0 \leqslant x \leqslant \frac{\pi}{2}$

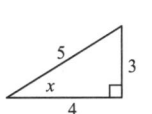

∴ $\csc x = \dfrac{1}{\sin x} = \dfrac{5}{3}$

$\sec x = \dfrac{1}{\cos x} = \dfrac{5}{4}$

$\cot x = \dfrac{1}{\tan x} = \dfrac{4}{3}$

b $\cos x = \frac{2}{3}$

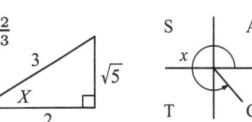

∴ $\sin x = -\dfrac{\sqrt{5}}{3}$ and $\tan x = -\dfrac{\sqrt{5}}{2}$

∴ $\csc x = -\dfrac{3}{\sqrt{5}}$

$\sec x = \dfrac{3}{2}$

$\cot x = -\dfrac{2}{\sqrt{5}}$

2 a $\sin(\frac{\pi}{3}) = \frac{\sqrt{3}}{2}$ **b** $\tan(\frac{2\pi}{3}) = -\sqrt{3}$ **c** $\cos(\frac{5\pi}{6}) = -\frac{\sqrt{3}}{2}$ **d** $\tan(\pi) = 0$

∴ $\csc(\frac{\pi}{3}) = \frac{2}{\sqrt{3}}$ ∴ $\cot(\frac{2\pi}{3}) = -\frac{1}{\sqrt{3}}$ ∴ $\sec(\frac{5\pi}{6}) = -\frac{2}{\sqrt{3}}$ ∴ $\cot(\pi)$ is undefined.

3 a $\cos x = \frac{3}{4}$

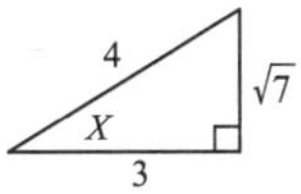

∴ $\sin x = -\dfrac{\sqrt{7}}{4}$

$\tan x = -\dfrac{\sqrt{7}}{3}$

$\csc x = -\dfrac{4}{\sqrt{7}}$

$\sec x = \dfrac{4}{3}$

$\cot x = -\dfrac{3}{\sqrt{7}}$

b $\sin x = -\frac{2}{3}$

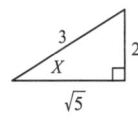

∴ $\cos x = -\dfrac{\sqrt{5}}{3}$

$\tan x = \dfrac{2}{\sqrt{5}}$

$\csc x = -\dfrac{3}{2}$

$\sec x = -\dfrac{3}{\sqrt{5}}$

$\cot x = \dfrac{\sqrt{5}}{2}$

c $\sec x = \frac{5}{2}$
$\therefore \cos x = \frac{2}{5}$
$\therefore \sin x = \frac{\sqrt{21}}{5}$
$\tan x = \frac{\sqrt{21}}{2}$
$\csc x = \frac{5}{\sqrt{21}}$
$\cot x = \frac{2}{\sqrt{21}}$

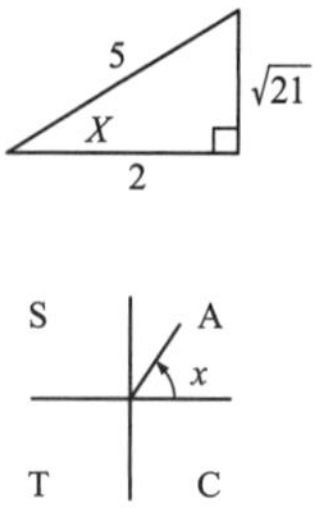

d $\csc x = 2$
$\therefore \sin x = \frac{1}{2}$
$\therefore \cos x = -\frac{\sqrt{3}}{2}$
$\tan x = -\frac{1}{\sqrt{3}}$
$\sec x = -\frac{2}{\sqrt{3}}$
$\cot x = -\sqrt{3}$

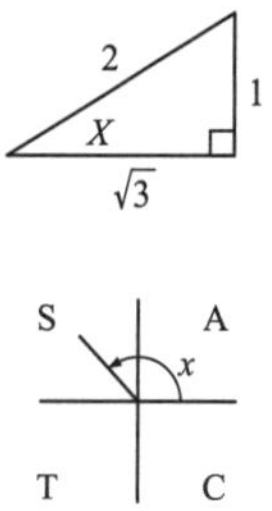

e $\tan \beta = \frac{1}{2}$
$\therefore \cot \beta = 2$
$\sin \beta = -\frac{1}{\sqrt{5}}$
$\cos \beta = -\frac{2}{\sqrt{5}}$
$\csc \beta = -\sqrt{5}$
$\sec \beta = -\frac{\sqrt{5}}{2}$

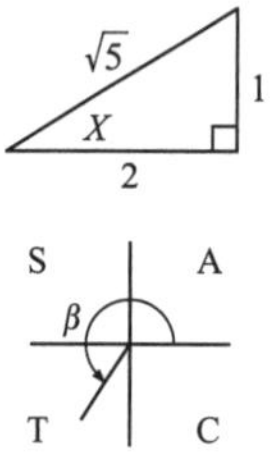

f $\cot \theta = \frac{4}{3}$
$\therefore \tan \theta = \frac{3}{4}$
$\therefore \sin \theta = -\frac{3}{5}$
$\cos \theta = -\frac{4}{5}$
$\csc \theta = -\frac{5}{3}$
$\sec \theta = -\frac{5}{4}$

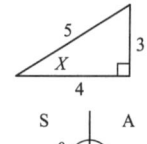

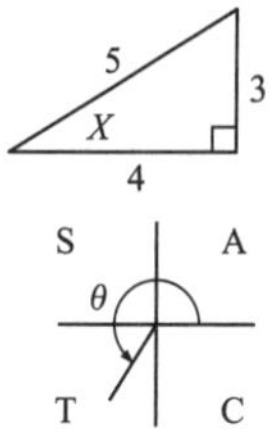

4 a $\tan x \cot x$
$= \frac{\sin x}{\cos x} \times \frac{\cos x}{\sin x}$
$= 1$

b $\sin x \csc x$
$= \sin x \times \frac{1}{\sin x}$
$= 1$

c $\csc x \cot x$
$= \frac{1}{\sin x} \times \frac{\cos x}{\sin x}$
$= \frac{\cos x}{\sin^2 x}$

d $\sin x \cot x$
$= \sin x \times \frac{\cos x}{\sin x}$
$= \cos x$

e $\frac{\cot x}{\csc x}$
$= \frac{\cos x}{\sin x} \div \frac{1}{\sin x}$
$= \frac{\cos x}{\sin x} \times \frac{\sin x}{1}$
$= \cos x$

f $\frac{2\sin x \cot x + 3\cos x}{\cot x}$
$= \frac{2\sin x \times \frac{\cos x}{\sin x} + 3\cos x}{\frac{\cos x}{\sin x}}$
$= (2\cos x + 3\cos x) \times \frac{\sin x}{\cos x}$
$= 5\cos x \times \frac{\sin x}{\cos x}$
$= 5\sin x$

5 a $y = \sec x$

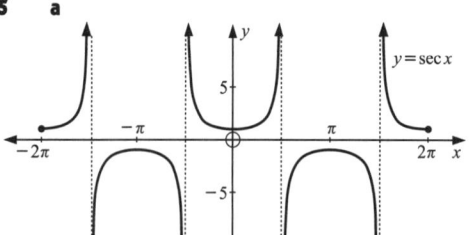

b $y = \cot x$

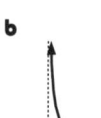

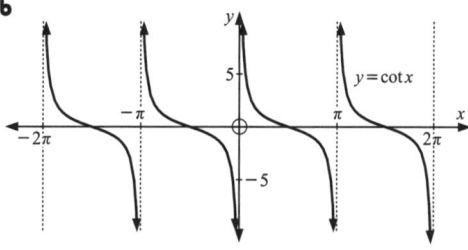

6 a $\sec x = 2$
$\therefore \cos x = \frac{1}{2}$
$\therefore x = \frac{\pi}{3}, \frac{5\pi}{3}$

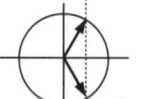

b $\csc x = -\sqrt{2}$
$\therefore \sin x = -\frac{1}{\sqrt{2}}$
$\therefore x = \frac{5\pi}{4}, \frac{7\pi}{4}$

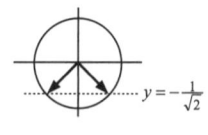

c $\cot x = 4$
$\therefore \tan x = \frac{1}{4}$

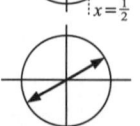

$\therefore x = \arctan\left(\frac{1}{4}\right) + k\pi$
$\therefore x \approx 0.245 \text{ or } 3.387$

d $\sec 2x = \frac{1}{3}$
$\therefore \cos 2x = 3$ which is impossible as all values of cosine lie between -1 and 1, $\therefore$ no solution exists.

e $\csc x = -\frac{2}{3}$
$\therefore\ \sin x = -\frac{3}{2}$ which is impossible as $-1 \leqslant \sin x \leqslant 1$
$\therefore$ no solutions exist.

f $\cot\left(2x - \frac{\pi}{4}\right) + 3 = 0$
$\therefore\ \cot\left(2x - \frac{\pi}{4}\right) = -3$
$\therefore\ \tan\left(2x - \frac{\pi}{4}\right) = -\frac{1}{3}$
$\therefore\ 2x - \frac{\pi}{4} = \arctan\left(-\frac{1}{3}\right) + k\pi$
$\therefore\ 2x - \frac{\pi}{4} \approx -0.3218 + k\pi$
$\therefore\ 2x \approx 0.4636 + k\pi$
$\therefore\ x \approx 0.232 + k\frac{\pi}{2}$
$\therefore\ x \approx 0.232,\ 1.80,\ 3.37,\ 4.94$

EXERCISE 12I

1 a $1 - \sin^2\theta$
$= (1 + \sin\theta)(1 - \sin\theta)$

b $3\tan^2\alpha - 2\tan\alpha$
$= \tan\alpha(3\tan\alpha - 2)$

c $\sec^2\beta - \csc^2\beta$
$= (\sec\beta + \csc\beta)(\sec\beta - \csc\beta)$

d $2\cot^2 x - 3\cot x + 1$
$= (2\cot x - 1)(\cot x - 1)$

e $2\sin^2 x + 7\sin x \cos x + 3\cos^2 x$
$= (2\sin x + \cos x)(\sin x + 3\cos x)$

2 a $3\sin^2\theta + 3\cos^2\theta$
$= 3(\sin^2\theta + \cos^2\theta)$
$= 3$

b $1 - \sec^2\beta$
$= 1 - \dfrac{1}{\cos^2\beta}$
$= \dfrac{\cos^2\beta - 1}{\cos^2\beta}$
$= \dfrac{-\sin^2\beta}{\cos^2\beta}$
$= -\tan^2\beta$

c $4 - 4\cos^2\theta$
$= 4(1 - \cos^2\theta)$
$= 4\sin^2\theta$

d $2\cos^2\alpha - 2$
$= 2(\cos^2\alpha - 1)$
$= -2\sin^2\alpha$

e $\dfrac{\tan^2\theta(\cot^2\theta + 1)}{\tan^2\theta + 1}$
$= \dfrac{\tan^2\theta\cot^2\theta + \tan^2\theta}{\tan^2\theta + 1}$
$= \dfrac{1 + \tan^2\theta}{\tan^2\theta + 1}$
$= 1$

f $\cos^2\alpha(\sec^2\alpha - 1)$
$= \cos^2\alpha\sec^2\alpha - \cos^2\alpha$
$= 1 - \cos^2\alpha$
$= \sin^2\alpha$

g $(2\sin\theta + 3\cos\theta)^2 + (3\sin\theta - 2\cos\theta)^2$
$= 4\sin^2\theta + 12\sin\theta\cos\theta + 9\cos^2\theta$
$\quad + 9\sin^2\theta - 12\sin\theta\cos\theta + 4\cos^2\theta$
$= 13\sin^2\theta + 13\cos^2\theta$
$= 13(\sin^2\theta + \cos^2\theta)$
$= 13$

h $(1 + \csc\theta)(\sin\theta - \sin^2\theta)$
$= \sin\theta - \sin^2\theta + \csc\theta\sin\theta - \csc\theta\sin^2\theta$
$= \sin\theta - \sin^2\theta + 1 - \sin\theta$
$= 1 - \sin^2\theta$
$= \cos^2\theta$

i $\sec A - \sin A \tan A - \cos A$
$= \dfrac{1}{\cos A} - \dfrac{\sin A \sin A}{\cos A} - \cos A$
$= \dfrac{1 - \sin^2 A - \cos^2 A}{\cos A}$
$= \dfrac{1 - (\sin^2 A + \cos^2 A)}{\cos A}$
$= 0$

j $1 - \dfrac{\cos^2\theta}{1 + \sin\theta}$
$= \dfrac{(1 + \sin\theta) - (1 - \sin^2\theta)}{1 + \sin\theta}$
$= \dfrac{1 + \sin\theta - 1 + \sin^2\theta}{1 + \sin\theta}$
$= \dfrac{\sin\theta\cancel{(1 + \sin\theta)}}{\cancel{1 + \sin\theta}}$
$= \sin\theta$

k $\quad \dfrac{1 + \cot \theta}{\csc \theta} - \dfrac{\sec \theta}{\tan \theta + \cot \theta}$

$= \sin \theta \left(1 + \dfrac{\cos \theta}{\sin \theta}\right) - \dfrac{1}{\cos \theta \left(\dfrac{\sin \theta}{\cos \theta} + \dfrac{\cos \theta}{\sin \theta}\right)}$

$= \sin \theta + \cos \theta - \dfrac{1}{\sin \theta + \dfrac{\cos^2 \theta}{\sin \theta}}$

$= \sin \theta + \cos \theta - \dfrac{\sin \theta}{\sin^2 \theta + \cos^2 \theta}$

$= \sin \theta + \cos \theta - \sin \theta$

$= \cos \theta$

l $\quad \dfrac{\cos^2 \beta - \sin^2 \beta}{\cos \beta - \sin \beta}$

$= \dfrac{(\cos \beta + \sin \beta)\cancel{(\cos \beta - \sin \beta)}}{\cancel{\cos \beta - \sin \beta}_{\,1}}$

$= \cos \beta + \sin \beta$

m $\quad \dfrac{\tan^2 \theta}{\sec \theta - 1} = \dfrac{\sec^2 \theta - 1}{\sec \theta - 1}$

$= \dfrac{(\sec \theta + 1)\cancel{(\sec \theta - 1)}}{\cancel{\sec \theta - 1}_{\,1}}$

$= \sec \theta + 1$

3 a $\sec A - \cos A = \dfrac{1}{\cos A} - \cos A$

$= \dfrac{1 - \cos^2 A}{\cos A}$

$= \dfrac{\sin^2 A}{\cos A}$

$= \dfrac{\sin A}{\cos A} \times \sin A$

$= \tan A \sin A$

b $\dfrac{\cos \theta}{1 - \sin \theta} = \dfrac{\cos \theta (1 + \sin \theta)}{(1 - \sin \theta)(1 + \sin \theta)}$

$= \dfrac{\cos \theta + \cos \theta \sin \theta}{1 - \sin^2 \theta}$

$= \dfrac{\cos \theta + \cos \theta \sin \theta}{\cos^2 \theta}$

$= \dfrac{1}{\cos \theta} + \dfrac{\sin \theta}{\cos \theta}$

$= \sec \theta + \tan \theta$

c $\dfrac{\cos \alpha}{1 - \tan \alpha} + \dfrac{\sin \alpha}{1 - \cot \alpha}$

$= \dfrac{\cos \alpha}{1 - \dfrac{\sin \alpha}{\cos \alpha}} + \dfrac{\sin \alpha}{1 - \dfrac{\cos \alpha}{\sin \alpha}}$

$= \dfrac{\cos \alpha}{\dfrac{\cos \alpha - \sin \alpha}{\cos \alpha}} + \dfrac{\sin \alpha}{\dfrac{\sin \alpha - \cos \alpha}{\sin \alpha}}$

$= \dfrac{\cos^2 \alpha}{\cos \alpha - \sin \alpha} + \dfrac{\sin^2 \alpha}{\sin \alpha - \cos \alpha}$

$= \dfrac{\cos^2 \alpha - \sin^2 \alpha}{\cos \alpha - \sin \alpha}$

$= \dfrac{(\cos \alpha + \sin \alpha)\cancel{(\cos \alpha - \sin \alpha)}}{\cancel{\cos \alpha - \sin \alpha}_{\,1}}$

$= \sin \alpha + \cos \alpha$

d $\dfrac{\sin \theta}{1 + \cos \theta} + \dfrac{1 + \cos \theta}{\sin \theta}$

$= \dfrac{\sin^2 \theta + (1 + \cos \theta)^2}{(1 + \cos \theta) \sin \theta}$

$= \dfrac{\sin^2 \theta + 1 + 2 \cos \theta + \cos^2 \theta}{(1 + \cos \theta) \sin \theta}$

$= \dfrac{2 + 2 \cos \theta}{(1 + \cos \theta) \sin \theta}$

$= \dfrac{2\cancel{(1 + \cos \theta)}}{\cancel{(1 + \cos \theta)} \sin \theta}$

$= \dfrac{2}{\sin \theta}$

$= 2 \csc \theta$

EXERCISE 12J

1 a $\sin(90° + \theta)$
$= \sin 90° \cos \theta + \cos 90° \sin \theta$
$= (1) \cos \theta + (0) \sin \theta$
$= \cos \theta$

b $\cos(90° + \theta)$
$= \cos 90° \cos \theta - \sin 90° \sin \theta$
$= (0) \cos \theta - (1) \sin \theta$
$= -\sin \theta$

c $\sin(180° - \alpha)$
$= \sin 180° \cos \alpha - \cos 180° \sin \alpha$
$= (0) \cos \alpha - (-1) \sin \alpha$
$= \sin \alpha$

d $\cos(\pi + \alpha)$
$= \cos \pi \cos \alpha - \sin \pi \sin \alpha$
$= (-1) \cos \alpha - (0) \sin \alpha$
$= -\cos \alpha$

e $\sin(2\pi - A)$
$= \sin 2\pi \cos A - \cos 2\pi \sin A$
$= (0)\cos A - (1)\sin A$
$= -\sin A$

f $\cos\left(\frac{3\pi}{2} - \theta\right)$
$= \cos\left(\frac{3\pi}{2}\right)\cos\theta + \sin\left(\frac{3\pi}{2}\right)\sin\theta$
$= (0)\cos\theta + (-1)\sin\theta$
$= -\sin\theta$

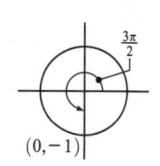

g $\tan(\frac{\pi}{4} + \theta)$
$= \frac{\tan\frac{\pi}{4} + \tan\theta}{1 - \tan\frac{\pi}{4}\tan\theta}$
$= \frac{1 + \tan\theta}{1 - \tan\theta}$

h $\tan(\theta - \frac{3\pi}{4})$
$= \frac{\tan\theta - \tan\frac{3\pi}{4}}{1 + \tan\theta\tan\frac{3\pi}{4}}$
$= \frac{\tan\theta - (-1)}{1 + \tan\theta(-1)}$
$= \frac{1 + \tan\theta}{1 - \tan\theta}$

i $\tan(\pi + \theta)$
$= \frac{\tan\pi + \tan\theta}{1 - \tan\pi\tan\theta}$
$= \frac{0 + \tan\theta}{1 - (0)\tan\theta}$
$= \tan\theta$

2 a $\sin\left(\theta + \frac{\pi}{3}\right)$
$= \sin\theta\cos\left(\frac{\pi}{3}\right) + \cos\theta\sin\left(\frac{\pi}{3}\right)$
$= \sin\theta \times \left(\frac{1}{2}\right) + \cos\theta \times \left(\frac{\sqrt{3}}{2}\right)$
$= \frac{1}{2}\sin\theta + \frac{\sqrt{3}}{2}\cos\theta$

b $\cos\left(\frac{2\pi}{3} - \theta\right)$
$= \cos\left(\frac{2\pi}{3}\right)\cos\theta + \sin\left(\frac{2\pi}{3}\right)\sin\theta$
$= \left(-\frac{1}{2}\right)\cos\theta + \left(\frac{\sqrt{3}}{2}\right)\sin\theta$
$= -\frac{1}{2}\cos\theta + \frac{\sqrt{3}}{2}\sin\theta$
$= \frac{\sqrt{3}}{2}\sin\theta - \frac{1}{2}\cos\theta$

c $\cos\left(\theta + \frac{\pi}{4}\right)$
$= \cos\theta\cos\left(\frac{\pi}{4}\right) - \sin\theta\sin\left(\frac{\pi}{4}\right)$
$= \frac{1}{\sqrt{2}}\cos\theta - \frac{1}{\sqrt{2}}\sin\theta$
$= -\frac{1}{\sqrt{2}}\sin\theta + \frac{1}{\sqrt{2}}\cos\theta$

d $\sin\left(\frac{\pi}{6} - \theta\right)$
$= \sin\left(\frac{\pi}{6}\right)\cos\theta - \cos\left(\frac{\pi}{6}\right)\sin\theta$
$= \frac{1}{2}\cos\theta - \frac{\sqrt{3}}{2}\sin\theta$
$= -\frac{\sqrt{3}}{2}\sin\theta + \frac{1}{2}\cos\theta$

3 a $\cos 2\theta\cos\theta + \sin 2\theta\sin\theta$
$= \cos(2\theta - \theta)$
$= \cos\theta$

b $\sin 2A\cos A + \cos 2A\sin A$
$= \sin(2A + A)$
$= \sin 3A$

c $\cos A\sin B - \sin A\cos B$
$= \sin B\cos A - \cos B\sin A$
$= \sin(B - A)$

d $\sin\alpha\sin\beta + \cos\alpha\cos\beta$
$= \cos\alpha\cos\beta + \sin\alpha\sin\beta$
$= \cos(\alpha - \beta)$

e $\sin\phi\sin\theta - \cos\phi\cos\theta$
$= -[\cos\phi\cos\theta - \sin\phi\sin\theta]$
$= -\cos(\phi + \theta)$

f $2\sin\alpha\cos\beta - 2\cos\alpha\sin\beta$
$= 2[\sin\alpha\cos\beta - \cos\alpha\sin\beta]$
$= 2\sin(\alpha - \beta)$

g $\frac{\tan 2\theta - \tan\theta}{1 + \tan 2\theta\tan\theta} = \tan(2\theta - \theta)$
$= \tan\theta$

h $\frac{\tan 2A + \tan A}{1 - \tan 2A\tan A} = \tan(2A + A)$
$= \tan 3A$

4 a $\frac{\sin 2\theta}{1 + \cos 2\theta} - \tan\theta$
$= \frac{\sin 2\theta}{1 + \cos 2\theta} - \frac{\sin\theta}{\cos\theta}$
$= \frac{\sin 2\theta\cos\theta - \sin\theta(1 + \cos 2\theta)}{(1 + \cos 2\theta)\cos\theta}$
$= \frac{\sin 2\theta\cos\theta - \sin\theta - \sin\theta\cos 2\theta}{(1 + \cos 2\theta)\cos\theta}$
$= \frac{(\sin 2\theta\cos\theta - \cos 2\theta\sin\theta) - \sin\theta}{(1 + \cos 2\theta)\cos\theta}$
$= \frac{\sin(2\theta - \theta) - \sin\theta}{(1 + \cos 2\theta)\cos\theta}$
$= 0$

b $\tan\theta + \cot 2\theta = \dfrac{\sin\theta}{\cos\theta} + \dfrac{\cos 2\theta}{\sin 2\theta}$

$= \dfrac{\sin\theta\sin 2\theta + \cos 2\theta\cos\theta}{\cos\theta\sin 2\theta}$

$= \dfrac{\cos 2\theta\cos\theta + \sin 2\theta\sin\theta}{\cos\theta\sin 2\theta}$

$= \dfrac{\cos(2\theta-\theta)}{\cos\theta\sin 2\theta}\ ^{\ 1}$

$= \csc 2\theta$

c $\dfrac{\sin 2\theta}{\sin\theta} - \dfrac{\cos 2\theta}{\cos\theta} = \dfrac{\sin 2\theta\cos\theta - \sin\theta\cos 2\theta}{\sin\theta\cos\theta}$

$= \dfrac{\sin(2\theta-\theta)}{\sin\theta\cos\theta}$

$= \dfrac{\sin\theta}{\sin\theta\cos\theta}\ ^{\ 1}$

$= \dfrac{1}{\cos\theta}$

$= \sec\theta$

5 a $\cos(\alpha+\beta)\cos(\alpha-\beta) - \sin(\alpha+\beta)\sin(\alpha-\beta)$
$= \cos\left[(\alpha+\beta)+(\alpha-\beta)\right]$
$= \cos 2\alpha$

b $\sin(\theta-2\phi)\cos(\theta+\phi) - \cos(\theta-2\phi)\sin(\theta+\phi)$
$= \sin\left[(\theta-2\phi)-(\theta+\phi)\right]$
$= \sin(-3\phi)$
$= -\sin 3\phi$

c $\cos\alpha\cos(\beta-\alpha) - \sin\alpha\sin(\beta-\alpha)$
$= \cos\left[\alpha+(\beta-\alpha)\right]$
$= \cos\beta$

6 a $\cos 75°$
$= \cos(45° + 30°)$
$= \cos 45°\cos 30° - \sin 45°\sin 30°$
$= \left(\dfrac{1}{\sqrt{2}}\right)\left(\dfrac{\sqrt{3}}{2}\right) - \left(\dfrac{1}{\sqrt{2}}\right)\left(\dfrac{1}{2}\right)$
$= \dfrac{\sqrt{3}-1}{2\sqrt{2}}$
$= \left(\dfrac{\sqrt{3}-1}{2\sqrt{2}}\right)\dfrac{\sqrt{2}}{\sqrt{2}}$
$= \dfrac{\sqrt{6}-\sqrt{2}}{4}$

b $\sin 105°$
$= \sin(60° + 45°)$
$= \sin 60°\cos 45° + \cos 60°\sin 45°$
$= \left(\dfrac{\sqrt{3}}{2}\right)\left(\dfrac{1}{\sqrt{2}}\right) + \left(\dfrac{1}{2}\right)\left(\dfrac{1}{\sqrt{2}}\right)$
$= \left(\dfrac{\sqrt{3}+1}{2\sqrt{2}}\right)\dfrac{\sqrt{2}}{\sqrt{2}}$
$= \dfrac{\sqrt{6}+\sqrt{2}}{4}$

c $\cos\left(\dfrac{13\pi}{12}\right)$
$= \cos\left(\dfrac{10\pi}{12}+\dfrac{3\pi}{12}\right)$
$= \cos\left(\dfrac{5\pi}{6}+\dfrac{\pi}{4}\right)$
$= \cos\left(\dfrac{5\pi}{6}\right)\cos\left(\dfrac{\pi}{4}\right) - \sin\left(\dfrac{5\pi}{6}\right)\sin\left(\dfrac{\pi}{4}\right)$
$= \left(-\dfrac{\sqrt{3}}{2}\right)\left(\dfrac{1}{\sqrt{2}}\right) - \left(\dfrac{1}{2}\right)\left(\dfrac{1}{\sqrt{2}}\right)$
$= \left(\dfrac{-\sqrt{3}-1}{2\sqrt{2}}\right)\dfrac{\sqrt{2}}{\sqrt{2}}$
$= \dfrac{-\sqrt{6}-\sqrt{2}}{4}$

7 a $\tan\left(\dfrac{5\pi}{12}\right)$
$= \tan\left(\dfrac{5\times 180°}{12}\right)$
$= \tan 75°$
$= \tan(45° + 30°)$
$= \dfrac{\tan 45° + \tan 30°}{1 - \tan 45°\tan 30°}$
$= \dfrac{1+\frac{1}{\sqrt{3}}}{1-(1)\left(\frac{1}{\sqrt{3}}\right)}$
$= \left(\dfrac{\sqrt{3}+1}{\sqrt{3}-1}\right)\left(\dfrac{\sqrt{3}+1}{\sqrt{3}+1}\right)$
$= \dfrac{3+\sqrt{3}+\sqrt{3}+1}{3-1}$
$= \dfrac{4+2\sqrt{3}}{2}$
$= 2+\sqrt{3}$

b $\tan 105°$
$= \tan(180° - 75°)$
$= \dfrac{\tan 180° - \tan 75°}{1 + \tan 180°\tan 75°}$
$= \dfrac{0-(2+\sqrt{3})}{1+(0)(2+\sqrt{3})}$ {using **a**}
$= -2-\sqrt{3}$

8 $\tan(A+B) = \dfrac{\tan A + \tan B}{1 - \tan A \tan B}$

$= \dfrac{\frac{2}{3} - \frac{1}{5}}{1 - (\frac{2}{3})(-\frac{1}{5})}$

$= \dfrac{\frac{10}{15} - \frac{3}{15}}{1 + \frac{2}{15}} = \dfrac{\frac{7}{15}}{\frac{17}{15}} = \dfrac{7}{17}$

9 $\tan(A + \frac{\pi}{4}) = \dfrac{\tan A + \tan \frac{\pi}{4}}{1 - \tan A \tan \frac{\pi}{4}}$

$= \dfrac{\frac{3}{4} + 1}{1 - (\frac{3}{4})(1)}$

$= \dfrac{\frac{7}{4}}{\frac{1}{4}} = 7$

10 a $\tan(A + \frac{\pi}{4})\tan(A - \frac{\pi}{4})$

$= \dfrac{\tan A + \tan \frac{\pi}{4}}{1 - \tan A \tan \frac{\pi}{4}} \times \dfrac{\tan A - \tan \frac{\pi}{4}}{1 + \tan A \tan \frac{\pi}{4}}$

$= \left(\dfrac{\tan A + 1}{1 - \tan A}\right)\left(\dfrac{\tan A - 1}{1 + \tan A}\right)$

$= \dfrac{\tan^2 A - 1}{1 - \tan^2 A}$

$= -1$

b $\dfrac{\tan(A+B) + \tan(A-B)}{1 - \tan(A+B)\tan(A-B)}$

$= \tan[(A+B) + (A-B)]$

$= \tan 2A$

11 $\dfrac{\tan 80° - \tan 20°}{1 + \tan 80° \tan 20°}$

$= \tan(80° - 20°)$

$= \tan 60° = \sqrt{3}$

12 $\tan(A+B) = \frac{3}{5}$

$\therefore \dfrac{\tan A + \tan B}{1 - \tan A \tan B} = \frac{3}{5}$

$\therefore \dfrac{\tan A + \frac{2}{3}}{1 - \tan A(\frac{2}{3})} = \frac{3}{5}$

$\therefore 5\tan A + \frac{10}{3} = 3 - 2\tan A$

$\therefore 7\tan A = -\frac{1}{3}$

$\therefore \tan A = -\frac{1}{21}$

13 $\tan(A-B)\tan(A+B) = 1$

$\therefore \left(\dfrac{\tan A - \tan B}{1 + \tan A \tan B}\right)\left(\dfrac{\tan A + \tan B}{1 - \tan A \tan B}\right) = 1$

$\therefore \dfrac{\tan^2 A - \tan^2 B}{1 - \tan^2 A \tan^2 B} = 1$

$\therefore \tan^2 A - \tan^2 B = 1 - \tan^2 A \tan^2 B$

$\therefore \tan^2 A(\tan^2 B + 1) = 1 + \tan^2 B$

$\therefore \tan^2 A = 1$

$\therefore \tan A = \pm 1$

14

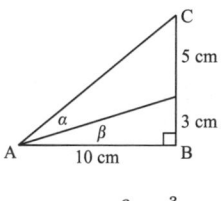

$\tan \beta = \frac{3}{10}$

$\tan(\alpha + \beta) = \frac{8}{10}$

$\therefore \dfrac{\tan \alpha + \tan \beta}{1 - \tan \alpha \tan \beta} = \frac{8}{10}$

$\therefore \dfrac{\tan \alpha + \frac{3}{10}}{1 - \tan \alpha(\frac{3}{10})} = \frac{4}{5}$

$\therefore 5\tan \alpha + \frac{15}{10} = 4 - \frac{12}{10}\tan \alpha$

$\therefore \frac{31}{5}\tan \alpha = \frac{5}{2}$

$\therefore \tan \alpha = \frac{25}{62}$

15

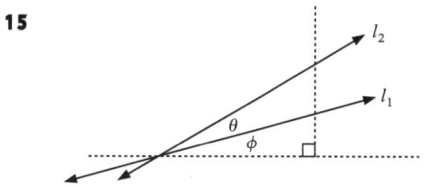

θ is the acute angle between the lines l_1 and l_2.

$\tan \phi = \frac{1}{2}$ {gradient of l_1}

$\tan(\theta + \phi) = \frac{2}{3}$ {gradient of l_2}

$\therefore \dfrac{\tan \theta + \tan \phi}{1 - \tan \theta \tan \phi} = \frac{2}{3}$

$\therefore \dfrac{\tan \theta + \frac{1}{2}}{1 - \tan \theta(\frac{1}{2})} = \frac{2}{3}$

$\therefore 3\tan \theta + \frac{3}{2} = 2 - \tan \theta$

$\therefore 4\tan \theta = \frac{1}{2}$

$\therefore \tan \theta = \frac{1}{8}$

$\therefore$ the tangent of the acute angle is $\frac{1}{8}$.

16 $\tan(A+B+C) = \tan[(A+B)+C]$

$$= \frac{\tan(A+B) + \tan C}{1 - \tan(A+B)\tan C}$$

$$= \frac{\frac{\tan A + \tan B}{1 - \tan A \tan B} + \tan C}{1 - \frac{\tan A + \tan B}{1 - \tan A \tan B} \times \tan C}$$

$$= \frac{\tan A + \tan B + \tan C(1 - \tan A \tan B)}{1 - \tan A \tan B - (\tan A + \tan B) \times \tan C} \quad \{\times \text{ top and bottom by } 1 - \tan A \tan B\}$$

$$= \frac{\tan A + \tan B + \tan C - \tan A \tan B \tan C}{1 - \tan A \tan B - \tan A \tan C - \tan B \tan C}$$

If A, B and C are the angles of a triangle then $A + B + C = 180°$
$\therefore \quad \tan(A + B + C) = 0$
$\therefore \quad \tan A + \tan B + \tan C - \tan A \tan B \tan C = 0$
$\therefore \quad \tan A + \tan B + \tan C = \tan A \tan B \tan C$

17 a $\sqrt{2}\cos\left(\theta + \frac{\pi}{4}\right)$
$= \sqrt{2}\left[\cos\theta \cos\left(\frac{\pi}{4}\right) - \sin\theta \sin\left(\frac{\pi}{4}\right)\right]$
$= \sqrt{2}\left[\frac{1}{\sqrt{2}}\cos\theta - \frac{1}{\sqrt{2}}\sin\theta\right]$
$= \cos\theta - \sin\theta$

b $2\cos\left(\theta - \frac{\pi}{3}\right)$
$= 2\left[\cos\theta \cos\left(\frac{\pi}{3}\right) + \sin\theta \sin\left(\frac{\pi}{3}\right)\right]$
$= 2\left[\frac{1}{2}\cos\theta + \frac{\sqrt{3}}{2}\sin\theta\right]$
$= \cos\theta + \sqrt{3}\sin\theta$

c $\cos(\alpha + \beta) - \cos(\alpha - \beta)$
$= \cos\alpha \cos\beta - \sin\alpha \sin\beta - [\cos\alpha \cos\beta + \sin\alpha \sin\beta]$
$= \cancel{\cos\alpha \cos\beta} - \sin\alpha \sin\beta - \cancel{\cos\alpha \cos\beta} - \sin\alpha \sin\beta$
$= -2\sin\alpha \sin\beta$

d $\cos(\alpha + \beta)\cos(\alpha - \beta)$
$= [\cos\alpha \cos\beta - \sin\alpha \sin\beta][\cos\alpha \cos\beta + \sin\alpha \sin\beta]$
$= \cos^2\alpha \cos^2\beta - \sin^2\alpha \sin^2\beta$
$= \cos^2\alpha \left[1 - \sin^2\beta\right] - \left[1 - \cos^2\alpha\right]\sin^2\beta$
$= \cos^2\alpha - \cancel{\cos^2\alpha \sin^2\beta} - \sin^2\beta + \cancel{\cos^2\alpha \sin^2\beta}$
$= \cos^2\alpha - \sin^2\beta$

18 $\tan\alpha = \frac{1}{3}$ and $\tan\beta = \frac{1}{2}$

$\therefore \quad \tan(\alpha + \beta) = \frac{\tan\alpha + \tan\beta}{1 - \tan\alpha \tan\beta}$

$= \frac{\frac{1}{3} + \frac{1}{2}}{1 - \left(\frac{1}{3}\right)\left(\frac{1}{2}\right)}$

$= \frac{\frac{5}{6}}{\frac{5}{6}} = 1$

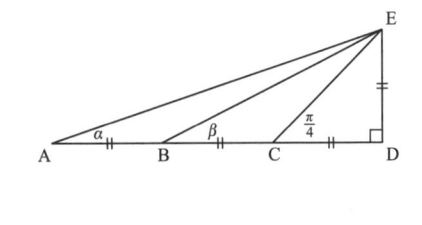

$\therefore \quad \alpha + \beta = \frac{\pi}{4} + k\pi, \quad k \in \mathbb{Z}$

But clearly both α and $\beta < \frac{\pi}{2}$
$\therefore \quad \alpha + \beta = \frac{\pi}{4}$

19 a $\sin(A+B) + \sin(A-B)$
$= \sin A \cos B + \cancel{\cos A \sin B} + \sin A \cos B - \cancel{\cos A \sin B}$
$= 2\sin A \cos B$

b Using **a**, $\sin A \cos B = \tfrac{1}{2}\sin(A+B) + \tfrac{1}{2}\sin(A-B)$

   i $\sin 3\theta \cos\theta$
$= \tfrac{1}{2}\sin(3\theta+\theta) + \tfrac{1}{2}\sin(3\theta-\theta)$
$= \tfrac{1}{2}\sin 4\theta + \tfrac{1}{2}\sin 2\theta$

   ii $\sin 6\alpha \cos\alpha$
$= \tfrac{1}{2}\sin(6\alpha+\alpha) + \tfrac{1}{2}\sin(6\alpha-\alpha)$
$= \tfrac{1}{2}\sin 7\alpha + \tfrac{1}{2}\sin 5\alpha$

   iii $2\sin 5\beta \cos\beta$
$= 2\left[\tfrac{1}{2}\sin(5\beta+\beta) + \tfrac{1}{2}\sin(5\beta-\beta)\right]$
$= \sin 6\beta + \sin 4\beta$

   iv $4\cos\theta \sin 4\theta$
$= 4\left[\sin 4\theta \cos\theta\right]$
$= 4\left[\tfrac{1}{2}\sin 5\theta + \tfrac{1}{2}\sin 3\theta\right]$
$= 2\sin 5\theta + 2\sin 3\theta$

   v $6\cos 4\alpha \sin 3\alpha$
$= 6\sin 3\alpha \cos 4\alpha$
$= 6\left[\tfrac{1}{2}\sin 7\alpha + \tfrac{1}{2}\sin(-\alpha)\right]$
$= 3\sin 7\alpha + 3\sin(-\alpha)$
$= 3\sin 7\alpha - 3\sin\alpha$

   vi $\tfrac{1}{3}\cos 5A \sin 3A$
$= \tfrac{1}{3}\sin 3A \cos 5A$
$= \tfrac{1}{3}\left[\tfrac{1}{2}\sin 8A + \tfrac{1}{2}\sin(-2A)\right]$
$= \tfrac{1}{6}\sin 8A - \tfrac{1}{6}\sin 2A$

20   **a** $\cos(A+B) + \cos(A-B)$
$= \cos A\cos B - \sin A\sin B + \cos A\cos B + \sin A\sin B$
$= 2\cos A\cos B$

   b $\therefore \; \cos A\cos B = \tfrac{1}{2}\cos(A+B) + \tfrac{1}{2}\cos(A-B)$

   i $\cos 4\theta \cos\theta$
$= \tfrac{1}{2}\cos 5\theta + \tfrac{1}{2}\cos 3\theta$

   ii $\cos 7\alpha \cos\alpha$
$= \tfrac{1}{2}\cos 8\alpha + \tfrac{1}{2}\cos 6\alpha$

   iii $2\cos 3\beta \cos\beta$
$= 2\left[\tfrac{1}{2}\cos 4\beta + \tfrac{1}{2}\cos 2\beta\right]$
$= \cos 4\beta + \cos 2\beta$

   iv $6\cos x\cos 7x$
$= 6\cos 7x\cos x$
$= 6\left[\tfrac{1}{2}\cos 8x + \tfrac{1}{2}\cos 6x\right]$
$= 3\cos 8x + 3\cos 6x$

   v $3\cos P\cos 4P$
$= 3\cos 4P\cos P$
$= 3\left[\tfrac{1}{2}\cos 5P + \tfrac{1}{2}\cos 3P\right]$
$= \tfrac{3}{2}\cos 5P + \tfrac{3}{2}\cos 3P$

   vi $\tfrac{1}{4}\cos 4x\cos 2x$
$= \tfrac{1}{4}\left[\tfrac{1}{2}\cos 6x + \tfrac{1}{2}\cos 2x\right]$
$= \tfrac{1}{8}\cos 6x + \tfrac{1}{8}\cos 2x$

21   **a** $\cos(A-B) - \cos(A+B)$
$= \cos A\cos B + \sin A\sin B - [\cos A\cos B - \sin A\sin B]$
$= \sin A\sin B + \sin A\sin B$
$= 2\sin A\sin B$

   b $\therefore \; \sin A\sin B = \tfrac{1}{2}\cos(A-B) - \tfrac{1}{2}\cos(A+B)$

   i $\sin 3\theta \sin\theta$
$= \tfrac{1}{2}\cos 2\theta - \tfrac{1}{2}\cos 4\theta$

   ii $\sin 6\alpha \sin\alpha$
$= \tfrac{1}{2}\cos 5\alpha - \tfrac{1}{2}\cos 7\alpha$

   iii $2\sin 5\beta \sin\beta$
$= 2\left[\tfrac{1}{2}\cos 4\beta - \tfrac{1}{2}\cos 6\beta\right]$
$= \cos 4\beta - \cos 6\beta$

   iv $4\sin\theta \sin 4\theta$
$= 4\sin 4\theta \sin\theta$
$= 4\left[\tfrac{1}{2}\cos 3\theta - \tfrac{1}{2}\cos 5\theta\right]$
$= 2\cos 3\theta - 2\cos 5\theta$

   v $10\sin 2A \sin 8A$
$= 10\sin 8A \sin 2A$
$= 10\left[\tfrac{1}{2}\cos 6A - \tfrac{1}{2}\cos 10A\right]$
$= 5\cos 6A - 5\cos 10A$

   vi $\tfrac{1}{5}\sin 3M \sin 7M$
$= \tfrac{1}{5}\sin 7M \sin 3M$
$= \tfrac{1}{5}\left[\tfrac{1}{2}\cos 4M - \tfrac{1}{2}\cos 10M\right]$
$= \tfrac{1}{10}\cos 4M - \tfrac{1}{10}\cos 10M$

22   (1) becomes $\sin A\cos A = \tfrac{1}{2}\sin 2A$

      (2) becomes $\cos^2 A = \tfrac{1}{2}\cos 2A + \tfrac{1}{2}\cos 0,$ $\therefore \; \cos^2 A = \tfrac{1}{2}\cos 2A + \tfrac{1}{2}$

      (3) becomes $\sin^2 A = \tfrac{1}{2}\cos 0 - \tfrac{1}{2}\cos 2A,$ $\therefore \; \sin^2 A = \tfrac{1}{2} - \tfrac{1}{2}\cos 2A$

23 **a** $A + B = S$ $\quad \therefore \quad 2A = S + D \quad \therefore \quad A = \frac{S+D}{2}$
   $A - B = D$ and $B = S - A = S - \left(\frac{S+D}{2}\right) = \frac{2S}{2} - \left(\frac{S+D}{2}\right) = \frac{2S-S-D}{2} = \frac{S-D}{2}$

b $\sin A \cos B = \frac{1}{2}\sin(A+B) + \frac{1}{2}\sin(A-B)$ becomes $\sin\left(\frac{S+D}{2}\right)\cos\left(\frac{S-D}{2}\right) = \frac{1}{2}\sin S + \frac{1}{2}\sin D$
   or $\sin S + \sin D = 2\sin\left(\frac{S+D}{2}\right)\cos\left(\frac{S-D}{2}\right)$ ...... (4)

c Replacing D by $(-D)$ in (4) gives
   $\sin S + \sin(-D) = 2\sin\left(\frac{S-D}{2}\right)\cos\left(\frac{S+D}{2}\right)$
   or $\sin S - \sin D = 2\cos\left(\frac{S+D}{2}\right)\sin\left(\frac{S-D}{2}\right)$

d $\cos A \cos B = \frac{1}{2}\cos(A+B) + \frac{1}{2}\cos(A-B)$ becomes
   $\cos\left(\frac{S+D}{2}\right)\cos\left(\frac{S-D}{2}\right) = \frac{1}{2}\cos S + \frac{1}{2}\cos D$
   or $\cos S + \cos D = 2\cos\left(\frac{S+D}{2}\right)\cos\left(\frac{S-D}{2}\right)$

e $\sin A \sin B = \frac{1}{2}\cos(A-B) - \frac{1}{2}\cos(A+B)$ becomes
   $\sin\left(\frac{S+D}{2}\right)\sin\left(\frac{S-D}{2}\right) = \frac{1}{2}\cos D - \frac{1}{2}\cos S$
   or $\cos D - \cos S = 2\sin\left(\frac{S+D}{2}\right)\sin\left(\frac{S-D}{2}\right)$
   or $\cos S - \cos D = -2\sin\left(\frac{S+D}{2}\right)\sin\left(\frac{S-D}{2}\right)$

24 **a** $\sin 5x + \sin x$
   $= 2\sin\left(\frac{5x+x}{2}\right)\cos\left(\frac{5x-x}{2}\right)$
   $= 2\sin 3x \cos 2x$

b $\cos 8A + \cos 2A$
   $= 2\cos\left(\frac{8A+2A}{2}\right)\cos\left(\frac{8A-2A}{2}\right)$
   $= 2\cos 5A \cos 3A$

c $\cos 3\alpha - \cos \alpha$
   $= -2\sin\left(\frac{3\alpha+\alpha}{2}\right)\sin\left(\frac{3\alpha-\alpha}{2}\right)$
   $= -2\sin 2\alpha \sin \alpha$

d $\sin 5\theta - \sin 3\theta$
   $= 2\cos\left(\frac{5\theta+3\theta}{2}\right)\sin\left(\frac{5\theta-3\theta}{2}\right)$
   $= 2\cos 4\theta \sin \theta$

e $\cos 7\alpha - \cos \alpha$
   $= -2\sin\left(\frac{7\alpha+\alpha}{2}\right)\sin\left(\frac{7\alpha-\alpha}{2}\right)$
   $= -2\sin 4\alpha \sin 3\alpha$

f $\sin 3\alpha + \sin 7\alpha$
   $= \sin 7\alpha + \sin 3\alpha$
   $= 2\sin\left(\frac{7\alpha+3\alpha}{2}\right)\cos\left(\frac{7\alpha-3\alpha}{2}\right)$
   $= 2\sin 5\alpha \cos 2\alpha$

g $\cos 2B - \cos 4B$
   $= -[\cos 4B - \cos 2B]$
   $= --2\sin\left(\frac{4B+2B}{2}\right)\sin\left(\frac{4B-2B}{2}\right)$
   $= 2\sin 3B \sin B$

h $\sin(x+h) - \sin x$
   $= 2\cos\left(\frac{x+h+x}{2}\right)\sin\left(\frac{x+h-x}{2}\right)$
   $= 2\cos\left(\frac{2x+h}{2}\right)\sin\left(\frac{h}{2}\right)$
   $= 2\cos\left(x + \frac{h}{2}\right)\sin\left(\frac{h}{2}\right)$

i $\cos(x+h) - \cos x$
   $= -2\sin\left(\frac{x+h+x}{2}\right)\sin\left(\frac{x+h-x}{2}\right)$
   $= -2\sin\left(\frac{2x+h}{2}\right)\sin\left(\frac{h}{2}\right)$
   $= -2\sin\left(x + \frac{h}{2}\right)\sin\left(\frac{h}{2}\right)$

EXERCISE 12K

1 **a** $\sin 2A = 2\sin A \cos A$
   $= 2(\frac{4}{5})(\frac{3}{5})$
   $= \frac{24}{25}$

b $\cos 2A = \cos^2 A - \sin^2 A$
   $= \frac{9}{25} - \frac{16}{25}$
   $= -\frac{7}{25}$

2 a $\cos 2A = 2\cos^2 A - 1$
$= 2(\frac{1}{3})^2 - 1$
$= 2 \times \frac{1}{9} - 1$
$= \frac{2}{9} - 1$
$= -\frac{7}{9}$

b $\cos 2\phi = 1 - 2\sin^2 \phi$
$= 1 - 2(-\frac{2}{3})^2$
$= 1 - 2(\frac{4}{9})$
$= 1 - \frac{8}{9}$
$= \frac{1}{9}$

3 a $\sin \alpha = -\frac{2}{3}$
α is in Q3
$\therefore \cos \alpha < 0$

$\cos^2 \alpha + \sin^2 \alpha = 1$
$\therefore \cos^2 \alpha + \frac{4}{9} = 1$
$\therefore \cos^2 \alpha = \frac{5}{9}$
$\therefore \cos \alpha = -\frac{\sqrt{5}}{3}$

$\sin 2\alpha = 2\sin\alpha\cos\alpha$
$= 2\left(-\frac{2}{3}\right)\left(-\frac{\sqrt{5}}{3}\right)$
$= \frac{4\sqrt{5}}{9}$

b $\cos \beta = \frac{2}{5}$
β is in Q4
$\therefore \sin \beta < 0$

$\cos^2 \beta + \sin^2 \beta = 1$
$\therefore \frac{4}{25} + \sin^2 \beta = 1$
$\therefore \sin^2 \beta = \frac{21}{25}$
$\therefore \sin \beta = -\frac{\sqrt{21}}{5}$

$\sin 2\beta = 2\sin\beta\cos\beta$
$= 2\left(-\frac{\sqrt{21}}{5}\right)\left(\frac{2}{5}\right)$
$= -\frac{4\sqrt{21}}{25}$

4 α is acute $\therefore \cos\alpha$ and $\sin\alpha$ are positive

a $\cos 2\alpha = 2\cos^2 \alpha - 1$
$\therefore -\frac{7}{9} = 2\cos^2 \alpha - 1$
$\therefore 2\cos^2 \alpha = \frac{2}{9}$
$\therefore \cos^2 \alpha = \frac{1}{9}$
$\therefore \cos \alpha = \frac{1}{3}$

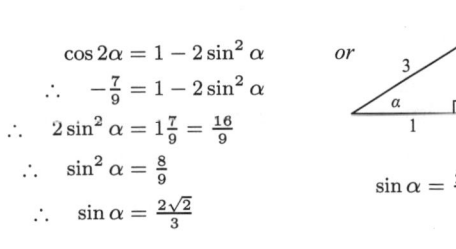

b $\cos 2\alpha = 1 - 2\sin^2 \alpha$
$\therefore -\frac{7}{9} = 1 - 2\sin^2 \alpha$
$\therefore 2\sin^2 \alpha = 1\frac{7}{9} = \frac{16}{9}$
$\therefore \sin^2 \alpha = \frac{8}{9}$
$\therefore \sin \alpha = \frac{2\sqrt{2}}{3}$

or

$\sin \alpha = \frac{2\sqrt{2}}{3}$

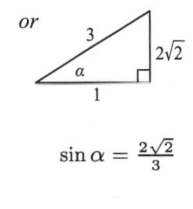

5 $\tan 2A = \frac{21}{20}$
$\therefore \frac{2\tan A}{1 - \tan^2 A} = \frac{21}{20}$
$\therefore 40\tan A = 21 - 21\tan^2 A$
$\therefore 21\tan^2 A + 40\tan A - 21 = 0$
$\therefore (7\tan A - 3)(3\tan A + 7) = 0$
$\therefore \tan A = \frac{3}{7}$ or $-\frac{7}{3}$
but A is obtuse $\therefore \tan A$ is negative
$\therefore \tan A = -\frac{7}{3}$

6 $\tan 2A = -\frac{12}{5}$
$\therefore \frac{2\tan A}{1 - \tan^2 A} = -\frac{12}{5}$
$\therefore 10\tan A = -12 + 12\tan^2 A$
$\therefore 12\tan^2 A - 10\tan A - 12 = 0$
$\therefore 2(6\tan^2 A - 5\tan A - 6) = 0$
$\therefore 2(3\tan A + 2)(2\tan A - 3) = 0$
$\therefore \tan A = -\frac{2}{3}$ or $\frac{3}{2}$
but A is acute $\therefore \tan A$ is positive
$\therefore \tan A = \frac{3}{2}$

7 $\tan(\frac{\pi}{4}) = 1$
$\therefore \tan(2 \times \frac{\pi}{8}) = 1$
$\therefore \frac{2\tan\frac{\pi}{8}}{1 - \tan^2(\frac{\pi}{8})} = 1$
$\therefore 2\tan(\frac{\pi}{8}) = 1 - \tan^2(\frac{\pi}{8})$
$\therefore \tan^2(\frac{\pi}{8}) + 2\tan(\frac{\pi}{8}) - 1 = 0$

$\therefore \tan(\frac{\pi}{8}) = \frac{-2 \pm \sqrt{2^2 - 4(1)(-1)}}{2}$
$= \frac{-2 \pm 2\sqrt{2}}{2}$
$= -1 \pm \sqrt{2}$
but $\frac{\pi}{8}$ is in Q1 $\therefore \tan(\frac{\pi}{8})$ is positive
$\therefore \tan(\frac{\pi}{8}) = \sqrt{2} - 1$

8 $\sin A = -\frac{1}{3}$
A is in Q3
$\therefore \cos A < 0$

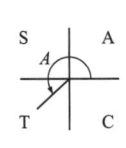

$\cos^2 A + \sin^2 A = 1$
$\therefore \cos^2 A + \frac{1}{9} = 1$
$\therefore \cos^2 A = \frac{8}{9}$
$\therefore \cos A = -\frac{2\sqrt{2}}{3}$

$\therefore \tan A = \frac{\sin A}{\cos A}$
$= \frac{-\frac{1}{3}}{-\frac{2\sqrt{2}}{3}}$
$= \frac{1}{2\sqrt{2}}$

$\cos B = \frac{1}{\sqrt{5}}$

B is in Q1

$\therefore \sin B > 0$

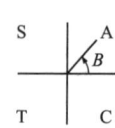

$\therefore \sin B = \frac{2}{\sqrt{5}}$

$\tan B = 2$

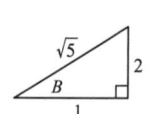

a $\tan(A+B)$
$= \frac{\tan A + \tan B}{1 - \tan A \tan B}$
$= \frac{\frac{1}{2\sqrt{2}} + 2}{1 - (\frac{1}{2\sqrt{2}})(2)} \times \left(\frac{2\sqrt{2}}{2\sqrt{2}}\right)$
$= \frac{1 + 4\sqrt{2}}{2\sqrt{2} - 2} \times \left(\frac{2\sqrt{2} + 2}{2\sqrt{2} + 2}\right)$
$= \frac{2\sqrt{2} + 2 + 16 + 8\sqrt{2}}{8 - 4}$
$= \frac{18 + 10\sqrt{2}}{4} = \frac{9 + 5\sqrt{2}}{2}$

b $\tan 2A = \frac{2\tan A}{1 - \tan^2 A}$
$= \frac{2(\frac{1}{2\sqrt{2}})}{1 - (\frac{1}{2\sqrt{2}})^2}$
$= \frac{\frac{1}{\sqrt{2}}}{1 - \frac{1}{8}}$
$= \frac{\frac{1}{\sqrt{2}}}{\frac{7}{8}}$
$= \frac{8}{7\sqrt{2}} \times \left(\frac{\sqrt{2}}{\sqrt{2}}\right)$
$= \frac{8\sqrt{2}}{14} = \frac{4\sqrt{2}}{7} \quad \left(\text{or } \frac{2\sqrt{8}}{7}\right)$

9 $\left[\cos(\frac{\pi}{12}) + \sin(\frac{\pi}{12})\right]^2$
$= \cos^2(\frac{\pi}{12}) + 2\cos(\frac{\pi}{12})\sin(\frac{\pi}{12}) + \sin^2(\frac{\pi}{12})$
$= 1 + 2\cos(\frac{\pi}{12})\sin(\frac{\pi}{12})$
$= 1 + \sin(\frac{\pi}{6}) \quad \{\sin 2A = 2\cos A \sin A\}$
$= 1 + \frac{1}{2}$
$= \frac{3}{2}$

10 a $2\sin\alpha\cos\alpha$
$= \sin 2\alpha$

b $4\cos\alpha\sin\alpha$
$= 2(2\sin\alpha\cos\alpha)$
$= 2\sin 2\alpha$

c $\sin\alpha\cos\alpha$
$= \frac{1}{2}(2\sin\alpha\cos\alpha)$
$= \frac{1}{2}\sin 2\alpha$

d $2\cos^2\beta - 1$
$= \cos 2\beta$

e $1 - 2\cos^2\phi$
$= -(2\cos^2\phi - 1)$
$= -\cos 2\phi$

f $1 - 2\sin^2 N$
$= \cos 2N$

g $2\sin^2 M - 1$
$= -(1 - 2\sin^2 M)$
$= -\cos 2M$

h $\cos^2\alpha - \sin^2\alpha$
$= \cos 2\alpha$

i $\sin^2\alpha - \cos^2\alpha$
$= -(\cos^2\alpha - \sin^2\alpha)$
$= -\cos 2\alpha$

j $2\sin 2A \cos 2A$
$= \sin 2(2A)$
$= \sin 4A$

k $2\cos 3\alpha \sin 3\alpha$
$= \sin 2(3\alpha)$
$= \sin 6\alpha$

l $2\cos^2 4\theta - 1$
$= \cos 2(4\theta)$
$= \cos 8\theta$

m $1 - 2\cos^2 3\beta$
$= -(2\cos^2 3\beta - 1)$
$= -\cos 2(3\beta)$
$= -\cos 6\beta$

n $1 - 2\sin^2 5\alpha$
$= \cos 2(5\alpha)$
$= \cos 10\alpha$

o $2\sin^2 3D - 1$
$= -(1 - 2\sin^2 3D)$
$= -\cos 2(3D)$
$= -\cos 6D$

p $\cos^2 2A - \sin^2 2A$
$= \cos 2(2A)$
$= \cos 4A$

q $\cos^2(\frac{\alpha}{2}) - \sin^2(\frac{\alpha}{2})$
$= \cos 2(\frac{\alpha}{2})$
$= \cos\alpha$

r $2\sin^2 3P - 2\cos^2 3P$
$= -2[\cos^2 3P - \sin^2 3P]$
$= -2\cos 2(3P)$
$= -2\cos 6P$

11 a $(\sin\theta + \cos\theta)^2$
$= \sin^2\theta + 2\sin\theta\cos\theta + \cos^2\theta$
$= \sin^2\theta + \cos^2\theta + 2\sin\theta\cos\theta$
$= 1 + \sin 2\theta$

b $\cos^4\theta - \sin^4\theta$
$= (\cos^2\theta + \sin^2\theta)(\cos^2\theta - \sin^2\theta)$
$= 1 \times \cos 2\theta$
$= \cos 2\theta$

12 a

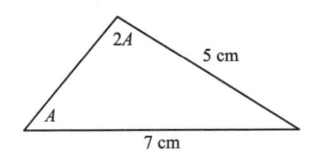

Using the sine rule,
$$\frac{\sin 2A}{7} = \frac{\sin A}{5}$$
$$\therefore \frac{2\sin A \cos A}{7} = \frac{\sin A}{5}$$
$$\therefore \cos A = \frac{7}{10}$$

b

Using the sine rule,
$$\frac{\sin 2A}{3} = \frac{\sin A}{2}$$
$$\therefore \frac{2\sin A \cos A}{3} = \frac{\sin A}{2}$$
$$\therefore \cos A = \frac{3}{4}$$

13 a $x \mapsto \tan x$

$\tan x = \dfrac{\sin x}{\cos x}$ is undefined when $\cos x = 0$
$\therefore$ when $x = \frac{\pi}{2} + k\pi$, $k \in \mathbb{Z}$
$\therefore$ domain of $x \mapsto \tan x$ is $\{x \mid x \neq \frac{\pi}{2} + k\pi,\ k \in \mathbb{Z}\}$
$\tan x$ can take any real value
$\therefore$ range of $x \mapsto \tan x$ is $\{y \mid y \text{ is in } \mathbb{R}\}$

b $x \mapsto \sec 2x$

$\sec 2x = \dfrac{1}{\cos 2x}$ is undefined when $\cos 2x = 0$
$\therefore 2x = \frac{\pi}{2} + k\pi,\ k \in \mathbb{Z}$
$\therefore x = \frac{\pi}{4} + \frac{k\pi}{2},\ k \in \mathbb{Z}$
$\therefore$ domain of $x \mapsto \sec 2x$ is $\{x \mid x \neq \frac{\pi}{4} + \frac{k\pi}{2},\ k \in \mathbb{Z}\}$
Now $-1 \leqslant \cos 2x \leqslant 1$
$\therefore \dfrac{1}{\cos 2x} \leqslant -1$ or $\dfrac{1}{\cos 2x} \geqslant 1$
$\therefore$ range of $x \mapsto \sec 2x$ is $\{y \mid y \geqslant 1 \text{ or } y \leqslant -1\}$

c $x \mapsto \cot 3x$

$\cot 3x = \dfrac{\cos 3x}{\sin 3x}$ is undefined when $\sin 3x = 0$
$\therefore 3x = k\pi,\ k \in \mathbb{Z}$
$\therefore x = \frac{k\pi}{3},\ k \in \mathbb{Z}$
$\therefore$ domain of $x \mapsto \cot 3x$ is $\{x \mid x \neq \frac{k\pi}{3},\ k \in \mathbb{Z}\}$
$\cot 3x$ can take any value
$\therefore$ range of $x \mapsto \cot 3x$ is $\{y \mid y \text{ is in } \mathbb{R}\}$

14 a $\frac{1}{2} - \frac{1}{2}\cos 2\theta$
$= \frac{1}{2} - \frac{1}{2}(1 - 2\sin^2\theta)$
$= \frac{1}{2} - \frac{1}{2} + \sin^2\theta$
$= \sin^2\theta$

b $\frac{1}{2} + \frac{1}{2}\cos 2\theta$
$= \frac{1}{2} + \frac{1}{2}(2\cos^2\theta - 1)$
$= \frac{1}{2} + \cos^2\theta - \frac{1}{2}$
$= \cos^2\theta$

15 a $\dfrac{\sin 2\theta}{1 - \cos 2\theta} = \dfrac{2\sin\theta\cos\theta}{1 - (1 - 2\sin^2\theta)}$

$= \dfrac{2\sin\theta\cos\theta}{1 - 1 + 2\sin^2\theta}$

$= \dfrac{2\sin\theta\cos\theta}{2\sin^2\theta}$

$= \dfrac{\cos\theta}{\sin\theta}$

$= \cot\theta$

b $\dfrac{\sin\theta + \sin 2\theta}{1 + \cos\theta + \cos 2\theta}$

$= \dfrac{\sin\theta + 2\sin\theta\cos\theta}{1 + \cos\theta + 2\cos^2\theta - 1}$

$= \dfrac{\sin\theta(1 + 2\cos\theta)}{\cos\theta(1 + 2\cos\theta)}$

$= \dfrac{\sin\theta}{\cos\theta}$

$= \tan\theta$

16 $\sqrt{3}\sin x + \cos x = k\sin(x + b)$
$\qquad\qquad\qquad = k[\sin x \cos b + \cos x \sin b]$
$\qquad\qquad\qquad = k\cos b \sin x + k\sin b \cos x$

Equating coefficients of $\sin x$ and $\cos x$,
$\qquad k\cos b = \sqrt{3}\quad$ and $\quad k\sin b = 1 \quad \ldots\ldots$ (1)
$\therefore\ k^2\cos^2 b = 3\quad$ and $\quad k^2\sin^2 b = 1\quad$ {squaring both sides}
$\therefore\ k^2(\cos^2 b + \sin^2 b) = 4\quad$ {adding the 2 equations}
$\qquad\therefore\ k^2 = 4$
$\qquad\therefore\ k = 2\quad \{k > 0\}$

Substituting $k = 2$ into (1) gives
$\qquad \cos b = \dfrac{\sqrt{3}}{2}\quad$ and $\quad \sin b = \dfrac{1}{2}$
$\qquad\therefore\ b = \dfrac{\pi}{6}$

17 If $\sin A = \sin B$, then $\sin A - \sin B = 0$
$\therefore\ 2\cos\tfrac{1}{2}(A + B)\sin\tfrac{1}{2}(A - B) = 0$
$\therefore\ \cos\tfrac{1}{2}(A + B) = 0\qquad$ or $\qquad \sin\tfrac{1}{2}(A - B) = 0$
$\therefore\ \tfrac{1}{2}(A + B) = \tfrac{\pi}{2} + k\pi\quad$ or $\quad \tfrac{1}{2}(A - B) = k\pi,\ k \in \mathbb{Z}$
$\therefore\ A + B = \pi + k2\pi\quad$ or $\quad A - B = k2\pi,\ k \in \mathbb{Z}$
$\therefore\ A + B = \pi + k2\pi\quad$ or $\quad A = B + k2\pi,\ k \in \mathbb{Z}$

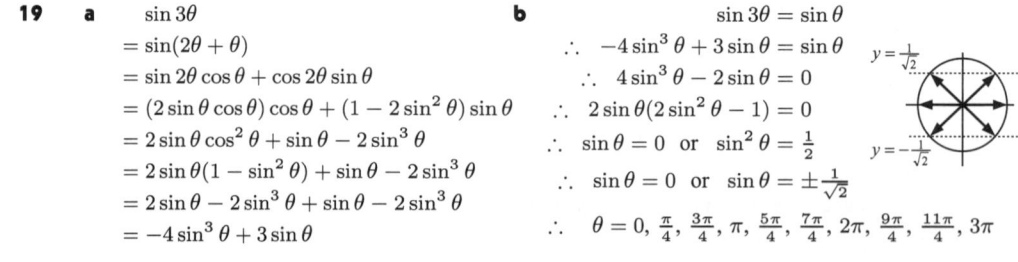

18 a $\cos 3\theta$
$= \cos(2\theta + \theta)$
$= \cos 2\theta \cos\theta - \sin 2\theta \sin\theta$
$= (2\cos^2\theta - 1)\cos\theta - (2\sin\theta\cos\theta)\sin\theta$
$= 2\cos^3\theta - \cos\theta - 2\sin^2\theta\cos\theta$
$= 2\cos^3\theta - \cos\theta - 2(1 - \cos^2\theta)\cos\theta$
$= 2\cos^3\theta - \cos\theta - 2\cos\theta + 2\cos^3\theta$
$= 4\cos^3\theta - 3\cos\theta$

b $8\cos^3\theta - 6\cos\theta + 1 = 0$
$\therefore\ 8\cos^3\theta - 6\cos\theta = -1$
$\therefore\ 4\cos^3\theta - 3\cos\theta = -\tfrac{1}{2}$
$\therefore\ \cos 3\theta = -\tfrac{1}{2}$
$\therefore\ 3\theta = -\tfrac{8\pi}{3}, -\tfrac{4\pi}{3}, -\tfrac{2\pi}{3},$
$\qquad \tfrac{2\pi}{3}, \tfrac{4\pi}{3}, \tfrac{8\pi}{3}$
$\{3\theta \in [-3\pi, 3\pi]\}$
$\therefore\ \theta = -\tfrac{8\pi}{9}, -\tfrac{4\pi}{9}, -\tfrac{2\pi}{9}, \tfrac{2\pi}{9}, \tfrac{4\pi}{9}, \tfrac{8\pi}{9}$

19 a $\sin 3\theta$
$= \sin(2\theta + \theta)$
$= \sin 2\theta \cos\theta + \cos 2\theta \sin\theta$
$= (2\sin\theta\cos\theta)\cos\theta + (1 - 2\sin^2\theta)\sin\theta$
$= 2\sin\theta\cos^2\theta + \sin\theta - 2\sin^3\theta$
$= 2\sin\theta(1 - \sin^2\theta) + \sin\theta - 2\sin^3\theta$
$= 2\sin\theta - 2\sin^3\theta + \sin\theta - 2\sin^3\theta$
$= -4\sin^3\theta + 3\sin\theta$

b $\sin 3\theta = \sin\theta$
$\therefore\ -4\sin^3\theta + 3\sin\theta = \sin\theta$
$\therefore\ 4\sin^3\theta - 2\sin\theta = 0$
$\therefore\ 2\sin\theta(2\sin^2\theta - 1) = 0$
$\therefore\ \sin\theta = 0\ $ or $\ \sin^2\theta = \tfrac{1}{2}$
$\therefore\ \sin\theta = 0\ $ or $\ \sin\theta = \pm\tfrac{1}{\sqrt{2}}$
$\therefore\ \theta = 0, \tfrac{\pi}{4}, \tfrac{3\pi}{4}, \pi, \tfrac{5\pi}{4}, \tfrac{7\pi}{4}, 2\pi, \tfrac{9\pi}{4}, \tfrac{11\pi}{4}, 3\pi$

20 The period of a function $f(x)$ is the smallest $p > 0$ such that
$\qquad\qquad f(x + p) = f(x)\quad$ for all x
$\qquad\therefore\ \sin[n(x + p)] = \sin(nx)$
$\qquad\therefore\ \sin(nx + np) = \sin(nx)$
$\therefore\ \sin(nx)\cos(np) + \cos(nx)\sin(np) = \sin(nx)$

Equating coefficients of $\sin(nx)$ and $\cos(nx)$,
$\cos(np) = 1$ and $\sin(np) = 0$
$\therefore \ np = 2k\pi, \quad k \in \mathbb{Z}$
$\therefore \ p = \dfrac{2k\pi}{n}, \quad k \in \mathbb{Z}$

The smallest $p > 0$ occurs when $k = 1$ $\therefore \ p = \dfrac{2\pi}{n}$

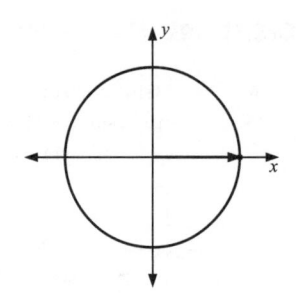

21 a $2\cos x - 5\sin x = k\cos(x+b)$
$ = k[\cos x \cos b - \sin x \sin b]$
$ = k\cos b \cos x - k\sin b \sin x$

Equating coefficients of $\cos x$ and $\sin x$,
$\quad k\cos b = 2$ and $k\sin b = 5$ ..... (1)
$\therefore \ k^2 \cos^2 b = 4$ and $k^2 \sin^2 b = 25$ {squaring both sides}
$\therefore \ k^2(\cos^2 b + \sin^2 b) = 29$ {adding the two equations}
$\therefore \ k^2 = 29$ $\therefore \ k = \sqrt{29}$ $\{k > 0\}$

Substituting $k = \sqrt{29}$ into (1) gives
$\cos b = \dfrac{2}{\sqrt{29}}$ and $\sin b = \dfrac{5}{\sqrt{29}}$
$\therefore \ b = \cos^{-1}\left(\dfrac{2}{\sqrt{29}}\right) \approx 1.19$

$\therefore \ 2\cos x - 5\sin x \approx \sqrt{29}\cos(x + 1.19)$

b $2\cos x - 5\sin x = -2$
$\therefore \ \sqrt{29}\cos(x + 1.19) \approx -2$
$\therefore \ \cos(x + 1.19) \approx -\dfrac{2}{\sqrt{29}}$
$\therefore \ x + 1.19 \approx 1.951, \ 4.33$
$\therefore \ x \approx 0.761, \ 3.14$ ← this solution is exactly π

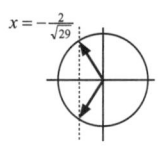

c $\tan x = \tan\left(2 \times \dfrac{x}{2}\right)$
$ = \dfrac{2\tan\left(\frac{x}{2}\right)}{1 - \tan^2\left(\frac{x}{2}\right)}$
$ = \dfrac{2t}{1 - t^2}$

Now $h^2 = (1 - t^2)^2 + (2t)^2$
$ = 1 - 2t^2 + t^4 + 4t^2$
$ = 1 + 2t^2 + t^4$
$\therefore \ h = 1 + t^2$

$\therefore \ \sin x = \dfrac{2t}{1 + t^2}$ and $\cos x = \dfrac{1 - t^2}{1 + t^2}$

d $2\cos x - 5\sin x = -2$
$\therefore \ 2\left(\dfrac{1 - t^2}{1 + t^2}\right) - 5\left(\dfrac{2t}{1 + t^2}\right) = -2$
$\therefore \ \dfrac{2 - 2t^2 - 10t}{1 + t^2} = -2$
$\therefore \ 2 - \cancel{2t^2} - 10t = -2 - \cancel{2t^2}$
$\therefore \ 4 = 10t$
$\therefore \ t = \dfrac{2}{5}$

So $\tan\left(\dfrac{x}{2}\right) = \dfrac{2}{5}$
$\therefore \ \dfrac{x}{2} \approx 0.3805$ $\left\{0 \leqslant \dfrac{x}{2} \leqslant \dfrac{\pi}{2}\right\}$
$\therefore \ x \approx 0.761$

The $x = \pi$ solution has been lost since t is undefined when $x = \pi$.

EXERCISE 12L

1 a $\quad 2\sin^2 x + \sin x = 0$
$\therefore \sin x(2\sin x + 1) = 0$
$\therefore \sin x = 0 \text{ or } -\tfrac{1}{2}$

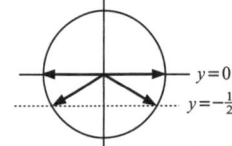

$\therefore x = 0, \pi, \tfrac{7\pi}{6}, \tfrac{11\pi}{6}, 2\pi$

b $\quad 2\cos^2 x = \cos x$
$\therefore 2\cos^2 x - \cos x = 0$
$\therefore \cos x(2\cos x - 1) = 0$
$\therefore \cos x = 0 \text{ or } \tfrac{1}{2}$

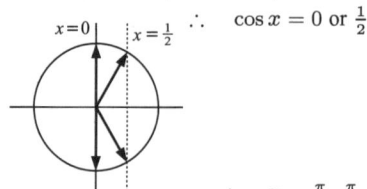

$\therefore x = \tfrac{\pi}{3}, \tfrac{\pi}{2}, \tfrac{3\pi}{2}, \tfrac{5\pi}{3}$

c $\quad 2\cos^2 x + \cos x - 1 = 0$
$\therefore (2\cos x - 1)(\cos x + 1) = 0$
$\therefore \cos x = \tfrac{1}{2} \text{ or } -1$

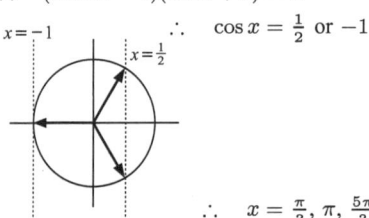

$\therefore x = \tfrac{\pi}{3}, \pi, \tfrac{5\pi}{3}$

d $\quad 2\sin^2 x + 3\sin x + 1 = 0$
$\therefore (2\sin x + 1)(\sin x + 1) = 0$
$\therefore \sin x = -\tfrac{1}{2} \text{ or } -1$

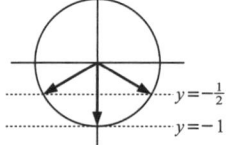

$\therefore x = \tfrac{7\pi}{6}, \tfrac{3\pi}{2}, \tfrac{11\pi}{6}$

e $\quad \sin^2 x = 2 - \cos x$
$\therefore 1 - \cos^2 x = 2 - \cos x$
$\therefore \cos^2 x - \cos x + 1 = 0$
where $\Delta = (-1)^2 - 4(1)(1)$
$= 1 - 4$
$= -3$
$\therefore$ no real solutions exist

f $\quad 3\tan x = \cot x$
$\therefore 3\tan^2 x = 1$
$\therefore \tan^2 x = \tfrac{1}{3}$
$\therefore \tan x = \pm\tfrac{1}{\sqrt{3}}$

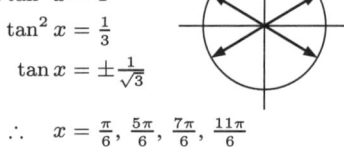

$\therefore x = \tfrac{\pi}{6}, \tfrac{5\pi}{6}, \tfrac{7\pi}{6}, \tfrac{11\pi}{6}$

g $\quad \sin 4x = \sin 2x$
$\therefore 2\sin 2x \cos 2x = \sin 2x$
$\therefore \sin 2x(2\cos 2x - 1) = 0$
$\therefore \sin 2x = 0 \text{ or } \cos 2x = \tfrac{1}{2}$

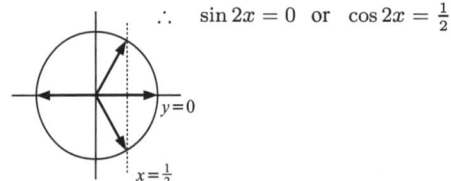

$\therefore 2x = 0, \tfrac{\pi}{3}, \pi, \tfrac{5\pi}{3}, 2\pi, \tfrac{7\pi}{3}, 3\pi, \tfrac{11\pi}{3}, 4\pi$
$\therefore x = 0, \tfrac{\pi}{6}, \tfrac{\pi}{2}, \tfrac{5\pi}{6}, \pi, \tfrac{7\pi}{6}, \tfrac{3\pi}{2}, \tfrac{11\pi}{6}, 2\pi$

h $\quad \sin x + \cos x = \sqrt{2}$
$\therefore (\sin x + \cos x)^2 = 2$
$\therefore \sin^2 x + 2\sin x \cos x + \cos^2 x = 2$
$\therefore 1 + \sin 2x = 2$
$\therefore \sin 2x = 1$
$\therefore 2x = \tfrac{\pi}{2}, \tfrac{5\pi}{2}$
$\therefore x = \tfrac{\pi}{4}, \tfrac{5\pi}{4}$

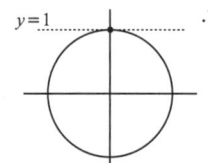

But when $x = \tfrac{5\pi}{4}$, $\sin x + \cos x = -\sqrt{2}$
$\therefore x = \tfrac{\pi}{4}$ is the only solution

2 a $\quad 2\sin x + \csc x = 3$
$\therefore 2\sin^2 x + 1 = 3\sin x$
$\therefore 2\sin^2 x - 3\sin x + 1 = 0$
$\therefore (2\sin x - 1)(\sin x - 1) = 0$
$\therefore \sin x = \tfrac{1}{2} \text{ or } 1$

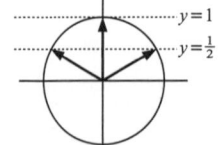

$\therefore x = \tfrac{\pi}{6}, \tfrac{\pi}{2}, \tfrac{5\pi}{6}$

b $\quad \sin 2x + \cos x - 2\sin x - 1 = 0$
$\therefore 2\sin x \cos x + \cos x - 2\sin x - 1 = 0$
$\therefore (2\sin x + 1)(\cos x - 1) = 0$
$\therefore \sin x = -\tfrac{1}{2} \text{ or } \cos x = 1$

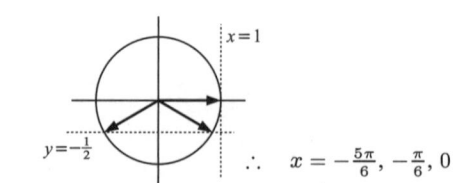

$\therefore x = -\tfrac{5\pi}{6}, -\tfrac{\pi}{6}, 0$

c $\tan^4 x - 2\tan^2 x - 3 = 0$
$\therefore \ (\tan^2 x - 3)(\tan^2 x + 1) = 0$
$\therefore \ \tan^2 x = 3 \text{ or } -1$
$\therefore \ \tan^2 x = \pm\sqrt{3}$

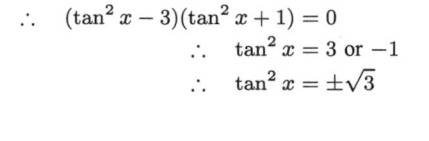

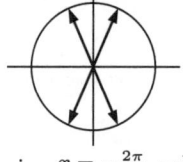

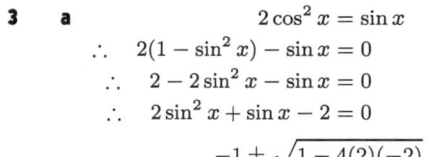

$\therefore \ x = -\frac{2\pi}{3}, -\frac{\pi}{3}, \frac{\pi}{3}, \frac{2\pi}{3}$

3 a $2\cos^2 x = \sin x$
$\therefore \ 2(1 - \sin^2 x) - \sin x = 0$
$\therefore \ 2 - 2\sin^2 x - \sin x = 0$
$\therefore \ 2\sin^2 x + \sin x - 2 = 0$
$\therefore \ \sin x = \dfrac{-1 \pm \sqrt{1 - 4(2)(-2)}}{2(2)}$
$\therefore \ \sin x = \dfrac{-1 \pm \sqrt{17}}{4} \approx 0.7808$
$\qquad \qquad \qquad \text{or } -1.281$

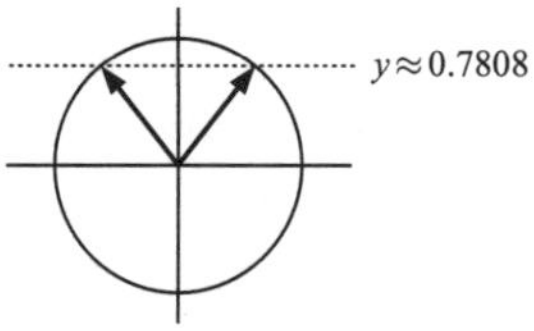

$\therefore \ \sin x \approx 0.7808 \ \text{ as }$
$\qquad -1 \leqslant \sin x \leqslant 1$
$\therefore \ x \approx \arcsin(0.7808) \ \text{ or } \ \pi - \arcsin(0.7808)$
$\therefore \ x \approx 0.896 \ \text{ or } \ 2.25$

b $\cos 2x + 5\sin x = 0$
$\therefore \ 1 - 2\sin^2 x + 5\sin x = 0$
$\therefore \ 2\sin^2 x - 5\sin x - 1 = 0$
$\therefore \ \sin x = \dfrac{5 \pm \sqrt{25 - 4(2)(-1)}}{2(2)}$
$= \dfrac{5 \pm \sqrt{33}}{4} \approx 2.6861 \text{ or } -0.1861$
$\therefore \ \sin x \approx -0.1861 \ \{\text{as } -1 \leqslant \sin x \leqslant 1\}$

$\therefore \ x \approx \pi + 0.1872$
$\quad \text{or } \ 2\pi - 0.1872$
$\therefore \ x \approx 3.33 \text{ or } 6.10$

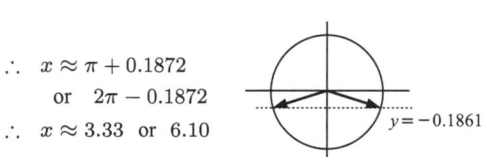

$y = -0.1861$

c $2\tan^2 x + 3\sec^2 x = 7$
$\therefore \ 2\tan^2 x + 3(\tan^2 x + 1) = 7$
$\therefore \ 5\tan^2 x + 3 = 7$
$\therefore \ 5\tan^2 x = 4$
$\therefore \ \tan^2 x = \frac{4}{5}$
$\therefore \ \tan x = \pm\frac{2}{\sqrt{5}}$

$\therefore \ x \approx 0.730, \ \pi - 0.730,$
$\qquad \pi + 0.730,$
$\qquad 2\pi - 0.730$
$\therefore \ x \approx 0.730, \ 2.41,$
$\qquad 3.87, \ 5.55$

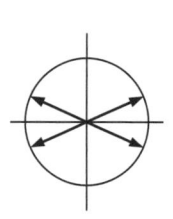

EXERCISE 12M

1 a $1 + \sin x + \sin^2 x + \sin^3 x + \ldots + \sin^{n-1} x$
is a geometric series with
$u_1 = 1, \ r = \sin x$

$\therefore \ \text{sum} = \dfrac{u_1(1 - r^n)}{1 - r}$
$= \dfrac{1(1 - \sin^n x)}{1 - \sin x}$
$= \dfrac{1 - \sin^n x}{1 - \sin x}$

b $S = \dfrac{u_1}{1 - r} = \dfrac{1}{1 - \sin x}$
as $-1 \leqslant \sin x \leqslant 1 \Rightarrow -1 \leqslant r \leqslant 1$

c If $S = \frac{2}{3}$, $\dfrac{1}{1 - \sin x} = \frac{2}{3}$
$\therefore \ 3 = 2 - 2\sin x$
$\therefore \ 2\sin x = -1$
$\therefore \ \sin x = -\frac{1}{2}$
$\therefore \ x = \frac{7\pi}{6} \text{ or } \frac{11\pi}{6}$

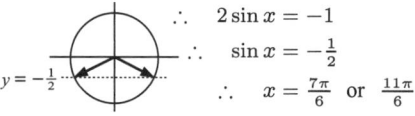

$y = -\frac{1}{2}$

2 a i $2\sin x(\cos x + \cos 3x)$
$= 2\sin x \cos x + 2\sin x \cos 3x$
$= \sin 2x + \sin 4x + \sin(-2x)$
$\{2\sin A \cos B = \sin(A+B) + \sin(A-B)\}$
$= \cancel{\sin 2x} + \sin 4x - \cancel{\sin 2x}$
$= \sin 4x$

ii $2\sin x(\cos x + \cos 3x + \cos 5x)$
$= 2\sin x(\cos x + \cos 3x) + 2\sin x \cos 5x$
$= \sin 4x + \sin 6x + \sin(-4x) \ \{\text{from I}\}$
$= \cancel{\sin 4x} + \sin 6x - \cancel{\sin 4x}$
$= \sin 6x$

b **i** $2\sin x(\cos x + \cos 3x + \cos 5x + \ldots + \cos 7x) = \sin 8x$

ii $2\sin x(\cos x + \cos 3x + \cos 5x + \ldots + \cos 19x) = \sin 20x$

$\therefore \cos x + \cos 3x + \cos 5x + \ldots + \cos 19x = \dfrac{\sin 20x}{2\sin x}$

c In general, $\cos x + \cos 3x + \cos 5x + \ldots + \cos(2n-1)x = \dfrac{\sin 2nx}{2\sin x}$

3 a i $\sin x \cos x \cos 2x$

$= \tfrac{1}{2}(2\sin x \cos x)\cos 2x$

$= \tfrac{1}{2}\sin 2x \cos 2x$

$= \tfrac{1}{4} 2\sin 2x \cos 2x$

$= \tfrac{1}{4}\sin 4x$ ......(1)

$= \dfrac{\sin(2^2 x)}{2^2}$

ii $(\sin x \cos x \cos 2x)\cos 4x$

$= \tfrac{1}{4}\sin 4x \cos 4x$ {from (1)}

$= \tfrac{1}{8}(2\sin 4x \cos 4x)$

$= \dfrac{\sin 8x}{8}$

$= \dfrac{\sin(2^3 x)}{2^3}$

b i $\dfrac{\sin(2^4 x)}{2^4}$

ii $\dfrac{\sin(2^6 x)}{2^6}$

c $\sin x \cos x \cos 2x \cos 4x \ldots \cos(2^n x) = \dfrac{\sin(2^{n+1} x)}{2^{n+1}}$

or $\cos x \cos 2x \cos 4x \ldots \cos(2^n x) = \dfrac{\sin(2^{n+1} x)}{2^{n+1} \sin x}$

4 a P_n is "$\cos\theta + \cos 3\theta + \cos 5\theta + \ldots + \cos(2n-1)\theta = \dfrac{\sin 2n\theta}{2\sin\theta}$", $n \in \mathbb{Z}^+$

Proof: (By the principle of mathematical induction)

(1) If $n = 1$, LHS $= \cos\theta$ and RHS $= \dfrac{\sin 2\theta}{2\sin\theta} = \dfrac{2\sin\theta\cos\theta}{2\sin\theta} = \cos\theta$ $\therefore P_1$ is true.

(2) If P_k is true, then

$\cos\theta + \cos 3\theta + \cos 5\theta + \ldots + \cos(2k-1)\theta = \dfrac{\sin 2k\theta}{2\sin\theta}$

$\therefore \cos\theta + \cos 3\theta + \cos 5\theta + \ldots + \cos(2k-1)\theta + \cos(2k+1)\theta$

$= \dfrac{\sin 2k\theta}{2\sin\theta} + \cos(2k+1)\theta$

$= \dfrac{\sin 2k\theta + 2\sin\theta\cos(2k+1)\theta}{2\sin\theta}$

$= \dfrac{\sin 2k\theta + \sin[\theta + (2k+1)\theta] + \sin[\theta - (2k+1)\theta]}{2\sin\theta}$

$= \dfrac{\sin 2k\theta + \sin(\theta + 2k\theta + \theta) + \sin(\theta - 2k\theta - \theta)}{2\sin\theta}$

$= \dfrac{\sin 2k\theta + \sin(2k\theta + 2\theta) + \sin(-2k\theta)}{2\sin\theta}$

$= \dfrac{\cancel{\sin 2k\theta} + \sin 2(k+1)\theta - \cancel{\sin 2k\theta}}{2\sin\theta}$

$= \dfrac{\sin 2(k+1)\theta}{2\sin\theta}$

Thus P_{k+1} is true whenever P_k is true and P_1 is true.

$\therefore P_n$ is true for all $n \in \mathbb{Z}^+$ {Principle of mathematical induction}

b $\cos\theta + \cos 3\theta + \cos 5\theta + \ldots + \cos 31\theta = \dfrac{\sin 32\theta}{2\sin\theta}$ {$n = 16$}

5 P_n is "$\sin\theta + \sin 3\theta + \sin 5\theta + \ldots + \sin(2n-1)\theta = \dfrac{1 - \cos 2n\theta}{2\sin\theta}$", $n \in \mathbb{Z}^+$

Proof: (By the principle of mathematical induction)

(1) If $n = 1$, LHS $= \sin\theta$ and RHS $= \dfrac{1 - \cos 2\theta}{2\sin\theta} = \dfrac{1 - (1 - 2\sin^2\theta)}{2\sin\theta} = \dfrac{2\sin^2\theta}{2\sin\theta} = \sin\theta$

$\therefore\ P_1$ is true.

(2) If P_k is true, then

$$\sin\theta + \sin 3\theta + \sin 5\theta + \ldots + \sin(2k-1)\theta = \dfrac{1 - \cos 2k\theta}{2\sin\theta}$$

$\therefore\ \sin\theta + \sin 3\theta + \sin 5\theta + \ldots + \sin(2k-1)\theta + \sin(2k+1)\theta$

$= \dfrac{1 - \cos 2k\theta}{2\sin\theta} + \sin(2k+1)\theta$

$= \dfrac{1 - \cos 2k\theta + 2\sin(2k+1)\theta \sin\theta}{2\sin\theta}$

$= \dfrac{1 - \cos 2k\theta + \cos[(2k+1)\theta - \theta] - \cos[(2k+1)\theta + \theta]}{2\sin\theta}$

$= \dfrac{1 - \cancel{\cos 2k\theta} + \cancel{\cos 2k\theta} - \cos[(2k+2)\theta]}{2\sin\theta}$

$= \dfrac{1 - \cos 2(k+1)\theta}{2\sin\theta}$

Thus P_{k+1} is true whenever P_k is true and P_1 is true.

$\therefore\ P_n$ is true for all $n \in \mathbb{Z}^+$ {Principle of mathematical induction}

Thus $\sin\frac{\pi}{7} + \sin\frac{3\pi}{7} + \sin\frac{5\pi}{7} + \ldots + \sin\frac{13\pi}{7}$ has $2n - 1 = 13$ and $\theta = \frac{\pi}{7}$

$\therefore\ n = 7$ and $\theta = \frac{\pi}{7}$

$\therefore\ $ the sum is $\dfrac{1 - \cos(2 \times 7 \times \frac{\pi}{7})}{2\sin\frac{\pi}{7}} = \dfrac{1 - \cos 2\pi}{2\sin\frac{\pi}{7}} = \dfrac{1 - 1}{2\sin\frac{\pi}{7}} = 0$

6 P_n is "$\cos x \times \cos 2x \times \cos 4x \times \cos 8x \times \ldots \times \cos(2^{n-1}x) = \dfrac{\sin(2^n x)}{2^n \times \sin x}$", $n \in \mathbb{Z}^+$

Proof: (By the principle of mathematical induction)

(1) If $n = 1$, LHS $= \cos x$, RHS $= \dfrac{\sin 2x}{2\sin x} = \dfrac{2\sin x \cos x}{2\sin x} = \cos x\ \ \therefore\ P_1$ is true.

(2) If P_k is true, then

$$\cos x \times \cos 2x \times \cos 4x \times \ldots \times \cos(2^{k-1}x) = \dfrac{\sin(2^k x)}{2^k \sin x}$$

$\therefore\ \cos x \times \cos 2x \times \cos 4x \times \ldots \times \cos(2^{k-1}x) \times \cos(2^k x)$

$= \dfrac{\sin(2^k x)}{2^k \sin x} \times \cos(2^k x)$

$= \dfrac{2\sin(2^k x)\cos(2^k x)}{2 \times 2^k \sin x}$

$= \dfrac{\sin(2 \times 2^k x)}{2^{k+1} \sin x}$ $\{2\sin\theta\cos\theta = \sin 2\theta\}$

$= \dfrac{\sin(2^{k+1} x)}{2^{k+1} \sin x}$

Thus P_{k+1} is true whenever P_k is true and P_1 is true.

$\therefore\ P_n$ is true for all $n \in \mathbb{Z}^+$ {Principle of mathematical induction}

7 P_n is "$\cos^2\theta + \cos^2 2\theta + \cos^2 3\theta + \ldots + \cos^2(n\theta) = \frac{1}{2}\left[n + \dfrac{\cos(n+1)\theta \sin n\theta}{\sin\theta}\right]$", $n \in \mathbb{Z}^+$

Proof: (By the principle of mathematical induction)

(1) If $n = 1$, LHS $= \cos^2\theta$, RHS $= \frac{1}{2}\left[1 + \dfrac{\cos 2\theta \sin\theta}{\sin\theta}\right]$

$\qquad\qquad\qquad\qquad\qquad\qquad = \frac{1}{2} + \frac{1}{2}(2\cos^2\theta - 1)$
$\qquad\qquad\qquad\qquad\qquad\qquad = \cos^2\theta \qquad \therefore \quad P_1$ is true.

(2) If P_k is true then

$$\cos^2\theta + \cos^2 2\theta + \cos^2 3\theta + \ldots + \cos^2(k\theta) = \frac{1}{2}\left[k + \dfrac{\cos(k+1)\theta \sin k\theta}{\sin\theta}\right]$$

$\therefore \quad \cos^2\theta + \cos^2 2\theta + \cos^2 3\theta + \ldots + \cos^2(k\theta) + \cos^2(k+1)\theta$

$= \frac{1}{2}\left[k + \dfrac{\cos(k+1)\theta \sin k\theta}{\sin\theta}\right] + \cos^2(k+1)\theta$

$= \frac{1}{2}\left[k + \dfrac{\cos(k+1)\theta \sin k\theta}{\sin\theta}\right] + \frac{1}{2} + \frac{1}{2}\cos 2(k+1)\theta \qquad \{\cos^2\theta = \frac{1}{2} + \frac{1}{2}\cos 2\theta\}$

$= \frac{1}{2}(k+1) + \dfrac{\cos(k+1)\theta \sin k\theta + \cos 2(k+1)\theta \sin\theta}{2\sin\theta}$

$= \frac{1}{2}(k+1) + $

$\qquad \dfrac{\frac{1}{2}\sin[k\theta + (k+1)\theta] + \frac{1}{2}\sin[k\theta - (k+1)\theta] + \frac{1}{2}\sin[\theta + 2(k+1)\theta] + \frac{1}{2}\sin[\theta - 2(k+1)\theta]}{2\sin\theta}$

$\qquad\qquad\qquad\qquad\qquad\qquad\qquad\qquad\qquad\qquad\qquad\qquad$ {products to sums formula}

$= \frac{1}{2}(k+1) + \dfrac{\frac{1}{2}\sin(2k+1)\theta + \frac{1}{2}\sin(-\theta) + \frac{1}{2}\sin(2k+3)\theta + \frac{1}{2}\sin(-2k-1)\theta}{2\sin\theta}$

$= \frac{1}{2}(k+1) + \dfrac{\frac{1}{2}\sin(2k+1)\theta - \frac{1}{2}\sin\theta + \frac{1}{2}\sin(2k+3)\theta - \frac{1}{2}\sin(2k+1)\theta}{2\sin\theta}$

$= \frac{1}{2}(k+1) + \dfrac{\frac{1}{2}\sin(2k+3)\theta - \frac{1}{2}\sin\theta}{2\sin\theta}$

$= \frac{1}{2}(k+1) + \dfrac{\cos\left[\frac{(2k+3)\theta + \theta}{2}\right]\sin\left[\frac{(2k+3)\theta - \theta}{2}\right]}{2\sin\theta} \qquad$ {factor formula}

$= \frac{1}{2}(k+1) + \dfrac{\cos(k+2)\theta \sin(k+1)\theta}{2\sin\theta}$

$= \frac{1}{2}\left[(k+1) + \dfrac{\cos(k+2)\theta \sin(k+1)\theta}{\sin\theta}\right]$

Thus P_{k+1} is true whenever P_k is true and P_1 is true.
$\therefore \quad P_n$ is true for all $n \in \mathbb{Z}^+$ {Principle of mathematical induction}

REVIEW SET 12A

1 This is the graph of $y = \sin x$ under a vertical stretch of factor 4.
The amplitude is 4.

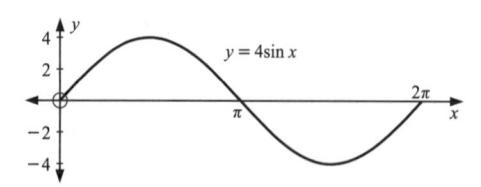

2 This is the graph of $y = \sin x$ under a horizontal compression of factor 3.
The period is $\frac{2\pi}{3}$.

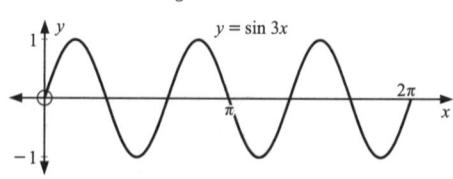

3 a period $= \dfrac{2\pi}{\frac{1}{3}} = 6\pi$

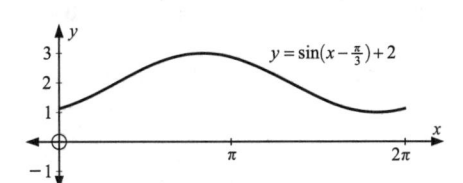

  b period $= \dfrac{\pi}{4}$

4 $y = \sin(x - \frac{\pi}{3}) + 2$

5

Month	1	2	3	4	5	6	7	8	9	10	11	12
Temp	31.5	31.8	29.5	25.4	21.5	18.8	17.7	18.3	20.1	22.4	25.5	28.8

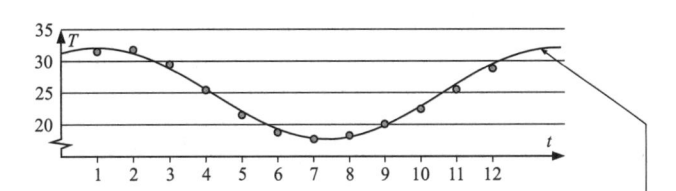

$T = A \sin B(t - C) + D$ period $= \dfrac{2\pi}{B} = 12$, $\therefore B = \dfrac{2\pi}{12} = \dfrac{\pi}{6}$

max. $= 31.8$
min. $= 17.7$ $\therefore A = \dfrac{\text{max.} - \text{min.}}{2} \approx \dfrac{31.8 - 17.7}{2} \approx 7.05$

$D = \dfrac{\text{max.} + \text{min.}}{2} \approx \dfrac{31.8 + 17.7}{2} \approx 24.75$

$C = \dfrac{7 + 14}{2} = 10.5$ {values of t at min. and max.}

So, $T \approx 7.05 \sin \frac{\pi}{6}(t - 10.5) + 24.75$

From technology, $T \approx 7.21 \sin(0.488t + 1.082) + 24.75$
  $\approx 7.21 \sin 0.488(t + 2.22) + 24.75$ Note: $2.22 - -10.5 \approx 12.7 \approx 12$

6 a $\sin x = 0.382$
  $\therefore x \approx 0.392, 2.75, 6.68$

  b $\tan\left(\frac{x}{2}\right) = -0.458$
  $\therefore x \approx 5.42$

7 a $\sin(x - 2.4) = 0.754$
  $\therefore x \approx 3.25, 4.69$

  b $\sin\left(x + \frac{\pi}{3}\right) = 0.6049$
  $\therefore x \approx 1.44, 5.89, 7.73$

8 a $2 \sin x = -1$, $x \in [0, 4\pi]$
  $\therefore \sin x = -\frac{1}{2}$

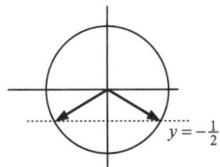

  $\therefore x = \left.\begin{array}{c}\frac{7\pi}{6}\\\frac{11\pi}{6}\end{array}\right\} + k2\pi$

  $\therefore x = \dfrac{7\pi}{6}, \dfrac{11\pi}{6}, \dfrac{19\pi}{6}, \dfrac{23\pi}{6}$

  b $\sqrt{2} \sin x - 1 = 0$, $x \in [-2\pi, 2\pi]$
  $\therefore \sin x = \dfrac{1}{\sqrt{2}}$

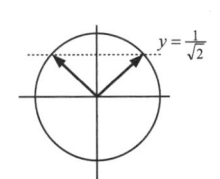

  $\therefore x = \left.\begin{array}{c}\frac{\pi}{4}\\\frac{3\pi}{4}\end{array}\right\} + k2\pi$

  $\therefore x = -\dfrac{7\pi}{4}, -\dfrac{5\pi}{4}, \dfrac{\pi}{4}, \dfrac{3\pi}{4}$

9 a $2\sin 3x + \sqrt{3} = 0$, $x \in [0, 2\pi]$

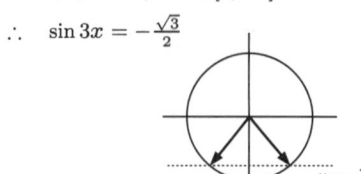

$\therefore \sin 3x = -\frac{\sqrt{3}}{2}$

$\therefore 3x = \left.\begin{array}{c}\frac{4\pi}{3}\\\frac{5\pi}{3}\end{array}\right\} + k2\pi$

$\therefore x = \left.\begin{array}{c}\frac{4\pi}{9}\\\frac{5\pi}{9}\end{array}\right\} + k\frac{2\pi}{3}$

$\therefore x = \frac{4\pi}{9}, \frac{5\pi}{9}, \frac{10\pi}{9}, \frac{11\pi}{9}, \frac{16\pi}{9}, \frac{17\pi}{9}$

b $\sec^2 x = \tan x + 1$, $x \in [0, 2\pi]$

$\therefore \tan^2 x + 1 = \tan x + 1$

$\therefore \tan x(\tan x - 1) = 0$

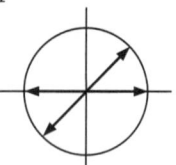

$\therefore \tan x = 0$ or 1

$\therefore x = 0, \frac{\pi}{4}, \pi, \frac{5\pi}{4}, 2\pi$

10 $P(t) = 5 + 2\sin\left(\frac{\pi t}{3}\right)$, $0 \leqslant t \leqslant 8$, where $P(t)$ is in thousands of water beetles.

a $P(0) = 5 + 2\sin 0$
$\quad = 5$

So, 5000 water beetles.

b Smallest $P = 5 + 2(-1) = 3$
Largest $P = 5 + 2(1) = 7$

$\therefore$ smallest is 3000 water beetles
largest is 7000 water beetles

c If population is > 6000,
then $P(t) > 6$

$\therefore 5 + 2\sin\left(\frac{\pi t}{3}\right) > 6$

$\therefore 2\sin\left(\frac{\pi t}{3}\right) > 1$

$\therefore \sin\left(\frac{\pi t}{3}\right) > \frac{1}{2}$

Using technology,
$0.5 < t < 2.5$ and $6.5 < t \leqslant 8$

REVIEW SET 12B

1 a $\sin^2 x - \sin x - 2 = 0$

$\therefore (\sin x - 2)(\sin x + 1) = 0$

$\therefore \sin x = 2$ or -1

But $\sin x$ values lie between -1 and 1 inclusive

$\therefore \sin x = -1$

$\therefore x = \frac{3\pi}{2} + k2\pi$

b $4\sin^2 x = 1$

$\therefore \sin^2 x = \frac{1}{4}$

$\therefore \sin x = \pm\frac{1}{2}$

$\therefore x = \left.\begin{array}{c}\frac{\pi}{6}\\\frac{5\pi}{6}\end{array}\right\} + k\pi$

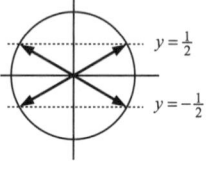

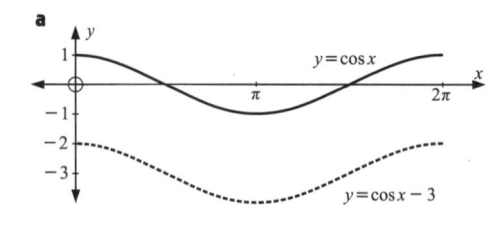

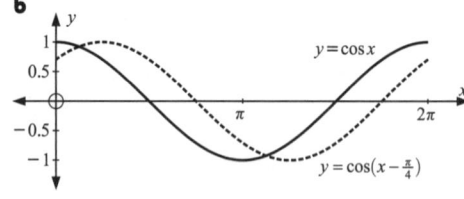

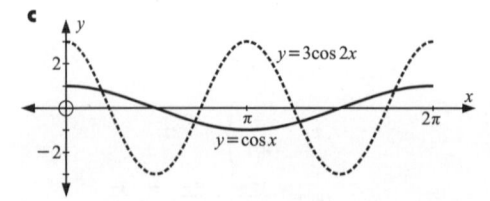

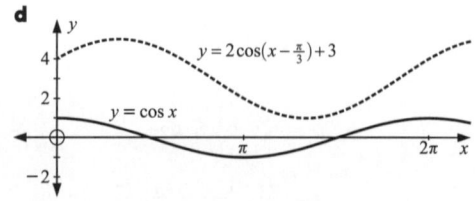

2 a $y = \cos x$, $y = \cos x - 3$

b $y = \cos x$, $y = \cos\left(x - \frac{\pi}{4}\right)$

c $y = 3\cos 2x$, $y = \cos x$

d $y = 2\cos\left(x - \frac{\pi}{3}\right) + 3$, $y = \cos x$

3 $P(t) = 40 + 12\sin\frac{2\pi}{7}\left(t - \frac{37}{12}\right)$ mg

   a $P(t)$ has a minimum of $40 + 12(-1)$
$= 28$ mg per m^3

   b when $\sin\frac{2\pi}{7}(t - \frac{37}{12}) = -1$

$\therefore \frac{2\pi}{7}(t - \frac{37}{12}) = \frac{3\pi}{2} + k2\pi$

$\therefore \frac{2}{7}(t - \frac{37}{12}) = \frac{3}{2} + k2$

So, $t - \frac{37}{12} = \frac{21}{4} + k7$

$\therefore t = 8\frac{1}{3} + k7$

$\therefore t = 1\frac{1}{3}, 8\frac{1}{3}, 15\frac{1}{3}$, and so on.

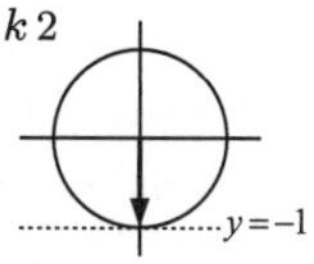

$\therefore$ on Mondays at 8.00 am
$\{1\frac{1}{3}$ days after midnight Saturday$\}$

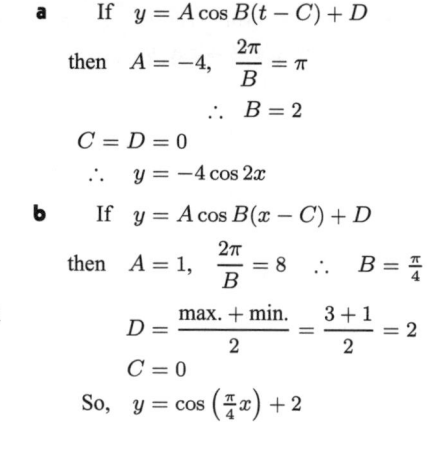

4 **a** If $y = A\cos B(t - C) + D$

then $A = -4$, $\frac{2\pi}{B} = \pi$

$\therefore B = 2$

$C = D = 0$

$\therefore y = -4\cos 2x$

  b If $y = A\cos B(x - C) + D$

then $A = 1$, $\frac{2\pi}{B} = 8$ $\therefore B = \frac{\pi}{4}$

$D = \frac{\text{max.} + \text{min.}}{2} = \frac{3+1}{2} = 2$

$C = 0$

So, $y = \cos\left(\frac{\pi}{4}x\right) + 2$

5 **a** $\cos x = 0.4379$, $0 \leqslant x \leqslant 10$

$\therefore x \approx 1.12, 5.17, 7.40$

  b $\cos(x - 2.4) = -0.6014$, $0 \leqslant x \leqslant 6$

$\therefore x \approx 0.184, 4.62$

6 **a** $\cos(165°)$
$= \cos(120° + 45°)$
$= \cos 120° \cos 45° - \sin 120° \sin 45°$
$= \left(-\frac{1}{2}\right)\left(\frac{1}{\sqrt{2}}\right) - \left(\frac{\sqrt{3}}{2}\right)\left(\frac{1}{\sqrt{2}}\right)$
$= \frac{-1 - \sqrt{3}}{2\sqrt{2}}$
$= \frac{-\sqrt{2} - \sqrt{6}}{4}$

  b $\tan(\frac{\pi}{12})$
$= \tan(\frac{3\pi}{12} - \frac{2\pi}{12})$
$= \frac{\tan(\frac{\pi}{4}) - \tan(\frac{\pi}{6})}{1 + \tan(\frac{\pi}{4})\tan(\frac{\pi}{6})}$
$= \frac{1 - \frac{1}{\sqrt{3}}}{1 + (1)(\frac{1}{\sqrt{3}})} \times \left(\frac{\sqrt{3}}{\sqrt{3}}\right)$
$= \frac{\sqrt{3} - 1}{\sqrt{3} + 1} \times \left(\frac{\sqrt{3} - 1}{\sqrt{3} - 1}\right)$
$= \frac{3 - 2\sqrt{3} + 1}{3 - 1}$
$= \frac{4 - 2\sqrt{3}}{2}$
$= 2 - \sqrt{3}$

7 **a** $\tan(x - \frac{\pi}{3}) = \frac{1}{\sqrt{3}}$, $x \in [0, 4\pi]$

$\therefore x - \frac{\pi}{3} = \frac{\pi}{6} + k\pi$

$\therefore x = \frac{\pi}{2} + k\pi$

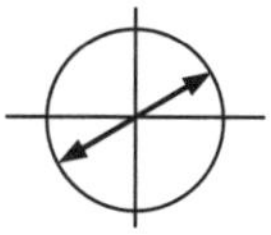

$\therefore x = \frac{\pi}{2}, \frac{3\pi}{2}, \frac{5\pi}{2}, \frac{7\pi}{2}$

  b $\cos(x + \frac{2\pi}{3}) = \frac{1}{2}$, $x \in [-2\pi, 2\pi]$

$x + \frac{2\pi}{3} = \left.\begin{array}{c}\frac{\pi}{3}\\\frac{5\pi}{3}\end{array}\right\} + k2\pi$

$\therefore x = \left.\begin{array}{c}-\frac{\pi}{3}\\\pi\end{array}\right\} + k2\pi$

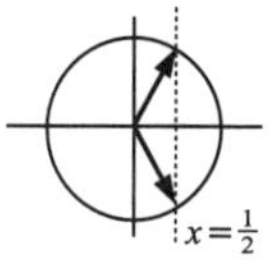

$\therefore x = -\pi, -\frac{\pi}{3}, \pi, \frac{5\pi}{3}$

8 **a** $\sqrt{2}\cos(x + \frac{\pi}{4}) - 1 = 0$, $x \in [0, 4\pi]$

$\therefore \cos(x + \frac{\pi}{4}) = \frac{1}{\sqrt{2}}$

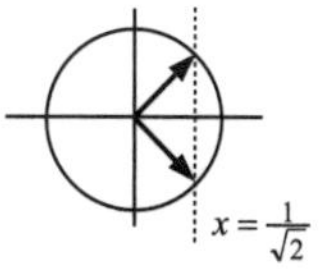

$\therefore x + \frac{\pi}{4} = \left.\begin{array}{c}\frac{\pi}{4}\\\frac{7\pi}{4}\end{array}\right\} + k2\pi$

$\therefore x = \left.\begin{array}{c}0\\\frac{3\pi}{2}\end{array}\right\} + k2\pi$

$\therefore x = 0, \frac{3\pi}{2}, 2\pi, \frac{7\pi}{2}, 4\pi$

  b $\tan 2x - \sqrt{3} = 0$, $x \in [0, 2\pi]$

$\therefore \tan 2x = \sqrt{3}$

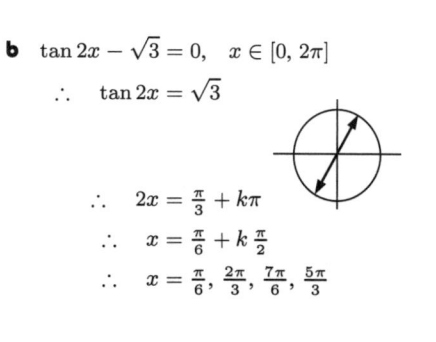

$\therefore 2x = \frac{\pi}{3} + k\pi$

$\therefore x = \frac{\pi}{6} + k\frac{\pi}{2}$

$\therefore x = \frac{\pi}{6}, \frac{2\pi}{3}, \frac{7\pi}{6}, \frac{5\pi}{3}$

9 **a** $\cos^3\theta + \sin^2\theta\cos\theta$
$= \cos\theta(\cos^2\theta + \sin^2\theta)$
$= \cos\theta(1)$
$= \cos\theta$

b $\dfrac{\cos^2\theta - 1}{\sin\theta}$
$= \dfrac{-(1 - \cos^2\theta)}{\sin\theta}$
$= -\dfrac{\sin^2\theta}{\sin\theta}$
$= -\sin\theta$

c $5 - 5\sin^2\theta$
$= 5(1 - \sin^2\theta)$
$= 5\cos^2\theta$

d $\dfrac{\sin^2\theta - 1}{\cos\theta}$
$= -\dfrac{(1 - \sin^2\theta)}{\cos\theta}$
$= -\dfrac{\cos^2\theta}{\cos\theta}$
$= -\cos\theta$

e $\cos^2\theta(\tan\theta + 1)^2 - 1$
$= \cos^2\theta(\tan^2\theta + 2\tan\theta + 1) - 1$
$= \cos^2\theta(\sec^2\theta + 2\tan\theta) - 1$
$= 1 + 2\cos^2\theta\left(\dfrac{\sin\theta}{\cos\theta}\right) - 1$
$= 2\sin\theta\cos\theta$
$= \sin 2\theta$

10 **a** $(2\sin\alpha - 1)^2$
$= 4\sin^2\alpha - 4\sin\alpha + 1$

b $(\cos\alpha - \sin\alpha)^2$
$= \cos^2\alpha - 2\sin\alpha\cos\alpha + \sin^2\alpha$
$= \cos^2\alpha + \sin^2\alpha - 2\sin\alpha\cos\alpha$
$= 1 - \sin 2\alpha$

REVIEW SET 12C

1 **a** $\dfrac{1 - \cos^2\theta}{1 + \cos\theta}$
$= \dfrac{(1 + \cos\theta)(1 - \cos\theta)}{1 + \cos\theta}$
$= 1 - \cos\theta$

b $\dfrac{\sin\alpha - \cos\alpha}{\sin^2\alpha - \cos^2\alpha}$
$= \dfrac{\sin\alpha - \cos\alpha}{(\sin\alpha + \cos\alpha)(\sin\alpha - \cos\alpha)}$
$= \dfrac{1}{\sin\alpha + \cos\alpha}$

c $\dfrac{4\sin^2\alpha - 4}{8\cos\alpha}$
$= \dfrac{-4(1 - \sin^2\alpha)}{8\cos\alpha}$
$= \dfrac{-4\cos^2\alpha}{8\cos\alpha}$
$= -\tfrac{1}{2}\cos\alpha$

2 **a** $\dfrac{\cos\theta}{1 + \sin\theta} + \dfrac{1 + \sin\theta}{\cos\theta}$
$= \dfrac{\cos^2\theta + (1 + \sin\theta)^2}{(1 + \sin\theta)\cos\theta}$
$= \dfrac{\cos^2\theta + 1 + 2\sin\theta + \sin^2\theta}{(1 + \sin\theta)\cos\theta}$
$= \dfrac{2 + 2\sin\theta}{(1 + \sin\theta)\cos\theta}$ $\{\cos^2\theta + \sin^2\theta = 1\}$
$= \dfrac{2(1 + \sin\theta)}{(1 + \sin\theta)\cos\theta}$
$= \dfrac{2}{\cos\theta} = 2\sec\theta$

b $\left(1 + \dfrac{1}{\cos\theta}\right)(\cos\theta - \cos^2\theta)$
$= \cos\theta - \cos^2\theta + 1 - \cos\theta$
$= 1 - \cos^2\theta$
$= \sin^2\theta$

3 **a** $\sin 2A = 2\sin A\cos A$
$= 2(\tfrac{5}{13})(\tfrac{12}{13})$
$= \tfrac{120}{169}$

b $\cos 2A = \cos^2 A - \sin^2 A$
$= (\tfrac{12}{13})^2 - (\tfrac{5}{13})^2$
$= \tfrac{144 - 25}{169}$
$= \tfrac{119}{169}$

4
$$\cos^2\alpha + \sin^2\alpha = 1$$
$$\therefore \cos^2\alpha + \tfrac{9}{16} = 1$$
$$\therefore \cos^2\alpha = \tfrac{7}{16}$$
$$\therefore \cos\alpha = \pm\tfrac{\sqrt{7}}{4}$$
But in Q3, $\cos\alpha < 0$
$$\therefore \cos\alpha = -\tfrac{\sqrt{7}}{4}$$

$$\sin 2\alpha = 2\sin\alpha\cos\alpha$$
$$= 2(-\tfrac{3}{4})(-\tfrac{\sqrt{7}}{4})$$
$$= \tfrac{3\sqrt{7}}{8}$$

5
$$\cos 2A = 1 - 2\sin^2 A$$
$$\therefore \cos x = 1 - 2\sin^2\left(\tfrac{x}{2}\right) \quad \{\text{letting } 2A = x,\ A = \tfrac{x}{2}\}$$
$$\therefore -\tfrac{3}{4} = 1 - 2\sin^2\left(\tfrac{x}{2}\right)$$
$$\therefore 2\sin^2\left(\tfrac{x}{2}\right) = \tfrac{7}{4}$$
$$\therefore \sin^2\left(\tfrac{x}{2}\right) = \tfrac{7}{8}$$
$$\therefore \sin\left(\tfrac{x}{2}\right) = \pm\tfrac{\sqrt{7}}{2\sqrt{2}}$$
But $\tfrac{\pi}{2} < \tfrac{x}{2} < \tfrac{3\pi}{4}$ (in Q2) $\quad \therefore \sin\left(\tfrac{x}{2}\right) = \tfrac{\sqrt{7}}{2\sqrt{2}}$

6 a **i** $\tan x = 4$
$\therefore x \approx 1.326 + k\pi$
$\therefore x \approx 1.33 + k\pi$

ii $\tan\left(\tfrac{x}{4}\right) = 4$
$\therefore \tfrac{x}{4} \approx 1.326 + k\pi$
$\therefore x \approx 5.30 + k4\pi$

iii $\tan(x - 1.5) = 4$
$\therefore x - 1.5 \approx 1.326 + k\pi$
$\therefore x \approx 2.83 + k\pi$

b **i** $\tan(x + \tfrac{\pi}{6}) = -\sqrt{3}$
$\therefore x + \tfrac{\pi}{6} = \tfrac{2\pi}{3} + k\pi$
$\therefore x = \tfrac{\pi}{2} + k\pi$

ii $\tan 2x = -\sqrt{3}$
$\therefore 2x = \tfrac{2\pi}{3} + k\pi$
$\therefore x = \tfrac{\pi}{3} + \tfrac{k\pi}{2}$

iii $\tan^2 x - 3 = 0$
$\therefore \tan x = \pm\sqrt{3}$
$\therefore x = \left.\begin{array}{c}\tfrac{\pi}{3}\\ \tfrac{2\pi}{3}\end{array}\right\} + k\pi$

c $3\tan(x - 1.2) = -2$
$\therefore \tan(x - 1.2) = -\tfrac{2}{3}$
$\therefore x - 1.2 \approx -0.588 + k\pi$
$\therefore x \approx 0.612 + k\pi$

7 $\tan\theta = -\tfrac{2}{3},\ \tfrac{\pi}{2} < \theta < \pi$
$\therefore \tfrac{\sin\theta}{\cos\theta} = -\tfrac{2}{3}$
$\therefore \sin\theta = -2k,\ \cos\theta = 3k$
but $\cos^2\theta + \sin^2\theta = 1$
$\therefore 9k^2 + 4k^2 = 1$
$\therefore 13k^2 = 1$
$\therefore k = \pm\tfrac{1}{\sqrt{13}}$

But in Q2,
$\sin\theta > 0,\ \cos\theta < 0$
$\therefore k = -\tfrac{1}{\sqrt{13}}$
$\therefore \sin\theta = \tfrac{2}{\sqrt{13}},\ \cos\theta = -\tfrac{3}{\sqrt{13}}$

8
$$\frac{\sin 2\alpha - \sin\alpha}{\cos 2\alpha - \cos\alpha + 1} = \frac{2\sin\alpha\cos\alpha - \sin\alpha}{2\cos^2\alpha - 1 - \cos\alpha + 1}$$
$$= \frac{\sin\alpha(2\cos\alpha - 1)}{\cos\alpha(2\cos\alpha - 1)} = \frac{\sin\alpha}{\cos\alpha} = \tan\alpha$$

9 a $\cos\left(\tfrac{3\pi}{2} - \theta\right)$
$= \cos\left(\tfrac{3\pi}{2}\right)\cos\theta + \sin\left(\tfrac{3\pi}{2}\right)\sin\theta$
$= (0)\cos\theta + (-1)\sin\theta$
$= -\sin\theta$

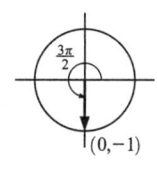

b $\sin\left(\theta + \frac{\pi}{2}\right)$
$= \sin\theta \cos\left(\frac{\pi}{2}\right) + \cos\theta \sin\left(\frac{\pi}{2}\right)$
$= \sin\theta(0) + \cos\theta(1)$
$= \cos\theta$

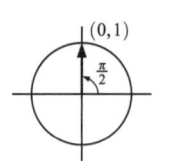

10 Let $BC = x$ m
$\therefore \tan\theta = \frac{x}{3}$, $\tan 2\theta = \frac{4}{3}$
$\therefore \frac{2\tan\theta}{1 - \tan^2\theta} = \frac{4}{3}$
$\therefore 6\tan\theta = 4 - 4\tan^2\theta$
$\therefore 2(2\tan^2\theta + 3\tan\theta - 2) = 0$
$\therefore 2(2\tan\theta - 1)(\tan\theta + 2) = 0$

$\therefore \tan\theta = \frac{1}{2}$ or -2
But θ is clearly acute,
so $\tan\theta > 0$
$\therefore \tan\theta = \frac{1}{2}$
$\therefore \frac{x}{3} = \frac{1}{2}$
$\therefore x = 1.5$
$\therefore BC = 1.5$ m

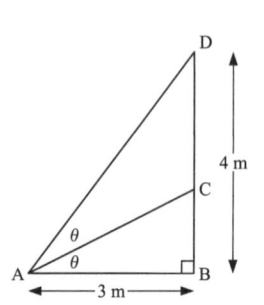

REVIEW SET 12D

1 a $\sqrt{2}\cos\left(\theta + \frac{\pi}{4}\right)$
$= \sqrt{2}\left[\cos\theta \cos\left(\frac{\pi}{4}\right) - \sin\theta \sin\left(\frac{\pi}{4}\right)\right]$
$= \sqrt{2}\left[\cos\theta \times \frac{1}{\sqrt{2}} - \sin\theta \times \frac{1}{\sqrt{2}}\right]$
$= \cos\theta - \sin\theta$

b $\cos\alpha \cos(\beta - \alpha) - \sin\alpha \sin(\beta - \alpha)$
$= \cos[\alpha + (\beta - \alpha)]$
$= \cos[\alpha + \beta - \alpha]$
$= \cos\beta$

2 a $\sin x = \frac{3}{4}$ 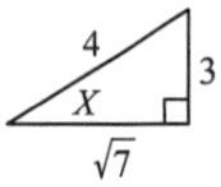 
$\therefore \cos x = -\frac{\sqrt{7}}{4}$

b $\sin 2x$
$= 2\sin x \cos x$
$= 2\left(\frac{3}{4}\right)\left(-\frac{\sqrt{7}}{4}\right)$
$= \frac{-3\sqrt{7}}{8}$

c $\cos 2x$
$= 1 - 2\sin^2 x$
$= 1 - 2\left(\frac{9}{16}\right)$
$= 1 - \frac{9}{8}$
$= -\frac{1}{8}$

d $\tan 2x$
$= \frac{\sin 2x}{\cos 2x}$
$= -\frac{3\sqrt{7}}{8} \div -\frac{1}{8}$
$= 3\sqrt{7}$

3 $\cos 2\theta = 1 - 2\sin^2\theta$
$\therefore \cos\left(\frac{\pi}{4}\right) = 1 - 2\sin^2\left(\frac{\pi}{8}\right)$ {letting $\theta = \frac{\pi}{8}$}
$\therefore \frac{1}{\sqrt{2}} = 1 - 2\sin^2\left(\frac{\pi}{8}\right)$
$\therefore 2\sin^2\left(\frac{\pi}{8}\right) = 1 - \frac{1}{\sqrt{2}} = \frac{\sqrt{2}-1}{\sqrt{2}}$
$\therefore \sin^2\left(\frac{\pi}{8}\right) = \frac{\sqrt{2}-1}{2\sqrt{2}} \times \frac{\sqrt{2}}{\sqrt{2}}$
$\therefore \sin^2\left(\frac{\pi}{8}\right) = \frac{2-\sqrt{2}}{4}$
$\therefore \sin\left(\frac{\pi}{8}\right) = \pm\frac{\sqrt{2-\sqrt{2}}}{2}$
But $\sin\left(\frac{\pi}{8}\right)$ is positive as $\frac{\pi}{8}$ is in quadrant 1.
$\therefore \sin\left(\frac{\pi}{8}\right) = \frac{1}{2}\sqrt{2-\sqrt{2}}$

4 $\alpha + \beta = \frac{\pi}{2}$ {angles of a $\triangle$}
$\therefore \beta = \frac{\pi}{2} - \alpha$

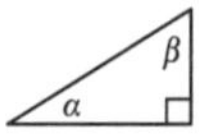

So, $\sin 2\beta = \sin(\pi - 2\alpha)$
$= \sin\pi \cos 2\alpha - \cos\pi \sin 2\alpha$
$= (0)\cos 2\alpha - (-1)\sin 2\alpha$
$= \sin 2\alpha$

5 a $(\sin\theta + \cos\theta)^2$
$= \sin^2\theta + 2\sin\theta\cos\theta + \cos^2\theta$
$= [\sin^2\theta + \cos^2\theta] + 2\sin\theta\cos\theta$
$= 1 + \sin 2\theta$

b $\csc(2x) + \cot(2x)$
$= \frac{1}{\sin 2x} + \frac{\cos 2x}{\sin 2x}$
$= \frac{1 + \cos 2x}{\sin 2x}$
$= \frac{\cancel{X} + 2\cos^2 x - \cancel{X}}{2\sin x \cos x}$
$= \frac{\cancel{2}\cos x \cancel{\cos x}}{\cancel{2}\sin x \cancel{\cos x}}$
$= \cot x$

6 a $2\cos(2x) + 1 = 0$

$\therefore \quad \cos(2x) = -\tfrac{1}{2}$

$\therefore \quad 2x = \left.\begin{array}{c}\tfrac{2\pi}{3}\\ \tfrac{4\pi}{3}\end{array}\right\} + k2\pi$

$\therefore \quad x = \left.\begin{array}{c}\tfrac{\pi}{3}\\ \tfrac{2\pi}{3}\end{array}\right\} + k\pi$

$\therefore \quad x = \tfrac{\pi}{3}, \tfrac{2\pi}{3}, \tfrac{4\pi}{3}, \tfrac{5\pi}{3}$

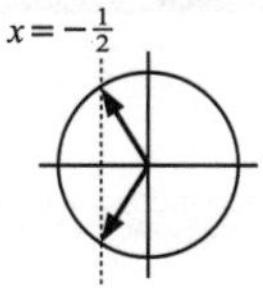

b $\sin 2x = -\sqrt{3}\cos 2x$

$\therefore \quad \dfrac{\sin 2x}{\cos 2x} = -\sqrt{3}$

$\therefore \quad \tan 2x = -\sqrt{3}$

$\therefore \quad 2x = \tfrac{2\pi}{3} + k\pi$

$\therefore \quad x = \tfrac{\pi}{3} + k\tfrac{\pi}{2}$

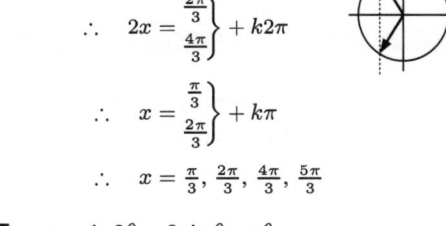

$\therefore \quad x = \tfrac{\pi}{3}, \tfrac{5\pi}{6}, \tfrac{4\pi}{3}, \tfrac{11\pi}{6}$

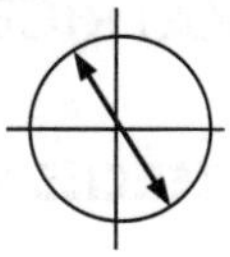

7 a $\sin 2\theta = 2\sin\theta\cos\theta$

$= 2\left(\dfrac{b}{c}\right)\left(\dfrac{a}{c}\right)$

$= \dfrac{2ab}{c^2}$

b $\cos 2\theta = \cos^2\theta - \sin^2\theta$

$= \left(\dfrac{a}{c}\right)^2 - \left(\dfrac{b}{c}\right)^2$

$= \dfrac{a^2 - b^2}{c^2}$

8 $\tan 2\alpha = \tfrac{4}{3}, \quad 0 < \alpha < \tfrac{\pi}{2}$

$\therefore \quad \dfrac{2\tan\alpha}{1 - \tan^2\alpha} = \tfrac{4}{3}$

$\therefore \quad 6\tan\alpha = 4 - 4\tan^2\alpha$

$\therefore \quad 4\tan^2\alpha + 6\tan\alpha - 4 = 0$

$\therefore \quad 2(2\tan^2\alpha + 3\tan\alpha - 2) = 0$

$\therefore \quad 2(2\tan\alpha - 1)(\tan\alpha + 2) = 0$

$\therefore \quad \tan\alpha = \tfrac{1}{2}$ or -2

But α is in quadrant 1.

$\therefore \quad \tan\alpha = \tfrac{1}{2}$

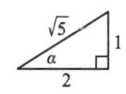

$\therefore \quad \sin\alpha = \tfrac{1}{\sqrt{5}}$

9 a By the sine rule, $\dfrac{\sin 2\alpha}{5} = \dfrac{\sin\alpha}{3}$

$\therefore \quad \dfrac{2\sin\alpha\cos\alpha}{\sin\alpha} = \tfrac{5}{3}$

$\therefore \quad 2\cos\alpha = \tfrac{5}{3} \quad \{\sin\alpha \neq 0\}$

$\therefore \quad \cos\alpha = \tfrac{5}{6}$

b Using the cosine rule

$3^2 = x^2 + 5^2 - 2 \times x \times 5 \times \cos\alpha$

$\therefore \quad 9 = x^2 + 25 - 10x\left(\tfrac{5}{6}\right)$

$\therefore \quad x^2 - \tfrac{25}{3}x + 16 = 0$

$\therefore \quad 3x^2 - 25x + 48 = 0$

c $(3x - 16)(x - 3) = 0$

$\therefore \quad x = \tfrac{16}{3}$ or 3

10 Let the shooter be x m from the wall.

$\therefore \quad \tan\alpha = \dfrac{20}{x}, \quad \tan 2\alpha = \dfrac{45}{x}$

$\therefore \quad \dfrac{2\tan\alpha}{1 - \tan^2\alpha} = \dfrac{45}{x}$

$\therefore \quad 2x\tan\alpha = 45 - 45\tan^2\alpha$

$\therefore \quad 2x\left(\dfrac{20}{x}\right) = 45 - 45\left(\dfrac{20}{x}\right)^2$

$\therefore \quad 40 = 45 - \dfrac{18\,000}{x^2}$

$\therefore \quad \dfrac{18\,000}{x^2} = 5$

$\therefore \quad x^2 = 3600$

$\therefore \quad x = 60$ So, the shooter is 60 m from the wall.

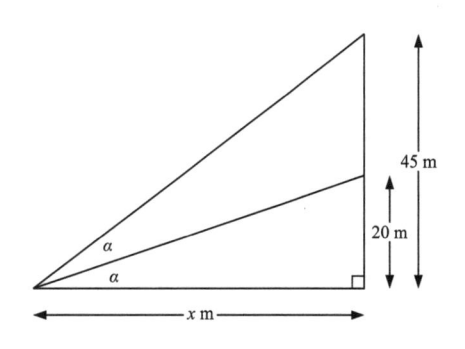

Chapter 13
MATRICES

EXERCISE 13A

1 **a** 1 row and 4 columns $\therefore$ 1×4 **b** 2 rows and 1 column $\therefore$ 2×1
   c 2 rows and 2 columns $\therefore$ 2×2 **d** 3 rows and 3 columns $\therefore$ 3×3

2 **a** $\begin{pmatrix} 2 & 1 & 6 & 1 \end{pmatrix}$ **b** $\begin{pmatrix} 1.95 \\ 2.35 \\ 0.15 \\ 0.95 \end{pmatrix}$ **c** $(2 \times 1.95) + (1 \times 2.35) + (6 \times 0.15) + (1 \times 0.95)$ represents the total cost of the groceries.

3
$$\begin{matrix} 200\text{ g} & 300\text{ g} & 500\text{ g} \\ \end{matrix}$$
$$\begin{pmatrix} 1000 & 1500 & 1250 \\ 1500 & 1000 & 1000 \\ 800 & 2300 & 1300 \\ 1200 & 1200 & 1200 \end{pmatrix} \begin{matrix} \text{week 1} \\ \text{week 2} \\ \text{week 3} \\ \text{week 4} \end{matrix}$$

4
$$\begin{matrix} \text{pies} & \text{pasties} & \text{rolls} & \text{buns} \end{matrix}$$
$$\begin{pmatrix} 40 & 50 & 55 & 40 \\ 25 & 65 & 44 & 30 \\ 35 & 40 & 40 & 35 \\ 35 & 40 & 35 & 50 \end{pmatrix} \begin{matrix} \text{Friday} \\ \text{Saturday} \\ \text{Sunday} \\ \text{Monday} \end{matrix} \text{ (in dozens)}$$

EXERCISE 13B.1

1 **a** $A + B = \begin{pmatrix} 3 & 4 \\ 5 & 2 \end{pmatrix} + \begin{pmatrix} 6 & -3 \\ -2 & 1 \end{pmatrix} = \begin{pmatrix} 9 & 1 \\ 3 & 3 \end{pmatrix}$

b $A + B + C = \begin{pmatrix} 9 & 1 \\ 3 & 3 \end{pmatrix} + \begin{pmatrix} -3 & 7 \\ -4 & -2 \end{pmatrix} = \begin{pmatrix} 6 & 8 \\ -1 & 1 \end{pmatrix}$

c $B + C = \begin{pmatrix} 6 & -3 \\ -2 & 1 \end{pmatrix} + \begin{pmatrix} -3 & 7 \\ -4 & -2 \end{pmatrix} = \begin{pmatrix} 3 & 4 \\ -6 & -1 \end{pmatrix}$

d $C + B - A = \begin{pmatrix} -3 & 7 \\ -4 & -2 \end{pmatrix} + \begin{pmatrix} 6 & -3 \\ -2 & 1 \end{pmatrix} - \begin{pmatrix} 3 & 4 \\ 5 & 2 \end{pmatrix} = \begin{pmatrix} 0 & 0 \\ -11 & -3 \end{pmatrix}$

2 **a** $P + Q = \begin{pmatrix} 3 & 5 & -11 \\ 10 & 2 & 6 \\ -2 & -1 & 7 \end{pmatrix} + \begin{pmatrix} 17 & -4 & 3 \\ -2 & 8 & -8 \\ 3 & -4 & 11 \end{pmatrix} = \begin{pmatrix} 20 & 1 & -8 \\ 8 & 10 & -2 \\ 1 & -5 & 18 \end{pmatrix}$

b $P - Q = \begin{pmatrix} 3 & 5 & -11 \\ 10 & 2 & 6 \\ -2 & -1 & 7 \end{pmatrix} - \begin{pmatrix} 17 & -4 & 3 \\ -2 & 8 & -8 \\ 3 & -4 & 11 \end{pmatrix} = \begin{pmatrix} -14 & 9 & -14 \\ 12 & -6 & 14 \\ -5 & 3 & -4 \end{pmatrix}$

c $Q - P = \begin{pmatrix} 17 & -4 & 3 \\ -2 & 8 & -8 \\ 3 & -4 & 11 \end{pmatrix} - \begin{pmatrix} 3 & 5 & -11 \\ 10 & 2 & 6 \\ -2 & -1 & 7 \end{pmatrix} = \begin{pmatrix} 14 & -9 & 14 \\ -12 & 6 & -14 \\ 5 & -3 & 4 \end{pmatrix}$

3 **a**
$$\begin{matrix} \text{Friday} & \text{Saturday} \end{matrix}$$
$$\begin{pmatrix} 85 \\ 92 \\ 52 \end{pmatrix} \begin{pmatrix} 102 \\ 137 \\ 49 \end{pmatrix}$$

b Total for Friday and Saturday $= \begin{pmatrix} 85 \\ 92 \\ 52 \end{pmatrix} + \begin{pmatrix} 102 \\ 137 \\ 49 \end{pmatrix} = \begin{pmatrix} 187 \\ 229 \\ 101 \end{pmatrix}$

4 **a** **i** Cost price   **ii** Selling price
$$\begin{pmatrix} 1.72 \\ 27.85 \\ 0.92 \\ 2.53 \\ 3.56 \end{pmatrix} \quad \begin{pmatrix} 1.79 \\ 28.75 \\ 1.33 \\ 2.25 \\ 3.51 \end{pmatrix}$$

b In order to find David's profit/loss matrix we subtract the cost price matrix from the selling price matrix.

c Profit/Loss matrix = $\begin{pmatrix} 1.79 \\ 28.75 \\ 1.33 \\ 2.25 \\ 3.51 \end{pmatrix} - \begin{pmatrix} 1.72 \\ 27.85 \\ 0.92 \\ 2.53 \\ 3.56 \end{pmatrix} = \begin{pmatrix} 0.07 \\ 0.90 \\ 0.41 \\ -0.28 \\ -0.05 \end{pmatrix}$

5 a Lou Rose $\begin{pmatrix} 23 & 19 \\ 17 & 29 \\ 31 & 24 \end{pmatrix}$ **b** Lou Rose $\begin{pmatrix} 18 & 25 \\ 7 & 13 \\ 36 & 19 \end{pmatrix}$ **c** Total sales for November and December
$= \begin{pmatrix} 23 & 19 \\ 17 & 29 \\ 31 & 24 \end{pmatrix} + \begin{pmatrix} 18 & 25 \\ 7 & 13 \\ 36 & 19 \end{pmatrix} = \begin{pmatrix} 41 & 44 \\ 24 & 42 \\ 67 & 43 \end{pmatrix}$

6 a $\begin{pmatrix} x & x^2 \\ 3 & -1 \end{pmatrix} = \begin{pmatrix} y & 4 \\ 3 & y+1 \end{pmatrix}$ 　　　　**b** $\begin{pmatrix} x & y \\ y & x \end{pmatrix} = \begin{pmatrix} -y & x \\ x & -y \end{pmatrix}$

Equating corresponding elements: 　　　　Equating corresponding elements:
$x = y,\ x^2 = 4$ and $-1 = y+1$ 　　　　$\left.\begin{array}{l} x = -y \\ y = x \end{array}\right\} \quad \therefore \quad y = 0,\ x = 0$
$\therefore \quad x = \pm 2$ and $y = -2$
But $x = y \quad \therefore \quad x = y = -2$

7 a $\mathbf{A} + \mathbf{B} = \begin{pmatrix} 2 & 1 \\ 3 & -1 \end{pmatrix} + \begin{pmatrix} -1 & 2 \\ 2 & 3 \end{pmatrix}$ 　　　　$\mathbf{B} + \mathbf{A} = \begin{pmatrix} -1 & 2 \\ 2 & 3 \end{pmatrix} + \begin{pmatrix} 2 & 1 \\ 3 & -1 \end{pmatrix}$

$= \begin{pmatrix} 2+(-1) & 1+2 \\ 3+2 & -1+3 \end{pmatrix}$ 　　　　$= \begin{pmatrix} -1+2 & 2+1 \\ 2+3 & 3+(-1) \end{pmatrix}$

$= \begin{pmatrix} 1 & 3 \\ 5 & 2 \end{pmatrix}$ 　　　　$= \begin{pmatrix} 1 & 3 \\ 5 & 2 \end{pmatrix}$

b $\mathbf{A} + \mathbf{B} = \mathbf{B} + \mathbf{A}$ for all 2×2 matrices $\mathbf{A}$ and $\mathbf{B}$ because addition of numbers is commutative.

8 a $(\mathbf{A} + \mathbf{B}) + \mathbf{C}$ 　　　　　　　　　　　　　　$\mathbf{A} + (\mathbf{B} + \mathbf{C})$

$= \left[\begin{pmatrix} -1 & 0 \\ 1 & 5 \end{pmatrix} + \begin{pmatrix} 3 & 4 \\ -1 & -2 \end{pmatrix}\right] + \begin{pmatrix} 4 & -1 \\ -1 & 3 \end{pmatrix}$ 　　$= \begin{pmatrix} -1 & 0 \\ 1 & 5 \end{pmatrix} + \left[\begin{pmatrix} 3 & 4 \\ -1 & -2 \end{pmatrix} + \begin{pmatrix} 4 & -1 \\ -1 & 3 \end{pmatrix}\right]$

$= \begin{pmatrix} 2 & 4 \\ 0 & 3 \end{pmatrix} + \begin{pmatrix} 4 & -1 \\ -1 & 3 \end{pmatrix}$ 　　　　$= \begin{pmatrix} -1 & 0 \\ 1 & 5 \end{pmatrix} + \begin{pmatrix} 7 & 3 \\ -2 & 1 \end{pmatrix}$

$= \begin{pmatrix} 6 & 3 \\ -1 & 6 \end{pmatrix}$ 　　　　　　　　　　$= \begin{pmatrix} 6 & 3 \\ -1 & 6 \end{pmatrix}$

b Let $\mathbf{A} = \begin{pmatrix} a & b \\ c & d \end{pmatrix}$, $\mathbf{B} = \begin{pmatrix} p & q \\ r & s \end{pmatrix}$ and $\mathbf{C} = \begin{pmatrix} w & x \\ y & z \end{pmatrix}$

$\therefore \quad (\mathbf{A} + \mathbf{B}) + \mathbf{C}$ 　　　　　　　　　　　$\mathbf{A} + (\mathbf{B} + \mathbf{C})$

$= \left[\begin{pmatrix} a & b \\ c & d \end{pmatrix} + \begin{pmatrix} p & q \\ r & s \end{pmatrix}\right] + \begin{pmatrix} w & x \\ y & z \end{pmatrix}$ 　　$= \begin{pmatrix} a & b \\ c & d \end{pmatrix} + \left[\begin{pmatrix} p & q \\ r & s \end{pmatrix} + \begin{pmatrix} w & x \\ y & z \end{pmatrix}\right]$

$= \begin{pmatrix} a+p & b+q \\ c+r & d+s \end{pmatrix} + \begin{pmatrix} w & x \\ y & z \end{pmatrix}$ 　　　$= \begin{pmatrix} a & b \\ c & d \end{pmatrix} + \begin{pmatrix} p+w & q+x \\ r+y & s+z \end{pmatrix}$

$= \begin{pmatrix} a+p+w & b+q+x \\ c+r+y & d+s+z \end{pmatrix}$ 　　　　　$= \begin{pmatrix} a+p+w & b+q+x \\ c+r+y & d+s+z \end{pmatrix}$

　　　　　　　　　　　　　　　　　　　　$= (\mathbf{A} + \mathbf{B}) + \mathbf{C}$

EXERCISE 13B.2

1 a $2B = 2\begin{pmatrix} 6 & 12 \\ 24 & 6 \end{pmatrix} = \begin{pmatrix} 12 & 24 \\ 48 & 12 \end{pmatrix}$ **b** $\frac{1}{3}B = \frac{1}{3}\begin{pmatrix} 6 & 12 \\ 24 & 6 \end{pmatrix} = \begin{pmatrix} 2 & 4 \\ 8 & 2 \end{pmatrix}$

c $\frac{1}{12}B = \frac{1}{12}\begin{pmatrix} 6 & 12 \\ 24 & 6 \end{pmatrix} = \begin{pmatrix} \frac{1}{2} & 1 \\ 2 & \frac{1}{2} \end{pmatrix}$ **d** $-\frac{1}{2}B = -\frac{1}{2}\begin{pmatrix} 6 & 12 \\ 24 & 6 \end{pmatrix} = \begin{pmatrix} -3 & -6 \\ -12 & -3 \end{pmatrix}$

2 a $A + B$

$= \begin{pmatrix} 2 & 3 & 5 \\ 1 & 6 & 4 \end{pmatrix} + \begin{pmatrix} 1 & 2 & 1 \\ 1 & 2 & 3 \end{pmatrix}$

$= \begin{pmatrix} 2+1 & 3+2 & 5+1 \\ 1+1 & 6+2 & 4+3 \end{pmatrix}$

$= \begin{pmatrix} 3 & 5 & 6 \\ 2 & 8 & 7 \end{pmatrix}$

b $A - B$

$= \begin{pmatrix} 2 & 3 & 5 \\ 1 & 6 & 4 \end{pmatrix} - \begin{pmatrix} 1 & 2 & 1 \\ 1 & 2 & 3 \end{pmatrix}$

$= \begin{pmatrix} 2-1 & 3-2 & 5-1 \\ 1-1 & 6-2 & 4-3 \end{pmatrix}$

$= \begin{pmatrix} 1 & 1 & 4 \\ 0 & 4 & 1 \end{pmatrix}$

c $2A + B$

$= 2\begin{pmatrix} 2 & 3 & 5 \\ 1 & 6 & 4 \end{pmatrix} + \begin{pmatrix} 1 & 2 & 1 \\ 1 & 2 & 3 \end{pmatrix}$

$= \begin{pmatrix} 4 & 6 & 10 \\ 2 & 12 & 8 \end{pmatrix} + \begin{pmatrix} 1 & 2 & 1 \\ 1 & 2 & 3 \end{pmatrix}$

$= \begin{pmatrix} 4+1 & 6+2 & 10+1 \\ 2+1 & 12+2 & 8+3 \end{pmatrix}$

$= \begin{pmatrix} 5 & 8 & 11 \\ 3 & 14 & 11 \end{pmatrix}$

d $3A - B$

$= 3\begin{pmatrix} 2 & 3 & 5 \\ 1 & 6 & 4 \end{pmatrix} - \begin{pmatrix} 1 & 2 & 1 \\ 1 & 2 & 3 \end{pmatrix}$

$= \begin{pmatrix} 6 & 9 & 15 \\ 3 & 18 & 12 \end{pmatrix} - \begin{pmatrix} 1 & 2 & 1 \\ 1 & 2 & 3 \end{pmatrix}$

$= \begin{pmatrix} 6-1 & 9-2 & 15-1 \\ 3-1 & 18-2 & 12-3 \end{pmatrix}$

$= \begin{pmatrix} 5 & 7 & 14 \\ 2 & 16 & 9 \end{pmatrix}$

3 a Increase of $15\% = 1.15$

$\begin{pmatrix} 30 & 40 & 40 & 60 \\ 50 & 40 & 30 & 75 \\ 40 & 40 & 50 & 50 \\ 10 & 20 & 20 & 15 \end{pmatrix} = \begin{pmatrix} 35 & 46 & 46 & 69 \\ 58 & 46 & 35 & 86 \\ 46 & 46 & 58 & 58 \\ 12 & 23 & 23 & 17 \end{pmatrix}$ rounded to the nearest whole number.

b Decrease of $15\% = 0.85$

$\begin{pmatrix} 30 & 40 & 40 & 60 \\ 50 & 40 & 30 & 75 \\ 40 & 40 & 50 & 50 \\ 10 & 20 & 20 & 15 \end{pmatrix} = \begin{pmatrix} 26 & 34 & 34 & 51 \\ 43 & 34 & 26 & 64 \\ 34 & 34 & 43 & 43 \\ 9 & 17 & 17 & 13 \end{pmatrix}$ rounded to the nearest whole number.

4 a Weekdays Weekends

$\begin{pmatrix} 75 \\ 27 \\ 102 \end{pmatrix} \quad \begin{pmatrix} 136 \\ 43 \\ 129 \end{pmatrix}$ DVD / VHS / games

b $\begin{pmatrix} 75 \\ 27 \\ 102 \end{pmatrix} + \begin{pmatrix} 136 \\ 43 \\ 129 \end{pmatrix} = \begin{pmatrix} 211 \\ 70 \\ 231 \end{pmatrix}$

c The sum matrix of **b** represents total weekly average hirings.

5 The matrix is $12F = 12\begin{pmatrix} 1 \\ 4 \\ 2 \\ 1 \end{pmatrix} = \begin{pmatrix} 12 \\ 48 \\ 24 \\ 12 \end{pmatrix}$

EXERCISE 13B.3

1 a $A + 2A = 3A$ **b** $3B - 3B = O$ **c** $C - 2C = -C$

d $-B + B = O$ **e** $2(A + B) = 2A + 2B$ **f** $-(A + B) = -A - B$

g $-(2A - C)$
$= -2A + C$

h $3A - (B - A)$
$= 3A - B + A$
$= 4A - B$

i $A + 2B - (A - B)$
$= A + 2B - A + B$
$= 3B$

2 a $\quad X + B = A$
$\therefore \quad X + B + (-B) = A + (-B)$
$\therefore \quad X + O = A - B$
$\therefore \quad X = A - B$

b $\quad B + X = C$
$\therefore \quad B + X + (-B) = C + (-B)$
$\therefore \quad O + X = C - B$
$\therefore \quad X = C - B$

c $\quad 4B + X = 2C$
$\therefore \quad 4B + X + (-4B) = 2C + (-4B)$
$\therefore \quad O + X = 2C - 4B$
$\therefore \quad X = 2C - 4B$

d $\quad 2X = A$
$\therefore \quad \frac{1}{2}(2X) = \frac{1}{2}A$
$\therefore \quad 1X = \frac{1}{2}A \quad \therefore \quad X = \frac{1}{2}A$

e $\quad 3X = B$
$\therefore \quad \frac{1}{3}(3X) = \frac{1}{3}B$
$\therefore \quad 1X = \frac{1}{3}B \quad \therefore \quad X = \frac{1}{3}B$

f $\quad A - X = B$
$\therefore \quad A - X + X = B + X$
$\therefore \quad A + O = B + X$
$\therefore \quad A = B + X$
and $\quad A + (-B) = B + X + (-B)$
$\therefore \quad A - B = X + O$
$\therefore \quad A - B = X$
$\therefore \quad X = A - B$

g $\quad \frac{1}{2}X = C$
$\therefore \quad 2(\frac{1}{2}X) = 2C$
$\therefore \quad 1X = 2C \quad \therefore \quad X = 2C$

h $\quad 2(X + A) = B$
$\therefore \quad \frac{1}{2}[2(X + A)] = \frac{1}{2}B$
$\therefore \quad 1(X + A) = \frac{1}{2}B$
$\therefore \quad X + A = \frac{1}{2}B$
$\therefore \quad X + A + (-A) = \frac{1}{2}B + (-A)$
$\therefore \quad X + O = \frac{1}{2}B - A$
$\therefore \quad X = \frac{1}{2}B - A$

i $\quad A - 4X = C$
$\therefore \quad A - 4X + 4X = C + 4X$
$\therefore \quad A + O = C + 4X$
$\therefore \quad A = C + 4X$
and $\quad A - C = 4X$
$\therefore \quad \frac{1}{4}(A - C) = \frac{1}{4}(4X)$
$\therefore \quad X = \frac{1}{4}(A - C)$

3 a If $\frac{1}{3}X = M$
then $3(\frac{1}{3}X) = 3M$
$\therefore \quad X = 3M = 3\begin{pmatrix} 1 & 2 \\ 3 & 6 \end{pmatrix} = \begin{pmatrix} 3 & 6 \\ 9 & 18 \end{pmatrix}$

b If $4X = N$ then $\frac{1}{4}(4X) = \frac{1}{4}N$
$\therefore \quad X = \frac{1}{4}N$
$\therefore \quad X = \frac{1}{4}\begin{pmatrix} 2 & -1 \\ 3 & 5 \end{pmatrix} = \begin{pmatrix} \frac{1}{2} & -\frac{1}{4} \\ \frac{3}{4} & \frac{5}{4} \end{pmatrix}$

c If $A - 2X = 3B$
then $A - 2X + 2X = 3B + 2X$
$\therefore \quad A = 3B + 2X$
$\therefore \quad A + (-3B) = 3B + 2X + (-3B)$
$\therefore \quad A - 3B = 2X$
$\therefore \quad \frac{1}{2}(A - 3B) = \frac{1}{2}(2X)$
$\therefore \quad \frac{1}{2}(A - 3B) = 1X$

$\therefore \quad X = \frac{1}{2}(A - 3B)$
$= \frac{1}{2}\left[\begin{pmatrix} 1 & 0 \\ -1 & 2 \end{pmatrix} - 3\begin{pmatrix} 1 & 4 \\ -1 & 1 \end{pmatrix}\right]$
$= \frac{1}{2}\begin{pmatrix} -2 & -12 \\ 2 & -1 \end{pmatrix} = \begin{pmatrix} -1 & -6 \\ 1 & -\frac{1}{2} \end{pmatrix}$

EXERCISE 13B.4

1 a $\begin{pmatrix} 3 & -1 \end{pmatrix}\begin{pmatrix} 5 \\ 4 \end{pmatrix} = (3 \times 5 + (-1) \times 4)$
$= (15 - 4)$
$= (11)$

b $\begin{pmatrix} 1 & 3 & 2 \end{pmatrix}\begin{pmatrix} 5 \\ 1 \\ 7 \end{pmatrix} = (1 \times 5 + 3 \times 1 + 2 \times 7)$
$= (5 + 3 + 14)$
$= (22)$

c $\begin{pmatrix} 6 & -1 & 2 & 3 \end{pmatrix}\begin{pmatrix} 1 \\ 0 \\ -1 \\ 4 \end{pmatrix} = (6 \times 1 + (-1) \times 0 + 2 \times (-1) + 3 \times 4)$
$= (6 + 0 - 2 + 12)$
$= (16)$

2 $\begin{pmatrix} w & x & y & z \end{pmatrix} \begin{pmatrix} 1 \\ 1 \\ 1 \\ 1 \end{pmatrix} = \begin{pmatrix} w+x+y+z \end{pmatrix}$

$\therefore$ $\frac{1}{4}(w+x+y+z)$, which is the average of w, x, y and z, can be represented as $\begin{pmatrix} w & x & y & z \end{pmatrix} \begin{pmatrix} \frac{1}{4} \\ \frac{1}{4} \\ \frac{1}{4} \\ \frac{1}{4} \end{pmatrix}$.

3 a $\mathbf{Q} = \begin{pmatrix} 4 \\ 3 \\ 2 \end{pmatrix}$, $\mathbf{P} = \begin{pmatrix} 27 & 35 & 39 \end{pmatrix}$

b total cost = $\mathbf{PQ} = \begin{pmatrix} 27 & 35 & 39 \end{pmatrix} \begin{pmatrix} 4 \\ 3 \\ 2 \end{pmatrix}$
$= (27 \times 4 + 35 \times 3 + 39 \times 2)$
$= (291)$ $\therefore$ total cost is \$291

4 a $\mathbf{P} = \begin{pmatrix} 10 & 6 & 3 & 1 \end{pmatrix}$

b total points = $\mathbf{PN} = \begin{pmatrix} 10 & 6 & 3 & 1 \end{pmatrix} \begin{pmatrix} 3 \\ 2 \\ 4 \\ 2 \end{pmatrix}$

$\mathbf{N} = \begin{pmatrix} 3 \\ 2 \\ 4 \\ 2 \end{pmatrix}$

$= (10 \times 3 + 6 \times 2 + 3 \times 4 + 1 \times 2)$
$= (30 + 12 + 12 + 2)$
$= (56)$ So, the number of points awarded is 56.

EXERCISE 13B.5

1 $\mathbf{A} = \begin{pmatrix} 4 & 2 & 1 \end{pmatrix}$ which is 1 row × 3 columns, $\mathbf{B} = \begin{pmatrix} 1 & 2 & 1 \\ 0 & 1 & 0 \end{pmatrix}$ which is 2 rows × 3 columns.

$\mathbf{AB}$ cannot be found because the number of columns in $\mathbf{A}$ does not equal the number of rows in $\mathbf{B}$.

2 $\mathbf{A}$ is $2 \times n$ and $\mathbf{B}$ is $m \times 3$.
  a We can find $\mathbf{AB}$ if the number of columns in $\mathbf{A}$ equals the number of rows in $\mathbf{B}$, $\therefore$ if $n = m$.
  b If $\mathbf{AB}$ can be found its order is 2×3.
  c $\mathbf{BA}$ cannot be found because the number of columns in $\mathbf{B}$ does not equal the number of rows in $\mathbf{A}$.

3 a i $\mathbf{A}$ is 2×2 and $\mathbf{B}$ is 1×2 $\therefore$ $\mathbf{AB}$ does not exist.
 (not equal)

  ii $\mathbf{B}$ is 1×2 and $\mathbf{A}$ is 2×2 $\quad \mathbf{BA} = \begin{pmatrix} 5 & 6 \end{pmatrix} \begin{pmatrix} 2 & 1 \\ 3 & 4 \end{pmatrix}$
  $\therefore$ $\mathbf{BA}$ is 1×2
  $= \begin{pmatrix} 5 \times 2 + 6 \times 3 & 5 \times 1 + 6 \times 4 \end{pmatrix}$
  $= \begin{pmatrix} 10 + 18 & 5 + 24 \end{pmatrix}$
  $= \begin{pmatrix} 28 & 29 \end{pmatrix}$

  b i $\mathbf{A}$ is 1×3 and $\mathbf{B}$ is 3×1, $\therefore$ $\mathbf{AB}$ is 1×1 and

  $\mathbf{AB} = \begin{pmatrix} 2 & 0 & 3 \end{pmatrix} \begin{pmatrix} 1 \\ 4 \\ 2 \end{pmatrix} = (2 \times 1 + 0 \times 4 + 3 \times 2) = (2 + 0 + 6) = (8)$

  ii $\mathbf{B}$ is 3×1 and $\mathbf{A}$ is 1×3, $\therefore$ $\mathbf{BA}$ is 3×3 and

  $\mathbf{BA} = \begin{pmatrix} 1 \\ 4 \\ 2 \end{pmatrix} \begin{pmatrix} 2 & 0 & 3 \end{pmatrix} = \begin{pmatrix} 1 \times 2 & 1 \times 0 & 1 \times 3 \\ 4 \times 2 & 4 \times 0 & 4 \times 3 \\ 2 \times 2 & 2 \times 0 & 2 \times 3 \end{pmatrix} = \begin{pmatrix} 2 & 0 & 3 \\ 8 & 0 & 12 \\ 4 & 0 & 6 \end{pmatrix}$

4 a $\begin{pmatrix} 1 & 2 & 1 \end{pmatrix} \begin{pmatrix} 2 & 3 & 1 \\ 0 & 1 & 0 \\ 1 & 0 & 2 \end{pmatrix}$ is 1×3 by 3×3 $\therefore$ resultant matrix is 1×3

$= \begin{pmatrix} 1 \times 2 + 2 \times 0 + 1 \times 1 & 1 \times 3 + 2 \times 1 + 1 \times 0 & 1 \times 1 + 2 \times 0 + 1 \times 2 \end{pmatrix}$

$= \begin{pmatrix} 2 + 0 + 1 & 3 + 2 + 0 & 1 + 0 + 2 \end{pmatrix}$

$= \begin{pmatrix} 3 & 5 & 3 \end{pmatrix}$

b $\begin{pmatrix} 1 & 0 & -1 \\ -1 & 1 & 0 \\ 0 & -1 & 1 \end{pmatrix} \begin{pmatrix} 2 \\ 3 \\ 4 \end{pmatrix}$ is 3×3 by 3×1 $\therefore$ resultant matrix is 3×1

$= \begin{pmatrix} 1 \times 2 + 0 \times 3 + (-1) \times 4 \\ (-1) \times 2 + 1 \times 3 + 0 \times 4 \\ 0 \times 2 + (-1) \times 3 + 1 \times 4 \end{pmatrix} = \begin{pmatrix} 2 + 0 - 4 \\ -2 + 3 + 0 \\ 0 - 3 + 4 \end{pmatrix} = \begin{pmatrix} -2 \\ 1 \\ 1 \end{pmatrix}$

5 a $C = \begin{pmatrix} 12.5 \\ 9.5 \end{pmatrix}$ $\quad$ $\begin{array}{cc} \text{adults} & \text{children} \end{array}$
$N = \begin{pmatrix} 2375 & 5156 \\ 2502 & 3612 \end{pmatrix} \begin{array}{l} \text{first day} \\ \text{second day} \end{array}$

b N is 2×2 and C is 2×1 $\therefore$ NC is 2×1

$NC = \begin{pmatrix} 2375 & 5156 \\ 2502 & 3612 \end{pmatrix} \begin{pmatrix} 12.5 \\ 9.5 \end{pmatrix} = \begin{pmatrix} 2375 \times 12.5 + 5156 \times 9.5 \\ 2502 \times 12.5 + 3612 \times 9.5 \end{pmatrix} = \begin{pmatrix} 29\,687.5 + 48\,982 \\ 31\,275 + 34\,314 \end{pmatrix}$

$= \begin{pmatrix} 78\,669.5 \\ 65\,589 \end{pmatrix} \begin{array}{l} \text{income from day 1} \\ \text{income from day 2} \end{array}$

c Total income $= \$78\,669.50 + \$65\,589 = \$144\,258.50$

6 a $\begin{array}{cc} \text{me} & \text{friend} \end{array}$
$R = \begin{pmatrix} 1 & 1 \\ 1 & 2 \\ 2 & 3 \end{pmatrix} \begin{array}{l} \text{hammers} \\ \text{screwdrivers} \\ \text{cans of paint} \end{array}$
$\quad$ **b** $P = \begin{pmatrix} 7 & 3 & 19 \\ 6 & 2 & 22 \end{pmatrix} \begin{array}{l} \text{store A} \\ \text{store B} \end{array}$

c P is 2×3 and R is 3×2, $\therefore$ PR is 2×2

$PR = \begin{pmatrix} 7 & 3 & 19 \\ 6 & 2 & 22 \end{pmatrix} \begin{pmatrix} 1 & 1 \\ 1 & 2 \\ 2 & 3 \end{pmatrix} = \begin{pmatrix} 7 \times 1 + 3 \times 1 + 19 \times 2 & 7 \times 1 + 3 \times 2 + 19 \times 3 \\ 6 \times 1 + 2 \times 1 + 22 \times 2 & 6 \times 1 + 2 \times 2 + 22 \times 3 \end{pmatrix}$

$\therefore$ $PR = \begin{pmatrix} 7 + 3 + 38 & 7 + 6 + 57 \\ 6 + 2 + 44 & 6 + 4 + 66 \end{pmatrix} = \begin{pmatrix} 48 & 70 \\ 52 & 76 \end{pmatrix}$

d My costs at Store A are €48; my friend's costs at Store B are €76.

e My costs at Store B are €52. Therefore I should shop at Store A, which is cheaper.

EXERCISE 13B.6

1 a $\begin{pmatrix} 16 & 18 & 15 \\ 13 & 21 & 16 \\ 10 & 22 & 24 \end{pmatrix}$ **b** $\begin{pmatrix} 10 & 6 & -7 \\ 9 & 3 & 0 \\ 4 & -4 & -10 \end{pmatrix}$ **c** $\begin{pmatrix} 22 & 0 & 132 & 176 & 198 \\ 44 & 154 & 88 & 110 & 0 \\ 176 & 44 & 88 & 88 & 132 \end{pmatrix}$ **d** $\begin{pmatrix} 115 \\ 136 \\ 46 \\ 106 \end{pmatrix}$

2 a $\begin{array}{ccc} \text{nights} & \text{breakfasts} & \text{dinners} \end{array}$
Numbers matrix $N = \begin{pmatrix} 3 & 3 & 2 \end{pmatrix}$

b Prices matrix $P = \begin{pmatrix} \text{Bay View} & \text{Terrace} & \text{Staunton Star} \\ 125 & 150 & 140 \\ 44 & 40 & 40 \\ 75 & 80 & 65 \end{pmatrix} \begin{array}{l} \text{room} \\ \text{breakfast} \\ \text{dinner} \end{array}$

c Total prices for each venue = numbers matrix × prices matrix = **NP**
   N is 1×3 and **P** is 3×3 $\therefore$ **NP** is 1×3

$$NP = \begin{pmatrix} 3 & 3 & 2 \end{pmatrix} \begin{pmatrix} 125 & 150 & 140 \\ 44 & 40 & 40 \\ 75 & 80 & 65 \end{pmatrix} = \begin{pmatrix} 657 & 730 & 670 \end{pmatrix} \quad \{\text{using technology}\}$$

$\therefore$ \$657 for Bay View, \$730 for Terrace, \$670 for Staunton Star.

d Total prices $= \begin{pmatrix} 2 & 1 & 1 \end{pmatrix} \begin{pmatrix} 125 & 150 & 140 \\ 44 & 40 & 40 \\ 75 & 80 & 65 \end{pmatrix} = \begin{pmatrix} 369 & 420 & 385 \end{pmatrix}$ $\{\text{using technology}\}$

$\therefore$ \$369 for Bay View, \$420 for Terrace, \$385 for Staunton Star.

e To include both scenarios we calculate

$$\begin{pmatrix} 3 & 3 & 2 \\ 2 & 1 & 1 \end{pmatrix} \begin{pmatrix} 125 & 150 & 140 \\ 44 & 40 & 40 \\ 75 & 80 & 65 \end{pmatrix} = \begin{pmatrix} 657 & 730 & 670 \\ 369 & 420 & 385 \end{pmatrix}, \text{ using technology}$$

3 Prices matrix $= \begin{pmatrix} 125 \\ 315 \\ 405 \\ 375 \end{pmatrix}$

Total income $= \dfrac{\text{numbers matrix}}{\times \text{ prices matrix}} = \begin{pmatrix} 50 & 42 & 18 & 65 \\ 65 & 37 & 25 & 82 \\ 120 & 29 & 23 & 75 \\ 42 & 36 & 19 & 72 \end{pmatrix} \begin{pmatrix} 125 \\ 315 \\ 405 \\ 375 \end{pmatrix} = \begin{pmatrix} 51\,145 \\ 60\,655 \\ 61\,575 \\ 51\,285 \end{pmatrix}$ $\{\text{using technology}\}$

$\therefore$ total income $= \$51\,145 + \$60\,655 + \$61\,575 + \$51\,285 = \$224\,660$

4 a Income matrix $\mathbf{I} = \begin{pmatrix} 125 & 195 & 225 \end{pmatrix}$, Cost matrix $\mathbf{C} = \begin{pmatrix} 85 & 120 & 130 \end{pmatrix}$,

Numbers (bookings) matrix $\mathbf{N} = \begin{pmatrix} 15 & 12 & 13 & 11 & 14 & 16 & 8 \\ 4 & 3 & 6 & 2 & 0 & 4 & 7 \\ 3 & 1 & 4 & 4 & 3 & 2 & 0 \end{pmatrix}$

Profit per day
$=$ (income from room) × (bookings per day) − (maintenance cost per room) × (bookings per day)
$= \mathbf{IN} - \mathbf{CN}$

$= \begin{pmatrix} 125 & 195 & 225 \end{pmatrix} \begin{pmatrix} 15 & 12 & 13 & 11 & 14 & 16 & 8 \\ 4 & 3 & 6 & 2 & 0 & 4 & 7 \\ 3 & 1 & 4 & 4 & 3 & 2 & 0 \end{pmatrix} - \begin{pmatrix} 85 & 120 & 130 \end{pmatrix} \begin{pmatrix} 15 & 12 & 13 & 11 & 14 & 16 & 8 \\ 4 & 3 & 6 & 2 & 0 & 4 & 7 \\ 3 & 1 & 4 & 4 & 3 & 2 & 0 \end{pmatrix}$

$= \begin{pmatrix} 1185 & 800 & 1350 & 970 & 845 & 1130 & 845 \end{pmatrix}$ $\{\text{using technology}\}$

$\therefore$ profit for the week $= \$1185 + \$800 + \$1350 + \$970 + \$845 + \$1130 + \$845 = \$7125$

b If the hotel maintained every room every day we would need to calculate
(income from room) × (bookings per day) − (maintenance costs per room) × (number of rooms)

$= \begin{pmatrix} 125 & 195 & 225 \end{pmatrix} \begin{pmatrix} 15 & 12 & 13 & 11 & 14 & 16 & 8 \\ 4 & 3 & 6 & 2 & 0 & 4 & 7 \\ 3 & 1 & 4 & 4 & 3 & 2 & 0 \end{pmatrix} - \begin{pmatrix} 85 & 120 & 130 \end{pmatrix} \begin{pmatrix} 20 & 20 & 20 & 20 & 20 & 20 & 20 \\ 15 & 15 & 15 & 15 & 15 & 15 & 15 \\ 5 & 5 & 5 & 5 & 5 & 5 & 5 \end{pmatrix}$

$\therefore$ using technology, profit per day $= \begin{pmatrix} -820 & -1840 & -455 & -1485 & -1725 & -920 & -1785 \end{pmatrix}$

$\therefore$ the profit per week would be $(-\$820) + \ldots + (-\$1785) = -\$9030$, or a loss of \$9030.

c Profit per room matrix = income per room matrix − cost per room matrix

$= \mathbf{I} - \mathbf{C} = \begin{pmatrix} 125 & 195 & 225 \end{pmatrix} - \begin{pmatrix} 85 & 120 & 130 \end{pmatrix}$

$= \begin{pmatrix} 40 & 75 & 95 \end{pmatrix}$

$\therefore$ the result in **a** can be calculated using:

$\begin{pmatrix} 40 & 75 & 95 \end{pmatrix} \begin{pmatrix} 15 & 12 & 13 & 11 & 14 & 16 & 8 \\ 4 & 3 & 6 & 2 & 0 & 4 & 7 \\ 3 & 1 & 4 & 4 & 3 & 2 & 0 \end{pmatrix}$ This checks using technology.

EXERCISE 13B.7

1 $AB = \begin{pmatrix} 1 & 0 \\ 1 & 2 \end{pmatrix} \begin{pmatrix} -1 & 1 \\ 0 & 3 \end{pmatrix} = \begin{pmatrix} -1+0 & 1+0 \\ -1+0 & 1+6 \end{pmatrix} = \begin{pmatrix} -1 & 1 \\ -1 & 7 \end{pmatrix}$

$BA = \begin{pmatrix} -1 & 1 \\ 0 & 3 \end{pmatrix} \begin{pmatrix} 1 & 0 \\ 1 & 2 \end{pmatrix} = \begin{pmatrix} -1+1 & 0+2 \\ 0+3 & 0+6 \end{pmatrix} = \begin{pmatrix} 0 & 2 \\ 3 & 6 \end{pmatrix}$

$AB \neq BA$ $\quad \therefore \quad$ in the general case AB does not necessarily equal BA.

2 $AO = \begin{pmatrix} a & b \\ c & d \end{pmatrix} \begin{pmatrix} 0 & 0 \\ 0 & 0 \end{pmatrix} = \begin{pmatrix} 0+0 & 0+0 \\ 0+0 & 0+0 \end{pmatrix} = \begin{pmatrix} 0 & 0 \\ 0 & 0 \end{pmatrix} = O$

$OA = \begin{pmatrix} 0 & 0 \\ 0 & 0 \end{pmatrix} \begin{pmatrix} a & b \\ c & d \end{pmatrix} = \begin{pmatrix} 0+0 & 0+0 \\ 0+0 & 0+0 \end{pmatrix} = \begin{pmatrix} 0 & 0 \\ 0 & 0 \end{pmatrix} = O \quad \therefore \quad AO = OA = O$

3 a Suppose $A = \begin{pmatrix} 1 & 2 \\ 3 & 4 \end{pmatrix}$, $B = \begin{pmatrix} 1 & 1 \\ 1 & 1 \end{pmatrix}$ and $C = \begin{pmatrix} 2 & 3 \\ 1 & 1 \end{pmatrix}$.

$A(B+C)$

$= \begin{pmatrix} 1 & 2 \\ 3 & 4 \end{pmatrix} \begin{pmatrix} 3 & 4 \\ 2 & 2 \end{pmatrix}$

$= \begin{pmatrix} 3+4 & 4+4 \\ 9+8 & 12+8 \end{pmatrix}$

$= \begin{pmatrix} 7 & 8 \\ 17 & 20 \end{pmatrix}$

$AB + AC$

$= \begin{pmatrix} 1 & 2 \\ 3 & 4 \end{pmatrix} \begin{pmatrix} 1 & 1 \\ 1 & 1 \end{pmatrix} + \begin{pmatrix} 1 & 2 \\ 3 & 4 \end{pmatrix} \begin{pmatrix} 2 & 3 \\ 1 & 1 \end{pmatrix}$

$= \begin{pmatrix} 1+2 & 1+2 \\ 3+4 & 3+4 \end{pmatrix} + \begin{pmatrix} 2+2 & 3+2 \\ 6+4 & 9+4 \end{pmatrix}$

$= \begin{pmatrix} 3 & 3 \\ 7 & 7 \end{pmatrix} + \begin{pmatrix} 4 & 5 \\ 10 & 13 \end{pmatrix}$

$= \begin{pmatrix} 7 & 8 \\ 17 & 20 \end{pmatrix}$

$= A(B+C)$

b $A = \begin{pmatrix} a & b \\ c & d \end{pmatrix}$, $B = \begin{pmatrix} p & q \\ r & s \end{pmatrix}$ and $C = \begin{pmatrix} w & x \\ y & z \end{pmatrix}$

$A(B+C) = \begin{pmatrix} a & b \\ c & d \end{pmatrix} \begin{pmatrix} p+w & q+x \\ r+y & s+z \end{pmatrix} = \begin{pmatrix} ap+aw+br+by & aq+ax+bs+bz \\ cp+cw+dr+dy & cq+cx+ds+dz \end{pmatrix}$

$AB + AC = \begin{pmatrix} a & b \\ c & d \end{pmatrix} \begin{pmatrix} p & q \\ r & s \end{pmatrix} + \begin{pmatrix} a & b \\ c & d \end{pmatrix} \begin{pmatrix} w & x \\ y & z \end{pmatrix}$

$= \begin{pmatrix} ap+br & aq+bs \\ cp+dr & cq+ds \end{pmatrix} + \begin{pmatrix} aw+by & ax+bz \\ cw+dy & cx+dz \end{pmatrix}$

$= \begin{pmatrix} ap+aw+br+by & aq+ax+bs+bz \\ cp+cw+dr+dy & cq+cx+ds+dz \end{pmatrix} = A(B+C)$

c Using the matrices in **a**,

$(AB)C = \begin{pmatrix} 3 & 3 \\ 7 & 7 \end{pmatrix} \begin{pmatrix} 2 & 3 \\ 1 & 1 \end{pmatrix}$

$= \begin{pmatrix} 6+3 & 9+3 \\ 14+7 & 21+7 \end{pmatrix}$

$= \begin{pmatrix} 9 & 12 \\ 21 & 28 \end{pmatrix}$

$A(BC) = \begin{pmatrix} 1 & 2 \\ 3 & 4 \end{pmatrix} \left[\begin{pmatrix} 1 & 1 \\ 1 & 1 \end{pmatrix} \begin{pmatrix} 2 & 3 \\ 1 & 1 \end{pmatrix} \right]$

$= \begin{pmatrix} 1 & 2 \\ 3 & 4 \end{pmatrix} \begin{pmatrix} 3 & 4 \\ 3 & 4 \end{pmatrix}$

$= \begin{pmatrix} 3+6 & 4+8 \\ 9+12 & 12+16 \end{pmatrix}$

$= \begin{pmatrix} 9 & 12 \\ 21 & 28 \end{pmatrix} = (AB)C$

d Using the matrices in **b**,

$$(AB)C = \begin{pmatrix} ap+br & aq+bs \\ cp+dr & cq+ds \end{pmatrix} \begin{pmatrix} w & x \\ y & z \end{pmatrix}$$

$$= \begin{pmatrix} apw+brw+aqy+bsy & apx+brx+aqz+bsz \\ cpw+drw+cqy+dsy & cpx+drx+cqz+dsz \end{pmatrix}$$

$$A(BC) = \begin{pmatrix} a & b \\ c & d \end{pmatrix} \left[\begin{pmatrix} p & q \\ r & s \end{pmatrix} \begin{pmatrix} w & x \\ y & z \end{pmatrix} \right] = \begin{pmatrix} a & b \\ c & d \end{pmatrix} \begin{pmatrix} pw+qy & px+qz \\ rw+sy & rx+sz \end{pmatrix}$$

$$= \begin{pmatrix} apw+brw+aqy+bsy & apx+brx+aqz+bsz \\ cpw+drw+cqy+dsy & cpx+drx+cqz+dsz \end{pmatrix} = (AB)C$$

4 a If $\begin{pmatrix} a & b \\ c & d \end{pmatrix} \begin{pmatrix} w & x \\ y & z \end{pmatrix} = \begin{pmatrix} a & b \\ c & d \end{pmatrix}$ then $\begin{pmatrix} aw+by & ax+bz \\ cw+dy & cx+dz \end{pmatrix} = \begin{pmatrix} a & b \\ c & d \end{pmatrix}$

$\therefore$ equating coefficients of corresponding elements: $w=1$, $y=0$, $x=0$, $z=1$
which checks with the coefficients in the second line. $\therefore$ $w=z=1$,
$x=y=0$ So, **X** is $\begin{pmatrix} 1 & 0 \\ 0 & 1 \end{pmatrix}$.

b In **a** we showed that $AX = A$ where $X = \begin{pmatrix} 1 & 0 \\ 0 & 1 \end{pmatrix}$.

$$XA = \begin{pmatrix} 1 & 0 \\ 0 & 1 \end{pmatrix} \begin{pmatrix} a & b \\ c & d \end{pmatrix} = \begin{pmatrix} a+0 & b+0 \\ 0+c & 0+d \end{pmatrix} = \begin{pmatrix} a & b \\ c & d \end{pmatrix} = A.$$

$\therefore$ $AI = IA = A$ for all 2×2 matrices **A** where $I = X = \begin{pmatrix} 1 & 0 \\ 0 & 1 \end{pmatrix}$.

5 a $A^2 = \begin{pmatrix} 2 & 1 \\ 3 & -2 \end{pmatrix} \begin{pmatrix} 2 & 1 \\ 3 & -2 \end{pmatrix}$ **b** $A^3 = \begin{pmatrix} 5 & -1 \\ 2 & 4 \end{pmatrix} \begin{pmatrix} 5 & -1 \\ 2 & 4 \end{pmatrix} \begin{pmatrix} 5 & -1 \\ 2 & 4 \end{pmatrix}$

$$= \begin{pmatrix} 4+3 & 2+(-2) \\ 6+(-6) & 3+4 \end{pmatrix} \qquad = \begin{pmatrix} 25+(-2) & -5+(-4) \\ 10+8 & -2+16 \end{pmatrix} \begin{pmatrix} 5 & -1 \\ 2 & 4 \end{pmatrix}$$

$$= \begin{pmatrix} 7 & 0 \\ 0 & 7 \end{pmatrix} \qquad\qquad = \begin{pmatrix} 23 & -9 \\ 18 & 14 \end{pmatrix} \begin{pmatrix} 5 & -1 \\ 2 & 4 \end{pmatrix}$$

$$= \begin{pmatrix} 115+(-18) & -23+(-36) \\ 90+28 & -18+56 \end{pmatrix} = \begin{pmatrix} 97 & -59 \\ 118 & 38 \end{pmatrix}$$

6 a $A = \begin{pmatrix} 1 & 2 \\ 3 & 4 \\ 5 & 6 \end{pmatrix}$ $\therefore$ A^2 is 3×2 by 3×2. $2 \neq 3$ so A^2 does not exist.

b We can square a matrix when the number of columns equals the number of rows, that is, if it is a square matrix.

7 $I^2 = \begin{pmatrix} 1 & 0 \\ 0 & 1 \end{pmatrix} \begin{pmatrix} 1 & 0 \\ 0 & 1 \end{pmatrix} = \begin{pmatrix} 1+0 & 0+0 \\ 0+0 & 0+1 \end{pmatrix} = \begin{pmatrix} 1 & 0 \\ 0 & 1 \end{pmatrix} = I$ $\therefore$ $I^3 = II^2 = II = I^2 = I$

EXERCISE 13B.8

1 a $A(A+I)$ **b** $(B+2I)B$ **c** $A(A^2 - 2A + I)$
      $= A^2 + AI$ $= B^2 + 2IB$ $= A^3 - 2A^2 + AI$
      $= A^2 + A$ $= B^2 + 2B$ $= A^3 - 2A^2 + A$

d $A(A^2 + A - 2I)$ **e** $(A+B)(C+D)$ **f** $(A+B)^2$
      $= A^3 + A^2 - 2AI$ $= (A+B)C + (A+B)D$ $= (A+B)(A+B)$
      $= A^3 + A^2 - 2A$ $= AC + BC + AD + BD$ $= (A+B)A + (A+B)B$
                                                         $= A^2 + BA + AB + B^2$

g $(A+B)(A-B)$
$= (A+B)A - (A+B)B$
$= A^2 + BA - AB - B^2$

h $(A+I)^2$
$= (A+I)(A+I)$
$= (A+I)A + (A+I)I$
$= A^2 + IA + AI + I^2$
$= A^2 + A + A + I$
$= A^2 + 2A + I$

i $(3I-B)^2$
$= (3I-B)(3I-B)$
$= (3I-B)3I - (3I-B)B$
$= 9I^2 - 3BI - 3IB + B^2$
$= 9I - 3B - 3B + B^2$
$= 9I - 6B + B^2$

2 a $A^2 = 2A - I$ $\therefore$ $A^3 = A \times A^2$
$= A(2A - I)$
$= 2A^2 - AI$
$= 2(2A - I) - A$
$= 4A - 2I - A$
$= 3A - 2I$

and $A^4 = A \times A^3$
$= A(3A - 2I)$
$= 3A^2 - 2AI$
$= 3(2A - I) - 2A$
$= 6A - 3I - 2A$
$= 4A - 3I$

b $B^2 = 2I - B$
$\therefore$ $B^3 = B \times B^2$
$= B(2I - B)$
$= 2BI - B^2$
$= 2B - (2I - B)$
$= 2B - 2I + B$
$= 3B - 2I$

and $B^4 = B \times B^3$
$= B(3B - 2I)$
$= 3B^2 - 2BI$
$= 3(2I - B) - 2B$
$= 6I - 3B - 2B$
$= 6I - 5B$

and $B^5 = B \times B^4$
$= B(6I - 5B)$
$= 6BI - 5B^2$
$= 6B - 5(2I - B)$
$= 6B - 10I + 5B$
$= 11B - 10I$

c $C^2 = 4C - 3I$ $C^3 = C \times C^2$
$= C(4C - 3I)$
$= 4C^2 - 3CI$
$= 4(4C - 3I) - 3C$
$= 16C - 12I - 3C$
$= 13C - 12I$

$C^5 = C^2 \times C^3$
$= (4C - 3I)(13C - 12I)$
$= (4C - 3I)13C - (4C - 3I)12I$
$= 52C^2 - 39IC - 48CI + 36I^2$
$= 52(4C - 3I) - 39C - 48C + 36I$
$= 208C - 156I - 87C + 36I$
$= 121C - 120I$

3 a If $A^2 = I$:
i $A(A + 2I)$
$= A^2 + 2AI$
$= I + 2A$

ii $(A - I)^2$
$= (A - I)(A - I)$
$= (A - I)A - (A - I)I$
$= A^2 - IA - AI + I^2$
$= I - A - A + I$
$= 2I - 2A$

iii $A(A + 3I)^2$
$= A(A + 3I)(A + 3I)$
$= A[(A + 3I)A + (A + 3I)3I]$
$= A(A^2 + 3IA + 3AI + 9I^2)$
$= A(I + 3A + 3A + 9I)$
$= A(10I + 6A)$
$= 10AI + 6A^2$
$= 10A + 6I$

b If $A^3 = I$, $A^2(A + I)^2 = A^2(A^2 + 2A + I)$
$= A^4 + 2A^3 + A^2I$
$= A(A^3) + 2A^3 + A^2I$
$= AI + 2I + A^2$
$= A^2 + A + 2I$

c If $A^2 = O$:
i $A(2A - 3I)$
$= 2A^2 - 3AI$
$= 2O - 3A$
$= -3A$

ii $A(A + 2I)(A - I)$
$= A[(A + 2I)A - (A + 2I)I]$
$= A(A^2 + 2IA - AI - 2I^2)$
$= A(O + A - 2I)$
$= A^2 - 2AI$
$= O - 2A$
$= -2A$

iii $A(A + I)^3$
$= A(A + I)(A + I)^2$
$= A(A + I)(A^2 + 2A + I)$
$= (A^2 + AI)(O + 2A + I)$
$= (O + A)(2A + I)$
$= 2A^2 + AI$
$= 2O + A$
$= A$

4 **a** $AB = \begin{pmatrix} 1 & 0 \\ 0 & 0 \end{pmatrix} \begin{pmatrix} 0 & 0 \\ 0 & 1 \end{pmatrix} = \begin{pmatrix} 0+0 & 0+0 \\ 0+0 & 0+0 \end{pmatrix} = \begin{pmatrix} 0 & 0 \\ 0 & 0 \end{pmatrix} = O$

 b $A^2 = \begin{pmatrix} \frac{1}{2} & \frac{1}{2} \\ \frac{1}{2} & \frac{1}{2} \end{pmatrix} \begin{pmatrix} \frac{1}{2} & \frac{1}{2} \\ \frac{1}{2} & \frac{1}{2} \end{pmatrix} = \begin{pmatrix} \frac{1}{4}+\frac{1}{4} & \frac{1}{4}+\frac{1}{4} \\ \frac{1}{4}+\frac{1}{4} & \frac{1}{4}+\frac{1}{4} \end{pmatrix} = \begin{pmatrix} \frac{1}{2} & \frac{1}{2} \\ \frac{1}{2} & \frac{1}{2} \end{pmatrix} = A$

 c $A^2 = A$
 $\therefore A^2 - A = O$
 $\therefore A(A - I) = O$
 $\therefore A = O$ or $A - I = O$
 $\therefore A = O$ or I

The argument contains a false step. As the example in **a** illustrates, $AB = O$ does not imply that $A = O$ or $B = O$. This is a property of real numbers that does not hold for matrices. Therefore it is false to say that if $A(A - I) = O$, then $A = O$ or $A - I$ equals O.

 d Let $A = \begin{pmatrix} a & b \\ c & d \end{pmatrix}$. If $A^2 = A$, $\begin{pmatrix} a & b \\ c & d \end{pmatrix}\begin{pmatrix} a & b \\ c & d \end{pmatrix} = \begin{pmatrix} a & b \\ c & d \end{pmatrix}$

$\therefore \begin{pmatrix} a^2 + bc & ab + bd \\ ac + cd & bc + d^2 \end{pmatrix} = \begin{pmatrix} a & b \\ c & d \end{pmatrix}$

Equating corresponding elements:

$a^2 + bc = a$ $\therefore$ $bc = a(1 - a)$ ...... (1)
$ab + bd = b$ $\therefore$ $b(a + d - 1) = 0$ ...... (2)
$ac + cd = c$ $\therefore$ $c(a + d - 1) = 0$ ...... (3)
$bc + d^2 = d$ $\therefore$ $bc = d(1 - d)$ ...... (4)

If $a + d - 1 \neq 0$ then from (2) and (3), $b = c = 0$.
$\therefore$ from (1) and (4), $a = 0$ or 1 and $d = 0$ or 1
$\therefore$ $a = 0, d = 0$ or $a = 1, d = 1$ or $a = 0, d = 1$ or $a = 1, d = 0$
where the last two cases are not possible as $a + d \neq 1$.

So, if $a = 0, d = 0$ then $A = \begin{pmatrix} 0 & 0 \\ 0 & 0 \end{pmatrix}$ and if $a = 1, d = 1$ then $A = \begin{pmatrix} 1 & 0 \\ 0 & 1 \end{pmatrix}$

If $a + d - 1 = 0$ then $d = 1 - a$ and $c = \dfrac{a - a^2}{b}$

So A is $\begin{pmatrix} a & b \\ \frac{a - a^2}{b} & 1 - a \end{pmatrix}$ provided $b \neq 0$.

5 Suppose $A = \begin{pmatrix} 1 & -1 \\ 1 & -1 \end{pmatrix}$.

$\therefore A^2 = \begin{pmatrix} 1 & -1 \\ 1 & -1 \end{pmatrix}\begin{pmatrix} 1 & -1 \\ 1 & -1 \end{pmatrix} = \begin{pmatrix} 1+(-1) & -1+1 \\ 1+(-1) & -1+1 \end{pmatrix} = \begin{pmatrix} 0 & 0 \\ 0 & 0 \end{pmatrix}$

$\therefore A \neq O$ but $A^2 = O$. So, "if $A^2 = O$ then $A = O$" is a false statement.

6 **a** Since $A^2 = aA + bI$, $\begin{pmatrix} 1 & 2 \\ -1 & 2 \end{pmatrix}\begin{pmatrix} 1 & 2 \\ -1 & 2 \end{pmatrix} = a\begin{pmatrix} 1 & 2 \\ -1 & 2 \end{pmatrix} + b\begin{pmatrix} 1 & 0 \\ 0 & 1 \end{pmatrix}$

$\therefore \begin{pmatrix} 1+(-2) & 2+4 \\ -1+(-2) & -2+4 \end{pmatrix} = \begin{pmatrix} a & 2a \\ -a & 2a \end{pmatrix} + \begin{pmatrix} b & 0 \\ 0 & b \end{pmatrix}$

$\therefore \begin{pmatrix} -1 & 6 \\ -3 & 2 \end{pmatrix} = \begin{pmatrix} a+b & 2a \\ -a & 2a+b \end{pmatrix}$

$\therefore a + b = -1$ and $2a = 6$
$\therefore a = 3$ and $b = -4$

Checking for consistency: $-a = -3$, $2a + b = 6 + (-4) = 2$ ✓
$\therefore A^2 = 3A - 4I$

b Since $\mathbf{A}^2 = a\mathbf{A} + b\mathbf{I}$, $\begin{pmatrix} 3 & 1 \\ 2 & -2 \end{pmatrix}\begin{pmatrix} 3 & 1 \\ 2 & -2 \end{pmatrix} = a\begin{pmatrix} 3 & 1 \\ 2 & -2 \end{pmatrix} + b\begin{pmatrix} 1 & 0 \\ 0 & 1 \end{pmatrix}$

$\therefore \begin{pmatrix} 9+2 & 3+(-2) \\ 6+(-4) & 2+4 \end{pmatrix} = \begin{pmatrix} 3a & a \\ 2a & -2a \end{pmatrix} + \begin{pmatrix} b & 0 \\ 0 & b \end{pmatrix}$

$\therefore \begin{pmatrix} 11 & 1 \\ 2 & 6 \end{pmatrix} = \begin{pmatrix} 3a+b & a \\ 2a & -2a+b \end{pmatrix}$

$\therefore \quad 3a + b = 11 \quad \text{and} \quad a = 1$
$\therefore \quad a = 1 \quad \text{and} \quad b = 8$

Checking for consistency $2a = 2(1) = 2$, $-2a + b = -2(1) + 8 = 6$ ✓
$\therefore \mathbf{A}^2 = \mathbf{A} + 8\mathbf{I}$

7 $\qquad \mathbf{A}^2 = p\mathbf{A} + q\mathbf{I}$

$\therefore \begin{pmatrix} 1 & 2 \\ -1 & -3 \end{pmatrix}\begin{pmatrix} 1 & 2 \\ -1 & -3 \end{pmatrix} = p\begin{pmatrix} 1 & 2 \\ -1 & -3 \end{pmatrix} + q\begin{pmatrix} 1 & 0 \\ 0 & 1 \end{pmatrix}$

$\therefore \begin{pmatrix} 1+(-2) & 2+(-6) \\ -1+3 & -2+9 \end{pmatrix} = \begin{pmatrix} p & 2p \\ -p & -3p \end{pmatrix} + \begin{pmatrix} q & 0 \\ 0 & q \end{pmatrix}$

$\therefore \begin{pmatrix} -1 & -4 \\ 2 & 7 \end{pmatrix} = \begin{pmatrix} p+q & 2p \\ -p & -3p+q \end{pmatrix}$

$\therefore \quad p + q = -1 \quad \text{and} \quad 2p = -4$
$\therefore \quad p = -2 \quad \text{and} \quad q = 1$

Checking for consistency $-p = -(-2) = 2$, $-3p + q = -3(-2) + 1 = 7$ ✓
$\therefore \mathbf{A}^2 = -2\mathbf{A} + \mathbf{I}$

a $\mathbf{A}^3 = \mathbf{A} \times \mathbf{A}^2$
$= \mathbf{A}(-2\mathbf{A} + \mathbf{I})$
$= -2\mathbf{A}^2 + \mathbf{AI}$
$= -2(-2\mathbf{A} + \mathbf{I}) + \mathbf{A}$
$= 4\mathbf{A} - 2\mathbf{I} + \mathbf{A}$
$= 5\mathbf{A} - 2\mathbf{I}$

b $\mathbf{A}^4 = \mathbf{A} \times \mathbf{A}^3$
$= \mathbf{A}(5\mathbf{A} - 2\mathbf{I})$
$= 5\mathbf{A}^2 - 2\mathbf{AI}$
$= 5(-2\mathbf{A} + \mathbf{I}) - 2\mathbf{A}$
$= -10\mathbf{A} + 5\mathbf{I} - 2\mathbf{A}$
$= -12\mathbf{A} + 5\mathbf{I}$

EXERCISE 13C.1

1 a $\begin{pmatrix} 5 & 6 \\ 2 & 3 \end{pmatrix}\begin{pmatrix} 3 & -6 \\ -2 & 5 \end{pmatrix} = \begin{pmatrix} 3 & 0 \\ 0 & 3 \end{pmatrix} = 3\mathbf{I}$

$\therefore \begin{pmatrix} 5 & 6 \\ 2 & 3 \end{pmatrix} \times \frac{1}{3}\begin{pmatrix} 3 & -6 \\ -2 & 5 \end{pmatrix} = \mathbf{I}$

$\therefore \begin{pmatrix} 5 & 6 \\ 2 & 3 \end{pmatrix}^{-1} = \frac{1}{3}\begin{pmatrix} 3 & -6 \\ -2 & 5 \end{pmatrix}$

$= \begin{pmatrix} 1 & -2 \\ -\frac{2}{3} & \frac{5}{3} \end{pmatrix}$

b $\begin{pmatrix} 3 & -4 \\ 1 & 2 \end{pmatrix}\begin{pmatrix} 2 & 4 \\ -1 & 3 \end{pmatrix} = \begin{pmatrix} 10 & 0 \\ 0 & 10 \end{pmatrix} = 10\mathbf{I}$

$\therefore \begin{pmatrix} 3 & -4 \\ 1 & 2 \end{pmatrix} \times \frac{1}{10}\begin{pmatrix} 2 & 4 \\ -1 & 3 \end{pmatrix} = \mathbf{I}$

$\therefore \begin{pmatrix} 3 & -4 \\ 1 & 2 \end{pmatrix}^{-1} = \frac{1}{10}\begin{pmatrix} 2 & 4 \\ -1 & 3 \end{pmatrix}$

$= \begin{pmatrix} 0.2 & 0.4 \\ -0.1 & 0.3 \end{pmatrix}$

2 a $|\mathbf{A}| = 12 - 14$
$= -2$

b $|\mathbf{A}| = 2 - 3$
$= -1$

c $|\mathbf{A}| = 0 - 0$
$= 0$

d $|\mathbf{A}| = 1 - 0$
$= 1$

3 a $\det \mathbf{B} = 12 - -14$
$= 26$

b $\det \mathbf{B} = 6 - 0$
$= 6$

c $\det \mathbf{B} = 0 - 1$
$= -1$

d $\det \mathbf{B} = a^2 - -a$
$= a^2 + a$

4 $A = \begin{pmatrix} 2 & -1 \\ -1 & -1 \end{pmatrix}$

a $|A| = 2(-1) - (-1)(-1)$
$= -3$

b $|A| = -3$
$\therefore |A|^2 = (-3)^2$
$= 9$

c $2A = 2\begin{pmatrix} 2 & -1 \\ -1 & -1 \end{pmatrix}$
$= \begin{pmatrix} 4 & -2 \\ -2 & -2 \end{pmatrix}$
$\therefore |2A| = 4(-2) - (-2)(-2)$
$= -12$

5 Let $A = \begin{pmatrix} a & b \\ c & d \end{pmatrix}$ then $kA = \begin{pmatrix} ka & kb \\ kc & kd \end{pmatrix}$ and $|kA| = ka(kd) - kb(kc)$
$= k^2(ad - bc)$
$= k^2|A|$

6 $A = \begin{pmatrix} a & b \\ c & d \end{pmatrix}$, $B = \begin{pmatrix} w & x \\ y & z \end{pmatrix}$

a $|A| = ad - bc$
and $|B| = wz - xy$

b $AB = \begin{pmatrix} a & b \\ c & d \end{pmatrix}\begin{pmatrix} w & x \\ y & z \end{pmatrix}$
$= \begin{pmatrix} aw + by & ax + bz \\ cw + dy & cx + dz \end{pmatrix}$
$\therefore |AB| = (aw + by)(cx + dz) - (ax + bz)(cw + dy)$

c Expanding brackets,
$|AB| = awcx + awdz + bycx + bydz - axcw - axdy - bzcw - bzdy$
$= wz(ad - bc) - xy(ad - bc)$
$= (ad - bc)(wz - xy)$
$= |A||B|$

7 $A = \begin{pmatrix} 1 & 2 \\ 3 & 4 \end{pmatrix}$, $B = \begin{pmatrix} -1 & 2 \\ 0 & 1 \end{pmatrix}$

a **i** $|A| = 1(4) - 2(3)$
$= 4 - 6$
$= -2$

ii $|2A| = 2^2|A|$
$= 4(-2)$
$= -8$

iii $|-A| = (-1)^2|A|$
$= 1(-2)$
$= -2$

iv $|B| = (-1)(1) - 2(0)$
$= -1$
$\therefore |-3B| = (-3)^2|B|$
$= 9(-1)$
$= -9$

v $|AB| = |A||B|$
$= (-2)(-1)$
$= 2$

b Check:

ii $2A = 2\begin{pmatrix} 1 & 2 \\ 3 & 4 \end{pmatrix} = \begin{pmatrix} 2 & 4 \\ 6 & 8 \end{pmatrix}$
$|2A| = 2(8) - 4(6) = -8$ ✓

iii $|-A| = \begin{pmatrix} -1 & -2 \\ -3 & -4 \end{pmatrix}$
$= (-1)(-4) - (-2)(-3) = -2$ ✓

iv $-3B = -3\begin{pmatrix} -1 & 2 \\ 0 & 1 \end{pmatrix}$
$= \begin{pmatrix} 3 & -6 \\ 0 & -3 \end{pmatrix}$
$|-3B| = (3)(-3) - (-6)(0)$
$= -9$ ✓

v $AB = \begin{pmatrix} 1 & 2 \\ 3 & 4 \end{pmatrix}\begin{pmatrix} -1 & 2 \\ 0 & 1 \end{pmatrix}$
$= \begin{pmatrix} -1+0 & 2+2 \\ -3+0 & 6+4 \end{pmatrix} = \begin{pmatrix} -1 & 4 \\ -3 & 10 \end{pmatrix}$
$|AB| = (-1)(10) - 4(-3) = 2$ ✓

8 **a** $\begin{pmatrix} 2 & 4 \\ -1 & 5 \end{pmatrix}^{-1} = \frac{1}{2(5) - 4(-1)}\begin{pmatrix} 5 & -4 \\ -(-1) & 2 \end{pmatrix} = \frac{1}{14}\begin{pmatrix} 5 & -4 \\ 1 & 2 \end{pmatrix}$

b $\begin{pmatrix} 1 & 0 \\ 1 & -1 \end{pmatrix}^{-1} = \frac{1}{1(-1) - 0(1)}\begin{pmatrix} -1 & 0 \\ -1 & 1 \end{pmatrix} = -\begin{pmatrix} -1 & 0 \\ -1 & 1 \end{pmatrix} = \begin{pmatrix} 1 & 0 \\ 1 & -1 \end{pmatrix}$

c $\begin{pmatrix} 2 & 4 \\ 1 & 2 \end{pmatrix}^{-1}$ does not exist, since $ad - bc = 2(2) - 4(1) = 0$

d $\begin{pmatrix} 1 & 0 \\ 0 & 1 \end{pmatrix}^{-1} = \dfrac{1}{1(1) - 0(0)} \begin{pmatrix} 1 & 0 \\ 0 & 1 \end{pmatrix} = \begin{pmatrix} 1 & 0 \\ 0 & 1 \end{pmatrix}$

e $\begin{pmatrix} 3 & 5 \\ -6 & -10 \end{pmatrix}^{-1}$ does not exist, since $ad - bc = 3(-10) - 5(-6) = 0$

f $\begin{pmatrix} -1 & 2 \\ 4 & 7 \end{pmatrix}^{-1} = \dfrac{1}{(-1)(7) - 2(4)} \begin{pmatrix} 7 & -2 \\ -4 & -1 \end{pmatrix} = -\dfrac{1}{15} \begin{pmatrix} 7 & -2 \\ -4 & -1 \end{pmatrix}$

g $\begin{pmatrix} 3 & 4 \\ -1 & 2 \end{pmatrix}^{-1} = \dfrac{1}{3(2) - (-1)(4)} \begin{pmatrix} 2 & -4 \\ -(-1) & 3 \end{pmatrix} = \dfrac{1}{10} \begin{pmatrix} 2 & -4 \\ 1 & 3 \end{pmatrix}$

h $\begin{pmatrix} -1 & -1 \\ 2 & 3 \end{pmatrix}^{-1} = \dfrac{1}{(-1)3 - (-1)2} \begin{pmatrix} 3 & -(-1) \\ -2 & -1 \end{pmatrix} = -\begin{pmatrix} 3 & 1 \\ -2 & -1 \end{pmatrix} = \begin{pmatrix} -3 & -1 \\ 2 & 1 \end{pmatrix}$

9 a **A** is 2×3 and **B** is 3×2 $\therefore$ **AB** is 2×2

$$\mathbf{AB} = \begin{pmatrix} 1 & 0 & 2 \\ -1 & 1 & 3 \end{pmatrix} \begin{pmatrix} -1 & 2 \\ -4 & 6 \\ 1 & -1 \end{pmatrix} = \begin{pmatrix} -1 + 0 + 2 & 2 + 0 + (-2) \\ 1 + (-4) + 3 & -2 + 6 + (-3) \end{pmatrix}$$

$$\therefore \mathbf{AB} = \begin{pmatrix} 1 & 0 \\ 0 & 1 \end{pmatrix} = \mathbf{I}$$

b **B** is 3×2 and **A** is 2×3 $\therefore$ **BA** is 3×3 whereas **AB** is 2×2. Hence **BA** $\neq$ **AB**, and **A** and **B** are not inverses. The inverse of a matrix **A** satisfies $\mathbf{A}^{-1}\mathbf{A} = \mathbf{A}\mathbf{A}^{-1}$. This requires that **A** has the same number of rows as columns, which means that **A** is a square matrix.

EXERCISE 13C.2

1 a $\left.\begin{array}{r} 3x - y = 8 \\ 2x + 3y = 6 \end{array}\right\}$ can be written as $\begin{pmatrix} 3 & -1 \\ 2 & 3 \end{pmatrix} \begin{pmatrix} x \\ y \end{pmatrix} = \begin{pmatrix} 8 \\ 6 \end{pmatrix}$

b $\left.\begin{array}{r} 4x - 3y = 11 \\ 3x + 2y = -5 \end{array}\right\}$ can be written as $\begin{pmatrix} 4 & -3 \\ 3 & 2 \end{pmatrix} \begin{pmatrix} x \\ y \end{pmatrix} = \begin{pmatrix} 11 \\ -5 \end{pmatrix}$

c $\left.\begin{array}{r} 3a - b = 6 \\ 2a + 7b = -4 \end{array}\right\}$ can be written as $\begin{pmatrix} 3 & -1 \\ 2 & 7 \end{pmatrix} \begin{pmatrix} a \\ b \end{pmatrix} = \begin{pmatrix} 6 \\ -4 \end{pmatrix}$

2 a $\left.\begin{array}{r} 2x - y = 6 \\ x + 3y = 14 \end{array}\right\}$ can be written as $\begin{pmatrix} 2 & -1 \\ 1 & 3 \end{pmatrix} \begin{pmatrix} x \\ y \end{pmatrix} = \begin{pmatrix} 6 \\ 14 \end{pmatrix}$

$\therefore \begin{pmatrix} x \\ y \end{pmatrix} = \begin{pmatrix} 2 & -1 \\ 1 & 3 \end{pmatrix}^{-1} \begin{pmatrix} 6 \\ 14 \end{pmatrix} = \dfrac{1}{7} \begin{pmatrix} 3 & 1 \\ -1 & 2 \end{pmatrix} \begin{pmatrix} 6 \\ 14 \end{pmatrix}$

$\therefore \begin{pmatrix} x \\ y \end{pmatrix} = \dfrac{1}{7} \begin{pmatrix} 18 + 14 \\ -6 + 28 \end{pmatrix} = \begin{pmatrix} \frac{32}{7} \\ \frac{22}{7} \end{pmatrix}$ and so $x = \dfrac{32}{7}$, $y = \dfrac{22}{7}$

b $\left.\begin{array}{r} 5x - 4y = 5 \\ 2x + 3y = -13 \end{array}\right\}$ can be written as $\begin{pmatrix} 5 & -4 \\ 2 & 3 \end{pmatrix} \begin{pmatrix} x \\ y \end{pmatrix} = \begin{pmatrix} 5 \\ -13 \end{pmatrix}$

$\therefore \begin{pmatrix} x \\ y \end{pmatrix} = \begin{pmatrix} 5 & -4 \\ 2 & 3 \end{pmatrix}^{-1} \begin{pmatrix} 5 \\ -13 \end{pmatrix} = \dfrac{1}{23} \begin{pmatrix} 3 & 4 \\ -2 & 5 \end{pmatrix} \begin{pmatrix} 5 \\ -13 \end{pmatrix}$

$\therefore \begin{pmatrix} x \\ y \end{pmatrix} = \dfrac{1}{23} \begin{pmatrix} 15 + (-52) \\ -10 + (-65) \end{pmatrix} = \begin{pmatrix} -\frac{37}{23} \\ -\frac{75}{23} \end{pmatrix}$ and so $x = -\dfrac{37}{23}$, $y = -\dfrac{75}{23}$

c $\left.\begin{array}{l}x - 2y = 7 \\ 5x + 3y = -2\end{array}\right\}$ can be written as $\begin{pmatrix} 1 & -2 \\ 5 & 3 \end{pmatrix}\begin{pmatrix} x \\ y \end{pmatrix} = \begin{pmatrix} 7 \\ -2 \end{pmatrix}$

$\therefore \begin{pmatrix} x \\ y \end{pmatrix} = \begin{pmatrix} 1 & -2 \\ 5 & 3 \end{pmatrix}^{-1}\begin{pmatrix} 7 \\ -2 \end{pmatrix} = \frac{1}{13}\begin{pmatrix} 3 & 2 \\ -5 & 1 \end{pmatrix}\begin{pmatrix} 7 \\ -2 \end{pmatrix}$

$\therefore \begin{pmatrix} x \\ y \end{pmatrix} = \frac{1}{13}\begin{pmatrix} 21 + (-4) \\ -35 + (-2) \end{pmatrix} = \begin{pmatrix} \frac{17}{13} \\ -\frac{37}{13} \end{pmatrix}$ and so $x = \frac{17}{13}$, $y = -\frac{37}{13}$

d $\left.\begin{array}{l}3x + 5y = 4 \\ 2x - y = 11\end{array}\right\}$ can be written as $\begin{pmatrix} 3 & 5 \\ 2 & -1 \end{pmatrix}\begin{pmatrix} x \\ y \end{pmatrix} = \begin{pmatrix} 4 \\ 11 \end{pmatrix}$

$\therefore \begin{pmatrix} x \\ y \end{pmatrix} = \begin{pmatrix} 3 & 5 \\ 2 & -1 \end{pmatrix}^{-1}\begin{pmatrix} 4 \\ 11 \end{pmatrix} = \frac{1}{-13}\begin{pmatrix} -1 & -5 \\ -2 & 3 \end{pmatrix}\begin{pmatrix} 4 \\ 11 \end{pmatrix}$

$\therefore \begin{pmatrix} x \\ y \end{pmatrix} = -\frac{1}{13}\begin{pmatrix} -4 + (-55) \\ -8 + 33 \end{pmatrix} = \begin{pmatrix} \frac{59}{13} \\ \frac{-25}{13} \end{pmatrix}$ and so $x = \frac{59}{13}$, $y = -\frac{25}{13}$

e $\left.\begin{array}{l}4x - 7y = 8 \\ 3x - 5y = 0\end{array}\right\}$ can be written as $\begin{pmatrix} 4 & -7 \\ 3 & -5 \end{pmatrix}\begin{pmatrix} x \\ y \end{pmatrix} = \begin{pmatrix} 8 \\ 0 \end{pmatrix}$

$\therefore \begin{pmatrix} x \\ y \end{pmatrix} = \begin{pmatrix} 4 & -7 \\ 3 & -5 \end{pmatrix}^{-1}\begin{pmatrix} 8 \\ 0 \end{pmatrix} = 1\begin{pmatrix} -5 & 7 \\ -3 & 4 \end{pmatrix}\begin{pmatrix} 8 \\ 0 \end{pmatrix}$

$\therefore \begin{pmatrix} x \\ y \end{pmatrix} = \begin{pmatrix} -40 + 0 \\ -24 + 0 \end{pmatrix}$ and so $x = -40$, $y = -24$

f $\left.\begin{array}{l}7x + 11y = 18 \\ 11x - 7y = -11\end{array}\right\}$ can be written as $\begin{pmatrix} 7 & 11 \\ 11 & -7 \end{pmatrix}\begin{pmatrix} x \\ y \end{pmatrix} = \begin{pmatrix} 18 \\ -11 \end{pmatrix}$

$\therefore \begin{pmatrix} x \\ y \end{pmatrix} = \begin{pmatrix} 7 & 11 \\ 11 & -7 \end{pmatrix}^{-1}\begin{pmatrix} 18 \\ -11 \end{pmatrix}$

$\therefore \begin{pmatrix} x \\ y \end{pmatrix} = \frac{1}{-170}\begin{pmatrix} -7 & -11 \\ -11 & 7 \end{pmatrix}\begin{pmatrix} 18 \\ -11 \end{pmatrix} = -\frac{1}{170}\begin{pmatrix} -126 + 121 \\ -198 - 77 \end{pmatrix}$

$\therefore \begin{pmatrix} x \\ y \end{pmatrix} = -\frac{1}{170}\begin{pmatrix} -5 \\ -275 \end{pmatrix} = \begin{pmatrix} \frac{1}{34} \\ \frac{55}{34} \end{pmatrix}$ and so $x = \frac{1}{34}$, $y = \frac{55}{34}$

3 a If $\mathbf{AX} = \mathbf{B}$ | If $\mathbf{XA} = \mathbf{B}$
then $\mathbf{A}^{-1}\mathbf{AX} = \mathbf{A}^{-1}\mathbf{B}$ {premultiply by $\mathbf{A}^{-1}$} | then $\mathbf{XAA}^{-1} = \mathbf{BA}^{-1}$ {postmultiply by $\mathbf{A}^{-1}$}
$\therefore \mathbf{IX} = \mathbf{A}^{-1}\mathbf{B}$ | $\therefore \mathbf{XI} = \mathbf{BA}^{-1}$
$\therefore \mathbf{X} = \mathbf{A}^{-1}\mathbf{B}$ | $\therefore \mathbf{X} = \mathbf{BA}^{-1}$

b i $\mathbf{X}\begin{pmatrix} 1 & 2 \\ 5 & -1 \end{pmatrix} = \begin{pmatrix} 14 & -5 \\ 22 & 0 \end{pmatrix}$

$\therefore \mathbf{X} = \begin{pmatrix} 14 & -5 \\ 22 & 0 \end{pmatrix}\begin{pmatrix} 1 & 2 \\ 5 & -1 \end{pmatrix}^{-1}$

$= \begin{pmatrix} 14 & -5 \\ 22 & 0 \end{pmatrix}\frac{1}{-11}\begin{pmatrix} -1 & -2 \\ -5 & 1 \end{pmatrix}$

$= -\frac{1}{11}\begin{pmatrix} -14 + 25 & -28 + (-5) \\ -22 + 0 & -44 + 0 \end{pmatrix}$

$= \begin{pmatrix} -1 & 3 \\ 2 & 4 \end{pmatrix}$

ii $\begin{pmatrix} 1 & 3 \\ 2 & -1 \end{pmatrix}\mathbf{X} = \begin{pmatrix} 1 & -3 \\ 4 & 2 \end{pmatrix}$

$\therefore \mathbf{X} = \begin{pmatrix} 1 & 3 \\ 2 & -1 \end{pmatrix}^{-1}\begin{pmatrix} 1 & -3 \\ 4 & 2 \end{pmatrix}$

$= \frac{1}{-7}\begin{pmatrix} -1 & -3 \\ -2 & 1 \end{pmatrix}\begin{pmatrix} 1 & -3 \\ 4 & 2 \end{pmatrix}$

$= -\frac{1}{7}\begin{pmatrix} -1 + (-12) & 3 + (-6) \\ -2 + 4 & 6 + 2 \end{pmatrix}$

$= \begin{pmatrix} \frac{13}{7} & \frac{3}{7} \\ -\frac{2}{7} & -\frac{8}{7} \end{pmatrix}$

4 a i $|A| = 0$ when $2k - (-6) = 0$ $\therefore$ $k = -3$ $\therefore$ A is singular when $k = -3$

   ii $A = \begin{pmatrix} k & 1 \\ -6 & 2 \end{pmatrix}$ $\therefore$ $A^{-1} = \dfrac{1}{2k+6} \begin{pmatrix} 2 & -1 \\ 6 & k \end{pmatrix}$, provided that $k \neq -3$

  b i $|A| = 0$ when $3k - 0 = 0$ $\therefore$ $k = 0$ $\therefore$ A is singular when $k = 0$

   ii $A = \begin{pmatrix} 3 & -1 \\ 0 & k \end{pmatrix}$ $\therefore$ $A^{-1} = \dfrac{1}{3k} \begin{pmatrix} k & 1 \\ 0 & 3 \end{pmatrix}$, provided that $k \neq 0$

  c i $|A| = 0$ when $k(k+1) - 2 = 0$
   $k^2 + k - 2 = 0$
   $(k-1)(k+2) = 0$
   $\therefore$ $k = 1$ or -2 $\therefore$ A is singular when $k = 1$ or -2

   ii $A = \begin{pmatrix} k+1 & 2 \\ 1 & k \end{pmatrix}$ $\therefore$ $A^{-1} = \dfrac{1}{k(k+1) - 2} \begin{pmatrix} k & -2 \\ -1 & k+1 \end{pmatrix}$,

   $= \dfrac{1}{(k+2)(k-1)} \begin{pmatrix} k & -2 \\ -1 & k+1 \end{pmatrix}$, provided that $k \neq -2$ or 1

5 a i $\begin{pmatrix} 2 & -3 \\ 4 & -1 \end{pmatrix} \begin{pmatrix} x \\ y \end{pmatrix} = \begin{pmatrix} 8 \\ 11 \end{pmatrix}$ **b i** $\begin{pmatrix} 2 & k \\ 4 & -1 \end{pmatrix} \begin{pmatrix} x \\ y \end{pmatrix} = \begin{pmatrix} 8 \\ 11 \end{pmatrix}$

   and $|A| = -2 - -12$ and $|A| = -2 - 4k$
   $= -2 + 12$
   $= 10$

   ii As $|A| \neq 0$, the system has a unique solution

   $\begin{pmatrix} x \\ y \end{pmatrix} = \begin{pmatrix} 2 & -3 \\ 4 & -1 \end{pmatrix}^{-1} \begin{pmatrix} 8 \\ 11 \end{pmatrix}$

   $= \tfrac{1}{10} \begin{pmatrix} -1 & 3 \\ -4 & 2 \end{pmatrix} \begin{pmatrix} 8 \\ 11 \end{pmatrix}$

   $= \tfrac{1}{10} \begin{pmatrix} 25 \\ -10 \end{pmatrix}$

   $= \begin{pmatrix} \tfrac{5}{2} \\ -1 \end{pmatrix}$

   $\therefore$ $x = \tfrac{5}{2}$, $y = -1$

   ii The system has a unique solution if
   $-2 - 4k \neq 0$ $\therefore$ $k \neq -\tfrac{1}{2}$

   $\begin{pmatrix} x \\ y \end{pmatrix} = \begin{pmatrix} 2 & k \\ 4 & -1 \end{pmatrix}^{-1} \begin{pmatrix} 8 \\ 11 \end{pmatrix}$

   $= \dfrac{1}{-2-4k} \begin{pmatrix} -1 & -k \\ -4 & 2 \end{pmatrix} \begin{pmatrix} 8 \\ 11 \end{pmatrix}$

   $= \dfrac{1}{-2-4k} \begin{pmatrix} -8 - 11k \\ -10 \end{pmatrix}$

   $\therefore$ $x = \dfrac{8+11k}{2+4k}$, $y = \dfrac{5}{1+2k}$, $k \neq -\tfrac{1}{2}$
   is the unique solution

   iii When $k = -\tfrac{1}{2}$, the equations are
   $\begin{cases} 2x - \tfrac{1}{2}y = 8 \\ 4x - y = 11 \end{cases}$ or $\begin{matrix} 4x - y = 16 \\ 4x - y = 11 \end{matrix}$

   So, we have no solutions (as the lines are parallel and so do not meet).

EXERCISE 13C.3

1 $A = \begin{pmatrix} 2 & 1 \\ 0 & 1 \end{pmatrix}$, $B = \begin{pmatrix} 1 & 2 \\ -1 & 0 \end{pmatrix}$ and $C = \begin{pmatrix} 0 & 3 \\ 1 & 2 \end{pmatrix}$

Since $AXB = C$,   and
then $A^{-1}AXB = A^{-1}C$ {premultiply by A^{-1}} $XBB^{-1} = A^{-1}CB^{-1}$ {postmultiply by B^{-1}}
   $\therefore$ $IXB = A^{-1}C$ $\therefore$ $XI = A^{-1}CB^{-1}$
   $\therefore$ $XB = A^{-1}C$ $\therefore$ $X = A^{-1}CB^{-1}$

$\therefore$ $X = \tfrac{1}{2} \begin{pmatrix} 1 & -1 \\ 0 & 2 \end{pmatrix} \begin{pmatrix} 0 & 3 \\ 1 & 2 \end{pmatrix} \tfrac{1}{2} \begin{pmatrix} 0 & -2 \\ 1 & 1 \end{pmatrix} = \tfrac{1}{4} \begin{pmatrix} 0 + (-1) & 3 + (-2) \\ 0 + 2 & 0 + 4 \end{pmatrix} \begin{pmatrix} 0 & -2 \\ 1 & 1 \end{pmatrix}$

$\therefore$ $X = \tfrac{1}{4} \begin{pmatrix} -1 & 1 \\ 2 & 4 \end{pmatrix} \begin{pmatrix} 0 & -2 \\ 1 & 1 \end{pmatrix} = \tfrac{1}{4} \begin{pmatrix} 0+1 & 2+1 \\ 0+4 & -4+4 \end{pmatrix} = \tfrac{1}{4} \begin{pmatrix} 1 & 3 \\ 4 & 0 \end{pmatrix} = \begin{pmatrix} \tfrac{1}{4} & \tfrac{3}{4} \\ 1 & 0 \end{pmatrix}$

2 a If $A = A^{-1}$, then $A^2 = AA = AA^{-1} = I$

b If $\begin{pmatrix} a & b \\ b & a \end{pmatrix}$ is its own inverse, then $\begin{pmatrix} a & b \\ b & a \end{pmatrix}\begin{pmatrix} a & b \\ b & a \end{pmatrix} = \begin{pmatrix} 1 & 0 \\ 0 & 1 \end{pmatrix}$

$$\therefore \begin{pmatrix} a^2 + b^2 & 2ab \\ 2ab & b^2 + a^2 \end{pmatrix} = \begin{pmatrix} 1 & 0 \\ 0 & 1 \end{pmatrix}$$

$\therefore \quad a^2 + b^2 = 1$ If $2ab = 0$, then $a = 0$ or $b = 0$
and $2ab = 0$ and $b^2 = 1$ and $a^2 = 1$

$\therefore \quad a = 0$ and $b = \pm 1$ $\therefore \quad a = \pm 1$ and $b = 0$

This gives four possible combinations: $\begin{pmatrix} 0 & 1 \\ 1 & 0 \end{pmatrix}, \begin{pmatrix} 0 & -1 \\ -1 & 0 \end{pmatrix}, \begin{pmatrix} 1 & 0 \\ 0 & 1 \end{pmatrix}, \begin{pmatrix} -1 & 0 \\ 0 & -1 \end{pmatrix}$

3 a $A = \begin{pmatrix} 1 & 2 \\ -1 & 0 \end{pmatrix}$ $\therefore \quad A^{-1} = \frac{1}{2}\begin{pmatrix} 0 & -2 \\ 1 & 1 \end{pmatrix} = \begin{pmatrix} 0 & -1 \\ \frac{1}{2} & \frac{1}{2} \end{pmatrix}$

$\therefore \quad (A^{-1})^{-1} = \frac{1}{\frac{1}{2}}\begin{pmatrix} \frac{1}{2} & 1 \\ -\frac{1}{2} & 0 \end{pmatrix} = \begin{pmatrix} 1 & 2 \\ -1 & 0 \end{pmatrix} = A$

b   If $A^{-1} = B$
then $(A^{-1})^{-1}(A^{-1}) = B^{-1}B = I$
and $(A^{-1})(A^{-1})^{-1} = BB^{-1} = I$

c We can deduce from **b** that $(A^{-1})^{-1} = A$ and A is the inverse of A^{-1}.

4 a $A = \begin{pmatrix} 1 & 1 \\ 2 & -1 \end{pmatrix}$, $B = \begin{pmatrix} 0 & 1 \\ 2 & -3 \end{pmatrix}$

i $A^{-1} = \frac{1}{-3}\begin{pmatrix} -1 & -1 \\ -2 & 1 \end{pmatrix} = \begin{pmatrix} \frac{1}{3} & \frac{1}{3} \\ \frac{2}{3} & -\frac{1}{3} \end{pmatrix}$ **ii** $B^{-1} = \frac{1}{-2}\begin{pmatrix} -3 & -1 \\ -2 & 0 \end{pmatrix} = \begin{pmatrix} \frac{3}{2} & \frac{1}{2} \\ 1 & 0 \end{pmatrix}$

iii $(AB)^{-1} = \left[\begin{pmatrix} 1 & 1 \\ 2 & -1 \end{pmatrix}\begin{pmatrix} 0 & 1 \\ 2 & -3 \end{pmatrix}\right]^{-1}$ **iv** $(BA)^{-1} = \left[\begin{pmatrix} 0 & 1 \\ 2 & -3 \end{pmatrix}\begin{pmatrix} 1 & 1 \\ 2 & -1 \end{pmatrix}\right]^{-1}$

$= \begin{pmatrix} 0+2 & 1+(-3) \\ 0+(-2) & 2+3 \end{pmatrix}^{-1}$ $= \begin{pmatrix} 0+2 & 0+(-1) \\ 2+(-6) & 2+3 \end{pmatrix}^{-1}$

$= \begin{pmatrix} 2 & -2 \\ -2 & 5 \end{pmatrix}^{-1}$ $= \begin{pmatrix} 2 & -1 \\ -4 & 5 \end{pmatrix}^{-1}$

$= \frac{1}{6}\begin{pmatrix} 5 & 2 \\ 2 & 2 \end{pmatrix}$ or $\begin{pmatrix} \frac{5}{6} & \frac{1}{3} \\ \frac{1}{3} & \frac{1}{3} \end{pmatrix}$ $= \frac{1}{6}\begin{pmatrix} 5 & 1 \\ 4 & 2 \end{pmatrix}$ or $\begin{pmatrix} \frac{5}{6} & \frac{1}{6} \\ \frac{2}{3} & \frac{1}{3} \end{pmatrix}$

v $A^{-1}B^{-1} = \begin{pmatrix} \frac{1}{3} & \frac{1}{3} \\ \frac{2}{3} & -\frac{1}{3} \end{pmatrix}\begin{pmatrix} \frac{3}{2} & \frac{1}{2} \\ 1 & 0 \end{pmatrix}$ **vi** $B^{-1}A^{-1} = \begin{pmatrix} \frac{3}{2} & \frac{1}{2} \\ 1 & 0 \end{pmatrix}\begin{pmatrix} \frac{1}{3} & \frac{1}{3} \\ \frac{2}{3} & -\frac{1}{3} \end{pmatrix}$

$= \begin{pmatrix} \frac{3}{6}+\frac{1}{3} & \frac{1}{6}+0 \\ \frac{6}{6}+(-\frac{1}{3}) & \frac{2}{6}+0 \end{pmatrix}$ $= \begin{pmatrix} \frac{3}{6}+\frac{2}{6} & \frac{3}{6}+(-\frac{1}{6}) \\ \frac{1}{3}+0 & \frac{1}{3}+0 \end{pmatrix}$

$= \begin{pmatrix} \frac{5}{6} & \frac{1}{6} \\ \frac{2}{3} & \frac{1}{3} \end{pmatrix}$ $= \begin{pmatrix} \frac{5}{6} & \frac{1}{3} \\ \frac{1}{3} & \frac{1}{3} \end{pmatrix}$

b Choose appropriate matrices and repeat question **a**.

c The results of **a** and **b** suggest that $(AB)^{-1} = B^{-1}A^{-1}$ and $(BA)^{-1} = A^{-1}B^{-1}$.

d $(AB)(B^{-1}A^{-1})$ and $(B^{-1}A^{-1})(AB)$ $\therefore \quad (AB)(B^{-1}A^{-1}) = (B^{-1}A^{-1})(AB) = I$
$= A(BB^{-1})A^{-1}$ $= B^{-1}(A^{-1}A)B$ $\therefore \quad AB$ and $B^{-1}A^{-1}$ are inverses.
$= AIA^{-1}$ $= B^{-1}IB$
$= AA^{-1} = I$ $= B^{-1}B = I$

5 $(kA)\left(\frac{1}{k}A^{-1}\right) = k \times \frac{1}{k}(AA^{-1}) = I$ also $\left(\frac{1}{k}A^{-1}\right)(kA) = \frac{1}{k} \times k(A^{-1}A) = I$

$\therefore \quad (kA)\left(\frac{1}{k}A^{-1}\right) = \left(\frac{1}{k}A^{-1}\right)(kA) = I$ $\therefore \quad kA$ and $\frac{1}{k}A^{-1}$ are inverses.

6 $X = AY$ and $Y = BZ$

a $X = AY = A(BZ) = ABZ$

b $(AB)^{-1}X = (AB)^{-1}ABZ$ {premultiply by $(AB)^{-1}$}
$(AB)^{-1}X = IZ$
$\therefore \quad Z = B^{-1}A^{-1}X$ {as $(AB)^{-1} = B^{-1}A^{-1}$}

7 If $A = \begin{pmatrix} 3 & 2 \\ -2 & -1 \end{pmatrix}$, let $A^2 = pA + qI$

$\therefore \quad \begin{pmatrix} 3 & 2 \\ -2 & -1 \end{pmatrix}\begin{pmatrix} 3 & 2 \\ -2 & -1 \end{pmatrix} = p\begin{pmatrix} 3 & 2 \\ -2 & -1 \end{pmatrix} + q\begin{pmatrix} 1 & 0 \\ 0 & 1 \end{pmatrix}$

$\therefore \quad \begin{pmatrix} 9+(-4) & 6+(-2) \\ -6+2 & -4+1 \end{pmatrix} = \begin{pmatrix} 3p & 2p \\ -2p & -p \end{pmatrix} + \begin{pmatrix} q & 0 \\ 0 & q \end{pmatrix}$

$\therefore \quad \begin{pmatrix} 5 & 4 \\ -4 & -3 \end{pmatrix} = \begin{pmatrix} 3p+q & 2p \\ -2p & -p+q \end{pmatrix}$

$\therefore \quad 5 = 3p + q$ and $4 = 2p$
$\therefore \quad p = 2$ and $q = -1$ and $A^2 = 2A - I$

Checking for consistency: $-2p = -2(2) = -4$ ✓
$-p + q = -2 + (-1) = -3$ ✓

Now $A^2 = 2A - I$
$\therefore \quad A^{-1}A^2 = A^{-1}2A - A^{-1}I$ {premultiplying by A^{-1}}
$\therefore \quad A^{-1}AA = 2A^{-1}A - A^{-1}$
$\therefore \quad IA = 2I - A^{-1}$
$\therefore \quad A = 2I - A^{-1}$
$\therefore \quad A^{-1} = 2I - A$

8 In each example we premultiply by A^{-1}.

a $A^2 = 4A - I$
$\therefore \quad A^{-1}A^2 = A^{-1}(4A - I)$
$\therefore \quad A^{-1}AA = 4A^{-1}A - A^{-1}I$
$\therefore \quad IA = 4I - A^{-1}$
$\therefore \quad A - 4I = -A^{-1}$
$\therefore \quad A^{-1} = 4I - A$

b $5A = I - A^2$
$\therefore \quad A^{-1}5A = A^{-1}(I - A^2)$
$\therefore \quad 5A^{-1}A = A^{-1}I - A^{-1}AA$
$\therefore \quad 5I = A^{-1} - IA$
$\therefore \quad 5I = A^{-1} - A$
$\therefore \quad A^{-1} = 5I + A$

c $2I = 3A^2 - 4A$
$\therefore \quad A^{-1}2I = A^{-1}3A^2 - A^{-1}4A$
$\therefore \quad 2A^{-1} = 3A^{-1}AA - 4A^{-1}A$
$\therefore \quad 2A^{-1} = 3IA - 4I$
$\therefore \quad 2A^{-1} = 3A - 4I$
$\therefore \quad A^{-1} = \frac{3}{2}A - 2I$

9 If $AB = A$ and $BA = B$,

then $A^2 = AA$
$= (AB)A$
$= A(BA)$ {associative rule}
$= AB$
$\therefore \quad A^2 = A$

$ab = ac$ implies that $b = c$ for non-zero real numbers, but this property does not hold for matrices.
Thus from $AB = AI = A$ it does not follow that $B = I$.

10   If $AB = AC$
then $A^{-1}AB = A^{-1}AC$ {premultiplying by A^{-1}}
$\therefore$ $IB = IC$
$\therefore$ $B = C$
So, if $AB = AC$ and $|A| \neq 0$
then $B = C$.

11 If $X = P^{-1}AP$ and $A^3 = I$
then $X^3 = (P^{-1}AP)(P^{-1}AP)(P^{-1}AP)$
$= (P^{-1}A)(PP^{-1})A(PP^{-1})AP$
   {associative rule}
$= P^{-1}AIAIAP$
$= P^{-1}AAAP$
$= P^{-1}A^3P$
$= P^{-1}IP$
$= P^{-1}P$ and so $X^3 = I$

12 If $aA^2 + bA + cI = O$
and $X = P^{-1}AP$ then
$aX^2 + bX + cI$
$= a(P^{-1}AP)(P^{-1}AP) + bP^{-1}AP + cI$
$= aP^{-1}A(PP^{-1})AP + bP^{-1}AP + cI$
$= aP^{-1}A^2P + bP^{-1}AP + cI$
$= P^{-1}(aA^2 + bA + cI)P$
$= P^{-1}OP$
$= O$

EXERCISE 13D.1

1 a $\begin{vmatrix} 2 & 3 & 0 \\ -1 & 2 & 1 \\ 2 & 0 & 5 \end{vmatrix} = 2\begin{vmatrix} 2 & 1 \\ 0 & 5 \end{vmatrix} - 3\begin{vmatrix} -1 & 1 \\ 2 & 5 \end{vmatrix} + 0\begin{vmatrix} -1 & 2 \\ 2 & 0 \end{vmatrix} = 2(10-0) - 3(-5-2) + 0 = 41$

b $\begin{vmatrix} -1 & 2 & -3 \\ 1 & 0 & 0 \\ -1 & 2 & 1 \end{vmatrix} = -1\begin{vmatrix} 0 & 0 \\ 2 & 1 \end{vmatrix} - 2\begin{vmatrix} 1 & 0 \\ -1 & 1 \end{vmatrix} + (-3)\begin{vmatrix} 1 & 0 \\ -1 & 2 \end{vmatrix}$
$= -1(0-0) - 2(1-0) - 3(2-0)$
$= -8$

c $\begin{vmatrix} 2 & 1 & 3 \\ -1 & 1 & 2 \\ 2 & 1 & 3 \end{vmatrix} = 2\begin{vmatrix} 1 & 2 \\ 1 & 3 \end{vmatrix} - 1\begin{vmatrix} -1 & 2 \\ 2 & 3 \end{vmatrix} + 3\begin{vmatrix} -1 & 1 \\ 2 & 1 \end{vmatrix}$
$= 2(3-2) - 1(-3-4) + 3(-1-2)$
$= 0$

d $\begin{vmatrix} 1 & 0 & 0 \\ 0 & 2 & 0 \\ 0 & 0 & 3 \end{vmatrix} = 1\begin{vmatrix} 2 & 0 \\ 0 & 3 \end{vmatrix} - 0\begin{vmatrix} 0 & 0 \\ 0 & 3 \end{vmatrix} + 0\begin{vmatrix} 0 & 2 \\ 0 & 0 \end{vmatrix} = 1(6-0) = 6$

e $\begin{vmatrix} 0 & 0 & 2 \\ 0 & 1 & 0 \\ 3 & 0 & 0 \end{vmatrix} = 0\begin{vmatrix} 1 & 0 \\ 0 & 0 \end{vmatrix} - 0\begin{vmatrix} 0 & 0 \\ 3 & 0 \end{vmatrix} + 2\begin{vmatrix} 0 & 1 \\ 3 & 0 \end{vmatrix} = 2(0-3) = -6$

f $\begin{vmatrix} 4 & 1 & 3 \\ -1 & 0 & 2 \\ -1 & 1 & 1 \end{vmatrix} = 4\begin{vmatrix} 0 & 2 \\ 1 & 1 \end{vmatrix} - 1\begin{vmatrix} -1 & 2 \\ -1 & 1 \end{vmatrix} + 3\begin{vmatrix} -1 & 0 \\ -1 & 1 \end{vmatrix}$
$= 4(0-2) - 1(-1--2) + 3(-1-0)$
$= -12$

2 a $\begin{vmatrix} x & 2 & 9 \\ 3 & 1 & 2 \\ -1 & 0 & x \end{vmatrix} = x\begin{vmatrix} 1 & 2 \\ 0 & x \end{vmatrix} - 2\begin{vmatrix} 3 & 2 \\ -1 & x \end{vmatrix} + 9\begin{vmatrix} 3 & 1 \\ -1 & 0 \end{vmatrix}$
$= x(x) - 2(3x - -2) + 9(1)$
$= x^2 - 6x - 4 + 9$
$= x^2 - 6x + 5$
$= (x-5)(x-1)$

The matrix is singular if its determinant is 0, which occurs when $x = 5$ or $x = 1$.

b This means that the matrix has an inverse for all x in $\mathbb{R}$, $x \neq 1$ or 5.

3 a $\begin{vmatrix} a & 0 & 0 \\ 0 & b & 0 \\ 0 & 0 & c \end{vmatrix} = a \begin{vmatrix} b & 0 \\ 0 & c \end{vmatrix} - 0 \begin{vmatrix} 0 & 0 \\ 0 & c \end{vmatrix} + 0 \begin{vmatrix} 0 & b \\ 0 & 0 \end{vmatrix} = a(bc - 0) = abc$

b $\begin{vmatrix} 0 & x & y \\ -x & 0 & z \\ -y & -z & 0 \end{vmatrix} = 0 \begin{vmatrix} 0 & z \\ -z & 0 \end{vmatrix} - x \begin{vmatrix} -x & z \\ -y & 0 \end{vmatrix} + y \begin{vmatrix} -x & 0 \\ -y & -z \end{vmatrix}$

$= -x(0 - -yz) + y(xz)$
$= -xyz + xyz$
$= 0$

c $\begin{vmatrix} a & b & c \\ b & c & a \\ c & a & b \end{vmatrix} = a \begin{vmatrix} c & a \\ a & b \end{vmatrix} - b \begin{vmatrix} b & a \\ c & b \end{vmatrix} + c \begin{vmatrix} b & c \\ c & a \end{vmatrix}$

$= a(cb - a^2) - b(b^2 - ac) + c(ba - c^2)$
$= abc - a^3 - b^3 + abc + abc - c^3$
$= 3abc - a^3 - b^3 - c^3$

4 $\begin{cases} x + 2y - 3z = 5 \\ 2x - y - z = 8 \\ kx + y + 2z = 14 \end{cases}$ has matrix equation $\underbrace{\begin{pmatrix} 1 & 2 & -3 \\ 2 & -1 & -1 \\ k & 1 & 2 \end{pmatrix}}_{\mathbf{A}} \underbrace{\begin{pmatrix} x \\ y \\ z \end{pmatrix}}_{\mathbf{X}} = \underbrace{\begin{pmatrix} 5 \\ 8 \\ 14 \end{pmatrix}}_{\mathbf{B}}$

$\therefore \ \mathbf{X} = \mathbf{A}^{-1}\mathbf{B}$ has a unique solution if $|\mathbf{A}| \neq 0$.

Now $\begin{vmatrix} 1 & 2 & -3 \\ 2 & -1 & -1 \\ k & 1 & 2 \end{vmatrix} = 1 \begin{vmatrix} -1 & -1 \\ 1 & 2 \end{vmatrix} - 2 \begin{vmatrix} 2 & -1 \\ k & 2 \end{vmatrix} + (-3) \begin{vmatrix} 2 & -1 \\ k & 1 \end{vmatrix}$

$= 1(-2 - -1) - 2(4 - -k) - 3(2 - -k)$
$= -1 - 8 - 2k - 6 - 3k$
$= -15 - 5k$

$\therefore$ there is a unique solution for all $k \neq -3$.

5 $\begin{cases} 2x - y - 4z = 8 \\ 3x - ky + z = 1 \\ 5x - y + kz = -2 \end{cases}$ has matrix equation $\underbrace{\begin{pmatrix} 2 & -1 & -4 \\ 3 & -k & 1 \\ 5 & -1 & k \end{pmatrix}}_{\mathbf{A}} \underbrace{\begin{pmatrix} x \\ y \\ z \end{pmatrix}}_{\mathbf{X}} = \underbrace{\begin{pmatrix} 8 \\ 1 \\ -2 \end{pmatrix}}_{\mathbf{B}}$

This has a unique solution if $|\mathbf{A}| \neq 0$.

Now $\begin{vmatrix} 2 & -1 & -4 \\ 3 & -k & 1 \\ 5 & -1 & k \end{vmatrix} = 2 \begin{vmatrix} -k & 1 \\ -1 & k \end{vmatrix} - (-1) \begin{vmatrix} 3 & 1 \\ 5 & k \end{vmatrix} + (-4) \begin{vmatrix} 3 & -k \\ 5 & -1 \end{vmatrix}$

$= 2(-k^2 - -1) + 1(3k - 5) - 4(-3 - -5k)$
$= -2k^2 + 2 + 3k - 5 + 12 - 20k$
$= -2k^2 - 17k + 9$
$= -(2k^2 + 17k - 9)$
$= -(2k - 1)(k + 9)$

$\therefore$ there is a unique solution for all $k \neq \frac{1}{2}$ or -9.

6 a $\begin{vmatrix} 1 & k & 3 \\ k & 1 & -1 \\ 3 & 4 & 2 \end{vmatrix} = 7 \quad \therefore \quad 1 \begin{vmatrix} 1 & -1 \\ 4 & 2 \end{vmatrix} - k \begin{vmatrix} k & -1 \\ 3 & 2 \end{vmatrix} + 3 \begin{vmatrix} k & 1 \\ 3 & 4 \end{vmatrix} = 7$

$\therefore \ 1(2 - -4) - k(2k - -3) + 3(4k - 3) = 7$
$\therefore \ 6 - 2k^2 - 3k + 12k - 9 = 7$
$\therefore \ 2k^2 - 9k + 10 = 0$
$\therefore \ (2k - 5)(k - 2) = 0$
and so $k = \frac{5}{2}$ or 2

b
$$\begin{vmatrix} k & 2 & 1 \\ 2 & k & 2 \\ 1 & 2 & k \end{vmatrix} = 0$$

$$\therefore \quad k \begin{vmatrix} k & 2 \\ 2 & k \end{vmatrix} - 2 \begin{vmatrix} 2 & 2 \\ 1 & k \end{vmatrix} + 1 \begin{vmatrix} 2 & k \\ 1 & 2 \end{vmatrix} = 0$$

$$\therefore \quad k(k^2 - 4) - 2(2k - 2) + (4 - k) = 0$$
$$\therefore \quad k^3 - 4k - 4k + 4 + 4 - k = 0$$
$$\therefore \quad k^3 - 9k + 8 = 0$$

Using technology there is one rational zero, $k = 1$

$$\therefore \quad (k - 1)(k^2 + k - 8) = 0$$

$$\therefore \quad k = 1 \quad \text{or} \quad k = \frac{-1 \pm \sqrt{1 - 4(1)(-8)}}{2} = \frac{-1 \pm \sqrt{33}}{2}$$

7 Using technology:

a $\begin{vmatrix} 1 & 2 & 3 & 1 \\ 2 & 0 & 1 & 2 \\ 3 & 1 & 4 & 0 \\ 1 & 2 & 0 & 5 \end{vmatrix} = 16$, inverse $= \begin{pmatrix} -\frac{21}{16} & -\frac{17}{16} & \frac{5}{4} & \frac{11}{16} \\ -\frac{17}{16} & -\frac{29}{16} & \frac{5}{4} & \frac{15}{16} \\ \frac{5}{4} & \frac{5}{4} & -1 & -\frac{3}{4} \\ \frac{11}{16} & \frac{15}{16} & -\frac{3}{4} & \frac{-5}{16} \end{pmatrix}$

b $\begin{vmatrix} 1 & 2 & 3 & 4 & 6 \\ 2 & 3 & 4 & 5 & 0 \\ 1 & 2 & 0 & 1 & 4 \\ 2 & 1 & 0 & 1 & 5 \\ 3 & 0 & 1 & 2 & 1 \end{vmatrix} = -34$, inverse $= \begin{pmatrix} -\frac{1}{2} & \frac{1}{2} & -1 & \frac{3}{2} & -\frac{1}{2} \\ -\frac{15}{34} & \frac{1}{2} & -\frac{4}{17} & \frac{29}{34} & -\frac{23}{34} \\ -\frac{29}{34} & \frac{3}{2} & -\frac{61}{17} & \frac{149}{34} & -\frac{83}{34} \\ \frac{39}{34} & -\frac{3}{2} & \frac{58}{17} & -\frac{157}{34} & \frac{87}{34} \\ \frac{1}{17} & 0 & -\frac{4}{17} & \frac{6}{17} & -\frac{3}{17} \end{pmatrix}$

8 a Let o, a, p, c, l represent (respectively) the cost (in dollars) of each orange, apple, pear, cabbage and lettuce. The system, in matrix form, becomes:

$$\underbrace{\begin{pmatrix} 1 & 2 & 1 & 1 & 1 \\ 2 & 1 & 2 & 1 & 1 \\ 1 & 2 & 3 & 1 & 1 \\ 2 & 2 & 1 & 1 & 3 \\ 3 & 3 & 5 & 2 & 2 \end{pmatrix}}_{\mathbf{A}} \underbrace{\begin{pmatrix} o \\ a \\ p \\ c \\ l \end{pmatrix}}_{\mathbf{X}} = \underbrace{\begin{pmatrix} 6.3 \\ 6.7 \\ 7.7 \\ 9.8 \\ 10.9 \end{pmatrix}}_{\mathbf{B}}$$

b $\mathbf{X} = \mathbf{A}^{-1}\mathbf{B}$
Using technology, $|\mathbf{A}| = 0$,
$\therefore \quad \mathbf{A}^{-1}$ does not exist and $\mathbf{X}$ cannot be found using this information.

c If the last line is amended, the matrix $\mathbf{A}$ becomes

$$\mathbf{A} = \begin{pmatrix} 1 & 2 & 1 & 1 & 1 \\ 2 & 1 & 2 & 1 & 1 \\ 1 & 2 & 3 & 1 & 1 \\ 2 & 2 & 1 & 1 & 3 \\ 3 & 1 & 2 & 2 & 1 \end{pmatrix} \quad \text{and} \quad \det \mathbf{A} = 6$$

$$\therefore \quad \mathbf{X} = \mathbf{A}^{-1}\mathbf{B} = \begin{pmatrix} 1 & 2 & 1 & 1 & 1 \\ 2 & 1 & 2 & 1 & 1 \\ 1 & 2 & 3 & 1 & 1 \\ 2 & 2 & 1 & 1 & 3 \\ 3 & 1 & 2 & 2 & 1 \end{pmatrix}^{-1} \begin{pmatrix} 6.3 \\ 6.7 \\ 7.7 \\ 9.8 \\ 9.2 \end{pmatrix} = \begin{pmatrix} 0.5 \\ 0.8 \\ 0.7 \\ 2 \\ 1.5 \end{pmatrix} \quad \text{\{using technology\}}$$

$\therefore$ oranges cost 50 cents, apples cost 80 cents, pears cost 70 cents, cabbages cost \$2.00, and lettuces cost \$1.50.

EXERCISE 13D.2

1 $\begin{pmatrix} 2 & 0 & 3 \\ 1 & 5 & 2 \\ 1 & -3 & 1 \end{pmatrix} \begin{pmatrix} -11 & 9 & 15 \\ -1 & 1 & 1 \\ 8 & -6 & -10 \end{pmatrix} = \begin{pmatrix} 2 & 0 & 0 \\ 0 & 2 & 0 \\ 0 & 0 & 2 \end{pmatrix} = 2\mathbf{I}$

$$\therefore \begin{pmatrix} 2 & 0 & 3 \\ 1 & 5 & 2 \\ 1 & -3 & 1 \end{pmatrix} \times \tfrac{1}{2} \begin{pmatrix} -11 & 9 & 15 \\ -1 & 1 & 1 \\ 8 & -6 & -10 \end{pmatrix} = I \quad \text{and so} \quad \begin{pmatrix} 2 & 0 & 3 \\ 1 & 5 & 2 \\ 1 & -3 & 1 \end{pmatrix}^{-1} = \begin{pmatrix} -\tfrac{11}{2} & \tfrac{9}{2} & \tfrac{15}{2} \\ -\tfrac{1}{2} & \tfrac{1}{2} & \tfrac{1}{2} \\ 4 & -3 & -5 \end{pmatrix}$$

2 **a** $A^{-1} = \begin{pmatrix} \tfrac{5}{4} & \tfrac{3}{4} & -\tfrac{7}{4} \\ -\tfrac{1}{4} & -\tfrac{3}{4} & \tfrac{3}{4} \\ -\tfrac{3}{4} & -\tfrac{1}{4} & \tfrac{5}{4} \end{pmatrix}$ **b** $A^{-1} = \begin{pmatrix} -\tfrac{11}{2} & \tfrac{9}{2} & \tfrac{15}{2} \\ -\tfrac{1}{2} & \tfrac{1}{2} & \tfrac{1}{2} \\ 4 & -3 & -5 \end{pmatrix}$

3 **a** $B^{-1} \approx \begin{pmatrix} 0.050\,23 & -0.011\,48 & -0.066\,34 \\ 4.212 \times 10^{-4} & 0.013\,53 & 0.027\,75 \\ -0.029\,90 & 0.039\,33 & 0.030\,06 \end{pmatrix} \approx \begin{pmatrix} 0.050 & -0.011 & -0.066 \\ 0.000 & 0.014 & 0.028 \\ -0.030 & 0.039 & 0.030 \end{pmatrix}$

b $B^{-1} \approx \begin{pmatrix} 1.596 & -0.9964 & -0.1686 \\ -3.224 & 1.925 & 0.6291 \\ 2.000 & -1.086 & -0.3958 \end{pmatrix} \approx \begin{pmatrix} 1.596 & -0.996 & -0.169 \\ -3.224 & 1.925 & 0.629 \\ 2.000 & -1.086 & -0.396 \end{pmatrix}$

4 Check that $AA^{-1} = I$ in **2**, and $BB^{-1} = I$ in **3**.

EXERCISE 13E

1 **a** $\left.\begin{array}{r} x - y - z = 2 \\ x + y + 3z = 7 \\ 9x - y - 3z = -1 \end{array}\right\}$ has matrix equation $\begin{pmatrix} 1 & -1 & -1 \\ 1 & 1 & 3 \\ 9 & -1 & -3 \end{pmatrix} \begin{pmatrix} x \\ y \\ z \end{pmatrix} = \begin{pmatrix} 2 \\ 7 \\ -1 \end{pmatrix}$

b $\left.\begin{array}{r} 2x + y - z = 3 \\ y + 2z = 6 \\ x - y + z = 13 \end{array}\right\}$ has matrix equation $\begin{pmatrix} 2 & 1 & -1 \\ 0 & 1 & 2 \\ 1 & -1 & 1 \end{pmatrix} \begin{pmatrix} x \\ y \\ z \end{pmatrix} = \begin{pmatrix} 3 \\ 6 \\ 13 \end{pmatrix}$

c $\left.\begin{array}{r} a + b - c = 7 \\ a - b + c = 6 \\ 2a + b - 3c = -2 \end{array}\right\}$ has matrix equation $\begin{pmatrix} 1 & 1 & -1 \\ 1 & -1 & 1 \\ 2 & 1 & -3 \end{pmatrix} \begin{pmatrix} a \\ b \\ c \end{pmatrix} = \begin{pmatrix} 7 \\ 6 \\ -2 \end{pmatrix}$

2 $AB = \begin{pmatrix} 2 & 1 & -1 \\ -1 & 2 & 1 \\ 0 & 6 & 1 \end{pmatrix} \begin{pmatrix} 4 & 7 & -3 \\ -1 & -2 & 1 \\ 6 & 12 & -5 \end{pmatrix}$

$= \begin{pmatrix} 8 - 1 - 6 & 14 - 2 - 12 & -6 + 1 + 5 \\ -4 - 2 + 6 & -7 - 4 + 12 & 3 + 2 - 5 \\ 0 - 6 + 6 & 0 - 12 + 12 & 0 + 6 - 5 \end{pmatrix}$

$= \begin{pmatrix} 1 & 0 & 0 \\ 0 & 1 & 0 \\ 0 & 0 & 1 \end{pmatrix}$ $\therefore AB = I$ and so $A = B^{-1}$

$\left.\begin{array}{r} 4a + 7b - 3c = -8 \\ -a - 2b + c = 3 \\ 6a + 12b - 5c = -15 \end{array}\right\}$ has matrix equation $\begin{pmatrix} 4 & 7 & -3 \\ -1 & -2 & 1 \\ 6 & 12 & -5 \end{pmatrix} \begin{pmatrix} a \\ b \\ c \end{pmatrix} = \begin{pmatrix} -8 \\ 3 \\ -15 \end{pmatrix}$

$\therefore \begin{pmatrix} a \\ b \\ c \end{pmatrix} = \begin{pmatrix} 4 & 7 & -3 \\ -1 & -2 & 1 \\ 6 & 12 & -5 \end{pmatrix}^{-1} \begin{pmatrix} -8 \\ 3 \\ -15 \end{pmatrix}$

$\therefore \begin{pmatrix} a \\ b \\ c \end{pmatrix} \approx \begin{pmatrix} 2 & 1 & -1 \\ -1 & 2 & 1 \\ 0 & 6 & 1 \end{pmatrix} \begin{pmatrix} -8 \\ 3 \\ -15 \end{pmatrix}$

$\therefore \begin{pmatrix} a \\ b \\ c \end{pmatrix} = \begin{pmatrix} -16 + 3 + 15 \\ 8 + 6 - 15 \\ 0 + 18 - 15 \end{pmatrix} = \begin{pmatrix} 2 \\ -1 \\ 3 \end{pmatrix}$ $\therefore a = 2, \; b = -1, \; c = 3$

3 $MN = \begin{pmatrix} 5 & 3 & -7 \\ -1 & -3 & 3 \\ -3 & -1 & 5 \end{pmatrix} \begin{pmatrix} 3 & 2 & 3 \\ 1 & -1 & 2 \\ 2 & 1 & 3 \end{pmatrix}$

$= \begin{pmatrix} 15+3-14 & 10-3-7 & 15+6-21 \\ -3-3+6 & -2+3+3 & -3-6+9 \\ -9-1+10 & -6+1+5 & -9-2+15 \end{pmatrix}$

$= \begin{pmatrix} 4 & 0 & 0 \\ 0 & 4 & 0 \\ 0 & 0 & 4 \end{pmatrix} = 4I \quad \therefore \quad (\tfrac{1}{4}M)N = I \text{ and so } \tfrac{1}{4}M = N^{-1}$

Now $\left.\begin{array}{r} 3u + 2v + 3w = 18 \\ u - v + 2w = 6 \\ 2u + v + 3w = 16 \end{array}\right\}$ has matrix equation $\begin{pmatrix} 3 & 2 & 3 \\ 1 & -1 & 2 \\ 2 & 1 & 3 \end{pmatrix} \begin{pmatrix} u \\ v \\ w \end{pmatrix} = \begin{pmatrix} 18 \\ 6 \\ 16 \end{pmatrix}$

$\therefore \quad \begin{pmatrix} u \\ v \\ w \end{pmatrix} = \begin{pmatrix} 3 & 2 & 3 \\ 1 & -1 & 2 \\ 2 & 1 & 3 \end{pmatrix}^{-1} \begin{pmatrix} 18 \\ 6 \\ 16 \end{pmatrix} = \tfrac{1}{4} \begin{pmatrix} 5 & 3 & -7 \\ -1 & -3 & 3 \\ -3 & -1 & 5 \end{pmatrix} \begin{pmatrix} 18 \\ 6 \\ 16 \end{pmatrix}$

$\therefore \quad \begin{pmatrix} u \\ v \\ w \end{pmatrix} = \tfrac{1}{4} \begin{pmatrix} 90+18-112 \\ -18-18+48 \\ -54-6+80 \end{pmatrix} = \tfrac{1}{4} \begin{pmatrix} -4 \\ 12 \\ 20 \end{pmatrix} = \begin{pmatrix} -1 \\ 3 \\ 5 \end{pmatrix} \quad \therefore \quad u = -1, \quad v = 3, \quad w = 5$

4 a $\begin{pmatrix} 3 & 2 & -1 \\ 1 & -1 & 2 \\ 2 & 3 & -1 \end{pmatrix} \begin{pmatrix} x \\ y \\ z \end{pmatrix} = \begin{pmatrix} 14 \\ -8 \\ 13 \end{pmatrix}$

Using technology, $x = \tfrac{23}{10}$, $y = \tfrac{13}{10}$, $z = -\tfrac{9}{2}$

$\therefore \quad \begin{pmatrix} x \\ y \\ z \end{pmatrix} = \begin{pmatrix} 3 & 2 & -1 \\ 1 & -1 & 2 \\ 2 & 3 & -1 \end{pmatrix}^{-1} \begin{pmatrix} 14 \\ -8 \\ 13 \end{pmatrix}$

b $\begin{pmatrix} 1 & -1 & -2 \\ 5 & 1 & 2 \\ 3 & -4 & -1 \end{pmatrix} \begin{pmatrix} x \\ y \\ z \end{pmatrix} = \begin{pmatrix} 4 \\ -6 \\ 17 \end{pmatrix}$

Using technology, $x = -\tfrac{1}{3}$, $y = -\tfrac{95}{21}$, $z = \tfrac{2}{21}$

$\therefore \quad \begin{pmatrix} x \\ y \\ z \end{pmatrix} = \begin{pmatrix} 1 & -1 & -2 \\ 5 & 1 & 2 \\ 3 & -4 & -1 \end{pmatrix}^{-1} \begin{pmatrix} 4 \\ -6 \\ 17 \end{pmatrix}$

c $\begin{pmatrix} 1 & 3 & -1 \\ 2 & 1 & 1 \\ 1 & -1 & -2 \end{pmatrix} \begin{pmatrix} x \\ y \\ z \end{pmatrix} = \begin{pmatrix} 15 \\ 7 \\ 0 \end{pmatrix}$

Using technology, $x = 2$, $y = 4$, $z = -1$

$\therefore \quad \begin{pmatrix} x \\ y \\ z \end{pmatrix} = \begin{pmatrix} 1 & 3 & -1 \\ 2 & 1 & 1 \\ 1 & -1 & -2 \end{pmatrix}^{-1} \begin{pmatrix} 15 \\ 7 \\ 0 \end{pmatrix}$

5 a $x = 2, \; y = -1, \; z = 5$ **b** $x = 4, \; y = -2, \; z = 1$
   c $x = 4, \; y = -3, \; z = 2$ **d** $x = 4, \; y = 6, \; z = -7$
   e $x = 3, \; y = 11, \; z = -7$ **f** $x \approx 0.326, \; y \approx 7.65, \; z \approx 4.16$

6 a Let x be the cost of a football in dollars,
        y be the cost of baseball in dollars, and
        z be the cost of a basketball in dollars.
  b Using technology, $x = 14$, $y = 11$, $z = 17$.
    Cost of 4 footballs and 5 baseballs is $4x + 5y = 4(14) + 5(11) = \$111$
    $\therefore$ amount left for basketballs is $\$315 - \$111 = \$204$
    Number of basketballs bought $= \tfrac{204}{17} = 12$

7 **a** System of equations is: $2x + 3y + 8z = 352$
$$x + 5y + 4z = 274$$
$$x + 2y + 11z = 351$$

  b Using technology, $x = 42$, $y = 28$, $z = 23$.
  So, the salaries are: manager €42 000, clerk €28 000 and labourer €23 000.

  c Salary bill is $3x + 8y + 37z$
$$= 3(42) + 8(28) + 37(23)$$
$$= 1201 \text{ thousands of euros} \quad \text{or} \quad €1\,201\,000$$

8 Let x be the cost in dollars of 1 kg of cashews,
    y be the cost in dollars of 1 kg of macadamias, and
    z be the cost in dollars of 1 kg of Brazil nuts.
The cost of 1 kg of mix A is $0.5x + 0.3y + 0.2z = 12.5$,
the cost of 1 kg of mix B is $0.2x + 0.4y + 0.4z = 12.4$,
the cost of 1 kg of mix C is $0.6x + 0.1y + 0.3z = 11.7$.
Using technology, $x = 12$, $y = 15$ and $z = 10$
So, the cost of 1 kg of cashews is \$12, the cost of 1 kg of macadamias is \$15 and the cost of 1 kg of Brazil nuts is \$10.
  Cost per kg of 400 g cashews, 200 g macadamias and 400 g Brazil nuts
$= 0.4 \times 12 + 0.2 \times 15 + 0.4 \times 10 \quad \text{dollars}$
$= \$11.80$

9 **a** Number of students who study Chemistry is $\frac{1}{3}p + \frac{1}{3}q + \frac{2}{5}r = 27$ ..... (1)
    number of students who study Maths is $\frac{1}{2}p + \frac{2}{3}q + \frac{1}{5}r = 35$ ..... (2)
    number of students who study Geography is $\frac{1}{4}p + \frac{1}{3}q + \frac{3}{5}r = 30$ ..... (3)
  The required system of equations is $5p + 5q + 6r = 405$ $\{(1) \times 15\}$
$$15p + 20q + 6r = 1050 \quad \{(2) \times 30\}$$
$$15p + 20q + 36r = 1800 \quad \{(3) \times 60\}$$

  b Using technology, $p = 24$, $q = 27$, $r = 25$.

10 **a** As t is the number of years after 2004, then
    profit in year 2004 is $P(0) = b + \dfrac{c}{4} = 160\,000$
    profit in year 2005 is $P(1) = a + b + \dfrac{c}{5} = 198\,000$
    profit in year 2006 is $P(2) = 2a + b + \dfrac{c}{6} = 240\,000$
    Using technology, $a = 50\,000$, $b = 100\,000$ and $c = 240\,000$.

  b Using the model given, the profit in 2003 would be
$$P(-1) = -a + b + \dfrac{c}{3} = -50\,000 + 100\,000 + 80\,000 = 130\,000$$
  $\therefore$ the profit would be £130 000, which fits the model.

  c Predicted profit in 2007 is $P(3) = 3a + b + \dfrac{c}{7} = 3(50\,000) + 100\,000 + \dfrac{240\,000}{7}$
$$\approx £284\,000$$
    Predicted profit in 2009 is $P(5) = 5a + b + \dfrac{c}{9} = 5(50\,000) + 100\,000 + \dfrac{240\,000}{9}$
$$\approx £377\,000$$

EXERCISE 13F.1

1 a In augmented matrix form, the system is:

$$\begin{pmatrix} 1 & -2 & | & 8 \\ 4 & 1 & | & 5 \end{pmatrix} \sim \begin{pmatrix} 1 & -2 & | & 8 \\ 0 & 9 & | & -27 \end{pmatrix} \leftarrow \text{Replace } R_2 \text{ with } R_2 - 4R_1$$

$$\begin{array}{rrr} 4 & 1 & 5 \\ -4 & 8 & -32 \\ \hline 0 & 9 & -27 \end{array}$$

From R_2, $9y = -27$ Now $x - 2y = 8$
$\therefore y = -3$ $\therefore x - 2(-3) = 8$
    $\therefore x = 2$

So, the solution is $x = 2$, $y = -3$.

b In augmented matrix form, the system is:

$$\begin{pmatrix} 4 & 5 & | & 21 \\ 5 & -3 & | & -20 \end{pmatrix} \sim \begin{pmatrix} 4 & 5 & | & 21 \\ 0 & -37 & | & -185 \end{pmatrix} \leftarrow \text{Replace } R_2 \text{ with } 4R_2 - 5R_1$$

$$\begin{array}{rrr} 20 & -12 & -80 \\ -20 & -25 & -105 \\ \hline 0 & -37 & -185 \end{array}$$

From R_2, $-37y = -185$ Now $4x + 5y = 21$
$\therefore y = 5$ $\therefore 4x + 25 = 21$
    $\therefore 4x = -4$
    $\therefore x = -1$

So, the solution is $x = -1$, $y = 5$.

c In augmented matrix form, the system is:

$$\begin{pmatrix} 3 & 1 & | & -10 \\ 2 & 5 & | & -24 \end{pmatrix} \sim \begin{pmatrix} 3 & 1 & | & -10 \\ 0 & 13 & | & -52 \end{pmatrix} \leftarrow \text{Replace } R_2 \text{ with } 3R_2 - 2R_1$$

$$\begin{array}{rrr} 6 & 15 & -72 \\ -6 & -2 & 20 \\ \hline 0 & 13 & -52 \end{array}$$

From R_2, $13y = -52$ Now $3x + y = -10$
$\therefore y = -4$ $\therefore 3x + (-4) = -10$
    $\therefore 3x = -6$
    $\therefore x = -2$

So, the solution is $x = -2$, $y = -4$.

2 a One equation is not a multiple of the other and their gradients are not the same, so the lines are intersecting.

b $x + y = 7$ can be written as $3x + 3y = 21$ and the other line is $3x + 3y = 1$,
$\therefore$ the lines are parallel.

c The lines intersect at $(2\frac{1}{2}, 2)$.

d $x - 2y = 4$ can be written as $2x - 4y = 8$, so the lines are coincident.

e The lines are intersecting.

f $3x - 4y = 5$ can be written as $-3x + 4y = -5$ and the other line is $-3x + 4y = 2$,
$\therefore$ the lines are parallel.

3 a $x + 2y = 3$ can be written as $2x + 4y = 6$, $\therefore$ the equations represent coincident lines. So, there are an infinite number of solutions (all the points on the line).

b As the second equation is an exact multiple of the first, it will give the same solutions as the first so it can be ignored.

c **i** If $x = t$, $t + 2y = 3$
$\therefore 2y = 3 - t$
$\therefore y = \dfrac{3-t}{2}$ $\therefore$ the solutions are $x = t$, $y = \dfrac{3-t}{2}$, $t \in \mathbb{R}$.

ii If $y = s$, $x + 2s = 3$
$\therefore x = 3 - 2s$ $\therefore$ the solutions are $x = 3 - 2s$, $y = s$, $s \in \mathbb{R}$.

4 a In augmented matrix form, the system is:

$$\begin{pmatrix} 2 & 3 & | & 5 \\ 2 & 3 & | & 11 \end{pmatrix} \sim \begin{pmatrix} 2 & 3 & | & 5 \\ 0 & 0 & | & 6 \end{pmatrix} \leftarrow \text{Replace } R_2 \text{ with } R_2 - R_1$$

$$\begin{array}{rrr} 2 & 3 & 11 \\ -2 & -3 & -5 \\ \hline 0 & 0 & 6 \end{array}$$

R_2 shows $0x + 0y = 6$ $\therefore$ there are no solutions {the lines are parallel}

b In augmented matrix form, the system is:

$$\begin{pmatrix} 2 & 3 & | & 5 \\ 4 & 6 & | & 10 \end{pmatrix} \sim \begin{pmatrix} 2 & 3 & | & 5 \\ 0 & 0 & | & 0 \end{pmatrix} \leftarrow \text{Replace } R_2 \text{ with } R_2 - 2R_1$$

$$\begin{array}{rrr} 4 & 6 & 10 \\ -4 & -6 & -10 \\ \hline 0 & 0 & 0 \end{array}$$

R_2 shows $0x + 0y = 0$, which is true for all x and y.
So, there are infinitely many solutions {the lines are coincident}.

5 a In augmented matrix form, the system is:

$$\begin{pmatrix} 3 & -1 & | & 2 \\ 6 & -2 & | & 4 \end{pmatrix} \sim \begin{pmatrix} 3 & -1 & | & 2 \\ 0 & 0 & | & 0 \end{pmatrix} \leftarrow \text{Replace } R_2 \text{ with } R_2 - 2R_1$$

$$\begin{array}{rrr} 6 & -2 & 4 \\ -6 & 2 & -4 \\ \hline 0 & 0 & 0 \end{array}$$

R_2 shows $0x + 0y = 0$, which is true for all x and y.
So, there are infinitely many solutions {the lines are coincident}.
Substitute $x = t$ in the first equation $3x - y = 2$
$\therefore$ $3t - y = 2$
$y = 3t - 2$
So, the solutions have form $x = t$, $y = 3t - 2$, t in $\mathbb{R}$.

b $3x - y = 2$ ...... (1)
$6x - 2y = k$ ...... (2)
If $k = 4$ then $6x - 2y = 4$, which is an exact multiple ($\times 2$) of equation (1), $\therefore$ the lines are coincident and there are an infinite number of solutions of the form $x = t$, $y = 3t - 2$, t in $\mathbb{R}$.
If $k \neq 4$ then the equations represent parallel lines $\therefore$ there are no solutions.

6 a In augmented matrix form, the system is:

$$\begin{pmatrix} 3 & -1 & | & 8 \\ 6 & -2 & | & k \end{pmatrix} \sim \begin{pmatrix} 3 & -1 & | & 8 \\ 0 & 0 & | & k - 16 \end{pmatrix} \leftarrow \text{Replace } R_2 \text{ with } R_2 - 2R_1$$

$$\begin{array}{rrr} 6 & -2 & k \\ -6 & 2 & -16 \\ \hline 0 & 0 & k-16 \end{array}$$

b If $k = 16$ there are infinitely many solutions.
c Substitute $x = t$ in $3x - y = 8$, then $3t - y = 8$ $\therefore$ $y = 3t - 8$.
The solutions are $x = t$, $y = 3t - 8$, t in $\mathbb{R}$.
d The system has no solutions when $k - 16 \neq 0$, $\therefore$ $k \neq 16$.

7 a In augmented matrix form, the system is:

$$\begin{pmatrix} 4 & 8 & | & 1 \\ 2 & -a & | & 11 \end{pmatrix} \sim \begin{pmatrix} 4 & 8 & | & 1 \\ 0 & -2a-8 & | & 21 \end{pmatrix} \leftarrow \text{Replace } R_2 \text{ with } 2R_2 - R_1$$

$$\begin{array}{rrr} 4 & -2a & 22 \\ -4 & -8 & -1 \\ \hline 0 & -2a-8 & 21 \end{array}$$

b A unique solution exists provided $-2a - 8 \neq 0$ $\therefore$ $a \neq -4$.
c From R_2, $(-2a - 8)y = 21$

$\therefore$ $y = \dfrac{-21}{2a + 8}$

and $4x + 8y = 1$

$\therefore$ $4x + 8\left(\dfrac{-21}{2a + 8}\right) = 1$

$\therefore$ $4x(2a + 8) - 168 = 2a + 8$
$\therefore$ $2x(2a + 8) - 84 = a + 4$
$\therefore$ $2x(2a + 8) = a + 88$

$\therefore$ $x = \dfrac{a + 88}{4a + 16}$

The solution is $x = \dfrac{a+88}{4a+16}$, $y = \dfrac{-21}{2a+8}$, $a \neq -4$.

d When $a = -4$ there are no solutions as the lines are parallel.

8 In augmented matrix form, the system is:

$\begin{pmatrix} m & 2 & | & 6 \\ 2 & m & | & 6 \end{pmatrix}$

$\sim \begin{pmatrix} m & 2 & | & 6 \\ 0 & m^2-4 & | & 6m-12 \end{pmatrix}$ ← Replace R_2 with $mR_2 - 2R_1$

$\begin{array}{ccc} 2m & m^2 & 6m \\ -2m & -4 & -12 \\ \hline 0 & m^2-4 & 6m-12 \end{array}$

A unique solution exists provided $m^2 - 4 \neq 0$.
So, there is a unique solution for all m except $m = \pm 2$.

a In R_2, $(m^2 - 4)y = 6m - 12$

$\therefore \; y = \dfrac{6(m-2)}{(m-2)(m+2)}$

$\therefore \; y = \dfrac{6}{m+2}$ provided $m \neq \pm 2$

Substituting in $mx + 2y = 6$

gives $mx + 2\left(\dfrac{6}{m+2}\right) = 6$

$\therefore \; m(m+2)x + 12 = 6(m+2)$
$\therefore \; m(m+2)x = 6m + 12 - 12$
$\therefore \; m(m+2)x = 6m$
$\therefore \; x = \dfrac{6}{m+2}$

So, the unique solution is $x = \dfrac{6}{m+2}$, $y = \dfrac{6}{m+2}$ when $m \neq \pm 2$.

b When $m = 2$, the equations are $2x + 2y = 6$ and $2x + 2y = 6$, $\therefore$ the lines are coincident. So, there are an infinite number of solutions of the form $x = t$, $y = \dfrac{6 - 2t}{2} = 3 - t$ for all t in $\mathbb{R}$.

When $m = -2$, the equations are $-2x + 2y = 6$ and $2x - 2y = 6$
or $-2x + 2y = -6$

$\therefore$ the lines are parallel and there are no solutions.

EXERCISE 13F.2

1 a In augmented matrix form, the system is:

$\begin{pmatrix} 1 & -2 & 5 & | & 1 \\ 2 & -4 & 8 & | & 2 \\ -3 & 6 & 7 & | & -3 \end{pmatrix}$

$\sim \begin{pmatrix} 1 & -2 & 5 & | & 1 \\ 0 & 0 & -2 & | & 0 \\ 0 & 0 & 22 & | & 0 \end{pmatrix}$ $\begin{array}{l} R_2 \to R_2 - 2R_1 \\ R_3 \to R_3 + 3R_1 \end{array}$

$\begin{array}{cccc} 2 & -4 & 8 & 2 \\ -2 & 4 & -10 & -2 \\ \hline 0 & 0 & -2 & 0 \end{array}$

$\begin{array}{cccc} -3 & 6 & 7 & -3 \\ 3 & -6 & 15 & 3 \\ \hline 0 & 0 & 22 & 0 \end{array}$

Rows 2 and 3 show $-2z = 0$ and $22z = 0$, so $z = 0$.
Row 1 becomes $x - 2y + 5(0) = 1$
let $y = t$, then $x - 2t = 1$
$\therefore \; x = 1 + 2t$

$\therefore$ there are infinitely many solutions of the form $x = 1 + 2t$, $y = t$, $z = 0$, $t \in \mathbb{R}$.

b In augmented matrix form, the system is:

$\begin{pmatrix} 1 & 4 & 11 & | & 7 \\ 1 & 6 & 17 & | & 9 \\ 1 & 4 & 8 & | & 4 \end{pmatrix}$

$\sim \begin{pmatrix} 1 & 4 & 11 & | & 7 \\ 0 & 2 & 6 & | & 2 \\ 0 & 0 & -3 & | & -3 \end{pmatrix}$ $\begin{array}{l} R_2 \to R_2 - R_1 \\ R_3 \to R_3 - R_1 \end{array}$

$\begin{array}{cccc} 1 & 6 & 17 & 9 \\ -1 & -4 & -11 & -7 \\ \hline 0 & 2 & 6 & 2 \end{array}$

$\begin{array}{cccc} 1 & 4 & 8 & 4 \\ -1 & -4 & -11 & -7 \\ \hline 0 & 0 & -3 & -3 \end{array}$

The last row gives $-3z = -3$ $\therefore$ $z = 1$
$\therefore$ in row 2, $2y + 6z = 2$ and in row 1, $x + 4y + 11z = 7$
$\therefore$ $2y + 6 = 2$ $\therefore$ $x + 4(-2) + 11(1) = 7$
$\therefore$ $y = -2$ $\therefore$ $x + 3 = 7$
$\therefore$ $x = 4$

Thus we have a unique solution $x = 4$, $y = -2$, $z = 1$.

c In augmented matrix form, the system is:

$$\begin{pmatrix} 2 & -1 & 3 & | & 17 \\ 2 & -2 & -5 & | & 4 \\ 3 & 2 & 2 & | & 10 \end{pmatrix}$$

$\sim \begin{pmatrix} 2 & -1 & 3 & | & 17 \\ 0 & -1 & -8 & | & -13 \\ 0 & 7 & -5 & | & -31 \end{pmatrix}$ $R_2 \to R_2 - R_1$
$R_3 \to 2R_3 - 3R_1$

$\sim \begin{pmatrix} 2 & -1 & 3 & | & 17 \\ 0 & -1 & -8 & | & -13 \\ 0 & 0 & -61 & | & -122 \end{pmatrix}$ $R_3 \to R_3 + 7R_2$

The last row gives $-61z = -122$ $\therefore$ $z = 2$
$\therefore$ in row 2, $-y - 8z = -13$ and in row 1, $2x - y + 3z = 17$
$\therefore$ $-y - 16 = -13$ $\therefore$ $2x + 3 + 6 = 17$
$\therefore$ $y = -3$ $\therefore$ $2x = 8$
$\therefore$ $x = 4$

Thus we have a unique solution $x = 4$, $y = -3$, $z = 2$.

d In augmented matrix form, the system is:

$$\begin{pmatrix} 2 & 3 & 4 & | & 1 \\ 5 & 6 & 7 & | & 2 \\ 8 & 9 & 10 & | & 4 \end{pmatrix}$$

$\sim \begin{pmatrix} 2 & 3 & 4 & | & 1 \\ 0 & -3 & -6 & | & -1 \\ 0 & -3 & -6 & | & 0 \end{pmatrix}$ $R_2 \to 2R_2 - 5R_1$
$R_3 \to R_3 - 4R_1$

$\sim \begin{pmatrix} 2 & 3 & 4 & | & 1 \\ 0 & -3 & -6 & | & -1 \\ 0 & 0 & 0 & | & 1 \end{pmatrix}$ $R_3 \to R_3 - R_2$

In row 3, $0z = 1$ which has no solution. $\therefore$ the system has no real solutions.

2 a In augmented matrix form, the system is:

$$\begin{pmatrix} 1 & 1 & 1 & | & 6 \\ 2 & 4 & 1 & | & 5 \\ 2 & 3 & 1 & | & 6 \end{pmatrix}$$

$\sim \begin{pmatrix} 1 & 1 & 1 & | & 6 \\ 0 & 2 & -1 & | & -7 \\ 0 & 1 & -1 & | & -6 \end{pmatrix}$ $R_2 \to R_2 - 2R_1$
$R_3 \to R_3 - 2R_1$

$\sim \begin{pmatrix} 1 & 1 & 1 & | & 6 \\ 0 & 2 & -1 & | & -7 \\ 0 & 0 & -1 & | & -5 \end{pmatrix}$ $R_3 \to 2R_3 - R_2$

The last row gives $-z = -5$ $\therefore$ $z = 5$
$\therefore$ in row 2, $2y - z = -7$ and in row 1, $x + y + z = 6$
$\therefore$ $2y - 5 = -7$ $\therefore$ $x - 1 + 5 = 6$
$\therefore$ $2y = -2$ $\therefore$ $x + 4 = 6$
$\therefore$ $y = -1$ $\therefore$ $x = 2$

Thus we have a unique solution $x = 2$, $y = -1$, $z = 5$.

b In augmented matrix form, the system is:

$$\begin{pmatrix} 1 & 2 & -1 & | & 4 \\ 3 & 2 & 1 & | & 7 \\ 5 & 2 & 3 & | & 11 \end{pmatrix}$$

$$\sim \begin{pmatrix} 1 & 2 & -1 & | & 4 \\ 0 & -4 & 4 & | & -5 \\ 0 & -8 & 8 & | & -9 \end{pmatrix} \quad \begin{matrix} R_2 \to R_2 - 3R_1 \\ R_3 \to R_3 - 5R_1 \end{matrix}$$

$$\sim \begin{pmatrix} 1 & 2 & -1 & | & 4 \\ 0 & -4 & 4 & | & -5 \\ 0 & 0 & 0 & | & 1 \end{pmatrix} \quad R_3 \to R_3 - 2R_2$$

$$\begin{array}{rrrr} 3 & 2 & 1 & 7 \\ -3 & -6 & 3 & -12 \\ \hline 0 & -4 & 4 & -5 \end{array}$$

$$\begin{array}{rrrr} 5 & 2 & 3 & 11 \\ -5 & -10 & 5 & -20 \\ \hline 0 & -8 & 8 & -9 \end{array}$$

$$\begin{array}{rrrr} 0 & -8 & 8 & -9 \\ 0 & 8 & -8 & 10 \\ \hline 0 & 0 & 0 & 1 \end{array}$$

In row 3, $0z = 1$ which has no solution. $\therefore$ the system has no real solutions.

c In augmented matrix form, the system is:

$$\begin{pmatrix} 2 & 4 & 1 & | & 1 \\ 3 & 5 & 0 & | & 1 \\ 5 & 13 & 7 & | & 4 \end{pmatrix}$$

$$\sim \begin{pmatrix} 2 & 4 & 1 & | & 1 \\ 0 & -2 & -3 & | & -1 \\ 0 & 6 & 9 & | & 3 \end{pmatrix} \quad \begin{matrix} R_2 \to 2R_2 - 3R_1 \\ R_3 \to 2R_3 - 5R_1 \end{matrix}$$

$$\sim \begin{pmatrix} 2 & 4 & 1 & | & 1 \\ 0 & -2 & -3 & | & -1 \\ 0 & 0 & 0 & | & 0 \end{pmatrix} \quad R_3 \to R_3 + 3R_2$$

$$\begin{array}{rrrr} 6 & 10 & 0 & 2 \\ -6 & -12 & -3 & -3 \\ \hline 0 & -2 & -3 & -1 \end{array}$$

$$\begin{array}{rrrr} 10 & 26 & 14 & 8 \\ -10 & -20 & -5 & -5 \\ \hline 0 & 6 & 9 & 3 \end{array}$$

$$\begin{array}{rrrr} 0 & 6 & 9 & 3 \\ 0 & -6 & -9 & -3 \\ \hline 0 & 0 & 0 & 0 \end{array}$$

The row of zeros indicates infinitely many solutions.

If we let $y = t$ in row 2, $-2t - 3z = -1$

$$\therefore \quad 3z = 1 - 2t$$

$$\therefore \quad z = \frac{1 - 2t}{3}$$

Thus in equation 1, $\quad 2x + 4t + \left(\dfrac{1 - 2t}{3}\right) = 1$

$$\therefore \quad 6x + 12t + 1 - 2t = 3$$

$$\therefore \quad 6x = 2 - 10t \quad \text{and so} \quad x = \frac{1 - 5t}{3}$$

$\therefore$ the solutions have form $\quad x = \dfrac{1 - 5t}{3}, \quad y = t, \quad z = \dfrac{1 - 2t}{3}, \quad$ for all t in $\mathbb{R}$.

3 In augmented matrix form, the system is $\begin{pmatrix} 1 & 2 & 1 & | & 3 \\ 2 & -1 & 4 & | & 1 \\ 1 & 7 & -1 & | & k \end{pmatrix}$

a
$$\begin{pmatrix} 1 & 2 & 1 & | & 3 \\ 2 & -1 & 4 & | & 1 \\ 1 & 7 & -1 & | & k \end{pmatrix}$$

$$\sim \begin{pmatrix} 1 & 2 & 1 & | & 3 \\ 0 & -5 & 2 & | & -5 \\ 0 & 5 & -2 & | & k - 3 \end{pmatrix} \quad \begin{matrix} R_2 \to R_2 - 2R_1 \\ R_3 \to R_3 - R_1 \end{matrix}$$

$$\sim \begin{pmatrix} 1 & 2 & 1 & | & 3 \\ 0 & -5 & 2 & | & -5 \\ 0 & 0 & 0 & | & k - 8 \end{pmatrix} \quad R_3 \to R_3 + R_2$$

$$\begin{array}{rrrr} 2 & -1 & 4 & 1 \\ -2 & -4 & -2 & -6 \\ \hline 0 & -5 & 2 & -5 \end{array}$$

$$\begin{array}{rrrr} 1 & 7 & -1 & k \\ -1 & -2 & -1 & -3 \\ \hline 0 & 5 & -2 & k - 3 \end{array}$$

b If $k - 8 \neq 0$, we have $0z \neq 0$, so the system is inconsistent and there are no solutions.

If $k - 8 = 0$, we have $0z = 0$, which is true for all z, so we have infinitely many solutions.

Let $z = t$ in row 2, then $-5y + 2t = -5 \quad \therefore \quad 5y = 2t + 5$

$$\therefore \quad y = \frac{2t + 5}{5}$$

and substituting in row 1, $\quad x + 2\left(\dfrac{2t+5}{5}\right) + t = 3$

$\therefore \quad x + \tfrac{4}{5}t + 2 + t = 3$

$\therefore \quad x = 1 - \tfrac{9}{5}t = \dfrac{5-9t}{5}$

$\therefore$ the solutions have form $\quad x = \dfrac{5-9t}{5}, \quad y = \dfrac{2t+5}{5}, \quad z = t, \quad t$ in $\mathbb{R}$.

c There is no unique solution because the system reduces to 2 equations in 3 unknowns when $k = 8$.

4 a In augmented matrix form, the system is:

$\begin{pmatrix} 1 & 2 & -2 & | & 5 \\ 1 & -1 & 3 & | & -1 \\ 1 & -7 & k & | & -k \end{pmatrix}$

$\sim \begin{pmatrix} 1 & 2 & -2 & | & 5 \\ 0 & -3 & 5 & | & -6 \\ 0 & -9 & k+2 & | & -k-5 \end{pmatrix} \begin{array}{l} R_2 \to R_2 - R_1 \\ R_3 \to R_3 - R_1 \end{array}$

$\sim \begin{pmatrix} 1 & 2 & -2 & | & 5 \\ 0 & -3 & 5 & | & -6 \\ 0 & 0 & k-13 & | & 13-k \end{pmatrix} R_3 \to R_3 - 3R_2$

$\begin{array}{cccc} 1 & -1 & 3 & -1 \\ -1 & -2 & 2 & -5 \\ 0 & -3 & 5 & -6 \end{array}$

$\begin{array}{cccc} 1 & -7 & k & -k \\ -1 & -2 & 2 & -5 \\ 0 & -9 & k+2 & -k-5 \end{array}$

$\begin{array}{cccc} 0 & -9 & k+2 & -k-5 \\ 0 & 9 & -15 & 18 \\ 0 & 0 & k-13 & 13-k \end{array}$

b If $k = 13$, row 3 is a row of zeros, so there are infinitely many solutions.

Let $z = t$ in row 2, then $\quad -3y + 5t = -6 \quad \therefore \quad 3y = 6 + 5t$

$\therefore \quad y = \dfrac{6+5t}{3}$

and substituting in row 1 gives $\quad x + 2\left(\dfrac{6+5t}{3}\right) - 2t = 5$

$\therefore \quad x + 4 + \tfrac{10}{3}t - 2t = 5$

$\therefore \quad x = 1 - \tfrac{4}{3}t = \dfrac{3-4t}{3}$

$\therefore$ there are infinitely many solutions of the form $\quad x = \dfrac{3-4t}{3}, \quad y = \dfrac{6+5t}{3}, \quad z = t, \quad t$ in $\mathbb{R}$.

c If $k \neq 13$, then $(k-13)z = 13-k \quad \therefore \quad z = \dfrac{13-k}{k-13} = -1$

From row 2, $\quad -3y + 5(-1) = -6 \quad \therefore \quad -3y - 5 = -6 \quad \therefore \quad y = \tfrac{1}{3}$

and from row 1, $\quad x + 2y - 2z = x + \tfrac{2}{3} + 2 = 5 \quad \therefore \quad x = 2\tfrac{1}{3}$

$\therefore$ the unique solution is $\quad x = \tfrac{7}{3}, \ y = \tfrac{1}{3}, \ z = -1$.

5 a In augmented matrix form, the system is:

$\begin{pmatrix} 1 & 3 & 3 & | & a-1 \\ 2 & -1 & 1 & | & 7 \\ 3 & -5 & a & | & 16 \end{pmatrix}$

$\sim \begin{pmatrix} 1 & 3 & 3 & | & a-1 \\ 0 & -7 & -5 & | & 9-2a \\ 0 & -14 & a-9 & | & 19-3a \end{pmatrix} \begin{array}{l} R_2 \to R_2 - 2R_1 \\ R_3 \to R_3 - 3R_1 \end{array}$

$\sim \begin{pmatrix} 1 & 3 & 3 & | & a-1 \\ 0 & -7 & -5 & | & 9-2a \\ 0 & 0 & a+1 & | & a+1 \end{pmatrix} R_3 \to R_3 - 2R_2$

$\begin{array}{cccc} 2 & -1 & 1 & 7 \\ -2 & -6 & -6 & -2a+2 \\ 0 & -7 & -5 & 9-2a \end{array}$

$\begin{array}{cccc} 3 & -5 & a & 16 \\ -3 & -9 & -9 & -3a+3 \\ 0 & -14 & a-9 & 19-3a \end{array}$

$\begin{array}{cccc} 0 & -14 & a-9 & 19-3a \\ 0 & 14 & 10 & 4a-18 \\ 0 & 0 & a+1 & a+1 \end{array}$

b If $a = -1$, row 3 is a row of zeros, so there are infinitely many solutions, as we have 2 equations in 3 unknowns.

Let $z = t$ in row 2, then $-7y - 5t = 9 - 2(-1)$ $\therefore$ $-7y - 5t = 11$

$$\therefore \quad y = \frac{-5t - 11}{7}$$

and substituting in row 1 gives $x + 3\left(\dfrac{-5t - 11}{7}\right) + 3t = (-1) - 1$

$$\therefore \quad x - \frac{15t}{7} - \frac{33}{7} + 3t = -2 \quad \text{and so,} \quad x = \frac{19}{7} - \frac{6t}{7}$$

$\therefore$ there are infinitely many solutions of form $x = \dfrac{19 - 6t}{7}$, $y = \dfrac{-5t - 11}{7}$, $z = t$, t in $\mathbb{R}$.

c If $a \neq -1$, then $(a+1)z = a+1$ $\therefore$ $z = 1$.

From row 2, $-7y - 5(1) = 9 - 2a$ $\therefore$ $-7y = -2a + 14$

$$y = \frac{2a - 14}{7}$$

and substituting in row 1 gives $x + 3\left(\dfrac{2a - 14}{7}\right) + 3(1) = a - 1$

$$\therefore \quad x + \frac{6a}{7} - 6 + 3 = a - 1$$

$$\therefore \quad x = \frac{a}{7} + 2 = \frac{a + 14}{7}$$

$\therefore$ the unique solution is $x = \dfrac{a + 14}{7}$, $y = \dfrac{2a - 14}{7}$, $z = 1$.

6 In augmented matrix form, the system is:

$$\begin{pmatrix} 2 & 1 & -1 & | & 3 \\ m & -2 & 1 & | & 1 \\ 1 & 2 & m & | & -1 \end{pmatrix}$$

$$\begin{array}{cccc} 2m & -4 & 2 & 2 \\ -2m & -m & m & -3m \\ \hline 0 & -m-4 & m+2 & -3m+2 \end{array}$$

$$\sim \begin{pmatrix} 2 & 1 & -1 & | & 3 \\ 0 & -m-4 & m+2 & | & -3m+2 \\ 0 & 3 & 2m+1 & | & -5 \end{pmatrix} \quad \begin{array}{l} R_2 \to 2R_2 - mR_1 \\ R_3 \to 2R_3 - R_1 \end{array}$$

$$\begin{array}{cccc} 2 & 4 & 2m & -2 \\ -2 & -1 & 1 & -3 \\ \hline 0 & 3 & 2m+1 & -5 \end{array}$$

$$\sim \begin{pmatrix} 2 & 1 & -1 & | & 3 \\ 0 & -m-4 & m+2 & | & -3m+2 \\ 0 & 0 & 2(m+1)(m+5) & | & -14(m+1) \end{pmatrix} \quad R_3 \to (m+4)R_3 + 3R_2$$

$$\begin{array}{cccc} 0 & 3m+12 & (m+4)(2m+1) & -5m-20 \\ 0 & -3m-12 & 3m+6 & -9m+6 \\ \hline 0 & 0 & 2m^2 + 12m + 10 & -14m - 14 \\ & & = 2(m^2 + 6m + 5) & = -14(m+1) \\ & & = 2(m+1)(m+5) & \end{array}$$

a If $m = -5$, row 3 becomes $0x + 0y + 0z = 56$
$\therefore$ the system is inconsistent and there are no solutions.

b If $m = -1$, row 3 is a row of zeros, so we have 2 equations in 3 unknowns.
$\therefore$ there are infinitely many solutions.

c If $m \neq -1$ and $m \neq -5$, then row 3 becomes
$2(m+1)(m+5)z = -14(m+1)$

$$\therefore \quad z = \frac{-7}{m+5} \quad \text{and substituting in row 2 gives}$$

$$-(m+4)y + (m+2)\left(\frac{-7}{m+5}\right) = -3m + 2$$

$$\therefore \quad -(m+4)(m+5)y - 7(m+2) = (-3m+2)(m+5)$$

$$\therefore \quad -(m+4)(m+5)y = -3m^2 - 13m + 10 + 7m + 14$$

$$\therefore \quad -(m+4)(m+5)y = -3m^2 - 6m + 24$$

$$\therefore \quad -(m+4)(m+5)y = -3(m^2 + 2m - 8)$$
$$\therefore \quad (m+4)(m+5)y = 3(m-2)(m+4)$$
$$\therefore \quad y = \frac{3(m-2)}{m+5}$$

and substituting in row 1 gives $\quad 2x + \frac{3(m-2)}{m+5} - \frac{-7}{m+5} = 3$

$$\therefore \quad 2x(m+5) + 3(m-2) + 7 = 3(m+5)$$
$$\therefore \quad 2x(m+5) + 3m - 6 + 7 = 3m + 15$$
$$\therefore \quad 2x(m+5) = 14$$
$$\therefore \quad x = \frac{7}{m+5}$$

$\therefore \quad$ the system has a unique solution for all m except $m = -5$ and $m = -1$, and the solution is $\quad x = \dfrac{7}{m+5}, \quad y = \dfrac{3(m-2)}{m+5}, \quad z = \dfrac{-7}{m+5}$.

7 a In augmented matrix form, the system is:

$$\begin{pmatrix} 1 & 3 & k & | & 2 \\ k & -2 & 3 & | & k \\ 4 & -3 & 10 & | & 5 \end{pmatrix}$$

$$\begin{array}{c|c} k & -2 & 3 & k \\ -k & -3k & -k^2 & -2k \\ \hline 0 & -2-3k & 3-k^2 & -k \end{array}$$

$$\sim \begin{pmatrix} 1 & 3 & k & | & 2 \\ 0 & -2-3k & 3-k^2 & | & -k \\ 0 & -15 & 10-4k & | & -3 \end{pmatrix} \begin{array}{l} R_2 \to R_2 - kR_1 \\ R_3 \to R_3 - 4R_1 \end{array}$$

$$\begin{array}{c|c} 4 & -3 & 10 & 5 \\ -4 & -12 & -4k & -8 \\ \hline 0 & -15 & 10-4k & -3 \end{array}$$

$$\sim \begin{pmatrix} 1 & 3 & k & | & 2 \\ 0 & -2-3k & 3-k^2 & | & -k \\ 0 & 0 & (3k+25)(k-1) & | & 6(k-1) \end{pmatrix} R_3 \to (3k+2)R_3 - 15R_2$$

$$\begin{array}{ccc} 0 & -15(3k+2) & (3k+2)(10-4k) & -3(3k+2) \\ 0 & 30+45k & 15k^2 - 45 & 15k \\ \hline 0 & 0 & -12k^2 + 22k + 20 + 15k^2 - 45 & 6k - 6 \\ & & = 3k^2 + 22k - 25 & = 6(k-1) \\ & & = (3k+25)(k-1) \end{array}$$

b If $k = 1$, row 3 is a row of zeros, so there are infinitely many solutions.

The system becomes $\begin{pmatrix} 1 & 3 & 1 & | & 2 \\ 0 & -5 & 2 & | & -1 \\ 0 & 0 & 0 & | & 0 \end{pmatrix}$. Let $z = t$ in row 2, then
$$-5y + 2t = -1$$
$$\therefore \quad -5y = -1 - 2t$$
$$\therefore \quad y = \frac{1+2t}{5}$$

and substituting in row 1 gives $\quad x + 3\left(\dfrac{1+2t}{5}\right) + t = 2$

$$\therefore \quad x + \tfrac{3}{5} + \tfrac{6}{5}t + t = 2$$
$$\therefore \quad x = \tfrac{7}{5} - \tfrac{11}{5}t = \frac{7-11t}{5}$$

$\therefore \quad$ the solutions are of the form $\quad x = \dfrac{7-11t}{5}, \quad y = \dfrac{1+2t}{5}, \quad z = t, \quad$ for all t in $\mathbb{R}$.

c If $k = -\tfrac{25}{3}$ the system is inconsistent $(0z = -56)$ $\therefore$ there are no real solutions.

d The system has a unique solution for all $k \neq 1$ or $-\tfrac{25}{3}$.

EXERCISE 13F.3

1 a In augmented matrix form, the system is:
$$\begin{pmatrix} 2 & 1 & 1 & | & 5 \\ 1 & -1 & 1 & | & 3 \end{pmatrix} \sim \begin{pmatrix} 2 & 1 & 1 & | & 5 \\ 0 & -3 & 1 & | & 1 \end{pmatrix} \quad R_2 \to 2R_2 - R_1$$

$$\begin{array}{cccc} 2 & -2 & 2 & 6 \\ -2 & -1 & -1 & -5 \\ \hline 0 & -3 & 1 & 1 \end{array}$$

Let $z = t$ in row 2, then $-3y + t = 1$ $\therefore$ $-3y = 1 - t$ $\therefore$ $y = \dfrac{t-1}{3}$

and substituting in equation 1 gives $2x + \left(\dfrac{t-1}{3}\right) + t = 5$

$\therefore \quad 2x + \tfrac{1}{3}t - \tfrac{1}{3} + t = 5$

$\therefore \quad 2x = \tfrac{16}{3} - \tfrac{4}{3}t$

$\therefore \quad x = \tfrac{8}{3} - \tfrac{2}{3}t = \dfrac{8-2t}{3}$

$\therefore$ the solutions are $x = \dfrac{8-2t}{3}, \quad y = \dfrac{t-1}{3}, \quad z = t, \quad t \in \mathbb{R}$.

b In augmented matrix form, the system is:
$$\begin{pmatrix} 3 & 1 & 2 & | & 10 \\ 1 & -2 & 1 & | & -4 \end{pmatrix} \sim \begin{pmatrix} 3 & 1 & 2 & | & 10 \\ 0 & -7 & 1 & | & -22 \end{pmatrix} \quad R_2 \to 3R_2 - R_1$$

$$\begin{array}{cccc} 3 & -6 & 3 & -12 \\ -3 & -1 & -2 & -10 \\ \hline 0 & -7 & 1 & -22 \end{array}$$

Let $z = t$ in row 2, then $-7y + t = -22$ $\therefore$ $-7y = -t - 22$

$\therefore \quad y = \dfrac{t+22}{7}$

and substituting in equation 1 gives $3x + \left(\dfrac{t+22}{7}\right) + 2t = 10$

$\therefore \quad 3x + \tfrac{1}{7}t + \tfrac{22}{7} + 2t = 10$

$\therefore \quad 3x = \tfrac{48}{7} - \tfrac{15}{7}t$

$\therefore \quad x = \tfrac{16}{7} - \tfrac{5}{7}t = \dfrac{16-5t}{7}$

$\therefore$ the solutions are $x = \dfrac{16-5t}{7}, \quad y = \dfrac{t+22}{7}, \quad z = t, \quad t \in \mathbb{R}$.

c In augmented matrix form, the system is:
$$\begin{pmatrix} 1 & 2 & 1 & | & 5 \\ 2 & 4 & 2 & | & 16 \end{pmatrix} \sim \begin{pmatrix} 1 & 2 & 1 & | & 5 \\ 0 & 0 & 0 & | & 6 \end{pmatrix} \quad R_2 \to R_2 - 2R_1$$

$$\begin{array}{cccc} 2 & 4 & 2 & 16 \\ -2 & -4 & -2 & -10 \\ \hline 0 & 0 & 0 & 6 \end{array}$$

Row 2 shows $0z = 6$ which has no solution

$\therefore$ the system is inconsistent and has no real solutions.

2 In augmented matrix form, the system is:
$$\begin{pmatrix} 1 & -3 & 1 & | & 0 \\ 2 & 1 & -2 & | & 0 \end{pmatrix} \sim \begin{pmatrix} 1 & -3 & 1 & | & 0 \\ 0 & 7 & -4 & | & 0 \end{pmatrix} \quad R_2 \to R_2 - 2R_1$$

$$\begin{array}{cccc} 2 & 1 & -2 & 0 \\ -2 & 6 & -2 & 0 \\ \hline 0 & 7 & -4 & 0 \end{array}$$

Let $z = t$ in row 2, then $7y - 4t = 0$ $\therefore$ $y = \tfrac{4}{7}t$

and substituting in equation 1 gives $x - 3(\tfrac{4}{7}t) + t = 0$ $\therefore$ $x = -t + \tfrac{12}{7}t = \tfrac{5}{7}t$

$\therefore$ the solution is $x = \tfrac{5}{7}t, \quad y = \tfrac{4}{7}t, \quad z = t \quad$ for t in $\mathbb{R}$

(or $x = 5s, \quad y = 4s, \quad z = 7s \quad$ for s in $\mathbb{R}$).

To solve the new system, substitute the solution of the first two equations into the third equation.

$\therefore \quad 3(\tfrac{5}{7}t) - (\tfrac{4}{7}t) + t = 18$ $\therefore$ $15t - 4t + 7t = 126$

$\therefore \quad 18t = 126$

$\therefore \quad t = 7$

$\therefore$ the solution is $x = 5, \, y = 4, \, z = 7$

3 In augmented matrix form, the system is:
$$\begin{pmatrix} 2 & 3 & 1 & | & 0 \\ 1 & -1 & 2 & | & 0 \end{pmatrix} \sim \begin{pmatrix} 2 & 3 & 1 & | & 0 \\ 0 & -5 & 3 & | & 0 \end{pmatrix} \quad R_2 \to 2R_2 - R_1$$

$$\begin{array}{rrrr} 2 & -2 & 4 & 0 \\ -2 & -3 & -1 & 0 \\ \hline 0 & -5 & 3 & 0 \end{array}$$

Let $z = t$ in row 2, then $-5y + 3t = 0$
$$\therefore \quad y = \tfrac{3}{5}t$$

and substituting in equation 1 gives $2x + 3(\tfrac{3}{5}t) + t = 0 \quad \therefore \quad 2x = -\tfrac{14}{5}t$
$$\therefore \quad x = -\tfrac{7}{5}t$$

$\therefore$ the solution is $x = -\tfrac{7}{5}t$, $y = \tfrac{3}{5}t$, $z = t$ for t in $\mathbb{R}$
  (or $x = -7s$, $y = 3s$, $z = 5s$ for s in $\mathbb{R}$).

To solve the new system, substitute the solution of the first two equations into the third equation.
$\therefore \quad a(-\tfrac{7}{5}t) + (\tfrac{3}{5}t) - t = 0 \quad \therefore \quad -7at + 3t - 5t = 0$
$$-7at - 2t = 0$$
$$\therefore \quad t(7a + 2) = 0$$
$$\therefore \quad t = 0 \text{ or } a = -\tfrac{2}{7}$$

If $a \neq -\tfrac{2}{7}$, then $t = 0$, so the solution is $x = 0$, $y = 0$, $z = 0$.
If $a = -\tfrac{2}{7}$, then the solution is $x = -\tfrac{7}{5}t$, $y = \tfrac{3}{5}t$, $z = t$ for t in $\mathbb{R}$
  (or $x = -7s$, $y = 3s$, $z = 5s$ for s in $\mathbb{R}$)

4 a $P(x) = ax^2 + bx + c$ in thousands of dollars where x is in thousands.
Profit is $8 \times \$1000$ when 1×1000 items are produced.
$\therefore \quad P(1) = a + b + c = 8$
and profit is $17 \times \$1000$ when 4×1000 items are produced.
$\therefore \quad P(4) = 16a + 4b + c = 17$
$\therefore \quad a + b + c = 8$ and $16a + 4b + c = 17$

b If $a = t$, $b = 3 - 5t$, $c = 5 + 4t$,
then $a + b + c = t + 3 - 5t + 5 + 4t = 8$ ✓
and $16a + 4b + c = 16t + 4(3 - 5t) + (5 + 4t) = 16t + 12 - 20t + 5 + 4t = 17$ ✓
$\therefore \quad a = t$, $b = 3 - 5t$, $c = 5 + 4t$ are the possible solutions for the system.

c Now $P(x) = tx^2 + (3 - 5t)x + (5 + 4t)$
and $P(2.5) = t(2.5)^2 + (3 - 5t)(2.5) + 5 + 4t$
$= 6.25t + 7.5 - 12.5t + 5 + 4t$
$= -2.25t + 12.5$

But $P(2.5) = 19.75 \quad \therefore \quad -2.25t + 12.5 = 19.75$
$$\therefore \quad -2.25t = 7.25$$
$$\therefore \quad t = -\frac{7.25}{2.25} = -\tfrac{29}{9}$$

$\therefore \quad a = -\tfrac{29}{9}$, $b = 3 - 5(-\tfrac{29}{9}) = \tfrac{172}{9}$ and $c = 5 + 4(-\tfrac{29}{9}) = -\tfrac{71}{9}$

$\therefore \quad P(x) = -\tfrac{29}{9}x^2 + \tfrac{172}{9}x - \tfrac{71}{9}$

d Now $P(x)$ is a quadratic with $a < 0$, so its shape is ⌒

$\therefore \quad P(x)$ has a maximum when $x = -\dfrac{b}{2a} = -\dfrac{\tfrac{172}{9}}{2(-\tfrac{29}{9})} = \tfrac{86}{29} \approx 2.966$.

$\therefore \quad 2966$ items should be produced to maximise the profit.
Now $P(2.966) \approx 20.448$, so the maximum profit is approximately $\$20\,448$.

EXERCISE 13G

1 a $\mathbf{M} = \begin{pmatrix} 1 & 2 \\ 0 & 1 \end{pmatrix}$

$\therefore \mathbf{M}^2 = \begin{pmatrix} 1 & 2 \\ 0 & 1 \end{pmatrix}\begin{pmatrix} 1 & 2 \\ 0 & 1 \end{pmatrix} = \begin{pmatrix} 1 & 4 \\ 0 & 1 \end{pmatrix}$

$\therefore \mathbf{M}^3 = \mathbf{M}^2\mathbf{M} = \begin{pmatrix} 1 & 4 \\ 0 & 1 \end{pmatrix}\begin{pmatrix} 1 & 2 \\ 0 & 1 \end{pmatrix} = \begin{pmatrix} 1 & 6 \\ 0 & 1 \end{pmatrix}$

$\therefore \mathbf{M}^4 = \mathbf{M}^3\mathbf{M} = \begin{pmatrix} 1 & 6 \\ 0 & 1 \end{pmatrix}\begin{pmatrix} 1 & 2 \\ 0 & 1 \end{pmatrix} = \begin{pmatrix} 1 & 8 \\ 0 & 1 \end{pmatrix}$

b P_n is: "If $\mathbf{M} = \begin{pmatrix} 1 & 2 \\ 0 & 1 \end{pmatrix}$ then $\mathbf{M}^n = \begin{pmatrix} 1 & 2n \\ 0 & 1 \end{pmatrix}$", $n \in \mathbb{Z}^+$.

c Proof: (By the principle of mathematical induction)

(1) If $n = 1$, $\mathbf{M}^1 = \begin{pmatrix} 1 & 2 \\ 0 & 1 \end{pmatrix} = \begin{pmatrix} 1 & 2(1) \\ 0 & 1 \end{pmatrix}$ $\therefore P_1$ is true.

(2) If P_k is true, then $\mathbf{M}^k = \begin{pmatrix} 1 & 2k \\ 0 & 1 \end{pmatrix}$

$\therefore \mathbf{M}^{k+1} = \mathbf{M}^k\mathbf{M}$

$= \begin{pmatrix} 1 & 2k \\ 0 & 1 \end{pmatrix}\begin{pmatrix} 1 & 2 \\ 0 & 1 \end{pmatrix}$

$= \begin{pmatrix} 1 & 2+2k \\ 0 & 1 \end{pmatrix}$

$= \begin{pmatrix} 1 & 2(k+1) \\ 0 & 1 \end{pmatrix}$

Thus, P_{k+1} is true whenever P_k is true and P_1 is true.
$\therefore P_n$ is true for all $n \in \mathbb{Z}^+$
{Principle of mathematical induction}

2 a $\mathbf{A} = \begin{pmatrix} 1 & 2 \\ 0 & 3 \end{pmatrix}$

$\therefore \mathbf{A}^2 = \begin{pmatrix} 1 & 2 \\ 0 & 3 \end{pmatrix}\begin{pmatrix} 1 & 2 \\ 0 & 3 \end{pmatrix} = \begin{pmatrix} 1 & 8 \\ 0 & 9 \end{pmatrix}$

$\therefore \mathbf{A}^3 = \mathbf{A}^2\mathbf{A} = \begin{pmatrix} 1 & 8 \\ 0 & 9 \end{pmatrix}\begin{pmatrix} 1 & 2 \\ 0 & 3 \end{pmatrix} = \begin{pmatrix} 1 & 26 \\ 0 & 27 \end{pmatrix}$

$\therefore \mathbf{A}^4 = \mathbf{A}^3\mathbf{A} = \begin{pmatrix} 1 & 26 \\ 0 & 27 \end{pmatrix}\begin{pmatrix} 1 & 2 \\ 0 & 3 \end{pmatrix} = \begin{pmatrix} 1 & 80 \\ 0 & 81 \end{pmatrix}$

$\therefore \mathbf{A}^5 = \mathbf{A}^4\mathbf{A} = \begin{pmatrix} 1 & 80 \\ 0 & 81 \end{pmatrix}\begin{pmatrix} 1 & 2 \\ 0 & 3 \end{pmatrix} = \begin{pmatrix} 1 & 242 \\ 0 & 243 \end{pmatrix}$

b P_n is "If $\mathbf{A} = \begin{pmatrix} 1 & 2 \\ 0 & 3 \end{pmatrix}$ then $\mathbf{A}^n = \begin{pmatrix} 1 & 3^n - 1 \\ 0 & 3^n \end{pmatrix}$", $n \in \mathbb{Z}^+$.

c Proof: (By the principle of mathematical induction)

(1) If $n = 1$, $\mathbf{A}^1 = \begin{pmatrix} 1 & 2 \\ 0 & 3 \end{pmatrix} = \begin{pmatrix} 1 & 3-1 \\ 0 & 3 \end{pmatrix}$ $\therefore P_1$ is true.

(2) If P_k is true, then $\mathbf{A}^k = \begin{pmatrix} 1 & 3^k - 1 \\ 0 & 3^k \end{pmatrix}$

$\therefore \mathbf{A}^{k+1} = \mathbf{A}^k\mathbf{A} = \begin{pmatrix} 1 & 3^k - 1 \\ 0 & 3^k \end{pmatrix}\begin{pmatrix} 1 & 2 \\ 0 & 3 \end{pmatrix}$

$= \begin{pmatrix} 1 & 2 + 3(3^k - 1) \\ 0 & 3^k \times 3 \end{pmatrix}$

$= \begin{pmatrix} 1 & 2 + 3^{k+1} - 3 \\ 0 & 3^{k+1} \end{pmatrix}$

$= \begin{pmatrix} 1 & 3^{k+1} - 1 \\ 0 & 3^{k+1} \end{pmatrix}$

Thus P_{k+1} is true whenever P_k is true and P_1 is true.
$\therefore P_n$ is true for all $n \in \mathbb{Z}^+$
{Principle of mathematical induction}

d If $n = -1$, $\begin{pmatrix} 1 & 3^{-1} - 1 \\ 0 & 3^{-1} \end{pmatrix} = \begin{pmatrix} 1 & -\frac{2}{3} \\ 0 & \frac{1}{3} \end{pmatrix}$

But $\mathbf{A}^{-1} = \frac{1}{3-0}\begin{pmatrix} 3 & -2 \\ 0 & 1 \end{pmatrix} = \frac{1}{3}\begin{pmatrix} 3 & -2 \\ 0 & 1 \end{pmatrix} = \begin{pmatrix} 1 & -\frac{2}{3} \\ 0 & \frac{1}{3} \end{pmatrix}$

So, the result is true when $n = -1$.

3 a $\mathbf{P} = \begin{pmatrix} 2 & 1 \\ -1 & 0 \end{pmatrix}$ $\therefore \mathbf{P}^3 = \begin{pmatrix} 3 & 2 \\ -2 & -1 \end{pmatrix}\begin{pmatrix} 2 & 1 \\ -1 & 0 \end{pmatrix} = \begin{pmatrix} 4 & 3 \\ -3 & -2 \end{pmatrix}$

$\therefore \mathbf{P}^2 = \begin{pmatrix} 2 & 1 \\ -1 & 0 \end{pmatrix}\begin{pmatrix} 2 & 1 \\ -1 & 0 \end{pmatrix} = \begin{pmatrix} 3 & 2 \\ -2 & -1 \end{pmatrix}$ $\therefore \mathbf{P}^4 = \begin{pmatrix} 4 & 3 \\ -3 & -2 \end{pmatrix}\begin{pmatrix} 2 & 1 \\ -1 & 0 \end{pmatrix} = \begin{pmatrix} 5 & 4 \\ -4 & -3 \end{pmatrix}$

b P_n is "If $\mathbf{P} = \begin{pmatrix} 2 & 1 \\ -1 & 0 \end{pmatrix}$ then $\mathbf{P}^n = \begin{pmatrix} n+1 & n \\ -n & 1-n \end{pmatrix}$", $n \in \mathbb{Z}^+$.

c Proof: (By the principle of mathematical induction)

(1) If $n = 1$, $\mathbf{P}^1 = \mathbf{P} = \begin{pmatrix} 2 & 1 \\ -1 & 0 \end{pmatrix}$ $\therefore P_1$ is true.

(2) If P_k is true then $\mathbf{P}^k = \begin{pmatrix} k+1 & k \\ -k & 1-k \end{pmatrix}$

$\therefore \mathbf{P}^{k+1} = \mathbf{P}^k \mathbf{P}$

$= \begin{pmatrix} k+1 & k \\ -k & 1-k \end{pmatrix}\begin{pmatrix} 2 & 1 \\ -1 & 0 \end{pmatrix}$

$= \begin{pmatrix} 2k+2-k & k+1+0 \\ -2k-1+k & -k+0 \end{pmatrix}$

$= \begin{pmatrix} k+2 & k+1 \\ -k-1 & -k \end{pmatrix}$

$= \begin{pmatrix} (k+1)+1 & (k+1) \\ -(k+1) & 1-(k+1) \end{pmatrix}$

Thus P_{k+1} is true whenever P_k is true and P_1 is true.
$\therefore P_n$ is true for all $n \in \mathbb{Z}^+$
{Principle of mathematical induction}

4 P_n is "If $u_1 = u_2 = 1$ and $u_{n+2} = u_n + u_{n+1}$ and $\mathbf{A} = \begin{pmatrix} 1 & 1 \\ 1 & 0 \end{pmatrix}$ then $\mathbf{A}^{n+1} = \begin{pmatrix} u_{n+2} & u_{n+1} \\ u_{n+1} & u_n \end{pmatrix}$" for $n \in \mathbb{Z}^+$.

Proof: (By the principle of mathematical induction)

(1) If $n = 1$, LHS $= \mathbf{A}^2 = \begin{pmatrix} 1 & 1 \\ 1 & 0 \end{pmatrix}\begin{pmatrix} 1 & 1 \\ 1 & 0 \end{pmatrix} = \begin{pmatrix} 2 & 1 \\ 1 & 1 \end{pmatrix}$

and RHS $= \begin{pmatrix} u_3 & u_2 \\ u_2 & u_1 \end{pmatrix} = \begin{pmatrix} 2 & 1 \\ 1 & 1 \end{pmatrix}$ $\therefore P_1$ is true.

(2) If P_k is true, then $\mathbf{A}^{k+1} = \begin{pmatrix} u_{k+2} & u_{k+1} \\ u_{k+1} & u_k \end{pmatrix}$

$\therefore \mathbf{A}^{k+2} = \mathbf{A}^{k+1}\mathbf{A} = \begin{pmatrix} u_{k+2} & u_{k+1} \\ u_{k+1} & u_k \end{pmatrix}\begin{pmatrix} 1 & 1 \\ 1 & 0 \end{pmatrix}$

$= \begin{pmatrix} u_{k+2} + u_{k+1} & u_{k+2} + 0 \\ u_{k+1} + u_k & u_{k+1} + 0 \end{pmatrix} = \begin{pmatrix} u_{k+3} & u_{k+2} \\ u_{k+2} & u_{k+1} \end{pmatrix}$

Thus P_{k+1} is true whenever P_k is true and P_1 is true.
$\therefore P_n$ is true for all $n \in \mathbb{Z}^+$ {Principle of mathematical induction}

REVIEW SET 13A

1 **a** $A + B$

$$= \begin{pmatrix} 3 & 2 \\ 0 & -1 \end{pmatrix} + \begin{pmatrix} 1 & 0 \\ -2 & 4 \end{pmatrix}$$

$$= \begin{pmatrix} 4 & 2 \\ -2 & 3 \end{pmatrix}$$

b $3A$

$$= 3 \begin{pmatrix} 3 & 2 \\ 0 & -1 \end{pmatrix}$$

$$= \begin{pmatrix} 9 & 6 \\ 0 & -3 \end{pmatrix}$$

c $-2B$

$$= -2 \begin{pmatrix} 1 & 0 \\ -2 & 4 \end{pmatrix}$$

$$= \begin{pmatrix} -2 & 0 \\ 4 & -8 \end{pmatrix}$$

d $A - B$

$$= \begin{pmatrix} 3 & 2 \\ 0 & -1 \end{pmatrix} - \begin{pmatrix} 1 & 0 \\ -2 & 4 \end{pmatrix}$$

$$= \begin{pmatrix} 2 & 2 \\ 2 & -5 \end{pmatrix}$$

e $B - 2A$

$$= \begin{pmatrix} 1 & 0 \\ -2 & 4 \end{pmatrix} - \begin{pmatrix} 6 & 4 \\ 0 & -2 \end{pmatrix}$$

$$= \begin{pmatrix} -5 & -4 \\ -2 & 6 \end{pmatrix}$$

f $3A - 2B$

$$= 3 \begin{pmatrix} 3 & 2 \\ 0 & -1 \end{pmatrix} - 2 \begin{pmatrix} 1 & 0 \\ -2 & 4 \end{pmatrix}$$

$$= \begin{pmatrix} 7 & 6 \\ 4 & -11 \end{pmatrix}$$

g AB

$$= \begin{pmatrix} 3 & 2 \\ 0 & -1 \end{pmatrix} \begin{pmatrix} 1 & 0 \\ -2 & 4 \end{pmatrix}$$

$$= \begin{pmatrix} -1 & 8 \\ 2 & -4 \end{pmatrix}$$

h BA

$$= \begin{pmatrix} 1 & 0 \\ -2 & 4 \end{pmatrix} \begin{pmatrix} 3 & 2 \\ 0 & -1 \end{pmatrix}$$

$$= \begin{pmatrix} 3 & 2 \\ -6 & -8 \end{pmatrix}$$

i A^{-1}

$$= \tfrac{1}{-3} \begin{pmatrix} -1 & -2 \\ 0 & 3 \end{pmatrix}$$

$$= \begin{pmatrix} \tfrac{1}{3} & \tfrac{2}{3} \\ 0 & -1 \end{pmatrix}$$

j A^2

$$= \begin{pmatrix} 3 & 2 \\ 0 & -1 \end{pmatrix} \begin{pmatrix} 3 & 2 \\ 0 & -1 \end{pmatrix}$$

$$= \begin{pmatrix} 9 & 4 \\ 0 & 1 \end{pmatrix}$$

k ABA
$= (AB)A$

$$= \begin{pmatrix} -1 & 8 \\ 2 & -4 \end{pmatrix} \begin{pmatrix} 3 & 2 \\ 0 & -1 \end{pmatrix}$$

$$= \begin{pmatrix} -3 & -10 \\ 6 & 8 \end{pmatrix}$$

l $(AB)^{-1}$

$$= \begin{pmatrix} -1 & 8 \\ 2 & -4 \end{pmatrix}^{-1}$$

$$= \tfrac{1}{4-16} \begin{pmatrix} -4 & -8 \\ -2 & -1 \end{pmatrix}$$

$$= \tfrac{1}{-12} \begin{pmatrix} -4 & -8 \\ -2 & -1 \end{pmatrix}$$

$$= \begin{pmatrix} \tfrac{1}{3} & \tfrac{2}{3} \\ \tfrac{1}{6} & \tfrac{1}{12} \end{pmatrix}$$

2 **a** Equating corresponding elements,
$a = -a$
$b - 2 = 3$
$c = 2 - c$ $\therefore$ $a = 0$, $b = 5$
$d = -4$ $c = 1$, $d = -4$

b Equating corresponding elements,
$3 + b = a$
$2a - a = 2$
$b + c = 2$ $\therefore$ $a = 2$, $b = -1$
$-2 + d = 6$ $c = 3$, $d = 8$

3 **a** $B - Y = A$
$\therefore$ $-Y = A - B$
$\therefore$ $Y = -(A - B)$
$\therefore$ $Y = B - A$

b $2Y + C = D$
$\therefore$ $2Y = D - C$
$\therefore$ $Y = \tfrac{1}{2}(D - C)$

c $AY = B$
$\therefore$ $A^{-1}AY = A^{-1}B$
$\therefore$ $IY = A^{-1}B$
$\therefore$ $Y = A^{-1}B$

d $YB = C$
$\therefore$ $YBB^{-1} = CB^{-1}$
$\therefore$ $YI = CB^{-1}$
$\therefore$ $Y = CB^{-1}$

e $C - AY = B$
$\therefore$ $-AY = B - C$
$\therefore$ $AY = C - B$
$\therefore$ $A^{-1}AY = A^{-1}(C - B)$
$\therefore$ $Y = A^{-1}(C - B)$

f $AY^{-1} = B$
$\therefore$ $A^{-1}AY^{-1} = A^{-1}B$
$\therefore$ $Y^{-1} = A^{-1}B$
$\therefore$ $(Y^{-1})^{-1} = (A^{-1}B)^{-1}$
$\therefore$ $Y = B^{-1}(A^{-1})^{-1}$
$\therefore$ $Y = B^{-1}A$

4 a $3x - 4y = 2$
         $5x + 2y = -1$

$\therefore \begin{pmatrix} 3 & -4 \\ 5 & 2 \end{pmatrix} \begin{pmatrix} x \\ y \end{pmatrix} = \begin{pmatrix} 2 \\ -1 \end{pmatrix}$

$\therefore \begin{pmatrix} x \\ y \end{pmatrix} = \begin{pmatrix} 3 & -4 \\ 5 & 2 \end{pmatrix}^{-1} \begin{pmatrix} 2 \\ -1 \end{pmatrix}$

$= \frac{1}{26} \begin{pmatrix} 2 & 4 \\ -5 & 3 \end{pmatrix} \begin{pmatrix} 2 \\ -1 \end{pmatrix}$

$= \frac{1}{26} \begin{pmatrix} 0 \\ -13 \end{pmatrix}$

$= \begin{pmatrix} 0 \\ -\frac{1}{2} \end{pmatrix}$

$\therefore \quad x = 0, \quad y = -\frac{1}{2}$

b $4x - y = 5$
         $2x + 3y = 9$

$\therefore \begin{pmatrix} 4 & -1 \\ 2 & 3 \end{pmatrix} \begin{pmatrix} x \\ y \end{pmatrix} = \begin{pmatrix} 5 \\ 9 \end{pmatrix}$

$\therefore \begin{pmatrix} x \\ y \end{pmatrix} = \begin{pmatrix} 4 & -1 \\ 2 & 3 \end{pmatrix}^{-1} \begin{pmatrix} 5 \\ 9 \end{pmatrix}$

$= \frac{1}{14} \begin{pmatrix} 3 & 1 \\ -2 & 4 \end{pmatrix} \begin{pmatrix} 5 \\ 9 \end{pmatrix}$

$= \frac{1}{14} \begin{pmatrix} 24 \\ 26 \end{pmatrix}$

$= \begin{pmatrix} \frac{12}{7} \\ \frac{13}{7} \end{pmatrix}$

$\therefore \quad x = \frac{12}{7}, \quad y = \frac{13}{7}$

This is possible because $\det \begin{pmatrix} 4 & -1 \\ 2 & 3 \end{pmatrix} \neq 0$.

c $\mathbf{X} \begin{pmatrix} 3 & 4 \\ 1 & 1 \end{pmatrix} = \begin{pmatrix} 5 & 4 \\ 0 & -2 \end{pmatrix}$

$\therefore \mathbf{X} = \begin{pmatrix} 5 & 4 \\ 0 & -2 \end{pmatrix} \begin{pmatrix} 3 & 4 \\ 1 & 1 \end{pmatrix}^{-1}$

$\therefore \mathbf{X} = \begin{pmatrix} 5 & 4 \\ 0 & -2 \end{pmatrix} \frac{1}{-1} \begin{pmatrix} 1 & -4 \\ -1 & 3 \end{pmatrix}$

$\therefore \mathbf{X} = \begin{pmatrix} 5 & 4 \\ 0 & -2 \end{pmatrix} \begin{pmatrix} -1 & 4 \\ 1 & -3 \end{pmatrix}$

$\therefore \mathbf{X} = \begin{pmatrix} -1 & 8 \\ -2 & 6 \end{pmatrix}$

d $\begin{pmatrix} 2 & 0 \\ -1 & 1 \end{pmatrix} \mathbf{X} = \begin{pmatrix} -1 \\ 2 \end{pmatrix}$

$\therefore \mathbf{X} = \begin{pmatrix} 2 & 0 \\ -1 & 1 \end{pmatrix}^{-1} \begin{pmatrix} -1 \\ 2 \end{pmatrix}$

$\therefore \mathbf{X} = \frac{1}{2} \begin{pmatrix} 1 & 0 \\ 1 & 2 \end{pmatrix} \begin{pmatrix} -1 \\ 2 \end{pmatrix}$

$\therefore \mathbf{X} = \frac{1}{2} \begin{pmatrix} -1 \\ 3 \end{pmatrix}$

$\therefore \mathbf{X} = \begin{pmatrix} -\frac{1}{2} \\ \frac{3}{2} \end{pmatrix}$

e $\begin{pmatrix} 1 & 1 \\ 1 & -2 \end{pmatrix} \mathbf{X} = \begin{pmatrix} 5 \\ 4 \end{pmatrix}$

$\therefore \mathbf{X} = \begin{pmatrix} 1 & 1 \\ 1 & -2 \end{pmatrix}^{-1} \begin{pmatrix} 5 \\ 4 \end{pmatrix}$

$\therefore \mathbf{X} = \frac{1}{-3} \begin{pmatrix} -2 & -1 \\ -1 & 1 \end{pmatrix} \begin{pmatrix} 5 \\ 4 \end{pmatrix}$

$\therefore \mathbf{X} = \frac{1}{-3} \begin{pmatrix} -14 \\ -1 \end{pmatrix}$

$\therefore \mathbf{X} = \begin{pmatrix} \frac{14}{3} \\ \frac{1}{3} \end{pmatrix}$

f $\begin{pmatrix} 1 & 1 \\ -1 & 1 \end{pmatrix} \mathbf{X} \begin{pmatrix} 2 & 1 \\ 1 & -1 \end{pmatrix} = \begin{pmatrix} 5 & 1 \\ 0 & 3 \end{pmatrix}$

$\therefore \mathbf{X} = \begin{pmatrix} 1 & 1 \\ -1 & 1 \end{pmatrix}^{-1} \begin{pmatrix} 5 & 1 \\ 0 & 3 \end{pmatrix} \begin{pmatrix} 2 & 1 \\ 1 & -1 \end{pmatrix}^{-1}$

$\therefore \mathbf{X} = \frac{1}{2} \begin{pmatrix} 1 & -1 \\ 1 & 1 \end{pmatrix} \begin{pmatrix} 5 & 1 \\ 0 & 3 \end{pmatrix} \frac{1}{-3} \begin{pmatrix} -1 & -1 \\ -1 & 2 \end{pmatrix}$

$= -\frac{1}{6} \begin{pmatrix} 5 & -2 \\ 5 & 4 \end{pmatrix} \begin{pmatrix} -1 & -1 \\ -1 & 2 \end{pmatrix}$

$= -\frac{1}{6} \begin{pmatrix} -3 & -9 \\ -9 & 3 \end{pmatrix}$

$= \begin{pmatrix} \frac{1}{2} & \frac{3}{2} \\ \frac{3}{2} & -\frac{1}{2} \end{pmatrix}$

5 a $2\mathbf{B} = 2 \begin{pmatrix} 2 & 4 \\ 0 & 1 \\ 3 & 2 \end{pmatrix} = \begin{pmatrix} 4 & 8 \\ 0 & 2 \\ 6 & 4 \end{pmatrix}$

b $\frac{1}{2}\mathbf{B} = \frac{1}{2} \begin{pmatrix} 2 & 4 \\ 0 & 1 \\ 3 & 2 \end{pmatrix} = \begin{pmatrix} 1 & 2 \\ 0 & \frac{1}{2} \\ \frac{3}{2} & 1 \end{pmatrix}$

c $\mathbf{AB} = \begin{pmatrix} 1 & 2 & 3 \end{pmatrix} \begin{pmatrix} 2 & 4 \\ 0 & 1 \\ 3 & 2 \end{pmatrix} = \begin{pmatrix} 11 & 12 \end{pmatrix}$

$1 \times \underset{\longleftarrow}{\widehat{3}} \quad \underset{\longrightarrow}{\widehat{3}} \times 2$

d $\mathbf{B}$ is $3 \times \widehat{2}$ and $\mathbf{A}$ is $\widehat{1} \times 3$ not equal $\therefore \mathbf{BA}$ does not exist.

6 a $P + Q$

$$= \begin{pmatrix} 1 & 2 \\ 1 & 0 \\ 2 & 3 \end{pmatrix} + \begin{pmatrix} 3 & 0 \\ 1 & 4 \\ 1 & 1 \end{pmatrix}$$

$$= \begin{pmatrix} 4 & 2 \\ 2 & 4 \\ 3 & 4 \end{pmatrix}$$

b $Q - P$

$$= \begin{pmatrix} 3 & 0 \\ 1 & 4 \\ 1 & 1 \end{pmatrix} - \begin{pmatrix} 1 & 2 \\ 1 & 0 \\ 2 & 3 \end{pmatrix}$$

$$= \begin{pmatrix} 2 & -2 \\ 0 & 4 \\ -1 & -2 \end{pmatrix}$$

c $\frac{3}{2}P - Q$

$$= \begin{pmatrix} \frac{3}{2} & 3 \\ \frac{3}{2} & 0 \\ 3 & \frac{9}{2} \end{pmatrix} - \begin{pmatrix} 3 & 0 \\ 1 & 4 \\ 1 & 1 \end{pmatrix}$$

$$= \begin{pmatrix} -\frac{3}{2} & 3 \\ \frac{1}{2} & -4 \\ 2 & \frac{7}{2} \end{pmatrix}$$

7 In augmented matrix form, the system is:

$$\begin{pmatrix} 1 & 4 & | & 2 \\ k & 3 & | & -6 \end{pmatrix} \sim \begin{pmatrix} 1 & 4 & | & 2 \\ 0 & 3-4k & | & -6-2k \end{pmatrix} \quad R_2 \to R_2 - kR_1$$

$$\begin{array}{ccc} k & 3 & -6 \\ -k & -4k & -2k \\ \hline 0 & 3-4k & -6-2k \end{array}$$

Row 2 gives $(3 - 4k)y = -6 - 2k$

$$\therefore \quad y = \frac{-2(3 + k)}{3 - 4k} \quad \text{which is not defined if } k = \frac{3}{4}$$

So the system has a unique solution for all $k \neq \frac{3}{4}$, k in $\mathbb{R}$.

If $k = \frac{3}{4}$, equation 2 becomes $\quad \frac{3}{4}x + 3y = -6$

$$\therefore \quad 3x + 12y = -24$$
$$\therefore \quad x + 4y = -8$$

which is the equation of a line parallel to $x + 4y = 2$ $\therefore$ there are no solutions.

8 In augmented matrix form, the system is:

$$\begin{pmatrix} 3 & -1 & 2 & | & 3 \\ 2 & 3 & -1 & | & -3 \\ 1 & -2 & 3 & | & 2 \end{pmatrix}$$

$$\sim \begin{pmatrix} 3 & -1 & 2 & | & 3 \\ 0 & 11 & -7 & | & -15 \\ 0 & -5 & 7 & | & 3 \end{pmatrix} \quad \begin{array}{l} R_2 \to 3R_2 - 2R_1 \\ R_3 \to 3R_3 - R_1 \end{array}$$

$$\sim \begin{pmatrix} 3 & -1 & 2 & | & 3 \\ 0 & 11 & -7 & | & -15 \\ 0 & 0 & 42 & | & -42 \end{pmatrix} \quad R_3 \to 11R_3 + 5R_2$$

$$\begin{array}{cccc} 6 & 9 & -3 & -9 \\ -6 & 2 & -4 & -6 \\ \hline 0 & 11 & -7 & -15 \end{array}$$

$$\begin{array}{cccc} 3 & -6 & 9 & 6 \\ -3 & 1 & -2 & -3 \\ \hline 0 & -5 & 7 & 3 \end{array}$$

$$\begin{array}{cccc} 0 & -55 & 77 & 33 \\ 0 & 55 & -35 & -75 \\ \hline 0 & 0 & 42 & -42 \end{array}$$

From row 3, $42z = -42 \quad \therefore \quad z = -1$

Substituting in row 2 gives $11y - 7(-1) = -15$ and from row 1, $3x - (-2) + 2(-1) = 3$

$$\therefore \quad 11y + 7 = -15 \qquad\qquad \therefore \quad 3x + 2 - 2 = 3$$
$$\therefore \quad 11y = -22 \qquad\qquad\qquad \therefore \quad x = 1$$
$$\therefore \quad y = -2$$

$\therefore \quad x = 1, \ y = -2, \ z = -1$

9 $x^2 + y^2 + ax + by + c = 0$

a $(-2, 4)$ lies on the circle $\qquad\qquad$ $(1, 3)$ lies on the circle

$\therefore \quad 4 + 16 - 2a + 4b + c = 0 \qquad \therefore \quad 1 + 9 + a + 3b + c = 0$

$\therefore \quad 2a - 4b - c = 20 \qquad\qquad\quad \therefore \quad a + 3b + c = -10$

In augmented matrix form, the system is:

$$\begin{pmatrix} 2 & -4 & -1 & | & 20 \\ 1 & 3 & 1 & | & -10 \end{pmatrix} \sim \begin{pmatrix} 2 & -4 & -1 & | & 20 \\ 0 & 10 & 3 & | & -40 \end{pmatrix} \quad R_2 \to 2R_2 - R_1$$

$$\begin{array}{cccc} 2 & 6 & 2 & -20 \\ -2 & 4 & 1 & -20 \\ \hline 0 & 10 & 3 & -40 \end{array}$$

Let $c = t$ in row 3, then $10b + 3t = -40$

$$\therefore \quad 10b = -3t - 40$$
$$\therefore \quad b = \frac{-3t - 40}{10}$$

and substituting in row 1 gives $2a - 4\left(\dfrac{-3t-40}{10}\right) - t = 20$

$\therefore\ 20a + 12t + 160 - 10t = 200$

$\therefore\ 20a = 40 - 2t \quad \therefore\ a = \dfrac{40-2t}{20}$

$\therefore\ a = 2 - \dfrac{t}{10},\quad b = -4 - \dfrac{3t}{10},\quad c = t \quad$ for all t in $\mathbb{R}$

(or $a = 2 - s,\ b = -4 - 3s,\ c = 10s\ $ for all s in $\mathbb{R}$).

b There are infinitely many solutions as we have 2 equations in 3 unknowns.

c If $(2, 2)$ is on the circle then $(2, 2)$ satisfies the equation of the circle.

$\therefore\ 2^2 + 2^2 + \left(\dfrac{20-t}{10}\right)(2) + \left(\dfrac{-3t-40}{10}\right)(2) + t = 0$

$\therefore\ 40 + 40 + 40 - 2t - 6t - 80 + 10t = 0$

$\therefore\ 2t = -40$

$\therefore\ t = -20$

and when $t = -20$, $a = 2 - \left(\dfrac{-20}{10}\right) = 4$, $b = -4 - \left(\dfrac{-60}{10}\right) = 2$, $c = -20$

$\therefore\ $ the equation of the circle is $\ x^2 + y^2 + 4x + 2y - 20 = 0$

10 In augmented matrix form, the system is:

$\begin{pmatrix} 2 & 3 & -4 & | & 13 \\ 1 & -1 & 3 & | & -1 \\ 3 & 7 & -11 & | & k \end{pmatrix}$

$\sim \begin{pmatrix} 1 & -1 & 3 & | & -1 \\ 2 & 3 & -4 & | & 13 \\ 3 & 7 & -11 & | & k \end{pmatrix} \quad R_1 \leftrightarrow R_2$

$\sim \begin{pmatrix} 1 & -1 & 3 & | & -1 \\ 0 & 5 & -10 & | & 15 \\ 0 & 10 & -20 & | & k+3 \end{pmatrix} \quad \begin{matrix} R_2 \to R_2 - 2R_1 \\ R_3 \to R_3 - 3R_1 \end{matrix}$

$\sim \begin{pmatrix} 1 & -1 & 3 & | & -1 \\ 0 & 5 & -10 & | & 15 \\ 0 & 0 & 0 & | & k-27 \end{pmatrix} \quad R_3 \to R_3 - 2R_2$

$\begin{array}{rrrr} 2 & 3 & -4 & 13 \\ -2 & 2 & -6 & 2 \\ \hline 0 & 5 & -10 & 15 \end{array}$

$\begin{array}{rrrr} 3 & 7 & -11 & k \\ -3 & 3 & -9 & 3 \\ \hline 0 & 10 & -20 & k+3 \end{array}$

$\begin{array}{rrrr} 0 & 10 & -20 & k+3 \\ 0 & -10 & 20 & -30 \\ \hline 0 & 0 & 0 & k-27 \end{array}$

If $k - 27 = 0$, or $k = 27$ we have a row of zeros.

$\therefore\ $ we have 2 equations in 3 unknowns which gives an infinite number of solutions.

Let $z = t$ in row 2 then $5y - 10t = 15$ and $x - (3 + 2t) + 3t = -1$

$\therefore\ y = 3 + 2t \qquad \therefore\ x - 3 - 2t + 3t = -1$

$\therefore\ x = 2 - t$

So, if $k = 27$ we have solutions of the form $x = 2 - t$, $y = 3 + 2t$, $z = t$ where t is in $\mathbb{R}$.

If $k \neq 27$ the system is inconsistent and there are no solutions.

11 In augmented matrix form, the system is:

$\begin{pmatrix} 3 & 1 & -1 & | & 0 \\ 1 & 1 & 2 & | & 0 \end{pmatrix} \sim \begin{pmatrix} 3 & 1 & -1 & | & 0 \\ 0 & 2 & 7 & | & 0 \end{pmatrix} \quad R_2 \to 3R_2 - R_1$

$\begin{array}{rrrr} 3 & 3 & 6 & 0 \\ -3 & -1 & 1 & 0 \\ \hline 0 & 2 & 7 & 0 \end{array}$

Let $z = t$ in row 2 then $2y + 7t = 0$, $\therefore\ y = -\tfrac{7}{2}t$ and $3x + (-\tfrac{7}{2}t) - t = 0$

$\therefore\ 3x = \tfrac{9}{2}t$

$\therefore\ x = \tfrac{3}{2}t$

$\therefore\ $ we have infinitely many solutions of the form $x = \tfrac{3}{2}t$, $y = -\tfrac{7}{2}t$, $z = t$ where t is in $\mathbb{R}$

(or $x = 3t$, $y = -7t$, $z = 2t$, $t \in \mathbb{R}$).

REVIEW SET 13B

1 $\begin{pmatrix} 1 & 0 \\ 1 & 1 \end{pmatrix} \begin{pmatrix} a & b \\ c & d \end{pmatrix} = \begin{pmatrix} 1 & 0 \\ 1 & 1 \end{pmatrix}$ $\therefore$ $a = 1$
$b = 0$
So, $a = 1$, $b = 0$, $c = 0$, $d = 1$

$\therefore \begin{pmatrix} a & b \\ a+c & b+d \end{pmatrix} = \begin{pmatrix} 1 & 0 \\ 1 & 1 \end{pmatrix}$ $a + c = 1$ $\therefore$ matrix is $\begin{pmatrix} 1 & 0 \\ 0 & 1 \end{pmatrix} = \mathbf{I}$
$b + d = 1$

2 a $\mathbf{AB} = \begin{pmatrix} 4 & 3 & 2 \end{pmatrix} \begin{pmatrix} 1 \\ 2 \\ 0 \end{pmatrix} = (10)$ **b** $\mathbf{BA} = \begin{pmatrix} 1 \\ 2 \\ 0 \end{pmatrix} \begin{pmatrix} 4 & 3 & 2 \end{pmatrix} = \begin{pmatrix} 4 & 3 & 2 \\ 8 & 6 & 4 \\ 0 & 0 & 0 \end{pmatrix}$

c $\mathbf{AC} = \begin{pmatrix} 4 & 3 & 2 \end{pmatrix} \begin{pmatrix} 1 & 2 & 3 \\ 3 & 2 & 1 \\ 1 & 2 & 3 \end{pmatrix} = \begin{pmatrix} 15 & 18 & 21 \end{pmatrix}$

d $\mathbf{CA}$ does not exist as $\mathbf{C}$ is 3×3 and $\mathbf{A}$ is 1×3.

e $\mathbf{CB} = \begin{pmatrix} 1 & 2 & 3 \\ 3 & 2 & 1 \\ 1 & 2 & 3 \end{pmatrix} \begin{pmatrix} 1 \\ 2 \\ 0 \end{pmatrix} = \begin{pmatrix} 5 \\ 7 \\ 5 \end{pmatrix}$

3 a $\mathbf{A}^{-1} = \dfrac{1}{42 - 40} \begin{pmatrix} 7 & -8 \\ -5 & 6 \end{pmatrix}$ **b** $\mathbf{A}^{-1}$ does not exist as $|\mathbf{A}| = -24 - -24 = 0$ **c** $\mathbf{A}^{-1} = \dfrac{1}{-3} \begin{pmatrix} -3 & -5 \\ 6 & 11 \end{pmatrix}$

$= \begin{pmatrix} \frac{7}{2} & -4 \\ -\frac{5}{2} & 3 \end{pmatrix}$ $= \begin{pmatrix} 1 & \frac{5}{3} \\ -2 & -\frac{11}{3} \end{pmatrix}$

4 $\mathbf{A} = 2\mathbf{A}^{-1}$ **a** $\mathbf{A}^2 = \mathbf{A} \times \mathbf{A}$ **b** $(\mathbf{A} - \mathbf{I})(\mathbf{A} + 3\mathbf{I}) = (\mathbf{A} - \mathbf{I})\mathbf{A} + (\mathbf{A} - \mathbf{I})3\mathbf{I}$
$= \mathbf{A}(2\mathbf{A}^{-1})$ $= \mathbf{A}^2 - \mathbf{I}\mathbf{A} + 3\mathbf{A}\mathbf{I} - 3\mathbf{I}^2$
$= 2\mathbf{A}\mathbf{A}^{-1}$ $= 2\mathbf{I} - \mathbf{A} + 3\mathbf{A} - 3\mathbf{I}$
$= 2\mathbf{I}$ $= 2\mathbf{A} - \mathbf{I}$

5 Sales matrix is $\begin{pmatrix} 42-27 & 54-31 \\ 36-28 & 27-15 \\ 34-28 & 30-22 \end{pmatrix} = \begin{pmatrix} 15 & 23 \\ 8 & 12 \\ 6 & 8 \end{pmatrix}$ Totals matrix is $\begin{pmatrix} 38 \\ 20 \\ 14 \end{pmatrix}$

Profit matrix is $\begin{pmatrix} 0.75 & 0.55 & 1.20 \end{pmatrix} \begin{pmatrix} 38 \\ 20 \\ 14 \end{pmatrix} = (56.3)$ $\therefore$ profit = \$56.30

6 $\mathbf{AB} = \begin{pmatrix} 1 & 2 & 3 \\ 2 & 5 & 7 \\ -2 & -4 & -5 \end{pmatrix} \begin{pmatrix} 3 & -2 & -1 \\ -4 & 1 & -1 \\ 2 & 0 & 1 \end{pmatrix} = \begin{pmatrix} 3-8+6 & -2+2+0 & -1-2+3 \\ 6-20+14 & -4+5+0 & -2-5+7 \\ -6+16-10 & 4-4+0 & 2+4-5 \end{pmatrix}$

$= \begin{pmatrix} 1 & 0 & 0 \\ 0 & 1 & 0 \\ 0 & 0 & 1 \end{pmatrix}$

$\mathbf{BA} = \begin{pmatrix} 3 & -2 & -1 \\ -4 & 1 & -1 \\ 2 & 0 & 1 \end{pmatrix} \begin{pmatrix} 1 & 2 & 3 \\ 2 & 5 & 7 \\ -2 & -4 & -5 \end{pmatrix} = \begin{pmatrix} 3-4+2 & 6-10+4 & 9-14+5 \\ -4+2+2 & -8+5+4 & -12+7+5 \\ 2+0-2 & 4+0-4 & 6+0-5 \end{pmatrix}$

$= \begin{pmatrix} 1 & 0 & 0 \\ 0 & 1 & 0 \\ 0 & 0 & 1 \end{pmatrix}$

$\therefore \mathbf{AB} = \mathbf{BA} = \mathbf{I}$ $\therefore \mathbf{A}^{-1} = \mathbf{B}$

7 Using technology, the solution of $2x + y + z = 8$ is $x = 2$, $y = 1$, $z = 3$
$4x - 7y + 3z = 10$
$3x - 2y - z = 1$

8 In augmented matrix form, the system is:

$$\begin{pmatrix} 1 & 2 & -3 & | & 3 \\ 6 & 3 & 2 & | & 4 \end{pmatrix} \sim \begin{pmatrix} 1 & 2 & -3 & | & 3 \\ 0 & -9 & 20 & | & -14 \end{pmatrix} \quad R_2 \to R_2 - 6R_1$$

6	3	2	4
-6	-12	18	-18
0	-9	20	-14

Letting $z = t$ in row 2, $\quad -9y + 20t = -14 \quad$ and in row 1, $\quad x + 2\left(\dfrac{14 + 20t}{9}\right) - 3t = 3$

$\therefore \quad -9y = -14 - 20t$

$\therefore \quad y = \dfrac{14 + 20t}{9}$

$\therefore \quad 9x + 28 + 40t - 27t = 27$

$\therefore \quad 9x = -1 - 13t$

$\therefore \quad x = \dfrac{-1 - 13t}{9}$

$\therefore$ there are infinitely many solutions of the form $\quad x = \dfrac{-1 - 13t}{9}, \quad y = \dfrac{14 + 20t}{9}, \quad z = t, \quad t \in \mathbb{R}$.

9 a In augmented matrix form, the system is:

$$\begin{pmatrix} 2 & -3 & | & 9 \\ m & -7 & | & n \end{pmatrix} \sim \begin{pmatrix} 2 & -3 & | & 9 \\ 3m - 14 & 0 & | & 3n - 63 \end{pmatrix} \quad R_2 \to 3R_2 - 7R_1$$

$$\sim \begin{pmatrix} 2 & -3 & | & 9 \\ 14 - 3m & 0 & | & 63 - 3n \end{pmatrix} \quad R_2 \to -R_2$$

$3m$	-21	$3n$
-14	21	-63
$3m - 14$	0	$3n - 63$

b The system has a unique solution when $\quad 14 - 3m \ne 0$, or when $m \ne \frac{14}{3}$.

(If $m = \frac{14}{3}$, there are either infinitely many solutions or no solutions, depending on the value of n.)

REVIEW SET 13C

1 In matrix form $\begin{pmatrix} k & 3 \\ 1 & k+2 \end{pmatrix} \begin{pmatrix} x \\ y \end{pmatrix} = \begin{pmatrix} -6 \\ 2 \end{pmatrix}$ has a unique solution if $\begin{vmatrix} k & 3 \\ 1 & k+2 \end{vmatrix} \ne 0$

$\therefore \quad k^2 + 2k - 3 \ne 0$

$\therefore \quad (k-1)(k+3) \ne 0$

$\therefore \quad k \ne 1$ or -3

If $k = 1$, the equations are: $\left. \begin{array}{l} x + 3y = -6 \\ x + 3y = 2 \end{array} \right\}$ parallel lines $\quad \therefore$ no solutions exist

If $k = -3$, the equations are: $\left. \begin{array}{l} -3x + 3y = -6 \\ x - y = 2 \end{array} \right\}$ coincident lines $\therefore$ infinitely many solutions

2 $\begin{vmatrix} x & 2 & 0 \\ 2 & x+1 & -2 \\ 0 & -2 & x+2 \end{vmatrix} = x \begin{vmatrix} x+1 & -2 \\ -2 & x+2 \end{vmatrix} - 2 \begin{vmatrix} 2 & -2 \\ 0 & x+2 \end{vmatrix} + 0 \begin{vmatrix} 2 & x+1 \\ 0 & -2 \end{vmatrix}$

$= x \left[(x+1)(x+2) - 4 \right] - 2 \left[2(x+2) - 0 \right]$

$= x(x^2 + 3x + 2 - 4) - 4(x+2)$

$= x(x^2 + 3x - 2) - 4x - 8$

$= x^3 + 3x^2 - 2x - 4x - 8$

$= x^3 + 3x^2 - 6x - 8$

$= (x+4)(x+1)(x-2) \quad$ {using technology}

$\therefore \quad (x+4)(x+1)(x-2) = 0$

$\therefore \quad x = -4, -1$ or 2

3 $A = \begin{pmatrix} -2 & 3 \\ 4 & -1 \end{pmatrix}$, $B = \begin{pmatrix} -7 & 9 \\ 9 & -3 \end{pmatrix}$, $C = \begin{pmatrix} -1 & 0 & 3 \\ 0 & 2 & 1 \end{pmatrix}$

a $2A - 2B = \begin{pmatrix} -4 & 6 \\ 8 & -2 \end{pmatrix} - \begin{pmatrix} -14 & 18 \\ 18 & -6 \end{pmatrix} = \begin{pmatrix} 10 & -12 \\ -10 & 4 \end{pmatrix}$

b A is 2×2 and C is 2×3 $\quad \therefore \quad AC$ is 2×3

$$AC = \begin{pmatrix} -2 & 3 \\ 4 & -1 \end{pmatrix} \begin{pmatrix} -1 & 0 & 3 \\ 0 & 2 & 1 \end{pmatrix} = \begin{pmatrix} 2+0 & 0+6 & -6+3 \\ -4+0 & 0-2 & 12-1 \end{pmatrix} = \begin{pmatrix} 2 & 6 & -3 \\ -4 & -2 & 11 \end{pmatrix}$$

c C is 2×3 and B is 2×2 $\quad \therefore \quad CB$ is not possible.

d $\qquad DA = B$
$\therefore \quad DAA^{-1} = BA^{-1}$ $\quad$ {postmultiplying by A^{-1}}
$\therefore \quad D = BA^{-1}$

$\therefore \quad D = \begin{pmatrix} -7 & 9 \\ 9 & -3 \end{pmatrix} \dfrac{1}{-2(-1) - 3(4)} \begin{pmatrix} -1 & -3 \\ -4 & -2 \end{pmatrix} = -\dfrac{1}{10} \begin{pmatrix} 7-36 & 21-18 \\ -9+12 & -27+6 \end{pmatrix}$

$\therefore \quad D = \begin{pmatrix} \frac{29}{10} & -\frac{3}{10} \\ -\frac{3}{10} & \frac{21}{10} \end{pmatrix}$

4 $\begin{pmatrix} 2 & -1 \\ 3 & 4 \end{pmatrix} X = \begin{pmatrix} 3 & 5 & 1 \\ -1 & 13 & 18 \end{pmatrix}$

$\therefore \quad X = \begin{pmatrix} 2 & -1 \\ 3 & 4 \end{pmatrix}^{-1} \begin{pmatrix} 3 & 5 & 1 \\ -1 & 13 & 18 \end{pmatrix}$

$= \dfrac{1}{11} \begin{pmatrix} 4 & 1 \\ -3 & 2 \end{pmatrix} \begin{pmatrix} 3 & 5 & 1 \\ -1 & 13 & 18 \end{pmatrix}$

$= \dfrac{1}{11} \begin{pmatrix} 11 & 33 & 22 \\ -11 & 11 & 33 \end{pmatrix}$

$\therefore \quad X = \begin{pmatrix} 1 & 3 & 2 \\ -1 & 1 & 3 \end{pmatrix}$

5 $\qquad 5A^2 - 6A = 3I$
$\therefore \quad A(5A - 6I) = 3I$
$\therefore \quad A \times \frac{1}{3}(5A - 6I) = I$
$\therefore \quad A^{-1} = \frac{5}{3}A - 2I$

6 a i If $AB = B$ then $ABB^{-1} = BB^{-1}$ provided B^{-1} exists.
$\therefore \quad A = I$ provided B^{-1} exists, $\quad \therefore \quad$ provided that $|B| \neq 0$.

ii $(A + B)^2 = (A + B)(A + B)$
$= A^2 + AB + BA + B^2$
$= A^2 + 2AB + B^2 \quad$ provided that $\quad AB = BA$.

b $M = \begin{pmatrix} k & 2 \\ 2 & k \end{pmatrix} \begin{pmatrix} k-1 & -2 \\ -3 & -k \end{pmatrix}$

$\therefore \quad |M| = \begin{vmatrix} k & 2 \\ 2 & k \end{vmatrix} \begin{vmatrix} k-1 & -2 \\ -3 & k \end{vmatrix} = (k^2 - 4)(k^2 - k - 6)$
$\qquad\qquad = (k+2)(k-2)(k+2)(k-3)$

Since M^{-1} exists, $|M| \neq 0$.
$\therefore \quad k$ is any real number $\neq 3$ or ± 2.

7 In augmented matrix form, the system is:

$\begin{pmatrix} 1 & -1 & -2 & | & -3 \\ t & 1 & -1 & | & 3t \\ 1 & 3 & t & | & 13 \end{pmatrix}$

$\sim \begin{pmatrix} 1 & -1 & -2 & | & -3 \\ 0 & 1+t & -1+2t & | & 6t \\ 0 & 4 & t+2 & | & 16 \end{pmatrix} \begin{matrix} R_2 \to R_2 - tR_1 \\ R_3 \to R_3 - R_1 \end{matrix}$

$\sim \begin{pmatrix} 1 & -1 & -2 & | & -3 \\ 0 & 1+t & -1+2t & | & 6t \\ 0 & 0 & t^2 - 5t + 6 & | & 16 - 8t \end{pmatrix} R_3 \to (1+t)R_3 - 4R_2$

Row 3 gives $(t-3)(t-2)z = -8(t-2)$ $\quad \therefore \quad z = \dfrac{-8(t-2)}{(t-3)(t-2)}$

$\begin{array}{rrrr} t & 1 & -1 & 3t \\ -t & t & 2t & 3t \\ \hline 0 & 1+t & -1+2t & 6t \end{array}$

$\begin{array}{rrrr} 1 & 3 & t & 13 \\ -1 & 1 & 2 & 3 \\ \hline 0 & 4 & t+2 & 16 \end{array}$

$\begin{array}{rrrr} 0 & 4+4t & t^2+3t+2 & 16+16t \\ 0 & -4-4t & 4-8t & -24t \\ \hline 0 & 0 & t^2 - 5t + 6 & 16 - 8t \end{array}$

If $t = 3$, there are no solutions, so there is no unique solution.
If $t = 2$, row 3 becomes a row of zeros so there are infinitely many solutions, so there is no unique solution.

The reduced matrix becomes $\begin{pmatrix} 1 & -1 & -2 & | & -3 \\ 0 & 3 & 3 & | & 12 \\ 0 & 0 & 0 & | & 0 \end{pmatrix}$.

Row 2 gives $3y + 3z = 12$, or $y + z = 4$.

Let $z = s$ ∴ $y = 4 - s$ and substituting in row 1 gives $\quad x - (4 - s) - 2s = -3$
$$\therefore \quad x - 4 + s - 2s = -3$$
$$\therefore \quad x = 1 + s$$

So, when $t = 2$, the solutions are of the form $x = 1 + s$, $y = 4 - s$, $z = s$ where s is in $\mathbb{R}$.

If $t \neq 2$ and $t \neq 3$, then $z = \dfrac{-8}{t-3}$.

Substituting in row 2 gives

$(1+t)y - \dfrac{8(-1+2t)}{t-3} = 6t$ and $x - \dfrac{2(3t-4)}{t-3} + \dfrac{2 \times 8}{t-3} = -3$

∴ $(t-3)(1+t)y + 8 - 16t = 6t(t-3)$ ∴ $(t-3)x - 6t + 8 + 16 = -3t + 9$

∴ $(t-3)(1+t)y = 6t^2 - 18t + 16t - 8$ ∴ $(t-3)x = 3t - 15$

∴ $y = \dfrac{2(3t^2 - t - 4)}{(t-3)(t+1)}$ ∴ $x = \dfrac{3(t-5)}{t-3}$

$= \dfrac{2(3t-4)(t+1)}{(t-3)(t+1)}$

$= \dfrac{2(3t-4)}{t-3}$

So if $t \neq 2$ or 3, then the unique solution is:
$x = \dfrac{3(t-5)}{t-3}$, $y = \dfrac{2(3t-4)}{t-3}$, $z = \dfrac{-8}{t-3}$ for t in $\mathbb{R}$.

8 a $s = at^2 + bt + c$
At $t = 1$, $s(1) = 63$ ∴ $a + b + c = 63$
At $t = 2$, $s(2) = 72$ ∴ $4a + 2b + c = 72$
At $t = 7$, $s(7) = 27$ ∴ $49a + 7b + c = 27$
Using technology, $a = -3$, $b = 18$, $c = 48$ and ∴ $s(t) = -3t^2 + 18t + 48$

b $s(0) = 48$ ∴ the height of the cliff is 48 m.

c The rock reaches sea level when $s(t) = 0$
∴ $-3(t^2 - 6t - 16) = 0$
∴ $-3(t - 8)(t + 2) = 0$
∴ $t = 8$ or -2
but $t \geqslant 0$, so it reaches sea level after 8 seconds.

REVIEW SET 13D

1 This system in matrix form is $\begin{pmatrix} 3 & -1 & 2 \\ 2 & 3 & -1 \\ 1 & -2 & 3 \end{pmatrix} \begin{pmatrix} x \\ y \\ z \end{pmatrix} = \begin{pmatrix} 8 \\ -3 \\ 9 \end{pmatrix}$

∴ $\begin{pmatrix} x \\ y \\ z \end{pmatrix} = \begin{pmatrix} 3 & -1 & 2 \\ 2 & 3 & -1 \\ 1 & -2 & 3 \end{pmatrix}^{-1} \begin{pmatrix} 8 \\ -3 \\ 9 \end{pmatrix}$

∴ $\begin{pmatrix} x \\ y \\ z \end{pmatrix} = \begin{pmatrix} 1 \\ -1 \\ 2 \end{pmatrix}$

So, $x = 1$, $y = -1$, $z = 2$. {using technology}

2 $\begin{vmatrix} a+b & c & c \\ a & b+c & a \\ b & b & c+a \end{vmatrix} = (a+b)\begin{vmatrix} b+c & a \\ b & c+a \end{vmatrix} - c\begin{vmatrix} a & a \\ b & c+a \end{vmatrix} + c\begin{vmatrix} a & b+c \\ b & b \end{vmatrix}$

$= (a+b)[(b+c)(c+a) - ab] - c[a(c+a) - ab] + c[ab - (b+c)b]$

$= (a+b)(bc + ab + c^2 + ac - ab) - ac^2 - a^2c + abc + abc - b^2c - bc^2$

$= abc + b^2c + ac^2 + bc^2 + a^2c + abc - ac^2 - a^2c + abc + abc - b^2c - bc^2$

$= 4abc$

3 If $A^2 = 5A + 2I$,

$\begin{aligned} A^3 &= A(5A + 2I) \\ &= 5A^2 + 2AI \\ &= 5(5A + 2I) + 2A \\ &= 25A + 10I + 2A \\ &= 27A + 10I \end{aligned}$
$\qquad\begin{aligned} A^4 &= A(27A + 10I) \\ &= 27A^2 + 10AI \\ &= 27(5A + 2I) + 10A \\ &= 135A + 54I + 10A \\ &= 145A + 54I \end{aligned}$
$\qquad\begin{aligned} A^5 &= A(145A + 54I) \\ &= 145A^2 + 54AI \\ &= 145(5A + 2I) + 54A \\ &= 725A + 290I + 54A \\ &= 779A + 290I \end{aligned}$

$\begin{aligned} A^6 &= A(779A + 290I) \\ &= 779A^2 + 290AI \\ &= 779(5A + 2I) + 290AI \\ &= 4185A + 1558I \end{aligned}$

4 a $C(0) = 80 \quad \therefore \quad a(0) + b(0) + c(0) + d = 80 \quad \therefore \quad d = 80$

b $C(1) = 100 \qquad \therefore \quad a + b + c + 80 = 100$
$C(2) = 148 \qquad \therefore \quad 8a + 4b + 2c + 80 = 148$
$C(4) = 376 \qquad \therefore \quad 64a + 16b + 4c + 80 = 376$

$\begin{pmatrix} 1 & 1 & 1 \\ 8 & 4 & 2 \\ 64 & 16 & 4 \end{pmatrix} \begin{pmatrix} a \\ b \\ c \end{pmatrix} = \begin{pmatrix} 20 \\ 68 \\ 296 \end{pmatrix}$

$\therefore \quad \begin{pmatrix} a \\ b \\ c \end{pmatrix} = \begin{pmatrix} 1 & 1 & 1 \\ 8 & 4 & 2 \\ 64 & 16 & 4 \end{pmatrix}^{-1} \begin{pmatrix} 20 \\ 68 \\ 296 \end{pmatrix} = \begin{pmatrix} 2 \\ 8 \\ 10 \end{pmatrix} \quad \{\text{using technology}\}$

$\therefore \quad a = 2, \quad b = 8, \quad c = 10$

5 $\qquad AXB = C$
$\therefore \quad A^{-1}AXBB^{-1} = A^{-1}CB^{-1}$
$\therefore \quad IXI = A^{-1}CB^{-1}$
$\therefore \quad X = A^{-1}CB^{-1}$

So $X = \begin{pmatrix} 1 & -3 \\ 2 & 1 \end{pmatrix}^{-1} \begin{pmatrix} -12 & -11 \\ -10 & -1 \end{pmatrix} \begin{pmatrix} -1 & 2 \\ 3 & 1 \end{pmatrix}^{-1}$

$\therefore \quad X = \begin{pmatrix} 0 & -2 \\ 1 & 1 \end{pmatrix} \quad \{\text{using technology}\}$

6 a $\begin{pmatrix} 2 & 1 & -1 \\ 3 & 2 & 5 \\ 1 & 1 & -3 \end{pmatrix} \begin{pmatrix} x \\ y \\ z \end{pmatrix} = \begin{pmatrix} 9 \\ 19 \\ 1 \end{pmatrix}$

$\therefore \quad \begin{pmatrix} x \\ y \\ z \end{pmatrix} = \begin{pmatrix} 2 & 1 & -1 \\ 3 & 2 & 5 \\ 1 & 1 & -3 \end{pmatrix}^{-1} \begin{pmatrix} 9 \\ 19 \\ 1 \end{pmatrix} = \begin{pmatrix} 6 \\ -2 \\ 1 \end{pmatrix}$

$\therefore \quad x = 6, \quad y = -2, \quad z = 1$

b $\begin{pmatrix} 2 & 1 & -1 \\ 3 & 2 & 1 \\ 1 & -3 & 0 \end{pmatrix} \begin{pmatrix} x \\ y \\ z \end{pmatrix} = \begin{pmatrix} 3 \\ 1 \\ 5 \end{pmatrix}$

$\therefore \quad \begin{pmatrix} x \\ y \\ z \end{pmatrix} = \begin{pmatrix} 2 & 1 & -1 \\ 3 & 2 & 1 \\ 1 & -3 & 0 \end{pmatrix}^{-1} \begin{pmatrix} 3 \\ 1 \\ 5 \end{pmatrix} = \begin{pmatrix} \frac{3}{2} \\ -\frac{7}{6} \\ -\frac{7}{6} \end{pmatrix}$

$\therefore \quad x = \frac{3}{2}, \quad y = -\frac{7}{6}, \quad z = -\frac{7}{6}$

7 In augmented matrix form, the system is:

$$\begin{pmatrix} k & 2 & | & 1 \\ 2 & k & | & -2 \end{pmatrix} \sim \begin{pmatrix} k & 2 & | & 1 \\ 0 & (k+2)(k-2) & | & -2(k+1) \end{pmatrix} \quad R_2 \to kR_2 - 2R_1$$

$$\begin{array}{ccc} 2k & k^2 & -2k \\ -2k & -4 & -2 \\ \hline 0 & k^2 - 4 & -2k - 2 \end{array}$$

Row 2 gives $(k+2)(k-2)y = -2(k+1)$ $\quad \therefore \quad y = \dfrac{-2(k+1)}{(k+2)(k-2)}$

If $k \neq \pm 2$, then substituting in row 1 gives

$$kx + 2\left(\dfrac{-2k-2}{(k+2)(k-2)}\right) = 1$$

$\therefore \quad k(k+2)(k-2)x - 4k - 4 = k^2 - 4$

$\therefore \quad x = \dfrac{k^2 + 4k}{k(k+2)(k-2)}$

$\quad = \dfrac{k+4}{(k+2)(k-2)}$

$\therefore$ if $k \neq \pm 2$, then the unique solution is $x = \dfrac{k+4}{(k+2)(k-2)}, \quad y = \dfrac{-2(k+1)}{(k+2)(k-2)}$

If $k = \pm 2$, then row 2 becomes $\quad 0z = -6 \quad$ or $\quad 0z = 2 \quad$ which has no solution, so the system has no solutions.

8 In augmented matrix form, the system is:

$$\begin{pmatrix} 2 & -3 & 1 & | & 10 \\ 4 & -6 & k & | & m \end{pmatrix} \sim \begin{pmatrix} 2 & -3 & 1 & | & 10 \\ 0 & 0 & k-2 & | & m-20 \end{pmatrix} \quad R_2 \to R_2 - 2R_1$$

$$\begin{array}{cccc} 4 & -6 & k & m \\ -4 & 6 & -2 & -20 \\ \hline 0 & 0 & k-2 & m-20 \end{array}$$

If $k = 2$ and $m = 20$, the last row is all zeros so there are an infinite number of solutions. Let $y = s$ and $z = t$ in equation 1.

The solutions are of the form $\quad x = \dfrac{10 + 3s - t}{2}, \quad y = s, \quad z = t \quad$ for all s, t in $\mathbb{R}$.

If $k = 2$ and $m \neq 20$, the system is inconsistent and there are no solutions.

If $k \neq 2$, then from row 2, $\quad z = \dfrac{m-20}{k-2}$.

Let $y = s$ in equation 1, then $\quad 2x - 3s + \dfrac{m-20}{k-2} = 10$

$\therefore \quad 2x = 10 + 3s - \dfrac{m-20}{k-2}$

$\therefore \quad x = \dfrac{10 + 3s - \frac{m-20}{k-2}}{2}$

So, there are an infinite number of solutions of the form

$$x = \dfrac{10 + 3s - \frac{m-20}{k-2}}{2}, \quad y = s, \quad z = \dfrac{m-20}{k-2}, \quad s \text{ is in } \mathbb{R}.$$

9 a In augmented matrix form, the system is: $\begin{pmatrix} 1 & 5 & -6 & | & 2 \\ k & 1 & -1 & | & 3 \\ 5 & -k & 3 & | & 7 \end{pmatrix}$

$\sim \begin{pmatrix} 1 & 5 & -6 & | & 2 \\ 0 & 1-5k & 6k-1 & | & 3-2k \\ 0 & -k-25 & 33 & | & -3 \end{pmatrix} \begin{array}{l} R_2 \to R_2 - kR_1 \\ R_3 \to R_3 - 5R_1 \end{array}$

$\begin{array}{ccc|c} k & 1 & -1 & 3 \\ -k & -5k & 6k & -2k \\ \hline 0 & 1-5k & 6k-1 & 3-2k \end{array}$

$\begin{array}{ccc|c} 5 & -k & 3 & 7 \\ -5 & -25 & 30 & -10 \\ \hline 0 & -k-25 & 33 & -3 \end{array}$

$\sim \begin{pmatrix} 1 & 5 & -6 & | & 2 \\ 0 & 1-5k & 6k-1 & | & 3-2k \\ 0 & 0 & 2(k-2)(3k-2) & | & -2(k-2)(k+18) \end{pmatrix} \quad R_3 \to (1-5k)R_3 + (k+25)R_2$

$\sim \begin{pmatrix} 1 & 5 & -6 & | & 2 \\ 0 & 1-5k & 6k-1 & | & 3-2k \\ 0 & 0 & (k-2)(3k-2) & | & -(k-2)(k+18) \end{pmatrix} \quad R_3 \to \tfrac{1}{2}R_3 \quad \text{as required}$

$\begin{array}{ccc} 0 & 5k^2 + 124k - 25 & 33 - 165k \\ 0 & -5k^2 - 124k + 25 & 6k^2 + 149k - 25 \\ \hline 0 & 0 & 6k^2 - 16k + 8 \\ & & = 2(3k^2 - 8k + 4) \end{array} \quad \begin{array}{c} -3 + 15k \\ -2k^2 - 47k + 75 \\ \hline -2k^2 - 32k + 72 \\ = -2(k^2 + 16k - 36) \end{array}$

b k has a unique solution provided $k \neq 2$ or $\tfrac{2}{3}$

c If $k = 2$, then row 3 becomes a row of zeros so there are infinitely many solutions.

The system becomes $\begin{pmatrix} 1 & 5 & -6 & | & 2 \\ 0 & -9 & 11 & | & -1 \\ 0 & 0 & 0 & | & 0 \end{pmatrix}$

Let $z = t$ in row 2, then $-9y + 11t = -1$

$\therefore \ y = \dfrac{1+11t}{9}$

Substituting in row 1 gives $x + 5\left(\dfrac{1+11t}{9}\right) - 6t = 2$

$\therefore \ 9x + 5 + 55t - 54t = 18$

$\therefore \ x = \dfrac{13-t}{9}$

So, the solutions are of the form $x = \dfrac{13-t}{9}, \ y = \dfrac{1+11t}{9}, \ z = t, \ $ where t is in $\mathbb{R}$.

d If $k = \tfrac{2}{3}$, then the system is inconsistent and there are no solutions.

REVIEW SET 13E

1 a Let €x be the cost of an opera ticket
€y be the cost of a play ticket
€z be the cost of a concert ticket

$\therefore \ 3x + 2y + 5z = 267$
$2x + 3y + z = 145$
$x + 5y + 4z = 230$

b So, $\begin{pmatrix} 3 & 2 & 5 \\ 2 & 3 & 1 \\ 1 & 5 & 4 \end{pmatrix} \begin{pmatrix} x \\ y \\ z \end{pmatrix} = \begin{pmatrix} 267 \\ 145 \\ 230 \end{pmatrix} \quad \therefore \quad \begin{pmatrix} x \\ y \\ z \end{pmatrix} = \begin{pmatrix} 3 & 2 & 5 \\ 2 & 3 & 1 \\ 1 & 5 & 4 \end{pmatrix}^{-1} \begin{pmatrix} 267 \\ 145 \\ 230 \end{pmatrix}$

$\therefore \ \begin{pmatrix} x \\ y \\ z \end{pmatrix} = \begin{pmatrix} 32 \\ 18 \\ 27 \end{pmatrix} \quad$ using technology

$\therefore \ $ the cost of each ticket is €32 for an opera, €18 for a play, €27 for a concert.

c Total cost $= 4 \times$ €$32 + 1 \times$ €$18 + 2 \times$ €27
$=$ €$128 +$ €$18 +$ €$54 =$ €200

2 $\begin{pmatrix} 2 & 1 & 1 \\ 4 & -7 & 3 \\ 3 & -2 & -1 \end{pmatrix} \begin{pmatrix} x \\ y \\ z \end{pmatrix} = \begin{pmatrix} 8 \\ 10 \\ 1 \end{pmatrix} \quad \therefore \quad \begin{pmatrix} x \\ y \\ z \end{pmatrix} = \begin{pmatrix} 2 & 1 & 1 \\ 4 & -7 & 3 \\ 3 & -2 & -1 \end{pmatrix}^{-1} \begin{pmatrix} 8 \\ 10 \\ 1 \end{pmatrix} = \begin{pmatrix} 2 \\ 1 \\ 3 \end{pmatrix}$

$\therefore \ x = 2, \ y = 1, \ z = 3 \ $ {using technology}

3 a $3\mathbf{A} = 3\begin{pmatrix} -3 & 2 & 2 \\ 1 & -1 & 0 \end{pmatrix} = \begin{pmatrix} -9 & 6 & 6 \\ 3 & -3 & 0 \end{pmatrix}$

  b $\mathbf{AB} = \begin{pmatrix} -3 & 2 & 2 \\ 1 & -1 & 0 \end{pmatrix}\begin{pmatrix} 2 & 4 \\ -3 & 1 \\ 1 & 2 \end{pmatrix} = \begin{pmatrix} -10 & -6 \\ 5 & 3 \end{pmatrix}$

  c $\mathbf{BA} = \begin{pmatrix} 2 & 4 \\ -3 & 1 \\ 1 & 2 \end{pmatrix}\begin{pmatrix} -3 & 2 & 2 \\ 1 & -1 & 0 \end{pmatrix} = \begin{pmatrix} -2 & 0 & 4 \\ 10 & -7 & -6 \\ -1 & 0 & 2 \end{pmatrix}$

  d $\mathbf{A}$ is 2×3 and $\mathbf{C}$ is 2×2 $\therefore$ $\mathbf{AC}$ does not exist.

  e $\mathbf{BC} = \begin{pmatrix} 2 & 4 \\ -3 & 1 \\ 1 & 2 \end{pmatrix}\begin{pmatrix} -2 & 5 \\ 1 & 3 \end{pmatrix} = \begin{pmatrix} 0 & 22 \\ 7 & -12 \\ 0 & 11 \end{pmatrix}$

4 $\mathbf{A} = \begin{pmatrix} 1 & 2 & 1 \\ 2 & 4 & 6 \\ 3 & 1 & 2 \end{pmatrix} \quad \mathbf{B} = \begin{pmatrix} -1 & 2 & -3 \\ 2 & -1 & 4 \\ 3 & 4 & 1 \end{pmatrix}$

  $\mathbf{AB} = \begin{pmatrix} 1 & 2 & 1 \\ 2 & 4 & 6 \\ 3 & 1 & 2 \end{pmatrix}\begin{pmatrix} -1 & 2 & -3 \\ 2 & -1 & 4 \\ 3 & 4 & 1 \end{pmatrix} = \begin{pmatrix} -1+4+3 & 2-2+4 & -3+8+1 \\ -2+8+18 & 4-4+24 & -6+16+6 \\ -3+2+6 & 6-1+8 & -9+4+2 \end{pmatrix}$

  $\therefore \mathbf{AB} = \begin{pmatrix} 6 & 4 & 6 \\ 24 & 24 & 16 \\ 5 & 13 & -3 \end{pmatrix}$

  $\therefore \det \mathbf{AB} = 6\begin{vmatrix} 24 & 16 \\ 13 & -3 \end{vmatrix} - 4\begin{vmatrix} 24 & 16 \\ 5 & -3 \end{vmatrix} + 6\begin{vmatrix} 24 & 24 \\ 5 & 13 \end{vmatrix}$

  $= 6(-72 - 208) - 4(-72 - 80) + 6(312 - 120)$
  $= 80$

  $\det \mathbf{A} = 1\begin{vmatrix} 4 & 6 \\ 1 & 2 \end{vmatrix} - 2\begin{vmatrix} 2 & 6 \\ 3 & 2 \end{vmatrix} + 1\begin{vmatrix} 2 & 4 \\ 3 & 1 \end{vmatrix}$

  $= 1(8 - 6) - 2(4 - 18) + 1(2 - 12)$
  $= 2 + 28 - 10$
  $= 20$

  and $\det \mathbf{B} = -1\begin{vmatrix} -1 & 4 \\ 4 & 1 \end{vmatrix} - 2\begin{vmatrix} 2 & 4 \\ 3 & 1 \end{vmatrix} + (-3)\begin{vmatrix} 2 & -1 \\ 3 & 4 \end{vmatrix}$

  $= -1(-1 - 16) - 2(2 - 12) - 3(8 - -3)$
  $= 17 + 20 - 33$
  $= 4$

  $\therefore \det \mathbf{A} \times \det \mathbf{B} = 20 \times 4 = 80 = \det(\mathbf{AB})$

5 If $\mathbf{A}^2 = \mathbf{A} - \mathbf{I}$ then $\mathbf{A}^3 = \mathbf{A}(\mathbf{A} - \mathbf{I}) = \mathbf{A}^2 - \mathbf{AI} = \mathbf{A} - \mathbf{I} - \mathbf{A} = -\mathbf{I}$
  $\mathbf{A}^4 = \mathbf{AA}^3 = \mathbf{A}(-\mathbf{I}) = -\mathbf{A}$
  $\mathbf{A}^5 = \mathbf{AA}^4 = \mathbf{A}(-\mathbf{A}) = -\mathbf{A}^2 = -(\mathbf{A} - \mathbf{I}) = \mathbf{I} - \mathbf{A}$
  $\mathbf{A}^6 = \mathbf{AA}^5 = \mathbf{A}(\mathbf{I} - \mathbf{A}) = \mathbf{AI} - \mathbf{A}^2 = \mathbf{A} - (\mathbf{A} - \mathbf{I}) = \mathbf{I}$
  $\mathbf{A}^7 = \mathbf{AA}^6 = \mathbf{AI} = \mathbf{A}$
  $\mathbf{A}^8 = \mathbf{AA}^7 = \mathbf{AA} = \mathbf{A}^2 = \mathbf{A} - \mathbf{I}$

  a $\mathbf{A}^{6n+3} = -\mathbf{I}$
    $\mathbf{A}^{6n+5} = \mathbf{I} - \mathbf{A}$

  b Now $\mathbf{A}^2 = \mathbf{A} - \mathbf{I}$
    $\therefore \mathbf{A}^{-1}\mathbf{AA} = \mathbf{A}^{-1}\mathbf{A} - \mathbf{A}^{-1}\mathbf{I}$ {premultiplying by $\mathbf{A}^{-1}$}
    $\therefore \mathbf{IA} = \mathbf{I} - \mathbf{A}^{-1}$
    $\therefore \mathbf{A}^{-1} = \mathbf{I} - \mathbf{A}$

c P_n is "$A^{6n+5} = I - A$" for all n in $\mathbb{Z}^+$.
Proof: (By the principle of mathematical induction)
(1) If $n = 1$, $A^{11} = A^5 A^6$
$= (I - A)I$
$= I - A$ $\therefore$ P_1 is true
(2) If P_k is true, then $A^{6k+5} = I - A$
$\therefore$ $A^{6(k+1)+5} = A^{6k+6+5}$
$= A^{6k+5} A^6$
$= (I - A)I$
$= I - A$
Thus P_{k+1} is true whenever P_k is true and P_1 is true.
$\therefore$ P_n is true for all $n \in \mathbb{Z}^+$ {Principle of mathematical induction}

6 a $\begin{pmatrix} a & b & 0 \\ b & 0 & a \\ 0 & 2 & b \end{pmatrix} \begin{pmatrix} 2 & 1 & 1 \\ 1 & 1 & 1 \\ 2 & 2 & 1 \end{pmatrix} = \begin{pmatrix} 2a+b & a+b & a+b \\ 2a+2b & 2a+b & a+b \\ 2+2b & 2+2b & 2+b \end{pmatrix}$

which is $\begin{pmatrix} 1 & 0 & 0 \\ 0 & 1 & 0 \\ 0 & 0 & 1 \end{pmatrix}$ if $a + b = 0$ and $2 + 2b = 0$
$\therefore$ $b = -1$ and $a = 1$.

The inverse is $\begin{pmatrix} 1 & -1 & 0 \\ -1 & 0 & 1 \\ 0 & 2 & -1 \end{pmatrix}$.

b Writing the system of equations in matrix form

$\begin{pmatrix} 2 & 1 & 1 \\ 1 & 1 & 1 \\ 2 & 2 & 1 \end{pmatrix} \begin{pmatrix} x \\ y \\ z \end{pmatrix} = \begin{pmatrix} 1 \\ 6 \\ 5 \end{pmatrix}$

$\therefore$ $\begin{pmatrix} 1 & -1 & 0 \\ -1 & 0 & 1 \\ 0 & 2 & -1 \end{pmatrix} \begin{pmatrix} 2 & 1 & 1 \\ 1 & 1 & 1 \\ 2 & 2 & 1 \end{pmatrix} \begin{pmatrix} x \\ y \\ z \end{pmatrix} = \begin{pmatrix} 1 & -1 & 0 \\ -1 & 0 & 1 \\ 0 & 2 & -1 \end{pmatrix} \begin{pmatrix} 1 \\ 6 \\ 5 \end{pmatrix}$

$\therefore$ $\begin{pmatrix} x \\ y \\ z \end{pmatrix} = \begin{pmatrix} -5 \\ 4 \\ 7 \end{pmatrix}$

$\therefore$ $x = -5$, $y = 4$, $z = 7$.

Chapter 14
VECTORS IN 2 AND 3 DIMENSIONS

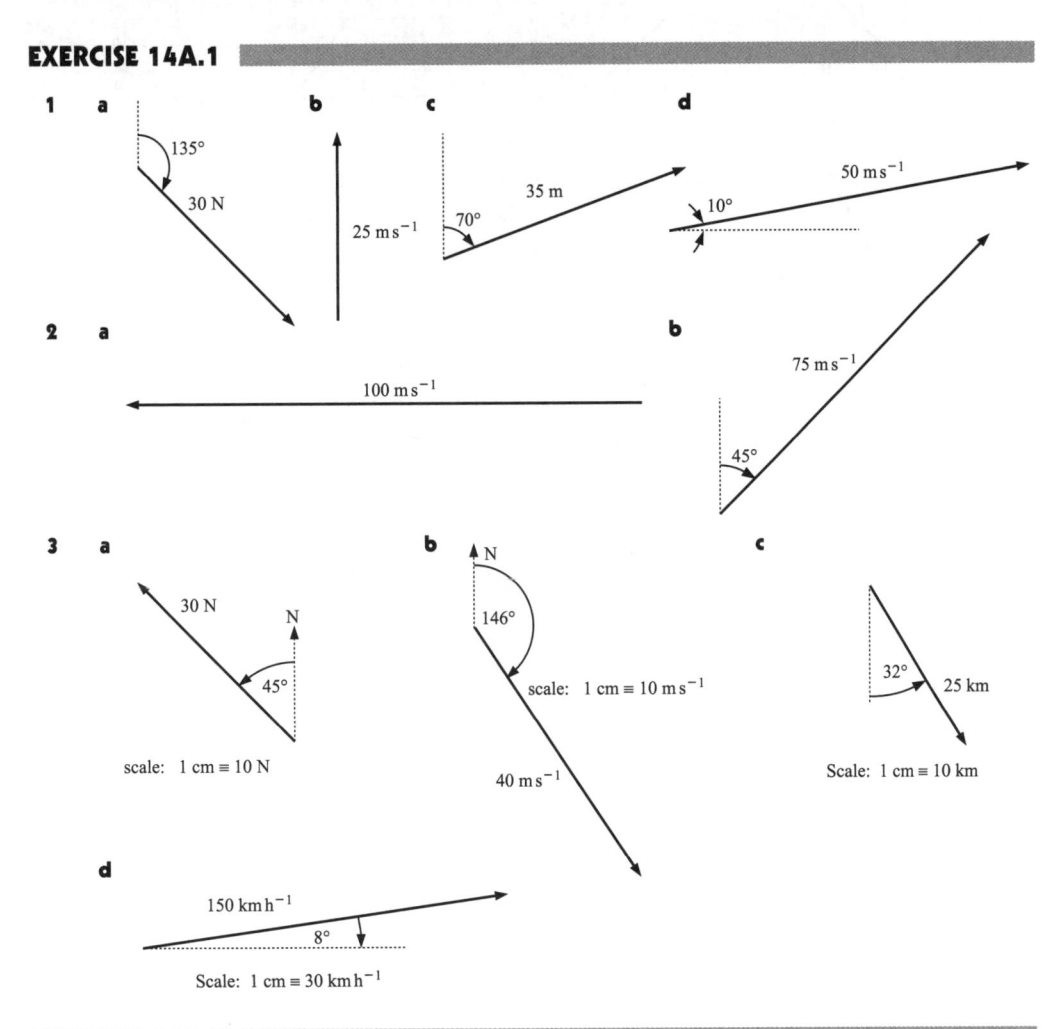

EXERCISE 14A.1

1 a, b, c, d [vector diagrams]

2 a, b [vector diagrams]

3 a, b, c, d [vector diagrams]

EXERCISE 14A.2

1 **a** If they are equal in magnitude, they have the same length. These are **p**, **q**, **s** and **t**.
   b Those parallel are **p**, **q**, **r** and **t**.
   c Those in the same direction are: **p** and **r**, **q** and **t**.
   d To be equal they must have the same direction and be equal in length $\therefore$ **q** = **t**.
   e **p** and **q** are negatives (equal length, but opposite direction). Likewise, **p** and **t** are negatives. We write **p** = −**q** and **p** = −**t**.

2 **a** True, as they have the same length and are parallel.
   b True, as they are sides of an equilateral triangle.
   c False, as they do not have the same direction.
   d False, as they have opposite directions.
   e True, as they have the same length and direction.
   f False, as they do not have the same direction.

EXERCISE 14B.1

1 a, b, 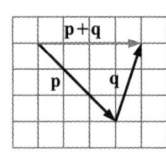 c, 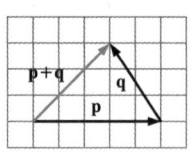 d, 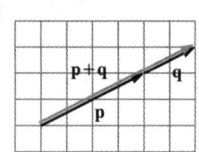 e, 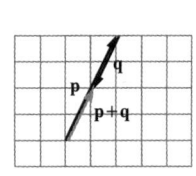 f — diagrams showing vector additions $\mathbf{p} + \mathbf{q}$

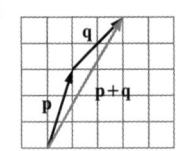

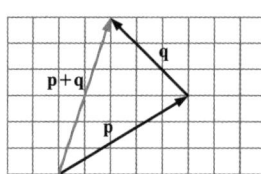

2 a $\overrightarrow{AB} + \overrightarrow{BC}$
$= \overrightarrow{AC}$

  b $\overrightarrow{BC} + \overrightarrow{CD}$
$= \overrightarrow{BD}$

  c $\overrightarrow{AB} + \overrightarrow{BC} + \overrightarrow{CD}$
$= \overrightarrow{AC} + \overrightarrow{CD}$
$= \overrightarrow{AD}$

  d $\overrightarrow{AC} + \overrightarrow{CB} + \overrightarrow{BD}$
$= \overrightarrow{AB} + \overrightarrow{BD}$
$= \overrightarrow{AD}$

3 a i, ii — diagrams   b yes

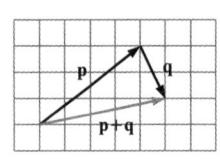

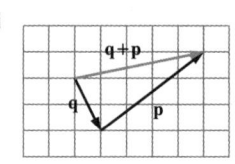

4 $\overrightarrow{PS} = \overrightarrow{PR} + \overrightarrow{RS}$
$= (\mathbf{a} + \mathbf{b}) + \mathbf{c}$

But $\overrightarrow{PS} = \overrightarrow{PQ} + \overrightarrow{QS}$
$= \mathbf{a} + (\mathbf{b} + \mathbf{c})$

$\therefore\ (\mathbf{a} + \mathbf{b}) + \mathbf{c} = \mathbf{a} + (\mathbf{b} + \mathbf{c})$ {as both are equal to $\overrightarrow{PS}$}

EXERCISE 14B.2

1 a, b, 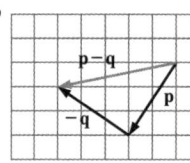 c, 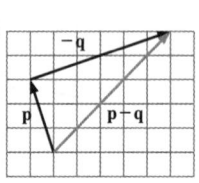 d — diagrams showing $\mathbf{p} - \mathbf{q}$

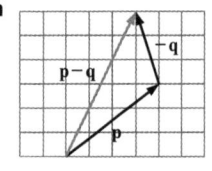

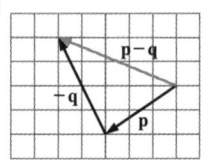

2 a, 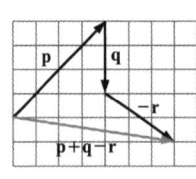 b, 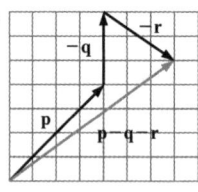 c — diagrams

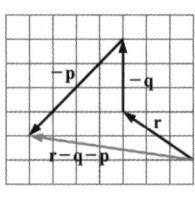

3 a $\overrightarrow{AC} + \overrightarrow{CB}$
$= \overrightarrow{AB}$

  b $\overrightarrow{AD} - \overrightarrow{BD}$
$= \overrightarrow{AD} + \overrightarrow{DB}$
$= \overrightarrow{AB}$

  c $\overrightarrow{AC} + \overrightarrow{CA}$
$= \overrightarrow{AA}$
$= \mathbf{0}$

  d $\overrightarrow{AB} + \overrightarrow{BC} + \overrightarrow{CD}$
$= \overrightarrow{AC} + \overrightarrow{CD}$
$= \overrightarrow{AD}$

  e $\overrightarrow{BA} - \overrightarrow{CA} + \overrightarrow{CB}$
$= \overrightarrow{BA} + \overrightarrow{AC} + \overrightarrow{CB}$
$= \overrightarrow{BC} + \overrightarrow{CB}$
$= \overrightarrow{BB}$
$= \mathbf{0}$

  f $\overrightarrow{AB} - \overrightarrow{CB} - \overrightarrow{DC}$
$= \overrightarrow{AB} + \overrightarrow{BC} + \overrightarrow{CD}$
$= \overrightarrow{AC} + \overrightarrow{CD}$
$= \overrightarrow{AD}$

4 a $t = r + s$ **b** $r = -s - t$ **c** $r = -p - q - s$ **d** $r = q - p + s$
   e $p = t + s + r - q$ **f** $p = -u + t + s - r - q$

5 a **i** $\overrightarrow{OB} = \overrightarrow{OA} + \overrightarrow{AB}$ **ii** $\overrightarrow{CA} = \overrightarrow{CB} + \overrightarrow{BA}$ **iii** $\overrightarrow{OC} = \overrightarrow{OA} + \overrightarrow{AB} + \overrightarrow{BC}$
           $= r + s$ $= -\overrightarrow{BC} - \overrightarrow{AB}$ $= r + s + t$
                                     $= -t - s$

   b **i** $\overrightarrow{AD} = \overrightarrow{AB} + \overrightarrow{BD}$ **ii** $\overrightarrow{BC} = \overrightarrow{BD} + \overrightarrow{DC}$ **iii** $\overrightarrow{AC} = \overrightarrow{AB} + \overrightarrow{BD} + \overrightarrow{DC}$
           $= p + q$ $= q + r$ $= p + q + r$

EXERCISE 14B.3

1 **a** Using the cosine rule,
         $V^2 = 20^2 + 6^2 - 2 \times 20 \times 6 \times \cos 135°$
         $\therefore\ V \approx 24.6$
         $\therefore$ the equivalent speed in still water is 24.6 km h^{-1}.

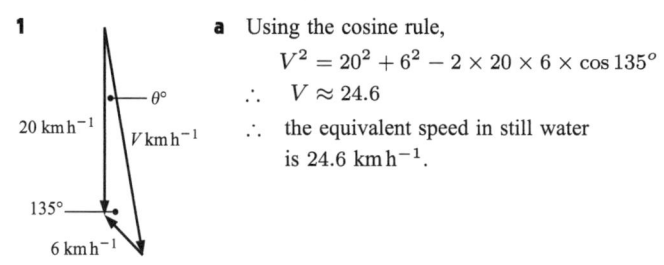

   b Using the sine rule,
         $\dfrac{\sin \theta}{6} \approx \dfrac{\sin 135°}{24.6}$
         $\therefore\ \theta \approx \sin^{-1}\left(\dfrac{6 \times \sin 135°}{24.6}\right)$
         $\therefore\ \theta \approx 9.93°$
         $\therefore$ the boat should head 9.93° east of south.

2 **a** $d^2 = 80^2 + 20^2$ {Pythagoras}
         $\therefore\ d = \sqrt{80^2 + 20^2}$ $\{d > 0\}$
         $\therefore\ d \approx 82.5$
         $\therefore$ the distance from X to Y is about 82.5 m.

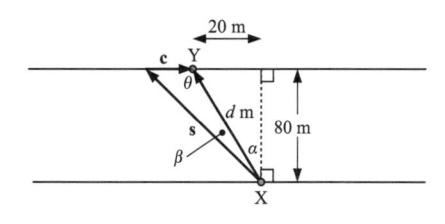

   c $\tan(\alpha + \beta) = \dfrac{20 + 0.3t}{80}$
         $\therefore\ 20 + 0.3t \approx 80 \tan(23.3°)$
         $\therefore\ t \approx \dfrac{80 \tan(23.3°) - 20}{0.3}$
         $\therefore\ t \approx 48.4$
         $\therefore$ Stephanie will take 48.4 seconds to cross the river.

   b $\alpha = \tan^{-1}\left(\dfrac{20}{80}\right) \approx 14.04°$
         $\therefore\ \theta \approx 90° + 14.04°$ {exterior angle of Δ}
         $\therefore\ \theta \approx 104.04°$
         In t seconds, Stephanie can swim $1.8t$ metres, and the current will move $0.3t$ metres.
         $\therefore\ |s| = 1.8t$ and $|c| = 0.3t$
         Using the sine rule,
         $\dfrac{\sin \beta}{0.3t} = \dfrac{\sin \theta}{1.8t}$
         $\therefore\ \beta \approx \sin^{-1}\left(\dfrac{0.3 \times \sin 104.04°}{1.8}\right)$
         $\therefore\ \beta \approx 9.31°$
         $\therefore\ \alpha + \beta \approx 23.3°$
         $\therefore$ Stephanie should head 23.3° west of north.

EXERCISE 14B.4

1 a   **b** 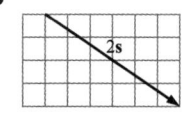   **c** 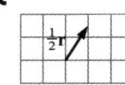   **d**

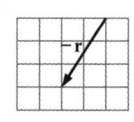

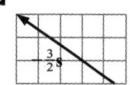

e 2r − s

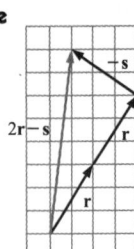

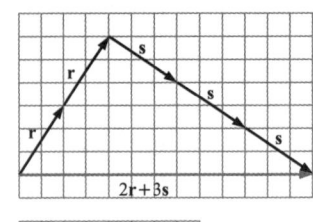

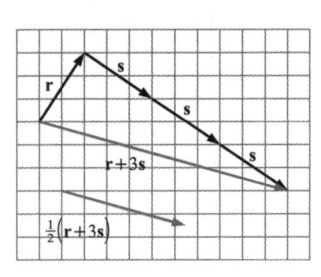

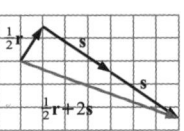

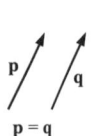

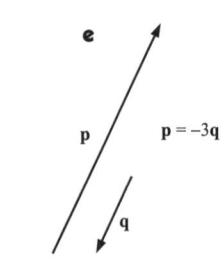

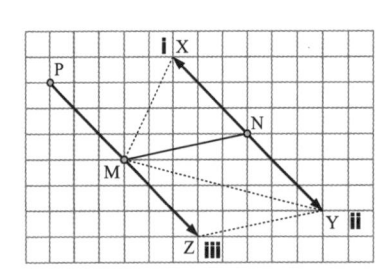

f 2r + 3s

g $\frac{1}{2}$r + 2s

h r + 3s, $\frac{1}{2}$(r + 3s)

2 a p = q **b** p = −q **c** p = 2q **d** p = $\frac{1}{3}$q **e** p = −3q

3 a (diagram) **b** a parallelogram

EXERCISE 14C.1

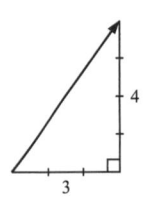

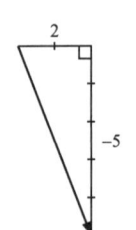

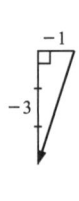

1 a (triangle with sides 3, 4) **b** (vector of length 2) **c** (triangle with sides 2, −5) **d** (triangle with sides −1, −3)

2 a $\binom{7}{3}$ **b** $\binom{-6}{0}$ **c** $\binom{2}{-5}$ **d** $\binom{0}{6}$ **e** $\binom{-6}{3}$ **f** $\binom{-5}{-5}$

EXERCISE 14C.2

1 a a + b
$= \binom{-3}{2} + \binom{1}{4}$
$= \binom{-2}{6}$

b b + a
$= \binom{1}{4} + \binom{-3}{2}$
$= \binom{-2}{6}$

c b + c
$= \binom{1}{4} + \binom{-2}{-5}$
$= \binom{-1}{-1}$

d c + b
$= \binom{-2}{-5} + \binom{1}{4}$
$= \binom{-1}{-1}$

e a + c
$= \binom{-3}{2} + \binom{-2}{-5}$
$= \binom{-5}{-3}$

f c + a
$= \binom{-2}{-5} + \binom{-3}{2}$
$= \binom{-5}{-3}$

g a + a
$= \binom{-3}{2} + \binom{-3}{2}$
$= \binom{-6}{4}$

h b + a + c
$= \binom{1}{4} + \binom{-3}{2} + \binom{-2}{-5}$
$= \binom{-2}{6} + \binom{-2}{-5}$
$= \binom{-4}{1}$

2 **a** $p - q$

$= \begin{pmatrix} -4 \\ 2 \end{pmatrix} - \begin{pmatrix} -1 \\ -5 \end{pmatrix}$

$= \begin{pmatrix} -3 \\ 7 \end{pmatrix}$

b $q - r$

$= \begin{pmatrix} -1 \\ -5 \end{pmatrix} - \begin{pmatrix} 3 \\ -2 \end{pmatrix}$

$= \begin{pmatrix} -4 \\ -3 \end{pmatrix}$

c $p + q - r$

$= \begin{pmatrix} -4 \\ 2 \end{pmatrix} + \begin{pmatrix} -1 \\ -5 \end{pmatrix} - \begin{pmatrix} 3 \\ -2 \end{pmatrix}$

$= \begin{pmatrix} -8 \\ -1 \end{pmatrix}$

d $p - q - r$

$= \begin{pmatrix} -4 \\ 2 \end{pmatrix} - \begin{pmatrix} -1 \\ -5 \end{pmatrix} - \begin{pmatrix} 3 \\ -2 \end{pmatrix}$

$= \begin{pmatrix} -6 \\ 9 \end{pmatrix}$

e $q - r - p$

$= \begin{pmatrix} -1 \\ -5 \end{pmatrix} - \begin{pmatrix} 3 \\ -2 \end{pmatrix} - \begin{pmatrix} -4 \\ 2 \end{pmatrix}$

$= \begin{pmatrix} 0 \\ -5 \end{pmatrix}$

f $r + q - p$

$= \begin{pmatrix} 3 \\ -2 \end{pmatrix} + \begin{pmatrix} -1 \\ -5 \end{pmatrix} - \begin{pmatrix} -4 \\ 2 \end{pmatrix}$

$= \begin{pmatrix} 6 \\ -9 \end{pmatrix}$

3 **a** $\overrightarrow{AC}$

$= \overrightarrow{AB} + \overrightarrow{BC}$

$= -\overrightarrow{BA} + \overrightarrow{BC}$

$= -\begin{pmatrix} 2 \\ -3 \end{pmatrix} + \begin{pmatrix} -3 \\ 1 \end{pmatrix}$

$= \begin{pmatrix} -5 \\ 4 \end{pmatrix}$

b $\overrightarrow{CB}$

$= \overrightarrow{CA} + \overrightarrow{AB}$

$= \begin{pmatrix} 2 \\ -1 \end{pmatrix} + \begin{pmatrix} -1 \\ 3 \end{pmatrix}$

$= \begin{pmatrix} 1 \\ 2 \end{pmatrix}$

c $\overrightarrow{SP}$

$= \overrightarrow{SR} + \overrightarrow{RQ} + \overrightarrow{QP}$

$= -\overrightarrow{RS} + \overrightarrow{RQ} - \overrightarrow{PQ}$

$= -\begin{pmatrix} -3 \\ 2 \end{pmatrix} + \begin{pmatrix} 2 \\ 1 \end{pmatrix} - \begin{pmatrix} -1 \\ 4 \end{pmatrix}$

$= \begin{pmatrix} 6 \\ -5 \end{pmatrix}$

4 **a** $\overrightarrow{AB} = \begin{pmatrix} b_1 - a_1 \\ b_2 - a_2 \end{pmatrix}$

$= \begin{pmatrix} 4 - 2 \\ 7 - 3 \end{pmatrix} = \begin{pmatrix} 2 \\ 4 \end{pmatrix}$

b $\overrightarrow{AB} = \begin{pmatrix} b_1 - a_1 \\ b_2 - a_2 \end{pmatrix}$

$= \begin{pmatrix} 1 - 3 \\ 4 - -1 \end{pmatrix} = \begin{pmatrix} -2 \\ 5 \end{pmatrix}$

c $\overrightarrow{AB} = \begin{pmatrix} b_1 - a_1 \\ b_2 - a_2 \end{pmatrix}$

$= \begin{pmatrix} 1 - -2 \\ 4 - 7 \end{pmatrix} = \begin{pmatrix} 3 \\ -3 \end{pmatrix}$

d $\overrightarrow{AB} = \begin{pmatrix} b_1 - a_1 \\ b_2 - a_2 \end{pmatrix}$

$= \begin{pmatrix} 3 - 2 \\ 0 - 5 \end{pmatrix} = \begin{pmatrix} 1 \\ -5 \end{pmatrix}$

e $\overrightarrow{AB} = \begin{pmatrix} b_1 - a_1 \\ b_2 - a_2 \end{pmatrix}$

$= \begin{pmatrix} 6 - 0 \\ -1 - 4 \end{pmatrix} = \begin{pmatrix} 6 \\ -5 \end{pmatrix}$

f $\overrightarrow{AB} = \begin{pmatrix} b_1 - a_1 \\ b_2 - a_2 \end{pmatrix}$

$= \begin{pmatrix} 0 - -1 \\ 0 - -3 \end{pmatrix} = \begin{pmatrix} 1 \\ 3 \end{pmatrix}$

EXERCISE 14C.3

1 **a** $-3p = -3\begin{pmatrix} 1 \\ 5 \end{pmatrix} = \begin{pmatrix} -3 \\ -15 \end{pmatrix}$

b $\frac{1}{2}q = \frac{1}{2}\begin{pmatrix} -2 \\ 4 \end{pmatrix} = \begin{pmatrix} -1 \\ 2 \end{pmatrix}$

c $2p + q = 2\begin{pmatrix} 1 \\ 5 \end{pmatrix} + \begin{pmatrix} -2 \\ 4 \end{pmatrix}$

$= \begin{pmatrix} 2 \\ 10 \end{pmatrix} + \begin{pmatrix} -2 \\ 4 \end{pmatrix}$

$= \begin{pmatrix} 0 \\ 14 \end{pmatrix}$

d $p - 2q = \begin{pmatrix} 1 \\ 5 \end{pmatrix} - 2\begin{pmatrix} -2 \\ 4 \end{pmatrix}$

$= \begin{pmatrix} 1 \\ 5 \end{pmatrix} - \begin{pmatrix} -4 \\ 8 \end{pmatrix}$

$= \begin{pmatrix} 5 \\ -3 \end{pmatrix}$

e $p - \frac{1}{2}r = \begin{pmatrix} 1 \\ 5 \end{pmatrix} - \begin{pmatrix} -\frac{3}{2} \\ -\frac{1}{2} \end{pmatrix}$

$= \begin{pmatrix} \frac{5}{2} \\ \frac{11}{2} \end{pmatrix}$

f $2p + 3r = 2\begin{pmatrix} 1 \\ 5 \end{pmatrix} + 3\begin{pmatrix} -3 \\ -1 \end{pmatrix}$

$= \begin{pmatrix} 2 \\ 10 \end{pmatrix} + \begin{pmatrix} -9 \\ -3 \end{pmatrix}$

$= \begin{pmatrix} -7 \\ 7 \end{pmatrix}$

g $2q - 3r = 2\begin{pmatrix} -2 \\ 4 \end{pmatrix} - 3\begin{pmatrix} -3 \\ -1 \end{pmatrix}$

$= \begin{pmatrix} -4 \\ 8 \end{pmatrix} - \begin{pmatrix} -9 \\ -3 \end{pmatrix}$

$= \begin{pmatrix} 5 \\ 11 \end{pmatrix}$

h $2p - q + \frac{1}{3}r = \begin{pmatrix} 2 \\ 10 \end{pmatrix} - \begin{pmatrix} -2 \\ 4 \end{pmatrix} + \begin{pmatrix} -1 \\ -\frac{1}{3} \end{pmatrix}$

$= \begin{pmatrix} 3 \\ \frac{17}{3} \end{pmatrix}$

2 **a** $= \begin{pmatrix} 8 \\ -1 \end{pmatrix}$ **b** $= \begin{pmatrix} 8 \\ -1 \end{pmatrix}$ **c** $= \begin{pmatrix} 8 \\ -1 \end{pmatrix}$

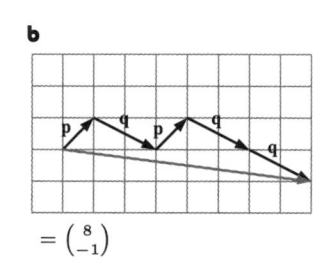

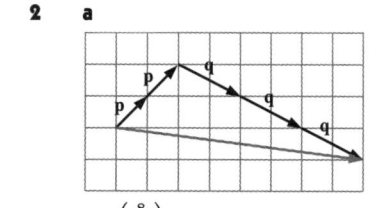

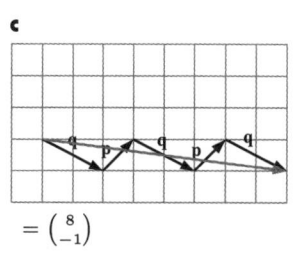

The vector expressions are equal, as each consists of **2p**s and **3q**s. Each expression is equal to $2p + 3q$.

EXERCISE 14C.4

1 a $|\mathbf{r}| = \sqrt{2^2 + 3^2}$
$= \sqrt{13}$ units

b $|\mathbf{s}| = \sqrt{(-1)^2 + 4^2}$
$= \sqrt{17}$ units

c $\mathbf{r} + \mathbf{s}$
$= \binom{2}{3} + \binom{-1}{4}$
$= \binom{1}{7}$
$\therefore |\mathbf{r} + \mathbf{s}|$
$= \sqrt{1^2 + 7^2}$
$= \sqrt{50}$ units

d $\mathbf{r} - \mathbf{s}$
$= \binom{2}{3} - \binom{-1}{4}$
$= \binom{3}{-1}$
$\therefore |\mathbf{r} - \mathbf{s}|$
$= \sqrt{3^2 + (-1)^2}$
$= \sqrt{10}$ units

e $\mathbf{s} - 2\mathbf{r}$
$= \binom{-1}{4} - \binom{4}{6}$
$= \binom{-5}{-2}$
$\therefore |\mathbf{s} - 2\mathbf{r}|$
$= \sqrt{(-5)^2 + (-2)^2}$
$= \sqrt{29}$ units

2 a $|\mathbf{p}| = \sqrt{1^2 + 3^2}$
$= \sqrt{10}$ units

b $2\mathbf{p} = \binom{2}{6}$
$\therefore |2\mathbf{p}| = \sqrt{2^2 + 6^2}$
$= \sqrt{4 + 36}$
$= \sqrt{40}$
$= 2\sqrt{10}$ units

c $-2\mathbf{p} = \binom{-2}{-6}$
$\therefore |-2\mathbf{p}| = \sqrt{(-2)^2 + (-6)^2}$
$= \sqrt{4 + 36}$
$= \sqrt{40}$
$= 2\sqrt{10}$ units

d $3\mathbf{p} = \binom{3}{9}$
$\therefore |3\mathbf{p}| = \sqrt{3^2 + 9^2}$
$= \sqrt{9 + 81}$
$= \sqrt{90}$
$= 3\sqrt{10}$ units

e $-3\mathbf{p} = \binom{-3}{-9}$
$\therefore |-3\mathbf{p}| = \sqrt{(-3)^2 + (-9)^2}$
$= \sqrt{9 + 81}$
$= \sqrt{90}$
$= 3\sqrt{10}$ units

f $|\mathbf{q}| = \sqrt{(-2)^2 + 4^2}$
$= \sqrt{4 + 16}$
$= \sqrt{20}$
$= 2\sqrt{5}$ units

g $4\mathbf{q} = \binom{-8}{16}$
$\therefore |4\mathbf{q}| = \sqrt{(-8)^2 + 16^2}$
$= \sqrt{64 + 256}$
$= \sqrt{320}$
$= 8\sqrt{5}$ units

h $-4\mathbf{q} = \binom{8}{-16}$
$\therefore |-4\mathbf{q}| = \sqrt{8^2 + (-16)^2}$
$= \sqrt{64 + 256}$
$= \sqrt{320}$
$= 8\sqrt{5}$ units

i $\tfrac{1}{2}\mathbf{q} = \binom{-1}{2}$
$\therefore \left|\tfrac{1}{2}\mathbf{q}\right| = \sqrt{(-1)^2 + 2^2}$
$= \sqrt{5}$ units

j $-\tfrac{1}{2}\mathbf{q} = \binom{1}{-2}$
$\therefore \left|-\tfrac{1}{2}\mathbf{q}\right| = \sqrt{1^2 + (-2)^2}$
$= \sqrt{5}$ units

3 $k\mathbf{a} = \begin{pmatrix} ka_1 \\ ka_2 \end{pmatrix}$ $\therefore |k\mathbf{a}| = \sqrt{(ka_1)^2 + (ka_2)^2}$
$= \sqrt{k^2 a_1^2 + k^2 a_2^2}$
$= \sqrt{k^2(a_1^2 + a_2^2)}$
$= \sqrt{k^2}\sqrt{a_1^2 + a_2^2}$
$= |k|\sqrt{a_1^2 + a_2^2} = |k|\,|\mathbf{a}|$

4 a $\overrightarrow{AB} = \binom{3-2}{5--1} = \binom{1}{6}$
$\therefore AB = \sqrt{1^2 + 6^2}$
$= \sqrt{37}$ units

b $\overrightarrow{BA} = \binom{2-3}{-1-5} = \binom{-1}{-6}$
$\therefore BA = \sqrt{(-1)^2 + (-6)^2}$
$= \sqrt{37}$ units

c $\overrightarrow{BC} = \binom{-1-3}{4-5} = \binom{-4}{-1}$
$\therefore BC = \sqrt{(-4)^2 + (-1)^2}$
$= \sqrt{17}$ units

d $\vec{DC} = \begin{pmatrix} -1--4 \\ 4--3 \end{pmatrix} = \begin{pmatrix} 3 \\ 7 \end{pmatrix}$ **e** $\vec{CA} = \begin{pmatrix} 2--1 \\ -1-4 \end{pmatrix} = \begin{pmatrix} 3 \\ -5 \end{pmatrix}$ **f** $\vec{DA} = \begin{pmatrix} 2--4 \\ -1--3 \end{pmatrix} = \begin{pmatrix} 6 \\ 2 \end{pmatrix}$

$\therefore DC = \sqrt{3^2 + 7^2}$ $\quad\therefore CA = \sqrt{3^2 + (-5)^2}$ $\quad\therefore DA = \sqrt{6^2 + 2^2}$
$= \sqrt{58}$ units $\qquad\qquad = \sqrt{34}$ units $\qquad\qquad = \sqrt{40}$
$\qquad\qquad\qquad\qquad\qquad\qquad\qquad\qquad\qquad\qquad\qquad = 2\sqrt{10}$ units

EXERCISE 14D

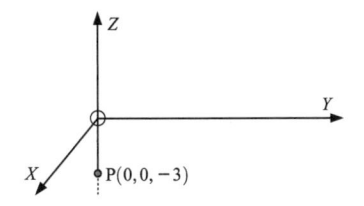

1 a $OP = \sqrt{0^2 + 0^2 + (-3)^2} = 3$ units

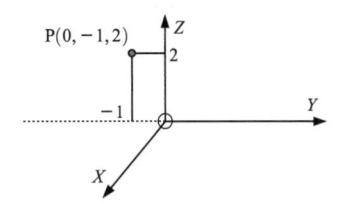

b $OP = \sqrt{0^2 + (-1)^2 + 2^2} = \sqrt{5}$ units

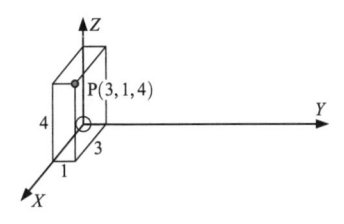

c $OP = \sqrt{3^2 + 1^2 + 4^2}$
$= \sqrt{26}$ units

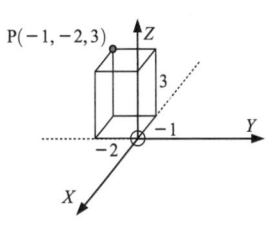

d $OP = \sqrt{(-1)^2 + (-2)^2 + 3^2}$
$= \sqrt{14}$ units

2 a i $AB = \sqrt{(0--1)^2 + (-1-2)^2 + (1-3)^2}$
$= \sqrt{1+9+4}$
$= \sqrt{14}$ units

ii Midpoint is at $\left(\dfrac{-1+0}{2}, \dfrac{2-1}{2}, \dfrac{3+1}{2}\right)$
which is $\left(-\tfrac{1}{2}, \tfrac{1}{2}, 2\right)$.

b i $AB = \sqrt{(2-0)^2 + (-1-0)^2 + (3-0)^2}$
$= \sqrt{4+1+9}$
$= \sqrt{14}$ units

ii Midpoint is at $\left(\dfrac{0+2}{2}, \dfrac{0-1}{2}, \dfrac{0+3}{2}\right)$
which is $\left(1, -\tfrac{1}{2}, \tfrac{3}{2}\right)$.

c i $AB = \sqrt{(-1-3)^2 + (0--1)^2 + (1--1)^2}$
$= \sqrt{16+1+4}$
$= \sqrt{21}$ units

ii Midpoint is at $\left(\dfrac{3-1}{2}, \dfrac{-1+0}{2}, \dfrac{-1+1}{2}\right)$
which is $\left(1, -\tfrac{1}{2}, 0\right)$.

d i $AB = \sqrt{(0-2)^2 + (1-0)^2 + (0--3)^2}$
$= \sqrt{4+1+9}$
$= \sqrt{14}$ units

ii Midpoint is at $\left(\dfrac{2+0}{2}, \dfrac{0+1}{2}, \dfrac{-3+0}{2}\right)$
which is $\left(1, \tfrac{1}{2}, -\tfrac{3}{2}\right)$.

3 $P(0, 4, 4)$, $Q(2, 6, 5)$, $R(1, 4, 3)$

$PQ = \sqrt{(2-0)^2 + (6-4)^2 + (5-4)^2}$
$= \sqrt{4+4+1}$
$= 3$

$PR = \sqrt{(1-0)^2 + (4-4)^2 + (3-4)^2}$
$= \sqrt{1+0+1}$
$= \sqrt{2}$

$QR = \sqrt{(1-2)^2 + (4-6)^2 + (3-5)^2}$
$= \sqrt{1+4+4}$
$= 3$ $\qquad \therefore$ $PQ = QR$ and so $\triangle PQR$ is isosceles.

4 a $A(2, -1, 7)$, $B(3, 1, 4)$, $C(5, 4, 5)$

$AB = \sqrt{(3-2)^2 + (1--1)^2 + (4-7)^2}$ $\qquad AC = \sqrt{(5-2)^2 + (4--1)^2 + (5-7)^2}$
$= \sqrt{1+4+9}$ $\qquad\qquad\qquad\qquad\qquad\qquad = \sqrt{9+25+4}$
$= \sqrt{14}$ $\qquad\qquad\qquad\qquad\qquad\qquad\qquad = \sqrt{38}$

$BC = \sqrt{(5-3)^2 + (4-1)^2 + (5-4)^2}$
$= \sqrt{4+9+1}$
$= \sqrt{14}$ $\qquad\qquad$ Since $AB = BC$, $\triangle ABC$ is isosceles.

b $A(0, 0, 3)$ $B(2, 8, 1)$ $C(-9, 6, 18)$

$AB = \sqrt{(2-0)^2 + (8-0)^2 + (1-3)^2}$ $\qquad AC = \sqrt{(-9-0)^2 + (6-0)^2 + (18-3)^2}$
$= \sqrt{4+64+4}$ $\qquad\qquad\qquad\qquad\qquad\qquad = \sqrt{81+36+225}$
$= \sqrt{72}$ $\qquad\qquad\qquad\qquad\qquad\qquad\qquad = \sqrt{342}$

$BC = \sqrt{(-9-2)^2 + (6-8)^2 + (18-1)^2}$
$= \sqrt{121+4+289}$
$= \sqrt{414}$ $\qquad\qquad$ Since $BC^2 = AB^2 + AC^2$, $\triangle ABC$ is right angled.

c $A(5, 6, -2)$ $B(6, 12, 9)$ $C(2, 4, 2)$

$AB = \sqrt{(6-5)^2 + (12-6)^2 + (9--2)^2}$ $\qquad AC = \sqrt{(2-5)^2 + (4-6)^2 + (2--2)^2}$
$= \sqrt{1+36+121}$ $\qquad\qquad\qquad\qquad\qquad = \sqrt{9+4+16}$
$= \sqrt{158}$ $\qquad\qquad\qquad\qquad\qquad\qquad = \sqrt{29}$

$BC = \sqrt{(2-6)^2 + (4-12)^2 + (2-9)^2}$
$= \sqrt{16+64+49}$
$= \sqrt{129}$ $\qquad\qquad$ Since $AB^2 = AC^2 + BC^2$, $\triangle ABC$ is right angled.

d $A(1, 0, -3)$ $B(2, 2, 0)$ $C(4, 6, 6)$

$AB = \sqrt{(2-1)^2 + (2-0)^2 + (0--3)^2}$ $\qquad AC = \sqrt{(4-1)^2 + (6-0)^2 + (6--3)^2}$
$= \sqrt{1^2 + 2^2 + 3^2}$ $\qquad\qquad\qquad\qquad\qquad = \sqrt{3^2 + 6^2 + 9^2}$
$= \sqrt{14}$ $\qquad\qquad\qquad\qquad\qquad\qquad\qquad = \sqrt{126}$

$BC = \sqrt{(4-2)^2 + (6-2)^2 + (6-0)^2}$ $\qquad\qquad = 3\sqrt{14}$
$= \sqrt{2^2 + 4^2 + 6^2}$
$= \sqrt{56}$
$= 2\sqrt{14}$

Since $AB + BC = AC$, the points A, B and C lie on a straight line, so they do not form a triangle.

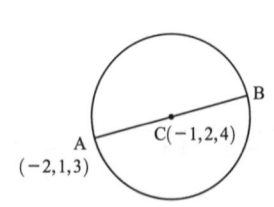

5 If B is (a, b, c) then $\dfrac{a-2}{2} = -1$, $\dfrac{b+1}{2} = 2$, $\dfrac{c+3}{2} = 4$

$\therefore$ $a = 0$, $b = 3$, $c = 5$
$\therefore$ B is $(0, 3, 5)$

$r = AC = \sqrt{(-1--2)^2 + (2-1)^2 + (4-3)^2}$
$= \sqrt{1+1+1}$
$= \sqrt{3}$ units

6 a $(0, y, 0)$ for any y

  b The distance between $(0, y, 0)$ and $B(-1, -1, 2)$ is $\sqrt{(-1)^2 + (-1-y)^2 + 2^2}$.

$$\therefore \quad \sqrt{1 + (y+1)^2 + 4} = \sqrt{14}$$
$$\therefore \quad (y+1)^2 = 9$$
$$\therefore \quad y + 1 = \pm 3$$
$$\therefore \quad y = -1 \pm 3$$
$$\therefore \quad y = -4 \text{ or } 2 \quad \therefore \text{ the two points are } (0, -4, 0) \text{ and } (0, 2, 0).$$

EXERCISE 14E.1

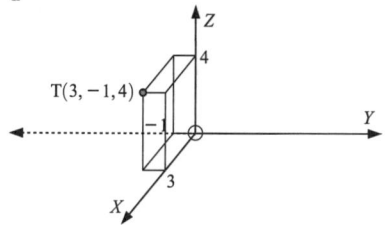

1 a
  Diagram showing $T(3, -1, 4)$ with axes X, Y, Z.

  b $\overrightarrow{OT} = \begin{pmatrix} 3 \\ -1 \\ 4 \end{pmatrix}$

  c $OT = \sqrt{(3-0)^2 + (-1-0)^2 + (4-0)^2}$
  $ = \sqrt{9 + 1 + 16}$
  $ = \sqrt{26}$ units

2 a $\overrightarrow{AB} = \begin{pmatrix} 1-(-3) \\ 0-1 \\ -1-2 \end{pmatrix} = \begin{pmatrix} 4 \\ -1 \\ -3 \end{pmatrix}$

  $\overrightarrow{BA} = \begin{pmatrix} -3-1 \\ 1-0 \\ 2-(-1) \end{pmatrix} = \begin{pmatrix} -4 \\ 1 \\ 3 \end{pmatrix}$

  b $|\overrightarrow{AB}| = \sqrt{4^2 + (-1)^2 + (-3)^2}$
  $\phantom{|\overrightarrow{AB}|} = \sqrt{26}$ units

  $|\overrightarrow{BA}| = \sqrt{(-4)^2 + 1^2 + 3^2}$
  $\phantom{|\overrightarrow{BA}|} = \sqrt{26}$ units

3 $\overrightarrow{OA} = \begin{pmatrix} 3 \\ 1 \\ 0 \end{pmatrix}$ $\overrightarrow{OB} = \begin{pmatrix} -1 \\ 1 \\ 2 \end{pmatrix}$ $\overrightarrow{AB} = \begin{pmatrix} -1-3 \\ 1-1 \\ 2-0 \end{pmatrix} = \begin{pmatrix} -4 \\ 0 \\ 2 \end{pmatrix}$

4 a The position vector of M from N
  $= \overrightarrow{NM} = \begin{pmatrix} 4-(-1) \\ -2-2 \\ -1-0 \end{pmatrix} = \begin{pmatrix} 5 \\ -4 \\ -1 \end{pmatrix}$.

  b The position vector of N from M
  $= \overrightarrow{MN} = \begin{pmatrix} -1-4 \\ 2-(-2) \\ 0-(-1) \end{pmatrix} = \begin{pmatrix} -5 \\ 4 \\ 1 \end{pmatrix}$.

  c $|\overrightarrow{MN}| = \sqrt{(-5)^2 + 4^2 + 1^2} = \sqrt{25 + 16 + 1} = \sqrt{42}$ units

5 a The position vector of A from O
  $= \overrightarrow{OA} = \begin{pmatrix} -1 \\ 2 \\ 5 \end{pmatrix}$.

  $\therefore \quad |\overrightarrow{OA}| = \sqrt{(-1)^2 + 2^2 + 5^2}$
  $\phantom{\therefore \quad |\overrightarrow{OA}|} = \sqrt{1 + 4 + 25}$
  $\phantom{\therefore \quad |\overrightarrow{OA}|} = \sqrt{30}$ units

  b The position vector of C from A
  $= \overrightarrow{AC} = \begin{pmatrix} -3-(-1) \\ 1-2 \\ 0-5 \end{pmatrix} = \begin{pmatrix} -2 \\ -1 \\ -5 \end{pmatrix}$.

  $\therefore \quad |\overrightarrow{AC}| = \sqrt{(-2)^2 + (-1)^2 + (-5)^2}$
  $\phantom{\therefore \quad |\overrightarrow{AC}|} = \sqrt{4 + 1 + 25}$
  $\phantom{\therefore \quad |\overrightarrow{AC}|} = \sqrt{30}$ units

  c The position vector of B from C
  $= \overrightarrow{CB} = \begin{pmatrix} 5 \\ -1 \\ 3 \end{pmatrix}$

  and $|\overrightarrow{CB}| = \sqrt{5^2 + (-1)^2 + 3^2}$
  $\phantom{\text{and } |\overrightarrow{CB}|} = \sqrt{25 + 1 + 9}$
  $\phantom{\text{and } |\overrightarrow{CB}|} = \sqrt{35}$ units

6

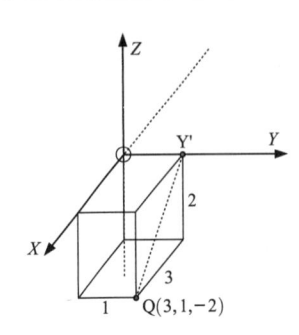

a The distance from Q to the Y-axis is the distance from Q to $Y'(0, 1, 0)$
$$\therefore \quad QY' = \sqrt{(3-0)^2 + (1-1)^2 + (-2-0)^2}$$
$$= \sqrt{9+4}$$
$$= \sqrt{13} \text{ units}$$

b The distance from Q to the origin is
$$QO = \sqrt{(3-0)^2 + (1-0)^2 + (-2-0)^2}$$
$$= \sqrt{9+1+4}$$
$$= \sqrt{14} \text{ units}$$

c The distance from Q to the ZOY plane is the distance from Q to $(0, 1, -2)$, which is 3 units.

EXERCISE 14E.2

1 a $\begin{pmatrix} a-4 \\ b-3 \\ c+2 \end{pmatrix} = \begin{pmatrix} 1 \\ 3 \\ -4 \end{pmatrix}$

$\therefore \begin{cases} a-4 = 1 \\ b-3 = 3 \\ c+2 = -4 \end{cases}$

$\therefore \quad a = 5, \quad b = 6, \quad c = -6$

b $\begin{pmatrix} a-5 \\ b-2 \\ c+3 \end{pmatrix} = \begin{pmatrix} 3-a \\ 2-b \\ 5-c \end{pmatrix}$

$\therefore \begin{cases} a-5 = 3-a \\ b-2 = 2-b \\ c+3 = 5-c \end{cases}$

$\therefore \quad 2a = 8, \quad 2b = 4, \quad 2c = 2$
$\therefore \quad a = 4, \quad b = 2, \quad c = 1$

2 a $2 \begin{pmatrix} 1 \\ 0 \\ 3a \end{pmatrix} = \begin{pmatrix} b \\ c-1 \\ 2 \end{pmatrix}$

$\therefore \begin{pmatrix} 2 \\ 0 \\ 6a \end{pmatrix} = \begin{pmatrix} b \\ c-1 \\ 2 \end{pmatrix}$

$\therefore \quad 6a = 2, \quad b = 2, \quad c-1 = 0$
$\therefore \quad a = \frac{1}{3}, \quad b = 2, \quad c = 1$

b $\begin{pmatrix} 2 \\ a \\ 3 \end{pmatrix} = \begin{pmatrix} b \\ a^2 \\ a+b \end{pmatrix}$

$\therefore \quad b = 2, \quad a^2 = a, \quad a+b = 3$
$\therefore \quad a = 1, \quad b = 2$

c $a \begin{pmatrix} 1 \\ 1 \\ 0 \end{pmatrix} + b \begin{pmatrix} 2 \\ 0 \\ -1 \end{pmatrix} + c \begin{pmatrix} 0 \\ 1 \\ 1 \end{pmatrix} = \begin{pmatrix} -1 \\ 3 \\ 3 \end{pmatrix}$

$\therefore \quad a + 2b = -1 \;\ldots\; (1), \quad a + c = 3 \;\ldots\; (2) \quad \text{and} \quad -b + c = 3 \;\ldots\; (3)$

$(1) - (2)$ gives: $2b - c = -4 \;\ldots\; (4)$

Adding (3) and (4) gives $b = -1$

$\therefore$ using (3), $c = 2$

and using (2), $a = 1$

$\therefore \quad a = 1, \quad b = -1, \quad c = 2$

3 $A(-1, 3, 4), \quad B(2, 5, -1), \quad C(-1, 2, -2), \quad D(r, s, t)$

a If $\overrightarrow{AC} = \overrightarrow{BD}$ then $\begin{pmatrix} -1-(-1) \\ 2-3 \\ -2-4 \end{pmatrix} = \begin{pmatrix} r-2 \\ s-5 \\ t+1 \end{pmatrix}$

$\therefore \quad r - 2 = 0, \quad s - 5 = -1 \quad \text{and} \quad t + 1 = -6 \quad \therefore \quad r = 2, \quad s = 4 \quad \text{and} \quad t = -7$

b If $\overrightarrow{AB} = \overrightarrow{DC}$ then $\begin{pmatrix} 2-(-1) \\ 5-3 \\ -1-4 \end{pmatrix} = \begin{pmatrix} -1-r \\ 2-s \\ -2-t \end{pmatrix}$

$\therefore \quad -1 - r = 3, \quad 2 - s = 2 \quad \text{and} \quad -2 - t = -5 \quad \therefore \quad r = -4, \quad s = 0 \quad \text{and} \quad t = 3$

4 a $\vec{AB} = \begin{pmatrix} 3-1 \\ -3-2 \\ 2-3 \end{pmatrix} = \begin{pmatrix} 2 \\ -5 \\ -1 \end{pmatrix}$ and $\vec{DC} = \begin{pmatrix} 7-5 \\ -4-1 \\ 5-6 \end{pmatrix} = \begin{pmatrix} 2 \\ -5 \\ -1 \end{pmatrix}$.

b ABCD is a parallelogram since its opposite sides are parallel and equal in length.

5 a Suppose S is at (x, y, z). $\vec{PQ} = \vec{SR}$ {opposite sides are parallel and equal in length}

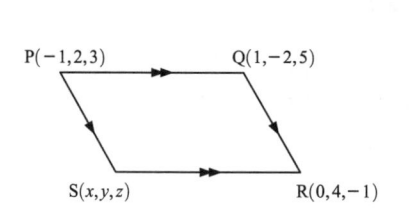

$\therefore \begin{pmatrix} 1-(-1) \\ -2-2 \\ 5-3 \end{pmatrix} = \begin{pmatrix} 0-x \\ 4-y \\ -1-z \end{pmatrix}$

$\therefore \begin{pmatrix} 2 \\ -4 \\ 2 \end{pmatrix} = \begin{pmatrix} -x \\ 4-y \\ -1-z \end{pmatrix}$

$\therefore -x = 2 \qquad 4 - y = -4 \qquad -1 - z = 2$
$\therefore x = -2 \qquad y = 8 \qquad z = -3$
$\therefore$ S is at $(-2, 8, -3)$.

b The midpoint of [PR] is $\left(\dfrac{-1+0}{2}, \dfrac{2+4}{2}, \dfrac{3+(-1)}{2}\right)$ which is $(-\tfrac{1}{2}, 3, 1)$.

The midpoint of [QS] is $\left(\dfrac{1+(-2)}{2}, \dfrac{-2+8}{2}, \dfrac{5+(-3)}{2}\right)$ which is $(-\tfrac{1}{2}, 3, 1)$.

So, [PR] and [QS] have the same midpoint. ✓

EXERCISE 14F.1

1 a $2\mathbf{x} = \mathbf{q}$
$\therefore \tfrac{1}{2}(2\mathbf{x}) = \tfrac{1}{2}\mathbf{q}$
$\therefore \mathbf{x} = \tfrac{1}{2}\mathbf{q}$

b $\tfrac{1}{2}\mathbf{x} = \mathbf{n}$
$\therefore 2(\tfrac{1}{2}\mathbf{x}) = 2\mathbf{n}$
$\therefore \mathbf{x} = 2\mathbf{n}$

c $-3\mathbf{x} = \mathbf{p}$
$\therefore 3\mathbf{x} = -\mathbf{p}$
$\therefore \tfrac{1}{3}(3\mathbf{x}) = -\tfrac{1}{3}\mathbf{p}$
$\therefore \mathbf{x} = -\tfrac{1}{3}\mathbf{p}$

d $\mathbf{q} + 2\mathbf{x} = \mathbf{r}$
$\therefore 2\mathbf{x} = \mathbf{r} - \mathbf{q}$
$\therefore \mathbf{x} = \tfrac{1}{2}(\mathbf{r} - \mathbf{q})$

e $4\mathbf{s} - 5\mathbf{x} = \mathbf{t}$
$\therefore -5\mathbf{x} = \mathbf{t} - 4\mathbf{s}$
$\therefore 5\mathbf{x} = 4\mathbf{s} - \mathbf{t}$
$\therefore \mathbf{x} = \tfrac{4}{5}\mathbf{s} - \tfrac{1}{5}\mathbf{t}$

f $4\mathbf{m} - \tfrac{1}{3}\mathbf{x} = \mathbf{n}$
$\therefore 4\mathbf{m} - \mathbf{n} = \tfrac{1}{3}\mathbf{x}$
$\therefore \mathbf{x} = 12\mathbf{m} - 3\mathbf{n}$
$\phantom{\therefore \mathbf{x}} = 3(4\mathbf{m} - \mathbf{n})$

2 a $2\mathbf{y} = \mathbf{r}$
$\therefore \mathbf{y} = \tfrac{1}{2}\mathbf{r}$
$= \tfrac{1}{2}\begin{pmatrix} -2 \\ 3 \end{pmatrix}$
$= \begin{pmatrix} -1 \\ \tfrac{3}{2} \end{pmatrix}$

b $\tfrac{1}{2}\mathbf{y} = \mathbf{s}$
$\therefore \mathbf{y} = 2\mathbf{s}$
$= 2\begin{pmatrix} 1 \\ 2 \end{pmatrix}$
$= \begin{pmatrix} 2 \\ 4 \end{pmatrix}$

c $\mathbf{r} + 2\mathbf{y} = \mathbf{s}$
$\therefore 2\mathbf{y} = \mathbf{s} - \mathbf{r}$
$\therefore \mathbf{y} = \tfrac{1}{2}\mathbf{s} - \tfrac{1}{2}\mathbf{r}$
$= \begin{pmatrix} \tfrac{1}{2} \\ 1 \end{pmatrix} - \begin{pmatrix} -1 \\ \tfrac{3}{2} \end{pmatrix}$
$= \begin{pmatrix} \tfrac{3}{2} \\ -\tfrac{1}{2} \end{pmatrix}$

d $3\mathbf{s} - 4\mathbf{y} = \mathbf{r}$
$\therefore 3\mathbf{s} - \mathbf{r} = 4\mathbf{y}$
$\therefore \mathbf{y} = \tfrac{3}{4}\mathbf{s} - \tfrac{1}{4}\mathbf{r}$
$= \begin{pmatrix} \tfrac{3}{4} \\ \tfrac{3}{2} \end{pmatrix} - \begin{pmatrix} -\tfrac{1}{2} \\ \tfrac{3}{4} \end{pmatrix}$
$= \begin{pmatrix} \tfrac{5}{4} \\ \tfrac{3}{4} \end{pmatrix}$

3 $k\mathbf{x} = \mathbf{a}$

$\therefore k\begin{pmatrix} x_1 \\ x_2 \end{pmatrix} = \begin{pmatrix} a_1 \\ a_2 \end{pmatrix}$

$\therefore kx_1 = a_1$ and $kx_2 = a_2$
$\therefore x_1 = \tfrac{1}{k}a_1$ and $x_2 = \tfrac{1}{k}a_2$

$\therefore \begin{pmatrix} x_1 \\ x_2 \end{pmatrix} = \begin{pmatrix} \tfrac{1}{k}a_1 \\ \tfrac{1}{k}a_2 \end{pmatrix} = \tfrac{1}{k}\begin{pmatrix} a_1 \\ a_2 \end{pmatrix}$ and so $\mathbf{x} = \tfrac{1}{k}\mathbf{a}$.

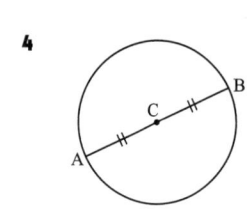

4

a $\vec{AC} = \begin{pmatrix} 1-3 \\ 4--2 \end{pmatrix} = \begin{pmatrix} -2 \\ 6 \end{pmatrix}$ ∴ B is $(1-2, 4+6)$ or $(-1, 10)$.

b $\vec{AC} = \begin{pmatrix} -1-0 \\ -2-5 \end{pmatrix} = \begin{pmatrix} -1 \\ -7 \end{pmatrix}$ ∴ B is $(-1-1, -2-7)$ or $(-2, -9)$.

c $\vec{AC} = \begin{pmatrix} 3--1 \\ 0--4 \end{pmatrix} = \begin{pmatrix} 4 \\ 4 \end{pmatrix}$ ∴ B is $(3+4, 0+4)$ or $(7, 4)$.

5

a M is $\left(\dfrac{3+-1}{2}, \dfrac{6+2}{2}\right)$

∴ M is $(1, 4)$

b $\vec{CA} = \begin{pmatrix} 3--4 \\ 6-1 \end{pmatrix} = \begin{pmatrix} 7 \\ 5 \end{pmatrix}$

$\vec{CM} = \begin{pmatrix} 1--4 \\ 4-1 \end{pmatrix} = \begin{pmatrix} 5 \\ 3 \end{pmatrix}$

$\vec{CB} = \begin{pmatrix} -1--4 \\ 2-1 \end{pmatrix} = \begin{pmatrix} 3 \\ 1 \end{pmatrix}$

c $\tfrac{1}{2}\vec{CA} + \tfrac{1}{2}\vec{CB}$

$= \tfrac{1}{2}\begin{pmatrix} 7 \\ 5 \end{pmatrix} + \tfrac{1}{2}\begin{pmatrix} 3 \\ 1 \end{pmatrix}$

$= \begin{pmatrix} 5 \\ 3 \end{pmatrix}$ which is $\vec{CM}$

6

a $2\mathbf{a} + \mathbf{x} = \mathbf{b}$

∴ $\mathbf{x} = \mathbf{b} - 2\mathbf{a}$

$= \begin{pmatrix} 2 \\ -2 \\ 1 \end{pmatrix} - 2\begin{pmatrix} -1 \\ 2 \\ 3 \end{pmatrix}$

$= \begin{pmatrix} 2 \\ -2 \\ 1 \end{pmatrix} - \begin{pmatrix} -2 \\ 4 \\ 6 \end{pmatrix}$

$= \begin{pmatrix} 4 \\ -6 \\ -5 \end{pmatrix}$

b $3\mathbf{x} - \mathbf{a} = 2\mathbf{b}$

∴ $3\mathbf{x} = \mathbf{a} + 2\mathbf{b}$

∴ $\mathbf{x} = \tfrac{1}{3}(\mathbf{a} + 2\mathbf{b})$

$= \tfrac{1}{3}\left[\begin{pmatrix} -1 \\ 2 \\ 3 \end{pmatrix} + 2\begin{pmatrix} 2 \\ -2 \\ 1 \end{pmatrix}\right]$

$= \tfrac{1}{3}\left[\begin{pmatrix} -1 \\ 2 \\ 3 \end{pmatrix} + \begin{pmatrix} 4 \\ -4 \\ 2 \end{pmatrix}\right]$

$= \tfrac{1}{3}\begin{pmatrix} 3 \\ -2 \\ 5 \end{pmatrix} = \begin{pmatrix} 1 \\ -\tfrac{2}{3} \\ \tfrac{5}{3} \end{pmatrix}$

c $2\mathbf{b} - 2\mathbf{x} = -\mathbf{a}$

∴ $\mathbf{a} + 2\mathbf{b} = 2\mathbf{x}$

∴ $\mathbf{x} = \tfrac{1}{2}(\mathbf{a} + 2\mathbf{b}) = \tfrac{1}{2}\begin{pmatrix} 3 \\ -2 \\ 5 \end{pmatrix}$ {using **b**}

$= \begin{pmatrix} \tfrac{3}{2} \\ -1 \\ \tfrac{5}{2} \end{pmatrix}$

7 $\vec{AB} = \vec{AO} + \vec{OB} = -\vec{OA} + \vec{OB} = -\begin{pmatrix} -2 \\ -1 \\ 1 \end{pmatrix} + \begin{pmatrix} 1 \\ 3 \\ -1 \end{pmatrix} = \begin{pmatrix} 2 \\ 1 \\ -1 \end{pmatrix} + \begin{pmatrix} 1 \\ 3 \\ -1 \end{pmatrix} = \begin{pmatrix} 3 \\ 4 \\ -2 \end{pmatrix}$

∴ $|\vec{AB}| = \sqrt{3^2 + 4^2 + (-2)^2} = \sqrt{9 + 16 + 4} = \sqrt{29}$ units

8 $\vec{OA} = \begin{pmatrix} 2 \\ 1 \\ -2 \end{pmatrix}$, $\vec{OB} = \begin{pmatrix} 0 \\ 3 \\ -4 \end{pmatrix}$, $\vec{OC} = \begin{pmatrix} 1 \\ -2 \\ 1 \end{pmatrix}$, $\vec{OD} = \begin{pmatrix} -2 \\ -3 \\ 2 \end{pmatrix}$

∴ $\vec{BD} = \vec{BO} + \vec{OD} = -\vec{OB} + \vec{OD} = -\begin{pmatrix} 0 \\ 3 \\ -4 \end{pmatrix} + \begin{pmatrix} -2 \\ -3 \\ 2 \end{pmatrix} = \begin{pmatrix} -2 \\ -6 \\ 6 \end{pmatrix}$

and $\vec{AC} = \vec{AO} + \vec{OC} = -\begin{pmatrix} 2 \\ 1 \\ -2 \end{pmatrix} + \begin{pmatrix} 1 \\ -2 \\ 1 \end{pmatrix} = \begin{pmatrix} -1 \\ -3 \\ 3 \end{pmatrix}$ ∴ $\vec{BD} = \begin{pmatrix} -2 \\ -6 \\ 6 \end{pmatrix} = 2\begin{pmatrix} -1 \\ -3 \\ 3 \end{pmatrix} = 2\vec{AC}$

9 $\vec{AB} = \begin{pmatrix} 2--1 \\ 3-5 \\ -3-2 \end{pmatrix} = \begin{pmatrix} 3 \\ -2 \\ -5 \end{pmatrix}$ ∴ C is $(2+3, 3-2, -3-5)$, or $(5, 1, -8)$,
D is $(5+3, 1-2, -8-5)$, or $(8, -1, -13)$,
E is $(8+3, -1-2, -13-5)$, or $(11, -3, -18)$.

10

a $\vec{AB} = \begin{pmatrix} 4-3 \\ 2--1 \end{pmatrix} = \begin{pmatrix} 1 \\ 3 \end{pmatrix}$ Now $\vec{AB} = \vec{DC}$
∴ sides [AB] and [DC] are equal in length and parallel.
$\vec{DC} = \begin{pmatrix} -1--2 \\ 4-1 \end{pmatrix} = \begin{pmatrix} 1 \\ 3 \end{pmatrix}$ This is sufficient to deduce that ABCD is a parallelogram.

b $\vec{AB} = \begin{pmatrix} -1-5 \\ 2-0 \\ 4-3 \end{pmatrix} = \begin{pmatrix} -6 \\ 2 \\ 1 \end{pmatrix}$ So $\vec{AB} = \vec{DC}$
∴ sides [AB] and [DC] are equal in length and parallel.
$\vec{DC} = \begin{pmatrix} 4-10 \\ -3--5 \\ 6-5 \end{pmatrix} = \begin{pmatrix} -6 \\ 2 \\ 1 \end{pmatrix}$ This is sufficient to deduce that ABCD is a parallelogram.

c $\vec{AB} = \begin{pmatrix} 1-2 \\ 4--3 \\ -1-2 \end{pmatrix} = \begin{pmatrix} -1 \\ 7 \\ -3 \end{pmatrix}$ So, $\vec{AB} \neq \vec{DC}$
∴ ABCD cannot be a parallelogram.
$\vec{DC} = \begin{pmatrix} -2--1 \\ 6--1 \\ -2-2 \end{pmatrix} = \begin{pmatrix} -1 \\ 7 \\ -4 \end{pmatrix}$

11 a Let D be (a, b).

Now $\vec{CD} = \vec{BA}$

∴ $\begin{pmatrix} a-8 \\ b--2 \end{pmatrix} = \begin{pmatrix} 3-2 \\ 0--1 \end{pmatrix}$

∴ $\begin{pmatrix} a-8 \\ b+2 \end{pmatrix} = \begin{pmatrix} 1 \\ 1 \end{pmatrix}$

∴ $a = 9, b = -1$

So, D is $(9, -1)$.

b Let R be (a, b, c).

Now $\vec{SR} = \vec{PQ}$

∴ $\begin{pmatrix} a-4 \\ b-0 \\ c-7 \end{pmatrix} = \begin{pmatrix} -2--1 \\ 5-4 \\ 2-3 \end{pmatrix}$

∴ $\begin{pmatrix} a-4 \\ b \\ c-7 \end{pmatrix} = \begin{pmatrix} -1 \\ 1 \\ -1 \end{pmatrix}$

∴ $a = 3, b = 1, c = 6$

So, R is $(3, 1, 6)$.

c Let X be (a, b, c).

Now $\vec{WX} = \vec{ZY}$

∴ $\begin{pmatrix} a--1 \\ b-5 \\ c-8 \end{pmatrix} = \begin{pmatrix} 3-0 \\ -2-4 \\ -2-6 \end{pmatrix}$

∴ $\begin{pmatrix} a+1 \\ b-5 \\ c-8 \end{pmatrix} = \begin{pmatrix} 3 \\ -6 \\ -8 \end{pmatrix}$

∴ $a = 2, b = -1, c = 0$

So, X is $(2, -1, 0)$.

12 a $\vec{BD} = \frac{1}{2}\vec{OA}$
$= \frac{1}{2}\mathbf{a}$

b $\vec{AB} = \vec{AO} + \vec{OB}$
$= -\mathbf{a} + \mathbf{b}$
$= \mathbf{b} - \mathbf{a}$

c $\vec{BA} = -\vec{AB}$
$= -(\mathbf{b} - \mathbf{a})$
$= -\mathbf{b} + \mathbf{a}$ or $\mathbf{a} - \mathbf{b}$

d $\vec{OD} = \vec{OB} + \vec{BD}$
$= \mathbf{b} + \frac{1}{2}\mathbf{a}$

e $\vec{AD} = \vec{AO} + \vec{OD}$
$= -\mathbf{a} + \mathbf{b} + \frac{1}{2}\mathbf{a}$
$= -\frac{1}{2}\mathbf{a} + \mathbf{b}$

f $\vec{DA} = -\vec{AD}$
$= \frac{1}{2}\mathbf{a} - \mathbf{b}$

13 a $\vec{AD} = \vec{AB} + \vec{BD} = \begin{pmatrix} -1 \\ 3 \\ 2 \end{pmatrix} + \begin{pmatrix} 0 \\ 2 \\ -3 \end{pmatrix} = \begin{pmatrix} -1 \\ 5 \\ -1 \end{pmatrix}$

b $\vec{CB} = \vec{CA} + \vec{AB} = -\vec{AC} + \vec{AB} = -\begin{pmatrix} 2 \\ -1 \\ 4 \end{pmatrix} + \begin{pmatrix} -1 \\ 3 \\ 2 \end{pmatrix} = \begin{pmatrix} -2 \\ 1 \\ -4 \end{pmatrix} + \begin{pmatrix} -1 \\ 3 \\ 2 \end{pmatrix} = \begin{pmatrix} -3 \\ 4 \\ -2 \end{pmatrix}$

c $\vec{CD} = \vec{CB} + \vec{BD} = \begin{pmatrix} -3 \\ 4 \\ -2 \end{pmatrix} + \begin{pmatrix} 0 \\ 2 \\ -3 \end{pmatrix}$ {using **b**} $= \begin{pmatrix} -3 \\ 6 \\ -5 \end{pmatrix}$

14 **a** $\mathbf{a}+\mathbf{b} = \begin{pmatrix} 2 \\ -1 \\ 1 \end{pmatrix} + \begin{pmatrix} 1 \\ 2 \\ -3 \end{pmatrix} = \begin{pmatrix} 3 \\ 1 \\ -2 \end{pmatrix}$ **b** $\mathbf{a}-\mathbf{b} = \begin{pmatrix} 2 \\ -1 \\ 1 \end{pmatrix} - \begin{pmatrix} 1 \\ 2 \\ -3 \end{pmatrix} = \begin{pmatrix} 1 \\ -3 \\ 4 \end{pmatrix}$

c $\mathbf{b}+2\mathbf{c} = \begin{pmatrix} 1 \\ 2 \\ -3 \end{pmatrix} + 2\begin{pmatrix} 0 \\ 1 \\ -3 \end{pmatrix} = \begin{pmatrix} 1 \\ 2 \\ -3 \end{pmatrix} + \begin{pmatrix} 0 \\ 2 \\ -6 \end{pmatrix} = \begin{pmatrix} 1 \\ 4 \\ -9 \end{pmatrix}$

d $\mathbf{a}-3\mathbf{c} = \begin{pmatrix} 2 \\ -1 \\ 1 \end{pmatrix} - 3\begin{pmatrix} 0 \\ 1 \\ -3 \end{pmatrix} = \begin{pmatrix} 2 \\ -1 \\ 1 \end{pmatrix} - \begin{pmatrix} 0 \\ 3 \\ -9 \end{pmatrix} = \begin{pmatrix} 2 \\ -4 \\ 10 \end{pmatrix}$

e $\mathbf{a}+\mathbf{b}+\mathbf{c} = \begin{pmatrix} 2 \\ -1 \\ 1 \end{pmatrix} + \begin{pmatrix} 1 \\ 2 \\ -3 \end{pmatrix} + \begin{pmatrix} 0 \\ 1 \\ -3 \end{pmatrix} = \begin{pmatrix} 3 \\ 2 \\ -5 \end{pmatrix}$

f $\mathbf{c}-\tfrac{1}{2}\mathbf{a} = \begin{pmatrix} 0 \\ 1 \\ -3 \end{pmatrix} - \tfrac{1}{2}\begin{pmatrix} 2 \\ -1 \\ 1 \end{pmatrix} = \begin{pmatrix} 0 \\ 1 \\ -3 \end{pmatrix} - \begin{pmatrix} 1 \\ -\tfrac{1}{2} \\ \tfrac{1}{2} \end{pmatrix} = \begin{pmatrix} -1 \\ \tfrac{3}{2} \\ -\tfrac{7}{2} \end{pmatrix}$

g $\mathbf{a}-\mathbf{b}-\mathbf{c} = \begin{pmatrix} 2 \\ -1 \\ 1 \end{pmatrix} - \begin{pmatrix} 1 \\ 2 \\ -3 \end{pmatrix} - \begin{pmatrix} 0 \\ 1 \\ -3 \end{pmatrix} = \begin{pmatrix} 1 \\ -4 \\ 7 \end{pmatrix}$

h $2\mathbf{b}-\mathbf{c}+\mathbf{a} = 2\begin{pmatrix} 1 \\ 2 \\ -3 \end{pmatrix} - \begin{pmatrix} 0 \\ 1 \\ -3 \end{pmatrix} + \begin{pmatrix} 2 \\ -1 \\ 1 \end{pmatrix} = \begin{pmatrix} 2 \\ 4 \\ -6 \end{pmatrix} - \begin{pmatrix} 0 \\ 1 \\ -3 \end{pmatrix} + \begin{pmatrix} 2 \\ -1 \\ 1 \end{pmatrix} = \begin{pmatrix} 4 \\ 2 \\ -2 \end{pmatrix}$

15 **a** $|\mathbf{a}| = \sqrt{(-1)^2 + 1^2 + 3^2}$
$= \sqrt{11}$ units

b $|\mathbf{b}| = \sqrt{1^2 + (-3)^2 + 2^2}$
$= \sqrt{14}$ units

c $|\mathbf{b}+\mathbf{c}| = \left| \begin{pmatrix} 1 \\ -3 \\ 2 \end{pmatrix} + \begin{pmatrix} -2 \\ 2 \\ 4 \end{pmatrix} \right| = \left| \begin{pmatrix} -1 \\ -1 \\ 6 \end{pmatrix} \right|$

$= \sqrt{(-1)^2 + (-1)^2 + 6^2}$
$= \sqrt{1+1+36}$
$= \sqrt{38}$ units

d $|\mathbf{a}-\mathbf{c}| = \left| \begin{pmatrix} -1 \\ 1 \\ 3 \end{pmatrix} - \begin{pmatrix} -2 \\ 2 \\ 4 \end{pmatrix} \right| = \left| \begin{pmatrix} 1 \\ -1 \\ -1 \end{pmatrix} \right|$

$= \sqrt{1^2 + (-1)^2 + (-1)^2}$
$= \sqrt{3}$ units

e $|\mathbf{a}|\mathbf{b} = \sqrt{11}\begin{pmatrix} 1 \\ -3 \\ 2 \end{pmatrix} = \begin{pmatrix} \sqrt{11} \\ -3\sqrt{11} \\ 2\sqrt{11} \end{pmatrix}$

f $\dfrac{1}{|\mathbf{a}|}\mathbf{a} = \dfrac{1}{\sqrt{11}}\begin{pmatrix} -1 \\ 1 \\ 3 \end{pmatrix} = \begin{pmatrix} -\tfrac{1}{\sqrt{11}} \\ \tfrac{1}{\sqrt{11}} \\ \tfrac{3}{\sqrt{11}} \end{pmatrix}$

16 **a** $r\begin{pmatrix} 1 \\ -1 \end{pmatrix} + s\begin{pmatrix} 2 \\ 5 \end{pmatrix} = \begin{pmatrix} -8 \\ -27 \end{pmatrix}$

$\therefore \begin{pmatrix} r+2s \\ -r+5s \end{pmatrix} = \begin{pmatrix} -8 \\ -27 \end{pmatrix}$

$\therefore \quad r+2s = -8 \quad \ldots\ldots (1)$
$ -r+5s = -27$
$\overline{\text{adding} \quad 7s = -35}$
$\therefore \quad s = -5$
and in (1) $\quad r + 2(-5) = -8$
$\therefore \quad r - 10 = -8$
$\therefore \quad r = 2$
So, $r = 2, \ s = -5$

b $r\begin{pmatrix} 2 \\ -3 \\ 1 \end{pmatrix} + s\begin{pmatrix} 1 \\ 7 \\ 2 \end{pmatrix} = \begin{pmatrix} 7 \\ -19 \\ 2 \end{pmatrix}$

$\therefore \begin{cases} 2r + s = 7 & \ldots\ldots (1) \\ -3r + 7s = -19 & \ldots\ldots (2) \\ r + 2s = 2 & \ldots\ldots (3) \end{cases}$

$\therefore \quad -4r - 2s = -14 \quad \{-2 \times (1)\}$
$ r + 2s = 2$
$\overline{\text{adding} \quad -3r = -12}$
$\therefore \quad r = 4$
In (1), $2(4) + s = 7 \quad \therefore \quad s = -1$
Checking in (2),
$\quad -3r + 7s = -3(4) + 7(-1) = -19 \ \checkmark$
$\therefore \quad r = 4, \ s = -1$ satisfies all equations.

EXERCISE 14F.2

1 **a** $\vec{AB} : \vec{BC} = 1 : 1$
   $\therefore$ B divides [AC] in the ratio $1 : 1$.

b $\vec{BC} : \vec{CF} = 1 : 3$
   $\therefore$ C divides [BF] in the ratio $1 : 3$.

c $\vec{FC} : \vec{CB} = 3 : 1$
   $\therefore$ C divides [FB] in the ratio $3 : 1$.

d $\vec{ED} : \vec{DA} = 1 : 3$
   $\therefore$ D divides [EA] in the ratio $1 : 3$.

e $\vec{AC} : \vec{CB} = -2 : 1$
   $\therefore$ C divides [AB] in the ratio $-2 : 1$.

f $\vec{DF} : \vec{FA} = -2 : 5$
   $\therefore$ F divides [DA] in the ratio $-2 : 5$.

2 a

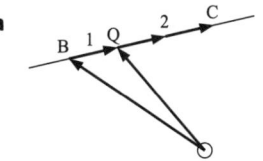

$\vec{BQ} : \vec{QC} = 1 : 2$
$\therefore \vec{BQ} = \tfrac{1}{3}\vec{BC}$
$\vec{OQ} = \vec{OB} + \vec{BQ}$
$\phantom{\vec{OQ}} = \vec{OB} + \tfrac{1}{3}\vec{BC}$

$= \begin{pmatrix} -1 \\ 2 \\ 0 \end{pmatrix} + \tfrac{1}{3}\begin{pmatrix} 1-(-1) \\ -1-2 \\ 4-0 \end{pmatrix}$

$= \begin{pmatrix} -1 \\ 2 \\ 0 \end{pmatrix} + \tfrac{1}{3}\begin{pmatrix} 2 \\ -3 \\ 4 \end{pmatrix}$

$= \begin{pmatrix} -\tfrac{1}{3} \\ 1 \\ \tfrac{4}{3} \end{pmatrix}$ $\therefore$ Q is $(-\tfrac{1}{3}, 1, \tfrac{4}{3})$.

b

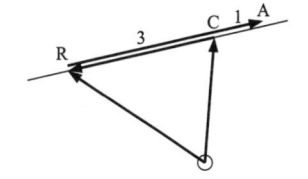

$\vec{CR} : \vec{RA} = -3 : 4$
$\therefore \vec{CR} = 3\vec{AC}$
$\vec{OR} = \vec{OC} + \vec{CR}$
$\phantom{\vec{OR}} = \vec{OC} + 3\vec{AC}$

$= \begin{pmatrix} 1 \\ -1 \\ 4 \end{pmatrix} + 3\begin{pmatrix} 1-3 \\ -1-1 \\ 4-1 \end{pmatrix}$

$= \begin{pmatrix} 1 \\ -1 \\ 4 \end{pmatrix} + 3\begin{pmatrix} -2 \\ -2 \\ 3 \end{pmatrix}$

$= \begin{pmatrix} -5 \\ -7 \\ 13 \end{pmatrix}$ $\therefore$ R is $(-5, -7, 13)$.

c

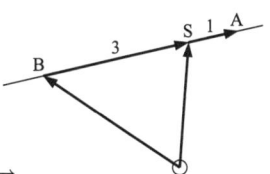

$\vec{BS} : \vec{SA} = 3 : 1$
$\therefore \vec{BS} = \tfrac{3}{4}\vec{BA}$
$\vec{OS} = \vec{OB} + \vec{BS}$
$\phantom{\vec{OS}} = \vec{OB} + \tfrac{3}{4}\vec{BA}$

$= \begin{pmatrix} -1 \\ 2 \\ 0 \end{pmatrix} + \tfrac{3}{4}\begin{pmatrix} 3-(-1) \\ 1-2 \\ 1-0 \end{pmatrix}$

$= \begin{pmatrix} -1 \\ 2 \\ 0 \end{pmatrix} + \tfrac{3}{4}\begin{pmatrix} 4 \\ -1 \\ 1 \end{pmatrix}$

$= \begin{pmatrix} 2 \\ \tfrac{5}{4} \\ \tfrac{3}{4} \end{pmatrix}$ $\therefore$ S is $(2, \tfrac{5}{4}, \tfrac{3}{4})$.

d

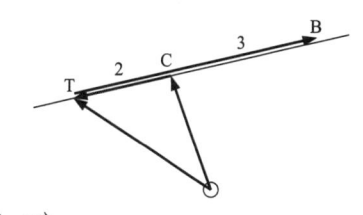

$\vec{CT} : \vec{TB} = -2 : 5$
$\therefore \vec{CT} = \tfrac{2}{3}\vec{BC}$
$\vec{OT} = \vec{OC} + \vec{CT}$
$\phantom{\vec{OT}} = \vec{OC} + \tfrac{2}{3}\vec{BC}$

$= \begin{pmatrix} 1 \\ -1 \\ 4 \end{pmatrix} + \tfrac{2}{3}\begin{pmatrix} 1-(-1) \\ -1-2 \\ 4-0 \end{pmatrix}$

$= \begin{pmatrix} 1 \\ -1 \\ 4 \end{pmatrix} + \tfrac{2}{3}\begin{pmatrix} 2 \\ -3 \\ 4 \end{pmatrix}$

$= \begin{pmatrix} \tfrac{7}{3} \\ -3 \\ \tfrac{20}{3} \end{pmatrix}$ $\therefore$ T is $(\tfrac{7}{3}, -3, \tfrac{20}{3})$.

e

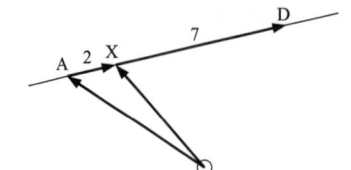

$\vec{AX} : \vec{XD} = 2 : 7$

$\therefore \vec{AX} = \frac{2}{9}\vec{AD}$

$\vec{OX} = \vec{OA} + \vec{AX}$

$= \vec{OA} + \frac{2}{9}\vec{AD}$

$= \begin{pmatrix} 3 \\ 1 \\ 1 \end{pmatrix} + \frac{2}{9} \begin{pmatrix} 3-3 \\ -2-1 \\ 4-1 \end{pmatrix}$

$= \begin{pmatrix} 3 \\ 1 \\ 1 \end{pmatrix} + \frac{2}{9} \begin{pmatrix} 0 \\ -3 \\ 3 \end{pmatrix}$

$= \begin{pmatrix} 3 \\ \frac{1}{3} \\ \frac{5}{3} \end{pmatrix}$ $\therefore$ X is $(3, \frac{1}{3}, \frac{5}{3})$.

f

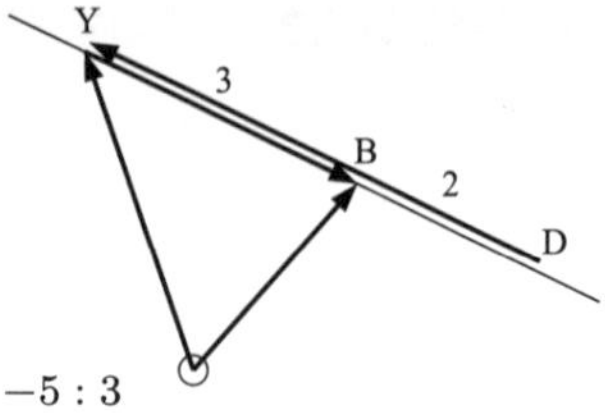

$\vec{DY} : \vec{YB} = -5 : 3$

$\therefore \vec{BY} = \frac{3}{2}\vec{DB}$

$\vec{OY} = \vec{OB} + \vec{BY}$

$= \vec{OB} + \frac{3}{2}\vec{DB}$

$= \begin{pmatrix} -1 \\ 2 \\ 0 \end{pmatrix} + \frac{3}{2} \begin{pmatrix} -1-3 \\ 2-(-2) \\ 0-4 \end{pmatrix}$

$= \begin{pmatrix} -1 \\ 2 \\ 0 \end{pmatrix} + \frac{3}{2} \begin{pmatrix} -4 \\ 4 \\ -4 \end{pmatrix}$

$= \begin{pmatrix} -7 \\ 8 \\ -6 \end{pmatrix}$ $\therefore$ Y is $(-7, 8, -6)$.

3 a

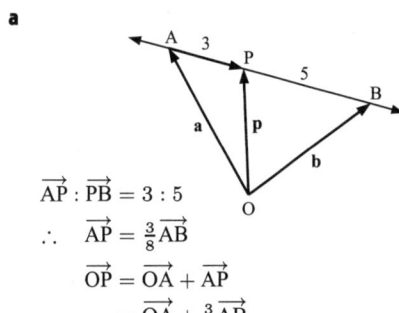

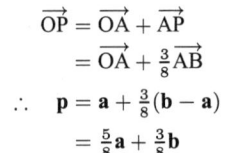

$\vec{AP} : \vec{PB} = 3 : 5$

$\therefore \vec{AP} = \frac{3}{8}\vec{AB}$

$\vec{OP} = \vec{OA} + \vec{AP}$

$= \vec{OA} + \frac{3}{8}\vec{AB}$

$\therefore \mathbf{p} = \mathbf{a} + \frac{3}{8}(\mathbf{b} - \mathbf{a})$

$= \frac{5}{8}\mathbf{a} + \frac{3}{8}\mathbf{b}$

b

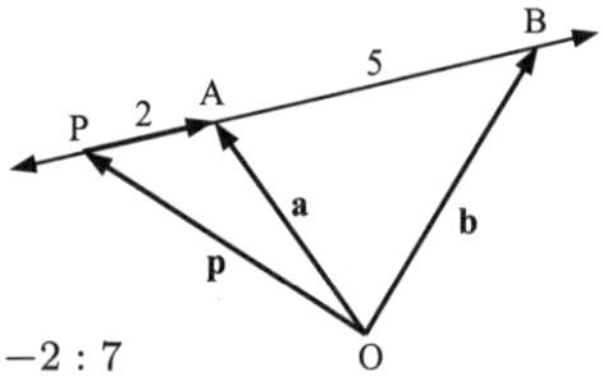

$\vec{AP} : \vec{PB} = -2 : 7$

$\therefore \vec{AP} = \frac{2}{5}\vec{BA}$

$\vec{OP} = \vec{OA} + \vec{AP}$

$= \vec{OA} + \frac{2}{5}\vec{BA}$

$\therefore \mathbf{p} = \mathbf{a} + \frac{2}{5}(\mathbf{a} - \mathbf{b})$

$= \frac{7}{5}\mathbf{a} - \frac{2}{5}\mathbf{b}$

c

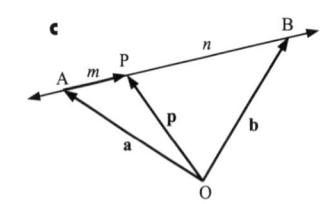

$\vec{AP} : \vec{PB} = m : n$

$\therefore \vec{AP} = \frac{m}{m+n}\vec{AB}$

$\therefore \vec{OP} = \vec{OA} + \vec{AP}$

$= \vec{OA} + \frac{m}{m+n}\vec{AB}$

$\therefore \mathbf{p} = \mathbf{a} + \frac{m}{m+n}(\mathbf{b} - \mathbf{a})$

$= \left(1 - \frac{m}{m+n}\right)\mathbf{a} + \frac{m}{m+n}\mathbf{b}$

$= \frac{n}{m+n}\mathbf{a} + \frac{m}{m+n}\mathbf{b}$

EXERCISE 14G

1 Since **a** and **b** are parallel, then $\mathbf{b} = k\mathbf{a}$. $\therefore \begin{pmatrix} -6 \\ r \\ s \end{pmatrix} = k \begin{pmatrix} 2 \\ -1 \\ 3 \end{pmatrix} = \begin{pmatrix} 2k \\ -k \\ 3k \end{pmatrix}$

$\therefore 2k = -6, \; r = -k, \; s = 3k$ $\therefore k = -3, \; r = 3, \; s = -9$

2 If $\begin{pmatrix} a \\ 2 \\ b \end{pmatrix}$ and $\begin{pmatrix} 3 \\ -1 \\ 2 \end{pmatrix}$ are parallel, then $\begin{pmatrix} a \\ 2 \\ b \end{pmatrix} = k \begin{pmatrix} 3 \\ -1 \\ 2 \end{pmatrix}$.

$\therefore 2 = -k, \; a = 3k, \; b = 2k$ $\therefore k = -2, \; a = -6 \text{ and } b = -4$

3 **a** Let the vector parallel to **a** be $k\mathbf{a}$.

$$\therefore\ k\mathbf{a} = k\begin{pmatrix} 2 \\ -1 \\ -2 \end{pmatrix} = \begin{pmatrix} 2k \\ -k \\ -2k \end{pmatrix}$$

Now $k\mathbf{a}$ has length $= 1$,

so $\sqrt{(2k)^2 + (-k)^2 + (-2k)^2} = 1$

$\therefore\ 4k^2 + k^2 + 4k^2 = 1$

$\therefore\ 9k^2 = 1$

$\therefore\ k = \pm\tfrac{1}{3}$

Choosing $k = \tfrac{1}{3}$, the vector is $\begin{pmatrix} \tfrac{2}{3} \\ -\tfrac{1}{3} \\ -\tfrac{2}{3} \end{pmatrix}$.

b Let the vector parallel to **b** be $k\mathbf{b}$.

$$\therefore\ k\mathbf{b} = k\begin{pmatrix} -2 \\ -1 \\ 2 \end{pmatrix} = \begin{pmatrix} -2k \\ -k \\ 2k \end{pmatrix}$$

Now $k\mathbf{b}$ has length $= 2$,

so $\sqrt{(-2k)^2 + (-k)^2 + (2k)^2} = 2$

$\therefore\ 4k^2 + k^2 + 4k^2 = 4$

$\therefore\ 9k^2 = 4$

$\therefore\ k = \pm\tfrac{2}{3}$

Choosing $k = \tfrac{2}{3}$, the vector is $\begin{pmatrix} -\tfrac{4}{3} \\ -\tfrac{2}{3} \\ \tfrac{4}{3} \end{pmatrix}$.

4 **a** $\overrightarrow{AB} = 3\overrightarrow{CD}$ means that $\overrightarrow{AB}$ is parallel to $\overrightarrow{CD}$ and 3 times its length.

b $\overrightarrow{RS} = -\tfrac{1}{2}\overrightarrow{KL}$ means that $\overrightarrow{RS}$ is parallel to $\overrightarrow{KL}$, half its length, and in the opposite direction.

c

$\overrightarrow{AB} = 2\overrightarrow{BC}$ means that A, B and C are collinear and the length of $\overrightarrow{AB}$ is twice the length of $\overrightarrow{BC}$.

d

$\overrightarrow{BC} = \tfrac{1}{3}\overrightarrow{AC}$ means that A, B and C are collinear and the length of $\overrightarrow{BC}$ is one third the length of $\overrightarrow{AC}$.

5 $\overrightarrow{OP} = \begin{pmatrix} 3 \\ 2 \\ -1 \end{pmatrix}$, $\overrightarrow{OQ} = \begin{pmatrix} 1 \\ 4 \\ -3 \end{pmatrix}$, $\overrightarrow{OR} = \begin{pmatrix} 2 \\ -1 \\ 2 \end{pmatrix}$, $\overrightarrow{OS} = \begin{pmatrix} -1 \\ -2 \\ 3 \end{pmatrix}$

a $\overrightarrow{PR} = \overrightarrow{PO} + \overrightarrow{OR} = -\begin{pmatrix} 3 \\ 2 \\ -1 \end{pmatrix} + \begin{pmatrix} 2 \\ -1 \\ 2 \end{pmatrix} = \begin{pmatrix} -1 \\ -3 \\ 3 \end{pmatrix}$

$\overrightarrow{QS} = \overrightarrow{QO} + \overrightarrow{OS} = -\begin{pmatrix} 1 \\ 4 \\ -3 \end{pmatrix} + \begin{pmatrix} -1 \\ -2 \\ 3 \end{pmatrix} = \begin{pmatrix} -2 \\ -6 \\ 6 \end{pmatrix} = 2\begin{pmatrix} -1 \\ -3 \\ 3 \end{pmatrix} = 2\overrightarrow{PR}$ and so [QS] ∥ [PR].

b Since $\overrightarrow{QS} = 2\overrightarrow{PR}$, $|\overrightarrow{QS}| = 2|\overrightarrow{PR}|$, and so [QS] is twice as long as [PR].

6 **a** $\overrightarrow{AB} = \begin{pmatrix} 4 - (-2) \\ 3 - 1 \\ 0 - 4 \end{pmatrix} = \begin{pmatrix} 6 \\ 2 \\ -4 \end{pmatrix} = 2\begin{pmatrix} 3 \\ 1 \\ -2 \end{pmatrix}$ $\therefore\ \overrightarrow{AB}$ is parallel to $\overrightarrow{BC}$, and since B is a common point, A, B and C are collinear.

$\overrightarrow{BC} = \begin{pmatrix} 19 - 4 \\ 8 - 3 \\ -10 - 0 \end{pmatrix} = \begin{pmatrix} 15 \\ 5 \\ -10 \end{pmatrix} = 5\begin{pmatrix} 3 \\ 1 \\ -2 \end{pmatrix}$

$\therefore$ A divides [CB] in the ratio $7 : 2$ externally.

b $\overrightarrow{RP} = \begin{pmatrix} 2 - (-1) \\ 1 - 7 \\ 1 - 4 \end{pmatrix} = \begin{pmatrix} 3 \\ -6 \\ -3 \end{pmatrix} = 3\begin{pmatrix} 1 \\ -2 \\ -1 \end{pmatrix}$ $\therefore\ \overrightarrow{RP}$ is parallel to $\overrightarrow{PQ}$, and since P is a common point, P, Q and R are collinear.

$\overrightarrow{PQ} = \begin{pmatrix} 5 - 2 \\ -5 - 1 \\ -2 - 1 \end{pmatrix} = \begin{pmatrix} 3 \\ -6 \\ -3 \end{pmatrix} = 3\begin{pmatrix} 1 \\ -2 \\ -1 \end{pmatrix}$

$\therefore$ Q divides [PR] in the ratio $1 : 2$ externally.

7 a

C(−13, a, b)   A(2, −3, 4)   B(11, −9, 7)

Since A, B and C are collinear, $\overrightarrow{CA}$ is parallel to $\overrightarrow{AB}$.

$$\therefore \begin{pmatrix} 15 \\ -3-a \\ 4-b \end{pmatrix} = k \begin{pmatrix} 9 \\ -6 \\ 3 \end{pmatrix}$$

$$\therefore \begin{cases} 15 = 9k \\ -3-a = -6k \\ 4-b = 3k \end{cases}$$

$\therefore k = \frac{5}{3}$

$\therefore a = -3 + 6k = -3 + 10 = 7$

$\therefore b = 4 - 3k = 4 - 5 = -1$

b

L(4, −3, 7)   K(1, −1, 0)   M(a, 2, b)

Since K, L and M are collinear, $\overrightarrow{LK}$ is parallel to $\overrightarrow{KM}$.

$$\therefore \begin{pmatrix} -3 \\ 2 \\ -7 \end{pmatrix} = k \begin{pmatrix} a-1 \\ 3 \\ b \end{pmatrix}$$

$$\therefore \begin{cases} k(a-1) = -3 \\ 3k = 2 \\ kb = -7 \end{cases}$$

$\therefore k = \frac{2}{3}$

$\therefore a - 1 = -\frac{3}{k} = -\frac{9}{2}$

$\therefore a = -\frac{7}{2}$

$\therefore b = -\frac{7}{k} = -\frac{21}{2}$

8 • Consider **a** not parallel to **b**:

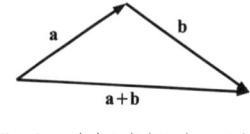

Clearly, $|\mathbf{a}| + |\mathbf{b}| > |\mathbf{a} + \mathbf{b}|$

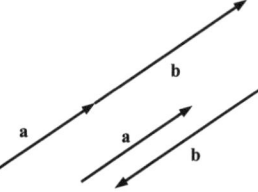

• Consider **a** parallel to **b**:

$|\mathbf{a}| + |\mathbf{b}| = |\mathbf{a} + \mathbf{b}|$

or

$|\mathbf{a}| + |\mathbf{b}| > |\mathbf{a} + \mathbf{b}|$

• If $\mathbf{a} = \mathbf{0}$, $\mathbf{b} \neq \mathbf{0}$, then $\mathbf{a} + \mathbf{b} = \mathbf{b}$ $\therefore |\mathbf{a}| + |\mathbf{b}| = 0 + |\mathbf{b}| = |\mathbf{b}| = |\mathbf{a} + \mathbf{b}|$
Similarly if $\mathbf{a} \neq \mathbf{0}$, $\mathbf{b} = \mathbf{0}$, then $\mathbf{a} + \mathbf{b} = \mathbf{a}$
$\therefore |\mathbf{a}| + |\mathbf{b}| = |\mathbf{a}| + 0 = |\mathbf{a}| = |\mathbf{a} + \mathbf{b}|$
If $\mathbf{a} = \mathbf{0}$ and $\mathbf{b} = \mathbf{0}$, then $\mathbf{a} + \mathbf{b} = \mathbf{0}$
$\therefore |\mathbf{a}| + |\mathbf{b}| = |\mathbf{a} + \mathbf{b}|$
Combining **all** possibilities, $|\mathbf{a}| + |\mathbf{b}| \geqslant |\mathbf{a} + \mathbf{b}|$, or $|\mathbf{a} + \mathbf{b}| \leqslant |\mathbf{a}| + |\mathbf{b}|$

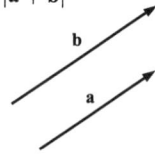

EXERCISE 14H

1 a $\mathbf{i} - \mathbf{j} + \mathbf{k} = \begin{pmatrix} 1 \\ -1 \\ 1 \end{pmatrix}$

$\therefore |\mathbf{i} - \mathbf{j} + \mathbf{k}| = \sqrt{3}$ units

b $3\mathbf{i} - \mathbf{j} + \mathbf{k} = \begin{pmatrix} 3 \\ -1 \\ 1 \end{pmatrix}$

$\therefore |3\mathbf{i} - \mathbf{j} + \mathbf{k}| = \sqrt{9 + 1 + 1} = \sqrt{11}$ units

c $\mathbf{i} - 5\mathbf{k} = \begin{pmatrix} 1 \\ 0 \\ -5 \end{pmatrix}$

$\therefore |\mathbf{i} - 5\mathbf{k}| = \sqrt{1 + 25}$
$= \sqrt{26}$ units

d $\frac{1}{2}(\mathbf{j} + \mathbf{k}) = \begin{pmatrix} 0 \\ \frac{1}{2} \\ \frac{1}{2} \end{pmatrix}$

$\therefore |\frac{1}{2}(\mathbf{j} + \mathbf{k})| = \sqrt{(\frac{1}{2})^2 + (\frac{1}{2})^2}$
$= \sqrt{\frac{1}{2}} = \frac{1}{\sqrt{2}}$ units

2 a length = 1
$\therefore \sqrt{0^2 + k^2} = 1$
$\therefore k^2 = 1$
$\therefore k = \pm 1$

b length = 1
$\therefore \sqrt{k^2 + 0} = 1$
$\therefore k^2 = 1$
$\therefore k = \pm 1$

c length = 1
$\therefore \sqrt{k^2 + 1} = 1$
$\therefore k^2 + 1 = 1$
$\therefore k^2 = 0$
$\therefore k = 0$

d length = 1
$$\therefore \sqrt{\left(\tfrac{1}{4}\right) + k^2 + \tfrac{1}{16}} = 1$$
$$\therefore \sqrt{k^2 + \tfrac{5}{16}} = 1$$
$$\therefore k^2 = \tfrac{11}{16} \quad \therefore k = \pm\tfrac{\sqrt{11}}{4}$$

e length = 1
$$\therefore \sqrt{k^2 + \tfrac{4}{9} + \tfrac{1}{9}} = 1$$
$$\therefore \sqrt{k^2 + \tfrac{5}{9}} = 1$$
$$\therefore k^2 = \tfrac{4}{9} \quad \therefore k = \pm\tfrac{2}{3}$$

3 a length
$= \sqrt{3^2 + 4^2}$
$= \sqrt{9+16}$
$= \sqrt{25}$
$= 5$ units

b length
$= \sqrt{2^2 + (-1)^2 + 1^2}$
$= \sqrt{4+1+1}$
$= \sqrt{6}$ units

c length
$= \sqrt{1^2 + 2^2 + (-2)^2}$
$= \sqrt{1+4+4}$
$= \sqrt{9}$
$= 3$ units

d length $= \sqrt{(-2.36)^2 + (5.65)^2} \approx 6.12$ units

4 a $\mathbf{i} + 2\mathbf{j}$ has length $\sqrt{1^2+2^2} = \sqrt{5}$ units $\quad \therefore$ unit vector $= \tfrac{1}{\sqrt{5}}(\mathbf{i}+2\mathbf{j})$

b $2\mathbf{i}-3\mathbf{k}$ has length $\sqrt{2^2+0^2+(-3)^2} = \sqrt{4+9} = \sqrt{13}$ units
$\therefore$ unit vector is $\tfrac{1}{\sqrt{13}}(2\mathbf{i}-3\mathbf{k})$

c $-2\mathbf{i}-5\mathbf{j}-2\mathbf{k}$ has length $\sqrt{(-2)^2+(-5)^2+(-2)^2} = \sqrt{4+25+4} = \sqrt{33}$ units
$\therefore$ unit vector is $\tfrac{1}{\sqrt{33}}(-2\mathbf{i}-5\mathbf{j}-2\mathbf{k})$

5 a $\begin{pmatrix} 2 \\ -1 \end{pmatrix}$ has length $\sqrt{2^2+(-1)^2} = \sqrt{5}$ units

$\therefore$ the unit vector in the same direction is $\tfrac{1}{\sqrt{5}}\begin{pmatrix} 2 \\ -1 \end{pmatrix}$

$\therefore$ the vector of length 3 units in the same direction is $\tfrac{3}{\sqrt{5}}\begin{pmatrix} 2 \\ -1 \end{pmatrix} = \begin{pmatrix} \tfrac{6}{\sqrt{5}} \\ -\tfrac{3}{\sqrt{5}} \end{pmatrix}$

b $\begin{pmatrix} -1 \\ -4 \end{pmatrix}$ has length $\sqrt{(-1)^2+(-4)^2} = \sqrt{17}$ units

$\therefore$ the unit vector in the opposite direction is $-\tfrac{1}{\sqrt{17}}\begin{pmatrix} -1 \\ -4 \end{pmatrix} = \tfrac{1}{\sqrt{17}}\begin{pmatrix} 1 \\ 4 \end{pmatrix}$

$\therefore$ the vector of length 2 units in the opposite direction is $\tfrac{2}{\sqrt{17}}\begin{pmatrix} 1 \\ 4 \end{pmatrix} = \begin{pmatrix} \tfrac{2}{\sqrt{17}} \\ \tfrac{8}{\sqrt{17}} \end{pmatrix}$

c $\begin{pmatrix} -1 \\ 4 \\ 1 \end{pmatrix}$ has length $\sqrt{(-1)^2+4^2+1^2} = \sqrt{18} = 3\sqrt{2}$ units

$\therefore$ the unit vector in the same direction is $\tfrac{1}{3\sqrt{2}}\begin{pmatrix} -1 \\ 4 \\ 1 \end{pmatrix}$

$\therefore$ the vector of length 6 units in the same direction is $\tfrac{6}{3\sqrt{2}}\begin{pmatrix} -1 \\ 4 \\ 1 \end{pmatrix} = \begin{pmatrix} -\sqrt{2} \\ 4\sqrt{2} \\ \sqrt{2} \end{pmatrix}$

d $\begin{pmatrix} -1 \\ -2 \\ -2 \end{pmatrix}$ has length $\sqrt{(-1)^2+(-2)^2+(-2)^2} = \sqrt{9} = 3$ units

$\therefore$ the unit vector in the opposite direction is $-\tfrac{1}{3}\begin{pmatrix} -1 \\ -2 \\ -2 \end{pmatrix} = \tfrac{1}{3}\begin{pmatrix} 1 \\ 2 \\ 2 \end{pmatrix}$

$\therefore$ the vector of length 5 units in the opposite direction is $\tfrac{5}{3}\begin{pmatrix} 1 \\ 2 \\ 2 \end{pmatrix} = \begin{pmatrix} \tfrac{5}{3} \\ \tfrac{10}{3} \\ \tfrac{10}{3} \end{pmatrix}$

EXERCISE 14I

1 a $\mathbf{q} \bullet \mathbf{p}$
$= \begin{pmatrix} -1 \\ 5 \end{pmatrix} \bullet \begin{pmatrix} 3 \\ 2 \end{pmatrix}$
$= -3 + 10$
$= 7$

b $\mathbf{q} \bullet \mathbf{r}$
$= \begin{pmatrix} -1 \\ 5 \end{pmatrix} \bullet \begin{pmatrix} -2 \\ 4 \end{pmatrix}$
$= 2 + 20$
$= 22$

c $\mathbf{q} \bullet (\mathbf{p} + \mathbf{r})$
$= \begin{pmatrix} -1 \\ 5 \end{pmatrix} \bullet \left[\begin{pmatrix} 3 \\ 2 \end{pmatrix} + \begin{pmatrix} -2 \\ 4 \end{pmatrix} \right]$
$= \begin{pmatrix} -1 \\ 5 \end{pmatrix} \bullet \begin{pmatrix} 1 \\ 6 \end{pmatrix}$
$= -1 + 30 = 29$

d $3\mathbf{r} \bullet \mathbf{q}$
$= 3 \begin{pmatrix} -2 \\ 4 \end{pmatrix} \bullet \begin{pmatrix} -1 \\ 5 \end{pmatrix}$
$= \begin{pmatrix} -6 \\ 12 \end{pmatrix} \bullet \begin{pmatrix} -1 \\ 5 \end{pmatrix}$
$= 6 + 60 = 66$

e $2\mathbf{p} \bullet 2\mathbf{p}$
$= 2 \begin{pmatrix} 3 \\ 2 \end{pmatrix} \bullet 2 \begin{pmatrix} 3 \\ 2 \end{pmatrix}$
$= \begin{pmatrix} 6 \\ 4 \end{pmatrix} \bullet \begin{pmatrix} 6 \\ 4 \end{pmatrix}$
$= 36 + 16 = 52$

f $\mathbf{i} \bullet \mathbf{p}$
$= \begin{pmatrix} 1 \\ 0 \end{pmatrix} \bullet \begin{pmatrix} 3 \\ 2 \end{pmatrix}$
$= 3 + 0$
$= 3$

g $\mathbf{q} \bullet \mathbf{j}$
$= \begin{pmatrix} -1 \\ 5 \end{pmatrix} \bullet \begin{pmatrix} 0 \\ 1 \end{pmatrix}$
$= 0 + 5$
$= 5$

h $\mathbf{i} \bullet \mathbf{i}$
$= \begin{pmatrix} 1 \\ 0 \end{pmatrix} \bullet \begin{pmatrix} 1 \\ 0 \end{pmatrix}$
$= 1 + 0$
$= 1$

2 a $\mathbf{a} \bullet \mathbf{b} = \begin{pmatrix} 2 \\ 1 \\ 3 \end{pmatrix} \bullet \begin{pmatrix} -1 \\ 1 \\ 1 \end{pmatrix}$
$= 2(-1) + 1(1) + 3(1)$
$= -2 + 1 + 3$
$= 2$

b $\mathbf{b} \bullet \mathbf{a} = \begin{pmatrix} -1 \\ 1 \\ 1 \end{pmatrix} \bullet \begin{pmatrix} 2 \\ 1 \\ 3 \end{pmatrix}$
$= (-1)(2) + 1(1) + 1(3)$
$= -2 + 1 + 3$
$= 2$

c $|\mathbf{a}|^2 = \left(\sqrt{2^2 + 1^2 + 3^2} \right)^2$
$= 14$

d $\mathbf{a} \bullet \mathbf{a} = \begin{pmatrix} 2 \\ 1 \\ 3 \end{pmatrix} \bullet \begin{pmatrix} 2 \\ 1 \\ 3 \end{pmatrix}$
$= 2(2) + 1(1) + 3(3)$
$= 14$

e $\mathbf{a} \bullet (\mathbf{b} + \mathbf{c})$
$= \begin{pmatrix} 2 \\ 1 \\ 3 \end{pmatrix} \bullet \left[\begin{pmatrix} -1 \\ 1 \\ 1 \end{pmatrix} + \begin{pmatrix} 0 \\ -1 \\ 1 \end{pmatrix} \right]$
$= \begin{pmatrix} 2 \\ 1 \\ 3 \end{pmatrix} \bullet \begin{pmatrix} -1 \\ 0 \\ 2 \end{pmatrix}$
$= 2(-1) + 1(0) + 3(2) = 4$

f $\mathbf{a} \bullet \mathbf{b} + \mathbf{a} \bullet \mathbf{c}$
$= 2 + \begin{pmatrix} 2 \\ 1 \\ 3 \end{pmatrix} \bullet \begin{pmatrix} 0 \\ -1 \\ 1 \end{pmatrix}$ {using **a**}
$= 2 + 2(0) + 1(-1) + 3(1)$
$= 4$

3 a $\mathbf{p} \bullet \mathbf{q}$
$= \begin{pmatrix} 3 \\ -1 \\ 2 \end{pmatrix} \bullet \begin{pmatrix} -2 \\ 1 \\ 3 \end{pmatrix}$
$= -6 - 1 + 6$
$= -1$

b If the angle between **p** and **q** is θ, then
$$\cos \theta = \frac{\mathbf{p} \bullet \mathbf{q}}{|\mathbf{p}||\mathbf{q}|} = \frac{-1}{\sqrt{3^2 + (-1)^2 + 2^2} \sqrt{(-2)^2 + 1^2 + 3^2}}$$
$$= \frac{-1}{\sqrt{14}\sqrt{14}}$$
$\therefore \theta = \arccos(-\frac{1}{14}) \approx 94.1°$

4 **a** $(\mathbf{i}+\mathbf{j}-\mathbf{k}) \bullet (2\mathbf{j}+\mathbf{k})$

$= \begin{pmatrix} 1 \\ 1 \\ -1 \end{pmatrix} \bullet \begin{pmatrix} 0 \\ 2 \\ 1 \end{pmatrix}$

$= 1(0) + 1(2) - 1(1) = 1$

b $\mathbf{i} \bullet \mathbf{i} = \begin{pmatrix} 1 \\ 0 \\ 0 \end{pmatrix} \bullet \begin{pmatrix} 1 \\ 0 \\ 0 \end{pmatrix}$

$= 1$

c $\mathbf{i} \bullet \mathbf{j} = \begin{pmatrix} 1 \\ 0 \\ 0 \end{pmatrix} \bullet \begin{pmatrix} 0 \\ 1 \\ 0 \end{pmatrix}$

$= 0$

5 $\mathbf{a} \bullet (\mathbf{b}+\mathbf{c})$

$= \begin{pmatrix} a_1 \\ a_2 \\ a_3 \end{pmatrix} \bullet \left[\begin{pmatrix} b_1 \\ b_2 \\ b_3 \end{pmatrix} + \begin{pmatrix} c_1 \\ c_2 \\ c_3 \end{pmatrix} \right]$

$= \begin{pmatrix} a_1 \\ a_2 \\ a_3 \end{pmatrix} \bullet \begin{pmatrix} b_1+c_1 \\ b_2+c_2 \\ b_3+c_3 \end{pmatrix}$

$= a_1(b_1+c_1) + a_2(b_2+c_2) + a_3(b_3+c_3)$
$= a_1 b_1 + a_1 c_1 + a_2 b_2 + a_2 c_2 + a_3 b_3 + a_3 c_3$
$= (a_1 b_1 + a_2 b_2 + a_3 b_3) + (a_1 c_1 + a_2 c_2 + a_3 c_3)$
$= \mathbf{a} \bullet \mathbf{b} + \mathbf{a} \bullet \mathbf{c}$

$\therefore \mathbf{p} \bullet (\mathbf{c}+\mathbf{d}) = \mathbf{p} \bullet \mathbf{c} + \mathbf{p} \bullet \mathbf{d}$

If we let $\mathbf{p} = \mathbf{a}+\mathbf{b}$,

then $(\mathbf{a}+\mathbf{b}) \bullet (\mathbf{c}+\mathbf{d})$
$= \mathbf{p} \bullet (\mathbf{c}+\mathbf{d})$
$= \mathbf{p} \bullet \mathbf{c} + \mathbf{p} \bullet \mathbf{d}$
$= (\mathbf{a}+\mathbf{b}) \bullet \mathbf{c} + (\mathbf{a}+\mathbf{b}) \bullet \mathbf{d}$
$= \mathbf{c} \bullet (\mathbf{a}+\mathbf{b}) + \mathbf{d} \bullet (\mathbf{a}+\mathbf{b})$
$= \mathbf{c} \bullet \mathbf{a} + \mathbf{c} \bullet \mathbf{b} + \mathbf{d} \bullet \mathbf{a} + \mathbf{d} \bullet \mathbf{b}$
$= \mathbf{a} \bullet \mathbf{c} + \mathbf{a} \bullet \mathbf{d} + \mathbf{b} \bullet \mathbf{c} + \mathbf{b} \bullet \mathbf{d}$

6 **a** $\begin{pmatrix} 3 \\ t \end{pmatrix} \bullet \begin{pmatrix} -2 \\ 1 \end{pmatrix} = 0$

$\therefore -6 + t = 0$
$\therefore t = 6$

b $\begin{pmatrix} t \\ t+2 \end{pmatrix} \bullet \begin{pmatrix} 3 \\ -4 \end{pmatrix} = 0$

$\therefore 3t - 4(t+2) = 0$
$\therefore 3t - 4t - 8 = 0$
$\therefore -t = 8$
$\therefore t = -8$

c $\begin{pmatrix} t \\ t+2 \end{pmatrix} \bullet \begin{pmatrix} 2-3t \\ t \end{pmatrix} = 0$

$\therefore 2t - 3t^2 + t^2 + 2t = 0$
$\therefore -2t^2 + 4t = 0$
$\therefore t^2 - 2t = 0$
$\therefore t(t-2) = 0$
$\therefore t = 0$ or 2

d $\begin{pmatrix} 3 \\ -1 \\ t \end{pmatrix} \bullet \begin{pmatrix} 2t \\ -3 \\ -4 \end{pmatrix} = 0 \quad \therefore 3(2t) + (-1)(-3) + t(-4) = 0$

$\therefore 6t + 3 - 4t = 0$
$\therefore 2t + 3 = 0 \quad \therefore t = -\frac{3}{2}$

7 **a** If $\mathbf{p} \parallel \mathbf{q}$ then $\begin{pmatrix} 3 \\ t \end{pmatrix} = k \begin{pmatrix} -2 \\ 1 \end{pmatrix}$ where $k \neq 0$ $\therefore 3 = -2k$ and $t = k$

$\therefore k = -\frac{3}{2}$ and $t = -\frac{3}{2}$

b If $\mathbf{r} \parallel \mathbf{s}$ then $\begin{pmatrix} t \\ t+2 \end{pmatrix} = k \begin{pmatrix} 3 \\ -4 \end{pmatrix}$ where $k \neq 0$ $\therefore t = 3k$ and $t+2 = -4k$

$\therefore t+2 = -4\left(\frac{t}{3}\right)$
$\therefore 3t + 6 = -4t$
$\therefore 7t = -6$
$\therefore t = -\frac{6}{7}$

c If $\mathbf{a} \parallel \mathbf{b}$ then $\begin{pmatrix} t \\ t+2 \end{pmatrix} = k \begin{pmatrix} 2-3t \\ t \end{pmatrix}$

$\therefore t = k(2-3t)$ and $t+2 = kt$

$\therefore \dfrac{t}{2-3t} = \dfrac{t+2}{t} \quad$ {equating ks}

$\therefore t^2 = (t+2)(2-3t)$
$\therefore t^2 = 2t - 3t^2 + 4 - 6t$
$\therefore 4t^2 + 4t - 4 = 0$
$\therefore t^2 + t - 1 = 0$ which has $\Delta = 1^2 - 4(1)(-1) = 5$

$\therefore t = \dfrac{-1 \pm \sqrt{5}}{2}$

d If $\mathbf{a} \parallel \mathbf{b}$ then $\begin{pmatrix} 3 \\ -1 \\ t \end{pmatrix} = k \begin{pmatrix} 2t \\ -3 \\ -4 \end{pmatrix}$ where $k \neq 0$

$\therefore \quad 3 = 2kt, \quad -1 = -3k \quad \text{and} \quad t = -4k$

$\therefore \quad k = \frac{1}{3} \quad \text{and} \quad 3 = \frac{2}{3}t, \quad t = -\frac{4}{3}$

$\therefore \quad t = \frac{9}{2} \quad \text{and} \quad -\frac{4}{3}$ simultaneously which is impossible.

$\therefore$ the vectors can never be parallel.

8

$\mathbf{a} \bullet \mathbf{b}$

$= \begin{pmatrix} 3 \\ 1 \\ 2 \end{pmatrix} \bullet \begin{pmatrix} -1 \\ 1 \\ 1 \end{pmatrix}$

$= 3(-1) + 1(1) + 2(1)$

$= 0$

$\mathbf{b} \bullet \mathbf{c}$

$= \begin{pmatrix} -1 \\ 1 \\ 1 \end{pmatrix} \bullet \begin{pmatrix} 1 \\ 5 \\ -4 \end{pmatrix}$

$= (-1)(1) + 1(5) + 1(-4)$

$= 0$

$\mathbf{a} \bullet \mathbf{c}$

$= \begin{pmatrix} 3 \\ 1 \\ 2 \end{pmatrix} \bullet \begin{pmatrix} 1 \\ 5 \\ -4 \end{pmatrix}$

$= (3)(1) + 1(5) + 2(-4)$

$= 0$

$\therefore$ $\mathbf{a}$, $\mathbf{b}$ and $\mathbf{c}$ are mutually perpendicular.

9 **a** $\begin{pmatrix} 1 \\ 1 \\ 5 \end{pmatrix} \bullet \begin{pmatrix} 2 \\ 3 \\ -1 \end{pmatrix} = 1(2) + 1(3) + 5(-1)$
$= 0$

$\therefore \begin{pmatrix} 1 \\ 1 \\ 5 \end{pmatrix}$ and $\begin{pmatrix} 2 \\ 3 \\ -1 \end{pmatrix}$ are perpendicular.

b $\begin{pmatrix} 3 \\ t \\ -2 \end{pmatrix} \bullet \begin{pmatrix} 1-t \\ -3 \\ 4 \end{pmatrix} = 0$

$\therefore \quad 3(1-t) + t(-3) + (-2)4 = 0$

$\therefore \quad 3 - 3t - 3t - 8 = 0$

$\therefore \quad -6t = 5$

$\therefore \quad t = -\frac{5}{6}$

10 We have three points: $A(5, 1, 2)$, $B(6, -1, 0)$, $C(3, 2, 0)$

Then $\overrightarrow{AB} = \begin{pmatrix} 1 \\ -2 \\ -2 \end{pmatrix}$, $\overrightarrow{AC} = \begin{pmatrix} -2 \\ 1 \\ -2 \end{pmatrix}$ and $\overrightarrow{BC} = \begin{pmatrix} -3 \\ 3 \\ 0 \end{pmatrix}$

Now $\overrightarrow{AB} \bullet \overrightarrow{AC} = \begin{pmatrix} 1 \\ -2 \\ -2 \end{pmatrix} \bullet \begin{pmatrix} -2 \\ 1 \\ -2 \end{pmatrix} = (-2) + (-2) + 4 = 0$

$\therefore$ $\overrightarrow{AB}$ is perpendicular to $\overrightarrow{AC}$ and so $\triangle ABC$ is right angled at A.

11 **a** $A(2,4,2)$ $B(-1,2,3)$

$D(0,5,5)$ $C(-3,3,6)$

$\overrightarrow{AB} = \begin{pmatrix} -3 \\ -2 \\ 1 \end{pmatrix}$ $\overrightarrow{BC} = \begin{pmatrix} -2 \\ 1 \\ 3 \end{pmatrix}$

$\overrightarrow{DC} = \begin{pmatrix} -3 \\ -2 \\ 1 \end{pmatrix}$ $\overrightarrow{AD} = \begin{pmatrix} -2 \\ 1 \\ 3 \end{pmatrix}$

$\therefore$ $\overrightarrow{AB}$ is parallel to $\overrightarrow{DC}$ and $\overrightarrow{BC}$ is parallel to $\overrightarrow{AD}$.

$\therefore$ ABCD is a parallelogram.

b $|\overrightarrow{AB}| = \sqrt{14}$ units and $|\overrightarrow{BC}| = \sqrt{14}$ units $\quad \therefore$ ABCD is a rhombus.

c $\overrightarrow{AC} \bullet \overrightarrow{BD} = \begin{pmatrix} -5 \\ -1 \\ 4 \end{pmatrix} \bullet \begin{pmatrix} 1 \\ 3 \\ 2 \end{pmatrix} = (-5) \times 1 + (-1) \times 3 + 4(2) = 0$

$\therefore$ $\overrightarrow{AC}$ is perpendicular to $\overrightarrow{BD}$ which illustrates that the diagonals of a rhombus are perpendicular.

12 a $x - y = 3$ has gradient $+\frac{1}{1}$ and so has direction vector $\binom{1}{1}$.

$3x + 2y = 11$ has gradient $-\frac{3}{2}$ and so has direction vector $\binom{2}{-3}$.

$\therefore \binom{1}{1} \bullet \binom{2}{-3} = \sqrt{1+1}\sqrt{4+9}\cos\theta$

$\therefore \ 2 - 3 = \sqrt{2}\sqrt{13}\cos\theta$

$\therefore \ \frac{-1}{\sqrt{26}} = \cos\theta$

$\therefore \ \theta \approx 101.3°$ $\therefore$ the angle is $101.3°$ or $78.7°$

b $y = x + 2$ has slope $1 = \frac{1}{1}$ $\therefore$ direction vector is $\binom{1}{1}$.

$y = 1 - 3x$ has slope $-3 = \frac{-3}{1}$ $\therefore$ direction vector is $\binom{1}{-3}$.

$\therefore \binom{1}{1} \bullet \binom{1}{-3} = \sqrt{1+1}\sqrt{1+9}\cos\theta$

$\therefore \ 1 - 3 = \sqrt{2}\sqrt{10}\cos\theta$

$\therefore \ \frac{-2}{\sqrt{20}} = \cos\theta$

$\therefore \ \theta \approx 116.6°$ $\therefore$ the angle is $116.6°$ or $63.4°$

c $y + x = 7$ has slope $-1 = \frac{-1}{1}$ $\therefore$ direction vector is $\binom{1}{-1}$.

$x - 3y + 2 = 0$ has slope $\frac{1}{3}$ $\therefore$ direction vector is $\binom{3}{1}$.

$\therefore \binom{1}{-1} \bullet \binom{3}{1} = \sqrt{1+1}\sqrt{9+1}\cos\theta$

$\therefore \ 3 - 1 = \sqrt{2}\sqrt{10}\cos\theta$

$\therefore \ \frac{2}{\sqrt{20}} = \cos\theta$

$\therefore \ \theta \approx 63.4°$ $\therefore$ the angle is $63.4°$ or $116.6°$

d $y = 2 - x$ has slope $-1 = \frac{-1}{1}$ $\therefore$ has direction vector $\binom{1}{-1}$.

$x - 2y = 7$ has slope $\frac{1}{2}$ $\therefore$ has direction vector $\binom{2}{1}$.

$\therefore \binom{1}{-1} \bullet \binom{2}{1} = \sqrt{1+1}\sqrt{4+1}\cos\theta$

$\therefore \ 2 - 1 = \sqrt{2}\sqrt{5}\cos\theta$

$\therefore \ \cos\theta = \frac{1}{\sqrt{10}}$

$\therefore \ \theta \approx 71.6°$ $\therefore$ the angle is $71.6°$ or $108.4°$

13 a $\mathbf{p} \bullet \mathbf{q} = |\mathbf{p}||\mathbf{q}|\cos\theta$
$= 2 \times 5 \times \cos 60°$
$= 5$

b $\mathbf{p} \bullet \mathbf{q} = |\mathbf{p}||\mathbf{q}|\cos\theta$
$= 6 \times 3 \times \cos 120°$
$= -9$

14 a $\binom{5}{2} \bullet \binom{-2}{5} = -10 + 10 = 0$, so $\binom{-2}{5}$ is one such vector.

$\therefore$ required vectors have form $k\binom{-2}{5}$, $k \neq 0$.   Note: $k\binom{2}{-5}$, $k \neq 0$ is also acceptable.

b $\binom{-1}{-2} \bullet \binom{-2}{1} = 2 - 2 = 0$, so $\binom{-2}{1}$ is one such vector.

$\therefore$ required vectors have form $k\binom{-2}{1}$, $k \neq 0$.

c $\binom{3}{-1} \bullet \binom{1}{3} = 3 - 3 = 0$, so $\binom{1}{3}$ is one such vector.

$\therefore$ required vectors have form $k\binom{1}{3}$, $k \neq 0$.

d $\binom{-4}{3} \bullet \binom{3}{4} = -12 + 12 = 0$, so $\binom{3}{4}$ is one such vector.

$\therefore$ required vectors have form $k\binom{3}{4}$, $k \neq 0$.

e $\binom{2}{0} \bullet \binom{0}{1} = 0 + 0 = 0$, so $\binom{0}{1}$ is one such vector.

$\therefore$ required vectors have form $k\binom{0}{1}$, $k \neq 0$.

15 Given $A(3, 0, 1)$, $B(-3, 1, 2)$ and $C(-2, 1, -1)$,

$\overrightarrow{BC} = \begin{pmatrix} 1 \\ 0 \\ -3 \end{pmatrix}$ and $\overrightarrow{BA} = \begin{pmatrix} 6 \\ -1 \\ -1 \end{pmatrix}$

$\therefore \cos\theta = \dfrac{\overrightarrow{BC} \bullet \overrightarrow{BA}}{|\overrightarrow{BC}||\overrightarrow{BA}|}$

$= \dfrac{\begin{pmatrix} 1 \\ 0 \\ -3 \end{pmatrix} \bullet \begin{pmatrix} 6 \\ -1 \\ -1 \end{pmatrix}}{\sqrt{1+9}\sqrt{36+1+1}}$

$= \dfrac{6+0+3}{\sqrt{10}\sqrt{38}}$

$= \dfrac{9}{\sqrt{380}}$ and so $\theta \approx 62.5°$

If $\overrightarrow{BA}$ and $\overrightarrow{CB}$ are used we would find the exterior angle of the triangle at B, which is $117.5°$.

16

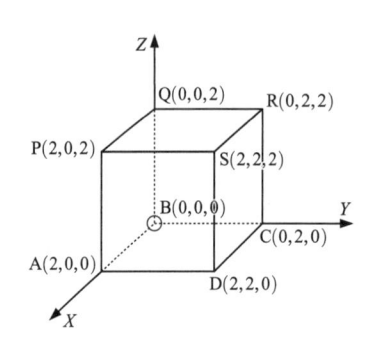

a Suppose the origin is at B.

Now $\overrightarrow{BA} = \begin{pmatrix} 2 \\ 0 \\ 0 \end{pmatrix}$ and $\overrightarrow{BS} = \begin{pmatrix} 2 \\ 2 \\ 2 \end{pmatrix}$

$\therefore \overrightarrow{BA} \bullet \overrightarrow{BS} = \begin{pmatrix} 2 \\ 0 \\ 0 \end{pmatrix} \bullet \begin{pmatrix} 2 \\ 2 \\ 2 \end{pmatrix} = 4+0+0 = 4$

$\therefore \cos A\widehat{B}S = \dfrac{4}{\sqrt{4+0+0}\sqrt{4+4+4}}$

$= \dfrac{4}{2 \times 2\sqrt{3}} = \dfrac{1}{\sqrt{3}}$

$\therefore A\widehat{B}S \approx 54.7°$

b Consider vectors away from B.

$\overrightarrow{BR} = \begin{pmatrix} 0 \\ 2 \\ 2 \end{pmatrix}$ and $\overrightarrow{BP} = \begin{pmatrix} 2 \\ 0 \\ 2 \end{pmatrix}$

$\overrightarrow{BR} \bullet \overrightarrow{BP} = \begin{pmatrix} 0 \\ 2 \\ 2 \end{pmatrix} \bullet \begin{pmatrix} 2 \\ 0 \\ 2 \end{pmatrix} = 0+0+4 = 4$

$\therefore \cos R\widehat{B}P = \dfrac{4}{\sqrt{0+4+4}\sqrt{4+0+4}}$

$= \dfrac{4}{\sqrt{8} \times \sqrt{8}}$

$= \dfrac{1}{2}$ and so $R\widehat{B}P = 60°$

c $\overrightarrow{BP} = \begin{pmatrix} 2 \\ 0 \\ 2 \end{pmatrix}$ and $\overrightarrow{BS} = \begin{pmatrix} 2 \\ 2 \\ 2 \end{pmatrix}$

$\therefore \overrightarrow{BP} \bullet \overrightarrow{BS} = \begin{pmatrix} 2 \\ 0 \\ 2 \end{pmatrix} \bullet \begin{pmatrix} 2 \\ 2 \\ 2 \end{pmatrix}$

$= 4+0+4 = 8$

$\therefore \cos P\widehat{B}S = \dfrac{8}{\sqrt{4+4}\sqrt{4+4+4}}$

$= \dfrac{8}{\sqrt{96}}$

$\therefore P\widehat{B}S \approx 35.3°$

17 Suppose the origin is at N.

a

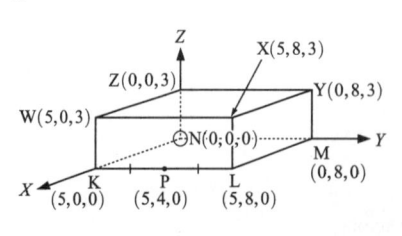

$\overrightarrow{NY} = \begin{pmatrix} 0 \\ 8 \\ 3 \end{pmatrix}$ and $\overrightarrow{NX} = \begin{pmatrix} 5 \\ 8 \\ 3 \end{pmatrix}$

$\overrightarrow{NY} \bullet \overrightarrow{NX} = \begin{pmatrix} 0 \\ 8 \\ 3 \end{pmatrix} \bullet \begin{pmatrix} 5 \\ 8 \\ 3 \end{pmatrix} = 0+64+9 = 73$

$\therefore \cos Y\widehat{N}X = \dfrac{73}{\sqrt{64+9}\sqrt{25+64+9}}$

$= \dfrac{73}{\sqrt{73}\sqrt{98}} = \sqrt{\dfrac{73}{98}}$

$\therefore Y\widehat{N}X \approx 30.3°$

b $\overrightarrow{NY} = \begin{pmatrix} 0 \\ 8 \\ 3 \end{pmatrix}$ and $\overrightarrow{NP} = \begin{pmatrix} 5 \\ 4 \\ 0 \end{pmatrix}$

$\overrightarrow{NY} \bullet \overrightarrow{NP} = \begin{pmatrix} 0 \\ 8 \\ 3 \end{pmatrix} \bullet \begin{pmatrix} 5 \\ 4 \\ 0 \end{pmatrix}$

$= 0 + 32 + 0$
$= 32$

$\therefore \cos Y\widehat{N}P = \dfrac{32}{\sqrt{64+9}\sqrt{25+16}}$

$= \dfrac{32}{\sqrt{73}\sqrt{41}}$

$\therefore Y\widehat{N}P \approx 54.2°$

18 a M is the midpoint of [BC]. $\therefore$ M is at $\left(\dfrac{2+1}{2}, \dfrac{2+3}{2}, \dfrac{2+1}{2}\right)$, which is $\left(\dfrac{3}{2}, \dfrac{5}{2}, \dfrac{3}{2}\right)$.

b Now $\overrightarrow{MD} = \begin{pmatrix} \frac{3}{2} \\ -\frac{1}{2} \\ -\frac{3}{2} \end{pmatrix}$ and $\overrightarrow{MA} = \begin{pmatrix} \frac{1}{2} \\ -\frac{3}{2} \\ -\frac{1}{2} \end{pmatrix}$

$\therefore \cos\theta = \dfrac{\overrightarrow{MD} \bullet \overrightarrow{MA}}{|\overrightarrow{MD}||\overrightarrow{MA}|} = \dfrac{\begin{pmatrix} \frac{3}{2} \\ -\frac{1}{2} \\ -\frac{3}{2} \end{pmatrix} \bullet \begin{pmatrix} \frac{1}{2} \\ -\frac{3}{2} \\ -\frac{1}{2} \end{pmatrix}}{\sqrt{\frac{9}{4}+\frac{1}{4}+\frac{9}{4}}\sqrt{\frac{1}{4}+\frac{9}{4}+\frac{1}{4}}}$

$\therefore \cos\theta = \dfrac{\frac{3}{4}+\frac{3}{4}+\frac{3}{4}}{\sqrt{\frac{19}{4}}\sqrt{\frac{11}{4}}} = \dfrac{\frac{9}{4}}{\frac{\sqrt{209}}{4}} = \dfrac{9}{\sqrt{209}}$ and so $\theta \approx 51.5°$

19 a $\begin{pmatrix} 2 \\ t \\ t-2 \end{pmatrix} \bullet \begin{pmatrix} t \\ 3 \\ t \end{pmatrix} = 0$ $\therefore 2t + 3t + t(t-2) = 0$
$\therefore 5t + t^2 - 2t = 0$
$\therefore t^2 + 3t = 0$
$\therefore t(t+3) = 0$ and so $t = 0$ or $t = -3$

b Given that $\mathbf{a} = \begin{pmatrix} 1 \\ 2 \\ 3 \end{pmatrix}$, $\mathbf{b} = \begin{pmatrix} 2 \\ 2 \\ r \end{pmatrix}$ and $\mathbf{c} = \begin{pmatrix} s \\ t \\ 1 \end{pmatrix}$ are mutually perpendicular,

$\mathbf{a} \bullet \mathbf{b} = 0$, $\mathbf{b} \bullet \mathbf{c} = 0$ and $\mathbf{a} \bullet \mathbf{c} = 0$

$\therefore \begin{pmatrix} 1 \\ 2 \\ 3 \end{pmatrix} \bullet \begin{pmatrix} 2 \\ 2 \\ r \end{pmatrix} = 0$ $\therefore 2 + 4 + 3r = 0$
$\therefore 3r = -6$
$\therefore r = -2$

and $\begin{pmatrix} 2 \\ 2 \\ -2 \end{pmatrix} \bullet \begin{pmatrix} s \\ t \\ 1 \end{pmatrix} = 0$ $\therefore 2s + 2t - 2 = 0$
$\therefore s + t = 1$ ...... (1)

and $\begin{pmatrix} 1 \\ 2 \\ 3 \end{pmatrix} \bullet \begin{pmatrix} s \\ t \\ 1 \end{pmatrix} = 0$ $\therefore s + 2t + 3 = 0$
$\therefore s + 2t = -3$ ...... (2)

(2) − (1) gives $t = -4$ and so $s = 5$ $\therefore r = -2$, $s = 5$ and $t = -4$

20 a Choose any vector in the direction of the X-axis, such as $\mathbf{i} = \begin{pmatrix} 1 \\ 0 \\ 0 \end{pmatrix}$.

Then $\cos\theta = \dfrac{\begin{pmatrix} 1 \\ 0 \\ 0 \end{pmatrix} \bullet \begin{pmatrix} 1 \\ 2 \\ 3 \end{pmatrix}}{\left|\begin{pmatrix} 1 \\ 0 \\ 0 \end{pmatrix}\right|\left|\begin{pmatrix} 1 \\ 2 \\ 3 \end{pmatrix}\right|} = \dfrac{1}{\sqrt{1}\sqrt{1+4+9}} = \dfrac{1}{\sqrt{14}}$ and so $\theta \approx 74.5°$.

b A line parallel to the Y-axis has direction vector $\mathbf{j} = \begin{pmatrix} 0 \\ 1 \\ 0 \end{pmatrix}$.

Then $\cos\theta = \dfrac{\begin{pmatrix} 0 \\ 1 \\ 0 \end{pmatrix} \bullet \begin{pmatrix} -1 \\ 1 \\ 3 \end{pmatrix}}{\sqrt{1}\sqrt{1+1+9}} = \dfrac{1}{\sqrt{11}}$ and so $\theta \approx 72.5°$.

21 We want vectors $\mathbf{a}$, $\mathbf{b}$ and $\mathbf{c}$ such that $\mathbf{a} \neq \mathbf{0}$, $\mathbf{a} \bullet \mathbf{b} = \mathbf{a} \bullet \mathbf{c}$ and $\mathbf{b} \neq \mathbf{c}$

For example, $\mathbf{a} = \begin{pmatrix} 1 \\ 0 \\ 0 \end{pmatrix}$, $\mathbf{b} = \begin{pmatrix} 0 \\ 1 \\ 0 \end{pmatrix}$, $\mathbf{c} = \begin{pmatrix} 0 \\ 0 \\ 1 \end{pmatrix}$

In this case, $\mathbf{a} \bullet \mathbf{b} = \mathbf{a} \bullet \mathbf{c} = 0$

22 **a** $|\mathbf{a}+\mathbf{b}|^2 + |\mathbf{a}-\mathbf{b}|^2 = (\mathbf{a}+\mathbf{b}) \bullet (\mathbf{a}+\mathbf{b}) + (\mathbf{a}-\mathbf{b}) \bullet (\mathbf{a}-\mathbf{b})$
$\qquad\qquad\qquad\quad = \mathbf{a}\bullet\mathbf{a} + \mathbf{a}\bullet\mathbf{b} + \mathbf{b}\bullet\mathbf{a} + \mathbf{b}\bullet\mathbf{b} + \mathbf{a}\bullet\mathbf{a} - \mathbf{a}\bullet\mathbf{b} - \mathbf{b}\bullet\mathbf{a} + \mathbf{b}\bullet\mathbf{b}$
$\qquad\qquad\qquad\quad = 2\mathbf{a}\bullet\mathbf{a} + 2\mathbf{b}\bullet\mathbf{b}$
$\qquad\qquad\qquad\quad = 2|\mathbf{a}|^2 + 2|\mathbf{b}|^2 \quad$ as required

b $|\mathbf{a}+\mathbf{b}|^2 - |\mathbf{a}-\mathbf{b}|^2 = (\mathbf{a}+\mathbf{b}) \bullet (\mathbf{a}+\mathbf{b}) - (\mathbf{a}-\mathbf{b}) \bullet (\mathbf{a}-\mathbf{b})$
$\qquad\qquad\qquad\quad = \mathbf{a}\bullet\mathbf{a} + \mathbf{a}\bullet\mathbf{b} + \mathbf{b}\bullet\mathbf{a} + \mathbf{b}\bullet\mathbf{b} - \mathbf{a}\bullet\mathbf{a} + \mathbf{a}\bullet\mathbf{b} + \mathbf{b}\bullet\mathbf{a} - \mathbf{b}\bullet\mathbf{b}$
$\qquad\qquad\qquad\quad = 2\mathbf{a}\bullet\mathbf{b} + 2\mathbf{b}\bullet\mathbf{a}$
$\qquad\qquad\qquad\quad = 4\mathbf{a}\bullet\mathbf{b} \quad$ as required $\quad\{$since $\mathbf{a}\bullet\mathbf{b} = \mathbf{b}\bullet\mathbf{a}\}$

23 We are given that $\mathbf{a} \neq \mathbf{b}$, $\mathbf{a} \neq \mathbf{0}$ and $\mathbf{b} \neq \mathbf{0}$

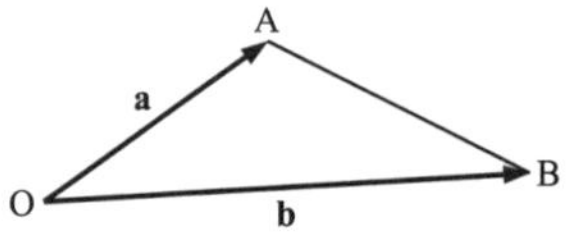

a $\qquad\qquad$ Now if $|\mathbf{a}+\mathbf{b}| = |\mathbf{a}-\mathbf{b}|$
$\qquad\qquad\qquad$ then $|\mathbf{a}+\mathbf{b}|^2 = |\mathbf{a}-\mathbf{b}|^2$
$\qquad\qquad\therefore\ (\mathbf{a}+\mathbf{b}) \bullet (\mathbf{a}+\mathbf{b}) = (\mathbf{a}-\mathbf{b}) \bullet (\mathbf{a}-\mathbf{b})$
$\qquad\therefore\ \mathbf{a}\bullet\mathbf{a} + \mathbf{a}\bullet\mathbf{b} + \mathbf{b}\bullet\mathbf{a} + \mathbf{b}\bullet\mathbf{b} = \mathbf{a}\bullet\mathbf{a} - \mathbf{a}\bullet\mathbf{b} - \mathbf{b}\bullet\mathbf{a} + \mathbf{b}\bullet\mathbf{b}$
$\qquad\qquad\therefore\ 2\mathbf{a}\bullet\mathbf{b} + 2\mathbf{b}\bullet\mathbf{a} = 0$
$\qquad\qquad\qquad\therefore\ 4\mathbf{a}\bullet\mathbf{b} = 0 \quad\{$as $\mathbf{a}\bullet\mathbf{b} = \mathbf{b}\bullet\mathbf{a}\}$
$\qquad\qquad\qquad\therefore\ \mathbf{a}\bullet\mathbf{b} = 0$, and since neither $\mathbf{a}$ nor $\mathbf{b} = \mathbf{0}$
$\qquad\qquad\qquad\qquad\mathbf{a}$ is perpendicular to $\mathbf{b}$.

b Consider the following diagram representing $\mathbf{a}$, $\mathbf{b}$, $\mathbf{a}+\mathbf{b}$ and $\mathbf{a}-\mathbf{b}$:

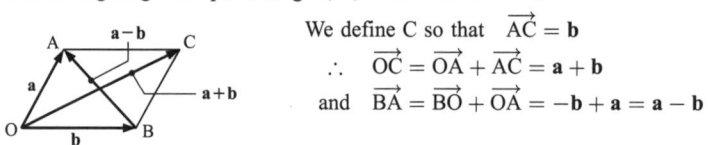

We define C so that $\overrightarrow{AC} = \mathbf{b}$
$\therefore\ \overrightarrow{OC} = \overrightarrow{OA} + \overrightarrow{AC} = \mathbf{a} + \mathbf{b}$
and $\overrightarrow{BA} = \overrightarrow{BO} + \overrightarrow{OA} = -\mathbf{b} + \mathbf{a} = \mathbf{a} - \mathbf{b}$

$\therefore\ \mathbf{a}+\mathbf{b}$ and $\mathbf{a}-\mathbf{b}$ represent the diagonals of the parallelogram OACB
But if $|\mathbf{a}+\mathbf{b}| = |\mathbf{a}-\mathbf{b}|$, then the diagonals must be equal in length.
This is only possible if OACB is a square or rectangle, which means that $\mathbf{a}$ is perpendicular to $\mathbf{b}$.

24 $(\mathbf{a}+\mathbf{b}) \bullet (\mathbf{a}-\mathbf{b}) = \mathbf{a}\bullet\mathbf{a} - \mathbf{a}\bullet\mathbf{b} + \mathbf{b}\bullet\mathbf{a} - \mathbf{b}\bullet\mathbf{b}$
$\qquad\qquad\qquad\quad = \mathbf{a}\bullet\mathbf{a} - \mathbf{b}\bullet\mathbf{b} \quad\{$since $\mathbf{a}\bullet\mathbf{b} = \mathbf{b}\bullet\mathbf{a}\}$
$\qquad\qquad\qquad\quad = |\mathbf{a}|^2 - |\mathbf{b}|^2$
$\qquad\qquad\qquad\quad = 9 - 16$
$\qquad\qquad\qquad\quad = -7$

25 The scalar product is only defined between two *vectors*.
Hence $\underbrace{(\mathbf{a}\bullet\mathbf{b})}_{\text{scalar}} \bullet \underbrace{\mathbf{c}}_{\text{vector}}\quad$ or $\quad\underbrace{\mathbf{a}}_{\text{vector}} \bullet \underbrace{(\mathbf{b}\bullet\mathbf{c})}_{\text{scalar}}$ is meaningless.

EXERCISE 14J.1

1 **a** $\begin{pmatrix} 2 \\ -3 \\ 1 \end{pmatrix} \times \begin{pmatrix} 1 \\ 4 \\ -2 \end{pmatrix} = \begin{vmatrix} i & j & k \\ 2 & -3 & 1 \\ 1 & 4 & -2 \end{vmatrix} = \begin{vmatrix} -3 & 1 \\ 4 & -2 \end{vmatrix} i - \begin{vmatrix} 2 & 1 \\ 1 & -2 \end{vmatrix} j + \begin{vmatrix} 2 & -3 \\ 1 & 4 \end{vmatrix} k$

$= (6 - 4)i - (-4 - 1)j + (8 - (-3))k$

$= 2i + 5j + 11k$

b $\begin{pmatrix} -1 \\ 0 \\ 2 \end{pmatrix} \times \begin{pmatrix} 3 \\ -1 \\ -2 \end{pmatrix} = \begin{vmatrix} i & j & k \\ -1 & 0 & 2 \\ 3 & -1 & -2 \end{vmatrix} = \begin{vmatrix} 0 & 2 \\ -1 & -2 \end{vmatrix} i - \begin{vmatrix} -1 & 2 \\ 3 & -2 \end{vmatrix} j + \begin{vmatrix} -1 & 0 \\ 3 & -1 \end{vmatrix} k$

$= (0 - (-2))i - (2 - 6)j + (1 - 0)k$

$= 2i + 4j + k$

c $(i + j - 2k) \times (i - k) = \begin{vmatrix} i & j & k \\ 1 & 1 & -2 \\ 1 & 0 & -1 \end{vmatrix} = \begin{vmatrix} 1 & -2 \\ 0 & -1 \end{vmatrix} i - \begin{vmatrix} 1 & -2 \\ 1 & -1 \end{vmatrix} j + \begin{vmatrix} 1 & 1 \\ 1 & 0 \end{vmatrix} k$

$= (-1 + 0)i - (-1 - (-2))j + (0 - 1)k$

$= -i - j - k$

d $(2i - k) \times (j + 3k) = \begin{vmatrix} i & j & k \\ 2 & 0 & -1 \\ 0 & 1 & 3 \end{vmatrix} = \begin{vmatrix} 0 & -1 \\ 1 & 3 \end{vmatrix} i - \begin{vmatrix} 2 & -1 \\ 0 & 3 \end{vmatrix} j + \begin{vmatrix} 2 & 0 \\ 0 & 1 \end{vmatrix} k$

$= (0 - (-1))i - (6 - 0)j + (2 - 0)k$

$= i - 6j + 2k$

2 If $a = \begin{pmatrix} 1 \\ 2 \\ 3 \end{pmatrix}$ and $b = \begin{pmatrix} -1 \\ 3 \\ -1 \end{pmatrix}$

then $a \times b = \begin{vmatrix} i & j & k \\ 1 & 2 & 3 \\ -1 & 3 & -1 \end{vmatrix} = \begin{vmatrix} 2 & 3 \\ 3 & -1 \end{vmatrix} i - \begin{vmatrix} 1 & 3 \\ -1 & -1 \end{vmatrix} j + \begin{vmatrix} 1 & 2 \\ -1 & 3 \end{vmatrix} k$

$= -11i - 2j + 5k$

$\therefore \ a \bullet (a \times b) = \begin{pmatrix} 1 \\ 2 \\ 3 \end{pmatrix} \bullet \begin{pmatrix} -11 \\ -2 \\ 5 \end{pmatrix}$ $\qquad b \bullet (a \times b) = \begin{pmatrix} -1 \\ 3 \\ -1 \end{pmatrix} \bullet \begin{pmatrix} -11 \\ -2 \\ 5 \end{pmatrix}$

$= -11 - 4 + 15 = 0 \qquad\qquad\qquad\qquad = 11 - 6 - 5 = 0$

$\therefore \ a \times b$ is perpendicular to both a and b.

3 **a** $i \times i = \begin{vmatrix} i & j & k \\ 1 & 0 & 0 \\ 1 & 0 & 0 \end{vmatrix} = 0, \quad j \times j = \begin{vmatrix} i & j & k \\ 0 & 1 & 0 \\ 0 & 1 & 0 \end{vmatrix} = 0, \quad k \times k = \begin{vmatrix} i & j & k \\ 0 & 0 & 1 \\ 0 & 0 & 1 \end{vmatrix} = 0$

b $i \times j = \begin{vmatrix} i & j & k \\ 1 & 0 & 0 \\ 0 & 1 & 0 \end{vmatrix} = k \qquad\qquad j \times i = \begin{vmatrix} i & j & k \\ 0 & 1 & 0 \\ 1 & 0 & 0 \end{vmatrix} = -k$

$j \times k = \begin{vmatrix} i & j & k \\ 0 & 1 & 0 \\ 0 & 0 & 1 \end{vmatrix} = i \qquad\qquad k \times j = \begin{vmatrix} i & j & k \\ 0 & 0 & 1 \\ 0 & 1 & 0 \end{vmatrix} = -i$

$i \times k = \begin{vmatrix} i & j & k \\ 1 & 0 & 0 \\ 0 & 0 & 1 \end{vmatrix} = -j \qquad\qquad k \times i = \begin{vmatrix} i & j & k \\ 0 & 0 & 1 \\ 1 & 0 & 0 \end{vmatrix} = j$

If a and b are vectors then $a \times a = 0$ and $a \times b = -(b \times a)$.

4 a $\mathbf{a} \times \mathbf{a} = \begin{vmatrix} \mathbf{i} & \mathbf{j} & \mathbf{k} \\ a_1 & a_2 & a_3 \\ a_1 & a_2 & a_3 \end{vmatrix} = \begin{vmatrix} a_2 & a_3 \\ a_2 & a_3 \end{vmatrix} \mathbf{i} - \begin{vmatrix} a_1 & a_3 \\ a_1 & a_3 \end{vmatrix} \mathbf{j} + \begin{vmatrix} a_1 & a_2 \\ a_1 & a_2 \end{vmatrix} \mathbf{k}$

$= 0 \times \mathbf{i} + 0 \times \mathbf{j} + 0 \times \mathbf{k}$
$= \mathbf{0}$

b $\mathbf{a} \times \mathbf{b} = \begin{vmatrix} \mathbf{i} & \mathbf{j} & \mathbf{k} \\ a_1 & a_2 & a_3 \\ b_1 & b_2 & b_3 \end{vmatrix} = \begin{vmatrix} a_2 & a_3 \\ b_2 & b_3 \end{vmatrix} \mathbf{i} - \begin{vmatrix} a_1 & a_3 \\ b_1 & b_3 \end{vmatrix} \mathbf{j} + \begin{vmatrix} a_1 & a_2 \\ b_1 & b_2 \end{vmatrix} \mathbf{k}$

$= (a_2 b_3 - a_3 b_2)\mathbf{i} - (a_1 b_3 - a_3 b_1)\mathbf{j} + (a_1 b_2 - a_2 b_1)\mathbf{k}$
$= -[(a_3 b_2 - a_2 b_3)\mathbf{i} - (a_3 b_1 - a_1 b_3)\mathbf{j} + (a_2 b_1 - a_1 b_2)\mathbf{k}]$

$= - \begin{vmatrix} \mathbf{i} & \mathbf{j} & \mathbf{k} \\ b_1 & b_2 & b_3 \\ a_1 & a_2 & a_3 \end{vmatrix}$

$= -\mathbf{b} \times \mathbf{a}$

5 a $\mathbf{b} \times \mathbf{c} = \begin{pmatrix} 2 \\ -1 \\ 1 \end{pmatrix} \times \begin{pmatrix} 0 \\ 1 \\ -2 \end{pmatrix} = \begin{vmatrix} \mathbf{i} & \mathbf{j} & \mathbf{k} \\ 2 & -1 & 1 \\ 0 & 1 & -2 \end{vmatrix} = \begin{vmatrix} -1 & 1 \\ 1 & -2 \end{vmatrix} \mathbf{i} - \begin{vmatrix} 2 & 1 \\ 0 & -2 \end{vmatrix} \mathbf{j} + \begin{vmatrix} 2 & -1 \\ 0 & 1 \end{vmatrix} \mathbf{k}$

$= \mathbf{i} + 4\mathbf{j} + 2\mathbf{k}$

$= \begin{pmatrix} 1 \\ 4 \\ 2 \end{pmatrix}$

b $\mathbf{a} \bullet (\mathbf{b} \times \mathbf{c}) = \begin{pmatrix} 1 \\ 3 \\ 2 \end{pmatrix} \bullet \begin{pmatrix} 1 \\ 4 \\ 2 \end{pmatrix} = 1 + 12 + 4 = 17$

c $\begin{vmatrix} 1 & 3 & 2 \\ 2 & -1 & 1 \\ 0 & 1 & -2 \end{vmatrix} = 1 \begin{vmatrix} -1 & 1 \\ 1 & -2 \end{vmatrix} - 3 \begin{vmatrix} 2 & 1 \\ 0 & -2 \end{vmatrix} + 2 \begin{vmatrix} 2 & -1 \\ 0 & 1 \end{vmatrix}$

$= 1(1) - 3(-4) + 2(2)$
$= 1 + 12 + 4$
$= 17$

7 a $\mathbf{a} \times \mathbf{b} = \begin{vmatrix} \mathbf{i} & \mathbf{j} & \mathbf{k} \\ 1 & 0 & 2 \\ 0 & -1 & 1 \end{vmatrix} = \begin{vmatrix} 0 & 2 \\ -1 & 1 \end{vmatrix} \mathbf{i} - \begin{vmatrix} 1 & 2 \\ 0 & 1 \end{vmatrix} \mathbf{j} + \begin{vmatrix} 1 & 0 \\ 0 & -1 \end{vmatrix} \mathbf{k}$

$= 2\mathbf{i} - \mathbf{j} - \mathbf{k}$

b $\mathbf{a} \times \mathbf{c} = \begin{vmatrix} \mathbf{i} & \mathbf{j} & \mathbf{k} \\ 1 & 0 & 2 \\ 2 & 0 & -1 \end{vmatrix} = \begin{vmatrix} 0 & 2 \\ 0 & -1 \end{vmatrix} \mathbf{i} - \begin{vmatrix} 1 & 2 \\ 2 & -1 \end{vmatrix} \mathbf{j} + \begin{vmatrix} 1 & 0 \\ 2 & 0 \end{vmatrix} \mathbf{k}$

$= 0\mathbf{i} + 5\mathbf{j} + 0\mathbf{k}$
$= 5\mathbf{j}$

c $(\mathbf{a} \times \mathbf{b}) + (\mathbf{a} \times \mathbf{c}) = 2\mathbf{i} - \mathbf{j} - \mathbf{k} + 5\mathbf{j}$ {using **a** and **b**}
$= 2\mathbf{i} + 4\mathbf{j} - \mathbf{k}$

d $\mathbf{a} \times (\mathbf{b} + \mathbf{c}) = \mathbf{a} \times (2\mathbf{i} - \mathbf{j})$

$= \begin{vmatrix} \mathbf{i} & \mathbf{j} & \mathbf{k} \\ 1 & 0 & 2 \\ 2 & -1 & 0 \end{vmatrix} = \begin{vmatrix} 0 & 2 \\ -1 & 0 \end{vmatrix} \mathbf{i} - \begin{vmatrix} 1 & 2 \\ 2 & 0 \end{vmatrix} \mathbf{j} + \begin{vmatrix} 1 & 0 \\ 2 & -1 \end{vmatrix} \mathbf{k}$

$= 2\mathbf{i} + 4\mathbf{j} - \mathbf{k}$

8 We suspect that $\mathbf{a} \times (\mathbf{b} + \mathbf{c}) = \mathbf{a} \times \mathbf{b} + \mathbf{a} \times \mathbf{c}$.

9 $\mathbf{a} \times (\mathbf{b} + \mathbf{c})$

$$= \begin{pmatrix} a_1 \\ a_2 \\ a_3 \end{pmatrix} \times \left[\begin{pmatrix} b_1 \\ b_2 \\ b_3 \end{pmatrix} + \begin{pmatrix} c_1 \\ c_2 \\ c_3 \end{pmatrix} \right] = \begin{vmatrix} \mathbf{i} & \mathbf{j} & \mathbf{k} \\ a_1 & a_2 & a_3 \\ b_1 + c_1 & b_2 + c_2 & b_3 + c_3 \end{vmatrix}$$

$$= \begin{vmatrix} a_2 & a_3 \\ b_2 + c_2 & b_3 + c_3 \end{vmatrix} \mathbf{i} - \begin{vmatrix} a_1 & a_3 \\ b_1 + c_1 & b_3 + c_3 \end{vmatrix} \mathbf{j} + \begin{vmatrix} a_1 & a_2 \\ b_1 + c_1 & b_2 + c_2 \end{vmatrix} \mathbf{k}$$

$$= (a_2(b_3 + c_3) - a_3(b_2 + c_2))\mathbf{i} - (a_1(b_3 + c_3) - a_3(b_1 + c_1))\mathbf{j} + (a_1(b_2 + c_2) - a_2(b_1 + c_1))\mathbf{k}$$

$$= (a_2 b_3 - a_3 b_2)\mathbf{i} - (a_1 b_3 - a_3 b_1)\mathbf{j} + (a_1 b_2 - a_2 b_1)\mathbf{k}$$
$$\quad + (a_2 c_3 - a_3 c_2)\mathbf{i} - (a_1 c_3 - a_3 c_1)\mathbf{j} + (a_1 c_2 - a_2 c_1)\mathbf{k}$$

$$= \begin{vmatrix} \mathbf{i} & \mathbf{j} & \mathbf{k} \\ a_1 & a_2 & a_3 \\ b_1 & b_2 & b_3 \end{vmatrix} + \begin{vmatrix} \mathbf{i} & \mathbf{j} & \mathbf{k} \\ a_1 & a_2 & a_3 \\ c_1 & c_2 & c_3 \end{vmatrix}$$

$$= \mathbf{a} \times \mathbf{b} + \mathbf{a} \times \mathbf{c} \quad \text{as required}$$

10 Now $\quad \mathbf{p} \times (\mathbf{c} + \mathbf{d}) = \mathbf{p} \times \mathbf{c} + \mathbf{p} \times \mathbf{d}$
$\therefore \quad$ if we let $\mathbf{p} = (\mathbf{a} + \mathbf{b})$,
then $\quad (\mathbf{a} + \mathbf{b}) \times (\mathbf{c} + \mathbf{d}) = \mathbf{p} \times (\mathbf{c} + \mathbf{d})$
$$= \mathbf{p} \times \mathbf{c} + \mathbf{p} \times \mathbf{d}$$
$$= (\mathbf{a} + \mathbf{b}) \times \mathbf{c} + (\mathbf{a} + \mathbf{b}) \times \mathbf{d}$$
$$= -\mathbf{c} \times (\mathbf{a} + \mathbf{b}) - \mathbf{d} \times (\mathbf{a} + \mathbf{b}) \qquad \{\text{since } \mathbf{x} \times \mathbf{y} = -\mathbf{y} \times \mathbf{x}\}$$
$$= -\mathbf{c} \times \mathbf{a} - \mathbf{c} \times \mathbf{b} - \mathbf{d} \times \mathbf{a} - \mathbf{d} \times \mathbf{b}$$
$$= \mathbf{a} \times \mathbf{c} + \mathbf{a} \times \mathbf{d} + \mathbf{b} \times \mathbf{c} + \mathbf{b} \times \mathbf{d} \qquad \{\text{since } \mathbf{x} \times \mathbf{y} = -\mathbf{y} \times \mathbf{x}\}$$

11 a $\quad \mathbf{a} \times (\mathbf{a} + \mathbf{b})$
$= \mathbf{a} \times \mathbf{a} + \mathbf{a} \times \mathbf{b}$
$= \mathbf{0} + \mathbf{a} \times \mathbf{b}$
$= \mathbf{a} \times \mathbf{b}$

b $\quad (\mathbf{a} + \mathbf{b}) \times (\mathbf{a} + \mathbf{b})$
$= \mathbf{a} \times \mathbf{a} + \mathbf{a} \times \mathbf{b} + \mathbf{b} \times \mathbf{a} + \mathbf{b} \times \mathbf{b}$
$= \mathbf{0} + \mathbf{a} \times \mathbf{b} + \mathbf{b} \times \mathbf{a} + \mathbf{0}$
$= \mathbf{a} \times \mathbf{b} + \mathbf{b} \times \mathbf{a}$
$= \mathbf{a} \times \mathbf{b} - \mathbf{a} \times \mathbf{b}$
$= \mathbf{0}$

c $\quad (\mathbf{a} + \mathbf{b}) \times (\mathbf{a} - \mathbf{b})$
$= \mathbf{a} \times \mathbf{a} - \mathbf{a} \times \mathbf{b} + \mathbf{b} \times \mathbf{a} - \mathbf{b} \times \mathbf{b}$
$= \mathbf{0} + \mathbf{b} \times \mathbf{a} + \mathbf{b} \times \mathbf{a} - \mathbf{0}$
$= 2(\mathbf{b} \times \mathbf{a})$

d $\mathbf{a}$ is perpendicular to $(\mathbf{a} \times \mathbf{b})$,
$2\mathbf{a}$ is perpendicular to $(\mathbf{a} \times \mathbf{b})$.
$\therefore \quad 2\mathbf{a} \bullet (\mathbf{a} \times \mathbf{b}) = 0$

12 a $\mathbf{a} \times \mathbf{b} = \begin{vmatrix} \mathbf{i} & \mathbf{j} & \mathbf{k} \\ 2 & -1 & 3 \\ 1 & 1 & 1 \end{vmatrix} = \begin{vmatrix} -1 & 3 \\ 1 & 1 \end{vmatrix} \mathbf{i} - \begin{vmatrix} 2 & 3 \\ 1 & 1 \end{vmatrix} \mathbf{j} + \begin{vmatrix} 2 & -1 \\ 1 & 1 \end{vmatrix} \mathbf{k} = -4\mathbf{i} + \mathbf{j} + 3\mathbf{k}$

$\therefore \quad$ the vectors are $\quad k(-4\mathbf{i} + \mathbf{j} + 3\mathbf{k}), \quad k \neq 0, \quad k \in \mathbb{R}$.

b $\mathbf{a} \times \mathbf{b} = \begin{vmatrix} \mathbf{i} & \mathbf{j} & \mathbf{k} \\ -1 & 3 & 4 \\ 5 & 0 & 2 \end{vmatrix} = \begin{vmatrix} 3 & 4 \\ 0 & 2 \end{vmatrix} \mathbf{i} - \begin{vmatrix} -1 & 4 \\ 5 & 2 \end{vmatrix} \mathbf{j} + \begin{vmatrix} -1 & 3 \\ 5 & 0 \end{vmatrix} \mathbf{k} = 6\mathbf{i} + 22\mathbf{j} - 15\mathbf{k}$

$\therefore \quad$ the vectors are $\quad k(6\mathbf{i} + 22\mathbf{j} - 15\mathbf{k}), \quad k \neq 0, \quad k \in \mathbb{R}$.

c $\mathbf{a} \times \mathbf{b} = \begin{vmatrix} \mathbf{i} & \mathbf{j} & \mathbf{k} \\ 1 & 1 & 0 \\ 1 & -1 & -1 \end{vmatrix} = \begin{vmatrix} 1 & 0 \\ -1 & -1 \end{vmatrix} \mathbf{i} - \begin{vmatrix} 1 & 0 \\ 1 & -1 \end{vmatrix} \mathbf{j} + \begin{vmatrix} 1 & 1 \\ 1 & -1 \end{vmatrix} \mathbf{k} = -\mathbf{i} + \mathbf{j} - 2\mathbf{k}$

$\therefore \quad$ the vectors are $\quad n(-\mathbf{i} + \mathbf{j} - 2\mathbf{k}), \quad n \neq 0, \quad n \in \mathbb{R}$.

d $\mathbf{a} \times \mathbf{b} = \begin{vmatrix} \mathbf{i} & \mathbf{j} & \mathbf{k} \\ 1 & -1 & -1 \\ 2 & 2 & -3 \end{vmatrix} = \begin{vmatrix} -1 & -1 \\ 2 & -3 \end{vmatrix} \mathbf{i} - \begin{vmatrix} 1 & -1 \\ 2 & -3 \end{vmatrix} \mathbf{j} + \begin{vmatrix} 1 & -1 \\ 2 & 2 \end{vmatrix} \mathbf{k} = 5\mathbf{i} + \mathbf{j} + 4\mathbf{k}$

$\therefore \quad$ the vectors are $\quad n(5\mathbf{i} + \mathbf{j} + 4\mathbf{k}), \quad n \neq 0, \quad n \in \mathbb{R}$.

13 $\mathbf{a} \times \mathbf{b} = \begin{vmatrix} \mathbf{i} & \mathbf{j} & \mathbf{k} \\ 2 & 3 & -1 \\ 1 & -2 & 2 \end{vmatrix} = \begin{vmatrix} 3 & -1 \\ -2 & 2 \end{vmatrix}\mathbf{i} - \begin{vmatrix} 2 & -1 \\ 1 & 2 \end{vmatrix}\mathbf{j} + \begin{vmatrix} 2 & 3 \\ 1 & -2 \end{vmatrix}\mathbf{k} = 4\mathbf{i} - 5\mathbf{j} - 7\mathbf{k}$

$\therefore$ the vectors $k(4\mathbf{i} - 5\mathbf{j} - 7\mathbf{k})$, $k \neq 0$ are all perpendicular to both **a** and **b**.
However, we require the vector to have length 5.

$\therefore \sqrt{(4k)^2 + (-5k)^2 + (-7k)^2} = 5$

$\therefore 16k^2 + 25k^2 + 49k^2 = 25$

$\therefore 90k^2 = 25$

$\therefore k^2 = \frac{25}{90} = \frac{5}{18}$

$\therefore k = \pm\frac{\sqrt{5}}{3\sqrt{2}} = \pm\frac{\sqrt{10}}{6}$ $\therefore$ the possible vectors are $\pm\frac{\sqrt{10}}{6}\begin{pmatrix} 4 \\ -5 \\ -7 \end{pmatrix}$.

14 a Given A(1, 3, 2), B(0, 2, −5) and C(3, 1, −4), $\overrightarrow{AB} = \begin{pmatrix} -1 \\ -1 \\ -7 \end{pmatrix}$ and $\overrightarrow{AC} = \begin{pmatrix} 2 \\ -2 \\ -6 \end{pmatrix}$.

$\therefore \mathbf{n} = \begin{vmatrix} \mathbf{i} & \mathbf{j} & \mathbf{k} \\ -1 & -1 & -7 \\ 2 & -2 & -6 \end{vmatrix} = \begin{vmatrix} -1 & -7 \\ -2 & -6 \end{vmatrix}\mathbf{i} - \begin{vmatrix} -1 & -7 \\ 2 & -6 \end{vmatrix}\mathbf{j} + \begin{vmatrix} -1 & -1 \\ 2 & -2 \end{vmatrix}\mathbf{k}$

$= (6 - 14)\mathbf{i} - (6 - -14)\mathbf{j} + (2 - -2)\mathbf{k}$

$= -8\mathbf{i} - 20\mathbf{j} + 4\mathbf{k}$

$= -4(2\mathbf{i} + 5\mathbf{j} - \mathbf{k})$

$\therefore 2\mathbf{i} + 5\mathbf{j} - \mathbf{k}$ is one vector perpendicular to the plane.

b Given P(2, 0, −1), Q(0, 1, 3) and R(1, −1, 1), $\overrightarrow{PQ} = \begin{pmatrix} -2 \\ 1 \\ 4 \end{pmatrix}$ and $\overrightarrow{PR} = \begin{pmatrix} -1 \\ -1 \\ 2 \end{pmatrix}$

$\therefore \mathbf{n} = \begin{vmatrix} \mathbf{i} & \mathbf{j} & \mathbf{k} \\ -2 & 1 & 4 \\ -1 & -1 & 2 \end{vmatrix} = \begin{vmatrix} 1 & 4 \\ -1 & 2 \end{vmatrix}\mathbf{i} - \begin{vmatrix} -2 & 4 \\ -1 & 2 \end{vmatrix}\mathbf{j} + \begin{vmatrix} -2 & 1 \\ -1 & -1 \end{vmatrix}\mathbf{k}$

$= 6\mathbf{i} + 3\mathbf{k}$

$= 3(2\mathbf{i} + \mathbf{k})$ and so $2\mathbf{i} + \mathbf{k}$ is one vector perpendicular to the plane.

EXERCISE 14J.2

1 a $\mathbf{i} \times \mathbf{k} = \begin{vmatrix} \mathbf{i} & \mathbf{j} & \mathbf{k} \\ 1 & 0 & 0 \\ 0 & 0 & 1 \end{vmatrix} = \begin{vmatrix} 0 & 0 \\ 0 & 1 \end{vmatrix}\mathbf{i} - \begin{vmatrix} 1 & 0 \\ 0 & 1 \end{vmatrix}\mathbf{j} + \begin{vmatrix} 1 & 0 \\ 0 & 0 \end{vmatrix}\mathbf{k} = 0\mathbf{i} - \mathbf{j} + 0\mathbf{k} = -\mathbf{j}$

$\mathbf{k} \times \mathbf{i} = \begin{vmatrix} \mathbf{i} & \mathbf{j} & \mathbf{k} \\ 0 & 0 & 1 \\ 1 & 0 & 0 \end{vmatrix} = \begin{vmatrix} 0 & 1 \\ 0 & 0 \end{vmatrix}\mathbf{i} - \begin{vmatrix} 0 & 1 \\ 1 & 0 \end{vmatrix}\mathbf{j} + \begin{vmatrix} 0 & 0 \\ 1 & 0 \end{vmatrix}\mathbf{k} = 0\mathbf{i} + \mathbf{j} + 0\mathbf{k} = \mathbf{j}$

b Using the RH rule these two results check.

c $\mathbf{i} \times \mathbf{k} = |\mathbf{i}||\mathbf{k}|\sin 90° \times (-\mathbf{j})$ {RH rule} $\mathbf{k} \times \mathbf{i} = |\mathbf{k}||\mathbf{i}|\sin 90° \times \mathbf{j}$ {RH rule}
$= 1 \times 1 \times 1 \times (-\mathbf{j})$ $= 1 \times 1 \times 1 \times \mathbf{j}$
$= -\mathbf{j}$ $= \mathbf{j}$

2 a $\mathbf{a} \cdot \mathbf{b} = 2 \times 1 + (-1) \times 0 + 3 \times (-1) = -1$ **b** $\cos\theta = \frac{\mathbf{a} \cdot \mathbf{b}}{|\mathbf{a}||\mathbf{b}|}$

$\mathbf{a} \times \mathbf{b} = \begin{vmatrix} \mathbf{i} & \mathbf{j} & \mathbf{k} \\ 2 & -1 & 3 \\ 1 & 0 & -1 \end{vmatrix}$

$= \begin{vmatrix} -1 & 3 \\ 0 & -1 \end{vmatrix}\mathbf{i} - \begin{vmatrix} 2 & 3 \\ 1 & -1 \end{vmatrix}\mathbf{j} + \begin{vmatrix} 2 & -1 \\ 1 & 0 \end{vmatrix}\mathbf{k}$

$= \mathbf{i} + 5\mathbf{j} + \mathbf{k}$

$= \frac{-1}{\sqrt{4+1+9}\sqrt{1+1}}$

$= \frac{-1}{\sqrt{14}\sqrt{2}}$

$= \frac{-1}{\sqrt{28}}$

c $\sin^2\theta + \cos^2\theta = 1$
$\therefore \sin^2\theta + \frac{1}{28} = 1$
$\therefore \sin^2\theta = \frac{27}{28}$
$\therefore \sin\theta = \pm\sqrt{\frac{27}{28}}$
But $0 \leqslant \theta \leqslant \pi$, so $\sin\theta = \sqrt{\frac{27}{28}}$

d $|\mathbf{a} \times \mathbf{b}| = |\mathbf{a}||\mathbf{b}|\sin\theta$
$\therefore \sin\theta = \frac{|\mathbf{a} \times \mathbf{b}|}{|\mathbf{a}||\mathbf{b}|}$
$= \frac{\sqrt{1^2 + 5^2 + 1^2}}{\sqrt{14}\sqrt{2}}$
$= \sqrt{\frac{27}{28}}$

3 $\mathbf{a} \times \mathbf{b} = \mathbf{0}$ $\therefore |\mathbf{a}||\mathbf{b}|\sin\theta \times \mathbf{u} = \mathbf{0}$
$\therefore |\mathbf{a}||\mathbf{b}|\sin\theta = 0$ {since $|\mathbf{a}| \neq 0$ and $|\mathbf{b}| \neq 0$, $\mathbf{u}$ exists and $\neq \mathbf{0}$}
$\therefore \sin\theta = 0$ {since $|\mathbf{a}| \neq 0$ and $|\mathbf{b}| \neq 0$}
$\therefore \theta = 0$ or π
$\therefore \mathbf{a}$ is parallel to $\mathbf{b}$

4 a $\overrightarrow{OA} = \begin{pmatrix} 2 \\ 3 \\ -1 \end{pmatrix}$ and $\overrightarrow{OB} = \begin{pmatrix} -1 \\ 1 \\ 2 \end{pmatrix}$

b $\overrightarrow{OA} \times \overrightarrow{OB} = \begin{vmatrix} \mathbf{i} & \mathbf{j} & \mathbf{k} \\ 2 & 3 & -1 \\ -1 & 1 & 2 \end{vmatrix} = \begin{vmatrix} 3 & -1 \\ 1 & 2 \end{vmatrix}\mathbf{i} - \begin{vmatrix} 2 & -1 \\ -1 & 2 \end{vmatrix}\mathbf{j} + \begin{vmatrix} 2 & 3 \\ -1 & 1 \end{vmatrix}\mathbf{k}$
$= 7\mathbf{i} - 3\mathbf{j} + 5\mathbf{k}$
$\therefore |\overrightarrow{OA} \times \overrightarrow{OB}| = \sqrt{7^2 + (-3)^2 + 5^2} = \sqrt{83}$ units

c Area $\triangle AOB = \frac{1}{2}|\overrightarrow{OA}||\overrightarrow{OB}|\sin\theta$
$= \frac{1}{2}|\overrightarrow{OA} \times \overrightarrow{OB}|$
$= \frac{1}{2}\sqrt{83}$ units²

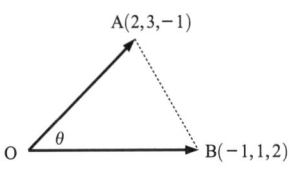

5

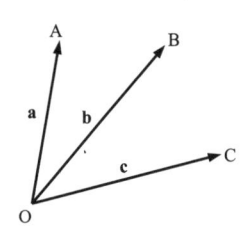

a $\mathbf{a} \times \mathbf{c} = \mathbf{b} \times \mathbf{c}$
$\therefore \mathbf{a} \times \mathbf{c} - \mathbf{b} \times \mathbf{c} = \mathbf{0}$
$\therefore (\mathbf{a} - \mathbf{b}) \times \mathbf{c} = \mathbf{0}$
$\therefore \overrightarrow{BA} \times \mathbf{c} = \mathbf{0}$
$\therefore \overrightarrow{OC}$ must be parallel to $\overrightarrow{AB}$.

b Since $\mathbf{a} + \mathbf{b} + \mathbf{c} = \mathbf{0}$,
$\mathbf{b} \times (\mathbf{a} + \mathbf{b} + \mathbf{c}) = \mathbf{b} \times \mathbf{0}$
$\therefore \mathbf{b} \times \mathbf{a} + \mathbf{b} \times \mathbf{b} + \mathbf{b} \times \mathbf{c} = \mathbf{0}$
$\therefore \mathbf{b} \times \mathbf{a} + \mathbf{b} \times \mathbf{c} = \mathbf{0}$
$\therefore \mathbf{a} \times \mathbf{b} = \mathbf{b} \times \mathbf{c}$
{since $\mathbf{a} \times \mathbf{b} = -\mathbf{b} \times \mathbf{a}$}

c $\mathbf{b} \times \mathbf{c} = \mathbf{c} \times \mathbf{a}$ where $\mathbf{c} \neq \mathbf{0}$
$\therefore \mathbf{b} \times \mathbf{c} = -\mathbf{a} \times \mathbf{c}$
$\therefore \mathbf{a} \times \mathbf{c} + \mathbf{b} \times \mathbf{c} = \mathbf{0}$
$\therefore (\mathbf{a} + \mathbf{b}) \times \mathbf{c} = \mathbf{0}$
$\therefore \mathbf{a} + \mathbf{b}$ is parallel to $\mathbf{c}$
$\therefore \mathbf{a} + \mathbf{b} = k\mathbf{c}$ for some scalar k.

EXERCISE 14J.3

1 a Given $A(2, 1, 1)$, $B(4, 3, 0)$ and $C(1, 3, -2)$, $\overrightarrow{AB} = \begin{pmatrix} 2 \\ 2 \\ -1 \end{pmatrix}$ and $\overrightarrow{AC} = \begin{pmatrix} -1 \\ 2 \\ -3 \end{pmatrix}$.

$\therefore \overrightarrow{AB} \times \overrightarrow{AC} = \begin{vmatrix} \mathbf{i} & \mathbf{j} & \mathbf{k} \\ 2 & 2 & -1 \\ -1 & 2 & -3 \end{vmatrix} = \begin{vmatrix} 2 & -1 \\ 2 & -3 \end{vmatrix}\mathbf{i} - \begin{vmatrix} 2 & -1 \\ -1 & -3 \end{vmatrix}\mathbf{j} + \begin{vmatrix} 2 & 2 \\ -1 & 2 \end{vmatrix}\mathbf{k}$
$= -4\mathbf{i} + 7\mathbf{j} + 6\mathbf{k}$

$\therefore$ area $= \frac{1}{2}|-4\mathbf{i} + 7\mathbf{j} + 6\mathbf{k}|$ {area $= \frac{1}{2}|\overrightarrow{AB} \times \overrightarrow{AC}|$}

$= \frac{1}{2}\sqrt{(-4)^2 + 7^2 + 6^2}$

$= \frac{1}{2}\sqrt{101}$ units²

b Given $A(0, 0, 0)$, $B(-1, 2, 3)$ and $C(1, 2, 6)$, $\overrightarrow{AB} = \begin{pmatrix} -1 \\ 2 \\ 3 \end{pmatrix}$ and $\overrightarrow{AC} = \begin{pmatrix} 1 \\ 2 \\ 6 \end{pmatrix}$.

$\therefore \overrightarrow{AB} \times \overrightarrow{AC} = \begin{vmatrix} \mathbf{i} & \mathbf{j} & \mathbf{k} \\ -1 & 2 & 3 \\ 1 & 2 & 6 \end{vmatrix} = \begin{vmatrix} 2 & 3 \\ 2 & 6 \end{vmatrix} \mathbf{i} - \begin{vmatrix} -1 & 3 \\ 1 & 6 \end{vmatrix} \mathbf{j} + \begin{vmatrix} -1 & 2 \\ 1 & 2 \end{vmatrix} \mathbf{k}$

$= 6\mathbf{i} + 9\mathbf{j} - 4\mathbf{k}$

$\therefore$ area $= \frac{1}{2}|6\mathbf{i} + 9\mathbf{j} - 4\mathbf{k}|$ {area $= \frac{1}{2}|\overrightarrow{AB} \times \overrightarrow{AC}|$}

$= \frac{1}{2}\sqrt{6^2 + 9^2 + (-4)^2}$

$= \frac{1}{2}\sqrt{133}$ units²

c Given $A(1, 3, 2)$, $B(2, -1, 0)$ and $C(1, 10, 6)$, $\overrightarrow{AB} = \begin{pmatrix} 1 \\ -4 \\ -2 \end{pmatrix}$ and $\overrightarrow{AC} = \begin{pmatrix} 0 \\ 7 \\ 4 \end{pmatrix}$.

$\therefore \overrightarrow{AB} \times \overrightarrow{AC} = \begin{vmatrix} \mathbf{i} & \mathbf{j} & \mathbf{k} \\ 1 & -4 & -2 \\ 0 & 7 & 4 \end{vmatrix} = \begin{vmatrix} -4 & -2 \\ 7 & 4 \end{vmatrix} \mathbf{i} - \begin{vmatrix} 1 & -2 \\ 0 & 4 \end{vmatrix} \mathbf{j} + \begin{vmatrix} 1 & -4 \\ 0 & 7 \end{vmatrix} \mathbf{k}$

$= -2\mathbf{i} - 4\mathbf{j} + 7\mathbf{k}$

$\therefore$ area $= \frac{1}{2}|-2\mathbf{i} - 4\mathbf{j} + 7\mathbf{k}| = \frac{1}{2}\sqrt{(-2)^2 + (-4)^2 + 7^2} = \frac{1}{2}\sqrt{69}$ units²

2 Given $A(-1, 2, 2)$, $B(2, -1, 4)$ and $C(0, 1, 0)$, $\overrightarrow{AB} = \begin{pmatrix} 3 \\ -3 \\ 2 \end{pmatrix}$ and $\overrightarrow{AC} = \begin{pmatrix} 1 \\ -1 \\ -2 \end{pmatrix}$.

$\therefore \overrightarrow{AB} \times \overrightarrow{AC} = \begin{vmatrix} \mathbf{i} & \mathbf{j} & \mathbf{k} \\ 3 & -3 & 2 \\ 1 & -1 & -2 \end{vmatrix} = \begin{vmatrix} -3 & 2 \\ -1 & -2 \end{vmatrix} \mathbf{i} - \begin{vmatrix} 3 & 2 \\ 1 & -2 \end{vmatrix} \mathbf{j} + \begin{vmatrix} 3 & -3 \\ 1 & -1 \end{vmatrix} \mathbf{k}$

$= 8\mathbf{i} + 8\mathbf{j}$

$\therefore$ area of parallelogram $= |8\mathbf{i} + 8\mathbf{j}| = \sqrt{8^2 + 8^2} = 8\sqrt{2}$ units²

3 a

A(−1,3,2)   B(2,0,4)

D(a,b,c)   C(−1,−2,5)

Suppose D is at (a, b, c).

Since $\overrightarrow{AB} = \overrightarrow{DC}$,

$\begin{pmatrix} 3 \\ -3 \\ 2 \end{pmatrix} = \begin{pmatrix} -1 - a \\ -2 - b \\ 5 - c \end{pmatrix}$

$\therefore -1 - a = 3$, $-2 - b = -3$ and $5 - c = 2$

$\therefore a = -4$, $b = 1$ and $c = 3$

$\therefore$ D is at $(-4, 1, 3)$.

b $\overrightarrow{BC} = \begin{pmatrix} -3 \\ -2 \\ 1 \end{pmatrix}$ and $\overrightarrow{BA} = \begin{pmatrix} -3 \\ 3 \\ -2 \end{pmatrix}$

$\therefore \overrightarrow{BC} \times \overrightarrow{BA} = \begin{vmatrix} \mathbf{i} & \mathbf{j} & \mathbf{k} \\ -3 & -2 & 1 \\ -3 & 3 & -2 \end{vmatrix} = \begin{vmatrix} -2 & 1 \\ 3 & -2 \end{vmatrix} \mathbf{i} - \begin{vmatrix} -3 & 1 \\ -3 & -2 \end{vmatrix} \mathbf{j} + \begin{vmatrix} -3 & -2 \\ -3 & 3 \end{vmatrix} \mathbf{k}$

$= \mathbf{i} - 9\mathbf{j} - 15\mathbf{k}$

$\therefore$ area $= |\mathbf{i} - 9\mathbf{j} - 15\mathbf{k}| = \sqrt{1^2 + (-9)^2 + (-15)^2} = \sqrt{307}$ units²

4 a Now $\vec{AB} = \begin{pmatrix} 1 \\ 2 \\ -1 \end{pmatrix}$, $\vec{AC} = \begin{pmatrix} -1 \\ 2 \\ -3 \end{pmatrix}$ and $\vec{AD} = \begin{pmatrix} -2 \\ 2 \\ 2 \end{pmatrix}$

∴ the volume of the tetrahedron

$= \frac{1}{6} \left| \vec{AB} \bullet \left(\vec{AC} \times \vec{AD} \right) \right|$

$= \frac{1}{6} \left\| \begin{matrix} 1 & 2 & -1 \\ -1 & 2 & -3 \\ -2 & 2 & 2 \end{matrix} \right\| = \frac{1}{6} \left| 1 \begin{vmatrix} 2 & -3 \\ 2 & 2 \end{vmatrix} - 2 \begin{vmatrix} -1 & -3 \\ -2 & 2 \end{vmatrix} - 1 \begin{vmatrix} -1 & 2 \\ -2 & 2 \end{vmatrix} \right|$

$= \frac{1}{6} |10 - 2(-8) - 1(2)|$

$= \frac{1}{6} |24| = 4$ units^3

b The total surface area of the tetrahedron is the sum of the four triangular faces forming it.

Face 1 $\vec{AB} \times \vec{AC} = \begin{vmatrix} \mathbf{i} & \mathbf{j} & \mathbf{k} \\ 1 & 2 & -1 \\ -1 & 2 & -3 \end{vmatrix} = \begin{vmatrix} 2 & -1 \\ 2 & -3 \end{vmatrix} \mathbf{i} - \begin{vmatrix} 1 & -1 \\ -1 & -3 \end{vmatrix} \mathbf{j} + \begin{vmatrix} 1 & 2 \\ -1 & 2 \end{vmatrix} \mathbf{k}$

$= -4\mathbf{i} + 4\mathbf{j} + 4\mathbf{k}$

∴ $A_1 = \frac{1}{2} |\vec{AB} \times \vec{AC}| = \frac{1}{2} \sqrt{4^2 + 4^2 + 4^2} = \frac{1}{2} \left(4\sqrt{3} \right) = 2\sqrt{3}$ units^2

Face 2 $\vec{AB} \times \vec{AD} = \begin{vmatrix} \mathbf{i} & \mathbf{j} & \mathbf{k} \\ 1 & 2 & -1 \\ -2 & 2 & 2 \end{vmatrix} = \begin{vmatrix} 2 & -1 \\ 2 & 2 \end{vmatrix} \mathbf{i} - \begin{vmatrix} 1 & -1 \\ -2 & 2 \end{vmatrix} \mathbf{j} + \begin{vmatrix} 1 & 2 \\ -2 & 2 \end{vmatrix} \mathbf{k}$

$= 6\mathbf{i} + 6\mathbf{k}$

∴ $A_2 = \frac{1}{2} |\vec{AB} \times \vec{AD}| = \frac{1}{2} \sqrt{6^2 + 6^2} = \frac{1}{2} 6\sqrt{2} = 3\sqrt{2}$ units^2

Face 3 $\vec{AC} \times \vec{AD} = \begin{vmatrix} \mathbf{i} & \mathbf{j} & \mathbf{k} \\ -1 & 2 & -3 \\ -2 & 2 & 2 \end{vmatrix} = \begin{vmatrix} 2 & -3 \\ 2 & 2 \end{vmatrix} \mathbf{i} - \begin{vmatrix} -1 & -3 \\ -2 & 2 \end{vmatrix} \mathbf{j} + \begin{vmatrix} -1 & 2 \\ -2 & 2 \end{vmatrix} \mathbf{k}$

$= 10\mathbf{i} + 8\mathbf{j} + 2\mathbf{k}$

∴ $A_3 = \frac{1}{2} |\vec{AC} \times \vec{AD}| = \frac{1}{2} \sqrt{10^2 + 8^2 + 2^2} = \frac{1}{2} \sqrt{168} = \sqrt{42}$ units^2

Face 4 $\vec{BC} \times \vec{BD} = \begin{vmatrix} \mathbf{i} & \mathbf{j} & \mathbf{k} \\ -2 & 0 & -2 \\ -3 & 0 & 3 \end{vmatrix} = \begin{vmatrix} 0 & -2 \\ 0 & 3 \end{vmatrix} \mathbf{i} - \begin{vmatrix} -2 & -2 \\ -3 & 3 \end{vmatrix} \mathbf{j} + \begin{vmatrix} -2 & 0 \\ -3 & 0 \end{vmatrix} \mathbf{k}$

$= 12\mathbf{j}$

∴ $A_4 = \frac{1}{2} |\vec{BC} \times \vec{BD}| = \frac{1}{2} \times 12 = 6$ units^2

∴ total surface area $= \left(\sqrt{42} + 2\sqrt{3} + 3\sqrt{2} + 6 \right)$ units^2

5 a Given A(3, 0, 0), B(0, 1, 0), C(1, 2, 3), O(0, 0, 0), we label the other vertices as shown.

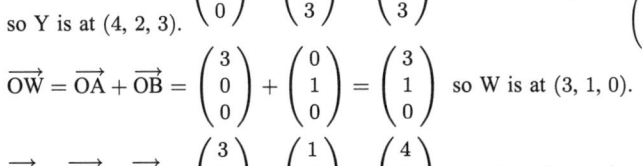

$\vec{OX} = \vec{OB} + \vec{OC} = \begin{pmatrix} 0 \\ 1 \\ 0 \end{pmatrix} + \begin{pmatrix} 1 \\ 2 \\ 3 \end{pmatrix} = \begin{pmatrix} 1 \\ 3 \\ 3 \end{pmatrix}$

so X is at (1, 3, 3).

$\vec{OY} = \vec{OA} + \vec{OC} = \begin{pmatrix} 3 \\ 0 \\ 0 \end{pmatrix} + \begin{pmatrix} 1 \\ 2 \\ 3 \end{pmatrix} = \begin{pmatrix} 4 \\ 2 \\ 3 \end{pmatrix}$

so Y is at (4, 2, 3).

$\vec{OW} = \vec{OA} + \vec{OB} = \begin{pmatrix} 3 \\ 0 \\ 0 \end{pmatrix} + \begin{pmatrix} 0 \\ 1 \\ 0 \end{pmatrix} = \begin{pmatrix} 3 \\ 1 \\ 0 \end{pmatrix}$ so W is at (3, 1, 0).

$\vec{OZ} = \vec{OW} + \vec{OC} = \begin{pmatrix} 3 \\ 1 \\ 0 \end{pmatrix} + \begin{pmatrix} 1 \\ 2 \\ 3 \end{pmatrix} = \begin{pmatrix} 4 \\ 3 \\ 3 \end{pmatrix}$ so Z is at (4, 3, 3).

b $\overrightarrow{BA} = \begin{pmatrix} 3 \\ -1 \\ 0 \end{pmatrix}$ and $\overrightarrow{BC} = \begin{pmatrix} 1 \\ 1 \\ 3 \end{pmatrix}$

$$\therefore \cos A\widehat{B}C = \frac{\overrightarrow{BA} \bullet \overrightarrow{BC}}{|\overrightarrow{BA}||\overrightarrow{BC}|} = \frac{\begin{pmatrix} 3 \\ -1 \\ 0 \end{pmatrix} \bullet \begin{pmatrix} 1 \\ 1 \\ 3 \end{pmatrix}}{\sqrt{3^2+(-1)^2+0^2}\sqrt{1^2+1^2+3^2}} = \frac{2}{\sqrt{110}}$$

$$\therefore \theta \approx 79.0°$$

c Volume $= \left\| \begin{matrix} 3 & 0 & 0 \\ 0 & 1 & 0 \\ 1 & 2 & 3 \end{matrix} \right\| = \left| 3 \begin{vmatrix} 1 & 0 \\ 2 & 3 \end{vmatrix} - 0 \begin{vmatrix} 0 & 0 \\ 1 & 3 \end{vmatrix} + 0 \begin{vmatrix} 0 & 1 \\ 1 & 2 \end{vmatrix} \right| = |3 \times 3| = 9$ units^3

6 Now $\overrightarrow{AB} = \begin{pmatrix} 3 \\ -1 \\ -1 \end{pmatrix}$ and $\overrightarrow{AC} = \begin{pmatrix} k+1 \\ 1 \\ -3 \end{pmatrix}$

Area of $\triangle ABC = \frac{1}{2}|\overrightarrow{AC} \times \overrightarrow{AB}|$

$$\therefore \sqrt{88} = \frac{1}{2} \left\| \begin{matrix} \mathbf{i} & \mathbf{j} & \mathbf{k} \\ k+1 & 1 & -3 \\ 3 & -1 & -1 \end{matrix} \right\| = \frac{1}{2} \left| \begin{vmatrix} 1 & -3 \\ -1 & -1 \end{vmatrix} \mathbf{i} - \begin{vmatrix} k+1 & -3 \\ 3 & -1 \end{vmatrix} \mathbf{j} + \begin{vmatrix} k+1 & 1 \\ 3 & -1 \end{vmatrix} \mathbf{k} \right|$$

$\therefore \sqrt{352} = |(-1-3)\mathbf{i} - (-(k+1)--9)\mathbf{j} + (-(k+1)-3)\mathbf{k}|$

$\therefore \sqrt{352} = |-4\mathbf{i} + (k-8)\mathbf{j} + (-k-4)\mathbf{k}|$

$\therefore \sqrt{352} = \sqrt{16+(k-8)^2+(-k-4)^2}$

$\therefore 352 = 16 + k^2 - 16k + 64 + k^2 + 8k + 16$

$\therefore 2k^2 - 8k - 256 = 0$

$\therefore k^2 - 4k - 128 = 0$

$\therefore k = \dfrac{4 \pm \sqrt{16+4(1)(128)}}{2} = 2 \pm \sqrt{132} = 2 \pm 2\sqrt{33}$

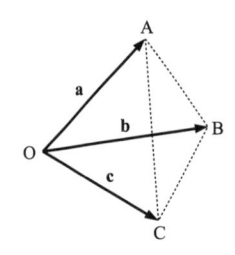

Diagram: $A(-1,1,2)$, $B(2,0,1)$, $C(k,2,-1)$

7 Total surface area S of the tetrahedron is the sum of the areas of the 4 triangular faces.

Now $\overrightarrow{AB} = \overrightarrow{AO} + \overrightarrow{OB} = -\mathbf{a} + \mathbf{b} = \mathbf{b} - \mathbf{a}$

and $\overrightarrow{AC} = \overrightarrow{AO} + \overrightarrow{OC} = -\mathbf{a} + \mathbf{c} = \mathbf{c} - \mathbf{a}$

$\therefore S = \frac{1}{2}|\mathbf{a} \times \mathbf{b}| + \frac{1}{2}|\mathbf{a} \times \mathbf{c}| + \frac{1}{2}|\mathbf{b} \times \mathbf{c}| + \frac{1}{2}|(\mathbf{b} - \mathbf{a}) \times (\mathbf{c} - \mathbf{a})|$

8 Now $\overrightarrow{BA} = \overrightarrow{BO} + \overrightarrow{OA} = -\mathbf{b} + \mathbf{a} = \mathbf{a} - \mathbf{b}$

and $\overrightarrow{BC} = \overrightarrow{BO} + \overrightarrow{OC} = -\mathbf{b} + \mathbf{c} = \mathbf{c} - \mathbf{b}$

$\therefore$ area $\triangle ABC = \frac{1}{2}|\overrightarrow{BA} \times \overrightarrow{BC}|$

$= \frac{1}{2}|(\mathbf{a} - \mathbf{b}) \times (\mathbf{c} - \mathbf{b})|$

$= \frac{1}{2}|(\mathbf{b} - \mathbf{a}) \times (\mathbf{c} - \mathbf{b})|$

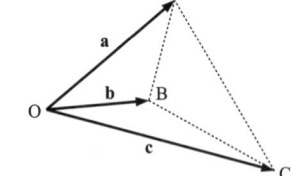

Now if A, B and C are collinear, then area $\triangle ABC = 0$

$\therefore (\mathbf{b} - \mathbf{a}) \times (\mathbf{c} - \mathbf{b}) = \mathbf{0}$

or $\overrightarrow{AB} = \overrightarrow{AO} + \overrightarrow{OB} = \mathbf{b} - \mathbf{a}$

$\overrightarrow{BC} = \overrightarrow{BO} + \overrightarrow{OC} = \mathbf{c} - \mathbf{b}$

If A, B and C are collinear, then $\overrightarrow{AB}$ is parallel to $\overrightarrow{BC}$

$\therefore \overrightarrow{AB} \times \overrightarrow{BC} = \mathbf{0} \quad \therefore (\mathbf{b} - \mathbf{a}) \times (\mathbf{c} - \mathbf{b}) = \mathbf{0}$

9 **a** $\mathbf{b} - \mathbf{a} = \overrightarrow{AB} = \begin{pmatrix} 1 \\ 3 \\ -2 \end{pmatrix}$ $\mathbf{c} - \mathbf{a} = \overrightarrow{AC} = \begin{pmatrix} 2 \\ 0 \\ -1 \end{pmatrix}$ $\mathbf{d} - \mathbf{a} = \overrightarrow{AD} = \begin{pmatrix} 3 \\ -1 \\ -1 \end{pmatrix}$

$\therefore$ $(\mathbf{b} - \mathbf{a}) \bullet (\mathbf{c} - \mathbf{a}) \times (\mathbf{d} - \mathbf{a})$

$= \begin{vmatrix} 1 & 3 & -2 \\ 2 & 0 & -1 \\ 3 & -1 & -1 \end{vmatrix} = 1 \begin{vmatrix} 0 & -1 \\ -1 & -1 \end{vmatrix} - 3 \begin{vmatrix} 2 & -1 \\ 3 & -1 \end{vmatrix} - 2 \begin{vmatrix} 2 & 0 \\ 3 & -1 \end{vmatrix}$

$= (-1) - 3(1) - 2(-2)$

$= 0$ and so A, B, C and D are coplanar.

b $\mathbf{q} - \mathbf{p} = \overrightarrow{PQ} = \begin{pmatrix} -2 \\ -1 \\ -1 \end{pmatrix}$ $\mathbf{r} - \mathbf{p} = \overrightarrow{PR} = \begin{pmatrix} 0 \\ 1 \\ -5 \end{pmatrix}$ $\mathbf{s} - \mathbf{p} = \overrightarrow{PS} = \begin{pmatrix} -1 \\ 1 \\ -4 \end{pmatrix}$

$\therefore$ $(\mathbf{q} - \mathbf{p}) \bullet (\mathbf{r} - \mathbf{p}) \times (\mathbf{s} - \mathbf{p})$

$= \begin{vmatrix} -2 & -1 & -1 \\ 0 & 1 & -5 \\ -1 & 1 & -4 \end{vmatrix} = -2 \begin{vmatrix} 1 & -5 \\ 1 & -4 \end{vmatrix} - (-1) \begin{vmatrix} 0 & -5 \\ -1 & -4 \end{vmatrix} - 1 \begin{vmatrix} 0 & 1 \\ -1 & 1 \end{vmatrix}$

$= -2(1) + 1(-5) - 1(1)$

$= -8$

$\neq 0$ and so P, Q, R and S are not coplanar.

10 $\mathbf{b} - \mathbf{a} = \overrightarrow{AB} = \begin{pmatrix} 2 \\ -1 \\ -2 \end{pmatrix}$ $\mathbf{c} - \mathbf{a} = \overrightarrow{AC} = \begin{pmatrix} -2 \\ k-1 \\ -1 \end{pmatrix}$ $\mathbf{d} - \mathbf{a} = \overrightarrow{AD} = \begin{pmatrix} -1 \\ 1 \\ -4 \end{pmatrix}$

$\therefore$ $(\mathbf{b} - \mathbf{a}) \bullet (\mathbf{c} - \mathbf{a}) \times (\mathbf{d} - \mathbf{a})$

$= \begin{vmatrix} 2 & -1 & -2 \\ -2 & k-1 & -1 \\ -1 & 1 & -4 \end{vmatrix} = 2 \begin{vmatrix} k-1 & -1 \\ 1 & -4 \end{vmatrix} - (-1) \begin{vmatrix} -2 & -1 \\ -1 & -4 \end{vmatrix} - 2 \begin{vmatrix} -2 & k-1 \\ -1 & 1 \end{vmatrix}$

$= 2(-4k + 4 + 1) + 1(8 - 1) - 2(-2 + k - 1)$

$= -8k + 10 + 7 - 2k + 6$

$= -10k + 23$

$\therefore$ A, B, C and D are coplanar when $k = \frac{23}{10}$.

REVIEW SET 14A

1 **a**

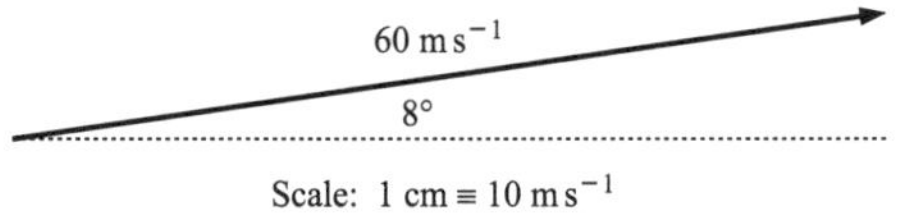

60 m s^{-1}

8°

Scale: 1 cm $\equiv$ 10 m s^{-1}

b

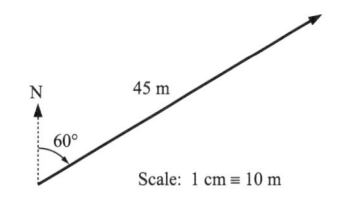

N   45 m

60°

Scale: 1 cm $\equiv$ 10 m

2 **a**

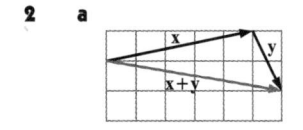

x, y, x+y

b

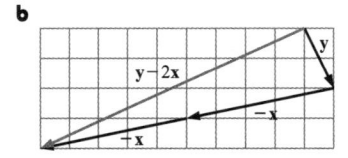

y, y−2x, −x, x

3 **a** $\overrightarrow{PR} + \overrightarrow{RQ}$
$= \overrightarrow{PQ}$

b $\overrightarrow{PS} + \overrightarrow{SQ} + \overrightarrow{QR}$
$= \overrightarrow{PQ} + \overrightarrow{QR}$
$= \overrightarrow{PR}$

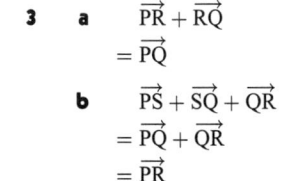

4 Dino's first displacement vector is $9\begin{pmatrix}\cos 246°\\\sin 246°\end{pmatrix}$. His second displacement vector is $6\begin{pmatrix}\cos 96°\\\sin 96°\end{pmatrix}$.

$\therefore$ Dino's resultant displacement vector is $\begin{pmatrix}9\cos 246°\\9\sin 246°\end{pmatrix} + \begin{pmatrix}6\cos 96°\\6\sin 96°\end{pmatrix} \approx \begin{pmatrix}-4.288\\-2.255\end{pmatrix}$

which has length $\sqrt{(-4.288)^2 + (-2.255)^2} \approx 4.845$.

$\therefore$ the resultant displacement vector $\approx 4.845\begin{pmatrix}-0.8851\\-0.4654\end{pmatrix} \leftarrow \cos\theta$

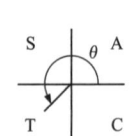

If $\cos\theta = -0.8850$ and $\sin\theta = -0.4654$, θ is in Quadrant 3

$\therefore \theta = 180° + \cos^{-1}(0.8850) \approx 207.7°$

$\therefore$ Dino is 4.84 km from the start at a bearing of 208°.

5 a $\vec{AB} - \vec{CB}$
$= \vec{AB} + \vec{BC}$
$= \vec{AC}$

b $\vec{AB} + \vec{BC} - \vec{DC}$
$= \vec{AC} + \vec{CD}$
$= \vec{AD}$

6 a If $\vec{AB} = \frac{1}{2}\vec{CD}$ then
[AB] $\parallel$ [CD] and $AB = \frac{1}{2}(CD)$

b If $\vec{AB} = 2\vec{AC}$ then
[AB] $\parallel$ [AC] and $AB = 2(AC)$
$\therefore$ A, B and C are collinear and $AB = 2(AC)$.
So, C is the midpoint of [AB].

7 a $\mathbf{p} + \mathbf{r} - \mathbf{q} = \mathbf{0}$
$\therefore \mathbf{p} + \mathbf{r} = \mathbf{q}$

b $\mathbf{l} + \mathbf{m} - \mathbf{n} + \mathbf{j} - \mathbf{k} = \mathbf{0}$
$\therefore \mathbf{l} + \mathbf{m} + \mathbf{j} = \mathbf{n} + \mathbf{k}$

8 a $\vec{OQ} = \vec{OR} + \vec{RQ} = \mathbf{r} + \mathbf{q}$

b $\vec{PQ} = \vec{PO} + \vec{OR} + \vec{RQ} = -\mathbf{p} + \mathbf{r} + \mathbf{q}$

c $\vec{ON} = \vec{OR} + \vec{RN} = \mathbf{r} + \frac{1}{2}\mathbf{q}$

d $\vec{MN} = \vec{MQ} + \vec{QN}$
$= \frac{1}{2}\vec{PQ} + \frac{1}{2}\vec{QR}$
$= \frac{1}{2}(-\mathbf{p} + \mathbf{r} + \mathbf{q}) + \frac{1}{2}(-\mathbf{q})$
$= -\frac{1}{2}\mathbf{p} + \frac{1}{2}\mathbf{r} + \frac{1}{2}\mathbf{q} - \frac{1}{2}\mathbf{q}$
$= \frac{1}{2}\mathbf{r} - \frac{1}{2}\mathbf{p}$

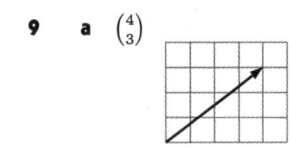

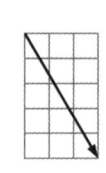

9 a $\begin{pmatrix}4\\3\end{pmatrix}$ **b** $\begin{pmatrix}3\\-5\end{pmatrix}$ **c** $\begin{pmatrix}0\\-4\end{pmatrix}$

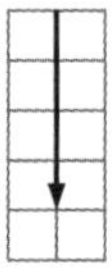

10 a $2\mathbf{p} + \mathbf{q}$
$= 2\begin{pmatrix}-3\\1\end{pmatrix} + \begin{pmatrix}2\\-4\end{pmatrix}$
$= \begin{pmatrix}-6\\2\end{pmatrix} + \begin{pmatrix}2\\-4\end{pmatrix}$
$= \begin{pmatrix}-4\\-2\end{pmatrix}$

b $\mathbf{q} - 3\mathbf{r}$
$= \begin{pmatrix}2\\-4\end{pmatrix} - 3\begin{pmatrix}1\\3\end{pmatrix}$
$= \begin{pmatrix}2\\-4\end{pmatrix} - \begin{pmatrix}3\\9\end{pmatrix}$
$= \begin{pmatrix}-1\\-13\end{pmatrix}$

c $\mathbf{p} - \mathbf{q} + \mathbf{r}$
$= \begin{pmatrix}-3\\1\end{pmatrix} - \begin{pmatrix}2\\-4\end{pmatrix} + \begin{pmatrix}1\\3\end{pmatrix}$
$= \begin{pmatrix}-5\\5\end{pmatrix} + \begin{pmatrix}1\\3\end{pmatrix}$
$= \begin{pmatrix}-4\\8\end{pmatrix}$

11 $\vec{SP}$
$= \vec{SR} + \vec{RQ} + \vec{QP}$
$= -\vec{RS} + \vec{RQ} - \vec{PQ}$
$= -\begin{pmatrix}2\\-3\end{pmatrix} + \begin{pmatrix}-1\\2\end{pmatrix} - \begin{pmatrix}-4\\1\end{pmatrix}$
$= \begin{pmatrix}1\\4\end{pmatrix}$

12 a $|\mathbf{r}| = \sqrt{4^2 + 1^2}$
$= \sqrt{17}$ units

c $\mathbf{r} + \mathbf{s} = \begin{pmatrix}4\\1\end{pmatrix} + \begin{pmatrix}-3\\2\end{pmatrix}$
$= \begin{pmatrix}1\\3\end{pmatrix}$
$\therefore |\mathbf{r} + \mathbf{s}| = \sqrt{1^2 + 3^2}$
$= \sqrt{10}$ units

b $|\mathbf{s}| = \sqrt{(-3)^2 + 2^2}$
$= \sqrt{13}$ units

d $2\mathbf{s} - \mathbf{r} = 2\begin{pmatrix}-3\\2\end{pmatrix} - \begin{pmatrix}4\\1\end{pmatrix}$
$= \begin{pmatrix}-10\\3\end{pmatrix}$
$\therefore |2\mathbf{s} - \mathbf{r}| = \sqrt{(-10)^2 + 3^2}$
$= \sqrt{109}$ units

13 a $\quad \overrightarrow{BC} = 2\overrightarrow{OA} = 2\mathbf{p}$

Now $\overrightarrow{AC} = \overrightarrow{AO} + \overrightarrow{OB} + \overrightarrow{BC}$
$= -\mathbf{p} + \mathbf{q} + 2\mathbf{p}$
$= \mathbf{p} + \mathbf{q}$

b $\quad \overrightarrow{OM} = \overrightarrow{OA} + \overrightarrow{AM}$
$= \mathbf{p} + \tfrac{1}{2}\overrightarrow{AC}$
$= \mathbf{p} + \tfrac{1}{2}(\mathbf{p} + \mathbf{q})$
$= \tfrac{3}{2}\mathbf{p} + \tfrac{1}{2}\mathbf{q}$

14 a $\quad \mathbf{p} - 3\mathbf{x} = \mathbf{0}$
$\therefore \quad \mathbf{p} = 3\mathbf{x}$
$\therefore \quad \tfrac{1}{3}\mathbf{p} = \mathbf{x}$
$\therefore \quad \mathbf{x} = \begin{pmatrix} -1 \\ \tfrac{1}{3} \end{pmatrix}$

b $\quad 2\mathbf{q} - \mathbf{x} = \mathbf{r}$
$\therefore \quad 2\mathbf{q} - \mathbf{r} = \mathbf{x}$
$\therefore \quad \mathbf{x} = 2\begin{pmatrix} 2 \\ -4 \end{pmatrix} - \begin{pmatrix} 3 \\ 2 \end{pmatrix}$
$\therefore \quad \mathbf{x} = \begin{pmatrix} 1 \\ -10 \end{pmatrix}$

15

$\overrightarrow{WY} = \begin{pmatrix} 3 - -3 \\ 4 - -1 \end{pmatrix} = \begin{pmatrix} 6 \\ 5 \end{pmatrix}$

$\overrightarrow{XZ} = \begin{pmatrix} 4 - -2 \\ 10 - 5 \end{pmatrix} = \begin{pmatrix} 6 \\ 5 \end{pmatrix}$

So, $\overrightarrow{WY} = \overrightarrow{XZ}$
$\therefore$ [WY] is parallel to [XZ] and they are equal in length. This is sufficient to deduce that WYZX is a parallelogram.

16 $\quad r \begin{pmatrix} -2 \\ 1 \end{pmatrix} + s \begin{pmatrix} 3 \\ -4 \end{pmatrix} = \begin{pmatrix} 13 \\ -24 \end{pmatrix}$

$\therefore \begin{pmatrix} -2r + 3s \\ r - 4s \end{pmatrix} = \begin{pmatrix} 13 \\ -24 \end{pmatrix}$

$\therefore \quad -2r + 3s = 13$
$\quad\quad r - 4s = -24 \quad \ldots \ldots (1)$
$\therefore \quad -2r + 3s = 13$
$\quad\quad 2r - 8s = -48 \quad \{2 \times (1)\}$
$\overline{\text{adding} \quad -5s = -35}$
$\therefore \quad s = 7$
and in (1) $r - 4(7) = -24$
$\therefore \quad r = -24 + 28$
$\therefore \quad r = 4 \quad \text{and} \quad s = 7$

17

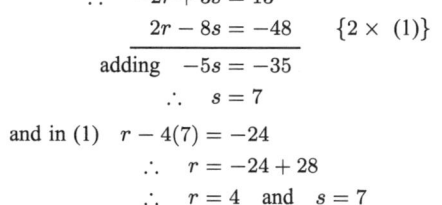

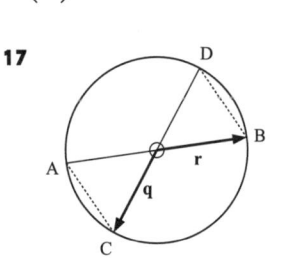

a $\overrightarrow{DB} = \overrightarrow{DO} + \overrightarrow{OB}$
$= \overrightarrow{OC} + \overrightarrow{OB}$
$= \mathbf{q} + \mathbf{r}$

b $\overrightarrow{AC} = \overrightarrow{AO} + \overrightarrow{OC}$
$= \overrightarrow{OB} + \overrightarrow{OC}$
$= \mathbf{r} + \mathbf{q}$

We see that $\overrightarrow{DB} = \overrightarrow{AC}$
$\therefore$ [DB] is parallel to [AC] and equal in length.

REVIEW SET 14B

1 a $\overrightarrow{PQ} = \begin{pmatrix} -1 - 2 \\ 7 - -5 \\ 9 - 6 \end{pmatrix} = \begin{pmatrix} -3 \\ 12 \\ 3 \end{pmatrix}$

b $PQ = \sqrt{(-3)^2 + 12^2 + 3^2}$
$= \sqrt{162}$ units

c

(2, −5, 6)

(2, 0, 0)

$\therefore$ distance
$= \sqrt{(2-2)^2 + (0 - -5)^2 + (0-6)^2}$
$= \sqrt{0 + 25 + 36}$
$= \sqrt{61}$ units

2 a $\mathbf{m} - \mathbf{n} + \mathbf{p} = \begin{pmatrix} 6 \\ -3 \\ 1 \end{pmatrix} - \begin{pmatrix} 2 \\ 3 \\ -4 \end{pmatrix} + \begin{pmatrix} -1 \\ 3 \\ 6 \end{pmatrix} = \begin{pmatrix} 3 \\ -3 \\ 11 \end{pmatrix}$

b $2\mathbf{n} - 3\mathbf{p} = 2\begin{pmatrix} 2 \\ 3 \\ -4 \end{pmatrix} - 3\begin{pmatrix} -1 \\ 3 \\ 6 \end{pmatrix} = \begin{pmatrix} 4 \\ 6 \\ -8 \end{pmatrix} - \begin{pmatrix} -3 \\ 9 \\ 18 \end{pmatrix} = \begin{pmatrix} 7 \\ -3 \\ -26 \end{pmatrix}$

c $\mathbf{m} + \mathbf{p} = \begin{pmatrix} 6 \\ -3 \\ 1 \end{pmatrix} + \begin{pmatrix} -1 \\ 3 \\ 6 \end{pmatrix} = \begin{pmatrix} 5 \\ 0 \\ 7 \end{pmatrix}$ $\therefore$ $|\mathbf{m} + \mathbf{p}| = \sqrt{25 + 0 + 49}$
$= \sqrt{74}$ units

3 $\overrightarrow{CB} = \overrightarrow{CA} + \overrightarrow{AB} = -\overrightarrow{AC} + \overrightarrow{AB} = \begin{pmatrix} 6 \\ -1 \\ 3 \end{pmatrix} + \begin{pmatrix} 2 \\ -7 \\ 4 \end{pmatrix} = \begin{pmatrix} 8 \\ -8 \\ 7 \end{pmatrix}$

4 The vectors are parallel, so $\begin{pmatrix} -12 \\ -20 \\ 2 \end{pmatrix} = k \begin{pmatrix} 3 \\ m \\ n \end{pmatrix}$ $\therefore$ $3k = -12$, $km = -20$, $kn = 2$
$\therefore$ $k = -4$, $m = 5$, $n = -\tfrac{1}{2}$

5 $\overrightarrow{PQ} = \begin{pmatrix} 4 - -6 \\ 6 - 8 \\ 8 - 2 \end{pmatrix} = \begin{pmatrix} 10 \\ -2 \\ 6 \end{pmatrix} = 2\begin{pmatrix} 5 \\ -1 \\ 3 \end{pmatrix}$ $\therefore$ both $\overrightarrow{PQ}$ and $\overrightarrow{QR}$ are parallel to $\begin{pmatrix} 5 \\ -1 \\ 3 \end{pmatrix}$

$\overrightarrow{QR} = \begin{pmatrix} 19 - 4 \\ 3 - 6 \\ 17 - 8 \end{pmatrix} = \begin{pmatrix} 15 \\ -3 \\ 9 \end{pmatrix} = 3\begin{pmatrix} 5 \\ -1 \\ 3 \end{pmatrix}$ $\therefore$ [PQ] || [QR] with Q common to both.
$\therefore$ P, Q, and R are collinear.

Now $\overrightarrow{PQ} : \overrightarrow{QR} = 2\begin{pmatrix} 5 \\ -1 \\ 3 \end{pmatrix} : 3\begin{pmatrix} 5 \\ -1 \\ 3 \end{pmatrix} = 2 : 3$.

$\therefore$ Q divides [PR] internally in the ratio 2 : 3.

6 As the vectors are perpendicular,

$\begin{pmatrix} -4 \\ t+2 \\ t \end{pmatrix} \bullet \begin{pmatrix} t \\ 1+t \\ -3 \end{pmatrix} = 0$

$\therefore$ $-4t + (t+2)(1+t) - 3t = 0$
$\therefore$ $-4t + t + t^2 + 2 + 2t - 3t = 0$
$\therefore$ $t^2 - 4t + 2 = 0$

$\therefore$ $t = \dfrac{4 \pm \sqrt{16 - 4(1)(2)}}{2}$

$\therefore$ $t = \dfrac{4 \pm \sqrt{8}}{2} = 2 \pm \sqrt{2}$

7 If θ is the angle then $\begin{pmatrix} 2 \\ -4 \\ 3 \end{pmatrix} \bullet \begin{pmatrix} -1 \\ 1 \\ 3 \end{pmatrix} = \sqrt{4 + 16 + 9}\sqrt{1 + 1 + 9} \cos\theta$

$\therefore$ $-2 - 4 + 9 = \sqrt{29}\sqrt{11} \cos\theta$

$\therefore$ $\dfrac{3}{\sqrt{29 \times 11}} = \cos\theta$ and so $\theta \approx 80.3°$

8 If D is the origin, (DA) the X-axis, (DC) the Y-axis and (DE) the Z-axis, then A is $(4, 0, 0)$, C is $(0, 8, 0)$ and G is $(4, 8, 5)$.

$\overrightarrow{AG} = \begin{pmatrix} 4 - 4 \\ 8 - 0 \\ 5 - 0 \end{pmatrix} = \begin{pmatrix} 0 \\ 8 \\ 5 \end{pmatrix}$ $\overrightarrow{AC} = \begin{pmatrix} 0 - 4 \\ 8 - 0 \\ 0 - 0 \end{pmatrix} = \begin{pmatrix} -4 \\ 8 \\ 0 \end{pmatrix}$

If the required angle is θ then $\begin{pmatrix} 0 \\ 8 \\ 5 \end{pmatrix} \bullet \begin{pmatrix} -4 \\ 8 \\ 0 \end{pmatrix} = \sqrt{0 + 64 + 25}\sqrt{16 + 64 + 0} \cos\theta$

$\therefore$ $0 + 64 + 0 = \sqrt{89}\sqrt{80} \cos\theta$

$\therefore$ $\cos\theta = \dfrac{64}{\sqrt{89 \times 80}}$ and so $\theta \approx 40.7°$

9 **a** $\overrightarrow{PQ} = \begin{pmatrix} -4 - 2 \\ 4 - 3 \\ 2 - -1 \end{pmatrix} = \begin{pmatrix} -6 \\ 1 \\ 3 \end{pmatrix}$ **b** $PQ = |\overrightarrow{PQ}| = \sqrt{36 + 1 + 9} = \sqrt{46}$ units

c The midpoint is at $\left(\dfrac{2 + -4}{2}, \dfrac{3 + 4}{2}, \dfrac{-1 + 2}{2}\right)$ which is $(-1, \tfrac{7}{2}, \tfrac{1}{2})$.

10 **a** $\mathbf{p} \bullet \mathbf{q} = \begin{pmatrix} -1 \\ 2 \\ 1 \end{pmatrix} \bullet \begin{pmatrix} 3 \\ -1 \\ 4 \end{pmatrix} = -3 - 2 + 4 = -1$

b $\mathbf{p} + 2\mathbf{q} - \mathbf{r} = \begin{pmatrix} -1 \\ 2 \\ 1 \end{pmatrix} + \begin{pmatrix} 6 \\ -2 \\ 8 \end{pmatrix} - \begin{pmatrix} 1 \\ 1 \\ 2 \end{pmatrix} = \begin{pmatrix} 4 \\ -1 \\ 7 \end{pmatrix}$

c $\mathbf{p} \bullet \mathbf{r} = |\mathbf{p}||\mathbf{r}|\cos\theta$ $\therefore \begin{pmatrix} -1 \\ 2 \\ 1 \end{pmatrix} \bullet \begin{pmatrix} 1 \\ 1 \\ 2 \end{pmatrix} = \sqrt{1+4+1}\sqrt{1+1+4}\cos\theta$

$\therefore -1 + 2 + 2 = \sqrt{6}\sqrt{6}\cos\theta$

$\therefore 3 = 6\cos\theta$

$\therefore \cos\theta = \frac{1}{2}$

$\therefore \theta = 60°$

11 $\overrightarrow{MK} = \begin{pmatrix} 3-4 \\ 1-1 \\ 4-3 \end{pmatrix} = \begin{pmatrix} -1 \\ 0 \\ 1 \end{pmatrix}$ $\overrightarrow{LK} = \begin{pmatrix} 3--2 \\ 1-1 \\ 4-3 \end{pmatrix} = \begin{pmatrix} 5 \\ 0 \\ 1 \end{pmatrix}$

$\overrightarrow{ML} = \begin{pmatrix} -2-4 \\ 1-1 \\ 3-3 \end{pmatrix} = \begin{pmatrix} -6 \\ 0 \\ 0 \end{pmatrix}$ $\overrightarrow{LM} = \begin{pmatrix} 4--2 \\ 1-1 \\ 3-3 \end{pmatrix} = \begin{pmatrix} 6 \\ 0 \\ 0 \end{pmatrix}$

$\overrightarrow{MK} \bullet \overrightarrow{ML} = |\overrightarrow{MK}||\overrightarrow{ML}|\cos M$ $\therefore \overrightarrow{LK} \bullet \overrightarrow{LM} = |\overrightarrow{LK}||\overrightarrow{LM}|\cos L$

$\therefore 6 + 0 + 0 = \sqrt{1+0+1}\sqrt{36+0+0}\cos M$ $\therefore 30 + 0 + 0 = \sqrt{25+0+1}\sqrt{36+0+0}\cos L$

$\therefore 6 = \sqrt{2} \times 6\cos M$ $\therefore 30 = \sqrt{26} \times 6 \cos L$

$\therefore \cos M = \frac{1}{\sqrt{2}}$ $\therefore \frac{5}{\sqrt{26}} = \cos L$

$\therefore M = 45°$ $\therefore L \approx 11.3°$

and $K \approx 180° - 45° - 11.3° \approx 123.7°$

12 If the angle is θ then $\begin{pmatrix} 3 \\ 1 \\ -2 \end{pmatrix} \bullet \begin{pmatrix} 2 \\ 5 \\ 1 \end{pmatrix} = \sqrt{9+1+4}\sqrt{4+25+1}\cos\theta$

$\therefore 6 + 5 - 2 = \sqrt{14}\sqrt{30}\cos\theta$

$\therefore \frac{9}{\sqrt{14 \times 30}} = \cos\theta$

$\therefore \theta \approx 64.0°$

13

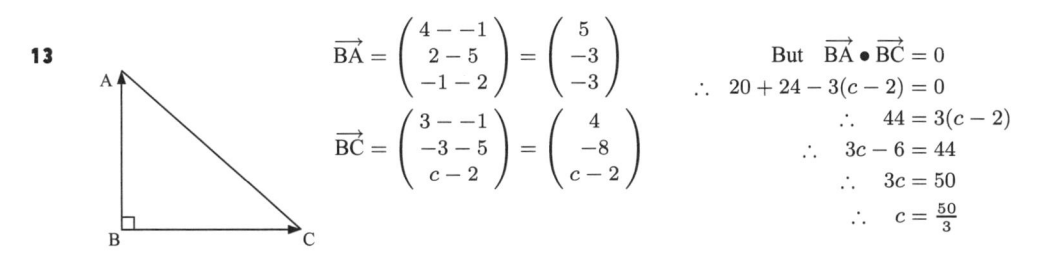

$\overrightarrow{BA} = \begin{pmatrix} 4--1 \\ 2-5 \\ -1-2 \end{pmatrix} = \begin{pmatrix} 5 \\ -3 \\ -3 \end{pmatrix}$ But $\overrightarrow{BA} \bullet \overrightarrow{BC} = 0$

$\therefore 20 + 24 - 3(c-2) = 0$

$\overrightarrow{BC} = \begin{pmatrix} 3--1 \\ -3-5 \\ c-2 \end{pmatrix} = \begin{pmatrix} 4 \\ -8 \\ c-2 \end{pmatrix}$ $\therefore 44 = 3(c-2)$

$\therefore 3c - 6 = 44$

$\therefore 3c = 50$

$\therefore c = \frac{50}{3}$

14 **a** $\mathbf{a} \bullet \mathbf{b}$ is a scalar, so in $\mathbf{a} \bullet \mathbf{b} \bullet \mathbf{c}$ we would be trying to find the scalar product of a scalar and a vector which is impossible.

b $\mathbf{a} \bullet \mathbf{b} \times \mathbf{c}$ does not need a bracket about the $\mathbf{b} \times \mathbf{c}$ as this must be performed first; if we try to find $\mathbf{a} \bullet \mathbf{b}$ first we get a scalar cross a vector which is impossible.

15 a $\begin{pmatrix} \frac{4}{7} \\ \frac{1}{k} \end{pmatrix}$ is a unit vector if

$\sqrt{\left(\frac{4}{7}\right)^2 + \left(\frac{1}{k}\right)^2} = 1$

$\therefore \quad \frac{16}{49} + \frac{1}{k^2} = 1$

$\therefore \quad \frac{1}{k^2} = \frac{33}{49}$

$\therefore \quad k = \pm \frac{7}{\sqrt{33}}$

b $\begin{pmatrix} k \\ k \end{pmatrix}$ is a unit vector if

$\sqrt{k^2 + k^2} = 1$

$\therefore \quad 2k^2 = 1$

$\therefore \quad k^2 = \frac{1}{2}$

$\therefore \quad k = \pm \frac{1}{\sqrt{2}}$

REVIEW SET 14C

1 a $\mathbf{p} \bullet \mathbf{q} = \begin{pmatrix} 3 \\ -2 \end{pmatrix} \bullet \begin{pmatrix} -1 \\ 5 \end{pmatrix}$
$= -3 + (-10)$
$= -13$

b $\mathbf{p} - \mathbf{r} = \begin{pmatrix} 3 \\ -2 \end{pmatrix} - \begin{pmatrix} -3 \\ 4 \end{pmatrix}$
$= \begin{pmatrix} 6 \\ -6 \end{pmatrix}$

$\therefore \quad \mathbf{q} \bullet (\mathbf{p} - \mathbf{r}) = \begin{pmatrix} -1 \\ 5 \end{pmatrix} \bullet \begin{pmatrix} 6 \\ -6 \end{pmatrix}$
$= -6 - 30$
$= -36$

2 LHS $= \mathbf{p} \bullet (\mathbf{q} - \mathbf{r})$
$= \begin{pmatrix} 3 \\ -2 \end{pmatrix} \bullet \left[\begin{pmatrix} -2 \\ 5 \end{pmatrix} - \begin{pmatrix} 1 \\ -3 \end{pmatrix} \right]$
$= \begin{pmatrix} 3 \\ -2 \end{pmatrix} \bullet \begin{pmatrix} -3 \\ 8 \end{pmatrix}$
$= -9 - 16$
$= -25$

RHS $= \mathbf{p} \bullet \mathbf{q} - \mathbf{p} \bullet \mathbf{r}$
$= \begin{pmatrix} 3 \\ -2 \end{pmatrix} \bullet \begin{pmatrix} -2 \\ 5 \end{pmatrix} - \begin{pmatrix} 3 \\ -2 \end{pmatrix} \bullet \begin{pmatrix} 1 \\ -3 \end{pmatrix}$
$= (-6 - 10) - (3 + 6)$
$= -16 - 9$
$= -25 \qquad \therefore \quad \text{LHS} = \text{RHS} \checkmark$

3 Since they are perpendicular

$\begin{pmatrix} 3 \\ 3 - 2t \end{pmatrix} \bullet \begin{pmatrix} t^2 + t \\ -2 \end{pmatrix} = 0$

$\therefore \quad 3(t^2 + t) - 2(3 - 2t) = 0$

$\therefore \quad 3t^2 + 3t - 6 + 4t = 0$

$\therefore \quad 3t^2 + 7t - 6 = 0$

$\therefore \quad (3t - 2)(t + 3) = 0$

$\therefore \quad t = \frac{2}{3} \text{ or } -3$

4 $\overrightarrow{AB} = \begin{pmatrix} -1 - 2 \\ 4 - 3 \end{pmatrix} = \begin{pmatrix} -3 \\ 1 \end{pmatrix}$

$\overrightarrow{AC} = \begin{pmatrix} 3 - 2 \\ k - 3 \end{pmatrix} = \begin{pmatrix} 1 \\ k - 3 \end{pmatrix}$

Now $\overrightarrow{AB} \bullet \overrightarrow{AC} = 0 \quad \{\text{as } \widehat{BAC} = 90°\}$

$\therefore \quad \begin{pmatrix} -3 \\ 1 \end{pmatrix} \bullet \begin{pmatrix} 1 \\ k - 3 \end{pmatrix} = 0$

$\therefore \quad -3 + k - 3 = 0$

$\therefore \quad k = 6$

5 One vector perpendicular to $\begin{pmatrix} -4 \\ 5 \end{pmatrix}$ is $\begin{pmatrix} 5 \\ 4 \end{pmatrix}$ as the dot product $= -20 + 20 = 0$

$\therefore$ all vectors have form $k \begin{pmatrix} 5 \\ 4 \end{pmatrix}$, $k \neq 0$.

6 $\overrightarrow{KL} = \begin{pmatrix} 3 - -2 \\ 2 - 1 \end{pmatrix} = \begin{pmatrix} 5 \\ 1 \end{pmatrix}$

$\overrightarrow{KM} = \begin{pmatrix} 1 - -2 \\ -3 - 1 \end{pmatrix} = \begin{pmatrix} 3 \\ -4 \end{pmatrix}$

Now $\overrightarrow{KL} \bullet \overrightarrow{KM} = |\overrightarrow{KL}||\overrightarrow{KM}| \cos K$

$\therefore \quad \begin{pmatrix} 5 \\ 1 \end{pmatrix} \bullet \begin{pmatrix} 3 \\ -4 \end{pmatrix} = \sqrt{25 + 1}\sqrt{9 + 16} \cos K$

$\therefore \quad 15 - 4 = \sqrt{26}\sqrt{25} \cos K$

$\therefore \quad \cos K = \frac{11}{5\sqrt{26}}$

$\therefore \quad K \approx 64.4°$

$\overrightarrow{LK} = -\overrightarrow{KL} = \begin{pmatrix} -5 \\ -1 \end{pmatrix}$

$\overrightarrow{LM} = \begin{pmatrix} 1 - 3 \\ -3 - 2 \end{pmatrix} = \begin{pmatrix} -2 \\ -5 \end{pmatrix}$

Now $\overrightarrow{LK} \bullet \overrightarrow{LM} = |\overrightarrow{LK}||\overrightarrow{LM}| \cos L$

$\therefore \quad \begin{pmatrix} -5 \\ -1 \end{pmatrix} \bullet \begin{pmatrix} -2 \\ -5 \end{pmatrix} = \sqrt{25 + 1}\sqrt{4 + 25} \cos L$

$\therefore \quad 10 + 5 = \sqrt{26}\sqrt{29} \cos L$

$\therefore \quad \cos L = \frac{15}{\sqrt{26 \times 29}}$

$\therefore \quad L \approx 56.9°$

$\therefore \quad M \approx 180° - 56.89° - 64.44° \approx 58.7°$

7 $4x - 5y = 11$ has gradient $\frac{4}{5}$ $\therefore$ it has direction vector $\begin{pmatrix} 5 \\ 4 \end{pmatrix}$.

$2x + 3y = 7$ has gradient $-\frac{2}{3}$ $\therefore$ it has direction vector $\begin{pmatrix} 3 \\ -2 \end{pmatrix}$.

If the angle is θ, $\begin{pmatrix} 5 \\ 4 \end{pmatrix} \bullet \begin{pmatrix} 3 \\ -2 \end{pmatrix} = \sqrt{5^2 + 4^2}\sqrt{3^2 + (-2)^2}\cos\theta$

$\therefore$ $15 - 8 = \sqrt{41}\sqrt{13}\cos\theta$

$\therefore$ $\dfrac{7}{\sqrt{41 \times 13}} = \cos\theta$

$\therefore$ $\theta \approx 72.3°$ $\therefore$ the angle is $72.3°$ (or $107.7°$)

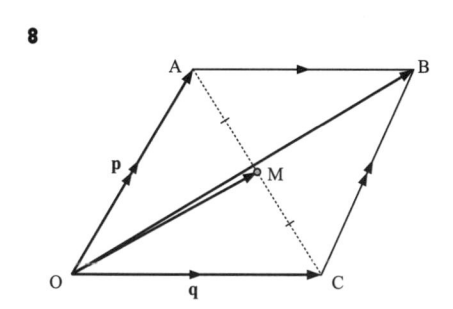

8 **a** **i** $\overrightarrow{OB}$
$= \overrightarrow{OA} + \overrightarrow{AB}$
$= \overrightarrow{OA} + \overrightarrow{OC}$
$= \mathbf{p} + \mathbf{q}$

ii $\overrightarrow{OM}$
$= \overrightarrow{OA} + \overrightarrow{AM}$
$= \overrightarrow{OA} + \frac{1}{2}\overrightarrow{AC}$
$= \mathbf{p} + \frac{1}{2}(\overrightarrow{AO} + \overrightarrow{OC})$
$= \mathbf{p} + \frac{1}{2}(-\mathbf{p} + \mathbf{q})$
$= \mathbf{p} - \frac{1}{2}\mathbf{p} + \frac{1}{2}\mathbf{q}$
$= \frac{1}{2}\mathbf{p} + \frac{1}{2}\mathbf{q}$

b We notice that $\overrightarrow{OM} = \frac{1}{2}\overrightarrow{OB}$

$\therefore$ [OM] $\parallel$ [OB] and $OM = \frac{1}{2}(OB)$

So, O, M and B are collinear (as O is common) and hence M is the midpoint of [OB].

9 **a** $\overrightarrow{AC} = \overrightarrow{AO} + \overrightarrow{OC}$ $\quad$ $\overrightarrow{BC} = \overrightarrow{BO} + \overrightarrow{OC}$
$= -\mathbf{p} + \mathbf{r}$ $\qquad\qquad$ $= -\mathbf{q} + \mathbf{r}$
$= \mathbf{r} - \mathbf{p}$ $\qquad\qquad$ $= \mathbf{r} - \mathbf{q}$

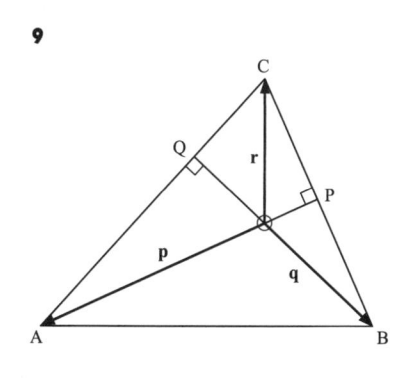

b $\quad$ [AP] $\perp$ [BC] $\qquad$ and $\qquad$ [BQ] $\perp$ [AC]
$\therefore$ $\mathbf{p} \perp \mathbf{r} - \mathbf{q}$ $\qquad\qquad$ $\therefore$ $\mathbf{q} \perp (\mathbf{r} - \mathbf{p})$
$\therefore$ $\mathbf{p} \bullet (\mathbf{r} - \mathbf{q}) = 0$ $\qquad$ $\therefore$ $\mathbf{q} \bullet (\mathbf{r} - \mathbf{p}) = 0$
$\therefore$ $\mathbf{p} \bullet \mathbf{r} - \mathbf{p} \bullet \mathbf{q} = 0$ $\qquad$ $\therefore$ $\mathbf{q} \bullet \mathbf{r} - \mathbf{q} \bullet \mathbf{p} = 0$
$\therefore$ $\mathbf{p} \bullet \mathbf{r} = \mathbf{p} \bullet \mathbf{q}$ $\qquad\qquad$ $\therefore$ $\mathbf{q} \bullet \mathbf{r} = \mathbf{p} \bullet \mathbf{q}$

c $\mathbf{r} \bullet \overrightarrow{AB} = \mathbf{r} \bullet (-\mathbf{p} + \mathbf{q})$
$= -\mathbf{r} \bullet \mathbf{p} + \mathbf{r} \bullet \mathbf{q}$
$= -\mathbf{p} \bullet \mathbf{q} + \mathbf{p} \bullet \mathbf{q}$ {from **b**}
$= 0$ $\quad$ and so $\mathbf{r} \perp \overrightarrow{AB}$ $\quad$ $\therefore$ [OC] $\perp$ [AB]

10 **a** $2\mathbf{a} - 3\mathbf{b} = 2\begin{pmatrix} 2 \\ -3 \\ 1 \end{pmatrix} - 3\begin{pmatrix} -1 \\ 2 \\ 3 \end{pmatrix} = \begin{pmatrix} 4 \\ -6 \\ 2 \end{pmatrix} - \begin{pmatrix} -3 \\ 6 \\ 9 \end{pmatrix} = \begin{pmatrix} 7 \\ -12 \\ -7 \end{pmatrix}$

b $\mathbf{a} - 3\mathbf{x} = \mathbf{b}$ $\quad$ $\therefore$ $\mathbf{a} - \mathbf{b} = 3\mathbf{x}$ $\quad$ $\therefore$ $\mathbf{x} = \frac{1}{3}(\mathbf{a} - \mathbf{b}) = \frac{1}{3}\begin{pmatrix} 3 \\ -5 \\ -2 \end{pmatrix} = \begin{pmatrix} 1 \\ -\frac{5}{3} \\ -\frac{2}{3} \end{pmatrix}$

11 $|\mathbf{a}| = 3$, $|\mathbf{b}| = \sqrt{7}$ and $\mathbf{a} \times \mathbf{b} = \begin{pmatrix} 1 \\ 2 \\ -3 \end{pmatrix}$

a $|\mathbf{a} \times \mathbf{b}| = |\mathbf{a}||\mathbf{b}|\sin\theta$
$\sqrt{1 + 4 + 9} = 3 \times \sqrt{7} \times \sin\theta$
$\sin\theta = \frac{\sqrt{14}}{3\sqrt{7}} = \frac{\sqrt{2}}{3}$
But $\cos^2\theta = 1 - \sin^2\theta$
$\therefore \cos\theta = \pm\frac{\sqrt{7}}{3}$

Hence $\mathbf{a} \bullet \mathbf{b} = |\mathbf{a}||\mathbf{b}|\cos\theta$
$= 3 \times \sqrt{7} \times (\pm\frac{\sqrt{7}}{3})$
$= \pm 7$

b   Area $\triangle OAB = \frac{1}{2}|\mathbf{a} \times \mathbf{b}|$
$= \frac{1}{2}\sqrt{14}$ units^2

c $V = \frac{1}{6}|\mathbf{c} \bullet (\mathbf{a} \times \mathbf{b})|$

Now $\mathbf{c} = \begin{pmatrix} 1 \\ -1 \\ 2 \end{pmatrix}$ and $\mathbf{a} \times \mathbf{b} = \begin{pmatrix} 1 \\ 2 \\ -3 \end{pmatrix}$

$\therefore V = \frac{1}{6}\left|\begin{pmatrix} 1 \\ -1 \\ 2 \end{pmatrix} \bullet \begin{pmatrix} 1 \\ 2 \\ -3 \end{pmatrix}\right|$
$= \frac{1}{6}|1 - 2 - 6|$
$= \frac{7}{6}$ units^3

REVIEW SET 14D

1 $\mathbf{a} = 3\mathbf{i} - \mathbf{j} + 2\mathbf{k}$, $\mathbf{b} = \mathbf{i} - 2\mathbf{k}$

a $3\mathbf{a} - 2\mathbf{b} = 3(3\mathbf{i} - \mathbf{j} + 2\mathbf{k}) - 2(\mathbf{i} - 2\mathbf{k})$
$= 9\mathbf{i} - 3\mathbf{j} + 6\mathbf{k} - 2\mathbf{i} + 4\mathbf{k}$
$= 7\mathbf{i} - 3\mathbf{j} + 10\mathbf{k}$

b $|\mathbf{a}| = \sqrt{3^2 + (-1)^2 + 2^2}$
$= \sqrt{14}$ units

2   Let $\mathbf{a} = \begin{pmatrix} a_1 \\ a_2 \\ a_3 \end{pmatrix}$ $\therefore$ $k\mathbf{a} = \begin{pmatrix} ka_1 \\ ka_2 \\ ka_3 \end{pmatrix}$ $\therefore$ $|k\mathbf{a}| = \sqrt{(ka_1)^2 + (ka_2)^2 + (ka_3)^2}$
$= \sqrt{k^2(a_1^2 + a_2^2 + a_3^2)}$
$= \sqrt{k^2}\sqrt{a_1^2 + a_2^2 + a_3^2}$
$= |k||\mathbf{a}|$

3   **a**   Given $P(-1, 2, 3)$ and $Q(4, 0, -1)$,
$\overrightarrow{PQ} = \begin{pmatrix} 5 \\ -2 \\ -4 \end{pmatrix}$

b   If the angle is α,
$|\overrightarrow{PQ}|\sqrt{1^2 + 0^2 + 0^2}\cos\alpha = \overrightarrow{PQ} \bullet \begin{pmatrix} 1 \\ 0 \\ 0 \end{pmatrix}$
$\therefore \sqrt{25 + 4 + 16}\cos\alpha = 5$
$\therefore \cos\alpha = \frac{5}{\sqrt{45}}$
$\therefore \alpha \approx 41.8°$

c

$Q(4,0,-1)$ $\xleftarrow{2x}$ $R(a,b,c)$ $\xleftarrow{x}$ $P(-1,2,3)$

$\overrightarrow{QR} = 2\overrightarrow{RP}$

$\begin{pmatrix} a - 4 \\ b \\ c + 1 \end{pmatrix} = 2\begin{pmatrix} -1 - a \\ 2 - b \\ 3 - c \end{pmatrix}$

$a - 4 = -2 - 2a$, $b = 4 - 2b$, $c + 1 = 6 - 2c$
$\therefore 3a = 2$ $\therefore 3b = 4$ $\therefore 3c = 5$
$\therefore a = \frac{2}{3}$ $\therefore b = \frac{4}{3}$ $\therefore c = \frac{5}{3}$

$\therefore$ R is at $(\frac{2}{3}, \frac{4}{3}, \frac{5}{3})$.

4

$Q(0,1,4)$, $R(a,-1,-2)$, $P(-1,2,1)$

Area of $\Delta = \frac{1}{2}|\vec{PQ} \times \vec{PR}| = \frac{1}{2}\left|\begin{pmatrix} 0--1 \\ 1-2 \\ 4-1 \end{pmatrix} \times \begin{pmatrix} a--1 \\ -1-2 \\ -2-1 \end{pmatrix}\right|$

$= \frac{1}{2}\left|\begin{pmatrix} 1 \\ -1 \\ 3 \end{pmatrix} \times \begin{pmatrix} a+1 \\ -3 \\ -3 \end{pmatrix}\right|$

$\therefore \quad \frac{1}{2}\left|\begin{vmatrix} i & j & k \\ 1 & -1 & 3 \\ a+1 & -3 & -3 \end{vmatrix}\right| = \sqrt{118}$

$\therefore \quad \left|\begin{vmatrix} -1 & 3 \\ -3 & -3 \end{vmatrix}i - \begin{vmatrix} 1 & 3 \\ a+1 & -3 \end{vmatrix}j + \begin{vmatrix} 1 & -1 \\ a+1 & -3 \end{vmatrix}k\right| = 2\sqrt{118}$

$|12i - (-3-3a-3)j + (-3+a+1)k| = 2\sqrt{118}$

$\therefore \quad \sqrt{144 + (3a+6)^2 + (a-2)^2} = 2\sqrt{118}$

$\therefore \quad 144 + 9a^2 + 36a + 36 + a^2 - 4a + 4 = 472$

$\therefore \quad 10a^2 + 32a - 288 = 0$

$\therefore \quad 5a^2 + 16a - 144 = 0$

$\therefore \quad (5a+36)(a-4) = 0$

$\therefore \quad a = -\frac{36}{5}$ or 4

5 a

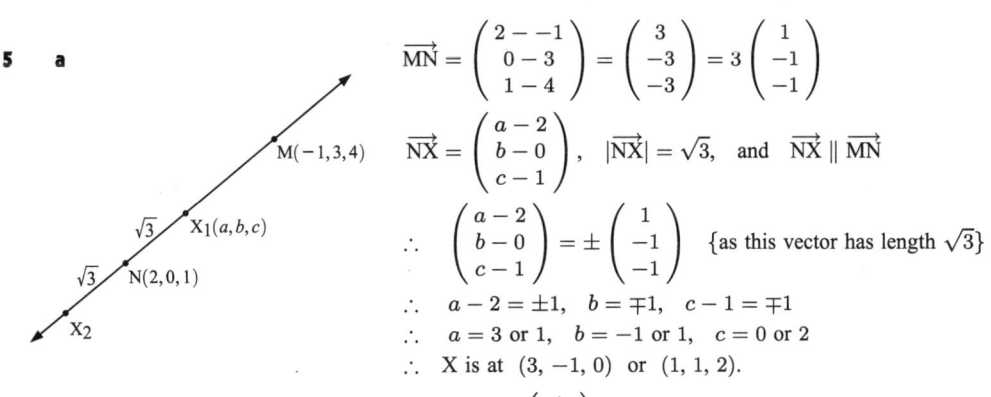

$M(-1,3,4)$, $X_1(a,b,c)$, $N(2,0,1)$, X_2

$\vec{MN} = \begin{pmatrix} 2--1 \\ 0-3 \\ 1-4 \end{pmatrix} = \begin{pmatrix} 3 \\ -3 \\ -3 \end{pmatrix} = 3\begin{pmatrix} 1 \\ -1 \\ -1 \end{pmatrix}$

$\vec{NX} = \begin{pmatrix} a-2 \\ b-0 \\ c-1 \end{pmatrix}$, $|\vec{NX}| = \sqrt{3}$, and $\vec{NX} \parallel \vec{MN}$

$\therefore \quad \begin{pmatrix} a-2 \\ b-0 \\ c-1 \end{pmatrix} = \pm\begin{pmatrix} 1 \\ -1 \\ -1 \end{pmatrix}$ {as this vector has length $\sqrt{3}$}

$\therefore \quad a-2 = \pm 1, \quad b = \mp 1, \quad c-1 = \mp 1$

$\therefore \quad a = 3$ or 1, $\quad b = -1$ or 1, $\quad c = 0$ or 2

$\therefore \quad X$ is at $(3, -1, 0)$ or $(1, 1, 2)$.

b The unit vector in the direction of $\vec{MN}$ is $\frac{1}{\sqrt{3}}\begin{pmatrix} 1 \\ -1 \\ -1 \end{pmatrix}$

$\therefore$ the required vector is $\frac{2}{\sqrt{3}}\begin{pmatrix} 1 \\ -1 \\ -1 \end{pmatrix}$ or $\begin{pmatrix} \frac{2}{\sqrt{3}} \\ -\frac{2}{\sqrt{3}} \\ -\frac{2}{\sqrt{3}} \end{pmatrix}$.

6 $\vec{BC} = \begin{pmatrix} -1-2 \\ -9-0 \\ 4-1 \end{pmatrix} = \begin{pmatrix} -3 \\ -9 \\ 3 \end{pmatrix}$ and $\vec{CA} = \begin{pmatrix} 1--1 \\ -3--9 \\ 2-4 \end{pmatrix} = \begin{pmatrix} 2 \\ 6 \\ -2 \end{pmatrix}$

$\therefore \quad -\frac{1}{3}\vec{BC} = \begin{pmatrix} 1 \\ 3 \\ -1 \end{pmatrix}$ and $\frac{1}{2}\vec{CA} = \begin{pmatrix} 1 \\ 3 \\ -1 \end{pmatrix}$

$\therefore \quad -\frac{1}{3}\vec{BC} = \frac{1}{2}\vec{CA}$ or $\vec{BC} = -\frac{3}{2}\vec{CA}$

$\therefore \quad [BC] \parallel [CA]$ so B, C and A are collinear.

For C divides [BA] we need $\vec{BC} : \vec{CA} = -3\begin{pmatrix} 1 \\ 3 \\ -1 \end{pmatrix} : 2\begin{pmatrix} 1 \\ 3 \\ -1 \end{pmatrix} = -3 : 2$

$\therefore$ C divides [BA] externally in the ratio $3 : 2$.

7

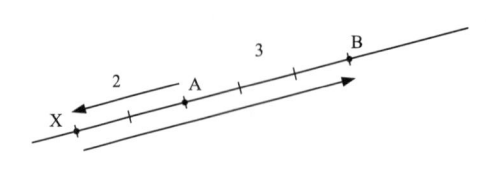

Let X divide [AB] externally in the ratio $2:5$.

$\therefore \vec{AX}:\vec{XB} = -2:5$

Now $\vec{OX} = \vec{OA} + \vec{AX}$

$= \vec{OA} + \frac{2}{3}\vec{BA}$

$= \begin{pmatrix} -2 \\ 3 \\ 5 \end{pmatrix} + \frac{2}{3}\begin{pmatrix} -2-3 \\ 3--1 \\ 5-1 \end{pmatrix}$

$= \begin{pmatrix} -2 \\ 3 \\ 5 \end{pmatrix} + \frac{2}{3}\begin{pmatrix} -5 \\ 4 \\ 4 \end{pmatrix}$

$= \begin{pmatrix} -2-\frac{10}{3} \\ 3+\frac{8}{3} \\ 5+\frac{8}{3} \end{pmatrix}$ or $\begin{pmatrix} -\frac{16}{3} \\ \frac{17}{3} \\ \frac{23}{3} \end{pmatrix}$

$\therefore$ X is $\left(-\frac{16}{3}, \frac{17}{3}, \frac{23}{3}\right)$.

8

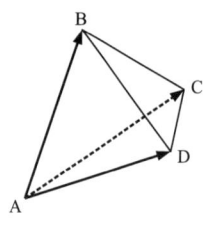

$\vec{AB} = \begin{pmatrix} -1-3 \\ 2-1 \\ 1-2 \end{pmatrix} = \begin{pmatrix} -4 \\ 1 \\ -1 \end{pmatrix}$

$\vec{AC} = \begin{pmatrix} -2-3 \\ 0-1 \\ 3-2 \end{pmatrix} = \begin{pmatrix} -5 \\ -1 \\ 1 \end{pmatrix}$

$\vec{AD} = \begin{pmatrix} 4-3 \\ 3-1 \\ -1-2 \end{pmatrix} = \begin{pmatrix} 1 \\ 2 \\ -3 \end{pmatrix}$

Volume

$= \frac{1}{6}|\vec{AB} \bullet (\vec{AC} \times \vec{AD})|$

$= \frac{1}{6}\begin{Vmatrix} -4 & 1 & -1 \\ -5 & -1 & 1 \\ 1 & 2 & -3 \end{Vmatrix}$ units^3

$= \frac{1}{6}\left|-4\begin{vmatrix} -1 & 1 \\ 2 & -3 \end{vmatrix} - 1\begin{vmatrix} -5 & 1 \\ 1 & -3 \end{vmatrix} - 1\begin{vmatrix} -5 & -1 \\ 1 & 2 \end{vmatrix}\right|$

$= \frac{1}{6}|-4(1) - 1(14) - 1(-9)|$

$= \frac{1}{6}|-9|$

$= 1\frac{1}{2}$ units^3

9 $\vec{AS}:\vec{SB} = -3:5$ and $\vec{CT}:\vec{TS} = 1:2$

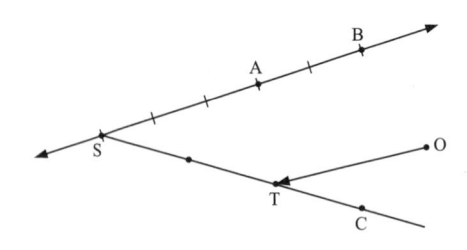

$\vec{OT} = \vec{OC} + \vec{CT}$

$= \mathbf{c} + \frac{1}{3}\vec{CS}$

$= \mathbf{c} + \frac{1}{3}(\vec{CB} + \vec{BS})$

$= \mathbf{c} + \frac{1}{3}(\vec{CO} + \vec{OB}) + \frac{1}{3} \times \frac{5}{2}\vec{BA}$

$= \mathbf{c} + \frac{1}{3}(-\mathbf{c} + \mathbf{b}) + \frac{5}{6}(\vec{BO} + \vec{OA})$

$= \mathbf{c} - \frac{1}{3}\mathbf{c} + \frac{1}{3}\mathbf{b} + \frac{5}{6}(-\mathbf{b} + \mathbf{a})$

$= \mathbf{c} - \frac{1}{3}\mathbf{c} + \frac{1}{3}\mathbf{b} - \frac{5}{6}\mathbf{b} + \frac{5}{6}\mathbf{a}$

$= \frac{5}{6}\mathbf{a} - \frac{1}{2}\mathbf{b} + \frac{2}{3}\mathbf{c}$

10 $\begin{pmatrix} 1 \\ r \\ 2 \end{pmatrix} \bullet \begin{pmatrix} 2 \\ 2 \\ -1 \end{pmatrix} = 0 \qquad \therefore 2 + 2r - 2 = 0$

$\therefore 2r = 0$

$\therefore r = 0$

So, we want a unit vector parallel to $\begin{pmatrix} 1 \\ 0 \\ 2 \end{pmatrix}$.

Now $\begin{pmatrix} 1 \\ 0 \\ 2 \end{pmatrix}$ has length $\sqrt{1+0+4} = \sqrt{5}$

∴ the vectors are $\pm \frac{1}{\sqrt{5}} \begin{pmatrix} 1 \\ 0 \\ 2 \end{pmatrix}$, which are $\frac{1}{\sqrt{5}}\mathbf{i} + \frac{2}{\sqrt{5}}\mathbf{k}$ or $-\frac{1}{\sqrt{5}}\mathbf{i} - \frac{2}{\sqrt{5}}\mathbf{k}$.

11 $\quad |\mathbf{u} \times \mathbf{v}| = |\mathbf{u}||\mathbf{v}|\sin\theta \qquad$ But $\cos^2\theta + \sin^2\theta = 1$

∴ $\sqrt{1+9+16} = 3 \times 5 \times \sin\theta \qquad$ ∴ $\cos^2\theta + \frac{26}{225} = 1$

∴ $\frac{\sqrt{26}}{15} = \sin\theta \qquad$ ∴ $\cos^2\theta = \frac{199}{225}$

∴ $\cos\theta = \pm\frac{\sqrt{199}}{15}$

So, if θ is acute, $\cos\theta = \frac{\sqrt{149}}{15}$ and $\mathbf{u} \bullet \mathbf{v} = |\mathbf{a}||\mathbf{b}|\cos\theta = 3 \times 5 \times \frac{\sqrt{199}}{15} = \sqrt{199}$
and if θ is obtuse, $\cos\theta = -\frac{\sqrt{199}}{15}$ and $\mathbf{u} \bullet \mathbf{v} = -\sqrt{199}$.

12 3 vectors are coplanar if the volume of the tetrahedron defined by them is 0.

∴ $\begin{vmatrix} 1 & 2 & -3 \\ 2 & 2 & 3 \\ 1 & 2-t & t+1 \end{vmatrix} = 0 \qquad$ ∴ $1\begin{vmatrix} 2 & 3 \\ 2-t & t+1 \end{vmatrix} - 2\begin{vmatrix} 2 & 3 \\ 1 & t+1 \end{vmatrix} - 3\begin{vmatrix} 2 & 2 \\ 1 & 2-t \end{vmatrix} = 0$

∴ $1(2t+2-6+3t) - 2(2t+2-3) - 3(4-2t-2) = 0$

∴ $5t - 4 - 4t + 2 - 6 + 6t = 0$

∴ $7t = 8$

∴ $t = \frac{8}{7}$

13

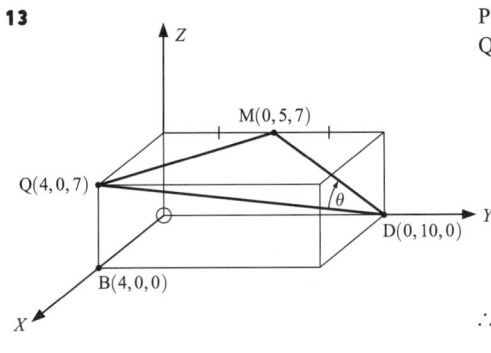

Placing a set of axes with origin at A, as shown, gives Q(4, 0, 7), M(0, 5, 7), D(0, 10, 0).

$\overrightarrow{DQ} = \begin{pmatrix} 4-0 \\ 0-10 \\ 7-0 \end{pmatrix} = \begin{pmatrix} 4 \\ -10 \\ 7 \end{pmatrix}$

$\overrightarrow{DM} = \begin{pmatrix} 0-0 \\ 5-10 \\ 7-0 \end{pmatrix} = \begin{pmatrix} 0 \\ -5 \\ 7 \end{pmatrix}$

$\overrightarrow{DQ} \bullet \overrightarrow{DM} = |\overrightarrow{DQ}||\overrightarrow{DM}|\cos\theta$

∴ $0 + 50 + 49 = \sqrt{16+100+49}\sqrt{0+25+49}\cos\theta$

∴ $99 = \sqrt{165}\sqrt{74}\cos\theta$

∴ $\cos\theta = \frac{99}{\sqrt{165 \times 74}}$

∴ $\theta \approx 26.4°$

REVIEW SET 14E

1 $\overrightarrow{AB} = \begin{pmatrix} 6 \\ 1 \\ -4 \end{pmatrix}$, $\overrightarrow{AC} = \begin{pmatrix} 0 \\ 2 \\ -7 \end{pmatrix}$, $\overrightarrow{BC} = \begin{pmatrix} -6 \\ 1 \\ -3 \end{pmatrix}$

∴ $AB = \sqrt{6^2 + 1^2 + (-4)^2} \qquad AC = \sqrt{0^2 + 2^2 + (-7)^2} \qquad BC = \sqrt{(-6)^2 + 1^2 + (-3)^2}$
$= \sqrt{53}$ units $\qquad\qquad\qquad = \sqrt{53}$ units $\qquad\qquad\qquad = \sqrt{46}$ units

∴ AB = AC, so ABC is an isosceles triangle.

2 $2\begin{pmatrix} s-1 \\ r+1 \\ t \end{pmatrix} = \begin{pmatrix} 4s \\ 3r \\ r \end{pmatrix} + \begin{pmatrix} r \\ -1 \\ s \end{pmatrix}$ $\therefore$ $\begin{pmatrix} 2s-2 \\ 2r+2 \\ 2t \end{pmatrix} = \begin{pmatrix} 4s+r \\ 3r-1 \\ r+s \end{pmatrix}$

$\therefore \begin{cases} 2s-2 = 4s+r \\ 2r+2 = 3r-1 \\ 2t = r+s \end{cases}$ and so $\begin{cases} r = -2s-2 & \dots (1) \\ r = 3 & \dots (2) \\ t = \dfrac{r+s}{2} & \dots (3) \end{cases}$

Substituting (2) into (1) gives $3 = -2s - 2$
$\therefore \quad s = -\dfrac{5}{2}$

Using (3), $t = \dfrac{3 - \frac{5}{2}}{2} = \dfrac{1}{4}$

$\therefore \quad r = 3, \quad s = -\dfrac{5}{2}, \quad t = \dfrac{1}{4}$

3 Let $Q(0, 0, z)$ be a point on the Z-axis.
$PQ = \sqrt{4^2 + (-2)^2 + (z-5)^2} = 6$
$\therefore \quad 16 + 4 + (z-5)^2 = 36$
$\therefore \quad (z-5)^2 = 16$
$\therefore \quad z - 5 = \pm 4$
$\therefore \quad z = 1 \text{ or } 9 \quad \therefore \quad Q \text{ is } (0, 0, 1) \text{ or } (0, 0, 9).$

4 a $\mathbf{a} - \mathbf{x} = 2\mathbf{b}$
$\therefore \quad \mathbf{x} = \mathbf{a} - 2\mathbf{b}$

$= \begin{pmatrix} -1 \\ 3 \\ -2 \end{pmatrix} - 2 \begin{pmatrix} 5 \\ -1 \\ 4 \end{pmatrix}$

$= \begin{pmatrix} -11 \\ 5 \\ -10 \end{pmatrix}$

b $\mathbf{b} - 2\mathbf{x} = -\mathbf{a}$
$\therefore \quad 2\mathbf{x} = \mathbf{a} + \mathbf{b}$
$\therefore \quad \mathbf{x} = \tfrac{1}{2}(\mathbf{a} + \mathbf{b})$

$= \tfrac{1}{2}\left[\begin{pmatrix} -1 \\ 3 \\ -2 \end{pmatrix} + \begin{pmatrix} 5 \\ -1 \\ 4 \end{pmatrix}\right]$

$= \begin{pmatrix} 2 \\ 1 \\ 1 \end{pmatrix}$

5 $\overrightarrow{JK} = \begin{pmatrix} 6 \\ -3 \\ -3 \end{pmatrix}$, $\overrightarrow{JL} = \begin{pmatrix} a+4 \\ b-1 \\ -1 \end{pmatrix}$

If J, K and L are collinear then $\overrightarrow{JK} \parallel \overrightarrow{JL}$

$\therefore \begin{pmatrix} 6 \\ -3 \\ -3 \end{pmatrix} = k \begin{pmatrix} a+4 \\ b-1 \\ -1 \end{pmatrix}$ for some $k \neq 0$ $\quad$ J(-4,1,3), L(a,b,2), K(2,-2,0)

$\therefore \quad k = 3$
$\therefore \quad a + 4 = 2 \text{ and } b - 1 = -1$
$\therefore \quad a = -2 \text{ and } b = 0$

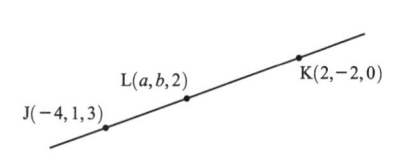

6 a $\mathbf{p} \bullet \mathbf{q}$

$= \begin{pmatrix} 2 \\ -1 \\ 4 \end{pmatrix} \bullet \begin{pmatrix} -1 \\ -4 \\ 2 \end{pmatrix}$

$= 2(-1) - 1(-4) + 4(2)$
$= 10$
$\therefore \quad |\mathbf{p} \bullet \mathbf{q}| = 10$

b If θ is the angle between $\mathbf{p}$ and $\mathbf{q}$ then
$\cos\theta = \dfrac{\mathbf{p} \bullet \mathbf{q}}{|\mathbf{p}||\mathbf{q}|}$

$= \dfrac{10}{\sqrt{2^2 + (-1)^2 + 4^2}\sqrt{(-1)^2 + (-4)^2 + 2^2}}$

$= \dfrac{10}{\sqrt{21}\sqrt{21}}$

$\therefore \quad \theta \approx 61.6°$

7 **a** $\begin{pmatrix} r \\ 4 \\ 3 \end{pmatrix} = k \begin{pmatrix} -5 \\ 10 \\ s \end{pmatrix}$

$\therefore \begin{cases} r = -5k \\ 4 = 10k \\ 3 = ks \end{cases}$

$\therefore \begin{cases} r = -5k \quad \text{.... (1)} \\ k = \frac{2}{5} \\ s = \dfrac{3}{k} \quad \text{.... (2)} \end{cases}$

Substituting $k = \frac{2}{5}$ into (1) and (2) gives

$r = -5(\frac{2}{5})$ and $s = \dfrac{3}{\frac{2}{5}}$

$\therefore r = -2$ and $s = \frac{15}{2}$

b $|3\mathbf{i} - 2\mathbf{j} + \mathbf{k}| = \sqrt{3^2 + (-2)^2 + 1^2} = \sqrt{14}$

$\therefore$ a unit vector in the direction $3\mathbf{i} - 2\mathbf{j} + \mathbf{k}$ is $\frac{1}{\sqrt{14}}(3\mathbf{i} - 2\mathbf{j} + \mathbf{k})$

$\therefore$ a vector 4 units long and parallel to $3\mathbf{i} - 2\mathbf{j} + \mathbf{k}$ is $\pm \frac{4}{\sqrt{14}}(3\mathbf{i} - 2\mathbf{j} + \mathbf{k})$.

8 **a** $\sqrt{k^2 + (\frac{1}{\sqrt{2}})^2 + (-k)^2} = 1$

$\therefore k^2 + \frac{1}{2} + k^2 = 1$

$\therefore 2k^2 = \frac{1}{2}$

$\therefore k^2 = \frac{1}{4}$

$\therefore k = \pm \frac{1}{2}$

b $\begin{pmatrix} 3 \\ 2 \\ -1 \end{pmatrix}$ has length $\sqrt{3^2 + 2^2 + (-1)^2} = \sqrt{14}$ units

$\therefore$ a unit vector in the opposite direction is $-\frac{1}{\sqrt{14}} \begin{pmatrix} 3 \\ 2 \\ -1 \end{pmatrix}$

$\therefore$ a vector of length 5 units in the opposite direction is $-\frac{5}{\sqrt{14}} \begin{pmatrix} 3 \\ 2 \\ -1 \end{pmatrix}$.

9 **a** $\mathbf{u} \bullet \mathbf{v}$

$= \begin{pmatrix} -4 \\ 2 \\ 1 \end{pmatrix} \bullet \begin{pmatrix} -1 \\ 3 \\ -2 \end{pmatrix}$

$= -4(-1) + 2(3) + 1(-2)$

$= 8$

b If θ is the angle between $\mathbf{u}$ and $\mathbf{v}$ then

$\cos \theta = \dfrac{\mathbf{u} \bullet \mathbf{v}}{|\mathbf{u}| \, |\mathbf{v}|}$

$= \dfrac{8}{\sqrt{(-4)^2 + 2^2 + 1^2} \sqrt{(-1)^2 + 3^2 + (-2)^2}}$

$= \dfrac{8}{\sqrt{21}\sqrt{14}}$

$\therefore \theta \approx 62.2°$

10 M is $\left(\dfrac{-2+2}{2}, \dfrac{1+5}{2}, \dfrac{-3-1}{2} \right)$ or $(0, 3, -2)$.

$\therefore \overrightarrow{MD} = \begin{pmatrix} 1 \\ -7 \\ 5 \end{pmatrix}$, $\overrightarrow{MC} = \begin{pmatrix} 3 \\ -6 \\ 4 \end{pmatrix}$

$\therefore \overrightarrow{MD} \bullet \overrightarrow{MC} = |\overrightarrow{MD}||\overrightarrow{MC}| \cos \theta$

$\therefore 3 + 42 + 20 = \sqrt{1 + 49 + 25}\sqrt{9 + 36 + 16} \cos \theta$

$\therefore 65 = \sqrt{75}\sqrt{61} \cos \theta$

$\therefore \theta \approx 16.1°$

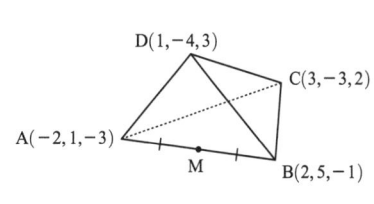

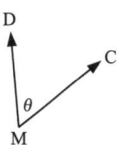

11 a $\overrightarrow{AB} = \begin{pmatrix} -2 \\ 1 \\ 2 \end{pmatrix}$, $\overrightarrow{AC} = \begin{pmatrix} 1 \\ -2 \\ 1 \end{pmatrix}$

$\overrightarrow{AB} \times \overrightarrow{AC} = \begin{vmatrix} \mathbf{i} & \mathbf{j} & \mathbf{k} \\ -2 & 1 & 2 \\ 1 & -2 & 1 \end{vmatrix} = \begin{vmatrix} 1 & 2 \\ -2 & 1 \end{vmatrix} \mathbf{i} - \begin{vmatrix} -2 & 2 \\ 1 & 1 \end{vmatrix} \mathbf{j} + \begin{vmatrix} -2 & 1 \\ 1 & -2 \end{vmatrix} \mathbf{k} = 5\mathbf{i} + 4\mathbf{j} + 3\mathbf{k}$

$\therefore$ the vectors $n(5\mathbf{i} + 4\mathbf{j} + 3\mathbf{k})$, $n \neq 0$ are perpendicular to the plane.
However, we require the vector to have length 10.

$\therefore \sqrt{(5n)^2 + (4n)^2 + (3n)^2} = 10$
$\therefore 25n^2 + 16n^2 + 9n^2 = 100$
$\therefore 50n^2 = 100$
$\therefore n^2 = 2$
$\therefore n = \pm\sqrt{2}$ $\therefore$ the possible vectors are $\pm\sqrt{2}\begin{pmatrix} 5 \\ 4 \\ 3 \end{pmatrix}$.

b Area of triangle ABC $= \frac{1}{2}|5\mathbf{i} + 4\mathbf{j} + 3\mathbf{k}|$
$= \frac{1}{2}\sqrt{5^2 + 4^2 + 3^2}$
$= \frac{1}{2}\sqrt{50}$
$= \frac{5}{2}\sqrt{2}$ units^2

c $\mathbf{b} - \mathbf{a} = \overrightarrow{AB} = \begin{pmatrix} -2 \\ 1 \\ 2 \end{pmatrix}$ $\quad \mathbf{c} - \mathbf{a} = \overrightarrow{AC} = \begin{pmatrix} 1 \\ -2 \\ 1 \end{pmatrix}$ $\quad \mathbf{d} - \mathbf{a} = \overrightarrow{AD} = \begin{pmatrix} -1 \\ 2 \\ k-1 \end{pmatrix}$

$\therefore (\mathbf{b} - \mathbf{a}) \bullet (\mathbf{c} - \mathbf{a}) \times (\mathbf{d} - \mathbf{a})$

$= \begin{vmatrix} -2 & 1 & 2 \\ 1 & -2 & 1 \\ -1 & 2 & k-1 \end{vmatrix} = -2\begin{vmatrix} -2 & 1 \\ 2 & k-1 \end{vmatrix} - 1\begin{vmatrix} 1 & 1 \\ -1 & k-1 \end{vmatrix} + 2\begin{vmatrix} 1 & -2 \\ -1 & 2 \end{vmatrix}$

$= -2(-2k + 2 - 2) - (k - 1 + 1) + 2(2 - 2)$
$= 4k - k$
$= 3k$

$\therefore$ A, B, C and D are coplanar when $3k = 0$ $\therefore$ $k = 0$

12 a $\begin{pmatrix} 2-t \\ 3 \\ t \end{pmatrix} \bullet \begin{pmatrix} t \\ 4 \\ t+1 \end{pmatrix} = 0$

$\therefore (2-t)t + 12 + t(t+1) = 0$
$\therefore 2t - t^2 + 12 + t^2 + t = 0$
$\therefore 3t + 12 = 0$
$\therefore t = -4$

b $\overrightarrow{KL} = \begin{pmatrix} -7 \\ 1 \\ 3 \end{pmatrix}$, $\overrightarrow{KM} = \begin{pmatrix} -2 \\ -2 \\ -1 \end{pmatrix}$, $\overrightarrow{LM} = \begin{pmatrix} 5 \\ -3 \\ -4 \end{pmatrix}$

Now $\overrightarrow{KM} \bullet \overrightarrow{LM} = \begin{pmatrix} -2 \\ -2 \\ -1 \end{pmatrix} \bullet \begin{pmatrix} 5 \\ -3 \\ -4 \end{pmatrix}$

$= -2(5) - 2(-3) - 1(-4)$
$= 0$

$\therefore$ [KM] and [LM] are perpendicular
$\therefore$ triangle KLM is right angled at M.

Chapter 15
COMPLEX NUMBERS

EXERCISE 15A.1

1

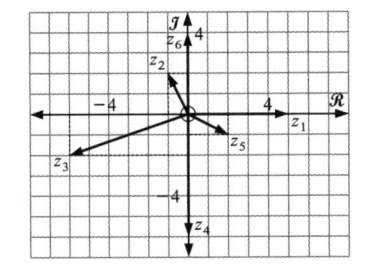

2 a
$$z + w = (1 + 2i) + (3 - i) = 4 + i$$ 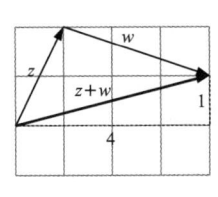

b 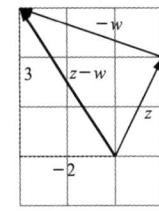
$$z - w = (1 + 2i) - (3 - i) = -2 + 3i$$

c 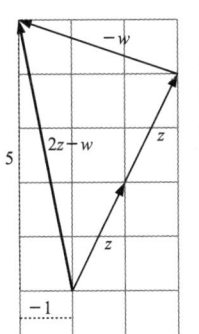
$$2z - w = 2(1 + 2i) - (3 - i) = 2 + 4i - 3 + i = -1 + 5i$$

d 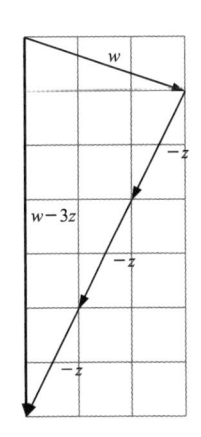
$$w - 3z = (3 - i) - 3(1 + 2i) = 3 - i - 3 - 6i = -7i$$

3 a 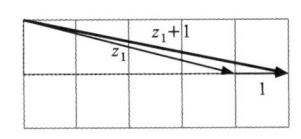
$$z_1 + 1 = 4 - i + 1 = 5 - i$$

b 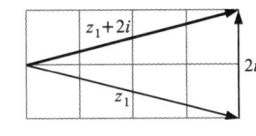
$$z_1 + 2i = 4 - i + 2i = 4 + i$$

c 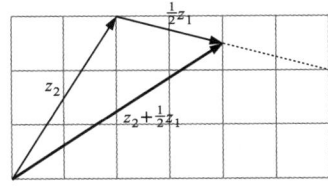
$$z_2 + \tfrac{1}{2}z_1 = (2 + 3i) + \tfrac{1}{2}(4 - i) = 2 + 3i + 2 - \tfrac{1}{2}i = 4 + \tfrac{5}{2}i$$

d 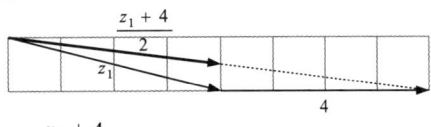
$$\frac{z_1 + 4}{2} = \frac{4 - i + 4}{2} = 4 - \tfrac{1}{2}i$$

4 a $3z$ is parallel to z and 3 times its length.

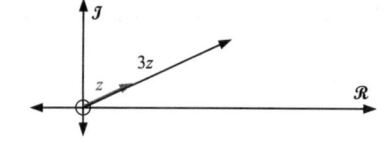

b $-2z$ is parallel to z, in the opposite direction and twice its length.

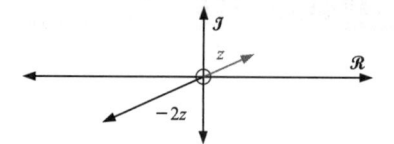

c Reflect z in a horizontal line through the start of z.

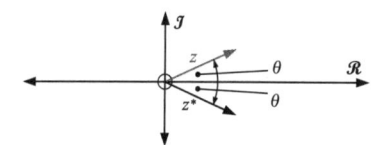

d Add $-z$ to $3i$.

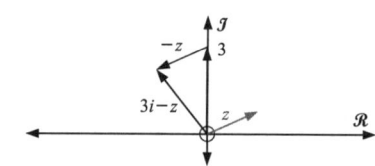

e Add $-z$ to 2.

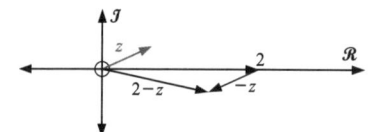

f Reflect z in a horizontal line through the start of z and then add i.

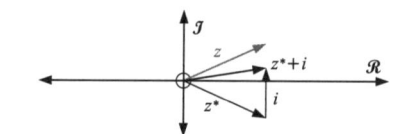

g Add z and 2 and find the vector $\frac{1}{3}$ of the length of the result.

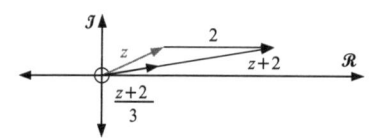

h Add z and -4 and find the vector $\frac{1}{2}$ of the length of the result.

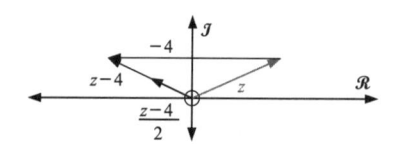

EXERCISE 15A.2

1 a

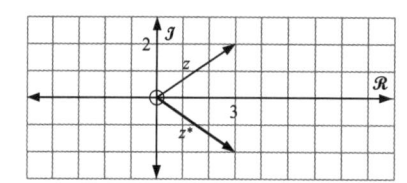

b

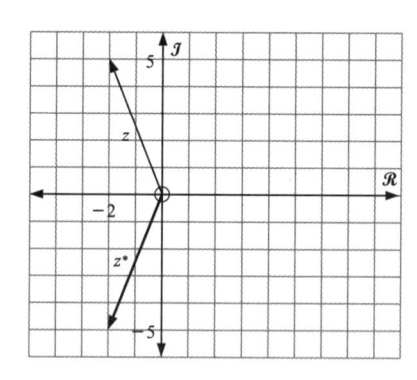

2

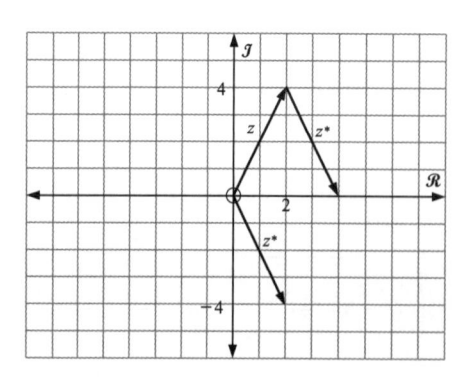

No matter where z is placed, $z + z^*$ lies on the real axis. So, $z + z^*$ is always real.

3

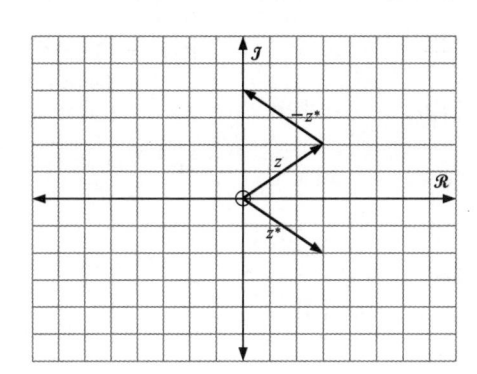

The resulting vector will always lie along the imaginary axis.
So, $z - z^*$ will be purely imaginary or zero.
When z is real, $z - z^* = 0$.

4 If z is real then z^* will also be real. In fact if $z = a$, $z^* = a$, so $z^* = z$ if z is real.

5

$(a+i)(3+bi) = 40 - 74i$
$\therefore \quad 3a + abi + 3i - b = 40 - 74i$
$\therefore \quad (3a - b) + i(ab + 3) = 40 - 74i$

Equating real and imaginary parts,
$3a - b = 40 \quad \therefore \quad b = 3a - 40 \quad \dots$ (1)
$ab + 3 = -74 \quad \dots$ (2)

Substituting (1) into (2) gives
$a(3a - 40) + 3 = -74$
$\therefore \quad 3a^2 - 40a + 77 = 0$
$\therefore \quad (3a - 7)(a - 11) = 0$
$\therefore \quad a = \frac{7}{3}$ or 11
$\therefore \quad a = 11 \quad \{a \in \mathbb{Z}\}$
and $\quad b = 3(11) - 40 \quad \{(1)\}$
$\quad \quad \quad = -7$

EXERCISE 15B.1

1
a $|3 - 4i|$
$= \sqrt{3^2 + (-4)^2}$
$= \sqrt{9 + 16}$
$= \sqrt{25}$
$= 5$

b $|5 + 12i|$
$= \sqrt{5^2 + 12^2}$
$= \sqrt{25 + 144}$
$= \sqrt{169}$
$= 13$

c $|-8 + 2i|$
$= \sqrt{(-8)^2 + 2^2}$
$= \sqrt{64 + 4}$
$= \sqrt{68}$
$= 2\sqrt{17}$

d $|3i|$
$= \sqrt{0^2 + 3^2}$
$= \sqrt{9}$
$= 3$

e $|-4|$
$= \sqrt{(-4)^2 + 0^2}$
$= \sqrt{16}$
$= 4$

2
a $|z|$
$= |2 + i|$
$= \sqrt{2^2 + 1^2}$
$= \sqrt{5}$

b $|z^*|$
$= |2 - i|$
$= \sqrt{2^2 + (-1)^2}$
$= \sqrt{5}$

c $|z^*|^2$
$= (\sqrt{5})^2$
$= 5$

d zz^*
$= (2 + i)(2 - i)$
$= 4 - i^2$
$= 5$

e $|zw|$
$= |(2 + i)(-1 + 3i)|$
$= |-2 + 6i - i + 3i^2|$
$= |-5 + 5i|$
$= \sqrt{(-5)^2 + 5^2}$
$= \sqrt{50}$ or $5\sqrt{2}$

f $|z||w|$
$= \sqrt{2^2 + 1^2}\sqrt{(-1)^2 + 3^2}$
$= \sqrt{5} \times \sqrt{10}$
$= \sqrt{50}$
$= 5\sqrt{2}$

g $\left|\dfrac{z}{w}\right|$

$= \left|\dfrac{2+i}{-1+3i}\right|$

$= \left|\dfrac{(2+i)}{(-1+3i)} \times \dfrac{(-1-3i)}{(-1-3i)}\right|$

$= \left|\dfrac{-2-6i-i-3i^2}{(-1)^2-(3i)^2}\right|$

$= \left|\dfrac{-2+3-7i}{10}\right|$

$= \left|\dfrac{1}{10} - \dfrac{7}{10}i\right|$

$= \sqrt{\left(\dfrac{1}{10}\right)^2 + \left(\dfrac{-7}{10}\right)^2}$

$= \sqrt{\dfrac{1+49}{100}}$

$= \sqrt{\dfrac{50}{100}}$

$= \dfrac{1}{\sqrt{2}}$

h $\dfrac{|z|}{|w|}$

$= \dfrac{\sqrt{5}}{\sqrt{10}}$

$= \sqrt{\dfrac{5}{10}}$

$= \dfrac{1}{\sqrt{2}}$

i $z^2 = (2+i)^2$
$= 4 + 4i + i^2$
$= 3 + 4i$

$\therefore \ |z^2| = \sqrt{3^2+4^2}$
$= \sqrt{25}$
$= 5$

j $|z|^2$
$= (\sqrt{5})^2$ {from **a**}
$= 5$

k $z^3 = z^2 \times z$
$= (3+4i)(2+i)$
$= 6 + 3i + 8i + 4i^2$
$= 2 + 11i$

$\therefore \ |z^3| = \sqrt{2^2 + 11^2}$
$= \sqrt{4+121}$
$= \sqrt{125}$
$= 5\sqrt{5}$

l $|z|^3$
$= (\sqrt{5})^3$ {from **a**}
$= \sqrt{125}$
$= 5\sqrt{5}$

3 Rules for Modulus

(1) $zz^* = |z|^2$ (2) $|z^*| = |z|$ (3) $|zw| = |z|\,|w|$

(4) $\left|\dfrac{z}{w}\right| = \dfrac{|z|}{|w|}$ (5) $|z^n| = |z|^n$

4 a Let $z = a + bi$

$\therefore \ |z^*| = |a-bi|$
$= \sqrt{a^2 + (-b)^2}$
$= \sqrt{a^2 + b^2}$
$= |a+bi|$
$= |z|$ as required

b Let $z = a + bi$

$\therefore \ zz^* = (a+bi)(a-bi)$
$= a^2 - b^2 i^2$
$= a^2 + b^2$
$= \left(\sqrt{a^2+b^2}\right)^2$
$= |z|^2$ as required

5 $z = \cos\theta + i\sin\theta$, $\therefore \ |z| = \sqrt{\cos^2\theta + \sin^2\theta}$
$= \sqrt{1}$
$= 1$

6 $\left|\dfrac{z}{w}\right| \times |w| = \left|\dfrac{z}{w} \times w\right|$ {using $|z_1|\,|z_2| = |z_1 z_2|$}
$= |z|$

$\therefore \ \left|\dfrac{z}{w}\right| \times |w| = |z|$

$\therefore \ \left|\dfrac{z}{w}\right| = \dfrac{|z|}{|w|}$ provided $w \neq 0$ {dividing both sides by $|w|$}

7 a i $|z_1 z_2 z_3| = |(z_1 z_2)z_3|$
$= |z_1 z_2|\,|z_3|$ {as $|zw| = |z|\,|w|$}
$= |z_1|\,|z_2|\,|z_3|$ {$|zw| = |z|\,|w|$ again}

Letting $z_1 = z_2 = z_3 = z$ we get the result that $|z^3| = |z \times z \times z|$
$= |z| \times |z| \times |z|$
$= |z|^3$

ii Now extending this result by the same argument
$$|z_1 z_2 z_3 z_4| = |(z_1 z_2 z_3) z_4|$$
$$= |z_1 z_2 z_3| |z_4|$$
$$= |z_1| |z_2| |z_3| |z_4|$$
and putting $z_1 = z_2 = z_3 = z_4 = z$ we get
$$\left|z^4\right| = |z \times z \times z \times z| = |z| \times |z| \times |z| \times |z| = |z|^4$$

b The generalisation of **a** is: $|z_1 z_2 z_3 .... z_n| = |z_1| |z_2| |z_3| .... |z_n|$ and that $|z^n| = |z|^n$

c P_n is "$|z_1 z_2 .... z_n| = |z_1| |z_2| .... |z_n|$" for $n \in \mathbb{Z}^+$.
Proof: (By the principle of mathematical induction)
(1) If $n = 1$ then LHS $= |z_1|$, RHS $= |z_1|$ $\therefore$ P_1 is true.
(2) If P_k is true then $\quad |z_1 z_2 .... z_k| = |z_1| |z_2| .... |z_k|$
$$|z_1 z_2 .... z_k z_{k+1}| = |(z_1 z_2 .... z_k) z_{k+1}|$$
$$= |z_1 z_2 .... z_k| |z_{k+1}| \quad \{|z| |w| = |zw|\}$$
$$= |z_1| |z_2| .... |z_k| |z_{k+1}| \quad \{P_k\}$$
$\therefore$ P_1 is true, and P_{k+1} is true whenever P_k is true.
$\therefore$ P_n is true for all $n \in \mathbb{Z}^+$ {Principle of mathematical induction}

d $|z_1 z_2 .... z_n| = |z_1| |z_2| .... |z_n|$
Letting $z_1 = z_2 = ... = z_n = z$ we have $|z^n| = |z|^n$

e If $z = 1 - i\sqrt{3}$ then $|z| = \sqrt{1^2 + (-\sqrt{3})^2}$ $\therefore$ $\left|z^{20}\right| = |z|^{20}$
$$= \sqrt{4} \qquad\qquad\qquad\qquad = 2^{20}$$
$$= 2 \qquad\qquad\qquad\qquad = 1\,048\,576$$

8 a $|2z|$
$= |2| |z|$
$= 2 \times 3$
$= 6$

b $|-3z|$
$= |-3| |z|$
$= 3 \times 3$
$= 9$

c $|(1 + 2i)z|$
$= |1 + 2i| \times |z|$
$= \sqrt{1 + 4} \times 3$
$= 3\sqrt{5}$

d $|iz|$
$= |i| |z|$
$= 1 \times 3$
$= 3$

e $\left|\dfrac{1}{z}\right|$
$= \dfrac{|1|}{|z|}$
$= \dfrac{1}{3}$

f $\left|\dfrac{2i}{z^2}\right|$
$= \dfrac{|2i|}{|z|^2}$
$= \dfrac{2}{3^2}$
$= \dfrac{2}{9}$

9 a $w = \dfrac{z+1}{z-1}$. Let $z = a + bi$, $\therefore$ $w = \dfrac{a + bi + 1}{a + bi - 1}$
$$= \dfrac{(a+1) + bi}{(a-1) + bi}$$
$$= \dfrac{(a+1) + bi}{(a-1) + bi} \times \dfrac{(a-1) - bi}{(a-1) - bi}$$
$$= \dfrac{(a+1)(a-1) - b(a+1)i + b(a-1)i - b^2 i^2}{(a-1)^2 - (bi)^2}$$
$$= \dfrac{a^2 - 1 - abi - bi + abi - bi + b^2}{(a-1)^2 + b^2}$$
$$= \left(\dfrac{a^2 + b^2 - 1}{(a-1)^2 + b^2}\right) + \left(\dfrac{-2b}{(a-1)^2 + b^2}\right) i$$

b $\quad \mathcal{Re}\,(w) = \dfrac{a^2+b^2-1}{(a-1)^2+b^2} = \dfrac{a^2+b^2-1}{a^2-2a+1+b^2} = \dfrac{a^2+b^2-1}{a^2+b^2-2a+1}$

Since $|z|=1$ $\quad \sqrt{a^2+b^2}=1$ $\quad \therefore \quad a^2+b^2=1$

$\therefore \quad \mathcal{Re}\,(w) = \dfrac{1-1}{1-2a+1} = 0 \quad$ provided $\quad a \neq 1$

If $a=1$, then $\mathcal{Re}\,(w)$ is undefined.

10
$$|z+9| = 3|z+1|$$
$$\therefore \quad |z+9|^2 = 9|z+1|^2$$
$$\therefore \quad (z+9)(z+9)^* = 9(z+1)(z+1)^* \qquad \{zz^* = |z|^2\}$$
$$\therefore \quad (z+9)(z^*+9) = 9(z+1)(z^*+1) \qquad \{(z \pm w)^* = z^* \pm w^*\}$$
$$\therefore \quad zz^* + 9z + 9z^* + 81 = 9zz^* + 9z + 9z^* + 9$$
$$\therefore \quad 72 = 8zz^*$$
$$\therefore \quad zz^* = 9$$
$$\therefore \quad |z|^2 = 9$$
$$\therefore \quad |z| = 3 \quad \{|z| > 0\}$$

11
$$\left|\dfrac{z+4}{z+1}\right| = 2$$
$$\therefore \quad \dfrac{|z+4|}{|z+1|} = 2 \qquad \left\{\left|\dfrac{z}{w}\right| = \dfrac{|z|}{|w|}\right\}$$
$$\therefore \quad |z+4| = 2|z+1|$$
$$\therefore \quad |z+4|^2 = 4|z+1|^2$$
$$\therefore \quad (z+4)(z+4)^* = 4(z+1)(z+1)^* \qquad \{zz^* = |z|^2\}$$
$$\therefore \quad (z+4)(z^*+4) = 4(z+1)(z^*+1) \qquad \{(z \pm w)^* = z^* \pm w^*\}$$
$$\therefore \quad zz^* + 4z + 4z^* + 16 = 4zz^* + 4z + 4z^* + 4$$
$$\therefore \quad 12 = 3zz^*$$
$$\therefore \quad zz^* = 4$$
$$\therefore \quad |z|^2 = 4$$
$$\therefore \quad |z| = 2 \qquad \{|z| > 0\}$$

12
$$|z+w| = |z-w|$$
$$\therefore \quad |z+w|^2 = |z-w|^2$$
$$\therefore \quad (z+w)(z+w)^* = (z-w)(z-w)^* \qquad \{zz^* = |z|^2\}$$
$$\therefore \quad (z+w)(z^*+w^*) = (z-w)(z^*-w^*) \qquad \{(z \pm w)^* = z^* \pm w^*\}$$
$$\therefore \quad zz^* + zw^* + wz^* + ww^* = zz^* - zw^* - wz^* + ww^*$$
$$\therefore \quad zw^* + wz^* = -zw^* - wz^*$$
$$\therefore \quad 2zw^* = -2wz^*$$
$$\therefore \quad \dfrac{z}{z^*} = -\dfrac{w}{w^*}$$

EXERCISE 15B.2

1 a $A(3, 6)$ $B(-1, 2)$ $z = 3+6i$ $w = -1+2i$

i $\quad z - w = (3+6i) - (-1+2i)$
$\qquad \qquad = 4 + 4i$

$\quad |z-w| = \sqrt{4^2+4^2}$
$\qquad \qquad = \sqrt{32}$
$\qquad \qquad = 4\sqrt{2}$

$\therefore \quad AB = 4\sqrt{2}$ units

ii $\quad \dfrac{z+w}{2} = \dfrac{(3+6i)+(-1+2i)}{2}$
$\qquad \qquad = \dfrac{2+8i}{2}$
$\qquad \qquad = 1+4i$, and so M is at $(1, 4)$

b $A(-4, 7)$ $B(1, -3)$ $z = -4 + 7i$ $w = 1 - 3i$

i $z - w = (-4 + 7i) - (1 - 3i)$
$= -5 + 10i$

$|z - w| = \sqrt{(-5)^2 + 10^2}$
$= \sqrt{125}$
$= 5\sqrt{5}$

$\therefore$ $AB = 5\sqrt{5}$ units

ii $\dfrac{z + w}{2} = \dfrac{(-4 + 7i) + (1 - 3i)}{2}$
$= \dfrac{-3 + 4i}{2}$
$= -\dfrac{3}{2} + 2i$

and so M is at $\left(-\dfrac{3}{2}, 2\right)$

2 a i $\overrightarrow{OQ} = z + w$ **ii** $\overrightarrow{PR} = w - z$

b In $\triangle OPQ$ $|z + w|$ represents the length of OQ, $|z| =$ length of OP and $|w|$ the length of PQ.
Now if w, z are not parallel we will form the $\triangle OPQ$ and this means $OQ < OP + PQ$
$\therefore$ $|z + w| < |z| + |w|$
If w and z are parallel then we form a straight line and $OQ = OP + PQ$
$\therefore$ $|z + w| = |z| + |w|$
Consequently $|z + w| \leqslant |z| + |w|$

c In $\triangle OPR$, the length of RP is represented by $|z - w|$. If w and z are not parallel, we form a triangle and $RP + OP > OR$. $\therefore$ $|z - w| + |z| > |w|$
$\therefore$ $|z - w| > |w| - |z|$
Equality will occur when w is parallel to z, in which case a straight line OPR is formed and
$|z - w| = |w| - |z|$
Consequently $|z - w| \geqslant |w| - |z|$

3 a $z \mapsto z^*$. Reflection in the real axis.
b $z \mapsto -z$. Rotation about O, anticlockwise π.
c $z \mapsto -z^*$. Reflection in the imaginary axis.
d $z \mapsto -iz$. Rotation about O, clockwise $\frac{\pi}{2}$.

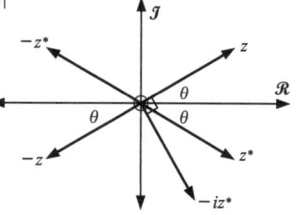

4 $\dfrac{50}{z^*} - \dfrac{10}{z} = 2 + 9i$, where $z = a + bi$

$\therefore$ $50z - 10z^* = (2 + 9i)(|z|^2)$
{multiply both sides by $zz^* = |z|^2$}
$\therefore$ $50(a + bi) - 10(a - bi) = (2 + 9i)(40)$ $\{|z| = 2\sqrt{10}\}$
$\therefore$ $40a + 60bi = 80 + 360i$

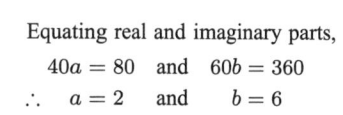

Equating real and imaginary parts,
$40a = 80$ and $60b = 360$
$\therefore$ $a = 2$ and $b = 6$
$\therefore$ $z = 2 + 6i$

EXERCISE 15B.3

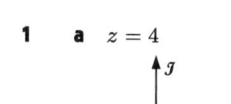

1 a $z = 4$ 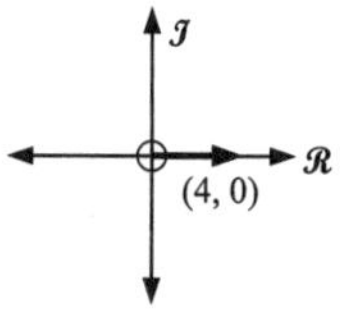
(4, 0)
arg $z = 0$
$|z| = 4$
$\therefore$ $z = 4$ cis 0

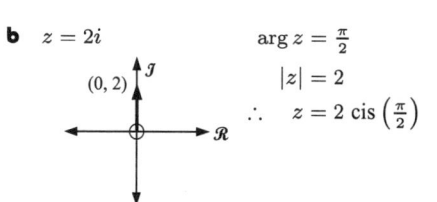

b $z = 2i$
(0, 2)
arg $z = \dfrac{\pi}{2}$
$|z| = 2$
$\therefore$ $z = 2$ cis $\left(\dfrac{\pi}{2}\right)$

c $z = -6$ 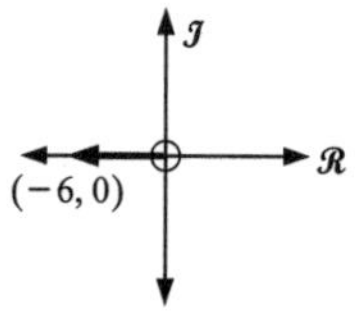
(-6, 0)
arg $z = \pi$
$|z| = 6$
$\therefore$ $z = 6$ cis π

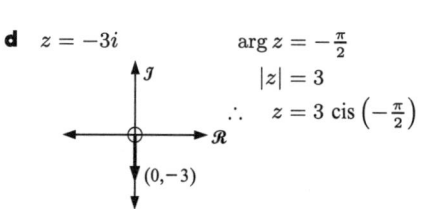

d $z = -3i$
(0, -3)
arg $z = -\dfrac{\pi}{2}$
$|z| = 3$
$\therefore$ $z = 3$ cis $\left(-\dfrac{\pi}{2}\right)$

e $z = 1 + i$ $\arg z = \frac{\pi}{4}$

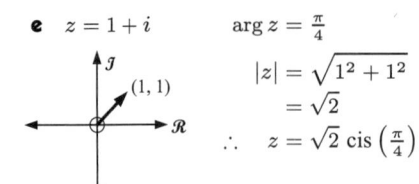

$|z| = \sqrt{1^2 + 1^2}$
$= \sqrt{2}$
$\therefore \quad z = \sqrt{2} \operatorname{cis}\left(\frac{\pi}{4}\right)$

f $z = 2 - 2i$ $\arg z = -\frac{\pi}{4}$

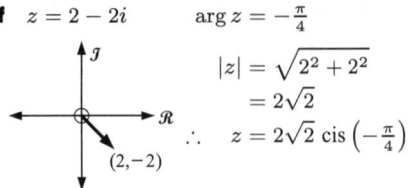

$|z| = \sqrt{2^2 + 2^2}$
$= 2\sqrt{2}$
$\therefore \quad z = 2\sqrt{2} \operatorname{cis}\left(-\frac{\pi}{4}\right)$

g $z = -\sqrt{3} + i,$ $\arg z = \frac{5\pi}{6}$

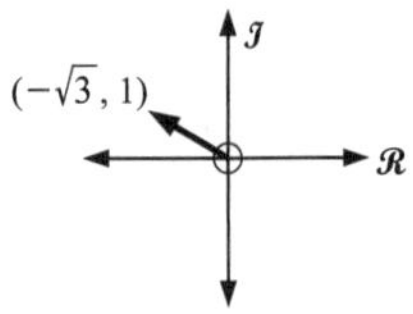

$|z| = \sqrt{(-\sqrt{3})^2 + 1^2}$
$= \sqrt{4}$
$= 2$
$\therefore \quad z = 2 \operatorname{cis}\left(\frac{5\pi}{6}\right)$

h $z = 2\sqrt{3} + 2i$ $\arg z = \frac{\pi}{6}$

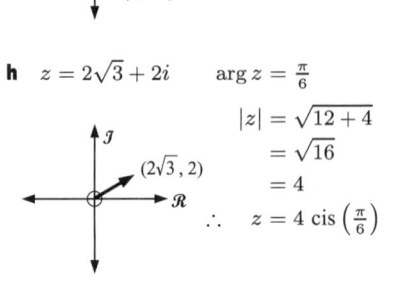

$|z| = \sqrt{12 + 4}$
$= \sqrt{16}$
$= 4$
$\therefore \quad z = 4 \operatorname{cis}\left(\frac{\pi}{6}\right)$

2 $z = 0 = 0 + 0i$ cannot be written in polar form. The vector representing $\overrightarrow{OP}$ has length zero, and an argument is not defined (no angle can be formed with the positive x-axis).

3 If $k = 0$ it is not possible.

If $k > 0$, $|z| = \sqrt{k^2 + k^2}$
$= k\sqrt{2}$
$\arg z = \frac{\pi}{4}$
$\therefore \quad z = k\sqrt{2} \operatorname{cis}\left(\frac{\pi}{4}\right)$

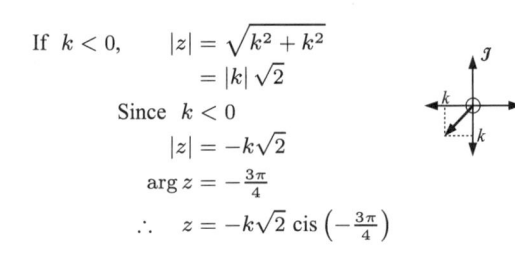

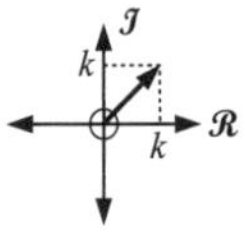

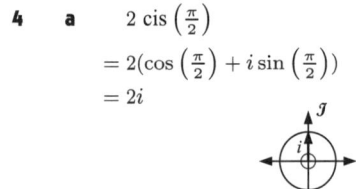

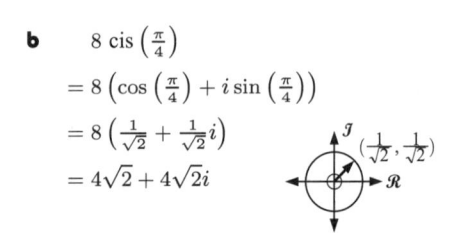

If $k < 0$, $|z| = \sqrt{k^2 + k^2}$
$= |k|\sqrt{2}$
Since $k < 0$
$|z| = -k\sqrt{2}$
$\arg z = -\frac{3\pi}{4}$
$\therefore \quad z = -k\sqrt{2} \operatorname{cis}\left(-\frac{3\pi}{4}\right)$

4 a $2 \operatorname{cis}\left(\frac{\pi}{2}\right)$
$= 2(\cos\left(\frac{\pi}{2}\right) + i\sin\left(\frac{\pi}{2}\right))$
$= 2i$

b $8 \operatorname{cis}\left(\frac{\pi}{4}\right)$
$= 8\left(\cos\left(\frac{\pi}{4}\right) + i\sin\left(\frac{\pi}{4}\right)\right)$
$= 8\left(\frac{1}{\sqrt{2}} + \frac{1}{\sqrt{2}}i\right)$
$= 4\sqrt{2} + 4\sqrt{2}i$

c $4 \operatorname{cis}\left(\frac{\pi}{6}\right)$
$= 4\left(\cos\left(\frac{\pi}{6}\right) + i\sin\left(\frac{\pi}{6}\right)\right)$
$= 4\left(\frac{\sqrt{3}}{2} + \frac{1}{2}i\right)$
$= 2\sqrt{3} + 2i$

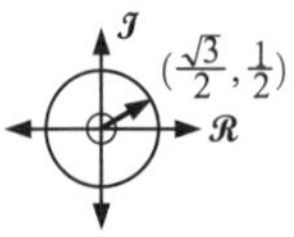

d $\sqrt{2} \operatorname{cis}\left(-\frac{\pi}{4}\right)$
$= \sqrt{2}\left(\cos\left(-\frac{\pi}{4}\right) + i\sin\left(-\frac{\pi}{4}\right)\right)$
$= \sqrt{2}\left(\frac{1}{\sqrt{2}} - \frac{1}{\sqrt{2}}i\right)$
$= 1 - i$

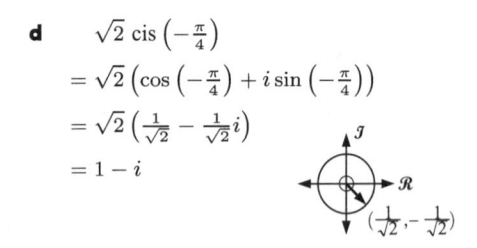

e $\sqrt{3} \operatorname{cis}\left(\frac{2\pi}{3}\right)$
$= \sqrt{3}\left(\cos\left(\frac{2\pi}{3}\right) + i\sin\left(\frac{2\pi}{3}\right)\right)$
$= \sqrt{3}\left(-\frac{1}{2} + \frac{\sqrt{3}}{2}i\right)$
$= -\frac{\sqrt{3}}{2} + \frac{3}{2}i$

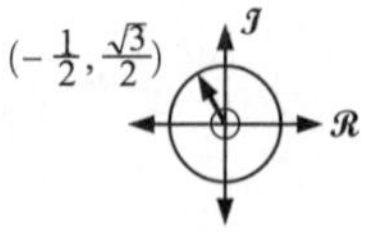

f $5 \operatorname{cis} \pi$
$= 5(\cos \pi + i \sin \pi)$
$= 5(-1)$
$= -5$

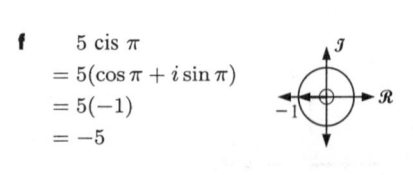

5 a cis 0
$= \cos 0 + i \sin 0$
$= 1$

b $|\text{cis } \theta|$
$= |\cos \theta + i \sin \theta|$
$= \sqrt{\cos^2 \theta + \sin^2 \theta}$
$= \sqrt{1}$
$= 1$

c cis $\alpha \times$ cis $\beta = (\cos \alpha + i \sin \alpha)(\cos \beta + i \sin \beta)$
$= \cos \alpha \cos \beta + i \cos \alpha \sin \beta + i \sin \alpha \cos \beta + i^2 \sin \alpha \sin \beta$
$= [\cos \alpha \cos \beta - \sin \alpha \sin \beta] + i [\sin \alpha \cos \beta + \sin \beta \cos \alpha]$
$= \cos (\alpha + \beta) + i \sin (\alpha + \beta)$
$= \text{cis } (\alpha + \beta)$

EXERCISE 15B.4

1 a cis θ cis 2θ
$= \text{cis } (\theta + 2\theta)$
$= \text{cis } 3\theta$

b $\dfrac{\text{cis } 3\theta}{\text{cis } \theta}$
$= \text{cis } (3\theta - \theta)$
$= \text{cis } 2\theta$

c $[\text{cis } \theta]^3$
$= (\text{cis } \theta)(\text{cis } \theta)(\text{cis } \theta)$
$= (\text{cis } 2\theta)(\text{cis } \theta)$
$= \text{cis } 3\theta$

d cis $\left(\dfrac{\pi}{18}\right) \times$ cis $\left(\dfrac{\pi}{9}\right)$
$= \text{cis } \left(\dfrac{\pi}{18} + \dfrac{\pi}{9}\right)$
$= \text{cis } \left(\dfrac{3\pi}{18}\right)$
$= \text{cis } \left(\dfrac{\pi}{6}\right)$
$= \dfrac{\sqrt{3}}{2} + \dfrac{1}{2}i$

e $2 \text{ cis } \left(\dfrac{\pi}{12}\right) \text{ cis } \left(\dfrac{\pi}{6}\right)$
$= 2 \text{ cis } \left(\dfrac{\pi}{12} + \dfrac{\pi}{6}\right)$
$= 2 \text{ cis } \left(\dfrac{3\pi}{12}\right)$
$= 2 \text{ cis } \left(\dfrac{\pi}{4}\right)$
$= 2 \left(\dfrac{1}{\sqrt{2}} + \dfrac{1}{\sqrt{2}}i\right)$
$= \sqrt{2} + i\sqrt{2}$

f $2 \text{ cis } \left(\dfrac{2\pi}{5}\right) \times 4 \text{ cis } \left(\dfrac{8\pi}{5}\right)$
$= 8 \text{ cis } \left(\dfrac{2\pi}{5} + \dfrac{8\pi}{5}\right)$
$= 8 \text{ cis } 2\pi$
$= 8$

g $\dfrac{4 \text{ cis } \left(\dfrac{\pi}{12}\right)}{2 \text{ cis } \left(\dfrac{7\pi}{12}\right)}$
$= 2 \text{ cis } \left(\dfrac{\pi}{12} - \dfrac{7\pi}{12}\right)$
$= 2 \text{ cis } \left(-\dfrac{6\pi}{12}\right)$
$= 2 \text{ cis } \left(-\dfrac{\pi}{2}\right)$
$= -2i$

h $\dfrac{\sqrt{32} \text{ cis } \left(\dfrac{\pi}{8}\right)}{\sqrt{2} \text{ cis } \left(\dfrac{-7\pi}{8}\right)}$
$= \dfrac{\sqrt{32}}{\sqrt{2}} \text{ cis } \left(\dfrac{\pi}{8} - \dfrac{-7\pi}{8}\right)$
$= \sqrt{16} \text{ cis } \left(\dfrac{8\pi}{8}\right)$
$= 4 \text{ cis } (\pi)$
$= -4$

i $\left[\sqrt{2} \text{ cis } \left(\dfrac{\pi}{8}\right)\right]^4$
$= \sqrt{2} \text{ cis } \left(\dfrac{\pi}{8}\right) \times \sqrt{2} \text{ cis } \left(\dfrac{\pi}{8}\right)$
$\quad \times \sqrt{2} \text{ cis } \left(\dfrac{\pi}{8}\right) \times \sqrt{2} \text{ cis } \left(\dfrac{\pi}{8}\right)$
$= (\sqrt{2})^4 \text{ cis } \left(\dfrac{\pi}{8} + \dfrac{\pi}{8} + \dfrac{\pi}{8} + \dfrac{\pi}{8}\right)$
$= 4 \text{ cis } \left(\dfrac{\pi}{2}\right)$
$= 4i$

2 a cis 17π
$= \text{cis } (\pi + 8(2\pi))$
$= \text{cis } \pi$
$= -1$

b cis (-37π)
$= \text{cis } (\pi - 19(2\pi))$
$= \text{cis } \pi$
$= -1$

c cis $\left(\dfrac{91\pi}{3}\right)$
$= \text{cis } \left(\dfrac{\pi}{3} + 15(2\pi)\right)$
$= \text{cis } \left(\dfrac{\pi}{3}\right)$
$= \dfrac{1}{2} + \dfrac{\sqrt{3}}{2}i$

3 a $z = 2 \text{ cis } \theta$
$|z| = 2$
$\arg z = \theta$

b $z^* = 2 \text{ cis } (-\theta)$

c $-z = 2 \text{ cis } (\theta + \pi)$

d $-z^* = 2 \text{ cis } (\pi - \theta)$

4 **a** $i = 1 \operatorname{cis}\left(\frac{\pi}{2}\right) = \operatorname{cis}\left(\frac{\pi}{2}\right)$ 	**b** $iz = \operatorname{cis}\left(\frac{\pi}{2}\right) \times r \operatorname{cis} \theta$
$$= r \operatorname{cis}\left(\theta + \frac{\pi}{2}\right)$$

c iz has the same length as z and its argument is $\frac{\pi}{2}$ more than the argument of z, so iz is an anticlockwise rotation of z about O through $\frac{\pi}{2}$ radians.

d $z \mapsto -iz$ $\quad -iz = \operatorname{cis}\left(-\frac{\pi}{2}\right) \times r \operatorname{cis} \theta$
$$= r \operatorname{cis}\left(\theta - \frac{\pi}{2}\right) \quad \text{So, a clockwise rotation of } \frac{\pi}{2} \text{ about O maps } z \text{ onto } -iz.$$

5 **a** $\cos \theta - i \sin \theta$ 	**b** $\sin \theta - i \cos \theta$
$= \cos(-\theta) + i \sin(-\theta)$	$= -i \cos \theta - i^2 \sin \theta$
$= \operatorname{cis}(-\theta)$	$= -i(\cos \theta + i \sin \theta)$
$\phantom{= \operatorname{cis}(-\theta)}$	$= \operatorname{cis}\left(-\frac{\pi}{2}\right) \operatorname{cis} \theta$
$\phantom{= \operatorname{cis}(-\theta)}$	$= \operatorname{cis}\left(\theta - \frac{\pi}{2}\right)$

If $z = r \operatorname{cis} \theta$ then $z^* = r \operatorname{cis}(-\theta)$ in polar form.

6 **a** Consider $\cos\left(\frac{\pi}{12}\right) + i \sin\left(\frac{\pi}{12}\right) = \operatorname{cis}\left(\frac{\pi}{12}\right)$
$$= \operatorname{cis}\left(\tfrac{4\pi}{12} - \tfrac{3\pi}{12}\right)$$
$$= \operatorname{cis}\left(\tfrac{\pi}{3} - \tfrac{\pi}{4}\right)$$
$$= \frac{\operatorname{cis}\left(\frac{\pi}{3}\right)}{\operatorname{cis}\left(\frac{\pi}{4}\right)}$$
$$= \left(\frac{\tfrac{1}{2} + i\tfrac{\sqrt{3}}{2}}{\tfrac{1}{\sqrt{2}} + i\tfrac{1}{\sqrt{2}}}\right) \times \frac{2}{2}$$
$$= \left(\frac{1 + i\sqrt{3}}{\sqrt{2} + i\sqrt{2}}\right)\left(\frac{\sqrt{2} - i\sqrt{2}}{\sqrt{2} - i\sqrt{2}}\right)$$
$$= \frac{\sqrt{2} - i\sqrt{2} + i\sqrt{6} - i^2\sqrt{6}}{2+2}$$
$$= \left(\frac{\sqrt{6} + \sqrt{2}}{4}\right) + \left(\frac{\sqrt{6} - \sqrt{2}}{4}\right)i$$

$\therefore \;\; \cos\left(\tfrac{\pi}{12}\right) = \dfrac{\sqrt{6}+\sqrt{2}}{4}, \quad \sin\left(\tfrac{\pi}{12}\right) = \dfrac{\sqrt{6}-\sqrt{2}}{4}$ {equating real and imaginary parts}

b Consider $\cos\left(\tfrac{11\pi}{12}\right) + i \sin\left(\tfrac{11\pi}{12}\right)$
$$= \operatorname{cis}\left(\tfrac{11\pi}{12}\right)$$
$$= \operatorname{cis}\left(\tfrac{3\pi}{12} + \tfrac{8\pi}{12}\right)$$
$$= \operatorname{cis}\left(\tfrac{\pi}{4} + \tfrac{2\pi}{3}\right)$$
$$= \operatorname{cis}\left(\tfrac{\pi}{4}\right) \times \operatorname{cis}\left(\tfrac{2\pi}{3}\right)$$
$$= \left(\tfrac{\sqrt{2}}{2} + i\tfrac{\sqrt{2}}{2}\right)\left(-\tfrac{1}{2} + i\tfrac{\sqrt{3}}{2}\right) \quad \{\tfrac{1}{\sqrt{2}} = \tfrac{1}{\sqrt{2}}\tfrac{\sqrt{2}}{\sqrt{2}} = \tfrac{\sqrt{2}}{2}\}$$
$$= -\tfrac{\sqrt{2}}{4} + i\tfrac{\sqrt{6}}{4} - i\tfrac{\sqrt{2}}{4} + i^2 \tfrac{\sqrt{6}}{4}$$
$$= \left(\tfrac{-\sqrt{2} - \sqrt{6}}{4}\right) + \left(\tfrac{\sqrt{6} - \sqrt{2}}{4}\right) i$$

$\therefore \;\; \cos\left(\tfrac{11\pi}{12}\right) = \dfrac{-\sqrt{2} - \sqrt{6}}{4}, \quad \sin\left(\tfrac{11\pi}{12}\right) = \dfrac{\sqrt{6} - \sqrt{2}}{4}$ {equating real and imaginary parts}

EXERCISE 15B.5

1 Let $z = R \operatorname{cis} \theta$ and $w = r \operatorname{cis} \phi$, $w \neq 0$

$$\frac{z}{w} = \frac{R \operatorname{cis} \theta}{r \operatorname{cis} \phi} = \frac{R}{r} \operatorname{cis}(\theta - \phi) \quad \ldots (*)$$

$$\therefore \quad \left|\frac{z}{w}\right| = \frac{R}{r} = \frac{|z|}{|w|}$$

also from (*), $\arg\left(\dfrac{z}{w}\right) = \theta - \phi = \arg z - \arg w$ if $w \neq 0$

$$\therefore \quad \arg\left(\frac{z}{w}\right) = \arg z - \arg w$$

2 a $z = 3 \operatorname{cis} \theta$

$\therefore \quad -z = -1 \times 3 \operatorname{cis} \theta$
$= \operatorname{cis}(\pi) \times 3 \operatorname{cis} \theta$
$= 3 \operatorname{cis}(\theta + \pi) \quad \therefore \quad |-z| = 3$ and $\arg(-z) = \theta + \pi$

b $z^* = 3 \operatorname{cis}(-\theta) \quad \therefore \quad |z^*| = 3$ and $\arg z^* = -\theta$

c $iz = \operatorname{cis}\left(\frac{\pi}{2}\right) \times 3 \operatorname{cis} \theta$
$= 3 \operatorname{cis}\left(\frac{\pi}{2} + \theta\right) \quad \therefore \quad |iz| = 3$ and $\arg(iz) = \theta + \frac{\pi}{2}$

d $(1+i)z = \sqrt{2} \operatorname{cis}\left(\frac{\pi}{4}\right) \times 3 \operatorname{cis} \theta$
$= 3\sqrt{2} \operatorname{cis}\left(\theta + \frac{\pi}{4}\right)$

$\therefore \quad |(1+i)z| = 3\sqrt{2}$ and $\arg[(1+i)z] = \theta + \frac{\pi}{4}$

3 a $z - 1 = z + (-1)$

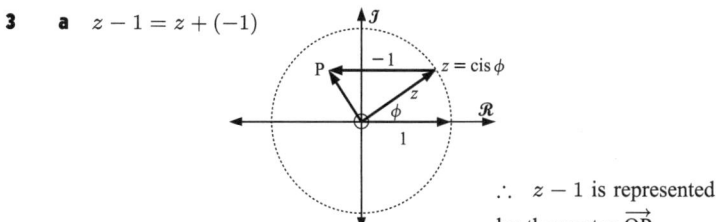

$\therefore \quad z - 1$ is represented by the vector $\overrightarrow{OP}$

Considering the $\triangle OZP$

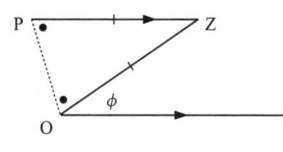

$\widehat{PZO} = \phi$ {alternate angles}
$OZ = ZP = 1$
$\therefore \quad \triangle OPZ$ is isosceles
$\therefore \quad \widehat{POZ} = \widehat{OPZ} = \alpha$

$\therefore \quad 2\alpha + \phi = \pi$ and so $\alpha = \dfrac{\pi - \phi}{2}$

$\therefore \quad \arg(z - 1) = \dfrac{\pi - \phi}{2} + \phi$
$= \frac{\pi}{2} - \frac{\phi}{2} + \phi$
$\arg(z - 1) = \frac{\pi}{2} + \frac{\phi}{2} \quad \ldots (*)$

Using the Cosine Rule in $\triangle OZP$
$OP^2 = 1^2 + 1^2 - 2(1)(1)\cos\phi$
$\therefore \quad OP^2 = 2 - 2\cos\phi$
$\therefore \quad OP^2 = 2 - 2\left(1 - 2\sin^2\left(\frac{\phi}{2}\right)\right)$
$\therefore \quad OP^2 = 2 - 2 + 4\sin^2\left(\frac{\phi}{2}\right)$
$\therefore \quad OP^2 = 4\sin^2\left(\frac{\phi}{2}\right)$
$\therefore \quad |z - 1| = 2\sin\left(\frac{\phi}{2}\right) \quad \ldots (**)$

b $z - 1 = 2\sin\left(\frac{\phi}{2}\right) \operatorname{cis}\left(\frac{\pi}{2} + \frac{\phi}{2}\right) \quad$ {using (*) and (**)}

c $(z - 1)^* = 2\sin\left(\frac{\phi}{2}\right) \operatorname{cis}\left(-\frac{\pi}{2} - \frac{\phi}{2}\right)$

4 **a** Now $z_2 - z_1 = \overrightarrow{AB}$
           $z_3 - z_2 = \overrightarrow{BC}$

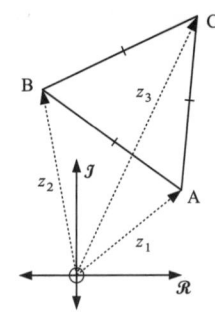

b $\left|\dfrac{z_2 - z_1}{z_3 - z_2}\right| = \dfrac{|z_2 - z_1|}{|z_3 - z_2|}$

$= \dfrac{|\overrightarrow{AB}|}{|\overrightarrow{BC}|}$

But $\triangle ABC$ is equilateral

$\therefore \ |\overrightarrow{AB}| = |\overrightarrow{BC}|$

$\therefore \ \left|\dfrac{z_2 - z_1}{z_3 - z_2}\right| = 1$

c Now $\arg\left(\dfrac{z_2 - z_1}{z_3 - z_2}\right) = \arg(z_2 - z_1) - \arg(z_3 - z_2)$

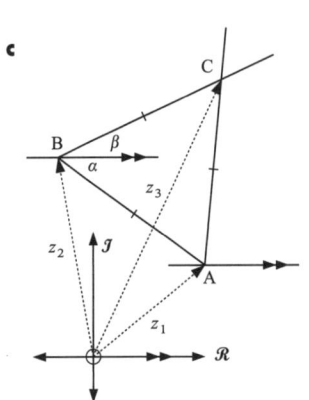

Since $z_2 - z_1 = \overrightarrow{AB}$ and $z_3 - z_2 = \overrightarrow{BC}$,

$\arg(z_2 - z_1) = \pi - \alpha$ {co-interior angles}

and $\arg(z_3 - z_2) = \beta$

$\therefore \ \arg\left(\dfrac{z_2 - z_1}{z_3 - z_2}\right) = (\pi - \alpha) - \beta$

$= \pi - (\alpha + \beta)$

But $\widehat{ABC} = \dfrac{\pi}{3}$ since the triangle is equilateral

$\therefore \ \alpha + \beta = \dfrac{\pi}{3}$

$\therefore \ \arg\left(\dfrac{z_2 - z_1}{z_3 - z_2}\right) = \pi - \dfrac{\pi}{3} = \dfrac{2\pi}{3}$

d $\left(\dfrac{z_2 - z_1}{z_3 - z_2}\right)^3 = \left(1\operatorname{cis}\left(\dfrac{2\pi}{3}\right)\right)^3 = 1(\operatorname{cis} 2\pi) = 1$

5 $\tan\dfrac{\pi}{6} = \dfrac{1}{X}$

$\therefore \ X = \dfrac{1}{\tan\dfrac{\pi}{6}}$

$\therefore \ X = \sqrt{3}$

$\therefore \ z = -\sqrt{3} - i$

$\therefore \ a = -\sqrt{3}$

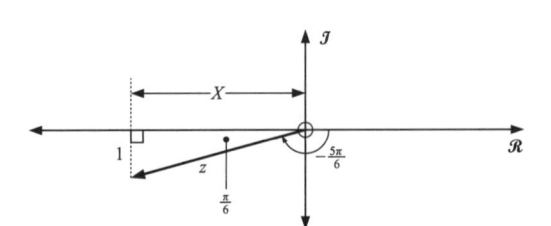

6 **a** $e^{i\theta} = \cos\theta + i\sin\theta$

$\therefore \ e^{i\pi} = \cos\pi + i\sin\pi$

$= -1 + i(0)$

$= -1$

$e^{i\frac{\pi}{2}} = \cos\dfrac{\pi}{2} + i\sin\dfrac{\pi}{2}$

$= 0 + i(1)$

$= i$

b $\operatorname{cis}\theta \operatorname{cis}\phi = e^{i\theta}e^{i\phi}$

$= e^{i(\theta+\phi)}$

$= \operatorname{cis}(\theta + \phi)$

$\dfrac{\operatorname{cis}\theta}{\operatorname{cis}\phi} = \dfrac{e^{i\theta}}{e^{i\phi}}$

$= e^{i(\theta-\phi)}$

$= \operatorname{cis}(\theta - \phi)$

c **i** $\sqrt{z} = (\operatorname{cis}\theta)^{\frac{1}{2}}$

$= \operatorname{cis}\left(\dfrac{\theta}{2}\right)$

$\therefore \ \arg(\sqrt{z}) = \dfrac{\theta}{2}$

ii $iz = \operatorname{cis}\dfrac{\pi}{2} \operatorname{cis}\theta$

$= \operatorname{cis}\left(\dfrac{\pi}{2} + \theta\right)$

$\therefore \ \arg(iz) = \dfrac{\pi}{2} + \theta$

iii $-iz^2 = \operatorname{cis}\left(-\dfrac{\pi}{2}\right)\operatorname{cis}^2\theta$

$= \operatorname{cis}\left(-\dfrac{\pi}{2}\right)\operatorname{cis} 2\theta$

$= \operatorname{cis}\left(2\theta - \dfrac{\pi}{2}\right)$

$\therefore \ \arg(-iz^2) = 2\theta - \dfrac{\pi}{2}$

iv $\dfrac{i}{z} = \dfrac{\operatorname{cis}\dfrac{\pi}{2}}{\operatorname{cis}\theta}$

$= \operatorname{cis}\left(\dfrac{\pi}{2} - \theta\right)$

$\therefore \ \arg\left(\dfrac{i}{z}\right) = \dfrac{\pi}{2} - \theta$

EXERCISE 15B.6

1 Using technology

    a $\sqrt{3}$ cis (2.5187)
          $\approx -1.41 + 1.01i$

    b $\sqrt{11}$ cis $\left(-\frac{3\pi}{8}\right)$
          $\approx 1.27 - 3.06i$

    c $2.836\,49$ cis $(-2.684\,32)$
          $\approx -2.55 - 1.25i$

2   **a** $3 - 4i$
          ≈ 5 cis (-0.927)

    b $-5 - 12i$
          ≈ 13 cis (-1.97)

    c $-11.6814 + 13.2697i$
          ≈ 17.7 cis (2.29)

3   **a** 3 cis $\left(\frac{\pi}{4}\right) + $ cis $\left(\frac{-3\pi}{4}\right)$

$= 3\cos\left(\frac{\pi}{4}\right) + 3i\sin\left(\frac{\pi}{4}\right) + \cos\left(\frac{-3\pi}{4}\right) + i\sin\left(\frac{-3\pi}{4}\right)$

$= 3\cos\left(\frac{\pi}{4}\right) + \cos\left(-\frac{3\pi}{4}\right) + i\left[3\sin\left(\frac{\pi}{4}\right) + \sin\left(-\frac{3\pi}{4}\right)\right]$

$= \left[\frac{3}{\sqrt{2}} - \frac{1}{\sqrt{2}}\right] + i\left[\frac{3}{\sqrt{2}} - \frac{1}{\sqrt{2}}\right]$

$= \sqrt{2} + i\sqrt{2}$

$= 2\left(\frac{1}{\sqrt{2}} + i\frac{1}{\sqrt{2}}\right)$

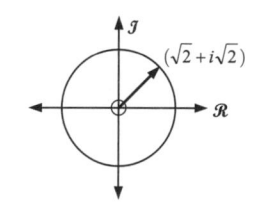

$= 2$ cis $\left(\frac{\pi}{4}\right)$

    b 2 cis $\left(\frac{2\pi}{3}\right) + 5$ cis $\left(\frac{-2\pi}{3}\right)$

$= 2\cos\left(\frac{2\pi}{3}\right) + 5\cos\left(\frac{-2\pi}{3}\right) + i\left[2\sin\left(\frac{2\pi}{3}\right) + 5\sin\left(\frac{-2\pi}{3}\right)\right]$

$= \left[-1 + \left(-\frac{5}{2}\right)\right] + i\left[\sqrt{3} + \left(\frac{-5\sqrt{3}}{2}\right)\right]$

$= -\frac{7}{2} - \frac{3\sqrt{3}}{2}i$

$\approx \sqrt{19}$ cis (-2.50)

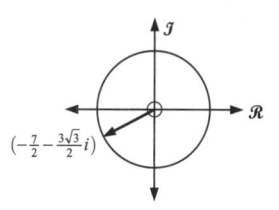

4   **a**   Sum of roots
$= 2$ cis $\left(\frac{2\pi}{3}\right) + 2$ cis $\left(\frac{4\pi}{3}\right)$
$= 2\left(-\frac{1}{2} + \frac{\sqrt{3}}{2}i\right) + 2\left(-\frac{1}{2} - \frac{\sqrt{3}}{2}i\right)$
$= -1 + \sqrt{3}i - 1 - \sqrt{3}i$
$= -2$

          Product of roots
$= 2$ cis $\left(\frac{2\pi}{3}\right) \times 2$ cis $\left(\frac{4\pi}{3}\right)$
$= 4$ cis $\left(\frac{6\pi}{3}\right)$
$= 4$ cis 0
$= 4$

$\therefore$ equations are $a\left(x^2 - (-2)x + 4\right) = 0$ or $a\left(x^2 + 2x + 4\right) = 0$, $a \neq 0$

    b   Sum of roots $= \sqrt{2}$ cis $\left(\frac{\pi}{4}\right) + \sqrt{2}$ cis $\left(-\frac{\pi}{4}\right)$
$= \sqrt{2}\left(\frac{1}{\sqrt{2}} + \frac{1}{\sqrt{2}}i\right) + \sqrt{2}\left(\frac{1}{\sqrt{2}} - \frac{1}{\sqrt{2}}i\right)$
$= (1 + i) + (1 - i) = 2$

Product of roots $= \sqrt{2}$ cis $\left(\frac{\pi}{4}\right) \times \sqrt{2}$ cis $\left(-\frac{\pi}{4}\right)$
$= 2$ cis $0 = 2$

$\therefore$ equations are $a(x^2 - 2x + 2) = 0$, $a \neq 0$

EXERCISE 15C

1   **a** $\left(\sqrt{2}\text{ cis}\left(\frac{\pi}{5}\right)\right)^{10}$
$= (\sqrt{2})^{10}$ cis $\left(\frac{10\pi}{5}\right)$
$= 2^5$ cis 2π
$= 2^5$
$= 32$

    b $\left(\text{cis}\left(\frac{\pi}{12}\right)\right)^{36}$
$= $ cis $\left(\frac{36\pi}{12}\right)$
$= $ cis 3π
$= $ cis π
$= -1$

    c $\left(\sqrt{2}\text{ cis}\left(\frac{\pi}{8}\right)\right)^{12}$
$= 2^6$ cis $\left(\frac{12\pi}{8}\right)$
$= 64$ cis $\left(\frac{3\pi}{2}\right)$
$= -64i$

d $\sqrt{5 \text{ cis}\left(\frac{\pi}{7}\right)}$
$= \left(5 \text{ cis}\left(\frac{\pi}{7}\right)\right)^{\frac{1}{2}}$
$= \sqrt{5} \text{ cis}\left(\frac{1}{2} \times \frac{\pi}{7}\right)$
$= \sqrt{5} \text{ cis}\left(\frac{\pi}{14}\right)$

e $\sqrt[3]{8 \text{ cis}\left(\frac{\pi}{2}\right)}$
$= \left(8 \text{ cis}\left(\frac{\pi}{2}\right)\right)^{\frac{1}{3}}$
$= 2 \text{ cis}\left(\frac{\pi}{6}\right)$
$= 2\left(\frac{\sqrt{3}}{2} + \frac{1}{2}i\right)$
$= \sqrt{3} + i$

f $\left(8 \text{ cis}\left(\frac{\pi}{5}\right)\right)^{\frac{5}{3}}$
$= 8^{\frac{5}{3}} \text{ cis}\left(\frac{5}{3} \times \frac{\pi}{5}\right)$
$= 2^5 \text{ cis}\left(\frac{\pi}{3}\right)$
$= 32\left(\frac{1}{2} + \frac{\sqrt{3}}{2}i\right)$
$= 16 + 16\sqrt{3}i$

2 a $(1+i)^{15}$
$= \left(\sqrt{2}\left(\frac{1}{\sqrt{2}} + \frac{1}{\sqrt{2}}i\right)\right)^{15}$
$= \left(\sqrt{2} \text{ cis}\left(\frac{\pi}{4}\right)\right)^{15}$
$= \sqrt{2}^{14}\sqrt{2} \text{ cis}\left(\frac{15\pi}{4}\right)$
$= 2^7\sqrt{2} \text{ cis}\left(\frac{7\pi}{4}\right)$
$= 128\sqrt{2}\left(\frac{1}{\sqrt{2}} - \frac{1}{\sqrt{2}}i\right)$
$= 128 - 128i$

b $(1 - i\sqrt{3})^{11}$
$= \left(2\left(\frac{1}{2} - \frac{\sqrt{3}}{2}i\right)\right)^{11}$
$= \left(2 \text{ cis}\left(-\frac{\pi}{3}\right)\right)^{11}$
$= 2^{11} \text{ cis}\left(\frac{-11\pi}{3}\right)$
$= 2048 \text{ cis}\left(\frac{\pi}{3}\right)$
$= 2048\left(\frac{1}{2} + \frac{\sqrt{3}}{2}i\right)$
$= 1024 + 1024\sqrt{3}i$

c $(\sqrt{2} - i\sqrt{2})^{-19}$
$= \left(2\left(\frac{1}{\sqrt{2}} - \frac{1}{\sqrt{2}}i\right)\right)^{-19}$
$= \left(2 \text{ cis}\left(-\frac{\pi}{4}\right)\right)^{-19}$
$= 2^{-19} \text{ cis}\left(\frac{19\pi}{4}\right)$
$= 2^{-19} \text{ cis}\left(\frac{3\pi}{4}\right)$
$= 2^{-19}\left(-\frac{1}{\sqrt{2}} + \frac{1}{\sqrt{2}}i\right)$
$= \frac{1}{524\,288}\left(-\frac{1}{\sqrt{2}} + \frac{1}{\sqrt{2}}i\right)$

d $(-1+i)^{-11}$
$= \left(\sqrt{2}\left(-\frac{1}{\sqrt{2}} + \frac{1}{\sqrt{2}}i\right)\right)^{-11}$
$= \left(\sqrt{2} \text{ cis}\left(\frac{3\pi}{4}\right)\right)^{-11}$
$= (\sqrt{2})^{-11} \text{ cis}\left(-\frac{33\pi}{4}\right)$
$= (\sqrt{2})^{-11} \text{ cis}\left(-\frac{\pi}{4}\right)$
$= (\sqrt{2})^{-11}\left(\frac{1}{\sqrt{2}} - \frac{1}{\sqrt{2}}i\right)$
$= (\sqrt{2})^{-12}(1 - i)$
$= \frac{1}{64}(1 - i)$

e $(\sqrt{3} - i)^{\frac{1}{2}}$
$= \left(2\left(\frac{\sqrt{3}}{2} - \frac{1}{2}i\right)\right)^{\frac{1}{2}}$
$= \left(2 \text{ cis}\left(-\frac{\pi}{6}\right)\right)^{\frac{1}{2}}$
$= 2^{\frac{1}{2}} \text{ cis}\left(-\frac{\pi}{12}\right)$
$= \sqrt{2} \text{ cis}\left(-\frac{\pi}{12}\right)$

f $(2 + 2i\sqrt{3})^{-\frac{5}{2}}$
$= \left(4\left(\frac{1}{2} + \frac{\sqrt{3}}{2}i\right)\right)^{-\frac{5}{2}}$
$= \left(4 \text{ cis}\left(\frac{\pi}{3}\right)\right)^{-\frac{5}{2}}$
$= 2^{-\frac{5}{2} \times 2} \text{ cis}\left(-\frac{5}{2} \times \frac{\pi}{3}\right)$
$= 2^{-5} \text{ cis}\left(-\frac{5\pi}{6}\right)$
$= \frac{1}{32}\left(-\frac{\sqrt{3}}{2} - \frac{1}{2}i\right)$
$= -\frac{1}{64}\left(\sqrt{3} + i\right)$

4 a $z = |z| \text{ cis } \theta$
$\sqrt{z} = (|z| \text{ cis } \theta)^{\frac{1}{2}}$
$\sqrt{z} = |z|^{\frac{1}{2}} \text{ cis}\left(\frac{\theta}{2}\right)$ {De Moivre}

b $-\frac{\pi}{2} < \phi \leqslant \frac{\pi}{2}$

c True: $\cos \phi \geqslant 0$ for all $-\frac{\pi}{2} < \phi \leqslant \frac{\pi}{2}$

5 If $z = r \text{ cis } \theta$, De Moivre's Theorem states that $z^n = r^n \text{ cis } n\theta$ for all rational values of n.
$\therefore \ |z^n| = r^n = |z|^n$ and $\arg(z^n) = n\theta = n \arg z$

6 $\text{cis}(-\theta) = \cos(-\theta) + i\sin(-\theta)$
$= \cos \theta - i \sin \theta$

$\therefore \ (\cos \theta - i \sin \theta)^{-3} = [\text{cis}(-\theta)]^{-3}$
$= \text{cis } 3\theta$ {De Moivre}

7 $z = 1 + i = \sqrt{2} \text{ cis}\left(\frac{\pi}{4}\right)$
$\therefore \ z^n = (\sqrt{2})^n \text{ cis}\left(\frac{n\pi}{4}\right)$ {De Moivre}
$= (\sqrt{2})^n \left[\cos\left(\frac{n\pi}{4}\right) + i \sin\left(\frac{n\pi}{4}\right)\right]$

a If z^n is real then $\sin\left(\frac{n\pi}{4}\right) = 0$ $\qquad \therefore \ \frac{n\pi}{4} = 0 + k\pi$
$\therefore \ n = 4k$ where k is any integer

b If z^n is purely imaginary then $\cos\left(\frac{n\pi}{4}\right) = 0$
$\therefore \ \frac{n\pi}{4} = \frac{\pi}{2} + k\pi$
$\therefore \ n = 2 + 4k$ where k is any integer

8 **a** $\quad z = 2 \text{ cis } \theta$
$\therefore \quad z^3 = 2^3 \text{ cis } 3\theta$
$\therefore \quad |z^3| = 8$
and $\arg z^3 = 3\theta$

b $\quad z = 2 \text{ cis } \theta$
$\therefore \quad z^2 = 4 \text{ cis } 2\theta$
$\therefore \quad iz^2 = i(4 \text{ cis } 2\theta)$
$\therefore \quad iz^2 = \text{cis}\left(\frac{\pi}{2}\right)(4 \text{ cis } 2\theta)$
$\therefore \quad iz^2 = 4 \text{ cis}\left(\frac{\pi}{2} + 2\theta\right)$
$\therefore \quad |iz^2| = 4$
and $\arg(iz^2) = \frac{\pi}{2} + 2\theta$

c $\quad z = 2 \text{ cis } \theta$
Now $\frac{1}{z} = z^{-1}$,
so $\frac{1}{z} = (2 \text{ cis } \theta)^{-1}$
$= \frac{1}{2} \text{ cis}(-\theta)$
$\therefore \quad \left|\frac{1}{z}\right| = \frac{1}{2}$
and $\arg\left(\frac{1}{z}\right) = -\theta$

d $\quad z = 2 \text{ cis } \theta$
Now $-\frac{i}{z^2} = -i \times z^{-2}$,
so $-\frac{i}{z^2} = \text{cis}\left(-\frac{\pi}{2}\right) \times (2 \text{ cis } \theta)^{-2}$
$= 2^{-2} \text{ cis}\left(-\frac{\pi}{2}\right) \text{ cis}(-2\theta)$
$= \frac{1}{4} \text{ cis}\left(-\frac{\pi}{2} - 2\theta\right)$
$\therefore \quad \left|-\frac{i}{z^2}\right| = \frac{1}{4}$ and $\arg\left(-\frac{i}{z^2}\right) = -\frac{\pi}{2} - 2\theta$

9 If $z = \text{cis } \theta$, then $\frac{z^2 - 1}{z^2 + 1} = \frac{(\text{cis } \theta)^2 - 1}{(\text{cis } \theta)^2 + 1}$
$= \frac{\text{cis } 2\theta - 1}{\text{cis } 2\theta + 1}$ {De Moivre}
$= \frac{\cos 2\theta + i \sin 2\theta - 1}{\cos 2\theta + i \sin 2\theta + 1}$
$= \frac{-2\left(\frac{1}{2} - \frac{1}{2}\cos 2\theta\right) + i \sin 2\theta}{2\left(\frac{1}{2} + \frac{1}{2}\cos 2\theta\right) + i \sin 2\theta}$
$= \frac{-2\sin^2 \theta + 2i \cos \theta \sin \theta}{2\cos^2 \theta + 2i \cos \theta \sin \theta}$
$= \frac{2\sin \theta(i \cos \theta + i^2 \sin \theta)}{2\cos \theta(\cos \theta + i \sin \theta)}$
$= \frac{i \sin \theta \text{ cis } \theta}{\cos \theta \text{ cis } \theta}$
$= i \tan \theta$

10 **a** $\quad \text{cis } 3\theta = \cos 3\theta + i \sin 3\theta$
But $\text{cis } 3\theta = (\text{cis } \theta)^3$ {De Moivre's Theorem}
$= (\cos \theta + i \sin \theta)^3$
$= \cos^3 \theta + 3 \cos^2 \theta(i \sin \theta) + 3 \cos \theta(i \sin \theta)^2 + (i \sin \theta)^3$
$= \left[\cos^3 \theta - 3 \cos \theta \sin^2 \theta\right] + i\left[3 \cos^2 \theta \sin \theta - \sin^3 \theta\right]$

i $\cos 3\theta = \cos^3 \theta - 3 \cos \theta \sin^2 \theta$
{equating real parts}
$= \cos^3 \theta - 3 \cos \theta(1 - \cos^2 \theta)$
$= \cos^3 \theta - 3 \cos \theta + 3 \cos^3 \theta$
$= 4 \cos^3 \theta - 3 \cos \theta$

ii $\sin 3\theta = 3 \cos^2 \theta \sin \theta - \sin^3 \theta$
{equating imaginary parts}
$= 3(1 - \sin^2 \theta) \sin \theta - \sin^3 \theta$
$= 3 \sin \theta - 3 \sin^3 \theta - \sin^3 \theta$
$= 3 \sin \theta - 4 \sin^3 \theta$

b $\tan 3\theta = \dfrac{\sin 3\theta}{\cos 3\theta} = \dfrac{3\sin\theta - 4\sin^3\theta}{4\cos^3\theta - 3\cos\theta}$ {using **a**}

$= \dfrac{\sin\theta(3 - 4\sin^2\theta)}{\cos\theta(4\cos^2\theta - 3)}$

$= \dfrac{\sin\theta\,[3(\cos^2\theta + \sin^2\theta) - 4\sin^2\theta]}{\cos\theta\,[4\cos^2\theta - 3(\cos^2\theta + \sin^2\theta)]}$ {$\cos^2\theta + \sin^2\theta = 1$}

$= \dfrac{\sin\theta(3\cos^2\theta - \sin^2\theta)}{\cos\theta(\cos^2\theta - 3\sin^2\theta)}$

$= \dfrac{3\sin\theta\cos^2\theta - \sin^3\theta}{\cos^3\theta - 3\sin^2\theta\cos\theta}$

$= \dfrac{3\,\dfrac{\sin\theta}{\cos\theta} - \dfrac{\sin^3\theta}{\cos^3\theta}}{1 - 3\,\dfrac{\sin^2\theta}{\cos^2\theta}}$ {$\div$ top and bottom by $\cos^3\theta$}

$= \dfrac{3\tan\theta - \tan^3\theta}{1 - 3\tan^2\theta}$

c i $4x^3 - 3x = -\dfrac{1}{\sqrt{2}}$

Let $x = \cos\theta$

$\therefore\ 4\cos^3\theta - 3\cos\theta = -\dfrac{1}{\sqrt{2}}$

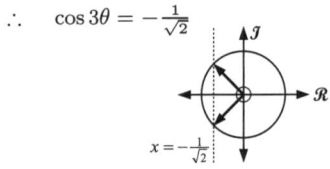

$\therefore\ \cos 3\theta = -\dfrac{1}{\sqrt{2}}$

$3\theta = \dfrac{3\pi}{4},\ \dfrac{5\pi}{4},\ \dfrac{11\pi}{4},\ \dfrac{13\pi}{4},\ \dfrac{19\pi}{4},\ \dfrac{21\pi}{4}$

$\{0 \leqslant 3\theta \leqslant 6\pi\}$

$\therefore\ \theta = \dfrac{\pi}{4},\ \dfrac{5\pi}{12},\ \dfrac{11\pi}{12},\ \dfrac{13\pi}{12},\ \dfrac{19\pi}{12},\ \dfrac{7\pi}{4}$

$\{0 \leqslant \theta \leqslant 2\pi\}$

$\therefore\ x = \cos\theta = \cos\dfrac{\pi}{4} = \dfrac{1}{\sqrt{2}}$ $\{= \cos\dfrac{7\pi}{4}\}$

or $\cos\dfrac{5\pi}{12}$ $\{= \cos\dfrac{19\pi}{12}\}$

or $\cos\dfrac{11\pi}{12}$ $\{= \cos\dfrac{13\pi}{12}\}$

ii $x^3 - 3\sqrt{3}x^2 - 3x + \sqrt{3} = 0$

$\therefore\ \sqrt{3} - 3\sqrt{3}x^2 = 3x - x^3$

$\therefore\ \sqrt{3}(1 - 3x^2) = 3x - x^3$

$\therefore\ \sqrt{3} = \dfrac{3x - x^3}{1 - 3x^2}$

Let $x = \tan\theta$

$\therefore\ \sqrt{3} = \dfrac{3\tan\theta - \tan^3\theta}{1 - 3\tan^2\theta}$

$\therefore\ \tan 3\theta = \sqrt{3}$

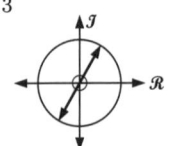

$3\theta = \dfrac{\pi}{3},\ \dfrac{4\pi}{3},\ \dfrac{7\pi}{3},\ \dfrac{10\pi}{3},\ \dfrac{13\pi}{3},\ \dfrac{16\pi}{3}$

$\{0 \leqslant 3\theta \leqslant 6\pi\}$

$\therefore\ \theta = \dfrac{\pi}{9},\ \dfrac{4\pi}{9},\ \dfrac{7\pi}{9},\ \dfrac{10\pi}{9},\ \dfrac{13\pi}{9},\ \dfrac{16\pi}{9}$

$\{0 \leqslant \theta \leqslant 2\pi\}$

$\therefore\ x = \tan\theta = \tan\dfrac{\pi}{9}$ $\{= \tan\dfrac{10\pi}{9}\}$

or $\tan\dfrac{4\pi}{9}$ $\{= \tan\dfrac{13\pi}{9}\}$

or $\tan\dfrac{7\pi}{9}$ $\{= \tan\dfrac{16\pi}{9}\}$

11 a

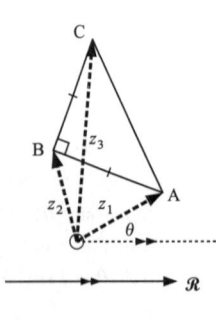

$\overrightarrow{BC} = \overrightarrow{BO} + \overrightarrow{OC} = -z_2 + z_3 = z_3 - z_2$

$\overrightarrow{BA} = \overrightarrow{BO} + \overrightarrow{OA} = -z_2 + z_1 = z_1 - z_2$

Now $\arg(\overrightarrow{BC}) - \arg(\overrightarrow{BA}) = \dfrac{\pi}{2}$

$\therefore\ \arg(z_3 - z_2) - \arg(z_1 - z_2) = \dfrac{\pi}{2}$

$\therefore\ \arg\left(\dfrac{z_3 - z_2}{z_1 - z_2}\right) = \dfrac{\pi}{2}$

Also $\left|\dfrac{z_3 - z_2}{z_1 - z_2}\right| = \dfrac{|z_3 - z_2|}{|z_1 - z_2|} = \dfrac{BC}{AB} = 1$

So, $\dfrac{z_3 - z_2}{z_1 - z_2}$ has modulus 1 and argument $\dfrac{\pi}{2}$

$\therefore \quad \dfrac{z_3 - z_2}{z_1 - z_2} = 1 \text{ cis } \dfrac{\pi}{2} = i$

$\therefore \quad \left(\dfrac{z_3 - z_2}{z_1 - z_2}\right)^2 = i^2 = -1 \quad$ and so $\quad \therefore \quad (z_1 - z_2)^2 = -(z_3 - z_2)^2$

b

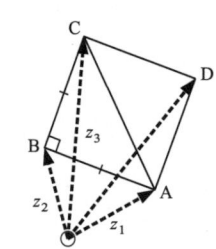

$\overrightarrow{BA} = \overrightarrow{CD}$ and $\overrightarrow{BA} = z_1 - z_2$

$\therefore \quad \overrightarrow{CD} = z_1 - z_2$

Now $\overrightarrow{OD} = \overrightarrow{OC} + \overrightarrow{CD}$

$\therefore \quad \overrightarrow{OD} = z_3 + z_1 - z_2$

$\therefore \quad z_3 + z_1 - z_2$ represents D.

12 $\cos 4\theta + i \sin 4\theta$
$= \text{cis } 4\theta$
$= (\text{cis } \theta)^4 \quad$ {De Moivre's theorem in reverse}
$= (\cos \theta + i \sin \theta)^4$
$= \cos^4 \theta + 4 \cos^3 \theta (i \sin \theta) + 6 \cos^2 \theta (i \sin \theta)^2 + 4 \cos \theta (i \sin \theta)^3 + (i \sin \theta)^4$
$= \cos^4 \theta + [4 \cos^3 \theta \sin \theta]i - 6 \cos^2 \theta \sin^2 \theta - [4 \cos \theta \sin^3 \theta]i + \sin^4 \theta$
$= [\cos^4 \theta - 6 \cos^2 \theta \sin^2 \theta + \sin^4 \theta] + [4 \cos^3 \theta \sin \theta - 4 \cos \theta \sin^3 \theta]i$

a Equating real parts gives $\cos 4\theta = \cos^4 \theta - 6 \cos^2 \theta (1 - \cos^2 \theta) + (1 - \cos^2 \theta)^2$
$\therefore \quad \cos 4\theta = \cos^4 \theta - 6 \cos^2 \theta + 6 \cos^4 \theta + 1 - 2 \cos^2 \theta + \cos^4 \theta$
$\therefore \quad \cos 4\theta = 8 \cos^4 \theta - 8 \cos^2 \theta + 1$

b Equating imaginary parts gives $\sin 4\theta = 4 \cos^3 \theta \sin \theta - 4 \cos \theta \sin^3 \theta$

13 a If $z = \text{cis } \theta$, then

$z^n + \dfrac{1}{z^n} = z^n + z^{-n}$
$= (\text{cis } \theta)^n + (\text{cis } \theta)^{-n}$
$= \text{cis } (n\theta) + \text{cis } (-n\theta)$
$= (\cos n\theta + i \sin n\theta) + (\cos(-n\theta) + i \sin(-n\theta))$
$= (\cos n\theta + i \sin n\theta + \cos n\theta - i \sin n\theta) \quad \{\cos(-\alpha) = \cos \alpha, \ \sin(-\alpha) = -\sin \alpha\}$
$= 2 \cos n\theta$

b In **a** if we let $n = 1$ we get $z + \dfrac{1}{z} = 2 \cos \theta$

c $\left(z + \dfrac{1}{z}\right)^3 = z^3 + 3z^2 \left(\dfrac{1}{z}\right) + 3z \left(\dfrac{1}{z}\right)^2 + \left(\dfrac{1}{z}\right)^3$

$\qquad = z^3 + 3z + \dfrac{3}{z} + \dfrac{1}{z^3}$

d From **c**, $\left(z + \dfrac{1}{z}\right)^3 = \left(z^3 + \dfrac{1}{z^3}\right) + 3 \left(z + \dfrac{1}{z}\right)$

Using **a** and **b**, $(2 \cos \theta)^3 = 2 \cos 3\theta + 3(2 \cos \theta)$
$\therefore \quad 8 \cos^3 \theta = 2 \cos 3\theta + 6 \cos \theta$
$\therefore \quad \cos^3 \theta = \tfrac{1}{4} \cos 3\theta + \tfrac{3}{4} \cos \theta$

e If we let $\theta = \dfrac{13\pi}{12}$ in **d** we get

$\cos^3 \left(\dfrac{13\pi}{12}\right) = \tfrac{1}{4} \cos \left(\dfrac{39\pi}{12}\right) + \tfrac{3}{4} \cos \left(\dfrac{13\pi}{12}\right)$

$\qquad = \tfrac{1}{4} \cos \left(\dfrac{13\pi}{4}\right) + \tfrac{3}{4} \cos \left(\dfrac{3\pi}{4} + \dfrac{\pi}{3}\right)$

$\qquad = \tfrac{1}{4} \cos \left(\dfrac{5\pi}{4}\right) + \tfrac{3}{4} \left[\cos \left(\dfrac{3\pi}{4}\right) \cos \left(\dfrac{\pi}{3}\right) - \sin \left(\dfrac{3\pi}{4}\right) \sin \left(\dfrac{\pi}{3}\right)\right]$

$$= \tfrac{1}{4}\left(-\tfrac{1}{\sqrt{2}}\right) + \tfrac{3}{4}\left[\left(-\tfrac{1}{\sqrt{2}}\right)\left(\tfrac{1}{2}\right) - \left(\tfrac{1}{\sqrt{2}}\right)\left(\tfrac{\sqrt{3}}{2}\right)\right]$$

$$= -\tfrac{1}{4\sqrt{2}} - \tfrac{3}{8\sqrt{2}} - \tfrac{3\sqrt{3}}{8\sqrt{2}}$$

$$= -\tfrac{1}{4\sqrt{2}}\left(\tfrac{2\sqrt{2}}{2\sqrt{2}}\right) - \tfrac{3}{8\sqrt{2}}\left(\tfrac{\sqrt{2}}{\sqrt{2}}\right) - \tfrac{3\sqrt{3}}{8\sqrt{2}}\left(\tfrac{\sqrt{2}}{\sqrt{2}}\right)$$

$$= \tfrac{-2\sqrt{2}-3\sqrt{2}-3\sqrt{6}}{16}$$

$$= \tfrac{-5\sqrt{2}-3\sqrt{6}}{16}$$

14 If $z = \text{cis}\,\theta$,

$$z^n - \tfrac{1}{z^n} = z^n - z^{-n}$$
$$= [\text{cis}\,\theta]^n - [\text{cis}\,\theta]^{-n}$$
$$= \text{cis}\,n\theta - \text{cis}(-n\theta) \quad \{\text{De Moivre}\}$$
$$= \cos n\theta + i\sin n\theta - [\cos(-n\theta) + i\sin(-n\theta)]$$
$$= \cos n\theta + i\sin n\theta - \cos(-n\theta) - i\sin(-n\theta)$$
$$= \cos n\theta + i\sin n\theta - \cos n\theta + i\sin n\theta$$
$$\quad \{\text{as } \cos(-\phi) = \cos\phi, \; \sin(-\phi) = -\sin\phi\}$$
$$= 2i\sin n\theta \quad \ldots \; (*)$$

If we let $n = 1$, $z - \tfrac{1}{z} = 2i\sin\theta$

$$\therefore \; [2i\sin\theta]^3 = \left(z - \tfrac{1}{z}\right)^3$$

$$\therefore \; 8i^3\sin^3\theta = z^3 + 3z^2\left(-\tfrac{1}{z}\right) + 3z\left(-\tfrac{1}{z}\right)^2 + \left(-\tfrac{1}{z}\right)^3$$

$$= z^3 - \tfrac{1}{z^3} - 3\left(z - \tfrac{1}{z}\right)$$

$$= 2i\sin 3\theta - 3 \times 2i\sin\theta \quad \{\text{using }(*)\}$$

$$\therefore \; -8i\sin^3\theta = 2i\sin 3\theta - 6i\sin\theta$$

$$\therefore \; \sin^3\theta = -\tfrac{1}{4}\sin 3\theta + \tfrac{3}{4}\sin\theta$$

$$\therefore \; \sin^3\theta = \tfrac{3}{4}\sin\theta - \tfrac{1}{4}\sin 3\theta$$

15 $\sin^3\theta\cos^3\theta = (\tfrac{3}{4}\sin\theta - \tfrac{1}{4}\sin 3\theta)(\tfrac{1}{4}\cos 3\theta + \tfrac{3}{4}\cos\theta) \quad \{\text{using }\mathbf{13\,d}\text{ and }\mathbf{14}\}$

$$= \tfrac{3}{16}\sin\theta\cos 3\theta + \tfrac{9}{16}\sin\theta\cos\theta - \tfrac{1}{16}\sin 3\theta\cos 3\theta - \tfrac{3}{16}\sin 3\theta\cos\theta$$

$$= \tfrac{3}{16}(\sin\theta\cos 3\theta - \sin 3\theta\cos\theta) + \tfrac{9}{32}(2\sin\theta\cos\theta) - \tfrac{1}{32}(2\sin 3\theta\cos 3\theta)$$

$$= \tfrac{3}{16}(\sin(\theta - 3\theta)) + \tfrac{9}{32}\sin 2\theta - \tfrac{1}{32}\sin 6\theta$$

$$= -\tfrac{3}{16}\sin 2\theta + \tfrac{9}{32}\sin 2\theta - \tfrac{1}{32}\sin 6\theta$$

$$= \tfrac{3}{32}\sin 2\theta - \tfrac{1}{32}\sin 6\theta$$

$$= \tfrac{1}{32}(3\sin 2\theta - \sin 6\theta)$$

EXERCISE 15D.1

1 **a** The cube roots of 1 are solutions to $z^3 = 1$, or $z^3 - 1 = 0$

Now $z = 1$ is a solution, so $z - 1$ is a factor.

$\therefore \; (z-1)(z^2 + z + 1) = 0$

$\therefore \; z = 1 \text{ or } \dfrac{-1 \pm \sqrt{1-4}}{2}$

$\therefore \; z = 1 \text{ or } -\tfrac{1}{2} \pm i\tfrac{\sqrt{3}}{2}$

1	1	0	0	-1
	0	1	1	1
	1	1	1	0

b $z^3 = 1$

$\therefore \ z^3 = 1 \text{ cis}(0 + k2\pi)$

$\therefore \ z = (1 \text{ cis}(k2\pi))^{\frac{1}{3}}$

$\therefore \ z = 1 \text{ cis}\left(\frac{k2\pi}{3}\right)$ {De Moivre}

$\therefore \ z = \text{cis } 0, \text{ cis}\left(\frac{2\pi}{3}\right) \text{ or cis}\left(\frac{4\pi}{3}\right)$ {when $k = 0, 1, 2$}

$\therefore \ z = 1, \ -\frac{1}{2} + i\frac{\sqrt{3}}{2}, \ -\frac{1}{2} - i\frac{\sqrt{3}}{2}$

2   **a** $z^3 = -8i$

$\therefore \ z^3 = 8 \text{ cis}\left(-\frac{\pi}{2} + k2\pi\right)$

$\therefore \ z = \left(8 \text{ cis}\left(-\frac{\pi}{2} + k2\pi\right)\right)^{\frac{1}{3}}$

$\therefore \ z = 8^{\frac{1}{3}} \text{ cis}\left(-\frac{\pi}{6} + \frac{k2\pi}{3}\right)$ {De Moivre}

$\therefore \ z = 2 \text{ cis}\left(-\frac{\pi}{6}\right), \ 2 \text{ cis}\left(\frac{3\pi}{6}\right) \text{ or } 2 \text{ cis}\left(\frac{7\pi}{6}\right)$ {when $k = 0, 1, 2$}

$\therefore \ z = 2\left(\frac{\sqrt{3}}{2} - \frac{1}{2}i\right), \ 2 \text{ cis}\frac{\pi}{2} \text{ or } 2\left(-\frac{\sqrt{3}}{2} - \frac{1}{2}i\right)$

$\therefore \ z = \sqrt{3} - i, \ 2i \text{ or } -\sqrt{3} - i$

b $z^3 = -27i$

$\therefore \ z^3 = 27 \text{ cis}\left(-\frac{\pi}{2} + k2\pi\right)$

$\therefore \ z = \left(27 \text{ cis}\left(-\frac{\pi}{2} + k2\pi\right)\right)^{\frac{1}{3}}$

$\therefore \ z = 27^{\frac{1}{3}} \text{ cis}\left(-\frac{\pi}{6} + \frac{k4\pi}{6}\right)$ {De Moivre}

$\therefore \ z = 3 \text{ cis}\left(-\frac{\pi}{6}\right), \ 3 \text{ cis}\left(\frac{3\pi}{6}\right) \text{ or } 3 \text{ cis}\left(\frac{7\pi}{6}\right)$ {when $k = 0, 1, 2$}

$\therefore \ z = 3\left(\frac{\sqrt{3}}{2} - \frac{1}{2}i\right), \ 3 \text{ cis}\frac{\pi}{2} \text{ or } 3\left(-\frac{\sqrt{3}}{2} - \frac{1}{2}i\right)$

$\therefore \ z = \frac{3\sqrt{3}}{2} - \frac{3}{2}i, \ 3i \text{ or } \frac{-3\sqrt{3}}{2} - \frac{3}{2}i$

3 $z^3 = -1$

$\therefore \ z^3 = 1 \text{ cis}(\pi + k2\pi)$

$\therefore \ z = (\text{cis}(\pi + k2\pi))^{\frac{1}{3}}$

$\therefore \ z = \text{cis}\left(\frac{\pi}{3} + \frac{k2\pi}{3}\right)$ {De Moivre}

$\therefore \ z = \text{cis}\left(\frac{\pi}{3}\right), \ \text{cis } \pi, \ \text{cis}\left(\frac{5\pi}{3}\right)$ {when $k = 0, 1, 2$}

$\therefore \ z = \frac{1}{2} + i\frac{\sqrt{3}}{2}, \ -1, \ \frac{1}{2} - i\frac{\sqrt{3}}{2}$

4   **a** $z^4 = 16$ $\therefore \ z^4 = 16 \text{ cis}(0 + k2\pi)$

$\therefore \ z = (16 \text{ cis}(k2\pi))^{\frac{1}{4}}$

$\therefore \ z = 16^{\frac{1}{4}} \text{ cis}\left(\frac{k\pi}{2}\right)$ {De Moivre}

$\therefore \ z = 2 \text{ cis}\left(\frac{k\pi}{2}\right)$

$\therefore \ z = 2 \text{ cis } 0, \ 2 \text{ cis}\left(\frac{\pi}{2}\right), \ 2 \text{ cis } \pi, \ 2 \text{ cis}\left(\frac{3\pi}{2}\right)$ {when $k = 0, 1, 2$ or 3}

$\therefore \ z = \pm 2 \text{ and } \pm 2i$

b $z^4 = -16$ $\therefore \ z^4 = 16 \text{ cis}(\pi + k2\pi)$

$\therefore \ z = (16 \text{ cis}(\pi + k2\pi))^{\frac{1}{4}}$

$\therefore \ z = 16^{\frac{1}{4}} \text{ cis}\left(\frac{\pi}{4} + \frac{k2\pi}{4}\right)$ {De Moivre}

$\therefore \ z = 2 \text{ cis}\left(\frac{\pi}{4}\right), \ 2 \text{ cis}\left(\frac{3\pi}{4}\right), \ 2 \text{ cis}\left(\frac{5\pi}{4}\right), \ 2 \text{ cis}\left(\frac{7\pi}{4}\right)$ {when $k = 0, 1, 2$ or 3}

$\therefore \ z = 2\left(\frac{1}{\sqrt{2}} + i\frac{1}{\sqrt{2}}\right), \ 2\left(-\frac{1}{\sqrt{2}} + i\frac{1}{\sqrt{2}}\right), \ 2\left(-\frac{1}{\sqrt{2}} - i\frac{1}{\sqrt{2}}\right), \ 2\left(\frac{1}{\sqrt{2}} - i\frac{1}{\sqrt{2}}\right)$

$\therefore \ z = \sqrt{2} \pm i\sqrt{2}, \ -\sqrt{2} \pm i\sqrt{2}$

5 $z^4 = -i$

$\therefore \ z^4 = \text{cis}\left(-\frac{\pi}{2} + k2\pi\right)$

$\therefore \ z = \left(\text{cis}\left(-\frac{\pi}{2} + k2\pi\right)\right)^{\frac{1}{4}}$

$\therefore \ z = \text{cis}\left(-\frac{\pi}{8} + \frac{k\pi}{2}\right)$ {De Moivre}

$\therefore \ z = \text{cis}\left(-\frac{\pi}{8} + \frac{k4\pi}{8}\right)$

$\therefore \ z = \text{cis}\left(-\frac{5\pi}{8}\right), \ \text{cis}\left(-\frac{\pi}{8}\right), \ \text{cis}\left(\frac{3\pi}{8}\right), \ \text{cis}\left(\frac{7\pi}{8}\right)$

     {when $k = -1, 0, 1, 2$}

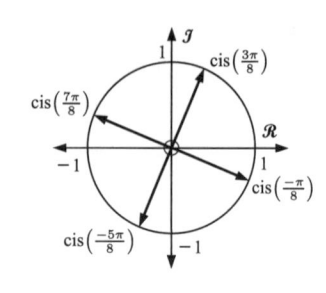

6 **a** $z^3 = 2 + 2i$

$\therefore \ z^3 = 2\sqrt{2}\ \text{cis}\left(\frac{\pi}{4} + k2\pi\right)$

$\therefore \ z = \left[2\sqrt{2}\ \text{cis}\left(\frac{\pi}{4} + k2\pi\right)\right]^{\frac{1}{3}}$

$\therefore \ z = (2\sqrt{2})^{\frac{1}{3}}\ \text{cis}\left(\frac{\pi}{12} + \frac{k2\pi}{3}\right)$ {De Moivre}

$\therefore \ z = \sqrt{2}\ \text{cis}\left(\frac{\pi}{12} + \frac{k8\pi}{12}\right)$

$\therefore \ z = \sqrt{2}\ \text{cis}\left(\frac{\pi}{12}\right), \ \sqrt{2}\ \text{cis}\left(\frac{3\pi}{4}\right) \ (\text{or } -1+i), \ \sqrt{2}\ \text{cis}\left(-\frac{7\pi}{12}\right)$

     {when $k = 0, 1, -1$}

b $z^3 = -2 + 2i$

$\therefore \ z^3 = 2\sqrt{2}\ \text{cis}\left(\frac{3\pi}{4} + k2\pi\right)$

$\therefore \ z = \left[2\sqrt{2}\ \text{cis}\left(\frac{3\pi}{4} + k2\pi\right)\right]^{\frac{1}{3}}$

$\therefore \ z = (2\sqrt{2})^{\frac{1}{3}}\ \text{cis}\left(\frac{\pi}{4} + \frac{k2\pi}{3}\right)$ {De Moivre}

$\therefore \ z = \sqrt{2}\ \text{cis}\left(\frac{3\pi}{12} + \frac{k8\pi}{12}\right)$

$\therefore \ z = \sqrt{2}\ \text{cis}\left(\frac{\pi}{4}\right) \ (\text{or } 1+i), \ \sqrt{2}\ \text{cis}\left(\frac{11\pi}{12}\right), \ \sqrt{2}\ \text{cis}\left(-\frac{5\pi}{12}\right)$

     {when $k = 0, 1, -1$}

c $z^2 = \frac{1}{2} + \frac{\sqrt{3}}{2}i$

$\therefore \ z^2 = \text{cis}\left(\frac{\pi}{3} + k2\pi\right)$

$\therefore \ z = \left[\text{cis}\left(\frac{\pi}{3} + k2\pi\right)\right]^{\frac{1}{2}}$

$\therefore \ z = \text{cis}\left(\frac{\pi}{6} + k\pi\right)$ {De Moivre}

$\therefore \ z = \text{cis}\left(\frac{\pi}{6} + \frac{k6\pi}{6}\right)$

$\therefore \ z = \text{cis}\left(\frac{\pi}{6}\right) \ (\text{or } \frac{\sqrt{3}}{2} + \frac{1}{2}i), \ \text{cis}\left(-\frac{5\pi}{6}\right) \ (\text{or } -\frac{\sqrt{3}}{2} - \frac{1}{2}i)$

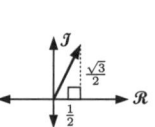

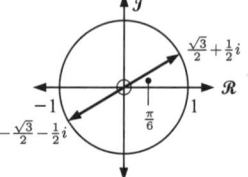

     {when $k = 0, -1$}

d $z^4 = \sqrt{3} + i$

$\therefore \ z^4 = 2\ \text{cis}\left(\frac{\pi}{6} + k2\pi\right)$

$\therefore \ z = \left[2\ \text{cis}\left(\frac{\pi}{6} + k2\pi\right)\right]^{\frac{1}{4}}$

$\therefore \ z = 2^{\frac{1}{4}}\ \text{cis}\left(\frac{\pi}{24} + \frac{k\pi}{2}\right)$ {De Moivre}

$\therefore \ z = \sqrt[4]{2}\ \text{cis}\left(\frac{\pi}{24} + \frac{k12\pi}{24}\right)$

$\therefore \ z = \sqrt[4]{2}\ \text{cis}\left(\frac{\pi}{24}\right), \ \sqrt[4]{2}\ \text{cis}\left(\frac{13\pi}{24}\right), \ \sqrt[4]{2}\ \text{cis}\left(-\frac{11\pi}{24}\right),$

     $\sqrt[4]{2}\ \text{cis}\left(-\frac{23\pi}{24}\right)$ {when $k = 0, 1, -1, -2$}

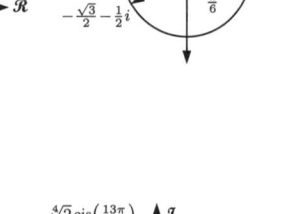

e $z^5 = -4 - 4i$
$\therefore z^5 = 4\sqrt{2} \operatorname{cis}\left(-\frac{3\pi}{4} + k2\pi\right)$
$\therefore z = \left[4\sqrt{2} \operatorname{cis}\left(-\frac{3\pi}{4} + k2\pi\right)\right]^{\frac{1}{5}}$
$\therefore z = (4\sqrt{2})^{\frac{1}{5}} \operatorname{cis}\left(-\frac{3\pi}{20} + \frac{k2\pi}{5}\right)$ {De Moivre}
$\therefore z = \sqrt{2} \operatorname{cis}\left(-\frac{3\pi}{20} + \frac{k8\pi}{20}\right)$
$\therefore z = \sqrt{2} \operatorname{cis}\left(-\frac{3\pi}{20}\right), \sqrt{2} \operatorname{cis}\left(\frac{\pi}{4}\right)$ (or $1+i$), $\sqrt{2} \operatorname{cis}\left(\frac{13\pi}{20}\right)$,
$\sqrt{2} \operatorname{cis}\left(-\frac{11\pi}{20}\right), \sqrt{2} \operatorname{cis}\left(-\frac{19\pi}{20}\right)$
{when $k = 0, 1, 2, -1, -2$}

f $z^3 = -2\sqrt{3} - 2i$
$\therefore z^3 = 4 \operatorname{cis}\left(-\frac{5\pi}{6} + k2\pi\right)$
$\therefore z = \left[4 \operatorname{cis}\left(-\frac{5\pi}{6} + k2\pi\right)\right]^{\frac{1}{3}}$
$\therefore z = 4^{\frac{1}{3}} \operatorname{cis}\left(-\frac{5\pi}{18} + \frac{k2\pi}{3}\right)$ {De Moivre}
$\therefore z = \sqrt[3]{4} \operatorname{cis}\left(-\frac{5\pi}{18} + \frac{k12\pi}{18}\right)$
$\therefore z = \sqrt[3]{4} \operatorname{cis}\left(-\frac{5\pi}{18}\right), \sqrt[3]{4} \operatorname{cis}\left(\frac{7\pi}{18}\right), \sqrt[3]{4} \operatorname{cis}\left(-\frac{17\pi}{18}\right)$
{when $k = 0, 1, -1$}

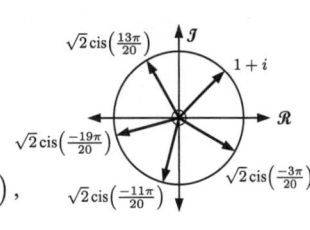

7 $z^4 + 1 = 0$
$\therefore z^4 = -1$
$\therefore z^4 = \operatorname{cis}(\pi + k2\pi)$
$\therefore z = [\operatorname{cis}(\pi + k2\pi)]^{\frac{1}{4}}$
$\therefore z = \operatorname{cis}\left(\frac{\pi}{4} + \frac{k\pi}{2}\right)$ {De Moivre}
$\therefore z = \operatorname{cis}\left(\frac{\pi}{4} + \frac{k2\pi}{4}\right)$
$\therefore z = \operatorname{cis}\left(\frac{\pi}{4}\right), \operatorname{cis}\left(\frac{3\pi}{4}\right), \operatorname{cis}\left(-\frac{\pi}{4}\right), \operatorname{cis}\left(-\frac{3\pi}{4}\right)$ {when $k = 0, 1, -1$ or -2}
$\therefore z = \frac{1}{\sqrt{2}} \pm \frac{1}{\sqrt{2}}i, -\frac{1}{\sqrt{2}} \pm \frac{1}{\sqrt{2}}i$

For the pair of roots $\frac{1}{\sqrt{2}} \pm \frac{1}{\sqrt{2}}i$,

sum $= \frac{1}{\sqrt{2}} + \frac{1}{\sqrt{2}}i + \frac{1}{\sqrt{2}} - \frac{1}{\sqrt{2}}i$ 　　product $= \left(\frac{1}{\sqrt{2}} + \frac{1}{\sqrt{2}}i\right)\left(\frac{1}{\sqrt{2}} - \frac{1}{\sqrt{2}}i\right)$
$= \frac{2}{\sqrt{2}} = \sqrt{2}$ 　　　　　　　　　　　　$= \frac{1}{2} + \frac{1}{2} = 1$

and so we have a quadratic factor of $z^2 - \sqrt{2}z + 1$
For the pair of roots $-\frac{1}{\sqrt{2}} \pm \frac{1}{\sqrt{2}}i$, sum $= -\sqrt{2}$ and product $= \frac{1}{2} + \frac{1}{2} = 1$
and so we have a quadratic factor of $z^2 + \sqrt{2}z + 1$
$\therefore z^4 + 1 = \left(z^2 - \sqrt{2}z + 1\right)\left(z^2 + \sqrt{2}z + 1\right)$

8 a $z = \dfrac{\left(\frac{\sqrt{3}}{2} - \frac{1}{2}i\right)^2}{\left(\cos\frac{\pi}{10} - i\sin\frac{\pi}{10}\right)^5 \left(\cos\frac{\pi}{30} + i\sin\frac{\pi}{30}\right)^{25}}$

$= \dfrac{\operatorname{cis}\left(-\frac{\pi}{6}\right)^2}{\left(\cos\left(-\frac{\pi}{10}\right) + i\sin\left(-\frac{\pi}{10}\right)\right)^5 \left(\cos\frac{\pi}{30} + i\sin\frac{\pi}{30}\right)^{25}}$

$= \dfrac{\operatorname{cis}\left(-\frac{\pi}{3}\right)}{\left(\operatorname{cis}\left(-\frac{\pi}{10}\right)\right)^5 \left(\operatorname{cis}\left(\frac{\pi}{30}\right)\right)^{25}}$

$= \dfrac{\operatorname{cis}\left(-\frac{\pi}{3}\right)}{\operatorname{cis}\left(-\frac{\pi}{2}\right) \operatorname{cis}\left(\frac{5\pi}{6}\right)}$

$= \dfrac{\operatorname{cis}\left(-\frac{\pi}{3}\right)}{\operatorname{cis}\left(\frac{\pi}{3}\right)}$

$= \operatorname{cis}\left(-\frac{2\pi}{3}\right)$

$\therefore |z| = 1, \quad \arg z = -\frac{2\pi}{3}$

b $z^3 = \left[\text{cis}\left(-\frac{2\pi}{3}\right)\right]^3$
$= \text{cis}(-2\pi)$ {De Moivre}
$= 1$
$\therefore$ z is a cube root of 1.

c $(1-2z)(2z^2-1) = 2z^2 - 1 - 4z^3 + 2z$
$= 2z^2 - 1 - 4(1) + 2z$ $\{z^3 = 1\}$
$= 2z^2 + 2z - 5$

Now $z^3 = 1$ $\therefore$ $z^2 = z^{-1}$, $z \neq 0$
$= \left[\text{cis}\left(-\frac{2\pi}{3}\right)\right]^{-1}$
$= \text{cis}\left(\frac{2\pi}{3}\right)$ {De Moivre}
$= z^*$
$\therefore$ $2z^2 + 2z - 5 = 2z^* + 2z - 5$
$= 2(z + z^*) - 5$

which is real as $z + z^*$ is always real.

9 a $-16i = 16 \text{ cis}\left(-\frac{\pi}{2}\right)$

b $z^4 = -16i$
$\therefore$ $z^4 = 16 \text{ cis}\left(-\frac{\pi}{2} + k2\pi\right)$
$\therefore$ $z = \left[16 \text{ cis}\left(-\frac{\pi}{2} + k2\pi\right)\right]^{\frac{1}{4}}$
$\therefore$ $z = 2 \text{ cis}\left(-\frac{\pi}{8} + \frac{k\pi}{2}\right)$ {De Moivre}
$\therefore$ $z = 2 \text{ cis}\left(-\frac{\pi}{8} + \frac{k4\pi}{8}\right)$
$\therefore$ $z = 2 \text{ cis}\left(-\frac{\pi}{8}\right)$, $2 \text{ cis}\left(\frac{3\pi}{8}\right)$, $2 \text{ cis}\left(\frac{7\pi}{8}\right)$, $2 \text{ cis}\left(-\frac{5\pi}{8}\right)$ {when $k = 0, 1, 2, -1$}

i The 4th root in the second quadrant is $z = 2 \text{ cis}\left(\frac{7\pi}{8}\right)$ $\{\frac{\pi}{2} < \frac{7\pi}{8} < \pi\}$

ii In Cartesian form, $z = 2\left[\cos\left(\frac{7\pi}{8}\right) + i \sin\left(\frac{7\pi}{8}\right)\right]$
$= 2 \cos\left(\frac{7\pi}{8}\right) + \left[2 \sin\left(\frac{7\pi}{8}\right)\right] i$

EXERCISE 15D.2

1 a i $(z+3)^3 = 1$
$\therefore$ $z + 3 = 1$, w or w^2 where $w = \text{cis}\left(\frac{2\pi}{3}\right)$
$\therefore$ $z + 3 = w^n$ where $n = 0, 1, 2$
$\therefore$ $z = w^n - 3$ where $n = 0, 1, 2$ and $w = \text{cis}\left(\frac{2\pi}{3}\right)$

ii $(z-1)^3 = 8$
$\therefore$ $\left[\frac{z-1}{2}\right]^3 = 1$
$\therefore$ $\frac{z-1}{2} = 1$, w or w^2 where $w = \text{cis}\left(\frac{2\pi}{3}\right)$
$\therefore$ $\frac{z-1}{2} = w^n$ where $n = 0, 1, 2$
$\therefore$ $z = 2w^n + 1$ where $n = 0, 1, 2$ and $w = \text{cis}\left(\frac{2\pi}{3}\right)$

iii $(2z-1)^3 = -1$
$\therefore$ $(2z-1)^3 = (-1)^3$
$\therefore$ $\left(\frac{2z-1}{-1}\right)^3 = 1$
$\therefore$ $(1-2z)^3 = 1$

$\therefore$ $1 - 2z = 1$, w, w^2 where $w = \text{cis}\left(\frac{2\pi}{3}\right)$
$\therefore$ $1 - 2z = w^n$ where $n = 0, 1, 2$
$\therefore$ $2z = 1 - w^n$
$\therefore$ $z = \frac{1 - w^n}{2}$ where $n = 0, 1, 2$ and $w = \text{cis}\left(\frac{2\pi}{3}\right)$

b The following represents the cube roots of unity:

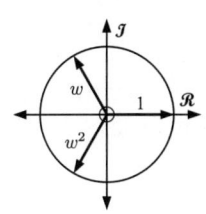

Adding these vectorially

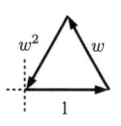

the resultant vector is **0**
$\therefore \ 1 + w + w^2 = 0$

2 a If $w = \text{cis}\left(\frac{\pi}{2}\right)$, $w^2 = \text{cis}\,\pi$
and $w^3 = \text{cis}\left(\frac{3\pi}{2}\right)$ {De Moivre}
$\therefore \ w = i, \ w^2 = -1$ and $w^3 = -i$
$\therefore \ 1, i, -1, -i$ can be written as
$1, w, w^2, w^3$, where $w = \text{cis}\left(\frac{\pi}{2}\right)$

b $1 + w + w^2 + w^3 = 1 + (i) + (-1) + (-i)$
$= 1 + i - 1 - i$
$= 0$

c Adding these vectorially

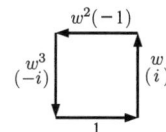

3 a The 5th roots of unity are the solutions to $z^5 = 1$.
$\therefore \ z^5 = \text{cis}\,(0 + k2\pi)$
$\therefore \ z^5 = \text{cis}\,(k2\pi)$
$\therefore \ z = [\text{cis}\,(k2\pi)]^{\frac{1}{5}}$
$\therefore \ z = \text{cis}\left(\frac{k2\pi}{5}\right)$ {De Moivre}
$\therefore \ z = \text{cis}\,0 = 1$ or
$\text{cis}\left(\frac{2\pi}{5}\right) = w$ or
$\text{cis}\left(\frac{4\pi}{5}\right) = \left(\text{cis}\,\frac{2\pi}{5}\right)^2 = w^2$ or
$\text{cis}\left(\frac{6\pi}{5}\right) = \left(\text{cis}\,\frac{2\pi}{5}\right)^3 = w^3$ or
$\text{cis}\left(\frac{8\pi}{5}\right) = \left(\text{cis}\,\frac{2\pi}{5}\right)^4 = w^4$ {when $k = 0, 1, 2, 3, 4$}

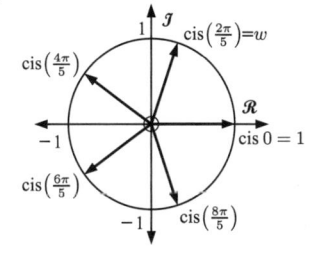

b Hence the five roots can be expressed as $1, w, w^2, w^3, w^4$ where $w = \text{cis}\left(\frac{2\pi}{5}\right)$

c $(1 + w + w^2 + w^3 + w^4)(1 - w)$
$= 1 + w + w^2 + w^3 + w^4 - w - w^2 - w^3 - w^4 - w^5$
$= 1 - w^5$
Since w is a solution of $z^5 = 1$, $1 - w^5 = 0$
$\therefore \ (1 + w + w^2 + w^3 + w^4)(1 - w) = 0$
But $w \neq 1$, so $1 + w + w^2 + w^3 + w^4 = 0$

d

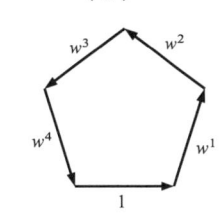

4 a The nth roots of unity are the solutions to $z^n = 1$
$z^n = 1$
$\therefore \ z^n = \text{cis}\,(0 + k2\pi)$
$\therefore \ z^n = \text{cis}\,(k2\pi)$
$\therefore \ z = [\text{cis}\,(k2\pi)]^{\frac{1}{n}}$
$\therefore \ z = \text{cis}\left(\frac{k2\pi}{n}\right)$ {De Moivre}
$\therefore \ z = \text{cis}\,0 = 1$ or
$\text{cis}\left(\frac{2\pi}{n}\right) = w$ or
$\text{cis}\left(\frac{4\pi}{n}\right) = \left(\text{cis}\left(\frac{2\pi}{n}\right)\right)^2 = w^2$ or
$\vdots$
$\text{cis}\left(\frac{2\pi}{n}(n-1)\right) = \left[\text{cis}\left(\frac{2\pi}{n}\right)\right]^{n-1} = w^{n-1}$ {letting $k = 0, 1, 2, 3, \ldots, n-1$}
$\therefore$ the n roots of $z^n = 1$ are $1, w, w^2, w^3, \ldots, w^{n-1}$ where $w = \text{cis}\left(\frac{2\pi}{n}\right)$

b Now $(1 + w + w^2 + \ldots + w^{n-1})(w - 1) = w^n - 1$
But w is a solution to $z^n - 1 = 0$ so $w^n - 1 = 0$
$\therefore$ $(1 + w + w^2 + \ldots + w^{n-1})(w - 1) = 0$
$\therefore$ since $w \neq 1$, $1 + w + w^2 + \ldots + w^{n-1} = 0$

5 Let $a = r \text{ cis } \theta$
$\therefore$ $z^n = r \text{ cis } (\theta + k2\pi)$
$\therefore$ $z^n = r \text{ cis } \theta \text{ cis } (k2\pi)$
$\therefore$ $z = [r \text{ cis } \theta \text{ cis } (k2\pi)]^{\frac{1}{n}}$
$\therefore$ $z = r^{\frac{1}{n}} \text{ cis } \left(\frac{\theta}{n}\right) \text{ cis } \left(\frac{k2\pi}{n}\right)$ {De Moivre}
$\therefore$ the n zeros of $z^n = a$ are $r^{\frac{1}{n}} \text{ cis } \left(\frac{\theta}{n}\right)$, $r^{\frac{1}{n}} \text{ cis } \left(\frac{\theta}{n}\right) \text{ cis } \left(\frac{2\pi}{n}\right)$, $r^{\frac{1}{n}} \text{ cis } \left(\frac{\theta}{n}\right) \text{ cis } \left(\frac{4\pi}{n}\right)$, ...,
$r^{\frac{1}{n}} \text{ cis } \left(\frac{\theta}{n}\right) \text{ cis } \left(\frac{2\pi}{n}(n-1)\right)$ {letting $k = 0, 1, 2, \ldots, n - 1$}
$\therefore$ the sum of the n zeros of z is

$r^{\frac{1}{n}} \text{ cis } \left(\frac{\theta}{n}\right) + r^{\frac{1}{n}} \text{ cis } \left(\frac{\theta}{n}\right) \text{ cis } \left(\frac{2\pi}{n}\right) + r^{\frac{1}{n}} \text{ cis } \left(\frac{\theta}{n}\right) \text{ cis } \left(\frac{4\pi}{n}\right) + \ldots + r^{\frac{1}{n}} \text{ cis } \left(\frac{\theta}{n}\right) \text{ cis } \left(\frac{2\pi}{n}(n-1)\right)$

$= r^{\frac{1}{n}} \text{ cis } \left(\frac{\theta}{n}\right) \underbrace{\left[1 + \text{cis } \left(\frac{2\pi}{n}\right) + \text{cis } \left(\frac{4\pi}{n}\right) + \ldots + \text{cis } \left(\frac{2\pi}{n}(n-1)\right)\right]}_{\text{These are the }n\text{th roots of unity, whose sum} = 0 \quad \{\text{using } \mathbf{4}\}}$

$= 0$

EXERCISE 15E

1 $z^2 - (2 + i)z + (3 + i) = 0$

$\therefore$ $z = \dfrac{2 + i \pm \sqrt{(2+i)^2 - 4(1)(3+i)}}{2}$

$= \dfrac{2 + i \pm \sqrt{4 + 4i - 1 - 12 - 4i}}{2}$

$= \dfrac{2 + i \pm \sqrt{-9}}{2}$

$= \dfrac{2 + i \pm 3i}{2}$

$= \dfrac{2 + 4i}{2}$ or $\dfrac{2 - 2i}{2}$

$= 1 + 2i$ or $1 - i$

2 a $z^* = -iz$
$\therefore$ $x - iy = -i(x + iy)$
$\therefore$ $x - iy = -ix + y$
Equating real and imaginary parts,
$x = y$ and $-y = -x$
$\therefore$ $y = x$

b $\arg(z - i) = \frac{\pi}{6}$
$\therefore$ $\arg(x + iy - i) = \frac{\pi}{6}$
$\therefore$ $\arg(x + (y - 1)i) = \frac{\pi}{6}$
$\therefore$ $\tan \frac{\pi}{6} = \frac{1}{\sqrt{3}} = \frac{y-1}{x}$
$\therefore$ $y - 1 = \frac{x}{\sqrt{3}}$
$\therefore$ $y = \frac{x}{\sqrt{3}} + 1$, $x > 0$

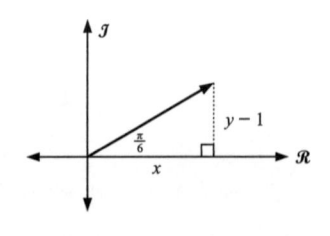

c $|z+3| + |z-3| = 8$

$\therefore \quad |z+3| = 8 - |z-3|$

$\therefore \quad |z+3|^2 = (8 - |z-3|)^2$

$\therefore \quad |z+3|^2 = 64 - 16|z-3| + |z-3|^2$

$\therefore \quad (z+3)(z+3)^* = 64 - 16|z-3| + (z-3)(z-3)^* \quad \{|z|^2 = zz^*\}$

$\therefore \quad (z+3)(z^*+3) = 64 - 16|z-3| + (z-3)(z^*-3) \quad \{(z \pm w)^* = z^* \pm w^*\}$

$\therefore \quad \cancel{zz^*} + 3z + 3z^* + \cancel{9} = 64 - 16|(x-3) + yi| + \cancel{zz^*} - 3z - 3z^* + \cancel{9}$

$\therefore \quad 6z + 6z^* = 64 - 16\sqrt{(x-3)^2 + y^2}$

$\therefore \quad 6(x+yi) + 6(x-yi) = 64 - 16\sqrt{(x-3)^2 + y^2}$

$\therefore \quad 12x - 64 = -16\sqrt{(x-3)^2 + y^2}$

$\therefore \quad 3x - 16 = -4\sqrt{(x-3)^2 + y^2}$

$\therefore \quad (3x-16)^2 = 16\left[(x-3)^2 + y^2\right]$

$\therefore \quad 9x^2 - 96x + 256 = 16(x^2 - 6x + 9 + y^2)$

$\therefore \quad 9x^2 - \cancel{96x} + 256 = 16x^2 - \cancel{96x} + 144 + 16y^2$

$\therefore \quad 112 = 7x^2 + 16y^2$

3 $(1+i)^{2n} = \binom{2n}{0}1^{2n}i^0 + \binom{2n}{1}1^{2n-1}i^1 + \binom{2n}{2}1^{2n-2}i^2 + \binom{2n}{3}1^{2n-3}i^3 + \ldots + \binom{2n}{2n}1^0 i^{2n}$

$= \binom{2n}{0} + \binom{2n}{1}i - \binom{2n}{2} - \binom{2n}{3}i + \ldots + \binom{2n}{2n}(-1)^n$

But $(1+i)^{2n} = \left(\sqrt{2} \text{ cis } \frac{\pi}{4}\right)^{2n}$

$= \left(2 \text{ cis } \frac{\pi}{2}\right)^n$

$= 2^n \text{ cis } \left(\frac{n\pi}{2}\right)$

$= 2^n \left[\cos\left(\frac{n\pi}{2}\right) + i\sin\left(\frac{n\pi}{2}\right)\right]$

So, $\binom{2n}{0} + \binom{2n}{1}i - \binom{2n}{2} - \binom{2n}{3}i + \ldots + \binom{2n}{2n}(-1)^n = 2^n \left[\cos\left(\frac{n\pi}{2}\right) + i\sin\left(\frac{n\pi}{2}\right)\right]$

Equating real parts,

$\binom{2n}{0} - \binom{2n}{2} + \binom{2n}{4} - \binom{2n}{6} + \ldots + (-1)^n \binom{2n}{2n} = 2^n \cos\left(\frac{n\pi}{2}\right), \quad n \in \mathbb{Z}^+$

4 $1 + \text{cis } \theta + \text{cis } 2\theta + \text{cis } 3\theta + \ldots + \text{cis } n\theta$

$= 1 + (\cos\theta + i\sin\theta) + (\cos 2\theta + i\sin 2\theta) + (\cos 3\theta + i\sin 3\theta) + \ldots + (\cos n\theta + i\sin n\theta)$

$= (1 + \cos\theta + \cos 2\theta + \cos 3\theta + \ldots + \cos n\theta) + i(\sin\theta + \sin 2\theta + \sin 3\theta + \ldots + \sin n\theta)$

$= \sum_{r=0}^{n} \cos r\theta + i \sum_{r=1}^{n} \sin r\theta$

$\therefore \quad \mathcal{R}e \, (1 + \text{cis } \theta + \text{cis } 2\theta + \text{cis } 3\theta + \ldots + \text{cis } n\theta) = \sum_{r=0}^{n} \cos r\theta \quad \ldots (1)$

Now $\quad 1 + \text{cis } \theta + \text{cis } 2\theta + \text{cis } 3\theta + \ldots + \text{cis } n\theta$

$= 1 + \text{cis } \theta + (\text{cis } \theta)^2 + (\text{cis } \theta)^3 + \ldots + (\text{cis } \theta)^n$

which is a geometric series with $u_1 = 1$, $r = \text{cis } \theta$

$\therefore \quad$ it has sum $\quad S_n = \dfrac{u_1(r^n - 1)}{r - 1}$

$\therefore \quad 1 + \text{cis } \theta + \text{cis } 2\theta + \ldots + \text{cis } n\theta = \dfrac{1(\text{cis } (n+1)\theta - 1)}{\text{cis } \theta - 1}$

$= \dfrac{\cos(n+1)\theta + i\sin(n+1)\theta - 1}{\cos\theta + i\sin\theta - 1}$

$= \left(\dfrac{\cos(n+1)\theta + i\sin(n+1)\theta - 1}{\cos\theta - 1 + i\sin\theta}\right)\left(\dfrac{\cos\theta - 1 - i\sin\theta}{\cos\theta - 1 - i\sin\theta}\right)$

$\therefore \; \mathcal{Re}\,(1 + \text{cis}\,\theta + \text{cis}\,2\theta + \ldots + \text{cis}\,n\theta)$

$= \dfrac{\cos(n+1)\theta\cos\theta - \cos(n+1)\theta + \sin(n+1)\theta\sin\theta - \cos\theta + 1}{(\cos\theta - 1)^2 + \sin^2\theta}$

$= \dfrac{[\cos(n+1)\theta\cos\theta + \sin(n+1)\theta\sin\theta] - \cos(n+1)\theta - \cos\theta + 1}{\cos^2\theta - 2\cos\theta + 1 + \sin^2\theta}$

$= \dfrac{\cos n\theta - \cos(n+1)\theta - \cos\theta + 1}{2 - 2\cos\theta}$ .... (2)

Equating (1) and (2) gives $\displaystyle\sum_{r=0}^{n} \cos r\theta = \dfrac{\cos n\theta - \cos(n+1)\theta - \cos\theta + 1}{2 - 2\cos\theta}$

5 $2\cos\left(\frac{\theta}{2}\right)\text{cis}\left(\frac{\theta}{2}\right) = 2\cos\left(\frac{\theta}{2}\right)\left[\cos\left(\frac{\theta}{2}\right) + i\sin\left(\frac{\theta}{2}\right)\right]$

$\qquad = 2\cos^2\left(\frac{\theta}{2}\right) + 2i\cos\left(\frac{\theta}{2}\right)\sin\left(\frac{\theta}{2}\right)$

$\qquad = \cos\theta + 1 + i\left(2\cos\left(\frac{\theta}{2}\right)\sin\left(\frac{\theta}{2}\right)\right) \qquad \left\{ \begin{array}{l} \cos 2X = 2\cos^2 X - 1 \\ \therefore \; 2\cos^2 X = \cos 2X + 1 \end{array} \right\}$

$\qquad = \cos\theta + 1 + i\sin\theta$

$\qquad = 1 + \text{cis}\,\theta$

Consider $(1 + \text{cis}\,\theta)^n = \binom{n}{0}1^n\,(\text{cis}\,\theta)^0 + \binom{n}{1}1^{n-1}\,(\text{cis}\,\theta)^1 + \binom{n}{2}1^{n-2}\,(\text{cis}\,\theta)^2 + \ldots + \binom{n}{n}1^0\,(\text{cis}\,\theta)^n$

$\qquad\qquad\qquad\quad = \binom{n}{0} + \binom{n}{1}\text{cis}\,\theta + \binom{n}{2}\text{cis}\,2\theta + \ldots + \binom{n}{n}\text{cis}\,n\theta$

$\therefore \; \mathcal{Re}\,[(1 + \text{cis}\,\theta)^n] = \binom{n}{0} + \binom{n}{1}\cos\theta + \binom{n}{2}\cos 2\theta + \ldots + \binom{n}{n}\cos n\theta$

$\qquad\qquad\qquad\quad = \displaystyle\sum_{r=0}^{n}\binom{n}{r}\cos(r\theta)$

So $\displaystyle\sum_{r=0}^{n}\binom{n}{r}\cos(r\theta) = \mathcal{Re}\,[(1 + \text{cis}\,\theta)^n]$

$\qquad\qquad\qquad = \mathcal{Re}\left[\left(2\cos\left(\frac{\theta}{2}\right)\text{cis}\left(\frac{\theta}{2}\right)\right)^n\right]$

$\qquad\qquad\qquad = \mathcal{Re}\left[2^n\cos^n\left(\frac{\theta}{2}\right)\text{cis}\left(\frac{n\theta}{2}\right)\right]$

$\qquad\qquad\qquad = 2^n\cos^n\left(\frac{\theta}{2}\right)\cos\left(\frac{n\theta}{2}\right)$

REVIEW SET 15A

1 $(i - \sqrt{3})^2 = i^2 - 2\sqrt{3}i + 3$
$\qquad\quad = 2 - 2\sqrt{3}i$
$\therefore \; (i - \sqrt{3})^4 = (2 - 2\sqrt{3}i)^2$
$\qquad\qquad\quad = 4 - 8\sqrt{3}i + 12i^2$
$\qquad\qquad\quad = -8 - 8\sqrt{3}i$

$\therefore \; (i - \sqrt{3})^5 = (-8 - 8\sqrt{3}i)(i - \sqrt{3})$
$\qquad\qquad\quad = -8i + 8\sqrt{3} + 8\sqrt{3} + 24i$
$\qquad\qquad\quad = 16\sqrt{3} + 16i$
$\therefore$ real part is $16\sqrt{3}$, imaginary part is 16.

2 a $|z - i| = |z + 1 + i|$ Since $z = x + iy$,
$\qquad |x + iy - i| = |x + iy + 1 + i|$
$\therefore \; |x + i(y - 1)| = |(x + 1) + i(y + 1)|$
$\therefore \; \sqrt{x^2 + (y - 1)^2} = \sqrt{(x + 1)^2 + (y + 1)^2}$
$\therefore \; x^2 + (y - 1)^2 = (x + 1)^2 + (y + 1)^2$
$\therefore \; x^2 + y^2 - 2y + 1 = x^2 + 2x + 1 + y^2 + 2y + 1$
$\therefore \; 1 - 2y = 2x + 2y + 2$
$\therefore \; 2x + 4y = -1$

b $z^* - iz = 0$
Since $z = x + iy$,
$x - iy - i(x + iy) = 0$
$\therefore \; x - iy - ix + y = 0$
$\therefore \; (x + y) - i(x + y) = 0$
$\therefore \; x + y = 0$
$\therefore \; y = -x$

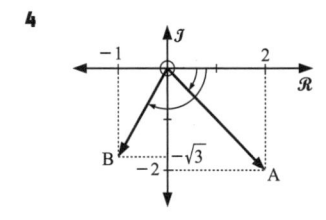

3
$$|z+16| = 4|z+1|$$
$$\therefore \quad |z+16|^2 = 16|z+1|^2$$
$$\therefore \quad (z+16)(z+16)^* = 16(z+1)(z+1)^* \quad \{|w|^2 = ww^*\}$$
$$\therefore \quad (z+16)(z^* + 16^*) = 16(z+1)(z^* + 1^*)$$
$$\therefore \quad zz^* + 16z + 16z^* + 256 = 16(zz^* + z + z^* + 1) \quad \{16^* = 16, \ 1^* = 1\}$$
$$\therefore \quad |z|^2 + \cancel{16z} + \cancel{16z^*} + 256 = 16|z|^2 + \cancel{16z} + \cancel{16z^*} + 16$$
$$240 = 15|z|^2$$
$$\therefore \quad |z|^2 = 16$$
$$\therefore \quad |z| = 4 \text{ as } |z| \geqslant 0$$

4

a $\arg \overrightarrow{OA} = \frac{-\pi}{4}$

$\arg \overrightarrow{OB} = \frac{-2\pi}{3}$

$\therefore \ \widehat{AOB} = \frac{2\pi}{3} - \frac{\pi}{4}$

$= \frac{5\pi}{12}$

b zw
$= 2\sqrt{2} \text{ cis}\left(\frac{-\pi}{4}\right) \times 2 \text{ cis}\left(\frac{-2\pi}{3}\right)$
$= 4\sqrt{2} \text{ cis}\left(\frac{-\pi}{4} + \frac{-2\pi}{3}\right)$
$= 4\sqrt{2} \text{ cis}\left(\frac{-11\pi}{12}\right)$
$\therefore \ \arg(zw) = \frac{-11\pi}{12}$

5 a $-5i = 5 \text{ cis}\left(-\frac{\pi}{2}\right)$

b $2 - 2i\sqrt{3} = 4\left(\frac{1}{2} - \frac{\sqrt{3}}{2}i\right)$
$= 4 \text{ cis}\left(-\frac{\pi}{3}\right)$

c $k - ki = -k\sqrt{2}\left(-\frac{1}{\sqrt{2}} + \frac{1}{\sqrt{2}}i\right)$
$= -k\sqrt{2} \text{ cis}\left(\frac{3\pi}{4}\right)$ which is in polar form since $k < 0$

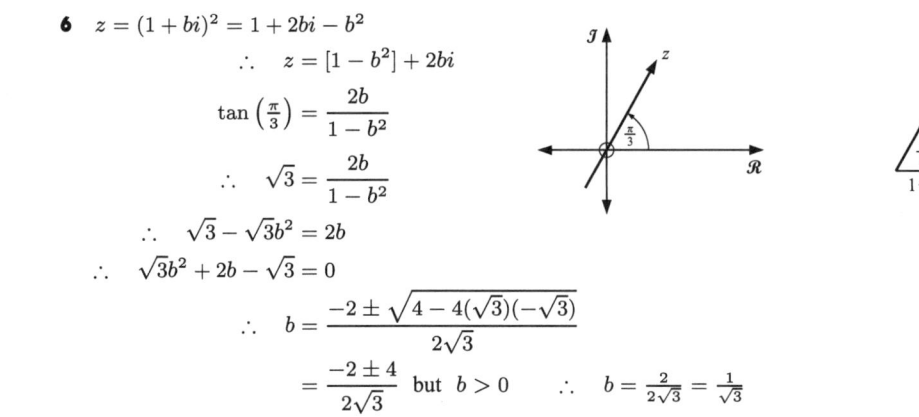

6 $z = (1 + bi)^2 = 1 + 2bi - b^2$
$$\therefore \quad z = [1 - b^2] + 2bi$$
$$\tan\left(\frac{\pi}{3}\right) = \frac{2b}{1 - b^2}$$
$$\therefore \quad \sqrt{3} = \frac{2b}{1 - b^2}$$
$$\therefore \quad \sqrt{3} - \sqrt{3}b^2 = 2b$$
$$\therefore \quad \sqrt{3}b^2 + 2b - \sqrt{3} = 0$$
$$\therefore \quad b = \frac{-2 \pm \sqrt{4 - 4(\sqrt{3})(-\sqrt{3})}}{2\sqrt{3}}$$
$$= \frac{-2 \pm 4}{2\sqrt{3}} \text{ but } b > 0 \quad \therefore \ b = \frac{2}{2\sqrt{3}} = \frac{1}{\sqrt{3}}$$

7 a $\text{cis } \theta \times \text{cis } \phi$
$= (\cos \theta + i \sin \theta)(\cos \phi + i \sin \phi)$
$= (\cos \theta \cos \phi - \sin \theta \sin \phi) + i(\sin \theta \cos \phi + \cos \theta \sin \phi)$
$= \cos(\theta + \phi) + i \sin(\theta + \phi)$
$= \text{cis}(\theta + \phi)$ as required

b $1 - i = \sqrt{2}\left(\frac{1}{\sqrt{2}} - \frac{1}{\sqrt{2}}i\right) = \sqrt{2} \text{ cis}\left(-\frac{\pi}{4}\right)$
$\therefore \ (1 - i)z = \sqrt{2} \text{ cis}\left(-\frac{\pi}{4}\right) \times 2\sqrt{2} \text{ cis } \alpha$
$= 4 \text{ cis}\left(\alpha - \frac{\pi}{4}\right) \quad \{\text{using } \mathbf{a}\}$
$\therefore \ \arg[(1 - i)z] = \alpha - \frac{\pi}{4}$

8 a $\left|\dfrac{z_1^2}{z_2^2}\right| = \dfrac{|z_1|^2}{|z_2|^2}$ But $|z_1| = |z_2|$ since the triangle is isosceles

$\therefore \left|\dfrac{z_1^2}{z_2^2}\right| = 1$

Also, $\arg\left(\dfrac{z_1^2}{z_2^2}\right)$

$= \arg(z_1^2) - \arg(z_2^2)$
$= 2\arg z_1 - 2\arg z_2$
$= 2(\arg z_1 - \arg z_2)$
$= 2 \times \dfrac{\pi}{2}$ since z_1 and z_2 are perpendicular
$= \pi$

a $\dfrac{z_1^2}{z_2^2} = \operatorname{cis} \pi = -1$ $\therefore z_1^2 = -z_2^2$ $\therefore z_1^2 + z_2^2 = 0$

9 $z = \sqrt[4]{a}\left(\cos\dfrac{\pi}{6} + i\sin\dfrac{\pi}{6}\right) = \sqrt[4]{a}\,\operatorname{cis}\dfrac{\pi}{6}$

$w = \sqrt[4]{b}\left(\cos\dfrac{\pi}{4} - i\sin\dfrac{\pi}{4}\right) = \sqrt[4]{b}\left(\cos\left(-\dfrac{\pi}{4}\right) + i\sin\left(-\dfrac{\pi}{4}\right)\right) = \sqrt[4]{b}\,\operatorname{cis}\left(-\dfrac{\pi}{4}\right)$

$\therefore \left(\dfrac{z}{w}\right)^4 = \dfrac{z^4}{w^4} = \dfrac{\left(\sqrt[4]{a}\,\operatorname{cis}\dfrac{\pi}{6}\right)^4}{\left(\sqrt[4]{b}\,\operatorname{cis}\left(-\dfrac{\pi}{4}\right)\right)^4}$

$= \dfrac{a\,\operatorname{cis}\dfrac{2\pi}{3}}{b\,\operatorname{cis}(-\pi)}$

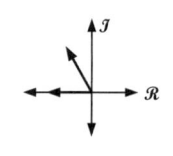

$= \dfrac{a\left(-\dfrac{1}{2} + \dfrac{\sqrt{3}}{2}i\right)}{b(-1)}$

$= \dfrac{a}{2b} - \dfrac{a\sqrt{3}}{2b}i$ $\therefore \operatorname{Re}\left(\left(\dfrac{z}{w}\right)^4\right) = \dfrac{a}{2b}$, $\operatorname{Im}\left(\left(\dfrac{z}{w}\right)^4\right) = -\dfrac{a\sqrt{3}}{2b}$

10 a The 5th roots of unity are the solutions to $z^5 = 1$.   **b**

$\therefore z^5 = \operatorname{cis}(0 + k2\pi)$
$\therefore z^5 = \operatorname{cis}(k2\pi)$
$\therefore z = [\operatorname{cis}(k2\pi)]^{\frac{1}{5}}$
$\therefore z = \operatorname{cis}\left(\dfrac{k2\pi}{5}\right)$ {De Moivre}
$\therefore z = \operatorname{cis} 0 = 1$ or
$\operatorname{cis}\left(\dfrac{2\pi}{5}\right) = w$ or
$\operatorname{cis}\left(\dfrac{4\pi}{5}\right) = \left(\operatorname{cis}\dfrac{2\pi}{5}\right)^2 = w^2$ or
$\operatorname{cis}\left(\dfrac{6\pi}{5}\right) = \left(\operatorname{cis}\dfrac{2\pi}{5}\right)^3 = w^3$ or
$\operatorname{cis}\left(\dfrac{8\pi}{5}\right) = \left(\operatorname{cis}\dfrac{2\pi}{5}\right)^4 = w^4$ {when $k = 0, 1, 2, 3, 4$}

Hence the five roots can be expressed as $1, w, w^2, w^3, w^4$ where $w = \operatorname{cis}\left(\dfrac{2\pi}{5}\right)$

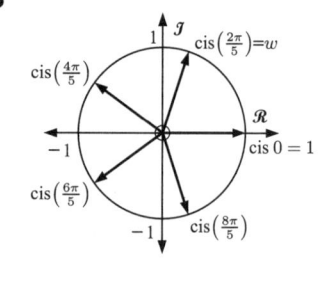

c $z^5 - 1 = (z - 1)(z^4 + z^3 + z^2 + z + 1)$ .... (1)
Also, since $1, w, w^2, w^3$ and w^4 are the solutions to $z^5 = 1$,
$z^5 - 1 = (z - 1)(z - w)(z - w^2)(z - w^3)(z - w^4)$ .... (2)
Equating (1) and (2),
$(z - 1)(z^4 + z^3 + z^2 + z + 1) = (z - 1)(z - w)(z - w^2)(z - w^3)(z - w^4)$
$\therefore z^4 + z^3 + z^2 + z + 1 = (z - w)(z - w^2)(z - w^3)(z - w^4)$

d $(2-w)(2-w^2)(2-w^3)(2-w^4) = 2^4 + 2^3 + 2^2 + 2 + 1$ {letting $z=2$}
$= 16 + 8 + 4 + 2 + 1$
$= 31$

11 The cube roots of $-8i$ are solutions to $z^3 = -8i$
$z^3 = 8 \text{ cis}\left(-\frac{\pi}{2} + k2\pi\right)$ where k is an integer
$\therefore \quad z = 8^{\frac{1}{3}} \text{ cis}\left(-\frac{\pi}{6} + \frac{k2\pi}{3}\right)$
$\therefore \quad z = 2 \text{ cis}\left(-\frac{\pi}{6} + \frac{k4\pi}{6}\right)$
$\therefore \quad z = 2 \text{ cis}\left(-\frac{\pi}{6}\right),\ 2 \text{ cis}\left(\frac{\pi}{2}\right),\ 2 \text{ cis}\left(-\frac{5\pi}{6}\right)$ {letting $k = 0,\ 1,\ -1$}
$\therefore \quad z = \sqrt{3} - i,\ 2i,\ -\sqrt{3} - i$

REVIEW SET 15B

1 $z_1 = \text{cis}\left(\frac{\pi}{6}\right)$ and $z_2 = \text{cis}\left(\frac{\pi}{4}\right)$

$\therefore \quad \left(\frac{z_1}{z_2}\right)^3 = \left[\frac{\text{cis}\left(\frac{\pi}{6}\right)}{\text{cis}\left(\frac{\pi}{4}\right)}\right]^3 = \left[\text{cis}\left(\frac{\pi}{6} - \frac{\pi}{4}\right)\right]^3$

$\therefore \quad \left(\frac{z_1}{z_2}\right)^3 = \left[\text{cis}\left(-\frac{\pi}{12}\right)\right]^3 = \text{cis}\left(-\frac{3\pi}{12}\right)$ {De Moivre}

$\therefore \quad \left(\frac{z_1}{z_2}\right)^3 = \text{cis}\left(-\frac{\pi}{4}\right) = \cos\left(-\frac{\pi}{4}\right) + i\sin\left(-\frac{\pi}{4}\right)$

$\therefore \quad \left(\frac{z_1}{z_2}\right)^3 = \frac{1}{\sqrt{2}} - \frac{1}{\sqrt{2}}i$

2 $z = 4 + i, \quad w = 2 - 3i$

a $2w^* - iz$
$= 2(2 + 3i) - i(4 + i)$
$= 4 + 6i - 4i - i^2$
$= 5 + 2i$

b $|w - z^*| = |(2 - 3i) - (4 - i)|$
$= |2 - 3i - 4 + i|$
$= |-2 - 2i|$
$= \sqrt{(-2)^2 + (-2)^2}$
$= \sqrt{8}$
$= 2\sqrt{2}$

c $|z^{10}| = |z|^{10}$
$= |4 + i|^{10}$
$= \left(\sqrt{16 + 1}\right)^{10}$
$= \sqrt{17}^{10}$
$= 17^5$

d $\arg(w - z) = \arg\left[(2 - 3i) - (4 + i)\right]$
$= \arg\left[-2 - 4i\right]$
≈ -2.03

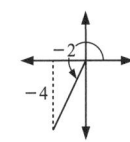

3 If $\dfrac{2 - 3i}{2a + bi} = 3 + 2i$, then $\dfrac{2 - 3i}{3 + 2i} = 2a + bi$

$\therefore \quad 2a + bi = \left(\dfrac{2 - 3i}{3 + 2i}\right)\left(\dfrac{3 - 2i}{3 - 2i}\right) = \dfrac{6 - 4i - 9i - 6}{9 + 4}$

$\therefore \quad 2a + bi = \dfrac{0 - 13i}{13} = 0 - i$

$\therefore \quad 2a = 0$ and $b = -1$ $\therefore \quad a = 0,\ b = -1$

4 a If $\arg z = \frac{\pi}{2}$, then we have a ray vertically upwards beginning at the origin.

If $\arg(z - i) = \frac{\pi}{2}$, the graph is translated $\begin{pmatrix} 0 \\ 1 \end{pmatrix}$, and we have a ray vertically upwards beginning at i.

$\therefore \ x = 0$, and geometrically we require $y > 1$.

b $\left|\dfrac{z+2}{z-2}\right| = 2, \quad \therefore \ \dfrac{|z+2|}{|z-2|} = 2$

$\therefore \ |z+2| = 2|z-2|$

If $z = x + iy$, then $\sqrt{(x+2)^2 + y^2} = 2\sqrt{(x-2)^2 + y^2}$

$\therefore \ (x+2)^2 + y^2 = 4(x-2)^2 + 4y^2$

$\therefore \ x^2 + 4x + 4 + y^2 = 4x^2 - 16x + 16 + 4y^2$

$\therefore \ 3x^2 + 3y^2 - 20x + 12 = 0$, which is a circle

5 $2 - 2\sqrt{3}i = 4\left(\frac{1}{2} - \frac{\sqrt{3}}{2}i\right)$

$= 4 \operatorname{cis}\left(-\frac{\pi}{3}\right)$

$\therefore \ (2 - 2\sqrt{3}i)^n = 4^n \operatorname{cis}\left(-\frac{n\pi}{3}\right) \qquad$ {De Moivre}

This is real if $\sin\left(-\frac{n\pi}{3}\right) = 0$

$\therefore \ -\frac{n\pi}{3} = k\pi, \ \ k$ an integer

$\therefore \ n = 3k$ where k is an integer

6 The cube roots of -27 are the solutions to $z^3 = -27$.

$\therefore \ z^3 = 27 \operatorname{cis}(\pi + k2\pi)$

$\therefore \ z = [27 \operatorname{cis}(\pi + k2\pi)]^{\frac{1}{3}}$

$\therefore \ z = 27^{\frac{1}{3}} \operatorname{cis}\left(\frac{\pi + k2\pi}{3}\right)$

$\therefore \ z = 3 \operatorname{cis}\left(\frac{\pi + k2\pi}{3}\right)$

$\therefore \ z = 3 \operatorname{cis}\left(\frac{\pi}{3}\right), \ 3 \operatorname{cis} \pi, \ 3 \operatorname{cis}\left(-\frac{\pi}{3}\right) \qquad$ {letting $k = 0, 1, -1$}

$\therefore \ z = 3(\frac{1}{2} + \frac{\sqrt{3}}{2}i), \ 3(-1 + 0i), \ 3(\frac{1}{2} - \frac{\sqrt{3}}{2}i)$

$\therefore \ z = -3$ or $\frac{3}{2} \pm \frac{3\sqrt{3}}{2}i$

7 a $z = 4 \operatorname{cis} \theta$

$z^3 = (4 \operatorname{cis} \theta)^3$

$= 4^3 \operatorname{cis} 3\theta$

$\therefore \ |z^3| = 64$

and $\arg(z^3) = 3\theta$

b $\dfrac{1}{z} = z^{-1}$

$= (4 \operatorname{cis} \theta)^{-1}$

$= 4^{-1} \operatorname{cis}(-\theta)$

$\therefore \ \left|\dfrac{1}{z}\right| = \frac{1}{4}$ and $\arg\left(\dfrac{1}{z}\right) = -\theta$

c If $z = 4 \operatorname{cis} \theta$

$z^* = 4 \operatorname{cis}(-\theta)$

$iz^* = \left(\operatorname{cis} \frac{\pi}{2}\right)(4 \operatorname{cis}(-\theta))$

$= 4 \operatorname{cis}\left(\frac{\pi}{2} - \theta\right)$

$\therefore \ |iz^*| = 4$ and $\arg(iz^*) = \frac{\pi}{2} - \theta$

8 a Let $z = r \operatorname{cis} \theta$

$\therefore \ z^n = r^n \operatorname{cis} n\theta \quad$ {De Moivre}

and so $\arg z^n = n\theta$

$\therefore \ \arg z^n = n \arg z$ as required

b $\left(\dfrac{z}{w}\right)^* = \left(\dfrac{a+bi}{c+di}\right)^*, \quad w \neq 0$ and also $\dfrac{z^*}{w^*} = \dfrac{a-bi}{c-di}, \quad w \neq 0$

$= \left(\dfrac{(a+bi)(c-di)}{(c+di)(c-di)}\right)^*$ $\qquad = \dfrac{(a-bi)(c+di)}{(c-di)(c+di)}$

$= \left(\dfrac{(ac+bd)+i(bc-ad)}{c^2+d^2}\right)^*$ $\qquad = \dfrac{(ac+bd)-i(bc-ad)}{c^2+d^2}$

$= \dfrac{(ac+bd)-i(bc-ad)}{c^2+d^2}$ $\qquad = \left(\dfrac{z}{w}\right)^*$

9 a $\cos 3\theta + i\sin 3\theta = \operatorname{cis} 3\theta = (\operatorname{cis}\theta)^3 \quad \therefore \quad n = 3$

b $\dfrac{1}{\cos 2\theta + i\sin 2\theta} \times \dfrac{\cos 2\theta - i\sin 2\theta}{\cos 2\theta - i\sin 2\theta}$ or $\dfrac{1}{\cos 2\theta + i\sin 2\theta} = \dfrac{1}{\operatorname{cis} 2\theta}$

$= \dfrac{\cos 2\theta - i\sin 2\theta}{\cos^2 2\theta + \sin^2 2\theta}$ $\qquad\qquad = (\operatorname{cis} 2\theta)^{-1}$

$= \cos 2\theta - i\sin 2\theta$ $\qquad\qquad = [(\operatorname{cis}\theta)^2]^{-1}$

$= \cos(-2\theta) + i\sin(-2\theta)$ $\qquad\qquad = (\operatorname{cis}\theta)^{-2}$

$= \operatorname{cis}(-2\theta)$ $\qquad\qquad \therefore \quad n = -2$

$= (\operatorname{cis}\theta)^{-2} \quad \therefore \quad n = -2$

c $\cos\theta - i\sin\theta$

$= \cos(-\theta) + i\sin(-\theta)$

$= \operatorname{cis}(-\theta)$

$= (\operatorname{cis}\theta)^{-1} \quad \therefore \quad n = -1$

10 The fifth roots of $2+2i$ are the solutions to $z^5 = 2+2i$

$\therefore \quad z^5 = 2\sqrt{2} \operatorname{cis}\left(\dfrac{\pi}{4} + k2\pi\right)$

$\therefore \quad z = \left[2^{\frac{3}{2}} \operatorname{cis}\left(\dfrac{\pi}{4} + k2\pi\right)\right]^{\frac{1}{5}}$

$\therefore \quad z = 2^{0.3} \operatorname{cis}\left(\dfrac{\pi}{20} + \dfrac{k2\pi}{5}\right) \quad$ {De Moivre}

$\therefore \quad z = 2^{0.3} \operatorname{cis}\left(\dfrac{\pi}{20} + \dfrac{k8\pi}{20}\right)$

$\therefore \quad z = 2^{0.3} \operatorname{cis}\left(\dfrac{\pi}{20}\right), \; 2^{0.3} \operatorname{cis}\left(\dfrac{9\pi}{20}\right), \; 2^{0.3} \operatorname{cis}\left(\dfrac{17\pi}{20}\right), \; 2^{0.3} \operatorname{cis}\left(-\dfrac{7\pi}{20}\right), \; 2^{0.3} \operatorname{cis}\left(-\dfrac{3\pi}{4}\right)$

(letting $k = 0, 1, 2, -1, -2$)

11 Let $z = x + iy \quad \therefore \quad z + \dfrac{1}{z} = (x+iy) + \dfrac{1}{x+iy} \times \dfrac{x-iy}{x-iy}$

$= (x+iy) + \dfrac{(x-iy)}{x^2+y^2}$

$= \dfrac{(x^2+y^2)(x+iy) + (x-iy)}{x^2+y^2}$

$= \dfrac{x^3 + ix^2y + xy^2 + y^3 i + x - iy}{x^2+y^2}$

$= \dfrac{x(x^2+y^2+1) + i(x^2+y^2-1)y}{x^2+y^2}$

which is real if $\dfrac{(x^2+y^2-1)y}{x^2+y^2} = 0 \quad \therefore \quad x^2+y^2-1=0 \quad \text{or} \quad y=0$

$\therefore \quad x^2+y^2 = 1 \quad \text{or} \quad y=0$

$\therefore \quad |z|^2 = 1 \quad \text{or} \quad y=0$

$\therefore \quad |z| = 1 \quad \text{or} \quad z \text{ is real}$

or Let $z = r\text{ cis }\theta$ $\therefore$ $z + \dfrac{1}{z} = r\text{ cis }\theta + \dfrac{1}{r}\text{ cis}(-\theta)$

$$= r\cos\theta + ir\sin\theta + \dfrac{1}{r}\cos(-\theta) + i \times \dfrac{1}{r}\sin(-\theta)$$

This is real if $r\sin\theta + \dfrac{1}{r}\sin(-\theta) = 0$

$\therefore$ $r\sin\theta - \dfrac{1}{r}\sin\theta = 0$

$\therefore$ $\sin\theta\left(r - \dfrac{1}{r}\right) = 0$

$\therefore$ $\sin\theta = 0$ or $r - \dfrac{1}{r} = 0$

$\therefore$ $\theta = 0$ or $r = 1$ $\{r \geqslant 0\}$

$\therefore$ $z = r$ (which is real) or $|z| = 1$

12 a If $z = \text{cis }\theta$
$ = \cos\theta + i\sin\theta$
$\therefore$ $|z| = \sqrt{\cos^2\theta + \sin^2\theta}$
$ = \sqrt{1}$
$ = 1$

b If $z = \text{cis }\theta$
then $z^* = \text{cis}(-\theta)$
$\therefore$ $zz^* = \text{cis }\theta\,\text{cis}(-\theta)$
$ = \text{cis}(\theta + (-\theta))$
$ = \text{cis }0$
$ = 1$ $\therefore$ $z^* = \dfrac{1}{z}$

c $z = \text{cis }\theta$
$\therefore$ $z^4 = (\text{cis }\theta)^4$
$\therefore$ $z^4 = \text{cis }4\theta$ {De Moivre}
$\therefore$ $z^4 = \cos 4\theta + i\sin 4\theta$ .... (1)

Also, $z^4 = (\cos\theta + i\sin\theta)^4$
$\therefore$ $z^4 = \cos^4\theta + 4\cos^3\theta i\sin\theta + 6\cos^2\theta i^2\sin^2\theta + 4\cos\theta i^3\sin^3\theta + i^4\sin^4\theta$
$\therefore$ $z^4 = \cos^4\theta + 4i\cos^3\theta\sin\theta - 6\cos^2\theta\sin^2\theta - 4i\cos\theta\sin^3\theta + \sin^4\theta$ .... (2)

Equating (1) and (2) gives
$\cos 4\theta + i\sin 4\theta = \cos^4\theta + 4i\cos^3\theta\sin\theta - 6\cos^2\theta\sin^2\theta - 4i\cos\theta\sin^3\theta + \sin^4\theta$

Equating real parts gives
$\cos 4\theta = \cos^4\theta - 6\cos^2\theta\sin^2\theta + \sin^4\theta$

$\therefore$ $\sin^4\theta = \cos 4\theta - \cos^4\theta + 6\cos^2\theta\sin^2\theta$
$ = \cos 4\theta - (1 - \sin^2\theta)^2 + 6(1 - \sin^2\theta)\sin^2\theta$
$ = \cos 4\theta - (1 - 2\sin^2\theta + \sin^4\theta) + 6\sin^2\theta - 6\sin^4\theta$
$ = \cos 4\theta - 1 + 2\sin^2\theta - \sin^4\theta + 6\sin^2\theta - 6\sin^4\theta$

$\therefore$ $8\sin^4\theta = \cos 4\theta - 1 + 8\sin^2\theta$
$ = \cos 4\theta - 1 + 8\left(\tfrac{1}{2} - \tfrac{1}{2}\cos 2\theta\right)$
$ = \cos 4\theta - 1 + 4 - 4\cos 2\theta$
$ = \cos 4\theta - 4\cos 2\theta + 3$

$\therefore$ $\sin^4\theta = \tfrac{1}{8}(\cos 4\theta - 4\cos 2\theta + 3)$

13 a If w is the root of $z^5 = 1$ with smallest positive argument, then $w = \text{cis}\left(\dfrac{2\pi}{5}\right)$ and $w^4 = \text{cis}\left(\dfrac{8\pi}{5}\right)$.

These have sum $= \cos\left(\dfrac{2\pi}{5}\right) + i\sin\left(\dfrac{2\pi}{5}\right) + \cos\left(\dfrac{8\pi}{5}\right) + i\sin\left(\dfrac{8\pi}{5}\right)$
$\phantom{\text{These have sum}} = \cos\left(\dfrac{2\pi}{5}\right) + i\sin\left(\dfrac{2\pi}{5}\right) + \cos\left(\dfrac{2\pi}{5}\right) - i\sin\left(\dfrac{2\pi}{5}\right)$
$\phantom{\text{These have sum}} = 2\cos\left(\dfrac{2\pi}{5}\right)$

and product $= \text{cis}\left(\dfrac{2\pi}{5}\right) \times \text{cis}\left(\dfrac{8\pi}{5}\right) = \text{cis}\left(\dfrac{10\pi}{5}\right) = \text{cis}2\pi = 1$

$\therefore$ a real quadratic with roots w, w^4 is $a\left(z^2 - 2\cos\left(\dfrac{2\pi}{5}\right)z + 1\right) = 0$, $a \neq 0$

b Let $\alpha = w + w^4$ and $\beta = w^2 + w^3$
Now we know that $1 + w + w^2 + w^3 + w^4 = 0$ .... (*)
$$1 + (w + w^4) + (w^2 + w^3) = 0$$
$$1 + \alpha + \beta = 0$$
$$\alpha + \beta = -1$$
and $\alpha\beta = (w + w^4)(w^2 + w^3)$
$$= w^3 + w^4 + w^6 + w^7$$
$$= w^3 + w^4 + w + w^2 \quad \{\text{as } w^5 = 1\}$$
$$= w + w^2 + w^3 + w^4$$
$$= -1 \quad \{\text{from } (*)\}$$

$\therefore$ the quadratic equation is $\quad a(z^2 + z - 1) = 0, \quad a \neq 0$

14 Consider the diagram which shows vectors w, z, $z + w$ and $z - w$.

Clearly OABC is a parallelogram with $\overrightarrow{OB} = z + w$ and $\overrightarrow{CA} = z - w$

If $|z + w| = |z - w|$, the diagonals are equal in length.

Hence, OABC is actually a rectangle and so $\widehat{COA}$ is a right angle $\therefore$ $\arg z$ and $\arg w$ differ by $\frac{\pi}{2}$.

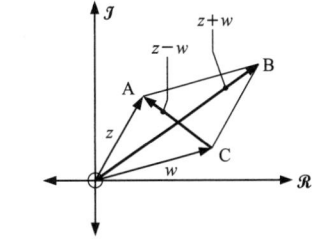

15 a $\quad |z| = |z + 4|$
$\therefore \quad |z|^2 = |z + 4|^2$
Let $z = x + yi$
$\therefore \quad |x + yi|^2 = |(x + 4) + yi|^2$
$\therefore \quad x^2 + y^2 = (x + 4)^2 + y^2$
$\therefore \quad \cancel{x^2} + \cancel{y^2} = \cancel{x^2} + 8x + 16 + \cancel{y^2}$
$\therefore \quad -8x = 16$
$\therefore \quad x = -2$
$\therefore$ the real part of z is -2.

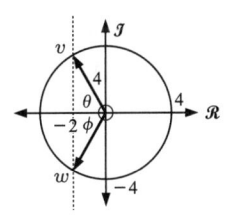

b i

ii In the diagram above, $\cos\theta = \frac{2}{4} = \frac{1}{2}$
$\therefore \quad \theta = \arccos(\frac{1}{2}) = \frac{\pi}{3}$
$\therefore \quad \arg v = \pi - \theta = \frac{2\pi}{3}$

iii $\cos\phi = \frac{2}{4} = \frac{1}{2}$
$\therefore \quad \phi = \arccos(\frac{1}{2}) = \frac{\pi}{3}$
$\therefore \quad \arg w = -\pi + \phi = -\frac{2\pi}{3}$

c i $v = 4 \operatorname{cis}\left(\frac{2\pi}{3}\right)$, $w = 4 \operatorname{cis}\left(-\frac{2\pi}{3}\right)$

$\therefore \quad \dfrac{v^m w}{i} = \dfrac{\left(4 \operatorname{cis}\left(\frac{2\pi}{3}\right)\right)^m 4 \operatorname{cis}\left(-\frac{2\pi}{3}\right)}{\operatorname{cis}\left(\frac{\pi}{2}\right)}$

$= \dfrac{4^m \operatorname{cis}\left(\frac{2m\pi}{3}\right) 4 \operatorname{cis}\left(-\frac{2\pi}{3}\right)}{\operatorname{cis}\left(\frac{\pi}{2}\right)}$

$= 4^{m+1} \operatorname{cis}\left(\dfrac{2m\pi}{3} - \dfrac{2\pi}{3} - \dfrac{\pi}{2}\right)$

$\therefore \quad \arg\left(\dfrac{v^m w}{i}\right) = \dfrac{2m\pi}{3} - \dfrac{2\pi}{3} - \dfrac{\pi}{2}$

$= \dfrac{4m\pi}{6} - \dfrac{4\pi}{6} - \dfrac{3\pi}{6}$

$= \dfrac{\pi(4m - 7)}{6}$

ii $\dfrac{v^m w}{i}$ is real when

$\arg\left(\dfrac{v^m w}{i}\right) = 0 + k\pi, \quad k \in \mathbb{Z}$

$\therefore \quad \dfrac{\pi(4m - 7)}{6} = k\pi$

$\therefore \quad 4m - 7 = 6k$

$\therefore \quad m = \dfrac{7 + 6k}{4}$

One such value of m is
$m = \frac{7}{4}$ {when $k = 0$}

REVIEW SET 15C

1 **a** $z = r \text{ cis } \theta$
  $z^* = r \text{ cis } (-\theta)$
  $\therefore$ T is a reflection in the real axis.

b $z = r \text{ cis } \theta$
  $-z = -r \text{ cis } \theta$
  $= \text{cis } \pi \times r \text{ cis } \theta$
  $= r \text{ cis } (\theta + \pi)$
  $\therefore$ T is a rotation of π about O.

c $z = r \text{ cis } \theta$
  $iz = ir \text{ cis } \theta$
  $= \text{cis}\left(\frac{\pi}{2}\right) r \text{ cis } \theta$
  $= r \text{ cis }\left(\theta + \frac{\pi}{2}\right)$
  $\therefore$ T is an anticlockwise rotation of $\frac{\pi}{2}$ about O.

2 Let $z = a + bi$ and $w = c + di$ $\quad \therefore \quad z + w = (a + c) + i(b + d)$, so $b + d = 0$ .... (1)
and $zw = (a + bi)(c + di)$
$= [ac - bd] + i[ad + bc]$
so, $ad + bc = 0$ .... (2)
From (1) $d = -b$ and in (2) $a(-b) + bc = 0$
$\therefore \quad b(c - a) = 0$
$\therefore \quad a = c$ as $b \neq 0$
So $z = a + bi$ and $w = a - bi$
$\therefore \quad z^* = a - bi = w$

3 If $(x + iy)^n = X + Yi$
$|(x + yi)^n| = |X + Yi|$
$|x + iy|^n = |X + Yi|$
$\left(\sqrt{x^2 + y^2}\right)^n = \sqrt{X^2 + Y^2}$
Squaring both sides, $X^2 + Y^2 = (x^2 + y^2)^n$

4 $|z - w|^2 + |z + w|^2 = (z - w)(z - w)^* + (z + w)(z + w)^*$
$= (z - w)(z^* - w^*) + (z + w)(z^* + w^*)$
$= zz^* - zw^* - wz^* + ww^* + zz^* + zw^* + wz^* + ww^*$
$= 2zz^* + 2ww^*$
$= 2|z|^2 + 2|w|^2$
$= 2\left(|z|^2 + |w|^2\right)$

5 **a** Since 1 is a root of $z^5 - 1 = 0$, we find that
$z^5 - 1 = (z - 1)(1 + z + z^2 + z^3 + z^4)$
$\therefore$ since α is a root,
$(\alpha - 1)(1 + \alpha + \alpha^2 + \alpha^3 + \alpha^4) = 0$
But $\alpha \neq 1$, so $1 + \alpha + \alpha^2 + \alpha^3 + \alpha^4 = 0$

1	1	0	0	0	0	-1
	0	1	1	1	1	1
	1	1	1	1	1	0

or Note that $1 + \alpha + \alpha^2 + \alpha^3 + \alpha^4$ is the sum of a geometric series.
Then $S_n = \dfrac{a(1 - r^n)}{1 - r} \quad a = 1, \; r = \alpha, \; n = 5$
$\therefore \quad S_5 = \dfrac{1(1 - \alpha^5)}{1 - \alpha}$ and $\alpha^5 = \text{cis}(2\pi) = 1$
$\therefore \quad 1 + \alpha + \alpha^2 + \alpha^3 + \alpha^4 = \dfrac{1(1 - 1)}{1 - \alpha} = 0$

b Now if $\left(\dfrac{z + 2}{z - 1}\right)^5 = 1$ then $\dfrac{z + 2}{z - 1} = 1, \; \alpha, \; \alpha^2, \; \alpha^3$ or α^4 where $\alpha = \text{cis}\left(\dfrac{2\pi}{5}\right)$
$\therefore \quad \dfrac{z + 2}{z - 1} = \alpha^n$ where $n = 0, \; 1, \; 2, \; 3, \; 4$
$\therefore \quad z + 2 = \alpha^n(z - 1)$

$\therefore \quad z + 2 = \alpha^n z - \alpha^n$

$\therefore \quad z(\alpha^n - 1) = \alpha^n + 2 \quad \text{and so} \quad z = \dfrac{\alpha^n + 2}{\alpha^n - 1}$

$\therefore$ roots of $\left(\dfrac{z+2}{z-1}\right)^5 = 1$ are $\dfrac{\alpha+2}{\alpha-1}, \dfrac{\alpha^2+2}{\alpha^2-1}, \dfrac{\alpha^3+2}{\alpha^3-1}, \dfrac{\alpha^4+2}{\alpha^4-1}$, where $\alpha = \text{cis}\left(\dfrac{2\pi}{5}\right)$

Note: The case where $n = 0$ requires $\dfrac{z+2}{z-1} = 1$, and so $z + 2 = z - 1$, which has no solution.

6

Since $\dfrac{|z+1|}{|z-1|} = 1$, then $|z+1| = |z-1|$

Letting $z = x + iy$,

$\therefore \quad |(x+1) + iy| = |(x-1) + iy|$

$\therefore \quad \sqrt{(x+1)^2 + y^2} = \sqrt{(x-1)^2 + y^2}$

Squaring both sides, we get $(x+1)^2 + y^2 = (x-1)^2 + y^2$

$\therefore \quad x^2 + 2x + 1 = x^2 - 2x + 1 \quad \therefore \quad 4x = 0 \quad \therefore \quad x = 0$

Therefore since $z \neq 0$, z is purely imaginary.

7 $w = \dfrac{1+z}{1+z^*} = \dfrac{1 + \text{cis } \phi}{1 + \text{cis}(-\phi)} \times \dfrac{\text{cis } \phi}{\text{cis } \phi}$

$= \dfrac{(1 + \text{cis } \phi) \text{ cis } \phi}{\text{cis } \phi + \text{cis } 0}$

$= \dfrac{(1 + \text{cis } \phi) \text{ cis } \phi}{1 + \text{cis } \phi}$

$= \text{cis } \phi$

8

$-1 + i\sqrt{3} = 2 \text{ cis}\left(\dfrac{2\pi}{3}\right)$

$\therefore \quad (-1 + i\sqrt{3})^m = 2^m \text{ cis}\left(\dfrac{m 2\pi}{3}\right) \quad \{\text{De Moivre}\}$

$= 2^m \left[\cos\left(\dfrac{m 2\pi}{3}\right) + i \sin\left(\dfrac{m 2\pi}{3}\right)\right]$

This is real provided $\sin\left(\dfrac{m 2\pi}{3}\right) = 0$

$\therefore \quad \dfrac{m 2\pi}{3} = 0 + k\pi$

$\therefore \quad m = \dfrac{3k}{2}$ where k is any integer

9 We first note that $\cos(A+B) + \cos(A-B) = 2 \cos A \cos B$

and $\sin(A+B) + \sin(A-B) = 2 \sin A \cos B$ .... (*)

Now $\text{cis } \theta + \text{cis } \phi = (\cos \theta + i \sin \theta) + (\cos \phi + i \sin \phi)$

$= (\cos \theta + \cos \phi) + i(\sin \theta + \sin \phi)$

$= \left[\cos\left(\dfrac{\theta+\phi}{2} + \dfrac{\theta-\phi}{2}\right) + \cos\left(\dfrac{\theta+\phi}{2} - \dfrac{\theta-\phi}{2}\right)\right]$

$\quad + i \left[\sin\left(\dfrac{\theta+\phi}{2} + \dfrac{\theta-\phi}{2}\right) + \sin\left(\dfrac{\theta+\phi}{2} - \dfrac{\theta-\phi}{2}\right)\right]$

$= 2 \cos\left(\dfrac{\theta+\phi}{2}\right) \cos\left(\dfrac{\theta-\phi}{2}\right) + 2i \sin\left(\dfrac{\theta+\phi}{2}\right) \cos\left(\dfrac{\theta-\phi}{2}\right) \quad \{\text{using } (*)\}$

$= 2 \cos\left(\dfrac{\theta-\phi}{2}\right) \text{cis}\left(\dfrac{\theta+\phi}{2}\right) \quad \text{as required.}$

Now $Z^5 = 1$ has solutions $Z = 1, \alpha, \alpha^2, \alpha^3, \alpha^4$ where $\alpha = \text{cis}\left(\frac{2\pi}{5}\right)$

$\therefore\ Z = \text{cis}\left(\frac{2n\pi}{5}\right)$ where $n = 0, 1, 2, 3, 4$

$\therefore\ $ if $\left(\frac{z+1}{z-1}\right)^5 = 1,$ then $\frac{z+1}{z-1} = \text{cis}\left(\frac{2n\pi}{5}\right)$

$\therefore\ z + 1 = \text{cis}\left(\frac{2n\pi}{5}\right)(z-1)$

$\therefore\ z(\text{cis}\left(\frac{2n\pi}{5}\right) - 1) = \text{cis}\left(\frac{2n\pi}{5}\right) + 1$

$\therefore\ z = \dfrac{\text{cis}\left(\frac{2n\pi}{5}\right) + 1}{\text{cis}\left(\frac{2n\pi}{5}\right) - 1}$

$\therefore\ z = \dfrac{\text{cis}\left(\frac{2n\pi}{5}\right) + \text{cis}\,0}{\text{cis}\left(\frac{2n\pi}{5}\right) + \text{cis}\,\pi}$

$\therefore\ z = \dfrac{2\cos\left(\frac{\frac{2n\pi}{5} - 0}{2}\right)\text{cis}\left[\frac{\frac{2n\pi}{5} + 0}{2}\right]}{2\cos\left(\frac{\frac{2n\pi}{5} - \pi}{2}\right)\text{cis}\left[\frac{\frac{2n\pi}{5} + \pi}{2}\right]}$ {using the above identity}

$\therefore\ z = \dfrac{\cos\frac{n\pi}{5}}{\cos\left(\frac{n\pi}{5} - \frac{\pi}{2}\right)}\,\text{cis}\left[\frac{n\pi}{5} - \left(\frac{n\pi}{5} + \frac{\pi}{2}\right)\right]$

$\therefore\ z = \dfrac{\cos\frac{n\pi}{5}}{\cos\left[\left(\frac{\pi}{2} - \frac{n\pi}{5}\right)\right]}\,\text{cis}\left(-\frac{\pi}{2}\right)$

$\therefore\ z = \dfrac{\cos\frac{n\pi}{5}}{\sin\frac{n\pi}{5}}(-i)$

$\therefore\ z = -i\cot\left(\frac{n\pi}{5}\right),\ n = 1, 2, 3, 4$ {excluding $n = 0$ since $\cot 0$ is undefined}

Now $\cot\left(\frac{n\pi}{5}\right) = -\cot\left(\pi - \frac{n\pi}{5}\right)$

$= -\cot\left(\frac{(5-n)\pi}{5}\right),\ n = 1, 2, 3, 4$

$= -\cot\left(\frac{n\pi}{5}\right),\ n = 4, 3, 2, 1$

$\therefore\ z = i\cot\left(\frac{n\pi}{5}\right),\ n = 1, 2, 3, 4$

10 The 3 cube roots of $-64i$ are the solutions to $z^3 = -64i$

$\therefore\ z^3 = 64\,\text{cis}\left(-\frac{\pi}{2} + k2\pi\right)$ for integer k

$\therefore\ z = \left[64\,\text{cis}\left(-\frac{\pi}{2} + k2\pi\right)\right]^{\frac{1}{3}}$

$\therefore\ z = 64^{\frac{1}{3}}\,\text{cis}\left(-\frac{\pi}{6} + \frac{k2\pi}{3}\right)$

$\therefore\ z = 4\,\text{cis}\left(-\frac{\pi}{6} + \frac{k4\pi}{6}\right)$

$\therefore\ z = 4\,\text{cis}\left(-\frac{\pi}{6}\right),\ 4\,\text{cis}\left(\frac{\pi}{2}\right),\ 4\,\text{cis}\left(-\frac{5\pi}{6}\right)$ {letting $k = 0, 1, -1$}

$\therefore\ z = 4\left(\frac{\sqrt{3}}{2} - \frac{1}{2}i\right),\ 4i,\ 4\,\text{cis}\left(-\frac{\sqrt{3}}{2} - \frac{1}{2}i\right)$

$\therefore\ z = 2\sqrt{3} - 2i,\ 4i,\ -2\sqrt{3} - 2i$

11 a $(2z)^{-1} = (2\,\text{cis}\,\theta)^{-1}$

$= 2^{-1}\,\text{cis}(-\theta)$

$\therefore\ \left|(2z)^{-1}\right| = \frac{1}{2}$ and $\arg\left[(2z)^{-1}\right] = -\theta$

b $1 - z = 1 - \text{cis } \theta$
$= (1 - \cos \theta) - i \sin \theta$
$\therefore |1 - z| = \sqrt{(1 - \cos \theta)^2 + \sin^2 \theta}$
$= \sqrt{1 - 2\cos \theta + \cos^2 \theta + \sin^2 \theta}$
$= \sqrt{2 - 2\cos \theta}$
$= \sqrt{4\left(\frac{1}{2} - \frac{1}{2}\cos \theta\right)}$
$= 2\sqrt{\sin^2\left(\frac{\theta}{2}\right)}$
$= 2\sin\left(\frac{\theta}{2}\right)$

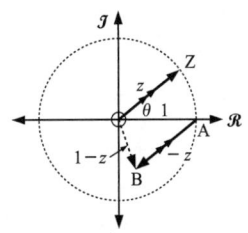

$\triangle OAB$ is isosceles since $|z| = 1$,
so we let $\widehat{AOB} = \widehat{ABO} = \phi$
Since $[OZ] \parallel [AB]$, $\widehat{OAB} = \theta$ {alternate $\angle$s}
$\therefore \phi + \phi + \theta = \pi$
$\therefore 2\phi = \pi - \theta$
$\phi = \frac{\pi}{2} - \frac{\theta}{2}$
But $\arg(1 - z) = -\phi$,
so $\arg(1 - z) = -\left(\frac{\pi}{2} - \frac{\theta}{2}\right)$
$= \frac{\theta}{2} - \frac{\pi}{2}$

12 $\{z \mid 2 \leqslant |z| \leqslant 5 \text{ and } -\frac{\pi}{4} < \arg z \leqslant \frac{\pi}{2}\}$

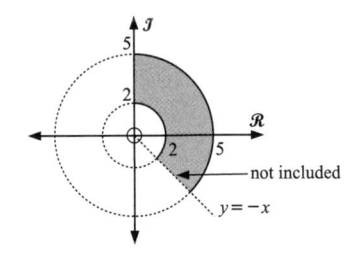

13 If $z = r \text{ cis } \theta$, then $|z| = r$ and $\arg z = \theta$
Now $\frac{1}{z} = (r \text{ cis } \theta)^{-1} = r^{-1} \text{ cis}(-\theta)$
$= \frac{1}{r} \text{ cis}(-\theta)$
$= \frac{1}{|z|} \text{ cis}(-\theta)$
$\therefore \left|\frac{1}{z}\right| = \frac{1}{|z|}$ (if $z \neq 0$), and $\arg\left(\frac{1}{z}\right) = -\theta$
$= -\arg z$

14 $z = \text{cis } \alpha$
$\therefore 1 + z = 1 + \text{cis } \alpha$
$= 1 + \cos \alpha + i \sin \alpha$
$= \left[1 + 2\cos^2\left(\frac{\alpha}{2}\right) - 1\right] + i\left[2\sin\left(\frac{\alpha}{2}\right)\cos\left(\frac{\alpha}{2}\right)\right]$
$= 2\cos^2\left(\frac{\alpha}{2}\right) + i\left[2\sin\left(\frac{\alpha}{2}\right)\cos\left(\frac{\alpha}{2}\right)\right]$
$= 2\cos\left(\frac{\alpha}{2}\right)\left[\cos\left(\frac{\alpha}{2}\right) + i\sin\left(\frac{\alpha}{2}\right)\right]$
$= 2\cos\left(\frac{\alpha}{2}\right) \text{cis}\left(\frac{\alpha}{2}\right)$
$\therefore |1 + z| = 2\cos\left(\frac{\alpha}{2}\right)$ and $\arg(1 + z) = \frac{\alpha}{2}$

15 a

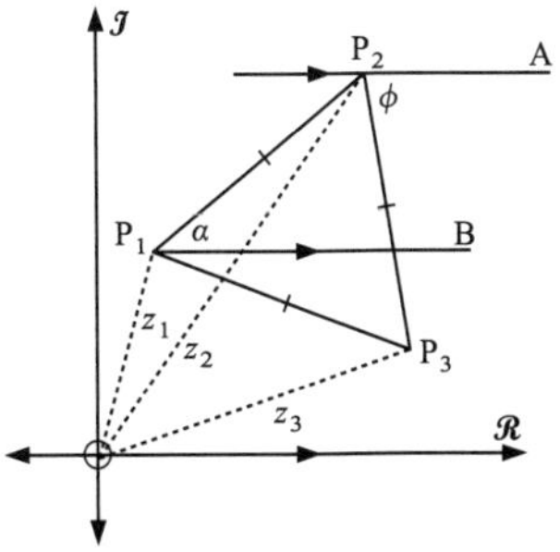

Now $z_2 - z_1 = \overrightarrow{P_1 P_2}$
so $\arg(z_2 - z_1) = \alpha$ as shown on the diagram alongside
$z_3 - z_2 = \overrightarrow{P_2 P_3}$
so $\arg(z_3 - z_2) = -\phi$
Now $\widehat{P_1 P_2 P_3} = \frac{\pi}{3}$ since the $\triangle$ is equilateral
$\therefore \alpha + \frac{\pi}{3} + \phi = \pi$ $\{(P_1 B) \parallel (P_2 A)$, co-interior angles$\}$
$\therefore \phi = -\alpha + \frac{2\pi}{3}$
$\therefore \arg(z_3 - z_2) = \alpha - \frac{2\pi}{3}$ as required

b $\left|\dfrac{z_2 - z_1}{z_3 - z_2}\right| = \dfrac{|\overrightarrow{P_1P_2}|}{|\overrightarrow{P_2P_3}|}$

$= 1$ since the Δ is equilateral

$\arg\left(\dfrac{z_2 - z_1}{z_3 - z_2}\right) = \arg(z_2 - z_1) - \arg(z_3 - z_2)$

$= \alpha - (\alpha - \tfrac{2\pi}{3})$ {part **a**}

$= \alpha - \alpha + \tfrac{2\pi}{3}$

$= \tfrac{2\pi}{3}$

16 If $z = 3 + i$ is a zero of $P(z)$, then $z^* = 3 - i$ is also a zero.
$\therefore$ the zeros of $P(z)$ are $3 \pm i$ and -3

$3 \pm i$ have sum $(3 + i) + (3 - i)$ and product $(3 + i)(3 - i)$
$= 6$ $= 9 + 1$
           $= 10$

$\therefore$ these zeros come from the quadratic factor $z^2 - 6z + 10$
$\therefore\ P(z) = z^3 + az^2 + bz + c = (z^2 - 6z + 10)(z + 3)$ {coefficient of z^3 is 1}
$= z^3 + 3z^2 - 6z^2 - 18z + 10z + 30$
$= z^3 - 3z^2 - 8z + 30$

$\therefore\ a = -3,\ b = -8,\ c = 30$

17 The fifth roots of unity are $1,\ w,\ w^2,\ w^3$ and w^4, where $w = \text{cis}\left(\tfrac{2\pi}{5}\right)$.

a $(2z - 1)^5 = 32$

$\therefore\ \dfrac{(2z - 1)^5}{2^5} = 1$

$\therefore\ \left(\dfrac{2z - 1}{2}\right)^5 = 1$

$\therefore\ \left(z - \tfrac{1}{2}\right)^5 = 1$

$\therefore\ z - \tfrac{1}{2} = 1,\ w,\ w^2,\ w^3$ or w^4

$\therefore\ z = \tfrac{3}{2},\ w + \tfrac{1}{2},\ w^2 + \tfrac{1}{2},$
$w^3 + \tfrac{1}{2}$ or $w^4 + \tfrac{1}{2}$

where $w = \text{cis}\left(\tfrac{2\pi}{5}\right)$

b $z^5 + 5z^4 + 10z^3 + 10z^2 + 5z = 0$
$\therefore\ z^5 + 5z^4 + 10z^3 + 10z^2 + 5z + 1 = 1$
$\therefore\ (z + 1)^5 = 1$

$\therefore\ z + 1 = 1,\ w,\ w^2,\ w^3,\ w^4$
$\therefore\ z = 0,\ w - 1,\ w^2 - 1,$
$w^3 - 1$ or $w^4 - 1$

where $w = \text{cis}\left(\tfrac{2\pi}{5}\right)$

c $(z + 1)^5 = (z - 1)^5$

$\therefore\ \dfrac{(z + 1)^5}{(z - 1)^5} = 1,\ z \neq 1$

$\therefore\ \left(\dfrac{z + 1}{z - 1}\right)^5 = 1$

$\therefore\ \dfrac{z + 1}{z - 1} = 1,\ w,\ w^2,\ w^3$ or w^4

$\dfrac{z + 1}{z - 1} = 1$ has no solutions as

$z + 1 \neq z - 1$ for any z

If $\dfrac{z + 1}{z - 1} = w^k,\ k = 1, 2, 3, 4$

$z + 1 = w^k z - w^k$

$\therefore\ z(1 - w^k) = -w^k - 1$

$\therefore\ z = \dfrac{-w^k - 1}{1 - w^k} = \dfrac{w^k + 1}{w^k - 1}$

$\therefore\ z = \dfrac{w + 1}{w - 1},\ \dfrac{w^2 + 1}{w^2 - 1},\ \dfrac{w^3 + 1}{w^3 - 1},\ \dfrac{w^4 + 1}{w^4 - 1}$

where $w = \text{cis}\left(\tfrac{2\pi}{5}\right)$

Chapter 16
LINES AND PLANES IN SPACE

EXERCISE 16A.1

1 a i $\begin{pmatrix} x \\ y \end{pmatrix} = \begin{pmatrix} 3 \\ -4 \end{pmatrix} + t \begin{pmatrix} 1 \\ 4 \end{pmatrix}$ **ii** $x = 3 + t, \ y = -4 + 4t, \ t \in \mathbb{R}$

   b i $\begin{pmatrix} x \\ y \end{pmatrix} = \begin{pmatrix} 5 \\ 2 \end{pmatrix} + t \begin{pmatrix} -8 \\ 2 \end{pmatrix}$ **ii** $x = 5 - 8t, \ y = 2 + 2t, \ t \in \mathbb{R}$

   c i $\begin{pmatrix} x \\ y \end{pmatrix} = \begin{pmatrix} -6 \\ 0 \end{pmatrix} + t \begin{pmatrix} 3 \\ 7 \end{pmatrix}$ **ii** $x = -6 + 3t, \ y = 7t, \ t \in \mathbb{R}$

   d i $\begin{pmatrix} x \\ y \end{pmatrix} = \begin{pmatrix} -1 \\ 11 \end{pmatrix} + t \begin{pmatrix} -2 \\ 1 \end{pmatrix}$ **ii** $x = -1 - 2t, \ y = 11 + t, \ t \in \mathbb{R}$

2 $x = -1 + 2\lambda, \ y = 4 - \lambda, \ \lambda \in \mathbb{R}$
  When $\lambda = 0$, $x = -1 + 2(0) = -1$ and $y = 4 - 0 = 4$ $\therefore$ the point is $(-1, 4)$.
  When $\lambda = 1$, $x = -1 + 2(1) = 1$ and $y = 4 - 1 = 3$ $\therefore$ the point is $(1, 3)$.
  When $\lambda = 3$, $x = -1 + 2(3) = 5$ and $y = 4 - 3 = 1$ $\therefore$ the point is $(5, 1)$.
  When $\lambda = -1$, $x = -1 + 2(-1) = -3$ and $y = 4 - -1 = 5$ $\therefore$ the point is $(-3, 5)$.
  When $\lambda = -4$, $x = -1 + 2(-4) = -9$ and $y = 4 - -4 = 8$ $\therefore$ the point is $(-9, 8)$.

3 a If $t + 2 = 3$ and $1 - 3t = -2$, we get $t = 1$ and $-3t = -3$ $\therefore$ $t = 1$
   Since $t = 1$ in each case, $(3, -2)$ lies on the line.
   If $t + 2 = 0$ and $1 - 3t = 6$, we get $t = -2$ and $-3t = 5$ $\therefore$ $t = -\frac{5}{3}$
   $\therefore$ $(0, 6)$ does not lie on the line.

   b If $(k, 4)$ lies on $x = 1 - 2t, \ y = 1 + t$, then
   $k = 1 - 2t$ and $4 = 1 + t$
   $\therefore$ $t = 3$
   and $k = 1 - 6 = -5$

4 a $x(0) = 1$ and $y(0) = 2$,
   $\therefore$ the initial position is $(1, 2)$

   c In 1 second, the
   x-step is 2 and y-step is -5, which is
   a distance of $\sqrt{2^2 + (-5)^2} = \sqrt{29}$ cm
   $\therefore$ the speed is $\sqrt{29}$ cm s^{-1}.

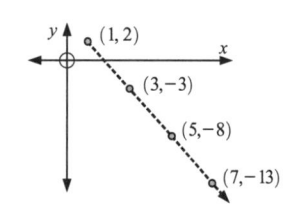

   b

   (graph showing points $(1,2)$, $(3,-3)$, $(5,-8)$, $(7,-13)$ on a line)

EXERCISE 16A.2

1 a The vector equation is $\begin{pmatrix} x \\ y \\ z \end{pmatrix} = \begin{pmatrix} 1 \\ 3 \\ -7 \end{pmatrix} + t \begin{pmatrix} 2 \\ 1 \\ 3 \end{pmatrix}, \ t \in \mathbb{R}$

   b The vector equation is $\begin{pmatrix} x \\ y \\ z \end{pmatrix} = \begin{pmatrix} 0 \\ 1 \\ 2 \end{pmatrix} + t \begin{pmatrix} 1 \\ 1 \\ -2 \end{pmatrix}, \ t \in \mathbb{R}$

   c Since the line is parallel to the X-axis, it has direction vector $\begin{pmatrix} 1 \\ 0 \\ 0 \end{pmatrix}$

   $\therefore$ the vector equation is $\begin{pmatrix} x \\ y \\ z \end{pmatrix} = \begin{pmatrix} -2 \\ 2 \\ 1 \end{pmatrix} + t \begin{pmatrix} 1 \\ 0 \\ 0 \end{pmatrix}, \ t \in \mathbb{R}$

2 **a** The parametric equations are:
$x = 5 + (-1)t, \ y = 2 + 2t, \ z = -1 + 6t$
$\therefore \ x = 5 - t, \ y = 2 + 2t, \ z = -1 + 6t, \ t \in \mathbb{R}$

b The parametric equations are:
$x = 0 + 2t, \ y = 2 + (-1)t, \ z = -1 + 3t$
$\therefore \ x = 2t, \ y = 2 - t, \ z = -1 + 3t, \ t \in \mathbb{R}$

c Since the line is perpendicular to the XOY plane, it has direction vector $\begin{pmatrix} 0 \\ 0 \\ 1 \end{pmatrix}$.

$\therefore$ the parametric equations are: $x = 3 + 0t, \ y = 2 + 0t, \ z = -1 + 1t$
$\therefore \ x = 3, \ y = 2, \ z = -1 + t, \ t \in \mathbb{R}$

3 **a** $\overrightarrow{AB} = \begin{pmatrix} -1 - 1 \\ 3 - 2 \\ 2 - 1 \end{pmatrix} = \begin{pmatrix} -2 \\ 1 \\ 1 \end{pmatrix}$ $\therefore \ x = 1 - 2t, \ y = 2 + t, \ z = 1 + t, \ t \in \mathbb{R}$

b $\overrightarrow{CD} = \begin{pmatrix} 3 - 0 \\ 1 - 1 \\ -1 - 3 \end{pmatrix} = \begin{pmatrix} 3 \\ 0 \\ -4 \end{pmatrix}$ $\therefore \ x = 3t, \ y = 1, \ z = 3 - 4t, \ t \in \mathbb{R}$

c $\overrightarrow{EF} = \begin{pmatrix} 1 - 1 \\ -1 - 2 \\ 5 - 5 \end{pmatrix} = \begin{pmatrix} 0 \\ -3 \\ 0 \end{pmatrix}$ $\therefore \ x = 1, \ y = 2 - 3t, \ z = 5, \ t \in \mathbb{R}$

d $\overrightarrow{GH} = \begin{pmatrix} 5 - 0 \\ -1 - 1 \\ 3 - -1 \end{pmatrix} = \begin{pmatrix} 5 \\ -2 \\ 4 \end{pmatrix}$ $\therefore \ x = 5t, \ y = 1 - 2t, \ z = -1 + 4t, \ t \in \mathbb{R}$

4 Given $x = 1 - \lambda, \ y = 3 + \lambda, \ z = 3 - 2\lambda$:

a The line meets the XOY plane when $z = 0$ $\therefore \ 3 - 2\lambda = 0$
$\therefore \ \lambda = \frac{3}{2}$
Then $x = 1 - \frac{3}{2} = -\frac{1}{2}$ and $y = 3 + \frac{3}{2} = \frac{9}{2}$, so the point is $\left(-\frac{1}{2}, \frac{9}{2}, 0\right)$.

b The line meets the YOZ plane when $x = 0$ $\therefore \ 1 - \lambda = 0$
$\therefore \ \lambda = 1$
Then $y = 3 + 1 = 4$ and $z = 3 - 2 = 1$, so the point is $(0, 4, 1)$.

c The line meets the XOZ plane when $y = 0$ $\therefore \ 3 + \lambda = 0$
$\therefore \ \lambda = -3$
Then $x = 1 - (-3) = 4$ and $z = 3 - 2(-3) = 9$, so the point is $(4, 0, 9)$.

5 Given a line with equations $x = 2 - \lambda, \ y = 3 + 2\lambda$ and $z = 1 + \lambda$,
the distance to the point $(1, 0, -2)$ is $\sqrt{(2 - \lambda - 1)^2 + (3 + 2\lambda - 0)^2 + (1 + \lambda + 2)^2}$.
But this distance $= 5\sqrt{3}$ units
$\therefore \ \sqrt{(1 - \lambda)^2 + (3 + 2\lambda)^2 + (\lambda + 3)^2} = 5\sqrt{3}$
$\therefore \ (1 - \lambda)^2 + (3 + 2\lambda)^2 + (\lambda + 3)^2 = 75$
$\therefore \ 1 - 2\lambda + \lambda^2 + 9 + 12\lambda + 4\lambda^2 + \lambda^2 + 6\lambda + 9 = 75$
$\therefore \ 6\lambda^2 + 16\lambda - 56 = 0$
$\therefore \ 3\lambda^2 + 8\lambda - 28 = 0$
$\therefore \ (3\lambda + 14)(\lambda - 2) = 0$
$\therefore \ \lambda = -\frac{14}{3}$ or $\lambda = 2$
When $\lambda = 2$ the point is $(0, 7, 3)$, and when $\lambda = -\frac{14}{3}$ the point is $\left(\frac{20}{3}, -\frac{19}{3}, -\frac{11}{3}\right)$.

6 a Let $A(1+\lambda, 2-\lambda, 3+\lambda)$ be a point on the line such that $\overrightarrow{PA}$ is perpendicular to the line.

Then $\overrightarrow{PA} = \begin{pmatrix} 1+\lambda-1 \\ 2-\lambda-1 \\ 3+\lambda-2 \end{pmatrix} = \begin{pmatrix} \lambda \\ 1-\lambda \\ 1+\lambda \end{pmatrix}$

and $PA = \sqrt{\lambda^2 + (1-\lambda)^2 + (1+\lambda)^2}$
$= \sqrt{\lambda^2 + (1-2\lambda+\lambda^2) + (1+2\lambda+\lambda^2)}$
$= \sqrt{3\lambda^2 + 2}$ units

$[PA]$ is perpendicular to the line when $PA^2 = 3\lambda^2 + 2$ is minimised, which occurs when $\lambda = -\dfrac{b}{2a} = -\dfrac{0}{6} = 0$

∴ A is at $(1+0, 2-0, 3+0)$
∴ the foot of the perpendicular is $(1, 2, 3)$.

b Let A be a point on the line such that $\overrightarrow{PA}$ is perpendicular to the line.
∴ A is at $(1+\mu, 2-\mu, 2\mu)$ for some μ.

Now $\overrightarrow{PA} = \begin{pmatrix} 1+\mu-2 \\ 2-\mu-1 \\ 2\mu-3 \end{pmatrix} = \begin{pmatrix} \mu-1 \\ 1-\mu \\ 2\mu-3 \end{pmatrix}$

and $PA = \sqrt{(\mu-1)^2 + (1-\mu)^2 + (2\mu-3)^2}$
$= \sqrt{\mu^2 - 2\mu + 1 + 1 - 2\mu + \mu^2 + 4\mu^2 - 12\mu + 9}$
$= \sqrt{6\mu^2 - 16\mu + 11}$ units

$[PA]$ is perpendicular to the line when $PA^2 = 6\mu^2 - 16\mu + 11$ is minimised, which occurs when $\mu = -\dfrac{b}{2a} = -\dfrac{-16}{12} = \frac{4}{3}$

∴ A is at $\left(1 + \frac{4}{3},\; 2 - \frac{4}{3},\; 2\left(\frac{4}{3}\right)\right)$
∴ the foot of the perpendicular is $\left(\frac{7}{3}, \frac{2}{3}, \frac{8}{3}\right)$.

EXERCISE 16A.3

1 l_1 has direction vector $\begin{pmatrix} 4 \\ -3 \end{pmatrix}$ and l_2 has direction vector $\begin{pmatrix} 5 \\ 4 \end{pmatrix}$. If θ is the angle between them,

$\cos\theta = \dfrac{\left|\begin{pmatrix} 4 \\ -3 \end{pmatrix} \bullet \begin{pmatrix} 5 \\ 4 \end{pmatrix}\right|}{\sqrt{16+9}\sqrt{25+16}} = \dfrac{|20+(-12)|}{\sqrt{25 \times 41}} = \dfrac{8}{\sqrt{25 \times 41}}$

∴ $\theta = \arccos\left(\dfrac{8}{\sqrt{25 \times 41}}\right) \approx 75.5°$

∴ the required angle measures $75.5°$.

2 l_1 has direction vector $\begin{pmatrix} 12 \\ 5 \end{pmatrix}$ and l_2 has direction vector $\begin{pmatrix} 3 \\ -4 \end{pmatrix}$. If θ is the angle between them,

$\cos\theta = \dfrac{\left|\begin{pmatrix} 12 \\ 5 \end{pmatrix} \bullet \begin{pmatrix} 3 \\ -4 \end{pmatrix}\right|}{\sqrt{144+25}\sqrt{9+16}} = \dfrac{|36+(-20)|}{13 \times 5} = \dfrac{16}{65}$

∴ $\theta = \arccos\left(\frac{16}{65}\right) \approx 75.7°$

3 Line 1 has direction vector $\begin{pmatrix} 5 \\ -2 \end{pmatrix}$ and line 2 has direction vector $\begin{pmatrix} 4 \\ 10 \end{pmatrix}$

and $\begin{pmatrix} 5 \\ -2 \end{pmatrix} \bullet \begin{pmatrix} 4 \\ 10 \end{pmatrix} = 20 + (-20) = 0$

∴ l_1 and l_2 are perpendicular

4 If $\dfrac{x-8}{3} = \dfrac{9-y}{16} = \dfrac{z-10}{7} = \lambda$ say, then $x = 8 + 3\lambda$, $y = 9 - 16\lambda$, $z = 10 + 7\lambda$

$\therefore$ line 1 has vector $\begin{pmatrix} 3 \\ -16 \\ 7 \end{pmatrix}$ and line 2 has vector $\begin{pmatrix} 3 \\ 8 \\ -5 \end{pmatrix}$. If θ is the angle between them,

$\cos\theta = \dfrac{\left|\begin{pmatrix} 3 \\ -16 \\ 7 \end{pmatrix} \bullet \begin{pmatrix} 3 \\ 8 \\ -5 \end{pmatrix}\right|}{\sqrt{9 + 256 + 49}\sqrt{9 + 64 + 25}} = \dfrac{|9 - 128 - 35|}{\sqrt{314}\sqrt{98}} = \dfrac{154}{\sqrt{314 \times 98}}$

$\therefore \theta \approx 28.6°$

EXERCISE 16B.1

1 a i When $t = 0$, $\begin{pmatrix} x \\ y \end{pmatrix} = \begin{pmatrix} -4 \\ 3 \end{pmatrix}$ **ii** The velocity vector is $\begin{pmatrix} 12 \\ 5 \end{pmatrix}$.   **iii** The speed is $\sqrt{12^2 + 5^2}$ $= 13 \text{ m s}^{-1}$
$\therefore$ the object is at $(-4, 3)$.

b i When $t = 0$, $\begin{pmatrix} x \\ y \end{pmatrix} = \begin{pmatrix} 0 \\ -6 \end{pmatrix}$ **ii** The velocity vector is $\begin{pmatrix} 3 \\ -4 \end{pmatrix}$.   **iii** The speed is $\sqrt{3^2 + (-4)^2}$ $= 5 \text{ m s}^{-1}$
$\therefore$ the object is at $(0, -6)$.

c i When $t = 0$, $\begin{pmatrix} x \\ y \end{pmatrix} = \begin{pmatrix} -2 \\ -7 \end{pmatrix}$ **ii** The velocity vector is $\begin{pmatrix} -6 \\ -4 \end{pmatrix}$.   **iii** The speed is $\sqrt{(-6)^2 + (-4)^2}$ $= \sqrt{36 + 16}$ $= \sqrt{52} \text{ m s}^{-1}$
$\therefore$ the object is at $(-2, -7)$.

2 a $\begin{pmatrix} 4 \\ -3 \end{pmatrix}$ has length $\sqrt{4^2 + (-3)^2} = 5$
$\therefore 30\begin{pmatrix} 4 \\ -3 \end{pmatrix}$ has length 150
$\therefore$ the velocity vector is $\begin{pmatrix} 120 \\ -90 \end{pmatrix}$.

b $\begin{pmatrix} 24 \\ 7 \end{pmatrix}$ has length $\sqrt{24^2 + 7^2} = 25$
$\therefore \tfrac{1}{2}\begin{pmatrix} 24 \\ 7 \end{pmatrix}$ has length 12.5
$\therefore$ the velocity vector is $\begin{pmatrix} 12 \\ 3.5 \end{pmatrix}$.

c $2\mathbf{i} + \mathbf{j} = \begin{pmatrix} 2 \\ 1 \end{pmatrix}$ has length $\sqrt{2^2 + 1^2} = \sqrt{5}$
$\therefore 10\sqrt{5}\begin{pmatrix} 2 \\ 1 \end{pmatrix}$ has length 50
$\therefore$ the velocity vector is $\begin{pmatrix} 20\sqrt{5} \\ 10\sqrt{5} \end{pmatrix}$.

d $-3\mathbf{i} + 4\mathbf{j} = \begin{pmatrix} -3 \\ 4 \end{pmatrix}$ has length $\sqrt{(-3)^2 + 4^2} = 5$
$\therefore 20\begin{pmatrix} -3 \\ 4 \end{pmatrix}$ has length 100
$\therefore$ the velocity vector is $\begin{pmatrix} -60 \\ 80 \end{pmatrix}$.

3 Yacht A: $\begin{pmatrix} x_A \\ y_A \end{pmatrix} = \begin{pmatrix} 4 \\ 5 \end{pmatrix} + t\begin{pmatrix} 1 \\ -2 \end{pmatrix}$ Yacht B: $\begin{pmatrix} x_B \\ y_B \end{pmatrix} = \begin{pmatrix} 1 \\ -8 \end{pmatrix} + t\begin{pmatrix} 2 \\ 1 \end{pmatrix}$, $t \geq 0$

a When $t = 0$, $\begin{pmatrix} x_A \\ y_A \end{pmatrix} = \begin{pmatrix} 4 \\ 5 \end{pmatrix}$ $\therefore$ A is at $(4, 5)$
and $\begin{pmatrix} x_B \\ y_B \end{pmatrix} = \begin{pmatrix} 1 \\ -8 \end{pmatrix}$ $\therefore$ B is at $(1, -8)$.

b For A, the velocity vector is $\begin{pmatrix} 1 \\ -2 \end{pmatrix}$, and for B it is $\begin{pmatrix} 2 \\ 1 \end{pmatrix}$.

c Speed of A $= \sqrt{1^2 + (-2)^2} = \sqrt{5}$ km h^{-1}. Speed of B $= \sqrt{2^2 + 1^2} = \sqrt{5}$ km h^{-1}.

d The distance between them is $D = \sqrt{[(1 + 2t) - (4 + t)]^2 + [(-8 + t) - (5 - 2t)]^2}$
$= \sqrt{(-3 + t)^2 + (-13 + 3t)^2}$
$= \sqrt{9 - 6t + t^2 + 169 - 78t + 9t^2}$
$= \sqrt{10t^2 - 84t + 178}$

This is a minimum when $10t^2 - 84t + 178$ is a minimum. This occurs when
$t = \dfrac{-b}{2a} = \dfrac{84}{20} = 4.2$ hours. $\therefore$ the time is 4 h 12 min after 6 am, or 10:12 am.

e A has direction vector $\begin{pmatrix} 1 \\ -2 \end{pmatrix}$ and B has direction vector $\begin{pmatrix} 2 \\ 1 \end{pmatrix}$.

Since $\begin{pmatrix} 1 \\ -2 \end{pmatrix} \bullet \begin{pmatrix} 2 \\ 1 \end{pmatrix} = 2 - 2 = 0$, the paths of the yachts are at right angles to each other.

4 a P has position $\begin{pmatrix} x_1 \\ y_1 \end{pmatrix} = \begin{pmatrix} -5 \\ 4 \end{pmatrix} + t\begin{pmatrix} 3 \\ -1 \end{pmatrix}$ and at $t = 0$, the time is 1:34 pm
$\therefore\ x_1(t) = -5 + 3t,\ y_1(t) = 4 - t$.

b Speed $= \sqrt{3^2 + (-1)^2} = \sqrt{10}$ km min^{-1}

c Q fires its torpedo after a minutes.
$\therefore$ at time t, its torpedo has travelled for $(t - a)$ minutes.
$\therefore\ \begin{pmatrix} x_2 \\ y_2 \end{pmatrix} = \begin{pmatrix} 15 \\ 7 \end{pmatrix} + (t - a)\begin{pmatrix} -4 \\ -3 \end{pmatrix},\ t > a$
$\therefore\ x_2(t) = 15 - 4(t - a)$ and $y_2(t) = 7 - 3(t - a)$

d They meet when $x_1(t) = x_2(t)$ and $y_1(t) = y_2(t)$
$\therefore\ -5 + 3t = 15 - 4(t - a)$ and $4 - t = 7 - 3(t - a)$
$\therefore\ 7t - 4a = 20$ ..... (1) and $2t - 3a = 3$ ..... (2)

Solving simultaneously, $21t - 12a = 60$ $3 \times (1)$
                          $-8t + 12a = -12$ $(-4) \times (2)$
adding $13t = 48$

$\therefore\ t = \frac{48}{13}$ and $7\left(\frac{48}{13}\right) - 4a = 20$
$\therefore\ t \approx 3.6923$ $\therefore\ 5.8462 = 4a$
$\therefore\ t \approx 3$ min 41.54 sec $\therefore\ a \approx 1.4615 \approx 1$ min 27.7 sec

So, as $a \approx 1.4615$, Q fired at 1:35:28 pm, and the explosion occurred at 1:37:42 pm.

5 a $|\mathbf{b}| = \sqrt{(-3)^2 + (-1)^2} = \sqrt{10}$

As the speed is $40\sqrt{10}$ km h^{-1}, the velocity vector is $40\begin{pmatrix} -3 \\ -1 \end{pmatrix} = \begin{pmatrix} -120 \\ -40 \end{pmatrix}$.

b $\begin{pmatrix} x \\ y \end{pmatrix} = \begin{pmatrix} 200 \\ 100 \end{pmatrix} + t\begin{pmatrix} -120 \\ -40 \end{pmatrix}$, $t \geqslant 0$ $\{t = 0$ at 12:00 noon$\}$

c At 1:00 pm, $t = 1$ and $\begin{pmatrix} x \\ y \end{pmatrix} = \begin{pmatrix} 200 - 120 \\ 100 - 40 \end{pmatrix} = \begin{pmatrix} 80 \\ 60 \end{pmatrix}$

d The distance from O(0, 0) to $P_1(80, 60)$ is $\left|\begin{pmatrix} 80 \\ 60 \end{pmatrix}\right| = \sqrt{80^2 + 60^2} = 100$ km,
which is when it becomes visible to radar. {within 100 km of O(0, 0)}

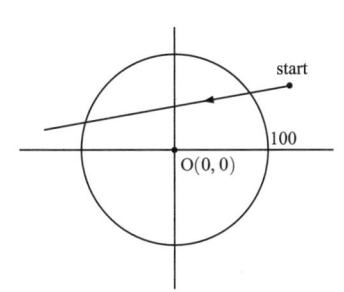

e A general point on the path is $P(200 - 120t, 100 - 40t)$.

Now $\overrightarrow{OP} = \begin{pmatrix} 200 - 120t \\ 100 - 40t \end{pmatrix}$,
and for the closest point $\overrightarrow{OP} \bullet \begin{pmatrix} -3 \\ -1 \end{pmatrix} = 0$
$\therefore\ -3(200 - 120t) - 1(100 - 40t) = 0$
$\therefore\ -700 + 400t = 0$
$\therefore\ t = \frac{7}{4} = 1\frac{3}{4}$ hours

The time when the aircraft is closest is 1:45 pm, and
at this time $\overrightarrow{OP} = \begin{pmatrix} 200 - 120(\frac{7}{4}) \\ 100 - 40(\frac{7}{4}) \end{pmatrix} = \begin{pmatrix} -10 \\ 30 \end{pmatrix}$
$\therefore\ d_{\min} = \sqrt{(-10)^2 + 30^2} \approx 31.6$ km

f It disappears from radar when $|\overrightarrow{OP}| = 100$ and $t > 1\frac{3}{4}$
$\therefore\ \sqrt{(200 - 120t)^2 + (100 - 40t)^2} = 100$
$\therefore\ 40\,000 - 48\,000t + 14\,400t^2 + 10\,000 - 8000t + 1600t^2 = 10\,000$
$\therefore\ 16\,000t^2 - 56\,000t + 40\,000 = 0$
$\therefore\ 16t^2 - 56t + 40 = 0$ $\{\div 1000\}$
$\therefore\ 2t^2 - 7t + 5 = 0$ $\{\div 8\}$
$\therefore\ (2t - 5)(t - 1) = 0$
$\therefore\ t = \frac{5}{2}$ {as $t > 1\frac{3}{4}$}

So, the aircraft disappears from the radar screen $2\frac{1}{2}$ hours after noon, or at 2:30 pm.

6 For A, $x_A(t) = 3 - t$, $y_A(t) = 2t - 4$ For B, $x_B(t) = 4 - 3t$, $y_B(t) = 3 - 2t$

a When $t = 0$, $x_A(0) = 3$, $y_A(0) = -4$ and $x_B(0) = 4$, $y_B(0) = 3$
∴ A is at $(3, -4)$. ∴ B is at $(4, 3)$.

b The velocity vector of A is $\begin{pmatrix} -1 \\ 2 \end{pmatrix}$ and the velocity vector of B is $\begin{pmatrix} -3 \\ -2 \end{pmatrix}$.

c If the angle is θ, $\begin{pmatrix} -1 \\ 2 \end{pmatrix} \bullet \begin{pmatrix} -3 \\ -2 \end{pmatrix} = \sqrt{1+4}\sqrt{9+4}\cos\theta$

∴ $3 - 4 = \sqrt{5}\sqrt{13}\cos\theta$

∴ $\frac{-1}{\sqrt{65}} = \cos\theta$ and so $\theta \approx 97.1°$

d If D is the distance between them, then

$D = \sqrt{[(4-3t)-(3-t)]^2 + [(3-2t)-(2t-4)]^2}$ and D is a minimum when
$= \sqrt{[1-2t]^2 + [7-4t]^2}$
$= \sqrt{1 - 4t + 4t^2 + 49 - 56t + 16t^2}$ $t = -\dfrac{b}{2a} = \dfrac{60}{40} = 1\tfrac{1}{2}$
$= \sqrt{20t^2 - 60t + 50}$ ∴ $t = 1.5$ hours

EXERCISE 16B.2

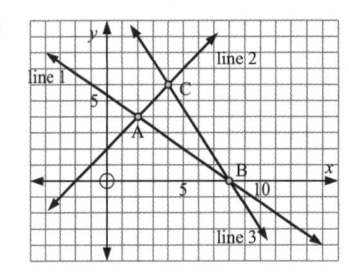

1 a

b A is $(2, 4)$, B is $(8, 0)$, C is $(4, 6)$

c $BC = \sqrt{(8-4)^2 + (0-6)^2} = \sqrt{16+36} = \sqrt{52}$ units

$AB = \sqrt{(8-2)^2 + (0-4)^2} = \sqrt{36+16} = \sqrt{52}$ units

∴ $BC = AB$ and so $\triangle ABC$ is isosceles.

d Line 1 and Line 2 meet at A.   Line 2 and Line 3 meet at C.

∴ $\begin{pmatrix} -1 \\ 6 \end{pmatrix} + \begin{pmatrix} 3r \\ -2r \end{pmatrix} = \begin{pmatrix} 0 \\ 2 \end{pmatrix} + s\begin{pmatrix} 1 \\ 1 \end{pmatrix}$ ∴ $\begin{pmatrix} 0 \\ 2 \end{pmatrix} + s\begin{pmatrix} 1 \\ 1 \end{pmatrix} = \begin{pmatrix} 10 \\ -3 \end{pmatrix} + t\begin{pmatrix} -2 \\ 3 \end{pmatrix}$

∴ $\begin{pmatrix} 3r-s \\ -2r-s \end{pmatrix} = \begin{pmatrix} 1 \\ -4 \end{pmatrix}$ ∴ $\begin{pmatrix} s+2t \\ s-3t \end{pmatrix} = \begin{pmatrix} 10 \\ -5 \end{pmatrix}$

∴ $3r - s = 1$ ∴ $s + 2t = 10$
and $2r + s = 4$ $-s + 3t = 5$
Adding, $5r = 5$ ∴ $r = 1$ Adding, $5t = 15$ ∴ $t = 3$

∴ $\begin{pmatrix} x \\ y \end{pmatrix} = \begin{pmatrix} -1 \\ 6 \end{pmatrix} + \begin{pmatrix} 3 \\ -2 \end{pmatrix} = \begin{pmatrix} 2 \\ 4 \end{pmatrix}$ ✓   ∴ $\begin{pmatrix} x \\ y \end{pmatrix} = \begin{pmatrix} 10 \\ -3 \end{pmatrix} + 3\begin{pmatrix} -2 \\ 3 \end{pmatrix} = \begin{pmatrix} 4 \\ 6 \end{pmatrix}$ ✓

Line 1 and Line 3 meet at B.

∴ $\begin{pmatrix} -1 \\ 6 \end{pmatrix} + r\begin{pmatrix} 3 \\ -2 \end{pmatrix} = \begin{pmatrix} 10 \\ -3 \end{pmatrix} + t\begin{pmatrix} -2 \\ 3 \end{pmatrix}$

∴ $\begin{pmatrix} 3r+2t \\ -2r-3t \end{pmatrix} = \begin{pmatrix} 11 \\ -9 \end{pmatrix}$

∴ $3r + 2t = 11$ ..... (1)
   $-2r - 3t = -9$ ..... (2)

∴ $9r + 6t = 33$ $\{3 \times (1)\}$
   $-4r - 6t = -18$ $\{2 \times (2)\}$

Adding, $5r = 15$
∴ $r = 3$

So, $\begin{pmatrix} x \\ y \end{pmatrix} = \begin{pmatrix} -1 \\ 6 \end{pmatrix} + 3\begin{pmatrix} 3 \\ -2 \end{pmatrix} = \begin{pmatrix} 8 \\ 0 \end{pmatrix}$ ✓

2 a

[Graph showing points A(−4, 6), D(1, 16), B(17, 15), C(22, 25) with lines]

b A(−4, 6), B(17, 15), C(22, 25), D(1, 16)

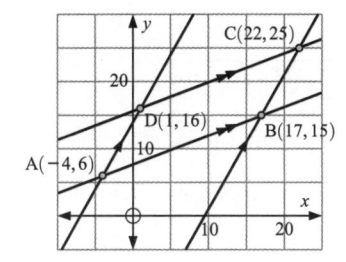

c Lines 1 and 2 meet at A.

$\therefore \begin{pmatrix} -4 \\ 6 \end{pmatrix} + r\begin{pmatrix} 7 \\ 3 \end{pmatrix} = \begin{pmatrix} -4 \\ 6 \end{pmatrix} + s\begin{pmatrix} 1 \\ 2 \end{pmatrix}$

$\therefore \begin{pmatrix} 7r-s \\ 3r-2s \end{pmatrix} = \begin{pmatrix} 0 \\ 0 \end{pmatrix}$

$\therefore \quad 7r - s = 0$ ..... (1)

and $3r - 2s = 0$

$\underline{-14r + 2s = 0 \quad \{-2 \times (1)\}}$

Adding, $-11r \quad = 0$

$\therefore \quad r = 0$

$\therefore \begin{pmatrix} x \\ y \end{pmatrix} = \begin{pmatrix} -4 \\ 6 \end{pmatrix}$ ✓

Lines 1 and 4 meet at B.

$\therefore \begin{pmatrix} -4 \\ 6 \end{pmatrix} + r\begin{pmatrix} 7 \\ 3 \end{pmatrix} = \begin{pmatrix} 22 \\ 25 \end{pmatrix} + u\begin{pmatrix} -1 \\ -2 \end{pmatrix}$

$\therefore \begin{pmatrix} 7r+u \\ 3r+2u \end{pmatrix} = \begin{pmatrix} 26 \\ 19 \end{pmatrix}$

$\therefore \quad 7r + u = 26$ ..... (1)

and $3r + 2u = 19$

$\underline{-14r - 2u = -52 \quad \{-2 \times (1)\}}$

Adding, $-11r \quad = -33$

$\therefore \quad r = 3$

$\therefore \begin{pmatrix} x \\ y \end{pmatrix} = \begin{pmatrix} -4 \\ 6 \end{pmatrix} + 3\begin{pmatrix} 7 \\ 3 \end{pmatrix} = \begin{pmatrix} 17 \\ 15 \end{pmatrix}$ ✓

Lines 3 and 4 meet at C.

$\therefore \begin{pmatrix} 22 \\ 25 \end{pmatrix} + t\begin{pmatrix} -7 \\ -3 \end{pmatrix} = \begin{pmatrix} 22 \\ 25 \end{pmatrix} + u\begin{pmatrix} -1 \\ -2 \end{pmatrix}$

$\therefore \begin{pmatrix} -7t+u \\ -3t+2u \end{pmatrix} = \begin{pmatrix} 0 \\ 0 \end{pmatrix}$

$\therefore \quad -7t + u = 0$ ..... (1)

and $-3t + 2u = 0$

$\underline{14t - 2u = 0 \quad \{-2 \times (1)\}}$

Adding, $11t \quad = 0$

$\therefore \quad t = 0$

$\therefore \begin{pmatrix} x \\ y \end{pmatrix} = \begin{pmatrix} 22 \\ 25 \end{pmatrix}$ ✓

Lines 2 and 3 meet at D.

$\therefore \begin{pmatrix} -4 \\ 6 \end{pmatrix} + s\begin{pmatrix} 1 \\ 2 \end{pmatrix} = \begin{pmatrix} 22 \\ 25 \end{pmatrix} + t\begin{pmatrix} -7 \\ -3 \end{pmatrix}$

$\therefore \begin{pmatrix} s+7t \\ 2s+3t \end{pmatrix} = \begin{pmatrix} 26 \\ 19 \end{pmatrix}$

$\therefore \quad s + 7t = 26$ ..... (1)

and $2s + 3t = 19$

$\underline{-2s - 14t = -52 \quad \{-2 \times (1)\}}$

Adding, $-11t = -33$

$\therefore \quad t = 3$

$\therefore \begin{pmatrix} x \\ y \end{pmatrix} = \begin{pmatrix} 22 \\ 25 \end{pmatrix} + 3\begin{pmatrix} -7 \\ -3 \end{pmatrix} = \begin{pmatrix} 1 \\ 16 \end{pmatrix}$ ✓

3 a Lines 1 and 3 meet at A.

$\therefore \begin{pmatrix} 0 \\ 2 \end{pmatrix} + r\begin{pmatrix} 2 \\ 1 \end{pmatrix} = \begin{pmatrix} 0 \\ 5 \end{pmatrix} + t\begin{pmatrix} 1 \\ -1 \end{pmatrix}$

$\therefore \begin{pmatrix} 2r-t \\ r+t \end{pmatrix} = \begin{pmatrix} 0 \\ 3 \end{pmatrix}$

$\therefore \quad 2r - t = 0$

$\underline{r + t = 3}$

Adding, $3r \quad = 3$

$\therefore \quad r = 1$

$\therefore \begin{pmatrix} x \\ y \end{pmatrix} = \begin{pmatrix} 0 \\ 2 \end{pmatrix} + \begin{pmatrix} 2 \\ 1 \end{pmatrix} = \begin{pmatrix} 2 \\ 3 \end{pmatrix}$

$\therefore$ A is (2, 3)

Lines 2 and 3 meet at C.

$\therefore \begin{pmatrix} 8 \\ 6 \end{pmatrix} + s\begin{pmatrix} -1 \\ -2 \end{pmatrix} = \begin{pmatrix} 0 \\ 5 \end{pmatrix} + t\begin{pmatrix} 1 \\ -1 \end{pmatrix}$

$\therefore \begin{pmatrix} -s-t \\ -2s+t \end{pmatrix} = \begin{pmatrix} -8 \\ -1 \end{pmatrix}$

$\therefore \quad -s - t = -8$

$\underline{-2s + t = -1}$

Adding, $-3s \quad = -9$

Lines 1 and 2 meet at B.

$\therefore \begin{pmatrix} 0 \\ 2 \end{pmatrix} + r\begin{pmatrix} 2 \\ 1 \end{pmatrix} = \begin{pmatrix} 8 \\ 6 \end{pmatrix} + s\begin{pmatrix} -1 \\ -2 \end{pmatrix}$

$\therefore \begin{pmatrix} 2r+s \\ r+2s \end{pmatrix} = \begin{pmatrix} 8 \\ 4 \end{pmatrix}$

$\therefore \quad -4r - 2s = -16$

$\underline{r + 2s = 4}$

Adding, $-3r \quad = -12$

$\therefore \quad r = 4$

$\therefore \begin{pmatrix} x \\ y \end{pmatrix} = \begin{pmatrix} 0 \\ 2 \end{pmatrix} + 4\begin{pmatrix} 2 \\ 1 \end{pmatrix} = \begin{pmatrix} 8 \\ 6 \end{pmatrix}$

$\therefore$ B is (8, 6)

$\therefore \quad s = 3$

$\therefore \begin{pmatrix} x \\ y \end{pmatrix} = \begin{pmatrix} 8 \\ 6 \end{pmatrix} + 3\begin{pmatrix} -1 \\ -2 \end{pmatrix} = \begin{pmatrix} 5 \\ 0 \end{pmatrix}$

$\therefore$ C is (5, 0)

b A(2, 3), B(8, 6), C(5, 0)

$AB = \sqrt{(8-2)^2 + (6-3)^2}$ $BC = \sqrt{(5-8)^2 + (0-6)^2}$
$= \sqrt{36 + 9}$ $= \sqrt{9 + 36}$
$= \sqrt{45}$ $= \sqrt{45}$

The two equal sides are [AB] and [BC] and they have length $\sqrt{45}$ units.

4 a Lines (QP) and (PR) meet at P.   Lines (QR) and (PR) meet at R.

$\therefore \begin{pmatrix} 3 \\ -1 \end{pmatrix} + r\begin{pmatrix} 14 \\ 10 \end{pmatrix} = \begin{pmatrix} 0 \\ 18 \end{pmatrix} + t\begin{pmatrix} 5 \\ -7 \end{pmatrix}$ $\therefore \begin{pmatrix} 3 \\ -1 \end{pmatrix} + s\begin{pmatrix} 17 \\ -9 \end{pmatrix} = \begin{pmatrix} 0 \\ 18 \end{pmatrix} + t\begin{pmatrix} 5 \\ -7 \end{pmatrix}$

$\therefore \begin{pmatrix} 14r - 5t \\ 10r + 7t \end{pmatrix} = \begin{pmatrix} -3 \\ 19 \end{pmatrix}$ $\therefore \begin{pmatrix} 17s - 5t \\ -9s + 7t \end{pmatrix} = \begin{pmatrix} -3 \\ 19 \end{pmatrix}$

$\therefore \quad 14r - 5t = -3 \quad ..... (1)$ $\therefore \quad 17s - 5t = -3 \quad ..... (1)$
$\quad\quad 10r + 7t = 19 \quad ..... (2)$ $\quad\quad -9s + 7t = 19 \quad ..... (2)$

$\therefore \quad 98r - 35t = -21 \quad \{7 \times (1)\}$ $\therefore \quad 119s - 35t = -21 \quad \{7 \times (1)\}$
$\quad\quad 50r + 35t = 95 \quad \{5 \times (2)\}$ $\quad\quad -45s + 35t = 95 \quad \{5 \times (2)\}$

Adding, $148r = 74$ Adding, $74s = 74$
$\therefore \quad r = \frac{1}{2}$ $\therefore \quad s = 1$

$\therefore \begin{pmatrix} x \\ y \end{pmatrix} = \begin{pmatrix} 3 \\ -1 \end{pmatrix} + \frac{1}{2}\begin{pmatrix} 14 \\ 10 \end{pmatrix} = \begin{pmatrix} 10 \\ 4 \end{pmatrix}$ $\therefore \begin{pmatrix} x \\ y \end{pmatrix} = \begin{pmatrix} 3 \\ -1 \end{pmatrix} + \begin{pmatrix} 17 \\ -9 \end{pmatrix} = \begin{pmatrix} 20 \\ -10 \end{pmatrix}$

$\therefore$ P is (10, 4) $\therefore$ R is (20, −10)

Lines (QP) and (PR) meet at Q.   **b** $\overrightarrow{PQ} = \begin{pmatrix} 3 - 10 \\ -1 - 4 \end{pmatrix} = \begin{pmatrix} -7 \\ -5 \end{pmatrix}$

$\begin{pmatrix} 3 \\ -1 \end{pmatrix} + r\begin{pmatrix} 14 \\ 10 \end{pmatrix} = \begin{pmatrix} 3 \\ -1 \end{pmatrix} + s\begin{pmatrix} 17 \\ -9 \end{pmatrix}$ $\overrightarrow{PR} = \begin{pmatrix} 20 - 10 \\ -10 - 4 \end{pmatrix} = \begin{pmatrix} 10 \\ -14 \end{pmatrix}$

$\therefore \quad r\begin{pmatrix} 14 \\ 10 \end{pmatrix} = s\begin{pmatrix} 17 \\ -9 \end{pmatrix}$ and $\overrightarrow{PQ} \bullet \overrightarrow{PR} = -70 + 70 = 0$

$\therefore \quad r = s = 0$ **c** [PQ] $\perp$ [PR] $\therefore \quad Q\hat{P}R = 90°$

So, $\begin{pmatrix} x \\ y \end{pmatrix} = \begin{pmatrix} 3 \\ -1 \end{pmatrix}$ **d** Area $= \frac{1}{2}|\overrightarrow{PQ}||\overrightarrow{PR}|$

$\therefore$ Q is (3, −1) $\quad\quad\quad = \frac{1}{2}\sqrt{49 + 25}\sqrt{100 + 196}$
$\quad\quad\quad = 74$ units^2

5 a Lines 1 and 4 meet at A.   Lines 1 and 2 meet at B.

$\therefore \begin{pmatrix} 2 \\ 5 \end{pmatrix} + r\begin{pmatrix} 4 \\ 1 \end{pmatrix} = \begin{pmatrix} 3 \\ 1 \end{pmatrix} + u\begin{pmatrix} -3 \\ 12 \end{pmatrix}$ $\therefore \begin{pmatrix} 2 \\ 5 \end{pmatrix} + r\begin{pmatrix} 4 \\ 1 \end{pmatrix} = \begin{pmatrix} 18 \\ 9 \end{pmatrix} + s\begin{pmatrix} -8 \\ 32 \end{pmatrix}$

$\therefore \begin{pmatrix} 4r + 3u \\ r - 12u \end{pmatrix} = \begin{pmatrix} 1 \\ -4 \end{pmatrix}$ $\therefore \begin{pmatrix} 4r + 8s \\ r - 32s \end{pmatrix} = \begin{pmatrix} 16 \\ 4 \end{pmatrix}$

$\therefore \quad 4r + 3u = 1$ $\therefore \quad 4r + 8s = 16 \quad ..... (1)$
$\quad\quad r - 12u = -4 \quad ..... (2)$ $\quad\quad r - 32s = 4 \quad ..... (2)$

$\therefore \quad 4r + 3u = 1$ $\therefore \quad r + 2s = 4 \quad \{(1) \div 4\}$
$\quad -4r + 48u = 16 \quad \{(-4) \times (2)\}$ $\quad -r + 32s = -4 \quad \{(-1) \times (2)\}$

Adding, $51u = 17$ Adding, $34s = 0$
$\therefore \quad u = \frac{1}{3}$ $\therefore \quad s = 0$

$\therefore \begin{pmatrix} x \\ y \end{pmatrix} = \begin{pmatrix} 3 \\ 1 \end{pmatrix} + \frac{1}{3}\begin{pmatrix} -3 \\ 12 \end{pmatrix} = \begin{pmatrix} 2 \\ 5 \end{pmatrix}$ $\therefore \begin{pmatrix} x \\ y \end{pmatrix} = \begin{pmatrix} 18 \\ 9 \end{pmatrix}$

$\therefore$ A is (2, 5) $\therefore$ B is (18, 9)

Lines 2 and 3 meet at C.

$\therefore \begin{pmatrix} 18 \\ 9 \end{pmatrix} + s \begin{pmatrix} -8 \\ 32 \end{pmatrix} = \begin{pmatrix} 14 \\ 25 \end{pmatrix} + t \begin{pmatrix} -8 \\ -2 \end{pmatrix}$

$\therefore \begin{pmatrix} -8s+8t \\ 32s+2t \end{pmatrix} = \begin{pmatrix} -4 \\ 16 \end{pmatrix}$

$\therefore \quad -8s + 8t = -4 \quad \ldots\ldots (1)$
$\quad\quad 32s + 2t = 16$

$\therefore \quad 2s - 2t = 1 \quad \{(1) \div -4\}$
$\quad\quad 32s + 2t = 16$

Adding, $34s \quad = 17$

$\therefore \quad s = \tfrac{1}{2}$

$\therefore \begin{pmatrix} x \\ y \end{pmatrix} = \begin{pmatrix} 18 \\ 9 \end{pmatrix} + \tfrac{1}{2} \begin{pmatrix} -8 \\ 32 \end{pmatrix} = \begin{pmatrix} 14 \\ 25 \end{pmatrix}$

$\therefore$ C is $(14, 25)$

b $\overrightarrow{AC} = \begin{pmatrix} 14-2 \\ 25-5 \end{pmatrix} = \begin{pmatrix} 12 \\ 20 \end{pmatrix}$

$\overrightarrow{DB} = \begin{pmatrix} 18--2 \\ 9-21 \end{pmatrix} = \begin{pmatrix} 20 \\ -12 \end{pmatrix}$

i $|\overrightarrow{AC}| = \sqrt{12^2 + 20^2} = \sqrt{544}$ units

ii $|\overrightarrow{DB}| = \sqrt{20^2 + (-12)^2} = \sqrt{544}$ units

iii $\overrightarrow{AC} \bullet \overrightarrow{DB} = 240 - 240 = 0$

Lines 3 and 4 meet at D.

$\therefore \begin{pmatrix} 14 \\ 25 \end{pmatrix} + t \begin{pmatrix} -8 \\ -2 \end{pmatrix} = \begin{pmatrix} 3 \\ 1 \end{pmatrix} + u \begin{pmatrix} -3 \\ 12 \end{pmatrix}$

$\therefore \begin{pmatrix} -8t+3u \\ -2t-12u \end{pmatrix} = \begin{pmatrix} -11 \\ -24 \end{pmatrix}$

$\therefore \quad -8t + 3u = -11 \quad \ldots\ldots (1)$
$\quad\quad -2t - 12u = -24 \quad \ldots\ldots (2)$

$\therefore \quad 16t - 6u = 22 \quad \{(-2) \times (1)\}$
$\quad\quad t + 6u = 12 \quad \{(2) \div -2\}$

Adding, $17t \quad = 34$

$\therefore \quad t = 2$

$\therefore \begin{pmatrix} x \\ y \end{pmatrix} = \begin{pmatrix} 14 \\ 25 \end{pmatrix} + 2 \begin{pmatrix} -8 \\ -2 \end{pmatrix} = \begin{pmatrix} -2 \\ 21 \end{pmatrix}$

$\therefore$ D is $(-2, 21)$

c The diagonals are perpendicular and equal in length, and as their midpoints are the same (at $(8, 15)$), ABCD is a square.

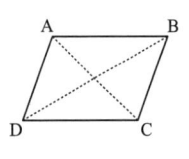

EXERCISE 16C

1 a Line 1 has direction vector $\begin{pmatrix} 2 \\ -1 \\ 1 \end{pmatrix}$ and line 2 has direction vector $\begin{pmatrix} 3 \\ -1 \\ 2 \end{pmatrix}$.

As one vector is not a scalar multiple of the other, the lines are not parallel.

Now $\quad 1 + 2t = -2 + 3s \quad\quad 2 - t = 3 - s \quad\quad 3 + t = 1 + 2s$

$\therefore \quad 2t - 3s = -3 \ldots (1) \quad \therefore \quad -t + s = 1 \ldots (2) \quad \therefore \quad t - 2s = -2 \ldots (3)$

Solving (2) and (3) simultaneously: $\quad -t + s = 1$
$\quad\quad\quad\quad\quad\quad\quad\quad\quad\quad\quad\quad\quad\quad\quad t - 2s = -2$
$\quad\quad\quad\quad\quad\quad\quad\quad\quad\quad\quad\quad\quad\quad\quad\overline{\quad -s = -1} \quad \therefore \quad s = 1$ and $t = 0$

and in (1), LHS $= 2t - 3s = 2(0) - 3(1) = -3$ ✓

$\therefore \quad s = 1, \quad t = 0$ satisfies all three equations

$\therefore$ the two lines meet at $(1, 2, 3) \quad$ {using $t = 0$ or $s = 1$}

The acute angle between the lines has $\quad \cos\theta = \dfrac{|6 + 1 + 2|}{\sqrt{4 + 1 + 1}\sqrt{9 + 1 + 4}} = \dfrac{9}{\sqrt{84}}$

and so $\quad \theta \approx 10.9°$

b Line 1 has direction vector $\begin{pmatrix} 2 \\ -12 \\ 12 \end{pmatrix}$ and line 2 has direction vector $\begin{pmatrix} 4 \\ 3 \\ -1 \end{pmatrix}$.

As one vector is not a scalar multiple of the other, the lines are not parallel.

Now $\quad -1 + 2\lambda = 4\mu - 3 \quad\quad 2 - 12\lambda = 3\mu + 2 \quad\quad 4 + 12\lambda = -\mu - 1$

$\therefore \quad 2\lambda - 4\mu = -2 \quad\quad\quad -12\lambda - 3\mu = 0 \quad\quad\quad 12\lambda + \mu = -5 \ldots\ldots (3)$

$\therefore \quad \lambda - 2\mu = -1 \ldots (1) \quad\quad \mu = -4\lambda \ldots (2)$

Solving (1) and (2) simultaneously: $\lambda - 2(-4\lambda) = -1$

$\therefore \quad 9\lambda = -1$

$\therefore \quad \lambda = -\tfrac{1}{9}$ and so $\mu = \tfrac{4}{9}$

In (3), $12\lambda + \mu = 12\left(-\tfrac{1}{9}\right) + \tfrac{4}{9} = -\tfrac{12}{9} + \tfrac{4}{9} = -\tfrac{8}{9}$, which is not -5.

Since the system is inconsistent, the lines do not intersect, so the lines are skew.

The acute angle between the lines has $\cos\theta = \dfrac{|8 - 36 - 12|}{\sqrt{292}\sqrt{26}} = \dfrac{40}{\sqrt{7592}}$ and so $\theta \approx 62.7°$.

c Line 1 has direction vector $\begin{pmatrix} 6 \\ 8 \\ 2 \end{pmatrix}$ and line 2 has direction vector $\begin{pmatrix} 3 \\ 4 \\ 1 \end{pmatrix}$.

As $\begin{pmatrix} 6 \\ 8 \\ 2 \end{pmatrix} = 2\begin{pmatrix} 3 \\ 4 \\ 1 \end{pmatrix}$ the two lines are parallel. Hence, $\theta = 0°$.

d In line 1 set $x = 2 - y = z + 2 = t$, so $x = t$, $y = 2 - t$ and $z = t - 2$.

Line 1 has direction vector $\begin{pmatrix} 1 \\ -1 \\ 1 \end{pmatrix}$ and line 2 has direction vector $\begin{pmatrix} 3 \\ -2 \\ 2 \end{pmatrix}$.

As one vector is not a scalar multiple of the other, the lines are not parallel.

Now $t = 1 + 3s$ ...... (1) $2 - t = -2 - 2s$ $-2 + t = 2s + \frac{1}{2}$

$-t + 2s = -4$ ...... (2) $t - 2s = 2\frac{1}{2}$ ...... (3)

Solving (1) and (2) simultaneously, $-(1 + 3s) + 2s = -4$

$\therefore \quad -s = -3$

$\therefore \quad s = 3$ and so $t = 1 + 3(3) = 10$

Substituting in (3), $t - 2s = 10 - 2(3) = 4 \neq 2\frac{1}{2}$

Since the system is inconsistent, the lines do not meet. $\therefore$ they are skew.

The acute angle between the lines has $\cos\theta = \dfrac{|3 + 2 + 2|}{\sqrt{1+1+1}\sqrt{9+4+4}} = \dfrac{7}{\sqrt{3}\sqrt{17}}$

$\therefore \quad \theta \approx 11.4°$

e Line 1 has direction vector $\begin{pmatrix} 1 \\ -1 \\ 2 \end{pmatrix}$ and line 2 has direction vector $\begin{pmatrix} 3 \\ -2 \\ 1 \end{pmatrix}$.

As one vector is not a scalar multiple of the other, the lines are not parallel.

$1 + \lambda = 2 + 3\mu$ $2 - \lambda = 3 - 2\mu$ $3 + 2\lambda = \mu - 5$

$\lambda - 3\mu = 1$ ...... (1) $-\lambda + 2\mu = 1$ ...... (2) $2\lambda - \mu = -8$ ...... (3)

Solving (1) and (2) simultaneously, $\lambda - 3\mu = 1$

$-\lambda + 2\mu = 1$

Adding, $-\mu = 2$

$\therefore \quad \mu = -2$ and $\lambda - 3(-2) = 1$ $\therefore \quad \lambda = -5$

Checking in (3), $2\lambda - \mu = 2(-5) - (-2) = -10 + 2 = -8$ ✓

Since $\mu = -2$, $\lambda = -5$ satisfies all three equations, the lines meet.

They meet at $x = 1 + (-5)$, $y = 2 - (-5)$, $z = 3 + 2(-5)$, or at $(-4, 7, -7)$.

The acute angle between the lines has $\cos\theta = \dfrac{|3 + 2 + 2|}{\sqrt{1+1+4}\sqrt{9+4+1}}$

$= \dfrac{7}{\sqrt{84}}$ and so $\theta \approx 40.2°$

f Line 1 has direction vector $\begin{pmatrix} -2 \\ 1 \\ 0 \end{pmatrix}$ and line 2 has direction vector $\begin{pmatrix} 4 \\ -2 \\ 0 \end{pmatrix}$.

Now $\begin{pmatrix} 4 \\ -2 \\ 0 \end{pmatrix} = -2\begin{pmatrix} -2 \\ 1 \\ 0 \end{pmatrix}$, so the lines are parallel and hence $\theta = 0°$.

2 $\begin{cases} 3x - y = 8 \\ 6x - 2y = k \end{cases} \equiv \begin{cases} 6x - 2y = 16 \\ 6x - 2y = k \end{cases}$ which are parallel as the gradient in each case is 3.

(1) If $k \neq 16$ the lines are parallel, so no solutions exist.

(2) If $k = 16$ the lines are coincident. There are infinitely many solutions of the form
$x = t$, $y = 3t - 8$, $t \in \mathbb{R}$.

3 $\begin{cases} 4x + 8y = 1 \\ 2x - ay = 11 \end{cases} \equiv \begin{cases} 4x + 8y = 1 \\ 4x - 2ay = 22 \end{cases}$

(1) If $-2a = 8$, $a = -4$, and the equations are $\begin{cases} 4x + 8y = 1 \\ 4x + 8y = 22 \end{cases}$

The lines are parallel, so no solutions exist.

(2) If $a \neq -4$, the lines are not parallel or coincident.
So, a unique solution exists.

$\begin{pmatrix} 4 & 8 & | & 1 \\ 2 & -a & | & 11 \end{pmatrix} \sim \begin{pmatrix} 2 & 4 & | & \frac{1}{2} \\ -2 & a & | & -11 \end{pmatrix} \quad \begin{matrix} R_1 \to \frac{1}{2}R_1 \\ R_2 \to -R_2 \end{matrix}$

$\sim \begin{pmatrix} 2 & 4 & | & \frac{1}{2} \\ 0 & a+4 & | & -10\frac{1}{2} \end{pmatrix} \quad R_2 \to R_1 + R_2$

The second equation is $(a+4)y = -\frac{21}{2}$ $\therefore$ $y = \dfrac{-21}{2(a+4)}$

and $4x + 8\left(\dfrac{-21}{2(a+4)}\right) = 1$

$\therefore \quad 4x - \dfrac{84}{a+4} = 1$

$\therefore \quad 4x = 1 + \dfrac{84}{a+4} = \dfrac{a+88}{a+4}$

$\therefore \quad x = \dfrac{a+88}{4(a+4)}$

$\therefore$ the lines intersect when $x = \dfrac{a+88}{4(a+4)}$, $y = \dfrac{-21}{2(a+4)}$, $a \neq -4$

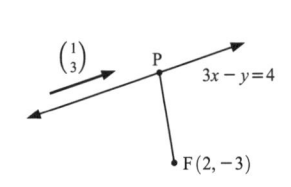

4

$3x - y = 4$, or $y = 3x - 4$ has gradient $3 = \frac{3}{1}$

$\therefore$ the direction vector is $\begin{pmatrix} 1 \\ 3 \end{pmatrix}$.

If $x = t$, $y = 3t - 4$.
So $P(t, 3t - 4)$ is a general point on the line.

Now $\overrightarrow{FP} = \begin{pmatrix} t - 2 \\ 3t - 4 - -3 \end{pmatrix} = \begin{pmatrix} t - 2 \\ 3t - 1 \end{pmatrix}$

But for shortest distance $\overrightarrow{FP} \perp \begin{pmatrix} 1 \\ 3 \end{pmatrix}$

$\therefore \quad \begin{pmatrix} t - 2 \\ 3t - 1 \end{pmatrix} \cdot \begin{pmatrix} 1 \\ 3 \end{pmatrix} = 0$

$\therefore \quad t - 2 + 9t - 3 = 0$

$\therefore \quad 10t = 5$

$\therefore \quad t = \frac{1}{2}$

$\therefore \quad \overrightarrow{FP} = \begin{pmatrix} -\frac{3}{2} \\ \frac{1}{2} \end{pmatrix}$ and $|\overrightarrow{FP}| = \sqrt{\frac{9}{4} + \frac{1}{4}}$

$= \sqrt{\frac{10}{4}}$

$= \frac{1}{2}\sqrt{10}$ units

Thus the shortest distance is $\frac{1}{2}\sqrt{10}$ units.

5 Let $A(2+3\lambda, -1+2\lambda, 4+\lambda)$ be a point on the line such that $\overrightarrow{PA}$ is perpendicular to the line.

Now $\overrightarrow{PA} = \begin{pmatrix} 2+3\lambda - 3 \\ -1+2\lambda - 0 \\ 4+\lambda - (-1) \end{pmatrix} = \begin{pmatrix} 3\lambda - 1 \\ 2\lambda - 1 \\ \lambda + 5 \end{pmatrix}$

$\mathbf{v} = \begin{pmatrix} 3 \\ 2 \\ 1 \end{pmatrix}$

and $\mathbf{v} = \begin{pmatrix} 3 \\ 2 \\ 1 \end{pmatrix}$ is the direction vector of the line.

$A(2+3\lambda, -1+2\lambda, 4+\lambda)$
$P(3, 0, -1)$

$\therefore$ since $\overrightarrow{PA} \bullet \mathbf{v} = 0$, $\begin{pmatrix} 3\lambda - 1 \\ 2\lambda - 1 \\ \lambda + 5 \end{pmatrix} \bullet \begin{pmatrix} 3 \\ 2 \\ 1 \end{pmatrix} = 0$

$\therefore \quad 3(3\lambda - 1) + 2(2\lambda - 1) + 1(\lambda + 5) = 0$
$\therefore \quad 9\lambda - 3 + 4\lambda - 2 + \lambda + 5 = 0$
$\therefore \quad 14\lambda = 0$
$\therefore \quad \lambda = 0$

$\therefore$ A is at $(2, -1, 4)$ and the distance $d = \sqrt{(2-3)^2 + (-1-0)^2 + (4-(-1))^2}$
$= \sqrt{1 + 1 + 25}$
$= \sqrt{27}$ or $3\sqrt{3}$ units

6 Let A be a point on the line such that $\overrightarrow{PA}$ is perpendicular to the line.
Then A is at $(1+2\lambda, -1+3\lambda, 2+\lambda)$ for some λ.

Now $\overrightarrow{PA} = \begin{pmatrix} 1+2\lambda - 1 \\ -1+3\lambda - 1 \\ 2+\lambda - 3 \end{pmatrix} = \begin{pmatrix} 2\lambda \\ 3\lambda - 2 \\ \lambda - 1 \end{pmatrix}$

$\mathbf{v} = \begin{pmatrix} 2 \\ 3 \\ 1 \end{pmatrix}$

$A(1+2\lambda, -1+3\lambda, 2+\lambda)$

and $\mathbf{v} = \begin{pmatrix} 2 \\ 3 \\ 1 \end{pmatrix}$ is the direction vector of the line.

$\therefore$ since $\overrightarrow{PA} \bullet \mathbf{v} = 0$, $\begin{pmatrix} 2\lambda \\ 3\lambda - 2 \\ \lambda - 1 \end{pmatrix} \bullet \begin{pmatrix} 2 \\ 3 \\ 1 \end{pmatrix} = 0$

$P(1, 1, 3)$

$\therefore \quad 4\lambda + 3(3\lambda - 2) + 1(\lambda - 1) = 0$
$\therefore \quad 4\lambda + 9\lambda - 6 + \lambda - 1 = 0$
$\therefore \quad 14\lambda = 7$
$\therefore \quad \lambda = \tfrac{1}{2}$

$\therefore$ A is at $\left(2, \tfrac{1}{2}, \tfrac{5}{2}\right)$ and the distance $d = \sqrt{(2-1)^2 + \left(\tfrac{1}{2}-1\right)^2 + \left(\tfrac{5}{2}-3\right)^2}$
$= \sqrt{1 + \tfrac{1}{4} + \tfrac{1}{4}} = \sqrt{\tfrac{3}{2}}$ units

7 a Line 1 has direction vector $\mathbf{u} = \begin{pmatrix} 2 \\ -1 \\ 3 \end{pmatrix}$ and line 2 has direction vector $\mathbf{v} = \begin{pmatrix} 1 \\ 1 \\ 1 \end{pmatrix}$.

$\mathbf{u} \times \mathbf{v} = \begin{vmatrix} \mathbf{i} & \mathbf{j} & \mathbf{k} \\ 2 & -1 & 3 \\ 1 & 1 & 1 \end{vmatrix} = \begin{vmatrix} -1 & 3 \\ 1 & 1 \end{vmatrix} \mathbf{i} - \begin{vmatrix} 2 & 3 \\ 1 & 1 \end{vmatrix} \mathbf{j} + \begin{vmatrix} 2 & -1 \\ 1 & 1 \end{vmatrix} \mathbf{k} = \begin{pmatrix} -4 \\ 1 \\ 3 \end{pmatrix}$

Let $A(1+2t, -t, 2+3t)$ and $B(s, s, s)$ be points on lines 1 and 2 respectively.

We require $\overrightarrow{AB} \parallel \mathbf{u} \times \mathbf{v}$, so $\overrightarrow{AB} = k \begin{pmatrix} -4 \\ 1 \\ 3 \end{pmatrix}$ for some scalar k

$\therefore \quad \begin{pmatrix} s - (1+2t) \\ s - (-t) \\ s - (2+3t) \end{pmatrix} = k \begin{pmatrix} -4 \\ 1 \\ 3 \end{pmatrix}$

$\therefore \quad s - 2t - 1 = -4k, \quad s + t = k, \quad s - 3t - 2 = 3k$

Using $k = s + t$, $\quad s - 2t - 1 = -4(s + t)$ and $\quad s - 3t - 2 = 3(s + t)$
$\therefore \quad 5s + 2t = 1$ and $\quad -2s - 6t = 2$

Solving simultaneously, $s = \frac{5}{13}$, $t = -\frac{6}{13}$ and so $k = s + t = -\frac{1}{13}$

$\therefore \quad \overrightarrow{AB} = -\frac{1}{13} \begin{pmatrix} -4 \\ 1 \\ 3 \end{pmatrix}$ and $|\overrightarrow{AB}| = \frac{1}{13}\sqrt{(-4)^2 + 1^2 + 3^2} = \frac{\sqrt{26}}{13}$

$\therefore$ the shortest distance between the skew lines is $\frac{\sqrt{26}}{13}$ units (or $\frac{2}{\sqrt{26}}$ units).

b Line 1 has direction vector $\mathbf{u} = \begin{pmatrix} -1 \\ 1 \\ -1 \end{pmatrix}$, and line 2 has direction vector $\mathbf{v} = \begin{pmatrix} 1 \\ -2 \\ 1 \end{pmatrix}$.

$\mathbf{u} \times \mathbf{v} = \begin{vmatrix} \mathbf{i} & \mathbf{j} & \mathbf{k} \\ -1 & 1 & -1 \\ 1 & -2 & 1 \end{vmatrix} = \begin{vmatrix} 1 & -1 \\ -2 & 1 \end{vmatrix} \mathbf{i} - \begin{vmatrix} -1 & -1 \\ 1 & 1 \end{vmatrix} \mathbf{j} + \begin{vmatrix} -1 & 1 \\ 1 & -2 \end{vmatrix} \mathbf{k}$

$= -\mathbf{i} + \mathbf{k}$

Let $A(1 - t, 1 + t, 3 - t)$ and $B(2 + s, 1 - 2s, s)$ be points on lines 1 and 2 respectively.
We require $\overrightarrow{AB} \parallel \mathbf{u} \times \mathbf{v}$

So $\overrightarrow{AB} = k \begin{pmatrix} -1 \\ 0 \\ 1 \end{pmatrix}$ for some scalar k, so $\begin{pmatrix} 2 + s - (1 - t) \\ 1 - 2s - (1 + t) \\ s - (3 - t) \end{pmatrix} = \begin{pmatrix} -k \\ 0 \\ k \end{pmatrix}$

which gives $\begin{cases} s + t + 1 = -k \\ -2s - t = 0 \\ s + t - 3 = k \end{cases}$

Using $t = -2s$, $s + (-2s) + 1 = -k$ and $s + (-2s) - 3 = k$
$\therefore \quad 1 - s = -k$ and $-3 - s = k$
$\therefore \quad 1 - s = -(-3 - s)$
$\therefore \quad -2s = 2$
$\therefore \quad s = -1$, $t = 2$ and $k = -3 - (-1) = -2$

$\therefore \quad \overrightarrow{AB} = -2 \begin{pmatrix} -1 \\ 0 \\ 1 \end{pmatrix}$ and $|\overrightarrow{AB}| = 2\sqrt{(-1)^2 + 1^2} = 2\sqrt{2}$ units

$\therefore$ the shortest distance between the skew lines is $2\sqrt{2}$ units.

8 a The lines intersect $\therefore$ the shortest distance $= 0$ units.

b Line 1 has direction vector $\mathbf{u} = \begin{pmatrix} 2 \\ -12 \\ 12 \end{pmatrix}$, and line 2 has $\mathbf{v} = \begin{pmatrix} 4 \\ 3 \\ -1 \end{pmatrix}$.

$\mathbf{u} \times \mathbf{v} = \begin{vmatrix} \mathbf{i} & \mathbf{j} & \mathbf{k} \\ 2 & -12 & 12 \\ 4 & 3 & -1 \end{vmatrix} = \begin{vmatrix} -12 & 12 \\ 3 & -1 \end{vmatrix} \mathbf{i} - \begin{vmatrix} 2 & 12 \\ 4 & -1 \end{vmatrix} \mathbf{j} + \begin{vmatrix} 2 & -12 \\ 4 & 3 \end{vmatrix} \mathbf{k}$

$= -24\mathbf{i} + 50\mathbf{j} + 54\mathbf{k} = -2(12\mathbf{i} - 25\mathbf{j} - 27\mathbf{k})$

Let $A(-1 + 2\lambda, 2 - 12\lambda, 4 + 12\lambda)$ and $B(4\mu - 3, 3\mu + 2, -\mu - 1)$ be points on lines 1 and 2 respectively.

We require $\overrightarrow{AB} \parallel \mathbf{u} \times \mathbf{v}$

Now $\overrightarrow{AB} = k \begin{pmatrix} 12 \\ -25 \\ -27 \end{pmatrix}$ for some scalar k, so $\begin{pmatrix} 4\mu - 3 - (-1 + 2\lambda) \\ 3\mu + 2 - (2 - 12\lambda) \\ -\mu - 1 - (4 + 12\lambda) \end{pmatrix} = \begin{pmatrix} 12k \\ -25k \\ -27k \end{pmatrix}$

which gives $\begin{cases} 4\mu - 2\lambda - 12k = 2 \\ 3\mu + 12\lambda + 25k = 0 \\ -\mu - 12\lambda + 27k = 5 \end{cases}$

Solving simultaneously using technology, $\mu = \frac{859}{1498}$, $\lambda = -\frac{223}{749}$, $k = \frac{111}{1498}$

$\therefore \overrightarrow{AB} = \frac{111}{1498}\begin{pmatrix} 12 \\ -25 \\ -27 \end{pmatrix}$ and $|\overrightarrow{AB}| = \frac{111}{1498}\sqrt{12^2 + (-25)^2 + (-27)^2}$

$\qquad = \frac{111}{1498}\sqrt{1498} = \frac{111}{\sqrt{1498}}$

$\therefore$ the shortest distance between the lines is $\frac{111}{\sqrt{1498}} \approx 2.87$ units.

c A point on line 1 is $A(0, 3, -1)$.

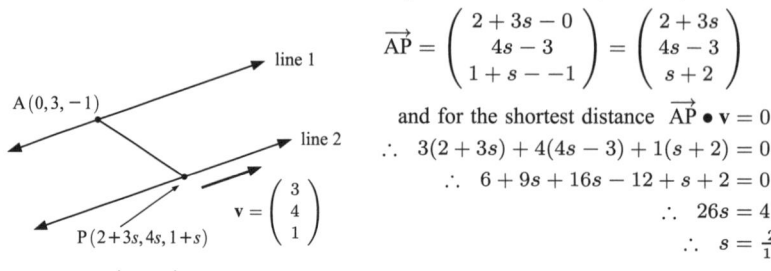

$\overrightarrow{AP} = \begin{pmatrix} 2 + 3s - 0 \\ 4s - 3 \\ 1 + s - -1 \end{pmatrix} = \begin{pmatrix} 2 + 3s \\ 4s - 3 \\ s + 2 \end{pmatrix}$

and for the shortest distance $\overrightarrow{AP} \bullet \mathbf{v} = 0$

$\therefore 3(2 + 3s) + 4(4s - 3) + 1(s + 2) = 0$

$\therefore 6 + 9s + 16s - 12 + s + 2 = 0$

$\therefore 26s = 4$

$\therefore s = \frac{2}{13}$

$\therefore \overrightarrow{AP} = \begin{pmatrix} \frac{32}{13} \\ -\frac{31}{13} \\ \frac{28}{13} \end{pmatrix}$ and $|\overrightarrow{AP}| = \sqrt{\left(\frac{32}{13}\right)^2 + \left(-\frac{31}{13}\right)^2 + \left(\frac{28}{13}\right)^2} = \frac{\sqrt{2769}}{13} \approx 4.05$ units

d Line 1 has direction vector $\mathbf{u} = \begin{pmatrix} 1 \\ -1 \\ 1 \end{pmatrix}$, and line 2 has direction vector $\mathbf{v} = \begin{pmatrix} 3 \\ -2 \\ 2 \end{pmatrix}$.

$\mathbf{u} \times \mathbf{v} = \begin{vmatrix} \mathbf{i} & \mathbf{j} & \mathbf{k} \\ 1 & -1 & 1 \\ 3 & -2 & 2 \end{vmatrix} = \begin{vmatrix} -1 & 1 \\ -2 & 2 \end{vmatrix}\mathbf{i} - \begin{vmatrix} 1 & 1 \\ 3 & 2 \end{vmatrix}\mathbf{j} + \begin{vmatrix} 1 & -1 \\ 3 & -2 \end{vmatrix}\mathbf{k}$

$= \mathbf{j} + \mathbf{k}$

Let $A(t, 2 - t, t - 2)$ and $B\left(1 + 3s, -2 - 2s, 2s + \frac{1}{2}\right)$ be points on lines 1 and 2 respectively.

We require $\overrightarrow{AB} \parallel \mathbf{u} \times \mathbf{v}$

So $\overrightarrow{AB} = k\begin{pmatrix} 0 \\ 1 \\ 1 \end{pmatrix}$ for some scalar k, so $\begin{pmatrix} 1 + 3s - t \\ -2 - 2s - (2 - t) \\ 2s + \frac{1}{2} - (t - 2) \end{pmatrix} = \begin{pmatrix} 0 \\ k \\ k \end{pmatrix}$

which gives $\begin{cases} 1 + 3s - t = 0 \\ t - 2s - 4 = k \\ 2s - t + \frac{5}{2} = k \end{cases}$

Equating ks, $t - 2s - 4 = 2s - t + \frac{5}{2}$

Using $t = 3s + 1$, $(3s + 1) - 2s - 4 = 2s - (3s + 1) + \frac{5}{2}$

$\therefore s - 3 = \frac{3}{2} - s$

$\therefore 2s = \frac{9}{2}$

$\therefore s = \frac{9}{4}$, $t = 3\left(\frac{9}{4}\right) + 1 = \frac{31}{4}$, $k = \frac{31}{4} - 2\left(\frac{9}{4}\right) - 4 = -\frac{3}{4}$

$\therefore \overrightarrow{AB} = -\frac{3}{4}\begin{pmatrix} 0 \\ 1 \\ 1 \end{pmatrix}$ and $|\overrightarrow{AB}| = \frac{3}{4}\sqrt{0^2 + 1^2 + 1^2} = \frac{3\sqrt{2}}{4}$

$\therefore$ the shortest distance between the lines is $\frac{3\sqrt{2}}{4}$ units.

e The lines intersect $\therefore$ the shortest distance $= 0$ units.

f The lines are parallel. Let A and P be as on the diagram.

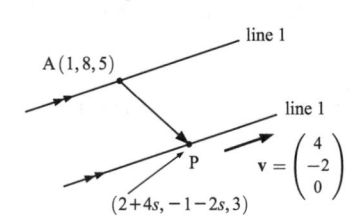

$$\overrightarrow{AP} = \begin{pmatrix} 2+4s-1 \\ -1-2s-8 \\ 3-5 \end{pmatrix} = \begin{pmatrix} 1+4s \\ -2s-9 \\ -2 \end{pmatrix}$$

and for the shortest distance

$$\overrightarrow{AP} \bullet \mathbf{v} = 0$$

$\therefore$ $(1+4s)(4) + (-2s-9)(-2) + 0 = 0$

$\therefore$ $4 + 16s + 4s + 18 = 0$

$\therefore$ $20s = -22$ and so $s = -1.1$

A$(1, 8, 5)$, line 1, P $(2+4s, -1-2s, 3)$, $\mathbf{v} = \begin{pmatrix} 4 \\ -2 \\ 0 \end{pmatrix}$

Thus $\overrightarrow{AP} = \begin{pmatrix} -3.4 \\ -6.8 \\ -2 \end{pmatrix}$ and $|\overrightarrow{AP}| = \sqrt{(-3.4)^2 + (-6.8)^2 + (-2)^2} \approx 7.86$ units

EXERCISE 16D

1 a Since $\mathbf{n} = \begin{pmatrix} 2 \\ -1 \\ 3 \end{pmatrix}$ and $(-1, 2, 4)$ lies on the plane, the equation is

$2x - y + 3z = 2(-1) - 2 + 3(4)$ or $2x - y + 3z = 8$.

b $\overrightarrow{AB} = \begin{pmatrix} 3 \\ 4 \\ 1 \end{pmatrix}$, and $(2, 3, 1)$ lies on the plane.

$\therefore$ a vector normal to the plane is

$3x + 4y + z = 3(2) + 4(3) + 1$

$\therefore$ $3x + 4y + z = 19$

c A$(1, 4, 2)$ $\overset{x}{\bullet}$ P(a, b, c) $\overset{2x}{\longrightarrow}$ B$(4, 1, -4)$

Now $2\overrightarrow{AP} = \overrightarrow{PB}$

$\therefore$ if P has coordinates (a, b, c), then $2\begin{pmatrix} a-1 \\ b-4 \\ c-2 \end{pmatrix} = \begin{pmatrix} 4-a \\ 1-b \\ -4-c \end{pmatrix}$

$\therefore$ $2a - 2 = 4 - a$ and $2b - 8 = 1 - b$ and $2c - 4 = -4 - c$

$\therefore$ $3a = 6$ $3b = 9$ $3c = 0$

$\therefore$ $a = 2$ $b = 3$ $c = 0$

$\therefore$ P is at $(2, 3, 0)$

$\overrightarrow{AB} = \begin{pmatrix} 3 \\ -3 \\ -6 \end{pmatrix} = 3\begin{pmatrix} 1 \\ -1 \\ -2 \end{pmatrix}$ so $\begin{pmatrix} 1 \\ -1 \\ -2 \end{pmatrix}$ is a normal vector to the plane.

$\therefore$ the plane is $x - y - 2z = 2 - 3 - 2(0)$ or $x - y - 2z = -1$

d The line $x = 1 + t$, $y = 2 - t$, $z = 3 + 2t$ has direction vector $\begin{pmatrix} 1 \\ -1 \\ 2 \end{pmatrix}$.

Also, letting $t = 0$, the point $(1, 2, 3)$ lies on the plane and we call this point B.

$\therefore$ $\overrightarrow{AB} = \begin{pmatrix} -2 \\ 0 \\ 2 \end{pmatrix}$ and so a vector normal to the plane is $\overrightarrow{AB} \times \begin{pmatrix} 1 \\ -1 \\ 2 \end{pmatrix}$

$\therefore$ $\mathbf{n} = \begin{vmatrix} \mathbf{i} & \mathbf{j} & \mathbf{k} \\ -2 & 0 & 2 \\ 1 & -1 & 2 \end{vmatrix} = \begin{vmatrix} 0 & 2 \\ -1 & 2 \end{vmatrix} \mathbf{i} - \begin{vmatrix} -2 & 2 \\ 1 & 2 \end{vmatrix} \mathbf{j} + \begin{vmatrix} -2 & 0 \\ 1 & -1 \end{vmatrix} \mathbf{k}$

$= 2\mathbf{i} + 6\mathbf{j} + 2\mathbf{k}$ or $2(\mathbf{i} + 3\mathbf{j} + \mathbf{k})$

$\therefore$ since A$(3, 2, 1)$ lies on the plane, it has equation $x + 3y + z = 3 + 3(2) + 1$

or $x + 3y + z = 10$

2 **a** $2x + 3y - z = 8$ has $\mathbf{n} = \begin{pmatrix} 2 \\ 3 \\ -1 \end{pmatrix}$ **b** $3x - y + 0z = 11$ has $\mathbf{n} = \begin{pmatrix} 3 \\ -1 \\ 0 \end{pmatrix}$

c $0x + 0y + z = 2$ has $\mathbf{n} = \begin{pmatrix} 0 \\ 0 \\ 1 \end{pmatrix}$ **d** $1x + 0y + 0z = 0$ has $\mathbf{n} = \begin{pmatrix} 1 \\ 0 \\ 0 \end{pmatrix}$

3 **a** The y-axis is perpendicular to the XOZ plane $\therefore$ a normal vector is $\begin{pmatrix} 0 \\ 1 \\ 0 \end{pmatrix}$

$\therefore$ since the origin lies on the plane, it has equation $y = 0$.

b Since the plane is perpendicular to the Z-axis, it has normal vector $\begin{pmatrix} 0 \\ 0 \\ 1 \end{pmatrix}$

$\therefore$ since $(2, -1, 4)$ lies on the plane, it has equation $z = 4$.

4 **a** **i** $\overrightarrow{AB} = \begin{pmatrix} 1 \\ 1 \\ -4 \end{pmatrix}$, $\overrightarrow{AC} = \begin{pmatrix} -1 \\ 0 \\ -2 \end{pmatrix}$, so $\mathbf{n} = \begin{pmatrix} x \\ y \\ z \end{pmatrix} = \begin{pmatrix} 0 \\ 2 \\ 6 \end{pmatrix} + \lambda \begin{pmatrix} 1 \\ 1 \\ -4 \end{pmatrix} + \mu \begin{pmatrix} -1 \\ 0 \\ -2 \end{pmatrix}$

ii If $\mathbf{n}$ is the normal vector, then

$\mathbf{n} = \overrightarrow{AB} \times \overrightarrow{AC} = \begin{vmatrix} \mathbf{i} & \mathbf{j} & \mathbf{k} \\ 1 & 1 & -4 \\ -1 & 0 & -2 \end{vmatrix} = \begin{vmatrix} 1 & -4 \\ 0 & -2 \end{vmatrix} \mathbf{i} - \begin{vmatrix} 1 & -4 \\ -1 & -2 \end{vmatrix} \mathbf{j} + \begin{vmatrix} 1 & 1 \\ -1 & 0 \end{vmatrix} \mathbf{k} = -2\mathbf{i} + 6\mathbf{j} + \mathbf{k}$

$\therefore$ since $A(0, 2, 6)$ lies on the plane, it has equation $-2x + 6y + z = -2(0) + 6(2) + 6$

$\therefore$ $-2x + 6y + z = 18$

b **i** $\overrightarrow{AB} = \begin{pmatrix} -3 \\ 3 \\ -2 \end{pmatrix}$, $\overrightarrow{AC} = \begin{pmatrix} -3 \\ -1 \\ -1 \end{pmatrix}$, so $\mathbf{n} = \begin{pmatrix} x \\ y \\ z \end{pmatrix} = \begin{pmatrix} 3 \\ 1 \\ 2 \end{pmatrix} + \lambda \begin{pmatrix} -3 \\ 3 \\ -2 \end{pmatrix} + \mu \begin{pmatrix} -3 \\ -1 \\ -1 \end{pmatrix}$

ii If $\mathbf{n}$ is the normal vector, then

$\mathbf{n} = \overrightarrow{AB} \times \overrightarrow{AC} = \begin{vmatrix} \mathbf{i} & \mathbf{j} & \mathbf{k} \\ -3 & 3 & -2 \\ -3 & -1 & -1 \end{vmatrix} = \begin{vmatrix} 3 & -2 \\ -1 & -1 \end{vmatrix} \mathbf{i} - \begin{vmatrix} -3 & -2 \\ -3 & -1 \end{vmatrix} \mathbf{j} + \begin{vmatrix} -3 & 3 \\ -3 & -1 \end{vmatrix} \mathbf{k}$

$= -5\mathbf{i} + 3\mathbf{j} + 12\mathbf{k}$

$\therefore$ since $C(0, 0, 1)$ lies on the plane, it has equation $-5x + 3y + 12z = 12$.

c **i** $\overrightarrow{AB} = \begin{pmatrix} -2 \\ -1 \\ -1 \end{pmatrix}$, $\overrightarrow{AC} = \begin{pmatrix} 2 \\ -3 \\ -3 \end{pmatrix}$, so $\mathbf{n} = \begin{pmatrix} x \\ y \\ z \end{pmatrix} = \begin{pmatrix} 2 \\ 0 \\ 3 \end{pmatrix} + \lambda \begin{pmatrix} -2 \\ -1 \\ -1 \end{pmatrix} + \mu \begin{pmatrix} 2 \\ -3 \\ -3 \end{pmatrix}$

ii If $\mathbf{n}$ is the normal vector, then

$\mathbf{n} = \overrightarrow{AB} \times \overrightarrow{AC} = \begin{vmatrix} \mathbf{i} & \mathbf{j} & \mathbf{k} \\ -2 & -1 & -1 \\ 2 & -3 & -3 \end{vmatrix} = \begin{vmatrix} -1 & -1 \\ -3 & -3 \end{vmatrix} \mathbf{i} - \begin{vmatrix} -2 & -1 \\ 2 & -3 \end{vmatrix} \mathbf{j} + \begin{vmatrix} -2 & -1 \\ 2 & -3 \end{vmatrix} \mathbf{k}$

$= -8\mathbf{j} + 8\mathbf{k}$ or $-8(\mathbf{j} - \mathbf{k})$

$\therefore$ since $A(2, 0, 3)$ lies on the plane, it has equation $y - z = -3$.

5 **a** The normal to $x - 3y + 4z = 8$ is $\begin{pmatrix} 1 \\ -3 \\ 4 \end{pmatrix}$, and this is the direction vector of the line.

$\therefore$ since the line passes through $(1, -2, 0)$, it has equation
$x = 1 + t$, $y = -2 - 3t$, $z = 4t$, t in $\mathbb{R}$.

b The normal to $x - y - 2z = 11$ is $\begin{pmatrix} 1 \\ -1 \\ -2 \end{pmatrix}$.

$\therefore$ since the line passes through $(3, 4, -1)$, it has equation
$x = 3 + t$, $y = 4 - t$, $z = -1 - 2t$, t in $\mathbb{R}$.

6 The line has direction vector $\vec{AB} = \begin{pmatrix} -1 \\ 3 \\ -3 \end{pmatrix}$.

$\therefore$ since the line passes through A(2, −1, 3), it has parametric equations
$$x = 2 - t, \quad y = -1 + 3t, \quad z = 3 - 3t, \quad t \text{ in } \mathbb{R}.$$
This line meets $x + 2y - z = 5$ when $(2 - t) + 2(-1 + 3t) - (3 - 3t) = 5$
$$\therefore \quad 2 - t - 2 + 6t - 3 + 3t = 5$$
$\therefore \quad 8t = 8 \quad \therefore \quad t = 1,$ and so they meet at (1, 2, 0).

7 The direction vector of the line is $\vec{PQ} = \begin{pmatrix} 1 \\ 2 \\ -5 \end{pmatrix}$.

$\therefore$ since it passes through P(1, −2, 4), it has parametric equations
$$x = 1 + t, \quad y = -2 + 2t, \quad z = 4 - 5t, \quad t \text{ in } \mathbb{R}.$$

a The line meets the YOZ plane when $x = 0$, or when $t = -1$.
This corresponds to the point (0, −4, 9).

b The line meets $y + z = 2$ when $-2 + 2t + 4 - 5t = 2$ $\therefore$ $-3t = 0$ $\therefore$ $t = 0$
This corresponds to the point (1, −2, 4).

c The line meets $\dfrac{x-3}{2} = \dfrac{y+2}{3} = \dfrac{z-30}{-1}$ when $\dfrac{1+t-3}{2} = \dfrac{-2+2t+2}{3} = \dfrac{4-5t-30}{-1}$

$\therefore \quad \dfrac{t-2}{2} = \dfrac{2t}{3} = 5t + 26$

$\therefore \quad 3t - 6 = 4t = 30t + 156$

$\therefore \quad 3t - 6 = 4t$ and $4t = 30t + 156$

$\therefore \quad t = -6$ and $-26t = 156$

$\therefore \quad t = -6$ is a common solution.

$\therefore$ the lines meet at the point corresponding to $t = -6$, which is (−5, −14, 34).

8 a The plane $2x + y - 2z = -11$ has $\mathbf{n} = \begin{pmatrix} 2 \\ 1 \\ -2 \end{pmatrix}$.

$\therefore$ the parametric equations of (AN) are $x = 1 + 2t, \; y = 0 + t, \; z = 2 - 2t, \; t \text{ in } \mathbb{R}.$
This line meets the plane when $2(1 + 2t) + t - 2(2 - 2t) = -11$
$\therefore \quad 2 + 4t + t - 4 + 4t = -11$
$\therefore \quad 9t = -9$
$\therefore \quad t = -1$

Thus N is (−1, −1, 4) and $\therefore$ $\vec{AN} = \begin{pmatrix} -2 \\ -1 \\ 2 \end{pmatrix}$ and $AN = \sqrt{(-2)^2 + (-1)^2 + 2^2}$
$= \sqrt{9} = 3$ units

b The plane $x - y + 3z = -10$ has $\mathbf{n} = \begin{pmatrix} 1 \\ -1 \\ 3 \end{pmatrix}$.

$\therefore$ the parametric equations of (AN) are $x = 2 + t, \; y = -1 - t, \; z = 3 + 3t, \; t \text{ in } \mathbb{R}.$
This line meets the plane when $(2 + t) - (-1 - t) + 3(3 + 3t) = -10$
$\therefore \quad 2 + t + 1 + t + 9 + 9t = -10$
$\therefore \quad 11t = -22$
$\therefore \quad t = -2$

$\therefore$ N is (0, 1, −3)

$\therefore \quad \vec{AN} = \begin{pmatrix} -2 \\ 2 \\ -6 \end{pmatrix}$ and $AN = \sqrt{(-2)^2 + 2^2 + (-6)^2} = \sqrt{44} = 2\sqrt{11}$ units

c The plane $4x - y - 2z = 8$ has $\mathbf{n} = \begin{pmatrix} 4 \\ -1 \\ -2 \end{pmatrix}$.

$\therefore$ the parametric equations of (AN) are
$$x = 1 + 4t, \quad y = -4 - t, \quad z = -3 - 2t, \quad t \text{ in } \mathbb{R}.$$
This line meets the plane when $4(1 + 4t) - (-4 - t) - 2(-3 - 2t) = 8$
$\therefore \quad 4 + 16t + 4 + t + 6 + 4t = 8$
$\therefore \quad 21t = -6$
$\therefore \quad t = -\frac{2}{7}$

$\therefore$ N is $\left(-\frac{1}{7}, -\frac{26}{7}, -\frac{17}{7}\right)$, $\therefore \overrightarrow{AN} = \begin{pmatrix} -\frac{8}{7} \\ \frac{2}{7} \\ \frac{4}{7} \end{pmatrix}$ and so $AN = \sqrt{\left(-\frac{8}{7}\right)^2 + \left(\frac{2}{7}\right)^2 + \left(\frac{4}{7}\right)^2}$
$= \sqrt{\frac{84}{49}} = 2\sqrt{\frac{3}{7}}$ units

9 The mirror image lies on the normal line to the plane through the object point.

Now $x + 2y + z = 1$ has $\mathbf{n} = \begin{pmatrix} 1 \\ 2 \\ 1 \end{pmatrix}$

$\therefore$ the normal at A has parametric equations $x = 3 + t, \ y = 1 + 2t, \ z = 2 + t, \ t \text{ in } \mathbb{R}$.
This line meets the plane when $(3 + t) + 2(1 + 2t) + 2 + t = 1$
$\therefore \quad 3 + t + 2 + 4t + 2 + t = 1$
$\therefore \quad 6t = -6$
$\therefore \quad t = -1$

$\therefore$ N is $(2, -1, 1)$

If A' is the mirror image of A, then $\overrightarrow{AN} = \overrightarrow{NA'}$

$\therefore$ letting A' have coordinates (a, b, c), $\begin{pmatrix} -1 \\ -2 \\ -1 \end{pmatrix} = \begin{pmatrix} a - 2 \\ b + 1 \\ c - 1 \end{pmatrix}$

$\therefore \quad a - 2 = -1, \ b + 1 = -2, \ c - 1 = -1$ and so A' is at $(1, -3, 0)$.

10 The plane $x + 4y - z = -2$ has normal $\mathbf{n} = \begin{pmatrix} 1 \\ 4 \\ -1 \end{pmatrix}$ which passes through $(3, 4, -1)$.

$\therefore$ the normal has parametric equations $x = 3 + t, \ y = 4 + 4t, \ z = -1 - t, \ t \text{ in } \mathbb{R}$ and will meet any of the coordinate axes if any two of the values of x, y, and z are zero at the same time.

$\therefore$ since $x = 0$ when $t = -3$ and $y = z = 0$ when $t = -1$, the normal meets the X-axis when $t = -1$, at the point $(2, 0, 0)$.

11 $\overrightarrow{AB} = \begin{pmatrix} -1 \\ -3 \\ -1 \end{pmatrix}$

a The normal $\mathbf{n}$ is perpendicular to both the X-axis and $\overrightarrow{AB}$.

Since the X-axis has direction vector $\begin{pmatrix} 1 \\ 0 \\ 0 \end{pmatrix}$,

$\mathbf{n} = \begin{vmatrix} \mathbf{i} & \mathbf{j} & \mathbf{k} \\ 1 & 0 & 0 \\ -1 & -3 & -1 \end{vmatrix}$

$= \begin{vmatrix} 0 & 0 \\ -3 & -1 \end{vmatrix} \mathbf{i} - \begin{vmatrix} 1 & 0 \\ -1 & -1 \end{vmatrix} \mathbf{j} + \begin{vmatrix} 1 & 0 \\ -1 & -3 \end{vmatrix} \mathbf{k}$

$= \mathbf{j} - 3\mathbf{k}$

Since $A(1, 2, 3)$ is in the plane, the plane has equation $y - 3z = 1(2) - 3(3)$

or $y - 3z = -7$

b The normal **n** is perpendicular to both the Y-axis and $\overrightarrow{AB}$.

Since the Y-axis has direction vector $\begin{pmatrix} 0 \\ 1 \\ 0 \end{pmatrix}$,

$$\mathbf{n} = \begin{vmatrix} \mathbf{i} & \mathbf{j} & \mathbf{k} \\ 0 & 1 & 0 \\ -1 & -3 & -1 \end{vmatrix}$$

$$= \begin{vmatrix} 1 & 0 \\ -3 & -1 \end{vmatrix} \mathbf{i} - \begin{vmatrix} 0 & 0 \\ -1 & -1 \end{vmatrix} \mathbf{j} + \begin{vmatrix} 0 & 1 \\ -1 & -3 \end{vmatrix} \mathbf{k}$$

$$= -\mathbf{i} + \mathbf{k}$$

Since $A(1, 2, 3)$ is in the plane, the plane has equation $-x + z = -1(1) + 1(3)$

or $-x + z = 2$

c The normal **n** is perpendicular to both the Z-axis and $\overrightarrow{AB}$.

Since the Z-axis has direction vector $\begin{pmatrix} 0 \\ 0 \\ 1 \end{pmatrix}$,

$$\mathbf{n} = \begin{vmatrix} \mathbf{i} & \mathbf{j} & \mathbf{k} \\ 0 & 0 & 1 \\ -1 & -3 & -1 \end{vmatrix}$$

$$= \begin{vmatrix} 0 & 1 \\ -3 & -1 \end{vmatrix} \mathbf{i} - \begin{vmatrix} 0 & 1 \\ -1 & -1 \end{vmatrix} \mathbf{j} + \begin{vmatrix} 0 & 0 \\ -1 & -3 \end{vmatrix} \mathbf{k}$$

$$= 3\mathbf{i} - \mathbf{j}$$

Since $A(1, 2, 3)$ is in the plane, the plane has equation $3x - y = 3(1) - 1(2)$

or $3x - y = 1$

12 Now $x - 1 = \dfrac{y-2}{2} = z + 3$ has direction vector $\begin{pmatrix} 1 \\ 2 \\ 1 \end{pmatrix}$

and $x + 1 = y - 3 = 2z + 5$ has direction vector $\begin{pmatrix} 1 \\ 1 \\ \frac{1}{2} \end{pmatrix}$ $\left\{ \text{since } 2z + 5 = \dfrac{z + \frac{5}{2}}{\frac{1}{2}} \right\}$

$\therefore$ a vector perpendicular to both lines is:

$$\begin{pmatrix} 1 \\ 2 \\ 1 \end{pmatrix} \times \begin{pmatrix} 1 \\ 1 \\ \frac{1}{2} \end{pmatrix} = \begin{vmatrix} \mathbf{i} & \mathbf{j} & \mathbf{k} \\ 1 & 2 & 1 \\ 1 & 1 & \frac{1}{2} \end{vmatrix} = \begin{vmatrix} 2 & 1 \\ 1 & \frac{1}{2} \end{vmatrix} \mathbf{i} - \begin{vmatrix} 1 & 1 \\ 1 & \frac{1}{2} \end{vmatrix} \mathbf{j} + \begin{vmatrix} 1 & 2 \\ 1 & 1 \end{vmatrix} \mathbf{k}$$

$$= 0\mathbf{i} + \tfrac{1}{2}\mathbf{j} - \mathbf{k}$$

$\therefore$ $\begin{pmatrix} 0 \\ 1 \\ -2 \end{pmatrix}$ is perpendicular to both lines.

A plane with normal $\begin{pmatrix} 0 \\ 1 \\ -2 \end{pmatrix}$ has equation $y - 2z = c$ for some c.

Now for line 1, $\dfrac{y-2}{2} = z+3$ and for line 2, $y-3 = 2z+5$

$\therefore\ y-2 = 2z+6$
$\therefore\ y-2z = 8$
$\therefore\ y-2z = 8$ also.

$\therefore\ y-2z = 8$ is a plane containing both lines, so the lines are coplanar.

13 **a** Since $A(1, 2, k)$ lies on $x+2y-2z = 8$, $1+2(2)-2k = 8$
$\therefore\ 1+4-2k = 8$
$\therefore\ -2k = 3$
$\therefore\ k = -\tfrac{3}{2}$

b Since $x+2y-2z = 8$, the plane has normal vector $\mathbf{n} = \begin{pmatrix} 1 \\ 2 \\ -2 \end{pmatrix}$.

$\therefore$ the normal from A has parametric equations
$$x = 1+t,\ \ y = 2+2t,\ \ z = -\tfrac{3}{2}-2t,\ \ t \in \mathbb{R}.$$
$\therefore$ points of the normal that are 6 units from A have
$$\sqrt{(1+t-1)^2 + (2+2t-2)^2 + (-\tfrac{3}{2}-2t+\tfrac{3}{2})^2} = 6$$
$\therefore\ \sqrt{t^2 + 4t^2 + 4t^2} = 6$
$\therefore\ 9t^2 = 36$
$\therefore\ t^2 = 4$
$\therefore\ t = \pm 2$

$\therefore$ B is $(3, 6, -\tfrac{11}{2})$ or $(-1, -2, \tfrac{5}{2})$.

14 **a** The normal from $A(3, 2, 1)$ to the plane has direction vector

$\mathbf{n} = (2\mathbf{i}+\mathbf{j}+\mathbf{k}) \times (4\mathbf{i}+2\mathbf{j}-2\mathbf{k}) = \begin{vmatrix} \mathbf{i} & \mathbf{j} & \mathbf{k} \\ 2 & 1 & 1 \\ 4 & 2 & -2 \end{vmatrix}$

$= \begin{vmatrix} 1 & 1 \\ 2 & -2 \end{vmatrix}\mathbf{i} - \begin{vmatrix} 2 & 1 \\ 4 & -2 \end{vmatrix}\mathbf{j} + \begin{vmatrix} 2 & 1 \\ 4 & 2 \end{vmatrix}\mathbf{k}$

$= -4\mathbf{i} + 8\mathbf{j}$

$\therefore$ if N is the foot of the normal from A, (AN)

has equation $\begin{pmatrix} x \\ y \\ z \end{pmatrix} = \begin{pmatrix} 3 \\ 2 \\ 1 \end{pmatrix} + t\begin{pmatrix} -4 \\ 8 \\ 0 \end{pmatrix}$

So, N has coordinates of the form $(3-4t,\ 2+8t,\ 1)$

But N lies on the plane $\therefore\ \begin{pmatrix} 3-4t \\ 2+8t \\ 1 \end{pmatrix} = \begin{pmatrix} 3 \\ 1 \\ 2 \end{pmatrix} + \lambda \begin{pmatrix} 2 \\ 1 \\ 1 \end{pmatrix} + \mu \begin{pmatrix} 4 \\ 2 \\ -2 \end{pmatrix}$

$\therefore\ \begin{cases} 3-4t = 3+2\lambda+4\mu \\ 2+8t = 1+\lambda+2\mu \\ 1 = 2+\lambda-2\mu \end{cases}$ and so $\begin{cases} 2\lambda+4\mu+4t = 0 \\ \lambda+2\mu-8t = 1 \\ \lambda-2\mu\ \ \ \ \ \ = -1 \end{cases}$

Solving simultaneously using technology gives $\lambda = -0.4,\ \ \mu = 0.3,\ \ t = -0.1$

$\therefore$ N is $(3-4(-0.1),\ 2+8(-0.1),\ 1)$ or $(3.4, 1.2, 1)$

$\therefore\ \overrightarrow{AN} = \begin{pmatrix} 3.4-3 \\ 1.2-2 \\ 1-1 \end{pmatrix} = \begin{pmatrix} 0.4 \\ -0.8 \\ 0 \end{pmatrix}$ and $|\overrightarrow{AN}| = \sqrt{(0.4)^2 + (0.8)^2 + 0^2} = \tfrac{2}{\sqrt{5}}$ units

b The normal from $A(1, 0, -2)$ to the plane has direction vector

$$\mathbf{n} = (3\mathbf{i} - \mathbf{j} + 2\mathbf{k}) \times (-\mathbf{i} + \mathbf{j} - \mathbf{k}) = \begin{vmatrix} \mathbf{i} & \mathbf{j} & \mathbf{k} \\ 3 & -1 & 2 \\ -1 & 1 & -1 \end{vmatrix}$$

$$= \begin{vmatrix} -1 & 2 \\ 1 & -1 \end{vmatrix}\mathbf{i} - \begin{vmatrix} 3 & 2 \\ -1 & -1 \end{vmatrix}\mathbf{j} + \begin{vmatrix} 3 & -1 \\ -1 & 1 \end{vmatrix}\mathbf{k}$$

$$= -\mathbf{i} + \mathbf{j} + 2\mathbf{k}$$

$\therefore$ (AN) has equation $\begin{pmatrix} x \\ y \\ z \end{pmatrix} = \begin{pmatrix} 1 \\ 0 \\ -2 \end{pmatrix} + t\begin{pmatrix} -1 \\ 1 \\ 2 \end{pmatrix}$

So, N has coordinates of the form $(1 - t, t, -2 + 2t)$

But N lies on the plane $\therefore$ $\begin{pmatrix} 1-t \\ t \\ -2+2t \end{pmatrix} = \begin{pmatrix} 1 \\ -1 \\ 1 \end{pmatrix} + \lambda\begin{pmatrix} 3 \\ -1 \\ 2 \end{pmatrix} + \mu\begin{pmatrix} -1 \\ 1 \\ -1 \end{pmatrix}$

$\therefore \begin{cases} 1 + 3\lambda - \mu = 1 - t \\ -1 - \lambda + \mu = t \\ 1 + 2\lambda - \mu = -2 + 2t \end{cases}$ and so $\begin{cases} 3\lambda - \mu + t = 0 \\ -\lambda + \mu - t = 1 \\ 2\lambda - \mu - 2t = -3 \end{cases}$

Solving simultaneously using technology gives $\lambda = \frac{1}{2}$, $\mu = 2\frac{1}{3}$, $t = \frac{5}{6}$

$\therefore$ N is $\left(1 - \frac{5}{6}, \frac{5}{6}, -2 + \frac{5}{3}\right)$ or $\left(\frac{1}{6}, \frac{5}{6}, -\frac{1}{3}\right)$

$\therefore \overrightarrow{AN} = \begin{pmatrix} \frac{1}{6} - 1 \\ \frac{5}{6} - 0 \\ -\frac{1}{3} - -2 \end{pmatrix} = \begin{pmatrix} -\frac{5}{6} \\ \frac{5}{6} \\ \frac{5}{3} \end{pmatrix}$ and $|\overrightarrow{AN}| = \sqrt{\frac{25}{36} + \frac{25}{36} + \frac{25}{9}} = \frac{5\sqrt{6}}{6}$ units

≈ 2.04 units

15 a If N is the point on the plane such that (NP) is a normal to it, then $\triangle NPQ$ is right angled at N. Draw a line parallel to $\mathbf{n}$ through Q.

Now θ is the angle between vectors $\mathbf{n}$ and $\overrightarrow{QP}$.

$\therefore \cos\theta = \frac{|\overrightarrow{QP} \bullet \mathbf{n}|}{|\overrightarrow{QP}||\mathbf{n}|}$ .... (1)

But $Q\hat{P}N = \theta$ {alternate angles}

$\therefore \cos\theta = \frac{d}{|\overrightarrow{QP}|}$ .... (2)

Equating (1) and (2), $\frac{d}{|\overrightarrow{QP}|} = \frac{|\overrightarrow{QP} \bullet \mathbf{n}|}{|\overrightarrow{QP}||\mathbf{n}|}$

$\therefore d = \frac{|\overrightarrow{QP} \bullet \mathbf{n}|}{|\mathbf{n}|}$

b Since Q is any point on the plane, it has coordinates (x, y, z) such that $Ax + By + Cz + D = 0$.

The normal vector to the plane is $\mathbf{n} = \begin{pmatrix} A \\ B \\ C \end{pmatrix}$.

$\therefore$ using **a**, $d = \frac{|\overrightarrow{QP} \bullet \mathbf{n}|}{|\mathbf{n}|} = \frac{\left|\begin{pmatrix} x_1 - x \\ y_1 - y \\ z_1 - z \end{pmatrix} \bullet \begin{pmatrix} A \\ B \\ C \end{pmatrix}\right|}{\sqrt{A^2 + B^2 + C^2}} = \frac{|Ax_1 - Ax + By_1 - By + Cz_1 - Cz|}{\sqrt{A^2 + B^2 + C^2}}$

$= \frac{|Ax_1 + By_1 + Cz_1 - (Ax + By + Cz)|}{\sqrt{A^2 + B^2 + C^2}}$

$= \frac{|Ax_1 + By_1 + Cz_1 + D|}{\sqrt{A^2 + B^2 + C^2}}$

c 8 a *check:* Given $A(1, 0, 2)$ and the plane $2x + y - 2z + 11 = 0$,
$$d = \frac{|2x_1 + y_1 - 2z_1 + 11|}{\sqrt{2^2 + 1^2 + (-2)^2}} = \frac{|2(1) + 1(0) - 2(2) + 11|}{\sqrt{9}} = \frac{9}{3} = 3 \text{ units}$$

8 b *check:* Given $A(2, -1, 3)$ and the plane $x - y + 3z = -10$,
$$d = \frac{|x_1 - y_1 + 3z_1 + 10|}{\sqrt{1^2 + (-1)^2 + 3^2}}$$
$$= \frac{|2 - (-1) + 3(3) + 10|}{\sqrt{11}}$$
$$= \frac{22}{\sqrt{11}} = 2\sqrt{11} \text{ units}$$

8 c *check:* Given $A(1, -4, -3)$ and the plane $4x - y - 2z = 8$,
$$d = \frac{|4x_1 - y_1 - 2z_1 - 8|}{\sqrt{4^2 + (-1)^2 + (-2)^2}}$$
$$= \frac{|4 - (-4) - 2(-3) - 8|}{\sqrt{21}}$$
$$= \frac{6}{\sqrt{21}} \text{ units or } 2\sqrt{\frac{3}{7}} \text{ units}$$

16 Using the formula derived in **15 b**,

a $d = \dfrac{|x_1 + 2y_1 - z_1 - 10|}{\sqrt{1^2 + 2^2 + (-1)^2}} = \dfrac{|0 + 2(0) - 0 - 10|}{\sqrt{6}} = \dfrac{10}{\sqrt{6}}$ units

b $d = \dfrac{|x_1 + y_1 - z_1 - 2|}{\sqrt{1^2 + 1^2 + (-1)^2}} = \dfrac{|1 + (-3) - 2 - 2|}{\sqrt{3}} = \dfrac{|-6|}{\sqrt{3}} = \dfrac{6}{\sqrt{3}}$ units or $2\sqrt{3}$ units

17 a First choose a point on the first plane $x + y + 2z = 4$, for example, $(0, 0, 2)$.
Using the formula obtained in **15 b** to calculate the distance from this point to the second plane,
$$d = \frac{|2x_1 + 2y_1 + 4z_1 + 11|}{\sqrt{2^2 + 2^2 + 4^2}} = \frac{|2(0) + 2(0) + 4(2) + 11|}{\sqrt{24}} = \frac{19}{\sqrt{24}} \text{ units.}$$

b Choose a point on the plane $ax + by + cz + d_1 = 0$, for example, $\left(0, 0, -\dfrac{d_1}{c}\right)$.
Using the formula obtained in **15 b** to calculate the distance from this point to the second plane,
$$d = \frac{|ax_1 + by_1 + cz_1 + d_2|}{\sqrt{a^2 + b^2 + c^2}} = \frac{\left|a(0) + b(0) + c\left(-\dfrac{d_1}{c}\right) + d_2\right|}{\sqrt{a^2 + b^2 + c^2}} = \frac{|d_2 - d_1|}{\sqrt{a^2 + b^2 + c^2}} \text{ units.}$$

18 The line $x = 2 + t$, $y = -1 + 2t$, $z = -3t$ has direction vector $\begin{pmatrix} 1 \\ 2 \\ -3 \end{pmatrix}$,

and $\begin{pmatrix} 11 \\ -4 \\ 1 \end{pmatrix}$ is a vector normal to the plane $11x - 4y + z = 0$.

But $\begin{pmatrix} 1 \\ 2 \\ -3 \end{pmatrix} \bullet \begin{pmatrix} 11 \\ -4 \\ 1 \end{pmatrix} = 11 - 8 - 3 = 0$

$\therefore$ these vectors are perpendicular and so the line is parallel to the plane.
Choose any point on the line, say $t = 0$, which corresponds to the point $(2, -1, 0)$.

Then the distance $d = \dfrac{|11x_1 - 4y_1 + z_1|}{\sqrt{11^2 + (-4)^2 + 1^2}} = \dfrac{|11(2) - 4(-1) + 0|}{\sqrt{138}} = \dfrac{26}{\sqrt{138}}$ units.

19 Since the planes are parallel to $2x - y + 2z = 5$, they have equation $2x - y + 2z = a$ for some a.
Choose any point on $2x - y + 2z = 5$, for example, $(0, -5, 0)$.
Then the distance from this point to the plane $2x - y + 2z = a$ is

$$d = \frac{|2x_1 - y_1 + 2z_1 - a|}{\sqrt{2^2 + (-1)^2 + 2^2}}$$

$\therefore \quad 2 = \dfrac{|2(0) - (-5) + 2(0) - a|}{3}$

$\therefore \quad 6 = |5 - a|$

$\therefore \quad 5 - a = \pm 6$

$\therefore \quad a = 5 \pm 6$

$\therefore \quad a = -1$ or $a = 11$

$\therefore \quad$ the planes are $2x - y + 2z = -1$
and $2x - y + 2z = 11$.

EXERCISE 16E

1 a $\mathbf{n} = \begin{pmatrix} 1 \\ -1 \\ 1 \end{pmatrix}$ and $\mathbf{d} = \begin{pmatrix} 4 \\ 3 \\ 1 \end{pmatrix}$ **b** $\mathbf{n} = \begin{pmatrix} 2 \\ -1 \\ 1 \end{pmatrix}$ and $\mathbf{d} = \begin{pmatrix} 1 \\ 3 \\ 1 \end{pmatrix}$

$\therefore \sin\phi = \dfrac{|\mathbf{n} \bullet \mathbf{d}|}{|\mathbf{n}|\,|\mathbf{d}|} = \dfrac{|4-3+1|}{\sqrt{3}\sqrt{26}} = \dfrac{2}{\sqrt{78}}$ $\therefore \sin\phi = \dfrac{|\mathbf{n} \bullet \mathbf{d}|}{|\mathbf{n}|\,|\mathbf{d}|} = \dfrac{|2-3+1|}{\sqrt{6}\sqrt{11}} = 0$

and so $\phi \approx 13.1°$ and so $\phi \approx 0°$

So, the line and plane are parallel.

c $\mathbf{n} = \begin{pmatrix} 3 \\ 4 \\ -1 \end{pmatrix}$ So, if $x - 4 = 3 - y = 2(z+1) = t$

or equivalently $x = 4+t$, $y = 3-t$, $z = -1 + \tfrac{1}{2}t$ then $\mathbf{d} = \begin{pmatrix} 1 \\ -1 \\ \tfrac{1}{2} \end{pmatrix}$.

$\therefore \sin\phi = \dfrac{|\mathbf{n}\bullet\mathbf{d}|}{|\mathbf{n}|\,|\mathbf{d}|} = \dfrac{|3 + (-4) + (-\tfrac{1}{2})|}{\sqrt{26}\sqrt{\tfrac{9}{4}}} = \dfrac{|-\tfrac{3}{2}|}{\tfrac{3}{2}\sqrt{26}} = \dfrac{1}{\sqrt{26}}$ and so $\phi \approx 11.3°$

d The plane has normal vector

$\mathbf{n} = \begin{vmatrix} \mathbf{i} & \mathbf{j} & \mathbf{k} \\ 3 & -4 & -1 \\ 1 & 1 & -2 \end{vmatrix} = \begin{vmatrix} -4 & -1 \\ 1 & -2 \end{vmatrix}\mathbf{i} - \begin{vmatrix} 3 & -1 \\ 1 & -2 \end{vmatrix}\mathbf{j} + \begin{vmatrix} 3 & -4 \\ 1 & 1 \end{vmatrix}\mathbf{k} = 9\mathbf{i} + 5\mathbf{j} + 7\mathbf{k}$

and the line has direction vector $\mathbf{d} = \mathbf{i} - \mathbf{j} + \mathbf{k}$

$\therefore \sin\phi = \dfrac{|\mathbf{n}\bullet\mathbf{d}|}{|\mathbf{n}|\,|\mathbf{d}|} = \dfrac{|9 - 5 + 7|}{\sqrt{81 + 25 + 49}\sqrt{1+1+1}} = \dfrac{11}{\sqrt{155}\sqrt{3}}$

$\therefore \phi \approx 30.7°$

2 a $\mathbf{n}_1 = \begin{pmatrix} 2 \\ -1 \\ 1 \end{pmatrix}$ and $\mathbf{n}_2 = \begin{pmatrix} 1 \\ 3 \\ 2 \end{pmatrix}$ **b** $\mathbf{n}_1 = \begin{pmatrix} 1 \\ -1 \\ 3 \end{pmatrix}$ and $\mathbf{n}_2 = \begin{pmatrix} 3 \\ 1 \\ -1 \end{pmatrix}$

$\therefore \cos\theta = \dfrac{|\mathbf{n}_1 \bullet \mathbf{n}_2|}{|\mathbf{n}_1|\,|\mathbf{n}_2|} = \dfrac{|2 - 3 + 2|}{\sqrt{6}\sqrt{14}} = \dfrac{1}{\sqrt{84}}$ $\therefore \cos\theta = \dfrac{|\mathbf{n}_1 \bullet \mathbf{n}_2|}{|\mathbf{n}_1|\,|\mathbf{n}_2|} = \dfrac{|3 - 1 - 3|}{\sqrt{11}\sqrt{11}} = \dfrac{1}{11}$

$\therefore \theta \approx 83.7°$ $\therefore \theta \approx 84.8°$

c $\mathbf{n}_1 = \begin{pmatrix} 3 \\ -1 \\ 1 \end{pmatrix}$ and $\mathbf{n}_2 = \begin{pmatrix} 2 \\ 4 \\ -1 \end{pmatrix}$ $\therefore \cos\theta = \dfrac{|\mathbf{n}_1 \bullet \mathbf{n}_2|}{|\mathbf{n}_1|\,|\mathbf{n}_2|} = \dfrac{|6 - 4 - 1|}{\sqrt{11}\sqrt{21}} = \dfrac{1}{\sqrt{231}}$

$\therefore \theta \approx 86.2°$

d $\mathbf{n}_1 = \begin{vmatrix} \mathbf{i} & \mathbf{j} & \mathbf{k} \\ -1 & 1 & -1 \\ 2 & -4 & 3 \end{vmatrix} = \begin{vmatrix} 1 & -1 \\ -4 & 3 \end{vmatrix}\mathbf{i} - \begin{vmatrix} -1 & -1 \\ 2 & 3 \end{vmatrix}\mathbf{j} + \begin{vmatrix} -1 & 1 \\ 2 & -4 \end{vmatrix}\mathbf{k}$

$= -\mathbf{i} + \mathbf{j} + 2\mathbf{k}$

$\mathbf{n}_2 = \begin{vmatrix} \mathbf{i} & \mathbf{j} & \mathbf{k} \\ -2 & -1 & -1 \\ 1 & 1 & 1 \end{vmatrix} = \begin{vmatrix} -1 & -1 \\ 1 & 1 \end{vmatrix}\mathbf{i} - \begin{vmatrix} -2 & -1 \\ 1 & 1 \end{vmatrix}\mathbf{j} + \begin{vmatrix} -2 & -1 \\ 1 & 1 \end{vmatrix}\mathbf{k}$

$= \mathbf{j} - \mathbf{k}$

$\therefore \cos\theta = \dfrac{|\mathbf{n}_1 \bullet \mathbf{n}_2|}{|\mathbf{n}_1|\,|\mathbf{n}_2|} = \dfrac{|-1(0) + 1(1) + 2(-1)|}{\sqrt{1+1+4}\sqrt{0+1+1}} = \dfrac{|1-2|}{\sqrt{6}\sqrt{2}} = \dfrac{1}{\sqrt{12}}$

$\therefore \theta \approx 73.2°$

e $\mathbf{n}_1 = \begin{pmatrix} 3 \\ -4 \\ 1 \end{pmatrix}$ and $\mathbf{n}_2 = \begin{vmatrix} \mathbf{i} & \mathbf{j} & \mathbf{k} \\ 3 & -1 & 0 \\ 2 & 1 & 1 \end{vmatrix} = \begin{vmatrix} -1 & 0 \\ 1 & 1 \end{vmatrix}\mathbf{i} - \begin{vmatrix} 3 & 0 \\ 2 & 1 \end{vmatrix}\mathbf{j} + \begin{vmatrix} 3 & -1 \\ 2 & 1 \end{vmatrix}\mathbf{k}$

$= -\mathbf{i} - 3\mathbf{j} + 5\mathbf{k}$

$$\therefore \quad \cos\theta = \frac{|\mathbf{n}_1 \bullet \mathbf{n}_2|}{|\mathbf{n}_1||\mathbf{n}_2|} = \frac{|(3)(-1) + (-4)(-3) + (1)(5)|}{\sqrt{9+16+1}\sqrt{1+9+25}} = \frac{14}{\sqrt{26 \times 35}}$$

$\therefore \quad \theta \approx 62.3°$

EXERCISE 16F

1 a Either (1) no solutions or (2) an infinite number of solutions.

b i They are parallel if
$a_1 = ka_2$
$b_1 = kb_2$
and $c_1 = kc_2$ for some k.

ii They are coincident if
$a_1 = ka_2$
$b_1 = kb_2$
$c_1 = kc_2$
and $d_1 = kd_2$ for some k.

c i $\begin{pmatrix} 1 & -3 & 2 & | & 8 \\ 3 & -9 & 2 & | & 4 \end{pmatrix} \sim \begin{pmatrix} 1 & -3 & 2 & | & 8 \\ 0 & 0 & -4 & | & -20 \end{pmatrix} \quad R_2 \to R_2 - 3R_1$

$\therefore \quad -4z = -20$ and $x - 3y + 2z = 8$ or $x = 3y - 2z + 8$
$\therefore \quad z = 5$ and if we let $y = t$, then $x = 3t - 2(5) + 8 = -2 + 3t$
$\therefore$ the planes meet in the line $x = -2 + 3t$, $y = t$, $z = 5$, t in $\mathbb{R}$

ii $\begin{pmatrix} 2 & 1 & 1 & | & 5 \\ 1 & -1 & 1 & | & 3 \end{pmatrix} \sim \begin{pmatrix} 2 & 1 & 1 & | & 5 \\ 0 & -3 & 1 & | & 1 \end{pmatrix} \quad R_2 \to 2R_2 - R_1$

$\therefore \quad -3y + z = 1$ and $2x + y + z = 5$
$\therefore$ if we let $y = t$, then $z = 1 + 3y = 1 + 3t$ and $2x = 5 - y - z$
$\qquad \qquad \qquad \qquad \qquad \qquad \qquad \qquad \qquad = 5 - t - (1 + 3t)$
$\qquad \qquad \qquad \qquad \qquad \qquad \qquad \qquad \qquad = 4 - 4t$
$\therefore \quad x = 2 - 2t$

$\therefore$ the planes meet in the line $x = 2 - 2t$, $y = t$, $z = 1 + 3t$, t in $\mathbb{R}$

iii $\begin{pmatrix} 1 & 2 & -3 & | & 6 \\ 3 & 6 & -9 & | & 18 \end{pmatrix} \sim \begin{pmatrix} 1 & 2 & -3 & | & 6 \\ 0 & 0 & 0 & | & 0 \end{pmatrix} \quad R_2 \to R_2 - 3R_1$

$\therefore$ there are infinitely many solutions, as the planes are coincident.
Let $y = s$ and $z = t$ in $x + 2y - 3z = 6$, $s, t \in \mathbb{R}$
$\therefore \quad x = 3t - 2s + 6$
$\therefore \quad x = 3t - 2s + 6$, $y = s$, $z = t$ is the general solution of the plane.

2 a $\begin{pmatrix} 1 & 2 & -1 & | & 6 \\ 2 & 4 & k & | & 12 \end{pmatrix}$
If $k = -2$, the two planes are coincident.
$\therefore$ infinitely many solutions.

$\sim \begin{pmatrix} 1 & 2 & -1 & | & 6 \\ 0 & 0 & k+2 & | & 0 \end{pmatrix} \quad R_2 \to R_2 - 2R_1$
If $k \neq -2$, the two planes meet in a line.
$\therefore$ infinitely many solutions.

b $\begin{pmatrix} 1 & -1 & 3 & | & 8 \\ 2 & -2 & 6 & | & k \end{pmatrix}$
If $k = 16$, the planes are coincident.
$\therefore$ infinitely many solutions.

$\sim \begin{pmatrix} 1 & -1 & 3 & | & 8 \\ 0 & 0 & 0 & | & k-16 \end{pmatrix} \quad R_2 \to R_2 - 2R_1$
If $k \neq 16$, the planes are parallel but not coincident.
$\therefore$ no solutions exist.

3 (1) $P_1 = P_2 = P_3$: infinitely many solutions where x, y and z are in terms of two parameters, s and t say. The solution is a plane.

(2) $P_1 = P_2$ are coincident and cut by P_3: infinitely many solutions where x, y and z are in terms of one parameter, t say. The solution is a line.

(3) $P_1 = P_2$ with P_3 parallel but not coincident: no solutions exist.

(4) P_1 and P_2 are parallel but not coincident, and P_3 cuts both planes: no solutions exist.

(5) P_1, P_2 and P_3 are all parallel but not coincident: no solutions exist.

(6) P_1, P_2 and P_3 meet in a unique point (a, b, c), so that $x = a$, $y = b$, $z = c$.

(7) P_1, P_2 and P_3 meet in a common line: infinitely many solutions where x, y and z are in terms of one parameter, t say.

(8) P_1, P_2 and P_3 are such that the line of intersection between any two is parallel to the third plane: no solutions exist.

4 **a** The system has augmented matrix

$$\begin{pmatrix} 1 & 1 & -1 & | & -5 \\ 1 & -1 & 2 & | & 11 \\ 4 & 1 & -5 & | & -18 \end{pmatrix}$$

$$\sim \begin{pmatrix} 1 & 1 & -1 & | & -5 \\ 0 & -2 & 3 & | & 16 \\ 0 & -3 & -1 & | & 2 \end{pmatrix} \begin{array}{l} R_2 \to R_2 - R_1 \\ R_3 \to R_3 - 4R_1 \end{array}$$

$$\sim \begin{pmatrix} 1 & 1 & -1 & | & -5 \\ 0 & -2 & 3 & | & 16 \\ 0 & 0 & -11 & | & -44 \end{pmatrix} R_3 \to 2R_3 - 3R_2$$

∴ the planes meet at the unique point $(1, -2, 4)$

b The system has augmented matrix

$$\begin{pmatrix} 1 & -1 & 2 & | & 1 \\ 2 & 1 & -1 & | & 8 \\ 5 & -2 & 5 & | & 11 \end{pmatrix}$$

$$\sim \begin{pmatrix} 1 & -1 & 2 & | & 1 \\ 0 & 3 & -5 & | & 6 \\ 0 & 3 & -5 & | & 6 \end{pmatrix} \begin{array}{l} R_2 \to R_2 - 2R_1 \\ R_3 \to R_3 - 5R_1 \end{array}$$

$$\sim \begin{pmatrix} 1 & -1 & 2 & | & 1 \\ 0 & 3 & -5 & | & 6 \\ 0 & 0 & 0 & | & 0 \end{pmatrix} R_3 \to R_3 - R_2$$

∴ the three planes meet in a common line

$x = \dfrac{9-t}{3}$, $y = \dfrac{5t+6}{3}$, $z = t$, t in $\mathbb{R}$

c The system has augmented matrix:

$$\begin{pmatrix} 1 & 2 & -1 & | & 8 \\ 2 & -1 & -1 & | & 5 \\ 3 & -4 & -1 & | & 2 \end{pmatrix}$$

$$\sim \begin{pmatrix} 1 & 2 & -1 & | & 8 \\ 0 & -5 & 1 & | & -11 \\ 0 & -10 & 2 & | & -22 \end{pmatrix} \begin{array}{l} R_2 \to R_2 - 2R_1 \\ R_3 \to R_3 - 3R_1 \end{array}$$

$$\sim \begin{pmatrix} 1 & 2 & -1 & | & 8 \\ 0 & -5 & 1 & | & -11 \\ 0 & 0 & 0 & | & 0 \end{pmatrix} R_3 \to R_3 - 2R_2$$

∴ the three planes meet in a common line

$x = 3t - 3$, $y = t$, $z = 5t - 11$, t in $\mathbb{R}$

d The system has augmented matrix:

$$\begin{pmatrix} 1 & -1 & 1 & | & 8 \\ 2 & -2 & 2 & | & 11 \\ 1 & 3 & -1 & | & -2 \end{pmatrix}$$

$$\sim \begin{pmatrix} 1 & -1 & 1 & | & 8 \\ 0 & 0 & 0 & | & -5 \\ 0 & 4 & -2 & | & -10 \end{pmatrix} \begin{array}{l} R_2 \to R_2 - 2R_1 \\ R_3 \to R_3 - R_1 \end{array}$$

Now $-11z = -44$ ∴ $z = 4$

and $-2y + 3z = 16$

∴ $-2y + 12 = 16$

∴ $-2y = 4$

∴ $y = -2$

and $x + y - z = -5$

∴ $x = -5 - (-2) + 4$

∴ $x = 1$

Let $z = t$

As $3y - 5z = 6$

$3y = 5t + 6$

∴ $y = \dfrac{5t+6}{3}$

But $x - y + 2z = 1$

∴ $x = 1 + \dfrac{5t+6}{3} - 2t$

∴ $x = \dfrac{3 + 5t + 6 - 6t}{3}$

∴ $x = \dfrac{9-t}{3}$

Let $y = t$

Now $-5y + z = -11$

∴ $z = -11 + 5t$

Also $x + 2y - z = 8$

∴ $x = 8 - 2y + z$

∴ $x = 8 - 2t - 11 + 5t$

∴ $x = -3 + 3t$

The first two planes are parallel and are cut by the third plane.

∴ the equations are inconsistent and there are no solutions.

e The system has augmented matrix:
$$\begin{pmatrix} 1 & 1 & -2 & | & 1 \\ 1 & -1 & 1 & | & 4 \\ 3 & 3 & -6 & | & 3 \end{pmatrix}$$

$$\sim \begin{pmatrix} 1 & 1 & -2 & | & 1 \\ 0 & -2 & 3 & | & 3 \\ 0 & 0 & 0 & | & 0 \end{pmatrix} \begin{array}{l} R_2 \to R_2 - R_1 \\ R_3 \to R_3 - 3R_1 \end{array}$$

There are two coincident planes cut by a third plane.
∴ infinitely many solutions in a line:
$$x = \frac{t+5}{2}, \quad y = \frac{3t-3}{2}, \quad z = t, \quad t \in \mathbb{R}$$

Let $z = t$

Now $-2y + 3z = 3$

∴ $2y = 3z - 3$

∴ $y = \dfrac{3t-3}{2}$

and as $x + y - 2z = 1$

∴ $x = 1 - y + 2z$

∴ $x = 1 - \dfrac{3t-3}{2} + 2t$

∴ $x = \dfrac{2 - 3t + 3 + 4t}{2}$

∴ $x = \dfrac{t+5}{2}$

f The system has augmented matrix:
$$\begin{pmatrix} 1 & -1 & -1 & | & 5 \\ 1 & 1 & 1 & | & 1 \\ 5 & -1 & 2 & | & 17 \end{pmatrix}$$

$$\sim \begin{pmatrix} 1 & -1 & -1 & | & 5 \\ 0 & 2 & 2 & | & -4 \\ 0 & 4 & 7 & | & -8 \end{pmatrix} \begin{array}{l} R_2 \to R_2 - R_1 \\ R_3 \to R_3 - 5R_1 \end{array}$$

$$\sim \begin{pmatrix} 1 & -1 & -1 & | & 5 \\ 0 & 2 & 2 & | & -4 \\ 0 & 0 & 3 & | & 0 \end{pmatrix} R_3 \to R_3 - 2R_2$$

∴ the planes meet at the unique point $(3, -2, 0)$.

Now $3z = 0$

∴ $z = 0$

As $2y + 2z = -4$

∴ $2y = -4$

∴ $y = -2$

and as $x - y - z = 5$

∴ $x = 5 + (-2) + 0$

∴ $x = 3$

5 The system has augmented matrix:
$$\begin{pmatrix} 1 & -1 & 3 & | & 1 \\ 2 & -3 & -1 & | & 3 \\ 3 & -5 & -5 & | & k \end{pmatrix}$$

$$\sim \begin{pmatrix} 1 & -1 & 3 & | & -1 \\ 0 & -1 & -7 & | & 1 \\ 0 & -2 & -14 & | & k-3 \end{pmatrix} \begin{array}{l} R_2 \to R_2 - 2R_1 \\ R_3 \to R_3 - 3R_1 \end{array}$$

$$\sim \begin{pmatrix} 1 & -1 & 3 & | & -1 \\ 0 & -1 & -7 & | & 1 \\ 0 & 0 & 0 & | & k-5 \end{pmatrix} R_3 \to R_3 - 2R_2$$

(1) If $k = 5$, the planes meet in a line {as we have a row of zeros}

Let $z = t$

Now $-y - 7z = 1$

∴ $y = -1 - 7t$

and $x - y + 3z = 1$

∴ $x = 1 + y - 3z$

∴ $x = 1 - 1 - 7t - 3t$

∴ $x = -10t$

∴ $x = -10t, \; y = -1 - 7t, \; z = t, \; t \in \mathbb{R}$

(2) If $k \neq 5$ there are no solutions.
Since no two planes are parallel, the line of intersection of any two planes is parallel to the third plane.

6 The augmented matrix is:
$$\begin{pmatrix} 1 & 2 & m & | & -1 \\ 2 & 1 & -1 & | & 3 \\ m & -2 & 1 & | & 1 \end{pmatrix}$$

$$\sim \begin{pmatrix} 1 & 2 & m & | & -1 \\ 0 & -3 & -1-2m & | & 5 \\ 0 & -2-2m & 1-m^2 & | & 1+m \end{pmatrix} \begin{array}{l} R_2 \to R_2 - 2R_1 \\ R_3 \to R_3 - mR_1 \end{array}$$

$$\sim \begin{pmatrix} 1 & 2 & m & | & -1 \\ 0 & -3 & -1-2m & | & 5 \\ 0 & 0 & -m^2-6m-5 & | & 7m+7 \end{pmatrix} R_3 \to -3R_3 - (-2-2m)R_2$$

0	$6+6m$	$3m^2-3$	$-3-3m$
0	$-6-6m$	$-4m^2-6m-2$	$10+10m$
0	0	$-m^2-6m-5$	$7+7m$

∴ $-(m^2 + 6m + 5)z = 7(m+1)$

∴ $-(m+5)(m+1)z = 7(m+1)$

(1) When $m \neq -1$ or -5, the system has a unique solution.
So, the three planes meet in a common point.

(2) When $m = -5$ we have $0z = -28$.
$\therefore$ the system is inconsistent, and there are no solutions.

The augmented matrix is: $\begin{pmatrix} 1 & 2 & -5 & | & -1 \\ 0 & -3 & 9 & | & 5 \\ 0 & 0 & 0 & | & -28 \end{pmatrix}$

The line of intersection of any two planes is parallel to the third plane.

(3) When $m = -1$, we have $\begin{pmatrix} 1 & 2 & -1 & | & -1 \\ 0 & -3 & 1 & | & 5 \\ 0 & 0 & 0 & | & 0 \end{pmatrix}$

So, the three planes meet in a common line {two coincident planes cut by the third}.

Let $z = t$, so $-3y + t = 5$ and hence $y = \dfrac{t-5}{3}$

Also, $x = -1 - 2y + z$

$= -1 - 2\left(\dfrac{t-5}{3}\right) + t$

$= -1 + \tfrac{1}{3}t + \tfrac{10}{3}$

$= \dfrac{t+7}{3}$

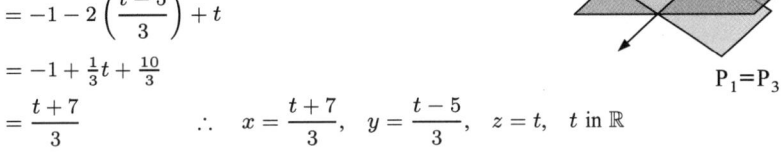

$\therefore\ x = \dfrac{t+7}{3},\ y = \dfrac{t-5}{3},\ z = t,\ t$ in $\mathbb{R}$

$P_1 = P_3$

7 P_1 meets P_2 where

$\begin{pmatrix} 2 \\ -1 \\ 0 \end{pmatrix} + \lambda \begin{pmatrix} 3 \\ 0 \\ 1 \end{pmatrix} + \mu \begin{pmatrix} 1 \\ 1 \\ -1 \end{pmatrix} = \begin{pmatrix} 3 \\ -1 \\ 3 \end{pmatrix} + r \begin{pmatrix} 2 \\ 0 \\ -1 \end{pmatrix} + s \begin{pmatrix} 1 \\ 1 \\ 0 \end{pmatrix}$

$\therefore \begin{cases} 2 + 3\lambda + \mu = 3 + 2r + s \\ -1 + \mu = -1 + s \\ \lambda - \mu = 3 - r \end{cases}$ which gives $\begin{cases} 3\lambda + \mu = 2r + s + 1 \\ \mu = s \\ \lambda - \mu = 3 - r \end{cases}$

If $\mu = a$ say, then $s = a$, $3\lambda + a = 2r + a + 1$, and $\lambda - a = 3 - r$

$\therefore\ r = 3 - \lambda + a$

$\therefore\ 3\lambda + a = 6 - 2\lambda + 2a + a + 1$

$\therefore\ 5\lambda = 2a + 7$

$\therefore\ \lambda = \dfrac{2a+7}{5}$ and $r = 3 + a - \dfrac{2a+7}{5}$

$\therefore\ r = \dfrac{3a+8}{5}$

$\therefore$ if $\mu = a$, $\lambda = \dfrac{2a+7}{5}$, $r = \dfrac{3a+8}{5}$, $s = a$ ...... (1)

P_2 meets P_3 where

$\begin{pmatrix} 3 \\ -1 \\ 3 \end{pmatrix} + r \begin{pmatrix} 2 \\ 0 \\ -1 \end{pmatrix} + s \begin{pmatrix} 1 \\ 1 \\ 0 \end{pmatrix} = \begin{pmatrix} 2 \\ -1 \\ 2 \end{pmatrix} + t \begin{pmatrix} 1 \\ -1 \\ 0 \end{pmatrix} - u \begin{pmatrix} 0 \\ -1 \\ 2 \end{pmatrix}$

$\therefore \begin{cases} 3 + 2r + s = 2 + t \\ -1 + s = -1 - t + u \\ 3 - r = 2 - 2u \end{cases}$ which gives $\begin{cases} 2r + s + 1 = t \\ s = u - t \\ 2u - r = -1 \end{cases}$

So, if $u = b$ say, then $r = 2b + 1$ and $4b + 2 + b - t + 1 = t$

$\therefore\ 5b + 3 = 2t$ and so $t = \dfrac{5b+3}{2}$

and $s = u - t = b - \dfrac{5b+3}{2} = \dfrac{-3b-3}{2}$

So, if $u = b$, $r = 2b + 1$, $t = \dfrac{5b+3}{2}$, $s = \dfrac{-3b-3}{2}$ ...... (2)

From (1) and (2), $\dfrac{3a+8}{5} = 2b+1$ and $a = \dfrac{-3b-3}{2}$

$\therefore \quad 3a + 8 = 10b + 5$ and $2a = -3b - 3$

$\therefore \quad \begin{cases} 3a - 10b = -3 \\ 2a + 3b = -3 \end{cases}$ which has solutions $a = -\dfrac{39}{29}$, $b = -\dfrac{3}{29}$

In (2), $u = -\dfrac{3}{29}$, $t = \dfrac{5\left(-\dfrac{3}{29}\right) + 3}{2} = 1\dfrac{7}{29}$ or $\dfrac{36}{29}$

$\therefore \quad \mathbf{r}_3 = \begin{pmatrix} 2 \\ -1 \\ 2 \end{pmatrix} + \dfrac{36}{29}\begin{pmatrix} 1 \\ -1 \\ 0 \end{pmatrix} + \dfrac{3}{29}\begin{pmatrix} 0 \\ -1 \\ 2 \end{pmatrix} = \begin{pmatrix} 3\tfrac{7}{29} \\ -2\tfrac{10}{29} \\ 2\tfrac{6}{29} \end{pmatrix} = \begin{pmatrix} \tfrac{94}{29} \\ -\tfrac{68}{29} \\ \tfrac{64}{29} \end{pmatrix}$

$\therefore$ all 3 planes meet at $\left(\dfrac{94}{29}, -\dfrac{68}{29}, \dfrac{64}{29}\right)$.

REVIEW SET 16A

1 a The vector equation is
$\begin{pmatrix} x \\ y \end{pmatrix} = \begin{pmatrix} -6 \\ 3 \end{pmatrix} + t\begin{pmatrix} 4 \\ -3 \end{pmatrix}$

b The parametric equations are
$x = -6 + 4t$, $y = 3 - 3t$, $t \in \mathbb{R}$

2 The vector equation is $\begin{pmatrix} x \\ y \end{pmatrix} = \begin{pmatrix} 0 \\ 8 \end{pmatrix} + t\begin{pmatrix} 5 \\ 4 \end{pmatrix}$, $t \in \mathbb{R}$

3 $(-3, m)$ lies on the line, so $\begin{pmatrix} -3 \\ m \end{pmatrix} = \begin{pmatrix} 18 \\ -2 \end{pmatrix} + \begin{pmatrix} -7t \\ 4t \end{pmatrix}$

$\therefore \quad -3 = 18 - 7t$ and $m = -2 + 4t$

$\therefore \quad 7t = 21$

$\therefore \quad t = 3$ and so $m = -2 + 4(3) = 10$

4 The direction vector is $\begin{pmatrix} 3 \\ -1 \end{pmatrix}$ which has length $\sqrt{3^2 + (-1)^2} = \sqrt{10}$ units

$\therefore \quad 2\sqrt{10}\begin{pmatrix} 3 \\ -1 \end{pmatrix}$ has length 20. So, the velocity vector is $\begin{pmatrix} 6\sqrt{10} \\ -2\sqrt{10} \end{pmatrix}$ or $2\sqrt{10}(3\mathbf{i} - \mathbf{j})$

5 a $x(0) = -4$ and $y(0) = 3$, so the initial position is $(-4, 3)$.
  b $x(4) = -4 + 8(4) = 28$ and $y(4) = 3 + 6(4) = 27$, so at $t = 4$ the position is $(28, 27)$.
  c The velocity vector is $\begin{pmatrix} 8 \\ 6 \end{pmatrix}$, so the speed is $\sqrt{8^2 + 6^2} = 10$ m s^{-1} **d** $\begin{pmatrix} 8 \\ 6 \end{pmatrix}$

6 a i The yacht is initially at $(-6, 10)$, so its initial position vector is $\begin{pmatrix} -6 \\ 10 \end{pmatrix}$ or $-6\mathbf{i} + 10\mathbf{j}$
  ii $-\mathbf{i} - 3\mathbf{j}$ has length $\sqrt{(-1)^2 + (-3)^2} = \sqrt{10}$
   $\therefore \quad 5(-\mathbf{i} - 3\mathbf{j})$ has length $5\sqrt{10}$
   $\therefore \quad$ the direction vector is $-5\mathbf{i} - 15\mathbf{j}$
  iii $\begin{pmatrix} x \\ y \end{pmatrix} = \begin{pmatrix} -6 \\ 10 \end{pmatrix} + t\begin{pmatrix} -5 \\ -15 \end{pmatrix}$ $\therefore \quad \begin{pmatrix} x \\ y \end{pmatrix} = -6\mathbf{i} + 10\mathbf{j} + t(-5\mathbf{i} - 15\mathbf{j})$
   $= (-6 - 5t)\mathbf{i} + (10 - 15t)\mathbf{j}$

b

$\overrightarrow{OP} = \begin{pmatrix} -6-5t \\ 10-15t \end{pmatrix}$ and $\overrightarrow{OP} \bullet \begin{pmatrix} -1 \\ -3 \end{pmatrix} = 0$

$\therefore \quad -1(-6 - 5t) - 3(10 - 15t) = 0$

$\therefore \quad 6 + 5t - 30 + 45t = 0$

$\therefore \quad 50t = 24$

$\therefore \quad t = 0.48$ h

(or 28.8 min)

O(0, 0), beacon, P(−6−5t, 10−15t), $\begin{pmatrix} -1 \\ -3 \end{pmatrix}$

c When $t = 0.48$, $\overrightarrow{OP} = \begin{pmatrix} -6-5(0.48) \\ 10-15(0.48) \end{pmatrix} = \begin{pmatrix} -8.4 \\ 2.8 \end{pmatrix}$

and OP $= \sqrt{(-8.4)^2 + (2.8)^2} \approx 8.85$ km

As the closest distance is 8.85 km and the radius is 8 km, the yacht will miss the reef.

7 a $\begin{pmatrix} x_1(t) \\ y_1(t) \end{pmatrix} = \begin{pmatrix} 2 \\ 4 \end{pmatrix} + t\begin{pmatrix} 1 \\ -3 \end{pmatrix}$ where $t \geqslant 0$. When $t = 0$, the time is 2:17 pm.

$\therefore\ x_1(t) = 2 + t, \quad y_1(t) = 4 - 3t$

b Likewise, $x_2(t) = 11 - (t - 2),\qquad y_2(t) = 3 + a(t - 2)$

$\therefore\ x_2(t) = 13 - t \qquad\qquad y_2(t) = [3 - 2a] + at, \quad t \geqslant 2$

c They meet where $2 + t = 13 - t$ and $4 - 3t = [3 - 2a] + at$

$\therefore\ 2t = 11$

$\therefore\ t = \frac{11}{2}$ $\therefore$ the time would be 2:17 pm plus $5\frac{1}{2}$ min, or 2:22:30 pm

d When $t = \frac{11}{2}$,

$4 - 3\left(\frac{11}{2}\right) = [3 - 2a] + a\left(\frac{11}{2}\right)$

$\therefore\ -\frac{25}{2} = 3 + \frac{7a}{2}$

$\therefore\ -25 = 6 + 7a$

$\therefore\ 7a = -31$

$\therefore\ a = -\frac{31}{7}$

Y18 has velocity vector $\begin{pmatrix} -1 \\ -\frac{31}{7} \end{pmatrix}$

with speed $= \sqrt{(-1)^2 + \left(-\frac{31}{7}\right)^2}$

≈ 4.54 units per minute

$\tan\alpha = \dfrac{1}{\frac{31}{7}} = \dfrac{7}{31}$

$\therefore\ \alpha = \tan^{-1}\left(\frac{7}{31}\right) \approx 12.7°$

$\therefore$ the direction is $180° + \alpha° \approx 192.7°$

So, the torpedo has speed 4.54 units per minute and direction 193°.

8 a Line 1 has direction vector $\begin{pmatrix} 5 \\ -2 \end{pmatrix}$ and line 4 has direction vector $\begin{pmatrix} -5 \\ 2 \end{pmatrix}$.

Now $\begin{pmatrix} 5 \\ -2 \end{pmatrix} = -\begin{pmatrix} -5 \\ 2 \end{pmatrix}$, so lines 1 and 4 are parallel, $\therefore$ [KL] $\parallel$ [MN].

b $\overrightarrow{KL} = a\begin{pmatrix} 5 \\ -2 \end{pmatrix}$, $\overrightarrow{NK} = b\begin{pmatrix} 4 \\ 10 \end{pmatrix}$, $\overrightarrow{MN} = c\begin{pmatrix} -5 \\ 2 \end{pmatrix}$ {for some constants a, b, c}

$\therefore\ \overrightarrow{KL} \bullet \overrightarrow{NK} = ab(20 - 20) = 0$ and $\overrightarrow{NK} \bullet \overrightarrow{MN} = bc(-20 + 20) = 0$

$\therefore$ [NK] is perpendicular to both [KL] and [MN].

c Lines 1 and 3 meet at K.

$\therefore\ \begin{pmatrix} 2 \\ 19 \end{pmatrix} + p\begin{pmatrix} 5 \\ -2 \end{pmatrix} = \begin{pmatrix} 3 \\ 7 \end{pmatrix} + r\begin{pmatrix} 4 \\ 10 \end{pmatrix}$

$\therefore\ \begin{pmatrix} 5p - 4r \\ -2p - 10r \end{pmatrix} = \begin{pmatrix} 1 \\ -12 \end{pmatrix}$

$\therefore\ 5p - 4r = 1$ ..... (1)

$\quad 2p + 10r = 12$ ..... (2)

$\therefore\ 25p - 20r = 5 \quad \{5 \times (1)\}$

$\quad 4p + 20r = 24 \quad \{2 \times (2)\}$

Adding, $\quad 29p \quad = 29$

$\therefore\ p = 1$ and $\begin{pmatrix} x \\ y \end{pmatrix} = \begin{pmatrix} 2 \\ 19 \end{pmatrix} + \begin{pmatrix} 5 \\ -2 \end{pmatrix} = \begin{pmatrix} 7 \\ 17 \end{pmatrix}$

$\therefore$ K is (7, 17).

Lines 2 and 4 meet at M.

$\therefore\ \begin{pmatrix} 33 \\ -5 \end{pmatrix} + q\begin{pmatrix} -11 \\ 16 \end{pmatrix} = \begin{pmatrix} 43 \\ -9 \end{pmatrix} + s\begin{pmatrix} -5 \\ 2 \end{pmatrix}$

$\therefore\ \begin{pmatrix} -11q + 5s \\ 16q - 2s \end{pmatrix} = \begin{pmatrix} 10 \\ -4 \end{pmatrix}$

$\therefore\ -11q + 5s = 10$ ..... (1)

$\quad 16q - 2s = -4$ ..... (2)

$\therefore\ -22q + 10s = 20 \quad \{2 \times (1)\}$

$\quad 80q - 10s = -20 \quad \{5 \times (2)\}$

Adding, $58q \quad = 0$

$\therefore\ q = 0$ and so $\begin{pmatrix} x \\ y \end{pmatrix} = \begin{pmatrix} 33 \\ -5 \end{pmatrix}$

$\therefore$ M is (33, −5).

Lines 1 and 2 meet at L.

$\therefore\ \begin{pmatrix} 2 \\ 19 \end{pmatrix} + p\begin{pmatrix} 5 \\ -2 \end{pmatrix} = \begin{pmatrix} 33 \\ -5 \end{pmatrix} + q\begin{pmatrix} -11 \\ 16 \end{pmatrix}$

$\therefore\ \begin{pmatrix} 5p + 11q \\ -2p - 16q \end{pmatrix} = \begin{pmatrix} 31 \\ -24 \end{pmatrix}$

$\therefore\ 5p + 11q = 31$ ..... (1)

$\quad -2p - 16q = -24$ ..... (2)

$\therefore\ 10p + 22q = 62 \quad \{2 \times (1)\}$

$\quad -10p - 80q = -120 \quad \{5 \times (2)\}$

Adding, $\ -58q = -58$

$\therefore\ q = 1$ and $\begin{pmatrix} x \\ y \end{pmatrix} = \begin{pmatrix} 33 \\ -5 \end{pmatrix} + \begin{pmatrix} -11 \\ 16 \end{pmatrix} = \begin{pmatrix} 22 \\ 11 \end{pmatrix}$

$\therefore$ L is (22, 11).

Lines 3 and 4 meet at N.

$\therefore\ \begin{pmatrix} 3 \\ 7 \end{pmatrix} + r\begin{pmatrix} 4 \\ 10 \end{pmatrix} = \begin{pmatrix} 43 \\ -9 \end{pmatrix} + s\begin{pmatrix} -5 \\ 2 \end{pmatrix}$

$\therefore\ \begin{pmatrix} 4r + 5s \\ 10r - 2s \end{pmatrix} = \begin{pmatrix} 40 \\ -16 \end{pmatrix}$

$\therefore\ 4r + 5s = 40$ ..... (1)

$\quad 10r - 2s = -16$ ..... (2)

$\therefore\ 8r + 10s = 80 \quad \{2 \times (1)\}$

$\quad 50r - 10s = -80 \quad \{5 \times (2)\}$

Adding, $58r \quad = 0$

$\therefore\ r = 0$ and so $\begin{pmatrix} x \\ y \end{pmatrix} = \begin{pmatrix} 3 \\ 7 \end{pmatrix}$

$\therefore$ N is (3, 7).

d

$K(7, 17)$, $L(22, 11)$, $N(3, 7)$, $M(33, -5)$

$KL = \sqrt{(22-7)^2 + (11-17)^2}$
$= \sqrt{225 + 36}$
$= \sqrt{261}$ units

$NM = \sqrt{(33-3)^2 + (-5-7)^2}$
$= \sqrt{900 + 144}$
$= \sqrt{1044}$ units

$KN = \sqrt{(7-3)^2 + (17-7)^2}$
$= \sqrt{16 + 100}$
$= \sqrt{116}$ units

$\therefore$ area $= \left(\dfrac{\sqrt{261} + \sqrt{1044}}{2}\right) \times \sqrt{116} = 261$ units^2

REVIEW SET 16B

1 $\mathbf{b} - \mathbf{a} = \overrightarrow{AB} = \begin{pmatrix} 2 \\ 1 \\ 8 \end{pmatrix}$, $\mathbf{c} - \mathbf{a} = \overrightarrow{AC} = \begin{pmatrix} -2 \\ 2 \\ -2 \end{pmatrix}$, $\mathbf{d} - \mathbf{a} = \overrightarrow{AD} = \begin{pmatrix} -3 \\ 0 \\ -9 \end{pmatrix}$

$\therefore (\mathbf{b} - \mathbf{a}) \bullet (\mathbf{c} - \mathbf{a}) \times (\mathbf{d} - \mathbf{a}) = \begin{vmatrix} 2 & 1 & 8 \\ -2 & 2 & -2 \\ -3 & 0 & -9 \end{vmatrix} = 2 \begin{vmatrix} 2 & -2 \\ 0 & -9 \end{vmatrix} - 1 \begin{vmatrix} -2 & -2 \\ -3 & -9 \end{vmatrix} + 8 \begin{vmatrix} -2 & 2 \\ -3 & 0 \end{vmatrix}$

$= 2(-18) - 1(12) + 8(6)$
$= 0$

$\therefore$ A, B, C and D are coplanar.

a We find the plane containing A, B and C.
The plane has normal

$\mathbf{n} = \overrightarrow{AB} \times \overrightarrow{AC} = \begin{vmatrix} \mathbf{i} & \mathbf{j} & \mathbf{k} \\ 2 & 1 & 8 \\ -2 & 2 & -2 \end{vmatrix} = \begin{vmatrix} 1 & 8 \\ 2 & -2 \end{vmatrix} \mathbf{i} - \begin{vmatrix} 2 & 8 \\ -2 & -2 \end{vmatrix} \mathbf{j} + \begin{vmatrix} 2 & 1 \\ -2 & 2 \end{vmatrix} \mathbf{k}$

$= -18\mathbf{i} - 12\mathbf{j} + 6\mathbf{k}$ or $-6[3\mathbf{i} + 2\mathbf{j} - \mathbf{k}]$

$\therefore$ since A lies on the plane, it has equation $3x + 2y - z = 3(1) + 2(0) + (-1)(4)$
$\therefore 3x + 2y - z = -1$

b The closest point on the plane to $E(3, 3, 2)$ is the foot of the normal from E.
The equation of the normal through E is $x = 3 + 3t$, $y = 3 + 2t$, $z = 2 - t$, and this intersects the plane when $3(3 + 3t) + 2(3 + 2t) - (2 - t) = -1$
$\therefore 9 + 9t + 6 + 4t - 2 + t = -1$
$\therefore 14t = -14$
$\therefore t = -1$

So, the nearest point is $(0, 1, 3)$.

2 a $\overrightarrow{AB} = \begin{pmatrix} -4 \\ 0 \\ 5 \end{pmatrix}$ $\therefore$ the line is $\begin{pmatrix} x \\ y \\ z \end{pmatrix} = \begin{pmatrix} 3 \\ 2 \\ -1 \end{pmatrix} + t \begin{pmatrix} -4 \\ 0 \\ 5 \end{pmatrix}$, $t \in \mathbb{R}$

b The equation of the plane is
$-4x + 0y + 5z = -4(-1) + 5(4)$
$\therefore -4x + 5z = 24$

P_2 (3, 2, −1)   A (3−4t, 2, −1+5t) P_1 B (−1, 2, 4)

c The distance from a point on the line to A is $d = \sqrt{(-4t)^2 + 0^2 + (5t)^2} = \sqrt{41t^2}$
$\therefore$ since $d = 2\sqrt{41}$ units, $\sqrt{41t^2} = 2\sqrt{41}$
$\therefore t^2 = 4$
$\therefore t = \pm 2$ $\therefore$ the points are $(-5, 2, 9)$ and $(11, 2, -11)$.

3 **a** $\mathbf{n} = \begin{pmatrix} 2 \\ -1 \\ -2 \end{pmatrix}$ and $\mathbf{l} = \begin{pmatrix} 1 \\ 2 \\ -1 \end{pmatrix}$

$\therefore \sin\phi = \dfrac{|2 + (-2) + 2|}{\sqrt{9}\sqrt{6}}$

$= \dfrac{2}{3\sqrt{6}}$

$\therefore \phi \approx 15.8°$

b The planes have normals

$\mathbf{n}_1 = \begin{pmatrix} 2 \\ -1 \\ -2 \end{pmatrix}$ and $\mathbf{n}_2 = \begin{pmatrix} 1 \\ 1 \\ 2 \end{pmatrix}$

$\therefore \cos\theta = \dfrac{|2 + (-1) + (-4)|}{\sqrt{9}\sqrt{6}}$

$= \dfrac{3}{3\sqrt{6}}$ or $\dfrac{1}{\sqrt{6}}$

$\therefore \theta \approx 65.9°$

4 **a** $\overrightarrow{AB} = \begin{pmatrix} 0 - 3 \\ 2 - -1 \\ -1 - 1 \end{pmatrix} = \begin{pmatrix} -3 \\ 3 \\ -2 \end{pmatrix}$ $\therefore \begin{pmatrix} x \\ y \\ z \end{pmatrix} = \begin{pmatrix} 3 \\ -1 \\ 1 \end{pmatrix} + t\begin{pmatrix} -3 \\ 3 \\ -2 \end{pmatrix}$, $t \in \mathbb{R}$

b If P divides [BA] in the ratio $2 : 5$, then $\overrightarrow{BP} : \overrightarrow{PA} = 2 : 5$

If P is (a, b, c) then $\begin{pmatrix} a - 0 \\ b - 2 \\ c - -1 \end{pmatrix} : \begin{pmatrix} 3 - a \\ -1 - b \\ 1 - c \end{pmatrix} = 2 : 5$

$\therefore 5\begin{pmatrix} a \\ b - 2 \\ c + 1 \end{pmatrix} = 2\begin{pmatrix} 3 - a \\ -1 - b \\ 1 - c \end{pmatrix}$

$\therefore \quad 5a = 6 - 2a,$ $5b - 10 = -2 - 2b,$ $5c + 5 = 2 - 2c$
$\therefore \quad 7a = 6,$ $7b = 8,$ $7c = -3$
$\therefore \quad a = \tfrac{6}{7},$ $b = \tfrac{8}{7},$ $c = -\tfrac{3}{7}$

So, P is $\left(\tfrac{6}{7}, \tfrac{8}{7}, \tfrac{-3}{7}\right)$.

5 Given $C(-3, 2, -1)$ and $D(0, 1, -4)$, $\overrightarrow{CD} = \begin{pmatrix} 3 \\ -1 \\ -3 \end{pmatrix}$

$\therefore$ the line passing through C and D has parametric equations
$x = -3 + 3t$, $y = 2 - t$, $z = -1 - 3t$

The line meets $2x - y + z = 3$ when $2(-3 + 3t) - (2 - t) + (-1 - 3t) = 3$
$\therefore \quad -6 + 6t - 2 + t - 1 - 3t = 3$
$\therefore \quad 4t = 12$
$\therefore \quad t = 3$

$\therefore$ they meet at $(6, -1, -10)$

6 **a** $\dfrac{x - 8}{3} = \dfrac{y + 9}{-16} = \dfrac{z - 10}{7}$ has direction vector $\begin{pmatrix} 3 \\ -16 \\ 7 \end{pmatrix}$

$x = 15 + 3t$, $y = 29 + 8t$, $z = 5 - 5t$ has direction vector $\begin{pmatrix} 3 \\ 8 \\ -5 \end{pmatrix}$

$\therefore$ since the direction vectors are not scalar multiples of each other, the lines are not parallel.

If they intersect then $\dfrac{15 + 3t - 8}{3} = \dfrac{29 + 8t + 9}{-16} = \dfrac{5 - 5t - 10}{7}$

$\therefore \quad t + \tfrac{7}{3} = -\tfrac{1}{2}t - \tfrac{38}{16} = -\tfrac{5}{7}t - \tfrac{5}{7}$

Now $t + \tfrac{7}{3} = -\tfrac{1}{2}t - \tfrac{38}{16}$ requires $\tfrac{3}{2}t = -\tfrac{19}{8} - \tfrac{7}{3} = -\tfrac{113}{24}$ $\therefore t = -\tfrac{113}{36}$

and $t + \tfrac{7}{3} = -\tfrac{5}{7}t - \tfrac{5}{7}$ requires $\tfrac{12}{7}t = -\tfrac{5}{7} - \tfrac{7}{3} = -\tfrac{64}{21}$ $\therefore t = -\tfrac{16}{9}$

Hence the lines do not intersect, and since they are not parallel, they are skew.

b If θ is the acute angle between the two lines, and $\mathbf{v}_1$ and $\mathbf{v}_2$ are their direction vectors,

then $\cos\theta = \dfrac{|\mathbf{v}_1 \bullet \mathbf{v}_2|}{|\mathbf{v}_1||\mathbf{v}_2|} = \dfrac{\left|\begin{pmatrix}3\\-16\\7\end{pmatrix} \bullet \begin{pmatrix}3\\8\\-5\end{pmatrix}\right|}{\sqrt{3^2+(-16)^2+7^2}\sqrt{3^2+8^2+(-5)^2}}$

$\therefore \cos\theta = \dfrac{|9-128-35|}{\sqrt{314}\sqrt{98}} = \dfrac{154}{\sqrt{30\,772}}$ and so $\theta \approx 28.6°$

c Let A and B be points on lines 1 and 2 respectively:
A is $(8+3s,\ -9-16s,\ 10+7s)$, and B is $(15+3t,\ 29+8t,\ 5-5t)$

The shortest distance between the two lines is when $\overrightarrow{AB} \parallel \mathbf{v}_1 \times \mathbf{v}_2$

$\mathbf{v}_1 \times \mathbf{v}_2 = \begin{vmatrix} \mathbf{i} & \mathbf{j} & \mathbf{k} \\ 3 & -16 & 7 \\ 3 & 8 & -5 \end{vmatrix} = \begin{vmatrix}-16 & 7 \\ 8 & -5\end{vmatrix}\mathbf{i} - \begin{vmatrix}3 & 7 \\ 3 & -5\end{vmatrix}\mathbf{j} + \begin{vmatrix}3 & -16 \\ 3 & 8\end{vmatrix}\mathbf{k}$

$= 24\mathbf{i} + 36\mathbf{j} + 72\mathbf{k}$ or $12(2\mathbf{i}+3\mathbf{j}+6\mathbf{k})$

So, $\overrightarrow{AB} = \begin{pmatrix}15+3t-(8+3s)\\29+8t-(-9-16s)\\5-5t-(10+7s)\end{pmatrix} = k\begin{pmatrix}2\\3\\6\end{pmatrix}$ $\therefore \begin{cases}3t-3s-2k=-7\\8t+16s-3k=-38\\-5t-7s-6k=5\end{cases}$

So, $t=-2,\ s=-1,\ k=2$ {using technology}

$\therefore \overrightarrow{AB} = \begin{pmatrix}15+3(-2)-(8+3(-1))\\29+8(-2)-(-9-16(-1))\\5-5(-2)-(10+7(-1))\end{pmatrix} = \begin{pmatrix}4\\6\\12\end{pmatrix}$ and distance $= \sqrt{16+36+144}$
$= 14$ units^2

7 a The distance of X$(-1, 1, 3)$ from $x-2y-2z=8$

is $d = \dfrac{|x_1-2y_1-2z_1-8|}{\sqrt{1^2+(-2)^2+(-2)^2}} = \dfrac{|-1-2-6-8|}{3} = \dfrac{|-17|}{3} = \dfrac{17}{3}$ units

b Since $2-x = y-3 = -\frac{1}{2}z$, $\dfrac{x-2}{-1} = \dfrac{y-3}{1} = \dfrac{z}{-2}$

$\therefore$ the line has direction vector $\mathbf{u} = \begin{pmatrix}-1\\1\\-2\end{pmatrix}$, and passes through $(2, 3, 0)$

$\therefore$ if P is a point on the line with coordinates $(2-t,\ 3+t,\ -2t)$, then

$\overrightarrow{QP} = \begin{pmatrix}2-t--1\\3+t-2\\-2t-3\end{pmatrix} = \begin{pmatrix}3-t\\1+t\\-2t-3\end{pmatrix}$

If P is chosen such that $\overrightarrow{QP}$ is perpendicular to the line, then $\mathbf{u} \bullet \overrightarrow{QP} = 0$

$\therefore \begin{pmatrix}-1\\1\\-2\end{pmatrix} \bullet \begin{pmatrix}3-t\\1+t\\-2t-3\end{pmatrix} = 0$ $\qquad \mathbf{u} = \begin{pmatrix}-1\\1\\-2\end{pmatrix}$

$\therefore -(3-t)+1(1+t)-2(-2t-3)=0$
$\therefore -3+t+1+t+4t+6=0$
$\therefore 6t = -4$
$\therefore t = -\frac{2}{3}$

$\therefore$ P is at $(2+\frac{2}{3},\ 3-\frac{2}{3},\ 2(\frac{2}{3}))$, so the foot of the perpendicular is at $(\frac{8}{3},\ \frac{7}{3},\ \frac{4}{3})$.

8 P(2, 0, 1), Q(3, 4, −2), R(−1, 3, 2)

a $\vec{PQ} = \begin{pmatrix} 1 \\ 4 \\ -3 \end{pmatrix}$

$|\vec{PQ}| = \sqrt{1 + 16 + 9} = \sqrt{26}$ units

and $\vec{QR} = \begin{pmatrix} -4 \\ -1 \\ 4 \end{pmatrix}$

b Since $\vec{PQ} = \begin{pmatrix} 1 \\ 4 \\ -3 \end{pmatrix}$ and P is at (2, 0, 1),

the line has equation
$x = 2 + t, \quad y = 0 + 4t, \quad z = 1 - 3t$
$\therefore \quad x = 2 + t, \quad y = 4t, \quad z = 1 - 3t, \quad t \in \mathbb{R}$

c vector equation of the plane is $\begin{pmatrix} x \\ y \\ z \end{pmatrix} = \begin{pmatrix} 2 \\ 0 \\ 1 \end{pmatrix} + \lambda \begin{pmatrix} 1 \\ 4 \\ -3 \end{pmatrix} + \mu \begin{pmatrix} -4 \\ -1 \\ 4 \end{pmatrix}, \quad \lambda, \mu \in \mathbb{R}$

9 a Given A(−1, 3, 2) and the plane $2x - y + 2z = 8$,

the distance from A to the plane is $d = \dfrac{|2x_1 - y_1 + 2z_1 - 8|}{\sqrt{2^2 + (-1)^2 + 2^2}}$

$= \dfrac{|2(-1) - 3 + 2(2) - 8|}{3}$

$= \dfrac{|-9|}{3} = 3$ units

b The point on the plane nearest A is the foot of the normal to the plane that passes through A.

Since the normal has direction vector $\begin{pmatrix} 2 \\ -1 \\ 2 \end{pmatrix}$ and passes through (−1, 3, 2),

it has equation $x = -1 + 2t, \quad y = 3 - t, \quad z = 2 + 2t, \quad t \in \mathbb{R}$
and meets the plane when $2(-1 + 2t) - (3 - t) + 2(2 + 2t) = 8$
$\therefore \quad -2 + 4t - 3 + t + 4 + 4t = 8$
$\therefore \quad 9t = 9$
$\therefore \quad t = 1$

$\therefore$ the point is (1, 2, 4).

c Call the foot of the perpendicular from A to the line X, so X has coordinates $(7 - 2t, -6 + t, 1 + 5t)$ for some t in $\mathbb{R}$. Then the shortest distance from A to the line is AX.

Now $\vec{AX} = \begin{pmatrix} 8 - 2t \\ t - 9 \\ -1 + 5t \end{pmatrix}$ and since the line has direction vector $\mathbf{u} = \begin{pmatrix} -2 \\ 1 \\ 5 \end{pmatrix}$,

$\mathbf{u} \bullet \vec{AX} = 0$

$\begin{pmatrix} -2 \\ 1 \\ 5 \end{pmatrix} \bullet \begin{pmatrix} 8 - 2t \\ t - 9 \\ -1 + 5t \end{pmatrix} = 0$

$-16 + 4t + t - 9 - 5 + 25t = 0$
$\therefore \quad 30t = 30$
$\therefore \quad t = 1$
$\therefore \quad |AX| = \sqrt{6^2 + (-8)^2 + 4^2}$
$= \sqrt{36 + 64 + 16}$
$= \sqrt{116}$ units

10 Given A(−1, 0, 2), B(0, −1, 1) and C(1, 2, −1)

a $\vec{AB} = \begin{pmatrix} 1 \\ -1 \\ -1 \end{pmatrix}$ and $\vec{AC} = \begin{pmatrix} 2 \\ 2 \\ -3 \end{pmatrix}$

$$\therefore \quad \mathbf{n} = \begin{vmatrix} \mathbf{i} & \mathbf{j} & \mathbf{k} \\ 1 & -1 & -1 \\ 2 & 2 & -3 \end{vmatrix} = \begin{vmatrix} -1 & -1 \\ 2 & -3 \end{vmatrix} \mathbf{i} - \begin{vmatrix} 1 & -1 \\ 2 & -3 \end{vmatrix} \mathbf{j} + \begin{vmatrix} 1 & -1 \\ 2 & 2 \end{vmatrix} \mathbf{k} = \begin{pmatrix} 5 \\ 1 \\ 4 \end{pmatrix}$$

$\therefore$ since A lies on the plane it has equation $\quad 5x + y + 4z = 5(-1) + 0 + 4(2)$
$$\therefore \quad 5x + y + 4z = 3$$

b Since the normal has direction $\begin{pmatrix} 5 \\ 1 \\ 4 \end{pmatrix}$ and passes through $(0, 0, 0)$, it has equation

$\quad x = 0 + 5t, \quad y = 0 + t, \quad z = 0 + 4t$
$\therefore \quad x = 5t, \quad\quad y = t, \quad\quad z = 4t, \quad t$ in $\mathbb{R}$

c The line meets the plane when $\quad 5(5t) + t + 4(4t) = 3$
$$\therefore \quad 25t + t + 16t = 3$$
$$\therefore \quad 42t = 3$$
$$\therefore \quad t = \tfrac{1}{14}$$

So, the line meets the plane at $(\tfrac{5}{14}, \tfrac{1}{14}, \tfrac{2}{7})$.

11 The system has augmented matrix:

$$\begin{pmatrix} 1 & -1 & 1 & | & 5 \\ 2 & 1 & -1 & | & -1 \\ 7 & 2 & k & | & -k \end{pmatrix}$$

$$\sim \begin{pmatrix} 1 & -1 & 1 & | & 5 \\ 0 & 3 & -3 & | & -11 \\ 0 & 9 & k-7 & | & -k-35 \end{pmatrix} \begin{array}{l} R_2 \to R_2 - 2R_1 \\ R_3 \to R_3 - 7R_1 \end{array}$$

$$\sim \begin{pmatrix} 1 & -1 & 1 & | & 5 \\ 0 & 3 & -3 & | & -11 \\ 0 & 0 & k+2 & | & -k-2 \end{pmatrix} \quad R_3 \to R_3 - 3R_2$$

Thus $(k+2)z = -(k+2)$

If $k \neq -2$ then $z = -1$, and as $3y - 3z = -11$,
$$\text{then} \quad 3y = -14$$
$$\therefore \quad y = -\tfrac{14}{3}$$
and $x - y + z = 5$,
$$\text{so} \quad x = 5 - \tfrac{14}{3} + 1 = \tfrac{4}{3}$$

$\therefore$ we have three planes that meet at the unique point $(\tfrac{4}{3}, -\tfrac{14}{3}, -1)$.

If $k = -2$, then the 3 planes meet in a common line and hence there are an infinite number of solutions.
In this case, let $z = t, \quad t$ in $\mathbb{R}$.
Now $3y - 3z = -11$, $\quad\quad\quad$ and as $x - y + z = 5$
$\quad \therefore \quad 3y = -11 + 3t \quad\quad\quad \therefore \quad x = 5 + y - z$
$\quad \therefore \quad y = -\tfrac{11}{3} + t \quad\quad\quad\quad \therefore \quad x = 5 - \tfrac{11}{3} + t - t$
$\quad\quad\quad\quad\quad\quad\quad\quad\quad\quad\quad\quad \therefore \quad x = \tfrac{4}{3}$
$\quad\quad\quad\quad\quad\quad\quad\quad\quad\quad\quad\quad \therefore \quad x = \tfrac{4}{3}, \quad y = -\tfrac{11}{3} + t, \quad z = t, \quad t$ in $\mathbb{R}$

12 a $\mathbf{p} \times \mathbf{q} = \begin{vmatrix} \mathbf{i} & \mathbf{j} & \mathbf{k} \\ 1 & -1 & 2 \\ 2 & 3 & -1 \end{vmatrix} = \begin{vmatrix} -1 & 2 \\ 3 & -1 \end{vmatrix} \mathbf{i} - \begin{vmatrix} 1 & 2 \\ 2 & -1 \end{vmatrix} \mathbf{j} + \begin{vmatrix} 1 & -1 \\ 2 & 3 \end{vmatrix} \mathbf{k}$

$$= -5\mathbf{i} + 5\mathbf{j} + 5\mathbf{k}$$
$$= 5 \begin{pmatrix} -1 \\ 1 \\ 1 \end{pmatrix}$$

b l has direction vector $\begin{pmatrix} 2 \\ 1 \\ m \end{pmatrix}$

$\therefore$ $\mathbf{p} \times \mathbf{q}$ is perpendicular to l if $\begin{pmatrix} -1 \\ 1 \\ 1 \end{pmatrix} \bullet \begin{pmatrix} 2 \\ 1 \\ m \end{pmatrix} = 0$

$\therefore \quad -2 + 1 + m = 0$

$\therefore \quad m = 1$

c P has normal vector $\mathbf{n} = \begin{pmatrix} -1 \\ 1 \\ 1 \end{pmatrix}$, and $(1, -2, 3)$ lies on the plane $\{$letting $\lambda = 0\}$

$\therefore$ P has equation $-x + y + z = -1 + (-2) + 3$

$\therefore \quad x - y - z = 0$

d A lies on the plane if $4 - t - 2 = 0$

$\therefore \quad t = 2$

e $\overrightarrow{AB} = \begin{pmatrix} 2 \\ -5 \\ 3 \end{pmatrix}$ and P has normal vector $\mathbf{n} = \begin{pmatrix} -1 \\ 1 \\ 1 \end{pmatrix}$

$\therefore$ if θ is the angle between $[AB]$ and P then $\sin \theta = \dfrac{\left| \begin{pmatrix} -1 \\ 1 \\ 1 \end{pmatrix} \bullet \begin{pmatrix} 2 \\ -5 \\ 3 \end{pmatrix} \right|}{\sqrt{(-1)^2 + 1^2 + 1^2} \sqrt{2^2 + (-5)^2 + 3^2}}$

$= \dfrac{|-2 - 5 + 3|}{\sqrt{3}\sqrt{38}} = \dfrac{4}{\sqrt{114}}$

REVIEW SET 16C

1 Given: $A(-1, 2, 3)$, $B(2, 0, -1)$ and $C(-3, 2, -4)$

a $\overrightarrow{AB} = \begin{pmatrix} 3 \\ -2 \\ -4 \end{pmatrix}$ $\overrightarrow{AC} = \begin{pmatrix} -2 \\ 0 \\ -7 \end{pmatrix}$ $\therefore$ a normal vector to the plane is

$\mathbf{n} = \begin{vmatrix} \mathbf{i} & \mathbf{j} & \mathbf{k} \\ -2 & 0 & -7 \\ 3 & -2 & -4 \end{vmatrix} = \begin{vmatrix} 0 & -7 \\ -2 & -4 \end{vmatrix} \mathbf{i} - \begin{vmatrix} -2 & -7 \\ 3 & -4 \end{vmatrix} \mathbf{j} + \begin{vmatrix} -2 & 0 \\ 3 & -2 \end{vmatrix} \mathbf{k}$

$= -14\mathbf{i} - 29\mathbf{j} + 4\mathbf{k}$

$\therefore$ since B lies on the plane, it has equation $14x + 29y - 4z = 14(2) + 29(0) - 4(-1)$

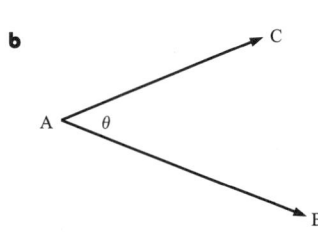

$\therefore \quad 14x + 29y - 4z = 32$

b $\cos \theta = \dfrac{|\overrightarrow{AB} \bullet \overrightarrow{AC}|}{|\overrightarrow{AB}||\overrightarrow{AC}|}$

$= \dfrac{|3 \times -2 + -2 \times 0 + -4 \times -7|}{\sqrt{9 + 4 + 16} \sqrt{4 + 0 + 49}}$

$= \dfrac{22}{\sqrt{29 \times 53}}$ and so $\theta \approx 55.9°$

c If D is at $(r, 1, -r)$ then $\overrightarrow{DB} = \begin{pmatrix} 2 - r \\ -1 \\ -1 + r \end{pmatrix}$

and $\overrightarrow{DC} = \begin{pmatrix} -3 - r \\ 1 \\ -4 + r \end{pmatrix}$

Now $B\widehat{D}C$ is a right angle, so $\overrightarrow{DB} \bullet \overrightarrow{DC} = 0$

$\therefore \quad (2-r)(-3-r) + (-1) + (-1+r)(-4+r) = 0$
$\therefore \quad -6 - 2r + 3r + r^2 - 1 + 4 - r - 4r + r^2 = 0$
$\therefore \quad 2r^2 - 4r - 3 = 0$
$\therefore \quad r = \dfrac{4 \pm \sqrt{16 + 24}}{4}$
$\therefore \quad r = \dfrac{2 \pm \sqrt{10}}{2}$

2 a $\overrightarrow{LM} = \begin{pmatrix} -2 \\ 2 \\ -2 \end{pmatrix} = -2 \begin{pmatrix} 1 \\ -1 \\ 1 \end{pmatrix}$

$\therefore$ since L lies on the line, it has parametric equations
$$x = 1 + t, \quad y = 0 - t, \quad z = 1 + t, \quad t \text{ in } \mathbb{R}$$
The line meets $x - 2y - 3z = 14$ if
$(1 + t) - 2(-t) - 3(1 + t) = 14$
$\therefore \quad 1 + t + 2t - 3 - 3t = 14$
$\therefore \quad -2 = 14$ which is absurd.
$\therefore$ the line and plane do not meet, but rather are parallel.

b The distance $d = \dfrac{|x_1 - 2y_1 - 3z_1 - 14|}{\sqrt{1 + 4 + 9}} = \dfrac{|1 - 2(0) - 3(1) - 14|}{\sqrt{14}} = \dfrac{16}{\sqrt{14}}$ units

3 a Given A$(-1, 2, 3)$, B$(1, 0, -1)$ and C$(1, 3, 0)$,

$\overrightarrow{AB} = \begin{pmatrix} 2 \\ -2 \\ -4 \end{pmatrix} = 2 \begin{pmatrix} 1 \\ -1 \\ -2 \end{pmatrix}$ and $\overrightarrow{AC} = \begin{pmatrix} 2 \\ 1 \\ -3 \end{pmatrix}$

$\therefore$ a normal to the plane containing A, B and C is

$\mathbf{n} = \begin{vmatrix} \mathbf{i} & \mathbf{j} & \mathbf{k} \\ 1 & -1 & -2 \\ 2 & 1 & -3 \end{vmatrix} = \begin{vmatrix} -1 & -2 \\ 1 & -3 \end{vmatrix} \mathbf{i} - \begin{vmatrix} 1 & -2 \\ 2 & -3 \end{vmatrix} \mathbf{j} + \begin{vmatrix} 1 & -1 \\ 2 & 1 \end{vmatrix} \mathbf{k} = 5\mathbf{i} - \mathbf{j} + 3\mathbf{k}$

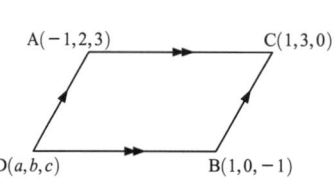

b Suppose D has coordinates (a, b, c).

$\therefore$ since $\overrightarrow{AD} = \overrightarrow{CB}$, $\begin{pmatrix} a + 1 \\ b - 2 \\ c - 3 \end{pmatrix} = \begin{pmatrix} 0 \\ -3 \\ -1 \end{pmatrix}$

$\therefore \quad a = -1, \quad b = -1$ and $c = 2$
$\therefore$ D is at $(-1, -1, 2)$

c From **a**, $\overrightarrow{AB}$ has direction vector $\begin{pmatrix} 1 \\ -1 \\ -2 \end{pmatrix}$

$\therefore$ the line through A and B has parametric equations
$$x = 1 + t, \quad y = 0 - t, \quad z = -1 - 2t, \quad t \text{ in } \mathbb{R}.$$
If $P(1 + t, -t, -1 - 2t)$ is the foot of the perpendicular,

then $\overrightarrow{CP} = \begin{pmatrix} t \\ -t - 3 \\ -1 - 2t \end{pmatrix}$ and $\overrightarrow{CP} \bullet \overrightarrow{AB} = 0$

$\therefore \quad \begin{pmatrix} t \\ -t - 3 \\ -1 - 2t \end{pmatrix} \bullet \begin{pmatrix} 1 \\ -1 \\ -2 \end{pmatrix} = 0$

$\therefore \quad t + t + 3 + 2 + 4t = 0$
$\therefore \quad 6t = -5$
$\therefore \quad t = -\frac{5}{6}$

$\therefore$ P is $(1 - \frac{5}{6}, \frac{5}{6}, -1 + \frac{10}{6})$ or $(\frac{1}{6}, \frac{5}{6}, \frac{2}{3})$

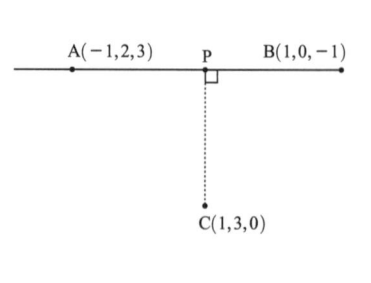

4 $x - 1 = \dfrac{y+2}{2} = \dfrac{z-3}{4}$ has direction vector $\begin{pmatrix} 1 \\ 2 \\ 4 \end{pmatrix}$ and $6x + 7y - 5z = 8$ has $\mathbf{n} = \begin{pmatrix} 6 \\ 7 \\ -5 \end{pmatrix}$.

Now $\begin{pmatrix} 1 \\ 2 \\ 4 \end{pmatrix} \bullet \begin{pmatrix} 6 \\ 7 \\ -5 \end{pmatrix} = 6 + 14 - 20 = 0$

∴ since these two vectors are perpendicular, the line is parallel to the plane.
Choose any point on the line, for example, $(1, -2, 3)$.

Then the distance from the line to the plane is $d = \dfrac{|6x_1 + 7y_1 - 5z_1 - 8|}{\sqrt{6^2 + 7^2 + (-5)^2}}$

$= \dfrac{|6(1) + 7(-2) - 5(3) - 8|}{\sqrt{110}}$

$= \dfrac{31}{\sqrt{110}}$ units

5 a $\dfrac{x-3}{2} = \dfrac{y-4}{1} = \dfrac{z+1}{-2}$ has direction vector $\mathbf{v}_1 = \begin{pmatrix} 2 \\ 1 \\ -2 \end{pmatrix}$

while $x = -1 + 3t$, $y = 2 + 2t$, $z = 3 - t$ has direction vector $\mathbf{v}_2 = \begin{pmatrix} 3 \\ 2 \\ -1 \end{pmatrix}$

∴ the lines are not parallel.

If the lines intersect, then $\dfrac{-1+3t-3}{2} = \dfrac{2+2t-4}{1} = \dfrac{3-t+1}{-2}$

∴ $\dfrac{3}{2}t - 2 = 2t - 2 = \dfrac{t}{2} - 2$

Now $t = 0$ satisfies this relation, so the lines intersect at $(-1, 2, 3)$.

b If θ is the acute angle between the lines, then

$\cos\theta = \dfrac{|\mathbf{v}_1 \bullet \mathbf{v}_2|}{|\mathbf{v}_1||\mathbf{v}_2|} = \dfrac{|2 \times 3 + 1 \times 2 + -2 \times -1|}{\sqrt{9}\sqrt{14}} = \dfrac{|6 + 2 + 2|}{3\sqrt{14}} = \dfrac{10}{3\sqrt{14}}$

6 a $\overrightarrow{AB} = \begin{pmatrix} -2 \\ 2 \\ -4 \end{pmatrix} = -2\begin{pmatrix} 1 \\ -1 \\ 2 \end{pmatrix}$

∴ since A lies on the line, it has equations $\begin{pmatrix} x \\ y \\ z \end{pmatrix} = \begin{pmatrix} 2 \\ -1 \\ 3 \end{pmatrix} + t\begin{pmatrix} 1 \\ -1 \\ 2 \end{pmatrix}$

b If C lies on (AB) and is 2 units from A, then C corresponds to t such that

$\sqrt{(t)^2 + (-t)^2 + (2t)^2} = 2$

∴ $\sqrt{6t^2} = 2$

∴ $6t^2 = 4$

∴ $t^2 = \dfrac{4}{6}$

∴ $t = \pm\dfrac{2}{\sqrt{6}}$

∴ C is $\left(2 + \dfrac{2}{\sqrt{6}}, -1 - \dfrac{2}{\sqrt{6}}, 3 + \dfrac{4}{\sqrt{6}}\right)$ or $\left(2 - \dfrac{2}{\sqrt{6}}, -1 + \dfrac{2}{\sqrt{6}}, 3 - \dfrac{4}{\sqrt{6}}\right)$

$A(2,-1,3)$ ←— 2 —→ $C(2+t,-1-t,3+2t)$

7 Given $A(-1, 2, 3)$, $B(1, 0, -1)$ and $C(0, -1, 5)$,

$\overrightarrow{AB} = \begin{pmatrix} 2 \\ -2 \\ -4 \end{pmatrix}$ and $\overrightarrow{AC} = \begin{pmatrix} 1 \\ -3 \\ 2 \end{pmatrix}$

∴ a normal to the plane is $\mathbf{n} = \begin{vmatrix} \mathbf{i} & \mathbf{j} & \mathbf{k} \\ 2 & -2 & -4 \\ 1 & -3 & 2 \end{vmatrix} = \begin{vmatrix} -2 & -4 \\ -3 & 2 \end{vmatrix}\mathbf{i} - \begin{vmatrix} 2 & -4 \\ 1 & 2 \end{vmatrix}\mathbf{j} + \begin{vmatrix} 2 & -2 \\ 1 & -3 \end{vmatrix}\mathbf{k}$

$= -16\mathbf{i} - 8\mathbf{j} - 4\mathbf{k}$ or $-4(4\mathbf{i} + 2\mathbf{j} + \mathbf{k})$

$\therefore$ the plane has equation $4x + 2y + z = 4(1) + 2(0) + 1(-1)$
$\therefore \quad 4x + 2y + z = 3$

Given the plane has normal $\mathbf{n} = \begin{pmatrix} 4 \\ 2 \\ 1 \end{pmatrix}$ and $\overrightarrow{AX} = \begin{pmatrix} 4 \\ 0 \\ 1 \end{pmatrix}$,

$\sin \phi = \dfrac{|\mathbf{n} \bullet \overrightarrow{AX}|}{|\mathbf{n}|\,|\overrightarrow{AX}|}$

$= \dfrac{|4 \times 4 + 2 \times 0 + 1 \times 1|}{\sqrt{21}\sqrt{17}}$

$= \dfrac{17}{\sqrt{21}\sqrt{17}}$ and so $\phi \approx 64.1°$

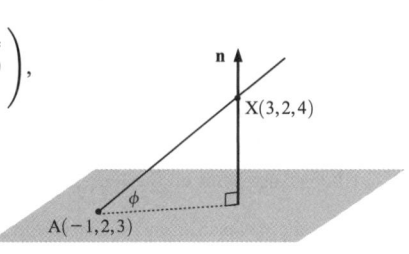

8 a All vectors normal to $x - y + z = 6$ have the form $t\begin{pmatrix} 1 \\ -1 \\ 1 \end{pmatrix} = \begin{pmatrix} t \\ -t \\ t \end{pmatrix}$, t in $\mathbb{R}$

$\therefore$ if the vector has length 3 units, $\sqrt{t^2 + t^2 + t^2} = 3$
$\therefore \quad 3t^2 = 9$
$\therefore \quad t^2 = 3$
$\therefore \quad t = \pm\sqrt{3}$

$\therefore$ the vectors are $\begin{pmatrix} \sqrt{3} \\ -\sqrt{3} \\ \sqrt{3} \end{pmatrix}$ and $\begin{pmatrix} -\sqrt{3} \\ \sqrt{3} \\ -\sqrt{3} \end{pmatrix}$

b Any vector parallel to $\mathbf{i} + r\mathbf{j} + 3\mathbf{k}$ has the form $t\begin{pmatrix} 1 \\ r \\ 3 \end{pmatrix} = \begin{pmatrix} t \\ rt \\ 3t \end{pmatrix}$, t in $\mathbb{R}$.

This is perpendicular to $\begin{pmatrix} 2 \\ -1 \\ 2 \end{pmatrix}$ if $\begin{pmatrix} 2 \\ -1 \\ 2 \end{pmatrix} \bullet \begin{pmatrix} t \\ rt \\ 3t \end{pmatrix} = 0$

$\therefore \quad 2t - rt + 6t = 0$
$\therefore \quad 8t - rt = 0$
$\therefore \quad t(8 - r) = 0$
$\therefore \quad t = 0$ or $r = 8$

But if $t = 0$, the vector has zero length.

$\therefore \quad r = 8$ and so a vector is $\begin{pmatrix} 1 \\ 8 \\ 3 \end{pmatrix}$.

$\therefore$ the unit vectors are $\mathbf{u} = \dfrac{1}{\sqrt{74}}\mathbf{i} + \dfrac{8}{\sqrt{74}}\mathbf{j} + \dfrac{3}{\sqrt{74}}\mathbf{k}$ or $-\dfrac{1}{\sqrt{74}}\mathbf{i} - \dfrac{8}{\sqrt{74}}\mathbf{j} - \dfrac{3}{\sqrt{74}}\mathbf{k}$

c The distance from the plane to A is $d = \dfrac{|2x_1 - y_1 + 2z_1 - k|}{\sqrt{9}}$

$\therefore \quad \dfrac{|2(-1) - (2) + 2(3) - k|}{3} = 3$

$\therefore \quad |2 - k| = 9$

$\therefore \quad 2 - k = 9$ or $k - 2 = 9$

$\therefore \quad k = -7$ or 11

9 If A is the origin, (AB) the X-axis, (AD) the Y-axis, and (AP) the Z-axis, then Q is $(4, 0, 7)$, D is $(0, 10, 0)$ and M is $(0, 5, 7)$.

Now $\overrightarrow{DQ} = \begin{pmatrix} 4 - 0 \\ 0 - 10 \\ 7 - 0 \end{pmatrix} = \begin{pmatrix} 4 \\ -10 \\ 7 \end{pmatrix}$ and $\overrightarrow{DM} = \begin{pmatrix} 0 - 0 \\ 5 - 10 \\ 7 - 0 \end{pmatrix} = \begin{pmatrix} 0 \\ -5 \\ 7 \end{pmatrix}$

So, if the required angle is θ, $\begin{pmatrix} 4 \\ -10 \\ 7 \end{pmatrix} \bullet \begin{pmatrix} 0 \\ -5 \\ 7 \end{pmatrix} = \sqrt{16+100+49}\sqrt{0+25+49}\cos\theta$

$\therefore \quad 0+50+49 = \sqrt{165}\sqrt{74}\cos\theta$

$\therefore \quad \dfrac{99}{\sqrt{165 \times 74}} = \cos\theta \quad \text{and so} \quad \theta \approx 26.4°$

10 a $\overrightarrow{PQ} = \begin{pmatrix} 4--1 \\ 0-2 \\ -1-3 \end{pmatrix}$

$= \begin{pmatrix} 5 \\ -2 \\ -4 \end{pmatrix}$

b For the X-axis, $\mathbf{v} = \begin{pmatrix} 1 \\ 0 \\ 0 \end{pmatrix}$

Now $\begin{pmatrix} 5 \\ -2 \\ -4 \end{pmatrix} \bullet \begin{pmatrix} 1 \\ 0 \\ 0 \end{pmatrix} = \sqrt{25+4+16}\sqrt{1+0+0}\cos\theta$

$\therefore \quad 5+0+0 = \sqrt{45}\cos\theta$

$\therefore \quad \cos\theta = \dfrac{5}{\sqrt{45}} \quad \text{and so} \quad \theta \approx 41.8°$

11 a $\overrightarrow{OM} = \overrightarrow{OB} + \tfrac{1}{2}\overrightarrow{BC}$

$= \overrightarrow{OB} + \tfrac{1}{2}(\overrightarrow{OC} - \overrightarrow{OB})$

$= \tfrac{1}{2}(\overrightarrow{OB} + \overrightarrow{OC})$

b $\overrightarrow{OP} = \tfrac{1}{3}(\overrightarrow{OA} + \overrightarrow{OB} + \overrightarrow{OC})$

$= \tfrac{1}{3}(\overrightarrow{OA} + 2 \times \tfrac{1}{2}(\overrightarrow{OB} + \overrightarrow{OC}))$

$= \tfrac{1}{3}(\overrightarrow{OA} + 2\overrightarrow{OM})$

c $\overrightarrow{AP} = \overrightarrow{OP} - \overrightarrow{OA}$

$= \tfrac{1}{3}(\overrightarrow{OA} + 2\overrightarrow{OM}) - \overrightarrow{OA}$

$= \tfrac{2}{3}(\overrightarrow{OM} - \overrightarrow{OA})$

$= \tfrac{2}{3}\overrightarrow{AM}$

$\therefore \quad \overrightarrow{AP} \parallel \overrightarrow{AM}$

$\therefore \quad$ P lies on [AM].

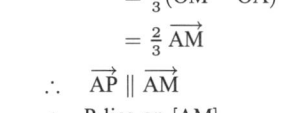

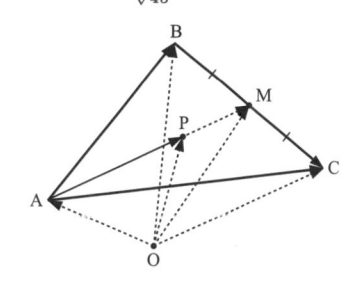

d The ratio in which P divides [AM]
$= AP : PM$
$= 2 : 1$

12 a The lines meet where

$\begin{pmatrix} 3 \\ -2 \\ -2 \end{pmatrix} + s\begin{pmatrix} -1 \\ 1 \\ 2 \end{pmatrix} = \begin{pmatrix} 3 \\ 0 \\ -1 \end{pmatrix} + t\begin{pmatrix} -1 \\ -1 \\ 1 \end{pmatrix}$

$\therefore \quad \begin{pmatrix} -s \\ s \\ 2s \end{pmatrix} = \begin{pmatrix} -t \\ -t+2 \\ t+1 \end{pmatrix}$

$\therefore \quad \begin{cases} -s = -t \Rightarrow s = t & \text{....} \ (1) \\ s = -t + 2 & \text{....} \ (2) \\ 2s = t + 1 & \text{....} \ (3) \end{cases}$

Substituting (1) into (2) gives

$t = -t + 2$

$\therefore \quad 2t = 2$

$\therefore \quad t = 1 \quad \text{and} \quad s = 1$

Checking with (3): $2(1) = 1+1$ ✓

$\therefore \quad \begin{pmatrix} x \\ y \\ z \end{pmatrix} = \begin{pmatrix} 3 \\ -2 \\ -2 \end{pmatrix} + 1\begin{pmatrix} -1 \\ 1 \\ 2 \end{pmatrix} = \begin{pmatrix} 2 \\ -1 \\ 0 \end{pmatrix}$

$\therefore \quad$ A is $(2, -1, 0)$

b $B(0, -3, 2)$ lies on l_2 if

$\begin{pmatrix} 3 \\ 0 \\ -1 \end{pmatrix} + t\begin{pmatrix} -1 \\ -1 \\ 1 \end{pmatrix} = \begin{pmatrix} 0 \\ -3 \\ 2 \end{pmatrix}$

for some $t \in \mathbb{R}$

$\therefore \quad \begin{cases} 3 - t = 0 \\ -t = -3 \\ -1 + t = 2 \end{cases}$

$t = 3$ satisfies all these equations

$\therefore \quad B(0, -3, 2)$ lies on l_2

c $\overrightarrow{BC} = \begin{pmatrix} 3 \\ 1 \\ -4 \end{pmatrix}$

$\therefore \quad$ the equation of the line (BC) is

$\mathbf{r} = \begin{pmatrix} 0 \\ -3 \\ 2 \end{pmatrix} + u\begin{pmatrix} 3 \\ 1 \\ -4 \end{pmatrix}, \quad u \in \mathbb{R}$

d $\overrightarrow{AB} = \begin{pmatrix} -2 \\ -2 \\ 2 \end{pmatrix}$, $\overrightarrow{AC} = \begin{pmatrix} 1 \\ -1 \\ -2 \end{pmatrix}$

∴ the plane containing A, B and C has normal vector

$$\mathbf{n} = \overrightarrow{AB} \times \overrightarrow{AC} = \begin{vmatrix} \mathbf{i} & \mathbf{j} & \mathbf{k} \\ -2 & -2 & 2 \\ 1 & -1 & -2 \end{vmatrix} = \begin{vmatrix} -2 & 2 \\ -1 & -2 \end{vmatrix} \mathbf{i} - \begin{vmatrix} -2 & 2 \\ 1 & -2 \end{vmatrix} \mathbf{j} + \begin{vmatrix} -2 & -2 \\ 1 & -1 \end{vmatrix} \mathbf{k}$$
$$= 6\mathbf{i} - 2\mathbf{j} + 4\mathbf{k}$$

∴ the equation is $6x - 2y + 4z = 6(2) - 2(-1) + 4(0) = 14$ {using A}

or $3x - y + 2z = 7$

e Area of triangle ABC
$= \tfrac{1}{2} |\overrightarrow{AB} \times \overrightarrow{AC}|$
$= \tfrac{1}{2} |6\mathbf{i} - 2\mathbf{j} + 4\mathbf{k}|$
$= \tfrac{1}{2} \sqrt{6^2 + (-2)^2 + 4^2}$
$= \tfrac{1}{2} \sqrt{56}$
$= \sqrt{14}$ units^2

f The normal to the plane has direction vector $\begin{pmatrix} 3 \\ -1 \\ 2 \end{pmatrix}$.

∴ the normal to the plane passing through $C(3, -2, -2)$ is

$$\begin{pmatrix} x \\ y \\ z \end{pmatrix} = \begin{pmatrix} 3 \\ -2 \\ -2 \end{pmatrix} + \lambda \begin{pmatrix} 3 \\ -1 \\ 2 \end{pmatrix}, \quad \lambda \in \mathbb{R}$$

$D(9, -4, 2)$ lies on this line if

$$\begin{pmatrix} 3 \\ -2 \\ -2 \end{pmatrix} + \lambda \begin{pmatrix} 3 \\ -1 \\ 2 \end{pmatrix} = \begin{pmatrix} 9 \\ -4 \\ 2 \end{pmatrix} \quad \text{for some } \lambda \in \mathbb{R}$$

∴ $\begin{cases} 3 + 3\lambda = 9 \\ -2 - \lambda = -4 \\ -2 + 2\lambda = 2 \end{cases}$

$\lambda = 2$ satisfies all three equations

∴ D lies on this line.

g $\overrightarrow{AB} = \begin{pmatrix} -2 \\ -2 \\ 2 \end{pmatrix}$, $\overrightarrow{AC} = \begin{pmatrix} 1 \\ -1 \\ -2 \end{pmatrix}$, $\overrightarrow{AD} = \begin{pmatrix} 7 \\ -3 \\ 2 \end{pmatrix}$

∴ volume of tetrahedron ABCD is $\tfrac{1}{6} \left| \overrightarrow{AB} \bullet \left(\overrightarrow{AC} \times \overrightarrow{AD} \right) \right|$

$= \tfrac{1}{6} \left\| \begin{matrix} -2 & -2 & 2 \\ 1 & -1 & -2 \\ 7 & -3 & 2 \end{matrix} \right\|$

$= \tfrac{1}{6} \left| -2 \begin{vmatrix} -1 & -2 \\ -3 & 2 \end{vmatrix} + 2 \begin{vmatrix} 1 & -2 \\ 7 & 2 \end{vmatrix} + 2 \begin{vmatrix} 1 & -1 \\ 7 & -3 \end{vmatrix} \right|$

$= \tfrac{1}{6} |-2(-8) + 2(16) + 2(4)|$

$= \tfrac{1}{6} |56| = \tfrac{28}{3}$ units^3

REVIEW SET 16D

1 a $\overrightarrow{AB} = \begin{pmatrix} 2-4 \\ 1-2 \\ 5--1 \end{pmatrix} = \begin{pmatrix} -2 \\ -1 \\ 6 \end{pmatrix}$ and $\overrightarrow{AC} = \begin{pmatrix} 9-4 \\ 4-2 \\ 1--1 \end{pmatrix} = \begin{pmatrix} 5 \\ 2 \\ 2 \end{pmatrix}$

∴ $\overrightarrow{AB} \bullet \overrightarrow{AC} = (-2)(5) + (-1)(2) + (6)(2) = -10 - 2 + 12 = 0$

∴ $\overrightarrow{AB} \perp \overrightarrow{AC}$

b $\mathbf{n} = \overrightarrow{AB} \times \overrightarrow{AC} = \begin{vmatrix} \mathbf{i} & \mathbf{j} & \mathbf{k} \\ -2 & -1 & 6 \\ 5 & 2 & 2 \end{vmatrix} = \begin{vmatrix} -1 & 6 \\ 2 & 2 \end{vmatrix} \mathbf{i} - \begin{vmatrix} -2 & 6 \\ 5 & 2 \end{vmatrix} \mathbf{j} + \begin{vmatrix} -2 & -1 \\ 5 & 2 \end{vmatrix} \mathbf{k}$

$= -14\mathbf{i} + 34\mathbf{j} + \mathbf{k}$

$\therefore$ the equation is $-14x + 34y + z = -14(4) + 34(2) + (-1) = 11$
$\therefore$ $14x - 34y - z = -11$

The distance $= \dfrac{|14(8) - 34(1) - (0) + 11|}{\sqrt{14^2 + (-34)^2 + (-1)^2}} = \dfrac{89}{\sqrt{1353}}$ units (≈ 2.42 units)

c The equation is $\begin{pmatrix} x \\ y \\ z \end{pmatrix} = \begin{pmatrix} 4 \\ 2 \\ -1 \end{pmatrix} + t \begin{pmatrix} -2 \\ -1 \\ 6 \end{pmatrix}$, $t \in \mathbb{R}$

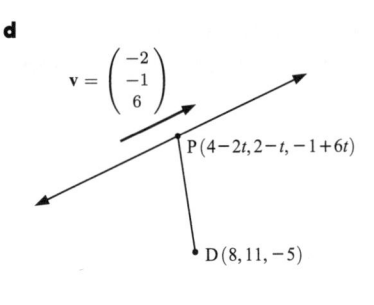

d

$\mathbf{v} = \begin{pmatrix} -2 \\ -1 \\ 6 \end{pmatrix}$

$P(4-2t, 2-t, -1+6t)$

$D(8, 11, -5)$

$\overrightarrow{DP} = \begin{pmatrix} 4 - 2t - 8 \\ 2 - t - 11 \\ -1 + 6t - -5 \end{pmatrix} = \begin{pmatrix} -4 - 2t \\ -9 - t \\ 4 + 6t \end{pmatrix}$

and $\overrightarrow{DP} \bullet \mathbf{v} = 0$

$\therefore$ $-2(-4 - 2t) - 1(-9 - t) + 6(4 + 6t) = 0$
$\therefore$ $8 + 4t + 9 + t + 24 + 36t = 0$
$\therefore$ $41t = -41$
$\therefore$ $t = -1$

$\therefore$ $\overrightarrow{DP} = \begin{pmatrix} -2 \\ -8 \\ -2 \end{pmatrix}$ and $|\overrightarrow{DP}| = \sqrt{4 + 64 + 4}$
$= \sqrt{72}$
$= 6\sqrt{2}$ units

2 a l_1 meets $2x + y - z = 2$ where $2(3t - 4) + (t + 2) - (2t - 1) = 2$
$\therefore$ $6t - 8 + t + 2 - 2t + 1 = 2$
$\therefore$ $5t = 7$
$\therefore$ $t = \frac{7}{5}$

$\therefore$ the lines meet at $\left(3(\frac{7}{5}) - 4, \frac{7}{5} + 2, 2(\frac{7}{5}) - 1\right)$
which is $(\frac{1}{5}, \frac{17}{5}, \frac{9}{5})$

b l_1 meets l_2 where $3t - 4 = \dfrac{t + 2 - 5}{2} = \dfrac{-(2t - 1) - 1}{2}$
$\therefore$ $6t - 8 = t - 3 = -2t$
$\therefore$ $5t = 5$ and $3t = 3$
$\therefore$ $t = 1$

So, l_1 and l_2 meet at $(-1, 3, 1)$.

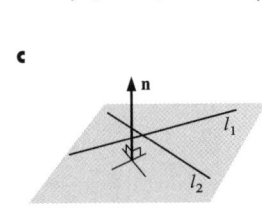

c

$\mathbf{n} = \begin{pmatrix} 3 \\ 1 \\ 2 \end{pmatrix} \times \begin{pmatrix} 1 \\ 2 \\ -2 \end{pmatrix} = \begin{vmatrix} \mathbf{i} & \mathbf{j} & \mathbf{k} \\ 3 & 1 & 2 \\ 1 & 2 & -2 \end{vmatrix}$

$= \begin{vmatrix} 1 & 2 \\ 2 & -2 \end{vmatrix} \mathbf{i} - \begin{vmatrix} 3 & 2 \\ 1 & -2 \end{vmatrix} \mathbf{j} + \begin{vmatrix} 3 & 1 \\ 1 & 2 \end{vmatrix} \mathbf{k} = -6\mathbf{i} + 8\mathbf{j} + 5\mathbf{k}$

$\therefore$ equation is $-6x + 8y + 5z = -6(-1) + 8(3) + 5(1)$
$\therefore$ $-6x + 8y + 5z = 35$
$\therefore$ $6x - 8y - 5z = -35$

3 a We substitute l_1 into the LHS of the plane's equation
$2(-2t + 2) + (t) + (3t + 1) = -4t + 4 + t + 3t + 1 = 5$ ✓
$\therefore$ the plane contains the line.

b If $x + ky + z = 3$ contains l_1 then $(-2t + 2) + k(t) + 3t + 1 = 3$
$\therefore$ $t[-2 + k + 3] + 2 + 1 = 3$
$\therefore$ $t[k + 1] = 0$
$\therefore$ $k = -1$ as $t \in \mathbb{R}$

c From **a** and **b**, both $2x + y + z = 5$ and $x - y + z = 3$ contain l_1.
So, substituting l_1 into plane 3 gives
$$-2(-2t + 2) + pt + 2(3t + 1) = q \quad \text{for all } t \text{ in } \mathbb{R}$$
$$\therefore \quad 4t - 4 + pt + 6t + 2 = q \quad \text{for all } t \text{ in } \mathbb{R}$$
$$\therefore \quad [10 + p]t - 2 = q \quad \text{for all } t$$
This equation has infinitely many solutions for t
when $10 + p = 0$ and $-2 = q$ {equating coefficients}
$\therefore \quad p = -10$ and $q = -2$

4 a

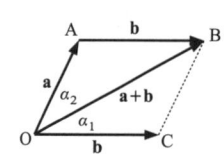

As **a** and **b** are unit vectors, OABC is a rhombus.
But the angles of a rhombus are bisected by its diagonals
$\therefore \quad \alpha_1 = \alpha_2$

b

$\vec{JH} = \begin{pmatrix} 9 - 7 \\ 5 - 3 \\ -5 - -4 \end{pmatrix} = \begin{pmatrix} 2 \\ 2 \\ -1 \end{pmatrix} \qquad \vec{JK} = \begin{pmatrix} 1 - 7 \\ 0 - 3 \\ 2 - -4 \end{pmatrix} = \begin{pmatrix} -6 \\ -3 \\ 6 \end{pmatrix}$

$\therefore \quad \mathbf{u}_1 = \dfrac{1}{\sqrt{4 + 4 + 1}} \begin{pmatrix} 2 \\ 2 \\ -1 \end{pmatrix} = \begin{pmatrix} \frac{2}{3} \\ \frac{2}{3} \\ -\frac{1}{3} \end{pmatrix}$

and $\mathbf{u}_2 = \dfrac{1}{\sqrt{36 + 9 + 36}} \begin{pmatrix} -6 \\ -3 \\ 6 \end{pmatrix} = \begin{pmatrix} -\frac{2}{3} \\ -\frac{1}{3} \\ \frac{2}{3} \end{pmatrix}$

and $\mathbf{u}_1 + \mathbf{u}_2 = \begin{pmatrix} 0 \\ \frac{1}{3} \\ \frac{1}{3} \end{pmatrix}$

$\therefore$ the line's equation is $\begin{pmatrix} x \\ y \\ z \end{pmatrix} = \begin{pmatrix} 7 \\ 3 \\ -4 \end{pmatrix} + t \begin{pmatrix} 0 \\ \frac{1}{3} \\ \frac{1}{3} \end{pmatrix}$, $t \in \mathbb{R}$

c $\vec{HK} = \begin{pmatrix} 1 - 9 \\ 0 - 5 \\ 2 - -5 \end{pmatrix} = \begin{pmatrix} -8 \\ -5 \\ 7 \end{pmatrix}$ so (HK) has equation $\begin{pmatrix} x \\ y \\ z \end{pmatrix} = \begin{pmatrix} 1 \\ 0 \\ 2 \end{pmatrix} + s \begin{pmatrix} -8 \\ -5 \\ 7 \end{pmatrix}$.

This line meets the first line where
$$7 = 1 - 8s, \quad 3 + \frac{t}{3} = -5s \quad \text{and} \quad -4 + \frac{t}{3} = 2 + 7s \quad \ldots\ldots (*)$$
$\therefore \quad 8s = -6 \quad \therefore \quad s = -\frac{3}{4}$ and so $3 + \frac{t}{3} = \frac{15}{4} \quad \therefore \quad \frac{t}{3} = \frac{3}{4} \quad \therefore \quad t = \frac{9}{4}$

In (*) LHS $= -4 + \dfrac{t}{3}$ RHS $= 2 + 7s$
$\qquad\qquad\quad = -4 + \frac{3}{4} \qquad\qquad = 2 + 7\left(-\frac{3}{4}\right)$
$\qquad\qquad\quad = -\frac{13}{4} \qquad\qquad\quad = \frac{8}{4} - \frac{21}{4}$
$\qquad\qquad\qquad\qquad\qquad\qquad\quad = -\frac{13}{4} \checkmark$

$\therefore \quad s = -\frac{3}{4}, \quad t = \frac{9}{4}$ satisfy all 3 equations

So, $\begin{pmatrix} x \\ y \\ z \end{pmatrix} = \begin{pmatrix} 1 \\ 0 \\ 2 \end{pmatrix} - \frac{3}{4} \begin{pmatrix} -8 \\ -5 \\ 7 \end{pmatrix} = \begin{pmatrix} 1 + 6 \\ 0 + \frac{15}{4} \\ 2 - \frac{21}{4} \end{pmatrix} = \begin{pmatrix} 7 \\ 3\frac{3}{4} \\ -3\frac{1}{4} \end{pmatrix} \quad \therefore$ M is $(7, 3\frac{3}{4}, -3\frac{1}{4})$.

5 If A is $(3, -1, -2)$ and B$(5, 3, -4)$ then $\overrightarrow{AB} = \begin{pmatrix} 5-3 \\ 3--1 \\ -4--2 \end{pmatrix} = \begin{pmatrix} 2 \\ 4 \\ -2 \end{pmatrix} = 2\begin{pmatrix} 1 \\ 2 \\ -1 \end{pmatrix}$

$\therefore$ the line has equation $\begin{pmatrix} x \\ y \\ z \end{pmatrix} = \begin{pmatrix} 3 \\ -1 \\ -2 \end{pmatrix} + t\begin{pmatrix} 1 \\ 2 \\ -1 \end{pmatrix}, \quad t \in \mathbb{R}$

and it meets $x^2 + y^2 + z^2 = 26$ where

$(3+t)^2 + (-1+2t)^2 + (-2-t)^2 = 26$

$\therefore \quad 9 + 6t + t^2 + 1 - 4t + 4t^2 + 4 + 4t + t^2 - 26 = 0$

$\therefore \quad 6t^2 + 6t - 12 = 0$

$\therefore \quad t^2 + t - 2 = 0$

$\therefore \quad (t+2)(t-1) = 0$

$\therefore \quad t = -2 \text{ or } 1$

$\therefore \begin{pmatrix} x \\ y \\ z \end{pmatrix} = \begin{pmatrix} 3 \\ -1 \\ -2 \end{pmatrix} - 2\begin{pmatrix} 1 \\ 2 \\ -1 \end{pmatrix} \quad \text{or} \quad \begin{pmatrix} 3 \\ -1 \\ -2 \end{pmatrix} + \begin{pmatrix} 1 \\ 2 \\ -1 \end{pmatrix}$

$\therefore$ the line meets the sphere at $(1, -5, 0)$ and $(4, 1, -3)$.

6 $\mathbf{n} = \begin{pmatrix} 2 \\ 2 \\ -1 \end{pmatrix} \quad \mathbf{l} = \begin{pmatrix} 1 \\ -2 \\ -1 \end{pmatrix}$

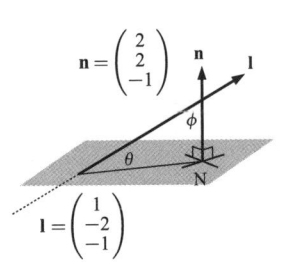

$\mathbf{n} \bullet \mathbf{l} = |\mathbf{n}| \, |\mathbf{l}| \cos \phi$

$\therefore \quad \cos \phi = \dfrac{\mathbf{n} \bullet \mathbf{l}}{|\mathbf{n}| \, |\mathbf{l}|}$

$\therefore \quad \sin \theta = \dfrac{|\mathbf{n} \bullet \mathbf{l}|}{|\mathbf{n}| \, |\mathbf{l}|} \quad \text{as} \quad \cos \phi = \cos\left(\dfrac{\pi}{2} - \theta\right) = \sin \theta$

$\qquad = \dfrac{|2 - 4 + 1|}{\sqrt{4+4+1}\sqrt{1+4+1}} = \dfrac{1}{\sqrt{54}}$

$\therefore \quad \theta \approx 7.82°$

7

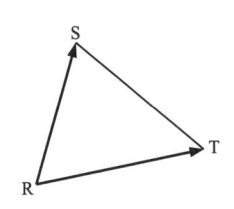

$\overrightarrow{RS} = \overrightarrow{RO} + \overrightarrow{OS} = \overrightarrow{OS} - \overrightarrow{OR}$

$\therefore \quad \overrightarrow{RS} = 2\mathbf{i} + \mathbf{j} + 2\mathbf{k} - 2\mathbf{i} + 2\mathbf{j} + \mathbf{k}$

$\qquad = 3\mathbf{j} + 3\mathbf{k}$

Likewise $\overrightarrow{RT} = \overrightarrow{OT} - \overrightarrow{OR} = \mathbf{i} + 2\mathbf{j} - \mathbf{k} - 2\mathbf{i} + 2\mathbf{j} + \mathbf{k}$

$\qquad = -\mathbf{i} + 4\mathbf{j}$

Now area $= \frac{1}{2} |\overrightarrow{RS} \times \overrightarrow{RT}|$

$= \frac{1}{2} \begin{Vmatrix} \mathbf{i} & \mathbf{j} & \mathbf{k} \\ 0 & 3 & 3 \\ -1 & 4 & 0 \end{Vmatrix}$

$= \frac{1}{2} \left| \begin{matrix} 3 & 3 \\ 4 & 0 \end{matrix} \right| \mathbf{i} - \left| \begin{matrix} 0 & 3 \\ -1 & 0 \end{matrix} \right| \mathbf{j} + \left| \begin{matrix} 0 & 3 \\ -1 & 4 \end{matrix} \right| \mathbf{k}$

$= \frac{1}{2} |-12\mathbf{i} - 3\mathbf{j} + 3\mathbf{k}|$

$= \frac{1}{2} \sqrt{144 + 9 + 9}$

$= \frac{1}{2} \sqrt{162}$

$= \frac{1}{2} 9\sqrt{2}$

$= \frac{9\sqrt{2}}{2}$ units^2

8 a X is $\left(\dfrac{4+10}{2}, \dfrac{4+2}{2}, \dfrac{-2+0}{2} \right)$ or $(7, 3, -1)$

If D is (a, b, c), $\overrightarrow{AD} = \begin{pmatrix} a-1 \\ b-3 \\ c--4 \end{pmatrix} = \begin{pmatrix} a-1 \\ b-3 \\ c+4 \end{pmatrix}$ and $\overrightarrow{BC} = \begin{pmatrix} 6 \\ -2 \\ 2 \end{pmatrix}$

Since $\overrightarrow{AD} = \overrightarrow{BC}$, $\quad a - 1 = 6, \quad b - 3 = -2, \quad c + 4 = 2$

$\therefore \quad a = 7, \quad\quad b = 1 \quad\quad c = -2 \quad \therefore$ D is $(7, 1, -2)$

b $\vec{OY} = \vec{OA} + \vec{AY} = \begin{pmatrix} 1 \\ 3 \\ -4 \end{pmatrix} + \frac{2}{3}\vec{AX} = \begin{pmatrix} 1 \\ 3 \\ -4 \end{pmatrix} + \frac{2}{3}\begin{pmatrix} 7-1 \\ 3-3 \\ -1--4 \end{pmatrix}$

$\therefore \vec{OY} = \begin{pmatrix} 1 \\ 3 \\ -4 \end{pmatrix} + \frac{2}{3}\begin{pmatrix} 6 \\ 0 \\ 3 \end{pmatrix} = \begin{pmatrix} 5 \\ 3 \\ -2 \end{pmatrix}$ and so Y is $(5, 3, -2)$

c $\vec{BY} = \begin{pmatrix} 5-4 \\ 3-4 \\ -2--2 \end{pmatrix} = \begin{pmatrix} 1 \\ -1 \\ 0 \end{pmatrix}$ and $\vec{BD} = \begin{pmatrix} 7-4 \\ 1-4 \\ -2--2 \end{pmatrix} = \begin{pmatrix} 3 \\ -3 \\ 0 \end{pmatrix}$

$\therefore \vec{BD} = 3\vec{BY} \quad \therefore \vec{BD} \parallel \vec{BY}$ and so B, D and Y are collinear

9 a $\mathbf{b} \times \mathbf{c} = \begin{vmatrix} \mathbf{i} & \mathbf{j} & \mathbf{k} \\ 1 & 1 & -1 \\ 2 & -1 & 1 \end{vmatrix} = \begin{vmatrix} 1 & -1 \\ -1 & 1 \end{vmatrix}\mathbf{i} - \begin{vmatrix} 1 & -1 \\ 2 & 1 \end{vmatrix}\mathbf{j} + \begin{vmatrix} 1 & 1 \\ 2 & -1 \end{vmatrix}\mathbf{k}$

$= -3\mathbf{j} - 3\mathbf{k}$

b $\mathbf{a} \times (\mathbf{b} \times \mathbf{c}) = \begin{vmatrix} \mathbf{i} & \mathbf{j} & \mathbf{k} \\ 3 & 2 & -1 \\ 0 & -3 & -3 \end{vmatrix} = \begin{vmatrix} 2 & -1 \\ -3 & -3 \end{vmatrix}\mathbf{i} - \begin{vmatrix} 3 & -1 \\ 0 & -3 \end{vmatrix}\mathbf{j} + \begin{vmatrix} 3 & 2 \\ 0 & -3 \end{vmatrix}\mathbf{k}$

$= -9\mathbf{i} + 9\mathbf{j} - 9\mathbf{k}$

and $\mathbf{b}(\mathbf{a} \bullet \mathbf{c}) - \mathbf{c}(\mathbf{a} \bullet \mathbf{b})$
$= [(3)(2) + (2)(-1) + (-1)(1)]\mathbf{b} - [(3)(1) + (2)(1) + (-1)(-1)]\mathbf{c}$
$= 3\mathbf{b} - 6\mathbf{c}$
$= 3(\mathbf{i} + \mathbf{j} - \mathbf{k}) - 6(2\mathbf{i} - \mathbf{j} + \mathbf{k})$
$= 3\mathbf{i} + 3\mathbf{j} - 3\mathbf{k} - 12\mathbf{i} + 6\mathbf{j} - 6\mathbf{k}$
$= -9\mathbf{i} + 9\mathbf{j} - 9\mathbf{k}$ ✓

10 a

$\mathbf{a} \perp \mathbf{b}$ **b** $\mathbf{a} \parallel \mathbf{b}$
$\therefore \mathbf{a} \bullet \mathbf{b} = 0$ $\therefore \mathbf{b} = k\mathbf{a}$ for some scalar k
$\therefore (1)(-t) + (2)(1+t) + (-2)(2t) = 0$
$\therefore -t + 2 + 2t - 4t = 0$ $\therefore \begin{pmatrix} -t \\ 1+t \\ 2t \end{pmatrix} = k\begin{pmatrix} 1 \\ 2 \\ -2 \end{pmatrix}$
$\therefore -3t = -2$
$\therefore t = \frac{2}{3}$ $\therefore -t = k, \; 1+t = 2k, \; 2t = -2k$
$\therefore 1 + t = 2(-t)$
$\therefore 1 = -3t$
$\therefore t = -\frac{1}{3}$

11 a The lines meet when

$\dfrac{(15 + 3\lambda) - 8}{3} = \dfrac{(29 + 8\lambda) + 9}{-16} = \dfrac{(5 - 5\lambda) - 10}{7}$ for some $\lambda \in \mathbb{R}$

$\therefore \dfrac{3\lambda + 7}{3} = \dfrac{8\lambda + 38}{-16} = \dfrac{-5\lambda - 5}{7}$

$\therefore -48\lambda - 112 = 24\lambda + 114$ and $56\lambda + 266 = 80\lambda + 80$
$\therefore -72\lambda = 226$ and $186 = 24\lambda$
$\therefore \lambda = -\dfrac{113}{36}$ and $\lambda = \dfrac{31}{4}$

$\therefore$ no value of λ satisfies both equations
$\therefore$ the lines do not meet

Their direction vectors are $\begin{pmatrix} 3 \\ -16 \\ 7 \end{pmatrix}$ and $\begin{pmatrix} 3 \\ 8 \\ -5 \end{pmatrix}$ $\therefore$ they are not parallel.

$\therefore$ line 1 and line 2 are skew.

b Line 3 is parallel to line 1 and so has direction vector $\begin{pmatrix} 3 \\ -16 \\ 7 \end{pmatrix}$.

∴ the plane containing lines 2 and 3 has normal vector

$$\mathbf{n} = \begin{vmatrix} \mathbf{i} & \mathbf{j} & \mathbf{k} \\ 3 & 8 & -5 \\ 3 & -16 & 7 \end{vmatrix} = \begin{vmatrix} 8 & -5 \\ -16 & 7 \end{vmatrix} \mathbf{i} - \begin{vmatrix} 3 & -5 \\ 3 & 7 \end{vmatrix} \mathbf{j} + \begin{vmatrix} 3 & 8 \\ 3 & -16 \end{vmatrix} \mathbf{k}$$

$$= -24\mathbf{i} - 36\mathbf{j} - 72\mathbf{k}$$

$$= -12(2\mathbf{i} + 3\mathbf{j} + 6\mathbf{k})$$

∴ the equation of the plane is $2x + 3y + 6z = 2(15) + 3(29) + 6(5)$

∴ $2x + 3y + 6z = 147$

c Since line 1 is parallel to line 3, line 1 is parallel to the plane containing lines 2 and 3.

∴ to find the shortest distance between lines 1 and 2, we choose a point on line 1 then find the shortest distance between this point and the plane.

$(8, -9, 10)$ is a point on line 1.

∴ distance $d = \dfrac{|2(8) + 3(-9) + 6(10) - 147|}{\sqrt{2^2 + 3^2 + 6^2}}$

$= \dfrac{|-98|}{\sqrt{49}}$

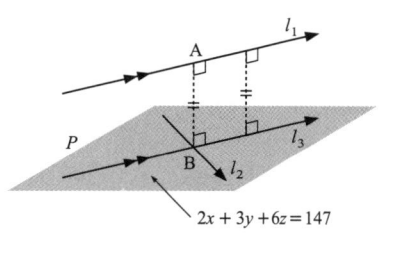

$= \dfrac{98}{7}$

$= 14$ units

d Let the common perpendicular meet lines 1 and 2 at A and B respectively.

A is $(8 + 3t, -9 - 16t, 10 + 7t)$ for some $t \in \mathbb{R}$

B is $(15 + 3\lambda, 29 + 8\lambda, 5 - 5\lambda)$ for some $\lambda \in \mathbb{R}$

The common perpendicular has direction vector $\begin{pmatrix} 2 \\ 3 \\ 6 \end{pmatrix}$

∴ we need to find values for t and λ so that

$$\overrightarrow{AB} = k \begin{pmatrix} 2 \\ 3 \\ 6 \end{pmatrix} \text{ for some scalar } k$$

∴ $\begin{pmatrix} 15 + 3\lambda - (8 + 3t) \\ 29 + 8\lambda - (-9 - 16t) \\ 5 - 5\lambda - (10 + 7t) \end{pmatrix} = k \begin{pmatrix} 2 \\ 3 \\ 6 \end{pmatrix}$

∴ $\begin{pmatrix} 7 + 3\lambda - 3t \\ 38 + 8\lambda + 16t \\ -5 - 5\lambda - 7t \end{pmatrix} = \begin{pmatrix} 2k \\ 3k \\ 6k \end{pmatrix}$

∴ $\begin{cases} 3\lambda - 3t - 2k = -7 \\ 8\lambda + 16t - 3k = -38 \\ -5\lambda - 7t - 6k = 5 \end{cases}$

Solving simultaneously using technology gives $\lambda = -2$, $t = -1$, $k = 2$.

∴ A is $(8 + 3(-1), -9 - 16(-1), 10 + 7(-1))$

and B is $(15 + 3(-2), 29 + 8(-2), 5 - 5(-2))$

∴ the common perpendicular meets lines 1 and 2 at $(5, 7, 3)$ and $(9, 13, 15)$.

Chapter 17
DESCRIPTIVE STATISTICS

EXERCISE 17A

1 a Heights can take any value from 170 cm to 205 cm, including decimal values such as 181.372 cm. The 'height' variable can take any real number between 170 and 205.

b *Heights of basketball players* (histogram, frequency vs height (cm), bars from 170 to 205)

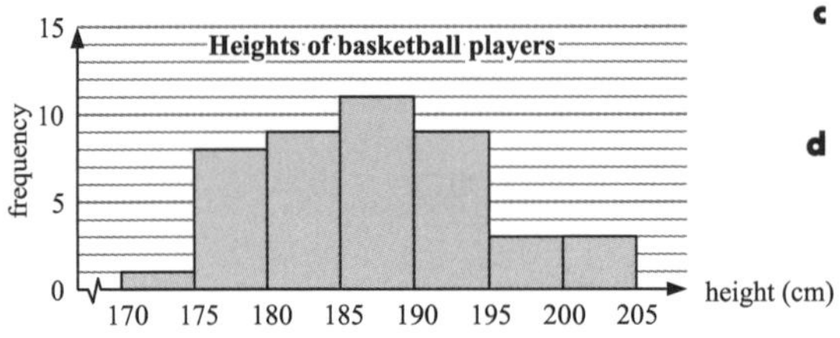

c The modal class is the class occurring most often. This is '185 - 190'.

d The distribution is slightly positively skewed, as there is more of a 'tail' to the right.

2 a The data is continuous numerical. Actual time is continuous and could be measured to the nearest millisecond. After it has been rounded to the nearest minute it becomes discrete numerical data.

b
Stem	Leaf
0	3 6 8 8 8 8
1	0 0 0 0 0 2 2 2 4 4 4 4 5 5 5 5 6 6 6 6 7 8 8 8 8 9
2	0 0 0 1 2 4 5 5 5 6 7 7 8
3	1 2 2 2 3 4 5 7 8
4	0 2 5 5 5 6

1 | 2 means 12 minutes

c The distribution is positively skewed, or skewed to the high end.

d The modal travelling time was between 10 and 20 min, if considering classes. The mode is actually 10.

3 a The data is discrete numerical, so a column graph should be used.

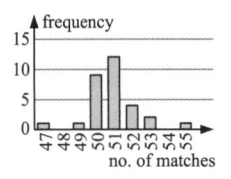

b The data is continuous, so a histogram should be used.

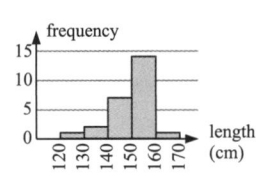

4 a *Seedling height* (histogram, frequency vs mm, from 300 to 450)

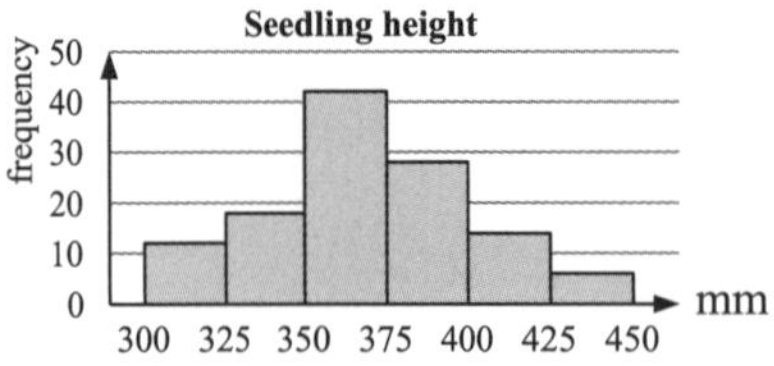

b Number which are $\geqslant 400$ mm is $14 + 6 = 20$ seedlings.

c % between 349 and 400 $= \dfrac{42 + 28}{120} \times 100\%$

$= \dfrac{70}{120} \times 100\%$

$\approx 58.3\%$

d i Number
$= \dfrac{12 + 18 + 42 + 28}{120} \times 1462$
$= \dfrac{100}{120} \times 1462$
≈ 1218 seedlings

ii Number
$= \dfrac{28 + 14}{120} \times 1462$
$= \dfrac{42}{120} \times 1462$
≈ 512 seedlings

EXERCISE 17B.1

1 a i mean $= \dfrac{2+3+3+3+4+\ldots+9+9}{23}$
$= \dfrac{129}{23}$
≈ 5.61

ii median = 12th score (when in order)
$= 6$

iii mode $= 6$ (6 occurs most often)

b i mean $= \dfrac{10+12+12+15+\ldots+20+21}{15}$
$= \dfrac{245}{15}$
≈ 16.3

ii median = 8th score (when in order)
$= 17$

iii mode $= 18$

c i mean $= \dfrac{22.4+24.6+21.8+\ldots+23.5}{11}$
$= \dfrac{273}{11}$
≈ 24.8

ii median = 6th score (when in order)
$= 24.9$

iii mode $= 23.5$

2 a mean of set A $= \dfrac{3+4+4+5+\ldots+10}{13}$
≈ 6.46

mean of set B $= \dfrac{3+4+4+5+\ldots+15}{13}$
≈ 6.85

b median of set A = 7th score = 7   median of set B = 7th score = 7

c The data sets are the same except for the last value, and the last value of set A is less than that of set B. So, the mean of set A is less than that of set B.

d The middle value of both data sets is the same, so the median is the same.

3 a mean $= \dfrac{23\,000+46\,000+23\,000+\ldots+32\,000}{10} = \$29\,300$

median = middle score when in order of size $= \dfrac{\$23\,000+\$24\,000}{2} = \$23\,500$

mode $= \$23\,000$

b The mode is unsatisfactory because it is the lowest salary. It does not take the higher values into account.

c The median is too close to the lower end of the distribution since the data is positively skewed. So the median is not a satisfactory measure of the middle.

4 a mean $= \dfrac{3+1+0+0+\ldots+1+0+0}{31} = \dfrac{99}{31} \approx 3.19$

median = 16th score (when in order) = 0

mode = 0 (most frequently occurring score)

b The median is not in the centre, as the data is very positively skewed.

c The mode is the lowest value. It does not take the higher values into account.

d Yes, 42 and 21.   **e** No, as this would ignore actual valid data.

5 a mean $= \dfrac{43+55+41+37}{4} = \dfrac{176}{4} = 44$ **b** another 44 points

c new mean $= \dfrac{43+55+41+37+25}{5} = 40.2$

d It will increase the new mean to 40.3 as 41 is greater than the old mean of 40.2.
$\left\{\dfrac{5 \times 40.2 + 41}{6} \approx 40.3\right\}$

6 mean $= \dfrac{\text{total}}{10}$ $\therefore$ $11.6 = \dfrac{\text{total}}{10}$ $\therefore$ total $= 11.6 \times 10 = 116$

7 mean $= \dfrac{\text{total}}{12}$ $\therefore$ $262 = \dfrac{\text{total}}{12}$ $\therefore$ total $= 262 \times 12 = 3144$ km

8 mean = $\dfrac{\text{total}}{12}$ ∴ $15\,467 = \dfrac{\text{total}}{12}$ ∴ total = $15\,467 \times 12 = \$185\,604$

9 $\dfrac{5+9+11+12+13+14+17+x}{8} = 12$

∴ $\dfrac{81+x}{8} = 12$

∴ $81 + x = 96$

∴ $x = 15$

10 $\dfrac{3+0+a+a+4+a+6+a+3}{9} = 4$

∴ $\dfrac{4a+16}{9} = 4$

∴ $4a + 16 = 36$

∴ $4a = 20$

∴ $a = 5$

11 $\dfrac{29+36+32+38+35+34+39+x}{8} = 35$

∴ $\dfrac{243+x}{8} = 35$

∴ $243 + x = 280$

∴ $x = 37$

So, her 8th result was 37.

12 Total for first 10 measurements = 10×15.7
$= 157$
Total for next 20 measurements = 20×14.3
$= 286$

∴ mean = $\dfrac{157+286}{30} \approx 14.8$

13 Scores were 5 7 9 9 10 a b where $a \leqslant b$ say.

mean = $\dfrac{5+7+9+9+10+a+b}{7} = 8$ ∴ $\dfrac{40+a+b}{7} = 8$

∴ $40 + a + b = 56$

∴ $a + b = 16$ $\{a \leqslant 12,\ b \leqslant 12\}$

Possibilities are:

a	5	6	7	8
b	11	10	9	8
	✗	✗	✓	✗

↑ reject as modes are 8 and 9
↑ reject as modes are 9 and 10
↑ reject as modes are 5 and 9

So, the missing results are 7 and 9.

EXERCISE 17B.2

1 a The mode is 1, as this is the result which occurs most often.

b The median is the average of the 15th and 16th scores
$= \dfrac{1+1}{2} = 1$

c

x	f	fx
0	4	0
1	12	12
2	11	22
3	3	9
$\sum$	30	43

mean = $\dfrac{\sum fx}{\sum f}$

$= \dfrac{43}{30}$

≈ 1.43

2 a i

x	f	fx
0	5	0
1	8	8
2	13	26
3	8	24
4	6	24
5	3	15
6	3	18
7	2	14
8	1	8
9	0	0
10	0	0
11	1	11
$\sum$	50	148

mean = $\dfrac{\sum fx}{\sum f}$

$= \dfrac{148}{50}$

$= 2.96$

ii median
= average of 25th and 26th scores
(when in order)

$= \dfrac{2+2}{2}$ $\left\{\begin{array}{l}\text{13 scores are 1 or 0}\\ \text{26 scores are 2, 1 or 0}\end{array}\right\}$

$= 2$

iii mode = 2 {occurs most often}

b

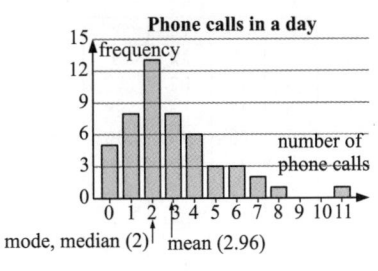

Phone calls in a day

[histogram showing frequency vs number of phone calls, with mode, median (2) and mean (2.96) marked]

c The distribution is positively skewed. 11 is an outlier.

d The mean takes into account the larger numbers of phone calls.

e The mean, as it best represents all the data.

3 a i mode = 49 {occurs most often}

ii median = average of 15th and 16th values (when in order)
$$= \frac{49 + 49}{2} = 49 \quad \{9 \text{ are } 47 \text{ or } 48 \text{ and the next } 11 \text{ are } 49\}$$

iii

x	f	fx
47	5	235
48	4	192
49	11	539
50	6	300
51	3	153
52	1	52
$\sum$	30	1471

mean $= \dfrac{\sum fx}{\sum f}$

$= \dfrac{1471}{30}$

≈ 49.0

b No, as they claim the average is 50 matches per box.

c The sample of only 30 is not large enough. The company could have won its case by arguing that a larger sample would have found an average of 50 matches per box.

4 a i

x	f	fx
1	5	5
2	28	56
3	15	45
4	8	32
5	2	10
6	1	6
$\sum$	59	154

mean $= \dfrac{\sum fx}{\sum f}$

$= \dfrac{154}{59}$

≈ 2.61

ii mode = 2 {occurs most often}

iii median = 30th score = 2

b This school has more children per family (2.61) than the average Australian family (2.2).

c Positive as the higher values are more spread out.

d The mean is higher than the mode and median.

5 a i mean $= \dfrac{53 + 55 + 56 + 60 + \ldots + 91}{17} = \dfrac{1175}{17} \approx 69.1$

ii median = 9th score (when in order) = 67

iii mode = 73 (73 is the only score occurring more than once)

b i mean $= \dfrac{3.7 + 4.0 + 4.4 + 4.8 + \ldots + 8.1}{23} = \dfrac{134.7}{23} \approx 5.86$

ii median = 12th score (when in order) = 5.8 **iii** mode = 6.7 {occurs most often}

6 a Without fertiliser

```
2 | ||
3 | ||||  ||||  |
4 | ||||  ||||  ||||  ||||
5 | ||||  ||||  ||||  ||||  ||||  ||||
6 | ||||  ||||  ||||  ||||  ||||  ||||  ||||  ||||  ||||  ||||  |
7 | ||||  ||||  ||||  ||||  ||||
8 | ||||  ||||  ||
9 | |
```

x	f	fx	cf
2	2	4	2
3	11	33	13
4	19	76	32
5	29	145	61
6	51	306	112
7	25	175	137
8	12	96	149
9	1	9	150

i mean $= \dfrac{\sum fx}{\sum f} = \dfrac{844}{150} \approx 5.63$ **ii** mode = 6 {occurs most often}

iii median = average of 75th and 76th scores $= \dfrac{6+6}{2} = 6$

b **With fertiliser**

3	||||		
4	＃＃ ＃＃ |||		
5	＃＃ ＃＃ |		
6	＃＃ ＃＃ ＃＃ ＃＃ ＃＃ |||		
7	＃＃ ＃＃ ＃＃ ＃＃ ＃＃ ＃＃ ＃＃ ＃＃ ＃＃ ||		
8	＃＃ ＃＃ ＃＃ ＃＃ ＃＃ ||		
9	＃＃ ＃＃ ||||		
10	||||		
11	|		
13	|		

x	f	fx	cf
3	4	12	4
4	13	52	17
5	11	55	28
6	28	168	56
7	47	329	103
8	27	216	130
9	14	126	144
10	4	40	148
11	1	11	149
13	1	13	150

i mean $= \dfrac{\sum fx}{\sum f} = \dfrac{1022}{150} \approx 6.81$ **ii** mode $= 7$ {occurs most often}

iii median $=$ average of 75th and 76th scores $= \dfrac{7+7}{2} = 7$

c The mean best represents the centre for this data.

d Yes, as 6.81 is significantly greater than 5.63.

    Note: The total yield of the crop may not have improved as, for example, the number of pods per plant may have decreased when using the fertiliser.

7 a mean selling price $= \dfrac{146\,400 + 127\,600 + 211\,000 + \,....\, + 162\,500}{10} = \$163\,770$

    median selling price $= \dfrac{\text{5th} + \text{6th}}{2} = \dfrac{146\,400 + 148\,000}{2} = \$147\,200$

    These figures differ by $16\,570$. There are more selling prices at the lower end of the market.

b **i** Use the mean as it tends to inflate the average house value of that district.

    ii Use the median as you want to buy at the lowest price possible.

8 a mean birth weight $= \dfrac{75 + 70 + 80 + \,....\, + 83}{8} = \dfrac{567}{8} \approx 70.9$ grams

b mean after 2 weeks $= \dfrac{210 + 200 + 200 + \,....\, + 230}{8} = \dfrac{1681}{8} \approx 210$ grams

c mean increase $\approx (210.13 - 70.88)$ grams ≈ 139 grams

9 The 31 scores in order are: {15 scores below 10}, 10.1, 10.4, 10.7, 10.9, {12 scores above 11}

    Median $=$ 16th score (when in order) $= 10.1$ cm

10 a

Brand A

x	f	fx
46	1	46
47	1	47
48	2	96
49	7	343
50	10	500
51	20	1020
52	15	780
53	3	159
55	1	55
$\sum$	60	3046

mean $= \dfrac{\sum fx}{\sum f} = \dfrac{3046}{60} \approx 50.8$

Brand B

x	f	fx
48	3	144
49	17	833
50	30	1500
51	7	357
52	2	104
53	1	53
54	1	54
$\sum$	61	3045

mean $= \dfrac{\sum fx}{\sum f} = \dfrac{3045}{61} \approx 49.9$

b Based on average contents, the C.P.S. should not prosecute either manufacturer. To the nearest match, the average contents for A is 51 and for B is 50.

11 Total for first 14 matches $= 14 \times 16.5$ goals $= 231$ goals

    $\therefore$ new average $= \dfrac{231 + 21 + 24}{16} = \dfrac{276}{16} = 17.25$ goals per game

12 The measurements are $7, 9, 11, 13, 14, 17, 19, a, b$ where $a \leqslant b$

mean $= \dfrac{7 + 9 + 11 + 13 + ... + a + b}{9} = \dfrac{90 + a + b}{9}$ $\therefore \dfrac{90 + a + b}{9} = 12$

$\therefore \; 90 + a + b = 108$

$\therefore \; a + b = 18$

If $b \geqslant 13$, then $a \leqslant 5$
If $b = 12$, then $a = 6$

 7 9 11 13 14 17 19
and the median $= 13$ $\;(\times)$
and the median $= 12$ $\;(\checkmark)$

The remaining cases are:

a	7	8	9
b	11	10	9
median	11	11	11

So, the other two data values are 6 and 12.

13 a i median salary
$= \dfrac{\text{10th} + \text{11th}}{2}$ {when in order}
$= \dfrac{35\,000 + 28\,000}{2}$
$= \$31\,500$

ii modal salary
$= \$28\,000$ {occurs most often}

iii

x	f	fx
50 000	1	50 000
42 000	3	126 000
35 000	6	210 000
28 000	10	280 000
$\sum$	20	666 000

mean $= \dfrac{\sum fx}{\sum f}$

$= \dfrac{666\,000}{20}$

$= \$33\,300$

b The mean, as it is the highest value.

EXERCISE 17B.3

1

x (midpoint)	f	fx
4.5	2	9
14.5	5	72.5
24.5	7	171.5
34.5	27	931.5
44.5	9	400.5
$\sum$	50	1585

$\therefore$ approximate mean result $= \dfrac{1585}{50}$
$= 31.7$

2 a 70

b $\approx 411\,000$ litres

c

midpoint (x)	f	fx
2499.5	4	9998
3499.5	4	13 998
4499.5	9	40 495.5
5499.5	14	76 993
6499.5	23	149 488.5
7499.5	16	119 992
$\sum$	70	410 965

Approximate mean

$= \dfrac{\sum fx}{\sum f}$

$= \dfrac{410\,965}{70}$

≈ 5870 litres

3 a $5 + 10 + 25 + 40 + 10 + 15 + 10 + 10 = 125$ people

b

midpoint (x)	frequency (f)	fx
85	5	425
95	10	950
105	25	2625
115	40	4600
125	10	1250
135	15	2025
145	10	1450
155	10	1550
$\sum$	125	14 875

Approximate mean

$= \dfrac{\sum fx}{\sum f}$

$= \dfrac{14\,875}{125}$

$= 119$ marks

c $\dfrac{15}{125}$ scored < 100

$\therefore \dfrac{3}{25}$ scored < 100

d 20% of 125 people $= 25$ people and 90 people scored < 130 for the test

$\therefore$ estimate is $130 + \dfrac{10}{15} \times 10 \approx 137$ marks

EXERCISE 17C

1

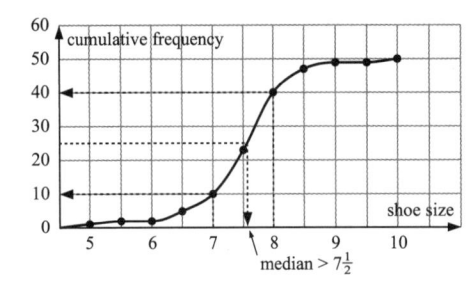

a Since the median is $> 7\frac{1}{2}$, and shoe size is *only* a multiple of $\frac{1}{2}$, median $= 8$.

b **i** 10 people had a shoe size 7 or less.
∴ $50 - 10 = 40$ people had a shoe size of $7\frac{1}{2}$ or more.
ii 40 people

2 a

Length (x cm)	Freq.	C. freq.
$24 \leqslant x < 27$	1	1
$27 \leqslant x < 30$	2	3
$30 \leqslant x < 33$	5	8
$33 \leqslant x < 36$	10	18
$36 \leqslant x < 39$	9	27
$39 \leqslant x < 42$	2	29
$42 \leqslant x < 45$	1	30

b

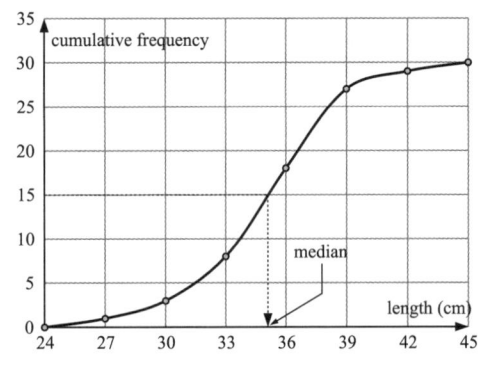

c median ≈ 35

d There are 30 data values. So, the median is the average of the 15th and 16th scores (when in order). In order they are:

24 27 28 30 31 31 32 32 33 33 33 33 34 34 34 35 35 35 36 .... and so on.

median $= \dfrac{34 + 35}{2} = 34.5$

So, the median from the graph is a good approximation.

3

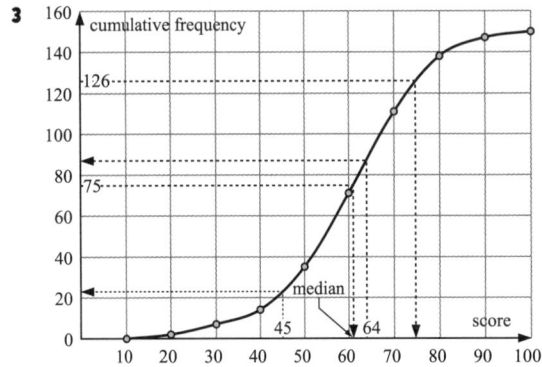

a Total frequency $= 150$
∴ median ≈ 61 {from the graph}

b When the score $= 64$,
CF ≈ 87 {from the graph}
∴ about 87 students scored less than 65.

c $\approx 36 + 40 = 76$ students scored between 50 and 70.

d For a pass mark of 45, CF ≈ 24.5
∴ 24 or 25 students failed the exam.

e 84% of $150 = 126$
So, for a CF of 126, the score value is 76.
So, the minimum credit mark would be 76.

4

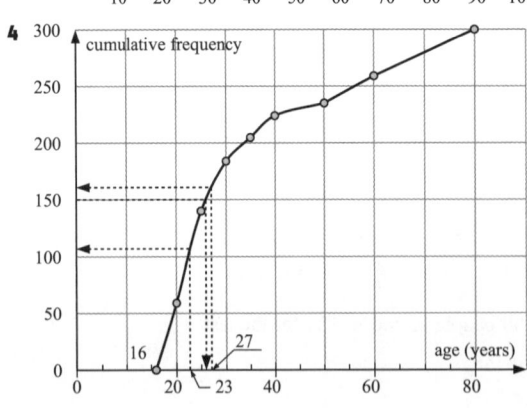

Total frequency $= 300$

a median ≈ 26 years {from the graph}

b when the age $= 23$, CF ≈ 108
and $\dfrac{108}{300} \times 100\% \approx 36\%$

c **i** when age is 27, CF ≈ 158
∴ P(age $\leqslant 27$) $= \dfrac{158}{300} = 0.527$

ii when age is 26 or less, CF ≈ 150 {**a**}
when age is 27 or less, CF ≈ 158 {**c ii**}
∴ 8 were 27 years old
∴ P(aged 27) $\approx \dfrac{8}{300} \approx 0.0267$

5

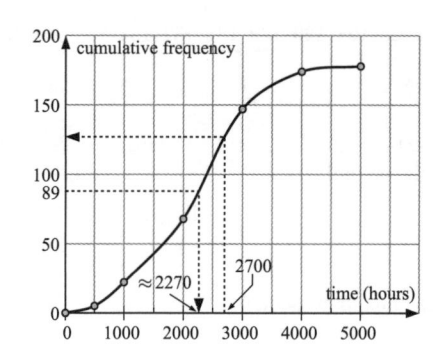

Total frequency = 178

a median ≈ 2270 hours

b For a life of 2700 hours CF ≈ 127

and $\dfrac{127}{178} \times 100\% \approx 71.3\%$

So, about 71.3% have a life ⩽ 2700 h

c For a life of 1500 h, CF ≈ 45

For a life of 2500 h, CF ≈ 108

and $108 - 45 = 63$

∴ ≈ 63 had a life between 1500 and 2500 hours.

EXERCISE 17D.1

1 a 2 3 3 3 4 4 4 5 5 5 5 6 6 6 6 6 7 7 8 8 8 9 9 $(n = 23)$
    ↑   ↑   ↑
    Q_1 median Q_3

  i median = 6   **ii** $Q_1 = 4$,   **iii** range   **iv** IQR
                              $Q_3 = 7$ $= 9 - 2$ $= Q_3 - Q_1$
                                                     $= 7$ $= 3$

  b 10 12 12 14 15 15 16 16 $\underbrace{17 \ 18}$ 18 18 18 19 20 21 22 24 $(n = 18)$
                      ↑   ↑   ↑
                     Q_1 median Q_3

  i median = 17.5   **ii** $Q_1 = 15$,   **iii** range   **iv** IQR
                              $Q_3 = 19$ $= 24 - 10$ $= Q_3 - Q_1$
                                                     $= 14$ $= 4$

  c 21.8 22.4 23.5 23.5 24.6 24.9 25.0 25.3 26.1 26.4 29.5 $(n = 11)$
                    ↑   ↑   ↑
                   Q_1 median Q_3

  i median = 24.9   **ii** $Q_1 = 23.5$,   **iii** range   **iv** IQR
                              $Q_3 = 26.1$ $= 29.5 - 21.8$ $= Q_3 - Q_1$
                                                     $= 7.7$ $= 2.6$

2 0 0 0 0.8 $\underbrace{1.4 \ 1.5}$ 1.6 1.9 2.1 $\underbrace{2.2 \ 2.7}$ 3.0 3.4 3.6 $\underbrace{3.8 \ 3.8}$ 4.5 4.8 5.2 5.2
↑   ↑   ↑   ↑   ↑
min Q_1 median Q_3 max

  a median $= \dfrac{2.2 + 2.7}{2}$ $Q_1 = 1.45$ **b** range $= 5.2 - 0$ IQR $= Q_3 - Q_1$
              $= 2.45$ $Q_3 = 3.8$ $= 5.2$ $= 3.8 - 1.45$
                                                                                                        $= 2.35$

  c i the median = 2.45 min   **ii** $Q_3 = 3.8$ min
     iii The minimum waiting time was 0 minutes and the maximum waiting time was 5.2 minutes.
          The waiting time was spread over 5.2 minutes.

3 3 4 7 9 10 13 14 16 17 18 20 20 23 25 26 29 29 29 31 33 37 38 42 $(n = 23)$
  ↑   ↑   ↑   ↑   ↑
 min Q_1 median Q_3 max

  a min = 3   **b** max = 42   **c** median = 20   **d** $Q_1 = 13$ **e** $Q_3 = 29$
  f range $= 42 - 3 = 39$ **g** IQR $= Q_3 - Q_1 = 29 - 13 = 16$

4 109 111 113 114 $\underbrace{114\ 118}$ 119 122 122 $\underbrace{124\ 124}$ 126 128 129 $\underbrace{129\ 131}$ 132 135 138 138 $(n = 20)$
 ↑   ↑   ↑   ↑   ↑
 min Q_1 median Q_3 max

    a   **i**   median = 124 cm   **b**   **i**   .... 124 cm tall   **c**   **i**   range = 138 − 109
         ii Q_3 = 130 cm,   **ii**   .... 130 cm tall   = 29 cm
             Q_1 = 116 cm   **ii**   IQR = $Q_3 - Q_1$
    d   the IQR = 14 cm   = 14 cm

5   **a**   **Without fertiliser** - See **Exercise 17B.2** solution to question **6**.
         i   range = 9 − 2 = 7   **ii**   median = 6
        iii   lower quartile = 38th score = 5   **iv**   upper quartile = 113th score = 7
         v   interquartile range = 7 − 5 = 2
   b   **With fertiliser**
         i   range = 13 − 3 = 10   **ii**   median = 7
        iii   lower quartile = 38th score = 6   **iv**   upper quartile = 113th score = 8
         v   interquartile range = 8 − 6 = 2

EXERCISE 17D.2

1   **a**   **i**   median = 35   **ii**   max. value = 78   **iii**   min. value = 13
         iv Q_3 = 53   **v** Q_1 = 26
   b   **i**   range = 78 − 13 = 65   **ii**   IQR = $Q_3 - Q_1$ = 53 − 26 = 27

2   **a**   highest mark was 98, lowest mark was 25   **b**   the median which is 70
   c Q_3 which is 85   **d** Q_1 = 55 and Q_3 = 85   **e**   range = 98 − 25 = 73
   f   IQR = $Q_3 - Q_1$ = 85 − 55 = 30
   g   The data is negatively skewed, so the mean will be slightly lower than the median of 70.
       ∴ mean ≈ 67, say.

3   **a**   **i**   3   4   5   5   5   6 $\underbrace{6\ 6}$ 7   7   8   8   9   10
             ↑   ↑   ↑   ↑   ↑
           min Q_1 median Q_3 max

            So, min = 3, Q_1 = 5, median = 6, Q_3 = 8, max = 10
        ii   **iii**   range = 10 − 3   **iv**   IQR = $Q_3 - Q_1$
                                                                                        = 7   = 8 − 5
                                                                                                                                            = 3
                   3   4   5   6   7   8   9   10

   b   **i**   0   1   2   3   4   5   6   6   7   7   7   8   8   8   8   8   9   9
               ↑   ↑   ↑   ↑   ↑
             min Q_1 median Q_3 max

            So, min = 0, Q_1 = 4, median = 7, Q_3 = 8, max = 9
        i   **ii**   range = 9 − 0   **iii**   IQR = $Q_3 - Q_1$
                                                                          = 9   = 8 − 4
                                                                                                             = 4
                   0   1   2   3   4   5   6   7   8   9

   c   **i**   min
             ↓
          117   120   123   126 $\underbrace{126\ 128}$ 130   131   131 $\underbrace{131\ 133}$ 135   135   137 $\underbrace{144\ 147}$ 147   149
          149   151
            ↑   ↑   ↑   ↑
          max Q_1 median Q_3

            So, min = 117, Q_1 = 127, median = 132, Q_3 = 145.5, max = 151

ii

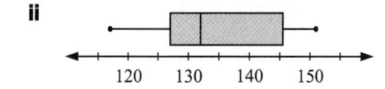

[box plot with scale 120, 130, 140, 150]

iii range
$= 151 - 117$
$= 34$

iv IQR $= Q_3 - Q_1$
$= 145.5 - 127$
$= 18.5$

4 a

Statistic	Year 9	Year 12
min value	1	6
Q_1	5	10
median	7.5	14
Q_3	10	16
max value	12	17.5

b For the year 9 group

  i range $= 12 - 1$
  $= 11$

  ii IQR $= 10 - 5$
  $= 5$

For the year 12 group

  i range $= 17.5 - 6$
  $= 11.5$

  ii IQR $= 16 - 10$
  $= 6$

  c i True, as indicated by the median.
  ii True, as Q_1 for year 9 $= 5$ and min for year 12 $= 6$.

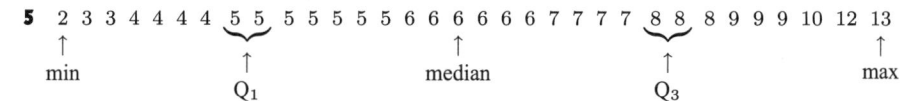

5 2 3 3 4 4 4 4 $\underbrace{5\ 5}$ 5 5 5 5 5 6 6 6 6 6 6 7 7 7 7 $\underbrace{8\ 8}$ 8 9 9 9 10 12 13

↑ min ↑ Q_1 ↑ median ↑ Q_3 ↑ max

a median $= 6$, $Q_1 = 5$, $Q_3 = 8$ **b** IQR $= 8 - 5 = 3$

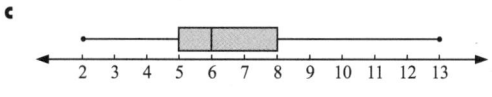

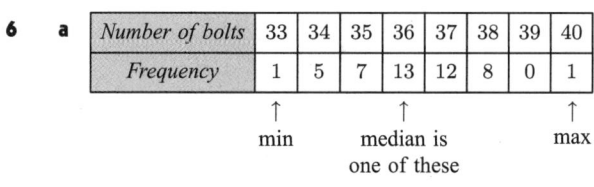

c

[box plot with scale 2 3 4 5 6 7 8 9 10 11 12 13]

6 a

Number of bolts	33	34	35	36	37	38	39	40
Frequency	1	5	7	13	12	8	0	1

↑ min   ↑ median is one of these   ↑ max

There are 47 scores
∴ median = 24th
$\left(\dfrac{47+1}{2} = 24\right)$

13 scores are 35 or less
26 scores are 36 or less
∴ median is 36

$Q_1 = 12$th $\left(\dfrac{23+1}{2} = 12\right)$ $Q_3 = 36$th
$= 35$ $= 37$

So, min $= 33$, $Q_1 = 35$, median $= 36$, $Q_3 = 37$, max $= 40$

b i range $= 40 - 33 = 7$
  ii IQR $= 37 - 35 = 2$

c

[box plot with scale 30 31 32 33 34 35 36 37 38 39 40 41]

7 a For $h = 5$, CF ≈ 9 ∴ 9 seedlings have height 5 cm or less

b For $h = 8$, CF ≈ 43 ∴ % taller than 8 cm $= \dfrac{60-43}{60} \times 100\% \approx 28.3\%$

c The approximate median occurs at CF $= 30$, ∴ median ≈ 7 cm.

d IQR $= Q_3 - Q_1 = (h$ when CF $= 45) - (h$ when CF $= 15)$
$\approx 8.3 - 5.9 \approx 2.4$ cm

e 90th percentile occurs when CF $= 90\%$ of $60 = 54$
∴ 90th percentile $= 10$
This means that 90% of the seedlings have a height of 10 cm or less.

8 a The lower quartile occurs when CF $= 25\%$ of $80 = 20$ ∴ $Q_1 = 27$ min
  b The median occurs when CF $= 50\%$ of $80 = 40$ ∴ median $= 29$ min
  c The upper quartile occurs when CF $= 75\%$ of $80 = 60$ ∴ $Q_3 \approx 31.3$ min
  d IQR $= Q_3 - Q_1 = 31.3 - 27 = 4.3$ min
  e For the 40th percentile, CF $= 40\%$ of $80 = 32$
  When CF $= 32$, $x \approx 28.2$ So, the 40th percentile is about 28 min 10 sec.

EXERCISE 17E

1 **a** $\bar{x} \approx 4.87$, $\text{Min}_x = 1$, $Q_1 = 3$, $Q_2 = 5$, $Q_3 = 7$, $\text{Max}_x = 9$

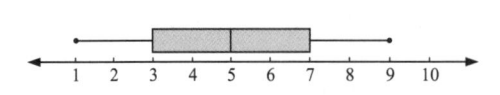

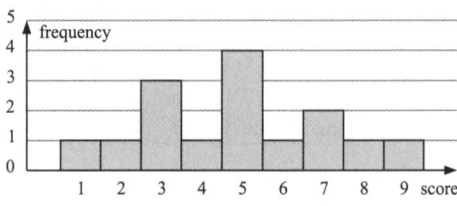

b [box plot from 1 to 9, median at 5]

c [frequency histogram of scores 1–9]

d $\bar{x} \approx 5.24$, $\text{Min}_x = 2$, $Q_1 = 4$, $Q_2 = 5$, $Q_3 = 6.5$, $\text{Max}_x = 9$

[parallel box plots: set 1 and set 2]

2 **a** discrete

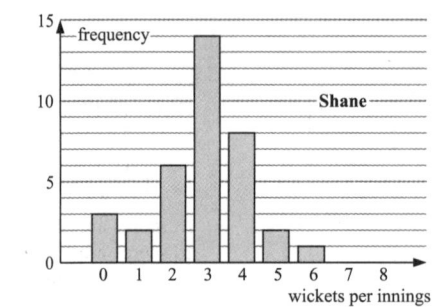

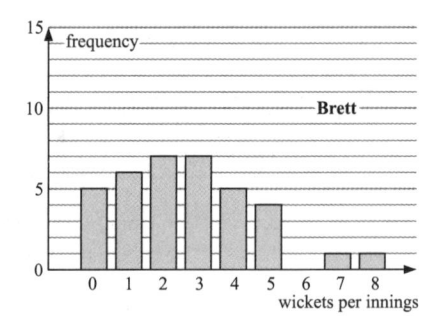

c [frequency histograms for Shane and Brett, wickets per innings]

d There are no outliers for Shane. Brett has outliers of 7 and 8 which must not be removed.

e Shane's distribution is reasonably symmetrical. Brett's distribution is positively skewed.

f Shane has a higher mean (≈ 2.89 wickets) compared with Brett (≈ 2.67 wickets). Shane has a higher median (3 wickets) compared with Brett (2.5 wickets). Shane's modal number of wickets is 3 (14 times) compared with Brett, who has a bi-modal distribution of 2 and 3 (7 times each).

g Shane's range is 6 wickets, compared with Brett's range of 8 wickets. Shane's IQR is 2 wickets, compared with Brett's IQR of 3 wickets. Brett's wicket taking shows greater spread or variability.

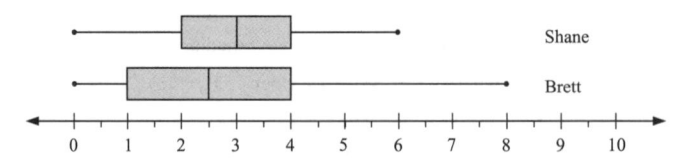

h [parallel box plots: Shane and Brett]

i Generally, Shane takes more wickets than Brett and is a more consistent bowler.

3 **a** continuous

c For the 'New type' globes, 191 hours could be considered an outlier. However, it could be a genuine piece of data, so we will include it in the analysis.

d The mean and median are $\approx 25\%$ and $\approx 19\%$ higher for the 'new type' of globe compared with the 'old type'.
The range is higher for the 'new type' of globe (but has been affected by the 191 hours).
The IQR for each type of globe is almost the same.

	Old type	New type
Mean	107	134
Median	110.5	132
Range	56	84
IQR	19	18.5

e

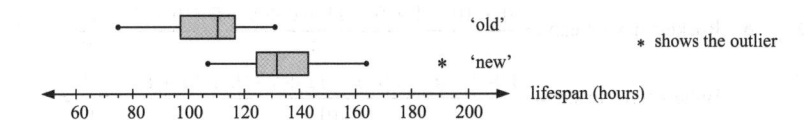

```
                    ┌──┬───┐
              •─────┤  │   ├─────•                    'old'
                    └──┴───┘
                       ┌────┬─┐
                    •──┤    │ ├──•         *          'new'       *  shows the outlier
                       └────┴─┘
              ←──┬────┬────┬────┬────┬────┬────┬────→  lifespan (hours)
                 60   80  100  120  140  160  180  200
```

f For the 'old type' of globe, the data is bunched to the right of the median, hence the distribution is negatively skewed. For the 'new type' of globe, the data is bunched to the left of the median, hence the distribution is positively skewed.

g The manufacturer's claim, that the 'new type' of globe has a 20% longer life than the 'old type' seems to be backed up by the 25% higher mean life and 19.5% higher median life.

EXERCISE 17F.1

1 a Looking at the graphs, Sample A appears to have the wider spread.

b Sample A:

x	f	fx
4	1	4
5	2	10
6	3	18
7	4	28
8	5	40
9	4	36
10	3	30
11	2	22
12	1	12
$\sum$	25	200

$\therefore$ mean $= \frac{200}{25} = 8$

Sample B:

x	f	fx
6	2	12
7	6	42
8	9	72
9	6	54
10	2	20
$\sum$	25	200

$\therefore$ mean $= \frac{200}{25} = 8$

c Sample A:

x	$x - \bar{x}$	$(x - \bar{x})^2$	f	$f(x - \bar{x})^2$
4	-4	16	1	16
5	-3	9	2	18
6	-2	4	3	12
7	-1	1	4	4
8	0	0	5	0
9	1	1	4	4
10	2	4	3	12
11	3	9	2	18
12	4	16	1	16
$\sum$				100

$\therefore s = \sqrt{\dfrac{\sum(x - \bar{x})^2}{n}} = \sqrt{\dfrac{100}{25}} = 2$

Sample B:

x	$x - \bar{x}$	$(x - \bar{x})^2$	f	$f(x - \bar{x})^2$
6	-2	4	2	8
7	-1	1	6	6
8	0	0	9	0
9	1	1	6	6
10	2	4	2	8
$\sum$				28

$\therefore s = \sqrt{\dfrac{\sum(x - \bar{x})^2}{n}} = \sqrt{\dfrac{28}{25}} \approx 1.06$

The standard deviation is higher for Sample A.

2 a Andrew: $\bar{x} = \dfrac{23 + 17 + \dots + 28 + 32}{8} = 25$

x	$x - \bar{x}$	$(x - \bar{x})^2$
23	-2	4
17	-8	64
31	6	36
25	0	0
25	0	0
19	-6	36
28	3	9
32	7	49
$\sum$		198

$\therefore s = \sqrt{\dfrac{\sum(x - \bar{x})^2}{n}} = \sqrt{\dfrac{198}{8}} \approx 4.97$

Brad: $\bar{x} = \dfrac{9 + 29 + \dots + 38 + 43}{8} = 30.5$

x	$x - \bar{x}$	$(x - \bar{x})^2$
9	-21.5	462.25
29	-1.5	2.25
41	10.5	110.25
26	-4.5	20.25
14	-16.5	272.25
44	13.5	182.25
38	7.5	56.25
43	12.5	156.25
$\sum$		1262

$\therefore s = \sqrt{\dfrac{\sum(x - \bar{x})^2}{n}} = \sqrt{\dfrac{1262}{8}} \approx 12.6$

b Andrew, as he has the smaller standard deviation.

3 a Rockets have mean $= \dfrac{0+10+1+9+11+0+8+5+6+7}{10} = \dfrac{57}{10} = 5.7$

Bullets have mean $= \dfrac{4+3+4+1+4+11+7+6+12+5}{10} = \dfrac{57}{10} = 5.7$

Rocket's range $= 11 - 0 = 11$ Bullet's range $= 12 - 1 = 11$

b We suspect the Rockets, as they have more high and low values.

c
Rockets

x	$(x - \bar{x})^2$
0	$(5.7)^2$
10	$(4.3)^2$
1	$(4.7)^2$
9	$(3.3)^2$
11	$(5.3)^2$
0	$(5.7)^2$
8	$(2.3)^2$
5	$(0.7)^2$
6	$(0.3)^2$
7	$(1.3)^2$
	152.1

$s = \sqrt{\dfrac{\sum(x-\bar{x})^2}{n}}$

$= \sqrt{\dfrac{152.1}{10}}$

$= 3.9$

↑ greater variability

Bullets

x	$(x - \bar{x})^2$
4	$(1.7)^2$
3	$(2.7)^2$
4	$(1.7)^2$
1	$(4.7)^2$
4	$(1.7)^2$
11	$(5.3)^2$
7	$(1.3)^2$
6	$(0.3)^2$
12	$(6.3)^2$
5	$(0.7)^2$
	108.1

$s = \sqrt{\dfrac{\sum(x-\bar{x})^2}{n}}$

$= \sqrt{\dfrac{108.1}{10}}$

≈ 3.29

d The standard deviation, as it takes all values into account, not just the lowest and highest.

4 a We suspect variability in standard deviation since the factors may change every day.

b **i** sample mean   **ii** sample standard deviation

c less variability in the volume of soft drink per can

5 a

x	$(x - \bar{x})^2$
79	10^2
64	5^2
59	10^2
71	2^2
68	1^2
68	1^2
74	5^2
483	256

$\bar{x} = \dfrac{\sum x}{n}$

$= \dfrac{483}{7} = 69$

$s = \sqrt{\dfrac{\sum(x-\bar{x})^2}{n}}$

$= \sqrt{\dfrac{256}{7}}$

≈ 6.05 kg

b

x	$(x - \bar{x})^2$
89	10^2
74	5^2
69	10^2
81	2^2
78	1^2
78	1^2
84	5^2
553	256

$\bar{x} = \dfrac{\sum x}{n}$

$= \dfrac{553}{7}$

$= 79$

$s \approx 6.05$ kg

c The distribution has simply shifted by 10 kg. The mean increases by 10 kg and the standard deviation remains the same. In general, changing the values by a constant does not affect standard deviation.

6 a

x	$(x - \bar{x})^2$
0.8	$(0.21)^2$
1.1	$(0.09)^2$
1.2	$(0.19)^2$
0.9	$(0.11)^2$
1.2	$(0.19)^2$
1.2	$(0.19)^2$
0.9	$(0.11)^2$
0.7	$(0.31)^2$
1.0	$(0.01)^2$
1.1	$(0.09)^2$
10.1	0.289

$\bar{x} = \dfrac{\sum x}{n}$

$= \dfrac{10.1}{10}$

$= 1.01$ kg

$= \sqrt{\dfrac{\sum(x-\bar{x})^2}{n}}$

$s = \sqrt{\dfrac{0.289}{10}}$

$= 0.17$ kg

b

x	$(x - \bar{x})^2$
1.6	$(0.42)^2$
2.2	$(0.18)^2$
2.4	$(0.38)^2$
1.8	$(0.22)^2$
2.4	$(0.38)^2$
2.4	$(0.38)^2$
1.8	$(0.22)^2$
1.4	$(0.62)^2$
2.0	$(0.02)^2$
2.2	$(0.18)^2$
20.2	1.156

$\bar{x} = \dfrac{\sum x}{n}$

$= \dfrac{20.2}{10}$

$= 2.02$ kg

$s = \sqrt{\dfrac{\sum(x-\bar{x})^2}{n}}$

$= \sqrt{\dfrac{1.156}{10}}$

$= 0.34$ kg

c Doubling the values doubles the mean and standard deviation.

7 mean $= \dfrac{1+3+5+7+4+5+p+q}{8} = 5$

$25 + p + q = 40$

$\therefore \quad p + q = 15$

$\therefore \quad q = 15 - p$

and $s = \sqrt{\dfrac{(-4)^2 + (-2)^2 + 0^2 + 2^2 + (-1)^2 + 0^2 + (p-5)^2 + (q-5)^2}{8}} = \sqrt{5.25}$

$\therefore \quad \dfrac{16 + 4 + 4 + 1 + (p-5)^2 + (15 - p - 5)^2}{8} = 5.25$

$\therefore \quad 25 + p^2 - 10p + 25 + 100 - 20p + p^2 = 42$

$\therefore \quad 2p^2 - 30p + 108 = 0$

$\therefore \quad p^2 - 15p + 54 = 0$

$\therefore \quad (p - 6)(p - 9) = 0$

$\therefore \quad p = 6$ or 9 and $q = 9$ or 6

But $p < q$ $\quad \therefore \quad p = 6, \ q = 9$

8 mean $= \dfrac{3 + 9 + 5 + 5 + 6 + 4 + a + 6 + b + 8}{10} = 6$

$\therefore \quad \dfrac{46 + a + b}{10} = 6$

$\therefore \quad 46 + a + b = 60$

$\therefore \quad a + b = 14$

$\therefore \quad b = 14 - a$

and $s = \sqrt{\dfrac{(-3)^2 + 3^2 + (-1)^2 + (-1)^2 + (-2)^2 + (a-6)^2 + (b-6)^2 + 2^2}{10}} = \sqrt{3.2}$

$\therefore \quad 9 + 9 + 1 + 1 + 4 + 4 + (a-6)^2 + (14 - a - 6)^2 = 32$

$\therefore \quad 28 + a^2 - 12a + 36 + 64 - 16a + a^2 = 32$

$\therefore \quad 2a^2 - 28a + 96 = 0$

$\therefore \quad a^2 - 14a + 48 = 0$

$\therefore \quad (a - 6)(a - 8) = 0$

$\therefore \quad a = 6$ or 8 and $b = 8$ or 6

But $a > b$ $\quad \therefore \quad a = 8, \ b = 6$

9 a $\displaystyle\sum_{i=1}^{n}(x_i - \overline{x})^2 = \sum_{i=1}^{n}(x_i{}^2) - 2\overline{x}\sum_{i=1}^{n}x_i + \sum_{i=1}^{n}(\overline{x})^2$

$\qquad \qquad \qquad \ \ = \displaystyle\sum_{i=1}^{n}(x_i{}^2) - 2\overline{x}(x_1 + x_2 + \ldots + x_n) + n(\overline{x})^2$

$\qquad \qquad \qquad \ \ = \displaystyle\sum_{i=1}^{n}(x_i{}^2) - 2\overline{x}(n\overline{x}) + n\overline{x}^2 \qquad \{\overline{x} = \dfrac{x_1 + x_2 + \ldots + x_n}{n}\}$

$\qquad \qquad \qquad \ \ = \displaystyle\sum_{i=1}^{n}(x_i{}^2) - n(\overline{x})^2$

b $s = \sqrt{\dfrac{\sum_{i=1}^{25}(x_i - \overline{x})^2}{25}} = 5.2$ $\therefore \sum_{i=1}^{25}(x_i)^2 - 25(\overline{x})^2 = 676$ {using **a**}

$\therefore \dfrac{\sum_{i=1}^{25}(x_i - \overline{x})^2}{25} = 27.04$ $\therefore 2568.25 - 25(\overline{x})^2 = 676$

$\therefore 1892.25 = 25(\overline{x})^2$

$\therefore \sum_{i=1}^{25}(x_i - \overline{x})^2 = 676$ $\therefore (\overline{x})^2 = 75.69$

$\therefore \overline{x} = 8.7$ {assuming positive data}

10 a $\overline{x} = \dfrac{0.8 + 0.6 + 0.7 + 0.8 + 0.4 + 2.8}{6}$

≈ 1.017

b $\overline{x} = \dfrac{0.8 + 0.6 + 0.7 + 0.8 + 0.4}{5}$

$= 0.66$

x	$(x - \overline{x})^2$
0.8	$(-0.217)^2$
0.6	$(-0.417)^2$
0.7	$(-0.317)^2$
0.8	$(-0.217)^2$
0.4	$(-0.617)^2$
2.8	$(1.783)^2$
$\sum$	3.928

x	$(x - \overline{x})^2$
0.8	$(0.14)^2$
0.6	$(-0.06)^2$
0.7	$(0.04)^2$
0.8	$(0.14)^2$
0.4	$(-0.26)^2$
$\sum$	0.112

$\therefore s = \sqrt{\dfrac{\sum(x - \overline{x})^2}{n}} \approx \sqrt{\dfrac{3.928}{6}}$

≈ 0.809

$\therefore s = \sqrt{\dfrac{\sum(x - \overline{x})^2}{n}} = \sqrt{\dfrac{0.112}{5}}$

≈ 0.150

c The extreme value greatly increases the standard deviation.

EXERCISE 17F.2

1 a $s = \sqrt{\text{variance}}$
$= \sqrt{45.9}$ kg
≈ 6.77 kg

b Unbiased estimate of μ is $\overline{x} = 93.8$ kg
Unbiased estimate of σ^2 is $\dfrac{87}{86} \times 45.9 \approx 46.4$ kg^2

2 a Using technology, $\overline{x} \approx 77.5$ g and $s_n \approx 7.44$ g
b Unbiased estimate of μ is $\overline{x} = 77.5$ g
Unbiased estimate of σ^2 is $\dfrac{17}{16} \times 7.445^2 \approx 58.9$ g^2

3 a Unbiased estimate of μ is $\overline{x} = \dfrac{\sum_{i=1}^{16} x_i}{16} = \dfrac{519}{16} \approx 32.4$ min

b $s_{16}^2 = \dfrac{\sum_{i=1}^{16}(x_i - \overline{x})^2}{16} = \dfrac{\sum_{i=1}^{16}(x_i)^2 - 16\overline{x}^2}{16}$ {using **Ex 17F.1 Q 9 a**}

$= \dfrac{16\,983 - 16 \times 32.4375^2}{16}$

≈ 9.246

$\therefore$ unbiased estimate of $\sigma^2 = \dfrac{16}{15} \times 9.246 \approx 9.86$ min^2

EXERCISE 17F.3

1 a

x	f	fx	$f(x-\bar{x})^2$
0	14	0	41.62
1	18	18	9.44
2	13	26	0.99
3	5	15	8.14
4	3	12	15.54
5	2	10	21.46
6	2	12	36.57
7	1	7	27.83
$\sum$	58	100	161.59

$$\bar{x} = \frac{\sum fx}{\sum f} = \frac{100}{58} \approx 1.72 \text{ children}$$

$$s = \sqrt{\frac{\sum f(x-\bar{x})^2}{\sum f}} \approx \sqrt{\frac{161.59}{58}} \approx 1.67 \text{ children}$$

b Unbiased estimate of μ is $\bar{x} \approx 1.72$ children
Unbiased estimate of σ^2 is $\frac{58}{57} \times (1.67)^2 \approx 2.83$ children^2

2 a

x	f	fx	$f(x-\bar{x})^2$
11	2	22	24.22
12	1	12	6.150
13	4	52	8.762
14	5	70	1.152
15	6	90	1.622
16	4	64	9.242
17	2	34	12.70
18	1	18	12.39
$\sum$	25	362	76.24

$$\bar{x} = \frac{\sum fx}{\sum f} = \frac{362}{25} \approx 14.5 \text{ years}$$

$$s = \sqrt{\frac{\sum f(x-\bar{x})^2}{\sum f}} = \sqrt{\frac{76.24}{25}} \approx 1.75 \text{ years}$$

b Unbiased estimate of μ is $\bar{x} \approx 14.5$ years
Unbiased estimate of σ^2 is $\frac{25}{24} \times (1.7463)^2 \approx 3.18$ years^2

3 a

x	f	fx	$f(x-\bar{x})^2$
33	1	33	18.24
35	5	175	25.78
36	7	252	11.31
37	13	481	0.95
38	12	456	6.38
39	8	312	23.92
40	2	80	14.90
$\sum$	48	1789	101.48

$$\bar{x} = \frac{\sum fx}{\sum f} = \frac{1789}{48} \approx 37.3 \text{ toothpicks}$$

$$s = \sqrt{\frac{\sum f(x-\bar{x})^2}{\sum f}} = \sqrt{\frac{101.48}{48}} \approx 1.45 \text{ toothpicks}$$

b Unbiased estimate of μ is $\bar{x} \approx 37.3$ toothpicks
Unbiased estimate of σ^2 is $\frac{48}{47} \times (1.454)^2 \approx 2.16$ toothpicks^2

4 a

Midpoint (x)	f	fx	$f(x-\bar{x})^2$
40.5	1	40.5	52.80
42.5	1	42.5	27.74
44.5	3	133.5	32.01
46.5	7	325.5	11.23
48.5	11	533.5	5.91
50.5	5	252.5	37.35
52.5	2	105	44.80
$\sum$	30	1433	211.87

$$\bar{x} = \frac{\sum fx}{\sum f} = \frac{1433}{30} \approx 47.8 \text{ cm}$$

$$s = \sqrt{\frac{\sum f(x-\bar{x})^2}{\sum f}} \approx \sqrt{\frac{211.87}{30}} \approx 2.66 \text{ cm}$$

b Unbiased estimate of μ is $\bar{x} \approx 47.8$ cm
Unbiased estimate of σ^2 is $\frac{30}{29} \times 2.657^2 \approx 7.31$ cm^2

5 a

Midpoint (x)	f	fx	$f(x-\bar{x})^2$
364.995	17	6204.9	10 881.53
374.995	38	14 249.8	8895.42
384.995	47	18 094.8	1320.23
394.995	57	22 514.7	1259.13
404.995	18	7289.9	3889.62
414.995	10	4150.0	6100.9
424.995	10	4250.0	12 040.9
434.995	3	1305.0	5994.27
$\sum$	200	78 059	50 382

$$\bar{x} = \frac{\sum fx}{\sum f} = \frac{78\,059}{200} \approx \$390.30$$

$$s = \sqrt{\frac{\sum f(x-\bar{x})^2}{\sum f}} = \sqrt{\frac{50\,382}{200}} \approx \$15.87$$

b Unbiased estimate of μ is $\bar{x} \approx \$390.30$

Unbiased estimate of σ^2 is $\frac{200}{199} \times \$15.87 \approx 253.18$ dollars^2

EXERCISE 17G

1

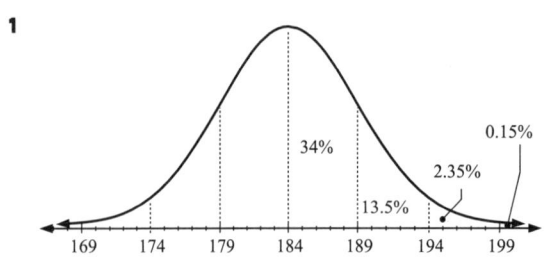

a $50\% + 34\% = 84\%$
So, 16% are above 189 cm.

b $50\% + 34\% = 84\%$
So, 84% are above 179 cm.

c $2 \times 34\% + 2 \times 13.5\% + 2.35\%$
$\approx 97.4\%$

d 0.15%

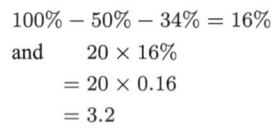

2

$100\% - 50\% - 34\% = 16\%$
and $\quad 20 \times 16\%$
$= 20 \times 0.16$
$= 3.2$

So, we expect less than 42 mm of rain on 3 occasions.

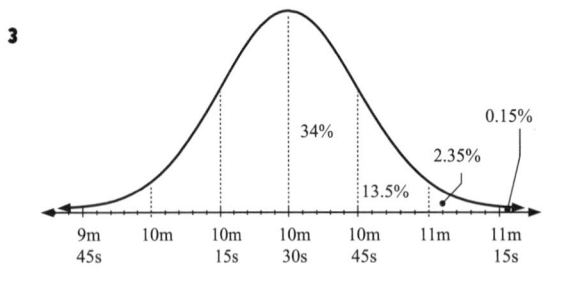

3

a $200 \times (2.35 + 0.15)\%$
$= 200 \times 2.5\%$
$= 5$ lifesavers

b $200 \times (0.15 + 2.35 + 13.5)\%$
$= 200 \times 16\%$
$= 32$ lifesavers

c $200 \times 68\% = 136$ lifesavers

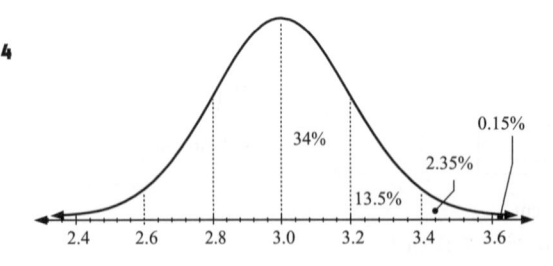

4

a $545 \times (50 + 34)\%$
$= 545 \times 0.84$
≈ 458 babies

b $545 \times (68 + 13.5)\%$
$= 545 \times 81.5\%$
≈ 444 babies

REVIEW SET 17A

1 a Diameter of bacteria colonies

```
0 | 4 8 9
1 | 3 5 5 7
2 | 1 1 5 6 8 8
3 | 0 1 2 3 4 5 5 6 6 7 7 9
4 | 0 1 2 7 9      Scale: 1 | 3 means 1.3 cm
```

b Using technology
  i median = 3.15 cm
  ii range = 4.9 − 0.4 = 4.5 cm

c The distribution is negatively skewed.

2 a highest = 97.5 m, lowest = 64.6 m

c

A frequency distribution table for distances thrown by Thabiso

distance (m)	tally	freq. (f)
60 - < 65	|	1
65 - < 70	|||	3
70 - < 75	|||||	5
75 - < 80	||	2
80 - < 85	||||| |||	8
85 - < 90	||||| |	6
90 - < 95	|||	3
95 - < 100	||	2
	Total	30

b The range = 97.5 − 64.5 = 33
So, if intervals of length 5 are used we need about 7 of them.
We choose 60 - < 65, 65 - < 70, 70 - < 75, and so on.

d Frequency histogram displaying the distance Thabiso throws a baseball

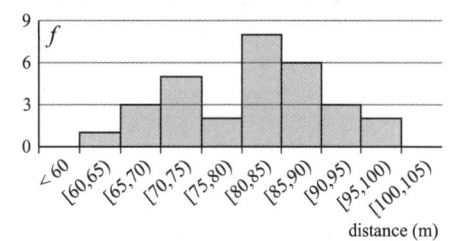

(histogram with bars at intervals [60,65), [65,70), [70,75), [75,80), [80,85), [85,90), [90,95), [95,100), [100,105); distance (m))

e Using technology:
  i $\bar{x} \approx 81.1$ m
  ii median ≈ 83.1 m

3 Mean $= \dfrac{5+6+8+3+a+b}{6} = 6$ $\therefore\ 22 + a + b = 36$
  $\therefore\ a + b = 14$
  $\therefore\ b = 14 - a$

and $s = \sqrt{\dfrac{(-1)^2 + 0^2 + 2^2 + (-3)^2 + (a-6)^2 + (b-6)^2}{6}} = \sqrt{3}$

$\therefore\ \dfrac{1 + 4 + 9 + (a-6)^2 + (8-a)^2}{6} = 3$

$\therefore\ 14 + a^2 - 12a + 36 + 64 - 16a + a^2 = 18$
$\therefore\ 2a^2 - 28a + 96 = 0$
$\therefore\ a^2 - 14a + 48 = 0$
$\therefore\ (a-6)(a-8) = 0$
$\therefore\ a = 6$ or 8 and $b = 8$ or 6
$\therefore\ a = 6,\ b = 8$ or $a = 8,\ b = 6$

4 a *(cumulative frequency graph with points, median line shown at approximately 25.9, score axis 0, 9.95, 19.95, 29.95, 39.95, 49.95)*

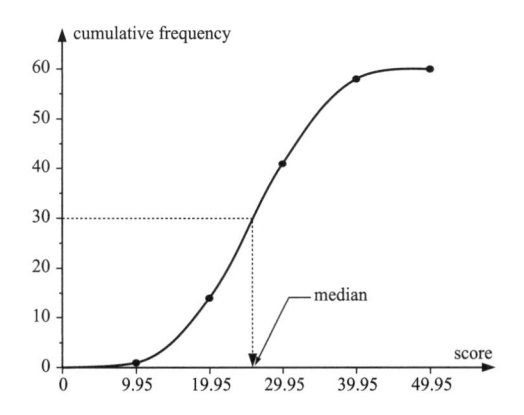

b median ≈ 25.9 (see graph)

c IQR $= Q_3 - Q_1$
 $=$ (score for CF of 45)
    $-$ (score for CF of 15)
 $\approx 32 - 20 \approx 12$

d

	f	midpt x	fx	$(x-\bar{x})^2$
0 - 9.9	1	4.95	4.95	441
10 - 19.9	13	14.95	194.35	121
20 - 29.9	27	24.95	673.65	1
30 - 39.9	17	34.95	594.15	81
40 - 49.9	2	44.95	89.9	361
	60		1557	

$$\bar{x} = \frac{\sum fx}{\sum x}$$
$$= \frac{1557}{60}$$
$$\approx 26.0$$

$$s = \sqrt{\frac{\sum f(x-\bar{x})^2}{\sum f}}$$
$$= \sqrt{\frac{4140}{60}}$$
$$\approx 8.31$$

5 a Using technology:

	Girls	Boys
shape	pos. skewed	approx. symm.
centre (median)	36.3 sec	34.9 sec
spread (range)	7.7 sec	4.9 sec

b The girls' distribution is positively skewed and the boys' distribution is approximately symmetrical. The median swim times for boys is 1.4 seconds lower than for girls but the range of the girls' swim times is 2.8 seconds higher than for boys. The analysis supports the conjecture that boys generally swim faster than girls with less spread of times.

6 a Reading from the boxplots

	A	B
Min	11	11.2
Q_1	11.6	12
Median	12	12.6
Q_3	12.6	13.2
Max	13	13.8

b i range of A
$= 13 - 11$
$= 2$

range of B
$= 13.8 - 11.2$
$= 2.6$

ii IQR of A
$= 12.6 - 11.6$
$= 1.0$

IQR of B
$= 13.2 - 12$
$= 1.2$

c i The members in squad A generally ran faster because their median time is lower.
ii The times in squad B are more varied because the range and IQR is higher.

7 Using technology: **a i** 101.5 **ii** 98 **iii** 105.5 **b** 7.5 **c** $\bar{x} = 100.2$, $s \approx 7.59$

8 a This question could be done using technology or

Litres (x)	f	fx	$f(x-\bar{x})^2$
17.5	5	87.5	1299.38
22.5	13	292.5	1607.71
27.5	17	467.5	636.87
32.5	29	942.5	36.42
37.5	27	1012.5	406.32
42.5	18	765	1419.16
47.5	7	332.5	1348.45
$\sum$	116	3900	6754.31

$$\bar{x} = \frac{\sum fx}{\sum f}$$
$$= \frac{3900}{116}$$
$$\approx 33.6 \text{ litres}$$

$$s = \sqrt{\frac{\sum f(x-\bar{x})^2}{\sum f}}$$
$$\approx \sqrt{\frac{6754.31}{116}}$$
$$\approx 7.63 \text{ litres}$$

b Unbiased estimate of μ is $\bar{x} \approx 33.6$ litres
Unbiased estimate of σ^2 is $\frac{116}{115} \times 7.63^2 \approx 58.7$ litres^2.

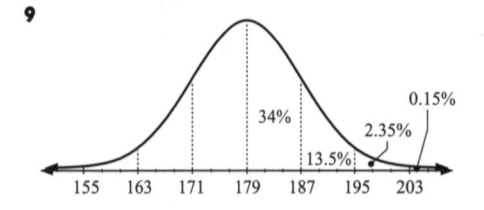

9

a % > 195 cm
$= (2.35 + 0.15)\%$
$= 2.5\%$

b % between 163 cm and 195 cm
$= 2 \times (34\% + 13.5\%)$
$= 95\%$

c % between 171 cm and 187 cm
$= 34\% + 34\% = 68\%$

10 a median = score for CF of 40
≈ 58.5 seconds

b IQR = (score for CF of 60) − (score for CF of 20)
$\approx 61.5 - 55.5$
≈ 6 seconds

11 a When $t = 20$, CF ≈ 108 and when $t = 10$, CF ≈ 20. So, approximately $108 - 20 \approx 88$ students spent between 10 and 20 minutes travelling to school.

b If 30% of students spent more than m minutes, 70% of students spent less than m minutes.
70% of 200 students = 140 students
When CF = 140, $t \approx 24$ minutes $\therefore$ $m \approx 24$.

REVIEW SET 17B

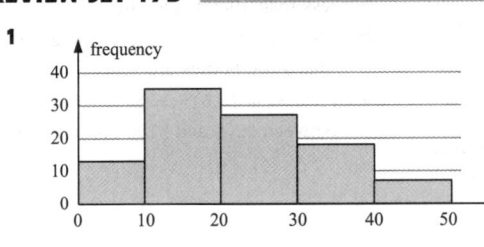

1 (frequency histogram)

2 Using technology, $\bar{x} \approx 49.6$, $s \approx 1.60$.
This does not justify the claim.
A much greater sample is needed.

3 Use technology or

Midpoint (x)	f	fx
274.5	14	3843
324.5	34	11 033
374.5	68	25 466
424.5	72	30 564
474.5	54	25 623
524.5	23	12 063.5
574.5	7	4021.5
Σ	272	112 614

$\bar{x} = \dfrac{\Sigma fx}{\Sigma f} = \dfrac{112\,614}{272}$
≈ 414 customers

4 116 118 120 122 127 128 132 135 ($n = 8$)
     ↑   ↑   ↑   ↑   ↑
    min Q_1 median Q_3 max

range = 135 − 116 $Q_1 = \dfrac{118 + 120}{2}$ $Q_3 = \dfrac{128 + 132}{2}$ $s \approx 6.38$ {technology}
= 19
= 119
= 130

5 11 12 12 13 14 14 15 15 15 16 17 17 18
      ↑   ↑   ↑   ↑   ↑
     min Q_1 median Q_3 max

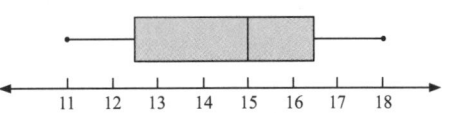

6 a Using technology with x values 74.995, 84.995, 94.995, and so on,
$\bar{x} \approx \$103.51$ and $s \approx \$19.40$

b Unbiased estimate of μ is $\bar{x} = \$103.50$
Unbiased estimate of σ^2 is $\dfrac{n}{n-1} \times \$19.40^2 \approx \dfrac{215}{214} \times \$19.40^2 \approx 378.15$ dollars^2

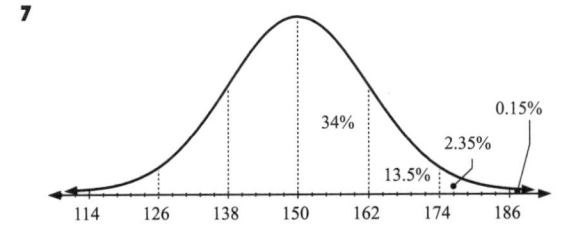

7
a 68%
b $2 \times (34 + 13.5) = 95\%$
c $2 \times 34 + 13.5 = 81.5\%$
d 13.5%

8

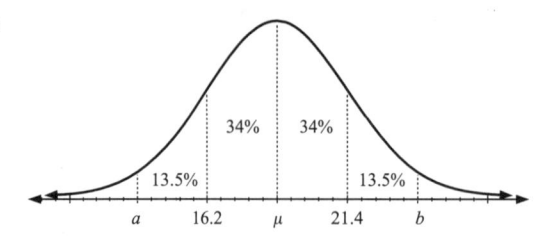

a $\mu = \dfrac{16.2 + 21.4}{2} = \dfrac{37.6}{2} = 18.8$
   $\sigma = 21.4 - 18.8 = 2.6$

b The middle 95% of data lies between a and b where $a = 16.2 - 2.6 = 13.6$ and $b = 21.4 + 2.6 = 24.0$
   $\therefore$ the middle 95% of data lies between 13.6 and 24.0

9

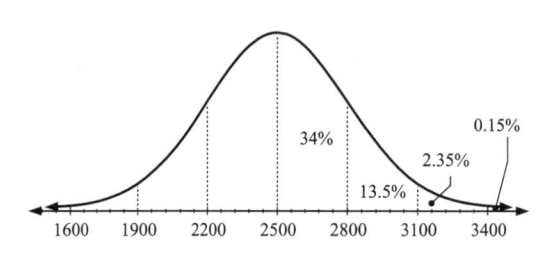

a $(50 - 34 - 13.5)\% = 2.5\%$ days when less than 1900 bottles are sold

b $(50 + 34)\% = 84\%$ days when more than 2200 bottles are sold

c $(2 \times 34 + 13.5)\% = 81.5\%$ days when between 2200 and 3100 bottles are sold

10 a

i mean $= \dfrac{\sum_{i=1}^{30} x_i}{30} = \dfrac{116.3}{30} \approx 3.877$ cm ≈ 3.88 cm

ii $s^2 = \dfrac{\sum_{i=1}^{30}(x_i - \overline{x})^2}{30} = \dfrac{\sum_{i=1}^{30}(x_i^2) - 30\overline{x}^2}{30}$

$\therefore \ s^2 = \dfrac{452.57 - 30 \times 3.877^2}{30} \approx 0.0571$ cm^2

b unbiased estimate of μ is $\overline{x} = 3.88$ cm

unbiased estimate of σ^2 is $\dfrac{n}{n-1} \times s^2 \approx \dfrac{30}{29} \times 0.571$

≈ 0.0591 cm^2

11 a mean $= \dfrac{7 + 5 + a + 8 + 1 + a + 4 + 6 + b}{9} = 5$

$\therefore \quad 2a + b + 31 = 45$
$\therefore \quad 2a + b = 14$
$\therefore \quad b = 14 - 2a$

and variance $= \dfrac{2^2 + 0^2 + (a-5)^2 + 3^2 + (-4)^2 + (a-5)^2 + (-1)^2 + 1^2 + (b-5)^2}{9} = 3\tfrac{7}{9}$

$\therefore \quad \dfrac{4 + (a-5)^2 + 9 + 16 + (a-5)^2 + 1 + 1 + (9-2a)^2}{9} = \dfrac{34}{9}$

$\therefore \quad 31 + a^2 - 10a + 25 + a^2 - 10a + 25 + 81 - 36a + 4a^2 = 34$

$\therefore \quad 6a^2 - 56a + 128 = 0$
$\therefore \quad 2(3a - 16)(a - 4) = 0$
$\therefore \quad a = 4$ or $\tfrac{16}{3}$
$\therefore \quad a = 4, \ b = 14 - 2(4) = 6 \quad \{a, b \in \mathbb{Z}^+\}$

$\therefore$ median $= 5$

b 1 4 4 4 5 6 6 7 8
        ↑   ↑   ↑
       Q_1 Q_2 Q_3

c IQR $= Q_3 - Q_1 = 6.5 - 4 = 2.5$

12 Let the number of marks be x.
- **a** When $x = 45$, CF ≈ 120
  $\therefore$ about 120 students scored 45 marks or less.
- **b** When CF $= 400$, $x \approx 65$
  $\therefore$ the median mark was about 65 marks.
- **c** When CF $= 200$, $x \approx 54$ and when CF $= 600$, $x \approx 75$
  $\therefore$ the middle 50% of results lie between 54 and 75 marks.
- **d** IQR $\approx 75 - 54 \approx 21$ marks
- **e** When $x = 55$, CF ≈ 215
  $\therefore$ about $\frac{215}{800} \approx 27\%$ of students scored less than 55
  $\therefore$ about 73% of students scored 55 or more
- **f** 10% of 800 students $= 80$ students
  When CF $= 800 - 80 = 720$, $x \approx 81$
  $\therefore$ a score of 81 marks is required for a 'distinction'.

Chapter 18
PROBABILITY

EXERCISE 18A

1 a P(inside a square) $\approx \dfrac{113}{145}$
≈ 0.78

  b P(on a line) $\approx \dfrac{32}{145}$
≈ 0.22

2 Total frequency $= 17 + 38 + 19 + 4 = 78$

  a P(20 to 39 seconds) $= \dfrac{38}{78} \approx 0.487$

  b P(> 60 seconds) $= \dfrac{4}{78} \approx 0.051$

  c P(between 20 and 59 seconds inclusive) $= \dfrac{38 + 19}{78} \approx 0.731$

3

Calls/day	No. of days
0	2
1	7
2	11
3	8
4	7
5	4
6	3
7	0
8	1

  a Survey lasted $2 + 7 + 11 + 8 + 7 + 4 + 3 + 0 + 1$
$= 43$ days

  b i P(0 calls)
$= \dfrac{2}{43}$
≈ 0.0465

  ii P($\geqslant 5$ calls)
$= \dfrac{4 + 3 + 0 + 1}{43}$
≈ 0.186

  iii P(< 3 calls)
$= \dfrac{2 + 7 + 11}{43}$
≈ 0.465

4 Total frequency
$= 37 + 81 + 48 + 17 + 6 + 1$
$= 190$

  a P(4 days gap)
$= \dfrac{17}{190}$
≈ 0.0895

  b P(at least 4 days gap)
$= \dfrac{17 + 6 + 1}{190}$
≈ 0.126

EXERCISE 18B

1 a {A, B, C, D}

  b {BB, BG, GB, GG}

  c {ABCD, ABDC, ACBD, ACDB, ADBC, ADCB, BACD, BADC, BCAD, BCDA, BDAC, BDCA, CABD, CADB, CBAD, CBDA, CDAB, CDBA, DABC, DACB, DBAC, DBCA, DCAB, DCBA}

  d {GGG, GGB, GBG, BGG, GBB, BGB, BBG, BBB}

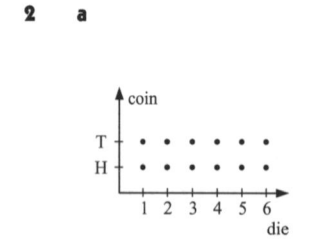

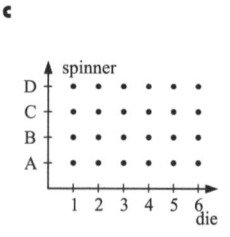

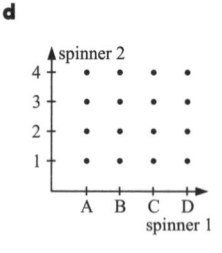

2 a coin vs die (T, H × 1–6) **b** die 2 vs die 1 (1–6 × 1–6) **c** spinner (A–D) vs die (1–6) **d** spinner 2 (1–4) vs spinner 1 (A–D)

3 a 5-cent, 10-cent tree: H→(H,T), T→(H,T)

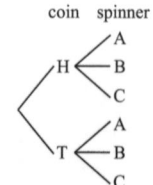

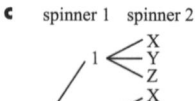

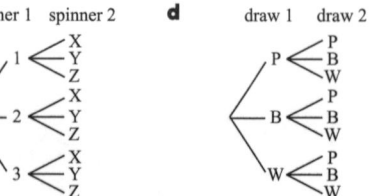

  b coin, spinner tree: H→(A,B,C), T→(A,B,C)

  c spinner 1, spinner 2 tree: 1→(X,Y,Z), 2→(X,Y,Z), 3→(X,Y,Z)

  d draw 1, draw 2 tree: P→(P,B,W), B→(P,B,W), W→(P,B,W)

EXERCISE 18C.1

1 Total number of marbles $= 5 + 3 + 7 = 15$
  a $P(\text{red}) = \frac{3}{15} = \frac{1}{5}$
  b $P(\text{green}) = \frac{5}{15} = \frac{1}{3}$
  c $P(\text{blue}) = \frac{7}{15}$
  d $P(\text{not red}) = \dfrac{5+7}{15} = \frac{12}{15}$ or $\frac{4}{5}$
  e $P(\text{neither green nor blue}) = P(\text{red}) = \frac{1}{5}$
  f $P(\text{green or red}) = \dfrac{5+3}{15} = \frac{8}{15}$

2
  a 8 are brown and so 4 are white.
  b **i** $P(\text{brown}) = \frac{8}{12} = \frac{2}{3}$
      ii $P(\text{white}) = \frac{4}{12} = \frac{1}{3}$

3
  a $P(\text{multiple of 4})$
     $= P(4, 8, 12, 16, 20, 24, 28, 32, 36)$
     $= \frac{9}{36}$
     $= \frac{1}{4}$
  b $P(\text{between 6 and 9 inclusive})$
     $= P(6, 7, 8 \text{ or } 9)$
     $= \frac{4}{36}$
     $= \frac{1}{9}$
  c $P(> 20)$
     $= P(21, 22, 23, 24, ..., 35, 36)$
     $= \dfrac{36 - 20}{36}$
     $= \frac{16}{36}$
     $= \frac{4}{9}$
  d $P(9)$
     $= \frac{1}{36}$
  e $P(\text{multiple of 13})$
     $= P(13 \text{ or } 26)$
     $= \frac{2}{36}$
     $= \frac{1}{18}$
  f $P(\text{odd multiple of 3})$
     $= P(3, 9, 15, 21, 27, \text{ or } 33)$
     $= \frac{6}{36}$
     $= \frac{1}{6}$
  g $P(\text{multiple of 4 and 6})$
     $= P(\text{multiple of 12})$
     $= P(12, 24, 36)$
     $= \frac{3}{36}$
     $= \frac{1}{12}$
  h $P(\text{multiple of 4 or 6})$
     $= P(4, 6, 8, 12, 16, 18, 20, 24, 28, 30, 32, 36)$
     $= \frac{12}{36}$
     $= \frac{1}{3}$

4
  a $P(\text{on Tuesday})$
     $= \frac{1}{7}$
  b $P(\text{on a weekend})$
     $= \frac{2}{7}$
  c $P(\text{in July})$
     $= \dfrac{4 \times 31}{365 \times 3 + 366}$ {over a 4 year period}
     $= \frac{124}{1461}$
  d $P(\text{in January or February})$
     $= \dfrac{4 \times 31 + 3 \times 28 + 1 \times 29}{3 \times 365 + 1 \times 366}$ {over a 4 year period}
     $= \frac{237}{1461} = \frac{79}{487}$

5 Let A denote Antti, K denote Kai and N denote Neda.
  Possible orders are: {AKN, ANK, KAN, KNA, NAK, NKA}
  a $P(\text{A in middle})$
     $= \frac{2}{6}$
     $= \frac{1}{3}$
  b $P(\text{A at left end})$
     $= \frac{2}{6}$
     $= \frac{1}{3}$
  c $P(\text{A at right end})$
     $= \frac{2}{6}$
     $= \frac{1}{3}$
  d $P(\text{K and N are together}) = \frac{4}{6} = \frac{2}{3}$

6 Let G denote 'a girl' and B denote 'a boy'.

  a Possible orders are: {GGG, GGB, GBG, BGG, GBB, BGB, BBG, BBB}

  b   **i**   P(all boys) = P(BBB) = $\frac{1}{8}$ **ii**   P(all girls) = P(GGG) = $\frac{1}{8}$

     iii   P(boy, then girl, then girl)   **iv**   P(2 girls and a boy)
         = P(BGG)   = P(GGB or GBG or BGG)
         = $\frac{1}{8}$ = $\frac{3}{8}$

     v   P(girl is eldest)   **vi**   P(at least one boy)
         = P(GGG or GBG or GBB or GGB)   = $\frac{7}{8}$ {all except GGG}
         = $\frac{4}{8}$ = $\frac{1}{2}$

7   **a**   {ABCD, ABDC, ACBD, ACDB, ADBC, ADCB, BACD, BADC, BCAD, BCDA, BDAC, BDCA, CABD, CADB, CBAD, CBDA, CDAB, CDBA, DABC, DACB, DBAC, DBCA, DCAB, DCBA}

  b **i**   P(A sits on one end) = $\frac{12}{24}$ = $\frac{1}{2}$

     ii   P(B sits on one of the two middle seats) = $\frac{12}{24}$ = $\frac{1}{2}$

     iii   P(A and B are together) = $\frac{12}{24}$ = $\frac{1}{2}$

     iv   P(A, B and C are together) = $\frac{12}{24}$ = $\frac{1}{2}$

EXERCISE 18C.2

1   [grid: 5 cent axis with H, T; 10 cent axis with H, T]

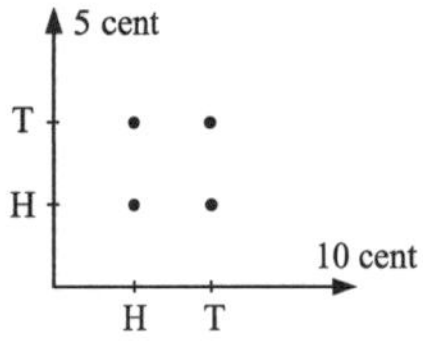

  a   P(2 heads) = $\frac{1}{4}$ **b**   P(2 tails) = $\frac{1}{4}$

  c   P(exactly 1 head)   **d**   P(at least one H)
     = P(HT or TH)   = P(HT or TH or HH)
     = $\frac{2}{4}$ or $\frac{1}{2}$ = $\frac{3}{4}$

2   **a**   [grid: coin (T, H) vs spinner (1–5), shaded region]   **b**   There are $2 \times 5 = 10$ possible outcomes.

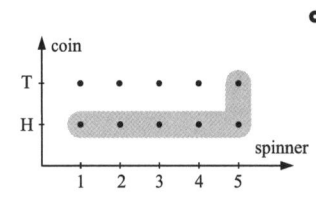

  c **i**   P(T and 3)   **ii**   P(H and even)
         = $\frac{1}{10}$ = P(H2 or H4)
                                                      = $\frac{2}{10}$ or $\frac{1}{5}$

     iii   P(an odd)   **iv**   P(H or 5)
         = P(H1, T1, H3, T3, H5, T5)   = $\frac{6}{10}$
         = $\frac{6}{10}$ = $\frac{3}{5}$ = $\frac{3}{5}$ {shaded}

3   **a**   P(two 3s)   **b**   P(5 and a 6)   **c**   P(5 or a 6)   [grid: die 1 vs die 2, shaded]
     = P((3, 3))   = P((5, 6), (6, 5))   = $\frac{20}{36}$
     = $\frac{1}{36}$ = $\frac{2}{36}$ = $\frac{5}{9}$
                     = $\frac{1}{18}$

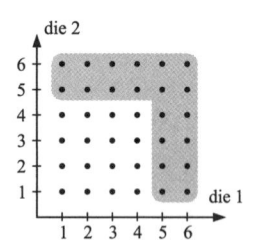

  d   P(at least one 6)   [grid: die 1 vs die 2]   **e**   P(exactly one 6)   [grid: die 1 vs die 2]
     = $\frac{11}{36}$ = $\frac{10}{36}$
                                                  = $\frac{5}{18}$

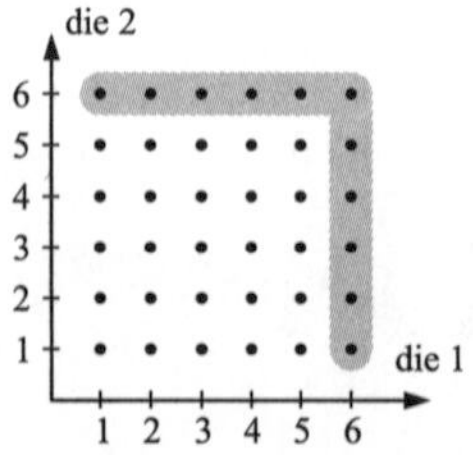

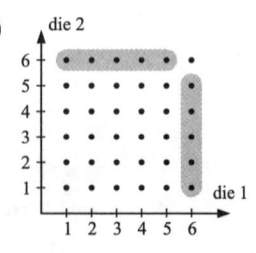

f P(no sixes)

$= \frac{25}{36}$

g P(sum of 7)

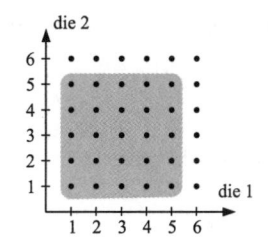

$= \frac{6}{36}$

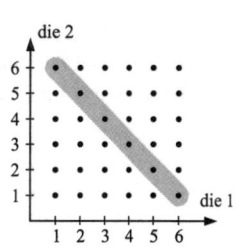

$= \frac{1}{6}$

h P(sum $>$ 8)

$= \frac{10}{36}$

$= \frac{5}{18}$

i P(sum of 7 or 11)

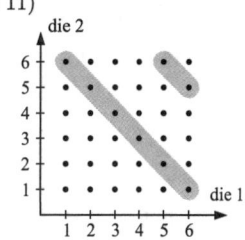

$= \frac{6+2}{36}$

$= \frac{2}{9}$

j P(sum no more than 8)

$= $ P(sum $\leqslant 8$)

$= \frac{26}{36}$

$= \frac{13}{18}$

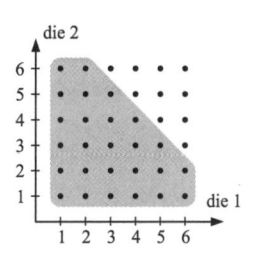

EXERCISE 18D.1

1 a P(rains on any one day)

$= \frac{6}{7}$

b P(rains on 2 successive days)

$= $ P(R and R)

$= \frac{6}{7} \times \frac{6}{7}$

$= \frac{36}{49}$

c P(rains on 3 successive days)

$= $ P(R and R and R)

$= \frac{6}{7} \times \frac{6}{7} \times \frac{6}{7}$ or $\frac{216}{343}$

2 a P(H, then H, then H)

$= $ P(H and H and H)

$= \frac{1}{2} \times \frac{1}{2} \times \frac{1}{2}$

$= \frac{1}{8}$

b P(T, then H, then T)

$= $ P(T and H and T)

$= \frac{1}{2} \times \frac{1}{2} \times \frac{1}{2}$

$= \frac{1}{8}$

3 Let A be the event of photocopier A malfunctioning and B be the event of photocopier B malfunctioning.

  a P(both malfunction)

  $= $ P(A and B)

  $= 0.08 \times 0.12$

  $= 0.0096$

  b P(both work)

  $= $ P(A' and B')

  $= 0.92 \times 0.88$

  $= 0.8096$

4 a P(they will be happy)

$= $ P(B, then G, then B, then G)

$= $ P(B and G and B and G)

$= \frac{1}{2} \times \frac{1}{2} \times \frac{1}{2} \times \frac{1}{2}$

$= \frac{1}{16}$

b P(they will be unhappy)

$= 1 - $ P(they will be happy)

$= 1 - \frac{1}{16}$

$= \frac{15}{16}$

5 Let J be the event of Jiri hitting the target and B be the event of Benita hitting the target.

a P(both hit)
$= P(JB)$
$= 0.7 \times 0.8$
$= 0.56$

b P(both miss)
$= P(J'B')$
$= 0.3 \times 0.2$
$= 0.06$

c P(J hits and B misses)
$= P(JB')$
$= 0.7 \times 0.2$
$= 0.14$

d P(B hits and J misses)
$= P(BJ')$
$= 0.8 \times 0.3$
$= 0.24$

6 Let H be the event the archer hits the target. $\therefore$ $P(H) = \frac{2}{5}$, $P(H') = \frac{3}{5}$

a P(3 hits)
$= P(HHH)$
$= \frac{2}{5} \times \frac{2}{5} \times \frac{2}{5}$
$= \frac{8}{125}$

b P(2 hits then a miss)
$= P(HHH')$
$= \frac{2}{5} \times \frac{2}{5} \times \frac{3}{5}$
$= \frac{12}{125}$

c P(all misses)
$= P(H'H'H')$
$= \frac{3}{5} \times \frac{3}{5} \times \frac{3}{5}$
$= \frac{27}{125}$

EXERCISE 18D.2

1 a P(all strawberry creams)
$= P(SSS)$
$= \frac{8}{12} \times \frac{7}{11} \times \frac{6}{10}$
$= \frac{14}{55}$

b P(none is a strawberry cream)
$= P(S'S'S')$
$= \frac{4}{12} \times \frac{3}{11} \times \frac{2}{10}$
$= \frac{1}{55}$

2 a P(both red)
$= P(RR)$
$= \frac{7}{10} \times \frac{6}{9}$
$= \frac{7}{15}$

b P(GR)
$= \frac{3}{10} \times \frac{7}{9}$
$= \frac{7}{30}$

c P(a green and a red)
$= P(GR \text{ or } RG)$
$= \frac{3}{10} \times \frac{7}{9} + \frac{7}{10} \times \frac{3}{9}$
$= \frac{7}{15}$

3 a P(wins first prize) $= \frac{3}{100}$

b P(wins 1st and 2nd)
$= P(WW)$
$= \frac{3}{100} \times \frac{2}{99}$
$\approx 0.000\,606$

c P(wins all 3)
$= P(WWW)$
$= \frac{3}{100} \times \frac{2}{99} \times \frac{1}{98}$
$\approx 0.000\,006\,18$

d P(wins none of them)
$= P(W'W'W')$
$= \frac{97}{100} \times \frac{96}{99} \times \frac{95}{98}$
≈ 0.912

4 a P(does not contain captain)
$= P(C'C'C')$
$= \frac{6}{7} \times \frac{5}{6} \times \frac{4}{5}$
$= \frac{4}{7}$

b P(does not contain captain or vice captain)
$= P(OOO)$ $\{O \equiv \text{other}\}$
$= \frac{5}{7} \times \frac{4}{6} \times \frac{3}{5}$
$= \frac{2}{7}$

EXERCISE 18E

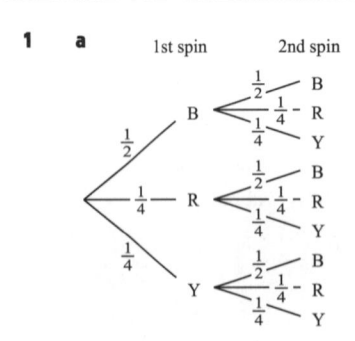

1 a

1st spin   2nd spin

B $\begin{cases} \frac{1}{2} - B \\ \frac{1}{4} - R \\ \frac{1}{4} - Y \end{cases}$

$\frac{1}{2}$

$\frac{1}{4}$ — R $\begin{cases} \frac{1}{2} - B \\ \frac{1}{4} - R \\ \frac{1}{4} - Y \end{cases}$

$\frac{1}{4}$

Y $\begin{cases} \frac{1}{2} - B \\ \frac{1}{4} - R \\ \frac{1}{4} - Y \end{cases}$

b P(both black)
$= P(BB)$
$= \frac{1}{2} \times \frac{1}{2}$
$= \frac{1}{4}$

c P(both yellow)
$= P(YY)$
$= \frac{1}{4} \times \frac{1}{4}$
$= \frac{1}{16}$

d P(both different)
= P(BR or BY or RB or RY or YB or YR)
= $\frac{1}{2} \times \frac{1}{4} + \frac{1}{2} \times \frac{1}{4} + \frac{1}{4} \times \frac{1}{2} + \frac{1}{4} \times \frac{1}{4}$
$\quad + \frac{1}{4} \times \frac{1}{2} + \frac{1}{4} \times \frac{1}{4}$
= $\frac{4}{8} + \frac{2}{16}$
= $\frac{5}{8}$

e P(B appears on either spin)
= P(BB or BR or BY or RB or YB)
= $\frac{1}{2} \times \frac{1}{2} + \frac{1}{2} \times \frac{1}{4} + \frac{1}{2} \times \frac{1}{4} + \frac{1}{4} \times \frac{1}{2}$
$\quad + \frac{1}{4} \times \frac{1}{2}$
= $4(\frac{1}{8}) + \frac{1}{4}$
= $\frac{3}{4}$

2

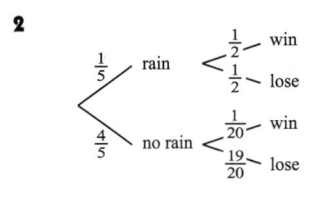

P(Mudlark wins)
= P(rain and win or no rain and win)
= $\frac{1}{5} \times \frac{1}{2} + \frac{4}{5} \times \frac{1}{20}$
= $\frac{1}{10} + \frac{4}{100}$
= $\frac{14}{100}$
= $\frac{7}{50}$

3 P(next is spoiled) = P(from A and spoiled or from B and spoiled)
= $0.4 \times 0.05 + 0.6 \times 0.02$
= $0.020 + 0.012$
= 0.032 (3.2%)

4

P(red)
= P(A and red or B and red)
= $\frac{1}{2} \times \frac{3}{5} + \frac{1}{2} \times \frac{1}{4}$
= $\frac{3}{10} + \frac{1}{8}$
= $\frac{17}{40}$

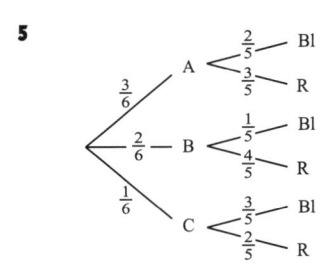

5

a P(blue) = P(A and Bl or B and Bl or C and Bl)
= $\frac{3}{6} \times \frac{2}{5} + \frac{2}{6} \times \frac{1}{5} + \frac{1}{6} \times \frac{3}{5}$
= $\frac{11}{30}$

b P(red) = 1 − P(blue)
= $1 - \frac{11}{30}$
= $\frac{19}{30}$

EXERCISE 18F

1

a P(different colours)
= P(PG or GP)
= $\frac{2}{7} \times \frac{5}{7} + \frac{5}{7} \times \frac{2}{7}$
= $\frac{20}{49}$

b P(different colours)
= P(PG or GP)
= $\frac{2}{7} \times \frac{5}{6} + \frac{5}{7} \times \frac{2}{6}$
= $\frac{20}{42}$ or $\frac{10}{21}$

2 **a** P(both odd)
= P(odd and odd)
= $\frac{3}{5} \times \frac{2}{4}$
= $\frac{3}{10}$

b P(both even)
= P(even and even)
= $\frac{2}{5} \times \frac{1}{4}$
= $\frac{1}{10}$

c P(one odd and other even)
= 1 − P(both odd) − P(both even)
= $1 - \frac{3}{10} - \frac{1}{10}$
= $\frac{6}{10}$
= $\frac{3}{5}$

3

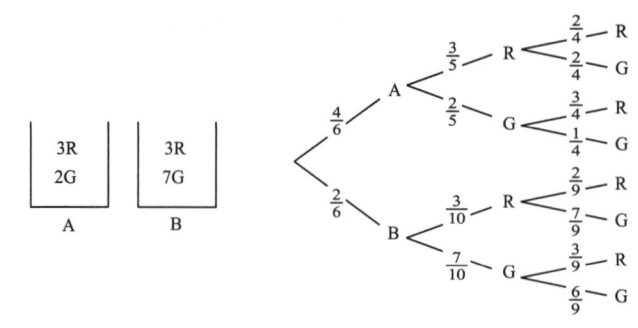

a P(both green)
= P(AGG or BGG)
= $\frac{4}{6} \times \frac{2}{5} \times \frac{1}{4} + \frac{2}{6} \times \frac{7}{10} \times \frac{6}{9}$
= $\frac{1}{15} + \frac{7}{45}$
= $\frac{10}{45}$
= $\frac{2}{9}$

b P(different in colour)
= $1 - $ P(both green) $-$ P(both red)
= $1 - \frac{2}{9} - $ P(ARR or BRR)
= $\frac{7}{9} - (\frac{4}{6} \times \frac{3}{5} \times \frac{2}{4} + \frac{2}{6} \times \frac{3}{10} \times \frac{2}{9})$
= $\frac{7}{9} - (\frac{1}{5} + \frac{1}{45})$
= $\frac{5}{9}$

4

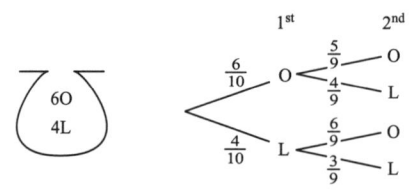

a P(both O)
= $\frac{6}{10} \times \frac{5}{9}$
= $\frac{1}{3}$

b P(both L)
= $\frac{4}{10} \times \frac{3}{9}$
= $\frac{2}{15}$

c P(OL)
= $\frac{6}{10} \times \frac{4}{9}$
= $\frac{4}{15}$

d P(LO)
= $\frac{4}{10} \times \frac{6}{9}$
= $\frac{4}{15}$

$\frac{1}{3} + \frac{2}{15} + \frac{4}{15} + \frac{4}{15}$
= $\frac{5}{15} + \frac{2}{15} + \frac{4}{15} + \frac{4}{15}$
= $\frac{15}{15}$ which is 1

The answer must be 1 as the four categories **a, b, c, d** are all the possibilities that could occur.

5

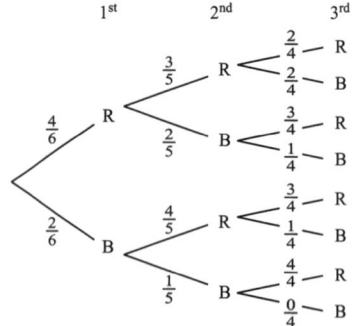

a P(all red)
= P(RRR)
= $\frac{4}{6} \times \frac{3}{5} \times \frac{2}{4}$
= $\frac{1}{5}$

b P(only two are red)
= P(RRB or RBR or BRR)
= $\frac{4}{6} \times \frac{3}{5} \times \frac{2}{4} + \frac{4}{6} \times \frac{2}{5} \times \frac{3}{4} + \frac{2}{6} \times \frac{4}{5} \times \frac{3}{4}$
= $3 \times (\frac{24}{6 \times 5 \times 4})$
= $\frac{3}{5}$

c P(at least two are red)
= P(all red or only two are red)
= $\frac{1}{5} + \frac{3}{5}$ {from **a** and **b**}
= $\frac{4}{5}$

6

P(marble from B is W)
= P(RW or WW)   {paths ticked}
= $\frac{3}{5} \times \frac{3}{9} + \frac{2}{5} \times \frac{5}{9}$
= $\frac{19}{45}$

7

a P(wins both)
= P(WW)
= $\frac{2}{100} \times \frac{1}{99}$
≈ 0.000 202

b P(wins neither)
= P(LL)
= $\frac{98}{100} \times \frac{97}{99}$
≈ 0.960

c P(wins at least one prize) = 1 − P(wins neither)
= $1 - \frac{98}{100} \times \frac{97}{99}$
≈ 0.0398

8

P(one white and one black)
= P(WB or BW)   {paths ticked}
= $\frac{7}{12} \times \frac{2}{11} + \frac{2}{12} \times \frac{7}{11}$
= $\frac{7}{33}$

9 There are $(n+7)$ markers in total.

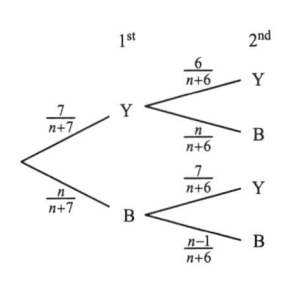

P(YY) = $\frac{3}{13}$

∴ $\frac{7}{n+7} \times \frac{6}{n+6} = \frac{3}{13}$

∴ $\frac{42}{n^2 + 13n + 42} = \frac{3}{13}$

∴ $546 = 3n^2 + 39n + 126$

∴ $3(n^2 + 13n - 140) = 0$

∴ $3(n-7)(n+20) = 0$

∴ $n = 7$ $\{n \geqslant 0\}$

∴ there are 7 blue markers in the bag.

EXERCISE 18G

1 a $(p+q)^4 = p^4 + 4p^3q + 6p^2q^2 + 4pq^3 + q^4$

  b P(3 heads) = $4p^3q$
   = $4 \left(\frac{1}{2}\right)^3 \left(\frac{1}{2}\right)$ {as $p = q = \frac{1}{2}$}
   = $\frac{1}{4}$

2 a $(p+q)^5 = p^5 + 5p^4q + 10p^3q^2 + 10p^2q^3 + 5pq^4 + q^5$

b **i** P(4H and 1T)
$= 5p^4q$
$= 5\left(\frac{1}{2}\right)^4\left(\frac{1}{2}\right)$
$= \frac{5}{32}$

ii P(2H and 3T)
$= 10p^2q^3$
$= 10\left(\frac{1}{2}\right)^2\left(\frac{1}{2}\right)^3$
$= \frac{10}{32}$
$= \frac{5}{16}$

iii P(HHHHT)
$= \left(\frac{1}{2}\right)^4 \times \frac{1}{2}$
$= \frac{1}{32}$

3 a $\left(\frac{2}{3} + \frac{1}{3}\right)^4 = \left(\frac{2}{3}\right)^4 + 4\left(\frac{2}{3}\right)^3\left(\frac{1}{3}\right) + 6\left(\frac{2}{3}\right)^2\left(\frac{1}{3}\right)^2 + 4\left(\frac{2}{3}\right)\left(\frac{1}{3}\right)^3 + \left(\frac{1}{3}\right)^4$

b $P(S) = \frac{2}{3}$, $P(S') = \frac{1}{3}$ S' represents a non-strawberry cream (or an almond centre)

i P(all S)
$= \left(\frac{2}{3}\right)^4$
$= \frac{16}{81}$

ii P(two of each)
$= 6\left(\frac{2}{3}\right)^2\left(\frac{1}{3}\right)^2$
$= \frac{8}{27}$

iii P(at least 2 strawberry creams)
$=$ P(all S or 3S, 1T or 2S, 2T)
$= \left(\frac{2}{3}\right)^4 + 4\left(\frac{2}{3}\right)^3\left(\frac{1}{3}\right) + 6\left(\frac{2}{3}\right)^2\left(\frac{1}{3}\right)^2$
$= \frac{16}{81} + \frac{32}{81} + \frac{24}{81}$
$= \frac{72}{81}$
$= \frac{8}{9}$

4 a $\left(\frac{3}{4} + \frac{1}{4}\right)^5 = \left(\frac{3}{4}\right)^5 + 5\left(\frac{3}{4}\right)^4\left(\frac{1}{4}\right)^1 + 10\left(\frac{3}{4}\right)^3\left(\frac{1}{4}\right)^2 + 10\left(\frac{3}{4}\right)^2\left(\frac{1}{4}\right)^3 + 5\left(\frac{3}{4}\right)\left(\frac{1}{4}\right)^4 + \left(\frac{1}{4}\right)^5$

b P(normal kiwi) $= \frac{3}{4}$, P(flat back) $= \frac{1}{4}$

i P(2 'flat backs')
$=$ P(3F's and 2Fs)
$= 10 \times \left(\frac{3}{4}\right)^3\left(\frac{1}{4}\right)^2$
$= \frac{135}{512}$

ii P(at least 3 are 'flat backs')
$=$ P(2F', 3F or 1F', 4F or 5F)
$= 10\left(\frac{3}{4}\right)^2\left(\frac{1}{4}\right)^3 + 5\left(\frac{3}{4}\right)\left(\frac{1}{4}\right)^4 + \left(\frac{1}{4}\right)^5$
$= \frac{53}{512}$ on simplifying

iii P(at most 3 normal kiwis) $= 1 -$ P(4 or 5 normal kiwis)
$= 1 -$ P(4F', 1F or 5F')
$= 1 - \left(5\left(\frac{3}{4}\right)^4\left(\frac{1}{4}\right) + \left(\frac{3}{4}\right)^5\right)$
$= \frac{47}{128}$

5 Let X be the event "Huy hits the target"

a Using the binomial expansion,
$P(X = 2) = 6\left(\frac{4}{5}\right)^2\left(\frac{1}{5}\right)^2 \approx 0.154$

b $P(X \geqslant 2)$
$= 1 - P(X \leqslant 1)$
$\approx 1 - \left(4\left(\frac{4}{5}\right)\left(\frac{1}{5}\right)^3 + \left(\frac{1}{5}\right)^4\right)$
≈ 0.973

6 Let X be the event "a light bulb is defective"

a $P(X = 2) \approx 0.0305$ {using technology}

b $P(X \geqslant 1)$
$= 1 - P(X = 0)$
$\approx 1 - 0.735$
≈ 0.265

7 If X is the event "Raj answers a question correctly", then X is binomial. There are $n = 10$ independent trials with probability $p = \frac{1}{5}$ of a corrrect answer for each.

P(Raj passes) $= P(X \geqslant 7)$
$= 1 - P(X \leqslant 6)$
$= 1 - 0.999\,136$
$\approx 0.000\,864$ {or about 9 in 10 000}

8 P(M wins a game against J) $= \frac{2}{3}$ $\therefore$ P(M wins) $= \frac{2}{3}$ P(J wins) $= \frac{1}{3}$
P(J wins a set 6 games to 4) $=$ P($\underbrace{\text{J wins 5 of the first 9 games}}$ **and** J wins the 10th game)

this is binomial with $n = 9$ trials of probability $p = \frac{1}{3}$

$\approx 0.1024 \times \frac{1}{3}$
≈ 0.0341

9 If there are n dice thrown, $P(\text{no sixes}) = \left(\frac{5}{6}\right)^n$

$\therefore \quad P(\text{at least 1 six}) = 1 - \left(\frac{5}{6}\right)^n$

$\therefore \quad$ need to find the smallest integer n such that $\quad 1 - \left(\frac{5}{6}\right)^n \geqslant 0.5$

$$\therefore \quad \left(\frac{5}{6}\right)^n \leqslant 0.5$$

$$\therefore \quad n \log\left(\frac{5}{6}\right) \leqslant \log(0.5)$$

$$\therefore \quad n \geqslant \frac{\log(0.5)}{\log\left(\frac{5}{6}\right)} \qquad \{\log\left(\frac{5}{6}\right) < 0\}$$

$$\therefore \quad n \geqslant 3.80$$

$\therefore \quad$ at least 4 dice are needed.

EXERCISE 18H.1

1 a $A = \{1, 2, 3, 6\}, \quad B = \{2, 4, 6, 8, 10\}$
 b **i** $n(A) = 4$ **ii** $A \cup B = \{1, 2, 3, 4, 6, 8, 10\}$ **iii** $A \cap B = \{2, 6\}$

2 a **b** 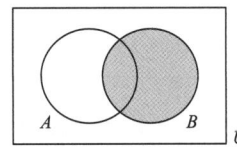 **c** 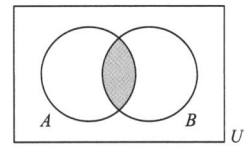 **d** 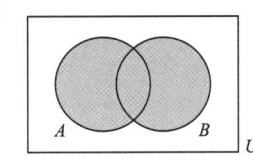 **e** 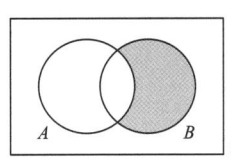 **f**

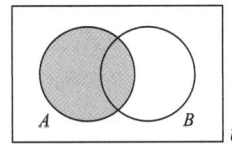

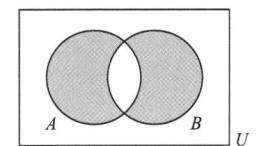

3 a Total number in the class $= 3 + 4 + 5 + 17 = 29$
 b Number who study both $= 17$ {the intersection}
 c Number who study at least one $= 5 + 17 + 4 = 26$ {the union}
 d Number who study only Chemistry $= 5$

4 a Total number in the survey $= 37 + 9 + 15 + 4 = 65$
 b Number who liked both $= 9$ {the intersection}
 c Number who liked neither $= 4$
 d Number who liked exactly one $= 37 + 15 = 52$

5 T represents those playing tennis
N represents those playing netball

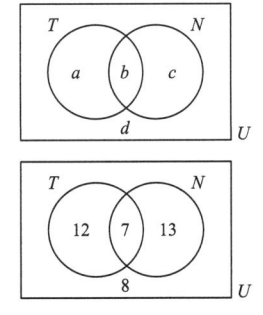

$$\therefore \quad \begin{cases} a + b + c + d = 40 \\ a + b = 19 \\ b + c = 20 \\ d = 8 \end{cases}$$

So, $a + b + c = 32$

$\therefore \quad 19 + c = 32 \quad$ and $\quad a + 20 = 32$

$\therefore \quad c = 13 \quad$ and $\quad a = 12$

Hence, $12 + b + 13 + 8 = 40$

$\therefore \quad b = 7$

a P(plays tennis)
$= \dfrac{12+7}{40}$
$= \dfrac{19}{40}$

b P(does not play netball)
$= \dfrac{12+8}{40}$
$= \dfrac{1}{2}$

c P(plays at least one)
$= \dfrac{12+7+13}{40}$
$= \dfrac{32}{40}$
$= \dfrac{4}{5}$

d P(plays one and only one)
$= \dfrac{12+13}{40}$
$= \dfrac{25}{40}$
$= \dfrac{5}{8}$

e P(plays netball, but not tennis) $= \dfrac{13}{40}$

f P(plays tennis given plays netball)
$= \dfrac{7}{7+13}$
$= \dfrac{7}{20}$

6

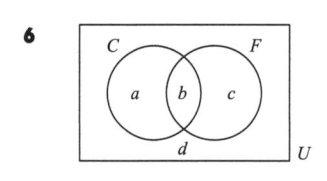

C represents men who gave chocolates.
F represents men who gave flowers.

$\therefore \begin{cases} a+b+c+d = 50 \\ a+b = 31 \\ b+c = 12 \\ b = 5 \end{cases}$

Thus $c = 7$, $a = 26$ and $26 + 5 + 7 + d = 50 \quad \therefore \quad d = 12$

a P(C or F)
$= \dfrac{26+5+7}{50}$
$= \dfrac{38}{50}$ or $\dfrac{19}{25}$

b P(C but not F)
$= \dfrac{26}{50}$
$= \dfrac{13}{25}$

c P(neither C nor F)
$= \dfrac{12}{50}$
$= \dfrac{6}{25}$

d P(F given that C')
$= \dfrac{7}{7+12}$
$= \dfrac{7}{19}$

7

Me represents children who had measles.
Mu represents children who had mumps.

$\therefore \begin{cases} a+b+c+d = 30 \\ a+b = 24 \\ b = 12 \\ a+b+c = 26 \end{cases}$

$\therefore \quad 26 + d = 30 \quad \therefore \quad d = 4$
$24 + c = 26 \quad \therefore \quad c = 2$
and $a + 12 + 2 = 26 \quad \therefore \quad a = 12$

a P(Mu)
$= \dfrac{14}{30}$
$= \dfrac{7}{15}$

b P(Mu, but not Me)
$= \dfrac{2}{30}$
$= \dfrac{1}{15}$

c P(neither Mu nor Me)
$= \dfrac{4}{30}$
$= \dfrac{2}{15}$

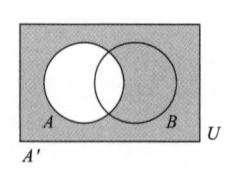

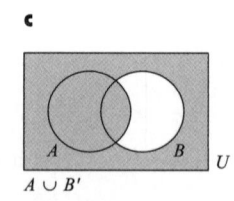

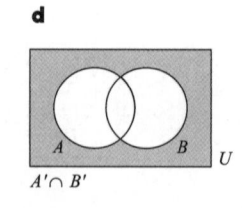

d P(Me given Mu)
$= \dfrac{12}{14}$
$= \dfrac{6}{7}$

8 **a** A' **b** $A' \cap B$ **c** $A \cup B'$ **d** $A' \cap B'$

9 a, b, c, d, e, f

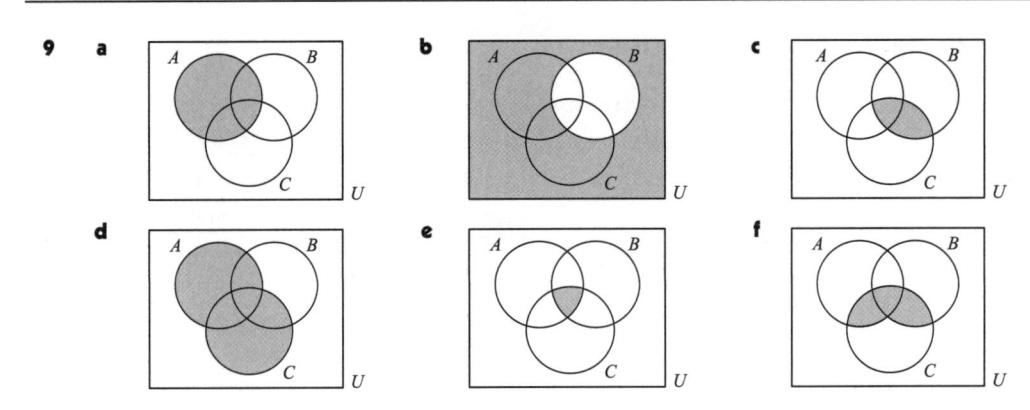

EXERCISE 18H.2

1 **a**

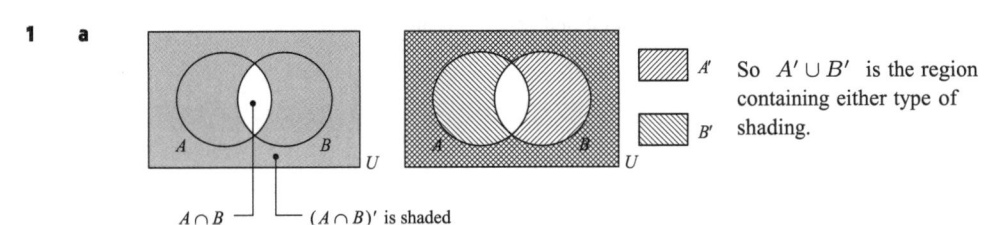

$A \cap B$ and $(A \cap B)'$ is shaded

So $A' \cup B'$ is the region containing either type of shading.

Thus, as the regions are the same, $(A \cap B)' = A' \cup B'$ is verified.

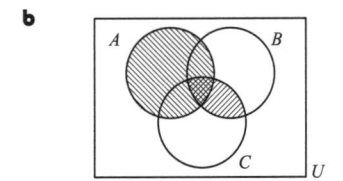

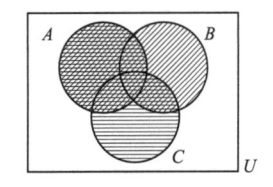

b

$A \cup (B \cap C)$ consists of the shaded region

$(A \cup B) \cap (A \cup C)$ consists of the 'double shaded' region.

As the two regions are identical
$A \cup (B \cap C) = (A \cup B) \cap (A \cup C)$ is verified.

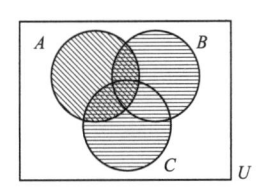

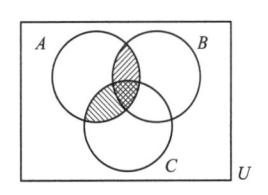

c

$A \cap (B \cup C)$ consists of the double shaded region

$(A \cap B) \cup (A \cap C)$ consists of the region shaded. (all forms ▨ and ▩)

As the regions are identical, $A \cap (B \cup C) = (A \cap B) \cup (A \cap C)$ is verified.

2 **a** $A = \{7, 14, 21, 28, 35, \ldots, 98\}$
$B = \{5, 10, 15, 20, 25, \ldots, 95\}$

i as $98 = 7 \times 14$, $n(A) = 14$

ii as $95 = 5 \times 19$, $n(B) = 19$

iii $A \cap B = \{35, 70\}$ $\therefore$ $n(A \cap B) = 2$

iv $A \cup B = \{5, 7, 10, 14, 15, 20, 21, 25, 28, 30, 35, 40, 42, 45, 49, 50, 55, 56, 60, 63, 65, 70,$
$75, 77, 80, 84, 85, 90, 91, 95, 98\}$ $\therefore$ $n(A \cup B) = 31$

b $n(A) + n(B) - n(A \cap B) = 14 + 19 - 2$
$ = 31$
$ = n(A \cup B)$ ✓

3 a i $P(B)$
$= \dfrac{n(B)}{n(U)}$
$= \dfrac{b+c}{a+b+c+d}$

ii $P(A \text{ and } B)$
$= \dfrac{n(A \cap B)}{n(U)}$
$= \dfrac{b}{a+b+c+d}$

iii $P(A \text{ or } B)$
$= \dfrac{n(A \cup B)}{n(U)}$
$= \dfrac{a+b+c}{a+b+c+d}$

iv $P(A) + P(B) - P(A \text{ and } B) = \dfrac{a+b+b+c-b}{a+b+c+d}$
$\phantom{P(A) + P(B) - P(A \text{ and } B)} = \dfrac{a+b+c}{a+b+c+d}$

b $P(A \text{ or } B) = P(A) + P(B) - P(A \text{ and } B)$ {using **iii** and **iv**}

EXERCISE 18I

1 a

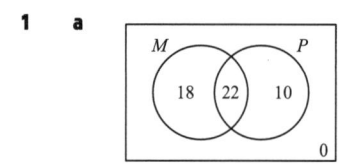

Venn diagram: M and P overlapping. M only: 18, intersection: 22, P only: 10, outside: 0.

So 22 study both.

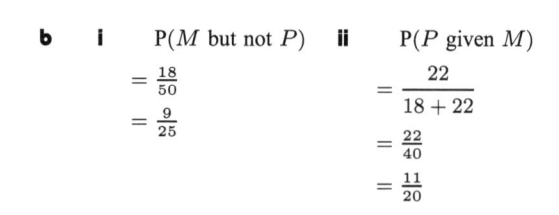

b i $P(M \text{ but not } P)$
$= \dfrac{18}{50}$
$= \dfrac{9}{25}$

ii $P(P \text{ given } M)$
$= \dfrac{22}{18+22}$
$= \dfrac{22}{40}$
$= \dfrac{11}{20}$

2

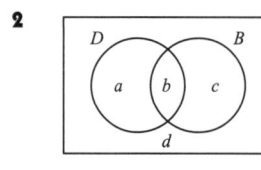

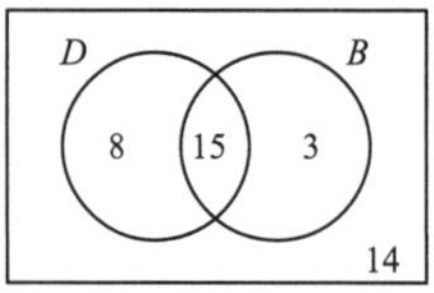

Venn diagram with regions a, b, c, d for D and B.

Second diagram: 8, 15, 3, 14.

$a + b + c + d = 40$ .... (1)
$a + b = 23$ .... (2)
$b + c = 18$ .... (3)
$a + b + c = 26$ .... (4)

∴ $d = 14$ {using (1) and (4)}
$23 + c = 26$ and $a + 18 = 26$
∴ $c = 3$ and $a = 8$
Thus $b = 18 - c = 15$

a $P(D \text{ and } B)$
$= \dfrac{15}{40}$
$= \dfrac{3}{8}$

b $P(\text{neither } D \text{ nor } B)$
$= \dfrac{14}{40}$
$= \dfrac{7}{20}$

c $P(D, \text{ but not } B)$
$= \dfrac{8}{40}$
$= \dfrac{1}{5}$

d $P(B \text{ given } D)$
$= \dfrac{15}{23}$

3

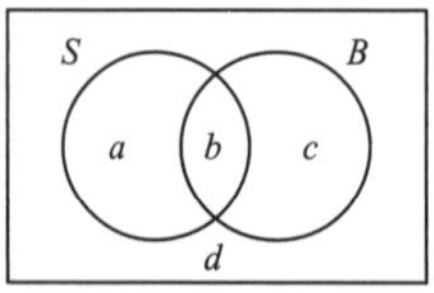

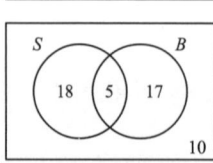

Venn diagram with regions a, b, c, d for S and B.

Second diagram: 18, 5, 17, 10.

$a + b + c + d = 50$
$a + b = 23$
$b + c = 22$
$b = 5$

∴ $c = 17$, $a = 18$
and $18 + 5 + 17 + d = 50$
∴ $d = 10$

a $P(\text{not } B)$
$= P(B')$
$= \dfrac{28}{50}$
$= \dfrac{14}{25}$

b $P(B \text{ or } S)$
$= \dfrac{18+5+17}{50}$
$= \dfrac{40}{50}$
$= \dfrac{4}{5}$

c P(neither B nor S)
$= \frac{10}{50}$
$= \frac{1}{5}$

d P(B, given S)
$= \frac{5}{18+5}$
$= \frac{5}{23}$

e P(S, given B')
$= \frac{18}{18+10}$
$= \frac{18}{28}$
$= \frac{9}{14}$

4

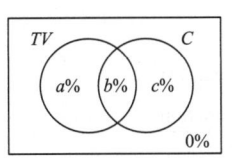

[Venn diagram: TV and C with regions $a\%$, $b\%$, $c\%$, and 0% outside]

$a + b + c = 100$
$a + b = 90$ $\therefore$ $c = 10$ and $a = 40$
$b + c = 60$ $\therefore$ $b = 50$

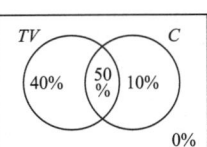

[Venn diagram: TV=40%, intersection=50%, C=10%, outside 0%]

P(TV, given C) $= \dfrac{50}{50+10} = \frac{5}{6}$ or $\approx 83.3\%$

5

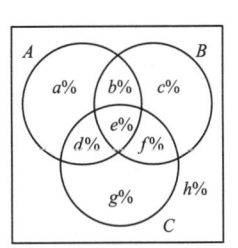

[Venn diagram with three circles A, B, C showing regions $a\%$, $b\%$, $c\%$, $d\%$, $e\%$, $f\%$, $g\%$, $h\%$]

$a + b + c + d + e + f + g + h = 100$
$a + b + d + e = 20$
$b + c + e + f = 16$
$d + e + f + g = 14$
$b + e = 8$
$d + e = 5$
$e + f = 4$
$e = 2$

$\therefore\ e = 2,\ f = 2,\ d = 3,\ b = 6,$ $\begin{cases} a + 6 + 3 + 2 = 20 \\ 6 + c + 2 + 2 = 16 \\ 3 + 2 + 2 + g = 14 \end{cases}$ $\therefore\ \begin{cases} a = 9 \\ c = 6 \\ g = 7 \end{cases}$

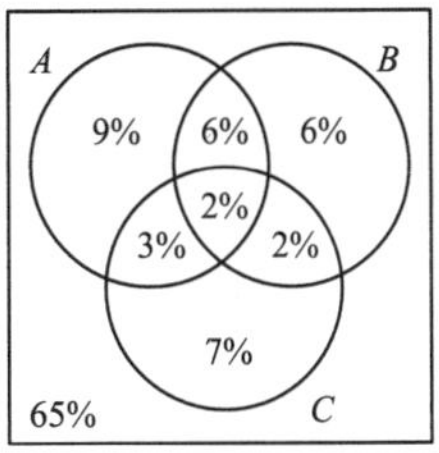

[Venn diagram with regions: A=9%, 6%, B=6%, 2%, 3%, 2%, 7%, outside 65%]

a P(none)
$= \frac{65}{100}$
$= \frac{13}{20}$

b P(at least one)
$= 1 - $ P(none)
$= 1 - \frac{13}{20}$
$= \frac{7}{20}$

c P(exactly one)
$= \dfrac{9+6+7}{100}$
$= \frac{22}{100}$
$= \frac{11}{50}$

d P(A or B)
$= \dfrac{9+6+6+3+2+2}{100}$
$= \frac{28}{100}$
$= \frac{7}{25}$

e P(A, given at least one)
$= \dfrac{9+6+2+3}{35}$
$= \frac{20}{35}$
$= \frac{4}{7}$

f P(C, given A or B or both)
$= \dfrac{3+2+2}{9+6+6+3+2+2}$
$= \frac{7}{28}$
$= \frac{1}{4}$

6

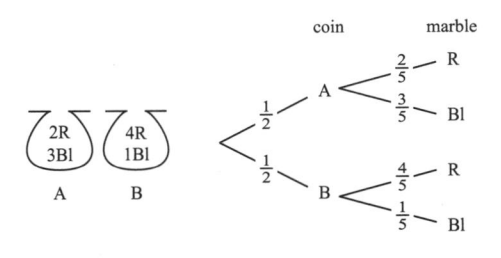

[Diagram: Bag A with 2R 3Bl, Bag B with 4R 1Bl]

[Tree diagram:
coin — marble
$\frac{1}{2}$ A → $\frac{2}{5}$ R, $\frac{3}{5}$ Bl
$\frac{1}{2}$ B → $\frac{4}{5}$ R, $\frac{1}{5}$ Bl]

a P(R) $= \frac{1}{2} \times \frac{2}{5} + \frac{1}{2} \times \frac{4}{5}$
$= \frac{3}{5}$

b P(B | R) $= \dfrac{P(B \cap R)}{P(R)}$
$= \dfrac{\frac{1}{2} \times \frac{4}{5}}{\frac{3}{5}}$
$= \frac{2}{3}$

7

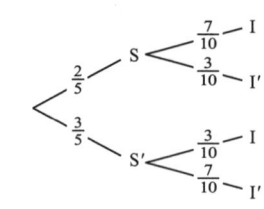

Tree diagram:
- S (2/5): I (7/10), I' (3/10)
- S' (3/5): I (3/10), I' (7/10)

a $P(I) = \frac{2}{5} \times \frac{7}{10} + \frac{3}{5} \times \frac{3}{10}$
$= \frac{23}{50}$ (or 0.46)

b $P(S \mid I) = \frac{P(S \cap I)}{P(I)}$
$= \frac{\frac{2}{5} \times \frac{7}{10}}{\frac{23}{50}}$
$= \frac{14}{23}$

8

Tree diagram:
- M (1/10): M (7/100), M' (93/100)
- M' (9/10): M (7/100), M' (93/100)

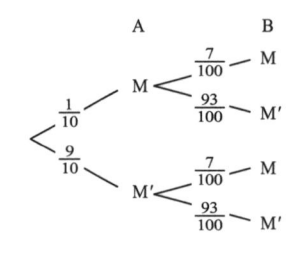

P(B | at least one malfunctions)
$= \frac{P(B \cap \text{at least one malfunctions})}{P(\text{at least one malfunctions})}$
$= \frac{\frac{1}{10} \times \frac{7}{100} + \frac{9}{10} \times \frac{7}{100}}{\frac{1}{10} \times \frac{7}{100} + \frac{1}{10} \times \frac{93}{100} + \frac{9}{10} \times \frac{7}{100}}$
$= \frac{7+63}{7+93+63}$
$= \frac{70}{163}$

9 $P(B) = 0.5$, $P(G) = 0.6$, $P(G \mid B) = 0.9$, where B is "the boy eats his lunch" and G is "the girl eats her lunch"

a P(both eat lunch)
$= P(B \cap G)$
$= P(G \mid B) \times P(B)$ $\quad \left\{ \text{as } P(G \mid B) = \frac{P(G \cap B)}{P(B)} \right\}$
$= 0.9 \times 0.5$
$= 0.45$

b $P(B \mid G)$
$= \frac{P(B \cap G)}{P(G)}$
$= \frac{0.45}{0.6}$
$= 0.75$

c P(at least one eats lunch)
$= P(B \cup G)$
$= P(B) + P(G) - P(B \cap G)$
$= 0.5 + 0.6 - 0.45$
$= 0.65$

10

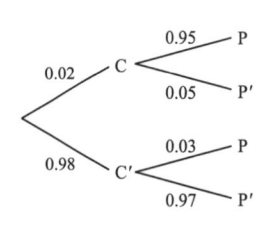

Tree diagram:
- C (0.02): P (0.95), P' (0.05)
- C' (0.98): P (0.03), P' (0.97)

a $P(P)$
$= 0.02 \times 0.95 + 0.98 \times 0.03$
$= 0.0484$

b $P(C \mid P)$
$= \frac{P(C \cap P)}{P(P)}$
$= \frac{0.02 \times 0.95}{0.0484}$
≈ 0.393

11 The coins are H, H T, T and H, T.
Any one of these 6 faces could be seen uppermost, $\therefore$ P(falls H) $= \frac{3}{6} = \frac{1}{2}$

Now P(HH coin | falls H) $= \frac{P(\text{HH coin} \cap \text{falls H})}{P(\text{falls H})}$
$= \frac{P(\text{HH})}{P(\text{falls H})}$
$= \frac{\frac{1}{3}}{\frac{1}{2}}$
$= \frac{2}{3}$

12 There are 7 teams above Tottenham and 12 teams below Tottenham.

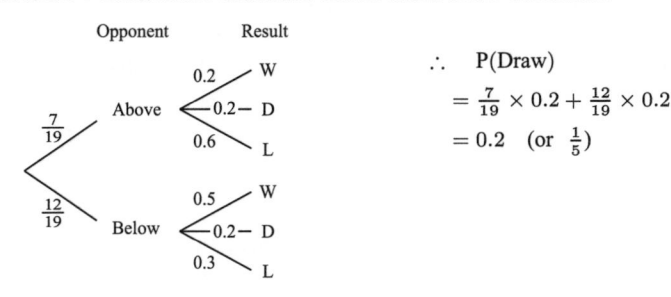

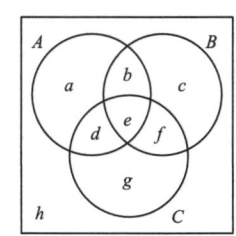

$\therefore$ P(Draw)
$= \frac{7}{19} \times 0.2 + \frac{12}{19} \times 0.2$
$= 0.2$ (or $\frac{1}{5}$)

13 $P(A \cup B \cup C) = \dfrac{a+b+c+d+e+f+g}{a+b+c+d+e+f+g+h}$

Now $P(A) + P(B) + P(C) - P(A \cap B) - P(A \cap C) - P(B \cap C) + P(A \cap B \cap C)$
$= \dfrac{(a+b+d+e) + (b+c+e+f) + (d+e+f+g) - (b+e) - (d+e) - (e+f) + e}{a+b+c+d+e+f+g+h}$
$= \dfrac{a+b+c+d+e+f+g}{a+b+c+d+e+f+g+h}$

$\therefore$ $P(A \cup B \cup C) = P(A) + P(B) + P(C) - P(A \cap B) - P(A \cap C) - P(B \cap C) + P(A \cap B \cap C)$

EXERCISE 18J

1 $P(R \cap S)$
$= P(R) + P(S) - P(R \cup S)$
$= 0.4 + 0.5 - 0.7$
$= 0.2$

Also, $P(R) \times P(S)$
$= 0.4 \times 0.5$
$= 0.2$

So, $P(R \cap S) = P(R) \times P(S)$ and hence R and S are independent events.

2 **a** $P(A \cap B)$
$= P(A) + P(B) - P(A \cup B)$
$= \frac{2}{5} + \frac{1}{3} - \frac{1}{2}$
$= \frac{7}{30}$

b $P(B \mid A)$
$= \dfrac{P(B \cap A)}{P(A)}$
$= \dfrac{\frac{7}{30}}{\frac{2}{5}}$
$= \frac{7}{12}$

c $P(A \mid B)$
$= \dfrac{P(A \cap B)}{P(B)}$
$= \dfrac{\frac{7}{30}}{\frac{1}{3}}$
$= \frac{7}{10}$

A and B are not independent as $P(A \mid B) \ne P(A)$.

3 **a** As X and Y are independent
$P(X \cap Y) = P(X) \times P(Y)$
$= 0.5 \times 0.7$
$= 0.35$
$\therefore$ P(both X and Y) $= 0.35$

b P(X or Y)
$= P(X \cup Y)$
$= P(X) + P(Y) - P(X \cap Y)$
$= 0.5 + 0.7 - 0.35$
$= 0.85$

d P(X but not Y)
$= 0.15$

c P(neither X nor Y)
$= 0.15$

e $P(X \mid Y) = \dfrac{P(X \cap Y)}{P(Y)} = \dfrac{0.35}{0.70} = \frac{1}{2}$

4 P(at least one solves it)
$= 1 - $ P(no-one solves it)
$= 1 - $ P(A' and B' and C')
$= 1 - \frac{2}{5} \times \frac{1}{3} \times \frac{1}{2}$
$= 1 - \frac{1}{15}$
$= \frac{14}{15}$

5 a P(at least one 6)
$= 1 - $ P(no 6s)
$= 1 - $ P($6'$ and $6'$ and $6'$)
$= 1 - \frac{5}{6} \times \frac{5}{6} \times \frac{5}{6}$
$= 1 - \frac{125}{216}$
$= \frac{91}{216}$

b P(at least one 6 in n throws)
$= 1 - (\frac{5}{6})^n$
So we want $1 - (\frac{5}{6})^n > 0.99$
$\therefore \quad -(\frac{5}{6})^n > -0.01$
$\therefore \quad (\frac{5}{6})^n < 0.01$
$\therefore \quad n \log(\frac{5}{6}) < \log(0.01)$
$\therefore \quad n > \frac{\log(0.01)}{\log(\frac{5}{6})} \quad \{$as $\log(\frac{5}{6}) < 0\}$
$\therefore \quad n > 25.2585$
$\therefore \quad n = 26$

6 A and B are independent, so $\quad P(A \cap B) = P(A)\,P(B) \quad$ ...... (1)
Now $\quad P(A' \cap B')$
$= 1 - P(A \cup B)$
$= 1 - [P(A) + P(B) - P(A \cap B)]$
$= 1 - P(A) - P(B) + P(A \cap B)$
$= 1 - P(A) - P(B) + P(A)\,P(B)$
$= [1 - P(A)][1 - P(B)]$
$= P(A')\,P(B') \qquad \therefore \quad A'$ and B' are also independent.

7 a i P(Karl wins on his third turn) $=$ P(4 non-aces, then an ace)
$= \left(\frac{12}{13}\right)^4 \times \left(\frac{1}{13}\right) \approx 0.0558$

ii P(Karl wins on his nth turn) $=$ P($2(n-1)$ non-aces, then an ace)
$= \left(\frac{12}{13}\right)^{2(n-1)} \times \frac{1}{13}$

$\therefore \quad$ P(Karl wins prior to his $(n+1)$th turn)
$=$ P(Karl wins on his 1st or 2nd or 3rd or .... or nth turn)
$= \left(\frac{12}{13}\right)^0 \times \frac{1}{13} + \left(\frac{12}{13}\right)^2 \times \frac{1}{13} + \left(\frac{12}{13}\right)^4 \times \frac{1}{13} + ... + \left(\frac{12}{13}\right)^{2(n-1)} \times \frac{1}{13}$
$= \frac{1}{13}\left(1 + \left(\frac{12}{13}\right)^2 + \left(\frac{12}{13}\right)^4 + ... + \left(\frac{12}{13}\right)^{2(n-1)}\right)$

geometric series with $u_1 = 1$, $r = \left(\frac{12}{13}\right)^2$, "$n$" $= n$

$= \frac{1}{13}\left(\frac{1 - \left(\frac{12}{13}\right)^{2n}}{1 - \left(\frac{12}{13}\right)^2}\right) = \frac{1}{13}\left(\frac{1 - \left(\frac{12}{13}\right)^{2n}}{\frac{25}{169}}\right)$

$= \frac{169}{13 \times 25}\left(1 - \left(\frac{12}{13}\right)^{2n}\right)$
$= \frac{13}{25}\left(1 - \left(\frac{12}{13}\right)^{2n}\right)$

iii As $n \to \infty$, $1 - \left(\frac{12}{13}\right)^{2n} \to 1$

$\therefore \quad \frac{13}{25}\left(1 - \left(\frac{12}{13}\right)^{2n}\right) \to \frac{13}{25}$

$\therefore$ P(Karl wins the game) $= \frac{13}{25}$

b Let X be the number of times Karl wins the game.
Then X is binomial with $n = 7$ trials of probability $p = \frac{13}{25}$.

$\therefore$ P(Karl will win more games than Hanna) $= P(X \geqslant 4)$
$= 1 - P(X \leqslant 3)$
$\approx 1 - 0.456$
≈ 0.544

8

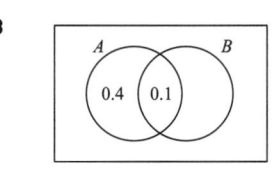

$\therefore \quad P(A) = 0.5$
and $P(A \cap B) = P(A) \times P(B)$ {A and B are independent}
$\therefore \quad 0.1 = 0.5 \times P(B)$
$\therefore \quad P(B) = 0.2$

Now $P(A \cup B') = P(A) + P(B') - P(A \cap B')$
$= 0.5 + 0.8 - 0.4$
$= 0.9$

9 a i $P(C \mid D) = \frac{P(C \cap D)}{P(D)}$, so $P(C \cap D) = P(C \mid D) P(D)$

Similarly, $P(C \cap D') = P(C \mid D') P(D')$

Now $P(C \cap D) + P(C \cap D') = P(C)$

$\therefore \quad P(C \mid D) P(D) + P(C \mid D') P(D') = P(C)$

$\therefore \quad \frac{6}{13} P(D) + \frac{3}{7}[1 - P(D)] = \frac{9}{20}$

$\therefore \quad \frac{6}{13} P(D) + \frac{3}{7} - \frac{3}{7} P(D) = \frac{9}{20}$

$\therefore \quad \frac{3}{91} P(D) = \frac{3}{140}$

$\therefore \quad P(D) = \frac{91}{140}$ or $\frac{13}{20}$

ii $P(C \cap D) = P(C \mid D) P(D) = \frac{6}{13} \times \frac{13}{20} = \frac{3}{10}$

Now $P(C' \cup D') = 1 - P(C \cap D)$
$= 1 - \frac{3}{10} = \frac{7}{10}$

b $P(C \cap D) = \frac{3}{10}$ and $P(C) P(D) = \frac{9}{20} \times \frac{13}{20} = \frac{117}{400}$

$\therefore \quad C$ and D are not independent as $P(C \cap D) \neq P(C) P(D)$

10 The man will step over the cliff in his first four steps if either:
(1) he steps towards the cliff on his first step
(2) he steps away from the cliff on his first step, but towards the cliff on his next two steps.

P(case (1)) $= \frac{2}{5}$

P(case (2)) $= \frac{3}{5} \times \left(\frac{2}{5}\right)^2 = \frac{12}{125}$

$\therefore$ P(the man steps over the cliff in his first four steps) $= \frac{2}{5} + \frac{12}{125} = \frac{62}{125}$

$\therefore$ P(the man does **not** step over the cliff in his first four steps) $= 1 - \frac{62}{125}$
$= \frac{63}{125}$

EXERCISE 18K

1 The total number of different committees is $\binom{11}{4}$.

The number of ways of X and Y being on a committee is $\binom{2}{2} \times \binom{9}{2}$.

$\therefore$ P(X and Y are on the committee) $= \dfrac{\binom{2}{2} \times \binom{9}{2}}{\binom{11}{2}} \approx 0.655$

2 AIDS and SAID are 2 of the 4! different orderings. $\quad\therefore$ P(AIDS or SAID) $= \dfrac{2}{4!} = \dfrac{1}{12}$

3 There are $\binom{12}{7}$ different teams that can be selected.

$\therefore$ P(captain and vice captain are chosen) $= \dfrac{\binom{2}{2} \times \binom{10}{5}}{\binom{12}{7}} \approx 0.318$

4 P(none of the golfers was killed) $= \dfrac{\binom{3}{0} \times \binom{19}{4}}{\binom{22}{4}} \approx 0.530$

5 | 5 | 4 | 3 | 2 | 1 | $\therefore$ there are 5! different possible seating arrangements.

  a | 2 | 3 | 2 | 1 | 1 | There are $2 \times 3!$ seating arrangements if K and J sit at the ends

  $\therefore$ P(K and J sit at the ends) $= \dfrac{2 \times 3!}{5!} = \dfrac{1}{10}$

  b K and J can sit together in 2! ways. They as a pair plus the other three people can then be ordered in 4! ways.

  $\therefore$ P(sit together) $= \dfrac{2! \times 4!}{5!} = \dfrac{2}{5}$

6 There are $\binom{16}{5}$ different committees possible.

  a P(all men)
  $= \dfrac{\binom{9}{5} \times \binom{7}{0}}{\binom{16}{5}}$
  $= 0.0288$

  b P(at least 3 men)
  $=$ P(3 men or 4 men or 5 men)
  $= \dfrac{\binom{9}{3}\binom{7}{2} + \binom{9}{4}\binom{7}{1} + \binom{9}{5}\binom{7}{0}}{\binom{16}{5}}$
  ≈ 0.635

  c P(at least one of each sex)
  $= 1 -$ P(no men or no women)
  $= 1 - \dfrac{\binom{9}{0}\binom{7}{5} + \binom{9}{5}\binom{7}{0}}{\binom{16}{5}}$
  ≈ 0.966

7 If there are no restrictions there are 6! different orderings possible. A, B and C can be ordered in 3! ways. This triple together with the 3 others can be ordered in 4! ways.

$\therefore$ P(A, B, C together) $= \dfrac{3! \times 4!}{6!} = \dfrac{1}{5}$

8 There are $\binom{14}{7}$ different committees possible.

  a P(only senior students) $= \dfrac{\binom{11}{7}\binom{3}{0}}{\binom{14}{7}} \approx 0.0962$

  b P(all three junior students chosen) $= \dfrac{\binom{11}{4}\binom{3}{3}}{\binom{14}{7}} \approx 0.0962$

EXERCISE 18L

1 (tree diagram: 0.65 → A; 0.35 → B; from A: 0.04 → U, 0.96 → U'; from B: 0.05 → U, 0.95 → U')

  a P(underfilled)
  $=$ P(A and U or B and U)
  $= 0.65 \times 0.04 + 0.35 \times 0.05$
  $= 0.0435$

  b P(A | U) $= \dfrac{P(A \cap U)}{P(U)}$
  $= \dfrac{0.65 \times 0.04}{0.0435}$
  ≈ 0.598

2 Tree diagram:
- F (0.54): C (0.02), C' (0.98)
- M (0.46): C (0.08), C' (0.92)

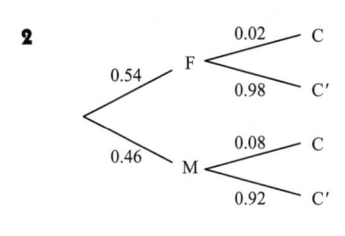

a $P(M \mid C) = \dfrac{P(C \mid M) \times P(M)}{P(C \mid M) \times P(M) + P(C \mid F) \times P(F)}$

$= \dfrac{0.08 \times 0.46}{0.08 \times 0.46 + 0.02 \times 0.54}$

≈ 0.773

b $P(F \mid C') = \dfrac{P(C' \mid F) \times P(F)}{P(C' \mid F) \times P(F) + P(C' \mid M) \times P(M)}$

$= \dfrac{0.98 \times 0.54}{0.98 \times 0.54 + 0.92 \times 0.46}$

≈ 0.556

3 Tree diagram (1st, 2nd):
- R ($\frac{3}{8}$): R ($\frac{2}{9}$), B ($\frac{7}{9}$)
- B ($\frac{5}{8}$): R ($\frac{5}{9}$), B ($\frac{4}{9}$)

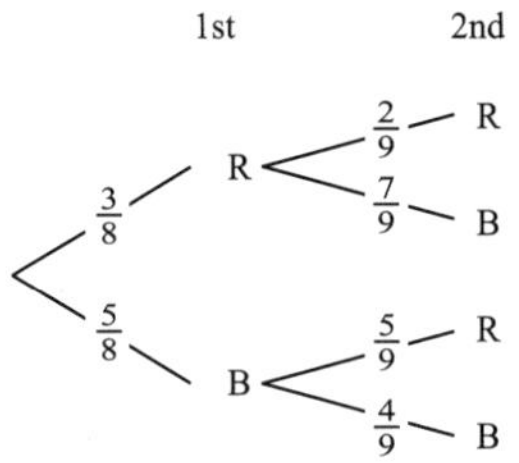

$P(BB \mid RR \text{ or } BB) = \dfrac{P(BB \cap (RR \text{ or } BB))}{P(RR \text{ or } BB)}$

$= \dfrac{P(BB)}{P(RR \text{ or } BB)}$

$= \dfrac{\frac{5}{8} \times \frac{4}{9}}{\frac{3}{8} \times \frac{2}{9} + \frac{5}{8} \times \frac{4}{9}}$

$= \dfrac{20}{26}$

$= \dfrac{10}{13}$

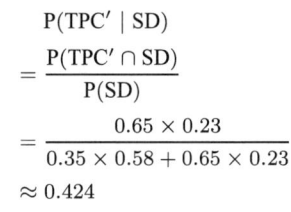

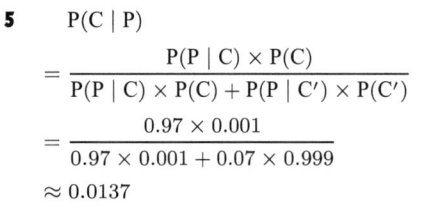

4 Tree diagram:
- TPC (0.35): SD (0.58), SD' (0.42)
- TPC' (0.65): SD (0.23), SD' (0.77)

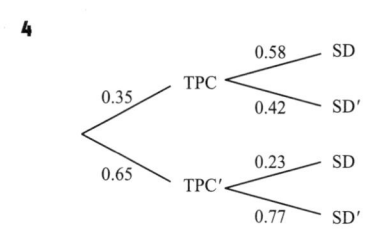

$P(TPC' \mid SD)$

$= \dfrac{P(TPC' \cap SD)}{P(SD)}$

$= \dfrac{0.65 \times 0.23}{0.35 \times 0.58 + 0.65 \times 0.23}$

≈ 0.424

5 $P(C \mid P)$

$= \dfrac{P(P \mid C) \times P(C)}{P(P \mid C) \times P(C) + P(P \mid C') \times P(C')}$

$= \dfrac{0.97 \times 0.001}{0.97 \times 0.001 + 0.07 \times 0.999}$

≈ 0.0137

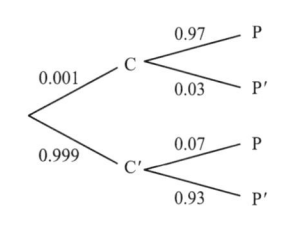

Tree diagram:
- C (0.001): P (0.97), P' (0.03)
- C' (0.999): P (0.07), P' (0.93)

6 Tree diagram:
- C (0.8): L (0.15), L' (0.85)
- B (0.2): L (0.25), L' (0.75)

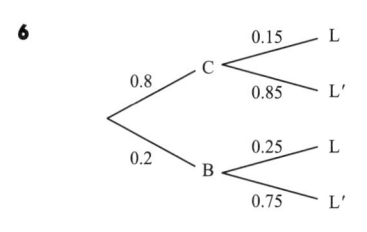

$P(B \mid L')$

$= \dfrac{P(L' \mid B) \times P(B)}{P(L' \mid B) \times P(B) + P(L' \mid C) \times P(C)}$

$= \dfrac{0.75 \times 0.2}{0.75 \times 0.2 + 0.85 \times 0.8}$

≈ 0.181 (or $\dfrac{15}{83}$)

7 Tree diagram (mother, father):
- M (0.99): F (0.98), F' (0.02)
- M' (0.01): F (0.98), F' (0.02)

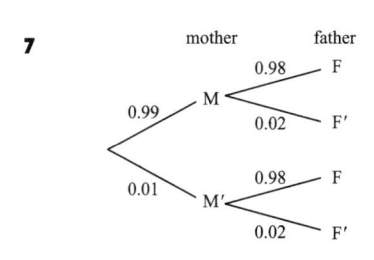

$P(M \mid \text{only 1 alive}) = \dfrac{P(M \cap (\text{only 1 alive}))}{P(\text{only 1 alive})}$

$= \dfrac{P(MF')}{P(MF' \text{ or } M'F)}$

$= \dfrac{0.99 \times 0.02}{0.99 \times 0.02 + 0.01 \times 0.98}$

≈ 0.669 (or $\dfrac{99}{148}$)

8

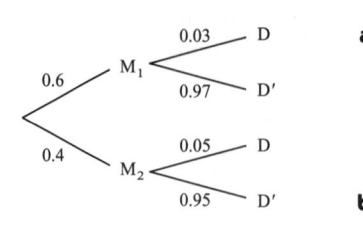

Tree diagram: 0.6 → M_1 → (0.03 → D, 0.97 → D'); 0.4 → M_2 → (0.05 → D, 0.95 → D')

a $P(M_1 \mid D) = \dfrac{P(D \mid M_1) \times P(M_1)}{P(D \mid M_1) \times P(M_1) + P(D \mid M_2) \times P(M_2)}$

$= \dfrac{0.03 \times 0.6}{0.03 \times 0.6 + 0.05 \times 0.4}$

$\approx 0.474 \quad$ (or $\tfrac{9}{19}$)

b $P(M_2 \mid D) = 1 - \tfrac{9}{19}$

$= \tfrac{10}{19}$

9 a $P(B) = P(B \text{ and in } A_1 \text{ or } B \text{ and in } A_2 \text{ or } B \text{ and in } A_3)$

$= P((B \cap A_1) \cup (B \cap A_2) \cup (B \cap A_3))$

$= P(B \cap A_1) + P(B \cap A_2) + P(B \cap A_3)$

as $B \cap A_1, \ B \cap A_2, \ B \cap A_3$ are disjoint

$= P(B \mid A_1) \, P(A_1) + P(B \mid A_2) \, P(A_2) + P(B \mid A_3) \, P(A_3)$

$\{\text{since } P(X \mid Y) = \dfrac{P(X \cap Y)}{P(Y)} \ \Rightarrow \ P(X \cap Y) = P(X \mid Y) \, P(Y)\}$

b $P(A_i \mid B) = \dfrac{P(A_i \cap B)}{P(B)} = \dfrac{P(B \mid A_i) \, P(A_i)}{P(B)}$

where $P(B) = P(B \mid A_1) \, P(A_1) + P(B \mid A_2) \, P(A_2) + P(B \mid A_3) \, P(A_3)$

$= \displaystyle\sum_{j=1}^{3} P(B \mid A_j) \, P(A_j)$

10

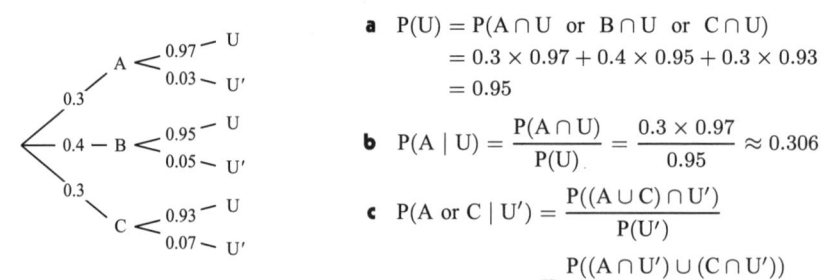

Tree diagram: 0.3 → A → (0.97 → U, 0.03 → U'); 0.4 → B → (0.95 → U, 0.05 → U'); 0.3 → C → (0.93 → U, 0.07 → U')

a $P(U) = P(A \cap U \text{ or } B \cap U \text{ or } C \cap U)$

$= 0.3 \times 0.97 + 0.4 \times 0.95 + 0.3 \times 0.93$

$= 0.95$

b $P(A \mid U) = \dfrac{P(A \cap U)}{P(U)} = \dfrac{0.3 \times 0.97}{0.95} \approx 0.306$

c $P(A \text{ or } C \mid U') = \dfrac{P((A \cup C) \cap U')}{P(U')}$

$= \dfrac{P((A \cap U') \cup (C \cap U'))}{1 - P(U)}$

$= \dfrac{0.3 \times 0.03 + 0.3 \times 0.07}{0.05}$

$= 0.6$

11

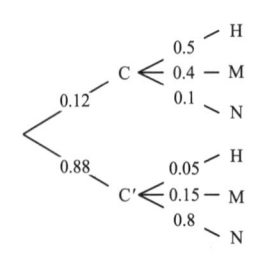

Tree diagram: 0.12 → C → (0.5 → H, 0.4 → M, 0.1 → N); 0.88 → C' → (0.05 → H, 0.15 → M, 0.8 → N)

a $P(H)$

$= P(C \cap H \text{ or } C' \cap H)$

$= 0.12 \times 0.5 + 0.88 \times 0.05$

$= 0.104$

b $P(C \mid M) = \dfrac{P(C \cap M)}{P(M)}$

$= \dfrac{0.12 \times 0.4}{0.12 \times 0.4 + 0.88 \times 0.15}$

≈ 0.267

c $P(C \mid N) = \dfrac{P(C \cap N)}{P(N)}$

$= \dfrac{0.12 \times 0.1}{0.12 \times 0.1 + 0.88 \times 0.8}$

≈ 0.0168

REVIEW SET 18A

1 ABCD, ABDC, ACBD, ACDB, ADBC, ADCB, BACD, BADC, BCAD, BCDA, BDAC, BDCA, CABD, CADB, CBAD, CBDA, CDAB, CDBA, DABC, DACB, DBAC, DBCA, DCAB, DCBA

   a There are 24 possible orderings.   **b**   P(exactly one person between A and C)
$\therefore$ P(A is next to C)
$= \frac{12}{24}$ {12 have A next to C}
$= \frac{1}{2}$

$= \frac{8}{24}$ {8 have one person between A and C}
$= \frac{1}{3}$

2

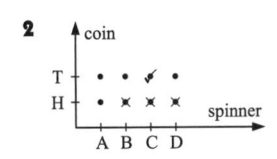

a Consonants are B, C and D
$\therefore$ P(H and a consonant)
$= \frac{3}{8}$ {those with a ×}

b P(T and C)
$= \frac{1}{8}$ {those with a ✓}

c P(T or vowel)
$= $ P(T or A)
$= $ P(T) + P(A) − P(T and A)
$= \frac{4}{8} + \frac{2}{8} - \frac{1}{8}$
$= \frac{5}{8}$

3

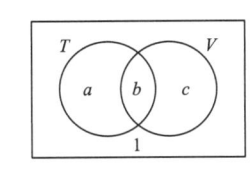

$a+b+c = 24$ $\therefore$ $13+c = 24$ and $a+14 = 24$
$a+b = 13$ $\therefore$ $c = 11$ and $a = 10$
$b+c = 14$
Also $b = 13 - a$
$= 3$

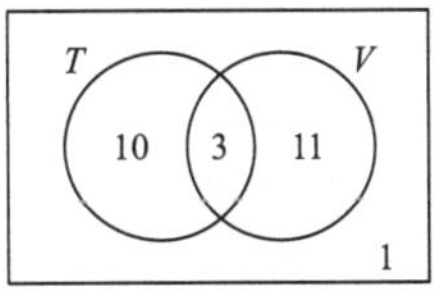

  a   P(T and V)
$= \frac{3}{25}$

  b   P(at least one)
$= 1 - $ P(neither)
$= 1 - \frac{1}{25}$
$= \frac{24}{25}$

  c   P(V | T')
$= \frac{11}{11+1}$
$= \frac{11}{12}$

4

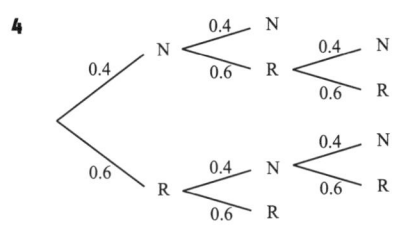

P(Niklas wins)
$= (0.4)(0.4) + (0.4)(0.6)(0.4) + (0.6)(0.4)(0.4)$
$= 0.352$

5   P(M) $= \frac{3}{5}$,   P(W) $= \frac{2}{3}$,   where M is the event "the man is alive in 25 years", and W is the event "the woman is alive in 25 years".

  a   P(M and W)
$= \frac{3}{5} \times \frac{2}{3}$
{assuming independence}
$= \frac{2}{5}$

  b   P(at least one)
$= $ P(M or W)
$= $ P(M) + P(W) − P(M and W)
$= \frac{3}{5} + \frac{2}{3} - \frac{2}{5}$
$= \frac{13}{15}$

  c   P(M' and W)
$= (1 - \frac{3}{5}) \times \frac{2}{3}$
$= \frac{2}{5} \times \frac{2}{3}$
$= \frac{4}{15}$

6 The 5 games are independent, so the binomial model applies.
P(M) $= \frac{4}{5}$,   P(M') $= \frac{1}{5}$

  a   P(M wins 3 games)
$= \binom{5}{3}(\frac{4}{5})^3(\frac{1}{5})^2$
≈ 0.205

  b   P(M wins 4 or 5 games)
$= \binom{5}{4}(\frac{4}{5})^4(\frac{1}{5})^1 + \binom{5}{5}(\frac{4}{5})^5$
≈ 0.737

7 a P(win first 3 prizes)
= P(WWW)
$= \frac{4}{500} \times \frac{3}{499} \times \frac{2}{498}$
$\approx 1.93 \times 10^{-7}$

b P(win at least one of the 3 prizes)
= 1 − P(wins none of them)
= 1 − P(W'W'W')
$= 1 - \frac{496}{500} \times \frac{495}{499} \times \frac{494}{498}$
≈ 0.0239

8

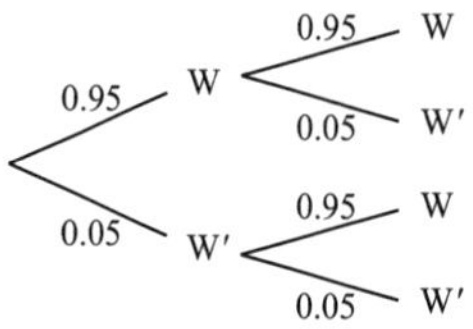

P(works on at least one day)
$= 0.95 \times 0.95 + 0.95 \times 0.05 + 0.05 \times 0.95$
$= 0.9975$

9 a P(all doctors) $= \dfrac{\binom{6}{5} \times \binom{4}{0}}{\binom{10}{5}} \approx 0.0238$

b P(at least 2 doctors) = 1 − P(1 doctor) $= 1 - \dfrac{\binom{6}{1} \times \binom{4}{4}}{\binom{10}{5}} \approx 0.976$

10 If there are no restrictions, there are 6! different orderings.

a

3	3	2	2	1	1
B	G	B	G	B	G

or

3	3	2	2	1	1
G	B	G	B	G	B

So, 36 + 36 consist of alternate sexes.

$\therefore$ P(alternate sexes) $= \dfrac{72}{6!} = \dfrac{1}{10}$

b The girls as a group can be ordered in 3! ways. This group plus the 3 boys can be ordered in 4! ways.

$\therefore$ P(girls are together) $= \dfrac{3! \times 4!}{6!} = \dfrac{1}{5}$

11

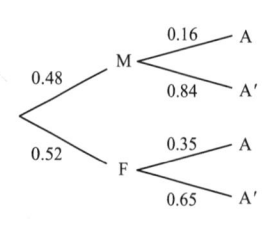

a P(A) = P(M ∩ A or F ∩ A)
$= 0.48 \times 0.16 + 0.52 \times 0.35$
$= 0.2588$ (≈ 0.259)

b P(F | A) $= \dfrac{P(F \cap A)}{P(A)}$
$= \dfrac{0.52 \times 0.35}{0.2588}$
≈ 0.703

REVIEW SET 18B

1 BBBB, BBBG, BBGB, BGBB, GBBB, BBGG, BGBG, BGGB, GBBG, GBGB, GGBB, BGGG, GBGG, GGBG, GGGB, GGGG

P(2B and 2G)
$= \dfrac{6}{16}$ ← 6 have 2B and 2G
$= \dfrac{3}{8}$

2

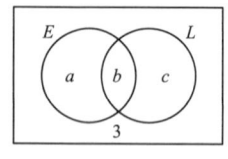

$a + b + c = 37$
$a + b = 22$
$b + c = 25$

$\therefore$ $22 + c = 37$ and $a + 25 = 37$
$\therefore$ $c = 15$ and $a = 12$
Hence, $b = 22 - a = 10$

a P(E and L)
$= \dfrac{10}{40}$
$= \dfrac{1}{4}$

b P(at least one)
$= \dfrac{12+10+15}{40}$
$= \dfrac{37}{40}$

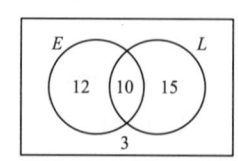

c P(E | L) $= \dfrac{10}{15+10} = \dfrac{10}{25} = \dfrac{2}{5}$

3 a P(both blue)
 = P(BB)
 = $\frac{5}{12} \times \frac{4}{11}$
 = $\frac{5}{33}$

b P(both same colour)
 = P(BB or RR or YY)
 = $\frac{5}{12} \times \frac{4}{11} + \frac{3}{12} \times \frac{2}{11} + \frac{4}{12} \times \frac{3}{11}$
 = $\frac{19}{66}$

c P(at least one R)
 = $1 - $ P(no reds)
 = $1 - $ P(R'R')
 = $1 - \frac{9}{12} \times \frac{8}{11}$
 = $1 - \frac{6}{11}$
 = $\frac{5}{11}$

d P(exactly one Y)
 = P(YY' or Y'Y)
 = $\frac{4}{12} \times \frac{8}{11} + \frac{8}{12} \times \frac{4}{11}$
 = $\frac{16}{33}$

4 a Two events are independent if the occurrence of each event does not influence the occurrence of the other. For A and B independent, $P(A) \times P(B) = P(A \text{ and } B)$.

b Two events, A and B, are disjoint if they have no common outcomes,
 $\therefore P(A \text{ and } B) = 0$ and so $P(A \text{ or } B) = P(A) + P(B)$.

5

```
          0.36   W
     R  <
0.25      0.64  W'

          0.36   W
0.75 R' <
          0.64  W'
```

a P(W and R)
 = 0.25×0.36
 = 0.09

b P(W or R)
 = P(W) + P(R) − P(W and R)
 = $0.36 + 0.25 - 0.09$
 = 0.52

 or P(W or R) = $1 - $ P(W'R')
 = $1 - 0.64 \times 0.75$
 = 0.52

6 $P(A) = 0.1$, $P(B) = 0.2$, $P(C) = 0.3$ $\therefore$ P(group solves it) = P(at least one solves it)
 = $1 - $ P(no-one solves it)
 = $1 - $ P(A' and B' and C')
 = $1 - (0.9 \times 0.8 \times 0.7)$
 = 0.496

7

```
            7/10  E
      C  <
  3/7       3/10  E'

            1/4   E
  4/7 C' <
            3/4   E'
```

a $P(E) = \frac{3}{7} \times \frac{7}{10} + \frac{4}{7} \times \frac{1}{4}$
 = $\frac{3}{10} + \frac{1}{7}$
 = $\frac{31}{70}$

b $P(C \mid E) = \dfrac{P(C \text{ and } E)}{P(E)}$
 = $\dfrac{\frac{3}{7} \times \frac{7}{10}}{\frac{31}{70}}$
 = $\frac{21}{31}$

8 a $\left(\frac{3}{5} + \frac{2}{5}\right)^4 = \underbrace{\left(\frac{3}{5}\right)^4}_{4B} + \underbrace{4\left(\frac{3}{5}\right)^3\left(\frac{2}{5}\right)}_{\substack{3B \\ 1B'}} + \underbrace{6\left(\frac{3}{5}\right)^2\left(\frac{2}{5}\right)^2}_{\substack{2B \\ 2B'}} + \underbrace{4\left(\frac{3}{5}\right)\left(\frac{2}{5}\right)^3}_{\substack{1B \\ 3B'}} + \underbrace{\left(\frac{2}{5}\right)^4}_{4B'}$

$P(B) = \frac{12}{20}$
 = $\frac{3}{5}$
$\therefore P(B') = \frac{2}{5}$

b i P(2 Blue inks)
 = P(2B and 2B')
 = $6\left(\frac{3}{5}\right)^2 \left(\frac{2}{5}\right)^2$
 = $\frac{6 \times 9 \times 4}{5^4}$
 = $\frac{216}{625}$

ii P(at most 2 Blue inks)
 = P(2B and 2B' or 1B and 3B' or 4B')
 = $6\left(\frac{3}{5}\right)^2\left(\frac{2}{5}\right)^2 + 4\left(\frac{3}{5}\right)\left(\frac{2}{5}\right)^3 + \left(\frac{2}{5}\right)^4$
 = $\frac{6 \times 9 \times 4 + 4 \times 3 \times 8 + 16}{625}$
 = $\frac{328}{625}$

9 a P(X wins) = $\frac{3}{5}$ P(Y wins) = $\frac{2}{5}$

Probability generator is $\left(\frac{3}{5}+\frac{2}{5}\right)^6$

$= \left(\frac{3}{5}\right)^6 + 6\left(\frac{3}{5}\right)^5\left(\frac{2}{5}\right) + 15\left(\frac{3}{5}\right)^4\left(\frac{2}{5}\right)^2 + 20\left(\frac{3}{5}\right)^3\left(\frac{2}{5}\right)^3 + 15\left(\frac{3}{5}\right)^2\left(\frac{2}{5}\right)^4 + 6\left(\frac{3}{5}\right)\left(\frac{2}{5}\right)^5 + \left(\frac{2}{5}\right)^6$

↑	↑	↑	↑	↑	↑	↑
X wins 6	X wins 5	X wins 4	X wins 3	X wins 2	X wins 1	X wins 0
	Y wins 1	Y wins 2	Y wins 3	Y wins 4	Y wins 5	Y wins 6

b i   P(Y wins 3)
$= 20(0.6)^3(0.4)^3$
≈ 0.276

ii   P(Y wins at least 5)
$= 6(0.6)^1(0.4)^5 + (0.4)^6$
≈ 0.0410

10 X = the number of goals scored

a   P(3 goals **then** 2 misses)
$= P(GGGG'G')$
$= (0.8)^3 \times (0.2)^2$
≈ 0.0205

b   P(3 goals and 2 misses)
$= P(X = 3)$
≈ 0.205

REVIEW SET 18C

1 a   P(M) × P(C) = 0.91 × 0.88
$= 0.8008$
and   P(M and C) = 0.85
∴ $P(M \cap C) \neq P(M)\,P(C)$,
so M and C are not independent.

b $P(M' \mid C) = \dfrac{P(M' \cap C)}{P(C)}$

Now $P(M' \cap C) + P(M \cap C) = P(C)$
∴ $P(M' \cap C) = P(C) - P(M \cap C)$
$= 0.88 - 0.85$
$= 0.03$
∴ $P(M' \mid C) = \frac{0.03}{0.88} = \frac{3}{88}$

2   There are $\binom{10}{5}$ different ways to choose the group.

∴   P(2 year 12, 2 year 11) $= \dfrac{\binom{3}{2}\binom{4}{2}\binom{3}{1}}{\binom{10}{5}}$

≈ 0.214 (or $\frac{3}{14}$)

3 a $b + c = 0.35$, $a + b + c = 0.8$ ∴ $a = 0.45$
Now $P(X)\,P(Y) = P(X \cap Y)$ {X, Y independent}
∴ $(0.45 + b)(0.35) = b$
∴ $0.1575 + 0.35b = b$
∴ $0.1575 = 0.65b$
∴ $b \approx 0.242$
∴ $P(X) = a + b \approx 0.692$

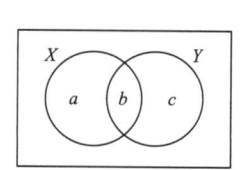

b $c = 0.35 - b \approx 0.108$
P(X or Y, but not both) $= a + c$
$\approx 0.45 + 0.108 \approx 0.558$

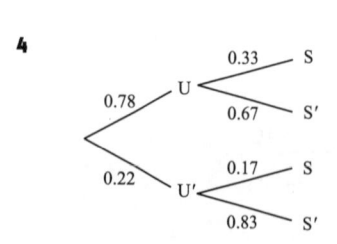

4

$P(U' \mid S) = \dfrac{P(U' \cap S)}{P(S)}$

$= \dfrac{0.22 \times 0.17}{0.22 \times 0.17 + 0.78 \times 0.33}$

≈ 0.127

5 Since $X' \cap Y' = \emptyset$, every element in the universal set is in either X or Y or both.
∴ we can construct the Venn diagram alongside:

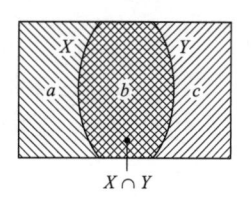

Now $P(X' \mid Y) = \frac{2}{3}$

∴ $\dfrac{P(X' \cap Y)}{P(Y)} = \dfrac{2}{3}$

∴ $P(X' \cap Y) = \frac{2}{3} \times P(Y)$

$= \frac{2}{3} \times \frac{5}{6}$

$= \frac{5}{9}$

So, $c = \frac{5}{9}$

and $P(Y) = b + c$

∴ $b = \frac{5}{6} - \frac{5}{9} = \frac{5}{18}$

∴ $a = 1 - b - c$

$= 1 - \frac{5}{18} - \frac{5}{9}$

$= \frac{1}{6}$

∴ $P(X) = a + b$

$= \frac{1}{6} + \frac{5}{18} = \frac{4}{9}$

6

$P(M \mid F) = \dfrac{P(M \cap F)}{P(F)}$

$= \dfrac{\frac{13}{28} \times \frac{4}{13}}{\frac{13}{28} \times \frac{4}{13} + \frac{15}{28} \times \frac{11}{15}}$

$= \frac{4}{15}$

7 Let L_i be the event that the salesman leaves his sunglasses in store i.

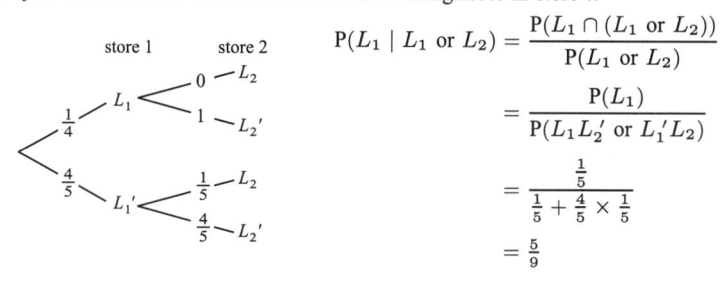

$P(L_1 \mid L_1 \text{ or } L_2) = \dfrac{P(L_1 \cap (L_1 \text{ or } L_2))}{P(L_1 \text{ or } L_2)}$

$= \dfrac{P(L_1)}{P(L_1 L_2' \text{ or } L_1' L_2)}$

$= \dfrac{\frac{1}{5}}{\frac{1}{5} + \frac{4}{5} \times \frac{1}{5}}$

$= \frac{5}{9}$

8 With n tosses, P(getting at least 4 heads) $= 1 - $ P(getting 3 or fewer heads)
We need to find n such that P(getting at least 4 heads) > 0.5.
So, $1 - \left(\binom{n}{0}\left(\frac{1}{2}\right)^n + \binom{n}{1}\left(\frac{1}{2}\right)^n + \binom{n}{2}\left(\frac{1}{2}\right)^n + \binom{n}{3}\left(\frac{1}{2}\right)^n\right) > 0.5$
Using technology, $n > 7$
∴ 8 coin tosses are needed.

9 a There are now 3 red and 5 blue balls remaining.
∴ $P(\text{blue}) = \frac{5}{8}$

b

$P(R_1 \mid R_2) = \dfrac{P(R_1 \cap R_2)}{P(R_2)}$

$= \dfrac{\frac{3}{9} \times \frac{2}{8}}{\frac{3}{9} \times \frac{2}{8} + \frac{6}{9} \times \frac{3}{8}}$

$= \frac{1}{4}$

c   added   drawn

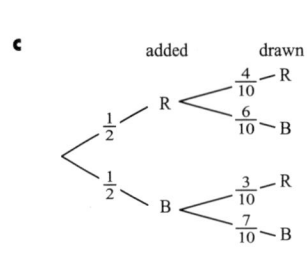

$\frac{1}{2}$ R $\begin{cases} \frac{4}{10} - R \\ \frac{6}{10} - B \end{cases}$

$\frac{1}{2}$ B $\begin{cases} \frac{3}{10} - R \\ \frac{7}{10} - B \end{cases}$

i P(red added | blue drawn) $= \dfrac{\text{P(red added} \cap \text{blue drawn)}}{\text{P(blue drawn)}}$

$= \dfrac{\frac{1}{2} \times \frac{6}{10}}{\frac{1}{2} \times \frac{6}{10} + \frac{1}{2} \times \frac{7}{10}}$

$= \dfrac{6}{13}$

ii P(blue added | blue drawn) $= 1 - \dfrac{6}{13}$

$= \dfrac{7}{13}$

10 a There are $\binom{52}{5}$ possible poker hands.

4 of these are a 'perfect' poker hand {10, J, Q, K, A of hearts, clubs, diamonds or spades}

$\therefore$ P('perfect' poker hand in any order) $= \dfrac{4}{\binom{52}{5}} \approx 1.54 \times 10^{-6}$

b When order is important, there are $52 \times 51 \times 50 \times 49 \times 48$ possible poker hands.
4 of these are a 'perfect' poker hand in the order 10, J, Q, K, A.

$\therefore$ P('perfect' poker hand in the order 10, J, Q, K, A) $= \dfrac{4}{52 \times 51 \times 50 \times 49 \times 48} \approx 1.28 \times 10^{-8}$

11

0.85 S $\begin{cases} 0.85 - S \\ 0.15 - T \checkmark \end{cases}$

0.15 T $\begin{cases} 0.85 - S \checkmark \\ 0.15 - T \end{cases}$

P(twins first | 3 children) $= \dfrac{\text{P(twins first} \cap \text{3 children)}}{\text{P(3 children)}}$

$= \dfrac{0.15 \times 0.85}{0.85 \times 0.15 + 0.15 \times 0.85}$

$= \dfrac{1}{2}$

REVIEW SET 18D

1 a Two events are independent if the occurrence of each event does not affect the occurrence of the other.

b A and B are independent $\Rightarrow$ $P(A \cap B) = P(A) P(B)$ ...... (1)

Now $P(A \cap B')$
$= P(A \cup B) - P(B)$ {see diagram}
$= P(A) + P(B) - P(A \cap B) - P(B)$
$= P(A) - P(A \cap B)$
$= P(A) - P(A) P(B)$ {from (1)}
$= P(A)[1 - P(B)]$
$= P(A) \times P(B')$ $\therefore$ A and B' are also independent.

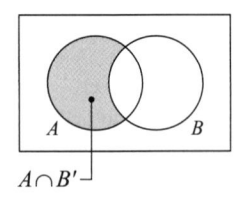

2 Let H_A be the probability that coin A lands heads up, and
H_B be the probability that coin B lands heads up.

P(a 'match') $= \frac{1}{2}$ $\therefore$ $H_A H_B + (1 - H_A)(1 - H_B) = \frac{1}{2}$

$\therefore$ $H_A H_B + 1 - H_A - H_B + H_A H_B = \frac{1}{2}$

$\therefore$ $2 H_A H_B - H_A - H_B + \frac{1}{2} = 0$

$\therefore$ $4 H_A H_B - 2 H_A - 2 H_B + 1 = 0$

$\therefore$ $(2 H_A - 1)(2 H_B - 1) = 0$

$\therefore$ $H_A = \frac{1}{2}$ or $H_B = \frac{1}{2}$

$\therefore$ at least one of the coins must be unbiased.

3 **a** $P(x) = \binom{n}{x} p^{n-x} q^x = \left(\dfrac{n!}{x!(n-x)!}\right) p^{n-x} q^x$

$\therefore\ P(x+1) = \binom{n}{x+1} p^{n-(x+1)} q^{x+1}$

$= \dfrac{n!}{(x+1)![n-(x+1)]!} p^{n-x-1} q^{x+1}$

$= \dfrac{n!}{(x+1)x!(n-x-1)!} \left(\dfrac{p^{n-x}}{p}\right) q^x \times q$

$= \dfrac{n!(n-x)}{(x+1)x!(n-x)!} p^{n-x} q^x \left(\dfrac{q}{p}\right)$

$= \left(\dfrac{n-x}{x+1}\right)\left(\dfrac{q}{p}\right)\left(\dfrac{n!}{x!(n-x)!}\right) p^{n-x} q^x$

$= \left(\dfrac{n-x}{x+1}\right)\left(\dfrac{q}{p}\right) P(x)$, where $P(0) = \binom{n}{0} p^{n-0} q^0 = p^n$

b $P(0) = p^n = \left(\dfrac{1}{2}\right)^5 = \dfrac{1}{32}$

$P(1) = \left(\dfrac{n-x}{x+1}\right)\left(\dfrac{q}{p}\right) P(0)$

$= \left(\dfrac{5-0}{0+1}\right)(1)\left(\dfrac{1}{32}\right)$ $\quad \{p = \tfrac{1}{2}$ and $q = 1 - p = \tfrac{1}{2} \quad \therefore\ \dfrac{q}{p} = 1\}$

$= \dfrac{5}{32}$

$P(2) = \left(\dfrac{5-1}{1+1}\right)(1)\left(\dfrac{5}{32}\right) = \dfrac{10}{32}$

$P(3) = \left(\dfrac{5-2}{2+1}\right)(1)\left(\dfrac{10}{32}\right) = \dfrac{10}{32}$

$P(4) = \left(\dfrac{5-3}{3+1}\right)(1)\left(\dfrac{10}{32}\right) = \dfrac{5}{32}$

$P(5) = \left(\dfrac{5-4}{4+1}\right)(1)\left(\dfrac{5}{32}\right) = \dfrac{1}{32}$

4 **a** $P(A \cup B) = P(A) + P(B) - P(A \cap B)$
$= P(A) + P(B) - P(A)\,P(B) \quad \{A$ and B are independent$\}$
$= 0.8 + 0.65 - 0.8 \times 0.65$
$= 0.93$

b $P(A \mid B) = P(A) \quad \{A$ and B are independent$\}$
$= 0.8$

c $P(A' \mid B') = \dfrac{P(A' \cap B')}{P(B')}$

$= \dfrac{1 - P(A \cup B)}{1 - P(B)}$

$= \dfrac{1 - 0.93}{1 - 0.65} = 0.2$

d $P(B \mid A) = P(B)$
$= 0.65$

5 With n tosses, P(getting at least 2 heads) $= 1 -$ P(getting at most 1 head)
We need to find n such that P(getting at least 2 heads) > 0.99
So, $1 - \left(\binom{n}{0}\left(\dfrac{1}{2}\right)^n + \binom{n}{1}\left(\dfrac{1}{2}\right)^n\right) > 0.99$
Using technology, $n \geqslant 11 \quad \{n \in \mathbb{Z}\}$
$\therefore\ n = 11$ is the smallest value of n.

6 a P(at least one component needs replacing) $= 1 -$ P(no components need replacing)

$$= 1 - \frac{19}{20} \times \frac{49}{50} \times \frac{99}{100}$$

$$= 0.07831$$

b P(exactly one component needs replacing) $= \frac{1}{20} \times \frac{49}{50} \times \frac{99}{100} + \frac{19}{20} \times \frac{1}{50} \times \frac{99}{100} + \frac{19}{20} \times \frac{49}{50} \times \frac{1}{100}$

$$= 0.07663$$

7 A Peter will win at least two consecutive games out of 3 serving first if

    (1) he wins the second game (served by John), **and**

    (2) he wins at least one of the other two games (served by Peter).

P(event 1) $= 1 - q$ {John loses his serve}

P(event 2) $= 1 -$ P(Peter loses both)

$$= 1 - (1-p)^2$$
$$= 1 - (1 - 2p + p^2)$$
$$= p(2-p)$$

$\therefore$ P(**A**) $= p(1-q)(2-p)$

B Peter will win at least two consecutive games out of 3 when John serves first if

    (1) he wins the second game (served by Peter), **and**

    (2) he wins at least one of the other two games (served by John).

P(event 1) $= p$ {Peter wins his serve}

P(event 2) $= 1 -$ P(Peter loses both)

$$= 1 - q^2$$
$$= (1-q)(1+q)$$

$\therefore$ P(**B**) $= p(1-q)(1+q)$

Now $p + q > 1$

$\therefore$ $q > 1 - p$

$\therefore$ $1 + q > 2 - p$

$\therefore$ P(**B**) > P(**A**), and so **B** is more likely than **A**.

8 There are $\binom{10}{4} = 210$ ways to select the four numbers.

a 2 cannot be the second largest number, as there is only 1 number smaller than 2.

$\therefore$ P($X = 2$) $= 0$

b There are $\binom{6}{2}\binom{1}{1}\binom{3}{1} = 45$ ways to choose the numbers so that $X = 7$.

    2 numbers below 7   7   1 number above 7 $\therefore$ P($X = 7$) $= \frac{45}{210} = \frac{3}{14}$

c There are $\binom{8}{2}\binom{1}{1}\binom{1}{1} = 28$ ways to choose the numbers so that $X = 9$.

    2 numbers below 9   9   10 $\therefore$ P($X = 9$) $= \frac{28}{210} = \frac{2}{15}$

9 If the sum of the numbers is even, then the numbers are either both even or both odd.

$\therefore$ P(both odd | sum even) $= \dfrac{\text{P(both odd} \cap \text{sum even)}}{\text{P(sum even)}}$

$$= \frac{\text{P(OO)}}{\text{P(OO or EE)}}$$

$$= \frac{\frac{5}{9} \times \frac{4}{8}}{\frac{5}{9} \times \frac{4}{8} + \frac{4}{9} \times \frac{3}{8}}$$

$$= \frac{5}{8}$$

10 P(hit) = $\frac{1}{3}$, P(miss) = $\frac{2}{3}$

Probability generator is

$\left(\frac{1}{3} + \frac{2}{3}\right)^5$

$= \left(\frac{1}{3}\right)^5 + 5\left(\frac{1}{3}\right)^4\left(\frac{2}{3}\right) + 10\left(\frac{1}{3}\right)^3\left(\frac{2}{3}\right)^2 + 10\left(\frac{1}{3}\right)^2\left(\frac{2}{3}\right)^3 + 5\left(\frac{1}{3}\right)\left(\frac{2}{3}\right)^4 + \left(\frac{2}{3}\right)^5$

$\quad\uparrow \qquad\quad \uparrow \qquad\qquad \uparrow \qquad\qquad \uparrow \qquad\qquad \uparrow \qquad\quad \uparrow$

$X = 5 \quad\ X = 4 \quad\ X = 3 \quad\ X = 2 \quad\ X = 1 \quad\ X = 0$

$\text{P}(X \text{ odd} \mid X \geqslant 2) = \dfrac{\text{P}(X \text{ odd} \cap X \geqslant 2)}{\text{P}(X \geqslant 2)}$

$= \dfrac{\text{P}(X = 3 \text{ or } 5)}{1 - \text{P}(X \leqslant 1)}$

$= \dfrac{10\left(\frac{1}{3}\right)^3\left(\frac{2}{3}\right)^2 + \left(\frac{1}{3}\right)^5}{1 - \left(5\left(\frac{1}{3}\right)\left(\frac{2}{3}\right)^4 + \left(\frac{2}{3}\right)^5\right)}$

≈ 0.313

11 P(any switch is closed) = $\frac{2}{3}$

Current will flow through a wire if all switches along that wire are closed.

∴ P(current flows through top wire) = $\left(\frac{2}{3}\right)^3$

P(current flows through bottom wire) = $\left(\frac{2}{3}\right)^2$

P(current flows through both wires) = P(all five switches closed)

$= \left(\frac{2}{3}\right)^5$

∴ P(current flows from A to B) = P(top) + P(bottom) − P(top and bottom)

$= \left(\frac{2}{3}\right)^3 + \left(\frac{2}{3}\right)^2 - \left(\frac{2}{3}\right)^5$

$= \frac{148}{243}$

12 a E and S are the only letters common to all three names.

∴ P(all letters are the same) = P(all Es) + P(all Ss)

$= \frac{1}{5} \times \frac{2}{6} \times \frac{1}{5} + \frac{1}{5} \times \frac{1}{6} \times \frac{1}{5}$

$= \frac{1}{50}$

b Exactly two letters will be the same if:

N is selected from JONES and EVANS	$\frac{1}{5} \times \frac{1}{5} = \frac{1}{25}$
E is selected from JONES and PETERS (but not EVANS)	$\frac{1}{5} \times \frac{2}{6} \times \frac{4}{5} = \frac{8}{150}$
E is selected from JONES and EVANS (but not PETERS)	$\frac{1}{5} \times \frac{1}{6} \times \frac{4}{5} = \frac{4}{150}$
E is selected from PETERS and EVANS (but not JONES)	$\frac{2}{6} \times \frac{1}{5} \times \frac{4}{5} = \frac{8}{150}$
S is selected from JONES and PETERS (but not EVANS)	$\frac{1}{5} \times \frac{1}{6} \times \frac{4}{5} = \frac{4}{150}$
S is selected from JONES and EVANS (but not PETERS)	$\frac{1}{5} \times \frac{1}{5} \times \frac{5}{6} = \frac{5}{150}$
S is selected from PETERS and EVANS (but not JONES)	$\frac{1}{6} \times \frac{1}{5} \times \frac{4}{5} = \frac{4}{150}$
	Total = $\frac{13}{50}$

∴ P(only two of the letters are the same) = $\frac{13}{50}$

Chapter 19
INTRODUCTION TO CALCULUS

EXERCISE 19A

1

a As $x \to 3$, $x + 4 \to 7$
$\therefore \lim_{x \to 3} (x + 4) = 7$

b As $x \to -1$, $5 - 2x \to 7$
$\therefore \lim_{x \to -1} (5 - 2x) = 7$

c As $x \to 4$, $3x - 1 \to 11$
$\therefore \lim_{x \to 4} (3x - 1) = 11$

d As $x \to 2$, $5x^2 - 3x + 2 \to 5(4) - 3(2) + 2 = 16$
$\therefore \lim_{x \to 2} (5x^2 - 3x + 2) = 16$

e As $h \to 0$, $h^2 \to 0$ and $1 - h \to 1$
$\therefore \lim_{h \to 0} h^2(1 - h) = 0 \times 1 = 0$

f As $x \to -1$, $1 - 2x \to 3$ and $x^2 + 1 \to 2$
$\therefore \lim_{x \to -1} \dfrac{1 - 2x}{x^2 + 1} = \dfrac{3}{2}$

g As $x \to 0$, $x^2 + 5 \to 5$
$\therefore \lim_{x \to 0} (x^2 + 5) = 5$

h As $x \to -2$, $\dfrac{4}{x} \to -2$
$\therefore \lim_{x \to -2} \dfrac{4}{x} = -2$

i $\dfrac{x^2 - 3x}{x} \begin{cases} = x - 3 & \text{if } x \neq 0 \\ \text{is undefined} & \text{if } x = 0 \end{cases}$

$\therefore \lim_{x \to 0} \dfrac{x^2 - 3x}{x}$
$= \lim_{x \to 0} (x - 3)$, $x \neq 0$
$= -3$

j $\dfrac{2h^2 + 6h}{h} \begin{cases} = 2h + 6 & \text{if } h \neq 0 \\ \text{is undefined} & \text{if } h = 0 \end{cases}$

$\therefore \lim_{h \to 0} \dfrac{2h^2 + 6h}{h}$
$= \lim_{h \to 0} (2h + 6)$, $h \neq 0$
$= 6$

k $\dfrac{h^3 - 8h}{h} \begin{cases} = h^2 - 8 & \text{if } h \neq 0 \\ \text{is undefined} & \text{if } h = 0 \end{cases}$

$\therefore \lim_{h \to 0} \dfrac{h^3 - 8h}{h}$
$= \lim_{h \to 0} (h^2 - 8)$, $h \neq 0$
$= -8$

l $\dfrac{x^2 - x}{x^2 - 1} = \dfrac{x(x - 1)}{(x + 1)(x - 1)}$
$\begin{cases} = \dfrac{x}{x + 1} & \text{if } x \neq 1 \\ \text{is undefined} & \text{if } x = 1 \end{cases}$

$\therefore \lim_{x \to 1} \dfrac{x^2 - x}{x^2 - 1}$
$= \lim_{x \to 1} \dfrac{x}{x + 1}$, $x \neq 1$
$= \dfrac{1}{2}$

m $\dfrac{x^2 - 2x}{x^2 - 4} = \dfrac{x(x - 2)}{(x + 2)(x - 2)}$
$\begin{cases} = \dfrac{x}{x + 2} & \text{if } x \neq 2 \\ \text{is undefined} & \text{if } x = 2 \end{cases}$

$\therefore \lim_{x \to 2} \dfrac{x^2 - 2x}{x^2 - 4}$
$= \lim_{x \to 2} \dfrac{x}{x + 2}$, $x \neq 2$
$= \dfrac{2}{4}$ or $\dfrac{1}{2}$

n $\dfrac{x^2 - x - 6}{x^2 - 5x + 6} = \dfrac{(x - 3)(x + 2)}{(x - 3)(x - 2)}$
$\begin{cases} = \dfrac{x + 2}{x - 2} & \text{if } x \neq 3 \\ \text{is undefined} & \text{if } x = 3 \end{cases}$

$\therefore \lim_{x \to 3} \dfrac{x^2 - x - 6}{x^2 - 5x + 6} = \lim_{x \to 3} \dfrac{x + 2}{x - 2}$, $x \neq 3$
$= 5$

o $\dfrac{2x^2 - 50}{3x^2 + 13x - 10} = \dfrac{2(x-5)(x+5)}{(3x-2)(x+5)}$

$\begin{cases} = \dfrac{2(x-5)}{3x-2} & \text{if } x \neq -5 \\ \text{is undefined} & \text{if } x = -5 \end{cases}$

$\therefore \lim\limits_{x \to -5} \dfrac{2x^2 - 50}{3x^2 + 13x - 10}$

$= \lim\limits_{x \to -5} \dfrac{2(x-5)}{3x-2}, \; x \neq -5$

$= \dfrac{-20}{-17}$ or $\dfrac{20}{17}$

q $\dfrac{x^3 - 8}{2x - 4} = \dfrac{(x-2)(x^2 + 2x + 4)}{2(x-2)}$

$\begin{cases} = \dfrac{x^2 + 2x + 4}{2} & \text{if } x \neq 2 \\ \text{is undefined} & \text{if } x = 2 \end{cases}$

$\therefore \lim\limits_{x \to 2} \dfrac{x^3 - 8}{2x - 4}$

$= \lim\limits_{x \to 2} \dfrac{x^2 + 2x + 4}{2}, \; x \neq 2$

$= 6$

p $\dfrac{x^3 - 1}{x^2 - 1} = \dfrac{(x-1)(x^2 + x + 1)}{(x-1)(x+1)}$

$\begin{cases} = \dfrac{x^2 + x + 1}{x + 1} & \text{if } x \neq 1 \\ \text{is undefined} & \text{if } x = 1 \end{cases}$

$\therefore \lim\limits_{x \to 1} \dfrac{x^3 - 1}{x^2 - 1}$

$= \lim\limits_{x \to 1} \dfrac{x^2 + x + 1}{x + 1}, \; x \neq 1$

$= \dfrac{3}{2}$

r $\dfrac{3x^2 + 5x - 2}{x^2 - 2x - 8} = \dfrac{(3x-1)(x+2)}{(x-4)(x+2)}$

$\begin{cases} = \dfrac{3x - 1}{x - 4} & \text{if } x \neq -2 \\ \text{is undefined} & \text{if } x = -2 \end{cases}$

$\therefore \lim\limits_{x \to -2} \dfrac{3x^2 + 5x - 2}{x^2 - 2x - 8}$

$= \lim\limits_{x \to -2} \dfrac{3x - 1}{x - 4}, \; x \neq -2$

$= \dfrac{-7}{-6}$ or $\dfrac{7}{6}$

2 As x gets larger and positive, $\dfrac{1}{x}$ gets smaller and closer to 0. $\quad \therefore \lim\limits_{x \to \infty} \dfrac{1}{x} = 0$

3 a $\lim\limits_{x \to \infty} \dfrac{3x - 2}{x + 1}$

$= \lim\limits_{x \to \infty} \dfrac{3 - \frac{2}{x}}{1 + \frac{1}{x}}$

$= \dfrac{3}{1}$

$= 3$

b $\lim\limits_{x \to \infty} \dfrac{1 - 2x}{3x + 2}$

$= \lim\limits_{x \to \infty} \dfrac{\frac{1}{x} - 2}{3 + \frac{2}{x}}$

$= -\dfrac{2}{3}$

c $\lim\limits_{x \to \infty} \dfrac{x}{1 - x}$

$= \lim\limits_{x \to \infty} \dfrac{1}{\frac{1}{x} - 1}$

$= \dfrac{1}{-1}$

$= -1$

d $\lim\limits_{x \to \infty} \dfrac{x^2 + 3}{x^2 - 1}$

$= \lim\limits_{x \to \infty} \dfrac{1 + \frac{3}{x^2}}{1 - \frac{1}{x^2}}$

$= \dfrac{1}{1}$

$= 1$

e $\lim\limits_{x \to \infty} \dfrac{x^2 - 2x + 4}{x^2 + x - 1}$

$= \lim\limits_{x \to \infty} \dfrac{1 - \frac{2}{x} + \frac{4}{x^2}}{1 + \frac{1}{x} - \frac{1}{x^2}}$

$= \dfrac{1}{1}$

$= 1$

f $\lim\limits_{x \to \infty} \dfrac{x^3 - 8}{3x^3 + x^2 - 8x - 4}$

$= \lim\limits_{x \to \infty} \dfrac{1 - \frac{8}{x^3}}{3 + \frac{1}{x} - \frac{8}{x^2} - \frac{4}{x^3}}$

$= \dfrac{1}{3}$

EXERCISE 19B

1 a $f(x) = \dfrac{3x - 2}{x + 3}$

$= \dfrac{3(x+3) - 9 - 2}{x + 3}$

$= 3 - \dfrac{11}{x + 3}$

$f(x)$ is undefined when $x = -3$

$\therefore \; x = -3$ is a vertical asymptote

As $|x| \to \infty, \; f(x) \to 3$

$\therefore \; y = 3$ is a horizontal asymptote

As $x \to -3$ (left), $f(x) \to \infty$

As $x \to -3$ (right), $f(x) \to -\infty$

As $x \to \infty, \; f(x) \to 3$ (below)

As $x \to -\infty, \; f(x) \to 3$ (above)

b $y = \dfrac{2x^2 + 10}{x} = 2x + \dfrac{10}{x}$

y is undefined when $x = 0$
$\therefore$ $x = 0$ is a vertical asymptote
As $|x| \to \infty$, $y \to 2x$
$\therefore$ $y = 2x$ is an oblique asymptote
As $x \to 0$ (left), $y \to -\infty$
As $x \to 0$ (right), $y \to \infty$
As $x \to \infty$, $y \to 2x$ (above)
As $x \to -\infty$, $y \to 2x$ (below)

d $y = \dfrac{x^2 - 1}{x^2 + 1} = \dfrac{x^2 + 1 - 2}{x^2 + 1}$

$= 1 - \dfrac{2}{x^2 + 1}$

y is defined for all $x \in \mathbb{R}$
$\therefore$ no vertical asymptotes exist
As $|x| \to \infty$, $y \to 1$
$\therefore$ $y = 1$ is a horizontal asymptote
As $x \to \infty$, $y \to 1$ (below)
As $x \to -\infty$, $y \to 1$ (below)

f $f(x) = \dfrac{x - 2}{x^2 + x - 2} = \dfrac{x - 2}{(x + 2)(x - 1)}$

$f(x)$ is undefined when $x = -2$ or 1
$\therefore$ $x = -2$ and $x = 1$ are vertical asymptotes

Now $f(x) = \dfrac{\frac{1}{x} - \frac{2}{x^2}}{1 + \frac{1}{x} - \frac{2}{x^2}}$

$\therefore$ as $|x| \to \infty$, $f(x) \to \frac{0}{1} = 0$
$\therefore$ $y = 0$ is a horizontal asymptote
As $x \to -2$ (left), $f(x) \to -\infty$
As $x \to -2$ (right), $f(x) \to \infty$
As $x \to 1$ (left), $f(x) \to \infty$
As $x \to 1$ (right), $f(x) \to -\infty$
As $x \to \infty$, $f(x) \to 0$ (above)
As $x \to -\infty$, $f(x) \to 0$ (below)

h $f(x) = e^{x - \frac{1}{x}}$

$f(x)$ is undefined when $x = 0$
$\therefore$ $x = 0$ is a vertical asymptote
As $x \to -\infty$, $f(x) \to 0$
$\therefore$ $y = 0$ is a horizontal asymptote
As $x \to 0$ (left), $f(x) \to \infty$
As $x \to 0$ (right), $f(x) \to 0$ (above)
As $x \to \infty$, $f(x) \to \infty$
As $x \to -\infty$, $f(x) \to 0$ (above)

c $W = 5000 - \dfrac{4900}{t^2 + 1}$, $t \geqslant 0$

W is defined for all $t \geqslant 0$
$\therefore$ no vertical asymptotes exist
As $t \to \infty$, $W \to 5000$
$\therefore$ $W = 5000$ is a horizontal asymptote
As $t \to \infty$, $W \to 5000$ (below)

e $f(x) = \dfrac{x}{x^2 + 1}$

$f(x)$ is defined for all $x \in \mathbb{R}$
$\therefore$ no vertical asymptotes exist

Now $f(x) = \dfrac{\frac{1}{x}}{1 + \frac{1}{x^2}}$

$\therefore$ as $|x| \to \infty$, $f(x) \to \frac{0}{1} = 0$
$\therefore$ $y = 0$ is a horizontal asymptote
As $x \to \infty$, $f(x) \to 0$ (above)
As $x \to -\infty$, $f(x) \to 0$ (below)

g $y = \dfrac{x^3 - 2}{x^2 + 1}$

$$\begin{array}{r}x\phantom{{}+x^2+1}\\x^2+1\,\overline{\smash{\big)}\,x^3 + 0x^2 + 0x - 2}\\\underline{x^3+x}\\-x-2\end{array}$$

$\therefore$ $y = x - \dfrac{x + 2}{x^2 + 1}$

x is defined for all $x \in \mathbb{R}$
$\therefore$ no vertical asymptotes exist
As $|x| \to \infty$, $y \to x$
$\therefore$ $y = x$ is an oblique asymptote
As $x \to \infty$, $y \to x$ (below)
As $x \to -\infty$, $y \to x$ (above)

i $y = x + \ln x$

y is undefined for $x \leqslant 0$
$\therefore$ $x = 0$ is a vertical asymptote
As $x \to 0$ (right), $y \to -\infty$

j $f(x) = e^{2x} - 7e^x + 12$

$f(x)$ is defined for all $x \in \mathbb{R}$
$\therefore$ no vertical asymptotes exist
As $x \to -\infty$, $f(x) \to 12$
$\therefore$ $y = 12$ is a horizontal asymptote
As $x \to -\infty$, $f(x) \to 12$ (below)

k $y = e^x - x$
  y is defined for all $x \in \mathbb{R}$
  $\therefore$ no vertical asymptotes exist
  As $x \to -\infty$, $y \to -x$
  $\therefore$ $y = -x$ is an oblique asymptote
  As $x \to \infty$, $y \to \infty$
  As $x \to -\infty$, $y \to -x$ (above)

l $y = \dfrac{1000}{1 + 2e^{-0.16t}}$
  y is defined for all $t \in \mathbb{R}$
  $\therefore$ no vertical asymptotes exist
  As $t \to \infty$, $y \to 1000$ and
  as $t \to -\infty$, $y \to 0$
  $\therefore$ $y = 0$ and $y = 1000$ are horizontal asymptotes.
  As $t \to \infty$, $y \to 1000$ (below)
  As $t \to -\infty$, $y \to 0$ (above)

EXERCISE 19C

1 a $\lim\limits_{\theta \to 0} \dfrac{\sin 2\theta}{\theta}$

$= \lim\limits_{\theta \to 0} \dfrac{\sin 2\theta}{2\theta} \times 2$

$= 2 \times \lim\limits_{2\theta \to 0} \dfrac{\sin 2\theta}{2\theta} \quad \{2\theta \to 0 \text{ as } \theta \to 0\}$

$= 2 \times 1$

$= 2$

b $\lim\limits_{\theta \to 0} \dfrac{\theta}{\sin \theta}$

$= \lim\limits_{\theta \to 0} \dfrac{1}{\frac{\sin \theta}{\theta}}$

$= \dfrac{1}{\lim\limits_{\theta \to 0} \frac{\sin \theta}{\theta}}$

$= \dfrac{1}{1}$

$= 1$

c $\lim\limits_{\theta \to 0} \dfrac{\tan \theta}{\theta}$

$= \lim\limits_{\theta \to 0} \dfrac{\sin \theta}{\theta} \times \dfrac{1}{\cos \theta}$

$= 1 \times \dfrac{1}{1}$

$= 1$

d $\lim\limits_{\theta \to 0} \dfrac{\sin \theta \sin 4\theta}{\theta^2}$

$= \lim\limits_{\theta \to 0} \left(\dfrac{\sin \theta}{\theta}\right) \lim\limits_{\theta \to 0} \left(\dfrac{\sin 4\theta}{\theta}\right)$

$= 1 \times \lim\limits_{\theta \to 0} \left(\dfrac{\sin 4\theta}{4\theta}\right) \times 4$

$= 4 \times \lim\limits_{4\theta \to 0} \left(\dfrac{\sin 4\theta}{4\theta}\right) \quad \{4\theta \to 0 \text{ as } \theta \to 0\}$

$= 4 \times 1$

$= 4$

e $\lim\limits_{h \to 0} \dfrac{\sin\left(\frac{h}{2}\right) \cos h}{h}$

$= \lim\limits_{h \to 0} \cos h \lim\limits_{h \to 0} \dfrac{\sin\left(\frac{h}{2}\right)}{h}$

$= 1 \times \lim\limits_{h \to 0} \dfrac{\sin\left(\frac{h}{2}\right)}{\frac{h}{2}} \times \dfrac{1}{2}$

$= \dfrac{1}{2} \times \lim\limits_{\frac{h}{2} \to 0} \dfrac{\sin\left(\frac{h}{2}\right)}{\frac{h}{2}} \quad \{\tfrac{h}{2} \to 0 \text{ as } h \to 0\}$

$= \dfrac{1}{2} \times 1$

$= \dfrac{1}{2}$

f $\lim\limits_{n \to \infty} n \sin\left(\dfrac{2\pi}{n}\right)$

$= \lim\limits_{\frac{1}{n} \to 0^+} \dfrac{\sin\left(\frac{2\pi}{n}\right)}{\frac{1}{n}} \quad \{\tfrac{1}{n} \to 0^+ \text{ as } n \to \infty\}$

$= \lim\limits_{\frac{1}{n} \to 0^+} \dfrac{\sin\left(\frac{2\pi}{n}\right)}{\frac{2\pi}{n}} \times 2\pi$

$= 2\pi \times \lim\limits_{\frac{2\pi}{n} \to 0^+} \dfrac{\sin\left(\frac{2\pi}{n}\right)}{\frac{2\pi}{n}} \quad \left\{\begin{array}{l} \frac{2\pi}{n} \to 0^+ \\ \text{as } \frac{1}{n} \to 0^+ \end{array}\right\}$

$= 2\pi \times 1$

$= 2\pi$

2 **a** The angle at the apex of each triangle $= \frac{2\pi}{n}$
{angles at a point}

$\therefore \quad$ area of each triangle $= \frac{1}{2}r^2 \sin\left(\frac{2\pi}{n}\right)$

$\therefore \quad$ area of the n triangles $S_n = \frac{1}{2}nr^2 \sin\left(\frac{2\pi}{n}\right)$

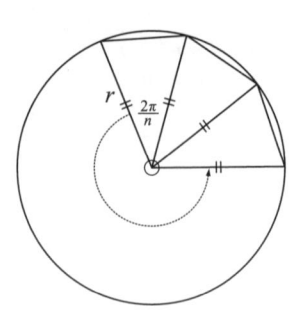

b **i** As the number of triangles increases, the triangles cover more of the circle. As $n \to \infty$, the triangles get closer to covering the whole circle.

$\therefore \quad \lim_{n \to \infty} S_n =$ area of the circle

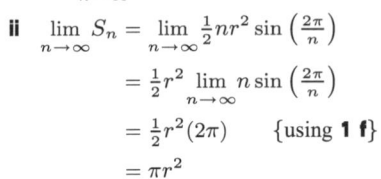

ii $\lim_{n \to \infty} S_n = \lim_{n \to \infty} \frac{1}{2}nr^2 \sin\left(\frac{2\pi}{n}\right)$

$= \frac{1}{2}r^2 \lim_{n \to \infty} n \sin\left(\frac{2\pi}{n}\right)$

$= \frac{1}{2}r^2 (2\pi) \quad$ {using **1 f**}

$= \pi r^2$

b Area of circle $= \pi r^2$

3 **a** $\cos(A+B) - \cos(A-B) = \cos A \cos B - \sin A \sin B - (\cos A \cos B + \sin A \sin B)$
$= \cos A \cos B - \sin A \sin B - \cos A \cos B - \sin A \sin B$
$= -2 \sin A \sin B$

b $\cos S - \cos D = \cos(A+B) - \cos(A-B)$
$\qquad \qquad = -2 \sin A \sin B \quad$ {using **a**}

Now $\quad S + D = A + B + A - B \quad$ and $\quad S - D = A + B - (A - B)$
$\qquad \qquad = 2A \qquad \qquad \qquad \qquad \qquad \qquad = 2B$

$\therefore \quad A = \dfrac{S+D}{2} \qquad \qquad \qquad \therefore \quad B = \dfrac{S-D}{2}$

So, $\cos S - \cos D = -2 \sin\left(\frac{S+D}{2}\right) \sin\left(\frac{S-D}{2}\right)$

c $\lim_{h \to 0} \dfrac{\cos(x+h) - \cos x}{h} = \lim_{h \to 0} \dfrac{-2 \sin\left[\frac{(x+h)+x}{2}\right] \sin\left[\frac{(x+h)-x}{2}\right]}{h} \quad \{x+h = S, \; x = D\}$

$= \lim_{h \to 0} \dfrac{-2 \sin\left(\frac{2x+h}{2}\right) \sin\left(\frac{h}{2}\right)}{h}$

$= -2 \lim_{h \to 0} \dfrac{\sin\left(x + \frac{h}{2}\right) \sin\left(\frac{h}{2}\right)}{h}$

$= -2 \lim_{h \to 0} \sin\left(x + \frac{h}{2}\right) \dfrac{\sin\left(\frac{h}{2}\right)}{\frac{h}{2}} \times \frac{1}{2}$

$= -1 \lim_{h \to 0} \sin\left(x + \frac{h}{2}\right) \lim_{\frac{h}{2} \to 0} \dfrac{\sin\left(\frac{h}{2}\right)}{\frac{h}{2}} \quad \{\frac{h}{2} \to 0 \text{ as } h \to 0\}$

$= -1 \lim_{h \to 0} \sin\left(x + \frac{h}{2}\right)$

$= -\sin x$

EXERCISE 19D.1

1 **a** [graph of $v(t)$ with values 100, 80, 60, 40, 20 on vertical axis and 0.2, 0.4, 0.6, 0.8, 1 on horizontal axis labelled time (h)]

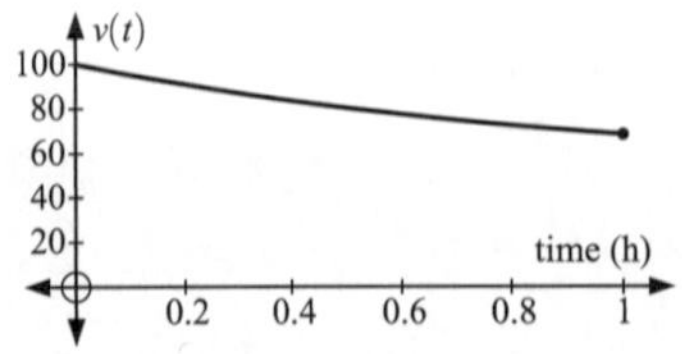

b From the graph, the speed is clearly decreasing, so the maximum speed occurs at $t = 0$, and the minimum speed occurs at $t = 1$.

$\therefore \quad$ maximum speed $= 50 + 50e^0 = 100 \text{ km h}^{-1}$
minimum speed $= 50 + 50e^{-1} \approx 68.4 \text{ km h}^{-1}$

c From **b**, we know that $v(t) \geqslant 68.4 \text{ km h}^{-1}$, and so for that hour the car will travel a distance of more than $68.4 \dfrac{\text{km}}{\text{hour}} \times 1 \text{ hour} = 68.4 \text{ km}$.

$\therefore$ since the car is initially 95 km from Adelaide, after 1 hour the distance of the car from Adelaide $d \leqslant 95 - 68.4 < 27$ km.

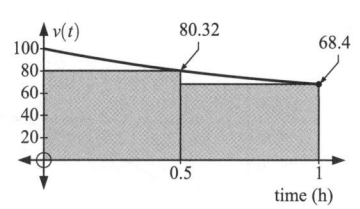

d

Using lower rectangles,
$A_L = 0.5 \times v(0.5) + 0.5 \times v(1)$
$\approx 0.5 \times 80.33 + 0.5 \times 68.39$
≈ 74.36

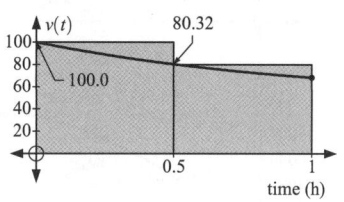

Using upper rectangles,
$A_U = 0.5 \times v(0) + 0.5 \times v(0.5)$
$\approx 0.5 \times 100 + 0.5 \times 80.32$
≈ 90.16

$\therefore\quad$ 74.36 km $<$ total distance travelled $<$ 90.16 km
$\therefore\quad$ $(95 - 90.16)$ km $<$ distance from Adelaide $< (95 - 74.36)$ km
$\therefore\quad$ 4.84 km $<$ distance from Adelaide $<$ 20.64 km

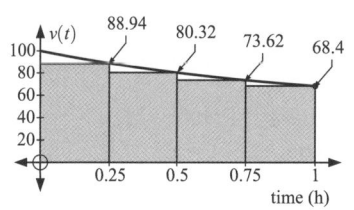

e

Using lower rectangles,
$A_L = 0.25 \times v(0.25) + 0.25 \times v(0.5)$
$\quad\quad + 0.25 \times v(0.75) + 0.25 \times v(1)$
$\approx 0.25 \times 88.94 + 0.25 \times 80.32$
$\quad\quad + 0.25 \times 73.62 + 0.25 \times 68.39$
≈ 77.82

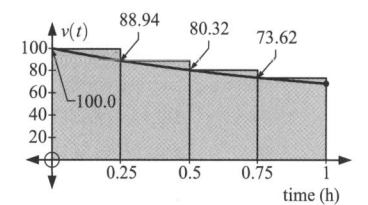

Using upper rectangles,
$A_U = 0.25 \times v(0) + 0.25 \times v(0.25)$
$\quad\quad + 0.25 \times v(0.5) + 0.25 \times v(0.75)$
$\approx 0.25 \times 100 + 0.25 \times 88.94$
$\quad\quad + 0.25 \times 80.32 + 0.25 \times 73.62$
≈ 85.72

$\therefore\quad$ 77.82 km $<$ total distance travelled $<$ 85.72 km
$\therefore\quad$ $(95 - 85.72)$ km $<$ distance from Adelaide $< (95 - 77.82)$ km
$\therefore\quad$ 9.28 km $<$ distance from Adelaide $<$ 17.18 km

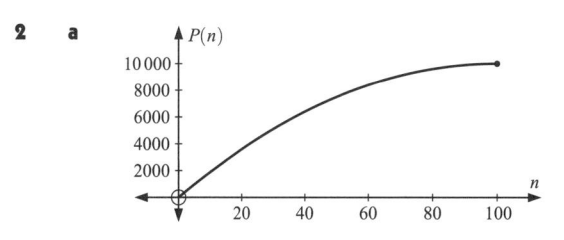

2 a

b From the graph, P is maximised when $n = 100$, and the maximum value of P is
$P(100) = 200(100) - 100^2 = 10\,000$
Thus $P(n) \leqslant 10\,000$ for $0 \leqslant n \leqslant 100$
$\therefore\quad$ the profit from selling 100 houses
$\quad\quad < 100 \times \$10\,000 = \$1\,000\,000$

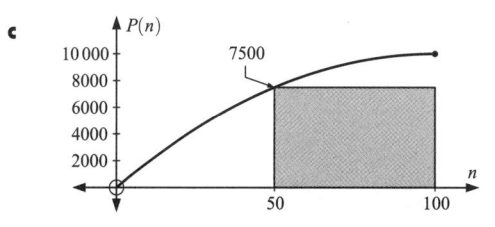

c

Using lower rectangles,
$A_L = 50 \times P(0) + 50 \times P(50)$
$\quad = 50 \times 0 + 50 \times 7500$
$\quad = 375\,000$

Using upper rectangles,
$$A_U = 50 \times P(50) + 50 \times P(100)$$
$$= 50 \times 7500 + 50 \times 10\,000$$
$$= 875\,000$$
$\therefore\ \$375\,000 <$ profit $< \$875\,000$

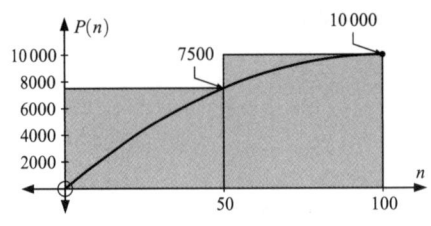

d

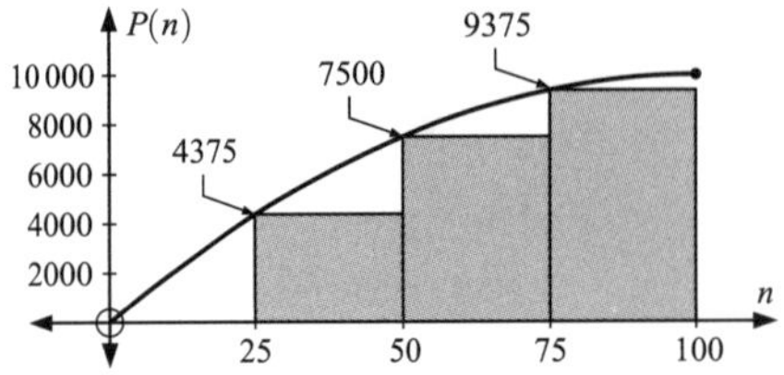

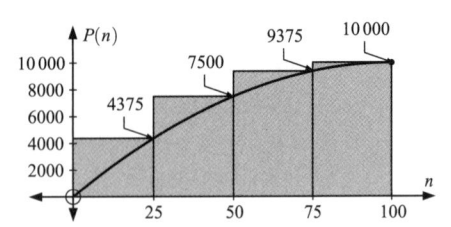

Using lower rectangles,
$$A_L = 25 \times P(0) + 25 \times P(25) + 25 \times P(50)$$
$$+ 25 \times P(75)$$
$$= 25 \times 0 + 25 \times 4375 + 25 \times 7500$$
$$+ 25 \times 9375$$
$$= 531\,250$$

Using upper rectangles,
$$A_U = 25 \times P(25) + 25 \times P(50)$$
$$+ 25 \times P(75) + 25 \times P(100)$$
$$= 25 \times 4375 + 25 \times 7500$$
$$+ 25 \times 9375 + 25 \times 10\,000$$
$$= 781\,250$$

$\therefore\ \$531\,250 <$ profit $< \$781\,250$

e If 100 intervals, each of width 1, were used, the upper sum
$$A_U = 1 \times P(1) + 1 \times P(2) + \ldots\ldots + 1 \times P(100)$$
would give the exact profit made by selling 100 houses.

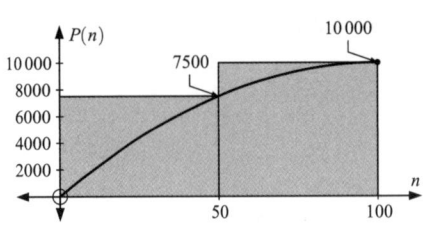

EXERCISE 19D.2

1 Using provided software,

n	A_L	A_U
10	2.1850	2.4850
25	2.2736	2.3936
50	2.3034	2.3634
100	2.3184	2.3484
500	2.3303	2.3363

A_L and A_U converge to $\frac{7}{3}$

2 a i

n	A_L	A_U
5	0.160 00	0.360 00
10	0.202 50	0.302 50
50	0.240 10	0.260 10
100	0.245 03	0.255 03
500	0.249 00	0.251 00
1000	0.249 50	0.250 50
10 000	0.249 95	0.250 05

ii

n	A_L	A_U
5	0.400 00	0.600 00
10	0.450 00	0.550 00
50	0.490 00	0.510 00
100	0.495 00	0.505 00
500	0.499 00	0.501 00
1000	0.499 50	0.500 50
10 000	0.499 95	0.500 05

iii

n	A_L	A_U
5	0.549 74	0.749 74
10	0.610 51	0.710 51
50	0.656 10	0.676 10
100	0.661 46	0.671 46
500	0.665 65	0.667 65
1000	0.666 16	0.667 16
10 000	0.666 62	0.666 72

iv

n	A_L	A_U
5	0.618 67	0.818 67
10	0.687 40	0.787 40
50	0.738 51	0.758 51
100	0.744 41	0.754 41
500	0.748 93	0.750 93
1000	0.749 47	0.750 47
10 000	0.749 95	0.750 05

b i A_L and A_U converge to $0.25 = \frac{1}{4} = \frac{1}{3+1}$

ii A_L and A_U converge to $0.5 = \frac{1}{2} = \frac{1}{1+1}$

iii A_L and A_U converge to $0.6\overline{6} = \frac{2}{3} = \frac{1}{\frac{1}{2}+1}$

iv A_L and A_U converge to $0.75 = \frac{3}{4} = \frac{1}{\frac{1}{3}+1}$

c From **b**, it appears that the area between the graph of $y = x^a$ and the x-axis for $0 \leqslant x \leqslant 1$ is $\dfrac{1}{a+1}$.

3 a

n	Rational bounds for π
10	$2.9045 < \pi < 3.3045$
50	$3.0983 < \pi < 3.1783$
100	$3.1204 < \pi < 3.1604$
200	$3.1312 < \pi < 3.1512$
1000	$3.1396 < \pi < 3.1436$
10 000	$3.1414 < \pi < 3.1418$

b $3\frac{10}{71} < \pi < 3\frac{1}{7}$ is approximately
$3.1408 < \pi < 3.1429$
From **a**, this is a better approximation than our estimate using $n = 10, 50, 100, 200, 1000$.
Only $n = 10\,000$ gives us a better estimate.

EXERCISE 19D.3

1 a

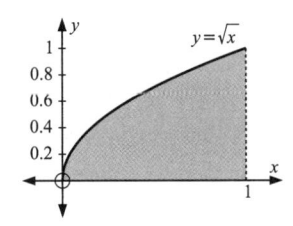

b

n	A_L	A_U
5	0.5497	0.7497
10	0.6105	0.7105
50	0.6561	0.6761
100	0.6615	0.6715
500	0.6656	0.6676

c $\int_0^1 \sqrt{x}\, dx \approx 0.67$

2 a

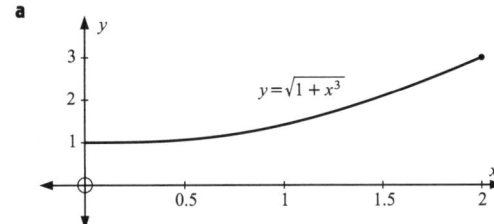

b

n	A_L	A_U
50	3.2016	3.2816
100	3.2214	3.2614
500	3.2373	3.2453

c $\int_0^2 \sqrt{1+x^3}\, dx \approx 3.24$

3 a

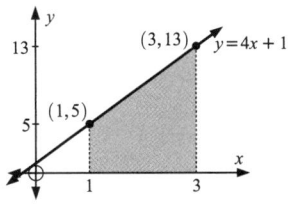

$\int_1^3 (1+4x)\, dx$
$=$ area of the shaded trap.
$= \left(\dfrac{5+13}{2}\right) \times 2$
$= 18$

b

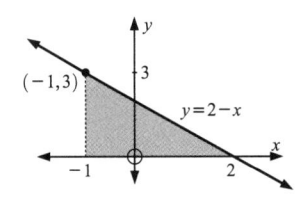

$\int_{-1}^2 (2-x)\, dx$
$=$ area of shaded triangle
$= \frac{1}{2}(3 \times 3)$
$= 4.5$

c

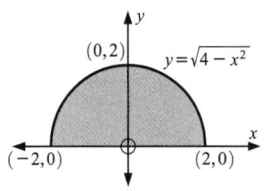

$\int_{-2}^2 \sqrt{4-x^2}\, dx$
$=$ area of semi-circle, radius 2
$= \frac{1}{2}\left(\pi \times 2^2\right)$
$= 2\pi$

REVIEW SET 19

1 **a** $\dfrac{x^2 - 4}{2 - x} = \dfrac{(x+2)(x-2)}{(2-x)}$

$\begin{cases} = -(x+2) & \text{if } x \neq 2 \\ \text{is undefined} & \text{if } x = 2 \end{cases}$

$\therefore \lim\limits_{x \to 2} \dfrac{x^2 - 4}{2 - x}$

$= \lim\limits_{x \to 2} -(x+2), \quad x \neq 2$

$= -4$

b $\dfrac{3x^2 - 12}{5x^2 + 10x} = \dfrac{3(x-2)(x+2)}{5x(x+2)}$

$\begin{cases} = \dfrac{3(x-2)}{5x} & \text{if } x \neq -2 \\ \text{is undefined} & \text{if } x = -2 \end{cases}$

$\therefore \lim\limits_{x \to -2} \dfrac{3x^2 - 12}{5x^2 + 10x}$

$= \lim\limits_{x \to -2} \dfrac{3(x-2)}{5x}, \quad x \neq -2$

$= \dfrac{-12}{-10}$ or $\dfrac{6}{5}$

c $\dfrac{\sqrt{x} - 2}{x - 4} = \dfrac{\sqrt{x} - 2}{(\sqrt{x} + 2)(\sqrt{x} - 2)}$

$\begin{cases} = \dfrac{1}{\sqrt{x} + 2} & \text{if } x \neq 4 \\ \text{is undefined} & \text{if } x = 4 \end{cases}$

$\therefore \lim\limits_{x \to 4} \dfrac{\sqrt{x} - 2}{x - 4}$

$= \lim\limits_{x \to 4} \dfrac{1}{\sqrt{x} + 2}, \quad x \neq 4$

$= \dfrac{1}{4}$

d $\dfrac{x^2 - 16}{x - 4} = \dfrac{(x+4)(x-4)}{x - 4}$

$\begin{cases} = x + 4 & \text{if } x \neq 4 \\ \text{is undefined} & \text{if } x = 4 \end{cases}$

$\therefore \lim\limits_{x \to 4} \dfrac{x^2 - 16}{x - 4}$

$= \lim\limits_{x \to 4} x + 4, \quad x \neq 4$

$= 8$

e $\dfrac{2x + 2}{x^2 - 1} = \dfrac{2(x+1)}{(x-1)(x+1)}$

$\begin{cases} = \dfrac{2}{x - 1} & \text{if } x \neq -1 \\ \text{is undefined} & \text{if } x = -1 \end{cases}$

$\therefore \lim\limits_{x \to -1} \dfrac{2x + 2}{x^2 - 1}$

$= \lim\limits_{x \to -1} \dfrac{2}{x - 1}, \quad x \neq -1$

$= \dfrac{2}{-2}$ or -1

f $\lim\limits_{x \to \infty} \dfrac{1 - 2x - x^2}{2x^2 - 4}$

$= \lim\limits_{x \to \infty} \dfrac{\dfrac{1}{x^2} - \dfrac{2}{x} - 1}{2 - \dfrac{4}{x^2}}$

$= \dfrac{-1}{2}$

2 **a** $y = \dfrac{x^2 + x - 2}{x - 2}$

$\begin{array}{r} x + 3 \\ x - 2 \,\overline{\smash{\big)}\, x^2 + x - 2} \\ \underline{x^2 - 2x} \\ 3x - 2 \\ \underline{3x - 6} \\ 4 \end{array}$

$\therefore y = x + 3 + \dfrac{4}{x - 2}$

y is undefined when $x = 2$

$\therefore x = 2$ is a vertical asymptote

As $|x| \to \infty$, $y \to x + 3$

$\therefore y = x + 3$ is an oblique asymptote

As $x \to 2$ (left), $y \to -\infty$

As $x \to 2$ (right), $y \to \infty$

As $x \to \infty$, $y \to x + 3$ (above)

As $x \to -\infty$, $y \to x + 3$ (below)

b $y = e^{x-2} - 3$
y is defined for all $x \in \mathbb{R}$
$\therefore$ no vertical asymptotes exist
As $x \to -\infty$, $y \to -3$
$\therefore$ $y = -3$ is a horizontal asymptote
As $x \to \infty$, $y \to \infty$
As $x \to -\infty$, $y \to -3$ (above)

c $y = \ln(x^2 + 3)$ has no asymptotes

d $f(x) = e^{-x} \ln x$
$f(x)$ is undefined for $x \leqslant 0$
$\therefore$ $x = 0$ is a vertical asymptote
As $x \to \infty$, $f(x) \to 0$
$\therefore$ $y = 0$ is a horizontal asymptote
As $x \to 0$ (right), $f(x) \to -\infty$
As $x \to \infty$, $f(x) \to 0$ (above)

e $y = x + \ln(2x - 3)$
y is undefined for $x \leqslant \frac{3}{2}$
$\therefore$ $x = \frac{3}{2}$ is a vertical asymptote
As $x \to \frac{3}{2}$ (right), $y \to -\infty$

f $x \mapsto \ln(-x) + 2$ $\therefore$ $y = \ln(-x) + 2$
y is undefined for $x \geqslant 0$
$\therefore$ $x = 0$ is a vertical asymptote
As $x \to 0$ (left), $y \to -\infty$

3 a $\lim\limits_{\theta \to 0} \dfrac{\sin 4\theta}{\theta}$

$= \lim\limits_{\theta \to 0} \dfrac{\sin 4\theta}{4\theta} \times 4$

$= 4 \lim\limits_{4\theta \to 0} \dfrac{\sin 4\theta}{4\theta}$ $\quad \{4\theta \to 0$ as $\theta \to 0\}$

$= 4 \times 1$
$= 4$

b $\lim\limits_{\theta \to 0} \dfrac{2\theta}{\sin 3\theta}$

$= \lim\limits_{\theta \to 0} \dfrac{3\theta}{\sin 3\theta} \times \dfrac{2}{3}$

$= \dfrac{2}{3} \lim\limits_{\theta \to 0} \dfrac{1}{\frac{\sin 3\theta}{3\theta}}$

$= \dfrac{2}{3} \dfrac{1}{\lim\limits_{3\theta \to 0} \frac{\sin 3\theta}{3\theta}}$ $\quad \{3\theta \to 0$ as $\theta \to 0\}$

$= \dfrac{2}{3} \times \dfrac{1}{1}$
$= \dfrac{2}{3}$

c $\lim\limits_{n \to \infty} n \sin\left(\dfrac{\pi}{n}\right)$

$= \lim\limits_{\frac{1}{n} \to 0} \dfrac{\sin\left(\frac{\pi}{n}\right)}{\frac{1}{n}}$ $\quad \{\frac{1}{n} \to 0$ as $n \to \infty\}$

$= \lim\limits_{\frac{1}{n} \to 0} \dfrac{\sin\left(\frac{\pi}{n}\right)}{\frac{\pi}{n}} \times \pi$

$= \pi \times \lim\limits_{\frac{\pi}{n} \to 0} \dfrac{\sin\left(\frac{\pi}{n}\right)}{\frac{\pi}{n}}$ $\quad \{\frac{\pi}{n} \to 0$ as $\frac{1}{n} \to 0\}$

$= \pi \times 1$
$= \pi$

4 a

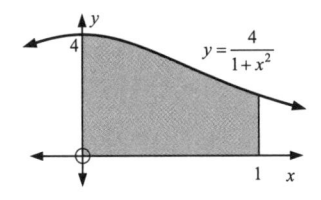

lower rectangles   upper rectangles

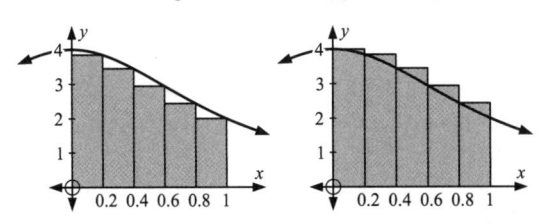

b

n	A_L	A_U
5	2.9349	3.3349
50	3.1215	3.1615
100	3.1316	3.1516
500	3.1396	3.1436

c $\displaystyle\int_0^1 \dfrac{4}{1+x^2}\, dx \approx 3.1416$

(the average of A_L and A_U for $n = 500$). This value agrees with π to 4 decimal places.

5 **a**

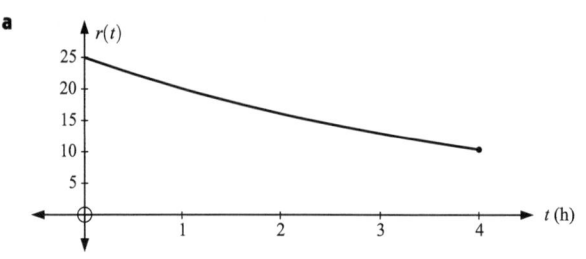

[Graph of $r(t)$ showing a decreasing exponential curve starting at 25 and ending near 10 at $t=4$]

b From the graph, the maximum value of r is $r(0) = 25e^{-0.22(0)} = 25$
and the minimum value of r is $r(4) = 25e^{-0.22(4)} \approx 10$
Thus $10 \leqslant r(t) \leqslant 25$ for $0 \leqslant t \leqslant 4$
$\therefore$ over four hours, (4×10) mg $\leqslant$ amount of caffeine eliminated from body $\leqslant (4 \times 25)$ mg
$\therefore$ 40 mg $\leqslant$ amount of caffeine eliminated from body $\leqslant$ 100 mg
Since the initial intake of caffeine was 110 mg,
$(110 - 100)$ mg $\leqslant$ amount of caffeine left in the body $\leqslant (110 - 40)$ mg
$\therefore$ 10 mg $\leqslant$ $\qquad\qquad Q(t) \qquad\qquad \leqslant$ 70 mg

c

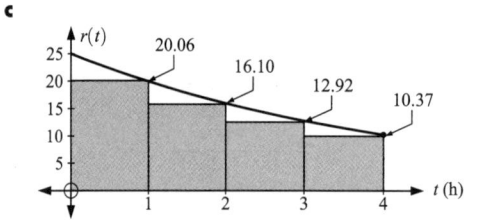

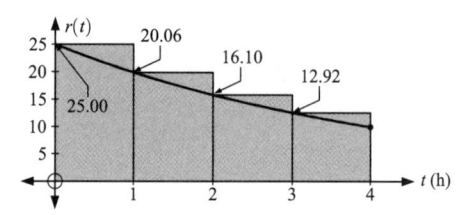

[Two bar graphs showing lower and upper rectangle approximations under curve $r(t)$. Lower rectangles have heights 20.06, 16.10, 12.92, 10.37. Upper rectangles have heights 25.00, 20.06, 16.10, 12.92.]

Using lower rectangles,
$A_L = 1 \times r(1) + 1 \times r(2) + 1 \times r(3)$
$\qquad + 1 \times r(4)$
$\approx 20.06 + 16.10 + 12.92 + 10.37$
≈ 59.5

Using upper rectangles,
$A_U = 1 \times r(0) + 1 \times r(1) + 1 \times r(2)$
$\qquad + 1 \times r(3)$
$\approx 25 + 20.06 + 16.10 + 12.92$
≈ 74.1

$\therefore \qquad$ 59.5 mg $<$ amount of caffeine eliminated from body $<$ 74.1 mg
$\therefore \quad (110 - 74.1)$ mg $<\quad$ amount of caffeine left in body $\quad< (110 - 59.5)$ mg
$\therefore \qquad$ 35.9 mg $<\qquad\qquad Q(t) \qquad\qquad <$ 50.5 mg

d Using more intervals of shorter width will improve the accuracy of the estimate in **c**.

6 $\quad \lim\limits_{h \to 0} \dfrac{2\cos\left(x + \frac{h}{2}\right)\sin\left(\frac{h}{2}\right)}{h}$

$= 2 \lim\limits_{h \to 0} \cos\left(x + \frac{h}{2}\right) \lim\limits_{h \to 0} \dfrac{\sin\left(\frac{h}{2}\right)}{h} \times \frac{1}{2}$

$= 1 \times \lim\limits_{h \to 0} \cos\left(x + \frac{h}{2}\right) \lim\limits_{\frac{h}{2} \to 0} \dfrac{\sin\left(\frac{h}{2}\right)}{\frac{h}{2}} \qquad \{\frac{h}{2} \to 0$ as $h \to 0\}$

$= 1 \times \lim\limits_{h \to 0} \cos\left(x + \frac{h}{2}\right)$

$= \cos x \qquad\qquad$ It is assumed that x and h are in radians.

7 **a** $\sin(A + B) - \sin(A - B) = \sin A \cos B + \cos A \sin B - (\sin A \cos B - \cos A \sin B)$
$\qquad\qquad\qquad\qquad\qquad\; = \sin A \cos B + \cos A \sin B - \sin A \cos B + \cos A \sin B$
$\qquad\qquad\qquad\qquad\qquad\; = 2 \cos A \sin B$

b $\sin S - \sin D = \sin(A + B) - \sin(A - B)$
$\qquad\qquad\quad\; = 2 \cos A \sin B \qquad$ {using **a**}

Now $S + D = A + B + (A - B)$ and $S - D = A + B - (A - B)$
$= 2A$ $= 2B$

$\therefore \quad A = \dfrac{S + D}{2}$ $\therefore \quad B = \dfrac{S - D}{2}$

$\therefore \quad \sin S - \sin D = 2 \cos\left(\dfrac{S+D}{2}\right) \sin\left(\dfrac{S-D}{2}\right)$

c $\lim\limits_{h \to 0} \dfrac{\sin(x+h) - \sin x}{h} = \lim\limits_{h \to 0} \dfrac{2 \cos\left[\frac{(x+h)+x}{2}\right] \sin\left[\frac{(x+h)-x}{2}\right]}{h}$ $\quad \{x + h = S, \ x = D\}$

$= \lim\limits_{h \to 0} \dfrac{2 \cos\left(\frac{2x+h}{2}\right) \sin\left(\frac{h}{2}\right)}{h}$

$= 2 \lim\limits_{h \to 0} \dfrac{\cos\left(x + \frac{h}{2}\right) \sin\left(\frac{h}{2}\right)}{h}$

$= 2 \lim\limits_{h \to 0} \cos\left(x + \frac{h}{2}\right) \dfrac{\sin\left(\frac{h}{2}\right)}{\frac{h}{2}} \times \frac{1}{2}$

$= 1 \lim\limits_{h \to 0} \cos\left(x + \frac{h}{2}\right) \lim\limits_{\frac{h}{2} \to 0} \dfrac{\sin\left(\frac{h}{2}\right)}{\frac{h}{2}}$ $\quad \{\frac{h}{2} \to 0 \text{ as } h \to 0\}$

$= \lim\limits_{h \to 0} \cos\left(x + \frac{h}{2}\right)$

$= \cos x$

8 a

b Since $f(x)$ is decreasing for $2 \leqslant x \leqslant 6$, the maximum value will occur at $x = 2$, and the minimum value will occur at $x = 6$.
$\therefore$ the maximum value $= f(2) = \frac{1}{2}$, and the minimum value $= f(6) = \frac{1}{6} \approx 0.167$
$\therefore$ using a single interval of length 4 to estimate the area,
$A_L = 4 \times \left(\frac{1}{6}\right) = \frac{2}{3}$ and $A_U = 4 \times \left(\frac{1}{2}\right) = 2$
$\therefore \quad \frac{2}{3} < \text{area} < 2$

c

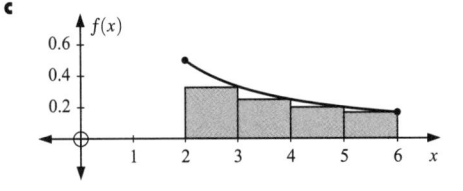

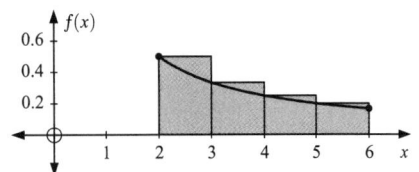

Using lower rectangles,
$A_L = 1 \times f(3) + 1 \times f(4) + 1 \times f(5) + 1 \times f(6)$
$= \frac{1}{3} + \frac{1}{4} + \frac{1}{5} + \frac{1}{6}$
$= 0.95$

Using upper rectangles,
$A_U = 1 \times f(2) + 1 \times f(3) + 1 \times f(4) + 1 \times f(5)$
$= \frac{1}{2} + \frac{1}{3} + \frac{1}{4} + \frac{1}{5}$
≈ 1.28

$\therefore \quad 0.95 < \text{area} < 1.28$

d Using more intervals of shorter width will improve the accuracy of the estimate in **c**.

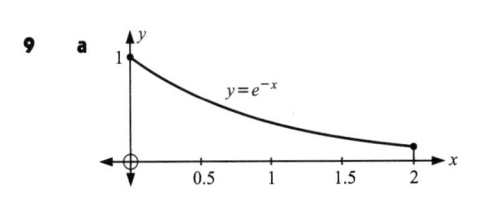

9 a

Each rectangle has width $\Delta x = \dfrac{2 - 0}{8} = 0.25$.

For $f(x) = e^{-x}$,
$f(0) = 1$, $\quad f(0.25) \approx 0.779$, $\quad f(0.5) \approx 0.607$,
$f(0.75) \approx 0.472$, $\quad f(1) \approx 0.368$, $\quad f(1.25) \approx 0.287$,
$f(1.5) \approx 0.223$, $\quad f(1.75) \approx 0.174$, $\quad f(2) \approx 0.135$.

b Upper bound $= 0.25 \,[f(0) + f(0.25) + f(0.5) + f(0.75) + f(1) + f(1.25) + f(1.5) + f(1.75)]$
$\approx 0.25(3.91)$
≈ 0.977 units^2

Lower bound $= 0.25 \,[f(0.25) + f(0.5) + f(0.75) + f(1) + f(1.25) + f(1.5) + f(1.75) + f(2)]$
$\approx 0.25(3.044)$
≈ 0.761 units^2

c Using technology, $A_U \approx 0.8733$ units^2, $A_L \approx 0.8560$ units^2.

10 a $\int_0^4 f(x)\,dx =$ area of semi-circle with radius 2
$= \frac{1}{2} \times \pi \times 2^2$
$= 2\pi$

b $\int_4^6 f(x)\,dx =$ area of square
$= 2 \times 2$
$= 4$

11 a Suppose P($\cos\theta$, $\sin\theta$) lies on the unit circle in the first quadrant.

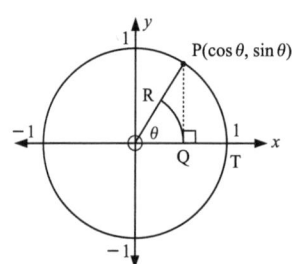

[PQ] is drawn perpendicular to the x-axis, and arc QR with centre O is drawn. Now,

area of sector OQR $\leqslant$ area $\triangle$OQP $\leqslant$ area sector OTP

$\therefore \quad \frac{1}{2}(OQ)^2 \times \theta \leqslant \frac{1}{2}(OQ)(PQ) \leqslant \frac{1}{2}(OT)^2 \times \theta$

$\therefore \quad \frac{1}{2}\theta\cos^2\theta \leqslant \frac{1}{2}\cos\theta\sin\theta \leqslant \frac{1}{2}\theta$

Dividing throughout by $\frac{1}{2}\theta\cos\theta$, which is > 0, $\quad \cos\theta \leqslant \dfrac{\sin\theta}{\theta} \leqslant \dfrac{1}{\cos\theta}$

Now as $\theta \to 0$, both $\cos\theta \to 1$ and $\dfrac{1}{\cos\theta} \to 1$

$\therefore \quad$ as $\theta \to 0$ (right), $\dfrac{\sin\theta}{\theta} \to 1$.

b If $f(\theta) = \dfrac{\sin\theta}{\theta}$, $f(-\theta) = \dfrac{\sin(-\theta)}{-\theta} = \dfrac{-\sin\theta}{-\theta} = \dfrac{\sin\theta}{\theta} = f(\theta)$

$\therefore \quad \dfrac{\sin\theta}{\theta}$ is an even function, so as $\theta \to 0$ (left), $\dfrac{\sin\theta}{\theta} \to 1$ also.

c Area of shaded segment
$=$ (area of sector) $-$ (area of triangle)
$= \frac{1}{2}r^2\theta - \frac{1}{2}r^2\sin\theta$
$= \frac{1}{2}r^2(\theta - \sin\theta)$

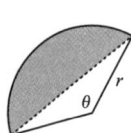

d As $\theta \to 0$, area of shaded segment $\to 0$
$\therefore \quad \frac{1}{2}r^2(\theta - \sin\theta) \to 0$
$\therefore \quad \theta - \sin\theta \to 0$
$\therefore \quad \theta \to \sin\theta$
$\therefore \quad \dfrac{\sin\theta}{\theta} \to 1$
$\therefore \quad \lim_{\theta \to 0} \dfrac{\sin\theta}{\theta} = 1$

12 a

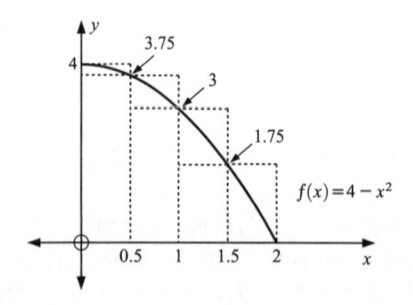

$A_U = 0.5\,[f(0) + f(0.5) + f(1) + f(1.5)]$
$= 0.5(4 + 3.75 + 3 + 1.75)$
$= 6.25$

$A_L = 0.5\,[f(0.5) + f(1) + f(1.5) + f(2)]$
$= 0.5(3.75 + 3 + 1.75 + 0)$
$= 4.25$

$\therefore \quad 4.25 < \int_0^2 (4 - x^2)\,dx < 6.25$

$\therefore \quad A = 4.25 = \frac{17}{4}, \quad B = 6.25 = \frac{25}{4}$

b an estimate of $\int_0^2 (4-x^2)\, dx = \dfrac{A+B}{2} = \dfrac{42}{8} = \dfrac{21}{4}$

13 a

(graph of $y = \sin^2 x$ from 0 to π, peaking at 1 at $x = \frac{\pi}{2}$)

b

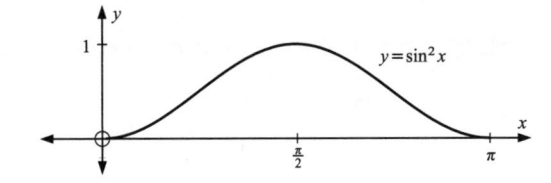

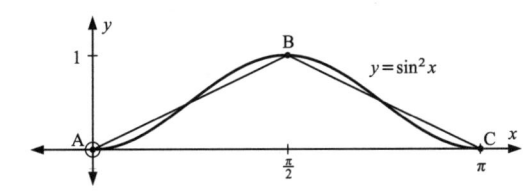

(same graph with triangle ABC inscribed: A at origin, B at $(\frac{\pi}{2}, 1)$, C at $(\pi, 0)$)

$\int_0^\pi \sin^2 x\, dx$ = area under the curve $y = \sin^2 x$ from $0 \leqslant x \leqslant \pi$
$\approx$ area of triangle ABC
$\approx \frac{1}{2} \times \pi \times 1$
$\approx \frac{\pi}{2}$

Chapter 20
DIFFERENTIAL CALCULUS

EXERCISE 20A

1 a $f(x) = x$

$$f'(x) = \lim_{h \to 0} \frac{f(x+h) - f(x)}{h}$$

$$= \lim_{h \to 0} \frac{(x+h) - x}{h}$$

$$= \lim_{h \to 0} \frac{h}{h}$$

$$= \lim_{h \to 0} 1 \quad \{\text{as } h \neq 0\}$$

$$= 1$$

b $f(x) = 5$

$$f'(x) = \lim_{h \to 0} \frac{f(x+h) - f(x)}{h}$$

$$= \lim_{h \to 0} \frac{5 - 5}{h}$$

$$= \lim_{h \to 0} \frac{0}{h}$$

$$= \lim_{h \to 0} 0 \quad \{\text{as } h \neq 0\}$$

$$= 0$$

c $f(x) = x^3 \quad \therefore \quad f'(x) = \lim_{h \to 0} \frac{f(x+h) - f(x)}{h}$

$$= \lim_{h \to 0} \frac{(x+h)^3 - x^3}{h}$$

$$= \lim_{h \to 0} \frac{x^3 + 3x^2h + 3xh^2 + h^3 - x^3}{h}$$

$$= \lim_{h \to 0} \frac{3x^2h + 3xh^2 + h^3}{h}$$

$$= \lim_{h \to 0} 3x^2 + 3xh + h^2 \quad \{\text{as } h \neq 0\}$$

$$= 3x^2$$

d $f(x) = x^4 \quad \therefore \quad f'(x) = \lim_{h \to 0} \frac{f(x+h) - f(x)}{h}$

$$= \lim_{h \to 0} \frac{(x+h)^4 - x^4}{h}$$

$$= \lim_{h \to 0} \frac{x^4 + 4x^3h + 6x^2h^2 + 4xh^3 + h^4 - x^4}{h}$$

$$= \lim_{h \to 0} \frac{4x^3h + 6x^2h^2 + 4xh^3 + h^4}{h}$$

$$= \lim_{h \to 0} 4x^3 + 6x^2h + 4xh^2 + h^3 \quad \{\text{as } h \neq 0\}$$

$$= 4x^3$$

2 a $f(x) = 2x + 5$

$\therefore \quad f'(x)$

$$= \lim_{h \to 0} \frac{f(x+h) - f(x)}{h}$$

$$= \lim_{h \to 0} \frac{(2(x+h) + 5) - (2x + 5)}{h}$$

$$= \lim_{h \to 0} \frac{2x + 2h + 5 - 2x - 5}{h}$$

$$= \lim_{h \to 0} \frac{2h}{h}$$

$$= \lim_{h \to 0} 2 \quad \{\text{as } h \neq 0\}$$

$$= 2$$

b $f(x) = x^2 - 3x$

$\therefore \quad f'(x)$

$$= \lim_{h \to 0} \frac{f(x+h) - f(x)}{h}$$

$$= \lim_{h \to 0} \frac{[(x+h)^2 - 3(x+h)] - [x^2 - 3x]}{h}$$

$$= \lim_{h \to 0} \frac{x^2 + 2xh + h^2 - 3x - 3h - x^2 + 3x}{h}$$

$$= \lim_{h \to 0} \frac{2xh + h^2 - 3h}{h}$$

$$= \lim_{h \to 0} 2x + h - 3 \quad \{\text{as } h \neq 0\}$$

$$= 2x - 3$$

c $f(x) = x^3 - 2x^2 + 3$

$f'(x) = \lim_{h \to 0} \dfrac{f(x+h) - f(x)}{h}$

$= \lim_{h \to 0} \dfrac{[(x+h)^3 - 2(x+h)^2 + 3] - [x^3 - 2x^2 + 3]}{h}$

$= \lim_{h \to 0} \dfrac{(x^3 + 3x^2h + 3xh^2 + h^3 - 2x^2 - 4xh - 2h^2 + 3) - (x^3 - 2x^2 + 3)}{h}$

$= \lim_{h \to 0} \dfrac{3x^2h + 3xh^2 + h^3 - 4xh - 2h^2}{h}$

$= \lim_{h \to 0} 3x^2 + 3xh + h^2 - 4x - 2h \quad \{\text{as } h \neq 0\}$

$= 3x^2 - 4x$

3 a $f(x) = \dfrac{1}{x+2}$

$\therefore f'(x)$

$= \lim_{h \to 0} \dfrac{f(x+h) - f(x)}{h}$

$= \lim_{h \to 0} \dfrac{\dfrac{1}{(x+h)+2} - \dfrac{1}{x+2}}{h}$

$= \lim_{h \to 0} \dfrac{(x+2) - (x+h+2)}{h(x+h+2)(x+2)}$

$= \lim_{h \to 0} \dfrac{-1 \cdot \cancel{h}}{\cancel{h}(x+2)(x+h+2)}$

$= \lim_{h \to 0} \dfrac{-1}{(x+2)(x+h+2)} \quad \{\text{as } h \neq 0\}$

$= \dfrac{-1}{(x+2)^2}$

b $f(x) = \dfrac{1}{2x-1}$

$\therefore f'(x)$

$= \lim_{h \to 0} \dfrac{f(x+h) - f(x)}{h}$

$= \lim_{h \to 0} \dfrac{\dfrac{1}{2(x+h)-1} - \dfrac{1}{2x-1}}{h}$

$= \lim_{h \to 0} \dfrac{(2x-1) - [2(x+h) - 1]}{h[2(x+h) - 1](2x-1)}$

$= \lim_{h \to 0} \dfrac{2x - 1 - 2x - 2h + 1}{h[2(x+h) - 1](2x-1)}$

$= \lim_{h \to 0} \dfrac{-2\cancel{h}}{\cancel{h}[2(x+h) - 1](2x-1)}$

$= \lim_{h \to 0} \dfrac{-2}{[2(x+h) - 1](2x-1)} \quad \{\text{as } h \neq 0\}$

$= \dfrac{-2}{(2x-1)^2}$

c $f(x) = \dfrac{1}{x^2}$

$\therefore f'(x) = \lim_{h \to 0} \dfrac{f(x+h) - f(x)}{h}$

$= \lim_{h \to 0} \dfrac{\dfrac{1}{(x+h)^2} - \dfrac{1}{x^2}}{h}$

$= \lim_{h \to 0} \dfrac{x^2 - (x+h)^2}{hx^2(x+h)^2}$

$= \lim_{h \to 0} \dfrac{[x + (x+h)][x - (x+h)]}{hx^2(x+h)^2}$

$= \lim_{h \to 0} \dfrac{(2x+h)(\cancel{-h})}{\cancel{h}x^2(x+h)^2}$

$= \lim_{h \to 0} \dfrac{-(2x+h)}{x^2(x+h)^2} \quad \{\text{as } h \neq 0\}$

$= \dfrac{-2x}{x^4}$

$= -\dfrac{2}{x^3}$

d $f(x) = \dfrac{1}{x^3}$

$\therefore f'(x) = \lim_{h \to 0} \dfrac{f(x+h) - f(x)}{h}$

$= \lim_{h \to 0} \dfrac{\dfrac{1}{(x+h)^3} - \dfrac{1}{x^3}}{h}$

$= \lim_{h \to 0} \dfrac{x^3 - (x+h)^3}{hx^3(x+h)^3}$

$= \lim_{h \to 0} \dfrac{x^3 - x^3 - 3x^2h - 3xh^2 - h^3}{hx^3(x+h)^3}$

$= \lim_{h \to 0} \dfrac{-3x^2h - 3xh^2 - h^3}{hx^3(x+h)^3}$

$= \lim_{h \to 0} \dfrac{-3x^2 - 3xh - h^2}{x^3(x+h)^3} \quad \{\text{as } h \neq 0\}$

$= \dfrac{-3x^2}{x^3 \times x^3}$

$= -\dfrac{3}{x^4}$

4 a $f(x) = \sqrt{x+2}$ $\quad \therefore \quad f'(x) = \lim_{h \to 0} \dfrac{f(x+h) - f(x)}{h}$

$$= \lim_{h \to 0} \dfrac{\sqrt{x+h+2} - \sqrt{x+2}}{h}$$

$$= \lim_{h \to 0} \dfrac{(\sqrt{x+2+h} - \sqrt{x+2})(\sqrt{x+2+h} + \sqrt{x+2})}{h(\sqrt{x+2+h} + \sqrt{x+2})}$$

$$= \lim_{h \to 0} \dfrac{(x+2+h) - (x+2)}{h(\sqrt{x+2+h} + \sqrt{x+2})}$$

$$= \lim_{h \to 0} \dfrac{1\!\!\!/\!h}{\!\!\!/\!h(\sqrt{x+2+h} + \sqrt{x+2})}$$

$$= \lim_{h \to 0} \dfrac{1}{\sqrt{x+2+h} + \sqrt{x+2}}$$

$$= \dfrac{1}{\sqrt{x+2} + \sqrt{x+2}}$$

$$= \dfrac{1}{2\sqrt{x+2}}$$

b $f(x) = \dfrac{1}{\sqrt{x}}$ $\quad \therefore \quad f'(x) = \lim_{h \to 0} \dfrac{f(x+h) - f(x)}{h}$

$$= \lim_{h \to 0} \dfrac{\dfrac{1}{\sqrt{x+h}} - \dfrac{1}{\sqrt{x}}}{h}$$

$$= \lim_{h \to 0} \dfrac{\sqrt{x} - \sqrt{x+h}}{h\sqrt{x+h} \times \sqrt{x}}$$

$$= \lim_{h \to 0} \dfrac{(\sqrt{x} - \sqrt{x+h})}{h\sqrt{x+h} \times \sqrt{x}} \left(\dfrac{\sqrt{x} + \sqrt{x+h}}{\sqrt{x} + \sqrt{x+h}} \right)$$

$$= \lim_{h \to 0} \dfrac{x - (x+h)}{h\sqrt{x+h} \times \sqrt{x}(\sqrt{x} + \sqrt{x+h})}$$

$$= \lim_{h \to 0} \dfrac{-\!\!\!/\!h}{\!\!\!/\!h\sqrt{x+h} \times \sqrt{x}(\sqrt{x} + \sqrt{x+h})}$$

$$= \lim_{h \to 0} \dfrac{-1}{\sqrt{x+h} \times \sqrt{x}(\sqrt{x} + \sqrt{x+h})}$$

$$= \dfrac{-1}{\sqrt{x} \times \sqrt{x} \times 2\sqrt{x}}$$

$$= \dfrac{-1}{2x\sqrt{x}}$$

c $f(x) = \sqrt{2x+1}$ $\quad \therefore \quad f'(x) = \lim_{h \to 0} \dfrac{f(x+h) - f(x)}{h}$

$$= \lim_{h \to 0} \dfrac{\sqrt{2(x+h)+1} - \sqrt{2x+1}}{h}$$

$$= \lim_{h \to 0} \dfrac{\sqrt{2(x+h)+1} - \sqrt{2x+1}}{h} \left(\dfrac{\sqrt{2(x+h)+1} + \sqrt{2x+1}}{\sqrt{2(x+h)+1} + \sqrt{2x+1}} \right)$$

$$= \lim_{h \to 0} \dfrac{[2(x+h)+1] - [2x+1]}{h(\sqrt{2(x+h)+1} + \sqrt{2x+1})}$$

$$= \lim_{h \to 0} \dfrac{2\!\!\!/\!h}{\!\!\!/\!h(\sqrt{2(x+h)+1} + \sqrt{2x+1})} \quad \{\text{as } h \neq 0\}$$

$$= \lim_{h \to 0} \frac{2}{(\sqrt{2(x+h)+1} + \sqrt{2x+1})}$$

$$= \frac{2}{2\sqrt{2x+1}}$$

$$= \frac{1}{\sqrt{2x+1}}$$

5

Function	Derivative	Function	Derivative	Function	Derivative
x^1	$1x^0 = 1$	x^{-1}	$-1x^{-2}$	$x^{\frac{1}{2}}$	$\frac{1}{2}x^{-\frac{1}{2}}$
x^2	$2x^1 = 2x$	x^{-2}	$-2x^{-3}$	$x^{-\frac{1}{2}}$	$-\frac{1}{2}x^{-\frac{3}{2}}$
x^3	$3x^2$	x^{-3}	$-3x^{-4}$		
x^4	$4x^3$				

If $f(x) = x^n$, $f'(x) = nx^{n-1}$

6 In order to prove this rule, we need the *binomial expansion* discussed in **Chapter 8**.

Now if $f(x) = x^n$,

then $f'(x) = \lim_{h \to 0} \dfrac{f(x+h) - f(x)}{h}$

$= \lim_{h \to 0} \dfrac{(x+h)^n - x^n}{h}$

$= \lim_{h \to 0} \dfrac{\left[\binom{n}{0}x^n + \binom{n}{1}x^{n-1}h + \binom{n}{2}x^{n-2}h^2 + \ldots + \binom{n}{n-1}xh^{n-1} + \binom{n}{n}h^n\right] - x^n}{h}$

{for $n \in \mathbb{Z}^+$ using the Binomial expansion}

$= \lim_{h \to 0} \dfrac{\left[x^n + nx^{n-1}h + \binom{n}{2}x^{n-2}h^2 + \ldots + \binom{n}{n-1}xh^{n-1} + h^n\right] - x^n}{h}$

$= \lim_{h \to 0} \dfrac{nx^{n-1}h + \binom{n}{2}x^{n-2}h^2 + \ldots + \binom{n}{n-1}xh^{n-1} + h^n}{h}$

$= \lim_{h \to 0} \left[nx^{n-1} + \binom{n}{2}x^{n-2}h + \ldots + \binom{n}{n-1}xh^{n-2} + h^{n-1}\right]$ {as $h \neq 0$}

$= nx^{n-1}$ for $n \in \mathbb{Z}^+$ as required

EXERCISE 20B

1 a $f(x) = 1 - x^2$
$\therefore\ f(2) = 1 - 2^2 = -3$

$f'(2) = \lim_{x \to 2} \dfrac{f(x) - f(2)}{x - 2}$

$= \lim_{x \to 2} \dfrac{(1 - x^2) - (-3)}{x - 2}$

$= \lim_{x \to 2} \dfrac{4 - x^2}{x - 2}$

$= \lim_{x \to 2} \dfrac{-(x+2)(x-2)}{x-2}$

$= \lim_{x \to 2} -(x+2)$ {as $x \neq 2$}

$= -4$

b $f(x) = 2x^2 + 5x$ at $x = -1$
$\therefore\ f(-1) = 2(-1)^2 + 5(-1) = -3$

$f'(-1) = \lim_{x \to -1} \dfrac{f(x) - f(-1)}{x - (-1)}$

$= \lim_{x \to -1} \dfrac{(2x^2 + 5x) - (-3)}{x + 1}$

$= \lim_{x \to -1} \dfrac{2x^2 + 5x + 3}{x + 1}$

$= \lim_{x \to -1} \dfrac{(2x+3)(x+1)}{x+1}$

$= \lim_{x \to -1} 2x + 3$ {as $x \neq -1$}

$= 1$

c $f(x) = 5 - 2x^2$ at $x = 3$

$\therefore$ $f(3) = 5 - 2(3)^2 = -13$

$f'(3) = \lim\limits_{x \to 3} \dfrac{f(x) - f(3)}{x - 3}$

$= \lim\limits_{x \to 3} \dfrac{(5 - 2x^2) - (-13)}{x - 3}$

$= \lim\limits_{x \to 3} \dfrac{18 - 2x^2}{x - 3}$

$= \lim\limits_{x \to 3} \dfrac{-2(x^2 - 9)}{x - 3}$

$= \lim\limits_{x \to 3} \dfrac{-2(x+3)\cancel{(x-3)}}{\cancel{x-3}}$

$= \lim\limits_{x \to 3} -2(x + 3)$ {as $x \neq 3$}

$= -2(6)$

$= -12$

d $f(x) = 3x + 5$ at $x = -2$

$\therefore$ $f(-2) = 3(-2) + 5 = -1$

$f'(-2) = \lim\limits_{x \to -2} \dfrac{f(x) - f(-2)}{x + 2}$ where

$= \lim\limits_{x \to -2} \dfrac{(3x + 5) - (-1)}{x + 2}$

$= \lim\limits_{x \to -2} \dfrac{3x + 6}{x + 2}$

$= \lim\limits_{x \to -2} \dfrac{3\cancel{(x+2)}}{\cancel{x+2}}$

$= \lim\limits_{x \to -2} 3$ {as $x \neq -2$}

$= 3$

2   **a** $f'(2) = \lim\limits_{x \to 2} \dfrac{f(x) - f(2)}{x - 2}$

$= \lim\limits_{x \to 2} \dfrac{\frac{4}{x} - \frac{4}{2}}{x - 2}$

$= \lim\limits_{x \to 2} \dfrac{8 - 4x}{2x(x - 2)}$

$= \lim\limits_{x \to 2} \dfrac{-4\cancel{(x-2)}}{2x\cancel{(x-2)}}$

$= \lim\limits_{x \to 2} \dfrac{-4}{2x}$ {as $x \neq 2$}

$= -\dfrac{4}{4}$

$= -1$

b $f'(-2) = \lim\limits_{x \to -2} \dfrac{f(x) - f(-2)}{x - (-2)}$

$= \lim\limits_{x \to -2} \dfrac{\frac{3}{x} - \frac{3}{-2}}{(x + 2)}$

$= \lim\limits_{x \to -2} \dfrac{-6 - 3x}{2x(x + 2)}$

$= \lim\limits_{x \to -2} \dfrac{-3\cancel{(x+2)}}{2x\cancel{(x+2)}}$

$= \lim\limits_{x \to -2} \dfrac{-3}{2x}$ {as $x \neq -2$}

$= \dfrac{-3}{-4}$

$= \dfrac{3}{4}$

c $f'(4) = \lim\limits_{x \to 4} \dfrac{f(x) - f(4)}{x - 4}$

$= \lim\limits_{x \to 4} \dfrac{\frac{1}{x^2} - \frac{1}{16}}{x - 4}$

$= \lim\limits_{x \to 4} \dfrac{16 - x^2}{16x^2(x - 4)}$

$= \lim\limits_{x \to 4} \dfrac{-(x+4)\cancel{(x-4)}}{16x^2\cancel{(x-4)}}$

$= \lim\limits_{x \to 4} \dfrac{-(x + 4)}{16x^2}$ {as $x \neq 4$}

$= \dfrac{-8}{256}$

$= -\dfrac{1}{32}$

d $f'(2) = \lim\limits_{x \to 2} \dfrac{f(x) - f(2)}{x - 2}$

$= \lim\limits_{x \to 2} \dfrac{\frac{4x}{x - 3} - \left(-\frac{8}{1}\right)}{x - 2}$

$= \lim\limits_{x \to 2} \dfrac{4x + 8(x - 3)}{(x - 2)(x - 3)}$

$= \lim\limits_{x \to 2} \dfrac{12\cancel{(x-2)}}{\cancel{(x-2)}(x - 3)}$

$= \lim\limits_{x \to 2} \dfrac{12}{x - 3}$ {as $x \neq 2$}

$= \dfrac{12}{-1}$

$= -12$

e $f'(5) = \lim\limits_{x \to 5} \dfrac{f(x) - f(5)}{(x - 5)}$

$= \lim\limits_{x \to 5} \dfrac{\dfrac{4x + 1}{x - 2} - \dfrac{7}{1}}{x - 5}$

$= \lim\limits_{x \to 5} \dfrac{4x + 1 - 7(x - 2)}{(x - 2)(x - 5)}$

$= \lim\limits_{x \to 5} \dfrac{4x + 1 - 7x + 14}{(x - 2)(x - 5)}$

$= \lim\limits_{x \to 5} \dfrac{-3x + 15}{(x - 2)(x - 5)}$

$= \lim\limits_{x \to 5} \dfrac{-3\cancel{(x - 5)}}{(x - 2)\cancel{(x - 5)}}$

$= \lim\limits_{x \to 5} \dfrac{-3}{x - 2}$ {as $x \neq 5$}

$= -\dfrac{3}{3}$

$= -1$

f $f'(-4) = \lim\limits_{x \to -4} \dfrac{f(x) - f(-4)}{x - (-4)}$

$= \lim\limits_{x \to -4} \dfrac{\dfrac{3x}{x^2 + 1} - \left(-\dfrac{12}{17}\right)}{x + 4}$

$= \lim\limits_{x \to -4} \dfrac{51x + 12(x^2 + 1)}{17(x^2 + 1)(x + 4)}$

$= \lim\limits_{x \to -4} \dfrac{12x^2 + 51x + 12}{17(x^2 + 1)(x + 4)}$

$= \lim\limits_{x \to -4} \dfrac{\cancel{(x + 4)}(12x + 3)}{17(x^2 + 1)\cancel{(x + 4)}}$

$= \lim\limits_{x \to -4} \dfrac{12x + 3}{17(x^2 + 1)}$ {$x \neq -4$}

$= -\dfrac{45}{17 \times 17}$

$= -\dfrac{45}{289}$

3 a $f(x) = \sqrt{x}$ and $f(4) = \sqrt{4} = 2$

$f'(4) = \lim\limits_{x \to 4} \dfrac{f(x) - f(4)}{x - 4}$

$= \lim\limits_{x \to 4} \dfrac{\sqrt{x} - 2}{x - 4}$

$= \lim\limits_{x \to 4} \dfrac{\cancel{\sqrt{x} - 2}}{(\sqrt{x} + 2)\cancel{(\sqrt{x} - 2)}}$

$= \lim\limits_{x \to 4} \dfrac{1}{(\sqrt{x} + 2)}$ {as $x \neq 4$}

$= \dfrac{1}{2 + 2}$

$= \dfrac{1}{4}$

b $f(x) = \sqrt{x}$ and $f\left(\dfrac{1}{4}\right) = \sqrt{\dfrac{1}{4}} = \dfrac{1}{2}$

$f'\left(\dfrac{1}{4}\right) = \lim\limits_{x \to \frac{1}{4}} \dfrac{f(x) - f\left(\frac{1}{4}\right)}{x - \frac{1}{4}}$

$= \lim\limits_{x \to \frac{1}{4}} \dfrac{\sqrt{x} - \frac{1}{2}}{x - \frac{1}{4}}$

$= \lim\limits_{x \to \frac{1}{4}} \dfrac{\cancel{(\sqrt{x} - \frac{1}{2})}}{(\sqrt{x} + \frac{1}{2})\cancel{(\sqrt{x} - \frac{1}{2})}}$

$= \lim\limits_{x \to \frac{1}{4}} \dfrac{1}{\sqrt{x} + \frac{1}{2}}$ {as $x \neq \frac{1}{4}$}

$= \dfrac{1}{\frac{1}{2} + \frac{1}{2}} = 1$

c $f(x) = \dfrac{2}{\sqrt{x}}$ and $f(9) = \dfrac{2}{3}$

$f'(9) = \lim\limits_{x \to 9} \dfrac{f(x) - f(9)}{x - 9}$

$= \lim\limits_{x \to 9} \dfrac{\frac{2}{\sqrt{x}} - \frac{2}{3}}{x - 9}$

$= \lim\limits_{x \to 9} \dfrac{2(3 - \sqrt{x})}{3\sqrt{x}(x - 9)}$

$= \lim\limits_{x \to 9} \dfrac{-2\cancel{(\sqrt{x} - 3)}}{3\sqrt{x}(\sqrt{x} + 3)\cancel{(\sqrt{x} - 3)}}$

$= \lim\limits_{x \to 9} \dfrac{-2}{3\sqrt{x}(\sqrt{x} + 3)}$ {$x \neq 9$}

$= \dfrac{-2}{3(3)(6)}$

$= -\dfrac{1}{27}$

d $f(x) = \sqrt{x - 6}$ and $f(10) = 2$

$f'(10) = \lim\limits_{x \to 10} \dfrac{f(x) - f(10)}{x - 10}$

$= \lim\limits_{x \to 10} \dfrac{\sqrt{x - 6} - 2}{x - 10}$

$= \lim\limits_{x \to 10} \dfrac{(\sqrt{x - 6} - 2)(\sqrt{x - 6} + 2)}{(x - 10)(\sqrt{x - 6} + 2)}$

$= \lim\limits_{x \to 10} \dfrac{x - 6 - 4}{(x - 10)(\sqrt{x - 6} + 2)}$

$= \lim\limits_{x \to 10} \dfrac{\cancel{x - 10}}{\cancel{(x - 10)}(\sqrt{x - 6} + 2)}$

$= \lim\limits_{x \to 10} \dfrac{1}{\sqrt{x - 6} + 2}$ {as $x \neq 10$}

$= \dfrac{1}{2 + 2} = \dfrac{1}{4}$

4 **a** $f(x) = x^2 + 3x - 4$ at $x = 3$

$f'(3) = \lim\limits_{h \to 0} \dfrac{f(3+h) - f(3)}{h}$ where $f(3) = 3^2 + 3(3) - 4 = 14$

$= \lim\limits_{h \to 0} \dfrac{[(3+h)^2 + 3(3+h) - 4] - 14}{h}$

$= \lim\limits_{h \to 0} \dfrac{9 + 6h + h^2 + 9 + 3h - 4 - 14}{h}$

$= \lim\limits_{h \to 0} \dfrac{9h + h^2}{h}$

$= \lim\limits_{h \to 0} 9 + h$ {as $h \neq 0$}

$= 9$

b $f(x) = 5 - 2x - 3x^2$ at $x = -2$

$f'(-2) = \lim\limits_{h \to 0} \dfrac{f(-2+h) - f(-2)}{h}$ where $f(-2) = 5 - 2(-2) - 3(4) = -3$

$= \lim\limits_{h \to 0} \dfrac{[5 - 2(-2+h) - 3(-2+h)^2] - (-3)}{h}$

$= \lim\limits_{h \to 0} \dfrac{5 + 4 - 2h - 12 + 12h - 3h^2 + 3}{h}$

$= \lim\limits_{h \to 0} \dfrac{10h - 3h^2}{h}$

$= \lim\limits_{h \to 0} 10 - 3h$ {as $h \neq 0$}

$= 10$

c $f(x) = \dfrac{1}{2x - 1}$

$\therefore \; f(-2) = \dfrac{1}{2(-2) - 1} = -\dfrac{1}{5}$

$f'(-2) = \lim\limits_{h \to 0} \dfrac{f(-2+h) - f(-2)}{h}$

$= \lim\limits_{h \to 0} \dfrac{\dfrac{1}{2(-2+h) - 1} - \left(-\dfrac{1}{5}\right)}{h}$

$= \lim\limits_{h \to 0} \dfrac{\dfrac{1}{2h - 5} + \dfrac{1}{5}}{h}$

$= \lim\limits_{h \to 0} \dfrac{5 + 1(2h - 5)}{5h(2h - 5)}$

$= \lim\limits_{h \to 0} \dfrac{2h}{5h(2h - 5)}$

$= \lim\limits_{h \to 0} \dfrac{2}{5(2h - 5)}$ {as $h \neq 0$}

$= -\dfrac{2}{25}$

d $f(x) = \dfrac{1}{x^2}$

$\therefore \; f(3) = \dfrac{1}{3^2} = \dfrac{1}{9}$

$f'(3) = \lim\limits_{h \to 0} \dfrac{f(3+h) - f(3)}{h}$

$= \lim\limits_{h \to 0} \dfrac{\dfrac{1}{(3+h)^2} - \dfrac{1}{9}}{h}$

$= \lim\limits_{h \to 0} \dfrac{9 - (3+h)^2}{9h(3+h)^2}$

$= \lim\limits_{h \to 0} \dfrac{9 - 9 - 6h - h^2}{9h(3+h)^2}$

$= \lim\limits_{h \to 0} \dfrac{-h(6+h)}{9h(3+h)^2}$

$= \lim\limits_{h \to 0} \dfrac{-(6+h)}{9(3+h)^2}$ {as $h \neq 0$}

$= \dfrac{-6}{81}$

$= -\dfrac{2}{27}$

e $f(x) = \sqrt{x}$

$\therefore \ f(4) = \sqrt{4} = 2$

$f'(4) = \lim\limits_{h \to 0} \dfrac{f(4+h) - f(4)}{h}$

$= \lim\limits_{h \to 0} \dfrac{\sqrt{4+h} - 2}{h}$

$= \lim\limits_{h \to 0} \dfrac{\sqrt{4+h} - 2}{h} \left(\dfrac{\sqrt{4+h} + 2}{\sqrt{4+h} + 2} \right)$

$= \lim\limits_{h \to 0} \dfrac{4 + h - 4}{h(\sqrt{4+h} + 2)}$

$= \lim\limits_{h \to 0} \dfrac{1\not{h}}{\not{h}(\sqrt{4+h} + 2)}$

$= \lim\limits_{h \to 0} \dfrac{1}{\sqrt{4+h} + 2} \quad \{\text{as } h \neq 0\}$

$= \tfrac{1}{4}$

f $f(x) = \dfrac{1}{\sqrt{x}}$

$\therefore \ f(1) = \dfrac{1}{\sqrt{1}} = 1$

$f'(1) = \lim\limits_{h \to 0} \dfrac{f(1+h) - f(1)}{h}$

$= \lim\limits_{h \to 0} \dfrac{\dfrac{1}{\sqrt{1+h}} - \dfrac{1}{1}}{h}$

$= \lim\limits_{h \to 0} \dfrac{1 - \sqrt{1+h}}{h\sqrt{1+h}}$

$= \lim\limits_{h \to 0} \dfrac{(1 - \sqrt{1+h})}{h\sqrt{1+h}} \left(\dfrac{1 + \sqrt{1+h}}{1 + \sqrt{1+h}} \right)$

$= \lim\limits_{h \to 0} \dfrac{1 - (1 + h)}{h(\sqrt{1+h})(1 + \sqrt{1+h})}$

$= \lim\limits_{h \to 0} \dfrac{-1\not{h}}{\not{h}\sqrt{1+h}(1 + \sqrt{1+h})}$

$= \lim\limits_{h \to 0} \dfrac{-1}{\sqrt{1+h}(1 + \sqrt{1+h})} \quad \{h \neq 0\}$

$= \dfrac{-1}{1(1+1)} = -\tfrac{1}{2}$

5 a $f(x) = x^3 \quad \therefore \ f'(2) = \lim\limits_{h \to 0} \dfrac{f(2+h) - f(2)}{h}$ where $f(2) = 2^3 = 8$

$= \lim\limits_{h \to 0} \dfrac{(2+h)^3 - 8}{h}$

$= \lim\limits_{h \to 0} \dfrac{8 + 12h + 6h^2 + h^3 - 8}{h}$

$= \lim\limits_{h \to 0} \dfrac{12h + 6h^2 + h^3}{h}$

$= \lim\limits_{h \to 0} \ 12 + 6h + h^2 \quad \{\text{as } h \neq 0\}$

$= 12$

b $f(x) = x^4 \quad \therefore \ f'(3) = \lim\limits_{h \to 0} \dfrac{f(3+h) - f(3)}{h}$ where $f(3) = 3^4 = 81$

$= \lim\limits_{h \to 0} \dfrac{(3+h)^4 - 3^4}{h}$

$= \lim\limits_{h \to 0} \dfrac{81 + 108h + 54h^2 + 12h^3 + h^4 - 81}{h}$

$= \lim\limits_{h \to 0} \dfrac{108h + 54h^2 + 12h^3 + h^4}{h}$

$= \lim\limits_{h \to 0} \ 108 + 54h + 12h^2 + h^3 \quad \{\text{as } h \neq 0\}$

$= 108$

EXERCISE 20C

1 a $f(x) = x^3$,

$\therefore \ f'(x) = 3x^2$

b $f(x) = 2x^3$,

$\therefore \ f'(x) = 3 \times 2x^2$

$= 6x^2$

c $f(x) = 7x^2$,

$\therefore \ f'(x) = 2 \times 7x$

$= 14x$

d $f(x) = x^2 + x$,
$\therefore \ f'(x) = 2x + 1$

e $f(x) = 4 - 2x^2$,
$\therefore \ f'(x) = 0 - 2 \times 2x$
$= -4x$

f $f(x) = x^2 + 3x - 5$,
$\therefore \ f'(x) = 2x + 3 - 0$
$= 2x + 3$

g $f(x) = x^3 + 3x^2 + 4x - 1$
$\therefore \ f'(x) = 3x^2 + 2(3x) + 4 - 0$
$= 3x^2 + 6x + 4$

h $f(x) = 5x^4 - 6x^2$
$\therefore \ f'(x) = 4(5x^3) - 2(6x)$
$= 20x^3 - 12x$

i $f(x) = \dfrac{3x - 6}{x} = 3 - 6x^{-1}$
$\therefore \ f'(x) = 0 - (-1) \times 6x^{-2}$
$= \dfrac{6}{x^2}$

j $f(x) = \dfrac{2x - 3}{x^2} = \dfrac{2x}{x^2} - \dfrac{3}{x^2}$
$= 2x^{-1} - 3x^{-2}$
$\therefore \ f'(x) = -2x^{-2} + 6x^{-3} = \dfrac{-2}{x^2} + \dfrac{6}{x^3}$

k $f(x) = \dfrac{x^3 + 5}{x} = x^2 + 5x^{-1}$
$\therefore \ f'(x) = 2x - 5x^{-2}$
$= 2x - \dfrac{5}{x^2}$

l $f(x) = \dfrac{x^3 + x - 3}{x}$
$= x^2 + 1 - 3x^{-1}$
$\therefore \ f'(x) = 2x + 0 + 3x^{-2}$
$= 2x + \dfrac{3}{x^2}$

m $f(x) = \dfrac{1}{\sqrt{x}} = x^{-\frac{1}{2}}$
$\therefore \ f'(x) = -\tfrac{1}{2} x^{-\frac{3}{2}} = \dfrac{-1}{2x\sqrt{x}}$

n $f(x) = (2x - 1)^2 = 4x^2 - 4x + 1$
$\therefore \ f'(x) = 8x - 4$

o $f(x) = (x + 2)^3$
$= x^3 + 3x^2(2) + 3x(2^2) + 2^3$
$= x^3 + 6x^2 + 12x + 8$
$\therefore \ f'(x) = 3x^2 + 12x + 12$

2

a $y = 2x^3 - 7x^2 - 1$
$\therefore \ \dfrac{dy}{dx} = 6x^2 - 14x$

b $y = \pi x^2$
$\therefore \ \dfrac{dy}{dx} = 2\pi x$

c $y = \dfrac{1}{5x^2} = \tfrac{1}{5} x^{-2}$
$\therefore \ \dfrac{dy}{dx} = -\tfrac{2}{5} x^{-3} = \dfrac{-2}{5x^3}$

d $y = 100x$
$\therefore \ \dfrac{dy}{dx} = 100$

e $y = 10(x + 1)$
$= 10x + 10$
$\therefore \ \dfrac{dy}{dx} = 10$

f $y = 4\pi x^3$
$\therefore \ \dfrac{dy}{dx} = 12\pi x^2$

3

a $\dfrac{d}{dx}(6x + 2)$
$= 6$

b $\dfrac{d}{dx}(x\sqrt{x})$
$= \dfrac{d}{dx}(x^{\frac{3}{2}})$
$= \tfrac{3}{2} x^{\frac{1}{2}}$
$= \tfrac{3}{2}\sqrt{x}$

c $\dfrac{d}{dx}(5 - x)^2$
$= \dfrac{d}{dx}(25 - 10x + x^2)$
$= -10 + 2x$
$= 2x - 10$

d $\dfrac{d}{dx}\left(\dfrac{6x^2 - 9x^4}{3x}\right)$
$= \dfrac{d}{dx}(2x - 3x^3)$
$= 2 - 9x^2$

e $\dfrac{d}{dx}\left(4x - \dfrac{1}{4x}\right)$
$= \dfrac{d}{dx}\left(4x - \tfrac{1}{4} x^{-1}\right)$
$= 4 + \tfrac{1}{4} x^{-2}$
$= 4 + \dfrac{1}{4x^2}$

f $\dfrac{d}{dx}(x(x + 1)(2x - 5))$
$= \dfrac{d}{dx}\left(x(2x^2 - 3x - 5)\right)$
$= \dfrac{d}{dx}\left(2x^3 - 3x^2 - 5x\right)$
$= 6x^2 - 6x - 5$

4 a Consider $y = x^2$ when $x = 2$

Now $\dfrac{dy}{dx} = 2x$

$\therefore$ when $x = 2$,

$\dfrac{dy}{dx} = 2(2) = 4$

$\therefore$ the tangent has gradient 4.

b Consider $y = \dfrac{8}{x^2}$ when $x = 9$

Now $y = 8x^{-2}$

$\therefore \dfrac{dy}{dx} = -16x^{-3} = -\dfrac{16}{x^3}$

$\therefore$ when $x = 9$, $\dfrac{dy}{dx} = -\dfrac{16}{729}$

$\therefore$ the tangent has gradient $-\dfrac{16}{729}$.

c Consider $y = 2x^2 - 3x + 7$ when $x = -1$

Now $\dfrac{dy}{dx} = 4x - 3$

$\therefore$ when $x = -1$,

$\dfrac{dy}{dx} = 4(-1) - 3 = -7$

$\therefore$ the tangent has gradient -7.

d Consider $y = \dfrac{2x^2 - 5}{x}$ when $x = 2$

Now $y = 2x - 5x^{-1}$

$\therefore \dfrac{dy}{dx} = 2 + 5x^{-2} = 2 + \dfrac{5}{x^2}$

$\therefore$ when $x = 2$, $\dfrac{dy}{dx} = 2 + \dfrac{5}{4} = \dfrac{13}{4}$

$\therefore$ the tangent has gradient $\dfrac{13}{4}$.

e Consider $y = \dfrac{x^2 - 4}{x^2}$ when $x = 4$

Now $y = 1 - 4x^{-2}$

$\therefore \dfrac{dy}{dx} = 0 + 8x^{-3} = \dfrac{8}{x^3}$

$\therefore$ when $x = 4$,

$\dfrac{dy}{dx} = \dfrac{8}{4^3} = \dfrac{1}{8}$

$\therefore$ the tangent has gradient $\dfrac{1}{8}$.

f Consider $y = \dfrac{x^3 - 4x - 8}{x^2}$ when $x = -1$

Now $y = x - 4x^{-1} - 8x^{-2}$

$\therefore \dfrac{dy}{dx} = 1 + 4x^{-2} + 16x^{-3}$

$= 1 + \dfrac{4}{x^2} + \dfrac{16}{x^3}$

$\therefore$ when $x = -1$, $\dfrac{dy}{dx} = 1 + 4 - 16 = -11$

$\therefore$ the tangent has gradient -11.

5 a $f(x) = 4\sqrt{x} + x = 4x^{\frac{1}{2}} + x$

$\therefore f'(x) = 4\left(\tfrac{1}{2}\right)x^{-\frac{1}{2}} + 1$

$= \dfrac{2}{\sqrt{x}} + 1$

b $f(x) = \sqrt[3]{x} = x^{\frac{1}{3}}$

$\therefore f'(x) = \tfrac{1}{3}x^{-\frac{2}{3}}$

$= \dfrac{1}{3\sqrt[3]{x^2}}$

c $f(x) = -\dfrac{2}{\sqrt{x}} = -2x^{-\frac{1}{2}}$

$\therefore f'(x) = -2(-\tfrac{1}{2})x^{-\frac{3}{2}}$

$= x^{-\frac{3}{2}}$

$= \dfrac{1}{x\sqrt{x}}$

d $f(x) = 2x - \sqrt{x} = 2x - x^{\frac{1}{2}}$

$\therefore f'(x) = 2 - \tfrac{1}{2}x^{-\frac{1}{2}}$

$= 2 - \dfrac{1}{2\sqrt{x}}$

e $f(x) = \dfrac{4}{\sqrt{x}} - 5 = 4x^{-\frac{1}{2}} - 5$

$\therefore f'(x) = 4(-\tfrac{1}{2})x^{-\frac{3}{2}}$

$= -2x^{-\frac{3}{2}}$ or $\dfrac{-2}{x\sqrt{x}}$

f $f(x) = 3x^2 - x\sqrt{x} = 3x^2 - x^{\frac{3}{2}}$

$\therefore f'(x) = 6x - \tfrac{3}{2}x^{\frac{1}{2}}$

$= 6x - \tfrac{3}{2}\sqrt{x}$

g $f(x) = \dfrac{5}{x^2\sqrt{x}} = 5x^{-\frac{5}{2}}$

$\therefore f'(x) = 5(-\tfrac{5}{2})x^{-\frac{7}{2}}$

$= -\tfrac{25}{2}x^{-\frac{7}{2}}$

$= \dfrac{-25}{2x^3\sqrt{x}}$

h $f(x) = 2x - \dfrac{3}{x\sqrt{x}} = 2x - 3x^{-\frac{3}{2}}$

$\therefore f'(x) = 2 - 3(-\tfrac{3}{2})x^{-\frac{5}{2}}$

$= 2 + \tfrac{9}{2}x^{-\frac{5}{2}}$

$= 2 + \dfrac{9}{2x^2\sqrt{x}}$

6 a $y = 4x - \dfrac{3}{x} = 4x - 3x^{-1}$ $\therefore$ $\dfrac{dy}{dx} = 4 + 3x^{-2} = 4 + \dfrac{3}{x^2}$

$\dfrac{dy}{dx}$ is the gradient function of $y = 4x - \dfrac{3}{x}$ from which the gradient at any point can be found.

b $S = 2t^2 + 4t$ m $\therefore$ $\dfrac{dS}{dt} = 4t + 4$ m s^{-1}

$\dfrac{dS}{dt}$ is the instantaneous rate of change in position at time t. It is the velocity function.

c $C = 1785 + 3x + 0.002x^2$ dollars.

$\dfrac{dC}{dx} = 3 + 2(0.002)x = 3 + 0.004x$ dollars per toaster

$\dfrac{dC}{dx}$ is the instantaneous rate of change in cost as the number of toasters changes.

EXERCISE 20D.1

1 a $f(x) = x^2$, $g(x) = 2x + 7$,
$\therefore$ $f(g(x)) = f(2x + 7) = (2x + 7)^2$

b $f(x) = 2x + 7$, $g(x) = x^2$,
$f(g(x)) = f(x^2) = 2x^2 + 7$

c $f(x) = \sqrt{x}$, $g(x) = 3 - 4x$,
$f(g(x)) = f(3 - 4x) = \sqrt{3 - 4x}$

d $f(x) = 3 - 4x$, $g(x) = \sqrt{x}$,
$f(g(x)) = f(\sqrt{x}) = 3 - 4\sqrt{x}$

e $f(x) = \dfrac{2}{x}$, $g(x) = x^2 + 3$,
$f(g(x)) = f(x^2 + 3) = \dfrac{2}{x^2 + 3}$

f $f(x) = x^2 + 3$, $g(x) = \dfrac{2}{x}$,
$f(g(x)) = f\left(\dfrac{2}{x}\right) = \left(\dfrac{2}{x}\right)^2 + 3 = \dfrac{4}{x^2} + 3$

2 a $f(g(x)) = (3x + 10)^3$ $\therefore$ $f(x) = x^3$, $g(x) = 3x + 10$

b $f(g(x)) = \dfrac{1}{2x + 4}$ $\therefore$ $f(x) = \dfrac{1}{x}$, $g(x) = 2x + 4$

c $f(g(x)) = \sqrt{x^2 - 3x}$ $\therefore$ $f(x) = \sqrt{x}$, $g(x) = x^2 - 3x$

d $f(g(x)) = \dfrac{10}{(3x - x^2)^3}$ $\therefore$ $f(x) = \dfrac{10}{x^3}$, $g(x) = 3x - x^2$ {other answers are possible for **2**}

EXERCISE 20D.2

1 a $\dfrac{1}{(2x - 1)^2}$
$= (2x - 1)^{-2}$
$= u^{-2}$,
where $u = 2x - 1$

b $\sqrt{x^2 - 3x}$
$= (x^2 - 3x)^{\frac{1}{2}}$
$= u^{\frac{1}{2}}$,
where $u = x^2 - 3x$

c $\dfrac{2}{\sqrt{2 - x^2}}$
$= 2(2 - x^2)^{-\frac{1}{2}}$
$= 2u^{-\frac{1}{2}}$,
where $u = 2 - x^2$

d $\sqrt[3]{x^3 - x^2}$
$= (x^3 - x^2)^{\frac{1}{3}}$
$= u^{\frac{1}{3}}$,
where $u = x^3 - x^2$

e $\dfrac{4}{(3 - x)^3}$
$= 4(3 - x)^{-3}$
$= 4u^{-3}$,
where $u = 3 - x$

f $\dfrac{10}{x^2 - 3}$
$= 10(x^2 - 3)^{-1}$
$= 10u^{-1}$,
where $u = x^2 - 3$

2 a $y = (4x - 5)^2$
$\therefore$ $y = u^2$ where $u = 4x - 5$

Now $\dfrac{dy}{dx} = \dfrac{dy}{du}\dfrac{du}{dx}$
$= 2u(4)$
$= 8u$
$= 8(4x - 5)$

b
$$y = \frac{1}{5-2x}$$
$$= u^{-1} \quad \text{where} \quad u = 5 - 2x$$
Now $\dfrac{dy}{dx} = \dfrac{dy}{du}\dfrac{du}{dx}$
$$= -u^{-2}(-2)$$
$$= \frac{2}{u^2}$$
$$= \frac{2}{(5-2x)^2}$$

c
$$y = \sqrt{3x - x^2}$$
$$\therefore \quad y = u^{\frac{1}{2}} \quad \text{where} \quad u = 3x - x^2$$
Now $\dfrac{dy}{dx} = \dfrac{dy}{du}\dfrac{du}{dx}$
$$= \tfrac{1}{2}u^{-\frac{1}{2}}(3 - 2x)$$
$$= \frac{(3-2x)}{2\sqrt{u}}$$
$$= \frac{3-2x}{2\sqrt{3x-x^2}}$$

d
$$y = (1-3x)^4$$
$$\therefore \quad y = u^4 \quad \text{where} \quad u = 1 - 3x$$
Now $\dfrac{dy}{dx} = \dfrac{dy}{du}\dfrac{du}{dx}$
$$= 4u^3(-3)$$
$$= -12u^3$$
$$= -12(1-3x)^3$$

e
$$y = 6(5-x)^3$$
$$\therefore \quad y = 6u^3 \quad \text{where} \quad u = 5 - x$$
Now $\dfrac{dy}{dx} = \dfrac{dy}{du}\dfrac{du}{dx}$
$$= 18u^2(-1)$$
$$= -18u^2$$
$$= -18(5-x)^2$$

f
$$y = \sqrt[3]{2x^3 - x^2}$$
$$\therefore \quad y = u^{\frac{1}{3}} \quad \text{where} \quad u = 2x^3 - x^2$$
Now $\dfrac{dy}{dx} = \dfrac{dy}{du}\dfrac{du}{dx}$
$$= \tfrac{1}{3}u^{-\frac{2}{3}}(6x^2 - 2x)$$
$$= \frac{6x^2 - 2x}{3\sqrt[3]{(2x^3 - x^2)^2}}$$

g
$$y = \frac{6}{(5x-4)^2}$$
$$\therefore \quad y = 6u^{-2} \quad \text{where} \quad u = 5x - 4$$
Now $\dfrac{dy}{dx} = \dfrac{dy}{du}\dfrac{du}{dx} = -12u^{-3}(5)$
$$= -\frac{60}{u^3}$$
$$= \frac{-60}{(5x-4)^3}$$

h
$$y = \frac{4}{3x - x^2}$$
$$\therefore \quad y = 4u^{-1} \quad \text{where} \quad u = 3x - x^2$$
Now $\dfrac{dy}{dx} = \dfrac{dy}{du}\dfrac{du}{dx} = -4u^{-2}(3 - 2x)$
$$= \frac{-4(3-2x)}{u^2}$$
$$= \frac{-4(3-2x)}{(3x-x^2)^2}$$

i
$$y = 2\left(x^2 - \frac{2}{x}\right)^3$$
$$\therefore \quad y = 2u^3 \quad \text{where} \quad u = x^2 - 2x^{-1}$$
Now $\dfrac{dy}{dx} = \dfrac{dy}{du}\dfrac{du}{dx}$
$$= 6u^2(2x + 2x^{-2})$$
$$= 6\left(x^2 - \frac{2}{x}\right)^2\left(2x + \frac{2}{x^2}\right)$$

3 a $y = \sqrt{1-x^2}$ at $x = \tfrac{1}{2}$
$$\therefore \quad y = \sqrt{u} \quad \text{where} \quad u = 1 - x^2$$
Now $\dfrac{dy}{dx} = \dfrac{dy}{du}\dfrac{du}{dx} = \tfrac{1}{2}u^{-\frac{1}{2}}(-2x)$
$$= \frac{-x}{\sqrt{u}}$$
$$= \frac{-x}{\sqrt{1-x^2}}$$
At $x = \tfrac{1}{2}$, $\dfrac{dy}{dx} = \dfrac{-\tfrac{1}{2}}{\sqrt{1-\tfrac{1}{4}}} = -\tfrac{1}{2}\left(\dfrac{2}{\sqrt{3}}\right)$
$\therefore$ gradient of tangent $= -\dfrac{1}{\sqrt{3}}$

b $y = (3x + 2)^6$ at $x = -1$
$$\therefore \quad y = u^6 \quad \text{where} \quad u = 3x + 2$$
Now $\dfrac{dy}{dx} = \dfrac{dy}{du}\dfrac{du}{dx}$
$$= 6u^5(3)$$
$$= 18u^5$$
$$= 18(3x+2)^5$$
At $x = -1$, $\dfrac{dy}{dx} = 18(-1)^5$
$\therefore$ gradient of tangent $= -18$

c $y = \dfrac{1}{(2x-1)^4}$ at $x = 1$

$\therefore \; y = u^{-4}$ where $u = 2x - 1$

Now $\dfrac{dy}{dx} = \dfrac{dy}{du}\dfrac{du}{dx} = -4u^{-5}(2)$

$= \dfrac{-8}{u^5}$

$= \dfrac{-8}{(2x-1)^5}$

At $x = 1$, $\dfrac{dy}{dx} = \dfrac{-8}{1^5}$

$\therefore$ gradient of tangent $= -8$

d $y = 6 \times \sqrt[3]{1-2x}$ at $x = 0$

$\therefore \; y = 6u^{\frac{1}{3}}$ where $u = 1 - 2x$

Now $\dfrac{dy}{dx} = \dfrac{dy}{du}\dfrac{du}{dx} = 6(\tfrac{1}{3})u^{-\frac{2}{3}}(-2)$

$= 2u^{-\frac{2}{3}}(-2)$

$= \dfrac{-4}{\sqrt[3]{u^2}}$

$= \dfrac{-4}{\sqrt[3]{(1-2x)^2}}$

At $x = 0$, $\dfrac{dy}{dx} = \dfrac{-4}{\sqrt[3]{1^2}}$

$\therefore$ gradient of tangent $= -4$

e $y = \dfrac{4}{x + 2\sqrt{x}}$ at $x = 4$

$\therefore \; y = 4u^{-1}$ where $u = x + 2x^{\frac{1}{2}}$

Now $\dfrac{dy}{dx} = \dfrac{dy}{du}\dfrac{du}{dx}$

$= -4u^{-2}(1 + x^{-\frac{1}{2}})$

$= -\dfrac{4}{u^2}\left(1 + \dfrac{1}{\sqrt{x}}\right)$

$= \dfrac{-4}{(x + 2\sqrt{x})^2}\left(1 + \dfrac{1}{\sqrt{x}}\right)$

At $x = 4$, $\dfrac{dy}{dx} = \dfrac{-4}{(4+4)^2}(1 + \tfrac{1}{2}) = -\dfrac{6}{64}$

$\therefore$ gradient of tangent $= -\dfrac{3}{32}$

f $y = \left(x + \dfrac{1}{x}\right)^3$ at $x = 1$

$\therefore \; y = u^3$ where $u = x + x^{-1}$

Now $\dfrac{dy}{dx} = \dfrac{dy}{du}\dfrac{du}{dx}$

$= 3u^2(1 - x^{-2})$

$= 3\left(x + \dfrac{1}{x}\right)^2\left(1 - \dfrac{1}{x^2}\right)$

At $x = 1$, $\dfrac{dy}{dx} = 3(1+1)^2(1-1)$

$\therefore$ gradient of tangent $= 0$

4 a $y = x^3 \quad \therefore \quad \dfrac{dy}{dx} = 3x^2$

$x = y^{\frac{1}{3}} \quad \therefore \quad \dfrac{dx}{dy} = \tfrac{1}{3}y^{-\frac{2}{3}}$

$\dfrac{dy}{dx}\dfrac{dx}{dy} = 3x^2\left(\tfrac{1}{3}\right)y^{-\frac{2}{3}}$

$= x^2(y)^{-\frac{2}{3}}$

$= x^2(x^3)^{-\frac{2}{3}} \quad$ {substituting $y = x^3$}

$= x^2(x^{-2})$

$= x^0$

$= 1 \quad$ as required

b We know that

$\dfrac{dy}{du}\dfrac{du}{dx} = \dfrac{dy}{dx} \quad$ {chain rule}

$\therefore \quad \dfrac{dy}{dx}\dfrac{dx}{dy} = \dfrac{dy}{dy}$

$= 1$

EXERCISE 20E.1

1 a $y = x^2(2x - 1)$ is the product of $u = x^2$ and $v = 2x - 1$

$\therefore \; u' = 2x$ and $v' = 2$

Now $\dfrac{dy}{dx} = u'v + uv' \quad$ {product rule}

$\therefore \quad \dfrac{dy}{dx} = 2x(2x - 1) + x^2(2)$

$= 2x(2x - 1) + 2x^2$

b $y = 4x(2x+1)^3$ is the product of $u = 4x$ and $v = (2x+1)^3$
$\therefore$ $u' = 4$ and $v' = 3(2x+1)^2 \times 2 = 6(2x+1)^2$

Now $\dfrac{dy}{dx} = u'v + uv'$ {product rule}

$\therefore$ $\dfrac{dy}{dx} = 4(2x+1)^3 + 24x(2x+1)^2$

c $y = x^2\sqrt{3-x}$ is the product of $u = x^2$ and $v = (3-x)^{\frac{1}{2}}$
$\therefore$ $u' = 2x$ and $v' = \frac{1}{2}(3-x)^{-\frac{1}{2}}(-1) = -\frac{1}{2}(3-x)^{-\frac{1}{2}}$

Now $\dfrac{dy}{dx} = u'v + uv'$ {product rule}

$\therefore$ $\dfrac{dy}{dx} = 2x(3-x)^{\frac{1}{2}} + x^2\left[-\frac{1}{2}(3-x)^{-\frac{1}{2}}\right]$

$= 2x\sqrt{3-x} - \dfrac{x^2}{2\sqrt{3-x}}$

d $y = \sqrt{x}(x-3)^2$ is the product of $u = x^{\frac{1}{2}}$ and $v = (x-3)^2$
$\therefore$ $u' = \frac{1}{2}x^{-\frac{1}{2}}$ and $v' = 2(x-3)^1$

Now $\dfrac{dy}{dx} = u'v + uv'$ {product rule}

$\therefore$ $\dfrac{dy}{dx} = \frac{1}{2}x^{-\frac{1}{2}}(x-3)^2 + 2\sqrt{x}(x-3)$

e $y = 5x^2(3x^2-1)^2$ is the product of $u = 5x^2$ and $v = (3x^2-1)^2$
$\therefore$ $u' = 10x$ and $v' = 2(3x^2-1)^1(6x) = 12x(3x^2-1)$

Now $\dfrac{dy}{dx} = u'v + uv'$ {product rule}

$\therefore$ $\dfrac{dy}{dx} = 10x(3x^2-1)^2 + 5x^2(12x)(3x^2-1)$

$= 10x(3x^2-1)^2 + 60x^3(3x^2-1)$

f $y = \sqrt{x}(x-x^2)^3$ is the product of $u = x^{\frac{1}{2}}$ and $v = (x-x^2)^3$
$\therefore$ $u' = \frac{1}{2}x^{-\frac{1}{2}}$ and $v' = 3(x-x^2)^2(1-2x)$

Now $\dfrac{dy}{dx} = u'v + uv'$ {product rule}

$\therefore$ $\dfrac{dy}{dx} = \frac{1}{2}x^{-\frac{1}{2}}(x-x^2)^3 + 3\sqrt{x}(x-x^2)^2(1-2x)$

2   **a** $y = x^4(1-2x)^2$ is the product of $u = x^4$ and $v = (1-2x)^2$
$\therefore$ $u' = 4x^3$ and $v' = 2(1-2x)^1(-2)$
$= -4(1-2x)$

Now $\dfrac{dy}{dx} = u'v + uv'$ {product rule}

$\therefore$ $\dfrac{dy}{dx} = 4x^3(1-2x)^2 - 4x^4(1-2x)$

At $x = -1$, $\dfrac{dy}{dx} = 4(-1)^3(3)^2 - 4(-1)^4(3) = -48$

$\therefore$ gradient of tangent $= -48$

b $y = \sqrt{x}(x^2-x+1)^2$ is the product of $u = x^{\frac{1}{2}}$ and $v = (x^2-x+1)^2$
$\therefore$ $u' = \frac{1}{2}x^{-\frac{1}{2}}$ and $v' = 2(x^2-x+1)(2x-1)$

Now $\dfrac{dy}{dx} = u'v + uv'$ {product rule}

$\therefore \quad \dfrac{dy}{dx} = \tfrac{1}{2}x^{-\frac{1}{2}}(x^2 - x + 1)^2 + 2\sqrt{x}(x^2 - x + 1)(2x - 1)$

At $x = 4$, $\dfrac{dy}{dx} = \tfrac{1}{2}(4)^{-\frac{1}{2}}(13)^2 + 2\sqrt{4}(13)(7) = 406\tfrac{1}{4}$

$\therefore$ gradient of tangent $= 406\tfrac{1}{4}$

c $y = x\sqrt{1 - 2x}$ is the product of $u = x$ and $v = (1 - 2x)^{\frac{1}{2}}$

$\therefore \quad u' = 1$ and $v' = \tfrac{1}{2}(1 - 2x)^{-\frac{1}{2}}(-2)$

$\qquad\qquad\qquad\qquad = -(1 - 2x)^{-\frac{1}{2}}$

Now $\dfrac{dy}{dx} = u'v + uv'$ {product rule}

$\therefore \quad \dfrac{dy}{dx} = \sqrt{1 - 2x} - \dfrac{x}{\sqrt{1 - 2x}}$

At $x = -4$, $\dfrac{dy}{dx} = \sqrt{9} - \dfrac{(-4)}{\sqrt{9}} = 3 + \tfrac{4}{3} = \tfrac{13}{3}$

$\therefore$ gradient of tangent $= \tfrac{13}{3}$

d $y = x^3\sqrt{5 - x^2}$ is the product of $u = x^3$ and $v = (5 - x^2)^{\frac{1}{2}}$

$\therefore \quad u' = 3x^2$ and $v' = \tfrac{1}{2}(5 - x^2)^{-\frac{1}{2}}(-2x)$

$\qquad\qquad\qquad\qquad = -x(5 - x^2)^{-\frac{1}{2}}$

Now $\dfrac{dy}{dx} = u'v + uv'$ {product rule}

$\therefore \quad \dfrac{dy}{dx} = 3x^2\sqrt{5 - x^2} - \dfrac{x^4}{\sqrt{5 - x^2}}$

At $x = 1$, $\dfrac{dy}{dx} = 3(1)^2\sqrt{4} - \dfrac{1}{\sqrt{4}} = 6 - \tfrac{1}{2} = \tfrac{11}{2}$

$\therefore$ gradient of tangent $= \tfrac{11}{2}$

3 $y = \sqrt{x}(3 - x)^2$ is the product of $u = x^{\frac{1}{2}}$ and $v = (3 - x)^2$

$\therefore \quad u' = \tfrac{1}{2}x^{-\frac{1}{2}}$ and $v' = 2(3 - x)^1(-1) = -2(3 - x)$

Now $\dfrac{dy}{dx} = u'v + uv'$ {product rule}

$\therefore \quad \dfrac{dy}{dx} = \dfrac{1}{2\sqrt{x}}(3 - x)^2 - 2\sqrt{x}(3 - x)$

$\qquad = \dfrac{(3 - x)^2 - (2\sqrt{x})(2\sqrt{x})(3 - x)}{2\sqrt{x}}$

$\qquad = \dfrac{(3 - x)[(3 - x) - 4x]}{2\sqrt{x}}$

$\qquad = \dfrac{(3 - x)(3 - 5x)}{2\sqrt{x}}$ as required

Tangents are horizontal when their gradients are 0.

$\dfrac{dy}{dx} = 0$ when $(3 - x)(3 - 5x) = 0$

$\therefore \quad 3 - x = 0$ or $3 - 5x = 0$

$\therefore \quad x = 3$ or $x = \tfrac{3}{5}$

EXERCISE 20E.2

1 a $y = \dfrac{1 + 3x}{2 - x}$ is a quotient where $u = 1 + 3x$ and $v = 2 - x$

$\therefore \quad u' = 3$ and $v' = -1$

Now $\dfrac{dy}{dx} = \dfrac{u'v - uv'}{v^2}$ {quotient rule}

$\therefore \quad \dfrac{dy}{dx} = \dfrac{3(2 - x) - (1 + 3x)(-1)}{(2 - x)^2} = \dfrac{7}{(2 - x)^2}$

b $y = \dfrac{x^2}{2x+1}$ is a quotient where $u = x^2$ and $v = 2x+1$

$\therefore$ $u' = 2x$ and $v' = 2$

Now $\dfrac{dy}{dx} = \dfrac{u'v - uv'}{v^2}$ {quotient rule}

$\therefore$ $\dfrac{dy}{dx} = \dfrac{2x(2x+1) - x^2(2)}{(2x+1)^2} = \dfrac{2x^2 + 2x}{(2x+1)^2}$

c $y = \dfrac{x}{x^2 - 3}$ is a quotient where $u = x$ and $v = x^2 - 3$

$\therefore$ $u' = 1$ and $v' = 2x$

Now $\dfrac{dy}{dx} = \dfrac{u'v - uv'}{v^2}$ {quotient rule}

$\therefore$ $\dfrac{dy}{dx} = \dfrac{1(x^2 - 3) - x(2x)}{(x^2 - 3)^2} = \dfrac{-3 - x^2}{(x^2 - 3)^2}$

d $y = \dfrac{\sqrt{x}}{1 - 2x}$ is a quotient where $u = x^{\frac{1}{2}}$ and $v = 1 - 2x$

$\therefore$ $u' = \tfrac{1}{2}x^{-\frac{1}{2}}$ and $v' = -2$

Now $\dfrac{dy}{dx} = \dfrac{u'v - uv'}{v^2}$ {quotient rule}

$\therefore$ $\dfrac{dy}{dx} = \dfrac{\tfrac{1}{2}x^{-\frac{1}{2}}(1 - 2x) - \sqrt{x}(-2)}{(1 - 2x)^2} = \dfrac{\tfrac{1}{2}x^{-\frac{1}{2}}(1 - 2x) + 2\sqrt{x}}{(1 - 2x)^2}$

e $y = \dfrac{x^2 - 3}{3x - x^2}$ is a quotient where $u = x^2 - 3$ and $v = 3x - x^2$

$\therefore$ $u' = 2x$ and $v' = 3 - 2x$

Now $\dfrac{dy}{dx} = \dfrac{u'v - uv'}{v^2}$ {quotient rule}

$\therefore$ $\dfrac{dy}{dx} = \dfrac{2x(3x - x^2) - (x^2 - 3)(3 - 2x)}{(3x - x^2)^2}$

$= \dfrac{6x^2 - 2x^3 - 3x^2 + 2x^3 + 9 - 6x}{(3x - x^2)^2} = \dfrac{3x^2 - 6x + 9}{(3x - x^2)^2}$

f $y = \dfrac{x}{\sqrt{1 - 3x}}$ is a quotient where $u = x$ and $v = (1 - 3x)^{\frac{1}{2}}$

$\therefore$ $u' = 1$ and $v' = -\tfrac{3}{2}(1 - 3x)^{-\frac{1}{2}}$

Now $\dfrac{dy}{dx} = \dfrac{u'v - uv'}{v^2}$ {quotient rule}

$\therefore$ $\dfrac{dy}{dx} = \dfrac{(1 - 3x)^{\frac{1}{2}} - x\left(-\tfrac{3}{2}(1 - 3x)^{-\frac{1}{2}}\right)}{1 - 3x} = \dfrac{(1 - 3x)^{\frac{1}{2}} + \tfrac{3}{2}x(1 - 3x)^{-\frac{1}{2}}}{1 - 3x}$

2 a $y = \dfrac{x}{1 - 2x}$ is a quotient where $u = x$ and $v = 1 - 2x$

$\therefore$ $u' = 1$ and $v' = -2$

Now $\dfrac{dy}{dx} = \dfrac{u'v - uv'}{v^2}$ {quotient rule}

$\therefore$ $\dfrac{dy}{dx} = \dfrac{1(1 - 2x) - x(-2)}{(1 - 2x)^2} = \dfrac{1}{(1 - 2x)^2}$

At $x = 1$, $\dfrac{dy}{dx} = \dfrac{1}{(1 - 2)^2} = \dfrac{1}{(-1)^2} = 1$

$\therefore$ the gradient of the tangent $= 1$

b $y = \dfrac{x^3}{x^2+1}$ is a quotient where $u = x^3$ and $v = x^2+1$

$\therefore\ u' = 3x^2$ and $v' = 2x$

Now $\dfrac{dy}{dx} = \dfrac{u'v - uv'}{v^2} = \dfrac{3x^2(x^2+1) - x^3(2x)}{(x^2+1)^2} = \dfrac{x^4 + 3x^2}{(x^2+1)^2}$

At $x = -1$, $\dfrac{dy}{dx} = \dfrac{1+3}{(1+1)^2} = \dfrac{4}{4} = 1$

$\therefore$ the gradient of the tangent $= 1$

c $y = \dfrac{\sqrt{x}}{2x+1}$ is a quotient where $u = x^{\frac{1}{2}}$ and $v = 2x + 1$

$\therefore\ u' = \tfrac{1}{2}x^{-\frac{1}{2}}$ and $v' = 2$

Now $\dfrac{dy}{dx} = \dfrac{u'v - uv'}{v^2} = \dfrac{\frac{1}{2\sqrt{x}}(2x+1) - \sqrt{x}(2)}{(2x+1)^2}$

At $x = 4$, $\dfrac{dy}{dx} = \dfrac{\frac{9}{4} - 4}{81} = \dfrac{\left(\frac{9}{4} - 4\right)}{81} \times \dfrac{4}{4} = \dfrac{9 - 16}{324}$

$\therefore$ the gradient of the tangent $= -\dfrac{7}{324}$

d $y = \dfrac{x^2}{\sqrt{x^2+5}}$ is a quotient where $u = x^2$ and $v = (x^2+5)^{\frac{1}{2}}$

$\therefore\ u' = 2x$ and $v' = \tfrac{1}{2}(x^2+5)^{-\frac{1}{2}}(2x)$

$\qquad\qquad\qquad\quad = x(x^2+5)^{-\frac{1}{2}}$

Now $\dfrac{dy}{dx} = \dfrac{u'v - uv'}{v^2} = \dfrac{2x\sqrt{x^2+5} - x^2\left(\dfrac{x}{\sqrt{x^2+5}}\right)}{(x^2+5)}$

At $x = -2$, $\dfrac{dy}{dx} = \dfrac{-4(3) - 4\left(\frac{-2}{3}\right)}{9} = \dfrac{\left(-12 + \frac{8}{3}\right)}{9} \times \dfrac{3}{3} = \dfrac{-36 + 8}{27}$

$\therefore$ the gradient of the tangent $= -\dfrac{28}{27}$

3 a $y = \dfrac{2\sqrt{x}}{1-x}$ is a quotient where $u = 2x^{\frac{1}{2}}$ and $v = 1 - x$

$\therefore\ u' = x^{-\frac{1}{2}}$ and $v' = -1$

Now $\dfrac{dy}{dx} = \dfrac{u'v - uv'}{v^2}$ {quotient rule}

$\therefore\ \dfrac{dy}{dx} = \dfrac{\frac{1}{\sqrt{x}}(1-x) - 2\sqrt{x}(-1)}{(1-x)^2} \times \left(\dfrac{\sqrt{x}}{\sqrt{x}}\right) = \dfrac{(1-x) + 2x}{\sqrt{x}(1-x)^2} = \dfrac{x+1}{\sqrt{x}(1-x)^2}$ as required

b i $\dfrac{dy}{dx} = 0$ when $x + 1 = 0$ $\therefore$ $x = -1$.

However $\dfrac{dy}{dx}$ is not defined for $x \leqslant 0$ because of the $\sqrt{x}$ term. Hence $\dfrac{dy}{dx}$ never equals 0.

ii $\dfrac{dy}{dx}$ is undefined when $x \leqslant 0$ and when $x = 1$.

4 a $y = \dfrac{x^2 - 3x + 1}{x + 2}$ is a quotient where $u = x^2 - 3x + 1$ and $v = x + 2$

$\therefore\ u' = 2x - 3$ and $v' = 1$

Now $\dfrac{dy}{dx} = \dfrac{u'v - uv'}{v^2}$ {quotient rule}

$\therefore \dfrac{dy}{dx} = \dfrac{(2x - 3)(x + 2) - (x^2 - 3x + 1)(1)}{(x + 2)^2}$

$= \dfrac{2x^2 + 4x - 3x - 6 - x^2 + 3x - 1}{(x + 2)^2}$

$= \dfrac{x^2 + 4x - 7}{(x + 2)^2}$ as required

b **i** $\dfrac{dy}{dx} = 0$ when $x^2 + 4x - 7 = 0$ $\therefore x = \dfrac{-4 \pm \sqrt{44}}{2} = -2 \pm \sqrt{11}$

ii $\dfrac{dy}{dx}$ is undefined when $(x + 2)^2 = 0$ $\therefore x = -2$

c $\dfrac{dy}{dx}$ is zero when the tangent to the function is horizontal. This occurs at the function's turning points or points of horizontal inflection.

$\dfrac{dy}{dx}$ is undefined at vertical asymptotes of the function.

EXERCISE 20F

1 a We seek the tangent to $y = x - 2x^2 + 3$ at $x = 2$.
When $x = 2$, $y = 2 - 2(2)^2 + 3 = -3$ $\therefore$ the point of contact is $(2, -3)$.
Now $\dfrac{dy}{dx} = 1 - 4x$, so at $x = 2$, $\dfrac{dy}{dx} = 1 - 8 = -7$

$\therefore$ the tangent has equation $\dfrac{y - (-3)}{x - 2} = -7$ $\therefore y + 3 = -7(x - 2)$
$\therefore y = -7x + 14 - 3$
$\therefore y = -7x + 11$

b We seek the tangent to $y = \sqrt{x} + 1 = x^{\frac{1}{2}} + 1$ at $x = 4$.
When $x = 4$, $y = \sqrt{4} + 1 = 3$ $\therefore$ the point of contact is $(4, 3)$.
Now $\dfrac{dy}{dx} = \dfrac{1}{2\sqrt{x}}$, so at $x = 4$, $\dfrac{dy}{dx} = \dfrac{1}{2\sqrt{4}} = \dfrac{1}{4}$

$\therefore$ the tangent has equation $\dfrac{y - 3}{x - 4} = \dfrac{1}{4}$ $\therefore 4y - 12 = x - 4$
$\therefore 4y = x + 8$

c We seek the tangent to $y = x^3 - 5x$ at $x = 1$.
When $x = 1$, $y = 1^3 - 5(1) = -4$ $\therefore$ the point of contact is $(1, -4)$.
Now $\dfrac{dy}{dx} = 3x^2 - 5$, so at $x = 1$, $\dfrac{dy}{dx} = 3 - 5 = -2$

$\therefore$ the tangent has equation $\dfrac{y - (-4)}{x - 1} = -2$ $\therefore y + 4 = -2x + 2$
$\therefore y = -2x - 2$

d We seek the tangent to $y = \dfrac{4}{\sqrt{x}}$ at $(1, 4)$. Now $y = \dfrac{4}{\sqrt{x}} = 4x^{-\frac{1}{2}}$

$\therefore \dfrac{dy}{dx} = -2x^{-\frac{3}{2}}$

At $x = 1$, $\dfrac{dy}{dx} = -2\left(1^{-\frac{3}{2}}\right) = -2$

$\therefore$ the tangent has equation $\dfrac{y - 4}{x - 1} = -2$ $\therefore y - 4 = -2x + 2$
$\therefore y = -2x + 6$

2 a We seek the normal to $y = x^2$ at $(3, 9)$.

Now $\dfrac{dy}{dx} = 2x$ so at $x = 3$, $\dfrac{dy}{dx} = 2(3) = 6 = \dfrac{6}{1}$

$\therefore$ the normal at $(3, 9)$ has gradient $-\dfrac{1}{6}$, so the equation of the normal is $\dfrac{y-9}{x-3} = -\dfrac{1}{6}$

$\therefore \quad 6y - 54 = -x + 3$

$\therefore \quad 6y = -x + 57$

b We seek the normal to $y = x^3 - 5x + 2$ at $x = -2$.

When $x = -2$, $y = (-2)^3 - 5(-2) + 2 = 4$ and so the point of contact is $(-2, 4)$.

Now $\dfrac{dy}{dx} = 3x^2 - 5$ so at $x = -2$, $\dfrac{dy}{dx} = 3(-2)^2 - 5 = 7$

$\therefore$ the normal at $(-2, 4)$ has gradient $-\dfrac{1}{7}$, so the equation of the normal is $\dfrac{y-4}{x-(-2)} = -\dfrac{1}{7}$

$\therefore \quad 7y - 28 = -(x + 2)$

$\therefore \quad 7y = -x + 26$

c We seek the normal to $y = \dfrac{5}{\sqrt{x}} - \sqrt{x}$ at $(1, 4)$.

Now $y = 5x^{-\frac{1}{2}} - x^{\frac{1}{2}}$ $\quad \therefore \quad \dfrac{dy}{dx} = -\dfrac{5}{2}x^{-\frac{3}{2}} - \dfrac{1}{2}x^{-\frac{1}{2}}$

$\therefore$ at $x = 1$, $\dfrac{dy}{dx} = -\dfrac{5}{2}\left(1^{-\frac{3}{2}}\right) - \dfrac{1}{2}\left(1^{-\frac{1}{2}}\right) = -\dfrac{5}{2} - \dfrac{1}{2} = -3$

$\therefore$ the normal at $(1, 4)$ has gradient $\dfrac{1}{3}$, so the equation of the normal is $\dfrac{y-4}{x-1} = \dfrac{1}{3}$

$\therefore \quad 3y - 12 = x - 1$

$\therefore \quad 3y = x + 11$

d We seek the normal to $y = 8\sqrt{x} - \dfrac{1}{x^2}$ at $x = 1$.

When $x = 1$, $y = 8\sqrt{1} - \dfrac{1}{1^2} = 7$ $\therefore$ the point of contact is $(1, 7)$.

Now $y = 8\sqrt{x} - \dfrac{1}{x^2} = 8x^{\frac{1}{2}} - x^{-2}$ $\quad \therefore \quad \dfrac{dy}{dx} = 4x^{-\frac{1}{2}} + 2x^{-3}$

$\therefore$ at $x = 1$, $\dfrac{dy}{dx} = 4 + 2 = 6$

$\therefore$ the normal at $(1, 7)$ has gradient $-\dfrac{1}{6}$, so the equation of the normal is $\dfrac{y-7}{x-1} = -\dfrac{1}{6}$

$\therefore \quad 6y - 42 = -x + 1$

$\therefore \quad 6y = -x + 43$

3 a $y = 2x^3 + 3x^2 - 12x + 1$ $\quad \therefore \quad \dfrac{dy}{dx} = 6x^2 + 6x - 12$

Horizontal tangents have gradient $= 0$ so $6x^2 + 6x - 12 = 0$

$\therefore \quad x^2 + x - 2 = 0$

$\therefore \quad (x + 2)(x - 1) = 0$

$\therefore \quad x = -2$ or $x = 1$

Now at $x = -2$, $y = 2(-2)^3 + 3(-2)^2 - 12(-2) + 1 = 21$

and at $x = 1$, $y = 2(1)^3 + 3(1)^2 - 12(1) + 1 = -6$

$\therefore$ the points of contact are $(-2, 21)$ and $(1, -6)$

$\therefore$ the tangents are $y = -6$ and $y = 21$.

b Now $y = 2\sqrt{x} + \dfrac{1}{\sqrt{x}} = 2x^{\frac{1}{2}} + x^{-\frac{1}{2}}$ Horizontal tangents have gradient $= 0$

$\therefore \dfrac{dy}{dx} = x^{-\frac{1}{2}} - \tfrac{1}{2}x^{-\frac{3}{2}}$

$= \dfrac{1}{\sqrt{x}} - \dfrac{1}{2x\sqrt{x}}$

$\therefore \dfrac{1}{\sqrt{x}} - \dfrac{1}{2x\sqrt{x}} = 0$

$\therefore \dfrac{2x - 1}{2x\sqrt{x}} = 0$

$\therefore 2x - 1 = 0$

$\therefore x = \tfrac{1}{2}$

Now at $x = \tfrac{1}{2}$, $y = \dfrac{2\left(\tfrac{1}{2}\right) + 1}{\sqrt{\tfrac{1}{2}}} = \dfrac{2}{\tfrac{1}{2}\sqrt{2}} = 2\sqrt{2}$

$\therefore$ the only horizontal tangent touches at the curve at $(\tfrac{1}{2}, 2\sqrt{2})$.

c Now $y = 2x^3 + kx^2 - 3$ When $x = 2$, $\dfrac{dy}{dx} = 4$

$\therefore \dfrac{dy}{dx} = 6x^2 + 2kx$ $\therefore 6(2)^2 + 2k(2) = 4$

$\therefore 24 + 4k = 4$

$\therefore 4k = -20$

$\therefore k = -5$

d Now $y = 1 - 3x + 12x^2 - 8x^3$ $\therefore \dfrac{dy}{dx} = -3 + 24x - 24x^2$

When $x = 1$, $\dfrac{dy}{dx} = -3 + 24 - 24 = -3$

$\therefore$ the tangent at $(1, 2)$ has gradient -3

The tangents to the curve with gradient 3 touch the curve when $-3 + 24x - 24x^2 = -3$

$\therefore 24x^2 - 24x = 0$

$\therefore 24x(x - 1) = 0$

$\therefore$ when $x = 0$ or $x = 1$

So the other x-value for which the tangent to the curve has gradient -3 is $x = 0$, and when $x = 0$, $y = 1 - 0 + 0 - 0 = 1$

$\therefore$ the tangent to the curve at $(0, 1)$ is parallel to the tangent at $(1, 2)$.

This tangent has equation $\dfrac{y - 1}{x - 0} = -3$ or $y = -3x + 1$.

4 a Now $y = x^2 + ax + b$ $\therefore \dfrac{dy}{dx} = 2x + a$

At $x = 1$, $\dfrac{dy}{dx} = 2 + a$

$\therefore$ the gradient of the tangent to the curve at $x = 1$ will be $2 + a$

However the equation of the tangent is $2x + y = 6$ or $y = -2x + 6$

and so the gradient of the tangent is -2. $\therefore 2 + a = -2$

$\therefore a = -4$

So, the curve is $y = x^2 - 4x + b$.

We also know that the tangent contacts the curve when $x = 1$.

$\therefore 1^2 - 4(1) + b = -2(1) + 6$

$\therefore 1 - 4 + b = 4$

$\therefore b = 7$ $\therefore a = -4,\ b = 7$

b Now $y = a\sqrt{x} + \dfrac{b}{\sqrt{x}} = ax^{\frac{1}{2}} + bx^{-\frac{1}{2}}$ $\therefore$ at $x = 4$, $\dfrac{dy}{dx} = \dfrac{a}{2}\left(4^{-\frac{1}{2}}\right) - \dfrac{b}{2}\left(4^{-\frac{3}{2}}\right)$

$\therefore \dfrac{dy}{dx} = \dfrac{a}{2}x^{-\frac{1}{2}} - \dfrac{b}{2}x^{-\frac{3}{2}}$

$= \dfrac{a}{2}\left(\dfrac{1}{2}\right) - \dfrac{b}{2}\left(\dfrac{1}{8}\right)$

$= \dfrac{a}{4} - \dfrac{b}{16}$

∴ the gradient of the tangent to the curve at $x = 4$ will be $\dfrac{a}{4} - \dfrac{b}{16} = \dfrac{4a-b}{16}$

However the equation of the *normal* is $4x + y = 22$, or $y = -4x + 22$

∴ the normal has gradient -4

∴ the tangent has gradient $\tfrac{1}{4}$, and so $\dfrac{4a-b}{16} = \tfrac{1}{4}$

∴ $4a - b = 4$

∴ $b = 4a - 4$ ...... (1)

Also, at $x = 4$ the normal line intersects the curve.

∴ $a\sqrt{4} + \dfrac{b}{\sqrt{4}} = -4(4) + 22$

∴ $2a + \dfrac{b}{2} = 6$

Consequently, $2a + \dfrac{4a-4}{2} = 6$ {using (1)}

∴ $2a + 2a - 2 = 6$

∴ $4a = 8$

∴ $a = 2$ and so $b = 4(2) - 4 = 4$ {from (1)}

5 a $y = \sqrt{2x+1}$

When $x = 4$, $y = \sqrt{2(4)+1} = 3$, so the point of contact is $(4, 3)$

Now $\dfrac{dy}{dx} = \tfrac{1}{2}(2x+1)^{-\frac{1}{2}}(2) = \dfrac{1}{\sqrt{2x+1}}$

∴ at $x = 4$, $\dfrac{dy}{dx} = \dfrac{1}{\sqrt{2(4)+1}} = \tfrac{1}{3}$

∴ the tangent has equation $\dfrac{y-3}{x-4} = \tfrac{1}{3}$ or $3y = x + 5$

b $y = \dfrac{1}{2-x} = (2-x)^{-1}$ ∴ at $x = -1$, $y = \dfrac{1}{2-(-1)} = \tfrac{1}{3}$

So the point of contact is $(-1, \tfrac{1}{3})$

Now $\dfrac{dy}{dx} = -1(2-x)^{-2}(-1) = \dfrac{1}{(2-x)^2}$

∴ at $x = -1$, $\dfrac{dy}{dx} = \dfrac{1}{(2-(-1))^2} = \tfrac{1}{9}$

∴ the tangent has equation $\dfrac{y-\tfrac{1}{3}}{x-(-1)} = \tfrac{1}{9}$ ∴ $9y - 3 = x + 1$ ∴ $9y = x + 4$

c We seek the tangent to $f(x) = \dfrac{x}{1-3x}$ at $(-1, -\tfrac{1}{4})$.

$f(x)$ is a quotient where $u = x$ and $v = 1 - 3x$ ∴ $u' = 1$ and $v' = -3$

Now $f'(x) = \dfrac{u'v - uv'}{v^2}$ {quotient rule}

∴ $f'(x) = \dfrac{1(1-3x) - x(-3)}{(1-3x)^2} = \dfrac{1}{(1-3x)^2}$

∴ $f'(-1) = \dfrac{1}{(1-3(-1))^2} = \tfrac{1}{16}$

∴ the tangent has equation $\dfrac{y-(-\tfrac{1}{4})}{x-(-1)} = \tfrac{1}{16}$ ∴ $16y + 4 = x + 1$

∴ $16y = x - 3$

d We seek the tangent to $f(x) = \dfrac{x^2}{1-x}$ at $(2, -4)$.

$f(x)$ is a quotient where $u = x^2$ and $v = 1 - x$ $\therefore$ $u' = 2x$ and $v' = -1$

Now $f'(x) = \dfrac{u'v - uv'}{v^2}$ {quotient rule}

$\therefore$ $f'(x) = \dfrac{2x(1-x) - x^2(-1)}{(1-x)^2} = \dfrac{2x - 2x^2 + x^2}{(1-x)^2} = \dfrac{2x - x^2}{(1-x)^2}$

$\therefore$ $f'(2) = \dfrac{2(2) - 2^2}{(1-2)^2} = \dfrac{4-4}{1} = 0$

As the tangent has gradient 0, it is horizontal.

$\therefore$ its equation is $y = c$

Since the contact point is $(2, -4)$, the tangent has equation $y = -4$.

6 a We seek the normal to $y = \dfrac{1}{(x^2+1)^2}$ at $(1, \tfrac{1}{4})$

As $y = (x^2+1)^{-2}$, $\dfrac{dy}{dx} = -2(x^2+1)^{-3}(2x) = \dfrac{-4x}{(x^2+1)^3}$

$\therefore$ at $x = 1$, $\dfrac{dy}{dx} = \dfrac{-4}{(1+1)^3} = \dfrac{-4}{8} = -\dfrac{1}{2}$

$\therefore$ the normal at $(1, \tfrac{1}{4})$ has gradient 2.

So the equation of the normal is $\dfrac{y - \tfrac{1}{4}}{x - 1} = 2$ $\therefore$ $y - \tfrac{1}{4} = 2x - 2$

$\therefore$ $y = 2x - \tfrac{7}{4}$

b $y = \dfrac{1}{\sqrt{3 - 2x}}$ $\therefore$ at $x = -3$, $y = \dfrac{1}{\sqrt{3 - 2(-3)}} = \dfrac{1}{3}$

$\therefore$ the point of contact is $(-3, \tfrac{1}{3})$

Now $y = (3 - 2x)^{-\frac{1}{2}}$

$\therefore$ $\dfrac{dy}{dx} = -\tfrac{1}{2}(3 - 2x)^{-\frac{3}{2}}(-2) = (3 - 2x)^{-\frac{3}{2}}$

$\therefore$ at $x = -3$, $\dfrac{dy}{dx} = (3 - 2(-3))^{-\frac{3}{2}} = 9^{-\frac{3}{2}} = 3^{-3} = \dfrac{1}{27}$

$\therefore$ the normal at $(-3, \tfrac{1}{3})$ has gradient -27.

So the equation of the normal is $\dfrac{y - \tfrac{1}{3}}{x - (-3)} = -27$ $\therefore$ $y - \tfrac{1}{3} = -27(x + 3)$

$\therefore$ $y = -27x - \dfrac{242}{3}$

c $f(x) = \sqrt{x}(1-x)^2$

Since $f(4) = \sqrt{4}(1-4)^2 = 18$, the point of contact is $(4, 18)$

Now $f(x)$ is a product where $u = x^{\frac{1}{2}}$ and $v = (1-x)^2$

$\therefore$ $u' = \tfrac{1}{2}x^{-\frac{1}{2}}$ and $v' = 2(1-x)(-1) = -2(1-x)$

Now $f'(x) = u'v + uv'$ {product rule}

$\therefore$ $f'(x) = \tfrac{1}{2}x^{-\frac{1}{2}}(1-x)^2 - x^{\frac{1}{2}}2(1-x)$

$\therefore$ $f'(4) = \dfrac{1}{2\sqrt{4}}(1-4)^2 - \sqrt{4}(2)(1-4) = \tfrac{1}{4}(9) - 2(2)(-3) = \dfrac{57}{4}$

$\therefore$ the normal at $(4, 18)$ has gradient $-\dfrac{4}{57}$.

So the equation of the normal is $\dfrac{y - 18}{x - 4} = -\dfrac{4}{57}$ $\therefore$ $57(y - 18) = -4(x - 4)$

$\therefore$ $57y = -4x + 1042$

d $f(x) = \dfrac{x^2 - 1}{2x + 3}$

Since $f(-1) = \dfrac{(-1)^2 - 1}{2(-1) + 3} = \dfrac{0}{1} = 0$ the point of contact is $(-1, 0)$.

Now $f(x)$ is a quotient where $u = x^2 - 1$ and $v = 2x + 3$

$\therefore\ u' = 2x$ and $v' = 2$

Now $f'(x) = \dfrac{u'v - uv'}{v^2} = \dfrac{2x(2x + 3) - (x^2 - 1)(2)}{(2x + 3)^2}$

$\therefore\ f'(-1) = \dfrac{2(-1)(-2 + 3) - ((-1)^2 - 1)(2)}{(2(-1) + 3)^2} = \dfrac{-2(1) - (0)(2)}{(1)^2} = -2$

$\therefore$ the normal at $(-1, 0)$ has gradient $\tfrac{1}{2}$.

So, the equation of the normal is $\dfrac{y - 0}{x - (-1)} = \tfrac{1}{2}$ or $2y = x + 1$

7 The tangent has equation $3x + y = 5$ or $y = -3x + 5$

$\therefore$ the tangent has gradient -3 ...... (1)

Also, at $x = -1$, $y = -3(-1) + 5 = 8$

$\therefore$ the tangent contacts the curve at $(-1, 8)$ ...... (2)

Now $y = a(1 - bx)^{\frac{1}{2}}$, so $\dfrac{dy}{dx} = \tfrac{1}{2}a(1 - bx)^{-\frac{1}{2}}(-b)$

$\therefore\ -3 = \tfrac{1}{2}a(1 + b)^{-\frac{1}{2}}(-b)$ {using (1)}

$\therefore\ 6 = \dfrac{ab}{\sqrt{1 + b}}$ ...... (3)

Using (2), $(-1, 8)$ must lie on the curve $y = a\sqrt{1 - bx}$.

$\therefore\ 8 = a\sqrt{1 + b}$ ...... (4)

$\therefore\ \dfrac{6\sqrt{1 + b}}{b} = \dfrac{8}{\sqrt{1 + b}}$ {equating a s in (3) and (4)}

$\therefore\ 6(1 + b) = 8b$

$\therefore\ 6 + 6b = 8b$

$\therefore\ 6 = 2b$

$\therefore\ b = 3$ and $a = \dfrac{8}{\sqrt{4}} = 4$

8 a Consider the tangent to $y = x^3$ at $x = 2$.

When $x = 2$, $y = 2^3 = 8$ so the point of contact is $(2, 8)$

Now $\dfrac{dy}{dx} = 3x^2$ and so at $x = 2$, $\dfrac{dy}{dx} = 3(2)^2 = 12$

$\therefore$ the tangent at $(2, 8)$ has gradient 12 and its equation is $\dfrac{y - 8}{x - 2} = 12$

$\therefore\ y - 8 = 12x - 24$

$\therefore\ y = 12x - 16$

$\therefore$ the tangent meets the curve where $12x - 16 = x^3$

$\therefore\ x^3 - 12x + 16 = 0$

Because the tangent touches the curve at $x = 2$, there must be a repeated solution at this point.

$\therefore\ (x - 2)^2$ must be a factor of this cubic

$\therefore\ (x - 2)^2(x + 4) = 0$

$\therefore$ the tangent meets the curve again when $x = -4$

When $x = -4$, $y = (-4)^3 = -64$

$\therefore$ the tangent meets the curve again at $(-4, -64)$.

b Consider the tangent to $y = -x^3 + 2x^2 + 1$ at $x = -1$.

When $x = -1$, $y = -(-1)^3 + 2(-1)^2 + 1 = 4$ and so the point of contact is $(-1, 4)$

Now $\dfrac{dy}{dx} = -3x^2 + 4x$ and so at $x = -1$, $\dfrac{dy}{dx} = -3(-1)^2 + 4(-1) = -7$

$\therefore$ the tangent at $(-1, 4)$ has gradient -7 and its equation is $\dfrac{y-4}{x-(-1)} = -7$

$\therefore \quad y - 4 = -7(x+1)$

$\therefore \quad y = -7x - 3$

$\therefore$ the tangent meets the curve where $-7x - 3 = -x^3 + 2x^2 + 1$

$\therefore \quad x^3 - 2x^2 - 7x - 4 = 0$

Because the tangent touches the curve at $x = -1$, there must be a repeated solution at this point.

$\therefore \ (x+1)^2$ must be a factor of this cubic

$\therefore \ (x+1)^2(x-4) = 0$

$\therefore$ the tangent meets the curve again when $x = 4$

When $x = 4$, $y = -(4)^3 + 2(4)^2 + 1 = -64 + 32 + 1 = -31$

$\therefore$ the tangent meets the curve again at $(4, -31)$.

c Consider the tangent to $y = x^3 + \dfrac{4}{x}$ at $x = 1$.

When $x = 1$, $y = 1^3 + \dfrac{4}{1} = 5$ and so the point of contact is $(1, 5)$

Now $\dfrac{dy}{dx} = 3x^2 - \dfrac{4}{x^2}$ and so at $x = 1$, $\dfrac{dy}{dx} = 3 - 4 = -1$

$\therefore$ the tangent at $(1, 5)$ has gradient -1 and its equation is $\dfrac{y-5}{x-1} = -1$

$\therefore \quad y - 5 = -x + 1$

$\therefore \quad y = -x + 6$

$\therefore$ the tangent meets the curve where $-x + 6 = x^3 + \dfrac{4}{x}$

$\therefore \quad x^3 + x - 6 + \dfrac{4}{x} = 0$

$\therefore \quad x^4 + x^2 - 6x + 4 = 0$

Using a graphics calculator, this quartic has a graph which touches the x-axis at $x = 1$, and has no other x-intercepts. So, the tangent *never* meets the curve again.

9 a Consider the tangent to $y = x^2 - x + 9$ at $x = a$.

When $x = a$, $y = a^2 - a + 9$, so the point of contact is $(a, a^2 - a + 9)$.

Now $\dfrac{dy}{dx} = 2x - 1$ and so at $x = a$, $\dfrac{dy}{dx} = 2a - 1$

$\therefore$ the gradient of the tangent at $(a, a^2 - a + 9)$ is $2a - 1$

$\therefore$ the equation of the tangent is $\dfrac{y - (a^2 - a + 9)}{x - a} = 2a - 1$

$\therefore \quad y - (a^2 - a + 9) = (2a - 1)(x - a)$

$\therefore \quad y = (2a - 1)x - 2a^2 + a + a^2 - a + 9$

$\therefore \quad y = (2a - 1)x - a^2 + 9$ .... (1)

But this tangent passes through $(0, 0)$, so $0 = a^2 - 9$

$\therefore \quad (a+3)(a-3) = 0$

$\therefore \quad a = \pm 3$

$\therefore$ the tangents are: At $a = 3$: $y = (2(3) - 1)x - 3^2 + 9$ {from (1)}

$\therefore \quad y = 5x$, with contact at $(3, 15)$.

At $a = -3$: $y = (2(-3) - 1)x - (-3)^2 + 9$ {from (1)}

$\therefore \quad y = -7x$, with contact at $(-3, 21)$.

b Let (a, a^3) lie on $y = x^3$.

Now $\dfrac{dy}{dx} = 3x^2$, so at $x = a$, $\dfrac{dy}{dx} = 3a^2$

∴ the gradient of the tangent at (a, a^3) is $3a^2$

∴ the equation of the tangent is $\dfrac{y - a^3}{x - a} = 3a^2$ or $y - a^3 = (3a^2)(x - a)$

But this tangent passes through $(-2, 0)$, so $\quad 0 - a^3 = 3a^2(-2 - a)$

$\therefore \quad -a^3 = -6a^2 - 3a^3$

$\therefore \quad 2a^3 + 6a^2 = 0$

$\therefore \quad 2a^2(a + 3) = 0$

$\therefore \quad a = 0 \text{ or } -3$

If $a = 0$, the tangent equation is $y = 0$, with contact point $(0, 0)$.

If $a = -3$, the tangent equation is $y - (-27) = 27(x + 3)$

$\therefore \quad y = 27x + 54$, with contact point $(-3, -27)$.

c Let $(a, \sqrt{a})$ lie on $y = \sqrt{x}$.

Now $\dfrac{dy}{dx} = \tfrac{1}{2}x^{-\frac{1}{2}} = \dfrac{1}{2\sqrt{x}}$, so at $x = a$, $\dfrac{dy}{dx} = \dfrac{1}{2\sqrt{a}}$

∴ the gradient of the tangent at $(a, \sqrt{a})$ is $\dfrac{1}{2\sqrt{a}}$

and the gradient of the normal at this point is $-2\sqrt{a}$.

∴ the normal has equation $\dfrac{y - \sqrt{a}}{x - a} = -2\sqrt{a}$

or $y - \sqrt{a} = -2\sqrt{a}(x - a)$.

But this normal passes through $(4, 0)$, so $\quad 0 - \sqrt{a} = -2\sqrt{a}(4 - a)$

$\therefore \quad 2\sqrt{a}(4 - a) - \sqrt{a} = 0$

$\therefore \quad \sqrt{a}(8 - 2a - 1) = 0$

$\therefore \quad \sqrt{a}(7 - 2a) = 0$

$\therefore \quad a = 0 \text{ or } \tfrac{7}{2}$

When $a = 0$, the normal has equation $y = 0$, with contact point $(0, 0)$.

When $a = \tfrac{7}{2}$, $y - \sqrt{\tfrac{7}{2}} = -2\sqrt{\tfrac{7}{2}}\left(x - \tfrac{7}{2}\right)$

$\therefore \quad \sqrt{2}y - \sqrt{7} = -2\sqrt{7}\left(x - \tfrac{7}{2}\right)$

$\therefore \quad \sqrt{2}y + 2\sqrt{7}x = 7\sqrt{7} + \sqrt{7}$

$\therefore \quad \sqrt{2}y + 2\sqrt{7}x = 8\sqrt{7}$

$\therefore \quad y = -\sqrt{14}x + 4\sqrt{14}$ with contact point $\left(\tfrac{7}{2}, \sqrt{\tfrac{7}{2}}\right)$.

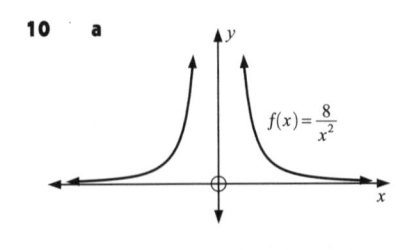

10 a

[Graph of $f(x) = \dfrac{8}{x^2}$]

b Let $\left(a, \dfrac{8}{a^2}\right)$ lie on $f(x) = \dfrac{8}{x^2} = 8x^{-2}$

Now $f'(x) = -16x^{-3} = -\dfrac{16}{x^3}$

$\therefore \quad f'(a) = -\dfrac{16}{a^3}$

∴ the gradient of the tangent at $\left(a, \dfrac{8}{a^2}\right)$ is $-\dfrac{16}{a^3}$

∴ the equation of the tangent is $\dfrac{y - \frac{8}{a^2}}{x - a} = -\dfrac{16}{a^3}$

$\therefore \quad a^3 y - 8a = -16x + 16a$

$\therefore \quad 16x + a^3 y = 24a$

c The tangent cuts the x-axis when $y = 0$

$\therefore \quad 16x = 24a$

$\therefore \quad x = \frac{3}{2}a$

$\therefore \quad$ A is $(\frac{3}{2}a, 0)$.

The tangent cuts the y-axis when $x = 0$

$\therefore \quad a^3 y = 24a$

$\therefore \quad y = \frac{24}{a^2}$

$\therefore \quad$ B is $\left(0, \frac{24}{a^2}\right)$.

d Area of triangle OAB

$= \left| \frac{1}{2} \times \left(\frac{3}{2}a\right) \times \left(\frac{24}{a^2}\right) \right|$

$= \frac{18}{|a|}$ units^2

As $a \to \infty$, $\frac{18}{a} \to 0$

$\therefore \quad$ area $\to 0$

11 a $f : x \mapsto \dfrac{x}{\sqrt{2 - x}}$

f is undefined when $2 - x \leqslant 0$

$\therefore \quad x \geqslant 2$

$\therefore \quad$ domain of f is $\{x \mid x < 2\}$

b $f(x) = \dfrac{x}{\sqrt{2 - x}} = x(2 - x)^{-\frac{1}{2}}$

is a product where $u = x$, $v = (2 - x)^{-\frac{1}{2}}$

$\therefore \quad u' = 1$, $v' = \frac{1}{2}(2 - x)^{-\frac{3}{2}}$

$\therefore \quad f'(x) = (2 - x)^{-\frac{1}{2}} + \frac{1}{2}x(2 - x)^{-\frac{3}{2}}$

$= \dfrac{1}{(2 - x)^{\frac{1}{2}}} + \dfrac{x}{2(2 - x)^{\frac{3}{2}}}$

$= \dfrac{2(2 - x) + x}{2(2 - x)^{\frac{3}{2}}}$

$= \dfrac{4 - x}{2(2 - x)^{\frac{3}{2}}}$ as required

c $f(x) = -1$ when $\dfrac{x}{\sqrt{2 - x}} = -1$

$\therefore \quad x = -\sqrt{2 - x}$

$\therefore \quad x^2 = 2 - x$

$\therefore \quad x^2 + x - 2 = 0$

$\therefore \quad (x + 2)(x - 1) = 0$

$\therefore \quad x = 1$ or -2

But $x = 1$ does not satisfy the original equation, so $x = -2$.

Now $f'(-2) = \dfrac{4 - (-2)}{2(2 - (-2))^{\frac{3}{2}}} = \dfrac{6}{16} = \dfrac{3}{8}$

$\therefore \quad$ the tangent at $(-2, -1)$ has gradient $\frac{3}{8}$

and the normal at this point has gradient $-\frac{8}{3}$.

$\therefore \quad$ the normal has equation $\dfrac{y + 1}{x + 2} = -\dfrac{8}{3}$

$\therefore \quad 3y + 3 = -8x - 16$

$\therefore \quad 8x + 3y = -19$

12 For $y = \sqrt{x + a} = (x + a)^{\frac{1}{2}}$,

$\dfrac{dy}{dx} = \frac{1}{2}(x + a)^{-\frac{1}{2}}$

$= \dfrac{1}{2\sqrt{x + a}}$

These graphs have the same gradient when

For $y = \sqrt{2x - x^2} = (2x - x^2)^{\frac{1}{2}}$,

$\dfrac{dy}{dx} = \frac{1}{2}(2x - x^2)^{-\frac{1}{2}}(2 - 2x)$

$= \dfrac{1 - x}{\sqrt{2x - x^2}}$

$\dfrac{1}{2\sqrt{x + a}} = \dfrac{1 - x}{\sqrt{2x - x^2}}$

$\therefore \quad \sqrt{2x - x^2} = 2(1 - x)\sqrt{x + a}$ ..... (1)

But we also know the graphs intersect at this point, so $\sqrt{2x - x^2} = \sqrt{x + a}$ ..... (2)

Comparing (1) and (2), $1 = 2(1 - x)$

$\therefore \quad 2x = 1$

$\therefore \quad x = \frac{1}{2}$

When $x = \frac{1}{2}$, $\sqrt{2x - x^2} = \sqrt{1 - \left(\frac{1}{2}\right)^2}$
$= \frac{\sqrt{3}}{2}$ ∴ the graphs intersect at $\left(\frac{1}{2}, \frac{\sqrt{3}}{2}\right)$

∴ when $x = \frac{1}{2}$, $\sqrt{x + a} = \frac{\sqrt{3}}{2}$

∴ $x + a = \frac{3}{4}$

∴ $\frac{1}{2} + a = \frac{3}{4}$

∴ $a = \frac{1}{4}$

So, $a = \frac{1}{4}$ and the point of intersection is $\left(\frac{1}{2}, \frac{\sqrt{3}}{2}\right)$.

13 The gradient of the line [PQ] is $\frac{-3 - 3}{6 - (-2)} = \frac{-6}{8} = -\frac{3}{4}$

∴ the equation of the tangent is $\frac{y - 3}{x + 2} = -\frac{3}{4}$ {tangent goes through P}

∴ $4y - 12 = -3x - 6$

∴ $y = -\frac{3}{4}x + \frac{3}{2}$

$y = \frac{b}{(x+1)^2} = b(x+1)^{-2}$

∴ $\frac{dy}{dx} = -2(b)(x+1)^{-3} = -\frac{3}{4}$ at the point of intersection

∴ $\frac{-2b}{(x+1)^3} = -\frac{3}{4}$

∴ $b = \frac{3}{8}(x+1)^3$ ...... (1)

The line [PQ] meets the curve where $-\frac{3}{4}x + \frac{3}{2} = \frac{b}{(x+1)^2}$

∴ $-\frac{3}{4}x + \frac{3}{2} = \frac{\frac{3}{8}(x+1)^3}{(x+1)^2}$ {using (1)}

∴ $-6x + 12 = 3(x + 1)$

∴ $9 = 9x$

∴ $x = 1$

and so $b = \frac{3}{8}(1+1)^3 = \frac{3}{8} \times 8 = 3$

EXERCISE 20G

1 a $f(x) = 3x^2 - 6x + 2$
∴ $f'(x) = 6x - 6$
∴ $f''(x) = 6$

b $f(x) = 2x^3 - 3x^2 - x + 5$
∴ $f'(x) = 6x^2 - 6x - 1$
∴ $f''(x) = 12x - 6$

c $f(x) = \frac{2}{\sqrt{x}} - 1 = 2x^{-\frac{1}{2}} - 1$
∴ $f'(x) = -x^{-\frac{3}{2}}$
$f''(x) = \frac{3}{2}x^{-\frac{5}{2}}$
$= \frac{3}{2\sqrt{x^5}}$

d $f(x) = \frac{2 - 3x}{x^2} = 2x^{-2} - 3x^{-1}$
∴ $f'(x) = -4x^{-3} + 3x^{-2}$
∴ $f''(x) = 12x^{-4} - 6x^{-3}$
$= \frac{12 - 6x}{x^4}$

e $f(x) = (1 - 2x)^3$
∴ $f'(x) = 3(1 - 2x)^2(-2)$
$= -6(1 - 2x)^2$
∴ $f''(x) = -12(1 - 2x)^1(-2) = 24(1 - 2x)$

f $f(x) = \dfrac{x+2}{2x-1}$ is a quotient with $u = x+2$ and $v = 2x-1$

$\therefore\ u' = 1$ and $v' = 2$

$\therefore\ f'(x) = \dfrac{1(2x-1) - 2(x+2)}{(2x-1)^2}$ {quotient rule}

$= \dfrac{-5}{(2x-1)^2}$

$= -5(2x-1)^{-2}$

$\therefore\ f''(x) = 10(2x-1)^{-3}(2) = \dfrac{20}{(2x-1)^3}$

2 a $y = x - x^3$

$\therefore\ \dfrac{dy}{dx} = 1 - 3x^2$

$\therefore\ \dfrac{d^2y}{dx^2} = -6x$

$\therefore\ \dfrac{d^3y}{dx^3} = -6$

b $y = x^2 - \dfrac{5}{x^2}$

$= x^2 - 5x^{-2}$

$\therefore\ \dfrac{dy}{dx} = 2x + 10x^{-3}$

$\therefore\ \dfrac{d^2y}{dx^2} = 2 - 30x^{-4} = 2 - \dfrac{30}{x^4}$

$\therefore\ \dfrac{d^3y}{dx^3} = 120x^{-5} = \dfrac{120}{x^5}$

c $y = 2 - \dfrac{3}{\sqrt{x}}$

$= 2 - 3x^{-\frac{1}{2}}$

$\therefore\ \dfrac{dy}{dx} = \tfrac{3}{2}x^{-\frac{3}{2}}$

$\therefore\ \dfrac{d^2y}{dx^2} = -\tfrac{9}{4}x^{-\frac{5}{2}}$

$\therefore\ \dfrac{d^3y}{dx^3} = \tfrac{45}{8}x^{-\frac{7}{2}}$

d $y = \dfrac{4-x}{x} = 4x^{-1} - 1$

$\therefore\ \dfrac{dy}{dx} = -4x^{-2}$

$\therefore\ \dfrac{d^2y}{dx^2} = 8x^{-3} = \dfrac{8}{x^3}$

$\therefore\ \dfrac{d^3y}{dx^3} = -24x^{-4} = -\dfrac{24}{x^4}$

e $y = (x^2 - 3x)^3$

$\therefore\ \dfrac{dy}{dx} = 3(x^2 - 3x)^2(2x - 3)$

$= (6x - 9)(x^2 - 3x)^2$

which is a product where $u = 6x - 9$

and $v = (x^2 - 3x)^2$

$\therefore\ u' = 6$ and $v' = 2(x^2 - 3x)^1(2x - 3)$

$\therefore\ \dfrac{d^2y}{dx^2} = 6(x^2 - 3x)^2$

$+ (6x - 9)(2)(x^2 - 3x)(2x - 3)$

$= 6(x^2 - 3x)\left[(x^2 - 3x) + (2x - 3)^2\right]$

$= 6(x^2 - 3x)(x^2 - 3x + 4x^2 - 12x + 9)$

$= 6(x^2 - 3x)(5x^2 - 15x + 9)$

which is a product where

$u = 6(x^2 - 3x)$ and $v = 5x^2 - 15x + 9$

$\therefore\ u' = 6(2x - 3)$ and $v' = 10x - 15$

$\therefore\ \dfrac{d^3y}{dx^3} = 6(2x - 3)(5x^2 - 15x + 9)$

$+ 6(x^2 - 3x)(10x - 15)$

f $y = x^2 - x + \dfrac{1}{1-x}$

$= x^2 - x + (1-x)^{-1}$

$\therefore\ \dfrac{dy}{dx} = 2x - 1 + (-1)(1-x)^{-2}(-1)$

$= 2x - 1 + (1-x)^{-2}$

$\therefore\ \dfrac{d^2y}{dx^2} = 2 - 2(1-x)^{-3}(-1)$

$= 2 + \dfrac{2}{(1-x)^3}$

$\therefore\ \dfrac{d^3y}{dx^3} = -6(1-x)^{-4}(-1)$

$= \dfrac{6}{(1-x)^4}$

3 a $f(x) = 2x^3 - 6x^2 + 5x + 1$
$\therefore\ f'(x) = 6x^2 - 12x + 5$
$\therefore\ f''(x) = 12x - 12$
So, $f''(x) = 0$
when $12x - 12 = 0$
$\therefore\ 12x = 12$
$\therefore\ x = 1$

b $f(x) = \dfrac{x}{x^2 + 2}$ is a quotient where
$u = x$ and $v = x^2 + 2$
$\therefore\ u' = 1,\ v' = 2x$
$\therefore\ f'(x) = \dfrac{1(x^2 + 2) - 2x^2}{(x^2 + 2)^2}$ {quotient rule}
$= \dfrac{2 - x^2}{(x^2 + 2)^2}$

This is another quotient, this time with
$u = 2 - x^2$ and $v = (x^2 + 2)^2$
$\therefore\ u' = -2x,\ v' = 2(x^2 + 2)(2x)$
$\therefore\ f''(x) = \dfrac{-2x(x^2 + 2)^2 - 4x(x^2 + 2)(2 - x^2)}{(x^2 + 2)^4}$
$= \dfrac{-2x(x^2 + 2)[x^2 + 2 + 2(2 - x^2)]}{(x^2 + 2)^4}$
$= \dfrac{-2x[-x^2 + 6]}{(x^2 + 2)^3} = \dfrac{2x[x^2 - 6]}{(x^2 + 2)^3}$

So, $f''(x) = 0$ when $2x[x^2 - 6] = 0$
$\therefore\ x = 0$ or $x^2 - 6 = 0$
$\therefore\ x = 0$ or $x = \pm\sqrt{6}$

4 a $y = \dfrac{1}{1 - x} = (1 - x)^{-1}$
$\therefore\ \dfrac{dy}{dx} = -(-1)(1 - x)^{-2} = \dfrac{1}{(1 - x)^2}$

b P_n is: "If $y = \dfrac{1}{1 - x}$ then $\dfrac{d^n y}{dx^n} = \dfrac{n!}{(1 - x)^{n+1}}$" for $n \in \mathbb{Z}^+$.

Proof: (By the principle of mathematical induction)

(1) Using **a**, $\dfrac{d^1 y}{dx^1} = \dfrac{dy}{dx} = \dfrac{1}{(1 - x)^2} = \dfrac{1!}{(1 - x)^{(1+1)}}$
$\therefore\ P_1$ is true.

(2) If P_k is true, then $\dfrac{d^k y}{dx^k} = \dfrac{k!}{(1 - x)^{k+1}}$
$= k!(1 - x)^{-(k+1)}$
$\therefore\ \dfrac{d^{k+1} y}{dx^{k+1}} = -k!(k + 1)(-1)(1 - x)^{-(k+1)-1}$
$= \dfrac{(k + 1)!}{(1 - x)^{(k+1)+1}}$

Hence P_{k+1} is true whenever P_k is true and P_1 is true
$\therefore\ P_n$ is true for $n \in \mathbb{Z}^+$ {Principle of mathematical induction}

REVIEW SET 20A

1 Consider $y = -2x^2$. When $x = -1$, $y = -2(-1)^2 = -2$, so the point of contact is $(-1, -2)$.
Now $\dfrac{dy}{dx} = -4x$
$\therefore$ at $x = -1$, $\dfrac{dy}{dx} = -4(-1) = 4$
$\therefore$ the tangent has equation $\dfrac{y - (-2)}{x - (-1)} = 4$ or $y = 4x + 2$.

2 a $y = 3x^2 - x^4$

$\therefore \dfrac{dy}{dx} = 6x - 4x^3$

b $y = \dfrac{x^3 - x}{x^2} = x - x^{-1}$

$\therefore \dfrac{dy}{dx} = 1 + x^{-2} = 1 + \dfrac{1}{x^2}$

3 $f(x) = x^2 + 2x \quad \therefore \quad f'(x) = \lim\limits_{h \to 0} \dfrac{f(x+h) - f(x)}{h}$

$= \lim\limits_{h \to 0} \dfrac{[(x+h)^2 + 2(x+h)] - [x^2 + 2x]}{h}$

$= \lim\limits_{h \to 0} \dfrac{2xh + h^2 + 2h}{h}$

$= \lim\limits_{h \to 0} 2x + 2 + h \quad \{\text{as } h \neq 0\}$

$= 2x + 2 \qquad$ Check: $f(x) = x^2 + 2x \quad \therefore \quad f'(x) = 2x + 2 \checkmark$

4 Consider $y = \dfrac{1 - 2x}{x^2}$. When $x = 1$, $y = \dfrac{1 - 2(1)}{1^2} = -1$, so the point of contact is $(1, -1)$.

Since $y = \dfrac{1}{x^2} - \dfrac{2}{x}$, $\dfrac{dy}{dx} = -2x^{-3} + 2x^{-2} = -\dfrac{2}{x^3} + \dfrac{2}{x^2}$

$\therefore$ at $x = 1$, $\dfrac{dy}{dx} = -2 + 2 = 0$

So, the tangent is a horizontal line, and the normal must be a vertical line of the form $x = k$.
As the normal passes through $(1, -1)$, its equation must be $x = 1$.

5 Consider the tangent to $y = 2x^3 + 4x - 1$ at $(1, 5)$.

$\dfrac{dy}{dx} = 6x^2 + 4 \quad \therefore \text{ at } x = 1, \quad \dfrac{dy}{dx} = 6(1)^2 + 4 = 10$

$\therefore$ the tangent has equation $\dfrac{y - 5}{x - 1} = 10 \quad$ or $\quad y = 10x - 5$

Now the tangent meets the curve again where $10x - 5 = 2x^3 + 4x - 1$

$\therefore \quad 2x^3 - 6x + 4 = 0$

$\therefore \quad x^3 - 3x + 2 = 0$

We know that $(x - 1)^2$ is a factor since the line is tangent to the curve at $x = 1$.
Consequently, $x^3 - 3x + 2 = (x - 1)^2(x + 2) = 0 \quad$ {since the constant term is 2}
Thus $x = -2$ is the other solution and when $x = -2$, $y = 2(-2)^3 + 4(-2) - 1 = -25$
$\therefore$ the tangent meets the curve again at $(-2, -25)$.

6 $y = \dfrac{ax + b}{\sqrt{x}} = a\sqrt{x} + \dfrac{b}{\sqrt{x}} = ax^{\frac{1}{2}} + bx^{-\frac{1}{2}}$

$\therefore \dfrac{dy}{dx} = \dfrac{a}{2}x^{-\frac{1}{2}} - \dfrac{b}{2}x^{-\frac{3}{2}} = \dfrac{a}{2\sqrt{x}} - \dfrac{b}{2x\sqrt{x}}$

The equation of the tangent at $x = 1$ is $2x - y = 1$

or $y = 2x - 1 \quad$ so the gradient of the tangent is 2

$\therefore$ at $x = 1$, $\dfrac{dy}{dx} = \dfrac{a}{2} - \dfrac{b}{2} = 2 \quad \therefore \quad a - b = 4$

$\therefore \quad a = b + 4 \quad \ldots \ldots (1)$

Also at $x = 1$, the tangent touches the curve $\quad \therefore \quad \dfrac{a(1) + b}{\sqrt{1}} = 2(1) - 1$

$\therefore \quad a + b = 1$

$\therefore \quad b + 4 + b = 1 \quad$ {using (1)}

$\therefore \quad 2b = -3$

$\therefore \quad b = -\dfrac{3}{2}$

and $\quad a = 4 - \dfrac{3}{2} = \dfrac{5}{2}$

7 Consider $y = 4(ax+1)^{-2}$.

When $x = 0$, $y = 4(0+1)^{-2} = 4$, so the point of contact is $(0, 4)$.

Now $\dfrac{dy}{dx} = -8(ax+1)^{-3}(a) = \dfrac{-8a}{(ax+1)^3}$ $\therefore$ at $x = 0$, $\dfrac{dy}{dx} = -8a$

$\therefore$ the tangent has equation $\dfrac{y-4}{x-0} = -8a$ or $y - 4 = -8ax$

This tangent passes through $(1, 0)$, so $0 - 4 = -8a(1)$ $\therefore$ $a = \frac{1}{2}$

8 Consider the normal to the curve $y = \dfrac{1}{\sqrt{x}}$ at $x = 4$.

When $x = 4$, $y = \frac{1}{\sqrt{4}} = \frac{1}{2}$, so the point of contact is $(4, \frac{1}{2})$.

Now $\dfrac{dy}{dx} = -\frac{1}{2}x^{-\frac{3}{2}}$ $\therefore$ at $x = 4$, $\dfrac{dy}{dx} = -\frac{1}{2}\left(4^{-\frac{3}{2}}\right) = -\frac{1}{2}\left(\frac{1}{8}\right) = -\frac{1}{16}$

$\therefore$ the normal at $(4, \frac{1}{2})$ has gradient 16.

So the equation is $\dfrac{y - \frac{1}{2}}{x - 4} = 16$

$\therefore$ $y - \frac{1}{2} = 16x - 64$

$\therefore$ $y = 16x - \frac{127}{2}$

9 a $M = (t^2 + 3)^4$

$\therefore$ $\dfrac{dM}{dt} = 4(t^2+3)^3(2t)$

$= 8t(t^2+3)^3$

b $A = \dfrac{\sqrt{t+5}}{t^2}$ is a quotient with

$u = (t+5)^{\frac{1}{2}}$ and $v = t^2$

$\therefore$ $u' = \frac{1}{2}(t+5)^{-\frac{1}{2}}$, $v' = 2t$

$\therefore$ $\dfrac{dA}{dt} = \dfrac{\frac{1}{2}(t+5)^{-\frac{1}{2}}(t^2) - (t+5)^{\frac{1}{2}}(2t)}{t^4}$

$= \dfrac{\frac{1}{2}t(t+5)^{-\frac{1}{2}} - 2(t+5)^{\frac{1}{2}}}{t^3}$

10 a $y = \dfrac{4}{\sqrt{x}} - 3x = 4x^{-\frac{1}{2}} - 3x$

$\therefore$ $\dfrac{dy}{dx} = -2x^{-\frac{3}{2}} - 3$

$= \dfrac{-2}{x\sqrt{x}} - 3$

b $y = \left(x - \dfrac{1}{x}\right)^4 = (x - x^{-1})^4$

$\therefore$ $\dfrac{dy}{dx} = 4(x - x^{-1})^3(1 + x^{-2})$

$= 4\left(x - \dfrac{1}{x}\right)^3\left(1 + \dfrac{1}{x^2}\right)$

c $y = \sqrt{x^2 - 3x} = (x^2 - 3x)^{\frac{1}{2}}$

$\therefore$ $\dfrac{dy}{dx} = \frac{1}{2}(x^2 - 3x)^{-\frac{1}{2}}(2x - 3)$

$= \dfrac{2x - 3}{2\sqrt{x^2 - 3x}}$

11 $y = \sqrt{5 - 4x} = (5 - 4x)^{\frac{1}{2}}$

a $\dfrac{dy}{dx} = \frac{1}{2}(5 - 4x)^{-\frac{1}{2}}(-4)$

$= -2(5 - 4x)^{-\frac{1}{2}}$

b $\dfrac{d^2y}{dx^2} = -2(-\frac{1}{2})(5 - 4x)^{-\frac{3}{2}}(-4)$

$= -4(5 - 4x)^{-\frac{3}{2}}$

c $\dfrac{d^3y}{dx^3} = -4(-\frac{3}{2})(5 - 4x)^{-\frac{5}{2}}(-4)$

$= -24(5 - 4x)^{-\frac{5}{2}}$

REVIEW SET 20B

1 a $y = 5x - 3x^{-1}$

$\therefore \dfrac{dy}{dx} = 5 + 3x^{-2} = 5 + \dfrac{3}{x^2}$

b $y = (3x^2 + x)^4$

$\therefore \dfrac{dy}{dx} = 4(3x^2 + x)^3(6x + 1)$

c $y = (x^2 + 1)(1 - x^2)^3$ is a product with $u = x^2 + 1$ and $v = (1 - x^2)^3$

$\therefore u' = 2x$ and $v' = 3(1 - x^2)^2(-2x)$

$\therefore \dfrac{dy}{dx} = 2x(1 - x^2)^3 - 6x(x^2 + 1)(1 - x^2)^2$ {product rule}

2 $y = x^3 - 3x^2 - 9x + 2 \quad \therefore \dfrac{dy}{dx} = 3x^2 - 6x - 9$

Horizontal tangents occur when $\dfrac{dy}{dx} = 0 \quad \therefore 3x^2 - 6x - 9 = 0$

$\therefore x^2 - 2x - 3 = 0$

$\therefore (x - 3)(x + 1) = 0$

$\therefore x = 3$ or $x = -1$

When $x = 3$, the horizontal tangent has equation $y = -25$.
When $x = -1$, the horizontal tangent has equation $y = 7$.

3 Consider $y = \dfrac{x+1}{x^2 - 2}$. When $x = 1$, $y = \dfrac{1+1}{1^2 - 2} = -2 \quad \therefore$ the point of contact is $(1, -2)$.

Now $y = \dfrac{x+1}{x^2 - 2}$ is a quotient with $u = x + 1$ and $v = x^2 - 2$

$\therefore u' = 1$ and $v' = 2x$

$\dfrac{dy}{dx} = \dfrac{1(x^2 - 2) - (x+1)(2x)}{(x^2 - 2)^2}$ {quotient rule}

$\therefore$ at $x = 1$, $\dfrac{dy}{dx} = \dfrac{(1^2 - 2) - (1+1)(2)}{(1^2 - 2)^2} = \dfrac{(-1) - 4}{1} = -5$

$\therefore$ the normal at $(1, -2)$ has gradient $\frac{1}{5}$

$\therefore$ the equation of the normal is $\dfrac{y - (-2)}{x - 1} = \frac{1}{5}$ or $5y = x - 11$.

4 a $f(x) = \dfrac{(x+3)^3}{\sqrt{x}}$ is a quotient with $u = (x+3)^3$ and $v = x^{\frac{1}{2}}$

$\therefore u' = 3(x+3)^2$ and $v' = \frac{1}{2}x^{-\frac{1}{2}}$

$\therefore f'(x) = \dfrac{3(x+3)^2 \sqrt{x} - \frac{1}{2}x^{-\frac{1}{2}}(x+3)^3}{x}$ {quotient rule}

b $f(x) = x^4 \sqrt{x^2 + 3}$ is a product with $u = x^4$ and $v = (x^2 + 3)^{\frac{1}{2}}$

$\therefore u' = 4x^3$ and $v' = \frac{1}{2}(x^2 + 3)^{-\frac{1}{2}}(2x) = x(x^2 + 3)^{-\frac{1}{2}}$

$\therefore f'(x) = 4x^3 \sqrt{x^2 + 3} + \dfrac{x^5}{\sqrt{x^2 + 3}}$ {product rule}

5 a $f(x) = 3x^2 - \dfrac{1}{x} = 3x^2 - x^{-1}$

$\therefore f'(x) = 6x + x^{-2}$

$\therefore f''(x) = 6 - 2x^{-3} = 6 - \dfrac{2}{x^3}$

b $f(x) = \sqrt{x} = x^{\frac{1}{2}}$

$\therefore f'(x) = \frac{1}{2}x^{-\frac{1}{2}}$

$\therefore f''(x) = -\frac{1}{4}x^{-\frac{3}{2}}$

6 Consider the tangent to $y = x^2\sqrt{1-x}$ at $x = -3$.
When $x = -3$, $y = (-3)^2\sqrt{1-(-3)} = 9\sqrt{4} = 18$,
$\therefore$ the point of contact is $(-3, 18)$.
Also, $y = x^2\sqrt{1-x}$ is a product with $u = x^2$ and $v = (1-x)^{\frac{1}{2}}$
$\therefore$ $u' = 2x$ and $v' = \frac{1}{2}(1-x)^{-\frac{1}{2}}(-1)$
$\therefore$ $\dfrac{dy}{dx} = 2x(1-x)^{\frac{1}{2}} - x^2(\frac{1}{2})(1-x)^{-\frac{1}{2}}$
$\therefore$ at $x = -3$, $\dfrac{dy}{dx} = 2(-3)(1-(-3))^{\frac{1}{2}} - (-3)^2(\frac{1}{2})(1-(-3))^{-\frac{1}{2}}$
$= -6(2) - 9(\frac{1}{2})(\frac{1}{2}) = -\frac{57}{4}$
$\therefore$ the tangent at $(-3, 18)$ has equation $\dfrac{y - 18}{x - (-3)} = -\dfrac{57}{4}$
$\therefore$ $4y - 72 = -57x - 171$
$\therefore$ $4y = -57x - 99$
Now when $x = 0$, $y = -\frac{99}{4}$ and when $y = 0$, $x = -\frac{99}{57}$
$\therefore$ the area of $\triangle OAB = \frac{1}{2}\left(\frac{99}{4}\right)\left(\frac{99}{57}\right) = \frac{3267}{152} \approx 21.5$ units^2

7 $y = x^3 + ax + b$ $\therefore$ $\dfrac{dy}{dx} = 3x^2 + a$
$\therefore$ at $x = 1$, $\dfrac{dy}{dx} = 3 + a$
The equation of the tangent at $x = 1$ is $y = 2x$, so the gradient is 2.
$\therefore$ $3 + a = 2$ and so $a = -1$
Also at $x = 1$, the tangent touches the curve.
$\therefore$ $x^3 + ax + b = 2x$ when $x = 1$
$\therefore$ $(1)^3 + (-1)(1) + b = 2(1)$
$\therefore$ $1 - 1 + b = 2$
$\therefore$ $b = 2$

8 $y = x^3 + ax^2 - 4x + 3$ $\therefore$ $\dfrac{dy}{dx} = 3x^2 + 2ax - 4$
The tangent at $x = 1$ is parallel to $y = 3x$, so when $x = 1$, $\dfrac{dy}{dx} = 3$
$\therefore$ $3 = 3(1)^2 + 2a(1) - 4$
$\therefore$ $2a = 4$
$\therefore$ $a = 2$
When $x = 1$, $y = 1^3 + 2(1)^2 - 4(1) + 3 = 2$
The contact point is $(1, 2)$ and since the gradient is 3, the tangent at $(1, 2)$ has equation
$\dfrac{y - 2}{x - 1} = 3$ $\therefore$ $y - 2 = 3x - 3$
$\therefore$ $y = 3x - 1$
The tangent meets the curve where $x^3 + 2x^2 - 4x + 3 = 3x - 1$
$\therefore$ $x^3 + 2x^2 - 7x + 4 = 0$
Since the line touches the curve at $x = 1$, $(x - 1)^2$ must be a factor.
Consequently, $x^3 + 2x^2 - 7x + 4 = (x - 1)^2(x + 4) = 0$ {since the constant term is 4}
$\therefore$ the curve cuts the tangent when $x = -4$.
When $x = 4$, $y = (-4)^3 + 2(-4)^2 - 4(-4) + 3 = -13$
$\therefore$ the curve cuts the tangent at $(-4, -13)$.

9 $f(x) = 2x^3 + Ax + B \quad \therefore \quad f'(x) = 6x^2 + A$

Now as the gradient at $(-2, 33)$ is 10,   Then, since $(-2, 33)$ lies on the curve,

$\therefore \quad f'(-2) = 10$ $f(-2) = 33$

$\therefore \quad 10 = 6(-2)^2 + A$ $\therefore \quad 2(-2)^3 - 14(-2) + B = 33$

$\therefore \quad A = -14$ $\therefore \quad -16 + 28 + B = 33$

$\therefore \quad f(x) = 2x^3 - 14x + B$ $\therefore \quad B = 21$

10 a $y = uv$

$\therefore \quad \dfrac{dy}{dx} = \left(\dfrac{du}{dx}\right)v + u\left(\dfrac{dv}{dx}\right) \quad$ {product rule}

$\therefore \quad \dfrac{d^2y}{dx^2} = \left[\left(\dfrac{d^2u}{dx^2}\right)v + \dfrac{du}{dx}\dfrac{dv}{dx}\right] + \left[\dfrac{du}{dx}\dfrac{dv}{dx} + u\left(\dfrac{d^2v}{dx^2}\right)\right] \quad$ {product rule}

$= \left(\dfrac{d^2u}{dx^2}\right)v + 2\dfrac{du}{dx}\dfrac{dv}{dx} + u\left(\dfrac{d^2v}{dx^2}\right)$

b $y = uvw = u(vw)$

$\therefore \quad \dfrac{dy}{dx} = \dfrac{du}{dx}(vw) + u\left[\dfrac{d}{dx}(vw)\right] \quad$ {product rule}

$= \dfrac{du}{dx}vw + u\left(\dfrac{dv}{dx}w + v\dfrac{dw}{dx}\right) \quad$ {product rule}

$= \dfrac{du}{dx}vw + u\dfrac{dv}{dx}w + uv\dfrac{dw}{dx}$

11 P_n is: "If $y = x^n$, then $\dfrac{dy}{dx} = nx^{n-1}$", $n \in \mathbb{Z}^+$.

Proof: (By the principle of mathematical induction)

(1) If $n = 1$, then $y = x$. This has gradient 1, so $\dfrac{dy}{dx} = 1 = 1x^0$. $\therefore \quad P_1$ is true.

(2) If P_k is true, then $y = x^k$ implies that $\dfrac{dy}{dx} = kx^{k-1}$

If $y = x^{k+1} = x^k x$,

then $\dfrac{dy}{dx} = \dfrac{d}{dx}\left(x^k\right)x + x^k \dfrac{d}{dx}(x) \quad$ {product rule}

$= kx^{k-1}x + x^k \times 1$

$= kx^k + x^k$

$= (k+1)x^k$

Hence P_{k+1} is true whenever P_k is true, and P_1 is true

$\therefore \quad P_n$ is true for all $n \in \mathbb{Z}^+$ {Principle of mathematical induction}

REVIEW SET 20C

1 a $y = x^3\sqrt{1-x^2}$ is a product where $u = x^3$ and $v = (1-x^2)^{\frac{1}{2}}$

$\therefore \quad u' = 3x^2$ and $v' = \tfrac{1}{2}(1-x^2)^{-\frac{1}{2}}(-2x) = -x(1-x^2)^{-\frac{1}{2}}$

$\therefore \quad \dfrac{dy}{dx} = 3x^2\sqrt{1-x^2} - \dfrac{x^4}{\sqrt{1-x^2}} \quad$ {product rule}

b $y = \dfrac{x^2 - 3x}{\sqrt{x+1}}$ is a quotient where $u = x^2 - 3x$ and $v = (x+1)^{\frac{1}{2}}$

$\therefore \quad u' = 2x - 3$ and $v' = \tfrac{1}{2}(x+1)^{-\frac{1}{2}}$

$\therefore \quad \dfrac{dy}{dx} = \dfrac{(2x-3)(x+1)^{\frac{1}{2}} - \tfrac{1}{2}(x^2-3x)(x+1)^{-\frac{1}{2}}}{x+1} \quad$ {quotient rule}

2 Consider $y = \dfrac{x+1}{x^2 - 2}$.

When $x = 1$, $y = \dfrac{1+1}{1^2 - 2} = -2$ ∴ the point of contact is $(1, -2)$

$y = \dfrac{x+1}{x^2 - 2}$ is a quotient with $u = x + 1$ and $v = x^2 - 2$

∴ $u' = 1$ and $v' = 2x$

∴ $\dfrac{dy}{dx} = \dfrac{1(x^2 - 2) - (x+1)2x}{(x^2 - 2)^2}$ {quotient rule}

∴ at $x = 1$, $\dfrac{dy}{dx} = \dfrac{(1-2) - 2(1+1)}{(1-2)^2} = \dfrac{-1 - 4}{1} = -5$

∴ the normal at $(1, -2)$ has gradient $\frac{1}{5}$.

So the normal has equation $\dfrac{y - (-2)}{x - 1} = \frac{1}{5}$ ∴ $5y + 10 = x - 1$
∴ $5y = x - 11$

3 $f(x) = 2x^4 - 4x^3 - 9x^2 + 4x + 7$

∴ $f'(x) = 8x^3 - 12x^2 - 18x + 4$

∴ $f''(x) = 24x^2 - 24x - 18$

So, $f''(x) = 0$ where $24x^2 - 24x - 18 = 0$

∴ $4x^2 - 4x - 3 = 0$

∴ $(2x + 1)(2x - 3) = 0$

∴ $x = -\frac{1}{2}$ or $x = \frac{3}{2}$

4 Consider the normal to $f(x) = \dfrac{3x}{1 + x}$ at $(2, 2)$.

$f(x)$ is a quotient with $u = 3x$ and $v = 1 + x$

∴ $u' = 3$ and $v' = 1$

∴ $f'(x) = \dfrac{3(1+x) - 1(3x)}{(1+x)^2} = \dfrac{3}{(1+x)^2}$ {quotient rule}

∴ $f'(2) = \dfrac{3}{9} = \dfrac{1}{3}$

∴ the normal at $(2, 2)$ has gradient -3

So, the equation of the normal is $\dfrac{y - 2}{x - 2} = -3$

∴ $y - 2 = -3(x - 2)$
∴ $y = -3x + 8$

When $x = 0$, $y = 8$ and when $y = 0$, $x = \frac{8}{3}$

∴ B and C are at $(0, 8)$ and $(\frac{8}{3}, 0)$,

and the distance BC $= \sqrt{\left(0 - \frac{8}{3}\right)^2 + (8 - 0)^2} = \sqrt{\frac{64}{9} + 64} = \sqrt{\frac{640}{9}} = \frac{8\sqrt{10}}{3}$ units

5 a $y = 3x^4 - \dfrac{2}{x} = 3x^4 - 2x^{-1}$

∴ $\dfrac{dy}{dx} = 12x^3 + 2x^{-2}$

∴ $\dfrac{d^2y}{dx^2} = 36x^2 - 4x^{-3}$

$= 36x^2 - \dfrac{4}{x^3}$

b $y = x^3 - x + \dfrac{1}{\sqrt{x}} = x^3 - x + x^{-\frac{1}{2}}$

∴ $\dfrac{dy}{dx} = 3x^2 - 1 - \frac{1}{2}x^{-\frac{3}{2}}$

∴ $\dfrac{d^2y}{dx^2} = 6x + \frac{3}{4}x^{-\frac{5}{2}}$

6 $y = \dfrac{x}{\sqrt{1-x}}$ at $x = -3$

When $x = -3$, $y = \dfrac{-3}{\sqrt{1-(-3)}} = -\dfrac{3}{2}$, so the point of contact is $(-3, -\dfrac{3}{2})$.

Now $y = \dfrac{x}{\sqrt{1-x}}$ is a quotient with $u = x$ and $v = (1-x)^{\frac{1}{2}}$

$\therefore \ u' = 1, \ v' = \dfrac{1}{2}(1-x)^{-\frac{1}{2}}(-1)$

$\therefore \ \dfrac{dy}{dx} = \dfrac{(1)\sqrt{1-x} - x(\frac{1}{2})(1-x)^{-\frac{1}{2}}(-1)}{1-x}$ {quotient rule}

At $x = -3$, $\dfrac{dy}{dx} = \dfrac{\sqrt{4} - (-3)(\frac{1}{2})(4)^{-\frac{1}{2}}(-1)}{4} = \dfrac{2 - 3(\frac{1}{2})(\frac{1}{2})}{4} = \dfrac{2 - \frac{3}{4}}{4} = \dfrac{5}{16}$

$\therefore$ the tangent at $(-3, -\dfrac{3}{2})$ has equation $\dfrac{y - (-\frac{3}{2})}{x - (-3)} = \dfrac{5}{16}$

$\therefore \ 16(y + \dfrac{3}{2}) = 5(x + 3)$
$16y + 24 = 5x + 15$
$\therefore \ 5x - 16y = 9$
$\therefore \ b = -16$ and $a = 9$

7 $f(x) = 3x^3 + Ax^2 + B$
$\therefore \ f'(x) = 9x^2 + 2Ax$

Since the tangent at $(-2, 14)$ has gradient 0, $f'(-2) = 0$
$\therefore \ 36 - 4A = 0$
$\therefore \ A = 9$

As the point $(-2, 14)$ lies on the curve, $14 = 3(-2)^3 + 9(-2)^2 + B$
$\therefore \ B = 14 + 24 - 36$
$\therefore \ B = 2$

$\therefore \ f'(x) = 9x^2 + 18x$
$\therefore \ f''(x) = 18x + 18$ and so $f''(-2) = -36 + 18 = -18$

8 $y = \dfrac{a}{(x+2)^2} = a(x+2)^{-2}$

The gradient of the line (AB) is $\dfrac{y_2 - y_1}{x_2 - x_1} = \dfrac{8 - 4}{0 - 2} = \dfrac{4}{-2} = -2$

$\therefore$ the equation of the tangent is $\dfrac{y - 8}{x - 0} = -2$ or $y = -2x + 8$

Now $\dfrac{dy}{dx} = -2a(x+2)^{-3}$, so for the given tangent, $-2a(x+2)^{-3} = -2$

$\therefore \ \dfrac{a}{(x+2)^3} = 1$

$\therefore \ a = (x+2)^3$ ..... (1)

The line (AB) meets the curve where $-2x + 8 = \dfrac{a}{(x+2)^2}$

$\therefore \ -2x + 8 = \dfrac{(x+2)^3}{(x+2)^2}$ {using (1)}

$\therefore \ -2x + 8 = x + 2$
$\therefore \ -3x = -6$
$\therefore \ x = 2$

and so $a = (2+2)^3 = 64$

9 The curves $y = \sqrt{3x+1}$ and $y = \sqrt{5x-x^2}$ meet when $\sqrt{3x+1} = \sqrt{5x-x^2}$
Squaring both sides, $3x + 1 = 5x - x^2$
$\therefore \quad x^2 - 2x + 1 = 0$
$\therefore \quad (x-1)^2 = 0$
$\therefore \quad x = 1$

When $x = 1$, $y = \sqrt{3+1} = 2$, so the curves meet at $(1, 2)$.

Now for $y = \sqrt{3x+1} = (3x+1)^{\frac{1}{2}}$ 　　Check: $y = \sqrt{5x-x^2} = (5x-x^2)^{\frac{1}{2}}$

$\dfrac{dy}{dx} = \tfrac{1}{2}(3x+1)^{-\frac{1}{2}}(3)$ 　　$\dfrac{dy}{dx} = \tfrac{1}{2}(5x-x^2)^{-\frac{1}{2}}(5-2x) = \dfrac{5-2x}{2\sqrt{5x-x^2}}$

$\therefore$ at $(1, 2)$, $\dfrac{dy}{dx} = \dfrac{3}{2(3+1)^{\frac{1}{2}}} = \dfrac{3}{4}$ 　　$\therefore$ at $(1, 2)$, $\dfrac{dy}{dx} = \dfrac{5-2}{2\sqrt{5-1}} = \dfrac{3}{4}$ ✓

$\therefore$ the curves have the same gradient of $\tfrac{3}{4}$ at their point of intersection.

The equation of the common tangent at $(1, 2)$ is $\dfrac{y-2}{x-1} = \dfrac{3}{4}$

$\therefore \quad 4(y-2) = 3(x-1)$
$\therefore \quad 4y = 3x + 5$

10 a

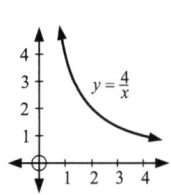

b For $f(x) = \dfrac{4}{x} = 4x^{-1}$,

$f'(x) = -4x^{-2} = -\dfrac{4}{x^2}$ 　and 　$f'(k) = -\dfrac{4}{k^2}$

$\therefore$ the gradient of the tangent to $f(x)$ at $\left(k, \dfrac{4}{k}\right)$ is $-\dfrac{4}{k^2}$

$\therefore$ the equation of the tangent is $\dfrac{y - \frac{4}{k}}{x - k} = -\dfrac{4}{k^2}$

$\therefore \quad yk^2 - 4k = -4x + 4k$
$\therefore \quad k^2 y = -4x + 8k$
$\therefore \quad y = -\dfrac{4}{k^2}x + \dfrac{8}{k}$

c $y = -\dfrac{4}{k^2}x + \dfrac{8}{k}$ cuts the x-axis when $y = 0$

$\therefore \quad -\dfrac{4}{k^2}x + \dfrac{8}{k} = 0$
$\therefore \quad \dfrac{4}{k^2}x = \dfrac{8}{k}$
$\therefore \quad x = 2k$ 　　$\therefore$ A is at $(2k, 0)$

$y = -\dfrac{4}{k^2}x + \dfrac{8}{k}$ cuts the y-axis when $x = 0$
$\therefore \quad y = \dfrac{8}{k}$ 　　$\therefore$ B is at $\left(0, \dfrac{8}{k}\right)$

d Area of triangle OAB $= \tfrac{1}{2}(2k)\left(\dfrac{8}{k}\right) = 8$ units^2

e The gradient of the tangent to $f(x)$ at $\left(k, \dfrac{4}{k}\right)$ is $-\dfrac{4}{k^2}$

$\therefore$ the gradient of the normal to $f(x)$ at $\left(k, \dfrac{4}{k}\right)$ is $\dfrac{k^2}{4}$

$\therefore$ the equation of the normal is $\dfrac{y - \frac{4}{k}}{x - k} = \dfrac{k^2}{4}$

$\therefore \quad 4y - \dfrac{16}{k} = k^2 x - k^3$

$$\therefore \quad 4ky - k^3x = 16 - k^4$$
This normal passes through $(1, 1)$, so $4k - k^3 = 16 - k^4$
$$\therefore \quad k^4 - k^3 + 4k - 16 = 0$$
$$\therefore \quad (k-2)(k+2)(k^2 - k + 4) = 0 \quad \{\text{using technology}\}$$
$$\therefore \quad k = \pm 2$$
But $k > 0$, so $k = 2$

11 P_n is "for $y = \dfrac{1}{2x+1}$, $\dfrac{d^n y}{dx^n} = \dfrac{(-2)^n n!}{(2x+1)^{n+1}}$", $n \in \mathbb{Z}^+$

Proof: (By the principle of mathematical induction)

(1) $y = \dfrac{1}{2x+1} = (2x+1)^{-1}$

$\therefore \quad \dfrac{dy}{dx} = -(2x+1)^{-2}(2) = \dfrac{-2}{(2x+1)^2}$

$\qquad = \dfrac{(-2)^1 1!}{(2x+1)^{1+1}} \qquad \therefore \quad P_1$ is true

(2) If P_k is true then $\dfrac{d^k y}{dx^k} = \dfrac{(-2)^k k!}{(2x+1)^{k+1}}$

Now $\dfrac{d^{k+1} y}{dx^{k+1}} = \dfrac{d}{dx}\left(\dfrac{d^k y}{dx^k}\right)$

$\qquad = \dfrac{d}{dx}\left(\dfrac{(-2)^k k!}{(2x+1)^{k+1}}\right) \quad \{\text{using } P_k\}$

$\qquad = \dfrac{d}{dx}\left[(-2)^k k! \, (2x+1)^{-(k+1)}\right]$

$\qquad = (-2)^k k! \, [-(k+1)] \, (2x+1)^{-(k+1)-1} \, (2)$

$\qquad = -2(-2)^k (k+1)! \, (2x+1)^{-(k+2)}$

$\qquad = \dfrac{(-2)^{k+1}(k+1)!}{(2x+1)^{(k+1)+1}}$

Thus P_{k+1} is true whenever P_k is true, and P_1 is true
$\therefore \quad P_n$ is true for all $n \in \mathbb{Z}^+$ {Principle of mathematical induction}

Chapter 21
APPLICATIONS OF DIFFERENTIAL CALCULUS

EXERCISE 21A

1 $P(t) = 2t^2 - 12t + 118$ thousand dollars, $t \geqslant 0$

  a $P(0) = \$118\,000$ is the current annual profit

  b $\dfrac{dP}{dt} = 4t - 12$ thousand dollars per year

  c $\dfrac{dP}{dt}$ is the rate of change in profit with time.

  d **i** The profit decreases when $\dfrac{dP}{dt} \leqslant 0$, which occurs when $4t - 12 \leqslant 0$
  $$\therefore \; 4t \leqslant 12$$
  $$\therefore \; t \leqslant 3$$
  But $t \geqslant 0$, so $0 \leqslant t \leqslant 3$ years.

  ii The profit increases when $\dfrac{dP}{dt} \geqslant 0$, which is for $t \geqslant 3$ years.

  e The profit function is a quadratic with $a > 0$ $\therefore$ the shape is $\smile$

  So, a minimum profit occurs when $\dfrac{dP}{dt} = 0$, which is when $t = 3$ years

  and $P(3) = 18 - 36 + 118 = 100$ thousand dollars or $\$100\,000$.

  f When $t = 4$, $\dfrac{dP}{dt} = 4$ thousand dollars per year.
  So, the profit is increasing at \$4000 per year after 4 years.
  When $t = 10$, $\dfrac{dP}{dt} = 28$ thousand dollars per year.
  So, the profit is increasing at \$28 000 per year after 10 years.
  When $t = 25$, $\dfrac{dP}{dt} = 88$ thousand dollars per year.
  So, the profit is increasing at \$88 000 per year after 25 years.

2 $V = 200(50 - t)^2$ m^3

  a average rate on $0 \leqslant t \leqslant 5$
  $= \dfrac{V(5) - V(0)}{5 - 0}$
  $= \dfrac{200(45)^2 - 200(50)^2}{5}$
  $= -19\,000$ m^3 per minute
  $\therefore$ leaving at 19 000 m^3 per minute

  b $V'(t) = 400(50 - t)^1 \times (-1)$
  $\therefore \; V'(5) = 400 \times 45 \times -1$
  $= -18\,000$ m^3 per minute
  $\therefore$ leaving at 18 000 m^3 per minute

3 $s(t) = 1.2 + 28.1t - 4.9t^2$ metres

  a When released, $t = 0$ and $s(0) = 1.2$ m $\therefore$ it is released 1.2 m above the ground.

  b $s'(t) = 28.1 - 9.8t$ m s^{-1} is the instantaneous velocity of the ball at the time t seconds after release.

  c When $s'(t) = 0$, $28.1 - 9.8t = 0$ $\therefore$ $t = \dfrac{28.1}{9.8} \approx 2.87$ seconds
  So, after 2.87 seconds the ball has stopped and reached its maximum height.

  d $s(2.867) = 1.2 + 28.1 \times 2.867 - 4.9 \times 2.867^2 \approx 41.5$ m
  So, the maximum height reached is about 41.5 m.

  e **i** $s'(0) = 28.1$ m s^{-1}
  ii $s'(2) = 28.1 - 19.6$
  $= 8.5$ m s^{-1}
  iii $s'(5) = 28.1 - 49$
  $= -20.9$ m s^{-1}

  If $s'(t) \geqslant 0$, the ball is travelling upwards. If $s'(t) \leqslant 0$, the ball is travelling downwards.

f $s(t) = 0$ when $1.2 + 28.1t - 4.9t^2 = 0$

$\therefore \quad 4.9t^2 - 28.1t - 1.2 = 0$

$\therefore \quad t = \dfrac{28.1 \pm \sqrt{28.1^2 - 4(4.9)(-1.2)}}{9.8} \approx -0.0424$ or 5.777

$\therefore$ the ball hits the ground after 5.78 seconds.

g $\dfrac{d^2s}{dt^2} = -9.8 \text{ m s}^{-2}$ and is the constant rate of change in $\dfrac{ds}{dt}$

$\therefore$ the instantaneous acceleration is constant at -9.8 m s^{-2} for the entire motion.

4 a $s(t) = bt - 4.9t^2$
$s'(t) = b - 9.8t$
$\therefore \quad s'(0) = b$
$\therefore$ the initial velocity is $b \text{ m s}^{-1}$

b Since $s(14.2) = 0$,
$b(14.2) - 4.9(14.2)^2 = 0$
$\therefore \quad 14.2\,[b - 4.9 \times 14.2] = 0$
$\therefore \quad b = 4.9 \times 14.2$
$\therefore \quad b = 69.58$
$\therefore$ the initial velocity is 69.6 m s^{-1}

EXERCISE 21B

1 $Q = 100 - 10\sqrt{t}, \quad t \geqslant 0$

a **i** At $t = 0$, $Q = 100$ units
ii At $t = 25$, $Q = 50$ units
iii At $t = 100$, $Q = 0$ units

b $\dfrac{dQ}{dt} = -5t^{-\frac{1}{2}} = -\dfrac{5}{\sqrt{t}}$

i At $t = 25$, $\dfrac{dQ}{dt} = -1$ unit per year
$\therefore$ decreasing at 1 unit per year

ii At $t = 50$, $\dfrac{dQ}{dt} = -\dfrac{5}{\sqrt{50}}$
$= -\dfrac{1}{\sqrt{2}}$ units per year
$\therefore$ decreasing at $\dfrac{1}{\sqrt{2}}$ units per year

c $\dfrac{dQ}{dt} = -\dfrac{5}{\sqrt{t}} \quad \therefore$ the skin *loses* the chemical at the rate $R = \dfrac{5}{\sqrt{t}} = 5t^{-\frac{1}{2}}$ units per year.

Now $\dfrac{dR}{dt} = -\dfrac{5}{2}t^{-\frac{3}{2}} = -\dfrac{5}{2t\sqrt{t}}$

Since $2t\sqrt{t} > 0$ for all $t > 0$, $\dfrac{dR}{dt} < 0$ for all $t > 0$.

$\therefore$ the rate at which the skin loses the chemical is decreasing for all $t > 0$.

2 $H = 20 - \dfrac{97.5}{t+5} \text{ m}, \quad t \geqslant 0$

a At planting, $t = 0$ $\therefore$ $H(0) = 20 - \dfrac{97.5}{0+5} = 0.5$ m

b $H(4) = 20 - \dfrac{97.5}{4+5} \approx 9.17$ m

$H(8) = 20 - \dfrac{97.5}{8+5} = 12.5$ m

$H(12) = 20 - \dfrac{97.5}{12+5} \approx 14.3$ m

c Now $\dfrac{dH}{dt} = 97.5(t+5)^{-2} = \dfrac{97.5}{(t+5)^2}$

When $t = 0$, $\dfrac{dH}{dt} = \dfrac{97.5}{25} = 3.9$ m yr^{-1}

When $t = 5$, $\dfrac{dH}{dt} = \dfrac{97.5}{100} = 0.975$ m yr^{-1}

When $t = 10$, $\dfrac{dH}{dt} = \dfrac{97.5}{225} \approx 0.433$ m yr^{-1}

d Now $\dfrac{dH}{dt} = \dfrac{97.5}{(t+5)^2}$

Since $(t+5)^2 > 0$ for all $t \geqslant 0$, $\dfrac{dH}{dt} > 0$ for all $t \geqslant 0$

$\therefore$ the height of the tree is always increasing, which means that the tree is always growing.

3 **a** $C(v) = \frac{1}{5}v^2 + 200\,000v^{-1}$ euros

    i At $v = 50$ km h^{-1}, $C = $ €4500
    ii At $v = 100$ km h^{-1}, $C = $ €4000

  b $\dfrac{dC}{dv} = \frac{2}{5}v - 200\,000v^{-2} = \frac{2}{5}v - \dfrac{200\,000}{v^2}$

    i At $v = 30$ km h^{-1},
    $\dfrac{dC}{dv} \approx -$€210 per km h^{-1}

    ii At $v = 90$ km h^{-1},
    $\dfrac{dC}{dv} \approx $ €11.3 per km h^{-1}

  c The cost is a minimum when $\dfrac{dC}{dv} = 0$, which occurs when $\frac{2}{5}v - \dfrac{200\,000}{v^2} = 0$

    $\therefore \ \frac{2}{5}v = \dfrac{200\,000}{v^2} \quad \therefore \ v^3 = 500\,000 \quad \therefore \ v \approx 79.4$ km h^{-1}

4 $y = \frac{1}{10}x(x-2)(x-3) = \frac{1}{10}(x^3 - 5x^2 + 6x)$

  a When $y = 0$, $x = 0$, 2 or 3
    $\therefore$ the lake is between 2 and 3 km from the shoreline.

  b $\dfrac{dy}{dx} = \frac{1}{10}(3x^2 - 10x + 6)$ When $x = \frac{1}{2}$, $\dfrac{dy}{dx} = \frac{7}{40} \quad \therefore$ land is sloping upwards.

    $= \frac{3}{10}x^2 - x + \frac{3}{5}$ When $x = \frac{3}{2}$, $\dfrac{dy}{dx} = -\frac{9}{40} \quad \therefore$ land is sloping downwards.

  c The deepest point of the lake occurs when the slope of the land is 0, which is when $\dfrac{dy}{dx} = 0$

    $\therefore \ \frac{1}{10}(3x^2 - 10x + 6) = 0$
    $\therefore \ 3x^2 - 10x + 6 = 0$
    $\therefore \ x = \dfrac{10 \pm \sqrt{100 - 72}}{6} = \dfrac{5 \pm \sqrt{7}}{3}$

    but it must be the value between 2 and 3 km, so $x = \dfrac{5 + \sqrt{7}}{3} \approx 2.549$ km

    The depth at this point is $y(2.549) \approx \frac{1}{10}(2.549)(0.549)(-0.451)$
    ≈ -0.06311 km
    ≈ 63.1 m below sea level.

5 **a** $V = 50\,000\left(1 - \dfrac{t}{80}\right)^2$, $0 \leqslant t \leqslant 80$

    $\therefore \ \dfrac{dV}{dt} = 2 \times 50\,000\left(1 - \dfrac{t}{80}\right)^1 \times \left(-\dfrac{1}{80}\right) = -1250\left(1 - \dfrac{t}{80}\right)$

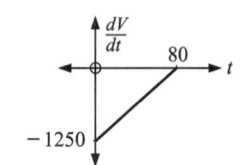

  b The outflow was fastest when $t = 0$, when the tap was first opened.

  c $\dfrac{dV}{dt} = -1250 + \dfrac{1250}{80}t \quad \therefore \ \dfrac{d^2V}{dt^2} = \dfrac{1250}{80} = \dfrac{125}{8}$

    Since $\dfrac{d^2V}{dt^2}$ is constant and positive, $\dfrac{dV}{dt}$ is constantly increasing
    $\therefore$ the outflow is decreasing at a constant rate.

6 **a** $\dfrac{dP}{dt} = aP\left(1 - \dfrac{P}{b}\right) - \left(\dfrac{c}{100}\right)P$ and when $\dfrac{dP}{dt} = 0$, the rate of change of population is zero, so the population is not changing and is stable.

  b If $a = 0.06$, $b = 24\,000$, $c = 5$ then

    $\dfrac{dP}{dt} = 0.06P\left(1 - \dfrac{P}{24\,000}\right) - \dfrac{5}{100}P$ Now for a stable population, $\dfrac{dP}{dt} = 0$

    $= 0.06P - 0.05P - \dfrac{0.06P^2}{24\,000}$ $\therefore \ P = 0$ or $\dfrac{P}{400\,000} = 0.01$

    $= P\left(0.01 - \dfrac{P}{400\,000}\right)$ $\therefore \ P = 0$ or 4000
    $\therefore$ the stable population is 4000 fish.

c If the harvest rate is 4%, then $\dfrac{dP}{dt} = 0.06P\left(1 - \dfrac{P}{24\,000}\right) - \dfrac{4}{100}P = P\left(0.02 - \dfrac{0.06P}{24\,000}\right)$

For a stable population, $\dfrac{dP}{dt} = 0$ and so $0 = P\left(0.02 - \dfrac{0.06P}{24\,000}\right)$

$\therefore \quad P = 0 \text{ or } \dfrac{0.06P}{24\,000} = 0.02$

$\therefore \quad P = 0 \text{ or } \dfrac{0.02 \times 24\,000}{0.06}$

$\therefore \quad P = 0 \text{ or } 8000$

$\therefore$ the stable population is 8000 fish

7 a $C(x) = 0.0003x^3 + 0.02x^2 + 4x + 2250$
$\therefore \quad C'(x) = 0.0009x^2 + 0.04x + 4$ dollars per pair

b $C'(220) = 0.0009(220)^2 + 0.04(220) + 4 = \$56.36$ per pair
This estimates the cost of making the 221st pair of jeans if 220 pairs are currently being made.

c $C(221) - C(220) \approx \$7348.98 - \$7292.40 \approx \$56.58$
This is the actual cost to make the extra pair of jeans (221 instead of 220).

d $C''(x) = 0.0018x + 0.04$

$C''(x) = 0$ when $0.0018x + 0.04 = 0 \quad \therefore \quad x = -\dfrac{0.04}{0.0018} \approx -22.2$

This is the point when the rate of change is a minimum. However, it is out of the bounds of our model, as we cannot make a negative quantity of jeans.

EXERCISE 21C.1

1 a $s(t) = t^2 + 3t - 2, \quad t \geqslant 0$
Average velocity
$= \dfrac{s(t_2) - s(t_1)}{t_2 - t_1}$
$= \dfrac{s(3) - s(1)}{3 - 1}$
$= \dfrac{16 - 2}{2}$
$= 7 \text{ m s}^{-1}$

c $\lim\limits_{h \to 0} \dfrac{s(1+h) - s(1)}{h}$
$= \lim\limits_{h \to 0} 5 + h$
$= 5 \text{ m s}^{-1}$
This is the *instantaneous velocity* at $t = 1$ second.

b Average velocity $= \dfrac{s(t_2) - s(t_1)}{t_2 - t_1}$
$= \dfrac{s(1+h) - s(1)}{(1+h) - 1}$
$= \dfrac{(1+h)^2 + 3(1+h) - 2 - 2}{h}$
$= \dfrac{2h + h^2 + 3h}{h}$
$= (5 + h) \text{ m s}^{-1}, \quad h \neq 0$

d Average velocity
$= \dfrac{s(t_2) - s(t_1)}{t_2 - t_1}$
$= \dfrac{s(t+h) - s(t)}{(t+h) - t}$
$= \dfrac{[(t+h)^2 + 3(t+h) - 2] - [t^2 + 3t - 2]}{h}$
$= \dfrac{2ht + h^2 + 3h}{h}$
$= (2t + 3 + h) \text{ m s}^{-1}, \quad h \neq 0$

Now $\lim\limits_{h \to 0} \dfrac{s(t+h) - s(t)}{h} = \lim\limits_{h \to 0} (2t + 3 + h)$
$= (2t + 3) \text{ m s}^{-1}$

This is the *instantaneous velocity* at t seconds.

2 a $s(t) = 5 - 2t^2$ cm

Average velocity $= \dfrac{s(t_2) - s(t_1)}{t_2 - t_1}$

$= \dfrac{s(5) - s(2)}{5 - 2}$

$= \dfrac{(-45) - (-3)}{3}$

$= -14$ cm s^{-1}

c $\lim\limits_{h \to 0} \dfrac{s(2+h) - s(2)}{h} = \lim\limits_{h \to 0} (-8 - 2h)$

$= -8$ cm s^{-1}

This is the *instantaneous velocity* when $t = 2$ seconds.

b Average velocity $= \dfrac{s(t_2) - s(t_1)}{t_2 - t_1}$

$= \dfrac{s(2+h) - s(2)}{(2+h) - 2}$

$= \dfrac{5 - 2(2+h)^2 + 3}{h}$

$= \dfrac{-8h - 2h^2}{h}$

$= (-8 - 2h)$ cm s^{-1}, $h \neq 0$

d $\lim\limits_{h \to 0} \dfrac{s(t+h) - s(t)}{h}$

$= \lim\limits_{h \to 0} \dfrac{[5 - 2(t+h)^2] - [5 - 2t^2]}{h}$

$= \lim\limits_{h \to 0} \dfrac{-4th - 2h^2}{h}$

$= \lim\limits_{h \to 0} (-4t - 2h)$

$= -4t$ cm s^{-1}

This is the *instantaneous velocity* at t seconds.

3 $v(t) = 2\sqrt{t} + 3$ cm s^{-1}, $t \geq 0$

a Average acceleration

$= \dfrac{v(t_2) - v(t_1)}{t_2 - t_1}$

$= \dfrac{v(4) - v(1)}{4 - 1}$

$= \dfrac{7 - 5}{3}$

$= \tfrac{2}{3}$ cm s^{-2}

c $\lim\limits_{h \to 0} \dfrac{v(1+h) - v(1)}{(1+h) - 1}$

$= \lim\limits_{h \to 0} \dfrac{[2\sqrt{1+h} + 3] - [2 + 3]}{h}$

$= \lim\limits_{h \to 0} \dfrac{2[\sqrt{1+h} - 1]}{h} \times \dfrac{\sqrt{1+h} + 1}{\sqrt{1+h} + 1}$

$= \lim\limits_{h \to 0} \dfrac{2h}{h(\sqrt{1+h} + 1)}$

$= \lim\limits_{h \to 0} \dfrac{2}{\sqrt{1+h} + 1}$

$= \tfrac{2}{2}$

$= 1$ cm s^{-2}

This is the *instantaneous acceleration* when $t = 1$ second.

b Average acceleration

$= \dfrac{v(t_2) - v(t_1)}{t_2 - t_1}$

$= \dfrac{v(1+h) - v(1)}{(1+h) - 1}$

$= \dfrac{[2\sqrt{1+h} + 3] - [2\sqrt{1} + 3]}{h}$

$= \dfrac{2\sqrt{1+h} - 2}{h}$ cm s^{-2}

d $\lim\limits_{h \to 0} \dfrac{v(t+h) - v(t)}{h}$

$= \lim\limits_{h \to 0} \dfrac{2\sqrt{t+h} - 2\sqrt{t}}{h}$

$= \lim\limits_{h \to 0} \dfrac{2(\sqrt{t+h} - \sqrt{t})}{h} \times \dfrac{\sqrt{t+h} + \sqrt{t}}{\sqrt{t+h} + t}$

$= \lim\limits_{h \to 0} \dfrac{2h}{h(\sqrt{t+h} + \sqrt{t})}$

$= \dfrac{2}{2\sqrt{t}}$

$= \dfrac{1}{\sqrt{t}}$ cm s^{-2}

This is the *instantaneous acceleration* at t seconds.

4 a This is the *instantaneous velocity* at $t = 4$ seconds.

  b This is the *instantaneous acceleration* at $t = 4$ seconds.

EXERCISE 21C.2

1 a $s(t) = t^2 - 4t + 3$ cm, $t \geqslant 0$ ∴ $v(t) = 2t - 4$ cm s^{-1} and $a(t) = 2$ cm s^{-2}.

$s(t)$: + − + at 1, 3 $v(t)$: − + at 2 $a(t)$: + at 0

b When $t = 0$, $s(0) = 3$ cm ∴ the object is 3 cm right of O and is moving to
$v(0) = -4$ cm s^{-1} the left with a velocity of 4 cm s^{-1} and slowing
$a(0) = 2$ cm s^{-2} down, its acceleration being 2 cm s^{-2} to the right.

c When $t = 2$, $s(2) = -1$ cm ∴ the object is 1 cm left of O, momentarily at rest,
$v(2) = 0$ cm s^{-1} but with acceleration 2 cm s^{-2} to the right.
$a(2) = 2$ cm s^{-2}

d The object reverses direction when $v(t) = 0$, which occurs at $t = 2$ seconds.
At $t = 2$, the particle is 1 cm left of O.

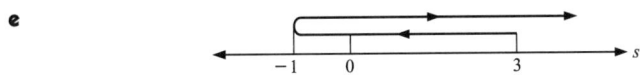

e [diagram from −1 to 3 on s-axis]

f Speed decreases when $v(t)$ and $a(t)$ have opposite signs, which is when $0 \leqslant t \leqslant 2$.

2 $s(t) = 98t - 4.9t^2$ m, $t \geqslant 0$

a $v(t) = 98 - 9.8t$ m s^{-1} $v(t)$: + − at 10
$a(t) = -9.8$ m s^{-2} $a(t)$: − at 0

b When $t = 0$, $s(0) = 0$ m, $v(0) = 98$ m s^{-1}

c When $t = 5$, $s(5) = 367.5$ m   The stone is 367.5 m above the ground, travelling
$v(5) = 49$ m s^{-1} upwards at 49 m s^{-1}, and slowing down.
$a(5) = -9.8$ m s^{-2}

When $t = 12$, $s(12) = 470.4$ m   The stone is 470.4 m above the ground and travelling
$v(12) = -19.6$ m s^{-1} downwards at 19.6 m s^{-1}, and increasing in speed.
$a(12) = -9.8$ m s^{-2}

d The maximum height is reached when $v(t) = 0$ m s^{-1} ∴ the maximum height is
∴ $98 - 9.8t = 0$ $s(10) = 98(10) - 4.9(100)$
∴ $9.8t = 98$ $= 980 - 490$
∴ $t = 10$ seconds $= 490$ m

e The stone is at ground level when $s(t) = 0$ which is at $98t - 4.9t^2 = 0$
∴ $4.9t(20 - t) = 0$
∴ $t = 0$ or 20 seconds
∴ it hits the ground after 20 seconds.

3 a $s(t) = 12t - 2t^3 - 1$ cm, $t \geqslant 0$ $v(t)$: + − at $\sqrt{2}$
∴ $v(t) = 12 - 6t^2$ cm s^{-1}
and $a(t) = -12t$ cm s^{-2} $a(t)$: − at 0

b When $t = 0$, $s(0) = -1$ cm   The particle is 1 cm left of O, moving right at
$v(0) = 12$ cm s^{-1} 12 cm s^{-1} with constant speed.
$a(0) = 0$ cm s^{-2}

c The particle reverses direction when $v(t) = 0$ which is at $t = \sqrt{2}$ seconds.
When $t = \sqrt{2}$, $s(\sqrt{2}) = 12\sqrt{2} - 2(2\sqrt{2}) - 1$
$= 8\sqrt{2} - 1$ ∴ the particle is $(8\sqrt{2} - 1)$ cm to the right of O.

d i From the sign diagrams in **a**, the speed increases for $t \geqslant \sqrt{2}$ seconds.
ii The velocity of the particle never increases $\{a(t) \leqslant 0\}$.

4 **a** $x(t) = t^3 - 9t^2 + 24t$ m, $t \geqslant 0$
$v(t) = 3t^2 - 18t + 24$ and $a(t) = 6t - 18$
$= 3(t^2 - 6t + 8)$ $= 6(t - 3)$ m s^{-2}
$= 3(t - 4)(t - 2)$ m s^{-1}

$v(t)$: $\boxed{+\ -\ +}$ at $2, 4$

$a(t)$: $\boxed{-\ +}$ at 3

b Reverses direction when $v(t) = 0$, which occurs at $t = 2$ and $t = 4$ seconds.
$x(2) = 8 - 36 + 48$ m and $x(4) = 64 - 144 + 96$
$= 20$ m $= 16$ m

c **i** The speed decreases when $v(t)$ and $a(t)$ have the opposite sign, which is when $0 \leqslant t \leqslant 2$ and $3 \leqslant t \leqslant 4$.
ii The velocity decreases when $a(t) \leqslant 0$, which is when $0 \leqslant t \leqslant 3$.

d When $t = 5$, $x(5) = 5^3 - 9(5)^2 + 24(5)$ $\therefore$ distance travelled $= 20 + 4 + 4$ m
$= 125 - 225 + 120$ $= 28$ m
$= 20$ m

5 **a** Let the equation be $s(t) = at^2 + bt + c$
$\therefore v(t) = 2at + b$
and $a(t) = 2a = g$ {gravitational acceleration}
$\therefore a = \tfrac{1}{2}g$
Also $v(t) = gt + b$
But, when $t = 0$, $v(0) = g \times 0 + b$
$\therefore v(0) = b$ $\therefore$ initial velocity is b
$\therefore v(t) = v(0) + gt$ as required

b Now when $t = 0$, $s(0) = 0$
$\therefore a \times 0^2 + b \times 0 + c = 0$
$\therefore c = 0$
and so $s(t) = \left(\tfrac{1}{2}g\right)t^2 + v(0)t$
$\therefore s(t) = v(0) \times t + \tfrac{1}{2}gt^2$ as required

EXERCISE 21D.1

1 **a** **i** $x \geqslant 0$ **ii** never

b **i** never **ii** $-2 < x \leqslant 3$

c **i** $x \leqslant 2$ **ii** $x \geqslant 2$

d **i** all real x **ii** never

e **i** $1 \leqslant x \leqslant 5$
 ii $x \leqslant 1$, $x \geqslant 5$

f **i** $2 \leqslant x < 4$, $x > 4$
 ii $x < 0$, $0 < x \leqslant 2$

2 a $f(x) = x^2$, $f'(x) = 2x$

Sign diagram of $f'(x)$: $\begin{array}{c} \xleftarrow{\quad - \quad | \quad + \quad}\rightarrow x \\ 0 \end{array}$

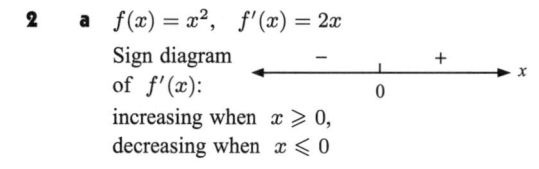

increasing when $x \geqslant 0$,
decreasing when $x \leqslant 0$

b $f(x) = -x^3$, $f'(x) = -3x^2$

Sign diagram of $f'(x)$: $\begin{array}{c} \xleftarrow{\quad - \quad | \quad - \quad}\rightarrow x \\ 0 \end{array}$

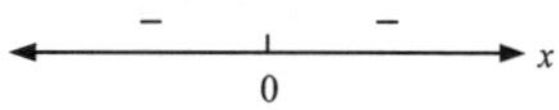

decreasing for all x

c $f(x) = 2x^2 + 3x - 4$, $f'(x) = 4x + 3$

Sign diagram of $f'(x)$: $\begin{array}{c} \xleftarrow{\quad - \quad | \quad + \quad}\rightarrow x \\ -\tfrac{3}{4} \end{array}$

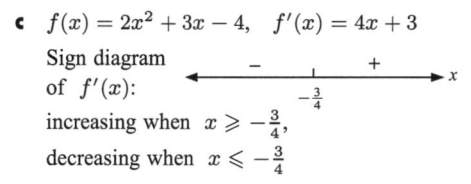

increasing when $x \geqslant -\tfrac{3}{4}$,
decreasing when $x \leqslant -\tfrac{3}{4}$

d $f(x) = \sqrt{x} = x^{\frac{1}{2}}$,

$f'(x) = \tfrac{1}{2}x^{-\frac{1}{2}} = \dfrac{1}{2\sqrt{x}}$

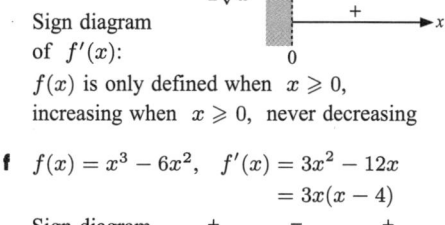

Sign diagram of $f'(x)$: $\begin{array}{c} \xleftarrow{\;\blacksquare\;|\;+\;}\rightarrow x \\ 0 \end{array}$

$f(x)$ is only defined when $x \geqslant 0$,
increasing when $x \geqslant 0$, never decreasing

e $f(x) = \dfrac{2}{\sqrt{x}} = 2x^{-\frac{1}{2}}$

$f'(x) = -x^{-\frac{3}{2}} = \dfrac{-1}{x\sqrt{x}}$

Sign diagram of $f'(x)$: $\begin{array}{c} \xleftarrow{\;\blacksquare\;|\;-\;}\rightarrow x \\ 0 \end{array}$

$f(x)$ is only defined for $x > 0$
never increasing, decreasing when $x > 0$

f $f(x) = x^3 - 6x^2$, $f'(x) = 3x^2 - 12x$
$ = 3x(x-4)$

Sign diagram of $f'(x)$: $\begin{array}{c} \xleftarrow{\;+\;|\;-\;|\;+\;}\rightarrow x \\ 0 4 \end{array}$

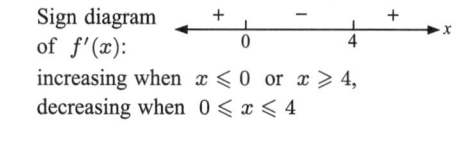

increasing when $x \leqslant 0$ or $x \geqslant 4$,
decreasing when $0 \leqslant x \leqslant 4$

g $f(x) = -2x^3 + 4x$
$f'(x) = -6x^2 + 4$
$ = -2(3x^2 - 2)$

Sign diagram of $f'(x)$: $\begin{array}{c} \xleftarrow{\;-\;|\;+\;|\;-\;}\rightarrow x \\ -\sqrt{\tfrac{2}{3}} \sqrt{\tfrac{2}{3}} \end{array}$

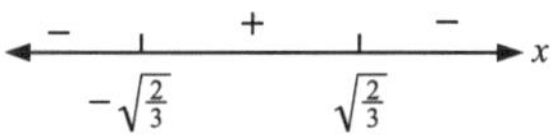

increasing for $-\sqrt{\tfrac{2}{3}} \leqslant x \leqslant \sqrt{\tfrac{2}{3}}$,
decreasing for $x \leqslant -\sqrt{\tfrac{2}{3}}$ or $x \geqslant \sqrt{\tfrac{2}{3}}$

h $f(x) = -4x^3 + 15x^2 + 18x + 3$
$f'(x) = -12x^2 + 30x + 18$
$ = -6(2x^2 - 5x - 3)$
$ = -6(2x+1)(x-3)$

Sign diagram of $f'(x)$: $\begin{array}{c} \xleftarrow{\;-\;|\;+\;|\;-\;}\rightarrow x \\ -\tfrac{1}{2} 3 \end{array}$

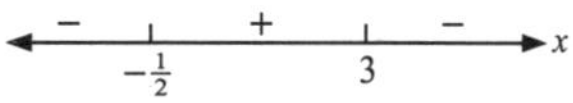

increasing when $-\tfrac{1}{2} \leqslant x \leqslant 3$,
decreasing when $x \leqslant -\tfrac{1}{2}$ and $x \geqslant 3$

i $f(x) = 3x^4 - 16x^3 + 24x^2 - 2$
$f'(x) = 12x^3 - 48x^2 + 48x$
$ = 12x(x^2 - 4x + 4)$
$ = 12x(x-2)^2$

Sign diagram of $f'(x)$: $\begin{array}{c} \xleftarrow{\;-\;|\;+\;|\;+\;}\rightarrow x \\ 0 2 \end{array}$

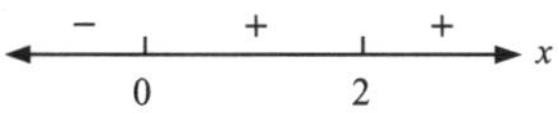

increasing when $x \geqslant 0$,
decreasing when $x \leqslant 0$

j $f(x) = 2x^3 + 9x^2 + 6x - 7$
$f'(x) = 6x^2 + 18x + 6$
$ = 6(x^2 + 3x + 1)$

$f'(x) = 0$ when $x = \dfrac{-3 \pm \sqrt{9-4}}{2} = \dfrac{-3 \pm \sqrt{5}}{2}$

Sign diagram of $f'(x)$: $\begin{array}{c} \xleftarrow{\;+\;|\;-\;|\;+\;}\rightarrow x \\ \tfrac{-3-\sqrt{5}}{2} \tfrac{-3+\sqrt{5}}{2} \end{array}$

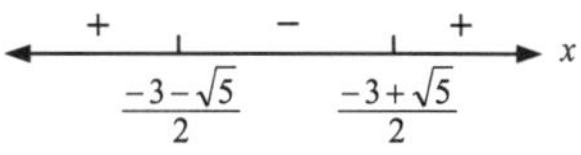

increasing for $x \leqslant \dfrac{-3-\sqrt{5}}{2}$ or $x \geqslant \dfrac{-3+\sqrt{5}}{2}$,
decreasing for $\dfrac{-3-\sqrt{5}}{2} \leqslant x \leqslant \dfrac{-3+\sqrt{5}}{2}$

k $f(x) = x^3 - 6x^2 + 3x - 1$,
$f'(x) = 3x^2 - 12x + 3$
$ = 3(x^2 - 4x + 1)$

$f'(x) = 0$ when $x = \dfrac{4 \pm \sqrt{16-4}}{2} = 2 \pm \sqrt{3}$

Sign diagram of $f'(x)$: $\begin{array}{c} \xleftarrow{\;+\;|\;-\;|\;+\;}\rightarrow x \\ 2-\sqrt{3} 2+\sqrt{3} \end{array}$

increasing when $x \leqslant 2 - \sqrt{3}$
or $x \geqslant 2 + \sqrt{3}$,
decreasing when $2 - \sqrt{3} \leqslant x \leqslant 2 + \sqrt{3}$

l $f(x) = x - 2\sqrt{x} = x - 2x^{\frac{1}{2}}$

$f'(x) = 1 - x^{-\frac{1}{2}} = 1 - \dfrac{1}{\sqrt{x}} = \dfrac{\sqrt{x}-1}{\sqrt{x}}$

Sign diagram of $f'(x)$: $\begin{array}{c} \xleftarrow{\;\blacksquare\;|\;-\;|\;+\;}\rightarrow x \\ 0 1 \end{array}$

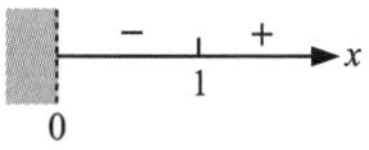

increasing when $x \geqslant 1$,
decreasing when $0 \leqslant x \leqslant 1$

m $f(x) = 3x^4 - 8x^3 - 6x^2 + 24x + 11$
$f'(x) = 12x^3 - 24x^2 - 12x + 24$
$\quad = 12(x^3 - 2x^2 - x + 2)$
Using technology, a root is -1,
$\therefore\ f'(x) = 12(x+1)(x^2 - 3x + 2)$
$\quad = 12(x+1)(x-1)(x-2)$
Sign diagram of $f'(x)$:

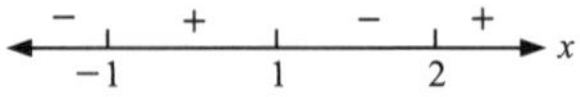

$\xleftarrow{\quad - \quad}\underset{-1}{|}\xrightarrow{\ +\ }\underset{1}{|}\xrightarrow{\ -\ }\underset{2}{|}\xrightarrow{\ +\ } x$

So, $f(x)$ is increasing for $-1 \leqslant x \leqslant 1$ and $x \geqslant 2$, and decreasing for $x \leqslant -1$ and $1 \leqslant x \leqslant 2$.

n $f(x) = x^4 - 4x^3 + 2x^2 + 4x + 1$,
$f'(x) = 4x^3 - 12x^2 + 4x + 4$
$\quad = 4(x^3 - 3x^2 + x + 1)$
Using technology, a root is 1,
$\therefore\ f'(x) = 4(x-1)(x^2 - 2x - 1)$
$f'(x) = 0$ when $x = 1$ or $x = \dfrac{2 \pm \sqrt{8}}{2}$
$\therefore\ x = 1$ or $x = 1 \pm \sqrt{2}$

Sign diagram of $f'(x)$:

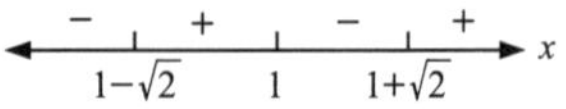

$\xleftarrow{\ -\ }\underset{1-\sqrt{2}}{|}\xrightarrow{\ +\ }\underset{1}{|}\xrightarrow{\ -\ }\underset{1+\sqrt{2}}{|}\xrightarrow{\ +\ } x$

So, $f(x)$ is increasing for $1 - \sqrt{2} \leqslant x \leqslant 1$ and $x \geqslant 1 + \sqrt{2}$, decreasing for $x \leqslant 1 - \sqrt{2}$ and $1 \leqslant x \leqslant 1 + \sqrt{2}$.

3 a i $f(x) = \dfrac{4x}{x^2 + 1}$ is a quotient with
$u = 4x$ and $v = x^2 + 1$
$\therefore\ u' = 4$ and $v' = 2x$
$\therefore\ f'(x) = \dfrac{4(x^2 + 1) - 4x \times 2x}{(x^2 + 1)^2}$
$\quad = \dfrac{4x^2 + 4 - 8x^2}{(x^2 + 1)^2}$
$\quad = \dfrac{4 - 4x^2}{(x^2 + 1)^2}$
$\quad = \dfrac{-4(x^2 - 1)}{(x^2 + 1)^2}$
$\quad = \dfrac{-4(x+1)(x-1)}{(x^2 + 1)^2}$

Sign diagram of $f'(x)$: $\xleftarrow{\ -\ }\underset{-1}{|}\xrightarrow{\ +\ }\underset{1}{|}\xrightarrow{\ -\ } x$

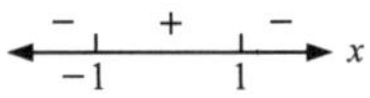

ii $f(x)$ is increasing for $-1 \leqslant x \leqslant 1$, decreasing for $x \leqslant -1$ and $x \geqslant 1$

c i $f(x) = \dfrac{-x^2 + 4x - 7}{x - 1}$ is a quotient with
$\therefore\ f'(x) = \dfrac{(-2x + 4)(x - 1) - (-x^2 + 4x - 7)(1)}{(x - 1)^2}$
$\quad = \dfrac{-2x^2 + 6x - 4 + x^2 - 4x + 7}{(x - 1)^2}$
$\quad = \dfrac{-x^2 + 2x + 3}{(x - 1)^2}$
$\quad = \dfrac{-(x^2 - 2x - 3)}{(x - 1)^2}$
$\quad = \dfrac{-(x + 1)(x - 3)}{(x - 1)^2}$

b i $f(x) = \dfrac{4x}{(x - 1)^2}$ is a quotient with
$u = 4x$ and $v = (x - 1)^2$
$\therefore\ u' = 4$ and $v' = 2(x - 1)$
$\therefore\ f'(x) = \dfrac{4(x - 1)^2 - 8x(x - 1)}{(x - 1)^4}$
$\quad = \dfrac{4(x - 1)((x - 1) - 2x)}{(x - 1)^4}$
$\quad = \dfrac{4(-1 - x)}{(x - 1)^3}$
$\quad = \dfrac{-4(x + 1)}{(x - 1)^3}$

Sign diagram of $f'(x)$:

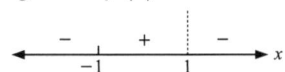

$\xleftarrow{\ -\ }\underset{-1}{|}\xrightarrow{\ +\ }\underset{1}{\vdots}\xrightarrow{\ -\ } x$

ii $f(x)$ is increasing for $-1 \leqslant x < 1$, decreasing for $x \leqslant -1$ and $x > 1$

$u = -x^2 + 4x - 7$ and $v = x - 1$
$\therefore\ u' = -2x + 4$ and $v' = 1$

Sign diagram of $f'(x)$:

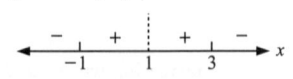

$\xleftarrow{\ -\ }\underset{-1}{|}\xrightarrow{\ +\ }\underset{1}{\vdots}\xrightarrow{\ +\ }\underset{3}{|}\xrightarrow{\ -\ } x$

ii $f(x)$ is increasing for $-1 \leqslant x < 1$ and $1 < x \leqslant 3$, and decreasing for $x \leqslant -1$ and $x \geqslant 3$.

4 **a** $f(x) = \dfrac{x^3}{x^2 - 1}$ is a quotient with $u = x^3$ and $v = x^2 - 1$
$\therefore$ $u' = 3x^2$ and $v' = 2x$

$\therefore$ $f'(x) = \dfrac{3x^2(x^2 - 1) - x^3 \times 2x}{(x^2 - 1)^2}$

$= \dfrac{3x^4 - 3x^2 - 2x^4}{(x^2 - 1)^2}$

$= \dfrac{x^2(x^2 - 3)}{(x^2 - 1)^2}$

$= \dfrac{x^2(x + \sqrt{3})(x - \sqrt{3})}{(x^2 - 1)^2}$

Sign diagram of $f'(x)$:

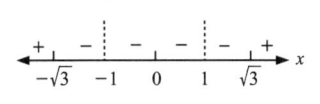

$\xleftarrow{\;+\;\;-\;\;-\;\;-\;\;-\;\;+\;}\to x$
$\qquad -\sqrt{3}\;-1\;\;0\;\;1\;\;\sqrt{3}$

$\therefore$ $f(x)$ is increasing for $x \leqslant -\sqrt{3}$ and $x \geqslant \sqrt{3}$, and decreasing for $-\sqrt{3} \leqslant x < -1$, $-1 < x < 1$ and $1 < x \leqslant \sqrt{3}$.

b $f(x) = x^2 + \dfrac{4}{x - 1} = x^2 + 4(x - 1)^{-1}$

$\therefore$ $f'(x) = 2x - 4(x - 1)^{-2} \times 1$

$= 2x - \dfrac{4}{(x - 1)^2}$

$= \dfrac{2x(x - 1)^2 - 4}{(x - 1)^2}$

$= \dfrac{2x(x^2 - 2x + 1) - 4}{(x - 1)^2}$

$= \dfrac{2x^3 - 4x^2 + 2x - 4}{(x - 1)^2}$

$= \dfrac{(x - 2)(2x^2 + 2)}{(x - 1)^2}$

Sign of $f'(x)$:

$\xleftarrow{\;-\;\;-\;\;+\;}\to x$
$\qquad\quad 1\;\;2$

$\therefore$ $f(x)$ is increasing for $x \geqslant 2$, and decreasing for $x < 1$ and $1 < x \leqslant 2$.

EXERCISE 21D.2

1 **a** A is a local minimum, B is a local maximum, C is a horizontal inflection.
   b $f'(x)$ has sign diagram:

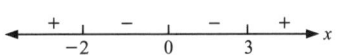

   $\xleftarrow{\;+\;\;-\;\;-\;\;+\;}\to x$
   $\qquad -2\;\;0\;\;3$

   c **i** $f(x)$ is increasing for $x \leqslant -2$ and $x \geqslant 3$ **ii** $f(x)$ is decreasing for $-2 \leqslant x \leqslant 3$.
   d $f(x)$ has sign diagram:

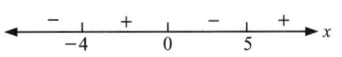

   $\xleftarrow{\;-\;\;+\;\;-\;\;+\;}\to x$
   $\qquad -4\;\;0\;\;5$

   e For **b** we have intervals where the function is increasing (+) or decreasing (−). For **d** we have intervals where the function is above (+) and below (−) the x-axis.

2 **a** $f(x) = x^2 - 2$ $\therefore$ $f'(x) = 2x$

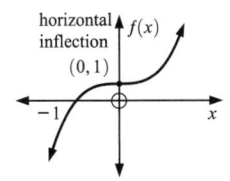

with sign diagram:

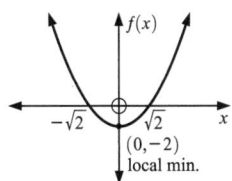

$\xleftarrow{\;-\;\;+\;}\to x$
$\qquad\;0$

local minimum at $(0, -2)$

$f(x)$, $-\sqrt{2}$, $\sqrt{2}$, $(0,-2)$ local min.

b $f(x) = x^3 + 1$ $\therefore$ $f'(x) = 3x^2$

with sign diagram:

$\xleftarrow{\;+\;\;+\;}\to x$
$\qquad\;0$

horizontal inflection at $(0, 1)$

horizontal inflection $f(x)$, $(0, 1)$, -1

c $f(x) = x^3 - 3x + 2$
$\therefore\ f'(x) = 3x^2 - 3$
$= 3(x^2 - 1)$
$= 3(x + 1)(x - 1)$

with sign diagram:

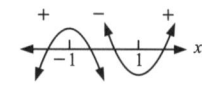

local maximum at $(-1, 4)$,
local minimum at $(1, 0)$

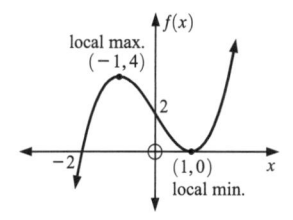

d $f(x) = x^4 - 2x^2$
$\therefore\ f'(x) = 4x^3 - 4x$
$= 4x(x^2 - 1)$
$= 4x(x + 1)(x - 1)$

with sign diagram:

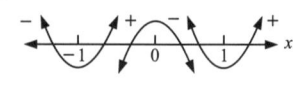

local minima at $(-1, -1)$ and $(1, -1)$,
local maximum at $(0, 0)$

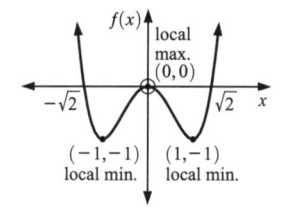

e $f(x) = x^3 - 6x^2 + 12x + 1$
$\therefore\ f'(x) = 3x^2 - 12x + 12$
$= 3(x^2 - 4x + 4)$
$= 3(x - 2)^2$

with sign diagram:

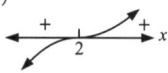

$\therefore$ horizontal inflection at $(2, 9)$

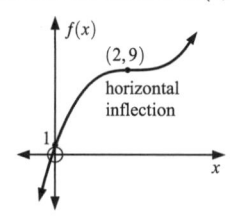

f $f(x) = \sqrt{x} + 2$
$\therefore\ f'(x) = \tfrac{1}{2}x^{-\tfrac{1}{2}}$
$= \dfrac{1}{2\sqrt{x}} \neq 0$

with sign diagram:

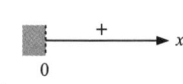

$\therefore$ no stationary points.

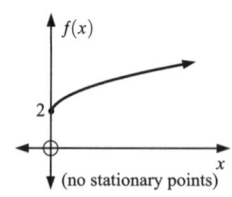

g $f(x) = x - \sqrt{x}$
$\therefore\ f'(x) = 1 - \tfrac{1}{2}x^{-\tfrac{1}{2}}$
$= 1 - \dfrac{1}{2\sqrt{x}}$
$= \dfrac{2\sqrt{x} - 1}{2\sqrt{x}}$

with sign diagram:

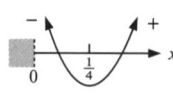

$f(x)$ is defined for all $x \geqslant 0$
local minimum at $(\tfrac{1}{4}, -\tfrac{1}{4})$

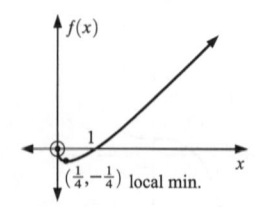

h $f(x) = x^4 - 6x^2 + 8x - 3$
$\therefore\ f'(x) = 4x^3 - 12x + 8$
$= 4(x^3 - 3x + 2)$
$= 4(x - 1)(x^2 + x - 2)$
$= 4(x - 1)(x + 2)(x - 1)$

with sign diagram:

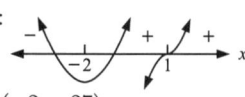

local minimum at $(-2, -27)$,
horizontal inflection at $(1, 0)$

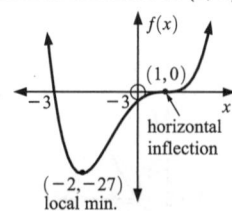

i $f(x) = 1 - x\sqrt{x} = 1 - x^{\frac{3}{2}}$

$\therefore \ f'(x) = -\frac{3}{2}x^{\frac{1}{2}} = \frac{-3\sqrt{x}}{2}$

with sign diagram:

$f(x)$ is only defined when $x \geqslant 0$
$\therefore$ local maximum at $(0, 1)$

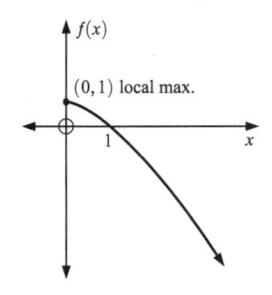

j $f(x) = x^4 - 2x^2 - 8$

$\therefore \ f'(x) = 4x^3 - 4x$
$= 4x(x^2 - 1)$
$= 4x(x+1)(x-1)$

with sign diagram:

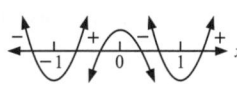

local minima at $(-1, -9)$ and $(1, -9)$,
local maximum at $(0, -8)$

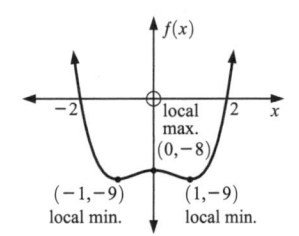

3 $f(x) = ax^2 + bx + c, \quad a \neq 0$
$\therefore \ f'(x) = 2ax + b$

$f(x)$ has a stationary point when $f'(x) = 0$

$\therefore \ x = -\dfrac{b}{2a}$

There is a local maximum when $a < 0$

and there is a local minimum when $a > 0$

4 $f(x) = 2x^3 + ax^2 - 24x + 1$
$\therefore \ f'(x) = 6x^2 + 2ax - 24$

But $f'(-4) = 0$, so $96 - 8a - 24 = 0$
$\therefore \ 72 = 8a$
$\therefore \ a = 9$

5 a $f(x) = x^3 + ax + b \quad \therefore \ f'(x) = 3x^2 + a$

When $x = -2, \ f'(x) = 0$
$\therefore \ 3x^2 + a = 0$
$\therefore \ 12 + a = 0$
$\therefore \ a = -12$

b $f'(x) = 3x^2 - 12$
$= 3(x^2 - 4)$
$= 3(x+2)(x-2)$

Also, $(-2, 3)$ is a point on the curve.
Using $f(x) = x^3 - 12x + b$
$\therefore \ 3 = -8 + 24 + b$
$\therefore \ b = -13$

$f'(x)$ has sign diagram:

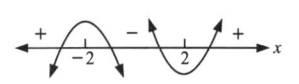

$\therefore$ there is a local maximum at $(-2, 3)$
and a local minimum at $(2, -29)$.

6 Let the cubic polynomial be
$P(x) = ax^3 + bx^2 + cx + d$
$\therefore \ P'(x) = 3ax^2 + 2bx + c \quad \text{....} \ (1)$

Now $(0, 2)$ lies on $P(x)$, so $P(0) = 2$
$\therefore \ a(0) + b(0) + c(0) + d = 2$
$\therefore \ d = 2$

The tangent at $(0, 2)$ is $y = 9x + 2$, so
$P'(0) = 9$
$\therefore \ 3a(0) + 2b(0) + c = 9$
$\therefore \ c = 9 \quad \text{....} \ (2)$

There is a stationary point at $(-1, -7)$, so
$P'(-1) = 0$

$\therefore \ 3a(-1)^2 + 2b(-1) + c = 0 \quad \{\text{using } (1)\}$
$\therefore \ 3a - 2b + c = 0$
So, using (2), $3a - 2b = -9 \quad \text{....} \ (3)$
Finally, $(-1, -7)$ lies on $P(x)$
$\therefore \ a(-1)^3 + b(-1)^2 + c(-1) + d = -7$
$\therefore \ -a + b - 9 + 2 = -7$
$\therefore \ a - b = 0$
$\therefore \ a = b$

So, using (3), $3a - 2a = -9$
$\therefore \ a = -9$
$\therefore \ a = b = -9$

$\therefore \ P(x) = -9x^3 - 9x^2 + 9x + 2$

7 **a** $f(x) = x^3 - 12x - 2$, for $-3 \leqslant x \leqslant 5$
∴ $f'(x) = 3x^2 - 12$
   $= 3(x+2)(x-2)$
which is 0 when $x = -2$ or 2

x	-3	-2	2	5
$f(x)$	7	14	-18	63

∴ the maximum value is 63 when $x = 5$, and the minimum value is -18, when $x = 2$.

b $f(x) = 4 - 3x^2 + x^3$, for $-2 \leqslant x \leqslant 3$
∴ $f'(x) = -6x + 3x^2$
   $= 3x(x-2)$
which is 0 when $x = 0$ or 2

x	-2	0	2	3
$f(x)$	-16	4	0	4

∴ maximum value is 4 when $x = 0$ or $x = 3$, minimum value is -16, when $x = -2$.

8 $C(x) = 0.0007x^3 - 0.1796x^2 + 14.663x + 160$ for $50 \leqslant x \leqslant 150$
$C'(x) = 0.0021x^2 - 0.3592x + 14.663$
$C'(x) = 0$ when $0.0021x^2 - 0.3592x + 14.663 = 0$
Using technology, $x \approx 103.74$ or $x \approx 67.30$

x	50	67.30	103.74	150
$C(x)$	531.65	546.73	529.80	680.95

∴ the maximum hourly cost is $680.95 when 150 hinges are made. The minimum hourly cost is $529.80 when 104 hinges are made.

EXERCISE 21E

1 **a** $y = \dfrac{2x}{x^2 - 4} = \dfrac{2x}{(x+2)(x-2)}$
has VAs when $x + 2 = 0$ and $x - 2 = 0$
∴ the VAs are $x = -2$ and $x = 2$.
As $|x| \to \infty$, $y \to 0$, so the HA is $y = 0$.

c $y = \dfrac{3x + 2}{x^2 + 1}$
$x^2 + 1 = 0$ has no real solutions, so there are no VAs.
As $|x| \to \infty$, $y \to 0$, so the HA is $y = 0$.

e $y = \dfrac{-x^2 + 2x - 1}{x^2 + x + 1} = \dfrac{-1 + \frac{2}{x} - \frac{1}{x^2}}{1 + \frac{1}{x} + \frac{1}{x^2}}$
Since $x^2 + x + 1 > 0$ for all x, there are no VAs.
As $|x| \to \infty$, $y \to -1$,
so the HA is $y = -1$.

f $y = \dfrac{3x^2 - x + 2}{(x+2)^2}$ has VA $x = -2$.
Now $y = \dfrac{3x^2 - x + 2}{x^2 + 4x + 4}$
$= \dfrac{3 - \frac{1}{x} + \frac{2}{x^2}}{1 + \frac{4}{x} + \frac{4}{x^2}}$
As $|x| \to \infty$, $y \to 3$, so the HA is $y = 3$.

b $y = \dfrac{1-x}{(x+2)^2}$
has VA $x + 2 = 0$ or $x = -2$.
As $|x| \to \infty$, $y \to 0$, so the HA is $y = 0$.

d $y = \dfrac{2x^2 - x + 2}{x^2 - 1} = \dfrac{2x^2 - x + 2}{(x+1)(x-1)}$
The VAs are $x = -1$ and $x = 1$.
We can also write $y = \dfrac{2 - \frac{1}{x} + \frac{2}{x^2}}{1 - \frac{1}{x^2}}$
As $|x| \to \infty$, $y \to 2$, so the HA is $y = 2$.

g $y = \dfrac{3x^3 + x^2 - 1}{x - 2}$
$= 3x^2 + 7x + 14 + \dfrac{27}{x - 2}$

$$\begin{array}{r}
3x^2 + 7x + 14 \\
x - 2 \overline{\smash{\big)}\, 3x^3 + x^2 - 1} \\
-(3x^3 - 6x^2) \\
\hline
7x^2 - 1 \\
-(7x^2 - 14x) \\
\hline
14x - 1 \\
-(14x - 28) \\
\hline
27
\end{array}$$

So, the VA is $x = 2$.
As $|x| \to \infty$, $y \to 3x^2 + 7x + 14$, so a parabolic asymptote is $y = 3x^2 + 7x + 14$.

h $y = \dfrac{2x^2 - 5x - 1}{x+1} = 2x - 7 + \dfrac{6}{x+1}$

$$\begin{array}{r} 2x - 7 \\ x+1 \overline{\smash{\big)} 2x^2 - 5x - 1 } \\ -(2x^2 + 2x) \\ \hline -7x - 1 \\ -(-7x - 7) \\ \hline 6 \end{array}$$

So, the VA is $x = -1$.
As $|x| \to \infty$, $y \to 2x - 7$, so an oblique asymptote is $y = 2x - 7$.

i $y = \dfrac{3x^2 + x}{2x - 1} = \dfrac{3}{2}x + \dfrac{5}{4} + \dfrac{5}{4(2x-1)}$

$$\begin{array}{r} \tfrac{3}{2}x + \tfrac{5}{4} \\ 2x-1 \overline{\smash{\big)} 3x^2 + x } \\ -(3x^2 - \tfrac{3}{2}x) \\ \hline \tfrac{5}{2}x \\ -(\tfrac{5}{2}x - \tfrac{5}{4}) \\ \hline \tfrac{5}{4} \end{array}$$

So, the VA is $x = \frac{1}{2}$.
As $|x| \to \infty$, $y \to \frac{3}{2}x + \frac{5}{4}$, so an oblique asymptote is $y = \frac{3}{2}x + \frac{5}{4}$.

2 a i $y = \dfrac{x^2 - x}{x^2 - x - 6} = \dfrac{x(x-1)}{(x-3)(x+2)}$

has VAs when $x - 3 = 0$, $x + 2 = 0$
$\therefore$ VAs are $x = 3$, $x = -2$

ii $\dfrac{dy}{dx} = \dfrac{(2x-1)(x^2 - x - 6) - (x^2 - x)(2x - 1)}{(x^2 - x - 6)^2}$

$= \dfrac{(2x-1)(x^2 - x - 6 - x^2 + x)}{(x^2 - x - 6)^2}$

$= \dfrac{-6(2x-1)}{(x^2 - x - 6)^2}$

iii When $x = 0$, $y = \frac{0}{-6} = 0$
$\therefore$ y-intercept is 0
When $y = 0$, $x(x-1) = 0$
$\therefore$ $x = 0$ or 1
$\therefore$ x-intercepts are 0 and 1

Also, since $y = \dfrac{1 - \frac{1}{x}}{1 - \frac{1}{x} - \frac{6}{x^2}}$

the HA is $y = 1$
{as $|x| \to \infty$, $y \to \frac{1}{1}$}

Turning points are when $f'(x) = 0$,
which occurs when $x = \frac{1}{2}$.
Sign diagram of $f'(x)$ is:

$\therefore$ there is a local maximum at $(\frac{1}{2}, \frac{1}{25})$.

iv

b i $y = \dfrac{x^2 - 1}{x^2 + 1} = \dfrac{(x+1)(x-1)}{x^2 + 1}$

has no VA as $x^2 + 1 = 0$ has no real solutions.

Since $y = \dfrac{1 - \frac{1}{x^2}}{1 + \frac{1}{x^2}}$ the HA is $y = 1$

{as $|x| \to \infty$, $y \to \frac{1}{1}$}

iii When $x = 0$, $y = \frac{-1}{1} = -1$
$\therefore$ y-intercept is -1
When $y = 0$, $(x+1)(x-1) = 0$
$\therefore$ $x = \pm 1$
$\therefore$ x-intercepts are ± 1

ii $\dfrac{dy}{dx} = \dfrac{2x(x^2 + 1) - (x^2 - 1)2x}{(x^2 + 1)^2}$

$= \dfrac{2x[x^2 + 1 - x^2 + 1]}{(x^2 + 1)^2}$

$= \dfrac{4x}{(x^2 + 1)^2}$

and has sign diagram

$\therefore$ there is a local minimum at $(0, -1)$.

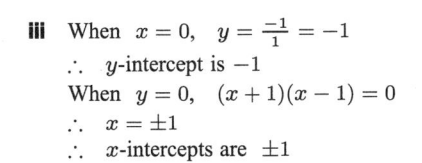

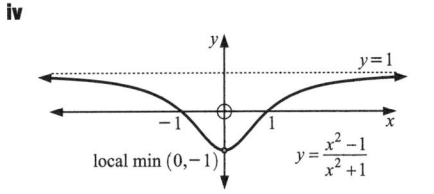

iv

c **i** $y = \dfrac{x^2 - 5x + 4}{x^2 + 5x + 4} = \dfrac{(x-1)(x-4)}{(x+1)(x+4)}$ has VAs when $x + 1 = 0$ and $x + 4 = 0$
$\therefore$ the VAs are $x = -1$, $x = -4$

Since $y = \dfrac{1 - \frac{5}{x} + \frac{4}{x^2}}{1 + \frac{5}{x} + \frac{4}{x^2}}$ the HA is $y = 1$ {as $|x| \to \infty$, $y \to \frac{1}{1}$}

ii $\dfrac{dy}{dx} = \dfrac{(2x-5)(x^2+5x+4) - (x^2-5x+4)(2x+5)}{(x+1)^2(x+4)^2}$

$= \dfrac{[2x^3 + 10x^2 + 8x - 5x^2 - 25x - 20] - [2x^3 + 5x^2 - 10x^2 - 25x + 8x + 20]}{(x+1)^2(x+4)^2}$

$= \dfrac{10x^2 - 40}{(x+1)^2(x+4)^2}$

$= \dfrac{10(x+2)(x-2)}{(x+1)^2(x+4)^2}$ which has sign diagram

$\therefore$ there is a local max at $\left(-2, \dfrac{4+10+4}{4-10+4}\right)$ or $(-2, -9)$

and a local min at $\left(2, \dfrac{4-10+4}{4+10+4}\right)$ or $(2, -\frac{1}{9})$.

iii When $x = 0$, $y = \frac{4}{4} = 1$
$\therefore$ the y-intercept is 1
When $y = 0$, $(x-1)(x-4) = 0$
$\therefore$ $x = 1$ or 4
$\therefore$ x-intercepts are 1, 4

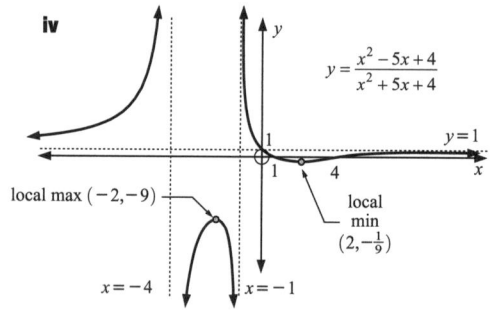

iv

d **i** $y = \dfrac{x^2 - 6x + 5}{(x+1)^2} = \dfrac{(x-1)(x-5)}{(x+1)^2}$ has VA $x + 1 = 0$ or $x = -1$,

and HA $y = 1$ {as $y = \dfrac{1 - \frac{6}{x} + \frac{5}{x^2}}{1 + \frac{2}{x} + \frac{1}{x^2}} \to \frac{1}{1}$ as $|x| \to \infty$}

ii $\dfrac{dy}{dx} = \dfrac{(2x-6)(x+1)^2 - (x^2 - 6x + 5) 2(x+1)^1(1)}{(x+1)^4}$

$= \dfrac{(x+1)[2x^2 - 4x - 6 - 2x^2 + 12x - 10]}{(x+1)^4}$

$= \dfrac{8x - 16}{(x+1)^3} = \dfrac{8(x-2)}{(x+1)^3}$ has sign diagram

$\therefore$ there is a local minimum at $\left(2, \dfrac{4-12+5}{3^2}\right)$ or $(2, -\frac{1}{3})$.

iii When $x = 0$, $y = \frac{5}{1} = 5$
$\therefore$ y-intercept is 5
When $y = 0$, $(x-1)(x-5) = 0$
$\therefore$ $x = 1$ or 5
$\therefore$ x-intercepts are 1, 5

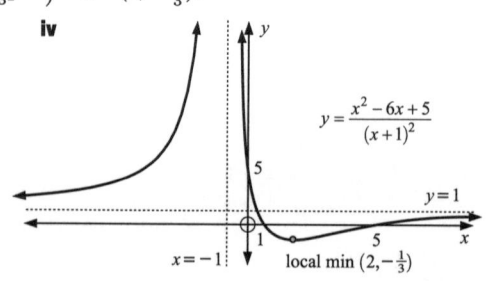

iv

3 **a** **i** $f(x) = \dfrac{4x}{x^2+1}$ has no VAs {as $x^2+1=0$ has no real solutions} and a HA of $y=0$ {as $|x| \to \infty$, $y \to 0$}

ii $f'(x) = \dfrac{4(x^2+1) - 4x(2x)}{(x^2+1)^2}$

$= \dfrac{4x^2 + 4 - 8x^2}{(x^2+1)^2}$

$= \dfrac{4 - 4x^2}{(x^2+1)^2}$

$= \dfrac{4(1+x)(1-x)}{(x^2+1)^2}$

and has sign diagram:

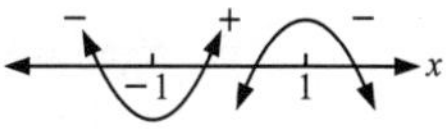

$\therefore$ local min. is $\left(-1, \dfrac{4(-1)}{1+1}\right)$ or $(-1, -2)$

and local max is $\left(1, \dfrac{4(1)}{1+1}\right)$ or $(1, 2)$.

iii When $x=0$, $f(0) = 0$
$\therefore$ y-intercept is 0

when $y=0$, $\dfrac{4x}{x^2+1} = 0$
$\therefore$ $x=0$ and so the x-intercept is 0

iv graph showing local max $(1, 2)$, local min $(-1, -2)$, $y = 0$, $y = \dfrac{4x}{x^2+1}$

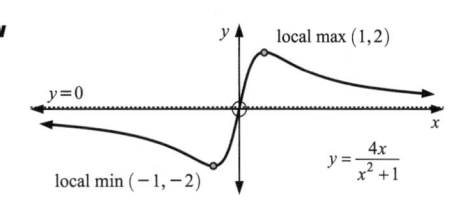

b **i** $f(x) = \dfrac{4x}{x^2 - 4x - 5} = \dfrac{4x}{(x-5)(x+1)}$

Vertical asymptotes occur when $(x-5)(x+1) = 0$,
$\therefore$ at $x = -1$ and $x = 5$.
Horizontal asymptote is $y = 0$
{as $|x| \to \infty$, $y \to 0$}

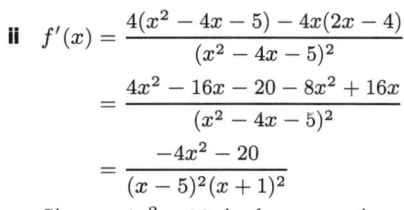

ii $f'(x) = \dfrac{4(x^2 - 4x - 5) - 4x(2x - 4)}{(x^2 - 4x - 5)^2}$

$= \dfrac{4x^2 - 16x - 20 - 8x^2 + 16x}{(x^2 - 4x - 5)^2}$

$= \dfrac{-4x^2 - 20}{(x-5)^2(x+1)^2}$

Since $-4x^2 - 20$ is always negative we have no turning points, and sign diagram is:

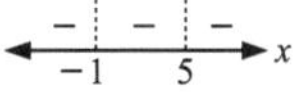

iii When $x=0$, $y = \dfrac{0}{-5} = 0$
$\therefore$ y-intercept is 0

When $y=0$, $\dfrac{4x}{x^2 - 4x - 5} = 0$
$\therefore$ $x = 0$
$\therefore$ x-intercept is 0

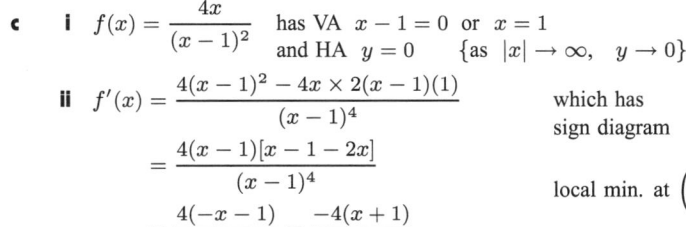

iv graph with $x = -1$, $x = 5$, $y = 0$, $y = \dfrac{4x}{x^2 - 4x - 5}$

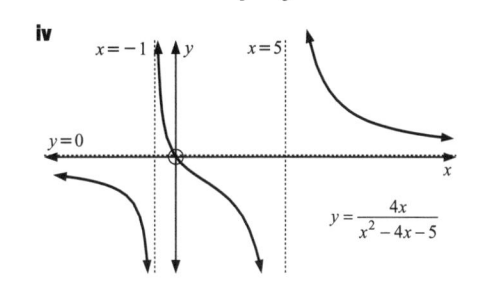

c **i** $f(x) = \dfrac{4x}{(x-1)^2}$ has VA $x - 1 = 0$ or $x = 1$ and HA $y = 0$ {as $|x| \to \infty$, $y \to 0$}

ii $f'(x) = \dfrac{4(x-1)^2 - 4x \times 2(x-1)(1)}{(x-1)^4}$

$= \dfrac{4(x-1)[x-1-2x]}{(x-1)^4}$

$= \dfrac{4(-x-1)}{(x-1)^3} = \dfrac{-4(x+1)}{(x-1)^3}$

which has sign diagram

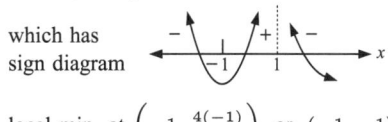

local min. at $\left(-1, \dfrac{4(-1)}{(-2)^2}\right)$ or $(-1, -1)$

iii When $x=0$, $y = \dfrac{0}{1} = 0$
$\therefore$ y-intercept is 0

When $y=0$, $\dfrac{4x}{(x-1)^2} = 0$
$\therefore$ x-intercept is 0

iv graph with $f(x) = \dfrac{4x}{(x-1)^2}$, $y = 0$, local min $(-1, -1)$, $x = 1$

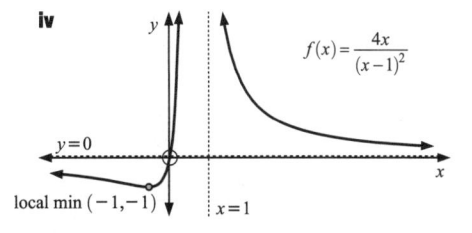

d **i** $f(x) = \dfrac{3x-3}{(x+2)^2}$ has a VA when $(x+2)^2 = 0$, so the VA is $x = -2$,

and HA $y = 0$ {as $|x| \to \infty$, $y \to 0$}

ii $f'(x) = \dfrac{3(x+2)^2 - 2(x+2)(3x-3)}{(x+2)^4}$

$= \dfrac{3(x+2) - 2(3x-3)}{(x+2)^3}$

$= \dfrac{3x + 6 - 6x + 6}{(x+2)^3}$

$= \dfrac{12 - 3x}{(x+2)^3} = \dfrac{-3(x-4)}{(x+2)^3}$

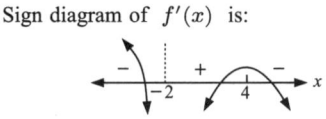

Sign diagram of $f'(x)$ is:

$\therefore$ there is a local maximum at $(4, \tfrac{1}{4})$.

iii When $x = 0$, $y = \dfrac{-3}{2^2} = -\dfrac{3}{4}$

$\therefore$ y-intercept is $-\dfrac{3}{4}$

When $y = 0$, $3x - 3 = 0$

$\therefore$ $x = 1$

$\therefore$ x-intercept is 1

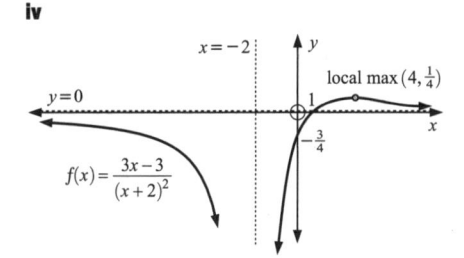

iv

4 a i $y = \dfrac{x^2 + 4x + 5}{x+2} = \dfrac{(x+2)^2 + 1}{x+2} = x + 2 + \dfrac{1}{x+2}$

$\therefore$ there is a vertical asymptote of $x = -2$ {as $x \to -2$, $|y| \to \infty$}

and an oblique asymptote of $y = x + 2$ {as $|x| \to \infty$, $y \to x + 2$}

ii $\dfrac{dy}{dx} = 1 - \dfrac{1}{(x+2)^2} = \dfrac{(x+2)^2 - 1}{(x+2)^2}$

$= \dfrac{x^2 + 4x + 3}{(x+2)^2}$

$= \dfrac{(x+1)(x+3)}{(x+2)^2}$

which has sign diagram

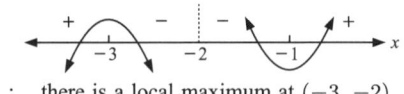

$\therefore$ there is a local maximum at $(-3, -2)$
and a local minimum at $(-1, 2)$

iii When $y = 0$, $x^2 + 4x + 5 = 0$

$\Delta = 4^2 - 4 \times 5 = -4$

$\therefore$ there are no real roots.

$\therefore$ there are no x-intercepts.

When $x = 0$, $y = \tfrac{5}{2}$

so the y-intercept is $\tfrac{5}{2}$

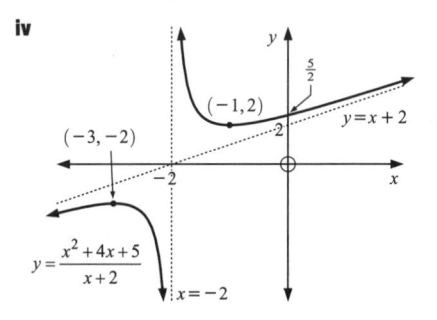

iv

b i $y = \dfrac{x^2 + 3x}{x+1} = \dfrac{(x+1)(x+2) - 2}{x+1} = x + 2 - \dfrac{2}{x+1}$

$\therefore$ there is a vertical asymptote of $x = -1$ {as $x \to -1$, $|y| \to \infty$}

and an oblique asymptote of $y = x + 2$ {as $|x| \to \infty$, $y \to x + 2$}

ii $\dfrac{dy}{dx} = 1 + \dfrac{2}{(x+1)^2}$

$= \dfrac{(x+1)^2 + 2}{(x+1)^2}$

$= \dfrac{x^2 + 2x + 3}{(x+1)^2}$

Now $x^2 + 2x + 3$ has $\Delta = 2^2 - 4 \times 3 = -8$

so $\dfrac{dy}{dx}$ is never zero.

$\therefore$ there are no turning points.

iii When $y = 0$, $x^2 + 3x = 0$
$\therefore \; x(x+3) = 0$
$\therefore \; x = -3$ or 0
So, the x-intercepts are -3 and 0
When $x = 0$, $y = 0$
so the y-intercept is 0

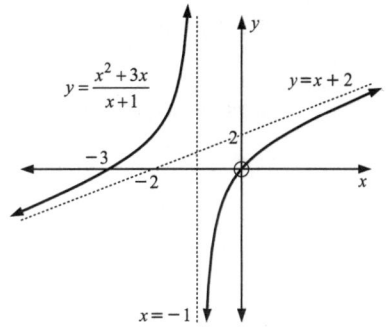

iv

[Graph showing $y = \dfrac{x^2+3x}{x+1}$ with oblique asymptote $y = x + 2$ and vertical asymptote $x = -1$]

c i $y = -2x + 1 - \dfrac{2}{x-2}$

has the vertical asymptote $x = 2$ {as $x \to 2$, $|y| \to \infty$}
and the oblique asymptote $y = -2x + 1$ {as $|x| \to \infty$, $y \to -2x + 1$}

ii $\dfrac{dy}{dx} = -2 + \dfrac{2}{(x-2)^2} = \dfrac{-2(x-2)^2 + 2}{(x-2)^2}$ which has sign diagram

$= \dfrac{-2x^2 + 8x - 6}{(x-2)^2}$

$= \dfrac{-2(x^2 - 4x + 3)}{(x-2)^2}$

$= \dfrac{-2(x-3)(x-1)}{(x-2)^2}$

[Sign diagram: $-$ at 1, $+$ between 1 and 2, $+$ between 2 and 3, $-$ after 3]

$\therefore$ there is a local minimum at $(1, 1)$
and a local maximum at $(3, -7)$.

iii When $y = 0$, $-2x + 1 - \dfrac{2}{x-2} = 0$

$\therefore \; \dfrac{(-2x+1)(x-2) - 2}{x-2} = 0$

$\therefore \; \dfrac{-2x^2 + 4x + x - 2 - 2}{x-2} = 0$

$\therefore \; \dfrac{-2x^2 + 5x - 4}{x-2} = 0$

$\therefore \; -2x^2 + 5x - 4 = 0$

$\therefore \; \Delta = 5^2 - 4(-2)(-4) < 0$

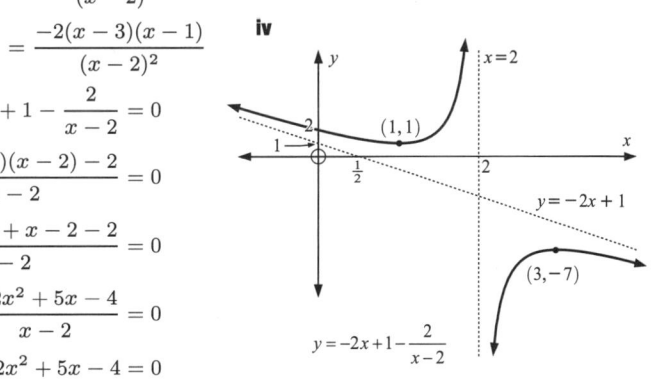

$\therefore$ there are no real roots, so there are no x-intercepts.

When $x = 0$, $y = -2(0) + 1 - \dfrac{2}{0-2} = 2$ so the y-intercept is 2.

iv

[Graph showing function with vertical asymptote $x=2$, oblique asymptote $y = -2x + 1$, local minimum $(1,1)$, local maximum $(3,-7)$]

d i $f(x) = \dfrac{x^3}{x^2 - 1} = \dfrac{x(x^2-1) + x}{x^2 - 1} = x + \dfrac{x}{(x+1)(x-1)}$

has vertical asymptotes $x = -1$ and $x = 1$ {as $x \to \pm 1$, $|y| \to \infty$}
and the oblique asymptote $y = x$ {as $|x| \to \infty$, $y \to x$}.

ii $f'(x) = \dfrac{3x^2(x^2 - 1) - x^3(2x)}{(x^2 - 1)^2}$ which has sign diagram:

$= \dfrac{3x^4 - 3x^2 - 2x^4}{(x+1)^2(x-1)^2}$

$= \dfrac{x^2(x^2 - 3)}{(x+1)^2(x-1)^2}$

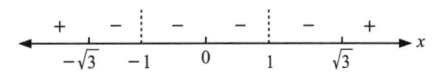

[Sign diagram: $+$ before $-\sqrt{3}$, $-$ between $-\sqrt{3}$ and -1, $-$ between -1 and 0, $-$ between 0 and 1, $-$ between 1 and $\sqrt{3}$, $+$ after $\sqrt{3}$]

$\therefore$ there is a local maximum at $(-\sqrt{3}, -\dfrac{3\sqrt{3}}{2})$,
a local minimum at $(\sqrt{3}, \dfrac{3\sqrt{3}}{2})$,
and a horizontal inflection at $(0, 0)$

iii When $y = 0$, $\dfrac{x^3}{x^2 - 1} = 0$

$\therefore \quad x = 0$

$\therefore$ the x-intercept is 0

when $x = 0$, $y = \dfrac{0^3}{0^2 - 1} = 0$

$\therefore$ the y-intercept is 0

iv

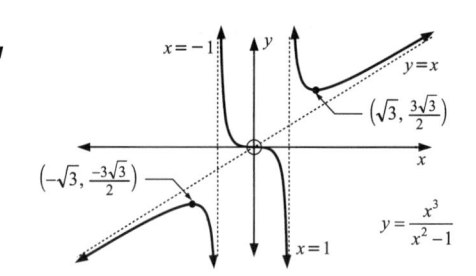

e i $f(x) = \dfrac{x^3}{x^2 + 1} = \dfrac{x(x^2 + 1) - x}{x^2 + 1} = x - \dfrac{x}{x^2 + 1}$

has no VAs {as $x^2 + 1 > 0$ for all real x}

and one oblique asymptote $y = x$ {as $|x| \to \infty$, $y \to x$}

ii $f'(x) = \dfrac{3x^2(x^2 + 1) - x^3(2x)}{(x^2 + 1)^2}$

$= \dfrac{3x^4 + 3x^2 - 2x^4}{(x^2 + 1)^2}$

$= \dfrac{x^2(x^2 + 3)}{(x^2 + 1)^2}$

which has sign diagram

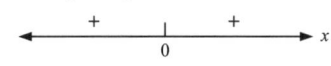

$\therefore$ there is a horizontal inflection at $(0, 0)$

iii When $y = 0$, $\dfrac{x^3}{x^2 + 1} = 0$

$\therefore \quad x = 0$

$\therefore$ the x-intercept is 0

when $x = 0$, $y = \dfrac{0^3}{0^2 + 1} = 0$

$\therefore$ the y-intercept is 0

iv

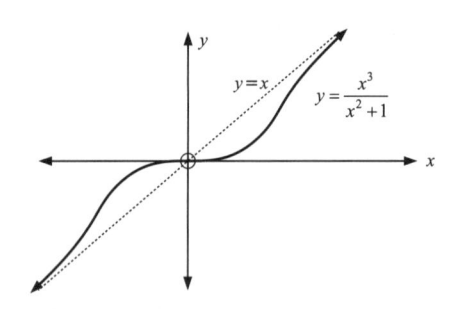

EXERCISE 21F

1 a $f(x) = x^2 + 3$
$\therefore \quad f'(x) = 2x$
$\therefore \quad f''(x) = 2$
Since $f''(x) \neq 0$,
no points of inflection exist.

b $f(x) = 2 - x^3$
$\therefore \quad f'(x) = -3x^2$
$\therefore \quad f''(x) = -6x$

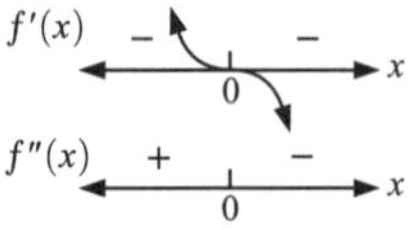

Now $f''(x) = 0$ when $x = 0$,
and $f'(0) = 0$
$\therefore$ there is a horizontal inflection at $(0, 2)$.

c $f(x) = x^3 - 6x^2 + 9x + 1$
$\therefore \quad f'(x) = 3x^2 - 12x + 9$
$= 3(x^2 - 4x + 3)$
$= 3(x - 3)(x - 1)$

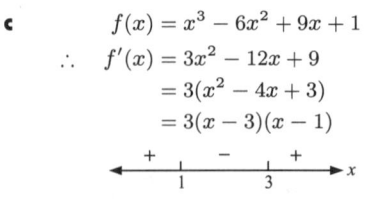

and $f''(x) = 6x - 12 = 6(x - 2)$
Now $f''(x) = 0$ when $x = 2$
and $f'(2) \neq 0$
$\therefore$ there is a non-horizontal inflection at $(2, 3)$

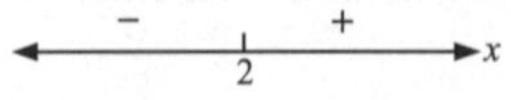

d $f(x) = x^3 + 6x^2 + 12x + 5$
$\therefore \quad f'(x) = 3x^2 + 12x + 12$
$= 3(x^2 + 4x + 4)$
$= 3(x + 2)^2$

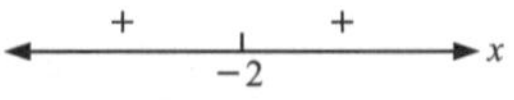

and $f''(x) = 6x + 12 = 6(x + 2)$
Now $f''(x) = 0$ when $x = -2$
and $f'(2) = 0$
$\therefore$ there is a horizontal inflection at $(-2, -3)$

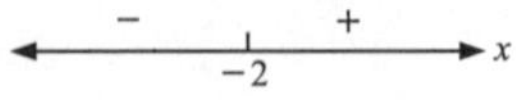

e $\quad f(x) = -3x^4 - 8x^3 + 2$
$\therefore \quad f'(x) = -12x^3 - 24x^2$
$\qquad = -12x^2(x+2)$

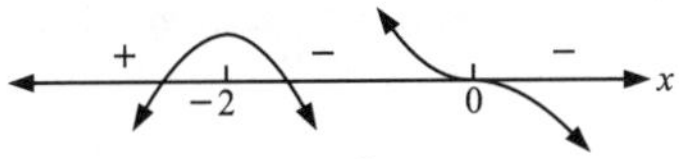

Sign diagram of $f'(x)$: $+$ at -2, $-$ at 0, $-$

and $f''(x) = -36x^2 - 48x$
$\qquad = -12x(3x+4)$

Sign diagram of $f''(x)$: $-$, $+$ at $-\frac{4}{3}$, $-$ at 0

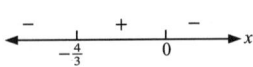

$\therefore$ there is a horizontal inflection at $(0, 2)$,
and a non-horizontal inflection at $\left(-\frac{4}{3}, \frac{310}{27}\right)$.

f $\quad f(x) = 3 - \dfrac{1}{\sqrt{x}} = 3 - x^{-\frac{1}{2}}$

$\therefore \quad f'(x) = \frac{1}{2}x^{-\frac{3}{2}}$

and $f''(x) = -\frac{3}{4}x^{-\frac{5}{2}} = \dfrac{-3}{4x^2\sqrt{x}}$

Now $f''(x) \neq 0$ for all x
$\therefore$ there are no points of inflection.

2 a $\quad f(x) = x^2$
$\therefore \quad f'(x) = 2x$ which has sign diagram: $-$ at 0, $+$
and $f''(x) = 2$

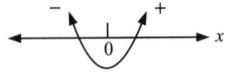

   i There is a local minimum at $(0, 0)$.
   ii There are no points of inflection as $f''(x) \neq 0$.
   iii $f(x)$ is increasing when $x \geqslant 0$, and decreasing when $x \leqslant 0$.
   iv $f(x)$ is concave up for all x as $f''(x) > 0$ for all x.

Graph of $f(x) = x^2$ with local min at $(0,0)$.

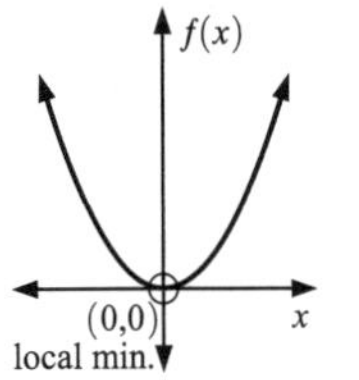

b $\quad f(x) = x^3$
$\therefore \quad f'(x) = 3x^2$ which has sign diagram: $+$, $+$ at 0
and $f''(x) = 6x$ which has sign diagram: $-$ at 0, $+$

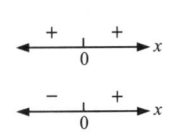

   i A horizontal inflection at $(0, 0)$.
   ii A horizontal inflection at $(0, 0)$.
   iii $f(x)$ is increasing for all x.
   iv $f(x)$ is concave up when $x \geqslant 0$, and concave down when $x \leqslant 0$.

Graph of $f(x) = x^3$ with horizontal inflection at $(0,0)$.

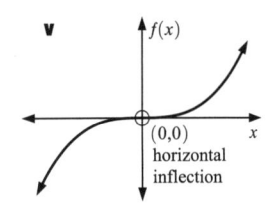

c $\quad f(x) = \sqrt{x}$
$\therefore \quad f'(x) = \frac{1}{2}x^{-\frac{1}{2}} = \dfrac{1}{2\sqrt{x}}$ which has sign diagram: $+$ at 0
and $f''(x) = -\frac{1}{4}x^{-\frac{3}{2}} = \dfrac{-1}{4x\sqrt{x}}$ which has sign diagram: $-$ at 0

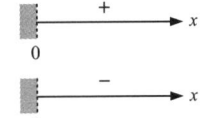

   i There are no stationary points as $f'(x) \neq 0$.
   ii There are no points of inflection as $f''(x) \neq 0$.
   iii $f(x)$ is increasing for all $x \geqslant 0$.
   iv $f(x)$ is concave down for all $x \geqslant 0$ as $f''(x) < 0$ for all $x > 0$.

Graph of $f(x) = \sqrt{x}$.

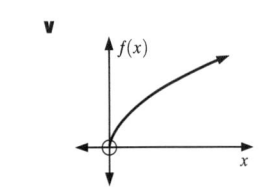

d $\quad f(x) = x^3 - 3x^2 - 24x + 1$
$\therefore \quad f'(x) = 3x^2 - 6x - 24$
$\qquad = 3(x^2 - 2x - 8)$
$\qquad = 3(x-4)(x+2)$ which has sign diagram: $+$ at -2, $-$ at 4, $+$
and $f''(x) = 6x - 6$
$\qquad = 6(x-1)$ which has sign diagram: $-$ at 1, $+$

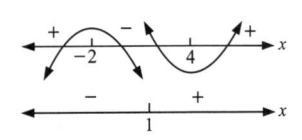

    i There is a local maximum at $(-2, 29)$, and a local minimum at $(4, -79)$.
    ii There is a non-horizontal inflection at $(1, -25)$.
    iii $f(x)$ is increasing for $x \leqslant -2$ and $x \geqslant 4$, and decreasing for $-2 \leqslant x \leqslant 4$.
    iv $f(x)$ is concave down for $x \leqslant 1$, and concave up for $x \geqslant 1$.

e $f(x) = 3x^4 + 4x^3 - 2$
    $\therefore \ f'(x) = 12x^3 + 12x^2$
    $= 12x^2(x+1)$ which has sign diagram:
  and $f''(x) = 36x^2 + 24x$
    $= 12x(3x+2)$ which has sign diagram:

    i There is a local minimum at $(-1, -3)$, and a horizontal inflection at $(0, -2)$.
    ii There is a non-horizontal inflection at $(-\frac{2}{3}, -\frac{70}{27})$ and a horizontal inflection at $(0, -2)$.
    iii $f(x)$ is increasing for $x \geqslant -1$, and decreasing for $x \leqslant -1$.
    iv $f(x)$ is concave down for $-\frac{2}{3} \leqslant x \leqslant 0$, and concave up for $x \leqslant -\frac{2}{3}$ and $x \geqslant 0$.

f $f(x) = (x-1)^4$
    $\therefore \ f'(x) = 4(x-1)^3$ which has sign diagram:
  and $f''(x) = 12(x-1)^2$ which has sign diagram:

    i There is a local minimum at $(1, 0)$.
    ii There are no points of inflection.
    iii $f(x)$ is increasing for $x \geqslant 1$, and decreasing for $x \leqslant 1$.
    iv $f(x)$ is concave up for all x.

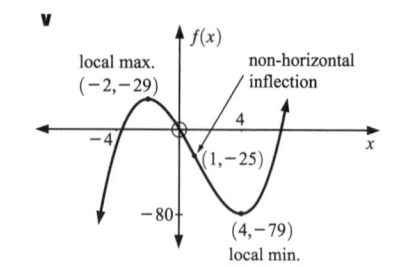

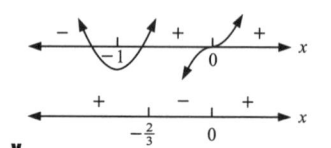

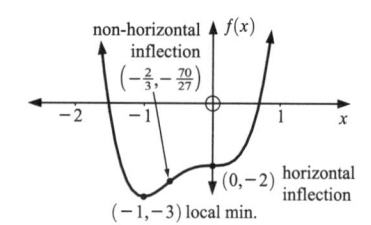

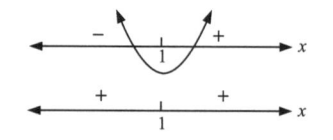

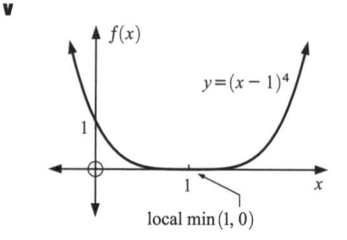

g $f(x) = x^4 - 4x^2 + 3$
    $f'(x) = 4x^3 - 8x = 4x(x^2 - 2)$
    $= 4x(x + \sqrt{2})(x - \sqrt{2})$ which has sign diagram:
    $f''(x) = 12x^2 - 8 = 4(3x^2 - 2)$
    $= 4(\sqrt{3}x + \sqrt{2})(\sqrt{3}x - \sqrt{2})$ which has sign diagram:

    i There is a local maximum at $(0, 3)$, and local minima at $(\sqrt{2}, -1)$ and $(-\sqrt{2}, -1)$.
    ii There are non-horizontal inflections at $(\sqrt{\frac{2}{3}}, \frac{7}{9})$ and $(-\sqrt{\frac{2}{3}}, \frac{7}{9})$.
    iii $f(x)$ is increasing for $-\sqrt{2} \leqslant x \leqslant 0$ and $x \geqslant \sqrt{2}$, and decreasing for $x \leqslant -\sqrt{2}$ and $0 \leqslant x \leqslant \sqrt{2}$.
    iv $f(x)$ is concave down for $-\sqrt{\frac{2}{3}} \leqslant x \leqslant \sqrt{\frac{2}{3}}$, and concave up for $x \leqslant -\sqrt{\frac{2}{3}}$ and $x \geqslant \sqrt{\frac{2}{3}}$.

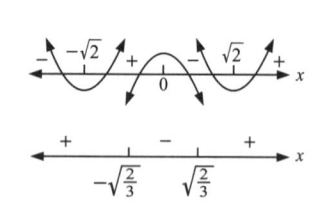

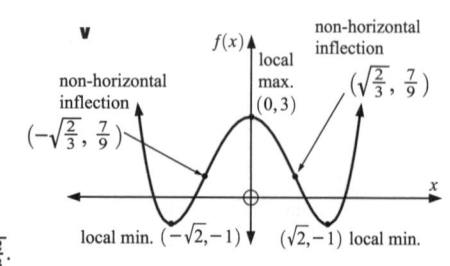

h $f(x) = 3 - \dfrac{4}{\sqrt{x}} = 3 - 4x^{-\frac{1}{2}}, \quad x > 0$

$\therefore \ f'(x) = 2x^{-\frac{3}{2}} = \dfrac{2}{x\sqrt{x}}$ with sign diagram: ![+ sign for x>0, 0]

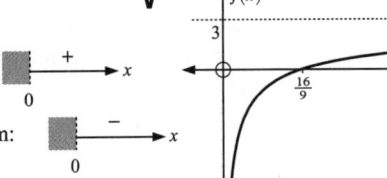

and $f''(x) = -3x^{-\frac{5}{2}} = -\dfrac{3}{x^2\sqrt{x}}$ with sign diagram: ![− sign for x>0, 0]

v (graph of $f(x)$ with horizontal asymptote at 3 and x-intercept at $\frac{16}{9}$)

i There are no stationary points as $f'(x) \neq 0$.
ii There are no points of inflection as $f''(x) \neq 0$.
iii $f(x)$ is increasing for all $x > 0$ as $f'(x) > 0$ for all x.
iv $f(x)$ is concave down for all $x > 0$ as $f''(x) < 0$ for all x.

3 a $f'(x) \geqslant 0$ for $x \leqslant -3$, and $f'(x) \leqslant 0$ for $x \geqslant -3$
$\therefore \ f(x)$ is increasing for $x \leqslant -3$, and decreasing for $x \geqslant -3$
$\therefore \ f(x)$ has a local maximum at $x = -3$
$f'(x)$ has a turning point at $x \approx -1.7$.
At this point, $f''(x) = 0$, but $f'(x) \neq 0$
$\therefore \ f(x)$ has a non-stationary inflection point here.
$f'(x)$ has another turning point at $x = 1$.
At this point, $f''(x) = 0$ and $f'(x) = 0$
$\therefore \ f(x)$ has a stationary inflection point at $x = 1$.
A possible graph of $f(x)$ is shown alongside:

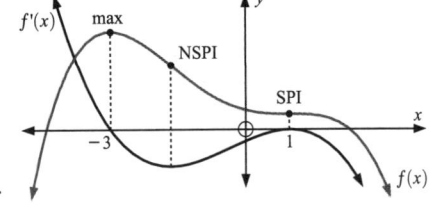

b $f'(x)$ has sign diagram ![− +2 + 4 −]

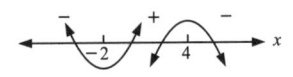

$\therefore \ f(x)$ has a local minimum at $x = -2$ and a local maximum at $x = 4$
$f'(x)$ has a turning point at $x \approx 1$.
At this point, $f''(x) = 0$, but $f'(x) \neq 0$
$\therefore \ f(x)$ has a non-stationary inflection point at $x \approx 1$.
A possible graph of $f(x)$ is shown alongside:

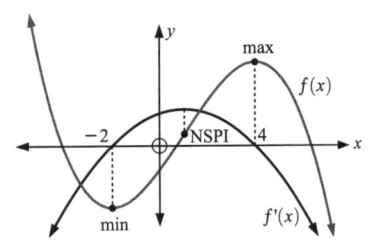

4 a $f(x)$ is quadratic, so $f'(x)$ will be linear and $f''(x)$ will be constant.
$f(x)$ is decreasing for $x \leqslant 1$ and increasing for $x \geqslant 1$
$\therefore \ f'(x) \leqslant 0$ for $x \leqslant 1$ and $f'(x) \geqslant 0$ for $x \geqslant 1$
$\therefore \ f'(x)$ is an increasing linear function which cuts the x-axis at 1.
As $f'(x)$ is increasing, $f''(x) > 0$.

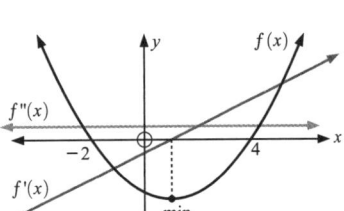

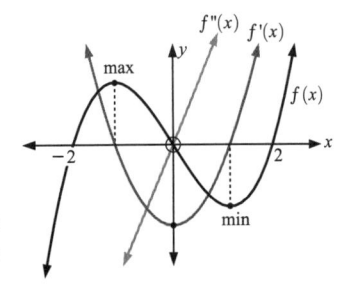

b $f(x)$ is cubic, so $f'(x)$ will be quadratic and $f''(x)$ will be linear.
$f(x)$ has turning points at $x \approx \pm 1$
$\therefore \ f'(x)$ cuts the x-axis at these points.
$f(x)$ has a non-stationary inflection point at $x = 0$
$\therefore \ f'(x)$ has a turning point at $x = 0$, and $f''(0) = 0$.
$f(x)$ is concave down for $x \leqslant 0$ and concave up for $x \geqslant 0$
$\therefore \ f'(x)$ is decreasing for $x \leqslant 0$ and increasing for $x \geqslant 0$
and $f''(x) \leqslant 0$ for $x \leqslant 0$ and $\geqslant 0$ for $x \geqslant 0$.

c $f(x)$ is cubic, so $f'(x)$ will be quadratic and $f''(x)$ will be linear.
$f(x)$ has turning points at $x \approx 1$ and $x = 3$
$\therefore$ $f'(x)$ cuts the x-axis at these points.
$f(x)$ has a non-stationary inflection point at $x \approx 2$
$\therefore$ $f'(x)$ has a turning point at $x \approx 2$, and $f''(2) = 0$
$f(x)$ is concave down for $x \leqslant 2$ and concave up for $x \geqslant 2$
$\therefore$ $f'(x)$ is decreasing for $x \leqslant 2$ and increasing for $x \geqslant 2$
and $f''(x) \leqslant 0$ for $x \leqslant 2$ and $\geqslant 0$ for $x \geqslant 2$.

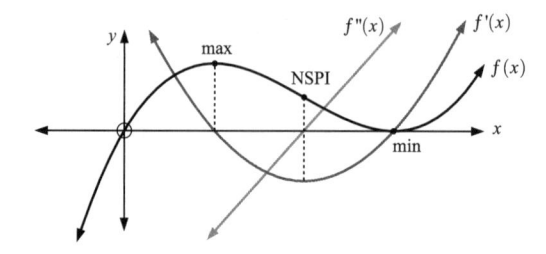

EXERCISE 21G

1 Suppose x fittings are produced daily.
$\therefore$ $C(x) = 1000 + 2x + \dfrac{5000}{x}$
$= 1000 + 2x + 5000x^{-1}$ euros
$\therefore$ $C'(x) = 2 - \dfrac{5000}{x^2}$
Now $C'(x) = 0$ when $x^2 = 2500$
$\therefore$ $x = 50$ {as $x > 0$}
Also, $C''(x) = 10\,000x^{-3} = \dfrac{10\,000}{x^3}$
which > 0 when $x > 0$.
$\therefore$ the cost is minimised when 50 fittings are produced.

3 $C(x) = \frac{1}{4}x^2 + 8x + 20$
$p(x) = 23 - \frac{1}{2}x$
Revenue $R(x) = xp(x) = 23x - \frac{1}{2}x^2$
Profit $P(x) = $ revenue $-$ cost
$= (23x - \frac{1}{2}x^2)$
$- (\frac{1}{4}x^2 + 8x + 20)$
$= -\frac{3}{4}x^2 + 15x - 20$
$\therefore$ $P'(x) = -\frac{3}{2}x + 15$
Now $P'(x) = 0$ when $x = \dfrac{15}{\frac{3}{2}} = 10$
$\therefore$ as $P''(x) = -\frac{3}{2} < 0$, P is maximised when 10 blankets per day are produced.

2 $C(x) = 720 + 4x + 0.02x^2$
$p(x) = 15 - 0.002x$
Revenue $R(x) = xp(x) = 15x - 0.002x^2$
Profit $P(x) = $ revenue $-$ cost
$= (15x - 0.002x^2)$
$- (720 + 4x + 0.02x^2)$
$= -0.022x^2 + 11x - 720$
$\therefore$ $P'(x) = -0.044x + 11$
Now $P'(x) = 0$ when $x = \dfrac{11}{0.044} = 250$
$\therefore$ as $P''(x) = -0.044 < 0$, P is maximised when 250 items are produced.

4 Cost per hour $=$ running costs $+$ other costs
$= \dfrac{v^2}{10} + 62.5$
Now cost per km $= \dfrac{\text{cost per hour}}{\text{km per hour}}$
$\therefore$ $C(v) = \dfrac{\dfrac{v^2}{10} + 62.5}{v}$
$\therefore$ $C(v) = \dfrac{v}{10} + \dfrac{62.5}{v} = 0.1v + 62.5v^{-1}$
$\therefore$ $C'(v) = 0.1 - 62.5v^{-2}$
Now $C'(v) = 0$ when $0.1 = \dfrac{62.5}{v^2}$
$\therefore$ $v^2 = 625$
$\therefore$ $v = 25$ {as $v > 0$}
Also, $C''(v) = 62.5 \times 2v^{-3} = \dfrac{125}{v^3}$
which is > 0 when $v > 0$
$\therefore$ minimum cost per km occurs when $v = 25$ km h^{-1}.

5 **a**

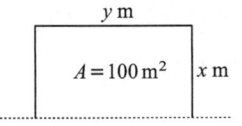

y m

$A = 100 \text{ m}^2$ x m

Now $xy = 100$

$\therefore y = \dfrac{100}{x}$

$\therefore L = 2x + y$

$\quad = 2x + \dfrac{100}{x}$

b

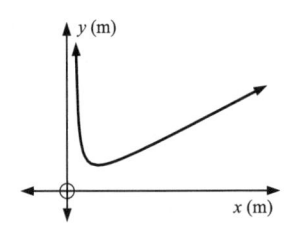

y (m)

x (m)

c $\dfrac{dL}{dx} = 2 - 100x^{-2} = 2 - \dfrac{100}{x^2}$

which is 0 when $\dfrac{100}{x^2} = 2$

$\therefore x^2 = 50$

$\therefore x = \sqrt{50} \quad \{x > 0\}$

$\dfrac{d^2L}{dt^2} = 200x^{-3} = \dfrac{200}{x^3} > 0 \text{ for } x > 0$

$\therefore L_{\min} = 2\sqrt{50} + \dfrac{100}{\sqrt{50}}$

$\quad = 2\sqrt{50} + 2\sqrt{50}$

$\quad = 4\sqrt{50}$

$\quad = 20\sqrt{2} \text{ m when } x = 5\sqrt{2} \text{ m}$

$\therefore \min L \approx 28.3 \text{ m when } x \approx 7.07 \text{ m}$

d

14.14 m

7.07 m

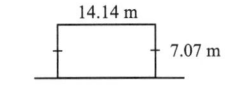

6 **a** Inner length of box $= 2x$ cm

b Volume $= 200$ cm^3

$\therefore x \times 2x \times h = 200$

$2x^2 h = 200$

$\therefore x^2 h = 100$

c From **b**, $h = \dfrac{100}{x^2}$.

Area of inner surface is

$A(x) = 2(2x \times x) + 2(2x \times h)$
$\qquad + 2(x \times h)$

$\quad = 4x^2 + 4xh + 2xh$

$\quad = 4x^2 + 6xh$

$\quad = 4x^2 + \dfrac{600}{x} \text{ cm}^2$

d

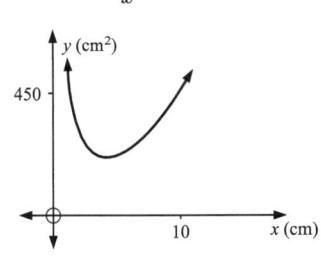

y (cm²)

450

10   x (cm)

e $A(x) = 4x^2 + 600x^{-1}$

$\therefore A'(x) = 8x - 600x^{-2}$

$\quad = 8x - \dfrac{600}{x^2}$

$\therefore A'(x) = 0$ when

$8x = \dfrac{600}{x^2}$

$\therefore 8x^3 = 600$

$\therefore x^3 = 75$

$\therefore x \approx 4.217$ cm

$A''(x) = 8 + 1200x^{-3}$

$\quad = 8 + \dfrac{1200}{x^3}$

$\therefore A''(x) > 0 \quad \{\text{as } x > 0\}$

$\therefore$ area is minimised when $x \approx 4.22$ cm

$\therefore A_{\min} \approx 4(4.217)^2 + \dfrac{600}{(4.217)}$

$\quad \approx 213 \text{ cm}^2$

f

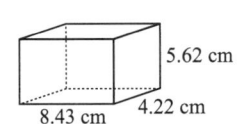

5.62 cm

8.43 cm   4.22 cm

7 **a** Volume of can $= \pi r^2 h$

$\therefore 1000 = \pi r^2 h$ (in cm)

$\therefore h = \dfrac{1000}{\pi r^2}$ cm

b Opening the can up we get:

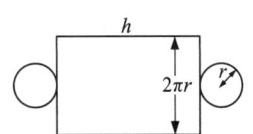

h

$2\pi r$ r

$\therefore A(r) = \pi r^2 + \pi r^2 + 2\pi rh$

$\quad = 2\pi r^2 + 2\pi rh$

$\quad = 2\pi r^2 + \dfrac{2000}{r} \text{ cm}^2$

c

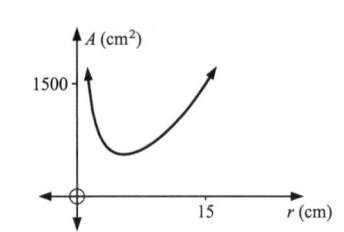

(Graph: A (cm²) with minimum near r = 15, value approximately 1500)

d $A(r) = 2\pi r^2 + 2000r^{-1}$

$A'(r) = 4\pi r - 2000r^{-2} = 4\pi r - \dfrac{2000}{r^2}$

So, $A'(r) = 0$ when $4\pi r = \dfrac{2000}{r^2}$

$r^3 = \dfrac{2000}{4\pi}$

$r = \sqrt[3]{\dfrac{500}{\pi}}$

$\therefore \quad r \approx 5.419$ cm

e

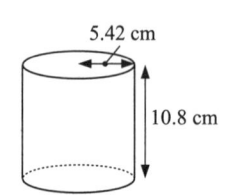

(Diagram: cylinder with radius labelled 5.42 cm and height 10.8 cm)

$A''(r) = 4\pi + 4000r^{-3} = 4\pi + \dfrac{4000}{r^3}$

and as $r > 0$, $A''(r) > 0$

$\therefore$ area is a minimum when $r \approx 5.42$ cm

and $h = \dfrac{1000}{\pi r^2} \approx 10.8$ cm

8 a

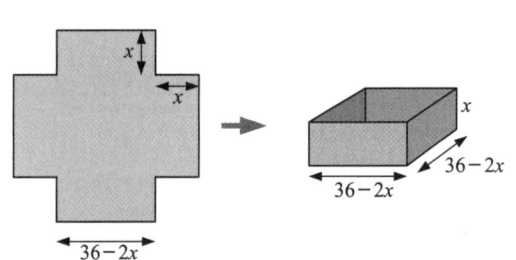

(Diagram: a plus-shaped net with squares of side x cut from the corners, folded into an open box with base $(36-2x) \times (36-2x)$ and height x)

The volume of the container is
$V = lbd$
$= x(36 - 2x)(36 - 2x)$
$\therefore \quad V = x(36 - 2x)^2$ cm³

b Using the product rule, $V'(x) = (36 - 2x)^2 - 4x(36 - 2x)$
$= (36 - 2x)[(36 - 2x) - 4x]$
$= (36 - 2x)(36 - 6x)$

$\therefore \quad V'(x) = 0$ when $x = 6$ or $x = 18$

Sign diagram of $V'(x)$ is:

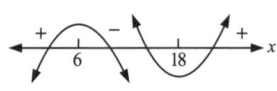

(Sign diagram: + on left, − between 6 and 18, + to the right of 18)

$\therefore$ the volume is maximised when $x = 6$ cm $\{0 \leqslant x \leqslant 18\}$

So, 6 cm × 6 cm squares should be cut out to maximise the volume.

9 a $P = 2\pi r + 2l$
$\therefore \quad 400 = 2\pi(x) + 2l$
$\therefore \quad 200 = \pi x + l$
$\therefore \quad l = 200 - \pi x$

Now clearly $x \geqslant 0$ and $l \geqslant 0$

$\therefore \quad \pi x \leqslant 200$

$\therefore \quad x \leqslant \dfrac{200}{\pi}$

So, $0 \leqslant x \leqslant \dfrac{200}{\pi}$

b Area $A = \pi r^2 + (2x) \times l$
$= \pi x^2 + 2xl$
$= \pi x^2 + 2x(200 - \pi x)$
$= \pi x^2 + 400x - 2\pi x^2$
$= 400x - \pi x^2$

c Now $\dfrac{dA}{dx} = 400 - 2\pi x$

which is 0 when $2\pi x = 400$

$\therefore \quad x = \dfrac{200}{\pi}$ and $l = 0$

Sign diagram of $A'(x)$:

(Sign diagram: + on left, − on right, with critical value at $\dfrac{200}{\pi}$)

$\therefore$ the area will be a maximum when the track is a circle.

10 a Arc $AC = \dfrac{\theta}{360} \times (2\pi r)$

$= \dfrac{\theta}{360}(2 \times \pi \times 10)$

$= \dfrac{\pi\theta}{18}$

b Now arc AC forms the base of the cone.

$\therefore\ 2\pi r = \dfrac{\pi\theta}{18}$ {from **a**}

$\therefore\ r = \dfrac{\theta}{36}$

c Height of cone $= \sqrt{10^2 - r^2}$ {Pythagoras}

$\therefore\ h = \sqrt{100 - \left(\dfrac{\theta}{36}\right)^2}$

d $V = \tfrac{1}{3}\pi r^2 h$

$= \tfrac{1}{3}\pi \left(\dfrac{\theta}{36}\right)^2 \sqrt{100 - \left(\dfrac{\theta}{36}\right)^2}$

$= \dfrac{\pi\theta^2}{3 \times 36^2} \sqrt{\dfrac{129\,600 - \theta^2}{36^2}}$

$= \dfrac{\pi\theta^2}{139\,968} \sqrt{129\,600 - \theta^2}$

e

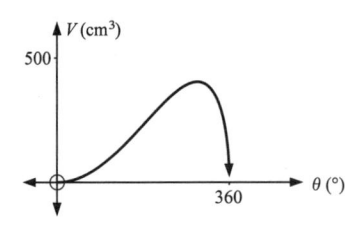

A graph with axes V (cm³) vs θ (°), showing a curve that rises from the origin to a maximum near 500 and then decreases to 0 at 360.

f Now $V'(\theta) = \dfrac{2\pi\theta}{139\,968}(129\,600 - \theta^2)^{\frac{1}{2}} + \dfrac{\pi\theta^2}{139\,968}\left(\tfrac{1}{2}\right)(129\,600 - \theta^2)^{-\frac{1}{2}}(-2\theta)$

$= \dfrac{\pi\theta}{139\,968}\left(\dfrac{2\sqrt{129\,600 - \theta^2}}{1} - \dfrac{\theta^2}{\sqrt{129\,600 - \theta^2}}\right)$

$= \dfrac{\pi\theta}{139\,968}\left(\dfrac{2(129\,600 - \theta^2) - \theta^2}{\sqrt{129\,600 - \theta^2}}\right)$

and $V'(\theta) = 0$ when $\theta = 0$ or $2(129\,600 - \theta^2) = \theta^2$

$259\,200 - 2\theta^2 = \theta^2$

$\therefore\ 3\theta^2 = 259\,200$

Sign diagram of $V'(\theta)$ is: a sign diagram with + from 0 to 293.9 and − from 293.9 to 360.

$\therefore\ \theta = \sqrt{86\,400}$ {as $\theta > 0$}

$\therefore\ \theta \approx 293.9$

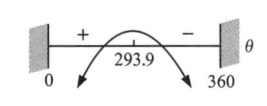

$\therefore$ maximum V occurs when $\theta \approx 294°$

11 a X must lie either between A and C or else at one of the two points. If $x = 0$, then he rows straight to the shore and runs to C. If $x = 6$, then he rows straight to C. $\therefore\ 0 \leqslant x \leqslant 6$

b Now $XC = 6 - x$

$\therefore$ the time to row from B to $X = \dfrac{BX}{8} = \dfrac{\sqrt{5^2 + x^2}}{8}$

and the time to run from X to $C = \dfrac{XC}{17} = \dfrac{6 - x}{17}$

$\therefore$ the total time $T(x) = \dfrac{\sqrt{25 + x^2}}{8} + \dfrac{6 - x}{17}$ hours

$= \tfrac{1}{8}(25 + x^2)^{\frac{1}{2}} + \tfrac{6}{17} - \tfrac{x}{17}$

c $\dfrac{dT}{dx} = \tfrac{1}{16}(25 + x^2)^{-\frac{1}{2}}(2x) - \tfrac{1}{17}$

$= \dfrac{x}{8\sqrt{25 + x^2}} - \tfrac{1}{17}$

Sign diagram of $\dfrac{dT}{dx}$: − from 0 to $\tfrac{8}{3}$, + from $\tfrac{8}{3}$ to 6.

So, $\dfrac{dT}{dx} = 0$ when $\dfrac{x}{8\sqrt{25 + x^2}} = \tfrac{1}{17}$

$17x = 8\sqrt{25 + x^2}$

$\therefore\ 289x^2 = 64(25 + x^2)$

$\therefore\ 225x^2 = 1600$

$\therefore\ x^2 = \dfrac{1600}{225}$

$\therefore\ x = \dfrac{40}{15} = \tfrac{8}{3}$ km

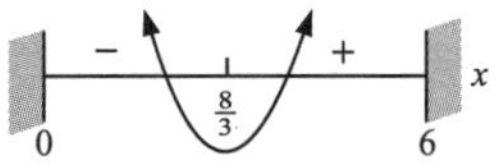

The time taken is minimised if Peter aims for X such that $x = \tfrac{8}{3}$ km.

12 Let $MX = x$ km, so $XN = 5 - x$ km

$\therefore\ AX = \sqrt{4 + x^2}$ km and $XB = \sqrt{1 + (5-x)^2}$ km {Pythagoras}

Now $P = AX + XB$

$\qquad = (4 + x^2)^{\frac{1}{2}} + (26 - 10x + x^2)^{\frac{1}{2}}$

$\therefore\ \dfrac{dP}{dx} = \frac{1}{2}(4 + x^2)^{-\frac{1}{2}}(2x) + \frac{1}{2}(26 - 10x + x^2)^{-\frac{1}{2}}(2x - 10)$

$\qquad = \dfrac{x}{\sqrt{4 + x^2}} + \dfrac{x - 5}{\sqrt{x^2 - 10x + 26}}$

Now $\dfrac{dP}{dx} = 0$ when $\dfrac{x}{\sqrt{4 + x^2}} = \dfrac{5 - x}{\sqrt{x^2 - 10x + 26}}$

$\therefore\ \dfrac{x^2}{4 + x^2} = \dfrac{(5 - x)^2}{x^2 - 10x + 26}$ {squaring both sides}

$\therefore\ x^2(x^2 - 10x + 26) = (4 + x^2)(25 - 10x + x^2)$

$\therefore\ x^4 - 10x^3 + 26x^2 = 100 - 40x + 4x^2 + 25x^2 - 10x^3 + x^4$

$\therefore\ 3x^2 - 40x + 100 = 0$

$\therefore\ (3x - 10)(x - 10) = 0$

$\therefore\ x = \dfrac{10}{3}$ {as x cannot be 10}

Sign diagram of $\dfrac{dP}{dx}$ is: $\begin{array}{c}\;-\quad+\\ \hline 0 \quad \frac{10}{3}\quad 5\end{array}$

$\therefore$ the minimum length pipeline occurs when $x = \dfrac{10}{3}$ km

13 $V = \pi r^2 h$

$\therefore\ 0.1 = \pi r^2 h$ {as 100 L = 0.1 m³}

$\therefore\ h = \dfrac{0.1}{\pi r^2}$

Now $A = \pi r^2 + (2\pi r)h = \pi r^2 + 2\pi r\left(\dfrac{0.1}{\pi r^2}\right)$

$\therefore\ A(r) = \pi r^2 + 0.2 r^{-1}$

$\therefore\ A'(r) = 2\pi r - 0.2 r^{-2}$

$\qquad = 2\pi r - \dfrac{0.2}{r^2}$

Now $A''(r) = 2\pi + 0.4 r^{-3} = 2\pi + \dfrac{0.4}{r^3}$ which is > 0 as $r > 0$

$\therefore$ the minimum area occurs when $r \approx 31.7$ cm and $h \approx \dfrac{1}{10\pi(31.69)} \approx 31.7$ cm

$\therefore\ r = h \approx 31.7$ cm

So, $A'(r) = 0$ when $2\pi r = \dfrac{0.2}{r^2}$

$\therefore\ r^3 = \dfrac{0.2}{2\pi}$

$\therefore\ r = \sqrt[3]{\dfrac{0.2}{2\pi}} \approx 0.3169$ m

$\therefore\ r \approx 31.7$ cm

14 Now $I \propto \dfrac{s}{d^2}$ where s is the power of the source and d is the distance from it

$\therefore\ I = \dfrac{ks}{d^2}$ where k is a constant

So, the intensity due to the 40 cp bulb $= \dfrac{40k}{x^2}$

and the intensity due to the 5 cp bulb $= \dfrac{5k}{(6 - x)^2}$

The total intensity $I = \dfrac{40k}{x^2} + \dfrac{5k}{(6-x)^2}$

$\qquad = k[40x^{-2} + 5(6 - x)^{-2}]$

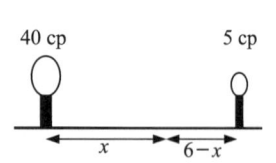

40 cp   5 cp

$\leftarrow x \rightarrow \leftarrow 6-x \rightarrow$

$\therefore\ \dfrac{dI}{dx} = k[-80 x^{-3} - 10(6 - x)^{-3}(-1)]$

$\qquad = k\left[\dfrac{-80}{x^3} + \dfrac{10}{(6-x)^3}\right]$

$\therefore \quad \dfrac{dI}{dx} = 0$ when $\dfrac{80}{x^3} = \dfrac{10}{(6-x)^3}$

$\therefore \quad 8(6-x)^3 = x^3$

$\therefore \quad 2(6-x) = x \quad$ {finding cube roots}

$\therefore \quad 12 - 2x = x$

$\therefore \quad x = 4$

Sign diagram of $\dfrac{dI}{dx}$ is:

$\therefore$ the darkest point occurs 4 m from the 40 cp lamp.

15 a $AB = x$ m

$\therefore \quad BC = (24 - x)$ m

$D(x) = \sqrt{x^2 + (24-x)^2} \quad$ {Pythagoras}

b $[D(x)]^2 = x^2 + (24-x)^2$

$\qquad = x^2 + 576 - 48x + x^2$

$\qquad = 2x^2 - 48x + 576$

$\therefore \quad \dfrac{d[D(x)]^2}{dx} = 4x - 48 \quad$ Sign diagram for $\dfrac{d[D(x)]^2}{dx}$:

$\therefore \quad \dfrac{d[D(x)]^2}{dx} = 0$ when $x = 12$

c When $AB = BC = 12$ m, $D(x)$ is a minimum, and the minimum $D(x) = 12\sqrt{2}$ m ≈ 17.0 m.

$D(x)$ is a maximum when either $x = 0$ or $x = 24$, when the pen ceases to exist and $D(x) = 24$ m.

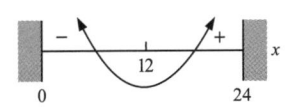

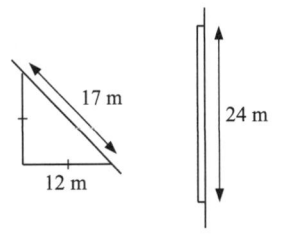

16 a Consider each boat's position t hours after 1.00 pm.

$\qquad AP = 12t \quad$ and $\quad BQ = 8t$

$\therefore \quad PB = 100 - 8t$

Using the cosine rule in $\triangle PAB$

$D(t)^2 = AP^2 + BP^2 - 2AP \times BP \cos 60°$

$\qquad = (12t)^2 + (100-8t)^2 - 2(12t)(100-8t)\tfrac{1}{2}$

$\qquad = 144t^2 + (100-8t)^2 - 12t(100-8t)$

$\qquad = 144t^2 + 10\,000 - 1600t + 64t^2 - 1200t + 96t^2$

$\qquad = 304t^2 - 2800t + 10\,000$

$\therefore \quad D(t) = \sqrt{304t^2 - 2800t + 10\,000}$

b Now $\dfrac{d[D(t)]^2}{dt} = 608t - 2800$

$\therefore \quad \dfrac{d[D(t)]^2}{dt} = 0$ when $t = \dfrac{2800}{608} \approx 4.605\,26$

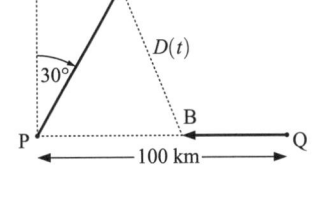

$\therefore \quad D(t)$ is a minimum when $t \approx 4.605\,26$ hours after 1.00 pm

and $[D(t)]^2_{\min} \approx 304\,(4.6053)^2 - 2800\,(4.6053) + 10\,000$

$\therefore \quad [D(t)]^2_{\min} \approx 3350$ km^2

c The ships are closest when $t = 4.605\,26$ hours which occurs when the time is 4 hours 36 minutes after 1.00 pm. So, the ships are closest at approximately 5.36 pm.

17 **a** As PAB and PRQ are similar.

$$\therefore \quad \frac{PA}{PR} = \frac{PB}{PQ} = \frac{AB}{RQ}$$

$$\therefore \quad \frac{x}{x+2} = \frac{1}{QR} \quad \text{and} \quad \therefore \quad QR = \frac{x+2}{x}$$

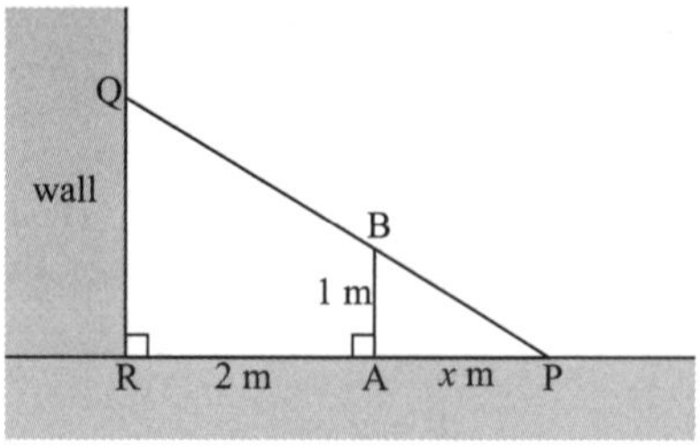

b Now $[L(x)]^2 = RP^2 + QR^2$ {Pythagoras}

$$= (x+2)^2 + \left(\frac{x+2}{x}\right)^2$$

$$= (x+2)^2 \times 1 + (x+2)^2 \times \frac{1}{x^2}$$

$$\therefore \quad [L(x)]^2 = (x+2)^2 \left(1 + \frac{1}{x^2}\right) \quad \text{as required}$$

c $[L(x)]^2 = (x+2)^2 \left(1 + x^{-2}\right)$

$$\therefore \quad \frac{d[L(x)]^2}{dx} = 2(x+2)\left(1+x^{-2}\right) + (x+2)^2 \left(-2x^{-3}\right) \quad \text{\{product rule\}}$$

$$= 2(x+2)\left(1+x^{-2} - (x+2)x^{-3}\right)$$

$$= 2(x+2)\left(1+x^{-2} - x^{-2} - 2x^{-3}\right)$$

$$= 2(x+2)\left(1 - \frac{2}{x^3}\right) = \frac{2(x+2)(x^3-2)}{x^3}$$

$$\therefore \quad \frac{d[L(x)]^2}{dx} = 0 \quad \text{when} \quad x = \sqrt[3]{2} \approx 1.2599 \quad \{\text{as } x > 0 \text{ and } L(x) > 0\}$$

d Sign diagram of $\frac{d[L(x)]^2}{dx}$ is:

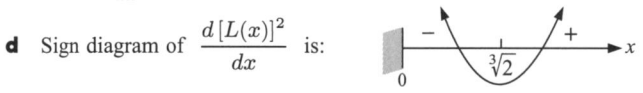

$\therefore$ the ladder is shortest when $x = \sqrt[3]{2}$ m and

its length at this time is $L = \sqrt{(x+2)^2 \left(1 + \frac{1}{x^2}\right)} = \sqrt{(\sqrt[3]{2}+2)^2 \left(1 + \frac{1}{2^{\frac{2}{3}}}\right)} \approx 4.16$ m

18 Suppose PN $= x$ m
$\therefore$ length of cable $=$ PA $+$ PB $+$ PC
$$\therefore \quad L = 8 - x + \sqrt{x^2 + 16} + \sqrt{x^2 + 25}$$
Using technology we graph and find the minimum
value of the function.
$\therefore$ the minimum length occurs when $x \approx 2.577\,98$
$\therefore$ P should be ≈ 2.58 m from N.

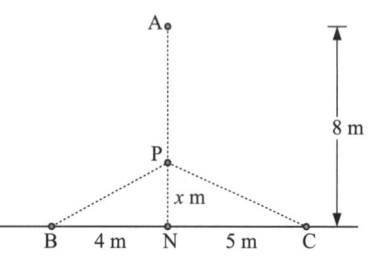

19 Suppose P has coordinates $(x, 8)$

$\therefore$ CP $= \sqrt{(x-3)^2 + (8-11)^2}$ $\quad$ AP $= \sqrt{(x-1)^2 + (8-2)^2}$

$\phantom{\therefore \text{ CP}} = \sqrt{x^2 - 6x + 9 + 9}$ $\quad\quad\quad\ \ = \sqrt{x^2 - 2x + 1 + 36}$

$\phantom{\therefore \text{ CP}} = \sqrt{x^2 - 6x + 18}$ $\quad\quad\quad\quad\ \ = \sqrt{x^2 - 2x + 37}$

BP $= \sqrt{(x-7)^2 + (8-3)^2}$

$\phantom{\text{BP}} = \sqrt{x^2 - 14x + 49 + 25}$

$\phantom{\text{BP}} = \sqrt{x^2 - 14x + 74}$

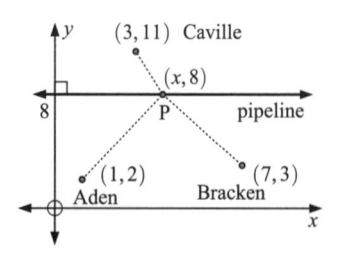

$\therefore$ the length of pipeline $L = \sqrt{x^2 - 6x + 18} + \sqrt{x^2 - 2x + 3} + \sqrt{x^2 - 14x + 74}$
We use technology to graph L and to find its minimum. This occurs when $x \approx 3.543\,66$,
$\therefore$ P is at $(3.54, 8)$.

20 $r^2 + h^2 = s^2$ {Pythagoras}

$\therefore \ h^2 = s^2 - r^2$

$\therefore \ h = \sqrt{s^2 - r^2}$

But $V = \frac{1}{3}\pi r^2 h$

$\therefore \ V = \frac{1}{3}\pi r^2 \sqrt{s^2 - r^2}$

$\therefore \ V^2 = \frac{\pi^2}{9} r^4 (s^2 - r^2)$

$= \frac{\pi^2}{9}(r^4 s^2 - r^6)$

$\therefore \ \frac{d(V^2)}{dr} = \frac{\pi^2}{9}(4r^3 s^2 - 6r^5)$

$= \frac{\pi^2}{9} 2r^3 (2s^2 - 3r^2)$

$\frac{d(V^2)}{dr} = 0$ when $2s^2 - 3r^2 = 0$

$\therefore \ 2s^2 = 3r^2$ {as $r > 0$}

$\therefore \ \frac{s^2}{r^2} = \frac{3}{2}$

$\therefore \ \frac{s}{r} = \sqrt{\frac{3}{2}}$

$\therefore \ s : r = \sqrt{\frac{3}{2}} : 1$

Sign diagram of $\frac{d(V^2)}{dr}$ is: $\xleftarrow[\ 0 \quad r=\sqrt{\frac{2}{3}}s \quad s\ ]{+ \quad - }\rightarrow r$

$\therefore \ V$ is a maximum when $s : r = \sqrt{\frac{3}{2}} : 1 = \sqrt{3} : \sqrt{2}$

21 a $\dfrac{x^2}{a^2} + \dfrac{y^2}{b^2} = 1$

$\therefore \ x^2 b^2 + y^2 a^2 = a^2 b^2$ {$\times$ by $a^2 b^2$}

$\therefore \ a^2 y^2 = a^2 b^2 - x^2 b^2$

$\therefore \ y^2 = \dfrac{a^2 b^2 - x^2 b^2}{a^2}$

$\therefore \ y = \pm \sqrt{\dfrac{a^2 b^2 - x^2 b^2}{a^2}}$

Since A lies in Q_1, $y > 0$

$\therefore \ y = \sqrt{\left(\dfrac{b^2}{a^2}\right)(a^2 - x^2)}$

$\therefore \ y = \dfrac{b}{a}\sqrt{a^2 - x^2}$

c $\dfrac{d(A^2)}{dx} = \dfrac{16b^2}{a^2}[2a^2 x - 4x^3]$

which is 0 when

$2a^2 x - 4x^3 = 0$

$\therefore \ 2x(a^2 - 2x^2) = 0$

$\therefore \ 2x^2 = a^2$ {as $x > 0$}

$\therefore \ x = \pm \dfrac{a}{\sqrt{2}}$

$\therefore \ x = \dfrac{a}{\sqrt{2}}$ {as x is in Q_1}

e   % occupied $= \dfrac{2ab}{\pi ab} \times 100\% = 63.7\%$

b   The seating area is $A = 2x \times 2y$

$= 4xy$

$= 4x\left[\dfrac{b}{a}\sqrt{a^2 - x^2}\right]$

$\therefore \ A(x) = \dfrac{4bx}{a}\sqrt{a^2 - x^2}$ as required

$\therefore \ A^2 = \dfrac{16b^2 x^2}{a^2}(a^2 - x^2)$

$= \dfrac{16b^2}{a^2}(a^2 x^2 - x^4)$

d   Sign diagram of $\dfrac{dA^2}{dx}$ is:

$\xleftarrow[\ 0 \quad \frac{a}{\sqrt{2}} \quad a\ ]{+ \quad - }\rightarrow x$

$\therefore \ $ maximum area occurs when $x = \dfrac{a}{\sqrt{2}}$

Max. area $= \dfrac{4b}{a} \cdot \dfrac{a}{\sqrt{2}} \sqrt{a^2 - \left(\dfrac{a}{\sqrt{2}}\right)^2}$

$= \dfrac{4b}{\sqrt{2}} \times \sqrt{\dfrac{a^2}{2}} = \dfrac{4b}{\sqrt{2}} \times \dfrac{a}{\sqrt{2}}$

$= 2ab$

EXERCISE 21H

1 a $\dfrac{d}{dx}(2y) = 2\dfrac{dy}{dx}$

b $\dfrac{d}{dx}(-3y) = -3\dfrac{dy}{dx}$

c $\dfrac{d}{dx}(y^3) = 3y^2 \dfrac{dy}{dx}$

d $\dfrac{d}{dx}\left(\dfrac{1}{y}\right) = \dfrac{d}{dx}(y^{-1}) = -y^{-2}\dfrac{dy}{dx}$

e $\dfrac{d}{dx}(y^4) = 4y^3 \dfrac{dy}{dx}$

f $\dfrac{d}{dx}(\sqrt{y}) = \dfrac{d}{dx}(y^{\frac{1}{2}}) = \frac{1}{2}y^{-\frac{1}{2}}\dfrac{dy}{dx}$

g $\dfrac{d}{dx}\left(\dfrac{1}{y^2}\right) = \dfrac{d}{dx}(y^{-2}) = -2y^{-3}\dfrac{dy}{dx}$

h $\dfrac{d}{dx}(xy) = y + x\dfrac{dy}{dx}$ {product rule}

i $\dfrac{d}{dx}(x^2y) = 2xy + x^2\dfrac{dy}{dx}$ {product rule}

j $\dfrac{d}{dx}(xy^2) = y^2 + x(2y)\dfrac{dy}{dx} = y^2 + 2xy\dfrac{dy}{dx}$ {product rule}

2 a Differentiating both sides of $x^2 + y^2 = 25$ with respect to x,

$2x + 2y\dfrac{dy}{dx} = 0$

$\therefore\ 2y\dfrac{dy}{dx} = -2x$

$\therefore\ \dfrac{dy}{dx} = -\dfrac{2x}{2y} = -\dfrac{x}{y}$

b Differentiating both sides of $x^2 + 3y^2 = 9$ with respect to x,

$2x + 6y\dfrac{dy}{dx} = 0$

$\therefore\ 6y\dfrac{dy}{dx} = -2x$

$\therefore\ \dfrac{dy}{dx} = -\dfrac{2x}{6y} = -\dfrac{x}{3y}$

c Differentiating both sides of $y^2 - x^2 = 8$ with respect to x,

$2y\dfrac{dy}{dx} - 2x = 0$

$\therefore\ 2y\dfrac{dy}{dx} = 2x$

$\therefore\ \dfrac{dy}{dx} = \dfrac{2x}{2y} = \dfrac{x}{y}$

d Differentiating both sides of $x^2 - y^3 = 10$ with respect to x,

$2x - 3y^2\dfrac{dy}{dx} = 0$

$\therefore\ 3y^2\dfrac{dy}{dx} = 2x$

$\therefore\ \dfrac{dy}{dx} = \dfrac{2x}{3y^2}$

e Differentiating both sides of $x^2 + xy = 4$ with respect to x,

$2x + \left(y + x\dfrac{dy}{dx}\right) = 0$ {product rule}

$\therefore\ x\dfrac{dy}{dx} = -2x - y$

$\therefore\ \dfrac{dy}{dx} = \dfrac{-2x - y}{x}$

f Differentiating both sides of $x^3 - 2xy = 5$ with respect to x,

$3x^2 - \left(2y + 2x\dfrac{dy}{dx}\right) = 0$ {product rule}

$\therefore\ 3x^2 - 2y = 2x\dfrac{dy}{dx}$

$\therefore\ \dfrac{dy}{dx} = \dfrac{3x^2 - 2y}{2x}$

3 a Differentiating both sides of $x + y^3 = 4y$ with respect to x,

$1 + 3y^2\dfrac{dy}{dx} = 4\dfrac{dy}{dx}$

When $y = 1$, $1 + 3\dfrac{dy}{dx} = 4\dfrac{dy}{dx}$

$\therefore\ \dfrac{dy}{dx} = 1$ at this point, and the gradient of the tangent is 1.

b $x + y = 8xy$. Now when $x = \frac{1}{2}$, $\frac{1}{2} + y = 4y$ $\therefore\ y = \frac{1}{6}$

Thus the point of contact is $(\frac{1}{2}, \frac{1}{6})$.

Differentiating both sides of $x + y = 8xy$ with respect to x,

$1 + \dfrac{dy}{dx} = 8y + 8x\dfrac{dy}{dx}$

So, at the point $(\frac{1}{2}, \frac{1}{6})$, $1 + \dfrac{dy}{dx} = 8(\frac{1}{6}) + 8(\frac{1}{2})\dfrac{dy}{dx}$

$\therefore\ 1 + \dfrac{dy}{dx} = \dfrac{4}{3} + 4\dfrac{dy}{dx}$

$\therefore\ -\dfrac{1}{3} = 3\dfrac{dy}{dx}$

$\therefore\ \dfrac{dy}{dx} = -\dfrac{1}{9}$ $\therefore$ the gradient of the tangent is $-\dfrac{1}{9}$.

4 **a** $$x^2 + y^2 = 25$$
$$\therefore \ 2x + 2y\frac{dy}{dx} = 0$$
$$\therefore \ 2 + 2\frac{dy}{dx}\frac{dy}{dx} + 2y\frac{d^2y}{dx^2} = 0$$
$$\therefore \ 2 + 2\left(-\frac{x}{y}\right)^2 + 2y\frac{d^2y}{dx^2} = 0 \ \{\frac{dy}{dx} = -\frac{x}{y}\}$$
$$\therefore \ 1 + \frac{x^2}{y^2} + y\frac{d^2y}{dx^2} = 0$$
$$\therefore \ y^2 + x^2 + y^3\frac{d^2y}{dx^2} = 0 \ \{\times y^2\}$$
$$\therefore \ 25 + y^3\frac{d^2y}{dx^2} = 0$$
$$\therefore \ \frac{d^2y}{dx^2} = \frac{-25}{y^3}$$

b $$x^2 + 3y^2 = 9$$
$$\therefore \ 2x + 6y\frac{dy}{dx} = 0$$
$$\therefore \ 2 + 6\frac{dy}{dx}\frac{dy}{dx} + 6y\frac{d^2y}{dx^2} = 0$$
$$\therefore \ 2 + 6\left(-\frac{x}{3y}\right)^2 + 6y\frac{d^2y}{dx^2} = 0 \ \{\frac{dy}{dx} = -\frac{x}{3y}\}$$
$$\therefore \ 1 + 3\left(\frac{x^2}{9y^2}\right) + 3y\frac{d^2y}{dx^2} = 0$$
$$\therefore \ 3y^2 + x^2 + 9y^3\frac{d^2y}{dx^2} = 0 \ \{\times 3y^2\}$$
$$\therefore \ 9 + 9y^3\frac{d^2y}{dx^2} = 0$$
$$\therefore \ \frac{d^2y}{dx^2} = \frac{-1}{y^3}$$

c $$y^2 - x^2 = 8$$
$$\therefore \ 2y\frac{dy}{dx} - 2x = 0$$
$$\therefore \ 2\frac{dy}{dx}\frac{dy}{dx} + 2y\frac{d^2y}{dx^2} - 2 = 0$$
$$\therefore \ 2\left(\frac{x}{y}\right)^2 + 2y\frac{d^2y}{dx^2} - 2 = 0 \ \{\frac{dy}{dx} = \frac{x}{y}\}$$
$$\therefore \ \frac{x^2}{y^2} + y\frac{d^2y}{dx^2} - 1 = 0$$
$$\therefore \ x^2 - y^2 + y^3\frac{d^2y}{dx^2} = 0 \ \{\times y^2\}$$
$$\therefore \ -8 + y^3\frac{d^2y}{dx^2} = 0$$
$$\therefore \ \frac{d^2y}{dx^2} = \frac{8}{y^3}$$

d $$x^2 - y^3 = 10$$
$$\therefore \ 2x - 3y^2\frac{dy}{dx} = 0$$
$$\therefore \ 2 - 6y\frac{dy}{dx}\frac{dy}{dx} - 3y^2\frac{d^2y}{dx^2} = 0$$
$$\therefore \ 2 - 6y\left(\frac{2x}{3y^2}\right)^2 - 3y^2\frac{d^2y}{dx^2} = 0 \ \{\frac{dy}{dx} = \frac{2x}{3y^2}\}$$
$$\therefore \ 2 - \frac{8x^2}{3y^3} - 3y^2\frac{d^2y}{dx^2} = 0$$
$$\therefore \ 6y^3 - 8x^2 - 9y^5\frac{d^2y}{dx^2} = 0 \ \{\times 3y^3\}$$
$$\therefore \ \frac{d^2y}{dx^2} = \frac{6y^3 - 8x^2}{9y^5}$$

e $$x^2 + xy = 4$$
$$\therefore \ 2x + \left(y + x\frac{dy}{dx}\right) = 0$$
$$\therefore \ 2 + \frac{dy}{dx} + \frac{dy}{dx} + x\frac{d^2y}{dx^2} = 0$$
$$\therefore \ 2 + 2\left(\frac{-2x - y}{x}\right) + x\frac{d^2y}{dx^2} = 0$$
$$\{\frac{dy}{dx} = \frac{-2x - y}{x}\}$$
$$\therefore \ 2x - 4x - 2y + x^2\frac{d^2y}{dx^2} = 0 \ \{\times x\}$$
$$\therefore \ \frac{d^2y}{dx^2} = \frac{2x + 2y}{x^2}$$
$$= \frac{2x^2 + 2xy}{x^3}$$
$$= \frac{8}{x^3} \ \{x^2 + xy = 4\}$$

f $$x^3 - 2xy = 5$$
$$\therefore \ 3x^2 - 2y - 2x\frac{dy}{dx} = 0$$
$$\therefore \ 6x - 2\frac{dy}{dx} - 2\frac{dy}{dx} - 2x\frac{d^2y}{dx^2} = 0$$
$$\therefore \ 6x - 4\left(\frac{3x^2 - 2y}{2x}\right) - 2x\frac{d^2y}{dx^2} = 0$$
$$\{\frac{dy}{dx} = \frac{3x^2 - 2y}{2x}\}$$
$$\therefore \ 6x - 6x + \frac{4y}{x} - 2x\frac{d^2y}{dx^2} = 0$$
$$\therefore \ 4y - 2x^2\frac{d^2y}{dx^2} = 0 \ \{\times x\}$$
$$\therefore \ \frac{d^2y}{dx^2} = \frac{4y}{2x^2}$$
$$\therefore \ \frac{d^2y}{dx^2} = \frac{2y}{x^2}$$

5 **a** $3V^2 + 2q = 2Vq$

Differentiating with respect to q,

$$\therefore\ 6V\frac{dV}{dq} + 2 = 2\frac{dV}{dq}q + 2V$$

$$\therefore\ \frac{dV}{dq}(6V - 2q) = 2V - 2$$

$$\therefore\ \frac{dV}{dq} = \frac{2V - 2}{6V - 2q}$$

$$= \frac{V - 1}{3V - q}$$

b $3V^2 + 2q = 2Vq$

Differentiating with respect to V,

$$6V + 2\frac{dq}{dV} = 2q + 2V\frac{dq}{dV}\ \ \ \ \ \dots\ (1)$$

$$\therefore\ (2 - 2V)\frac{dq}{dV} = 2q - 6V$$

$$\therefore\ \frac{dq}{dV} = \frac{2q - 6V}{2 - 2V} = \frac{q - 3V}{1 - V}\ \ \ \ \ \dots\ (2)$$

Now differentiating (1) with respect to V,

$$6 + 2\frac{d^2q}{dV^2} = 2\frac{dq}{dV} + 2\frac{dq}{dV} + 2V\frac{d^2q}{dV^2}$$

$$\therefore\ (2 - 2V)\frac{d^2q}{dV^2} = 4\frac{dq}{dV} - 6$$

$$= 4\left(\frac{q - 3V}{1 - V}\right) - 6\ \ \{\text{using (2)}\}$$

$$= \frac{4q - 12V - 6(1 - V)}{1 - V}$$

$$= \frac{4q - 6V - 6}{1 - V}$$

$$\therefore\ \frac{d^2q}{dV^2} = \frac{4q - 6V - 6}{(2 - 2V)(1 - V)}$$

$$= \frac{2q - 3V - 3}{(1 - V)^2}$$

REVIEW SET 21A

1 **a** $s(t) = 2t^3 - 9t^2 + 12t - 5$ cm, $t \geqslant 0$

$v(t) = 6t^2 - 18t + 12$
$= 6(t^2 - 3t + 2)$
$= 6(t - 2)(t - 1)$ cm s^{-1}

and $a(t) = 12t - 18$
$= 6(2t - 3)$ cm s^{-2}

$v(t)$: $\quad\ +\quad\ -\quad\ +$
$\qquad\qquad\ 1\qquad 2 \to t$

$a(t)$: $\quad\ -\quad\ +$
$\qquad 0\quad \frac{3}{2} \to t$

b When $t = 0$, $s(0) = -5$ cm
$v(0) = 12$ cm s^{-1}
$a(0) = -18$ cm s^{-2}

c When $t = 2$, $s(2) = -1$ cm
$v(2) = 0$ cm s^{-1}
$a(2) = 6$ cm s^{-2}

$\therefore$ when $t = 2$, the particle is 1 cm to the left of O, instantaneously at rest and increasing in speed towards O.

d The particle changes direction when $t = 1$ and $t = 2$, at $s(1) = 0$ cm, $s(2) = -1$ cm.

e
$\qquad\quad -5\qquad\quad -1\ 0 \to s$

f The speed is increasing when $1 \leqslant t \leqslant \frac{3}{2}$ and $t \geqslant 2$
$\{v(t)$ and $a(t)$ have the same sign$\}$

2 $C(v) = \dfrac{v^2}{30} + \dfrac{9000}{v}$ dollars per hour

a **i** For $t = 2$ hours at $v = 45$ km h^{-1},

$$\text{cost} = \left(\frac{45^2}{30} + \frac{9000}{45}\right) \times 2\ \text{dollars}$$

$$= \$535.00$$

ii For $t = 5$ hours at $v = 64$ km h^{-1},

$$\text{cost} = \left(\frac{64^2}{30} + \frac{9000}{64}\right) \times 5\ \text{dollars}$$

$$\approx \$1385.79$$

$$\approx \$1390$$

b $C'(v) = \dfrac{2v}{30} - 9000v^{-2} = \dfrac{v}{15} - \dfrac{9000}{v^2}$

i For $v = 50$ km h^{-1}

$\therefore\ C'(50) = \dfrac{50}{15} - \dfrac{9000}{50^2}$

$\approx -\$0.267$ per km h^{-1}

ii For $v = 66$ km h^{-1}

$\therefore\ C'(66) = \dfrac{66}{15} - \dfrac{9000}{66^2}$

$= \$2.33$ per km h^{-1}

c Now $C'(v) = \dfrac{v}{15} - \dfrac{9000}{v^2} = \dfrac{v^3 - 135\,000}{15v^2}$

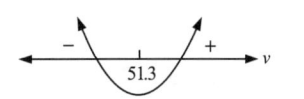

$\therefore\ C'(v) = 0$ when $v^3 = 135\,000$

$\therefore\ v \approx 51.3$

$\therefore$ minimum cost occurs when $v \approx 51.3$ km h^{-1}

Sign diagram: $-$ | $+$ at 51.3

3 a $f(x) = 2x^3 - 3x^2 - 36x + 7$

$\therefore\ f'(x) = 6x^2 - 6x - 36$

$= 6(x^2 - x - 6)$

$= 6(x-3)(x+2)$ with sign diagram: $+\ -2\ -\ 3\ +$

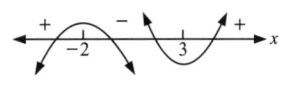

Now $f(-2) = 51$, $f(3) = -74$, so there is a local maximum at $(-2, 51)$, and a local minimum at $(3, -74)$.

$f''(x) = 12x - 6$

$= 6(2x - 1)$ with sign diagram: $-\ \tfrac{1}{2}\ +$

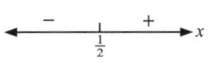

Now $f(\tfrac{1}{2}) = -\tfrac{23}{2}$, so there is a non-horizontal inflection at $(\tfrac{1}{2}, -\tfrac{23}{2})$.

b $f(x)$ is increasing when $x \leqslant -2$ or $x \geqslant 3$, and decreasing when $-2 \leqslant x \leqslant 3$.

c $f(x)$ is concave up when $x \geqslant \tfrac{1}{2}$, and concave down when $x \leqslant \tfrac{1}{2}$.

d local max $(-2, 51)$, non-horizontal inflection $(\tfrac{1}{2}, -11\tfrac{1}{2})$, local min $(3, -74)$

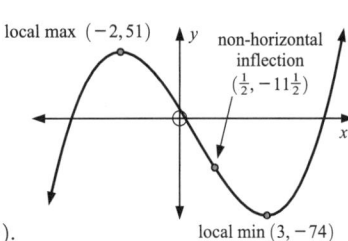

4 a Now if OD $= x$, the coordinates of C are $(x, k - x^2)$.

$\therefore$ the area of ABCD $= 2x \times (k - x^2)$

$\therefore\ A = 2kx - 2x^3,\ x > 0$

b Now $\dfrac{dA}{dx} = 2k - 6x^2$

But $\dfrac{dA}{dx} = 0$ when AD $= 2\sqrt{3}$, and this occurs when $x = \sqrt{3}$

$\therefore\ 2k - 6(\sqrt{3})^2 = 0$

$\therefore\ 2k - 18 = 0$

$\therefore\ 2k = 18$

$\therefore\ k = 9$

Check: $\dfrac{dA}{dx} = 18 - 6x^2$

$= 6(3 - x^2)$

$= 6(\sqrt{3} + x)(\sqrt{3} - x)$

$\dfrac{dA}{dx}$ has sign diagram: $0\ +\ \sqrt{3}\ -$

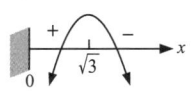

$\therefore$ the maximum occurs when $x = \sqrt{3}$ and AD $= 2\sqrt{3}$.

5 a Volume $= lbd$

$\therefore\ x^2 y = 1$

$\therefore\ y = \dfrac{1}{x^2},\ x > 0$

b area $= x^2 + 4xy$

$\therefore$ cost $= (x^2 + 4xy) \times 2$

$\therefore\ C = 2x^2 + 8xy$

$= 2x^2 + \dfrac{8}{x}$ dollars {using **a**}

c $\dfrac{dC}{dx} = 4x - 8x^{-2}$

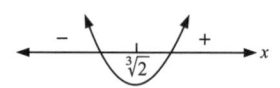

$= 4x - \dfrac{8}{x^2}$

$= \dfrac{4(x^3 - 2)}{x^2}$

So, $\dfrac{dC}{dx} = 0$ when $x = \sqrt[3]{2}$ m

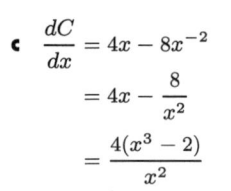

$\dfrac{dC}{dx}$ has sign diagram: $\underset{\sqrt[3]{2}}{- \;\;\; +} \to x$

The minimum cost is when $x = \sqrt[3]{2} \approx 1.26$ m

$\therefore\ y = \dfrac{1}{x^2} \approx 0.630$

and the box is 1.26 m by 1.26 m by 0.630 m.

6 a Differentiating $x^2 y + 2xy^3 = -18$ with respect to x,

$2xy + x^2 \dfrac{dy}{dx} + 2y^3 + 6xy^2 \dfrac{dy}{dx} = 0$

$\therefore\ \dfrac{dy}{dx}(x^2 + 6xy^2) = -2xy - 2y^3$

$\therefore\ \dfrac{dy}{dx} = \dfrac{-2y(x + y^2)}{x(x + 6y^2)}$

b At $(1, -2)$, $\dfrac{dy}{dx} = \dfrac{-2(-2)(1 + (-2)^2)}{1(1 + 6(-2)^2)} = \dfrac{4 \times 5}{25} = \dfrac{4}{5}$

$\therefore$ the tangent has equation $\dfrac{y - (-2)}{x - 1} = \dfrac{4}{5}$ $\therefore\ y + 2 = \dfrac{4}{5}x - \dfrac{4}{5}$ $\therefore\ y = \dfrac{4}{5}x - \dfrac{14}{5}$

7 At $x = A$, $f'(x) = 0$ and $f''(x) = 0$
$\therefore\ f(x)$ has a stationary inflection point at $x = A$.
At $x = B$, $f''(x) = 0$ but $f'(x) \neq 0$
$\therefore\ f(x)$ has a non-stationary inflection point at $x = B$.
$f'(x)$ is above the x-axis for $x \leqslant C$, and below the x-axis for $x \geqslant C$
$\therefore\ f(x)$ is increasing for $x \leqslant C$ and decreasing for $x \geqslant C$, so $f(x)$ has a local maximum at $x = C$.

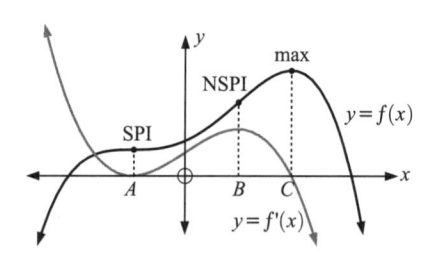

REVIEW SET 21B

1 a $AC = 2x$ m
Now ABC is an isosceles triangle.
$\therefore\ XC = x$
But $BC^2 = BX^2 + XC^2$ {Pythagoras}
$\therefore\ 2500 = BX^2 + x^2$
$\therefore\ BX = \sqrt{2500 - x^2}$
$\therefore\ A(x) = \tfrac{1}{2}(2x)\sqrt{2500 - x^2} = x\sqrt{2500 - x^2}$

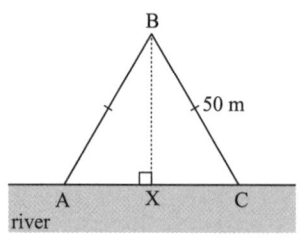

b Now $[A(x)]^2 = x^2(2500 - x^2)$
$\therefore\ A^2 = 2500x^2 - x^4$

$\therefore\ \dfrac{d(A^2)}{dx} = 5000x - 4x^3$

$= 4x(1250 - x^2)$

$= 4x(\sqrt{1250} + x)(\sqrt{1250} - x)$

Sign diagram for $\dfrac{d(A^2)}{dx}$ is: $\underset{0 \quad\quad 25\sqrt{2}}{+ \quad\quad -} \to x$

$\therefore$ maximum area occurs when $x = 25\sqrt{2}$ m ≈ 35.4 m
The corresponding maximum area $= 1250$ m^2.

2 a $s(t) = 15t - \dfrac{60}{(t-1)^2}$ cm, $t \geqslant 0$

$= 15t - 60(t-1)^{-2}$ cm

$\therefore \quad v(t) = 15 + 120(t-1)^{-3}$ cm s^{-1}

$\therefore \quad a(t) = -360(t-1)^{-4}$ cm s^{-2}

c $v(t) = 15 + \dfrac{120}{(t-1)^3}$ cm s^{-1}

$v(t) = 0$ when $15 + \dfrac{120}{(t-1)^3} = 0$

$\therefore \quad 15(t-1)^3 + 120 = 0$

$\therefore \quad (t-1)^3 = -8$

$\therefore \quad t = -1$

$a(t) = -360(t-1)^{-4} = \dfrac{-360}{(t-1)^4}$ cm s^{-2}

where $(t-1)^4$ is always positive. $\therefore \quad a(t) < 0$ for all $t > 0$

The speed increases for $0 \leqslant t < 1$ when $v(t)$ and $a(t)$ have the same sign.

b When $t = 3$, $s(t) = 30$ cm

$v(t) = 30$ cm s^{-1}

$a(t) = -22.5$ cm s^{-2}

The particle is 30 cm right of O, travelling right at 30 cm s^{-1}, and is slowing down at 22.5 cm s^{-2}.

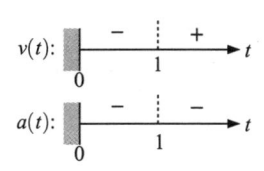

$v(t)$: (sign diagram: − on $0 < t < 1$, + on $t > 1$)

$a(t)$: (sign diagram: − on $0 < t < 1$, − on $t > 1$)

3 Suppose the sheet is bent x cm from each end. To maximise the water carried we need to maximise the area of cross-section.

$A = x(24 - 2x)$, $0 \leqslant x \leqslant 12$

$= 24x - 2x^2$

$\therefore \quad \dfrac{dA}{dx} = 24 - 4x$

So, $\dfrac{dA}{dx} = 0$ when $x = 6$, and $\dfrac{dA}{dx}$ has sign diagram:

The maximum water is held when $x = 6$ cm

$\therefore \quad$ the bends must be made 6 cm from each end.

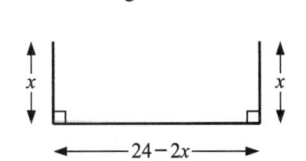

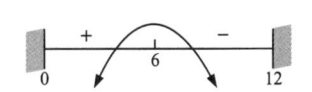

4 a $(2, -1)$ lies on the curve, so

$k = 2^2 - 2(2)(-1)^2 + (-1)^3$

$= 4 - 4 - 1$

$= -1$

c At $(2, -1)$, $\dfrac{dy}{dx} = \dfrac{2(1-2)}{(-1)(-3 - 4 \times 2)}$

$= -\dfrac{2}{11}$

$\therefore \quad$ the gradient of the normal is $\dfrac{11}{2}$

and its equation is $\dfrac{y - (-1)}{x - 2} = \dfrac{11}{2}$

$\therefore \quad y + 1 = \dfrac{11}{2}x - 11$

$\therefore \quad y = \dfrac{11}{2}x - 12$

or $11x - 2y = 24$

b $x^2 - 2xy^2 + y^3 = -1$

Differentiating with respect to x,

$2x - 2y^2 - 4xy \dfrac{dy}{dx} + 3y^2 \dfrac{dy}{dx} = 0$

$\therefore \quad \dfrac{dy}{dx}(3y^2 - 4xy) = 2y^2 - 2x$

$\therefore \quad \dfrac{dy}{dx} = \dfrac{2(y^2 - x)}{y(3y - 4x)}$

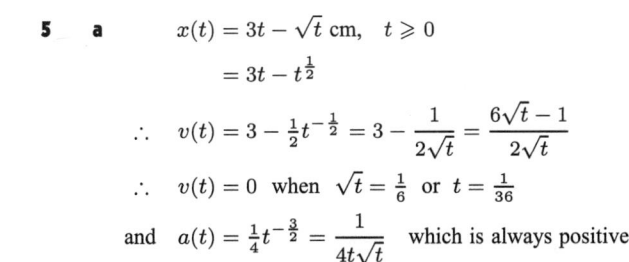

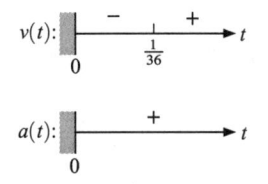

5 a $x(t) = 3t - \sqrt{t}$ cm, $t \geqslant 0$

$= 3t - t^{\frac{1}{2}}$

$\therefore \quad v(t) = 3 - \dfrac{1}{2}t^{-\frac{1}{2}} = 3 - \dfrac{1}{2\sqrt{t}} = \dfrac{6\sqrt{t} - 1}{2\sqrt{t}}$

$\therefore \quad v(t) = 0$ when $\sqrt{t} = \dfrac{1}{6}$ or $t = \dfrac{1}{36}$

and $a(t) = \dfrac{1}{4}t^{-\frac{3}{2}} = \dfrac{1}{4t\sqrt{t}}$ which is always positive

$v(t)$: (sign diagram: − on $0 < t < \tfrac{1}{36}$, + on $t > \tfrac{1}{36}$)

$a(t)$: (sign diagram: + for $t > 0$)

b As $t \to 0^+$, $x \to 0$ cm
$$v \to -\infty \text{ cm s}^{-1}$$
$$a \to \infty \text{ cm s}^{-2}$$
$\therefore$ the particle is at O, moving left and slowing down.

c When $t = 9$, $x(9) = 24$ cm, $v(9) = \frac{17}{6}$ cm s^{-1}, $a(9) = \frac{1}{108}$ cm s^{-2}
the particle is 24 cm right of O, moving right at $\frac{17}{6}$ cm s^{-1} and increasing its speed.

d The particle reverses direction when $t = \frac{1}{36}$ seconds.
$x\left(\frac{1}{36}\right) = \frac{3}{36} - \frac{1}{6} = -\frac{3}{36} = -\frac{1}{12}$ $\therefore$ it is $\frac{1}{12} \approx 0.0833$ cm to the left of O.

e The particle's speed decreases when $v(t)$ and $a(t)$ have different signs, which occurs when $0 < t \leqslant \frac{1}{36}$.

6 $f(x) = \dfrac{x^2 - 1}{x^2 + 1}$

a $f(x)$ cuts the x-axis when $y = 0$
$\therefore$ $x^2 - 1 = 0$ $\therefore$ $x = \pm 1$
which occurs at $(1, 0)$ and $(-1, 0)$
$f(x)$ cuts the y-axis when $x = 0$, at $(0, -1)$.

b As $x^2 \geqslant 0$, $x^2 + 1$ can never be 0.
$\therefore$ there are no vertical asymptotes.

c $f'(x) = \dfrac{2x(x^2 + 1) - (x^2 - 1)2x}{(x^2 + 1)^2}$
$= \dfrac{4x}{(x^2 + 1)^2}$

Sign diagram of $f'(x)$ is: $\xleftarrow{\quad - \quad 0 \quad + \quad} x$

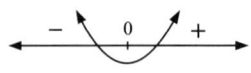

$\therefore$ there is a local minimum at $(0, -1)$

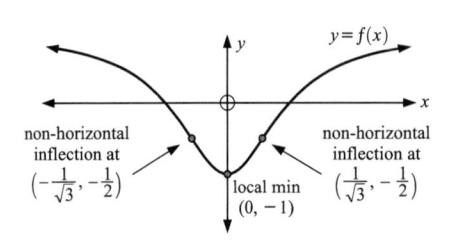

d $f''(x) = \dfrac{4(x^2 + 1)^2 - 4x \times 2(x^2 + 1)(2x)}{(x^2 + 1)^4}$
$= \dfrac{4(x^2 + 1) - 16x^2}{(x^2 + 1)^3}$
$= \dfrac{4 - 12x^2}{(x^2 + 1)^3}$
$= \dfrac{4(1 + \sqrt{3}x)(1 - \sqrt{3}x)}{(x^2 + 1)^3}$

$\therefore$ $f''(x) = 0$ when $x = \pm\frac{1}{\sqrt{3}}$

Sign diagram of $f''(x)$ is: $\xleftarrow{\quad - \quad -\frac{1}{\sqrt{3}} \quad + \quad \frac{1}{\sqrt{3}} \quad - \quad} x$

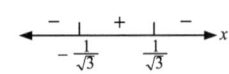

$\therefore$ $f(x)$ has non-stationary inflections at $x = \pm\sqrt{\frac{1}{3}}$.

e Graph of $y = f(x)$ with non-horizontal inflection at $\left(-\frac{1}{\sqrt{3}}, -\frac{1}{2}\right)$, local min $(0, -1)$, non-horizontal inflection at $\left(\frac{1}{\sqrt{3}}, -\frac{1}{2}\right)$.

7 $f(x)$ has a turning point at $x = 0$
$\therefore$ $f'(0) = 0$
As $|x| \to \infty$, $f(x)$ becomes closer to horizontal so $|f'(x)| \to 0$.

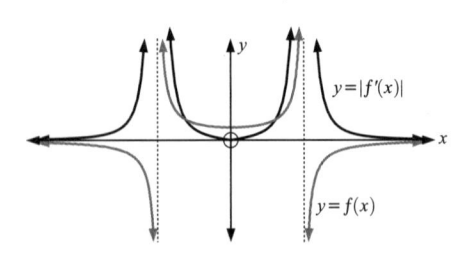

Graph of $y = |f'(x)|$ and $y = f(x)$.

REVIEW SET 21C

1 $f(x) = x^3 - 4x^2 + 4x$
$= x(x^2 - 4x + 4)$
$= x(x - 2)^2$

a $f(x)$ cuts the y-axis when $x = 0$, at $(0, 0)$
$f(x)$ cuts the x-axis when $y = 0$ $\therefore$ $x(x - 2)^2 = 0$
$\therefore$ $x = 0$ or 2
$\therefore$ it cuts the x-axis at $(0, 0)$ and $(2, 0)$.

b $f'(x) = 3x^2 - 8x + 4$
$= (3x - 2)(x - 2)$
which is 0 when $x = \frac{2}{3}$ or 2

Sign diagram of $f'(x)$ is:

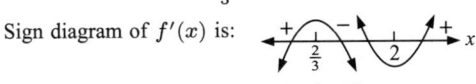

$\begin{array}{ccccc} + & & - & & + \\ \hline & \frac{2}{3} & & 2 & \end{array} \to x$

$\therefore$ there is a local maximum at $(\frac{2}{3}, \frac{32}{27})$,
and a local minimum at $(2, 0)$

$f''(x) = 6x - 8 = 2(3x - 4)$

Sign diagram of $f''(x)$ is:

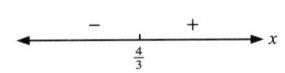

$\begin{array}{ccc} - & & + \\ \hline & \frac{4}{3} & \end{array} \to x$

$\therefore$ there is a non-horizontal inflection at $(\frac{4}{3}, \frac{16}{27})$

c Graph showing $y = f(x)$ with axis intercept at $(0,0)$, local max $(\frac{2}{3}, \frac{32}{27})$, non-horizontal inflection $(\frac{4}{3}, \frac{16}{27})$, local min $(2, 0)$.

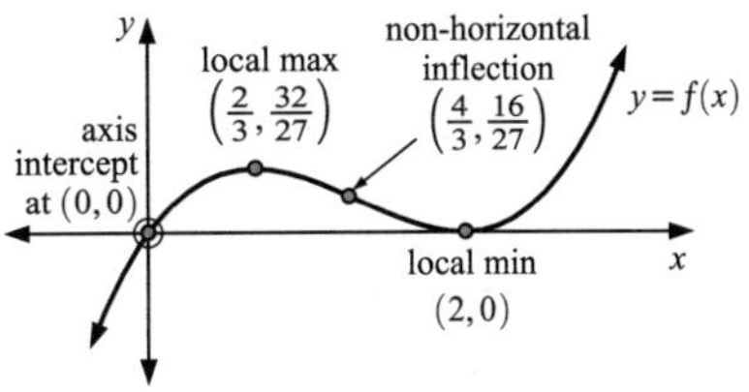

2 a $P = 200$ m
But $P = 2x + 2y + \pi x$
$\therefore \quad 200 = 2x + 2y + \pi x$
$\therefore \quad 2y = 200 - 2x - \pi x$
$\therefore \quad y = 100 - x - \frac{\pi}{2}x$

b Area of lawn $= 2x \times y + \frac{1}{2}\pi x^2$
$= 2x\left[100 - x - \frac{\pi}{2}x\right] + \frac{1}{2}\pi x^2$
$= 200x - 2x^2 - \pi x^2 + \frac{1}{2}\pi x^2$
$= 200x - 2x^2 - \frac{\pi}{2}x^2$
$\therefore \quad A = 200x - \left(2 + \frac{\pi}{2}\right)x^2$ m²

c $\frac{dA}{dx} = 200 - 2\left(2 + \frac{\pi}{2}\right)x = 200 - (4 + \pi)x$

$\therefore \quad \frac{dA}{dx} = 0$ when $(4 + \pi)x = 200$ $\quad \therefore \quad x = \frac{200}{4 + \pi}$

and the sign diagram for $\frac{dA}{dx}$ is:

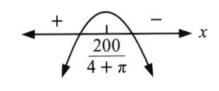

$\begin{array}{ccc} + & & - \\ \hline & \frac{200}{4+\pi} & \end{array} \to x$

$\therefore$ maximum area occurs when $x = \frac{200}{4 + \pi} \approx 28.0$ m

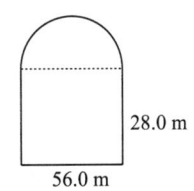

(Diagram: shape with dimensions 28.0 m and 56.0 m)

3 a $f(x) = \frac{x^2 + 2x}{x - 2} = \frac{(x - 2)(x + 4) + 8}{x - 2} = x + 4 + \frac{8}{x - 2}$

$\therefore$ there is a vertical asymptote of $x = 2$ $\quad$ {as $x \to 2$, $|f(x)| \to \infty$}
and an oblique asymptote of $y = x + 4$ $\quad$ {as $|x| \to \infty$, $f(x) \to x + 4$}

b $f'(x) = 1 - \frac{8}{(x - 2)^2} = \frac{(x - 2)^2 - 8}{(x - 2)^2}$

$= \frac{x^2 - 4x - 4}{(x - 2)^2}$

$\therefore \quad f'(x) = 0$ when $x^2 - 4x - 4 = 0$

$\therefore \quad x = \frac{4 \pm \sqrt{(-4)^2 - 4(-4)}}{2} = 2 \pm 2\sqrt{2}$

$\therefore \quad f'(x)$ has sign diagram

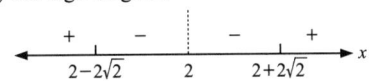

$\begin{array}{ccccc} + & & - & & + \\ \hline & 2-2\sqrt{2} & 2 & 2+2\sqrt{2} & \end{array} \to x$

Now $f(2 + 2\sqrt{2}) = 2 + 2\sqrt{2} + 4 + \frac{8}{2\sqrt{2}}$
$= 6 + 2\sqrt{2} + 2\sqrt{2}$
$= 6 + 4\sqrt{2}$

and $f(2 - 2\sqrt{2}) = 2 - 2\sqrt{2} + 4 + \frac{8}{-2\sqrt{2}}$
$= 6 - 2\sqrt{2} - 2\sqrt{2}$
$= 6 - 4\sqrt{2}$

$\therefore$ $f(x)$ has a local maximum at $(2 - 2\sqrt{2}, 6 - 4\sqrt{2})$ and a local minimum at $(2 + 2\sqrt{2}, 6 + 4\sqrt{2})$.

c When $f(x) = 0$, $x^2 + 2x = 0$
$\therefore \quad x(x + 2) = 0$
$\therefore \quad x = -2$ or 0

$\therefore$ the x-intercepts are -2 and 0
Also, $f(0) = 0$, so the y-intercept is 0

d

[Graph showing function with local max at $(2-2\sqrt{2}, 6-4\sqrt{2})$, local min at $(2+2\sqrt{2}, 6+4\sqrt{2})$, asymptote $y = x+4$, vertical asymptote $x=2$, function $y = \dfrac{x^2+2x}{x-2}$]

e $f(x) = p$ has two real distinct roots if
$p < 6 - 4\sqrt{2}$ or $p > 6 + 4\sqrt{2}$.

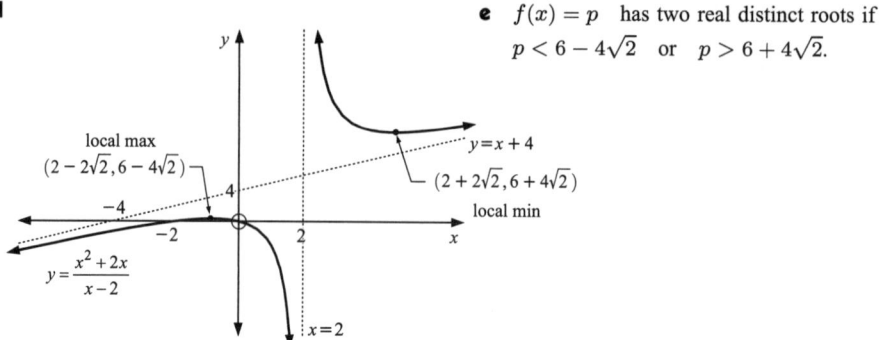

4 a

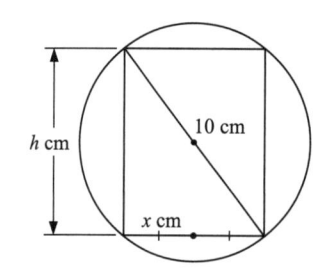

[Diagram of cylinder inscribed in sphere of diameter 10 cm, with height h cm and base radius x cm]

Let the height of the cylinder be h cm.

$\therefore \quad (2x)^2 + h^2 = 10^2$ {Pythagoras}

$\therefore \quad h = \sqrt{100 - 4x^2}$

$\therefore \quad V(x) = $ area of base $\times$ height

$\qquad = \pi x^2 \times \sqrt{100 - 4x^2}$

So, $V(x) = \pi x^2 \sqrt{100 - 4x^2}$ cm^3

b Now $V^2 = \pi^2 x^4 (100 - 4x^2)$
$\qquad\quad = \pi^2 (100x^4 - 4x^6)$

$\therefore \quad \dfrac{d(V^2)}{dx} = \pi^2 (400x^3 - 24x^5)$

$\qquad\qquad\quad = 8\pi^2 x^3 (50 - 3x^2)$

$\qquad\qquad\quad = 8\pi^2 x^3 (\sqrt{50} + \sqrt{3}x)(\sqrt{50} - \sqrt{3}x)$

$\therefore \quad \dfrac{d(V^2)}{dx} = 0$ when $x = \sqrt{\dfrac{50}{3}}$ {as $x > 0$}

and $\dfrac{d(V^2)}{dx}$ has sign diagram:

[Sign diagram: + for $0 < x < \sqrt{50/3}$, − for $x > \sqrt{50/3}$]

$\therefore$ maximum V occurs when $x = \sqrt{\dfrac{50}{3}} \approx 4.08$

$\therefore$ radius ≈ 4.08 cm, height $= \sqrt{100 - 4\left(\dfrac{50}{3}\right)} \approx 5.77$ cm

5 a $\triangle$s LQX and XPM are similar.

$\therefore \quad \dfrac{LQ}{XP} = \dfrac{LX}{XM} = \dfrac{QX}{PM}$

$\therefore \quad \dfrac{LQ}{1} = \dfrac{8}{PM}$

$\therefore \quad LQ = \dfrac{8}{PM}$

$\therefore \quad LQ = \dfrac{8}{x}$ km

b $L(x) = LX + XM$

$\qquad = \sqrt{\left(\dfrac{8}{x}\right)^2 + 8^2} + \sqrt{1^2 + x^2}$

$\qquad = 8\sqrt{\dfrac{1}{x^2} + 1} + \sqrt{x^2 + 1}$

$\qquad = \dfrac{8}{x}\sqrt{1 + x^2} + 1\sqrt{1 + x^2}$

$\qquad = \sqrt{x^2 + 1}\left(\dfrac{8}{x} + 1\right)$

$\therefore \quad L(x) = \sqrt{x^2 + 1}\left(1 + \dfrac{8}{x}\right)$

and $L^2 = (x^2 + 1)\left(1 + \dfrac{8}{x}\right)^2$

c $\dfrac{d[L(x)]^2}{dx} = 2x\left(1+\dfrac{8}{x}\right)^2 + (x^2+1)2\left(1+\dfrac{8}{x}\right)\left(-\dfrac{8}{x^2}\right)$ {product rule}

$= 2\left(1+\dfrac{8}{x}\right)\left[x\left(1+\dfrac{8}{x}\right) - (x^2+1)\left(\dfrac{8}{x^2}\right)\right]$

$= 2\left(1+\dfrac{8}{x}\right)\left[x + 8 - 8 - \dfrac{8}{x^2}\right]$

$= 2\left(\dfrac{x+8}{x}\right)\left(\dfrac{x^3-8}{x^2}\right)$

$\dfrac{d[L(x)]^2}{dx} = 0$ when $x = -8$ or $x^3 = 8$, but $x > 0$ so $\dfrac{d[L(x)]^2}{dx} = 0$ when $x = 2$

The sign diagram for $\dfrac{d[L(x)]^2}{dx}$ is: [sign diagram: − then + with critical point at 2, 0 at left]

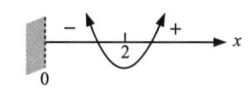

$\therefore$ minimum $L(x)$ occurs when $x = 2$ and the shortest length is $\sqrt{2^2+1}\left(1+\dfrac{8}{2}\right) = 5\sqrt{5}$
≈ 11.2 km

6 When the box is manufactured its base is $(2k - 2x)$ by $(k - 2x)$ and height is x cm.

$\therefore V = x(2k - 2x)(k - 2x)$
$\therefore V = x(2k^2 - 4kx - 2xk + 4x^2)$
$= 2k^2x - 6kx^2 + 4x^3$
$\therefore \dfrac{dV}{dx} = 2k^2 - 12kx + 12x^2$
$= 2(6x^2 - 6kx + k^2)$

So, $\dfrac{dV}{dx} = 0$ when $x = \dfrac{6k \pm \sqrt{36k^2 - 4(6)k^2}}{12}$

$= \dfrac{6k \pm k\sqrt{12}}{12}$

$= \dfrac{k}{2} \pm \dfrac{k}{\sqrt{12}}$

$= \dfrac{k}{2} - \dfrac{k}{2\sqrt{3}}$ {as $x \leqslant \dfrac{k}{2}$}

$= \dfrac{k}{2}\left(1 - \dfrac{1}{\sqrt{3}}\right)$

The sign diagram of $\dfrac{dV}{dx}$ is: [sign diagram: + then − with critical points at $\frac{k}{2}(1-\frac{1}{\sqrt{3}})$ and $\frac{k}{2}$]

$\therefore$ maximum capacity occurs when $x = \dfrac{k}{2}\left(1 - \dfrac{1}{\sqrt{3}}\right)$.

7 At $x = B$, $f''(x) = 0$ but $f'(x) \neq 0$
$\therefore$ $f(x)$ has a non-stationary inflection point at $x = B$.
$f'(x)$ is above the x-axis for $x \leqslant A$ and $x \geqslant C$, and below the x-axis for $A \leqslant x \leqslant C$
$\therefore$ $f(x)$ is increasing for $x \leqslant A$, decreasing for $A \leqslant x \leqslant C$, then increasing for $x \geqslant C$
$\therefore$ $f(x)$ has a local maximum at $x = A$ and a local minimum at $x = C$.

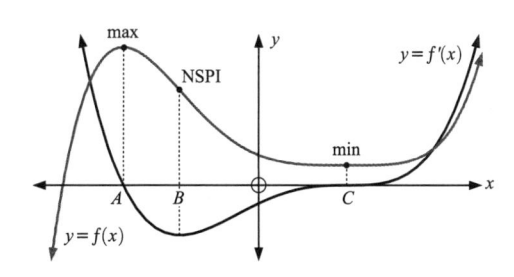

Chapter 22
DERIVATIVES OF EXPONENTIAL AND LOGARITHMIC FUNCTIONS

EXERCISE 22A

1 a $f(x) = e^{4x}$
$\therefore f'(x) = 4e^{4x}$

b $f(x) = e^x + 3$
$\therefore f'(x) = e^x + 0$
$= e^x$

c $f(x) = \exp(-2x)$
$= e^{-2x}$
$\therefore f'(x) = -2e^{-2x}$

d $f(x) = e^{\frac{x}{2}}$
$\therefore f'(x) = \frac{1}{2}e^{\frac{x}{2}}$

e $f(x) = 2e^{-\frac{x}{2}}$
$\therefore f'(x) = 2e^{-\frac{x}{2}}\left(-\frac{1}{2}\right)$
$= -e^{-\frac{x}{2}}$

f $f(x) = 1 - 2e^{-x}$
$\therefore f'(x) = 0 - 2e^{-x}(-1)$
$= 2e^{-x}$

g $f(x) = 4e^{\frac{x}{2}} - 3e^{-x}$
$\therefore f'(x) = 4e^{\frac{x}{2}}\left(\frac{1}{2}\right) - 3e^{-x}(-1)$
$= 2e^{\frac{x}{2}} + 3e^{-x}$

h $f(x) = \dfrac{e^x + e^{-x}}{2} = \frac{1}{2}(e^x + e^{-x})$
$\therefore f'(x) = \frac{1}{2}(e^x + e^{-x}(-1))$
$= \frac{1}{2}(e^x - e^{-x})$

i $f(x) = e^{-x^2}$
$\therefore f'(x) = e^{-x^2}(-2x)$
$= -2xe^{-x^2}$

j $f(x) = e^{\frac{1}{x}}$
$\therefore f'(x) = e^{\frac{1}{x}}\left(-\dfrac{1}{x^2}\right)$
$= -\dfrac{e^{\frac{1}{x}}}{x^2}$

k $f(x) = 10\left(1 + e^{2x}\right)$
$= 10 + 10e^{2x}$
$\therefore f'(x) = 0 + 10e^{2x}(2)$
$= 20e^{2x}$

l $f(x) = 20\left(1 - e^{-2x}\right)$
$= 20 - 20e^{-2x}$
$\therefore f'(x) = 0 - 20e^{-2x}(-2)$
$= 40e^{-2x}$

m $f(x) = e^{2x+1}$
$\therefore f'(x) = e^{2x+1}(2)$
$= 2e^{2x+1}$

n $f(x) = e^{\frac{x}{4}}$
$\therefore f'(x) = e^{\frac{x}{4}}\left(\frac{1}{4}\right)$
$= \frac{1}{4}e^{\frac{x}{4}}$

o $f(x) = e^{1-2x^2}$
$\therefore f'(x) = e^{1-2x^2}(-4x)$
$= -4xe^{1-2x^2}$

p $f(x) = e^{-0.02x}$
$\therefore f'(x) = e^{-0.02x} \times (-0.02)$
$= -0.02e^{-0.02x}$

2 a $f(x) = xe^x$
$\therefore f'(x) = 1e^x + xe^x$ {product rule}
$= e^x + xe^x$

b $f(x) = x^3 e^{-x}$
$\therefore f'(x) = 3x^2 e^{-x} + x^3(-e^{-x})$
{product rule}
$= 3x^2 e^{-x} - x^3 e^{-x}$

c $f(x) = \dfrac{e^x}{x}$
$\therefore f'(x) = \dfrac{e^x x - e^x(1)}{x^2}$ {quotient rule}
$= \dfrac{xe^x - e^x}{x^2}$

d $f(x) = \dfrac{x}{e^x}$
$\therefore f'(x) = \dfrac{1e^x - xe^x}{(e^x)^2}$ {quotient rule}
$= \dfrac{e^x(1-x)}{(e^x)^2} = \dfrac{1-x}{e^x}$

e $f(x) = x^2 e^{3x}$
$\therefore f'(x) = 2xe^{3x} + 3x^2 e^{3x}$ {product rule}

f $f(x) = \dfrac{e^x}{\sqrt{x}}$
$\therefore f'(x) = \dfrac{e^x \sqrt{x} - \dfrac{e^x}{2\sqrt{x}}}{(\sqrt{x})^2}$ {quotient rule}
$= \dfrac{xe^x - \frac{1}{2}e^x}{x\sqrt{x}}$

g $f(x) = \sqrt{x}e^{-x}$

$\therefore\ f'(x) = \dfrac{1}{2\sqrt{x}}e^{-x} - \sqrt{x}e^{-x}$

{product rule}

h $f(x) = \dfrac{e^x + 2}{e^{-x} + 1}$

$\therefore\ f'(x) = \dfrac{e^x(e^{-x} + 1) - (e^x + 2)\left(-e^{-x}\right)}{(e^{-x} + 1)^2}$

{product rule}

$= \dfrac{1 + e^x + 1 + 2e^{-x}}{(e^{-x} + 1)^2}$

$= \dfrac{2 + e^x + 2e^{-x}}{(e^{-x} + 1)^2}$

3 a $f(x) = (e^x + 2)^4$

$= u^4$ where $u = e^x + 2$

$\dfrac{dy}{dx} = \dfrac{dy}{du}\dfrac{du}{dx}$ {chain rule}

$= 4u^3(e^x)$

$\therefore\ f'(x) = 4(e^x + 2)^3(e^x)$

$= 4e^x(e^x + 2)^3$

b $f(x) = \dfrac{1}{1 - e^{-x}}$

$= u^{-1}$ where $u = 1 - e^{-x}$

$\dfrac{dy}{dx} = \dfrac{dy}{du}\dfrac{du}{dx}$ {chain rule}

$= -u^{-2}(e^{-x})$

$\therefore\ f'(x) = -\dfrac{e^{-x}}{(1 - e^{-x})^2}$

c $f(x) = \sqrt{e^{2x} + 10}$

$= u^{\frac{1}{2}}$ where $u = e^{2x} + 10$

$\dfrac{dy}{dx} = \dfrac{dy}{du}\dfrac{du}{dx}$ {chain rule}

$= \tfrac{1}{2}u^{-\frac{1}{2}}(2e^{2x})$

$\therefore\ f'(x) = \dfrac{e^{2x}}{\sqrt{e^{2x} + 10}}$

d $f(x) = \dfrac{1}{(1 - e^{3x})^2}$

$= u^{-2}$ where $u = 1 - e^{3x}$

$\dfrac{dy}{dx} = \dfrac{dy}{du}\dfrac{du}{dx}$ {chain rule}

$= -2u^{-3}(-3e^{3x}) = \dfrac{6e^{3x}}{u^3}$

$\therefore\ f'(x) = \dfrac{6e^{3x}}{(1 - e^{3x})^3}$

e $f(x) = \dfrac{1}{\sqrt{1 - e^{-x}}}$

$= u^{-\frac{1}{2}}$ where $u = 1 - e^{-x}$

$\dfrac{dy}{dx} = \dfrac{dy}{du}\dfrac{du}{dx}$ {chain rule}

$= -\tfrac{1}{2}u^{-\frac{3}{2}}(e^{-x})$

$= \dfrac{-e^{-x}}{2u^{\frac{3}{2}}}$

$\therefore\ f'(x) = \dfrac{-e^{-x}}{2(1 - e^{-x})^{\frac{3}{2}}}$

f $f(x) = x\sqrt{1 - 2e^{-x}}$

$= xu^{\frac{1}{2}}$ where $u = 1 - 2e^{-x}$

$\therefore\ f'(x) = 1u^{\frac{1}{2}} + x \times \tfrac{1}{2}u^{-\frac{1}{2}}\dfrac{du}{dx}$

{product rule and chain rule}

$= 1\sqrt{u} + x\tfrac{1}{2}u^{-\frac{1}{2}}2e^{-x}$

$= \dfrac{\sqrt{1 - 2e^{-x}}}{1} + \dfrac{xe^{-x}}{\sqrt{1 - 2e^{-x}}}$

$\therefore\ f'(x) = \dfrac{1 - 2e^{-x} + xe^{-x}}{\sqrt{1 - 2e^{-x}}}$

4 a $y = Ae^{kx}$

i $\dfrac{dy}{dx} = Ae^{kx}(k)$

$= k(Ae^{kx})$

$= ky$

ii $\dfrac{d^2y}{dx^2} = k\dfrac{dy}{dx}$ {differentiating **i**}

$= k(ky)$

$= k^2y$

b Prediction: $\dfrac{d^ny}{dx^n} = k^ny$

P_n is "if $y = Ae^{kx}$, then $\dfrac{d^ny}{dx^n} = k^ny$", $n \in \mathbb{Z}^+$.

Proof: (By the principle of mathematical induction)

(1) If $n = 1$, $\dfrac{d^1y}{dx^1} = \dfrac{dy}{dx} = ky = k^1y$ {from **a i**} $\therefore\ P_1$ is true.

(2) If P_m is true, then $\dfrac{d^m y}{dx^m} = k^m y$

Now $\dfrac{d^{m+1} y}{dx^{m+1}} = \dfrac{d}{dx}\left(\dfrac{d^m y}{dx^m}\right)$

$= \dfrac{d}{dx}(k^m y)$ {using P_m}

$= k^m \dfrac{dy}{dx}$

$= k^m (ky)$

$= k^{m+1} y$

Thus P_{m+1} is true whenever P_m is true, and P_1 is true

∴ P_n is true for all $n \in \mathbb{Z}^+$ {Principle of mathematical induction}

5 $y = 2e^{3x} + 5e^{4x}$ ∴ $\dfrac{dy}{dx} = 6e^{3x} + 20e^{4x}$ and $\dfrac{d^2 y}{dx^2} = 18e^{3x} + 80e^{4x}$

Now $\dfrac{d^2 y}{dx^2} - 7\dfrac{dy}{dx} + 12y = \left(18e^{3x} + 80e^{4x}\right) - 7\left(6e^{3x} + 20e^{4x}\right) + 12\left(2e^{3x} + 5e^{4x}\right)$

$= 18e^{3x} + 80e^{4x} - 42e^{3x} - 140e^{4x} + 24e^{3x} + 60e^{4x}$

$= e^{3x}[18 - 42 + 24] + e^{4x}[80 - 140 + 60]$

$= e^{3x}(0) + e^{4x}(0)$

$= 0$

∴ $\dfrac{d^2 y}{dx^2} - 7\dfrac{dy}{dx} + 12y = 0$

6 $x^3 e^{3y} + 4x^2 y^3 = 27e^{-2x}$

∴ $3x^2 e^{3y} + x^3\left(3e^{3y}\dfrac{dy}{dx}\right) + 8xy^3 + 4x^2\left(3y^2\dfrac{dy}{dx}\right) = 27(-2e^{-2x})$ {product rule}

∴ $\dfrac{dy}{dx}(3x^3 e^{3y} + 12x^2 y^2) = -54e^{-2x} - 3x^2 e^{3y} - 8xy^3$

∴ $\dfrac{dy}{dx} = \dfrac{-54e^{-2x} - 3x^2 e^{3y} - 8xy^3}{3x^3 e^{3y} + 12x^2 y^2}$

$= \dfrac{-(54e^{-2x} + 3x^2 e^{3y} + 8xy^3)}{3x^2(xe^{3y} + 4y^2)}$

7 a $y = xe^{-x}$

∴ $\dfrac{dy}{dx} = 1e^{-x} - xe^{-x}$ {product rule}

$= e^{-x}(1 - x)$

$= \dfrac{1 - x}{e^x}$ which has sign diagram:

∴ at $x = 1$, $y = 1e^{-1} = \dfrac{1}{e}$ we have a maximum turning point.

∴ we have a local maximum at $(1, \dfrac{1}{e})$.

b $y = x^2 e^x$

∴ $\dfrac{dy}{dx} = 2xe^x + x^2 e^x$ {product rule}

$= xe^x(2 + x)$ which has sign diagram:

∴ at $x = -2$, $y = 4e^{-2}$, we have a maximum turning point
and at $x = 0$, $y = 0$, we have a minimum turning point.

∴ we have a local maximum at $(-2, \dfrac{4}{e^2})$, and a local minimum at $(0, 0)$.

c $\quad y = \dfrac{e^x}{x}$

$\therefore \quad \dfrac{dy}{dx} = \dfrac{e^x x - e^x(1)}{x^2}$ {quotient rule}

$\quad = \dfrac{e^x(x-1)}{x^2}$ which has sign diagram:

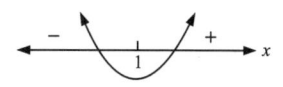

$\therefore$ at $x = 1$, $y = \dfrac{e^1}{1} = e$ we have a minimum turning point.

$\therefore$ we have a local minimum at $(1, e)$.

d $\quad y = e^{-x}(x+2)$

$\therefore \quad \dfrac{dy}{dx} = -e^{-x}(x+2) + e^{-x}$ {product rule}

$\quad = e^{-x}(-x - 2 + 1)$

$\quad = e^{-x}(-x - 1)$ which has sign diagram:

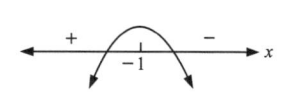

$\therefore$ at $x = -1$, $y = e(-1+2) = e$ we have a maximum turning point.

$\therefore$ we have a local maximum at $(-1, e)$.

EXERCISE 22B

1 a $\quad N = 50e^{2t}$
$\therefore \quad \ln N = \ln(50e^{2t})$
$\quad = \ln 50 + \ln e^{2t}$ $\quad \{\ln ab = \ln a + \ln b\}$
$\therefore \quad \ln N = \ln 50 + 2t$ $\quad \{\ln e^n = n\}$

b $\quad P = 8.69e^{-0.0541t}$
$\therefore \quad \ln P = \ln(8.69e^{-0.0541t})$
$\quad = \ln 8.69 + \ln e^{-0.0541t}$
$\therefore \quad \ln P = \ln 8.69 - 0.0541t$

c $\quad S = a^2 e^{-kt}$
$\therefore \quad \ln S = \ln(a^2 e^{-kt})$
$\quad = \ln a^2 + \ln e^{-kt}$
$\therefore \quad \ln S = 2\ln a - kt \quad \{\ln a^n = n \ln a\}$

2 a $\ln e^2 = 2\ln e$
$\quad = 2(1)$
$\quad = 2$

b $\ln \sqrt{e} = \ln e^{\frac{1}{2}}$
$\quad = \frac{1}{2}\ln e$
$\quad = \frac{1}{2}$

c $\ln\left(\dfrac{1}{e}\right) = \ln e^{-1}$
$\quad = -1\ln e$
$\quad = -1$

d $\ln\left(\dfrac{1}{\sqrt{e}}\right)$
$\quad = \ln e^{-\frac{1}{2}}$
$\quad = -\frac{1}{2}\ln e$
$\quad = -\frac{1}{2}(1)$
$\quad = -\frac{1}{2}$

e $e^{\ln 3} = 3$

f $e^{2\ln 3} = e^{\ln 3^2}$
$\quad = e^{\ln 9}$
$\quad = 9$

g $e^{-\ln 5} = e^{\ln 5^{-1}}$
$\quad = e^{\ln \frac{1}{5}}$
$\quad = \frac{1}{5}$

h $e^{-2\ln 2} = e^{\ln 2^{-2}}$
$\quad = e^{\ln \frac{1}{4}}$
$\quad = \frac{1}{4}$

3 a Let $2 = e^x$
$\therefore \quad \ln 2 = x$
$\therefore \quad 2 = e^{\ln 2}$

b Let $10 = e^x$
$\therefore \quad \ln 10 = x$
$\therefore \quad 10 = e^{\ln 10}$

c Let $a = e^x$
$\therefore \quad \ln a = x$
$\therefore \quad a = e^{\ln a}$

d Let $a^x = e^k$
$\therefore \quad \ln a^x = k$
$\therefore \quad x \ln a = k$
$\therefore \quad a^x = e^{x \ln a}$

4 a $\quad e^x = 2$
$\therefore \quad \ln e^x = \ln 2$
$\therefore \quad x = \ln 2$

b $e^x = -2$ has no solutions
as $e^x > 0$ for all x

c $e^x = 0$ has no solutions
as $e^x > 0$ for all x

d $e^{2x} = 2e^x$
$\therefore \; e^x(e^x - 2) = 0$
$\therefore \;\; e^x = 2 \;\; \{\text{as } e^x > 0\}$
$\therefore \;\;\; x = \ln 2$

e $e^x = e^{-x}$
$\therefore \;\; x = -x$
$\therefore \; 2x = 0$
$\therefore \;\; x = 0$

f $e^{2x} - 5e^x + 6 = 0$
$\therefore \; (e^x - 3)(e^x - 2) = 0$
$\therefore \;\; e^x = 3 \text{ or } 2$
$\therefore \;\; x = \ln 3 \text{ or } \ln 2$

g $e^x + 2 = 3e^{-x}$
$\therefore \;\; e^{2x} + 2e^x = 3 \;\; \{\times e^x\}$
$\therefore \;\; e^{2x} + 2e^x - 3 = 0$
$\therefore \; (e^x + 3)(e^x - 1) = 0$
$\therefore \;\; e^x = -3 \text{ or } 1$
$\therefore \;\; e^x = 1 \;\; \{\text{as } e^x > 0\}$
$\therefore \;\; x = \ln 1$
$\therefore \;\; x = 0$

h $1 + 12e^{-x} = e^x$
$\therefore \;\; e^x + 12 = e^{2x} \;\; \{\times e^x\}$
$\therefore \; e^{2x} - e^x - 12 = 0$
$\therefore \; (e^x - 4)(e^x + 3) = 0$
$\therefore \;\; e^x = 4 \text{ or } -3$
$\therefore \;\; e^x = 4 \;\; \{\text{as } e^x > 0\}$
$\therefore \;\; x = \ln 4$

i $e^x + e^{-x} = 3$
$\therefore \;\; e^{2x} + 1 = 3e^x \;\; \{\times e^x\}$
$\therefore \; e^{2x} - 3e^x + 1 = 0$
$\therefore \;\; e^x = \dfrac{3 \pm \sqrt{9 - 4}}{2}$
$\therefore \;\; e^x = \dfrac{3 \pm \sqrt{5}}{2}$
$\therefore \;\; x = \ln\left(\dfrac{3 + \sqrt{5}}{2}\right) \text{ or } \ln\left(\dfrac{3 - \sqrt{5}}{2}\right)$
$\approx 0.962 \text{ or } -0.962$

5 a $y = 2^x$
$\therefore \; \dfrac{dy}{dx} = 2^x \ln 2$

b $y = 5^x$
$\therefore \; \dfrac{dy}{dx} = 5^x \ln 5$

c $y = x\, 2^x$
$\therefore \; \dfrac{dy}{dx} = \dfrac{d}{dx}(x) 2^x + x\, \dfrac{d}{dx}(2^x)$
              {product rule}
$= 2^x + x\, 2^x \ln 2$

d $y = x^3 6^{-x} = \dfrac{x^3}{6^x}$
$\therefore \; \dfrac{dy}{dx} = \dfrac{\dfrac{d}{dx}(x^3) 6^x - x^3 \dfrac{d}{dx}(6^x)}{6^{2x}}$
              {quotient rule}
$= \dfrac{3x^2 6^x - x^3 \times 6^x \ln 6}{6^{2x}}$
$= \dfrac{x^2(3 - x \ln 6)}{6^x}$

e $y = \dfrac{2^x}{x}$
$\therefore \; \dfrac{dy}{dx} = \dfrac{\dfrac{d}{dx}(2^x)x - 2^x \dfrac{d}{dx}(x)}{x^2}$
              {quotient rule}
$= \dfrac{2^x \ln 2 \times x - 2^x}{x^2}$
$= \dfrac{2^x(x \ln 2 - 1)}{x^2}$

f $y = \dfrac{x}{3^x}$
$\therefore \; \dfrac{dy}{dx} = \dfrac{\dfrac{d}{dx}(x) 3^x - x \dfrac{d}{dx}(3^x)}{3^{2x}}$
              {quotient rule}
$= \dfrac{3^x - x \times 3^x \ln 3}{3^{2x}}$
$= \dfrac{1 - x \ln 3}{3^x}$

6 **a** $y_1 = e^x$ and $y_2 = e^{2x} - 6$
meet when $y_1 = y_2$
$\therefore\ e^x = e^{2x} - 6$
$\therefore\ e^{2x} - e^x - 6 = 0$
$\therefore\ (e^x - 3)(e^x + 2) = 0$
$\therefore\ e^x = 3$ or -2
$\therefore\ e^x = 3$ {as $e^x > 0$}
$\therefore\ x = \ln 3$ and $y = e^x = 3$
$\therefore\ $ they meet at $(\ln 3, 3)$.

b $y_1 = 2e^x + 1$ and $y_2 = 7 - e^x$
meet when $y_1 = y_2$
$\therefore\ 2e^x + 1 = 7 - e^x$
$\therefore\ 3e^x = 6$
$\therefore\ e^x = 2$
$\therefore\ x = \ln 2$ and $y = 7 - e^x = 5$
$\therefore\ $ they meet at $(\ln 2, 5)$.

c $y_1 = 3 - e^x$ and $y_2 = 5e^{-x} - 3$
meet when $y_1 = y_2$
$\therefore\ 3 - e^x = 5e^{-x} - 3$
$\therefore\ 3e^x - e^{2x} = 5 - 3e^x$ $\{\times e^x\}$
$\therefore\ e^{2x} - 6e^x + 5 = 0$
$\therefore\ (e^x - 5)(e^x - 1) = 0$
$\therefore\ e^x = 1$ or 5
$\therefore\ x = 0$ or $\ln 5$

When $x = 0$, $y = 3 - e^0 = 3 - 1 = 2$
When $x = \ln 5$, $y = 3 - e^{\ln 5} = 3 - 5 = -2$
$\therefore\ $ they meet at $(0, 2)$ and $(\ln 5, -2)$.

7 **a** x-intercepts occur when $y = 0$
For $f(x) = e^x - 3$, $e^x - 3 = 0$
$\therefore\ e^x = 3$
$\therefore\ x = \ln 3$

$\therefore\ f(x)$ has x-intercept $\ln 3$
and $g(x)$ has x-intercept $\ln \frac{5}{3}$.

y-intercepts occur when $x = 0$
Now $f(0) = e^0 - 3 = -2$ and $g(0) = 3 - \dfrac{5}{e^0} = 3 - 5 = -2$
$\therefore\ $ both $f(x)$ and $g(x)$ have y-intercept -2.

and for $g(x) = 3 - \dfrac{5}{e^x}$, $3 - \dfrac{5}{e^x} = 0$
$\therefore\ \dfrac{3e^x - 5}{e^x} = 0$
$\therefore\ 3e^x - 5 = 0$
$\therefore\ e^x = \dfrac{5}{3}$
$\therefore\ x = \ln \dfrac{5}{3}$

b As $x \to \infty$, $f(x) \to \infty$
$x \to -\infty$, $f(x) \to -3$ (above)

As $x \to \infty$, $g(x) \to 3$ (below)
$x \to -\infty$, $g(x) \to -\infty$

c $f(x)$ and $g(x)$ meet when
$e^x - 3 = 3 - 5e^{-x}$
$\therefore\ e^{2x} - 3e^x = 3e^x - 5$ $\{\times e^x\}$
$\therefore\ e^{2x} - 6e^x + 5 = 0$
$\therefore\ (e^x - 5)(e^x - 1) = 0$
$\therefore\ e^x = 5$ or 1
$\therefore\ x = \ln 5$ or 0
Now $f(\ln 5) = e^{\ln 5} - 3 = 5 - 3 = 2$
and $f(0) = -2$
$\therefore\ f(x)$ and $g(x)$ meet at $(0, -2)$ and $(\ln 5, 2)$.

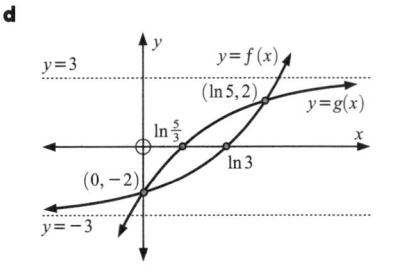

d

8 **a** Consider $y = e^x - 3e^{-x}$
It cuts the x-axis at P when $y = 0$
$\therefore\ e^x - 3e^{-x} = 0$
$\therefore\ e^{2x} - 3 = 0$ $\{\times e^x\}$
$\therefore\ e^{2x} = 3$
$\therefore\ 2x = \ln 3$
$\therefore\ x = \tfrac{1}{2} \ln 3$

and the y-axis at Q when $x = 0$
$\therefore\ y = e^0 - 3e^0$
$= 1 - 3$
$= -2$

$\therefore\ $ P is $(\tfrac{1}{2} \ln 3, 0)$ and Q is $(0, -2)$.

b $\dfrac{dy}{dx} = e^x + 3e^{-x}$

$= e^x + \dfrac{3}{e^x}$

Since $e^x > 0$ for all x,

$\dfrac{dy}{dx} > 0$ for all x

$\therefore$ the function is increasing for all x

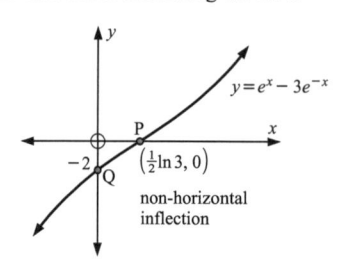

c $\dfrac{dy}{dx} = e^x + 3x^{-x}$

$\therefore \dfrac{d^2y}{dx^2} = e^x - 3e^{-x}$

$= y$

Above x-axis $y > 0$ $\therefore \dfrac{d^2y}{dx^2} > 0$

$\therefore$ the function is concave up

Below x-axis $y < 0$ $\therefore \dfrac{d^2y}{dx^2} < 0$

$\therefore$ the function is concave down

$\therefore$ a non-horizontal inflection occurs when $y = 0$

d

[Graph showing $y = e^x - 3e^{-x}$ with point P at $(\frac{1}{2}\ln 3, 0)$, Q marked, intercept at -2, and non-horizontal inflection labeled]

9 a Consider $y = 4^x - 2^x$.

The x-intercept occurs when $y = 0$

$\therefore 4^x - 2^x = 0$

$\therefore 2^x(2^x - 1) = 0$

$\therefore 2^x = 1$ $\{2^x > 0\}$

$\therefore x = 0$

and the y-intercept occurs when $x = 0$

$\therefore y = 4^0 - 2^0$

$= 1 - 1$

$= 0$

$\therefore$ the x-intercept is 0 and the y-intercept is 0.

b As $x \to \infty$, $y \to \infty$ and as $x \to -\infty$, $y \to 0$ (below)

c $\dfrac{dy}{dx} = 4^x \ln 4 - 2^x \ln 2$

$= 2^x 2^x \times 2 \ln 2 - 2^x \ln 2$

$= 2^x \ln 2(2^{x+1} - 1)$

$\therefore \dfrac{dy}{dx} = 0$ when $2^{x+1} = 1$ and $y = 4^{-1} - 2^{-1}$

$\therefore x + 1 = 0$ $\quad = \dfrac{1}{4} - \dfrac{1}{2}$

$\therefore x = -1$ $\quad = -\dfrac{1}{4}$

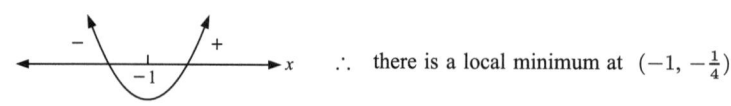

[Sign diagram: $-$ to the left of -1, $+$ to the right]

$\therefore$ there is a local minimum at $(-1, -\dfrac{1}{4})$

d $\dfrac{dy}{dx} = (\ln 4)4^x - (\ln 2)2^x$

$\therefore \dfrac{d^2y}{dx^2} = \ln 4\,(4^x \ln 4) - \ln 2\,(2^x \ln 2)$

$= 4^x(2\ln 2)^2 - 2^x(\ln 2)^2$

$= 2^x(\ln 2)^2(4 \times 2^x - 1)$

$\therefore \dfrac{d^2y}{dx^2} = 0$ when $4 \times 2^x - 1 = 0$

$\therefore 2^x = \dfrac{1}{4}$

$\therefore x = -2$

When $x = -2$, $y = 4^{-2} - 2^{-2}$

$= \dfrac{1}{16} - \dfrac{1}{4}$

$= -\dfrac{3}{16}$

$\therefore$ there is a non-stationary inflection point at $(-2, -\dfrac{3}{16})$

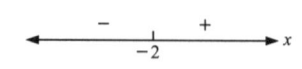

[Sign diagram: $-$ to the left of -2, $+$ to the right]

$\therefore$ y is concave down for $x \leqslant -2$, and concave up for $x \geqslant -2$

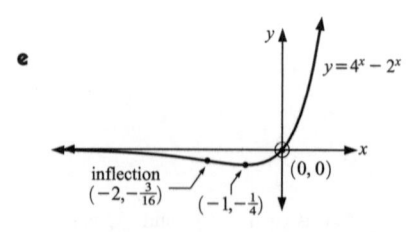

e

[Graph of $y = 4^x - 2^x$ showing inflection at $(-2, -\frac{3}{16})$, minimum at $(-1, -\frac{1}{4})$, and passing through $(0, 0)$]

EXERCISE 22C

1 **a** $y = \ln(7x)$ or $y = \ln(7x)$

$\therefore\ y = \ln 7 + \ln x$

$\therefore\ \dfrac{dy}{dx} = \dfrac{7}{7x} \leftarrow f'(x) \atop \leftarrow f(x)$

$\therefore\ \dfrac{dy}{dx} = 0 + \dfrac{1}{x} = \dfrac{1}{x}$

$= \dfrac{1}{x}$

b $y = \ln(2x + 1)$

$\therefore\ \dfrac{dy}{dx} = \dfrac{2}{2x+1} \leftarrow f'(x) \atop \leftarrow f(x)$

c $y = \ln(x - x^2)$

$\therefore\ \dfrac{dy}{dx} = \dfrac{1 - 2x}{x - x^2} \leftarrow f'(x) \atop \leftarrow f(x)$

d $y = 3 - 2\ln x$

$\therefore\ \dfrac{dy}{dx} = 0 - 2\left(\dfrac{1}{x}\right)$

$= -\dfrac{2}{x}$

e $y = x^2 \ln x$

$\therefore\ \dfrac{dy}{dx} = 2x \ln x + x^2 \left(\dfrac{1}{x}\right)$

$= 2x \ln x + x$

f $y = \dfrac{\ln x}{2x}$

$\therefore\ \dfrac{dy}{dx} = \dfrac{\left(\dfrac{1}{x}\right) 2x - \ln x (2)}{(2x)^2}$

$= \dfrac{2 - 2\ln x}{4x^2}$

$= \dfrac{1 - \ln x}{2x^2}$

g $y = e^x \ln x$

$\therefore\ \dfrac{dy}{dx} = e^x \ln x + \dfrac{e^x}{x}$

h $y = (\ln x)^2$

$\therefore\ \dfrac{dy}{dx} = 2(\ln x)^1 \left(\dfrac{1}{x}\right)$

$= \dfrac{2\ln x}{x}$

i $y = \sqrt{\ln x} = (\ln x)^{\frac{1}{2}}$

$\therefore\ \dfrac{dy}{dx} = \tfrac{1}{2}(\ln x)^{-\frac{1}{2}}\left(\dfrac{1}{x}\right)$

$= \dfrac{1}{2x\sqrt{\ln x}}$

j $y = e^{-x} \ln x$

$\therefore\ \dfrac{dy}{dx} = -e^{-x} \ln x + e^{-x}\left(\dfrac{1}{x}\right)$

$= \dfrac{e^{-x}}{x} - e^{-x}\ln x$

k $y = \sqrt{x} \ln 2x$

$\therefore\ \dfrac{dy}{dx} = \dfrac{1}{2\sqrt{x}} \ln 2x + \sqrt{x}\left(\dfrac{1}{x}\right)$

$= \dfrac{\ln 2x}{2\sqrt{x}} + \dfrac{1}{\sqrt{x}}$

l $y = \dfrac{2\sqrt{x}}{\ln x}$

$\therefore\ \dfrac{dy}{dx} = \dfrac{\dfrac{1}{\sqrt{x}} \ln x - 2\sqrt{x}\left(\dfrac{1}{x}\right)}{(\ln x)^2}$

$= \dfrac{\dfrac{1}{\sqrt{x}} \ln x - \dfrac{2}{\sqrt{x}}}{(\ln x)^2}$

$= \dfrac{\ln x - 2}{\sqrt{x}(\ln x)^2}$

2 **a** $y = x \ln 5$

$\therefore\ \dfrac{dy}{dx} = \ln 5$

b $y = \ln(x^3) = 3\ln x$

$\therefore\ \dfrac{dy}{dx} = 3\left(\dfrac{1}{x}\right) = \dfrac{3}{x}$

c $y = \ln(x^4 + x)$

$\therefore\ \dfrac{dy}{dx} = \dfrac{4x^3 + 1}{x^4 + x}$

d $y = \ln(10 - 5x)$

$\therefore\ \dfrac{dy}{dx} = \dfrac{-5}{10 - 5x} = \dfrac{1}{x - 2}$

e $y = [\ln(2x + 1)]^3$

$\therefore\ \dfrac{dy}{dx} = 3[\ln(2x + 1)]^2 \times \dfrac{2}{2x + 1}$

$= \dfrac{6[\ln(2x + 1)]^2}{2x + 1}$

f $y = \dfrac{\ln(4x)}{x}$

$\therefore\ \dfrac{dy}{dx} = \dfrac{\left(\dfrac{4}{4x}\right)x - \ln(4x) \times 1}{x^2}$

$= \dfrac{1 - \ln(4x)}{x^2}$

g $y = \ln\left(\dfrac{1}{x}\right)$
$= -\ln x$
$\therefore \dfrac{dy}{dx} = -\dfrac{1}{x}$

h $y = \ln(\ln x)$
$\therefore \dfrac{dy}{dx} = \dfrac{\frac{1}{x}}{\ln x} = \dfrac{1}{x \ln x}$

i $y = \dfrac{1}{\ln x} = [\ln x]^{-1}$
$\therefore \dfrac{dy}{dx} = -1[\ln x]^{-2} \times \dfrac{1}{x}$
$= \dfrac{-1}{x[\ln x]^2}$

3 a $y = \ln\sqrt{1-2x}$
$= \ln(1-2x)^{\frac{1}{2}}$
$= \tfrac{1}{2}\ln(1-2x)$
$\therefore \dfrac{dy}{dx} = \tfrac{1}{2} \times \dfrac{-2}{1-2x}$
$= \dfrac{1}{2x-1}$

b $y = \ln\left(\dfrac{1}{2x+3}\right)$
$= -\ln(2x+3)$
$\therefore \dfrac{dy}{dx} = -\dfrac{2}{2x+3}$

c $y = \ln(e^x \sqrt{x})$
$= \ln e^x + \ln x^{\frac{1}{2}}$
$= \ln e^x + \tfrac{1}{2}\ln x$
$= x + \tfrac{1}{2}\ln x$
$\therefore \dfrac{dy}{dx} = 1 + \tfrac{1}{2}\left(\dfrac{1}{x}\right)$
$\therefore \dfrac{dy}{dx} = 1 + \dfrac{1}{2x}$

d $y = \ln(x\sqrt{2-x})$
$= \ln x + \ln(2-x)^{\frac{1}{2}}$
$= \ln x + \tfrac{1}{2}\ln(2-x)$
$\therefore \dfrac{dy}{dx} = \dfrac{1}{x} + \tfrac{1}{2}\left(\dfrac{-1}{2-x}\right)$
$= \dfrac{1}{x} - \dfrac{1}{2(2-x)}$

e $y = \ln\left(\dfrac{x+3}{x-1}\right)$
$= \ln(x+3) - \ln(x-1)$
$\therefore \dfrac{dy}{dx} = \dfrac{1}{x+3} - \dfrac{1}{x-1}$

f $y = \ln\left(\dfrac{x^2}{3-x}\right)$
$= \ln x^2 - \ln(3-x)$
$= 2\ln x - \ln(3-x)$
$\therefore \dfrac{dy}{dx} = \dfrac{2}{x} - \dfrac{-1}{3-x}$
$= \dfrac{2}{x} + \dfrac{1}{3-x}$

g $f(x) = \ln\big((3x-4)^3\big)$
$= 3\ln(3x-4)$
$\therefore f'(x) = 3 \times \dfrac{3}{3x-4}$
$= \dfrac{9}{3x-4}$

h $f(x) = \ln\big(x(x^2+1)\big)$
$= \ln x + \ln(x^2+1)$
$\therefore f'(x) = \dfrac{1}{x} + \dfrac{2x}{x^2+1}$

i $f(x) = \ln\left(\dfrac{x^2+2x}{x-5}\right)$
$= \ln(x^2+2x) - \ln(x-5)$
$f'(x) = \dfrac{2x+2}{x^2+2x} - \dfrac{1}{x-5}$

4 a For this question, we remember that $\log_a x = \dfrac{\log_e x}{\log_e a} = \dfrac{\ln x}{\ln a}$

 i $y = \log_2 x = \dfrac{\ln x}{\ln 2}$
$\therefore \dfrac{dy}{dx} = \dfrac{1}{x \ln 2}$

 ii $y = \log_{10} x = \dfrac{\ln x}{\ln 10}$
$\therefore \dfrac{dy}{dx} = \dfrac{1}{x \ln 10}$

 iii $y = x\log_3 x = \dfrac{x \ln x}{\ln 3}$
Since $\ln 3$ is a constant,
$\therefore \dfrac{dy}{dx} = \dfrac{\frac{d}{dx}(x)\ln x + x\frac{d}{dx}(\ln x)}{\ln 3}$
$= \dfrac{\ln x + x\left(\frac{1}{x}\right)}{\ln 3}$
$= \dfrac{1+\ln x}{\ln 3} = \dfrac{1}{\ln 3} + \log_3 x$

b $y = 2^x$
$= (e^{\ln 2})^x$
$= e^{x \ln 2}$
$\therefore \dfrac{dy}{dx} = e^{x \ln 2} \times \ln 2$
$= 2^x \ln 2$

c $y = a^x$
$= (e^{\ln a})^x$
$= e^{x \ln a}$
$\therefore \dfrac{dy}{dx} = e^{x \ln a} \times \ln a$
$= a^x \ln a$

5 $f(x) = \ln(2x - 1) - 3$

  a $f(x) = 0$ when $\ln(2x - 1) = 3$
$$\therefore \quad 2x - 1 = e^3$$
$$\therefore \quad 2x = e^3 + 1$$
$$\therefore \quad x = \frac{e^3 + 1}{2} \approx 10.54 \quad \therefore \quad \text{the } x\text{-intercept is } \frac{e^3 + 1}{2}$$

  b $f(0)$ cannot be found as $\ln(-1)$ is not defined. $\therefore$ there is no y-intercept.

  c $f'(x) = \dfrac{2}{2x - 1}$ $\therefore$ $f'(1) = \dfrac{2}{2 - 1} = 2$ $\therefore$ gradient of tangent $= 2$

  d $\ln(2x - 1)$ has meaning provided $2x - 1 > 0$ $\therefore$ $2x > 1$ and so $x > \frac{1}{2}$
$$\therefore \quad f(x) \text{ has meaning provided } x > \tfrac{1}{2}$$

  e $f'(x) = 2(2x - 1)^{-1}$ **f** $f(x)$, $x = \frac{1}{2}$
$$\therefore \quad f''(x) = -2(2x - 1)^{-2}(2)$$
$$= \frac{-4}{(2x-1)^2}, \quad x > \frac{1}{2}$$
$$\therefore \text{ provided } x > \tfrac{1}{2}, \quad f''(x) < 0$$
$$\therefore f(x) \text{ is concave down when } f(x) \text{ has meaning.}$$

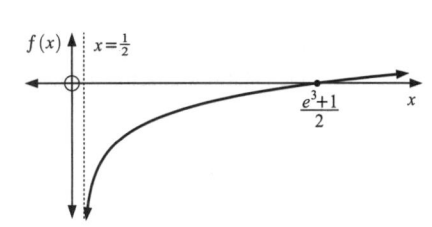

6 Consider $f(x) = \dfrac{\ln x}{x}$

$$\therefore \quad f'(x) = \frac{\left(\frac{1}{x}\right)x - \ln x(1)}{x^2} = \frac{1 - \ln x}{x^2}$$

$$\therefore \quad f'(x) = 0 \text{ when } 1 - \ln x = 0$$
$$\therefore \quad \ln x = 1 \qquad \text{Sign diagram of } f'(x) \text{ is:}$$ 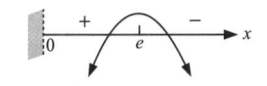
$$\therefore \quad x = e$$

Now $f(e) = \dfrac{\ln e}{e} = \dfrac{1}{e}$

$\therefore$ there is a local maximum at $\left(e, \dfrac{1}{e}\right)$

$\therefore \quad f(x) \leqslant \dfrac{1}{e}$ for all x, and so $\dfrac{\ln x}{x} \leqslant \dfrac{1}{e}$ for all $x > 0$

7 $f(x) = x - \ln x$

$\therefore \quad f'(x) = 1 - \dfrac{1}{x} = \dfrac{x - 1}{x}$ and the sign diagram of $f'(x)$ is:

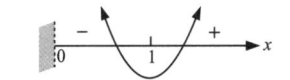

$\therefore \quad f(x)$ has a minimum turning point at $(1, 1 - \ln 1)$ or $(1, 1)$
$$\therefore \quad f(x) \geqslant 1 \text{ for all } x > 0$$
$$\therefore \quad x - \ln x \geqslant 1$$
$$\therefore \quad \ln x \leqslant x - 1 \text{ for all } x > 0$$

8 $e^{2a} \ln b^2 - a^3 b + \ln(ab) = 21$

$$\therefore \quad \left(2e^{2a} \frac{da}{db}\right) \ln b^2 + e^{2a} \left(\frac{2b}{b^2}\right) - \left(3a^2 \frac{da}{db}\right) b - a^3 + \frac{\frac{da}{db} \times b + a}{ab} = 0$$

$$\therefore \quad 4abe^{2a} \ln b \frac{da}{db} + 2ae^{2a} - 3a^3 b^2 \frac{da}{db} - a^4 b + b \frac{da}{db} + a = 0 \quad \{\times ab\}$$

$$\therefore \quad \frac{da}{db}\left(4abe^{2a} \ln b - 3a^3 b^2 + b\right) = a^4 b - 2ae^{2a} - a$$

$$\therefore \quad \frac{da}{db} = \frac{a^4 b - 2ae^{2a} - a}{4abe^{2a} \ln b - 3a^3 b^2 + b}$$

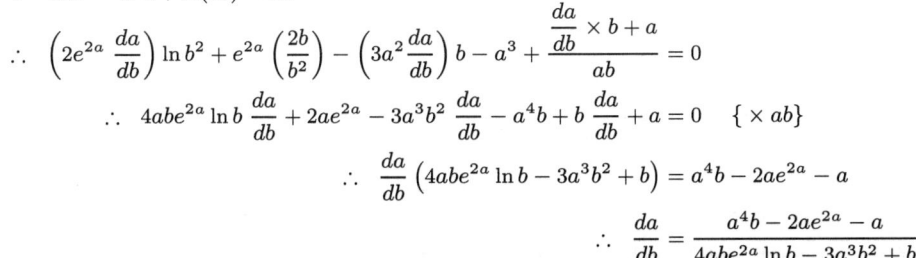

EXERCISE 22D

1 $f(x) = e^{-x}$
$\therefore \ f(1) = e^{-1}$
$\therefore \ $ the point of contact is $(1, \dfrac{1}{e})$.
Now $f'(x) = -e^{-x}$
$\therefore \ f'(1) = -e^{-1} = \dfrac{-1}{e}$
So, the gradient of the tangent is $\dfrac{-1}{e}$

$\therefore \ $ the tangent has equation $\dfrac{y - \dfrac{1}{e}}{x - 1} = -\dfrac{1}{e}$

$\therefore \ e\left(y - \dfrac{1}{e}\right) = -(x - 1)$
$\therefore \ ey - 1 = -x + 1$
$\therefore \ x + ey = 2$
or $y = -\dfrac{1}{e}x + \dfrac{2}{e}$

2 $y = \ln(2 - x)$
so when $x = -1, \ y = \ln 3$
$\therefore \ $ the point of contact is $(-1, \ln 3)$.
Now $\dfrac{dy}{dx} = \dfrac{-1}{2 - x}$
$\therefore \ $ when $x = -1, \ \dfrac{dy}{dx} = -\dfrac{1}{2+1} = -\dfrac{1}{3}$
So, the gradient of the tangent is $-\dfrac{1}{3}$.

$\therefore \ $ tangent has equation $\dfrac{y - \ln 3}{x + 1} = -\dfrac{1}{3}$

$\therefore \ 3(y - \ln 3) = -(x + 1)$
$\therefore \ 3y - 3\ln 3 = -x - 1$
$\therefore \ x + 3y = 3\ln 3 - 1$

3 $y = x^2 e^x$ so when $x = 1, \ y = e$
$\therefore \ $ the point of contact is $(1, e)$.
Now $\dfrac{dy}{dx} = 2xe^x + x^2 e^x$
$\therefore \ $ when $x = 1, \ \dfrac{dy}{dx} = 2e + e = 3e$
$\therefore \ $ the tangent has equation $\dfrac{y - e}{x - 1} = 3e$
$\therefore \ y - e = 3ex - 3e$
$\therefore \ y - 3ex = -2e$
$\therefore \ 3ex - y = 2e$

The tangent cuts the x-axis when
$y = 0$
$\therefore \ 3ex = 2e$
$\therefore \ x = \dfrac{2}{3}$
and the y-axis when
$x = 0$
$\therefore \ -y = 2e$
$\therefore \ y = -2e$
So, A is $(\dfrac{2}{3}, 0)$ and B is $(0, -2e)$.

4 $y = \ln \sqrt{x}$
$= \ln x^{\frac{1}{2}}$
$= \frac{1}{2} \ln x$

$\therefore \ $ when $y = -1, \ -1 = \frac{1}{2} \ln x$
$\therefore \ \ln x = -2$
$\therefore \ x = e^{-2}$
$\therefore \ x = \dfrac{1}{e^2}$
$\therefore \ $ the point of contact is $\left(\dfrac{1}{e^2}, -1\right)$

Now $\dfrac{dy}{dx} = \dfrac{1}{2} \cdot \dfrac{1}{x} = \dfrac{1}{2x}$, so at the point of contact, $\dfrac{dy}{dx} = \dfrac{1}{2e^{-2}} = \dfrac{e^2}{2}$

$\therefore \ $ the tangent has gradient $\dfrac{e^2}{2}$ and the normal has gradient $-\dfrac{2}{e^2}$

$\therefore \ $ the normal has equation $\dfrac{y + 1}{x - \dfrac{1}{e^2}} = -\dfrac{2}{e^2}$

$\therefore \ e^2(y + 1) = -2\left(x - \dfrac{1}{e^2}\right)$
$\therefore \ e^2 y + e^2 = -2x + \dfrac{2}{e^2}$
$\therefore \ 2x + e^2 y = -e^2 + \dfrac{2}{e^2}$ or $y = -\dfrac{2}{e^2}x + \dfrac{2}{e^4} - 1$

5 $y = e^x$ so when $x = a$, $y = e^a$
∴ the point of contact is (a, e^a).

Now $\dfrac{dy}{dx} = e^x$

∴ at the point (a, e^a), $\dfrac{dy}{dx} = e^a$

∴ the tangent has equation $\dfrac{y - e^a}{x - a} = e^a$

or $y - e^a = e^a(x - a)$ .... (*)

Since the tangent passes through the origin, $(0, 0)$ must satisfy (*)

∴ $0 - e^a = e^a(0 - a)$
∴ $-e^a = -ae^a$
∴ $e^a(a - 1) = 0$
∴ $a = 1$ {as $e^a > 0$}

So the equation of the tangent is
$y - e = ex - e$ or $y = ex$.

6 a $f(x) = \ln x$ is defined for all $x > 0$.

b $f'(x) = \dfrac{1}{x}$ which is > 0 for all $x > 0$ ∴ $f(x)$ is increasing on $x > 0$.

$f''(x) = -x^{-2} = \dfrac{-1}{x^2}$ which is < 0 for all $x > 0$ ∴ $f(x)$ is concave down on $x > 0$.

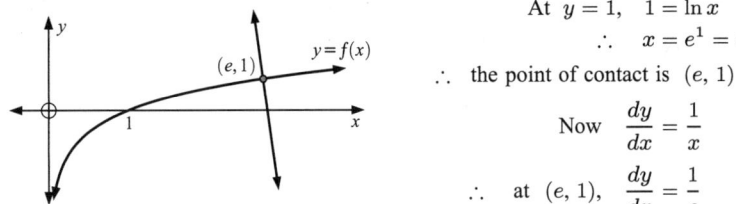

c

[Graph showing $y = f(x)$ passing through $(e, 1)$ and 1 on x-axis]

At $y = 1$, $1 = \ln x$
∴ $x = e^1 = e$
∴ the point of contact is $(e, 1)$

Now $\dfrac{dy}{dx} = \dfrac{1}{x}$

∴ at $(e, 1)$, $\dfrac{dy}{dx} = \dfrac{1}{e}$

∴ the gradient of the tangent is $\dfrac{1}{e}$, and the gradient of the normal is $-e$

∴ the equation of the normal is $\dfrac{y - 1}{x - e} = -e$ ∴ $y - 1 = -e(x - e)$
∴ $y - 1 = -ex + e^2$
∴ $ex + y = 1 + e^2$

7 $y = 3e^{-x}$ and $y = 2 + e^x$ meet when $3e^{-x} = 2 + e^x$
∴ $3 = 2e^x + e^{2x}$ $\{\times e^x\}$
∴ $e^{2x} + 2e^x - 3 = 0$
∴ $(e^x + 3)(e^x - 1) = 0$
∴ $e^x = -3$ or 1
∴ $e^x = 1$ and $x = 0$ {as $e^x > 0$}

Now when $x = 0$, $y = 3e^0 = 3$, so the graphs meet at $(0, 3)$.

For $y = 2 + e^x$, $\dfrac{dy}{dx} = e^x$,

so at the point $(0, 3)$, $\dfrac{dy}{dx} = e^0 = 1$

∴ the gradient of the tangent at this point is 1
If θ is the angle between the tangent and the x-axis, then $\tan \theta = 1$
∴ $\theta = 45°$

∴ the angle between the tangents
$\approx (180 - (71.57 + 45))° \approx 63.43°$

For $y = 3e^{-x}$, $\dfrac{dy}{dx} = -3e^{-x}$,

so at the point $(0, 3)$, $\dfrac{dy}{dx} = -3$

∴ the gradient of the tangent at this point is -3
If ϕ is the angle between the tangent and the x-axis, then

$\tan \phi = 3$
∴ $\phi = \tan^{-1}(3) \approx 71.6°$

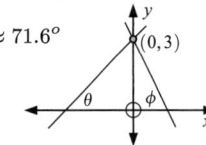

[Diagram showing angles θ and ϕ with point $(0, 3)$]

8 a $W = 20e^{-kt}$ so when $t = 50$ hours, $W = 10$ g
∴ $20e^{-50k} = 10$
∴ $e^{-50k} = \tfrac{1}{2}$
∴ $-50k = \ln \tfrac{1}{2} = -\ln 2$ ∴ $k = \tfrac{1}{50} \ln 2 \approx 0.0139$

b **i** When $t = 0$,
$W = 20e^0$
$= 20$ g

ii When $t = 24$,
$W = 20e^{-24k}$
$= 20e^{-24\frac{\ln 2}{50}}$
≈ 14.3 g

iii When $t = 1$ week
$= 7 \times 24$ hours
$= 168$ hours
$W = 20e^{-168\frac{\ln 2}{50}}$
≈ 1.95 g

c When $W = 1$ g, $\quad 20e^{-\frac{\ln 2}{50} \times t} = 1$
$\therefore \quad e^{-\frac{\ln 2}{50} \times t} = 0.05$
$\therefore \quad -\frac{\ln 2}{50} \times t = \ln 0.05$
$\therefore \quad t = \dfrac{-50 \ln 0.05}{\ln 2} \approx 216$ hours

d $\dfrac{dW}{dt}$
$= 20e^{-kt}(-k)$
$= \left(-20\dfrac{\ln 2}{50}\right) \times e^{-\frac{\ln 2}{50}t}$

i When $t = 100$ hours,
$\dfrac{dW}{dt} = \left(\dfrac{-20 \ln 2}{50}\right)e^{-2\ln 2}$
≈ -0.0693 g h^{-1}

ii When $t = 1000$ hours,
$\dfrac{dW}{dt} = \left(\dfrac{-20 \ln 2}{50}\right)e^{-20\ln 2}$
$\approx -2.64 \times 10^{-7}$ g h^{-1}

e $\dfrac{dW}{dt} = -k(20e^{-kt}) = -kW \quad \therefore \quad \dfrac{dW}{dt} \propto W$

9 $T = 5 + 95e^{-kt}$ °C

a $T = 20$°C when $t = 15$
$\therefore \quad 20 = 5 + 95e^{-15k}$
$\therefore \quad 15 = 95e^{-15k}$
$\therefore \quad \ln\left(\dfrac{15}{95}\right) = -15k$
$\therefore \quad k = \dfrac{\ln\left(\frac{15}{95}\right)}{-15} \approx 0.123$

b When $t = 0$,
$T = 5 + 95e^0$
$= 5 + 95$
$= 100$°C

c $\dfrac{dT}{dt} = 0 + 95e^{-kt}(-k)$
$= -(95e^{-kt})k$
$= -k(T-5)$

d $\dfrac{dT}{dt} = -95e^{-kt} \times k \approx -11.6902e^{-0.1231t}$

  i When $t = 0$, $\dfrac{dT}{dt} \approx -11.69$, so the temperature is decreasing at 11.7°C min^{-1}.

  ii When $t = 10$, $\dfrac{dT}{dt} \approx -11.6902e^{-1.231} \approx -3.415$,
  so the temperature is decreasing at 3.42°C min^{-1}.

  iii When $t = 20$, $\dfrac{dT}{dt} \approx -11.6902e^{-2.461} \approx -0.998$,
  so the temperature is decreasing at 0.998°C min^{-1}.

10 $H(t) = 20\ln(3t+2) + 30$ cm, $t \geqslant 0$

a The shrubs were planted when $t = 0$. $H(0) = 20\ln(2) + 30 \approx 43.9$ cm

b When $H = 1$ m $= 100$ cm,
$20\ln(3t+2) + 30 = 100$
$\therefore \quad 20\ln(3t+2) = 70$
$\therefore \quad \ln(3t+2) = 3.5$
$\therefore \quad 3t+2 = e^{3.5}$
$\therefore \quad 3t = e^{3.5} - 2$
$\therefore \quad t = \dfrac{e^{3.5}-2}{3}$ years
$\therefore \quad t \approx 10.4$ years

c $\dfrac{dH}{dt} = 20 \times \dfrac{3}{(3t+2)} = \dfrac{60}{3t+2}$ cm year^{-1}

  i When $t = 3$, $\dfrac{dH}{dt} = \dfrac{60}{11} \approx 5.4545$
  $\therefore$ it is growing at 5.45 cm year^{-1}

  ii When $t = 10$, $\dfrac{dH}{dt} = \dfrac{60}{32} = 1.875$
  $\therefore$ it is growing at 1.88 cm year^{-1}

11 **a** $A = s(1 - e^{-kt})$, $t \geq 0$
When $t = 0$, $A = s(1 - e^0)$
$= s(1 - 1)$
$= 0$

b When $t = 3$, $A = 5$ and $s = 10$
$\therefore \quad 5 = 10(1 - e^{-3k})$
$\therefore \quad 0.5 = 1 - e^{-3k}$
$\therefore \quad e^{-3k} = 0.5$
$\therefore \quad e^{3k} = 2$
$\therefore \quad 3k = \ln 2$
$\therefore \quad k = \frac{1}{3} \ln 2 \approx 0.231$

c $\dfrac{dA}{dt} = ske^{-kt}$

$\therefore$ when $t = 5$ and $s = 10$,

$\dfrac{dA}{dt} = 10 \left(\frac{1}{3} \ln 2\right) \left(e^{-\frac{5}{3} \ln 2}\right)$

≈ 0.728 litres per hour

d $\dfrac{dA}{dt} = ske^{-kt}$
$= k\left(se^{-kt}\right)$
$= -k\left(-se^{-kt}\right)$
$= -k(A - s)$

$\therefore \quad \dfrac{dA}{dt} \propto (A - s)$

12 Consider $f(x) = \dfrac{e^x}{x}$.

a $e^x \neq 0$ for all x, so $f(x) \neq 0$ and there is no x-intercept.

$f(0) = \dfrac{e^0}{0}$ is undefined, so there is also no y-intercept.

b As $x \to +\infty$ $f(x) \to \infty$, and as $x \to -\infty$, $f(x) \to 0$ (below)

$\left(\begin{array}{l}\text{As } x \to 0 \text{ (above)}, \ y \to +\infty, \text{ and as } x \to 0 \text{ (below)}, \ y \to -\infty \\ \therefore \ x = 0 \text{ is a vertical asymptote.}\end{array}\right)$

c Using the quotient rule, $f'(x) = \dfrac{e^x x - e^x(1)}{x^2} = \dfrac{e^x(x - 1)}{x^2}$

with sign diagram:

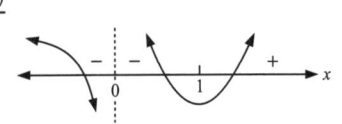

$f(1) = \dfrac{e^1}{1} = e$, so there is a local minimum at $(1, e)$.

d

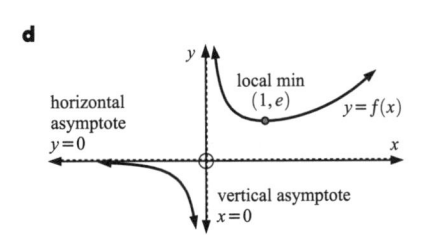

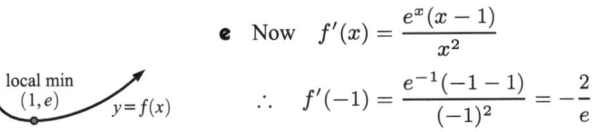

horizontal asymptote $y = 0$

local min $(1, e)$

$y = f(x)$

vertical asymptote $x = 0$

e Now $f'(x) = \dfrac{e^x(x - 1)}{x^2}$

$\therefore \quad f'(-1) = \dfrac{e^{-1}(-1 - 1)}{(-1)^2} = -\dfrac{2}{e}$

$\therefore$ the gradient of the tangent is $= -\dfrac{2}{e}$

When $x = -1$, $y = \dfrac{e^{-1}}{-1} = -\dfrac{1}{e}$

$\therefore$ the equation of tangent is $\dfrac{y - \left(-\frac{1}{e}\right)}{x - (-1)} = -\dfrac{2}{e}$

$\therefore \quad \dfrac{y + \frac{1}{e}}{x + 1} = -\dfrac{2}{e}$

$\therefore \quad e\left(y + \dfrac{1}{e}\right) = -2(x + 1)$

$ey + 1 = -2x - 2$

$\therefore \quad ey = -2x - 3$

13 **a** $s(t) = 100t + 200e^{-\frac{t}{5}}$ cm, $t \geq 0$
$v(t) = 100 - 40e^{-\frac{t}{5}}$ cm s^{-1}
$a(t) = 8e^{-\frac{t}{5}}$ cm s^{-2}

b When $t = 0$, $s(0) = 200$ cm
$v(0) = 60$ cm s^{-1}
$a(0) = 8$ cm s^{-2}

c As $t \to +\infty$, $e^{-\frac{t}{5}} \to 0$,
$\therefore \quad v(t) \to 100$ cm s^{-1} (below)

d

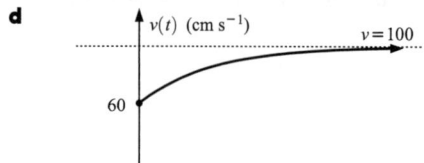

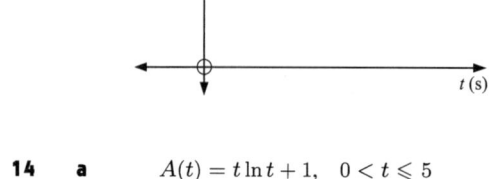

graph of v(t) (cm s⁻¹) vs t(s), showing curve rising from 60 asymptotically to v = 100

e When $v(t) = 80 \text{ cm s}^{-1}$,

$$100 - 40e^{-\frac{t}{5}} = 80$$
$$\therefore \quad -40e^{-\frac{t}{5}} = -20$$
$$\therefore \quad e^{-\frac{t}{5}} = 0.5$$
$$\therefore \quad -\frac{t}{5} = \ln 0.5$$
$$\therefore \quad t = -5\ln 0.5 \approx 3.47 \text{ s}$$

14 a $\quad A(t) = t\ln t + 1, \quad 0 < t \leqslant 5$

$\therefore \quad A'(t) = \ln t + t \times \dfrac{1}{t} + 0 \quad$ {product rule}

$\quad = \ln t + 1$

$\therefore \quad A'(t) = 0$ when $\ln t = -1$

$\therefore \quad t = e^{-1}$

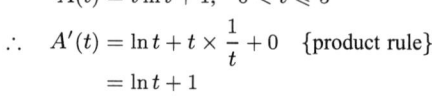

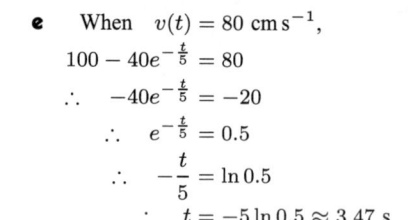

and the sign diagram of $A'(t)$ is: *sign diagram: − on (0, e⁻¹), + on (e⁻¹, ∞)*

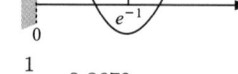

$\therefore \quad A(t)$ is a minimum when $t = \dfrac{1}{e} \approx 0.3679$ years

$\therefore$ the child's memorising ability is a minimum at 4.41 months old.

b *graph of A(t) with minimum at $(e^{-1}, 0.632)$ and endpoint $(5, 5\ln 5 + 1)$*

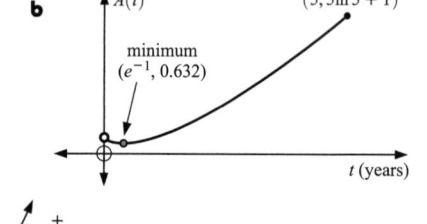

15 a $\quad f(x) = \dfrac{1}{\sqrt{2\pi}} e^{-\frac{1}{2}x^2}$

$\therefore \quad f'(x) = \dfrac{1}{\sqrt{2\pi}} e^{-\frac{1}{2}x^2}(-x)$

$\quad = \dfrac{-x}{\sqrt{2\pi}} e^{-\frac{1}{2}x^2}$

$\therefore \quad f'(x) = 0$ when $x = 0$

$f'(x)$ has sign diagram: *+ on (−∞, 0), − on (0, ∞)*

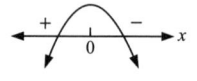

Now $f(0) = \dfrac{1}{\sqrt{2\pi}}$

so there is a local maximum at $\left(0, \dfrac{1}{\sqrt{2\pi}}\right)$.

The function is increasing for $x \leqslant 0$ and decreasing for $x \geqslant 0$.

b $\quad f'(x) = \dfrac{-x}{\sqrt{2\pi}} e^{-\frac{1}{2}x^2} = \dfrac{1}{\sqrt{2\pi}}\left(-xe^{-\frac{1}{2}x^2}\right)$

$\therefore \quad f''(x) = \dfrac{1}{\sqrt{2\pi}}\left((-1)e^{-\frac{1}{2}x^2} + (-x)e^{-\frac{1}{2}x^2}(-x)\right) \quad$ {product rule}

$\quad = \dfrac{1}{\sqrt{2\pi}} e^{-\frac{1}{2}x^2}(x^2 - 1)$

$\quad = \dfrac{1}{\sqrt{2\pi}} e^{-\frac{1}{2}x^2}(x+1)(x-1) \quad$ which has sign diagram: *+ on (−∞,−1), − on (−1,1), + on (1,∞)*

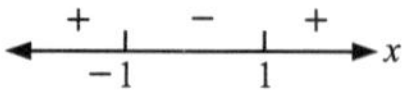

Now $f(1) = \dfrac{1}{\sqrt{2\pi}} e^{-\frac{1}{2}} = \dfrac{1}{\sqrt{2e\pi}}$ and $f(-1) = \dfrac{1}{\sqrt{2e\pi}}$

$\therefore$ there are points of inflection at $\left(1, \dfrac{1}{\sqrt{2e\pi}}\right)$ and $\left(-1, \dfrac{1}{\sqrt{2e\pi}}\right)$.

c As $x \to \infty$, $e^{-\frac{1}{2}x^2} \to 0$ (above),

$\therefore \quad f(x) \to 0$ (above)

As $x \to -\infty$, $e^{-\frac{1}{2}x^2} \to 0$ (above),

$\therefore \quad f(x) \to 0$ (above)

d *graph of $y = \dfrac{1}{\sqrt{2\pi}} e^{-\frac{1}{2}x^2}$ showing local max at $\left(0, \dfrac{1}{\sqrt{2\pi}}\right)$ and non-horizontal inflections at $\left(-1, \dfrac{1}{\sqrt{2e\pi}}\right)$ and $\left(1, \dfrac{1}{\sqrt{2e\pi}}\right)$*

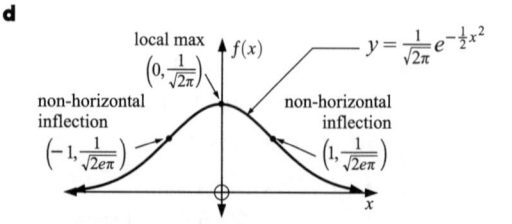

16 $\quad C(x) = 4\ln x + \left(\dfrac{30-x}{10}\right)^2, \quad x \geqslant 10$

$\therefore\ C'(x) = \dfrac{4}{x} + 2\left(\dfrac{30-x}{10}\right)\left(-\dfrac{1}{10}\right)$

$ = \dfrac{4}{x} - \dfrac{30-x}{50}$

$ = \dfrac{200 - x(30-x)}{50x}$

$ = \dfrac{200 - 30x + x^2}{50x}$

$ = \dfrac{(x-10)(x-20)}{50x}$

$C'(x)$ has sign diagram:

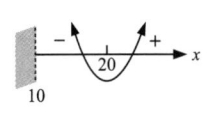

$\therefore$ the minimum cost occurs when $x = 20$ or when 20 kettles per day are produced.

17 Let coordinates of D be $(x, 0)$ where $x > 0$.

$\therefore$ the coordinates of C are (x, e^{-x^2}).

$\therefore$ area ABCD $= 2xe^{-x^2}$

$\therefore\ \dfrac{dA}{dx} = 2e^{-x^2} + 2xe^{-x^2}(-2x) \quad$ {product rule}

$\phantom{\therefore\ \dfrac{dA}{dx}} = 2e^{-x^2}\left(1 - 2x^2\right)$

$\phantom{\therefore\ \dfrac{dA}{dx}} = 2e^{-x^2}(1 + \sqrt{2}x)(1 - \sqrt{2}x)$

and $\dfrac{dA}{dx}$ has sign diagram:

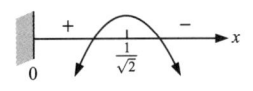

$\therefore$ area is a maximum when $x = \dfrac{1}{\sqrt{2}}$

and so C is $\left(\dfrac{1}{\sqrt{2}},\ e^{-\frac{1}{2}}\right)$.

18 $\quad P(x) = R(x) - C(x)$

$\therefore\ P(x) = \left[1000\ln\left(1 + \dfrac{x}{400}\right) + 600\right] - [x(1.5) + 300]$

$ = 1000\ln(1 + 0.0025x) - 1.5x + 300$

$\therefore\ P'(x) = 1000\left(\dfrac{0.0025}{1 + 0.0025x}\right) - 1.5 = \dfrac{2.5}{1 + 0.0025x} - 1.5$

$\therefore\ P'(x) = 0$ when $\dfrac{2.5}{1 + 0.0025x} = \dfrac{3}{2}$

$\therefore\ 3 + 0.0075x = 5$

$\therefore\ 0.0075x = 2$

$\therefore\ x = \dfrac{2}{0.0075} \approx 266.7$

Sign diagram of $P'(x)$:

Now $P(266) \approx 410.83$ and $P(267) \approx 410.83$

$\therefore$ to maximise the profit, 266 or 267 torches per day should be produced.

19 a $y = ax^2$, $a > 0$ touches $y = \ln x$ when $ax^2 = \ln x$

If the curves touch when $x = b$ then $ab^2 = \ln b$ .... (1)

Now for $y = ax^2$, $\dfrac{dy}{dx} = 2ax$ and for $y = \ln x$, $\dfrac{dy}{dx} = \dfrac{1}{x}$

$\therefore$ when $x = b$, $\dfrac{dy}{dx} = 2ab$ $\quad\therefore$ when $x = b$, $\dfrac{dy}{dx} = \dfrac{1}{b}$

Since the curves touch each other, they share a common tangent. $\quad\therefore\ \dfrac{1}{b} = 2ab$ .... (2)

b Now $ab^2 = \dfrac{1}{2}$ {from (2)}

and $ab^2 = \ln b$ {from (1)}

$\therefore\ \ln b = \dfrac{1}{2}$

$\therefore\ b = e^{\frac{1}{2}} = \sqrt{e}$

When $x = b = \sqrt{e}$, $y = \ln x = \ln e^{\frac{1}{2}} = \dfrac{1}{2}$

$\therefore$ the point of contact is $(\sqrt{e},\ \dfrac{1}{2})$.

c $a = \dfrac{1}{2b^2}$ {from (2)}

$\therefore\ a = \dfrac{1}{2(\sqrt{e})^2} = \dfrac{1}{2e}$

d The tangent has gradient $2ab = 2\left(\dfrac{1}{2e}\right)\sqrt{e} = \dfrac{1}{\sqrt{e}}$ and passes through $(\sqrt{e}, \tfrac{1}{2})$

$\therefore$ tangent is $\dfrac{y - \tfrac{1}{2}}{x - \sqrt{e}} = \dfrac{1}{\sqrt{e}}$ $\therefore$ $y - \tfrac{1}{2} = \dfrac{1}{\sqrt{e}}(x - \sqrt{e})$

$\therefore$ $y - \tfrac{1}{2} = \dfrac{1}{\sqrt{e}}x - 1$

$\therefore$ $y = xe^{-\tfrac{1}{2}} - \tfrac{1}{2}$

20 $P(t) = \dfrac{50\,000}{1 + 1000e^{-0.5t}}, \quad 0 \leqslant t \leqslant 25$

$= 50\,000(1 + 1000e^{-0.5t})^{-1}$

$\therefore$ $P'(t) = -50\,000(1 + 1000e^{-0.5t})^{-2}\left(-500e^{-0.5t}\right)$

$= 2.5 \times 10^7 e^{-0.5t}(1 + 1000e^{-0.5t})^{-2}$

The wasp population is growing the fastest when $\dfrac{dP}{dt}$ is a maximum.

Using technology, the graph of $P'(t)$ can be drawn and the maximum obtained. The maximum occurs when $t \approx 13.8$ weeks.

21 $f(t) = ate^{bt^2} = (at)e^{bt^2}$

$\therefore$ $f'(t) = ae^{bt^2} + ate^{bt^2}(2bt) = ae^{bt^2}(1 + 2bt^2)$ {product rule}

$\therefore$ $f'(t) = 0$ when $1 + 2bt^2 = 0$

But when know $f(t)$ is a maximum when $t = 2$, so $1 + 8b = 0$

$\therefore$ $b = -\tfrac{1}{8}$ and $f(t) = ate^{-\tfrac{t^2}{8}}$

Also, $f(2) = 1$ so $2ae^{-\tfrac{4}{8}} = 1$

$\therefore$ $ae^{-\tfrac{1}{2}} = \tfrac{1}{2}$ and so $a = \dfrac{\sqrt{e}}{2}$

22 $f(x) = e^{ax}(x + 1), \quad a \in \mathbb{R}$

a $f'(x) = ae^{ax}(x + 1) + e^{ax}(1)$ {product rule}
$= e^{ax}(a[x + 1] + 1)$

b $f''(x) = ae^{ax}(a[x + 1] + 1) + e^{ax}(a)$ {product rule}
$= ae^{ax}(a[x + 1] + 1 + 1)$
$= ae^{ax}(a[x + 1] + 2)$

c If $f^{(k)}(x) = a^{k-1}e^{ax}(a[x + 1] + k)$
then $f^{(k+1)}(x) = a^{k-1}ae^{ax}(a[x + 1] + k) + a^{k-1}e^{ax}(a)$ {product rule}
$= a^k e^{ax}(a[x + 1] + k) + a^k e^{ax}$
$= a^k e^{ax}(a[x + 1] + [k + 1])$

23 $f(x) = e^{-x}(x + 2)$

a i $f'(x) = -e^{-x}(x + 2) + e^{-x}(1)$
$= -e^{-x}(x + 2 - 1)$
$= -e^{-x}(x + 1)$

ii $f''(x) = e^{-x}(x + 1) - e^{-x}(1)$
$= e^{-x}(x + 1 - 1)$
$= e^{-x}(x)$

iii $f'''(x) = -e^{-x}(x) + e^{-x}(1)$
$= -e^{-x}(x - 1)$

iv $f^{(4)}(x) = e^{-x}(x - 1) - e^{-x}(1)$
$= e^{-x}(x - 1 - 1)$
$= e^{-x}(x - 2)$

b $f^{(n)}(x) = (-1)^n e^{-x}(x - (n - 2))$
$= (-1)^n e^{-x}(x - n + 2)$

- P_n is "for $f(x) = e^{-x}(x+2)$, $f^{(n)}(x) = (-1)^n e^{-x}(x-n+2)$", $n \in \mathbb{Z}^+$

  Proof: (By the principle of mathematical induction)

  (1) For $n=1$, $f'(x) = -e^{-x}(x+1)$ {using **a i**}
  $= (-1)^1 e^{-x}(x-1+2)$ $\therefore$ P_1 is true.

  (2) If P_k is true then $f^{(k)}(x) = (-1)^k e^{-x}(x-k+2)$
  $\therefore$ $f^{(k+1)}(x) = (-1)^k(-1)e^{-x}(x-k+2) + (-1)^k e^{-x}(1)$ {product rule}
  $= (-1)^{k+1} e^{-x}(x-k+2) + (-1)(-1)^k e^{-x}(-1)$
  $= (-1)^{k+1} e^{-x}(x-k+2-1)$
  $= (-1)^{k+1} e^{-x}(x-(k+1)+2)$

  Thus P_{k+1} is true whenever P_k is true
  $\therefore$ since P_1 is true, P_n is true for all $n \in \mathbb{Z}^+$ {Principle of mathematical induction}

24 a $f(x) = xe^{ax}$
$f'(x) = e^{ax} + x(ae^{ax})$
$= e^{ax}(ax+1)$

$f''(x) = ae^{ax}(ax+1) + e^{ax}(a)$
$= ae^{ax}(ax+1+1)$
$= ae^{ax}(ax+2)$

$f'''(x) = a^2 e^{ax}(ax+2) + ae^{ax}(a)$
$= a^2 e^{ax}(ax+2+1)$
$= a^2 e^{ax}(ax+3)$

$f^{(4)}(x) = a^3 e^{ax}(ax+3) + a^2 e^{ax}(a)$
$= a^3 e^{ax}(ax+3+1)$
$= a^3 e^{ax}(ax+4)$

b $f^{(n)}(x) = a^{n-1} e^{ax}(ax+n)$

c P_n is "for $f(x) = xe^{ax}$, $f^{(n)}(x) = a^{n-1} e^{ax}(ax+n)$", $n \in \mathbb{Z}^+$

   Proof: (By the principle of mathematical induction)

(1) For $n=1$, $f'(x) = e^{ax}(ax+1)$ {using **a**}
$= a^{1-1} e^{ax}(ax+1)$ $\therefore$ P_1 is true.

(2) If P_k is true then $f^{(k)}(x) = a^{k-1} e^{ax}(ax+k)$
$\therefore$ $f^{(k+1)}(x) = a^{k-1}(a)e^{ax}(ax+k) + a^{k-1} e^{ax}(a)$ {product rule}
$= a^k e^{ax}(ax+k) + a^k e^{ax}$
$= a^{(k+1)-1} e^{ax}(ax+[k+1])$

Thus P_{k+1} is true whenever P_k is true
$\therefore$ since P_1 is true, P_n is true for all $n \in \mathbb{Z}^+$ {Principle of mathematical induction}

EXERCISE 22E

1 a

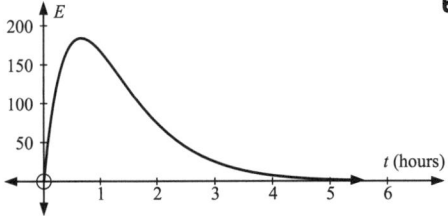

b   **i** When $t = 0.5$,
$E = 750(0.5)e^{-1.5 \times 0.5}$
≈ 177 units

    ii When $t = 2$,
$E = 750(2)e^{-1.5 \times 2}$
≈ 74.7 units

c $E'(t) = 750 \times e^{-1.5t} + 750t(-1.5)e^{-1.5t}$ {product rule}
$= 750 e^{-1.5t}(1 - 1.5t)$

$\therefore$ $E'(t) = 0$ when $t = \dfrac{1}{1.5} = \dfrac{2}{3}$

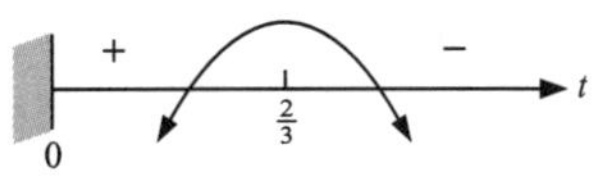

$\therefore$ the drug is most effective when $t = \dfrac{2}{3}$ hours $= 40$ minutes.

d   **i** Using technology, E first reaches 100 units when $t \approx 0.1728$ hours, or ≈ 10 minutes.
$\therefore$ the operation can commence 10 minutes after the injection.

ii Using technology, E returns to 100 units when $t \approx 1.695$ hours.
∴ the length of time that $E > 100$ is $\approx (1.695 - 0.1728)$ hours ≈ 1.52 hours
≈ 91 minutes.

e $E''(t) = 750(-1.5)e^{-1.5t}(1 - 1.5t) + 750e^{-1.5t}(-1.5)$ {product rule}
$= -1125e^{-1.5t}(2 - 1.5t)$

∴ $E''(t) = 0$ when $t = \dfrac{2}{1.5} = \dfrac{4}{3}$ hours

This is the time at which the effectiveness is decreasing the fastest.

2 a i $f(t) = Ate^{-bt}$
∴ $f'(t) = A \times e^{-bt} + At \times (-b)e^{-bt}$
$= Ae^{-bt}(1 - bt)$

∴ $f'(t) = 0$ when $bt = 1$ or $t = \dfrac{1}{b}$

∴ $f(t)$ has a local maximum at $t = \dfrac{1}{b}$.

ii $f'(t) = Ae^{-bt}(1 - bt)$
∴ $f''(t) = A(-b)e^{-bt}(1 - bt) + Ae^{-bt}(-b)$
$= -Abe^{-bt}(2 - bt)$

∴ $f''(t) = 0$ when $bt = 2$ or $t = \dfrac{2}{b}$

∴ $f(t)$ has a point of inflection at $t = \dfrac{2}{b}$.

b in question **1**, $b = 1.5$
∴ $f(t)$ has a local maximum at $t = \dfrac{1}{1.5} = \dfrac{2}{3}$, the same result as **1 c**

$f(t)$ has a point of inflection at $t = \dfrac{2}{1.5} = \dfrac{4}{3}$, the same result as **1 e**.

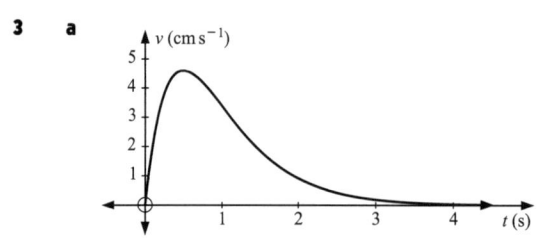

3 a

b $a(t) = v'(t)$
$= 25 \times e^{-2t} + 25t(-2)e^{-2t}$
$= 25(1 - 2t)e^{-2t}$ cm s^{-2}

c $v'(t) = 0$ when $1 - 2t = 0$
∴ $t = \dfrac{1}{2}$

∴ the velocity is increasing for $0 \leqslant t \leqslant \dfrac{1}{2}$

d $v'(t) = 25(1 - 2t)e^{-2t}$
∴ $v''(t) = 25(-2) \times e^{-2t} + 25(1 - 2t) \times -2e^{-2t}$
$= -50e^{-2t}(2 - 2t)$

∴ $v''(t) = 0$ when $t = 1$
∴ the point of inflection of the velocity function is at $(1, 3.38)$.
This is when the velocity is decreasing the fastest.

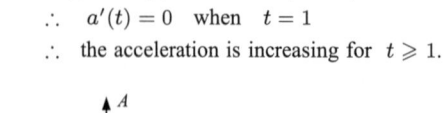

e $a'(t) = v''(t) = -50e^{-2t}(2 - 2t)$
∴ $a'(t) = 0$ when $t = 1$
∴ the acceleration is increasing for $t \geqslant 1$.

4 a

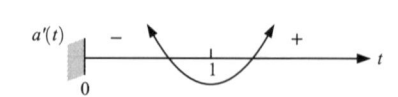

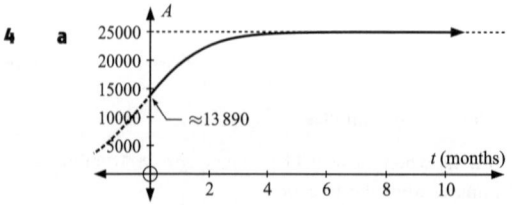

b When $t = 0$, $A(0) = \dfrac{25\,000}{1 + 0.8e^0}$
$\approx 13\,900$ ants

c When $t = 3$, $A(3) = \dfrac{25\,000}{1 + 0.8e^{-3}}$
$\approx 24\,000$ ants

d As $t \to \infty$, $e^{-t} \to 0$, and so

$A(t)$ approaches $\dfrac{25\,000}{1+0} = 25\,000$

∴ the population size is limited to 25 000

e $A(t) = \dfrac{25\,000}{1+0.8e^{-t}} = 24\,500$

∴ $25\,000 = 24\,500 + 19\,600e^{-t}$

∴ $e^{-t} = \dfrac{500}{19\,600}$

∴ $t = -\ln\left(\dfrac{500}{19\,600}\right) \approx 3.67$ months

5 a When $t = 0$,

$B(0) = \dfrac{C}{1+0.5e^0} = \dfrac{C}{1.5} = \dfrac{2C}{3}$ bees

b When $t = 1$, $B(1) = \dfrac{C}{1+0.5e^{-1.73}}$

$\approx \dfrac{C}{1.089} \approx 0.919C$

∴ % increase $= \left(\dfrac{0.919C - \frac{2}{3}C}{\frac{2}{3}C}\right) \times 100\%$

$\approx 37.8\%$ increase

c As $t \to \infty$, $e^{-1.73t} \to 0$, and so

$B(t)$ approaches $\dfrac{C}{1+0} = C$

∴ the population is limited to C bees.

d $B(2) = \dfrac{C}{1+0.5e^{-1.73 \times 2}} = 4500$

∴ $\dfrac{C}{1.016} = 4500$

∴ $C \approx 4570.7$

∴ from **a**, initial population $= \dfrac{2C}{3} \approx 3050$ bees

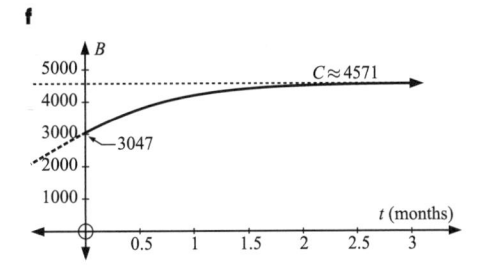

e $B(t) = C(1+0.5e^{-1.73t})^{-1}$

∴ $B'(t) = -C(1+0.5e^{-1.73t})^{-2}$
$\times (0.5(-1.73)e^{-1.73t})$

$= \dfrac{0.865Ce^{-1.73t}}{(1+0.5e^{-1.73t})^2}$

$= \dfrac{0.865C}{e^{1.73t}(1+0.5e^{-1.73})^2}$

Since $C > 0$, $B'(t) > 0$ for all t

∴ $B(t)$ is increasing over time.

f

Graph showing B vs t (months), with horizontal asymptote $C \approx 4571$, value 3047 marked near t near origin, axis marks at 0.5, 1, 1.5, 2, 2.5, 3; B axis marks at 1000, 2000, 3000, 4000, 5000.

6 a Consider $f(t) = \dfrac{C}{1+Ae^{-bt}}$

As $t \to \infty$, $e^{-bt} \to 0$ and so $1+Ae^{-bt} \to 1$ and $f(t) \to C$

∴ $f(t) = C$ is its horizontal asymptote

b $f(t) = C(1+Ae^{-bt})^{-1}$

∴ $f'(t) = -C(1+Ae^{-bt})^{-2} \times (-Abe^{-bt})$

$= AbCe^{-bt}(1+Ae^{-bt})^{-2} = AbC\dfrac{e^{-bt}}{(1+Ae^{-bt})^2}$

∴ $f''(t) = AbC\left[\dfrac{(-be^{-bt})(1+Ae^{-bt})^2 - (e^{-bt})(2(1+Ae^{-bt})(-Abe^{-bt}))}{(1+Ae^{-bt})^4}\right]$

$= AbC\left[\dfrac{-be^{-bt}(1+Ae^{-bt}) + 2Abe^{-2bt}}{(1+Ae^{-bt})^3}\right]$

$= Ab^2Ce^{-bt}\left[\dfrac{-1-Ae^{-bt}+2Ae^{-bt}}{(1+Ae^{-bt})^3}\right]$

$= Ab^2Ce^{-bt}\left[\dfrac{Ae^{-bt}-1}{(1+Ae^{-bt})^3}\right]$

$\therefore\ f''(t) = 0$ when $Ae^{-bt} = 1$

But when $Ae^{-bt} = 1$, $f(t) = \dfrac{C}{1 + Ae^{-bt}} = \dfrac{C}{1+1} = \dfrac{C}{2}$

$\therefore\ f(t)$ has a point of inflection with y-coordinate $\dfrac{C}{2}$.

REVIEW SET 22A

1 a $y = e^{x^3+2}$
   $= e^u$ where $u = x^3 + 2$

   $\therefore\ \dfrac{dy}{dx} = \dfrac{dy}{du}\dfrac{du}{dx}$ {chain rule}

   $= e^u \times 3x^2$
   $= 3x^2 e^u$
   $= 3x^2 e^{x^3+2}$

b $y = \dfrac{e^x}{x^2}$

   $\therefore\ \dfrac{dy}{dx} = \dfrac{e^x x^2 - e^x(2x)}{x^4}$ {quotient rule}

   $= \dfrac{xe^x(x-2)}{x^4}$

   $= \dfrac{e^x(x-2)}{x^3}$

c Consider $\ln(2y+1) = xe^y$

Differentiating with respect to x, $\dfrac{d}{dx}(\ln(2y+1)) = \dfrac{d}{dx}(xe^y)$

$\therefore\ \dfrac{2}{2y+1}\dfrac{dy}{dx} = \dfrac{d}{dx}(x)e^y + x\dfrac{d}{dx}(e^y)$

$\therefore\ \dfrac{2}{2y+1}\dfrac{dy}{dx} = e^y + xe^y\dfrac{dy}{dx}$

$\therefore\ \dfrac{dy}{dx}\left(\dfrac{2}{2y+1} - xe^y\right) = e^y$

$\therefore\ \dfrac{dy}{dx}(2 - xe^y(2y+1)) = e^y(2y+1)$

$\therefore\ \dfrac{dy}{dx} = \dfrac{e^y(2y+1)}{2 - xe^y(2y+1)}$

2 $y = e^{-x^2}$ so when $x = 1$,

$y = e^{-x^2} = e^{-1} = \dfrac{1}{e}$

$\therefore$ the point of contact is $\left(1, \dfrac{1}{e}\right)$

Now $\dfrac{dy}{dx} = -2xe^{-x^2}$

$\therefore$ when $x = 1$, $\dfrac{dy}{dx} = -2e^{-1}$

$\therefore$ the gradient of the tangent is $-\dfrac{2}{e}$

and the gradient of the normal is $\dfrac{e}{2}$

$\therefore$ the equation of the normal is $\dfrac{y - \dfrac{1}{e}}{x - 1} = \dfrac{e}{2}$

$\therefore\ 2\left(y - \dfrac{1}{e}\right) = e(x-1)$

$\therefore\ 2y - \dfrac{2}{e} = ex - e$

$\therefore\ 2ey - 2 = e^2 x - e^2$

$\therefore\ e^2 x - 2ey = e^2 - 2$ or $y = \dfrac{e}{2}x - \dfrac{e}{2} + \dfrac{1}{e}$

3 The graphs meet when $e^x + 3 = 9 - 5e^{-x}$

$\therefore\ e^{2x} + 3e^x = 9e^x - 5$ $\{\times e^x\}$

$\therefore\ e^{2x} - 6e^x + 5 = 0$

$\therefore\ (e^x - 5)(e^x - 1) = 0$

$\therefore\ e^x = 5$ or $e^x = 1$

$\therefore\ x = \ln 5$ or 0

When $x = \ln 5$, $y = 5 + 3 = 8$
and when $x = 0$, $y = 1 + 3 = 4$

$\therefore$ the graphs meet at $(\ln 5, 8)$ and $(0, 4)$

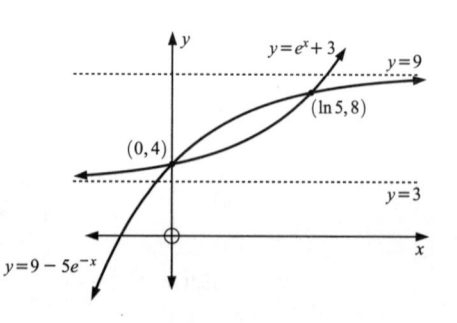

4 **a** $f(x) = \dfrac{e^x}{x-1}$ has no x-intercepts since e^x is never 0.

Now $f(0) = \dfrac{e^0}{-1} = -1$ so the y-intercept is -1.

b $f(x)$ is defined for all $x \neq 1$.

c $f'(x) = \dfrac{e^x(x-1) - e^x(1)}{(x-1)^2}$ {quotient rule}

$= \dfrac{e^x(x-2)}{(x-1)^2}$ and has sign diagram:

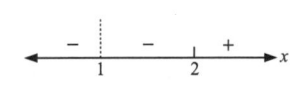

$\qquad\qquad\qquad\qquad\qquad\qquad\qquad\qquad\qquad\quad \underset{1\quad\ 2}{\xleftarrow{\ -\ \vdots\ -\ \vdots\ +\ }\!\!\to x}$

$\therefore$ $f(x)$ is decreasing for $x < 1$ and $1 < x \leqslant 2$, and increasing for $x \geqslant 2$.

$f''(x) = \dfrac{[e^x(x-2) + e^x(1)](x-1)^2 - e^x(x-2)[2(x-1)^1(1)]}{(x-1)^4}$ {product and quotient rules}

$= \dfrac{[e^x(x-2+1)(x-1)^2] - 2e^x(x-2)(x-1)}{(x-1)^4}$

$= \dfrac{e^x(x-1)(x-1)^2 - 2e^x(x-2)(x-1)}{(x-1)^4}$

$= \dfrac{e^x(x-1)[(x-1)^2 - 2(x-2)]}{(x-1)^4}$

$= \dfrac{e^x(x-1)[x^2 - 2x + 1 - 2x + 4]}{(x-1)^4}$

$= \dfrac{e^x(x^2 - 4x + 5)}{(x-1)^3}$ where the quadratic term has $\Delta < 0$

The sign diagram of $f''(x)$ is: $\underset{\quad 1}{\xleftarrow{\ -\ \vdots\ +\ }\!\!\to x}$ $\therefore$ $f(x)$ is concave down for all $x < 1$ and concave up for all $x > 1$.

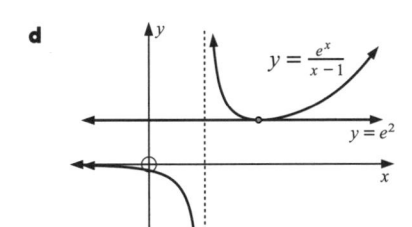

Now $f(2) = \dfrac{e^2}{2-1} = e^2$

Using **c** we have a local minimum at $(2,\ e^2)$

$\therefore$ the tangent at $x = 2$ is horizontal and is $y = e^2$.

d Graph showing $y = \dfrac{e^x}{x-1}$ with horizontal asymptote $y = e^2$ indicated and vertical asymptote $x = 1$.

5 $H(t) = 60 + 40\ln(2t + 1)$ cm, $t \geqslant 0$

a When first planted, $t = 0$ $\therefore$ $H(0) = 60 + 40\ln(1) = 60 + 40(0) = 60$ cm.

b **i** When $H(t) = 150$ cm,

$\therefore$ $60 + 40\ln(2t+1) = 150$

$\therefore$ $40\ln(2t+1) = 90$

$\therefore$ $\ln(2t+1) = \tfrac{90}{40} = 2.25$

$\therefore$ $2t + 1 = e^{2.25}$

$\therefore$ $2t = e^{2.25} - 1$

$\therefore$ $t = \tfrac{1}{2}(e^{2.25} - 1)$

$\therefore$ $t \approx 4.24$ years

ii When $H(t) = 300$ cm,

$\therefore$ $60 + 40\ln(2t+1) = 300$

$\therefore$ $40\ln(2t+1) = 240$

$\therefore$ $\ln(2t+1) = 6$

$\therefore$ $2t + 1 = e^6$

$\therefore$ $2t = e^6 - 1$

$\therefore$ $t = \tfrac{1}{2}(e^6 - 1)$

$\therefore$ $t \approx 201$ years

c $H'(t) = 40\left(\dfrac{2}{2t+1}\right) = \dfrac{80}{2t+1}$ cm per year

i When $t = 2$, $H'(2) = \tfrac{80}{5} = 16$ cm per year

ii When $t = 20$, $H'(20) = \tfrac{80}{41} \approx 1.95$ cm per year

6 $s(t) = 80e^{-\frac{t}{10}} - 40t$ metres, $t \geqslant 0$

a $v(t) = s'(t) = -8e^{-\frac{t}{10}} - 40$ m s^{-1}
$a(t) = v'(t) = 0.8e^{-\frac{t}{10}}$ m s^{-2}

b When $t = 0$, $s(0) = 80$ m
$v(0) = -48$ m s^{-1}
$a(0) = 0.8$ m s^{-2}

c As $t \to \infty$, $e^{-\frac{t}{10}} \to 0$ $\therefore$ $v(t) \to -40$ m s^{-1} (below)

d

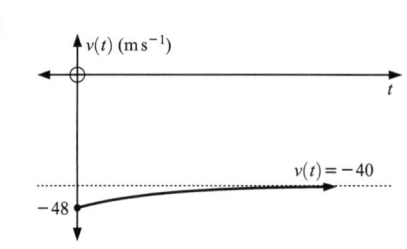

$v(t)$ (m s^{-1})

$v(t) = -40$

-48

e When $v(t) = -44$ m s^{-1}
$\therefore -8e^{-\frac{t}{10}} - 40 = -44$
$\therefore -8e^{-\frac{t}{10}} = -4$
$\therefore e^{-\frac{t}{10}} = 0.5$
$\therefore -\frac{t}{10} = \ln 0.5$
$\therefore t = -10\ln 0.5$
$\therefore t \approx 6.93$ seconds

7 Let the coordinates of B be $(x, 0)$
$\therefore$ the coordinates of A are (x, e^{-2x})
$\therefore$ the area OBAC is $A = xe^{-2x}$
$\therefore \dfrac{dA}{dx} = (1)e^{-2x} + x(-2e^{-2x})$ {product rule}
$= e^{-2x}(1 - 2x)$
$= \dfrac{1 - 2x}{e^{2x}}$ and has sign diagram:

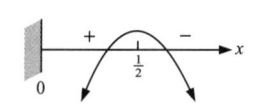

There is a local maximum when $x = \frac{1}{2}$
and when $x = \frac{1}{2}$, $y = e^{-2(\frac{1}{2})} = e^{-1} = \dfrac{1}{e}$

$\therefore$ the coordinates of A are $\left(\dfrac{1}{2}, \dfrac{1}{e}\right)$

8 $P(x) = R(x) - C(x)$
$= \left[200\ln\left(1 + \dfrac{x}{100}\right) + 1000\right] - \left[(x - 100)^2 + 200\right]$
$= 200\ln(1 + 0.01x) - (x - 100)^2 + 800$

$\dfrac{dP}{dx} = 200\left(\dfrac{0.01}{1 + 0.01x}\right) - 2(x - 100)^1$

$= \dfrac{2}{1 + 0.01x} - \dfrac{2(x - 100)}{1}$

$= \dfrac{2 - 2(x - 100)(1 + 0.01x)}{1 + 0.01x}$

$= \dfrac{2 - 2(x + 0.01x^2 - 100 - x)}{1 + 0.01x}$

$= \dfrac{2 - 0.02x^2 + 200}{1 + 0.01x}$

$= \dfrac{202 - 0.02x^2}{1 + 0.01x}$

$\therefore \dfrac{dP}{dx} = 0$ when $0.02x^2 = 202$
$\therefore x^2 = 10\,100$
$\therefore x = \sqrt{10\,100}$ {as $x > 0$}
$\therefore x \approx 100.49$

and the sign diagram of $\dfrac{dP}{dx}$ is:

$\therefore$ maximum profit occurs when $x \approx 100.49$

Now $P(100) = \$938.63$ and $P(101) = \$938.63$
$\therefore$ maximum daily profit of $\$938.63$ when 100 or 101 shirts are made.

9 $y = \ln(x^2 + 3)$

$\therefore \dfrac{dy}{dx} = \dfrac{2x}{x^2 + 3}$

When $x = 0$, $\dfrac{dy}{dx} = 0$ so the gradient of the tangent at this point is 0.

But when $x = 0$, $y = \ln(0 + 3) = \ln 3$

$\therefore$ the tangent is $y = \ln 3$ which does not cut the x-axis.

10 a $y = x2^x$
$\therefore \ln y = \ln(x2^x)$
$\therefore \ln y = \ln x + x \ln 2$
$\therefore \dfrac{1}{y}\dfrac{dy}{dx} = \dfrac{1}{x} + \ln 2$
$\therefore \dfrac{dy}{dx} = y\left(\dfrac{1}{x} + \ln 2\right)$
$= x 2^x \left(\dfrac{1}{x} + \ln 2\right)$
$= 2^x (1 + x \ln 2)$

b $y = \dfrac{(x^2 + 2)(x - 3)}{1 - x^3}$

$\therefore \ln y = \ln\left[\dfrac{(x^2 + 2)(x - 3)}{1 - x^3}\right]$

$\therefore \ln y = \ln(x^2 + 2) + \ln(x - 3) - \ln(1 - x^3)$

$\therefore \dfrac{1}{y}\dfrac{dy}{dx} = \dfrac{2x}{x^2 + 2} + \dfrac{1}{x - 3} - \dfrac{-3x^2}{1 - x^3}$

$\therefore \dfrac{dy}{dx} = y\left[\dfrac{2x}{x^2 + 2} + \dfrac{1}{x - 3} + \dfrac{3x^2}{1 - x^3}\right]$

$= \dfrac{(x^2 + 2)(x - 3)}{1 - x^3}\left[\dfrac{2x}{x^2 + 2} + \dfrac{1}{x - 3} + \dfrac{3x^2}{1 - x^3}\right]$

REVIEW SET 22B

1 a $y = \ln(x^3 - 3x)$

$\therefore \dfrac{dy}{dx} = \dfrac{3x^2 - 3}{x^3 - 3x}$

b $y = \ln\left(\dfrac{x + 3}{x^2}\right)$
$= \ln(x + 3) - \ln x^2$
$= \ln(x + 3) - 2 \ln x$

$\therefore \dfrac{dy}{dx} = \dfrac{1}{x + 3} - \dfrac{2}{x}$

c Consider $e^{x+y} = \ln(y^2 + 1)$.
Differentiating with respect to x,

$\left(1 + \dfrac{dy}{dx}\right) e^{x+y} = \dfrac{2y}{y^2 + 1} \dfrac{dy}{dx}$

$\therefore \left(1 + \dfrac{dy}{dx}\right) e^{x+y}(y^2 + 1) = 2y \dfrac{dy}{dx}$

$\therefore e^{x+y}(y^2 + 1) = \dfrac{dy}{dx}(2y - e^{x+y}(y^2 + 1))$

$\therefore \dfrac{dy}{dx} = \dfrac{e^{x+y}(y^2 + 1)}{2y - e^{x+y}(y^2 + 1)}$

d $y = x^{x^2}$

$\therefore \ln y = \ln x^{x^2}$
$\therefore \ln y = x^2 \ln x$

Differentiating with respect to x,

$\dfrac{1}{y}\dfrac{dy}{dx} = 2x \ln x + x^2 \left(\dfrac{1}{x}\right)$

$\therefore \dfrac{dy}{dx} = y(2x \ln x + x)$
$= x^{x^2}(2x \ln x + x)$
$= x^{x^2 + 1}(2 \ln x + 1)$

2 $y = \ln(x^4 + 3)$

$\therefore \dfrac{dy}{dx} = \dfrac{4x^3}{x^4 + 3}$

$\therefore$ when $x = 1$, $\dfrac{dy}{dx} = \dfrac{4(1)^3}{1^4 + 3} = 1$ and $y = \ln(1^4 + 3) = \ln 4$

$\therefore$ the tangent has equation $\dfrac{y - \ln 4}{x - 1} = 1$ or $y = x - 1 + \ln 4$

Now when $x = 0$, $y = \ln 4 - 1$, so the tangent cuts the y-axis at $(0, \ln 4 - 1)$.

3 a $e^{2x} = 3e^x$
$\therefore\ e^{2x} - 3e^x = 0$
$\therefore\ e^x(e^x - 3) = 0$
$\therefore\ e^x = 0$ or 3
$\therefore\ e^x = 3$ {as $e^x > 0$}
$\therefore\ x = \ln 3$

b $e^{2x} - 7e^x + 12 = 0$
$\therefore\ (e^x - 3)(e^x - 4) = 0$
$\therefore\ e^x = 3$ or 4
$\therefore\ x = \ln 3$ or $\ln 4$

4 $f(x) = e^x - x$

a $f'(x) = e^x - 1$
so $f'(x) = 0$ when $e^x = 1$
$\therefore\ x = 0$

Sign diagram of $f'(x)$ is:

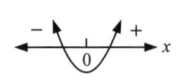

Now $f(0) = e^0 - 0 = 1$
$\therefore$ there is a local minimum at $(0, 1)$.

c $f''(x) = e^x$
$\therefore\ f''(x) > 0$ for all x
$\therefore\ f(x)$ is concave up for all x

b As $x \to \infty$, $e^x \to \infty$ faster than x
$\therefore\ f(x) \to \infty$
As $x \to -\infty$, $e^x \to 0$
$\therefore\ f(x) \to -x$ (from above)

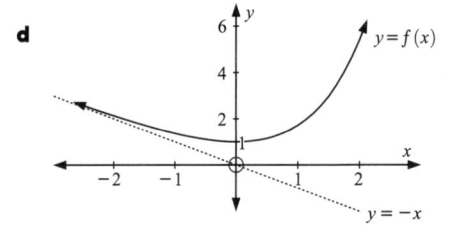

d

e Since a local minimum exists at $(0, 1)$,
$f(x) \geqslant 1$ for all x
$\therefore\ e^x - x \geqslant 1$
$\therefore\ e^x \geqslant x + 1$ for all x

5 a $f(x) = \ln(e^x + 3)$
$\therefore\ y = \ln u$ where $u = e^x + 3$
$\therefore\ \dfrac{dy}{dx} = \dfrac{dy}{du}\dfrac{du}{dx}$ {chain rule}
$= \dfrac{1}{u} \times e^x$
$= \dfrac{e^x}{u}$
$\therefore\ f'(x) = \dfrac{e^x}{e^x + 3}$

b $f(x) = \ln\left[\dfrac{(x+2)^3}{x}\right]$
$= \ln(x+2)^3 - \ln x$
$= 3\ln(x+2) - \ln x$
$\therefore\ f'(x) = \dfrac{3}{x+2} - \dfrac{1}{x}$
$= \dfrac{3x - (x+2)}{x(x+2)}$
$= \dfrac{2x - 2}{x(x+2)}$

6 a $3e^x - 5 = -2e^{-x}$
$\therefore\ 3e^{2x} - 5e^x = -2$ { $\times e^x$ }
$\therefore\ 3e^{2x} - 5e^x + 2 = 0$
$\therefore\ (3e^x - 2)(e^x - 1) = 0$
$\therefore\ e^x = \tfrac{2}{3}$ or 1
$\therefore\ x = \ln \tfrac{2}{3}$ or 0

b $2\ln x - 3\ln\left(\dfrac{1}{x}\right) = 10$
$\therefore\ 2\ln x - 3\ln(x^{-1}) = 10$
$\therefore\ 2\ln x + 3\ln x = 10$
$\therefore\ 5\ln x = 10$
$\therefore\ \ln x = 2$
$\therefore\ x = e^2$

7 a $s(t) = 25t - 10\ln t$ cm, $t \geq 1$

$\therefore\ v(t) = 25 - \dfrac{10}{t}$ cm min^{-1}

$\therefore\ a(t) = 10t^{-2}$

$= \dfrac{10}{t^2}$ cm min^{-2}

b When $t = e$,
$s(e) = 25e - 10\ln e = 25e - 10$
≈ 58.0 cm

$v(e) = 25 - \dfrac{10}{e}$ cm min^{-1}
≈ 21.3 cm min^{-1}

$a(e) = \dfrac{10}{e^2}$ cm min$^{-2} \approx 1.35$ cm min^{-2}

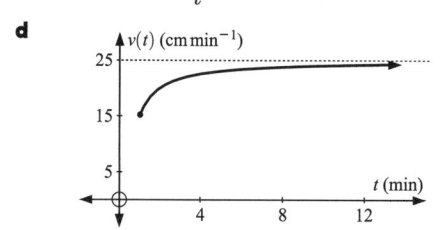

c As $t \to \infty$, $\dfrac{10}{t} \to 0$ $\therefore\ v(t) \to 25$ cm min^{-1} (below)

d

e When $v(t) = 12$ cm min^{-1},

$25 - \dfrac{10}{t} = 12$

$\therefore\ \dfrac{10}{t} = 13$

$\therefore\ t = \dfrac{10}{13}$ minutes

8 $C(x) = 10\ln x + \left(20 - \dfrac{x}{10}\right)^2 = 10\ln x + 400 - 4x + \dfrac{x^2}{100}$

$\therefore\ C'(x) = \dfrac{10}{x} - 4 + \dfrac{x}{50} = \dfrac{500 - 200x + x^2}{50x}$

$\therefore\ C'(x) = 0$ when $x^2 - 200x + 500 = 0$

$\therefore\ x = \dfrac{200 \pm \sqrt{38\,000}}{2}$

≈ 2.53 or 197.47

But $x \geq 50$, so $x \approx 197.47$

Now $C''(x) = -10x^{-2} + \dfrac{1}{50}$

$\therefore\ C''(197.47) = -10(197.47)^{-2} + 0.02 \approx 0.02$ which is > 0

$\therefore$ the minimum cost is when $x \approx 197.47$

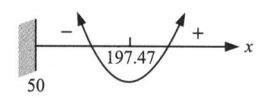

$C(197) \approx 52.92$ and $C(198) \approx 52.92$

$\therefore$ the manufacturer needs to produce 197 or 198 clocks per day to minimise costs.

9 Let the coordinates of A be $(x, 0)$

$\therefore$ the coordinates of P are (x, ae^{-x})

OAPB has perimeter $P = 2(x + ae^{-x})$
$= 2x + 2ae^{-x}$

$\therefore\ \dfrac{dP}{dx} = 2 - 2ae^{-x}$

$= 2\left(1 - \dfrac{a}{e^x}\right)$

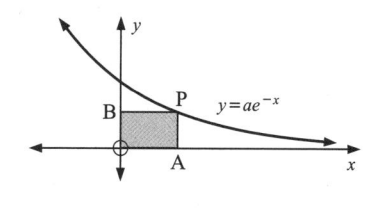

Now $\dfrac{dP}{dx} = 0$ when $1 = \dfrac{a}{e^x}$

$\therefore\ e^x = a$

$\therefore\ x = \ln a$

$\therefore$ there is a local minimum when $x = \ln a$

When $x = \ln a$, $y = ae^{-(\ln a)} = \dfrac{a}{e^{\ln a}} = 1$

$\therefore$ rectangle OAPB has minimum perimeter when P is at $(\ln a, 1)$.

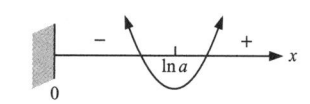

10 a $f(x) = x + \ln x$ is defined when $x > 0$

b $f'(x) = 1 + \frac{1}{x} = \frac{x+1}{x}$ which has sign diagram

$\therefore$ $f(x)$ is increasing for all $x > 0$.

$f''(x) = -\frac{1}{x^2}$ which has sign diagram

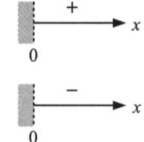

$\therefore$ $f(x)$ is concave down for all $x > 0$.

c

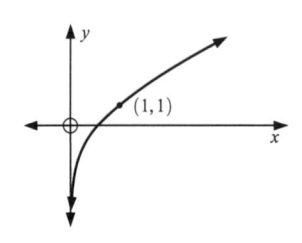

$f(1) = 1 + \ln(1) = 1$

$\therefore$ (1, 1) is the point of contact.

$f'(1) = \frac{1+1}{1} = 2$

$\therefore$ the tangent at $x = 1$ has gradient 2 and the normal has gradient $-\frac{1}{2}$

$\therefore$ the normal has equation $\frac{y-1}{x-1} = -\frac{1}{2}$

$\therefore$ $2y - 2 = -x + 1$

$\therefore$ $x + 2y = 3$

Chapter 23
DERIVATIVES OF CIRCULAR FUNCTIONS AND RELATED RATES

EXERCISE 23A

1

a $y = \sin(2x)$
$\therefore \dfrac{dy}{dx} = \cos(2x)\dfrac{d}{dx}(2x)$
$= 2\cos(2x)$

b $y = \sin x + \cos x$
$\therefore \dfrac{dy}{dx} = \cos x - \sin x$

c $y = \cos(3x) - \sin x$
$\therefore \dfrac{dy}{dx} = -\sin(3x) \times 3 - \cos x$
$= -3\sin(3x) - \cos x$

d $y = \sin(x+1)$
$\therefore \dfrac{dy}{dx} = \cos(x+1)\dfrac{d}{dx}(x+1)$
$= 1\cos(x+1)$
$= \cos(x+1)$

e $y = \cos(3-2x)$
$\therefore \dfrac{dy}{dx} = -\sin(3-2x) \times -2$
$= 2\sin(3-2x)$

f $y = \tan(5x)$
$\therefore \dfrac{dy}{dx} = \sec^2(5x) \times 5$
$= 5\sec^2(5x)$

g $y = \sin\left(\dfrac{x}{2}\right) - 3\cos x$
$\therefore \dfrac{dy}{dx} = \tfrac{1}{2}\cos\left(\dfrac{x}{2}\right) + 3\sin x$

h $y = 3\tan(\pi x)$
$\therefore \dfrac{dy}{dx} = 3 \times \sec^2(\pi x) \times \pi$
$= 3\pi \sec^2(\pi x)$

i $y = 4\sin x - \cos(2x)$
$\therefore \dfrac{dy}{dx} = 4\cos x + \sin(2x) \times 2$
$= 4\cos x + 2\sin(2x)$

2

a $y = x^2 + \cos x$
$\therefore \dfrac{dy}{dx} = 2x - \sin x$

b $y = \tan x - 3\sin x$
$\therefore \dfrac{dy}{dx} = \sec^2 x - 3\cos x$

c $y = e^x \cos x$
$\therefore \dfrac{dy}{dx} = e^x \cos x + e^x(-\sin x)$
$= e^x \cos x - e^x \sin x$

d $y = e^{-x}\sin x$
$\therefore \dfrac{dy}{dx} = -e^{-x}\sin x + e^{-x}\cos x$

e $y = \ln(\sin x)$
$\therefore \dfrac{dy}{dx} = \dfrac{\cos x}{\sin x}$
$= \cot x$

f $y = e^{2x}\tan x$
$\therefore \dfrac{dy}{dx} = 2e^{2x}\tan x + e^{2x}\sec^2 x$

g $y = \sin(3x)$
$\therefore \dfrac{dy}{dx} = 3\cos(3x)$

h $y = \cos(\tfrac{x}{2})$
$\therefore \dfrac{dy}{dx} = -\tfrac{1}{2}\sin(\tfrac{x}{2})$

i $y = 3\tan(2x)$
$\therefore \dfrac{dy}{dx} = 3 \times \sec^2(2x) \times 2$
$= 6\sec^2(2x)$

j $y = x\cos x$
$\therefore \dfrac{dy}{dx} = 1 \times \cos x + x(-\sin x)$
$= \cos x - x\sin x$

k $\quad y = \dfrac{\sin x}{x}$

$\therefore \dfrac{dy}{dx} = \dfrac{(\cos x)(x) - \sin x \times 1}{x^2}$

$\quad = \dfrac{x\cos x - \sin x}{x^2}$

l $\quad y = x\tan x$

$\therefore \dfrac{dy}{dx} = 1 \times \tan x + x \times \sec^2 x$

$\quad = \tan x + x\sec^2 x$

3 a $\quad y = \sin(x^2)$

$\therefore \dfrac{dy}{dx} = 2x\cos(x^2)$

b $\quad y = \cos\left(\sqrt{x}\right)$

$\quad = \cos(x^{\frac{1}{2}})$

$\therefore \dfrac{dy}{dx} = -\sin(x^{\frac{1}{2}}) \times \tfrac{1}{2}x^{-\frac{1}{2}}$

$\quad = -\dfrac{1}{2\sqrt{x}}\sin(\sqrt{x})$

c $\quad y = \sqrt{\cos x}$

$\quad = (\cos x)^{\frac{1}{2}}$

$\therefore \dfrac{dy}{dx} = \tfrac{1}{2}(\cos x)^{-\frac{1}{2}} \times (-\sin x)$

$\quad = -\dfrac{\sin x}{2\sqrt{\cos x}}$

d $\quad y = \sin^2 x$

$\quad = (\sin x)^2$

$\therefore \dfrac{dy}{dx} = 2\sin x \cos x$

e $\quad y = \cos^3 x$

$\quad = (\cos x)^3$

$\therefore \dfrac{dy}{dx} = 3\cos^2 x \times (-\sin x)$

$\quad = -3\sin x \cos^2 x$

f $\quad y = \cos x \sin(2x)$

$\therefore \dfrac{dy}{dx} = (-\sin x)\sin(2x) + \cos x(2\cos(2x))$

$\quad = -\sin x \sin(2x) + 2\cos x \cos(2x)$

g $\quad y = \cos(\cos x)$

$\therefore \dfrac{dy}{dx} = -\sin(\cos x) \times (-\sin x)$

$\quad = \sin x \sin(\cos x)$

h $\quad y = \cos^3(4x)$

$\quad = (\cos(4x))^3$

$\therefore \dfrac{dy}{dx} = 3(\cos(4x))^2 \times (-4\sin(4x))$

$\quad = -12\sin(4x)\cos^2(4x)$

i $\quad y = \csc x$

$\quad = (\sin x)^{-1}$

$\therefore \dfrac{dy}{dx} = -1(\sin x)^{-2} \times \cos x$

$\quad = -\dfrac{\cos x}{\sin^2 x}$

j $\quad y = \sec(2x)$

$\quad = (\cos(2x))^{-1}$

$\therefore \dfrac{dy}{dx} = -1(\cos(2x))^{-2} \times (-2\sin(2x))$

$\quad = \dfrac{2\sin(2x)}{\cos^2(2x)}$

k $\quad y = \dfrac{2}{\sin^2(2x)}$

$\quad = 2(\sin(2x))^{-2}$

$\therefore \dfrac{dy}{dx} = -4(\sin(2x))^{-3} \times 2\cos(2x)$

$\quad = -\dfrac{8\cos(2x)}{\sin^3(2x)}$

l $\quad y = 8\cot^3\left(\tfrac{x}{2}\right) = 8\left[\tan\left(\tfrac{x}{2}\right)\right]^{-3}$

$\therefore \dfrac{dy}{dx} = -24\left[\tan\left(\tfrac{x}{2}\right)\right]^{-4} \times \tfrac{1}{2} \times \sec^2\left(\tfrac{x}{2}\right)$

$\quad = \dfrac{-12}{\cos^2\left(\tfrac{x}{2}\right)\tan^4\left(\tfrac{x}{2}\right)}$

4 a If $y = \sin x$, then $\dfrac{dy}{dx} = \cos x$, $\dfrac{d^2y}{dx^2} = -\sin x$, $\dfrac{d^3y}{dx^3} = -\cos x$ and $\dfrac{d^4y}{dx^4} = \sin x$

b Successive derivatives will cycle through the pattern, so $\dfrac{d^n y}{dx^n}$ may only take the values found in **a**.

$\sin x \to -\cos x \to -\sin x \to \cos x \to \sin x$ (cycle)

5 a If $y = \sin(2x + 3)$, then $\dfrac{dy}{dx} = 2\cos(2x + 3)$ and $\dfrac{d^2y}{dx^2} = -4\sin(2x + 3)$

$\therefore \ \dfrac{d^2y}{dx^2} + 4y = -4\sin(2x + 3) + 4\sin(2x + 3) = 0$

b If $y = 2\sin x + 3\cos x$, then $y' = 2\cos x - 3\sin x$ and $y'' = -2\sin x - 3\cos x$

$\therefore \ y'' + y = -2\sin x - 3\cos x + 2\sin x + 3\cos x = 0$

c $y = \dfrac{\cos x}{1 + \sin x}$ $\therefore \ \dfrac{dy}{dx} = \dfrac{(-\sin x)(1 + \sin x) - \cos x(\cos x)}{(1 + \sin x)^2}$

$= \dfrac{-\sin x - \sin^2 x - \cos^2 x}{(1 + \sin x)^2}$

$= \dfrac{-1 - \sin x}{(1 + \sin x)^2} \quad \{\sin^2 x + \cos^2 x = 1\}$

$= -\dfrac{(1 + \sin x)}{(1 + \sin x)^2} = \dfrac{-1}{1 + \sin x}$

Since $\dfrac{-1}{1 + \sin x}$ never equals 0, there are no horizontal tangents.

6 a $y = \sin x$ $\therefore \ \dfrac{dy}{dx} = \cos x$

When $x = 0$, $\dfrac{dy}{dx} = \cos 0 = 1$

$\therefore$ the tangent has equation $\dfrac{y - 0}{x - 0} = 1$

or $y = x$

b $y = \tan x$ $\therefore \ \dfrac{dy}{dx} = \sec^2 x$

When $x = 0$, $\dfrac{dy}{dx} = \dfrac{1}{\cos^2 0} = 1$

$\therefore$ the tangent has equation $\dfrac{y - 0}{x - 0} = 1$

or $y = x$

c $y = \cos x$ $\therefore \ \dfrac{dy}{dx} = -\sin x$

When $x = \tfrac{\pi}{6}$, $y = \tfrac{\sqrt{3}}{2}$

and $\dfrac{dy}{dx} = -\sin \tfrac{\pi}{6} = -\tfrac{1}{2}$

So, the normal has gradient 2,

and its equation is $\dfrac{y - \tfrac{\sqrt{3}}{2}}{x - \tfrac{\pi}{6}} = 2$

$\therefore \ y - \tfrac{\sqrt{3}}{2} = 2x - \tfrac{\pi}{3}$

$\therefore \ 2x - y = \tfrac{\pi}{3} - \tfrac{\sqrt{3}}{2}$

d $y = \csc(2x) = (\sin(2x))^{-1}$

$\therefore \ \dfrac{dy}{dx} = -1(\sin(2x))^{-2} \times 2\cos(2x)$

$= -\dfrac{2\cos(2x)}{(\sin(2x))^2}$

When $x = \tfrac{\pi}{4}$, $y = 1$

and $\dfrac{dy}{dx} = -\dfrac{2\cos \tfrac{\pi}{2}}{\left(\sin \tfrac{\pi}{2}\right)^2} = 0$

$\therefore$ the gradient of the normal is undefined, so the normal is $x = \tfrac{\pi}{4}$.

7 $d = 9.3 + 6.8\cos(0.507t)$ m

$\therefore \ \dfrac{dd}{dt} = -6.8\sin(0.507t) \times 0.507$

$= -3.4476\sin(0.507t)$

a When $t = 8$, $\dfrac{dd}{dt} \approx 2.731 > 0$

$\therefore$ the tide is rising.

b When $t = 8$, the tide is rising at the rate of 2.73 m per hour.

8 a $V(t) = 340\sin(100\pi t)$

$\therefore \ \dfrac{dV}{dt} = 340\cos(100\pi t) \times 100\pi$

$= 34\,000\pi \cos(100\pi t)$

When $t = 0.01$,

$\dfrac{dV}{dt} = 34\,000\pi \times \cos \pi$

$= -34\,000\pi$ units per second

b When $V(t)$ is a maximum, $\dfrac{dV}{dt}$ must be 0 units per second.

9 **a** The distance from $A(-x, 0)$ to $P(\cos t, \sin t)$ is fixed at 2 m.
$\therefore \ (\cos t + x)^2 + \sin^2 t = 2^2$ {triangle APQ}
$\therefore \ (\cos t + x)^2 = 4 - \sin^2 t$
$\therefore \ x + \cos t = \pm\sqrt{4 - \sin^2 t}$
$\therefore$ since $x > 0$, $x = \sqrt{4 - \sin^2 t} - \cos t$

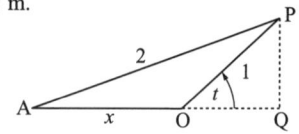

b Now $\dfrac{dx}{dt} = \tfrac{1}{2}(4 - \sin^2 t)^{-\frac{1}{2}}(-2\sin t \cos t) + \sin t$

$= \dfrac{-\sin t \cos t}{\sqrt{4 - \sin^2 t}} + \sin t$

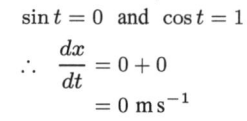

i When $t = 0$ s,
$\sin t = 0$ and $\cos t = 1$
$\therefore \ \dfrac{dx}{dt} = 0 + 0$
$= 0 \text{ ms}^{-1}$

ii When $t = \tfrac{\pi}{2}$ s,
$\sin t = 1$ and $\cos t = 0$
$\therefore \ \dfrac{dx}{dt} = 0 + \sin\tfrac{\pi}{2}$
$= 1 \text{ ms}^{-1}$

iii When $t = \tfrac{2\pi}{3}$ s,
$\sin t = \tfrac{\sqrt{3}}{2}$ and $\cos t = -\tfrac{1}{2}$
$\therefore \ \dfrac{dx}{dt} = \dfrac{-\tfrac{\sqrt{3}}{2}(-\tfrac{1}{2})}{\sqrt{4 - \tfrac{3}{4}}} + \dfrac{\sqrt{3}}{2}$
$\approx 1.11 \text{ ms}^{-1}$

10 **a** If $f(x) = \sin x$ then $f'(x) = \cos x$
Stationary points occur when $f'(x) = 0$,
which is when $x = \tfrac{\pi}{2}, \tfrac{3\pi}{2}$
Sign diagram for $f'(x)$ is:

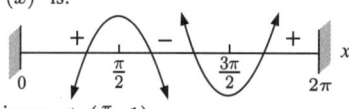

There is a local maximum at $(\tfrac{\pi}{2}, 1)$
and a local minimum at $(\tfrac{3\pi}{2}, -1)$.

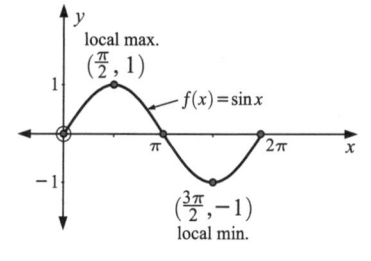

b If $f(x) = \cos(2x)$ then $f'(x) = -2\sin(2x)$
$\therefore \ f'(x) = 0$ when $-2\sin(2x) = 0$
$\therefore \ \sin(2x) = 0$
$\therefore \ 2x = k\pi$ for any integer k
$\therefore \ x = \dfrac{k\pi}{2}$
On the domain $0 \leqslant x \leqslant 2\pi$, $f'(x) = 0$
when $x = 0, \tfrac{\pi}{2}, \pi, \tfrac{3\pi}{2}$ and 2π.
Sign diagram for $f'(x)$ is:

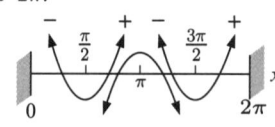

There are local maxima at $(0, 1)$, $(\pi, 1)$, $(2\pi, 1)$
and local minima at $(\tfrac{\pi}{2}, -1)$, $(\tfrac{3\pi}{2}, -1)$.

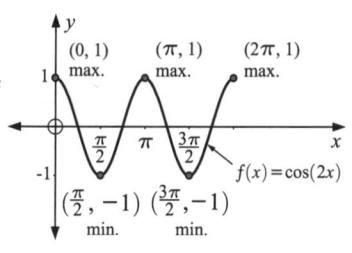

c If $f(x) = \sin^2 x$ then $f'(x) = 2\sin x \cos x = \sin(2x)$
$\therefore \ f'(x) = 0$ when $\sin(2x) = 0$
Using **b**, we know on the domain $0 \leqslant x \leqslant 2\pi$
that $f'(x) = 0$ when $x = 0, \tfrac{\pi}{2}, \pi, \tfrac{3\pi}{2}$ and 2π.
Sign diagram for $f'(x)$ is:

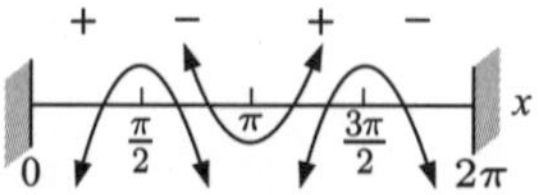

There are local minima at $(0, 0)$, $(\pi, 0)$, $(2\pi, 0)$
and local maxima at $(\tfrac{\pi}{2}, 1)$, $(\tfrac{3\pi}{2}, 1)$.

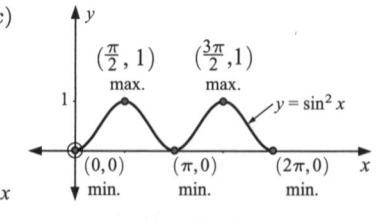

11 a $f(x) = \sec x$ for $0 \leqslant x \leqslant 2\pi$

$ = \dfrac{1}{\cos x}$

$\therefore$ $f(x)$ is undefined whenever $\cos x = 0$

which is when $x = \dfrac{\pi}{2}$ or $\dfrac{3\pi}{2}$.

b $f(x) = (\cos x)^{-1}$

$\therefore$ $f'(x) = -1(\cos x)^{-2}(-\sin x)$

$ = \dfrac{\sin x}{\cos^2 x}$

$\therefore$ $f'(x) = 0$ when $\sin x = 0$

which is when $x = 0,\ \pi,\ 2\pi$

Sign diagram for $f'(x)$ is:

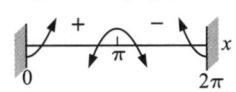

There are local minima at $(0, 1)$, $(2\pi, 1)$ and a local maximum at $(\pi, -1)$.

c $f(x) = \dfrac{1}{\cos x}$

$\therefore$ $f(x + 2\pi) = \dfrac{1}{\cos(x + 2\pi)}$

$ = \dfrac{1}{\cos x}$

$ = f(x)$

Now 2π is the smallest positive value of p such that $f(x + p) = f(x)$.

$\therefore$ $f(x)$ has a period of 2π.

d

12 $y = \sin(2x) + 2\cos x$

$\therefore$ $\dfrac{dy}{dx} = 2\cos(2x) + (-2\sin x)$

$\phantom{\therefore \dfrac{dy}{dx}} = 2[1 - 2\sin^2 x] - 2\sin x$

$\phantom{\therefore \dfrac{dy}{dx}} = 2 - 4\sin^2 x - 2\sin x$

Sign diagram for $\dfrac{dy}{dx}$ is:

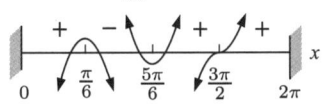

There is a local maximum at $\left(\dfrac{\pi}{6}, \dfrac{3\sqrt{3}}{2}\right)$, a local minimum at $\left(\dfrac{5\pi}{6}, -\dfrac{3\sqrt{3}}{2}\right)$, and a stationary inflection at $\left(\dfrac{3\pi}{2}, 0\right)$.

At the stationary points, $\dfrac{dy}{dx} = 0$

$\therefore$ $-4\sin^2 x - 2\sin x + 2 = 0$

$\therefore$ $2\sin^2 x + \sin x - 1 = 0$

$\therefore$ $(2\sin x - 1)(\sin x + 1) = 0$

$\therefore$ $\sin x = \dfrac{1}{2}$ or $\sin x = -1$

$\therefore$ $x = \dfrac{\pi}{6},\ \dfrac{5\pi}{6}$ or $x = \dfrac{3\pi}{2}$

13 $x(t) = 1 - 2\cos t$ cm

$\therefore$ $v(t) = x'(t) = 2\sin t$

$\therefore$ $a(t) = v'(t) = 2\cos t$

a When $t = 0$,

$x(0) = 1 - 2\cos 0$

$ = -1$ cm

$v(0) = 2\sin 0$

$ = 0$ cm s^{-1}

$a(0) = 2\cos 0$

$ = 2$ cm s^{-2}

b When $t = \dfrac{\pi}{4}$,

$x\left(\dfrac{\pi}{4}\right) = 1 - \dfrac{2}{\sqrt{2}}$

$\phantom{x\left(\dfrac{\pi}{4}\right)} = 1 - \sqrt{2}$ cm

$v\left(\dfrac{\pi}{4}\right) = \dfrac{2}{\sqrt{2}} = \sqrt{2}$ cm s^{-1}

$a\left(\dfrac{\pi}{4}\right) = \dfrac{2}{\sqrt{2}} = \sqrt{2}$ cm s^{-2}

The particle is $(\sqrt{2} - 1)$ cm left of the origin, moving right at $\sqrt{2}$ cm s^{-1} with increasing speed.

c We need to look for the points where the velocity equals zero
If $v(t) = 2\sin t = 0$
then $\sin t = 0$
$\therefore \ t = 0, \pi, 2\pi \quad (0 \leqslant t \leqslant 2\pi)$

$v(t):$ $\begin{array}{c} + - \\ \hline 0 \pi 2\pi\end{array}$ t

The particle reverses direction when $t = 0, \pi, 2\pi$.

At $t = 0$, $x(0) = -1$ cm.
At $t = \pi$, $x(\pi) = 3$ cm.
At $t = 2\pi$, $x(2\pi) = -1$ cm.

d The particle's speed is increasing when $v(t) = 2\sin t$ and $a(t) = 2\cos t$ have the same sign.
If $a(t) = 2\cos t = 0$
then $\cos t = 0$
$t = \frac{\pi}{2}, \frac{3\pi}{2} \quad (0 \leqslant t \leqslant 2\pi)$

$a(t):$ $\begin{array}{c} + \phantom{\frac{\pi}{2}} - \phantom{\frac{3\pi}{2}} + \\ \hline 0 \frac{\pi}{2} \frac{3\pi}{2} 2\pi\end{array}$ t

$\therefore$ the particle's speed is increasing when $0 \leqslant t \leqslant \frac{\pi}{2}$ and $\pi \leqslant t \leqslant \frac{3\pi}{2}$.

EXERCISE 23B

1 a $\quad y = (\cos x)^{-1} = \sec x$

$\therefore \dfrac{dy}{dx} = -\dfrac{(-\sin x)}{\cos^2 x}$ {chain rule}

$\phantom{\therefore \dfrac{dy}{dx}} = \dfrac{\tan x}{\cos x}$

$\phantom{\therefore \dfrac{dy}{dx}} = \sec x \tan x$

$\therefore \dfrac{d}{dx}(\sec x) = \sec x \tan x \quad$ as required

b $\quad y = \cot x = \dfrac{\cos x}{\sin x}$

$\therefore \dfrac{dy}{dx} = \dfrac{\dfrac{d}{dx}(\cos x)\sin x - \cos x \dfrac{d}{dx}(\sin x)}{\sin^2 x}$

{quotient rule}

$\phantom{\therefore \dfrac{dy}{dx}} = \dfrac{-\sin x \times \sin x - \cos x \times \cos x}{\sin^2 x}$

$\phantom{\therefore \dfrac{dy}{dx}} = \dfrac{-(\sin^2 x + \cos^2 x)}{\sin^2 x}$

$\phantom{\therefore \dfrac{dy}{dx}} = -\csc^2 x \quad$ as required

2 a $\quad y = x \sec x$

$\therefore \dfrac{dy}{dx} = \sec x + x \sec x \tan x$

{product rule}

$\phantom{\therefore \dfrac{dy}{dx}} = \sec x(x\tan x + 1)$

c $\quad y = 4\sec(2x)$

$\therefore \dfrac{dy}{dx} = 4\sec(2x)\tan(2x)(2)$

$\phantom{\therefore \dfrac{dy}{dx}} = 8\sec(2x)\tan(2x)$

e $\quad y = x^2 \csc x$

$\therefore \dfrac{dy}{dx} = 2x \csc x + x^2(-\csc x \cot x) \quad$ {product rule}

$\phantom{\therefore \dfrac{dy}{dx}} = x\csc x \, (2 - x\cot x)$

f $\quad y = x\sqrt{\csc x} = x(\csc x)^{\frac{1}{2}}$

$\therefore \dfrac{dy}{dx} = (\csc x)^{\frac{1}{2}} + \tfrac{1}{2}x(\csc x)^{-\frac{1}{2}}(-\csc x \cot x)$

$\phantom{\therefore \dfrac{dy}{dx}} = (\csc x)^{\frac{1}{2}} - \tfrac{1}{2}x(\csc x)^{\frac{1}{2}}\cot x$

$\phantom{\therefore \dfrac{dy}{dx}} = \sqrt{\csc x}\left(1 - \tfrac{1}{2}x\cot x\right)$

b $\quad y = e^x \cot x$

$\therefore \dfrac{dy}{dx} = e^x \cot x + e^x(-\csc^2 x)$

{product rule}

$\phantom{\therefore \dfrac{dy}{dx}} = e^x(\cot x - \csc^2 x)$

d $\quad y = e^{-x}\cot\left(\tfrac{x}{2}\right)$

$\therefore \dfrac{dy}{dx} = -e^{-x}\cot\left(\tfrac{x}{2}\right) + e^{-x}\left(-\csc^2\left(\tfrac{x}{2}\right)\right)\left(\tfrac{1}{2}\right)$

{product rule}

$\phantom{\therefore \dfrac{dy}{dx}} = -e^{-x}\left(\cot\left(\tfrac{x}{2}\right) + \tfrac{1}{2}\csc^2\left(\tfrac{x}{2}\right)\right)$

g $\quad y = \ln(\sec x)$

$\therefore \quad \dfrac{dy}{dx} = \dfrac{\frac{d}{dx}(\sec x)}{\sec x}$

$\phantom{\therefore \quad \dfrac{dy}{dx}} = \dfrac{\sec x \tan x}{\sec x} = \tan x$

i $\quad y = \dfrac{\cot x}{\sqrt{x}} = x^{-\frac{1}{2}} \cot x$

$\therefore \quad \dfrac{dy}{dx} = -\frac{1}{2} x^{-\frac{3}{2}} \cot x + x^{-\frac{1}{2}}(-\csc^2 x)$ {product rule}

$\phantom{\therefore \quad \dfrac{dy}{dx}} = -\dfrac{\cot x + 2x \csc^2 x}{2x\sqrt{x}}$

$\phantom{\therefore \quad \dfrac{dy}{dx}} = -\dfrac{\cos x \sin x + 2x}{2x\sqrt{x} \sin^2 x}$

h $\quad y = x \csc(x^2)$

$\therefore \quad \dfrac{dy}{dx} = \csc(x^2) + x\left[-\csc(x^2) \cot(x^2)\right](2x)$ {product rule}

$\phantom{\therefore \quad \dfrac{dy}{dx}} = \csc(x^2)(1 - 2x^2 \cot(x^2))$

3 a $\quad y = \sec x \quad \therefore \quad \dfrac{dy}{dx} = \sec x \tan x$

When $x = \frac{\pi}{4}$, $y = \sec \frac{\pi}{4} = \dfrac{1}{\cos \frac{\pi}{4}} = \sqrt{2}$

and $\dfrac{dy}{dx} = \sec \frac{\pi}{4} \tan \frac{\pi}{4} = \sqrt{2} \times 1 = \sqrt{2}$

$\therefore$ the tangent has equation $\dfrac{y - \sqrt{2}}{x - \frac{\pi}{4}} = \sqrt{2}$

$\therefore \quad y - \sqrt{2} = x\sqrt{2} - \dfrac{\pi\sqrt{2}}{4}$

$\therefore \quad y = x\sqrt{2} - \dfrac{\pi\sqrt{2}}{4} + \sqrt{2}$

b $\quad y = \cot\left(\dfrac{x}{2}\right) \quad \therefore \quad \dfrac{dy}{dx} = -\csc^2\left(\dfrac{x}{2}\right)\left(\dfrac{1}{2}\right)$

When $x = \frac{\pi}{3}$, $\frac{x}{2} = \frac{\pi}{6}$

$\therefore \quad y = \cot\left(\frac{\pi}{6}\right) = \sqrt{3}$

and $\dfrac{dy}{dx} = -\dfrac{1}{2 \sin^2\left(\frac{\pi}{6}\right)} = -\dfrac{1}{2\left(\frac{1}{2}\right)^2} = -2$

$\therefore$ the tangent has equation $\dfrac{y - \sqrt{3}}{x - \frac{\pi}{3}} = -2$

$\therefore \quad y - \sqrt{3} = -2x + \dfrac{2\pi}{3}$

$\therefore \quad y = -2x + \dfrac{2\pi}{3} + \sqrt{3}$

4 a $\quad y = \csc x \quad \therefore \quad \dfrac{dy}{dx} = -\csc x \cot x$

When $x = \frac{\pi}{6}$, $y = \dfrac{1}{\sin \frac{\pi}{6}} = 2$ and $\dfrac{dy}{dx} = -\csc \frac{\pi}{6} \cot \frac{\pi}{6} = -2\sqrt{3}$

$\therefore$ the normal has gradient $\dfrac{1}{2\sqrt{3}}$

and its equation is $\dfrac{y - 2}{x - \frac{\pi}{6}} = \dfrac{1}{2\sqrt{3}} \quad \therefore \quad 2\sqrt{3}y - 4\sqrt{3} = x - \frac{\pi}{6}$

$\therefore \quad x - 2\sqrt{3}y = \frac{\pi}{6} - 4\sqrt{3}$

b $\quad y = \sqrt{\sec\left(\frac{x}{3}\right)} = \left(\sec\left(\frac{x}{3}\right)\right)^{\frac{1}{2}} \quad \therefore \quad \dfrac{dy}{dx} = \frac{1}{2}\left(\sec\left(\frac{x}{3}\right)\right)^{-\frac{1}{2}} \sec\left(\frac{x}{3}\right) \tan\left(\frac{x}{3}\right)\left(\frac{1}{3}\right)$

$\phantom{\therefore \quad \dfrac{dy}{dx}} = \dfrac{\sqrt{\sec\left(\frac{x}{3}\right)} \tan\left(\frac{x}{3}\right)}{6}$

When $x = \pi$, $\dfrac{x}{3} = \dfrac{\pi}{3}$

$\therefore \quad y = \dfrac{1}{\sqrt{\cos\left(\frac{\pi}{3}\right)}} = \dfrac{1}{\sqrt{\frac{1}{2}}} = \sqrt{2}$

and $\dfrac{dy}{dx} = \dfrac{\sqrt{\sec\left(\frac{\pi}{3}\right)} \tan\left(\frac{\pi}{3}\right)}{6} = \dfrac{\sqrt{2}\sqrt{3}}{6} = \dfrac{1}{\sqrt{6}}$

$\therefore$ the normal has gradient $-\sqrt{6}$

and its equation is $\dfrac{y - \sqrt{2}}{x - \pi} = -\sqrt{6} \quad \therefore \quad y - \sqrt{2} = -x\sqrt{6} + \pi\sqrt{6}$

$\therefore \quad \sqrt{6}x + y = \pi\sqrt{6} + \sqrt{2}$

EXERCISE 23C.1

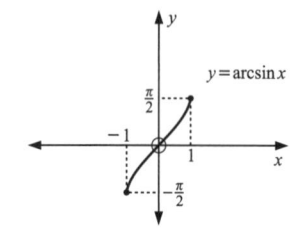

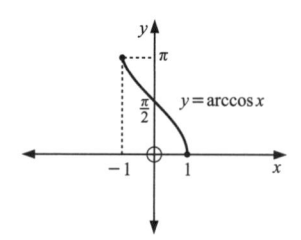

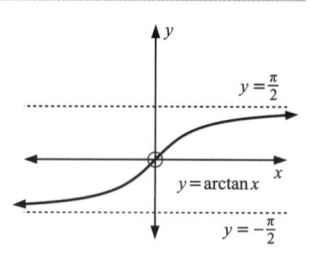

1 [Graphs of $y = \arcsin x$, $y = \arccos x$, and $y = \arctan x$]

2
- **a** $\arccos(1) = 0$
- **b** $\arcsin(-1) = -\frac{\pi}{2}$
- **c** $\arctan(1) = \frac{\pi}{4}$
- **d** $\arctan(-1) = -\frac{\pi}{4}$
- **e** $\arcsin\left(\frac{1}{2}\right) = \frac{\pi}{6}$
- **f** $\arccos\left(-\frac{\sqrt{3}}{2}\right) = \frac{5\pi}{6}$
- **g** $\arctan(\sqrt{3}) = \frac{\pi}{3}$
- **h** $\arccos\left(-\frac{1}{\sqrt{2}}\right) = \frac{3\pi}{4}$
- **i** $\arctan\left(-\frac{1}{\sqrt{3}}\right) = -\frac{\pi}{6}$
- **j** $\sin^{-1}(-0.767) \approx -0.874$
- **k** $\cos^{-1}(0.327) \approx 1.24$
- **l** $\tan^{-1}(-50) \approx -1.55$

3
- **a** If $\arcsin x = \frac{\pi}{3}$ then $x = \sin(\frac{\pi}{3}) = \frac{\sqrt{3}}{2}$
- **b** If $\arctan(3x) = -\frac{\pi}{4}$ then $3x = \tan\left(-\frac{\pi}{4}\right) = -1$ $\quad \therefore \quad x = -\frac{1}{3}$

4 Let $\theta = \arctan(5)$ $\quad \therefore \quad \tan\theta = 5$
and $\phi = \arctan(\frac{2}{3})$ $\quad \therefore \quad \tan\phi = \frac{2}{3}$

Now $\tan(\theta - \phi) = \dfrac{\tan\theta - \tan\phi}{1 + \tan\theta\tan\phi}$

$= \dfrac{5 - \frac{2}{3}}{1 + 5 \times \frac{2}{3}} = \dfrac{\frac{13}{3}}{\frac{13}{3}} = 1$

But $\tan\left(\frac{\pi}{4}\right) = 1$, so $\theta - \phi = \frac{\pi}{4}$

$\therefore \quad \arctan(5) - \arctan(\frac{2}{3}) = \frac{\pi}{4}$

5 a Let $\theta = \arctan(\frac{1}{5})$ $\quad \therefore \quad \tan\theta = \frac{1}{5}$
and $\phi = \arctan(\frac{2}{3})$ $\quad \therefore \quad \tan\phi = \frac{2}{3}$

Now $\tan(\theta + \phi) = \dfrac{\tan\theta + \tan\phi}{1 - \tan\theta\tan\phi}$

$= \dfrac{\frac{1}{5} + \frac{2}{3}}{1 - (\frac{1}{5})(\frac{2}{3})}$

$= \dfrac{\frac{13}{15}}{\frac{13}{15}} = 1$

But $\tan\left(\frac{\pi}{4}\right) = 1$, so $\theta + \phi = \frac{\pi}{4}$

$\therefore \quad \arctan(\frac{1}{5}) + \arctan(\frac{2}{3}) = \frac{\pi}{4}$

b Let $\theta = \arctan(\frac{4}{3})$ $\quad \therefore \quad \tan\theta = \frac{4}{3}$
and $\phi = \arctan(\frac{1}{2})$ $\quad \therefore \quad \tan\phi = \frac{1}{2}$

Now $\tan 2\phi = \dfrac{2\tan\phi}{1 - \tan^2\phi}$

$= \dfrac{2(\frac{1}{2})}{1 - (\frac{1}{2})^2}$

$= \dfrac{1}{\frac{3}{4}} = \frac{4}{3}$

But $\tan\theta = \frac{4}{3}$, so $\theta = 2\phi$

$\therefore \quad \arctan(\frac{4}{3}) = 2\arctan(\frac{1}{2})$

6 Let $\theta = \arctan(\frac{1}{5})$ $\quad \therefore \quad \tan\theta = \frac{1}{5}$
and $\phi = \arctan(\frac{1}{239})$ $\quad \therefore \quad \tan\phi = \frac{1}{239}$

Now $\tan 2\theta = \dfrac{2\tan\theta}{1 - \tan^2\theta} = \dfrac{2(\frac{1}{5})}{1 - (\frac{1}{5})^2} = \dfrac{\frac{2}{5}}{\frac{24}{25}} = \frac{5}{12}$

$\therefore \quad \tan 4\theta = \dfrac{2\tan 2\theta}{1 - \tan^2 2\theta} = \dfrac{2(\frac{5}{12})}{1 - (\frac{5}{12})^2} = \dfrac{\frac{5}{6}}{\frac{119}{144}} = \frac{120}{119}$

Now $\tan(4\theta - \phi) = \dfrac{\tan 4\theta - \tan \phi}{1 + \tan 4\theta \tan \phi}$

$= \dfrac{\frac{120}{119} - \frac{1}{239}}{1 + (\frac{120}{119})(\frac{1}{239})}$

$= \dfrac{120 \times 239 - 119}{119 \times 239 + 120}$

$= 1$

But $\tan(\frac{\pi}{4}) = 1$

$\therefore \quad 4\theta - \phi = \frac{\pi}{4}$

$\therefore \quad 4\arctan(\frac{1}{5}) - \arctan(\frac{1}{239}) = \frac{\pi}{4}$

EXERCISE 23C.2

1 If $y = \arccos x$ then $x = \cos y$

$\therefore \quad \dfrac{dx}{dy} = -\sin y = -\sqrt{1 - \cos^2 y} = -\sqrt{1 - x^2}$

$\therefore \quad \dfrac{dy}{dx} = -\dfrac{1}{\sqrt{1 - x^2}}, \quad x \in \,]-1,\,1[$

2 If $y = \arctan x$ then $x = \tan y$

$\therefore \quad 1 = \sec^2 y \, \dfrac{dy}{dx}$ {differentiating with respect to x}

$\therefore \quad 1 = (1 + \tan^2 y) \, \dfrac{dy}{dx}$

$\therefore \quad 1 = (1 + x^2) \, \dfrac{dy}{dx}$ and so $\dfrac{dy}{dx} = \dfrac{1}{1 + x^2}, \quad x \in \mathbb{R}$

3 a $y = \arctan(2x)$

$\therefore \quad \dfrac{dy}{dx} = 2 \times \dfrac{1}{1 + (2x)^2} = \dfrac{2}{1 + 4x^2}$

b $y = \arccos(3x)$

$\therefore \quad \dfrac{dy}{dx} = 3 \times \left(\dfrac{-1}{\sqrt{1 - (3x)^2}}\right) = -\dfrac{3}{\sqrt{1 - 9x^2}}$

c $y = \arcsin\left(\frac{x}{4}\right)$

$\therefore \quad \dfrac{dy}{dx} = \frac{1}{4} \times \dfrac{1}{\sqrt{1 - \left(\frac{x}{4}\right)^2}}$

$= \dfrac{1}{4\sqrt{1 - \frac{x^2}{16}}}$

$= \dfrac{1}{\sqrt{16 - x^2}}$

d $y = \arccos\left(\frac{x}{5}\right)$

$\therefore \quad \dfrac{dy}{dx} = \frac{1}{5} \times \left(\dfrac{-1}{\sqrt{1 - \left(\frac{x}{5}\right)^2}}\right)$

$= -\dfrac{1}{5\sqrt{1 - \frac{x^2}{25}}}$

$= -\dfrac{1}{\sqrt{25 - x^2}}$

e $y = \arctan(x^2)$

$\therefore \quad \dfrac{dy}{dx} = 2x \times \dfrac{1}{1 + (x^2)^2}$

$= \dfrac{2x}{1 + x^4}$

f $y = \arccos(\sin x)$

$\therefore \quad \dfrac{dy}{dx} = \cos x \times \left(-\dfrac{1}{\sqrt{1 - \sin^2 x}}\right)$

$= -\dfrac{\cos x}{\cos x}$

$= -1$

4 a $y = x \arcsin x$

$\therefore \quad \dfrac{dy}{dx} = \arcsin x + x \left(\dfrac{1}{\sqrt{1 - x^2}}\right)$ {product rule}

$= \arcsin x + \dfrac{x}{\sqrt{1 - x^2}}$

b $y = e^x \arccos x$ $\therefore$ $\dfrac{dy}{dx} = e^x \arccos x + e^x \left(-\dfrac{1}{\sqrt{1-x^2}}\right)$ {product rule}

$$= e^x \arccos x - \dfrac{e^x}{\sqrt{1-x^2}}$$

c $y = e^{-x} \arctan x$ $\therefore$ $\dfrac{dy}{dx} = -e^{-x} \arctan x + e^{-x}\left(\dfrac{1}{1+x^2}\right)$ {product rule}

$$= -e^{-x} \arctan x + \dfrac{e^{-x}}{1+x^2}$$

5 a $y = \arcsin\left(\dfrac{x}{a}\right)$

$\therefore$ $\dfrac{dy}{dx} = \dfrac{1}{a} \cdot \dfrac{1}{\sqrt{1-\left(\dfrac{x}{a}\right)^2}}$

$$= \dfrac{1}{a\sqrt{1-\dfrac{x^2}{a^2}}}$$

$$= \dfrac{1}{\sqrt{a^2-x^2}} \quad \text{as required,}$$

and this is defined for $x \in \,]-a,\,a[\,$.

b $y = \arctan\left(\dfrac{x}{a}\right)$

$\therefore$ $\dfrac{dy}{dx} = \dfrac{1}{a} \times \dfrac{1}{1+\left(\dfrac{x}{a}\right)^2}$

$$= \dfrac{a}{a^2} \times \dfrac{1}{1+\dfrac{x^2}{a^2}}$$

$$= \dfrac{a}{a^2+x^2} \quad \text{as required,}$$

and this is defined for $x \in \mathbb{R}$.

c $y = \arccos\left(\dfrac{x}{a}\right)$

$\therefore$ $\dfrac{dy}{dx} = \dfrac{1}{a} \times -\dfrac{1}{\sqrt{1-\left(\dfrac{x}{a}\right)^2}} = -\dfrac{1}{a\sqrt{1-\dfrac{x^2}{a^2}}}$

$$= -\dfrac{1}{\sqrt{a^2-x^2}} \quad \text{and this is defined for } x \in \,]-a,\,a[\,.$$

6 a $\tan\alpha = \dfrac{2}{x}$ and $\tan(\alpha+\theta) = \dfrac{3}{x}$

b Now $\theta = (\alpha+\theta) - \alpha = \arctan\left(\dfrac{3}{x}\right) - \arctan\left(\dfrac{2}{x}\right)$

c $\dfrac{d\theta}{dx} = \left(-\dfrac{3}{x^2}\right) \times \dfrac{1}{1+\left(\dfrac{3}{x}\right)^2} - \left(-\dfrac{2}{x^2}\right) \times \dfrac{1}{1+\left(\dfrac{2}{x}\right)^2}$

$$= -\dfrac{3}{x^2+9} + \dfrac{2}{x^2+4}$$

$$= \dfrac{2}{x^2+4} - \dfrac{3}{x^2+9} \quad \text{as required}$$

So, $\dfrac{d\theta}{dx} = 0$ when $2(x^2+9) - 3(x^2+4) = 0$

$\therefore \quad 2x^2 + 18 - 3x^2 - 12 = 0$

$\therefore \quad x^2 = 6$

$\therefore \quad x = \sqrt{6} \quad \{x > 0\}$

and $\dfrac{d\theta}{dx}$ has sign diagram: $\xrightarrow[0\sqrt{6}]{+-}\,x$

d The maximum viewing angle occurs when $x = \sqrt{6}$, which is when Sonia is $\sqrt{6}$ m from the wall.

EXERCISE 23D

1

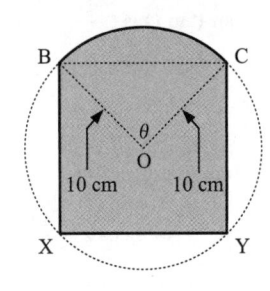

Using the cosine rule in $\triangle BCO$,
$$BC^2 = 10^2 + 10^2 - 2 \times 10 \times 10 \cos \theta$$
$$\therefore \quad BC = \sqrt{200 - 200 \cos \theta}$$
$$\therefore \quad XY = \sqrt{200 - 200 \cos \theta} \quad \text{also}$$
Now $BY^2 = BX^2 + XY^2$ {Pythagoras}
$$\therefore \quad 400 = BX^2 + (200 - 200 \cos \theta)$$
$$\therefore \quad BX^2 = 200 + 200 \cos \theta$$
$$\therefore \quad BX = \sqrt{200 + 200 \cos \theta}$$

The shaded area is equal to the area of the sector plus $\frac{3}{4}$ of the area of BCYX.
$$\therefore \quad A = \tfrac{1}{2}(10)^2 \theta + \tfrac{3}{4}[BX \times BC]$$
$$= 50\theta + \tfrac{3}{4}\sqrt{200 + 200\cos\theta}\sqrt{200 - 200\cos\theta}$$
$$= 50\theta + \tfrac{3}{4} \times 200\sqrt{1 + \cos\theta}\sqrt{1 - \cos\theta}$$
$$= 50\theta + 150\sqrt{1 - \cos^2 \theta}$$
$$= 50\theta + 150 \sin \theta$$
$$= 50(\theta + 3\sin\theta) \quad \text{as required}$$
$$\therefore \quad \frac{dA}{d\theta} = 50 + 150 \cos \theta = 50(1 + 3 \cos \theta),$$

which is zero when $\cos \theta = -\tfrac{1}{3}$
$$\therefore \quad \theta \approx 109.5°$$

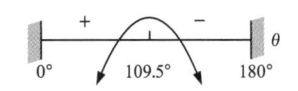

The sign diagram of $\dfrac{dA}{d\theta}$ is:

Since $0° < \theta < 180°$, A is maximised when $\theta \approx 109.5°$.

2 a

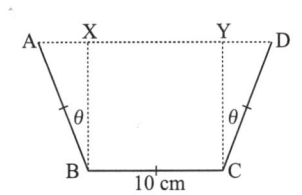

The triangles have height $10 \cos \theta$ and width $10 \sin \theta$.
$$\therefore \quad \text{area } A$$
$$= \text{area of } \triangle\text{s} + \text{area of rectangle}$$
$$= 2 \times \tfrac{1}{2} \times 10 \cos \theta \times 10 \sin \theta + 10 \times 10 \cos \theta$$
$$= 100 \sin \theta \cos \theta + 100 \cos \theta$$
$$= 100 \cos \theta (1 + \sin \theta)$$

b $\dfrac{dA}{d\theta} = 100(-\sin\theta(1 + \sin\theta) + \cos\theta \times \cos\theta)$
$$= 100(-\sin\theta - \sin^2\theta + \cos^2\theta)$$
$$= 100(-\sin\theta - \sin^2\theta + 1 - \sin^2\theta)$$
$$= -100(2\sin^2\theta + \sin\theta - 1)$$
$$= -100(2\sin\theta - 1)(\sin\theta + 1)$$
$$\therefore \quad \dfrac{dA}{d\theta} = 0 \quad \text{when} \quad 2\sin\theta - 1 = 0 \quad \text{or} \quad \sin\theta + 1 = 0$$
$$\therefore \quad \sin\theta = \tfrac{1}{2} \quad \text{or} \quad \sin\theta = -1$$

c Using **b**, $\dfrac{dA}{d\theta} = 0$ when $\theta = \tfrac{\pi}{6}, \tfrac{5\pi}{6}$ or $\tfrac{3\pi}{2}$.

But $0 \leqslant \theta \leqslant \tfrac{\pi}{2}$, so the sign diagram for $\dfrac{dA}{d\theta}$ is:

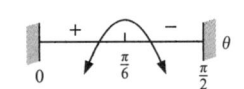

So, the maximum area occurs when $\theta = \tfrac{\pi}{6} = 30°$

3

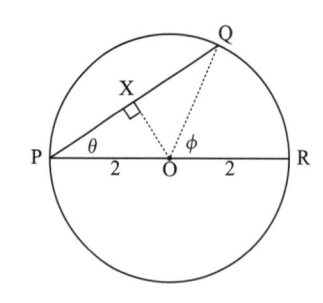

$\dfrac{PX}{2} = \cos\theta \quad \therefore \quad PQ = 2PX = 4\cos\theta$

$\therefore$ the time taken to row from P to Q is $\dfrac{4\cos\theta}{3}$ hours

Now $\phi = 2\theta$ {angle at the centre}

But, arc length $QR_{arc} = 2\phi$

$\therefore \quad QR_{arc} = 4\theta$

and the time taken to walk from Q to R is $\dfrac{4\theta}{5}$

$\therefore$ the total time from P to R, $T = \dfrac{4}{3}\cos\theta + \dfrac{4\theta}{5}$

$\therefore \quad \dfrac{dT}{d\theta} = -\dfrac{4}{3}\sin\theta + \dfrac{4}{5}$

$\therefore \quad \dfrac{dT}{d\theta} = 0$ when $-\dfrac{4}{3}\sin\theta = -\dfrac{4}{5}$

and the sign diagram of $\dfrac{dT}{d\theta}$ is:

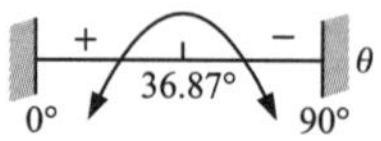

$\therefore \quad \sin\theta = \dfrac{3}{5}$

$\therefore \quad \theta \approx 0.6435$ radians

$\therefore \quad \theta \approx 36.87°$

So the maximum time occurs when $\theta \approx 36.87°$
and the maximum time is $\quad \dfrac{4}{3}\cos 0.6435 + \dfrac{4}{5} \times 0.6435$

≈ 1.581 hours

≈ 1 hour 34 min 53 sec

4 a $\tan\theta = \dfrac{2}{AX}$ and $\sin\theta = \dfrac{2}{BX}$

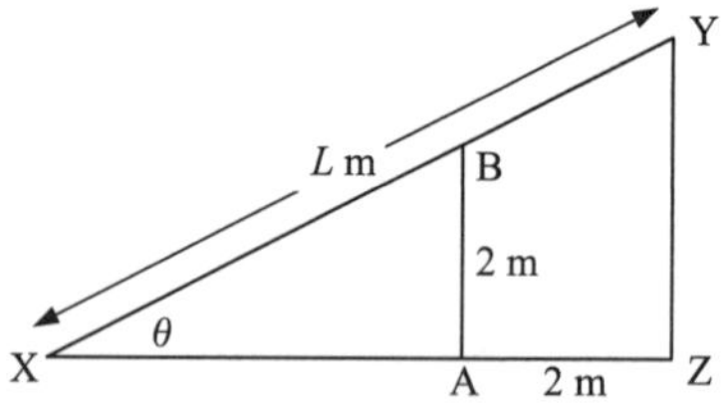

$\therefore \quad AX = \dfrac{2}{\tan\theta} = \dfrac{2\cos\theta}{\sin\theta}$ and $BX = \dfrac{2}{\sin\theta}$

From the similar $\triangle$s, $\dfrac{L}{BX} = \dfrac{AX+2}{AX} = 1 + \dfrac{2}{AX}$

$\therefore \quad L = BX + \dfrac{2BX}{AX}$

$= \dfrac{2}{\sin\theta} + \dfrac{2\left(\dfrac{2}{\sin\theta}\right)}{\left(\dfrac{2\cos\theta}{\sin\theta}\right)}$

$= \dfrac{2}{\sin\theta} + 2\left(\dfrac{2}{\sin\theta}\right)\left(\dfrac{\sin\theta}{2\cos\theta}\right)$

$= 2\sec\theta + 2\csc\theta$, as required

b Now $L = 2\sec\theta + 2\csc\theta$

$\therefore \quad \dfrac{dL}{d\theta} = 2\sec\theta\tan\theta - 2\csc\theta\cot\theta$

$= \dfrac{2\sin\theta}{\cos^2\theta} - \dfrac{2\cos\theta}{\sin^2\theta}$

$= \dfrac{2\sin^3\theta - 2\cos^3\theta}{\sin^2\theta\cos^2\theta}$

c Now $\dfrac{dL}{d\theta} = 0$ when $2\sin^3\theta - 2\cos^3\theta = 0$

$\therefore \quad 2\sin^3\theta = 2\cos^3\theta$

$\therefore \quad \tan^3\theta = 1$

$\therefore \quad \tan\theta = 1$

$\therefore$ since $0 < \theta < 90°$, $\theta = 45°$

Sign diagram of $\dfrac{dL}{d\theta}$ is:

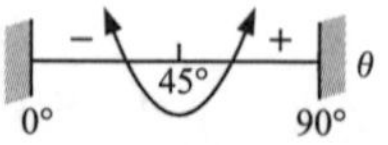

$\therefore$ the ladder is shortest when $\theta = 45°$

$\therefore \quad \sec\theta = \sqrt{2}$ and $\csc\theta = \sqrt{2}$

$\therefore \quad L_{min} = 2\sqrt{2} + 2\sqrt{2} = 4\sqrt{2}$ m

5

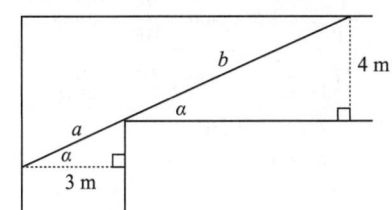

$\cos \alpha = \dfrac{3}{a}$ and $\sin \alpha = \dfrac{4}{b}$

$\therefore \quad a = 3 \sec \alpha$ and $b = 4 \csc \alpha$

Now $L = a + b$

$\therefore \quad L = 3 \sec \alpha + 4 \csc \alpha$

$\therefore \quad \dfrac{dL}{d\alpha} = 3 \sec \alpha \tan \alpha - 4 \csc \alpha \cot \alpha$

$= \dfrac{3 \sin \alpha}{\cos^2 \alpha} - \dfrac{4 \cos \alpha}{\sin^2 \alpha}$

$= \dfrac{3 \sin^3 \alpha - 4 \cos^3 \alpha}{\cos^2 \alpha \sin^2 \alpha}$

$\therefore \quad \dfrac{dL}{d\alpha} = 0$ when $3 \sin^3 \alpha - 4 \cos^3 \alpha = 0$

$\therefore \quad 3 \sin^3 \alpha = 4 \cos^3 \alpha$

$\therefore \quad \tan^3 \alpha = \dfrac{4}{3}$

$\therefore \quad \tan \alpha = \sqrt[3]{\dfrac{4}{3}}$

$\therefore \quad \alpha \approx 47.74°$

Sign diagram of $\dfrac{dL}{d\alpha}$ is:

$\therefore$ AB is minimised when $\alpha = 47.74°$ and $L = 3 \sec \alpha + 4 \csc \alpha \approx 9.87$ m

6

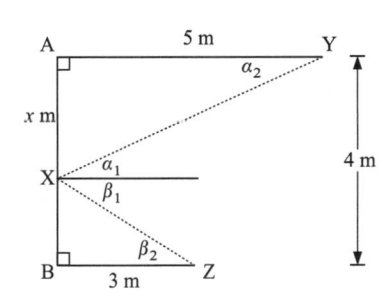

Now $\alpha_1 = \alpha_2$ and $\beta_1 = \beta_2$ {alternate angles}

$\therefore \quad \theta = \alpha + \beta$

Let AX $= x$ m

$\therefore$ XB $= (4 - x)$ m

$\therefore \quad \tan \alpha = \dfrac{x}{5}$ and $\tan \beta = \dfrac{4 - x}{3}$

Now $\tan \theta = \tan(\alpha + \beta)$

$= \dfrac{\tan \alpha + \tan \beta}{1 - \tan \alpha \tan \beta}$

$= \dfrac{\dfrac{x}{5} + \dfrac{4-x}{3}}{1 - \dfrac{x}{5}\left(\dfrac{4-x}{3}\right)} \times \dfrac{15}{15}$

$= \dfrac{3x + 20 - 5x}{15 - x(4-x)} = \dfrac{20 - 2x}{x^2 - 4x + 15}$

Differentiating both sides with respect to x

$\sec^2 \theta \dfrac{d\theta}{dx} = \dfrac{-2(x^2 - 4x + 15) - (20 - 2x)(2x - 4)}{(x^2 - 4x + 15)^2}$ {chain and quotient rules}

$= \dfrac{-2x^2 + 8x - 30 - 40x + 80 + 4x^2 - 8x}{(x^2 - 4x + 15)^2}$

$= \dfrac{2x^2 - 40x + 50}{(x^2 - 4x + 15)^2}$

$\therefore \quad \dfrac{d\theta}{dx} = 2 \cos^2 \theta \, \dfrac{x^2 - 20x + 25}{(x^2 - 4x + 15)^2}$

Now by inspection, $\theta < 90°$, so $\dfrac{d\theta}{dx} = 0$ when $x^2 - 20x + 25 = 0$

$\therefore \quad x \approx 1.3397$ or $x \approx 18.660$ (where 18.660 is not physically possible)

$\therefore \quad x \approx 1.34$ m from A

Sign diagram for $\dfrac{d\theta}{dx}$ is:

$\therefore \quad \theta$ is a maximum when $x \approx 1.34$ m from A.

7 a

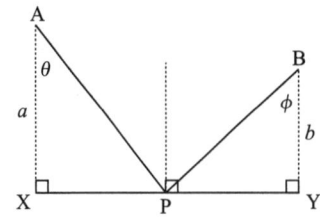

$\dfrac{a}{AP} = \cos\theta$ and $\dfrac{b}{BP} = \cos\phi$

$\therefore\ AP = \dfrac{a}{\cos\theta}$ and $BP = \dfrac{b}{\cos\phi}$

Now $L = AP + BP$

$\therefore\ L = a\sec\theta + b\sec\phi$

b $L = a\sec\theta + b\sec\phi$

$\dfrac{dL}{d\theta} = a(\sec\theta\tan\theta) + b\left(\sec\phi\tan\phi\,\dfrac{d\phi}{d\theta}\right)$

$= \dfrac{a\sin\theta}{\cos^2\theta} + \dfrac{b\sin\phi}{\cos^2\phi}\dfrac{d\phi}{d\theta}$ as required

c Now $\dfrac{XP}{a} = \tan\theta$ and $\dfrac{YP}{b} = \tan\phi$

$\therefore\ XP = a\tan\theta$ and $YP = b\tan\phi$

$\therefore\ XY = a\tan\theta + b\tan\phi$

But XY is a fixed distance,

so $a\tan\theta + b\tan\phi = c$ {c a constant}

$\therefore\ a\sec^2\theta + b\sec^2\phi\,\dfrac{d\phi}{d\theta} = 0$ {differentiating with respect to θ}

$\therefore\ b\sec^2\phi\,\dfrac{d\phi}{d\theta} = -a\sec^2\theta$

$\therefore\ \dfrac{d\phi}{d\theta} = -\dfrac{a\sec^2\theta}{b\sec^2\phi}$

$= -\dfrac{a\cos^2\phi}{b\cos^2\theta}$ as required.

d $\dfrac{dL}{d\theta} = \dfrac{a\sin\theta}{\cos^2\theta} + \dfrac{b\sin\phi}{\cos^2\phi}\left(\dfrac{-a\cos^2\phi}{b\cos^2\theta}\right)$ {using **b** and **c**}

$= \dfrac{a\sin\theta}{\cos^2\theta} - \dfrac{a\sin\phi}{\cos^2\theta}$

$= \dfrac{a(\sin\theta - \sin\phi)}{\cos^2\theta}$

$\therefore\ \dfrac{dL}{d\theta} = 0$ when $\sin\theta - \sin\phi = 0$

$\therefore\ \sin\theta = \sin\phi$

$\therefore\ \theta = \phi$ {since $\theta, \phi \in [0, \tfrac{\pi}{2}]$}

e Sign diagram of $\dfrac{dL}{d\theta}$ is:

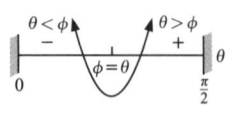

$\therefore\ AP + PB$ is a minimum when $\theta = \phi$

$\therefore$ it will be cheapest for the pump house to be located at the point such that $\theta = \phi$.

EXERCISE 23E

1 $ab^3 = 40$ $\therefore\ \dfrac{da}{dt}b^3 + a(3b^2)\dfrac{db}{dt} = 0$

Particular case: When $a = 5$, $b = 2$ and $\dfrac{db}{dt} = +1$, so $8\dfrac{da}{dt} + 5(12)(1) = 0$

$\therefore\ \dfrac{da}{dt} = -\dfrac{60}{8} = -7.5$

$\therefore\ a$ decreases at 7.5 units per second

2 $A = LB = 100$ cm^2 $\therefore \dfrac{dL}{dt}B + L\dfrac{dB}{dt} = 0$

Particular case:

When a square, $L = B = 10$ cm and $\dfrac{dL}{dt} = -1$

$\therefore \quad 10\dfrac{dB}{dt} + 10(-1) = 0$

$\therefore \quad \dfrac{dB}{dt} = 1$ cm min^{-1}

$\therefore$ the breadth is increasing at 1 cm min^{-1}.

3 $A = \pi r^2$ $\therefore \dfrac{dA}{dt} = 2\pi r \dfrac{dr}{dt} = 2\pi r$ $\left\{\text{since } \dfrac{dr}{dt} = 1 \text{ m s}^{-1}\right\}$

Particular cases:

a When $t = 2$ and $r = 2$, $\dfrac{dA}{dt} = 2\pi(2) = 4\pi$ m^2 per second

b When $t = 4$ and $r = 4$, $\dfrac{dA}{dt} = 2\pi(4) = 8\pi$ m^2 per second

4 $V = \tfrac{4}{3}\pi r^3$ $\therefore \dfrac{dV}{dt} = 4\pi r^2 \dfrac{dr}{dt} = 6\pi$ m^3 min^{-1}

$\therefore \dfrac{dr}{dt} = \dfrac{6\pi}{4\pi r^2} = \dfrac{3}{2r^2}$ m min^{-1}

Now $A = 4\pi r^2$

$\therefore \dfrac{dA}{dt} = 8\pi r \dfrac{dr}{dt} = 8\pi r \times \dfrac{3}{2r^2}$

Particular case: When $r = 2$, $\dfrac{dA}{dt} = \dfrac{8\pi \times 2 \times 3}{2 \times 4}$ m^2 min^{-1} $= 6\pi$ m^2 min^{-1}

$\therefore$ the surface area is increasing at 6π m^2 per minute.

5 $pV^{\frac{3}{2}} = 400$ $\therefore \dfrac{dp}{dt}V^{\frac{3}{2}} + \tfrac{3}{2}pV^{\frac{1}{2}}\dfrac{dV}{dt} = 0$

Particular case: When $p = 50$ Nm^{-2}, $V^{\frac{3}{2}} = 8$ and so $V = 4$

$\therefore \quad 3(8) + \tfrac{3}{2}(50)(2)\dfrac{dV}{dt} = 0$ $\left\{\text{as } \dfrac{dp}{dt} = +3 \text{ Nm}^{-2}\right\}$

$\therefore \quad \dfrac{dV}{dt} = -\dfrac{24}{150}$ m^3 min^{-1}

$\therefore$ the volume is decreasing at 0.16 m^3 per minute.

6 $V = \tfrac{1}{3}\pi r^2 h$ and $r = 3h$

$\therefore \quad V = \tfrac{1}{3}\pi(3h)^2 h = 3\pi h^3$ .... (*)

Particular case: After 1 min, the volume $V = 3\pi(20)^3$ cm^3 $= 24\,000\pi$ cm^3

$\therefore \dfrac{dV}{dt} = 24\,000\pi$ cm^3 min^{-1}

But $\dfrac{dV}{dt} = 9\pi h^2 \dfrac{dh}{dt}$ {from (*)}

$\therefore$ when $h = 20$, $24\,000\pi = 9\pi \times (20^2) \times \dfrac{dh}{dt}$

$\therefore \dfrac{dh}{dt} = \dfrac{24\,000\pi}{400 \times 9\pi} = \dfrac{20}{3}$ cm min^{-1}

$\therefore$ the height is rising at $\dfrac{20}{3}$ cm per minute.

7 $\theta = 30°$ $\therefore \dfrac{x}{h} = \tan 30°$

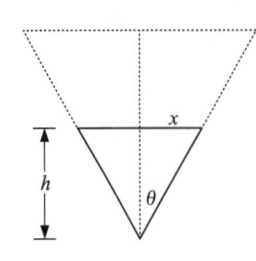

$\therefore x = h\tan 30° = \dfrac{h}{\sqrt{3}}$

$\therefore V = \dfrac{h}{\sqrt{3}} \times h \times 600 = 200\sqrt{3}h^2 \text{ cm}^3$

$\therefore \dfrac{dV}{dt} = 400\sqrt{3}h\,\dfrac{dh}{dt}$

Particular case: When $h = 20$, $-100\,000 = 400\sqrt{3}(20)\,\dfrac{dh}{dt}$ $\left\{\dfrac{dV}{dt} = -0.1 \text{ m}^3 = -100\,000 \text{ cm}^3\right\}$

$\therefore \dfrac{dh}{dt} = \dfrac{-100\,000}{400\sqrt{3} \times 20} = -\dfrac{25}{6}\sqrt{3} \text{ cm min}^{-1}$

$\therefore$ the water level is falling at $\dfrac{25\sqrt{3}}{6}$ cm per minute

8 Let P_1 in the diagram be the faster jet and P_2 be the slower jet. Let y m be the distance that P_2 is ahead of P_1, and x m be the distance between them.

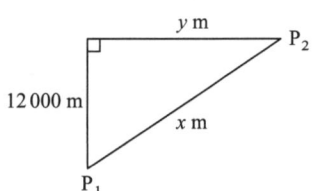

Now $x^2 = y^2 + (12\,000)^2$ {Pythagoras}

$\therefore 2x\,\dfrac{dx}{dt} = 2y\,\dfrac{dy}{dt}$

Particular case:

As P_1 is behind P_2, it is catching up at a rate of 50 m s^{-1}.

$\therefore \dfrac{dy}{dt} = -50$ m s^{-1}

When $y = 5000$, $x = 13\,000$

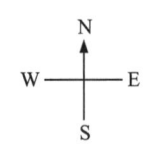

$\therefore 26\,000 \times \dfrac{dx}{dt} = 10\,000 \times (-50)$

$\dfrac{dx}{dt} = \dfrac{10}{26} \times (-50) = -\dfrac{250}{13}$ m s^{-1}

$\therefore$ their separation is decreasing at $\dfrac{250}{13}$ m s^{-1}.

9 Let S m be the height of the person's shadow and x m be the person's distance from the building. $\triangle ABC$ and $\triangle AXY$ are similar.

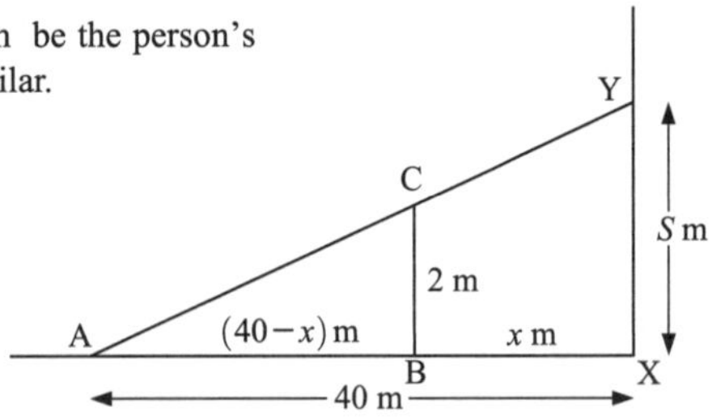

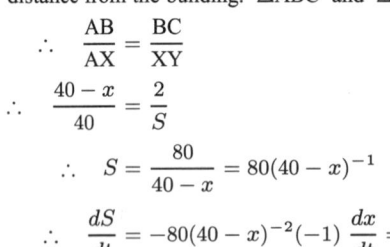

$\therefore \dfrac{AB}{AX} = \dfrac{BC}{XY}$

$\therefore \dfrac{40-x}{40} = \dfrac{2}{S}$

$\therefore S = \dfrac{80}{40-x} = 80(40-x)^{-1}$

$\therefore \dfrac{dS}{dt} = -80(40-x)^{-2}(-1)\,\dfrac{dx}{dt} = \dfrac{80}{(40-x)^2}\,\dfrac{dx}{dt}$

But $\dfrac{dx}{dt} = -1$ m s^{-1}, so $\dfrac{dS}{dt} = -\dfrac{80}{(40-x)^2}$

Particular cases:

a When $x = 20$ m, $\dfrac{dS}{dt} = -\dfrac{80}{(40-20)^2} = -\dfrac{80}{400} = -0.2$

$\therefore$ the person's shadow is shortening at 0.2 m s^{-1}

b When $x = 10$ m, $\dfrac{dS}{dt} = -\dfrac{80}{(40-10)^2} = -\dfrac{80}{900} = -\dfrac{8}{90}$

$\therefore$ the person's shadow is shortening at $\dfrac{8}{90}$ m s^{-1}

10

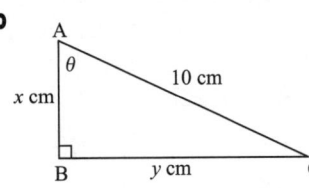

$$\cos \theta = \frac{x}{10}$$

$$\therefore \ -\sin \theta \ \frac{d\theta}{dt} = \frac{1}{10} \ \frac{dx}{dt} \quad \{\text{differentiating with respect to } t\}$$

If the length AB increases at 0.1 cm s^{-1}, $\frac{dx}{dt} = 0.1$ cm s^{-1}

Particular case: When ABC is isosceles, $\theta = 45°$

$$\therefore \ \sin \theta = \frac{1}{\sqrt{2}}$$

$$\therefore \ -\frac{1}{\sqrt{2}} \ \frac{d\theta}{dt} = \frac{1}{10} \times 0.1$$

$$\therefore \ \frac{d\theta}{dt} = -\frac{\sqrt{2}}{100} \text{ radians s}^{-1}$$

$\therefore$ $\widehat{CAB}$ is decreasing at $\frac{\sqrt{2}}{100}$ radians per second.

11

$$\tan E = \frac{5000}{x} = 5000x^{-1}$$

Differentiating with respect to t,

$$\sec^2 E \ \frac{dE}{dt} = -5000x^{-2} \ \frac{dx}{dt}$$

Now $\frac{dx}{dt} = 200$ m s^{-1},

$$\therefore \ \frac{1}{\cos^2 E} \ \frac{dE}{dt} = -5000 \times \frac{1}{x^2} \times 200$$

$$\therefore \ \frac{dE}{dt} = -1\,000\,000 \times \frac{\cos^2 E}{x^2}$$

Particular cases:

a When $E = 60°$, $\cos E = \frac{1}{2}$

and $\tan E = \sqrt{3} = \frac{5000}{x}$

$$\therefore \ x = \frac{5000}{\sqrt{3}}$$

$$\therefore \ \frac{dE}{dt} = -1\,000\,000 \times \frac{\left(\frac{1}{2}\right)^2}{\left(\frac{5000}{\sqrt{3}}\right)^2}$$

$$= -0.03$$

$\therefore$ the angle of elevation is decreasing at 0.03 radians per second

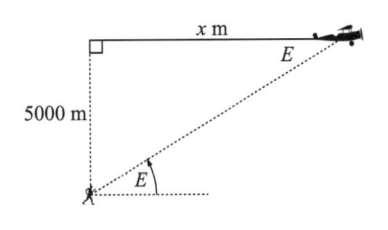

b When $E = 30°$, $\cos E = \frac{\sqrt{3}}{2}$

and $\tan E = \frac{1}{\sqrt{3}} = \frac{5000}{x}$

$$\therefore \ x = 5000\sqrt{3}$$

$$\therefore \ \frac{dE}{dt} = -1\,000\,000 \times \frac{\left(\frac{\sqrt{3}}{2}\right)^2}{\left(5000\sqrt{3}\right)^2}$$

$$= -0.01$$

$\therefore$ the angle of elevation is decreasing at 0.01 radians per second

12

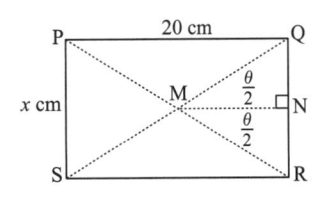

Let N be the midpoint of [QR] in isosceles triangle QMR

$\therefore$ MN $= 10$ cm

Let QR $= x$ cm and let $\widehat{QMR} = \theta$.

In triangle MNQ, $\tan\left(\frac{\theta}{2}\right) = \frac{QN}{MN} = \frac{\frac{x}{2}}{10} = \frac{x}{20}$

$$\therefore \ \tfrac{1}{2}\sec^2\left(\frac{\theta}{2}\right) \frac{d\theta}{dt} = \frac{1}{20} \ \frac{dx}{dt}$$

$$\therefore \ \frac{d\theta}{dt} = \tfrac{1}{10} \cos^2\left(\frac{\theta}{2}\right) \frac{dx}{dt}$$

where $\frac{dx}{dt} = 2$ cm s^{-1}

Particular case: When $x = 15$ cm, $\tan\left(\dfrac{\theta}{2}\right) = \dfrac{15}{20} = \dfrac{3}{4}$

$\therefore \quad \cos\left(\dfrac{\theta}{2}\right) = \dfrac{4}{5}$

$\therefore \quad \dfrac{d\theta}{dt} = \dfrac{1}{10}\left(\dfrac{4}{5}\right)^2 2 = 0.128$

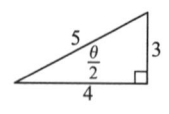

$\therefore \quad \theta$ is increasing at 0.128 radians per second

13 Let $QR = x$ cm and the angle at P be θ.

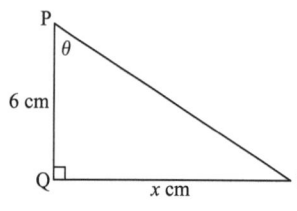

Then $\tan\theta = \dfrac{x}{6}$

$\therefore \quad \sec^2\theta \, \dfrac{d\theta}{dt} = \dfrac{1}{6}\dfrac{dx}{dt}$

$\therefore \quad \dfrac{d\theta}{dt} = \dfrac{\cos^2\theta}{6}\dfrac{dx}{dt}$ where $\dfrac{dx}{dt} = 2$ cm min^{-1}

Particular case: When $x = 8$ cm, $PR = 10$ cm

Now $\cos\theta = \dfrac{6}{10}$, so $\dfrac{d\theta}{dt} = \left(\dfrac{6}{10}\right)^2 \times \dfrac{1}{6} \times 2 = 0.12$

$\therefore \quad$ the angle at P is increasing at a rate of 0.12 radians per minute.

14 Let x and y be the distances the cyclists A and B have travelled respectively at time t, and let z be the distance between them.

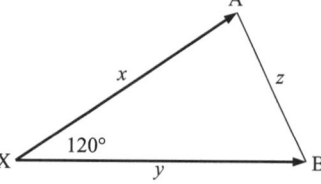

So, $z^2 = x^2 + y^2 - 2xy\cos 120°$ {cosine rule}

$\therefore \quad z^2 = x^2 + y^2 + xy$ .... (1)

$\therefore \quad 2z\dfrac{dz}{dt} = 2x\dfrac{dx}{dt} + 2y\dfrac{dy}{dt} + \dfrac{dx}{dt}y + x\dfrac{dy}{dt}$ .... (2)

Particular case:

After 2 minutes, $t = 120$ s, $x = 1440$ m, $y = 1920$ m, $\dfrac{dx}{dt} = 12$ m s^{-1}, and $\dfrac{dy}{dt} = 16$ m s^{-1}.

Using (1), $z^2 = 1440^2 + 1920^2 + 1440 \times 1920 = 8\,524\,800$

$\therefore \quad z = \sqrt{8\,524\,800} = 480\sqrt{37}$

$\therefore \quad 2\left(480\sqrt{37}\right)\dfrac{dz}{dt} = 2880(12) + 3840(16) + (12)1920 + 1440(16)$ {using (2)}

$\therefore \quad 960\sqrt{37}\,\dfrac{dz}{dt} = 142\,080$

$\therefore \quad \dfrac{dz}{dt} = \dfrac{148}{\sqrt{37}} = 4\sqrt{37} \approx 24.33$

$\therefore \quad$ the distance between the cyclists is increasing at 24.3 m s^{-1}.

15 Let $AP = l$ cm and let $A\widehat{O}P = \theta$

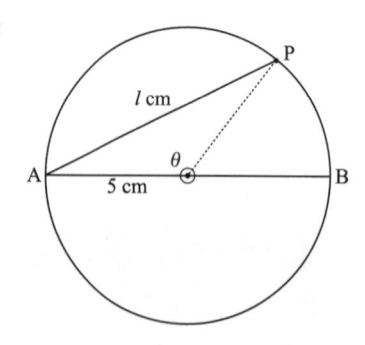

$\therefore \quad l^2 = 5^2 + 5^2 - 2 \times 5 \times 5\cos\theta$ {cosine rule}

$\therefore \quad l^2 = 50 - 50\cos\theta$

$\therefore \quad 2l\dfrac{dl}{dt} = 50\sin\theta\,\dfrac{d\theta}{dt}$

$\therefore \quad \dfrac{dl}{dt} = \dfrac{25\sin\theta}{l}\dfrac{d\theta}{dt}$

Now the point moves at one revolution every 10 seconds.

$\therefore \quad \dfrac{d\theta}{dt} = \dfrac{2\pi}{10} = \dfrac{\pi}{5}$ radians per second

Particular cases:

a If $AP = l = 5$ cm, $\dfrac{dl}{dt} > 0$,

then $\theta = \dfrac{\pi}{3}$ {$\triangle APO$ is equilateral}

$\therefore \dfrac{dl}{dt} = \dfrac{25 \sin(\frac{\pi}{3})}{5} \times \dfrac{\pi}{5}$

$= \dfrac{\sqrt{3}}{2}\pi$ cm s^{-1}

b If P is at B, then $l = 10$ cm

and $\theta = \pi$

$\therefore \dfrac{dl}{dt} = \dfrac{25 \sin \pi}{10} \times \dfrac{\pi}{5}$

$= 0$ cm s^{-1}

16

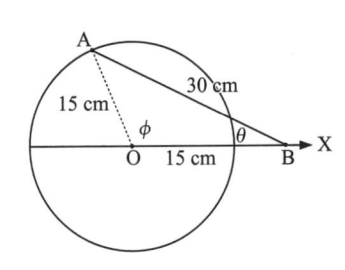

Let $\widehat{AOB} = \phi$ and $\widehat{ABO} = \theta$

Now $\dfrac{d\phi}{dt} = -100$ revolutions per second
{negative for clockwise rotation}

$\therefore \dfrac{d\phi}{dt} = -200\pi$ radians per second

Also, $\dfrac{30}{\sin \phi} = \dfrac{15}{\sin \theta}$ {sine rule}

$\therefore \sin \phi = 2 \sin \theta$

$\therefore \cos \phi \dfrac{d\phi}{dt} = 2 \cos \theta \dfrac{d\theta}{dt}$

$\therefore \dfrac{d\theta}{dt} = \dfrac{1}{2} \dfrac{\cos \phi}{\cos \theta} \dfrac{d\phi}{dt}$ where $\dfrac{d\phi}{dt} = -200\pi$ ^{c} s^{-1}

Particular cases:

a When $\widehat{AOX} = 120°$, $\phi = \dfrac{2\pi}{3}$

$\therefore \cos \phi = -\dfrac{1}{2}$ and $\sin \phi = \dfrac{\sqrt{3}}{2}$

$\therefore \sin \theta = \dfrac{1}{2} \sin \phi$

$= \dfrac{1}{2}\left(\dfrac{\sqrt{3}}{2}\right)$

$= \dfrac{\sqrt{3}}{4}$

$\therefore \cos \theta = \dfrac{\sqrt{13}}{4}$

$\therefore \dfrac{d\theta}{dt} = \dfrac{1}{2} \times \dfrac{-\frac{1}{2}}{\frac{\sqrt{13}}{4}} \times (-200\pi) = \dfrac{200\pi}{\sqrt{13}}$

$\therefore \widehat{ABO}$ is increasing at $\dfrac{200\pi}{\sqrt{13}}$ radians per second.

b When $\widehat{AOX} = 180°$, $\phi = \pi$,

$\therefore \cos \phi = -1$ and $\sin \phi = 0$

$\therefore \sin \theta = 0$ and $\cos \theta = 1$

$\therefore \dfrac{d\theta}{dt} = \dfrac{1}{2} \times \dfrac{-1}{1} \times (-200\pi)$

$= 100\pi$

$\therefore \widehat{ABO}$ is increasing at 100π radians per second.

17

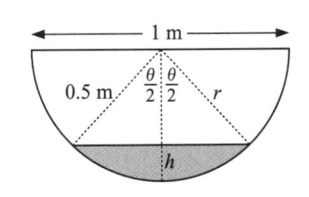

Denote the radius of the semicircle $r = \dfrac{1}{2}$ m.

Let h be the depth and V be the volume of water in the trough at time t.

a The cross-sectional area of water in the trough

$=$ area of sector $-$ area of triangle

$= \dfrac{1}{2}r^2\theta - \dfrac{1}{2}r^2 \sin \theta$

$= \dfrac{1}{2}r^2(\theta - \sin \theta)$

$= \dfrac{1}{8}(\theta - \sin \theta)$

$\therefore$ the volume of water,

$V =$ area of water $\times$ length of trough

$= \dfrac{1}{8}(\theta - \sin \theta) \times 8$

$= \theta - \sin \theta$ as required

b Now $\dfrac{dV}{dt} = \dfrac{d\theta}{dt} - \cos\theta \dfrac{d\theta}{dt}$

$\therefore \dfrac{dV}{dt} = \dfrac{d\theta}{dt}(1 - \cos\theta)$

But $\dfrac{dV}{dt} = 0.1$ m^3 min^{-1}

$\therefore \dfrac{d\theta}{dt} = \dfrac{0.1}{1 - \cos\theta}$ ....(1)

Also, $\cos\left(\dfrac{\theta}{2}\right) = \dfrac{\frac{1}{2} - h}{\frac{1}{2}} = 1 - 2h$

Differentiating with respect to t,

$-\sin\left(\dfrac{\theta}{2}\right) \times \dfrac{1}{2}\dfrac{d\theta}{dt} = -2\dfrac{dh}{dt}$

$\therefore \dfrac{dh}{dt} = \dfrac{1}{4}\sin\left(\dfrac{\theta}{2}\right)\dfrac{d\theta}{dt}$ ....(2)

Particular case:

When $h = 0.25$ m, $\cos\left(\dfrac{\theta}{2}\right) = \dfrac{r-h}{r} = \dfrac{\frac{1}{2} - \frac{1}{4}}{\frac{1}{2}} = \dfrac{\frac{1}{4}}{\frac{1}{2}} = \dfrac{1}{2}$

$\therefore \sin\left(\dfrac{\theta}{2}\right) = \dfrac{\sqrt{3}}{2}$ and $\cos\theta = 2\cos^2\left(\dfrac{\theta}{2}\right) - 1 = 2\left(\dfrac{1}{2}\right)^2 - 1 = -\dfrac{1}{2}$

Using (1), $\dfrac{d\theta}{dt} = \dfrac{0.1}{1 - \left(-\frac{1}{2}\right)} = \dfrac{1}{15}$ $\therefore$ θ is increasing at $\dfrac{1}{15}$ radians per minute.

Using (2), $\dfrac{dh}{dt} = \dfrac{1}{4}\sin\left(\dfrac{\theta}{2}\right)\dfrac{d\theta}{dt}$

$= \dfrac{1}{4} \times \dfrac{\sqrt{3}}{2} \times \dfrac{1}{15}$

$= \dfrac{\sqrt{3}}{120}$ $\therefore$ h is increasing at $\dfrac{\sqrt{3}}{120}$ metres per minute.

REVIEW SET 23A

1 a $\dfrac{d}{dx}(\sin(5x)\ln x) = \dfrac{d}{dx}(\sin(5x))\ln x + \sin(5x)\dfrac{d}{dx}(\ln x)$ {product rule}

$= 5\cos(5x)\ln x + \dfrac{\sin(5x)}{x}$

b $\dfrac{d}{dx}(\sin x \cos(2x)) = \dfrac{d}{dx}(\sin x)\cos(2x) + \sin x \dfrac{d}{dx}(\cos(2x))$ {product rule}

$= \cos x \cos(2x) + \sin x(-2\sin(2x))$

$= \cos x \cos(2x) - 2\sin x \sin(2x)$

c $\dfrac{d}{dx}(e^{-2x}\tan x) = \dfrac{d}{dx}(e^{-2x})\tan x + e^{-2x}\dfrac{d}{dx}(\tan x)$ {product rule}

$= -2e^{-2x}\tan x + e^{-2x}\sec^2 x$

2 $y = x\tan x$ $\therefore$ $\dfrac{dy}{dx} = 1 \times \tan x + x \times \sec^2 x$

Now $\cos\dfrac{\pi}{4} = \dfrac{1}{\sqrt{2}}$ and $\tan\dfrac{\pi}{4} = 1$

$\therefore$ at $x = \dfrac{\pi}{4}$, $y = \dfrac{\pi}{4}$ and $\dfrac{dy}{dx} = 1 + \dfrac{\pi}{4}\left(\sqrt{2}\right)^2 = 1 + \dfrac{\pi}{2}$

$\therefore$ the equation of the tangent is $\dfrac{y - \frac{\pi}{4}}{x - \frac{\pi}{4}} = 1 + \dfrac{\pi}{2}$

$\therefore$ $y - \dfrac{\pi}{4} = (1 + \dfrac{\pi}{2})(x - \dfrac{\pi}{4})$

$= x - \dfrac{\pi}{4} + \dfrac{\pi}{2}x - \dfrac{\pi^2}{8}$

$\therefore$ $y = (1 + \dfrac{\pi}{2})x - \dfrac{\pi^2}{8}$

$\therefore$ $2y = (2 + \pi)x - \dfrac{\pi^2}{4}$

$\therefore$ $(2 + \pi)x - 2y = \dfrac{\pi^2}{4}$ as required

3 a $f(x) = 3\sin x - 4\cos(2x)$
$\therefore\ f'(x) = 3\cos x + 8\sin(2x)$ and $f''(x) = -3\sin x + 16\cos(2x)$

b $f(x) = x^{\frac{1}{2}}\cos(4x)$
$\therefore\ f'(x) = \frac{1}{2}x^{-\frac{1}{2}}\cos(4x) + x^{\frac{1}{2}}(-4\sin(4x))$ {product rule}
$= \frac{1}{2}x^{-\frac{1}{2}}\cos(4x) - 4x^{\frac{1}{2}}\sin(4x)$

and $f''(x) = -\frac{1}{4}x^{-\frac{3}{2}}\cos(4x) + \frac{1}{2}x^{-\frac{1}{2}}(-4\sin 4x)) - \left[2x^{-\frac{1}{2}}\sin(4x) + 4x^{\frac{1}{2}} \times 4\cos(4x)\right]$
$= -\frac{1}{4}x^{-\frac{3}{2}}\cos(4x) - 4x^{-\frac{1}{2}}\sin(4x) - 16x^{\frac{1}{2}}\cos(4x)$

4 a $x(t) = 3 + \sin(2t)$ cm, $t \geqslant 0$ s $\qquad \therefore\ x(0) = 3$ cm
$x'(t) = 0 + 2\cos(2t)$ cm s^{-1} $\qquad x'(0) = 2$ cm s^{-1}
$x''(t) = -4\sin(2t)$ cm s^{-2} $\qquad x''(0) = 0$ cm s^{-2}
$\therefore\ $ initially the particle is 3 cm right of O, moving right at a speed of 2 cm s^{-1}.

b $x'(t) = 0$ when $2\cos(2t) = 0$
$\therefore\ \cos(2t) = 0$
$\therefore\ 2t = \frac{\pi}{2} + k\pi$
For the interval $0 \leqslant t \leqslant \pi$, $t = \frac{\pi}{4}$ or $\frac{3\pi}{4}$

$\therefore\ $ the particle reverses direction at $t = \frac{\pi}{4}, \frac{3\pi}{4}$

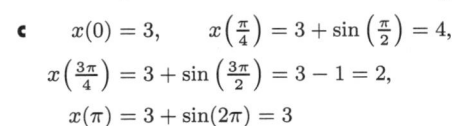

c $x(0) = 3$, $x\left(\frac{\pi}{4}\right) = 3 + \sin\left(\frac{\pi}{2}\right) = 4$,
$x\left(\frac{3\pi}{4}\right) = 3 + \sin\left(\frac{3\pi}{2}\right) = 3 - 1 = 2$,
$x(\pi) = 3 + \sin(2\pi) = 3$
$\therefore\ $ the total distance travelled $= 1 + 2 + 1 = 4$ cm.

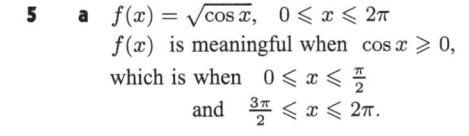

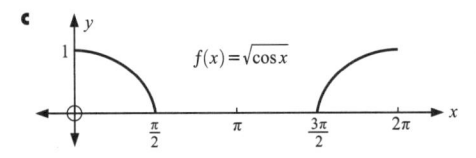

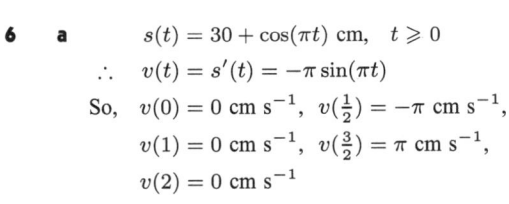

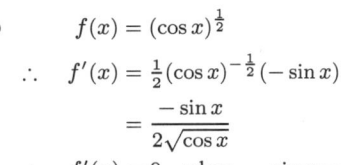

5 a $f(x) = \sqrt{\cos x}$, $0 \leqslant x \leqslant 2\pi$
$f(x)$ is meaningful when $\cos x \geqslant 0$,
which is when $0 \leqslant x \leqslant \frac{\pi}{2}$
and $\frac{3\pi}{2} \leqslant x \leqslant 2\pi$.

b $f(x) = (\cos x)^{\frac{1}{2}}$
$\therefore\ f'(x) = \frac{1}{2}(\cos x)^{-\frac{1}{2}}(-\sin x)$
$= \dfrac{-\sin x}{2\sqrt{\cos x}}$
$\therefore\ f'(x) = 0$ when $-\sin x = 0$
For $0 \leqslant x \leqslant 2\pi$, this is when $x = 0, \pi, 2\pi$.
Sign diagram for $f'(x)$ is:

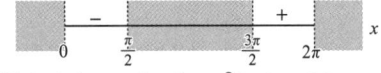

$f(x)$ is increasing for $\frac{3\pi}{2} \leqslant x \leqslant 2\pi$
and decreasing for $0 \leqslant x \leqslant \frac{\pi}{2}$.

c

6 a $s(t) = 30 + \cos(\pi t)$ cm, $t \geqslant 0$
$\therefore\ v(t) = s'(t) = -\pi\sin(\pi t)$
So, $v(0) = 0$ cm s^{-1}, $v(\frac{1}{2}) = -\pi$ cm s^{-1},
$v(1) = 0$ cm s^{-1}, $v(\frac{3}{2}) = \pi$ cm s^{-1},
$v(2) = 0$ cm s^{-1}

Sign diagram of $v(t)$ is:

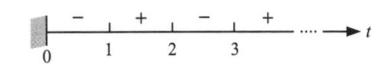

b The cork is falling when $v(t) \leqslant 0$, which is for $0 \leqslant t \leqslant 1$, $2 \leqslant t \leqslant 3$, ...
$\therefore\ $ the cork is falling for $2n \leqslant t \leqslant 2n + 1$, $n \in \mathbb{N}$.

7 a $(3\cos\theta, 2\sin\theta)$ lies on the curve

$\therefore \quad x = 3\cos\theta \quad$ and $\quad y = 2\sin\theta$

$\therefore \quad x^2 = 9\cos^2\theta \quad$ and $\quad y^2 = 4\sin^2\theta$

$\therefore \quad \dfrac{x^2}{9} + \dfrac{y^2}{4} = \cos^2\theta + \sin^2\theta = 1$

$\therefore \quad$ the curve has equation $\dfrac{x^2}{9} + \dfrac{y^2}{4} = 1$

b $\dfrac{x^2}{9} + \dfrac{y^2}{4} = 1$

$\therefore \quad \dfrac{2x}{9} + \dfrac{2y}{4}\dfrac{dy}{dx} = 0$

$\therefore \quad \dfrac{dy}{dx} = \left(\dfrac{2}{y}\right)\left(-\dfrac{2x}{9}\right)$

$= -\dfrac{4x}{9y} = -\dfrac{4 \times 3\cos\theta}{9 \times 2\sin\theta}$

$= -\dfrac{2\cos\theta}{3\sin\theta}$

c The tangent has gradient $-\dfrac{2\cos\theta}{3\sin\theta}$ and passes through $(3\cos\theta, 2\sin\theta)$.

$\therefore \quad$ the tangent has equation $\dfrac{y - 2\sin\theta}{x - 3\cos\theta} = -\dfrac{2\cos\theta}{3\sin\theta}$

$\therefore \quad 3y\sin\theta - 6\sin^2\theta = -2x\cos\theta + 6\cos^2\theta$

$\therefore \quad 2x\cos\theta + 3y\sin\theta = 6 \quad \{\sin^2\theta + \cos^2\theta = 1\}$

The tangent meets the x-axis when $y = 0$

$\therefore \quad 2x\cos\theta = 6$

$\therefore \quad x = \dfrac{3}{\cos\theta}$

$\therefore \quad$ A is at $\left(\dfrac{3}{\cos\theta}, 0\right)$

The tangent meets the y-axis when $x = 0$

$\therefore \quad 3y\sin\theta = 6$

$\therefore \quad y = \dfrac{2}{\sin\theta}$

$\therefore \quad$ B is at $\left(0, \dfrac{2}{\sin\theta}\right)$

$\therefore \quad$ triangle OAB has area $A = \left|\dfrac{1}{2}\left(\dfrac{3}{\cos\theta}\right)\left(\dfrac{2}{\sin\theta}\right)\right| = \left|\dfrac{6}{\sin 2\theta}\right|$ .... (*)

$\therefore \quad A^2 = 36(\sin 2\theta)^{-2}$

$\therefore \quad \dfrac{d(A^2)}{d\theta} = -72(\sin 2\theta)^{-3} \times 2\cos 2\theta = -\dfrac{144\cos 2\theta}{\sin^3 2\theta}$

Since $0 \leqslant \theta \leqslant 2\pi$, $0 \leqslant 2\theta \leqslant 4\pi$

$\therefore \quad \dfrac{d(A^2)}{d\theta} = 0$ when $\theta = \dfrac{\pi}{4}, \dfrac{3\pi}{4}, \dfrac{5\pi}{4}$ and $\dfrac{7\pi}{4}$,

and is undefined when $\theta = 0, \dfrac{\pi}{2}, \pi, \dfrac{3\pi}{2}$ and 2π.

Sign diagram for $\dfrac{d(A^2)}{d\theta}$ is:

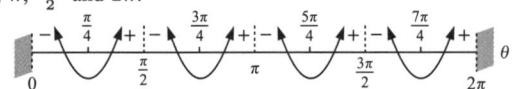

```
       −  π/4  +  π/2  −  3π/4  +  π  −  5π/4  +  3π/2  −  7π/4  +
   0                                                                    2π
```

$\therefore \quad$ there are local minima at $\theta = \dfrac{\pi}{4}, \dfrac{3\pi}{4}, \dfrac{5\pi}{4}, \dfrac{7\pi}{4}$

For all of these values of θ, $\sin 2\theta = -1$ or 1.

$\therefore \quad A = 6 \quad \{\text{using }(*)\}$

$\therefore \quad$ the smallest area of triangle OAB is 6 units^2, and this occurs when $\theta = \dfrac{\pi}{4}, \dfrac{3\pi}{4}, \dfrac{5\pi}{4}$ or $\dfrac{7\pi}{4}$.

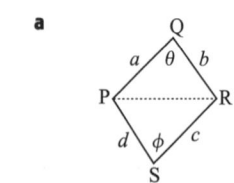

8 a

Using the cosine rule: in $\triangle PQR$, $PR^2 = a^2 + b^2 - 2ab\cos\theta$

in $\triangle PSR$, $PR^2 = c^2 + d^2 - 2cd\cos\phi$

$\therefore \quad a^2 + b^2 - 2ab\cos\theta = c^2 + d^2 - 2cd\cos\phi$

Now a, b, c and d are constants, so differentiating with respect to ϕ,

$\therefore \quad 2ab\sin\theta \dfrac{d\theta}{d\phi} = 2cd\sin\phi$

$\therefore \quad \dfrac{d\theta}{d\phi} = \dfrac{2cd\sin\phi}{2ab\sin\theta} = \dfrac{cd\sin\phi}{ab\sin\theta}$ as required

b Area of quadrilateral, A = area of $\triangle PQR$ + area of $\triangle PSR$

$$= \tfrac{1}{2}ab\sin\theta + \tfrac{1}{2}cd\sin\phi$$

$$\therefore \quad \frac{dA}{d\phi} = \tfrac{1}{2}ab\cos\theta\,\frac{d\theta}{d\phi} + \tfrac{1}{2}cd\cos\phi$$

$$= \tfrac{1}{2}ab\cos\theta\left(\frac{cd\sin\phi}{ab\sin\theta}\right) + \tfrac{1}{2}cd\cos\phi \quad \{\text{using } \mathbf{a}\}$$

$$= \tfrac{1}{2}cd\left[\frac{\cos\theta\sin\phi}{\sin\theta} + \cos\phi\right]$$

$$= \frac{cd}{2\sin\theta}(\sin\phi\cos\theta + \cos\phi\sin\theta)$$

$$= \frac{cd}{2\sin\theta}\sin(\phi + \theta)$$

$$\therefore \quad \frac{dA}{d\phi} = 0 \text{ when } \sin(\phi + \theta) = 0, \text{ which is when } \phi + \theta = \pi$$

$\therefore$ the area of PQRS is a maximum when the opposite angles are supplementary, which occurs when PQRS is a cyclic quadrilateral.

9 a $\sin\theta = \dfrac{NA}{x} = \dfrac{1}{x}$

$\therefore \quad \dfrac{1}{x^2} = \sin^2\theta$

$\therefore$ at A, $I = \dfrac{\sqrt{8}\cos\theta}{x^2} = \sqrt{8}\cos\theta\sin^2\theta$

b $\dfrac{dI}{d\theta} = \sqrt{8}(-\sin\theta)\sin^2\theta + \sqrt{8}\cos\theta(2\sin\theta\cos\theta)$

$\phantom{\dfrac{dI}{d\theta}} = \sqrt{8}\sin\theta[2\cos^2\theta - \sin^2\theta]$

$\phantom{\dfrac{dI}{d\theta}} = \sqrt{8}\sin\theta[2(1 - \sin^2\theta) - \sin^2\theta]$

$\phantom{\dfrac{dI}{d\theta}} = \sqrt{8}\sin\theta[2 - 3\sin^2\theta]$

$\dfrac{dI}{d\theta} = 0$ when $\sin\theta = \sqrt{\tfrac{2}{3}}$, $0 < \theta < \tfrac{\pi}{2}$

and the sign diagram of $\dfrac{dI}{d\theta}$ is:

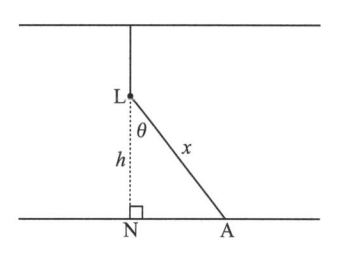

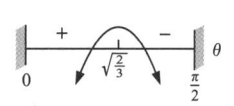

$\therefore$ the maximum illumination at A is obtained when $\sin\theta = \sqrt{\tfrac{2}{3}}$.

$\therefore \quad x = \dfrac{1}{\sin\theta} = \sqrt{\tfrac{3}{2}}$

$\therefore \quad h = \sqrt{x^2 - NA^2} = \sqrt{\tfrac{3}{2} - 1} = \tfrac{1}{\sqrt{2}}$

$\therefore$ the bulb is $\dfrac{1}{\sqrt{2}}$ m above the floor.

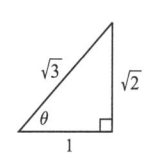

REVIEW SET 23B

1 a $y = \dfrac{x}{\sqrt{\sec x}} = x(\cos x)^{\frac{1}{2}}$ $\quad \therefore \quad \dfrac{dy}{dx} = (\cos x)^{\frac{1}{2}} + x \times \tfrac{1}{2}(\cos x)^{-\frac{1}{2}}(-\sin x)$ $\quad \{\text{product rule}\}$

$$= \sqrt{\cos x} - \dfrac{x\sin x}{2\sqrt{\cos x}}$$

b $y = e^x \cot(2x)$ $\quad \therefore \quad \dfrac{dy}{dx} = e^x\cot(2x) + e^x \times 2\left(-\csc^2(2x)\right)$ $\quad \{\text{product rule}\}$

$$= e^x\left(\cot(2x) - 2\csc^2(2x)\right)$$

c $y = \arccos\left(\tfrac{x}{2}\right)$ $\quad \therefore \quad \dfrac{dy}{dx} = \tfrac{1}{2} \times \left(\dfrac{-1}{\sqrt{1 - \left(\tfrac{x}{2}\right)^2}}\right) = -\dfrac{1}{2\sqrt{1 - \tfrac{x^2}{4}}} = -\dfrac{1}{\sqrt{4 - x^2}}$

2 a $y = \sec x$ $\quad \therefore \quad \dfrac{dy}{dx} = \sec x \tan x$

When $x = \frac{\pi}{3}$, $y = \sec \frac{\pi}{3} = 2$

and $\dfrac{dy}{dx} = \sec \frac{\pi}{3} \tan \frac{\pi}{3} = 2\sqrt{3}$

$\therefore$ the tangent has equation

$$\dfrac{y-2}{x - \frac{\pi}{3}} = 2\sqrt{3}$$

$\therefore \quad y - 2 = 2\sqrt{3}x - \dfrac{2\pi}{\sqrt{3}}$

$\therefore \quad y = 2\sqrt{3}x - \dfrac{2\pi}{\sqrt{3}} + 2$

b $y = \arctan x$ $\quad \therefore \quad \dfrac{dy}{dx} = \dfrac{1}{1 + x^2}$.

When $x = \sqrt{3}$, $y = \arctan \sqrt{3} = \frac{\pi}{3}$

and $\dfrac{dy}{dx} = \dfrac{1}{1 + (\sqrt{3})^2} = \dfrac{1}{1+3} = \dfrac{1}{4}$

$\therefore$ the normal has gradient -4, so its equation is

$$\dfrac{y - \frac{\pi}{3}}{x - \sqrt{3}} = -4$$

$\therefore \quad y - \frac{\pi}{3} = -4x + 4\sqrt{3}$

$\therefore \quad y = -4x + 4\sqrt{3} + \frac{\pi}{3}$

3 Let l m be the length of rope and x m be the distance of the boat from the jetty.

Then $x^2 + 5^2 = l^2$

$\therefore \quad 2x \dfrac{dx}{dt} = 2l \dfrac{dl}{dt}$

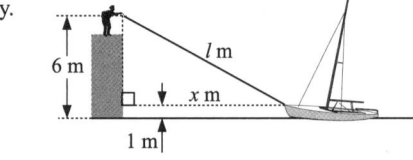

Particular case:

When $x = 15$ m, $l = \sqrt{15^2 + 5^2} = \sqrt{250}$ and $\dfrac{dl}{dt} = -20$ m min^{-1}

$\therefore \quad 2(15) \dfrac{dx}{dt} = 2\sqrt{250}(-20)$

$\therefore \quad \dfrac{dx}{dt} = -\dfrac{40\sqrt{250}}{30} \approx -21.1$

$\therefore$ the boat is approaching the jetty at 21.1 metres per minute.

4 Let t be the number of seconds after A passes through X. In this time, A travels $5t$ m.

B passes through X when $t = 3$.

$\therefore$ for $t > 3$, B is $4(t - 3)$ m from X.

Using the cosine rule,

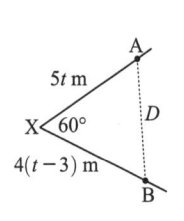

$D^2 = 25t^2 + 16(t-3)^2 - 2 \times 5t \times 4(t-3) \times \cos 60°$

$\quad = 25t^2 + 16(t-3)^2 - 20t(t-3)$

$\therefore \quad 2D \dfrac{dD}{dt} = 50t + 32(t-3) - 20(t-3) - 20t$

When $5t = 20$, $t = 4$ and $D^2 = 25 \times 16 + 16 - 20 \times 4 = 336$

$\therefore \quad 2\sqrt{336} \dfrac{dD}{dt} = 200 + 32 - 20 - 80 = 132$

$\therefore \quad \dfrac{dD}{dt} = \dfrac{66}{\sqrt{336}} \approx 3.60$ m s^{-1}

5 a $f(x) = \arcsin x + \arccos x$

$\therefore \quad f'(x) = \dfrac{1}{\sqrt{1-x^2}} + \dfrac{-1}{\sqrt{1-x^2}} = 0$

$\therefore \quad f(x)$ is a constant

We can see this by letting $\theta = \arcsin x$ and $\phi = \arccos x$

$\therefore \quad \sin \theta = x \qquad$ and $\quad \cos \phi = x$

$\therefore \quad \sin \theta = \cos \phi$

$\therefore \quad \sin \theta = \sin(\frac{\pi}{2} - \phi) \qquad \{\cos \phi = \sin(\frac{\pi}{2} - \phi)\}$

$\therefore \quad \theta = \frac{\pi}{2} - \phi \qquad \{\theta, \frac{\pi}{2} - \phi \in [-\frac{\pi}{2}, \frac{\pi}{2}]\}$

$\therefore \quad \theta + \phi = \frac{\pi}{2}$

$\therefore \quad \arcsin x + \arccos x = \frac{\pi}{2}$ for all $x \in [-1, 1]$.

b Let $\theta = \arctan\left(\dfrac{1-a}{1+a}\right)$ and $\phi = \arctan a$

$\therefore \ \tan\theta = \dfrac{1-a}{1+a}$ and $\tan\phi = a$

Now $\tan(\theta+\phi) = \dfrac{\tan\theta + \tan\phi}{1 - \tan\theta\tan\phi} = \dfrac{\dfrac{1-a}{1+a} + a}{1 - \left(\dfrac{1-a}{1+a}\right)a} = \dfrac{1-a+a(1+a)}{(1+a)-(1-a)a} = \dfrac{a^2+1}{a^2+1} = 1$

But $\tan(\tfrac{\pi}{4}) = 1$, so $\theta + \phi = \tfrac{\pi}{4}$

$\therefore \ \arctan\left(\dfrac{1-a}{1+a}\right) + \arctan a = \tfrac{\pi}{4}$

c Let $\alpha = \arctan(\tfrac{1}{2})$, $\beta = \arctan(\tfrac{1}{5})$ and $\gamma = \arctan(\tfrac{1}{8})$,

$\therefore \ \tan\alpha = \tfrac{1}{2}$, $\tan\beta = \tfrac{1}{5}$ and $\tan\gamma = \tfrac{1}{8}$

Now $\tan(\alpha+\beta) = \dfrac{\tan\alpha + \tan\beta}{1 - \tan\alpha\tan\beta} = \dfrac{\tfrac{1}{2} + \tfrac{1}{5}}{1 - (\tfrac{1}{2})(\tfrac{1}{5})} = \dfrac{\tfrac{7}{10}}{\tfrac{9}{10}} = \tfrac{7}{9}$

$\therefore \ \tan(\alpha+\beta+\gamma) = \tan[(\alpha+\beta)+\gamma]$

$= \dfrac{\tan(\alpha+\beta) + \tan\gamma}{1 - \tan(\alpha+\beta)\tan\gamma} = \dfrac{\tfrac{7}{9} + \tfrac{1}{8}}{1 - (\tfrac{7}{9})(\tfrac{1}{8})} = \dfrac{\tfrac{65}{72}}{\tfrac{65}{72}} = 1$

But $\tan(\tfrac{\pi}{4}) = 1$, so $\alpha + \beta + \gamma = \tfrac{\pi}{4}$

$\therefore \ \arctan(\tfrac{1}{2}) + \arctan(\tfrac{1}{5}) + \arctan(\tfrac{1}{8}) = \tfrac{\pi}{4}$

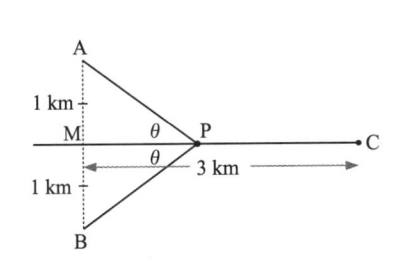

6 a The length of cable required
$= (PA + PB + PC)$ km

  i If P is at M, then $PA = PB = 1$ km
  and $PC = 3$ km
  $\therefore \ 5$ km of cable is required

  ii If P is at C, then
  $PA = PB = \sqrt{1^2 + 3^2} = \sqrt{10}$ km
  and $PC = 0$ km
  $\therefore \ 2\sqrt{10}$ km of cable is required

b Now $\sin\theta = \dfrac{1}{AP} = \dfrac{1}{BP}$ and $\tan\theta = \dfrac{1}{MP}$

$\therefore \ AP = BP = \dfrac{1}{\sin\theta}$ and $MP = \dfrac{1}{\tan\theta} = \cot\theta$

$\therefore \ AP + BP + CP = \dfrac{2}{\sin\theta} + (CM - MP)$ $\quad \therefore \ L = 2\csc\theta + 3 - \cot\theta$ as required

c Since $L = 2\csc\theta + 3 - \cot\theta$, $\dfrac{dL}{d\theta} = 2(-\csc\theta\cot\theta) - (-\csc^2\theta)$

$= \dfrac{-2\cos\theta}{\sin^2\theta} + \dfrac{1}{\sin^2\theta}$

$= \dfrac{1 - 2\cos\theta}{\sin^2\theta}$ as required

$\therefore \ \dfrac{dL}{d\theta} = 0$ if $\cos\theta = \tfrac{1}{2}$

$\therefore \ \theta = \tfrac{\pi}{3}$ and sign diagram of $\dfrac{dL}{d\theta}$ is:

$\therefore \ $ the minimum length of cable is required when $\theta = \tfrac{\pi}{3}$

When $\theta = \tfrac{\pi}{3}$, $\sin\theta = \tfrac{\sqrt{3}}{2}$ and $\tan\theta = \sqrt{3}$,

$\therefore \ \csc\theta = \tfrac{2}{\sqrt{3}}$ and $\cot\theta = \tfrac{1}{\sqrt{3}}$

so $L_{\min} = \tfrac{4}{\sqrt{3}} + 3 - \tfrac{1}{\sqrt{3}} = (3 + \sqrt{3})$ km as required

7

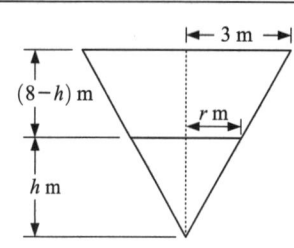

a Volume $V = \frac{1}{3}\pi r^2 h$

Using similar triangles $\dfrac{h}{r} = \dfrac{8}{3}$

$\therefore\ h = \dfrac{8r}{3}$

$\therefore\ V(r) = \frac{1}{3}\pi r^2 \left(\dfrac{8r}{3}\right) = \dfrac{8\pi}{9}r^3\ \text{m}^3$

b *Particular case:* When $h = 5$, $r = \dfrac{3h}{8} = \dfrac{15}{8}$ and $\dfrac{dV}{dt} = -0.2 = -\dfrac{1}{5}\ \text{m}^3\ \text{min}^{-1}$

Now $\dfrac{dV}{dt} = \dfrac{8\pi}{3}r^2\dfrac{dr}{dt}$ $\quad\therefore\ -\dfrac{1}{5} = \dfrac{8\pi}{3}\left(\dfrac{15}{8}\right)^2 \dfrac{dr}{dt}$

$\therefore\ -\dfrac{1}{5} = \dfrac{225}{24}\pi\dfrac{dr}{dt}$

$\therefore\ \dfrac{dr}{dt} = -\dfrac{8}{375\pi}$

$\therefore\ \dfrac{dr}{dt} = -0.006\,79$

$\therefore$ the radius is decreasing at $0.006\,79$ m per minute

8

a Using the cosine rule for $\triangle$BPO,

$\text{BP}^2 = r^2 + (a+r)^2 - 2r(a+r)\cos\theta$

$\therefore\ \text{BP} = \sqrt{r^2 + (a+r)^2 - 2r(a+r)\cos\theta}$

$\therefore$ time taken to travel from B to P

$= \dfrac{\text{distance}}{\text{speed}}$

$= \dfrac{\sqrt{r^2 + (a+r)^2 - 2r(a+r)\cos\theta}}{v}$

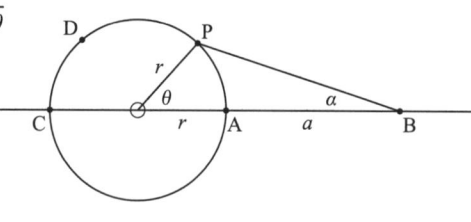

Now arc $\text{AP} = r\theta$

$\therefore$ arc PC = (perimeter of semi-circle) $-$ arc AP

$= \frac{1}{2} \times 2\pi r - r\theta$

$= r(\pi - \theta)$

$\therefore$ the time taken to travel from P to C $= \dfrac{\text{distance}}{\text{speed}} = \dfrac{r(\pi - \theta)}{w}$

The total time for the journey $T = \dfrac{\sqrt{r^2 + (a+r)^2 - 2r(a+r)\cos\theta}}{v} + \dfrac{r(\pi - \theta)}{w}$

b $T = \dfrac{w\,[r^2 + (a+r)^2 - 2r(a+r)\cos\theta]^{\frac{1}{2}} + rv(\pi - \theta)}{vw}$

$\therefore\ \dfrac{dT}{d\theta} = \dfrac{\frac{1}{2}w\,[r^2 + (a+r)^2 - 2r(a+r)\cos\theta]^{-\frac{1}{2}}(2r(a+r)\sin\theta) - rv}{vw}$

$= \dfrac{2r(a+r)\sin\theta}{2v\sqrt{r^2 + (a+r)^2 - 2r(a+r)\cos\theta}} - \dfrac{rv}{vw}$

$= \dfrac{r(a+r)\sin\theta}{v \times \text{BP}} - \dfrac{rv}{vw}$

Now $\dfrac{\text{BP}}{\sin\theta} = \dfrac{r}{\sin\alpha}$ {sine rule}

$\therefore\ \text{BP} = \dfrac{r\sin\theta}{\sin\alpha}$

$$\therefore \quad \frac{dT}{d\theta} = \frac{r(a+r)\sin\theta}{v \times \dfrac{r\sin\theta}{\sin\alpha}} - \frac{rv}{vw}$$

$$= \frac{a+r}{v}\sin\alpha - \frac{rv}{vw}$$

$$= \frac{a+r}{v}\left(\sin\alpha - \frac{rv}{(a+r)w}\right)$$

c Now $a+r \neq 0$ so $\dfrac{dT}{d\theta} = 0$ when $\sin\alpha - \dfrac{rv}{(a+r)w} = 0$

$$\therefore \quad \sin\alpha = \frac{rv}{(a+r)w}$$

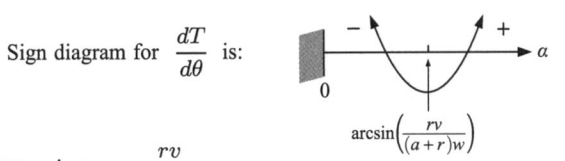

Sign diagram for $\dfrac{dT}{d\theta}$ is:

$\qquad\qquad\qquad\qquad 0 \qquad \arcsin\left(\dfrac{rv}{(a+r)w}\right)$

$\therefore \;\; T$ is minimised when $\sin\alpha = \dfrac{rv}{(a+r)w}$

Chapter 24
INTEGRATION

EXERCISE 24A

1 a i $\dfrac{d}{dx}(x^2) = 2x$

$\therefore \dfrac{d}{dx}\left(\tfrac{1}{2}x^2\right) = x$

$\therefore$ the antiderivative of x is $\tfrac{1}{2}x^2$

ii $\dfrac{d}{dx}(x^3) = 3x^2$

$\therefore \dfrac{d}{dx}\left(\tfrac{1}{3}x^3\right) = x^2$

$\therefore$ the antiderivative of x^2 is $\tfrac{1}{3}x^3$

iii $\dfrac{d}{dx}(x^6) = 6x^5$

$\therefore \dfrac{d}{dx}\left(\tfrac{1}{6}x^6\right) = x^5$

$\therefore$ the antiderivative of x^5 is $\tfrac{1}{6}x^6$

iv $\dfrac{d}{dx}(x^{-1}) = -x^{-2}$

$\therefore \dfrac{d}{dx}(-x^{-1}) = x^{-2}$

$\therefore$ the antiderivative of x^{-2} is $-x^{-1}$ or $-\dfrac{1}{x}$

v $\dfrac{d}{dx}(x^{-3}) = -3x^{-4}$

$\therefore \dfrac{d}{dx}\left(-\tfrac{1}{3}x^{-3}\right) = x^{-4}$

$\therefore$ the antiderivative of x^{-4} is $-\tfrac{1}{3}x^{-3}$

vi $\dfrac{d}{dx}\left(x^{\frac{4}{3}}\right) = \tfrac{4}{3}x^{\frac{1}{3}}$

$\therefore \dfrac{d}{dx}\left(\tfrac{3}{4}x^{\frac{4}{3}}\right) = x^{\frac{1}{3}}$

$\therefore$ the antiderivative of $x^{\frac{1}{3}}$ is $\tfrac{3}{4}x^{\frac{4}{3}}$

vii $\dfrac{d}{dx}\left(x^{\frac{1}{2}}\right) = \tfrac{1}{2}x^{-\frac{1}{2}}$

$\therefore \dfrac{d}{dx}\left(2x^{\frac{1}{2}}\right) = x^{-\frac{1}{2}}$

$\therefore$ the antiderivative of of $x^{-\frac{1}{2}}$ is $2x^{\frac{1}{2}} = 2\sqrt{x}$

b the antiderivative of x^n is $\dfrac{x^{n+1}}{n+1}$

2 a i $\dfrac{d}{dx}(e^{2x}) = 2e^{2x}$

$\therefore \dfrac{d}{dx}\left(\tfrac{1}{2}e^{2x}\right) = e^{2x}$

$\therefore$ the antiderivative of e^{2x} is $\tfrac{1}{2}e^{2x}$

ii $\dfrac{d}{dx}(e^{5x}) = 5e^{5x}$

$\therefore \dfrac{d}{dx}\left(\tfrac{1}{5}e^{5x}\right) = e^{5x}$

$\therefore$ the antiderivative of e^{5x} is $\tfrac{1}{5}e^{5x}$

iii $\dfrac{d}{dx}\left(e^{\frac{1}{2}x}\right) = \tfrac{1}{2}e^{\frac{1}{2}x}$

$\therefore \dfrac{d}{dx}\left(2e^{\frac{1}{2}x}\right) = e^{\frac{1}{2}x}$

$\therefore$ the antiderivative of $e^{\frac{1}{2}x}$ is $2e^{\frac{1}{2}x}$

iv $\dfrac{d}{dx}(e^{0.01x}) = 0.01e^{0.01x}$

$\therefore \dfrac{d}{dx}(100e^{0.01x}) = e^{0.01x}$

$\therefore$ the antiderivative of $e^{0.01x}$ is $100e^{0.01x}$

v $\dfrac{d}{dx}(e^{\pi x}) = \pi e^{\pi x}$

$\therefore \dfrac{d}{dx}\left(\tfrac{1}{\pi}e^{\pi x}\right) = e^{\pi x}$

$\therefore$ the antiderivative of $e^{\pi x}$ is $\tfrac{1}{\pi}e^{\pi x}$

vi $\dfrac{d}{dx}\left(e^{\frac{x}{3}}\right) = \tfrac{1}{3}e^{\frac{x}{3}}$

$\therefore \dfrac{d}{dx}\left(3e^{\frac{x}{3}}\right) = e^{\frac{x}{3}}$

$\therefore$ the antiderivative of $e^{\frac{x}{3}}$ is $3e^{\frac{x}{3}}$

b the antiderivative of e^{kx} is $\dfrac{1}{k}e^{kx}$

3 **a** $\dfrac{d}{dx}(x^3 + x^2) = 3x^2 + 2x$ **b** $\dfrac{d}{dx}(e^{3x+1}) = 3e^{3x+1}$

$\therefore \dfrac{d}{dx}\left(\dfrac{2x^3}{} + 2x^2\right) = 6x^2 + 4x$ $\therefore \dfrac{d}{dx}\left(\tfrac{1}{3}e^{3x+1}\right) = e^{3x+1}$

$\therefore$ the antiderivative of $6x^2 + 4x$ $\therefore$ the antiderivative of e^{3x+1} is $\tfrac{1}{3}e^{3x+1}$
is $2x^3 + 2x^2$

c $\dfrac{d}{dx}(x\sqrt{x}) = \dfrac{d}{dx}(x^{\frac{3}{2}}) = \tfrac{3}{2}x^{\frac{1}{2}}$ **d** $\dfrac{d}{dx}((2x+1)^4) = 4(2x+1)^3 \times 2$

$= \tfrac{3}{2}\sqrt{x}$ $= 8(2x+1)^3$

$\therefore \dfrac{d}{dx}\left(\tfrac{2}{3}x\sqrt{x}\right) = \sqrt{x}$ $\therefore \dfrac{d}{dx}\left(\tfrac{1}{8}(2x+1)^4\right) = (2x+1)^3$

$\therefore$ the antiderivative of $\sqrt{x}$ is $\tfrac{2}{3}x\sqrt{x}$ $\therefore$ the antiderivative of $(2x+1)^3$ is $\tfrac{1}{8}(2x+1)^4$

EXERCISE 24B

1 **a** $\int_a^a f(x)\,dx = F(a) - F(a) = 0$ **b** The antiderivative of c is cx.

$\int_a^a f(x)\,dx$ = area of the strip between $\therefore \int_a^b c\,dx = F(b) - F(a)$
$x = a$ and $x = a$. $= cb - ca$
This strip has 0 width, so its area = 0. $= c(b - a)$

c $\int_b^a f(x)\,dx = F(a) - F(b)$ **d** If $\dfrac{d}{dx}F(x) = f(x)$ then
$= -[F(b) - F(a)]$
$= -\int_a^b f(x)\,dx$ $\dfrac{d}{dx}cF(x) = cf(x)$

$\therefore \int_a^b cf(x)\,dx = cF(b) - cF(a)$
$= c[F(b) - F(a)]$
$= c\int_a^b f(x)\,dx$

e $\int_a^b (f(x) + g(x))\,dx = [F(b) + G(b)] - [F(a) + G(a)]$
$= [F(b) - F(a)] + [G(b) - G(a)]$
$= \int_a^b f(x)\,dx + \int_a^b g(x)\,dx$

2 **a** $f(x) = x^3$ has antiderivative $F(x) = \dfrac{x^4}{4}$ **b** $f(x) = x^3$ has antiderivative $F(x) = \dfrac{x^4}{4}$

$\therefore$ area $= \int_0^1 x^3\,dx$ $\therefore$ area $= \int_1^2 x^3\,dx$
$= F(1) - F(0)$ $= F(2) - F(1)$
$= \tfrac{1}{4} - 0$ $= \tfrac{16}{4} - \tfrac{1}{4}$
$= \tfrac{1}{4}$ units^2 $= 3\tfrac{3}{4}$ units^2

c $f(x) = x^2 + 3x + 2$ has antiderivative   **d** $f(x) = \sqrt{x} = x^{\frac{1}{2}}$ has antiderivative

$F(x) = \dfrac{x^3}{3} + \dfrac{3x^2}{2} + 2x$ $F(x) = \dfrac{x^{\frac{3}{2}}}{\tfrac{3}{2}} = \tfrac{2}{3}x\sqrt{x}$

$\therefore$ area $= \int_1^3 (x^2 + 3x + 2)\,dx$ $\therefore$ area $= \int_0^2 \sqrt{x}\,dx$
$= F(3) - F(1)$ $= F(2) - F(0)$
$= \left(\tfrac{27}{3} + \tfrac{27}{2} + 6\right) - \left(\tfrac{1}{3} + \tfrac{3}{2} + 2\right)$ $= \tfrac{2}{3} \times 2\sqrt{2} - 0$
$= 24\tfrac{2}{3}$ units^2 $= \tfrac{4\sqrt{2}}{3}$ units^2

e $f(x) = e^x$ has antiderivative $F(x) = e^x$
$$\therefore \text{ area} = \int_0^{1.5} e^x \, dx$$
$$= F(1.5) - F(0)$$
$$= e^{1.5} - e^0$$
$$= e^{1.5} - 1$$
$$\approx 3.48 \text{ units}^2$$

g $f(x) = x^3 + 2x^2 + 7x + 4$ has antiderivative
$$F(x) = \frac{x^4}{4} + \frac{2x^3}{3} + \frac{7x^2}{2} + 4x$$
$$\therefore \text{ area} = \int_1^{1.25} x^3 + 2x^2 + 7x + 4 \, dx$$
$$= F(1.25) - F(1)$$
$$= [12.381\,18 - 8.416\,67]$$
$$\approx 3.96 \text{ units}^2$$

f $f(x) = \frac{1}{\sqrt{x}} = x^{-\frac{1}{2}}$ has antiderivative
$$F(x) = \frac{x^{\frac{1}{2}}}{\frac{1}{2}} = 2\sqrt{x}$$
$$\therefore \text{ area} = \int_1^4 \frac{1}{\sqrt{x}} \, dx$$
$$= F(4) - F(1)$$
$$= 2\sqrt{4} - 2\sqrt{1}$$
$$= 2 \text{ units}^2$$

3 Using technology:

a area $= \int_0^{1.5} e^{x^2} \, dx \approx 4.06$ units^2

b area $= \int_2^4 (\ln x)^2 \, dx \approx 2.41$ units^2

c area $= \int_1^2 \sqrt{9 - x^2} \, dx \approx 2.58$ units^2

4 a If $\dfrac{d}{dx} F(x) = f(x)$ then $\dfrac{d}{dx}(-F(x)) = -f(x)$
$$\therefore \int_a^b (-f(x)) \, dx = -F(b) - (-F(a))$$
$$= -(F(b) - F(a))$$
$$= -\int_a^b f(x) \, dx$$

b Since $y = -f(x)$ is a reflection of $y = f(x)$ in the x-axis,

shaded area = area between the x-axis and $y = -f(x)$ from $x = a$ to $x = b$
$$= \int_a^b (-f(x)) \, dx$$
$$= -\int_a^b f(x) \, dx \quad \{\text{using a}\}$$

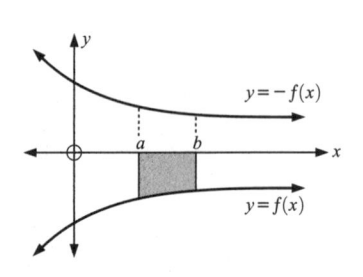

c i $\int_0^1 (-x^2) \, dx = -\int_0^1 x^2 \, dx$

Now $f(x) = x^2$ has antiderivative
$$F(x) = \tfrac{1}{3}x^3$$
$$\therefore \int_0^1 (-x^2) \, dx = -(F(1) - F(0))$$
$$= -\left(\tfrac{1}{3} - 0\right)$$
$$= -\tfrac{1}{3}$$

ii $\int_0^1 (x^2 - x) \, dx = -\int_0^1 (x - x^2) \, dx$

$\{x^2 - x \leqslant 0$ for all $x \in [0, 1]\}$

Now $f(x) = x - x^2$ has antiderivative
$$F(x) = \tfrac{1}{2}x^2 - \tfrac{1}{3}x^3$$
$$\therefore \int_0^1 (x^2 - x) \, dx = -(F(1) - F(0))$$
$$= -\left(\tfrac{1}{2} - \tfrac{1}{3} - (0 - 0)\right)$$
$$= -\tfrac{1}{6}$$

iii $\int_{-2}^0 3x \, dx = -\int_{-2}^0 -3x \, dx$

Now $f(x) = -3x$ has antiderivative
$$F(x) = -\tfrac{3}{2}x^2$$

$$\therefore \int_{-2}^0 3x \, dx = -(F(0) - F(-2))$$
$$= -(0 - (-6))$$
$$= -6$$

d $\int_0^2 \left(-\sqrt{4-x^2}\right) dx = -\int_0^2 \sqrt{4-x^2}\, dx$

Now $f(x) = \sqrt{4-x^2}$ is the top half of a circle with radius 2 units and centre (0, 0).

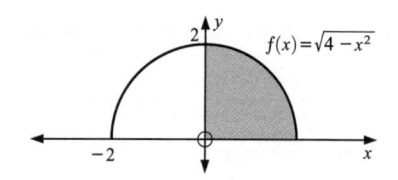

$\therefore \int_0^2 \left(-\sqrt{4-x^2}\right) dx = -\int_0^2 \sqrt{4-x^2}\, dx$
$= -\text{(shaded area)}$
$= -\frac{1}{4} \times \pi \times 2^2$
$= -\pi$

EXERCISE 24C.1

1 If $y = x^7$ then $\dfrac{dy}{dx} = 7x^6$

$\therefore \int 7x^6\, dx = x^7 + c_1$

$\therefore 7\int x^6\, dx = x^7 + c_1$

$\therefore \int x^6\, dx = \frac{1}{7}x^7 + c$

2 If $y = x^3 + x^2$ then $\dfrac{dy}{dx} = 3x^2 + 2x$

$\therefore \int 3x^2 + 2x\, dx = x^3 + x^2 + c$

3 If $y = e^{2x+1}$ then $\dfrac{dy}{dx} = 2e^{2x+1}$

$\therefore \int 2e^{2x+1}\, dx = e^{2x+1} + c_1$

$\therefore 2\int e^{2x+1}\, dx = e^{2x+1} + c_1$

$\therefore \int e^{2x+1}\, dx = \frac{1}{2}e^{2x+1} + c$

4 If $y = (2x+1)^4$

then $\dfrac{dy}{dx} = 4(2x+1)^3 \times 2 = 8(2x+1)^3$

$\therefore \int 8(2x+1)^3\, dx = (2x+1)^4 + c_1$

$\therefore 8\int (2x+1)^3\, dx = (2x+1)^4 + c_1$

$\therefore \int (2x+1)^3\, dx = \frac{1}{8}(2x+1)^4 + c$

5 If $y = x\sqrt{x} = x^{\frac{3}{2}}$

then $\dfrac{dy}{dx} = \frac{3}{2}x^{\frac{1}{2}} = \frac{3}{2}\sqrt{x}$

$\therefore \int \frac{3}{2}\sqrt{x}\, dx = x\sqrt{x} + c_1$

$\therefore \frac{3}{2}\int \sqrt{x}\, dx = x\sqrt{x} + c_1$

$\therefore \int \sqrt{x}\, dx = \frac{2}{3}x\sqrt{x} + c$

6 If $y = \dfrac{1}{\sqrt{x}} = x^{-\frac{1}{2}}$

then $\dfrac{dy}{dx} = -\frac{1}{2}x^{-\frac{3}{2}} = -\frac{1}{2}\left(\dfrac{1}{x\sqrt{x}}\right)$

$\therefore \int -\frac{1}{2}\left(\dfrac{1}{x\sqrt{x}}\right) dx = \dfrac{1}{\sqrt{x}} + c_1$

$\therefore -\frac{1}{2}\int \dfrac{1}{x\sqrt{x}}\, dx = \dfrac{1}{\sqrt{x}} + c_1$

$\therefore \int \dfrac{1}{x\sqrt{x}}\, dx = -\dfrac{2}{\sqrt{x}} + c$

7 Suppose $F(x)$ is the antiderivative of $f(x)$ and $G(x)$ is the antiderivative of $g(x)$.

$\therefore \dfrac{d}{dx}(F(x) + G(x)) = f(x) + g(x)$

$\therefore \int (f(x) + g(x))\, dx$
$= F(x) + G(x) + c$
$= (F(x) + c_1) + (G(x) + c_2)$
$= \int f(x)\, dx + \int g(x)\, dx$

8 $y = \sqrt{1-4x} = (1-4x)^{\frac{1}{2}}$

$\therefore \dfrac{dy}{dx} = \frac{1}{2}(1-4x)^{-\frac{1}{2}}(-4)$
$= -2(1-4x)^{-\frac{1}{2}}$

$\therefore \int \dfrac{-2}{\sqrt{1-4x}}\, dx = \sqrt{1-4x} + c_1$

$\therefore -2\int \dfrac{1}{\sqrt{1-4x}}\, dx = \sqrt{1-4x} + c_1$

$\therefore \int \dfrac{1}{\sqrt{1-4x}}\, dx = -\frac{1}{2}\sqrt{1-4x} + c$

9 $\dfrac{d}{dx}(\ln(5 - 3x + x^2)) = \dfrac{2x - 3}{5 - 3x + x^2}$

$\therefore \displaystyle\int \dfrac{2x - 3}{5 - 3x + x^2}\,dx = \ln\left|5 - 3x + x^2\right| + c_1$

Now $5 - 3x + x^2 > 0$ for all x,
 as $a > 0$ and $\Delta = -11 < 0$.

$\therefore \displaystyle\int \dfrac{4x - 6}{5 - 3x + x^2}\,dx = 2\ln(5 - 3x + x^2) + c$

10 $\dfrac{d}{dx}(2^x) = \dfrac{d}{dx}(e^{\ln 2})^x$
$= e^{(\ln 2)x} \times \ln 2$
$= 2^x \ln 2$

$\therefore \displaystyle\int 2^x \ln 2\,dx = 2^x + c_1$

$\therefore \ln 2 \displaystyle\int 2^x\,dx = 2^x + c_1$

$\therefore \displaystyle\int 2^x\,dx = \dfrac{2^x}{\ln 2} + c$

11 $\dfrac{d}{dx}(x \ln x) = 1 \times \ln x + x \times \dfrac{1}{x}$
$= \ln x + 1$

$\therefore \displaystyle\int (\ln x + 1)\,dx = x \ln x + c_1$

$\therefore \displaystyle\int \ln x\,dx + x = x \ln x + c_1$

$\therefore \displaystyle\int \ln x\,dx = x \ln x - x + c$

EXERCISE 24C.2

1 a $\displaystyle\int (x^4 - x^2 - x + 2)\,dx$
$= \tfrac{1}{5}x^5 - \tfrac{1}{3}x^3 - \tfrac{1}{2}x^2 + 2x + c$

b $\displaystyle\int (\sqrt{x} + e^x)\,dx$
$= \displaystyle\int (x^{\frac{1}{2}} + e^x)\,dx$
$= \dfrac{x^{\frac{3}{2}}}{\frac{3}{2}} + e^x + c$
$= \tfrac{2}{3}x^{\frac{3}{2}} + e^x + c$

c $\displaystyle\int \left(3e^x - \dfrac{1}{x}\right)dx$
$= 3e^x - \ln|x| + c$

d $\displaystyle\int \left(x\sqrt{x} - \dfrac{2}{x}\right)dx$
$= \displaystyle\int \left(x^{\frac{3}{2}} - \dfrac{2}{x}\right)dx$
$= \dfrac{x^{\frac{5}{2}}}{\frac{5}{2}} - 2\ln|x| + c$
$= \tfrac{2}{5}x^{\frac{5}{2}} - 2\ln|x| + c$

e $\displaystyle\int \left(\dfrac{1}{x\sqrt{x}} + \dfrac{4}{x}\right)dx$
$= \displaystyle\int \left(x^{-\frac{3}{2}} + \dfrac{4}{x}\right)dx$
$= \dfrac{x^{-\frac{1}{2}}}{-\frac{1}{2}} + 4\ln|x| + c$
$= -\dfrac{2}{\sqrt{x}} + 4\ln|x| + c$

f $\displaystyle\int (\tfrac{1}{2}x^3 - x^4 + x^{\frac{1}{3}})\,dx$
$= \tfrac{1}{2}\dfrac{x^4}{4} - \dfrac{x^5}{5} + \dfrac{x^{\frac{4}{3}}}{\frac{4}{3}} + c$
$= \tfrac{1}{8}x^4 - \tfrac{1}{5}x^5 + \tfrac{3}{4}x^{\frac{4}{3}} + c$

g $\displaystyle\int \left(x^2 + \dfrac{3}{x}\right)dx$
$= \dfrac{x^3}{3} + 3\ln|x| + c$

h $\displaystyle\int \left(\dfrac{1}{2x} + x^2 - e^x\right)dx$
$= \tfrac{1}{2}\ln|x| + \dfrac{x^3}{3} - e^x + c$

i $\displaystyle\int \left(5e^x + \tfrac{1}{3}x^3 - \dfrac{4}{x}\right)dx$
$= 5e^x + \tfrac{1}{3}\dfrac{x^4}{4} - 4\ln|x| + c$
$= 5e^x + \tfrac{1}{12}x^4 - 4\ln|x| + c$

2 a $\displaystyle\int (x^2 + 3x - 2)\,dx$
$= \dfrac{x^3}{3} + \dfrac{3x^2}{2} - 2x + c$

b $\displaystyle\int \left(\sqrt{x} - \dfrac{1}{\sqrt{x}}\right)dx$
$= \displaystyle\int x^{\frac{1}{2}} - x^{-\frac{1}{2}}\,dx$
$= \dfrac{x^{\frac{3}{2}}}{\frac{3}{2}} - \dfrac{x^{\frac{1}{2}}}{\frac{1}{2}} + c$
$= \tfrac{2}{3}x^{\frac{3}{2}} - 2x^{\frac{1}{2}} + c$

c $\displaystyle\int \left(2e^x - \dfrac{1}{x^2}\right)dx$
$= \displaystyle\int (2e^x - x^{-2})\,dx$
$= 2e^x - \dfrac{x^{-1}}{-1} + c$
$= 2e^x + \dfrac{1}{x} + c$

d $\int \left(\dfrac{1-4x}{x\sqrt{x}}\right) dx$

$= \int \left(\dfrac{1}{x\sqrt{x}} - \dfrac{4}{\sqrt{x}}\right) dx$

$= \int (x^{-\frac{3}{2}} - 4x^{-\frac{1}{2}}) dx$

$= \dfrac{x^{-\frac{1}{2}}}{-\frac{1}{2}} - \dfrac{4x^{\frac{1}{2}}}{\frac{1}{2}} + c$

$= -\dfrac{2}{\sqrt{x}} - 8\sqrt{x} + c$

e $\int (2x+1)^2 \, dx$

$= \int (4x^2 + 4x + 1) \, dx$

$= \dfrac{4x^3}{3} + \dfrac{4x^2}{2} + x + c$

$= \tfrac{4}{3}x^3 + 2x^2 + x + c$

f $\int \dfrac{x^2 + x - 3}{x} dx$

$= \int \left(x + 1 - \dfrac{3}{x}\right) dx$

$= \dfrac{x^2}{2} + x - 3\ln|x| + c$

g $\int \dfrac{2x-1}{\sqrt{x}} dx$

$= \int \left(2x^{\frac{1}{2}} - x^{-\frac{1}{2}}\right) dx$

$= \dfrac{2x^{\frac{3}{2}}}{\frac{3}{2}} - \dfrac{x^{\frac{1}{2}}}{\frac{1}{2}} + c$

$= \tfrac{4}{3}x^{\frac{3}{2}} - 2x^{\frac{1}{2}} + c$

h $\int \dfrac{x^2 - 4x + 10}{x^2 \sqrt{x}} dx$

$= \int \left(\dfrac{x^2}{x^2\sqrt{x}} - \dfrac{4x}{x^2\sqrt{x}} + \dfrac{10}{x^2\sqrt{x}}\right) dx$

$= \int \left(x^{-\frac{1}{2}} - 4x^{-\frac{3}{2}} + 10x^{-\frac{5}{2}}\right) dx$

$= \dfrac{x^{\frac{1}{2}}}{\frac{1}{2}} - \dfrac{4x^{-\frac{1}{2}}}{-\frac{1}{2}} + \dfrac{10x^{-\frac{3}{2}}}{-\frac{3}{2}} + c$

$= 2\sqrt{x} + \dfrac{8}{\sqrt{x}} - \dfrac{20}{3x\sqrt{x}} + c$

i $\int (x+1)^3 \, dx$

$= \int (x^3 + 3x^2 + 3x + 1) \, dx$

$= \tfrac{1}{4}x^4 + x^3 + \tfrac{3}{2}x^2 + x + c$

3 a $\dfrac{dy}{dx} = 6$

$\therefore \ y = \int 6 \, dx$

$\therefore \ y = 6x + c$

b $\dfrac{dy}{dx} = 4x^2$

$\therefore \ y = \int 4x^2 \, dx$

$\therefore \ y = \tfrac{4}{3}x^3 + c$

c $\dfrac{dy}{dx} = 5x - x^2$

$\therefore \ y = \int (5x - x^2) \, dx$

$\therefore \ y = \tfrac{5}{2}x^2 - \tfrac{1}{3}x^3 + c$

d $\dfrac{dy}{dx} = \dfrac{1}{x^2} = x^{-2}$

$\therefore \ y = \int x^{-2} \, dx$

$\therefore \ y = \dfrac{x^{-1}}{-1} + c$

$\therefore \ y = -\dfrac{1}{x} + c$

e $\dfrac{dy}{dx} = 2e^x - 5$

$\therefore \ y = \int (2e^x - 5) \, dx$

$\therefore \ y = 2e^x - 5x + c$

f $\dfrac{dy}{dx} = 4x^3 + 3x^2$

$\therefore \ y = \int (4x^3 + 3x^2) \, dx$

$= \dfrac{4x^4}{4} + \dfrac{3x^3}{3} + c$

$\therefore \ y = x^4 + x^3 + c$

4 a $\dfrac{dy}{dx} = (1-2x)^2$

$\therefore \ y = \int (1-2x)^2 \, dx$

$= \int (1 - 4x + 4x^2) \, dx$

$= x - \dfrac{4x^2}{2} + \dfrac{4x^3}{3} + c$

$= x - 2x^2 + \tfrac{4}{3}x^3 + c$

b $\dfrac{dy}{dx} = \sqrt{x} - \dfrac{2}{\sqrt{x}}$

$= x^{\frac{1}{2}} - 2x^{-\frac{1}{2}}$

$\therefore \ y = \int (x^{\frac{1}{2}} - 2x^{-\frac{1}{2}}) \, dx$

$= \dfrac{x^{\frac{3}{2}}}{\frac{3}{2}} - \dfrac{2x^{\frac{1}{2}}}{\frac{1}{2}} + c$

$= \tfrac{2}{3}x^{\frac{3}{2}} - 4x^{\frac{1}{2}} + c$

c $\dfrac{dy}{dx} = \dfrac{x^2 + 2x - 5}{x^2}$ $\therefore\ y = \int \left(1 + 2x^{-1} - 5x^{-2}\right) dx$

$\phantom{\dfrac{dy}{dx}} = 1 + 2x^{-1} - 5x^{-2}$ $ = x + 2\ln|x| - \dfrac{5x^{-1}}{-1} + c$

$ = x + 2\ln|x| + \dfrac{5}{x} + c$

5 a $f'(x) = x^3 - 5x + 3$

$\therefore\ f(x) = \int (x^3 - 5x + 3)\, dx$

$ = \dfrac{x^4}{4} - \dfrac{5x^2}{2} + 3x + c$

b $f'(x) = 2\sqrt{x}(1 - 3x)$

$ = 2x^{\frac{1}{2}} - 6x^{\frac{3}{2}}$

$\therefore\ f(x) = \int (2x^{\frac{1}{2}} - 6x^{\frac{3}{2}})\, dx$

$ = \dfrac{2x^{\frac{3}{2}}}{\frac{3}{2}} - \dfrac{6x^{\frac{5}{2}}}{\frac{5}{2}} + c$

$ = \tfrac{4}{3}x^{\frac{3}{2}} - \tfrac{12}{5}x^{\frac{5}{2}} + c$

c $f'(x) = 3e^x - \dfrac{4}{x}$

$\therefore\ f(x) = \int \left(3e^x - \dfrac{4}{x}\right) dx$

$ = 3e^x - 4\ln|x| + c$

6 a $f'(x) = 2x - 1$

$\therefore\ f(x) = \int (2x - 1)\, dx$

$ = \dfrac{2x^2}{2} - x + c$

$ = x^2 - x + c$

But $f(0) = 3$, so $0 - 0 + c = 3$

$\therefore\ c = 3$

$\therefore\ f(x) = x^2 - x + 3$

b $f'(x) = 3x^2 + 2x$

$\therefore\ f(x) = \int (3x^2 + 2x)\, dx$

$ = \dfrac{3x^3}{3} + \dfrac{2x^2}{2} + c$

$ = x^3 + x^2 + c$

But $f(2) = 5$, so $8 + 4 + c = 5$

$\therefore\ c = -7$

$\therefore\ f(x) = x^3 + x^2 - 7$

c $f'(x) = e^x + \dfrac{1}{\sqrt{x}} = e^x + x^{-\frac{1}{2}}$

$\therefore\ f(x) = \int (e^x + x^{-\frac{1}{2}})\, dx$

$ = e^x + 2x^{\frac{1}{2}} + c$

But $f(1) = 1$, so $e^1 + 2 + c = 1$

$\therefore\ c = -1 - e$

$\therefore\ f(x) = e^x + 2\sqrt{x} - 1 - e$

d $f'(x) = x - \dfrac{2}{\sqrt{x}} = x - 2x^{-\frac{1}{2}}$

$\therefore\ f(x) = \int (x - 2x^{-\frac{1}{2}})\, dx$

$ = \dfrac{x^2}{2} - \dfrac{2x^{\frac{1}{2}}}{\frac{1}{2}} + c$

$ = \tfrac{1}{2}x^2 - 4\sqrt{x} + c$

But $f(1) = 2$, so $\tfrac{1}{2} - 4 + c = 2$

$\therefore\ c = \tfrac{11}{2}$

$\therefore\ f(x) = \tfrac{1}{2}x^2 - 4\sqrt{x} + \tfrac{11}{2}$

7 a Given: $f''(x) = 2x + 1$, $f'(1) = 3$, $f(2) = 7$

$\therefore\ f'(x) = \int (2x + 1)\, dx$

$ = \dfrac{2x^2}{2} + x + c$

$ = x^2 + x + c$

But $f'(1) = 3$ so $1 + 1 + c = 3$

$\therefore\ c = 1$

$\therefore\ f'(x) = x^2 + x + 1$

Then $f(x) = \int (x^2 + x + 1)\, dx$

$ = \dfrac{x^3}{3} + \dfrac{x^2}{2} + x + k$

But $f(2) = 7$ so $\tfrac{8}{3} + 2 + 2 + k = 7$

$\therefore\ k = 7 - 4 - \tfrac{8}{3}$

$\therefore\ k = \tfrac{1}{3}$

$\therefore\ f(x) = \tfrac{1}{3}x^3 + \tfrac{1}{2}x^2 + x + \tfrac{1}{3}$

b Given: $f''(x) = 15\sqrt{x} + \dfrac{3}{\sqrt{x}}$, $f'(1) = 12$, $f(0) = 5$

Now $f''(x) = 15x^{\frac{1}{2}} + 3x^{-\frac{1}{2}}$

$\therefore\ f'(x) = \dfrac{15x^{\frac{3}{2}}}{\frac{3}{2}} + \dfrac{3x^{\frac{1}{2}}}{\frac{1}{2}} + c$

$= 10x^{\frac{3}{2}} + 6x^{\frac{1}{2}} + c$

But $f'(1) = 12$ so $10 + 6 + c = 12$

$\therefore\ c = -4$

$\therefore\ f'(x) = 10x^{\frac{3}{2}} + 6x^{\frac{1}{2}} - 4$

Then $f(x) = \dfrac{10x^{\frac{5}{2}}}{\frac{5}{2}} + \dfrac{6x^{\frac{3}{2}}}{\frac{3}{2}} - 4x + k$

$= 4x^{\frac{5}{2}} + 4x^{\frac{3}{2}} - 4x + k$

But $f(0) = 5$ so $k = 5$

$\therefore\ f(x) = 4x^{\frac{5}{2}} + 4x^{\frac{3}{2}} - 4x + 5$

c Given: $f''(x) = 2x$ and that $(1, 0)$ and $(0, 5)$ lie on the curve

Now $f'(x) = \dfrac{2x^2}{2} + c = x^2 + c$

$\therefore\ f(x) = \dfrac{x^3}{3} + cx + k$

But $f(0) = 5$ so $0 + 0 + k = 5$ and so $k = 5$

and $f(1) = 0$ so $\frac{1}{3} + c + 5 = 0$ and so $c = -5\frac{1}{3}$

$\therefore\ f(x) = \frac{1}{3}x^3 - \frac{16}{3}x + 5$

EXERCISE 24D

1 a $\int (2x+5)^3\, dx$

$= \frac{1}{2} \times \dfrac{(2x+5)^4}{4} + c$

$= \frac{1}{8}(2x+5)^4 + c$

b $\int \dfrac{1}{(3-2x)^2}\, dx$

$= \int (3-2x)^{-2}\, dx$

$= \dfrac{1}{-2} \times \dfrac{(3-2x)^{-1}}{-1} + c$

$= \dfrac{1}{2(3-2x)} + c$

c $\int \dfrac{4}{(2x-1)^4}\, dx$

$= \int 4(2x-1)^{-4}\, dx$

$= 4(\tfrac{1}{2}) \times \dfrac{(2x-1)^{-3}}{-3} + c$

$= -\tfrac{2}{3}(2x-1)^{-3} + c$

d $\int (4x-3)^7\, dx$

$= \tfrac{1}{4} \times \dfrac{(4x-3)^8}{8} + c$

$= \tfrac{1}{32}(4x-3)^8 + c$

e $\int \sqrt{3x-4}\, dx$

$= \int (3x-4)^{\frac{1}{2}}\, dx$

$= \tfrac{1}{3} \times \dfrac{(3x-4)^{\frac{3}{2}}}{\frac{3}{2}} + c$

$= \tfrac{2}{9}(3x-4)^{\frac{3}{2}} + c$

f $\int \dfrac{10}{\sqrt{1-5x}}\, dx$

$= \int 10(1-5x)^{-\frac{1}{2}}\, dx$

$= 10(\tfrac{1}{-5}) \times \dfrac{(1-5x)^{\frac{1}{2}}}{\frac{1}{2}} + c$

$= -4(1-5x)^{\frac{1}{2}} + c$

g $\int 3(1-x)^4\, dx$

$= 3\int (1-x)^4\, dx$

$= 3(\tfrac{1}{-1}) \times \dfrac{(1-x)^5}{5} + c$

$= -\tfrac{3}{5}(1-x)^5 + c$

h $\int \dfrac{4}{\sqrt{3-4x}}\, dx$

$= \int 4(3-4x)^{-\frac{1}{2}}\, dx$

$= 4(\tfrac{1}{-4}) \times \dfrac{(3-4x)^{\frac{1}{2}}}{\frac{1}{2}} + c$

$= -2\sqrt{3-4x} + c$

2 a $\dfrac{dy}{dx} = \sqrt{2x-7} = (2x-7)^{\frac{1}{2}}$

$\therefore\ y = \tfrac{1}{2} \times \dfrac{(2x-7)^{\frac{3}{2}}}{\frac{3}{2}} + c$

$= \tfrac{1}{3}(2x-7)^{\frac{3}{2}} + c$

But $y = 11$ when $x = 8$

$\therefore\ \tfrac{1}{3}(16-7)^{\frac{3}{2}} + c = 11$

$\therefore\ \tfrac{1}{3}(27) + c = 11$

$\therefore\ 9 + c = 11$ and so $c = 2$

$\therefore\ y = \tfrac{1}{3}(2x-7)^{\frac{3}{2}} + 2$

b $f(x)$ has gradient function $f'(x) = \dfrac{4}{\sqrt{1-x}} = 4(1-x)^{-\frac{1}{2}}$

$\therefore\ f(x) = 4(\frac{1}{-1}) \times \dfrac{(1-x)^{\frac{1}{2}}}{\frac{1}{2}} + c$ But $y = -11$ when $x = -3$

$= -8\sqrt{1-x} + c$

$\therefore\ -8\sqrt{1-(-3)} + c = -11$

$\therefore\ -8\sqrt{4} + c = -11$

$\therefore\ -16 + c = -11$ and so $c = 5$

$\therefore\ f(x) = 5 - 8\sqrt{1-x}$

Now $f(-8) = 5 - 8\sqrt{1-(-8)} = 5 - 8(3) = -19$, so the point is $(-8, -19)$.

3 a $\int 3(2x-1)^2\, dx$
$= 3\int (2x-1)^2\, dx$
$= 3(\frac{1}{2})\dfrac{(2x-1)^3}{3} + c$
$= \frac{1}{2}(2x-1)^3 + c$

b $\int (x^2 - x)^2\, dx$
$= \int (x^4 - 2x^3 + x^2)\, dx$
$= \dfrac{x^5}{5} - \dfrac{2x^4}{4} + \dfrac{x^3}{3} + c$
$= \frac{1}{5}x^5 - \frac{1}{2}x^4 + \frac{1}{3}x^3 + c$

c $\int (1 - 3x)^3\, dx$
$= (\frac{1}{-3})\dfrac{(1-3x)^4}{4} + c$
$= -\frac{1}{12}(1-3x)^4 + c$

d $\int (1 - x^2)^2\, dx$
$= \int (1 - 2x^2 + x^4)\, dx$
$= x - \frac{2}{3}x^3 + \frac{1}{5}x^5 + c$

e $\int 4\sqrt{5-x}\, dx$
$= 4\int (5-x)^{\frac{1}{2}}\, dx$
$= 4(\frac{1}{-1})\dfrac{(5-x)^{\frac{3}{2}}}{\frac{3}{2}} + c$
$= -\frac{8}{3}(5-x)^{\frac{3}{2}} + c$

f $\int (x^2 + 1)^3\, dx$
$= \int (x^6 + 3x^4 + 3x^2 + 1)\, dx$
$= \dfrac{x^7}{7} + \dfrac{3x^5}{5} + \dfrac{3x^3}{3} + x + c$
$= \frac{1}{7}x^7 + \frac{3}{5}x^5 + x^3 + x + c$

4 a $\int (2e^x + 5e^{2x})\, dx$
$= 2e^x + 5(\frac{1}{2})e^{2x} + c$
$= 2e^x + \frac{5}{2}e^{2x} + c$

b $\int (3e^{5x-2})\, dx$
$= 3(\frac{1}{5})e^{5x-2} + c$
$= \frac{3}{5}e^{5x-2} + c$

c $\int (e^{7-3x})\, dx$
$= \frac{1}{-3}e^{7-3x} + c$
$= -\frac{1}{3}e^{7-3x} + c$

d $\int \dfrac{1}{2x-1}\, dx$
$= \frac{1}{2}\ln|2x-1| + c$

e $\int \dfrac{5}{1-3x}\, dx$
$= 5\int \dfrac{1}{1-3x}\, dx$
$= 5(\frac{1}{-3})\ln|1-3x| + c$
$= -\frac{5}{3}\ln|1-3x| + c$

f $\int \left(e^{-x} - \dfrac{4}{2x+1}\right) dx$
$= \frac{1}{-1}e^{-x} - 4(\frac{1}{2})\ln|2x+1| + c$
$= -e^{-x} - 2\ln|2x+1| + c$

g $\int (e^x + e^{-x})^2\, dx$
$= \int \left(e^{2x} + 2 + e^{-2x}\right) dx$
$= \frac{1}{2}e^{2x} + 2x + (\frac{1}{-2})e^{-2x} + c$
$= \frac{1}{2}e^{2x} + 2x - \frac{1}{2}e^{-2x} + c$

h $\int (e^{-x} + 2)^2\, dx$
$= \int \left(e^{-2x} + 4e^{-x} + 4\right) dx$
$= \frac{1}{-2}e^{-2x} + 4(\frac{1}{-1})e^{-x} + 4x + c$
$= -\frac{1}{2}e^{-2x} - 4e^{-x} + 4x + c$

i $\int \left(x - \dfrac{5}{1-x}\right) dx = \dfrac{x^2}{2} - 5(\frac{1}{-1})\ln|1-x| + c$
$= \frac{1}{2}x^2 + 5\ln|1-x| + c$

5 a $\dfrac{dy}{dx} = (1 - e^x)^2$
$= 1 - 2e^x + e^{2x}$
$\therefore\ y = x - 2e^x + \frac{1}{2}e^{2x} + c$

b $\dfrac{dy}{dx} = 1 - 2x + \dfrac{3}{x+2}$
$\therefore\ y = x - \dfrac{2x^2}{2} + 3\ln|x+2| + c$
$= x - x^2 + 3\ln|x+2| + c$

c $\dfrac{dy}{dx} = e^{-2x} + \dfrac{4}{2x-1}$

$\therefore\ y = \dfrac{1}{-2}e^{-2x} + 4(\tfrac{1}{2})\ln|2x-1| + c$

$ = -\tfrac{1}{2}e^{-2x} + 2\ln|2x-1| + c$

6 Differentiating Tracy's answer gives

$\dfrac{d}{dx}\left(\tfrac{1}{4}\ln|4x| + c\right) = \tfrac{1}{4}\left(\dfrac{1}{4x}\right) \times 4 + 0$

$\phantom{\dfrac{d}{dx}\left(\tfrac{1}{4}\ln|4x| + c\right)} = \dfrac{1}{4x}$

Differentiating Nadine's answer gives

$\dfrac{d}{dx}\left(\tfrac{1}{4}\ln|x| + c\right) = \tfrac{1}{4}\left(\dfrac{1}{x}\right) + 0$

$\phantom{\dfrac{d}{dx}\left(\tfrac{1}{4}\ln|x| + c\right)} = \dfrac{1}{4x}$

Both answers give the correct derivative and both are correct. This result occurs because $\log 4x = \log 4 + \log x$. Their answers differ by a constant which is accounted for by c.

7 a $f'(x) = 2e^{-2x}$

$\therefore\ f(x) = 2(\tfrac{1}{-2})e^{-2x} + c$

$ = -e^{-2x} + c$

But $f(0) = 3$ so $-e^0 + c = 3$

$\therefore\ c = 4$

$\therefore\ f(x) = -e^{-2x} + 4$

b $f'(x) = 2x - \dfrac{2}{1-x}$

$\therefore\ f(x) = \dfrac{2x^2}{2} - \dfrac{2}{-1}\ln|1-x| + c$

$ = x^2 + 2\ln|1-x| + c$

But $f(-1) = 3$ so $1 + 2\ln|2| + c = 3$

$\therefore\ c = 2 - 2\ln 2$

$\therefore\ f(x) = x^2 + 2\ln|1-x| + 2 - 2\ln 2$

c $f'(x) = \sqrt{x} + \tfrac{1}{2}e^{-4x}$

$ = x^{\tfrac{1}{2}} + \tfrac{1}{2}e^{-4x}$

$\therefore\ f(x) = \dfrac{x^{\tfrac{3}{2}}}{\tfrac{3}{2}} + \tfrac{1}{2}(\tfrac{1}{-4})e^{-4x} + c$

$ = \tfrac{2}{3}x^{\tfrac{3}{2}} - \tfrac{1}{8}e^{-4x} + c$

But $f(1) = 0$

$\therefore\ \tfrac{2}{3} - \tfrac{1}{8}e^{-4} + c = 0$

$\therefore\ c = \tfrac{1}{8}e^{-4} - \tfrac{2}{3}$

$\therefore\ f(x) = \tfrac{2}{3}x^{\tfrac{3}{2}} - \tfrac{1}{8}e^{-4x} + \tfrac{1}{8}e^{-4} - \tfrac{2}{3}$

8 $\dfrac{3}{x+2} - \dfrac{1}{x-2} = \dfrac{3(x-2) - 1(x+2)}{(x+2)(x-2)}$

$\phantom{\dfrac{3}{x+2} - \dfrac{1}{x-2}} = \dfrac{3x - 6 - x - 2}{x^2 - 4}$

$\phantom{\dfrac{3}{x+2} - \dfrac{1}{x-2}} = \dfrac{2x - 8}{x^2 - 4}$

$\therefore\ \displaystyle\int \dfrac{2x-8}{x^2-4}\,dx = \int \left(\dfrac{3}{x+2} - \dfrac{1}{x-2}\right) dx$

$\phantom{\therefore\ \displaystyle\int \dfrac{2x-8}{x^2-4}\,dx} = 3\ln|x+2| - \ln|x-2| + c$

9 $\dfrac{1}{2x-1} - \dfrac{1}{2x+1} = \dfrac{1(2x+1) - 1(2x-1)}{(2x-1)(2x+1)}$

$\phantom{\dfrac{1}{2x-1} - \dfrac{1}{2x+1}} = \dfrac{2x+1-2x+1}{(2x-1)(2x+1)}$

$\phantom{\dfrac{1}{2x-1} - \dfrac{1}{2x+1}} = \dfrac{2}{4x^2-1}$

$\therefore\ \displaystyle\int \dfrac{2}{4x^2-1}\,dx$

$= \displaystyle\int \left(\dfrac{1}{2x-1} - \dfrac{1}{2x+1}\right) dx$

$= \tfrac{1}{2}\ln|2x-1| - \tfrac{1}{2}\ln|2x+1| + c$

EXERCISE 24E

1 a Let $u = x^3 + 1$, $\dfrac{du}{dx} = 3x^2$

$\therefore\ \displaystyle\int 3x^2(x^3+1)^4\,dx = \int u^4 \dfrac{du}{dx}\,dx$

$ = \displaystyle\int u^4\,du$

$ = \tfrac{1}{5}u^5 + c$

$ = \tfrac{1}{5}(x^3+1)^5 + c$

b Let $u = x^2 + 3$, $\dfrac{du}{dx} = 2x$

$\therefore \ \displaystyle\int \dfrac{2x}{\sqrt{x^2+3}}\,dx$

$= \displaystyle\int \left((x^2+3)^{-\frac{1}{2}} \times 2x\right) dx$

$= \displaystyle\int u^{-\frac{1}{2}} \dfrac{du}{dx}\,dx$

$= \displaystyle\int u^{-\frac{1}{2}}\,du$

$= \dfrac{u^{\frac{1}{2}}}{\frac{1}{2}} + c$

$= 2\sqrt{u} + c$

$= 2\sqrt{x^2+3} + c$

c Let $u = x^3 + x$, $\dfrac{du}{dx} = 3x^2 + 1$

$\therefore \ \displaystyle\int \sqrt{x^3+x}\,(3x^2+1)\,dx$

$= \displaystyle\int \sqrt{u}\,\dfrac{du}{dx}\,dx$

$= \displaystyle\int u^{\frac{1}{2}}\,du$

$= \dfrac{u^{\frac{3}{2}}}{\frac{3}{2}} + c$

$= \tfrac{2}{3} u^{\frac{3}{2}} + c$

$= \tfrac{2}{3}(x^3+x)^{\frac{3}{2}} + c$

d Let $u = 2 + x^4$, $\dfrac{du}{dx} = 4x^3$

$\therefore \ \displaystyle\int 4x^3(2+x^4)^3\,dx$

$= \displaystyle\int u^3 \dfrac{du}{dx}\,dx$

$= \displaystyle\int u^3\,du$

$= \dfrac{u^4}{4} + c$

$= \tfrac{1}{4}(2+x^4)^4 + c$

e Let $u = x^3 + 2x + 1$ $\ \therefore\ \dfrac{du}{dx} = 3x^2 + 2$

$\therefore \ \displaystyle\int (x^3+2x+1)^4(3x^2+2)\,dx$

$= \displaystyle\int u^4 \dfrac{du}{dx}\,dx$

$= \displaystyle\int u^4\,du$

$= \dfrac{u^5}{5} + c$

$= \tfrac{1}{5}(x^3+2x+1)^5 + c$

f Let $u = 3x^3 - 1$, $\dfrac{du}{dx} = 9x^2$

$\therefore \ \displaystyle\int \dfrac{x^2}{(3x^3-1)^4}\,dx$

$= \displaystyle\int (3x^3-1)^{-4} \times x^2\,dx$

$= \tfrac{1}{9} \displaystyle\int (3x^3-1)^{-4} \times 9x^2\,dx$

$= \tfrac{1}{9} \displaystyle\int u^{-4} \dfrac{du}{dx}\,dx$

$= \tfrac{1}{9} \displaystyle\int u^{-4}\,du$

$= \tfrac{1}{9}\dfrac{u^{-3}}{-3} + c = -\dfrac{1}{27(3x^3-1)^3} + c$

g Let $u = 1 - x^2$, $\dfrac{du}{dx} = -2x$

$\therefore \ \displaystyle\int \dfrac{x}{(1-x^2)^5}\,dx$

$= -\tfrac{1}{2}\displaystyle\int (1-x^2)^{-5} \times (-2x)\,dx$

$= -\tfrac{1}{2}\displaystyle\int u^{-5} \dfrac{du}{dx}\,dx$

$= -\tfrac{1}{2}\displaystyle\int u^{-5}\,du$

$= -\tfrac{1}{2}\dfrac{u^{-4}}{-4} + c$

$= \dfrac{1}{8(1-x^2)^4} + c$

h Let $u = x^2 + 4x - 3$, $\dfrac{du}{dx} = 2x + 4$

$\therefore \ \displaystyle\int \dfrac{x+2}{(x^2+4x-3)^2}\,dx$

$= \tfrac{1}{2} \displaystyle\int (x^2+4x-3)^{-2}(2x+4)\,dx$

$= \tfrac{1}{2} \displaystyle\int u^{-2} \dfrac{du}{dx}\,dx$

$= \tfrac{1}{2} \displaystyle\int u^{-2}\,du$

$= \tfrac{1}{2}\dfrac{u^{-1}}{-1} + c$

$= \dfrac{-1}{2(x^2+4x-3)} + c$

i Let $u = x^2 + x$, $\dfrac{du}{dx} = 2x + 1$

$\therefore \ \displaystyle\int x^4(x+1)^4(2x+1)\,dx$

$= \displaystyle\int (x^2+x)^4(2x+1)\,dx$

$= \displaystyle\int u^4 \dfrac{du}{dx}\,dx$

$= \displaystyle\int u^4\,du$

$= \tfrac{1}{5}u^5 + c$

$= \tfrac{1}{5}(x^2+x)^5 + c$

2 a Let $u = 1 - 2x$, $\dfrac{du}{dx} = -2$

$\therefore \int -2e^{1-2x}\,dx = \int e^u \dfrac{du}{dx}\,dx$
$= \int e^u\,du$
$= e^u + c$
$= e^{1-2x} + c$

b Let $u = x^2$, $\dfrac{du}{dx} = 2x$

$\therefore \int 2xe^{x^2}\,dx = \int e^u \dfrac{du}{dx}\,dx$
$= \int e^u\,du$
$= e^u + c$
$= e^{x^2} + c$

c Let $u = x^3 + 1$, $\dfrac{du}{dx} = 3x^2$

$\therefore \int x^2 e^{x^3+1}\,dx$
$= \tfrac{1}{3}\int (3x^2)e^{x^3+1}\,dx$
$= \tfrac{1}{3}\int e^u \dfrac{du}{dx}\,dx$
$= \tfrac{1}{3}\int e^u\,du$
$= \tfrac{1}{3}e^u + c$
$= \tfrac{1}{3}e^{x^3+1} + c$

d Let $u = \sqrt{x}$, $\dfrac{du}{dx} = \dfrac{1}{2\sqrt{x}}$

$\therefore \int \dfrac{e^{\sqrt{x}}}{\sqrt{x}}\,dx = 2\int \dfrac{e^{\sqrt{x}}}{2\sqrt{x}}\,dx$
$= 2\int e^u \dfrac{du}{dx}\,dx$
$= 2\int e^u\,du$
$= 2e^u + c$
$= 2e^{\sqrt{x}} + c$

e Let $u = x - x^2$, $\dfrac{du}{dx} = 1 - 2x$

$\therefore \int (2x - 1)e^{x-x^2}\,dx$
$= -\int (1 - 2x)e^{x-x^2}\,dx$
$= -\int e^u \dfrac{du}{dx}\,dx$
$= -\int e^u\,du$
$= -e^u + c$
$= -e^{x-x^2} + c$

f Let $u = \dfrac{x-1}{x} = 1 - x^{-1}$

$\therefore \dfrac{du}{dx} = 0 - (-1)x^{-2} = \dfrac{1}{x^2}$

$\therefore \int \dfrac{e^{\frac{x-1}{x}}}{x^2}\,dx = \int e^u \dfrac{du}{dx}\,dx$
$= \int e^u\,du$
$= e^u + c$
$= e^{\frac{x-1}{x}} + c$

3 a Let $u = x^2 + 1$, $\dfrac{du}{dx} = 2x$

$\therefore \int \dfrac{2x}{x^2+1}\,dx = \int \dfrac{1}{x^2+1}(2x)\,dx$
$= \int \dfrac{1}{u}\dfrac{du}{dx}\,dx$
$= \int \dfrac{1}{u}\,du$
$= \ln|u| + c$
$= \ln(x^2 + 1) + c$ {as $x^2 + 1 > 0$}

b Let $u = 2 - x^2$, $\dfrac{du}{dx} = -2x$

$\therefore \int \dfrac{x}{2 - x^2}\,dx = -\tfrac{1}{2}\int \dfrac{1}{2-x^2}(-2x)\,dx$
$= -\tfrac{1}{2}\int \dfrac{1}{u}\dfrac{du}{dx}\,dx$
$= -\tfrac{1}{2}\int \dfrac{1}{u}\,du$
$= -\tfrac{1}{2}\ln|u| + c$
$= -\tfrac{1}{2}\ln\left|2 - x^2\right| + c$

c Let $u = x^2 - 3x$, $\dfrac{du}{dx} = 2x - 3$

$\therefore \int \dfrac{2x - 3}{x^2 - 3x}\,dx$
$= \int \dfrac{1}{x^2 - 3x}(2x - 3)\,dx$
$= \int \dfrac{1}{u}\dfrac{du}{dx}\,dx$
$= \int \dfrac{1}{u}\,du$
$= \ln|u| + c$
$= \ln\left|x^2 - 3x\right| + c$

d Let $u = x^3 - x$, $\dfrac{du}{dx} = 3x^2 - 1$

$\therefore \int \dfrac{6x^2 - 2}{x^3 - x}\,dx$
$= 2\int \dfrac{1}{x^3 - 3x}(3x^2 - 1)\,dx$
$= 2\int \dfrac{1}{u}\dfrac{du}{dx}\,dx$
$= 2\int \dfrac{1}{u}\,du$
$= 2\ln|u| + c$
$= 2\ln\left|x^3 - x\right| + c$

e   Let $u = 5x - x^2$, $\dfrac{du}{dx} = 5 - 2x$

$\therefore \displaystyle\int \dfrac{4x - 10}{5x - x^2}\, dx$

$= -2 \displaystyle\int \dfrac{1}{5x - x^2}(5 - 2x)\, dx$

$= -2 \displaystyle\int \dfrac{1}{u}\dfrac{du}{dx}\, dx$

$= -2 \displaystyle\int \dfrac{1}{u}\, du$

$= -2 \ln|u| + c$

$= -2 \ln\left|5x - x^2\right| + c$

f   Let $u = x^3 - 3x$, $\dfrac{du}{dx} = 3x^2 - 3$

$\therefore \displaystyle\int \dfrac{1 - x^2}{x^3 - 3x}\, dx$

$= -\tfrac{1}{3} \displaystyle\int \dfrac{1}{x^3 - 3x}(3x^2 - 3)\, dx$

$= -\tfrac{1}{3} \displaystyle\int \dfrac{1}{u}\dfrac{du}{dx}\, dx$

$= -\tfrac{1}{3} \displaystyle\int \dfrac{1}{u}\, du$

$= -\tfrac{1}{3} \ln|u| + c$

$= -\tfrac{1}{3} \ln\left|x^3 - 3x\right| + c$

4   **a**   Let $u = 3 - x^3$, $\dfrac{du}{dx} = -3x^2$

$\therefore f(x) = \displaystyle\int x^2(3 - x^3)^2\, dx$

$= -\tfrac{1}{3} \displaystyle\int (-3x^2)(3 - x^3)^2\, dx$

$= -\tfrac{1}{3} \displaystyle\int u^2 \dfrac{du}{dx}\, dx$

$= -\tfrac{1}{3} \displaystyle\int u^2\, du$

$= -\tfrac{1}{3} \times \dfrac{u^3}{3} + c$

$= -\tfrac{1}{9}(3 - x^3)^3 + c$

b   Let $u = \ln x$, $\dfrac{du}{dx} = \dfrac{1}{x}$

$\therefore f(x) = \displaystyle\int \dfrac{4}{x \ln x}\, dx$

$= 4 \displaystyle\int \dfrac{1}{\ln x} \times \dfrac{1}{x}\, dx$

$= 4 \displaystyle\int u^{-1} \dfrac{du}{dx}\, dx$

$= 4 \displaystyle\int \dfrac{1}{u}\, du$

$= 4 \ln|u| + c$

$= 4 \ln|\ln x| + c$

c   Let $u = 1 - x^2$, $\dfrac{du}{dx} = -2x$

$\therefore f(x) = \displaystyle\int x\sqrt{1 - x^2}\, dx$

$= -\tfrac{1}{2} \displaystyle\int (-2x)\sqrt{1 - x^2}\, dx$

$= -\tfrac{1}{2} \displaystyle\int \sqrt{u}\, \dfrac{du}{dx}\, dx$

$= -\tfrac{1}{2} \displaystyle\int u^{\frac{1}{2}}\, du$

$= -\tfrac{1}{2}\, \dfrac{u^{\frac{3}{2}}}{\frac{3}{2}} + c = -\tfrac{1}{3} u^{\frac{3}{2}} + c$

$= -\tfrac{1}{3}(1 - x^2)^{\frac{3}{2}} + c$

d   Let $u = 1 - x^2$, $\dfrac{du}{dx} = -2x$

$\therefore f(x) = \displaystyle\int x e^{1 - x^2}\, dx$

$= -\tfrac{1}{2} \displaystyle\int (-2x) e^{1 - x^2}\, dx$

$= -\tfrac{1}{2} \displaystyle\int e^u \dfrac{du}{dx}\, dx$

$= -\tfrac{1}{2} \displaystyle\int e^u\, du$

$= -\tfrac{1}{2} e^u + c$

$= -\tfrac{1}{2} e^{1 - x^2} + c$

e   Let $u = x^3 - x$, $\dfrac{du}{dx} = 3x^2 - 1$

$\therefore f(x) = \displaystyle\int \dfrac{1 - 3x^2}{x^3 - x}\, dx$

$= -\displaystyle\int \dfrac{3x^2 - 1}{x^3 - x}\, dx$

$= -\displaystyle\int \dfrac{1}{u} \dfrac{du}{dx}\, dx$

$= -\displaystyle\int \dfrac{1}{u}\, du = -\ln|u| + c$

$= -\ln\left|x^3 - x\right| + c$

f   Let $u = \ln x$, $\dfrac{du}{dx} = \dfrac{1}{x}$

$\therefore f(x) = \displaystyle\int \dfrac{(\ln x)^3}{x}\, dx$

$= \displaystyle\int u^3 \dfrac{du}{dx}\, dx$

$= \displaystyle\int u^3\, du$

$= \dfrac{u^4}{4} + c$

$= \tfrac{1}{4}(\ln x)^4 + c$

EXERCISE 24F.1

1 **a** $\int (3\sin x - 2)\, dx$
$= -3\cos x - 2x + c$

b $\int (4x - 2\cos x)\, dx$
$= 2x^2 - 2\sin x + c$

c $\int (2\sqrt{x} + 4\sec^2 x)\, dx$
$= \int (2x^{\frac{1}{2}} + 4\sec^2 x)\, dx$
$= \frac{4}{3}x^{\frac{3}{2}} + 4\tan x + c$

d $\int (\sec^2 x + 2\sin x)\, dx$
$= \tan x - 2\cos x + c$

e $\int \left(\frac{x}{2} - \sec^2 x\right) dx$
$= \frac{x^2}{4} - \tan x + c$

f $\int (\sin x - 2\cos x + e^x)\, dx$
$= -\cos x - 2\sin x + e^x + c$

g $\int (x^2 \sqrt{x} - 10\sin x)\, dx$
$= \int (x^{\frac{5}{2}} - 10\sin x)\, dx$
$= \frac{2}{7}x^{\frac{7}{2}} + 10\cos x + c$

h $\int \left(\frac{x(x-1)}{3} + \cos x\right) dx$
$= \int \left(\frac{x^2}{3} - \frac{x}{3} + \cos x\right) dx$
$= \frac{x^3}{9} - \frac{x^2}{6} + \sin x + c$

i $\int (5\sec^2 x - \sin x + 2\sqrt{x})\, dx$
$= \int (5\sec^2 x - \sin x + 2x^{\frac{1}{2}})\, dx$
$= 5\tan x + \cos x + \frac{4}{3}x^{\frac{3}{2}} + c$

2 **a** $\int (\sqrt{x} + \frac{1}{2}\cos x)\, dx$
$= \int (x^{\frac{1}{2}} + \frac{1}{2}\cos x)\, dx$
$= \frac{2}{3}x^{\frac{3}{2}} + \frac{1}{2}\sin x + c$

b $\int (\theta - \sin\theta)\, d\theta$
$= \frac{\theta^2}{2} + \cos\theta + c$

c $\int \left(t\sqrt{t} + 2\sec^2 t\right) dt$
$= \int (t^{\frac{3}{2}} + 2\sec^2 t)\, dt$
$= \frac{2}{5}t^{\frac{5}{2}} + 2\tan t + c$

d $\int (2e^t - 4\sin t)\, dt$
$= 2e^t + 4\cos t + c$

e $\int \left(3\cos t - \frac{1}{t}\right) dt$
$= 3\sin t - \ln|t| + c$

f $\int \left(3 - \frac{2}{\theta} + \sec^2\theta\right) d\theta$
$= 3\theta - 2\ln|\theta| + \tan\theta + c$

3 **a** $\frac{d}{dx}(e^x \sin x) = e^x \sin x + e^x \cos x$
$\therefore \int e^x(\sin x + \cos x)\, dx = \int (e^x \sin x + e^x \cos x)\, dx$
$= e^x \sin x + c$

b $\frac{d}{dx}\left(e^{-x} \sin x\right) = -e^{-x}\sin x + e^{-x}\cos x$
$= \frac{\cos x - \sin x}{e^x}$
$\therefore \int \frac{\cos x - \sin x}{e^x}\, dx = e^{-x}\sin x + c$

c $\frac{d}{dx}(x\cos x) = \cos x + x(-\sin x)$
$= \cos x - x\sin x$
$\therefore \int (\cos x - x\sin x)\, dx = x\cos x + c_1$
$\therefore \int \cos x\, dx - \int x\sin x\, dx = x\cos x + c_1$
$\therefore \sin x - \int x\sin x\, dx = x\cos x + c_1$
$\therefore \int x\sin x\, dx = -x\cos x + \sin x + c$

d $\frac{d}{dx}(\sec x) = \sec x \tan x \quad \therefore \int \tan x \sec x\, dx = \sec x + c$

4 a $f'(x) = x^2 - 4\cos x$

$\therefore\ f(x) = \int (x^2 - 4\cos x)\, dx$

$= \dfrac{x^3}{3} - 4\sin x + c$

But $f(0) = 3$

$\therefore\ 0 - 4\sin(0) + c = 3$

$\therefore\ c = 3$

$\therefore\ f(x) = \dfrac{x^3}{3} - 4\sin x + 3$

b $f'(x) = 2\cos x - 3\sin x$

$\therefore\ f(x) = \int (2\cos x - 3\sin x)\, dx$

$= 2\sin x + 3\cos x + c$

But $f(\tfrac{\pi}{4}) = \tfrac{1}{\sqrt{2}}$

$\therefore\ 2\sin\tfrac{\pi}{4} + 3\cos\tfrac{\pi}{4} + c = \tfrac{1}{\sqrt{2}}$

$\therefore\ 2(\tfrac{1}{\sqrt{2}}) + 3(\tfrac{1}{\sqrt{2}}) + c = \tfrac{1}{\sqrt{2}}$

$\therefore\ c = -\tfrac{4}{\sqrt{2}}$

$\therefore\ c = -2\sqrt{2}$

$\therefore\ f(x) = 2\sin x + 3\cos x - 2\sqrt{2}$

c $f'(x) = \sqrt{x} - 2\sec^2 x$

$\therefore\ f(x) = \int (x^{\frac{1}{2}} - 2\sec^2 x)\, dx$

$= \tfrac{2}{3}x^{\frac{3}{2}} - 2\tan x + c$

But $f(\pi) = 0$

$\therefore\ \tfrac{2}{3}\pi^{\frac{3}{2}} - 2\tan\pi + c = 0$

$\therefore\ c = -\tfrac{2}{3}\pi^{\frac{3}{2}}$

$\therefore\ f(x) = \tfrac{2}{3}x^{\frac{3}{2}} - 2\tan x - \tfrac{2}{3}\pi^{\frac{3}{2}}$

EXERCISE 24F.2

1 a $\int \sin(3x)\, dx$

$= -\tfrac{1}{3}\cos(3x) + c$

b $\int 2\cos(4x)\, dx$

$= 2 \times \tfrac{1}{4}\sin(4x) + c$

$= \tfrac{1}{2}\sin(4x) + c$

c $\int \sec^2(2x)\, dx$

$= \tfrac{1}{2}\tan(2x) + c$

d $\int 3\cos\left(\tfrac{x}{2}\right) dx$

$= 6\sin\left(\tfrac{x}{2}\right) + c$

e $\int (3\sin(2x) - e^{-x})\, dx$

$= -\tfrac{3}{2}\cos(2x) + e^{-x} + c$

f $\int \left[e^{2x} - 2\sec^2\left(\tfrac{x}{2}\right)\right] dx$

$= \tfrac{1}{2}e^{2x} - 2 \times 2\tan\left(\tfrac{x}{2}\right) + c$

$= \tfrac{1}{2}e^{2x} - 4\tan\left(\tfrac{x}{2}\right) + c$

g $\int 2\sin\left(2x + \tfrac{\pi}{6}\right) dx$

$= -\tfrac{2}{2}\cos\left(2x + \tfrac{\pi}{6}\right) + c$

$= -\cos\left(2x + \tfrac{\pi}{6}\right) + c$

h $\int -3\cos\left(\tfrac{\pi}{4} - x\right) dx$

$= -3 \times (-1)\sin\left(\tfrac{\pi}{4} - x\right) + c$

$= 3\sin\left(\tfrac{\pi}{4} - x\right) + c$

i $\int 4\sec^2\left(\tfrac{\pi}{3} - 2x\right) dx$

$= 4 \times (-\tfrac{1}{2})\tan\left(\tfrac{\pi}{3} - 2x\right) + c$

$= -2\tan\left(\tfrac{\pi}{3} - 2x\right) + c$

j $\int \cos(2x) + \sin(2x)\, dx$

$= \tfrac{1}{2}\sin(2x) - \tfrac{1}{2}\cos(2x) + c$

k $\int 2\sin(3x) + 5\cos(4x)\, dx$

$= -\tfrac{2}{3}\cos(3x) + \tfrac{5}{4}\sin(4x) + c$

l $\int \tfrac{1}{2}\cos(8x) - 3\sin x\, dx$

$= \tfrac{1}{2}(\tfrac{1}{8})\sin(8x) + 3\cos x + c$

$= \tfrac{1}{16}\sin(8x) + 3\cos x + c$

2 a $\int \cos^2 x\, dx$

$= \int (\tfrac{1}{2} + \tfrac{1}{2}\cos(2x))\, dx$

$= \tfrac{1}{2}x + \tfrac{1}{4}\sin(2x) + c$

b $\int \sin^2 x\, dx$

$= \int (\tfrac{1}{2} - \tfrac{1}{2}\cos(2x))\, dx$

$= \tfrac{1}{2}x - \tfrac{1}{4}\sin(2x) + c$

c $\int (1 + \cos^2(2x))\, dx$

$= \int (1 + \tfrac{1}{2} + \tfrac{1}{2}\cos(4x))\, dx$

$= \int (\tfrac{3}{2} + \tfrac{1}{2}\cos(4x))\, dx$

$= \tfrac{3}{2}x + \tfrac{1}{8}\sin(4x) + c$

d $\int (3 - \sin^2(3x))\, dx$

$= \int (3 - (\tfrac{1}{2} - \tfrac{1}{2}\cos(6x)))\, dx$

$= \int (\tfrac{5}{2} + \tfrac{1}{2}\cos(6x))\, dx$

$= \tfrac{5}{2}x + \tfrac{1}{12}\sin(6x) + c$

e $\quad \int \frac{1}{2}\cos^2(4x)\,dx$
$= \int \frac{1}{2}(\frac{1}{2} + \frac{1}{2}\cos(8x))\,dx$
$= \int (\frac{1}{4} + \frac{1}{4}\cos(8x))\,dx$
$= \frac{1}{4}x + \frac{1}{32}\sin(8x) + c$

f $\quad \int (1+\cos x)^2\,dx$
$= \int (1 + 2\cos x + \cos^2 x)\,dx$
$= \int (1 + 2\cos x + \frac{1}{2} + \frac{1}{2}\cos(2x))\,dx$
$= \int \left(\frac{3}{2} + 2\cos x + \frac{1}{2}\cos(2x)\right)\,dx$
$= \frac{3}{2}x + 2\sin x + \frac{1}{4}\sin(2x) + c$

3 $\quad \cos^2\theta = \frac{1}{2} + \frac{1}{2}\cos(2\theta) \quad \therefore \quad \cos^4 x = (\frac{1}{2} + \frac{1}{2}\cos(2x))^2$
$= \frac{1}{4} + \frac{1}{2}\cos(2x) + \frac{1}{4}\cos^2(2x)$
$= \frac{1}{4} + \frac{1}{2}\cos(2x) + \frac{1}{4}(\frac{1}{2} + \frac{1}{2}\cos(4x))$
$= \frac{1}{4} + \frac{1}{2}\cos(2x) + \frac{1}{8} + \frac{1}{8}\cos(4x)$
$= \frac{1}{8}\cos(4x) + \frac{1}{2}\cos(2x) + \frac{3}{8}$ as required

$\therefore \int \cos^4 x\,dx = \int (\frac{1}{8}\cos(4x) + \frac{1}{2}\cos(2x) + \frac{3}{8})\,dx$
$= \frac{1}{32}\sin(4x) + \frac{1}{4}\sin(2x) + \frac{3}{8}x + c$

4 a Let $u = \sin x$, $\dfrac{du}{dx} = \cos x$

$\therefore \int \sin^4 x \cos x\,dx = \int u^4 \dfrac{du}{dx}\,dx$
$= \int u^4\,du$
$= \dfrac{u^5}{5} + c$
$= \frac{1}{5}\sin^5 x + c$

b Let $u = \cos x$, $\dfrac{du}{dx} = -\sin x$

$\therefore \int \dfrac{\sin x}{\sqrt{\cos x}}\,dx = -\int \dfrac{-\sin x}{\sqrt{\cos x}}\,dx$
$= -\int u^{-\frac{1}{2}} \dfrac{du}{dx}\,dx$
$= -\int u^{-\frac{1}{2}}\,du$
$= -\dfrac{u^{\frac{1}{2}}}{\frac{1}{2}} + c$
$= -2\sqrt{\cos x} + c$

c Let $u = \cos x$, $\dfrac{du}{dx} = -\sin x$

$\therefore \int \dfrac{\sin x}{\cos x}\,dx = -\int \dfrac{-\sin x}{\cos x}\,dx$
$= -\int \dfrac{1}{u}\dfrac{du}{dx}\,dx$
$= -\int \dfrac{1}{u}\,du = -\ln|u| + c$
$= -\ln|\cos x| + c$

d Let $u = \sin x$, $\dfrac{du}{dx} = \cos x$

$\therefore \int \sqrt{\sin x}\cos x\,dx = \int u^{\frac{1}{2}}\dfrac{du}{dx}\,dx$
$= \int u^{\frac{1}{2}}\,du$
$= \frac{2}{3}u^{\frac{3}{2}} + c$
$= \frac{2}{3}(\sin x)^{\frac{3}{2}} + c$

e Let $u = 2 + \sin x$, $\dfrac{du}{dx} = \cos x$

$\therefore \int \dfrac{\cos x}{(2+\sin x)^2}\,dx = \int u^{-2}\dfrac{du}{dx}\,dx$
$= \int u^{-2}\,du$
$= -u^{-1} + c$
$= \dfrac{-1}{2+\sin x} + c$

f Let $u = \cos x$, $\dfrac{du}{dx} = -\sin x$

$\therefore \int \dfrac{\sin x}{\cos^3 x}\,dx = -\int \dfrac{-\sin x}{\cos^3 x}\,dx$
$= -\int u^{-3}\dfrac{du}{dx}\,dx$
$= -\int u^{-3}\,du$
$= \dfrac{-u^{-2}}{-2} + c$
$= \frac{1}{2}u^{-2} + c$
$= \dfrac{1}{2\cos^2 x} + c$

g Let $u = 1 - \cos x$, $\dfrac{du}{dx} = \sin x$

$\therefore \displaystyle\int \dfrac{\sin x}{1 - \cos x}\, dx = \int \dfrac{1}{u} \dfrac{du}{dx}\, dx$

$\phantom{\therefore \int \dfrac{\sin x}{1-\cos x}dx} = \displaystyle\int \dfrac{1}{u}\, du$

$\phantom{\therefore \int \dfrac{\sin x}{1-\cos x}dx} = \ln|u| + c$

$\phantom{\therefore \int \dfrac{\sin x}{1-\cos x}dx} = \ln|1 - \cos x| + c$

h Let $u = \sin(2x) - 3$, $\dfrac{du}{dx} = 2\cos(2x)$

$\therefore \displaystyle\int \dfrac{\cos(2x)}{\sin(2x) - 3}\, dx = \tfrac{1}{2}\int \dfrac{2\cos(2x)}{\sin(2x) - 3}\, dx$

$\phantom{\therefore \int \dfrac{\cos(2x)}{\sin(2x)-3}dx} = \tfrac{1}{2}\displaystyle\int \dfrac{1}{u}\dfrac{du}{dx}\, dx$

$\phantom{\therefore \int \dfrac{\cos(2x)}{\sin(2x)-3}dx} = \tfrac{1}{2}\displaystyle\int \dfrac{1}{u}\, du$

$\phantom{\therefore \int \dfrac{\cos(2x)}{\sin(2x)-3}dx} = \tfrac{1}{2}\ln|u| + c$

$\phantom{\therefore \int \dfrac{\cos(2x)}{\sin(2x)-3}dx} = \tfrac{1}{2}\ln|\sin(2x) - 3| + c$

i Let $u = x^2$, $\dfrac{du}{dx} = 2x$

$\therefore \displaystyle\int x \sin(x^2)\, dx = \tfrac{1}{2}\int (2x)\sin(x^2)\, dx$

$ = \tfrac{1}{2}\displaystyle\int \sin u \dfrac{du}{dx}\, dx$

$ = \tfrac{1}{2}\displaystyle\int \sin u\, du$

$ = \tfrac{1}{2}(-\cos u) + c$

$ = -\tfrac{1}{2}\cos(x^2) + c$

j Now $\displaystyle\int \dfrac{\sin^3 x}{\cos^5 x}\, dx = \int \tan^3 x \sec^2 x\, dx$

Let $u = \tan x$, $\dfrac{du}{dx} = \sec^2 x$

$\therefore \displaystyle\int \dfrac{\sin^3 x}{\cos^5 x}\, dx = \int u^3 \dfrac{du}{dx}\, dx$

$\phantom{\therefore \int \dfrac{\sin^3 x}{\cos^5 x}dx} = \displaystyle\int u^3\, du$

$\phantom{\therefore \int \dfrac{\sin^3 x}{\cos^5 x}dx} = \dfrac{u^4}{4} + c$

$\phantom{\therefore \int \dfrac{\sin^3 x}{\cos^5 x}dx} = \dfrac{\tan^4 x}{4} + c$

k Let $u = \csc(2x)$,

$\dfrac{du}{dx} = -\csc(2x)\cot(2x) \times 2$

Now $\displaystyle\int \csc^3(2x)\cot(2x)\, dx$

$= \displaystyle\int \csc^2(2x)\csc(2x)\cot(2x)\, dx$

$= \displaystyle\int u^2 \left(-\tfrac{1}{2}\dfrac{du}{dx}\right) dx$

$= -\tfrac{1}{2}\displaystyle\int u^2 \dfrac{du}{dx}\, dx$

$= -\tfrac{1}{2}\displaystyle\int u^2\, du$

$= -\tfrac{1}{2}\left(\dfrac{u^3}{3}\right) + c$

$= -\tfrac{1}{6}\csc^3(2x) + c$

l $\displaystyle\int \cos^3 x\, dx = \int \cos^2 x \cos x\, dx$

$ = \displaystyle\int (1 - \sin^2 x)\cos x\, dx$

Let $u = \sin x$, $\dfrac{du}{dx} = \cos x$

$\therefore \displaystyle\int \cos^3 x\, dx = \int (1 - u^2)\dfrac{du}{dx}\, dx$

$ = \displaystyle\int (1 - u^2)\, du$

$ = u - \dfrac{u^3}{3} + c$

$ = \sin x - \dfrac{\sin^3 x}{3} + c$

$ = \sin x - \tfrac{1}{3}\sin^3 x + c$

5 a $\displaystyle\int \sin^5 x\, dx = \int \sin^4 x \sin x\, dx$

$ = \displaystyle\int (1 - \cos^2 x)^2 \sin x\, dx$

$ = \displaystyle\int (1 - 2\cos^2 x + \cos^4 x)\sin x\, dx$

Let $u = \cos x$, $\dfrac{du}{dx} = -\sin x$

$\therefore \displaystyle\int \sin^5 x\, dx = -\int (1 - 2u^2 + u^4)\dfrac{du}{dx}\, dx$

$ = -\displaystyle\int (1 - 2u^2 + u^4)\, du$

$ = -u + \tfrac{2}{3}u^3 - \tfrac{1}{5}u^5 + c$

$ = -\cos x + \tfrac{2}{3}\cos^3 x - \tfrac{1}{5}\cos^5 x + c$

b $\displaystyle\int \sin^4 x \cos^3 x \, dx = \int \sin^4 x \cos^2 x \cos x \, dx$
$= \int \sin^4 x (1 - \sin^2 x) \cos x \, dx$
$= \int (\sin^4 x - \sin^6 x) \cos x \, dx$

Let $u = \sin x$, $\dfrac{du}{dx} = \cos x$

$\therefore \displaystyle\int \sin^4 x \cos^3 x \, dx = \int (u^4 - u^6) \dfrac{du}{dx} dx$
$= \int (u^4 - u^6) \, du$
$= \tfrac{1}{5} u^5 - \tfrac{1}{7} u^7 + c$
$= \tfrac{1}{5} \sin^5 x - \tfrac{1}{7} \sin^7 x + c$

6 a Let $u = \cos x$, $\dfrac{du}{dx} = -\sin x$

$\therefore f(x) = \displaystyle\int \sin x \, e^{\cos x} \, dx$
$= -\displaystyle\int e^{\cos x} (-\sin x) \, dx$
$= -\displaystyle\int e^u \dfrac{du}{dx} dx$
$= -\displaystyle\int e^u \, du$
$= -e^u + c$
$= -e^{\cos x} + c$

b Let $u = \sin(2x)$, $\dfrac{du}{dx} = 2\cos(2x)$

$\therefore f(x) = \displaystyle\int \sin^3(2x) \cos(2x) \, dx$
$= \tfrac{1}{2} \displaystyle\int \sin^3(2x) (2\cos(2x)) \, dx$
$= \tfrac{1}{2} \displaystyle\int u^3 \dfrac{du}{dx} dx$
$= \tfrac{1}{2} \displaystyle\int u^3 \, du$
$= \tfrac{1}{2} \times \dfrac{u^4}{4} + c$
$= \tfrac{1}{8} \sin^4(2x) + c$

c Let $u = \sin x - \cos x$,
$\dfrac{du}{dx} = \cos x + \sin x$

$\therefore f(x) = \displaystyle\int \dfrac{\sin x + \cos x}{\sin x - \cos x} \, dx$
$= \displaystyle\int \dfrac{1}{u} \dfrac{du}{dx} \, dx$
$= \displaystyle\int \dfrac{1}{u} \, du$
$= \ln|u| + c$
$= \ln|\sin x - \cos x| + c$

d Let $u = \tan x$,
$\therefore \dfrac{du}{dx} = \sec^2 x = \dfrac{1}{\cos^2 x}$

$\therefore \displaystyle\int \dfrac{e^{\tan x}}{\cos^2 x} \, dx = \int e^u \left(\dfrac{du}{dx}\right) dx$
$= \displaystyle\int e^u \, du$
$= e^u + c$
$= e^{\tan x} + c$

7 a $\displaystyle\int \cot x \, dx = \int \dfrac{\cos x}{\sin x} \, dx$

Let $u = \sin x$, $\dfrac{du}{dx} = \cos x$

$\therefore \displaystyle\int \cot x \, dx = \int \dfrac{1}{u} \dfrac{du}{dx} \, dx$
$= \displaystyle\int \dfrac{1}{u} \, du$
$= \ln|u| + c$
$= \ln|\sin x| + c$

b $\displaystyle\int \cot(3x) \, dx = \int \dfrac{\cos(3x)}{\sin(3x)} \, dx$

Let $u = \sin(3x)$, $\dfrac{du}{dx} = 3\cos(3x)$

$\therefore \displaystyle\int \cot(3x) \, dx = \tfrac{1}{3} \int \dfrac{3\cos(3x)}{\sin(3x)} \, dx$
$= \tfrac{1}{3} \displaystyle\int \dfrac{1}{u} \dfrac{du}{dx} \, dx$
$= \tfrac{1}{3} \displaystyle\int \dfrac{1}{u} \, du$
$= \tfrac{1}{3} \ln|u| + c$
$= \tfrac{1}{3} \ln|\sin(3x)| + c$

c Let $u = \cot x = \dfrac{\cos x}{\sin x}$,

$\dfrac{du}{dx} = \dfrac{-\sin^2 x - \cos^2 x}{\sin^2 x} = -\dfrac{1}{\sin^2 x}$

$= -\csc^2 x$

$\therefore \int \csc^2 x \, dx = -\int -\csc^2 x \, dx$

$= -\int 1 \dfrac{du}{dx} dx$

$= -\int 1 \, du$

$= -u + c$

$= -\cot x + c$

e $\int \csc x \cot x \, dx = \int \dfrac{1}{\sin x} \dfrac{\cos x}{\sin x} dx$

Let $u = \sin x$, $\dfrac{du}{dx} = \cos x$

$\therefore \int \csc x \cot x \, dx = \int \dfrac{1}{u^2} \dfrac{du}{dx} dx$

$= \int u^{-2} \, du$

$= \dfrac{u^{-1}}{-1} + c$

$= -\dfrac{1}{\sin x} + c = -\csc x + c$

g $\int \csc\left(\tfrac{x}{2}\right) \cot\left(\tfrac{x}{2}\right) dx = \int \dfrac{1}{\sin\left(\tfrac{x}{2}\right)} \dfrac{\cos\left(\tfrac{x}{2}\right)}{\sin\left(\tfrac{x}{2}\right)} dx$

Let $u = \sin\left(\tfrac{x}{2}\right)$, $\dfrac{du}{dx} = \tfrac{1}{2} \cos\left(\tfrac{x}{2}\right)$

$\therefore \int \csc\left(\tfrac{x}{2}\right) \cot\left(\tfrac{x}{2}\right) dx = 2 \int \dfrac{1}{u^2} \dfrac{du}{dx} dx$

$= 2 \int u^{-2} \, du$

$= 2 \dfrac{u^{-1}}{-1} + c$

$= \dfrac{-2}{\sin\left(\tfrac{x}{2}\right)} + c$

$= -2 \csc\left(\tfrac{x}{2}\right) + c$

d $\int \sec x \tan x \, dx = \int \dfrac{1}{\cos x} \dfrac{\sin x}{\cos x} dx$

Let $u = \cos x$, $\dfrac{du}{dx} = -\sin x$

$\therefore \int \sec x \tan x \, dx = -\int \dfrac{1}{u^2} \dfrac{du}{dx} dx$

$= -\int u^{-2} \, du$

$= -\dfrac{u^{-1}}{(-1)} + c$

$= \dfrac{1}{\cos x} + c = \sec x + c$

f $\int \tan(3x) \sec(3x) \, dx = \int \dfrac{\sin(3x)}{\cos(3x)} \dfrac{1}{\cos(3x)} dx$

Let $u = \cos(3x)$, $\dfrac{du}{dx} = -3\sin(3x)$

$\therefore \int \tan(3x) \sec(3x) \, dx = -\tfrac{1}{3} \int \dfrac{1}{u^2} \dfrac{du}{dx} dx$

$= -\tfrac{1}{3} \int u^{-2} \, du$

$= -\tfrac{1}{3} \times \dfrac{u^{-1}}{-1} + c$

$= \tfrac{1}{3} \dfrac{1}{\cos(3x)} + c$

$= \tfrac{1}{3} \sec(3x) + c$

h $\int \sec^3 x \sin x \, dx = \int (\cos x)^{-3} \sin x \, dx$

Let $u = \cos x$, $\dfrac{du}{dx} = -\sin x$

$\therefore \int \sec^3 x \sin x \, dx = -\int \sec^3 x (-\sin x) \, dx$

$= -\int u^{-3} \dfrac{du}{dx} dx$

$= -\int u^{-3} \, du$

$= \tfrac{1}{2} u^{-2} + c = \dfrac{1}{2\cos^2 x} + c$

i Let $u = \cot x$, $\dfrac{du}{dx} = -\csc^2 x$ {see **c**}

$\therefore \int \dfrac{\csc^2 x}{\sqrt{\cot x}} dx = -\int \dfrac{-\csc^2 x}{\sqrt{\cot x}} dx$

$= -\int \dfrac{1}{\sqrt{u}} \dfrac{du}{dx} dx$

$= -\int u^{-\tfrac{1}{2}} \, du$

$= -2u^{\tfrac{1}{2}} + c$

$= -2\sqrt{\cot x} + c$

EXERCISE 24G.1

1 a $\int_0^1 x^3 \, dx = \left[\dfrac{x^4}{4}\right]_0^1$

$= \tfrac{1}{4} - 0$

$= \tfrac{1}{4}$

b $\int_0^2 (x^2 - x) \, dx = \left[\dfrac{x^3}{3} - \dfrac{x^2}{2}\right]_0^2$

$= \left(\tfrac{8}{3} - 2\right) - (0 - 0)$

$= \tfrac{2}{3}$

c $\int_0^1 e^x \, dx = [e^x]_0^1$

$= e^1 - e^0$

$= e - 1$

≈ 1.72

d $\int_1^4 \left(x - \dfrac{3}{\sqrt{x}}\right) dx$

$= \int_1^4 (x - 3x^{-\frac{1}{2}}) dx$

$= \left[\dfrac{x^2}{2} - \dfrac{3x^{\frac{1}{2}}}{\frac{1}{2}}\right]_1^4$

$= \left[\dfrac{x^2}{2} - 6\sqrt{x}\right]_1^4$

$= \left[\dfrac{16}{2} - 12\right] - \left(\dfrac{1}{2} - 6\right)$

$= 1\dfrac{1}{2}$

e $\int_4^9 \dfrac{x-3}{\sqrt{x}} dx$

$= \int_4^9 (x^{\frac{1}{2}} - 3x^{-\frac{1}{2}}) dx$

$= \left[\dfrac{x^{\frac{3}{2}}}{\frac{3}{2}} - \dfrac{3x^{\frac{1}{2}}}{\frac{1}{2}}\right]_4^9$

$= \left[\dfrac{2}{3}x^{\frac{3}{2}} - 6x^{\frac{1}{2}}\right]_4^9$

$= \left[\dfrac{2}{3}(27) - 6(3)\right] - \left[\dfrac{2}{3}(8) - 6(2)\right]$

$= (18 - 18) - \left(\dfrac{16}{3} - 12\right)$

$= 6\dfrac{2}{3}$

f $\int_1^3 \dfrac{1}{x} dx = [\ln |x|]_1^3$

$= \ln 3 - \ln 1$
$= \ln 3 - 0$
$= \ln 3$
≈ 1.10

g $\int_1^2 (e^{-x} + 1)^2 dx$

$= \int_1^2 (e^{-2x} + 2e^{-x} + 1) dx$

$= \left[\left(\dfrac{1}{-2}\right)e^{-2x} + 2\left(\dfrac{1}{-1}\right)e^{-x} + x\right]_1^2$

$= \left[-\dfrac{e^{-2x}}{2} - 2e^{-x} + x\right]_1^2$

$= \left(-\dfrac{e^{-4}}{2} - 2e^{-2} + 2\right)$
$ - \left(-\dfrac{e^{-2}}{2} - 2e^{-1} + 1\right)$

≈ 1.52

h $\int_2^6 \dfrac{1}{\sqrt{2x-3}} dx = \int_2^6 (2x-3)^{-\frac{1}{2}} dx$

$= \left[\dfrac{1}{2} \dfrac{(2x-3)^{\frac{1}{2}}}{\frac{1}{2}}\right]_2^6$

$= \left[\sqrt{2x-3}\right]_2^6$

$= \sqrt{9} - \sqrt{1}$

$= 2$

i $\int_0^1 e^{1-x} dx = \left[\left(\dfrac{1}{-1}\right)e^{1-x}\right]_0^1$

$= \left(\dfrac{e^0}{-1}\right) - \left(\dfrac{e^1}{-1}\right)$

$= -1 + e$

≈ 1.72

2 a $\int_0^{\frac{\pi}{6}} \cos x \, dx$

$= [\sin x]_0^{\frac{\pi}{6}}$

$= \sin \dfrac{\pi}{6} - \sin 0$

$= \dfrac{1}{2}$

b $\int_{\frac{\pi}{3}}^{\frac{\pi}{2}} \sin x \, dx$

$= [-\cos x]_{\frac{\pi}{3}}^{\frac{\pi}{2}}$

$= -\cos \dfrac{\pi}{2} + \cos \dfrac{\pi}{3}$

$= \dfrac{1}{2}$

c $\int_{\frac{\pi}{4}}^{\frac{\pi}{3}} \sec^2 x \, dx$

$= [\tan x]_{\frac{\pi}{4}}^{\frac{\pi}{3}}$

$= \tan \dfrac{\pi}{3} - \tan \dfrac{\pi}{4}$

$= \sqrt{3} - 1$

d $\int_0^{\frac{\pi}{6}} \sin(3x) \, dx$

$= \left[-\dfrac{1}{3}\cos(3x)\right]_0^{\frac{\pi}{6}}$

$= -\dfrac{1}{3}[\cos \dfrac{\pi}{2} - \cos 0]$

$= -\dfrac{1}{3}[0 - 1]$

$= \dfrac{1}{3}$

e $\int_0^{\frac{\pi}{4}} \cos^2 x \, dx$

$= \int_0^{\frac{\pi}{4}} \left(\dfrac{1}{2} + \dfrac{1}{2}\cos(2x)\right) dx$

$= \left[\dfrac{x}{2} + \dfrac{1}{4}\sin(2x)\right]_0^{\frac{\pi}{4}}$

$= \left[\dfrac{\pi}{8} + \dfrac{1}{4}\sin \dfrac{\pi}{2}\right] - 0$

$= \dfrac{\pi}{8} + \dfrac{1}{4}$

f $\int_0^{\frac{\pi}{2}} \sin^2 x \, dx$

$= \int_0^{\frac{\pi}{2}} \left(\dfrac{1}{2} - \dfrac{1}{2}\cos(2x)\right) dx$

$= \left[\dfrac{x}{2} - \dfrac{1}{4}\sin(2x)\right]_0^{\frac{\pi}{2}}$

$= \left[\dfrac{\pi}{4} - \dfrac{1}{4}\sin \pi\right] - 0$

$= \dfrac{\pi}{4}$

3 a In $\int_1^2 \dfrac{x}{(x^2+2)^2} dx$

we let $u = x^2 + 2$, $\dfrac{du}{dx} = 2x$

when $x = 1$, $u = 3$
when $x = 2$, $u = 6$

$\therefore \int_1^2 \dfrac{x}{(x^2+2)^2} dx = \int_1^2 u^{-2} \left(\dfrac{1}{2}\dfrac{du}{dx}\right) dx$

$= \dfrac{1}{2}\int_3^6 u^{-2} du$

$= \dfrac{1}{2}\left[\dfrac{u^{-1}}{-1}\right]_3^6 = \dfrac{1}{2}\left[-\dfrac{1}{6} - \left(-\dfrac{1}{3}\right)\right]$

$= \dfrac{1}{12}$

b In $\int_0^1 x^2 e^{x^3+1}\, dx$

we let $u = x^3 + 1$, $\dfrac{du}{dx} = 3x^2$

when $x = 0$, $u = 1$
when $x = 1$, $u = 2$

$\therefore \int_0^1 x^2 e^{x^3+1}\, dx = \int_0^1 e^u \left(\dfrac{1}{3}\dfrac{du}{dx}\right) dx$

$= \dfrac{1}{3}\int_1^2 e^u\, du$

$= \dfrac{1}{3}[e^u]_1^2$

$= \dfrac{1}{3}(e^2 - e)$

≈ 1.56

c In $\int_0^3 x\sqrt{x^2 + 16}\, dx$

we let $u = x^2 + 16$, $\dfrac{du}{dx} = 2x$

when $x = 0$, $u = 16$
when $x = 3$, $u = 25$

$\therefore \int_0^3 x\sqrt{x^2 + 16}\, dx$

$= \dfrac{1}{2}\int_0^3 2x\sqrt{x^2 + 16}\, dx$

$= \dfrac{1}{2}\int_0^3 u^{\frac{1}{2}}\dfrac{du}{dx}\, dx$

$= \dfrac{1}{2}\int_{16}^{25} u^{\frac{1}{2}}\, du$

$= \dfrac{1}{2}\left[\dfrac{u^{\frac{3}{2}}}{\frac{3}{2}}\right]_{16}^{25}$

$= \dfrac{1}{2}\times\dfrac{2}{3}\left[u^{\frac{3}{2}}\right]_{16}^{25}$

$= \dfrac{1}{3}(125 - 64) = 20\dfrac{1}{3}$

d In $\int_1^2 x e^{-2x^2}\, dx$

we let $u = -2x^2$, $\dfrac{du}{dx} = -4x$

when $x = 1$, $u = -2$
when $x = 2$, $u = -8$

$\therefore \int_1^2 x e^{-2x^2}\, dx$

$= -\dfrac{1}{4}\int_1^2 -4x e^{-2x^2}\, dx$

$= -\dfrac{1}{4}\int_1^2 e^u \dfrac{du}{dx}\, dx$

$= -\dfrac{1}{4}\int_{-2}^{-8} e^u\, du$

$= -\dfrac{1}{4}[e^u]_{-2}^{-8}$

$= -\dfrac{1}{4}(e^{-8} - e^{-2})$

≈ 0.0337

e In $\int_2^3 \dfrac{x}{2 - x^2}\, dx$

we let $u = 2 - x^2$, $\dfrac{du}{dx} = -2x$

when $x = 2$, $u = -2$
when $x = 3$, $u = -7$

$\therefore \int_2^3 \dfrac{x}{2 - x^2}\, dx = -\dfrac{1}{2}\int_2^3 \dfrac{1}{u}\dfrac{du}{dx}\, dx$

$= -\dfrac{1}{2}\int_{-2}^{-7}\dfrac{1}{u}\, du$

$= -\dfrac{1}{2}[\ln|u|]_{-2}^{-7}$

$= -\dfrac{1}{2}(\ln 7 - \ln 2)$

$= -\dfrac{1}{2}\ln\left(\dfrac{7}{2}\right)$

≈ -0.626

f In $\int_1^2 \dfrac{\ln x}{x}\, dx$

we let $u = \ln x$, $\dfrac{du}{dx} = \dfrac{1}{x}$

when $x = 1$, $u = 0$
when $x = 2$, $u = \ln 2$

$\therefore \int_1^2 \dfrac{\ln x}{x}\, dx = \int_1^2 u\dfrac{du}{dx}\, dx$

$= \int_0^{\ln 2} u\, du$

$= \left[\dfrac{u^2}{2}\right]_0^{\ln 2}$

$= \dfrac{(\ln 2)^2}{2} - 0$

≈ 0.240

g In $\int_0^1 \dfrac{1 - 3x^2}{1 - x^3 + x}\, dx$

we let $u = 1 - x^3 + x$,

$\dfrac{du}{dx} = -3x^2 + 1$

when $x = 0$, $u = 1$
when $x = 1$, $u = 1$

$\therefore \int_0^1 \dfrac{1 - 3x^2}{1 - x^3 + x}\, dx = \int_0^1 \dfrac{1}{u}\dfrac{du}{dx}\, dx$

$= \int_1^1 \dfrac{1}{u}\, du$

$= 0$

h In $\int_2^4 \dfrac{6x^2 - 4x + 4}{x^3 - x^2 + 2x} dx$

we let $u = x^3 - x^2 + 2x$,

$\dfrac{du}{dx} = 3x^2 - 2x + 2$

when $x = 2, \ u = 8$

when $x = 4, \ u = 56$

$\therefore \int_2^4 \dfrac{6x^2 - 4x + 4}{x^3 - x^2 + 2x} dx$

$= 2 \int_2^4 \dfrac{3x^2 - 2x + 2}{x^3 - x^2 + 2x} dx$

$= 2 \int_2^4 \dfrac{1}{u} \dfrac{du}{dx} dx$

$= 2 \int_8^{56} \dfrac{1}{u} du$

$= 2 [\ln |u|]_8^{56}$

$= 2(\ln 56 - \ln 8)$

$= 2 \ln 7 \approx 3.89$

i In $\int_0^1 (x^2 + 2x)^n (x+1) dx$

we let $u = x^2 + 2x$, $\dfrac{du}{dx} = 2x + 2$

when $x = 0, \ u = 0$

when $x = 1, \ u = 3$

$\therefore \int_0^1 (x^2 + 2x)^n (x+1) dx$

$= \tfrac{1}{2} \int_0^1 (x^2 + 2x)^n (2x + 2) dx$

$= \tfrac{1}{2} \int_0^1 u^n \dfrac{du}{dx} dx$

$= \tfrac{1}{2} \int_0^3 u^n du$

If $n \neq -1$,

the integral $= \tfrac{1}{2} \left[\dfrac{u^{n+1}}{n+1} \right]_0^3 = \tfrac{1}{2} \left(\dfrac{3^{n+1}}{n+1} \right)$

If $n = -1$,

the integral $= \tfrac{1}{2} \int_0^3 \dfrac{1}{u} du = \tfrac{1}{2} [\ln |u|]_0^3$

which is undefined as $\ln 0$ is not defined

4 a Let $u = \cos x$, $\dfrac{du}{dx} = -\sin x$

when $x = 0, \ u = \cos 0 = 1$

when $x = \tfrac{\pi}{3}, \ u = \cos \tfrac{\pi}{3} = \tfrac{1}{2}$

$\therefore \int_0^{\frac{\pi}{3}} \dfrac{\sin x}{\sqrt{\cos x}} dx = -\int_0^{\frac{\pi}{3}} \dfrac{-\sin x}{\sqrt{\cos x}} dx$

$= -\int_0^{\frac{\pi}{3}} u^{-\frac{1}{2}} \dfrac{du}{dx} dx$

$= \int_{\frac{1}{2}}^1 u^{-\frac{1}{2}} du = \left[2u^{\frac{1}{2}} \right]_{\frac{1}{2}}^1$

$= 2\sqrt{1} - 2\sqrt{\tfrac{1}{2}}$

$= 2 - \sqrt{2}$

b Let $u = \sin x$, $\dfrac{du}{dx} = \cos x$

when $x = 0, \ u = \sin 0 = 0$

when $x = \tfrac{\pi}{6}, \ u = \sin \tfrac{\pi}{6} = \tfrac{1}{2}$

$\therefore \int_0^{\frac{\pi}{6}} \sin^2 x \cos x \, dx = \int_0^{\frac{\pi}{6}} u^2 \dfrac{du}{dx} dx$

$= \int_0^{\frac{1}{2}} u^2 du$

$= \left[\dfrac{u^3}{3} \right]_0^{\frac{1}{2}}$

$= \tfrac{1}{3} (\tfrac{1}{2})^3$

$= \tfrac{1}{24}$

c Let $u = \cos x$, $\dfrac{du}{dx} = -\sin x$

when $x = 0, \ u = \cos 0 = 1$ and when $x = \tfrac{\pi}{4}, \ u = \cos \tfrac{\pi}{4} = \tfrac{1}{\sqrt{2}}$

$\therefore \int_0^{\frac{\pi}{4}} \tan x \, dx = \int_0^{\frac{\pi}{4}} \dfrac{\sin x}{\cos x} dx$

$= -\int_0^{\frac{\pi}{4}} \dfrac{1}{u} \dfrac{du}{dx} dx$

$= -\int_1^{\frac{1}{\sqrt{2}}} \dfrac{1}{u} du$

$= \int_{\frac{1}{\sqrt{2}}}^1 \dfrac{1}{u} du$

$= \left[\ln |u| \right]_{\frac{1}{\sqrt{2}}}^1 = \ln 1 - \ln \tfrac{1}{\sqrt{2}} = \ln \sqrt{2} = \tfrac{1}{2} \ln 2$

d Let $u = \sin x$, $\dfrac{du}{dx} = \cos x$

when $x = \dfrac{\pi}{6}$, $u = \sin \dfrac{\pi}{6} = \dfrac{1}{2}$

when $x = \dfrac{\pi}{2}$, $u = \sin \dfrac{\pi}{2} = 1$

$\therefore \displaystyle\int_{\frac{\pi}{6}}^{\frac{\pi}{2}} \cot x \, dx = \int_{\frac{\pi}{6}}^{\frac{\pi}{2}} \dfrac{\cos x}{\sin x} \, dx$

$= \displaystyle\int_{\frac{\pi}{6}}^{\frac{\pi}{2}} \dfrac{1}{u} \dfrac{du}{dx} \, dx$

$= \displaystyle\int_{\frac{1}{2}}^{1} \dfrac{1}{u} \, du$

$= [\ln|u|]_{\frac{1}{2}}^{1}$

$= \ln 1 - \ln \dfrac{1}{2}$

$= \ln 2$

e Let $u = 1 - \sin x$, $\dfrac{du}{dx} = -\cos x$

when $x = 0$, $u = 1 - \sin 0 = 1$

when $x = \dfrac{\pi}{6}$, $u = 1 - \sin \dfrac{\pi}{6} = \dfrac{1}{2}$

$\therefore \displaystyle\int_{0}^{\frac{\pi}{6}} \dfrac{\cos x}{1 - \sin x} \, dx = -\int_{0}^{\frac{\pi}{6}} \dfrac{-\cos x}{1 - \sin x} \, dx$

$= -\displaystyle\int_{0}^{\frac{\pi}{6}} \dfrac{1}{u} \dfrac{du}{dx} \, dx$

$= -\displaystyle\int_{1}^{\frac{1}{2}} \dfrac{1}{u} \, du$

$= \displaystyle\int_{\frac{1}{2}}^{1} \dfrac{1}{u} \, du$

$= [\ln|u|]_{\frac{1}{2}}^{1}$

$= \ln 1 - \ln \dfrac{1}{2}$

$= \ln 2$

f Let $u = \tan x$, $\dfrac{du}{dx} = \sec^2 x$

when $x = 0$, $u = \tan 0 = 0$

when $x = \dfrac{\pi}{4}$, $u = \tan \dfrac{\pi}{4} = 1$

$\therefore \displaystyle\int_0^{\frac{\pi}{4}} \sec^2 x \tan^3 x \, dx = \int_0^{\frac{\pi}{4}} u^3 \dfrac{du}{dx} \, dx$

$= \displaystyle\int_0^1 u^3 \, du$

$= \left[\dfrac{u^4}{4}\right]_0^1$

$= \dfrac{1}{4}$

EXERCISE 24G.2

1 **a** $\displaystyle\int_1^4 \sqrt{x} \, dx = 4.67$

$\displaystyle\int_1^4 (-\sqrt{x}) \, dx = -4.67$

b $\displaystyle\int_0^1 x^7 \, dx = 0.125 = \dfrac{1}{8}$

$\displaystyle\int_0^1 (-x^7) \, dx = -0.125 = -\dfrac{1}{8}$

2 **a** $\displaystyle\int_0^1 x^2 \, dx = \dfrac{1}{3}$ **b** $\displaystyle\int_1^2 x^2 \, dx = \dfrac{7}{3}$ **c** $\displaystyle\int_0^2 x^2 \, dx = \dfrac{8}{3}$ **d** $\displaystyle\int_0^1 3x^2 \, dx = 1$

3 **a** $\displaystyle\int_0^2 (x^3 - 4x) \, dx = -4$ **b** $\displaystyle\int_2^3 (x^3 - 4x) \, dx = 6\dfrac{1}{4}$ **c** $\displaystyle\int_0^3 (x^3 - 4x) \, dx = 2\dfrac{1}{4}$

4 **a** $\displaystyle\int_0^1 x^2 \, dx = \dfrac{1}{3}$ **b** $\displaystyle\int_0^1 \sqrt{x} \, dx = \dfrac{2}{3}$ **c** $\displaystyle\int_0^1 (x^2 + \sqrt{x}) \, dx = 1$

We see that $\displaystyle\int_0^1 (x^2 + \sqrt{x}) \, dx = \int_0^1 x^2 \, dx + \int_0^1 \sqrt{x} \, dx$.

In general, $\displaystyle\int_a^b f(x) \, dx + \int_a^b g(x) \, dx = \int_a^b (f(x) + g(x)) \, dx$

5 **a** $\displaystyle\int_0^3 f(x) \, dx = 2 + 3 + 1.5 = 6.5$ **b** $\displaystyle\int_3^7 f(x) \, dx = -\left(\dfrac{3}{2} + 3 + \dfrac{5}{2} + 2\right) = -9$

c $\displaystyle\int_2^4 f(x) \, dx = 1.5 - 1.5 = 0$ **d** $\displaystyle\int_0^7 f(x) \, dx = 6.5 - 9 = -2.5$

6 **a** $\displaystyle\int_0^4 f(x) \, dx = \dfrac{1}{2}\pi(2)^2 = 2\pi$ **b** $\displaystyle\int_4^6 f(x) \, dx = -(2 \times 2) = -4$

c $\displaystyle\int_6^8 f(x) \, dx = \dfrac{1}{2}\pi(1)^2 = \dfrac{\pi}{2}$ **d** $\displaystyle\int_0^8 f(x) \, dx = 2\pi + (-4) + \dfrac{\pi}{2} = \dfrac{5\pi}{2} - 4$

7 **a** $\displaystyle\int_2^4 f(x) \, dx + \int_4^7 f(x) \, dx$

$= \displaystyle\int_2^7 f(x) \, dx$

b $\displaystyle\int_1^3 g(x) \, dx + \int_3^8 g(x) \, dx + \int_8^9 g(x) \, dx$

$= \displaystyle\int_1^9 g(x) \, dx$

8 **a** $\int_1^3 f(x)\,dx + \int_3^6 f(x)\,dx = \int_1^6 f(x)\,dx$

$\therefore \int_3^6 f(x)\,dx = \int_1^6 f(x)\,dx - \int_1^3 f(x)\,dx$

$= (-3) - 2$

$= -5$

b $\int_0^2 f(x)\,dx + \int_2^4 f(x)\,dx + \int_4^6 f(x)\,dx = \int_0^6 f(x)\,dx$

$\therefore \int_2^4 f(x)\,dx = \int_0^6 f(x)\,dx - \int_4^6 f(x)\,dx - \int_0^2 f(x)\,dx$

$= (7) - (-2) - (5)$

$= 4$

REVIEW SET 24A

1 **a** $\displaystyle\int \frac{4}{\sqrt{x}}\,dx = 4\int x^{-\frac{1}{2}}\,dx$

$= 4\dfrac{x^{\frac{1}{2}}}{\frac{1}{2}} + c = 8\sqrt{x} + c$

b $\displaystyle\int \frac{3}{1-2x}\,dx = 3\int \frac{1}{1-2x}\,dx$

$= 3(\frac{1}{-2})\ln|1-2x| + c$

$= -\frac{3}{2}\ln|1-2x| + c$

c Let $u = 1 - x^2$, $\dfrac{du}{dx} = -2x$

$\therefore \int xe^{1-x^2}\,dx = -\frac{1}{2}\int e^{1-x^2}(-2x)\,dx$

$= -\frac{1}{2}\int e^u \dfrac{du}{dx}\,dx$

$= -\frac{1}{2}\int e^u\,du$

$= -\frac{1}{2}e^u + c$

$= -\frac{1}{2}e^{1-x^2} + c$

d $\int e^{4-3x}\,dx = \frac{1}{-3}e^{4-3x} + c$

$= -\frac{1}{3}e^{4-3x} + c$

2 **a** Let $u = \sin x$, $\dfrac{du}{dx} = \cos x$

$\therefore \int \sin^7 x \cos x\,dx = \int u^7 \dfrac{du}{dx}\,dx$

$= \int u^7\,du$

$= \dfrac{u^8}{8} + c$

$= \dfrac{\sin^8 x}{8} + c$

c Let $u = \sin x$, $\dfrac{du}{dx} = \cos x$

$\therefore \int e^{\sin x} \cos x\,dx = \int e^u \dfrac{du}{dx}\,dx$

$= \int e^u\,du$

$= e^u + c$

$= e^{\sin x} + c$

b Let $u = \cos 2x$, $\dfrac{du}{dx} = -2\sin 2x$

$\therefore \int \tan 2x\,dx = \int \dfrac{\sin 2x}{\cos 2x}\,dx$

$= -\frac{1}{2}\int \dfrac{-2\sin 2x}{\cos 2x}\,dx$

$= -\frac{1}{2}\int \dfrac{1}{u}\dfrac{du}{dx}\,dx$

$= -\frac{1}{2}\int \dfrac{1}{u}\,du$

$= -\frac{1}{2}\ln|u| + c$

$= -\frac{1}{2}\ln|\cos(2x)| + c$

3 **a** $\int_{-5}^{-1} \sqrt{1-3x}\,dx = \int_{-5}^{-1}(1-3x)^{\frac{1}{2}}\,dx$

$= \left[\dfrac{1}{-3} \times \dfrac{(1-3x)^{\frac{3}{2}}}{\frac{3}{2}}\right]_{-5}^{-1}$

$= -\dfrac{2}{9}\left[(1-3x)^{\frac{3}{2}}\right]_{-5}^{-1} = -\dfrac{2}{9}\left[4^{\frac{3}{2}} - 16^{\frac{3}{2}}\right] = -\dfrac{2}{9}[8 - 64] = 12\dfrac{4}{9}$

b In $\displaystyle\int_0^1 \frac{4x^2}{(x^3+2)^3}\,dx$

we let $u = x^3 + 2$, $\dfrac{du}{dx} = 3x^2$

when $x = 0$, $u = 2$
when $x = 1$, $u = 3$

$\displaystyle\therefore \int_0^1 \frac{4x^2}{(x^3+2)^3}\,dx = \frac{4}{3}\int_0^1 \frac{3x^2}{(x^2+2)^3}\,dx$

$= \dfrac{4}{3}\displaystyle\int_0^1 \dfrac{1}{u^3}\dfrac{du}{dx}\,dx$

$= \dfrac{4}{3}\displaystyle\int_2^3 u^{-3}\,du$

$= \dfrac{4}{3}\left[\dfrac{u^{-2}}{-2}\right]_2^3 = -\dfrac{2}{3}\left[\dfrac{1}{u^2}\right]_2^3$

$= -\dfrac{2}{3}\left[\dfrac{1}{9} - \dfrac{1}{4}\right]$

$= \dfrac{5}{54}$

4 $y = \sqrt{x^2 - 4} = (x^2 - 4)^{\frac{1}{2}}$

$\therefore \dfrac{dy}{dx} = \dfrac{1}{2}\left(x^2 - 4\right)^{-\frac{1}{2}} \times 2x$

$= \dfrac{x}{(x^2-4)^{\frac{1}{2}}}$

$= \dfrac{x}{\sqrt{x^2-4}}$

$\therefore \displaystyle\int \dfrac{x}{\sqrt{x^2-4}}\,dx = \sqrt{x^2-4} + c$

5 Given: $f''(x) = 18x + 10$, $f(0) = -1$, $f(1) = 13$

$f'(x) = \int (18x + 10)\,dx$
$= 9x^2 + 10x + c$

$\therefore f(x) = 3x^3 + 5x^2 + cx + d$

But $f(0) = -1$ so $d = -1$

$\therefore f(x) = 3x^3 + 5x^2 + cx - 1$

And $f(1) = 13$ so $3 + 5 + c - 1 = 13$

$\therefore c + 7 = 13$

$\therefore c = 6$

$\therefore f(x) = 3x^3 + 5x^2 + 6x - 1$

6 a $\displaystyle\int_0^{\frac{\pi}{3}} \cos^2\left(\dfrac{x}{2}\right)\,dx$

$= \displaystyle\int_0^{\frac{\pi}{3}} \left(\dfrac{1}{2} + \dfrac{1}{2}\cos x\right)\,dx$

$= \left[\dfrac{1}{2}x + \dfrac{1}{2}\sin x\right]_0^{\frac{\pi}{3}}$

$= \dfrac{\pi}{6} + \dfrac{1}{2}\left(\dfrac{\sqrt{3}}{2}\right) - 0 - 0$

$= \dfrac{\pi}{6} + \dfrac{\sqrt{3}}{4}$

b Let $u = \cos x$, $\dfrac{du}{dx} = -\sin x$

when $x = 0$, $u = \cos 0 = 1$
when $x = \dfrac{\pi}{4}$, $u = \cos\dfrac{\pi}{4} = \dfrac{1}{\sqrt{2}}$

$\therefore \displaystyle\int_0^{\frac{\pi}{4}} \tan x\,dx$

$= \displaystyle\int_0^{\frac{\pi}{4}} \dfrac{\sin x}{\cos x}\,dx$

$= -\displaystyle\int_0^{\frac{\pi}{4}} \dfrac{-\sin x}{\cos x}\,dx$

$= -\displaystyle\int_0^{\frac{\pi}{4}} \dfrac{1}{u}\dfrac{du}{dx}\,dx$

$= -\displaystyle\int_1^{\frac{1}{\sqrt{2}}} \dfrac{1}{u}\,du$

$= \displaystyle\int_{\frac{1}{\sqrt{2}}}^1 \dfrac{1}{u}\,du$

$= [\ln|u|]_{\frac{1}{\sqrt{2}}}^1$

$= \ln 1 - \ln\dfrac{1}{\sqrt{2}}$

$= \dfrac{1}{2}\ln 2$

7 a $\dfrac{4x-3}{2x+1} = \dfrac{2(2x+1) - 5}{2x+1} = 2 + \dfrac{-5}{2x+1}$ $\therefore A = 2$, $B = -5$

b $\displaystyle\int_0^2 \dfrac{4x-3}{2x+1}\,dx = \displaystyle\int_0^2 \left(2 - 5\left(\dfrac{1}{2x+1}\right)\right)\,dx$

$= \left[2x - 5\left(\dfrac{1}{2}\right)\ln|2x+1|\right]_0^2$

$= [4 - \dfrac{5}{2}\ln 5] - [0 - \dfrac{5}{2}\ln 1]$

$= 4 - \dfrac{5}{2}\ln 5$

≈ -0.0236

8 a $\displaystyle\int_3^4 \frac{1}{\sqrt{2x+1}}\, dx$

$= \int_3^4 (2x+1)^{-\frac{1}{2}}\, dx$

$= \left[\dfrac{(2x+1)^{\frac{1}{2}}}{\frac{1}{2}}\cdot\dfrac{1}{2}\right]_3^4$

$= \left[\sqrt{2x+1}\right]_3^4$

$= \sqrt{9} - \sqrt{7}$

$= 3 - \sqrt{7}$

b Let $u = x^3 + 1$, $\dfrac{du}{dx} = 3x^2$

when $x = 0$, $u = 1$

when $x = 1$, $u = 2$

$\therefore\ \int_0^1 x^2 e^{x^3+1}\, dx = \frac{1}{3}\int_0^1 3x^2 e^{x^3+1}\, dx$

$= \frac{1}{3}\int_0^1 e^u \dfrac{du}{dx}\, dx$

$= \frac{1}{3}\int_1^2 e^u\, du$

$= \frac{1}{3}\times [e^u]_1^2$

$= \frac{1}{3}(e^2 - e)$

9 $y = \ln(\sec x),\ \sec x > 0$

$\therefore\ \dfrac{dy}{dx} = \dfrac{\sec x\tan x}{\sec x} = \tan x$

$\therefore\ \int \tan x\, dx = \ln(\sec x) + c,\ \sec x > 0$

10 $\displaystyle\int_0^a e^{1-2x}\, dx = \dfrac{e}{4}$

$\therefore\ \left[\dfrac{1}{-2}e^{1-2x}\right]_0^a = \dfrac{e}{4}$

$\therefore\ \left(-\tfrac{1}{2}e^{1-2a}\right) - \left(-\tfrac{1}{2}e^1\right) = \dfrac{e}{4}$

$\therefore\ -\tfrac{1}{2}e^{1-2a} + \dfrac{e}{2} = \dfrac{e}{4}$

$\therefore\ \tfrac{1}{2}e^{1-2a} = \dfrac{e}{4}$

$\therefore\ e^{1-2a} = \dfrac{e}{2}$

$\therefore\ 1 - 2a = \ln\left(\dfrac{e}{2}\right) = \ln e - \ln 2$

$\therefore\ 1 - 2a = 1 - \ln 2$

$\therefore\ 2a = \ln 2$

$\therefore\ a = \tfrac{1}{2}\ln 2$

$\therefore\ a = \ln 2^{\frac{1}{2}}$

$\therefore\ a = \ln\sqrt{2}$

11 $\dfrac{d}{dx}(e^{-2x}\sin x) = -2e^{-2x}\sin x + e^{-2x}\cos x$ {product rule}

$= e^{-2x}(\cos x - 2\sin x)$

$\therefore\ \int_0^{\frac{\pi}{2}} e^{-2x}(\cos x - 2\sin x)\, dx = \left[e^{-2x}\sin x\right]_0^{\frac{\pi}{2}}$

$= e^{-\pi}(1) - e^0(0) = e^{-\pi}$

REVIEW SET 24B

1 a $\int \left(2e^{-x} - \dfrac{1}{x} + 3\right) dx$

$= -2e^{-x} - \ln|x| + 3x + c$

b $\int \left(\sqrt{x} - \dfrac{1}{\sqrt{x}}\right)^2 dx$

$= \int \left(x - 2 + \dfrac{1}{x}\right) dx$

$= \dfrac{x^2}{2} - 2x + \ln|x| + c$

c $\int (3 + e^{2x-1})^2\, dx$

$= \int (9 + 6e^{2x-1} + e^{4x-2})\, dx$

$= 9x + 3e^{2x-1} + \tfrac{1}{4}e^{4x-2} + c$

2 a $\int_1^2 (x^2 - 1)^2\, dx$

$= \int_1^2 (x^4 - 2x^2 + 1)\, dx$

$= \left[\dfrac{x^5}{5} - \dfrac{2x^3}{3} + x\right]_1^2$

$= \left(\dfrac{32}{5} - \dfrac{16}{3} + 2\right) - \left(\dfrac{1}{5} - \dfrac{2}{3} + 1\right) = \dfrac{31}{5} - \dfrac{14}{3} + 1 = 2\dfrac{8}{15}$

b In $\int_1^2 x(x^2-1)^2 \, dx$

we let $u = x^2 - 1$, $\dfrac{du}{dx} = 2x$

when $x = 1$, $u = 0$
when $x = 2$, $u = 3$

$\therefore \int_1^2 x(x^2-1)^2 \, dx = \frac{1}{2}\int 2x(x^2-1)^2 \, dx$
$= \frac{1}{2}\int_1^2 u^2 \dfrac{du}{dx} \, dx$
$= \frac{1}{2}\int_0^3 u^2 \, du$
$= \frac{1}{2}\left[\dfrac{u^3}{3}\right]_0^3$
$= \frac{1}{2}\left(\dfrac{27}{3} - 0\right)$
$= 4\frac{1}{2}$

3 a $\int 4\sin^2\left(\dfrac{x}{2}\right) \, dx$
$= \int 4\left(\dfrac{1}{2} - \dfrac{1}{2}\cos x\right) \, dx$
$= \int (2 - 2\cos x) \, dx$
$= 2x - 2\sin x + c$

b $\int (2 - \cos x)^2 \, dx$
$= \int (4 - 4\cos x + \cos^2 x) \, dx$
$= \int (4 - 4\cos x + \frac{1}{2} + \frac{1}{2}\cos 2x) \, dx$
$= \frac{9}{2}x - 4\sin x + \frac{1}{4}\sin 2x + c$

4 $f(x) = (3x^2 + x)^3$
$\therefore f'(x) = 3(3x^2 + x)^2 (6x + 1)$
$\therefore \int 3(3x^2 + x)^2(6x+1) \, dx = (3x^2 + x)^3 + c_1$
$\therefore 3\int (3x^2 + x)^2(6x+1) \, dx = (3x^2 + x)^3 + c_1$
$\therefore \int (3x^2 + x)^2(6x+1) \, dx = \frac{1}{3}(3x^2 + x)^3 + c$

5 $f'(x) = x^2 - 3x + 2$
$\therefore f(x) = \dfrac{x^3}{3} - \dfrac{3x^2}{2} + 2x + c$
But $f(1) = 3$
so $\frac{1}{3} - \frac{3}{2} + 2 + c = 3$
$\therefore c = 1 - \frac{1}{3} + 1\frac{1}{2}$
$\therefore c = 2\frac{1}{6}$
$\therefore f(x) = \frac{1}{3}x^3 - \frac{3}{2}x^2 + 2x + 2\frac{1}{6}$

6 $y = \sin(x^2)$
$\therefore \dfrac{dy}{dx} = \cos(x^2) \times 2x$
$\therefore \int 2x\cos(x^2) \, dx = \sin(x^2) + c_1$
$\therefore 2\int x\cos(x^2) \, dx = \sin(x^2) + c_1$
$\therefore \int x\cos(x^2) \, dx = \frac{1}{2}\sin(x^2) + c$

7 $\int_2^3 \dfrac{1}{\sqrt{3x-4}} \, dx = \int_2^3 (3x-4)^{-\frac{1}{2}} \, dx$
$= \left[\dfrac{1}{3}\dfrac{(3x-4)^{\frac{1}{2}}}{\frac{1}{2}}\right]_2^3$
$= \left[\dfrac{2}{3}\sqrt{3x-4}\right]_2^3$
$= \dfrac{2}{3}\sqrt{5} - \dfrac{2}{3}\sqrt{2}$
$= \dfrac{2}{3}(\sqrt{5} - \sqrt{2})$

8 a $f''(x) = 3x^2 + 2x$
$\therefore f'(x) = \dfrac{3x^3}{3} + \dfrac{2x^2}{2} + c$
$= x^3 + x^2 + c$
$\therefore f(x) = \dfrac{x^4}{4} + \dfrac{x^3}{3} + cx + d$
But $f(0) = 3$ so $d = 3$
$\therefore f(x) = \dfrac{x^4}{4} + \dfrac{x^3}{3} + cx + 3$
Also, $f(2) = 3$ so $4 + \frac{8}{3} + 2c + 3 = 3$
$\therefore \dfrac{20}{3} = -2c$
$\therefore c = -\dfrac{10}{3}$
$\therefore f(x) = \frac{1}{4}x^4 + \frac{1}{3}x^3 - \frac{10}{3}x + 3$

b Now $f'(2) = 2^3 + 2^2 - \dfrac{10}{3}$
$= 12 - \dfrac{10}{3}$
$= \dfrac{26}{3}$
$\therefore$ the normal has gradient $-\dfrac{3}{26}$
$\therefore$ equation is $\dfrac{y-3}{x-2} = -\dfrac{3}{26}$
$\therefore y - 3 = -\dfrac{3}{26}(x - 2)$
$\therefore y = -\dfrac{3}{26}x + \dfrac{6}{26} + 3$
or $3x + 26y = 84$

9 Let $u = \sin\theta$, $\dfrac{du}{d\theta} = \cos\theta$

when $\theta = \dfrac{\pi}{6}$, $\sin\theta = \sin\dfrac{\pi}{6} = \dfrac{1}{2}$

when $\theta = \dfrac{\pi}{2}$, $\sin\theta = \sin\dfrac{\pi}{2} = 1$

$\therefore \displaystyle\int_{\frac{\pi}{6}}^{\frac{\pi}{2}} \cot\theta\, d\theta = \int_{\frac{\pi}{6}}^{\frac{\pi}{2}} \dfrac{\cos\theta}{\sin\theta}\, d\theta$

$= \displaystyle\int_{\frac{\pi}{6}}^{\frac{\pi}{2}} \dfrac{1}{u}\dfrac{du}{d\theta}\, d\theta$

$= \displaystyle\int_{\frac{1}{2}}^{1} \dfrac{1}{u}\, du$

$= [\ln|u|]_{\frac{1}{2}}^{1}$

$= \ln 1 - \ln\dfrac{1}{2}$

$= \ln 2$

10
$$\begin{array}{r|rrrr} 2 & 1 & 0 & -3 & 2 \\ & 0 & 2 & 4 & 2 \\ \hline & 1 & 2 & 1 & 4 \end{array}$$

$\therefore \dfrac{x^3 - 3x + 2}{x - 2} = x^2 + 2x + 1 + \dfrac{4}{x - 2}$

$\therefore A = 1,\ B = 2,\ C = 1,\ D = 4$

$\therefore \displaystyle\int \dfrac{x^3 - 3x + 2}{x - 2}\, dx$

$= \displaystyle\int \left(x^2 + 2x + 1 + \dfrac{4}{x - 2}\right) dx$

$= \dfrac{x^3}{3} + \dfrac{2x^2}{2} + x + 4\ln|x - 2| + c$

$= \tfrac{1}{3}x^3 + x^2 + x + 4\ln|x - 2| + c$

or $\displaystyle\int \dfrac{x^3 - 3x + 2}{x - 2}\, dx$

$= \displaystyle\int \left((x + 1)^2 + \dfrac{4}{x - 2}\right) dx$

$= \dfrac{(x + 1)^3}{3} + 4\ln|x - 2| + c$

11 a $\displaystyle\int \dfrac{1}{x + 2}\, dx - \int \dfrac{2}{x - 1}\, dx = \ln|x + 2| - 2\ln|x - 1| + c_1 = \ln\left(\dfrac{|x + 2|}{(x - 1)^2}\right) + c_1$

b $\dfrac{1}{x + 2} - \dfrac{2}{x - 1} = \dfrac{(x - 1) - 2(x + 2)}{(x + 2)(x - 1)}$

$= \dfrac{-x - 5}{(x + 2)(x - 1)}$

$= -\dfrac{x + 5}{(x + 2)(x - 1)}$

$\therefore \displaystyle\int \dfrac{x + 5}{(x + 2)(x - 1)}\, dx$

$= -\left[\displaystyle\int \dfrac{1}{x + 2}\, dx - \int \dfrac{2}{x - 1}\, dx\right]$

$= -\ln\left(\dfrac{|x + 2|}{(x - 1)^2}\right) + c$

$= \ln\left(\dfrac{(x - 1)^2}{|x + 2|}\right) + c$

12 a $\dfrac{A}{x} + \dfrac{B}{x + 1} + \dfrac{C}{x - 1}$

$= \dfrac{A(x^2 - 1) + Bx(x - 1) + Cx(x + 1)}{x(x + 1)(x - 1)}$

$= \dfrac{Ax^2 - A + Bx^2 - Bx + Cx^2 + Cx}{x(x^2 - 1)}$

$= \dfrac{x^2(A + B + C) + x(C - B) - A}{x(x^2 - 1)}$

$= \dfrac{x^2(-A - B - C) + x(B - C) + A}{x(1 - x^2)}$

So, if $\dfrac{A}{x} + \dfrac{B}{x + 1} + \dfrac{C}{x - 1} = \dfrac{4}{x(1 - x^2)}$, then

$A = 4,\quad B - C = 0$ and $-A - B - C = 0$

$\therefore B = C$

$\therefore -4 - 2B = 0$

So, $A = 4,\ B = -2,\ C = -2$

b $\displaystyle\int \dfrac{4}{x(1 - x^2)}\, dx = \int \left(\dfrac{4}{x} - \dfrac{2}{x + 1} - \dfrac{2}{x - 1}\right) dx$

$= 4\ln|x| - 2\ln|x + 1| - 2\ln|x - 1| + c$

c $\displaystyle\int_2^4 \frac{4}{x(1-x^2)}\,dx = [4\ln|x| - 2\ln|x+1| - 2\ln|x-1|]_2^4$
$= 4\ln 4 - 2\ln 5 - 2\ln 3 - 4\ln 2 + 2\ln 3 + 2\ln 1$
$= \ln\left(\dfrac{4^4}{5^2 \times 2^4}\right) = \ln\left(\dfrac{16}{25}\right)$

REVIEW SET 24C

1 a $\dfrac{dy}{dx} = (x^2 - 1)^2$
$\therefore\ y = \int (x^2 - 1)^2\,dx$
$= \int (x^4 - 2x^2 + 1)\,dx$
$= \tfrac{1}{5}x^5 - \tfrac{2}{3}x^3 + x + c$

b $\dfrac{dy}{dx} = 400 - 20e^{-\frac{x}{2}}$
$\therefore\ y = \int (400 - 20e^{-\frac{x}{2}})\,dx$
$= 400x - \dfrac{20e^{-\frac{x}{2}}}{-\frac{1}{2}} + c$
$= 400x + 40e^{-\frac{x}{2}} + c$

2 a $\displaystyle\int_{-2}^0 \dfrac{4}{2x-1}\,dx$

$= 4\displaystyle\int_{-2}^0 \dfrac{1}{2x-1}\,dx$

$= 4\left[\left(\tfrac{1}{2}\right)\ln|2x-1|\right]_{-2}^0$

$= 2[\ln|2x-1|]_{-2}^0$

$= 2[\ln|-1| - \ln|-5|]$

$= 2[0 - \ln 5]$

$= -2\ln 5$

≈ -3.22

b In $\displaystyle\int_0^1 \dfrac{10x}{\sqrt{3x^2+1}}\,dx$

we let $u = 3x^2 + 1$, $\dfrac{du}{dx} = 6x$

when $x = 0$, $u = 1$, when $x = 1$, $u = 4$.

$\therefore\ \displaystyle\int_0^1 \dfrac{10x}{\sqrt{3x^2+1}}\,dx = \tfrac{5}{3}\displaystyle\int_0^1 \dfrac{6x}{\sqrt{3x^2+1}}\,dx$

$= \tfrac{5}{3}\displaystyle\int_0^1 u^{-\frac{1}{2}}\dfrac{du}{dx}\,dx$

$= \tfrac{5}{3}\displaystyle\int_1^4 u^{-\frac{1}{2}}\,du$

$= \tfrac{5}{3}\left[\dfrac{u^{\frac{1}{2}}}{\frac{1}{2}}\right]_1^4$

$= \tfrac{10}{3}\left(\sqrt{4} - \sqrt{1}\right) = \tfrac{10}{3}$

3 Let $u = \cos x$, $\dfrac{du}{dx} = -\sin x$

$\therefore\ \displaystyle\int \dfrac{\sin x}{\cos^4 x}\,dx = -\int \dfrac{-\sin x}{\cos^4 x}\,dx$

$= -\int u^{-4}\dfrac{du}{dx}\,dx$

$= -\int u^{-4}\,du$

$= \dfrac{u^{-3}}{3} + c = \dfrac{1}{3\cos^3 x} + c$

4 $\dfrac{d}{dx}(\ln x)^2 = 2(\ln x)^1 \left(\dfrac{1}{x}\right)$
$= \dfrac{2\ln x}{x}$

$\therefore\ \displaystyle\int \dfrac{2\ln x}{x}\,dx = (\ln x)^2 + c_1$

$\therefore\ \displaystyle\int \dfrac{\ln x}{x}\,dx = \tfrac{1}{2}(\ln x)^2 + c$

5 $f''(x) = 4x^2 - 3$

$\therefore\ f'(x) = \dfrac{4x^3}{3} - 3x + c$

But $f'(0) = 6$ so $c = 6$

$\therefore\ f'(x) = \dfrac{4x^3}{3} - 3x + 6$

$\therefore\ f(x) = \dfrac{4}{3}\dfrac{x^4}{4} - \dfrac{3x^2}{2} + 6x + d$
$= \tfrac{1}{3}x^4 - \tfrac{3}{2}x^2 + 6x + d$

But $f(2) = 3$, so $\tfrac{16}{3} - 6 + 12 + d = 3$

$\therefore\ d = -3 - \tfrac{16}{3} = -\tfrac{25}{3}$

$\therefore\ f(x) = \tfrac{1}{3}x^4 - \tfrac{3}{2}x^2 + 6x - \tfrac{25}{3}$

and $f(3) = 27 - \tfrac{27}{2} + 18 - \tfrac{25}{3}$
$= 23\tfrac{1}{6}$

6   If $y = x\tan x$ then $\dfrac{dy}{dx} = \tan x + x\sec^2 x$

$\therefore \int (\tan x + x\sec^2 x)\,dx = x\tan x + c$

$\therefore \int \tan x\,dx + \int x\sec^2 x\,dx = x\tan x + c$

$\therefore -\ln|\cos x| + \int x\sec^2 x\,dx = x\tan x + c$ {see **Ex 24F.2, Q 4 c**}

$\therefore \int x\sec^2 x\,dx = x\tan x + \ln|\cos x| + c$

7   If $n \neq -1$, $\int (2x+3)^n\,dx = \dfrac{1}{2}\dfrac{(2x+3)^{n+1}}{n+1} + c = \dfrac{(2x+3)^{n+1}}{2(n+1)} + c$

If $n = -1$, $\int (2x+3)^{-1}\,dx = \int \dfrac{1}{2x+3}\,dx = \tfrac{1}{2}\ln|2x+3| + c$

So, $\int (2x+3)^n\,dx = \begin{cases} \dfrac{(2x+3)^{n+1}}{2(n+1)} + c & \text{if } n \neq -1 \\ \tfrac{1}{2}\ln|2x+3| + c & \text{if } n = -1 \end{cases}$

8 a $(e^x + 2)^3$
$= (e^x)^3 + 3(e^x)^2(2) + 3(e^x)(2)^2 + (2)^3$
$= e^{3x} + 6e^{2x} + 12e^x + 8$

b $\int_0^1 (e^x + 2)^3\,dx$
$= \left[\tfrac{1}{3}e^{3x} + 3e^{2x} + 12e^x + 8x\right]_0^1$
$= \left(\tfrac{1}{3}e^3 + 3e^2 + 12e + 8\right) - \left(\tfrac{1}{3} + 3 + 12\right)$
$= \tfrac{1}{3}e^3 + 3e^2 + 12e - 7\tfrac{1}{3} \approx 54.1$

c   Using technology, $\int_0^1 (e^x + 2)^3\,dx \approx 54.1$

9 a $\int_0^{\pi/6} \sin^2\left(\tfrac{x}{2}\right)\,dx$
$= \int_0^{\pi/6} \left(\tfrac{1}{2} - \tfrac{1}{2}\cos x\right)\,dx$
$= \left[\tfrac{1}{2}x - \tfrac{1}{2}\sin x\right]_0^{\pi/6}$
$= \tfrac{\pi}{12} - \tfrac{1}{2}\left(\tfrac{1}{2}\right) - 0 + 0$
$= \tfrac{\pi}{12} - \tfrac{1}{4}$

b   Let $u = \tan x$, $\dfrac{du}{dx} = \sec^2 x$

when $x = \tfrac{\pi}{4}$, $u = \tan\tfrac{\pi}{4} = 1$

when $x = \tfrac{\pi}{3}$, $y = \tan\tfrac{\pi}{3} = \sqrt{3}$

$\therefore \int_{\pi/4}^{\pi/3} \dfrac{\sec^2 x}{\tan x}\,dx = \int_{\pi/4}^{\pi/3} \dfrac{1}{u}\dfrac{du}{dx}\,dx$

$= \int_1^{\sqrt{3}} \dfrac{1}{u}\,du$

$= [\ln|u|]_1^{\sqrt{3}}$

$= \ln\sqrt{3} - \ln 1$

$= \tfrac{1}{2}\ln 3$

10 $f'(x) = 2\sqrt{x} + \dfrac{a}{\sqrt{x}}$

$= 2x^{\frac{1}{2}} + ax^{-\frac{1}{2}}$

$\therefore f(x) = \tfrac{4}{3}x^{\frac{3}{2}} + 2ax^{\frac{1}{2}} + c$

$= \dfrac{4x\sqrt{x}}{3} + 2a\sqrt{x} + c$

Now $f(0) = 2$ so $c = 2$

$\therefore f(x) = \dfrac{4x\sqrt{x}}{3} + 2a\sqrt{x} + 2$

Also, $f(1) = 4$ so $\tfrac{4}{3} + 2a + 2 = 4$

$\therefore 2a = \tfrac{2}{3}$

$\therefore a = \tfrac{1}{3}$

$\therefore f'(x) = 2\sqrt{x} + \dfrac{1}{3\sqrt{x}} = \dfrac{6x+1}{3\sqrt{x}}$

Now $f(x)$ is only defined for $x > 0$,
so $f'(x) > 0$ for all x in the domain.
$\therefore$ the function has no stationary points.

11
$$\int_a^{2a} (x^2 + ax + 2)\, dx = \frac{73a}{2}$$

$$\therefore\ \left[\frac{x^3}{3} + \frac{ax^2}{2} + 2x\right]_a^{2a} = \frac{73a}{2}$$

$$\therefore\ \left(\frac{8a^3}{3} + \frac{a}{2}(4a^2) + 4a\right) - \left(\frac{a^3}{3} + \frac{a^3}{2} + 2a\right) = \frac{73a}{2}$$

$$\frac{8a^3}{3} + 2a^3 + 4a - \frac{a^3}{3} - \frac{a^3}{2} - 2a = \frac{73a}{2}$$

$$\therefore\ 16a^3 + 12a^3 + 24a - 2a^3 - 3a^3 - 12a = 219a$$

$$\therefore\ 23a^3 - 207a = 0$$

$$\therefore\ 23a(a^2 - 9) = 0$$

$$\therefore\ 23a(a+3)(a-3) = 0$$

$$\therefore\ a = 0 \ \text{or}\ a = \pm 3$$

12
$$\frac{d}{dx}\left(\frac{e^{1-x}}{x^2}\right) = \frac{-e^{1-x}x^2 - e^{1-x}(2x)}{x^4} \quad \{\text{quotient rule}\}$$

$$= -\frac{e^{1-x}(x+2)}{x^3}$$

$$\therefore\ \int_1^2 \frac{e^{1-x}(x+2)}{x^3}\, dx = -\int_1^2 -\frac{e^{1-x}(x+2)}{x^3}\, dx$$

$$= -\left[\frac{e^{1-x}}{x^2}\right]_1^2$$

$$= -\left(\frac{e^{-1}}{4} - \frac{e^0}{1}\right)$$

$$= 1 - \frac{1}{4e}$$

13 Let $u = \cos x$, $\dfrac{du}{dx} = -\sin x$

$$\therefore\ \int \frac{\sin x}{\sqrt{\cos^n x}}\, dx = -\int \frac{-\sin x}{\sqrt{\cos^n x}}\, dx$$

$$= -\int \frac{1}{\sqrt{u^n}} \frac{du}{dx}\, dx$$

$$= -\int u^{-\frac{n}{2}}\, du$$

$$= -\frac{u^{1-\frac{n}{2}}}{1-\frac{n}{2}} + c \quad \text{provided}\ n \neq 2$$

$$= \frac{\cos^{1-\frac{n}{2}} x}{\frac{n}{2} - 1} + c$$

If $n = 2$, $\displaystyle\int \frac{\sin x}{\sqrt{\cos^2 x}}\, dx = \int \frac{\sin x}{\cos x}\, dx$

$$= \int \tan x\, dx$$

$$= -\ln|\cos x| + c \quad \{\text{see Ex 24F.2 Q 4 c}\}$$

So, the integral is defined for all n.

Chapter 25
APPLICATIONS OF INTEGRATION

EXERCISE 25A

1 a

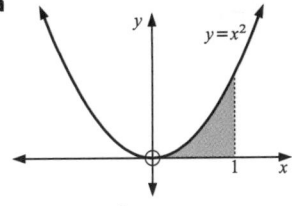

Area $= \int_0^1 x^2 \, dx$

$= \left[\dfrac{x^3}{3}\right]_0^1$

$= \dfrac{1}{3} - 0$

$= \dfrac{1}{3}$ units^2

b

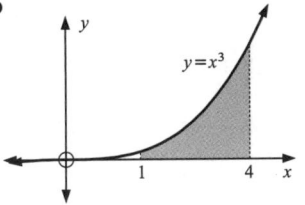

Area $= \int_1^4 x^3 \, dx$

$= \left[\dfrac{x^4}{4}\right]_1^4$

$= \dfrac{256}{4} - \dfrac{1}{4}$

$= 63\dfrac{3}{4}$ units^2

c

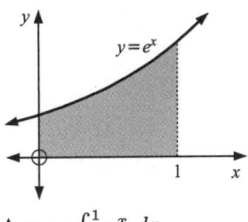

Area $= \int_0^1 e^x \, dx$

$= [e^x]_0^1$

$= e - 1$

≈ 1.72 units^2

d The graph cuts the x-axis at $y = 0$.

$\therefore \quad 6 + x - x^2 = 0$

$\therefore \quad (3-x)(2+x) = 0$

$\therefore \quad x = 3$ or -2

The x-intercepts are 3 and -2.

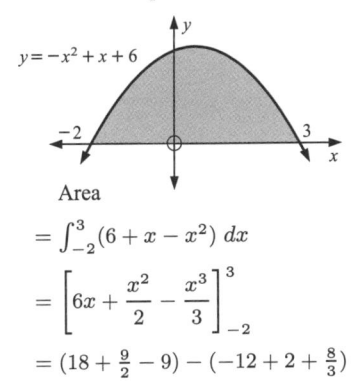

Area

$= \int_{-2}^{3} (6 + x - x^2) \, dx$

$= \left[6x + \dfrac{x^2}{2} - \dfrac{x^3}{3}\right]_{-2}^{3}$

$= (18 + \dfrac{9}{2} - 9) - (-12 + 2 + \dfrac{8}{3})$

$= 20\dfrac{5}{6}$ units^2

e

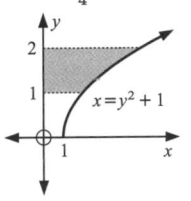

Area

$= \int_1^2 x \, dy$

$= \int_1^2 (y^2 + 1) \, dy$

$= \left[\dfrac{y^3}{3} + y\right]_1^2$

$= \left(\dfrac{8}{3} + 2\right) - \left(\dfrac{1}{3} + 1\right)$

$= 3\dfrac{1}{3}$ units^2

f

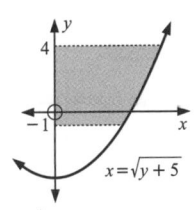

Area

$= \int_{-1}^{4} x \, dy$

$= \int_{-1}^{4} (y+5)^{\frac{1}{2}} \, dy$

$= \left[\dfrac{(y+5)^{\frac{3}{2}}}{\frac{3}{2}}\right]_{-1}^{4}$

$= \left[\dfrac{2}{3}(y+5)^{\frac{3}{2}}\right]_{-1}^{4}$

$= \dfrac{2}{3}(9)^{\frac{3}{2}} - \dfrac{2}{3}(4)^{\frac{3}{2}}$

$= \dfrac{2}{3}(27 - 8)$

$= \dfrac{2}{3} \times 19$

$= 12\dfrac{2}{3}$ units^2

2 a

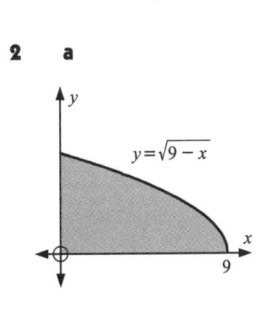

Area

$= \int_0^9 \left((9-x)^{\frac{1}{2}} - 0\right) dx$

$= \int_0^9 (9-x)^{\frac{1}{2}} \, dx$

$= \left[\left(\dfrac{1}{-1}\right) \dfrac{(9-x)^{\frac{3}{2}}}{\frac{3}{2}}\right]_0^9$

$= -\dfrac{2}{3}\left[(9-x)^{\frac{3}{2}}\right]_0^9$

$= -\dfrac{2}{3}[0 - 27]$

$= 18$ units^2

b

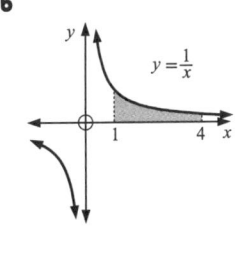

Area

$= \int_1^4 \left(\dfrac{1}{x} - 0\right) dx$

$= \int_1^4 \dfrac{1}{x} \, dx$

$= [\ln |x|]_1^4$

$= \ln 4 - \ln 1$

$= \ln 4 - 0$

≈ 1.39 units^2

c

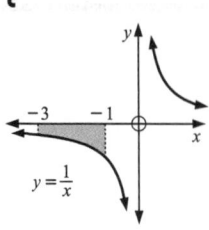

Area
$$= \int_{-3}^{-1} \left(0 - \frac{1}{x}\right) dx$$
$$= -\int_{-3}^{-1} \left(\frac{1}{x}\right) dx$$
$$= -[\ln|x|]_{-3}^{-1}$$
$$= -(\ln 1 - \ln 3)$$
$$= 0 + \ln 3$$
$$\approx 1.10 \text{ units}^2$$

d

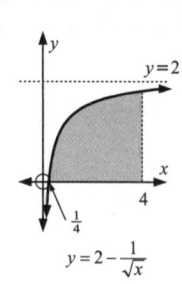

Area
$$= \int_{\frac{1}{4}}^{4} \left(2 - \frac{1}{\sqrt{x}} - 0\right) dx$$
$$= \int_{\frac{1}{4}}^{4} \left(2 - x^{-\frac{1}{2}}\right) dx$$
$$= \left[2x - \frac{x^{\frac{1}{2}}}{\frac{1}{2}}\right]_{\frac{1}{4}}^{4}$$
$$= \left[2x - 2\sqrt{x}\right]_{\frac{1}{4}}^{4}$$
$$= (8 - 4) - (\tfrac{1}{2} - 1)$$
$$= 4\tfrac{1}{2} \text{ units}^2$$

e

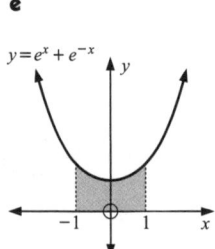

Area
$$= \int_{-1}^{1} (e^x + e^{-x}) dx$$
$$= [e^x - e^{-x}]_{-1}^{1}$$
$$= (e - e^{-1}) - (e^{-1} - e)$$
$$= 2e - \frac{2}{e}$$
$$\approx 4.70 \text{ units}^2$$

f $y = e^x$ or $x = \ln y$

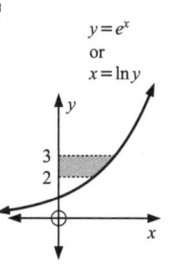

Area
$$= \int_{2}^{3} (x - 0) dy$$
$$= \int_{2}^{3} \ln y \, dy$$
$$= [y \ln y - y]_{2}^{3}$$
$$= (3 \ln 3 - 3)$$
$$\quad - (2 \ln 2 - 2)$$
$$= \ln 27 - \ln 4 - 1$$
$$= \ln\left(\tfrac{27}{4}\right) - 1 \text{ units}^2$$
$$\approx 0.910 \text{ units}^2$$

3 a

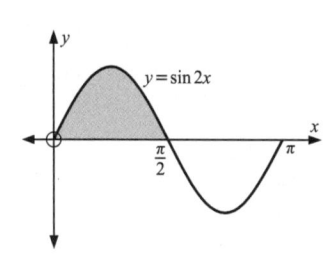

The period is $\frac{2\pi}{2} = \pi$
$\therefore$ the first positive x-intercept is $\frac{\pi}{2}$
The required area $= \int_0^{\frac{\pi}{2}} \sin(2x) \, dx$
$$= \left[\tfrac{1}{2}(-\cos(2x))\right]_0^{\frac{\pi}{2}}$$
$$= -\tfrac{1}{2}[\cos(2x)]_0^{\frac{\pi}{2}}$$
$$= -\tfrac{1}{2}(\cos \pi - \cos 0)$$
$$= 1 \text{ unit}^2$$

b

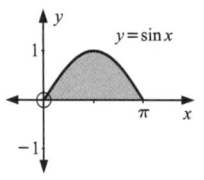

$$A = \int_0^{\pi} \sin x \, dx$$
$$= [-\cos x]_0^{\pi}$$
$$= [-\cos \pi + \cos 0]$$
$$= -(-1) + 1$$
$$= 2 \text{ units}^2$$

c Since $\sin^2 x \geq 0$ always, the function never drops below the x-axis.
$$\therefore A = \int_0^{\pi} \sin^2 x \, dx$$
$$= \int_0^{\pi} \left(\tfrac{1}{2} - \tfrac{1}{2}\cos(2x)\right) dx$$
$$= \left[\tfrac{x}{2} - \tfrac{1}{4}\sin(2x)\right]_0^{\pi}$$
$$= \left[\tfrac{\pi}{2} - \tfrac{1}{4}\sin(2\pi)\right] - [0 - \tfrac{1}{4}\sin 0]$$
$$= \tfrac{\pi}{2} \text{ units}^2$$

4 a The curve cuts the x-axis when $y = 0$.
$\therefore \quad x^2 + x - 2 = 0$
$\therefore \quad (x+2)(x-1) = 0$
$\therefore \quad x = -2 \text{ or } 1$
$\therefore$ the x-intercepts are -2 and 1

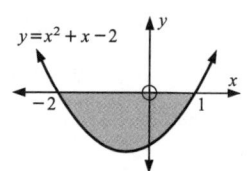

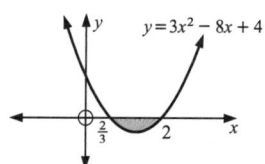

Area $= \int_{-2}^{1} [0 - (x^2 + x - 2)] \, dx$
$= \int_{-2}^{1} (-x^2 - x + 2) \, dx$
$= \left[-\dfrac{x^3}{3} - \dfrac{x^2}{2} + 2x \right]_{-2}^{1}$
$= (-\tfrac{1}{3} - \tfrac{1}{2} + 2) - (\tfrac{8}{3} - 2 - 4)$
$= 4\tfrac{1}{2}$ units^2

b The curve cuts the x-axis at $(0, 0)$.

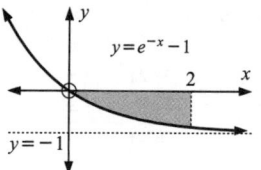

Area $= \int_0^2 [0 - (e^{-x} - 1)] \, dx$
$= \int_0^2 (1 - e^{-x}) \, dx$
$= \left[x + e^{-x} \right]_0^2$
$= \left(2 + \dfrac{1}{e^2} \right) - (0 + e^0)$
$= 1 + \dfrac{1}{e^2}$
≈ 1.14 units^2

c The curve cuts the x-axis when $y = 0$.
$\therefore \quad 3x^2 - 8x + 4 = 0$
$\therefore \quad (3x - 2)(x - 2) = 0$
$\therefore \quad x = 2 \text{ or } \tfrac{2}{3}$
$\therefore$ the x-intercepts are 2 and $\tfrac{2}{3}$.

Area $= \int_{\frac{2}{3}}^{2} [0 - (3x^2 - 8x + 4)] \, dx$
$= \int_{\frac{2}{3}}^{2} (-3x^2 + 8x - 4) \, dx$
$= \left[-x^3 + 4x^2 - 4x \right]_{\frac{2}{3}}^{2}$
$= (-8 + 16 - 8) - (-\tfrac{8}{27} + \tfrac{16}{9} - \tfrac{8}{3})$
$= 1\tfrac{5}{27}$ units^2

d The curve cuts the x-axis when $y = 0$.
$\therefore \quad x^3 - 4x = 0$
$\therefore \quad x(x^2 - 4) = 0$
$\therefore \quad x(x+2)(x-2) = 0$
$\therefore$ the x-intercepts are 0 and ± 2

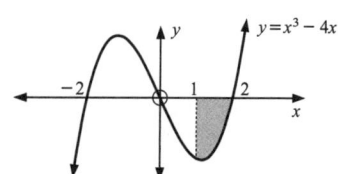

Area $= \int_1^2 [0 - y_L] \, dx$
$= \int_1^2 (-x^3 + 4x) \, dx$
$= \left[-\dfrac{x^4}{4} + 2x^2 \right]_1^2$
$= (-4 + 8) - (-\tfrac{1}{4} + 2)$
$= 2\tfrac{1}{4}$ units^2

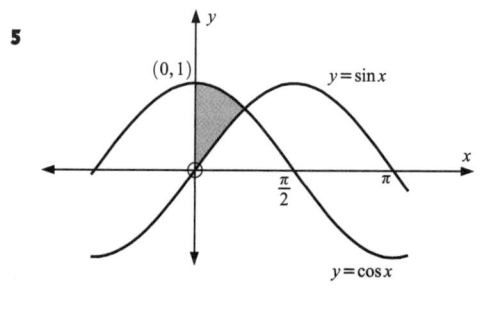

5 The curves $y = \cos x$ and $y = \sin x$ meet when $x = \dfrac{\pi}{4}$.
$\therefore \quad A = \int_0^{\frac{\pi}{4}} (\cos x - \sin x) \, dx$
$= \left[\sin x + \cos x \right]_0^{\frac{\pi}{4}}$
$= (\sin \tfrac{\pi}{4} + \cos \tfrac{\pi}{4}) - (\sin 0 + \cos 0)$
$= \left(\dfrac{1}{\sqrt{2}} + \dfrac{1}{\sqrt{2}} \right) - (0 + 1)$
$= (\sqrt{2} - 1)$ units^2

6 a $y = x^2 - 2x$ meets $y = 3$ when
$$x^2 - 2x = 3$$
$$\therefore \quad x^2 - 2x - 3 = 0$$
$$\therefore \quad (x-3)(x+1) = 0$$
$$\therefore \quad x = 3 \text{ or } -1$$

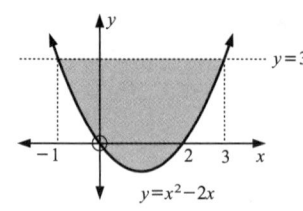

$A = \int_{-1}^{3} [3 - (x^2 - 2x)] \, dx$

$= \int_{-1}^{3} (3 + 2x - x^2) \, dx$

$= \left[3x + x^2 - \dfrac{x^3}{3} \right]_{-1}^{3}$

$= (9 + 9 - 9) - (-3 + 1 + \tfrac{1}{3})$

$= 10\tfrac{2}{3}$ units^2

b i

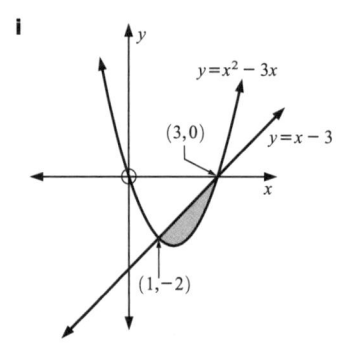

ii The graphs meet where $x - 3 = x^2 - 3x$
$\therefore \quad x^2 - 3x - x + 3 = 0$
$\therefore \quad x^2 - 4x + 3 = 0$
$\therefore \quad (x-1)(x-3) = 0$
$\therefore \quad x = 1$ or 3
$\therefore$ the graphs meet at $(1, -2)$ and $(3, 0)$

iii Area $= \int_{1}^{3} [(x - 3) - (x^2 - 3x)] \, dx$

$= \int_{1}^{3} (-3 + 4x - x^2) \, dx$

$= \left[-3x + 2x^2 - \dfrac{x^3}{3} \right]_{1}^{3}$

$= (-9 + 18 - 9) - (-3 + 2 - \tfrac{1}{3})$

$= 1\tfrac{1}{3}$ units^2

c $y = \sqrt{x}$ meets $y = x^2$ where
$$\sqrt{x} = x^2$$
$$\therefore \quad x = x^4$$
$$\therefore \quad x^4 - x = 0$$
$$\therefore \quad x(x^3 - 1) = 0$$
$$\therefore \quad x(x-1)(x^2 + x + 1) = 0$$
$$\therefore \quad x = 0 \text{ or } 1$$

The factor $(x^2 + x + 1)$ has no real root since $\Delta = -3$ which is < 0.

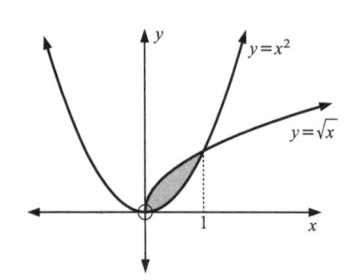

Area $= \int_{0}^{1} \left(\sqrt{x} - x^2 \right) dx$

$= \int_{0}^{1} (x^{\frac{1}{2}} - x^2) \, dx$

$= \left[\dfrac{2}{3} x^{\frac{3}{2}} - \dfrac{x^3}{3} \right]_{0}^{1}$

$= \tfrac{2}{3} - \tfrac{1}{3}$

$= \tfrac{1}{3}$ unit^2

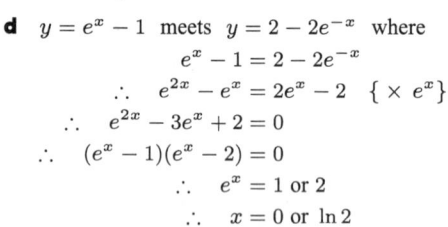

d $y = e^x - 1$ meets $y = 2 - 2e^{-x}$ where
$$e^x - 1 = 2 - 2e^{-x}$$
$$\therefore \quad e^{2x} - e^x = 2e^x - 2 \quad \{ \times e^x \}$$
$$\therefore \quad e^{2x} - 3e^x + 2 = 0$$
$$\therefore \quad (e^x - 1)(e^x - 2) = 0$$
$$\therefore \quad e^x = 1 \text{ or } 2$$
$$\therefore \quad x = 0 \text{ or } \ln 2$$
$\therefore$ the graphs meet at $(0, 0)$ and $(\ln 2, 1)$

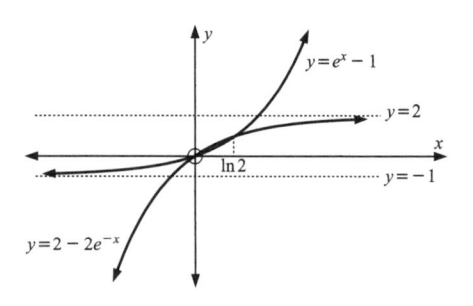

$A = \int_{0}^{\ln 2} [(2 - 2e^{-x}) - (e^x - 1)] \, dx$

$= \int_{0}^{\ln 2} (3 - e^x - 2e^{-x}) \, dx$

$= \left[3x - e^x + 2e^{-x} \right]_{0}^{\ln 2}$

$= (3 \ln 2 - 2 + 1) - (0 - 1 + 2)$

$= 3 \ln 2 - 2$

≈ 0.0794 units^2

e $y = 2e^x$ meets $y = e^{2x}$ where
$$2e^x = e^{2x}$$
$$\therefore \ e^{2x} - 2e^x = 0$$
$$\therefore \ e^x(e^x - 2) = 0$$
$$\therefore \ e^x = 2 \quad \{e^x > 0 \text{ for all } x\}$$
$$\therefore \ x = \ln 2$$

Area $= \int_0^{\ln 2}(2e^x - e^{2x})\,dx$

$= \left[2e^x - \tfrac{1}{2}e^{2x}\right]_0^{\ln 2}$

$= (4 - 2) - (2 - \tfrac{1}{2})$

$= \tfrac{1}{2}$ unit^2

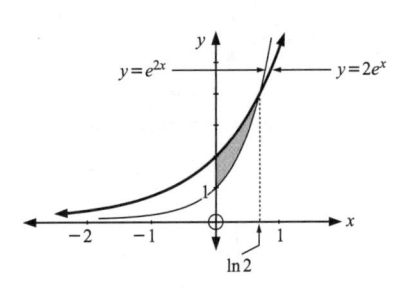

7 $y = 2x$ meets $y^2 = 4x$ where
$$(2x)^2 = 4x$$
$$\therefore \ 4x^2 = 4x$$
$$\therefore \ 4x^2 - 4x = 0$$
$$\therefore \ 4x(x-1) = 0$$
$$\therefore \ x = 0 \text{ or } 1$$

The upper part of $y^2 = 4x$
is $y = \sqrt{4x}$
or $y = 2\sqrt{x}$

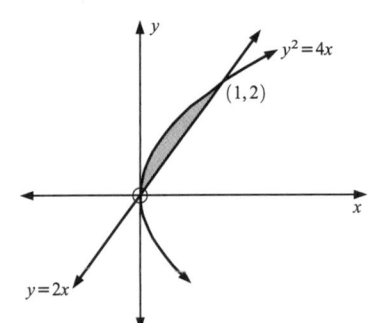

Area
$= \int_0^1 (2\sqrt{x} - 2x)\,dx$
$= \int_0^1 (2x^{\frac{1}{2}} - 2x)\,dx$
$= \left[\tfrac{4}{3}x^{\frac{3}{2}} - x^2\right]_0^1$
$= \tfrac{4}{3} - 1$
$= \tfrac{1}{3}$ unit^2

8 a Point A has y-coordinate 1 and lies on the graph of $y = \tan x$ on the interval $[0, \tfrac{\pi}{2}[$.
At this point, $\tan x = 1 \quad \therefore \ x = \tfrac{\pi}{4} \quad \therefore$ A is at $(\tfrac{\pi}{4}, 1)$.

b Consider $\tan x = \dfrac{\sin x}{\cos x} \qquad \therefore$ area $= \int_0^{\frac{\pi}{4}} \tan x \, dx$

Let $u = \cos x$, $\dfrac{du}{dx} = -\sin x$

When $x = 0$, $u = \cos 0 = 1$

When $x = \tfrac{\pi}{4}$, $u = \cos \tfrac{\pi}{4} = \tfrac{1}{\sqrt{2}}$

$= -\int_0^{\frac{\pi}{4}} \dfrac{-\sin x}{\cos x}\,dx$

$= -\int_0^{\frac{\pi}{4}} \dfrac{1}{u}\dfrac{du}{dx}\,dx$

$= -\int_1^{\frac{1}{\sqrt{2}}} \dfrac{1}{u}\,du$

$= \int_{\frac{1}{\sqrt{2}}}^1 \dfrac{1}{u}\,du$

$= [\ln|u|]_{\frac{1}{\sqrt{2}}}^1$

$= \ln 1 - \ln \tfrac{1}{\sqrt{2}}$

$= \ln \sqrt{2}$

$= \tfrac{1}{2}\ln 2$ units^2

9 a Now $x^2 + y^2 = 9 \quad \therefore \ y^2 = 9 - x^2$
$$\therefore \ y = \pm\sqrt{9 - x^2}$$

In the upper half of the circle all y-values are $\geqslant 0$

$\therefore \ y = +\sqrt{9 - x^2}$ is the required equation.

b The shaded area is A where $A = \int_0^3 \sqrt{9 - x^2}\,dx$
This is a quarter of the area of a circle with radius 3 units.

$\therefore \ A = \tfrac{1}{4}(\pi \times 3^2) = \tfrac{9}{4}\pi \approx 7.07$ units^2

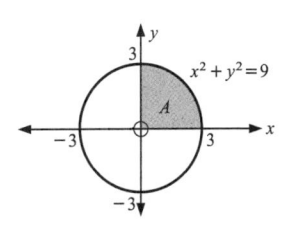

10 a $f(x) = x^3 - 9x$
$= x(x^2 - 9)$
$= x(x+3)(x-3)$
$\therefore\ y = f(x)$ cuts the x-axis at $0, \pm 3$

Area $= \int_{-3}^{0}(x^3 - 9x)\,dx + \int_{0}^{3}[0 - (x^3 - 9x)]\,dx$

$= \left[\dfrac{x^4}{4} - \dfrac{9x^2}{2}\right]_{-3}^{0} + \left[-\dfrac{x^4}{4} + \dfrac{9x^2}{2}\right]_{0}^{3}$

$= (0 - [\tfrac{81}{4} - \tfrac{81}{2}]) + ([-\tfrac{81}{4} + \tfrac{81}{2}] - 0)$

$= 40\tfrac{1}{2}$ units^2

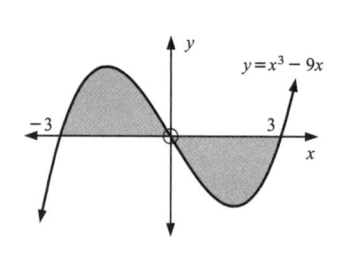

b $f(x) = -x(x-2)(x-4)$
$= -x^3 + 6x^2 - 8x$
$\therefore\ y = f(x)$ cuts the x-axis at $0, 2$ and 4

Area $= \int_{0}^{2}[0 - (-x^3 + 6x^2 - 8x)]\,dx$
$\qquad + \int_{2}^{4}(-x^3 + 6x^2 - 8x)\,dx$

$= \int_{0}^{2}(x^3 - 6x^2 + 8x)\,dx + \int_{2}^{4}(-x^3 + 6x^2 - 8x)\,dx$

$= \left[\dfrac{x^4}{4} - 2x^3 + 4x^2\right]_{0}^{2} + \left[-\dfrac{x^4}{4} + 2x^3 - 4x^2\right]_{2}^{4}$

$= ([4 - 16 + 16] - 0) + ([-64 + 128 - 64] - [-4 + 16 - 16])$

$= 8$ units^2

c $f(x) = x^4 - 5x^2 + 4$
$= (x^2 - 1)(x^2 - 4)$
$= (x+1)(x-1)(x+2)(x-2)$
$\therefore\ y = f(x)$ cuts the x-axis at $\pm 1, \pm 2$

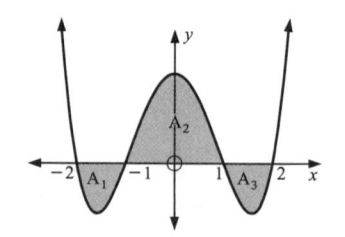

$A_1 = \int_{-2}^{-1}[0 - (x^4 - 5x^2 + 4)]\,dx$

$= \int_{-2}^{-1}(-x^4 + 5x^2 - 4)\,dx$

$= \left[-\dfrac{x^5}{5} + \dfrac{5x^3}{3} - 4x\right]_{-2}^{-1}$

$= (\tfrac{1}{5} - \tfrac{5}{3} + 4) - (\tfrac{32}{5} - \tfrac{40}{3} + 8)$

$= \tfrac{22}{15}$ units^2

$A_2 = \int_{-1}^{1}(x^4 - 5x^2 + 4)\,dx$

$= \left[\dfrac{x^5}{5} - \dfrac{5x^3}{3} + 4x\right]_{-1}^{1}$

$= (\tfrac{1}{5} - \tfrac{5}{3} + 4) - (-\tfrac{1}{5} + \tfrac{5}{3} - 4)$

$= \tfrac{76}{15}$ units^2

By symmetry, $A_3 = A_1$ $\quad\therefore\ A = \tfrac{22}{15} + \tfrac{76}{15} + \tfrac{22}{15} = \tfrac{120}{15} = 8$ units^2

11 a $y = \sin(2x)$ is the curve C_1
$y = \sin x$ is the curve C_2

b The curves meet when $\sin(2x) = \sin x$
$\therefore\ 2\sin x \cos x - \sin x = 0$
$\therefore\ \sin x(2\cos x - 1) = 0$
$\therefore\ \sin x = 0$ or $\cos x = \tfrac{1}{2}$
$\therefore\ x$-coordinate of A $= \tfrac{\pi}{3}$
$\therefore\ $A is at $(\tfrac{\pi}{3}, \tfrac{\sqrt{3}}{2})$

c Area $= \int_0^{\frac{\pi}{3}} (\sin(2x) - \sin x)\, dx + \int_{\frac{\pi}{3}}^{\pi} (\sin x - \sin(2x))\, dx$

$= \left[-\frac{1}{2}\cos(2x) + \cos x\right]_0^{\frac{\pi}{3}} + \left[-\cos x + \frac{1}{2}\cos(2x)\right]_{\frac{\pi}{3}}^{\pi}$

$= \left(-\frac{1}{2}\cos\frac{2\pi}{3} + \cos\frac{\pi}{3}\right) - \left(-\frac{1}{2}\cos 0 + \cos 0\right) + \left(-\cos\pi + \frac{1}{2}\cos 2\pi\right)$
$\quad - \left(-\cos\frac{\pi}{3} + \frac{1}{2}\cos\frac{2\pi}{3}\right)$

$= (\frac{1}{4} + \frac{1}{2}) - (-\frac{1}{2} + 1) + (1 + \frac{1}{2}) - (-\frac{1}{2} - \frac{1}{4})$

$= 2\frac{1}{2}$ units^2

12 a i The graphs meet where $\quad x^3 - 4x = 3x + 6$
$\therefore \quad x^3 - 7x - 6 = 0$
$\therefore \quad (x+2)(x^2 - 2x - 3) = 0 \quad$ {diagram shows intersection at -2}
$\therefore \quad (x+2)(x+1)(x-3) = 0$
$\therefore \quad x = -2, -1 \text{ or } 3$

$\therefore \quad$ area $= \int_{-2}^{-1} ([x^3 - 4x] - [3x + 6])\, dx + \int_{-1}^{3} ([3x + 6] - [x^3 - 4x])\, dx$

$= \int_{-2}^{-1} (x^3 - 7x - 6)\, dx + \int_{-1}^{3} (-x^3 + 7x + 6)\, dx$

ii Area $= \int_{-2}^{3} |x^3 - 7x - 6|\, dx$

b Using technology, area $= 32\frac{3}{4}$ units^2

13 a The graphs meet where $\quad x^3 - 5x = 2x^2 - 6$
$\therefore \quad x^3 - 2x^2 - 5x + 6 = 0$
$\therefore \quad (x-1)(x^2 - x - 6) = 0$
$\therefore \quad (x-1)(x-3)(x+2) = 0$
$\therefore \quad x = -2, 1 \text{ or } 3$

So, area $= \int_{-2}^{3} |x^3 - 2x^2 - 5x + 6|\, dx = 21\frac{1}{12}$ units^2 {technology}

b The graphs meet where $\quad -x^3 + 3x^2 + 6x - 8 = 5x - 5$
$\therefore \quad x^3 - 3x^2 - x + 3 = 0$
$\therefore \quad (x-1)(x^2 - 2x - 3) = 0$
$\therefore \quad (x-1)(x-3)(x+1) = 0$
$\therefore \quad x = -1, 1 \text{ or } 3$

So, area $= \int_{-1}^{3} |x^3 - 3x^2 - x + 3|\, dx = 8$ units^2 {technology}

c The graphs meet where $\quad 2x^3 - 3x^2 + 18 = x^3 + 10x - 6$
$\therefore \quad x^3 - 3x^2 - 10x + 24 = 0$
$\therefore \quad (x-2)(x^2 - x - 12) = 0$
$\therefore \quad (x-2)(x-4)(x+3) = 0$
$\therefore \quad x = -3, 2 \text{ or } 4$

So, area $= \int_{-3}^{4} |x^3 - 3x^2 - 10x + 24|\, dx = 101\frac{3}{4}$ units^2 {technology}

14

a $\int_1^7 f(x)\, dx\quad$ only gives us the correct area provided that $f(x)$ is positive on the interval $1 \leqslant x \leqslant 7$. But $f(x)$ is not positive for $3 \leqslant x \leqslant 5$, so $\int_1^7 f(x)\, dx = A_1 - A_2 + A_3$ which is *not* the shaded area.

b shaded area $= \int_1^3 f(x)\, dx + \int_3^5 [0 - f(x)]\, dx + \int_5^7 f(x)\, dx$

$= \int_1^3 f(x)\, dx - \int_3^5 f(x)\, dx + \int_5^7 f(x)\, dx$

15 a $y = \cos(2x)$ is the curve C_2 and $y = \cos^2 x$ is the curve C_1

b Point A lies on $y = \cos(2x)$. When $x = 0$, $y = \cos 0 = 1$. $\therefore$ A is at $(0, 1)$.
Point B lies on $y = \cos(2x)$. When $x = \frac{\pi}{4}$, $y = \cos \frac{\pi}{2} = 0$. $\therefore$ B is at $(\frac{\pi}{4}, 0)$.
Point C lies on $y = \cos^2 x$. When $x = \frac{\pi}{2}$, $y = \cos^2 \frac{\pi}{2} = 0$. $\therefore$ C is at $(\frac{\pi}{2}, 0)$.
Point D lies on $y = \cos(2x)$. When $x = \frac{3\pi}{4}$, $y = \cos \frac{3\pi}{2} = 0$. $\therefore$ D is at $(\frac{3\pi}{4}, 0)$.
Point E lies where the curves meet. Now $\cos(2\pi) = \cos^2 \pi = 1$. $\therefore$ E is at $(\pi, 1)$.

c $A = \int_0^\pi (\cos^2 x - \cos(2x))\, dx$

$= \int_0^\pi \left(\frac{1}{2} + \frac{1}{2}\cos(2x) - \cos(2x)\right) dx$

$= \int_0^\pi \left(\frac{1}{2} - \frac{1}{2}\cos(2x)\right) dx$

$= \left[\frac{x}{2} - \frac{1}{4}\sin(2x)\right]_0^\pi = \left(\frac{\pi}{2} - 0\right) - (0 - 0) = \frac{\pi}{2}$ units^2

16 a The graphs meet when $e^{-x^2} = x^2 - 1$
$\therefore x = \pm 1.1307$ {technology}

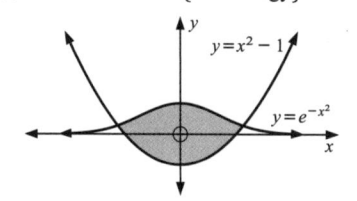

$\therefore$ area $= \int_{-1.1307}^{1.1307} [e^{-x^2} - (x^2 - 1)]\, dx$

≈ 2.88 units^2 {technology}

b The graphs meet when $x^x = 4x - \frac{1}{10}x^4$
$\therefore x \approx 0.1832$ or 2.2696 {technology}

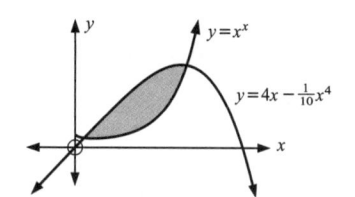

$\therefore$ area $= \int_{0.1832}^{2.2696} (4x - \frac{1}{10}x^4 - x^x)\, dx$

≈ 4.97 units^2 {technology}

17 Area $= \int_1^k \frac{1}{1+2x}\, dx = 0.2$ units^2

$\therefore \left[\frac{1}{2}\ln|1+2x|\right]_1^k = 0.2$

$\therefore [\ln|1+2x|]_1^k = 0.4$

$\therefore \ln|1+2k| - \ln 3 = 0.4$

$\therefore \ln(1+2k) - \ln 3 = 0.4$ {since $k > 0$}

$\therefore \ln\left(\frac{1+2k}{3}\right) = 0.4$

$\therefore \frac{1+2k}{3} = e^{0.4}$

$\therefore 1 + 2k = 3e^{0.4}$

$\therefore k = \frac{3e^{0.4} - 1}{2} \approx 1.7377$

18 Area $= \int_0^b \sqrt{x}\, dx$

$\therefore \int_0^b x^{\frac{1}{2}}\, dx = 1$

$\therefore \left[\frac{2}{3}x^{\frac{3}{2}}\right]_0^b = 1$

$\therefore \frac{2}{3}b\sqrt{b} - 0 = 1$

$\therefore b\sqrt{b} = \frac{3}{2}$

$\therefore b^{\frac{3}{2}} = 1.5$

$\therefore b = (1.5)^{\frac{2}{3}} \approx 1.3104$

19 $y = x^2$ meets $y = k$ where $x^2 = k$

$\therefore x = \pm\sqrt{k}$

Now, the area $= \int_0^{\sqrt{k}} (k - x^2)\, dx$

$\therefore \int_0^{\sqrt{k}} (k - x^2)\, dx = 2.4$

$\therefore \left[kx - \frac{x^3}{3}\right]_0^{\sqrt{k}} = 2.4$

$\therefore k\sqrt{k} - \frac{k\sqrt{k}}{3} - 0 = 2.4$

$\therefore \frac{2k\sqrt{k}}{3} = 2.4$

$\therefore k^{\frac{3}{2}} = 3.6$

$\therefore k = (3.6)^{\frac{2}{3}} \approx 2.3489$

20 By symmetry, the area bounded by $x = 0$ and $x = a$ is $\frac{1}{2}(6a)$ units^2.

$\therefore \int_0^a (x^2 + 2)\, dx = 3a$

$\therefore \left[\dfrac{x^3}{3} + 2x\right]_0^a = 3a$

$\therefore \dfrac{a^3}{3} + 2a - 0 = 3a$

$\therefore a^3 + 6a = 9a$

$\therefore a^3 - 3a = 0$

$\therefore a(a^2 - 3) = 0$

$\therefore a = 0$ or $\pm\sqrt{3}$ $\therefore a = \sqrt{3}$ {as $a > 0$}

EXERCISE 25B.1

1

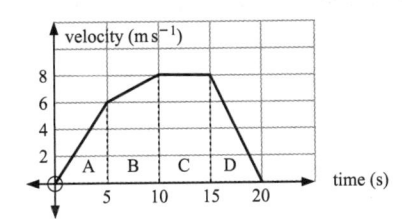

Total distance travelled
= area A + area B + area C + area D
$= \frac{1}{2}(5 \times 6) + \left(\dfrac{6+8}{2}\right)5 + 5 \times 8 + \frac{1}{2}(5 \times 8)$
$= 15 + 35 + 40 + 20$
$= 110$ m

2

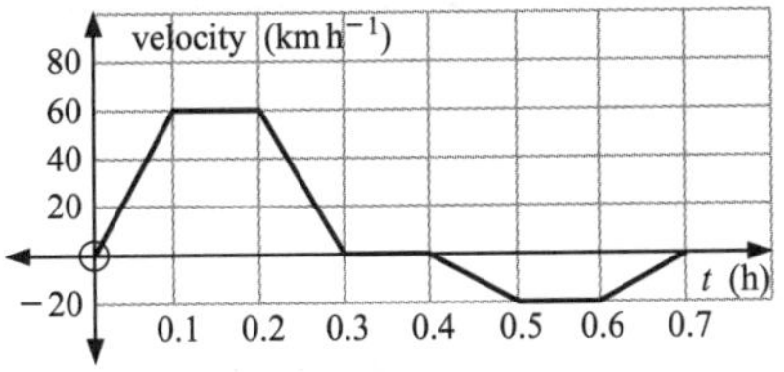

a **i** The graph above the t-axis indicates that the velocity is positive and the car is travelling forwards.

ii The graph below the t-axis indicates that the velocity is negative and the car is travelling backwards.

b Total distance travelled = area above the t-axis + area below the t-axis
$= \left(\dfrac{0.1}{2} + 0.1 + \dfrac{0.1}{2}\right) 60 + \left(\dfrac{0.1}{2} + 0.1 + \dfrac{0.1}{2}\right) 20$
$= 12 + 4$
$= 16$ km

c Final displacement = area above the t-axis − area below the t-axis
$= 12 - 4$
$= 8$ km from the starting point in the positive direction

3

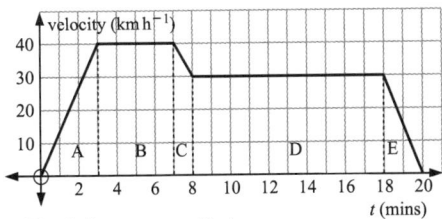

Total distance travelled
= area A + area B + area C + area D + area E
$= \dfrac{1}{60}\left[\frac{1}{2}(3 \times 40) + (40 \times 4) + \left(\dfrac{40+30}{2}\right)1 + (10 \times 30) + \frac{1}{2}(2 \times 30)\right]$
$= \dfrac{1}{60}[60 + 160 + 35 + 300 + 30]$
$= 9.75$ km

{the factor $\frac{1}{60}$ accounts for the fact that the times are in minutes while the speeds are in km h^{-1}}

EXERCISE 25B.2

1 a $v(t) = 1 - 2t$ cm s^{-1}, $t \geqslant 0$
$v(t) = s'(t) = 1 - 2t$ which has sign diagram: 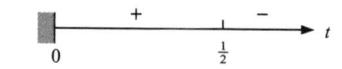
$\therefore$ a direction reversal occurs at $t = \frac{1}{2}$.

Now $s(t) = \int (1 - 2t)\, dt = t - \dfrac{2t^2}{2} + c = t - t^2 + c$

$\therefore$ $s(0) = c$ $\therefore$ motion diagram is:
and $s(\frac{1}{2}) = \frac{1}{4} + c$
and $s(1) = c$

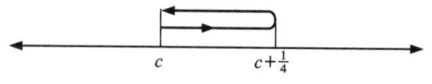

$\therefore$ total distance travelled $= (c + \frac{1}{4} - c) + (c + \frac{1}{4} - c)$
$= \frac{1}{2}$ cm

b Displacement   **or**   **a** total distance travelled   **b** displacement
$= s(1) - s(0)$ $= \int_0^1 |1 - 2t|\, dt$ $= \int_0^1 (1 - 2t)\, dt$
$= c - c$ $= 0.5$ cm $= \left[t - t^2\right]_0^1$
$= 0$ cm $= 0 - 0$
                                                                                  $= 0$ cm

2 a $v(t) = t^2 - t - 2$ cm s^{-1}, $t \geqslant 0$
$v(t) = s'(t) = t^2 - t - 2$ which has
$= (t - 2)(t + 1)$ sign diagram: 
$\therefore$ a direction reversal occurs at $t = 2$.

Now $s(t) = \int (t^2 - t - 2)\, dt = \dfrac{t^3}{3} - \dfrac{t^2}{2} - 2t + c$

$s(0) = c$
$s(2) = c - \frac{10}{3}$ $\therefore$ motion diagram is:
$s(3) = c - \frac{3}{2}$

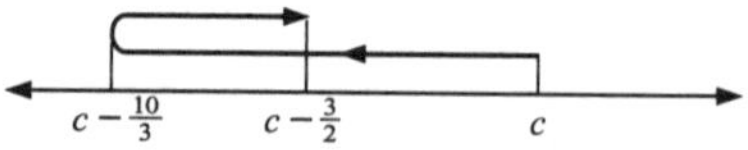

$\therefore$ total distance travelled $= \left(c - [c - \frac{10}{3}]\right) + \left(c - \frac{3}{2} - [c - \frac{10}{3}]\right)$
$= \frac{10}{3} - \frac{3}{2} + \frac{10}{3}$
$= \frac{31}{6}$
$= 5\frac{1}{6}$ cm

b Displacement $= s(3) - s(0)$ **or**   **a** total distance travelled   **b** displacement
$= c - \frac{3}{2} - c$ $= \int_0^3 |t^2 - t - 2|\, dt$ $= \int_0^3 (t^2 - t - 2)\, dt$
$= -\frac{3}{2}$ cm ≈ 5.17 cm $= -1.5$ cm

3 $x'(t) = 16t - 4t^3$ units s^{-1}, $t \geqslant 0$
$= 4t(4 - t^2)$
$= 4t(2 + t)(2 - t)$ which has sign diagram: 
$\therefore$ a direction reversal occurs at $t = 2$.
Now $x(t) = \int (16t - 4t^3)\, dt = 8t^2 - t^4 + c$

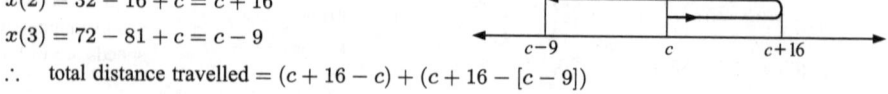

a $x(0) = c$ $\therefore$ motion diagram for $0 \leqslant t \leqslant 3$ is:
$x(2) = 32 - 16 + c = c + 16$
$x(3) = 72 - 81 + c = c - 9$
$\therefore$ total distance travelled $= (c + 16 - c) + (c + 16 - [c - 9])$
$= 41$ units

b $x(1) = 7 + c = c + 7$ $\therefore$ motion diagram for $1 \leqslant t \leqslant 3$ is:

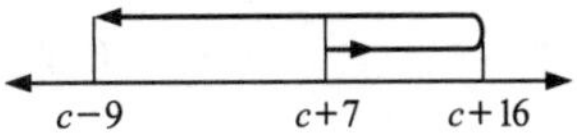

$\therefore$ total distance travelled $= (c + 16 - [c + 7]) + (c + 16 - [c - 9])$
$= 34$ units

or **a**   total distance travelled   **b**   total distance travelled
$= \int_0^3 |16t - 4t^3| \, dt$ $= \int_1^3 |16t - 4t^3| \, dt$
$= 41$ units $= 34$ units

4   **a** $v(t) = \cos t \text{ m s}^{-1}, \ t \geqslant 0$
$\therefore v(t)$ has sign diagram:

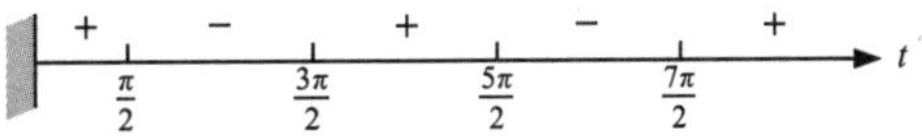

$\therefore$ a direction reversal occurs at $t = \frac{\pi}{2}, \frac{3\pi}{2}, \frac{5\pi}{2}, \frac{7\pi}{2}, \ldots$

$s(t) = \int \cos t \, dt = \sin t + c$

$\therefore \quad s(0) = c$
$s\left(\frac{\pi}{2}\right) = c + 1$
$s\left(\frac{3\pi}{2}\right) = c - 1$
$s\left(\frac{5\pi}{2}\right) = c + 1$
$s\left(\frac{7\pi}{2}\right) = c - 1$

The motion diagram is:

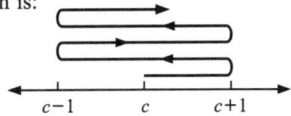

$\therefore$ the particle oscillates between the points $(c - 1)$ and $(c + 1)$.

b   distance $= (c + 1) - (c - 1)$
$= 2$ units

EXERCISE 25B.3

1 $v(t) = 50 - 10e^{-0.5t} \text{ m s}^{-1}, \ t \geqslant 0$

a $v(0) = 50 - \dfrac{10}{e^0} = 50 - 10 = 40 \text{ m s}^{-1}$ **b** $v(3) = 50 - \dfrac{10}{e^{1.5}} \approx 47.8 \text{ m s}^{-1}$

c   The velocity reaches 45 m s^{-1} **d** $v(t) = 50 - \dfrac{10}{e^{\frac{t}{2}}}$
when $45 = 50 - 10e^{-0.5t}$
$\therefore \quad 10e^{-\frac{t}{2}} = 5$ As $t \to \infty$, $\dfrac{10}{e^{\frac{t}{2}}} \to 0^+$
$\therefore \quad e^{\frac{t}{2}} = 2$ $\therefore \quad v(t) \to 50 \text{ m s}^{-1}$ (below)
$\therefore \quad \dfrac{t}{2} = \ln 2$
$\therefore \quad t = 2 \ln 2 \approx 1.39$ s

e $a(t) = v'(t)$ **f**
$= -10e^{-0.5t}(-0.5)$
$= 5e^{-0.5t} \text{ m s}^{-2}$
$= \dfrac{5}{e^{0.5t}} \text{ m s}^{-2}$

$\therefore \quad a(t) > 0$ for all t $\{e^x > 0$ for all $x\}$
$\therefore$ the acceleration is always positive

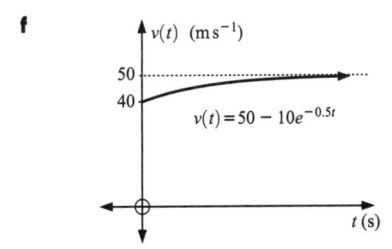

g   total distance travelled $= \int_0^3 (50 - 10e^{-0.5t}) \, dt$
$= \left[50t + 20e^{-0.5t}\right]_0^3$
$= 150 + 20e^{-1.5} - 20$
≈ 134 m

2 $a(t) = \dfrac{t}{10} - 3 \text{ ms}^{-2}$

$\therefore\ v(t) = \displaystyle\int \left(\dfrac{t}{10} - 3\right) dt$

$= \dfrac{t^2}{20} - 3t + c$

But $v(0) = 45$ $\therefore\ c = 45$

Now $v(t) = \dfrac{t^2}{20} - 3t + 45$

$= \dfrac{t^2 - 60t + 900}{20}$

$= \dfrac{(t-30)^2}{20}$

The total distance travelled in the first minute

$= \displaystyle\int_0^{60} \left|\dfrac{(t-30)^2}{20}\right| dt$

$= \dfrac{1}{20}\displaystyle\int_0^{60} |(t-30)^2|\ dt$

$= \dfrac{1}{20}\displaystyle\int_0^{60} (t-30)^2\ dt$ $\quad$ {as $(t-30)^2 \geqslant 0$}

$= \dfrac{1}{20}\left[\dfrac{(t-30)^3}{3}\right]_0^{60}$

$= \dfrac{1}{60}\left((30)^3 - (-30)^3\right)$

$= \dfrac{1}{60}(30^3 + 30^3)$

$= 900$ m

3 $a(t) = 4e^{-\frac{t}{20}} \text{ ms}^{-2}$

$\therefore\ v(t) = \displaystyle\int 4e^{-\frac{t}{20}}\ dt$

$= 4 \cdot \dfrac{1}{-\frac{1}{20}} e^{-\frac{t}{20}} + c$

$= -80e^{-\frac{t}{20}} + c$

Now $v(0) = 20 \text{ ms}^{-1}$

$\therefore\ c = 100$

$\therefore\ v(t) = 100 - 80e^{-\frac{t}{20}}$

a As $t \to \infty$, $e^{-\frac{t}{20}} \to 0$ (above) $\quad \therefore\ v(t) \to 100$ (below)

$\therefore$ the body approaches a limiting velocity of 100 ms^{-1}

b The total distance travelled $= \displaystyle\int_0^{10} (100 - 80e^{-\frac{t}{20}})\ dt$ $\quad$ {$v(t) > 0$ for $0 \leqslant t \leqslant 10$}

$= [100t + 1600e^{-\frac{t}{20}}]_0^{10}$

$= 1000 + 1600e^{-\frac{1}{2}} - 1600$

≈ 370 m

EXERCISE 25C

1 The marginal cost is $C'(x)$ and $C'(x) = 3.15 + 0.004x$ € per gadget

$\therefore\ C(x) = \displaystyle\int (3.15 + 0.004x)\ dx$

$= 3.15x + 0.002x^2 + c$

But $C(0) = 450$ so $c = 450$

$\therefore\ C(x) = 3.15x + 0.002x^2 + 450$ euros

$\therefore\ C(800) = 3.15(800) + 0.002(800)^2 + 450$

$= €4250$

So, the total cost is €4250.

2 **a** The marginal profit is $P'(x)$ and $P'(x) = 15 - 0.03x$ dollars per plate

$\therefore\ P(x) = \displaystyle\int (15 - 0.03x)\ dx$

$= 15x - 0.015x^2 + c$

But $P(0) = -650$ so $c = -650$

$\therefore\ P(x) = 15x - 0.015x^2 - 650$ dollars

b The maximum profit occurs when $P'(x) = 0$, which is when $15 - 0.03x = 0$

$\therefore\ 0.03x = 15$

$\therefore\ x = \dfrac{15}{0.03}$

$\therefore\ x = 500$

Now $P''(x) = -0.03 < 0$ ∴ the profit is at a maximum when $x = 500$.
The maximum profit $= P(500) = 15(500) - 0.015(500)^2 - 650$
$= \$3100$

c In order for a profit to be made, $P(x)$ must be greater than 0
∴ $15x - 0.015x^2 - 650 > 0$
Using technology, the x-intercepts of $P(x)$ are $x_1 = 45.39$ and $x_2 = 954.6$
Since we cannot produce part plates, a profit is made for $46 \leqslant x \leqslant 954$.

3 $E'(t) = 350(80 + 0.15t)^{0.8} - 120(80 + 0.15t)$ calories per day

Total energy needs over the first week $= \int_0^7 E'(t)\,dt$

$= \int_0^7 [350(80 + 0.15t)^{0.8} - 120(80 + 0.15t)]\,dt$

$= \left[\frac{1}{0.15} \times \frac{350(80 + 0.15t)^{1.8}}{1.8} - 9600t - 9t^2 \right]_0^7$

$\approx 14\,400$ calories

4 $\dfrac{dT}{dx} = \dfrac{-20}{x^{0.63}} = -20x^{-0.63}$ ∴ $T = \int -20x^{-0.63}\,dx$

$= \dfrac{-20x^{0.37}}{0.37} + c$

Now when $x = 3$, $T = 100$

∴ $\dfrac{-20(3^{0.37})}{0.37} + c = 100$

∴ $c = 100 + \dfrac{20(3^{0.37})}{0.37} \approx 181.1639$

∴ $T \approx \dfrac{-20x^{0.37}}{0.37} + 181.1639$

So, when $x = 6$, $T \approx -104.8925 + 181.1639 \approx 76.27$

∴ the outer surface temperature is about $76.3°C$

5 a $\dfrac{d^2y}{dx^2} = -\tfrac{1}{10}(1-x)^2$

∴ $\dfrac{dy}{dx} = \int -\tfrac{1}{10}(1-x)^2\,dx$

$= -\tfrac{1}{10}(\tfrac{1}{-1}) \times \dfrac{(1-x)^3}{3} + c$

$= \tfrac{1}{30}(1-x)^3 + c$

But when $x = 0$, the tangent is horizontal

∴ when $x = 0$, $\dfrac{dy}{dx} = 0$

∴ $\tfrac{1}{30}(1-0)^3 + c = 0$

∴ $c = -\tfrac{1}{30}$

∴ $\dfrac{dy}{dx} = \tfrac{1}{30}(1-x)^3 - \tfrac{1}{30}$

∴ $y = \int [\tfrac{1}{30}(1-x)^3 - \tfrac{1}{30}]\,dx$

$= \tfrac{1}{30}(\tfrac{1}{-1})\dfrac{(1-x)^4}{4} - \tfrac{1}{30}x + d$

$= -\dfrac{(1-x)^4}{120} - \dfrac{x}{30} + d$

Also, when $x = 0$, $y = 0$

∴ $-\tfrac{1}{120} - 0 + d = 0$

∴ $d = \tfrac{1}{120}$

∴ $y = \dfrac{1}{120} - \dfrac{(1-x)^4}{120} - \dfrac{x}{30}$

b Maximum deflection occurs at the right hand end where $x \approx 1$
and at $x \approx 1$, $y \approx \tfrac{1}{120} - 0 - \tfrac{1}{30} \approx -0.025$ m
∴ the maximum deflection is about 2.5 cm.

6 a $\dfrac{d^2y}{dx^2} = \dfrac{1}{100}\left(2x - \dfrac{x^2}{2}\right) = \dfrac{1}{50}x - \dfrac{1}{200}x^2$

$\therefore \quad \dfrac{dy}{dx} = \int (\dfrac{1}{50}x - \dfrac{1}{200}x^2)\,dx = \dfrac{1}{100}x^2 - \dfrac{1}{600}x^3 + c$

The sag, $y = \int (\dfrac{1}{100}x^2 - \dfrac{1}{600}x^3 + c)\,dx$

$\therefore \quad y = \dfrac{1}{300}x^3 - \dfrac{1}{2400}x^4 + cx + d$

Now when $x = 0$, $y = 0$ $\therefore$ $0 - 0 + 0 + d = 0$

$\therefore \quad d = 0$

$\therefore \quad y = \dfrac{1}{300}x^3 - \dfrac{1}{2400}x^4 + cx$

Also, when $x = 4$, $y = 0$ $\therefore$ $\dfrac{1}{300}(4^3) - \dfrac{1}{2400}(4^4) + 4c = 0$

$\therefore \quad 4c = \dfrac{1}{2400}(4^4) - \dfrac{1}{300}(4^3)$

$\therefore \quad c = \dfrac{1}{2400}(4^3) - \dfrac{1}{300}(4^2)$

$\therefore \quad c = -\dfrac{2}{75}$

$\therefore \quad y = \left(\dfrac{1}{300}x^3 - \dfrac{1}{2400}x^4 - \dfrac{2}{75}x\right)$ m

b The maximum sag occurs when $\dfrac{dy}{dx} = 0$ $\therefore$ $\dfrac{1}{100}x^2 - \dfrac{1}{600}x^3 - \dfrac{2}{75} = 0$

$\therefore \quad 6x^2 - x^3 - 16 = 0$

Using technology, the three solutions are $x = -1.464$, 2 and 5.464
But the maximum lies between 0 and 4, so it must occur when $x = 2$.

When $x = 2$, $y = \dfrac{1}{300}(2^3) - \dfrac{1}{2400}(2^4) - \dfrac{2}{75}(2)$

$\approx -0.033\,33$ m

≈ -3.333 cm $\therefore$ the maximum sag is ≈ 3.33 cm

c At the point 1 m from P, $x = 3$ m, so $y = \dfrac{1}{300}(3^3) - \dfrac{1}{2400}(3^4) - \dfrac{2}{75}(3)$

$= -0.023\,75$ m

$= -2.375$ cm $\therefore$ the sag is 2.375 cm

d At the point 1 m from P, $x = 3$ m, so $\dfrac{dy}{dx} = \dfrac{1}{100}(3^2) - \dfrac{1}{600}(3^3) - \dfrac{2}{75} \approx 0.0183$

$\therefore$ the angle θ that the plank makes with the horizontal is such that $\tan\theta \approx 0.0183$
$\therefore$ $\theta \approx \tan^{-1}(0.0183) \approx 1.05°$

7 The cost per unit volume, $\dfrac{dC}{dV} = \dfrac{1}{2}x^2 + 4$ dollars per m³ (at depth x).

Since the volume of a well x m deep is $V = \pi r^2 x$, $\dfrac{dV}{dx} = \pi r^2$

Now $\dfrac{dC}{dx} = \dfrac{dC}{dV}\dfrac{dV}{dx}$ {chain rule}

$\therefore \quad \dfrac{dC}{dx} = \left(\dfrac{1}{2}x^2 + 4\right)\pi r^2$

$\therefore \quad C = \displaystyle\int \dfrac{dC}{dx}\,dx$

$= \int [\pi r^2(\tfrac{1}{2}x^2 + 4)]\,dx$

$= \pi r^2\left(\dfrac{x^3}{6} + 4x\right) + c$

So, the cost of digging a well h metres deep

$= \pi r^2\left(\dfrac{h^3}{6} + 4h\right) + c$

Now if the initial cost $= C_0$ when $h = 0$,
$\pi r^2(\tfrac{0}{6} + 0) + c = C_0$

$\therefore \quad c = C_0$

$\therefore \quad C(h) = \pi r^2\left(\dfrac{h^3 + 24h}{6}\right) + C_0$

8 $y = \sin x$, $0 \leqslant x \leqslant \pi$

$\therefore \quad \dfrac{dy}{dx} = \cos x$

$\therefore \quad L = \int_0^\pi \sqrt{1 + \cos^2 x} \, dx \approx 3.820 \, 20$ units {technology}

9 **a** The yield Y per unit area A is proportional to $\dfrac{1}{\sqrt{x+4}}$.

$\therefore \quad \dfrac{dY}{dA} \propto \dfrac{1}{\sqrt{x+4}}$

$\therefore \quad \dfrac{dY}{dA} = \dfrac{k}{\sqrt{x+4}}$ for some constant k.

b The shaded area $A = \text{length} \times \text{width}$

$\therefore \quad A = (4 - 2p)x$

$\therefore \quad \dfrac{dA}{dx} = 4 - 2p$

Now $\dfrac{dY}{dx} = \dfrac{dY}{dA} \dfrac{dA}{dx}$ {chain rule}

$\therefore \quad \dfrac{dY}{dx} = \dfrac{k}{\sqrt{x+4}} \times (4 - 2p)$

$\therefore \quad \dfrac{dY}{dx} = \dfrac{k(4 - 2p)}{\sqrt{x+4}}$

c $\dfrac{dY}{dx}$ is the instantaneous rate of change of the yield with respect to the distance x from the canal.

$\therefore \quad \text{total yield} = Y = \int_0^p \dfrac{dY}{dx} \, dx = \int_0^p \dfrac{k(4-2p)}{\sqrt{x+4}} \, dx$

d Using **c**, $Y = k(4 - 2p) \int_0^p (x+4)^{-\frac{1}{2}} \, dx$

$= k(4 - 2p) \times \left[\dfrac{(x+4)^{\frac{1}{2}}}{\frac{1}{2}} \right]_0^p$

$= 2k(4 - 2p) \left[\sqrt{x+4} \right]_0^p$

$= 4k(2 - p) \left[\sqrt{p+4} - \sqrt{4} \right]$

$\therefore \quad Y = 4k(2 - p)\left(\sqrt{p+4} - 2 \right)$

e Using technology to graph Y and find its maximum, we find that the maximum occurs when $p \approx 0.9735$ km

$\therefore$ the orchard is 0.974 km $\times$ 2.05 km

REVIEW SET 25A

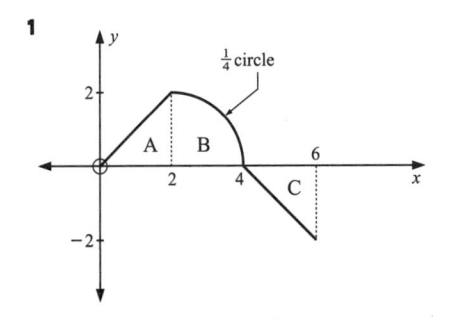

1

a $\int_0^4 f(x) \, dx =$ area of triangle + area of $\frac{1}{4}$ circle

$= \frac{1}{2}(2 \times 2) + \frac{1}{4}\pi(2)^2$

$= 2 + \pi$

b $\int_4^6 f(x) \, dx = -$area of triangle below x-axis

$= -\frac{1}{2}(2 \times 2)$

$= -2$

c $\int_0^6 f(x) \, dx = \int_0^4 f(x) \, dx + \int_4^6 f(x) \, dx$

$= (2 + \pi) + (-2)$

$= \pi$

2 **a** shaded area $= \int_a^b [f(x) - g(x)]\,dx + \int_b^c [g(x) - f(x)]\,dx + \int_c^d [f(x) - g(x)]\,dx$

b shaded area $= \int_a^d |f(x) - g(x)|\,dx$

3 $a(t) = 6t - 30$ cm s^{-2}

$\therefore\ v(t) = \int (6t - 30)\,dt$
$= 3t^2 - 30t + c$

But $v(0) = 27$ so $c = 27$

$\therefore\ v(t) = 3t^2 - 30t + 27$ cm s^{-1}

$\therefore\ s(t) = \int (3t^2 - 30t + 27)\,dt$
$= t^3 - 15t^2 + 27t + d$

But $s(0) = 0$ so $d = 0$

$\therefore\ s(t) = t^3 - 15t^2 + 27t$

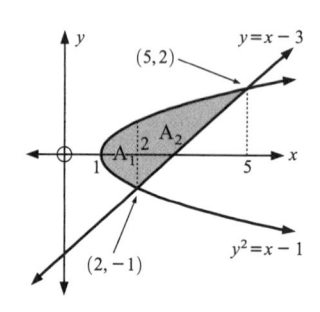

Also, $v(t) = 3t^2 - 30t + 27$
$= 3(t^2 - 10t + 9)$
$= 3(t - 1)(t - 9)$

which has sign diagram:

(sign diagram: + from 0 to 1, − from 1 to 9, + after 9)

The particle comes to rest for the second time at $t = 9$ seconds.

$\therefore$ the total distance travelled
$= \int_0^9 |3t^2 - 30t + 27|$ cm $= 269$ cm

4 a

(figure showing curves $y^2 = x - 1$ and $y = x - 3$ meeting at $(5, 2)$ and $(2, -1)$, with regions A_1 and A_2 shaded)

$y^2 = x - 1$ meets $y = x - 3$ where
$x - 1 = (x - 3)^2$
$\therefore\ x - 1 = x^2 - 6x + 9$
$\therefore\ x^2 - 7x + 10 = 0$
$\therefore\ (x - 5)(x - 2) = 0$
$\therefore\ x = 2$ or $x = 5$

$\therefore$ the graphs meet at $(5, 2)$ and $(2, -1)$

b Area $= A_1 + A_2$

$= 2\int_1^2 (x-1)^{\frac{1}{2}}\,dx + \int_2^5 [(x-1)^{\frac{1}{2}} - (x-3)]\,dx$

$= 2\left[\tfrac{2}{3}(x-1)^{\frac{3}{2}}\right]_1^2 + \left[\tfrac{2}{3}(x-1)^{\frac{3}{2}} - \dfrac{x^2}{2} + 3x\right]_2^5$

$= 2\left[\tfrac{2}{3} - 0\right] + \left[(\tfrac{2}{3}(8) - \tfrac{25}{2} + 15) - (\tfrac{2}{3} - 2 + 6)\right] = 4\tfrac{1}{2}$ units^2

5 $y = k$ meets $y = x^2$ where $x^2 = k$ $\therefore\ x = \pm\sqrt{k}$

By symmetry, $\int_0^{\sqrt{k}} (k - x^2)\,dx = \tfrac{1}{2} \times 5\tfrac{1}{3} = \tfrac{1}{2} \times \tfrac{16}{3}$

$\therefore\ \left[kx - \dfrac{x^3}{3}\right]_0^{\sqrt{k}} = \tfrac{8}{3}$

$\therefore\ k\sqrt{k} - \dfrac{k\sqrt{k}}{3} = \tfrac{8}{3}$

$\therefore\ \tfrac{2}{3}k\sqrt{k} = \tfrac{8}{3}$

$\therefore\ k\sqrt{k} = 4$

$\therefore\ k^{\frac{3}{2}} = 4$

$\therefore\ k = 4^{\frac{2}{3}} = \sqrt[3]{16}$

6

(figure showing $y = e^x$ and $y = \ln x$ with point $(0, e)$, region A' above, region B below, and point $(e, 0)$)

$y = e^x$ and $y = \ln x$ are inverse functions, so they are symmetrical about $y = x$

$\therefore$ area A = area A'

But area A' + area B = area of rectangle

$\therefore$ area A + area B $= e \times 1 = e$

Since area A $= \int_1^e \ln x\,dx$

and area B $= \int_0^1 e^x\,dx$,

$\int_1^e \ln x\,dx + \int_0^1 e^x\,dx = e$

7 $v(t) = \dfrac{100}{(t+2)^2} = 100(t+2)^{-2}$ m s^{-1}

  a At $t = 0$, $v(0) = \dfrac{100}{2^2} = 25$ m s^{-1}.   At $t = 3$, $v(3) = \dfrac{100}{5^2} = 4$ m s^{-1}.

  b As $t \to +\infty$, $v(t) \to 0$ m s^{-1} (above)

  c

  d As $v(t)$ is always positive, the boat is always travelling forwards.

$$s(t) = \int v(t)\, dt$$
$$= \int 100(t+2)^{-2}\, dt$$
$$= -100(t+2)^{-1} + c$$
$$= \dfrac{-100}{t+2} + c$$

$\therefore\ s(0) = c - 50$ m

$\therefore\ $ when the boat has travelled 30 m,
$$s(t) = c - 20$$
$\therefore\ c - 20 = \dfrac{-100}{t+2} + c$

$\therefore\ \dfrac{-100}{t+2} = -20$

$\therefore\ t + 2 = 5$

$\therefore\ t = 3$ seconds

  e $a(t) = v'(t)$
$$= -200(t+2)^{-3}$$
$$= \dfrac{-200}{(t+2)^3} \text{ m s}^{-2}$$

  f $\dfrac{dv}{dt} = \dfrac{-200}{(t+2)^3} = -\dfrac{1}{5}\dfrac{1000}{(t+2)^3}$

$$= -\dfrac{1}{5}\left(\dfrac{100}{(t+2)^2}\right)^{\frac{3}{2}}$$
$$= -\dfrac{1}{5}v^{\frac{3}{2}}$$

$\therefore\ \dfrac{dv}{dt} = -kv^{\frac{3}{2}}$ where $k = \dfrac{1}{5}$

8 $y = x^3$ meets $y = 7x^2 - 10x$
when $x^3 = 7x^2 - 10x$
$\therefore\ x^3 - 7x^2 + 10x = 0$
$\therefore\ x(x^2 - 7x + 10) = 0$
$\therefore\ x(x-2)(x-5) = 0$
$\therefore\ x = 0$, 2 or 5

$\therefore\ $ total area $= \int_0^5 |x^3 - 7x^2 + 10x|\, dx$
$= 21\tfrac{1}{12}$ units^2

9 The area between $x = 0$ and $x = a$ is 2 units^2.

$\therefore\ \int_0^a e^x\, dx = 2$
$\therefore\ [e^x]_0^a = 2$
$\therefore\ e^a - e^0 = 2$
$\therefore\ e^a = 3$
$\therefore\ a = \ln 3$

The area between $x = a = \ln 3$ and $x = b$ is 2 units^2.

$\therefore\ \int_{\ln 3}^b e^x\, dx = 2$
$\therefore\ [e^x]_{\ln 3}^b = 2$
$\therefore\ e^b - e^{\ln 3} = 2$
$\therefore\ e^b - 3 = 2$
$\therefore\ e^b = 5$
$\therefore\ b = \ln 5$

10 $\dfrac{d^2y}{dx^2} = k(L-x)^2$

$\therefore\ \dfrac{dy}{dx} = \int k(L-x)^2\, dx = \dfrac{-k(L-x)^3}{3} + c$

But when $x = 0$ the tangent is horizontal and so $\dfrac{dy}{dx} = 0$.

$\therefore\ \dfrac{-kL^3}{3} + c = 0$ and so $c = \dfrac{kL^3}{3}$

$$\therefore \quad \frac{dy}{dx} = \frac{-k(L-x)^3}{3} + \frac{kL^3}{3}$$

$$\therefore \quad y = \int \left(\frac{-k(L-x)^3}{3} + \frac{kL^3}{3} \right) dx$$

$$= \frac{k(L-x)^4}{12} + \frac{kL^3}{3}x + d$$

But when $x = 0$, $y = 0$

$$\therefore \quad \frac{kL^4}{12} + d = 0$$

$$\therefore \quad d = -\frac{kL^4}{12}$$

$$\therefore \quad y = \frac{k(L-x)^4}{12} + \frac{kL^3 x}{3} - \frac{kL^4}{12}$$

The greatest deflection occurs when $x \approx L$

$$\therefore \quad y \approx \frac{k(0)^4}{12} + \frac{kL^4}{3} - \frac{kL^4}{12} = \frac{kL^4}{4}$$

$\therefore$ the greatest deflection is about $\dfrac{kL^4}{4}$ metres.

11 The graphs meet when $\frac{2}{\pi}x = \sin x$

$\therefore \quad x = -\frac{\pi}{2}, 0, \frac{\pi}{2}$ {using technology}

$\therefore \quad$ area $= \int_{-\frac{\pi}{2}}^{0} (\frac{2}{\pi}x - \sin x)\, dx + \int_{0}^{\frac{\pi}{2}} (\sin x - \frac{2}{\pi}x)\, dx$

$$= \left[\frac{x^2}{\pi} + \cos x \right]_{-\frac{\pi}{2}}^{0} + \left[-\cos x - \frac{x^2}{\pi} \right]_{0}^{\frac{\pi}{2}}$$

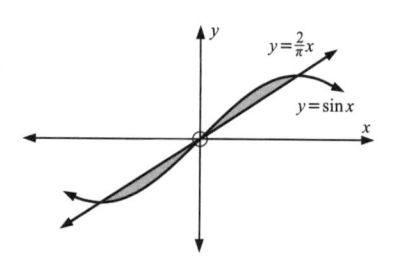

$= (0 + 1) - (\frac{\pi}{4} + 0) + (0 - \frac{\pi}{4}) - (-1 - 0)$

$= (2 - \frac{\pi}{2})$ units^2

12 a The graphs meet when $\cos 2x = e^{3x}$

Using technology, $x \approx -0.7292$

$\therefore \quad b \approx -0.7292$

b Shaded area $= \int_{-0.7292}^{0} (\cos 2x - e^{3x})\, dx \approx 0.2009$ units^2 {using technology}

13 a $\dfrac{d}{dx}[\ln(\tan x + \sec x)] = \dfrac{\sec^2 x + \sec x \tan x}{\tan x + \sec x}$

$= \sec x$

$\therefore \quad \int \sec x\, dx = \ln|\tan x + \sec x| + c$

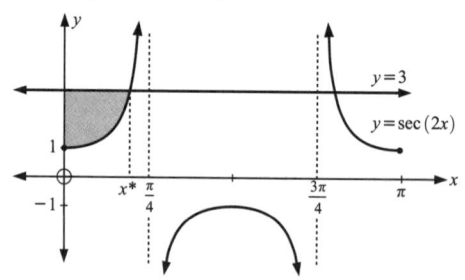

b i

ii $y = \sec(2x)$ and $y = 3$ meet when $\sec(2x) = 3$

$\therefore \quad \cos(2x) = \frac{1}{3}$

$\therefore \quad x^* \approx 0.615$ {see the graph}

$\therefore \quad$ shaded area $\approx$ (rectangle area) $- \int_{0}^{0.615} \sec(2x)\, dx$

$\approx 0.615 \times 3 - \left[\frac{1}{2} \ln|\tan(2x) + \sec(2x)| \right]_{0}^{0.615}$

$\approx 1.846 - \left[\frac{1}{2} \ln|\tan(1.23) + \sec(1.23)| - \frac{1}{2} \ln|0 + 1| \right]$

≈ 0.965 units^2

REVIEW SET 25B

1 $v(t) = 2t - 3t^2 = t(2 - 3t)$ which has sign diagram:

Now $s(t) = \int (2t - 3t^2)\, dt$
$= t^2 - t^3 + c$ metres

and so $s(0) = c$

$s(\tfrac{2}{3}) = \tfrac{4}{9} - \tfrac{8}{27} + c = c + \tfrac{4}{27}$ with motion diagram:

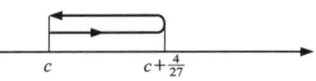

$s(1) = 1 - 1 + c = c$

∴ total distance travelled $= (c + \tfrac{4}{27} - c) + (c + \tfrac{4}{27} - c) = \tfrac{8}{27}$ m ≈ 29.6 cm

or total distance travelled $= \int_0^1 |2t - 3t^2|\, dt \approx 0.296$ m

2 $y = x^2 + 4x + 1$ meets $y = 3x + 3$ where $x^2 + 4x + 1 = 3x + 3$
∴ $x^2 + x - 2 = 0$
∴ $(x + 2)(x - 1) = 0$
∴ $x = -2$ or 1

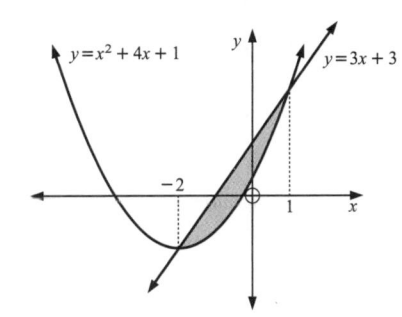

∴ area $= \int_{-2}^{1} [(3x + 3) - (x^2 + 4x + 1)]\, dx$

$= \int_{-2}^{1} (-x^2 - x + 2)\, dx$

$= \left[-\dfrac{x^3}{3} - \dfrac{x^2}{2} + 2x \right]_{-2}^{1}$

$= \left(-\tfrac{1}{3} - \tfrac{1}{2} + 2 \right) - \left(\tfrac{8}{3} - 2 - 4 \right)$

$= -\tfrac{1}{3} - \tfrac{1}{2} + 2 - \tfrac{8}{3} + 2 + 4$

$= 4\tfrac{1}{2}$ units^2

3 $y = \sqrt{4 - x^2}$ is a semi-circle above the x-axis with centre O and radius 2.

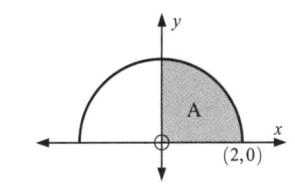

Now $\int_0^2 \sqrt{4 - x^2}\, dx$

$=$ shaded area

$= \tfrac{1}{4}$ of the area of a circle of radius 2 units

$= \tfrac{1}{4}\pi (2^2)$

$= \pi$ units^2

4 $\dfrac{dI}{dt} = -\dfrac{100}{t^2},\ t \geqslant 0.2$ seconds

∴ $I(t) = \int \dfrac{dI}{dt}\, dt = \int -100 t^{-2}\, dt = 100 t^{-1} + c$

Now $I(2) = 150$ milliamps, so $\dfrac{100}{2} + c = 150$ and so $c = 100$

∴ $I(t) = \left(\dfrac{100}{t} + 100 \right)$ milliamps

a $I(20) = \dfrac{100}{20} + 100$
$= 105$ milliamps

b As $t \to \infty$,
$I(t) \to 100$ milliamps (above)

5 $\int_{-1}^{3} f(x)\, dx$ gives us the correct area only if $f(x)$ is non-negative on the interval $-1 \leqslant x \leqslant 3$.

In this case $f(x)$ is negative for $1 < x < 3$, so $\int_{-1}^{3} f(x)\, dx$ does not provide the correct answer.

The shaded area which is below the x-axis is given by $\int_1^3 [0 - f(x)]\, dx = -\int_1^3 f(x)\, dx$.

6 a $f(x) = \dfrac{x}{1+x^2}$ $\therefore$ $f'(x) = \dfrac{1(1+x^2) - x(2x)}{(1+x^2)^2}$ {quotient rule}

$$= \dfrac{1+x^2 - 2x^2}{(1+x^2)^2}$$

$$= \dfrac{1-x^2}{(1+x^2)^2} \quad \text{which has sign diagram:}$$

$$= \dfrac{(1+x)(1-x)}{(1+x^2)^2}$$

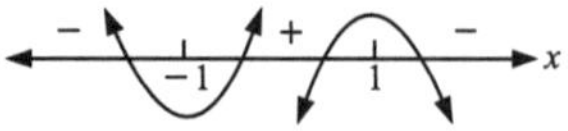

$\therefore$ there is a local minimum at $(-1, -\tfrac{1}{2})$ and a local maximum at $(1, \tfrac{1}{2})$.

b As $x \to \infty$, $f(x) \to 0$ (above).
As $x \to -\infty$, $f(x) \to 0$ (below).

c $f(x) = \dfrac{x}{1+x^2}$, $(1, \tfrac{1}{2})$ local max.
local min. $(-1, -\tfrac{1}{2})$

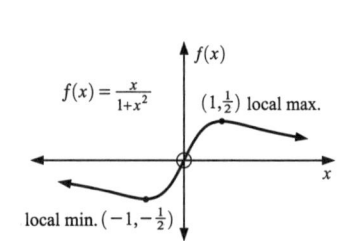

d Area $= \displaystyle\int_{-2}^{0} \left[0 - \dfrac{x}{1+x^2}\right] dx$

$= \displaystyle\int_{-2}^{0} \dfrac{-x}{1+x^2}\, dx$

Let $u = 1 + x^2$, $\dfrac{du}{dx} = 2x$

when $x = 0$, $u = 1$
when $x = -2$, $u = 5$

$\therefore \displaystyle\int_{-2}^{0} \dfrac{-x}{1+x^2}\, dx = -\tfrac{1}{2}\displaystyle\int_{-2}^{0} \dfrac{2x}{1+x^2}\, dx$

$= -\tfrac{1}{2}\displaystyle\int_{-2}^{0} \dfrac{1}{u}\dfrac{du}{dx}\, dx$

$= -\tfrac{1}{2}\displaystyle\int_{5}^{1} \dfrac{1}{u}\, du$

$= -\tfrac{1}{2}\left[\ln|u|\right]_{5}^{1} = -\tfrac{1}{2}(0 - \ln 5) = \tfrac{1}{2}\ln 5$ units^2 (≈ 0.805 units^2)

7 The coordinates of B are $(2, 4+k)$
$\therefore$ area rectangle OABC $= 2 \times (4+k)$
$= 8 + 2k$
$\therefore$ since the two shaded regions are equal in area,
each area is $4 + k$ units^2.

$\therefore \displaystyle\int_{0}^{2}(x^2 + k)\, dx = 4 + k$

$\therefore \left[\dfrac{x^3}{3} + kx\right]_{0}^{2} = 4 + k$

$\therefore \tfrac{8}{3} + 2k = 4 + k$

$\therefore k = 4 - \tfrac{8}{3}$

$\therefore k = \tfrac{4}{3}$

8 a

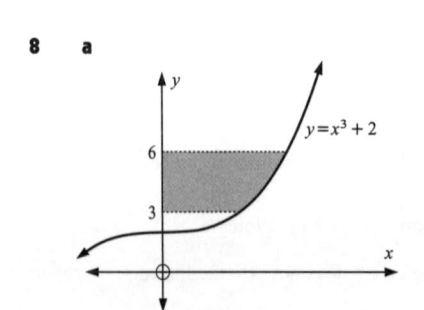

b $y = x^3 + 2$
$\therefore x^3 = y - 2$
$\therefore x = (y-2)^{\frac{1}{3}}$

c Area $= \displaystyle\int_{3}^{6} x\, dy$

$= \displaystyle\int_{3}^{6}(y-2)^{\frac{1}{3}}\, dy$

$= \left[\dfrac{(y-2)^{\frac{4}{3}}}{\tfrac{4}{3}}\right]_{3}^{6}$

$= \tfrac{3}{4}\left(4^{\frac{4}{3}} - 1^{\frac{4}{3}}\right)$

$= \tfrac{3}{4}\left(4\sqrt[3]{4} - 1\right)$ units^2

≈ 4.01 units^2

9 $y = 2x^3 - 9x$ meets $y = 3x^2 - 10$ when $2x^3 - 9x = 3x^2 - 10$
$\therefore \quad 2x^3 - 3x^2 - 9x + 10 = 0$
$\therefore \quad (x-1)(2x^2 - x - 10) = 0$
$\therefore \quad (x-1)(2x-5)(x+2) = 0$
$\therefore \quad x = -2, 1$ or $\frac{5}{2}$

$\therefore$ total area $= \int_{-2}^{\frac{5}{2}} |2x^3 - 3x^2 - 9x + 10| \, dx$
≈ 31.2 units^2

10 a

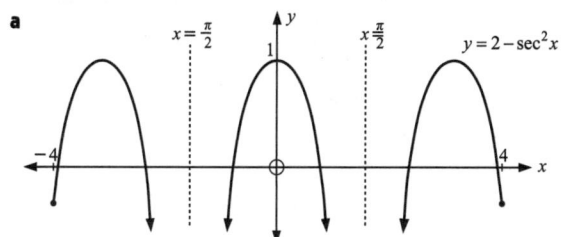

b $f(x) = 2 - \sec^2 x$ is undefined when $\cos x = 0$.
On the domain $x \in [-4, 4]$ this is when $x = -\frac{\pi}{2}, \frac{\pi}{2}$.
$\therefore$ the vertical asymptotes are $x = -\frac{\pi}{2}$ and $x = \frac{\pi}{2}$

c When $y = 0$, $2 - \sec^2 x = 0$
$\therefore \cos^2 x = \frac{1}{2}$
$\therefore \cos x = \pm \frac{1}{\sqrt{2}}$
$\therefore x = -\frac{5\pi}{4}, -\frac{3\pi}{4}, -\frac{\pi}{4}, \frac{\pi}{4}, \frac{3\pi}{4}, \frac{5\pi}{4}$ {for $x \in [-4, 4]$}
$\therefore$ the x-intercepts are $-\frac{5\pi}{4}, -\frac{3\pi}{4}, -\frac{\pi}{4}, \frac{\pi}{4}, \frac{3\pi}{4}, \frac{5\pi}{4}$
When $x = 0$, $y = 2 - \sec^2(0) = 2 - 1^2 = 1$
$\therefore$ the y-intercept is 1.

d area
$= \int_{-\frac{\pi}{4}}^{\frac{\pi}{4}} (2 - \sec^2 x) \, dx$
$= [2x - \tan x]_{-\frac{\pi}{4}}^{\frac{\pi}{4}}$
$= \left(\frac{\pi}{2} - 1\right) - \left(-\frac{\pi}{2} - (-1)\right)$
$= (\pi - 2)$ units^2

11 $\frac{dT}{dx} = \frac{k}{x} = kx^{-1}$
$\therefore T = k \ln x + c \quad \{x > 0\}$
When $x = r_1$, $T = T_0$
$\therefore k \ln r_1 + c = T_0$
$\therefore c = T_0 - k \ln r_1$

$\therefore T = k \ln x + T_0 - k \ln r_1$
$= T_0 + k \ln \left(\frac{x}{r_1}\right)$
So, when $x = r_2$,
$T = T_0 + k \ln \left(\frac{r_2}{r_1}\right)$
$\therefore$ the outer surface has temperature $T_0 + k \ln \left(\frac{r_2}{r_1}\right)$

12 area $= \int_0^{\frac{\pi}{3}} \tan x \, dx$
$= [-\ln |\cos x|]_0^{\frac{\pi}{3}}$ {see **Exercise 24F.2 Q 4 c**}
$= -\ln \cos \frac{\pi}{3} + \ln \cos 0$
$= -\ln(\frac{1}{2}) + \ln 1$
$= \ln 2$ units^2

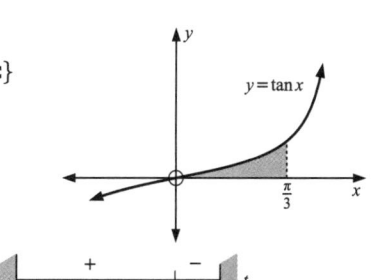

13 $v(t) = \sin t$ which has sign diagram

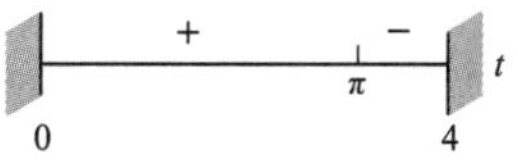

Now $s(t) = \int \sin t \, dt$
$= -\cos t + c$ metres
$\therefore s(0) = -1 + c$
$s(\pi) = 1 + c$
$s(4) = -\cos 4 + c \approx c + 0.654$
$\therefore$ total distance travelled $= [(c+1) - (c-1)] + [(c+1) - (c+0.654)]$ 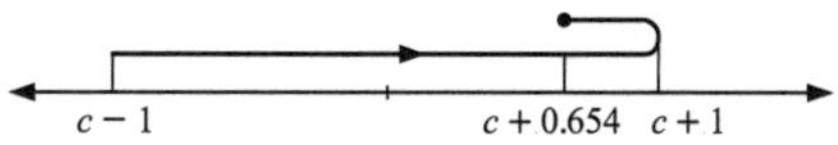
≈ 2.35 m

REVIEW SET 25C

1 a $v(t) = t^2 - 6t + 8$ m s^{-1}, $t \geq 0$
$= (t-4)(t-2)$ which has sign diagram:

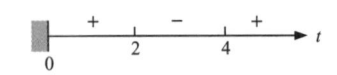

b Now $s(t) = \int (t^2 - 6t + 8)\, dt = \dfrac{t^3}{3} - 3t^2 + 8t + c$

$\therefore\ s(0) = c$
$s(2) = c + 6\frac{2}{3}$ the motion diagram is:
$s(4) = c + 5\frac{1}{3}$
$s(5) = c + 6\frac{2}{3}$

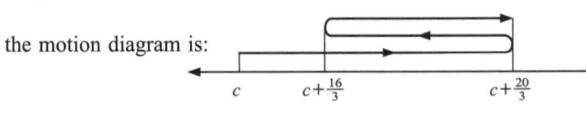

The particle moves in the positive direction initially. When $t = 2$, $6\frac{2}{3}$ m from its starting point, it changes direction. It changes direction again when $t = 4$, $5\frac{1}{3}$ m from its starting point. When $t = 5$ it is $6\frac{2}{3}$ m from its starting point.

c After 5 seconds, the particle is $6\frac{2}{3}$ m to the right of its starting point.

d The total distance travelled $= (c + \frac{20}{3} - c) + [(c + \frac{20}{3}) - (c + \frac{16}{3})] + [(c + \frac{20}{3}) - (c + \frac{16}{3})]$
$= 9\frac{1}{3}$ m

2 $x = \ln\left(\dfrac{y+3}{2}\right)$

$\therefore\ \dfrac{y+3}{2} = e^x$

$\therefore\ y = 2e^x - 3$

When $y = 3$, $x = \ln\left(\dfrac{3+3}{2}\right)$

$\therefore\ x = \ln 3$

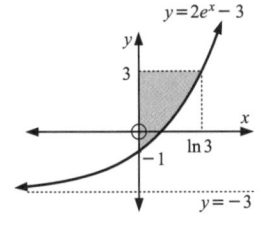

Area $= \int_0^{\ln 3} (3 - [2e^x - 3])\, dx$
$= \int_0^{\ln 3} (6 - 2e^x)\, dx$
$= [6x - 2e^x]_0^{\ln 3}$
$= (6\ln 3 - 2e^{\ln 3}) - (0 - 2)$
$= (6\ln 3 - 2 \times 3 + 2)$
$= 6\ln 3 - 4$ units^2
≈ 2.59 units^2

3 a The shaded area $= \int_0^2 ax(x-2)\, dx$
$= 4$ units^2

$\therefore\ \int_0^2 (ax^2 - 2ax)\, dx = 4$

$\therefore\ \left[\dfrac{ax^3}{3} - ax^2\right]_0^2 = 4$

$\therefore\ \left(\dfrac{8a}{3} - 4a\right) - 0 = 4$

$\therefore\ \dfrac{8a}{3} - \dfrac{12a}{3} = 4$

$\therefore\ -\dfrac{4a}{3} = 4$

$\therefore\ a = -3$

$\therefore\ y = -3x(x-2)$

b Suppose A has coordinates $(k, -3k(k-2))$.

$\therefore$ gradient of [OA] $= \dfrac{-3k(k-2) - 0}{k - 0}$
$= -3(k-2)$

$\therefore$ equation of [OA] is $y = -3(k-2)x$

If [OA] divides the shaded region into equal areas,

$\int_0^k [-3x(x-2) - (-3(k-2)x)]\, dx = 2$

$\therefore\ \int_0^k (-3x^2 + 6x + 3kx - 6x)\, dx = 2$

$\therefore\ \int_0^k (-3x^2 + 3kx)\, dx = 2$

$\therefore\ \left[-x^3 + \dfrac{3kx^2}{2}\right]_0^k = 2$

$\therefore\ -k^3 + \dfrac{3k^3}{2} = 2$

$\therefore\ \dfrac{k^3}{2} = 2$

$\therefore\ k^3 = 4$

$\therefore\ k = \sqrt[3]{4}$

$\therefore$ the x-coordinate of A is $\sqrt[3]{4}$

4 a From the graph,
area $\triangle OBX <$ area under the curve $<$ area OXYZ
$\therefore \quad \frac{1}{2}\pi(1) < \int_0^\pi \sin x \, dx < \pi(1)$
$\therefore \quad \frac{\pi}{2} < \int_0^\pi \sin x \, dx < \pi$

b If we partition the diagram as shown:
Area $1 = \frac{1}{2}\left(\frac{\pi}{4}\right)\left(\frac{\sqrt{2}}{2}\right) = \frac{\pi\sqrt{2}}{16}$
Area $2 = \frac{\pi\sqrt{2}}{16}$
Area $3 = \frac{\pi}{2} \times \frac{\sqrt{2}}{2} = \frac{\pi\sqrt{2}}{4}$
Area $4 = \frac{1}{2}\left(\frac{\pi}{2}\right)\left(1 - \frac{\sqrt{2}}{2}\right) = \frac{\pi}{4}\left(1 - \frac{\sqrt{2}}{2}\right)$

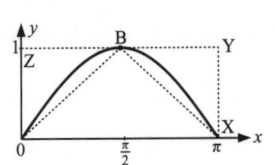

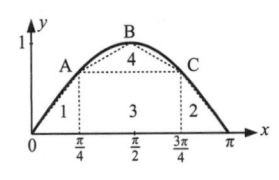

The area under the arch is slightly larger than the total area of the 4 sections.
Total area of the sections $= \frac{\pi\sqrt{2}}{16} + \frac{\pi\sqrt{2}}{16} + \frac{\pi\sqrt{2}}{4} + \frac{\pi}{4}\left(1 - \frac{\sqrt{2}}{2}\right)$
$= \frac{\pi\sqrt{2} + \pi\sqrt{2} + 4\pi\sqrt{2} + 4\pi - 2\pi\sqrt{2}}{16}$
$= \frac{4\pi + 4\pi\sqrt{2}}{16}$
$= \frac{\pi + \pi\sqrt{2}}{4}$
$= \frac{\pi}{4}(1 + \sqrt{2})$ units^2

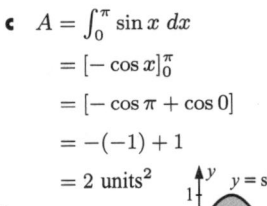

$\therefore$ the area under the arch is slightly more than $\frac{\pi}{4}(1 + \sqrt{2})$ units^2.

c $A = \int_0^\pi \sin x \, dx$
$= [-\cos x]_0^\pi$
$= [-\cos \pi + \cos 0]$
$= -(-1) + 1$
$= 2$ units^2

5 a A is the *upper half* of a circle centre $(2, 0)$ and radius 2.
$\therefore \quad (x - 2)^2 + (y - 0)^2 = 2^2$
$(x - 2)^2 + y^2 = 4$
$y^2 = 4 - (x - 2)^2$
$y^2 = 4 - x^2 + 4x - 4$
$y^2 = 4x - x^2$
$\therefore \quad y = \pm\sqrt{4x - x^2}$

So, $y = \sqrt{4x - x^2}$
or $y = -\sqrt{4x - x^2}$

Since A is the upper half of the circle,
$y_A = \sqrt{4x - x^2}$

b Now B is the *lower half* of a circle centre $(5, 0)$ and radius 1.
$\therefore \quad (x - 5)^2 + (y - 0)^2 = 1^2$
$(x - 5)^2 + y^2 = 1$
$y^2 = 1 - (x - 5)^2$
$y^2 = 1 - x^2 + 10x - 25$
$\therefore \quad y = \pm\sqrt{10x - x^2 - 24} \quad \therefore \quad y_B = -\sqrt{10x - x^2 - 24}$

c $\int_0^4 y_A \, dx$
$= \frac{1}{2}\pi r^2$ where $r = 2$
$= \frac{1}{2}\pi(2)^2$
$= 2\pi$

$\int_4^6 y_B \, dx$
$= -\frac{1}{2}\pi r^2$ where $r = 1$
$= -\frac{1}{2}\pi(1)^2$
$= -\frac{\pi}{2}$

d $\int_0^6 f(x) \, dx$
$= \int_0^4 y_A \, dx + \int_4^6 y_B \, dx$
$= 2\pi + \left(-\frac{\pi}{2}\right)$
$= \frac{3\pi}{2}$

6 The line $y = mx + c$ passes through $(-1, 0)$. $\quad \therefore \quad 0 = -m + c$
$\therefore \quad c = m$
$\therefore \quad$ the line is $y = cx + c$

The curve and the line meet when $cx + c = -x^2 + 2x + 3$
$\therefore \quad x^2 + (c - 2)x + (c - 3) = 0$
$\therefore \quad (x + 1)(x + [c - 3]) = 0 \qquad$ {we know $x = -1$ is a solution}
$\therefore \quad x = -1$ or $3 - c$

If we let $a = 3 - c$, the enclosed area $= \int_{-1}^{a}[(-x^2 + 2x + 3) - (3 - a)(x + 1)] \, dx$

$= \int_{-1}^{a}[-x^2 + (a - 1)x + a] \, dx$

$= \left[-\dfrac{x^3}{3} + \dfrac{(a-1)x^2}{2} + ax\right]_{-1}^{a}$

$= \left(-\dfrac{a^3}{3} + \dfrac{(a-1)a^2}{2} + a^2\right) - \left(\dfrac{1}{3} + \dfrac{(a-1)}{2} - a\right)$

$= -\dfrac{1}{3}a^3 + \dfrac{1}{2}a^3 - \dfrac{1}{2}a^2 + a^2 - \dfrac{1}{3} - \dfrac{1}{2}a + \dfrac{1}{2} + a$

$= \dfrac{1}{6}a^3 + \dfrac{1}{2}a^2 + \dfrac{1}{2}a + \dfrac{1}{6}$

But this area is 4.5 units^2, so $\dfrac{1}{6}a^3 + \dfrac{1}{2}a^2 + \dfrac{1}{2}a + \dfrac{1}{6} = \dfrac{9}{2}$

$\therefore \quad a^3 + 3a^2 + 3a + 1 = 27$
$\therefore \quad a^3 + 3a^2 + 3a - 26 = 0$
$\therefore \quad (a - 2)(a^2 + 5a + 13) = 0$

The quadratic has $\Delta < 0$, so there are no real solutions.
$\therefore \quad a = 2$ and so $c = 1$ and $m = 1$
$\therefore$ the line has equation $y = x + 1$.

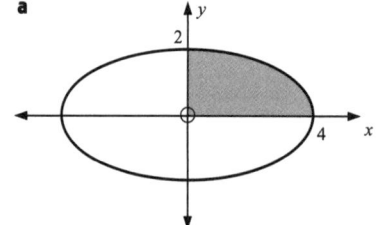

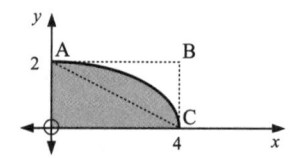

7 a

b

Now area $\triangle AOC <$ shaded area $<$ area ABCO

$\therefore \quad \dfrac{1}{2}(2 \times 4) < \int_0^4 \dfrac{1}{2}\sqrt{16 - x^2} \, dx < 2 \times 4$

$\therefore \quad 4 < \int_0^4 \dfrac{1}{2}\sqrt{16 - x^2} \, dx < 8$

$\therefore \quad 8 < \int_0^4 \sqrt{16 - x^2} \, dx < 16$

8 The curves meet when
$x^3 + x^2 + 2x + 6 = 7x^2 - x - 4$
$\therefore \quad x^3 - 6x^2 + 3x + 10 = 0$
$\therefore \quad (x + 1)(x^2 - 7x + 10) = 0$
$\therefore \quad (x + 1)(x - 2)(x - 5) = 0$
$\therefore \quad x = -1, 2$ or 5
$\therefore$ area enclosed
$= \int_{-1}^{5} |x^3 - 6x^2 + 3x + 10| \, dx$
$= 40\dfrac{1}{2}$ units^2

9 Consider the graph of $y = \sin^3 x$, $0 \leqslant x \leqslant \pi$

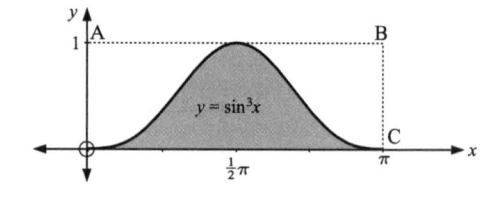

Now $\int_0^{\pi} \sin^3 x \, dx =$ shaded area
But the shaded area $<$ area of rectangle ABCO
$\therefore \quad \int_0^{\pi} \sin^3 x \, dx < \pi$
$\therefore \quad \int_0^{\pi} \sin^3 x \, dx < 4$

10 a

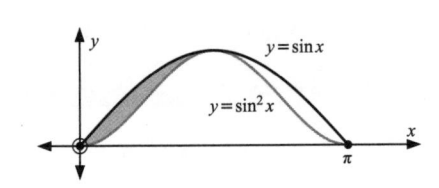

[Graph showing $y=\sin x$ and $y=\sin^2 x$ on $[0, \pi]$]

b Area $= \int_0^{\frac{\pi}{2}} (\sin x - \sin^2 x)\, dx$

$= \int_0^{\frac{\pi}{2}} (\sin x - (\frac{1}{2} - \frac{1}{2}\cos 2x))\, dx$

$= \int_0^{\frac{\pi}{2}} (\sin x + \frac{1}{2}\cos 2x - \frac{1}{2})\, dx$

$= \left[-\cos x + \frac{1}{4}\sin 2x - \frac{1}{2}x\right]_0^{\frac{\pi}{2}}$

$= \left(0 + \frac{1}{4}(0) - \frac{\pi}{4}\right) - (-1 + 0 - 0)$

$= \left(1 - \frac{\pi}{4}\right)$ units^2

11

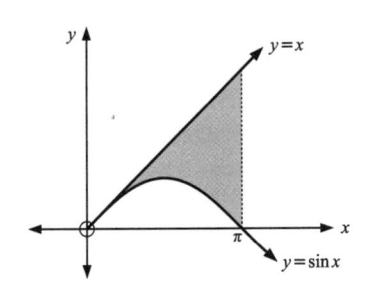

[Graph showing $y=x$ and $y=\sin x$ with shaded region]

Required area $=$ area of Δ $-$ area under sine curve

$= \frac{1}{2}\pi \times \pi - \int_0^{\pi} \sin x\, dx$

$= \frac{\pi^2}{2} - [-\cos x]_0^{\pi}$

$= \frac{\pi^2}{2} - [-\cos \pi + \cos 0]$

$= \left(\frac{\pi^2}{2} - 2\right)$ units^2

12 $\int_0^m \sin x\, dx = \frac{1}{2}$

$\therefore\ [-\cos x]_0^m = \frac{1}{2}$

$\therefore\ -\cos m + \cos 0 = \frac{1}{2}$

$\therefore\ \cos m = \frac{1}{2}$

$\therefore\ m = \frac{\pi}{3}\quad \{0 < m < \frac{\pi}{2}\}$

13 a The graphs meet where

$x^2 = \sin x$

$\therefore\ x = 0$ or $\approx 0.8767\ \{$using technology$\}$

$\therefore\ a \approx 0.8767$

b area $= \int_0^{0.8767} (\sin x - x^2)\, dx$

≈ 0.1357 units$^2\ \{$using technology$\}$

14 a Amount at time $T = P_0 +$ interest

$= P_0 + \int_0^T P_0 r e^{rt}\, dt$

$= P_0 + \left[P_0 e^{rt}\right]_0^T$

$= P_0 + P_0 e^{rT} - P_0 e^0$

$= P_0 e^{rT}$

b $P_0 e^{0.08T} = 2P_0$

$\therefore\ e^{0.08T} = 2$

$\therefore\ 0.08T = \ln 2$

$\therefore\ T = \dfrac{\ln 2}{0.08}$

$\therefore\ T \approx 8.66$

$\therefore$ at a rate of 8% p.a., an investment would take 8.66 years to double.

c $P_0 = 55,\ T = 2007 - 1940 = 67,\ P_{67} = 196\,000$

$\therefore\ 55 e^{67r} = 196\,000$

$\therefore\ e^{67r} = \dfrac{196\,000}{55}$

$\therefore\ 67r = \ln\left(\dfrac{196\,000}{55}\right)$

$\therefore\ r = \dfrac{1}{67}\ln\left(\dfrac{196\,000}{55}\right) \approx 0.1221\quad \therefore$ the interest rate required is 12.2% p.a.

Chapter 26
VOLUMES OF REVOLUTION

EXERCISE 26A

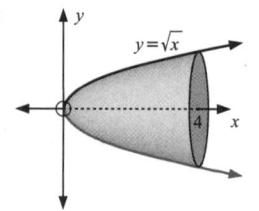

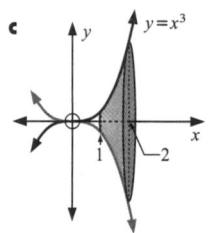

1 a ($y = 2x$, region to $x=3$)

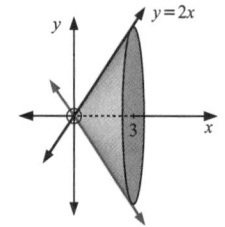

Volume $= \pi \int_0^3 (2x)^2 \, dx$
$= 4\pi \int_0^3 x^2 \, dx$
$= 4\pi \left[\frac{1}{3}x^3\right]_0^3$
$= 4\pi(9 - 0)$
$= 36\pi$ units^3

b ($y = \sqrt{x}$, region to $x=4$)

Volume $= \pi \int_0^4 (\sqrt{x})^2 \, dx$
$= \pi \int_0^4 x \, dx$
$= \pi \left[\frac{1}{2}x^2\right]_0^4$
$= \pi(8 - 0)$
$= 8\pi$ units^3

c ($y = x^3$, region from $x=1$ to 2)

Volume $= \pi \int_1^2 (x^3)^2 \, dx$
$= \pi \int_1^2 x^6 \, dx$
$= \pi \left[\frac{1}{7}x^7\right]_1^2$
$= \pi \left(\frac{128}{7} - \frac{1}{7}\right)$
$= \frac{127\pi}{7}$ units^3

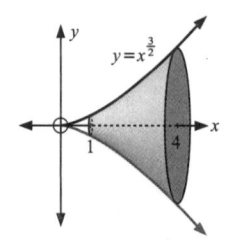

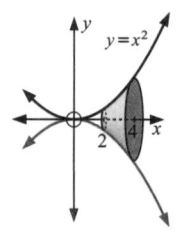

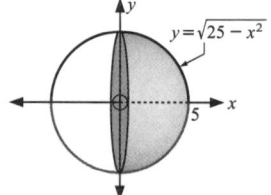

d ($y = x^{\frac{3}{2}}$, region from $x=1$ to 4)

Volume $= \pi \int_1^4 (x^{\frac{3}{2}})^2 \, dx$
$= \pi \int_1^4 x^3 \, dx$
$= \pi \left[\frac{1}{4}x^4\right]_1^4$
$= \pi \left(\frac{256}{4} - \frac{1}{4}\right)$
$= \frac{255\pi}{4}$ units^3

e ($y = x^2$, region from $x=2$ to 4)

Volume $= \pi \int_2^4 (x^2)^2 \, dx$
$= \pi \int_2^4 x^4 \, dx$
$= \pi \left[\frac{1}{5}x^5\right]_2^4$
$= \pi \left(\frac{1024}{5} - \frac{32}{5}\right)$
$= \frac{992\pi}{5}$ units^3

f ($y = \sqrt{25 - x^2}$, region from $x=0$ to 5)

Volume $= \pi \int_0^5 (25 - x^2) \, dx$
$= \pi \left[25x - \frac{x^3}{3}\right]_0^5$
$= \pi \left(125 - \frac{125}{3}\right)$
$= \pi \left(\frac{2}{3}\right) 125$
$= \frac{250\pi}{3}$ units^3

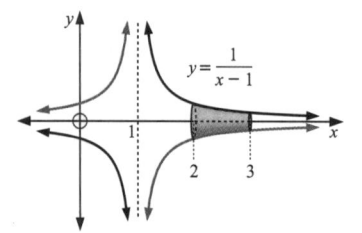

g ($y = \frac{1}{x-1}$, region from $x=2$ to 3)

Volume $= \pi \int_2^3 \left(\frac{1}{x-1}\right)^2 \, dx$
$= \pi \int_2^3 (x-1)^{-2} \, dx$
$= \pi \left[-\frac{1}{x-1}\right]_2^3$
$= \pi \left(-\frac{1}{2} + 1\right)$
$= \frac{\pi}{2}$ units^3

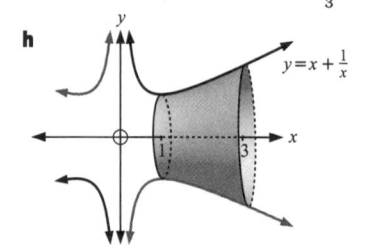

h ($y = x + \frac{1}{x}$, region from $x=1$ to 3)

Volume $= \pi \int_1^3 \left(x + \frac{1}{x}\right)^2 \, dx$
$= \pi \int_1^3 \left(x^2 + 2 + x^{-2}\right) \, dx$
$= \pi \left[\frac{x^3}{3} + 2x - \frac{1}{x}\right]_1^3$
$= \pi \left[9 + 6 - \frac{1}{3} - \left(\frac{1}{3} + 2 - 1\right)\right]$
$= \frac{40\pi}{3}$ units^3

2 a Volume $= \pi \int_1^3 \left(\dfrac{x^3}{x^2+1}\right)^2 dx$

$\approx 5.926\pi$ {using technology}

≈ 18.6 units^3

b Volume $= \pi \int_0^2 \left(e^{\sin x}\right)^2 dx$

$\approx 9.613\pi$ {using technology}

≈ 30.2 units^3

3 a $V = \pi \int_0^6 \left(\dfrac{x}{2}+4\right)^2 dx$

$= \pi \int_0^6 \left(\tfrac{1}{4}x^2 + 4x + 16\right) dx$

$= \pi \left[\dfrac{x^3}{12} + \dfrac{4x^2}{2} + 16x\right]_0^6$

$= \pi(18 + 72 + 96) - 0$

$= 186\pi$ units^3

c $V = \pi \int_0^4 (e^x)^2 dx$

$= \pi \int_0^4 e^{2x} dx$

$= \pi \left[\tfrac{1}{2}e^{2x}\right]_0^4$

$= \pi \left(\tfrac{1}{2}e^8 - \tfrac{1}{2}\right)$

$= \tfrac{\pi}{2}(e^8 - 1)$ units^3

b $V = \pi \int_1^2 (x^2+3)^2 dx$

$= \pi \int_1^2 (x^4 + 6x^2 + 9) dx$

$= \pi \left[\dfrac{x^5}{5} + \dfrac{6x^3}{3} + 9x\right]_1^2$

$= \pi \left[\left(\tfrac{32}{5} + 16 + 18\right) - \left(\tfrac{1}{5} + 2 + 9\right)\right]$

$= \pi \left(\dfrac{146}{5}\right)$

$= \dfrac{146\pi}{5}$ units^3

4 a Volume $= \pi \int_5^8 y^2 dx$

$= \pi \int_5^8 (64 - x^2) dx$

$= \pi \left[64x - \dfrac{x^3}{3}\right]_5^8$

$= \pi \left[\left(512 - \dfrac{512}{3}\right) - \left(320 - \dfrac{125}{3}\right)\right]$

$= 63\pi$ units^3

b 63π cm$^3 \approx 198$ cm^3

5 a a cone of base radius r and height h

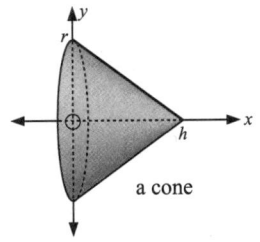

a cone

b [AB] has gradient $= \dfrac{r-0}{0-h} = -\dfrac{r}{h}$

$\therefore$ its equation is $y = -\dfrac{r}{h}x + r$

c $V = \pi \int_0^h \left(\dfrac{-r}{h}x + r\right)^2 dx$

$= \pi r^2 \int_0^h \left(-\dfrac{x}{h} + 1\right)^2 dx$

$= \pi r^2 \int_0^h \left(\dfrac{x^2}{h^2} - \dfrac{2x}{h} + 1\right) dx$

$= \pi r^2 \left[\dfrac{x^3}{3h^2} - \dfrac{2x^2}{2h} + x\right]_0^h$

$= \pi r^2 \left[\left(\dfrac{h}{3} - h + h\right) - 0\right]$

$= \tfrac{1}{3}\pi r^2 h$ units^3

6 a a sphere of radius r

b $V = \pi \int_{-r}^r y^2 dx = 2\pi \int_0^r (r^2 - x^2) dx$

$= 2\pi \left[r^2 x - \dfrac{x^3}{3}\right]_0^r$

$= 2\pi \left(r^3 - \dfrac{r^3}{3} - 0\right)$

$= 2\pi \times \tfrac{2}{3}r^3$

$= \tfrac{4}{3}\pi r^3$ units^3

7

a

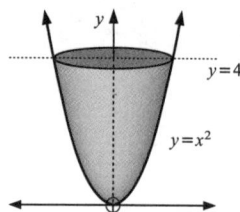

Volume $= \pi \int_0^4 x^2 \, dy$
$= \pi \int_0^4 y \, dy$
$= \pi \left[\dfrac{y^2}{2}\right]_0^4$
$= \pi(8-0)$
$= 8\pi$ units^3

b

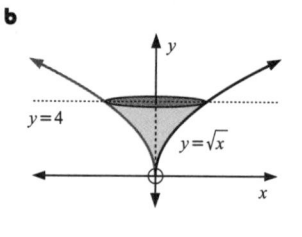

Volume $= \pi \int_0^4 x^2 \, dy$
$= \pi \int_0^4 y^4 \, dy$
$= \pi \left[\dfrac{y^5}{5}\right]_0^4$
$= \pi \left(\dfrac{4^5}{5} - 0\right)$
$= \dfrac{1024}{5}\pi$ units^3

c $y = \ln x$ or $x = e^y$

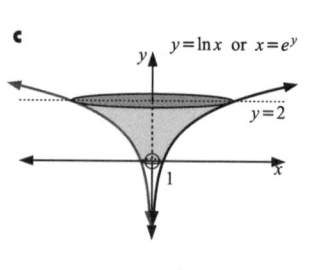

Volume $= \pi \int_0^2 x^2 \, dy$
$= \pi \int_0^2 (e^y)^2 \, dy$
$= \pi \int_0^2 e^{2y} \, dy$
$= \pi \left[\tfrac{1}{2} e^{2y}\right]_0^2$
$= \pi \left(\tfrac{1}{2} e^4 - \tfrac{1}{2}\right)$
$= \tfrac{\pi}{2}(e^4 - 1)$ units^3

d

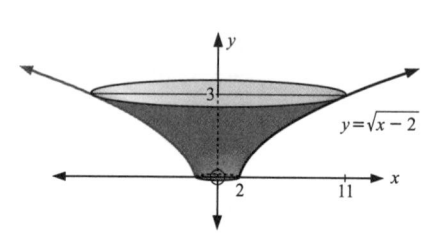

When $x = 2$, $y = 0$
When $x = 11$, $y = 3$
Now $y = \sqrt{x-2}$
$\therefore \quad y^2 = x - 2$
$\therefore \quad x = y^2 + 2$
$\therefore$ volume $= \pi \int_0^3 x^2 \, dy$
$= \pi \int_0^3 (y^2 + 2)^2 \, dy$
$= \pi \int_0^3 (y^4 + 4y^2 + 4) \, dy$
$= \pi \left[\dfrac{y^5}{5} + \dfrac{4}{3}y^3 + 4y\right]_0^3$
$= \pi \left(\dfrac{3^5}{5} + 36 + 12 - 0\right)$
$= \dfrac{483}{5}\pi$ units^3

e

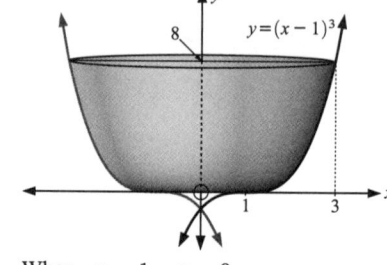

When $x = 1$, $y = 0$
When $x = 3$, $y = 8$
Now $y = (x-1)^3$
$\therefore \quad x - 1 = y^{\frac{1}{3}}$
$\therefore \quad x = y^{\frac{1}{3}} + 1$
$\therefore$ volume $= \pi \int_0^8 x^2 \, dy$
$= \pi \int_0^8 (y^{\frac{1}{3}} + 1)^2 \, dy$
$= \pi \int_0^8 \left(y^{\frac{2}{3}} + 2y^{\frac{1}{3}} + 1\right) dy$
$= \left[\tfrac{3}{5} y^{\frac{5}{3}} + \tfrac{3}{2} y^{\frac{4}{3}} + y\right]_0^8$
$= \pi \left(\tfrac{3}{5} \times 32 + \tfrac{3}{2} \times 16 + 8 - 0\right)$
$= \dfrac{256}{5}\pi$ units^3

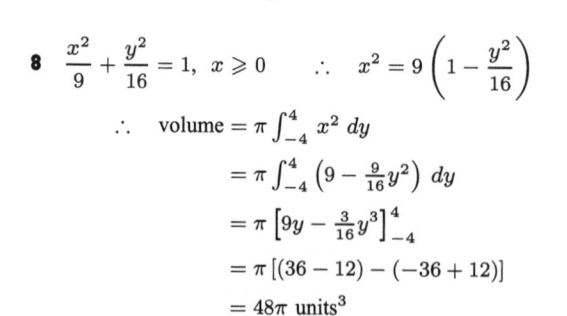

8 $\dfrac{x^2}{9} + \dfrac{y^2}{16} = 1$, $x \geqslant 0$ $\quad \therefore \quad x^2 = 9\left(1 - \dfrac{y^2}{16}\right)$

$\therefore$ volume $= \pi \int_{-4}^4 x^2 \, dy$
$= \pi \int_{-4}^4 \left(9 - \tfrac{9}{16} y^2\right) dy$
$= \pi \left[9y - \tfrac{3}{16} y^3\right]_{-4}^4$
$= \pi \left[(36 - 12) - (-36 + 12)\right]$
$= 48\pi$ units^3

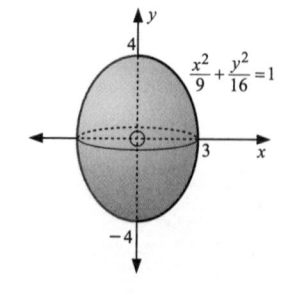

9 a

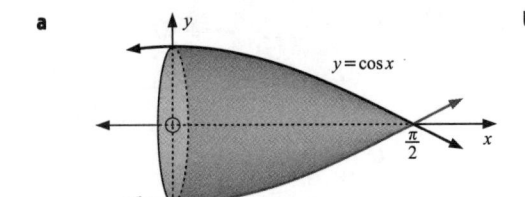

Volume $= \pi \int_0^{\frac{\pi}{2}} (\cos x)^2 \, dx$
$= \pi \int_0^{\frac{\pi}{2}} \cos^2 x \, dx$
$= \pi \int_0^{\frac{\pi}{2}} \left(\frac{1}{2} + \frac{1}{2}\cos(2x)\right) dx$
$= \pi \left[\frac{1}{2}x + \frac{1}{2}\left(\frac{1}{2}\right)\sin(2x)\right]_0^{\frac{\pi}{2}}$
$= \pi \left[\frac{\pi}{4} + \frac{1}{4}\sin \pi - 0\right]$
$= \frac{\pi^2}{4}$ units^3

b

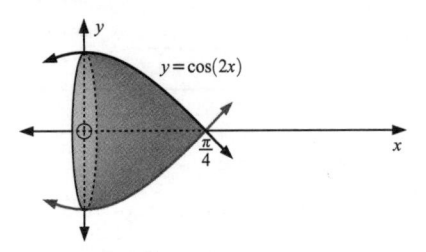

Volume $= \pi \int_0^{\frac{\pi}{4}} \cos^2(2x) \, dx$
$= \pi \int_0^{\frac{\pi}{4}} \left(\frac{1}{2} + \frac{1}{2}\cos(4x)\right) dx$
$= \pi \left[\frac{1}{2}x + \frac{1}{2}\left(\frac{1}{4}\right)\sin(4x)\right]_0^{\frac{\pi}{4}}$
$= \pi \left[\frac{\pi}{8} + \frac{1}{8}\sin \pi - 0\right]$
$= \frac{\pi^2}{8}$ units^3

c

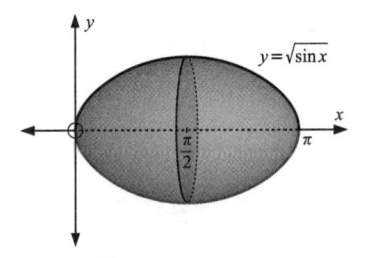

Volume $= \pi \int_0^{\pi} \sin x \, dx$
$= \pi \left[-\cos x\right]_0^{\pi}$
$= \pi \left[-\cos \pi - -\cos 0\right]$
$= \pi(2)$
$= 2\pi$ units^3

d

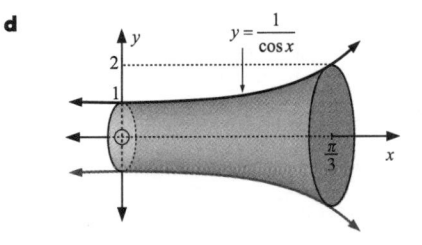

Volume $= \pi \int_0^{\frac{\pi}{3}} \frac{1}{\cos^2 x} \, dx$
$= \pi \left[\tan x\right]_0^{\frac{\pi}{3}}$
$= \pi \left(\tan \frac{\pi}{3} - \tan 0\right)$
$= \pi(\sqrt{3} - 0)$
$= \pi\sqrt{3}$ units^3

e

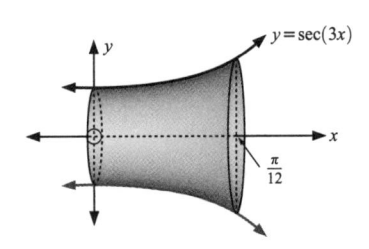

Volume $= \pi \int_0^{\frac{\pi}{12}} \sec^2(3x) \, dx$
$= \pi \left[\frac{1}{3}\tan(3x)\right]_0^{\frac{\pi}{12}}$
$= \frac{\pi}{3}\left(\tan\left(\frac{\pi}{4}\right) - 0\right)$
$= \frac{\pi}{3}$ units^3

f

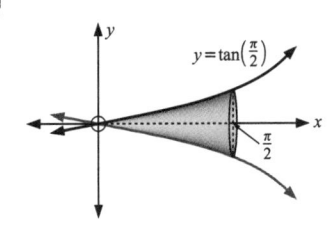

Volume $= \pi \int_0^{\frac{\pi}{2}} \tan^2\left(\frac{x}{2}\right) dx$
$= \pi \int_0^{\frac{\pi}{2}} \left(\sec^2\left(\frac{x}{2}\right) - 1\right) dx$
$= \pi \left[2\tan\left(\frac{x}{2}\right) - x\right]_0^{\frac{\pi}{2}}$
$= \pi \left(2\tan\frac{\pi}{4} - \frac{\pi}{2} - 0\right)$
$= \pi(2 - \frac{\pi}{2})$ units^3

10 a

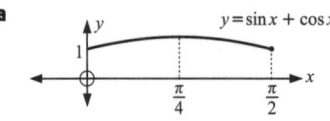

[Graph: $y = \sin x + \cos x$ from 0 to $\pi/2$, with marks at $\pi/4$ and $\pi/2$]

b Volume
$= \pi \int_0^{\frac{\pi}{4}} (\sin x + \cos x)^2 \, dx$
$= \pi \int_0^{\frac{\pi}{4}} (\sin^2 x + 2 \sin x \cos x + \cos^2 x) \, dx$
$= \pi \int_0^{\frac{\pi}{4}} (1 + \sin(2x)) \, dx$
$= \pi \left[x - \frac{1}{2} \cos(2x) \right]_0^{\frac{\pi}{4}}$
$= \pi \left[\left(\frac{\pi}{4} - \frac{1}{2} \cos\left(\frac{\pi}{2}\right) \right) - \left(0 - \frac{1}{2} \cos 0 \right) \right]$
$= \pi \left(\frac{\pi}{4} + \frac{1}{2} \right)$ units^3

11 a

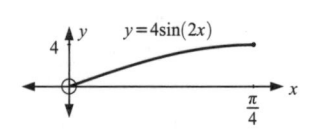

[Graph: $y = 4\sin(2x)$ from 0 to $\pi/4$]

b Volume
$= \pi \int_0^{\frac{\pi}{4}} (4 \sin(2x))^2 \, dx$
$= 16\pi \int_0^{\frac{\pi}{4}} \sin^2(2x) \, dx$
$= 16\pi \int_0^{\frac{\pi}{4}} \left(\frac{1}{2} - \frac{1}{2} \cos(4x) \right) dx$
$= 16\pi \left[\frac{x}{2} - \frac{1}{2} \left(\frac{1}{4} \right) \sin(4x) \right]_0^{\frac{\pi}{4}}$
$= 16\pi \left[\left(\frac{\pi}{8} - \frac{1}{8} \sin \pi \right) - \left(0 - \frac{1}{8} \sin 0 \right) \right]$
$= 2\pi^2$ units^3

EXERCISE 26B

1 a The graphs meet where $4 - x^2 = 3$
$\therefore \quad x^2 = 1$
$\therefore \quad x = \pm 1$
$\therefore$ A is at $(-1, 3)$ and B is at $(1, 3)$.

b $V = \pi \int_{-1}^{1} ((4 - x^2)^2 - 3^2) \, dx$
$= \pi \int_{-1}^{1} (16 - 8x^2 + x^4 - 9) \, dx$
$= \pi \int_{-1}^{1} (x^4 - 8x^2 + 7) \, dx$
$= \pi \left[\frac{x^5}{5} - \frac{8x^3}{3} + 7x \right]_{-1}^{1}$
$= \pi \left(\frac{1}{5} - \frac{8}{3} + 7 - \left(\frac{-1}{5} - \frac{-8}{3} - 7 \right) \right)$
$= \frac{136\pi}{15}$ units^3

2 a The graphs meet where $e^{\frac{x}{2}} = e$
$\therefore \quad e^{\frac{x}{2}} = e^1$
$\therefore \quad \frac{x}{2} = 1$
$\therefore \quad x = 2$
$\therefore$ A is at $(2, e)$.

b $V = \pi \int_0^2 \left(e^2 - \left(e^{\frac{x}{2}} \right)^2 \right) dx$
$= \pi \int_0^2 (e^2 - e^x) \, dx$
$= \pi \left[e^2 x - e^x \right]_0^2$
$= \pi \left[2e^2 - e^2 - (0 - 1) \right]$
$= \pi \left[e^2 + 1 \right]$ units^3

3 a The graphs meet where $x = \frac{1}{x}$
$\therefore \quad x^2 = 1$
$\therefore \quad x = \pm 1$
$\therefore \quad x = 1$ {as $x > 0$}
$\therefore$ A is at $(1, 1)$.

b $V = \pi \int_1^2 \left(x^2 - \left(\frac{1}{x} \right)^2 \right) dx$
$= \pi \int_1^2 \left(x^2 - x^{-2} \right) dx$
$= \pi \left[\frac{x^3}{3} - \frac{x^{-1}}{-1} \right]_1^2$
$= \pi \left[\left(\frac{8}{3} + \frac{1}{2} \right) - \left(\frac{1}{3} + 1 \right) \right]$
$= \frac{11\pi}{6}$ units^3

4 The graphs meet where $x^2 - 4x + 6 = 6 - x$
$\therefore \quad x^2 - 3x = 0$
$\therefore \quad x(x - 3) = 0$
$\therefore \quad x = 0$ or 3

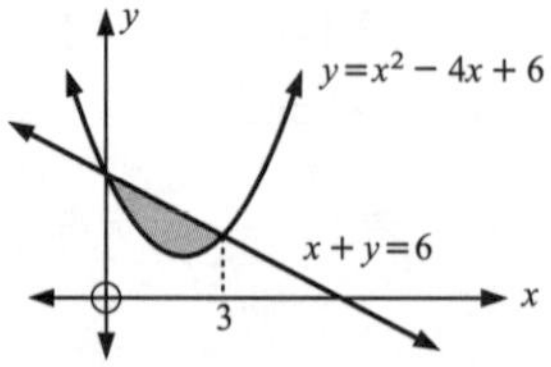

[Graph: parabola $y = x^2 - 4x + 6$ and line $x + y = 6$, shaded region between them]

$\therefore\ V = \pi \int_0^3 [(6-x)^2 - (x^2-4x+6)^2]\ dx$

$= \pi \int_0^3 [(36 - 12x + x^2) - (x^4 - 4x^3 + 6x^2 - 4x^3 + 16x^2 - 24x + 6x^2 - 24x + 36)]\ dx$

$= \pi \int_0^3 (-x^4 + 8x^3 - 27x^2 + 36x)\ dx$

$= \pi \left[-\dfrac{x^5}{5} + 2x^4 - 9x^3 + 18x^2 \right]_0^3$

$= \pi \left(-\dfrac{3^5}{5} + 2(3^4) - 9(27) + 18(9) - 0 \right)$

$= \dfrac{162}{5}\pi$ units^3

5 a The curves meet where $\sqrt{x-4} = 1$
$\therefore\ x - 4 = 1$
$\therefore\ x = 5$
$\therefore$ A is at (5, 1).

b $V = \pi \int_5^8 \left(\left(\sqrt{x-4} \right)^2 - 1^2 \right) dx$

$= \pi \int_5^8 (x - 4 - 1)\ dx$

$= \pi \int_5^8 (x - 5)\ dx$

$= \pi \left[\dfrac{x^2}{2} - 5x \right]_5^8$

$= \pi \left[(32 - 40) - \left(\dfrac{25}{2} - 25 \right) \right]$

$= \dfrac{9\pi}{2}$ units^3

6 a $x^2 + (y-3)^2 = 4$
$\therefore\ (y-3)^2 = 4 - x^2$
$\therefore\ y - 3 = \pm\sqrt{4 - x^2}$
$\therefore\ y = 3 \pm \sqrt{4 - x^2}$

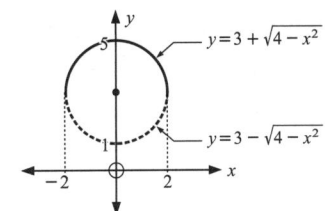

b

c $V = \pi \int_{-2}^{2} \left[\left(3 + \sqrt{4-x^2}\right)^2 - \left(3 - \sqrt{4-x^2}\right)^2 \right] dx$

$= 2\pi \int_0^2 \left[\left(3 + \sqrt{4-x^2}\right)^2 - \left(3 - \sqrt{4-x^2}\right)^2 \right] dx$

$= 2\pi \int_0^2 \left[\left(9 + 6\sqrt{4-x^2} + 4 - x^2\right) - \left(9 - 6\sqrt{4-x^2} + 4 - x^2\right) \right] dx$

$= 2\pi \int_0^2 12\sqrt{4 - x^2}\ dx$

$= 24\pi \int_0^2 \sqrt{4 - x^2}\ dx$

Let $x = 2\sin u$, $\dfrac{dx}{du} = 2\cos u$. When $x = 0$, $u = 0$, when $x = 2$, $u = \dfrac{\pi}{2}$.

$\therefore\ V = 24\pi \int_0^2 \sqrt{4 - (2\sin u)^2}\ dx$

$= 24\pi \int_0^{\frac{\pi}{2}} \sqrt{4 - 4\sin^2 u}\ \dfrac{dx}{du}\ du$

$= 48\pi \int_0^{\frac{\pi}{2}} \sqrt{1 - \sin^2 u}\ (2\cos u)\ du$

$= 48\pi \int_0^{\frac{\pi}{2}} 2\cos^2 u\ du$ $\qquad \{\sqrt{1 - \sin^2 u} = \cos u\}$

$= 48\pi \int_0^{\frac{\pi}{2}} (1 + \cos 2u)\ du$

$= 48\pi \left[u + \dfrac{1}{2}\sin 2u \right]_0^{\frac{\pi}{2}}$

$= 48\pi \left(\dfrac{\pi}{2} + \dfrac{1}{2}(0) - 0 \right)$

$= 24\pi^2$ units^3 (≈ 237 units^3)

7 Since the chord is parallel to the y-axis, the y-coordinate of P is $\dfrac{r}{2}$.

When $y = \dfrac{r}{2}$, $x^2 + \left(\dfrac{r}{2}\right)^2 = r^2$

$\therefore \quad x^2 = \dfrac{3}{4}r^2$

$\therefore \quad x = \pm\dfrac{\sqrt{3}}{2}r$

$\therefore \quad$ the coordinates of P are $\left(\dfrac{\sqrt{3}}{2}r, \dfrac{r}{2}\right)$.

$\therefore \quad V = 2\pi \int_0^{\frac{r}{2}} \left[(r^2 - y^2) - \dfrac{3}{4}r^2\right] dy$

$= 2\pi \left[r^2 y - \dfrac{y^3}{3} - \dfrac{3}{4}r^2 y\right]_0^{\frac{r}{2}}$

$= 2\pi \left(\dfrac{r^3}{2} - \dfrac{r^3}{24} - \dfrac{3r^3}{8} - 0\right)$

$= 2\pi \left(\dfrac{r^3}{12}\right) = \dfrac{\pi r^3}{6}$ units^3

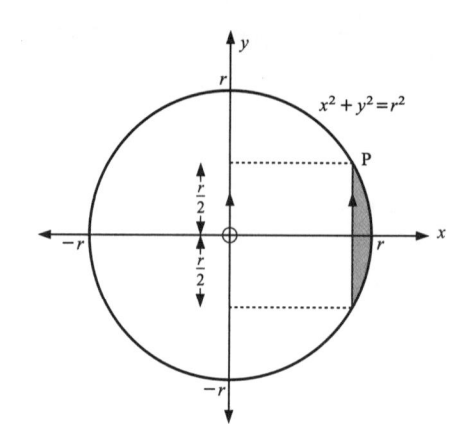

8 When $y = 3$, $x^2 + 3^2 = r^2$

$\therefore \quad x^2 = r^2 - 9$

$\therefore \quad x = \pm\sqrt{r^2 - 9}$

$\therefore \quad$ the coordinates of P are $(\sqrt{r^2 - 9}, 3)$.

$\therefore \quad V = 2\pi \int_0^3 [(r^2 - y^2) - (r^2 - 9)] \, dy$

$= 2\pi \int_0^3 (9 - y^2) \, dy$

$= 2\pi \left[9y - \dfrac{y^3}{3}\right]_0^3$

$= 2\pi(27 - 9 - 0)$

$= 36\pi$ units^3, no matter what the value of r is.

$\therefore \quad$ the volume is independent of r.

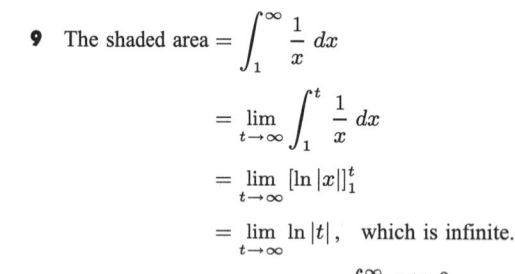

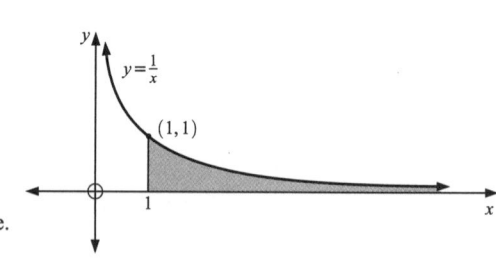

9 The shaded area $= \displaystyle\int_1^\infty \dfrac{1}{x} \, dx$

$= \displaystyle\lim_{t \to \infty} \int_1^t \dfrac{1}{x} \, dx$

$= \displaystyle\lim_{t \to \infty} [\ln|x|]_1^t$

$= \displaystyle\lim_{t \to \infty} \ln|t|$, which is infinite.

The volume of revolution $= \pi \displaystyle\int_1^\infty \left(\dfrac{1}{x}\right)^2 dx$

$= \pi \displaystyle\lim_{t \to \infty} \int_1^t x^{-2} \, dx$

$= \pi \displaystyle\lim_{t \to \infty} \left[-\dfrac{1}{x}\right]_1^t$

$= \pi \displaystyle\lim_{t \to \infty} \left(-\dfrac{1}{t} + 1\right)$

$= \pi$, which is finite.

REVIEW SET 26

1 a

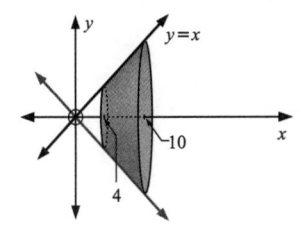

$V = \pi \int_4^{10} x^2 \, dx$

$= \pi \left[\dfrac{x^3}{3}\right]_4^{10}$

$= \pi \left(\dfrac{1000}{3} - \dfrac{64}{3}\right)$

$= \dfrac{936\pi}{3} = 312\pi$ units^3

b

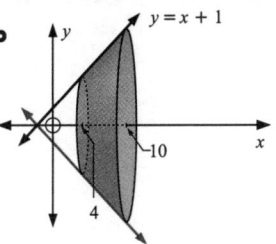

$V = \pi \int_4^{10} (x+1)^2 \, dx$

$= \pi \left[\dfrac{(x+1)^3}{3}\right]_4^{10}$

$= \pi \left(\dfrac{11^3}{3} - \dfrac{5^3}{3}\right)$

$= \dfrac{1206\pi}{3} = 402\pi$ units^3

c

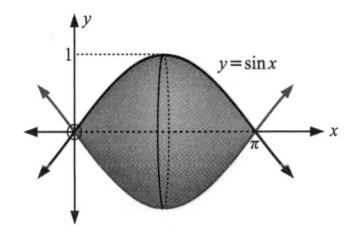

$V = \pi \int_0^{\pi} \sin^2 x \, dx$

$= \pi \int_0^{\pi} \left(\dfrac{1}{2} - \dfrac{1}{2}\cos(2x)\right) dx$

$= \pi \left[\dfrac{1}{2}x - \dfrac{1}{2}\left(\dfrac{1}{2}\right)\sin(2x)\right]_0^{\pi}$

$= \pi \left[\dfrac{1}{2}\pi - \dfrac{1}{4}\sin 2\pi - 0\right]$

$= \dfrac{\pi^2}{2}$ units^3

d

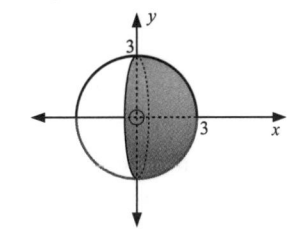

$V = \pi \int_0^3 (9 - x^2) \, dx$

$= \pi \left[9x - \dfrac{x^3}{3}\right]_0^3$

$= \pi \left[27 - \dfrac{27}{3} - 0\right]$

$= 18\pi$ units^3

2 a $y = \cos(2x)$ meets the x-axis where $2x = \dfrac{\pi}{2}$, or $x = \dfrac{\pi}{4}$.

$\therefore \ V = \pi \int_{\frac{\pi}{16}}^{\frac{\pi}{4}} \cos^2(2x) \, dx = \pi \int_{\frac{\pi}{16}}^{\frac{\pi}{4}} \left(\dfrac{1}{2} + \dfrac{1}{2}\cos(4x)\right) dx$

$= \pi \left[\dfrac{1}{2}x + \dfrac{1}{8}\sin(4x)\right]_{\frac{\pi}{16}}^{\frac{\pi}{4}}$

$= \pi \left[\left(\dfrac{\pi}{8} + \dfrac{1}{8}\sin\pi\right) - \left(\dfrac{\pi}{32} + \dfrac{1}{8}\sin\left(\dfrac{\pi}{4}\right)\right)\right]$

$= \pi \left(\dfrac{\pi}{8} - \dfrac{\pi}{32} - \dfrac{1}{8}\left(\dfrac{1}{\sqrt{2}}\right)\right)$

$= \pi \left(\dfrac{3\pi}{32} - \dfrac{1}{8\sqrt{2}}\right)$ units^3

b $V = \pi \int_0^2 (e^{-x} + 4)^2 \, dx$

$= \pi \int_0^2 \left(e^{-2x} + 8e^{-x} + 16\right) dx$

$= \pi \left[\dfrac{1}{-2}e^{-2x} + \dfrac{8}{-1}e^{-x} + 16x\right]_0^2$

$= \pi \left[\left(-\dfrac{1}{2}e^{-4} - 8e^{-2} + 32\right) - \left(-\dfrac{1}{2} - 8\right)\right]$

$= \pi \left(\dfrac{81}{2} - \dfrac{1}{2e^4} - \dfrac{8}{e^2}\right)$ units^3

≈ 124 units^3

3

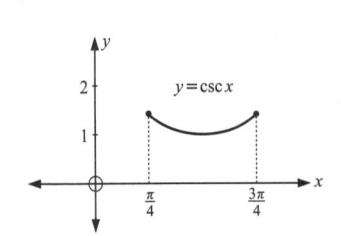

$$V = \pi \int_{\frac{\pi}{4}}^{\frac{3\pi}{4}} \csc^2 x \, dx$$
$$= \pi \left[-\cot x\right]_{\frac{\pi}{4}}^{\frac{3\pi}{4}}$$
$$= \pi \left(-\cot\left(\frac{3\pi}{4}\right) - -\cot\left(\frac{\pi}{4}\right)\right)$$
$$= \pi (-(-1) + 1)$$
$$= 2\pi \text{ units}^3$$

4 a

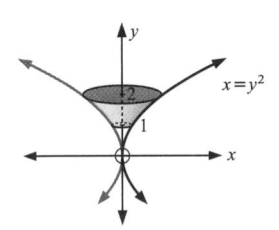

$$V = \pi \int_1^2 x^2 \, dy$$
$$= \pi \int_1^2 y^4 \, dy$$
$$= \pi \left[\frac{y^5}{5}\right]_1^2$$
$$= \pi \left(\frac{32}{5} - \frac{1}{5}\right)$$
$$= \frac{31\pi}{5} \text{ units}^3$$

b

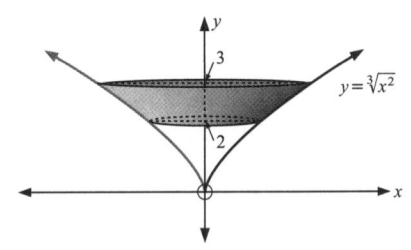

$$y = \sqrt[3]{x^2} \quad \therefore \quad x^2 = y^3$$
$$V = \pi \int_2^3 x^2 \, dy$$
$$= \pi \int_2^3 y^3 \, dy$$
$$= \pi \left[\frac{y^4}{4}\right]_2^3$$
$$= \pi \left(\frac{81}{4} - \frac{16}{4}\right)$$
$$= \frac{65\pi}{4} \text{ units}^3$$

c When $x = 1$, $y = 1$, and when $x = 2$, $y = 8$

Also, since $y = x^3$ $\therefore$ $x^2 = y^{\frac{2}{3}}$

Hence $V = \pi \int_1^8 x^2 \, dy$
$$= \pi \int_1^8 y^{\frac{2}{3}} \, dy$$
$$= \pi \left[\frac{3}{5} y^{\frac{5}{3}}\right]_1^8$$
$$= \pi \left(\frac{3}{5}(32) - \frac{3}{5}(1)\right)$$
$$= \frac{93\pi}{5} \text{ units}^3$$

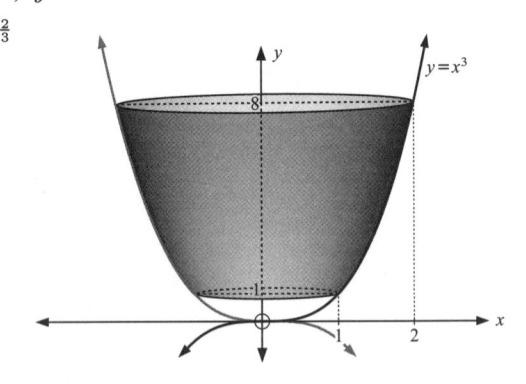

5 $y = x^2$ and $y = 4$ meet where $x^2 = 4$
$$\therefore \quad x = \pm 2$$
But $x > 0$, so $x = 2$

Hence $V = \pi \int_0^2 (4^2 - (x^2)^2) \, dx$
$$= \pi \int_0^2 (16 - x^4) \, dx$$
$$= \pi \left[16x - \frac{x^5}{5}\right]_0^2$$
$$= \pi \left(32 - \frac{32}{5} - 0\right)$$
$$= \frac{128\pi}{5} \text{ units}^3$$

6 $y = \sin x$ and $y = \cos x$ meet where $\sin x = \cos x$

$\therefore \quad \dfrac{\sin x}{\cos x} = 1$

$\therefore \quad \tan x = 1$

$\therefore \quad x = \dfrac{\pi}{4}$

Hence $V = \pi \int_0^{\frac{\pi}{4}} (\cos^2 x - \sin^2 x)\, dx$

$= \pi \int_0^{\frac{\pi}{4}} \cos(2x)\, dx$

$= \pi \left[\tfrac{1}{2}\sin(2x)\right]_0^{\frac{\pi}{4}}$

$= \pi \left(\tfrac{1}{2}\sin\left(\tfrac{\pi}{2}\right) - \tfrac{1}{2}\sin 0\right)$

$= \pi \left(\tfrac{1}{2}(1) - 0\right)$

$= \dfrac{\pi}{2}$ units^3

7 a $V = \tfrac{1}{3}\pi r^2 h$

$= \tfrac{1}{3}\pi \times 4^2 \times 8$

$= \tfrac{1}{3}\pi \times 128$

$= \dfrac{128\pi}{3}$ units^3

b

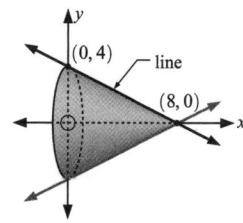

gradient $= \dfrac{0-4}{8-0} = -\dfrac{1}{2}$

$\therefore$ the line has equation $y = -\tfrac{1}{2}x + 4$

$\therefore \quad V = \pi \int_0^8 \left(-\tfrac{1}{2}x + 4\right)^2 dx$

$= \pi \int_0^8 \left(\dfrac{x^2}{4} - 4x + 16\right) dx$

$= \pi \left[\dfrac{x^3}{12} - \dfrac{4x^2}{2} + 16x\right]_0^8$

$= \pi \left(\dfrac{128}{3} - 128 + 128 - 0\right)$

$= \dfrac{128\pi}{3}$ units^3 ✓

8

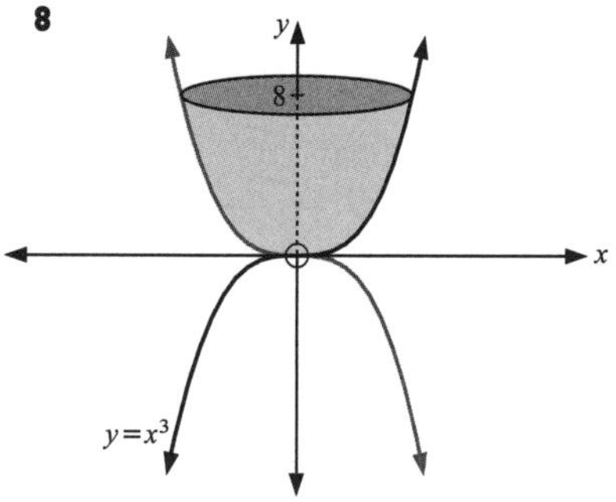

Now $x^3 = y$

$\therefore \quad (x^3)^{\frac{2}{3}} = y^{\frac{2}{3}}$

$\therefore \quad x^2 = y^{\frac{2}{3}}$

Volume $V = \pi \int_0^8 x^2\, dy$

$= \pi \int_0^8 y^{\frac{2}{3}}\, dy$

$= \pi \left[\dfrac{y^{\frac{5}{3}}}{\frac{5}{3}}\right]_0^8$

$= \dfrac{3\pi}{5}\left(8^{\frac{5}{3}} - 0^{\frac{5}{3}}\right)$

$= \dfrac{3\pi}{5} \times (2^3)^{\frac{5}{3}}$

$= \dfrac{3\pi}{5} \times 2^5$

$= \dfrac{96\pi}{5}$ units^3

Chapter 27
FURTHER INTEGRATION AND DIFFERENTIAL EQUATIONS

EXERCISE 27A

1 a $\displaystyle\int \frac{4}{\sqrt{1-x^2}}\, dx$
$= 4\int \frac{1}{\sqrt{1-x^2}}\, dx$
$= 4\arcsin\left(\frac{x}{1}\right) + c$
$= 4\arcsin(x) + c$

b $\displaystyle\int \frac{3}{\sqrt{4-x^2}}\, dx$
$= 3\int \frac{1}{\sqrt{4-x^2}}\, dx$
$= 3\arcsin\left(\frac{x}{2}\right) + c$

c $\displaystyle\int \frac{1}{x^2+16}\, dx$
$= \frac{1}{4}\arctan\left(\frac{x}{4}\right) + c$

d $\displaystyle\int \frac{1}{4x^2+1}\, dx$
$= \frac{1}{4}\int \frac{1}{x^2+(\frac{1}{2})^2}\, dx$
$= \frac{1}{4}\left(\frac{1}{\frac{1}{2}}\right)\arctan\left(\frac{x}{\frac{1}{2}}\right) + c$
$= \frac{1}{2}\arctan(2x) + c$

e $\displaystyle\int \frac{1}{\sqrt{1-4x^2}}\, dx$
$= \frac{1}{2}\int \frac{1}{\sqrt{\frac{1}{4}-x^2}}\, dx$
$= \frac{1}{2}\arcsin\left(\frac{x}{\frac{1}{2}}\right) + c$
$= \frac{1}{2}\arcsin(2x) + c$

f $\displaystyle\int \frac{2}{\sqrt{4-9x^2}}\, dx$
$= 2\int \frac{1}{\sqrt{4-9x^2}}\, dx$
$= \frac{2}{3}\int \frac{1}{\sqrt{\frac{4}{9}-x^2}}\, dx$
$= \frac{2}{3}\arcsin\left(\frac{3x}{2}\right) + c$

g $\displaystyle\int \frac{1}{4+2x^2}\, dx$
$= \frac{1}{2}\int \frac{1}{2+x^2}\, dx$
$= \frac{1}{2}\left(\frac{1}{\sqrt{2}}\right)\arctan\left(\frac{x}{\sqrt{2}}\right) + c$
$= \frac{1}{2\sqrt{2}}\arctan\left(\frac{x}{\sqrt{2}}\right) + c$

h $\displaystyle\int \frac{5}{9+4x^2}\, dx$
$= \frac{5}{4}\int \frac{1}{\frac{9}{4}+x^2}\, dx$
$= \frac{5}{4}\left(\frac{1}{\frac{3}{2}}\right)\arctan\left(\frac{x}{\frac{3}{2}}\right) + c$
$= \frac{5}{6}\arctan\left(\frac{2x}{3}\right) + c$

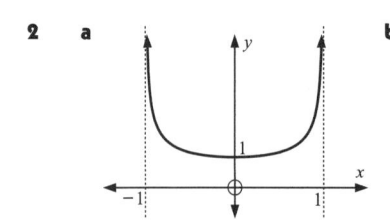

2 a

b i If $f(x) = \dfrac{1}{\sqrt{1-x^2}}$ then $f(-x) = \dfrac{1}{\sqrt{1-(-x)^2}}$
$= \dfrac{1}{\sqrt{1-x^2}}$
$= f(x)$ for all x
$\therefore\ f(x)$ is an even function, and so it is symmetric about the y-axis.

ii $f(x)$ is defined when $1 - x^2 > 0$
$\therefore\ x^2 - 1 < 0$
$\therefore\ (x+1)(x-1) < 0$

$\therefore\ x \in\ ]-1,\ 1\ [$

c Area $= \displaystyle\int_0^{\frac{1}{2}} \frac{1}{\sqrt{1-x^2}}\, dx$
$= [\arcsin(x)]_0^{\frac{1}{2}}$
$= \arcsin(\frac{1}{2}) - \arcsin(0)$
$= \frac{\pi}{6} - 0$
$= \frac{\pi}{6}$ units^2

EXERCISE 27B

1 **a** Let $u = x - 3$, $\dfrac{du}{dx} = 1$

$\therefore \ x = u + 3$

$\therefore \ \int x\sqrt{x-3}\,dx$

$= \int (u+3)\sqrt{u}\,\dfrac{du}{dx}\,dx$

$= \int \left(u^{\frac{3}{2}} + 3u^{\frac{1}{2}}\right) du$

$= \dfrac{u^{\frac{5}{2}}}{\frac{5}{2}} + \dfrac{3u^{\frac{3}{2}}}{\frac{3}{2}} + c$

$= \tfrac{2}{5}u^{\frac{5}{2}} + 2u^{\frac{3}{2}} + c$

$= \tfrac{2}{5}(x-3)^{\frac{5}{2}} + 2(x-3)^{\frac{3}{2}} + c$

b Let $u = x + 1$, $\dfrac{du}{dx} = 1$

$\therefore \ x = u - 1$

$\therefore \ \int x^2\sqrt{x+1}\,dx$

$= \int (u-1)^2 \sqrt{u}\,\dfrac{du}{dx}\,dx$

$= \int (u^2 - 2u + 1)u^{\frac{1}{2}}\,du$

$= \int \left(u^{\frac{5}{2}} - 2u^{\frac{3}{2}} + u^{\frac{1}{2}}\right) du$

$= \dfrac{u^{\frac{7}{2}}}{\frac{7}{2}} - \dfrac{2u^{\frac{5}{2}}}{\frac{5}{2}} + \dfrac{u^{\frac{3}{2}}}{\frac{3}{2}} + c$

$= \tfrac{2}{7}u^{\frac{7}{2}} - \tfrac{4}{5}u^{\frac{5}{2}} + \tfrac{2}{3}u^{\frac{3}{2}} + c$

$= \tfrac{2}{7}(x+1)^{\frac{7}{2}} - \tfrac{4}{5}(x+1)^{\frac{5}{2}} + \tfrac{2}{3}(x+1)^{\frac{3}{2}} + c$

c Let $u = 3 - x^2$, $\dfrac{du}{dx} = -2x$

$\therefore \ \int x^3 \sqrt{3-x^2}\,dx$

$= -\tfrac{1}{2} \int x^2 \sqrt{3-x^2}\,(-2x)\,dx$

$= -\tfrac{1}{2} \int x^2 \sqrt{3-x^2}\,\dfrac{du}{dx}\,dx$

$= -\tfrac{1}{2} \int (3-u)\sqrt{u}\,du$

$= -\tfrac{1}{2} \int \left(3u^{\frac{1}{2}} - u^{\frac{3}{2}}\right) du$

$= -\tfrac{1}{2} \left[\dfrac{3u^{\frac{3}{2}}}{\frac{3}{2}} - \dfrac{u^{\frac{5}{2}}}{\frac{5}{2}}\right] + c$

$= -\tfrac{1}{2} \left[2u^{\frac{3}{2}} - \tfrac{2}{5}u^{\frac{5}{2}}\right] + c$

$= -u^{\frac{3}{2}} + \tfrac{1}{5}u^{\frac{5}{2}} + c$

$= -\left(3-x^2\right)^{\frac{3}{2}} + \tfrac{1}{5}\left(3-x^2\right)^{\frac{5}{2}} + c$

d Let $u = t^2 + 2$, $\dfrac{du}{dt} = 2t$

$\therefore \ \int t^3 \sqrt{t^2+2}\,dt$

$= \tfrac{1}{2} \int t^2 \sqrt{t^2+2}\,(2t)\,dt$

$= \tfrac{1}{2} \int t^2 \sqrt{t^2+2}\,\dfrac{du}{dt}\,dt$

$= \tfrac{1}{2} \int (u-2)\sqrt{u}\,du$

$= \tfrac{1}{2} \int \left(u^{\frac{3}{2}} - 2u^{\frac{1}{2}}\right) du$

$= \tfrac{1}{2} \left[\dfrac{u^{\frac{5}{2}}}{\frac{5}{2}} - \dfrac{2u^{\frac{3}{2}}}{\frac{3}{2}}\right] + c$

$= \tfrac{1}{5}u^{\frac{5}{2}} - \tfrac{2}{3}u^{\frac{3}{2}} + c$

$= \tfrac{1}{5}\left(t^2+2\right)^{\frac{5}{2}} - \tfrac{2}{3}\left(t^2+2\right)^{\frac{3}{2}} + c$

e Let $u = \sqrt{x-1}$, $\dfrac{du}{dx} = \tfrac{1}{2}(x-1)^{-\frac{1}{2}}(1)$

$\therefore \ x = u^2 + 1$, $\dfrac{du}{dx} = \dfrac{1}{2\sqrt{x-1}}$

$\therefore \ \int \dfrac{\sqrt{x-1}}{x}\,dx = 2\int \dfrac{x-1}{x}\,\dfrac{1}{2\sqrt{x-1}}\,dx$

$= 2 \int \dfrac{u^2}{u^2+1}\,\dfrac{du}{dx}\,dx$

$= 2 \int \dfrac{u^2}{u^2+1}\,du$

$= 2 \int \left(1 - \dfrac{1}{u^2+1}\right) du$

$= 2(u - \arctan u) + c$

$= 2\sqrt{x-1} - 2\arctan \sqrt{x-1} + c$

2 a Let $u = x - 1$, $\dfrac{du}{dx} = 1$

when $x = 4$, $u = 3$
when $x = 3$, $u = 2$

$\therefore \int_3^4 x\sqrt{x-1}\, dx$

$= \int_2^3 (u+1)\sqrt{u}\, du$

$= \int_2^3 (u^{\frac{3}{2}} + u^{\frac{1}{2}})\, du$

$= \left[\dfrac{u^{\frac{5}{2}}}{\frac{5}{2}} + \dfrac{u^{\frac{3}{2}}}{\frac{3}{2}}\right]_2^3$

$= \left(\tfrac{2}{5}(3)^{\frac{5}{2}} + \tfrac{2}{3}(3)^{\frac{3}{2}}\right) - \left(\tfrac{2}{5}(2)^{\frac{5}{2}} + \tfrac{2}{3}(2)^{\frac{3}{2}}\right)$

$= \tfrac{2}{5}(9\sqrt{3}) + \tfrac{2}{3}(3\sqrt{3}) - \tfrac{2}{5}(4\sqrt{2}) - \tfrac{2}{3}(2\sqrt{2})$

$= \left(\tfrac{18}{5} + 2\right)\sqrt{3} - \left(\tfrac{8}{5} + \tfrac{4}{3}\right)\sqrt{2}$

$= \dfrac{28\sqrt{3}}{5} - \dfrac{44\sqrt{2}}{15}$

b Let $u = x + 6$, $\dfrac{du}{dx} = 1$

when $x = 3$, $u = 9$
when $x = 0$, $u = 6$

$\therefore \int_0^3 x\sqrt{x+6}\, dx$

$= \int_6^9 (u - 6)\sqrt{u}\, du$

$= \int_6^9 (u^{\frac{3}{2}} - 6u^{\frac{1}{2}})\, du$

$= \left[\dfrac{u^{\frac{5}{2}}}{\frac{5}{2}} - \dfrac{6u^{\frac{3}{2}}}{\frac{3}{2}}\right]_6^9$

$= \left(\tfrac{2}{5}(9)^{\frac{5}{2}} - 4(9)^{\frac{3}{2}}\right) - \left(\tfrac{2}{5}(6)^{\frac{5}{2}} - 4(6)^{\frac{3}{2}}\right)$

$= \tfrac{2}{5}(3^5) - 4(3^3) - \tfrac{2}{5} \times 36\sqrt{6} + 4 \times 6\sqrt{6}$

$= \dfrac{486}{5} - 108 - \dfrac{72}{5}\sqrt{6} + 24\sqrt{6}$

$= -\dfrac{54}{5} + \dfrac{48}{5}\sqrt{6}$

$= \tfrac{1}{5}(48\sqrt{6} - 54)$

c Let $u = x - 2$, $\dfrac{du}{dx} = 1$

when $x = 5$, $u = 3$
when $x = 2$, $u = 0$

$\therefore \int_2^5 x^2\sqrt{x-2}\, dx = \int_0^3 (u+2)^2\sqrt{u}\, du$

$= \int_0^3 (u^2 + 4u + 4)\sqrt{u}\, du$

$= \int_0^3 (u^{\frac{5}{2}} + 4u^{\frac{3}{2}} + 4u^{\frac{1}{2}})\, du$

$= \left[\dfrac{u^{\frac{7}{2}}}{\frac{7}{2}} + \dfrac{4u^{\frac{5}{2}}}{\frac{5}{2}} + \dfrac{4u^{\frac{3}{2}}}{\frac{3}{2}}\right]_0^3$

$= \tfrac{2}{7}(3)^{\frac{7}{2}} + \tfrac{8}{5}(3)^{\frac{5}{2}} + \tfrac{8}{3}(3)^{\frac{3}{2}} - 0$

$= \tfrac{2}{7}(27\sqrt{3}) + \tfrac{8}{5}(9\sqrt{3}) + \tfrac{8}{3}(3\sqrt{3})$

$= \dfrac{1054}{35}\sqrt{3}$

3 a Let $x = 3\tan\theta$, $\dfrac{dx}{d\theta} = 3\sec^2\theta$

$\therefore \int \dfrac{x^2}{9 + x^2}\, dx$

$= \int \dfrac{9\tan^2\theta}{9 + 9\tan^2\theta} \, 3\sec^2\theta\, d\theta$

$= 3\int \dfrac{\tan^2\theta}{1 + \tan^2\theta}\sec^2\theta\, d\theta$

$= 3\int \tan^2\theta\, d\theta \quad \{\sec^2\theta = 1 + \tan^2\theta\}$

$= 3\int (\sec^2\theta - 1)\, d\theta$

$= 3\tan\theta - 3\theta + c$

$= x - 3\arctan\left(\dfrac{x}{3}\right) + c$

b Let $x = \sin\theta$, $\dfrac{dx}{d\theta} = \cos\theta$

$\therefore \int \dfrac{x^2}{\sqrt{1 - x^2}}\, dx$

$= \int \dfrac{\sin^2\theta}{\sqrt{1 - \sin^2\theta}}\cos\theta\, d\theta$

$= \int \dfrac{\sin^2\theta}{\cos\theta}\cos\theta\, d\theta$

$= \int \sin^2\theta\, d\theta$

$= \int \left(\tfrac{1}{2} - \tfrac{1}{2}\cos 2\theta\right) d\theta$

$= \tfrac{1}{2}\theta - \tfrac{1}{2}(\tfrac{1}{2})\sin 2\theta + c$

$= \tfrac{1}{2}\theta - \tfrac{1}{2}\sin\theta\cos\theta + c$

$= \tfrac{1}{2}\arcsin x - \tfrac{1}{2}x\sqrt{1 - x^2} + c$

$\{\text{since } \cos\theta = \sqrt{1 - \sin^2\theta}\}$

c $\int \dfrac{2x}{x^2+9}\,dx$ has the form $\int \dfrac{f'(x)}{f(x)}\,dx$.

$\therefore \int \dfrac{2x}{x^2+9}\,dx$

$= \ln\left|x^2+9\right| + c$

$= \ln(x^2+9) + c \quad \{x^2+9 > 0 \text{ for all } x\}$

e Let $x = 2\sec\theta$, $\dfrac{dx}{d\theta} = 2\sec\theta\tan\theta$

$\therefore \int \dfrac{\sqrt{x^2-4}}{x}\,dx$

$= \int \dfrac{\sqrt{4\sec^2\theta - 4}}{2\sec\theta}\, 2\sec\theta\tan\theta\,d\theta$

$= \dfrac{2}{2}\int \dfrac{\sqrt{\sec^2\theta - 1}}{\sec\theta} \times 2\sec\theta\tan\theta\,d\theta$

$= 2\int \sqrt{\sec^2\theta - 1}\,\tan\theta\,d\theta$

$= 2\int \tan\theta\tan\theta\,d\theta \quad \{\sec^2\theta - 1 = \tan^2\theta\}$

$= 2\int \tan^2\theta\,d\theta$

$= 2\int (\sec^2\theta - 1)\,d\theta$

$= 2\tan\theta - 2\theta + c$

$= 2\dfrac{\sqrt{x^2-4}}{2} - 2\arccos\left(\dfrac{2}{x}\right) + c$

$= \sqrt{x^2-4} - 2\arccos\left(\dfrac{2}{x}\right) + c$

d Let $u = \ln x$, $\dfrac{du}{dx} = \dfrac{1}{x}$

$\therefore \int \dfrac{4\ln x}{x(1+[\ln x]^2)}\,dx$

$= \int \dfrac{4u}{1+u^2}\dfrac{du}{dx}\,dx$

$= 2\int \dfrac{2u}{1+u^2}\,du$

which has the form $\int \dfrac{f'(x)}{f(x)}\,dx$.

$\therefore$ the integral

$= 2\ln\left|1+u^2\right| + c$

$= 2\ln(1+u^2) + c \quad \{1+u^2 > 0\}$

$= 2\ln\left(1+[\ln x]^2\right) + c$

f $\int \sin x \cos 2x\,dx$

$= \int \sin x(2\cos^2 x - 1)\,dx$

$= 2\int \cos^2 x \sin x\,dx - \int \sin x\,dx$

$= -2\int [\cos x]^2(-\sin x)\,dx - \int \sin x\,dx$

$= -2\dfrac{[\cos x]^3}{3} - (-\cos x) + c$

$= -\dfrac{2}{3}\cos^3 x + \cos x + c$

$= \cos x - \dfrac{2}{3}\cos^3 x + c$

g $\int \dfrac{1}{\sqrt{9-4x^2}}\,dx = \dfrac{1}{2}\int \dfrac{1}{\sqrt{\dfrac{9}{4}-x^2}}\,dx$

Let $x = \dfrac{3}{2}\sin\theta$, so $\dfrac{dx}{d\theta} = \dfrac{3}{2}\cos\theta$

$\therefore$ the integral

$= \dfrac{1}{2}\int \dfrac{1}{\sqrt{\dfrac{9}{4}-\dfrac{9}{4}\sin^2\theta}} \cdot \dfrac{3}{2}\cos\theta\,d\theta$

$= \dfrac{1}{2}\int \dfrac{1}{\dfrac{3}{2}\sqrt{1-\sin^2\theta}} \times \dfrac{3}{2}\cos\theta\,d\theta$

$= \dfrac{1}{2}\int \dfrac{\cos\theta}{\cos\theta}\,d\theta$

$= \dfrac{1}{2}\int 1\,d\theta$

$= \dfrac{1}{2}\theta + c$

$= \dfrac{1}{2}\arcsin\left(\dfrac{2x}{3}\right) + c \quad \{\text{since } \sin\theta = \dfrac{2x}{3}\}$

h $\int \dfrac{x^3}{1+x^2}\,dx$

$= \int \dfrac{x(1+x^2) - x}{1+x^2}\,dx$

$= \int \left(x - \dfrac{x}{1+x^2}\right)dx$

$= \int \left(x - \dfrac{1}{2}\left(\dfrac{2x}{1+x^2}\right)\right)dx$

$= \dfrac{x^2}{2} - \dfrac{1}{2}\ln\left|1+x^2\right| + c$

$= \dfrac{x^2}{2} - \dfrac{1}{2}\ln(1+x^2) + c \quad \{\text{as } 1+x^2 > 0\}$

i Let $u = \ln x$, $\dfrac{du}{dx} = \dfrac{1}{x}$

$\therefore \displaystyle\int \dfrac{1}{x(9 + 4[\ln x]^2)} \, dx$

$= \displaystyle\int \dfrac{1}{9 + 4u^2} \dfrac{du}{dx} \, dx$

$= \displaystyle\int \dfrac{1}{9 + 4u^2} \, du$

$= \dfrac{1}{4} \displaystyle\int \dfrac{1}{u^2 + \frac{9}{4}} \, du$

$= \dfrac{1}{4} \left(\dfrac{1}{\frac{3}{2}}\right) \arctan\left(\dfrac{u}{\frac{3}{2}}\right) + c$

$= \dfrac{1}{6} \arctan\left(\dfrac{2u}{3}\right) + c$

$= \dfrac{1}{6} \arctan\left(\dfrac{2\ln x}{3}\right) + c$

j Let $x = 4\tan\theta$, $\dfrac{dx}{d\theta} = 4\sec^2\theta$

$\therefore \displaystyle\int \dfrac{1}{x(x^2 + 16)} \, dx$

$= \displaystyle\int \dfrac{1}{4\tan\theta(16\tan^2\theta + 16)} \times 4\sec^2\theta \, d\theta$

$= \displaystyle\int \dfrac{1}{4\tan\theta \times 16\sec^2\theta} \times 4\sec^2\theta \, d\theta$

$= \dfrac{1}{16} \displaystyle\int \dfrac{1}{\tan\theta} \, d\theta$

$= \dfrac{1}{16} \displaystyle\int \dfrac{\cos\theta}{\sin\theta} \, d\theta$

$= \dfrac{1}{16} \ln|\sin\theta| + c \quad \left\{\text{form } \dfrac{f'(\theta)}{f(\theta)}\right\}$

$= \dfrac{1}{16} \ln\left|\dfrac{x}{\sqrt{x^2 + 16}}\right| + c$

$= \dfrac{1}{16} \ln\left(\dfrac{|x|}{\sqrt{x^2 + 16}}\right) + c$

k Let $x = 4\sin\theta$, $\dfrac{dx}{d\theta} = 4\cos\theta$

$\therefore \displaystyle\int \dfrac{1}{x^2\sqrt{16 - x^2}} \, dx$

$= \displaystyle\int \dfrac{1}{16\sin^2\theta\sqrt{16 - 16\sin^2\theta}} \, 4\cos\theta \, d\theta$

$= \displaystyle\int \dfrac{1}{16\sin^2\theta \times 4\cos\theta} \, 4\cos\theta \, d\theta$

$= \dfrac{1}{16} \displaystyle\int \dfrac{1}{\sin^2\theta} \, d\theta$

$= \dfrac{1}{16} \displaystyle\int \csc^2\theta \, d\theta$

$= \dfrac{1}{16}(-\cot\theta) + c$

$= -\dfrac{1}{16} \cot\theta + c$

$= -\dfrac{1}{16} \dfrac{\sqrt{16 - x^2}}{x} + c$

$= -\dfrac{\sqrt{16 - x^2}}{16x} + c$

l Let $x = 2\sin\theta$, $\dfrac{dx}{d\theta} = 2\cos\theta$

$\therefore \displaystyle\int x^2\sqrt{4 - x^2} \, dx$

$= \displaystyle\int 4\sin^2\theta \sqrt{4 - 4\sin^2\theta} \, 2\cos\theta \, d\theta$

$= \displaystyle\int 4\sin^2\theta \, 2\cos\theta \, 2\cos\theta \, d\theta$

$= 4 \displaystyle\int 4\sin^2\theta \cos^2\theta \, d\theta$

$= 4 \displaystyle\int \sin^2(2\theta) \, d\theta$

$= 4 \displaystyle\int \left(\tfrac{1}{2} - \tfrac{1}{2}\cos(4\theta)\right) d\theta$

$= 2\theta - 2(\tfrac{1}{4})\sin(4\theta) + c$

$= 2\theta - \tfrac{1}{2}\sin(4\theta) + c$

Now $\sin\theta = \dfrac{x}{2}$, $\cos\theta = \dfrac{\sqrt{4 - x^2}}{2}$

$\therefore \sin 2\theta = 2\left(\dfrac{x}{2}\right)\dfrac{\sqrt{4 - x^2}}{2} = \dfrac{x\sqrt{4 - x^2}}{2}$

and $\cos 2\theta = \cos^2\theta - \sin^2\theta$

$= \dfrac{4 - x^2}{4} - \dfrac{x^2}{4}$

$= \dfrac{4 - 2x^2}{4}$

$\therefore \sin 4\theta = 2\left(\dfrac{x\sqrt{4 - x^2}}{2}\right)\left(\dfrac{4 - 2x^2}{4}\right)$

$= \dfrac{x\sqrt{4 - x^2}(2 - x^2)}{2}$

$\therefore \displaystyle\int x^2\sqrt{4 - x^2} \, dx$

$= 2\arcsin\left(\dfrac{x}{2}\right) - \tfrac{1}{4}x\sqrt{4 - x^2}(2 - x^2) + c$

EXERCISE 27C

1 a We integrate by parts with
$$u = x \qquad v' = e^x$$
$$u' = 1 \qquad v = e^x$$
$$\therefore \int xe^x \, dx = xe^x - \int 1e^x \, dx$$
$$= xe^x - e^x + c$$

c We integrate by parts with
$$u = \ln x \qquad v' = x^2$$
$$u' = \frac{1}{x} \qquad v = \frac{x^3}{3}$$
$$\therefore \int x^2 \ln x \, dx$$
$$= \ln x \left(\frac{x^3}{3}\right) - \int \frac{1}{x} \frac{x^3}{3} \, dx$$
$$= \frac{x^3 \ln x}{3} - \frac{1}{3} \int x^2 \, dx$$
$$= \frac{x^3 \ln x}{3} - \frac{1}{3} \frac{x^3}{3} + c$$
$$= \tfrac{1}{3} x^3 \ln x - \tfrac{1}{9} x^3 + c$$

e We integrate by parts with
$$u = x \qquad v' = \cos 2x$$
$$u' = 1 \qquad v = \tfrac{1}{2} \sin 2x$$
$$\therefore \int x \cos 2x \, dx$$
$$= x(\tfrac{1}{2} \sin 2x) - \int \tfrac{1}{2} \sin 2x \, dx$$
$$= \tfrac{1}{2} x \sin 2x - \tfrac{1}{2}(-\tfrac{1}{2}) \cos 2x + c$$
$$= \tfrac{1}{2} x \sin 2x + \tfrac{1}{4} \cos 2x + c$$

g $\int \ln x \, dx = \int 1 \times \ln x \, dx$
So, we integate by parts with
$$u = \ln x \qquad v' = 1$$
$$u' = \frac{1}{x} \qquad v = x$$
$$\therefore \int \ln x \, dx = x \ln x - \int \left(\frac{1}{x}\right) x \, dx$$
$$= x \ln x - \int 1 \, dx$$
$$= x \ln x - x + c$$

i $\int \arctan x \, dx = \int 1 \arctan x \, dx$
So, we integrate by parts with
$$u = \arctan x \qquad v' = 1$$
$$u' = \frac{1}{x^2 + 1} \qquad v = x$$

b We integrate by parts with
$$u = x \qquad v' = \sin x$$
$$u' = 1 \qquad v = -\cos x$$
$$\therefore \int x \sin x \, dx$$
$$= x(-\cos x) - \int 1(-\cos x) \, dx$$
$$= -x \cos x + \int \cos x \, dx$$
$$= -x \cos x + \sin x + c$$

d We integrate by parts with
$$u = x \qquad v' = \sin 3x$$
$$u' = 1 \qquad v = -\tfrac{1}{3} \cos 3x$$
$$\therefore \int x \sin 3x \, dx$$
$$= x(-\tfrac{1}{3} \cos 3x) - \int \left(-\tfrac{1}{3} \cos 3x\right) dx$$
$$= -\tfrac{1}{3} x \cos 3x + \tfrac{1}{3}(\tfrac{1}{3}) \sin 3x + c$$
$$= -\tfrac{1}{3} x \cos 3x + \tfrac{1}{9} \sin 3x + c$$

f We integrate by parts with
$$u = x \qquad v' = \sec^2 x$$
$$u' = 1 \qquad v = \tan x$$
$$\therefore \int x \sec^2 x \, dx$$
$$= x \tan x - \int \tan x \, dx$$
$$= x \tan x + \int \frac{-\sin x}{\cos x} \, dx$$
$$= x \tan x + \ln|\cos x| + c$$

h $\int (\ln x)^2 \, dx = \int (\ln x)(\ln x) \, dx$
So, we integrate by parts with
$$u = \ln x \qquad v' = \ln x$$
$$u' = \frac{1}{x} \qquad v = x \ln x - x \quad \{\text{using \textbf{g}}\}$$
$$\therefore \int (\ln x)^2 \, dx$$
$$= \ln x (x \ln x - x) - \int \frac{1}{x}(x \ln x - x) \, dx$$
$$= x(\ln x)^2 - x \ln x - \int (\ln x - 1) \, dx$$
$$= x(\ln x)^2 - x \ln x - [x \ln x - x] + x + c$$
$$= x(\ln x)^2 - 2x \ln x + 2x + c$$

$$\therefore \int \arctan x \, dx$$
$$= x \arctan x - \int \frac{x}{x^2 + 1} \, dx$$
$$= x \arctan x - \tfrac{1}{2} \int \frac{2x}{x^2 + 1} \, dx$$
$$= x \arctan x - \tfrac{1}{2} \ln |x^2 + 1| + c$$
$$= x \arctan x - \tfrac{1}{2} \ln(x^2 + 1) + c \quad \{\text{as } x^2 + 1 > 0\}$$

2 **a** We integrate by parts with $\quad u = x^2 \quad v' = e^{-x}$
$\qquad\qquad\qquad\qquad\qquad\quad u' = 2x \quad v = -e^{-x}$

$\therefore \quad \int x^2 e^{-x} \, dx = -x^2 e^{-x} - \int 2x(-e^{-x}) \, dx$
$\qquad\qquad\qquad = -x^2 e^{-x} + 2 \int x e^{-x} \, dx$

We integrate by parts again, this time with $\quad u = x \quad v' = e^{-x}$
$\qquad\qquad\qquad\qquad\qquad\qquad\qquad\qquad\quad u' = 1 \quad v = -e^{-x}$

$\therefore \quad \int x^2 e^{-x} \, dx = -x^2 e^{-x} + 2\left[x(-e^{-x}) - \int -e^{-x} \, dx\right]$
$\qquad\qquad\qquad = -x^2 e^{-x} - 2x e^{-x} + 2 \int e^{-x} \, dx$
$\qquad\qquad\qquad = -x^2 e^{-x} - 2x e^{-x} - 2 e^{-x} + c$

b We integrate by parts with $\quad u = e^x \quad v' = \cos x$
$\qquad\qquad\qquad\qquad\qquad\quad u' = e^x \quad v = \sin x$

$\therefore \quad \int e^x \cos x \, dx = e^x \sin x - \int e^x \sin x \, dx$

We again integrate by parts with $\quad u = e^x \quad v' = \sin x$
$\qquad\qquad\qquad\qquad\qquad\qquad\quad u' = e^x \quad v = -\cos x$

$\therefore \quad \int e^x \cos x \, dx = e^x \sin x - \left[-e^x \cos x - \int e^x(-\cos x) \, dx\right] + c_1$
$\qquad\qquad\qquad = e^x \sin x + e^x \cos x - \int e^x \cos x \, dx + c_1$

$\therefore \quad 2 \int e^x \cos x \, dx = e^x(\sin x + \cos x) + c_1$

$\therefore \quad \int e^x \cos x \, dx = \tfrac{1}{2} e^x(\sin x + \cos x) + c$

c We integrate by parts with $\quad u = e^{-x} \quad v' = \sin x$
$\qquad\qquad\qquad\qquad\qquad\quad u' = -e^{-x} \quad v = -\cos x$

$\therefore \quad \int e^{-x} \sin x \, dx = -e^{-x} \cos x - \int -e^{-x}(-\cos x) \, dx$
$\qquad\qquad\qquad = -e^{-x} \cos x - \int e^{-x} \cos x \, dx$

We integrate by parts again, this time with $\quad u = e^{-x} \quad v' = \cos x$
$\qquad\qquad\qquad\qquad\qquad\qquad\qquad\qquad\quad u' = -e^{-x} \quad v = \sin x$

$\therefore \quad \int e^{-x} \sin x \, dx = -e^{-x} \cos x - \left[e^{-x} \sin x - \int -e^{-x} \sin x \, dx\right] + c_1$
$\qquad\qquad\qquad = -e^{-x} \cos x - e^{-x} \sin x - \int e^{-x} \sin x \, dx + c_1$

$\therefore \quad 2 \int e^{-x} \sin x \, dx = -e^{-x}(\sin x + \cos x) + c_1$

$\therefore \quad \int e^{-x} \sin x \, dx = -\tfrac{1}{2} e^{-x}(\sin x + \cos x) + c$

d We integrate by parts with $\quad u = x^2 \quad v' = \sin x$
$\qquad\qquad\qquad\qquad\qquad\quad u' = 2x \quad v = -\cos x$

$\therefore \quad \int x^2 \sin x \, dx = -x^2 \cos x - \int -2x \cos x \, dx$
$\qquad\qquad\qquad = -x^2 \cos x + \int 2x \cos x \, dx$

We integrate by parts again, this time with $\quad u = 2x \quad v' = \cos x$
$\qquad\qquad\qquad\qquad\qquad\qquad\qquad\qquad\quad u' = 2 \quad v = \sin x$

$\therefore \quad \int x^2 \sin x \, dx = -x^2 \cos x + \left[2x \sin x - \int 2 \sin x \, dx\right]$
$\qquad\qquad\qquad = -x^2 \cos x + 2x \sin x - 2 \int \sin x \, dx$
$\qquad\qquad\qquad = -x^2 \cos x + 2x \sin x - 2(-\cos x) + c$
$\qquad\qquad\qquad = -x^2 \cos x + 2x \sin x + 2 \cos x + c$

3 **a** We integrate by parts with $\quad a = u^2 \quad b' = e^u$
$\qquad\qquad\qquad\qquad\qquad\quad a' = 2u \quad b = e^u$

$\therefore \quad \int u^2 e^u \, du = u^2 e^u - \int 2u e^u \, du$
$\qquad\qquad\qquad = u^2 e^u - 2 \int u e^u \, du$

We integrate by parts again, this time with $\quad a = u \quad b' = e^u$
$\qquad\qquad\qquad\qquad\qquad\qquad\qquad\qquad\qquad a' = 1 \quad b = e^u$

$\therefore \int u^2 e^u \, du = u^2 e^u - 2 \left[u e^u - \int e^u \, du \right]$
$\qquad\qquad\quad = u^2 e^u - 2u e^u + 2 e^u + c$

b Let $u = \ln x$, $\dfrac{du}{dx} = \dfrac{1}{x} = \dfrac{1}{e^u}$ $\quad\therefore \int (\ln x)^2 \, dx = \int u^2 e^u \, du$
$\qquad\qquad\qquad\qquad\qquad\qquad\qquad\qquad = u^2 e^u - 2u e^u + 2 e^u + c \quad \{\text{using } \mathbf{a}\}$
$\qquad\qquad\qquad\qquad\qquad\qquad\qquad\qquad = (\ln x)^2 e^{\ln x} - 2 \ln x \, e^{\ln x} + 2 e^{\ln x} + c$
$\qquad\qquad\qquad\qquad\qquad\qquad\qquad\qquad = x(\ln x)^2 - 2x \ln x + 2x + c$

4 a We integrate by parts with $\quad a = u \quad b' = \sin u$
$\qquad\qquad\qquad\qquad\qquad\qquad\qquad a' = 1 \quad b = -\cos u$

$\therefore \int u \sin u \, du = -u \cos u - \int -\cos u \, du$
$\qquad\qquad\qquad = -u \cos u + \sin u + c$

b Let $u^2 = 2x$, $2u \dfrac{du}{dx} = 2$ $\quad \therefore \int \sin \sqrt{2x} \, dx = \int \sin u \, (u \, du)$
$\qquad\qquad \therefore \dfrac{du}{dx} = \dfrac{1}{u}$ $\qquad\qquad\qquad\qquad\qquad = \int u \sin u \, du$
$\qquad\qquad\qquad\qquad\qquad\qquad\qquad\qquad\qquad = -u \cos u + \sin u + c$
$\qquad\qquad\qquad\qquad\qquad\qquad\qquad\qquad\qquad = -\sqrt{2x} \cos \sqrt{2x} + \sin \sqrt{2x} + c$

5 Let $u^2 = 3x$, $2u \dfrac{du}{dx} = 3$ $\qquad$ We integrate by parts with $\quad a = u \quad b' = \cos u$
$\qquad\qquad\qquad\qquad\qquad\qquad\qquad\qquad\qquad\qquad\qquad\qquad\qquad a' = 1 \quad b = \sin u$
$\therefore \dfrac{du}{dx} = \dfrac{3}{2u}$ $\qquad\qquad\qquad \therefore \int \cos \sqrt{3x} \, dx = \tfrac{2}{3} \left[u \sin u - \int \sin u \, du \right]$
$\therefore \int \cos \sqrt{3x} \, dx = \int \cos u \left(\dfrac{2u}{3} \right) du$ $\qquad\qquad\qquad = \tfrac{2}{3} u \sin u - \tfrac{2}{3} (-\cos u) + c$
$\qquad\qquad\qquad = \tfrac{2}{3} \int u \cos u \, du$ $\qquad\qquad\qquad\qquad\quad = \tfrac{2}{3} \sqrt{3x} \sin \sqrt{3x} + \tfrac{2}{3} \cos \sqrt{3x} + c$

EXERCISE 27D

1 a $\int \dfrac{e^x + e^{-x}}{e^x - e^{-x}} \, dx$ has the form $\int \dfrac{f'(x)}{f(x)} \, dx$. $\quad$ **b** $\int 7^x \, dx = \dfrac{1}{\ln 7} \int 7^x \ln 7 \, dx$

$\therefore \int \dfrac{e^x + e^{-x}}{e^x - e^{-x}} \, dx = \ln \left| e^x - e^{-x} \right| + c$ $\qquad\qquad\qquad\qquad = \dfrac{7^x}{\ln 7} + c$

c $\int (3x+5)^5 \, dx = \tfrac{1}{3} \dfrac{(3x+5)^6}{6} + c$ $\quad$ **d** $\int \dfrac{\sin x}{2 - \cos x} \, dx$ has the form $\int \dfrac{f'(x)}{f(x)} \, dx$.

$\qquad\qquad\qquad\quad = \dfrac{(3x+5)^6}{18} + c$ $\qquad\qquad \therefore \int \dfrac{\sin x}{2 - \cos x} \, dx = \ln |2 - \cos x| + c$
$\qquad\qquad\qquad\qquad\qquad\qquad\qquad\qquad\qquad\qquad\qquad = \ln (2 - \cos x) + c$

e We integrate by parts with $\qquad\qquad$ **f** $\int \cot 2x \, dx$
$\qquad\qquad u = x \quad v' = \sec^2 x$
$\qquad\qquad u' = 1 \quad v = \tan x$ $\qquad\qquad\qquad\qquad = \int \dfrac{\cos 2x}{\sin 2x} \, dx$

$\therefore \int x \sec^2 x \, dx$
$\qquad = x \tan x - \int \tan x \, dx$ $\qquad\qquad\qquad\qquad = \tfrac{1}{2} \int \dfrac{2 \cos 2x}{\sin 2x} \, dx$

$\qquad = x \tan x + \int \dfrac{-\sin x}{\cos x} \, dx$ $\qquad\qquad\qquad \left\{ \text{which has form } \int \dfrac{f'(x)}{f(x)} \, dx \right\}$

$\qquad \left\{ \text{which has form } \int \dfrac{f'(x)}{f(x)} \, dx \right\}$ $\qquad\qquad = \tfrac{1}{2} \ln |\sin 2x| + c$

$\qquad = x \tan x + \ln |\cos x| + c$

g Let $u = x+3$, $\dfrac{du}{dx} = 1$

$\therefore \int x(x+3)^3\,dx$
$= \int (u-3)u^3\,du$
$= \int (u^4 - 3u^3)\,du$
$= \dfrac{u^5}{5} - \dfrac{3u^4}{4} + c$
$= \tfrac{1}{5}(x+3)^5 - \tfrac{3}{4}(x+3)^4 + c$

h $\displaystyle \int \dfrac{(x+1)^3}{x}\,dx$

$= \int \dfrac{x^3 + 3x^2 + 3x + 1}{x}\,dx$

$= \int \left(x^2 + 3x + 3 + \dfrac{1}{x}\right)\,dx$

$= \tfrac{1}{3}x^3 + \tfrac{3}{2}x^2 + 3x + \ln|x| + c$

i We integrate by parts with $\quad u = x^2 \quad v' = e^{-x}$
$\qquad\qquad\qquad\qquad\qquad\quad u' = 2x \quad v = -e^{-x}$

$\therefore \int x^2 e^{-x}\,dx = x^2(-e^{-x}) - \int 2x(-e^{-x})\,dx$
$\qquad\qquad\qquad\;\; = -x^2 e^{-x} + 2\int x e^{-x}\,dx$

We integrate by parts again, this time with $\quad u = x \quad v' = e^{-x}$
$\qquad\qquad\qquad\qquad\qquad\qquad\qquad\qquad\quad u' = 1 \quad v = -e^{-x}$

$\therefore \int x^2 e^{-x}\,dx = -x^2 e^{-x} + 2\left[x(-e^{-x}) - \int -e^{-x}\,dx\right]$
$\qquad\qquad\qquad\;\; = -x^2 e^{-x} - 2x e^{-x} + 2\int e^{-x}\,dx$
$\qquad\qquad\qquad\;\; = -x^2 e^{-x} - 2x e^{-x} - 2e^{-x} + c$

j Let $u = 1 - x$, $\dfrac{du}{dx} = -1$

$\therefore \int x\sqrt{1-x}\,dx$
$= \int (1-u)\sqrt{u}\,(-du)$
$= \int (u-1)u^{\frac{1}{2}}\,du$
$= \int (u^{\frac{3}{2}} - u^{\frac{1}{2}})\,du$
$= \tfrac{2}{5}u^{\frac{5}{2}} - \tfrac{2}{3}u^{\frac{3}{2}} + c$
$= \tfrac{2}{5}(1-x)^{\frac{5}{2}} - \tfrac{2}{3}(1-x)^{\frac{3}{2}} + c$

k Let $x = \sin\theta$, $\dfrac{dx}{d\theta} = \cos\theta$

$\therefore \int x^2\sqrt{1-x^2}\,dx$
$= \int \sin^2\theta\sqrt{1-\sin^2\theta}\,\cos\theta\,d\theta$
$= \tfrac{1}{4}\int 4\sin^2\theta \cos^2\theta\,d\theta$
$= \tfrac{1}{4}\int \sin^2(2\theta)\,d\theta$
$= \tfrac{1}{4}\int \left(\tfrac{1}{2} - \tfrac{1}{2}\cos(4\theta)\right)\,d\theta$
$= \tfrac{1}{4}\left(\tfrac{1}{2}\theta - \tfrac{1}{8}\sin 4\theta\right) + c$
$= \tfrac{1}{8}\theta - \tfrac{1}{32}\sin 4\theta + c$

Now $\sin\theta = x$, $\cos\theta = \sqrt{1-x^2}$

$\therefore \sin 2\theta = 2x\sqrt{1-x^2}$

and $\cos 2\theta = 1 - 2\sin^2\theta = 1 - 2x^2$

$\therefore \sin 4\theta = 2\left(2x\sqrt{1-x^2}\right)\left(1-2x^2\right)$
$\qquad\quad\;\; = 4x\sqrt{1-x^2}(1-2x^2)$

$\therefore \int x^2\sqrt{1-x^2}\,dx$
$= \tfrac{1}{8}\arcsin x - \tfrac{1}{32}\left(4x\sqrt{1-x^2}(1-2x^2)\right) + c$
$= \tfrac{1}{8}\arcsin x - \tfrac{1}{8}x\sqrt{1-x^2}(1-2x^2) + c$

l Let $x = 2\sec\theta$, $\dfrac{dx}{d\theta} = 2\sec\theta\tan\theta$

$\therefore \int \dfrac{3}{x\sqrt{x^2 - 4}}\,dx$

$= \int \dfrac{3}{2\sec\theta\sqrt{4\sec^2\theta - 4}}\,2\sec\theta\tan\theta\,d\theta$

$= \int \dfrac{3\tan\theta}{2\sqrt{\sec^2\theta - 1}}\,d\theta$

$= \int \tfrac{3}{2}\,d\theta \quad \{\sqrt{\sec^2\theta - 1} = \tan\theta\}$

$= \tfrac{3}{2}\theta + c$

Now $x = \dfrac{2}{\cos\theta}$ so $\cos\theta = \dfrac{2}{x}$

$\therefore \int \dfrac{3}{x\sqrt{x^2 - 4}}\,dx = \tfrac{3}{2}\arccos\left(\dfrac{2}{x}\right) + c$

m Let $u = x - 3$, $\dfrac{du}{dx} = 1$

$\therefore \int x^2 \sqrt{x-3}\, dx$

$= \int (u+3)^2 \sqrt{u}\, du$

$= \int (u^2 + 6u + 9)\, u^{\frac{1}{2}}\, du$

$= \int (u^{\frac{5}{2}} + 6u^{\frac{3}{2}} + 9u^{\frac{1}{2}})\, du$

$= \tfrac{2}{7} u^{\frac{7}{2}} + \tfrac{12}{5} u^{\frac{5}{2}} + 6 u^{\frac{3}{2}} + c$

$= \tfrac{2}{7}(x-3)^{\frac{7}{2}} + \tfrac{12}{5}(x-3)^{\frac{5}{2}} + 6(x-3)^{\frac{3}{2}} + c$

n Let $u = \cos x$, $\dfrac{du}{dx} = -\sin x$

$\therefore \int \tan^3 x\, dx$

$= \int \dfrac{\sin^3 x}{\cos^3 x}\, dx$

$= \int \dfrac{\sin x (1 - \cos^2 x)}{\cos^3 x}\, dx$

$= \int \left(\dfrac{1}{\cos x} - \dfrac{1}{\cos^3 x}\right)(-\sin x)\, dx$

$= \int (u^{-1} - u^{-3})\, du$

$= \ln|u| + \dfrac{1}{2u^2} + c$

$= \ln|\cos x| + \dfrac{1}{2\cos^2 x} + c$

o Let $u = x + 2$, $\dfrac{du}{dx} = 1$

$\therefore \int \dfrac{\ln(x+2)}{(x+2)^2}\, dx = \int u^{-2} \ln u\, du$

We integrate by parts with

$a = \ln u \quad b' = u^{-2}$

$a' = \dfrac{1}{u} \quad b = -\dfrac{1}{u}$

$\therefore \int \dfrac{\ln(x+2)}{(x+2)^2}\, dx = -\dfrac{\ln u}{u} - \int -u^{-2}\, du$

$= -\dfrac{\ln u}{u} - \dfrac{1}{u} + c$

$= -\dfrac{\ln u + 1}{u} + c$

$= -\dfrac{\ln(x+2) + 1}{x+2} + c$

p $\dfrac{1}{x^2 + 2x + 3} = \dfrac{1}{(x+1)^2 + 2}$

$= \dfrac{1}{(x+1)^2 + (\sqrt{2})^2}$

We let $x + 1 = \sqrt{2} \tan \theta$, $\dfrac{dx}{d\theta} = \sqrt{2} \sec^2 \theta$

$\therefore \int \dfrac{1}{x^2 + 2x + 3}\, dx$

$= \int \dfrac{1}{(x+1)^2 + (\sqrt{2})^2}\, dx$

$= \int \dfrac{1}{2 \tan^2 \theta + 2} (\sqrt{2} \sec^2 \theta\, d\theta)$

$= \int \dfrac{\sqrt{2} \sec^2 \theta}{2 \sec^2 \theta}\, d\theta = \int \dfrac{1}{\sqrt{2}}\, d\theta$

$= \tfrac{1}{\sqrt{2}} \theta + c$

Now $\tan \theta = \dfrac{x+1}{\sqrt{2}}$, so $\theta = \arctan\left(\dfrac{x+1}{\sqrt{2}}\right)$

$\therefore \int \dfrac{1}{x^2 + 2x + 3}\, dx = \tfrac{1}{\sqrt{2}} \arctan\left(\dfrac{x+1}{\sqrt{2}}\right) + c$

2 a Let $x = 3 \tan \theta$ so $\dfrac{dx}{d\theta} = 3 \sec^2 \theta$

$\therefore \int \dfrac{1}{x^2 + 9}\, dx$

$= \int \dfrac{1}{9 \tan^2 \theta + 9} \times 3 \sec^2 \theta\, d\theta$

$= \int \dfrac{3 \sec^2 \theta}{9 (\tan^2 \theta + 1)}\, d\theta$

$= \int \tfrac{1}{3}\, d\theta \quad \{\tan^2 \theta + 1 = \sec^2 \theta\}$

$= \tfrac{1}{3} \theta + c$

$= \tfrac{1}{3} \arctan\left(\tfrac{x}{3}\right) + c$

b Let $x = \sin^2 \theta$, $\dfrac{dx}{d\theta} = 2 \sin \theta \cos \theta$

$\therefore \int \dfrac{4}{\sqrt{x} \sqrt{1-x}}\, dx$

$= \int \dfrac{4}{\sqrt{\sin^2 \theta} \sqrt{1 - \sin^2 \theta}} \times 2 \sin \theta \cos \theta\, d\theta$

$= \int \dfrac{8 \sin \theta \cos \theta}{\sin \theta \cos \theta}\, d\theta$

$= \int 8\, d\theta$

$= 8 \theta + c$

$= 8 \arcsin(\sqrt{x}) + c$

c Let $u = 2x$, $\dfrac{du}{dx} = 2$ $\therefore$ $\int \ln(2x)\, dx = \dfrac{1}{2} \int \ln(2x) \times 2\, dx$

$= \dfrac{1}{2} \int \ln u\, du$

$= \dfrac{1}{2}(u \ln u - u) + c$ {**Ex. 27C Q 1 g**}

$= \dfrac{1}{2}(2x) \ln(2x) - \dfrac{1}{2}(2x) + c$

$= x \ln(2x) - x + c$

d We integrate by parts with $\quad u = e^{-x} \quad v' = \cos x$
$\phantom{\text{We integrate by parts with}}\quad u' = -e^{-x} \quad v = \sin x$

$\therefore \int e^{-x} \cos x\, dx = e^{-x} \sin x + \int e^{-x} \sin x\, dx$

We integrate by parts again, this time with $\quad u = e^{-x} \quad v' = \sin x$
$\phantom{\text{We integrate by parts again, this time with}}\quad u' = -e^{-x} \quad v = -\cos x$

$\therefore \int e^{-x} \cos x\, dx = e^{-x} \sin x - e^{-x} \cos x - \int e^{-x} \cos x\, dx + c_1$

$\therefore \ 2 \int e^{-x} \cos x\, dx = e^{-x}(\sin x - \cos x) + c_1$

$\therefore \ \int e^{-x} \cos x\, dx = \dfrac{1}{2} e^{-x}(\sin x - \cos x) + c$

e Let $x = \tan \theta$, $\dfrac{dx}{d\theta} = \sec^2 \theta$

$\therefore \int \dfrac{1}{x(1 + x^2)}\, dx$

$= \int \dfrac{1}{\tan \theta (1 + \tan^2 \theta)} \times \sec^2 \theta\, d\theta$

$= \int \dfrac{1}{\tan \theta}\, d\theta \quad \{1 + \tan^2 \theta = \sec^2 \theta\}$

$= \int \dfrac{\cos \theta}{\sin \theta}\, d\theta$

$= \ln |\sin \theta| + c$

$= \ln \left| \dfrac{x}{\sqrt{x^2 + 1}} \right| + c$

f Let $x = \tan \theta$, $\dfrac{dx}{d\theta} = \sec^2 \theta$

$\therefore \int \dfrac{\arctan x}{1 + x^2}\, dx$

$= \int \dfrac{\arctan(\tan \theta)}{1 + \tan^2 \theta} \sec^2 \theta\, d\theta$

$= \int \dfrac{\theta \times \sec^2 \theta}{\sec^2 \theta}\, d\theta$

$= \int \theta\, d\theta$

$= \dfrac{1}{2} \theta^2 + c$

$= \dfrac{1}{2} \arctan^2 x + c$

g Let $x = 3 \sin \theta$, $\dfrac{dx}{d\theta} = 3 \cos \theta$

$\therefore \int \sqrt{9 - x^2}\, dx = \int \sqrt{9 - 9 \sin^2 \theta} \times 3 \cos \theta\, d\theta$

$\phantom{\therefore \int \sqrt{9 - x^2}\, dx}= 9 \int \cos^2 \theta\, d\theta$

$\phantom{\therefore \int \sqrt{9 - x^2}\, dx}= 9 \int \left(\dfrac{1}{2} + \dfrac{1}{2} \cos 2\theta \right) d\theta$

$\phantom{\therefore \int \sqrt{9 - x^2}\, dx}= 9 \left(\dfrac{1}{2} \theta + \dfrac{1}{4} \sin 2\theta \right) + c$

$\phantom{\therefore \int \sqrt{9 - x^2}\, dx}= \dfrac{9}{2} \theta + \dfrac{9}{4} \sin 2\theta + c$

Now $\sin \theta = \dfrac{x}{3}$, so $\cos \theta = \dfrac{\sqrt{9 - x^2}}{3}$

$\therefore \ \sin 2\theta = 2 \left(\dfrac{x}{3} \right) \dfrac{\sqrt{9 - x^2}}{3} = \dfrac{2x \sqrt{9 - x^2}}{9}$

$\therefore \ \int \sqrt{9 - x^2}\, dx = \dfrac{9}{2} \arcsin \left(\dfrac{x}{3} \right) + \dfrac{9}{4} \left(\dfrac{2x \sqrt{9 - x^2}}{9} \right) + c$

$\phantom{\therefore \int \sqrt{9 - x^2}\, dx}= \dfrac{9}{2} \arcsin \left(\dfrac{x}{3} \right) + \dfrac{x \sqrt{9 - x^2}}{2} + c$

FURTHER INTEGRATION AND DIFFERENTIAL EQUATIONS

h $\int \dfrac{(\ln x)^2}{x^2}\, dx = \int x^{-2} (\ln x)^2\, dx$

We integrate by parts with $u = (\ln x)^2 \quad v' = x^{-2}$
$$u' = \dfrac{2\ln x}{x} \qquad v = -\dfrac{1}{x}$$

$\therefore \int \dfrac{(\ln x)^2}{x^2}\, dx = -\dfrac{(\ln x)^2}{x} - \int \left(\dfrac{2\ln x}{x}\right)\left(-\dfrac{1}{x}\right) dx$

$\qquad = -\dfrac{(\ln x)^2}{x} + 2\int x^{-2} \ln x\, dx$

We integrate by parts again, this time with $u = \ln x \quad v' = x^{-2}$
$$u' = \dfrac{1}{x} \qquad v = -\dfrac{1}{x}$$

$\therefore \int \dfrac{(\ln x)^2}{x^2}\, dx = \dfrac{-(\ln x)^2}{x} + 2\left(-\dfrac{\ln x}{x} - \int -x^{-2}\, dx\right)$

$\qquad = \dfrac{-(\ln x)^2}{x} - \dfrac{2\ln x}{x} - 2\left(\dfrac{1}{x}\right) + c$

$\qquad = -\dfrac{(\ln x)^2 + 2\ln x + 2}{x} + c$

i Let $u = x - 3$, $\dfrac{du}{dx} = 1$

$\therefore \int \dfrac{x}{\sqrt{x-3}}\, dx = \int \dfrac{u+3}{\sqrt{u}}\, du$

$\qquad = \int \left(u^{\frac{1}{2}} + 3u^{-\frac{1}{2}}\right) du$

$\qquad = \tfrac{2}{3} u^{\frac{3}{2}} + 6u^{\frac{1}{2}} + c$

$\qquad = \tfrac{2}{3}(x-3)^{\frac{3}{2}} + 6\sqrt{x-3} + c$

j We integrate by parts with $u = \sin 4x \quad v' = \cos x$
$$u' = 4\cos 4x \qquad v = \sin x$$

$\therefore \int \sin 4x \cos x\, dx = \sin 4x \sin x - 4\int \cos 4x \sin x\, dx$

We integrate by parts again, this time with $u = \cos 4x \quad v' = \sin x$
$$u' = -4\sin 4x \qquad v = -\cos x$$

$\therefore \int \sin 4x \cos x\, dx = \sin 4x \sin x - 4\left[-\cos 4x \cos x - \int 4\sin 4x \cos x\, dx\right] + c_1$

$\qquad = \sin 4x \sin x + 4\cos 4x \cos x + 16\int \sin 4x \cos x\, dx + c_1$

$\therefore -15 \int \sin 4x \cos x\, dx = \sin 4x \sin x + 4\cos 4x \cos x + c_1$

$\therefore \int \sin 4x \cos x\, dx = -\tfrac{1}{15}(\sin 4x \sin x + 4\cos 4x \cos x) + c$

k $\dfrac{2x+3}{x^2 - 2x + 5} = \dfrac{2x-2}{x^2 - 2x + 5} + \dfrac{5}{x^2 - 2x + 5}$

$\therefore \int \dfrac{2x+3}{x^2 - 2x + 5}\, dx = \int \dfrac{2x-2}{x^2 - 2x + 5}\, dx + \int \dfrac{5}{x^2 - 2x + 5}\, dx$

Now $\int \dfrac{2x-2}{x^2 - 2x + 5}\, dx$ has the form $\int \dfrac{f'(x)}{f(x)}\, dx$,

so $\int \dfrac{2x-2}{x^2 - 2x + 5}\, dx = \ln\left|x^2 - 2x + 5\right| + c$

$\qquad = \ln(x^2 - 2x + 5) + c \quad$ since $x^2 - 2x + 5 > 0$

For $\int \dfrac{5}{x^2 - 2x + 5}\, dx$ we let $x - 1 = 2\tan\theta$, $\dfrac{dx}{d\theta} = 2\sec^2 \theta$

$$\therefore \int \frac{5}{x^2 - 2x + 5}\, dx = \int \frac{5}{(2\tan\theta)^2 + 4} \times 2\sec^2\theta\, d\theta$$

$$= \int \frac{10\sec^2\theta}{4(\tan^2\theta + 1)}\, d\theta$$

$$= \int \tfrac{5}{2}\, d\theta \quad \{\tan^2\theta + 1 = \sec^2\theta\}$$

$$= \tfrac{5}{2}\theta + c$$

$$= \tfrac{5}{2}\arctan\left(\frac{x-1}{2}\right) + c$$

So, $\displaystyle\int \frac{2x+3}{x^2 - 2x + 5}\, dx = \ln(x^2 - 2x + 5) + \tfrac{5}{2}\arctan\left(\dfrac{x-1}{2}\right) + c$

l Let $u = \sin x$, $\dfrac{du}{dx} = \cos x$

$$\therefore \int \cos^3 x\, dx = \int \cos^2 x \cos x\, dx$$

$$= \int (1 - \sin^2 x)\cos x\, dx$$

$$= \int (1 - u^2)\, du$$

$$= u - \frac{u^3}{3} + c$$

$$= \sin x - \tfrac{1}{3}\sin^3 x + c$$

m $\displaystyle\int \frac{x+4}{x^2 + 4}\, dx = \tfrac{1}{2}\int \frac{2x}{x^2 + 4}\, dx + \int \frac{4}{x^2 + 4}\, dx$

$$= \tfrac{1}{2}\ln|x^2 + 4| + \int \frac{4}{x^2 + 2^2}\, dx \quad \text{where } x^2 + 4 > 0$$

Let $x = 2\tan\theta$, $\dfrac{dx}{d\theta} = 2\sec^2\theta$

$$\therefore \int \frac{x+4}{x^2 + 4}\, dx = \tfrac{1}{2}\ln(x^2 + 4) + \int \frac{4}{4\tan^2\theta + 4} \times 2\sec^2\theta\, d\theta$$

$$= \tfrac{1}{2}\ln(x^2 + 4) + \int \frac{8\sec^2\theta}{4(\tan^2\theta + 1)}\, d\theta$$

$$= \tfrac{1}{2}\ln(x^2 + 4) + \int 2\, d\theta$$

$$= \tfrac{1}{2}\ln(x^2 + 4) + 2\theta + c$$

$$= \tfrac{1}{2}\ln(x^2 + 4) + 2\arctan\left(\frac{x}{2}\right) + c$$

n Let $x = 2\sin\theta$, $\dfrac{dx}{d\theta} = 2\cos\theta$

$$\therefore \int \frac{1 - 2x}{\sqrt{4 - x^2}}\, dx = \int \frac{1 - 4\sin\theta}{\sqrt{4 - 4\sin^2\theta}}\,(2\cos\theta)\, d\theta$$

$$= \int \frac{1 - 4\sin\theta}{2\sqrt{1 - \sin^2\theta}}\,(2\cos\theta)\, d\theta$$

$$= \int \frac{1 - 4\sin\theta}{2\cos\theta}\,(2\cos\theta)\, d\theta$$

$$= \int (1 - 4\sin\theta)\, d\theta$$

$$= \theta + 4\cos\theta + c$$

$$= \arcsin\left(\frac{x}{2}\right) + 4\left(\frac{\sqrt{4 - x^2}}{2}\right) + c$$

$$= \arcsin\left(\frac{x}{2}\right) + 2\sqrt{4 - x^2} + c$$

FURTHER INTEGRATION AND DIFFERENTIAL EQUATIONS

o Let $u = 2 - x$, $\dfrac{du}{dx} = -1$

$\therefore \displaystyle\int \dfrac{x^3}{(2-x)^3}\,dx$

$= \displaystyle\int \dfrac{(2-u)^3}{u^3}(-du)$

$= \displaystyle\int \dfrac{(u-2)^3}{u^3}\,du$

$= \displaystyle\int \dfrac{u^3 - 6u^2 + 12u - 8}{u^3}\,du$

$= \displaystyle\int \left(1 - \dfrac{6}{u} + 12u^{-2} - 8u^{-3}\right) du$

$= u - 6\ln|u| - 12u^{-1} + 4u^{-2} + c$

$= (2-x) - 6\ln|2-x| - \dfrac{12}{2-x} + \dfrac{4}{(2-x)^2} + c$

p Let $u = \sin x$, $\dfrac{du}{dx} = \cos x$

$\therefore \displaystyle\int \sin^5 x \cos^5 x \, dx$

$= \displaystyle\int \sin^5 x\,(1 - \sin^2 x)(1 - \sin^2 x)\cos x \, dx$

$= \displaystyle\int u^5(1-u^2)(1-u^2)\,du$

$= \displaystyle\int u^5(1 - 2u^2 + u^4)\,du$

$= \displaystyle\int (u^5 - 2u^7 + u^9)\,du$

$= \dfrac{u^6}{6} - \dfrac{u^8}{4} + \dfrac{u^{10}}{10} + c$

$= \dfrac{\sin^6 x}{6} - \dfrac{\sin^8 x}{4} + \dfrac{\sin^{10} x}{10} + c$

EXERCISE 27E.1

1 a $\dfrac{dy}{dx} = 5y$ $\quad\therefore\quad \dfrac{1}{y}\dfrac{dy}{dx} = 5$

$\therefore \displaystyle\int \dfrac{1}{y}\dfrac{dy}{dx}\,dx = \int 5\,dx$

$\therefore \displaystyle\int \dfrac{1}{y}\,dy = \int 5\,dx$

$\therefore \ln|y| = 5x + c$

$\therefore y = Ae^{5x}$

b $\dfrac{dM}{dt} = -2M$ $\quad\therefore\quad \dfrac{1}{M}\dfrac{dM}{dt} = -2$

$\therefore \displaystyle\int \dfrac{1}{M}\dfrac{dM}{dt}\,dt = \int -2\,dt$

$\therefore \displaystyle\int \dfrac{1}{M}\,dM = \int -2\,dt$

$\therefore \ln|M| = -2t + c$

$\therefore M = Ae^{-2t}$

c $\dfrac{dy}{dx} = \dfrac{2}{y}$ $\quad\therefore\quad y\dfrac{dy}{dx} = 2$

$\therefore \displaystyle\int y\dfrac{dy}{dx}\,dx = \int 2\,dx$

$\therefore \displaystyle\int y\,dy = \int 2\,dx$

$\therefore \tfrac{1}{2}y^2 = 2x + a$

$\therefore y^2 = 4x + c$

d $\dfrac{dP}{dt} = 3\sqrt{P}$ $\quad\therefore\quad \dfrac{1}{\sqrt{P}}\dfrac{dP}{dt} = 3$

$\therefore \displaystyle\int \dfrac{1}{\sqrt{P}}\dfrac{dP}{dt}\,dt = \int 3\,dt$

$\therefore \displaystyle\int \dfrac{1}{\sqrt{P}}\,dP = \int 3\,dt$

$\therefore 2\sqrt{P} = 3t + a$

$\therefore \sqrt{P} = \tfrac{3}{2}t + c$

e $\dfrac{dQ}{dt} = 2Q + 3$

$\therefore \dfrac{1}{2Q+3}\dfrac{dQ}{dt} = 1$

$\therefore \displaystyle\int \dfrac{1}{2Q+3}\dfrac{dQ}{dt}\,dt = \int 1\,dt$

$\therefore \displaystyle\int \dfrac{1}{2Q+3}\,dQ = \int 1\,dt$

$\therefore \tfrac{1}{2}\ln|2Q+3| = t + a$

$\ln|2Q+3| = 2t + 2a$

$\therefore 2Q + 3 = ce^{2t}$

$\therefore Q = Ae^{2t} - \tfrac{3}{2}$

f $\dfrac{dQ}{dt} = \dfrac{1}{2Q+3}$

$\therefore (2Q+3)\dfrac{dQ}{dt} = 1$

$\therefore \displaystyle\int (2Q+3)\dfrac{dQ}{dt}\,dt = \int 1\,dt$

$\therefore \displaystyle\int (2Q+3)\,dQ = \int 1\,dt$

$\therefore Q^2 + 3Q = t + a$

$\therefore t = Q^2 + 3Q + c$

2 a
$$\frac{dy}{dx} = 4y$$
$$\therefore \quad \frac{1}{y}\frac{dy}{dx} = 4$$
$$\therefore \quad \int \frac{1}{y}\frac{dy}{dx}\,dx = \int 4\,dx$$
$$\therefore \quad \int \frac{1}{y}\,dy = \int 4\,dx$$
$$\therefore \quad \ln|y| = 4x + c$$
$$\therefore \quad y = Ae^{4x}$$
But when $x = 0$, $y = 10$
$$\therefore \quad A = 10$$
$$\therefore \quad y = 10e^{4x}$$

b
$$\frac{dM}{dt} = -3M$$
$$\therefore \quad \frac{1}{M}\frac{dM}{dt} = -3$$
$$\therefore \quad \int \frac{1}{M}\frac{dM}{dt}\,dt = \int -3\,dt$$
$$\therefore \quad \int \frac{1}{M}\,dM = \int -3\,dt$$
$$\therefore \quad \ln|M| = -3t + c$$
$$\therefore \quad M = Ae^{-3t}$$
But $M(0) = 20$, so $A = 20$
$$\therefore \quad M = 20e^{-3t}$$

c
$$\frac{dy}{dt} = \frac{\sqrt{y}}{3}$$
$$\therefore \quad \frac{1}{\sqrt{y}}\frac{dy}{dt} = \frac{1}{3}$$
$$\therefore \quad \int \frac{1}{\sqrt{y}}\frac{dy}{dt}\,dt = \int \frac{1}{3}\,dt$$
$$\therefore \quad \int \frac{1}{\sqrt{y}}\,dy = \int \frac{1}{3}\,dt$$
$$\therefore \quad 2\sqrt{y} = \tfrac{1}{3}t + c$$
$$\therefore \quad 6\sqrt{y} = t + 3c$$
But when $t = 24$, $y = 9$
$$\therefore \quad 18 = 24 + 3c$$
$$\therefore \quad 3c = -6$$
$$\therefore \quad 6\sqrt{y} = t - 6$$
$$\therefore \quad \sqrt{y} = \tfrac{1}{6}t - 1$$

d
$$\frac{dP}{dn} = 2P + 3$$
$$\therefore \quad \frac{1}{2P+3}\frac{dP}{dn} = 1$$
$$\therefore \quad \int \frac{1}{2P+3}\frac{dP}{dn}\,dn = \int 1\,dn$$
$$\therefore \quad \int \frac{1}{2P+3}\,dP = \int dn$$
$$\therefore \quad \tfrac{1}{2}\ln|2P+3| = n + c$$
$$\therefore \quad \ln|2P+3| = 2n + 2c$$
$$\therefore \quad 2P + 3 = Ae^{2n}$$
$$\therefore \quad 2P = Ae^{2n} - 3$$
$$\therefore \quad P = Be^{2n} - \tfrac{3}{2}$$
But when $n = 0$, $P = 2$
$$\therefore \quad 2 = B - \tfrac{3}{2}$$
$$\therefore \quad B = \tfrac{7}{2}$$
$$\therefore \quad P = \tfrac{7}{2}e^{2n} - \tfrac{3}{2}$$

e
$$\frac{dy}{dx} = k\sqrt{y}$$
$$\therefore \quad \frac{1}{\sqrt{y}}\frac{dy}{dx} = k$$
$$\therefore \quad \int \frac{1}{\sqrt{y}}\frac{dy}{dx}\,dx = \int k\,dx$$
$$\therefore \quad \int \frac{1}{\sqrt{y}}\,dy = \int k\,dx$$
$$\therefore \quad 2\sqrt{y} = kx + c$$
But $y(4) = 1$, so $4k + c = 2$
and $y(5) = 4$, so $5k + c = 4$
$$\therefore \quad k = 2 \text{ and } c = -6$$
$$\therefore \quad 2\sqrt{y} = 2x - 6$$
$$\therefore \quad y = (x-3)^2$$

3
$$\frac{dy}{dx} = 2y$$
$$\therefore \quad \frac{1}{y}\frac{dy}{dx} = 2$$
$$\therefore \quad \int \frac{1}{y}\frac{dy}{dx}\,dx = \int 2\,dx$$
$$\therefore \quad \int \frac{1}{y}\,dy = \int 2\,dx$$
$$\therefore \quad \ln|y| = 2x + c$$
$$\therefore \quad y = Ae^{2x}$$
So, the curve is an exponential function.

4 a $\quad \dfrac{dp}{dt} = -\tfrac{1}{2}p$

$\therefore \quad \dfrac{1}{p}\dfrac{dp}{dt} = -\tfrac{1}{2}$

$\therefore \quad \displaystyle\int \dfrac{1}{p}\dfrac{dp}{dt}\,dt = \int -\tfrac{1}{2}\,dt$

$\therefore \quad \displaystyle\int \dfrac{1}{p}\,dp = \int -\tfrac{1}{2}\,dt$

$\therefore \quad \ln|p| = -\tfrac{1}{2}t + c$

$\therefore \quad p = Ae^{-\frac{1}{2}t}$

But when $t = 0$, $p = 10$,

$\therefore \quad A = 10$

$\therefore \quad p = 10e^{-\frac{1}{2}t}$

$\therefore$ when $t = 2$, $p = \dfrac{10}{e}$

b $\quad \dfrac{dM}{dr} = 8 - 2M$

$\therefore \quad \dfrac{1}{8-2M}\dfrac{dM}{dr} = 1$

$\therefore \quad \displaystyle\int \dfrac{1}{8-2M}\dfrac{dM}{dr}\,dr = \int 1\,dr$

$\therefore \quad \displaystyle\int \dfrac{1}{8-2M}\,dM = \int 1\,dr$

$\therefore \quad -\tfrac{1}{2}\ln|8-2M| + c = r$

But when $r = 0$, $M = 2$

$\therefore \quad -\tfrac{1}{2}\ln|8-4| + c = 0$

$\therefore \quad c = \tfrac{1}{2}\ln 4 = \ln 4^{\frac{1}{2}} = \ln 2$

$\therefore$ when $M = 3.5$, $r = -\tfrac{1}{2}\ln|8-7| + \ln 2$

$\therefore \quad r = -\tfrac{1}{2}\ln 1 + \ln 2 = \ln 2$

5 $\quad \dfrac{ds}{dt} + ks = 0$

$\therefore \quad \dfrac{ds}{dt} = -ks$

$\therefore \quad \dfrac{1}{s}\dfrac{ds}{dt} = -k$

$\therefore \quad \displaystyle\int \dfrac{1}{s}\dfrac{ds}{dt}\,dt = \int -k\,dt$

$\therefore \quad \displaystyle\int \dfrac{1}{s}\,ds = \int -k\,dt$

$\therefore \quad \ln|s| = -kt + c$

$\therefore \quad s = Ae^{-kt}$ ...... (*)

Now $s(0) = 50$, so $A = 50$

and $s(3) = 20$, so $50e^{-3k} = 20$

$\therefore \quad e^{-3k} = \tfrac{20}{50} = 0.4$

Using (*), $s = 50(e^{-3k})^{\frac{t}{3}}$,

$\therefore \quad s = 50\,(0.4)^{\frac{t}{3}}$ as required

6 a $\quad xy' = 3y$

$\therefore \quad x\dfrac{dy}{dx} = 3y$

$\therefore \quad \dfrac{1}{y}\dfrac{dy}{dx} = \dfrac{3}{x}$

$\therefore \quad \displaystyle\int \dfrac{1}{y}\dfrac{dy}{dx}\,dx = \int \dfrac{3}{x}\,dx$

$\therefore \quad \displaystyle\int \dfrac{1}{y}\,dy = \int \dfrac{3}{x}\,dx$

$\therefore \quad \ln|y| = 3\ln|x| + c$

$\quad = \ln|x^3| + c$

$\therefore \quad y = Ax^3$

b $\quad xy = 4y'$

$\therefore \quad xy = 4\dfrac{dy}{dx}$

$\therefore \quad x = \dfrac{4}{y}\dfrac{dy}{dx}$

$\therefore \quad \displaystyle\int x\,dx = \int \dfrac{4}{y}\dfrac{dy}{dx}\,dx$

$\therefore \quad \displaystyle\int x\,dx = \int \dfrac{4}{y}\,dy$

$\therefore \quad \dfrac{x^2}{2} = 4\ln|y| + c$

$\therefore \quad \dfrac{x^2}{8} + d = \ln|y|$

$\therefore \quad y = Ae^{\frac{x^2}{8}}$

c $\quad y' = ye^x$

$\therefore \quad \dfrac{dy}{dx} = ye^x$

$\therefore \quad \dfrac{1}{y}\dfrac{dy}{dx} = e^x$

$\therefore \quad \displaystyle\int \dfrac{1}{y}\dfrac{dy}{dx}\,dx = \int e^x\,dx$

$\therefore \quad \displaystyle\int \dfrac{1}{y}\,dy = \int e^x\,dx$

$\therefore \quad \ln|y| = e^x + c$

$\therefore \quad y = Ae^{e^x}$

d $\quad y' = xe^y$

$\therefore \quad \dfrac{dy}{dx} = xe^y$

$\therefore \quad e^{-y}\dfrac{dy}{dx} = x$

$\therefore \quad \displaystyle\int e^{-y}\dfrac{dy}{dx}\,dx = \int x\,dx$

$\therefore \quad \displaystyle\int e^{-y}\,dy = \int x\,dx$

$\therefore \quad -e^{-y} = \dfrac{x^2}{2} + c_1$

$\therefore \quad e^{-y} = -\dfrac{x^2}{2} - c_1$

$\therefore \quad -y = \ln\left(-\dfrac{x^2}{2} + c\right)$

$\therefore \quad y = -\ln\left(-\dfrac{x^2}{2} + c\right)$, $x \in\,]-\sqrt{2c},\sqrt{2c}\,[$

7 $\dfrac{dz}{dr} = z + zr^2 = z(1+r^2)$

$\therefore \dfrac{1}{z}\dfrac{dz}{dr} = 1 + r^2$

$\therefore \int \dfrac{1}{z}\dfrac{dz}{dr}\, dr = \int (1+r^2)\, dr$

$\therefore \int \dfrac{1}{z}\, dz = \int (1+r^2)\, dr$

$\therefore \ln|z| = r + \dfrac{r^3}{3} + c$

$\therefore z = Ae^{r+\frac{r^3}{3}}$

But $z(0) = 1$, so $1 = Ae^0$

$\therefore A = 1$

$\therefore z = e^{r + \frac{r^3}{3}}$

8 $\dfrac{dy}{dx} = -2xy$

$\therefore \dfrac{1}{y}\dfrac{dy}{dx} = -2x$

$\therefore \int \dfrac{1}{y}\dfrac{dy}{dx}\, dx = \int -2x\, dx$

$\therefore \int \dfrac{1}{y}\, dy = \int -2x\, dx$

$\therefore \ln|y| = -x^2 + c$

$\therefore y = Ae^{-x^2}$

But $y(0) = 1$, so $A = 1$

$\therefore y = e^{-x^2}$

9 $ye^x \dfrac{dy}{dx} = x$

$\therefore y\dfrac{dy}{dx} = xe^{-x}$

$\therefore \int y\dfrac{dy}{dx}\, dx = \int xe^{-x}\, dx$

We integrate the RHS by parts with

$u = x \qquad v' = e^{-x}$
$u' = 1 \qquad v = -e^{-x}$

$\therefore \int y\, dy = -xe^{-x} - \int -e^{-x}\, dx$

$\therefore \dfrac{y^2}{2} = -xe^{-x} - e^{-x} + c_1$

$\therefore y^2 = c - 2(x+1)e^{-x}$

But $y(0) = 2$,

so $4 = c - 2e^0$

$\therefore c = 6$

$\therefore y^2 = 6 - 2(x+1)e^{-x}$

$\therefore y = \sqrt{6 - 2(x+1)e^{-x}} \quad \{y > 0\}$

10 $(1+x)\dfrac{dy}{dx} = 2xy$

$\therefore \dfrac{1}{y}\dfrac{dy}{dx} = \dfrac{2x}{1+x}$

$\therefore \dfrac{1}{y}\dfrac{dy}{dx} = 2 - \dfrac{2}{1+x}$

$\therefore \int \dfrac{1}{y}\dfrac{dy}{dx}\, dx = \int \left(2 - \dfrac{2}{1+x}\right) dx$

$\therefore \int \dfrac{1}{y}\, dy = \int \left(2 - \dfrac{2}{1+x}\right) dx$

$\therefore \ln|y| = 2x - 2\ln|x+1| + c$

$\therefore \ln\left|y(x+1)^2\right| = 2x + c$

$\therefore |y|(x+1)^2 = e^{2x+c}$

$\therefore y = Ae^{2x}(x+1)^{-2}$

But $y(0) = e^2$

$\therefore e^2 = Ae^0 \times 1$

$\therefore A = e^2$

$\therefore y = \dfrac{e^{2x+2}}{(x+1)^2}$

11 $(1+x^2)\dfrac{dy}{dx} = 2xy$

$\therefore \dfrac{1}{y}\dfrac{dy}{dx} = \dfrac{2x}{1+x^2}$

$\therefore \int \dfrac{1}{y}\dfrac{dy}{dx}\, dx = \int \dfrac{2x}{1+x^2}\, dx$

$\therefore \int \dfrac{1}{y}\, dy = \int \dfrac{2x}{1+x^2}\, dx$

$\therefore \ln|y| = \ln|x^2+1| + c$

But $y(2) = 10$

$\therefore \ln 10 = \ln 5 + c$

$\therefore c = \ln\left(\dfrac{10}{5}\right) = \ln 2$

$\therefore \ln|y| = \ln|x^2+1| + \ln 2$

$\therefore \ln|y| = \ln\left(2(x^2+1)\right) \qquad \{x^2+1 > 0\}$

$\therefore y = 2(x^2+1)$

$\therefore y = 2x^2 + 2$

12 $\dfrac{dy}{dx} = 4x + xy^2 = x(4 + y^2)$

$\therefore \ \dfrac{1}{y^2 + 4} \dfrac{dy}{dx} = x$

$\therefore \ \displaystyle\int \dfrac{1}{y^2 + 4} \dfrac{dy}{dx} dx = \int x\, dx$

$\therefore \ \displaystyle\int \dfrac{1}{y^2 + 4} dy = \int x\, dx$

Let $y = 2\tan\theta, \ \dfrac{dy}{d\theta} = 2\sec^2\theta$

$\therefore \ \displaystyle\int \dfrac{2\sec^2\theta}{4\tan^2\theta + 4} d\theta = \int x\, dx$

$\therefore \ \displaystyle\int \dfrac{2\sec^2\theta}{4(\tan^2\theta + 1)} d\theta = \int x\, dx$

$\therefore \ \displaystyle\int \tfrac{1}{2} d\theta = \int x\, dx$

$\therefore \ \tfrac{1}{2}\theta = \tfrac{1}{2}x^2 + c_1$

$\therefore \ \tfrac{1}{2}\arctan\left(\dfrac{y}{2}\right) = \tfrac{1}{2}x^2 + c_1$

$\therefore \ \arctan\left(\dfrac{y}{2}\right) = x^2 + c$

$\therefore \ \dfrac{y}{2} = \tan(x^2 + c)$

$\therefore \ y = 2\tan(x^2 + c)$

But $y(0) = 2$, so $2 = 2\tan c$

$\therefore \ c = \dfrac{\pi}{4}$

$\therefore \ y = 2\tan\left(x^2 + \dfrac{\pi}{4}\right)$

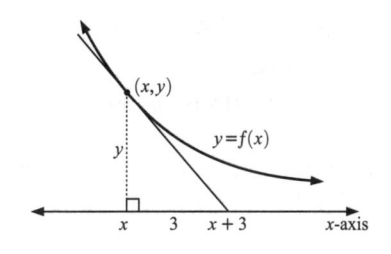

13

$\dfrac{dy}{dx} = -\dfrac{y}{3}$

$\therefore \ \dfrac{1}{y}\dfrac{dy}{dx} = -\dfrac{1}{3}$

$\therefore \ \displaystyle\int \dfrac{1}{y}\dfrac{dy}{dx} dx = \int -\tfrac{1}{3} dx$

$\therefore \ \displaystyle\int \dfrac{1}{y} dy = \int -\tfrac{1}{3} dx$

$\therefore \ \ln|y| = -\tfrac{1}{3}x + c$

$\therefore \ y = Ae^{-\frac{1}{3}x}$

But $y(0) = 2$, so $2 = Ae^0$

$\therefore \ A = 2$

$\therefore \ f(x) = 2e^{-\frac{x}{3}}$

14 $\dfrac{dy}{dx} = \dfrac{x}{y}$

$\therefore \ y\dfrac{dy}{dx} = x$

$\therefore \ \displaystyle\int y\dfrac{dy}{dx} dx = \int x\, dx$

$\therefore \ \displaystyle\int y\, dy = \int x\, dx$

$\therefore \ \dfrac{y^2}{2} = \dfrac{x^2}{2} + c$

$\therefore \ x^2 - y^2 = -2c$

The curve passes through $(5, -4)$, so $5^2 - (-4)^2 = -2c$

$\therefore \ -2c = 9$

$\therefore \ x^2 - y^2 = 9$

If $(a, 3)$ lies on the curve, then $a^2 - 3^2 = 9$

$\therefore \ a^2 = 18$

$\therefore \ a = \pm 3\sqrt{2}$

15 a $\dfrac{dy}{dx} = y^2(1 + x)$

$\therefore \ \dfrac{1}{y^2}\dfrac{dy}{dx} = 1 + x$

$\therefore \ \displaystyle\int \dfrac{1}{y^2}\dfrac{dy}{dx} dx = \int (1+x)\, dx$

$\therefore \ \displaystyle\int y^{-2} dy = \int (1+x)\, dx$

$\therefore \ -\dfrac{1}{y} = x + \tfrac{1}{2}x^2 + c$

$\therefore \ y = \dfrac{1}{-x - \tfrac{1}{2}x^2 - c}$

But $(1, 2)$ lies on the curve,

so $\dfrac{1}{-1 - \tfrac{1}{2} - c} = 2$

$\therefore \ \tfrac{1}{2} = -\tfrac{3}{2} - c$

$\therefore \ c = -2$

$\therefore \ y = \dfrac{1}{2 - x - \tfrac{1}{2}x^2}$

$\therefore \ y = \dfrac{-2}{x^2 + 2x - 4}$

b When $x^2 + 2x - 4 = 0$, $x = \dfrac{-2 \pm \sqrt{4 - 4(1)(-4)}}{2} = \dfrac{-2 \pm 2\sqrt{5}}{2} = -1 \pm \sqrt{5}$

$\therefore$ the VAs are $x = -1 + \sqrt{5}$, $x = -1 - \sqrt{5}$,
and the HA is $y = 0$ {as $|x| \to \infty$, $y \to 0$}

16 a At any point (x, y), the product of the gradients of the curves is $-\dfrac{x}{y} \times \dfrac{y}{x} = -1$

$\therefore$ the solution curves are always at right angles.

b For $\dfrac{dy}{dx} = -\dfrac{x}{y}$ $\qquad\qquad\qquad\qquad \dfrac{dy}{dx} = \dfrac{y}{x}$

$\therefore \int y \dfrac{dy}{dx}\, dx = \int -x\, dx \qquad\qquad \therefore \int \dfrac{1}{y} \dfrac{dy}{dx}\, dx = \int \dfrac{1}{x}\, dx$

$\therefore \int y\, dy = \int -x\, dx \qquad\qquad\qquad \int \dfrac{1}{y}\, dy = \int \dfrac{1}{x}\, dx$

$\therefore \dfrac{y^2}{2} = -\dfrac{x^2}{2} + a \qquad\qquad\qquad \therefore \ln|y| = \ln|x| + a$

$\therefore x^2 + y^2 = c \qquad\qquad\qquad\qquad \therefore \ln\left|\dfrac{y}{x}\right| = a$

This represents a circle with centre $(0, 0)$
and radius $\sqrt{c}$ .... (1) $\qquad\qquad \therefore \dfrac{y}{x} = \pm e^a = k$, say

$\qquad\qquad\qquad\qquad\qquad\qquad\qquad \therefore y = kx$ .... (2)

This represents a line with gradient k that passes through $(0, 0)$.

Any line passing through the centre of a circle will include a diameter of the circle and therefore be normal to the tangent of the circle at the points of intersection. This is why the solution curves in **a** were at right angles.

17 acceleration $a \propto$ velocity v $\qquad\qquad$ Also, when $t = 4$, $v = 6$,

$\therefore \dfrac{dv}{dt} = kv$ for some constant k $\qquad$ so $6 = 4e^{4k}$

$\therefore \dfrac{1}{v}\dfrac{dv}{dt} = k \qquad\qquad\qquad\qquad \therefore e^{4k} = \dfrac{3}{2}$

$\therefore \int \dfrac{1}{v}\dfrac{dv}{dt}\, dt = \int k\, dt \qquad\qquad \therefore k = \dfrac{1}{4}\ln\dfrac{3}{2}$

$\therefore \int \dfrac{1}{v}\, dv = \int k\, dt \qquad\qquad\qquad \therefore v = 4e^{\frac{1}{4}\ln\frac{3}{2}t}$

$\therefore \ln|v| = kt + c \qquad\qquad\qquad\qquad \therefore v = 4\left(\dfrac{3}{2}\right)^{\frac{t}{4}}$ m s^{-1}

$\therefore v = \pm e^{kt+c} \qquad\qquad\qquad\qquad$ When $t = 5$, $v = 4\left(\dfrac{3}{2}\right)^{\frac{5}{4}}$

$\therefore v = Ae^{kt} \qquad\qquad\qquad\qquad\qquad \therefore v \approx 6.64$ m s^{-1}

When $t = 0$, $v = 4$, so $A = 4$

18 $\dfrac{dw}{dt} \propto w$ so $\dfrac{dw}{dt} = kw$ for some k $\qquad$ If there was weight w_0 of sugar at time 0,
then $A = w_0$

$\therefore \dfrac{1}{w}\dfrac{dw}{dt} = k \qquad\qquad\qquad\qquad \therefore w = w_0 e^{kt}$

$\therefore \int \dfrac{1}{w}\dfrac{dw}{dt}\, dt = \int k\, dt \qquad\qquad$ When $t = 10$, $w = 0.2w_0$,
so $w_0 e^{10k} = 0.2 w_0$

$\therefore \int \dfrac{1}{w}\, dw = \int k\, dt \qquad\qquad\qquad \therefore e^{10k} = 0.2$

$\therefore \ln w = kt + c$ {since $w \geqslant 0$} $\qquad$ But $w = w_0\left(e^{10k}\right)^{\frac{t}{10}}$,

$\therefore w = Ae^{kt} \qquad\qquad\qquad\qquad\qquad$ so $w = w_0 \times 0.2^{\frac{t}{10}}$

$\qquad\qquad\qquad\qquad\qquad\qquad \therefore$ when $t = 30$, $w = w_0 \times 0.2^3$

$\qquad\qquad\qquad\qquad\qquad\qquad\qquad \therefore w = 0.008 w_0$

So, 0.8% is remaining

Mathematics HL (2nd edn), Chapter 27
FURTHER INTEGRATION AND DIFFERENTIAL EQUATIONS

19
$$\frac{dI}{dt} = -kI$$
$$\therefore \quad \frac{1}{I}\frac{dI}{dt} = -k$$
$$\therefore \quad \int \frac{1}{I}\frac{dI}{dt}\,dt = -\int k\,dt$$
$$\therefore \quad \int \frac{1}{I}\,dI = -\int k\,dt$$
$$\therefore \quad \ln|I| = -kt + c$$
$$\therefore \quad I = Ae^{-kt}$$

If $I(0) = I_0$, then $A = I_0$
$$\therefore \quad I = I_0 e^{-kt}$$

When $t = 1$, $I = 0.1I_0$,
so $I_0 e^{-k} = 0.1 I_0$
$$\therefore \quad e^{-k} = 0.1$$
$$\therefore \quad I = I_0 0.1^t$$
$\therefore$ when $I = 0.001 I_0$,
$$0.001 I_0 = I_0 0.1^t$$
$$\therefore \quad t = 3$$
$\therefore$ the current will take 3 seconds to drop to 0.1% of its original value.

20 a
$$\frac{dv}{dt} = g - 4v$$
$$\therefore \quad \frac{1}{g-4v}\frac{dv}{dt} = 1$$
$$\therefore \quad \int \frac{1}{g-4v}\frac{dv}{dt}\,dt = \int 1\,dt$$
$$\therefore \quad \int \frac{1}{g-4v}\,dv = \int 1\,dt$$
$$\therefore \quad -\tfrac{1}{4}\ln|g-4v| = t + c$$
$$\therefore \quad \ln|g-4v| = -4t - 4c$$
$$\therefore \quad g - 4v = Ae^{-4t}$$
$$\therefore \quad 4v = g - Ae^{-4t}$$

Since the metal is released from rest,
$$v(0) = 0$$
$$\therefore \quad g - A = 0$$
$$\therefore \quad A = g$$
$$\therefore \quad 4v = g - ge^{-4t}$$
$$\therefore \quad v = \frac{g}{4}(1 - e^{-4t}) \quad \text{as required}$$

As $t \to \infty$, $e^{-4t} \to 0$
$$\therefore \quad v(t) \to \frac{g}{4}\ \text{m s}^{-1}$$
$\therefore$ there is a limiting velocity of $\dfrac{g}{4}\ \text{m s}^{-1}$

b $v = \dfrac{g}{10}$ when $\dfrac{g}{10} = \dfrac{g}{4}(1 - e^{-4t})$
$$\therefore \quad 1 - e^{-4t} = \tfrac{4}{10}$$
$$\therefore \quad e^{-4t} = \tfrac{3}{5}$$
$$\therefore \quad -4t = \ln \tfrac{3}{5}$$
$$\therefore \quad t = -\tfrac{1}{4}\ln \tfrac{3}{5} \approx 0.128 \text{ seconds}$$

21 a Suppose V_0 is the initial volume of water in the lake, and $V(t)$ is the total amount of water that has evaporated at time t. The volume of water remaining in the lake is $(V_0 - V)$.

Hence $\dfrac{dV}{dt} \propto (V_0 - V)$ or $\dfrac{dV}{dt} = k(V_0 - V)$

b
$$\frac{1}{V_0 - V}\frac{dV}{dt} = k$$
$$\therefore \quad \int \frac{1}{V_0 - V}\frac{dV}{dt}\,dt = \int k\,dt$$
$$\therefore \quad \int \frac{1}{V_0 - V}\,dV = \int k\,dt$$
$$\therefore \quad -\ln|V_0 - V| = kt + c$$
$$\therefore \quad \ln|V_0 - V| = -kt - c$$
$$\therefore \quad V_0 - V = Ae^{-kt}$$
But $V(0) = 0$, so $A = V_0$

After 20 days, $V = \tfrac{1}{2}V_0$
$$\therefore \quad V_0 - \tfrac{1}{2}V_0 = V_0 e^{-20k}$$
$$\therefore \quad e^{-20k} = \tfrac{1}{2}$$
$$\therefore \quad V_0 - V = V_0 \left(e^{-20k}\right)^{\frac{t}{20}} = V_0 \left(\tfrac{1}{2}\right)^{\frac{t}{20}}$$
$$\therefore \quad V = V_0 \left(1 - 0.5^{\frac{t}{20}}\right)$$

Hence after 50 days without rain,
$V = V_0(1 - 0.5^{2.5}) \approx 0.8232\,V_0$
$\therefore$ 82.3% has evaporated and 17.7% remains.

22 Let V be the volume of water in the tank and h be the water depth.

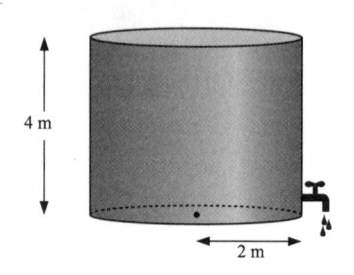

Then $\dfrac{dV}{dt} \propto \sqrt{h}$,

$\therefore \dfrac{dV}{dt} = k\sqrt{h}$ for some k

We know that $V = \pi r^2 h$
where $r = 2$ m is the radius of the tank.

Hence $V = 4\pi h$ and $\dfrac{dV}{dh} = 4\pi$

Now $\dfrac{dV}{dt} = \dfrac{dV}{dh} \times \dfrac{dh}{dt}$ {chain rule}

so $k\sqrt{h} = 4\pi \times \dfrac{dh}{dt}$

$\therefore \dfrac{1}{\sqrt{h}} \dfrac{dh}{dt} = \dfrac{k}{4\pi}$

$\therefore \int \dfrac{1}{\sqrt{h}} \dfrac{dh}{dt} \, dt = \int \dfrac{k}{4\pi} \, dt$

$\therefore \int \dfrac{1}{\sqrt{h}} \, dh = \int \dfrac{k}{4\pi} \, dt$

$\therefore 2\sqrt{h} = \dfrac{k}{4\pi} t + c$

Initially the tank is full, so $h(0) = 4$

$\therefore 4 = 0 + c$

$\therefore 2\sqrt{h} = \dfrac{k}{4\pi} t + 4$

Also, $h(2) = 1$, so $2 = \dfrac{k}{4\pi} \times 2 + 4$

$\therefore \dfrac{k}{4\pi} = -1$

$\therefore k = -4\pi$

$\therefore 2\sqrt{h} = 4 - t$

$\therefore$ the tank is empty when $t = 4$,
so it takes 4 hours to empty.

23 a $V = \tfrac{1}{3}\pi h^2(3r - h) = \pi h^2 r - \tfrac{1}{3}\pi h^3$

$\therefore$ for fixed r, $\dfrac{dV}{dh} = 2\pi hr - \pi h^2$

Now $\dfrac{dV}{dt} = \dfrac{dV}{dh} \times \dfrac{dh}{dt}$ {chain rule}

$\therefore$ since $\dfrac{dV}{dt} = -r^2$,

$-r^2 = (2\pi hr - \pi h^2)\dfrac{dh}{dt}$

$\therefore \dfrac{dh}{dt} = \dfrac{r^2}{\pi h^2 - 2\pi hr}$

b $(\pi h^2 - 2\pi hr)\dfrac{dh}{dt} = r^2$

$\therefore \int (\pi h^2 - 2\pi hr)\dfrac{dh}{dt} \, dt = \int r^2 \, dt$

$\therefore \int (\pi h^2 - 2\pi hr) \, dh = \int r^2 \, dt$

$\therefore \tfrac{1}{3}\pi h^3 - \pi h^2 r = r^2 t + c$

If $r = 10$ and the bowl is initially full,
then $h = 10$ when $t = 0$.

$\therefore \dfrac{1000}{3}\pi - 1000\pi = c$ $\therefore c = -\dfrac{2000}{3}\pi$

$\therefore 100t = \tfrac{1}{3}\pi h^3 - 10\pi h^2 + \dfrac{2000}{3}\pi$

$\therefore t = \dfrac{\pi}{300} h^3 - \dfrac{\pi}{10} h^2 + \dfrac{2000}{300}\pi$

$\therefore t = \dfrac{\pi}{300}[h^3 - 30h^2 + 2000]$

$\therefore$ when $h = 5$, $t = \dfrac{1375\pi}{300} \approx 14.4$ hours

24 $\dfrac{dT}{dt} \propto (T - T_m)$

$\therefore \dfrac{dT}{dt} = k(T - T_m)$ for some k

$\therefore \dfrac{1}{T - T_m} \dfrac{dT}{dt} = k$

$\therefore \int \dfrac{1}{T - T_m} \, dT = \int k \, dt$

$\therefore \ln|T - T_m| = kt + c$

$\therefore T - T_m = Ae^{kt}$

Given $T_m = 5°C$ and that $T(0) = 100°C$,
$Ae^0 = 100 - 5$

$\therefore A = 95$

Also, since $T(1) = 80$, $95e^k = 80 - 5 = 75$

$\therefore e^k = \dfrac{15}{19}$

$\therefore T - 5 = 95\left(\dfrac{15}{19}\right)^t$

$\therefore T = 5 + 95\left(\dfrac{15}{19}\right)^t$

So, $T = 10°C$ when $10 = 5 + 95\left(\dfrac{15}{19}\right)^t$

$\therefore \left(\dfrac{15}{19}\right)^t = \dfrac{5}{95} = \dfrac{1}{19}$

$\therefore t \ln \dfrac{15}{19} = \ln \dfrac{1}{19}$

$\therefore t = \dfrac{\ln \frac{1}{19}}{\ln \frac{15}{19}}$

$\therefore t \approx 12.5$ minutes

25 From question **24**, a general solution to Newton's Law of Cooling is $T - T_m = Ae^{kt}$.
We assume $t = 0$ to be 6 am, so $T(0) = 13$.
Then since $T_m = 5°C$, $Ae^0 = 13 - 5 = 8$
$\therefore A = 8$
$\therefore T = 5 + 8e^{kt}$

Also, $T(3) = 9$, so $8e^{3k} = 4$
$\therefore e^{3k} = \frac{1}{2}$

$\therefore T = 5 + 8(e^{3k})^{\frac{t}{3}}$
$= 5 + 8(\frac{1}{2})^{\frac{t}{3}}$

$\therefore$ the temperature was 37°C when
$5 + 8\left(\frac{1}{2}\right)^{\frac{t}{3}} = 37$
$\therefore \left(\frac{1}{2}\right)^{\frac{t}{3}} = \frac{32}{8} = 4$
$\therefore \frac{t}{3} = -2$
$\therefore t = -6$ hours

So, the time of death was 6 hours before 6 am, or midnight.

EXERCISE 27E.2

1 $\frac{dy}{dx} - 2xe^x = y$ so $\frac{dy}{dx} = 2xe^x + y$

Let $y = ue^x$ so $\frac{dy}{dx} = \frac{du}{dx}e^x + ue^x$

$\therefore 2xe^x + ue^x = \frac{du}{dx}e^x + ue^x$

$\therefore \frac{du}{dx}e^x = 2xe^x$

$\therefore \frac{du}{dx} = 2x$

$\therefore \int \frac{du}{dx} dx = \int 2x \, dx$

$\therefore \int 1 \, du = \int 2x \, dx$

$\therefore u = x^2 + c$

But $y = ue^x$, so $\frac{y}{e^x} = x^2 + c$

$\therefore y = e^x(x^2 + c)$

2 If $y = ue^x$, then $\frac{dy}{dx} = \frac{du}{dx}e^x + ue^x$

$\left(\frac{dy}{dx}\right)^2 = y^2 + 2e^x y + e^{2x}$

$\therefore \left[\frac{du}{dx}e^x + ue^x\right]^2 = u^2 e^{2x} + 2e^x(ue^x) + e^{2x}$

$\therefore \left[\frac{du}{dx}e^x\right]^2 + 2ue^{2x}\frac{du}{dx} + u^2 e^{2x}$
$= u^2 e^{2x} + 2ue^{2x} + e^{2x}$

$\therefore \left(\frac{du}{dx}\right)^2 e^{2x} + 2ue^{2x}\left(\frac{du}{dx}\right) = 2ue^{2x} + e^{2x}$

$\therefore \left(\frac{du}{dx}\right)^2 + 2u\frac{du}{dx} = 2u + 1$

$\therefore \left(\frac{du}{dx}\right)^2 + 2u\frac{du}{dx} - 2u - 1 = 0$

$\therefore \left(\frac{du}{dx} - 1\right)\left(\frac{du}{dx} + 2u + 1\right) = 0$

$\therefore \frac{du}{dx} = 1$ or $-2u - 1$

If $\frac{du}{dx} = 1$ then

$\int \frac{du}{dx} dx = \int 1 \, dx$

$\therefore \int 1 \, du = \int 1 \, dx$

$\therefore u = x + c$

$\therefore \frac{y}{e^x} = x + c$

$\therefore y = e^x(x + c)$

or, if $\frac{du}{dx} = -2u - 1$ then

$\int \frac{1}{2u+1} \frac{du}{dx} dx = \int -1 \, dx$

$\therefore \int \frac{1}{2u+1} du = \int -1 \, dx$

$\therefore \frac{1}{2}\ln|2u+1| = -x + c$

$\therefore 2u + 1 = Ae^{-2x}$

$\therefore \frac{2y}{e^x} + 1 = Ae^{-2x}$

$\therefore 2y + e^x = Ae^{-x}$

$\therefore y = \frac{Ae^{-x} - e^x}{2}$

Hence $y = e^x(x + c)$ or $y = \frac{Ae^{-x} - e^x}{2}$.

3 $4xy \dfrac{dy}{dx} = -x^2 - y^2$, $x > 0$

Let $y = ux$ so $\dfrac{dy}{dx} = \dfrac{du}{dx} x + u$

$\therefore\ 4x(ux)\left[\dfrac{du}{dx} x + u\right] = -x^2 - u^2 x^2$

$\therefore\ 4ux^2\left[\dfrac{du}{dx} x + u\right] = -x^2 - u^2 x^2$

$\therefore\ 4u\left[\dfrac{du}{dx} x + u\right] = -1 - u^2$

$\therefore\ x \dfrac{du}{dx} + u = \dfrac{-u^2 - 1}{4u}$

$\therefore\ x \dfrac{du}{dx} = \dfrac{-u^2 - 1 - 4u^2}{4u}$

$\therefore\ x \dfrac{du}{dx} = \dfrac{-5u^2 - 1}{4u}$

$\therefore\ \dfrac{4u}{5u^2 + 1} \dfrac{du}{dx} = -\dfrac{1}{x}$

$\therefore\ \displaystyle\int \dfrac{4u}{5u^2 + 1} \dfrac{du}{dx}\, dx = \int -\dfrac{1}{x}\, dx$

$\therefore\ \displaystyle\int \dfrac{4u}{5u^2 + 1}\, du = -\int \dfrac{1}{x}\, dx$

$\therefore\ \dfrac{4}{10} \displaystyle\int \dfrac{10u}{5u^2 + 1}\, du = -\int \dfrac{1}{x}\, dx$

$\therefore\ \tfrac{2}{5} \ln|5u^2 + 1| = -\ln|x| + c_1$

$\therefore\ \ln|5u^2 + 1| = -\tfrac{5}{2}\ln|x| + c$

$\therefore\ \dfrac{5y^2}{x^2} + 1 = A x^{-\frac{5}{2}}$

$\therefore\ \dfrac{x^2 + 5y^2}{x^2} = A x^{-\frac{5}{2}}$

$\therefore\ \sqrt{x}\,(x^2 + 5y^2) = A$

$\therefore\ x\,(x^2 + 5y^2)^2 = k$

4 $x \dfrac{dy}{dx} - y = 4x^2 y$

Let $y = ux$ so $\dfrac{dy}{dx} = \dfrac{du}{dx} x + u$

$\therefore\ x\left[\dfrac{du}{dx} x + u\right] - ux = 4x^2(ux)$

$\therefore\ \dfrac{du}{dx} x^2 + ux - ux = 4ux^3$

$\therefore\ \dfrac{du}{dx} x^2 = 4ux^3$

$\therefore\ \dfrac{du}{dx} = 4ux$

$\therefore\ \dfrac{1}{u} \dfrac{du}{dx} = 4x$

$\therefore\ \displaystyle\int \dfrac{1}{u} \dfrac{du}{dx}\, dx = \int 4x\, dx$

$\therefore\ \displaystyle\int \dfrac{1}{u}\, du = \int 4x\, dx$

$\therefore\ \ln|u| = \dfrac{4x^2}{2} + c$

$\therefore\ u = A e^{2x^2}$

But $y = ux$, so $\dfrac{y}{x} = A e^{2x^2}$

$\therefore\ y = A x e^{2x^2}$

REVIEW SET 27A

1 Let $u = 4 - x$, $\dfrac{du}{dx} = -1$

$\therefore\ \displaystyle\int x^2 \sqrt{4 - x}\, dx$
$= \displaystyle\int (4 - u)^2 \sqrt{u}\,(-du)$
$= -\displaystyle\int (16 - 8u + u^2) u^{\frac{1}{2}}\, du$
$= -\displaystyle\int (16 u^{\frac{1}{2}} - 8 u^{\frac{3}{2}} + u^{\frac{5}{2}})\, du$
$= -\left(\dfrac{16 u^{\frac{3}{2}}}{\frac{3}{2}} - \dfrac{8 u^{\frac{5}{2}}}{\frac{5}{2}} + \dfrac{u^{\frac{7}{2}}}{\frac{7}{2}}\right) + c$
$= -\tfrac{32}{3} u^{\frac{3}{2}} + \tfrac{16}{5} u^{\frac{5}{2}} - \tfrac{2}{7} u^{\frac{7}{2}} + c$
$= -\tfrac{32}{3}(4 - x)^{\frac{3}{2}} + \tfrac{16}{5}(4 - x)^{\frac{5}{2}}$
$\qquad - \tfrac{2}{7}(4 - x)^{\frac{7}{2}} + c$

2 $\displaystyle\int \arctan x\, dx = \int 1 \cdot \arctan x\, dx$

so we integrate by parts with $u = \arctan x$, $v' = 1$

$u' = \dfrac{1}{x^2 + 1}$, $v = x$

$\therefore\ \displaystyle\int \arctan x\, dx$

$= x \arctan x - \displaystyle\int \dfrac{1}{x^2 + 1}\,(x)\, dx$

$= x \arctan x - \tfrac{1}{2} \displaystyle\int \dfrac{2x}{x^2 + 1}\, dx$

$= x \arctan x - \tfrac{1}{2} \ln|x^2 + 1| + c$

$= x \arctan x - \tfrac{1}{2} \ln(x^2 + 1) + c \quad \{x^2 + 1 > 0\}$

Check: $\dfrac{d}{dx}\left(x \arctan x - \tfrac{1}{2}\ln(x^2 + 1) + c\right)$

$= \arctan x + \dfrac{x}{x^2 + 1} - \tfrac{1}{2} \cdot \dfrac{2x}{x^2 + 1}$

$= \arctan x \quad \checkmark$

FURTHER INTEGRATION AND DIFFERENTIAL EQUATIONS

3 a We integrate by parts with $\quad u = e^{-x} \quad v' = \cos x$
$\qquad\qquad\qquad\qquad\qquad\qquad u' = -e^{-x} \quad v = \sin x$

$\therefore \int e^{-x} \cos x \, dx = e^{-x} \sin x - \int -e^{-x} \sin x \, dx$
$\qquad\qquad\qquad\quad = e^{-x} \sin x + \int e^{-x} \sin x \, dx$

We integrate by parts again, this time with $\quad u = e^{-x} \quad v' = \sin x$
$\qquad\qquad\qquad\qquad\qquad\qquad\qquad\qquad u' = -e^{-x} \quad v = -\cos x$

$\therefore \int e^{-x} \cos x \, dx = e^{-x} \sin x + e^{-x}(-\cos x) - \int (-e^{-x})(-\cos x) \, dx + c_1$
$\qquad\qquad\qquad\quad = e^{-x} \sin x - e^{-x} \cos x - \int e^{-x} \cos x \, dx + c_1$

$\therefore \ 2 \int e^{-x} \cos x \, dx = e^{-x}(\sin x - \cos x) + c_1$
$\therefore \ \int e^{-x} \cos x \, dx = \tfrac{1}{2} e^{-x}(\sin x - \cos x) + c$

b We integrate by parts with $\quad u = x^2 \quad v' = e^x$
$\qquad\qquad\qquad\qquad\qquad u' = 2x \quad v = e^x$

$\therefore \int x^2 e^x \, dx = x^2 e^x - \int 2x e^x \, dx$

We integrate by parts again, this time with $\quad u = 2x \quad v' = e^x$
$\qquad\qquad\qquad\qquad\qquad\qquad\qquad\qquad u' = 2 \quad v = e^x$

$\therefore \int x^2 e^x \, dx = x^2 e^x - \left[2x e^x - \int 2 e^x \, dx \right]$
$\qquad\qquad\quad = x^2 e^x - 2x e^x + 2 \int e^x \, dx$
$\qquad\qquad\quad = x^2 e^x - 2x e^x + 2 e^x + c$
$\qquad\qquad\quad = e^x (x^2 - 2x + 2) + c$

c Let $u = 9 - x^2$, $\dfrac{du}{dx} = -2x$

$\therefore \int \dfrac{x^3}{\sqrt{9 - x^2}} \, dx$

$= -\dfrac{1}{2} \int \dfrac{x^2}{\sqrt{9 - x^2}} (-2x) \, dx$

$= -\dfrac{1}{2} \int \dfrac{9 - u}{\sqrt{u}} \dfrac{du}{dx} \, dx$

$= -\dfrac{1}{2} \int \dfrac{9 - u}{\sqrt{u}} \, du$

$= -\dfrac{1}{2} \int \left(9u^{-\frac{1}{2}} - u^{\frac{1}{2}} \right) du$

$= -\dfrac{1}{2} \left[\dfrac{9u^{\frac{1}{2}}}{\frac{1}{2}} - \dfrac{u^{\frac{3}{2}}}{\frac{3}{2}} \right] + c$

$= -9 u^{\frac{1}{2}} + \tfrac{1}{3} u^{\frac{3}{2}} + c$

$= -9 \sqrt{9 - x^2} + \tfrac{1}{3} \left(9 - x^2 \right)^{\frac{3}{2}} + c$

4 $\quad y' = -\dfrac{2 e^x}{y}$

$\therefore \ y \dfrac{dy}{dx} = -2 e^x$

$\therefore \ \int y \, dy = \int -2 e^x \, dx$

$\therefore \ \dfrac{y^2}{2} = -2 e^x + c$

But $y(0) = 4$, so $\dfrac{16}{2} = -2 e^0 + c$

$\therefore \ c = 10$

$\therefore \ \dfrac{y^2}{2} = -2 e^x + 10$

$\therefore \ y^2 = 20 - 4 e^x$

5 $\quad L \dfrac{dI}{dt} = E - RI$

Using $R = 4$, $L = 0.2$ and $E = 20$,

$\tfrac{1}{5} \dfrac{dI}{dt} = 20 - 4I = 4(5 - I)$

$\therefore \ \dfrac{1}{5 - I} \dfrac{dI}{dt} = 20$

$\therefore \ \int \dfrac{1}{5 - I} \dfrac{dI}{dt} \, dt = \int 20 \, dt$

$\therefore \ \int \dfrac{1}{5 - I} \, dI = \int 20 \, dt$

$\therefore \ -\ln |5 - I| = 20 t + c$

But $I(0) = 0$, so $c = -\ln 5$

$\therefore \ 20 t = \ln 5 - \ln |5 - I|$

$\therefore \ t = \dfrac{1}{20} \ln \left| \dfrac{5}{5 - I} \right|$

The current is 0.5 amps when $t = \dfrac{1}{20} \ln (\dfrac{5}{4.5})$

$t \approx 0.005\,27$ s

6

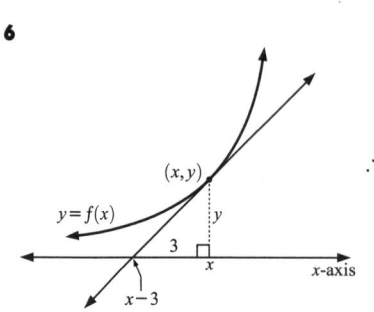

$\dfrac{dy}{dx} = \dfrac{y}{3}$

$\therefore \dfrac{1}{y}\dfrac{dy}{dx} = \dfrac{1}{3}$

$\therefore \int \dfrac{1}{y}\dfrac{dy}{dx}\,dx = \int \dfrac{1}{3}\,dx$

$\therefore \int \dfrac{1}{y}\,dy = \int \dfrac{1}{3}\,dx$

$\therefore \ln|y| = \dfrac{1}{3}x + c$

$\therefore y = Ae^{\frac{1}{3}x}$

But when $x = 0$, $y = 3$

$\therefore 3 = Ae^0$

$\therefore A = 3$

So, $f(x) = 3e^{\frac{1}{3}x}$

7 Letting $y = ux$, $\dfrac{dy}{dx} = \dfrac{du}{dx}x + u$

So, $2xy\dfrac{dy}{dx} = x^2 + y^2$ becomes

$2x(ux)\left[\dfrac{du}{dx}x + u\right] = x^2 + (ux)^2$

$\therefore 2ux^2\left[x\dfrac{du}{dx} + u\right] = x^2 + u^2x^2$

$\therefore 2u\left[x\dfrac{du}{dx} + u\right] = 1 + u^2 \quad \{\div x^2\}$

$\therefore x\dfrac{du}{dx} + u = \dfrac{1+u^2}{2u}$

$\therefore x\dfrac{du}{dx} = \dfrac{1-u^2}{2u}$

$\therefore \dfrac{2u}{1-u^2}\dfrac{du}{dx} = \dfrac{1}{x}$

$\therefore \int \dfrac{2u}{1-u^2}\dfrac{du}{dx}\,dx = \int \dfrac{1}{x}\,dx$

$\therefore \int \dfrac{2u}{1-u^2}\,du = \int \dfrac{1}{x}\,dx$

$\therefore -\int \dfrac{-2u}{1-u^2}\,du = \int \dfrac{1}{x}\,dx$

$\therefore -\ln|1-u^2| = \ln|x| + c$

$\therefore \ln|x(1-u^2)| = -c$

$\therefore x(1-u^2) = A$

$\therefore x\left(1 - \dfrac{y^2}{x^2}\right) = A$

$\therefore x\left(\dfrac{x^2 - y^2}{x^2}\right) = A$

$\therefore x^2 - y^2 = Ax$

If $y = 2$ when $x = 1$,
then $1^2 - 2^2 = A$

$\therefore A = -3$

$\therefore x^2 - y^2 = -3x$

$\therefore y^2 = x^2 + 3x$

8 a   cis θ cis ϕ
$= e^{i\theta} \times e^{i\phi}$
$= e^{i\theta + i\phi}$
$= e^{i(\theta + \phi)}$
$= \text{cis}(\theta + \phi)$

b $(\text{cis }\theta)^n$
$= \left(e^{i\theta}\right)^n$
$= e^{i\theta n}$
$= e^{i(n\theta)}$
$= \text{cis } n\theta$

REVIEW SET 27B

1 a $\displaystyle\int \dfrac{5}{\sqrt{9 - x^2}}\,dx$

$= 5\displaystyle\int \dfrac{1}{\sqrt{3^2 - x^2}}\,dx$

$= 5 \arcsin\left(\dfrac{x}{3}\right) + c$

b $\displaystyle\int \dfrac{1}{9 + 4x^2}\,dx$

$= \dfrac{1}{4}\displaystyle\int \dfrac{1}{\frac{9}{4} + x^2}\,dx$

$= \dfrac{1}{4}\left(\dfrac{1}{\frac{3}{2}}\right)\arctan\left(\dfrac{x}{\frac{3}{2}}\right) + c$

$= \dfrac{1}{6}\arctan\left(\dfrac{2x}{3}\right) + c$

c Let $u = x - 5$, $\dfrac{du}{dx} = 1$

when $x = 10$, $u = 5$, and when $x = 7$, $u = 2$

$\therefore \int_7^{10} x\sqrt{x-5}\,dx = \int_2^5 (u+5)\sqrt{u}\,du$

$= \int_2^5 (u^{\frac{3}{2}} + 5u^{\frac{1}{2}})\,du$

$= \left[\dfrac{u^{\frac{5}{2}}}{\frac{5}{2}} + \dfrac{5u^{\frac{3}{2}}}{\frac{3}{2}}\right]_2^5$

$= \dfrac{2}{5}\left(5^{\frac{5}{2}}\right) + \dfrac{10}{3}\left(5^{\frac{3}{2}}\right) - \left[\dfrac{2}{5}\left(2^{\frac{5}{2}}\right) + \dfrac{10}{3}\left(2^{\frac{3}{2}}\right)\right]$

$= \dfrac{2}{5}(25\sqrt{5}) + \dfrac{10}{3}(5\sqrt{5}) - \dfrac{2}{5}(4\sqrt{2}) - \dfrac{10}{3}(2\sqrt{2})$

$= 10\sqrt{5} + \dfrac{50}{3}\sqrt{5} - \dfrac{8}{5}\sqrt{2} - \dfrac{20}{3}\sqrt{2}$

$= \dfrac{80}{3}\sqrt{5} - \dfrac{124}{15}\sqrt{2}$

2 a We integrate by parts with

$u = x \quad v' = \cos x$
$u' = 1 \quad v = \sin x$

$\therefore \int x \cos x\,dx$
$= x \sin x - \int \sin x\,dx$
$= x \sin x - (-\cos x) + c$
$= x \sin x + \cos x + c$

b Let $x = 2\sec\theta$, $\dfrac{dx}{d\theta} = 2\sec\theta\tan\theta$

$\therefore \int \dfrac{\sqrt{x^2-4}}{x}\,dx$

$= \int \dfrac{\sqrt{4\sec^2\theta - 4}}{2\sec\theta} \times 2\sec\theta\tan\theta\,d\theta$

$= \int \sqrt{4(\sec^2\theta - 1)}\,\tan\theta\,d\theta$

$= \int 2\tan\theta\tan\theta\,d\theta$

$= 2\int \tan^2\theta\,d\theta$

$= 2\int (\sec^2\theta - 1)\,d\theta$

$= 2[\tan\theta - \theta] + c$

$= 2\tan\theta - 2\theta + c$

$= 2\left(\dfrac{\sqrt{x^2-4}}{2}\right) - 2\arccos\left(\dfrac{2}{x}\right) + c$

$= \sqrt{x^2-4} - 2\arccos\left(\dfrac{2}{x}\right) + c$

3 $\dfrac{dy}{dx} = \dfrac{1}{y+2}$

$\therefore (y+2)\dfrac{dy}{dx} = 1$

$\therefore \int (y+2)\,dy = \int 1\,dx$

$\therefore \dfrac{y^2}{2} + 2y = x + c$

But when $x = 0$, $y = 0$

$\therefore c = 0$

$\therefore \dfrac{y^2}{2} + 2y = x$

$\therefore y^2 + 4y = 2x$

$\therefore (y+2)^2 = 2x + 4$

$\therefore y + 2 = \pm\sqrt{2x+4}$

However, since $y = 0$ when $x = 0$,

$y + 2 = +\sqrt{2x+4}$

$\therefore y = \sqrt{2x+4} - 2$

4 $\dfrac{dy}{dx} = \dfrac{2x}{\cos y}$

$\therefore \cos y\dfrac{dy}{dx} = 2x$

$\therefore \int \cos y\,dy = \int 2x\,dx$

$\therefore \sin y = x^2 + c$

But $y(1) = \dfrac{\pi}{2}$, so $\sin\left(\dfrac{\pi}{2}\right) = 1 + c$

$\therefore c = 0$

$\therefore \sin y = x^2$

$\therefore y = \arcsin\left(x^2\right) \quad$ as required.

5 **a** Since the uniformly inclined plane has highest point P and a 5 m horizontal base,

it has gradient $\dfrac{dy}{dx} = -\dfrac{y}{5}$

$\therefore \quad \dfrac{1}{y}\dfrac{dy}{dx} = -\dfrac{1}{5}$

$\therefore \quad \displaystyle\int \dfrac{1}{y}\dfrac{dy}{dx}\,dx = \int -\dfrac{1}{5}\,dx$

$\therefore \quad \displaystyle\int \dfrac{1}{y}\,dy = \int -\dfrac{1}{5}\,dx$

$\therefore \quad \ln|y| = -\dfrac{1}{5}x + c$

$\therefore \quad y = Ae^{-\frac{1}{5}x}$

Now when $x = 0$, $y = 10$,

so $A = 10$

$\therefore \quad y = 10e^{-\frac{1}{5}x}$ as required.

b $x = 30$ m at L

$\therefore \quad y = 10e^{-\frac{30}{5}}$

$= 10e^{-6}$

≈ 0.0248 m

c $\dfrac{dy}{dx} = -\dfrac{y}{5}$

$\therefore$ the gradient at H $= -\dfrac{10}{5} = -2$

and the gradient at L $\approx -\dfrac{0.024\,79}{5}$

$\approx -0.004\,96$

6 **a** Letting $N(t)$ be the number of bacteria at time t,

$\dfrac{dN}{dt} = kN$ for some constant k.

b Using **a**, $\dfrac{1}{N}\dfrac{dN}{dt} = k$

$\therefore \quad \displaystyle\int \dfrac{1}{N}\,dN = \int k\,dt$

$\therefore \quad \ln|N| = kt + c$

$\therefore \quad N = Ae^{kt}$

The initial population was $N(0) = 10^5$, so $A = 10^5$

$\therefore \quad N = 10^5 e^{kt}$

Since the population doubles every 37 minutes, $10^5 e^{k(t+37)} = 2 \times 10^5 e^{kt}$

$\therefore \quad e^{kt} e^{37k} = 2e^{kt}$

$\therefore \quad (e^k)^{37} = 2$

$\therefore \quad e^k = 2^{\frac{1}{37}}$

$\therefore \quad N = 10^5 (2^{\frac{1}{37}})^t$

$\therefore \quad N = 10^5 \times 2^{\frac{t}{37}}$

After 4 hours or 240 minutes, the population is $N(240) = 10^5 \times 2^{\frac{240}{37}}$

$\approx 8.97 \times 10^6$ bacteria

7 **a** $\dfrac{dy}{dx} = (y-1)^2(2+x)$

$\therefore \quad (y-1)^{-2}\dfrac{dy}{dx} = 2 + x$

$\therefore \quad \displaystyle\int (y-1)^{-2}\dfrac{dy}{dx}\,dx = \int (2+x)\,dx$

$\therefore \quad \int (y-1)^{-2}\,dy = \int (2+x)\,dx$

$\therefore \quad -(y-1)^{-1} = 2x + \dfrac{x^2}{2} + c$

But the curve passes through $(-1, 2)$,

so $-2 + \dfrac{1}{2} + c = -1$

$\therefore \quad c = \dfrac{1}{2}$

$\therefore \quad -\dfrac{1}{y-1} = 2x + \dfrac{x^2}{2} + \dfrac{1}{2}$

$\therefore \quad y - 1 = -\dfrac{1}{\frac{x^2}{2} + 2x + \frac{1}{2}}$

$= -\dfrac{2}{x^2 + 4x + 1}$

$\therefore \quad y = 1 - \dfrac{2}{x^2 + 4x + 1}$

b As $x \to \pm\infty$, $y \to 1$
$\therefore\ y = 1$ is a horizontal asymptote.
The function is undefined when $x^2 + 4x + 1 = 0$,
which is when $x = \dfrac{-4 \pm \sqrt{16 - 4}}{2} = -2 \pm \sqrt{3}$.
$\therefore\ $ the vertical asymptotes are $x = -2 + \sqrt{3}$ and $x = -2 - \sqrt{3}$.

8 If V is the volume of water in the tank, then $\dfrac{dV}{dt} \propto V$

$$\therefore\ \frac{1}{V}\frac{dV}{dt} = k \quad \text{for some constant } k$$

$$\therefore\ \int \frac{1}{V}\, dV = \int k\, dt$$

$$\therefore\ \ln|V| = kt + c$$

$$\therefore\ V = Ae^{kt}$$

At time zero, the tank is full. If we call this volume V_0, then $A = V_0$

$$\therefore\ V = V_0 e^{kt}$$

After 20 minutes, the tank is half full, so $V_0 e^{20k} = \tfrac{1}{2} V_0$

$$\therefore\ (e^k)^{20} = \tfrac{1}{2}$$

$$\therefore\ e^k = (\tfrac{1}{2})^{\frac{1}{20}}$$

$$\therefore\ V = V_0 \left(\tfrac{1}{2}\right)^{\frac{t}{20}}$$

So, after one hour, the volume present is $V(60) = V_0(\tfrac{1}{2})^3 = \tfrac{1}{8} V_0$
Hence $\tfrac{1}{8}$ of the water remains.

Chapter 28
STATISTICAL DISTRIBUTIONS OF DISCRETE RANDOM VARIABLES

EXERCISE 28A

1 **a** The quantity of fat in a lamb chop is a continuous random variable.
  b The mark out of 50 for a Geography test is a discrete random variable.
  c The weight of a seventeen-year-old student is a continuous random variable.
  d The volume of water in a cup of coffee is a continuous random variable.
  e The number of trout in a lake is a discrete random variable.
  f The number of hairs on a cat is a discrete random variable.
  g The length of hairs on a horse is a continuous random variable.
  h The height of a sky-scraper is a continuous random variable.

2 **a** **i** The random variable is the height of water in the rain gauge.
    ii $0 \leqslant x \leqslant 200$ mm   **iii** The variable is a continuous random variable.
  b **i** The random variable is the stopping distance.
    ii $0 \leqslant x \leqslant 50$ m   **iii** The variable is a continuous random variable.
  c **i** The random variable is the number of times that the switch is turned on or off before it fails.
    ii $1 \leqslant x \leqslant 2000$ switches   **iii** The variable is a discrete random variable.

3 **a** Since x is the number of weighing devices that are accurate, $x = 0, 1, 2, 3$ or 4.
  b
```
                              YYNN
                              YNYN
              YYYN    YNNY    NNNY
              YYNY    NYYN    NNYN
              YNYY    NYNY    NYNN
    YYYY      NYYY    NNYY    YNNN    NNNN
   (x = 4)   (x = 3) (x = 2) (x = 1) (x = 0)
```
  c **i** If two are accurate then $x = 2$.
    ii If at least two are accurate then 2, 3 or 4 are accurate $\therefore$ $x = 2, 3$ or 4.

4 **a** If 3 coins are tossed then the number of heads x can be 0, 1, 2 or 3.
  b Suppose H represents heads, T represents tails. **c** $P(x = 0) = \frac{1}{8}$ $P(x = 1) = \frac{3}{8}$
```
              HHT    TTH
              HTH    THT
    HHH       THH    HTT     TTT
   (x = 3)  (x = 2) (x = 1) (x = 0)
```
  $P(x = 2) = \frac{3}{8}$ $P(x = 3) = \frac{1}{8}$

  d

EXERCISE 28B

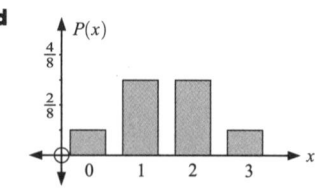

1 **a** $\sum_{x=0}^{2} P(x) = 1$ **b** $\sum_{x=0}^{3} P(x) = 1$
  $\therefore$ $0.3 + k + 0.5 = 1$ $\therefore$ $k + 2k + 3k + k = 1$
  $\therefore$ $k = 0.2$ $\therefore$ $7k = 1$
       $\therefore$ $k = \frac{1}{7}$

2 a $P(2) = 0.1088$ (from table)

b Since this is a probability distribution, $\sum P(i) = 1$
$$\therefore \quad a + 0.3333 + 0.1088 + 0.0084 + 0.0007 + 0.0000 = 1$$
$$\therefore \quad a + 0.4512 = 1$$
$$\therefore \quad a = 0.5488$$
This is the probability that Jason does not hit a home run in a game.

c $P(1) + P(2) + P(3) + P(4) + P(5) = 0.3333 + 0.1088 + 0.0084 + 0.0007 + 0.0000$
$$= 0.4512$$
This represents the probability that Jason hits *at least one* home run in a game.

d

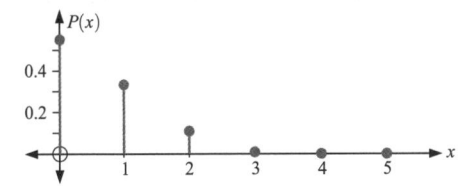

3 a Sum of probabilities $\sum P(i) = 0.2 + 0.3 + 0.4 + 0.2 = 1.1$
Since this sum $\neq 1$, this is not a valid probability distribution.

b $P(5) = -0.2$, so not all of the probabilities lie in $0 \leqslant P(i) \leqslant 1$.
$\therefore$ this is not a valid probability distribution.

4 a The random variable represents the number of hits that Sally has in each game.
$$0.07 + 0.14 + k + 0.46 + 0.08 + 0.02 = 1 \quad \{\text{since } \sum P(i) = 1\}$$
$$\therefore \quad k + 0.77 = 1$$
$$\therefore \quad k = 0.23$$

b i $P(X \geqslant 2)$
$= P(X = 2 \text{ or } X = 3 \text{ or } X = 4 \text{ or } X = 5)$
$= P(2) + P(3) + P(4) + P(5)$
$= 0.23 + 0.46 + 0.08 + 0.02$
$= 0.79$

ii $P(1 \leqslant X \leqslant 3)$
$= P(1) + P(2) + P(3)$
$= 0.14 + 0.23 + 0.46$
$= 0.83$

5 a When rolling a die twice, the sample space is:

	1	2	3	4	5	6
6	(6, 1)	(6, 2)	(6, 3)	(6, 4)	(6, 5)	(6, 6)
5	(5, 1)	(5, 2)	(5, 3)	(5, 4)	(5, 5)	(5, 6)
4	(4, 1)	(4, 2)	(4, 3)	(4, 4)	(4, 5)	(4, 6)
3	(3, 1)	(3, 2)	(3, 3)	(3, 4)	(3, 5)	(3, 6)
2	(2, 1)	(2, 2)	(2, 3)	(2, 4)	(2, 5)	(2, 6)
1	(1, 1)	(1, 2)	(1, 3)	(1, 4)	(1, 5)	(1, 6)

roll 1 (vertical), roll 2 (horizontal)

b $P(0) = 0 \qquad P(1) = 0$
$P(2) = \frac{1}{36} \qquad P(3) = \frac{2}{36}$
$P(4) = \frac{3}{36} \qquad P(5) = \frac{4}{36}$
$P(6) = \frac{5}{36} \qquad P(7) = \frac{6}{36}$
$P(8) = \frac{5}{36} \qquad P(9) = \frac{4}{36}$
$P(10) = \frac{3}{36} \qquad P(11) = \frac{2}{36}$
$P(12) = \frac{1}{36}$

c

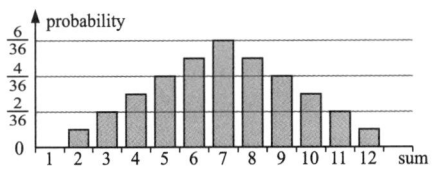

6 a $P(x) = k(x+2), \quad x = 1, 2, 3$
$\therefore \quad P(1) = 3k, \quad P(2) = 4k, \quad P(3) = 5k$
Since this is a probability distribution, $\sum P(i) = 3k + 4k + 5k$
$$\therefore \quad 12k = 1 \quad \{\text{as } \sum P(i) = 1\}$$
$$\therefore \quad k = \frac{1}{12}$$

b $P(x) = \dfrac{k}{x+1}$, $x = 0, 1, 2, 3$

$\therefore\ P(0) = k$, $P(1) = \dfrac{k}{2}$,

$P(2) = \dfrac{k}{3}$, $P(3) = \dfrac{k}{4}$.

Since $\sum P(i) = 1$, $k + \dfrac{k}{2} + \dfrac{k}{3} + \dfrac{k}{4} = 1$

$\therefore\ \dfrac{12k + 6k + 4k + 3k}{12} = 1$

$\therefore\ \dfrac{25k}{12} = 1$

$\therefore\ k = \dfrac{12}{25}$

7 a $P(x) = k\left(\dfrac{1}{3}\right)^x \left(\dfrac{2}{3}\right)^{4-x}$, $x = 0, 1, 2, 3, 4$

$P(0) = k\left(\dfrac{1}{3}\right)^0 \left(\dfrac{2}{3}\right)^4 = \dfrac{16k}{81}$ $P(1) = k\left(\dfrac{1}{3}\right)^1 \left(\dfrac{2}{3}\right)^3 = \dfrac{8k}{81}$ $P(2) = k\left(\dfrac{1}{3}\right)^2 \left(\dfrac{2}{3}\right)^2 = \dfrac{4k}{81}$

$P(3) = k\left(\dfrac{1}{3}\right)^3 \left(\dfrac{2}{3}\right)^1 = \dfrac{2k}{81}$ $P(4) = k\left(\dfrac{1}{3}\right)^4 \left(\dfrac{2}{3}\right)^0 = \dfrac{k}{81}$

b Since $\sum P(i) = 1$,

$\therefore\ \dfrac{16k}{81} + \dfrac{8k}{81} + \dfrac{4k}{81} + \dfrac{2k}{81} + \dfrac{k}{81} = 1$

$\therefore\ \dfrac{31k}{81} = 1$

$\therefore\ k = \dfrac{81}{31}$

$\therefore\ k \approx 2.61$

$\therefore\ P(X \geqslant 2) = P(2) + P(3) + P(4)$

$= \dfrac{4k}{81} + \dfrac{2k}{81} + \dfrac{k}{81}$

$= \dfrac{7k}{81} = \dfrac{7}{81} \times \dfrac{81}{31}$

$= \dfrac{7}{31}\ (\approx 0.226)$

8 a P(no faulty component)
$= P(X = 0)$
$= P(0)$
$= \binom{10}{0}(0.04)^0(0.96)^{10-0}$
$= (0.96)^{10}$
≈ 0.665

b P(at least one faulty component)
$= 1 - \text{P(none are faulty)}$
$\approx 1 - 0.6648$
≈ 0.335

9 a

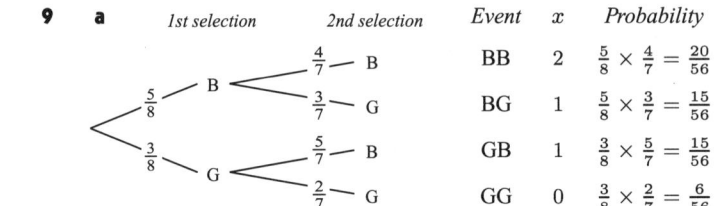

1st selection	2nd selection	Event	x	Probability
$\frac{5}{8}$ B	$\frac{4}{7}$ B	BB	2	$\frac{5}{8} \times \frac{4}{7} = \frac{20}{56}$
	$\frac{3}{7}$ G	BG	1	$\frac{5}{8} \times \frac{3}{7} = \frac{15}{56}$
$\frac{3}{8}$ G	$\frac{5}{7}$ B	GB	1	$\frac{3}{8} \times \frac{5}{7} = \frac{15}{56}$
	$\frac{2}{7}$ G	GG	0	$\frac{3}{8} \times \frac{2}{7} = \frac{6}{56}$

x	0	1	2
$P(X = x)$	$\frac{3}{28}$	$\frac{15}{28}$	$\frac{10}{28}$

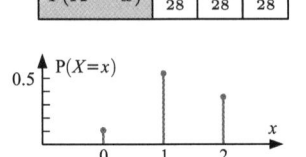

b

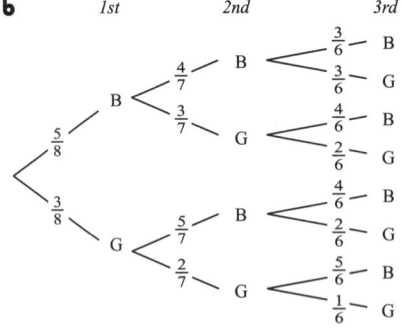

1st	2nd	3rd	Event	x	Probability
B $\frac{5}{8}$	B $\frac{4}{7}$	B $\frac{3}{6}$	BBB	3	$\frac{5}{8} \times \frac{4}{7} \times \frac{3}{6} = \frac{10}{56}$
		G $\frac{3}{6}$	BBG	2	$\frac{5}{8} \times \frac{4}{7} \times \frac{3}{6} = \frac{10}{56}$
	G $\frac{3}{7}$	B $\frac{4}{6}$	BGB	2	$\frac{5}{8} \times \frac{3}{7} \times \frac{4}{6} = \frac{10}{56}$
		G $\frac{2}{6}$	BGG	1	$\frac{5}{8} \times \frac{3}{7} \times \frac{2}{6} = \frac{5}{56}$
G $\frac{3}{8}$	B $\frac{5}{7}$	B $\frac{4}{6}$	GBB	2	$\frac{3}{8} \times \frac{5}{7} \times \frac{4}{6} = \frac{10}{56}$
		G $\frac{2}{6}$	GBG	1	$\frac{3}{8} \times \frac{5}{7} \times \frac{2}{6} = \frac{5}{56}$
	G $\frac{2}{7}$	B $\frac{5}{6}$	GGB	1	$\frac{3}{8} \times \frac{2}{7} \times \frac{5}{6} = \frac{5}{56}$
		G $\frac{1}{6}$	GGG	0	$\frac{3}{8} \times \frac{2}{7} \times \frac{1}{6} = \frac{1}{56}$

x	0	1	2	3
$P(X = x)$	$\frac{1}{56}$	$\frac{15}{56}$	$\frac{30}{56}$	$\frac{10}{56}$

10 a

Die 2 table:
Die 1 \ Die 2	1	2	3	4	5	6
1	2	3	4	5	6	7
2	3	4	5	6	7	8
3	4	5	6	7	8	9
4	5	6	7	8	9	10
5	6	7	8	9	10	11
6	7	8	9	10	11	12

36 sample points

b $P(D = 7) = \frac{6}{36} = \frac{1}{6}$

c

x	2	3	4	5	6	7	8	9	10	11	12
$P(x)$	$\frac{1}{36}$	$\frac{2}{36}$	$\frac{3}{36}$	$\frac{4}{36}$	$\frac{5}{36}$	$\frac{6}{36}$	$\frac{5}{36}$	$\frac{4}{36}$	$\frac{3}{36}$	$\frac{2}{36}$	$\frac{1}{36}$

d $P(D \geqslant 8 \mid D \geqslant 6) = \dfrac{P(D \geqslant 8 \cap D \geqslant 6)}{P(D \geqslant 6)}$

$= \dfrac{P(D \geqslant 8)}{P(D \geqslant 6)}$

$= \dfrac{15}{36} \div \dfrac{26}{36}$

$= \dfrac{15}{26}$

11 $P(X = x) = \dfrac{(0.2)^x e^{-0.2}}{x!}$

a i $P(X = 0)$
$= \dfrac{(0.2)^0 e^{-0.2}}{0!}$
$\approx 0.818\,73$
≈ 0.819

ii $P(X = 1)$
$= \dfrac{(0.2)^1 e^{-0.2}}{1!}$
$\approx 0.163\,75$
≈ 0.164

iii $P(X = 2)$
$= \dfrac{(0.2)^2 e^{-0.2}}{2!}$
$\approx 0.016\,37$
≈ 0.0164

b $P(X \geqslant 3)$
$= 1 - P(X \leqslant 2)$
$= 1 - P(X = 0 \text{ or } X = 1 \text{ or } X = 2)$
$\approx 1 - (0.818\,73 + 0.163\,75 + 0.016\,37)$
$\approx 0.001\,15$

12 a

Die 1 \ Die 2	1	2	3	4	5	6
1	0	1	2	3	4	5
2	1	0	1	2	3	4
3	2	1	0	1	2	3
4	3	2	1	0	1	2
5	4	3	2	1	0	1
6	5	4	3	2	1	0

b

n	0	1	2	3	4	5
$P(N = n)$	$\frac{6}{36}$	$\frac{10}{36}$	$\frac{8}{36}$	$\frac{6}{36}$	$\frac{4}{36}$	$\frac{2}{36}$

c $P(N = 3) = \frac{6}{36} = \frac{1}{6}$

d $P(N \geqslant 3 \mid N \geqslant 1)$
$= \dfrac{P(N \geqslant 3 \cap N \geqslant 1)}{P(N \geqslant 1)}$
$= \dfrac{P(N \geqslant 3)}{P(N \geqslant 1)}$
$= \dfrac{12}{36} \div \dfrac{30}{36}$
$= \dfrac{2}{5}$

EXERCISE 28C

1 P(rain) = 0.28 ∴ we would expect rain on 0.28 × 365.25 ≈ 102 days a year.

2 a P(HHH)
$= \frac{1}{2} \times \frac{1}{2} \times \frac{1}{2}$
$= \frac{1}{8}$

b For 200 tosses, we expect $200 \times \frac{1}{8} = 25$ to be '3 heads'.

3 P(double) = P(1,1 or 2,2 or 3,3 or 4,4 or 5,5 or 6,6)
$= \frac{6}{36}$ {6 of the possible 36 outcomes}
$= \frac{1}{6}$

∴ when rolling the dice 180 times, we expect $180 \times \frac{1}{6} = 30$ doubles.

4

result	win
H	$2
T	−$1

For playing *once*,

we would expect to win $\frac{1}{2} \times \$2 + \frac{1}{2} \times (-\$1) = \$0.50$

∴ for 3 games we would expect to win $1.50.

5 Udo could expect to see snow falling on $\frac{3}{7} \times 5 \times 7 = 15$ days.

6 a $165 + 87 + 48 = 300$ **i**   P(A)   **ii**   P(B)   **iii**   P(C)

$\approx \frac{165}{300} = 0.55$ $\approx \frac{87}{300} = 0.29$ $\approx \frac{48}{300} = 0.16$

b   **i**   We expect $7500 \times 0.55 = 4125$ to vote for A.
     ii   We expect $7500 \times 0.29 = 2175$ to vote for B.
     iii   We expect $7500 \times 0.16 = 1200$ to vote for C.

7 a Expect to win $\frac{1}{6} \times \$1 + \frac{1}{6} \times \$2 + \frac{1}{6} \times \$3 + \frac{1}{6} \times \$4 + \frac{1}{6} \times \$5 + \frac{1}{6} \times \$6$

$= \frac{1}{6} \times \$21 = \$3.50$

b No, as on each occasion he would expect to lose an average of $0.50.

8 a   **i**   P(wins $10)   **ii**   P(wins $4)   **iii**   P(wins $1)

= P(rolls a 6)   = P(rolls 4 or 5)   = P(rolls 1, 2 or 3)

$= \frac{1}{6}$ $= \frac{2}{6}$ (or $\frac{1}{3}$) $= \frac{3}{6}$ (or $\frac{1}{2}$)

b   **i**   Expectation   **ii**   Expectation   **iii**   Expectation

$= \frac{2}{6} \times \$4$ $= \frac{3}{6} \times \$1$ $= \frac{1}{6} \times \$10 + \frac{2}{6} \times \$4 + \frac{3}{6} \times \$1$

$\approx \$1.33$ $= \$0.50$ $= \frac{1}{6}(\$21) = \$3.50$

c It costs $4 to play and the expected return is $3.50.
     ∴ you expect to lose $0.50 per game.

d Over 100 games you expect to lose $100 \times \$0.50 = \$50$.

9

result	win
HH	$10
HT or TH	$3
TT	−$5

a Expectation $= \frac{1}{4} \times \$10 + \frac{2}{4} \times \$3 + \frac{1}{4} \times (-\$5) = \$2.75$

b Expected win per game (payout) $= \$2.75$

∴ the organiser would charge $\$2.75 + \$1.00 = \$3.75$ to play each game.

EXERCISE 28D.1

1

x_i	0	1	2	3	4	5	> 5
$P(x_i)$	0.54	0.26	0.15	k	0.01	0.01	0.00

a $0.54 + 0.26 + 0.15 + k + 0.01 + 0.01 = 1$

∴ $k + 0.97 = 1$

∴ $k = 0.03$

b $\mu = \sum x_i p_i$

$= 0 \times 0.54 + 1 \times 0.26 + \ldots\ldots + 5 \times 0.01$

$= 0.26 + 0.30 + 0.09 + 0.04 + 0.05$

$= 0.74$ So, over a long period the mean number of deaths per dozen crayfish is 0.74.

c $\sigma = \sqrt{\sum(x_i - \mu)^2 p_i}$

$= \sqrt{(0 - 0.74)^2 \times 0.54 + (1 - 0.74)^2 \times 0.26 + \ldots\ldots + (5 - 0.74)^2 \times 0.01}$

≈ 0.996

STATISTICAL DISTRIBUTIONS OF DISCRETE RANDOM VARIABLES

2 $P(x) = \dfrac{x^2 + x}{20}$ for $x = 1, 2, 3$

x_i	1	2	3
$P(x_i) = p_i$	$\frac{2}{20} = 0.1$	$\frac{6}{20} = 0.3$	$\frac{12}{20} = 0.6$

$\mu = \sum x_i p_i$
$= 1 \times 0.1 + 2 \times 0.3 + 3 \times 0.6$
$= 2.5$

$\sigma = \sqrt{\sum(x_i - \mu)^2 p_i}$
$= \sqrt{(1-2.5)^2 \times 0.1 + (2-2.5)^2 \times 0.3 + (3-2.5)^2 \times 0.6}$
≈ 0.671

3 a $P(x) = \binom{3}{x}(0.4)^x(0.6)^{3-x}$ for $x = 0, 1, 2, 3$

$\therefore \quad P(0) = \binom{3}{0}(0.4)^0(0.6)^3 \qquad P(1) = \binom{3}{1}(0.4)^1(0.6)^2 \qquad P(2) = \binom{3}{2}(0.4)^2(0.6)^1$
$\qquad \qquad = (0.6)^3 \qquad \qquad \qquad = 3(0.4)(0.6)^2 \qquad \qquad \quad = 3(0.16)(0.6)$
$\qquad \qquad = 0.216 \qquad \qquad \qquad = 0.432 \qquad \qquad \qquad \quad = 0.288$

$P(3) = \binom{3}{3}(0.4)^3(0.6)^0$
$\qquad = 1(0.4)^3$
$\qquad = 0.064$

x_i	0	1	2	3
$P(x_i)$	0.216	0.432	0.288	0.064

b $\mu = \sum x_i p_i = 0(0.216) + 1(0.432) + 2(0.288) + 3(0.064) = 1.2$

$\sigma = \sqrt{\sum(x_i - \mu)^2 p_i}$
$\quad = \sqrt{(0-1.2)^2(0.216) + (1-1.2)^2(0.432) + (2-1.2)^2 \times 0.288 + (3-1.2)^2 \times 0.064}$
$\quad \approx 0.849$

4 $\sigma = \sqrt{\sum(x_i - \mu)^2 p_i}$
$\therefore \sigma^2 = \sum(x_i - \mu)^2 p_i$
$\quad = (x_1 - \mu)^2 p_1 + (x_2 - \mu)^2 p_2 + \dots + (x_n - \mu)^2 p_n$
$\quad = (x_1^2 - 2x_1\mu + \mu^2)p_1 + (x_2^2 - 2x_2\mu + \mu^2)p_2 + \dots + (x_n^2 - 2x_n\mu + \mu^2)p_n$
$\quad = (x_1^2 p_1 + x_2^2 p_2 + x_3^2 p_3 + \dots + x_n^2 p_n) - 2\mu(x_1 p_1 + x_2 p_2 + \dots + x_n p_n)$
$\qquad + \mu^2(p_1 + p_2 + p_3 + \dots + p_n)$

Now $p_1 + p_2 + \dots + p_n = 1$
$\therefore \sigma^2 = \sum x_i^2 p_i - 2\mu(\sum x_i p_i) + \mu^2(1)$
$\quad = \sum x_i^2 p_i - 2\mu(\mu) + \mu^2 \qquad \{\text{since } \sum x_i p_i = \mu\}$
$\quad = \sum x_i^2 p_i - \mu^2$

5 a

x_i	1	2	3	4	5
$P(x_i)$	0.1	0.2	0.4	0.2	0.1

b $\mu = \sum x_i p_i$
$\quad = 1(0.1) + 2(0.2) + \dots + 5(0.1)$
$\quad = 0.1 + 0.4 + 1.2 + 0.8 + 0.5$
$\quad = 3$

$\sigma = \sqrt{\sum(x_i - \mu)^2 p_i}$
$\quad = \sqrt{\sum x_i^2 p_i - \mu^2}$
$\quad = \sqrt{1^2(0.1) + 2^2(0.2) + \dots + 5^2(0.1) - (3.0)^2}$
$\quad = \sqrt{0.1 + 0.8 + 3.6 + 3.2 + 2.5 - 9}$
$\quad = \sqrt{1.2}$
$\quad \approx 1.10$

c **i** $P(\mu - \sigma < X < \mu + \sigma)$
$= P(3 - 1.095 < X < 3 + 1.095)$
$= P(1.905 < X < 4.095)$
$= P(X = 2, 3, 4)$
$= 0.2 + 0.4 + 0.2$
$= 0.8$

ii $P(\mu - 2\sigma < X < \mu + 2\sigma)$
$= P(3 - 2.19 < X < 3 + 2.19)$
$= P(0.81 < X < 5.19)$
$= P(X = 1, 2, 3, 4 \text{ or } 5)$
$= 0.1 + 0.2 + 0.4 + 0.2 + 0.1$
$= 1$

6 Let X be the payout, so $x = \$20\,000, \$8000, \text{ or } \$0$.
$\therefore$ the probability distribution is

x_i	20 000	8000	0
$P(x_i) = p_i$	0.0025	0.03	0.9675

The expectation is $\mu = \sum x_i p_i = 20\,000(0.0025) + 8000(0.03) + 0(0.9675)$
$= \$290$

The company expects to pay out $290 on average in the long run
$\therefore$ the company should charge $290 + $100 = $390.

7

Die 2

	1	2	3	4	5	6
1	1	2	3	4	5	6
2	2	2	3	4	5	6
3	3	3	3	4	5	6
4	4	4	4	4	5	6
5	5	5	5	5	5	6
6	6	6	6	6	6	6

Die 1

a

m_i	1	2	3	4	5	6
$P(m_i)$	$\frac{1}{36}$	$\frac{3}{36}$	$\frac{5}{36}$	$\frac{7}{36}$	$\frac{9}{36}$	$\frac{11}{36}$

b $\mu = \sum m_i p_i$
$= 1\left(\frac{1}{36}\right) + 2\left(\frac{3}{36}\right) + 3\left(\frac{5}{36}\right) + \ldots + 6\left(\frac{11}{36}\right)$
$= \frac{1}{36} + \frac{6}{36} + \frac{15}{36} + \frac{28}{36} + \frac{45}{36} + \frac{66}{36}$
$= \frac{161}{36}$
≈ 4.47

$\sigma = \sqrt{\sum m_i^2 p_i - \mu^2}$
$= \sqrt{1^2\left(\frac{1}{36}\right) + 2^2\left(\frac{3}{36}\right) + \ldots + 6^2\left(\frac{11}{36}\right) - \left(\frac{161}{36}\right)^2}$
$\approx \sqrt{1.971\,45}$
≈ 1.40

8 Examples are:

(1) Tossing one coin, where X is the number of 'heads' resulting. $x = 0$ or 1

x	0	1
$P(x)$	$\frac{1}{2}$	$\frac{1}{2}$

(2) Rolling one die, where X is the number on the uppermost face. $x = 1, 2, 3, 4, 5$ or 6

x	1	2	3	4	5	6
$P(x)$	$\frac{1}{6}$	$\frac{1}{6}$	$\frac{1}{6}$	$\frac{1}{6}$	$\frac{1}{6}$	$\frac{1}{6}$

9 **1** In 100 trials the expected frequencies are:

x_i	0	1	2	3	4	5	> 5
f_i	54	26	15	3	1	1	0

$\therefore$ median $=$ middle score $= \dfrac{\text{50th score} + \text{51st score}}{2} = \dfrac{0 + 0}{2} = 0$

mode $= 0$ {most frequently occurring score}

2 In 100 trials the expected frequencies are:

x_i	1	2	3
f_i	10	30	60

$\therefore$ median $=$ middle score $= \dfrac{\text{50th score} + \text{51st score}}{2} = \dfrac{3 + 3}{2} = 3$

mode $= 3$ {most frequently occurring score}

3 In 100 trials the expected frequencies are:

x_i	0	1	2	3
f_i	22	43	29	6

$\therefore$ median = middle score = $\dfrac{\text{50th score} + \text{51st score}}{2} = \dfrac{1+1}{2} = 1$

mode = 1 {most frequently occurring score}

5 In 100 trials the expected frequencies are:

x_i	1	2	3	4	5
f_i	10	20	40	20	10

$\therefore$ median = middle score = $\dfrac{\text{50th score} + \text{51st score}}{2} = \dfrac{3+3}{2} = 3$

mode = 3 {most frequently occurring score}

7 In 36 trials the expected frequencies are:

m_i	1	2	3	4	5	6
f_i	1	3	5	7	9	11

$\therefore$ median = middle score = $\dfrac{\text{18th score} + \text{19th score}}{2} = \dfrac{5+5}{2} = 5$

mode = 6 {most frequently occurring score}

EXERCISE 28D.2

1 a mean of $X = E(X)$
$= \sum x p_x$
$= 2(0.3) + 3(0.3) + 4(0.2) + 5(0.1) + 6(0.1)$
$= 3.4$

b $E(X^2) = \sum x^2 p_x = 4(0.3) + 9(0.3) + 16(0.2) + 25(0.1) + 36(0.1) = 13.2$
Now $\text{Var}(X) = E(X^2) - \{E(X)\}^2$
$= 13.2 - (3.4)^2$
$= 1.64$

c $\sigma = \sqrt{\text{Var}(X)} \approx 1.28$

2 a $\sum p_x = 1$
$\therefore \quad 0.2 + k + 0.4 + 0.1 = 1$
$\therefore \quad k = 0.3$

b $E(X) = \sum x p_x$
$= 5(0.2) + 6(0.3) + 7(0.4) + 8(0.1)$
$= 6.4$

c $\text{Var}(X) = \sum x^2 p_x - \{E(X)\}^2$
$= 25(0.2) + 36(0.3) + 49(0.4) + 64(0.1) - 6.4^2$
$= 0.84$

3 a $E(X)$
$= \sum x p_x$
$= 1(0.4) + 2(0.3) + 3(0.2) + 4(0.1)$
$= 2$

b $E(X^2)$
$= \sum x^2 p_x$
$= 1(0.4) + 4(0.3) + 9(0.2) + 16(0.1)$
$= 5$

c $\text{Var}(X)$
$= E(X^2) - \{E(X)\}^2$
$= 5 - 2^2$
$= 1$

d $\sigma = \sqrt{\text{Var}(X)}$
$= \sqrt{1}$
$= 1$

e $E(X+1)$
$= E(X) + E(1)$
$= 2 + 1$
$= 3$

f $\text{Var}(X+1)$
$= \text{E}\left((X+1)^2\right) - \{\text{E}(X+1)\}^2$
$= \text{E}\left(X^2 + 2X + 1\right) - 3^2$
$= \text{E}(X^2) + 2\,\text{E}(X) + \text{E}(1) - 9$
$= 5 + 2(2) + 1 - 9$
$= 1$

g $\text{E}(2X^2 + 3X - 7)$
$= 2\,\text{E}(X^2) + 3\,\text{E}(X) - \text{E}(7)$
$= 2(5) + 3(2) - 7$
$= 9$

4 a $\text{E}(X) = 2.8$
$\therefore\ 1(0.2) + 2a + 3(0.3) + 4b = 2.8$
$\therefore\ 0.2 + 2a + 0.9 + 4b = 2.8$
$\therefore\ 2a + 4b = 1.7$ .... (1)
Also, $0.2 + a + 0.3 + b = 1$
$\therefore\ b = 0.5 - a$ .... (2)

Substituting (2) into (1) gives
$2a + 4(0.5 - a) = 1.7$
$\therefore\ 2a + 2 - 4a = 1.7$
$\therefore\ -2a = -0.3$
$\therefore\ a = 0.15$
and $b = 0.5 - 0.15$
$= 0.35$

b $\text{E}(X^2) = \sum x^2 p_x$
$= 1(0.2) + 4(0.15) + 9(0.3) + 16(0.35)$
$= 9.1$
$\therefore\ \text{Var}(X) = \text{E}(X)^2 - \{\text{E}(X)\}^2$
$= 9.1 - 2.8^2$
$= 1.26$

5 a $\text{P}(X = 0) = a(0) = 0$
$\text{P}(X = 1) = a(-7) = -7a$
$\text{P}(X = 2) = a(-12) = -12a$
$\text{P}(X = 3) = a(-15) = -15a$
$\text{P}(X = 4) = a(-16) = -16a$
$\text{P}(X = 5) = a(-15) = -15a$
$\text{P}(X = 6) = a(-12) = -12a$
$\text{P}(X = 7) = a(-7) = -7a$
$\text{P}(X = 8) = a(0) = 0$

$\therefore\ 2(-7a - 12a - 15a) - 16a = 1$
$\therefore\ a(-84) = 1$
$\therefore\ a = -\frac{1}{84}$

b $\text{E}(X) = \sum x p_x$
$= 1\left(\frac{7}{84}\right) + 2\left(\frac{12}{84}\right) + 3\left(\frac{15}{84}\right) + 4\left(\frac{16}{84}\right) + 5\left(\frac{15}{84}\right) + 6\left(\frac{12}{84}\right) + 7\left(\frac{7}{84}\right)$
$= \frac{336}{84} = 4$

c $\text{E}(X^2) = \sum x^2 p_x$
$= 1\left(\frac{7}{84}\right) + 4\left(\frac{12}{84}\right) + 9\left(\frac{15}{84}\right) + 16\left(\frac{16}{84}\right) + 25\left(\frac{15}{84}\right) + 36\left(\frac{12}{84}\right) + 49\left(\frac{7}{84}\right)$
$= \frac{1596}{84} = 19$
$\therefore\ \text{Var}(X) = \text{E}(X^2) - \{\text{E}(X)\}^2$
$= 19 - 4^2$
$= 3$
$\therefore\ \sigma = \sqrt{\text{Var}(X)} = \sqrt{3}$

6 a $\left(\frac{1}{2} + \frac{1}{2}\right)^4 = \left(\frac{1}{2}\right)^4 + 4\left(\frac{1}{2}\right)^3\left(\frac{1}{2}\right)^1 + 6\left(\frac{1}{2}\right)^2\left(\frac{1}{2}\right)^2 + 4\left(\frac{1}{2}\right)^1\left(\frac{1}{2}\right)^3 + \left(\frac{1}{2}\right)^4$
$= \frac{1}{16} + \frac{4}{16} + \frac{6}{16} + \frac{4}{16} + \frac{1}{16}$

So, the probability distribution for X, the number of heads occurring, is:

x	0	1	2	3	4
$P(x)$	$\frac{1}{16}$	$\frac{4}{16}$	$\frac{6}{16}$	$\frac{4}{16}$	$\frac{1}{16}$

b i $E(X) = \sum xp_x = 0\left(\frac{1}{16}\right) + 1\left(\frac{4}{16}\right) + 2\left(\frac{6}{16}\right) + 3\left(\frac{4}{16}\right) + 4\left(\frac{1}{16}\right) = 2$

$\therefore$ mean $= 2$

ii $E(X^2) = \sum x^2 p_x = 0\left(\frac{1}{16}\right) + 1\left(\frac{4}{16}\right) + 4\left(\frac{6}{16}\right) + 9\left(\frac{4}{16}\right) + 16\left(\frac{1}{16}\right) = 5$

$\therefore \ \sigma = \sqrt{\text{Var}(X)} = \sqrt{E(X^2) - \{E(X)\}^2} = \sqrt{5 - 2^2} = 1$

7 a $P(0 \text{ bitter, 3 not bitter}) = \dfrac{\binom{2}{0}\binom{8}{3}}{\binom{10}{3}} = \dfrac{42}{90} = \dfrac{7}{15}$

$P(1 \text{ bitter, 2 not bitter}) = \dfrac{\binom{2}{1}\binom{8}{2}}{\binom{10}{3}} = \dfrac{7}{15}$

$P(2 \text{ bitter, 1 not bitter}) = \dfrac{\binom{2}{2}\binom{8}{1}}{\binom{10}{3}} = \dfrac{6}{90} = \dfrac{1}{15}$

x	0	1	2
$P(x)$	$\frac{7}{15}$	$\frac{7}{15}$	$\frac{1}{15}$

b i $E(X)$

$= 0\left(\frac{7}{15}\right) + 1\left(\frac{7}{15}\right) + 2\left(\frac{1}{15}\right)$

$= \frac{9}{15}$

$= 0.6$

$\therefore$ mean $= 0.6$ bitter almonds

ii $E(X^2) = 0^2\left(\frac{7}{15}\right) + 1^2\left(\frac{7}{15}\right) + 2^2\left(\frac{1}{15}\right) = \frac{11}{15}$

$\therefore$ Var$(X) = E(X^2) - \{E(X)\}^2$

$= \frac{11}{15} - \left(\frac{3}{5}\right)^2$

$= \frac{11}{15} - \frac{9}{25}$

≈ 0.3733 and so $\sigma \approx 0.611$

8 a $E(Y) = 0.9$

$\therefore \ -1(0.1) + 0(a) + 1(0.3) + 2b = 0.9$

$\therefore \ 0.2 + 2b = 0.9$ Also, $0.1 + a + 0.3 + b = 1$

$\therefore \ 2b = 0.7$ $\therefore \ a = 1 - 0.1 - 0.3 - 0.35$

$\therefore \ b = 0.35$ $\therefore \ a = 0.25$

b $E(Y^2) = (-1)^2(0.1) + 0^2(0.25) + 1^2(0.3) + 2^2(0.35) = 1.8$

$\therefore$ Var$(Y) = E(Y^2) - \{E(Y)\}^2 = 1.8 - 0.9^2 = 0.99$

9 $\frac{1}{6} + \frac{1}{3} + \frac{1}{12} + a + \frac{1}{6} = 1$ $E(X) = 1\left(\frac{1}{6}\right) + 2\left(\frac{1}{3}\right) + 3\left(\frac{1}{12}\right) + 4\left(\frac{1}{4}\right) + 5\left(\frac{1}{6}\right) = \frac{35}{12}$

$\therefore \ a = \frac{1}{4}$ $E(X^2) = 1^2\left(\frac{1}{6}\right) + 2^2\left(\frac{1}{3}\right) + 3^2\left(\frac{1}{12}\right) + 4^2\left(\frac{1}{4}\right) + 5^2\left(\frac{1}{6}\right) = \frac{125}{12}$

$\therefore$ Var$(X) = E(X^2) - \{E(X)\}^2$

$= \frac{125}{12} - \left(\frac{35}{12}\right)^2$

$= \frac{1500}{144} - \frac{1225}{144}$

$= \frac{275}{144} \approx 1.91$

EXERCISE 28D.3

1 X has mean 6 and standard deviation 2.

$E(Y) = E(2X + 5)$ $\qquad$ Var$(Y) = $ Var$(2X + 5)$

$\quad = 2E(X) + E(5)$ $\qquad \qquad = 2^2 \text{Var}(X)$

$\quad = 2 \times 6 + 5$ $\qquad \qquad = 4 \times 2^2$

$\quad = 17$ $\qquad \qquad = 16$

$\therefore$ mean of Y distribution is 17 $\qquad \therefore$ standard deviation of Y distribution is $\sqrt{16} = 4$

2 a $E(aX + b) = E(aX) + E(b)$ {using $E(A + B) = E(A) + E(B)$}

$\quad = a E(X) + E(b)$ {using $E(kX) = k E(X)$}

$\quad = a E(X) + b$ {using $E(k) = k$, k a constant}

b **i** $E(Y) = E(3X + 4)$ **ii** $E(Y) = E(-2X + 1)$ **iii** $E(Y) = E\left(\dfrac{4X - 2}{3}\right)$
$= 3E(X) + 4 = -2E(X) + 1 = E\left(\tfrac{4}{3}X - \tfrac{2}{3}\right)$
$= 3(3) + 4 = -2(3) + 1 = \tfrac{4}{3}E(X) - \tfrac{2}{3}$
$= 13 = -5 = \tfrac{4}{3}(3) - \tfrac{2}{3} = 3\tfrac{1}{3}$

3 X has mean 5 and standard deviation 2.

  a   **i** $E(Y) = E(2X + 3) = 2E(X) + 3 = 2 \times 5 + 3 = 13$
        ii $\text{Var}(Y) = \text{Var}(2X + 3) = 2^2\,\text{Var}(X) = 4 \times 2^2 = 16$

  b   **i** $E(Y) = E(-2X + 3) = -2E(X) + 3 = -2 \times 5 + 3 = -7$
        ii $\text{Var}(Y) = \text{Var}(-2X + 3) = (-2)^2\,\text{Var}(X) = 4 \times 2^2 = 16$

  c $Y = \dfrac{X - 5}{2} = \tfrac{1}{2}X - \tfrac{5}{2}$

        i $E(Y) = E\left(\tfrac{1}{2}X - \tfrac{5}{2}\right) = \tfrac{1}{2}E(X) - \tfrac{5}{2} = \tfrac{1}{2} \times 5 - \tfrac{5}{2} = 0$
        ii $\text{Var}(Y) = \text{Var}\left(\tfrac{1}{2}X - \tfrac{5}{2}\right) = \left(\tfrac{1}{2}\right)^2 \text{Var}(X) = \tfrac{1}{4} \times 2^2 = 1$

4 $Y = 2X + 3$

  a $E(Y) = E(2X + 3)$ **b** $E(Y^2) = E(4X^2 + 12X + 9)$
       $= 2E(X) + 3 = 4E(X^2) + 12E(X) + 9$

  c $\text{Var}(Y) = E(Y^2) - \{E(Y)\}^2$
            $= \left[4E(X^2) + 12E(X) + 9\right] - \left[(2E(X) + 3)^2\right]$
            $= 4E(X^2) + 12E(X) + 9 - \left[4\{E(X)\}^2 + 12E(X) + 9\right]$
            $= 4E(X^2) - 4\{E(X)\}^2$

5 $\text{Var}(aX + b) = E\left((aX + b)^2\right) - \{E(aX + b)\}^2$
                 $= E\left(a^2X^2 + 2abX + b^2\right) - \{aE(X) + b\}^2$
                 $= a^2E(X^2) + 2ab\,E(X) + b^2 - \left[a^2\{E(X)\}^2 + 2ab\,E(X) + b^2\right]$
                 $= a^2E(X^2) + 2ab\,E(X) + b^2 - a^2\{E(X)\}^2 - 2ab\,E(X) - b^2$
                 $= a^2\left(E(X^2) - \{E(X)\}^2\right)$
                 $= a^2\,\text{Var}(X)$

EXERCISE 28E.1

1   **a**   The binomial distribution applies, as tossing a coin has two possible outcomes (a tail or a head) and each toss is independent of every other toss.

     b   The binomial distribution applies, as this is equivalent to tossing one coin 100 times.

     c   The binomial distribution applies as we can draw out a red or a blue marble with the same chances each time.

     d   The binomial distribution does not apply as the result of each draw is dependent upon the results of previous draws.

     e   The binomial distribution does not apply, assuming that ten bolts are drawn without replacement, as we do not have a repetition of independent trials.

2 X is the random variable for the number working night-shift.
     $\therefore \;\; X = 0, 1, 2, 3, 4, 5, 6, 7 \;$ and $\; X \sim B(7, 0.35)$.

     a $P(X = 3)$ **b** $P(X < 4)$ **c**   P(at least 4 work night-shift)
        $= \binom{7}{3}(0.35)^3(0.65)^4 = P(X \leqslant 3) = P(X \geqslant 4)$
        $\approx 0.268 \approx 0.800 = 1 - P(X \leqslant 3)$
        $ \approx 1 - 0.800$
        $ \approx 0.200$

3 X is the number of faulty items.
$\therefore\ X = 0, 1, 2, 3, ..., 12$ and $X \sim B(12, 0.06)$.

  a $P(X = 0)$
$= \binom{12}{0}(0.06)^0(0.94)^{12}$
≈ 0.476

  b   P(at most one is faulty)
$= P(X \leqslant 1)$
≈ 0.840

  c   P(at least 2 are faulty)
$= P(X \geqslant 2)$
$= 1 - P(X \leqslant 1)$
≈ 0.160 {from **b**}

  d   P(less than 4 are faulty)
$= P(X < 4)$
$= P(X \leqslant 3)$
≈ 0.996

4 X is the random variable for the number of times in a week when the bus is on time. Since it is late 2 in every 5 days, and on time 3 in every 5 days,
$X = 0, 1, 2, 3, 4, 5, 6$ or 7 and $X \sim B(7, 0.6)$.

  a $P(X = 7)$
$= \binom{7}{7}(0.6)^7(0.4)^0$
≈ 0.0280

  b   P(on time only on Monday)
$= 0.6 \times (0.4)^6$
≈ 0.00246

  c $P(X = 6)$
$= \binom{7}{6}(0.6)^6(0.4)$
≈ 0.131

  d $P(X \geqslant 4)$
$= 1 - P(X \leqslant 3)$
$\approx 1 - 0.290$
≈ 0.710

5 X is the random variable for the number of students with the flu.
$\therefore\ X = 0, 1, 2, 3, ..., 25$ and $X \sim B(25, 0.3)$.

  a $P(X \geqslant 2)$
$= 1 - P(X \leqslant 1)$
$\approx 1 - 0.00157$
≈ 0.998

  b   P(test cancelled)
$= P(X \geqslant 6)$ {20% of 25 = 5}
$= 1 - P(X \leqslant 5)$
$\approx 1 - 0.193$
≈ 0.807

EXERCISE 28E.2

1 $X \sim B(6, p)$

  a   If $p = 0.5$, $X \sim B(6, 0.5)$

    i $\mu = np = 6 \times 0.5 = 3$ and $\sigma = \sqrt{npq} = \sqrt{6 \times 0.5 \times 0.5} \approx 1.225$

    ii $P(X = 0)$ $P(X = 1)$ $P(X = 2)$ $P(X = 3)$
$= \binom{6}{0}(0.5)^0(0.5)^6$ $= \binom{6}{1}(0.5)^1(0.5)^5$ $= \binom{6}{2}(0.5)^2(0.5)^4$ $= \binom{6}{3}(0.5)^3(0.5)^3$
≈ 0.0156 ≈ 0.0938 ≈ 0.2344 ≈ 0.3125

$P(X = 4)$ $P(X = 5)$ $P(X = 6)$
$= \binom{6}{4}(0.5)^4(0.5)^2$ $= \binom{6}{5}(0.5)^5(0.5)^1$ $= \binom{6}{6}(0.5)^6(0.5)^0$
≈ 0.2344 ≈ 0.0938 ≈ 0.0156

x_i	0	1	2	3
$P(x_i)$	0.0156	0.0938	0.2344	0.3125
x_i	4	5	6	
$P(x_i)$	0.2344	0.0938	0.0156	

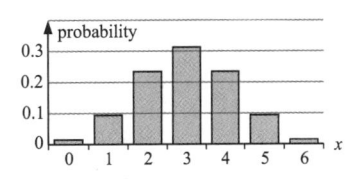

    iii   The distribution is bell-shaped.

b If $p = 0.2$, $X \sim B(6, 0.2)$

  i $\mu = np = 6 \times 0.2 = 1.2$ and $\sigma = \sqrt{npq} = \sqrt{6 \times 0.2 \times 0.8} \approx 0.980$

  ii

  $P(X = 0)$ $= \binom{6}{0}(0.2)^0(0.8)^6$ ≈ 0.2621

  $P(X = 1)$ $= \binom{6}{1}(0.2)^1(0.8)^5$ ≈ 0.3932

  $P(X = 2)$ $= \binom{6}{2}(0.2)^2(0.8)^4$ ≈ 0.2458

  $P(X = 3)$ $= \binom{6}{3}(0.2)^3(0.8)^3$ ≈ 0.0819

  $P(X = 4)$ $= \binom{6}{4}(0.2)^4(0.8)^2$ ≈ 0.0154

  $P(X = 5)$ $= \binom{6}{5}(0.2)^5(0.8)^1$ ≈ 0.0015

  $P(X = 6)$ $= \binom{6}{6}(0.2)^6(0.8)^0$ ≈ 0.0001

x_i	0	1	2	3	4	5	6
$P(x_i)$	0.2621	0.3932	0.2458	0.0819	0.0154	0.0015	0.0001

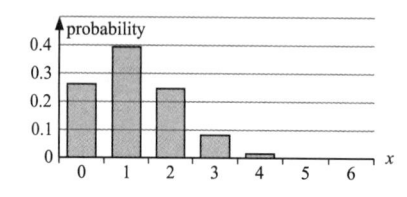

  iii The distribution is skewed to the right, or positively skewed.

c If $p = 0.8$, $X \sim B(6, 0.8)$

  i $\mu = np = 6 \times 0.8 = 4.8$ and $\sigma = \sqrt{npq} = \sqrt{6 \times 0.8 \times 0.2} \approx 0.980$

  ii

  $P(X = 0)$ $= \binom{6}{0}(0.8)^0(0.2)^6$ ≈ 0.0001

  $P(X = 1)$ $= \binom{6}{1}(0.8)^1(0.2)^5$ ≈ 0.0015

  $P(X = 2)$ $= \binom{6}{2}(0.8)^2(0.2)^4$ ≈ 0.0154

  $P(X = 3)$ $= \binom{6}{3}(0.8)^3(0.2)^3$ ≈ 0.0819

  $P(X = 4)$ $= \binom{6}{4}(0.8)^4(0.2)^2$ ≈ 0.2458

  $P(X = 5)$ $= \binom{6}{5}(0.8)^5(0.2)^1$ ≈ 0.3932

  $P(X = 6)$ $= \binom{6}{6}(0.8)^6(0.2)^0$ ≈ 0.2621

x_i	0	1	2	3	4	5	6
$P(x_i)$	0.0001	0.0015	0.0154	0.0819	0.2458	0.3932	0.2621

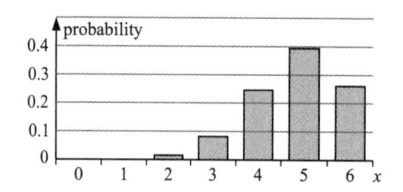

  iii This distribution is the exact reflection of **b**. It is skewed to the left or negatively skewed.

2 Number of tosses, $n = 10$
  X is the number of heads obtained. $\therefore$ $X \sim B(10, 0.5)$

  $\mu = np$ $\sigma = \sqrt{npq}$
  $ = 10 \times 0.5$ $ = \sqrt{10 \times 0.5 \times 0.5}$
  $ = 5$ $ \approx 1.58$

3 a $X \sim B(3, p)$

  $P(X = 0) = \binom{3}{0}p^0 q^3$ $P(X = 1) = \binom{3}{1}p^1 q^2$ $P(X = 2) = \binom{3}{2}p^2 q^1$
  $ = q^3$ $ = 3pq^2$ $ = 3p^2 q$

  $P(X = 3) = \binom{3}{3}p^3 q^0$
  $ = p^3$

x_i	0	1	2	3
$P(x_i)$	q^3	$3pq^2$	$3p^2 q$	p^3

b $\mu = \sum x_i p_i$
$= 0q^3 + 1 \times 3pq^2 + 2 \times 3p^2q + 3p^3$
$= 3p(1-p)^2 + 6p^2(1-p) + 3p^3$
$= 3p(1 - 2p + p^2) + 6p^2 - 6p^3 + 3p^3$
$= 3p - 6p^2 + 3p^3 + 6p^2 - 6p^3 + 3p^3$
$= 3p$ as required

c $\sigma^2 = \sum x_i^2 p_i - \mu^2$
$= 0^2 \times q^3 + 1^2 \times 3pq^2 + 2^2 \times 3p^2q + 3^2p^3 - (3p)^2$
$= 3p(1-p)^2 + 12p^2(1-p) + 9p^2(p-1)$
$= (1-p)\left[3p(1-p) + 12p^2 - 9p^2\right]$
$= (1-p)\left[3p - 3p^2 + 3p^2\right]$
$= 3p(1-p)$
$= 3pq$ $\therefore$ $\sigma = \sqrt{3pq}$ as required

4 X is the number of defective bolts in the sample.
$X \sim B(30, 0.04)$ $\mu = np$ and $\sigma = \sqrt{npq}$
$= 30 \times 0.04$ $= \sqrt{30 \times 0.04 \times 0.96}$
$= 1.2$ ≈ 1.07

5 X is the number of groups that do not arrive.
$X \sim B(5, 0.13)$ $\mu = np$ and $\sigma = \sqrt{npq}$
$= 5 \times 0.13$ $= \sqrt{5 \times 0.13 \times 0.87}$
$= 0.65$ ≈ 0.752

EXERCISE 28F

1 a mean $= \dfrac{\sum fx}{\sum f} = \dfrac{0 + 18 + 24 + 18 + 12 + 0 + 6}{52} = \dfrac{78}{52} = 1.5$

b Using $m = 1.5$, we find $p_x = \dfrac{(1.5)^x e^{-1.5}}{x!}$, $x = 0, 1, 2, 3, ...$

So, we can obtain: $p_0 = \dfrac{(1.5)^0 e^{-1.5}}{0!} \approx 0.2231$ $\therefore$ $52p_0 \approx 11.6$

$p_1 = \dfrac{(1.5)^1 e^{-1.5}}{1!} \approx 0.3347$ $\therefore$ $52p_1 \approx 17.4$

$p_2 = \dfrac{(1.5)^2 e^{-1.5}}{2!} \approx 0.2510$ $\therefore$ $52p_2 \approx 13.1$

$p_3 = \dfrac{(1.5)^3 e^{-1.5}}{3!} \approx 0.1255$ $\therefore$ $52p_3 \approx 6.5$

$p_4 = \dfrac{(1.5)^4 e^{-1.5}}{4!} \approx 0.0471$ $\therefore$ $52p_4 \approx 2.4$

$p_5 = \dfrac{(1.5)^5 e^{-1.5}}{5!} \approx 0.0141$ $\therefore$ $52p_5 \approx 0.7$

$p_6 = \dfrac{(1.5)^6 e^{-1.5}}{6!} \approx 0.0035$ $\therefore$ $52p_6 \approx 0.2$

Comparison:

x	0	1	2	3	4	5	6
f	12	18	12	6	3	0	1
$52p_x$	11.6	17.4	13.1	6.5	2.4	0.7	0.2

The fit is excellent.

2 a Standard deviation $= 2.67$

i mean $= \sigma^2$
$= 2.67^2$
≈ 7.13

ii $m \approx 7.13$

$\therefore$ $p_x \approx \dfrac{(7.13)^x e^{-7.13}}{x!}$ where $x = 0, 1, 2, 3, 4, 5, ...$

b **i** $P(X = 2)$

$$= \frac{(7.1289)^2 e^{-7.1289}}{2!}$$

≈ 0.0204

ii $P(X \leqslant 3)$

≈ 0.0753

iii $P(X \geqslant 5)$
$= 1 - P(X \leqslant 4)$
$\approx 1 - 0.162$
≈ 0.838

iv $P(X \geqslant 3 \mid X \geqslant 1)$

$$= \frac{P(X \geqslant 3 \cap X \geqslant 1)}{P(X \geqslant 1)}$$

$$= \frac{P(X \geqslant 3)}{P(X \geqslant 1)}$$

$$= \frac{1 - P(X \leqslant 2)}{1 - P(X = 0)}$$

$$\approx \frac{1 - 0.0269}{1 - 0.0008}$$

≈ 0.974

3 a $\bar{x} = \dfrac{1 \times 156 + 2 \times 132 + 3 \times 75 + 4 \times 33 + 5 \times 9 + 6 \times 3 + 7 \times 1}{91 + 156 + 132 + 75 + 33 + 9 + 3 + 1}$

$= \dfrac{847}{500}$

$= 1.694$

b Using $m = 1.694$, we find $p_x = \dfrac{(1.694)^x e^{-1.694}}{x!}$ where $x = 0, 1, 2, 3, 4, \ldots$.

So, we can obtain: $500p_0 = 500 \times 1.694^0 \times e^{-1.694} \times \frac{1}{0!} \approx 91.9$

$500p_1 = 500 \times 1.694^1 \times e^{-1.694} \times \frac{1}{1!} \approx 155.7$

$500p_2 = 500 \times 1.694^2 \times e^{-1.694} \times \frac{1}{2!} \approx 131.8$

$500p_3 = 500 \times 1.694^3 \times e^{-1.694} \times \frac{1}{3!} \approx 74.4$

$500p_4 = 500 \times 1.694^4 \times e^{-1.694} \times \frac{1}{4!} \approx 31.5$

$500p_5 = 500 \times 1.694^5 \times e^{-1.694} \times \frac{1}{5!} \approx 10.7$

$500p_6 = 500 \times 1.694^6 \times e^{-1.694} \times \frac{1}{6!} \approx 3.0$

$500p_7 = 500 \times 1.694^7 \times e^{-1.694} \times \frac{1}{7!} \approx 0.7$

Comparison:

x	0	1	2	3	4	5	6	7
f	91	156	132	75	33	9	3	1
$500p_x$	92	156	132	74	32	11	3	1

The fit is excellent.

c $\text{Var}(X)$

$= E(X^2) - \{E(X)\}^2$

$= \sum x^2 p_x - (1.694)^2$

$= 1 \times \frac{156}{500} + 4 \times \frac{132}{500} + 9 \times \frac{75}{500} + 16 \times \frac{33}{500} + 25 \times \frac{9}{500} + 36 \times \frac{3}{500} + 49 \times \frac{1}{500} - (1.694)^2$

≈ 1.6683

$\therefore \ \sigma \approx 1.29$ and $\sqrt{m} = \sqrt{1.694} \approx 1.30$ $\quad \therefore \ \sigma$ is very close to $\sqrt{m}$

4 $p_x = \dfrac{3^x e^{-3}}{x!}$ where $x = 0, 1, 2, 3, 4, 5, \ldots$

a $P(X = 0)$

$= \dfrac{3^0 e^{-3}}{0!}$

≈ 0.0498

b $P(X \geqslant 3)$

$= 1 - P(X \leqslant 2)$

$\approx 1 - 0.423$

≈ 0.577

STATISTICAL DISTRIBUTIONS OF DISCRETE RANDOM VARIABLES

c   P(some requests are refused)
$= P(X \geqslant 5)$
$= 1 - P(X \leqslant 4)$
$\approx 1 - 0.815$
≈ 0.185

d $P(X \geqslant 4 \mid X \geqslant 2)$
$= \dfrac{P(X \geqslant 4 \cap X \geqslant 2)}{P(X \geqslant 2)}$
$= \dfrac{P(X \geqslant 4)}{P(X \geqslant 2)}$
$= \dfrac{1 - P(X \leqslant 3)}{1 - P(X \leqslant 1)}$
$\approx \dfrac{1 - 0.647\,23}{1 - 0.199\,14} \approx 0.440$

5 $P(X = x) = \dfrac{m^x e^{-m}}{x!}$ where $x = 0, 1, 2, 3, 4, ...$

a   If $P(X = 1) + P(X = 2) = P(X = 3)$,

then $\dfrac{me^{-m}}{1!} + \dfrac{m^2 e^{-m}}{2!} = \dfrac{m^3 e^{-m}}{3!}$

$\therefore \; m + \dfrac{m^2}{2} = \dfrac{m^3}{6}$ $\{\div e^{-m}\}$

$\therefore \; 6m + 3m^2 = m^3$

$\therefore \; m(m^2 - 3m - 6) = 0$ where $m \neq 0$

$\therefore \; m^2 - 3m - 6 = 0$

$\therefore \; m = \dfrac{3 \pm \sqrt{9 - 4(1)(-6)}}{2} = \dfrac{3 \pm \sqrt{33}}{2}$

But $m > 0$, so $m = \dfrac{3 + \sqrt{33}}{2}$

b   **i** $P(X \geqslant 3)$
$= 1 - P(X \leqslant 2)$
$\approx 1 - 0.494$
≈ 0.506

    ii $P(X \leqslant 4 \mid X \geqslant 2)$
$= \dfrac{P(X \leqslant 4 \cap X \geqslant 2)}{P(X \geqslant 2)}$
$= \dfrac{P(X = 2, 3 \text{ or } 4)}{P(X \geqslant 2)}$
$= \dfrac{P(X \leqslant 4) - P(X \leqslant 1)}{1 - P(X \leqslant 1)}$
$\approx \dfrac{0.8629 - 0.248\,66}{1 - 0.248\,66}$
≈ 0.818

6   Let X be the number of aerofoils which disintegrate from a sample of 100.
Each aerofoil has a 2% chance of disintegrating, so $m = E(X) = 0.02 \times 100 = 2$

$\therefore \; P(X = x) = \dfrac{2^x e^{-2}}{x!}$ where $x = 0, 1, 2, 3, ...$

a $P(X = 1) = \dfrac{2^1 e^{-2}}{1!} = \dfrac{2}{e^2} \approx 0.271$

b $P(X = 2) = \dfrac{2^2 e^{-2}}{2!} = \dfrac{4}{2e^2} \approx 0.271$

c $P(X \leqslant 2) = P(X = 0) + P(X = 1) + P(X = 2)$

$= \dfrac{2^0 e^{-2}}{0!} + \dfrac{2^1 e^{-2}}{1!} + \dfrac{2^2 e^{-2}}{2!}$

$= \dfrac{1}{e^2} + \dfrac{2}{e^2} + \dfrac{2}{e^2}$

$= \dfrac{5}{e^2} \approx 0.677$

7 **a** A person who drives 10 times per week will drive $10 \times 52 = 520$ times in one year.
Let X be the number of fatalities from driving 520 times.
$$m = E(X) = 0.0002 \times 520 = 0.104$$
$$\therefore \quad P(X = x) = \frac{0.104^x e^{-0.104}}{x!}$$
$$\therefore \quad P(X = 0) = \frac{0.104^0 e^{-0.104}}{0!} \approx 0.901 \quad \therefore \text{ the probability of surviving is } 0.901.$$

b P(driving for n years and surviving) $= (0.901)^n$
$\therefore$ we need to find n such that $(0.901)^n = 0.5$
$$\therefore \quad n \log 0.901 = \log 0.5$$
$$\therefore \quad n = \frac{\log 0.5}{\log 0.901} \approx 6.66$$
$\therefore$ you can drive for 6 years and still have a better than even chance of surviving.

8 Let X be the number of flaws in 1 metre of material.
$m = 1.7 \quad \therefore \quad P(X = x) = \dfrac{1.7^x e^{-1.7}}{x!}, \quad x = 0, 1, 2, 3, \ldots$

a $P(X = 3) = \dfrac{1.7^3 e^{-1.7}}{3!} \approx 0.150$

b P(at least one flaw in 2 metres)
$= 1 - $ P(no flaws in 2 metres)
$= 1 - (P(X = 0))^2$
$\approx 1 - (0.1827)^2$
≈ 0.967

c $P(X = 0) \approx 0.183$
$P(X = 1) \approx 0.311$
$P(X = 2) \approx 0.264$
$P(X = 3) \approx 0.150$
$P(X = 4) \approx 0.064$
Finding the highest of the probabilities, the mode is 1 flaw per metre.

9 **a** $P(Y = y) = \dfrac{m^y e^{-m}}{y!}, \quad y = 0, 1, 2, 3, \ldots$
$P(Y = 3) = P(Y = 1) + 2P(Y = 2)$
$$\therefore \quad \frac{m^3 e^{-m}}{3!} = \frac{m^1 e^{-m}}{1!} + 2\frac{m^2 e^{-m}}{2!}$$
$$\therefore \quad \frac{m^3}{6} = m + m^2 \quad \{\times e^m\}$$
$$\therefore \quad m^3 = 6m + 6m^2$$
$$\therefore \quad m(m^2 - 6m - 6) = 0 \text{ where } m \neq 0$$
$$\therefore \quad m^2 - 6m - 6 = 0$$
$$\therefore \quad m = \frac{6 \pm \sqrt{36 - 4(1)(-6)}}{2}$$
$$= 3 \pm \sqrt{15}$$
But $m > 0$, so $m = 3 + \sqrt{15}$
≈ 6.8730

b $P(1 < Y < 5)$
$= P(Y \leqslant 4) - P(Y \leqslant 1)$
≈ 0.177

c $P(2 \leqslant Y \leqslant 6 \mid Y \geqslant 4)$
$= \dfrac{P(2 \leqslant Y \leqslant 6 \cap Y \geqslant 4)}{P(Y \geqslant 4)}$
$= \dfrac{P(4 \leqslant Y \leqslant 6)}{P(Y \geqslant 4)}$
$= \dfrac{P(Y \leqslant 6) - P(Y \leqslant 3)}{1 - P(Y \leqslant 3)}$
≈ 0.417

10 $P(U = u) = \dfrac{x^u e^{-x}}{u!}$ where $u = 0, 1, 2, 3, \ldots$

a $y = P(U = 0, 1 \text{ or } 2)$
$= P(U = 0) + P(U = 1) + P(U = 2)$
$= \dfrac{x^0 e^{-x}}{0!} + \dfrac{x^1 e^{-x}}{1!} + \dfrac{x^2 e^{-x}}{2!}$
$= e^{-x} + xe^{-x} + \tfrac{1}{2}x^2 e^{-x}$
$\therefore \quad y = e^{-x}(1 + x + \tfrac{1}{2}x^2)$

b

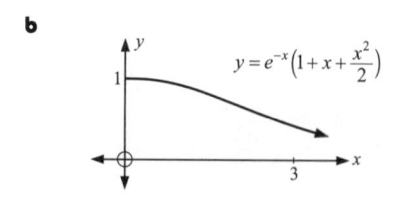

c $y = e^{-x}(1 + x + \frac{1}{2}x^2)$

∴ $\frac{dy}{dx} = -e^{-x}(1 + x + \frac{1}{2}x^2) + e^{-x}(1 + x)$

$= -e^{-x} - xe^{-x} - \frac{1}{2}x^2 e^{-x} + e^{-x} + xe^{-x}$

$= -\frac{1}{2}x^2 e^{-x}$

Since $x^2 e^{-x} > 0$, $\frac{dy}{dx} < 0$ for all $x > 0$.

∴   as the mean x increases, $y = P(U \leqslant 2)$ decreases.

REVIEW SET 28A

1 a $P(x) = \dfrac{a}{x^2 + 1}$ for $a = 0, 1, 2, 3$

x_i	0	1	2	3
$P(x_i)$	a	$\dfrac{a}{2}$	$\dfrac{a}{5}$	$\dfrac{a}{10}$

Now $a + \dfrac{a}{2} + \dfrac{a}{5} + \dfrac{a}{10} = 1$ {as $\sum P(x_i) = 1$}

∴ $10a + 5a + 2a + a = 10$

∴ $18a = 10$

∴ $a = \frac{5}{9}$

b $P(X \geqslant 1) = P(X = 1, 2 \text{ or } 3)$ or $P(X \geqslant 1) = 1 - P(X < 1)$

$= P(X = 1) + P(X = 2) + P(X = 3)$ $= 1 - P(X = 0)$

$= \frac{5}{18} + \frac{1}{9} + \frac{5}{90}$ $= 1 - \frac{5}{9}$

$= \frac{4}{9}$ $= \frac{4}{9}$

2 a $P(x) = \binom{4}{x}\left(\frac{1}{2}\right)^x \left(\frac{1}{2}\right)^{4-x}$ $P(2) = \binom{4}{2}\left(\frac{1}{2}\right)^2 \left(\frac{1}{2}\right)^2 = 0.375$

∴ $P(0) = \binom{4}{0}\left(\frac{1}{2}\right)^0 \left(\frac{1}{2}\right)^4 = 0.0625$ $P(3) = \binom{4}{3}\left(\frac{1}{2}\right)^3 \left(\frac{1}{2}\right)^1 = 0.25$

$P(1) = \binom{4}{1}\left(\frac{1}{2}\right)^1 \left(\frac{1}{2}\right)^3 = 0.25$ $P(4) = \binom{4}{4}\left(\frac{1}{2}\right)^4 \left(\frac{1}{2}\right)^0 = 0.0625$

x_i	0	1	2	3	4
$P(x_i)$	0.0625	0.25	0.375	0.25	0.0625

b $\mu = \sum x_i P(x_i)$

$= 0 \times 0.0625 + 1 \times 0.25 + 2 \times 0.375 + 3 \times 0.25 + 4 \times 0.0625$

$= 2$

$\sigma = \sqrt{\sum (x_i - \mu)^2 P(x_i)}$

$= \sqrt{(-2)^2 (0.0625) + (-1)^2 (0.25) + 0^2 (0.375) + 1^2 (0.25) + 2^2 (0.0625)}$

$= 1$

3 X is the number of defectives. Then $X \sim B(10, 0.18)$. $X = 0, 1, 2, 3, \ldots, 10$.

a $P(X = 1)$ **b** $P(X = 2)$ **c** $P(X \geqslant 2)$

$= \binom{10}{1}(0.18)^1 (0.82)^9$ $= \binom{10}{2}(0.18)^2 (0.82)^8$ $= 1 - P(X \leqslant 1)$

≈ 0.302 ≈ 0.298 $\approx 1 - 0.439$

≈ 0.561

4 Let X be the number of defective toothbrushes.

∴ $X \sim B(120, 0.04)$,   **a** $\mu = np$ **b** $\sigma = \sqrt{npq}$

$n = 120$, $p = 0.04$, $q = 0.96$ $= 120 \times 0.04$ $= \sqrt{120 \times 0.04 \times 0.96}$

$= 4.8$ ≈ 2.15

5

Result	Pays
1, 3, 5	$2
2	$3
4	$6
6	$9

a Expected return $= \frac{3}{6} \times \$2 + \frac{1}{6} \times \$3 + \frac{1}{6} \times \$6 + \frac{1}{6} \times \$9$

$\qquad = \frac{1}{6}(\$24)$

$\qquad = \$4$

b For a $5 amount to play the game, the club expects a $1 return per game
∴ for 75 people, the return expected is $75.

6 a $\frac{1}{3} + \frac{1}{6} + \frac{1}{4} + y = 1$

∴ $y = \frac{1}{4}$

∴ the probability of obtaining the number 24 is $\frac{1}{4}$.

b $E(X) = 6\left(\frac{1}{3}\right) + 12\left(\frac{1}{6}\right) + x\left(\frac{1}{4}\right) + 24\left(\frac{1}{4}\right) = 14$

∴ $2 + 2 + \frac{x}{4} + 6 = 14$

∴ $\frac{x}{4} = 4$

∴ $x = 16$

So, the fourth number is 16.

c In 24 trials the expected frequencies are:

Number	6	12	16	24
Frequency	8	4	6	6

∴ median = middle score = $\frac{\text{12th score} + \text{13th score}}{2} = \frac{12 + 16}{2} = 14$

mode = 6 {most frequently occurring score}

7 $P(X = 0) + P(X = 1) + P(X = 2) + \ldots = 1$

∴ $a\left(\frac{5}{6}\right)^0 + a\left(\frac{5}{6}\right)^1 + a\left(\frac{5}{6}\right)^2 + \ldots = 1$

∴ $a\underbrace{\left(1 + \frac{5}{6} + \left(\frac{5}{6}\right)^2 + \ldots\right)}_{} = 1$

infinite geometric series with $u_1 = 1$, $r = \frac{5}{6}$

∴ $a\left(\frac{1}{1 - \frac{5}{6}}\right) = 1$

∴ $a(6) = 1$

∴ $a = \frac{1}{6}$

8 a P(hot water unit fails within one year) = P(all 20 components fail)

$\qquad = (0.85)^{20}$

$\qquad \approx 0.0388$

b P(hot water unit with n components fails within one year) $= 0.85^n$

∴ P(hot water unit with n components is operating after one year) $= 1 - 0.85^n$

∴ we need to find the smallest integer n such that $1 - 0.85^n \geqslant 0.98$

∴ $0.85^n \leqslant 0.02$

∴ $n \log 0.85 \leqslant \log 0.02$

∴ $n \geqslant \frac{\log 0.02}{\log 0.85}$ {$\log 0.85 < 0$}

∴ $n \geqslant 24.1$

∴ at least 25 solar components are needed.

9 a $P(X = 3) = 0.22689$

∴ $\binom{7}{3} p^3 (1-p)^{7-3} = 0.22689$

∴ $35 p^3 (1-p)^4 = 0.22689$

∴ $p \approx 0.300$ or 0.564 {using technology}

∴ $p \approx 0.300$ {smallest p}

b $P(X \leqslant 4) \approx 0.850$

10 a Let X be the number of customers arriving at the shop in a 15 minute period.

$$X \sim \text{Po}(20) \quad \therefore \quad P(X = x) = \frac{20^x e^{-20}}{x!}, \quad \text{where } x = 0, 1, 2, 3, ...$$

$$P(X = 15) = \frac{20^{15} e^{-20}}{15!} \approx 0.0516$$

b Let Y be the number of customers arriving at the shop in a 10 minute period.

$\therefore$ Y has mean $m = \frac{10}{15} \times 20 = \frac{40}{3}$

$\therefore$ $Y \sim \text{Po}\left(\frac{40}{3}\right)$

$P(Y > 10) = 1 - P(Y \leqslant 10)$
$\approx 1 - 0.224$
$\approx 0.776 < 0.8$

$\therefore$ the probability that more than 10 customers will arrive at the shop in a 10 minute period is *not* greater than 80%.

$\therefore$ the manager will not hire an extra shop assistant.

11 a $P(X = x) = \dfrac{m^x e^{-m}}{x!}$, $x = 0, 1, 2, \ldots$

Now $P(X = 1) = P(2 \leqslant x \leqslant 4)$

$\therefore P(X = 1) = P(X = 2) + P(X = 3) + P(X = 4)$

$\therefore \dfrac{me^{-m}}{1!} = \dfrac{m^2 e^{-m}}{2!} + \dfrac{m^3 e^{-m}}{3!} + \dfrac{m^4 e^{-m}}{4!}$

$\therefore m = \dfrac{m^2}{2} + \dfrac{m^3}{6} + \dfrac{m^4}{24} \quad \{\times e^m\}$

$\therefore 24m = 12m^2 + 4m^3 + m^4$

$\therefore m(m^3 + 4m^2 + 12m - 24) = 0$ where $m \neq 0$

$\therefore m \approx 1.28$ {using technology}

b $P(X \geqslant 2) = 1 - P(X \leqslant 1)$
$\approx 1 - 0.634$
≈ 0.366

i mean of $X = m \approx 1.28$

standard deviation $= \sqrt{m} \approx 1.13$

ii $Y = \dfrac{X + 1}{2} = \frac{1}{2}X + \frac{1}{2}$

$\therefore$ mean of $Y = E(Y)$
$= E\left(\frac{1}{2}X + \frac{1}{2}\right)$
$= \frac{1}{2}E(X) + E(\frac{1}{2})$
≈ 1.14

Now, $\text{Var}(X) \approx 1.28$
and $\text{Var}(Y) = \text{Var}(\frac{1}{2}X)$
$\approx (\frac{1}{2})^2 \times 1.28$
≈ 0.320

$\therefore \sigma_Y \approx \sqrt{0.320}$
≈ 0.566

REVIEW SET 28B

1 a $P(x_i) = k \left(\frac{3}{4}\right)^x \left(\frac{1}{4}\right)^{3-x}$ for $x = 0, 1, 2, 3$

$P(0) = k \left(\frac{3}{4}\right)^0 \left(\frac{1}{4}\right)^3 = \dfrac{k}{64}$

$P(1) = k \left(\frac{3}{4}\right)^1 \left(\frac{1}{4}\right)^2 = \dfrac{3k}{64}$

$P(2) = k \left(\frac{3}{4}\right)^2 \left(\frac{1}{4}\right)^1 = \dfrac{9k}{64}$

$P(3) = k \left(\frac{3}{4}\right)^3 \left(\frac{1}{4}\right)^0 = \dfrac{27k}{64}$

x_i	0	1	2	3
$P(x_i)$	$\dfrac{k}{64}$	$\dfrac{3k}{64}$	$\dfrac{9k}{64}$	$\dfrac{27k}{64}$

Now $\dfrac{k}{64} + \dfrac{3k}{64} + \dfrac{9k}{64} + \dfrac{27k}{64} = 1$ {as $\sum P(x_i) = 1$}

$\therefore \dfrac{40k}{64} = 1$

$\therefore k = 1.6$

b $P(X \geqslant 1) = 1 - P(X = 0) = 1 - \dfrac{k}{64}$
$= 1 - \dfrac{1.6}{64}$
$= 0.975$

2 X is the number of X-rays which show the fracture, then $X = 0, 1, 2, 3, 4$ and $X \sim B(4, 0.96)$.

  a $P(X = 4)$
$= \binom{4}{4}(0.96)^4(0.04)^0$
≈ 0.849

  b $P(X = 0)$
$= \binom{4}{0}(0.96)^0(0.04)^4$
$\approx 2.56 \times 10^{-6}$

  c $P(X \geq 3)$
$= 1 - P(X \leq 2)$
$\approx 1 - 0.00910$
≈ 0.991

  d $P(X = 1)$
$= \binom{4}{1}(0.96)^1(0.04)^3$
≈ 0.000246

3

x_i	0	1	2	3	4
$P(x_i)$	0.10	0.30	0.45	0.10	k

  a   If this is a probability distribution then $\sum P(x_i) = 1$
$\therefore \quad 1 = 0.1 + 0.3 + 0.45 + 0.1 + k$
$\therefore \quad k = 1 - 0.95$
$\therefore \quad k = 0.05$

  b $\mu = \sum x_i p_i$
$= 0(0.1) + 1(0.3) + 2(0.45) + 3(0.1) + 4(0.05)$
$= 0 + 0.3 + 0.9 + 0.3 + 0.2$
$= 1.7$

$\sigma^2 = \sum x_i^2 p_i - \mu^2$
$= 0^2(0.1) + 1^2(0.3) + 2^2(0.45) + 3^2(0.1) + 4^2(0.05) - (1.7)^2$
$= 0.3 + 1.8 + 0.9 + 0.8 - 2.89$
$= 0.91 \qquad \therefore \quad \sigma = \sqrt{0.91} \approx 0.954$

4 Let X denote the number of cases of netballers needing knee surgery.
$\therefore \quad X \sim B(487, 0.0132)$ with $n = 487$, $p = 0.0132$, $q = 0.9868$
$\therefore \quad \mu = np \qquad\qquad \sigma = \sqrt{npq}$
$\quad\quad = 487 \times 0.0132 \qquad = \sqrt{487 \times 0.0132 \times 0.9868}$
$\quad\quad \approx 6.43 \qquad\qquad \approx 2.52$

5 Let X be the number of mistakes made by the first author.
$\therefore \quad X$ has mean $m = 1 \times \frac{20}{200} = 0.1$
$\therefore \quad X \sim Po(0.1)$
Let Y be the number of mistakes made by the second author.
$\therefore \quad Y$ has mean $m = 3 \times \frac{40}{200} = 0.6$
$\therefore \quad Y \sim Po(0.6)$
$\therefore \quad P$(authors made 2 or more mistakes between them)
$= 1 - P$(authors made 0 or 1 mistakes between them)
$= 1 - P(X = 0, Y = 0 \text{ or } X = 1, Y = 0 \text{ or } X = 0, Y = 1)$
$= 1 - \left[\dfrac{0.1^0 e^{-0.1}}{0!} \times \dfrac{0.6^0 e^{-0.6}}{0!} + \dfrac{0.1^1 e^{-0.1}}{1!} \times \dfrac{0.6^0 e^{-0.6}}{0!} + \dfrac{0.1^0 e^{-0.1}}{0!} \times \dfrac{0.6^1 e^{-0.6}}{1!} \right]$
≈ 0.156

6 Let X be the number of sixes obtained.
$\therefore \quad X \sim B(1200, 0.4)$ with $n = 1200$, $p = 0.4$, $q = 0.6$

  a   mean of $X = np$
$= 1200 \times 0.4$
$= 480$

  b   standard deviation of $X = \sqrt{npq}$
$= \sqrt{1200 \times 0.4 \times 0.6}$
≈ 17.0

7 $P(X = x) = k\left(x + \dfrac{1}{x}\right)$

a $P(X = 1) = k(1 + \frac{1}{1}) = 2k$

$P(X = 2) = k(2 + \frac{1}{2}) = \frac{5}{2}k$

$P(X = 3) = k(3 + \frac{1}{3}) = \frac{10}{3}k$

$P(X = 4) = k(4 + \frac{1}{4}) = \frac{17}{4}k$

Now $\sum P(x_i) = 1$

$\therefore 2k + \frac{5}{2}k + \frac{10}{3}k + \frac{17}{4}k = 1$

$\therefore \frac{145}{12}k = 1$

$\therefore k = \dfrac{12}{145}$

b Using $k = \dfrac{12}{145}$ we obtain:

x	1	2	3	4
$P(x)$	$\frac{24}{145}$	$\frac{30}{145}$	$\frac{40}{145}$	$\frac{51}{145}$

$\therefore E(X) = 1\left(\frac{24}{145}\right) + 2\left(\frac{30}{145}\right) + 3\left(\frac{40}{145}\right) + 4\left(\frac{51}{145}\right) = \frac{408}{145}$

$E(X^2) = 1^2\left(\frac{24}{145}\right) + 2^2\left(\frac{30}{145}\right) + 3^2\left(\frac{40}{145}\right) + 4^2\left(\frac{51}{145}\right) = \frac{264}{29}$

$\therefore \text{Var}(X) = E(X^2) - \{E(X)\}^2$

$= \dfrac{264}{29} - \left(\dfrac{408}{145}\right)^2$

≈ 1.19

c In 145 trials the expected frequencies are:

x	1	2	3	4
$P(x)$	24	30	40	51

$\therefore$ median = middle score = 73rd score = 3

mode = 4 {most frequently occurring score}

8 a For a Poisson random variable X,

$E(X) = \text{Var}(X) = m$

$\therefore 5m = 2m^2 - 12$

$\therefore 2m^2 - 5m - 12 = 0$

$\therefore (2m + 3)(m - 4) = 0$

$\therefore m = 4$ {as $m > 0$}

$\therefore$ the mean of X is 4.

b $P(X = x) = \dfrac{4^x e^{-4}}{x!}$, $x = 0, 1, 2, 3, ...$

$\therefore P(X < 3) = \dfrac{4^0 e^{-4}}{0!} + \dfrac{4^1 e^{-4}}{1!} + \dfrac{4^2 e^{-4}}{2!}$

$= e^{-4}(1 + 4 + 8)$

$= \dfrac{13}{e^4} \approx 0.238$

9 $P(X > 2) \approx 0.070\,198$

$\therefore P(X \leqslant 2) \approx 1 - 0.070\,198$

$\therefore P(X = 0, 1 \text{ or } 2) \approx 0.929\,802$

$\therefore \binom{10}{0}p^0(1-p)^{10} + \binom{10}{1}p^1(1-p)^9 + \binom{10}{2}p^2(1-p)^8 \approx 0.929\,802$

$\therefore (1-p)^{10} + 10p(1-p)^9 + 45p^2(1-p)^8 \approx 0.929\,802$

Using technology and the domain $0 \leqslant p \leqslant 1$, we find $p \approx 0.100$

$\therefore P(X < 2) = P(X \leqslant 1)$

≈ 0.736

10 $P(Y > 3) \approx 0.033\,768\,97$

$\therefore P(Y \leqslant 3) \approx 1 - 0.033\,768\,97$

$\therefore P(Y = 0, 1, 2 \text{ or } 3) \approx 0.966\,231\,03$

$\therefore \dfrac{m^0 e^{-m}}{0!} + \dfrac{m^1 e^{-m}}{1!} + \dfrac{m^2 e^{-m}}{2!} + \dfrac{m^3 e^{-m}}{3!} \approx 0.966\,231\,03$

$\therefore e^{-m}\left(1 + m + \dfrac{m^2}{2} + \dfrac{m^3}{6}\right) \approx 0.966\,231\,03$

Using technology on the domain $m > 0$, we find $m = 1.2$

$$\therefore \quad P(Y < 3) = P(Y \leqslant 2)$$
$$\approx 0.879$$

11 X has mean μ and standard deviation σ.
$\therefore \quad E(X) = \mu$ and $\sigma^2 = \text{Var}(X) = E(X^2) - \{E(X)\}^2$
Now $Y = aX + b \quad \therefore \quad$ mean of $Y = E(Y)$
$$= E(aX + b)$$
$$= E(aX) + E(b)$$
$$= a\,E(X) + b$$
$$= a\mu + b$$

Also, $\text{Var}(aX + b) = E\left((aX + b)^2\right) - \{E(aX + b)\}^2$
$$= E\left(a^2 X^2 + 2abX + b^2\right) - \{a\,E(X) + b\}^2$$
$$= a^2\,E(X^2) + 2ab\,E(X) + b^2 - \left[a^2\,\{E(X)\}^2 + 2ab\,E(X) + b^2\right]$$
$$= a^2\,E(X^2) + 2ab\,E(X) + b^2 - a^2\,\{E(X)\}^2 - 2ab\,E(X) - b^2$$
$$= a^2\left(E(X^2) - \{E(X)\}^2\right)$$
$$= a^2 \sigma^2$$

$\therefore \quad$ standard deviation of $Y = \sqrt{a^2 \sigma^2}$
$$= \sqrt{a^2}\,\sigma \quad \{\text{since } \sigma > 0\}$$
$$= |a|\sigma$$

Chapter 29
STATISTICAL DISTRIBUTIONS OF CONTINUOUS RANDOM VARIABLES

EXERCISE 29A

1 a $\int_0^4 ax(x-4)\, dx = 1$

$\therefore\ a\int_0^4 (x^2 - 4x)\, dx = 1$

$\therefore\ a\left[\dfrac{x^3}{3} - \dfrac{4x^2}{2}\right]_0^4 = 1$

$\therefore\ a\left(\dfrac{64}{3} - 32\right) = 1$

$\therefore\ a\left(\dfrac{-32}{3}\right) = 1$

$\therefore\ a = -\dfrac{3}{32}$

b $f(x) = -\dfrac{3}{32}x(x-4),\ \ 0 \leqslant x \leqslant 4$

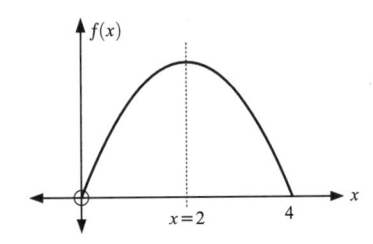

ii mode $= 2$ {symmetry of graph}

iii If $\int_0^m -\dfrac{3}{32}x(x-4)\, dx = \dfrac{1}{2}$

then $\int_0^m (x^2 - 4x)\, dx = -\dfrac{16}{3}$

$\therefore\ \left[\dfrac{x^3}{3} - \dfrac{4x^2}{2}\right]_0^m = -\dfrac{16}{3}$

$\therefore\ \dfrac{m^3}{3} - 2m^2 - 0 = -\dfrac{16}{3}$

$\therefore\ m^3 - 6m^2 = -16$

$\therefore\ m^3 - 6m^2 + 16 = 0$

$\therefore\ (m-2)(m^2 - 4m - 8) = 0$

$\therefore\ m = 2\ \ \text{or}\ \ \dfrac{4 \pm \sqrt{16 + 32}}{2}$

$\therefore\ m = 2\ \ \text{or}\ \ 2 \pm 2\sqrt{3}$

$\therefore\ m = 2\ \ \{\text{as } 0 < m < 4\}$

$\therefore\ \text{the median is } 2$

c i $\mu = \int_0^4 x f(x)\, dx$

$= \int_0^4 -\dfrac{3}{32}x^2(x-4)\, dx$

$= -\dfrac{3}{32}\int_0^4 (x^3 - 4x^2)\, dx$

$= -\dfrac{3}{32}\left[\dfrac{1}{4}x^4 - \dfrac{4}{3}x^3\right]_0^4$

$= -\dfrac{3}{32}\left(\dfrac{1}{4}(4)^4 - \dfrac{4}{3}(4)^3\right)$

$= -\dfrac{3}{32}\left(4^3 - \dfrac{4}{3} \times 4^3\right)$

$= -\dfrac{3}{32}\left(-\dfrac{64}{3}\right) = 2$

iv $\int_0^4 x^2 f(x)\, dx$

$= \int_0^4 -\dfrac{3}{32}x^3(x-4)\, dx$

$= -\dfrac{3}{32}\int_0^4 (x^4 - 4x^3)\, dx$

$= -\dfrac{3}{32}\left[\dfrac{1}{5}x^5 - x^4\right]_0^4$

$= -\dfrac{3}{32}\left(\dfrac{4}{5}(4)^4 - 4^4\right)$

$= -\dfrac{3}{32}\left(-\dfrac{256}{5}\right) = \dfrac{24}{5}$

$\therefore\ \text{Var}(X) = \dfrac{24}{5} - 2^2 = \dfrac{4}{5}$

2 a $\int_0^b -0.2x(x-b)\, dx = 1$

$\therefore\ -0.2\int_0^b (x^2 - bx)\, dx = 1$

$\therefore\ \left[\dfrac{1}{3}x^3 - \dfrac{1}{2}bx^2\right]_0^b = -5$

$\therefore\ \dfrac{1}{3}b^3 - \dfrac{1}{2}b^3 - 0 = -5$

$\therefore\ 2b^3 - 3b^3 = -30$

$\therefore\ -b^3 = -30$

$\therefore\ b^3 = 30$

$\therefore\ b = \sqrt[3]{30}$

b i $\mu = \int_0^{\sqrt[3]{30}} -0.2x^2(x - \sqrt[3]{30})\, dx$

≈ 1.5536 {using technology}

≈ 1.55

ii $\int_0^{\sqrt[3]{30}} x^2 f(x)\, dx$

$= \int_0^{\sqrt[3]{30}} -0.2x^3(x - \sqrt[3]{30})\, dx$

≈ 2.8965 {using technology}

$\therefore\ \text{Var}(X) \approx 2.8965 - \mu^2$

≈ 0.483

3 a $\int_0^3 ke^{-x}\, dx = 1$

$\therefore\ k\int_0^3 e^{-x}\, dx = 1$

$\therefore\ k\left[\dfrac{e^{-x}}{-1}\right]_0^3 = 1$

$\therefore\ k(-e^{-3} - (-1)) = 1$

$\therefore\ k(1 - e^{-3}) = 1$

$\therefore\ k \approx 1.0524$

b If m is the median then

$\int_0^m ke^{-x}\, dx = \tfrac{1}{2}$

$\therefore\ \int_0^m e^{-x}\, dx = \dfrac{1}{2k}$

$\therefore\ \left[\dfrac{e^{-x}}{-1}\right]_0^m = \dfrac{1}{2k}$

$\therefore\ -e^{-m} - (-1) = \dfrac{1}{2k}$

$\therefore\ e^{-m} \approx 1 - \dfrac{1}{2(1.0524)}$

$\therefore\ e^{-m} \approx 0.524\,89$

$\therefore\ -m \approx \ln(0.524\,89)$

$\therefore\ m \approx 0.645$

4 a $\int_0^5 kx^2(x - 6)\, dx = 1$

$\therefore\ k\int_0^5 (x^3 - 6x^2)\, dx = 1$

$\therefore\ k\left[\tfrac{1}{4}x^4 - \tfrac{6}{3}x^3\right]_0^5 = 1$

$\therefore\ k\left(\dfrac{625}{4} - 250\right) = 1$

$\therefore\ k\left(\dfrac{-375}{4}\right) = 1$

$\therefore\ k = -\dfrac{4}{375}$

b $f(x) = -\dfrac{4}{375}x^2(x - 6)$

$= -\dfrac{4}{375}(x^3 - 6x^2)$

$\therefore\ f'(x) = -\dfrac{4}{375}(3x^2 - 12x)$

$\therefore\ f'(x) = 0$ when $3x(x - 4) = 0$

$\therefore\ x = 0$ or 4

$f'(x)$ has sign diagram:

```
        +       -
|───────|───────|  x
0       4       5
```

There is a maximum when $x = 4$, so the mode is 4.

c If m is the median,

then $\int_0^m -\dfrac{4}{375}x^2(x - 6)\, dx = \tfrac{1}{2}$

$\therefore\ \int_0^m (x^3 - 6x^2)\, dx = -\dfrac{375}{8}$

$\therefore\ \left[\tfrac{1}{4}x^4 - \tfrac{6}{3}x^3\right]_0^m = -\dfrac{375}{8}$

$\therefore\ \tfrac{1}{4}m^4 - 2m^3 = -\dfrac{375}{8}$

$\therefore\ 2m^4 - 16m^3 + 375 = 0$

Using technology, $m \approx 3.46$

d $\mu = \int_0^5 x f(x)\, dx$

$= \int_0^5 -\dfrac{4}{375}x^3(x - 6)\, dx$

$= 3\tfrac{1}{3}$ {using technology}

e $E(X^2) = \int_0^5 x^2 f(x)\, dx$

$= \int_0^5 -\dfrac{4}{375}x^4(x - 6)\, dx$

$= 12\tfrac{2}{9}$ {using technology}

$\therefore\ \mathrm{Var}(X) = 12\tfrac{2}{9} - \left(3\tfrac{1}{3}\right)^2 = 1\tfrac{1}{9}$

5 a Y is a continuous random variable if $5 - 12y \geqslant 0$ for all $0 \leqslant y \leqslant k$ and $\int_0^k (5 - 12y)\, dy = 1$.
Since $f(y) = 5 - 12y$ is a decreasing function, $f(k) = 5 - 12k$ is the smallest value of $f(y)$ on $0 \leqslant y \leqslant k$.

$\therefore\ 5 - 12k \geqslant 0$

$\therefore\ 12k \leqslant 5$

$\therefore\ k \leqslant \tfrac{5}{12}$ So, $k \leqslant \tfrac{5}{12}$ and $\int_0^k (5 - 12y)\, dy = 1$

b

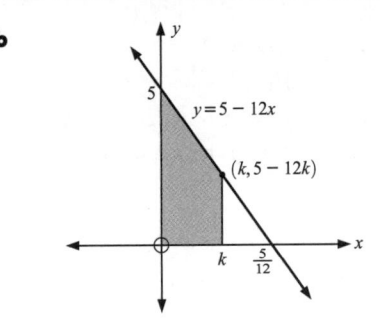

$\int_0^k (5 - 12y)\, dy = $ shaded area $= 1$

$\therefore \quad k \times \left(\dfrac{5 + (5 - 12k)}{2} \right) = 1$

$\therefore \quad k(5 - 6k) = 1$

$\therefore \quad 5k - 6k^2 = 1$

$\therefore \quad 6k^2 - 5k + 1 = 0$

$\therefore \quad (3k - 1)(2k - 1) = 0$

$\therefore \quad k = \tfrac{1}{3}$ or $\tfrac{1}{2}$

But $k \leqslant \tfrac{5}{12}$, so $k = \tfrac{1}{3}$

c If $k = \tfrac{1}{2}$, the graph $f(y) = 5 - 12y$ falls below the horizontal axis.

d $\mu = \int_0^{\frac{1}{3}} y\, f(y)\, dy$

$= \int_0^{\frac{1}{3}} (5y - 12y^2)\, dy$

$= \left[\tfrac{5}{2} y^2 - 4y^3 \right]_0^{\frac{1}{3}}$

$= \tfrac{5}{2} \left(\tfrac{1}{9} \right) - 4 \left(\tfrac{1}{27} \right)$

$= \tfrac{7}{54}$

If $\int_0^m (5 - 12y)\, dy = \tfrac{1}{2}$

then $\left[5y - 6y^2 \right]_0^m = \tfrac{1}{2}$

$\therefore \quad 5m - 6m^2 = \tfrac{1}{2}$

$\therefore \quad 12m^2 - 10m + 1 = 0$

$\therefore \quad m = \dfrac{5 \pm \sqrt{13}}{12}$

But $m < \tfrac{5}{12}$, so $m = \dfrac{5 - \sqrt{13}}{12} \approx 0.116$

$\therefore$ the median ≈ 0.116

6 a $\int_a^b k\, dx = 1$

$\therefore \quad [kx]_a^b = 1$

$\therefore \quad bk - ak = 1$

$\therefore \quad k = \dfrac{1}{b - a}$

c $\int_a^b kx^2\, dx = \dfrac{1}{b - a} \left[\dfrac{x^3}{3} \right]_a^b$

$= \dfrac{1}{b - a} \left(\dfrac{b^3}{3} - \dfrac{a^3}{3} \right)$

$= \tfrac{1}{3} \dfrac{b^3 - a^3}{b - a}$

$= \tfrac{1}{3} \dfrac{(b - a)(b^2 + ab + a^2)}{(b - a)}$

$= \dfrac{a^2 + ab + b^2}{3}$

$\therefore \quad \mathrm{Var}(X) = \dfrac{a^2 + ab + b^2}{3} - \left(\dfrac{a + b}{2} \right)^2$

$= \dfrac{4(a^2 + ab + b^2) - 3(a + b)^2}{12}$

$= \dfrac{4a^2 + 4ab + 4b^2 - 3a^2 - 6ab - 3b^2}{12}$

$= \dfrac{a^2 - 2ab + b^2}{12}$

$= \dfrac{(a - b)^2}{12}$

$\therefore \quad \sigma_X = \sqrt{\dfrac{(a - b)^2}{12}} = \dfrac{b - a}{\sqrt{12}}$ {as $b > a$}

b $\mu = \int_a^b kx\, dx$

$= \dfrac{1}{b - a} \left[\tfrac{1}{2} x^2 \right]_a^b$

$= \dfrac{1}{b - a} \left(\tfrac{1}{2} b^2 - \tfrac{1}{2} a^2 \right)$

$= \tfrac{1}{2} \dfrac{(b - a)(b + a)}{(b - a)}$

$\therefore \quad $ mean $= \dfrac{a + b}{2}$

If $\int_a^m k\, dx = \tfrac{1}{2}$ then $[kx]_a^m = \tfrac{1}{2}$

$\therefore \quad \dfrac{m}{b - a} - \dfrac{a}{b - a} = \tfrac{1}{2}$

$\therefore \quad m - a = \dfrac{b - a}{2}$

$\therefore \quad m = a + \dfrac{b - a}{2}$

$= \dfrac{a + b}{2}$

$\therefore \quad $ median $= \dfrac{a + b}{2}$

The mode is undefined as the function is constant for all $a \leqslant x \leqslant b$.

7 a If $\int_0^m 2e^{-2x}\, dx = \frac{1}{2}$

then $\left[-e^{-2x}\right]_0^m = \frac{1}{2}$

$\therefore\ -e^{-2m} - (-e^0) = \frac{1}{2}$

$\therefore\ \frac{1}{2} = e^{-2m}$

$\therefore\ -2m = \ln\frac{1}{2}$

$\therefore\ m = -\frac{1}{2}\ln\frac{1}{2} \approx 0.347$

b $f(x) = 2e^{-2x}$

$\therefore\ f'(x) = -4e^{-2x}$

$\therefore\ f'(x) < 0$ for all $x \geqslant 0 \quad \{e^{-2x} > 0\}$

$\therefore\ f(x)$ is always decreasing for $x \geqslant 0$

$\therefore\ $ the mode $= 0$

8 a $\int_0^a 6\cos 3x\, dx = 1$

$\therefore\ [2\sin 3x]_0^a = 1$

$\therefore\ 2\sin 3a - 2\sin 0 = 1$

$\therefore\ \sin 3a = \frac{1}{2}$

$\therefore\ 3a = \frac{\pi}{6}$

$\therefore\ a = \frac{\pi}{18}$

b $\mu = \int_0^{\frac{\pi}{18}} 6x\cos 3x\, dx$

We integrate by parts with $u = 6x \quad v' = \cos 3x$
$\qquad\qquad\qquad\qquad\qquad\qquad u' = 6 \quad v = \frac{1}{3}\sin 3x$

$\therefore\ \int 6x\cos 3x\, dx = 2x\sin 3x - \int 2\sin 3x\, dx$

$\qquad\qquad\qquad\qquad = 2x\sin 3x + \frac{2}{3}\cos 3x + c$

$\therefore\ \mu = \int_0^{\frac{\pi}{18}} 6x\cos 3x\, dx$

$= \left[2x\sin 3x + \frac{2}{3}\cos 3x\right]_0^{\frac{\pi}{18}}$

$= \left(\frac{\pi}{9}\sin\frac{\pi}{6} + \frac{2}{3}\cos\frac{\pi}{6}\right) - \left(0 + \frac{2}{3}\cos 0\right)$

$= \frac{\pi}{9}\left(\frac{1}{2}\right) + \frac{2}{3}\left(\frac{\sqrt{3}}{2}\right) - \frac{2}{3}$

$= \frac{\pi}{18} + \frac{\sqrt{3}-2}{3}$

≈ 0.0852

c If k is the 20th percentile of X,

then $\int_0^k 6\cos 3x\, dx = 0.2$

$\therefore\ [2\sin 3x]_0^k = 0.2$

$\therefore\ 2\sin 3k - 2\sin 0 = 0.2$

$\therefore\ \sin 3k = 0.1$

$\therefore\ 3k \approx 0.100$

$\therefore\ k \approx 0.0334$

So, the 20th percentile of $X \approx 0.0334$

d $E(X^2) = \int_0^{\frac{\pi}{18}} 6x^2\cos 3x\, dx$

$\approx 0.009\,773 \quad$ {using technology}

$\therefore\ \text{Var}(X) \approx 0.009\,773 - (0.0852)^2$

$\approx 0.002\,511$

$\therefore\ \sigma_X \approx \sqrt{0.002\,511}$

≈ 0.0501

9 $P\left(X \leqslant \frac{2}{3}\right) = \frac{1}{243}$

$\therefore\ \int_0^{\frac{2}{3}} ax^4\, dx = \frac{1}{243}$

$\therefore\ \left[\frac{1}{5}ax^5\right]_0^{\frac{2}{3}} = \frac{1}{243}$

$\therefore\ \frac{1}{5}a \times \left(\frac{2}{3}\right)^5 = \frac{1}{243}$

$\therefore\ \frac{1}{5}a \times \frac{32}{243} = \frac{1}{243}$

$\therefore\ a = \frac{5}{32}$

So, $\int_0^k \frac{5}{32}x^4\, dx = 1$

$\therefore\ \left[\frac{1}{32}x^5\right]_0^k = 1$

$\therefore\ \frac{1}{32}k^5 = 1$

$\therefore\ k^5 = 32$

$\therefore\ k = 2$

10 a

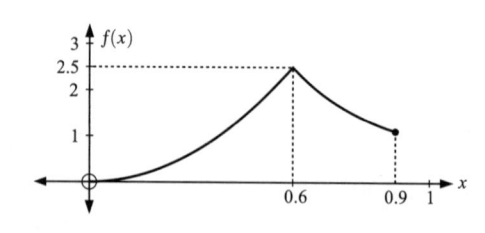

Mathematics HL (2nd edn), Chapter 29
STATISTICAL DISTRIBUTIONS OF CONTINUOUS RANDOM VARIABLES

b From the graph in **a**, $f(x) \geqslant 0$ for all $x \in [0, 0.9]$.

Also, the area under the curve $= \int_0^{0.6} \frac{125}{18} x^2 \, dx + \int_{0.6}^{0.9} \frac{9}{10x^2} \, dx$

$= \left[\frac{125}{54} x^3 \right]_0^{0.6} + \left[-\frac{9}{10x} \right]_{0.6}^{0.9}$

$= \frac{125}{54} \left(\frac{3}{5} \right)^3 + \left(-\frac{9}{9} \right) - \left(-\frac{9}{6} \right)$

$= \frac{1}{2} - 1 + \frac{3}{2}$

$= 1$ as required.

c $\mu = \int_0^{0.9} x f(x) \, dx$

$= \int_0^{0.6} \frac{125}{18} x^3 \, dx + \int_{0.6}^{0.9} \frac{9}{10x} \, dx$

$= \left[\frac{125}{72} x^4 \right]_0^{0.6} + \left[\frac{9}{10} \ln x \right]_{0.6}^{0.9}$

$= \frac{125}{72} (0.6)^4 + \frac{9}{10} \ln(0.9) - \frac{9}{10} \ln(0.6)$

≈ 0.590

d $E(X^2) = \int_0^{0.9} x^2 f(x) \, dx$

$= \int_0^{0.6} \frac{125}{18} x^4 \, dx + \int_{0.6}^{0.9} \frac{9}{10} \, dx$

$= \left[\frac{25}{18} x^5 \right]_0^{0.6} + \left[\frac{9}{10} x \right]_{0.6}^{0.9}$

$= \frac{25}{18} \left(\frac{3}{5} \right)^5 + \frac{9}{10} \left(\frac{9}{10} \right) - \frac{9}{10} \left(\frac{3}{5} \right)$

$= \frac{189}{500}$

$\therefore \text{Var}(X) \approx \frac{189}{500} - 0.58992^2$

≈ 0.0300

$\therefore \sigma_X \approx \sqrt{0.029\,996}$

≈ 0.173

From the calculations in **b**,

$\int_0^{0.6} f(x) \, dx = \int_{0.6}^{0.9} f(x) \, dx = \frac{1}{2}$

$\therefore$ median $= 0.6$

From the graph in **a**, the highest value of $f(x)$ occurs at $x = 0.6$

$\therefore$ mode $= 0.6$

e

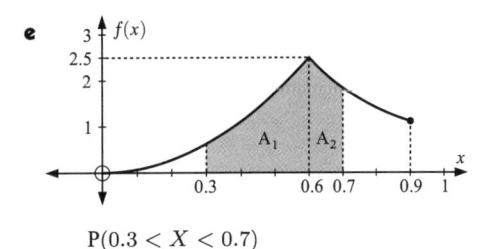

$P(0.3 < X < 0.7)$
$=$ shaded area
$= A_1 + A_2$

$= \int_{0.3}^{0.6} \frac{125}{18} x^2 \, dx + \int_{0.6}^{0.7} \frac{9}{10x^2} \, dx$

$= \left[\frac{125}{54} x^3 \right]_{0.3}^{0.6} + \left[-\frac{9}{10x} \right]_{0.6}^{0.7}$

$= \frac{125}{54} (0.6^3 - 0.3^3) + \left(-\frac{9}{7} \right) - \left(-\frac{9}{6} \right)$

≈ 0.652

$\therefore$ it takes between 0.3 hours ($= 18$ minutes) and 0.7 hours ($= 42$ minutes) to perform the task 65.2% of the time.

EXERCISE 29B.1

1

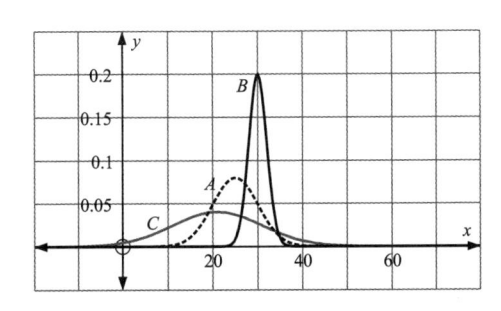

2 a/b As a result of random variations in the production process, the mean volume or diameter is likely to be the frequently occurring value. We expect variations around the mean to occur symmetrically.

3

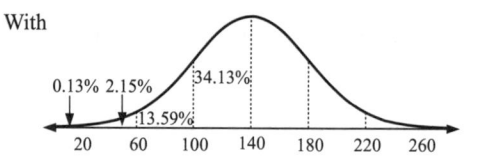

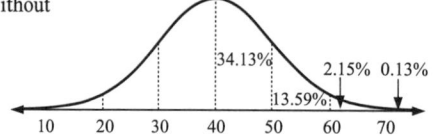

a P(without and < 50)
$\approx 50\% + 34.13\%$
$\approx 84.1\%$

b P(with and < 60)
$\approx 0.13\% + 2.15\%$
$\approx 2.28\%$

c i P(with and $20 \leqslant x \leqslant 60$)
$\approx 2.15\%$

ii P(without and $20 \leqslant x \leqslant 60$)
$\approx 2(34.13\% + 13.59\%)$
$\approx 95.4\%$

d i P(with and $x \geqslant 60$)
$\approx 13.59\% + 34.13\% + 50\%$
$\approx 97.7\%$

ii P(without and $x \geqslant 60$)
$\approx 2.15\% + 0.13\%$
$\approx 2.28\%$

4

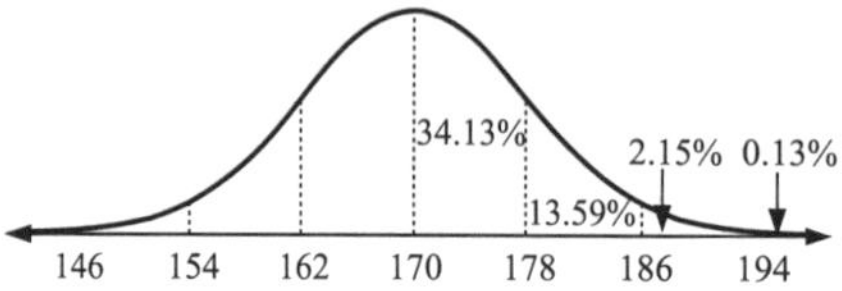

a i P($162 < x < 170$) $\approx 34.1\%$

ii P($170 < x < 186$) $\approx 34.13\% + 13.59\%$
$\approx 47.7\%$

b i P($178 < x < 186$)
$\approx 13.59\%$
≈ 0.136

ii P($x < 162$)
$\approx 1 - (0.5 + 0.3413)$
≈ 0.159

iii P($x < 154$)
$\approx 0.0215 + 0.0013$
≈ 0.0228

iv P($x > 162$)
$\approx 1 - 0.159$ {using **b ii**}
≈ 0.841

5

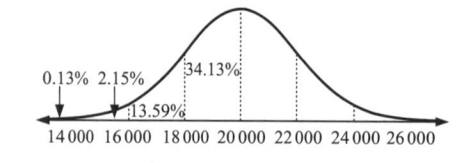

a P($x < 18\,000$)
$\approx 1 - 0.5 - 0.3413$
≈ 0.1587
$\therefore$ we expect that less than $18\,000$ bottles are filled on $260 \times 0.1587 \approx 41$ days.

b P($x > 16\,000$)
$\approx 0.1359 + 0.3413 + 0.5$
≈ 0.9772
$\therefore$ we expect that over $16\,000$ bottles are filled on $260 \times 0.9772 \approx 254$ days.

c P($18\,000 \leqslant x \leqslant 24\,000$)
$\approx 0.3413 \times 2 + 0.1359$
≈ 0.8185
$\therefore$ we expect that between $18\,000$ and $24\,000$ bottles are filled on 260×0.8185
≈ 213 days.

EXERCISE 29B.2

1 a 0.341 **b** 0.383 **c** 0.106

2 a 0.341 **b** 0.264 **c** 0.212 **d** 0.945 **e** 0.579 **f** 0.383

3 a $P(X < a) = 0.378$
$\therefore \ a \approx 21.4$

b $P(X \geqslant a) = 0.592$
$\therefore \ P(X < a) = 1 - 0.592 = 0.408$
$\therefore \ a \approx 21.8$

c $P(23 - a < X < 23 + a) = 0.427$
$\therefore \ P(23 < X < 23 + a) = \frac{1}{2}(0.427) = 0.2135$
$\therefore \ P(X < 23 + a) = 0.5 + 0.2135 = 0.7135$
$\therefore \ 23 + a \approx 25.82$
$\therefore \ a \approx 2.82$

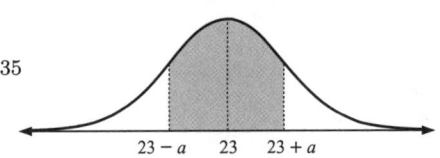

EXERCISE 29C.1

1 a $E\left(\dfrac{X-\mu}{\sigma}\right) = E\left(\dfrac{1}{\sigma}X - \dfrac{\mu}{\sigma}\right)$
$= \dfrac{1}{\sigma}E(X) - \dfrac{\mu}{\sigma}$
$= \dfrac{1}{\sigma}\mu - \dfrac{\mu}{\sigma}$
$= 0$

b $\mathrm{Var}\left(\dfrac{X-\mu}{\sigma}\right) = \mathrm{Var}\left(\dfrac{1}{\sigma}X - \dfrac{\mu}{\sigma}\right)$
$= \left(\dfrac{1}{\sigma}\right)^2 \mathrm{Var}(X)$
$= \dfrac{1}{\sigma^2} \times \sigma^2$
$= 1$

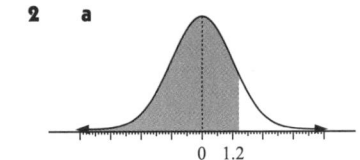

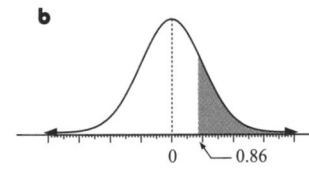

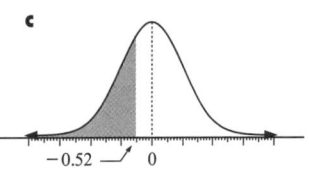

2 a
$P(Z \leqslant 1.2)$
≈ 0.8849
≈ 0.885

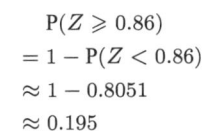

b
$P(Z \geqslant 0.86)$
$= 1 - P(Z < 0.86)$
$\approx 1 - 0.8051$
≈ 0.195

c
$P(Z \leqslant -0.52)$
≈ 0.3015
≈ 0.302

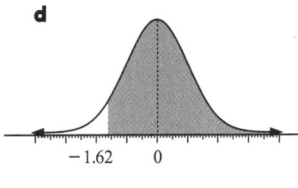

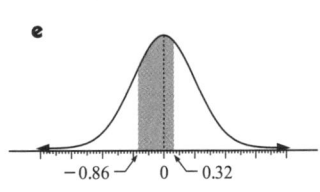

d
$P(Z \geqslant -1.62)$
$= 1 - P(Z < -1.62)$
$\approx 1 - 0.0526$
≈ 0.947

e
$P(-0.86 < Z < 0.32)$
$= P(Z < 0.32) - P(Z \leqslant -0.86)$
$\approx 0.6255 - 0.1949$
≈ 0.431

3 a $P(Z \geqslant 0.837) \approx 0.201$
c $P(Z \geqslant -0.876) \approx 0.809$
e $P(-2.367 \leqslant Z \leqslant -0.6503) \approx 0.249$

b $P(Z \leqslant 0.0614) \approx 0.524$
d $P(-0.3862 \leqslant Z \leqslant 0.2506) \approx 0.249$

4 a $P(-0.5 < Z < 0.5) \approx 0.383$

b $P(-1.960 < Z < 1.960) \approx 0.950$

5 a $P(Z \leqslant a) = 0.95$
$\therefore \quad a \approx 1.64$ {searching in tables or using technology}

b $P(Z \geqslant a) = 0.90$
$\therefore \quad 1 - P(Z < a) = 0.90$
$\therefore \quad P(Z < a) = 0.1$
$\therefore \quad a \approx -1.28 - \frac{3}{18}(0.01)$
$\therefore \quad a \approx -1.282$
$\therefore \quad a \approx -1.28$

6 a For Physics, $Z = \dfrac{83 - 78}{10.8} \approx 0.463$ For Chemistry, $Z = \dfrac{77 - 72}{11.6} \approx 0.431$

For Maths, $Z = \dfrac{84 - 74}{10.1} \approx 0.990$ For German, $Z = \dfrac{91 - 86}{9.6} \approx 0.521$

For Biology, $Z = \dfrac{72 - 62}{12.2} \approx 0.820$

b Maths, Biology, German, Physics, Chemistry

7 Z-score for algebra $= \dfrac{56 - 50.2}{15.8} \approx 0.3671$ Z-score for geometry $= \dfrac{x - 58.7}{18.7}$

$\therefore$ we need to solve $\dfrac{x - 58.7}{18.7} = 0.3671$

$\therefore \quad x - 58.7 \approx 6.86$

$\therefore \quad x \approx 65.6$ So, Pedro needs a result of 65.6%.

EXERCISE 29C.2

1 X is normal with mean 70, standard deviation 4.

a $P(X \geqslant 74)$
$= P\left(\dfrac{X - 70}{4} \geqslant \dfrac{74 - 70}{4}\right)$
$= P(Z \geqslant 1)$
$= 1 - P(Z < 1)$
$\approx 1 - 0.8413$
≈ 0.159

b $P(X \leqslant 68)$
$= P\left(\dfrac{X - 70}{4} \geqslant \dfrac{68 - 70}{4}\right)$
$= P(Z \leqslant -\tfrac{1}{2})$
≈ 0.309

c $P(60.6 \leqslant X \leqslant 68.4)$
$= P\left(\dfrac{60.6 - 70}{4} \leqslant \dfrac{X - 70}{4} \leqslant \dfrac{68.4 - 70}{4}\right)$
$= P(-2.35 \leqslant Z \leqslant -0.4)$
$\approx 0.3446 - 0.0094$
≈ 0.335

2 X is normal with mean 58.3 and standard deviation 8.96.

a $P(X \geqslant 61.8)$
$= P\left(\dfrac{X - 58.3}{8.96} \geqslant \dfrac{61.8 - 58.3}{8.96}\right)$
$= P(Z \geqslant 0.390\,625)$
≈ 0.348

b $P(X \leqslant 54.2)$
$= P\left(\dfrac{X - 58.3}{8.96} \leqslant \dfrac{54.2 - 58.3}{8.96}\right)$
$\approx P(Z \leqslant -0.4576)$
≈ 0.324

c $P(50.67 \leqslant X \leqslant 68.92)$
$= P\left(\dfrac{50.67 - 58.3}{8.96} \leqslant \dfrac{X - 58.3}{8.96} \leqslant \dfrac{68.92 - 58.3}{8.96}\right)$
$\approx P(-0.851\,56 \leqslant Z \leqslant 1.1853)$
≈ 0.685

3 L is normal with mean 50.2 mm and standard deviation 0.93 mm.

   a $P(L \geqslant 50)$

$$= P\left(\frac{L - 50.2}{0.93} \geqslant \frac{50 - 50.2}{0.93}\right)$$

$$\approx P(Z \geqslant -0.2151)$$

$$\approx 0.585$$

   b $P(L \leqslant 51)$

$$= P\left(\frac{L - 50.2}{0.93} \leqslant \frac{51 - 50.2}{0.93}\right)$$

$$\approx P(Z \leqslant 0.8602)$$

$$\approx 0.805$$

   c $P(49 \leqslant L \leqslant 50.5)$

$$= P\left(\frac{49 - 50.2}{0.93} \leqslant \frac{L - 50.2}{0.93} \leqslant \frac{50.5 - 50.2}{0.93}\right)$$

$$= P(-1.2903 \leqslant Z \leqslant 0.3226)$$

$$\approx 0.528$$

EXERCISE 29C.3

1 **a** $P(Z \leqslant k) = 0.81$

      $\therefore\ k \approx 0.87 + \frac{22}{28}(0.01)$

      $\therefore\ k \approx 0.878$

  b $P(Z \leqslant k) = 0.58$

      $\therefore\ k \approx 0.20 + \frac{7}{39}(0.01)$

      $\therefore\ k \approx 0.202$

  c $P(Z \leqslant k) = 0.17$

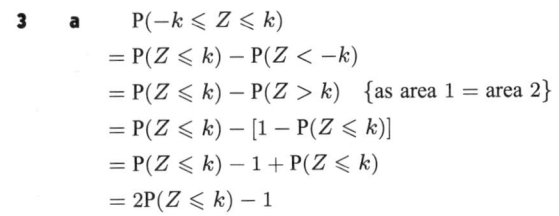

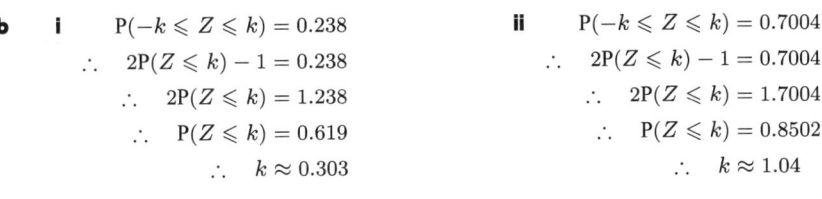

      $\therefore\ k \approx -0.96 + \frac{15}{26}(0.01)$

      $\therefore\ k \approx -0.954$

2 **a** $P(Z \leqslant k) = 0.384$

      $\therefore\ k \approx -0.295$

  b $P(Z \leqslant k) = 0.878$

      $\therefore\ k \approx 1.17$

  c $P(Z \leqslant k) = 0.1384$

      $\therefore\ k \approx -1.09$

3 **a** $P(-k \leqslant Z \leqslant k)$

$$= P(Z \leqslant k) - P(Z < -k)$$

$$= P(Z \leqslant k) - P(Z > k) \quad \{\text{as area 1 = area 2}\}$$

$$= P(Z \leqslant k) - [1 - P(Z \leqslant k)]$$

$$= P(Z \leqslant k) - 1 + P(Z \leqslant k)$$

$$= 2P(Z \leqslant k) - 1$$

  b **i** $P(-k \leqslant Z \leqslant k) = 0.238$

        $\therefore\ 2P(Z \leqslant k) - 1 = 0.238$

        $\therefore\ 2P(Z \leqslant k) = 1.238$

        $\therefore\ P(Z \leqslant k) = 0.619$

        $\therefore\ k \approx 0.303$

    ii $P(-k \leqslant Z \leqslant k) = 0.7004$

        $\therefore\ 2P(Z \leqslant k) - 1 = 0.7004$

        $\therefore\ 2P(Z \leqslant k) = 1.7004$

        $\therefore\ P(Z \leqslant k) = 0.8502$

        $\therefore\ k \approx 1.04$

4 **a** $P(X \leqslant k) = 0.9$

      $\therefore\ k \approx 79.1$ {using technology}

  b $P(X \geqslant k) = 0.8$

      $\therefore\ P(X < k) = 0.2$

      $\therefore\ k \approx 31.3$ {using technology}

EXERCISE 29D

1 Let X be the length of a bolt in cm.
Then X is normally distributed with $\mu = 19.8$ and $\sigma = 0.3$.
$\therefore\ P(19.7 < X < 20) \approx 0.378$

2 Let X be the money collected in dollars.
Then X is normally distributed with $\mu = 40$ and $\sigma = 6$.

  a $P(30.00 < X < 50.00) \approx 0.904$

                       $\approx 90.4\%$

  b $P(X \geqslant 50) \approx 0.0478$

          $\approx 4.78\%$

3 Let X be the result of the Physics test.
Then X is normally distributed with $\mu = 46$ and $\sigma = 25$.
We need to find k such that $P(X \geqslant k) = 0.07$
$$\therefore \quad 1 - P(X < k) = 0.07$$
$$\therefore \quad P(X < k) = 0.93$$
$$\therefore \quad k \approx 82.894$$
$$\therefore \quad k \approx 83 \quad \{\text{assuming } k \text{ is an integer}\}$$
So, the lowest score to get an A would be 83.

4 Let X be the length of an eel in cm.
Then X is normally distributed with $\mu = 41$ and $\sigma = \sqrt{11}$.
  a $P(X \geqslant 50) \approx 0.00333$
  b $P(40 \leqslant X \leqslant 50) \approx 0.615$
  $$\approx 61.5\%$$
  c $P(X \geqslant 45) \approx 0.114$
  So, we would expect $200 \times 0.114 \approx 23$ eels to be at least 45 cm long.

5
$$P(X \geqslant 35) = 0.32 \quad \text{and} \quad P(X \leqslant 8) = 0.26$$
$$\therefore \quad P(X < 35) = 0.68 \qquad \therefore \quad P\left(\frac{X-\mu}{\sigma} \leqslant \frac{8-\mu}{\sigma}\right) = 0.26$$
$$\therefore \quad P\left(\frac{X-\mu}{\sigma} < \frac{35-\mu}{\sigma}\right) = 0.68 \qquad \therefore \quad P\left(Z \leqslant \frac{8-\mu}{\sigma}\right) = 0.26$$
$$\therefore \quad P\left(Z < \frac{35-\mu}{\sigma}\right) = 0.68 \qquad \therefore \quad \frac{8-\mu}{\sigma} \approx -0.6433$$
$$\therefore \quad \frac{35-\mu}{\sigma} \approx 0.4677 \qquad \therefore \quad 8 - \mu \approx -0.6433\sigma \quad .... \text{ (2)}$$
$$\therefore \quad 35 - \mu \approx 0.4677\sigma \quad .... \text{ (1)}$$
Solving (1) and (2) simultaneously, $35 - 0.4677\sigma \approx 8 + 0.6433\sigma$
$$\therefore \quad 27 \approx 1.111\sigma$$
$$\therefore \quad \sigma \approx 24.3 \quad \text{and} \quad \mu = 35 - 0.4677 \times 24.3$$
$$\therefore \quad \mu \approx 23.6$$
So, $\mu \approx 23.6$ and $\sigma \approx 24.3$

6 a Let the mean be μ and standard deviation be σ.
Then $P(X \geqslant 80) = 0.1$ and $P(X \leqslant 30) = 0.15$
$$\therefore \quad P(X < 80) = 0.9$$
$$\therefore \quad P\left(\frac{X-\mu}{\sigma} < \frac{80-\mu}{\sigma}\right) = 0.9 \qquad \therefore \quad P\left(\frac{X-\mu}{\sigma} \leqslant \frac{30-\mu}{\sigma}\right) = 0.15$$
$$\therefore \quad P\left(Z < \frac{80-\mu}{\sigma}\right) = 0.9 \qquad \therefore \quad P\left(Z \leqslant \frac{30-\mu}{\sigma}\right) = 0.15$$
$$\therefore \quad \frac{80-\mu}{\sigma} \approx 1.2816 \qquad \therefore \quad \frac{30-\mu}{\sigma} \approx -1.0364$$
$$\therefore \quad 80 - \mu \approx 1.2816\sigma \quad .... \text{ (1)} \qquad \therefore \quad 30 - \mu \approx -1.0364\sigma \quad .... \text{ (2)}$$
Solving (1) and (2) simultaneously, $(80 - \mu) - (30 - \mu) \approx 1.2816\sigma + 1.0364\sigma$
$$50 \approx 2.318\sigma$$
$$\therefore \quad \sigma \approx \frac{50}{2.318} \approx 21.57$$
Using (1), $80 - \mu \approx 1.2816 \times 21.57 \approx 27.6$
$$\therefore \quad \mu \approx 52.36$$
$$\therefore \quad \mu \approx 52.4 \quad \text{and} \quad \sigma \approx 21.6$$

b Let X be the result of the mathematics exam.
   X is normally distributed with mean μ and standard deviation σ.
   We know that $P(X \geq 80) = 0.1$ and $P(X \leq 30) = 0.15$.
   So, from **a**, $\mu \approx 52.36$ and $\sigma \approx 21.57$.
   If part marks can be given, $P(X > 50) \approx 0.544$
   $$\approx 54.4\%$$
   If only integer marks can be given, $P(X \geq 51) \approx 0.525$
   $$\approx 52.5\%$$

7 a Let the mean be μ and standard deviation be σ and X be the diameter in cm.
   $\therefore \quad P(X < 1.94) = 0.02 \qquad$ and $\qquad P(X > 2.06) = 0.03$
   $\therefore \quad P\left(\dfrac{X-\mu}{\sigma} < \dfrac{1.94-\mu}{\sigma}\right) = 0.02 \qquad \therefore \quad P\left(\dfrac{X-\mu}{\sigma} > \dfrac{2.06-\mu}{\sigma}\right) = 0.03$
   $\therefore \quad P\left(Z < \dfrac{1.94-\mu}{\sigma}\right) = 0.02 \qquad \therefore \quad P\left(Z > \dfrac{2.06-\mu}{\sigma}\right) = 0.03$
   $\therefore \quad \dfrac{1.94-\mu}{\sigma} \approx -2.054 \qquad\qquad \therefore \quad P\left(Z \leq \dfrac{2.06-\mu}{\sigma}\right) = 0.97$
   $\therefore \quad 1.94 - \mu \approx -2.054\sigma \quad \text{.... (1)} \qquad\qquad \dfrac{2.06-\mu}{\sigma} \approx 1.881$
   $$2.06 - \mu \approx 1.881\sigma \quad \text{.... (2)}$$

   Solving (1) and (2) simultaneously, $(2.06 - \mu) - (1.94 - \mu) = 1.881\sigma + 2.054\sigma$
   $\therefore \quad 3.935\sigma = 0.12$
   $\therefore \quad \sigma \approx 0.0305$

   Using (1), $1.94 - \mu \approx -2.054 \times 0.0305 \approx -0.0626$
   $\therefore \quad \mu \approx 2.00$
   $\therefore \quad \mu \approx 2.00$ and $\sigma \approx 0.0305$

b Let Y be the number of tokens which will not operate the machine. This is a binomial situation with the probability $p = 0.02 + 0.03 = 0.05$ of failure to operate and $n = 20$. So, $Y \sim B(20, 0.05)$.
   $\therefore \quad$ P(at most one will not operate) $= P(Y \leq 1)$
   $$\approx 0.736$$

REVIEW SET 29A

1 If random variable X is the arm length in cm then X is normally distributed with $\mu = 64$ and $\sigma = 4$.

   a i $P(60 < X < 72)$ $\qquad\qquad$ **ii** $P(X > 60)$
   $\qquad \approx 2 \times 34.13\% + 13.59\% \qquad\qquad \approx 50\% + 34.13\%$
   $\qquad \approx 81.9\% \qquad\qquad\qquad\qquad\quad \approx 84.1\%$

   b $P(56 < X < 68) \approx 2 \times 0.3413 + 0.1359$
   $\qquad\qquad\qquad\qquad \approx 0.819$

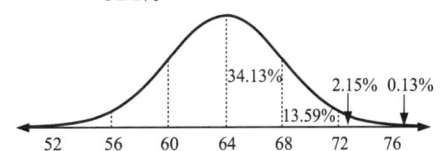

2 Let X be the rod length in mm.
   X is normally distributed with mean μ and $\sigma = 3$.
   Now $\quad P(X < 25) = 0.02$
   $\therefore \quad P\left(\dfrac{X-\mu}{3} < \dfrac{25-\mu}{3}\right) = 0.02 \qquad \therefore \quad \dfrac{25-\mu}{3} \approx -2.0537$
   $\therefore \quad P\left(Z < \dfrac{25-\mu}{3}\right) = 0.02 \qquad\qquad \therefore \quad 25 - \mu \approx -6.161$
   $\qquad\qquad\qquad\qquad\qquad\qquad\qquad\qquad \therefore \quad \mu \approx 31.2$
   $\therefore \quad$ the mean rod length is 31.2 mm.

3 a $\int_0^2 ax(x-3)\,dx = 1$

$\therefore\ a\int_0^2 (x^2 - 3x)\,dx = 1$

$\therefore\ a\left[\frac{1}{3}x^3 - \frac{3}{2}x^2\right]_0^2 = 1$

$\therefore\ a\left[\frac{8}{3} - 6\right] = 1$

$\therefore\ a\left(-\frac{10}{3}\right) = 1$

$\therefore\ a = -\frac{3}{10}$

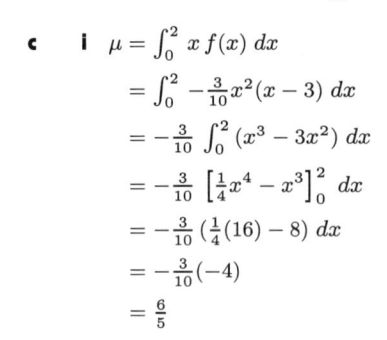

b

y, $f(x) = -\frac{3}{10}x(x-3)$, quadratic, 1.5, 2, 3, x

c i $\mu = \int_0^2 x f(x)\,dx$

$= \int_0^2 -\frac{3}{10}x^2(x-3)\,dx$

$= -\frac{3}{10}\int_0^2 (x^3 - 3x^2)\,dx$

$= -\frac{3}{10}\left[\frac{1}{4}x^4 - x^3\right]_0^2 dx$

$= -\frac{3}{10}\left(\frac{1}{4}(16) - 8\right)dx$

$= -\frac{3}{10}(-4)$

$= \frac{6}{5}$

ii $f(x)$ has maximum value when $x = 1.5$

$\therefore$ the mode $= 1.5$

iv $E(X^2) = \int_0^2 x^2 f(x)\,dx$

$= \int_0^2 -\frac{3}{10}x^3(x-3)\,dx$

$= 1.68$ {using technology}

$\therefore\ \text{Var}(X) = E(X^2) - \{E(X)\}^2$

$= 1.68 - (1.2)^2$

$= 0.24$

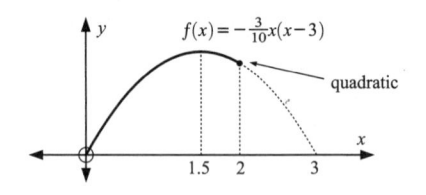

iii If the median is m, then

$\int_0^m f(x)\,dx = \frac{1}{2}$

$\int_0^m -\frac{3}{10}x(x-3)\,dx = \frac{1}{2}$

$\therefore\ \int_0^m (x^2 - 3x)\,dx = -\frac{5}{3}$

$\left[\frac{1}{3}x^3 - \frac{3}{2}x^2\right]_0^m = -\frac{5}{3}$

$\therefore\ \frac{1}{3}m^3 - \frac{3}{2}m^2 + \frac{5}{3} = 0$

$\therefore\ 2m^3 - 9m^2 + 10 = 0$

$\therefore\ m \approx -0.957,\ 1.24,\ 4.22$

  {using technology}

But $0 \leqslant m \leqslant 2$, so $m \approx 1.24$

d $P(1 \leqslant x \leqslant 2)$

$= \int_1^2 -\frac{3}{10}x(x-3)\,dx$

$= 0.65$ {using technology}

4 Let X be the volume of drink in mL.
Then X is normally distributed with $\mu = 376$.
Now $P(X < 375) = 0.023$

$\therefore\ P\left(\frac{X - 376}{\sigma} < \frac{375 - 376}{\sigma}\right) = 0.023$

$\therefore\ P\left(Z < \frac{-1}{\sigma}\right) = 0.023$

$\therefore\ -\frac{1}{\sigma} \approx -1.995$

$\therefore\ \sigma \approx 0.501$

$\therefore$ the standard deviation is 0.501 mL

5 $P(|Z| > k) = 0.376$

$\therefore\ P(Z > k\ \text{or}\ Z < -k) = 0.376$

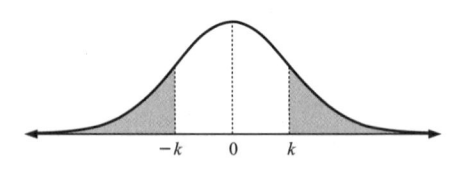

$-k$, 0, k

$\therefore\ P(Z < -k) = \frac{1}{2}(0.376) = 0.188$

$\therefore\ -k \approx -0.885$

$\therefore\ k \approx 0.885$

6 $P(|X - \mu| < 0.524) = P(-0.524 < X - \mu < 0.524)$

$= P\left(\frac{-0.524}{2} < \frac{X - \mu}{2} < \frac{0.524}{2}\right)$

$= P(-0.262 < Z < 0.262)$

≈ 0.207 {using technology}

7 Let X be the marks in the examination. Then X is normally distributed with $\mu = 49$ and $\sigma = 15$.
  a $P(X \geqslant 45) \approx 0.6051$
  So, $2376 \times 0.6051 \approx 1438$ students passed the examination.
  b Let k be the minimum mark required for a '7'.
  $\therefore \quad P(X \geqslant k) = 0.07$
  $\therefore \quad P(X < k) = 1 - 0.07 = 0.93$
  $\therefore \quad k \approx 71.1$
  $\therefore \quad k \approx 71$ (to the nearest integer)
  So the minimum mark required to obtain a '7' is 71 marks.
  c Let L and U be the lower and upper quartiles of the distribution.
  $\therefore \quad P(X \leqslant L) = 0.25$ and $P(X \leqslant U) = 0.75$
  $\therefore \quad L \approx 38.88$ {using technology} $\therefore \quad U \approx 59.12$ {using technology}
  $\therefore \quad$ the interquartile range $= U - L \approx 59.12 - 38.88 \approx 20.2$ marks

8 Let X be the length of the rods. X is normally distributed with $\sigma = 6$.
  Now $P(X \geqslant 89.52) = 0.0563$
  $\therefore \quad P(X < 89.52) = 1 - 0.0563$
  $\therefore \quad P\left(\dfrac{X - \mu}{6} < \dfrac{89.52 - \mu}{6}\right) = 0.9437$
  $\therefore \quad P\left(Z < \dfrac{89.52 - \mu}{6}\right) = 0.9437$
  $\therefore \quad \dfrac{89.52 - \mu}{6} \approx 1.5866$
  $\therefore \quad 89.52 - \mu \approx 9.52$
  $\therefore \quad \mu \approx 80.0$
  So, the mean is 80.0 cm.

  Since the normal distribution is symmetrical and bell-shaped, the median and modal lengths are also 80.0 cm.

9 a $\int_0^k e^{-\frac{1}{2}x}\, dx = 1$
  $\therefore \quad \left[-2e^{-\frac{1}{2}x}\right]_0^k = 1$
  $\therefore \quad -2e^{-\frac{k}{2}} - (-2e^0) = 1$
  $\therefore \quad 2e^{-\frac{k}{2}} = 1$
  $\therefore \quad e^{-\frac{k}{2}} = \frac{1}{2}$
  $\therefore \quad -\dfrac{k}{2} = \ln \frac{1}{2}$
  $\therefore \quad k = -2\ln\frac{1}{2} = \ln 4$

  b $P(\frac{1}{4} < X < \frac{7}{8})$
  $= \int_{\frac{1}{4}}^{\frac{7}{8}} e^{-\frac{1}{2}x}\, dx$
  $= \left[-2e^{-\frac{1}{2}x}\right]_{\frac{1}{4}}^{\frac{7}{8}}$
  $= -2e^{-\frac{7}{16}} - (-2e^{-\frac{1}{8}})$
  ≈ 0.474

  c Consider $\mu = \int_0^{\ln 4} xe^{-\frac{1}{2}x}\, dx$.
  We integrate by parts with $u = x \quad v' = e^{-\frac{1}{2}x}$
  $u' = 1 \quad v = -2e^{-\frac{1}{2}x}$
  $\therefore \quad \int xe^{-\frac{1}{2}x}\, dx$
  $= -2xe^{-\frac{1}{2}x} - \int -2e^{-\frac{1}{2}x}\, dx$
  $= -2xe^{-\frac{1}{2}x} - 4e^{-\frac{1}{2}x} + c$
  $= 2e^{-\frac{1}{2}x}(-x - 2) + c \quad \ldots \text{ (*)}$

So, $\mu = \int_0^{\ln 4} xe^{-\frac{1}{2}x}\, dx = \left[2e^{-\frac{1}{2}x}(-x-2)\right]_0^{\ln 4}$

$ = 2e^{-\frac{1}{2}\ln 4}(-\ln 4 - 2) - 2e^0(-2)$

$ = 2(\frac{1}{2})(-\ln 4 - 2) + 4$

$ = 2 - \ln 4$

Now consider $E(X^2) = \int_0^{\ln 4} x^2 e^{-\frac{1}{2}x}\, dx$.

We integrate by parts with $\quad u = x^2 \quad v' = e^{-\frac{1}{2}x}$

$ u' = 2x \quad v = -2e^{-\frac{1}{2}x}$

$\therefore \int x^2 e^{-\frac{1}{2}x}\, dx = -2x^2 e^{-\frac{1}{2}x} + 4\int xe^{-\frac{1}{2}x}\, dx$

$\phantom{\therefore \int x^2 e^{-\frac{1}{2}x}\, dx} = -2x^2 e^{-\frac{1}{2}x} + 4(2e^{-\frac{1}{2}x}(-x-2)) + c \quad \{\text{using } (*)\}$

$\phantom{\therefore \int x^2 e^{-\frac{1}{2}x}\, dx} = 2e^{-\frac{1}{2}x}(-x^2 - 4x - 8) + c$

$\therefore E(X^2) = \int_0^{\ln 4} x^2 e^{-\frac{1}{2}x}\, dx$

$ = \left[2e^{-\frac{1}{2}x}(-x^2 - 4x - 8)\right]_0^{\ln 4}$

$ = 2e^{-\frac{1}{2}\ln 4}\left(-(\ln 4)^2 - 4\ln 4 - 8\right) - 2e^0(-8)$

$ = 2(\frac{1}{2})(-(\ln 4)^2 - 4\ln 4 - 8) + 16$

$ = 8 - 4\ln 4 - (\ln 4)^2$

$\therefore \text{Var}(X) = E(X^2) - \{E(X)\}^2$

$\phantom{\therefore \text{Var}(X)} = E(X^2) - \mu^2$

$\phantom{\therefore \text{Var}(X)} = 8 - 4\ln 4 - (\ln 4)^2 - (2 - \ln 4)^2$

$\phantom{\therefore \text{Var}(X)} = 8 - 4\ln 4 - (\ln 4)^2 - (4 - 4\ln 4 + (\ln 4)^2)$

$\phantom{\therefore \text{Var}(X)} = 4 - 2(\ln 4)^2$

10 $ P(X < 90) \approx 0.975$

$\therefore P\left(\dfrac{X-50}{\sigma} < \dfrac{90-50}{\sigma}\right) \approx 0.975$

$\therefore P\left(Z < \dfrac{40}{\sigma}\right) \approx 0.975 \qquad$ So, the shaded area $= P(X \geq 80)$

$\therefore \dfrac{40}{\sigma} \approx 1.959\,96 \approx 0.0708$

$\therefore \sigma \approx 20.409$

REVIEW SET 29B

1 X is the contents of the container in mL.
X is normally distributed with $\mu = 377$ and $\sigma = 4.2$.

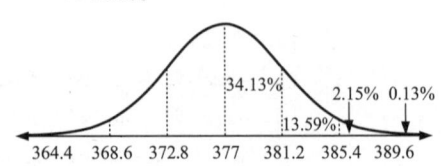

a i $\quad P(X < 368.6)$
$ \approx 2.15\% + 0.13\%$
$ \approx 2.28\%$

ii $\quad P(372.8 < X < 389.6)$
$ \approx 2 \times 34.13\% + 13.59\% + 2.15\%$
$ \approx 84.0\%$

b $\quad P(364.4 < X < 381.2)$
$ \approx 2 \times 0.3413 + 0.1359 + 0.0215$
$ \approx 0.840$

2 X is the life of a battery in weeks.
   X is normally distributed with $\mu = 33.2$ and $\sigma = 2.8$.
   a $P(X \geqslant 35) \approx 0.260$
   b We need to find k such that $P(X \leqslant k) = 0.08$
   $$\therefore \quad k \approx 29.3$$
   So, the manufacturer can expect that no more than 8% will fail for a maximum of 29.3 weeks.

3 Let X denote the mass of a Coffin Bay Oyster. X is distributed normally with a mean of 38.6 and a standard deviation of 6.3.

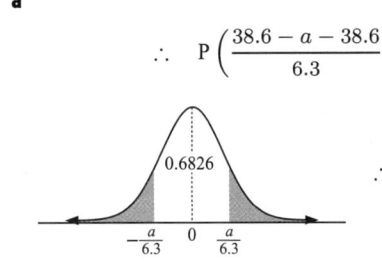

   a
   $$P(38.6 - a \leqslant X \leqslant 38.6 + a) = 0.6826$$
   $$\therefore \quad P\left(\frac{38.6 - a - 38.6}{6.3} \leqslant \frac{X - 38.6}{6.3} \leqslant \frac{38.6 + a - 38.6}{6.3}\right) = 0.6826$$
   $$\therefore \quad P\left(-\frac{a}{6.3} \leqslant Z \leqslant \frac{a}{6.3}\right) = 0.6826$$
   $$\therefore \text{ by symmetry, } P\left(Z \leqslant -\frac{a}{6.3}\right) = \frac{1 - 0.6826}{2}$$
   $$\therefore \quad P\left(Z \leqslant -\frac{a}{6.3}\right) = 0.1587 \quad \ldots \quad (*)$$
   $$\therefore \quad -\frac{a}{6.3} \approx -0.9998$$
   $$\therefore \quad a \approx 6.30 \text{ g}$$

   b
   $$P(X \geqslant b) = 0.8413$$
   $$\therefore \quad P(X < b) = 0.1587$$
   $$\therefore \quad P\left(\frac{X - 38.6}{6.3} < \frac{b - 38.6}{6.3}\right) = 0.1587$$
   $$\therefore \quad P\left(Z < \frac{b - 38.6}{6.3}\right) = 0.1587$$
   Comparing with $(*)$, $\frac{b - 38.6}{6.3} = -\frac{a}{6.3}$
   $$\therefore \quad b - 38.6 \approx -6.30$$
   $$\therefore \quad b \approx 32.3 \text{ g}$$

4 $f(x) = ax^2(2 - x)$ for $0 < x < 2$

   a Since $f(x)$ is a probability distribution function the area under the curve is 1.
   $$\therefore \quad \int_0^2 ax^2(2 - x)\, dx = 1$$
   $$\therefore \quad a \int_0^2 (2x^2 - x^3)\, dx = 1$$
   $$\therefore \quad a \left[\frac{2}{3}x^3 - \frac{1}{4}x^4\right]_0^2 = 1$$
   $$\therefore \quad a \left[\left(\frac{16}{3} - \frac{16}{4}\right) - 0\right] = 1$$
   $$\therefore \quad a \left(\frac{4}{3}\right) = 1$$
   $$\therefore \quad a = \frac{3}{4}$$

   b The mode is the most frequently occurring score, which is the value of x when $f(x)$ is a maximum.
   $$f(x) = \frac{3}{4}\left(2x^2 - x^3\right)$$
   $$f'(x) = \frac{3}{4}\left(4x - 3x^2\right)$$
   $$= \frac{3}{4}x(4 - 3x)$$
   which has sign diagram: $-\;|\;+\;|\;-$ at $0,\ \frac{4}{3}$
   $\therefore \quad f(x)$ is a maximum when $x = \frac{4}{3}$
   $\therefore$ the mode is $\frac{4}{3}$.

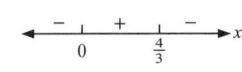

   c If the median is m, then,
   $$\int_0^m \frac{3}{4}x^2(2 - x)\, dx = \frac{1}{2}$$
   $$\frac{3}{4}\int_0^m (2x^2 - x^3)\, dx = \frac{1}{2}$$
   $$\therefore \quad \left[\frac{2}{3}x^3 - \frac{1}{4}x^4\right]_0^m = \frac{2}{3}$$
   $$\therefore \quad \frac{2}{3}m^3 - \frac{1}{4}m^4 = \frac{2}{3}$$
   Using technology, $m \approx 1.2285$
   So, the median is approximately 1.23.

   d $P(0.6 < x < 1.2)$
   $$= \int_{0.6}^{1.2} \frac{3}{4}x^2(2 - x)\, dx$$
   $$= \int_{0.6}^{1.2} \left(\frac{3}{2}x^2 - \frac{3}{4}x^3\right) dx$$
   $$= \left[\frac{1}{2}x^3 - \frac{3}{16}x^4\right]_{0.6}^{1.2}$$
   $$= \frac{(1.2)^3}{2} - \frac{3(1.2)^4}{16} - \frac{(0.6)^3}{2} + \frac{3(0.6)^4}{16}$$
   $$= 0.3915$$

5 **a** T is the lifetime in years of a solar cell component.

$\therefore \ P(T \leqslant 1) = \int_0^1 0.4e^{-0.4t} \, dt$

$ = \left[-e^{-0.4t}\right]_0^1$

$ = -e^{-0.4} - (-e^0)$

$ = 1 - e^{-0.4}$

$ \approx 0.329\,68$

b Let X be the number of components not working after one year.

Then $X \sim B(5, 0.329\,68)$

$\therefore$ P(solar cell still operates)
$= P(X \leqslant 2)$ {at least 3 work}
$=$ binomcdf(5, 0.329 68, 2)
≈ 0.796

6 **a** Consider the integral $\displaystyle\int_0^1 \frac{4}{1+x^2} \, dx$.

Let $x = \tan\theta$, $\dfrac{dx}{d\theta} = \sec^2\theta$

When $x = 0$, $\theta = 0$, and when $x = 1$, $\theta = \dfrac{\pi}{4}$

$\therefore \ \displaystyle\int_0^1 \frac{4}{1+x^2} \, dx = \int_0^{\frac{\pi}{4}} \frac{4}{1+\tan^2\theta}\sec^2\theta \, d\theta$

$\phantom{\therefore \ \int_0^1 \frac{4}{1+x^2} \, dx} = \int_0^{\frac{\pi}{4}} 4 \, d\theta \quad \{1+\tan^2\theta = \sec^2\theta\}$

$\phantom{\therefore \ \int_0^1 \frac{4}{1+x^2} \, dx} = [4\theta]_0^{\frac{\pi}{4}} = \pi$

$\therefore \ \displaystyle\int_0^1 \frac{4}{1+x^2} \, dx \neq 1$, and so $f(x)$ cannot be a probability density function.

b $k f(x) = \begin{cases} \dfrac{4k}{1+x^2} & \text{for } 0 \leqslant x \leqslant 1 \\ 0 & \text{otherwise.} \end{cases}$

For a probability density function, $\displaystyle\int_0^1 \frac{4k}{1+x^2} \, dx = 1$

$\therefore \ k \displaystyle\int_0^1 \frac{4}{1+x^2} \, dx = 1$

$\therefore \ k(\pi) = 1$

$\therefore \ k = \dfrac{1}{\pi}$

c $\mu = \dfrac{1}{\pi} \displaystyle\int_0^1 \frac{4x}{1+x^2} \, dx$

$ = \dfrac{2}{\pi} \displaystyle\int_0^1 \frac{2x}{1+x^2} \, dx$

$ = \dfrac{2}{\pi} \left[\ln(1+x^2)\right]_0^1 \quad \{\text{as } 1+x^2 > 0\}$

$ = \dfrac{2}{\pi}(\ln 2 - \ln 1)$

$ = \dfrac{2}{\pi} \ln 2$

$E(X^2) = \dfrac{4}{\pi} \displaystyle\int_0^1 \frac{x^2}{1+x^2} \, dx$

$ = \dfrac{4}{\pi} \displaystyle\int_0^1 \left(1 - \frac{1}{1+x^2}\right) dx$

$ = \dfrac{4}{\pi} \displaystyle\int_0^1 1 \, dx - \dfrac{4}{\pi} \displaystyle\int_0^1 \frac{1}{1+x^2} \, dx$

$ = \dfrac{4}{\pi}[x]_0^1 - \dfrac{4}{\pi}[\arctan x]_0^1$

$ = \dfrac{4}{\pi} - \dfrac{4}{\pi} \times \dfrac{\pi}{4}$

$ = \dfrac{4}{\pi} - 1$

$\therefore \ \text{Var}(X) = E(X^2) - \mu^2$

$\phantom{\therefore \ \text{Var}(X)} = \dfrac{4}{\pi} - 1 - \left(\dfrac{2}{\pi} \ln 2\right)^2$

$\phantom{\therefore \ \text{Var}(X)} = \dfrac{4}{\pi} - 1 - \left(\dfrac{2\ln 2}{\pi}\right)^2$

7 a $\int_0^2 ax(4-x^2)\,dx = 1$

$\therefore\ a\int_0^2 (4x - x^3)\,dx = 1$

$\therefore\ a\left[2x^2 - \dfrac{x^4}{4}\right]_0^2 = 1$

$\therefore\ a(8-4) = 1$

$\therefore\ a = \dfrac{1}{4}$

b The mode is the value of x when $f(x)$ is a maximum.

$f(x) = \dfrac{1}{4}x(4-x^2) = x - \dfrac{1}{4}x^3$

$\therefore\ f'(x) = 1 - \dfrac{3}{4}x^2$

$\therefore\ f'(x) = 0$ when $x^2 = \dfrac{4}{3}$

$\therefore\ x = \dfrac{2}{\sqrt{3}}\quad \{0 \leqslant x \leqslant 2\}$

$\therefore$ the mode is $\dfrac{2}{\sqrt{3}}$

c If the median is m, then

$\int_0^m (x - \dfrac{1}{4}x^3)\,dx = \dfrac{1}{2}$

$\therefore\ \left[\dfrac{x^2}{2} - \dfrac{x^4}{16}\right]_0^m = \dfrac{1}{2}$

$\therefore\ \dfrac{m^2}{2} - \dfrac{m^4}{16} = \dfrac{1}{2}$

$\therefore\ m^4 - 8m^2 + 8 = 0$

Using technology, $m \approx 1.08$

So, the median ≈ 1.08.

d $\mu = \int_0^2 (x^2 - \dfrac{1}{4}x^4)\,dx$

$= \left[\dfrac{x^3}{3} - \dfrac{x^5}{20}\right]_0^2$

$= \dfrac{8}{3} - \dfrac{32}{20}$

$= \dfrac{16}{15}$

8 Let X be the heights of 18 year old boys. X is normally distributed with $\mu = 187$.

Now $P(X > 193) = 0.15$

$\therefore\ P(X \leqslant 193) = 0.85$

$\therefore\ P\left(\dfrac{X - 187}{\sigma} \leqslant \dfrac{193 - 187}{\sigma}\right) = 0.85$

$\therefore\ P\left(Z \leqslant \dfrac{6}{\sigma}\right) = 0.85$

$\therefore\ \dfrac{6}{\sigma} \approx 1.0364$

$\therefore\ \sigma \approx 5.789$

So, $P(X > 185) \approx 0.635$

$\therefore$ the probability that two 18 year old boys are taller than 185 cm $\approx 0.635^2$

≈ 0.403

9 a $P(X \leqslant 30) = 0.0832$ and $P(X \geqslant 90) = 0.101$

$\therefore\ P\left(\dfrac{X - \mu}{\sigma} \leqslant \dfrac{30 - \mu}{\sigma}\right) \approx 0.0832$

$\therefore\ P\left(Z \leqslant \dfrac{30 - \mu}{\sigma}\right) \approx 0.0832$

$\therefore\ \dfrac{30 - \mu}{\sigma} \approx -1.383\,864$

$\therefore\ 30 - \mu \approx -1.383\,864\sigma$ ...... (1)

$\therefore\ P(X < 90) = 0.899$

$\therefore\ P\left(\dfrac{X - \mu}{\sigma} < \dfrac{90 - \mu}{\sigma}\right) = 0.899$

$\therefore\ P\left(Z < \dfrac{90 - \mu}{\sigma}\right) = 0.899$

$\therefore\ \dfrac{90 - \mu}{\sigma} \approx 1.275\,874$

$\therefore\ 90 - \mu = 1.275\,874\sigma$ ...... (2)

Solving (1) and (2) simultaneously,

$(90 - \mu) - (30 - \mu) \approx 1.275\,874\sigma - (-1.383\,864\sigma)$

$\therefore\ 60 \approx 2.6597\sigma$

$\therefore\ \sigma \approx 22.559$

Using (2), $90 - \mu \approx 1.275\,874(22.559)$
$\therefore \quad \mu \approx 90 - 1.275\,874(22.559)$
$\qquad \approx 61.218$

b $P(|X - \mu| > 7) = P(X - 61.218 > 7 \text{ or } X - 61.218 < -7)$
$\qquad = P(X > 68.218 \text{ or } X < 54.218)$
$\qquad \approx 0.378 + 0.378$
$\qquad \approx 0.756$

10 a $\int_0^k f(x)\,dx = 1$

$\therefore \quad \int_0^2 \frac{x}{5}\,dx + \int_2^k \frac{8}{5x^2}\,dx = 1$

$\therefore \quad \left[\frac{x^2}{10}\right]_0^2 + \left[-\frac{8}{5x}\right]_2^k = 1$

$\therefore \quad \frac{4}{10} + \left(-\frac{8}{5k}\right) - \left(-\frac{8}{10}\right) = 1$

$\therefore \quad -\frac{8}{5k} = -\frac{2}{10}$

$\therefore \quad 10k = 80$

$\therefore \quad k = 8$

b If m is the median of X, then $\int_0^m f(x)\,dx = \frac{1}{2}$

$\therefore$ since $\int_0^2 \frac{x}{5}\,dx < \frac{1}{2}$,

$\int_0^2 \frac{x}{5}\,dx + \int_2^m \frac{8}{5x^2}\,dx = \frac{1}{2}$

$\therefore \quad \frac{4}{10} + \left[-\frac{8}{5x}\right]_2^m = \frac{1}{2}$

$\therefore \quad \frac{4}{10} + \left(-\frac{8}{5m}\right) - \left(-\frac{8}{10}\right) = \frac{1}{2}$

$\therefore \quad -\frac{8}{5m} = -\frac{7}{10}$

$\therefore \quad 35m = 80$

$\therefore \quad m = \frac{16}{7}$

$\therefore$ the median is $2\frac{2}{7}$

c $\mu = \int_0^8 x\,f(x)\,dx$

$\quad = \int_0^2 \frac{x^2}{5}\,dx + \int_2^8 \frac{8}{5x}\,dx$

$\quad = \left[\frac{x^3}{15}\right]_0^2 + \left[\frac{8}{5}\ln|x|\right]_2^8$

$\quad = \frac{8}{15} + \frac{8}{5}\ln 8 - \frac{8}{5}\ln 2$

$\quad \approx 2.75$

$E(X^2) = \int_0^8 x^2 f(x)\,dx$

$\quad = \int_0^2 \frac{x^3}{5}\,dx + \int_2^8 \frac{8}{5}\,dx$

$\quad = \left[\frac{x^4}{20}\right]_0^2 + \left[\frac{8}{5}x\right]_2^8$

$\quad = \frac{16}{20} + \frac{64}{5} - \frac{16}{5}$

$\quad = \frac{52}{5}$

$\therefore \quad \text{Var}(X) = E(X^2) - \mu^2$

$\qquad \approx \frac{52}{5} - 2.751^2$

$\qquad \approx 2.83$

Chapter 30
MISCELLANEOUS QUESTIONS

EXERCISE 30

1 a $(-1+i\sqrt{2})^3 = (-1)^3 + 3(-1)^2 i\sqrt{2} + 3(-1)(i\sqrt{2})^2 + (i\sqrt{2})^3$
$= -1 + 3\sqrt{2}i + 6 - 2\sqrt{2}i$
$= 5 + i\sqrt{2}$

b $|5+i\sqrt{2}| = \sqrt{25+2} = \sqrt{27} = (\sqrt{3})^3$
$\arg(5+i\sqrt{2}) = \theta = \arctan\left(\frac{\sqrt{2}}{5}\right)$
$\therefore \ 5+i\sqrt{2} = \left(\sqrt{3}\right)^3 \text{cis}\left[\arctan\left(\frac{\sqrt{2}}{5}\right)\right]$
$\therefore \ a = \sqrt{3}, \ \theta = \arctan\left(\frac{\sqrt{2}}{5}\right)$

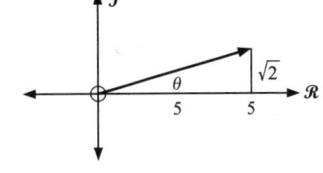

c $z^3 = 5 + i\sqrt{2} = \left(\sqrt{3}\right)^3 \text{cis}\left[\arctan\left(\frac{\sqrt{2}}{5}\right)\right]$
$\therefore \ z = \sqrt{3}\,\text{cis}\left[\dfrac{\arctan\left(\frac{\sqrt{2}}{5}\right) + k2\pi}{3}\right]$ where $k = 0, 1, 2$ {De Moivre}

d From **a**, one of the solutions to $z^3 = 5 + i\sqrt{2}$ is
$z = -1 + i\sqrt{2}$
$\therefore \ z = \sqrt{3}\,\text{cis}\,\phi$
$\therefore \ z = \sqrt{3}\,\text{cis}\left[\arccos\left(\frac{-1}{\sqrt{3}}\right)\right]$ 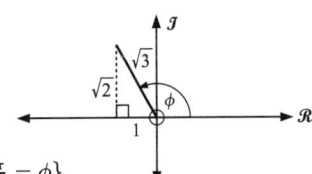
This corresponds to the solution in **c** where $k = 1$ $\{\frac{\theta}{3} + \frac{2\pi}{3} = \phi\}$

Equating arguments gives: $\dfrac{\arctan\left(\frac{\sqrt{2}}{5}\right) + 2\pi}{3} = \arccos\left(\frac{-1}{\sqrt{3}}\right)$

$\therefore \ \arctan\left(\frac{\sqrt{2}}{5}\right) + 2\pi = 3\arccos\left(\frac{-1}{\sqrt{3}}\right)$

2 a $|-2-2i| = \sqrt{4+4} = \sqrt{8} = (\sqrt{2})^3$ and $\arg(-2-2i) = \frac{-3\pi}{4}$
So, when $z^3 = -2 - 2i$, $z^3 = (\sqrt{2})^3 \text{cis}\left(\frac{-3\pi}{4} + k2\pi\right)$
$\therefore \ z = \sqrt{2}\,\text{cis}\left(\frac{-\pi}{4} + k\frac{2\pi}{3}\right)$, $k = 0, 1, 2$ {De Moivre}
$\therefore$ the cube roots are: $\sqrt{2}\,\text{cis}\left(-\frac{\pi}{4}\right)$, $\sqrt{2}\,\text{cis}\left(\frac{5\pi}{12}\right)$, $\sqrt{2}\,\text{cis}\left(\frac{13\pi}{12}\right)$

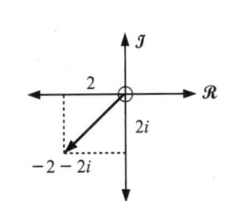

b

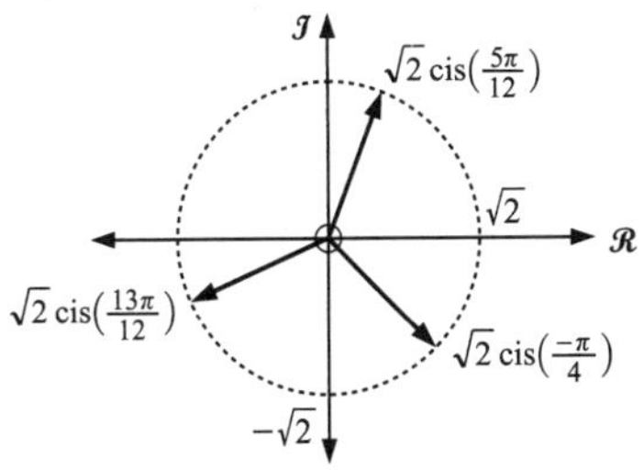

c $\alpha_1 + \alpha_2 + \alpha_3$
$= \sqrt{2}\left[\text{cis}\left(\frac{-\pi}{4}\right) + \text{cis}\left(\frac{5\pi}{12}\right) + \text{cis}\left(\frac{13\pi}{12}\right)\right]$
$= \sqrt{2}\left[a^{-3} + a^5 + a^{13}\right]$ where $a = \text{cis}\left(\frac{\pi}{12}\right)$
$= \sqrt{2}a^{-3}\left[1 + a^8 + a^{16}\right]$
$= \sqrt{2}a^{-3}\left[\dfrac{(a^8)^3 - 1}{a^8 - 1}\right]$ {sum of a geometric series}
$= \dfrac{\sqrt{2}}{a^3}\left[\dfrac{a^{24} - 1}{a^8 - 1}\right]$
$= \dfrac{\sqrt{2}}{a^3}\left[\dfrac{\left[\text{cis}\left(\frac{\pi}{12}\right)\right]^{24} - 1}{a^8 - 1}\right] = \dfrac{\sqrt{2}}{a^3}\left[\dfrac{\text{cis}(2\pi) - 1}{a^8 - 1}\right]$
$= 0$

d Let $z^n = \beta \operatorname{cis}(0 + k2\pi)$ {as $\operatorname{cis}(0 + k2\pi) = 1$}

$\therefore \ z = \beta^{\frac{1}{n}} \left[\operatorname{cis}\left(\frac{k2\pi}{n}\right)\right], \quad k = 0, 1, 2, 3, \ldots, n-1$ {De Moivre}

$\therefore \ z = \beta^{\frac{1}{n}} \operatorname{cis} 0, \ \beta^{\frac{1}{n}} \operatorname{cis}\left(\frac{2\pi}{n}\right), \ \beta^{\frac{1}{n}} \operatorname{cis}\left(\frac{4\pi}{n}\right), \ldots, \beta^{\frac{1}{n}} \operatorname{cis}\left(\frac{(n-1)2\pi}{n}\right)$

$\therefore \ z = \beta^{\frac{1}{n}}, \ \beta^{\frac{1}{n}}\alpha, \ \beta^{\frac{1}{n}}\alpha^2, \ \beta^{\frac{1}{n}}\alpha^3, \ldots, \beta^{\frac{1}{n}}\alpha^{n-1}$ where $\alpha = \operatorname{cis}\left(\frac{2\pi}{n}\right)$

The sum of these zeros is

$\beta^{\frac{1}{n}}\left[1 + \alpha + \alpha^2 + \alpha^3 + \ldots + \alpha^{n-1}\right]$

$= \beta^{\frac{1}{n}}\left[\frac{1-\alpha^n}{1-\alpha}\right]$ {sum of a geometric series with $u_1 = 1$, $r = \alpha$, "n" $= n$}

$= \beta^{\frac{1}{n}}\left[\frac{1-\operatorname{cis} 2\pi}{1-\alpha}\right]$ {since $\alpha^n = \left[\operatorname{cis}\left(\frac{2\pi}{n}\right)\right]^n = \operatorname{cis} 2\pi$}

$= \beta^{\frac{1}{n}}(0)$ {as $\operatorname{cis} 2\pi = 1$}

$= 0$

3 a $(1-i)^2 = 1 - 2i + i^2 = -2i$

$\therefore \ (1-i)^{4n} = \left[(1-i)^2\right]^{2n} = (-2i)^{2n} = \left[(-2i)^2\right]^n = (-4)^n$

b $(1-i)^{16} = (1-i)^{4\times 4} = (-4)^4 = 256$ {using $(1-i)^{4n} = (-4)^n$}

c If $z^{16} = 256$ we have a polynomial with real coefficients.
From **b**, $1 - i$ is one solution and so $1 + i$ must also be a solution {Theorem of real polynomials}
Thus $z = 1 \pm i$ are two solutions of $z^{16} = 256$.

4 a $z = \frac{-1 + i\sqrt{3}}{4}$ $w = \frac{\sqrt{2} + i\sqrt{2}}{4}$

$= \frac{1}{2}\left(-\frac{1}{2} + i\frac{\sqrt{3}}{2}\right)$ $= \frac{1}{2}\left(\frac{1}{\sqrt{2}} + i\frac{1}{\sqrt{2}}\right)$

$= \frac{1}{2}\operatorname{cis}\left(\frac{2\pi}{3}\right)$ $= \frac{1}{2}\operatorname{cis}\left(\frac{\pi}{4}\right)$

$= \frac{1}{2}\left(\cos\frac{2\pi}{3} + i\sin\frac{2\pi}{3}\right)$ $= \frac{1}{2}(\cos\frac{\pi}{4} + i\sin\frac{\pi}{4})$

b $zw = \frac{1}{2}\operatorname{cis}\left(\frac{2\pi}{3}\right) \times \frac{1}{2}\operatorname{cis}\left(\frac{\pi}{4}\right)$

$= \frac{1}{4}\operatorname{cis}\left(\frac{2\pi}{3} + \frac{\pi}{4}\right)$

$= \frac{1}{4}\operatorname{cis}\left(\frac{11\pi}{12}\right)$

$= \frac{1}{4}\left(\cos\left(\frac{11\pi}{12}\right) + i\sin\left(\frac{11\pi}{12}\right)\right)$

c $zw = \frac{1}{16}(-1 + i\sqrt{3})(\sqrt{2} + i\sqrt{2}) = \frac{1}{16}\left(\left[-\sqrt{2} - \sqrt{6}\right] + i\left[\sqrt{6} - \sqrt{2}\right]\right)$

Equating real and imaginary parts of zw gives $\cos\left(\frac{11\pi}{12}\right) = \frac{-\sqrt{2}-\sqrt{6}}{4}$ and $\sin\left(\frac{11\pi}{12}\right) = \frac{\sqrt{6}-\sqrt{2}}{4}$.

5 $S_n = n^3 + 2n - 1$

Now $u_n = S_n - S_{n-1}, \quad n > 1$

$= n^3 + 2n - 1 - \left[(n-1)^3 + 2(n-1) - 1\right]$

$= n^3 + 2n - 1 - \left[n^3 - 3n^2 + 3n - 1\right] - 2n + 2 + 1$

$= \cancel{n^3} + \cancel{2n} - \cancel{1} - \cancel{n^3} + 3n^2 - 3n + \cancel{1} - \cancel{2n} + 3$

$= 3n^2 - 3n + 3, \quad n > 1$

and $u_1 = S_1 = 2$

$\therefore \ u_1 = 2, \ u_n = 3n^2 - 3n + 3, \ n > 1$

6 At any point $A(x, y)$, $\dfrac{dy}{dx} = \dfrac{y - 0}{x - (x - \frac{1}{2})} = 2y$

$\therefore \ \dfrac{1}{y} \dfrac{dy}{dx} = 2$

$\therefore \ \displaystyle\int \dfrac{1}{y} \dfrac{dy}{dx} dx = \int 2 \, dx$

$\therefore \ \displaystyle\int \dfrac{1}{y} dy = \int 2 \, dx$

$\therefore \ \ln |y| = 2x + c$

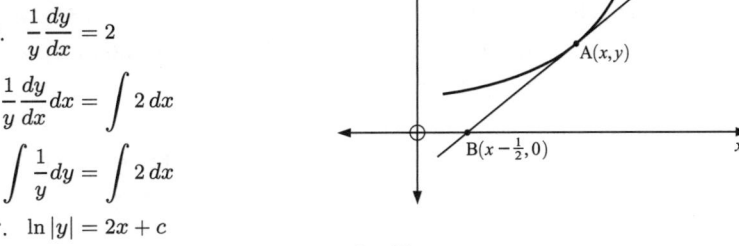

$\therefore \ |y| = e^c e^{2x}$

$\therefore \ y = \pm e^c e^{2x}$

$\quad = A e^{2x}$

But $C\left(0, \dfrac{1}{e}\right)$ lies on this curve,

so $\dfrac{1}{e} = A e^0$ and hence $A = \dfrac{1}{e}$

So, the curve is $y = \dfrac{1}{e} e^{2x}$ or $y = e^{2x - 1}$

7 P lies on the unit circle, so $OQ = \cos \theta$ and $PQ = \sin \theta$

In $\triangle OP_1 Q_1$, $OP_1 = OQ = \cos \theta$

So, $\sin \theta = \dfrac{P_1 Q_1}{\cos \theta}$ and $\cos \theta = \dfrac{OQ_1}{\cos \theta}$

$\therefore \ OQ_1 = \cos^2 \theta$ and $P_1 Q_1 = \sin \theta \cos \theta$

Likewise in $\triangle OP_2 Q_2$, $\sin \theta = \dfrac{P_2 Q_2}{\cos^2 \theta}$ and $\cos \theta = \dfrac{OQ_2}{\cos^2 \theta}$

$\therefore \ OQ_2 = \cos^3 \theta$ and $P_2 Q_2 = \sin \theta \cos^2 \theta$

Thus $PQ + P_1 Q_1 + P_2 Q_2 + P_3 Q_3 + \ldots$

$= \sin \theta + \sin \theta \cos \theta + \sin \theta \cos^2 \theta + \sin \theta \cos^3 \theta + \ldots$

$= \sin \theta (1 + \cos \theta + \cos^2 \theta + \cos^3 \theta + \ldots)$

$= \sin \theta \left(\dfrac{1}{1 - \cos \theta}\right)$ $\quad$ {sum of an infinite geometric series with $|r| = |\cos \theta| \leqslant 1$}

$= \dfrac{\sin \theta}{1 - \cos \theta}$

$= \dfrac{2 \sin\left(\frac{\theta}{2}\right) \cos\left(\frac{\theta}{2}\right)}{2 \sin^2 \left(\frac{\theta}{2}\right)} = \cot\left(\dfrac{\theta}{2}\right)$

8 We integrate by parts with $\quad u = \arctan x \quad v' = x$

$\qquad\qquad\qquad\qquad\qquad u' = \dfrac{1}{1 + x^2} \quad v = \dfrac{x^2}{2}$

$\therefore \ \displaystyle\int x \arctan x \, dx$

$= \arctan x \left(\dfrac{x^2}{2}\right) - \displaystyle\int \dfrac{x^2}{2(1 + x^2)} dx$

$= \tfrac{1}{2} x^2 \arctan x - \tfrac{1}{2} \displaystyle\int \dfrac{1 + x^2 - 1}{1 + x^2} dx$

$= \tfrac{1}{2} x^2 \arctan x - \tfrac{1}{2} \displaystyle\int \left(1 - \dfrac{1}{1 + x^2}\right) dx$

$= \tfrac{1}{2} x^2 \arctan x - \dfrac{x}{2} + \tfrac{1}{2} \arctan x + c$

Check:

$\dfrac{d}{dx} \left(\tfrac{1}{2} x^2 \arctan x - \tfrac{1}{2} x + \tfrac{1}{2} \arctan x + c\right)$

$= x \arctan x + \tfrac{1}{2} x^2 \left(\dfrac{1}{1 + x^2}\right) - \tfrac{1}{2} + \tfrac{1}{2} \left(\dfrac{1}{1 + x^2}\right) + 0$

$= x \arctan x + \dfrac{\tfrac{1}{2} x^2 - \tfrac{1}{2}(1 + x^2) + \tfrac{1}{2}}{1 + x^2}$

$= x \arctan x + \dfrac{0}{1 + x^2}$

$= x \arctan x \quad \checkmark$

9 a $\log_2(x^2 - 2x + 1) = 1 + \log_2(x - 1)$
$\therefore \log_2(x - 1)^2 - \log_2(x - 1) = 1$
$\therefore 2\log_2(x - 1) - \log_2(x - 1) = 1$
$\therefore \log_2(x - 1) = 1$
$\therefore x - 1 = 2^1$
$\therefore x = 3$

b $3^{2x+1} = 5(3^x) + 2$
$\therefore 3(3^x)^2 - 5(3^x) - 2 = 0$
$\therefore 3m^2 - 5m - 2 = 0 \quad \{m = 3^x\}$
$\therefore (3m + 1)(m - 2) = 0$
$\therefore m = -\tfrac{1}{3}$ or 2
$\therefore 3^x = -\tfrac{1}{3}$ or $3^x = 2$
The first equation is impossible as $3^x > 0$ for all x.
$\therefore 3^x = 2$
$\therefore x = \dfrac{\ln 2}{\ln 3} \approx 0.631$

10 Consider $\dfrac{3x - 1}{|x + 1|} > 2$.
If $x = -1$, LHS is undefined, so $x = -1$ is not a solution.
If $x \neq -1$, $|x + 1| > 0$ and so $3x - 1 > 2|x + 1|$.
So, if $x > -1$, $\quad 3x - 1 > 2x + 2 \quad \therefore x > 3$
$\quad\;\;$ if $x < -1$, $\quad 3x - 1 > -2x - 2 \quad \therefore 5x > -1$ and so $x > -\tfrac{1}{5}$, which is impossible.
Thus, $x > 3$ is the solution.

11 $\sin^2 x + \sin x - 2 = 0$, $\quad -2\pi \leqslant x \leqslant 2\pi$
$\therefore (\sin x + 2)(\sin x - 1) = 0$
$\therefore \sin x = -2$ or 1
$\therefore \sin x = 1 \quad \{$as $-1 \leqslant \sin x \leqslant 1\}$
$\therefore x = \tfrac{\pi}{2} + k2\pi, \; k \in \mathbb{Z}$
$\therefore x = -\tfrac{3\pi}{2}$ or $\tfrac{\pi}{2}$

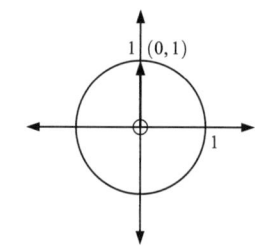

12 $f(x) = \ln x$ has inverse $f^{-1}(x) = e^x$.
$g(x) = 3 + x$ has inverse given by $\quad x = 3 + y$
$\qquad\qquad\qquad\qquad\qquad\qquad\qquad \therefore y = x - 3 \quad$ so $\quad g^{-1}(x) = x - 3$.

a $f^{-1}(2) \times g^{-1}(2)$
$= e^2 \times -1$
$= -e^2$

b $(f \circ g)(x) = f(g(x)) = f(3 + x)$
$\qquad\qquad\qquad\qquad\quad = \ln(3 + x)$
$\therefore$ the inverse of $(f \circ g)(x)$ is $x = \ln(3 + y)$
$\therefore 3 + y = e^x$
$\therefore y = e^x - 3$
So, $(f \circ g)^{-1}(x) = e^x - 3$
and $(f \circ g)^{-1}(2) = e^2 - 3$

13 $\sin \theta = -\tfrac{7}{25}$

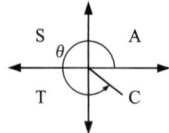

a $\cos \theta$
$= \sqrt{1 - \sin^2 \theta}$
$= \sqrt{1 - \tfrac{49}{625}}$
$= \tfrac{24}{25}$

b $\tan \theta$
$= \dfrac{\sin \theta}{\cos \theta}$
$= -\tfrac{7}{25} \div \tfrac{24}{25}$
$= -\tfrac{7}{24}$

c $\sin 2\theta$
$= 2 \sin \theta \cos \theta$
$= 2 \left(\tfrac{-7}{25}\right)\left(\tfrac{24}{25}\right)$
$= -\tfrac{336}{625}$

d $\sec 2\theta$
$= \dfrac{1}{\cos 2\theta}$
$= \dfrac{1}{2\cos^2 \theta - 1}$
$= \dfrac{1}{2\left(\tfrac{24}{25}\right)^2 - 1}$
$= \dfrac{625}{527}$

14 $\sqrt{3}\cos x \csc x + 1 = 0$, $0 \leqslant x \leqslant 2\pi$

$\therefore\ \sqrt{3}\cos x \left(\dfrac{1}{\sin x}\right) = -1$

$\therefore\ \dfrac{\cos x}{\sin x} = -\dfrac{1}{\sqrt{3}}$

$\therefore\ \tan x = -\sqrt{3}$

$\therefore\ x = \dfrac{2\pi}{3}$ or $\dfrac{5\pi}{3}$

15 Let X be the number of snails.

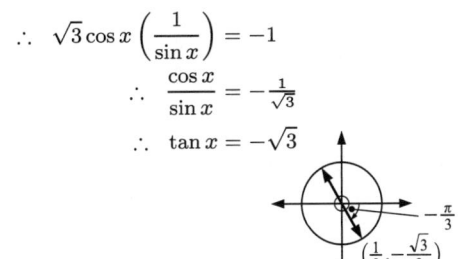

$\mu = \sigma^2 = m$ and $\sigma = d$ $\therefore\ m = d^2$

Now $P(X = 8) = \frac{1}{2}P(X = 7)$

where $P(X = x) = \dfrac{m^x e^{-m}}{x!} = \dfrac{d^{2x} e^{-d^2}}{x!}$

$\therefore\ \dfrac{d^{16} e^{-d^2}}{8!} = \dfrac{1}{2} \dfrac{d^{14} e^{-d^2}}{7!}$

$\therefore\ \dfrac{d^2}{8} = \dfrac{1}{2}$

$\therefore\ d = 2$ {as $d > 0$}

16

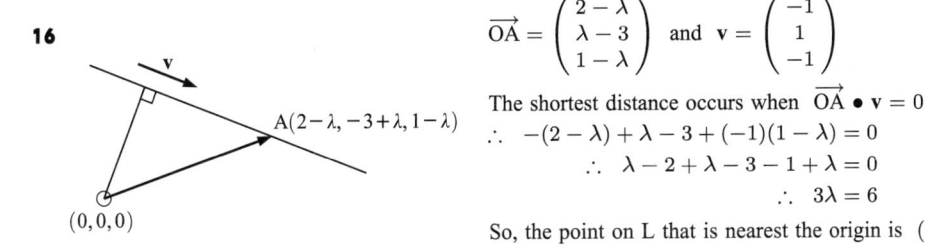

$\overrightarrow{OA} = \begin{pmatrix} 2-\lambda \\ \lambda - 3 \\ 1 - \lambda \end{pmatrix}$ and $\mathbf{v} = \begin{pmatrix} -1 \\ 1 \\ -1 \end{pmatrix}$

The shortest distance occurs when $\overrightarrow{OA} \bullet \mathbf{v} = 0$

$\therefore\ -(2 - \lambda) + \lambda - 3 + (-1)(1 - \lambda) = 0$

$\therefore\ \lambda - 2 + \lambda - 3 - 1 + \lambda = 0$

$\therefore\ 3\lambda = 6$ $\therefore\ \lambda = 2$

So, the point on L that is nearest the origin is $(0, -1, -1)$.

17 $f'(x) > 0$ and $f''(x) < 0$ for all x

$\therefore\ f(x)$ is increasing and concave downwards for all x.

a $f(2) = 1$ and $f'(2) = 2$

$\therefore\ (2, 1)$ lies on the curve and the tangent at this point has gradient 2

$\therefore\ $ the equation of the tangent is $y = 2x + c$

and $1 = 2(2) + c$, so $c = -3$

$\therefore\ $ the tangent has equation $y = 2x - 3$.

b

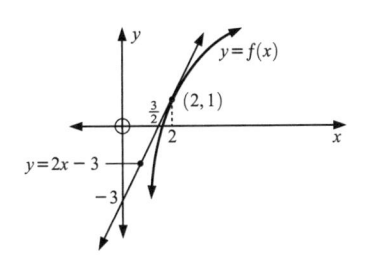

c As $f(x)$ is increasing it has *at most one* zero. But $f(x)$ is also concave downwards for all x, so it always lies below the tangent shown. So, for $x < \frac{3}{2}$, the tangent's y-values are negative and so $f(x)$ is also negative. Thus $f(x)$ has *exactly one* zero.

d From the graph, the x-intercept of $y = f(x)$ lies inside $]\frac{3}{2}, 2[$.

18 P_n is "$2n^3 - 3n^2 + n + 31 \geqslant 0$" for $n \in \mathbb{Z}$, $n \geqslant -2$.

Proof: (By the principle of mathematical induction)

(1) If $n = -2$, $2(-2)^3 - 3(-2)^2 + (-2) + 31 = -16 - 12 - 2 + 31 = 1$ which is $\geqslant 0$

$\therefore\ P_{-2}$ is true.

(2) If P_k is assumed true then $2k^3 - 3k^2 + k + 31 \geqslant 0$

Thus $2(k+1)^3 - 3(k+1)^2 + (k+1) + 31$

$= 2(k^3 + 3k^2 + 3k + 1) - 3(k^2 + 2k + 1) + k + 32$

$= \left[2k^3 - 3k^2 + k + 31\right] + 6k^2 + 6k + 2 - 6k - 3 + 1$

$= \underbrace{\left[2k^3 - 3k^2 + k + 31\right]}_{\geqslant 0 \text{ \{using } P_k\}} + \underbrace{6k^2}_{\geqslant 0 \text{ as } k^2 \geqslant 0 \text{ for all } k}$

$\geqslant 0$

Thus P_{k+1} is true whenever P_k is true.

$\therefore\ $ since P_{-2} is true, P_n is true for all $n \in \mathbb{Z}$, $n \geqslant -2$ {Principle of mathematical induction}

19 P_n is "$\sum_{r=1}^{n} r3^r = \frac{3}{4}[(2n-1)3^n + 1]$" for $n \in \mathbb{Z}^+$.

Proof: (By the principle of mathematical induction)

(1) If $n = 1$, LHS $= \sum_{r=1}^{1} r3^r = 1(3)^1 = 3$

RHS $= \frac{3}{4}[(1)3^1 + 1] = \frac{3}{4} \times 4 = 3$ ∴ P_1 is true.

(2) If P_k is assumed true, then $\sum_{r=1}^{k}(r3^r) = \frac{3}{4}\left[(2k-1)3^k + 1\right]$

Thus $\sum_{r=1}^{k+1} r3^r = \sum_{r=1}^{k} r3^r + (k+1)3^{k+1}$

$= \frac{3}{4}\left[(2k-1)3^k + 1\right] + (k+1)3^{k+1}$ {using P_k}

$= \frac{3}{4}\left[(2k-1)3^k + 1 + \frac{4}{3}(k+1)3^{k+1}\right]$

$= \frac{3}{4}\left[(2k-1)3^k + 1 + (4k+4)3^k\right]$

$= \frac{3}{4}\left[(6k+3)3^k + 1\right]$

$= \frac{3}{4}\left[(2k+1)3^{k+1} + 1\right]$

$= \frac{3}{4}\left[(2(k+1)-1)3^{k+1} + 1\right]$

Thus P_{k+1} is true whenever P_k is true.

∴ since P_1 is true, P_n is true for all $n \in \mathbb{Z}^+$ {Principle of mathematical induction}

20 P_n is "$\dfrac{1}{a(a+1)} + \dfrac{1}{(a+1)(a+2)} + \dfrac{1}{(a+2)(a+3)} + \ldots + \dfrac{1}{(a+n-1)(a+n)} = \dfrac{n}{a(a+n)}$" for $n \in \mathbb{Z}^+$.

Proof: (By the principle of mathematical induction)

(1) If $n = 1$, LHS $= \dfrac{1}{a(a+1)}$ and RHS $= \dfrac{1}{a(a+1)}$ ∴ P_1 is true.

(2) If P_k is assumed true then

$\dfrac{1}{a(a+1)} + \dfrac{1}{(a+1)(a+2)} + \ldots + \dfrac{1}{(a+k-1)(a+k)} = \dfrac{k}{a(a+k)}$

Thus $\dfrac{1}{a(a+1)} + \dfrac{1}{(a+1)(a+2)} + \ldots + \dfrac{1}{(a+k-1)(a+k)} + \dfrac{1}{(a+k)(a+k+1)}$

$= \dfrac{k}{a(a+k)} + \dfrac{1}{(a+k)(a+k+1)}$ {using P_k}

$= \dfrac{k}{a(a+k)}\left(\dfrac{a+k+1}{a+k+1}\right) + \dfrac{1}{(a+k)(a+k+1)}\left(\dfrac{a}{a}\right)$

$= \dfrac{ak + k^2 + k + a}{a(a+k)(a+k+1)}$

$= \dfrac{(a+k)(k+1)}{a(a+k)(a+k+1)}$

$= \dfrac{k+1}{a(a+[k+1])}$

Thus P_{k+1} is true whenever P_k is true.

∴ since P_1 is true, P_n is true for all $n \in \mathbb{Z}^+$ {Principle of mathematical induction}

21 P_n is "$x^n - y^n$ has factor $x - y$" for $n \in \mathbb{Z}^+$.

Proof: (By the principle of mathematical induction)

(1) If $n = 1$, $x^1 - y^1$ has factor $x - y$ ✓ ∴ P_1 is true.

(2) If P_k is assumed true then $x^k - y^k = (x-y)f_k(x, y)$, where $f_k(x, y)$ is another factor.

Now $x^{k+1} - y^{k+1} = x(x^k - y^k) + xy^k - y^{k+1}$
$= x(x-y)f_k(x, y) + y^k(x-y)$
$= (x-y)\left[xf_k(x, y) + y^k\right]$
$\equiv (x-y)f_{k+1}(x, y)$

$\therefore$ $x^{k+1} - y^{k+1}$ has factor $x - y$.
Thus P_{k+1} is true whenever P_k is true.
$\therefore$ since P_1 is true, P_n is true for all $n \in \mathbb{Z}^+$ {Principle of mathematical induction}

22 P_n is "$3(5^{2n+1}) + 2^{3n+1}$ is divisible by 17" for $n \in \mathbb{Z}^+$.
Proof: (By the principle of mathematical induction)
(1) If $n = 1$, $3(5^3) + 2^{3+1} = 391 = 17 \times 23$ where $23 \in \mathbb{Z}$ $\therefore$ P_1 is true.
(2) If P_k is assumed true, then $3(5^{2k+1}) + 2^{3k+1} = 17A$ for some $A \in \mathbb{Z}$
Thus $3(5^{2(k+1)+1}) + 2^{3(k+1)+1}$
$= 3(5^{2k+1+2}) + 2^{3k+1+3}$
$= 3 \times 25 \times 5^{2k+1} + 8 \times 2^{3k+1}$
$= 25\left(17A - 2^{3k+1}\right) + 8 \times 2^{3k+1}$ {by rearranging and substituting P_k}
$= 25 \times 17 \times A + (8 - 25)2^{3k+1}$
$= 25 \times 17 \times A - 17 \times 2^{3k+1}$
$= 17\left(25A - 2^{3k+1}\right)$ where $25A - 2^{3k+1} \in \mathbb{Z}$

Thus P_{k+1} is true whenever P_k is true.
$\therefore$ since P_1 is true, P_n is true for all $n \in \mathbb{Z}^+$ {Principle of mathematical induction}

23 a P_n is: "$(1+x)^n = 1 + \binom{n}{1}x + \binom{n}{2}x^2 + \dots + \binom{n}{n}x^n$" for $n \in \mathbb{Z}^+$.
Proof: (By the principle of mathematical induction)
(1) If $n = 1$, LHS $= (1+x)^1 = 1+x$
RHS $= 1 + \binom{1}{1}x = 1+x$ $\therefore$ P_1 is true.
(2) If P_k is assumed true, then
$(1+x)^k = 1 + \binom{k}{1}x + \binom{k}{2}x^2 + \dots + \binom{k}{k}x^k$
Thus $(1+x)^{k+1} = \left[1 + \binom{k}{1}x + \binom{k}{2}x^2 + \dots + \binom{k}{k}x^k\right][1+x]$
$= 1 + \binom{k}{1}x + \binom{k}{2}x^2 + \binom{k}{3}x^3 + \dots + \binom{k}{k}x^k$
$\qquad + x + \binom{k}{1}x^2 + \binom{k}{2}x^3 + \dots + \binom{k}{k-1}x^k + \binom{k}{k}x^{k+1}$
$= 1 + \left[\binom{k}{1} + \binom{k}{0}\right]x + \left[\binom{k}{2} + \binom{k}{1}\right]x^2 + \dots$
$\qquad + \left[\binom{k}{k} + \binom{k}{k-1}\right]x^k + \binom{k}{k}x^{k+1}$
$= 1 + \binom{k+1}{1}x + \binom{k+1}{2}x^2 + \dots + \binom{k+1}{k}x^k + \binom{k+1}{k+1}x^{k+1}$
{Using Pascal's Rule and $\binom{k+1}{k+1} = \binom{k}{k} = 1$}

Thus P_{k+1} is true whenever P_k is true.
$\therefore$ since P_1 is true, P_n is true for all $n \in \mathbb{Z}^+$ {Principle of mathematical induction}

b Letting $x = \dfrac{b}{a}$, $\left(1 + \dfrac{b}{a}\right)^n = 1 + \binom{n}{1}\dfrac{b}{a} + \binom{n}{2}\dfrac{b^2}{a^2} + \dots + \binom{n}{n}\dfrac{b^n}{a^n}$, $n \in \mathbb{Z}^+$

$\therefore$ $a^n\left(1 + \dfrac{b}{a}\right)^n = a^n + \binom{n}{1}a^{n-1}b + \binom{n}{2}a^{n-2}b^2 + \dots + \binom{n}{n}b^n$

$\therefore$ $\left[a\left(1 + \dfrac{b}{a}\right)\right]^n = a^n + \binom{n}{1}a^{n-1}b + \binom{n}{2}a^{n-2}b^2 + \dots + \binom{n}{n}b^n$

$\therefore$ $(a+b)^n = a^n + \binom{n}{1}a^{n-1}b + \binom{n}{2}a^{n-2}b^2 + \dots + \binom{n}{n}b^n$

24 P_n is "$\dfrac{1}{\sin 2x} + \dfrac{1}{\sin 4x} + \dfrac{1}{\sin 8x} + \ldots + \dfrac{1}{\sin(2^n x)} = \cot x - \cot(2^n x)$" for $n \in \mathbb{Z}^+$.

Proof: (By the principle of mathematical induction)

(1) If $n = 1$, LHS $= \dfrac{1}{\sin 2x}$ and RHS $= \cot x - \cot 2x$

$$= \dfrac{\cos x}{\sin x} - \dfrac{\cos 2x}{\sin 2x}$$

$$= \dfrac{\cos x}{\sin x}\left(\dfrac{2\cos x}{2\cos x}\right) - \dfrac{\cos 2x}{\sin 2x}$$

$$= \dfrac{2\cos^2 x - \cos 2x}{\sin 2x}$$

$$= \dfrac{2\cos^2 x - [2\cos^2 x - 1]}{\sin 2x}$$

$$= \dfrac{1}{\sin 2x}$$

$\therefore$ P_1 is true.

(2) If P_k is true, $\dfrac{1}{\sin 2x} + \dfrac{1}{\sin 4x} + \ldots + \dfrac{1}{\sin(2^k x)} = \cot x - \cot(2^k x)$

$\therefore \dfrac{1}{\sin 2x} + \dfrac{1}{\sin 4x} + \ldots + \dfrac{1}{\sin(2^k x)} + \dfrac{1}{\sin(2^{k+1} x)}$

$= \cot x - \cot(2^k x) + \dfrac{1}{\sin(2^{k+1} x)}$

$= \cot x + \dfrac{1}{\sin(2^{k+1} x)} - \dfrac{\cos(2^k x)}{\sin(2^k x)}\left(\dfrac{2\cos(2^k x)}{2\cos(2^k x)}\right)$

$= \cot x + \dfrac{1}{\sin(2^{k+1} x)} - \dfrac{2\cos^2(2^k x)}{\sin(2^{k+1} x)}$

$= \cot x + \dfrac{1 - 2\cos^2(2^k x)}{\sin(2^{k+1} x)}$

$= \cot x + \dfrac{-\cos(2^{k+1} x)}{\sin(2^{k+1} x)}$ $\{\cos 2\theta = 2\cos^2 \theta - 1\}$

$= \cot x - \cot(2^{k+1} x)$

Thus P_{k+1} is true whenever P_k is true.

$\therefore$ since P_1 is true, P_n is true for all $n \in \mathbb{Z}^+$ {Principle of mathematical induction}

25 As $y^2 = 4x$, $2y\dfrac{dy}{dx} = 4$ and so $\dfrac{dy}{dx} = \dfrac{2}{y}$.

But the tangent has gradient m, so at the point of contact, $m = \dfrac{2}{y}$ or $y = \dfrac{2}{m}$.

So, the y-coordinate of the point of contact is $\dfrac{2}{m}$.

The x-coordinate of the point of contact is $\dfrac{y^2}{4} = \dfrac{4}{m^2} \div 4 = \dfrac{1}{m^2}$

$\therefore$ the point of contact is $\left(\dfrac{1}{m^2}, \dfrac{2}{m}\right)$.

This point lies on $y = mx + c$, so $\dfrac{2}{m} = m\left(\dfrac{1}{m^2}\right) + c$

$\therefore \dfrac{2}{m} = \dfrac{1}{m} + c$

$\therefore c = \dfrac{1}{m}$

26 **a** Since $\dfrac{x^2}{a^2} + \dfrac{y^2}{b^2} = 1$, $y^2 = b^2\left(1 - \dfrac{x^2}{a^2}\right) = \dfrac{b^2}{a^2}(a^2 - x^2)$

$$\therefore\ y = \pm\dfrac{b}{a}\sqrt{a^2 - x^2}$$

$y = \dfrac{b}{a}\sqrt{a^2 - x^2}$ is the top half of the ellipse

$\therefore\ $ shaded area $= \int_0^a y\,dx = \int_0^a \dfrac{b}{a}\sqrt{a^2 - x^2}\,dx$

$\qquad\qquad\qquad = \dfrac{b}{a}\int_0^a \sqrt{a^2 - x^2}\,dx$

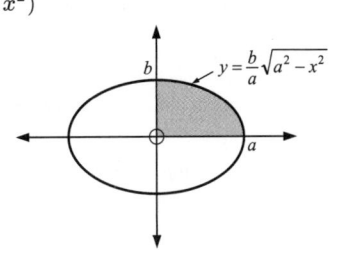

b Let $x = a\sin\theta$, $\dfrac{dx}{d\theta} = a\cos\theta$

when $x = 0$, $\sin\theta = 0$, $\theta = 0$
when $x = a$, $\sin\theta = 1$, $\theta = \dfrac{\pi}{2}$

$\therefore\ $ shaded area $= \dfrac{b}{a}\int_0^{\frac{\pi}{2}} \sqrt{a^2 - a^2\sin^2\theta}\ a\cos\theta\,d\theta$

$\qquad\qquad\qquad = b\int_0^{\frac{\pi}{2}} a\sqrt{1 - \sin^2\theta}\cos\theta\,d\theta$

$\qquad\qquad\qquad = ab\int_0^{\frac{\pi}{2}} \cos^2\theta\,d\theta$

$\qquad\qquad\qquad = ab\int_0^{\frac{\pi}{2}} \left(\tfrac{1}{2} + \tfrac{1}{2}\cos 2\theta\right)d\theta$

$\qquad\qquad\qquad = ab\left[\tfrac{1}{2}\theta + \tfrac{1}{4}\sin 2\theta\right]_0^{\frac{\pi}{2}}$

$\qquad\qquad\qquad = ab\left(\tfrac{\pi}{4} + \tfrac{1}{4}\sin\pi - 0 - 0\right)$

$\qquad\qquad\qquad = \dfrac{\pi ab}{4}$

$\therefore\ $ area of ellipse $= 4 \times$ shaded area $= \pi ab$

c Volume $= 2\pi \int_0^a y^2\,dx$

$\qquad\qquad = 2\pi \dfrac{b^2}{a^2}\int_0^a (a^2 - x^2)\,dx$

$\qquad\qquad = 2\pi \dfrac{b^2}{a^2}\left[a^2 x - \dfrac{x^3}{3}\right]_0^a$

$\qquad\qquad = 2\pi \dfrac{b^2}{a^2}\left(a^3 - \dfrac{a^3}{3} - 0\right)$

$\qquad\qquad = 2\pi \times \dfrac{b^2}{a^2} \times \dfrac{2a^3}{3}$

$\qquad\qquad = \tfrac{4}{3}\pi a b^2$

(**Note:** When $a = b$, $V = \tfrac{4}{3}\pi a^3$, which is the volume of a sphere of radius a.)

27 Now $f(x) = (a_1 x - b_1)^2 + (a_2 x - b_2)^2 + \ldots + (a_n x - b_n)^2$
is the sum of squares, so $f(x) \geqslant 0$ for all x.

But $f(x) = \sum_{i=1}^{n}(a_i x - b_i)^2$

$\qquad = \left(\sum_{i=1}^{n} a_i^2\right)x^2 - 2\left(\sum_{i=1}^{n} a_i b_i\right)x + \left(\sum_{i=1}^{n} b_i^2\right)$

Since $f(x) \geqslant 0$ for all x, the discriminant must be non-positive.

Hence $\left(2\sum_{i=1}^{n} a_i b_i\right)^2 - 4\left(\sum_{i=1}^{n} a_i^2\right)\left(\sum_{i=1}^{n} b_i^2\right) \leqslant 0$

$\therefore\ 4\left(\sum_{i=1}^{n} a_i^2\right)\left(\sum_{i=1}^{n} b_i^2\right) \geqslant 4\left(\sum_{i=1}^{n} a_i b_i\right)^2$

$\therefore\ \left(\sum_{i=1}^{n} a_i^2\right)\left(\sum_{i=1}^{n} b_i^2\right) \geqslant \left(\sum_{i=1}^{n} a_i b_i\right)^2$

28 Since $\dfrac{x^2}{a^2} + \dfrac{y^2}{b^2} = 1$, $\quad b^2x^2 + a^2y^2 = a^2b^2 \quad \ldots\ (*)$

$\therefore\ b^2(2x) + a^2(2y)\dfrac{dy}{dx} = 0$

$\therefore\ $ at the point (x_1, y_1), $\quad \dfrac{dy}{dx} = -\dfrac{b^2x}{a^2y} = -\dfrac{b^2x_1}{a^2y_1}$

$\therefore\ $ the equation of the tangent is $\dfrac{y - y_1}{x - x_1} = \dfrac{-b^2x_1}{a^2y_1}$

$\therefore\ a^2y_1y - a^2y_1^2 = -b^2x_1x + b^2x_1^2$

$\therefore\ a^2y_1y + b^2x_1x = b^2x_1^2 + a^2y_1^2$

As (x_1, y_1) lies on the curve, $b^2x_1^2 + a^2y_1^2 = a^2b^2 \quad$ {from $(*)$}

$\therefore\ $ the equation of the tangent is $b^2x_1x + a^2y_1y = a^2b^2$

$\qquad\qquad$ or $\left(\dfrac{x_1}{a^2}\right)x + \left(\dfrac{y_1}{b^2}\right)y = 1 \quad$ {dividing throughout by a^2b^2}

29 a $\sin 2A + \sin 2B + \sin 2C$

$= \sin 2A + \sin 2B + \sin(2\pi - 2A - 2B) \qquad$ {as $A + B + C = \pi$}

$= \sin 2A + \sin 2B - \sin(2A + 2B) \qquad\qquad\ $ {$\sin(2\pi - \theta) = -\sin\theta$}

$= \sin 2A + \sin 2B - [\sin 2A \cos 2B + \cos 2A \sin 2B]$

$= \sin 2A(1 - \cos 2B) + \sin 2B(1 - \cos 2A)$

$= 2\sin A \cos A(2\sin^2 B) + 2\sin B \cos B\left(2\sin^2 A\right) \quad$ {$\cos 2\theta = 1 - 2\sin^2\theta$}

$= 4\sin A \cos A \sin^2 B + 4\sin^2 A \sin B \cos B$

$= 4\sin A \sin B\,[\sin B \cos A + \cos B \sin A]$

$= 4\sin A \sin B \sin(A + B)$

$= 4\sin A \sin B \sin(\pi - C) \qquad\qquad\qquad\qquad\ \ $ {$\sin(\pi - \theta) = \sin\theta$}

$= 4\sin A \sin B \sin C$

b $\tan A + \tan B + \tan C$

$= \tan A + \tan B + \tan(\pi - (A + B))$

$= \tan A + \tan B - \tan(A + B) \qquad\qquad$ {$\tan(\pi - \theta) = -\tan\theta$}

$= \dfrac{\tan A + \tan B}{1} - \dfrac{\tan A + \tan B}{1 - \tan A \tan B}$

$= \dfrac{(\tan A + \tan B)(1 - \tan A \tan B) - (\tan A + \tan B)}{1 - \tan A \tan B}$

$= \dfrac{\cancel{\tan A} + \cancel{\tan B} - \tan^2 A \tan B - \tan A \tan^2 B - \cancel{\tan A} - \cancel{\tan B}}{1 - \tan A \tan B}$

$= -\tan A \tan B \dfrac{(\tan A + \tan B)}{1 - \tan A \tan B}$

$= -\tan A \tan B \tan(A + B)$

$= \tan A \tan B \tan(\pi - (A + B)) \qquad\qquad$ {$\tan(\pi - \theta) = -\tan\theta$}

$= \tan A \tan B \tan C$

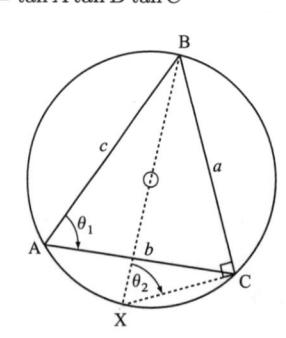

30 a Draw diameter BOX and join [CX].

Now $\theta_1 = \theta_2 \qquad$ {angles in the same segment theorem}

and $\widehat{BCX} = 90° \qquad$ {angle in a semi-circle theorem}

Now the area is $\tfrac{1}{2}bc \sin \theta_1 = \tfrac{1}{2}bc \sin \theta_2$

$\qquad\qquad\qquad\qquad = \tfrac{1}{2}bc\,\dfrac{a}{BX}$

$\qquad\qquad\qquad\qquad = \tfrac{1}{2}bc \times \dfrac{a}{2r}$

$\qquad\qquad\qquad\qquad = \dfrac{abc}{4r}$

b
$$\sin A = \cos B + \cos C$$
$$\therefore \sin(\pi - [B+C]) = \cos B + \cos C$$
$$\therefore \sin[B+C] = \cos B + \cos C$$
$$\therefore 2\sin\left(\frac{B+C}{2}\right)\cos\left(\frac{B+C}{2}\right) = 2\cos\left(\frac{B+C}{2}\right)\cos\left(\frac{B-C}{2}\right)$$
$$\therefore 2\cos\left(\frac{B+C}{2}\right)\left[\sin\left(\frac{B+C}{2}\right) - \cos\left(\frac{B-C}{2}\right)\right] = 0$$
$$\therefore \cos\left(\frac{B+C}{2}\right) = 0 \text{ .... (1)} \quad \text{or} \quad \sin\left(\frac{B+C}{2}\right) = \cos\left(\frac{B-C}{2}\right) \text{ .... (2)}$$

In (1), $\frac{B+C}{2} = \frac{\pi}{2} + k\pi$
$$\therefore B + C = \pi + k2\pi, \ k \in \mathbb{Z}$$
$$\therefore B + C = \pi, 3\pi, -\pi, \text{ and so on, all of which are impossible.}$$

In (2), $\sin\left(\frac{B+C}{2}\right) = \sin\left(\frac{\pi}{2} - \frac{B-C}{2}\right) \quad \{\cos\theta = \sin\left(\frac{\pi}{2} - \theta\right)\}$
$$\therefore \frac{B+C}{2} = \frac{\pi - B + C}{2} \quad \text{or} \quad \frac{B+C}{2} = \pi - \left(\frac{\pi - B + C}{2}\right)$$
$$\therefore B + \cancel{C} = \pi - B + \cancel{C} \quad \text{or} \quad \cancel{B} + C = 2\pi - \pi + \cancel{B} - C$$
$$\therefore B = \frac{\pi}{2} \quad \text{or} \quad C = \frac{\pi}{2}$$
$\therefore$ the triangle is right angled at B or C.

31

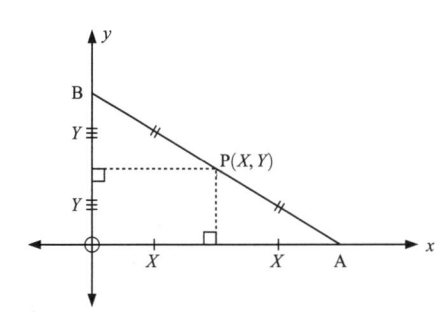

Let $P(X, Y)$ be the midpoint of [AB].
$\therefore$ A is at $(2X, 0)$ and B is at $(0, 2Y)$.
Let [AB] have fixed length l units.
$$\therefore (2X)^2 + (2Y)^2 = l^2$$
$$\therefore X^2 + Y^2 = \left(\frac{l}{2}\right)^2$$
which is the equation of a circle, centre $(0, 0)$ and radius $\frac{l}{2}$ units.

32 a Suppose $\sqrt{14 - 4\sqrt{6}} = a + b\sqrt{6}$ where $a, b \in \mathbb{Z}$ .... (∗)
$$\therefore a^2 + 2ab\sqrt{6} + 6b^2 = 14 - 4\sqrt{6} \quad \{\text{squaring both sides}\}$$
$$\therefore a^2 + 6b^2 = 14 \text{ and } ab = -2$$
$$\therefore a^2 + 6\left(\frac{-2}{a}\right)^2 = 14$$
$$\therefore a^2 + \frac{24}{a^2} - 14 = 0$$
$$\therefore a^4 - 14a^2 + 24 = 0$$
$$\therefore (a^2 - 2)(a^2 - 12) = 0$$
$$\therefore a^2 = 2 \text{ or } 12$$
$$\therefore a = \pm\sqrt{2} \text{ or } \pm 2\sqrt{3} \text{ which is a contradiction to (∗)}$$

Hence the supposition is false, and so $\sqrt{14 - 4\sqrt{6}}$ cannot be written in the form $a + b\sqrt{6}$ with $a, b \in \mathbb{Z}$.

b As $\sqrt{6} = \sqrt{2}\sqrt{3}$ we try $\sqrt{14 - 4\sqrt{6}} = a\sqrt{3} + b\sqrt{2}$ where $a, b \in \mathbb{Z}$.
$$\therefore 3a^2 + 2b^2 + 2ab\sqrt{6} = 14 - 4\sqrt{6}$$
$$\therefore 3a^2 + 2b^2 = 14 \text{ and } ab = -2$$

$$\therefore\ 3a^2 + 2\left(\frac{-2}{a}\right)^2 - 14 = 0$$

$$\therefore\ 3a^2 + \frac{8}{a^2} - 14 = 0$$

$$\therefore\ 3a^4 - 14a^2 + 8 = 0$$

$$\therefore\ (a^2 - 4)(3a^2 - 2) = 0$$

$$\therefore\ a^2 = 4 \text{ or } \tfrac{2}{3}$$

Since $a \in \mathbb{Z}$, $a = \pm 2$ and so $b = -\dfrac{2}{a} = \mp 1$

$\therefore\ \sqrt{14 - 4\sqrt{6}} = 2\sqrt{3} - \sqrt{2}$ or $-2\sqrt{3} + \sqrt{2}$

We reject the second one as it is negative. So, $\sqrt{14 - 4\sqrt{6}} = 2\sqrt{3} - \sqrt{2}$.

33 Given: $(1+x)^n = \binom{n}{0} + \binom{n}{1}x + \binom{n}{2}x^2 + \binom{n}{3}x^3 + \dots + \binom{n}{n}x^n$, $n \in \mathbb{Z}^+$ .... (*)

a Differentiating both sides gives:

$$n(1+x)^{n-1} = \binom{n}{1} + 2\binom{n}{2}x + 3\binom{n}{3}x^2 + \dots + n\binom{n}{n}x^{n-1}$$

Letting $x = 1$, $\binom{n}{1} + 2\binom{n}{2} + 3\binom{n}{3} + \dots + n\binom{n}{n} = n\,2^{n-1}$

b $\binom{n}{0} + 2\binom{n}{1} + 3\binom{n}{2} + \dots + (n+1)\binom{n}{n}$

$= \left[\binom{n}{0} + \binom{n}{1} + \binom{n}{2} + \dots + \binom{n}{n}\right] + \left[\binom{n}{1} + 2\binom{n}{2} + \dots + n\binom{n}{n}\right]$

$= 2^n + n2^{n-1}\quad$ {letting $x=1$ in (*), and using **a**}

$= (n+2)2^{n-1}$

c We notice that $\dfrac{1}{r+1}\binom{n}{r} = \dfrac{1}{r+1}\left(\dfrac{n!}{r!(n-r)!}\right) = \dfrac{n!}{(r+1)!(n-r)!}$

$= \left[\dfrac{n!}{(r+1)!(n-r)!}\right]\dfrac{n+1}{n+1}$

$= \dfrac{1}{n+1}\left[\dfrac{(n+1)!}{(r+1)!(n-r)!}\right]$

$= \dfrac{1}{n+1}\binom{n+1}{r+1}$

$\therefore\ \frac{1}{1}\binom{n}{0} + \frac{1}{2}\binom{n}{1} + \frac{1}{3}\binom{n}{2} + \dots + \frac{1}{n+1}\binom{n}{n}$

$= \frac{1}{n+1}\binom{n+1}{1} + \frac{1}{n+1}\binom{n+1}{2} + \frac{1}{n+1}\binom{n+1}{3} + \dots + \frac{1}{n+1}\binom{n+1}{n+1}$

$= \frac{1}{n+1}\left[\binom{n+1}{1} + \binom{n+1}{2} + \binom{n+1}{3} + \dots + \binom{n+1}{n+1}\right]$

$= \frac{1}{n+1}\left[(1+1)^{n+1} - \binom{n+1}{0}\right]\quad$ {using (*) with n replaced by $n+1$, $x=1$}

$= \dfrac{2^{n+1} - 1}{n+1}$

34 a $\dfrac{Ax+B}{x^2+5} + \dfrac{C}{x-1} = \dfrac{Ax+B}{x^2+5} - \dfrac{C}{1-x}$

$= \dfrac{(Ax+B)(1-x) - C(x^2+5)}{(x^2+5)(1-x)}$

$= \dfrac{-(A+C)x^2 + (A-B)x + (B-5C)}{(x^2+5)(1-x)}$

So, if $\dfrac{x+5}{(x^2+5)(1-x)} = \dfrac{Ax+B}{x^2+5} + \dfrac{C}{x-1}\quad$ for all x then

$-(A+C) = 0$, $A - B = 1$ and $B - 5C = 5$

Solving these simultaneously gives $A = 1$, $B = 0$, $C = -1$

b $\displaystyle\int_2^4 \frac{x+5}{(x^2+5)(1-x)}\,dx = \int_2^4 \left(\frac{x}{x^2+5} - \frac{1}{x-1}\right) dx$

$\displaystyle = \tfrac{1}{2}\int_2^4 \frac{2x}{x^2+5}\,dx - \int_2^4 \frac{1}{x-1}\,dx$

$= \tfrac{1}{2}\left[\ln|x^2+5|\right]_2^4 - [\ln|x-1|]_2^4$

$= \tfrac{1}{2}(\ln 21 - \ln 9) - (\ln 3 - \ln 1)$

$= \tfrac{1}{2}\ln\left(\tfrac{7}{3}\right) - \ln 3$

$= \tfrac{1}{2}(\ln 7 - \ln 3) - \ln 3 = \tfrac{1}{2}\ln 7 - \tfrac{3}{2}\ln 3$

35 a Let $\dfrac{1}{n(n+2)} = \dfrac{A}{n} + \dfrac{B}{n+2} = \dfrac{A(n+2)+Bn}{n(n+2)}$ for all n

$\therefore \dfrac{1}{n(n+2)} = \dfrac{(A+B)n + 2A}{n(n+2)}$ for all n

$\therefore A+B = 0$ and $2A = 1$

$\therefore A = \tfrac{1}{2},\ B = -\tfrac{1}{2}$

b $\dfrac{1}{1\times 3} + \dfrac{1}{2\times 4} + \dfrac{1}{3\times 5} + \ldots + \dfrac{1}{n(n+2)}$

$= \dfrac{\tfrac{1}{2}}{1} - \dfrac{\tfrac{1}{2}}{3} + \dfrac{\tfrac{1}{2}}{2} - \dfrac{\tfrac{1}{2}}{4} + \dfrac{\tfrac{1}{2}}{3} - \dfrac{\tfrac{1}{2}}{5} + \dfrac{\tfrac{1}{2}}{4} - \dfrac{\tfrac{1}{2}}{6} + \ldots + \dfrac{\tfrac{1}{2}}{n-1} - \dfrac{\tfrac{1}{2}}{n+1} + \dfrac{\tfrac{1}{2}}{n} - \dfrac{\tfrac{1}{2}}{n+2}$

$= \dfrac{1}{2} + \dfrac{1}{4} - \dfrac{1}{2n+2} - \dfrac{1}{2n+4}$ {as all other terms cancel}

$= \dfrac{3}{4} - \dfrac{1}{2n+2} - \dfrac{1}{2n+4}$

c $\displaystyle\sum_{r=1}^{\infty} \dfrac{1}{r(r+2)} = \lim_{n\to\infty} \sum_{r=1}^{n} \dfrac{1}{r(r+2)} = \lim_{n\to\infty}\left(\dfrac{3}{4} - \dfrac{1}{2n+2} - \dfrac{1}{2n+4}\right) = \dfrac{3}{4}$

d P_n is "$\dfrac{1}{1\times 3} + \dfrac{1}{2\times 4} + \dfrac{1}{3\times 5} + \ldots + \dfrac{1}{n(n+2)} = \dfrac{3}{4} - \dfrac{1}{2n+2} - \dfrac{1}{2n+4}$" for $n \in \mathbb{Z}^+$.

Proof: (By the principle of mathematical induction)

(1) If $n = 1$, LHS $= \dfrac{1}{1\times 3} = \dfrac{1}{3}$, RHS $= \dfrac{3}{4} - \dfrac{1}{4} - \dfrac{1}{6} = \dfrac{1}{3}$ ✓

(2) If P_k is assumed true then

$\dfrac{1}{1\times 3} + \dfrac{1}{2\times 4} + \dfrac{1}{3\times 5} + \ldots + \dfrac{1}{k(k+2)} = \dfrac{3}{4} - \dfrac{1}{2k+2} - \dfrac{1}{2k+4}$

So, $\dfrac{1}{1\times 3} + \dfrac{1}{2\times 4} + \dfrac{1}{3\times 5} + \ldots + \dfrac{1}{k(k+2)} + \dfrac{1}{(k+1)(k+3)}$

$= \dfrac{3}{4} - \dfrac{1}{2k+2} - \dfrac{1}{2k+4} + \dfrac{1}{(k+1)(k+3)}$

$= \dfrac{3}{4} - \dfrac{1}{2k+4} + \dfrac{1}{(k+1)(k+3)} - \dfrac{1}{2(k+1)}$

$= \dfrac{3}{4} - \dfrac{1}{2k+4} + \dfrac{2-(k+3)}{2(k+1)(k+3)}$

$= \dfrac{3}{4} - \dfrac{1}{2k+4} + \dfrac{-\cancel{(k+1)}}{2\cancel{(k+1)}(k+3)}$

$= \dfrac{3}{4} - \dfrac{1}{2k+4} - \dfrac{1}{2k+6}$

$= \dfrac{3}{4} - \dfrac{1}{2(k+1)+2} - \dfrac{1}{2(k+1)+4}$

Thus P_{k+1} is true whenever P_k is true.

Since P_1 is true, P_n is true for all $n \in \mathbb{Z}^+$ {Principle of mathematical induction}

36 a Let $x = \sin\theta$, $\dfrac{dx}{d\theta} = \cos\theta$

$\therefore \displaystyle\int \dfrac{x}{\sqrt{1-x^2}}\,dx = \int \dfrac{\sin\theta}{\cos\theta}\cos\theta\,d\theta$

$\qquad\qquad\qquad = \displaystyle\int \sin\theta\,d\theta$

$\qquad\qquad\qquad = -\cos\theta + c$

$\qquad\qquad\qquad = -\sqrt{1-\sin^2\theta} + c$

$\qquad\qquad\qquad = -\sqrt{1-x^2} + c$

b $\displaystyle\int \dfrac{1+x}{1+x^2}\,dx$

$= \displaystyle\int \dfrac{1}{1+x^2}\,dx + \int \dfrac{x}{1+x^2}\,dx$

$= \displaystyle\int \dfrac{1}{1+x^2}\,dx + \dfrac{1}{2}\int \dfrac{2x}{1+x^2}\,dx$

$= \arctan x + \dfrac{1}{2}\ln\left|1+x^2\right| + c$

$= \arctan x + \dfrac{1}{2}\ln\left(1+x^2\right) + c$

$\qquad\qquad\qquad\qquad\{x^2+1 > 0\}$

c Let $x = \sin\theta$, $\dfrac{dx}{d\theta} = \cos\theta$

$\therefore \displaystyle\int \dfrac{1}{\sqrt{1-x^2}}\,dx = \int \dfrac{1}{\sqrt{1-\sin^2\theta}}\cos\theta\,d\theta$

$\qquad\qquad\qquad = \displaystyle\int \dfrac{1}{\cos\theta}\cos\theta\,d\theta$

$\qquad\qquad\qquad = \displaystyle\int 1\,d\theta = \theta + c = \arcsin x + c$

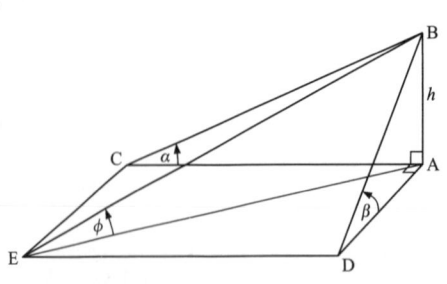

37 Suppose the pole has height h and the angle of elevation of B from E is ϕ.

$\tan\alpha = \dfrac{h}{AC}, \quad \tan\beta = \dfrac{h}{AD}, \quad \tan\phi = \dfrac{h}{AE}$

$\therefore\ AC = h\cot\alpha,\ AD = h\cot\beta,\ AE = h\cot\phi$

But $AE^2 = AC^2 + AD^2$ {Pythagoras}

$\therefore\ h^2\cot^2\phi = h^2\cot^2\alpha + h^2\cot^2\beta$

$\therefore\ \cot^2\phi = \cot^2\alpha + \cot^2\beta$

$\therefore\ \cot\phi = \sqrt{\cot^2\alpha + \cot^2\beta}\quad\{\cot\phi > 0\}$

$\therefore\ \phi = \operatorname{arccot}\left(\sqrt{\cot^2\alpha + \cot^2\beta}\right)$

38 a $\cos 4\theta + i\sin 4\theta = \operatorname{cis} 4\theta$

$\qquad\qquad\qquad = (\operatorname{cis}\theta)^4$ {De Moivre}

$\qquad\qquad\qquad = (C+iS)^4$ where $C = \cos\theta$ and $S = \sin\theta$

$\qquad\qquad\qquad = C^4 + 4C^3(iS) + 6C^2(iS)^2 + 4C(iS)^3 + (iS)^4$

$\qquad\qquad\qquad = (C^4 - 6C^2S^2 + S^4) + i(4C^3S - 4CS^3)$

Equating real and imaginary parts, $\sin 4\theta = 4C^3S - 4CS^3$ and $\cos 4\theta = C^4 - 6C^2S^2 + S^4$.

Hence, $\tan 4\theta = \dfrac{\sin 4\theta}{\cos 4\theta} = \dfrac{4C^3S - 4CS^3}{C^4 - 6C^2S^2 + S^4}$

$\qquad\qquad = \dfrac{4\left(\dfrac{S}{C}\right) - 4\left(\dfrac{S}{C}\right)^3}{1 - 6\left(\dfrac{S}{C}\right)^2 + \left(\dfrac{S}{C}\right)^4}$ {dividing all terms by C^4}

$\qquad\qquad = \dfrac{4\tan\theta - 4\tan^3\theta}{1 - 6\tan^2\theta + \tan^4\theta}$

b $x^4 + 4x^3 - 6x^2 - 4x + 1 = 0$.

If we let $x = \tan\theta$ then $\tan^4\theta + 4\tan^3\theta - 6\tan^2\theta - 4\tan\theta + 1 = 0$

$\therefore\ 1 - 6\tan^2\theta + \tan^4\theta = 4\tan\theta - 4\tan^3\theta$

$\therefore\ \dfrac{4\tan\theta - 4\tan^3\theta}{1 - 6\tan^2\theta + \tan^4\theta} = 1$

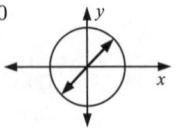

$\therefore \tan 4\theta = 1$ {by **a**}

$\therefore 4\theta = \frac{\pi}{4} + k\pi, \; k \in \mathbb{Z}$

$\therefore \theta = \frac{\pi}{16} + \frac{k\pi}{4}$ Thus $x = \tan\left(\frac{\pi}{16}\right), \; \tan\left(\frac{5\pi}{16}\right), \; \tan\left(\frac{9\pi}{16}\right), \; \tan\left(\frac{13\pi}{16}\right)$.

39 a Consider $1 + a \operatorname{cis}\theta + a^2 \operatorname{cis} 2\theta + a^3 \operatorname{cis} 3\theta + \ldots + a^n \operatorname{cis} n\theta$ .... (1)
$= 1 + a[\operatorname{cis}\theta]^1 + a^2[\operatorname{cis}\theta]^2 + a^3[\operatorname{cis}\theta]^3 + \ldots + a^n[\operatorname{cis}\theta]^n$

which is a geometric series with $u_1 = 1, \; r = a \operatorname{cis}\theta$ and has $n+1$ terms. So, its sum is:

$= \dfrac{1\left[\dfrac{(a\operatorname{cis}\theta)^{n+1} - 1}{a\operatorname{cis}\theta - 1}\right]}{}$

$= \dfrac{a^{n+1}\operatorname{cis}(n+1)\theta - 1}{a\operatorname{cis}\theta - 1}$

$= \dfrac{a^{n+1}[\cos(n+1)\theta + i\sin(n+1)\theta] - 1}{a\cos\theta + ai\sin\theta - 1}$

$= \left[\dfrac{a^{n+1}\cos(n+1)\theta - 1 + ia^{n+1}\sin(n+1)\theta}{a\cos\theta - 1 + ia\sin\theta}\right]\left[\dfrac{a\cos\theta - 1 - ia\sin\theta}{a\cos\theta - 1 - ia\sin\theta}\right]$

$= \dfrac{(a^{n+1}\cos(n+1)\theta - 1 + ia^{n+1}\sin(n+1)\theta)(a\cos\theta - 1 - ia\sin\theta)}{(a\cos\theta - 1)^2 + a^2\sin^2\theta}$ .... (2)

Equating the real parts of (1) and (2) gives

$1 + a\cos\theta + a^2\cos 2\theta + a^3\cos 3\theta + \ldots + a^n(\cos n\theta)$

$= \dfrac{(a^{n+1}\cos(n+1)\theta - 1)(a\cos\theta - 1) + a^{n+2}\sin(n+1)\theta\sin\theta}{a^2\cos^2\theta - 2a\cos\theta + 1 + a^2\sin^2\theta}$

$= \dfrac{a^{n+2}\cos(n+1)\theta\cos\theta - a\cos\theta - a^{n+1}\cos(n+1)\theta + 1 + a^{n+2}\sin(n+1)\theta\sin\theta}{a^2 - 2a\cos\theta + 1}$

$= \dfrac{a^{n+2}[\cos(n+1)\theta\cos\theta + \sin(n+1)\theta\sin\theta] - a\cos\theta - a^{n+1}\cos(n+1)\theta + 1}{a^2 - 2a\cos\theta + 1}$

$= \dfrac{a^{n+2}\cos n\theta - a\cos\theta - a^{n+1}\cos(n+1)\theta + 1}{a^2 - 2a\cos\theta + 1}$

$= \dfrac{a^{n+1}(a\cos n\theta - \cos(n+1)\theta) - a\cos\theta + 1}{a^2 - 2a\cos\theta + 1}$

b Equating the imaginary parts of (1) and (2) gives

$a\sin\theta + a^2\sin 2\theta + a^3\sin 3\theta + \ldots + a^n\sin n\theta$

$= \dfrac{(a^{n+1}\sin(n+1)\theta)(a\cos\theta - 1) - a\sin\theta(a^{n+1}\cos(n+1)\theta - 1)}{a^2 - 2a\cos\theta + 1}$

$= \dfrac{a^{n+2}\sin(n+1)\theta\cos\theta - a^{n+1}\sin(n+1)\theta - a^{n+2}\cos(n+1)\theta\sin\theta + a\sin\theta}{a^2 - 2a\cos\theta + 1}$

$= \dfrac{a^{n+2}(\sin(n+1)\theta\cos\theta - \cos(n+1)\theta\sin\theta) - a^{n+1}\sin(n+1)\theta + a\sin\theta}{a^2 - 2a\cos\theta + 1}$

$= \dfrac{a^{n+2}\sin n\theta - a^{n+1}\sin(n+1)\theta + a\sin\theta}{a^2 - 2a\cos\theta + 1}$

$= \dfrac{a^{n+1}(a\sin n\theta - \sin(n+1)\theta) + a\sin\theta}{a^2 - 2a\cos\theta + 1}$

40 a Suppose $e^x = a_0 + a_1 x + a_2 x^2 + a_3 x^3 + a_4 x^4 + a_5 x^5 + \ldots$ .... (1)

By successive differentiation of both sides, we find:

$e^x = a_1 + 2a_2 x + 3a_3 x^2 + 4a_4 x^3 + 5a_5 x^4 + \ldots$ .... (2)

and $e^x = 2a_2 + 6a_3 x + 12a_4 x^2 + 20a_5 x^3 + 30a_6 x^4 + \ldots$ .... (3)

and $e^x = 6a_3 + 24a_4 x + 60a_5 x^2 + 120a_6 x^3 + 210a_7 x^4 + \ldots$ .... (4)

and $e^x = 24a_4 + 120a_5 x + 360a_6 x^2 + \ldots$ .... (5)

Letting $x = 0$ in (1) to (5) gives $1 = a_0$, $1 = a_1$, $1 = 2a_2$, $1 = 6a_3$, $1 = 24a_4$, ...

Thus $a_0 = 1$, $a_1 = 1$, $a_2 = \frac{1}{2}$, $a_3 = \frac{1}{6}$, $a_4 = \frac{1}{24}$, ...

$\therefore \quad a_0 = \frac{1}{0!}, \quad a_1 = \frac{1}{1!}, \quad a_2 = \frac{1}{2!}, \quad a_3 = \frac{1}{3!}, \quad a_4 = \frac{1}{4!}, \quad ....$

b Conjecture: $e^x = \sum_{n=0}^{\infty} \frac{x^n}{n!}$

c When $x = 1$, $e = \sum_{n=0}^{\infty} \frac{1}{n!} = 1 + 1 + \frac{1}{2!} + \frac{1}{3!} + \frac{1}{4!} + \frac{1}{5!} + ...$

$\approx 2.718\,281\,828 ....$ (adding the first 13 terms)

which checks with the calculator result.

41 a $\dfrac{P}{a-x} + \dfrac{Q}{a+x} = \dfrac{P(a+x) + Q(a-x)}{(a-x)(a+x)} = \dfrac{[P-Q]x + [P+Q]a}{a^2 - x^2}$

So, if $\dfrac{1}{a^2 - x^2} = \dfrac{P}{a-x} + \dfrac{Q}{a+x}$ for all x, then $P - Q = 0$ and $[P+Q]a = 1$

Thus $P = Q$ and so $P = Q = \dfrac{1}{2a}$

b $\displaystyle\int \dfrac{1}{a^2 - x^2}\, dx = \int \left(\dfrac{\frac{1}{2a}}{a-x} + \dfrac{\frac{1}{2a}}{a+x} \right) dx = \dfrac{1}{2a} \int \left(\dfrac{1}{a-x} + \dfrac{1}{a+x} \right) dx$

$= \dfrac{1}{2a} \left(-\ln|a-x| + \ln|a+x| \right) + c$

$= \dfrac{1}{2a} \ln \left| \dfrac{a+x}{a-x} \right| + c \quad$ provided $x \neq -a$

c $\dfrac{a+x}{a-x}$ has sign diagram

$\xrightarrow{-|+\vdots-}{x}$
$-aa$

So, $\dfrac{d}{dx}\left[\dfrac{1}{2a} \ln \left| \dfrac{a+x}{a-x} \right| + c \right] = \begin{cases} \dfrac{d}{dx}\left[\dfrac{1}{2a} \ln \left(\dfrac{a+x}{a-x} \right) \right] & \text{if } -a < x < a \\ \dfrac{d}{dx}\left[\dfrac{1}{2a} \ln \left(-\dfrac{a+x}{a-x} \right) \right] & \text{if } x < -a \text{ or } x > a \end{cases}$

$= \begin{cases} \dfrac{1}{2a}\dfrac{d}{dx}[\ln(a+x) - \ln(a-x)] & \text{if } -a < x < a \\ \dfrac{1}{2a}\dfrac{d}{dx}[\ln(a+x) - \ln(x-a)] & \text{if } x > a \\ \dfrac{1}{2a}\dfrac{d}{dx}[\ln(-a-x) - \ln(a-x)] & \text{if } x < -a \end{cases}$

$= \begin{cases} \dfrac{1}{2a}\left[\dfrac{1}{a+x} - \dfrac{-1}{a-x} \right] & \text{if } -a < x < a \\ \dfrac{1}{2a}\left[\dfrac{1}{a+x} - \dfrac{1}{x-a} \right] & \text{if } x > a \\ \dfrac{1}{2a}\left[\dfrac{-1}{-a-x} - \dfrac{-1}{a-x} \right] & \text{if } x < -a \end{cases}$

$= \dfrac{1}{2a} \left(\dfrac{1}{a+x} + \dfrac{1}{a-x} \right)$

$= \dfrac{1}{2a} \times \dfrac{a - x + a + x}{(a+x)(a-x)}$

$= \dfrac{1}{2a} \times \dfrac{2a}{a^2 - x^2} = \dfrac{1}{a^2 - x^2} \quad$ as required.

42 **a** $\operatorname{cis}\theta + \operatorname{cis}\phi = \cos\theta + i\sin\theta + \cos\phi + i\sin\phi$

$\phantom{\operatorname{cis}\theta + \operatorname{cis}\phi} = [\cos\theta + \cos\phi] + i[\sin\theta + \sin\phi]$

$\phantom{\operatorname{cis}\theta + \operatorname{cis}\phi} = 2\cos\left(\dfrac{\theta+\phi}{2}\right)\cos\left(\dfrac{\theta-\phi}{2}\right) + i2\sin\left(\dfrac{\theta+\phi}{2}\right)\cos\left(\dfrac{\theta-\phi}{2}\right)$

$\phantom{\operatorname{cis}\theta + \operatorname{cis}\phi} = 2\cos\left(\dfrac{\theta-\phi}{2}\right)\left[\cos\left(\dfrac{\theta+\phi}{2}\right) + i\sin\left(\dfrac{\theta+\phi}{2}\right)\right]$

$\phantom{\operatorname{cis}\theta + \operatorname{cis}\phi} = 2\cos\left(\dfrac{\theta-\phi}{2}\right)\operatorname{cis}\left(\dfrac{\theta+\phi}{2}\right)$

b $|\operatorname{cis}\theta + \operatorname{cis}\phi| = 2\left|\cos\left(\dfrac{\theta-\phi}{2}\right)\right|$ and $\arg(\operatorname{cis}\theta + \operatorname{cis}\phi) = \dfrac{\theta+\phi}{2}$

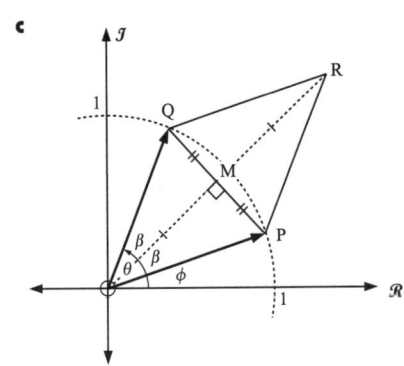

c Let $\overrightarrow{OP} = \operatorname{cis}\phi$ and $\overrightarrow{OQ} = \operatorname{cis}\theta$, $\theta > \phi$

We complete rhombus OPRQ, where the diagonals bisect each other at right angles.

$\overrightarrow{OR} = \overrightarrow{OP} + \overrightarrow{PR} = \overrightarrow{OP} + \overrightarrow{OQ} = \operatorname{cis}\phi + \operatorname{cis}\theta$

Since $\theta = \phi + 2\beta$, $\beta = \dfrac{\theta-\phi}{2}$

Now $\arg\overrightarrow{OR} = \phi + \beta = \dfrac{\theta+\phi}{2}$

and $|\overrightarrow{OR}| = 2(OM)$ where $\cos\beta = \dfrac{OM}{OP} = OM$

$\therefore\ |\overrightarrow{OR}| = 2\cos\left(\dfrac{\theta-\phi}{2}\right)$

Note: If θ and ϕ are interchanged, $|\overrightarrow{OR}| = 2\cos\left(\dfrac{\phi-\theta}{2}\right)$.

Thus $|\overrightarrow{OR}|$ is actually $2\left|\cos\left(\dfrac{\theta-\phi}{2}\right)\right|$.

d $\left(\dfrac{z+1}{z-1}\right)^5 = 1 \quad \therefore\ \dfrac{z+1}{z-1} = 1,\ \alpha,\ \alpha^2,\ \alpha^3,\ \text{and}\ \alpha^4$ where $\alpha = \operatorname{cis}\left(\dfrac{2\pi}{5}\right)$

$\therefore\ \dfrac{z+1}{z-1} = \alpha^k$ where $k = 0, 1, 2, 3, 4$ and $\alpha = \operatorname{cis}\left(\dfrac{2\pi}{5}\right)$

$\therefore\ z = \dfrac{1+\alpha^k}{\alpha^k - 1}$ {making z the subject}

$\therefore\ z = \dfrac{\operatorname{cis} 0 + \left[\operatorname{cis}\left(\frac{2\pi}{5}\right)\right]^k}{\left[\operatorname{cis}\left(\frac{2\pi}{5}\right)\right]^k + \operatorname{cis}\pi}$ {as $\operatorname{cis}\pi = -1$}

$\therefore\ z = \dfrac{\operatorname{cis}\left(\frac{2\pi k}{5}\right) + \operatorname{cis} 0}{\operatorname{cis}\left(\frac{2\pi k}{5}\right) + \operatorname{cis}\pi}$

$\therefore\ z = \dfrac{2\cos\left(\frac{\pi k}{5}\right)\operatorname{cis}\left(\frac{\pi k}{5}\right)}{2\cos\left(\frac{\left(\frac{2\pi k}{5}\right)-\pi}{2}\right)\operatorname{cis}\left(\frac{\left(\frac{2\pi k}{5}\right)+\pi}{2}\right)}$

$\therefore\ z = \dfrac{\cos\left(\frac{\pi k}{5}\right)}{\cos\left(\frac{\pi k}{5} - \frac{\pi}{2}\right)}\operatorname{cis}\left(\frac{\pi k}{5} - \frac{\pi k}{5} - \frac{\pi}{2}\right)$

$\therefore\ z = \dfrac{\cos\left(\frac{\pi k}{5}\right)}{\sin\left(\frac{\pi k}{5}\right)}\operatorname{cis}\left(-\frac{\pi}{2}\right)$ $\{\cos(\theta - \frac{\pi}{2}) = \sin\theta\}$

$\therefore\ z = \cot\left(\frac{\pi k}{5}\right) \times -i$

$\therefore\ z = -i\cot\left(\frac{\pi k}{5}\right)$ for $k = 0, 1, 2, 3, 4$

However $\cot 0$ is undefined, so we reject the solution when $k = 0$

$\therefore\ z = -i\cot\left(\frac{k\pi}{5}\right)$ where $k = 1, 2, 3, 4$.

43 a Let $z = |z|\operatorname{cis}\theta$, $\therefore \dfrac{1}{z} = \dfrac{\operatorname{cis} 0}{|z|\operatorname{cis}\theta} = \dfrac{1}{|z|}\operatorname{cis}(-\theta)$

$\therefore z + \dfrac{1}{z} = |z|\operatorname{cis}\theta + \dfrac{1}{|z|}\operatorname{cis}(-\theta)$

$= |z|(\cos\theta + i\sin\theta) + \dfrac{1}{|z|}(\cos\theta - i\sin\theta)$

$= \cos\theta\left(|z| + \dfrac{1}{|z|}\right) + i\sin\theta\left(|z| - \dfrac{1}{|z|}\right)$

Now $z + \dfrac{1}{z}$ is real, $\therefore \sin\theta = 0$ or $|z| - \dfrac{1}{|z|} = 0$

$\therefore \theta = k\pi$ or $|z| = 1$

$\therefore z$ is real or $|z| = 1$

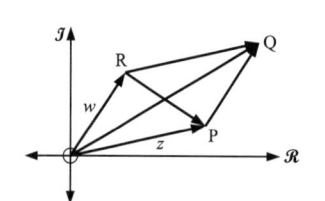

b If $z = \overrightarrow{OP}$ and $w = \overrightarrow{OR}$ then
$\overrightarrow{RP} = z - w$ and $\overrightarrow{OQ} = z + w$ in parallelogram OPQR.
So, if $|z + w| = |z - w|$ the diagonals are equal in length, which is only possible when the parallelogram is a rectangle.

Thus, $\widehat{POR} = \dfrac{\pi}{2}$, so $\arg w - \arg z = \dfrac{\pi}{2}$

If P and R were interchanged then $\arg z - \arg w = \dfrac{\pi}{2}$

Thus, the arguments differ by $\dfrac{\pi}{2}$.

c If $z = r\operatorname{cis}\theta$
$z^4 = [r\operatorname{cis}\theta]^4$
$= r^4\operatorname{cis} 4\theta$
{De Moivre}

$\dfrac{1}{z} = \dfrac{1}{r\operatorname{cis}\theta}$
$= \dfrac{1}{r\operatorname{cis}\theta}\left(\dfrac{\operatorname{cis}(-\theta)}{\operatorname{cis}(-\theta)}\right)$
$= \dfrac{1}{r}\dfrac{\operatorname{cis}(-\theta)}{\operatorname{cis} 0}$
$= \dfrac{1}{r}\operatorname{cis}(-\theta)$

$iz^* = \operatorname{cis}\left(\dfrac{\pi}{2}\right)(r\operatorname{cis}(-\theta))$
$= r\operatorname{cis}\left(\dfrac{\pi}{2} - \theta\right)$

44 Suppose the common root is α and the other roots are β and γ.
$\therefore x^2 + ax + bc = (x - \alpha)(x - \beta)$ and $x^2 + bx + ca = (x - \alpha)(x - \gamma)$
Thus $\alpha + \beta = -a$ and $\alpha + \gamma = -b$ so $(\alpha + \beta)(\alpha + \gamma) = ab$ .... (1)
Also, $\alpha\beta = bc$ and $\alpha\gamma = ca$ so $\alpha^2\beta\gamma = abc^2$ .... (2)
Now α is a common root of both equations $\therefore \alpha^2 + a\alpha + bc = 0$ .... (3) and
$\alpha^2 + b\alpha + ca = 0$ .... (4)
Subtracting (4) from (3), $(a - b)\alpha - (a - b)c = 0$
$\therefore (a - b)(\alpha - c) = 0$
$\therefore a = b$ or $\alpha = c$

But if $a = b$, both equations are the same, and so the equations would have two common roots
$\therefore \alpha = c$ .... (5)
Using (2), $\alpha^2\beta\gamma = abc^2$
$\therefore c^2\beta\gamma = abc^2$
$\therefore \beta\gamma = ab$ .... (6)
Using (1), $\alpha^2 + \alpha(\beta + \gamma) + \beta\gamma = ab$
$\therefore c^2 + c(\beta + \gamma) = 0$ {using (5), (6)}
$\therefore \beta + \gamma = -c$ .... (7)
From (6) and (7), β and γ are the roots of $x^2 + cx + ab = 0$.

45 If $x = a^{\frac{1}{3}} + b^{\frac{1}{3}}$ then $x^3 = (a^{\frac{1}{3}} + b^{\frac{1}{3}})^3$

$\therefore x^3 = (a^{\frac{1}{3}})^3 + 3(a^{\frac{1}{3}})^2 b^{\frac{1}{3}} + 3(a^{\frac{1}{3}})(b^{\frac{1}{3}})^2 + (b^{\frac{1}{3}})^3$

$\therefore x^3 = a + b + 3a^{\frac{1}{3}} b^{\frac{1}{3}} (a^{\frac{1}{3}} + b^{\frac{1}{3}})$

$\therefore x^3 = 3(ab)^{\frac{1}{3}} x + (a + b)$

$x^3 = 6x + 6$ is of the above form where $(ab)^{\frac{1}{3}} = 2$ and $a + b = 6$

$\therefore ab = 8$ and $a + b = 6$

$\therefore a = 2, b = 4$ or $a = 4, b = 2$.

Thus $x = 4^{\frac{1}{3}} + 2^{\frac{1}{3}}$ is a root of $x^3 = 6x + 6$
The graph of $f(x) = x^3 - 6x - 6$ is:

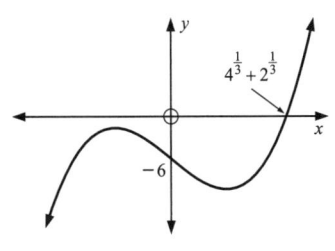

As a cubic has at most two turning points, it is clear that $x = \sqrt[3]{4} + \sqrt[3]{2}$ is the only real zero of $f(x) = x^3 - 6x - 6$, and hence is the only real solution of $x^3 = 6x + 6$.

46 $\log_y 16y - \log_{16y} y = \frac{8}{3}$ {as $x = 16y$}

$\therefore \dfrac{\log 16y}{\log y} - \dfrac{\log y}{\log 16y} - \dfrac{8}{3} = 0$

$\therefore m - \dfrac{1}{m} - \dfrac{8}{3} = 0$ {letting $\dfrac{\log 16y}{\log y} = m$}

$\therefore 3m^2 - 8m - 3 = 0$ {$\times 3m$}

$\therefore (3m + 1)(m - 3) = 0$

$\therefore m = \dfrac{\log 16y}{\log y} = -\dfrac{1}{3}$ or 3

$\therefore \log 16y = -\dfrac{1}{3} \log y$ or $\log 16y = 3 \log y$

$\therefore 16y = y^{-\frac{1}{3}}$ or $16y = y^3$

$\therefore y^{\frac{4}{3}} = \dfrac{1}{16}$ or $y(y^2 - 16) = 0$

$\therefore y = \left(\pm \dfrac{1}{2}\right)^3$ or $y = 0$ or ± 4

$\therefore y = \dfrac{1}{8}$ or 4 {as y is a base, $y > 0$}

$\therefore y = \dfrac{1}{8}, x = 2$ or $y = 4, x = 64$

47 Let the roots be $a - 3b, a - b, a + b, a + 3b$
$a - b$ and $a + b$ have sum $2a$ and product $a^2 - b^2$
$a - 3b$ and $a + 3b$ have sum $2a$ and product $a^2 - 9b^2$

$\therefore x^4 - (3m + 2)x^2 + m^3 = [x^2 - 2ax + (a^2 - b^2)] [x^2 - 2ax + (a^2 - 9b^2)]$

Equating coefficients of x^3 gives $0 = -2a - 2a = -4a$ $\therefore a = 0$

Thus $x^4 - (3m + 2)x^2 + m^2 = (x^2 - b^2)(x^2 - 9b^2)$
$= x^4 - 10b^2 x^2 + 9b^4$

Equating coefficients, $3m + 2 = 10b^2$ and $m^2 = 9b^4$

$\therefore m = \pm 3b^2$

$\therefore 3m + 2 = 10 \left(\pm \dfrac{m}{3}\right)$

$\therefore 9m + 6 = \pm 10m$

$\therefore m = 6$ or $-\dfrac{6}{19}$

48 If k is the third root then $x^3 + ax^2 + bx + c = (x - \alpha)(x - \beta)(x - k)$
$$= x^3 - [\alpha + \beta + k]x^2 + [\alpha\beta + \alpha k + \beta k]x - \alpha\beta k$$

Equating coefficients: $a = -(\alpha + \beta + k)$ .... (1)
$\qquad\qquad\qquad\quad b = \alpha\beta + \alpha k + \beta k$ .... (2)
$\qquad\qquad\qquad\quad c = -\alpha\beta k$ and so $k = -\dfrac{c}{\alpha\beta}$ .... (3)

So, $(\alpha\beta)^3 - b(\alpha\beta)^2 + ac(\alpha\beta) - c^2$
$= (\alpha\beta)^3 - [\alpha\beta + \alpha k + \beta k](\alpha\beta)^2 - \alpha\beta c(\alpha + \beta + k) - c^2$ $\quad$ {using (1) and (2)}
$= (\alpha\beta)^3 - (\alpha\beta)^3 - (\alpha + \beta)k(\alpha\beta)^2 - \alpha\beta c(\alpha + \beta + k) - c^2$
$= -(\alpha + \beta)(-\dfrac{c}{\alpha\beta})(\alpha\beta)^2 - \alpha\beta c(\alpha + \beta - \dfrac{c}{\alpha\beta}) - c^2$ $\quad$ {using (3)}
$= -(\alpha + \beta)(-c\alpha\beta) - \alpha\beta c(\alpha + \beta) + c^2 - c^2$
$= 0$ and so $\alpha\beta$ is a root of $x^3 - bx^2 + acx - c^2 = 0$

49 Since $x = 1 - y^2$, $\quad (1 - y^2)^2 + 3(1 - y^2)y + 9 = 0$
$\therefore\quad 1 - 2y^2 + y^4 + 3y - 3y^3 + 9 = 0$
$\therefore\quad y^4 - 3y^3 - 2y^2 + 3y + 10 = 0$

Using technology there are two real solutions,
$y = 2$ and $y \approx 2.939$
When $y = 2$, $x = -3$ and when $y \approx 2.939$, $x \approx -7.64$.
So, $x = -3$ and $x \approx -7.64$ are the solutions.

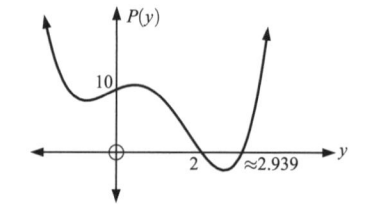

50 a $\dfrac{1}{1 + \sqrt{2}} + \dfrac{1}{\sqrt{2} + \sqrt{3}} + \dfrac{1}{\sqrt{3} + \sqrt{4}} + \ldots + \dfrac{1}{\sqrt{99} + \sqrt{100}}$

$= \dfrac{1}{1 + \sqrt{2}}\left(\dfrac{1 - \sqrt{2}}{1 - \sqrt{2}}\right) + \dfrac{1}{\sqrt{2} + \sqrt{3}}\left(\dfrac{\sqrt{2} - \sqrt{3}}{\sqrt{2} - \sqrt{3}}\right) + \dfrac{1}{\sqrt{3} + \sqrt{4}}\left(\dfrac{\sqrt{3} - \sqrt{4}}{\sqrt{3} - \sqrt{4}}\right) + \ldots$
$\qquad + \dfrac{1}{\sqrt{99} + \sqrt{100}}\left(\dfrac{\sqrt{99} - \sqrt{100}}{\sqrt{99} - \sqrt{100}}\right)$

$= \dfrac{1 - \sqrt{2}}{1 - 2} + \dfrac{\sqrt{2} - \sqrt{3}}{2 - 3} + \dfrac{\sqrt{3} - \sqrt{4}}{3 - 4} + \ldots + \dfrac{\sqrt{99} - \sqrt{100}}{99 - 100}$
$= -\left(1 - \sqrt{2} + \sqrt{2} - \sqrt{3} + \sqrt{3} - \sqrt{4} + \ldots + \sqrt{99} - \sqrt{100}\right)$
$= -(1 - 10)$
$= 9$

b Using the same technique, $\dfrac{1}{1 + \sqrt{2}} + \dfrac{1}{\sqrt{2} + \sqrt{3}} + \dfrac{1}{\sqrt{3} + \sqrt{4}} + \ldots + \dfrac{1}{\sqrt{n} + \sqrt{n+1}}$
$= -\left(1 - \sqrt{n + 1}\right)$
$= \sqrt{n + 1} - 1$

51 Since $x > y > z > 0$, $\dfrac{1}{x} < \dfrac{1}{y} < \dfrac{1}{z}$
$\therefore\quad \dfrac{1}{z} - \dfrac{1}{y} = \dfrac{1}{y} - \dfrac{1}{x}$ and so $\dfrac{1}{x} + \dfrac{1}{z} = \dfrac{2}{y}$
$\therefore\quad \dfrac{x + z}{xz} = \dfrac{2}{y}$
$\therefore\quad xy + yz = 2xz$ .... (*)
Now $(x - y + z)^2 = x^2 + y^2 + z^2 - 2xy + 2xz - 2yz$
$\qquad\qquad\qquad = x^2 + y^2 + z^2 - 2(xy + yz) + 2xz$

$\therefore \quad (x-y+z)^2 = x^2 + y^2 + z^2 - 4xz + 2xz \quad$ {using (*)}
$ = x^2 - 2xz + z^2 + y^2$
$ = (x-z)^2 + y^2$

Hence $x-z$, y and $x-y+z$ form the sides of a right angled triangle.

52 Let n be the number of years after winter 1969 and let u_n be the number of trees at time n.
Each summer, 10% die out and 100 new ones are planted, so $u_{n+1} = 0.9u_n + 100$.
We also know that $u_{11} = 1200$, since there were 1200 trees in 1980.
We hence have a sequence of the form $u_{n+1} = au_n + b$, $n = 1, 2, 3, 4, 5, ...$
Now $u_2 = au_1 + b$
$u_3 = au_2 + b = a(au_1 + b) + b = a^2 u_1 + ab + b$
$u_4 = au_3 + b = a(a^2 u_1 + ab + b) + b = a^3 u_1 + a^2 b + ab + b$ and so on.
This suggests: $u_{n+1} = a^n u_1 + b(1 + a + a^2 + ... + a^{n-1})$
$\therefore \quad u_{n+1} = a^n u_1 + b\left(\dfrac{1-a^n}{1-a}\right) \quad$ {sum of a geometric series}

a In this case $a = 0.9$ and $b = 100$
$\therefore \quad u_{n+1} = (0.9)^n u_1 + 100\left(\dfrac{1-(0.9)^n}{1-0.9}\right)$
$\therefore \quad u_{n+1} = (0.9)^n u_1 + 1000(1-(0.9)^n)$
But $u_{11} = (0.9)^{10} u_1 + 1000(1-(0.9)^{10}) = 1200$
$\therefore \quad 0.348\,68 u_1 + 651.32 \approx 1200$
$\therefore \quad u_1 \approx \dfrac{548.68}{0.348\,68} \approx 1574$ trees
$\therefore$ there were about 1574 trees at the end of winter in 1970.

b As n gets large, $(0.9)^n \to 0$ and $1-(0.9)^n \to 1$
$\therefore \quad u_{n+1} \to 1000$
This indicates a stable number of trees at 1000.

53 a Let u_n be the amount still owing after n quarters and let R be the repayment each quarter.
Each quarter, interest is charged at $\dfrac{12\%}{4} = 3\%$, so $u_{n+1} = 1.03u_n - R$.
From **52**, $u_{n+1} = (1.03)^n u_1 - R\left(\dfrac{1-(1.03)^n}{1-1.03}\right)$
We want $u_{n+1} = 0$, $u_1 = 20\,000$ and $n = 40$
Thus $(1.03)^{40} \times 20\,000 + \dfrac{100R}{3}\left(1-(1.03)^{40}\right) = 0$
$\therefore \quad 65\,240.756 \approx R \times 75.401\,26$
$\therefore \quad R \approx 865.25$
So, repayments of $\$865.25$ each quarter are required.

b From **a** $0 = \left(1+\dfrac{r}{100m}\right)^{mn} P - R\left(\dfrac{1-\left(1+\dfrac{r}{100m}\right)^{mn}}{-\dfrac{r}{100m}}\right)$

$\therefore \quad R\left(\dfrac{1-\left(1+\dfrac{r}{100m}\right)^{mn}}{-\dfrac{r}{100m}}\right) = P\left(1+\dfrac{r}{100m}\right)^{mn}$

$\therefore \quad R = \dfrac{P\left(1+\dfrac{r}{100m}\right)^{mn}\left(-\dfrac{r}{100m}\right)}{1-\left(1+\dfrac{r}{100m}\right)^{mn}} = \dfrac{P\left(\dfrac{r}{100m}\right)\left(1+\dfrac{r}{100m}\right)^{mn}}{\left(1+\dfrac{r}{100m}\right)^{mn}-1}$

54 Each rectangle is determined by choosing the two pairs of opposite sides.

This can be done in $\binom{m+2}{2} \times \binom{n+2}{2} = \dfrac{(m+2)(m+1)(n+2)(n+1)}{4}$ ways.

55   **a** We select the captain first and then the other 10 from the remaining 21.

   This can be done in $\binom{11}{1}\binom{21}{10} = 3\,879\,876$ ways.

   b This identity can be established using the general solution of **a**, using n instead of 11. The number of choices is therefore $\binom{n}{1}\binom{2n-1}{n-1}$ .... (1).

   We can do this count in a different way.

   Suppose we select i members from A and $n-i$ from B. There are i ways of choosing the captain from A.

   So, we have $\quad i \times \binom{n}{i}\binom{n}{n-i}\quad$ selections where $i = 1, 2, 3, 4, ..., n$

   $= i\binom{n}{i}^2 \quad$ {as $\binom{n}{i} = \binom{n}{n-i}$ by Pascal's rule}

   Thus the total number of ways is $\quad 1\binom{n}{1}^2 + 2\binom{n}{2}^2 + 3\binom{n}{3}^2 + ... + n\binom{n}{n}^2$ .... (2)

   From (1) and (2), $\quad 1\binom{n}{1}^2 + 2\binom{n}{2}^2 + 3\binom{n}{3}^2 + ... + n\binom{n}{n}^2 = n\binom{2n-1}{n-1}$.

56 The two numbers selected are different and there are $\binom{n}{2}$ different selections.

Of these $(1, 4), (2, 8), (3, 12), ..., (\frac{n}{4}, n)$ are the different outcomes where one is 4 times the other. There are $\frac{n}{4}$ of these.

$\therefore$ P(one is 4 times the other) $= \dfrac{\frac{n}{4}}{\binom{n}{2}} = \dfrac{\frac{n}{4}}{\frac{n(n-1)}{2}} = \dfrac{1}{2(n-1)}$

57 If X is the number of seedlings in a selected row, then $X \sim B(10, \frac{1}{2})$.

P(randomly selected row has *at least* 8 seedlings) $= P(X = 8, 9 \text{ or } 10)$

$= \dfrac{\binom{10}{8} + \binom{10}{9} + \binom{10}{10}}{2^{10}}$

$= \dfrac{56}{1024} \text{ or } \dfrac{7}{128}$

$\therefore$ P(randomly selected row has *less than* 8 seedlings) $= 1 - \dfrac{7}{128} = \dfrac{121}{128}$

$\therefore$ P(*all 10 rows* have *less than* 8 seedlings) $= \left(\dfrac{121}{128}\right)^{10}$

$\therefore$ P(row with maximum germination contains *at least* 8 seedlings) $\approx 1 - \left(\dfrac{121}{128}\right)^{10} \approx 0.430$

58 A is the event of a family having at most one boy in n children.
B is the event of a family having every child the same sex in n children.

$P(A) = P(0B \text{ and } nG \text{ or } 1B \text{ and } (n-1)G)$
$= \binom{n}{0}\left(\dfrac{1}{2}\right)^n + \binom{n}{1}\left(\dfrac{1}{2}\right)^1\left(\dfrac{1}{2}\right)^{n-1}$
$= \left(\dfrac{1}{2}\right)^n + n\left(\dfrac{1}{2}\right)^n$
$= \left(\dfrac{1}{2}\right)^n (n+1)$

$P(B) = P(0B \text{ and } nG \text{ or } nB \text{ and } 0G)$
$= \binom{n}{0}\left(\dfrac{1}{2}\right)^n + \binom{n}{n}\left(\dfrac{1}{2}\right)^n$
$= 2\left(\dfrac{1}{2}\right)^n$

$P(A \cap B) = P(0B \text{ and } nG) = \left(\dfrac{1}{2}\right)^n$

A and B are independent when
$P(A \cap B) = P(A)P(B)$
$\therefore \left(\dfrac{1}{2}\right)^n = \left(\dfrac{1}{2}\right)^n (n+1) \times 2\left(\dfrac{1}{2}\right)^n$
$\therefore 1 = 2(n+1)\left(\dfrac{1}{2}\right)^n$
$\therefore 2^n = 2(n+1)$
$\therefore 2^{n-1} = n+1$
$\therefore n = 3 \quad \{n > 1\}$

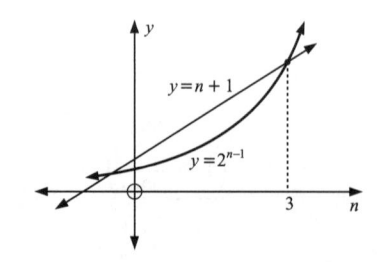

59 Let P(A hits) $= 2p$ and P(B hits) $= p$
Now P(at least one hits) $= \frac{1}{2}$, so P(both miss) $= \frac{1}{2}$
$$\therefore (1 - 2p)(1 - p) = \frac{1}{2}$$
$$\therefore 4p^2 - 6p + 1 = 0$$
$$\therefore p = \frac{3 \pm \sqrt{5}}{4}$$
$$\therefore p = \frac{3 - \sqrt{5}}{4} \quad \left\{\text{since } \frac{3 + \sqrt{5}}{4} > 1\right\}$$
$$\therefore 2p = \frac{3 - \sqrt{5}}{2} \approx 0.382$$
$$\therefore \text{P}(A \text{ hits}) \approx 0.382$$

60 We assume that the typist would know that the coefficients $a = 1$ and $b = 1$ are excluded, so we assume $a \neq 1$ and $b \neq 1$.
Thus a and b are from $\{2, 3, 4, 5, 6, 7, 8, 9\}$, but c is from $\{1, 2, 3, 4, 5, 6, 7, 8, 9\}$
$\therefore$ the total number of guesses is $8 \times 8 \times 9 = 576$.
For real roots, $b^2 - 4ac \geqslant 0$ and so $ac \leqslant \dfrac{b^2}{4}$.

If $b = 2$, $ac \leqslant 1$	which is impossible.	0 solutions
If $b = 3$, $ac \leqslant 2\frac{1}{4}$	$\therefore a = 2$, $c = 1$.	1 solution
If $b = 4$, $ac \leqslant 4$	$\therefore a = 2$, $c = 1$ or 2; $a = 3$, $c = 1$; $a = 4$, $c = 1$.	4 solutions

The number of solutions is best shown in a table:

b values $\Big\{$

	max. ac	a values: 2	3	4	5	6	7	8	9	Total
2	1	0	0	0	0	0	0	0	0	0
3	$2\frac{1}{4}$	1	0	0	0	0	0	0	0	1
4	4	2	1	1	0	0	0	0	0	4
5	$6\frac{1}{4}$	3	2	1	1	1	0	0	0	8
6	9	4	3	2	1	1	1	1	1	14
7	$12\frac{1}{4}$	6	4	3	2	2	1	1	1	20
8	16	8	5	4	3	2	2	2	1	27
9	$20\frac{1}{4}$	9	6	5	4	3	2	2	2	33
										107

$\therefore$ P(real roots) $= \dfrac{107}{576}$

61 Let X arrive x hours after 1 pm, $0 \leqslant x \leqslant 1$
and Y arrive y hours after 1 pm, $0 \leqslant y \leqslant 1$.
They meet provided $-\frac{1}{2} < x - y < \frac{1}{2}$
as the difference between their arrival times is not more than half an hour.

$\therefore$ P(they meet) $= \dfrac{\text{shaded area}}{\text{area of square}} = \dfrac{\frac{3}{4}}{1} = \dfrac{3}{4}$.

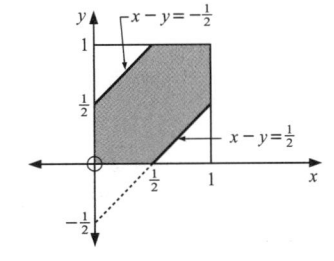

62 After labelling the triangles,
$\triangle ABC$ and $\triangle ABD$ are isosceles   {equal base angles}
and $B\hat{D}C = 2\alpha$ {exterior angle of $\triangle ABD$}
$\therefore$ $\triangle BDC$ is isosceles   {equal base angles}
Thus $AD = BD = BC = x$, say.
If we let $AE = EB = 1$ unit, then $AC = 2$ and $DC = 2 - x$.
Now $\triangle ABC$ and $\triangle BCD$ are similar   {equiangular}

$\therefore \dfrac{AB}{BC} = \dfrac{BC}{CD}$ and so $\dfrac{2}{x} = \dfrac{x}{2-x}$

$\therefore x^2 + 2x - 4 = 0$

$\therefore x = -1 \pm \sqrt{5}$

$\therefore x = \sqrt{5} - 1$ {as x must be > 0}

But $5\alpha = 180°$ {angle sum of a triangle}

$\therefore \alpha = 36°$

and in $\triangle BED$, $\cos 36° = \dfrac{1}{\sqrt{5}-1} = \dfrac{1}{\sqrt{5}-1}\left(\dfrac{\sqrt{5}+1}{\sqrt{5}+1}\right) = \dfrac{1+\sqrt{5}}{4}$.

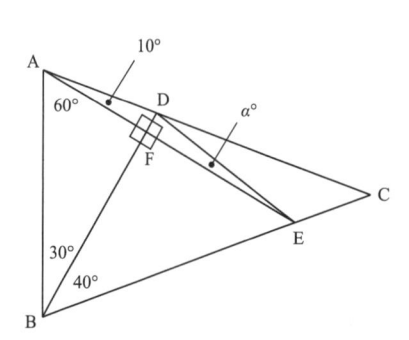

63
We notice that $A\hat{F}B = 90°$ {angles in a $\triangle$}

$\therefore \tan 30° = \dfrac{AF}{BF}$, $\tan 40° = \dfrac{EF}{BF}$, $\tan 10° = \dfrac{DF}{AF}$

Now $\tan \alpha = \dfrac{DF}{EF} = \dfrac{DF}{AF} \times \dfrac{AF}{BF} \times \dfrac{BF}{EF}$

$= \dfrac{\tan 10° \times \tan 30°}{\tan 40°}$

$\therefore \alpha = \arctan\left(\dfrac{\tan 10° \times \tan 30°}{\tan 40°}\right)$

$\therefore \alpha \approx 6.92°$

64 $\tan A + \tan B + \tan C = \tan A \tan B \tan C$

$\therefore \tan A + \tan B = \tan C(\tan A \tan B - 1)$ .... (1)

Suppose $\tan A \tan B = 1$ .... (2)

Then $\tan A + \tan B + \tan C = \tan C$

$\therefore \tan A + \tan B = 0$

$\therefore \tan A = -\tan B$

$\therefore \tan A = -\dfrac{1}{\tan A}$ {using (2)}

$\therefore \tan^2 A = -1$ which is impossible

$\therefore \tan A \tan B \neq 1$, and the supposition (2) is false.

So, using (1), $\dfrac{\tan A + \tan B}{1 - \tan A \tan B} = -\tan C$

$\therefore \tan(A + B) = \tan(-C)$

$\therefore A + B = -C + k\pi$, $k \in \mathbb{Z}$ {equal tans are π apart}

$\therefore A + B + C = k\pi$, $k \in \mathbb{Z}$

65 Let $\arctan\left(\frac{1}{7}\right) = \alpha$ and $\arctan\left(\frac{1}{3}\right) = \beta$ where $\alpha, \beta \in \left]-\frac{\pi}{2}, \frac{\pi}{2}\right[$

$\therefore \tan\alpha = \frac{1}{7}$ and $\tan\beta = \frac{1}{3}$

Since $\tan\alpha, \tan\beta > 0$ and $\alpha, \beta \in \left]-\frac{\pi}{2}, \frac{\pi}{2}\right[$, we know that actually $\alpha, \beta \in \left[0, \frac{\pi}{2}\right[$.

From the diagrams we see that $\alpha, \beta \in \left]0, \frac{\pi}{4}\right[$.

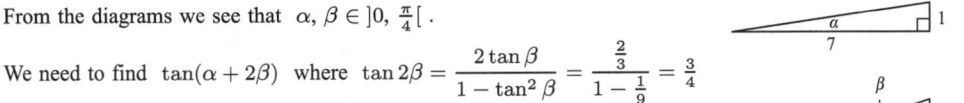

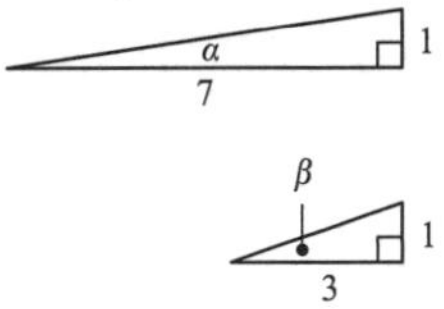

We need to find $\tan(\alpha + 2\beta)$ where $\tan 2\beta = \dfrac{2\tan\beta}{1 - \tan^2\beta} = \dfrac{\frac{2}{3}}{1 - \frac{1}{9}} = \dfrac{3}{4}$

Now $\tan(\alpha + 2\beta) = \dfrac{\tan\alpha + \tan 2\beta}{1 - \tan\alpha \tan 2\beta} = \dfrac{\frac{1}{7} + \frac{3}{4}}{1 - \frac{3}{28}} = 1$

$\therefore \alpha + 2\beta = \frac{\pi}{4} + k\pi, \ k \in \mathbb{Z}$

$\therefore \alpha + 2\beta = \frac{\pi}{4}$, the only solution satisfying $\alpha, \beta \in \left]0, \frac{\pi}{4}\right[$.

66 Consider a model of the mountain. We cut the model along [CT] and flatten it out. To make AB as short as possible, [AB] is a straight line on a sector of a circle.

The circumference of the cone's base is equal to the arc length of the sector, so

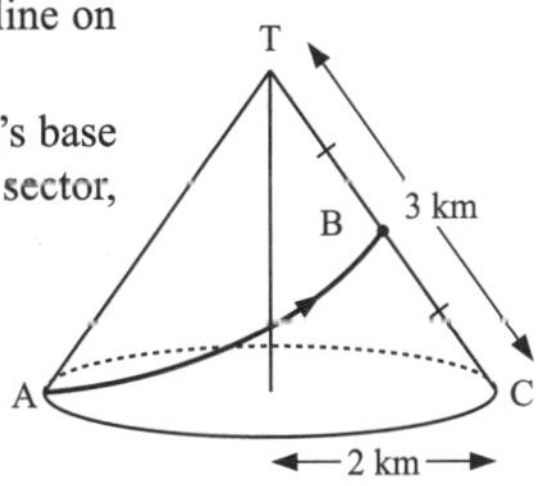

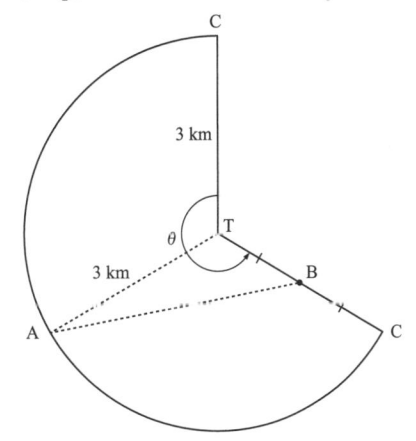

$2\pi \times 2 = \theta \times 3$

$\therefore \theta = \frac{4\pi}{3}$

Thus $\widehat{ATB} = \frac{1}{2}\theta = \frac{2\pi}{3}$

and $AB^2 = 3^2 + \left(\frac{3}{2}\right)^2 - 2 \times 3 \times \frac{3}{2} \cos\left(\frac{2\pi}{3}\right)$

$= 9 + \frac{9}{4} - 9\left(-\frac{1}{2}\right)$

$\therefore AB = \sqrt{\frac{63}{4}} \approx 3.97$ km

67 a

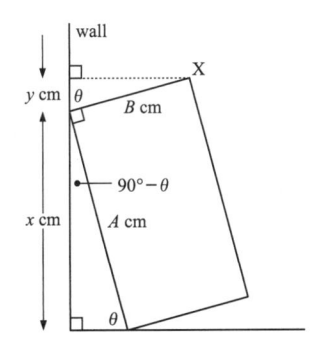

$\sin\theta = \dfrac{x}{A}$ and $\cos\theta = \dfrac{y}{B}$

$\therefore x = A\sin\theta$ and $y = B\cos\theta$

$\therefore H = x + y = A\sin\theta + B\cos\theta$

b H must be $\leqslant$ diagonal of refrigerator

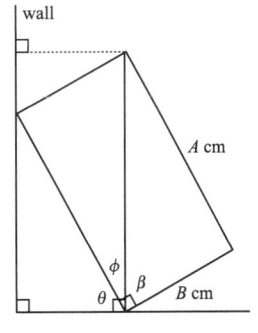

$\therefore A\sin\theta + B\cos\theta \leqslant \sqrt{A^2 + B^2}$

with equality when H is the diagonal

In this case, $\phi = \frac{\pi}{2} - \theta$

and $\beta = \frac{\pi}{2} - \phi = \theta$

$\therefore \tan\theta = \tan\beta = \dfrac{A}{B}$.

68

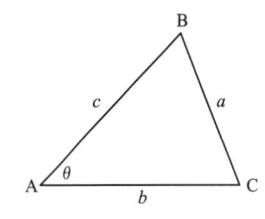

Area of $\triangle ABC$, $A = \tfrac{1}{2}bc\sin A$

$\therefore\ A^2 = \tfrac{1}{4}b^2c^2\sin^2\theta$

$= \tfrac{1}{4}b^2c^2\left(1 - \cos^2\theta\right)$

$= \dfrac{b^2c^2}{4}\left(1 - \left[\dfrac{b^2+c^2-a^2}{2bc}\right]^2\right)$

$= \dfrac{b^2c^2}{4}\left(1 + \dfrac{b^2+c^2-a^2}{2bc}\right)\left(1 - \dfrac{b^2+c^2-a^2}{2bc}\right)$

$= \dfrac{b^2c^2}{4}\left(\dfrac{2bc+b^2+c^2-a^2}{2bc}\right)\left(\dfrac{2bc-b^2-c^2+a^2}{2bc}\right)$

$= \tfrac{1}{16}\left((b+c)^2 - a^2\right)\left(a^2 - (b-c)^2\right)$

$= \tfrac{1}{16}(b+c-a)(b+c+a)(a-b+c)(a+b-c)$

$= \left(\dfrac{a+b+c}{2}\right)\left(\dfrac{b+c-a}{2}\right)\left(\dfrac{a+c-b}{2}\right)\left(\dfrac{a+b-c}{2}\right)$

$= s(s-a)(s-b)(s-c)$ where $s = \dfrac{a+b+c}{2}$

Thus $A = \sqrt{s(s-a)(s-b)(s-c)}$ where $s = \dfrac{a+b+c}{2}$.

69 a $y = \ln(\tan x)$

$\therefore\ \dfrac{dy}{dx} = \dfrac{\sec^2 x}{\tan x}$

$= \dfrac{1}{\cos^2 x} \times \dfrac{\cos x}{\sin x}$

$= \dfrac{1}{\sin x \cos x}\left(\dfrac{2}{2}\right)$

$= \dfrac{2}{\sin 2x}$

$= 2\csc(2x)$

$\therefore\ k = 2$

b Area $= \displaystyle\int_{\frac{\pi}{6}}^{\frac{\pi}{3}} \csc(2x)\, dx$

$= \left[\tfrac{1}{2}\ln(\tan x)\right]_{\frac{\pi}{6}}^{\frac{\pi}{3}}$

$= \tfrac{1}{2}\ln(\sqrt{3}) - \tfrac{1}{2}\ln\left(\tfrac{1}{\sqrt{3}}\right)$

$= \tfrac{1}{2}\ln(3^{\frac{1}{2}}) - \tfrac{1}{2}\ln(3^{-\frac{1}{2}})$

$= \tfrac{1}{4}\ln 3 + \tfrac{1}{4}\ln 3$

$= \tfrac{1}{2}\ln 3$ units^2

70 a

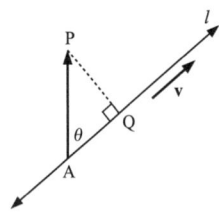

Let angle $PAQ = \theta$

$\therefore\ \sin\theta = \dfrac{PQ}{|\overrightarrow{AP}|}$

$\therefore\ PQ = |\overrightarrow{AP}|\sin\theta$

$= \dfrac{|\overrightarrow{AP}|\,|\mathbf{v}|\sin\theta}{|\mathbf{v}|}$

$= \dfrac{|\overrightarrow{AP}\times\mathbf{v}|}{|\mathbf{v}|}$

{as $|\mathbf{a}|\,|\mathbf{b}|\sin\theta = |\mathbf{a}\times\mathbf{b}|$}

b P is at $(2, -1, 3)$.

A is at $(-1, 1, 2)$ and $\mathbf{v} = \begin{pmatrix} 3 \\ -1 \\ 1 \end{pmatrix}$

$\overrightarrow{AP} \times \mathbf{v} = \begin{pmatrix} 3 \\ -2 \\ 1 \end{pmatrix} \times \begin{pmatrix} 3 \\ -1 \\ 1 \end{pmatrix}$

$= \begin{vmatrix} \mathbf{i} & \mathbf{j} & \mathbf{k} \\ 3 & -2 & 1 \\ 3 & -1 & 1 \end{vmatrix}$

$= \begin{vmatrix} -2 & 1 \\ -1 & 1 \end{vmatrix}\mathbf{i} - \begin{vmatrix} 3 & 1 \\ 3 & 1 \end{vmatrix}\mathbf{j} + \begin{vmatrix} 3 & -2 \\ 3 & -1 \end{vmatrix}\mathbf{k}$

$= -\mathbf{i} + 3\mathbf{k}$

$\therefore\ |\overrightarrow{AP}\times\mathbf{v}| = \sqrt{1+0+9} = \sqrt{10}$ units

$\therefore\ PQ = \dfrac{\sqrt{10}}{\sqrt{9+1+1}} = \sqrt{\tfrac{10}{11}}$ units

≈ 0.953 units

71 Area $= \int_a^{a+2} x^2 \, dx = \frac{31}{6}$

$\therefore \left[\frac{x^3}{3}\right]_a^{a+2} = \frac{31}{6}$

$\therefore \frac{(a+2)^3}{3} - \frac{a^3}{3} = \frac{31}{6}$

$\therefore \frac{\cancel{a^3} + 6a^2 + 12a + 8 - \cancel{a^3}}{3} = \frac{31}{6}$

$\therefore 12a^2 + 24a + 16 = 31$

$\therefore 12a^2 + 24a - 15 = 0$

$\therefore 4a^2 + 8a - 5 = 0$

$\therefore (2a - 1)(2a + 5) = 0$

$a = \frac{1}{2}$ or $-\frac{5}{2}$

But $a > 0$, so $a = \frac{1}{2}$

72 $\frac{dy}{dx} = x \csc y = \frac{x}{\sin y}$

$\therefore \sin y \, \frac{dy}{dx} = x$

$\therefore \int \sin y \, \frac{dy}{dx} \, dx = \int x \, dx$

$\therefore \int \sin y \, dy = \int x \, dx$

$\therefore -\cos y = \frac{x^2}{2} + c$

But when $x = 2$, $y = 0$

$\therefore -1 = 2 + c$

$\therefore c = -3$

$\therefore \cos y = 3 - \frac{x^2}{2}$

$\therefore y = \arccos\left(3 - \frac{1}{2}x^2\right)$

73 $\frac{d}{dx}(\tan^3 x) = 3(\tan x)^2 \times \sec^2 x$

$= 3 \frac{\sin^2 x}{\cos^2 x} \cdot \frac{1}{\cos^2 x}$

$= 3(1 - \cos^2 x) \sec^4 x$

$= 3 \sec^4 x - 3 \sec^2 x$

$\therefore \int (3 \sec^4 x - 3 \sec^2 x) \, dx = \tan^3 x + c_1$

$\therefore 3 \int \sec^4 x \, dx - 3 \tan x + c_2 = \tan^3 x + c_1$

$\therefore 3 \int \sec^4 x \, dx = 3 \tan x + \tan^3 x + c_3$

$\therefore \int \sec^4 x \, dx = \tan x + \frac{1}{3} \tan^3 x + c$

74 If X and Y are independent events then $P(X \cap Y) = P(X)P(Y)$

Thus $P((A \cap B) \cap (A \cup B)) = P(A \cap B) \, P(A \cup B)$

$\therefore P(A \cap B) = P(A \cap B) \, P(A \cup B)$ {since $A \cap B \subseteq A \cup B$}

$\therefore P(A \cap B) = 0$ or $P(A \cup B) = 1$

$\therefore$ A and B are disjoint or either A or B must occur.

75 a $L = \int_0^1 \sqrt{1 + (2x)^2} \, dx$

≈ 1.48 units   {using technology}

b $y = \sin x$, so $\frac{dy}{dx} = \cos x$

$\therefore L = \int_0^\pi \sqrt{1 + \cos^2 x} \, dx$

≈ 3.82 units   {using technology}

76 a i $(A \cup B) \cap A'$
$= A' \cap (A \cup B)$
$= (A' \cap A) \cup (A' \cap B)$
$= \varnothing \cup (A' \cap B)$
$= A' \cap B$

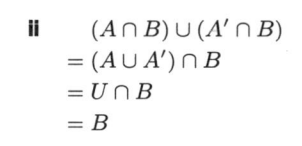

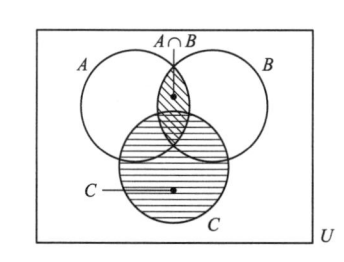

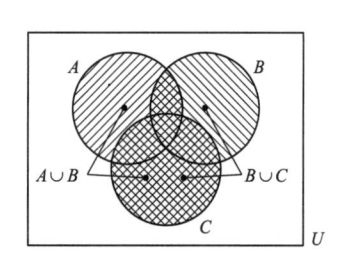

ii $(A \cap B) \cup (A' \cap B)$
$= (A \cup A') \cap B$
$= U \cap B$
$= B$

b

$(A \cap B) \cup C$ includes all that is shaded.

$(A \cup B) \cap (B \cup C)$ includes all parts double shaded.

As the shadings match, the identity is verified.

c **i** $P(A' \cap B')$
$= P((A \cup B)')$
$= 1 - P(A \cup B)$
$= 1 - [P(A) + P(B) - P(A \cap B)]$
$= 1 - P(A) - P(B) + P(A)P(B)$
$= [1 - P(A)][1 - P(B)]$
$= P(A')P(B')$
$\therefore$ A' and B' are independent

ii $P(A \cap B')$
$= P(A) - P(A \cap B)$
$= P(A) - P(A)P(B)$
$= P(A)[1 - P(B)]$
$= P(A)P(B')$
$\therefore$ A and B' are independent

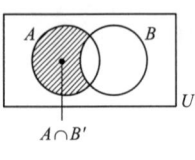

77 $(3 - i\sqrt{2})^4 = 3^4 + 4(3^3)(-i\sqrt{2}) + 6(3^2)(-i\sqrt{2})^2 + 4(3)(-i\sqrt{2})^3 + (-i\sqrt{2})^4$
$= 81 - 108\sqrt{2}i - 108 + 24\sqrt{2}i + 4$
$= -23 - 84\sqrt{2}i$

78 $\sin\theta \cos\theta = \frac{1}{4}$
$\therefore \frac{1}{2}\sin 2\theta = \frac{1}{4}$
$\therefore \sin 2\theta = \frac{1}{2}$
$\therefore 2\theta = \frac{\pi}{6} + k2\pi$ or $\frac{5\pi}{6} + k2\pi$
$\therefore 2\theta = \frac{\pi}{6}, -\frac{11\pi}{6}, \frac{5\pi}{6}, -\frac{7\pi}{6}$ {as $-2\pi \leqslant 2\theta \leqslant 2\pi$}
$\therefore \theta = -\frac{11\pi}{12}, -\frac{7\pi}{12}, \frac{\pi}{12}, \frac{5\pi}{12}$

79 Now $2z + w = i$, so $6z + 3w = 3i$
Also, $z - 3w = 7 - 10i$
$\therefore 7z = 7 - 7i$
$\therefore z = 1 - i$

$\therefore w = i - 2z$
$= i - 2 + 2i$
$= -2 + 3i$
Thus $z + w = -1 + 2i$

80 $(x+1)^2 \dfrac{dy}{dx} = 2xy$

$\therefore \dfrac{1}{y}\dfrac{dy}{dx} = \dfrac{2x}{(x+1)^2}$ {$x > -1$}

$\therefore \displaystyle\int \dfrac{1}{y}\dfrac{dy}{dx}\,dx = \int \dfrac{2(x+1) - 2}{(x+1)^2}\,dx = \int \left[\dfrac{2}{x+1} - 2(x+1)^{-2}\right] dx$

$\therefore \ln|y| = 2\ln|x+1| - 2\dfrac{(x+1)^{-1}}{-1} + c$

$\therefore \ln|y| = \ln(x+1)^2 + \dfrac{2}{x+1} + c$

$\therefore \ln\left|\dfrac{y}{(x+1)^2}\right| = \dfrac{2}{x+1} + c$

$\therefore \left|\dfrac{y}{(x+1)^2}\right| = e^{\frac{2}{x+1} + c}$

$\therefore \dfrac{y}{(x+1)^2} = \pm e^c e^{\frac{2}{x+1}} = A e^{\frac{2}{x+1}}$

But when $x = 1$, $y = 4$, so $\dfrac{4}{2^2} = A e^{\frac{2}{2}}$ $\therefore A = \dfrac{1}{e}$

$\therefore \dfrac{y}{(x+1)^2} = e^{\frac{2}{x+1} - 1} = e^{\frac{1-x}{x+1}}$

$\therefore y = (x+1)^2 e^{\frac{1-x}{x+1}}$

81 **a** $f(x) = \ln(x(x-2))$ is defined when $x(x-2) > 0$

```
    +    |    -    |    +
  ―――――――0―――――――――2――――――― x
```

$\therefore\ x < 0$ or $x > 2$
So the domain is $x \in\ ]-\infty,\ 0[\ \cup\ ]2,\ \infty[$

b $f(x) = \ln x + \ln(x-2)$ {log law}
$\therefore\ f'(x) = \dfrac{1}{x} + \dfrac{1}{x-2}$

c $f'(3) = \frac{1}{3} + 1 = \frac{4}{3}$ at $(3, \ln 3)$
$\therefore$ the tangent has equation
$$\dfrac{y - \ln 3}{x - 3} = \dfrac{4}{3}$$
$\therefore\ 4x - 12 = 3y - 3\ln 3$
$\therefore\ 4x - 3y = 12 - 3\ln 3$

82 **a**

```
   | 3G |     | 4G |
   | 4B |     | 3B |
    (1)        (2)
```

P(both same colour)
= P(GG or BB)
$= \frac{3}{7} \times \frac{4}{7} + \frac{4}{7} \times \frac{3}{7}$
$= \frac{24}{49}$

b P(G from (2) | both different)
$= \dfrac{\text{P(G from (2)} \cap \text{both different)}}{\text{P(both different)}}$
$= \dfrac{\text{P(G from (2) and B from (1))}}{1 - \frac{24}{49}}$
$= \dfrac{\frac{4}{7} \times \frac{4}{7}}{\frac{25}{49}}$
$= \dfrac{16}{25}$

83 **a** $\mathbf{A}^3 = \mathbf{A}$
$\therefore\ |\mathbf{A}^3| = |\mathbf{A}|$
$\therefore\ |\mathbf{A}|^3 = |\mathbf{A}|$
$\therefore\ |\mathbf{A}|^3 - |\mathbf{A}| = 0$
$\therefore\ |\mathbf{A}|(|\mathbf{A}|^2 - 1) = 0$
$\therefore\ |\mathbf{A}| = 0$ or ± 1

b $\mathbf{A}^3 = \mathbf{A}$
$\therefore\ \mathbf{A}^3\mathbf{A}^{-1} = \mathbf{A}\mathbf{A}^{-1}$ if $|\mathbf{A}| \ne 0$
$\therefore\ \mathbf{A}^2\mathbf{A}\mathbf{A}^{-1} = \mathbf{I}$
$\therefore\ \mathbf{A}^2 = \mathbf{I}$
$\therefore\ \mathbf{A}^2\mathbf{A}^{-1} = \mathbf{I}\mathbf{A}^{-1}$
$\therefore\ \mathbf{A}(\mathbf{A}\mathbf{A}^{-1}) = \mathbf{A}^{-1}$
$\therefore\ \mathbf{A} = \mathbf{A}^{-1}$
So, provided $|\mathbf{A}| \ne 0$, $\mathbf{A}^{-1} = \mathbf{A}$

84 $\dfrac{P(x)}{(x-a)^2} = Q(x) + \dfrac{bx + c}{(x-a)^2}$ {the division process}

$\therefore\ P(x) = Q(x)(x-a)^2 + bx + c$
$\therefore\ P(a) = Q(a) \times 0 + ab + c = ab + c$ .... (1)
Also, $P'(x) = Q'(x)(x-a)^2 + Q(x)2(x-a) + b$
$\therefore\ P'(a) = 0 + 0 + b = b$ .... (2)
So, the remainder is $bx + c = bx + (ab + c) - ab$
$= P'(a)\,x + P(a) - a\,P'(a)$ {using (1) and (2)}
$= P'(a)(x - a) + P(a)$

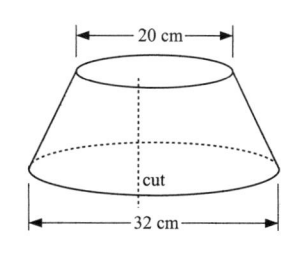

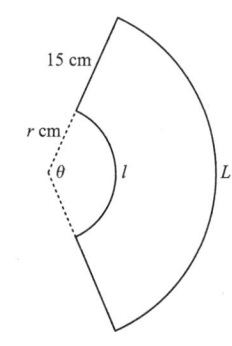

85

$l = 2\pi(10) = 20\pi$
$L = 2\pi(16) = 32\pi$
But $l = r\theta$ and $L = (r+15)\theta$
$\therefore\ r\theta = 20\pi$ and $(r+15)\theta = 32\pi$
Thus $20\pi + 15\theta = 32\pi$
$\therefore\ 15\theta = 12\pi$
$\therefore\ \theta = \frac{4\pi}{5}{}^c = 144°$
and $r\left(\frac{4\pi}{5}\right) = 20\pi$
$\therefore\ r = 25$
$\therefore\ r = 25$ and $\theta = 144°$

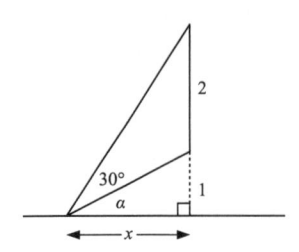

86 $\tan\alpha = \dfrac{1}{x}$ and $\tan(\alpha + 30°) = \dfrac{3}{x}$

$\therefore\ \dfrac{\tan\alpha + \tan 30°}{1 - \tan\alpha\tan 30°} = \dfrac{3}{x}$

$\therefore\ \dfrac{\dfrac{1}{x} + \dfrac{1}{\sqrt{3}}}{} = \dfrac{3}{x}\left(1 - \dfrac{1}{x}\dfrac{1}{\sqrt{3}}\right) = \dfrac{3}{x} - \dfrac{\sqrt{3}}{x^2}$

$\therefore\ \dfrac{1}{\sqrt{3}} - \dfrac{2}{x} + \dfrac{\sqrt{3}}{x^2} = 0$

$\therefore\ x^2 - 2\sqrt{3}x + 3 = 0 \quad \{\times \sqrt{3}x^2\}$

$\therefore\ (x - \sqrt{3})^2 = 0$

$\therefore\ x = \sqrt{3} \approx 1.73$

So, she is $\sqrt{3}$ m or 1.73 m from the wall.

87 We draw the smaller circle in another position, and deliberately do not put P on the x-axis, but close to it.

We let $\widehat{XOP} = \alpha$ and M be the centre of the smaller circle.

We join [MP] and let $\widehat{MOP} = \theta$

$\therefore\ \widehat{QMP} = 2\theta$ {angle at the centre theorem}

Now arc QX = arc QP, since both represent the distance the smaller circle has been rolled.

$\therefore\ r(\theta + \alpha) = \dfrac{r}{2}(2\theta)$

$\therefore\ r\theta + r\alpha = r\theta$

$\therefore\ r\alpha = 0$

$\therefore\ \alpha = 0$ as $r \neq 0$

$\therefore$ P lies on the x-axis.

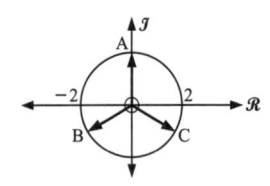

88 a $-8i = 8(-i) = 8\operatorname{cis}\left(-\dfrac{\pi}{2}\right)$

b As $z^3 = -8i$,

$z^3 = 8\operatorname{cis}\left(-\dfrac{\pi}{2} + k2\pi\right),\ k \in \mathbb{Z}$

$\therefore\ z = 8^{\frac{1}{3}}\operatorname{cis}\left(\dfrac{-\dfrac{\pi}{2} + k2\pi}{3}\right)$ {De Moivre}

$\therefore\ z = 2\operatorname{cis}\left(\dfrac{-\pi + k4\pi}{6}\right)$

$\therefore\ z = 2\operatorname{cis}\left(-\dfrac{\pi}{6}\right),\ 2\operatorname{cis}\left(\dfrac{\pi}{2}\right),\ 2\operatorname{cis}\left(-\dfrac{5\pi}{6}\right)$

$\{k = 0, 1, -1\}$

c We let A, B and C be the points corresponding to z_1, z_2, z_3 say.

d If $z_1 = 2\operatorname{cis}\left(-\dfrac{\pi}{6}\right)$,

$z_1^2 = 4\operatorname{cis}\left(-\dfrac{\pi}{3}\right)$ and

$z_2 z_3 = 2\operatorname{cis}\left(\dfrac{\pi}{2}\right) \times 2\operatorname{cis}\left(-\dfrac{5\pi}{6}\right)$

$= 4\operatorname{cis}\left(\dfrac{\pi}{2} - \dfrac{5\pi}{6}\right)$

$= 4\operatorname{cis}\left(-\dfrac{\pi}{3}\right)$

$= z_1^2$

If $z_1 = 2\operatorname{cis}\left(\dfrac{\pi}{2}\right)$,

$z_1^2 = (2i)^2 = -4$ and

$z_2 z_3 = 2\operatorname{cis}\left(\dfrac{-5\pi}{6}\right) \times 2\operatorname{cis}\left(\dfrac{-\pi}{6}\right)$

$= 4\operatorname{cis}\left(\dfrac{-5\pi}{6} + \dfrac{-\pi}{6}\right)$

$= 4\operatorname{cis}(-\pi)$

$= -4 = z_1^2$

If $z_1 = 2\operatorname{cis}\left(-\dfrac{5\pi}{6}\right)$,

$z_1^2 = 4\operatorname{cis}\left(-\dfrac{5\pi}{3}\right)$ and

$z_2 z_3 = 2\operatorname{cis}\left(-\dfrac{\pi}{6}\right) \times 2\operatorname{cis}\left(\dfrac{\pi}{2}\right)$

$= 4\operatorname{cis}\left(\dfrac{\pi}{2} - \dfrac{\pi}{6}\right)$

$= 4\operatorname{cis}\dfrac{\pi}{3}$

$= 4\operatorname{cis}\left(-\dfrac{5\pi}{3}\right) = z_1^2$

e $z_1 z_2 z_3 = z_1(z_2 z_3)$

$= z_1 \times z_1^2$ {from **d**}

$= z_1^3$

$= -8i$ {as z_1 is a root of $z^3 = -8i$}

89 a Let $z = R \operatorname{cis} \theta$
$\therefore \ iz = \operatorname{cis} \frac{\pi}{2} \times R \operatorname{cis} \theta$
$\therefore \ iz = R \operatorname{cis} \left(\frac{\pi}{2} + \theta\right)$
$\therefore \ \arg(iz) = \frac{\pi}{2} + \theta$

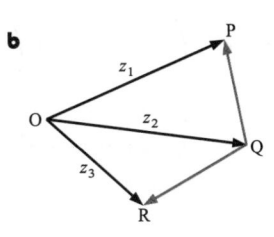

b

$z_3 - z_2 = \overrightarrow{QR}$
$z_1 - z_2 = \overrightarrow{QP}$
Now $i(z_3 - z_2) = z_1 - z_2$
$\therefore \ i\overrightarrow{QR} = \overrightarrow{QP}$
$\therefore \ \overrightarrow{QR} \perp \overrightarrow{QP} \ \{\text{from } \mathbf{a}\}$
$\therefore \ \widehat{PQR}$ is a right angle.
Also $|\overrightarrow{QP}| = |i\overrightarrow{QR}| = |i||\overrightarrow{QR}|$
$\therefore \ QP = 1 \times QR = QR$
$\therefore \ \triangle PQR$ is right angled and isosceles.

90 a $z = re^{i\theta} = r \operatorname{cis} \theta$
$\therefore \ z + \frac{1}{z} = r \operatorname{cis} \theta + \frac{1}{r \operatorname{cis} \theta}$
$= r \operatorname{cis} \theta + \frac{1}{r} \operatorname{cis}(-\theta)$
$= r[\cos \theta + i \sin \theta] + \frac{1}{r}[\cos \theta - i \sin \theta]$
$= \left(r + \frac{1}{r}\right) \cos \theta + i \left(r - \frac{1}{r}\right) \sin \theta$
Thus $a = \left(r + \frac{1}{r}\right) \cos \theta$ and $b = \left(r - \frac{1}{r}\right) \sin \theta$

b If $z + \frac{1}{z}$ is real then
$\left(r - \frac{1}{r}\right) \sin \theta = 0$
$\therefore \ r - \frac{1}{r} = 0$ or $\sin \theta = 0$
$\therefore \ r^2 = 1$ or $\sin \theta = 0$
$\therefore \ r = 1$ or $\theta = k\pi, k \in \mathbb{Z}$ $\{r > 0\}$
$\therefore \ r = 1$ or z is real and non-zero

91 a

P(current flows)
$= P((1) \text{ closed} \cup (2) \text{ closed})$
$= P((1) \text{ closed}) + P((2) \text{ closed})$
$\quad - P((1) \text{ and } (2) \text{ closed})$
$= p^2 + p^2 - p^4$
$= 2p^2 - p^4$

b We need to solve $2p^2 - p^4 > \frac{1}{2}$
We graph $y = 2x^2 - x^4$ in $[0, 1]$.

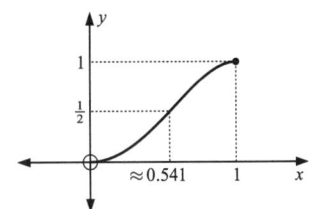

So, for $2p^2 - p^4 > \frac{1}{2}$, $p > 0.541$
$\therefore$ the least value of p is ≈ 0.541

92 a $\mathbf{A}^2 = \begin{pmatrix} 2 & 1 \\ 0 & 2 \end{pmatrix} \begin{pmatrix} 2 & 1 \\ 0 & 2 \end{pmatrix} = \begin{pmatrix} 4 & 4 \\ 0 & 4 \end{pmatrix}$ and $\mathbf{A}^3 = \begin{pmatrix} 4 & 4 \\ 0 & 4 \end{pmatrix} \begin{pmatrix} 2 & 1 \\ 0 & 2 \end{pmatrix} = \begin{pmatrix} 8 & 12 \\ 0 & 8 \end{pmatrix}$

b Proof: (By the principle of mathematical induction)

P_n is "If $\mathbf{A} = \begin{pmatrix} 2 & 1 \\ 0 & 2 \end{pmatrix}$ then $\mathbf{A}^n = \begin{pmatrix} 2^n & n2^{n-1} \\ 0 & 2^n \end{pmatrix}$" for $n \in \mathbb{Z}^+$.

(1) If $n = 1$, $\mathbf{A}^1 = \begin{pmatrix} 2 & 1 \\ 0 & 2 \end{pmatrix} = \begin{pmatrix} 2^1 & 1(2^0) \\ 0 & 2^1 \end{pmatrix}$ $\therefore \ P_1$ is true.

(2) If P_k is assumed true then $\mathbf{A}^k = \begin{pmatrix} 2^k & k2^{k-1} \\ 0 & 2^k \end{pmatrix}$

Now $\mathbf{A}^{k+1} = \mathbf{A}^k \mathbf{A} = \begin{pmatrix} 2^k & k2^{k-1} \\ 0 & 2^k \end{pmatrix} \begin{pmatrix} 2 & 1 \\ 0 & 2 \end{pmatrix}$ {using P_k}

$= \begin{pmatrix} 2^{k+1} + 0 & 2^k + k2^k \\ 0 + 0 & 0 + 2^{k+1} \end{pmatrix}$

$= \begin{pmatrix} 2^{k+1} & (k+1)2^k \\ 0 & 2^{k+1} \end{pmatrix}$

Thus P_{k+1} is true whenever P_k is true.

$\therefore$ since P_1 is true, P_n is true for all $n \in \mathbb{Z}^+$. {Principle of mathematical induction}

93 $(1+x)^n = 1 + \binom{n}{1}x + \binom{n}{2}x^2 + \binom{n}{3}x^3 + \ldots + \binom{n}{n}x^n$ .... (1)

$(1+x)^2(1+x)^{n-2} = (1 + 2x + 1x^2)\left[1 + \binom{n-2}{1}x + \binom{n-2}{2}x^2 + \ldots + \binom{n-2}{n-2}x^{n-2}\right]$ .... (2)

In (1), the coefficient of x^r is $\binom{n}{r}$

In (2), the coefficient of x^r is $1 \times \binom{n-2}{r} + 2\binom{n-2}{r-1} + 1\binom{n-2}{r-2}$

Equating these gives $\binom{n}{r} = \binom{n-2}{r} + 2\binom{n-2}{r-1} + \binom{n-2}{r-2}$

94 a P(stopped at least once)
$= 1 - $ P(never stopped in n intersections)
$= 1 - (1-p)^n$

b $P(A_k \mid B_k) = \dfrac{P(A_k \cap B_k)}{P(B_k)}$

$= \dfrac{P(A_k)}{P(B_k)}$

$= \dfrac{\binom{n}{k}p^k(1-p)^{n-k}}{\sum_{r=k}^{n}\binom{n}{r}p^r(1-p)^{n-r}}$

c If A_1 and B_1 are independent then
$P(A_1 \mid B_1) = P(A_1)$

$\therefore \dfrac{\binom{n}{1}p(1-p)^{n-1}}{1-(1-p)^n} = \binom{n}{1}p(1-p)^{n-1}$

$\therefore \ 1 - (1-p)^n = 1$

$\therefore \ (1-p)^n = 0$

$\therefore \ p = 1$

d If $P(A_2 \mid B_2) = P(A_1)$ and $n = 2$,

$\dfrac{\binom{2}{2}p^2}{\binom{2}{2}p^2} = \binom{2}{1}p(1-p)$

$\therefore \ 1 = 2p(1-p)$

$\therefore \ 2p^2 - 2p + 1 = 0$

where $\Delta = 4 - 4(2)(1) < 0$

$\therefore$ there are no real solutions

95 a The number of ways of selecting 2 females from n is $\binom{n}{2}$

and the number of ways of selecting 1 male from n is $\binom{n}{1}$

$\therefore$ there are $\binom{n}{2}\binom{n}{1} = n\binom{n}{2}$ ways of selecting 2 females and 1 male.

b The number of ways of selecting 3 females from n is $\binom{n}{3}$.

c The total number of ways of selecting a committee of 3 from $2n$ people is $\binom{2n}{3}$.

As there are equal numbers of male and female members, exactly half of these committees will have more females than males.

$\therefore$ total number of committees with more females than males $= \frac{1}{2}\binom{2n}{3}$.

$\therefore$ using **a** and **b**, $n\binom{n}{2} + \binom{n}{3} = \frac{1}{2}\binom{2n}{3}$.

d i If $n = 6$,
P(Mrs Jones is on the committee)
$$= \frac{\binom{1}{1}\binom{5}{1}\binom{6}{1} + \binom{1}{1}\binom{5}{2}\binom{6}{0}}{\frac{1}{2}\binom{12}{3}}$$
$$= \frac{30 + 10}{110}$$
$$= \frac{4}{11}$$

ii P(Mr Jones is on | Mrs Jones is on)
$$= \frac{\text{P(Mr Jones is on} \cap \text{Mrs Jones is on)}}{\text{P(Mrs Jones is on)}}$$
$$= \frac{\text{P(both are on)}}{\text{P(Mrs Jones is on)}}$$
$$= \frac{\binom{2}{2}\binom{5}{1}\binom{5}{0}}{\frac{1}{2}\binom{12}{3}} \div \frac{4}{11}$$
$$= \frac{5}{110} \times \frac{11}{4}$$
$$= \frac{1}{8}$$

96 a

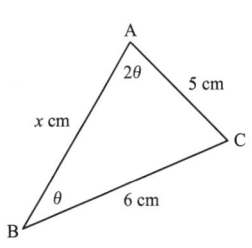

Let the angle at B be θ and at A be 2θ.

By the sine rule: $\dfrac{\sin 2\theta}{6} = \dfrac{\sin \theta}{5}$

$\therefore \dfrac{2\sin\theta \cos\theta}{\sin\theta} = \dfrac{6}{5}$

$\therefore \cos\theta = \dfrac{3}{5}$ .... (*) {as $\sin\theta \neq 0$}

b Let $AB = x$ cm.
Using the cosine rule,
$$5^2 = x^2 + 6^2 - 2x(6)\cos\theta$$
$\therefore 25 = x^2 + 36 - 12x\left(\dfrac{3}{5}\right)$
$\therefore x^2 - \dfrac{36}{5}x + 11 = 0$
$5x^2 - 36x + 55 = 0$
$\therefore (x - 5)(5x - 11) = 0$
$\therefore x = 5$ or $\dfrac{11}{5}$
$\therefore AB = 5$ cm or 2.2 cm

c If $AB = 5$ we have an isosceles triangle
$\therefore 4\theta = 180°$
$\therefore \theta = 45°$
which contradicts (*)
as $\cos 45° = \dfrac{1}{\sqrt{2}} \neq \dfrac{3}{5}$.

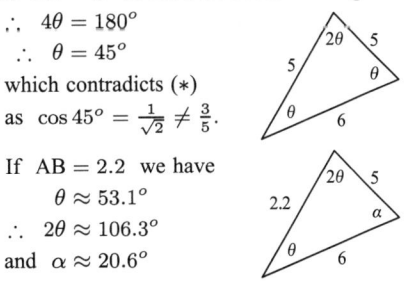

If $AB = 2.2$ we have
$\theta \approx 53.1°$
$\therefore 2\theta \approx 106.3°$
and $\alpha \approx 20.6°$

$\therefore AB = 2.2$ is the only valid solution.

97 Proof: (By contradiction)
Suppose neither equation has real roots
$\therefore b_1^2 - 4c_1 < 0$ and $b_2^2 - 4c_2 < 0$
$\therefore b_1^2 + b_2^2 < 4c_1 + 4c_2$
$\therefore b_1^2 + b_2^2 < 4(c_1 + c_2)$
$\therefore b_1^2 + b_2^2 < 2b_1 b_2$ {given $b_1 b_2 = 2(c_1 + c_2)$}
$\therefore b_1^2 - 2b_1 b_2 + b_2^2 < 0$
$\therefore (b_1 - b_2)^2 < 0$
which is a contradiction as no perfect square of real numbers can be negative.
Thus the supposition is false and so at least one of the equations has real roots.

98 a
$$(2 - \sqrt{3})^{n+1} = a_{n+1} - b_{n+1}\sqrt{3}$$ {replacing n by $n+1$}
$\therefore a_{n+1} - b_{n+1}\sqrt{3} = (2 - \sqrt{3})^n(2 - \sqrt{3})$
$= (a_n - b_n\sqrt{3})(2 - \sqrt{3})$
$= (2a_n + 3b_n) - (a_n + 2b_n)\sqrt{3}$
$\therefore a_{n+1} = 2a_n + 3b_n$ and $b_{n+1} = a_n + 2b_n$

b $(2-\sqrt{3})^1 = a_1 - b_1\sqrt{3}$ $\qquad\qquad (2-\sqrt{3})^2 = a_2 - b_2\sqrt{3}$
   $\therefore\ a_1 = 2,\ b_1 = 1$ $\qquad\qquad\therefore\ 7 - 4\sqrt{3} = a_2 - b_2\sqrt{3}$
   $\therefore\ a_1^2 - 3b_1^2 = 4 - 3(1) = 1$ $\qquad\therefore\ a_2 = 7,\ b_2 = 4$

   $(2-\sqrt{3})^3 = a_3 - b_3\sqrt{3}$ $\qquad\therefore\ a_2^2 - 3b_2^2 = 49 - 3(16) = 1$
   $\therefore\ 26 - 15\sqrt{3} = a_3 - b_3\sqrt{3}$
   $\therefore\ a_3 = 26,\ b_3 = 15$
   $\therefore\ a_3^2 - 3b_3^2 = 676 - 3(225) = 1$

c P_n is: "If $(2-\sqrt{3})^n = a_n - b_n\sqrt{3}$, $a_n, b_n \in \mathbb{Z}$, then $a_n^2 - 3b_n^2 = 1$" for $n \in \mathbb{Z}^+$.

d Proof: (By the principle of mathematical induction)
   (1) If $n = 1$, $a_1^2 - 3b_1^2 = 1$ was shown in **b**. $\therefore\ P_1$ is true.
   (2) If P_k is assumed true then $a_k^2 - 3b_k^2 = 1$
   Now $a_{k+1}^2 - 3b_{k+1}^2 = (2a_k + 3b_k)^2 - 3(a_k + 2b_k)^2$ {from **a**}
   $\qquad\qquad\qquad\quad = 4a_k^2 + 12a_k b_k + 9b_k^2 - 3\left(a_k^2 + 4a_k b_k + 4b_k^2\right)$
   $\qquad\qquad\qquad\quad = a_k^2 - 3b_k^2$
   $\qquad\qquad\qquad\quad = 1$ {using P_k}
   Thus P_{k+1} is true whenever P_k is true.
   $\therefore$ since P_1 is true, P_n is true for all $n \in \mathbb{Z}$ {Principle of mathematical induction}

99 P_n is "If u_n is defined by $u_1 = u_2 = 1$ and $u_{n+2} = u_{n+1} + u_n$ then $u_n \leqslant 2^n$" for $n \in \mathbb{Z}^+$.
Proof: (By the principle of mathematical induction)
   (1) If $n = 1$ or 2, $u_1 = u_2 = 1$ and so $u_1, u_2 \leqslant 2^1$ $\therefore\ P_1$ and P_2 are true.
   (2) If P_k is assumed true then $u_k \leqslant 2^k$
   Now $u_{k+1} = u_k + u_{k-1},\ k \geqslant 2$
   $\therefore\ u_{k+1} \leqslant u_k + u_k$ {the sequence $\{u_n\}$ is increasing, so $u_{k-1} \leqslant u_k$ for all $k \in \mathbb{Z}$}
   $\therefore\ u_{k+1} \leqslant 2u_k$
   $\therefore\ u_{k+1} \leqslant 2(2^k)$ {by P_k}
   $\therefore\ u_{k+1} \leqslant 2^{k+1}$
   Thus P_{k+1} is true whenever P_k is true, for $k \geqslant 2$.
   $\therefore$ since P_1 and P_2 are true, P_n is true for all $n \in \mathbb{Z}^+$ {Principle of mathematical induction}

100 P_n is "$\left(1 - \dfrac{1}{2^2}\right)\left(1 - \dfrac{1}{3^2}\right)\left(1 - \dfrac{1}{4^2}\right) \cdots \left(1 - \dfrac{1}{n^2}\right) = \dfrac{n+1}{2n}$" for $n \in \mathbb{Z}^+,\ n \geqslant 2$.
Proof: (By the principle of mathematical induction)
   (1) If $n = 2$, LHS $= 1 - \dfrac{1}{2^2} = \dfrac{3}{4}$ and RHS $= \dfrac{2+1}{2(2)} = \dfrac{3}{4}$ $\therefore\ P_2$ is true.
   (2) If P_k is assumed true then
   $$\left(1 - \dfrac{1}{2^2}\right)\left(1 - \dfrac{1}{3^2}\right) \cdots \left(1 - \dfrac{1}{k^2}\right) = \dfrac{k+1}{2k}$$
   $$\therefore\ \left(1 - \dfrac{1}{2^2}\right)\left(1 - \dfrac{1}{3^2}\right) \cdots \left(1 - \dfrac{1}{k^2}\right)\left(1 - \dfrac{1}{(k+1)^2}\right) = \dfrac{k+1}{2k}\left(1 - \dfrac{1}{(k+1)^2}\right)$$
   $$= \dfrac{k+1}{2k}\left(\dfrac{(k+1)^2 - 1}{(k+1)^2}\right)$$
   $$= \dfrac{k+1}{2k} \times \dfrac{k^2 + 2k}{(k+1)^2}$$
   $$= \dfrac{k(k+2)}{2k(k+1)} = \dfrac{(k+1) + 1}{2(k+1)}$$

Thus P_{k+1} is true whenever P_k is true.
∴ since P_2 is true, P_n is true for all $n \geqslant 2$ {Principle of mathematical induction}

101 a $y = x^3 - 12x^2 + 45x$

∴ $\dfrac{dy}{dx} = 3x^2 - 24x + 45$
$= 3(x^2 - 8x + 15)$
$= 3(x - 3)(x - 5)$

which is 0 when $x = 3$ or 5

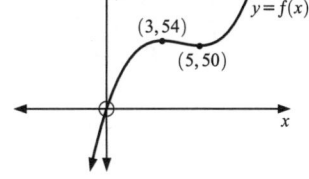

The sign diagram is:

local maximum at $(3, 54)$
local minimum at $(5, 50)$

b $y = x^3 - 12x^2 + 45x$ meets $y = k$ where $x^3 - 12x^2 + 45x = k$.
Now $y = k$ is a horizontal line, so for 3 real roots we need to observe where $y = k$ meets the curve in 3 places.
Thus $50 < k < 54$.

102 a If $z = \text{cis}\,\theta$, then $z^n + \dfrac{1}{z^n} = 2\cos n\theta$, $n \in \mathbb{Z}^+$ {see **Ex 15C 13 a**}

So, with $n = 1$, $z + \dfrac{1}{z} = 2\cos\theta$

∴ $\left(z + \dfrac{1}{z}\right)^3 = 8\cos^3\theta$

∴ $z^3 + 3z + \dfrac{3}{z} + \dfrac{1}{z^3} = 8\cos^3\theta$

∴ $\cos^3\theta = \tfrac{1}{8}\left[z^3 + \dfrac{1}{z^3} + 3\left(z + \dfrac{1}{z}\right)\right]$

$= \tfrac{1}{8}[2\cos 3\theta + 6\cos\theta]$

$= \tfrac{3}{4}\cos\theta + \tfrac{1}{4}\cos 3\theta$ .... (*)

b We let $y = mx$ in $x^3 - 3x + 1 = 0$

∴ $\left(\dfrac{y}{m}\right)^3 - 3\left(\dfrac{y}{m}\right) + 1 = 0$

∴ $y^3 - 3m^2 y + m^3 = 0$

So, for $m^2 = \tfrac{1}{4}$, the equation becomes $y^3 - \tfrac{3}{4}y \pm \tfrac{1}{8} = 0$

Choosing $m = \tfrac{1}{2}$, we have $y^3 - \tfrac{3}{4}y + \tfrac{1}{8} = 0$

So, if $y = \cos\theta$, $\cos^3\theta - \tfrac{3}{4}\cos\theta = -\tfrac{1}{8}$

∴ $\tfrac{1}{4}\cos 3\theta = -\tfrac{1}{8}$ {using (*)}

∴ $\cos 3\theta = -\tfrac{1}{2}$

∴ $3\theta = \tfrac{2\pi}{3} + k2\pi$ or $\tfrac{-2\pi}{3} + k2\pi$

∴ $\theta = \tfrac{2\pi}{9} + \tfrac{k6\pi}{9}$ or $\tfrac{-2\pi}{9} + k\tfrac{6\pi}{9}$

Now $x = \dfrac{y}{m} = \dfrac{\cos\theta}{\tfrac{1}{2}} = 2\cos\theta$

∴ $x = 2\cos\left(\tfrac{2\pi}{9}\right)$, $2\cos\left(\tfrac{8\pi}{9}\right)$, $2\cos\left(\tfrac{14\pi}{9}\right)$

≈ 1.53, -1.88, 0.347

As these are all different, they are the required roots.
(Any solution of 3 consecutive values of θ will generate these roots when decimalised.)

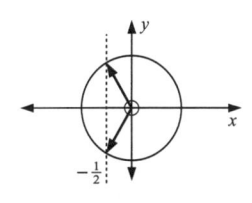

103 **a** Using the cosine rule,
$$y^2 = x^2 + 8^2 - 2(x)(8)\cos\theta$$
$$\therefore\ y^2 = x^2 + 64 - 16x\cos\theta$$
But $x + y + 8 = 20$
$$\therefore\ y = 12 - x$$
Hence, $(12 - x)^2 = x^2 + 64 - 16x\cos\theta$
$$\therefore\ 144 - 24x + x^2 = x^2 + 64 - 16x\cos\theta$$
$$\therefore\ 16x\cos\theta = 24x - 80$$
$$\therefore\ \cos\theta = \frac{3x - 10}{2x}$$

b The area, $A = \frac{1}{2}(8x)\sin\theta = 4x\sin\theta$
$$\therefore\ A^2 = 16x^2\sin^2\theta$$
$$= 16x^2(1 - \cos^2\theta)$$
$$= 16x^2\left(1 - \left(\frac{3x - 10}{2x}\right)^2\right)$$
$$= 16x^2\left(1 - \frac{9x^2 - 60x + 100}{4x^2}\right)$$
$$= 16x^2 - 36x^2 + 240x - 400$$
$$= -20x^2 + 240x - 400$$
$$= -20(x^2 - 12x + 20)$$

c A^2 is a quadratic in x with $a = -20$ and so the shape is ⌒

Thus it has a maximum value when $x = \dfrac{-b}{2a} = \dfrac{-240}{-40} = 6$

$$\therefore\ A^2_{\max} = -20(36 - 72 + 20) = 320$$
So, $A_{\max} = \sqrt{320} = 8\sqrt{5}$ cm^2 when $x = y = 6$ $\therefore$ the triangle is isosceles.

104 **a** $\mathbf{A}^1 = \begin{pmatrix} 2 & 1 \\ 0 & 1 \end{pmatrix}$, $\mathbf{A}^2 = \begin{pmatrix} 2 & 1 \\ 0 & 1 \end{pmatrix}\begin{pmatrix} 2 & 1 \\ 0 & 1 \end{pmatrix} = \begin{pmatrix} 4 & 3 \\ 0 & 1 \end{pmatrix}$

$$\mathbf{A}^3 = \begin{pmatrix} 4 & 3 \\ 0 & 1 \end{pmatrix}\begin{pmatrix} 2 & 1 \\ 0 & 1 \end{pmatrix} = \begin{pmatrix} 8 & 7 \\ 0 & 1 \end{pmatrix}$$

$$\mathbf{A}^4 = \begin{pmatrix} 8 & 7 \\ 0 & 1 \end{pmatrix}\begin{pmatrix} 2 & 1 \\ 0 & 1 \end{pmatrix} = \begin{pmatrix} 16 & 15 \\ 0 & 1 \end{pmatrix}$$

So, we predict: $\mathbf{A}^n = \begin{pmatrix} 2^n & 2^n - 1 \\ 0 & 1 \end{pmatrix}$ for all $n \in \mathbb{Z}^+$

b P_n is "if $\mathbf{A} = \begin{pmatrix} 2 & 1 \\ 0 & 1 \end{pmatrix}$ then $\mathbf{A}^n = \begin{pmatrix} 2^n & 2^n - 1 \\ 0 & 1 \end{pmatrix}$" for all $n \in \mathbb{Z}^+$.

Proof: (By the principle of mathematical induction)

(1) If $n = 1$, $\mathbf{A}^1 = \begin{pmatrix} 2 & 1 \\ 0 & 1 \end{pmatrix} = \begin{pmatrix} 2^1 & 2^1 - 1 \\ 0 & 1 \end{pmatrix}$ $\therefore\ P_1$ is true.

(2) If P_k is assumed true then $\mathbf{A}^k = \begin{pmatrix} 2^k & 2^k - 1 \\ 0 & 1 \end{pmatrix}$

$$\therefore\ \mathbf{A}^{k+1} = \mathbf{A}^k \mathbf{A} = \begin{pmatrix} 2^k & 2^k - 1 \\ 0 & 1 \end{pmatrix}\begin{pmatrix} 2 & 1 \\ 0 & 1 \end{pmatrix}$$

$$= \begin{pmatrix} 2^{k+1} + 0 & 2^k + 2^k - 1 \\ 0 + 0 & 0 + 1 \end{pmatrix}$$

$$= \begin{pmatrix} 2^{k+1} & 2^{k+1} - 1 \\ 0 & 1 \end{pmatrix}$$

Thus P_{k+1} is true whenever P_k is true.
$\therefore$ since P_1 is true, P_n is true for all $n \in \mathbb{Z}$ {Principle of mathematical induction}

c $S_n = \mathbf{A} + \mathbf{A}^2 + \mathbf{A}^3 + \ldots + \mathbf{A}^n$

$$= \begin{pmatrix} 2 & 1 \\ 0 & 1 \end{pmatrix} + \begin{pmatrix} 2^2 & 2^2 - 1 \\ 0 & 1 \end{pmatrix} + \begin{pmatrix} 2^3 & 2^3 - 1 \\ 0 & 1 \end{pmatrix} + \ldots + \begin{pmatrix} 2^n & 2^n - 1 \\ 0 & 1 \end{pmatrix}$$

$$= \begin{pmatrix} 2^1 + 2^2 + 2^3 + \ldots + 2^n & 2^1 - 1 + 2^2 - 1 + 2^3 - 1 + \ldots + 2^n - 1 \\ 0 + 0 + 0 + \ldots + 0 & 1 + 1 + 1 + \ldots + 1 \end{pmatrix}$$

Using the sum of a geometric series formula, $2^1 + 2^2 + 2^3 + ... + 2^n = \dfrac{2(2^n - 1)}{2 - 1} = 2^{n+1} - 2$

$\therefore\ \mathbf{S}_n = \begin{pmatrix} 2^{n+1} - 2 & 2^{n+1} - 2 - n \\ 0 & n \end{pmatrix}$

$\therefore\ \mathbf{S}_{20} = \begin{pmatrix} 2^{21} - 2 & 2^{21} - 2 - 20 \\ 0 & 20 \end{pmatrix} = \begin{pmatrix} 2\,097\,150 & 2\,097\,130 \\ 0 & 20 \end{pmatrix}$

105 $\displaystyle\sum_{n=1}^{m} f(n) = m^3 + 3m$

$\therefore\ f(1) + f(2) + f(3) + ... + f(m) = m^3 + 3m$

$\therefore\ f(1) + f(2) + f(3) + ... + f(m-1) = (m-1)^3 + 3(m-1)$

Thus $(m-1)^3 + 3(m-1) + f(m) = m^3 + 3m$

Hence $m^3 - 3m^2 + 3m - 1 + 3m - 3 + f(m) = m^3 + 3m$

$\therefore\ f(m) = 3m^2 - 3m + 4$

Hence $f(n) = 3n^2 - 3n + 4$ {replacing m by n}

106

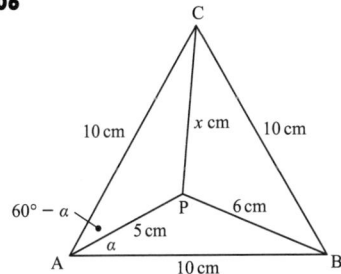

Using the cosine rule in $\triangle ABP$,

$\cos \alpha = \dfrac{5^2 + 10^2 - 6^2}{2(5)(10)} = \dfrac{89}{100} = 0.89$

$\therefore\ \alpha \approx 27.127°$

$\therefore\ 60° - \alpha \approx 32.873°$

So, in $\triangle APC$, $x^2 = 10^2 + 5^2 - 2(10)(5) \cos 32.873°$

$\therefore\ x^2 \approx 41.012\,7$

$\therefore\ x \approx 6.40$

Thus P is about 6.40 cm from C.

107

a $P(X < 85) \approx 0.16$
From the diagram,
$P(90 < X < 95) \approx 0.34$

b As roughly 34% of scores lie between μ and $\mu + \sigma$ for the normal distribution then $\sigma \approx 5$.

108 $X \sim N(90, \sigma^2)$

a $P(X < 88) \approx 0.289\,25$

$\therefore\ P\left(\dfrac{X - 90}{\sigma} < \dfrac{88 - 90}{\sigma}\right) \approx 0.289\,25$

$\therefore\ P\left(Z < \dfrac{-2}{\sigma}\right) \approx 0.289\,25$

$\therefore\ \dfrac{-2}{\sigma} \approx -0.555\,577$

$\therefore\ \sigma \approx 3.599\,86$

b $P(X < 89 \text{ or } X > 91)$
$= 1 - P(89 \leqslant X \leqslant 91)$
$\approx 1 - 0.219$
≈ 0.781

109

$P(M \mid HL) = \dfrac{P(M \cap HL)}{P(HL)}$

$= \dfrac{\frac{38}{78} \times \frac{17}{38}}{\frac{38}{78} \times \frac{17}{38} + \frac{40}{78} \times \frac{15}{40}}$

$= \dfrac{17}{32}$

110 Let F be the event of a faulty chip.
$\therefore$ $P(F) = 0.03$ and $P(F') = 0.97$
If X is the number which are faulty then $X \sim B(500, 0.03)$
So, $P(5 \leqslant X \leqslant 10) = P(X \leqslant 10) - P(X \leqslant 4)$ {1% is 5, 2% is 10}
$\approx 0.114\,787 - 0.000\,754$
≈ 0.114

111 a For 2 metres of rope, $m = 1.4$
$P(2 \text{ flaws}) = \dfrac{1.4^2 e^{-1.4}}{2!}$
≈ 0.242

b For 4 metres of rope, $m = 2.8$
$P(\text{at least 2 flaws}) = 1 - P(X \leqslant 1)$
$\approx 1 - 0.231$
≈ 0.769

112 $X \sim N(\mu, 2.83^2)$
$\therefore$ $P(-4 < X - \mu < 4) = P\left(\dfrac{-4}{2.83} < \dfrac{X - \mu}{2.83} < \dfrac{4}{2.83}\right)$
$= P(-1.4134 < Z < 1.4134)$
≈ 0.842

113 $P(X = x) = a\left(\dfrac{2}{5}\right)^x$ where $x = 0, 1, 2, 3, 4, 5, ...$
$\therefore$ $a\left(\dfrac{2}{5}\right)^0 + a\left(\dfrac{2}{5}\right)^1 + a\left(\dfrac{2}{5}\right)^2 + ... = 1$ $\{\sum P(x) = 1\}$
$\therefore$ $a\left(1 + \dfrac{2}{5} + \left(\dfrac{2}{5}\right)^2 + ...\right) = 1$
$\therefore$ $a\left(\dfrac{1}{1 - \frac{2}{5}}\right) = 1$ {sum of an infinite geometric series}
$\therefore$ $\dfrac{a}{\frac{3}{5}} = 1$
$\therefore$ $a = \dfrac{3}{5}$

114 As A and B are independent, $P(A \mid B) = P(A)$ and $P(B \mid A) = P(B)$
$\therefore$ $P(A) = \dfrac{1}{4}$ and $P(B) = \dfrac{2}{5}$
and $P(A \cap B) = P(A)P(B) = \dfrac{1}{4} \times \dfrac{2}{5} = \dfrac{1}{10}$
So, $P(A \cup B') = 1 - P(B) + P(A \cap B)$
$= 1 - \dfrac{2}{5} + \dfrac{1}{10}$
$= \dfrac{7}{10}$

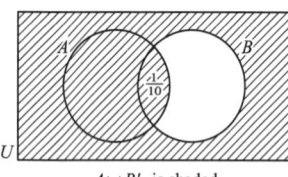

$A \cup B'$ is shaded

115 a As the sum of the probabilities must be 1,
$\dfrac{1}{12} + k + \dfrac{1}{4} + \dfrac{1}{3} = 1$
$\therefore$ $k + \dfrac{1 + 3 + 4}{12} = 1$
$\therefore$ $k = 1 - \dfrac{2}{3}$
$\therefore$ $k = \dfrac{1}{3}$

b Let X be the number of 2s when the die is rolled 2400 times.
So, $X \sim B(2400, \dfrac{1}{3})$
mean $= np$ standard deviation
$= 2400 \times \dfrac{1}{3}$ $= \sqrt{npq}$
$= 800$ $= \sqrt{2400 \times \dfrac{1}{3} \times \dfrac{2}{3}}$
$= \dfrac{\sqrt{4800}}{3}$
$= \dfrac{40\sqrt{3}}{3}$

116 $f(n) = \begin{cases} 0.6e^{-0.6n}, & n \geq 0 \\ 0 & \text{otherwise} \end{cases}$

    a   P(lasts at least a year)
          $= P(N \geq 1)$
          $= 1 - P(0 \leq N < 1)$
          $= 1 - \int_0^1 0.6e^{-0.6n}\,dn$
          $\approx 0.548\,81 \approx 0.549$

    b   P(cell fails within one year)
          $= P(\text{all components fail in one year})$
          $\approx (1 - 0.548\,81)^8$
          $\approx 0.001\,72$

117 $P(X = x) = \dfrac{m^x e^{-m}}{x!}$ for $x = 0, 1, 2, 3, 4, \ldots$ where $m = \text{mean} = \text{variance} = \sigma^2$

     Thus $P(X = x) = \dfrac{\sigma^{2x} e^{-\sigma^2}}{x!}$

     But $P(X = 2) - P(X = 1) = 3P(X = 0)$

     $\therefore \quad \dfrac{\sigma^4 e^{-\sigma^2}}{2!} - \dfrac{\sigma^2 e^{-\sigma^2}}{1!} = \dfrac{3\sigma^0 e^{-\sigma^2}}{0!}$

     $\therefore \quad \dfrac{\sigma^4}{2} - \sigma^2 = 3$

     $\therefore \quad \sigma^4 - 2\sigma^2 - 6 = 0$

     $\therefore \quad \sigma^2 = \dfrac{2 \pm \sqrt{4 - 4(1)(-6)}}{2} = \dfrac{2 \pm \sqrt{28}}{2} = 1 \pm \sqrt{7}$

     But $\sigma^2 > 0$, so $\sigma^2 = 1 + \sqrt{7}$ and $\sigma > 0$ so $\sigma = \sqrt{1 + \sqrt{7}}$

118 Using technology, $\bar{x} \approx 375.01$ and $s_n \approx 0.189\,983$

    a   An unbiased estimate of μ is $\bar{x} \approx 375$ mL

    b   An unbiased estimate of σ^2 is $\dfrac{n}{n-1} s_n^2 \approx \dfrac{80}{79} \times 0.189\,983^2 \approx 0.0366$

119 $\sum_{i=1}^{25} x_i = 1650$ and $\sum_{i=1}^{25} x_i^2 = 115\,492$

    a   An unbiased estimate of μ is $\bar{x} = \dfrac{\sum_{i=1}^{25} x_i}{25} = \dfrac{1650}{25} = 66$

    b $\sum_{i=1}^{25} (x_i - \bar{x})^2 = \sum_{i=1}^{25} x_i^2 - n\bar{x}^2 = 115\,492 - 25 \times 66^2 = 6592$

     Now $s_n^2 = \dfrac{\sum_{i=1}^{25}(x_i - \bar{x})^2}{25} = \dfrac{6592}{25} = 263.68$

     $\therefore$ an unbiased estimate of σ^2 is $\dfrac{n}{n-1} s_n^2 = \dfrac{25}{24} \times 263.68$
                                                    ≈ 275

120   **a** $\int \ln x \, dx = \int 1 \ln x \, dx$

        We integrate by parts with $u = \ln x$ $v' = 1$
                                        $u' = \dfrac{1}{x}$ $v = x$

        $\therefore \int \ln x \, dx = x \ln x - \int \left(\dfrac{1}{x}\right) x \, dx$
                           $= x \ln x - \int 1 \, dx$
                           $= x \ln x - x + c$

        Check: $\dfrac{d}{dx}(x \ln x - x + c)$
                 $= 1 \ln x + x\left(\dfrac{1}{x}\right) - 1 + 0$
                 $= \ln x + 1 - 1$
                 $= \ln x \checkmark$

b For $f(x)$ to be a pdf, $\int_1^k f(x)\,dx = 1$ $\therefore$ $\int_1^k \ln x\,dx = 1$

$\therefore$ $[x \ln x - x]_1^k = 1$ {using **a**}

$\therefore$ $(k \ln k - k) - (0 - 1) = 1$

$\therefore$ $k(\ln k - 1) = 0$

$\therefore$ $k = 0$ or $\ln k = 1$

$\therefore$ $k = 0$ or e

But $k \geqslant 1$, so $k = e$

c If the median was m, we would need to solve $\int_1^m \ln x\,dx = \frac{1}{2}$.

121 The diagonals [AC] and [BD] intersect at right angles.
Let $BD = x$. Using the cosine rule,
$$x^2 = a^2 + a^2 - 2aa\cos 2\theta$$
$$\therefore\ x^2 = 2a^2(1 - \cos 2\theta) \ \ ....\ (1)$$
But $\sin \theta = \dfrac{\frac{x}{2}}{a} = \dfrac{x}{2a}$
$$\therefore\ x^2 = 4a^2 \sin^2 \theta \ \ ....\ (2)$$
From (1) and (2), $2a^2(1 - \cos 2\theta) = 4a^2 \sin^2 \theta$
$$\therefore\ 1 - \cos 2\theta = 2 \sin^2 \theta$$
$$\therefore\ \sin^2 \theta = \tfrac{1}{2} - \tfrac{1}{2}\cos 2\theta$$
and $\cos^2 \theta = 1 - \sin^2 \theta$
$$= 1 - \left(\tfrac{1}{2} - \tfrac{1}{2}\cos 2\theta\right)$$
$$\therefore\ \cos^2 \theta = \tfrac{1}{2} + \tfrac{1}{2}\cos 2\theta$$

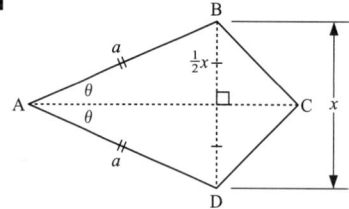

122 Draw [DN] $\perp$ [BC] in isosceles $\triangle BCD$.
$\therefore$ $BN = NC = a$ say and so $AB = BC = 2a$
If $DN = h$, then $\tan \alpha = \dfrac{DN}{AN} = \dfrac{h}{3a}$
and $\tan \theta = \dfrac{h}{a}$
$\therefore$ $3 \tan \alpha = \tan \theta$

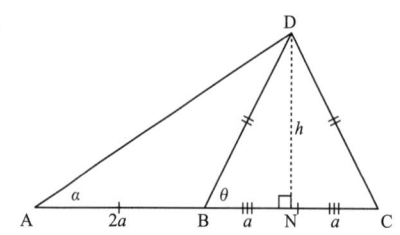

123 a As $O\widehat{P}Q = \theta$, $P\widehat{O}N = 90° - \theta$ and so $N\widehat{O}Q = \theta$
So, $\cos \theta = \dfrac{X}{d}$ and $\sin \theta = \dfrac{Y}{d}$
$\therefore$ $X = d\cos \theta$ and $Y = d\sin \theta$
But $\sin \theta = \dfrac{d}{b}$ and $\cos \theta = \dfrac{b}{3}$
$\therefore$ $\sin \theta \cos \theta = \left(\dfrac{d}{b}\right)\left(\dfrac{b}{3}\right) = \dfrac{d}{3}$
$\therefore$ $d = 3 \sin \theta \cos \theta$
Thus $X = 3 \sin \theta \cos^2 \theta$ and $Y = 3 \sin^2 \theta \cos \theta$
$\therefore$ N is at $(3\sin \theta \cos^2 \theta,\ 3\sin^2 \theta \cos \theta)$.

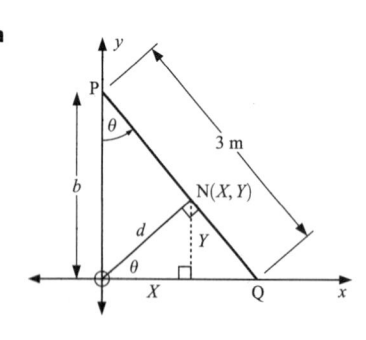

b a 'four leaf clover'

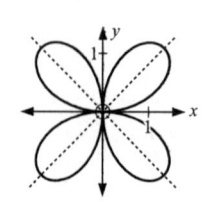

124 **a** $u_1 = \dfrac{1}{\sin\theta} - \sin\theta = \dfrac{1-\sin^2\theta}{\sin\theta} = \dfrac{\cos^2\theta}{\sin\theta}$

$u_4 = \dfrac{1}{\cos\theta} - \cos\theta = \dfrac{1-\cos^2\theta}{\cos\theta} = \dfrac{\sin^2\theta}{\cos\theta}$

$\therefore \dfrac{u_2}{u_1} = \dfrac{\cos\theta}{\left(\dfrac{\cos^2\theta}{\sin\theta}\right)} = \tan\theta$, $\dfrac{u_3}{u_2} = \dfrac{\sin\theta}{\cos\theta} = \tan\theta$ and $\dfrac{u_4}{u_3} = \dfrac{\left(\dfrac{\sin^2\theta}{\cos\theta}\right)}{\sin\theta} = \dfrac{\sin\theta}{\cos\theta} = \tan\theta$

So, the sequence is geometric with $u_1 = \dfrac{\cos^2\theta}{\sin\theta}$ and $r = \tan\theta$

$\therefore u_n = u_1 r^{n-1} = \dfrac{\cos^2\theta}{\sin\theta} \times (\tan\theta)^{n-1} = \dfrac{\cos\theta}{\tan\theta} \times \tan^{n-1}\theta$

$\therefore u_n = \cos\theta \tan^{n-2}\theta$

b $u_1 = 1$, $u_2 = \cos^1\theta$, $u_3 = \cos^3\theta$, $u_4 = \cos^7\theta$, $u_5 = \cos^{15}\theta$
We notice that $u_5 = u_4^2 \cos\theta$, $u_4 = u_3^2\cos\theta$, $u_3 = u_2^2\cos\theta$, $u_2 = u_1^2\cos\theta$,
suggesting that $u_1 = 1$ and $u_{n+1} = u_n^2\cos\theta$ for all $n\in\mathbb{Z}^+$.

125 **a** $u_3 = u_1 + 2d = \dfrac{1}{k}$ .... (1)   So, $u_1 + 3d - u_1 - 2d = k - \dfrac{1}{k}$

$u_4 = u_1 + 3d = k$

$u_6 = u_1 + 5d = k^2 + 1$ $\therefore d = k - \dfrac{1}{k}$ .... (2)

and $u_1 + 5d - u_1 - 3d = k^2 + 1 - k$

$\therefore 2d = k^2 + 1 - k$ .... (3)

From (2) and (3), $k^2 - k + 1 = 2k - \dfrac{2}{k}$

$\therefore k^3 - 3k^2 + k + 2 = 0$

$\therefore (k-2)(k^2 - k - 1) = 0$

$\therefore k = 2$ or $\dfrac{1\pm\sqrt{1-4(1)(-1)}}{2} = \dfrac{1\pm\sqrt{5}}{2}$ But $k\in\mathbb{Q}$, so $k = 2$.

b Using (2), $d = 2 - \tfrac{1}{2} = \tfrac{3}{2}$ Now $u_n = u_1 + (n-1)d$

$\therefore$ using (1), $u_1 + 2\left(\tfrac{3}{2}\right) = \tfrac{1}{2}$ $\therefore u_n = -\tfrac{5}{2} + (n-1)\tfrac{3}{2}$

$\therefore u_1 = -\tfrac{5}{2}$ $\therefore u_n = \tfrac{3}{2}n - 4$ for all $n\in\mathbb{Z}^+$

126 **a**   Let $PC = a$ units

So, $\sin\theta = \dfrac{PZ}{a}$

$\therefore PZ = a\sin\theta$ .... (1)

and $\sin(60° - \theta) = \dfrac{PY}{a}$

$\therefore PY = a\sin(60° - \theta)$ .... (2)

Now $M\widehat{P}C = 30° + 30° + \theta$

$\qquad = 60° + \theta$

so in $\triangle CMP$, $\sin(60° + \theta) = \dfrac{CM}{a}$

$\therefore CM = a\sin(60° + \theta)$ .... (3)

Also, in triangle ACN, $\sin 60° = \dfrac{CN}{2k}$

$\therefore CN = 2k\left(\dfrac{\sqrt{3}}{2}\right) = \sqrt{3}k$ .... (4)

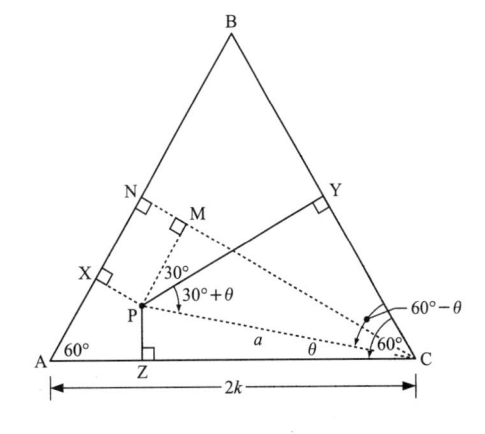

$\therefore$ PX = NM = CN − CM
$= k\sqrt{3} - a\sin(60° + \theta)$ {using (3) and (4)}

Thus PX + PY + PZ $= k\sqrt{3} - a\sin(60° + \theta) + a\sin(60° - \theta) + a\sin\theta$ {using (1) and (2)}
$= k\sqrt{3} + a[\sin\theta + \sin(60° - \theta) - \sin(60° + \theta)]$
$= k\sqrt{3} + a[\sin\theta - \sin\theta]$
$= k\sqrt{3}$ for all θ, which is a constant.

b If P is at A, PX + PY + PZ = altitude from A to [BC] + 0 + 0
$= AC\sin 60° = k\sqrt{3}$ ✓

c

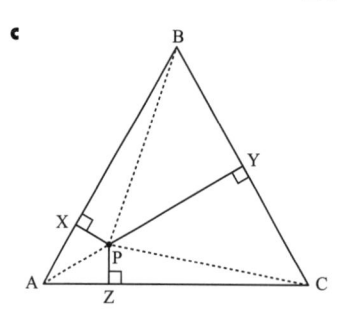

Area $\triangle ABC$ = area $\triangle ABP$ + area $\triangle BCP$ + area $\triangle ACP$
$= \frac{1}{2}(2kPX) + \frac{1}{2}(2kPY) + \frac{1}{2}(2kPZ)$
$= k(PX + PY + PZ)$ .... (5)

But area $\triangle ABC = \frac{1}{2}(2k)(\sqrt{3}k) = k^2\sqrt{3}$ .... (6)

From (5) and (6), PX + PY + PZ = $k\sqrt{3}$.

127 a $\theta_1 = \theta_2$ and $\phi_1 = \phi_2$ {equal alternate angles}

Now $\tan\theta = \dfrac{PN}{b}$ and $\tan\phi = \dfrac{PM}{a}$

$\therefore$ PN = $b\tan\theta$ and PM = $a\tan\phi$

But MN is constant, so we let
$b\tan\theta + a\tan\phi = k$

Differentiating with respect to θ gives

$b\sec^2\theta + a\sec^2\phi \dfrac{d\phi}{d\theta} = 0$

$\therefore \dfrac{d\phi}{d\theta} = \dfrac{-b\sec^2\theta}{a\sec^2\phi} = \dfrac{-b\cos^2\phi}{a\cos^2\theta}$

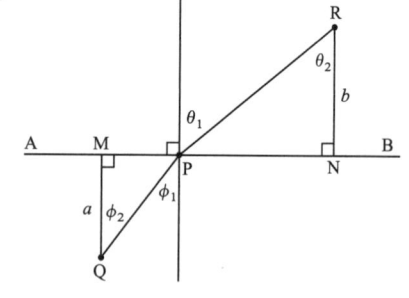

b Now speed = $\dfrac{\text{distance}}{\text{time}}$ $\therefore$ time = $\dfrac{\text{distance}}{\text{speed}}$

$\therefore$ the total time T to travel from R to P to Q is given by

$T = \dfrac{PR}{v_1} + \dfrac{PQ}{v_2}$

$= \dfrac{b}{v_1 \cos\theta} + \dfrac{a}{v_2 \cos\phi}$ {since $\cos\theta = \dfrac{b}{PR}$, $\cos\phi = \dfrac{a}{PQ}$}

$= \dfrac{b}{v_1}[\cos\theta]^{-1} + \dfrac{a}{v_2}[\cos\phi]^{-1}$

$\therefore \dfrac{dT}{d\theta} = -\dfrac{b}{v_1}[\cos\theta]^{-2} \times -\sin\theta - \dfrac{a}{v_2}[\cos\phi]^{-2} \times -\sin\phi \dfrac{d\phi}{d\theta}$

$= \dfrac{b\sin\theta}{v_1 \cos^2\theta} + \dfrac{a\sin\phi}{v_2 \cos^2\phi}\left(\dfrac{-b\cos^2\phi}{a\cos^2\theta}\right)$ {from **a**}

$= \dfrac{b\sin\theta}{v_1 \cos^2\theta} - \dfrac{b\sin\phi}{v_2 \cos^2\theta}$

$= \dfrac{b}{\cos^2\theta}\left[\dfrac{\sin\theta}{v_1} - \dfrac{\sin\phi}{v_2}\right]$

$\therefore \dfrac{dT}{d\theta} = 0$ when $\dfrac{\sin\theta}{v_1} = \dfrac{\sin\phi}{v_2}$, or when $\dfrac{\sin\theta}{\sin\phi} = \dfrac{v_1}{v_2}$.

So, there is only one case when $\dfrac{dT}{d\theta} = 0$.

The question is whether we have a minimum or a maximum T in this case.

We construct the following sign diagram for $\dfrac{dT}{d\theta}$:

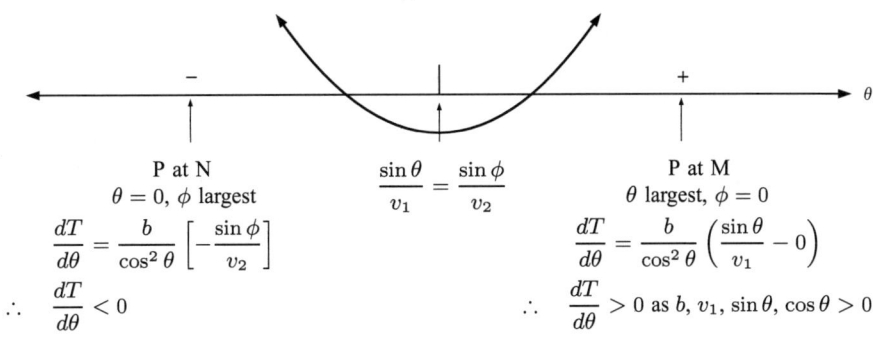

P at N	$\dfrac{\sin\theta}{v_1} = \dfrac{\sin\phi}{v_2}$	P at M
$\theta = 0$, ϕ largest		θ largest, $\phi = 0$
$\dfrac{dT}{d\theta} = \dfrac{b}{\cos^2\theta}\left[-\dfrac{\sin\phi}{v_2}\right]$		$\dfrac{dT}{d\theta} = \dfrac{b}{\cos^2\theta}\left(\dfrac{\sin\theta}{v_1} - 0\right)$
$\therefore \dfrac{dT}{d\theta} < 0$		$\therefore \dfrac{dT}{d\theta} > 0$ as $b, v_1, \sin\theta, \cos\theta > 0$

$\therefore$ the minimum value of T occurs when $\dfrac{dT}{d\theta} = 0$.

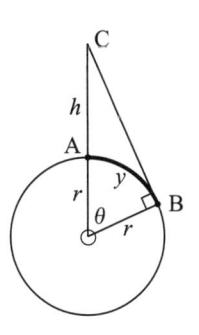

128 a Let the arc length AB be y

$\therefore y = r\theta$ ....(1) and $\cos\theta = \dfrac{r}{r+h}$

$= r(r+h)^{-1}$ ....(2)

We differentiate (1) and (2) with r as a constant:

$\dfrac{dy}{dt} = r\dfrac{d\theta}{dt} \quad \therefore \dfrac{d\theta}{dt} = \dfrac{1}{r}\dfrac{dy}{dt}$ ....(3)

and $-\sin\theta \dfrac{d\theta}{dt} = -r(r+h)^{-2}\dfrac{dh}{dt}$

$\therefore \sin\theta \left(\dfrac{1}{r}\dfrac{dy}{dt}\right) = \dfrac{r}{(r+h)^2}\dfrac{dh}{dt}$ {using (3)}

But $r+h = \dfrac{r}{\cos\theta}$, so $\sin\theta\left(\dfrac{1}{r}\dfrac{dy}{dt}\right) = r\left(\dfrac{\cos^2\theta}{r^2}\right)\dfrac{dh}{dt}$

$\therefore \dfrac{dy}{dt} = \dfrac{\cos^2\theta}{\sin\theta}\dfrac{dh}{dt}$

b The rocket has velocity $\dfrac{dh}{dt}$.

$\therefore \dfrac{dh}{dt} = r\sin t$ for $t \in [0, \pi]$

$\therefore h = \int r\sin t\, dt = -r\cos t + c$

But when $t = 0$, $h = 0$

$\therefore c = r$

So, $h = r(1 - \cos t)$

Now when $t = \dfrac{\pi}{2}$, $\cos t = 0$ and $h = r$.

This means that the rocket is r km above the earth's surface.

c At $t = \dfrac{\pi}{2}$, we have:

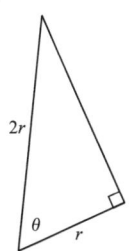

$\cos\theta = \dfrac{r}{2r} = \dfrac{1}{2}$

$\therefore \theta = \dfrac{\pi}{3}$ and $\sin\theta = \dfrac{\sqrt{3}}{2}$

$\therefore \dfrac{dy}{dt} \approx \dfrac{\left(\dfrac{1}{2}\right)^2}{\dfrac{\sqrt{3}}{2}} \times 6000 \times \sin\left(\dfrac{\pi}{2}\right)$ {using **a**, $\dfrac{dh}{dt} = r\sin t$}

$\approx \dfrac{1}{4} \times \dfrac{2}{\sqrt{3}} \times 6000 \times 1$

$\approx \dfrac{3000}{\sqrt{3}}$

$\approx 1000\sqrt{3}$ km h^{-1}

129 The discriminant, $\Delta = 1^2 - 4(m-1)(-m)$
$= 1 + 4m(m-1)$
$= 4m^2 - 4m + 1$
$= (2m-1)^2$
$\geqslant 0$ for all $0 < m < 1$

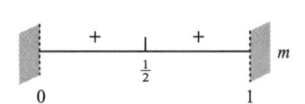

So, the roots are always real.

sum of roots $= \dfrac{-b}{a} = \dfrac{-1}{m-1}$ which is positive since $m - 1 < 0$ for all $0 < m < 1$

product of roots $= \dfrac{c}{a} = \dfrac{-m}{m-1}$ which is positive since $-m < 0$ for all $0 < m < 1$.

As the sum and product of the roots are both positive, both roots are positive.

130 a $\sin 15°$
$= \sin(45° - 30°)$
$= \sin 45° \cos 30° - \cos 45° \sin 30°$
$= \left(\dfrac{1}{\sqrt{2}}\right)\left(\dfrac{\sqrt{3}}{2}\right) - \left(\dfrac{1}{\sqrt{2}}\right)\left(\dfrac{1}{2}\right)$
$= \left(\dfrac{\sqrt{3}-1}{2\sqrt{2}}\right)\dfrac{\sqrt{2}}{\sqrt{2}} = \dfrac{\sqrt{6}-\sqrt{2}}{4}$

b $\cos^2 165° + \cos^2 285°$
$= [\cos(180° - 15°)]^2 + [\cos(270° + 15°)]^2$
$= (-\cos 15°)^2 + (\sin 15°)^2$
$\{\cos(\pi - \theta) = -\cos\theta \text{ and } \cos\left(\dfrac{3\pi}{2} + \theta\right) = \sin\theta\}$
$= \cos^2 15° + \sin^2 15°$
$= 1$

131 $3 \sec 2x = \cot 2x + 3 \tan 2x$, $-\pi \leqslant x \leqslant \pi$

$\therefore \dfrac{3}{\cos 2x} = \dfrac{\cos 2x}{\sin 2x} + 3 \dfrac{\sin 2x}{\cos 2x}$, $-2\pi \leqslant 2x \leqslant 2\pi$

Multiplying all terms by $\sin 2x \cos 2x$ gives:
$3 \sin 2x = \cos^2 2x + 3 \sin^2 2x$
$\therefore 3 \sin 2x = 1 - \sin^2 2x + 3 \sin^2 2x$
$\therefore 2 \sin^2 2x - 3 \sin 2x + 1 = 0$
$\therefore (2 \sin 2x - 1)(\sin 2x - 1) = 0$
$\therefore \sin 2x = \tfrac{1}{2}$ or 1
$\therefore 2x = \dfrac{-11\pi}{6}, \dfrac{-3\pi}{2}, \dfrac{-7\pi}{6}, \dfrac{\pi}{6}, \dfrac{\pi}{2}$ or $\dfrac{5\pi}{6}$
$\therefore x = \dfrac{-11\pi}{12}, \dfrac{-3\pi}{4}, \dfrac{-7\pi}{12}, \dfrac{\pi}{12}, \dfrac{\pi}{4}$ or $\dfrac{5\pi}{12}$.

132 $4 \sin x = \sqrt{3} \csc x + 2 - 2\sqrt{3}$ where $0 \leqslant x \leqslant 2\pi$

$\therefore 4 \sin x = \dfrac{\sqrt{3}}{\sin x} + 2 - 2\sqrt{3}$

$\therefore 4 \sin^2 x + (2\sqrt{3} - 2) \sin x - \sqrt{3} = 0$

$\therefore (2 \sin x + \sqrt{3})(2 \sin x - 1) = 0$

$\therefore \sin x = -\dfrac{\sqrt{3}}{2}$ or $\dfrac{1}{2}$

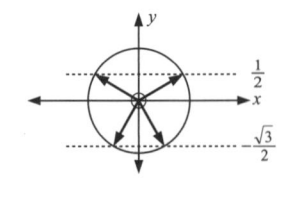

$\therefore x = \dfrac{\pi}{6}, \dfrac{5\pi}{6}, \dfrac{4\pi}{3}, \dfrac{5\pi}{3}$

133 Let the terms of the geometric series be x, rx and r^2x, where r is the common ratio.

$\therefore x + rx + r^2x = 39$ .... (1)

But x, $\tfrac{5}{3}rx$ and r^2x are arithmetic, so $\tfrac{5}{3}rx - x = r^2x - \tfrac{5}{3}rx$

$\therefore \tfrac{10}{3}rx - x = r^2x$

$\therefore \tfrac{10}{3}r - 1 = r^2$

$\therefore 3r^2 - 10r + 3 = 0$

$\therefore (3r - 1)(r - 3) = 0$

$\therefore r = \tfrac{1}{3}$ or 3

Now from (1), $x = \dfrac{39}{1+r+r^2}$

$\therefore$ when $r = \frac{1}{3}$, $x = \dfrac{39}{1 + \frac{1}{3} + \frac{1}{9}} = 27$, and when $r = 3$, $x = \dfrac{39}{1+3+9} = 3$

$\therefore$ the smallest possible value of the first term is 3.

134 $\log_3(x-k) + \log_3(x+2) = 1$
$\therefore \log_3(x-k)(x+2) = 1$
$\therefore (x-k)(x+2) = 3^1 = 3$
$\therefore x^2 + [2-k]x - 2k - 3 = 0$

This quadratic in x has $\Delta = (2-k)^2 - 4(1)(-2k-3)$
$= 4 - 4k + k^2 + 8k + 12$
$= k^2 + 4k + 16$
$= (k+2)^2 + 12$

Since $(k+2)^2 \geqslant 0$, $\Delta \geqslant 0$ for all k
$\therefore$ the original equation has a real solution for all real k.

135 a $8^{2x+3} = 4\sqrt[3]{2}$
$\therefore 2^{3(2x+3)} = 2^2 \times 2^{\frac{1}{3}}$
$\therefore 6x + 9 = \frac{7}{3}$
$\therefore 18x + 27 = 7$
$\therefore 18x = -20$
$\therefore x = -1\frac{1}{9}$

b $3^{2x+1} + 8(3^x) = 3$
$\therefore 3(3^x)^2 + 8(3^x) - 3 = 0$
$\therefore 3m^2 + 8m - 3 = 0$ where $m = 3^x$
$\therefore (3m-1)(m+3) = 0$ where $m = 3^x$
$\therefore m = \frac{1}{3}$ or -3
But $m = 3^x > 0$, so $3^x = \frac{1}{3} = 3^{-1}$
$\therefore x = -1$

c $\ln(\ln x) = 1$
$\therefore \ln x = e^1 = e$
$\therefore x = e^e$

d $\log_{\frac{1}{9}} x = \log_9 5$
$\therefore \dfrac{\log x}{\log \left(\frac{1}{9}\right)} = \dfrac{\log 5}{\log 9}$
$\therefore \dfrac{\log x}{-\log 9} = \dfrac{\log 5}{\log 9}$
$\therefore \log x = -\log 5 = \log(5^{-1})$
$\therefore x = 5^{-1} = \frac{1}{5}$

136 a $(0.5)^{x+1} > 0.125$
$\therefore (0.5)^{x+1} > (0.5)^3$
But $y = (0.5)^{x+1}$ is decreasing,
so $x + 1 < 3$
$\therefore x < 2$

c $4^x + 2^{x+3} < 48$
$\therefore (2^x)^2 + 8(2^x) - 48 < 0$
$(2^x + 12)(2^x - 4) < 0$
where $2^x + 12 > 0$ for all x
$\therefore 2^x - 4 < 0$
$\therefore 2^x < 2^2$
But $y = 2^x$ is increasing,
$\therefore x < 2$

b $\left(\frac{2}{3}\right)^x > \left(\frac{3}{2}\right)^{x-1}$
$\therefore \left(\frac{2}{3}\right)^x > \left(\frac{2}{3}\right)^{1-x}$
$\therefore \dfrac{\left(\frac{2}{3}\right)^x}{\left(\frac{2}{3}\right)^{1-x}} > 1$
$\therefore \left(\frac{2}{3}\right)^{x-1+x} > 1$
$\therefore \left(\frac{2}{3}\right)^{2x-1} > \left(\frac{2}{3}\right)^0$
But $y = \left(\frac{2}{3}\right)^x$ is decreasing,
$\therefore 2x - 1 < 0$
$\therefore x < \frac{1}{2}$

137 $x^2 + y^2 = 52xy$
$\therefore x^2 - 2xy + y^2 = 50xy$
$\therefore (x-y)^2 = 50xy$
$\therefore \dfrac{(x-y)^2}{25} = 2xy$
$\therefore \left(\dfrac{x-y}{5}\right)^2 = 2xy$

$\therefore \log\left(\dfrac{x-y}{5}\right)^2 = \log(2xy)$
$\therefore 2\log\left(\dfrac{x-y}{5}\right) = \log x + \log 2y$
$\therefore \log\left(\dfrac{x-y}{5}\right) = \frac{1}{2}(\log x + \log 2y)$

138 $z = \cos\theta + i\sin\theta = \text{cis}\,\theta$ has modulus 1 and argument θ.
$z^2 = [\text{cis}\,\theta]^2 = \text{cis}\,2\theta$ {De Moivre}
$\therefore\ z^2$ has modulus 1 and argument 2θ

$1 - z^2$ is found using vector subtraction on the diagram.

$\triangle OAB$ is isosceles as $OA = BA = 1$
Hence $\alpha_1 = \alpha_2$ {isosceles $\triangle$ theorem}

As z^2 and $-z^2$ are parallel,
$\widehat{OAB} = 2\theta$ {equal alternate angles}

Thus $2\alpha + 2\theta = \pi$ and so $\alpha = \frac{\pi}{2} - \theta$
Now $\arg(1 - z^2) = -\alpha_1 = \theta - \frac{\pi}{2}$
and $\sin\theta = \frac{m}{1} = m$
$\therefore\ |1 - z^2| = 2m = 2\sin\theta$
{$\sin\theta > 0$, as $0 < \theta < \frac{\pi}{4}$}
So, $1 - z^2$ has argument $\theta - \frac{\pi}{2}$ and modulus $2\sin\theta$.

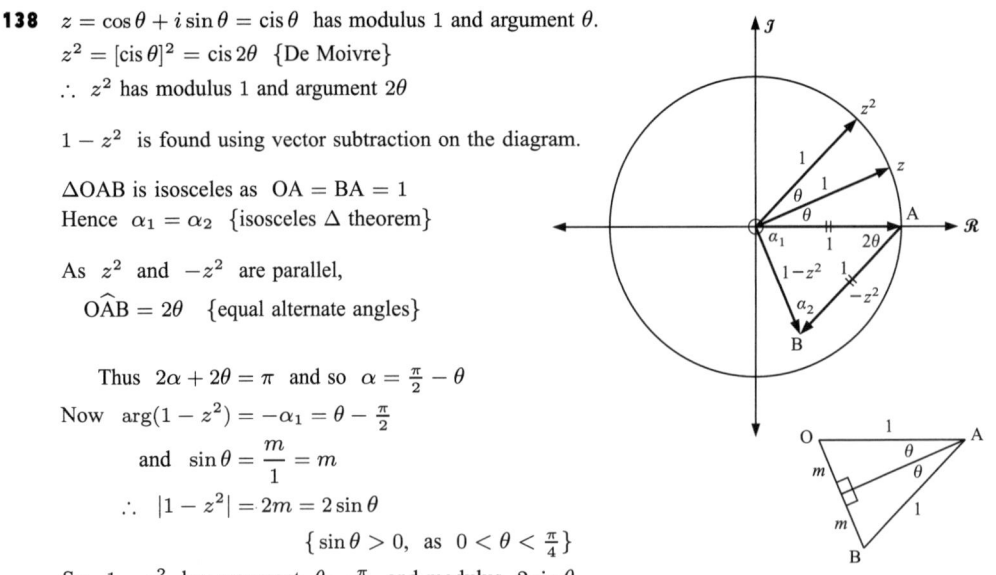

139 $\dfrac{58}{9(3-7i)} = \dfrac{58}{9(3-7i)}\left(\dfrac{3+7i}{3+7i}\right)$

$= \dfrac{58(3+7i)}{9(9+49)}$

$= \dfrac{3+7i}{9}$

Thus, $z^2 = 1 + i + \dfrac{3+7i}{9} = \dfrac{12+16i}{9}$

$\therefore\ z = \pm\dfrac{\sqrt{12+16i}}{3}$

We now let $\sqrt{12+16i} = c + di,\ c > 0$
$\therefore\ 12 + 16i = c^2 - d^2 + 2cdi$
$\therefore\ c^2 - d^2 = 12$ and $cd = 8$
$\therefore\ c = 4,\ d = 2$ or $c = -4,\ d = -2$ {as $c > 0$}
$\therefore\ z = \pm\dfrac{4+2i}{3}$
$\therefore\ z = \frac{4}{3} + \frac{2}{3}i$ or $-\frac{4}{3} - \frac{2}{3}i$

140 $4^x = 8^y$ and $9^y = \dfrac{243}{3^x}$
$\therefore\ (2^2)^x = (2^3)^y$ and $(3^2)^y \times 3^x = 3^5$
$\therefore\ 2x = 3y$ and $2y + x = 5$
{equating indices}
Solving these simultaneously gives
$2(5 - 2y) = 3y$
$\therefore\ 10 = 7y$
$\therefore\ y = \frac{10}{7}$
So, $2x = 3\left(\frac{10}{7}\right)$
$\therefore\ x = \frac{15}{7}$
So, $x = 2\frac{1}{7},\ y = 1\frac{3}{7}$.

141 $w = \dfrac{z-1}{z^*+1} = \dfrac{a+bi-1}{a-bi+1} = \dfrac{[a-1]+bi}{[a+1]-bi}$

$\therefore\ w = \left(\dfrac{[a-1]+bi}{[a+1]-bi}\right)\left(\dfrac{[a+1]+bi}{[a+1]+bi}\right)$

$= \dfrac{[a^2-1-b^2] + i\,[2ab]}{[a+1]^2 + b^2}$

So, w is purely imaginary when
$a^2 - b^2 - 1 = 0$ and $2ab \neq 0$
$\therefore\ a^2 - b^2 = 1$ and $ab \neq 0$

142 $x = \log_3 y^2\quad \therefore\ y^2 = 3^x = (81^{\frac{1}{4}})^x = 81^{\frac{x}{4}}$

$\therefore\ y = (81^{\frac{x}{4}})^{\frac{1}{2}} = 81^{\frac{x}{8}}$

$\therefore\ 81 = y^{\frac{8}{x}}$ and so $\log_y 81 = \dfrac{8}{x}$.

143 a

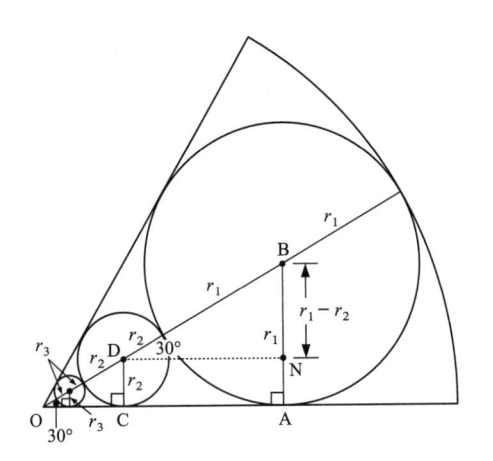

$\sin 30° = \dfrac{r_1}{10 - r_1}$ {in $\triangle OAB$}

$\therefore \ \dfrac{1}{2} = \dfrac{r_1}{10 - r_1} \quad \therefore \ r_1 = \dfrac{10}{3}$

In $\triangle DBN$, $\sin 30° = \dfrac{r_1 - r_2}{r_1 + r_2} = \dfrac{1}{2}$

$\therefore \ 2r_1 - 2r_2 = r_1 + r_2$

$\therefore \ r_1 = 3r_2$

$\therefore \ r_2 = \tfrac{1}{3} r_1$

So, in successive circles, radii are reduced by a factor of 3.

$\therefore \ r_2 = \dfrac{10}{9}, \ r_3 = \dfrac{10}{27}, \ r_4 = \dfrac{10}{81}$, and so on.

Thus the total area of the circles $= \pi r_1^2 + \pi r_2^2 + \pi r_3^2 + \pi r_4^2 + \ldots$

$= \pi \left(\left(\dfrac{10}{3}\right)^2 + \left(\dfrac{10}{9}\right)^2 + \left(\dfrac{10}{27}\right)^2 + \left(\dfrac{10}{81}\right)^2 + \ldots \right)$

$= \pi \times \left(\dfrac{10}{3}\right)^2 \left[1 + \left(\dfrac{1}{3}\right)^2 + \left(\dfrac{1}{3}\right)^4 + \left(\dfrac{1}{3}\right)^6 + \ldots \right]$

$= \pi \times \dfrac{100}{9} \times \left(\dfrac{1}{1 - \tfrac{1}{9}} \right)$

$= \dfrac{25\pi}{2}$ units^2

b We let $\dfrac{\alpha}{2}$ replace $30°$ in the calculations of **a**, and let $a = \sin\left(\dfrac{\alpha}{2}\right)$.

In this case $a = \dfrac{r_1}{10 - r_1}$, and so $r_1 = \dfrac{10a}{1 + a}$

Now $a = \dfrac{r_1 - r_2}{r_1 + r_2}$ {using $\triangle DBN$}

$\therefore \ a(r_1 + r_2) = r_1 - r_2$

$\therefore \ r_2(a + 1) = r_1(1 - a)$

$\therefore \ r_2 = r_1 \left(\dfrac{1 - a}{a + 1}\right) = \dfrac{10a}{1 + a} \left(\dfrac{1 - a}{a + 1}\right) = \dfrac{10a(1 - a)}{(a + 1)^2}$

Thus $r_3 = r_2 \left(\dfrac{1 - a}{a + 1}\right) = \dfrac{10a(1 - a)^2}{(a + 1)^3}$, and so on.

$\therefore$ total area $= \pi(r_1^2 + r_2^2 + r_3^2 + r_4^2 + \ldots)$

$= \pi \left[\left(\dfrac{10a}{1 + a}\right)^2 + \left(\dfrac{10a(1 - a)}{(1 + a)^2}\right)^2 + \left(\dfrac{10a(1 - a)^2}{(1 + a)^3}\right)^2 + \ldots \right]$

$= \pi \dfrac{100a^2}{(1 + a)^2} \left[1 + \left(\dfrac{1 - a}{1 + a}\right)^2 + \left(\dfrac{1 - a}{1 + a}\right)^4 + \ldots \right]$

This is the sum of an infinite geometric series which converges since $\left| \dfrac{1 - \sin\left(\tfrac{\alpha}{2}\right)}{1 + \sin\left(\tfrac{\alpha}{2}\right)} \right| < 1$.

$\therefore$ total area $= \pi \times \dfrac{100a^2}{(1 + a)^2} \times \dfrac{1}{1 - \left(\dfrac{1 - a}{1 + a}\right)^2}$

$= \pi \times \dfrac{100a^2}{(1 + a)^2 - (1 - a)^2}$

$= \pi \times \dfrac{100a^2}{4a} = 25\pi a = 25\pi \sin\left(\dfrac{\alpha}{2}\right)$ units^2

144 Let $x^2 + ax + b$ have zeros α and 2α

$\therefore$ the sum of the zeros $= 3\alpha = \dfrac{-a}{1}$ and the product of the zeros $= 2\alpha^2 = \dfrac{b}{1}$

$\therefore \alpha = \dfrac{-a}{3}$ and $2\alpha^2 = b$

$\therefore 2\left(\dfrac{a^2}{9}\right) = b$ and so $2a^2 = 9b$

145 As the cubic has real coefficients, both $2+i$ and $2-i$ are roots.
These have sum 4 and product $4+1 = 5$, and so come from the quadratic factor $z^2 - 4z + 5$.
Thus $z^3 + az^2 + bz + 15 = (z^2 - 4z + 5)(z + 3)$
$\therefore z^3 + az^2 + bz + 15 = z^3 - z^2 - 7z + 15$
$\therefore a = -1$ and $b = -7$ {equating coefficients}

146 By the Remainder theorem, $P(1) = -3$ and $P(-3) = -15$ where $P(x) = x^n + ax^2 - 6$
$\therefore (1)^n + a(1)^2 - 6 = -3$ and $(-3)^n + a(-3)^2 - 6 = -15$
$\therefore 1 + a - 6 = -3$ and $(-3)^n + 9a = -9$
$\therefore a = 2$ and $(-3)^n = -27$
$\therefore n = 3$

147 $\dfrac{P(x)}{x(2x-3)} = Q(x) + \dfrac{ax+b}{x(2x-3)}$ {division process}

$\therefore P(x) = Q(x)[x(2x-3)] + ax + b$

a If $Q(x) = ax + b$, $P(x) = x(ax+b)(2x-3) + ax + b$
$\therefore P(x) = (ax+b)(2x^2 - 3x + 1)$

b Factorising the quadratic, $P(x) = (ax+b)(2x-1)(x-1)$

c Now $P(0) = 7$ so $b(-1)(-1) = 7$ $\therefore b = 7$
and $P(2) = 39$ so $(2a+7)(3)(1) = 39$ $\therefore 2a + 7 = 13$ and so $a = 3$
Thus $P(x) = (3x+7)(2x^2 - 3x + 1)$

148 $f(x) = 2x^3 - x^2 - 8x - 5$
$= (x+1)(2x^2 - 3x - 5)$
$= (x+1)(2x-5)(x+1)$
$= (x+1)^2(2x-5)$ which has sign diagram: $\quad - \ \underset{-1}{|} \ - \ \underset{\frac{5}{2}}{|} \ + \ \longrightarrow x$

$\therefore f(x) \geqslant 0$ for $x = -1$ or $x \geqslant \dfrac{5}{2}$

149 The x-intercepts -3 and $-\dfrac{1}{4}$ indicate that $(x+3)$ and $(4x+1)$ are factors of $f(x)$.
$f(x)$ touches the x-axis at $\dfrac{3}{2}$, so $(2x-3)^2$ is also a factor of $f(x)$.
Thus, the quartic has the form $f(x) = a(x+3)(4x+1)(2x-3)^2$, where $a \neq 0$.
But $f(0) = 9$, so $a(3)(1)(-3)^2 = 9$
$\therefore a = \dfrac{1}{3}$
$\therefore f(x) = \dfrac{1}{3}(x+3)(4x+1)(2x-3)^2$

150 a As a is real, $p(x)$ has all real coefficients.
By the theorem on real polynomials, $-2+i$ and $-2-i$ are both zeros.
These have sum -4 and product $4+1 = 5$, so come from the quadratic factor $x^2 + 4x + 5$.

b Hence, $p(x) = x^3 + (5+4a)x + 5a = (x^2 + 4x + 5)(x + a)$ {comparing constant terms}
$\therefore x^3 + (5+4a)x + 5a = x^3 + [a+4]x^2 + [4a+5]x + 5a$
$\therefore a + 4 = 0$ {equating coefficients of x^2}
$\therefore a = -4$ and the real zero is $-a$ which is 4.

151 $h(x) = x^3 - 6tx^2 + 11t^2x - 6t^3$

  a $h(t) = t^3 - 6t^3 + 11t^3 - 6t^3 = 0$
    $\therefore$ $x = t$ is a zero of $h(x)$.

  b By inspection, $h(x) = (x - t)(x^2 - 5tx + 6t^2)$
    $\therefore$ $h(x) = (x - t)(x - 2t)(x - 3t)$

  c $y = x^3 + 6x^2$ meets $y = -6 - 11x$ where $x^3 + 6x^2 = -6 - 11x$
    $\therefore$ $x^3 + 6x^2 + 11x + 6 = 0$ which is $h(x)$ when $t = -1$
    $\therefore$ $x = t, 2t$ or $3t$, which correspond to $x = -1, -2$ or -3.
    So, the graphs meet at $(-1, 5), (-2, 16)$ and $(-3, 27)$.

152 **a** **i** Since $P(x)$ is a real polynomial, both $1 + ki$ and $1 - ki$ are zeros, $k \in \mathbb{Z}$.
      These have sum 2 and product $1 + k^2$ and therefore come from the quadratic factor
      $x^2 - 2x + 1 + k^2$.

    ii By comparison with $P(x)$, $1 + k^2$ is a factor of -10.
      $\therefore$ $1 + k^2 = \pm 1, \pm 2, \pm 5, \pm 10$ where $k \in \mathbb{Z}$
      $\therefore$ $k^2 = 0, 1, 4, 9$
      $\therefore$ $k = 0, \pm 1, \pm 2, \pm 3$

  b As p and q are integer zeros, they come from
    $(x - p)(x - q) = x^2 - (p + q)x + pq$
    $\therefore$ pq is a factor of -10
    The possibilities are as shown in the table:

$1 + k^2$	pq
1	-10
2	-5
5	-2
10	-1

  c Without loss of generality we assume $p > q$. Then as $p + q = -1$, the only possibility is $p = 1$,
    $q = -2$, and $1 + k^2 = 5$ $\therefore$ $k = \pm 2$
    $\therefore$ $P(x) = (x - 1)(x + 2)(x - 1 - 2i)(x - 1 + 2i)$
    So, the zeros of $P(x)$ are $1, -2, 1 + 2i$ and $1 - 2i$.

153 Since the polynomial is real, $1 \pm 2i$ and $\pm ai$ are zeros, $a \neq 0$.
  $1 \pm 2i$ have sum 2 and product $1 + 4 = 5$ and so come from $z^2 - 2z + 5$
  $\pm ai$ have sum 0 and product a^2 and so come from $z^2 + a^2$
  $\therefore$ $P(z) = k(z^2 - 2z + 5)(z^2 + a^2)$
  But $k = 1$ and $P(0) = 1(5)(a^2) = 10$ so $a^2 = 2$
    $\therefore$ $P(z) = (z^2 - 2z + 5)(z^2 + 2)$

154 **a** $y = f(x - 2) + 1$ is a translation of $y = f(x)$ through $\begin{pmatrix} 2 \\ 1 \end{pmatrix}$. $\therefore$ A$(-2, 3) \to$ A$'(0, 4)$.

  b $y = 2f(x - 2)$ is obtained from $y = f(x)$ by a translation through $\begin{pmatrix} 2 \\ 0 \end{pmatrix}$ followed by a vertical
    stretch with scale factor $k = 2$. $\therefore$ A$(-2, 3) \to$ A$'(0, 3) \to$ A$''(0, 6)$.

  c Consider $y = -|f(x)| - 2$. When $x = -2$, $y = -|f(-2)| - 2 = -3 - 2 = -5$
    $\therefore$ A$(-2, 3) \to$ A$'(-2, -5)$.

  d $y = f(2x - 3) = f\left(2\left(x - \tfrac{3}{2}\right)\right)$.
    It is obtained from $y = f(x)$ by a horizontal compression with scale factor $k = 2$ followed by a
    translation through $\begin{pmatrix} \frac{3}{2} \\ 0 \end{pmatrix}$. $\therefore$ A$(-2, 3) \to$ A$'(-1, 3) \to$ A$''(\tfrac{1}{2}, 3)$.

  e Consider $y = \dfrac{1}{f(x)}$. When $x = -2$, $y = \dfrac{1}{f(-2)} = \tfrac{1}{3}$. $\therefore$ A$(-2, 3) \to$ A$'(-2, \tfrac{1}{3})$.

  f Consider $y = f^{-1}(x)$. For an inverse function, the point is reflected in the line $y = x$.
    $\therefore$ A$(-2, 3) \to$ A$'(3, -2)$.

155 **a**

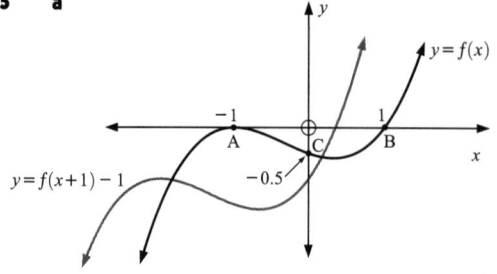

$A(-1, 0) \to A'(-2, -1)$
$B(1, 0) \to B'(0, -1)$
$C(0, -\frac{1}{2}) \to C'(-1, -\frac{3}{2})$

b

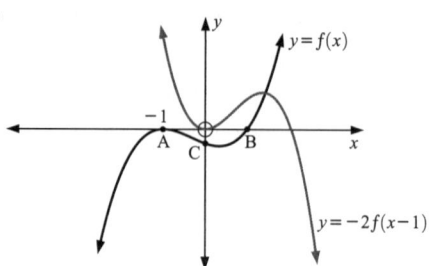

$A(-1, 0) \to A'(0, 0)$
$B(1, 0) \to B'(2, 0)$
$C(0, -\frac{1}{2}) \to C'(1, 1)$

c

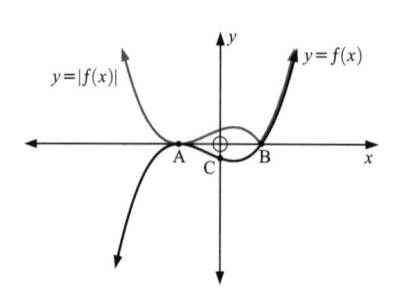

$A(-1, 0) \to A'(-1, 0)$
$B(1, 0) \to B'(1, 0)$
$C(0, -\frac{1}{2}) \to C'(0, \frac{1}{2})$

d

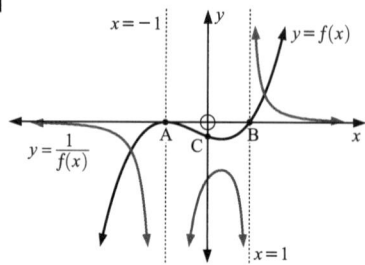

$A(-1, 0) \to$ VA, $x = -1$
$B(1, 0) \to$ VA, $x = 1$
$C(0, -\frac{1}{2}) \to C'(0, -2)$

156 **a** Zeros are $3 \pm 2i$ with sum 6 and product $9 + 4 = 13$
$\therefore \ f(x) = a(x^2 - 6x + 13), \ a \neq 0$
But $f(0) = -13$, so $a = -1$
$\therefore \ f(x) = -x^2 + 6x - 13$

b $f(x) = -1(x^2 - 6x + 13)$
$= -1\left([x-3]^2 + 13 - 9\right)$
$= -(x-3)^2 - 4$

157

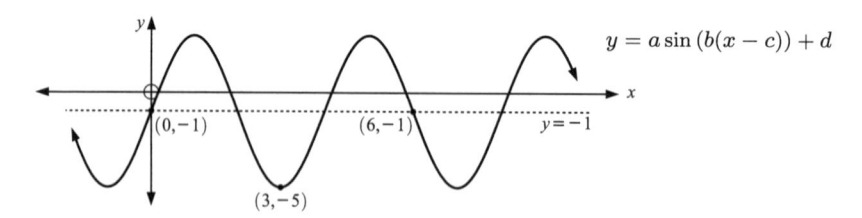

$y = a \sin(b(x-c)) + d$

The amplitude $= a = 4$.   The period $= 4 = \dfrac{2\pi}{b}$ $\therefore \ b = \dfrac{\pi}{2}$

The basic sine curve has been translated through $\begin{pmatrix} 0 \\ -1 \end{pmatrix}$. $\therefore \ c = 0, \ d = -1$

Thus $y = 4\sin\left(\dfrac{\pi}{2}x\right) - 1$

Check: $y(3) = 4\sin\left(\dfrac{3\pi}{2}\right) - 1 = 4(-1) - 1 = -5$ ✓
$y(6) = 4\sin(3\pi) - 1 = 4(0) - 1 = -1$ ✓

158 In matrix form the system is: $\begin{pmatrix} 1 & 3 & -1 \\ 2 & 1 & 1 \\ 1 & -1 & -2 \end{pmatrix} \begin{pmatrix} x \\ y \\ z \end{pmatrix} = \begin{pmatrix} 15 \\ 7 \\ 0 \end{pmatrix}$

$\therefore \begin{pmatrix} x \\ y \\ z \end{pmatrix} = \begin{pmatrix} 1 & 3 & -1 \\ 2 & 1 & 1 \\ 1 & -1 & -2 \end{pmatrix}^{-1} \begin{pmatrix} 15 \\ 7 \\ 0 \end{pmatrix}$

$= \begin{pmatrix} -\frac{1}{17} & \frac{7}{17} & \frac{4}{17} \\ \frac{5}{17} & -\frac{1}{17} & -\frac{3}{17} \\ -\frac{3}{17} & \frac{4}{17} & -\frac{5}{17} \end{pmatrix} \begin{pmatrix} 15 \\ 7 \\ 0 \end{pmatrix}$

$= \begin{pmatrix} 2 \\ 4 \\ -1 \end{pmatrix}$ Thus, $x = 2$, $y = 4$, $z = -1$.

159 a

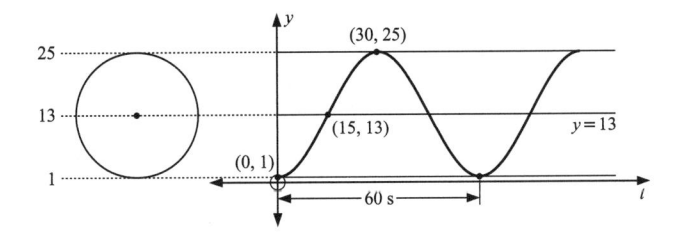

We model the Ferris wheel using $h(t) = a + b\sin(c(t - d))$.

The amplitude $= b = 12$. The period $= \dfrac{2\pi}{c} = 60$ $\therefore$ $c = \dfrac{\pi}{30}$

The basic sine curve has been translated through $\begin{pmatrix} 15 \\ 13 \end{pmatrix}$. $\therefore$ $d = 15$, $a = 13$

Thus $h(t) = 12\sin\left(\dfrac{\pi}{30}(t - 15)\right) + 13$

Check: $h(0) = 12\sin\left(\dfrac{-\pi}{2}\right) + 13 = 12(-1) + 13 = 1$ ✓

$h(30) = 12\sin\left(\dfrac{\pi}{2}\right) + 13 = 12(1) + 13 = 25$ ✓

b When $t = 91$, $h(91) = 12\sin\left(\dfrac{\pi \times 76}{30}\right) + 13 \approx 24.9$ m

160 a The line meets the plane where
$2(-4 + 3\lambda) + (2 + \lambda) - (-1 + 2\lambda) = 2$
$\therefore \; -8 + 6\lambda + 2 + \lambda + 1 - 2\lambda = 2$
$\therefore \; 5\lambda - 5 = 2$
$\therefore \; \lambda = \dfrac{7}{5}$

$\therefore$ the point of intersection is $\left(\dfrac{1}{5}, \dfrac{17}{5}, \dfrac{9}{5}\right)$.

c The lines meet where
$-4 + 3\lambda = \dfrac{2 + \lambda - 5}{2} = \dfrac{-(-1 + 2\lambda) - 1}{2}$

$\therefore \; -4 + 3\lambda = \underbrace{\dfrac{\lambda - 3}{2}}_{} = -\lambda$

$-8 + 6\lambda = \lambda - 3$ Check: $\lambda - 3 = -2\lambda$
$\therefore \; 5\lambda = 5$ $\therefore \; 3\lambda = 3$
$\therefore \; \lambda = 1$ $\therefore \; \lambda = 1$

So, they meet at $(-1, 3, 1)$.

b l_1 has $\mathbf{v}_1 = \begin{pmatrix} 3 \\ 1 \\ 2 \end{pmatrix}$.

l_2 has $\mathbf{v}_2 = \begin{pmatrix} 1 \\ 2 \\ -2 \end{pmatrix}$.

Since $\mathbf{v}_2$ is **not** a multiple of $\mathbf{v}_1$, l_1 and l_2 are not parallel.

d Normal vector $\mathbf{n} = \mathbf{v}_1 \times \mathbf{v}_2$

$= \begin{vmatrix} \mathbf{i} & \mathbf{j} & \mathbf{k} \\ 3 & 1 & 2 \\ 1 & 2 & -2 \end{vmatrix}$

$= \mathbf{i}(-6) - \mathbf{j}(-8) + \mathbf{k}(5)$

$= -6\mathbf{i} + 8\mathbf{j} + 5\mathbf{k}$

$\therefore$ the equation of the plane is
$-6x + 8y + 5z = -6(-1) + 8(3) + 5(1)$
$\therefore \; -6x + 8y + 5z = 35$
$\therefore \; 6x - 8y - 5z = -35$

161

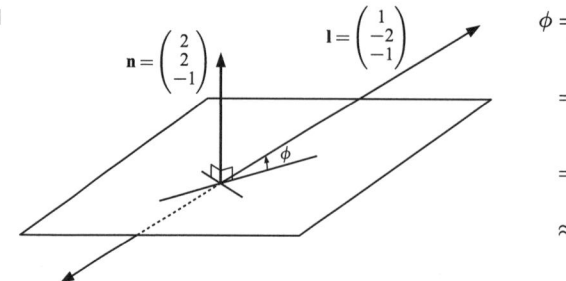

$\mathbf{n} = \begin{pmatrix} 2 \\ 2 \\ -1 \end{pmatrix}$, $\mathbf{l} = \begin{pmatrix} 1 \\ -2 \\ -1 \end{pmatrix}$

$\phi = \arcsin\left(\dfrac{|\mathbf{n} \bullet \mathbf{l}|}{|\mathbf{n}| \, |\mathbf{l}|}\right)$

$= \arcsin\left(\dfrac{|2 - 4 + 1|}{\sqrt{4+4+1}\sqrt{1+4+1}}\right)$

$= \arcsin\left(\dfrac{1}{3\sqrt{6}}\right)$

$\approx 7.82°$

162 a $\begin{pmatrix} 1 & -2 & 3 & | & 1 \\ 1 & p & 2 & | & 0 \\ -2 & p^2 & -4 & | & q \end{pmatrix}$

b $\sim \begin{pmatrix} 1 & -2 & 3 & | & 1 \\ 0 & p+2 & -1 & | & -1 \\ 0 & p^2-4 & 2 & | & q+2 \end{pmatrix}$ $\begin{array}{l} R_2 \to R_2 - R_1 \\ R_3 \to R_3 + 2R_1 \end{array}$

$\begin{array}{cccc} 0 & p^2-4 & 2 & q+2 \\ 0 & -(p^2-4) & p-2 & p-2 \\ 0 & 0 & p & p+q \end{array}$

$\sim \begin{pmatrix} 1 & -2 & 3 & | & 1 \\ 0 & p+2 & -1 & | & -1 \\ 0 & 0 & p & | & p+q \end{pmatrix}$ $R_3 \to R_3 - (p-2)R_2$

c i For a unique solution, $p \neq 0$.
  ii There are no solutions if $p = 0$, $q \neq 0$.
  iii There are infinitely many solutions when $p = q = 0$.

d When $p = q = 0$ the augmented matrix is $\begin{pmatrix} 1 & -2 & 3 & | & 1 \\ 0 & 2 & -1 & | & -1 \\ 0 & 0 & 0 & | & 0 \end{pmatrix}$ ← this equation is $2y - z = -1$.

Letting $y = t$, $z = 1 + 2t$.
Using $x - 2y + 3z = 1$, we find $x - 2(t) + 3(1 + 2t) = 1$
$\therefore \ x - 2t + 3 + 6t = 1$
$\therefore \ x = -2 - 4t$

So, $x = -2 - 4t$, $y = t$, $z = 1 + 2t$, $t \in \mathbb{R}$.

163 a Substituting $x = -2t + 2$, $y = t$, and $z = 3t + 1$ into $2x + y + z$, we get:
$2(-2t + 2) + t + 3t + 1$
$= -4t + 4 + t + 3t + 1$
$= 5$ ✓
$\therefore$ the line lies in the plane.

b If $x + ky + z = 3$ contains l_1 then
$(-2t + 2) + k(t) + (3t + 1) = 3$
$\therefore \ -2t + kt + 3t = 3 - 2 - 1$
$\therefore \ t(k + 1) = 0$
$\therefore \ k = -1$
as t is not necessarily equal to 0.

c From **a** and **b**, both $2x + y + z = 5$ and $x - y + z = 3$ contain l_1.
The solution of the system of 3 equations is where l_1 meets the third plane.
$\therefore \ 2(-2t + 2) + p(t) + 2(3t + 1) = q$
$\therefore \ -4t + 4 + pt + 6t + 2 = q$
$\therefore \ t(p + 2) = q - 6$
Now t can be any real number. So, we have infinitely many solutions when $p + 2 = 0$ and $q - 6 = 0$.
$\therefore \ p = -2$, $q = 6$

d With $p = -2$, $q = 6$, the system has augmented matrix
$\begin{pmatrix} 2 & 1 & 1 & | & 5 \\ 1 & -1 & 1 & | & 3 \\ 2 & -2 & 2 & | & 6 \end{pmatrix}$

$\sim \begin{pmatrix} 2 & 1 & 1 & | & 5 \\ 1 & -1 & 1 & | & 3 \\ 0 & 0 & 0 & | & 0 \end{pmatrix}$ $R_3 \to R_3 - 2R_2$

The row of all zeros and the fact that the first two rows are not multiples indicates there are infinitely many solutions.

164 $AB = \begin{pmatrix} 2 & 1 & -1 \\ -1 & 2 & 1 \\ 0 & 6 & 1 \end{pmatrix} \begin{pmatrix} 4 & 7 & -3 \\ -1 & -2 & 1 \\ 6 & 12 & -5 \end{pmatrix} = \begin{pmatrix} 1 & 0 & 0 \\ 0 & 1 & 0 \\ 0 & 0 & 1 \end{pmatrix} = I$

Now $\begin{pmatrix} 4 & 7 & -3 \\ -1 & -2 & 1 \\ 6 & 12 & -5 \end{pmatrix} \begin{pmatrix} a \\ b \\ c \end{pmatrix} = \begin{pmatrix} -8 \\ 3 \\ -15 \end{pmatrix}$

$\therefore \begin{pmatrix} a \\ b \\ c \end{pmatrix} = \begin{pmatrix} 4 & 7 & -3 \\ -1 & -2 & 1 \\ 6 & 12 & -5 \end{pmatrix}^{-1} \begin{pmatrix} -8 \\ 3 \\ -15 \end{pmatrix}$

$= \begin{pmatrix} 2 & 1 & -1 \\ -1 & 2 & 1 \\ 0 & 6 & 1 \end{pmatrix} \begin{pmatrix} -8 \\ 3 \\ -15 \end{pmatrix}$ {since $B^{-1} = A$}

$= \begin{pmatrix} 2 \\ -1 \\ 3 \end{pmatrix}$

$\therefore a = 2, \ b = -1, \ c = 3$

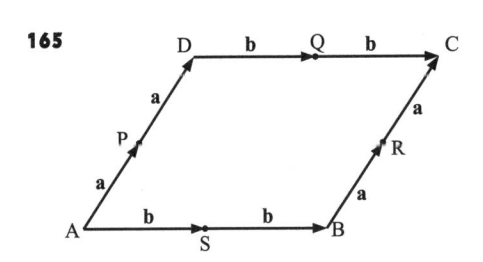

165 Using the vectors given, $\overrightarrow{PQ} = \mathbf{a} + \mathbf{b} = \overrightarrow{SR}$
$\overrightarrow{QR} = \mathbf{b} - \mathbf{a} = \overrightarrow{PS}$
$\therefore$ [PQ] $\parallel$ [SR] and [QR] $\parallel$ [PS]
$\therefore$ PQRS is a parallelogram
But $\overrightarrow{PQ} \bullet \overrightarrow{QR} = (\mathbf{a} + \mathbf{b}) \bullet (\mathbf{b} - \mathbf{a})$
$= \mathbf{a} \bullet \mathbf{b} - \mathbf{a} \bullet \mathbf{a} + \mathbf{b} \bullet \mathbf{b} - \mathbf{b} \bullet \mathbf{a}$
$= \mathbf{b} \bullet \mathbf{b} - \mathbf{a} \bullet \mathbf{a}$ {as $\mathbf{a} \bullet \mathbf{b} = \mathbf{b} \bullet \mathbf{a}$}
$= |\mathbf{b}|^2 - |\mathbf{a}|^2$ {as $\mathbf{x} \bullet \mathbf{x} = |\mathbf{x}|^2$}
$= 0$ as $|\mathbf{a}| = |\mathbf{b}|$
$\therefore \widehat{PQR}$ is a right angle
So, PQRS is a rectangle.

166 a $\mathbf{a} \times \mathbf{b} = \begin{vmatrix} \mathbf{i} & \mathbf{j} & \mathbf{k} \\ 1 & 1 & -3 \\ 0 & 1 & 2 \end{vmatrix} = \begin{vmatrix} 1 & -3 \\ 1 & 2 \end{vmatrix} \mathbf{i} - \begin{vmatrix} 1 & -3 \\ 0 & 2 \end{vmatrix} \mathbf{j} + \begin{vmatrix} 1 & 1 \\ 0 & 1 \end{vmatrix} \mathbf{k}$

$= 5\mathbf{i} - 2\mathbf{j} + \mathbf{k}$

b $|\mathbf{a} \times \mathbf{b}| = \sqrt{25 + 4 + 1} = \sqrt{30}$ units

$\therefore \frac{1}{\sqrt{30}}(5\mathbf{i} - 2\mathbf{j} + \mathbf{k})$ is a unit vector perpendicular to both $\mathbf{a}$ and $\mathbf{b}$.

$\therefore$ the required vector is $\frac{5}{\sqrt{30}}(5\mathbf{i} - 2\mathbf{j} + \mathbf{k}) = \frac{\sqrt{30}}{6}(5\mathbf{i} - 2\mathbf{j} + \mathbf{k})$

167 $\overrightarrow{TR} = \mathbf{r} - \mathbf{t}$
$= 2\mathbf{i} - 2\mathbf{j} + \mathbf{k} - \mathbf{i} - 2\mathbf{j} + \mathbf{k}$
$= \mathbf{i} - 4\mathbf{j} + 2\mathbf{k}$
$\overrightarrow{TS} = \mathbf{s} - \mathbf{t}$
$= 3\mathbf{i} + \mathbf{j} + 2\mathbf{k} - \mathbf{i} - 2\mathbf{j} + \mathbf{k}$
$= 2\mathbf{i} - \mathbf{j} + 3\mathbf{k}$

$\therefore$ area $\triangle RST$
$= \frac{1}{2} |\overrightarrow{TR} \times \overrightarrow{TS}|$
$= \frac{1}{2} \begin{Vmatrix} \mathbf{i} & \mathbf{j} & \mathbf{k} \\ 1 & -4 & 2 \\ 2 & -1 & 3 \end{Vmatrix}$
$= \frac{1}{2} |-10\mathbf{i} + \mathbf{j} + 7\mathbf{k}|$
$= \frac{1}{2}\sqrt{100 + 1 + 49}$
$= \frac{1}{2}\sqrt{150}$
$= \frac{5}{2}\sqrt{6}$ units^2

168 **a** $\overrightarrow{AD} = \overrightarrow{BC}$

$\therefore \begin{pmatrix} a-1 \\ b-3 \\ c+4 \end{pmatrix} = \begin{pmatrix} 6 \\ -2 \\ 2 \end{pmatrix}$

$\therefore a = 7, \ b = 1, \ c = -2$

$\therefore$ D is at $(7, 1, -2)$, X is at $(7, 3, -1)$

Now $\overrightarrow{OY} = \overrightarrow{OA} + \frac{2}{3}\overrightarrow{AX}$

$= \begin{pmatrix} 1 \\ 3 \\ -4 \end{pmatrix} + \frac{2}{3}\begin{pmatrix} 6 \\ 0 \\ 3 \end{pmatrix} = \begin{pmatrix} 5 \\ 3 \\ -2 \end{pmatrix}$

So, Y is at $(5, 3, -2)$.

b $\overrightarrow{BY} = \begin{pmatrix} 5-4 \\ 3-4 \\ -2+2 \end{pmatrix} = \begin{pmatrix} 1 \\ -1 \\ 0 \end{pmatrix}$ and $\overrightarrow{BD} = \begin{pmatrix} 7-4 \\ 1-4 \\ -2+2 \end{pmatrix} = \begin{pmatrix} 3 \\ -3 \\ 0 \end{pmatrix}$

$\therefore \overrightarrow{BD} = 3\overrightarrow{BY}$

$\therefore$ [BD] || [BY] and BD = 3(BY)

Since B is common to both [BD] and [BY], B, D and Y are collinear.

169 **a** $\mathbf{b} \times \mathbf{c} = \begin{vmatrix} \mathbf{i} & \mathbf{j} & \mathbf{k} \\ 1 & 1 & -1 \\ 2 & -1 & 1 \end{vmatrix} = \mathbf{i}(0) - \mathbf{j}(3) + \mathbf{k}(-3) = -3\mathbf{j} - 3\mathbf{k}$

b LHS = $\mathbf{a} \times (\mathbf{b} \times \mathbf{c}) = \begin{vmatrix} \mathbf{i} & \mathbf{j} & \mathbf{k} \\ 3 & 2 & -1 \\ 0 & -3 & -3 \end{vmatrix}$

$= \mathbf{i}(-9) - \mathbf{j}(-9) + \mathbf{k}(-9)$
$= -9\mathbf{i} + 9\mathbf{j} - 9\mathbf{k}$

RHS = $\mathbf{b}(\mathbf{a} \bullet \mathbf{c}) - \mathbf{c}(\mathbf{a} \bullet \mathbf{b})$
$= 3\mathbf{b} - 6\mathbf{c}$
$= 3\mathbf{i} + 3\mathbf{j} - 3\mathbf{k} - 12\mathbf{i} + 6\mathbf{j} - 6\mathbf{k}$
$= -9\mathbf{i} + 9\mathbf{j} - 9\mathbf{k}$

170 **a** Since **p** and **q** perpendicular,
$\mathbf{p} \bullet \mathbf{q} = 0$
$\therefore -t + 2 + 2t - 4t = 0$
$\therefore 3t = 2$
$\therefore t = \frac{2}{3}$

b Since **p** and **q** parallel,
$\mathbf{q} = k\mathbf{p}$ for some scalar k
$\therefore \begin{pmatrix} -t \\ 1+t \\ 2t \end{pmatrix} = \begin{pmatrix} k \\ 2k \\ -2k \end{pmatrix}$
$\therefore k = -t$ and $2k = 1 + t = -2t$
$\therefore 3t = -1$
$\therefore t = -\frac{1}{3}$

171 **a** A and B are mutually exclusive if $A \cap B = \emptyset$. In this case $P(A \cap B) = 0$, so $x = 0$.

b If A and B are independent, then $P(A \cap B) = P(A)P(B)$
$\therefore x = (0.3 + x)(0.2 + x)$
$\therefore x = 0.06 + 0.5x + x^2$
$\therefore x^2 - 0.5x + 0.06 = 0$
$\therefore (x - 0.2)(x - 0.3) = 0$
$\therefore x = 0.2$ or 0.3

172 **a**
$|1 - 4x| > \frac{1}{3}|2x - 1|$
$\therefore 3|1 - 4x| > |2x - 1|$
$\therefore 9(1 - 4x)^2 > (2x - 1)^2$
$\therefore 9(1 - 4x)^2 - (2x - 1)^2 > 0$
$\therefore [3(1 - 4x) + (2x - 1)][3(1 - 4x) - (2x - 1)] > 0$
$\therefore (-10x + 2)(-14x + 4) > 0$

Sign diagram:

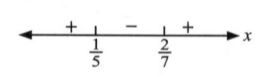

$\therefore x < \frac{1}{5}$ or $x > \frac{2}{7}$

b $\quad \dfrac{x-2}{6-5x-x^2} \leqslant 0$ $\qquad$ Sign diagram: $\underset{-6 \quad\quad 1 \quad 2}{\overset{-\;\;+\;\;-\;\;+}{\longleftrightarrow} x}$

$\therefore \quad \dfrac{x-2}{x^2+5x-6} \geqslant 0$

$\therefore \quad \dfrac{x-2}{(x-1)(x+6)} \geqslant 0 \qquad\qquad \therefore \; -6 < x < 1 \text{ or } x \geqslant 2$

173 The average number of amoebas in 10 mL of water, $m = 4$. $\therefore \; X \sim \text{Po}(4)$
  a $P(X \leqslant 5) \approx 0.785$
  b If Y is the number of days where no more than 5 amoebas are collected then $Y \sim B(20, 0.785\,13)$.
  $P(Y > 10) = 1 - P(Y \leqslant 10)$
  $\approx 1 - 0.004\,52$
  ≈ 0.995

174 $\dfrac{dy}{dx} = \cos^2 x = \tfrac{1}{2} + \tfrac{1}{2}\cos 2x$

$\therefore \; y = \int \left(\tfrac{1}{2} + \tfrac{1}{2}\cos 2x\right) dx$

$\therefore \; y = \tfrac{1}{2}x + \tfrac{1}{4}\sin 2x + c$

But $y(0) = 4$, so $4 = 0 + 0 + c$

Thus $y = \tfrac{1}{2}x + \tfrac{1}{4}\sin 2x + 4$

175 $\qquad xy\dfrac{dy}{dx} = 1 + y^2$

$\therefore \; \dfrac{y}{1+y^2}\dfrac{dy}{dx} = \dfrac{1}{x}$

$\therefore \; \int \dfrac{y}{1+y^2}\dfrac{dy}{dx}\,dx = \int \dfrac{1}{x}\,dx$

$\therefore \; \tfrac{1}{2}\int \dfrac{2y}{1+y^2}\,dy = \int \dfrac{1}{x}\,dx$

$\therefore \; \tfrac{1}{2}\ln|1+y^2| = \ln|x| + c$

But $1 + y^2$ is certainly positive,
so $\ln\sqrt{1+y^2} = \ln|x| + c$

$\therefore \; \ln\left|\dfrac{\sqrt{1+y^2}}{x}\right| = c$

$\therefore \; \dfrac{\sqrt{1+y^2}}{x} = \pm e^c = d$

$\{d \text{ a constant}\}$

Now when $x = 2$, $y = 0$, so $\tfrac{1}{2} = d$

$\therefore \; \dfrac{\sqrt{1+y^2}}{x} = \tfrac{1}{2}$

$\therefore \; \sqrt{1+y^2} = \tfrac{1}{2}x$

$\therefore \; 1 + y^2 = \tfrac{1}{4}x^2$

$\therefore \; y^2 = \tfrac{1}{4}x^2 - 1$

176 Now $L\dfrac{dI}{dt} + RI = E$

where E, L, and R are constants

$\therefore \; L\dfrac{dI}{dt} = E - RI$

$\therefore \; \dfrac{1}{E - RI}\dfrac{dI}{dt} = \dfrac{1}{L}$

$\therefore \; \int \dfrac{1}{E - RI}\dfrac{dI}{dt}\,dt = \int \dfrac{1}{L}\,dt$

$\therefore \; \dfrac{1}{-R}\ln|E - RI| = \dfrac{1}{L}t + c$

$\therefore \; \ln|E - RI| = -\dfrac{R}{L}t + d$

$\therefore \; |E - RI| = e^{-\frac{R}{L}t + d}$

$\therefore \; E - RI = \pm e^d e^{-\frac{R}{L}t}$

$\qquad\qquad\qquad = A e^{-\frac{R}{L}t}$

$\{A \text{ a constant}\}$

But when $t = 0$, $I = 0$,

so $E - 0 = A e^0$

$\therefore \; A = E$

$\therefore \; E - RI = E e^{-\frac{R}{L}t}$

$\therefore \; RI = E\left(1 - e^{-\frac{R}{L}t}\right)$

$\therefore \; I = \dfrac{E}{R}\left(1 - e^{-\frac{R}{L}t}\right)$

177 If the population size is M, then

$$\frac{dM}{dt} \propto M$$

$$\therefore \quad \frac{dM}{dt} = kM$$

So, $\frac{1}{M}\frac{dM}{dt} = k$

$$\therefore \quad \int \frac{1}{M}\frac{dM}{dt}\,dt = \int k\,dt$$

$$\therefore \quad \ln|M| = kt + c$$

$$\therefore \quad |M| = e^{kt+c}$$

$$\therefore \quad M = \pm e^c e^{kt}$$

$$\therefore \quad M = Ae^{kt}$$

Now when $t = 0$, $M = 2$, so $2 = Ae^0 = A$

Thus $M = 2e^{kt}$

Also, when $t = 4$, $M = 180$

$$\therefore \quad 180 = 2e^{4k}$$

$$\therefore \quad 90 = (e^k)^4$$

$$\therefore \quad e^k = 90^{\frac{1}{4}}$$

$$\therefore \quad M = 2(90)^{\frac{t}{4}}$$

So, when $t = 9$, $M = 2(90)^{2.25}$

$\approx 49\,900$ guinea pigs.

178 a $\dfrac{1}{y} + \dfrac{1}{P-y} = \dfrac{1}{y}\left(\dfrac{P-y}{P-y}\right) + \dfrac{1}{P-y}\left(\dfrac{y}{y}\right)$

$= \dfrac{P-y+y}{y(P-y)}$

$= \dfrac{P}{y(P-y)}$

b $\dfrac{dy}{dt} = ky\left(1 - \dfrac{y}{P}\right) = ky\left(\dfrac{P-y}{P}\right)$

$$\therefore \quad \dfrac{P}{y(P-y)}\dfrac{dy}{dt} = k$$

$$\therefore \quad \int \left(\dfrac{1}{y} + \dfrac{1}{P-y}\right)\dfrac{dy}{dt}\,dt = \int k\,dt$$

$$\therefore \quad \int \left(\dfrac{1}{y} + \dfrac{1}{P-y}\right)dy = \int k\,dt$$

$$\therefore \quad \ln|y| - \ln|P-y| = kt + c$$

$$\therefore \quad \ln\left|\dfrac{y}{P-y}\right| = kt + c$$

$$\therefore \quad \dfrac{y}{P-y} = \pm e^c e^{kt}$$

$$\therefore \quad \dfrac{P-y}{y} = \pm e^{-c} e^{-kt}$$

$= Ae^{-kt}$

Now $P = 624$, so $\dfrac{624-y}{y} = Ae^{-kt}$

When $t = 0$, $y = 2$, so $\dfrac{624-2}{2} = Ae^0$

$$\therefore \quad 311 = Ae^0$$

$$\therefore \quad A = 311$$

When $t = 1$, $y = 12$, so $\dfrac{612}{12} = 311e^{-k}$

$$\therefore \quad e^{-k} = \dfrac{51}{311}$$

So, $\dfrac{624}{y} - 1 = 311\left(\dfrac{51}{311}\right)^t$

$$\therefore \quad \dfrac{624}{y} = 1 + 311\left(\dfrac{51}{311}\right)^t$$

$$\therefore \quad y = \dfrac{624}{1 + 311\left(\dfrac{51}{311}\right)^t}$$

c i As $t \to \infty$, $y \to 624$
As time goes on, all of the people will hear the rumour, so the total number of people is 624.

ii When $t = 2$,

$y = \dfrac{624}{1 + 311\left(\dfrac{51}{311}\right)^2} \approx 66.6$

So, about 67 have heard it.

iii 90% of $624 \approx 562$

$\therefore$ we need to solve $\dfrac{624}{1 + 311\left(\dfrac{51}{311}\right)^t} = 562$

$$\therefore \quad 1 + 311\left(\dfrac{51}{311}\right)^t \approx 1.110\,32$$

$$\therefore \quad \left(\dfrac{51}{311}\right)^t \approx 0.000\,354\,7$$

$$\therefore \quad t \approx \dfrac{\log(0.000\,354\,7)}{\log\left(\dfrac{51}{311}\right)}$$

$t \approx 4.394$ hours

$\therefore$ 90% of the people have heard the rumour at 4:24 pm (to the nearest minute).

179 **a** $1 + i = \sqrt{2} \text{ cis } \frac{\pi}{4} = \sqrt{2} e^{i\frac{\pi}{4}}$

$\sqrt{3} - i = 2 \text{ cis}\left(-\frac{\pi}{6}\right) = 2e^{i\left(-\frac{\pi}{6}\right)}$

$\therefore \quad \dfrac{-1-i}{\sqrt{3}-i} = \dfrac{\sqrt{2}e^{i\left(-\frac{3\pi}{4}\right)}}{2e^{i\left(-\frac{\pi}{6}\right)}}$

$= \frac{1}{\sqrt{2}} e^{i\left(-\frac{3\pi}{4} + \frac{\pi}{6}\right)}$

$= \frac{1}{\sqrt{2}} e^{i\left(-\frac{7\pi}{12}\right)}$

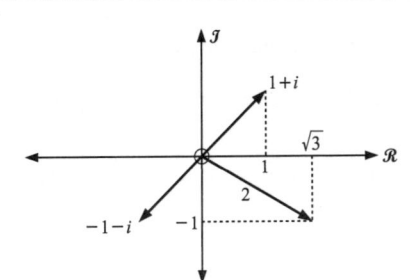

b $z^n = \left(\frac{1}{\sqrt{2}}\right)^n e^{i\left(-\frac{7\pi n}{12}\right)}$ which is real when $-\dfrac{7\pi n}{12} = 0 + k\pi$

$\therefore \quad n = 0 - \dfrac{12k}{7}, \; k \in \mathbb{Z}$

$\therefore$ the smallest positive integer is $n = 12$ when $k = -7$.

180 **a** There are $12! = 479\,001\,600$ possible orders.

    b **i** There are $\binom{4}{2} \times 2! = 12$ ways to place I and E amongst the last 4, and the other 10 are ordered in 10! ways.
$\therefore$ the total number is $12 \times 10! = 43\,545\,600$ ways.

        ii The 3 can be together in 2 ways (PIL or LIP) and this group together with the other 9 can be ordered in 10! ways.
$\therefore$ the total number is $2 \times 10! = 7\,257\,600$ ways.

        iii Istvan will be between Paul and Laszlo in $\frac{1}{3}$ of all possible cases, since each of them will be the 'middle student' $\frac{1}{3}$ of the time.
$\therefore$ the total number of ways $= \frac{1}{3}$ of $12! = 159\,667\,200$ ways.

        iv The students can be arranged in the form
$$\left.\begin{array}{l} \text{A x x x H x x x x x x x} \quad \text{in 10! ways} \\ \text{H x x x A x x x x x x x} \quad \text{in 10! ways} \\ \text{x A x x x H x x x x x x} \quad \text{in 10! ways} \\ \quad\vdots \\ \text{x x x x x x x H x x x A} \quad \text{in 10! ways} \end{array}\right\} 8 \times 2 = 16 \text{ like these}$$
$\therefore$ the total number of ways $= 16 \times 10! = 58\,060\,800$ ways.

    c **i** There are $\binom{12}{4}$ ways to choose the first group, $\binom{8}{4}$ ways to choose the second group, and $\binom{4}{4}$ ways to choose the third group. The order of groups is not important, so we divide by 3!.
So, there are $\frac{1}{3!} \binom{12}{4}\binom{8}{4}\binom{4}{4} = 5775$ ways.

        ii There are $\binom{2}{2}\binom{10}{2}$ ways to choose the group with Ben and Marton. There are then $\binom{8}{4}$ ways to choose the second group, and $\binom{4}{4}$ ways to choose the third group. The order of groups 2 and 3 is not important, so we divide by 2!.
So, there are $\frac{1}{2!}\binom{2}{2}\binom{10}{2}\binom{8}{4}\binom{4}{4} = 1575$ ways.

181 $v(t) = \cos\left(\frac{1}{3}t\right)$ cm s^{-1}

Now $\cos\left(\frac{1}{3}t\right) = 0$ when $\frac{1}{3}t = \frac{\pi}{2} + k\pi$

$\therefore \quad t = \frac{3\pi}{2} + 3k\pi$

So, for $0 \leqslant t \leqslant 10\pi$, the graph is:

Now $\int \cos\left(\frac{1}{3}t\right) dt = 3\sin\left(\frac{1}{3}t\right) + c$

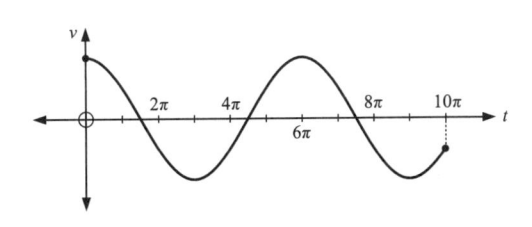

∴ the total distance travelled

$$= \int_0^{\frac{3\pi}{2}} \cos(\tfrac{1}{3}t)\,dt - \int_{\frac{3\pi}{2}}^{\frac{9\pi}{2}} \cos(\tfrac{1}{3}t)\,dt + \int_{\frac{9\pi}{2}}^{\frac{15\pi}{2}} \cos(\tfrac{1}{3}t)\,dt - \int_{\frac{15\pi}{2}}^{10\pi} \cos(\tfrac{1}{3}t)\,dt$$

$$= \big[3\sin(\tfrac{1}{3}t)\big]_0^{\frac{3\pi}{2}} - \big[3\sin(\tfrac{1}{3}t)\big]_{\frac{3\pi}{2}}^{\frac{9\pi}{2}} + \big[3\sin(\tfrac{1}{3}t)\big]_{\frac{9\pi}{2}}^{\frac{15\pi}{2}} - \big[3\sin(\tfrac{1}{3}t)\big]_{\frac{15\pi}{2}}^{10\pi}$$

$$= 3\sin\tfrac{\pi}{2} - 3\sin 0 - 3\sin\tfrac{3\pi}{2} + 3\sin\tfrac{\pi}{2} + 3\sin\tfrac{5\pi}{2} - 3\sin\tfrac{3\pi}{2} - 3\sin\tfrac{10\pi}{3} + 3\sin\tfrac{5\pi}{2}$$

$$= 3 - 0 + 3 + 3 + 3 + 3 - 3(-\tfrac{\sqrt{3}}{2}) + 3$$

$$= 18 + \tfrac{3\sqrt{3}}{2} \approx 20.6 \text{ cm}$$

182 **a** If there are no restrictions there are $\binom{16}{6} = 8008$ possible choices.

b $\binom{7}{2}\binom{6}{2}\binom{3}{2} + \binom{7}{2}\binom{6}{3}\binom{3}{1} + \binom{7}{2}\binom{6}{4}\binom{3}{0} + \binom{7}{3}\binom{6}{2}\binom{3}{1} + \binom{7}{3}\binom{6}{3}\binom{3}{0} + \binom{7}{4}\binom{6}{2}\binom{3}{0}$
$= 5320$ possible choices

c $\binom{1}{1}\binom{3}{1}\binom{12}{4} + \binom{1}{1}\binom{3}{2}\binom{12}{3} + \binom{1}{1}\binom{3}{3}\binom{12}{2} = 2211$ possible choices

183
$$\binom{n}{3} = 3\binom{n-1}{2} - \binom{n-1}{1}$$

∴ $\dfrac{n(n-1)(n-2)}{6} - \dfrac{3(n-1)(n-2)}{2} + (n-1) = 0$

∴ $\dfrac{n-1}{6}\big(n(n-2) - 9(n-2) + 6\big) = 0$

∴ $(n-1)(n^2 - 2n - 9n + 18 + 6) = 0$

∴ $(n-1)(n^2 - 11n + 24) = 0$

∴ $(n-1)(n-3)(n-8) = 0$

∴ $n = 1, 3$ or 8

But $n \geqslant 3$, $n - 1 \geqslant 2$ and $n - 1 \geqslant 1$, so $n \geqslant 3$

∴ $n = 3$ or 8

184 **a**
$$T_{r+1} = \binom{8}{r}(2x^3)^{8-r}\left(\dfrac{-1}{2x}\right)^r \quad \text{where } r = 0, 1, 2, 3, \ldots, 8$$

$$= \binom{8}{r} 2^{8-r} x^{24-3r} \left(\dfrac{-1}{2}\right)^r x^{-r}$$

$$= \binom{8}{r} 2^{8-r} \left(\dfrac{-1}{2}\right)^r x^{24-4r}$$

We require $24 - 4r = 12$, so $4r = 12$ or $r = 3$

∴ $T_4 = \binom{8}{3} 2^5 \left(\dfrac{-1}{2}\right)^3 x^{12}$

∴ the coefficient of x^{12} is $-\binom{8}{3} 2^2 = -224$

b $(1+2x)^5(2-x)^6 = \big[1 + \binom{5}{1}2x + \binom{5}{2}(2x)^2 + \ldots\big]\big[2^6 - \binom{6}{1}2^5 x + \binom{6}{2}2^4 x^2 - \ldots\big]$

The coefficient of x^2 is $\quad 1 \times \binom{6}{2} 2^4 + \binom{5}{1} 2 \times (-1)\binom{6}{1} 2^5 + \binom{5}{2} 2^2 \times 2^6$
$= 240 - 1920 + 2560 = 880$

c $(1 + 2x - 3x^2)^4$
$= \big([1+2x] - 3x^2\big)^4$
$= (1+2x)^4 + 4(1+2x)^3(-3x^2) + \underbrace{6(1+2x)^2(-3x^2)^2 + \ldots}_{\text{all terms have order higher than } x^3}$

$= 1 + \binom{4}{1}(2x) + \binom{4}{2}(2x)^2 + \binom{4}{3}(2x)^3 + (2x)^4 - 12x^2\left(1 + \binom{3}{1}(2x) + \ldots\right) + \ldots$

∴ the coefficient of x^3 is $4 \times 2^3 - 12 \times 3 \times 2 = -40$

185 $f(x) = e^{\sin^2 x}$, $x \in [0, \pi]$

a $f'(x) = e^{\sin^2 x} \times 2\sin x \cos x$
$= e^{\sin^2 x} \sin 2x$

which is 0 when $\sin 2x = 0$
$\therefore\ 2x = 0 + k\pi$
$\therefore\ x = 0 + \dfrac{k\pi}{2}$
$\therefore\ x = 0, \dfrac{\pi}{2}, \pi$

Sign diagram:

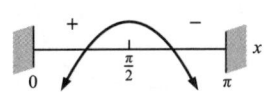

$\therefore\ f(x)$ has maximum value when $x = \dfrac{\pi}{2}$, and this value is e.

b $f''(x) = e^{\sin^2 x} \times \sin 2x \sin 2x + e^{\sin^2 x} 2 \cos 2x$
$= e^{\sin^2 x}(\sin^2 2x + 2\cos 2x)$

So, $\sin^2 2x + 2\cos 2x = 0$ needs to be solved.

c $\sin^2 2x + 2\cos 2x = 0$
$\therefore\ 1 - \cos^2 2x + 2\cos 2x = 0$
$\therefore\ \cos^2 2x - 2\cos 2x - 1 = 0$
$\therefore\ \cos 2x = \dfrac{2 \pm \sqrt{4 - 4(1)(-1)}}{2} = \dfrac{2 \pm 2\sqrt{2}}{2} = 1 \pm \sqrt{2}$
$\therefore\ \cos 2x = 1 - \sqrt{2}$ {as $1 + \sqrt{2} > 1$}
$\therefore\ x \approx 0.999$ or 2.14

$\therefore$ the points of inflection are $(0.999, 2.03)$ and $(2.14, 2.03)$.

186
$\log_x 4 + \log_2 x = 3$
$\therefore\ \dfrac{\log 4}{\log x} + \dfrac{\log x}{\log 2} - 3 = 0$
$\therefore\ \log 4 \log 2 + (\log x)^2 - 3\log 2 \log x = 0$
$\therefore\ (\log x)^2 - 3\log 2(\log x) + \log 4 \log 2 = 0$
$\therefore\ (\log x)^2 - 3\log 2(\log x) + 2(\log 2)^2 = 0$
$\therefore\ (\log x - 2\log 2)(\log x - \log 2) = 0$
$\therefore\ \log x = 2\log 2$ or $\log 2$
$\therefore\ x = 4$ or 2

187 $\displaystyle\int_0^a \dfrac{x}{x^2+1}\,dx = 3$
$\therefore\ \dfrac{1}{2}\displaystyle\int_0^a \dfrac{2x}{x^2+1}\,dx = 3$
$\therefore\ \left[\ln|x^2+1|\right]_0^a = 6$
$\therefore\ \ln|a^2+1| - \ln 1 = 6$
$\therefore\ \ln(a^2+1) = 6$ $\{a^2+1 > 0\}$
$\therefore\ a^2 + 1 = e^6$
$\therefore\ a^2 = e^6 - 1$
$\therefore$ since $a > 0$, $a = \sqrt{e^6 - 1}$

188
$\tan 2A = \dfrac{3}{2}$
$\therefore\ \dfrac{2\tan A}{1 - \tan^2 A} = \dfrac{3}{2}$
$\therefore\ 4\tan A = 3 - 3\tan^2 A$
$\therefore\ 3\tan^2 A + 4\tan A - 3 = 0$
$\therefore\ \tan A = \dfrac{-4 \pm \sqrt{16 - 4(3)(-3)}}{6}$
$= -\dfrac{2}{3} \pm \dfrac{\sqrt{13}}{3}$

But A is acute, so $\tan A > 0$.
$\therefore\ \tan A = \dfrac{\sqrt{13} - 2}{3}$

189 $\dfrac{a + b + 26}{5} = 8$ {as the mean is 8}
$\therefore\ a + b = 14$ .... (1)

But $\dfrac{\sum(x_i - \bar{x})^2}{n} = 8$ also,

so $\dfrac{(a-8)^2 + (b-8)^2 + 4 + 25 + 1}{5} = 8$

Using (1), $(a-8)^2 + (6-a)^2 + 30 = 40$
$\therefore\ a^2 - 16a + 64 + 36 - 12a + a^2 - 10 = 0$
$\therefore\ 2a^2 - 28a + 90 = 0$
$\therefore\ a^2 - 14a + 45 = 0$
$\therefore\ (a - 9)(a - 5) = 0$
$\therefore\ a = 5$ or 9

When $a = 5$, $b = 9$, and when $a = 9$, $b = 5$.
As $b > a$, $a = 5$, $b = 9$

190

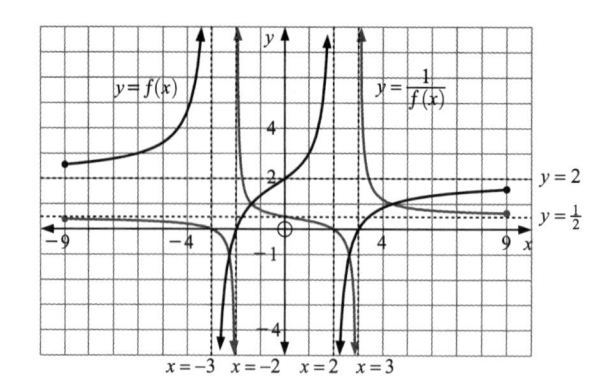

[Graph showing $y = f(x)$ and $y = \frac{1}{f(x)}$ with asymptotes $x = -3$, $x = -2$, $x = 2$, $x = 3$, and horizontal asymptotes $y = 2$ and $y = \frac{1}{2}$]

191 $|\mathbf{A}| = (x-1)\begin{vmatrix} 3-x & -2 \\ 5 & -8 \end{vmatrix} - (-2)\begin{vmatrix} -4 & -2 \\ -2 & -8 \end{vmatrix} + 5\begin{vmatrix} -4 & 3-x \\ -2 & 5 \end{vmatrix}$

$= (x-1)(-24 + 8x + 10) + 2(32 - 4) + 5(-20 + 6 - 2x)$
$= (x-1)(8x - 14) + 2(28) + 5(-2x - 14)$
$= 8x^2 - 32x$
$= 8x(x - 4)$ So, $\mathbf{A}$ is singular when $|\mathbf{A}| = 0$, which occurs when $x = 0$ or 4.

192 Since $\mathbf{A}$ is its own inverse, $\mathbf{A} = \mathbf{A}^{-1}$
$\therefore \mathbf{A}\mathbf{A} = \mathbf{A}\mathbf{A}^{-1}$ {premultiplying by $\mathbf{A}$}
$\therefore \mathbf{A}^2 = \mathbf{I}$

$\therefore \begin{pmatrix} a & -1 \\ b & 2 \end{pmatrix}\begin{pmatrix} a & -1 \\ b & 2 \end{pmatrix} = \begin{pmatrix} 1 & 0 \\ 0 & 1 \end{pmatrix}$

$\therefore a^2 - b = 1$, $-a - 2 = 0$, $ab + 2b = 0$, $-b + 4 = 1$
$\therefore a = -2$ and $b = 3$ Check: $a^2 - b = 4 - 3 = 1$ ✓
$ab + 2b = -6 + 6 = 0$ ✓

So, $\mathbf{A}^{11} = (\mathbf{A}^2)^5 \mathbf{A} = \mathbf{I}^5 \mathbf{A} = \mathbf{I}\mathbf{A} = \mathbf{A} = \begin{pmatrix} -2 & -1 \\ 3 & 2 \end{pmatrix}$.

193 $\dfrac{z+u}{z-u} = \dfrac{x + 2i + 3 + iy}{x + 2i - 3 - iy}$

$= \dfrac{(x+3) + i(y+2)}{(x-3) - i(y-2)} \times \dfrac{(x-3) + i(y-2)}{(x-3) + i(y-2)}$

$= \dfrac{[(x^2 - 9) - (y^2 - 4)] + i\,[(x+3)(y-2) + (y+2)(x-3)]}{(x-3)^2 + (y-2)^2}$

This is purely imaginary when $x^2 - 9 - y^2 + 4 = 0$ and $(x+3)(y-2) + (y+2)(x-3) \neq 0$
$\therefore x^2 - y^2 = 5$ and $xy - 2x + 3y - 6 + xy - 3y + 2x - 6 \neq 0$
$\therefore 2xy \neq 12$
$\therefore xy \neq 6$

Since $x^2 = 5 + y^2$ where $y^2 \geqslant 0$, $x^2 \geqslant 5$.
So, $x \geqslant \sqrt{5}$ or $x \leqslant -\sqrt{5}$, and the smallest positive x is $\sqrt{5}$.

194 As $P(x)$ is a real polynomial, both $1 - 2i$ and $1 + 2i$ are zeros. These have sum 2 and product $1 + 4 = 5$.
$\therefore P(x)$ has a quadratic factor $x^2 - 2x + 5$
$\therefore P(x) = (x^2 - 2x + 5)(x^2 + ax + 10)$
$\therefore$ the coefficient of x^3 is $a - 2$
So, $a - 2 = 0$
$\therefore a = 2$

Check:

		1	-2	5
×		1	2	10
		10	-20	50
	2	-4	10	
1	-2	5		
1	0	11	-10	50 ✓

Thus $P(x) = (x^2 - 2x + 5)(x^2 + 2x + 10)$ where

$x^2 + 2x + 10$ has zeros $\dfrac{-2 \pm \sqrt{4 - 4(1)(10)}}{2} = \dfrac{-2 \pm 6i}{2} = -1 \pm 3i$

So, the other three zeros are $1 + 2i$, $-1 + 3i$ and $-1 - 3i$.

195

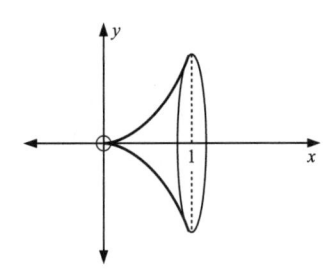

Volume $= \pi \int_0^1 y^2 \, dx$

$= \pi \int_0^1 x^2 e^{2x^3} \, dx$

$= \dfrac{\pi}{6} \int_0^1 e^{2x^3} (6x^2) \, dx$

$= \dfrac{\pi}{6} \left[e^{2x^3} \right]_0^1$

$= \dfrac{\pi}{6}(e^2 - 1)$ units^3

196 $f(x) = 3x^2 - 12x + 5$
$= 3(x^2 - 4x + 4) + 5 - 12$
$= 3(x - 2)^2 - 7$

$g(x) = -3x^2 + 18x - 10$
$= -3(x^2 - 6x + 9) - 10 + 27$
$= -3(x - 3)^2 + 17$

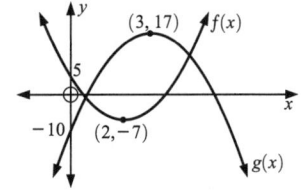

$g(x) = -3(x - 3)^2 + 17$
$= -(3(x - 1 - 2)^2 - 7 - 10)$
$= -(f(x - 1)^2 - 10)$

So, we translate $y = f(x)$ through $\begin{pmatrix} 1 \\ -10 \end{pmatrix}$ and then reflect the result in the x-axis.

197

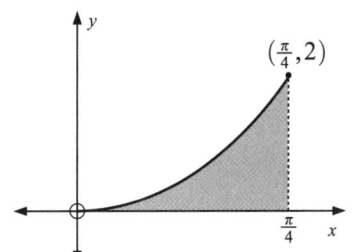

Area $= \int_0^{\frac{\pi}{4}} \tan^2 x + 2\sin^2 x \, dx$

$= \int_0^{\frac{\pi}{4}} \sec^2 x - 1 + 2\left(\frac{1}{2} - \frac{1}{2}\cos 2x\right) dx$

$= \int_0^{\frac{\pi}{4}} \sec^2 x - \cos 2x \, dx$

$= \left[\tan x - \frac{1}{2}\sin 2x \right]_0^{\frac{\pi}{4}}$

$= \left(1 - \frac{1}{2}\right) - (0 - 0)$

$= \frac{1}{2}$ unit^2

198 Let $\theta = \arcsin x$

$\therefore \ x = \sin \theta$

$\therefore \ \sin(2 \arcsin x)$
$= \sin 2\theta$
$= 2 \sin \theta \cos \theta$
$= 2x\sqrt{1 - x^2}$

$\therefore \ \int_0^1 \sin(2 \arcsin x) \, dx$
$= \int_0^1 2x(1 - x^2)^{\frac{1}{2}} \, dx$
$= -\int_0^1 (1 - x^2)^{\frac{1}{2}}(-2x) \, dx$

Let $u = 1 - x^2$, $\dfrac{du}{dx} = -2x$

when $x = 0$, $u = 1$
when $x = 1$, $u = 0$

$\therefore \ \int_0^1 \sin(2 \arcsin x) \, dx = -\int_1^0 u^{\frac{1}{2}} \dfrac{du}{dx} \, dx$

$= \int_0^1 u^{\frac{1}{2}} \, du$

$= \left[\frac{2}{3} u^{\frac{3}{2}} \right]_0^1$

$= \left(\frac{2}{3} - 0 \right)$

$= \frac{2}{3}$ unit^2

199 The system has augmented matrix

$\begin{pmatrix} 2 & -1 & 3 & | & 4 \\ 2 & 1 & a+3 & | & 10-a \\ 4 & 6 & a^2+6 & | & a^2 \end{pmatrix} = \begin{pmatrix} 2 & -1 & 3 & | & 4 \\ 0 & 2 & a & | & 6-a \\ 0 & 8 & a^2 & | & a^2-8 \end{pmatrix}$ $\begin{matrix} R_2 \to R_2 - R_1 \\ R_3 \to R_3 - 2R_1 \end{matrix}$

$= \begin{pmatrix} 2 & -1 & 3 & | & 4 \\ 0 & 2 & a & | & 6-a \\ 0 & 0 & a^2-4a & | & a^2+4a-32 \end{pmatrix}$ $R_3 \to R_3 - 4R_2$

The last equation is $a(a-4)z = (a+8)(a-4)$

a The system has no solutions if the LHS $= 0$ and the RHS $\neq 0$.
This occurs when $a = 0$, since we get $0z = -32$.

b The system has infinitely many solutions if the last equation has the form $0z = 0$, which is true for any real number z. This occurs when $a = 4$.

The augmented matrix becomes $\begin{pmatrix} 2 & -1 & 3 & | & 4 \\ 0 & 2 & 4 & | & 2 \\ 0 & 0 & 0 & | & 0 \end{pmatrix}$ Letting $z = t$, $2y + 4t = 2$
$$\therefore \ y + 2t = 1$$
$$\therefore \ y = 1 - 2t$$
and so $2x - (1 - 2t) + 3t = 4$
$$\therefore \ 2x - 1 + 2t + 3t = 4$$
$$\therefore \ x = \frac{5 - 5t}{2}$$

$\therefore$ when $a = 4$, there are infinitely many solutions of the form
$$x = \frac{5 - 5t}{2}, \ y = 1 - 2t, \ z = t, \ t \in \mathbb{R}.$$

c The system has a unique solution for all other values of a. So, $a \neq 0$ or 4.

In this case $z = \dfrac{a+8}{a}$

$\therefore \ 2y + a\left(\dfrac{a+8}{a}\right) = 6 - a$ and $2x + a + 1 + 3\left(\dfrac{a+8}{a}\right) = 4$

$\therefore \ 2y = 6 - a - a - 8$ $\therefore \ 2x = 4 - a - 1 - 3 - \dfrac{24}{a}$

$\quad\quad\quad = -2a - 2$ $\quad\quad\quad\quad = -a - \dfrac{24}{a}$

$\therefore \ y = -a - 1$ $\therefore \ x = -\dfrac{a}{2} - \dfrac{12}{a}$

$\therefore$ when $a \neq 0$ or 4, there is a unique solution of the form
$$x = -\frac{a}{2} - \frac{12}{a}, \ y = -a - 1, \ z = \frac{a+8}{a}$$

When $a = 2$, the solution is $x = -7$, $y = -3$, $z = 5$.

200 $f(x) = \dfrac{x^2 + 1}{(x+1)^2}$

a Vertical asymptote is $x = -1$.
Horizontal asymptote is $y = 1$.

b $f'(x) = \dfrac{2x(x+1)^2 - (x^2+1)2(x+1)^1}{(x+1)^4}$

$\quad\quad = \dfrac{2x(x+1) - 2(x^2+1)}{(x+1)^3}$

$\quad\quad = \dfrac{2(x-1)}{(x+1)^3}$

which has sign diagram:

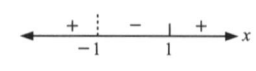

$\xleftarrow{\quad + \ \vdots \ - \ | \ + \quad}\to x$
$\quad\quad\quad -1 \quad\ 1$

$\therefore$ there is a local minimum at $(1, \frac{1}{2})$.

c $f''(x) = \dfrac{2(x+1)^3 - 2(x-1)3(x+1)^2}{(x+1)^6}$

$\quad\quad = \dfrac{2(x+1) - 6(x-1)}{(x+1)^4}$

$\quad\quad = \dfrac{-4x + 8}{(x+1)^4}$

which has sign diagram:

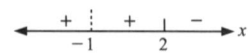

$\xleftarrow{\quad + \ \vdots \ + \ | \ - \quad}\to x$
$\quad\quad\quad -1 \quad\ 2$

A change of sign about $x = 2$ indicates that $(2, \frac{5}{9})$ is a point of inflection.

d

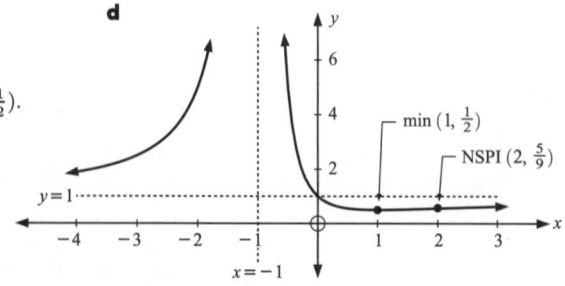

201 **a** $\quad a = \tfrac{1}{2}v^2$

$\therefore \dfrac{dv}{dt} = \tfrac{1}{2}v^2$

$\therefore v^{-2}\dfrac{dv}{dt} = \tfrac{1}{2}$

$\therefore \int v^{-2}\dfrac{dv}{dt}\,dt = \int \tfrac{1}{2}\,dt$

$\therefore \int v^{-2}\,dv = \int \tfrac{1}{2}\,dt$

$\therefore \dfrac{v^{-1}}{-1} = \tfrac{1}{2}t + c$

$\therefore -\dfrac{1}{v} = \dfrac{t}{2} + c$

But when $t = 0$, $v = -1$

$\therefore 1 = c$

So, $-\dfrac{1}{v} = \dfrac{t}{2} + 1 = \dfrac{t+2}{2}$

$\therefore v = \dfrac{-2}{t+2}$

b

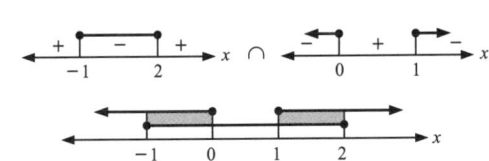

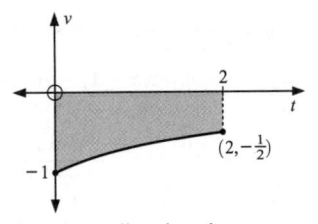

$\therefore$ there is no direction change
total distance travelled = shaded area

$= -\displaystyle\int_0^2 \dfrac{-2}{t+2}\,dt$

$= 2\left[\ln|t+2|\right]_0^2$

$= 2\ln 4 - 2\ln 2$

$= 2\ln 2^2 - 2\ln 2$

$= 4\ln 2 - 2\ln 2$

$= 2\ln 2$

≈ 1.39 units

202 For $f(x)$ to be defined we require that

$-1 \leqslant 1 + x - x^2 \leqslant 1$

$\therefore x^2 - x - 2 \leqslant 0$ and $x - x^2 \leqslant 0$

$\therefore (x-2)(x+1) \leqslant 0$ and $x(1-x) \leqslant 0$

$\therefore x \in [-1, 0] \cup [1, 2]$

$f(x) = \arccos u$ where $u = 1 + x - x^2$

$f'(x) = f'(u)\dfrac{du}{dx}$

$= \dfrac{-1}{\sqrt{1-u^2}}(1 - 2x)$

$= \dfrac{2x - 1}{\sqrt{1 - (1 + x - x^2)^2}}$

203

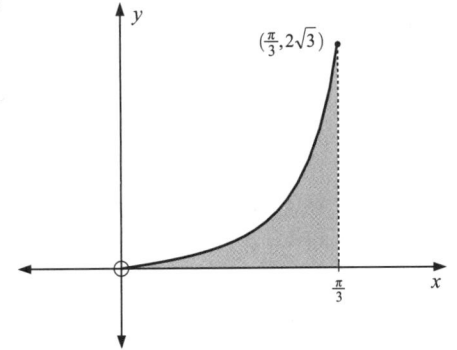

Area $= \displaystyle\int_0^{\pi/3} \dfrac{\tan x}{\cos 2x + 1}\,dx$

$= \displaystyle\int_0^{\pi/3} \dfrac{\tan x}{2\cos^2 x - 1 + 1}\,dx$

$= \tfrac{1}{2}\displaystyle\int_0^{\pi/3} \tan x \sec^2 x\,dx$

$= \tfrac{1}{2}\left[\dfrac{(\tan x)^2}{2}\right]_0^{\pi/3}$ $\quad \left\{\dfrac{d}{dx}\tan x = \sec^2 x\right\}$

$= \tfrac{1}{4}\left((\sqrt{3})^2 - 0^2\right)$

$= \tfrac{3}{4}$ unit^2

204 $y = \dfrac{\tan x}{\sin(2x) + 1} = \dfrac{\sin x}{\cos x(\sin 2x + 1)}$ is undefined if $\cos x = 0$ or $\sin 2x = -1$

$\therefore x = \tfrac{\pi}{2} + k\pi, \ k \in \mathbb{Z}$ or $2x = -\tfrac{\pi}{2} + k2\pi, \ k \in \mathbb{Z}$

$\therefore x = -\tfrac{\pi}{2}, -\tfrac{\pi}{4}, \tfrac{\pi}{2}, \tfrac{3\pi}{4}$ for $x \in [-\pi, \pi]$

$\therefore$ the vertical asymptotes are: $x = -\tfrac{\pi}{2}, \ x = -\tfrac{\pi}{4}, \ x = \tfrac{\pi}{2}, \ x = \tfrac{3\pi}{4}$.

There are no horizontal asymptotes.

205 $y = \dfrac{\sin x}{\tan x + 1}$, $-\pi \leqslant x \leqslant \dfrac{\pi}{2}$

$\therefore \dfrac{dy}{dx} = \dfrac{\cos x(\tan x + 1) - \sin x \sec^2 x}{(\tan x + 1)^2}$

$\therefore \dfrac{dy}{dx} = \dfrac{\sin x + \cos x - \dfrac{\sin x}{\cos^2 x}}{(\tan x + 1)^2}$

which is 0 when $\sin x + \cos x = \dfrac{\sin x}{\cos^2 x}$

$\therefore \sin x \cos^2 x + \cos^3 x = \sin x$

$\therefore \cos^3 x = \sin x(1 - \cos^2 x)$

$\therefore \cos^3 x = \sin^3 x$

$\therefore \tan^3 x = 1$

$\therefore \tan x = 1$

$\therefore x = \dfrac{\pi}{4},\ -\dfrac{3\pi}{4}$

$\therefore$ the stationary points are at $\left(\dfrac{\pi}{4},\ \dfrac{\sqrt{2}}{4}\right)$
and $\left(-\dfrac{3\pi}{4},\ -\dfrac{\sqrt{2}}{4}\right)$.

206 $\dfrac{u_1}{1 - r} = 49$ and $u_1 r = 10$

$\therefore \dfrac{10}{r} = 49(1 - r)$

$\therefore 10 = 49r - 49r^2$

$\therefore 49r^2 - 49r + 10 = 0$

$\therefore (7r - 2)(7r - 5) = 0$

$\therefore r = \dfrac{2}{7}$ or $\dfrac{5}{7}$

When $r = \dfrac{2}{7}$, $u_1 = 35$.

When $r = \dfrac{5}{7}$, $u_1 = 14$.

Thus $S_3 = \dfrac{35\left(1 - \left(\frac{2}{7}\right)^3\right)}{1 - \frac{2}{7}} = 47\dfrac{6}{7}$

or $S_3 = \dfrac{14\left(1 - \left(\frac{5}{7}\right)^3\right)}{1 - \frac{5}{7}} = 31\dfrac{1}{7}$

207 a $(f \circ g)(x) = f(g(x))$

$= f\left(\dfrac{x+1}{x-2}\right)$

$= 2\left(\dfrac{x+1}{x-2}\right) + 1$

$= \dfrac{2x + 2 + x - 2}{x - 2}$

$= \dfrac{3x}{x - 2}$

b $y = \dfrac{x+1}{x-2}$ has inverse $x = \dfrac{y+1}{y-2}$

$\therefore xy - 2x = y + 1$

$\therefore y(x - 1) = 2x + 1$

$\therefore y = \dfrac{2x + 1}{x - 1}$

$\therefore f^{-1}(x) = \dfrac{2x + 1}{x - 1}$

208 a $x^2 - 3xy + y^2 = 7$

$\therefore 2x - \left[3y + 3x\dfrac{dy}{dx}\right] + 2y\dfrac{dy}{dx} = 0$

$\therefore 2x - 3y + (2y - 3x)\dfrac{dy}{dx} = 0$

$\therefore \dfrac{dy}{dx} = \dfrac{3y - 2x}{2y - 3x}$

b We need to find where $\dfrac{3y - 2x}{2y - 3x} = \dfrac{2}{3}$

$\therefore 9y - 6x = 4y - 6x$

$\therefore 5y = 0$

$\therefore y = 0$

$\therefore x^2 = 7$ and so $x = \pm\sqrt{7}$

$\therefore$ the points are $(\sqrt{7},\ 0)$ and $(-\sqrt{7},\ 0)$.

209 a i If A and B are mutually exclusive then
$P(A \cup B) = P(A) + P(B) = \dfrac{1}{3} + \dfrac{2}{7} = \dfrac{13}{21}$

ii If A and B are independent then
$P(A \cup B) = P(A) + P(B) - P(A)P(B)$
$= \dfrac{1}{3} + \dfrac{2}{7} - \dfrac{1}{3} \times \dfrac{2}{7} = \dfrac{11}{21}$

b $P(A \mid B) = \dfrac{P(A \cap B)}{P(B)} = \dfrac{P(A) + P(B) - P(A \cup B)}{P(B)} = \dfrac{\left(\frac{13}{21} - \frac{3}{7}\right)}{\frac{2}{7}} \cdot \dfrac{21}{21} = \dfrac{4}{6} = \dfrac{2}{3}$

210 a l_1 can be written in the form $x = 8 + 3\lambda,\ y = -13 - 5\lambda,\ z = -3 - 2\lambda$

Substituting into l_2 gives: $\dfrac{8 + 3\lambda + 10}{6} = \dfrac{-13 - 5\lambda - 7}{-5} = \dfrac{-3 - 2\lambda - 11}{-5}$

$\therefore \dfrac{3\lambda + 18}{6} = \dfrac{-20 - 5\lambda}{-5} = \dfrac{-2\lambda - 14}{-5}$

$$\therefore \quad \frac{\lambda+6}{2} = \lambda+4 = \frac{2\lambda+14}{5}$$

$\therefore \quad \lambda+6 = 2\lambda+8 \quad$ and $\quad 5\lambda+20 = 2\lambda+14$
$\qquad \therefore \quad \lambda = -2 \quad$ and $\quad 3\lambda = -6$

So, $\lambda = -2$ is a common solution.
Substituting $\lambda = -2$, $x = 2$, $y = -3$, $z = 1$, so they meet at A(2, -3, 1).

b l_1 meets $3x+2y-z = -2$ where $3(8+3\lambda)+2(-13-5\lambda)-(-3-2\lambda) = -2$
$$\therefore \quad 24+9\lambda-26-10\lambda+3+2\lambda = -2$$
$$\therefore \quad \lambda+1 = -2$$
$$\therefore \quad \lambda = -3$$

So, B is at $(-1, 2, 3)$.

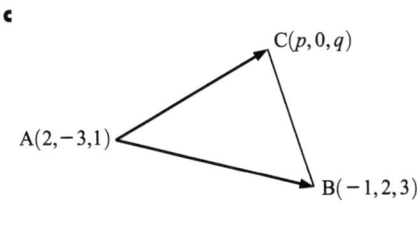

c

$\overrightarrow{AB} = \begin{pmatrix} -3 \\ 5 \\ 2 \end{pmatrix}$, $\overrightarrow{AC} = \begin{pmatrix} p-2 \\ 3 \\ q-1 \end{pmatrix}$

C$(p, 0, q)$

A$(2, -3, 1)$

B$(-1, 2, 3)$

$\therefore \quad$ Area $\triangle ABC = \frac{1}{2}|\overrightarrow{AB} \times \overrightarrow{AC}|$

$= \frac{1}{2}\left\| \begin{array}{ccc} \mathbf{i} & \mathbf{j} & \mathbf{k} \\ -3 & 5 & 2 \\ p-2 & 3 & q-1 \end{array} \right\| = \frac{\sqrt{3}}{2}$

But C lies on $3x+2y-z = -2$
$$\therefore \quad 3p-q = -2$$
$$\therefore \quad q = 3p+2$$

Thus $\left\| \begin{array}{ccc} \mathbf{i} & \mathbf{j} & \mathbf{k} \\ -3 & 5 & 2 \\ p-2 & 3 & 3p+1 \end{array} \right\| = \sqrt{3}$

$\therefore \quad |(15p-1)\mathbf{i}-(1-11p)\mathbf{j}+(1-5p)\mathbf{k}| = \sqrt{3}$
$\therefore \quad \sqrt{(15p-1)^2+(1-11p)^2+(1-5p)^2} = \sqrt{3}$
$\therefore \quad 225p^2-30p+1+1-22p+121p^2+1-10p+25p^2 = 3$
$$\therefore \quad 371p^2-62p = 0$$
$$\therefore \quad p(371p-62) = 0$$
$$\therefore \quad p = 0 \text{ or } \tfrac{62}{371}$$

211 $\qquad \log_a(x+2) = \log_a x + 2$
$\therefore \quad \log_a(x+2) - \log_a x = 2$
$\therefore \quad \log_a\left(\dfrac{x+2}{x}\right) = 2$
$\therefore \quad \dfrac{x+2}{x} = a^2$
$\therefore \quad 1 + \dfrac{2}{x} = a^2$
$\therefore \quad \dfrac{2}{x} = a^2 - 1$
$\therefore \quad$ since $a > 1$, $x = \dfrac{2}{a^2-1}$

212 $\qquad (x^2+1)\dfrac{dy}{dx} = y+1$

$\therefore \quad \dfrac{1}{y+1}\dfrac{dy}{dx} = \dfrac{1}{x^2+1}$

$\therefore \quad \int \dfrac{1}{y+1}\dfrac{dy}{dx}\,dx = \int \dfrac{1}{x^2+1}\,dx$

$\therefore \quad \int \dfrac{1}{y+1}\,dy = \int \dfrac{1}{x^2+1}\,dx$

$\therefore \quad \ln|y+1| = \arctan x + c$
$\therefore \quad y+1 = \pm e^c e^{\arctan x}$
$\therefore \quad y = Ae^{\arctan x} - 1$

But when $x = 0$, $y = 2$
so $2 = Ae^{\arctan 0} - 1$
$\therefore \quad 3 = A$
So, $y = 3e^{\arctan x} - 1$

213 We integrate by parts with $\quad u = x^2 \quad v' = \sin x$
$\qquad\qquad\qquad\qquad\qquad\qquad u' = 2x \quad v = -\cos x$

$\therefore \int x^2 \sin x \, dx = x^2(-\cos x) - \int -\cos x \,(2x) \, dx$
$\qquad\qquad\qquad = -x^2 \cos x + 2\int x \cos x \, dx$

We again integrate by parts, this time with $\quad u = x \quad v' = \cos x$
$\qquad\qquad\qquad\qquad\qquad\qquad\qquad\qquad u' = 1 \quad v = \sin x$

$\therefore \int x^2 \sin x \, dx = -x^2 \cos x + 2\left[x \sin x - \int \sin x \, dx\right]$
$\qquad\qquad\qquad = -x^2 \cos x + 2x \sin x - 2(-\cos x) + c$
$\qquad\qquad\qquad = -x^2 \cos x + 2x \sin x + 2\cos x + c$

214 Let $f(x) = ax + b$
$\therefore f(2x+3) = a(2x+3) + b$
$\qquad\qquad = 2ax + [3a + b]$
So, $2a = 5$ and $3a + b = -7$
$\therefore a = \frac{5}{2}$ and $\frac{15}{2} + b = -7$
$\qquad\qquad\qquad \therefore b = -\frac{29}{2}$
$\therefore f(x) = \frac{5}{2}x - \frac{29}{2}$ or $\frac{5x - 29}{2}$

To obtain $f^{-1}(x)$ we use $x = \frac{5y - 29}{2}$
$\therefore 2x = 5y - 29$
$\qquad y = \frac{2x + 29}{5}$
So, $f^{-1}(x) = \frac{2x + 29}{5}$

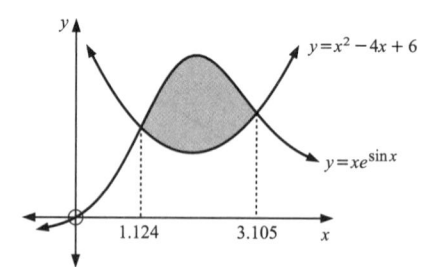

215 Using technology, the graphs intersect when
$x \approx 1.124$ and 3.105

$\therefore$ area $= \int_{1.124}^{3.105} (xe^{\sin x} - x^2 + 4x - 6) \, dx$
$\qquad\qquad \approx 3.76$ units^2 {using technology}

216
$$e^{xy} + xy^2 - \sin y = 2$$
$$e^{xy}\left(1y + x\frac{dy}{dx}\right) + 1y^2 + x\left(2y\frac{dy}{dx}\right) - \cos y \frac{dy}{dx} = 0$$
$$\frac{dy}{dx}(xe^{xy} + 2xy - \cos y) = -y^2 - ye^{xy}$$
$$\therefore \frac{dy}{dx} = \frac{-y^2 - ye^{xy}}{xe^{xy} + 2xy - \cos y}$$

217 To solve $\dfrac{|2x - 1| + 3}{|x + 3| - 2} < -x$ we plot

$y = \dfrac{|2x - 1| + 3}{|x + 3| - 2}$ and $y = -x$ on the same set of axes.

We suppose the graphs intersect when $x = a$.
So, the solutions are $x < a$ or $-5 < x < -1$, and we need to find the value of a.

Clearly $a < -5$, and with $x < -5$, $2x - 1 < 0$ and $x + 3 < 0$.

So, a is a solution of $\dfrac{-(2x - 1) + 3}{-(x + 3) - 2} = -x$

$\therefore \dfrac{-2x + 4}{-x - 5} = -x$

$\therefore 4 - 2x = x^2 + 5x$

$\therefore x^2 + 7x - 4 = 0$

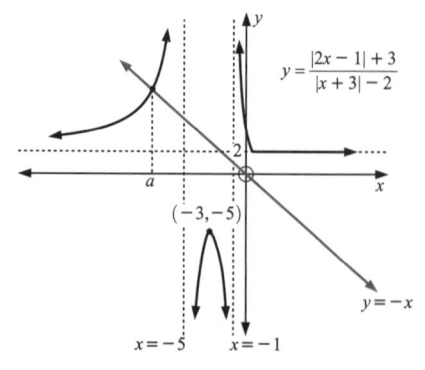

$\therefore x = \dfrac{-7 \pm \sqrt{65}}{2}, \quad x < -5$

Thus $x < \dfrac{-\sqrt{65} - 7}{2}$ or $-5 < x < -1$

218 Let $u = \sqrt{x+2}$, so $u^2 = x+2$

$\therefore \ 2u \dfrac{du}{dx} = 1$

$\therefore \ \displaystyle\int \dfrac{x}{1+\sqrt{x+2}}\, dx = \int \left(\dfrac{u^2-2}{1+u}\right) 2u\, du$

$\quad = \displaystyle\int \dfrac{2u^3 - 4u}{u+1}\, du$

$\quad = \displaystyle\int \left(2u^2 - 2u - 2 + \dfrac{2}{u+1}\right) du$

$\quad = \dfrac{2u^3}{3} - \dfrac{2u^2}{2} - 2u + 2\ln|u+1| + c$

$\quad = \dfrac{2}{3}(x+2)^{\frac{3}{2}} - x - 2 - 2\sqrt{x+2} + 2\ln(\sqrt{x+2}+1) + c$

$$\begin{array}{r} 2u^2 - 2u - 2 \\ u+1 \overline{\smash{\big)}\ 2u^3 + 0u^2 - 4u + 0} \\ \underline{-(2u^3 + 2u^2)} \\ -2u^2 - 4u + 0 \\ \underline{-(-2u^2 - 2u)} \\ -2u + 0 \\ \underline{-(-2u - 2)} \\ 2 \end{array}$$

219 $\sin(xy) + y^2 = x$

$\therefore \ \cos(xy)\left[1y + x\dfrac{dy}{dx}\right] + 2y\dfrac{dy}{dx} = 1$

$\therefore \ \dfrac{dy}{dx}(x\cos(xy) + 2y) = 1 - y\cos(xy)$

$\therefore \ \dfrac{dy}{dx} = \dfrac{1 - y\cos(xy)}{x\cos(xy) + 2y}$

220 a $x = 3 + a\lambda$, $y = -2 - \lambda$, $z = 2 + 2\lambda$

meets $\dfrac{x-4}{2} = 1 - y = \dfrac{z+2}{3}$ where

$\dfrac{3 + a\lambda - 4}{2} = 1 + 2 + \lambda = \dfrac{2 + 2\lambda + 2}{3}$

$\therefore \ \dfrac{a\lambda - 1}{2} = \lambda + 3 = \dfrac{2\lambda + 4}{3}$

$\therefore \ 3\lambda + 9 = 2\lambda + 4$

$\therefore \ \lambda = -5$

Hence $\dfrac{-5a - 1}{2} = -2$

$\therefore \ 5a + 1 = 4$

$\therefore \ a = \dfrac{3}{5}$

and P is $\left(3 + \dfrac{3}{5}(-5),\ -2 + 5,\ 2 + 2(-5)\right)$

or $(0, 3, -8)$.

b l_1 has direction vector $\begin{pmatrix} 3 \\ -5 \\ 10 \end{pmatrix} = \mathbf{v}_1$

l_2 has direction vector $\begin{pmatrix} 2 \\ -1 \\ 3 \end{pmatrix} = \mathbf{v}_2$

$\{$as $\dfrac{x-4}{2} = \dfrac{y-1}{-1} = \dfrac{z+2}{3}\}$

Now $\cos\theta = \dfrac{|\mathbf{v}_1 \bullet \mathbf{v}_2|}{|\mathbf{v}_1||\mathbf{v}_2|}$ $\{$as θ is acute$\}$

$\quad = \dfrac{|6 + 5 + 30|}{\sqrt{9+25+100}\sqrt{4+1+9}}$

$\quad = \dfrac{41}{\sqrt{134}\sqrt{14}}$

$\therefore \ \theta \approx 18.8°$

c $\mathbf{n} = \mathbf{v}_1 \times \mathbf{v}_2$

$\quad = \begin{vmatrix} \mathbf{i} & \mathbf{j} & \mathbf{k} \\ 3 & -5 & 10 \\ 2 & -1 & 3 \end{vmatrix}$

$\quad = \begin{vmatrix} -5 & 10 \\ -1 & 3 \end{vmatrix} \mathbf{i} - \begin{vmatrix} 3 & 10 \\ 2 & 3 \end{vmatrix} \mathbf{j} + \begin{vmatrix} 3 & -5 \\ 2 & -1 \end{vmatrix} \mathbf{k}$

$\quad = -5\mathbf{i} + 11\mathbf{j} + 7\mathbf{k}$

$\therefore \ $ the plane has equation $5x - 11y - 7z = 5(3) - 11(-2) - 7(2)$

$\therefore \ 5x - 11y - 7z = 23$

221 $y = ax + 2$ meets $y = 3x^2 - 2x + 5$
when $3x^2 - 2x + 5 = ax + 2$
$\therefore \ 3x^2 - [2+a]x + 3 = 0$
This has 2 distinct solutions when $\Delta > 0$
$\therefore \ (2+a)^2 - 4(3)(3) > 0$
$\therefore \ (a+2)^2 - 36 > 0$
$\therefore \ (a+2+6)(a+2-6) > 0$
$\therefore \ (a+8)(a-4) > 0$

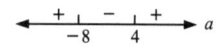

$\therefore \ a < -8$ or $a > 4$

222 $h = 2r$
$V = \frac{1}{3}\pi r^2 h$
$\therefore \ V = \frac{\pi}{3}r^2(2r)$
$\therefore \ V = \frac{2\pi}{3}r^3$

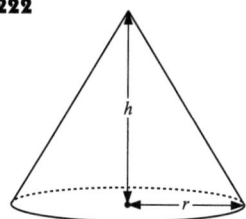

So, $\dfrac{dV}{dt} = 2\pi r^2 \dfrac{dr}{dt}$

Particular case:

When $h = 20$ cm, $r = 10$ cm
and $\dfrac{dV}{dt} = 5$ cm^3 s^{-1}

$\therefore \ 5 = 2\pi(10^2)\dfrac{dr}{dt}$

$\therefore \ 5 = 200\pi \dfrac{dr}{dt}$

$\therefore \ \dfrac{dr}{dt} = \dfrac{1}{40\pi}$ cm s^{-1}

223

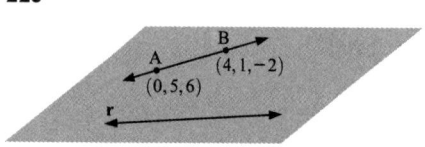

$\overrightarrow{AB} = \begin{pmatrix} 4 \\ -4 \\ -8 \end{pmatrix} = 4\begin{pmatrix} 1 \\ -1 \\ -2 \end{pmatrix}$

$\therefore$ the first line has equation $x = t$, $y = 5 - t$, $z = 6 - 2t$

The lines are not parallel as the direction vectors of the lines are not multiples of each other.
For the lines to be coplanar, they must intersect.

The first line meets the second line where $\begin{pmatrix} 0 \\ 5 \\ 6 \end{pmatrix} + t\begin{pmatrix} 1 \\ -1 \\ -2 \end{pmatrix} = \begin{pmatrix} a \\ 3 \\ 2 \end{pmatrix} + s\begin{pmatrix} 2 \\ -1 \\ 1 \end{pmatrix}$

$\therefore \ t = a + 2s$, $\underbrace{5 - t = 3 - s}$, and $\underbrace{6 - 2t = 2 + s}$
$\therefore \ s = t - 2$ $\therefore \ s + 2t = 4$

Thus $t - 2 + 2t = 4$
$\therefore \ 3t = 6$
$\therefore \ t = 2$ and $s = 0$
$\therefore$ the lines are coplanar if $2 = a + 2(0)$
$\therefore \ a = 2$

224 **a**

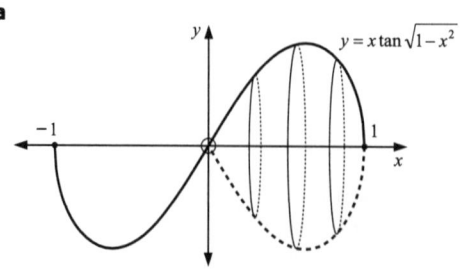

b $V = \pi \int_0^1 (x\tan\sqrt{1-x^2})^2 \, dx$

225 $f(x) = xe^{1-2x^2}$

a $f'(x) = 1e^{1-2x^2} + xe^{1-2x^2}(-4x)$
$= e^{1-2x^2}(1 - 4x^2)$
$f''(x) = -4xe^{1-2x^2}(1 - 4x^2) + e^{1-2x^2}(-8x)$
$= e^{1-2x^2}(-4x + 16x^3 - 8x)$
$= e^{1-2x^2}(16x^3 - 12x)$

b $f'(x) = e^{1-2x^2}(1 + 2x)(1 - 2x)$

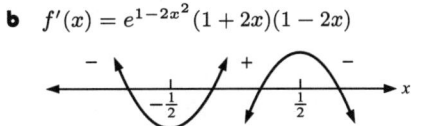

∴ there is a local minimum at $(-\frac{1}{2}, -\frac{\sqrt{e}}{2})$
and a local maximum at $(\frac{1}{2}, \frac{\sqrt{e}}{2})$.

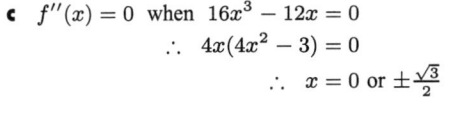

c $f''(x) = 0$ when $16x^3 - 12x = 0$
∴ $4x(4x^2 - 3) = 0$
∴ $x = 0$ or $\pm\frac{\sqrt{3}}{2}$

d As $x \to \infty$, $f(x) \to 0$ (above).
As $x \to -\infty$, $f(x) \to 0$ (below).

e

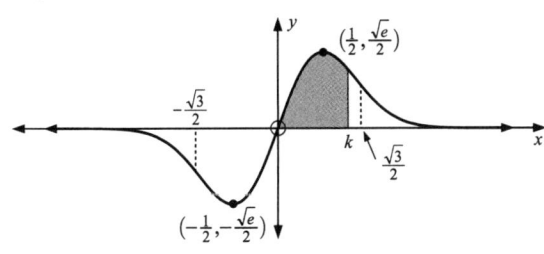

f If $\int_0^k xe^{1-2x^2}\,dx = \frac{e-1}{4}$
then $\frac{1}{-4}\int_0^k e^{1-2x^2}(-4x)\,dx = \frac{e-1}{4}$
∴ $\left[e^{1-2x^2}\right]_0^k = 1 - e$
∴ $e^{1-2k^2} - e = 1 - e$
∴ $e^{1-2k^2} = 1$
∴ $1 - 2k^2 = 0$
∴ $k = \pm\frac{1}{\sqrt{2}}$
But $k > 0$, so $k = \frac{1}{\sqrt{2}}$

226 a If $x = 1 + \lambda$, $y = -1 + a\lambda$, $z = 2 - \lambda$ lies on $3x - ky + z = 3$, then
$3(1 + \lambda) - k(-1 + a\lambda) + 2 - \lambda = 3$ for all λ
∴ $3 + 3\lambda + k - ak\lambda + 2 - \lambda = 3$
∴ $(3 + k + 2) + \lambda(3 - ak - 1) = 3$
∴ $k + 5 = 3$ and $2 - ak = 0$
∴ $k = -2$ and $2 + 2a = 0$
∴ $k = -2$ and $a = -1$

b P_2 has normal vector $\mathbf{n}_2 = \begin{pmatrix} 2 \\ -1 \\ -4 \end{pmatrix}$

P_1 has normal vector $\mathbf{n}_1 = \begin{pmatrix} 3 \\ 2 \\ 1 \end{pmatrix}$

Now $\mathbf{n}_1 \bullet \mathbf{n}_2 = 6 - 2 - 4 = 0$
∴ $\mathbf{n}_1 \perp \mathbf{n}_2$ and so $P_1 \perp P_2$.

c We need to solve $\begin{cases} 2x - y - 4z = 9 \\ 3x + 2y + z = 3 \end{cases}$

$\begin{pmatrix} 2 & -1 & -4 & | & 9 \\ 3 & 2 & 1 & | & 3 \end{pmatrix}$

$\sim \begin{pmatrix} 2 & -1 & -4 & | & 9 \\ 0 & 7 & 14 & | & -21 \end{pmatrix}$ $R_2 \to 2R_2 - 3R_1$

The second equation simplifies to $y + 2z = -3$
If $z = t$ then $y = -3 - 2t$
and $2x + 3 + 2t - 4t = 9$
∴ $2x = 6 + 2t$
∴ $x = 3 + t$

So, l_2 has equation
$x = 3 + t$, $y = -3 - 2t$, $z = t$, $t \in \mathbb{R}$.

d l_1 and l_2 meet when $\quad 1 + \lambda = 3 + t, \quad -1 - \lambda = -3 - 2t, \quad 2 - \lambda = t$
∴ $\lambda = 2 + t, \qquad\qquad \lambda = 2 + 2t, \qquad\quad \lambda = 2 - t$

∴ $2 + t = 2 + 2t = 2 - t$
The common solution is $t = 0$, so l_1 and l_2 meet at $(3, -3, 0)$.

e $l_1 = \begin{pmatrix} 1 \\ -1 \\ -1 \end{pmatrix}$ and $l_2 = \begin{pmatrix} 1 \\ -2 \\ 1 \end{pmatrix}$ $\cos\theta = \dfrac{|l_1 \bullet l_2|}{|l_1||l_2|} = \dfrac{|1+2-1|}{\sqrt{3}\sqrt{6}} = \dfrac{2}{\sqrt{18}}$

$\therefore\ \theta = \arccos\left(\dfrac{2}{\sqrt{18}}\right) \approx 61.9°$

227 We choose two quadratic factors with complex roots, in this case $\pm 2i$, $\pm i$.
These come from quadratics $x^2 + 4$ and $x^2 + 1$, both of which are positive for all x.
$\therefore\ f(x) = -(x^2 + 4)(x^2 + 1)$ is negative for all x.
$\therefore\ f(x) = -x^4 - 5x^2 - 4$.

228 As a, b, and c are real, all the coefficients of $P(z)$ are real.
Consequently $-3 + 2i$ and $-3 - 2i$ are both zeros.
They have sum -6 and product $9 + 4 = 13$.
$\therefore\ z^2 + 6z + 13$ is a factor of $P(z)$.
Thus $P(z) = (z + 2)(z^2 + 6z + 13)$
$= z^3 + 8z^2 + 25z + 26$
$\therefore\ a = 8,\ b = 25$ and $c = 26$
If $P(z) \geqslant 0$ then $(z + 2)(z^2 + 6z + 13) \geqslant 0$.
Now $z^2 + 6z + 13 > 0$ for all z, since its roots are complex and it has shape $\smile$
$\therefore\ P(z) \geqslant 0$ provided $z + 2 \geqslant 0$
$\therefore\ z \geqslant -2$

229 $f(x) = 2\tan(3(x - 1)) + 4,\ x \in [-1, 1]$

a $y = \tan nx$ has period $\dfrac{\pi}{n}$, so $f(x)$ has period $= \dfrac{\pi}{3}$

b Asymptotes are solutions of $\cos(3(x - 1)) = 0$
$\therefore\ 3(x - 1) = \dfrac{\pi}{2} + k\pi$
$\therefore\ x - 1 = \dfrac{\pi}{6} + \dfrac{k\pi}{3}$
$\therefore\ x = 1 + \dfrac{\pi}{6} + \dfrac{k\pi}{3}$

For the domain $-1 \leqslant x \leqslant 1$, asymptotes are $x \approx -0.571$ and $x \approx 0.476$.

c $y = \tan x\ \to\ y = \tan(3x)\ \to\ y = 2\tan(3x)\ \to\ y = 2\tan(3(x - 1)) + 4$
We have a horizontal stretch with scale factor $\frac{1}{3}$, followed by a vertical stretch with scale factor 2, followed by a translation through $\begin{pmatrix} 1 \\ 4 \end{pmatrix}$.

d The domain is $x \in [-1, 1]$ but $x \neq -0.571$ or 0.476.
The range is $y \in \mathbb{R}$.

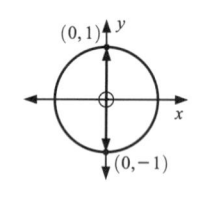